12th Conference of the European Chapter of the Association for Computational Linguistics 2009

(EACL 2009)

Athens, Greece
30 March - 3 April 2009

ISBN: 978-1-63266-013-8

Printed from e-media with permission by:

Curran Associates, Inc.
57 Morehouse Lane
Red Hook, NY 12571

Some format issues inherent in the e-media version may also appear in this print version.

Printed by Curran Associates, Inc. (2014)

For permission requests, please contact the Association for Computational Linguistics at the address below.

Association for Computational Linguistics
209 N. Eighth Street
Stroudsburg, Pennsylvania 18360

Phone: 1-570-476-8006
Fax: 1-570-476-0860

acl@aclweb.org

Additional copies of this publication are available from:

Curran Associates, Inc.
57 Morehouse Lane
Red Hook, NY 12571 USA
Phone: 845-758-0400
Fax: 845-758-2634
Email: curran@proceedings.com
Web: www.proceedings.com

EACL 2009

Proceedings of the 12th Conference of the European Chapter of the Association for Computational Linguistics

30 March – 3 April 2009
Megaron Athens International Conference Centre
Athens, Greece

Production and Manufacturing by
TEHNOGRAFIA DIGITAL PRESS, 7 Ektoros Street, 152 35 Vrilissia, Athens, Greece

Platinum Sponsors:

Gold Sponsors:

Silver Sponsors:

Bronze Sponsors:

Supporters:

Bag Supporter:

Preface: General Chair

Welcome to the 12th Conference of the European Chapter of the Association for Computational Linguistics—EACL 2009. This is the largest ever EACL in terms of the number of papers being presented. There are also ten workshops, four tutorials, a demos session and a student research workshop. I hope that you will enjoy this full and diverse programme.

This is the first time that an EACL conference that is not held jointly with ACL has had a General Chair. Having a General Chair is the EACL Board's strategy for ensuring continuity in the organisation of their conferences, now that the triennial EACLs are not synchronised with the biennial changes to personnel on the board. My job as General Chair is to liaise between the organising team and the EACL board, and to offer advice when needed. What an easy job it has been! And that is thanks wholly to the fantastic people who have done all the hard work to make this conference happen. I could not have asked for a better team of people. I would like to thank them all.

First, the Programme Committee, chaired by Claire Gardent and Joakim Nivre, attracted a record number of submissions. Thanks to their efforts, we have our largest ever main programme. I am very excited by the sheer breadth of topics and methodologies that are to be presented at this conference. It was a total pleasure to deal with the Programme Chairs – Joakim especially often offered me valuable advice on many matters concerning the conference, particularly electronic publication. I can't thank Claire and Joakim enough for all they have done to make this EACL conference a success. I would also like to thank Ann Copestake and Franciska de Jong for agreeing to be the keynote speakers.

For the first time, the three ACL conferences coordinated the call for workshop proposals. This gave proposers more flexibility in choosing the location for their workshops. The Workshop Chairs for EACL, Miriam Butt and Steve Clark, coordinated with the workshop chairs for NAACL 2009 and ACL 2009 in reviewing all the workshop proposals. This coordination inevitably makes the task more complex. But the whole process ran very smoothly thanks to their careful and diligent work. I'm very grateful to Steve and Miriam for putting together a very exciting and broad workshop programme for EACL.

As is traditional, the student research workshop was organised by the student members of the EACL board – Vera Demberg, Yanjun Ma and Nils Reiter. Their job is very demanding; they essentially do everything that programme chairs do, only on a slightly smaller scale. They issued the call, organised a fantastic team of reviewers, assigned papers, coordinated and mediated among reviewers, and finally constructed a schedule consisting of four parallel sessions. They did a brilliant job, and with very little help from me. I owe them a huge debt of thanks.

The Tutorial Chairs, Emiel Krahmer and David Weir, could be viewed as victims of their own success! Their efforts to attract tutorial proposals produced a record number of submissions; many more excellent proposals than we could accommodate. We have a very strong programme of four tutorials, and I thank the tutorials team for all their careful and thoughtful work.

The task of producing both the electronic and hard copy versions of the conference materials has become extremely complex as the conference has increased in size and diversity. The Publications Chairs, Kemal Oflazer and David Schlangen, somehow make it look easy. Thanks to them and Ion Androutsopoulous, the member of the local organising team who liaised with them, we have all the materials delivered on time and in good order.

In these depressing economic times, being a Sponsorship Chair is a challenging task, and for the most part a thankless one. This year, for the first time, the three ACL conferences coordinated applications for sponsorship funds. This allowed companies to sponsor ACL, EACL and NAACL in one package. The Sponsorship Chairs are Josef van Genabith and Philipp Koehn for Europe, Hitoshi Isahara and Kim-Teng Lua for Asia, and Nicolas Nikolov for the US. They issued hundreds of applications to companies all over the world. While sponsorship income is generally lower than in previous years, I am convinced it would be much lower still, if they had not coordinated their efforts this way, and done such a thorough job of asking everyone and anyone for money. I am really grateful to them.

We received a record number of submissions to the demos session, making it necessary for the Demos Chair, Jörn Kreutel, to recruit additional reviewers at the last minute. I would like to thank him for overcoming the reviewing problems so quickly and efficiently, and thank also the team of reviewers for doing such a great job.

I would also like to thank Priscilla Rassmussen, who has been a very valuable source of information and advice for me over the last 3 years. I have really appreciated her thoughtful suggestions and her help in keeping me informed about ACL protocols.

Last, but definitely not least, the local organising team have been nothing short of spectacular. The Local Chair, Vangelis Karkaletsis, has been working for over two years on an overwhelming number of tasks, ranging from finding the conference venue and liaising with its management, through dealing with special dietary requirements, to acquiring local sponsorship. Vangelis has always been accessible to me, to other members of the organising team, and to delegates. I simply don't know where he gets his energy from, but I wish he could bottle it and sell it. Thanks to him, my job as General Chair has been stress free. I owe him a huge debt.

Vangelis has been backed by the Co-chairs Stelios Piperidis and Ion Androutsopoulos. Stelios also has boundless energy and his effortless charm makes him very effective at persuading people to part with money (what an asset!). I am particularly impressed with the achievements of Vangelis and Stelios in attracting local sponsors, achieving their sponsorship targets even in the current financial climate. Ion's responsibilities have centred largely on publications and publicity, in particular liaising with the Publications Chairs. In spite of the sheer complexity of the task, thanks to him everything has run smoothly. Ion's careful attention to detail has been a really valuable asset on many fronts. The Local Chair and Co-chairs have been backed up by a strong team of local organisers; there are just too many of them for me to thank individually here. I have always felt that the conference has been in excellent hands; every member of the local organising team is highly competent, unflappable, and professional to the last. I thank them all.

We have also received unwavering support from the academic institutions to which our three local co-chairs belong: NCSR Demokritos, Athens University of Economics and Business, and the Institute for Language and Speech Processing. These institutions have subsidised expenses directly that are associated with secretarial work and the travel costs of invited speakers and tutors. They have also provided all sorts of support that are essentially hidden costs, in administration, publicity, web design and maintenance, and much much more. This conference simply wouldn't happen without this help, and I thank them all.

I very much hope that EACL 2009 offers you the opportunity to engage in stimulating debate with fellow researchers in computational linguisitcs. And I hope to see you again next year in Uppsala at the jointly held meeting with ACL.

Alex Lascarides
General Chair
March 2009

Preface: Program Chairs

We are delighted to present you with this volume containing the papers accepted for presentation at the 12th Conference of the European Chapter of the Association for Computational Linguistics, held in Athens, Greece, from March 30th till April 3rd 2009.

EACL 2009 received yet another record-breaking number of submissions, with 360 valid submissions against 264 for EACL 2006 and 181 for EACL 2003. Thanks to the new policy adopted by EACL regarding modes of presentation, we were nonetheless able to accept 100 papers (of which 2 were later withdrawn), achieving a healthy acceptance rate of 28% against only 20% in 2006 and 27% in 2003. Indeed, in 2009, the EACL conference will renew its format by having the main conference papers presented either as regular talks or as posters, with posters getting both a ten-minute quick-fire presentation in a thematic session and a one-hour discussion period in a traditional poster session. EACL 2009 will thus feature 41 posters and 57 talks, all with equal status in terms of quality and appearance in the proceedings. Not only does this move towards a balanced mix of traditional talks, quick-fire presentations and poster sessions allow us to maintain a reasonable acceptance rate, we also believe that it will increase interaction between researchers and contribute to a more lively scientific exchange.

The increased number of submissions naturally comes with an increased reviewing load and we are greatly indebted to the 11 area chairs who recruited 449 reviewers and managed the reviewing process in their areas. Each paper submission was reviewed by three reviewers, who were furthermore encouraged to discuss any divergences they might have, and the papers in each area were ranked by the area chair. The final selection was made by the program co-chairs after an independent check of all reviews and discussions with the area chairs.

In addition to the main conference program, EACL 2009 will feature the now traditional Student Research Workshop, 10 workshops, 4 tutorials and a demo session with 18 presentations. We are also fortunate to have Ann Copestake, University of Cambridge, and Franciska de Jong, University of Twente, as invited speakers. Ann Copestake will speak about "Slacker semantics: why superficiality, dependency and avoidance of commitment can be the right way to go" and Franciska de Jong will discuss "NLP and the humanities: the revival of an old liaison."

An event of this size is a highly collaborative effort and we are grateful to all those who helped us construct the main conference program: the authors for submitting their research results; the reviewers for delivering their reviews and discussing them whenever there was some disagreement; and the area chairs for managing the review process in their area.

Thanks are due to the START people, Rich Gerber and Paolo Gai, for responding to questions quickly and for modifying START whenever this was needed, and to the local organizing committee chairs, Vangelis Karkaletsis, Ion Androutsopoulos and Stelios Piperidis, for their patient cooperation with us over many organisational issues. We are also grateful to the Student Research Workshop chairs, Vera Demberg, Yanjun Ma and Nils Reiter, and to the NAACL HLT program chairs, Michael Collins, Lucy Vanderwende, Doug Oard and Shri Narayanan, for smooth collaboration in the handling of double submissions.

Finally, we are indebted to the General Chair, Alex Lascarides, for her lively guidance and support throughout the whole process, and to the two Publication Chairs, David Schlangen and Kemal Oflazer, for putting together the conference proceedings.

Wishing you a very enjoyable time at EACL 2009!

Claire Gardent and Joakim Nivre
EACL 2009 Program Chairs

EACL 2009 Organizers

General Chair:

Alex Lascarides, University of Edinburgh (UK)

Programme Chairs:

Claire Gardent, CNRS/LORIA Nancy (France)
Joakim Nivre, Uppsala University and Växjö University (Sweden)

Invited Speakers:

Ann Copestake, University of Cambridge (UK)
Franciska de Jong, University of Twente (The Netherlands)

Workshop Chairs:

Miriam Butt, University of Konstanz (Germany)
Stephen Clark, University of Cambridge (UK)

Tutorial Chairs:

Emiel Krahmer, University of Tilburg (The Netherlands)
David Weir, University of Sussex (UK)

Student Research Workshop Chairs:

Vera Demberg, University of Edinburgh (UK)
Yanjun Ma, Dublin City University (Ireland)
Nils Reiter, Heidelberg University (Germany)

Demos Chair:

Jörn Kreutel, Semantic Edge (Germany)

Publications Chairs:

Kemal Oflazer, Sabancı University (Turkey)
David Schlangen, University of Potsdam (Germany)

Sponsorship Chairs:

Josef van Genabith, Dublin City University (Ireland)
Philipp Koehn, University of Edinburgh (UK)
Hitoshi Isihara, NICT (Japan)
Kim-Teng Lua, National University of Singapore (Singapore)
Nicolas Nicolov, JD Powers (USA)
Vangelis Karkaletsis, NCSR Demokritos (Greece)
Stelios Piperidis, Institute for Language and Speech Processing (Greece)

Local Chairs:

Vangelis Karkaletsis, NCSR Demokritos (Greece)
Ion Androutsopoulos, Athens University of Economics and Business (Greece)
Stelios Piperidis, Institute for Language and Speech Processing (Greece)

Local Organizing Team:

Dimitrios Galanis, Athens University of Economics and Business (Greece)
Maria Gavrilidou, Institute for Language and Speech Processing (Greece)
Georgios Gianakopoulos, NCSR Demokritos (Greece)
Elias Iosif, NCSR Demokritos (Greece)
Pythagoras Karampiperis, NCSR Demokritos (Greece)
Stasinos Konstantopoulos, NCSR Demokritos (Greece)
Gerasimos Lampouras, Athens University of Economics and Business (Greece)
Prodromos Malakasiotis, Athens University of Economics and Business (Greece)
Stella Markantonatou, Institute for Language and Speech Processing (Greece)
Evgenia Pantouvaki, NCSR Demokritos (Greece)
Anastasios Patrikakos, Institute for Language and Speech Processing (Greece)
Georgios Petasis, NCSR Demokritos (Greece)
Kostas Stamatakis, NCSR Demokritos (Greece)
Georgios Tsatsaronis, NCSR Demokritos and Athens University of Economics and Business (Greece)

EACL 2009 Program Committee

Program Chairs:

Claire Gardent, CNRS/LORIA Nancy (France)
Joakim Nivre, Uppsala University and Växjö University (Sweden)

Area Chairs:

Anja Belz, University of Brighton (UK)
Sabine Buchholz, Toshiba Research Europe (UK)
Chris Callison-Burch, Johns Hopkins University (USA)
Philipp Cimiano, Delft University of Technology (The Netherlands)
Maarten de Rijke, University of Amsterdam (The Netherlands)
Anna Korhonen, University of Cambridge (UK)
Kimmo Koskenniemi, University of Helsinki (Finland)
Bernardo Magnini, FBK-irst (Italy)
Stephan Oepen, University of Oslo (Norway)
Richard Power, The Open University (UK)
Giuseppe Riccardi, University of Trento (Italy)

Program Committee Members:

Anne Abeillé, Omri Abend, Meni Adler, Eneko Agirre, David Ahn, Lars Ahrenberg, Amparo Albalate, Mikhail Alexandrov, Enrique Alfonseca, Gianni Amati, Saba Amsalu, Mohammed Attia, Nathalie Aussenac-Gilles

Tim Baldwin. Krisztian Balog, Srinivas Bangalore, Marco Baroni, Roberto Basili, John Bateman, Frederic Bechet, Abdelmajid Ben Hamadou, Emily Bender, Anton Benz, Jonathan Berant, Sabine Bergler, Raffaella Bernardi, Delphine Bernhard, Nicola Bertoldi, Rahul Bhagat, Ergun Biçici, Eckhard Bick, Tamás Biró, Philippe Blache, Xavier Blanco, Phil Blunsom, Rens Bod, Bernd Bohnet, Dan Bohus, Ondrej Bojar, Gemma Boleda, Francis Bond, Johan Bos, Mohand Boughanem, Gosse Bouma, Antonio Branco, Thorsten Brants, Chris Brew, Christopher Brewster, Ted Briscoe, Paul Buitelaar, Harry Bunt, Aljoscha Burchardt, Donna Byron

Aoife Cahill, Zoraida Callejas, Nicoletta Calzolari, Sandra Carberry, Marine Carpuat, Xavier Carreras, John Carroll, Francisco Casacuberta, Mauro Cettolo, Nouha Chaâbane, Yee Seng Chan, Ming-Wei Chang, Eugene Charniak, Ciprian Chelba, Stanley Chen, Colin Cherry, David Chiang, Massimiliano Ciaramita, Stephen Clark, James Clarke, Trevor Cohn, Michael Connor, Bonaventura Coppola, Stephen Cox, Nick Craswell, Montserrat Cuadros, James Curran, James Cussens

Walter Daelemans, Ido Dagan, Robert Dale, Hercules Dalianis, Geraldine Damnati, Noa Danon, Hal Daumé III, Dmitry Davidov, Guy De Pauw, Thierry Declerck, Rodolfo Delmonte, David DeVault, Giuseppe Di Fabbrizio, Mona Diab, Anne Diekema, Christine Doran, Qing Dou, Markus Dreyer, Amit Dubey, Chris Dyer, Helge Dyvik

Markus Egg, Andreas Eisele, Elisabet Engdahl, Katrin Erk, Maxine Eskenazi, Cristina España, Roger Evans, Stefan Evert

Afsaneh Fazly, Marcello Federico, Christiane Fellbaum, Raquel Fernández, Olivier Ferret, Dan Flickinger, George Foster, Jennifer Foster, Mary Ellen Foster, Anette Frank, Alex Fraser, Fumiyo Fukumoto

Aldo Gangemi, Nikesh Garera, Albert Gatt, Dale Gerdemann, Ulrich Germann, Dafydd Gibbon, Daniel Gildea, Jesus Gimenez, Kevin Gimpel, Jonathan Ginzburg, Roxana Girju, Alfio Gliozzo, John Goldsmith, Julio Gonzalo, Allen Gorin, Genevieve Gorrell, Brigitte Grau, Mark Greenwood, Gregory Grefenstette, David Griol, Claire Grover, Iryna Gurevych

Ben Hachey, Lamia Hadrich Belguith, Udo Hahn, Dilek Hakkani-Tür, Keith Hall, Greg Hanneman, Sanda Harabagiu, Donna Harman, Sasa Hasan, Kenneth Heafield, Ulrich Heid, James Henderson, John Henderson, Iris Hendrickx, Gerhard Heyer, Andrew Hickl, Djoerd Hiemstra, Erhard Hinrichs, Graeme Hirst, Jerry Hobbs, Julia Hockenmaier, Deirdre Hogan, Mark Hopkins, Veronique Hoste, Arvi Hurskainen, Rebecca Hwa

Nancy Ide, Diana Inkpen, Neil Ireson, Amy Isard, Alexei Ivanov

Guillaume Jacquet, Jerom Janssen, Sittichai Jiampojamarn, Valentin Jijkoun, Richard Johansson, Sofie Johansson Kokkinakis, Rie Johnson (formerly, Ando), Michael Johnston, Kristiina Jokinen, Doug Jones, Gareth Jones, Aravind Joshi

Heiki Kaalep, Laura Kallmeyer, Min-Yen Kan, Viggo Kann, Damianos Karakos, Jussi Karlgren, Fred Karlsson, Lauri Karttunen, Martin Kay, Simon Keizer, Jaana Kekalainen, Frank Keller, Bernd Kiefer, Adam Kilgarriff, Tracy King, Kevin Knight, Alistair Knott, Philipp Koehn, Dimitrios Kokkinakis, Alexander Koller, Greg Kondrak, Valia Kordoni, Zornitsa Kozareva, Bob Krovetz, Yuval Krymolowski, Taku Kudo, Sandra Kübler, Peter Kühnlein, Marco Kuhlmann, Jonas Kuhn, Roland Kuhn, Shankar Kumar, Jeff Kuo, Oren Kurland, Sadao Kurohashi, Olivia Kwong

Tore Langholm, Guy Lapalme, Mirella Lapata, Alberto Lavelli, Alon Lavie, Gary Lee, Fabrice Lefevre, Jochen Leidner, Oliver Lemon, Alessandro Lenci, Piroska Lendvai, Ian Lewin, Zhifei Li, Frank Liberato, Jimmy Lin, Krister Lindén, Kenneth Litkowski, Peter Ljunglöf, Birte Loenneker-Rodman, Adam Lopez

Nitin Madnani, Thomas Mandl, Inderjeet Mani, Daniel Marcu, Katja Markert, Lluís Màrquez Villodre, Erwin Marsi, Colin Matheson, Lambert Mathias, Yuji Matsumoto, Takuya Matsuzak, Arne Mauseri, Diana McCarthy, David McClosky, Ryan McDonald, Michael McTear, Ben Medlock, Paola Merlo, Slim Mesfar, Donald Metzler, Jeffrey Micher, Rada Mihalcea, Maria Milosavljevic, Wolfgang Minker, Yusuke Miyao, Sien Moens, Dan Moldovan, Simonetta Montemagni, Christof Monz, Bob Moore, Roser Morante, Alessandro Moschitti, Smaranda Muresan, Stefan Müller

Vivi Nastase, Sven Naumann, Roberto Navigli, Mark-Jan Nederhof, Ani Nenkova, Günter Neumann, Hermann Ney, Hwee Tou Ng, Patrik Nguyen, Rodney Nielsen, Sergei Nirenburg, Malvina Nissim, Tadashi Nomoto

Diarmuid Ó Séaghdha, Franz-Josef Och, Kemal Oflazer, Alessandro Oltramari, Constantin Orasan, Csaba Oravecz, Miles Osborne, Rainer Osswald, Lilja Øvrelid

Sebastian Padó, Tim Paek, Patrick Pantel, Rebecca Passonneau, Catherine Pelachaud, Anselmo Peñas, Gerald Penn, Marco Pennacchiotti, Wim Peters, Kay Peterson, Emanuele Pianta, Paul Piwek, Massimo Poesio, Thierry Poibeau, Alexandros Potamianos, Judita Preiss, Laurent Prevot, James Pustejovsky

Lizhen Qu, Silvia Quarteroni, Chris Quirk

Jan Raab, Aarne Ranta, Ari Rappoport, Christian Raymond, Gisela Redeker, Ehud Reiter, Martin Reynaert, Sebastian Riedel, Verena Rieser, Stefan Riezler, German Rigau, Michael Riley, Brian Roark, Laurent Romary, Barbara Rosario, Mike Rosner, Dan Roth, Salim Roukos

Kenji Sagae, Patrick Saint-Dizier, Emilio Sanchis, Diana Santos, Giorgio Satta, Jacques Savoy, David Schlangen, Judith Schlesinger, Helmut Schmid, Sabine Schulte im Walde, Donia Scott,

Frédérique Segond, Satoshi Sekine, Libin Shen, Wade Shen, Eyal Shnarch, Börkur Sigurbjörnsson, Max Silberztein, Rui Sousa Silva, Khalil Sima'an, Michel Simard, Kiril Simov, Vivek Srikumar, Inguna Skadina, David Smith, Noah Smith, Rion Snow, Radu Soricut, Caroline Sporleder, Manfred Stede, Mark Steedman, Josef Steinberger, Svetlana Stenchikova, Amanda Stent, Mark Stevenson, Suzanne Stevenson, Matthew Stone, Carlo Strapparava, Michael Strube, Eiichiro Sumita, Mihai Surdeanu

Maite Taboada, David Talbot, Thora Tenbrink, Simone Teufel, Jörg Tiedemann, Christoph Tillmann, Ivan Titov, Takenobu Tokunaga, Kristina Toutanova, Trond Trosterud, Theodora Tsikrika, Dan Tufiş, Juho Tupakka, Gokhan Tur, Peter Turney

Nicola Ueffing

Antal van den Bosch, Lelka van der Sluis, Marieke van Erp, Josef van Genabith, Hans van Halteren, Gertjan van Noord, Menno van Zaanen, Keith Vander Linden, Lucy Vanderwende, Tamás Váradi, Sebastian Varges, Tony Veale, Paola Velardi, Karin Verspoor, Jose Luis Vicedo, Barbora Vidova-Hladka, Simona Vietri, Laure Vieu, Aline Villavicencio, Eric Villemonte de la Clergerie, Dusko Vitas, Andreas Vlachos, Carl Vogel, Clare Voss, Piek Vossen, Atro Voutilainen

Qin Iris Wang, Nigel Ward, Taro Watanabe, Andy Way, Gabe Webster, Richard Wicentowski, Sandra Williams, Jason Williams, Shuly Wintner, Yuk Wah Wong, Jeremy Wright, Dekai Wu

Fei Xia

Alexander Yeh, Anssi Yli-Jyrä, Kai Yu, Deniz Yuret

Fabio Massimo Zanzotto, Sina Zarrieß, Richard Zens, Torsten Zesch, Yi Zhang, Imed Zitouni, Ingrid Zukerman

Table of Contents

Slacker semantics: why superficiality, dependency and avoidance of commitment can be the right way to go

Ann Copestake
Computer Laboratory, University of Cambridge
15 JJ Thomson Avenue, Cambridge, UK
aac@cl.cam.ac.uk

Abstract

This paper discusses computational compositional semantics from the perspective of grammar engineering, in the light of experience with the use of Minimal Recursion Semantics in DELPH-IN grammars. The relationship between argument indexation and semantic role labelling is explored and a semantic dependency notation (DMRS) is introduced.

1 Introduction

The aim of this paper is to discuss work on compositional semantics from the perspective of grammar engineering, which I will take here as the development of (explicitly) linguistically-motivated computational grammars. The paper was written to accompany an invited talk: it is intended to provide background and further details for those parts of the talk which are not covered in previous publications. It consists of an brief introduction to our approach to computational compositional semantics, followed by details of two contrasting topics which illustrate the grammar engineering perspective. The first of these is argument indexing and its relationship to semantic role labelling, the second is semantic dependency structure.

Standard linguistic approaches to compositional semantics require adaptation for use in broad-coverage computational processing. Although some of the adaptations are relatively trivial, others have involved considerable experimentation by various groups of computational linguists. Perhaps the most important principle is that semantic representations should be a good match for syntax, in the sense of capturing all and only the information available from syntax and productive morphology, while nevertheless abstracting over semantically-irrelevant idiosyncratic detail. Compared to much of the linguistics literature, our analyses are relatively superficial, but this is essentially because the broad-coverage computational approach prevents us from over-committing on the basis of the information available from the syntax. One reflection of this are the formal techniques for scope underspecification which have been developed in computational linguistics. The implementational perspective, especially when combined with a requirement that grammars can be used for generation as well as parsing, also forces attention to details which are routinely ignored in theoretical linguistic studies. This is particularly true when there are interactions between phenomena which are generally studied separately. Finally, our need to produce usable systems disallows some appeals to pragmatics, especially those where analyses are radically underspecified to allow for syntactic and morphological effects found only in highly marked contexts.[1]

In a less high-minded vein, sometimes it is right to be a slacker: life (or at least, project funding) is too short to implement all ideas within a grammar in their full theoretical glory. Often there is an easy alternative which conveys the necessary information to a consumer of the semantic representations. Without this, grammars would never stabilise.

Here I will concentrate on discussing work which has used Minimal Recursion Semantics (MRS: Copestake et al. (2005)) or Robust Minimal Recursion Semantics (RMRS: Copestake (2003)). The (R)MRS approach has been adopted as a common framework for the DELPH-IN initiative (Deep Linguistic Processing with HPSG: http://www.delph-in.net) and the work discussed here has been done by and in collaboration with researchers involved in DELPH-IN.

The programme of developing computational compositional semantics has a large number of aspects. It is important that the semantics has a logically-sound interpretation (e.g., Koller and Lascarides (2009), Thater (2007)), is cross-

[1] For instance, we cannot afford to underspecify number on nouns because of examples such as *The hash browns is getting angry* (from Pollard and Sag (1994) p.85).

Proceedings of the 12th Conference of the European Chapter of the ACL, pages 1–9,
Athens, Greece, 30 March – 3 April 2009. ©2009 Association for Computational Linguistics

linguistically adequate (e.g., Bender (2008)) and is compatible with generation (e.g., Carroll et al. (1999), Carroll and Oepen (2005)). Ideally, we want support for shallow as well as deep syntactic analysis (which was the reason for developing RMRS), enrichment by deeper analysis (including lexical semantics and anaphora resolution, both the subject of ongoing work), and (robust) inference. The motivation for the development of dependency-style representations (including Dependency MRS (DMRS) discussed in §4) has been to improve ease of use for consumers of the representation and human annotators, as well as use in statistical ranking of analyses/realisations (Fujita et al. (2007), Oepen and Lønning (2006)). Integration with distributional semantic techniques is also of interest.

The belated 'introduction' to MRS in Copestake et al. (2005) primarily covered formal representation of complete utterances. Copestake (2007a) described uses of (R)MRS in applications. Copestake et al. (2001) and Copestake (2007b) concern the algebra for composition. What I want to do here is to concentrate on less abstract issues in the syntax-semantics interface. I will discuss two cases where the grammar engineering perspective is important and where there are some conclusions about compositional semantics which are relevant beyond DELPH-IN. The first, argument indexing (§3), is a relatively clear case in which the constraints imposed by grammar engineering have a significant effect on choice between plausible alternatives. I have chosen to talk about this both because of its relationship with the currently popular task of semantic role labelling and because the DELPH-IN approach is now fairly stable after a quite considerable degree of experimentation. What I am reporting is thus a perspective on work done primarily by Flickinger within the English Resource Grammar (ERG: Flickinger (2000)) and by Bender in the context of the Grammar Matrix (Bender et al., 2002), though I've been involved in many of the discussions. The second main topic (§4) is new work on a semantic dependency representation which can be derived from MRS, extending the previous work by Oepen (Oepen and Lønning, 2006). Here, the motivation came from an engineering perspective, but the nature of the representation, and indeed the fact that it is possible at all, reveals some interesting aspects of semantic composition in the grammars.

2 The MRS and RMRS languages

This paper concerns only representations which are output by deep grammars, which use MRS, but it will be convenient to talk in terms of RMRS and to describe the RMRSs that are constructed under those assumptions. Such RMRSs are interconvertible with MRSs.[2] The description is necessarily terse and contains the minimal detail necessary to follow the remainder of the paper.

An RMRS is a description of a set of trees corresponding to scoped logical forms. Fig 1 shows an example of an RMRS and its corresponding scoped form (only one for this example). RMRS is a 'flat' representation, consisting of a bag of **elementary predications** (EP), a set of **argument relations**, and a set of constraints on the possible linkages of the EPs when the RMRS is resolved to scoped form. Each EP has a predicate, a **label** and a unique **anchor** and may have a distinguished (ARG0) argument (EPs are written here as label:anchor:pred(arg0)). Label sharing between EPs indicates conjunction (e.g., in Fig 1, *big*, *angry* and *dog* share the label l2). Argument relations relate non-arg0 arguments to the corresponding EP via the anchor. Argument names are taken from a fixed set (discussed in §3). Argument values may be variables (e.g., e8, x4: variables are the only possibility for values of ARG0), constants (strings such as "London"), or **holes** (e.g. h5), which indicate scopal relationships. Variables have sortal properties, indicating tense, number and so on, but these are not relevant for this paper. Variables corresponding to unfilled (syntactically optional) arguments are unique in the RMRS, but otherwise variables must correspond to the ARG0 of an EP (since I am only considering RMRSs from deep grammars here).

Constraints on possible scopal relationships between EPs may be explicitly specified in the grammar via relationships between holes and labels. In particular **qeq** constraints (the only type considered here) indicate that, in the scoped forms, a label must either plug a hole directly or be connected to it via a chain of quantifiers. Hole arguments (other than the BODY of a quantifier) are always linked to a label via a qeq or other constraint (in a deep grammar RMRS). Variables survive in the models of RMRSs (i.e., the fully scoped trees) whereas holes and labels do not.

[2]See Flickinger and Bender (2003) and Flickinger et al. (2003) for the use of MRS in DELPH-IN grammars.

l1:a1:_some_q, BV(a1,x4), RSTR(a1,h5), BODY(a1,h6), h5 qeq l2,
l2:a2:_big_a_1(e8), ARG1(a2,x4), l2:a3:_angry_a_1(e9), ARG1(a3,x4), l2:a4:_dog_n_1(x4),
l4:a5:_bark_v_1(e2), ARG1(a5,x4), l4:a6:_loud_a_1(e10), ARG1(a6,e2)

_some_q(x4,_big_a_1(e8,x4) ∧ _angry_a_1(e9, x4) ∧ _dog_n_1(x4),_bark_v_1(e2,x4) ∧ _loud_a_1(e10,e2))

Figure 1: RMRS and scoped form for 'Some big angry dogs bark loudly'. Tense and number are omitted.

The naming convention for predicates corresponding to lexemes is: _ stem _ major sense tag, optionally followed by _ and minor sense tag (e.g., _loud_a_1). Major sense tags correspond roughly to traditional parts of speech. There are also non-lexical predicates such as 'poss' (though none occur in Fig 1).[3] MRS varies from RMRS in that the arguments are all directly associated with the EP and thus no anchors are necessary.

I have modified the definition of RMRS given in Copestake (2007b) to make the ARG0 argument optional. Here I want to add the additional constraint that the ARG0 of an EP is unique to it (i.e., not the ARG0 of any other EP). I will term this the **characteristic variable** property. This means that, for every variable, there is a unique EP which has that variable as its ARG0. I will assume for this paper that all EPs, apart from quantifier EPs, have such an ARG0.[4] The characteristic variable property is one that has emerged from working with large-scale constraint-based grammars.

A few concepts from the MRS algebra are also necessary to the discussion. Composition can be formalised as functor-argument combination where the argument phrase's **hook** fills a **slot** in the functor phrase, thus instantiating an RMRS argument relation. The hook consists of an **index** (a variable), an **external argument** (also a variable) and an **ltop** (local top: the label corresponding to the topmost node in the current partial tree, ignoring quantifiers). The syntax-semantics interface requires that the appropriate hook and slots be set up (mostly lexically in a DELPH-IN grammar) and that each application of a rule specifies the slot to be used (e.g., MOD for modification). In a lexical entry, the ARG0 of the EP provides the hook index, and, apart from quantifiers, the hook ltop is the EP's label. In intersective combination, the ltops of the hooks will be equated. In scopal combination, a hole argument in a slot is specified to be qeq to the ltop of the argument phrase and the ltop of the functor phrase supplies the new hook's ltop.

By thinking of qeqs as links in an RMRS graph (rather than in terms of their logical behaviour as constraints on the possible scoped forms), an RMRS can be treated as consisting of a set of trees with nodes consisting of EPs grouped via intersective relationships: there will be a backbone tree (headed by the overall ltop and including the main verb if there is one), plus a separate tree for each quantified NP. For instance, in Fig 1, the third line contains the EPs corresponding to the (single node) backbone tree and the first two lines show the EPs comprising the tree for the quantified NP (one node for the quantifier and one for the N′ which it connects to via the RSTR and its qeq).

3 Arguments and roles

I will now turn to the representation of arguments in MRS and their relationship to semantic roles. I want to discuss the approach to argument labelling in some detail, because it is a reasonably clear case where the desiderata for broad-coverage semantics which were discussed in §1 led us to a syntactically-driven approach, as opposed to using semantically richer roles such as AGENT, GOAL and INSTRUMENT.

An MRS can, in fact, be written using a conventional predicate-argument representation. A representation which uses ordered argument labels can be recovered from this in the obvious way. E.g., l:like_v_1(e,x,y) is equivalent to l:a:like_v_1(e), ARG1(a,x), ARG2(a,y). A fairly large inventory of argument labels is actually used in the DELPH-IN grammars (e.g., RSTR, BODY). To recover these from the conventional predicate-argument notation requires a look up in a semantic interface component (the SEM-I, Flickinger et al. (2005)). But open-class predicates use the ARGn convention, where n is 0,1,2,3 or 4 and the discussion here

[3] In fact, most of the choices about semantics made by grammar writers concern the behaviour of constructions and thus these non-lexical predicates, but this would require another paper to discuss.

[4] I am simplifying for expository convenience. In current DELPH-IN grammars, quantifiers have an ARG0 which corresponds to the bound variable. This should not be the characteristic variable of the quantifier (it is the characteristic variable of a nominal EP), since its role in the scoped forms is as a notational convenience to avoid lambda expressions. I will call it the BV argument here.

only concerns these.[5]

Arguably, the DELPH-IN approach is Davidsonian rather than neo-Davidsonian in that, even in the RMRS form, the arguments are related to the predicate via the anchor which plays no other role in the semantics. Unlike the neo-Davidsonian use of the event variable to attach arguments, this allows the same style of representation to be used uniformly, including quantifiers, for instance. Arguments can omitted completely without syntactic ill-formedness of the RMRS, but this is primarily relevant to shallower grammars. A semantic predicate, such as like_v_1, is a logical predicate and as such is expected to have the same arity wherever it occurs in the DELPH-IN grammars. Thus models for an MRS may be defined in a language with or without argument labels.

The ordering of arguments for open class lexemes is lexically specified on the basis of the syntactic obliqueness hierarchy (Pollard and Sag, 1994). ARG1 corresponds to the subject in the base (non-passivised) form ('deep subject'). Argument numbering is consecutive in the base form, so no predicate with an ARG3 is lexically missing an ARG2, for instance. An ARG3 may occur without an instantiated ARG2 when a syntactically optional argument is missing (e.g., *Kim gave to the library*), but this is explicit in the linearised form (e.g., _give_v(e,x,u,y)).

The full statement of how the obliqueness hierarchy (and thus the labelling) is determined for lexemes has to be made carefully and takes us too far into discussion of syntax to explain in detail here. While the majority of cases are straightforward, a few are not (e.g., because they depend on decisions about which form is taken as the base in an alternation). However, all decisions are made at the level of lexical types: adding an entry for a lexeme for a DELPH-IN grammar only requires working out its lexical type(s) (from syntactic behaviour and very constrained semantic notions, e.g., control). The actual assignment of arguments to an utterance is just a consequence of parsing. Argument labelling is thus quite different from PropBank (Palmer et al., 2005) role labelling despite the unfortunate similarity of the PropBank naming scheme.

It follows from the fixed arity of predicates that lexemes with different numbers of arguments should be given different predicate symbols. There is usually a clear sense distinction when this occurs. For instance, we should distinguish between the 'depart' and 'bequeath' senses of *leave* because the first takes an ARG1 and an ARG2 (optional) and the second ARG1, ARG2 (optional), ARG3. We do not draw sense distinctions where there is no usage which the grammar could disambiguate.

Of course, there are obvious engineering reasons for preferring a scheme that requires minimal additional information in order to assign argument labels. Not only does this simplify the job of the grammar writer, but it makes it easier to construct lexical entries automatically and to integrate RMRSs derived from shallower systems. However, grammar engineers respond to consumers: if more detailed role labelling had a clear utility and required an analysis at the syntax level, we would want to do it in the grammar. The question is whether it is practically possible.

Detailed discussion of the linguistics literature would be out of place here. I will assume that Dowty (1991) is right in the assertion that there is no small (say, less than 10) set of role labels which can also be used to link the predicate to its arguments in compositionally constructed semantics (i.e., argument-indexing in Dowty's terminology) such that each role label can be given a consistent individual semantic interpretation. For our purposes, a consistent semantic interpretation involves entailment of one or more useful real world propositions (allowing for exceptions to the entailment for unusual individual sentences).

This is not a general argument against rich role labels in semantics, just their use as the means of argument-indexation. It leaves open uses for grammar-internal purposes, e.g., for defining and controlling alternations. The earliest versions of the ERG experimented with a version of Davis's (2001) approach to roles for such reasons: this was not continued, but for reasons irrelevant here. Roles are still routinely used for argument indexation in linguistics papers (without semantic interpretation). The case is sometimes made that more mnemonic argument labelling helps human interpretation of the notation. This may be true of semantics papers in linguistics, which tend to concern groups of similar lexemes. It is not true of a collaborative computational linguistics project in which broad coverage is being attempted: names

[5] ARG4 occurs very rarely, at least in English (the verb *bet* being perhaps the clearest case).

can only be mnemonic if they carry some meaning and if the meaning cannot be consistently applied this leads to endless trouble.

What I want to show here is how problems arise even when very limited semantic generalisations are attempted about the nature of just one or two argument labels, when used in broad-coverage grammars. Take the quite reasonable idea that a semantically consistent labelling for intransitives and related causatives is possible (cf PropBank). For instance, *water* might be associated with the same argument label in the following examples:

(1) Kim boiled the water.

(2) The water boiled.

Using (simplified) RMRS representations, this might amount to:

(3) l:a:boil_v(e), a:ARG1(k), a:ARG2(x), water(x)

(4) l:a:boil_v(e), a:ARG2(x), water(x)

Such an approach was used for a time in the ERG with unaccusatives. However, it turns out to be impossible to carry through consistently for causative alternations.

Consider the following examples of *gallop*: [6]

(5) Michaela galloped the horse to the far end of the meadow, ...

(6) With that Michaela nudged the horse with her heels and off the horse galloped.

(7) Michaela declared, "I shall call him Lightning because he runs as fast as lightning." And with that, off she galloped.

If only a single predicate is involved, e.g., gallop_v, and the causative has an ARG1 and an ARG2, then what about the two intransitive cases? If the causative is treated as obligatorily transitive syntactically, then (6) and (7) presumably both have an ARG2 subject. This leads to Michaela having a different role label in (5) and (7), despite the evident similarity of the real world situation. Furthermore, the role labels for intransitive movement verbs could only be predicted by a consumer of the semantics who knew whether or not a causative form existed. The causative may be rare, as with *gallop*, where the intransitive use is clearly the base case. Alternatively, if (7) is treated as a causative intransitive, and thus has a subject labelled ARG1, there is a systematic unresolvable ambiguity and the generalisation that the subjects in both intransitive sentences are moving is lost.

Gallop is an not isolated case in having a volitional intransitive use: it applies to most (if not all) motion verbs which undergo the causative alternation. To rescue this account, we would need to apply it only to true lexical anti-causatives. It is not clear whether this is doable (even the standard example *sink* can be used intransitively of deliberate movement) but from a slacker perspective, at this point we should decide to look for an easier approach.

The current ERG captures the causative relationship by using systematic sense labelling:

(8) Kim boiled the water.
l:a:boil_v_cause(e), a:ARG1(k), a:ARG2(x), water(x)

(9) The water boiled.
l:a:boil_v_1(e), a:ARG1(x), water(x)

This is not perfect, but it has clear advantages. It allows inferences to be made about ARG1 and ARG2 of _cause verbs. In general, inferences about arguments may be made with respect to particular verb classes. This lends itself to successive refinement in the grammars: the decision to add a standardised sense label, such as _cause, does not require changes to the type system, for instance. If we decide that we can identify true anti-causatives, we can easily make them a distinguished class via this convention. Conversely, in the situation where causation has not been recognised, and the verb has been treated as a single lexeme having an optional ARG2, the semantics is imperfect but at least the imperfection is local.

In fact, determining argument labelling by the obliqueness hierarchy still allows generalisations to be made for all verbs. Dowty (1991) argues for the notion of proto-agent (p-agt) and proto-patient (p-pat) as cluster concepts. Proto-agent properties include volitionality, sentience, causation of an event and movement relative to another participant. Proto-patient properties include being causally affected and being stationary relative to another participant. Dowty claims that generalisations about which arguments are lexicalised as subject, object and indirect object/oblique can be expressed in terms of relative numbers of p-agt and p-pat properties. If this is correct, then we can,

[6] http://www.thewestcoast.net/bobsnook/kid/horses.htm.

for example, predict that the ARG1 of any predicate in a DELPH-IN grammar will not have fewer p-agt properties than the ARG2 of that predicate.[7]

As an extreme alternative, we could use labels which were individual to each predicate, such as LIKER and LIKED (e.g., Pollard and Sag (1994)). For such role labels to have a consistent meaning, they would have to be lexeme-specific: e.g., LEAVER1 ('departer') versus LEAVER2 ('bequeather'). However this does nothing for semantic generalisation, blocks the use of argument labels in syntactic generalisations and leads to an extreme proliferation of lexical types when using typed feature structure formalisms (one type would be required per lexeme). The labels add no additional information and could trivially be added automatically to an RMRS if this were useful for human readers. Much more interesting is the use of richer lexical semantic generalisations, such as those employed in FrameNet (Baker et al., 1998). In principle, at least, we could (and should) systematically link the ERG to FrameNet, but this would be a form of semantic enrichment mediated via the SEM-I (cf Roa et al. (2008)), and not an alternative technique for argument indexation.

4 Dependency MRS

The second main topic I want to address is a form of semantic dependency structure (DMRS: see `wiki.delph-in.net` for the evolving details). There are good engineering reasons for producing a dependency style representation with links between predicates and no variables: ease of readability for consumers of the representation and for human annotators, parser comparison and integration with distributional lexical semantics being the immediate goals. Oepen has previously produced **elementary dependencies** from MRSs but the procedure (partially sketched in Oepen and Lønning (2006)) was not intended to produce complete representations. It turns out that a DMRS can be constructed which can be demonstrated to be interconvertible with RMRS, has a simple graph structure and minimises redundancy in the representation. What is surprising is that this can be done for a particular class of grammars without making use of the evident clues to syntax in the predicate names. The characteristic variable property discussed in §2 is crucial: its availability allows a partial replication of composition, with DMRS links being relatable to functor-argument combinations in the MRS algebra. I should emphasize that, unlike MRS and RMRS, DMRS is not intended to have a direct logical interpretation.

An example of a DMRS is given in Fig 2. Links relate nodes corresponding to RMRS predicates. Nodes have unique identifiers, not shown here. Directed link labels are of the form ARG/H, ARG/EQ or ARG/NEQ, where ARG corresponds to an RMRS argument label. H indicates a qeq relationship, EQ label equality and NEQ label inequality, as explained more fully below. Undirected /EQ arcs also sometimes occur (see §4.3). The ltop is indicated with a *.

4.1 RMRS-to-DMRS

In order to transform an RMRS into a DMRS, we will treat the RMRS as made up of three subgraphs:

Label equality graph. Each EP in an RMRS has a label, which may be shared with any number of other EPs. This can be captured in DMRS via a graph linking EPs: if this is done exhaustively, there would be $n(n-1)/2$ binary non-directional links. E.g., for the RMRS in Fig 1, we need to link _big_a_1, _angry_a_1 and _dog_n_1 and this takes 3 links. Obviously the effect of equality could be captured by a smaller number of links, assuming transitivity: but to make the RMRS-to-DMRS conversion deterministic, we need a method for selecting canonical links.

Hole-to-label qeq graph. A qeq in RMRS links a hole to a label which labels a set of EPs. There is thus a $1:1$ mapping between holes and labels which can be converted to a $1:n$ mapping between holes and the EPs which share the label. By taking the EP with the hole as the origin, we can construct an EP-to-EP graph, using the argument name as a label for the link: of course, such links are asymmetric and thus the graph is directed. e.g., _some_q has RSTR links to each of _big_a_1, _angry_a_1 and _dog_n_1. Reducing this to a $1:1$ mapping between EPs, which we would ideally like for DMRS, requires a canonical method of selecting a **head** EP from the set of target EPs (as does the selection of the ltop).

Variable graph. For the conversion to DMRS, we will rely on the characteristic variable prop-

[7] Sanfilippo (1990) originally introduced Dowty's ideas into computational linguistics, but this relative behaviour cannot be correctly expressed simply by using p-agt and p-pat directly for argument indexation as he suggested. It is incorrect for examples like (2) to be labelled as p-agt, since they have no agentive properties.

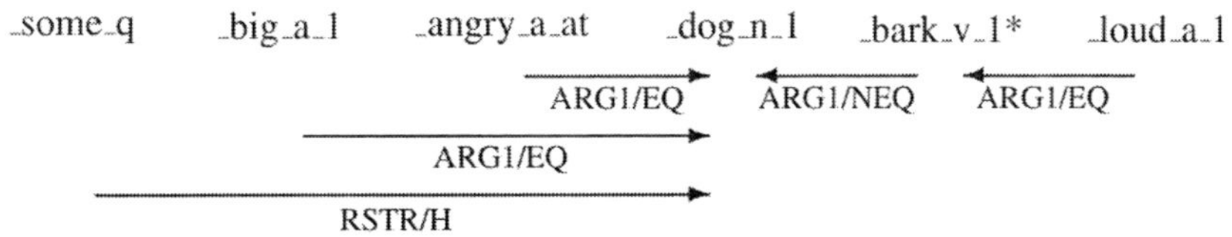

Figure 2: DMRS for 'Some big angry dogs bark loudly.'

erty, that every variable has a unique EP associated with it via its ARG0. Any non-hole argument of an EP will have a value which is the ARG0 of some other EP, or which is unbound (i.e., not found elsewhere in the RMRS) in which case we ignore it. Thus we can derive a graph between EPs, such that each link is labelled with an argument position and points to a unique EP. I will talk about an EP's 'argument EPs', to refer to the set of EPs its arguments point to in this graph.

The three EP graphs can be combined to form a dependency structure. But this has an excessive number of links due to the label equality and qeq components. We need deterministic techniques for removing the redundancy. These can utilise the variable graph, since this is already minimal.

The first strategy is to combine the label equality and variable links when they connect the same two EPs. For instance, we combine the ARG1 link between _big_a_1, and _dog_n_1 with the label equality link to give a link labelled ARG1/EQ. We then test the connectivity of the ARG/EQ links on the assumption of transitivity and remove any redundant links from the label graph. This usually removes all label equality links: one case where it does not is discussed in §4.3. Variable graph links with no corresponding label equality are annotated ARG/NEQ, while links arising from the qeq graph are labelled ARG/H. This retains sufficient information to allow the reconstruction of the three graphs in DMRS-to-RMRS conversion.

In order to reduce the number of links arising from the qeq graph, we make use of the variable graph to select a head from a set of EPs sharing a label. It is not essential that there should be a unique head, but it is desirable. The next section outlines how head selection works: despite not using any directly syntactic properties, it generally recovers the syntactic head.

4.2 Head selection in the qeq graph

Head selection uses one principle and one heuristic, both of which are motivated by the compositional properties of the grammar. The principle is that qeq links from an EP should parallel any comparable variable links. If an EP has two arguments, one of which is a variable argument which links to EP′ and the other a hole argument which has a value corresponding to a set of EPs including EP′, EP′ is chosen as the head of that set.

This essentially follows from the composition rules: in an algebra operation giving rise to a qeq, the argument phrase supplies a hook consisting of an index (normally, the ARG0 of the head EP) and an ltop (normally, the label of the head EP). Thus if a variable argument corresponds to EP′, EP′ will have been the head of the corresponding phrase and is thus the choice of head in the DMRS. This most frequently arises with quantifiers, which have both a BV and a RSTR argument: the RSTR argument can be taken as linking to the EP which has an ARG0 equal to the BV (i.e., the head of the N′). If this principle applies, it will select a unique head. In fact, in this special case, we drop the BV link from the final DMRS because it is entirely predictable from the RSTR link.

In the case where there is no variable argument, we use the heuristic which generally holds in DELPH-IN grammars that the EPs which we wish to distinguish as heads in the DMRS do not share labels with their DMRS argument EPs (in contrast to intersective modifiers, which always share labels with their argument EPs). Heads may share labels with PPs which are syntactically arguments, but these have a semantics like PP modifiers, where the head is the preposition's EP argument. NP arguments are generally quantified and quantifiers scope freely. AP, VP and S syntactic arguments are always scopal. PPs which are not modifier-like are either scopal (small clauses) or NP-like (case marking Ps) and free-scoping. Thus, somewhat counter-intuitively, we can select the head EP from the set of EPs which share a label by looking for an EP which has no argument EPs in that set.

4.3 Some properties of DMRS

The MRS-to-DMRS procedure deterministically creates a unique DMRS. A converse DMRS-to-MRS procedure recreates the MRS (up to label, anchor

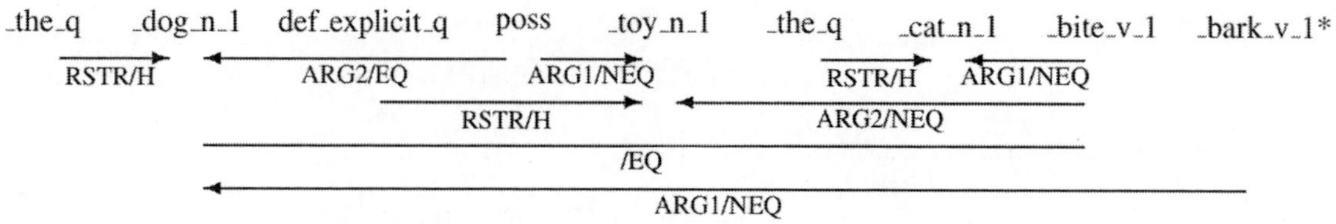

Figure 3: DMRS for 'The dog whose toy the cat bit barked.'

and variable renaming), though requiring the SEM-I to add the uninstantiated optional arguments.

I claimed above that DMRSs are an idealisation of semantic composition. A pure functor-argument application scheme would produce a tree which could be transformed into a structure where no dependent had more than one head. But in DMRS the notion of functor/head is more complex as determiners and modifiers provide slots in the RMRS algebra but not the index of the result. Composition of a verb (or any other functor) with an NP argument gives rise to a dependency between the verb and the head noun in the N′. The head noun provides the index of the NP's hook in composition, though it does not provide the ltop, which comes from the quantifier. However, because this ltop is not equated with any label, there is no direct link between the verb and the determiner. Thus the noun will have a link from the determiner and from the verb.

Similarly, if the constituents in composition were continuous, the adjacency condition would hold, but this does not apply because of the mechanisms for long-distance dependencies and the availability of the external argument in the hook.[8]

DMRS indirectly preserves the information about constituent structure which is essential for semantic interpretation, unlike some syntactic dependency schemes. In particular, it retains information about a quantifier's N′, since this forms the restrictor of the generalised quantifier (for instance *Most white cats are deaf* has different truth conditions from *Most deaf cats are white*). An interesting example of nominal modification is shown in Fig 3. Notice that *whose* has a decomposed semantics combining two non-lexeme predicates def_explicit_q and poss. Unusually, the relative clause has a gap which is not an argument of its semantic head (it's an argument of poss rather than bite_v_1). This means that when the relative clause is combined with the gap filler, the label equality and the argument instantiation correspond to different EPs. Thus there is a label equality which cannot be combined with an argument link and has to be represented by an undirected /EQ arc.

[8]Given that non-local effects are relatively circumscribed, it is possible to require adjacency in some parts of the DMRS. This leads to a technique for recording underspecification of noun compound bracketing, for instance.

5 Related work and conclusion

Hobbs (1985) described a philosophy of computational compositional semantics that is in some respects similar to that presented here. But, as far as I am aware, the Core Language Engine book (Alshawi, 1992) provided the first detailed description of a truly computational approach to compositional semantics: in any case, Steve Pulman provided my own introduction to the idea. Currently, the ParGram project also undertakes large-scale multilingual grammar engineering work: see Crouch and King (2006) and Crouch (2006) for an account of the semantic composition techniques now being used. I am not aware of any other current grammar engineering activities on the ParGram or DELPH-IN scale which build bidirectional grammars for multiple languages.

Overall, what I have tried to do here is to give a flavour of how compositional semantics and syntax interact in computational grammars. Analyses which look simple have often taken considerable experimentation to arrive at when working on a large-scale, especially when attempting cross-linguistic generalisations. The toy examples that can be given in papers like this one do no justice to this, and I would urge readers to try out the grammars and software and, perhaps, to join in.

Acknowledgements

Particular thanks to Emily Bender, Dan Flickinger and Alex Lascarides for detailed comments at very short notice! I am also grateful to many other colleagues, especially from DELPH-IN and in the Cambridge NLIP research group. This work was supported by the Engineering and Physical Sciences Research Council [grant numbers EP/C010035/1, EP/F012950/1].

References

Hiyan Alshawi, editor. 1992. *The Core Language Engine*. MIT Press.

Collin F. Baker, Charles J. Fillmore, and John B. Lowe. 1998. The Berkeley FrameNet project. In *Proc. ACL-98*, pages 86–90, Montreal, Quebec, Canada. Association for Computational Linguistics.

Emily Bender, Dan Flickinger, and Stephan Oepen. 2002. The Grammar Matrix: An open-source starter-kit for the rapid development of cross-linguistically consistent broad-coverage precision grammars. In *Proc. Workshop on Grammar Engineering and Evaluation, Coling 2002*, pages 8–14, Taipei, Taiwan.

Emily Bender. 2008. Evaluating a crosslinguistic grammar resource: A case study of Wambaya. In *Proc. ACL-08*, pages 977–985, Columbus, Ohio, USA.

John Carroll and Stephan Oepen. 2005. High efficiency realization for a wide-coverage unification grammar. In *Proc. IJCNLP05, Springer Lecture Notes in Artificial Intelligence, Volume 3651*, pages 165–176, Jeju Island, Korea.

John Carroll, Ann Copestake, Dan Flickinger, and Victor Poznanski. 1999. An efficient chart generator for (semi-)lexicalist grammars. In *Proc. 7th European Workshop on Natural Language Generation (EWNLG'99)*, pages 86–95, Toulouse.

Ann Copestake, Alex Lascarides, and Dan Flickinger. 2001. An algebra for semantic construction in constraint-based grammars. In *Proc. ACL-01*, Toulouse.

Ann Copestake, Dan Flickinger, Ivan A. Sag, and Carl Pollard. 2005. Minimal Recursion Semantics: an introduction. *Research on Language and Computation*, 3(2-3):281–332.

Ann Copestake. 2003. Report on the design of RMRS. DeepThought project deliverable.

Ann Copestake. 2007a. Applying robust semantics. In *Proc. PACLING 2007 — 10th Conference of the Pacific Association for Computational Linguistics*, pages 1–12, Melbourne.

Ann Copestake. 2007b. Semantic composition with (Robust) Minimal Recursion Semantics. In *Proc. Workshop on Deep Linguistic Processing, ACL 2007*, Prague.

Dick Crouch and Tracy Holloway King. 2006. Semantics via F-structure rewriting. In Miriam Butt and Tracy Holloway King, editors, *Proc. LFG06 Conference*, Universitat Konstanz. CSLI Publications.

Dick Crouch. 2006. Packed rewriting for mapping semantics and KR. In *Intelligent Linguistic Architectures Variations on Themes by Ronald M. Kaplan*, pages 389–416. CSLI Publications.

Anthony Davis. 2001. *Linking by Types in the Hierarchical Lexicon*. CSLI Publications.

David Dowty. 1991. Thematic proto-roles and argument selection. *Language*, 67(3):547–619.

Dan Flickinger and Emily Bender. 2003. Compositional semantics in a multilingual grammar resource. In *Proc. Workshop on Ideas and Strategies for Multilingual Grammar Development, ESSLLI 2003*, pages 33–42, Vienna.

Dan Flickinger, Emily Bender, and Stephan Oepen. 2003. MRS in the LinGO Grammar Matrix: A practical user's guide. http://tinyurl.com/crf5z7.

Dan Flickinger, Jan Tore Lønning, Helge Dyvik, Stephan Oepen, and Francis Bond. 2005. SEM-I rational MT — enriching deep grammars with a semantic interface for scalable machine translation. In *Proc. MT Summit X*, Phuket, Thailand.

Dan Flickinger. 2000. On building a more efficient grammar by exploiting types. *Natural Language Engineering*, 6(1):15–28.

Sanae Fujita, Francis Bond, Stephan Oepen, and Takaaki Tanaka. 2007. Exploiting semantic information for HPSG parse selection. In *Proc. Workshop on Deep Linguistic Processing, ACL 2007*, Prague.

Jerry Hobbs. 1985. Ontological promiscuity. In *Proc. ACL-85*, pages 61–69, Chicago, IL.

Alexander Koller and Alex Lascarides. 2009. A logic of semantic representations for shallow parsing. In *Proc. EACL-2009*, Athens.

Stephan Oepen and Jan Tore Lønning. 2006. Discriminant-based MRS banking. In *Proc. LREC-2006*, Genoa, Italy.

Martha Palmer, Dan Gildea, and Paul Kingsbury. 2005. The Proposition Bank: A corpus annotated with semantic roles. *Computational Linguistics*, 31(1).

Carl Pollard and Ivan Sag. 1994. *Head-driven Phrase Structure Grammar*. University of Chicago Press, Chicago.

Sergio Roa, Valia Kordoni, and Yi Zhang. 2008. Mapping between compositional semantic representations and lexical semantic resources: Towards accurate deep semantic parsing. In *Proc. ACL-08*, pages 189–192, Columbus, Ohio. Association for Computational Linguistics.

Antonio Sanfilippo. 1990. *Grammatical Relations, Thematic Roles and Verb Semantics*. Ph.D. thesis, Centre for Cognitive Science, University of Edinburgh.

Stefan Thater. 2007. *Minimal Recursion Semantics as Dominance Constraints: Graph-Theoretic Foundation and Application to Grammar Engineering*. Ph.D. thesis, Universität des Saarlandes.

NLP and the humanities: the revival of an old liaison

Franciska de Jong
University of Twente
Enschede, The Netherlands
fdejong@ewi.utwente.nl

Abstract

This paper present an overview of some emerging trends in the application of NLP in the domain of the so-called Digital Humanities and discusses the role and nature of metadata, the annotation layer that is so characteristic of documents that play a role in the scholarly practises of the humanities. It is explained how metadata are the key to the added value of techniques such as text and link mining, and an outline is given of what measures could be taken to increase the chances for a bright future for the old ties between NLP and the humanities. There is no data like metadata!

1 Introduction

The humanities and the field of natural language processing (NLP) have always had common playgrounds. The liaison was never constrained to linguistics; also philosophical, philological and literary studies have had their impact on NLP , and there have always been dedicated conferences and journals for the humanities and the NLP community of which the journal Computers and the Humanities (1966-2004) is probably known best. Among the early ideas on how to use machines to do things with text that had been done manually for ages is the plan to build a concordance for ancient literature, such as the works of St Thomas Aquinas (Schreibman et al., 2004). which was expressed already in the late 1940s. Later on humanities researchers started thinking about novel tasks for machines, things that were not feasible without the power of computers, such as authorship discovery. For NLP the units of processing gradually became more complex and shifted from the character level to units for which string processing is an insufficient basis. At some stage syntactic parsers and generators were seen as a method to prove the correctness of linguistic theories. Nowadays semantic layers can be analysed at much more complex levels of granularity. Not just phrases and sentences are processed, but also entire documents or even document collections including those involving multimodal features. And in addition to NLP for information carriers, also language-based interaction has grown into a matured field, and applications in other domains than the humanities now seem more dominant. The impact of the wide range of functionalities that involve NLP in all kinds of information processing tasks is beyond what could be imagined 60 years ago and has given rise to the outreach of NLP in many domains, but during a long period the humanities were one of the few valuable playgrounds.

Even though the humanities have been able to conduct NLP-empowered research that would have been impossible without the the early tools and resources already for many decades, the more recent introduction of statistical methods in langauge is affecting research practises in the humanities at yet another scale. An important explanation for this development is of course the wide scale digitisation that is taken up in the humanities. All kinds of initiatives for converting analogue resources into data sets that can be stored in digital repositories have been initiated. It is widely known that "*There is no data like more data*" (Mercer, 1985), and indeed the volumes of digital humanities resources have reached the level required for adequate performance of all kinds of tasks that require the training of statistical models. In addition, ICT-enabled methodologies and types of collaboration are being developed and have given rise to new epistemic cultures. Digital Humanities (sometimes also referred to as Computational Humanities) are a trend, and digital scholarship seems a prerequisite for a successful research career. But in itself the growth of digi-

Proceedings of the 12th Conference of the European Chapter of the ACL, pages 10–15,
Athens, Greece, 30 March – 3 April 2009.

tal resources is not the main factor that makes the humanities again a good testbed for NLP. A key aspect is the nature and role of metadata in the humanities. In the next section the role of metadata in the humanities and the the ways in which they can facilitate and enhance the application of text and data mining tools will be described in more detail. The paper takes the position that for the humanities a variant of Mercer's saying is even more true. *There is no data like metadata*!

The relation between NLP and the humanities is worth reviewing, as a closer look into the way in which techniques such as text and link mining can demonstrate that the potential for mutual impact has gained in strength and diversity, and that important lessons can be learned for other application areas than the humanities. This renewed liaison with the now digital humanities can help NLP to set up an innovative research agenda which covers a wide range of topics including semantic analysis, integration of multimodal information, language-based interaction, performance evaluation, service models, and usability studies. The further and combined exploration of these topics will help to develop an infrastructure that will also allow content and data-driven research domains in the humanities to renew their field and to exploit the additional potential coming from the ongoing and future digitisation efforts, as well as the richness in terms of available metadata. To name a few fields of scholarly research: art history, media studies, oral history, archeology, archiving studies, they all have needs that can be served in novel ways by the mature branches that NLP offers today. After a sketch in section 2 of the role of metadata, so crucial for the interaction between the humanities and NLP, a rough overview of relevant initiatives will be given. Inspired by some telling examples, it will be outlined what could be done to increase the chances for a bright future for the old ties, and how other domains can benefit as well from the reinvention of the old common playground between NLP and the humanities.

2 Metadata in the Humanities

Digital text, but also multimedia content, can be mined for the occurrence of patterns at all kinds of layers, and based on techniques for information extraction and classification, documents can be annotated automatically with a variety of labels, including indications of topic, event types, authorship, stylistics, etc. Automatically generated annotations can be exploited to support to what is often called the semantic access to content, which is typically seen as more powerful than plain full text search, but in principle also includes conceptual search and navigation.

The data used in research in the domain of the humanities comes from a variety of sources: archives, musea (or in general cultural heritage collections), libraries, etc. As a testbed for NLP these collections are particularly challenging because of the combination of complexity increasing features, such as language and spelling change over time, diversity in orthography, noisy content (due to errors introduced during data conversion, e.g., OCR or transcription of spoken word material), wider than average stylistic variation and cross-lingual and cross-media links. They are also particularly attractive because of the available metadata or annotation records, which are the reflection of analytical and comparative scholarly processes. In addition, there is a wide diversity of annotation types to be found in the domain (cf. the annotation dimensions distinguished by (Marshall, 1998)), and the field has developed modelling procedures to exploit this diversity (McCarty, 2005) and visualisation tools (Unsworth, 2005).

2.1 Metadata for Text

For many types of textual data automatically generated annotations are the sole basis for semantic search, navigation and mining. For humanities and cultural heritage collections, automatically generated annotation is often an addition to the catalogue information traditionally produced by experts in the field. The latter kind of manually produced metadataa is often specified in accordance to controlled key word lists and metadata schemata agreed for the domain. NLP tagging is then an add on to a semantic layer that in itself can already be very rich and of high quality. More recently initiatives and support tools for so-called social tagging have been proposed that can in principle circumvent the costly annotation by experts, and that could be either based on free text annotation or on the application of so-called folksonomies as a replacement for the traditional taxonomies. Digital librarians have initiated the development of platforms aiming at the integration of the various annotation processes and at sharing tools that can help to realise an infrastructure for distributed annotation. But whatever the genesis is of annotations capturing the semantics of an entire document, they are a very valuable source for the training of automatic classifiers. And traditionally, textual resources in the humanities have lots of it, partly because the mere art of annotating texts has been invented in this domain.

2.2 Metadata for Multimedia

Part of the resources used as basis for scholarly research is non-textual. Apart from numeric data resources, which are typically strongly structured in database-like environments, there is a growing amount of audiovisual material that is of interest to humanities researchers. Various kinds of multimedia collections can be a primary source of information for humanities researchers, in particular if there is a substantial amount of spoken word content, e.g., broadcast news archives, and even more prominently: oral history collections.

It is commonly agreed that accessibility of heterogeneous audiovisual archives can be boosted by indexing not just via the classical metadata, but by enhancing indexing mechanisms through the exploitation of the spoken audio. For several types of audiovisual data, transcription of the speech segments can be a good basis for a time-coded index. Research has shown that the quality of the automatically generated speech transcriptions, and as a consequence also the index quality, can increase if the language models applied have been optimised to both the available metadata (in particular on the named entities in the annotations) *and* the collateral sources available (Huijbregts et al., 2007). 'Collateral data is the term used for secondary information objects that relate to the primary documents, e.g., reviews, program guide summaries, biographies, all kinds of textual publications, etc. This requires that primary sources have been annotated with links to these secondary materials. These links can be pointers to source locations *within the collection*, but also links to related documents from *external sources*. In laboratory settings the amount of collateral data is typically scarce, but in real life spoken word archives, experts are available to identify and collect related (textual) content that can help to turn generic language models into domain specific models with higher accuracy.

2.3 Metadata for Surprise Data

The quality of automatically generated content annotations in real life settings is lagging behind in comparison to experimental settings. This is of course an obstacle for the uptake of technology, but a number of pilot projects with collections from the humanities domain show us what can be done to overcome the obstacles. This can be illustrated again with the situation in the field of spoken document retrieval.

For many A/V collections with a spoken audio track, metadata is not or only sparsely available, which is why this type of collection is often only searchable by linear exploration. Although there is common agreement that speech-based, automatically generated annotation of audiovisual archives may boost the semantic access to fragments of spoken word archives enormously (Goldman et al., 2005; Garofolo et al., 2000; Smeaton et al., 2006), success stories for real life archives are scarce. (Exceptions can be found in research projects in the broadcast news and cultural heritage domains, such as MALACH (Byrne et al., 2004), and systems such as SpeechFind (Hansen et al., 2005).) In lab conditions the focus is usually on data that (i) have well-known characteristics (e.g, news content), often learned along with annual benchmark evaluations,[1] (ii) form a relatively homogeneous collection, (iii) are based on tasks that hardly match the needs of real users, and (iv) are annotated in large quantities for training purposes. In real life however, the exact characteristics of archival data are often unknown, and are far more heterogeneous in nature than those found in laboratory settings. Language models for realistic audio sets, sometimes referred to as *surprise data* (Huijbregts, 2008), can benefit from a clever use of this contextual information.

Surprise data sets are increasingly being taken into account in research agendas in the field focusing on multimedia indexing and search (de Jong et al., 2008). In addition to the fact that they are less homogenous, and may come with links to related documents, real user needs may be available from query logs, and as a consequence they are an interesting challenge for cross-media indexing strategies targeting aggregated collections. Sur-

[1]E.g., evaluation activities such as those organised by NIST, the National Institute of Standards, e.g., TREC for search tasks involving text, TRECVID for video search, Rich Transcription for the analysis of speech data, etc. `http://www.nist.gov/`

prise data are therefore an ideal source for the development of best practises for the application of tools for exploiting collateral content and metadata. The exploitation of available contextual information for surprise content and the organisation of this dual annotation process can be improved, but in principle joining forces between NLP technologies and the capacity of human annotators is attractive. On the one hand for the improved access to the content, on the other hand for an innovation of the NLP research agenda.

3 Ingredients for a Novel Knowledge-driven Workflow

A crucial condition for the revival of the common playground for NLP and the humanities is the availability of representatives of communities that could use the outcome, either in the development of services to their users or as end users. These representatives may be as diverse and include e.g., archivists, scholars with a research interest in a collection, collection keepers in libraries and musea, developers of educational materials, but in spite of the divergence that can be attributed to such groups, they have a few important characteristics in common: they have a deep understanding of the structure, semantic layers and content of collections, and in developing new road maps and novel ways of working, the pressure they encounter to be cost-effective is modest. They are the first to understand that the technical solutions and business models of the popular web search engines are not directly applicable to their domain in which the workflow is typically knowledge-driven and labour-intensive. Though with the introduction of new technologies the traditional role of documentalists as the primary source of high quality annotations may change, the availability of their expertise is likely to remain one of the major success factors in the realisation of a digital infrastructure that is as rich source as the repositories from the analogue era used to be.

All kinds of coordination bodies and action plans exist to further the field of Digital Humanities, among which The Alliance of Digital Humanities Organizations `http://www.digitalhumanities.org/` and HASTAC (`https://www.hastac.org/`) and Digital Arts an Humanities `www.arts-humanities.net`, and dedicated journals and events have emerged, such as the LaTeCH workshop series. In part they can build on results of initiatives for collaboration and harmonisation that were started earlier, e.g., as Digital Libraries support actions or as coordinated actions for the international community of cultural heritage institutions. But in order to reinforce the liaison between NLP and the humanities continued attention, support and funding is needed for the following:

Coordination of coherent platforms (both local and international) for the interaction between the communities involved that stimulate the exchange of expertise, tools, experience and guidelines. Good examples hereof exist already in several domains, e.g., the field of broadcast archiving (IST project PrestoSpace; `www.prestospace.org/`), the research area of Oral History, all kinds of communities and platforms targeting the accessibility of cultural heritage collections (e.g., CATCH; `http://www.nwo.nl/catch`), but the long-term sustainability of accessible interoperable institutional networks remains a concern.

Infrastructural facilities for the support of researchers and developers of NLP tools; such facilities should support them in finetuning the instruments they develop to the needs of scholarly research. CLARIN (`http://www.clarin.eu/`) is a promising initiative in the EU context that is aiming to cover exactly this (and more) for the social sciences and the humanities.

Open access, source and standards to increase the chances for inter-institutional collaboration and exchange of content and tools in accordance with the policies of the *de facto* leading bodies, such as TEI (`http://www.tei-c.org/`) and OAI (`http://www.openarchives.org/`).

Metadata schemata that can accommodate NLP-specific features:

- automatically generated labels and summaries
- reliability scores
- indications of the suitability of items for training purposes

Exchange mechanisms for best practices e.g., of building and updating training data, the use of annotation tools and the analysis of query logs.

Protocols and tools for the mark-up of content, the specification of links between collections, the handling of IPR and privacy issues, etc.

Service centers that can offer heavy processing facilities (e.g. named entity extraction or speech transcription) for collections kept in technically modestly equipped environments hereof.

User Interfaces that can flexibly meet the needs of scholarly users for expressing their information needs, and for visualising relationships between interactive information elements (e.g., timelines and maps).

Pilot projects in which researchers from various backgrounds collaborate in analysing a specific digital resource as a central object in order to learn to understand how the interfaces between their fields can be opened up. An interesting example is the the project Veteran Tapes (`http://www.surffoundation.nl/smartsite.dws?id=14040`). This initiative is linked to the interview collection which is emerging as a result for the Dutch Veterans Interview-project, which aims at collecting 1000 interviews with a representative group of veterans of all conflicts and peace-missions in which The Netherlands were involved. The research results will be integrated in a web-based fashion to form what is called an *enriched publication*.

Evaluation frameworks that will trigger contributions to the enhancement en tuning of what NLP has to offer to the needs of the humanities. These frameworks should include benchmarks addressing tasks and user needs that are more realistic than most of the existing performance evaluation frameworks. This will require close collaboration between NLP developers and scholars.

4 Conclusion

The assumption behind presenting these issues as priorities is that NLP-empowered use of digital content by humanities scholars will be beneficial to both communities. NLP can use the testbed of the Digital Humanities for the further shaping of that part of the research agenda that covers the role of NLP in information handling, and in particular those avenues that fall under the concept of mining. By focussing on the integration of metadata in the models underlying the mining tools and searching for ways to increase the involvement of metadata generators, both experts and 'amateurs', important insights are likely to emerge that could help to shape agendas for the role of NLP in other disciplines. Examples are the role of NLP in the study of recorded meeting content, in the field of social studies, or the organisation and support of tagging communities in the biomedical domain, both areas where manual annotation by experts used to be common practise, and both areas where mining could be done with aggregated collections.

Equally important are the benefits for the humanities. The added value of metadata-based mining technology for enhanced indexing is not so much in the cost-reduction as in the wider usability of the materials, and in the impulse this may bring for sharing collections that otherwise would too easily be considered as of no general importance. Furthermore the evolution of digital texts from 'book surrogates' towards the rich semantic layers and networks generated by text and/or media mining tools that take all available metadata into account should help the fields involved in not just answering their research questions more efficiently, but also in opening up grey literature for research purposes and in scheduling entirely new questions for which the availability of such networks are a *conditio sine qua non*.

Acknowledgments

Part of what is presented in this paper has been inspired by collaborative work with colleagues. In particular I would like to thank Willemijn Heeren, Roeland Ordelman and Stef Scagliola for their role in the genesis of ideas and insights.

References

W. Byrne, D.Doermann, M. Franz, S. Gustman, J. Hajic, D. Oard, M. Picheny, J. Psutka, B. Ramabhadran, D. Soergel, T. Ward, and W-J. Zhu. 2004. Automatic recognition of spontaneous speech for access to multilingual oral history archives. *IEEE Transactions on Speech and Audio Processing*, 12(4).

F. M. G. de Jong, D. W. Oard, W. F. L. Heeren, and R. J. F. Ordelman. 2008. Access to recorded interviews: A research agenda. *ACM Journal on Computing and Cultural Heritage (JOCCH)*, 1(1):3:1–3:27, June.

J.S. Garofolo, C.G.P. Auzanne, and E.M Voorhees. 2000. The TREC SDR Track: A Success Story. In *8th Text Retrieval Conference*, pages 107–129, Washington.

J. Goldman, S. Renals, S. Bird, F. M. G. de Jong, M. Federico, C. Fleischhauer, M. Kornbluh, L. Lamel, D. W. Oard, C. Stewart, and R. Wright. 2005. Accessing the spoken word. *International Journal on Digital Libraries*, 5(4):287–298.

J.H.L. Hansen, R. Huang, B. Zhou, M. Deadle, J.R. Deller, A. R. Gurijala, M. Kurimo, and P. Angkititrakul. 2005. Speechfind: Advances in spoken document retrieval for a national gallery of the spoken word. *IEEE Transactions on Speech and Audio Processing*, 13(5):712–730.

M.A.H. Huijbregts, R.J.F. Ordelman, and F.M.G. de Jong. 2007. Annotation of heterogeneous multimedia content using automatic speech recognition. In *Proceedings of SAMT 2007*, volume 4816 of *Lecture Notes in Computer Science*, pages 78–90, Berlin. Springer Verlag.

M.A.H. Huijbregts. 2008. *Segmentation, Diarization and Speech Transcription: Surprise Data Unraveled*. Phd thesis, University of Twente.

C. Marshall. 1998. Toward an ecology of hypertext annotation. In *Proceedings of the ninth ACM conference on Hypertext and hypermedia : links, objects, time and space—structure in hypermedia systems (HYPERTEXT '98)*, pages 40–49, Pittsburgh, Pennsylvania.

W. McCarty. 2005. *Humanities Computing*. Basingstoke, Palgrave Macmillan.

S. Schreibman, R. Siemens, and J. Unsworth (eds.). 2004. *A Companion to Digital Humanities*. Blackwell.

A.F. Smeaton, P. Over, and W. Kraaij. 2006. Evaluation campaigns and trecvid. In *8th ACM SIGMM International Workshop on Multimedia Information Retrieval (MIR2006)*.

J. Unsworth. 2005. *New Methods for Humanities Research. The 2005 Lyman Award Lecture*. National Humanities Center, NC.

On the use of Comparable Corpora to improve SMT performance

Sadaf Abdul-Rauf and **Holger Schwenk**
LIUM, University of Le Mans, FRANCE
Sadaf.Abdul-Rauf@lium.univ-lemans.fr

Abstract

We present a simple and effective method for extracting parallel sentences from comparable corpora. We employ a statistical machine translation (SMT) system built from small amounts of parallel texts to translate the source side of the non-parallel corpus. The target side texts are used, along with other corpora, in the language model of this SMT system. We then use information retrieval techniques and simple filters to create French/English parallel data from a comparable news corpora. We evaluate the quality of the extracted data by showing that it significantly improves the performance of an SMT systems.

1 Introduction

Parallel corpora have proved be an indispensable resource in Statistical Machine Translation (SMT). A parallel corpus, also called bitext, consists in bilingual texts aligned at the sentence level. They have also proved to be useful in a range of natural language processing applications like automatic lexical acquisition, cross language information retrieval and annotation projection.

Unfortunately, parallel corpora are a limited resource, with insufficient coverage of many language pairs and application domains of interest. The performance of an SMT system heavily depends on the parallel corpus used for training. Generally, more bitexts lead to better performance. Current resources of parallel corpora cover few language pairs and mostly come from one domain (proceedings of the Canadian or European Parliament, or of the United Nations). This becomes specifically problematic when SMT systems trained on such corpora are used for general translations, as the language jargon heavily used in these corpora is not appropriate for everyday life translations or translations in some other domain.

One option to increase this scarce resource could be to produce more human translations, but this is a very expensive option, in terms of both time and money. In recent work less expensive but very productive methods of creating such sentence aligned bilingual corpora were proposed. These are based on generating "parallel" texts from already available "almost parallel" or "not much parallel" texts. The term "comparable corpus" is often used to define such texts.

A comparable corpus is a collection of texts composed independently in the respective languages and combined on the basis of similarity of content (Yang and Li, 2003). The raw material for comparable documents is often easy to obtain but the alignment of individual documents is a challenging task (Oard, 1997). Multilingual news reporting agencies like AFP, Xinghua, Reuters, CNN, BBC etc. serve to be reliable producers of huge collections of such comparable corpora. Such texts are widely available from LDC, in particular the Gigaword corpora, or over the WEB for many languages and domains, e.g. Wikipedia. They often contain many sentences that are reasonable translations of each other, thus potential parallel sentences to be identified and extracted.

There has been considerable amount of work on bilingual comparable corpora to learn word translations as well as discovering parallel sentences. Yang and Lee (2003) use an approach based on dynamic programming to identify potential parallel sentences in title pairs. Longest common sub sequence, edit operations and match-based score functions are subsequently used to determine confidence scores. Resnik and Smith (2003) propose their STRAND web-mining based system and show that their approach is able to find large numbers of similar document pairs.

Works aimed at discovering parallel sentences

Proceedings of the 12th Conference of the European Chapter of the ACL, pages 16–23,
Athens, Greece, 30 March – 3 April 2009. ©2009 Association for Computational Linguistics

French: *Au total, 1,634 million d'électeurs doivent désigner les 90 députés de la prochaine législature parmi 1.390 candidats présentés par 17 partis, dont huit sont représentés au parlement.*
Query: *In total, 1,634 million voters will designate the 90 members of the next parliament among 1.390 candidates presented by 17 parties, eight of which are represented in parliament.*
Result: *Some 1.6 million voters were registered to elect the 90 members of the legislature from 1,390 candidates from 17 parties, eight of which are represented in parliament,* ***several civilian organisations and independent lists.***

French: *"Notre implication en Irak rend possible que d'autres pays membres de l'Otan, comme l'Allemagne par exemple, envoient un plus gros contingent" en Afghanistan, a estimé M.Belka au cours d'une conférence de presse.*
Query: *"Our involvement in Iraq makes it possible that other countries members of NATO, such as Germany, for example, send a larger contingent in Afghanistan, "said Mr.Belka during a press conference.*
Result: *"Our involvement in Iraq makes it possible for other NATO members, like Germany for example, to send troops, to send a bigger contingent to your country, "Belka said at a press conference,* ***with Afghan President Hamid Karzai.***

French: *De son côté, Mme Nicola Duckworth, directrice d'Amnesty International pour l'Europe et l'Asie centrale, a déclaré que les ONG demanderaient à M.Poutine de mettre fin aux violations des droits de l'Homme dans le Caucase du nord.*
Query: *For its part, Mrs Nicole Duckworth, director of Amnesty International for Europe and Central Asia, said that NGOs were asking Mr Putin to put an end to human rights violations in the northern Caucasus.*
Result: *Nicola Duckworth, head of Amnesty International's Europe and Central Asia department, said the non-governmental organisations (NGOs) would call on Putin to put an end to human rights abuses in the North Caucasus,* ***including the war-torn province of Chechnya.***

Figure 1: Some examples of a French source sentence, the SMT translation used as query and the potential parallel sentence as determined by information retrieval. Bold parts are the extra tails at the end of the sentences which we automatically removed.

include (Utiyama and Isahara, 2003), who use cross-language information retrieval techniques and dynamic programming to extract sentences from an English-Japanese comparable corpus. They identify similar article pairs, and then, treating these pairs as parallel texts, align their sentences on a sentence pair similarity score and use DP to find the least-cost alignment over the document pair. Fung and Cheung (2004) approach the problem by using a cosine similarity measure to match foreign and English documents. They work on "very non-parallel corpora". They then generate all possible sentence pairs and select the best ones based on a threshold on cosine similarity scores. Using the extracted sentences they learn a dictionary and iterate over with more sentence pairs. Recent work by Munteanu and Marcu (2005) uses a bilingual lexicon to translate some of the words of the source sentence. These translations are then used to query the database to find matching translations using information retrieval (IR) techniques. Candidate sentences are determined based on word overlap and the decision whether a sentence pair is parallel or not is performed by a maximum entropy classifier trained on parallel sentences. Bootstrapping is used and the size of the learned bilingual dictionary is increased over iterations to get better results.

Our technique is similar to that of (Munteanu and Marcu, 2005) but we bypass the need of the bilingual dictionary by using proper SMT translations and instead of a maximum entropy classifier we use simple measures like the word error rate (WER) and the translation error rate (TER) to decide whether sentences are parallel or not. Using the full SMT sentences, we get an added advantage of being able to detect one of the major errors of this technique, also identified by (Munteanu and Marcu, 2005), i.e, the cases where the initial sentences are identical but the retrieved sentence has a tail of extra words at sentence end. We try to counter this problem as detailed in 4.1.

We apply this technique to create a parallel corpus for the French/English language pair using the LDC Gigaword comparable corpus. We show that we achieve significant improvements in the BLEU score by adding our extracted corpus to the already available human-translated corpora.

This paper is organized as follows. In the next section we first describe the baseline SMT system trained on human-provided translations only. We then proceed by explaining our parallel sentence selection scheme and the post-processing. Section 4 summarizes our experimental results and the paper concludes with a discussion and perspectives of this work.

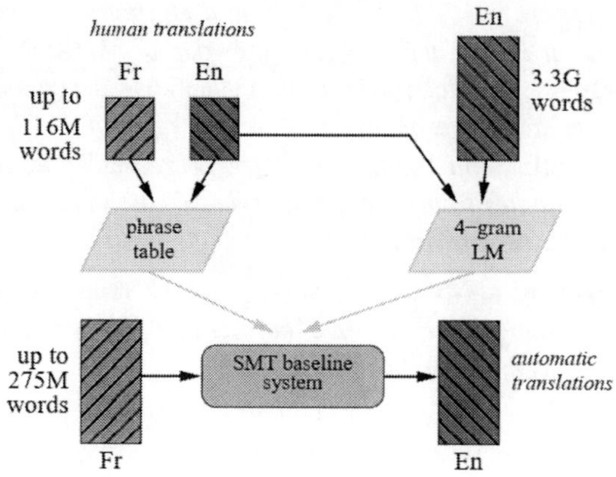

Figure 2: Using an SMT system used to translate large amounts of monolingual data.

2 Baseline SMT system

The goal of SMT is to produce a target sentence e from a source sentence f. Among all possible target language sentences the one with the highest probability is chosen:

$$e^* = \arg\max_e \Pr(e|f) \quad (1)$$
$$= \arg\max_e \Pr(f|e)\Pr(e) \quad (2)$$

where $\Pr(f|e)$ is the translation model and $\Pr(e)$ is the target language model (LM). This approach is usually referred to as the *noisy source-channel* approach in SMT (Brown et al., 1993). Bilingual corpora are needed to train the translation model and monolingual texts to train the target language model.

It is today common practice to use phrases as translation units (Koehn et al., 2003; Och and Ney, 2003) instead of the original word-based approach. A phrase is defined as a group of source words $\tilde{f}$ that should be translated together into a group of target words $\tilde{e}$. The translation model in phrase-based systems includes the phrase translation probabilities in both directions, i.e. $P(\tilde{e}|\tilde{f})$ and $P(\tilde{f}|\tilde{e})$. The use of a maximum entropy approach simplifies the introduction of several additional models explaining the translation process :

$$e^* = \arg\max Pr(e|f)$$
$$= \arg\max_e \{exp(\sum_i \lambda_i h_i(e,f))\} \quad (3)$$

The feature functions h_i are the system models and the λ_i weights are typically optimized to maximize a scoring function on a development set (Och and Ney, 2002). In our system fourteen features functions were used, namely phrase and lexical translation probabilities in both directions, seven features for the lexicalized distortion model, a word and a phrase penalty, and a target language model.

The system is based on the Moses SMT toolkit (Koehn et al., 2007) and constructed as follows. First, Giza++ is used to perform word alignments in both directions. Second, phrases and lexical reorderings are extracted using the default settings of the Moses SMT toolkit. The 4-gram back-off target LM is trained on the English part of the bitexts and the Gigaword corpus of about 3.2 billion words. Therefore, it is likely that the target language model includes at least some of the translations of the French Gigaword corpus. We argue that this is a key factor to obtain good quality translations. The translation model was trained on the news-commentary corpus (1.56M words)[1] and a bilingual dictionary of about 500k entries.[2] This system uses only a limited amount of human-translated parallel texts, in comparison to the bitexts that are available in NIST evaluations. In a different versions of this system, the Europarl (40M words) and the Canadian Hansard corpus (72M words) were added.

In the framework of the EuroMatrix project, a test set of general news data was provided for the shared translation task of the third workshop on

[1] Available at `http://www.statmt.org/wmt08/shared-task.html`

[2] The different conjugations of a verb and the singular and plural form of adjectives and nouns are counted as multiple entries.

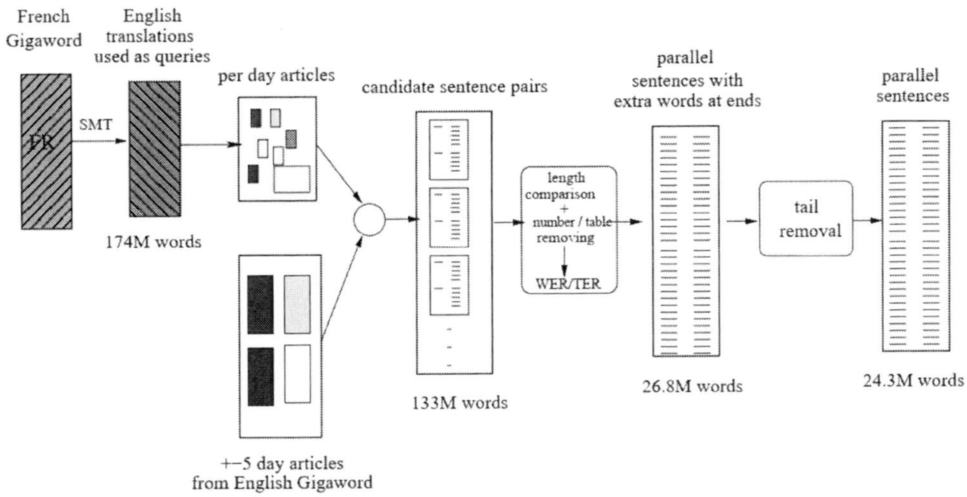

Figure 3: Architecture of the parallel sentence extraction system.

SMT (Callison-Burch et al., 2008), called *newstest2008* in the following. The size of this corpus amounts to 2051 lines and about 44 thousand words. This data was randomly split into two parts for development and testing. Note that only one reference translation is available. We also noticed several spelling errors in the French source texts, mainly missing accents. These were mostly automatically corrected using the Linux spell checker. This increased the BLEU score by about 1 BLEU point in comparison to the results reported in the official evaluation (Callison-Burch et al., 2008). The system tuned on this development data is used translate large amounts of text of French Gigaword corpus (see Figure 2). These translations will be then used to detect potential parallel sentences in the English Gigaword corpus.

3 System Architecture

The general architecture of our parallel sentence extraction system is shown in figure 3. Starting from comparable corpora for the two languages, French and English, we propose to translate French to English using an SMT system as described above. These translated texts are then used to perform information retrieval from the English corpus, followed by simple metrics like WER and TER to filter out good sentence pairs and eventually generate a parallel corpus. We show that a parallel corpus obtained using this technique helps considerably to improve an SMT system.

We shall also be trying to answer the following question over the course of this study: do we need to use the best possible SMT systems to be able to retrieve the correct parallel sentences or any ordinary SMT system will serve the purpose ?

3.1 System for Extracting Parallel Sentences from Comparable Corpora

LDC provides large collections of texts from multilingual news reporting agencies. We identified agencies that provided news feeds for the languages of our interest and chose AFP for our study.[3]

We start by translating the French AFP texts to English using the SMT systems discussed in section 2. In our experiments we considered only the most recent texts (2002-2006, 5.5M sentences; about 217M French words). These translations are then treated as queries for the IR process. The design of our sentence extraction process is based on the heuristic that considering the corpus at hand, we can safely say that a news item reported on day X in the French corpus will be most probably found in the day X-5 and day X+5 time period. We experimented with several window sizes and found the window size of ±5 days to be the most accurate in terms of time and the quality of the retrieved sentences.

Using the ID and date information for each sentence of both corpora, we first collect all sentences from the SMT translations corresponding to the same day (query sentences) and then the corresponding articles from the English Gigaword cor-

[3]LDC corpora LDC2007T07 (English) and LDC2006T17 (French).

pus (search space for IR). These day-specific files are then used for information retrieval using a robust information retrieval system. The Lemur IR toolkit (Ogilvie and Callan, 2001) was used for sentence extraction. The top 5 scoring sentences are returned by the IR process. We found no evidence that retrieving more than 5 top scoring sentences helped get better sentences. At the end of this step, we have for each query sentence 5 potentially matching sentences as per the IR score.

The information retrieval step is the most time consuming task in the whole system. The time taken depends upon various factors like size of the index to search in, length of the query sentence etc. To give a time estimate, using a ± 5 day window required 9 seconds per query vs 15 seconds per query when a ± 7 day window was used. The number of results retrieved per sentence also had an impact on retrieval time with 20 results taking 19 seconds per query, whereas 5 results taking 9 seconds per query. Query length also affected the speed of the sentence extraction process. But with the problem at we could differentiate among important and unimportant words as nouns, verbs and sometimes even numbers (year, date) could be the keywords. We, however did place a limit of approximately 90 words on the queries and the indexed sentences. This choice was motivated by the fact that the word alignment toolkit Giza++ does not process longer sentences.

A Krovetz stemmer was used while building the index as provided by the toolkit. English stop words, i.e. frequently used words, such as "a" or "the", are normally not indexed because they are so common that they are not useful to query on. The stop word list provided by the IR Group of University of Glasgow[4] was used.

The resources required by our system are minimal : translations of one side of the comparable corpus. We will be showing later in section 4.2 of this paper that with an SMT system trained on small amounts of human-translated data we can 'retrieve' potentially good parallel sentences.

3.2 Candidate Sentence Pair Selection

Once we have the results from information retrieval, we proceed on to decide whether sentences are parallel or not. At this stage we choose the best scoring sentence as determined by the toolkit and pass the sentence pair through further filters. Gale and Church (1993) based their align program on the fact that longer sentences in one language tend to be translated into longer sentences in the other language, and that shorter sentences tend to be translated into shorter sentences. We also use the same logic in our initial selection of the sentence pairs. A sentence pair is selected for further processing if the length ratio is not more than 1.6. A relaxed factor of 1.6 was chosen keeping in consideration the fact that French sentences are longer than their respective English translations. Finally, we discarded all sentences that contain a large fraction of numbers. Typically, those are tables of sport results that do not carry useful information to train an SMT.

Sentences pairs conforming to the previous criteria are then judged based on WER (Levenshtein distance) and translation error rate (TER). WER measures the number of operations required to transform one sentence into the other (insertions, deletions and substitutions). A zero WER would mean the two sentences are identical, subsequently lower WER sentence pairs would be sharing most of the common words. However two correct translations may differ in the order in which the words appear, something that WER is incapable of taking into account as it works on word to word basis. This shortcoming is addressed by TER which allows block movements of words and thus takes into account the reorderings of words and phrases in translation (Snover et al., 2006). We used both WER and TER to choose the most suitable sentence pairs.

4 Experimental evaluation

Our main goal was to be able to create an additional parallel corpus to improve machine translation quality, especially for the domains where we have less or no parallel data available. In this section we report the results of adding these extracted parallel sentences to the already available human-translated parallel sentences.

We conducted a range of experiments by adding our extracted corpus to various combinations of already available human-translated parallel corpora. We experimented with WER and TER as filters to select the best scoring sentences. Generally, sentences selected based on TER filter showed better BLEU and TER scores than their WER counter parts. So we chose TER filter as standard for

[4] http://ir.dcs.gla.ac.uk/resources/linguistic_utils/stop_words

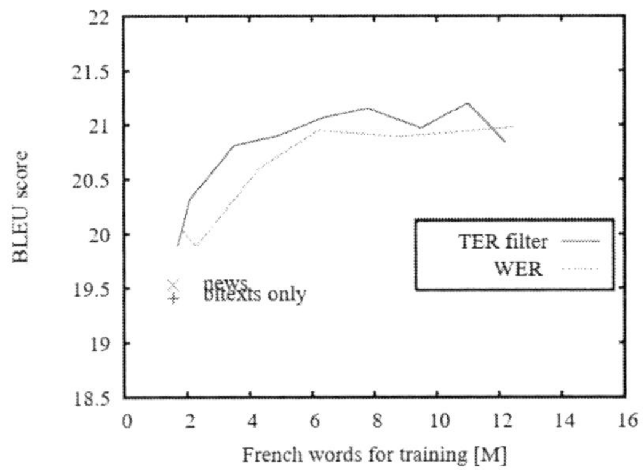

Figure 4: BLEU scores on the Test data using an WER or TER filter.

our experiments with limited amounts of human translated corpus. Figure 4 shows this WER vs TER comparison based on BLEU and TER scores on the test data in function of the size of training data. These experiments were performed with only 1.56M words of human-provided translations (news-commentary corpus).

4.1 Improvement by sentence tail removal

Two main classes of errors common in such tasks: firstly, cases where the two sentences share many common words but actually convey different meaning, and secondly, cases where the two sentences are (exactly) parallel except at sentence ends where one sentence has more information than the other. This second case of errors can be detected using WER as we have both the sentences in English. We detected the extra insertions at the end of the IR result sentence and removed them. Some examples of such sentences along with tails detected and removed are shown in figure 1. This resulted in an improvement in the SMT scores as shown in table 1.

This technique worked perfectly for sentences having TER greater than 30%. Evidently these are the sentences which have longer tails which result in a lower TER score and removing them improves performance significantly. Removing sentence tails evidently improved the scores especially for larger data, for example for the data size of 12.5M we see an improvement of 0.65 and 0.98 BLEU points on dev and test data respectively and 1.00 TER points on test data (last line table 1).

The best BLEU score on the development data is obtained when adding 9.4M words of automatically aligned bitexts (11M in total). This corresponds to an increase of about 2.88 points BLEU on the development set and an increase of 2.46 BLEU points on the test set (19.53 → 21.99) as shown in table 2, first two lines. The TER decreased by 3.07%.

Limit TER filter	Word tail removal	Words (M)	BLEU Dev data	BLEU Test data	TER Test data
0		1.56	19.41	19.53	63.17
10	no	1.58	19.62	19.59	63.11
	yes		19.56	19.51	63.24
20	no	1.7	19.76	19.89	62.49
	yes		**19.81**	19.75	62.80
30	no	2.1	20.29	20.32	62.16
	yes		20.16	20.22	**62.02**
40	no	3.5	20.93	20.81	61.80
	yes		**21.23**	**21.04**	**61.49**
45	no	4.9	20.98	20.90	62.18
	yes		**21.39**	**21.49**	**60.90**
50	no	6.4	21.12	21.07	61.31
	yes		**21.70**	**21.70**	**60.69**
55	no	7.8	21.30	21.15	61.23
	yes		**21.90**	**21.78**	**60.41**
60	no	9.8	21.42	20.97	61.46
	yes		**21.96**	**21.79**	**60.33**
65	no	11	21.34	21.20	61.02
	yes		**22.29**	**21.99**	**60.10**
70	no	12.2	21.21	20.84	61.24
	yes		**21.86**	**21.82**	**60.24**

Table 1: Effect on BLEU score of removing extra sentence tails from otherwise parallel sentences.

Adding the dictionary improves the baseline system (second line in Table 2), but it is not necessary any more once we have the automatically extracted data.

Having had very promising results with our previous experiments, we proceeded onto experimentation with larger human-translated data sets. We added our extracted corpus to the collection of News-commentary (1.56M) and Europarl (40.1M) bitexts. The corresponding SMT experiments yield an improvement of about 0.2 BLEU points on the Dev and Test set respectively (see table 2).

4.2 Effect of SMT quality

Our motivation for this approach was to be able to improve SMT performance by 'creating' parallel texts for domains which do not have enough or any parallel corpora. Therefore only the news-

Bitexts	total words	BLEU score Dev	BLEU score Test	TER Test
News	1.56M	19.41	19.53	63.17
News+Extracted	11M	**22.29**	**21.99**	**60.10**
News+dict	2.4M	20.44	20.18	61.16
News+dict+Extracted	13.9M	**22.40**	**21.98**	**60.11**
News+Eparl+dict	43.3M	22.27	22.35	59.81
News+Eparl+dict+Extracted	51.3M	**22.47**	**22.56**	59.83

Table 2: Summary of BLEU scores for the best systems on the Dev-data with the news-commentary corpus and the bilingual dictionary.

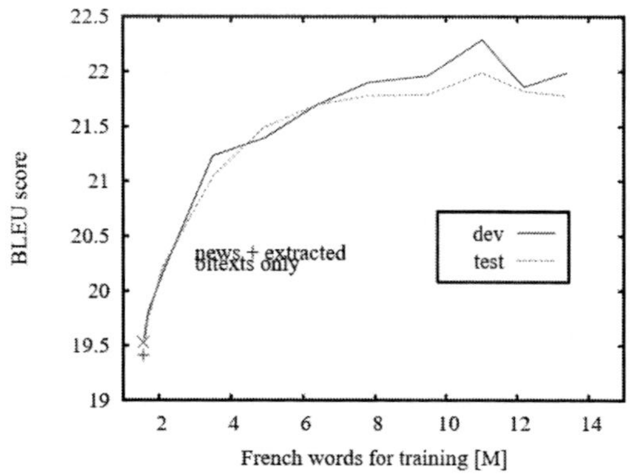

Figure 5: BLEU scores when using news-commentary bitexts and our extracted bitexts filtered using TER.

commentary bitext and the bilingual dictionary were used to train an SMT system that produced the queries for information retrieval. To investigate the impact of the SMT quality on our system, we built another SMT system trained on large amounts of human-translated corpora (116M), as detailed in section 2. Parallel sentence extraction was done using the translations performed by this big SMT system as IR queries. We found no experimental evidence that the improved automatic translations yielded better alignments of the comaprable corpus. It is however interesting to note that we achieve almost the same performance when we add 9.4M words of autoamticallly extracted sentence as with 40M of human-provided (out-of domain) translations (second versus fifth line in Table 2).

5 Conclusion and discussion

Sentence aligned parallel corpora are essential for any SMT system. The amount of in-domain parallel corpus available accounts for the quality of the translations. Not having enough or having no in-domain corpus usually results in bad translations for that domain. This need for parallel corpora, has made the researchers employ new techniques and methods in an attempt to reduce the dire need of this crucial resource of the SMT systems. Our study also contributes in this regard by employing an SMT itself and information retrieval techniques to produce additional parallel corpora from easily available comparable corpora.

We use automatic translations of comparable corpus of one language (source) to find the corresponding parallel sentence from the comparable corpus in the other language (target). We only used a limited amount of human-provided bilingual resources. Starting with about a total 2.6M words of sentence aligned bilingual data and a bilingual dictionary, large amounts of monolingual data are translated. These translations are then employed to find the corresponding matching sentences in the target side corpus, using information retrieval methods. Simple filters are used to determine whether the retrieved sentences are parallel or not. By adding these retrieved parallel sentences to already available human translated parallel corpora we were able to improve the BLEU score on the test set by almost 2.5 points. Almost one point BLEU of this improvement was obtained by removing additional words at the end of the aligned sentences in the target language.

Contrary to the previous approaches as in (Munteanu and Marcu, 2005) which used small amounts of in-domain parallel corpus as an initial resource, our system exploits the target language side of the comparable corpus to attain the same goal, thus the comparable corpus itself helps to better extract possible parallel sentences. The Gigaword comparable corpora were used in this paper, but the same approach can be extended to extract parallel sentences from huge amounts of corpora available on the web by identifying comparable articles using techniques such as (Yang and Li, 2003) and (Resnik and Y, 2003).

This technique is particularly useful for language pairs for which very little parallel corpora exist. Other probable sources of comparable corpora to be exploited include multilingual encyclopedias like Wikipedia, encyclopedia Encarta etc. There also exist domain specific comparable corpora (which are probably potentially parallel), like the documentations that are done in the national/regional language as well as English, or the translations of many English research papers in French or some other language used for academic proposes.

We are currently working on several extensions of the procedure described in this paper. We will investigate whether the same findings hold for other tasks and language pairs, in particular translating from Arabic to English, and we will try to compare our approach with the work of Munteanu and Marcu (2005). The simple filters that we are currently using seem to be effective, but we will also test other criteria than the WER and TER. Finally, another interesting direction is to iterate the process. The extracted additional bitexts could be used to build an SMT system that is better optimized on the Gigaword corpus, to translate again all the sentence from French to English, to perform IR and the filtering and to extract new, potentially improved, parallel texts. Starting with some million words of bitexts, this process may allow to build at the end an SMT system that achieves the same performance than we obtained using about 40M words of human-translated bitexts (news-commentary + Europarl).

6 Acknowledgments

This work was partially supported by the Higher Education Commission, Pakistan through the HEC Overseas Scholarship 2005 and the French Government under the project INSTAR (ANR JCJC06 143038). Some of the baseline SMT systems used in this work were developed in a cooperation between the University of Le Mans and the company SYSTRAN.

References

P. Brown, S. Della Pietra, Vincent J. Della Pietra, and R. Mercer. 1993. The mathematics of statistical machine translation. *Computational Linguistics*, 19(2):263–311.

Chris Callison-Burch, Cameron Fordyce, Philipp Koehn, Christof Monz, and Josh Schroeder. 2008. Further meta-evaluation of machine translation. In *Third Workshop on SMT*, pages 70–106.

Pascale Fung and Percy Cheung. 2004. Mining very-non-parallel corpora: Parallel sentence and lexicon extraction via bootstrapping and em. In Dekang Lin and Dekai Wu, editors, *EMNLP*, pages 57–63, Barcelona, Spain, July. Association for Computational Linguistics.

William A. Gale and Kenneth W. Church. 1993. A program for aligning sentences in bilingual corpora. *Computational Linguistics*, 19(1):75–102.

Philipp Koehn, Franz Josef Och, and Daniel Marcu. 2003. Statistical phrased-based machine translation. In *HLT/NACL*, pages 127–133.

Philipp Koehn et al. 2007. Moses: Open source toolkit for statistical machine translation. In *ACL, demonstration session*.

Dragos Stefan Munteanu and Daniel Marcu. 2005. Improving machine translation performance by exploiting non-parallel corpora. *Computational Linguistics*, 31(4):477–504.

Douglas W. Oard. 1997. Alternative approaches for cross-language text retrieval. In *In AAAI Symposium on Cross-Language Text and Speech Retrieval. American Association for Artificial Intelligence*.

Franz Josef Och and Hermann Ney. 2002. Discriminative training and maximum entropy models for statistical machine translation. In *ACL*, pages 295–302.

Franz Josef Och and Hermann Ney. 2003. A systematic comparison of various statistical alignement models. *Computational Linguistics*, 29(1):19–51.

Paul Ogilvie and Jamie Callan. 2001. Experiments using the Lemur toolkit. In *In Proceedings of the Tenth Text Retrieval Conference (TREC-10)*, pages 103–108.

Philip Resnik and Noah A. Smith Y. 2003. The web as a parallel corpus. *Computational Linguistics*, 29:349–380.

Matthew Snover, Bonnie Dorr, Richard Schwartz, Linnea Micciulla, and John Makhoul. 2006. A study of translation edit rate with targeted human annotation. In *ACL*.

Masao Utiyama and Hitoshi Isahara. 2003. Reliable measures for aligning Japanese-English news articles and sentences. In Erhard Hinrichs and Dan Roth, editors, *ACL*, pages 72–79.

Christopher C. Yang and Kar Wing Li. 2003. Automatic construction of English/Chinese parallel corpora. *J. Am. Soc. Inf. Sci. Technol.*, 54(8):730–742.

Contextual Phrase-Level Polarity Analysis using Lexical Affect Scoring and Syntactic N-grams

Apoorv Agarwal
Department of Computer Science
Columbia University
New York, USA
aa2644@columbia.edu

Fadi Biadsy
Department of Computer Science
Columbia University
New York, USA
fadi@cs.columbia.edu

Kathleen R. Mckeown
Department of Computer Science
Columbia University
New York, USA
kathy@cs.columbia.edu

Abstract

We present a classifier to predict contextual polarity of subjective phrases in a sentence. Our approach features lexical scoring derived from the Dictionary of Affect in Language (DAL) and extended through WordNet, allowing us to automatically score the vast majority of words in our input avoiding the need for manual labeling. We augment lexical scoring with n-gram analysis to capture the effect of context. We combine DAL scores with syntactic constituents and then extract n-grams of constituents from all sentences. We also use the polarity of all syntactic constituents within the sentence as features. Our results show significant improvement over a majority class baseline as well as a more difficult baseline consisting of lexical n-grams.

1 Introduction

Sentiment analysis is a much-researched area that deals with identification of positive, negative and neutral opinions in text. The task has evolved from document level analysis to sentence and phrasal level analysis. Whereas the former is suitable for classifying news (e.g., editorials vs. reports) into positive and negative, the latter is essential for question-answering and recommendation systems. A recommendation system, for example, must be able to recommend restaurants (or movies, books, etc.) based on a variety of features such as food, service or ambience. Any single review sentence may contain both positive and negative opinions, evaluating different features of a restaurant. Consider the following sentence (1) where the writer expresses opposing sentiments towards food and service of a restaurant. In tasks such as this, therefore, it is important that sentiment analysis be done at the phrase level.

(1) The Taj has great food but I found their service to be lacking.

Subjective phrases in a sentence are carriers of sentiments in which an experiencer expresses an attitude, often towards a target. These subjective phrases may express neutral or polar attitudes depending on the context of the sentence in which they appear. Context is mainly determined by content and structure of the sentence. For example, in the following sentence (2), the underlined subjective phrase seems to be negative, but in the larger context of the sentence, it is positive.[1]

(2) The robber entered the store but his efforts were crushed when the police arrived on time.

Our task is to predict contextual polarity of subjective phrases in a sentence. A traditional approach to this problem is to use a prior polarity lexicon of words to first set priors on target phrases and then make use of the syntactic and semantic information in and around the sentence to make the final prediction. As in earlier approaches, we also use a lexicon to set priors, but we explore new uses of a Dictionary of Affect in Language (DAL) (Whissel, 1989) extended using WordNet (Fellbaum, 1998). We augment this approach with n-gram analysis to capture the effect of context. We present a system for classification of neutral versus positive versus negative and positive versus negative polarity (as is also done by (Wilson et al., 2005)). Our approach is novel in the use of following features:

- **Lexical scores derived from DAL and extended through WordNet**: The Dictionary of Affect has been widely used to aid in interpretation of emotion in speech (Hirschberg

[1]We assign polarity to phrases based on Wiebe (Wiebe et al., 2005); the polarity of all examples shown here is drawn from annotations in the MPQA corpus. Clearly the assignment of polarity chosen in this corpus depends on general cultural norms.

Proceedings of the 12th Conference of the European Chapter of the ACL, pages 24–32,
Athens, Greece, 30 March – 3 April 2009.

et al., 2005). It contains numeric scores assigned along axes of pleasantness, activeness and concreteness. We introduce a method for setting numerical priors on words using these three axes, which we refer to as a "scoring scheme" throughout the paper. This scheme has high coverage of the phrases for classification and requires no manual intervention when tagging words with prior polarities.

- **N-gram Analysis: exploiting automatically derived polarity of syntactic constituents** We compute polarity for each syntactic constituent in the input phrase using lexical affect scores for its words and extract n-grams over these constituents. N-grams of syntactic constituents tagged with polarity provide patterns that improve prediction of polarity for the subjective phrase.

- **Polarity of Surrounding Constituents:** We use the computed polarity of syntactic constituents surrounding the phrase we want to classify. These features help to capture the effect of context on the polarity of the subjective phrase.

We show that classification of subjective phrases using our approach yields better accuracy than two baselines, a majority class baseline and a more difficult baseline of lexical n-gram features.

We also provide an analysis of how the different component DAL scores contribute to our results through the introduction of a "norm" that combines the component scores, separating polar words that are less subjective (e.g., *Christmas* , *murder*) from neutral words that are more subjective (e.g., *most, lack*).

Section 2 presents an overview of previous work, focusing on phrasal level sentiment analysis. Section 3 describes the corpus and the gold standard we used for our experiments. In section 4, we give a brief description of DAL, discussing its utility and previous uses for emotion and for sentiment analysis. Section 5 presents, in detail, our polarity classification framework. Here we describe our scoring scheme and the features we extract from sentences for classification tasks. Experimental set-up and results are presented in Section 6. We conclude with Section 7 where we also look at future directions for this research.

2 Literature Survey

The task of sentiment analysis has evolved from document level analysis (e.g., (Turney., 2002); (Pang and Lee, 2004)) to sentence level analysis (e.g., (Hu and Liu., 2004); (Kim and Hovy., 2004); (Yu and Hatzivassiloglou, 2003)). These researchers first set priors on words using a prior polarity lexicon. When classifying sentiment at the sentence level, other types of clues are also used, including averaging of word polarities or models for learning sentence sentiment.

Research on contextual phrasal level sentiment analysis was pioneered by Nasukawa and Yi (2003), who used manually developed patterns to identify sentiment. Their approach had high precision, but low recall. Wilson et al., (2005) also explore contextual phrasal level sentiment analysis, using a machine learning approach that is closer to the one we present. Both of these researchers also follow the traditional approach and first set priors on words using a prior polarity lexicon. Wilson et al. (2005) use a lexicon of over 8000 subjectivity clues, gathered from three sources ((Riloff and Wiebe, 2003); (Hatzivassiloglou and McKeown, 1997) and The General Inquirer[2]). Words that were not tagged as positive or negative were manually labeled. Yi et al. (2003) acquired words from GI, DAL and WordNet. From DAL, only words whose pleasantness score is one standard deviation away from the mean were used. Nasukawa as well as other researchers (Kamps and Marx, 2002)) also manually tag words with prior polarities. All of these researchers use categorical tags for prior lexical polarity; in contrast, we use quantitative scores, making it possible to use them in computation of scores for the full phrase.

While Wilson et al. (2005) aim at phrasal level analysis, their system actually only gives "each clue instance its own label" [p. 350]. Their gold standard is also at the clue level and assigns a value based on the clue's appearance in different expressions (e.g., if a clue appears in a mixture of negative and neutral expressions, its class is negative). They note that they do not determine subjective expression boundaries and for this reason, they classify at the word level. This approach is quite different from ours, as we compute the polarity of the full phrase. The average length of the subjective phrases in the corpus was 2.7 words, with a standard deviation of 2.3. Like Wilson et al.

[2]http://www.wjh.harvard.edu/ inquirer

(2005) we do not attempt to determine the boundary of subjective expressions; we use the labeled boundaries in the corpus.

3 Corpus

We used the Multi-Perspective Question-Answering (MPQA version 1.2) Opinion corpus (Wiebe et al., 2005) for our experiments. We extracted a total of 17,243 subjective phrases annotated for contextual polarity from the corpus of 535 documents (11,114 sentences). These subjective phrases are either "direct subjective" or "expressive subjective". "Direct subjective" expressions are explicit mentions of a private state (Quirk et al., 1985) and are much easier to classify. "Expressive subjective" phrases are indirect or implicit mentions of private states and therefore are harder to classify. Approximately one third of the phrases we extracted were direct subjective with non-neutral expressive intensity whereas the rest of the phrases were expressive subjective. In terms of polarity, there were 2779 positive, 6471 negative and 7993 neutral expressions. Our Gold Standard is the manual annotation tag given to phrases in the corpus.

4 DAL

DAL is an English language dictionary built to measure emotional meaning of texts. The samples employed to build the dictionary were gathered from different sources such as interviews, adolescents' descriptions of their emotions and university students' essays. Thus, the 8742 word dictionary is broad and avoids bias from any one particular source. Each word is given three kinds of scores (pleasantness – also called evaluation, *ee*, activeness, *aa* and imagery, *ii*) on a scale of 1 (low) to 3 (high). Pleasantness is a measure of polarity. For example, in Table 1, *affection* is given a pleasantness score of 2.77 which is closer to 3.0 and is thus a highly positive word. Likewise, activeness is a measure of the activation or arousal level of a word, which is apparent from the activeness scores of *slug* and *energetic* in the table. The third score, imagery, is a measure of the ease with which a word forms a mental picture. For example, *affect* cannot be imagined easily and therefore has a score closer to 1, as opposed to *flower* which is a very concrete and therefore has an imagery score of 3.

A notable feature of the dictionary is that it has different scores for various inflectional forms of a word (*affect* and *affection*) and thus, morphological parsing, and the possibility of resulting errors, is avoided. Moreover, Cowie et al., (2001) showed that the three scores are uncorrelated; this implies that each of the three scores provide complementary information.

Word	*ee*	*aa*	*ii*
Affect	1.75	1.85	1.60
Affection	2.77	2.25	2.00
Slug	1.00	1.18	2.40
Energetic	2.25	3.00	3.00
Flower	2.75	1.07	3.00

Table 1: DAL scores for words

The dictionary has previously been used for detecting deceptive speech (Hirschberg et al., 2005) and recognizing emotion in speech (Athanaselis et al., 2006).

5 The Polarity Classification Framework

In this section, we present our polarity classification framework. The system takes a sentence marked with a subjective phrase and identifies the most likely contextual polarity of this phrase. We use a logistic regression classifier, implemented in Weka, to perform two types of classification: Three way (positive, negative, vs. neutral) and binary (positive vs. negative). The features we use for classification can be broadly divided into three categories: I. Prior polarity features computed from DAL and augmented using WordNet (Section 5.1). II. lexical features including POS and word n-gram features (Section 5.3), and III. the combination of DAL scores and syntactic features to allow both n-gram analysis and polarity features of neighbors (Section 5.4).

5.1 Scoring based on DAL and WordNet

DAL is used to assign three prior polarity scores to each word in a sentence. If a word is found in DAL, scores of pleasantness *(ee)*, activeness *(aa)*, and imagery *(ii)* are assigned to it. Otherwise, a list of the word's synonyms and antonyms is created using WordNet. This list is sequentially traversed until a match is found in DAL or the list ends, in which case no scores are assigned. For example, *astounded*, a word absent in DAL, was scored by using its synonym *amazed*. Similarly, *in-humane* was scored using the reverse polarity of its antonym *humane*, present in DAL. These scores are Z-Normalized using the mean and standard deviation measures given in the dictionary's manual (Whissel, 1989). It should be noted that in our current implementation all function words are given zero scores since they typically do not demonstrate any polarity. The next step is to boost these normalized scores depending on how far they lie from the mean. The reason for doing this is to be able to differentiate between phrases like "fairly decent advice" and "excellent advice". Without boosting, the pleasantness scores of both phrases are almost the same. To boost the score, we multiply it by the number of standard deviations it lies from the mean.

After the assignment of scores to individual words, we handle local negations in a sentence by using a simple finite state machine with two states: RETAIN and INVERT. In the INVERT state, the sign of the pleasantness score of the current word is inverted, while in the RETAIN state the sign of the score stays the same. Initially, the first word in a given sentence is fed to the RETAIN state. When a negation (e.g., not, no, never, cannot, didn't) is encountered, the state changes to the INVERT state. While in the INVERT state, if 'but' is encountered, it switches back to the RETAIN state. In this machine we also take care of "not only" which serves as an intensifier rather than negation (Wilson et al., 2005). To handle phrases like "no better than evil" and "could not be clearer", we also switch states from INVERT to RETAIN when a comparative degree adjective is found after 'not'. For example, the words in phrase in Table (2) are given positive pleasantness scores labeled with positive prior polarity.

Phrase	has	no	greater	desire
POS	VBZ	DT	JJR	NN
(ee)	0	0	3.37	0.68
State	RETAIN	INVERT	RETAIN	RETAIN

Table 2: Example of scoring scheme using DAL

We observed that roughly 74% of the content words in the corpus were directly found in DAL. Synonyms of around 22% of the words in the corpus were found to exist in DAL. Antonyms of only 1% of the words in the corpus were found in DAL. Our system failed to find prior semantic orientations of roughly 3% of the total words in the corpus. These were rarely occurring words like *apartheid*, *apocalyptic* and *ulterior*. We assigned zero scores for these words.

In our system, we assign three DAL scores, using the above scheme, for the subjective phrase in a given sentence. The features are (1) μ_{ee}, the mean of the pleasantness scores of the words in the phrase, (2) μ_{aa}, the mean of the activeness scores of the words in the phrase, and similarly (3) μ_{ii}, the mean of the imagery scores.

5.2 Norm

We gave each phrase another score, which we call the *norm*, that is a combination of the three scores from DAL. Cowie et al. (2001) suggest a mechanism of mapping emotional states to a 2-D continuous space using an Activation-Evaluation space (AE) representation. This representation makes use of the pleasantness and activeness scores from DAL and divides the space into four quadrants: "delightful", "angry", "serene", and "depressed". Whissel (2008), observes that tragedies, which are easily imaginable in general, have higher imagery scores than comedies. Drawing on these approaches and our intuition that neutral expressions tend to be more subjective, we define the norm in the following equation (1).

$$norm = \frac{\sqrt{ee^2 + aa^2}}{ii} \tag{1}$$

Words of interest to us may fall into the following four broad categories:

1. **High AE score and high imagery:** These are words that are highly polar and less subjective (e.g., *angel* and *lively*).
2. **Low AE score and low imagery:** These are highly subjective neutral words (e.g., *generally* and *ordinary*).
3. **High AE score and low imagery:** These are words that are both highly polar and subjective (e.g., *succeed* and *good*).
4. **Low AE score and high imagery:** These are words that are neutral and easily imaginable (e.g., *car* and *door*).

It is important to differentiate between these categories of words, because highly subjective words may change orientation depending on context; less subjective words tend to retain their prior orientation. For instance, in the example sentence from Wilson et al.(2005)., the underlined phrase seems negative, but in the context it is positive. Since a subjective word like *succeed* depends on "what" one succeeds in, it may change its polarity accordingly. In contrast, less subjective words, like *angel*, do not depend on the context in which they are used; they evoke the same connotation as their prior polarity.

(3) They haven't succeeded and will never succeed in breaking the will of this valiant people.

As another example, AE space scores of *goodies* and *good* turn out to be the same. What differentiates one from the another is the imagery score, which is higher for the former. Therefore, value of the norm is lower for *goodies* than for *good*. Unsurprisingly, this feature always appears in the top 10 features when the classification task contains neutral expressions as one of the classes.

5.3 Lexical Features

We extract two types of lexical features, part of speech (POS) tags and n-gram word features. We count the number of occurrences of each POS in the subjective phrase and represent each POS as an integer in our feature vector.[3] For each subjective phrase, we also extract a subset of unigram, bigrams, and trigrams of words (selected automatically, see Section 6). We represent each n-gram feature as a binary feature. These types of features were used to approximate standard n-gram language modeling (LM). In fact, we did experiment with a standard trigram LM, but found that it did not improve performance. In particular, we trained two LMs, one on the polar subjective phrases and another on the neutral subjective phrases. Given a sentence, we computed two perplexities of the two LMs on the subjective phrase in the sentence and added them as features in our feature vectors. This procedure provided us with significant improvement over a chance baseline but did not outperform our current system. We speculate that this was caused by the split of training data into two parts, one for training the LMs and another for training the classifier. The resulting small quantity of training data may be the reason for bad performance. Therefore, we decided to back off to only binary n-gram features as part of our feature vector.

[3]We use the Stanford Tagger to assign parts of speech tags to sentences. (Toutanova and Manning, 2000)

5.4 Syntactic Features

In this section, we show how we can combine the DAL scores with syntactic constituents. This process involves two steps. First, we chunk each sentence to its syntactic constituents (NP, VP, PP, JJP, and Other) using a CRF Chunker.[4] If the marked-up subjective phrase does not contain complete chunks (i.e., it partially overlaps with other chunks), we expand the subjective phrase to include the chunks that it overlaps with. We term this expanded phrase as the *target phrase*, see Figure 1.

Second, each chunk in a sentence is then assigned a 2-D AE space score as defined by Cowie et al., (2001) by adding the individual AE space scores of all the words in the chunk and then normalizing it by the number of words. At this point, we are only concerned with the polarity of the chunk (i.e., whether it is positive or negative or neutral) and imagery will not help in this task; the AE space score is determined from pleasantness and activeness alone. A threshold, determined empirically by analyzing the distributions of positive (pos), negative (neg) and neutral (neu) expressions, is used to define ranges for these classes of expressions. This enables us to assign each chunk a prior semantic polarity. Having the semantic orientation (positive, negative, neutral) and phrasal tags, the sentence is then converted to a sequence of encodings $[Phrasal - Tag]_{polarity}$. We mark each phrase that we want to classify as a "target" to differentiate it from the other chunks and attach its encoding. As mentioned, if the target phrase partially overlaps with chunks, it is simply expanded to subsume the chunks. This encoding is illustrated in Figure 1.

After these two steps, we extract a set of features that are used in classifying the target phrase. These include n-grams of chunks from the all sentences, minimum and maximum pleasantness scores from the chunks in the target phrase itself, and the syntactic categories that occur in the context of the target phrase. In the remainder of this section, we describe how these features are extracted.

We extract unigrams, bigrams and trigrams of chunks from all the sentences. For example, we may extract a bigram from Figure 1 of $[VP]_{neu}$ followed by $[PP]^{target}_{neg}$. Similar to the lexical

[4]Xuan-Hieu Phan, "CRFChunker: CRF English Phrase Chunker", http://crfchunker.sourceforge.net/, 2006.

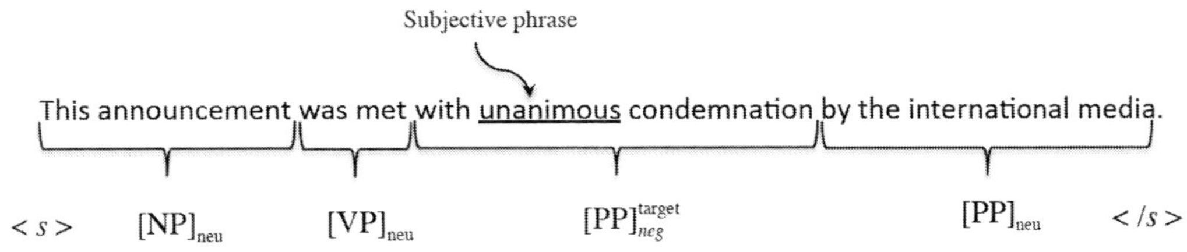

Figure 1: Converting a sentence with a subjective phrase to a sequence of chunks with their types and polarities

n-grams, for the sentence containing the target phrase, we add binary values in our feature vector such that the value is 1 if the sentence contains that chunk n-gram.

We also include two features related to the target phrase. The target phrase often consists of many chunks. To detect if a chunk of the target phrase is highly polar, minimum and maximum pleasantness scores over all the chunks in the target phrase are noted.

In addition, we add features which attempt to capture contextual information using the prior semantic polarity assigned to each chunk both within the target phrase itself and within the context of the target phrase. In cases where the target phrase is in the beginning of the sentence or at the end, we simply assign zero scores. Then we compute the frequency of each syntactic type (i.e., NP, VP, PP, JJP) and polarity (i.e., positive, negative, neutral) to the left of the target, to the right of the target and for the target. This additional set of contextual features yields 36 features in total: three polarities: {positive, negative, neutral} * three contexts: {left, target, right} * four chunk syntactic types: {NP, VP, PP, JJP}.

The full set of features captures different types of information. N-grams look for certain patterns that may be specific to either polar or neutral sentiments. Minimum and maximum scores capture information about the target phrase standalone. The last set of features incorporate information about the neighbors of the target phrase. We performed feature selection on this full set of n-gram related features and thus, a small subset of these n-gram related features, selected automatically (see section 6) were used in the experiments.

6 Experiments and Results

Subjective phrases from the MPQA corpus were used in 10-fold cross-validation experiments. The MPQA corpus includes gold standard tags for each phrase. A logistic classifier was used for two polarity classification tasks, positive versus negative versus neutral and positive versus negative. We report accuracy, and F-measure for both balanced and unbalanced data.

Feature Types	Accuracy	Pos.*	Neg.*	Neu.*
Chance baseline	33.33%	-	-	-
N-gram baseline	59.05%	0.602	0.578	0.592
DAL scores only	59.66%	0.635	0.635	0.539
+ POS	60.55%	0.621	0.542	0.655
+ Chunks	64.72%	0.681	0.665	0.596
+ N-gram (all)	67.51%	0.703	0.688	0.632
All (unbalanced)	70.76%	0.582	0.716	0.739

Table 3: Results of 3 way classification (Positive, Negative, and Neutral). In the unbalanced case, majority class baseline is 46.3% (*F-Measure).

Feature Types	Accuracy	Pos.*	Neg.*
Chance baseline	50%	-	-
N-gram baseline	73.21%	0.736	0.728
DAL scores only	77.02%	0.763	0.728
+ POS	79.02%	0.788	0.792
+ Chunks	80.72%	0.807	0.807
+ N-gram (all)	82.32%	0.802	0.823
All (unbalanced)	84.08%	0.716	0.889

Table 4: Positive vs. Negative classification results. Baseline is the majority class. In the unbalanced case, majority class baseline is 69.74%. (* F-Measure)

6.1 Positive versus Negative versus Neutral

Table 3 shows results for a 3-way classifier. For the balanced data-set, each class has 2799 instances and hence the chance baseline is 33%. For the unbalanced data-set, there are 2799 instances of positive, 6471 instances of negative and 7993 instances of neutral phrases and thus the baseline is about 46%. Results show that the accuracy increases as more features are added. It may be seen from the table that prior polarity scores do not do well alone, but when used in conjunction with other features they play an important role in achieving an accuracy much higher than both baselines (chance and lexical n-grams). To re-

(A)

The MDC leader said systematic cheating, new laws and sheer obstruction spoiling tactics, rigid – (B) as well as political (C) violence and intimidation –were just some of the irregularities practiced by the authorities in the run-up to, and during the polls.

(a)

… as well as political violence and intimidation …

$[\text{Other}]_{neu}^{target}$ $[\text{Other}]_{neu}^{target}$ $[\text{Other}]_{neu}^{target}$ $[\text{NP}]_{neg}$

(b)

Figure 2: (a) An example sentence with three annotated subjective phrases in the same sentence. (b) Part of the sentence with the target phrase (B) and their chunks with prior polarities.

confirm if prior polarity scores add value, we experimented by using all features except the prior polarity scores and noticed a drop in accuracy by about 4%. This was found to be true for the other classification task as well. The table shows that parts of speech and lexical n-grams are good features. A significant improvement in accuracy (over 4%, p-value = $4.2e$-15) is observed when chunk features (i.e., n-grams of constituents and polarity of neighboring constituents) are used in conjunction with prior polarity scores and part of speech features.[5] This improvement may be explained by the following observation. The bigram "$[Other]_{neu}^{target}$ $[NP]_{neu}$" was selected as a top feature by the Chi-square feature selector. So were unigrams, $[Other]_{neu}^{target}$ and $[Other]_{neg}^{target}$. We thus learned n-gram patterns that are characteristic of neutral expressions (the just mentioned bigram and the first of the unigrams) as well as a pattern found mostly in negative expressions (the latter unigram). It was surprising to find another top chunk feature, the bigram "$[Other]_{neu}^{target}$ $[NP]_{neg}$" (i.e., a neutral chunk of syntactic type "Other" preceding a negative noun phrase), present in neutral expressions six times more than in polar expressions. An instance where these chunk features could have been responsible for the correct prediction of a target phrase is shown in Figure 2. Figure 2(a) shows an example sentence from the MPQA corpus, which has three annotated subjective phrases. The manually labeled polarity of phrases (A) and (C) is negative and that of (B) is neutral. Figure 2(b) shows the relevant chunk bigram which is used to predict the contextual polarity of the target phrase (B).

It was interesting to see that the top 10 features consisted of all categories (i.e., prior DAL scores, lexical n-grams and POS, and syntactic) of features. In this and the other experiment, pleasantness, activation and the norm were among the top 5 features. We ran a significance test to show the importance of the norm feature in our classification task and observed that it exerted a significant increase in accuracy (2.26%, p-value = $1.45e$-5).

6.2 Positive versus Negative

Table 4 shows results for positive versus negative classification. We show results for both balanced and unbalanced data-sets. For balanced, there are 2779 instances of each class. For the unbalanced data-set, there are 2779 instances of positive and 6471 instances of neutral, thus our chance baseline is around 70%. As in the earlier classification, accuracy and F-measure increase as we add features. While the increase of adding the chunk features, for example, is not as great as in the previous classification, it is nonetheless significant (p-value = 0.0018) in this classification task. The smaller increase lends support to our hypothesis that polar expressions tend to be less subjective and thus are less likely to be affected by contextual polarity. Another thing that supports our hypothesis that neutral expressions are more subjective is the fact that the rank of imagery (*ii*), dropped significantly in this classification task as compared to the previous classification task. This implies that imagery has a much lesser role to play when we are dealing with non-neutral expressions.

[5] We use the binomial test procedure to test statistical significance throughout the paper.

7 Conclusion and Future Work

We present new features (DAL scores, norm scores computed using DAL, n-gram over chunks with polarity) for phrasal level sentiment analysis. They work well and help in achieving high accuracy in a three-way classification of positive, negative and neutral expressions. We do not require any manual intervention during feature selection, and thus our system is fully automated. We also introduced a 3-D representation that maps different classes to spatial coordinates.

It may seem to be a limitation of our system that it requires accurate expression boundaries. However, this is not true for the following two reasons: first, Wiebe et al., (2005) declare that while marking the span of subjective expressions and hand annotating the MPQA corpus, the annotators were not trained to mark accurate expression boundaries. The only constraint was that the subjective expression should be within the mark-ups for all annotators. Second, we expanded the marked subjective phrase to subsume neighboring phrases at the time of chunking.

A limitation of our scoring scheme is that it does not handle polysemy, since words in DAL are not provided with their parts of speech. Statistics show, however, that most words occurred with primarily one part of speech only. For example, "will" occurred as modal 1272 times in the corpus, whereas it appeared 34 times as a noun. The case is similar for "like" and "just", which mostly occur as a preposition and an adverb, respectively. Also, in our state machine, we haven't accounted for the impact of connectives such as "but" or "although"; we propose drawing on work in argumentative orientation to do so ((Anscombre and Ducrot, 1983); (Elhadad and McKeown, 1990)).

For future work, it would be interesting to do subjectivity and intensity classification using the same scheme and features. Particularly, for the task of subjectivity analysis, we speculate that the imagery score might be useful for tagging chunks with "subjective" and "objective" instead of positive, negative, and neutral.

Acknowledgments

This work was supported by the National Science Foundation under the KDD program. Any opinions, ndings, and conclusions or recommendations expressed in this paper are those of the authors and do not necessarily reect the views of the National Science Foundation. score.

We would like to thank Julia Hirschberg for useful discussion. We would also like to acknowledge Narayanan Venkiteswaran for implementing parts of the system and Amal El Masri, Ashleigh White and Oliver Elliot for their useful comments.

References

J.C. Anscombre and O. Ducrot. 1983. Philosophie et langage. l'argumentation clans la langue. Bruxelles: Pierre Mardaga.

T. Athanaselis, S. Bakamidis, , and L. Dologlou. 2006. Automatic recognition of emotionally coloured speech. In *Proceedings of World Academy of Science, Engineering and Technology, volume 12, ISSN 1307-6884.*

R. Cowie, E. Douglas-Cowie, N. Tsapatsoulis, G. Votsis, S. Kollias, and W. Fellenz et al. 2001. Emotion recognition in human-computer interaction. In *IEEE Signal Processing Magazine, 1, 32-80.*

M. Elhadad and K. R. McKeown. 1990. Generating connectives. In *Proceedings of the 13th conference on Computational linguistics*, pages 97–101, Morristown, NJ, USA. Association for Computational Linguistics.

C. Fellbaum. 1998. Wordnet, an electronic lexical database. In *MIT press.*

V. Hatzivassiloglou and K. McKeown. 1997. Predicting the semantic orientation of adjectives. In *Proceedings of ACL.*

J. Hirschberg, S. Benus, J.M. Brenier, F. Enos, and S. Friedman. 2005. Distinguishing deceptive from non-deceptive speech. In *Proceedings of Interspeech, 1833-1836.*

M. Hu and B. Liu. 2004. Mining and summarizing customer reviews. In *Proceedings of KDD.*

J. Kamps and M. Marx. 2002. Words with attitude. In *1st International WordNet Conference.*

S. M. Kim and E. Hovy. 2004. Determining the sentiment of opinions. In *In Coling.*

T. Nasukawa and J. Yi. 2003. Sentiment analysis: Capturing favorability using natural language processing. In *Proceedings of K-CAP.*

B. Pang and L. Lee. 2004. A sentimental education: Sentiment analysis using subjectivity analysis using subjectivity summarization based on minimum cuts. In *Proceedings of ACL.*

R. Quirk, S. Greenbaum, G. Leech, and J. Svartvik. 1985. A comprehensive grammar of the english language. Longman, New York.

E. Riloff and J. Wiebe. 2003. Learning extraction patterns for subjective expressions. In *Proceedings of EMNLP*.

K. Toutanova and C. D. Manning. 2000. Enriching the knowledge sources used in a maximum entropy part-of-speech tagger. In *Proceedings of the Joint SIGDAT Conference on Empirical Methods in Natural Language Processing and Very Large Corpora (EMNLP/VLC-2000), pp. 63-70.*

P. Turney. 2002. Thumbs up or thumbs down? semantic orientation applied to unsupervised classification of reviews. In *Proceedings of ACL*.

C. M. Whissel. 1989. The dictionary of affect in language. In *R. Plutchik and H. Kellerman, editors, Emotion: theory research and experience, volume 4, Acad. Press.*, London.

C. M. Whissell. 2008. A psychological investigation of the use of shakespeare=s emotional language: The case of his roman tragedies. In *Edwin Mellen Press.*, Lewiston, NY.

J. Wiebe, T. Wilson, and C. Cardie. 2005. Annotating expressions of opinions and emotions in language. In *Language Resources and Evaluation, volume 39, issue 2-3, pp. 165-210.*

T. Wilson, J. Wiebe, and P. Hoffman. 2005. Recognizing contextual polarity in phrase level sentiment analysis. In *Proceedings of ACL*.

J. Yi, T. Nasukawa, R. Bunescu, and W. Niblack. 2003. Sentiment analyzer: Extracting sentiments about a given topic using natural language processing techniques. In *Proceedings of IEEE ICDM*.

H. Yu and V. Hatzivassiloglou. 2003. Towards answering opinion questions: Separating facts from opinions and identifying the polarity of opinion sentences. In *Proceedings of EMNLP*.

Personalizing PageRank for Word Sense Disambiguation

Eneko Agirre and Aitor Soroa
IXA NLP Group
University of the Basque Country
Donostia, Basque Contry
{e.agirre,a.soroa}@ehu.es

Abstract

In this paper we propose a new graph-based method that uses the knowledge in a LKB (based on WordNet) in order to perform unsupervised Word Sense Disambiguation. Our algorithm uses the full graph of the LKB efficiently, performing better than previous approaches in English all-words datasets. We also show that the algorithm can be easily ported to other languages with good results, with the only requirement of having a wordnet. In addition, we make an analysis of the performance of the algorithm, showing that it is efficient and that it could be tuned to be faster.

1 Introduction

Word Sense Disambiguation (WSD) is a key enabling-technology that automatically chooses the intended sense of a word in context. Supervised WSD systems are the best performing in public evaluations (Palmer et al., 2001; Snyder and Palmer, 2004; Pradhan et al., 2007) but they need large amounts of hand-tagged data, which is typically very expensive to build. Given the relatively small amount of training data available, current state-of-the-art systems only beat the simple most frequent sense (MFS) baseline[1] by a small margin. As an alternative to supervised systems, knowledge-based WSD systems exploit the information present in a lexical knowledge base (LKB) to perform WSD, without using any further corpus evidence.

Traditional knowledge-based WSD systems assign a sense to an ambiguous word by comparing each of its senses with those of the surrounding context. Typically, some semantic similarity metric is used for calculating the relatedness among senses (Lesk, 1986; McCarthy et al., 2004). One of the major drawbacks of these approaches stems from the fact that senses are compared in a pairwise fashion and thus the number of computations can grow exponentially with the number of words. Although alternatives like simulated annealing (Cowie et al., 1992) and conceptual density (Agirre and Rigau, 1996) were tried, most of past knowledge based WSD was done in a suboptimal word-by-word process, i.e., disambiguating words one at a time.

Recently, graph-based methods for knowledge-based WSD have gained much attention in the NLP community (Sinha and Mihalcea, 2007; Navigli and Lapata, 2007; Mihalcea, 2005; Agirre and Soroa, 2008). These methods use well-known graph-based techniques to find and exploit the structural properties of the graph underlying a particular LKB. Because the graph is analyzed as a whole, these techniques have the remarkable property of being able to find globally optimal solutions, given the relations between entities. Graph-based WSD methods are particularly suited for disambiguating word sequences, and they manage to exploit the interrelations among the senses in the given context. In this sense, they provide a principled solution to the exponential explosion problem, with excellent performance.

Graph-based WSD is performed over a graph composed by senses (nodes) and relations between pairs of senses (edges). The relations may be of several types (lexico-semantic, coocurrence relations, etc.) and may have some weight attached to

[1]This baseline consists of tagging all occurrences in the test data with the sense of the word that occurs more often in the training data

Proceedings of the 12th Conference of the European Chapter of the ACL, pages 33–41,
Athens, Greece, 30 March – 3 April 2009.

them. The disambiguation is typically performed by applying a ranking algorithm over the graph, and then assigning the concepts with highest rank to the corresponding words. Given the computational cost of using large graphs like WordNet, many researchers use smaller subgraphs built online for each target context.

In this paper we present a novel graph-based WSD algorithm which uses the full graph of WordNet efficiently, performing significantly better that previously published approaches in English all-words datasets. We also show that the algorithm can be easily ported to other languages with good results, with the only requirement of having a wordnet. The algorithm is publicly available[2] and can be applied easily to sense inventories and knowledge bases different from WordNet. Our analysis shows that our algorithm is efficient compared to previously proposed alternatives, and that a good choice of WordNet versions and relations is fundamental for good performance.

The paper is structured as follows. We first describe the PageRank and Personalized PageRank algorithms. Section 3 introduces the graph based methods used for WSD. Section 4 shows the experimental setting and the main results, and Section 5 compares our methods with related experiments on graph-based WSD systems. Section 6 shows the results of the method when applied to a Spanish dataset. Section 7 analyzes the performance of the algorithm. Finally, we draw some conclusions in Section 8.

2 PageRank and Personalized PageRank

The celebrated PageRank algorithm (Brin and Page, 1998) is a method for ranking the vertices in a graph according to their relative structural importance. The main idea of PageRank is that whenever a link from v_i to v_j exists in a graph, a vote from node i to node j is produced, and hence the rank of node j increases. Besides, the strength of the vote from i to j also depends on the rank of node i: the more important node i is, the more strength its votes will have. Alternatively, PageRank can also be viewed as the result of a random walk process, where the final rank of node i represents the probability of a random walk over the graph ending on node i, at a sufficiently large time.

Let G be a graph with N vertices $v_1, \dots, v_N$ and d_i be the outdegree of node i; let M be a $N \times N$ transition probability matrix, where $M_{ji} = \frac{1}{d_i}$ if a link from i to j exists, and zero otherwise. Then, the calculation of the *PageRank vector* $\mathbf{Pr}$ over G is equivalent to resolving Equation (1).

$$\mathbf{Pr} = cM\mathbf{Pr} + (1-c)\mathbf{v} \qquad (1)$$

In the equation, $\mathbf{v}$ is a $N \times 1$ vector whose elements are $\frac{1}{N}$ and c is the so called *damping factor*, a scalar value between 0 and 1. The first term of the sum on the equation models the voting scheme described in the beginning of the section. The second term represents, loosely speaking, the probability of a surfer randomly jumping to any node, e.g. without following any paths on the graph. The damping factor, usually set in the $[0.85..0.95]$ range, models the way in which these two terms are combined at each step.

The second term on Eq. (1) can also be seen as a smoothing factor that makes any graph fulfill the property of being aperiodic and irreducible, and thus guarantees that PageRank calculation converges to a unique stationary distribution.

In the traditional PageRank formulation the vector $\mathbf{v}$ is a stochastic normalized vector whose element values are all $\frac{1}{N}$, thus assigning equal probabilities to all nodes in the graph in case of random jumps. However, as pointed out by (Haveliwala, 2002), the vector $\mathbf{v}$ can be non-uniform and assign stronger probabilities to certain kinds of nodes, effectively biasing the resulting PageRank vector to prefer these nodes. For example, if we concentrate all the probability mass on a unique node i, all random jumps on the walk will return to i and thus its rank will be high; moreover, the high rank of i will make all the nodes in its vicinity also receive a high rank. Thus, the importance of node i given by the initial distribution of $\mathbf{v}$ spreads along the graph on successive iterations of the algorithm.

In this paper, we will use *traditional PageRank* to refer to the case when a uniform $\mathbf{v}$ vector is used in Eq. (1); and whenever a modified $\mathbf{v}$ is used, we will call it *Personalized PageRank*. The next section shows how we define a modified $\mathbf{v}$.

PageRank is actually calculated by applying an iterative algorithm which computes Eq. (1) successively until convergence below a given threshold is achieved, or, more typically, until a fixed number of iterations are executed.

Regarding PageRank implementation details, we chose a damping value of 0.85 and finish the calculation after 30 iterations. We did not try other

[2] `http://ixa2.si.ehu.es/ukb`

damping factors. Some preliminary experiments with higher iteration counts showed that although sometimes the node ranks varied, the relative order among particular word synsets remained stable after the initial iterations (cf. Section 7 for further details). Note that, in order to discard the effect of *dangling nodes* (i.e. nodes without outlinks) we slightly modified Eq. (1). For the sake of brevity we omit the details, which the interested reader can check in (Langville and Meyer, 2003).

3 Using PageRank for WSD

In this section we present the application of PageRank to WSD. If we were to apply the traditional PageRank over the whole WordNet we would get a context-independent ranking of word senses, which is not what we want. Given an input piece of text (typically one sentence, or a small set of contiguous sentences), we want to disambiguate all open-class words in the input taken the rest as context. In this framework, we need to rank the senses of the target words according to the other words in the context. Theare two main alternatives to achieve this:

- To create a subgraph of WordNet which connects the senses of the words in the input text, and then apply traditional PageRank over the subgraph.
- To use Personalized PageRank, initializing v with the senses of the words in the input text

The first method has been explored in the literature (cf. Section 5), and we also presented a variant in (Agirre and Soroa, 2008) but the second method is novel in WSD. In both cases, the algorithms return a list of ranked senses for each target word in the context. We will see each of them in turn, but first we will present some notation and a preliminary step.

3.1 Preliminary step

A LKB is formed by a set of concepts and relations among them, and a dictionary, i.e., a list of words (typically, word lemmas) each of them linked to at least one concept of the LKB. Given any such LKB, we build an undirected graph $G = (V, E)$ where nodes represent LKB concepts (v_i), and each relation between concepts v_i and v_j is represented by an undirected edge $e_{i,j}$.

In our experiments we have tried our algorithms using three different LKBs:

- *MCR16 + Xwn*: The Multilingual Central Repository (Atserias et al., 2004b) is a lexical knowledge base built within the MEANING project[3]. This LKB comprises the original WordNet 1.6 synsets and relations, plus some relations from other WordNet versions automatically mapped[4] into version 1.6: WordNet 2.0 relations and eXtended WordNet relations (Mihalcea and Moldovan, 2001) (gold, silver and normal relations). The resulting graph has $99,632$ vertices and $637,290$ relations.
- *WNet17 + Xwn*: WordNet 1.7 synset and relations and eXtended WordNet relations. The graph has $109,359$ vertices and $620,396$ edges
- *WNet30 + gloss*: WordNet 3.0 synset and relations, including manually disambiguated glosses . The graph has $117,522$ vertices and $525,356$ relations.

Given an input text, we extract the list W_i $i = 1 \dots m$ of content words (i.e. nouns, verbs, adjectives and adverbs) which have an entry in the dictionary, and thus can be related to LKB concepts. Let $Concepts_i = \{v_1, \dots, v_{i_m}\}$ be the i_m associated concepts of word W_i in the LKB graph. Note that monosemous words will be related to just one concept, whereas polysemous words may be attached to several. As a result of the disambiguation process, every concept in $Concepts_i$, $i = 1, \dots, m$ receives a score. Then, for each target word to be disambiguated, we just choose its associated concept in G with maximal score.

In our experiments we build a context of at least 20 content words for each sentence to be disambiguated, taking the sentences immediately before and after it in the case that the original sentence was too short.

3.2 Traditional PageRank over Subgraph (Spr)

We follow the algorithm presented in (Agirre and Soroa, 2008), which we explain here for completeness. The main idea of the subgraph method is to extract the subgraph of G_{KB} whose vertices and relations are particularly relevant for a given input

[3] http://nipadio.lsi.upc.es/nlp/meaning

[4] We use the freely available WordNet mappings from http://www.lsi.upc.es/~nlp/tools/download-map.php

context. Such a subgraph is called a "disambiguation subgraph" G_{D}, and it is built in the following way. For each word W_i in the input context and each concept $v_i \in Concepts_i$, a standard breath-first search (BFS) over G_{KB} is performed, starting at node v_i. Each run of the BFS calculates the minimum distance paths between v_i and the rest of concepts of G_{KB}. In particular, we are interested in the minimum distance paths between v_i and the concepts associated to the rest of the words in the context, $v_j \in \bigcup_{j \neq i} Concepts_j$. Let mdp_{v_i} be the set of these shortest paths.

This BFS computation is repeated for every concept of every word in the input context, storing mdp_{v_i} accordingly. At the end, we obtain a set of minimum length paths each of them having a different concept as a source. The disambiguation graph G_D is then just the union of the vertices and edges of the shortest paths, $G_D = \bigcup_{i=1}^{m} \{mdp_{v_j} / v_j \in Concepts_i\}$.

The disambiguation graph G_D is thus a subgraph of the original G_{KB} graph obtained by computing the shortest paths between the concepts of the words co-occurring in the context. Thus, we hypothesize that it captures the most relevant concepts and relations in the knowledge base for the particular input context.

Once the G_D graph is built, we compute the traditional PageRank algorithm over it. The intuition behind this step is that the vertices representing the correct concepts will be more relevant in G_D than the rest of the possible concepts of the context words, which should have less relations on average and be more isolated.

As usual, the disambiguation step is performed by assigning to each word W_i the associated concept in $Concepts_i$ which has maximum rank. In case of ties we assign all the concepts with maximum rank. Note that the standard evaluation script provided in the Senseval competitions treats multiple senses as if one was chosen at random, i.e. for evaluation purposes our method is equivalent to breaking ties at random.

3.3 Personalized PageRank (Ppr and Ppr_w2w)

As mentioned before, personalized PageRank allows us to use the full LKB. We first insert the context words into the graph G as nodes, and link them with directed edges to their respective concepts. Then, we compute the personalized PageRank of the graph G by concentrating the initial probability mass uniformly over the newly introduced word nodes. As the words are linked to the concepts by directed edges, they act as source nodes injecting mass into the concepts they are associated with, which thus become relevant nodes, and spread their mass over the LKB graph. Therefore, the resulting personalized PageRank vector can be seen as a measure of the structural relevance of LKB concepts in the presence of the input context.

One problem with Personalized PageRank is that if one of the target words has two senses which are related by semantic relations, those senses reinforce each other, and could thus dampen the effect of the other senses in the context. With this observation in mind we devised a variant (dubbed *Ppr_w2w*), where we build the graph for each target word in the context: for each target word W_i, we concentrate the initial probability mass in the senses of the words surrounding W_i, but not in the senses of the target word itself, so that context words increase its relative importance in the graph. The main idea of this approach is to avoid biasing the initial score of concepts associated to target word W_i, and let the surrounding words decide which concept associated to W_i has more relevance. Contrary to the other two approaches, *Ppr_w2w* does not disambiguate all target words of the context in a single run, which makes it less efficient (cf. Section 7).

4 Evaluation framework and results

In this paper we will use two datasets for comparing graph-based WSD methods, namely, the Senseval-2 (S2AW) and Senseval-3 (S3AW) all words datasets (Snyder and Palmer, 2004; Palmer et al., 2001), which are both labeled with WordNet 1.7 tags. We did not use the Semeval dataset, for the sake of comparing our results to related work, none of which used Semeval data. Table 1 shows the results as recall of the graph-based WSD system over these datasets on the different LKBs. We detail overall results, as well as results per PoS, and the confidence interval for the overall results. The interval was computed using bootstrap resampling with 95% confidence.

The table shows that *Ppr_w2w* is consistently the best method in both datasets and for all LKBs. *Ppr* and *Spr* obtain comparable results, which is remarkable, given the simplicity of the *Ppr* algo-

Senseval-2 All Words dataset							
LKB	Method	All	N	V	Adj.	Adv.	Conf. interval
MCR16 + Xwn	Ppr	51.1	64.9	38.1	57.4	47.5	[49.3, 52.6]
MCR16 + Xwn	Ppr_w2w	53.3	64.5	38.6	**58.3**	48.1	[52.0, 55.0]
MCR16 + Xwn	Spr	52.7	64.8	35.3	56.8	50.2	[51.3, 54.4]
WNet17 + Xwn	Ppr	56.8	71.1	33.4	55.9	67.1	[55.0, 58.7]
WNet17 + Xwn	Ppr_w2w	**58.6**	70.4	**38.9**	**58.3**	70.1	[56.7, 60.3]
WNet17 + Xwn	Spr	56.7	66.8	37.7	57.6	**70.8**	[55.0, 58.2]
WNet30 + gloss	Ppr	53.5	70.0	28.6	53.9	55.1	[51.8, 55.2]
WNet30 + gloss	Ppr_w2w	55.8	**71.9**	34.4	53.8	57.5	[54.1, 57.8]
WNet30 + gloss	Spr	54.8	68.9	35.1	55.2	56.5	[53.2, 56.3]
MFS		60.1	71.2	39.0	61.1	75.4	[58.6, 61.9]
SMUaw		68.6	78.0	52.9	69.9	81.7	
Senseval-3 All Words dataset							
LKB	Method	All	N	V	Adj.	Adv.	
MCR16 + Xwn	Ppr	54.3	60.9	45.4	56.5	**92.9**	[52.3, 56.1]
MCR16 + Xwn	Ppr_w2w	55.8	63.2	46.2	57.5	**92.9**	[53.7, 57.7]
MCR16 + Xwn	Static	53.7	59.5	45.0	57.8	**92.9**	[51.8, 55.7]
WNet17 + Xwn	Ppr	56.1	62.6	46.0	60.8	**92.9**	[54.0, 58.1]
WNet17 + Xwn	Ppr_w2w	**57.4**	**64.1**	46.9	**62.6**	**92.9**	[55.5, 59.3]
WNet17 + Xwn	Spr	56.20	61.6	**47.3**	61.8	**92.9**	[54.8, 58.2]
WNet30 + gloss	Ppr	48.5	52.2	41.5	54.2	78.6	[46.7, 50.6]
WNet30 + gloss	Ppr_w2w	51.6	59.0	40.2	57.2	78.6	[49.9, 53.3]
WNet30 + gloss	Spr	45.4	54.1	31.4	52.5	78.6	[43.7, 47.4]
MFS		62.3	69.3	53.6	63.7	92.9	[60.2, 64.0]
GAMBL		65.2	70.8	59.3	65.3	100	

Table 1: Results (as recall) on Senseval-2 and Senseval-3 all words tasks. We also include the MFS baseline and the best results of supervised systems at competition time (SMUaw,GAMBL).

rithm, compared to the more elaborate algorithm to construct the graph. The differences between methods are not statistically significant, which is a common problem on this relatively small datasets (Snyder and Palmer, 2004; Palmer et al., 2001).

Regarding LKBs, the best results are obtained using WordNet 1.7 and eXtended WordNet. Here the differences are in many cases significant. These results are surprising, as we would expect that the manually disambiguated gloss relations from WordNet 3.0 would lead to better results, compared to the automatically disambiguated gloss relations from the eXtended WordNet (linked to version 1.7). The lower performance of WNet30+gloss can be due to the fact that the Senseval all words data set is tagged using WordNet 1.7 synsets. When using a different LKB for WSD, a mapping to WordNet 1.7 is required. Although the mapping is cited as having a correctness on the high 90s (Daude et al., 2000), it could have introduced sufficient noise to counteract the benefits of the hand-disambiguated glosses.

Table 1 also shows the most frequent sense (MFS), as well as the best supervised systems (Snyder and Palmer, 2004; Palmer et al., 2001) that participated in each competition (SMUaw and GAMBL, respectively). The MFS is a baseline for supervised systems, but it is considered a difficult competitor for unsupervised systems, which rarely come close to it. In this case the MFS baseline was computed using previously availabel training data like SemCor. Our best results are close to the MFS in both Senseval-2 and Senseval-3 datasets. The results for the supervised system are given for reference, and we can see that the gap is relatively small, specially for Senseval-3.

5 Comparison to Related work

In this section we will briefly describe some graph-based methods for knowledge-based WSD. The methods here presented cope with the problem of sequence-labeling, i.e., they disambiguate all the words coocurring in a sequence (typically, all content words of a sentence). All the methods rely on the information represented on some LKB, which typically is some version of WordNet, sometimes enriched with proprietary relations. The results on our datasets, when available, are shown in Table 2. The table also shows the performance of supervised systems.

The TexRank algorithm (Mihalcea, 2005) for WSD creates a complete weighted graph (e.g. a graph where every pair of distinct vertices is connected by a weighted edge) formed by the synsets of the words in the input context. The weight

Senseval-2 All Words dataset					
System	All	N	V	Adj.	Adv.
Mih05	54.2	57.5	36.5	56.7	70.9
Sihna07	56.4	65.6	32.3	**61.4**	60.2
Tsatsa07	49.2	–	–	–	–
Spr	56.6	66.7	37.5	57.6	**70.8**
Ppr	56.8	**71.1**	33.4	55.9	67.1
Ppr_w2w	**58.6**	70.4	**38.9**	58.3	70.1
MFS	60.1	71.2	39.0	61.1	75.4
Senseval-3 All Words dataset					
System	All	N	V	Adj.	Adv.
Mih05	52.2	-	-	-	-
Sihna07	52.4	60.5	40.6	54.1	**100.0**
Nav07	-	61.9	36.1	**62.8**	-
Spr	56.2	61.6	**47.3**	61.8	92.9
Ppr	56.1	62.6	46.0	60.8	92.9
Ppr_w2w	**57.4**	**64.1**	46.9	62.6	92.9
MFS	62.3	69.3	53.6	63.7	92.9
Nav05	60.4	-	-	-	-

Table 2: Comparison with related work. Note that Nav05 uses the MFS.

of the links joining two synsets is calculated by executing Lesk's algorithm (Lesk, 1986) between them, i.e., by calculating the overlap between the words in the glosses of the correspongind senses. Once the complete graph is built, the PageRank algorithm is executed over it and words are assigned to the most relevant synset. In this sense, PageRank is used an alternative to simulated annealing to find the optimal pairwise combinations. The method was evaluated on the Senseval-3 dataset, as shown in row Mih05 on Table 2.

(Sinha and Mihalcea, 2007) extends their previous work by using a collection of semantic similarity measures when assigning a weight to the links across synsets. They also compare different graph-based centrality algorithms to rank the vertices of the complete graph. They use different similarity metrics for different POS types and a voting scheme among the centrality algorithm ranks. Here, the Senseval-3 corpus was used as a development data set, and we can thus see those results as the upper-bound of their method.

We can see in Table 2 that the methods presented in this paper clearly outperform both Mih05 and Sin07. This result suggests that analyzing the LKB structure as a whole is preferable than computing pairwise similarity measures over synsets. The results of various in-house made experiments replicating (Mihalcea, 2005) also confirm this observation. Note also that our methods are simpler than the combination strategy used in (Sinha and Mihalcea, 2007), and that we did not perform any parameter tuning as they did.

In (Navigli and Velardi, 2005) the authors develop a knowledge-based WSD method based on lexical chains called structural semantic interconnections (SSI). Although the system was first designed to find the meaning of the words in WordNet glosses, the authors also apply the method for labeling text sequences. Given a text sequence, SSI first identifies monosemous words and assigns the corresponding synset to them. Then, it iteratively disambiguates the rest of terms by selecting the senses that get the strongest interconnection with the synsets selected so far. The interconnection is calculated by searching for paths on the LKB, constrained by some hand-made rules of possible semantic patterns. The method was evaluated on the Senseval-3 dataset, as shown in row Nav05 on Table 2. Note that the method labels an instance with the most frequent sense of the word if the algorithm produces no output for that instance, which makes comparison to our system unfair, specially given the fact that the MFS performs better than SSI. In fact it is not possible to separate the effect of SSI from that of the MFS. For this reason we place this method close to the MFS baseline in Table 2.

In (Navigli and Lapata, 2007), the authors perform a two-stage process for WSD. Given an input context, the method first explores the whole LKB in order to find a subgraph which is particularly relevant for the words of the context. Then, they study different graph-based centrality algorithms for deciding the relevance of the nodes on the subgraph. As a result, every word of the context is attached to the highest ranking concept among its possible senses. The *Spr* method is very similar to (Navigli and Lapata, 2007), the main difference lying on the initial method for extracting the context subgraph. Whereas (Navigli and Lapata, 2007) apply a depth-first search algorithm over the LKB graph —and restrict the depth of the subtree to a value of 3—, *Spr* relies on shortest paths between word synsets. Navigli and Lapata don't report overall results and therefore, we can't directly compare our results with theirs. However, we can see that on a PoS-basis evaluation our results are consistently better for nouns and verbs (especially the *Ppr_w2w* method) and rather similar for adjectives.

(Tsatsaronis et al., 2007) is another example of a two-stage process, the first one consisting on finding a relevant subgraph by performing a BFS

Spanish Semeval07		
LKB	Method	Acc.
Spanish Wnet + Xnet*	Ppr	78.4
Spanish Wnet + Xnet*	Ppr_w2w	79.3
–	MFS	84.6
–	Supervised	85.10

Table 3: Results (accuracy) on Spanish Semeval07 dataset, including MFS and the best supervised system in the competition.

search over the LKB. The authors apply a spreading activation algorithm over the subgraph for node ranking. Edges of the subgraph are weighted according to its type, following a tf.idf like approach. The results show that our methods clearly outperform Tsatsa07. The fact that the *Spr* method works better suggests that the traditional PageRank algorithm is a superior method for ranking the subgraph nodes.

As stated before, all methods presented here use some LKB for performing WSD. (Mihalcea, 2005) and (Sinha and Mihalcea, 2007) use WordNet relations as a knowledge source, but neither of them specify which particular version did they use. (Tsatsaronis et al., 2007) uses WordNet 1.7 enriched with eXtended WordNet relations, just as we do. Both (Navigli and Velardi, 2005; Navigli and Lapata, 2007) use WordNet 2.0 as the underlying LKB, albeit enriched with several new relations, which are manually created. Unfortunately, those manual relations are not publicly available, so we can't directly compare their results with the rest of the methods. In (Agirre and Soroa, 2008) we experiment with different LKBs formed by combining relations of different MCR versions along with relations extracted from SemCor, which we call supervised and unsupervised relations, respectively. The unsupervised relations that yielded bests results are also used in this paper (c.f Section 3.1).

6 Experiments on Spanish

Our WSD algorithm can be applied over non-english texts, provided that a LKB for this particular language exists. We have tested the graph-algorithms proposed in this paper on a Spanish dataset, using the Spanish WordNet as knowledge source (Atserias et al., 2004a).

We used the Semeval-2007 Task 09 dataset as evaluation gold standard (Màrquez et al., 2007). The dataset contains examples of the 150 most frequent nouns in the CESS-ECE corpus, manually annotated with Spanish WordNet synsets. It is split into a train and test part, and has an "all words" shape i.e. input consists on sentences, each one having at least one occurrence of a target noun. We ran the experiment over the test part (792 instances), and used the train part for calculating the MFS baseline. We used the Spanish WordNet as LKB, enriched with eXtended WordNet relations. It contains 105, 501 nodes and 623, 316 relations. The results in Table 3 are consistent with those for English, with our algorithm approaching MFS performance. Note that for this dataset the supervised algorithm could barely improve over the MFS, suggesting that for this particular dataset MFS is particularly strong.

Method	Time
Ppr	26m46
Spr	119m7
Ppr_w2w	164m4

Table 4: Elapsed time (in minutes) of the algorithms when applied to the Senseval-2 dataset.

7 Performance analysis

Table 4 shows the time spent by the different algorithms when applied to the Senseval-2 all words dataset, using the WNet17 + Xwn as LKB. The dataset consists on 2473 word instances appearing on 476 different sentences. The experiments were done on a computer with four 2.66 Ghz processors and 16 Gb memory. The table shows that the time elapsed by the algorithms varies between 30 minutes for the *Ppr* method (which thus disambiguates circa 82 instances per minute) to almost 3 hours spent by the *Ppr_w2w* method (circa 15 instances per minute). The *Spr* method lies in between, requiring 2 hours for completing the task, but its overall performance is well below the PageRank based *Ppr_w2w* method. Note that the algorithm is coded in C++ for greater efficiency, and uses the Boost Graph Library.

Regarding PageRank calculation, we have tried different numbers of iterations, and analyze the rate of convergence of the algorithm. Figure 1 depicts the performance of the *Ppr_w2w* method for different iterations of the algorithm. As before, the algorithm is applied over the MCR17 + Xwn LKB, and evaluated on the Senseval-2 all words dataset. The algorithm converges very quickly: one sole iteration suffices for achieving a relatively high per-

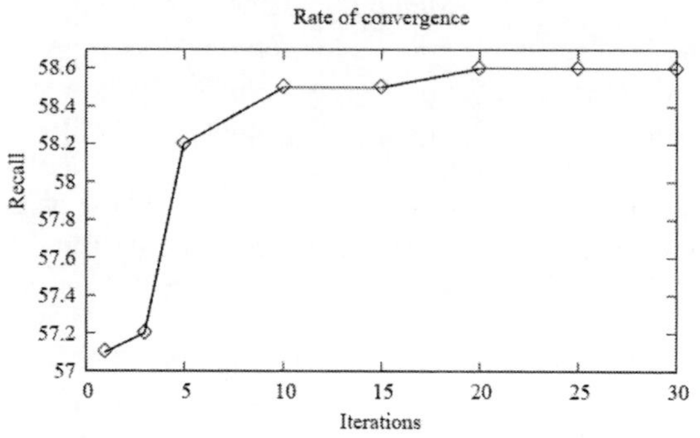

Figure 1: Rate of convergence of PageRank algorithm over the MCR17 + Xwn LKB.

formance, and 20 iterations are enough for achieving convergence. The figure shows that, depending on the LKB complexity, the user can tune the algorithm and lower the number of iterations, thus considerably reducing the time required for disambiguation.

8 Conclusions

In this paper we propose a new graph-based method that uses the knowledge in a LKB (based on WordNet) in order to perform unsupervised Word Sense Disambuation. Our algorithm uses the full graph of the LKB efficiently, performing better than previous approaches in English all-words datasets. We also show that the algorithm can be easily ported to other languages with good results, with the only requirement of having a wordnet. Both for Spanish and English the algorithm attains performances close to the MFS.

The algorithm is publicly available[5] and can be applied easily to sense inventories and knowledge bases different from WordNet. Our analysis shows that our algorithm is efficient compared to previously proposed alternatives, and that a good choice of WordNet versions and relations is fundamental for good performance.

Acknowledgments

This work has been partially funded by the EU Commission (project KYOTO ICT-2007-211423) and Spanish Research Department (project KNOW TIN2006-15049-C03-01).

References

E. Agirre and G. Rigau. 1996. Word sense disambiguation using conceptual density. In *In Proceedings of the 16th International Conference on Computational Linguistics*, pages 16–22.

E. Agirre and A. Soroa. 2008. Using the multilingual central repository for graph-based word sense disambiguation. In *Proceedings of LREC '08*, Marrakesh, Morocco.

J. Atserias, G. Rigau, and L. Villarejo. 2004a. Spanish wordnet 1.6: Porting the spanish wordnet across princeton versions. In *In Proceedings of LREC '04*.

J. Atserias, L. Villarejo, G. Rigau, E. Agirre, J. Carroll, B. Magnini, and P. Vossen. 2004b. The meaning multilingual central repository. In *In Proceedings of GWC*, Brno, Czech Republic.

S. Brin and L. Page. 1998. The anatomy of a large-scale hypertextual web search engine. *Computer Networks and ISDN Systems*, 30(1-7).

J. Cowie, J. Guthrie, and L. Guthrie. 1992. Lexical disambiguation using simulated annealing. In *HLT '91: Proceedings of the workshop on Speech and Natural Language*, pages 238–242, Morristown, NJ, USA.

J. Daude, L. Padro, and G. Rigau. 2000. Mapping WordNets using structural information. In *Proceedings of ACL'2000*, Hong Kong.

T. H. Haveliwala. 2002. Topic-sensitive pagerank. In *WWW '02: Proceedings of the 11th international conference on World Wide Web*, pages 517–526, New York, NY, USA. ACM.

A. N. Langville and C. D. Meyer. 2003. Deeper inside pagerank. *Internet Mathematics*, 1(3):335–380.

M. Lesk. 1986. Automatic sense disambiguation using machine readable dictionaries: how to tell a pine cone from an ice cream cone. In *SIGDOC '86: Proceedings of the 5th annual international conference on Systems documentation*, pages 24–26, New York, NY, USA. ACM.

L. Màrquez, L. Villarejo, M. A. Martí, and M. Taulé. 2007. Semeval-2007 task 09: Multilevel semantic annotation of catalan and spanish. In *Proceedings of SemEval-2007*, pages 42–47, Prague, Czech Republic, June.

D. McCarthy, R. Koeling, J. Weeds, and J. Carroll. 2004. Finding predominant word senses in untagged text. In *ACL '04: Proceedings of the 42nd Annual Meeting on Association for Computational Linguistics*, page 279, Morristown, NJ, USA. Association for Computational Linguistics.

R. Mihalcea and D. I. Moldovan. 2001. eXtended WordNet: Progress report. In *in Proceedings of NAACL Workshop on WordNet and Other Lexical Resources*, pages 95–100.

R. Mihalcea. 2005. Unsupervised large-vocabulary word sense disambiguation with graph-based algorithms for sequence data labeling. In *Proceedings of HLT05*, Morristown, NJ, USA.

[5] http://ixa2.si.ehu.es/ukb

R. Navigli and M. Lapata. 2007. Graph connectivity measures for unsupervised word sense disambiguation. In *IJCAI*.

R. Navigli and P. Velardi. 2005. Structural semantic interconnections: A knowledge-based approach to word sense disambiguation. *IEEE Trans. Pattern Anal. Mach. Intell.*, 27(7):1075–1086.

M. Palmer, C. Fellbaum, S. Cotton, L. Delfs, and H.T. Dang. 2001. English tasks: All-words and verb lexical sample. In *Proc. of SENSEVAL-2: Second International Workshop on Evaluating Word Sense Disambiguation Systems*, Tolouse, France, July.

S. Pradhan, E. Loper, D. Dligach, and M.Palmer. 2007. Semeval-2007 task-17: English lexical sample srl and all words. In *Proceedings of SemEval-2007*, pages 87–92, Prague, Czech Republic, June.

R. Sinha and R. Mihalcea. 2007. Unsupervised graph-based word sense disambiguation using measures of word semantic similarity. In *Proceedings of the IEEE International Conference on Semantic Computing (ICSC 2007)*, Irvine, CA, USA.

B. Snyder and M. Palmer. 2004. The English all-words task. In *ACL 2004 Senseval-3 Workshop*, Barcelona, Spain, July.

G. Tsatsaronis, M. Vazirgiannis, and I. Androutsopoulos. 2007. Word sense disambiguation with spreading activation networks generated from thesauri. In *IJCAI*.

Supervised Domain Adaption for WSD

Eneko Agirre and Oier Lopez de Lacalle
IXA NLP Group
University of the Basque Country
Donostia, Basque Contry
{e.agirre,oier.lopezdelacalle}@ehu.es

Abstract

The lack of positive results on supervised domain adaptation for WSD have cast some doubts on the utility of hand-tagging general corpora and thus developing generic supervised WSD systems. In this paper we show for the first time that our WSD system trained on a general source corpus (BNC) and the target corpus, obtains up to 22% error reduction when compared to a system trained on the target corpus alone. In addition, we show that as little as 40% of the target corpus (when supplemented with the source corpus) is sufficient to obtain the same results as training on the full target data. The key for success is the use of unlabeled data with SVD, a combination of kernels and SVM.

1 Introduction

In many Natural Language Processing (NLP) tasks we find that a large collection of manually-annotated text is used to train and test supervised machine learning models. While these models have been shown to perform very well when tested on the text collection related to the training data (what we call the **source** domain), the performance drops considerably when testing on text from other domains (called **target** domains).

In order to build models that perform well in new (target) domains we usually find two settings (Daumé III, 2007). In the semi-supervised setting, the training hand-annotated text from the source domain is supplemented with unlabeled data from the target domain. In the supervised setting, we use training data from both the source and target domains to test on the target domain.

In (Agirre and Lopez de Lacalle, 2008) we studied semi-supervised Word Sense Disambiguation (WSD) adaptation, and in this paper we focus on supervised WSD adaptation. We compare the performance of similar supervised WSD systems on three different scenarios. In the **source to target scenario** the WSD system is trained on the source domain and tested on the target domain. In the **target scenario** the WSD system is trained and tested on the target domain (using cross-validation). In the **adaptation scenario** the WSD system is trained on both source and target domain and tested in the target domain (also using cross-validation over the target data). The source to target scenario represents a weak baseline for domain adaptation, as it does not use any examples from the target domain. The target scenario represents the hard baseline, and in fact, if the domain adaptation scenario does not yield better results, the adaptation would have failed, as it would mean that the source examples are not useful when we do have hand-labeled target examples.

Previous work shows that current state-of-the-art WSD systems are not able to obtain better results on the adaptation scenario compared to the target scenario (Escudero et al., 2000; Agirre and Martínez, 2004; Chan and Ng, 2007). This would mean that if a user of a generic WSD system (i.e. based on hand-annotated examples from a generic corpus) would need to adapt it to a specific domain, he would be better off throwing away the generic examples and hand-tagging domain examples directly. This paper will show that domain adaptation is feasible, even for difficult domain-related words, in the sense that generic corpora can be reused when deploying WSD systems in specific domains. We will also show that, given the source corpus, our technique can save up to 60% of effort when tagging domain-related occurrences.

We performed on a publicly available corpus which was designed to study the effect of domains in WSD (Koeling et al., 2005). It comprises 41

Proceedings of the 12th Conference of the European Chapter of the ACL, pages 42–50,
Athens, Greece, 30 March – 3 April 2009.

nouns which are highly relevant in the SPORTS and FINANCES domains, with 300 examples for each. The use of two target domains strengthens the conclusions of this paper.

Our system uses Singular Value Decomposition (SVD) in order to find correlations between terms, which are helpful to overcome the scarcity of training data in WSD (Gliozzo et al., 2005). This work explores how this ability of SVD and a combination of the resulting feature spaces improves domain adaptation. We present two ways to combine the reduced spaces: kernel combination with Support Vector Machines (SVM), and k Nearest-Neighbors (k-NN) combination.

The paper is structured as follows. Section 2 reviews prior work in the area. Section 3 presents the data sets used. In Section 4 we describe the learning features, including the application of SVD, and in Section 5 the learning methods and the combination. The experimental results are presented in Section 6. Section 7 presents the discussion and some analysis of this paper and finally Section 8 draws the conclusions.

2 Prior work

Domain adaptation is a practical problem attracting more and more attention. In the supervised setting, a recent paper by Daumé III (2007) shows that a simple feature augmentation method for SVM is able to effectively use both labeled target and source data to provide the best domain-adaptation results in a number of NLP tasks. His method improves or equals over previously explored more sophisticated methods (Daumé III and Marcu, 2006; Chelba and Acero, 2004). The feature augmentation consists in making three version of the original features: a general, a source-specific and a target-specific versions. That way the augmented source contains the general and source-specific version and the augmented target data general and specific versions. The idea behind this is that target domain data has twice the influence as the source when making predictions about test target data. We reimplemented this method and show that our results are better.

Regarding WSD, some initial works made a basic analysis of domain adaptation issues. Escudero et al. (2000) tested the supervised adaptation scenario on the DSO corpus, which had examples from the Brown corpus and Wall Street Journal corpus. They found that the source corpus did not help when tagging the target corpus, showing that tagged corpora from each domain would suffice, and concluding that hand tagging a large general corpus would not guarantee robust broad-coverage WSD. Agirre and Martínez (2000) used the DSO corpus in the supervised scenario to show that training on a subset of the source corpora that is topically related to the target corpus does allow for some domain adaptation.

More recently, Chan and Ng (2007) performed supervised domain adaptation on a manually selected subset of 21 nouns from the DSO corpus. They used active learning, count-merging, and predominant sense estimation in order to save target annotation effort. They showed that adding just 30% of the target data to the source examples the same precision as the full combination of target and source data could be achieved. They also showed that using the source corpus allowed to significantly improve results when only 10%-30% of the target corpus was used for training. Unfortunately, no data was given about the target corpus results, thus failing to show that domain-adaptation succeeded. In followup work (Zhong et al., 2008), the feature augmentation approach was combined with active learning and tested on the OntoNotes corpus, on a large domain-adaptation experiment. They reduced significantly the effort of hand-tagging, but only obtained domain-adaptation for smaller fractions of the source and target corpus. Similarly to these works we show that we can save annotation effort on the target corpus, but, in contrast, we do get domain adaptation when using the full dataset. In a way our approach is complementary, and we could also apply active learning to further reduce the number of target examples to be tagged.

Though not addressing domain adaptation, other works on WSD also used SVD and are closely related to the present paper. Ando (2006) used Alternative Structured Optimization. She first trained one linear predictor for each target word, and then performed SVD on 7 carefully selected submatrices of the feature-to-predictor matrix of weights. The system attained small but consistent improvements (no significance data was given) on the Senseval-3 lexical sample datasets using SVD and unlabeled data.

Gliozzo et al. (2005) used SVD to reduce the space of the term-to-document matrix, and then computed the similarity between train and test instances using a mapping to the reduced space (similar to our SMA method in Section 4.2). They combined other knowledge sources into a complex kernel using SVM. They report improved performance on a number of languages in the Senseval-3 lexical sample dataset. Our present paper differs from theirs in that we propose an additional method to use SVD (the OMT method), and that we focus on domain adaptation.

In the semi-supervised setting, Blitzer et al. (2006) used Structural Correspondence Learning and unlabeled data to adapt a Part-of-Speech tagger. They carefully select so-called 'pivot features' to learn linear predictors, perform SVD on the weights learned by the predictor, and thus learn correspondences among features in both source and target domains. Our technique also uses SVD, but we directly apply it to all features, and thus avoid the need to define pivot features. In preliminary work we unsuccessfully tried to carry along the idea of pivot features to WSD. On the contrary, in (Agirre and Lopez de Lacalle, 2008) we show that methods closely related to those presented in this paper produce positive semi-supervised domain adaptation results for WSD.

The methods used in this paper originated in (Agirre et al., 2005; Agirre and Lopez de Lacalle, 2007), where SVD over a feature-to-documents matrix improved WSD performance with and without unlabeled data. The use of several k-NN classifiers trained on a number of reduced and original spaces was shown to get the best results in the Senseval-3 dataset and ranked second in the SemEval 2007 competition. The present paper extends this work and applies it to domain adaptation.

3 Data sets

The dataset we use was designed for domain-related WSD experiments by Koeling et al. (2005), and is publicly available. The examples come from the BNC (Leech, 1992) and the SPORTS and FINANCES sections of the Reuters corpus (Rose et al., 2002), comprising around 300 examples (roughly 100 from each of those corpora) for each of the 41 nouns. The nouns were selected because they were salient in either the SPORTS or FINANCES domains, or because they had senses linked to those domains. The occurrences were hand-tagged with the senses from WordNet (WN) version 1.7.1 (Fellbaum, 1998). In our experiments the BNC examples play the role of general **source** corpora, and the FINANCES and SPORTS examples the role of two specific domain **target** corpora.

Compared to the DSO corpus used in prior work (cf. Section 2) this corpus has been explicitly created for domain adaptation studies. DSO contains texts coming from the Brown corpus and the Wall Street Journal, but the texts are not classified according to specific domains (e.g. Sports, Finances), which make DSO less suitable to study domain adaptation. The fact that the selected nouns are related to the target domain makes the (Koeling et al., 2005) corpus more demanding than the DSO corpus, because one would expect the performance of a generic WSD system to drop when moving to the domain corpus for domain-related words (cf. Table 1), while the performance would be similar for generic words.

In addition to the labeled data, we also use unlabeled data coming from the three sources used in the labeled corpus: the 'written' part of the BNC (89.7M words), the FINANCES part of Reuters (32.5M words), and the SPORTS part (9.1M words).

4 Original and SVD features

In this section, we review the features and two methods to apply SVD over the features.

4.1 Features

We relied on the usual features used in previous WSD work, grouped in three main sets. **Local collocations** comprise the bigrams and trigrams formed around the target word (using either lemmas, word-forms, or PoS tags) , those formed with the previous/posterior lemma/word-form in the sentence, and the content words in a $\pm$4-word window around the target. **Syntactic dependencies** use the object, subject, noun-modifier, preposition, and sibling lemmas, when available. Finally, **Bag-of-words features** are the lemmas of the content words in the whole context, plus the salient bigrams in the context (Pedersen, 2001). We refer to these features as **original features**.

4.2 SVD features

Apart from the original space of features, we have used the so called **SVD features**, obtained from the projection of the feature vectors into the reduced space (Deerwester et al., 1990). Basically, we set a term-by-document or feature-by-example matrix M from the corpus (see section below for more details). SVD decomposes M into three matrices, $M = U\Sigma V^T$. If the desired number of dimensions in the reduced space is p, we select p rows from Σ and V, yielding Σ_p and V_p respectively. We can map any feature vector $\vec{t}$ (which represents either a train or test example) into the p-dimensional space as follows: $\vec{t_p} = \vec{t}^T V_p \Sigma_p^{-1}$. Those mapped vectors have p dimensions, and each of the dimensions is what we call a SVD feature. We have explored two different variants in order to build the reduced matrix and obtain the SVD features, as follows.

Single Matrix for All target words (SVD-SMA). The method comprises the following steps: (i) extract bag-of-word features (terms in this case) from unlabeled corpora, (ii) build the term-by-document matrix, (iii) decompose it with SVD, and (iv) map the labeled data (train/test). This technique is very similar to previous work on SVD (Gliozzo et al., 2005; Zelikovitz and Hirsh, 2001). The dimensionality reduction is performed once, over the whole unlabeled corpus, and it is then applied to the labeled data of each word. The reduced space is constructed only with terms, which correspond to bag-of-words features, and thus discards the rest of the features. Given that the WSD literature shows that all features are necessary for optimal performance (Pradhan et al., 2007), we propose the following alternative to construct the matrix.

One Matrix per Target word (SVD-OMT). For each word: (i) construct a corpus with its occurrences in the labeled and, if desired, unlabeled corpora, (ii) extract all features, (iii) build the feature-by-example matrix, (iv) decompose it with SVD, and (v) map all the labeled training and test data for the word. Note that this variant performs one SVD process for each target word separately, hence its name.

When building the SVD-OMT matrices we can use only the training data (TRAIN) or both the train and unlabeled data (+UNLAB). When building the SVD-SMA matrices, given the small size of the individual word matrices, we always use both the train and unlabeled data (+UNLAB). Regarding the amount of data, based also on previous work, we used 50% of the available data for OMT, and the whole corpora for SMA. An important parameter when doing SVD is the number of dimensions in the reduced space (p). We tried two different values for p (25 and 200) in the BNC domain, and set a dimension for each classifier/matrix combination.

4.3 Motivation

The motivation behind our method is that although the train and test feature vectors overlap sufficiently in the usual WSD task, the domain difference makes such overlap more scarce. SVD implicitly finds correlations among features, as it maps related features into nearby regions in the reduced space. In the case of SMA, SVD is applied over the joint term-by-document matrix of labeled (and possibly unlabeled corpora), and it thus can find correlations among closely related words (e.g. *cat* and *dog*). These correlations can help reduce the gap among bag-of-words features from the source and target examples. In the case of OMT, SVD over the joint feature-by-example matrix of labeled and unlabeled examples of a word allows to find correlations among features that show similar occurrence patterns in the source and target corpora for the target word.

5 Learning methods

k-NN is a memory based learning method, where the neighbors are the k most similar labeled examples to the test example. The similarity among instances is measured by the cosine of their vectors. The test instance is labeled with the sense obtaining the maximum sum of the weighted vote of the k most similar contexts. We set k to 5 based on previous results published in (Agirre and Lopez de Lacalle, 2007).

Regarding SVM, we used linear kernels, but also purpose-built kernels for the reduced spaces and the combinations (cf. Section 5.2). We used the default soft margin (C=0). In previous experiments we learnt that C is very dependent on the feature set and training data used. As we will experiment with different features and training datasets, it did not make sense to optimize it across all settings.

We will now detail how we combined the original and SVD features in each of the machine learning methods.

5.1 k-NN combinations

Our k-NN combination method (Agirre et al., 2005; Agirre and Lopez de Lacalle, 2007) takes advantage of the properties of k-NN classifiers and exploit the fact that a classifier can be seen as k points (number of nearest neighbor) each casting one vote. This makes easy to combine several classifiers, one for each feature space. For instance, taking two k-NN classifiers of $k = 5$, C_1 and C_2, we can combine them into a single $k = 10$ classifier, where five votes come from C_1 and five from C_2. This allows to smoothly combine classifiers from different feature spaces.

In this work we built three single k-NN classifiers trained on OMT, SMA and the original features, respectively. In order to combine them we weight each vote by the inverse ratio of its position in the rank of the single classifier, $(k - r_i + 1)/k$, where r_i is the rank.

5.2 Kernel combination

The basic idea of kernel methods is to find a suitable mapping function (ϕ) in order to get a better generalization. Instead of doing this mapping explicitly, kernels give the chance to do it inside the algorithm. We will formalize it as follows. First, we define the mapping function $\phi : \mathcal{X} \rightarrow \mathcal{F}$. Once the function is defined, we can use it in the kernel function in order to become an implicit function $K(\mathbf{x}, \mathbf{z}) = \langle \phi(\mathbf{x}) \cdot \phi(\mathbf{z}) \rangle$, where $\langle \cdot \rangle$ denotes a inner product between vectors in the feature space. This way, we can very easily define mappings representing different information sources and use this mappings in several machine learning algorithm. In our work we use SVM.

We defined three individual kernels (OMT, SMA and original features) and the combined kernel.

The **original feature kernel** (K_{Orig}) is given by the identity function over the features $\phi : \mathcal{X} \rightarrow \mathcal{X}$, defining the following kernel:

$$K_{Orig}(\mathbf{x_i}, \mathbf{x_j}) = \frac{\langle \mathbf{x_i} \cdot \mathbf{x_j} \rangle}{\sqrt{\langle \mathbf{x_i} \cdot \mathbf{x_i} \rangle \langle \mathbf{x_j} \cdot \mathbf{x_j} \rangle}}$$

where the denominator is used to normalize and avoid any kind of bias in the combination.

The **OMT kernel** (K_{Omt}) and **SMA kernel** (K_{Sma}) are defined using OMT and SMA projection matrices, respectively (cf. Section 4.2). Given the OMT function mapping $\phi_{omt} : \mathbb{R}^m \rightarrow \mathbb{R}^p$, where m is the number of the original features and p the reduced dimensionality, then we define $K_{Omt}(\mathbf{x_i}, \mathbf{x_j})$ as follows (K_{Sma} is defined similarly):

$$\frac{\langle \phi_{omt}(\mathbf{x_i}) \cdot \phi_{omt}(\mathbf{x_j}) \rangle}{\sqrt{\langle \phi_{omt}(\mathbf{x_i}) \cdot \phi_{omt}(\mathbf{x_i}) \rangle \langle \phi_{omt}(\mathbf{x_j}) \cdot \phi_{omt}(\mathbf{x_j}) \rangle}}$$

BNC $\rightarrow \mathcal{X}$	SPORTS	FINANCES
MFS	39.0	51.2
k-NN	51.7	60.4
SVM	**53.9**	**62.9**

Table 1: Source to target results: Train on BNC, test on SPORTS and FINANCES.

Finally, we define the kernel combination:

$$K_{Comb}(\mathbf{x_i}, \mathbf{x_j}) = \sum_{l=1}^{n} \frac{K_l(\mathbf{x_i}, \mathbf{x_j})}{\sqrt{K_l(\mathbf{x_i}, \mathbf{x_i}) K_l(\mathbf{x_j}, \mathbf{x_j})}}$$

where n is the number of single kernels explained above, and l the index for the kernel type.

6 Domain adaptation experiments

In this section we present the results in our two reference scenarios (source to target, target) and our reference scenario (domain adaptation). Note that all methods presented here have full coverage, i.e. they return a sense for all test examples, and therefore precision equals recall, and suffices to compare among systems.

6.1 Source to target scenario: BNC $\rightarrow \mathcal{X}$

In this scenario our supervised WSD systems are trained on the general source corpus (BNC) and tested on the specific target domains separately (SPORTS and FINANCES). We do not perform any kind of adaptation, and therefore the results are those expected for a generic WSD system when applied to domain-specific texts.

Table 1 shows the results for k-NN and SVM trained with the original features on the BNC. In addition, we also show the results for the Most Frequent Sense baseline (MFS) taken from the BNC. The second column denotes the accuracies obtained when testing on SPORTS, and the third column the accuracies for FINANCES. The low accuracy obtained with MFS, e.g. 39.0 of precision in SPORTS, shows the difficulty of this task. Both classifiers improve over MFS. These classifiers are weak baselines for the domain adaptation system.

6.2 Target scenario $\mathcal{X} \rightarrow \mathcal{X}$

In this scenario we lay the harder baseline which the domain adaptation experiments should improve on (cf. next section). The WSD systems are trained and tested on each of the target corpora (SPORTS and FINANCES) using 3-fold cross-validation.

$\mathcal{X} \rightarrow \mathcal{X}$	SPORTS		FINANCES	
	TRAIN	+UNLAB	TRAIN	+UNLAB
MFS	77.8	-	82.3	-
k-NN	84.5	-	87.1	-
SVM	85.1	-	87.0	-
k-NN-OMT	85.0	86.1	87.3	87.6
SVM-OMT	82.9	85.1	85.3	86.4
k-NN-SMA	-	81.1	-	83.2
SVM-SMA	-	81.3	-	84.1
k-NN-COMB	86. 0	**86.7**	87.9	**88.6**
SVM-COMB	-	86.5	-	88.5

Table 2: Target results: train and test on SPORTS, train and test on FINANCES, using 3-fold cross-validation.

Table 2 summarizes the results for this scenario. TRAIN denotes that only tagged data was used to train, +UNLAB denotes that we added unlabeled data related to the source corpus when computing SVD. The rows denote the classifier and the feature spaces used, which are organized in four sections. On the top rows we show the three baseline classifiers on the original features. The two sections below show the results of those classifiers on the reduced dimensions, OMT and SMA (cf. Section 4.2). Finally, the last rows show the results of the combination strategies (cf. Sections 5.1 and 5.2). Note that some of the cells have no result, because that combination is not applicable (e.g. using the train and unlabeled data in the original space).

First of all note that the results for the baselines (MFS, SVM, k-NN) are much larger than those in Table 1, showing that this dataset is specially demanding for supervised WSD, and particularly difficult for domain adaptation experiments. These results seem to indicate that the examples from the source general corpus could be of little use when tagging the target corpora. Note specially the difference in MFS performance. The priors of the senses are very different in the source and target corpora, which is a well-known shortcoming for supervised systems. Note the high results of the baseline classifiers, which leave small room for improvement.

The results for the more sophisticated methods show that SVD and unlabeled data helps slightly, except for k-NN-OMT on SPORTS. SMA decreases the performance compared to the classifiers trained on original features. The best improvements come when the three strategies are combined in one, as both the kernel and k-NN combinations obtain improvements over the respective single classifiers. Note that both the k-NN and SVM combinations perform similarly.

BNC + $\mathcal{X}$ $\rightarrow \mathcal{X}$	SPORTS		FINANCES	
	TRAIN	+ UNLAB	TRAIN	+ UNLAB
BNC $\rightarrow \mathcal{X}$	53.9	-	62.9	-
$\mathcal{X} \rightarrow \mathcal{X}$	86.0	86.7	87.9	88.5
MFS	68.2	-	73.1	-
k-NN	81.3	-	86.0	-
SVM	84.7	-	87.5	-
k-NN-OMT	84.0	84.7	87.5	86.0
SVM-OMT	85.1	84.7	84.2	85.5
k-NN-SMA	-	77.1	-	81.6
SVM-SMA	-	78.1	-	80.7
k-NN-COMB	84.5	87.2	88.1	88.7
SVM-COMB	-	**88.4**	-	**89.7**
SVM-AUG	85.9	-	88.1	-

Table 3: Domain adaptation results: Train on BNC and SPORTS, test on SPORTS (same for FINANCES).

In the combination strategy we show that unlabeled data helps slightly, because instead of only combining OMT and original features we have the opportunity to introduce SMA. Note that it was not our aim to improve the results of the basic classifiers on this scenario, but given the fact that we are going to apply all these techniques in the domain adaptation scenario, we need to show these results as baselines. That is, in the next section we will try to obtain results which improve significantly over the best results in this section.

6.3 Domain adaptation scenario BNC + $\mathcal{X} \rightarrow \mathcal{X}$

In this last scenario we try to show that our WSD system trained on both source (BNC) and target (SPORTS and FINANCES) data performs better than the one trained on the target data alone. We also use 3-fold cross-validation for the target data, but the entire source data is used in each turn. The unlabeled data here refers to the combination of unlabeled source and target data.

The results are presented in table 3. Again, the columns denote if unlabeled data has been used in the learning process. The rows correspond to classifiers and the feature spaces involved. The first rows report the best results in the previous scenarios: BNC $\rightarrow \mathcal{X}$ for the source to target scenario, and $\mathcal{X} \rightarrow \mathcal{X}$ for the target scenario. The rest of the table corresponds to the domain adaptation scenario. The rows below correspond to MFS and the baseline classifiers, followed by the OMT and SMA results, and the combination results. The last row shows the results for the feature augmentation algorithm (Daumé III, 2007).

	SPORTS	FINANCES
BNC $\rightarrow \mathcal{X}$		
MFS	39.0	51.2
SVM	53.9	62.9
$\mathcal{X} \rightarrow \mathcal{X}$		
MFS	77.8	82.3
SVM	85.1	87.0
k-NN-COMB (+UNLAB)	86.7	88.6
BNC $+\mathcal{X} \rightarrow \mathcal{X}$		
MFS	68.2	73.1
SVM	84.7	87.5
SVM-AUG	85.9	88.1
SVM-COMB (+UNLAB)	**88.4**	**89.7**

Table 4: The most important results in each scenario.

Focusing on the results, the table shows that MFS decreases with respect to the target scenario (cf. Table 2) when the source data is added, probably caused by the different sense distributions in BNC and the target corpora. The baseline classifiers (k-NN and SVM) are not able to improve over the baseline classifiers on the target data alone, which is coherent with past research, and shows that straightforward domain adaptation does not work.

The following rows show that our reduction methods on themselves (OMT, SMA used by k-NN and SVM) also fail to perform better than in the target scenario, but the combinations using unlabeled data (k-NN-COMB and specially SVM-COMB) do manage to improve the best results for the target scenario, showing that we were able to attain domain adaptation. The feature augmentation approach (SVM-AUG) does improve slightly over SVM in the target scenario, but not over the best results in the target scenario, showing the difficulty of domain adaptation for WSD, at least on this dataset.

7 Discussion and analysis

Table 4 summarizes the most important results. The kernel combination method with unlabeled data on the adaptation scenario reduces the error on 22.1% and 17.6% over the baseline SVM on the target scenario (SPORTS and FINANCES respectively), and 12.7% and 9.0% over the k-NN combination method on the target scenario. These gains are remarkable given the already high baseline, specially taking into consideration that the 41 nouns are closely related to the domains. The differences, including SVM-AUG, are statistically significant according to the Wilcoxon test with $p < 0.01$.

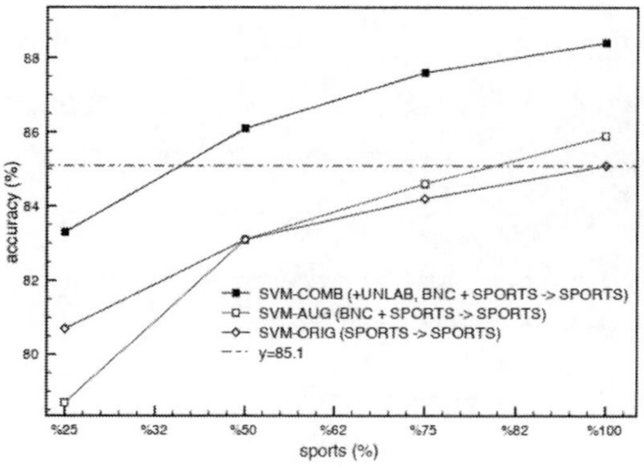

Figure 1: Learning curves for SPORTS. The $\mathcal{X}$ axis denotes the amount of SPORTS data and the Y axis corresponds to accuracy.

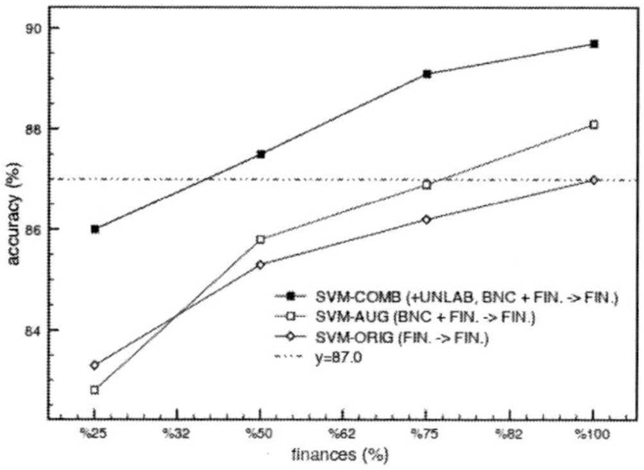

Figure 2: Learning curves for FINANCES. The X axis denotes the amount of FINANCES data and Y axis corresponds to the accuracy.

In addition, we carried extra experiments to examine the learning curves, and to check, given the source examples, how many additional examples from the target corpus are needed to obtain the same results as in the target scenario using all available examples. We fixed the source data and used increasing amounts of target data. We show the original SVM on the target scenario, and SVM-COMB (+UNLAB) and SVM-AUG as the domain adaptation approaches. The results are shown in figure 1 for SPORTS and figure 2 for FINANCES. The horizontal line corresponds to the performance of SVM on the target domain. The point where the learning curves cross the horizontal line show that our domain adaptation method needs only around 40% of the target data in order to get the same performance as the baseline SVM on the target data. The learning curves also shows that the domain adaptation kernel combination approach, no matter the amount of target data, is always above the rest of the classifiers, showing the robustness of our approach.

8 Conclusion and future work

In this paper we explore supervised domain adaptation for WSD with positive results, that is, whether hand-labeling general domain (source) text is worth the effort when training WSD systems that are to be applied to specific domains (targets). We performed several experiments in three scenarios. In the first scenario (source to target scenario), the classifiers were trained on source domain data (the BNC) and tested on the target domains, composed by the SPORTS and FINANCES sections of Reuters. In the second scenario (target scenario) we set the main baseline for our domain adaptation experiment, training and testing our classifiers on the target domain data. In the last scenario (domain adaptation scenario), we combine both source and target data for training, and test on the target data.

We report results in each scenario for k-NN and SVM classifiers, for reduced features obtained using SVD over the training data, for the use of unlabeled data, and for k-NN and SVM combinations of all.

Our results show that our best domain adaptation strategy (using kernel combination of SVD features and unlabeled data related to the training data) yields statistically significant improvements: up to 22% error reduction compared to SVM on the target domain data alone. We also show that our domain adaptation method only needs 40% of the target data (in addition to the source data) in order to get the same results as SVM on the target alone.

We obtain coherent results in two target scenarios, and consistent improvement at all levels of the learning curves, showing the robustness or our findings. We think that our dataset, which comprises examples for 41 nouns that are closely related to the target domains, is specially demanding, as one would expect the performance of a generic WSD system to drop when moving to the domain corpus, **specially** on domain-related words, while we could expect the performance to be similar for generic or unrelated words.

In the future we would like to evaluate our method on other datasets (e.g. DSO or OntoNotes), to test whether the positive results are confirmed. We would also like to study word-by-word behaviour, in order to assess whether target examples are really necessary for words which are less related to the domain.

Acknowledgments

This work has been partially funded by the EU Commission (project KYOTO ICT-2007-211423) and Spanish Research Department (project KNOW TIN2006-15049-C03-01). Oier Lopez de Lacalle has a PhD grant from the Basque Government.

References

Eneko Agirre and Oier Lopez de Lacalle. 2007. Ubc-alm: Combining k-nn with svd for wsd. In *Proceedings of the Fourth International Workshop on Semantic Evaluations (SemEval-2007)*, pages 342–345, Prague, Czech Republic, June. Association for Computational Linguistics.

Eneko Agirre and Oier Lopez de Lacalle. 2008. On robustness and domain adaptation using SVD for word sense disambiguation. In *Proceedings of the 22nd International Conference on Computational Linguistics (Coling 2008)*, pages 17–24, Manchester, UK, August. Coling 2008 Organizing Committee.

Eneko Agirre and David Martínez. 2004. The effect of bias on an automatically-built word sense corpus. *Proceedings of the 4rd International Conference on Languages Resources and Evaluations (LREC)*.

E. Agirre, O.Lopez de Lacalle, and David Martínez. 2005. Exploring feature spaces with svd and unlabeled data for Word Sense Disambiguation. In *Proceedings of the Conference on Recent Advances on Natural Language Processing (RANLP'05)*, Borovets, Bulgaria.

Rie Kubota Ando. 2006. Applying alternating structure optimization to word sense disambiguation. In *Proceedings of the 10th Conference on Computational Natural Language Learning (CoNLL)*, pages 77–84, New York City.

John Blitzer, Ryan McDonald, and Fernando Pereira. 2006. Domain adaptation with structural correspondence learning. In *Proceedings of the 2006 Conference on Empirical Methods in Natural Language Processing*, pages 120–128, Sydney, Australia, July. Association for Computational Linguistics.

Yee Seng Chan and Hwee Tou Ng. 2007. Domain adaptation with active learning for word sense disambiguation. In *Proceedings of the 45th Annual Meeting of the Association of Computational Linguistics*, pages 49–56, Prague, Czech Republic, June. Association for Computational Linguistics.

Ciprian Chelba and Alex Acero. 2004. Adaptation of maximum entropy classifier: Little data can help a lot. In *Proceedings of of th Conference on Empirical Methods in Natural Language Processing (EMNLP)*, Barcelona, Spain.

Hal Daumé III and Daniel Marcu. 2006. Domain adaptation for statistical classifiers. *Journal of Artificial Intelligence Research*, 26:101–126.

Hal Daumé III. 2007. Frustratingly easy domain adaptation. In *Proceedings of the 45th Annual Meeting of the Association of Computational Linguistics*, pages 256–263, Prague, Czech Republic, June. Association for Computational Linguistics.

Scott Deerwester, Susan Dumais, Goerge Furnas, Thomas Landauer, and Richard Harshman. 1990. Indexing by Latent Semantic Analysis. *Journal of the American Society for Information Science*, 41(6):391–407.

Gerard Escudero, Lluiz Márquez, and German Rigau. 2000. An Empirical Study of the Domain Dependence of Supervised Word Sense Didanbiguation Systems. *Proceedings of the joint SIGDAT Conference on Empirical Methods in Natural Language Processing and Very Large Corpora, EMNLP/VLC.*

C. Fellbaum. 1998. *WordNet: An Electronic Lexical Database*. MIT Press.

Alfio Massimiliano Gliozzo, Claudio Giuliano, and Carlo Strapparava. 2005. Domain Kernels for Word Sense Disambiguation. *43nd Annual Meeting of the Association for Computational Linguistics. (ACL-05).*

R. Koeling, D. McCarthy, and J. Carroll. 2005. Domain-specific sense distributions and predominant sense acquisition. In *Proceedings of the Human Language Technology Conference and Conference on Empirical Methods in Natural Language Processing. HLT/EMNLP*, pages 419–426, Ann Arbor, Michigan.

G. Leech. 1992. 100 million words of English: the British National Corpus. *Language Research*, 28(1):1–13.

David Martínez and Eneko Agirre. 2000. One Sense per Collocation and Genre/Topic Variations. *Conference on Empirical Method in Natural Language.*

T. Pedersen. 2001. A Decision Tree of Bigrams is an Accurate Predictor of Word Sense. In *Proceedings of the Second Meeting of the North American Chapter of the Association for Computational Linguistics (NAACL-01)*, Pittsburgh, PA.

Sameer Pradhan, Edward Loper, Dmitriy Dligach, and Martha Palmer. 2007. Semeval-2007 task-17: English lexical sample, srl and all words. In *Proceedings of the Fourth International Workshop on Semantic Evaluations (SemEval-2007)*, pages 87–92, Prague, Czech Republic.

Tony G. Rose, Mark Stevenson, and Miles Whitehead. 2002. The reuters corpus volumen 1 from yesterday's news to tomorrow's language resources. In *Proceedings of the Third International Conference on Language Resources and Evaluation (LREC-2002)*, pages 827–832, Las Palmas, Canary Islands.

Sarah Zelikovitz and Haym Hirsh. 2001. Using LSI for text classification in the presence of background text. In Henrique Paques, Ling Liu, and David Grossman, editors, *Proceedings of CIKM-01, 10th ACM International Conference on Information and Knowledge Management*, pages 113–118, Atlanta, US. ACM Press, New York, US.

Zhi Zhong, Hwee Tou Ng, and Yee Seng Chan. 2008. Word sense disambiguation using OntoNotes: An empirical study. In *Proceedings of the 2008 Conference on Empirical Methods in Natural Language Processing*, pages 1002–1010, Honolulu, Hawaii, October. Association for Computational Linguistics.

Clique-Based Clustering for improving Named Entity Recognition systems

Julien Ah-Pine
Xerox Research Centre Europe
6, chemin de Maupertuis
38240 Meylan, France
julien.ah-pine@xrce.xerox.com

Guillaume Jacquet
Xerox Research Centre Europe
6, chemin de Maupertuis
38240 Meylan, France
guillaume.jacquet@xrce.xerox.com

Abstract

We propose a system which builds, in a semi-supervised manner, a resource that aims at helping a NER system to annotate corpus-specific named entities. This system is based on a distributional approach which uses syntactic dependencies for measuring similarities between named entities. The specificity of the presented method however, is to combine a clique-based approach and a clustering technique that amounts to a soft clustering method. Our experiments show that the resource constructed by using this clique-based clustering system allows to improve different NER systems.

1 Introduction

In Information Extraction domain, named entities (NEs) are one of the most important textual units as they express an important part of the meaning of a document. Named entity recognition (NER) is not a new domain (see MUC[1] and ACE[2] conferences) but some new needs appeared concerning NEs processing. For instance the NE *Oxford* illustrates the different ambiguity types that are interesting to address:

- intra-annotation ambiguity: Wikipedia lists more than 25 cities named *Oxford* in the world
- systematic inter-annotation ambiguity: the name of cities could be used to refer to the university of this city or the football club of this city. This is the case for *Oxford* or *Newcastle*
- non-systematic inter-annotation ambiguity: *Oxford* is also a company unlike *Newcastle*.

The main goal of our system is to act in a complementary way with an existing NER system, in order to enhance its results. We address two kinds of issues: first, we want to detect and correctly annotate corpus-specific NEs[3] that the NER system could have missed; second, we want to correct some wrong annotations provided by the existing NER system due to ambiguity. In section 3, we give some examples of such corrections.

The paper is organized as follows. We present, in section 2, the global architecture of our system and from §2.1 to §2.6, we give details about each of its steps. In section 3, we present the evaluation of our approach when it is combined with other classic NER systems. We show that the resulting hybrid systems perform better with respect to F-measure. In the best case, the latter increased by 4.84 points. Furthermore, we give examples of successful correction of NEs annotation thanks to our approach. Then, in section 4, we discuss about related works. Finally we sum up the main points of this paper in section 5.

2 Description of the system

Given a corpus, the main objectives of our system are: to *detect* potential NEs; to *compute the possible annotations* for each NE and then; to *annotate* each occurrence of these NEs with the *right annotation* by analyzing its local context.

We assume that this corpus dependent approach allows an easier NE annotation. Indeed, even if a NE such as *Oxford* can have many annotation types, it will certainly have less annotation possibilities in a specific corpus.

Figure 1 presents the global architecture of our system. The most important part concerns steps 3 (§2.3) and 4 (§2.4). The aim of these subprocesses is to group NEs which have the same annotation with respect to a given context. On the one hand, clique-based methods (see §2.3 for

[1] http://www-nlpir.nist.gov/related_projects/muc/
[2] http://www.nist.gov/speech/tests/ace

[3] In our definition a corpus-specific NE is the one which does not appear in a classic NEs lexicon. Recent news articles for instance, are often constituted of NEs that are not in a classic NEs lexicon.

Proceedings of the 12th Conference of the European Chapter of the ACL, pages 51–59,
Athens, Greece, 30 March – 3 April 2009.

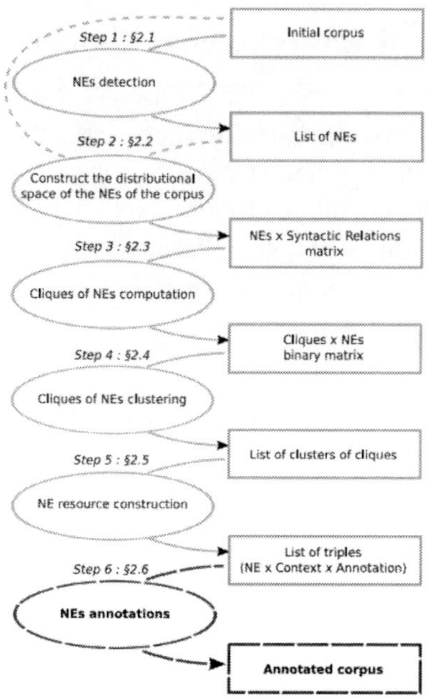

Figure 1: General description of our system

details on cliques) are interesting as they allow the same NE to be in different cliques. In other words, cliques allow to represent the different possible annotations of a NE. The clique-based approach drawback however, is the over production of cliques which corresponds to an artificial over production of possible annotations for a NE. On the other hand, clustering methods aim at structuring a data set and such techniques can be seen as data compression processes. However, a simple NEs hard clustering doesn't allow a NE to be in several clusters and thus to express its different annotations. Then, our proposal is to combine both methods in a clique-based clustering framework. This combination leads to a soft-clustering approach that we denote CBC system. The following paragraphs, from 2.1 to 2.6, describe the respective steps mentioned in Figure 1.

2.1 Detection of potential Named Entities

Different methods exist for detecting potential NEs. In our system, we used some lexico-syntactic constraints to extract expressions from a corpus because it allows to detect some corpus-specific NEs. In our approach, a potential NE is a noun starting with an upper-case letter or a noun phrase which is (see (Ehrmann and Jacquet, 2007) for similar use):

- a governor argument of an attribute syntactic relation with a noun as governee argument (e.g. *president* $\xrightarrow{attribute}$ *George Bush*)
- a governee argument of a modifier syntactic relation with a noun as a governor argument (e.g. *company* $\xleftarrow{modifier}$ *Coca-Cola*).

The list of potential NEs extracted from the corpus will be denoted $\mathbb{NE}$ and the number of NEs $|\mathbb{NE}|$.

2.2 Distributional space of NEs

The distributional approach aims at evaluating a distance between words based on their syntactic distribution. This method assumes that words which appear in the same contexts are semantically similar (Harris, 1951).

To construct the *distributional space* associated to a corpus, we use a robust parser (in our experiments, we used XIP parser (Aït et al., 2002)) to extract chunks (i.e. nouns, noun phrases, ...) and syntactic dependencies between these chunks. Given this parser's output, we identify triple instances. Each triple has the form $w_1.R.w_2$ where w_1 and w_2 are chunks and R is a syntactic relation (Lin, 1998), (Kilgarriff et al., 2004).

One triple gives two contexts ($1.w_1.R$ and $2.w_2.R$) and two chunks (w_1 and w_2). Then, we only select chunks w which belong to $\mathbb{NE}$. Each point in the distributional space is a NE and each dimension is a syntactic context. $\mathbb{CT}$ denotes the set of all syntactic contexts and $|\mathbb{CT}|$ represents its cardinal.

We illustrate this construction on the sentence *"provide Albania with food aid"*. We obtain the three following triples (note that *aid* and *food aid* are considered as two different chunks):

provide_VERB•I-OBJ•Albania_NOUN
provide_VERB•PREP_WITH•aid_NOUN
provide_VERB•PREP_WITH•food aid_NP

From these triples, we have the following chunks and contexts[4]:

Chunks:	Contexts:
provide_VERB	**1.provide_VERB.I-OBJ**
Albania_NOUN	1.provide_VERB.PREP_WITH
aid_NOUN	2.Albania_NOUN.I-OBJ
food aid_NP	2.aid_NOUN.PREP_WITH
	2.food aid_NP.PREP_WITH

According to the NEs detection method described previously, we only keep the chunks and contexts which are in **bold** in the above table.

[4]In the context 1.VERB:provide.I-OBJ, the figure 1 means that the verb *provide* is the governor argument of the Indirect OBJect relation.

We also use an heuristic in order to reduce the over production of chunks and contexts: in our experiments for example, each NE and each context should appear more than 10 times in the corpus for being considered.

D is the resulting ($|\mathbb{NE}| \times |\mathbb{CT}|$) NE-Context matrix where $e_i : i = 1, \ldots, |\mathbb{NE}|$ is a NE and $c_j : j = 1, \ldots, |\mathbb{CT}|$ is a syntactic context. Then we have:

$$D(e_i, c_j) = \text{Nb. of occ. of } c_j \text{ associated to } e_i \quad (1)$$

2.3 Cliques of NEs computation

A clique in a graph is a set of pairwise adjacent nodes which is equivalent to a complete subgraph. A maximal clique is a clique that is not a subset of any other clique. Maximal cliques computation was already employed for semantic space representation (Ploux and Victorri, 1998). In this work, cliques of lexical units are used to represent a precise meaning. Similarly, we compute cliques of NEs in order to represent a precise annotation.

For example, *Oxford* is an ambiguous NE but a clique such as <*Cambridge, Oxford, Edinburgh University, Edinburgh, Oxford University*> allows to focus on the specific annotation <organization> (see (Ehrmann and Jacquet, 2007) for similar use).

Given the distributional space described in the previous paragraph, we use a probabilistic framework for computing similarities between NEs. The approach that we propose is inspired from the language modeling framework introduced in the information retrieval field (see for example (Lavrenko and Croft, 2003)). Then, we construct cliques of NEs based on these similarities.

2.3.1 Similarity measures between NEs

We first compute the maximum likelihood estimation for a NE e_i to be associated with a context c_j: $P_{ml}(c_j|e_i) = \frac{D(e_i,c_j)}{|e_i|}$, where $|e_i| = \sum_{j=1}^{|\mathbb{CT}|} D(e_i, c_j)$ is the total occurrences of the NE e_i in the corpus.

This leads to sparse data which is not suitable for measuring similarities. In order to counter this problem, we use the Jelinek-Mercer smoothing method: $D'(e_i, c_j) = \lambda P_{ml}(c_j|e_i) + (1 - \lambda)P_{ml}(c_j|\mathbb{CORP})$ where $\mathbb{CORP}$ is the corpus and $P_{ml}(c_j|\mathbb{CORP}) = \frac{\sum_i D(e_i,c_j)}{\sum_{i,j} D(e_i,c_j)}$. In our experiments we took $\lambda = 0.5$.

Given D', we then use the cross-entropy as a similarity measure between NEs. Let us denote by s this similarity matrix, we have:

$$s(e_i, e'_i) = - \sum_{c_j \in \mathbb{CT}} D'(e_i, c_j) \log(D'(e_{i'}, c_j)) \quad (2)$$

2.3.2 From similarity matrix to adjacency matrix

Next, we convert s into an adjacency matrix denoted $\hat{s}$. In a first step, we binarize s as follows. Let us denote $\{e^i_1, \ldots, e^i_{|\mathbb{NE}|}\}$, the list of NEs ranked according to the descending order of their similarity with e_i. Then, $L(e_i)$ is the list of NEs which are considered as the nearest neighbors of e_i according to the following definition:

$$L(e_i) = \quad (3)$$
$$\{e^i_1, ..., e^i_p : \frac{\sum_{i'=1}^{p} s(e_i, e^i_{i'})}{\sum_{i'=1}^{|\mathbb{NE}|} s(e_i, e_{i'})} \leq a; p \leq b\}$$

where $a \in [0, 1]$ and $b \in \{1, \ldots, |\mathbb{NE}|\}$. $L(e_i)$ gathers the most significant nearest neighbors of e_i by choosing the ones which bring the a most relevant similarities providing that the neighborhood's size doesn't exceed b. This approach can be seen as a flexible k-nearest neighbor method. In our experiments we chose $a = 20\%$ and $b = 10$.

Finally, we symmetrize the similarity matrix as follows and we obtain $\hat{s}$:

$$\hat{s}(e_i, e_{i'}) = \begin{cases} 1 & \text{if } e_{i'} \in L(e_i) \text{ or } e_i \in L(e_{i'}) \\ 0 & \text{otherwise} \end{cases} \quad (4)$$

2.3.3 Cliques computation

Given $\hat{s}$, the adjacency matrix between NEs, we compute the set of maximal cliques of NEs denoted $\mathbb{CLI}$. Then, we construct the matrix T of general term:

$$T(cli_k, e_i) = \begin{cases} 1 & \text{if } e_i \in cli_k \\ 0 & \text{otherwise} \end{cases} \quad (5)$$

where cli_k is an element of $\mathbb{CLI}$. T will be the input matrix for the clustering method.

In the following, we also use cli_k for denoting the vector represented by $(T(cli_k, e_1), \ldots, T(cli_k, e_{|\mathbb{NE}|}))$.

Figure 2 shows some cliques which contain *Oxford* that we can obtain with this method. This figure also illustrates the over production of cliques since at least cli8, cli10 and cli12 can be annotated as <organization>.

```
cli1 : Wembley_NOUN;Heathrow_NOUN;Oxford_NOUN;Twickenham_NOUN
cli2 : Hampstead_NOUN;Chelsea_NOUN;Oxford_NOUN
cli3 : Hammersmith_NOUN;Leeds_NOUN;Chelsea_NOUN;Oxford_NOUN
cli4 : Norwich_NOUN;Waterloo_NOUN;Oxford_NOUN;Worcester_NOUN
cli5 : Sunderland_NOUN;Liverpool_NOUN;Leeds_NOUN;Chelsea_NOUN;Oxford_NOUN
cli6 : Bolton_NOUN;Oxford_NOUN;Worcester_NOUN
cli7 : Birmingham_NOUN;Coventry_NOUN;Ayr_NOUN;Oxford_NOUN
cli8 : Bristol_NOUN;Cambridge_NOUN;Edinburgh_NOUN;Henley_NOUN;Oxford_NOUN
cli9 : Leeds_NOUN;Southampton_NOUN;Highbury_NOUN;Oxford_NOUN
cli10: Cambridge_NOUN;Leeds_NOUN;Highbury_NOUN;Oxford_NOUN
cli11: Oxfordshire_NOUN;London_NOUN;Oxford_NOUN
cli12: Edinburgh University_NP;Cambridge_NOUN;Edinburgh_NOUN;Oxford_NOUN
cli13: Paris_NOUN;Hollywood_NOUN;London_NOUN;Oxford_NOUN
cli14: Glasgow_NOUN;Piccadilly_NOUN;London_NOUN;Oxford_NOUN
cli15: Cambridge_NOUN;Harvard_NOUN;London_NOUN;Oxford_NOUN
cli16: Warwick_NOUN;Salisbury_NOUN;Oxford_NOUN
cli17: Birmingham_NOUN;Nottingham_NOUN;Middlesex_NOUN;Oxford_NOUN
```

Figure 2: Examples of cliques containing *Oxford*

2.4 Cliques clustering

We use a clustering technique in order to group cliques of NEs which are mutually highly similar. The clusters of cliques which contain a NE allow to find the different possible annotations of this NE.

This clustering technique must be able to construct "pure" clusters in order to have precise annotations. In that case, it is desirable to avoid fixing the number of clusters. That's the reason why we propose to use the Relational Analysis approach described below.

2.4.1 The Relational Analysis approach

We propose to apply the *Relational Analysis approach* (RA) which is a clustering model that doesn't require to fix the number of clusters (Michaud and Marcotorchino, 1980), (Bédécarrax and Warnesson, 1989). This approach takes as input a similarity matrix. In our context, since we want to cluster cliques of NEs, the corresponding similarity matrix S between cliques is given by the *dot products* matrix taken from T: $S = T \cdot T'$. The general term of this similarity matrix is: $S(cli_k, cli_{k'}) = S_{kk'} = \langle cli_k, cli_{k'} \rangle$. Then, we want to maximize the following clustering function:

$$\Delta(S, X) = \sum_{k,k'=1}^{|\mathbb{CLI}|} \underbrace{\left(S_{kk'} - \frac{\sum_{(k'',k''')\in \mathbb{S}^+} S_{k''k'''}}{|\mathbb{S}^+|} \right)}_{cont_{kk'}} X_{kk'} \quad (6)$$

where $\mathbb{S}^+ = \{(cli_k, cli_{k'}) : S_{kk'} > 0\}$.

In other words, cli_k and $cli_{k'}$ have more chances to be in the same cluster providing that their similarity measure, $S_{kk'}$, is greater or equal to the mean average of positive similarities.

X is the solution we are looking for. It is a binary relational matrix with general term: $X_{kk'} = 1$, if cli_k is in the same cluster as $cli_{k'}$; and $X_{kk'} = 0$, otherwise. X represents an equivalence relation. Thus, it must respect the following properties:

- binarity: $X_{kk'} \in \{0, 1\}; \forall k, k'$,
- reflexivity: $X_{kk} = 1; \forall k$,
- symmetry: $X_{kk'} - X_{k'k} = 0; \forall k, k'$,
- transitivity: $X_{kk'} + X_{k'k''} - X_{kk''} \leq 1; \forall k, k', k''$.

As the objective function is linear with respect to X and as the constraints that X must respect are linear equations, we can solve the clustering problem using an integer linear programming solver. However, this problem is NP-hard. As a result, in practice, we use heuristics for dealing with large data sets.

2.4.2 The Relational Analysis heuristic

The presented heuristic is quite similar to another algorithm described in (Hartigan, 1975) known as the "leader" algorithm. But unlike this last approach which is based upon euclidean distances and inertial criteria, the RA heuristic aims at maximizing the criterion given in (6). A sketch of this heuristic is given in Algorithm 1, (see (Marcotorchino and Michaud, 1981) for further details).

Algorithm 1 RA heuristic

Require: $nbitr$ = number of iterations; $\kappa_{\max}$ = maximal number of clusters; S the similarity matrix
$m \leftarrow \frac{\sum_{(k,k')\in \mathbb{S}^+} S_{kk'}}{|\mathbb{S}^+|}$
Take the first clique cli_k as the first element of the first cluster
$\kappa = 1$ where κ is the current number of cluster
for $q = 1$ to $nbitr$ **do**
  for $k = 1$ to $|\mathbb{CLI}|$ **do**
    for $l = 1$ to κ **do**
      Compute the contribution of clique cli_k with cluster clu_l: $cont_l = \sum_{cli_{k'} \in clu_l} (S_{kk'} - m)$
    end for
    clu_{l^*} is the cluster id which has the highest contribution with clique cli_k and $cont_{l^*}$ is the corresponding contribution value
    if $(cont_{l^*} < (S_{kk} - m)) \wedge (\kappa < \kappa_{\max})$ **then**
      Create a new cluster where clique cli_k is the first element and $\kappa \leftarrow \kappa + 1$
    else
      Assign clique cli_k to cluster clu_{l^*}
      if the cluster where was taken cli_k before its new assignment, is empty **then**
        $\kappa \leftarrow \kappa - 1$
      end if
    end if
  end for
end for

We have to provide a number of iterations

or/and a delta threshold in order to have an approximate solution in a reasonable processing time. Besides, it is also required a maximum number of clusters but since we don't want to fix this parameter, we put by default $\kappa_{\max} = |\mathbb{CLI}|$.

Basically, this heuristic has a $O(nbitr \times \kappa_{\max} \times |\mathbb{CLI}|)$ computation cost. In general terms, we can assume that $nbitr << |\mathbb{CLI}|$, but not $\kappa_{\max} << |\mathbb{CLI}|$. Thus, in the worst case, the algorithm has a $O(\kappa_{\max} \times |\mathbb{CLI}|)$ computation cost.

Figure 3 gives some examples of clusters of cliques[5] obtained using the RA approach.

num clu	more significant NEs		more significant contexts	
4	Oxford_NOUN	497	1.be_VERB.AT	77.17
	London_NOUN	291	1.area_NOUN.MOD	63.56
	Liverpool_NOUN	252	1.have_VERB.AT	50.66
	Manchester_NOUN	240	1.move_VERB.TO	48.23
	Newcastle_NOUN	166	1.member_NOUN.FOR	44.76
	Leeds_NOUN	135	1.magistrate_NOUN.MOD	42.19
	Edinburgh_NOUN	131	1.go_VERB.TO	41.91
	Birmingham_NOUN	125	1.live_VERB.IN	41.47
	Glasgow_NOUN	123	1.be_VERB.NEAR	41.05
58	Cambridge_NOUN	26	1.study_VERB.AT	8.76
	Oxford_NOUN	26	1.professor_NOUN.AT	8.25
	London_NOUN	7	1.student_NOUN.AT	7.27
	Edinburgh University_NOUN	6	1.graduate_NOUN.MOD	7.24
	Edinburgh_NOUN	5	1.attend_VERB.AT	6.06
	Oxford University_NOUN	5	1.be_VERB.AT	5.93
	Westminster_NOUN	4	1.degree_NOUN.MOD	5.70
	Glastonbury_NOUN	4	1.teach_VERB.AT	5.62
	Cheltenham_NOUN	4	1.educate_VERB.AT	4.88
95	Wembley_NOUN	11	1.beat_VERB.AT	4.71
	Ibrox_NOUN	10	1.play_VERB.AT	4.51
	Twickenham_NOUN	9	1.final_NOUN.AT	4.27
	Elland_NOUN road_NOUN	6	1.win_VERB.AT	4.13
	Highbury_NOUN	5	1.match_NOUN.AT	4.00
	Oxford_NOUN	5	1.game_NOUN.AT	3.52
	Wimbledon_NOUN	4	1.face_VERB.AT	3.49
	Cheltenham_NOUN	4	1.crowd_NOUN.AT	3.18
	Ascot_NOUN	3	1.the_DET game_NOUN.AT	2.84

Figure 3: Examples of clusters of cliques (only the NEs are represented) and their associated contexts

2.5 NE resource construction using the CBC system's outputs

Now, we want to exploit the clusters of cliques in order to annotate NE occurrences. Then, we need to construct a NE resource where for each pair (NE x syntactic context) we have an annotation. To this end, we need first, to assign a cluster to each pair (NE x syntactic context) (§2.5.1) and second, to assign each cluster an annotation (§2.5.2).

2.5.1 Cluster assignment to each pair (NE x syntactic context)

For each cluster clu_l we provide a score $F_c(c_j, clu_l)$ for each context c_j and a score $F_e(e_i, clu_l)$ for each NE e_i. These scores[6] are given by:

$$F_c(c_j, clu_l) = \sum_{e_i \in clu_l} \frac{D(e_i, c_j)}{\sum_{i=1}^{|\mathbb{NE}|} D(e_i, c_j)} \sum_{e_i \in clu_l} \mathbf{1}_{\{D(e_i,c_j) \neq 0\}} \quad (7)$$

where $\mathbf{1}_{\{P\}}$ equals 1 if P is true and 0 otherwise.

$$F_e(e_i, clu_l) = \#(clu_l, e_i) \quad (8)$$

Given a NE e_i and a syntactic context c_j, we now introduce the contextual cluster assignment matrix $A_{ctxt}(e_i, c_j)$ as follows: $A_{ctxt}(e_i, c_j) = clu^*$ where: $clu^* = \text{Argmax}_{\{clu_l : clu_l \ni e_i ; F_e(e_i, clu_l) > 1\}} F_c(c_j, clu_l)$.

In other words, clu^* is the cluster for which we find more than one occurrence of e_i and the highest score related to the context c_j.

Furthermore, we compute a default cluster assignment matrix A_{def}, which does not depend on the local context: $A_{def}(e_i) = clu^\bullet$ where: $clu^\bullet = \text{Argmax}_{\{clu_l : clu_l \ni \{cli_k : cli_k \ni e_i\}\}} |cli_k|$.

In other words, $clu^\bullet$ is the cluster containing the biggest clique cli_k containing e_i.

2.5.2 Clusters annotation

So far, the different steps that we have introduced were unsupervised. In this paragraph, our aim is to give a correct annotation to each cluster (hence, to all NEs in this cluster). To this end, we need some annotation seeds and we propose two different semi-supervised approaches (regarding the classification given in (Nadeau and Sekine, 2007)). The first one is the manual annotation of some clusters. The second one proposes an automatic cluster annotation and assumes that we have some NEs that are already annotated.

Manual annotation of clusters This method is fastidious but it is the best way to match the corpus data with a specific guidelines for annotating NEs. It also allows to identify new types of annotation. We used the ACE2007 guidelines for manually annotating each cluster. However, our CBC system leads to a high number of clusters of cliques and we can't annotate each of them. Fortunately, it also leads to a distribution of the clusters' size (number of cliques by cluster) which is

[5] We only represent the NEs and their frequency in the cluster which corresponds to the number of cliques which contain the NEs. Furthermore, we represent the most relevant contexts for this cluster according to equation (7) introduced in the following.

[6] For data fusion tasks in information retrieval field, the scoring method in equation (7) is denoted CombMNZ (Fox and Shaw, 1994). Other scoring approaches can be used see for example (Cucchiarelli and Velardi, 2001).

similar to a Zipf distribution. Consequently, in our experiments, if we annotate the 100 biggest clusters, we annotate around eighty percent of the detected NEs (see §3).

Automatic annotation of clusters We suppose in this context that many NEs in $\mathbb{NE}$ are already annotated. Thus, under this assumption, we have in each cluster provided by the CBC system, both annotated and non-annotated NEs. Our goal is to exploit the available annotations for *refining the annotation* of a cluster by implicitly taking into account the syntactic contexts and for *propagating the available annotations* to NEs which have no annotation.

Given a cluster clu_l of cliques, $\#(clu_l, e_i)$ is the weight of the NE e_i in this cluster: it is the number of cliques in clu_l that contain e_i. For all annotations a_p in the set of all possible annotations $\mathbb{AN}$, we compute its associated score in cluster clu_l: it is the sum of the weights of NEs in clu_l that is annotated a_p.

Then, if the maximal annotation score is greater than a simple majority (half) of the total votes[7], we assign the corresponding annotation to the cluster. We precise that the annotation <none>[8] is processed in the same way as any other annotations. Thus, a cluster can be globally annotated <none>. The limit of this automatic approach is that it doesn't allow to annotate new NE types than the ones already available.

In the following, we will denote by $\mathbf{A_{clu}}(clu_l)$ the annotation of the cluster clu_l.

The cluster annotation matrix $\mathbf{A_{clu}}$ associated to the contextual cluster assignment matrix A_{ctxt} and the default cluster assignment matrix A_{def} introduced previously will be called the CBC system's NE resource (or shortly the NE resource).

2.6 NEs annotation processes using the NE resource

In this paragraph, we describe how, given the CBC system's NE resource, we annotate occurrences of NEs in the studied corpus with respect to its local context. We precise that for an occurrence of a NE e_i its associated local context is the set of syntactical dependencies c_j in which e_i is involved.

[7] The total votes number is given by $\sum_{e_i \in clu_l} \#(clu_l, e_i)$.

[8] The NEs which don't have any annotation.

2.6.1 NEs annotation process for the CBC system

Given a NE occurrence and its local context we can use $A_{ctxt}(e_i, c_j)$ and $A_{def}(e_i)$ in order to get the default annotation $\mathbf{A_{clu}}(A_{def}(e_i))$ and the list of contextual annotations $\{\mathbf{A_{clu}}(A_{ctxt}(e_i, c_j))\}_j$.

Then for annotating this NE occurrence using our NE resource, we apply the following rules:

- if the list of contextual annotations $\{\mathbf{A_{clu}}(A_{ctxt}(e_i, c_j))\}_j$ is conflictual, we annotate the NE occurrence as <none>,
- if the list of contextual annotations is non-conflictual, then we use the corresponding annotation to annotate the NE occurrence
- if the list of contextual annotations is empty, we use the default annotation $\mathbf{A_{clu}}(A_{def}(e_i))$.

The NE resource plus the annotation process described in this paragraph lead to a NER system based on the CBC system. This NER system will be called CBC-NER system and it will be tested in our experiments both alone and as a complementary resource.

2.6.2 NEs annotation process for an hybrid system

We place ourselves into an hybrid situation where we have two NER systems (NER 1 + NER 2) which provide two different lists of annotated NEs. We want to combine these two systems when annotating NEs occurrences.

Therefore, we resolve any conflicts by applying the following rules:

- If the same NE occurrence has two different annotations from the two systems then there are two cases. If one of the two system is CBC-NER system then we take its annotation; otherwise we take the annotation provided by the NER system which gave the best precision.
- If a NE occurrence is included in another one we only keep the biggest one and its annotation. For example, if *Jacques Chirac* is annotated <person> by one system and *Chirac* by <person> by the other system, then we only keep the first annotation.
- If two NE occurrences are contiguous and have the same annotation, we merge the two NEs in one NE occurrence.

3 Experiments

The system described in this paper rather target corpus-specific NE annotation. Therefore, our experiments will deal with a corpus of recent news articles (see (Shinyama and Sekine, 2004) for motivations regarding our corpus choice) rather than well-known annotated corpora. Our corpus is constituted of news in English published on the web during two weeks in June 2008. This corpus is constituted of around 300,000 words (10Mb) which doesn't represent a very large corpus. These texts were taken from various press sources and they involve different themes (sports, technology, ...). We extracted randomly a subset of articles and manually annotated 916 NEs (in our experiments, we deal with three types of annotation namely <person>, <organization> and <location>). This subset constitutes our test set.

In our experiments, first, we applied the XIP parser (Aït et al., 2002) to the whole corpus in order to construct the frequency matrix D given by (1). Next, we computed the similarity matrix between NEs according to (2) in order to obtain $\hat{s}$ defined by (4). Using the latter, we computed cliques of NEs that allow us to obtain the assignment matrix T given by (5). Then we applied the clustering heuristic described in Algorithm 1. At this stage, we want to build the NE resource using the clusters of cliques. Therefore, as described in §2.5, we applied two kinds of clusters annotations: the manual and the automatic processes. For the first one, we manually annotated the 100 biggest clusters of cliques. For the second one, we exploited the annotations provided by XIP NER (Brun and Hagège, 2004) and we propagated these annotations to the different clusters (see §2.5.2).

The different materials that we obtained constitute the CBC system's NE resource. Our aim now is to exploit this resource and to show that it allows to improve the performances of different classic NER systems.

The different NER systems that we tested are the following ones:

- CBC-NER system M (in short CBC M) based on the CBC system's NE resource using the manual cluster annotation (line 1 in Table 1),
- CBC-NER system A (in short CBC A) based on the CBC system's NE resource using the automatic cluster annotation (line 1 in Table 1),
- XIP NER or in short XIP (Brun and Hagège, 2004) (line 2 in Table 1),
- Stanford NER (or in short Stanford) associated to the following model provided by the tool and which was trained on different news corpora (CoNLL, MUC6, MUC7 and ACE): ner-eng-ie.crf-3-all2008-distsim.ser.gz (Finkel et al., 2005) (line 3 in Table 1),
- GATE NER or in short GATE (Cunningham et al., 2002) (line 4 in Table 1),
- and several hybrid systems which are given by the combination of pairs taken among the set of the three last-mentioned NER systems (lines 5 to 7 in Table 1). Notice that these baseline hybrid systems use the annotation combination process described in §2.6.1.

	Systems	Prec.	Rec.	F-me.
1	*CBC-NER system M*	*71.67*	*23.47*	*35.36*
	CBC-NER system A	*70.66*	*32.86*	*44.86*
	XIP NER	*77.77*	*56.55*	*65.48*
2	XIP + CBC M	78.41	60.26	**68.15**
	XIP + CBC A	76.31	60.48	67.48
	Stanford NER	*67.94*	*68.01*	*67.97*
3	Stanford + CBC M	69.40	71.07	70.23
	Stanford + CBC A	70.09	72.93	**71.48**
	GATE NER	*63.30*	*56.88*	*59.92*
4	GATE + CBC M	66.43	61.79	64.03
	GATE + CBC A	66.51	63.10	**64.76**
	Stanford + XIP	*72.85*	*75.87*	*74.33*
5	Stanford + XIP + CBC M	72.94	77.70	75.24
	Stanford + XIP + CBC A	73.55	78.93	**76.15**
	GATE + XIP	*69.38*	*66.04*	*67.67*
6	GATE + XIP + CBC M	69.62	67.79	68.69
	GATE + XIP + CBC A	69.87	69.10	**69.48**
	GATE + Stanford	*63.12*	*69.32*	*66.07*
7	GATE + Stanford + CBC M	65.09	72.05	68.39
	GATE + Stanford + CBC A	65.66	73.25	**69.25**

Table 1: Results given by different hybrid NER systems and coupled with the CBC-NER system

In Table 1 we first reported in each line, the results given by each system when they are applied alone (figures in italics). These performances represent our baselines. Second, we tested for each baseline system, an extended hybrid system that integrates the CBC-NER systems (with respect to the combination process detailed in §2.6.2).

The first two lines of Table 1 show that the two CBC-NER systems alone lead to rather poor results. However, our aim is to show that the CBC-NER system is, despite its low performances alone, complementary to other basic NER systems. In other words, we want to show that the exploitation of the CBC system's NE resource is beneficial and non-redundant compared to other baseline NER systems.

This is actually what we obtained in Table 1 as for each line from 2 to 7, the extended hybrid systems that integrate the CBC-NER systems (M or

A) always perform better than the baseline either in terms of precision[9] or recall. For each line, we put in bold the best performance according to the F-measure.

These results allow us to show that the NE resource built using the CBC system is *complementary* to any baseline NER systems and that it allows to improve the results of the latter.

In order to illustrate why the CBC-NER systems are beneficial, we give below some examples taken from the test corpus for which the CBC system A had allowed to improve the performances by respectively disambiguating or correcting a wrong annotation or detecting corpus-specific NEs.

First, in the sentence "From the start, his parents, *Lourdes* and Hemery, were with him.", the baseline hybrid system Stanford + XIP annotated the ambiguous NE "*Lourdes*" as <location> whereas Stanford + XIP + CBC A gave the correct annotation <person>.

Second, in the sentence "Got 3 percent chance of survival, what ya gonna do?" The back read, "A) Fight Through, b) Stay Strong, c) Overcome Because I Am a *Warrior*.", the baseline hybrid system Stanford + XIP annotated "*Warrior*" as <organization> whereas Stanford + XIP + CBC A corrected this annotation with <none>.

Finally, in the sentence "*Matthew*, also a favorite to win in his fifth and final appearance, was stunningly eliminated during the semifinal round Friday when he misspelled "secernent".", the baseline hybrid system Stanford + XIP didn't give any annotation to "*Matthew*" whereas Stanford + XIP + CBC A allowed to give the annotation <person>.

4 Related works

Many previous works exist in NEs recognition and classification. However, most of them do not build a NEs resource but exploit external gazetteers (Bunescu and Pasca, 2006), (Cucerzan, 2007).

A recent overview of the field is given in (Nadeau and Sekine, 2007). According to this paper, we can classify our method in the category of semi-supervised approaches. Our proposal is close to (Cucchiarelli and Velardi, 2001) as it uses syntactic relations (§2.2) and as it relies on existing NER systems (§2.6.2). However, the particularity of our method concerns the clustering of cliques of NEs that allows both to represent the different annotations of the NEs and to group the latter with respect to one precise annotation according to a local context.

Regarding this aspect, (Lin and Pantel, 2001) and (Ngomo, 2008) also use a clique computation step and a clique merging method. However, they do not deal with ambiguity of lexical units nor with NEs. This means that, in their system, a lexical unit can be in only one merged clique.

From a methodological point of view, our proposal is also close to (Ehrmann and Jacquet, 2007) as the latter proposes a system for NEs fine-grained annotation, which is also corpus dependent. However, in the present paper we use all syntactic relations for measuring the similarity between NEs whereas in the previous mentioned work, only specific syntactic relations were exploited. Moreover, we use clustering techniques for dealing with the issue related to over production of cliques.

In this paper, we construct a NE resource from the corpus that we want to analyze. In that context, (Pasca, 2004) presents a lightly supervised method for acquiring NEs in arbitrary categories from unstructured text of Web documents. However, Pasca wants to improve web search whereas we aim at annotating specific NEs of an analyzed corpus. Besides, as we want to focus on corpus-specific NEs, our work is also related to (Shinyama and Sekine, 2004). In this work, the authors found a significant correlation between the similarity of the time series distribution of a word and the likelihood of being a NE. This result motivated our choice to test our approach on recent news articles rather than on well-known annotated corpora.

5 Conclusion

We propose a system that allows to improve NE recognition. The core of this system is a clique-based clustering method based upon a distributional approach. It allows to extract, analyze and discover highly relevant information for corpus-specific NEs annotation. As we have shown in our experiments, this system combined with another one can lead to strong improvements. Other applications are currently addressed in our team using this approach. For example, we intend to use the concept of clique-based clustering as a soft clustering method for other issues.

[9] Except for XIP+CBC A in line 2 where the precision is slightly lower than XIP's one.

References

S. Aït, J.P. Chanod, and C. Roux. 2002. Robustness beyond shallowness: incremental dependency parsing. *NLE Journal*.

C. Bédécarrax and I. Warnesson. 1989. Relational analysis and dictionnaries. In *Proceedings of ASMDA 1988*, pages 131–151. Wiley, London, New-York.

C. Brun and C. Hagège. 2004. Intertwining deep syntactic processing and named entity detection. In *Proceedings of ESTAL 2004*, Alicante, Spain.

R. Bunescu and M. Pasca. 2006. Using encyclopedic knowledge for named entity disambiguation. In *Proceedings of EACL 2006*.

A. Cucchiarelli and P. Velardi. 2001. Unsupervised Named Entity Recognition using syntactic and semantic contextual evidence. *Computational Linguistics*, 27(1).

S. Cucerzan. 2007. Large-scale named entity disambiguation based on wikipedia data. In *Proceedings of EMNLP/CoNLL 2007*, Prague, Czech Republic.

H. Cunningham, D. Maynard, K. Bontcheva, and V. Tablan. 2002. GATE: A framework and graphical development environment for robust NLP tools and applications. In *Proceedings of ACL 2002*, Philadelphia.

M. Ehrmann and G. Jacquet. 2007. Vers une double annotation des entités nommées. *Traitement Automatique des Langues*, 47(3).

J.R. Finkel, T. Grenager, and C. Manning. 2005. Incorporating non-local information into information extraction systems by gibbs sampling. In *Proceedings of ACL 2005*.

E.A. Fox and J.A. Shaw. 1994. Combination of multiple searches. In *Proceedings of the 3rd NIST TREC Conference*, pages 105–109.

Z. Harris. 1951. *Structural Linguistics*. University of Chicago Press.

J.A. Hartigan. 1975. *Clustering Algorithms*. John Wiley and Sons.

A. Kilgarriff, P. Rychly, P. Smr, and D. Tugwell. 2004. The sketch engine. In *In Proceedings of EURALEX 2004*.

V. Lavrenko and W.B. Croft. 2003. Relevance models in information retrieval. In W.B. Croft and J. Lafferty (Eds), editors, *Language modeling in information retrieval*. Springer.

D. Lin and P. Pantel. 2001. Induction of semantic classes from natural language text. In *Proceedings of ACM SIGKDD*.

D. Lin. 1998. Using collocation statistics in information extraction. In *Proceedings of MUC-7*.

J.F. Marcotorchino and P. Michaud. 1981. Heuristic approach of the similarity aggregation problem. *Methods of operation research*, 43:395–404.

P. Michaud and J.F. Marcotorchino. 1980. Optimisation en analyse de données relationnelles. In *Data Analysis and informatics*. North Holland Amsterdam.

D. Nadeau and S. Sekine. 2007. A survey of Named Entity Recognition and Classification. *Lingvisticae Investigationes*, 30(1).

A. C. Ngonga Ngomo. 2008. Signum a graph algorithm for terminology extraction. In *Proceedings of CICLING 2008*, Haifa, Israel.

M. Pasca. 2004. Acquisition of categorized named entities for web search. In *Proceedings of CIKM 2004*, New York, NY, USA.

S. Ploux and B. Victorri. 1998. Construction d'espaces sémantiques à l'aide de dictionnaires de synonymes. *TAL*, 39(1).

Y. Shinyama and S. Sekine. 2004. Named Entity Discovery using comparable news articles. In *Proceedings of COLING 2004*, Geneva.

Correcting Automatic Translations through Collaborations between MT and Monolingual Target-Language Users

Joshua S. Albrecht and **Rebecca Hwa** and **G. Elisabeta Marai**
Department of Computer Science
University of Pittsburgh
{jsa8,hwa,marai}@cs.pitt.edu

Abstract

Machine translation (MT) systems have improved significantly; however, their outputs often contain too many errors to communicate the intended meaning to their users. This paper describes a collaborative approach for mediating between an MT system and users who do not understand the source language and thus cannot easily detect translation mistakes on their own. Through a visualization of multiple linguistic resources, this approach enables the users to correct difficult translation errors and understand translated passages that were otherwise baffling.

1 Introduction

Recent advances in machine translation (MT) have given us some very good translation systems. They can automatically translate between many languages for a variety of texts; and they are widely accessible to the public via the web. The quality of the MT outputs, however, is not reliably high. People who do not understand the source language may be especially baffled by the MT outputs because they have little means to recover from translation mistakes.

The goal of this work is to help *monolingual target-language* users to obtain better translations by enabling them to identify and overcome errors produced by the MT system. We argue for a human-computer collaborative approach because both the users and the MT system have gaps in their abilities that the other could compensate. To facilitate this collaboration, we propose an interface that mediates between the user and the MT system. It manages additional NLP tools for the source language and translation resources so that the user can explore this extra information to gain enough understanding of the source text to correct MT errors. The interactions between the users and the MT system may, in turn, offer researchers insights into the translation process and inspirations for better translation models.

We have conducted an experiment in which we asked non-Chinese speakers to correct the outputs of a Chinese-English MT system for several short passages of different genres. They performed the correction task both with the help of the visualization interface and without. Our experiment addresses the following questions:

- To what extent can the visual interface help the user to understand the source text?
- In what way do factors such as the user's backgrounds, the properties of source text, and the quality of the MT system and other NLP resources impact that understanding?
- What resources or strategies are more helpful to the users? What research directions do these observations suggest in terms of improving the translation models?

Through qualitative and quantitative analysis of the user actions and timing statistics, we have found that users of the interface achieved a more accurate understanding of the source texts and corrected more difficult translation mistakes than those who were given the MT outputs alone. Furthermore, we observed that some users made better use of the interface for certain genres, such as sports news, suggesting that the translation model may be improved by a better integration of document-level contexts.

Proceedings of the 12th Conference of the European Chapter of the ACL, pages 60–68,
Athens, Greece, 30 March – 3 April 2009. ©2009 Association for Computational Linguistics

2 Collaborative Translation

The idea of leveraging human-computer collaborations to improve MT is not new; computer-aided translation, for instance, was proposed by Kay (1980). The focus of these efforts has been on improving the performance of professional translators. In contrast, our intended users cannot read the source text.

These users do, however, have the world knowledge and the language model to put together coherent sentences in the target-language. From the MT research perspective, this raises an interesting question: given that they are missing a *translation model*, what would it take to make these users into effective "decoders?" While some translation mistakes are recoverable from a strong language model alone, and some might become readily apparent if one can choose from some possible phrasal translations; the most difficult mistakes may require greater contextual knowledge about the source. Consider the range of translation resources available to an MT decoder–which ones might the users find informative, handicapped as they are for not knowing the source language? Studying the users' interactions with these resources may provide insights into how we might build a better translation model and a better decoder.

In exploring the collaborative approach, the design considerations for facilitating human computer interaction are crucial. We chose to make available relatively few resources to prevent the users from becoming overwhelmed by the options. We also need to determine how to present the information from the resources so that the users can easily interpret them. This is a challenge because the Chinese processing tools and the translation resources are imperfect themselves. The information should be displayed in such a way that conflicting analyses between different resources are highlighted.

3 Prototype Design

We present an overview of our prototype for a collaborative translation interface, named *The Chinese Room*[1]. A screen-shot is shown in Figure 1. It

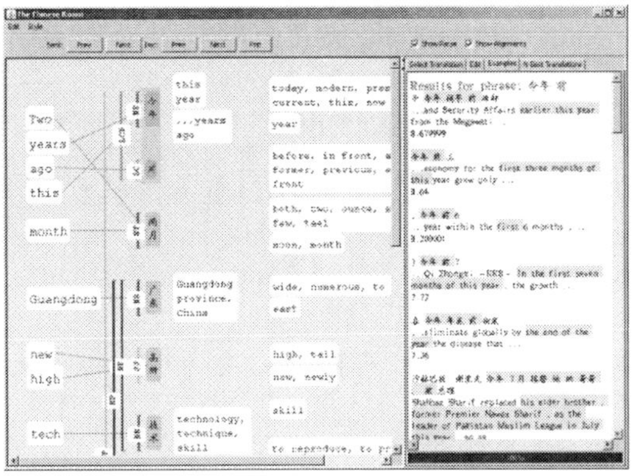

Figure 1: A screen-shot of the visual interface. It consists of two main regions. The left pane is a workspace for users to explore the sentence; the right pane provides multiple tabs that offer additional functionalities.

is a graphical environment that supports five main sources of information and functionalities. The space separates into two regions. On the left pane is a large workspace for the user to explore the source text one sentence at a time. On the right pane are tabbed panels that provide the users with access to a document view of the MT outputs as well as additional functionalities for interpreting the source. In our prototype, the MT output is obtained by querying Google's Translation API[2]. In the interest of exploiting user interactions as a diagnostic tool for improving MT, we chose information sources that are commonly used by modern MT systems.

First, we display the word alignments between MT output and segmented Chinese[3]. Even without knowing the Chinese characters, the users can visually detect potential misalignments and poor word reordering. For instance, the automatic translation shown in Figure 1 begins: *Two years ago this month...* It is fluent but incorrect. The crossed alignments offer users a clue that "two" and "months" should not have been split up. Users can also explore alternative orderings by dragging the English tokens around.

Second, we make available the glosses for words and characters from a bilingual dictionary[4].

[1]The inspiration for the name of our system came from Searle's thought experiment(Searle, 1980). We realize that there are major differences between our system and Searle's description. Importantly, our users get to insert their knowledge rather than purely operate based on instructions. We felt the name was nonetheless evocative in that the user requires additional resources to process the input "squiggles."

[2]http://code.google.com/apis/translate/research

[3]The Chinese segmentation is obtained as a by-product of Google's translation process.

[4]We used the Chinese-English Translation Lexi-

The placement of the word gloss presents a challenge because there are often alternative Chinese segmentations. We place glosses for multi-character words in the column closer to the source. When the user mouses over each definition, the corresponding characters are highlighted, helping the user to notice potential mis-segmentation in the Chinese.

Third, the Chinese sentence is annotated with its parse structure[5]. Constituents are displayed as brackets around the source sentence. They have been color-coded into four major types (noun phrase, verb phrases, prepositional phrases, and other). Users can collapse and expand the brackets to keep the workspace uncluttered as they work through the Chinese sentence. This also indicates to us which fragments held the user's focus.

Fourth, based on previous studies reporting that automatic translations may improve when given decomposed source inputs (Mellebeek et al., 2005), we allow the users to select a substring from the source text for the MT system to translate. We display the N-best alternatives in the *Translation Tab.* The list is kept short; its purpose is less for reranking but more to give the users a sense of the kinds of hypotheses that the MT system is considering.

Fifth, users can select a substring from the source text and search for source sentences from a bilingual corpus and a monolingual corpus that contain phrases similar to the query[6]. The retrieved sentences are displayed in the *Example Tab.* For sentences from the bilingual corpus, human translations for the queried phrase are highlighted. For sentences retrieved from the monolingual corpus, their automatic translations are provided. If the users wished to examine any of the retrieved translation pairs in detail, they can push it onto the sentence workspace.

4 Experimental Methodology

We asked eight non-Chinese speakers to correct the machine translations of four short Chinese passages, with an average length of 11.5 sentences. Two passages are news articles and two are excerpts of a fictional work. Each participant was instructed to correct the translations for one news article and one fictional passage using all the resources made available by *The Chinese Room* and the other two passages without. To keep the experimental conditions as similar as possible, we provided them with a restricted version of the interface (see Figure 2 for a screen-shot) in which all additional functionalities except for the *Document View Tab* are disabled. We assigned each person to alternate between working with the full and the restricted versions of the system; half began without, and the others began with. Thus, every passage received four sets of corrections made collaboratively with the system and four sets of corrections made based solely on the participants' internal language models. All together, there are 184 participant corrected sentences (11.5 sentences $\times$ 4 passages $\times$ 4 participants) for each condition.

The participants were asked to complete each passage in one sitting. Within a passage, they could work on the sentences in any arbitrary order. They could also elect to "pass" any part of a sentence if they found it too difficult to correct. Timing statistics were automatically collected while they made their corrections. We interviewed each participant for qualitative feedbacks after all four passages were corrected.

Next, we asked two bilingual speakers to evaluate all the corrected translations. The outcomes between different groups of users are compared,

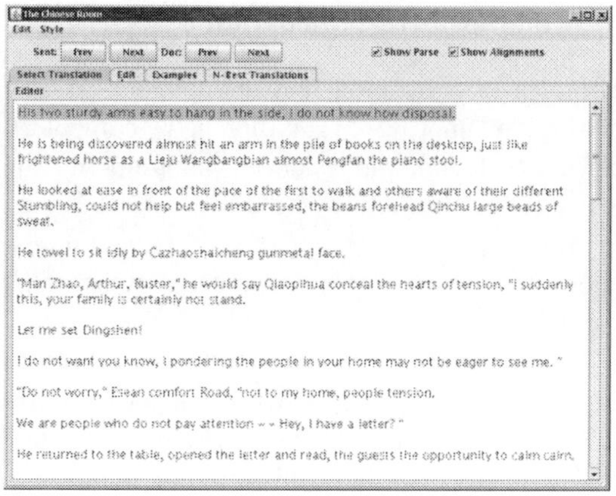

Figure 2: The interface for users who are correcting translations without help; they have access to the document view, but they do not have access to any of the other resources.

con released by the LDC; for a handful of characters that serve as function words, we added the functional definitions using an online dictionary http://www.mandarintools.com/worddict.html.

[5]It is automatically generated by the Stanford Parser for Chinese (Klein and Manning, 2003).

[6]We used Lemur (2006) for the information retrieval back-end; the parallel corpus is from the Federal Broadcast Information Service corpus; the monolingual corpus is from the Chinese Gigaword corpus.

and the significance of the difference is determined using the two-sample t-test assuming unequal variances. We require 90% confidence (alpha=0.1) as the cut-off for a difference to be considered statistically significant; when the difference can be established with higher confidence, we report that value. In the following subsections, we describe the conditions of this study in more details.

Participants' Background For this study, we strove to maintain a relatively heterogeneous population; participants were selected to be varied in their exposures to NLP, experiences with foreign languages, as well as their age and gender. A summary of their backgrounds is shown in Table 1.

Prior to the start of the study, the participants received a 20 minute long presentational tutorial about the basic functionalities supported by our system, but they did not have an opportunity to explore the system on their own. This helps us to determine whether our interface is intuitive enough for new users to pick up quickly.

Data The four passages used for this study were chosen to span a range of difficulties and genre types. The easiest of the four is a news article about a new Tamagotchi-like product from Bandai. It was taken from a webpage that offers bilingual news to help Chinese students to learn English. A harder news article is taken from a past NIST Chinese-English MT Evaluation; it is about Michael Jordan's knee injury. For a different genre, we considered two fictional excerpts from the first chapter of *Martin Eden*, a novel by Jack London that has been professionally translated into Chinese[7]. One excerpt featured a short dialog, while the other one was purely descriptive.

Evaluation of Translations Bilingual human judges are presented with the source text as well as the parallel English text for reference. Each judge is then shown a set of candidate translations (the original MT output, an alternative translation by a bilingual speaker, and corrected translations by the participants) in a randomized order. Since the human corrected translations are likely to be fluent, we have instructed the judges to concentrate more on the adequacy of the meaning conveyed. They are asked to rate each sentence on an absolute scale of 1-10 using the guideline in Table 2. To reduce the biases in the rating scales of different judges, we normalized the judges' scores, following standard practices in MT evaluation (Blatz et al., 2003). Post normalization, the correlation coefficient between the judges is 0.64. The final assessment score for each translated sentence is the average of judges' scores, on a scale of 0-1.

[7]We chose an American story so as to not rely on a user's knowledge about Chinese culture. The participants confirmed that they were not familiar with the chosen story.

Table 2: The guideline used by bilingual judges for evaluating the translation quality of the MT outputs and the participants' corrections.

9-10	The meaning of the Chinese sentence is fully conveyed in the translation.
7-8	Most of the meaning is conveyed.
5-6	Misunderstands the sentence in a major way; or has many small mistakes.
3-4	Very little meaning is conveyed.
1-2	The translation makes no sense at all.

5 Results

The results of human evaluations for the user experiment are summarized in Table 3, and the corresponding timing statistics (average minutes spent editing a sentence) is shown in Table 4. We observed that typical MT outputs contain a range of errors. Some are primarily problems in fluency such that the participants who used the restricted interface, which provided no additional resources other than the *Document View Tab*, were still able to improve the MT quality from 0.35 to 0.42. On the other hand, there are also a number of more serious errors that require the participants to gain some level of understanding of the source in order to correct them. The participants who had access to the full collaborative interface were able to improve the quality from 0.35 to 0.53, closing the gap between the MT and the bilingual translations by 36.9%. These differences are all statistically significant (with >98% confidence).

The higher quality of corrections does require the participants to put in more time. Overall, the participants took 2.5 times as long when they have the interface than when they do not. This may be partly because the participants have more sources of information to explore and partly because the participants tended to "pass" on fewer sentences. The average Levenshtein edit distance (with words as the atomic unit, and with the score normalized to the interval [0,1]) between the original MT out-

Table 1: A summary of participants' background. ‡User5 recognizes some simple Kanji characters, but does not have enough knowledge to gain any additional information beyond what the MT system and the dictionary already provided.

	User1	User2	User3	User4	User5‡	User6	User7	User8
NLP background	intro	grad	none	none	intro	grad	intro	none
Native English	yes	no	yes	yes	yes	yes	yes	yes
Other Languages	French (beginner)	multiple (fluent)	none	none	Japanese (beginner)	none	none	Greek (beginner)
Gender	M	F	F	M	M	M	F	M
Education	Ugrad	PhD	PhD	Ugrad	Ugrad	PhD	Ugrad	Ugrad

puts and the corrected sentences made by participants using *The Chinese Room* is 0.59; in contrast, the edit distance is shorter, at 0.40, when participants correct MT outputs directly. The timing statistics are informative, but they reflect the interactions of many factors (e.g., the difficulty of the source text, the quality of the machine translation, the background and motivation of the user). Thus, in the next few subsections, we examine how these factors correlate with the quality of the participant corrections.

5.1 Impact of Document Variation

Since the quality of MT varies depending on the difficulty and genre of the source text, we investigate how these factors impact our participants' performances. Columns 3-6 of Table 3 (and Table 4) compare the corrected translations on a per-document basis.

Of the four documents, the baseline MT system performed the best on the product announcement. Because the article is straight-forward, participants found it relatively easy to guess the intended translation. The major obstacle is in detecting and translating Chinese transliteration of Japanese names, which stumped everyone. The quality difference between the two groups of participants on this document was not statistically significant. Relatedly, the difference in the amount of time spent is the smallest for this document; participants using *The Chinese Room* took about 1.5 times longer.

The other news article was much more difficult. The baseline MT made many mistakes, and both groups of participants spent longer on sentences from this article than the others. Although sports news is fairly formulaic, participants who only read MT outputs were baffled, whereas those who had access to additional resources were able to recover from MT errors and produced good quality translations.

Finally, as expected, the two fictional excerpts were the most challenging. Since the participants were not given any information about the story, they also have little context to go on. In both cases, participants who collaborated with *The Chinese Room* made higher quality corrections than those who did not. The difference is statistically significant at 97% confidence for the first excerpt, and 93% confidence for the second. The differences in time spent between the two groups are greater for these passages because the participants who had to make corrections without help tended to give up more often.

5.2 Impact of Participants' Background

We further analyze the results by separating the participants into two groups according to four factors: whether they were familiar with NLP, whether they studied another language, their gender, and their education level.

Exposure to NLP One of our design objectives for *The Chinese Room* is accessibility by a diverse population of end-users, many of whom may not be familiar with human language technologies. To determine how prior knowledge of NLP may impact a user's experience, we analyze the experimental results with respect to the participants' background. In columns 2 and 3 of Table 5, we compare the quality of the corrections made by the two groups. When making corrections on their own, participants who had been exposed to NLP held a significant edge (0.35 vs. 0.47). When both groups of participants used *The Chinese Room*, the difference is reduced (0.51 vs. 0.54) and is not statistically significant. Because all the participants were given the same short tutorial prior to the start of the study, we are optimistic that the interface is intuitive for many users.

None of the other factors distinguished one

Table 3: Averaged human judgments of the translation quality of the four different approaches: automatic MT, corrections by participants without help, corrections by participants using *The Chinese Room*, and translation produced by a bilingual speaker. The second column reports score for all documents; columns 3-6 show the per-document scores.

	Overall	News (product)	News (sports)	Story1	Story2
Machine translation	0.35	0.45	0.30	0.25	0.26
Corrections without The Chinese Room	0.42	0.56	0.35	0.33	0.41
Corrections with The Chinese Room	0.53	0.55	0.62	0.42	0.49
Bilingual translation	0.83	0.83	0.73	0.92	0.88

Table 4: The average amount of time (minutes) participants spent on correcting a sentence.

	Overall	News (product)	News (sports)	Story1	Story2
Corrections without The Chinese Room	2.5	1.9	3.2	2.9	2.3
Corrections with The Chinese Room	6.3	2.9	8.7	6.5	8.5

Table 6: The quality of the corrections produced by four participants using The Chinese Room for the sports news article.

User1	0.57
User2	0.46
User5	0.70
User6	0.73
bilingual translator	0.73

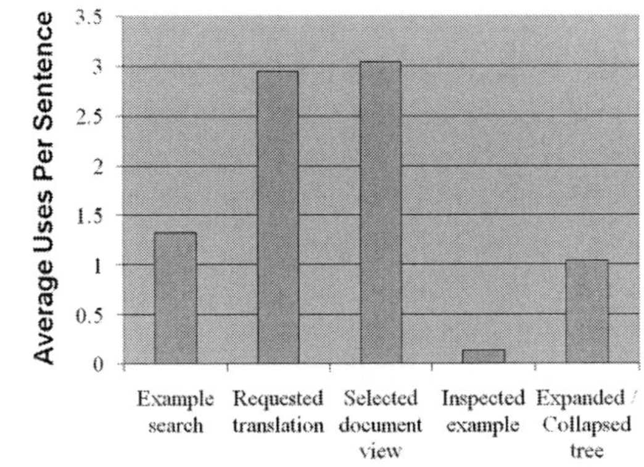

Figure 3: This graph shows the average counts of access per sentence for different resources.

group of participants from the others. The results are summarized in columns 4-9 of Table 5. In each case, the two groups had similar levels of performance, and the differences between their corrections were not statistically significant. This trend holds for both when they were collaborating with the system and when editing on their own.

Prior Knowledge Another factor that may impact the success of the outcome is the user's knowledge about the domain of the source text. An example from our study is the sports news article. Table 6 lists the scores that the four participants who used *The Chinese Room* received for their corrected translations for that passage (averaged over sentences). User5 and User6 were more familiar with the basketball domain; with the help of the system, they produced translations that were comparable to those from the bilingual translator (the differences are not statistically significant).

5.3 Impact of Available Resources

Post-experiment, we asked the participants to describe the strategies they developed for collaborating with the system. Their responses fall into three main categories:

Divide and Conquer Some users found the syntactic trees helpful in identifying phrasal units for N-best re-translations or example searches. For longer sentences, they used the constituent collapse feature to help them reduce clutter and focus on a portion of the sentence.

Example Retrieval Using the search interface, users examined the highlighted query terms to determine whether the MT system made any segmentation errors. Sometimes, they used the examples to arbitrate whether they should trust any of the dictionary glosses or the MT's lexical choices. Typically, though, they did not attempt to inspect the example translations in detail.

Document Coherence and Word Glosses Users often referred to the document view to determine the context for the sentence they are editing. Together with the word glosses and other

Table 5: A comparison of translation quality, grouped by four characteristics of participant backgrounds: their level of exposure to NLP, exposure to another language, their gender, and education level.

	No NLP	NLP	No 2nd Lang.	2nd Lang.	Female	Male	Ugrad	PhD
without The Chinese Room	0.35	0.47	0.41	0.43	0.41	0.43	0.41	0.45
with The Chinese Room	0.51	0.54	0.56	0.51	0.50	0.55	0.52	0.54

resources, the discourse level clues helped to guide users to make better lexical choices than when they made corrections without the full system, relying on sentence coherence alone.

Figure 3 compares the average access counts (per sentence) of different resources (aggregated over all participants and documents). The option of inspect retrieved examples in detail (i.e., bring them up on the sentence workspace) was rarely used. The inspiration for this feature was from work on translation memory (Macklovitch et al., 2000); however, it was not as informative for our participants because they experienced a greater degree of uncertainty than professional translators.

6 Discussion

The results suggest that collaborative translation is a promising approach. Participant experiences were generally positive. Because they felt like they understood the translations better, they did not mind putting in the time to collaborate with the system. Table 7 shows some of the participants' outputs. Although there are some translation errors that cannot be overcome with our current system (e.g., transliterated names), the participants taken as a collective performed surprisingly well. For many mistakes, even when the users cannot correct them, they recognized a problem; and often, one or two managed to intuit the intended meaning with the help of the available resources. As an upper-bound for the effectiveness of the system, we construct a combined "oracle" user out of all 4 users that used the interface for each sentence. The oracle user's average score is 0.70; in contrast, an oracle of users who did not use the system is 0.54 (cf. the MT's overall of 0.35 and the bilingual translator's overall of 0.83). This suggests *The Chinese Room* affords a potential for human-human collaboration as well.

The experiment also made clear some limitations of the current resources. One is domain dependency. Because NLP technologies are typically trained on news corpora, their bias toward the news domain may mislead our users. For example, there is a Chinese character (pronounced *mei3*) that could mean either "beautiful" or "the United States." In one of the passages, the intended translation should have been: *He was responsive to beauty...* but the corresponding MT output was *He was sensitive to the United States...* Although many participants suspected that it was wrong, they were unable to recover from this mistake because the resources (the searchable examples, the part-of-speech tags, and the MT system) did not offer a viable alternative. This suggests that collaborative translation may serve as a useful diagnostic tool to help MT researchers verify ideas about what types of models and data are useful in translation. It may also provide a means of data collection for MT training. To be sure, there are important challenges to be addressed, such as participation incentive and quality assurance, but similar types of collaborative efforts have been shown fruitful in other domains (Cosley et al., 2007). Finally, the statistics of user actions may be useful for translation evaluation. They may be informative features for developing automatic metrics for sentence-level evaluations (Kulesza and Shieber, 2004).

7 Related Work

While there have been many successful computer-aided translation systems both for research and as commercial products (Bowker, 2002; Langlais et al., 2000), collaborative translation has not been as widely explored. Previous efforts such as *DerivTool* (DeNeefe et al., 2005) and *Linear B* (Callison-Burch, 2005) placed stronger emphasis on improving MT. They elicited more in-depth interactions between the users and the MT system's phrase tables. These approaches may be more appropriate for users who are MT researchers themselves. In contrast, our approach focuses on providing intuitive visualization of a variety of information sources for users who may not be MT-savvy. By tracking the types of information they consulted, the portions of translations they selected to modify, and the portions of the source

Table 7: Some examples of translations corrected by the participants and their scores.

	Score	Translation
MT	0.34	He is being discovered almost hit an arm in the pile of books on the desktop, just like frightened horse as a Lieju Wangbangbian almost Pengfan the piano stool.
without The Chinese Room	0.26	Startled, he almost knocked over a pile of book on his desk, just like a frightened horse as a Lieju Wangbangbian almost Pengfan the piano stool.
with The Chinese Room	0.78	He was nervous, and when one of his arms nearly hit a stack of books on the desktop, he startled like a horse, falling back and almost knocking over the piano stool.
Bilingual Translator	0.93	Feeling nervous, he discovered that one of his arms almost hit the pile of books on the table. Like a frightened horse, he stumbled aside, almost turning over a piano stool.
MT	0.50	Bandai Group, a spokeswoman for the U.S. to be SIN-West said: "We want to bring women of all ages that 'the flavor of life'."
without The Chinese Room	0.67	SIN-West, a spokeswoman for the U.S. Bandai Group declared: "We want to bring to women of all ages that 'flavor of life'."
with The Chinese Room	0.68	West, a spokeswoman for the U.S. Toy Manufacturing Group, and soon to be Vice President-said: "We want to bring women of all ages that 'flavor of life'."
Bilingual Translator	0.75	"We wanted to let women of all ages taste the 'flavor of life'," said Bandai's spokeswoman Kasumi Nakanishi.

text they attempted to understand, we may alter the design of our translation model. Our objective is also related to that of cross-language information retrieval (Resnik et al., 2001). This work can be seen as providing the next step in helping users to gain some understanding of the information in the documents once they are retrieved.

By facilitating better collaborations between MT and target-language readers, we can naturally increase human annotated data for exploring alternative MT models. This form of symbiosis is akin to the paradigm proposed by von Ahn and Dabbish (2004). They designed interactive games in which the player generated data could be used to improve image tagging and other classification tasks (von Ahn, 2006). While our interface does not have the entertainment value of a game, its application serves a purpose. Because users are motivated to understand the documents, they may willingly spend time to collaborate and make detailed corrections to MT outputs.

8 Conclusion

We have presented a collaborative approach for mediating between an MT system and monolingual target-language users. The approach encourages users to combine evidences from complementary information sources to infer alternative hypotheses based on their world knowledge. Experimental evidences suggest that the collaborative effort results in better translations than either the original MT or uninformed human edits. Moreover, users who are knowledgeable in the document domain were enabled to correct translations with a quality approaching that of a bilingual speaker. From the participants' feedbacks, we learned that the factors that contributed to their understanding include: document coherence, syntactic constraints, and re-translation at the phrasal level. We believe that the collaborative translation approach can provide insights about the translation process and help to gather training examples for future MT development.

Acknowledgments

This work has been supported by NSF Grants IIS-0710695 and IIS-0745914. We would like to thank Jarrett Billingsley, Ric Crabbe, Joanna Drummund, Nick Farnan, Matt Kaniaris Brian Madden, Karen Thickman, Julia Hockenmaier, Pauline Hwa, and Dorothea Wei for their help with the experiment. We are also grateful to Chris Callison-Burch for discussions about collaborative translations and to Adam Lopez and the anonymous reviewers for their comments and suggestions on this paper.

References

John Blatz, Erin Fitzgerald, George Foster, Simona Gandrabur, Cyril Goutte, Alex Kulesza, Alberto Sanchis, and Nicola Ueffing. 2003. Confidence estimation for machine translation. Technical Report Natural Language Engineering Workshop Final Report, Johns Hopkins University.

Lynne Bowker. 2002. *Computer-Aided Translation Technology*. University of Ottawa Press, Ottawa, Canada.

Chris Callison-Burch. 2005. Linear B System description for the 2005 NIST MT Evaluation. In *The Proceedings of Machine Translation Evaluation Workshop*.

Dan Cosley, Dan Frankowski, Loren Terveen, and John Riedl. 2007. Suggestbot: using intelligent task routing to help people find work in wikipedia. In *IUI '07: Proceedings of the 12th international conference on Intelligent user interfaces*, pages 32–41.

Steve DeNeefe, Kevin Knight, and Hayward H. Chan. 2005. Interactively exploring a machine translation model. In *Proceedings of the ACL Interactive Poster and Demonstration Sessions*, pages 97–100, Ann Arbor, Michigan, June.

Martin Kay. 1980. The proper place of men and machines in language translation. Technical Report CSL-80-11, Xerox. Later reprinted in *Machine Translation*, vol. 12 no.(1-2), 1997.

Dan Klein and Christopher D. Manning. 2003. Fast exact inference with a factored model for natural language parsing. *Advances in Neural Information Processing Systems*, 15.

Alex Kulesza and Stuart M. Shieber. 2004. A learning approach to improving sentence-level MT evaluation. In *Proceedings of the 10th International Conference on Theoretical and Methodological Issues in Machine Translation (TMI)*, Baltimore, MD, October.

Philippe Langlais, George Foster, and Guy Lapalme. 2000. Transtype: a computer-aided translation typing system. In *Workshop on Embedded Machine Translation Systems*, pages 46–51, May.

Lemur. 2006. Lemur toolkit for language modeling and information retrieval. The Lemur Project is a collaborative project between CMU and UMASS.

Elliott Macklovitch, Michel Simard, and Philippe Langlais. 2000. Transsearch: A free translation memory on the world wide web. In *Proceedings of the Second International Conference on Language Resources & Evaluation (LREC)*.

Bart Mellebeek, Anna Khasin, Josef van Genabith, and Andy Way. 2005. Transbooster: Boosting the performance of wide-coverage machine translation systems. In *Proceedings of the 10th Annual Conference of the European Association for Machine Translation (EAMT)*, pages 189–197.

Philip S. Resnik, Douglas W. Oard, and Gina-Anne Levow. 2001. Improved cross-language retrieval using backoff translation. In *Human Language Technology Conference (HLT-2001)*, San Diego, CA, March.

John R. Searle. 1980. Minds, brains, and programs. *Behavioral and Brain Sciences*, 3:417–457.

Luis von Ahn and Laura Dabbish. 2004. Labeling images with a computer game. In *CHI '04: Proceedings of the SIGCHI conference on Human factors in computing systems*, pages 319–326, New York, NY, USA. ACM.

Luis von Ahn. 2006. Games with a purpose. *Computer*, 39(6):92–94.

Incremental Parsing with Parallel Multiple Context-Free Grammars

Krasimir Angelov
Chalmers University of Technology
Göteborg, Sweden
krasimir@chalmers.se

Abstract

Parallel Multiple Context-Free Grammar (PMCFG) is an extension of context-free grammar for which the recognition problem is still solvable in polynomial time. We describe a new parsing algorithm that has the advantage to be incremental and to support PMCFG directly rather than the weaker MCFG formalism. The algorithm is also top-down which allows it to be used for grammar based word prediction.

1 Introduction

Parallel Multiple Context-Free Grammar (PMCFG) (Seki et al., 1991) is one of the grammar formalisms that have been proposed for the syntax of natural languages. It is an extension of context-free grammar (CFG) where the right hand side of the production rule is a tuple of strings instead of only one string. Using tuples the grammar can model discontinuous constituents which makes it more powerful than context-free grammar. In the same time PMCFG has the advantage to be parseable in polynomial time which makes it attractive from computational point of view.

A parsing algorithm is incremental if it reads the input one token at the time and calculates all possible consequences of the token, before the next token is read. There is substantial evidence showing that humans process language in an incremental fashion which makes the incremental algorithms attractive from cognitive point of view.

If the algorithm is also top-down then it is possible to predict the next word from the sequence of preceding words using the grammar. This can be used for example in text based dialog systems or text editors for controlled language where the user might not be aware of the grammar coverage. In this case the system can suggest the possible continuations.

A restricted form of PMCFG that is still stronger than CFG is Multiple Context-Free Grammar (MCFG). In Seki and Kato (2008) it has been shown that MCFG is equivalent to string-based Linear Context-Free Rewriting Systems and Finite-Copying Tree Transducers and it is stronger than Tree Adjoining Grammars (Joshi and Schabes, 1997). Efficient recognition and parsing algorithms for MCFG have been described in Nakanishi et al. (1997), Ljunglöf (2004) and Burden and Ljunglöf (2005). They can be used with PMCFG also but it has to be approximated with overgenerating MCFG and post processing is needed to filter out the spurious parsing trees.

We present a parsing algorithm that is incremental, top-down and supports PMCFG directly. The algorithm exploits a view of PMCFG as an infinite context-free grammar where new context-free categories and productions are generated during parsing. It is trivial to turn the algorithm into statistical by attaching probabilities to each rule.

In Ljunglöf (2004) it has been shown that the **Grammatical Framework** (GF) formalism (Ranta, 2004) is equivalent to PMCFG. The algorithm was implemented as part of the GF interpreter and was evaluated with the **resource grammar library** (Ranta, 2008) which is the largest collection of grammars written in this formalism. The incrementality was used to build a help system which suggests the next possible words to the user.

Section 2 gives a formal definition of PMCFG. In section 3 the procedure for "linearization" i.e. the derivation of string from syntax tree is defined. The definition is needed for better understanding of the formal proofs in the paper. The algorithm introduction starts with informal description of the idea in section 4 and after that the formal rules are given in section 5. The implementation details are outlined in section 6 and after that there are some comments on the evaluation in section 7. Section 8 gives a conclusion.

2 PMCFG definition

Definition 1 *A parallel multiple context-free grammar is an 8-tuple* $G = (N, T, F, P, S, d, r, a)$ *where:*

- N *is a finite set of categories and a positive integer* $d(A)$ *called dimension is given for each* $A \in N$.
- T *is a finite set of terminal symbols which is disjoint with* N.
- F *is a finite set of functions where the arity* $a(f)$ *and the dimensions* $r(f)$ *and* $d_i(f)$ $(1 \leq i \leq a(f))$ *are given for every* $f \in F$. *For every positive integer* d, $(T^*)^d$ *denote the set of all d-tuples*

Proceedings of the 12th Conference of the European Chapter of the ACL, pages 69–76,
Athens, Greece, 30 March – 3 April 2009.

of strings over T. Each function $f \in F$ is a total mapping from $(T^*)^{d_1(f)} \times (T^*)^{d_2(f)} \times \cdots \times (T^*)^{d_{a(f)}(f)}$ to $(T^*)^{r(f)}$, defined as:

$$f := (\alpha_1, \alpha_2, \ldots, \alpha_{r(f)})$$

Here α_i is a sequence of terminals and $\langle k; l \rangle$ pairs, where $1 \leq k \leq a(f)$ is called argument index and $1 \leq l \leq d_k(f)$ is called constituent index.

- *P is a finite set of productions of the form:*

  $$A \rightarrow f[A_1, A_2, \ldots, A_{a(f)}]$$

  where $A \in N$ is called result category, $A_1, A_2, \ldots, A_{a(f)} \in N$ are called argument categories and $f \in F$ is the function symbol. For the production to be well formed the conditions $d_i(f) = d(A_i)$ $(1 \leq i \leq a(f))$ and $r(f) = d(A)$ must hold.

- *S is the start category and $d(S) = 1$.*

We use the same definition of PMCFG as is used by Seki and Kato (2008) and Seki et al. (1993) with the minor difference that they use variable names like x_{kl} while we use $\langle k; l \rangle$ to refer to the function arguments. As an example we will use the $a^n b^n c^n$ language:

$$S \rightarrow c[N]$$
$$N \rightarrow s[N]$$
$$N \rightarrow z[]$$

$$c := (\langle 1;1 \rangle\ \langle 1;2 \rangle\ \langle 1;3 \rangle)$$
$$s := (a\ \langle 1;1 \rangle, b\ \langle 1;2 \rangle, c\ \langle 1;3 \rangle)$$
$$z := (\epsilon, \epsilon, \epsilon)$$

Here the dimensions are $d(S) = 1$ and $d(N) = 3$ and the arities are $a(c) = a(s) = 1$ and $a(z) = 0$. ϵ is the empty string.

3 Derivation

The derivation of a string in PMCFG is a two-step process. First we have to build a syntax tree of a category S and after that to linearize this tree to string. The definition of a syntax tree is recursive:

Definition 2 *$(f\ t_1 \ldots t_{a(f)})$ is a tree of category A if t_i is a tree of category B_i and there is a production:*
$A \rightarrow f[B_1 \ldots B_{a(f)}]$
The abstract notation for "t is a tree of category A" is $t : A$. When $a(f) = 0$ then the tree does not have children and the node is called leaf.

The linearization is bottom-up. The functions in the leaves do not have arguments so the tuples in their definitions already contain constant strings. If the function has arguments then they have to be linearized and the results combined. Formally this can be defined as a function $\mathcal{L}$ applied to the syntax tree:

$$\mathcal{L}(f\ t_1\ t_2 \ldots t_{a(f)}) = (x_1, x_2 \ldots x_{r(f)})$$
$$\text{where } x_i = \mathcal{K}(\mathcal{L}(t_1), \mathcal{L}(t_2) \ldots \mathcal{L}(t_{a(f)}))\ \alpha_i$$
$$\text{and } f := (\alpha_1, \alpha_2 \ldots \alpha_{r(f)}) \in F$$

The function uses a helper function $\mathcal{K}$ which takes the already linearized arguments and a sequence α_i of terminals and $\langle k; l \rangle$ pairs and returns a string. The string is produced by simple substitution of each $\langle k; l \rangle$ with the string for constituent l from argument k:

$$\mathcal{K}\ \sigma\ (\beta_1 \langle k_1; l_1 \rangle \beta_2 \langle k_2; l_2 \rangle \ldots \beta_n) = \beta_1 \sigma_{k_1 l_1} \beta_2 \sigma_{k_2 l_2} \ldots \beta_n$$

where $\beta_i \in T^*$. The recursion in $\mathcal{L}$ terminates when a leaf is reached.

In the example $a^n b^n c^n$ language the function z does not have arguments and it corresponds to the base case when $n = 0$. Every application of s over another tree $t : N$ increases n by one. For example the syntax tree $(s\ (s\ z))$ will produce the tuple (aa, bb, cc). Finally the application of c combines all elements in the tuple in a single string i.e. $c\ (s\ (s\ z))$ will produce the string $aabbcc$.

4 The Idea

Although PMCFG is not context-free it can be approximated with an overgenerating context-free grammar. The problem with this approach is that the parser produces many spurious parse trees that have to be filtered out. A direct parsing algorithm for PMCFG should avoid this and a careful look at the difference between PMCFG and CFG gives an idea. The context-free approximation of $a^n b^n c^n$ is the language $a^* b^* c^*$ with grammar:

$$S \rightarrow ABC$$
$$A \rightarrow \epsilon \mid aA$$
$$B \rightarrow \epsilon \mid bB$$
$$C \rightarrow \epsilon \mid cC$$

The string "$aabbcc$" is in the language and it can be derived with the following steps:

$$\begin{aligned} & S \\ \Rightarrow\ & ABC \\ \Rightarrow\ & aABC \\ \Rightarrow\ & aaABC \\ \Rightarrow\ & aaBC \\ \Rightarrow\ & aabBC \\ \Rightarrow\ & aabbBC \\ \Rightarrow\ & aabbC \\ \Rightarrow\ & aabbcC \\ \Rightarrow\ & aabbccC \\ \Rightarrow\ & aabbcc \end{aligned}$$

The grammar is only an approximation because there is no enforcement that we will use only equal number of reductions for A, B and C. This can be guaranteed if we replace B and C with new categories B' and C' after the derivation of A:

$$B' \to bB'' \qquad C' \to cC''$$
$$B'' \to bB''' \qquad C'' \to cC'''$$
$$B''' \to \epsilon \qquad C''' \to \epsilon$$

In this case the only possible derivation from $aaB'C'$ is $aabbcc$.

The PMCFG parser presented in this paper works like context-free parser, except that during the parsing it generates fresh categories and rules which are specializations of the originals. The newly generated rules are always versions of already existing rules where some category is replaced with new more specialized category. The generation of specialized categories prevents the parser from recognizing phrases that are otherwise withing the scope of the context-free approximation of the original grammar.

5 Parsing

The algorithm is described as a deductive process in the style of (Shieber et al., 1995). The process derives a set of items where each item is a statement about the grammatical status of some substring in the input.

The inference rules are in natural deduction style:

$$\frac{X_1 \ldots X_n}{Y} < \text{side conditions on } X_1, \ldots, X_n >$$

where the premises X_i are some items and Y is the derived item. We assume that $w_1 \ldots w_n$ is the input string.

5.1 Deduction Rules

The deduction system deals with three types of items: active, passive and production items.

Productions In Shieber's deduction systems the grammar is a constant and the existence of a given production is specified as a side condition. In our case the grammar is incrementally extended at runtime, so the set of productions is part of the deduction set. The productions from the original grammar are axioms and are included in the initial deduction set.

Active Items The active items represent the partial parsing result:

$[^k_j A \to f[\vec{B}]; l : \alpha \bullet \beta]\,, \quad j \le k$

The interpretation is that there is a function f with a corresponding production:

$$A \to f[\vec{B}]$$
$$f := (\gamma_1, \ldots \gamma_{l-1}, \alpha\beta, \ldots \gamma_{r(f)})$$

such that the tree $(f\ t_1 \ldots t_{a(f)})$ will produce the substring $w_{j+1} \ldots w_k$ as a prefix in constituent l for any sequence of arguments $t_i : B_i$. The sequence α is the part that produced the substring:

$$\mathcal{K}(\mathcal{L}(t_1), \mathcal{L}(t_2) \ldots \mathcal{L}(t_{a(f)}))\ \alpha = w_{j+1} \ldots w_k$$

and β is the part that is not processed yet.

Passive Items The passive items are of the form:

$[^k_j A; l; N]\,, \quad j \le k$

and state that there exists at least one production:

$$A \to f[\vec{B}]$$
$$f := (\gamma_1, \gamma_2, \ldots \gamma_{r(f)})$$

and a tree $(f\ t_1 \ldots t_{a(f)}) : A$ such that the constituent with index l in the linearization of the tree is equal to $w_{j+1} \ldots w_k$. Contrary to the active items in the passive the whole constituent is matched:

$$\mathcal{K}(\mathcal{L}(t_1), \mathcal{L}(t_2) \ldots \mathcal{L}(t_{a(f)}))\ \gamma_l = w_{j+1} \ldots w_k$$

Each time when we complete an active item, a passive item is created and at the same time we create a new category N which accumulates all productions for A that produce the $w_{j+1} \ldots w_k$ substring from constituent l. All trees of category N must produce $w_{j+1} \ldots w_k$ in the constituent l.

There are six inference rules (see figure 1).

The INITIAL PREDICT rule derives one item spanning the $0 - 0$ range for each production with the start category S on the left hand side. The $\text{rhs}(f, l)$ function returns the constituent with index l of function f.

In the PREDICT rule, for each active item with dot before a $\langle d; r\rangle$ pair and for each production for B_d, a new active item is derived where the dot is in the beginning of constituent r in g.

When the dot is before some terminal s and s is equal to the current terminal w_k then the SCAN rule derives a new item where the dot is moved to the next position.

INITIAL PREDICT

$$\frac{S \to f[\vec{B}]}{[^0_0 S \to f[\vec{B}]; 1 : \bullet\alpha]} \quad S \text{ - start category}, \alpha = \text{rhs}(f, 1)$$

PREDICT

$$\frac{B_d \to g[\vec{C}] \qquad [^k_j A \to f[\vec{B}]; l : \alpha \bullet \langle d; r\rangle\ \beta]}{[^k_k B_d \to g[\vec{C}]; r : \bullet\gamma]} \quad \gamma = \text{rhs}(g, r)$$

SCAN

$$\frac{[^k_j A \to f[\vec{B}]; l : \alpha \bullet s\ \beta]}{[^{k+1}_j A \to f[\vec{B}]; l : \alpha\ s \bullet \beta]} \quad s = w_{k+1}$$

COMPLETE

$$\frac{[^k_j A \to f[\vec{B}]; l : \alpha\bullet]}{N \to f[\vec{B}] \qquad [^k_j A; l; N]} \quad N = (A, l, j, k)$$

COMBINE

$$\frac{[^u_j A \to f[\vec{B}]; l : \alpha \bullet \langle d; r\rangle\ \beta] \qquad [^k_u B_d; r; N]}{[^k_j A \to f[\vec{B}\{d := N\}]; l : \alpha\ \langle d; r\rangle \bullet \beta]}$$

Figure 1: Deduction Rules

When the dot is at the end of an active item then it is converted to passive item in the COMPLETE rule. The category N in the passive item is a fresh category created for each unique (A, l, j, k) quadruple. A new production is derived for N which has the same function and arguments as in the active item.

The item in the premise of COMPLETE was at some point predicted in PREDICT from some other item. The COMBINE rule will later replace the occurence A in the original item (the premise of PREDICT) with the specialization N.

The COMBINE rule has two premises: one active item and one passive. The passive item starts from position u and the only inference rule that can derive items with different start positions is PREDICT. Also the passive item must have been predicted from active item where the dot is before $\langle d; r\rangle$, the category for argument number d must have been B_d and the item ends at u. The active item in the premise of COMBINE is such an item so it was one of the items used to predict the passive one. This means that we can move the dot after $\langle d; r\rangle$ and the d-th argument is replaced with its specialization N.

If the string β contains another reference to the d-th argument then the next time when it has to be predicted the rule PREDICT will generate active items, only for those productions that were successfully used to parse the previous constituents. If a context-free approximation was used this would have been equivalent to unification of the redundant subtrees. Instead this is done at runtime which also reduces the search space.

The parsing is successful if we had derived the $[^n_0 S; 1; S']$ item, where n is the length of the text, S is the start category and S' is the newly created category.

The parser is incremental because all active items span up to position k and the only way to move to the next position is the SCAN rule where a new symbol from the input is consumed.

5.2 Soundness

The parsing system is sound if every derivable item represents a valid grammatical statement under the interpretation given to every type of item.

The derivation in INITIAL PREDICT and PREDICT is sound because the item is derived from existing production and the string before the dot is empty so:

$$\mathcal{K}\ \sigma\ \epsilon = \epsilon$$

The rationale for SCAN is that if

$$\mathcal{K}\ \sigma\ \alpha = w_{j-1} \dots w_k$$

and $s = w_{k+1}$ then

$$\mathcal{K}\ \sigma\ (\alpha\ s) = w_{j-1} \dots w_{k+1}$$

If the item in the premise is valid then it is based on existing production and function and so will be the item in the consequent.

In the COMPLETE rule the dot is at the end of the string. This means that $w_{j+1} \dots w_k$ will be not just a prefix in constituent l of the linearization but the full string. This is exactly what is required in the semantics of the passive item. The passive item is derived from a valid active item so there is at least one production for A. The category N is unique for each (A, l, j, k) quadruple so it uniquely identifies the passive item in which it is placed. There might be many productions that can produce the passive item but all of them should be able to generate $w_{j+1} \dots w_k$ and they are exactly the productions that are added to N. From all this arguments it follows that COMPLETE is sound.

The COMBINE rule is sound because from the active item in the premise we know that:

$$\mathcal{K}\ \sigma\ \alpha = w_{j+1} \dots w_u$$

for every context σ built from the trees:

$$t_1 : B_1;\ t_2 : B_2;\ \dots t_{a(f)} : B_{a(f)}$$

From the passive item we know that every production for N produces the $w_{u+1} \dots w_k$ in r. From that follows that

$$\mathcal{K}\ \sigma'\ (\alpha\langle d; r\rangle) = w_{j+1} \dots w_k$$

where σ' is the same as σ except that B_d is replaced with N. Note that the last conclusion will not hold if we were using the original context because B_d is a more general category and can contain productions that does not derive $w_{u+1} \dots w_k$.

5.3 Completeness

The parsing system is complete if it derives an item for every valid grammatical statement. In our case we have to prove that for every possible parse tree the corresponding items will be derived.

The proof for completeness requires the following lemma:

Lemma 1 *For every possible syntax tree*

$$(f\ t_1 \dots t_{a(f)}) : A$$

with linearization

$$\mathcal{L}(f t_1 \dots t_{a(f)}) = (x_1, x_2 \dots x_{d(A)})$$

where $x_l = w_{j+1} \dots w_k$*, the system will derive an item* $[^k_j A; l; A']$ *if the item* $[^k_j A \to f[\vec{B}]; l : \bullet\alpha_l]$ *was predicted before that. We assume that the function definition is:*

$$f := (\alpha_1, \alpha_2 \dots \alpha_{r(f)})$$

The proof is by induction on the depth of the tree. If the tree has only one level then the function f does not have arguments and from the linearization definition and from the premise in the lemma it follows that $\alpha_l = w_{j+1} \dots w_k$. From the active item in the lemma by applying iteratively the SCAN rule and finally the COMPLETE rule the system will derive the requested item.

If the tree has subtrees then we assume that the lemma is true for every subtree and we prove it for the whole tree. We know that

$$\mathcal{K}\ \sigma\ \alpha_l = w_{j+1} \dots w_k$$

Since the function $\mathcal{K}$ does simple substitution it is possible for each $\langle d; s \rangle$ pair in α_l to find a new range in the input string $j' - k'$ such that the lemma to be applicable for the corresponding subtree $t_d : B_d$. The terminals in α_l will be processed by the SCAN rule. Rule PREDICT will generate the active items required for the subtrees and the COMBINE rule will consume the produced passive items. Finally the COMPLETE rule will derive the requested item for the whole tree.

From the lemma we can prove the completeness of the parsing system. For every possible tree $t : S$ such that $\mathcal{L}(t) = (w_1 \dots w_n)$ we have to prove that the $[^n_0 S; 1; S']$ item will be derived. Since the top-level function of the tree must be from production for S the INITIAL PREDICT rule will generate the active item in the premise of the lemma. From this and from the assumptions for t it follows that the requested passive item will be derived.

5.4 Complexity

The algorithm is very similar to the Earley (1970) algorithm for context-free grammars. The similarity is even more apparent when the inference rules in this paper are compared to the inference rules for the Earley algorithm presented in Shieber et al. (1995) and Ljunglöf (2004). This suggests that the space and time complexity of the PMCFG parser should be similar to the complexity of the Earley parser which is $\mathcal{O}(n^2)$ for space and $\mathcal{O}(n^3)$ for time. However we generate new categories and productions at runtime and this have to be taken into account.

Let the $\mathcal{P}(j)$ function be the maximal number of productions generated from the beginning up to the state where the parser has just consumed terminal number j. $\mathcal{P}(j)$ is also the upper limit for the number of categories created because in the worst case there will be only one production for each new category.

The active items have two variables that directly depend on the input size - the start index j and the end index k. If an item starts at position j then there are $(n - j + 1)$ possible values for k because $j \leq k \leq n$. The item also contains a production and there are $\mathcal{P}(j)$ possible choices for it. In total there are:

$$\sum_{j=0}^{n} (n - j + 1)\mathcal{P}(j)$$

possible choices for one active item. The possibilities for all other variables are only a constant factor. The $\mathcal{P}(j)$ function is monotonic because the algorithm only adds new productions and never removes. From that follows the inequality:

$$\sum_{j=0}^{n} (n - j + 1)\mathcal{P}(j) \leq \mathcal{P}(n) \sum_{i=0}^{n} (n - j + 1)$$

which gives the approximation for the upper limit:

$$\mathcal{P}(n)\frac{n(n+1)}{2}$$

The same result applies to the passive items. The only difference is that the passive items have only a category instead of a full production. However the upper limit for the number of categories is the same. Finally the upper limit for the total number of active, passive and production items is:

$$\mathcal{P}(n)(n^2 + n + 1)$$

The expression for $\mathcal{P}(n)$ is grammar dependent but we can estimate that it is polynomial because the set of productions corresponds to the compact representation of all parse trees in the context-free approximation of the grammar. The exponent however is grammar dependent. From this we can expect that asymptotic space complexity will be $\mathcal{O}(n^e)$ where e is some parameter for the grammar. This is consistent with the results in Nakanishi et al. (1997) and Ljunglöf (2004) where the exponent also depends on the grammar.

The time complexity is proportional to the number of items and the time needed to derive one item. The time is dominated by the most complex rule which in this algorithm is COMBINE. All variables that depend on the input size are present both in the premises and in the consequent except u. There are n possible values for u so the time complexity is $\mathcal{O}(n^{e+1})$.

5.5 Tree Extraction

If the parsing is successful we need a way to extract the syntax trees. Everything that we need is already in the set of newly generated productions. If the goal item is $[^n_0 S; 0; S']$ then every tree t of category S' that can be constructed is a syntax tree for the input sentence (see definition 2 in section 3 again).

Note that the grammar can be erasing; i.e., there might be productions like this:

$$S \rightarrow f[B_1, B_2, B_3]$$
$$f := (\langle 1; 1 \rangle \langle 3; 1 \rangle)$$

There are three arguments but only two of them are used. When the string is parsed this will generate a new specialized production:

$$S' \rightarrow f[B'_1, B_2, B'_3]$$

Here S,B_1 and B_3 are specialized to S', B'_1 and B'_3 but the B_2 category is still the same. This is correct because actually any subtree for the second argument will produce the same result. Despite this it is sometimes useful to know which parts of the tree were used and which were not. In the GF interpreter such unused branches are replaced by meta variables. In this case the tree extractor should check whether the category also exists in the original set of categories N in the grammar.

Just like with the context-free grammars the parsing algorithm is polynomial but the chart can contain exponential or even infinite number of trees. Despite this the chart is a compact finite representation of the set of trees.

6 Implementation

Every implementation requires a careful design of the data structures in the parser. For efficient access the set of items is split into four subsets: $\mathbb{A}$, $\mathbb{S}_j$, $\mathbb{C}$ and $\mathbb{P}$. $\mathbb{A}$ is the agenda i.e. the set of active items that have to be analyzed. $\mathbb{S}_j$ contains items for which the dot is before an argument reference and which span up to position j. $\mathbb{C}$ is the set of possible continuations i.e. a set of items for which the dot is just after a terminal. $\mathbb{P}$ is the set of productions. In addition the set $\mathbb{F}$ is used internally for the generatation of fresh categories. The sets $\mathbb{C}$, $\mathbb{S}_j$ and $\mathbb{F}$ are used as association maps. They contain associations like $k \mapsto v$ where k is the key and v is the value. All maps except $\mathbb{F}$ can contain more than one value for one and the same key.

The pseudocode of the implementation is given in figure 2. There are two procedures *Init* and *Compute*.

Init computes the initial values of $\mathbb{S}$, $\mathbb{P}$ and $\mathbb{A}$. The initial agenda $\mathbb{A}$ is the set of all items that can be predicted from the start category S (INITIAL PREDICT rule).

Compute consumes items from the current agenda and applies the SCAN, PREDICT, COMBINE or COMPLETE rule. The case statement matches the current item against the patterns of the rules and selects the proper rule. The PREDICT and COMBINE rules have two premises so they are used in two places. In both cases one of the premises is related to the current item and a loop is needed to find item matching the other premis.

The passive items are not independent entities but are just the combination of key and value in the set $\mathbb{F}$. Only the start position of every item is kept because the end position for the interesting passive items is always the current position and the active items are either in the agenda if they end at the current position or they are in the $\mathbb{S}_j$ set if they end at position j. The active items also keep only the dot position in the constituent because the constituent definition can be retrieved from the grammar. For this reason the runtime representation of the items is $[j; A \to f[\vec{B}]; l; p]$ where j is the start position of the item and p is the dot position inside the constituent.

The *Compute* function returns the updated $\mathbb{S}$ and $\mathbb{P}$ sets and the set of possible continuations $\mathbb{C}$. The set of continuations is a map indexed by a terminal and the values are active items. The parser computes the set of continuations at each step and if the current terminal is one of the keys the set of values for it is taken as an agenda for the next step.

Language	Productions	Constituents
Bulgarian	3516	75296
English	1165	8290
German	8078	21201
Swedish	1496	8793

Table 1: GF Resource Grammar Library size in number of PMCFG productions and discontinuous constituents

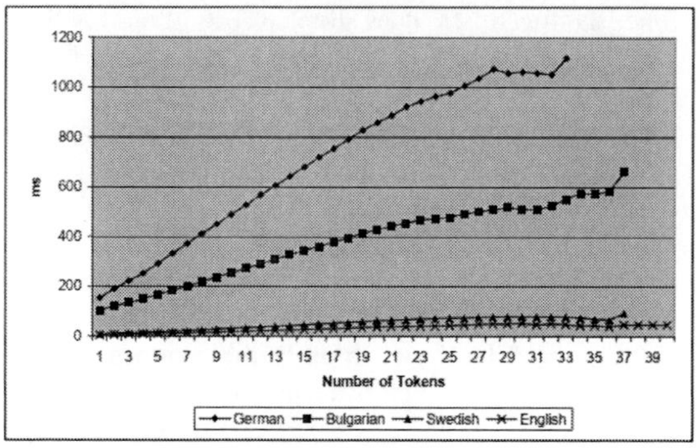

Figure 3: Parser performance in miliseconds per token

7 Evaluation

The algorithm was evaluated with four languages from the GF resource grammar library (Ranta, 2008): Bulgarian, English, German and Swedish. These grammars are not primarily intended for parsing but as a resource from which smaller domain dependent grammars are derived for every application. Despite this, the resource grammar library is a good benchmark for the parser because these are the biggest GF grammars.

The compiler converts a grammar written in the high-level GF language to a low-level PMCFG grammar which the parser can use directly. The sizes of the grammars in terms of number of productions and number of unique discontinuous constituents are given on table 1. The number of constituents roughly corresponds to the number of productions in the context-free approximation of the grammar. The parser performance in terms of miliseconds per token is shown in figure 3. In the evaluation 34272 sentences were parsed and the average time for parsing a given number of tokens is drawn in the chart. As it can be seen, although the theoretical complexity is polynomial, the real-time performance for practically interesting grammars tends to be linear.

8 Conclusion

The algorithm has proven useful in the GF system. It accomplished the initial goal to provide suggestions

```
procedure Init() {
  k = 0
  S_i = ∅,   for every i
  P = the set of productions P in the grammar

  A = ∅
  forall S → f[B⃗] ∈ P do    // INITIAL PREDICT
    A = A + [0; S → f[B⃗]; 1; 0]

  return (S, P, A)
}


procedure Compute(k, (S, P, A)) {
  C = ∅
  F = ∅
  while A ≠ ∅ do {
    let x ∈ A,   x ≡ [j; A → f[B⃗]; l; p]
    A = A − x
    case the dot in x is {
      before s ∈ T ⇒ C = C + (s ↦ [j; A → f[B⃗]; l; p + 1])    // SCAN

      before ⟨d; r⟩  ⇒ if ((B_d, r) ↦ (x, d)) ∉ S_k then {
                          S_k = S_k + ((B_d, r) ↦ (x, d))
                          forall B_d → g[C⃗] ∈ P do    // PREDICT
                            A = A + [k; B_d → g[C⃗]; r; 0]
                        }
                        forall (k; B_d, r) ↦ N ∈ F do    // COMBINE
                          A = A + [j; A → f[B⃗{d := N}]; l; p + 1]

      at the end     ⇒ if ∃N.((j, A, l) ↦ N ∈ F) then {
                          forall (N, r) ↦ (x′, d′) ∈ S_k do      // PREDICT
                            A = A + [k; N → f[B⃗]; r; 0]
                        } else {
                          generate fresh N      // COMPLETE
                          F = F + ((j, A, l) ↦ N)
                          forall (A, l) ↦ ([j′; A′ → f′[B⃗′]; l′; p′], d) ∈ S_j do    // COMBINE
                            A = A + [j′; A′ → f′[B⃗′{d := N}]; l′; p′ + 1]
                        }
                        P = P + (N → f[B⃗])
    }
  }

  return (S, P, C)
}
```

Figure 2: Pseudocode of the parser implementation

in text based dialog systems and in editors for controlled languages. Additionally the algorithm has properties that were not envisaged in the beginning. It works with PMCFG directly rather that by approximation with MCFG or some other weaker formalism.

Since the Linear Context-Free Rewriting Systems, Finite-Copying Tree Transducers and Tree Adjoining Grammars can be converted to PMCFG, the algorithm presented in this paper can be used with the converted grammar. The approach to represent context-dependent grammar as infinite context-free grammar might be applicable to other formalisms as well. This will make it very attractive in applications where some of the other formalisms are already in use.

References

Håkan Burden and Peter Ljunglöf. 2005. Parsing linear context-free rewriting systems. In *Proceedings of the Ninth International Workshop on Parsing Technologies (IWPT)*, pages 11–17, October.

Jay Earley. 1970. An efficient context-free parsing algorithm. *Commun. ACM*, 13(2):94–102.

Aravind Joshi and Yves Schabes. 1997. Tree-adjoining grammars. In Grzegorz Rozenberg and Arto Salomaa, editors, *Handbook of Formal Languages. Vol 3: Beyond Words*, chapter 2, pages 69–123. Springer-Verlag, Berlin/Heidelberg/New York.

Peter Ljunglöf. 2004. *Expressivity and Complexity of the Grammatical Framework*. Ph.D. thesis, Department of Computer Science, Gothenburg University and Chalmers University of Technology, November.

Ryuichi Nakanishi, Keita Takada, and Hiroyuki Seki. 1997. An Efficient Recognition Algorithm for Multiple ContextFree Languages. In *Fifth Meeting on Mathematics of Language*. The Association for Mathematics of Language, August.

Aarne Ranta. 2004. Grammatical Framework: A Type-Theoretical Grammar Formalism. *Journal of Functional Programming*, 14(2):145–189, March.

Aarne Ranta. 2008. GF Resource Grammar Library. `digitalgrammars.com/gf/lib/`.

Hiroyuki Seki and Yuki Kato. 2008. On the Generative Power of Multiple Context-Free Grammars and Macro Grammars. *IEICE-Transactions on Info and Systems*, E91-D(2):209–221.

Hiroyuki Seki, Takashi Matsumura, Mamoru Fujii, and Tadao Kasami. 1991. On multiple context-free grammars. *Theoretical Computer Science*, 88(2):191–229, October.

Hiroyuki Seki, Ryuichi Nakanishi, Yuichi Kaji, Sachiko Ando, and Tadao Kasami. 1993. Parallel Multiple Context-Free Grammars, Finite-State Translation Systems, and Polynomial-Time Recognizable Subclasses of Lexical-Functional Grammars. In *31st Annual Meeting of the Association for Computational Linguistics*, pages 130–140. Ohio State University, Association for Computational Linguistics, June.

Stuart M. Shieber, Yves Schabes, and Fernando C. N. Pereira. 1995. Principles and Implementation of Deductive Parsing. *Journal of Logic Programming*, 24(1&2):3–36.

Data-driven semantic analysis for multilingual WSD and lexical selection in translation

Marianna Apidianaki
National Centre for Language Technology
School of Computing, Dublin City University
Dublin 9, Ireland
mapidianaki@computing.dcu.ie

Abstract

A common way of describing the senses of ambiguous words in multilingual Word Sense Disambiguation (WSD) is by reference to their translation equivalents in another language. The theoretical soundness of the senses induced in this way can, however, be doubted. This type of cross-lingual sense identification has implications for multilingual WSD and MT evaluation as well. In this article, we first present some arguments in favour of a more thorough analysis of the semantic information that may be induced by the equivalents of ambiguous words found in parallel corpora. Then, we present an unsupervised WSD method and a lexical selection method that exploit the results of a data-driven sense induction method. Finally, we show how this automatically acquired information can be exploited for a multilingual WSD and MT evaluation more sensitive to lexical semantics.

1 Word senses in a bi-(multi-)lingual context

1.1 Cross-lingual sense determination for WSD

Determining the senses of ambiguous words by reference to their translational equivalents constitutes a common practice in multilingual WSD: the candidate senses of an ambiguous word, from which one has to be selected during WSD, correspond to its equivalents in another language. This empirical approach to sense identification circumvents the need for predefined sense inventories and their disadvantages for automatic WSD.[1] The first to adopt it were Brown *et al.* (1991), who represented the two main senses of a SL word by its two most frequent translations in the target language (TL). Further promoted by Resnik and Yarowsky (2000) and endorsed in the multilingual tasks of the Senseval (Chklovski *et al.*, 2004) and Semeval (Jin *et al.*, 2007) exercises, this conception of senses is still found in recent works on the integration of WSD in MT.

From these works, only that of Carpuat and Wu (2005) exploits an external hand-crafted sense inventory. The use of an external resource, not related to the training corpus of their Statistical Machine Translation (SMT) system, turned out to be one of the causes of the observed deterioration of translation quality. In later works on the subject, which show a more or less important improvement in translation quality, SL word senses are considered as directly reflected in their equivalents found in a parallel training corpus (Cabezas and Resnik, 2005; Carpuat and Wu, 2007; Chan *et al.*, 2007). Nevertheless, the theoretical soundness of these senses is not really addressed.

1.2 Advantages of cross-lingual sense determination

Cross-lingual sense induction offers a standard criterion for sense delimitation: the translation equivalents of ambiguous words are supposed to reveal their hidden meanings (Resnik, 2004). Additional advantages become evident in MT: when the candidate senses of an ambiguous word consist of its possible translations, identifying the sense carried by a new instance of the word coincides with its translation. Conceiving WSD

[1] Such as the high granularity, the great number and the striking similarity of the described senses, and their irrelevance to the domains of the processed texts (Edmonds and Kilgarriff, 2002).

Proceedings of the 12th Conference of the European Chapter of the ACL, pages 77–85, as lexical selection thus seems natural (Vickrey *et al.*, 2005): it appears that there is no reason to pass through senses in order to arrive to translations. A correct translation may be attained even without WSD, as in the case of parallel ambiguities where the SL and TL words are similarly ambiguous (Resnik and Yarowsky, 2000).[2]

1.3 Disadvantages of cross-lingual sense determination

However, this conception of senses is not theoretically sound, as translation equivalents do not always constitute valid sense indicators. This is often neglected in an attempt to render the sense inventory as close as possible to the training corpus of the SMT system. So, translation equivalents are considered as straightforward indicators of SL senses.

This approach assumes and results in some type of uniformity regarding the nature of the induced senses: clear-cut (e.g. homonymic) and finer sense distinctions are all handled in the same way. Moreover, senses are enumerated without any description of their possible relations. For instance, a SL word *w* having three equivalents (*a*, *b* and *c*) is considered to have three distinct senses (described as '*w-a*', '*w-b*' et '*w-c*)'.

The assumption of biunivocal (one-to-one) correspondences between senses and equivalents disregards the fact that semantically similar equivalents may be used to translate the same sense of a SL word in context. However, this constitutes a common practice in translation and an advised technique for translators, in order to avoid repetitions in the translated texts. The phenomenon of translation ambiguity may pose some problems as well: it may not need to be resolved during translation but should be considered in multilingual WSD. Resolving this kind of ambiguity could also improve the quality of the results of applications such as multilingual information retrieval.

1.4 Impact of cross-lingually defined senses on evaluation

Ignoring the relations between word senses may raise further problems during WSD evaluation, as errors concerning close or distant senses are considered as equally important. Thus, if a WSD algorithm selects a sense which is slightly different from the one effectively carried by an instance of an ambiguous word, but not totally wrong, this is directly considered as a false choice. A differing weighting of WSD errors would be preferable in these cases, if sense distance information was available (Resnik and Yarowsky, 2000).

When WSD coincides with lexical selection in MT, the equivalents of a SL word (*w*) are perceived to be its candidate senses. The sense assigned to a new instance of *w* is considered to be correct if it corresponds to the reference translation (i.e. the translation of that instance in the test corpus). This strict requirement of exact correspondence constitutes one of the main critics addressed to MT evaluation metrics (Cabezas and Resnik, 2005; Callison-Burch, 2006; Chan *et al.*, 2007) and is one of the main reasons that methods have been developed which go beyond pure string matching (Owczarzak *et al.*, 2007).

A central issue in MT evaluation is the high correlation of the metrics with human judgements of translation quality, which puts the accent on the identification of sense correspondences. Here too, it is essential to penalize errors relatively to their importance and so information relative to the semantics of the equivalents should be available. In the next section we will show how this information can be acquired using a data-driven sense induction method.

2 Data-driven semantic analysis in a bilingual context

We propose to explore the semantic relations of the equivalents of ambiguous words using a parallel corpus and to exploit these relations for SL sense induction. A data-driven sense acquisition method based on this type of relations is presented in Apidianaki (2008). The theoretical assumptions underlying this approach are the distributional hypotheses of meaning (Harris, 1954) and of semantic similarity (Miller and Charles, 1989), and that of sense correspondence between words in translation relation in real texts.

Our training corpus is the English (EN)–Greek (GR) part of the lemmatized and POS-tagged INTERA corpus (Gavrilidou *et al.*, 2004) which contains approximately four million words. The corpus has been sentence- and word-aligned at the level of tokens and types (Simard and Langlais, 2003). Two bilingual lexicons (one

[2] A typical example is that of the ambiguous English noun *interest* whose "personal" and "financial" senses are translated by the same word in French (*intérêt*).

for each translation direction: EN–GR/GR–EN are built from the alignment of word types. In these lexicons, each SL word (w) is associated with the set of the equivalents to which it is aligned, as shown hereafter:

implication: {*συνέπεια* (consequence), *επίπτωση* (impact), *επιπλοκή* (complication)}

variation: {*διακύμανση* (fluctuation), *μεταβολή* (alteration), *τροποποίηση* (modification)}

The words in parentheses describe the senses of the Greek equivalents. In order to eliminate the noise present in the lexicons, two filters are used: a POS-filter, that keeps only the correspondences between words of the same category[3] and an intersection filter, which discards the translation correspondences not found in both translation lexicons. A lexical sample of 150 ambiguous English nouns having more than two equivalents is then created from the EN–GR lexicon[4]. At this stage, the semantic relations possibly existing between the equivalents are not yet evident, and so no conclusions can be extracted concerning the distinctiveness of the senses they can induce on the SL words.

The core component of the sense induction method used is a semantic similarity calculation which aims at discovering the relations between the equivalents of a SL ambiguous word (w). First, the translation units (TUs)[5] in which w appears in the SL sentence(s) are extracted from the training corpus and are then grouped by reference to w's equivalents. For instance, if w is translated by a, b and c, three sets of TUs are formed (where w is translated by a ('*w-a*' TUs), by b ('*w-b*' TUs), etc.).

The SL context features corresponding to each equivalent (i.e. the set of lemmatized content words surrounding w in the SL side of the TUs corresponding to the equivalent) are extracted and treated as a 'bag of words'. This distributional information serves to calculate the equivalents' similarity using a variation of the Weighted Jaccard coefficient (Grefenstette, 1994). The similarity calculation is described in detail in Apidianaki (2008).

Each retained context feature is assigned a weight relatively to each equivalent, which serves to define its relevance for the estimation of the equivalents' similarity. The equivalents are compared in a pairwise manner and a similarity score is assigned to each pair. Two equivalents are considered as semantically related if the instances of w they translate in the training corpus occur in "similar enough" contexts. The pertinence of their relation is judged by comparing its score to a threshold, equal to the mean of the scores assigned to all the pairs of equivalents of w.

The results of this calculation are exploited by a clustering algorithm which takes as input the set of equivalents of w and outputs clusters of similar equivalents illustrating its senses (Apidianaki, 2008). Clustered equivalents are semantically related[6] and considered as translating the same SL sense, while isolated ones translate distinct senses.

The same calculation is performed by reference to the TL contexts of the equivalents, i.e. using the lemmatized content words surrounding the equivalents in the TL side of the corresponding TUs sets. Contrary to the SL results, the TL ones are not used for clustering. The TL distributional information relative to the clustered equivalents and acquired at this stage will be used for lexical selection, as we will show later in this paper.

The sense clusters created for a word serve to identify its senses. We describe the senses acquired for the nouns *implication* and *variation*:

implication:
{*συνέπεια, επίπτωση*}: the "impact" sense
{*επιπλοκή*}: the "complication" sense

variation:
{*διακύμανση*}: the "fluctuation" sense
{*μεταβολή, τροποποίηση*}: the "alteration" sense

The sense induction method presented above thus permits the automatic creation of a sense inventory from a parallel corpus. In what follows, we will show how this can be exploited for WSD.

3 Unsupervised WSD based on the semantic clustering

The method described in section 2 provides, as a by-product, information that can be exploited by an unsupervised WSD classifier. In the case of a one-equivalent cluster, this information corresponds to the set of the equivalent's

[3] The noun equivalents of nouns, the verb equivalents of verbs, etc.

[4] Here we focus on nouns but the method is applicable to words of other POS categories.

[5] A translation unit contains up to 2 sentences of each language linked by an alignment.

[6] Most often near-synonyms but they may be linked by other relations (hyperonymy, hyponymy, etc.).

features, retained from the corresponding SL contexts of *w*. In the case of bigger clusters, it consists of the SL context features that reveal the equivalents' similarities: for a cluster of two equivalents, it consists of their assimilative contexts (i.e. the features they share)[7]; for a cluster of more than 2 equivalents, it consists of the intersection of the common features of the pairs of equivalents found in the cluster.

As we have already said, each retained context feature is assigned a weight relatively to each equivalent. Here are the weighted features characterizing the clusters of *variation* :

{διακύμανση}: *significant* (2.04), *range* (0.76), *pharmacokinetics*(1.89), *individual* (1.89), *affect* (1.89), *insulin* (1.89), *woman* (1.89), *year* (1.49), *man* (1.19), *considerable* (1.19), *member* (1.12), *old* (0.76), *Ireland* (0.76), *case* (0.72), *increase* (0.76), *group* (0.76), *states* (0.71), *external* (0.76), *good* (0.76), *expectancy* (0.76), *Spain* (0.76), *pressure* (0.76), *Europe* (0.76)

{τροποποίηση, μεταβολή} : *minor* (2.25/1.83), *human* (2.01/1.13), *number* (0.73/1.16)[8]

In order to disambiguate a new instance of a word *w*, cooccurrence information coming from its context is compared to the sets of features characterizing the clusters. The new context must thus be lemmatized and POS-tagged as well. Here is an example of a new instance of *variation*:

a. "*Although certain regions have been faced with an exodus of their endogenous population, most of the coastal zones are experiencing an increase in overall demographic pressure, as well as significant seasonal* ***variations*** *in employment, essentially linked to tourism.*"

The features retained from this context are the lemmas of the content words (nouns, verbs and adjectives) surrounding *w*. If common features (CFs) are found between this context and just one cluster of *w*, this is selected as describing the sense of the new instance. On the contrary, if CFs with more than one cluster are found, a score is given to each *context-cluster* association. This score corresponds to the mean of the weights of the CFs relatively to each equivalent of the cluster and is given by the following formula.

$$\frac{\sum_{i=1}^{e}\sum_{j=1}^{f} w\,(equivalent_i\,,\,feature_j)}{e*f}$$

In this formula, *e* is the number of the equivalents of a cluster and *f* is the number of its CFs with the new context. The cluster with the highest score is retained; it describes the sense carried by the new instance *of w* and could be used as its sense tag. The only cluster having CFs with the context of *variation* in (a) and is thus selected is {*διακύμανση*} (CFs : *increase, pressure, significant*).

If any instances remain ambiguous at the end of the WSD process (i.e. no associations are established with the sense clusters), a small modification could increase the method's coverage. If *w* has clusters of more than two equivalents, it is possible to use the assimilative contexts of the pairs of equivalents instead of their intersection. The coverage of the WSD method would be increased in this way, as the sets of assimilative contexts would contain more features than their intersection, and so it would become more probable to find CFs with the new contexts and to establish '*context-cluster*' associations.

4 Semantics-sensitive WSD evaluation

4.1 The notion of *enriched precision*

In this section, we will present the evaluation of the proposed WSD method and we will show how the clustering information can be exploited at this stage.[9] The new instances of the nouns of our lexical sample, used for evaluation, come from our test corpus, the sentence aligned EN–GR part of EUROPARL (Koehn, 2005). The TUs containing the ambiguous nouns are extracted from the corpus. Lacking a gold-standard for evaluation, we exploit information relative to translations.

In the multilingual tasks of Senseval and Semeval (Ckhlovski *et al.*, 2004; Jin *et al.*, 2007), the translations of the words in the parallel test corpus are considered as their sense tags. Here, we consider that the equivalent translating an ambiguous SL word in context (called *reference translation*) points to a sense described by a cluster. Consequently, what is being evaluated is the capacity of the WSD

[7] Term used in the study of paraphrase (Fuchs, 1994).

[8] The two scores in parentheses correspond, respectively, to the score of the feature by reference to the first and the second equivalent of the cluster.

[9] Some of the equivalents of *w* found in the training corpus and contained in the clusters may not be used in the test corpus. The evaluation concerns only those that are found in the test corpus.

method to predict this sense. The sense proposed for an instance of an ambiguous word is considered as **correct** if a) a 1-equivalent cluster is selected and the equivalent corresponds to the reference, or b) if a bigger cluster containing the reference is selected. Otherwise, the proposed sense is **false**.

In the multilingual tasks where translations are regarded as sense tags, the proposed senses are considered as correct only if they correspond exactly to the reference translation. This is the principle of *precision*, underlying most of the existing MT evaluation metrics. From a quantitative point of view, this strict criterion has a negative impact on the WSD evaluation results. From a qualitative point of view, it ignores the fact that different equivalents may correspond to the same source sense and that an ambiguous word in context can have more than one good translation.

The use of the sense clusters during WSD evaluation offers the possibility of capturing the semantic relations between the equivalents of ambiguous words, acquired during learning. In this case, the evaluation could be considered as based on a principle of *enriched precision* that exploits the paradigmatic relations of TL words.

4.2. Evaluation metrics

The metrics used for WSD evaluation are the following:

$$recall = \frac{number\ of\ correct\ predictions}{number\ of\ new\ instances}$$

$$precision = \frac{number\ of\ correct\ predictions}{number\ of\ predictions}$$

The obtained results are compared to those of a baseline method. The baseline most often used in Senseval is that of the most frequent sense (i.e. the first sense given for a word in a predefined sense inventory). This is a very powerful heuristic because of the asymmetric distribution of word senses in real texts. Our baseline consists of choosing the most frequent equivalent (i.e. the one that translates w most frequently in the training corpus) as illustrating the sense of all its new instances. The asymmetric distribution of senses is, however, reflected at the level of the equivalents used to translate them: the most frequent equivalent in the training corpus is often the one that translates most of the instances of w in the test corpus.

The baseline score corresponds to both recall and precision, as a prediction is made for all the new instances. This score is calculated, for each w, on the basis of the number of its instances for which the proposed sense is correct. This number coincides with the frequency of the most frequent equivalent of w in the test corpus. In order to facilitate the comparison between our results and the baseline, we use the *f-measure* (*f-score*) that combines precision and recall in a unique measure:

$$f-score = \frac{2*(precision*recall)}{precision + recall}$$

We evaluate here the performance of our WSD method on the 150 ambiguous nouns of our sample. We observe that the *f-score* of our method easily overcomes the results of the baseline.

baseline	51.42%
enriched *f*-score	76.99%

The difference between these scores indicates the positive impact of the clustering information on the WSD results. As the senses are situated at a higher level of abstraction, the correspondences with the reference are established at a more abstract level than that of exact unigram correspondences.

Our results can be compared to those obtained in the multilingual lexical sample tasks of Senseval and SemEval. This comparison seems interesting although these tasks concern words of different parts of speech (nouns, verbs and adjectives). The systems participating at the multilingual English–Hindi lexical sample task of Senseval-3 are all supervised and they all perform better than the baseline (Chklovski *et al.*, 2004). This is interpreted by the authors as an indication of the clarity of the sense distinctions performed using translations, which provide sufficient information for the training of supervised classifiers. The systems performed better on the sense-tagged part of the data, showing that sense information may be helpful for the task of targeted word translation. In the English–Chinese lexical sample task of SemEval the unsupervised systems perform worse than the baseline, contrary to the supervised ones (Jin *et al.*, 2007).

5 Capturing semantic similarity during translation

5.1 Lexical selection based on WSD

In the experiments reported here, *lexical selection* refers to the translation of ambiguous SL nouns in context and not to that of whole sentences. Lexical selection is thus considered as a *blank-filling* task (Vickrey *et al.*, 2005): the equivalents translating the SL nouns in the TL sentences of the test TUs are automatically replaced by a blank which has to be filled by the WSD or the lexical selection method. We give an example of a test TU containing the noun *implication*.

> b) "*Any change to the current situation must be preceded by a rigorous study of its various* ***implications****, with the objective always being to guarantee a high-quality public service and to retain the current public operators and existing jobs.*" / "*Επίσης, σε οποιαδήποτε μεταβολή της σημερινής κατάστασης θα πρέπει πάντα να προηγείται μία εμπεριστατωμένη μελέτη των διαφορετικών* **[...]** *έχοντας διαρκώς κατά νου το στόχο της διασφάλισης μίας ποιοτικής δημόσιας υπηρεσίας, της διατήρησης των σημερινών δημοσίων φορέων παροχής υπηρεσιών και της κατοχύρωσης των σημερινών θέσεων εργασίας.*"

If a one-equivalent cluster is selected by the WSD method, this equivalent is retained as the translation of the SL word (cf. (*a*), section 3). On the contrary, when a bigger sense cluster is proposed, the most adequate equivalent for the TL context has to be selected. This is done by the lexical selection method, which filters the cluster and fills the blank in the TL sentence with the best translation according to the TL context.

The cluster retained during WSD as describing the sense of *implication* in (b) is {*συνέπεια, επίπτωση*}. Most often the clustered equivalents are near-synonyms translating the same source sense, but almost never absolute synonyms interchangeable in all TL contexts. Consequently, the cluster can be filtered by considering their differences.

In order to judge the equivalents' adequacy in the new TL context, the lexical selection method compares information coming from this context to information learned during training. Given that the training was performed on a lemmatized and POS-tagged corpus, the new TL context must be lemmatized and POS-tagged as well, in order to retain only the lemmas of the content words[10].

The information acquired during training and exploited here concerns the context features that differentiate the equivalents in the TL, as shown by the semantic similarity calculation in the TL side of the training corpus (cf. section 2). The differentiating contexts of the equivalents characterize the sense clusters as well, as was the case with their assimilative contexts.[11]

The equivalent retained by the lexical selection method for *implication* in the example (b) is *συνέπεια*. This differs from the reference translation (*επίπτωση*) but is closely related to it. Thus, it is a semantically plausible translation that can be used in this TL context.

In a real Statistical Machine Translation (SMT) system, the clusters could be filtered by the language model, on the basis of word sequence probabilities in translations. In this way, the most probable translation in the TL context, among the semantically pertinent alternatives included in the cluster suggested during WSD, would be selected.

5.2 Evaluation of the lexical selection

The lexical selection method has been applied to the WSD results on our lexical sample. The reference translations, found in the test corpus, serve for evaluation here as well. We calculate the results of this method first using the principle of *strict precision* (i.e. looking for exact correspondences with the reference) and then on the basis of *enriched precision* (i.e. exploiting the clustering information).

The sense clusters serve here to estimate the semantic proximity of the proposed translation to the reference, in cases of no exact correspondence. Thus, a translation which is semantically similar to the reference is considered to be correct if they are both found in the cluster proposed during WSD. This renders the evaluation more flexible and significantly increases the quantity of semantically pertinent translations compared to the baseline.

The strict and enriched *f*-scores are estimated by considering as correct (score = 1) every translation that is pertinent according to the corresponding evaluation principles. The

[10] Our test corpus has been tagged and lemmatized using the TreeTagger (Schmid, 1994).

[11] The SL contextual information exploited for WSD.

results indicate the increase in pertinent translations.

baseline	52.14%
strict - *f-score*	48.37%
enriched *f-score*	77.79%

We observe that the strict *f-score* is lower than the baseline. This happens because our method proposes equivalents semantically similar to the reference for some instances for which the baseline predictions are correct. However, these pertinent predictions are not taken into account by the principle of strict precision. This is the case in example (b): the baseline prediction (*επίπτωση*) for this instance of *implication* corresponds to the reference while the suggestion of our method (*συνέπεια*), even though semantically pertinent, is not considered as correct according to the principle of strict precision and is not rewarded.

Nevertheless, it would be preferable to weigh differently the predictions related to the reference, by taking into account the strength of their relation. These predictions could be considered as *almost correct* and they could be, at the same time, penalized less than translations having a different sense and less rewarded than exact correspondences to the reference.

For this to be done, a measure capable of capturing the semantic distance would be needed. Using a weighted coefficient is essential in tasks implicating semantics, not only in WSD (Resnik and Yarowsky, 2000) but also in tasks such as the estimation of inter-annotator agreement in semantic annotation (Artstein and Poesio, 2008). The common element between these tasks is that the distances between the categories (word senses) should be weighted, so that the WSD errors or the divergences between annotators be treated differently.

We envisaged the possibility of weighting differently the proposed translations on the basis of their relation to the reference, by using as distance measure their similarity score in the TL. A semantically pertinent translation different from the reference was assigned a score equal to the similarity score of the two equivalents in the TL. A problem that we encountered, and that made us fall back to the solution of a uniform weighting of semantically pertinent translations, is that the comparison of these results to the baseline was not representative of the effective improvement (the great increase in the number of pertinent translation predictions) brought about by exploiting the clustering information. This happens because all the correct suggestions of the baseline are weighted by a score equal to 1, while the score of translations semantically related to the reference is always lower than 1, given that absolute synonyms are very rare in natural language.

We envisage the elaboration of a more sophisticated coefficient for weighting semantically pertinent translations, that will permit a more conclusive comparison with the baseline. This coefficient could take into account not only the similarity score between a proposed translation and the reference but also the number of the SL word's candidate translations, the number of its senses and their distinctiveness, as well as the number of the equivalents similar to the reference and their scores.

Before concluding, we would like to take a look at the way the concern for lexical semantics is manifested and taken into account in existing MT evaluation metrics.

5.3 Semantic similarity in existing MT evaluation metrics

Lexical semantic relations are supposed to be captured in BLEU by the use of multiple reference translations (Papineni *et al.,* 2002). Finding many references for evaluation is, however, rather problematic (Callison-Burch, 2006).

In METEOR (Banerjee and Lavie, 2005), such relations are detected by exploiting WordNet (Miller *et al.*, 1990). More precisely, the number of pertinent translations is increased using synset information: a translation is correct not only if it corresponds to the reference, but also if it is semantically similar to it, i.e. found in the same synset.

One of the limitations of this metric is that the words being tested for synonymy are not disambiguated; that is what Banerjee and Lavie call "a poor-man's synonymy detection algorithm". Consequently, the WN-Synonymy module used maps two unigrams together simply if at least one sense of each word belongs to the same WordNet synset.

Another problem is that the metric is strongly dependent on a predefined sense inventory. Given that such resources are publicly available for very few languages, the synonymy module often is not operational and is omitted.

Lavie and Agarwal (2007) envisage the possibility of developing new synonymy modules for languages other than English, which would be based on alternative methods and could replace WordNet.

In the previous sections, we showed how the information acquired by an unsupervised sense induction method can help to account for the words' semantic similarity. The created sense clusters, grouping semantically similar equivalents, can be compared to WordNet synsets. This kind of semantic information, extracted directly from text data, can constitute an alternative to the use of predefined sense inventories. A clear advantage of a metric based on the results of unsupervised semantic analysis, in comparison to one dependent on a predefined resource, is that it is language-independent and may be used for evaluation in languages where semantic resources are not available.

6 Conclusion and perspectives

In this paper, we have presented the advantages and weaknesses of cross-lingual sense determination, often used in multilingual WSD and MT. We have put forward some arguments towards a more thorough semantic analysis of the translation equivalents of ambiguous words that serve as sense indicators, and we have shown how it could be of use in multilingual WSD and MT.

The data-driven sense induction method used identifies the senses of ambiguous English nouns by clustering their translation equivalents according to their semantic similarity. Exploiting the sense inventory built in this way proves of benefit in multilingual WSD and lexical selection in MT. Their evaluation becomes more flexible as well, as it becomes possible to capture the semantic relations between the translations of ambiguous words.

The problem of strictness of the MT evaluation metrics can thus be overcome without the need for a predefined inventory. This would allow for a more conclusive estimation of the effect of WSD in SMT. The integration of the cluster-based WSD method into a real SMT system and the evaluation of its impact on translation quality constitute the main perspectives of the work presented in this article and the object of future work.

Acknowledgments

I would like to thank Philippe Langlais for the word alignment and Andy Way for useful comments. This research is funded by SFI grant 05/IN/1732.

References

Marianna Apidianaki. 2008. *Translation-oriented Sense Induction Based on Parallel Corpora*, In Proceedings of the 6th Conference on Language Resources and Evaluation (LREC), Marrakech, Morocco.

Ron Artstein and Massimo Poesio. 2008. *Inter-coder Agreement for Computational Linguistics*, Computational Linguistics 34(4): 555-596.

Satanjeev Banerjee and Alon Lavie. 2005. *METEOR: An Automatic Metric for MT Evaluation with Improved Correlation with Human Judgments*. In Proceedings of the Workshop on Intrinsic and Extrinsic Evaluation Measures for MT and/or Summarization, 43rd Annual Meeting of the Association for Computational Linguistics (ACL), Ann Arbor, Michigan, 65-72.

Peter F. Brown, Stephen A. Della Pietra, Vincent J. Della Pietra and Robert L. Mercer. 1991. *Word-sense disambiguation using statistical methods*. In 29th Annual Meeting of the Association for Computational Linguistics (ACL), Berkeley, California, 264-270.

Clara Cabezas and Philip Resnik. 2005. *Using WSD Techniques for Lexical Selection in Statistical Machine Translation*. Technical Report CS-TR-4736/LAMP-TR-124/UMIACS-TR-2005-42.

Chris Callison-Burch, Miles Osborne and Philipp Koehn. 2006. *Re-evaluating the Role of BLEU in Machine Translation Research*. In Proceedings of the 11th Conference of the European Chapter of the Association for Computational Linguistics (EACL), Trento, Italy, 249-256.

Marine Carpuat and Dekai Wu. 2005. *Word Sense Disambiguation vs. Statistical Machine Translation*. In 43rd Annual Meeting of the Association for Computational Linguistics (ACL). Ann Arbor, Michigan, 387-394.

Marine Carpuat and Dekai Wu. 2007. *Improving Statistical Machine Translation using Word Sense Disambiguation*. In Proceedings of the Joint Conference on Empirical Methods in Natural Language Processing and Computational Natural Language Learning (EMNLP-CoNLL), Prague, Czech Republic, 61-72.

Yee Seng Chan, Hwee Tou Ng and David Chiang. 2007. *Word Sense Disambiguation Improves Statistical Machine Translation*. In 45th Annual

Meeting of the Association for Computational Linguistics, Prague, Czech Republic, 33-40.

Timothy Chklovski, Rada Mihalcea, Ted Pedersen and Amruta Purandare. 2004. *The senseval-3 multilingual English-Hindi lexical sample task.* Senseval-3, Third International Workshop on Evaluating Word Sense Disambiguation Systems, Barcelona, Spain, 5-8.

Philip Edmonds and Adam Kilgarriff. 2002. *Introduction to the special issue on evaluating word sense disambiguation systems.* Natural Language Engineering 8(4): 279-291.

Catherine, Fuchs. 1994. Paraphrase et énonciation. Editions Ophrys, Paris.

Maria Gavrilidou, Peny Labropoulou, Elina Desipri, Voula Giouli, Vasilis Antonopoulos and Stelios Piperidis. 2004. *Building parallel corpora for eContent professionals.* In Proceedings of the Workshop on Multilingual Linguistic Resources, 20th International Conference on Computational Linguistics (COLING), Geneva, Switzerland, 90-93.

Gregory Grefenstette. 1994. Explorations in Automatic Thesaurus Discovery. Kluwer Academic Publishers, Boston/Dordrecht/London.

Zellig Harris. 1954. Distributional Structure. *Word*, 10: 146-162.

Peng Jin, Yunfang Wu and Shiwen Yu. 2007. *SemEval-2007 Task 5: Multilingual Chinese-English Lexical Sample*, In Proceedings of the 4th International Workshop on Semantic Evaluations (SemEval 2007), Prague, Czech Republic, 19-23.

Philipp Koehn. 2005. *Europarl: A Parallel Corpus for Statistical Machine Translation.* In Proceedings of MT Summit X, Phuket, Thailand, 79-86.

Alon Lavie and Abhaya Agarwal. 2007. *METEOR: An Automatic Metric for MT Evaluation with High Levels of Correlation with Human Judgments.* In Proceedings of the 2nd Workshop on Statistical Machine Translation, 45th Meeting of the Association for Computational Linguistics (ACL), Prague, Czech Republic, 228-231.

George A. Miller, Richard Beckwith, Christiane Fellbaum, Derek Groos and Katherine Miller. 1990. *Introduction to WordNet: An On-line Lexical Database.* International Journal of Lexicography 3(4): 235-312.

George A. Miller and Walter G. Charles. 1991. *Contextual correlates of semantic similarity.* Language and Cognitive Processes 6(1): 1-28.

Karolina Owczarzak, Josef van Genabith and Andy Way. 2007. *Labelled Dependencies in Machine Translation Evaluation.* In Proceedings of the 2nd Workshop on Statistical Machine Translation, 45th Meeting of the Association for Computational Linguistics (ACL), Prague, Czech Republic, 104-111.

Kishore Papineni, Salim Roukos, Todd Ward and Wei-Jing Zhu. 2002. BLEU: a Method for Automatic Evaluation of Machine Translation. In 40th Annual Meeting of the Association for Computational Linguistics, Philadelphia, PA., 311-318.

Philip Resnik. 2004. *Exploiting Hidden Meanings: Using Bilingual Text for Monolingual Annotation.* In Gelbukh, A. (ed.), Lecture Notes in Computer Science 2945: Computational Linguistics and Intelligent Text Processing: Proceedings of the 5th International Conference CICLing, Seoul, Korea, 283-299.

Philip Resnik and David Yarowsk. 2000. *Distinguishing Systems and Distinguishing Senses: New Evaluation Methods for Word Sense Disambiguation*, Natural Language Engineering 5(3): 113-133.

Helmut Schmid. 1994. *Probabilistic Part-of-Speech Tagging Using Decision Trees.* In Proceedings of the International Conference on New Methods in Language Processing, Manchester, 44-49.

David Vickrey, Luke Biewald, Marc Teyssier and Daphne Koller. 2005. *Word-Sense Disambiguation for Machine Translation.* In Proceedings of the Joint Conference on Human Language Technology / Empirical Methods in Natural Language Processing (HLT-EMNLP), Vancouver, Canada, 771-778.

Syntactic Phrase Reordering for English-to-Arabic Statistical Machine Translation

Ibrahim Badr **Rabih Zbib** **James Glass**
Computer Science and Artificial Intelligence Lab
Massachusetts Institute of Technology
Cambridge, MA 02139, USA
{iab02, rabih, glass}@csail.mit.edu

Abstract

Syntactic Reordering of the source language to better match the phrase structure of the target language has been shown to improve the performance of phrase-based Statistical Machine Translation. This paper applies syntactic reordering to English-to-Arabic translation. It introduces reordering rules, and motivates them linguistically. It also studies the effect of combining reordering with Arabic morphological segmentation, a preprocessing technique that has been shown to improve Arabic-English and English-Arabic translation. We report on results in the news text domain, the UN text domain and in the spoken travel domain.

1 Introduction

Phrase-based Statistical Machine Translation has proven to be a robust and effective approach to machine translation, providing good performance without the need for explicit linguistic information. Phrase-based SMT systems, however, have limited capabilities in dealing with long distance phenomena, since they rely on local alignments. Automatically learned reordering models, which can be conditioned on lexical items from both the source and the target, provide some limited reordering capability when added to SMT systems.

One approach that explicitly deals with long distance reordering is to reorder the source side to better match the target side, using predefined rules. The reordered source is then used as input to the phrase-based SMT system. This approach indirectly incorporates structure information since the reordering rules are applied on the parse trees of the source sentence. Obviously, the same reordering has to be applied to both training data and test data. Despite the added complexity of parsing the data, this technique has shown improvements, especially when good parses of the source side exist. It has been successfully applied to German-to-English and Chinese-to-English SMT (Collins et al., 2005; Wang et al., 2007).

In this paper, we propose the use of a similar approach for English-to-Arabic SMT. Unlike most other work on Arabic translation, our work is in the direction of the more morphologically complex language, which poses unique challenges. We propose a set of syntactic reordering rules on the English source to align it better to the Arabic target. The reordering rules exploit systematic differences between the syntax of Arabic and the syntax of English; they specifically address two syntactic constructs. The first is the Subject-Verb order in independent sentences, where the preferred order in written Arabic is Verb-Subject. The second is the noun phrase structure, where many differences exist between the two languages, among them the order of adjectives, compound nouns and genitive constructs, as well as the way definiteness is marked. The implementation of these rules is fairly straightforward since they are applied to the parse tree. It has been noted in previous work (Habash, 2007) that syntactic reordering does not improve translation if the parse quality is not good enough. Since in this paper our source language is English, the parses are more reliable, and result in more correct reorderings. We show that using the reordering rules results in gains in the translation scores and study the effect of the training data size on those gains.

This paper also investigates the effect of using morphological segmentation of the Arabic target

Proceedings of the 12th Conference of the European Chapter of the ACL, pages 86–93,
Athens, Greece, 30 March – 3 April 2009. ©2009 Association for Computational Linguistics

in combination with the reordering rules. Morphological segmentation has been shown to benefit Arabic-to-English (Habash and Sadat, 2006) and English-to-Arabic (Badr et al., 2008) translation, although the gains tend to decrease with increasing training data size.

Section 2 provides linguistic motivation for the paper. It describes the rich morphology of Arabic, and its implications on SMT. It also describes the syntax of the verb phrase and noun phrase in Arabic, and how they differ from their English counterparts. In Section 3, we describe some of the relevant previous work. In Section 4, we present the preprocessing techniques used in the experiments. Section 5 describes the translation system, the data used, and then presents and discusses the experimental results from three domains: news text, UN data and spoken dialogue from the travel domain. The final section provides a brief summary and conclusion.

2 Arabic Linguistic Issues

2.1 Arabic Morphology

Arabic has a complex morphology compared to English. The Arabic noun and adjective are inflected for gender and number; the verb is inflected in addition for tense, voice, mood and person. Various clitics can attach to words as well: Conjunctions, prepositions and possessive pronouns attach to nouns, and object pronouns attach to verbs. The example below shows the decomposition into stems and clitics of the Arabic verb phrase *wsyqAblhm*[1] and noun phrase *wbydh*, both of which are written as one word:

(1) a. w+ s+ yqAbl +hm
and will meet-3SM them
and he will meet them

b. w+ b+ yd +h
and with hand his
and with his hand

An Arabic corpus will, therefore, have more surface forms than an equivalent English corpus, and will also be sparser. In the LDC news corpora used in this paper (see Section 5.2), the average English sentence length is 33 words compared to the Arabic 25 words.

[1] All examples in this paper are written in the Buckwalter Transliteration System (*http://www.qamus.org/transliteration.htm*)

Although the Arabic language family consists of many dialects, none of them has a standard orthography. This affects the consistency of the orthography of Modern Standard Arabic (MSA), the only written variety of Arabic. Certain characters are written inconsistently in different data sources: Final *'y'* is sometimes written as *'Y'* (*Alif mqSwrp*), and initial *Alif hamza* (The Buckwalter characters '<' and '{') are written as bare *alif* (*A*). Arabic is usually written without the diacritics that denote short vowels. This creates an ambiguity at the word level, since a word can have more than one reading. These factors adversely affect the performance of Arabic-to-English SMT, especially in the English-to-Arabic direction.

Simple pattern matching is not enough to perform morphological analysis and decomposition, since a certain string of characters can, in principle, be either an affixed morpheme or part of the base word itself. Word-level linguistic information as well as context analysis are needed. For example the written form *wly* can mean either *ruler* or *and for me*, depending on the context. Only in the latter case should it be decomposed.

2.2 Arabic Syntax

In this section, we describe a number of syntactic facts about Arabic which are relevant to the reordering rules described in Section 4.2.

Clause Structure

In Arabic, the main sentence usually has the order Verb-Subject-Object (VSO). The order Subject-Verb-Object (SVO) also occurs, but is less frequent than VSO. The verb agrees with the subject in gender and number in the SVO order, but only in gender in the VSO order (Examples 2c and 2d).

(2) a. Akl AlwId AltfAHp
ate-3SM the-boy the-apple
the boy ate the apple

b. AlwId Akl AltfAHp
the-boy ate-3SM the-apple
the boy ate the apple

c. Akl AlAwlAd AltfAHAt
ate-3SM the-boys the-apples
the boys ate the apples

d. AlAwlAd AklwA AltfAHAt
the-boys ate-3PM the-apples
the boys ate the apples

In a dependent clause, the order must be SVO, as illustrated by the ungrammaticality of Example 3b below. As we discuss in more detail later, this distinction between dependent and independent clauses has to be taken into account when the syntactic reordering rules are applied.

(3) a. qAl An Alwld Akl AltfAHp
said-3SM that the-boy ate the-apple
he said that the boy ate the apple

b. *qAl An Akl Alwld AltfAHp
said-3SM that ate the-boy the-apple
he said that the boy ate the apple

Another pertinent fact is that the negation particle has to always preceed the verb:

(4) lm yAkl Alwld AltfAHp
not eat-3SM the-boy the-apple
the boy did not eat the apple

Noun Phrase

The Arabic noun phrase can have constructs that are quite different from English. The adjective in Arabic follows the noun that it modifies, and it is marked with the definite article, if the head noun is definite:

(5) AlbAb Alkbyr
the-door the-big
the big door

The Arabic equivalent of the English possessive, compound nouns and the *of*-relationship is the Arabic *idafa* construct, which compounds two or more nouns. Therefore, N_1*'s* N_2 and N_2 *of* N_1 are both translated as N_2 N_1 in Arabic. As Example 6b shows, this construct can also be chained recursively.

(6) a. bAb Albyt
door the-house
the house's door

b. mftAH bAb Albyt
key door the-house
The key to the door of the house

Example 6 also shows that an *idafa* construct is made definite by adding the definite article *Al-* to the last noun in the noun phrase. Adjectives follow the *idafa* noun phrase, regardless of which noun in the chain they modify. Thus, Example 7 is ambiguous in that the adjective *kbyr (big)* can modify any of the preceding three nouns. The same is true for relative clauses that modify a noun.

(7) mftAH bAb Albyt Alkbyr
key door the-house the-big

These and other differences between the Arabic and English syntax are likely to affect the quality of automatic alignments, since corresponding words will occupy positions in the sentence that are far apart, especially when the relevant words (e.g. the verb and its subject) are separated by subordinate clauses. In such cases, the lexicalized distortion models used in phrase-based SMT do not have the capability of performing reorderings correctly. This limitation adversely affects the translation quality.

3 Previous Work

Most of the work in Arabic machine translation is done in the Arabic-to-English direction. The other direction, however, is also important, since it opens the wealth of information in different domains that is available in English to the Arabic speaking world. Also, since Arabic is a morphologically richer language, translating into Arabic poses unique issues that are not present in the opposite direction. The only works on English-to-Arabic SMT that we are aware of are Badr et al. (2008), and Sarikaya and Deng (2007). Badr et al. show that using segmentation and recombination as pre- and post- processing steps leads to significant gains especially for smaller training data corpora. Sarikaya and Deng use Joint Morphological-Lexical Language Models to rerank the output of an English-to-Arabic MT system. They use regular expression-based segmentation of the Arabic so as not to run into recombination issues on the output side.

Similarly, for Arabic-to-English, Lee (2004), and Habash and Sadat (2006) show that various segmentation schemes lead to improvements that decrease with increasing parallel corpus size. They use a trigram language model and the Arabic morphological analyzer MADA (Habash and Rambow, 2005) respectively, to segment the Arabic side of their corpora. Other work on Arabic-to-English SMT tries to address the word reordering problem. Habash (2007) automatically learns syntactic reordering rules that are then applied to the Arabic side of the parallel corpora. The words are aligned in a sentence pair, then the Arabic sentence is parsed to extract reordering rules based on how the constituents in the parse tree are reordered on the English side. No significant improvement is shown with reordering when compared to a baseline that uses a non-lexicalized distance reordering model. This is attributed in the paper to the poor quality of parsing.

Syntax-based reordering as a preprocessing step has been applied to many language pairs other than English-Arabic. Most relevant to the approach in this paper are Collins et al. (2005) and Wang et al. (2007). Both parse the source side and then reorder the sentence based on predefined, linguistically motivated rules. Significant gain is reported for German-to-English and Chinese-to-English translation. Both suggest that reordering as a preprocessing step results in better alignment, and reduces the reliance on the distortion model. Popovic and Ney (2006) use similar methods to reorder German by looking at the POS tags for German-to-English and German-to-Spanish. They show significant improvements on test set sentences that do get reordered as well as those that don't, which is attributed to the improvement of the extracted phrases. (Xia and McCord, 2004) present a similar approach, with a notable difference: the re-ordering rules are automatically learned from aligning parse trees for both the source and target sentences. They report a 10% relative gain for English-to-French translation. Although target-side parsing is optional in this approach, it is needed to take full advantage of the approach. This is a bigger issue when no reliable parses are available for the target language, as is the case in this paper. More generally, the use of automatically-learned rules has the advantage of readily applicable to different language pairs. The use of deterministic, pre-defined rules, however, has the advantage of being linguistically motivated, since differences between the two languages are addressed explicitly. Moreover, the implementation of pre-defined transfer rules based on target-side parses is relatively easy and cheap to implement in different language pairs.

Generic approaches for translating from English to more morphologically complex languages have been proposed. Koehn and Hoang (2007) propose Factored Translation Models, which extend phrase-based statistical machine translation by allowing the integration of additional morphological features at the word level. They demonstrate improvements for English-to-German and English-to-Czech. Tighter integration of features is claimed to allow for better modeling of the morphology and hence is better than using pre-processing and post-processing techniques. Avramidis and Koehn (2008) enrich the English side by adding a feature to the Factored Model that models noun case agreement and verb person conjugation, and show that it leads to a more grammatically correct output for English-to-Greek and English-to-Czech translation. Although Factored Models are well equipped for handling languages that differ in terms of morphology, they still use the same distortion reordering model as a phrase-based MT system.

4 Preprocessing Techniques

4.1 Arabic Segmentation and Recombination

It has been shown previously work (Badr et al., 2008; Habash and Sadat, 2006) that morphological segmentation of Arabic improves the translation performance for both Arabic-to-English and English-to-Arabic by addressing the problem of sparsity of the Arabic side. In this paper, we use segmented and non-segmented Arabic on the target side, and study the effect of the combination of segmentation with reordering.

As mentioned in Section 2.1, simple pattern matching is not enough to decompose Arabic words into stems and affixes. Lexical information and context are needed to perform the decomposition correctly. We use the Morphological Analyzer MADA (Habash and Rambow, 2005) to decompose the Arabic source. MADA uses SVM-based classifiers of features (such as POS, number, gender, etc.) to score the different analyses of a given word in context. We apply morphological decomposition before aligning the training data. We split the conjunction and preposition prefixes, as well as possessive and object pronoun suffixes. We then glue the split morphemes into one prefix and one suffix, such that any given word is split into at most three parts: *prefix+ stem +suffix*. Note that plural markers and subject pronouns are not split. For example, the word *wlAwlAdh ('and for his children')* is segmented into *wl+ AwlAd +P:3MS*.

Since training is done on segmented Arabic, the output of the decoder must be recombined into its original surface form. We follow the approach of Badr et. al (2008) in combining the Arabic output, which is a non-trivial task for several reasons. First, the ending of a stem sometimes changes when a suffix is attached to it. Second, word endings are normalized to remove orthographic inconsistency between different sources (Section 2.1). Finally, some words can recombine into more than one grammatically correct form. To address these issues, a lookup table is derived from the training data that maps the segmented form of the word to its original form. The table is also useful in recombining words that are erroneously segmented. If a certain word does not occur in the table, we back off to a set of manually defined recombination rules. Word ambiguity is resolved by picking the more frequent surface form.

4.2 Arabic Reordering Rules

This section presents the syntax-based rules used for re-ordering the English source to better match the syntax of the Arabic target. These rules are motivated by the Arabic syntactic facts described in Section 2.2.

Much like Wang et al. (2007), we parse the English side of our corpora and reorder using predefined rules. Reordering the English can be done more reliably than other source languages, such as Arabic, Chinese and German, since the state-of-the-art English parsers are considerably better than parsers of other languages. The following rules for reordering at the sentence level and the noun phrase level are applied to the English parse tree:

1. **NP:** All nouns, adjectives and adverbs in the noun phrase are inverted. This rule is motivated by the order of the adjective with respect to its head noun, as well as the *idafa* construct (see Examples 6 and 7 in Section 2.2. As a result of applying this rule, the phrase *the blank computer screen* becomes *the screen computer blank* .

2. **PP:** All prepositional phrases of the form $N_1 of N_2 ... of N_n$ are transformed to $N_1 N_2 ... N_n$. All N_i are also made indefinite, and the definite article is added to N_n, the last noun in the chain. For example, the phrase *the general chief of staff of the armed forces* becomes *general chief staff the armed forces*. We also move all adjectives in the top noun phrase to the end of the construct. So *the real value of the Egyptian pound* becomes *value the Egyptian pound real*. This rule is motivated by the *idafa* construct and its properties (see Example 6).

3. **the:** The definite article *the* is replicated before adjectives (see Example 5 above). So *the blank computer screen* becomes *the blank the computer the screen*. This rule is applied after **NP** rule abote. Note that we do not replicate *the* before proper names.

4. **VP:** This rule transforms SVO sentences to VSO. All verbs are reordered on the condition that they have their own subject noun phrase and are not in the participle form, since in these cases the Arabic subject occurs before the verb participle. We also check that the verb is not in a relative clause with a *that* complementizer (Example 3 above). The following example illustrates all these cases: *the health minister stated that 11 police officers were wounded in clashes with the demonstrators* → *stated the health minister that 11 police officers were wounded in clashes with the demonstrators*. If the verb is negated, the negative particle is moved with the verb (Example 4. Finally, if the object of the reordered verb is a pronoun, it is reordered with the verb. Example: *the authorities gave us all the necessary help* becomes *gave us the authorities all the necessary help*.

The transformation rules 1, 2 and 3 are applied in this order, since they interact although they do not conflict. So, *the real value of the Egyptian pound* → *value the Egyptian the pound the real* The VP reordering rule is independent.

5 Experiments

5.1 System description

For the English source, we first tokenize using the Stanford Log-linear Part-of-Speech Tagger (Toutanova et al., 2003). We then proceed to split the data into smaller sentences and tag them using Ratnaparkhi's Maximum Entropy Tagger (Ratnaparkhi, 1996). We parse the data using the Collins Parser (Collins, 1997), and then tag person, location and organization names using the Stanford Named Entity Recognizer (Finkel et al., 2005). On the Arabic side, we normalize the data by changing final *'Y'* to *'y'*, and changing the various forms of *Alif hamza* to bare *Alif*, since these characters are written inconsistently in some Arabic sources. We then segment the data using MADA according to the scheme explained in Section 4.1.

The English source is aligned to the segmented Arabic target using the standard MOSES (MOSES, 2007) configuration of GIZA++ (Och and Ney, 2000), which is IBM Model 4, and decoding is done using the phrase-based SMT system MOSES. We use a maximum phrase length of 15 to account for the increase in length of the segmented Arabic. We also use a lexicalized bidirectional reordering model conditioned on both the source and target sides, with a distortion limit set to 6. We tune using Och's algorithm (Och, 2003) to optimize weights for the distortion model, language model, phrase translation model and word penalty over the BLEU metric (Papineni et al., 2001). For the segmented Arabic experiments, we experiment with tuning using non-segmented Arabic as a reference. This is done by recombining the output before each tuning iteration is scored and has been shown by Badr et. al (2008) to perform better than using segmented Arabic as reference.

5.2 Data Used

We report results on three domains: newswire text, UN data and spoken dialogue from the travel domain. It is important to note that the sentences in the travel domain are much shorter than in the news domain, which simplifies the alignment as well as reordering during decoding. Also, since the travel domain contains spoken Arabic, it is more biased towards the Subject-Verb-Object sentence order than the Verb-Subject-Object order more common in the news domain. Also note that since most of our data was originally intended for Arabic-to-English translation, our test and tuning sets have only one reference, and therefore, the BLEU scores we report are lower than typical scores reported in the literature on Arabic-to-English.

The news training data consists of several LDC corpora[2]. We construct a test set by randomly picking 2000 sentences. We pick another 2000 sentences randomly for tuning. Our final training set consists of 3 million English words. We also test on the NIST MT 05 "test set while tuning on both the NIST MT 03 and 04 test sets. We use the first English reference of the NIST test sets as the source, and the Arabic source as our reference. For

Scheme	RandT		MT 05	
	S	NoS	S	NoS
Baseline	21.6	21.3	23.88	23.44
VP	21.9	21.5	23.98	23.58
NP	21.9	21.8		
NP+PP	21.8	21.5	23.72	23.68
NP+PP+VP	22.2	21.8	23.74	23.16
NP+PP+VP+The	21.3	21.0		

Table 1: Translation Results for the News Domain in terms of the BLEU Metric.

the language model, we use 35 million words from the LDC Arabic Gigaword corpus, plus the Arabic side of the 3 million word training corpus. Experimentation with different language model orders shows that the optimal model orders are 4-grams for the baseline system and 6-grams for the segmented Arabic. The average sentence length is 33 for English, 25 for non-segmented Arabic and 36 for segmented Arabic.

To study the effect of syntactic reordering on larger training data sizes, we use the UN English-Arabic parallel text (LDC2003T05). We experiment with two training data sizes: 30 million and 3 million words. The test and tuning sets are comprised of 1500 and 500 sentences respectively, chosen at random.

For the spoken domain, we use the BTEC 2007 Arabic-English corpus. The training set consists of 200K words, the test set has 500 sentences and the tuning set has 500 sentences. The language model consists of the Arabic side of the training data. Because of the significantly smaller data size, we use a trigram LM for the baseline, and a 4-gram for segmented Arabic. In this case, the average sentence length is 9 for English, 8 for Arabic, and 10 for segmented Arabic.

5.3 Translation Results

The translation scores for the News domain are shown in Table 1. The notation used in the table is as follows:

- **S:** Segmented Arabic
- **NoS:** Non-Segmented Arabic
- **RandT:** Scores for test set where sentences were picked at random from NEWS data
- **MT 05:** Scores for the NIST MT 05 test set

The reordering notation is explained in Section 4.2. All results are in terms of the BLEU met-

[2] LDC2003E05 LDC2003E09 LDC2003T18 LDC2004E07 LDC2004E08 LDC2004E11 LDC2004E72 LDC2004T18 LDC2004T17 LDC2005E46 LDC2005T05 LDC2007T24

	S		NoS	
	Short	**Long**	**Short**	**Long**
Baseline	22.57	25.22	22.40	24.33
VP	22.95	25.05	22.95	24.02
NP+PP	22.71	24.76	23.16	24.067
NP+PP+VP	22.84	24.62	22.53	24.56

Table 2: Translation Results depending on sentence length for NIST test set.

Scheme	**Score**	**% Oracle reord**
VP	25.76	59%
NP+PP	26.07	58%
NP+PP+VP	26.17	53%

Table 3: Oracle scores for combining baseline system with other reordered systems.

ric. It is important to note that the gain that we report in terms of BLEU are more significant that comparable gains on test sets that have multiple references, since our test sets have only one reference. Any amount of gain is a result of additional n-gram precision with one reference. We note that the gain achieved from the reordering of the non-segmented and segmented systems are comparable. Replicating *the* before adjectives hurts the scores, possibly because it increases the sentence length noticeably, and thus deteriorates the alignments' quality. We note that the gains achieved by reordering on the NIST test set are smaller than the improvements on the random test set. This is due to the fact that the sentences in the NIST test set are longer, which adversely affects the parsing quality. The average English sentence length is 33 words in the NIST test set, while the random test set has an average sentence length of 29 words. Table 2 shows the reordering gains of the non-segmented Arabic by sentence length. Short sentences are sentences that have less that 40 words of English, while long sentences have more than 40 words. Out of the 1055 sentence in the NIST test set 719 are short and 336 are long. We also report oracle scores in Table 3 for combining the baseline system with the reordering systems, as well as the percentage of oracle sentences produced by the reordered system. The oracle score is computed by starting with the reordered system's candidate translations and iterating over all the sentences one by one: we replace each sentence with its corresponding baseline system translation then

Scheme	**30M**	**3M**
Baseline	32.17	28.42
VP	32.46	28.60
NP+PP	31.73	28.80

Table 4: Translation Results on segmentd UN data in terms of the BLEU Metric.

compute the total BLEU score of the entire set. If the score improves, then the sentence in question is replaced with the baseline system's translation, otherwise it remains unchanged and we move on to the next one.

In Table 4, we report results on the UN corpus for different training data sizes. It is important to note that although gains from VP reordering stay constant when scaled to larger training sets, gains from NP+PP reordering diminish. This is due to the fact that NP reordering tend to be more localized then VP reorderings. Hence with more training data the lexicalized reordering model becomes more effective in reordering NPs.

In Table 5, we report results on the BTEC corpus for different segmentation and reordering scheme combinations. We should first point out that all sentences in the BTEC corpus are short, simple and easy to align. Hence, the gain introduced by reordering might not be enough to offset the errors introduced by the parsing. We also note that spoken Arabic usually prefers the Subject-Verb-Object sentence order, rather than the Verb-Subject-Object sentence order of written Arabic. This explains the fact that no gain is observed when the verb phrase is reordered. Noun phrase reordering produces a significant gain with non-segmented Arabic. Replicating the definite article *the* in the noun phrase does not create alignment problems as is the case with the newswire data, since the sentences are considerably shorter, and hence the 0.74 point gain observed on the segmented Arabic system. That gain does not translate to the non-segmented Arabic system since in that case the definite article *Al* remains attached to its head word.

6 Conclusion

This paper presented linguistically motivated rules that reorder English to look like Arabic. We showed that these rules produce significant gains. We also studied the effect of the interaction between Arabic morphological segmentation and

Scheme	S	NoS
Baseline	29.06	25.4
VP	26.92	23.49
NP	27.94	26.83
NP+PP	28.59	26.42
The	29.8	25.1

Table 5: Translation Results for the Spoken Language Domain in the BLEU Metric.

syntactic reordering on translation results, as well as how they scale to bigger training data sizes.

Acknowledgments

We would like to thank Michael Collins, Ali Mohammad and Stephanie Seneff for their valuable comments.

References

Eleftherios Avramidis, and Philipp Koehn 2008. *Enriching Morphologically Poor Languages for Statistical Machine Translation.* In Proc. of ACL/HLT.

Ibrahim Badr, Rabih Zbib, and James Glass 2008. *Segmentation for English-to-Arabic Statistical Machine Translation.* In Proc. of ACL/HLT.

Michael Collins 1997. *Three Generative, Lexicalized Models for Statistical Parsing.* In Proc. of ACL.

Michael Collins, Philipp Koehn, and Ivona Kucerova 2005. *Clause Restructuring for Statistical Machine Translation.* In Proc. of ACL.

Jenny Rose Finkel, Trond Grenager, and Christopher Manning 2005. *Incorporating Non-local Information into Information Extraction Systems by Gibbs Sampling.* In Proc. of ACL.

Nizar Habash, 2007. *Syntactic Preprocessing for Statistical Machine Translation.* In Proc. of the Machine Translation Summit (MT-Summit).

Nizar Habash and Owen Rambow, 2005. *Arabic Tokenization, Part-of-Speech Tagging and Morphological Disambiguation in One Fell Swoop.* In Proc. of ACL.

Nizar Habash and Fatiha Sadat, 2006. *Arabic Preprocessing Schemes for Statistical Machine Translation.* In Proc. of HLT.

Philipp Koehn and Hieu Hoang, 2007. *Factored Translation Models.* In Proc. of EMNLP/CNLL.

Young-Suk Lee, 2004. *Morphological Analysis for Statistical Machine Translation.* In Proc. of EMNLP.

MOSES, 2007. *A Factored Phrase-based Beam-search Decoder for Machine Translation.* URL: http://www.statmt.org/moses/.

Franz Och 2003. *Minimum Error Rate Training in Statistical Machine Translation.* In Proc. of ACL.

Franz Och and Hermann Ney 2000. *Improved Statistical Alignment Models.* In Proc. of ACL.

Kishore Papineni, Salim Roukos, Todd Ward, and Wei-Jing Zhu 2001. *BLUE: a Method for Automatic Evaluation of Machine Translation.* In Proc. of ACL.

Maja Popovic and Hermann Ney 2006. *POS-based Word Reordering for Statistical Machine Translation.* In Proc. of NAACL LREC.

Adwait Ratnaparkhi 1996. *A Maximum Entropy Model for Part-of-Speech Tagging.* In Proc. of EMNLP.

Ruhi Sarikaya and Yonggang Deng 2007. *Joint Morphological-Lexical Language Modeling for Machine Translation.* In Proc. of NAACL HLT.

Kristina Toutanova, Dan Klein, Christopher Manning, and Yoram Singer. 2003. *Feature-Rich Part-of-Speech Tagging with a Cyclic Dependency Network.* In Proc. of NAACL HLT.

Chao Wang, Michael Collins, and Philipp Koehn 2007. *Chinese Syntactic Reordering for Statistical Machine Translation.* In Proc. of EMNLP.

Fei Xia and Michael McCord 2004. Improving a Statistical MT System with Automatically Learned Rewrite Patterns. In COLING.

Incremental Parsing Models for Dialog Task Structure

Srinivas Bangalore and **Amanda J. Stent**
AT&T Labs – Research, Inc., 180 Park Avenue,
Florham Park, NJ 07932, USA
{srini,stent}@research.att.com

Abstract

In this paper, we present an integrated model of the two central tasks of dialog management: interpreting user actions and generating system actions. We model the interpretation task as a classification problem and the generation task as a prediction problem. These two tasks are interleaved in an incremental parsing-based dialog model. We compare three alternative parsing methods for this dialog model using a corpus of human-human spoken dialog from a catalog ordering domain that has been annotated for dialog acts and task/subtask information. We contrast the amount of context provided by each method and its impact on performance.

1 Introduction

Corpora of spoken dialog are now widely available, and frequently come with annotations for tasks/games, dialog acts, named entities and elements of syntactic structure. These types of information provide rich clues for building dialog models (Grosz and Sidner, 1986). Dialog models can be built offline (for dialog mining and summarization), or online (for dialog management).

A dialog manager is the component of a dialog system that is responsible for interpreting user actions in the dialog context, and for generating system actions. Needless to say, a dialog manager operates incrementally as the dialog progresses. In typical commercial dialog systems, the interpretation and generation processes operate independently of each other, with only a small amount of shared context. By contrast, in this paper we describe a dialog model that (1) tightly integrates interpretation and generation, (2) makes explicit the type and amount of shared context, (3) includes the task structure of the dialog in the context, (4) can be trained from dialog data, and (5) runs incrementally, parsing the dialog as it occurs and interleaving generation and interpretation.

At the core of our model is a parser that incrementally builds the dialog task structure as the dialog progresses. In this paper, we experiment with three different incremental tree-based parsing methods. We compare these methods using a corpus of human-human spoken dialogs in a catalog ordering domain that has been annotated for dialog acts and task/subtask information. We show that all these methods outperform a baseline method for recovering the dialog structure.

The rest of this paper is structured as follows: In Section 2, we review related work. In Section 3, we present our view of the structure of task-oriented human-human dialogs. In Section 4, we present the parsing approaches included in our experiments. In Section 5, we describe our data and experiments. Finally, in Section 6, we present conclusions and describe our current and future work.

2 Related Work

There are two threads of research that are relevant to our work: work on parsing (written and spoken) discourse, and work on plan-based dialog models.

Discourse Parsing Discourse parsing is the process of building a hierarchical model of a discourse from its basic elements (sentences or clauses), as one would build a parse of a sentence from its words. There has now been considerable work on discourse parsing using statistical bottom-up parsing (Soricut and Marcu, 2003), hierarchical agglomerative clustering (Sporleder and Lascarides, 2004), parsing from lexicalized tree-adjoining grammars (Cristea, 2000), and rule-based approaches that use rhetorical relations and discourse cues (Forbes et al., 2003; Polanyi et al., 2004; LeThanh et al., 2004). With the exception of Cristea (2000), most of this research has been limited to non-incremental parsing of textual monologues where, in contrast to incremental dialog parsing, predicting a system action is not relevant.

The work on discourse parsing that is most similar to ours is that of Baldridge and Lascarides (2005). They used a probabilistic head-driven parsing method (described in (Collins, 2003)) to construct rhetorical structure trees for a spoken dialog corpus. However, their parser was

Proceedings of the 12th Conference of the European Chapter of the ACL, pages 94–102,
Athens, Greece, 30 March – 3 April 2009. ©2009 Association for Computational Linguistics

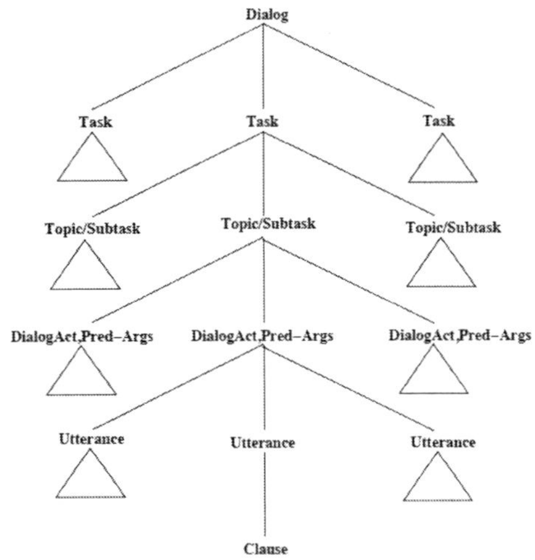

Figure 1: A schema of a shared plan tree for a dialog.

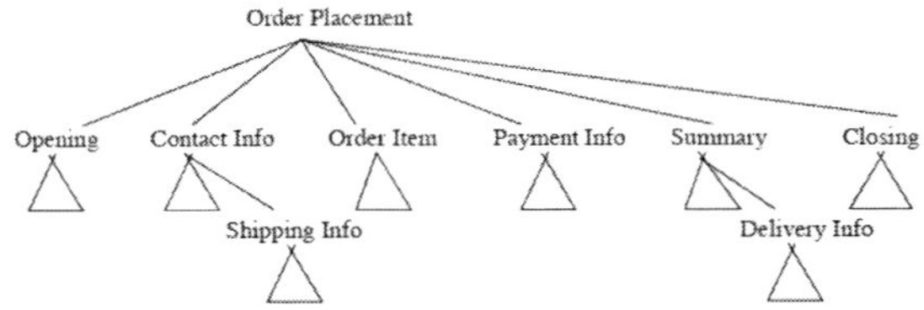

Figure 2: Sample output (subtask tree) from a parse-based model for the catalog ordering domain.

not incremental; it used global features such as the number of turn changes. Also, it focused strictly in interpretation of input utterances; it could not predict actions by either dialog partner.

In contrast to other work on discourse parsing, we wish to use the parsing process directly for dialog management (rather than for information extraction or summarization). This influences our approach to dialog modeling in two ways. First, the subtask tree we build represents the functional task structure of the dialog (rather than the rhetorical structure of the dialog). Second, our dialog parser must be entirely incremental.

Plan-Based Dialog Models Plan-based approaches to dialog modeling, like ours, operate directly on the dialog's task structure. The process of task-oriented dialog is treated as a special case of AI-style plan recognition (Sidner, 1985; Litman and Allen, 1987; Rich and Sidner, 1997; Carberry, 2001; Bohus and Rudnicky, 2003; Lochbaum, 1998). Plan-based dialog models are used for both interpretation of user utterances and prediction of agent actions. In addition to the hand-crafted models listed above, researchers have built stochastic plan recognition models for interaction, including ones based on Hidden Markov Models (Bui, 2003; Blaylock and Allen, 2006) and on probabilistic context-free grammars (Alexandersson and Reithinger, 1997; Pynadath and Wellman, 2000).

In this area, the work most closely related to ours is that of Barrett and Weld (Barrett and Weld, 1994), who build an incremental bottom-up parser to parse plans. Their parser, however, was not probabilistic or targeted at dialog processing.

3 Dialog Structure

We consider a task-oriented dialog to be the result of incremental creation of a shared plan by the participants (Lochbaum, 1998). The shared plan is represented as a single tree T that incorporates the task/subtask structure, dialog acts, syntactic structure and lexical content of the dialog, as shown in Figure 1. A task is a sequence of subtasks $ST \in S$. A subtask is a sequence of dialog acts $DA \in D$. Each dialog act corresponds to one clause spoken by one speaker, customer (c^u) or agent (c^a) (for which we may have acoustic, lexical, syntactic and semantic representations).

Figure 2 shows the subtask tree for a sample dialog in our domain (catalog ordering). An *order placement* task is typically composed of the sequence of subtasks *opening, contact-information, order-item, related-offers, summary*. Subtasks can be nested; the nesting can be as deep as five levels in our data. Most often the nesting is at the leftmost or rightmost frontier of the subtask tree.

As the dialog proceeds, an utterance from a participant is accommodated into the subtask tree in an incremental manner, much like an incremental syntactic parser accommodates the next word into a partial parse tree (Alexandersson and Reithinger, 1997). An illustration of the incremental evolution of dialog structure is shown in Figure 4. However, while a syntactic parser processes input from a single source, our dialog parser parses user-system *exchanges*: user utterances are interpreted, while system utterances are generated. So the steps taken by our dialog parser to incorporate an utterance into the subtask tree depend on whether the utterance was produced by the *agent* or the *user* (as shown in Figure 3).

User utterances Each user turn is split into clauses (utterances). Each clause is supertagged

Interpretation of a user's utterance:

$$DAC : da_i^u = \underset{d^u \in D}{argmax}\ P(d^u | c_i^u, ST_{i-k}^{i-1}, DA_{i-k}^{i-1}, c_{i-k}^{i-1}) \quad (1)$$

$$STC : st_i^u = \underset{s^u \in S}{argmax}\ P(s^u | da_i^u, c_i^u, ST_{i-k}^{i-1}, DA_{i-k}^{i-1}, c_{i-k}^{i-1}) \quad (2)$$

Generation of an agent's utterance:

$$STP : st_i^a = \underset{s^a \in S}{argmax}\ P(s^a | ST_{i-k}^{i-1}, DA_{i-k}^{i-1}, c_{i-k}^{i-1}) \quad (3)$$

$$DAP : da_i^a = \underset{d^a \in D}{argmax}\ P(d^a | st_i^a, ST_{i-k}^{i-1}, DA_{i-k}^{i-1}, c_{i-k}^{i-1}) \quad (4)$$

Table 1: Equations used for modeling dialog act and subtask labeling of agent and user utterances. c_i^u/c_i^a = the words, syntactic information and named entities associated with the ith utterance of the dialog, spoken by user/agent u/a. da_i^u/da_i^a = the dialog act of the ith utterance, spoken by user/agent u/a. st_i^u/st_i^a = the subtask label of the ith utterance, spoken by user/agent u/a. DA_{i-k}^{i-1} represents the dialog act tags for utterances $i-1$ to $i-k$.

and labeled with named entities[1]. Interpretation of the clause (c_i^u) involves assigning a dialog act label (da_i^u) and a subtask label (st_i^u). We use ST_{i-k}^{i-1}, DA_{i-k}^{i-1}, and c_{i-k}^{i-1} to represent the sequence of preceeding k subtask labels, dialog act labels and clauses respectively. The dialog act label da_i^u is determined from information about the clause and (a kth order approximation of) the subtask tree so far ($T_{i-1} = (ST_{i-k}^{i-1}, DA_{i-k}^{i-1}, c_{i-k}^{i-1})$), as shown in Equation 1 (Table 1). The subtask label st_i^u is determined from information about the clause, its dialog act and the subtask tree so far, as shown in Equation 2. Then, the clause is incorporated into the subtask tree.

Agent utterances In contrast, a dialog system starts planning an agent utterance by identifying the subtask to contribute to next, st_i^a, based on the subtask tree so far ($T_{i-1} = (ST_{i-k}^{i-1}, DA_{i-k}^{i-1}, c_{i-k}^{i-1})$), as shown in Equation 3 (Table 1) . Then, it chooses the dialog act of the utterance, da_i^a, based on the subtask tree so far and the chosen subtask for the utterance, as shown in Equation 4. Finally, it generates an utterance, c_i^a, to realize its communicative intent (represented as a subtask and dialog act pair, with associated named entities)[2].

Note that the current clause c_i^u is used in the

[1]This results in a syntactic parse of the clause and could be done incrementally as well.

[2]We do not address utterance realization in this paper.

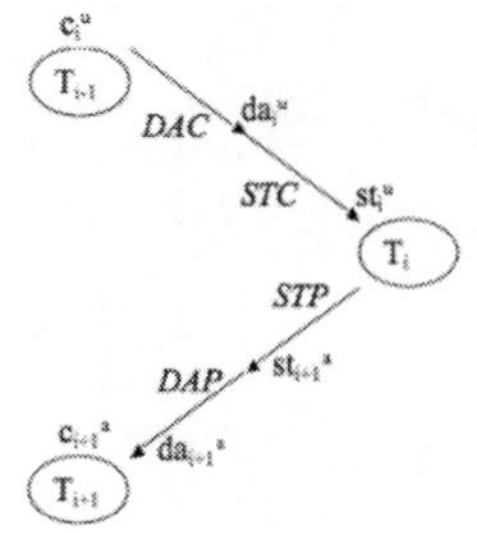

Figure 3: Dialog management process

conditioning context of the interpretation model (for user utterances), but the corresponding clause for the agent utterance c_i^a is to be predicted and hence is not part of conditioning context in the generation model.

4 Dialog Parsing

A dialog parser can produce a "shallow" or "deep" tree structure. A shallow parse is one in which utterances are grouped together into subtasks, but the dominance relations among subtasks are not tracked. We call this model a *chunk-based* dialog model (Bangalore et al., 2006). The chunk-based model has limitations. For example, dominance relations among subtasks are important for dialog processes such as anaphora resolution (Grosz and Sidner, 1986). Also, the chunk-based model is representationally inadequate for center-embedded nestings of subtasks, which do occur in our domain, although less frequently than the more prevalent "tail-recursive" structures.

We use the term *parse-based* dialog model to refer to deep parsing models for dialog which not only segment the dialog into chunks but also predict dominance relations among chunks. For this paper, we experimented with three alternative methods for building parse-based models: **shift-reduce**, **start-complete** and **connection path**. Each of these operates on the subtask tree for the dialog incrementally, from left-to-right, with access only to the preceding dialog context, as shown in Figure 4. They differ in the parsing actions and the data structures used by the parser; this has implications for robustness to errors. The instructions to reconstruct the parse are either entirely encoded in the stack (in the shift-reduce method), or entirely in the parsing actions (in the start-complete and connection path methods). For each of the four types of parsing action required to build the parse tree (see Table 1), we construct

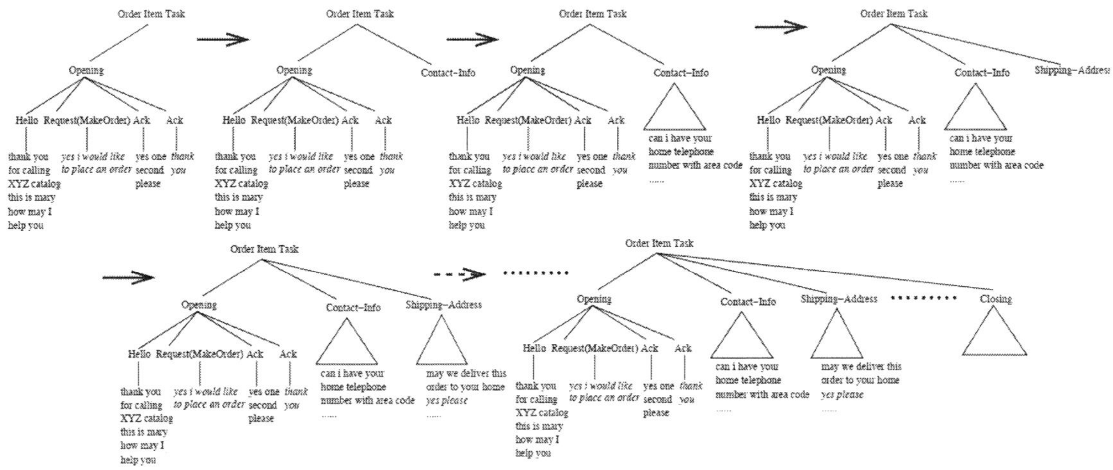

Figure 4: An illustration of incremental evolution of dialog structure

a feature vector containing contextual information for the parsing action (see Section 5.1). These feature vectors and the associated parser actions are used to train maximum entropy models (Berger et al., 1996). These models are then used to incrementally incorporate the utterances for a new dialog into that dialog's subtask tree as the dialog progresses, as shown in Figure 3.

4.1 Shift-Reduce Method

In this method, the subtask tree is recovered through a right-branching shift-reduce parsing process (Hall et al., 2006; Sagae and Lavie, 2006). The parser shifts each utterance on to the stack. It then inspects the stack and decides whether to do one or more reduce actions that result in the creation of subtrees in the subtask tree. The parser maintains two data structures – a stack and a tree. The actions of the parser change the contents of the stack and create nodes in the dialog tree structure. The actions for the parser include *unary-reduce-X*, *binary-reduce-X* and *shift*, where X is each of the non-terminals (subtask labels) in the tree. *Shift* pushes a token representing the utterance onto the stack; *binary-reduce-X* pops two tokens off the stack and pushes the non-terminal X; and *unary-reduce-X* pops one token off the stack and pushes the non-terminal X. Each type of *reduce* action creates a constituent *X* in the dialog tree and the tree(s) associated with the reduced elements as subtree(s) of *X*. At the end of the dialog, the output is a binary branching subtask tree.

Consider the example subdialog *A: would you like a free magazine? U: no.* The processing of this dialog using our shift-reduce dialog parser would proceed as follows: the STP model predicts *shift* for st^a; the DAP model predicts *YNP(Promotions)* for da^a; the generator outputs *would you like a free magazine?*; and the parser shifts a token representing this utterance onto the stack. Then, the customer says *no*. The DAC model classifies da^u as *No*; the STC model classifies st^u as *shift* and *binary-reduce-special-offer*; and the parser shifts a token representing the utterance onto the stack, before popping the top two elements off the stack and adding the subtree for *special-order* into the dialog's subtask tree.

4.2 Start-Complete Method

In the shift-reduce method, the dialog tree is constructed as a side effect of the actions performed on the stack: each reduce action on the stack introduces a non-terminal in the tree. By contrast, in the start-complete method the instructions to build the tree are directly encoded in the parser actions. A stack is used to maintain the global parse state. The actions the parser can take are similar to those described in (Ratnaparkhi, 1997). The parser must decide whether to join each new terminal onto the existing left-hand edge of the tree, or start a new subtree. The actions for the parser include *start-X*, *n-start-X*, *complete-X*, *u-complete-X* and *b-complete-X*, where X is each of the non-terminals (subtask labels) in the tree. *Start-X* pushes a token representing the current utterance onto the stack; *n-start-X* pushes non-terminal X onto the stack; *complete-X* pushes a token representing the current utterance onto the stack, then pops the top two tokens off the stack and pushes the non-terminal X; *u-complete-X* pops the top token off the stack and pushes the non-terminal X; and *b-complete-X* pops the top two tokens off the stack and pushes the non-terminal X. This method produces a dialog subtask tree directly, rather than producing an equivalent binary-branching tree.

Consider the same subdialog as before, *A: would you like a free magazine? U: no.* The processing of this dialog using our start-complete dialog parser would proceed as follows: the STP model predicts *start-special-offer* for st^a; the DAP model predicts *YNP(Promotions)* for da^a; the generator outputs *would you like a free magazine?*; and the parser shifts a token representing this utterance onto the stack. Then, the customer says *no*. The DAC model classifies da^u as *No*; the STC model classifies st^u as *complete-special-offer*; and the parser shifts a token representing the utterance onto the stack, before popping the top two elements off the stack and adding the subtree for *special-order* into the dialog's subtask tree.

4.3 Connection Path Method

In contrast to the shift-reduce and the start-complete methods described above, the connection path method does not use a stack to track the global state of the parse. Instead, the parser directly predicts the *connection path* (path from the root to the terminal) for each utterance. The collection of connection paths for all the utterances in a dialog defines the parse tree. This encoding was previously used for incremental sentence parsing by (Costa et al., 2001). With this method, there are many more choices of decision for the parser (195 decisions for our data) compared to the shift-reduce (32) and start-complete (82) methods.

Consider the same subdialog as before, *A: would you like a free magazine? U: no.* The processing of this dialog using our connection path dialog parser would proceed as follows. First, the STP model predicts *S-special-offer* for st^a; the DAP model predicts *YNP(Promotions)* for da^a; the generator outputs *would you like a free magazine?*; and the parser adds a subtree rooted at *special-offer*, with one terminal for the current utterance, into the top of the subtask tree. Then, the customer says *no*. The DAC model classifies da^u as *No* and the STC model classifies st^u as *S-special-offer*. Since the right frontier of the subtask tree has a subtree matching this path, the parser simply incorporates the current utterance as a terminal of the *special-offer* subtree.

Type	Task/subtask labels
Call-level	call-forward, closing, misc-other, opening, out-of-domain, sub-call
Task-level	check-availability, contact-info, delivery-info, discount, order-change, order-item, order-problem, payment-info, related-offer, shipping-address, special-offer, summary

Table 2: Task/subtask labels in CHILD

Type	Subtype
Ask	Info
Explain	Catalog, CC_Related, Discount, Order_Info
	Order_Problem, Payment_Rel, Product_Info
	Promotions, Related_Offer, Shipping
Convers- -ational	Ack, Goodbye, Hello, Help, Hold, YoureWelcome, Thanks, Yes, No, Ack,
	Repeat, Not(Information)
Request	Code, Order_Problem, Address, Catalog,
	CC_Related, Change_Order, Conf, Credit,
	Customer_Info, Info, Make_Order, Name,
	Order_Info, Order_Status, Payment_Rel,
	Phone_Number, Product_Info, Promotions,
	Shipping, Store_Info
YNQ	Address, Email, Info, Order_Info,
	Order_Status,Promotions, Related_Offer

Table 3: Dialog act labels in CHILD

5 Data and Experiments

To evaluate our parse-based dialog model, we used 817 two-party dialogs from the CHILD corpus of telephone-based dialogs in a catalog-purchasing domain. Each dialog was transcribed by hand; all numbers (telephone, credit card, etc.) were removed for privacy reasons. The average dialog in this data set had 60 turns. The dialogs were automatically segmented into utterances and automatically annotated with part-of-speech tag and supertag information and named entities. They were annotated by hand for dialog acts and tasks/subtasks. The dialog act and task/subtask labels are given in Tables 2 and 3.

5.1 Features

In our experiments we used the following features for each utterance: (a) the speaker ID; (b) unigrams, bigrams and trigrams of the words; (c) unigrams, bigrams and trigrams of the part of speech tags; (d) unigrams, bigrams and trigrams of the supertags; (e) binary features indicating the presence or absence of particular types of named entity; (f) the dialog act (determined by the parser); (g) the task/subtask label (determined by the parser); and (h) the parser stack at the current utterance (determined by the parser). Each input feature vector for agent subtask prediction has these features for up to three utterances of left-hand context (see Equation 3). Each input feature vector for dialog act prediction has the same features as for agent subtask prediction, plus the actual or predicted subtask label (see Equation 4). Each input feature vector for dialog act interpretation has features a-h for up to three utterances of left-hand context, plus the current utterance (see Equation 1). Each input feature vector for user subtask classification has the same features as for user dialog act interpretation, plus the actual or classified dialog act (see Equation 2).

The label for each input feature vector is the parsing action (for subtask classification and prediction) or the dialog act label (for dialog act classification and prediction). If more than one parsing action takes place on a particular utterance (e.g. a shift and then a reduce), the feature vector is repeated twice with different stack contents.

5.2 Training Method

We randomly selected roughly 90% of the dialogs for training, and used the remainder for testing.

We separately trained models for: user dialog act classification (DAC, Equation 1); user task/subtask classification (STC, Equation 2); agent task/subtask prediction (STP, Equation 3); and agent dialog act prediction (DAP, Equation 4). In order to estimate the conditional distributions shown in Table 1, we use the general technique of choosing the MaxEnt distribution that properly estimates the average of each feature over the training data (Berger et al., 1996). We use the machine learning toolkit LLAMA (Haffner, 2006), which encodes multiclass classification problems using binary MaxEnt classifiers to increase the speed of training and to scale the method to large data sets.

5.3 Decoding Method

The decoding process for the three parsing methods is illustrated in Figure 3 and has four stages: STP, DAP, DAC, and STC. As already explained, each of these steps in the decoding process is modeled as either a prediction task or a classification task. The decoder constructs an input feature vector depending on the amount of context being used. This feature vector is used to query the appropriate classifier model to obtain a vector of labels with weights. The parser action labels (STP and STC) are used to extend the subtask tree. For example, in the shift-reduce method, *shift* results in a push action on the stack, while *reduce-X* results in popping the top two elements off the stack and pushing *X* on to the stack. The dialog act labels (DAP and DAC) are used to label the leaves of the subtask tree (the utterances).

The decoder can use n-best results from the classifier to enlarge the search space. In order to manage the search space effectively, the decoder uses a beam pruning strategy. The decoding process proceeds until the end of the dialog is reached. In this paper, we assume that the end of the dialog is given to the decoder[3].

Given that the classifiers are error-prone in their assignment of labels, the parsing step of the decoder needs to be robust to these errors. We exploit the state of the stack in the different methods to rule out incompatible parser actions (e.g. a *reduce-X* action when the stack has one element, a *shift* action on an already shifted utterance). We also use n-best results to alleviate the impact of classification errors. Finally, at the end of the dialog, if there are unattached constituents on the stack, the decoder attaches them as sibling constituents to produce a rooted tree structure. These constraints contribute to robustness, but cannot be used with the connection path method, since any connection path (parsing action) suggested by the classifier can be incorporated into the incremental parse tree. Consequently, in the connection path method there are fewer opportunities to correct the errors made by the classifiers.

5.4 Evaluation Metrics

We evaluate dialog act classification and prediction by comparing the automatically assigned dialog act tags to the reference dialog act tags. For these tasks we report accuracy. We evaluate subtask classification and prediction by comparing the subtask trees output by the different parsing methods to the reference subtask tree. We use the labeled crossing bracket metric (typically used in the syntactic parsing literature (Harrison et al., 1991)), which computes recall, precision and crossing brackets for the constituents (subtrees) in a hypothesized parse tree given the reference parse tree. We report F-measure, which is a combination of recall and precision.

For each task, performance is reported for 1, 3,

[3]This is an unrealistic assumption if the decoder is to serve as a dialog model. We expect to address this limitation in future work.

5, and 10-best dynamic decoding as well as oracle (Or) and for 0, 1 and 3 utterances of context.

5.5 Results

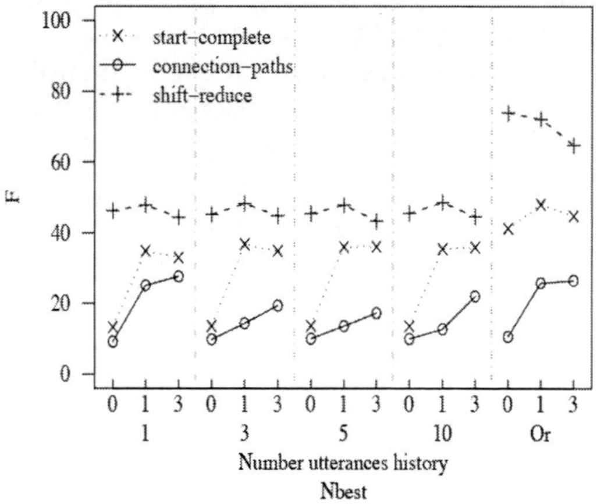

Figure 5: Performance of parse-based methods for subtask tree building

Figure 5 shows the performance of the different methods for determining the subtask tree of the dialog. Wider beam widths do not lead to improved performance for any method. One utterance of context is best for shift-reduce and start-join; three is best for the connection path method. The shift-reduce method performs the best. With 1 utterance of context, its 1-best f-score is 47.86, as compared with 34.91 for start-complete, 25.13 for the connection path method, and 21.32 for the chunk-based baseline. These performance differences are statistically significant at $p < .001$. However, the best performance for the shift-reduce method is still significantly worse than oracle.

All of the methods are subject to some 'stickiness', a certain preference to stay within the current subtask rather than starting a new one. Also, all of the methods tended to perform poorly on parsing subtasks that occur rarely (e.g. *call-forward, order-change*) or that occur at many different locations in the dialog (e.g. *out-of-domain, order-problem, check-availability*). For example, the shift-reduce method did not make many *shift* errors but did frequently *b-reduce* on an incorrect non-terminal (indicating trouble identifying subtask boundaries). Some non-terminals most likely to be labeled incorrectly by this method (for both agent and user) are: *call-forward, order-change, summary, order-problem, opening* and *out-of-domain*.

Similarly, the start-complete method frequently mislabeled a non-terminal in a *complete* action, e.g. *misc-other, check-availability, summary* or *contact-info*. It also quite frequently mislabeled nonterminals in *n-start* actions, e.g. *order-item, contact-info* or *summary*. Both of these errors indicate trouble identifying subtask boundaries.

It is harder to analyze the output from the connection path method. This method is more likely to mislabel tree-internal nodes than those immediately above the leaves. However, the same non-terminals show up as error-prone for this method as for the others: *out-of-domain, check-availability, order-problem* and *summary*.

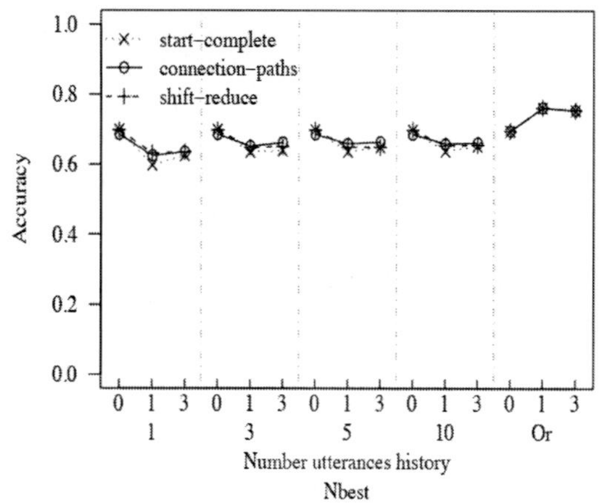

Figure 6: Performance of dialog act assignment to user's utterances.

Figure 6 shows accuracy for classification of user dialog acts. Wider beam widths do not lead to signficantly improved performance for any method. Zero utterances of context gives the highest accuracy for all methods. All methods perform fairly well, but no method significantly outperforms any other: with 0 utterances of context, 1-best accuracy is .681 for the connection path method, .698 for the start-complete method and .698 for the shift-reduce method. We note that these results are competitive with those reported in the literature (e.g. (Poesio and Mikheev, 1998; Serafin and Eugenio, 2004)), although the dialog corpus and the label sets are different.

The most common errors in dialog act classification occur with dialog acts that occur 40 times or fewer in the testing data (out of 3610 testing utterances), and with *Not(Information)*.

Figure 7 shows accuracy for prediction of agent dialog acts. Performance for this task is lower than

Speaker	Utterance	Shift-Reduce	Start-Complete	Connection Path
A	This is Sally	shift, *Hello*	start-opening, *Hello*	opening_S, *Hello*
A	How may I help you	shift, binary-reduce-out-of-domain, *Hello*	complete-opening, *Hello*	opening_S, *Hello*
B	Yes	*Not(Information)*, shift, binary-reduce-out-of-domain	*Not(Information)*, complete-opening	*Not(Information)*, opening_S
B	Um I would like to place an order please	*Rquest(Make-Order)*, shift, binary-reduce-opening	*Rquest(Make-Order)*, complete-opening, n-start-S	*Rquest(Make-Order)*, opening_S
A	May I have your telephone number with the area code	shift, *Acknowledge*	start-contact-info, *Acknowledge*	contact-info_S, *Request(Phone-Number)*
B	Uh the phone number is [number]	*Explain(Phone-Number)*, shift, binary-reduce-contact-info	*Explain(Phone-Number)*, complete-contact-info	*Explain(Phone-Number)*, contact-info_S

Table 4: Dialog extract with subtask tree building actions for three parsing methods

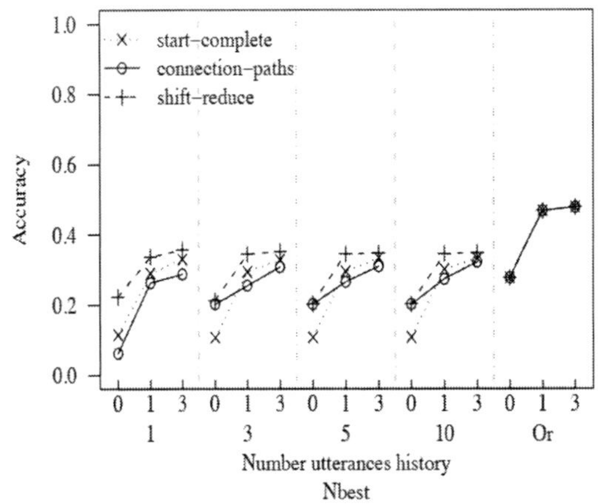

Figure 7: Performance of dialog act prediction used to generate agent utterances.

that for dialog act classification because this is a prediction task. Wider beam widths do not generally lead to improved performance for any method. Three utterances of context generally gives the best performance. The shift-reduce method performs significantly better than the connection path method with a beam width of 1 ($p < .01$), but not at larger beam widths; there are no other significant performance differences between methods at 3 utterances of context. With 3 utterances of context, 1-best accuracies are .286 for the connection path method, .329 for the start-complete method and .356 for the shift-reduce method.

The most common errors in dialog act prediction occur with rare dialog acts, *Not(Information)*, and the prediction of *Acknowledge* at the start of a turn (we did not remove grounding acts from the data). With the shift-reduce method, some *YNQ* acts are commonly mislabeled. With all methods, dialog acts pertaining to *Order-Info* and *Product-Info* acts are commonly mislabeled, which could potentially indicate that these labels require a subtle distinction between information pertaining to an order and information pertaining to a product.

Table 4 shows the parsing actions performed by each of our methods on the dialog snippet presented in Figure 4. For this example, the connection path method's output is correct in all cases.

6 Conclusions and Future Work

In this paper, we present a parsing-based model of task-oriented dialog that tightly integrates interpretation and generation using a subtask tree representation, can be trained from data, and runs incrementally for use in dialog management. At the core of this model is a parser that incrementally builds the dialog task structure as it interprets user actions and generates system actions. We experiment with three different incremental parsing methods for our dialog model. Our proposed shift-reduce method is the best-performing so far, and performance of this method for dialog act classification and task/subtask modeling is good enough to be usable. However, performance of all the methods for dialog act prediction is too low to be useful at the moment. In future work, we will explore improved models for this task that make use of global information about the task (e.g. whether each possible subtask has yet been completed; whether required and optional task-related concepts such as *shipping address* have been filled). We will also separate grounding and task-related behaviors in our model.

References

J. Alexandersson and N. Reithinger. 1997. Learning dialogue structures from a corpus. In *Proceedings of Eurospeech*.

J. Baldridge and A. Lascarides. 2005. Probabilistic head-driven parsing for discourse. In *Proceedings of CoNLL*.

S. Bangalore, G. Di Fabbrizio, and A. Stent. 2006. Learning the structure of task-driven human-human dialogs. In *Proceedings of COLING/ACL*.

A. Barrett and D. Weld. 1994. Task-decomposition via plan parsing. In *Proceedings of AAAI*.

A. Berger, S.D. Pietra, and V.D. Pietra. 1996. A Maximum Entropy Approach to Natural Language Processing. *Computational Linguistics*, 22(1):39–71.

N. Blaylock and J. F. Allen. 2006. Hierarchical instantiated goal recognition. In *Proceedings of the AAAI Workshop on Modeling Others from Observations*.

D. Bohus and A. Rudnicky. 2003. RavenClaw: Dialog management using hierarchical task decomposition and an expectation agenda. In *Proceedings of Eurospeech*.

H.H. Bui. 2003. A general model for online probabalistic plan recognition. In *Proceedings of IJCAI*.

S. Carberry. 2001. Techniques for plan recognition. *User Modeling and User-Adapted Interaction*, 11(1–2):31–48.

M. Collins. 2003. Head-driven statistical models for natural language parsing. *Computational Linguistics*, 29(4):589–638.

F. Costa, V. Lombardo, P. Frasconi, and G. Soda. 2001. Wide coverage incremental parsing by learning attachment preferences. In *Proceedings of the Conference of the Italian Association for Artificial Intelligence (AIIA)*.

D. Cristea. 2000. An incremental discourse parser architecture. In *Proceedings of the 2nd International Conference on Natural Language Processing*.

K. Forbes, E. Miltsakaki, R. Prasad, A. Sarkar, A. Joshi, and B. Webber. 2003. D-LTAG system: Discourse parsing with a lexicalized tree-adjoining grammar. *Journal of Logic, Language and Information*, 12(3):261–279.

B.J. Grosz and C.L. Sidner. 1986. Attention, intentions and the structure of discourse. *Computational Linguistics*, 12(3):175–204.

P. Haffner. 2006. Scaling large margin classifiers for spoken language understanding. *Speech Communication*, 48(3–4):239–261.

J. Hall, J. Nivre, and J. Nilsson. 2006. Discriminative classifiers for deterministic dependency parsing. In *Proceedings of COLING/ACL*.

P. Harrison, S. Abney, D. Fleckenger, C. Gdaniec, R. Grishman, D. Hindle, B. Ingria, M. Marcus, B. Santorini, and T. Strzalkowski. 1991. Evaluating syntax performance of parser/grammars of English. In *Proceedings of the Workshop on Evaluating Natural Language Processing Systems, ACL*.

H. LeThanh, G. Abeysinghe, and C. Huyck. 2004. Generating discourse structures for written texts. In *Proceedings of COLING*.

D. Litman and J. Allen. 1987. A plan recognition model for subdialogs in conversations. *Cognitive Science*, 11(2):163–200.

K. Lochbaum. 1998. A collaborative planning model of intentional structure. *Computational Linguistics*, 24(4):525–572.

M. Poesio and A. Mikheev. 1998. The predictive power of game structure in dialogue act recognition: experimental results using maximum entropy estimation. In *Proceedings of ICSLP*.

L. Polanyi, C. Culy, M. van den Berg, G. L. Thione, and D. Ahn. 2004. A rule based approach to discourse parsing. In *Proceedings of SIGdial*.

D.V. Pynadath and M.P. Wellman. 2000. Probabilistic state-dependent grammars for plan recognition. In *Proceedings of UAI*.

A. Ratnaparkhi. 1997. A linear observed time statistical parser based on maximum entropy models. In *Proceedings of EMNLP*.

C. Rich and C.L. Sidner. 1997. COLLAGEN: When agents collaborate with people. In *Proceedings of the First International Conference on Autonomous Agents*.

K. Sagae and A. Lavie. 2006. A best-first probabilistic shift-reduce parser. In *Proceedings of COLING/ACL*.

R. Serafin and B. Di Eugenio. 2004. FLSA: Extending latent semantic analysis with features for dialogue act classification. In *Proceedings of ACL*.

C.L. Sidner. 1985. Plan parsing for intended response recognition in discourse. *Computational Intelligence*, 1(1):1–10.

R. Soricut and D. Marcu. 2003. Sentence level discourse parsing using syntactic and lexical information. In *Proceedings of NAACL/HLT*.

C. Sporleder and A. Lascarides. 2004. Combining hierarchical clustering and machine learning to predict high-level discourse structure. In *Proceedings of COLING*.

Bayesian Word Sense Induction

Samuel Brody
Dept. of Biomedical Informatics
Columbia University
samuel.brody@dbmi.columbia.edu

Mirella Lapata
School of Informatics
University of Edinburgh
mlap@inf.ed.ac.uk

Abstract

Sense induction seeks to automatically identify word senses directly from a corpus. A key assumption underlying previous work is that the context surrounding an ambiguous word is indicative of its meaning. Sense induction is thus typically viewed as an unsupervised clustering problem where the aim is to partition a word's contexts into different classes, each representing a word sense. Our work places sense induction in a Bayesian context by modeling the contexts of the ambiguous word as samples from a multinomial distribution over senses which are in turn characterized as distributions over words. The Bayesian framework provides a principled way to incorporate a wide range of features beyond lexical co-occurrences and to systematically assess their utility on the sense induction task. The proposed approach yields improvements over state-of-the-art systems on a benchmark dataset.

1 Introduction

Sense induction is the task of discovering automatically all possible senses of an ambiguous word. It is related to, but distinct from, word sense disambiguation (WSD) where the senses are assumed to be known and the aim is to identify the intended meaning of the ambiguous word in context.

Although the bulk of previous work has been devoted to the disambiguation problem[1], there are good reasons to believe that sense induction may be able to overcome some of the issues associated with WSD. Since most disambiguation methods assign senses according to, and with the aid of, dictionaries or other lexical resources, it is difficult to adapt them to new domains or to languages where such resources are scarce. A related problem concerns the granularity of the sense distinctions which is fixed, and may not be entirely suitable for different applications. In contrast, when sense distinctions are inferred directly from the data, they are more likely to represent the task and domain at hand. There is little risk that an important sense will be left out, or that irrelevant senses will influence the results. Furthermore, recent work in machine translation (Vickrey et al., 2005) and information retrieval (Véronis, 2004) indicates that induced senses can lead to improved performance in areas where methods based on a fixed sense inventory have previously failed (Carpuat and Wu, 2005; Voorhees, 1993).

Sense induction is typically treated as an unsupervised clustering problem. The input to the clustering algorithm are instances of the ambiguous word with their accompanying contexts (represented by co-occurrence vectors) and the output is a grouping of these instances into classes corresponding to the induced senses. In other words, contexts that are grouped together in the same class represent a specific word sense. In this paper we adopt a novel Bayesian approach and formalize the induction problem in a generative model. For each ambiguous word we first draw a distribution over senses, and then generate context words according to this distribution. It is thus assumed that different senses will correspond to distinct lexical distributions. In this framework, sense distinctions arise naturally through the generative process: our model postulates that the observed data (word contexts) are explicitly intended to communicate a latent structure (their meaning).

Our work is related to Latent Dirichlet Allocation (LDA, Blei et al. 2003), a probabilistic model of text generation. LDA models each document using a mixture over K topics, which are in turn characterized as distributions over words.

[1] Approaches to WSD are too numerous to list; We refer the interested reader to Agirre et al. (2007) for an overview of the state of the art.

Proceedings of the 12th Conference of the European Chapter of the ACL, pages 103–111,
Athens, Greece, 30 March – 3 April 2009.

The words in the document are generated by repeatedly sampling a topic according to the topic distribution, and selecting a word given the chosen topic. Whereas LDA generates words from *global topics* corresponding to the whole document, our model generates words from *local topics* chosen based on a context window around the ambiguous word. Document-level topics resemble general domain labels (e.g., *finance*, *education*) and cannot faithfully model more fine-grained meaning distinctions. In our work, therefore, we create an individual model for every (ambiguous) word rather than a global model for an entire document collection. We also show how multiple information sources can be straightforwardly integrated without changing the underlying probabilistic model. For instance, besides lexical information we may want to consider parts of speech or dependencies in our sense induction problem. This is in marked contrast with previous LDA-based models which mostly take only word-based information into account. We evaluate our model on a recently released benchmark dataset (Agirre and Soroa, 2007) and demonstrate improvements over the state-of-the-art.

The remainder of this paper is structured as follows. We first present an overview of related work (Section 2) and then describe our Bayesian model in more detail (Sections 3 and 4). Section 5 describes the resources and evaluation methodology used in our experiments. We discuss our results in Section 6, and conclude in Section 7.

2 Related Work

Sense induction is typically treated as a clustering problem, where instances of a target word are partitioned into classes by considering their co-occurring contexts. Considerable latitude is allowed in selecting and representing the co-occurring contexts. Previous methods have used first or second order co-occurrences (Purandare and Pedersen, 2004; Schütze, 1998), parts of speech (Purandare and Pedersen, 2004), and grammatical relations (Pantel and Lin, 2002; Dorow and Widdows, 2003). The size of the context window also varies, it can be a relatively small, such as two words before and after the target word (Gauch and Futrelle, 1993), the sentence within which the target is found (Bordag, 2006), or even larger, such as the 20 surrounding words on either side of the target (Purandare and Pedersen, 2004).

In essence, each instance of a target word is represented as a feature vector which subsequently serves as input to the chosen clustering method. A variety of clustering algorithms have been employed ranging from k-means (Purandare and Pedersen, 2004), to agglomerative clustering (Schütze, 1998), and the Information Bottleneck (Niu et al., 2007). Graph-based methods have also been applied to the sense induction task. In this framework words are represented as nodes in the graph and vertices are drawn between the target and its co-occurrences. Senses are induced by identifying highly dense subgraphs (hubs) in the co-occurrence graph (Véronis, 2004; Dorow and Widdows, 2003).

Although LDA was originally developed as a generative topic model, it has recently gained popularity in the WSD literature. The inferred document-level topics can help determine coarse-grained sense distinctions. Cai et al. (2007) propose to use LDA's word-topic distributions as features for training a supervised WSD system. In a similar vein, Boyd-Graber and Blei (2007) infer LDA topics from a large corpus, however for unsupervised WSD. Here, LDA topics are integrated with McCarthy et al.'s (2004) algorithm. For each target word, a topic is sampled from the document's topic distribution, and a word is generated from that topic. Also, a distributional neighbor is selected based on the topic and distributional similarity to the generated word. Then, the word sense is selected based on the word, neighbor, and topic. Boyd-Graber et al. (2007) extend the topic modeling framework to include WordNet senses as a latent variable in the word generation process. In this case the model discovers both the topics of the corpus and the senses assigned to each of its words.

Our own model is also inspired by LDA but crucially performs word sense induction, not disambiguation. Unlike the work mentioned above, we do not rely on a pre-existing list of senses, and do not assume a correspondence between our automatically derived sense-clusters and those of any given inventory.[2] A key element in these previous attempts at adapting LDA for WSD is the tendency to remain at a high level, document-like, setting. In contrast, we make use of much smaller units of text (a few sentences, rather than a full document), and create an individual model for each (ambiguous) word type. Our induced senses are few in number (typically less than ten). This is in marked contrast to tens, and sometimes hundreds,

[2]Such a mapping is only performed to enable evaluation and comparison with other approaches (see Section 5).

of topics commonly used in document-modeling tasks.

Unlike many conventional clustering methods (e.g., Purandare and Pedersen 2004; Schütze 1998), our model is probabilistic; it specifies a probability distribution over possible values, which makes it easy to integrate and combine with other systems via mixture or product models. Furthermore, the Bayesian framework allows the incorporation of several information sources in a principled manner. Our model can easily handle an arbitrary number of feature classes (e.g., parts of speech, dependencies). This functionality in turn enables us to evaluate which linguistic information matters for the sense induction task. Previous attempts to handle multiple information sources in the LDA framework (e.g., Griffiths et al. 2005; Barnard et al. 2003) have been task-specific and limited to only two layers of information. Our model provides this utility in a general framework, and could be applied to other tasks, besides sense induction.

3 The Sense Induction Model

The core idea behind sense induction is that contextual information provides important cues regarding a word's meaning. The idea dates back to (at least) Firth (1957) ("You shall know a word by the company it keeps"), and underlies most WSD and lexicon acquisition work to date. Under this premise, we should expect different senses to be signaled by different lexical distributions.

We can place sense induction in a probabilistic setting by modeling the context words around the ambiguous target as samples from a multinomial sense distribution. More formally, we will write $P(s)$ for the distribution over senses s of an ambiguous target in a specific context window and $P(w|s)$ for the probability distribution over context words w given sense s. Each word w_i in the context window is generated by first sampling a sense from the sense distribution, then choosing a word from the sense-context distribution. $P(s_i = j)$ denotes the probability that the jth sense was sampled for the ith word token and $P(w_i|s_i = j)$ the probability of context word w_i under sense j. The model thus specifies a distribution over words within a context window:

$$P(w_i) = \sum_{j=1}^{S} P(w_i|s_i = j)P(s_i = j) \quad (1)$$

where S is the number of senses. We assume that each target word has C contexts and each context c

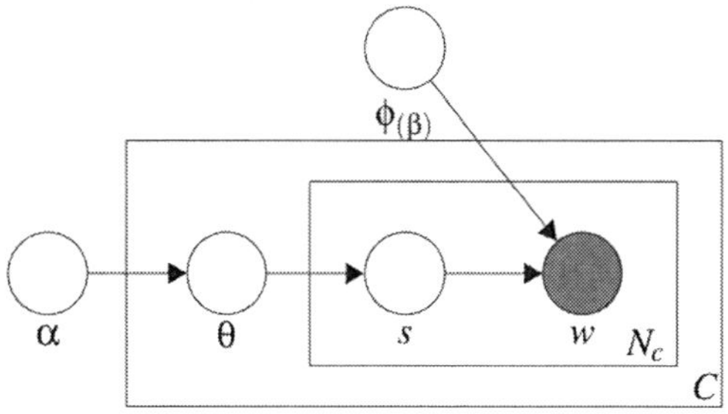

Figure 1: Bayesian sense induction model; shaded nodes represent observed variables, unshaded nodes indicate latent variables. Arrows indicate conditional dependencies between variables, whereas plates (the rectangles in the figure) refer to repetitions of sampling steps. The variables in the lower right corner refer to the number of samples.

consists of N_c word tokens. We shall write $\phi^{(j)}$ as a shorthand for $P(w_i|s_i = j)$, the multinomial distribution over words for sense j, and $\theta^{(c)}$ as a shorthand for the distribution of senses in context c.

Following Blei et al. (2003) we will assume that the mixing proportion over senses θ is drawn from a Dirichlet prior with parameters α. The role of the hyperparameter α is to create a smoothed sense distribution. We also place a symmetric Dirichlet β on ϕ (Griffiths and Steyvers, 2002). The hyperparmeter β can be interpreted as the prior observation count on the number of times context words are sampled from a sense before any word from the corpus is observed. Our model is represented in graphical notation in Figure 1.

The model sketched above only takes word information into account. Methods developed for supervised WSD often use a variety of information sources based not only on words but also on lemmas, parts of speech, collocations and syntactic relationships (Lee and Ng, 2002). The first idea that comes to mind, is to use the same model while treating various features as word-like elements. In other words, we could simply assume that the contexts we wish to model are the union of all our features. Although straightforward, this solution is undesirable. It merges the distributions of distinct feature categories into a single one, and is therefore conceptually incorrect, and can affect the performance of the model. For instance, parts-of-speech (which have few values, and therefore high probability), would share a distribution with words (which are much sparser). Layers containing more elements (e.g. 10 word window) would overwhelm

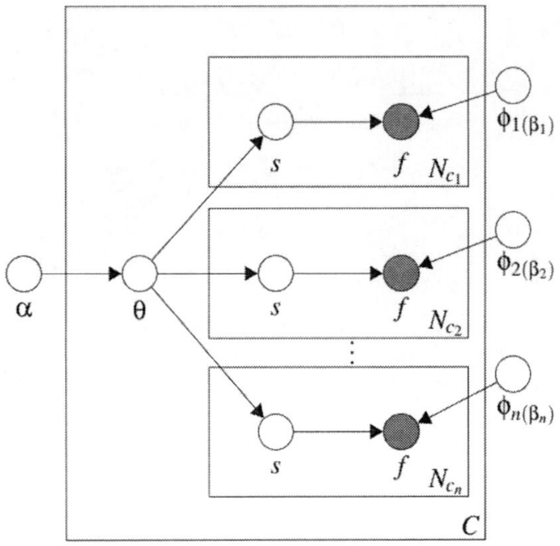

Figure 2: Extended sense induction model; inner rectangles represent different sources (layers) of information. All layers share the same, instance-specific, sense distribution (θ), but each have their own (multinomial) sense-feature distribution (ϕ). Shaded nodes represent observed features f; these can be words, parts of speech, collocations or dependencies.

smaller ones (e.g. 1 word window).

Our solution is to treat each information source (or feature type) individually and then combine all of them together in a unified model. Our underlying assumption is that the context window around the target word can have multiple representations, all of which share the same sense distribution. We illustrate this in Figure 2 where each inner rectangle (layer) corresponds to a distinct feature type. We will naively assume independence between multiple layers, even though this is clearly not the case in our task. The idea here is to model each layer as faithfully as possible to the empirical data while at the same time combining information from all layers in estimating the sense distribution of each target instance.

4 Inference

Our inference procedure is based on Gibbs sampling (Geman and Geman, 1984). The procedure begins by randomly initializing all unobserved random variables. At each iteration, each random variable s_i is sampled from the conditional distribution $P(s_i|\overline{s}_{-i})$ where $\overline{s}_{-i}$ refers to all variables other than s_i. Eventually, the distribution over samples drawn from this process will converge to the unconditional joint distribution $P(\overline{s})$ of the unobserved variables (provided certain criteria are fulfilled).

In our model, each element in each layer is a variable, and is assigned a sense label (see Figure 2, where distinct layers correspond to different representations of the context around the target word). From these assignments, we must determine the sense distribution of the instance as a whole. This is the purpose of the Gibbs sampling procedure. Specifically, in order to derive the update function used in the Gibbs sampler, we must provide the conditional probability of the i-th variable being assigned sense s_i in layer l, given the feature value f_i of the context variable and the current sense assignments of all the other variables in the data ($\overline{s}_{-i}$):

$$p(s_i|\overline{s}_{-i},\overline{f}) \propto p(f_i|\overline{s},\overline{f}_{-i},\beta) \cdot p(s_i|\overline{s}_{-i},\alpha) \tag{2}$$

The probability of a single sense assignment, s_i, is proportional to the product of the likelihood (of feature f_i, given the rest of the data) and the prior probability of the assignment.

$$\begin{aligned} &p(f_i|\overline{s},\overline{f}_{-i},\beta) = \\ &\int p(f_i|l,\overline{s},\phi) \cdot p(\phi|\overline{f}_{-i},\beta_l)d\phi = \frac{\#(f_i,s_i)+\beta_l}{\#(s_i)+V_l \cdot \beta_l} \end{aligned} \tag{3}$$

For the likelihood term $p(f_i|\overline{s},\overline{f}_{-i},\beta)$, integrating over all possible values of the multinomial feature-sense distribution ϕ gives us the rightmost term in Equation 3, which has an intuitive interpretation. The term $\#(f_i,s_i)$ indicates the number of times the feature-value f_i was assigned sense s_i in the rest of the data. Similarly, $\#(s_i)$ indicates the number of times the sense assignment s_i was observed in the data. β_l is the Dirichlet prior for the feature-sense distribution ϕ in the current layer l, and V_l is the size of the vocabulary of that layer, i.e., the number of possible feature values in the layer. Intuitively, the probability of a feature-value given a sense is directly proportional to the number of times we have seen that value and that sense-assignment together in the data, taking into account a pseudo-count prior, expressed through β. This can also be viewed as a form of smoothing.

A similar approach is taken with regards to the prior probability $p(s_i|\overline{s}_{-i},\alpha)$. In this case, however, all layers must be considered:

$$p(s_i|\overline{s}_{-i},\alpha) = \sum_l \lambda_l \cdot p(s_i|l,\overline{s}_{-i},\alpha_l) \tag{4}$$

Here λ_l is the weight for the contribution of layer l, and α_l is the portion of the Dirichlet prior for the sense distribution θ in the current layer. Treating each layer individually, we integrate over the possible values of θ, obtaining a similar count-based term:

$$p(s_i|l, \bar{s}_{-i}, \alpha_l) = \int p(s_i|l, \bar{s}_{-i}, \theta) \cdot p(\theta|\bar{f}_{-i}, \alpha_l) d\theta = \frac{\#l(s_i) + \alpha_l}{\#l + S \cdot \alpha_l} \quad (5)$$

where $\#l(s_i)$ indicates the number of elements in layer l assigned the sense s_i, $\#l$ indicates the number of elements in layer l, i.e., the size of the layer and S the number of senses.

To distribute the pseudo counts represented by α in a reasonable fashion among the layers, we define $\alpha_l = \frac{\#l}{\#m} \cdot \alpha$ where $\#m = \sum_l \#l$, i.e., the total size of the instance. This distributes α according to the relative size of each layer in the instance.

$$p(s_i|l, \bar{s}_{-i}, \alpha_l) = \frac{\#l(s_i) + \frac{\#l}{\#m} \cdot \alpha}{\#l + S \cdot \frac{\#l}{\#m} \cdot \alpha} = \frac{\#m \cdot \frac{\#l(s_i)}{\#l} + \alpha}{\#m + S \cdot \alpha} \quad (6)$$

Placing these values in Equation 4 we obtain the following:

$$p(s_i|\bar{s}_{-i}, \alpha) = \frac{\#m \cdot \sum_l \lambda_l \cdot \frac{\#l(s_i)}{\#l} + \alpha}{\#m + S \cdot \alpha} \quad (7)$$

Putting it all together, we arrive at the final update equation for the Gibbs sampling:

$$p(s_i|\bar{s}_{-i}, \bar{f}) \propto \frac{\#(f_i, s_i) + \beta_l}{\#(s_i) + V_l \cdot \beta_l} \cdot \frac{\#m \cdot \sum_l \lambda_l \cdot \frac{\#l(s_i)}{\#l} + \alpha}{\#m + S \cdot \alpha} \quad (8)$$

Note that when dealing with a single layer, Equation 8 collapses to:

$$p(s_i|\bar{s}_{-i}, \bar{f}) \propto \frac{\#(f_i, s_i) + \beta}{\#(s_i) + V \cdot \beta} \cdot \frac{\#m(s_i) + \alpha}{\#m + S \cdot \alpha} \quad (9)$$

where $\#m(s_i)$ indicates the number of elements (e.g., words) in the context window assigned to sense s_i. This is identical to the update equation in the original, word-based LDA model.

The sampling algorithm gives direct estimates of s for every context element. However, in view of our task, we are more interested in estimating θ, the sense-context distribution which can be obtained as in Equation 7, but taking into account all sense assignments, without removing assignment i. Our system labels each instance with the single, most probable sense.

5 Evaluation Setup

In this section we discuss our experimental set-up for assessing the performance of the model presented above. We give details on our training procedure, describe our features, and explain how our system output was evaluated.

Data In this work, we focus solely on inducing senses for nouns, since they constitute the largest portion of content words. For example, nouns represent 45% of the content words in the British National Corpus. Moreover, for many tasks and applications (e.g., web queries, Jansen et al. 2000) nouns are the most frequent and most important part-of-speech.

For evaluation, we used the Semeval-2007 benchmark dataset released as part of the sense induction and discrimination task (Agirre and Soroa, 2007). The dataset contains texts from the Penn Treebank II corpus, a collection of articles from the first half of the 1989 Wall Street Journal (WSJ). It is hand-annotated with OntoNotes senses (Hovy et al., 2006) and has 35 nouns. The average noun ambiguity is 3.9, with a high (almost 80%) skew towards the predominant sense. This is not entirely surprising since OntoNotes senses are less fine-grained than WordNet senses.

We used two corpora for training as we wanted to evaluate our model's performance across different domains. The British National Corpus (BNC) is a 100 million word collection of samples of written and spoken language from a wide range of sources including newspapers, magazines, books (both academic and fiction), letters, and school essays as well as spontaneous conversations. This served as our out-of-domain corpus, and contained approximately 730 thousand instances of the 35 target nouns in the Semeval lexical sample. The second, in-domain, corpus was built from selected portions of the Wall Street Journal. We used all articles (excluding the Penn Treebank II portion used in the Semeval dataset) from the years 1987-89 and 1994 to create a corpus of similar size to the BNC, containing approximately 740 thousand instances of the target words.

Additionally, we used the Senseval 2 and 3 lexical sample data (Preiss and Yarowsky, 2001; Mihalcea and Edmonds, 2004) as development sets, for experimenting with the hyper-parameters of our model (see Section 6).

Evaluation Methodology Agirre and Soroa (2007) present two evaluation schemes for assessing sense induction methods. Under the first scheme, the system output is compared to the gold standard using standard clustering evaluation metrics (e.g., purity, entropy). Here, no attempt is made to match the induced senses against the labels of the gold standard. Under the second scheme, the gold standard is partitioned into a test and training corpus. The latter is used to derive a mapping of the induced senses to the gold standard labels. The mapping is then used to calculate the system's F-Score on the test corpus.

Unfortunately, the first scheme failed to discriminate among participating systems. The one-cluster-per-word baseline outperformed all systems, except one, which was only marginally better. The scheme ignores the actual labeling and due to the dominance of the first sense in the data, encourages a single-sense approach which is further amplified by the use of a coarse-grained sense inventory. For the purposes of this work, therefore, we focused on the second evaluation scheme. Here, most of the participating systems outperformed the most-frequent-sense baseline, and the rest obtained only slightly lower scores.

Feature Space Our experiments used a feature set designed to capture both immediate local context, wider context and syntactic context. Specifically, we experimented with six feature categories: ±10-word window (10w), ±5-word window (5w), collocations (1w), word n-grams (ng), part-of-speech n-grams (pg) and dependency relations (dp). These features have been widely adopted in various WSD algorithms (see Lee and Ng 2002 for a detailed evaluation). In all cases, we use the lemmatized version of the word(s).

The Semeval workshop organizers provided a small amount of context for each instance (usually a sentence or two surrounding the sentence containing the target word). This context, as well as the text in the training corpora, was parsed using RASP (Briscoe and Carroll, 2002), to extract part-of-speech tags, lemmas, and dependency information. For instances containing more than one occurrence of the target word, we disambiguate the first occurrence. Instances which were not correctly recognized by the parser (e.g., a target word labeled with the wrong lemma or part-of-speech), were automatically assigned to the largest sense-cluster.[3]

[3]This was the case for less than 1% of the instances.

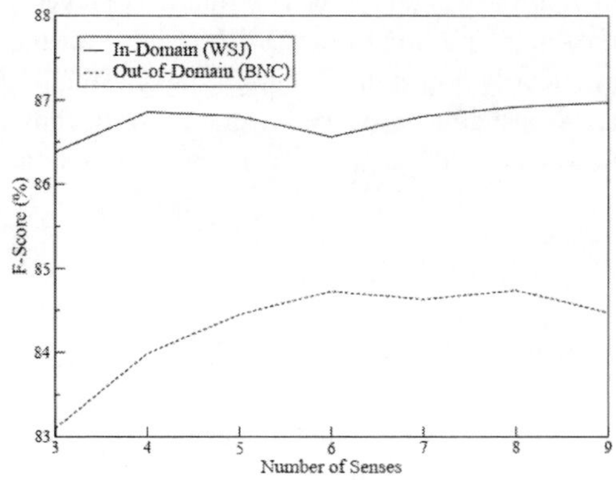

Figure 3: Model performance with varying number of senses on the WSJ and BNC corpora.

6 Experiments

Model Selection The framework presented in Section 3 affords great flexibility in modeling the empirical data. This however entails that several parameters must be instantiated. More precisely, our model is conditioned on the Dirichlet hyperparameters α and β and the number of senses S. Additional parameters include the number of iterations for the Gibbs sampler and whether or not the layers are assigned different weights.

Our strategy in this paper is to fix α and β and explore the consequences of varying S. The value for the α hyperparameter was set to 0.02. This was optimized in an independent tuning experiment which used the Senseval 2 (Preiss and Yarowsky, 2001) and Senseval 3 (Mihalcea and Edmonds, 2004) datasets. We experimented with α values ranging from 0.005 to 1. The β parameter was set to 0.1 (in all layers). This value is often considered optimal in LDA-related models (Griffiths and Steyvers, 2002). For simplicity, we used uniform weights for the layers. The Gibbs sampler was run for 2,000 iterations. Due to the randomized nature of the inference procedure, all reported results are average scores over ten runs.

Our experiments used the same number of senses for all the words, since tuning this number individually for each word would be prohibitive. We experimented with values ranging from three to nine senses. Figure 3 shows the results obtained for different numbers of senses when the model is trained on the WSJ (in-domain) and BNC (out-of-domain) corpora, respectively. Here, we are using the optimal combination of layers for each system (which we discuss in the following section in de-

Senses of *drug* (WSJ)
1. U.S., administration, federal, against, war, dealer
2. patient, people, problem, doctor, company, abuse
3. company, million, sale, maker, stock, inc.
4. administration, food, company, approval, FDA
Senses of *drug* (BNC)
1. patient, treatment, effect, anti-inflammatory
2. alcohol, treatment, patient, therapy, addiction
3. patient, new, find, effect, choice, study
4. test, alcohol, patient, abuse, people, crime
5. trafficking, trafficker, charge, use, problem
6. abuse, against, problem, treatment, alcohol
7. people, wonder, find, prescription, drink, addict
8. company, dealer, police, enforcement, patient

Table 1: Senses inferred for the word *drug* from the WSJ and BNC corpora.

tail). For the model trained on WSJ, performance peaks at four senses, which is similar to the average ambiguity in the test data. For the model trained on the BNC, however, the best results are obtained using twice as many senses. Using fewer senses with the BNC-trained system can result in a drop in accuracy of almost 2%. This is due to the shift in domain. As the sense-divisions of the learning domain do not match those of the target domain, finer granularity is required in order to encompass all the relevant distinctions.

Table 1 illustrates the senses inferred for the word *drug* when using the in-domain and out-of-domain corpora, respectively. The most probable words for each sense are also shown. Firstly, note that the model infers some plausible senses for *drug* on the WSJ corpus (top half of Table 1). Sense 1 corresponds to the "enforcement" sense of *drug*, Sense 2 refers to "medication", Sense 3 to the "drug industry" and Sense 4 to "drugs research". The inferred senses for *drug* on the BNC (bottom half of Table 1) are more fine grained. For example, the model finds distinct senses for "medication" (Sense 1 and 7) and "illegal substance" (Senses 2, 4, 6, 7). It also finds a separate sense for "drug dealing" (Sense 5) and "enforcement" (Sense 8). Because the BNC has a broader focus, finer distinctions are needed to cover as many senses as possible that are relevant to the target domain (WSJ).

Layer Analysis We next examine which individual feature categories are most informative in our sense induction task. We also investigate whether their combination, through our layered model (see Figure 2), yields performance improvements. We used 4 senses for the system trained on WSJ and 8 for the system trained on the BNC (α was set to 0.02 and β to 0.1)

1-Layer		5-Layers		Combination	
10w	86.9	-10w	83.1	**10w+5w**	**87.3%**
5w	86.8	-5w	83.0	5w+pg	83.9%
1w	84.6	-1w	83.0	1w+ng	83.2%
ng	83.6	-ng	83.0	10w+pg	83.3%
pg	82.5	-pg	82.7	1w+pg	84.5%
dp	82.2	-dp	84.7	10w+pg+dep	82.2%
MFS	80.9	all	83.3	MFS	80.9%

Table 2: Model performance (F-score) on the WSJ with one layer (left), five layers (middle), and selected combinations of layers (right).

Table 2 (left side) shows the performance of our model when using only one layer. The layer composed of words co-occurring within a $\pm$10-word window (10w), and representing wider, topical, information gives the highest scores on its own. It is followed by the $\pm$5 (5w) and $\pm$1 (1w) word windows, which represent more immediate, local context. Part-of-speech n-grams (pg) and word n-grams (ng), on their own, achieve lower scores, largely due to over-generalization and data sparseness, respectively. The lowest-scoring single layer is the dependency layer (dp), with performance only slightly above the most-frequent-sense baseline (MFS). Dependency information is very informative when present, but extremely sparse.

Table 2 (middle) also shows the results obtained when running the layered model with all but one of the layers as input. We can use this information to determine the contribution of each layer by comparing to the combined model with all layers (all). Because we are dealing with multiple layers, there is an element of overlap involved. Therefore, each of the word-window layers, despite relatively high informativeness on its own, does not cause as much damage when it is absent, since the other layers compensate for the topical and local information. The absence of the word n-gram layer, which provides specific local information, does not make a great impact when the 1w and pg layers are present. Finally, we can see that the extremely sparse dependency layer is detrimental to the multi-layer model as a whole, and its removal *increases* performance. The sparsity of the data in this layer means that there is often little information on which to base a decision. In these cases, the layer contributes a close-to-uniform estimation

1-Layer		5-Layers		Combination	
10w	84.6	-10w	83.3	**10w+5w**	**85.5%**
5w	84.6	-5w	82.8	5w+pg	83.5%
1w	83.6	-1w	83.5	1w+ng	83.5%
pg	83.1	-pg	83.2	10w+pg	83.4%
ng	82.8	-ng	82.9	1w+pg	84.1%
dp	81.1	-dp	84.7	10w+pg+dep	81.7%
MFS	80.9	all	84.1	MFS	80.9%

Table 3: Model performance (F-score) on the BNC with one layer (left), five layers (middle), and selected combinations of layers (right).

of the sense distribution, which confuses the combined model.

Other layer combinations obtained similar results. Table 2 (right side) shows the most informative two and three layer combinations. Again, dependencies tend to decrease performance. On the other hand, combining features that have similar performance on their own is beneficial. We obtain the best performance overall with a two layered model combining topical (+10w) and local (+5w) contexts.

Table 3 replicates the same suite of experiments on the BNC corpus. The general trends are similar. Some interesting differences are apparent, however. The sparser layers, notably word n-grams and dependencies, fare comparatively worse. This is expected, since the more precise, local, information is likely to vary strongly across domains. Even when both domains refer to the same sense of a word, it is likely to be used in a different immediate context, and local contextual information learned in one domain will be less effective in the other. Another observable difference is that the combined model without the dependency layer does slightly better than each of the single layers. The 1w+pg combination improves over its components, which have similar individual performance. Finally, the best performing model on the BNC also combines two layers capturing wider (10w) and more local (5w) contextual information (see Table 3, right side).

Comparison to State-of-the-Art Table 4 compares our model against the two best performing sense induction systems that participated in the Semeval-2007 competition. IR2 (Niu et al., 2007) performed sense induction using the Information Bottleneck algorithm, whereas UMND2 (Pedersen, 2007) used *k*-means to cluster second order co-occurrence vectors associated with the target word. These models and our own model significantly outperform the most-frequent-sense baseline ($p < 0.01$ using a χ^2 test). Our best system (10w+5w on WSJ) is significantly better than UMND2 ($p < 0.01$) and quantitatively better than IR2, although the difference is not statistically significant.

System	F-Score
10w, 5w (WSJ)	87.3
I2R	86.8
UMND2	84.5
MFS	80.9

Table 4: Comparison of the best-performing Semeval-07 systems against our model.

7 Discussion

This paper presents a novel Bayesian approach to sense induction. We formulated sense induction in a generative framework that describes how the contexts surrounding an ambiguous word might be generated on the basis of latent variables. Our model incorporates features based on lexical information, parts of speech, and dependencies in a principled manner, and outperforms state-of-the-art systems. Crucially, the approach is not specific to the sense induction task and can be adapted for other applications where it is desirable to take multiple levels of information into account. For example, in document classification, one could consider an accompanying image and its caption as possible additional layers to the main text.

In the future, we hope to explore more rigorous parameter estimation techniques. Goldwater and Griffiths (2007) describe a method for integrating hyperparameter estimation into the Gibbs sampling procedure using a prior over possible values. Such an approach could be adopted in our framework, as well, and extended to include the layer weighting parameters, which have strong potential for improving the model's performance. In addition, we could allow an infinite number of senses and use an infinite Dirichlet model (Teh et al., 2006) to automatically determine how many senses are optimal. This provides an elegant solution to the model-order problem, and eliminates the need for external cluster-validation methods.

Acknowledgments The authors acknowledge the support of EPSRC (grant EP/C538447/1). We are grateful to Sharon Goldwater for her feedback on earlier versions of this work.

References

Agirre, Eneko, Lluís Màrquez, and Richard Wicentowski, editors. 2007. *Proceedings of the SemEval-2007*. Prague, Czech Republic.

Agirre, Eneko and Aitor Soroa. 2007. Semeval-2007 task 02: Evaluating word sense induction and discrimination systems. In *Proceedings of SemEval-2007*. Prague, Czech Republic, pages 7–12.

Barnard, K., P. Duygulu, D. Forsyth, N. De Freitas, D. M. Blei, and M. I. Jordan. 2003. Matching words and pictures. *J. of Machine Learning Research* 3(6):1107–1135.

Blei, David M., Andrew Y. Ng, and Michael I. Jordan. 2003. Latent dirichlet allocation. *Journal of Machine Learning Research* 3:993–1022.

Bordag, Stefan. 2006. Word sense induction: Triplet-based clustering and automatic evaluation. In *Proceedings of the 11th EACL*. Trento, Italy, pages 137–144.

Boyd-Graber, Jordan and David Blei. 2007. Putop: Turning predominant senses into a topic model for word sense disambiguation. In *Proceedings of SemEval-2007*. Prague, Czech Republic, pages 277–281.

Boyd-Graber, Jordan, David Blei, and Xiaojin Zhu. 2007. A topic model for word sense disambiguation. In *Proceedings of the EMNLP-CoNLL*. Prague, Czech Republic, pages 1024–1033.

Briscoe, Ted and John Carroll. 2002. Robust accurate statistical annotation of general text. In *Proceedings of the 3rd LREC*. Las Palmas, Gran Canaria, pages 1499–1504.

Cai, J. F., W. S. Lee, and Y. W. Teh. 2007. Improving word sense disambiguation using topic features. In *Proceedings of the EMNLP-CoNLL*. Prague, Czech Republic, pages 1015–1023.

Carpuat, Marine and Dekai Wu. 2005. Word sense disambiguation vs. statistical machine translation. In *Proceedings of the 43rd ACL*. Ann Arbor, MI, pages 387–394.

Dorow, Beate and Dominic Widdows. 2003. Discovering corpus-specific word senses. In *Proceedings of the 10th EACL*. Budapest, Hungary, pages 79–82.

Firth, J. R. 1957. *A Synopsis of Linguistic Theory 1930-1955*. Oxford: Philological Society.

Gauch, Susan and Robert P. Futrelle. 1993. Experiments in automatic word class and word sense identification for information retrieval. In *Proceedings of the 3rd Annual Symposium on Document Analysis and Information Retrieval*. Las Vegas, NV, pages 425–434.

Geman, S. and D. Geman. 1984. Stochastic relaxation, Gibbs distribution, and Bayesian restoration of images. *IEEE Transactions on Pattern Analysis and Machine Intelligence* 6(6):721–741.

Goldwater, Sharon and Tom Griffiths. 2007. A fully Bayesian approach to unsupervised part-of-speech tagging. In *Proceedings of the 45th ACL*. Prague, Czech Republic, pages 744–751.

Griffiths, Thomas L., Mark Steyvers, David M. Blei, and Joshua B. Tenenbaum. 2005. Integrating topics and syntax. In Lawrence K. Saul, Yair Weiss, and Léon Bottou, editors, *Advances in Neural Information Processing Systems 17*, MIT Press, Cambridge, MA, pages 537–544.

Griffiths, Tom L. and Mark Steyvers. 2002. A probabilistic approach to semantic representation. In *Proeedings of the 24th Annual Conference of the Cognitive Science Society*. Fairfax, VA, pages 381–386.

Hovy, Eduard, Mitchell Marcus, Martha Palmer, Lance Ramshaw, and Ralph Weischedel. 2006. Ontonotes: The 90% solution. In *Proceedings of the HLT, Companion Volume: Short Papers*. Association for Computational Linguistics, New York City, USA, pages 57–60.

Jansen, B. J., A. Spink, and A. Pfaff. 2000. Linguistic aspects of web queries.

Lee, Yoong Keok and Hwee Tou Ng. 2002. An empirical evaluation of knowledge sources and learning algorithms for word sense disambiguation. In *Proceedings of the EMNLP*. Morristown, NJ, USA, pages 41–48.

McCarthy, Diana, Rob Koeling, Julie Weeds, and John Carroll. 2004. Finding predominant senses in untagged text. In *Proceedings of the 42nd ACL*. Barcelona, Spain, pages 280–287.

Mihalcea, Rada and Phil Edmonds, editors. 2004. *Proceedings of the SENSEVAL-3*. Barcelona.

Niu, Zheng-Yu, Dong-Hong Ji, and Chew-Lim Tan. 2007. I2r: Three systems for word sense discrimination, chinese word sense disambiguation, and english word sense disambiguation. In *Proceedings of the Fourth International Workshop on Semantic Evaluations (SemEval-2007)*. Association for Computational Linguistics, Prague, Czech Republic, pages 177–182.

Pantel, Patrick and Dekang Lin. 2002. Discovering word senses from text. In *Proceedings of the 8th KDD*. New York, NY, pages 613–619.

Pedersen, Ted. 2007. Umnd2 : Senseclusters applied to the sense induction task of senseval-4. In *Proceedings of SemEval-2007*. Prague, Czech Republic, pages 394–397.

Preiss, Judita and David Yarowsky, editors. 2001. *Proceedings of the 2nd International Workshop on Evaluating Word Sense Disambiguation Systems*. Toulouse, France.

Purandare, Amruta and Ted Pedersen. 2004. Word sense discrimination by clustering contexts in vector and similarity spaces. In *Proceedings of the CoNLL*. Boston, MA, pages 41–48.

Schütze, Hinrich. 1998. Automatic word sense discrimination. *Computational Linguistics* 24(1):97–123.

Teh, Y. W., M. I. Jordan, M. J. Beal, and D. M. Blei. 2006. Hierarchical Dirichlet processes. *Journal of the American Statistical Association* 101(476):1566–1581.

Véronis, Jean. 2004. Hyperlex: lexical cartography for information retrieval. *Computer Speech & Language* 18(3):223–252.

Vickrey, David, Luke Biewald, Marc Teyssier, and Daphne Koller. 2005. Word-sense disambiguation for machine translation. In *Proceedings of the HLT/EMNLP*. Vancouver, pages 771–778.

Voorhees, Ellen M. 1993. Using wordnet to disambiguate word senses for text retrieval. In *Proceedings of the 16th SIGIR*. New York, NY, pages 171–180.

Human Evaluation of a German Surface Realisation Ranker

Aoife Cahill
Institut für Maschinelle Sprachverarbeitung (IMS)
University of Stuttgart
70174 Stuttgart, Germany
aoife.cahill@ims.uni-stuttgart.de

Martin Forst
Palo Alto Research Center
3333 Coyote Hill Road
Palo Alto, CA 94304, USA
mforst@parc.com

Abstract

In this paper we present a human-based evaluation of surface realisation alternatives. We examine the relative rankings of naturally occurring corpus sentences and automatically generated strings chosen by statistical models (language model, log-linear model), as well as the naturalness of the strings chosen by the log-linear model. We also investigate to what extent preceding context has an effect on choice. We show that native speakers do accept quite some variation in word order, but there are also clearly factors that make certain realisation alternatives more natural.

1 Introduction

An important component of research on surface realisation (the task of generating strings for a given abstract representation) is evaluation, especially if we want to be able to compare across systems. There is consensus that exact match with respect to an actually observed corpus sentence is too strict a metric and that BLEU score measured against corpus sentences can only give a rough impression of the quality of the system output. It is unclear, however, what kind of metric would be most suitable for the evaluation of string realisations, so that, as a result, there have been a range of automatic metrics applied including *inter alia* exact match, string edit distance, NIST SSA, BLEU, NIST, ROUGE, generation string accuracy, generation tree accuracy, word accuracy (Bangalore et al., 2000; Callaway, 2003; Nakanishi et al., 2005; Velldal and Oepen, 2006; Belz and Reiter, 2006).

It is not always clear how appropriate these metrics are, especially at the level of individual sentences. Using automatic evaluation metrics cannot be avoided, but ideally, a metric for the evaluation of realisation rankers would rank alternative realisations in the same way as native speakers of the language for which the surface realisation system is developed, and not only globally, but also at the level of individual sentences.

Another major consideration in evaluation is what to take as the gold standard. The easiest option is to take the original corpus string that was used to produce the abstract representation from which we generate. However, there may well be other realisations of the same input that are as suitable in the given context. Reiter and Sripada (2002) argue that while we should take advantage of large corpora in NLG, we also need to take care that we do not introduce errors by learning from incorrect data present in corpora.

In order to better understand what makes good evaluation data (and metrics), we designed and implemented an experiment in which human judges evaluated German string realisations. The main aims of this experiment were: (i) to establish how much variation in German word order is acceptable for human judges, (ii) to find an automatic evaluation metric that mirrors the findings of the human evaluation, (iii) to provide detailed feedback for the designers of the surface realisation ranking model and (iv) to establish what effect preceding context has on the choice of realisation. In this paper, we concentrate on points (i) and (iv).

The remainder of the paper is structured as follows: In Section 2 we outline the realisation ranking system that provided the data for the experiment. In Section 3 we outline the design of the experiment and in Section 4 we present our findings. In Section 5 we relate this to other work and finally we conclude in Section 6.

2 A Realisation Ranking System for German

We take the realisation ranking system for German described in Cahill et al. (2007) and present the output to human judges. One goal of this series of experiments is to examine whether the results

Proceedings of the 12th Conference of the European Chapter of the ACL, pages 112–120,
Athens, Greece, 30 March – 3 April 2009. ©2009 Association for Computational Linguistics

based on automatic evaluation metrics published in that paper are confirmed in an evaluation by humans. Another goal is to collect data that will allow us and other researchers[1] to explore more fine-grained and reliable automatic evaluation metrics for realisation ranking.

The system presented by Cahill et al. (2007) ranks the strings generated by a hand-crafted broad-coverage Lexical Functional Grammar (Bresnan, 2001) for German (Rohrer and Forst, 2006) on the basis of a given input f-structure. In these experiments, we use f-structures from their held-out and test sets, of which 96% can be associated with surface realisations by the grammar. F-structures are attribute-value matrices representing grammatical functions and morphosyntactic features; roughly speaking, they are predicate-argument structures. In LFG, f-structures are assumed to be a crosslinguistically relatively parallel syntactic representation level, alongside the more surface-oriented c-structures, which are context-free trees. Figure 1 shows the f-structure[2] associated with TIGER Corpus sentence 8609, glossed in (1), as well as the 4 string realisations that the German LFG generates from this f-structure. The LFG is reversible, i.e. the same grammar is used for parsing as for generation. It is a hand-crafted grammar, and has been carefully constructed to only parse (and therefore generate) grammatical strings.[3]

(1) Williams war in der britischen Politik äußerst umstritten.
Williams was in the British politics extremely controversial.
'Williams was extremely controversial in British politics.'

The ranker consists of a log-linear model that is based on linguistically informed structural features as well as a trigram language model, whose score is integrated into the model simply as an additional feature. The log-linear model is trained on corpus data, in this case sentences from the TIGER Corpus (Brants et al., 2002), for which f-structures are available; the observed corpus sentences are considered as references whose probability is to be maximised during the training process.

The output of the realisation ranker is evaluated in terms of exact match and BLEU score, both measured against the actually observed corpus sentences. In addition to the figures achieved by the ranker, the corresponding figures achieved by the employed trigram language model on its own are given as a baseline, and the exact match figure of the best possible string selection is given as an upper bound.[4] We summarise these figures in Table 1.

	Exact Match	BLEU score
Language model	27%	0.7306
Log-linear model	37%	0.7939
Upper bound	62%	–

Table 1: Results achieved by trigram LM ranker and log-linear model ranker in Cahill et al. (2007)

By means of these figures, Cahill et al. (2007) show that a log-linear model based on structural features and a language model score performs considerably better realisation ranking than just a language model. In our experiments, presented in detail in the following section, we examine whether human judges confirm this and how natural and/or acceptable the selection performed by the realisation ranker under consideration is for German native speakers.

3 Experiment Design

The experiment was divided into three parts. Each part took between 30 and 45 minutes to complete, and participants were asked to leave some time (e.g. a week) between each part. In total, 24 participants completed the experiment. All were native German speakers (mostly from South-Western Germany) and almost all had a linguistic background. Table 2 gives a breakdown of the items in each part of the experiment.[5]

[1] The data is available for download from http://www.ims.uni-stuttgart.de/projekte/pargram/geneval/data/

[2] Note that only grammatical functions are displayed; morphosyntactic features are omitted due to space constraints. Also note that the discourse function TOPIC was ignored in generation.

[3] A ranking mechanism based on so-called optimality marks can lead to a certain "asymmetry" between parsing and generation in the sense that not all sentences that can be associated with a certain f-structure are necessarily generated from this same f-structure. E.g. the sentence *Williams war äußerst umstritten in der britischen Politik.* can be parsed into the f-structure in Figure 1, but it is not generated because an optimality mark penalizes the extraposition of PPs to the right of a clause. Only few optimality marks were used in the process of generating the data for our experiments, so that the bias they introduce should not be too noticeable.

[4] The observed corpus sentence can be (re)generated from the corresponding f-structure for only 62% of the sentences used, usually because of differences in punctuation. Hence this exact match upper bound. An upper bound in terms of BLEU score cannot be computed because BLEU score is computed on entire corpora rather than individual sentences.

[5] Experiments 3a and 3b contained the same items as experiments 1a and 1b.

"Williams war in der britischen Politik äußerst umstritten."

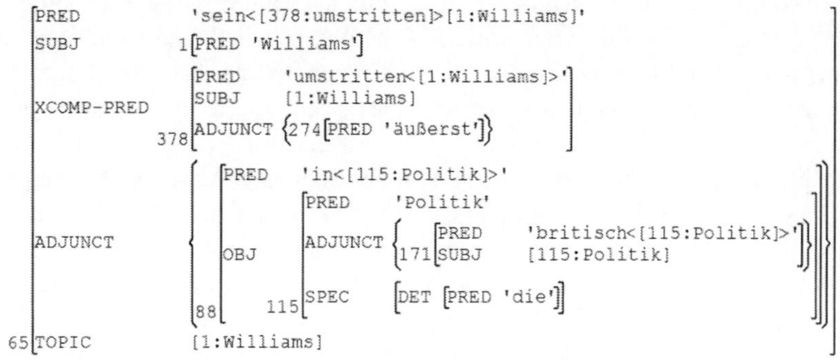

Williams war in der britischen Politik äußerst umstritten.
In der britischen Politik war Williams äußerst umstritten.
Äußerst umstritten war Williams in der britischen Politik.
Äußerst umstritten war in der britischen Politik Williams.

Figure 1: F-structure associated with (1) and strings generated from it.

	Exp 1a	Exp 1b	Exp 2
Num. items	44	52	41
Avg. sent length	14.4	12.1	9.4

Table 2: Statistics for each experiment part

3.1 Part 1

The aim of part 1 of the experiment was twofold. First, to identify the relative rankings of the systems evaluated in Cahill et al. (2007) according to the human judges, and second to evaluate the quality of the strings as chosen by the log-linear model of Cahill et al. (2007). To these ends, part 1 was further subdivided into two tasks: 1a and b.

Task 1a: During the first task, participants were presented with alternative realisations for an input f-structure (but not shown the original f-structure) and asked to rank them in order of how natural sounding they were, 1 being the best and 3 being the worst.[6] Each item contained three alternatives, (i) the original string found in TIGER, (ii) the string chosen as most likely by the trigram language model, and (iii) the string chosen as most likely by the log-linear model. Only items where each system chose a different alternative were chosen from the evaluation data of Cahill et al. (2007). The three alternatives were presented in random order for each item, and the items were presented in random order for each participant. Some items were presented randomly to participants more than once as a sanity check, and in total for Part 1a, participants made 52 ranking judgements on 44 items. Figure 2 shows a screen shot of what the participant was presented with for this task.

Task 1b: In the second task of part 1, participants were presented with the string chosen by the log-linear model as being the most likely and asked to evaluate it on a scale from 1 to 5 on how natural sounding it was, 1 being very unnatural or marked and 5 being completely natural. Figure 3 shows a screen shot of what the participant saw during the experiment. Again some random items were presented to the participant more than once, and the items themselves were presented in random order. In total, the participants made 58 judgements on 52 items.

3.2 Part 2

In the second part of the experiment, participants were presented between 4 and 8 alternative surface realisations for an input f-structure, as well as some preceding context. This preceding context was automatically determined using information from the export release of the TIGER treebank and was not hand-checked for relevance.[7] The participants were then asked to choose the realisation that they felt fit best given the preceding sentences.

[6]Joint rankings were not allowed, i.e. the participants were forced to make strict ranking decisions, and in hindsight this may have introduced some noise into the data.

[7]The export release of the TIGER treebank includes an article ID for each sentence. Unfortunately, this is not completely reliable for determining relevant context, since an article can also contain several short news snippets which are completely unrelated. Paragraph boundaries are not marked. This leads to some noise, which unfortunately is difficult to measure objectively

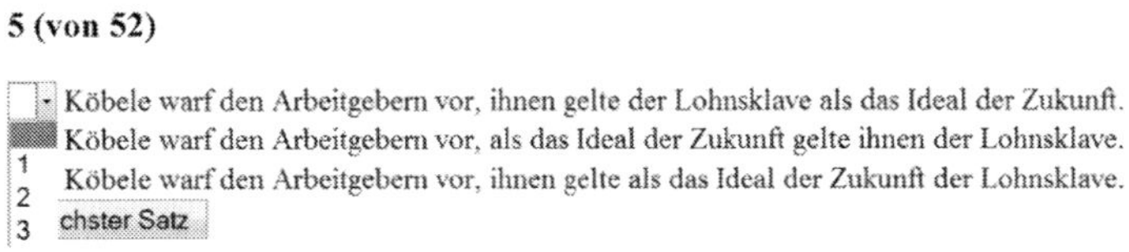

Figure 2: Screenshot of Part 1a of the Experiment

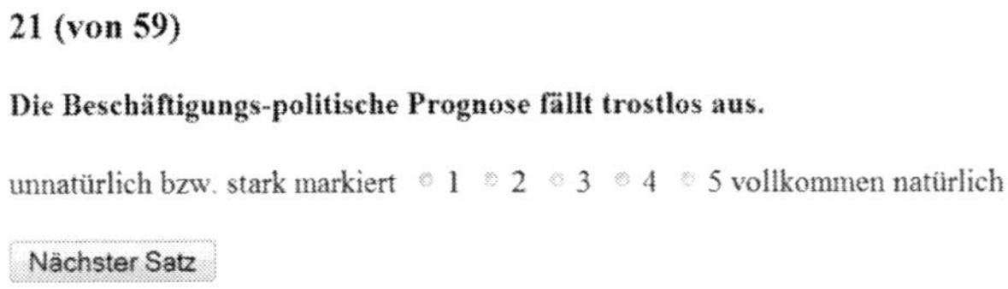

Figure 3: Screenshot of Part 1b of the Experiment

	Total			Average
	Rank 1	Rank 2	Rank 3	Rank
Original String	817	366	65	1.40
LL String	303	593	352	2.04
LM String	128	289	831	2.56

Table 3: Task 1a: Ranks for each system

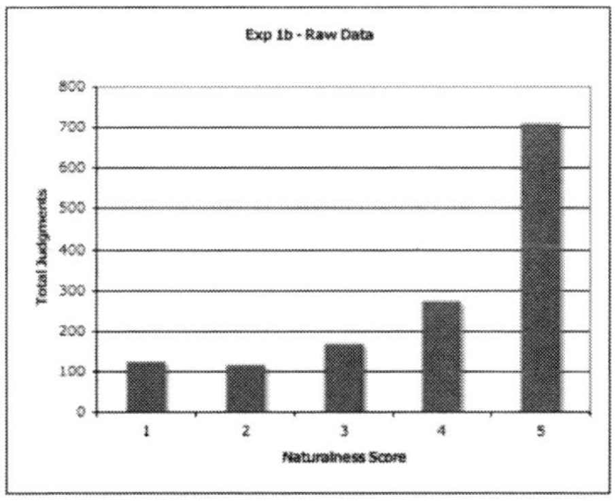

Figure 5: Task 1b: Naturalness scores for strings chosen by log-linear model, 1=worst

The items were presented in random order, and the list of alternatives were presented in random order to each participant. Some items were randomly presented more than once, resulting in 50 judgements on 41 items. Figure 4 shows a screen shot of what the participant saw.

3.3 Part 3

Part 3 of the experiment was identical to Part 1, except that now, rather than the participants being presented with sentences in isolation, they were given some preceding context. The context was determined automatically, in the same way as in Part 2. The items themselves were the same as in Part 1. The aim of this part of the experiment was to see what effect preceding context had on judgements.

4 Results

In this section we present the result and analysis of the experiments outlined above.

4.1 How good were the strings?

The data collected in Experiment 1a showed the overall human relative ranking of the three systems. We calculate the total numbers of each rank for each system. Table 3 summarises the results. The original string is the string found in the TIGER Corpus, the LM String is the string chosen as being most likely by the trigram language model and the LL String is the string chosen as being most likely by the log-linear model.

Table 3 confirms the overall relative rankings of the three systems as determined using BLEU scores. The original TIGER strings are ranked best (average 1.4), the strings chosen by the log-linear model are ranked better than the strings chosen by the language model (average 2.65 vs 2.04).

In Experiment 1b, the aim was to find out how acceptable the strings chosen by the log-linear model were, although they were not the same as the original string. Figure 5 summarises the data. The graph shows that the majority of strings chosen by the log-linear model ranked very highly on the naturalness scale.

4.2 Did the human judges agree with the original authors?

In Experiment 2, the aim was to find out how often the human judges chose the same string as the original author (given alternatives generated by the LFG grammar). Most items had between 4 and 6 alternative strings. In 70% of all items, the human judges chose the same string as the original author. However, the remaining 30% of the time, the human judges picked an alternative as being the

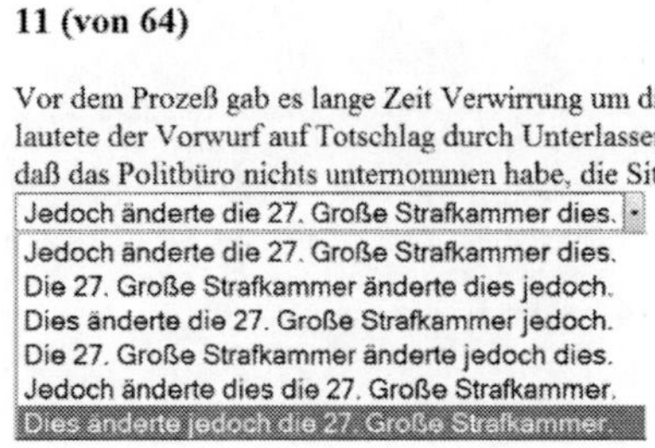

Figure 4: Screenshot of Part 2 of the Experiment

most fitting in the given context.[8] This suggests that there is quite some variation in what native German speakers will accept, but that this variation is by no means random, as indicated by 70% of choices being the same string as the original author's.

Figure 6 shows for each bin of possible alternatives, the percentage of items with a given number of choices made. For example, for the items with 4 possible alternatives, over 70% of the time, the judges chose between only 2 of them. For the items with 5 possible alternatives, in 10% of those items the human judges chose only 1 of those alternatives; in 30% of cases, the human judges all chose the same 2 solutions, and for the remaining 60% they chose between only 3 of the 5 possible alternatives. These figures indicate that although judges could not always agree on one best string, often they were only choosing between 2 or 3 of the possible alternatives. This suggests that, on the one hand, native speakers do accept quite some variation, but that, on the other hand, there are clearly factors that make certain realisation alternatives more preferable than others.

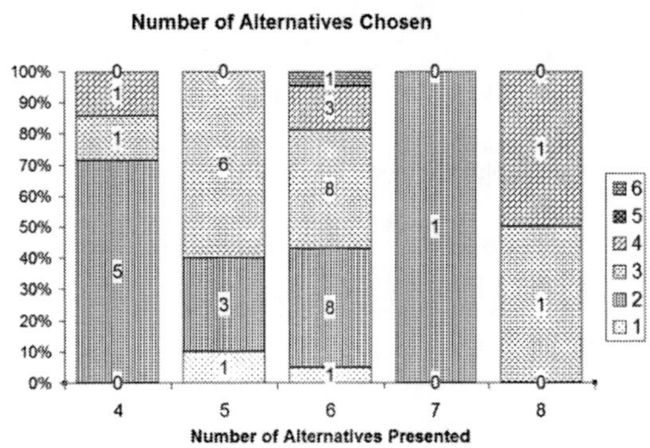

Figure 6: Exp 2: Number of Alternatives Chosen

[8]Recall that almost all strings presented to the judges were grammatical.

The graph in Figure 6 shows that only in two cases did the human judges choose from among all possible alternatives. In one case, there were 4 possible alternatives and in the other 6. The original sentence that had 4 alternatives is given in (2). The four alternatives that participants were asked to choose from are given in Table 4, with the frequency of each choice. The original sentence that had 6 alternatives is given in (3). The six alternatives generated by the grammar and the frequencies with which they were chosen is given in Table 5.

(2) Die Brandursache blieb zunächst unbekannt.
The cause of fire remained initially unknown.
'The cause of the fire remained unknown initially.'

Alternative	Freq.
Zunächst blieb die Brandursache unbekannt.	2
Die Brandursache blieb zunächst unbekannt.	24
Unbekannt blieb die Brandursache zunächst.	1
Unbekannt blieb zunächst die Brandursache.	1

Table 4: The 4 alternatives given by the grammar for (2) and their frequencies

Tables 4 and 5 tell different stories. On the one hand, although each of the 4 alternatives was chosen at least once from Table 4, there is a clear preference for one string (and this is also the original string from the TIGER Corpus). On the other hand, there is no clear preference[9] for any one of the alternatives in Table 5, and, in fact, the alternative that was selected most frequently by the participants is not the original string. Interestingly, out of the 41 items presented to participants, the original string was chosen by the majority of participants in 36 cases. Again, this confirms the hypothesis that there is a certain amount of acceptable variation for native speakers but there are clear preferences for certain strings over others.

[9]Although it is clear that alternative 2 is dispreferred.

(3) Die Unternehmensgruppe Tengelmann fördert mit einem sechsstelligen Betrag die Arbeit im brandenburgischen
The group of companies Tengelmann assists with a 6-figure sum the work in of-Brandenburg
Biosphärenreservat Schorfheide.
biosphere reserve Schorfheide.

'The Tengelmann group of companies is supporting the work at the biosphere reserve in Schorfheide, Brandenburg, with a 6-figure sum.'

Alternative	Freq.
Mit einem sechsstelligen Betrag fördert die Unternehmensgruppe Tengelmann die Arbeit im brandenburgischen Biosphärenreservat Schorfheide.	7
Mit einem sechsstelligen Betrag fördert die Arbeit im brandenburgischen Biosphärenreservat Schorfheide die Unternehmensgruppe Tengelmann.	1
Die Arbeit im brandenburgischen Biosphärenreservat Schorfheide fördert die Unternehmensgruppe Tengelmann mit einem sechsstelligen Betrag.	4
Die Arbeit im brandenburgischen Biosphärenreservat Schorfheide fördert mit einem sechsstelligen Betrag die Unternehmensgruppe Tengelmann.	5
Die Unternehmensgruppe Tengelmann fördert die Arbeit im brandenburgischen Biosphärenreservat Schorfheide mit einem sechsstelligen Betrag.	5
Die Unternehmensgruppe Tengelmann fördert mit einem sechsstelligen Betrag die Arbeit im brandenburgischen Biosphärenreservat Schorfheide.	5

Table 5: The 6 alternatives given by the grammar for (3) and their frequencies

4.3 Effects of context

As explained in Section 3.1, Part 3 of our experiment was identical to Part 1, except that the participants could see some preceding context. The aim of this part was to investigate to what extent discourse factors influence the way in which human judges evaluate the output of the realisation ranker. In Task 3a, we expected the original strings to be ranked (even) higher in context than out of context; consequently, the ranks of the realisations selected by the log-linear and the language model would have to go down. With respect to Task 3b, we had no particular expectation, but were just interested in seeing whether some preceding context would affect the evaluation results for the strings selected as most probable by the log-linear model ranker in any way.

Table 6 summarises the results of Task 3a. It shows that, at least overall, our expectation that the original corpus sentences would be ranked higher within context than out of context was not borne out. Actually, they were ranked a bit lower than they were when presented in isolation, and the only realisations that are ranked slightly higher overall are the ones selected by the trigram LM.

The overall results of Task 3b are presented in Figure 7. Interestingly, although we did not expect any particular effect of preceding context on the way the participants would rate the realisations selected by the log-linear model, the naturalness scores were higher in the condition with context (Task 3b) than in the one without context

	Total			Average
	Rank 1	Rank 2	Rank 3	Rank
Original String	810 (-7)	365 (-1)	71 (+6)	1.41 (+0.01)
LL String	274 (-29)	615 (+22)	357 (+5)	2.07 (+0.03)
LM String	162 (+34)	266 (-23)	818 (-13)	2.53 (-0.03)

Table 6: Task 3a: Ranks for each system (compared to ranks in Task 1a)

(Task 1b). One explanation might be that sentences in some sort of default order are generally rated higher in context than out of context, simply because the context makes sentences less surprising.

Since, contrary to our expectations, we could not detect a clear effect of context in the overall results of Task 3a, we investigated how the average ranks of the three alternatives presented for individual items differ between Task 1a and Task 3a. An example of an original corpus sentence which many participants ranked higher in context than in isolation is given in (4a.). The realisations selected by the the log-linear model and the trigram LM are given in (4b.) and (4c.) respectively, and the context shown to the participants is given above these alternatives. We believe that the context has this effect because it prepares the reader for the structure with the sentence-initial predicative participle *entscheidend*; usually, these elements appear rather in clause-final position.

In contrast, (5a) is an example of a corpus

(4) -2 Betroffen sind die Antibabypillen Femovan, Lovelle, [...] und Dimirel.
Concerned are the contraceptive pills Femovan, Lovelle, [...], and Dimirel.

-1 Das Bundesinstitut schließt nicht aus, daß sich die Thrombose-Warnung als grundlos erweisen könnte.
The federal institute excludes not that the thrombosis warning as unfounded turn out could.

a. Entscheidend sei die [...] abschließende Bewertung, sagte Jürgen Beckmann vom Institut dem ZDF.
Decisive is the [...] final evaluation, said Jürgen Beckmann of the institute the ZDF.

b. Die [...] abschließende Bewertung sei entscheidend, sagte Jürgen Beckmann vom Institut dem ZDF.

c. Die [...] abschließende Bewertung sei entscheidend, sagte dem ZDF Jürgen Beckmann vom Institut.

(5) -2 Im konkreten Fall darf der Kurde allerdings trotz der Entscheidung der Bundesrichter nicht in die
In the concrete case may the Kurd however despite the decision of the federal judges not to the
Türkei abgeschoben werden, weil ihm dort nach den Feststellungen der Vorinstanz
Turkey deported be because him there according to the conclusions of the court of lower instance
politische Verfolgung droht.
political persecution threatens.

-1 Es besteht Abschiebeschutz nach dem Ausländergesetz.
It exists deportation protection according to the foreigner law.

a. Der 9. Senat [...] äußerte sich in seiner Entscheidung nicht zur Verfassungsgemäßheit der
The 9th senate [...] expressed itself in its decision not to the constitutionality of the
Drittstaatenregelung.
third-country rule.

b. In seiner Entscheidung äußerte sich der 9. Senat [...] nicht zur Verfassungsgemäßheit der Drittstaatenregelung.

c. Der 9. Senat [...] äußerte sich in seiner Entscheidung zur Verfassungsgemäßheit der Drittstaatenregelung nicht.

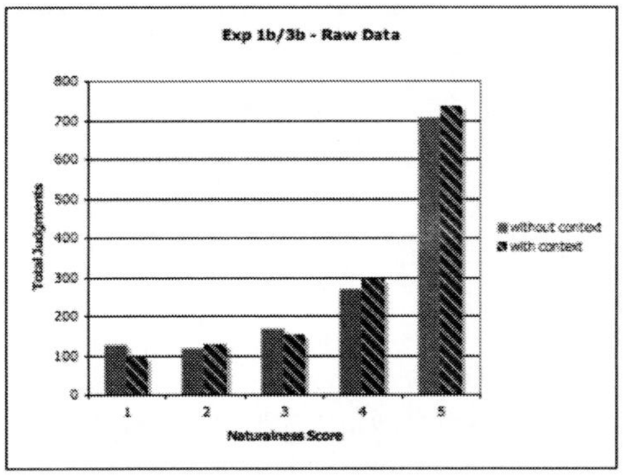

Figure 7: Tasks 1b and 3b: Naturalness scores for strings chosen by log-linear model, presented without and with context

sentence which our participants tended to rank lower in context than in isolation. Actually, the human judges preferred the realisation selected by the trigram LM to the original sentence and the realisation chosen by the log-linear model in both conditions, but this preference was even reinforced when context was available. One explanation might be that the two preceding sentences are precisely about the decision to which the initial phrase of variant (5b) refers, which ensures a smooth flow of the discourse.

4.4 Inter-Annotator Agreement

We measure two types of annotator agreement. First we measure how well each annotator agrees with him/herself. This is done by evaluating what percentage of the time an annotator made the same choice when presented with the same item choices (recall that as described in Section 3, a number of items were presented randomly more than once to each participant). The results are given in Table 7. The results show that in between 70% and 74% of cases, judges make the same decision when presented with the same data. We found this to be a surprisingly low number and think that it is most likely due to the acceptable variation in word order for speakers. Another measure of agreement is how well the individual participants agree with each other. In order to establish this, we calculate an average Spearman's correlation coefficient (non-parametric Pearson's correlation coefficient) between each participant for each experiment. The results are summarised in Table 8. Although these figures indicate a high level of inter-annotator agreement, more tests are required to establish exactly what these figures mean for each experiment.

5 Related Work

The work that is most closely related to what is presented in this paper is that of Velldal (2008). In

Experiment	Agreement (%)
Part 1a	77.43
Part 1b	71.05
Part 2	74.32
Part 3a	72.63
Part 3b	70.89

Table 7: How often did a participant make the same choice?

Experiment	Spearman coefficient
Part 1a	0.62
Part 1b	0.60
Part 2	0.58
Part 3a	0.61
Part 3b	0.51

Table 8: Inter-Annotator Agreement for each experiment

his thesis several models of realisation ranking are presented and evaluated against the original corpus text. Chapter 8 describes a small human-based experiment, where 7 native English speakers rank the output of 4 systems. One system is the original text, another is a randomly chosen baseline, another is a string chosen by a log-linear model and the fourth is one chosen by a language model. Joint rankings were allowed. The results presented in Velldal (2008) mirror our findings in Experiments 1a and 3a, that native speakers rank the original strings higher than the log-linear model strings which are ranked higher than the language model strings. In both cases, the log-linear models include the language model score as a feature in the log-linear model. Nakanishi et al. (2005) report that they achieve the best BLEU scores when they do not include the language model score in their log-linear model, but they also admit that their language model was not trained on enough data.

Belz and Reiter (2006) carry out a comparison of automatic evaluation metrics against human domain experts and human non-experts in the domain of weather forecast statements. In their evaluations, the NIST score correlated more closely than BLEU or ROUGE to the human judgements. They conclude that more than 4 reference texts are needed for automatic evaluation of NLG systems.

6 Conclusion and Outlook to Future Work

In this paper, we have presented a human-based experiment to evaluate the output of a realisation ranking system for German. We evaluated the original corpus text, and strings chosen by a language model and a log-linear model. We found that, at a global level, the human judgements mirrored the relative rankings of the three system according to the BLEU score. In terms of naturalness, the strings chosen by the log-linear model were generally given 4 or 5, indicating that although the log-linear model might not choose the same string as the original author had written, the strings it was choosing were mostly very natural strings.

When presented with all alternatives generated by the grammar for a given input f-structure, the human judges chose the same string as the original author 70% of the time. In 5 out of 41 cases, the majority of judges chose a string other than the original string. These figures show that native speakers accept some variation in word order, and so caution should be exercised when using corpus-derived reference data. The observed acceptable variation was often linked to information structural considerations, and further experiments will be carried out to investigate this relationship between word order and information structure.

In examining the effect of preceding context, we found that overall context had very little effect. At the level of individual sentences, however, clear tendencies were observed, but there were some sentences which were judged better in context and others which were ranked lower. This again indicates that corpus-derived reference data should be used with caution.

An obvious next step is to examine how well automatic metrics correlate with the human judgements collected, not only at an individual sentence level, but also at a global level. This can be done using statistical techniques to correlate the human judgements with the scores from the automatic metrics. We will also examine the sentences that were consistently judged to be of poor quality, so that we can provide feedback to the developers of the log-linear model in terms of possible additional features for disambiguation.

Acknowledgments

We are extremely grateful to all of our participants for taking part in this experiment. This work was partly funded by the Collaborative Research Centre (SFB 732) at the University of Stuttgart.

References

Srinivas Bangalore, Owen Rambow, and Steve Whittaker. 2000. Evaluation metrics for generation. In *Proceedings of the First International Natural Language Generation Conference (INLG2000)*, pages 1–8, Mitzpe Ramon, Israel.

Anja Belz and Ehud Reiter. 2006. Comparing automatic and human evaluation of NLG systems. In *Proceedings of the 11th Conference of the European Chapter of the Association for Computational Linguistics*, pages 313–320, Trento, Italy.

Sabine Brants, Stefanie Dipper, Silvia Hansen, Wolfgang Lezius, and George Smith. 2002. The TIGER treebank. In *Proceedings of the Workshop on Treebanks and Linguistic Theories*, Sozopol, Bulgaria.

Joan Bresnan. 2001. *Lexical-Functional Syntax*. Blackwell, Oxford.

Aoife Cahill, Martin Forst, and Christian Rohrer. 2007. Stochastic Realisation Ranking for a Free Word Order Language. In *Proceedings of the Eleventh European Workshop on Natural Language Generation*, pages 17–24, Saarbrücken, Germany, June. DFKI GmbH. Document D-07-01.

Charles Callaway. 2003. Evaluating Coverage for Large Symbolic NLG Grammars. In *Proceedings of the 18th International Joint Conference on Artificial Intelligence (IJCAI 2003)*, pages 811–817, Acapulco, Mexico.

Hiroko Nakanishi, Yusuke Miyao, and Jun'ichi Tsujii. 2005. Probabilistic models for disambiguation of an HPSG-based chart generator. In *Proceedings of IWPT 2005*.

Ehud Reiter and Somayajulu Sripada. 2002. Should Corpora Texts Be Gold Standards for NLG? In *Proceedings of INLG-02*, pages 97–104, Harriman, NY.

Christian Rohrer and Martin Forst. 2006. Improving coverage and parsing quality of a large-scale LFG for German. In *Proceedings of the Language Resources and Evaluation Conference (LREC-2006)*, Genoa, Italy.

Erik Velldal and Stephan Oepen. 2006. Statistical ranking in tactical generation. In *Proceedings of the 2006 Conference on Empirical Methods in Natural Language Processing*, Sydney, Australia.

Erik Velldal. 2008. *Empirical Realization Ranking*. Ph.D. thesis, University of Oslo.

Large-Coverage Root Lexicon Extraction for Hindi

Cohan Sujay Carlos **Monojit Choudhury** **Sandipan Dandapat**
Microsoft Research India
monojitc@microsoft.com

Abstract

This paper describes a method using morphological rules and heuristics, for the automatic extraction of large-coverage lexicons of stems and root word-forms from a raw text corpus. We cast the problem of high-coverage lexicon extraction as one of stemming followed by root word-form selection. We examine the use of POS tagging to improve precision and recall of stemming and thereby the coverage of the lexicon. We present accuracy, precision and recall scores for the system on a Hindi corpus.

1 Introduction

Large-coverage morphological lexicons are an essential component of morphological analysers. Morphological analysers find application in language processing systems for tasks like tagging, parsing and machine translation. While raw text is an abundant and easily accessible linguistic resource, high-coverage morphological lexicons are scarce or unavailable in Hindi as in many other languages (Clément et al., 2004). Thus, the development of better algorithms for the extraction of morphological lexicons from raw text corpora is a task of considerable importance.

A root word-form lexicon is an intermediate stage in the creation of a morphological lexicon. In this paper, we consider the problem of extracting a large-coverage root word-form lexicon for the Hindi language, a highly inflectional and moderately agglutinative Indo-European language spoken widely in South Asia.

Since a POS tagger, another basic tool, was available along with POS tagged data to train it, and since the error patterns indicated that POS tagging could greatly improve the accuracy of the lexicon, we used the POS tagger in our experiments on lexicon extraction.

Previous work in morphological lexicon extraction from a raw corpus often does not achieve very high precision and recall (de Lima, 1998; Oliver and Tadić, 2004). In some previous work the process of lexicon extraction involves incremental or post-construction manual validation of the entire lexicon (Clément et al., 2004; Sagot, 2005; Forsberg et al., 2006; Sagot et al., 2006; Sagot, 2007).

Our method attempts to improve on and extend the previous work by increasing the precision and recall of the system to such a point that manual validation might even be rendered unnecessary. Yet another difference, to our knowledge, is that in our method we cast the problem of lexicon extraction as two subproblems: that of stemming and following it, that of root word-form selection.

The input resources for our system are as follows: a) raw text corpus, b) morphological rules, c) POS tagger and d) word-segmentation labelled data. We output a stem lexicon and a root word-form lexicon.

We take as input a raw text corpus and a set of morphological rules. We first run a stemming algorithm that uses the morphological rules and some heuristics to obtain a stem dictionary. We then create a root dictionary from the stem dictionary.

The last two input resources are optional but when a POS tagger is utilized, the F-score (harmonic mean of precision and recall) of the root lexicon can be as high as 94.6%.

In the rest of the paper, we provide a brief overview of the morphological features of the Hindi language, followed by a description of our method including the specification of rules, the corpora and the heuristics for stemming and root word-form selection. We then evaluate the system with and without the POS tagger.

Proceedings of the 12th Conference of the European Chapter of the ACL, pages 121–129,
Athens, Greece, 30 March – 3 April 2009. ©2009 Association for Computational Linguistics

2 Hindi Orthography and Morphology

There are some features peculiar to Hindi orthography and to the character encoding system that we use. These need to be compensated for in the system. It was also found that Hindi's inflectional morphology has certain characteristics that simplify the word segmentation rules.

2.1 Orthography

Hindi is written in the partially-phonemic Devanagari script. Most consonant clusters that occur in the language are represented by characters and ligatures, while a very few are represented as diacritics. Vowels that follow consonants or consonant clusters are marked with diacritics. However, each consonant in the Devanagari script also carries an implicit vowel `a`[1] unless its absence is marked by a special diacritic "halant". Vowels are represented by vowel characters when they occur at the head of a word or after another vowel.

The `y` sound sometimes does not surface in the pronunciation when it occurs between two vowels. So suffixes where the `y` is followed by `e` or `I` can be written in two ways, with or without the `y` sound in them. For instance the suffix `ie` can also be written as `iye`.

Certain stemming rules will therefore need to be duplicated in order to accommodate the different spelling possibilities and the different vowel representations in Hindi. The character encoding also plays a small but significant role in the ease of stemming of Hindi word-forms.

2.2 Unicode Representation

We used Unicode to encode Hindi characters. The Unicode representation of Devanagari treats simple consonants and vowels as separate units and so makes it easier to match substrings at consonant-vowel boundaries. Ligatures and diacritical forms of consonants are therefore represented by the same character code and they can be equated very simply.

However, when using Unicode as the character encoding, it must be borne in mind that there are different character codes for the vowel diacritics and for the vowel characters for one and the same vowel sound, and that the long and short forms of the vowels are represented by different codes. These artifacts of the character encoding need to be compensated for when using substring matches to identify the short vowel sound as being part of the corresponding prolonged vowel sound and when stemming.

[1]In the discussion in Section 2 and in Table 1 and Table 2, we have used a loose phonetic transcription that resembles ITRANS (developed by Avinash Chopde http://www.aczoom.com/itrans/).

Word Form	**Derivational Segmentation**	**Root**
karnA	kar + nA	kar
karAnA	kar + A + nA	kar
karvAnA	kar + vA + nA	kar
Word Form	**Inflectional Segmentation**	**Root**
karnA	kar + nA	kar
karAnA	karA + nA	karA
karvAnA	karvA + nA	karvA

Table 1: Morpheme Segmentation

laDkA	**Nominative**	**Oblique**
Singular	laDkA	laDke
Plural	laDke	laDkon

laDkI	**Nominative**	**Oblique**
Singular	laDkI	laDkI
Plural	laDkI	laDkiyAn

Table 2: Sample Paradigms

2.3 Morphology

The inflectional morphology of Hindi does not permit agglutination. This helps keep the number of inflectional morphological rules manageable. However, the derivational suffixes are agglutinative, leading to an explosion in the number of root word-forms in the inflectional root lexicon.

The example in Table 1 shows that verbs can take one of the two causative suffixes `A` and `vA`. These being derivational suffixes are not stemmed in our system and cause the verb lexicon to be larger than it would have otherwise.

2.4 Paradigms

Nouns, verbs and adjectives are the main POS categories that undergo inflection in Hindi according to regular paradigm rules.

For example, Hindi nouns inflect for case and number. The inflections for the paradigms that the words `laDkA` (meaning boy) and `laDkI` (meaning girl) belong to are shown in Table 2. The root word-forms are `laDkA` and `laDkI` respectively (the singular and nominative forms).

Hindi verbs are inflected by gender, number, person, mood and tense. Hindi adjectives take inflections for gender and case. The number of inflected forms in different POS categories varies considerably, with verbs tending to have a lot more inflections than other POS categories.

3 System Description

In order to construct a morphological lexicon, we used a rule-based approach combined with heuristics for stem and root selection. When used in concert with a POS tagger, they could extract a very accurate morphological lexicon from a raw text corpus. Our system therefore consists of the following components:

1. A raw text corpus in the Hindi language large enough to contain a few hundred thousand unique word-forms and a smaller labelled corpus to train a POS tagger with.
2. A list of rules comprising suffix strings and constraints on the word-forms and POS categories that they can be applied to.
3. A stemmer that uses the above rules, and some heuristics to identify and reduce inflected word-forms to stems.
4. A POS tagger to identify the POS category or categories that the word forms in the raw text corpus can belong to.
5. A root selector that identifies a root word-form and its paradigm from a stem and a set of inflections of the stem.

The components of the system are described in more detail below.

3.1 Text Corpora

Rules alone are not always sufficient to identify the best stem or root for a word-form, when the words being stemmed have very few inflectional forms or when a word might be stemmed in one of many ways. In that case, a raw text corpus can provide important clues for identifying them.

The raw text corpus that we use is the Web-Duniya corpus which consists of 1.4 million sentences of newswire and 21.8 million words. The corpus, being newswire, is clearly not balanced. It has a preponderance of third-person forms whereas first and second person inflectional forms are under-represented.

Name	POS	Paradigm Suffixes	Root
`laDkA`	noun	{'A','e','on'}	'A'
`laDkI`	noun	{'I','iyAn'}	'I'
`dho`	verb	{'','yogI','nA',...}	''
`chal`	verb	{'','ogI','nA',...}	''

Table 3: Sample Paradigm Suffix Sets

Since Hindi word boundaries are clearly marked with punctuation and spaces, tokenization was an easy task. The raw text corpus yielded approximately 331000 unique word-forms. When words beginning with numbers were removed, we were left with about 316000 unique word-forms of which almost half occurred only once in the corpus.

In addition, we needed a corpus of 45,000 words labelled with POS categories using the IL-POST tagset (Sankaran et al., 2008) for the POS tagger.

3.2 Rules

The morphological rules input into the system are used to recognize word-forms that together belong to a paradigm. Paradigms can be treated as a set of suffixes that can be used to generate inflectional word-forms from a stem. The set of suffixes that constitutes a paradigm defines an equivalence class on the set of unique word-forms in the corpus.

For example, the `laDkA` paradigm in Table 2 would be represented by the set of suffix strings {'A', 'e', 'on'} derived from the word-forms `laDkA`, `laDke` and `laDkon`. A few paradigms are listed in Table 3.

The suffix set formalism of a paradigm closely resembles the one used in a previous attempt at unsupervised paradigm extraction (Zeman, 2007) but differs from it in that Zeman (2007) considers the set of word-forms that match the paradigm to be a part of the paradigm definition.

In our system, we represent the morphological rules by a list of suffix add-delete rules. Each rule in our method is a five-tuple $\{\alpha, \beta, \gamma, \delta, \epsilon\}$ where:

- α is the suffix string to be matched for the rule to apply.
- β is the portion of the suffix string after which the stem ends.
- γ is a POS category in which the string α is a valid suffix.

α	β	γ	δ	ϵ
'A'	''	Noun	N1	'A'
'on'	''	Noun	N1,N3	'A'
'e'	''	Noun	N1	'A'
'oyogI'	'o'	Verb	V5	'o'

Table 4: Sample Paradigm Rules

Word Form	α **Match**	**Stem**	**Root**
`laDkA`	`laDk + A`	`laDk`	`laDkA`
`laDkon`	`laDk + on`	`laDk`	`laDkA`
`laDke`	`laDk + e`	`laDk`	`laDkA`
`dhoyogI`	`dh + oyogI`	`dh + o`	`dho`

Table 5: Rule Application

- δ is a list of paradigms that contain the suffix string α.
- ϵ is the root suffix

The sample paradigm rules shown in Table 4 would match the words `laDkA`, `laDkon`, `laDke` and `dhoyogI` respectively and cause them to be stemmed and assigned roots as shown in Table 5.

The rules by themselves can identify word-and-paradigm entries from the raw text corpus if a sufficient number of inflectional forms were present. For instance, if the words `laDkA` and `laDkon` were present in the corpus, by taking the intersection of the paradigms associated with the matching rules in Table 4, it would be possible to infer that the root word-form was `laDkA` and that the paradigm was N1.

We needed to create about 300 rules for Hindi. The rules could be stored in a list indexed by the suffix in the case of Hindi because the number of possible suffixes was small. For highly agglutinative languages, such as Tamil and Malayalam, which can have thousands of suffixes, it would be necessary to use a Finite State Machine representation of the rules.

3.3 Suffix Evidence

We define the term 'suffix evidence' for a potential stem as the number of word-forms in the corpus that are composed of a concatenation of the stem and any valid suffix. For instance, the suffix evidence for the stem `laDk` is 2 if the word-forms `laDkA` and `laDkon` are the only word-forms with the prefix `laDk` that exist in the corpus and `A` and `on` are both valid suffixes.

BSE	**Word-forms**	**Accuracy**
1	20.5%	79%
2	20.0%	70%
3	13.2%	70%
4	10.8%	81%
5 & more	35.5%	80%

Table 6: % Frequency and Accuracy by BSE

BSE	**Nouns**	**Verbs**	**Others**
1	292	6	94
2	245	2	136
3	172	15	66
4	120	16	71
5 & more	103	326	112

Table 7: Frequency by POS Category

Table 6 presents word-form counts for different suffix evidence values for the WebDuniya corpus. Since the real stems for the word-forms were not known, the prefix substring with the highest suffix evidence was used as the stem. We shall call this heuristically selected stem the best-suffix-evidence stem and its suffix evidence as the best-suffix-evidence (BSE).

It will be seen from Table 6 that about 20% of the words have a BSE of only 1. Altogether about 40% of the words have a BSE of 1 or 2. Note that all words have a BSE of atleast 1 since the empty string is also considered a valid suffix. The fraction is even higher for nouns as shown in Table 7.

It must be noted that the number of nouns with a BSE of 5 or more is in the hundreds only because of erroneous concatenations of suffixes with stems. Nouns in Hindi do not usually have more than four inflectional forms.

The scarcity of suffix evidence for most word-forms poses a huge obstacle to the extraction of a high-coverage lexicon because :

1. There are usually multiple ways to pick a stem from word-forms with a BSE of 1 or 2.
2. Spurious stems cannot be detected easily when there is no overwhelming suffix evidence in favour of the correct stem.

3.4 Gold Standard

The gold standard consists of one thousand word-forms picked at random from the intersection of the unique word-forms in the unlabelled Web-Duniya corpus and the POS labelled corpus. Each word-form in the gold standard was manually examined and a stem and a root word-form found for it.

For word-forms associated with multiple POS categories, the stem and root of a word-form were listed once for each POS category because the segmentation of a word could depend on its POS category. There were 1913 word and POS category combinations in the gold standard.

The creation of the stem gold standard needed some arbitrary choices which had to be reflected in the rules as well. These concerned some words which could be stemmed in multiple ways. For instance, the noun `laDkI` meaning 'girl' could be segmented into the morphemes `laDk` and `I` or allowed to remain unsegmented as `laDkI`. This is because by doing the former, the stems of both `laDkA` and `laDkI` could be conflated whereas by doing the latter, they could be kept separate from each other. We arbitrarily made the choice to keep nouns ending in `I` unsegmented and made our rules reflect that choice.

A second gold standard consisting of 1000 word-forms was also created to be used in evaluation and as training data for supervised algorithms. The second gold standard contained 1906 word and POS category combinations. Only word-forms that did not appear in the first gold standard were included in the second one.

3.5 Stemmer

Since the list of valid suffixes is given, the stemmer does not need to discover the stems in the language but only learn to apply the right one in the right place. We experimented with three heuristics for finding the right stem for a word-form. The heuristics were:

- Longest Suffix Match (LSM) - Picking the longest suffix that can be applied to the word-form.

- Highest Suffix Evidence (HSE) - Picking the suffix which yields the stem with the highest value for suffix evidence.

- Highest Suffix Evidence with Supervised Rule Selection (HSE + Sup) - Using labelled data to modulate suffix matching.

3.5.1 Longest Suffix Match (LSM)

In the LSM heuristic, when multiple suffixes can be applied to a word-form to stem it, we choose the longest one. Since Hindi has concatenative morphology with only postfix inflection, we only need to find one matching suffix to stem it. It is claimed in the literature that the method of using the longest suffix match works better than random suffix selection (Sarkar and Bandyopadhyay, 2008). This heuristic was used as the baseline for our experiments.

3.5.2 Highest Suffix Evidence (HSE)

In the HSE heuristic, which has been applied before to unsupervised morphological segmentation (Goldsmith, 2001), stemming (Pandey and Siddiqui, 2008), and automatic paradigm extraction (Zeman, 2007), when multiple suffixes can be applied to stem a word-form, the suffix that is picked is the one that results in the stem with the highest suffix evidence. In our case, when computing the suffix evidence, the following additional constraint is applied: all the suffixes used to compute the suffix evidence score for any stem must be associated with the same POS category.

For example, the suffix `yon` is only applicable to nouns, whereas the suffix `ta` is only applicable to verbs. These two suffixes will therefore never be counted together in computing the suffix evidence for a stem. The algorithm for determining the suffix evidence computes the suffix evidence once for each POS category and then returns the maximum.

In the absence of this constraint, the accuracy drops as the size of the raw word corpus increases.

3.5.3 HSE and Supervised Rule Selection (HSE + Sup)

The problem with the aforementioned heuristics is that there are no weights assigned to rules. Since the rules for the system were written to be as general and flexible as possible, false positives were commonly encountered. We propose a very simple supervised learning method to circumvent this problem.

The training data used was a set of 1000 word-forms sampled, like the gold standard, from the unique word-forms in the intersection of the raw text corpus and the POS labelled corpus. The set of word-forms in the training data was disjoint from the set of word-forms in the gold standard.

Rules	Accur	Prec	Recall	F-Score
Rules1	73.65%	68.25%	69.4%	68.8%
Rules2	75.0%	69.0%	77.6%	73.0%

Table 8: Comparison of Rules

Gold 1	Accur	Prec	Recall	F-Score
LSM	71.6%	65.8%	66.1%	65.9%
HSE	76.7%	70.6%	77.9%	74.1%
HSE+Sup	78.0%	72.3%	79.8%	75.9%

Gold 2	Accur	Prec	Recall	F-Score
LSM	75.7%	70.7%	72.7%	71.7%
HSE	75.0%	69.0%	77.6%	73.0%
HSE+Sup	75.3%	69.3%	78.0%	73.4%

Table 9: Comparison of Heuristics

The feature set consisted of two features: the last character (or diacritic) of the word-form, and the suffix. The POS category was an optional feature and used when available. If the number of incorrect splits exceeded the number of correct splits given a feature set, the rule was assigned a weight of 0, else it was given a weight of 1.

3.5.4 Comparison

We compare the performance of our rules with the performance of the Lightweight Stemmer for Hindi (Ramanathan and Rao, 2003) with a reported accuracy of 81.5%. The scores we report in Table 8 are the average of the LSM scores on the two gold standards. The stemmer using the standard rule-set (Rules1) does not perform as well as the Lightweight Stemmer. We then handcrafted a different set of rules (Rules2) with adjustments to maximize its performance. The accuracy was better than Rules1 but not quite equal to the Lightweight Stemmer. However, since our gold standard is different from that used to evaluate the Lightweight Stemmer, the comparison is not necessarily very meaningful.

As shown in Table 9, in F-score comparisons, HSE seems to outperform LSM and HSE+Sup seems to outperform HSE, but the improvement in performance is not very large in the case of the second gold standard. In terms of accuracy scores, LSM outperforms HSE and HSE+Sup when evaluated against the second gold standard.

POS	Correct	Incorrect	POS Errors
Noun	749	231	154
Verb	324	108	0
Adjective	227	49	13
Others	136	82	35

Table 10: Errors by POS Category

3.5.5 Error Analysis

Table 10 lists the number of correct stems, incorrect stems, and finally a count of those incorrect stems that the HSE+Sup heuristic would have gotten right if the POS category had been available. From the numbers it appears that a sizeable fraction of the errors, especially with noun word-forms, is caused when a suffix of the wrong POS category is applied to a word-form. Moreover, prior work in Bangla (Sarkar and Bandyopadhyay, 2008) indicates that POS category information could improve the accuracy of stemming.

Assigning POS categories to word-forms requires a POS tagger and a substantial amount of POS labelled data as described below.

3.5.6 POS Tagging

The POS tagset used was the hierarchical tagset IL-POST (Sankaran et al., 2008). The hierarchical tagset supports broad POS categories like nouns and verbs, less broad POS types like common and proper nouns and finally, at its finest granularity, attributes like gender, number, case and mood.

We found that with a training corpus of about 45,000 tagged words (2366 sentences), it was possible to produce a reasonably accurate POS tagger[2], use it to label the raw text corpus with broad POS tags, and consequently improve the accuracy of stemming. For our experiments, we used both the full training corpus of 45,000 words and a subset of the same consisting of about 20,000 words. The POS tagging accuracies obtained were approximately 87% and 65% respectively.

The reason for repeating the experiment using the 20,000 word subset of the training data was to demonstrate that a mere 20,000 words of labelled data, which does not take a very great amount of

[2]The Part-of-Speech tagger used was an implementation of a Cyclic Dependency Network Part-of-Speech tagger (Toutanova et al., 2003). The following feature set was used in the tagger: tag of previous word, tag of next word, word prefixes and suffixes of length exactly four, bigrams and the presence of numbers or symbols.

time and effort to create, can produce significant improvements in stemming performance.

In order to assign tags to the words of the gold standard, sentences from the raw text corpus containing word-forms present in the gold standard were tagged using a POS tagger. The POS categories assigned to each word-form were then read off and stored in a table.

Once POS tags were associated with all the words, a more restrictive criterion for matching a rule to a word-form could be used to calculate the BSE in order to determine the stem of the word-form. When searching for rules, and consequently the suffixes, to be applied to a word-form, only rules whose γ value matches the word-form's POS category were considered. We shall call the HSE heuristic that uses POS information in this way HSE+Pos.

3.6 Root Selection

The stem lexicon obtained by the process described above had to be converted into a root word-form lexicon. A root word-form lexicon is in some cases more useful than a stem lexicon, for the following reasons:

1. Morphological lexicons are traditionally indexed by root word-forms

2. Multiple root word-forms may map to one stem and be conflated.

3. Tools that use the morphological lexicon may expect the lexicon to consist of roots instead of stems.

4. Multiple root word-forms may map to one stem and be conflated.

5. Stems are entirely dependent on the way stemming rules are crafted. Roots are independent of the stemming rules.

The stem lexicon can be converted into a root lexicon using the raw text corpus and the morphological rules that were used for stemming, as follows:

1. For any word-form and its stem, list all rules that match.

2. Generate all the root word-forms possible from the matching rules and stems.

3. From the choices, select the root word-form with the highest frequency in the corpus.

Relative frequencies of word-forms have been used in previous work to detect incorrect affix attachments in Bengali and English (Dasgupta and Ng, 2007). Our evaluation of the system showed that relative frequencies could be very effective predictors of root word-forms when applied within the framework of a rule-based system.

4 Evaluation

The goal of our experiment was to build a high-coverage morphological lexicon for Hindi and to evaluate the same. Having developed a multi-stage system for lexicon extraction with a POS tagging step following by stemming and root word-form discovery, we proceeded to evaluate it as follows.

The stemming and the root discovery module were evaluated against the gold standard of 1000 word-forms. In the first experiment, the precision and recall of stemming using the HSE+Pos algorithm were measured at different POS tagging accuracies.

In the second experiment the root word-form discovery module was provided the entire raw word corpus to use in determining the best possible candidate for a root and tested using the gold standard. The scores obtained reflect the performance of the overall system.

For stemming, the recall was calculated as the fraction of stems and suffixes in the gold standard that were returned by the stemmer for each word-form examined. The precision was calculated as the fraction of stems and suffixes returned by the stemmer that matched the gold standard. The F-score was calculated as the harmonic mean of the precision and recall.

The recall of the root lexicon was measured as the fraction of gold standard roots that were in the lexicon. The precision was calculated as the fraction of roots in the lexicon that were also in the gold standard. Accuracy was the percentage of gold word-forms' roots that were matched exactly.

In order to approximately estimate the accuracy of a stemmer or morphological analyzer that used such a lexicon, we also calculated the accuracy weighted by the frequency of the word-forms in a small corpus of running text. The gold standard tokens were seen in this corpus about 4400 times. We only considered content words (nouns, verbs, adjectives and adverbs) in this calculation.

Gold1	Accur	Prec	Recall	F-Sco
POS	86.7%	82.4%	86.2%	84.2%
Sup+POS	88.2%	85.2%	87.3%	86.3%
Gold2	**Accur**	**Prec**	**Recall**	**F-Sco**
POS	81.8%	77.8%	82.0%	79.8%
Sup+POS	83.5%	80.2%	82.6%	81.3%

Table 11: Stemming Performance Comparisons

Gold 1	Accur	Prec	Recall	F-Sco
No POS	76.7%	70.6%	77.9%	74.1%
65% POS	82.3%	77.5%	81.4%	79.4%
87% POS	85.4%	80.8%	85.1%	82.9%
Gold POS	86.7%	82.4%	86.2%	84.2%

Table 12: Stemming Performance at Different POS Tagger Accuracies

5 Results

The performance of our system using POS tag information is comparable to that obtained by Sarkar and Bandyopadhyay (2008). Sarkar and Bandyopadhyay (2008) obtained stemming accuracies of 90.2% for Bangla using gold POS tags. So in the comparisons in Table 11, we use gold POS tags (row two) and also supervised learning (row three) using the other gold corpus as the labelled training corpus. We present the scores for the two gold standards separately. It must be noted that Sarkar and Bandyopadhyay (2008) conducted their experiments on Bangla, and so the results are not exactly comparable.

We also evaluate the performance of stemming using HSE with POS tagging by a real tagger at two different tagging accuracies - approximately 65% and 87% - as shown in Table 12. We compare the performance with gold POS tags and a baseline system which does not use POS tags. We do not use labelled training data for this section of the experiments and only evaluate against the first gold standard.

Table 13 compares the F-scores for root discovery at different POS tagging accuracies against a baseline which excludes the use of POS tags altogether. There seems to be very little prior work that we can use for comparison here. To our knowledge, the closest comparable work is a system built by Oliver and Tadić (2004) in order to enlarge a Croatian Morphological Lexicon. The overall performance reported by Tadić et al was as follows: (precision=86.13%, recall=35.36%, F1=50.14%).

Gold 1	Accur	Prec	Recall	F-Sco
No POS	71.7%	77.6%	78.8%	78.1%
65% POS	82.5%	87.2%	88.9%	88.0%
87% POS	87.0%	94.1%	95.3%	94.6%
Gold POS	89.1%	95.4%	97.9%	96.6%

Table 13: Root Finding Accuracy

Gold 1	Stemming	Root Finding
65% POS	85.6%	87.0%
87% POS	87.5%	90.6%
Gold POS	88.5%	90.2%

Table 14: Weighted Stemming and Root Finding Accuracies (only Content Words)

Lastly, Table 14 shows the accuracy of stemming and root finding weighted by the frequencies of the words in a running text corpus. This was calculated only for content words.

6 Conclusion

We have described a system for automatically constructing a root word-form lexicon from a raw text corpus. The system is rule-based and utilizes a POS tagger. Though preliminary, our results demonstrate that it is possible, using this method, to extract a high-precision and high-recall root word-form lexicon. Specifically, we show that with a POS tagger capable of labelling word-forms with POS categories at an accuracy of about 88%, we can extract root word-forms with an accuracy of about 87% and a precision and recall of 94.1% and 95.3% respectively.

Though the system has been evaluated on Hindi, the techniques described herein can probably be applied to other inflectional languages. The rules selected by the system and applied to the word-forms also contain information that can be used to determine the paradigm membership of each root word-form. Further work could evaluate the accuracy with which we can accomplish this task.

7 Acknowledgements

We would like to thank our colleagues Priyanka Biswas, Kalika Bali and Shalini Hada, of Microsoft Research India, for their assistance in the creation of the Hindi root and stem gold standards.

References

Lionel Clément, Benoît Sagot and Bernard Lang. 2004. Morphology based automatic acquisition of large-coverage lexica. In *Proceedings of LREC 2004*, Lisbon, Portugal.

Sajib Dasgupta and Vincent Ng. 2007. High-Performance, Language-Independent Morphological Segmentation. In *Main Proceedings of NAACL HLT 2007*, Rochester, NY, USA.

Markus Forsberg, Harald Hammarström and Aarne Ranta. 2006. Morphological Lexicon Extraction from Raw Text Data. In *Proceedings of the 5th International Conference on Advances in Natural Language Processing, FinTAL*, Finland.

John A. Goldsmith. 2001. Linguistica: An Automatic Morphological Analyzer. In *Arika Okrent and John Boyle, editors, CLS 36: The Main Session, volume 36-1*, Chicago Linguistic Society, Chicago.

Erika de Lima. 1998. Induction of a Stem Lexicon for Two-Level Morphological Analysis. In *Proceedings of the Joint Conferences on New Methods in Language Processing and Computational Natural Language Learning, NeMLaP3/CoNLL98, pp 267-268*, Sydney, Australia.

Antoni Oliver, Marko Tadić. 2004. Enlarging the Croatian Morphological Lexicon by Automatic Lexical Acquisition from Raw Corpora. In *Proceedings of LREC 2004*, Lisbon, Portugal.

Amaresh Kumar Pandey and Tanveer J. Siddiqui. 2008. An Unsupervised Hindi Stemmer with Heuristic Improvements. In *Proceedings of the Second Workshop on Analytics for Noisy Unstructured Text Data, AND 2008, pp 99-105*, Singapore.

A Ramanathan and D. D. Rao. 2003. A Lightweight Stemmer for Hindi. Presented at *EACL 2003*, Budapest, Hungary.

Benoît Sagot. 2005. Automatic Acquisition of a Slovak Lexicon from a Raw Corpus. In *Lecture Notes in Artificial Intelligence 3658, Proceedings of TSD'05*, Karlovy Vary, Czech Republic.

Benoît Sagot. 2007. Building a Morphosyntactic Lexicon and a Pre-Syntactic Processing Chain for Polish. In *Proceedings of LTC 2007*, Poznań, Poland.

Benoît Sagot, Lionel Clément, Éric Villemonte de la Clergerie and Pierre Boullier. 2006. The Lefff 2 Syntactic Lexicon for French: Architecture, Acquisition, Use. In *Proceedings of LREC'06*, Genoa, Italy.

Baskaran Sankaran, Kalika Bali, Monojit Choudhury, Tanmoy Bhattacharya, Pushpak Bhattacharyya, Girish Nath Jha, S. Rajendran, K. Saravanan, L. Sobha and K.V. Subbarao. 2008. A Common Parts-of-Speech Tagset Framework for Indian Languages. In *Proceedings of the Sixth International Language Resources and Evaluation (LREC'08)*, Marrakech, Morocco.

Sandipan Sarkar and Sivaji Bandyopadhyay. 2008. Design of a Rule-based Stemmer for Natural Language Text in Bengali. In *Proceedings of the IJCNLP-08 Workshop on NLP for Less Privileged Languages*, Hyderabad, India.

Kristina Toutanova, Dan Klein, Christopher D. Manning and Yoram Singer. 2003. Feature-Rich Part-of-Speech Tagging with a Cyclic Dependedependency Network In *Proceedings of HLT-NAACL 2003 pages 252-259.*

Daniel Zeman. 2007. Unsupervised Acquisition of Morphological Paradigms from Tokenized Text. In *Working Notes for the Cross Language Evaluation Forum CLEF 2007 Workshop*, Budapest, Hungary.

Lexical Morphology in Machine Translation: a Feasibility Study

Bruno Cartoni
University of Geneva
cartonib@gmail.com

Abstract

This paper presents a feasibility study for implementing lexical morphology principles in a machine translation system in order to solve unknown words. Multilingual symbolic treatment of word-formation is seducing but requires an in-depth analysis of every step that has to be performed. The construction of a prototype is firstly presented, highlighting the methodological issues of such approach. Secondly, an evaluation is performed on a large set of data, showing the benefits and the limits of such approach.

1 Introduction

Formalising morphological information to deal with morphologically constructed unknown words in machine translation seems attractive, but raises many questions about the resources and the prerequisites (both theoretical and practical) that would make such symbolic treatment efficient and feasible. In this paper, we describe the prototype we built to evaluate the feasibility of such approach. We focus on the knowledge required to build such system and on its evaluation. First, we delimit the issue of neologisms amongst the other unknown words (section 2), and we present the few related work done in NLP research (section 3). We then explain why implementing morphology in the context of machine translation (MT) is a real challenge and what kind of aspects need to be taken into account (section 4), and we show that translating constructed neologisms is not only a mechanical decomposition but requires more fine-grained analysis. We then describe the methodology developed to build up a prototyped *translator* of constructed neologisms (section 5) with all the extensions that have to be made, especially in terms of resources. Finally, we concentrate on the evaluation of each step of the process and on the global evaluation of the entire approach (section 6). This last evaluation highlights a set of methodological criteria that are needed to exploit lexical morphology in machine translation.

2 Issues

Unknown words are a problematic issue in any NLP tool. Depending on the studies (Ren and Perrault 1992; Maurel 2004), it is estimated that between 5 and 10 % of the words of a text written in "standard" language are unknown to lexical resources. In a MT context (analysis-transfer-generation), unknown words remain not only unanalysed but they cannot be translated, and sometimes they also stop the translation of the whole sentence.

Usually, three main groups of unknown words are distinguished: proper names, errors, and neologisms, and the possible solution highly depends on the type of unknown word to be solved. In this paper, we concentrate on neologisms which are constructed following a morphological process.

The processing of unknown "constructed neologisms" in NLP can be done by simple guessing (based on the sequence of final letters). This option can be efficient enough when the task is only tagging, but in a multilingual context (like in MT), dealing with constructed neologisms implies a transfer and a generation process that require a more complex formalisation and implementation. In the project presented in this paper, we propose to implement lexical morphology phenomena in MT.

3 Related work

Implementing lexical morphology in a MT context has seldom been investigated in the past, probably because many researchers share the following view: "Though the idea of providing rules for translating derived words may seem attractive, it raises many problems and so it is currently more of a research goal for MT than a practical possibility" (Arnold, Balkan et al. 1994). As far as we know, the only related project is described in (Gdaniec, Manandise et al. 2001), where they describe a project of implementation of rules for dealing with constructed words in the IBM MT system.

Proceedings of the 12th Conference of the European Chapter of the ACL, pages 130–138,
Athens, Greece, 30 March – 3 April 2009. ©2009 Association for Computational Linguistics

Even in monolingual contexts, lexical morphology is not very often implemented in NLP. Morphological analyzers like the ones described in (Porter 1980; Byrd 1983; Byrd, Klavans et al. 1989; Namer 2005) propose more or less deeper lexical analyses, to exploit that dimension of the lexicon.

4 Proposed solution

Since morphological processes are regular and exist in many languages, we propose an approach where constructed neologisms in source language (SL) can be analysed and their translation generated in a target language (TL) through the transfer of the constructional information.

For example, a constructed neologism in one language (e.g. *ricostruire* in Italian) should firstly be analysed, i.e. find (i) the rule that produced it (in this case <reiteration rule>) and (ii) the lexeme-base which it is constructed on (*costruire,* with all morphosyntactic and translational information). Secondly, through a transfer mechanism (of both the rule and the base), a translation can be generated by rebuilding a constructed word, (in French *reconstruire,* Eng: to rebuild). On a theoretical side, the whole process is formalised into bilingual Lexeme Formation Rules (LFR), as explained below in section 4.3.

Although this approach seems to be simple and attractive, feasibility studies and evaluation should be carefully performed. To do so, we built a system to translate neologisms from one language into another. In order to delimit the project and to concentrate on methodological issues, we focused on the prefixation process and on two related languages (Italian and French). Prefixation is, after suffixation, the most productive process of neologism, and prefixes can be more easily processed in terms of character strings. Regarding the language, we choose to deal with the translation of Italian constructed neologisms into French. These two languages are historically and morphologically related and are consequently more "neighbours" in terms of neologism coinage.

In the following, we firstly describe precisely the phenomena that have to be formalized and then the prototype built up for the experiment.

4.1 Phenomena to be formalized

Like in any MT project, the formalisation work has to face different issues of contrastivity, i.e. highlighting the divergences and the similarities between the two languages.

In the two languages chosen for the experiment, few divergences were found in the way they construct prefixed neologisms. However, in some cases, although the morphosemantic process is similar, the item used to build it up (i.e. the affixes) is not always the same. For example, to coin nouns of the spatial location "before", where Italian uses the prefix *retro,* French uses *rétro* and *arrière*. A deeper analysis shows that Italian *retro* is used with all types of nouns, whereas in French, *rétro* only forms processual nouns (derived from verbs, like *rétrovision, rétroprojection*). For the other type of nouns (generally locative nouns), *arrière* is used (*arrière-cabine, arrière-cour).*

Other problematic issues appear when there is more than one prefix for the same LFR. For example, the rule for "indeterminate plurality" provides in both languages a set of two prefixes (*multi/pluri* in Italian and *multi/pluri* in French) with no known restrictions for selecting one or the other (e.g. both *pluridimensionnel* and *multidimensionnel* are acceptable in French). For these cases, further empirical research have to be performed to identify restrictions on the rule.

Another important divergence is found in the prefixation of relational adjectives. Relational adjectives are derived from nouns and designate a relation between the entity denoted by the noun they are derived from and the entity denoted by the noun they modify. Consequently, in a prefixation such as *anticostituzionale*, the formal base is a relational adjective (*costituzionale*), but the semantic base is the noun the adjective is derived from (*costituzione*). The constructed word *anticostituzionale* can be paraphrased as "*against the constitution*". Moreover, when the relational adjective does not exist, prefixation is possible on a nominal base to create an adjective (*squadra antidroga*). In cases where the adjective does exist, both forms are possible and seem to be equally used, like in the Italian *collaborazione interuniversità / collaborazione interuniversitaria*. From a contrastive point of view, the prefixation of relational adjectives exists in both languages (Italian and French) and in both these languages prefixing a noun to create an adjective is also possible (*anticostituzione* (Adj)). But we notice an important discrepancy in the possibility of constructing relational adjectives (a rough estimation performed on a large bilingual dictionary (Garzanti IT-FR (2006)) shows that more than 1 000 Italian relational adjectives have no equivalent in French (and are generally translated with a prepositional phrase).

All these divergences require an in-dept analysis but can be overcome only if the formalism and the implementation process are done following a rigorous methodology.

4.2 The prototype

In order to evaluate the approach described above and to concretely investigate the ins and outs of such implementation, we built up a prototype of a machine translation system specialized for constructed neologisms. This prototype is composed of two modules. The first one checks every unknown word to see if it is potentially constructed, and if so, performs a morphological analysis to individualise the lexeme-base and the rule that coined it. The second module is the actual translation module, which analyses the constructed neologism and generates a possible translation.

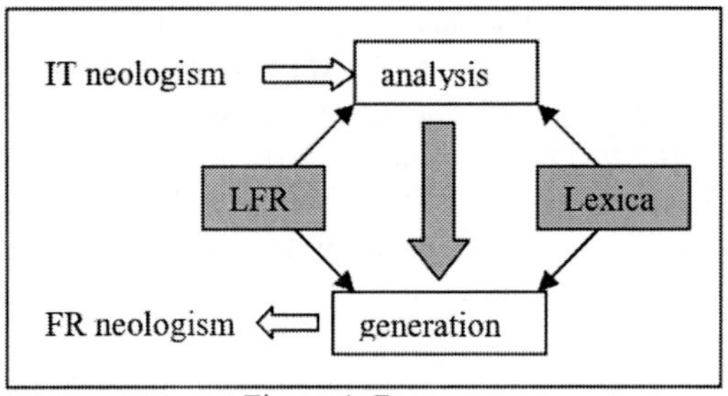

Figure 1: Prototype

The whole prototype relies on one hand on lexical resources (two monolingual and one bilingual) and on a set of bilingual Lexeme Formation Rules (LFR). These two sets of information helps the analysis and the generation steps. When a neologism is looked-up, the system checks if it is constructed with one of the LFRs and if the lexeme-base is in the lexicon. If it is the case, the transfer brings the relevant morphological and lexical information in the target language. The generation step constructs the translation equivalent, using the information provided by the LFR and the lexical resources. Consequently, the whole system relies on the quality of both the lexical resources and the LFR.

4.3 Bilingual Lexeme Formation Rules

The whole morphological process in the system is formalised through bilingual Lexeme Formation Rules. Their representation is inspired by (Fradin 2003) as shown in figure 2 in the rule of reiterativity.

Such rules match together two monolingual rules (to be read in columns). Each monolingual rule describes a process that applies a series of instructions on the different sections of the lexeme : the surface section (G and F), the syntactic category (SX) and the semantic (S) sections. In this theoretical framework, affixation is only one of the instructions of the rule (the graphemic and phonological modification), and consequently, affixes are called "exponent" of the rule.

	Italian		*French*
	input		input
(G)	V_{it}		V_{fr}
(F)	$/V_{it}/$		$/V_{fr}/$
(SX)	cat :v		cat :v
(S)	V_{it}'(...)		V_{fr}'(...)
	↕	↔	↕
	output		output
(G)	riV_{it}		reV_{fr}
(F)	/ri/⊕/V_{it}/		/ʀə/⊕/V_{fr}/
(SX)	cat :v		cat :v
(S)	reiterativity (V_{it}'(...))		reiterativity (V_{fr}'(...))

where $V_{it}' = V_{fr}'$, translation equivalent

Figure 2: Bilingual LFR of reiterativity

This formalisation is particularly useful in a bilingual context for rules that have more than one prefix in both languages: more than one affix can be declared in one single rule, the selection being made according to different constraints or restrictions. For example, the rule for "indeterminate plurality" explained in section 4.1 can be formalised as follows:

	Italian		*French*
	input		input
(G)	X_{it}		X_{fr}
(F)	$/X_{it}/$		$/X_{fr}/$
(SX)	cat :n		cat :n
(S)	X_{it}'(...)		X_{fr}'(...)
	↕	↔	↕
	output		output
(G)	multi/pluriX_{it}		multi/pluriX_{fr}
(F)	/multi/pluri/⊕/X_{it}/		/mʏlti/plʏri/⊕/X_{fr}/
(SX)	cat :n		cat :n
(S)	indet. plur. (X_{it}'(...))		indet. plur. (X_{fr}'(...))

where $X_{it}' = X_{fr}'$, translation equivalent

Figure 3: Bilingual LFR of indeterminate plurality

In this kind of rules with "multiple exponents", the two possible prefixes are declared in the surface section (G and F). The selection is a monolingual issue and cannot be done at the theoretical level.

Such rules have been formalised and implemented for the 56 productive prefixes of Italian (Iacobini 2004)[1], with their French translation equivalent. However, finding the translation equivalent for each rule requires specific studies

[1] i.e. *a, ad, anti, arci, auto, co, contro, de, dis, ex, extra, in, inter, intra, iper, ipo, macro, maxi, mega, meta, micro, mini, multi, neo, non, oltre, onni, para, pluri, poli, post, pre, pro, retro, ri, s, semi, sopra, sotto, sovra, stra, sub, super, trans, ultra, vice, mono, uni, bi, di, tri, quasi, pseudo.*

of the morphological system of both languages in a contrastive perspective.

The following section briefly summarises the contrastive analysis that has been performed to acquire this type of contrastive knowledge.

4.4 Knowledge acquisition of bilingual LFR

As in any MT system, the acquisition of bilingual knowledge is an important issue. In morphology, the method should be particularly accurate to prevent any methodological bias. To formalise translation rules for prefixed neologisms, we adopt a meaning-to-form approach, i.e. discovering how a constructed meaning is morphologically realised in two languages.

We build up a *tertium comparationis* (a neutral platform, see (James 1980) for details) that constitute a semantic typology of prefixation processes. This typology aims to be universal and therefore applicable to all the languages concerned. On a practical point of view, the typology has been built up by summing up various descriptions of prefixation in various languages (Montermini 2002; Iacobini 2004; Amiot 2005). We end up with six main classes*: location, evaluation, quantitative, modality, negation and ingressive*. The classes are then subdivided according to sub-meanings: for example, *location* is subdivided in *temporal* and *spatial*, and within *spatial location,* a distinction is made between different positions (*before, above, below, in front, ...*).

Prefixes of both languages are then literally "projected" (or classified) onto the *tertium*. For each terminal sub-class, we have a clear picture of the prefixes involved in both languages. For example, the LFR presented in figure 1 is the result of the projection of the Italian prefix (*ri*) and the French one (*re*) on the sub-class *reiterativity,* which is a sub-class of *modality*.

At the end of the comparison, we end up with more than 100 LFRs (one rule can be reiterated according the different input and output categories). From a computing point of view, constraints have to be specified and the lexicon has to be adapted consequently.

5 Implementation

Implementation of the LFR is set up as a database, from where the program takes the information to perform the analysis, the transfer and the generation of the neologisms. In our approach, LFRs are simply declared in a tab format database, easily accessible and modifiable by the user, as shown below:

```
arci  a      a  2.1.2   archi
arci  n      n  2.1.2   archi
[...]
pro   a_rel  a  1.1.10  pro
pro   n      a  1.1.10  pro
[...]
ri    v      v  6.1     re
ri    n_dev  n  6.1     re
[...]
```

Figure 4: Implemented LFRs

Implemented LFRs describe (i) the surface form of the Italian prefix to be analysed, (ii) the category of the base, (iii) the category of the derived lexeme (*the output*), (iv) a reference to the rule implied and (v) the French prefix(es) for the generation.

The surface form in (i) should sometimes take into account the different allomorphs of one prefix. Consequently, the rule has to be reiterated in order to be able to recognize any forms (e.g. the prefix *in* has different forms according to the initial letter of the base, and four rules have to be implemented for the four allomorphs (*in, il, im, ir*)). In some other cases, the initial consonant is doubled, and the algorithm has to take this phenomenon into account.

In (ii), the information of the category of the base has been "overspecified", to differentiate qualitative and relational adjectives, and deverbal nouns and the other ones (`a_rel/a` or `n_dev/n`). These overspecifications have two objectives: optimizing the analysis performance (reducing the noise of homographic character strings that look like constructed neologisms but that are only misspellings - see below in the evaluation section), and refining the analysis, i.e. selecting the appropriate LFR and, consequently, the appropriate translation.

To identify relational adjectives and deverbal nouns, the monolingual lexicon that supports the analysis step has to be extended. Thereafter, we present the symbolic method we used to perform such extension.

5.1 Extension of the monolingual lexicon

Our MT prototype relies on lexical resources: it aims at dealing with unknown words that are not in a Reference lexicon and these unknown words are analyzed with lexical material that is in this lexicon.

From a practical point of view, our prototype is based on two very large monolingual databases (*Mmorph* (Bouillon, Lehmann *et al.* 1998)) for Italian and French, that contain only morpho-syntactic information, and on one bilingual lexicon that has been built semi-automatically for the use of the experiment. But the monolingual lexica have to be adapted to provide specific information necessary for dealing with morphological process.

As stated above, identifying the prefix and the base is not enough to provide a proper analysis of constructed neologisms which is detailed enough to be translated. The main information that is essential for the achievement of the process is the category of the base, which has to be sometimes "overspecified". Obviously, the Italian reference lexicon does not contain such information. Consequently, we looked for a simple way to automatically extend the Italian lexicon. For example, we looked for a way to automatically link **relational adjectives** with their noun bases.

Our approach tries to take advantage of only the lexicon, without the use of any larger resources. To extend the Italian lexicon, we simply built a routine based on the typical suffixes of relational adjectives (in Italian: *-ale, -are, -ario, -ano, -ico, -ile, -ino, -ivo, -orio, -esco, -asco, -iero, -izio, -aceo* (Wandruszka 2004)). For every adjective ending with one of these suffixes, the routine looks up if the potential base corresponds to a noun in the rest of the lexicon (modulo some morphographemic variations). For example, the routine is able to find links between adjectives and base nouns such as *ambientale* and *ambiente, aziendale* and *azienda, cortisonica* and *cortisone* or *contestuale* and *contesto.* Unfortunately, this kind of automatic implementation does not find links between adjectives made from the learned root of the noun, (*prandiale → pranzo, bellico → guerra*).

This automatic extension has been evaluated. Out of a total of more than 68 000 adjective forms in the lexicon, we identified 8 466 relational adjectives. From a "recall" perspective, it is not easy to evaluate the coverage of this extension because of the small number of resources containing relational adjectives that could be used as a gold standard.

A similar extension is performed for the deverbal aspect, for the lexicon should also distinguish **deverbal noun**. From a morphological point of view, deverbalisation can be done trough two main productive processes: conversion (*a command → to command*) and suffixation. If the first one is relatively difficult to implement, the second one can be easily captured using the typical suffixes of such processes. Consequently, we considere that any noun ending with suffixes like *ione, aggio,*or *mento* are deverbal.

Thanks to this extended lexicon, overspecified input categories (like `a_rel` for *relational adjective* or `n_dev` for *deverbal noun*) can be stated and exploited in the implemented LFR as shown in figure 4.

5.2 Applying LFRs to translate neologisms

Once the prototyped MT system was built and the lexicon adapted, it was applied to a set of neologisms (see section 6 for details). For example, unknown Italian neologisms such as *arci-contento, ridescrizione, deitalianizzare,* were automatically translated in French: *archi-content, redescription, désitalianiser.*

The divergences existing in the LFR of <locative position before> are correctly dealt with, thanks to the correct analysis of the base. For example, in the neologism *retrobottega,* the lexeme-base is correctly identified as a locative noun, and the French equivalent is constructed with the appropriate prefix (*arrière-boutique*), while in *retrodiffusione,* the base is analysed as *deverbal,* and the French equivalent is correctly generated (*rétrodiffusion*).

For the analysis of relational adjectives, the overspecification of the LFRs and the extension of the lexicon are particularly useful when there is no French equivalent for Italian relational adjectives because the corresponding construction is not possible in the French morphological system. For example, the Italian relational adjective *aziendale* (from the noun *azienda,* Eng: company) has no adjectival equivalent in French. The Italian prefixed adjective *interaziendale* can only be translated in French by using a noun as the base (*interentreprise*). This translation equivalent can be found only if the base noun of the Italian adjective is found (*interaziendale, inter+aziendale → azienda, azienda = entreprise, → interentreprise*). The same process has been applied for the translation of *precongressuale, post-transfuzionale* by *précongrès, post-transfusion.*

Obviously, all the mechanisms formalised in this prototype should be carefully evaluated.

6 Evaluation

The advantages of this approach should be carefully evaluated from two points of view: the evaluation of the performance of each step and of the feasibility and portability of the system.

6.1 corpus

As previously stated, the system is intended to solve neologisms that are unknown from a lexicon with LFRs that exploit information contained in the lexicon. To evaluate the performance of our system, we built up a corpus of unknown words by confronting a large Italian corpus from journalistic domain (*La Repubblica Online* (Baroni, Bernardini et al. 2004)) with our reference lexicon for this language (see section 4.1 above). We obtained a set of unknown words that contains neologisms, but also proper names and erroneous items. This set is submitted to the various steps of the system, where constructed neologisms are recognised, analysed and translated.

6.2 Evaluation of the performance of the analysis

As we previously stated, the analysis step can actually be divided into two tasks. First of all, the program has to identify, among the unknown words, which of them are morphologically constructed (and so analysable by the LFRs); secondly, the program has to analyse the constructed neologisms, i.e matching them with the correct LFRs and isolating the correct base-words.

For the first task, we obtain a list of 42 673 potential constructed neologisms. Amongst those, there are a number of erroneous words that are homographic to a constructed neologism. For example, the item *progesso,* a misspelling of *progresso* (Eng: *progress*), is erroneously analysed as the prefixation of *gesso* (eng: *plaster*) with the LFR in *pro.*

In the second part of the processing, LFRs are concretely applied to the potential neologisms (i.e. constraints on categories and on overspecified category, phonological constraints). This stage retains 30 376 neologisms. A manual evaluation is then performed on these outputs. Globally, 71.18 % of the analysed words are actually neologisms. But the performance is not the same for every rule. Most of them are very efficient: among all the rules for the 56 Italian prefixes, only 7 cause too many erroneous analyses, and should be excluded - mainly rules with very short prefixes (like *a, di, s*), that cause mistakes due to homograph.

As explained above, some of the rules are strongly specified, (i.e. very constrained), so we also evaluate the consequence of some constraints, not only in terms of improved performance but also in terms of loss of information. Indeed, some of the constraints specified in the rule exclude some neologisms (false negatives). For example, the modality LFRs with *co* and *ri* have been overspecified, requiring deverbal base-noun (and not just a noun). Adding this constraint improves the performance of the analysis (i.e. the number of correct lexemes analysed), respectively from 69.48 % to 96 % and from 91.21 % to 99.65 %. Obviously, the number of false negatives (i.e. correct neologisms excluded by the constraint) is very large (between 50 % and 75 % of the excluded items).

In this situation, the question is to decide whether the gain obtained by the constraints (the improved performance) is more important than the un-analysed items. In this context, we prefer to keep the more constrained rule. Un-analysed items remain unknown words, and the output of the analysis is almost perfect, which is an important condition for the rest of the process (i.e. transfer and generation).

6.3 Evaluation of the performance of the generation

Generation can also be evaluated according to two points of view: the correctness of the generated items, and the improvement brought by the solved words to the quality of the translated sentence.

To evaluate the first aspect, many procedures can be put in place. The correctness of constructed words could be evaluated by human judges, but this kind of approach would raise many questions and biases: people that are not expert of morphology would judge the correctness according to their degree of *acceptability* which varies between judges and is particularly sensitive when neologism is concerned. Questions of homogeneity in terms of knowledge of the domain and of the language are also raised.

Because of these difficulties, we prefer to centre the evaluation on the existence of the generated neologisms in a corpus. For neologisms, the most adequate corpus is the Internet, even if the use of such an uncontrolled resource requires some precautions (see (Fradin, Dal et al. 2007) for a complete debate on the use of web resources in morphology).

Concretely, we use the robot Golf (Thomas 2008) that sends each generated neologism automatically as a request on a search engine (here Google©) and reports the number of occurrences as captured by Google. This robot can be parameterized, for instance by selecting the appropriate language.

Because of the uncontrolled aspect of the resource, we distinguish three groups of reported frequencies: 0 occurrence, less than 5 occurrences and more than 5. The threshold of 5 helps to distinguish confirmed existence of neologism (> 5) from unstable appearances (< 5), that are closed to hapax phenomena.

The table below summarizes some results for some prefixed neologisms.

Prefix	tested forms	0 occ.	< 5 occ.	> 5 occ.
ri	391	8.2 %	5.6 %	86.2 %
anti	1120	8.6 %	19.9 %	71.5 %
de	114	2.6 %	3.5 %	93.9 %
super	951	28 %	30 %	42 %
pro	166	6.6 %	29.5 %	63.9 %
...				

Table 1 : Some evaluation results

Globally, most of the generated prefixed neologisms have been found in corpus, and most of the time with more than 5 occurrences. Unfound items are very useful, because they help to point out difficulties or miss-formalised processes. Most of the unfound neologisms were ill-analysed items in Italian. Others were due to misuses of hyphens in the generation. Indeed, in the program, we originally implemented the use of the hyphen in French following the established norm (i.e. a hyphen is required when the prefix ends with a vowel and the base starts with a vowel). But following this "norm", some forms were not found in corpus (for example *antibraconnier* (Eng: *antipoacher*) reports 0 occurrence). When re-generated with a hyphen, it reports 63 occurrences. This last point shows that in neology, usage does not stick always to the norm.

The other problem raised by unknown words is that they decrease the quality of the translation of the entire sentence. To evaluate the impact of the translated unknown words on the translated sentence, we built up a test-suite of sentences, each of them containing one prefixed neologism (in bold in table 2). We then submitted the sentences to a commercial MT system (Systran©) and recorded the translation and counted the number of mistakes (FR1 in table 2 below). On a second step, we "feed" the lexicon of the translation system with the neologisms and their translation (generated by our prototype) and resubmit the same sentences to the system (FR2 in table 2).

For the 60 sentences of the test-suit (21 with an unknown verb, 19 with an unknown adjective and 20 with a unknown noun), we then counted the number of errors before and after the introduction of the neologisms in the lexicon, as shown below (errors are underlined).

IT	Le **defiscalizzazioni** logiche di 17 Euro sono previste	
FR1	Le defiscalizzazioni logiques de 17 Euro sont prévus	2
FR2	Les défiscalisations logiques de 17 Euro sont prévues	0

Table 2: Example of a tested sentence

For a global view of the evaluation, we classified in the table below the number of sentences according to the number of errors "removed" thanks to the resolution of the unknown word.

	0	-1	-2	-3
Nouns		10	8	2
Adjectives		18	1	
Verbs	2	14	3	2

Table 3: Reduction of the number of errors/sentence

Most of the improvements concern only a reduction of 1, i.e. only the unknown word has been solved. But it should be noticed that improvement is more impressive when the unknown words are nouns or verbs, probably because these categories influence much more items in the sentence in terms of agreement.

In two cases (involving verbs), errors are corrected because of the translation of the unknown words, but at the same time, two other errors are caused by it. This problem comes from the fact that adding new words in the lexicon of the system requires sometimes more information (such as valency) to provide a proper syntaxctic generation of the sentence.

6.4 Evaluation of feasibility and portability

The relatively good results obtained by the prototype are very encouraging. They mainly show that if the analysis step is performed correctly, the rest of the process can be done with not much further work. But at the end of such a feasibility study, it is useful to look objectively for the conditions that make such results possible.

The good quality of the result can be explained by the important preliminary work done (i) in the extension/specialisation of the lexicon, and (ii) in the setting up of the LFRs. The acquisition of the contrastive knowledge in a MT context is indeed the most essential issue in this kind of approach. The methodology we proposed here for setting these LFR proves to be useful for the linguist to acquire this specific type of knowledge.

Lexical morphology is often considered as not regular enough to be exploited in NLP. The evaluation performed in this study shows that it is not the case, especially in neologism. But in some cases, it is no use to ask for the impossible, and simply give up implementing the most inefficient rules.

We also show that the efficient analysis step is probably the main condition to make the whole system work. This step should be implemented with as much constraints as possible, to provide an output without errors. Such implementation requires proper evaluation of the impact of every constraint.

It should also be stated that such implementation (and especially knowledge acquisition) is time-consuming, and one can legitimately ask if machine-learning methods would do the job. The number of LFRs being relatively restrained in producing neologisms, we can say that the effort of manual formalisation is worthwhile for the benefits that should be valuable on the long term. Another aspect of the feasibility is closely related to questions of "interoperability", because such implementation should be done within existing MT programs, and not independently as it was for this feasibility study.

Other questions of portability should also be considered. As we stated, we chose two morphologically related languages on purpose: they present less divergences to deal with and allow concentrating on the method. However, the proposed method (especially that contrastive knowledge acquisition) can clearly be ported to another pair of languages (at least inflexional languages). It should also be noticed that the same approach can be applied to other types of construction. We mainly think here of suffixation, but one can imagine to use LFRs with other elements of formation (like combining forms, that tend to be very "international", and consequently the material for many neologisms). Moreover, the way the rules are formalised and the algorithm designed allow easy reversibility and modification.

7 Conclusion

This feasibility study presents the benefit of implementing lexical morphology principles in a MT system. It presents all the issues raised by formalization and implementation, and shows in a quantitative manner how those principles are useful to partly solve unknown words in machine translation.

From a broader perspective, we show the benefits of such implementation in a MT system, but also the method that should be used to formalise this special kind of information. We also emphasize the need for in-dept work of knowledge acquisition before actually building up the system, especially because contrastive morphological data are not as obvious as other linguistic dimensions.

Moreover, the evaluation step clearly states that the analysis module is the most important issue in dealing with lexical morphology in multilingual context.

The multilingual approach of morphology also paves the way for other researches, either in representation of word-formation or in exploitation of multilingual dimension in NLP systems.

References

(2006) *Garzanti francese : francese-italiano, italiano-francese.* I grandi dizionari Garzanti. Milano, Garzanti Linguistica.

Amiot, D. (2005) *Between compounding and derivation: elements of word formation corresponding to prepositions.* Morphology and its Demarcations. W. U. Dressler, R. Dieter and F. Rainer. Amsterdam, John Benjamins Publishing Company: 183-195.

Arnold, D., L. Balkan, R. L. Humphrey, S. Meijer and L. Sadler (1994) *Machine Translation. An Introductory Guide.* Manchester, NCC Blackwell.

Baroni, M., S. Bernardini, F. Comastri, L. Piccioni, A. Volpi, G. Aston and M. Mazzoleni (2004) *Introducing the "la Repubblica" corpus: A large, annotated, TEI(XML)-compliant corpus of newspaper Italian.* Proceedings of LREC 2004, Lisbon: 1771-1774.

Bouillon, P., S. Lehmann, S. Manzi and D. Petitpierre (1998) *Développement de lexiques à grande échelle.* Proceedings of Colloque des journées LTT de TUNIS, Tunis: 71-80.

Byrd, R. J. (1983) *Word Formation in Natural Language Processing Systems.* IJCAI: 704-706.

Byrd, R. J., J. L. Klavans, M. Aronoff and F. Anshen (1989) *Computer methods for morphological analysis* Proceedings of 24th annual meeting on Association for Computational Linguistics, New York, New York Association for Computational Linguistics: 120-127

Fradin, B., G. Dal, N. Grabar, F. Namer, S. Lignon, D. Tribout and P. Zweigenbaum (2007) *Remarques sur l'usage des corpus en morphologie.* Langages 167.

Gdaniec, C., E. Manandise and M. C. McCord (2001) *Derivational Morphology to the Rescue: How It Can Help Resolve Unfound Words in MT.* Proceedings of MT Summit VIII, Santiago Di Compostella: 127-131.

Iacobini, C. (2004) *I prefissi*. La formazione delle parole in italiano. M. Grossmann and F. Rainer. Tübingen, Niemeyer: 99-163.

James, C. (1980) *Contrastive analysis*. Burnt Mill, Longman.

Maurel, D. (2004) *Les mots inconnus sont-ils des noms propres?* Proceedings of JADT 2004, Louvain-la-Neuve

Montermini, F. (2002) *Le système préfixal en italien contemporain*, Université de Paris X-Nanterre, Università degli Studi di Bologna: 355.

Namer, F. (2005) *La morphologie constructionnelle du français et les propriétés sémantiques du lexique: traitement automatique et modélisation*. UMR 7118 ATILF. Nancy, Université de Nancy 2.

Porter, M. (1980) *An algorithm for suffix stripping*. Program 14: 130-137.

Ren, X. and F. Perrault (1992) *The Typology of Unknown Words: An experimental Study of Two Corpora*. Proceedings of Coling 92, Nantes: 408-414.

Thomas, C. (2008) "Google Online Lexical Frequencies User Manual (Version 0.9.0)." Retrieved 04.02.2008, from http://www.craigthomas.ca/docs/golf-0.9.0-manual.pdf.

Wandruszka, U. (2004) *Derivazione aggettivale*. La Formazione delle Parole in Italiano. M. Grossman and F. Rainer. Tübingen, Niemeyer.

Predicting the fluency of text with shallow structural features: case studies of machine translation and human-written text

Jieun Chae
University of Pennsylvania
chaeji@seas.upenn.edu

Ani Nenkova
University of Pennsylvania
nenkova@seas.upenn.edu

Abstract

Sentence fluency is an important component of overall text readability but few studies in natural language processing have sought to understand the factors that define it. We report the results of an initial study into the predictive power of surface syntactic statistics for the task; we use fluency assessments done for the purpose of evaluating machine translation. We find that these features are weakly but significantly correlated with fluency. Machine and human translations can be distinguished with accuracy over 80%. The performance of pairwise comparison of fluency is also very high—over 90% for a multi-layer perceptron classifier. We also test the hypothesis that the learned models capture general fluency properties applicable to human-written text. The results do not support this hypothesis: prediction accuracy on the new data is only 57%. This finding suggests that developing a dedicated, task-independent corpus of fluency judgments will be beneficial for further investigations of the problem.

1 Introduction

Numerous natural language applications involve the task of producing fluent text. This is a core problem for surface realization in natural language generation (Langkilde and Knight, 1998; Bangalore and Rambow, 2000), as well as an important step in machine translation. Considerations of sentence fluency are also key in sentence simplification (Siddharthan, 2003), sentence compression (Jing, 2000; Knight and Marcu, 2002; Clarke and Lapata, 2006; McDonald, 2006; Turner and Charniak, 2005; Galley and McKeown, 2007), text re-generation for summarization (Daumé III and Marcu, 2004; Barzilay and McKeown, 2005; Wan et al., 2005) and headline generation (Banko et al., 2000; Zajic et al., 2007; Soricut and Marcu, 2007).

Despite its importance for these popular applications, the factors contributing to sentence level fluency have not been researched indepth. Much more attention has been devoted to discourse-level constraints on adjacent sentences indicative of coherence and good text flow (Lapata, 2003; Barzilay and Lapata, 2008; Karamanis et al., to appear).

In many applications fluency is assessed in combination with other qualities. For example, in machine translation evaluation, approaches such as BLEU (Papineni et al., 2002) use n-gram overlap comparisons with a model to judge overall "goodness", with higher n-grams meant to capture fluency considerations. More sophisticated ways to compare a system production and a model involve the use of syntax, but even in these cases fluency is only indirectly assessed and the main advantage of the use of syntax is better estimation of the *semantic* overlap between a model and an output. Similarly, the metrics proposed for text generation by (Bangalore et al., 2000) (simple accuracy, generation accuracy) are based on string-edit distance from an ideal output.

In contrast, the work of (Wan et al., 2005) and (Mutton et al., 2007) directly sets as a goal the assessment of sentence-level fluency, regardless of content. In (Wan et al., 2005) the main premise is that syntactic information from a parser can more robustly capture fluency than language models, giving more direct indications of the degree of ungrammaticality. The idea is extended in (Mutton et al., 2007), where four parsers are used

Proceedings of the 12th Conference of the European Chapter of the ACL, pages 139–147,
Athens, Greece, 30 March – 3 April 2009.

and artificially generated sentences with varying level of fluency are evaluated with impressive success. The fluency models hold promise for actual improvements in machine translation output quality (Zwarts and Dras, 2008). In that work, only simple parser features are used for the prediction of fluency, but no actual syntactic properties of the sentences. But certainly, problems with sentence fluency are expected to be manifested in syntax. We would expect for example that syntactic tree features that capture common parse configurations and that are used in discriminative parsing (Collins and Koo, 2005; Charniak and Johnson, 2005; Huang, 2008) should be useful for predicting sentence fluency as well. Indeed, early work has demonstrated that syntactic features, and branching properties in particular, are helpful features for automatically distinguishing human translations from machine translations (Corston-Oliver et al., 2001). The exploration of branching properties of human and machine translations was motivated by the observations during failure analysis that MT system output tends to favor right-branching structures over noun compounding. Branching preference mismatch manifest themselves in the English output when translating from languages whose branching properties are radically different from English. Accuracy close to 80% was achieved for distinguishing human translations from machine translations.

In our work we continue the investigation of sentence level fluency based on features that capture surface statistics of the syntactic structure in a sentence. We revisit the task of distinguishing machine translations from human translations, but also further our understanding of fluency by providing comprehensive analysis of the association between fluency assessments of translations and surface syntactic features. We also demonstrate that based on the same class of features, it is possible to distinguish fluent machine translations from disfluent machine translations. Finally, we test the models on human written text in order to verify if the classifiers trained on data coming from machine translation evaluations can be used for general predictions of fluency and readability.

For our experiments we use the evaluations of Chinese to English translations distributed by LDC (catalog number LDC2003T17), for which both machine and human translations are available. Machine translations have been assessed by evaluators for fluency on a five point scale (5: flawless English; 4: good English; 3: non-native English; 2: disfluent English; 1: incomprehensible). Assessments by different annotators were averaged to assign overall fluency assessment for each machine-translated sentence. For each segment (sentence), there are four human and three machine translations.

In this setting we address four tasks with increasing difficulty:

- Distinguish human and machine translations.
- Distinguish fluent machine translations from poor machine translations.
- Distinguish the better (in terms of fluency) translation among two translations of the same input segment.
- Use the models trained on data from MT evaluations to predict potential fluency problems of human-written texts (from the Wall Street Journal).

Even for the last most challenging task results are promising, with prediction accuracy almost 10% better than a random baseline. For the other tasks accuracies are high, exceeding 80%.

It is important to note that the purpose of our study is not evaluation of machine translation per se. Our goal is more general and the interest is in finding predictors of sentence fluency. No general corpora exist with fluency assessments, so it seems advantageous to use the assessments done in the context of machine translation for preliminary investigations of fluency. Nevertheless, our findings are also potentially beneficial for sentence-level evaluation of machine translation.

2 Features

Perceived sentence fluency is influenced by many factors. The way the sentence fits in the context of surrounding sentences is one obvious factor (Barzilay and Lapata, 2008). Another well-known factor is vocabulary use: the presence of uncommon difficult words are known to pose problems to readers and to render text less readable (Collins-Thompson and Callan, 2004; Schwarm and Ostendorf, 2005). But these discourse- and vocabulary-level features measure properties at granularities different from the sentence level.

Syntactic sentence level features have not been investigated as a stand-alone class, as has been done for the other types of features. This is why we constrain our study to syntactic features alone, and do not discuss discourse and language model features that have been extensively studied in prior work on coherence and readability.

In our work, instead of looking at the syntactic structures present in the sentences, e.g. the syntactic rules used, we use surface statistics of phrase length and types of modification. The sentences were parsed with Charniak's parser (Charniak, 2000) in order to calculate these features.

Sentence length is the number of words in a sentence. Evaluation metrics such as BLEU (Papineni et al., 2002) have a built-in preference for shorter translations. In general one would expect that shorter sentences are easier to read and thus are perceived as more fluent. We added this feature in order to test directly the hypothesis for brevity preference.

Parse tree depth is considered to be a measure of sentence complexity. Generally, longer sentences are syntactically more complex but when sentences are approximately the same length the larger parse tree depth can be indicative of increased complexity that can slow processing and lead to lower perceived fluency of the sentence.

Number of fragment tags in the sentence parse Out of the 2634 total sentences, only 165 contained a fragment tag in their parse, indicating the presence of ungrammaticality in the sentence. Fragments occur in headlines (e.g. "Cheney willing to hold bilateral talks if Arafat observes U.S. cease-fire arrangement") but in machine translation the presence of fragments can signal a more serious problem.

Phrase type proportion was computed for prepositional phrases (PP), noun phrases (NP) and verb phrases (VP). The length in number of words of each phrase type was counted, then divided by the sentence length. Embedded phrases were also included in the calculation: for example a noun phrase (NP1 ... (NP2)) would contribute $length(NP1) + length(NP2)$ to the phrase length count.

Average phrase length is the number of words comprising a given type of phrase, divided by the number of phrases of this type. It was computed for PP, NP, VP, ADJP, ADVP. Two versions of the features were computed—one with embedded phrases included in the calculation and one just for the largest phrases of a given type. *Normalized average phrase length* is computed for PP, NP and VP and is equal to the average phrase length of given type divided by the sentence length. These were computed only for the largest phrases.

Phrase type rate was also computed for PPs, VPs and NPs and is equal to the number of phrases of the given type that appeared in the sentence, divided by the sentence length. For example, the sentence "The boy caught a huge fish this morning" will have NP phrase number equal to 3/8 and VP phrase number equal to 1/8.

Phrase length The number of words in a PP, NP, VP, without any normalization; it is computed only for the largest phrases. *Normalized phrase length* is the average phrase length (for VPs, NPs, PPs) divided by the sentence length. This was computed both for longest phrase (where embedded phrases of the same type were counted only once) and for each phrase regardless of embedding.

Length of NPs/PPs contained in a VP The average number of words that constitute an NP or PP within a verb phrase, divided by the length of the verb phrase. Similarly, the *length of PP in NP* was computed.

Head noun modifiers Noun phrases can be very complex, and the head noun can be modified in variety of ways—pre-modifiers, prepositional phrase modifiers, apposition. The length in words of these modifiers was calculated. Each feature also had a variant in which the modifier length was divided by the sentence length. Finally, two more features on total modification were computed: one was the sum of all modifier lengths, the other the sum of normalized modifier length.

3 Feature analysis

In this section, we analyze the association of the features that we described above and fluency. Note that the purpose of the analysis is not feature selection—all features will be used in the later experiments. Rather, the analysis is performed in order to better understand which factors are predictive of good fluency.

The distribution of fluency scores in the dataset is rather skewed, with the majority of the sentences rated as being of average fluency 3 as can be seen in Table 1.

Pearson's correlation between the fluency ratings and features are shown in Table 2. First of all, fluency and adequacy as given by MT evaluators

Fluency score	The number of sentences
$1 \leq$ fluency < 2	7
$1 \leq$ fluency < 2	295
$2 \leq$ fluency < 3	1789
$3 \leq$ fluency < 4	521
$4 \leq$ fluency < 5	22

Table 1: Distribution of fluency scores.

are highly correlated (0.7). This is surprisingly high, given that separate fluency and adequacy assessments were elicited with the idea that these are qualities of the translations that are independent of each other. Fluency was judged directly by the assessors, while adequacy was meant to assess the content of the sentence compared to a human gold-standard. Yet, the assessments of the two aspects were often the same—readability/fluency of the sentence is important for understanding the sentence. Only after the assessor has understood the sentence can (s)he judge how it compares to the human model. One can conclude then that a model of fluency/readability that will allow systems to produce fluent text is key for developing a successful machine translation system.

The next feature most strongly associated with fluency is sentence length. Shorter sentences are easier and perceived as more fluent than longer ones, which is not surprising. Note though that the correlation is actually rather weak. It is only one of various fluency factors and has to be accommodated alongside the possibly conflicting requirements shown by the other features. Still, length considerations reappear at sub-sentential (phrasal) levels as well.

Noun phrase length for example has almost the same correlation with fluency as sentence length does. The longer the noun phrases, the less fluent the sentence is. Long noun phrases take longer to interpret and reduce sentence fluency/readability. Consider the following example:

- *[The dog]* jumped over the fence and fetched the ball.
- *[The big dog in the corner]* fetched the ball.

The long noun phrase is more difficult to read, especially in subject position. Similarly the length of the verb phrases signal potential fluency problems:

- Most of the US allies in Europe publicly *[object to invading Iraq]$_{VP}$*.
- But this *[is dealing against some recent remarks of Japanese financial minister, Masajuro Shiokawa]$_{VP}$*.

VP distance (the average number of words separating two verb phrases) is also negatively correlated with sentence fluency. In machine translations there is the obvious problem that they might not include a verb for long stretches of text. But even in human written text, the presence of more verbs can make a difference in fluency (Bailin and Grafstein, 2001). Consider the following two sentences:

- In his state of the Union address, Putin also **talked** about the national development plan for this fiscal year and the domestic and foreign policies.
- Inside the courtyard of the television station, a reception team of 25 people **was formed to attend** to those who **came to make** donations in person.

The next strongest correlation is with unnormalized verb phrase length. In fact in terms of correlations, in turned out that it was best not to normalize the phrase length features at all. The normalized versions were also correlated with fluency, but the association was lower than for the direct count without normalization.

Parse tree depth is the final feature correlated with fluency with correlation above 0.1.

4 Experiments with machine translation data

4.1 Distinguishing human from machine translations

In this section we use all the features discussed in Section 2 for several classification tasks. Note that while we discussed the high correlation between fluency and adequacy, we do not use adequacy in the experiments that we report from here on.

For all experiments we used four of the classifiers in Weka—decision tree (J48), logistic regression, support vector machines (SMO), and multilayer perceptron. All results are for 10-fold cross validation.

We extracted the 300 sentences with highest fluency scores, 300 sentences with lowest fluency scores among machine translations and 300 randomly chosen human translations. We then tried the classification task of distinguishing human and machine translations with different fluency quality (highest fluency scores vs. lowest fluency score). We expect that low fluency MT will be more easily

adequacy 0.701(0.00)	**sentence length** -0.132(0.00)	**unnormalized NP length** -0.124(0.00)	**VP distance** -0.116(0.00)
unnormalized VP length -0.109(0.00)	**Max Tree depth** -0.106(0.00)	**phrase length** -0.105(0.00)	**avr. NP length (embedded)** -0.097(0.00)
avr. VP length (embedded) -0.094(0.00)	**SBAR length** -0.086(0.00)	**avr. largest NP length** -0.084(0.00)	**Unnormalized PP** -0.082(0.00)
avr PP length (embedded) -0.070(0.00)	**SBAR count** -0.069(0.001)	**PP length in VP** -0.066(0.001)	**Normalized PP1** 0.065(0.001)
NP length in VP -0.058(0.003)	**PP length** -0.054(0.006)	**normalized VP length** 0.054(0.005)	**PP length in NP** 0.053(0.006)
Fragment -0.049(0.011)	**avr. ADJP length (embedded)** -0.046(0.019)	**avr. largest VP length** -0.038(0.052)	

Table 2: Pearson's correlation coefficient between fluency and syntactic phrasing features. P-values are given in parenthesis.

	worst 300 MT	best 300 MT	total MT (5920)
SMO	86.00%	78.33%	82.68%
Logistic reg.	77.16%	79.33%	82.68%
MLP	78.00%	82%	86.99%
Decision Tree(J48)	71.67 %	81.33%	86.11%

Table 3: Accuracy for the task of distinguishing machine and human translations.

distinguished from human translation in comparison with machine translations rated as having high fluency.

Results are shown in Table 3. Overall the best classifier is the multi-layer perceptron. On the task using all available data of machine and human translations, the classification accuracy is 86.99%. We expected that distinguishing the machine translations from the human ones will be harder when the best translations are used, compared to the worse translations, but this expectation is fulfilled only for the support vector machine classifier.

The results in Table 3 give convincing evidence that the surface structural statistics can distinguish very well between fluent and non-fluent sentences when the examples come from human and machine-produced text respectively. If this is the case, will it be possible to distinguish between good and bad machine translations as well? In order to answer this question, we ran one more binary classification task. The two classes were the 300 machine translations with highest and lowest fluency respectively. The results are not as good as those for distinguishing machine and human translation, but still significantly outperform a random baseline. All classifiers performed similarly on the task, and achieved accuracy close to 61%.

4.2 Pairwise fluency comparisons

We also considered the possibility of pairwise comparisons for fluency: given two sentences, can we distinguish which is the one scored more highly for fluency. For every two sentences, the feature for the pair is the difference of features of the individual sentences.

There are two ways this task can be set up. First, we can use all assessed translations and make pairings for every two sentences with different fluency assessment. In this setting, the question being addressed is *Can sentences with differing fluency be distinguished?*, without regard to the sources of the sentence. The harder question is *Can a more fluent translation be distinguished from a less fluent translation of the same sentence?*

The results from these experiments can be seen in Table 4. When any two sentences with different fluency assessments are paired, the prediction accuracy is very high: 91.34% for the multi-layer perceptron classifier. In fact all classifiers have accuracy higher than 80% for this task. The surface statistics of syntactic form are powerful enough to distinguishing sentences of varying fluency.

The task of pairwise comparison for translations of the same input is more difficult: doing well on this task would be equivalent to having a reliable measure for ranking different possible translation variants.

In fact, the problem is *much* more difficult as

Task	J48	Logistic Regression	SMO	MLP
Any pair	89.73%	82.35%	82.38%	91.34%
Same Sentence	67.11%	70.91%	71.23%	69.18%

Table 4: Accuracy for pairwise fluency comparison. "Same sentence" are comparisons constrained between different translations of the same sentences, "any pair" contains comparisons of sentences with different fluency over the entire data set.

can be seen in the second row of Table 4. Logistic regression, support vector machines and multi-layer perceptron perform similarly, with support vector machine giving the best accuracy of 71.23%. This number is impressively high, and significantly higher than baseline performance. The results are about 20% lower than for prediction of a more fluent sentence when the task is not constrained to translation of the same sentence.

4.3 Feature analysis: differences among tasks

In the previous sections we presented three variations involving fluency predictions based on syntactic phrasing features: distinguishing human from machine translations, distinguishing good machine translations from bad machine translations, and pairwise ranking of sentences with different fluency. The results differ considerably and it is interesting to know whether the same kind of features are useful in making the three distinctions.

In Table 5 we show the five features with largest weight in the support vector machine model for each task. In many cases, certain features appear to be important only for particular tasks. For example the number of prepositional phrases is an important feature only for ranking different versions of *the same sentence* but is not important for other distinctions. The number of appositions is helpful in distinguishing human translations from machine translations, but is not that useful in the other tasks. So the predictive power of the features is very directly related to the variant of fluency distinctions one is interested in making.

5 Applications to human written text

5.1 Identifying hard-to-read sentences in Wall Street Journal texts

The goal we set out in the beginning of this paper was to derive a predictive model of sentence fluency from data coming from MT evaluations. In the previous sections, we demonstrated that indeed structural features can enable us to perform this task very accurately *in the context of machine translation*. But will the models conveniently trained on data from MT evaluation be at all capable to identify sentences in human-written text that are not fluent and are difficult to understand?

To answer this question, we performed an additional experiment on 30 Wall Street Journal articles from the Penn Treebank that were previously used in experiments for assessing overall text quality (Pitler and Nenkova, 2008). The articles were chosen at random and comprised a total of 290 sentences. One human assessor was asked to read each sentence and mark the ones that seemed disfluent because they were hard to comprehend. These were sentences that needed to be read more than once in order to fully understand the information conveyed in them. There were 52 such sentences. The assessments served as a gold-standard against which the predictions of the fluency models were compared.

Two models trained on machine translation data were used to predict the status of each sentence in the WSJ articles. One of the models was that for distinguishing human translations from machine translations (human vs machine MT), the other was the model for distinguishing the 300 best from the 300 worst machine translations (good vs bad MT). The classifiers used were decision trees for human vs machine distinction and support vector machines for good vs bad MT. For the first model sentences predicted to belong to the "human translation" class are considered fluent; for the second model fluent sentences are the ones predicted to be in the "best MT" class.

The results are shown in Table 6. The two models vastly differ in performance. The model for distinguishing machine translations from human translations is the better one, with accuracy of 57%. For both, prediction accuracy is much lower than when tested on data from MT evaluations. These findings indicate that building a new

MT vs HT	good MT vs Bad MT	Ranking	Same sentence Ranking
unnormalized PP	SBAR count	avr. NP lengt	normalized NP length
PP length in VP	Unnormalized VP length	normalized PP length	PP count
avr. NP length	post attribute length	NP count	normalized NP length
# apposition	VP count	normalized NP length	max tree depth
SBAR length	sentence length	normalized VP length	avr. phrase length

Table 5: The five features with highest weights in the support vector machine model for the different tasks.

Model	Acc	P	R
human vs machine trans.	57%	0.79	0.58
good MT vs bad MT	44%	0.57	0.44

Table 6: Accuracy, precision and recall (for fluent class) for each model when test on WSJ sentences. The gold-standard is assessment by a single reader of the text.

corpus for the finer fluency distinctions present in human-written text is likely to be more beneficial than trying to leverage data from existing MT evaluations.

Below, we show several example sentences on which the assessor and the model for distinguishing human and machine translations (dis)agreed.

Model and assessor agree that sentence is problematic:

(1.1) The Soviet legislature approved a 1990 budget yesterday that halves its huge deficit with cuts in defense spending and capital outlays while striving to improve supplies to frustrated consumers.

(1.2) Officials proposed a cut in the defense budget this year to 70.9 billion rubles (US$114.3 billion) from 77.3 billion rubles (US$125 billion) as well as large cuts in outlays for new factories and equipment.

(1.3) Rather, the two closely linked exchanges have been drifting apart for some years, with a nearly five-year-old moratorium on new dual listings, separate and different listing requirements, differing trading and settlement guidelines and diverging national-policy aims.

The model predicts the sentence is good, but the assessor finds it problematic:

(2.1) Moody's Investors Service Inc. said it lowered the ratings of some $145 million of Pinnacle debt because of "accelerating deficiency in liquidity," which it said was evidenced by Pinnacle's elimination of dividend payments.

(2.2) Sales were higher in all of the company's business categories, with the biggest growth coming in sales of foodstuffs such as margarine, coffee and frozen food, which rose 6.3%.

(2.3) Ajinomoto predicted sales in the current fiscal year ending next March 31 of 480 billion yen, compared with 460.05 billion yen in fiscal 1989.

The model predicts the sentences are bad, but the assessor considered them fluent:

(3.1) The sense grows that modern public bureaucracies simply don't perform their assigned functions well.

(3.2) Amstrad PLC, a British maker of computer hardware and communications equipment, posted a 52% plunge in pre-tax profit for the latest year.

(3.3) At current allocations, that means EPA will be spending $300 billion on itself.

5.2 Correlation with overall text quality

In our final experiment we focus on the relationship between sentence fluency and overall text quality. We would expect that the presence of disfluent sentences in text will make it appear less well written. Five annotators had previously assess the overall text quality of each article on a scale from 1 to 5 (Pitler and Nenkova, 2008). The average of the assessments was taken as a single number describing the article. The correlation between this number and the percentage of fluent sentences in the article according to the different models is shown in Table 7.

The correlation between the percentage of fluent sentences in the article as given by the human assessor and the overall text quality is rather low, 0.127. The positive correlation would suggest that the more hard to read sentence appear in a text, the higher the text would be rated overall, which is surprising. The predictions from the model for distinguishing good and bad machine translations very close to zero, but negative which corresponds better to the intuitive relationship between the two.

Note that none of the correlations are actually significant for the small dataset of 30 points.

6 Conclusion

We presented a study of sentence fluency based on data from machine translation evaluations. These data allow for two types of comparisons: human (fluent) text and (not so good) machine-generated

Fluency given by	Correlation
human	0.127
human vs machine trans. model	-0.055
good MT vs bad MT model	0.076

Table 7: Correlations between text quality assessment of the articles and the percentage of fluent sentences according to different models.

text, and levels of fluency in the automatically produced text. The distinctions were possible even when based solely on features describing syntactic phrasing in the sentences.

Correlation analysis reveals that the structural features are significant but weakly correlated with fluency. Interestingly, the features correlated with fluency levels in machine-produced text are not the same as those that distinguish between human and machine translations. Such results raise the need for caution when using assessments for machine produced text to build a general model of fluency. The captured phenomena in this case might be different than these from comparing human texts with differing fluency. For future research it will be beneficial to build a dedicated corpus in which *human-produced* sentences are assessed for fluency.

Our experiments show that basic fluency distinctions can be made with high accuracy. Machine translations can be distinguished from human translations with accuracy of 87%; machine translations with low fluency can be distinguished from machine translations with high fluency with accuracy of 61%. In pairwise comparison of sentences with different fluency, accuracy of predicting which of the two is better is 90%. Results are not as high but still promising for comparisons in fluency of translations of the same text. The prediction becomes better when the texts being compared exhibit larger difference in fluency quality.

Admittedly, our pilot experiments with human assessment of text quality and sentence level fluency are small, so no big generalizations can be made. Still, they allow some useful observations that can guide future work. They do show that for further research in automatic recognition of fluency, new annotated corpora developed specially for the task will be necessary. They also give some evidence that sentence-level fluency is only weakly correlated with overall text quality. Discourse apects and language model features that have been extensively studied in prior work are indeed much more indicative of overall text quality (Pitler and Nenkova, 2008). We leave direct comparison for future work.

References

A. Bailin and A. Grafstein. 2001. The linguistic assumptions underlying readability formulae: a critique. *Language and Communication*, 21:285–301.

S. Bangalore and O. Rambow. 2000. Exploiting a probabilistic hierarchical model for generation. In *COLING*, pages 42–48.

S. Bangalore, O. Rambow, and S. Whittaker. 2000. Evaluation metrics for generation. In *INLG'00: Proceedings of the first international conference on Natural language generation*, pages 1–8.

M. Banko, V. Mittal, and M. Witbrock. 2000. Headline generation based on statistical translation. In *Proceedings of the 38th Annual Meeting of the Association for Co mputational Linguistics.*

R. Barzilay and M. Lapata. 2008. Modeling local coherence: An entity-based approach. *Computational Linguistics*, 34(1):1–34.

R. Barzilay and K. McKeown. 2005. Sentence fusion for multidocument news summarization. *Computational Linguistics*, 31(3).

E. Charniak and M. Johnson. 2005. Coarse-to-fine n-best parsing and maxent discriminative reranking. In *Proceedings of the 43rd Annual Meeting of the Association for Computational Linguistics (ACL'05)*, pages 173–180.

Eugene Charniak. 2000. A maximum-entropy-inspired parser. In *NAACL-2000.*

J. Clarke and M. Lapata. 2006. Models for sentence compression: A comparison across domains, training requirements and evaluation measures. In *ACL:COLING'06*, pages 377–384.

M. Collins and T. Koo. 2005. Discriminative reranking for natural language parsing. *Comput. Linguist.*, 31(1):25–70.

K. Collins-Thompson and J. Callan. 2004. A language modeling approach to predicting reading difficulty. In *Proceedings of HLT/NAACL'04.*

S. Corston-Oliver, M. Gamon, and C. Brockett. 2001. A machine learning approach to the automatic evaluation of machine translation. In *Proceedings of 39th Annual Meeting of the Association for Computational Linguistics*, pages 148–155.

H. Daumé III and D. Marcu. 2004. Generic sentence fusion is an ill-defined summarization task. In *Proceedings of the Text Summarization Branches Out Workshop at ACL.*

M. Galley and K. McKeown. 2007. Lexicalized markov grammars for sentence compression. In *Proceedings of Human Language Technologies: The Annual Conference of the North American Chapter of the Association for Computational Linguistics (NAACL-HLT)*.

Liang Huang. 2008. Forest reranking: Discriminative parsing with non-local features. In *Proceedings of ACL-08: HLT*, pages 586–594.

H. Jing. 2000. Sentence simplification in automatic text summarization. In *Proceedings of the 6th Applied NLP Conference, ANLP'2000*.

N. Karamanis, M. Poesio, C. Mellish, and J. Oberlander. (to appear). Evaluating centering for information ordering using corpora. *Computational Linguistics*.

K. Knight and D. Marcu. 2002. Summarization beyond sentence extraction: A probabilistic approach to sentence compression. *Artificial Intelligence*, 139(1).

I. Langkilde and K. Knight. 1998. Generation that exploits corpus-based statistical knowledge. In *COLING-ACL*, pages 704–710.

Mirella Lapata. 2003. Probabilistic text structuring: Experiments with sentence ordering. In *Proceedings of ACL'03*.

R. McDonald. 2006. Discriminative sentence compression with soft syntactic evidence. In *EACL'06*.

A. Mutton, M. Dras, S. Wan, and R. Dale. 2007. Gleu: Automatic evaluation of sentence-level fluency. In *ACL'07*, pages 344–351.

K. Papineni, S. Roukos, T. Ward, and W. Zhu. 2002. BLEU: A method for automatic evaluation of machine translation. In *Proceedings of ACL*.

E. Pitler and A. Nenkova. 2008. Revisiting readability: A unified framework for predicting text quality. In *Proceedings of the 2008 Conference on Empirical Methods in Natural Language Processing*, pages 186–195.

S. Schwarm and M. Ostendorf. 2005. Reading level assessment using support vector machines and statistical language models. In *Proceedings of ACL'05*, pages 523–530.

A. Siddharthan. 2003. *Syntactic simplification and Text Cohesion*. Ph.D. thesis, University of Cambridge, UK.

R. Soricut and D. Marcu. 2007. Abstractive headline generation using widl-expressions. *Inf. Process. Manage.*, 43(6):1536–1548.

J. Turner and E. Charniak. 2005. Supervised and unsupervised learning for sentence compression. In *ACL'05*.

S. Wan, R. Dale, and M. Dras. 2005. Searching for grammaticality: Propagating dependencies in the viterbi algorithm. In *Proceedings of the Tenth European Workshop on Natural Language Generation (ENLG-05)*.

D. Zajic, B. Dorr, J. Lin, and R. Schwartz. 2007. Multi-candidate reduction: Sentence compression as a tool for document summarization tasks. *Inf. Process. Manage.*, 43(6):1549–1570.

S. Zwarts and M. Dras. 2008. Choosing the right translation: A syntactically informed classification approach. In *Proceedings of the 22nd International Conference on Computational Linguistics (Coling 2008)*, pages 1153–1160.

EM Works for Pronoun Anaphora Resolution

Eugene Charniak and Micha Elsner
Brown Laboratory for Linguistic Information Processing (BLLIP)
Brown University
Providence, RI 02912
{ec,melsner}@cs.brown.edu

Abstract

We present an algorithm for pronoun-anaphora (in English) that uses Expectation Maximization (EM) to learn virtually all of its parameters in an unsupervised fashion. While EM frequently fails to find good models for the tasks to which it is set, in this case it works quite well. We have compared it to several systems available on the web (all we have found so far). Our program significantly outperforms all of them. The algorithm is fast and robust, and has been made publically available for downloading.

1 Introduction

We present a new system for resolving (personal) pronoun anaphora[1]. We believe it is of interest for two reasons. First, virtually all of its parameters are learned via the expectation-maximization algorithm (EM). While EM has worked quite well for a few tasks, notably machine translations (starting with the IBM models 1-5 (Brown et al., 1993), it has not had success in most others, such as part-of-speech tagging (Merialdo, 1991), named-entity recognition (Collins and Singer, 1999) and context-free-grammar induction (numerous attempts, too many to mention). Thus understanding the abilities and limitations of EM is very much a topic of interest. We present this work as a positive data-point in this ongoing discussion.

Secondly, and perhaps more importantly, is the system's performance. Remarkably, there are very few systems for actually *doing* pronoun anaphora available on the web. By emailing the corpora-list the other members of the list pointed us to four. We present a head to head evaluation and find that our performance is significantly better than the competition.

[1]The system, the Ge corpus, and the model described here can be downloaded from http://bllip.cs.brown.edu/download/emPronoun.tar.gz.

2 Previous Work

The literature on pronominal anaphora is quite large, and we cannot hope to do justice to it here. Rather we limit ourselves to particular papers and systems that have had the greatest impact on, and similarity to, ours.

Probably the closest approach to our own is Cherry and Bergsma (2005), which also presents an EM approach to pronoun resolution, and obtains quite successful results. Our work improves upon theirs in several dimensions. Firstly, they do not distinguish antecedents of non-reflexive pronouns based on syntax (for instance, subjects and objects). Both previous work (cf. Tetreault (2001) discussed below) and our present results find these distinctions extremely helpful. Secondly, their system relies on a separate preprocessing stage to classify non-anaphoric pronouns, and mark the gender of certain NPs (Mr., Mrs. and some first names). This allows the incorporation of external data and learning systems, but conversely, it requires these decisions to be made sequentially. Our system classifies non-anaphoric pronouns jointly, and learns gender without an external database. Next, they only handle third-person pronouns, while we handle first and second as well. Finally, as a demonstration of EM's capabilities, its evidence is equivocal. Their EM requires careful initialization — sufficiently careful that the EM version only performs 0.4% better than the initialized program alone. (We can say nothing about relative performance of their system vs. ours since we have been able to access neither their data nor code.)

A quite different unsupervised approach is Kehler et al. (2004a), which uses self-training of a discriminative system, initialized with some con-

Proceedings of the 12th Conference of the European Chapter of the ACL, pages 148–156,
Athens, Greece, 30 March – 3 April 2009. ©2009 Association for Computational Linguistics

servative number and gender heuristics. The system uses the conventional ranking approach, applying a maximum-entropy classifier to pairs of pronoun and potential antecedent and selecting the best antecedent. In each iteration of self-training, the system labels the training corpus and its decisions are treated as input for the next training phase. The system improves substantially over a Hobbs baseline. In comparison to ours, their feature set is quite similar, while their learning approach is rather different. In addition, their system does not classify non-anaphoric pronouns,

A third paper that has significantly influenced our work is that of (Haghighi and Klein, 2007). This is the first paper to treat all noun phrase (NP) anaphora using a generative model. The success they achieve directly inspired our work. There are, however, many differences between their approach and ours. The most obvious is our use of EM rather than theirs of Gibbs sampling. However, the most important difference is the choice of training data. In our case it is a very large corpus of parsed, but otherwise unannotated text. Their system is trained on the ACE corpus, and requires explicit annotation of all "markables" — things that are or have antecedents. For pronouns, only anaphoric pronouns are so marked. Thus the system does not learn to recognize non-anaphoric pronouns — a significant problem. More generally it follows from this that the system only works (or at least works with the accuracy they achieve) when the input data is so marked. These markings not only render the non-anaphoric pronoun situation moot, but also significantly restrict the choice of possible antecedent. Only perhaps one in four or five NPs are markable (Poesio and Vieira, 1998).

There are also several papers which treat coference as an unsupervised clustering problem (Cardie and Wagstaff, 1999; Angheluta et al., 2004). In this literature there is no generative model at all, and thus this work is only loosely connected to the above models.

Another key paper is (Ge et al., 1998). The data annotated for the Ge research is used here for testing and development data. Also, there are many overlaps between their formulation of the problem and ours. For one thing, their model is generative, although they do not note this fact, and (with the partial exception we are about to mention) they obtain their probabilities from hand annotated data rather than using EM. Lastly, they learn their gender information (the probability of that a pronoun will have a particular gender given its antecedent) using a truncated EM procedure. Once they have derived all of the other parameters from the training data, they go through a larger corpus of unlabeled data collecting estimated counts of how often each word generates a pronoun of a particular gender. They then normalize these probabilities and the result is used in the final program. This is, in fact, a single iteration of EM.

Tetreault (2001) is one of the few papers that use the (Ge et al., 1998) corpus used here. They achieve a very high 80% correct, but this is given hand-annotated number, gender and syntactic binding features to filter candidate antecedents and also ignores non-anaphoric pronouns.

We defer discussion of the systems against which we were able to compare to Section 7 on evaluation.

3 Pronouns

We briefly review English pronouns and their properties. First we only concern ourselves with "personal" pronouns: "I", "you", "he", "she", "it", and their variants. We ignore, e.g., relative pronouns ("who", "which", etc.), deictic pronouns ("this", "that") and others.

Personal pronouns come in four basic types:

subject "I", "she", etc. Used in subject position.

object "me", "her" etc. Used in non-subject position.

possessive "my" "her", and

reflexive "myself", "herself" etc. Required by English grammar in certain constructions — e.g., "I kicked myself."

The system described here handles all of these cases.

Note that the type of a pronoun is not connected with its antecedent, but rather is completely determined by the role it plays in it's sentence.

Personal pronouns are either anaphoric or non-anaphoric. We say that a pronoun is anaphoric when it is coreferent with another piece of text in the same discourse. As is standard in the field we distinguish between a referent and an antecedent. The referent is the thing in the world that the pronoun, or, more generally, noun phrase (NP), denotes. Anaphora on the other hand is a relation between pieces of text. It follows from this that non-anaphoric pronouns come in two basic varieties — some have a referent, but because the referent is not mentioned in the text[2] there is no anaphoric relation to other text. Others have no referent (*expletive* or *pleonastic* pronouns, as in "It seems that ..."). For the purposes of this article we do not distinguish the two.

Personal pronouns have three properties other than their type:

person first ("I","we"), second ("you") or third ("she","they") person,

number singular ("I","he") or plural ("we", "they"), and

gender masculine ("he"), feminine ("she") or neuter ("they").

These are critical because it is these properties that our generative model generates.

4 The Generative Model

Our generative model ignores the generation of most of the discourse, only generating a pronoun's person, number,and gender features along with the governor of the pronoun and the syntactic relation between the pronoun and the governor. (Informally, a word's governor is the head of the phrase above it. So the governor of both "I" and "her" in "I saw her" is "saw".

We first decide if the pronoun is anaphoric based upon a distribution p(anaphoric). (Actually this is a bit more complex, see the discussion in Section 5.3.) If the pronoun is anaphoric we then select a possible antecedent. Any NP in the current or two previous sentences is considered. We select the antecedent based upon a distribution p(anaphora|context). The nature of the "context" is discussed below. Then given the antecedent we generative the pronoun's person according to p(person|antecedent), the pronoun's gender according to p(gender|antecedent), number, p(number|antecedent) and governor/relation-to-governor from p(governor/relation|antecedent).

To generate a non-anaphoric third person singular "it" we first guess that the non-anaphoric pronouns is "it" according to p("it"|non-anaphoric). and then generate the governor/relation according to p(governor/relation|non-anaphoric-it);

Lastly we generate any other non-anaphoric pronouns and their governor with a fixed probability p(other). (Strictly speaking, this is mathematically invalid, since we do not bother to normalize over all the alternatives; a good topic for future research would be exploring what happens when we make this part of the model truly generative.)

One inelegant part of the model is the need to scale the p(governor/rel|antecedent) probabilities. We smooth them using Kneser-Ney smoothing, but even then their dynamic range (a factor of 10^6) greatly exceeds those of the other parameters. Thus we take their nth root. This n is the last of the model parameters.

5 Model Parameters

5.1 Intuitions

All of our distributions start with uniform values. For example, gender distributions start with the probability of each gender equal to one-third. From this it follows that on the first EM iteration all antecedents will have the same probability of generating a pronoun. At first glance then, the EM process might seem to be futile. In this section we hope to give some intuitions as to why this is not the case.

As is typically done in EM learning, we start the process with a much simpler generative model, use a few EM iterations to learn its parameters, and gradually expose the data to more and more complex models, and thus larger and larger sets of parameters.

The first model only learns the probability of an antecedent generating the pronoun given what sentence it is in. We train this model through four iterations before moving on to more complex ones.

As noted above, all antecedents initially have the same probability, but this is not true after the first iteration. To see how the probabilities diverge, and diverge correctly, consider the first sentence of a news article. Suppose it starts "President Bush announced that he ..." In this situation there is only one possible antecedent, so the expectation that "he" is generated by the NP in the same sentence is 1.0. Contrast this with the situation in the third and subsequent sentences. It is only then that we have expectation for sentences two back generating the pronoun. Furthermore, typically by this point there will be, say, twenty NPs to share the

[2] Actually, as in most previous work, we only consider referents realized by NPs. For more general approaches see Byron (2002).

probability mass, so each one will only get an increase of 0.05. Thus on the first iteration only the first two sentences have the power to move the distributions, but they do, and they make NPs in the current sentence very slightly more likely to generate the pronoun than the sentence one back, which in turn is more likely than the ones two back.

This slight imbalance is reflected when EM readjusts the probability distribution at the end of the first iteration. Thus for the second iteration everyone contributes to subsequent imbalances, because it is no longer the case the all antecedents are equally likely. Now the closer ones have higher probability so forth and so on.

To take another example, consider how EM comes to assign gender to various words. By the time we start training the gender assignment probabilities the model has learned to prefer nearer antecedents as well as ones with other desirable properties. Now suppose we consider a sentence, the first half of which has no pronouns. Consider the gender of the NPs in this half. Given no further information we would expect these genders to distribute themselves accord to the prior probability that any NP will be masculine, feminine, etc. But suppose that the second half of the sentence has a feminine pronoun. Now the genders will be skewed with the probability of one of them being feminine being much larger. Thus in the same way these probabilities will be moved from equality, and should, in general be moved correctly.

5.2 Parameters Learned by EM

Virtually all model parameters are learned by EM. We use the parsed version of the North-American News Corpus. This is available from the (McClosky et al., 2008). It has about 800,000 articles, and 500,000,000 words.

The least complicated parameter is the probability of gender given word. Most words that have a clear gender have this reflected in their probabilities. Some examples are shown in Table 1. We can see there that EM gets "Paul", "Paula", and "Wal-mart" correct. "Pig" has no obvious gender in English, and the probabilities reflect this. On the other hand "Piggy" gets feminine gender. This is no doubt because of "Miss Piggy" the puppet character. "Waist" the program gets wrong. Here the probabilities are close to gender-of-pronoun priors. This happens for a (comparatively small) class of pronouns that, in fact, are probably never an antecedent, but are nearby random pronouns. Because of their non-antecedent proclivities, this sort of mistake has little effect.

Word	Male	Female	Neuter
paul	0.962	0.002	0.035
paula	0.003	0.915	0.082
pig	0.445	0.170	0.385
piggy	0.001	0.853	0.146
wal-mart	0.016	0.007	0.976
waist	0.380	0.155	0.465

Table 1: Words and their probabilities of generating masculine, feminine and neuter pronouns

antecedent	p(singular|antecedent)
Singular	0.939048
Plural	0.0409721
Not NN or NNP	0.746885

Table 2: The probability of an antecedent generation a singular pronoun as a function of its number

Next consider p(number|antecedent), that is the probability that a given antecedent will generate a singular or plural pronoun. This is shown in Table 2. Since we are dealing with parsed text, we have the antecedent's part-of-speech, so rather than the antecedent we get the number from the part of speech: "NN" and "NNP" are singular, "NNS" and "NNPS" are plural. Lastly, we have the probability that an antecedent which is not a noun will have a singular pronoun associated with it. Note that the probability that a singular antecedent will generate a singular pronoun is not one. This is correct, although the exact number probably is too low. For example, "IBM" may be the antecedent of both "we" and "they", and vice versa.

Next we turn to p(person|antecedent), predicting whether the pronoun is first, second or third person given its antecedent. We simplify this by noting that we know the person of the antecedent (everything except "I" and "you" and their variants are third person), so we compute p(person|person). Actually we condition on one further piece of information, if either the pronoun or the antecedent is being quoted. The idea is that an "I" in quoted material may be the same person as "John Doe" outside of quotes, if Mr. Doe is speaking. Indeed, EM picks up on this as is illustrated in Tables 3 and 4. The first gives the situation when neither antecedent nor pronoun is within a quotation. The high numbers along the

	Person of Pronoun		
Person of Ante	First	Second	Third
First	0.923	0.076	0.001
Second	0.114	0.885	0.001
Third	0.018	0.015	0.967

Table 3: Probability of an antecedent generating a first,second or third person pronoun as a function of the antecedents person

	Person of Pronoun		
Person of Ante	First	Second	Third
First	0.089	0.021	0.889
Second	0.163	0.132	0.705
Third	0.025	0.011	0.964

Table 4: Same, but when the antecedent is in quoted material but the pronoun is not

diagonal (0.923, 0.885, and 0.967) show the expected like-goes-to-like preferences. Contrast this with Table 4 which gives the probabilities when the antecedent is in quotes but the pronoun is not. Here we see all antecedents being preferentially mapped to third person (0.889, 0.705, and 0.964).

We save p(antecedent|context) till last because it is the most complicated. Given what we know about the context of the pronoun not all antecedent positions are equally likely. Some important conditioning events are:

- the exact position of the sentence relative to the pronoun (0, 1, or 2 sentences back),
- the position of the head of the antecedent within the sentence (bucketed into 6 bins). For the current sentence position is measured backward from the pronoun. For the two previous sentences it is measure forward from the start of the sentence.
- syntactic positions — generally we expect NPs in subject position to be more likely antecedents than those in object position, and those more likely than other positions (e.g., object of a preposition).
- position of the pronoun — for example the subject of the previous sentence is very likely to be the antecedent if the pronoun is very early in the sentence, much less likely if it is at the end.
- type of pronoun — reflexives can only be bound within the same sentence, while subject and object pronouns may be anywhere. Possessives may be in previous sentences but this is not as common.
- type of antecedent. Intuitively other pronouns and proper nouns are more likely to be antecedents than common nouns and NPs headed up by things other than nouns.

Part of Speech	pron	proper	common
	0.094	0.057	0.032
Word Position	bin 0	bin 2	bin 5
	0.111	0.007	0.0004
Syntactic Type	subj	other	object
	0.068	0.045	0.037

Table 5: Geometric mean of the probability of the antecedent when holding everything expect the stated feature of the antecedent constant

All told this comes to 2592 parameters (3 sentences, 6 antecedent word positions, 3 syntactic positions, 4 pronoun positions, 3 pronoun types, and 4 antecedent types). It is impossible to say if EM is setting all of these correctly. There are too many of them and we do not have knowledge or intuitions about most all of them. However, all help performance on the development set, and we can look at a few where we do have strong intuitions. Table 5 gives some examples. The first two rows are devoted to the probabilities of particular kind of antecedent (pronouns, proper nouns, and common nouns) generating a pronoun, holding everything constant except the type of antecedent. The numbers are the geometric mean of the probabilities in each case. The probabilities are ordered according to, at least my, intuition with pronoun being the most likely (0.094), followed by proper nouns (0.057), followed by common nouns (0.032), a fact also noted by (Haghighi and Klein, 2007). When looking at the probabilities as a function of word position again the EM derived probabilities accord with intuition, with bin 0 (the closest) more likely than bin 2 more likely than bin 5. The last two lines have the only case where we have found the EM probability not in accord with our intuitions. We would have expected objects of verbs to be more likely to generate a pronoun than the catch-all "other" case. This proved not to be the case. On the other hand, the two are much closer in probabilities than any of the other, more intuitive, cases.

5.3 Parameters Not Set by EM

There are a few parameters not set by EM.

Several are connected with the well known syntactic constraints on the use of reflexives. A simple version of this is built in. Reflexives must have an antecedent in same sentence, and generally cannot be coreferent-referent with the subject of the sentence.

There are three system parameters that we set by hand to optimize performance on the development set. The first is n. As noted above, the distribution p(governor/relation|antecedent) has a much greater dynamic range than the other probability distributions and to prevent it from, in essence, completely determining the answer, we take its nth root. Secondly, there is a probability of generating a non-anaphoric "it". Lastly we have a probability of generating each of the other non-monotonic pronouns along with (the nth root of) their governor. These parameters are 6, 0.1, and 0.0004 respectively.

6 Definition of Correctness

We evaluate all programs according to Mitkov's "resolution etiquette" scoring metric (also used in Cherry and Bergsma (2005)), which is defined as follows: if N is the number of non-anaphoric pronouns correctly identified, A the number of anaphoric pronouns correctly linked to their antecedent, and P the total number of pronouns, then a pronoun-anaphora program's percentage correct is $\frac{N+A}{P}$.

Most papers dealing with pronoun coreference use this simple ratio, or the variant that ignores non-anaphoric pronouns. It has appeared under a number of names: *success* (Yang et al., 2006), *accuracy* (Kehler et al., 2004a; Angheluta et al., 2004) and *success rate* (Tetreault, 2001). The other occasionally-used metric is the MUC score restricted to pronouns, but this has well-known problems (Bagga and Baldwin, 1998).

To make the definition perfectly concrete, however, we must resolve a few special cases. One is the case in which a pronoun x correctly says that it is coreferent with another pronoun y. However, the program misidentifies the antecedent of y. In this case (sometimes called *error chaining* (Walker, 1989)), both x and y are to be scored as wrong, as they both end up in the wrong coreferential chain. We believe this is, in fact, the standard (Mitkov, personal communication), although there are a few papers (Tetreault, 2001; Yang et al., 2006) which do the opposite and many which simply do not discuss this case.

One more issue arises in the case of a system attempting to perform complete NP anaphora[3]. In these cases the coreferential chains they create may not correspond to any of the original chains. In these cases, we call a pronoun correctly resolved if it is put in a chain including at least one correct non-pronominal antecedent. This definition cannot be used in general, as putting all NPs into the same set would give a perfect score. Fortunately, the systems we compare against do not do this – they seem more likely to over-split than under-split. Furthermore, if they do take some inadvertent advantage of this definition, it helps them and puts our program at a possible disadvantage, so it is a more-than-fair comparison.

7 Evaluation

To develop and test our program we use the dataset annotated by Niyu Ge (Ge et al., 1998). This consists of sections 0 and 1 of the Penn treebank. Ge marked every personal pronoun and all noun phrases that were coreferent with these pronouns. We used section 0 as our development set, and section 1 for testing. We reparsed the sentences using the Charniak and Johnson parser (Charniak and Johnson, 2005) rather than using the gold-parses that Ge marked up. We hope thereby to make the results closer to those a user will experience. (Generally the gold trees perform about 0.005 higher than the machine parsed version.) The test set has 1119 personal pronouns of which 246 are non-anaphoric. Our selection of this dataset, rather than the widely used MUC-6 corpus, is motivated by this large number of pronouns.

We compared our results to four currently-available anaphora programs from the web. These four were selected by sending a request to a commonly used mailing list (the "corpora-list") asking for such programs. We received four leads: JavaRAP, Open-NLP, BART and GuiTAR. Of course, these systems represent the best available work, not the state of the art. We presume that more recent supervised systems (Kehler et al., 2004b; Yang et al., 2004; Yang et al., 2006) per-

[3]Of course our system does not attempt NP coreference resolution, nor does JavaRAP. The other three comparison systems do.

form better. Unfortunately, we were unable to obtain a comparison unsupervised learning system at all.

Only one of the four is explicitly aimed at personal-pronoun anaphora — RAP (Resolution of Anaphora Procedure) (Lappin and Leass, 1994). It is a non-statistical system originally implemented in Prolog. The version we used is JavaRAP, a later reimplementation in Java (Long Qiu and Chua, 2004). It only handles third person pronouns.

The other three are more general in that they handle all NP anaphora. The GuiTAR system (Poesio and Kabadjov, 2004) is designed to work in an "off the shelf" fashion on general text GUITAR resolves pronouns using the algorithm of (Mitkov et al., 2002), which filters candidate antecedents and then ranks them using morphosyntactic features. Due to a bug in version 3, GUITAR does not currently handle possessive pronouns.GUITAR also has an optional discourse-new classification step, which cannot be used as it requires a discontinued Google search API.

OpenNLP (Morton et al., 2005) uses a maximum-entropy classifier to rank potential antecedents for pronouns. However despite being the best-performing (on pronouns) of the existing systems, there is a remarkable lack of published information on its innards.

BART (Versley et al., 2008) also uses a maximum-entropy model, based on Soon et al. (2001). The BART system also provides a more sophisticated feature set than is available in the basic model, including tree-kernel features and a variety of web-based knowledge sources. Unfortunately we were not able to get the basic version working. More precisely we were able to run the program, but the results we got were substantially lower than any of the other models and we believe that the program as shipped is not working properly.

Some of these systems provide their own preprocessing tools. However, these were bypassed, so that all systems ran on the Charniak parse trees (with gold sentence segmentation). Systems with named-entity detectors were allowed to run them as a preprocess. All systems were run using the models included in their standard distribution; typically these models are trained on annotated news articles (like MUC-6), which should be relatively similar to our WSJ documents.

System	Restrictions	Performance
GuiTAR	No Possessives	0.534
JavaRap	Third Person	0.529
Open-NLP	None	0.593
Our System	None	0.686

Table 6: Performance of Evaluated Systems on Test Data

The performance of the remaining systems is given in Table 6. The two programs with restrictions were only evaluated on the pronouns the system was capable of handling.

These results should be approached with some caution. In particular it is possible that the results for the systems other than ours are underestimated due to errors in the evaluation. Complications include the fact all of the four programs all have different output conventions. The better to catch such problems the authors independently wrote two scoring programs.

Nevertheless, given the size of the difference between the results of our system and the others, the conclusion that ours has the best performance is probably solid.

8 Conclusion

We have presented a generative model of pronoun-anaphora in which virtually all of the parameters are learned by expectation maximization. We find it of interest first as an example of one of the few tasks for which EM has been shown to be effective, and second as a useful program to be put in general use. It is, to the best of our knowledge, the best-performing system available on the web. To down-load it, go to (to be announced).

The current system has several obvious limitation. It does not handle cataphora (antecedents occurring after the pronoun), only allows antecedents to be at most two sentences back, does not recognize that a conjoined NP can be the antecedent of a plural pronoun, and has a very limited grasp of pronominal syntax. Perhaps the largest limitation is the programs inability to recognize the speaker of a quoted segment. The result is a very large fraction of first person pronouns are given incorrect antecedents. Fixing these problems would no doubt push the system's performance up several percent.

However the most critical direction for future research is to push the approach to handle full NP anaphora. Besides being of the greatest importance in its own right, it would also allow us to add one piece of information we currently neglect in our pronominal system — the more times a document refers to an entity the more likely it is to do so again.

9 Acknowledgements

We would like to thank the authors and maintainers of the four systems against which we did our comparison, especially Tom Morton, Mijail Kabadjov and Yannick Versley. Making your system freely available to other researchers is one of the best ways to push the field forward. In addition, we thank three anonymous reviewers.

References

Roxana Angheluta, Patrick Jeuniaux, Rudradeb Mitra, and Marie-Francine Moens. 2004. Clustering algorithms for noun phrase coreference resolution. In *Proceedings of the 7es Journes internationales d'Analyse statistique des Donnes Textuelles*, pages 60–70, Louvain La Neuve, Belgium, March 10–12.

Amit Bagga and Breck Baldwin. 1998. Algorithms for scoring coreference chains. In *In The First International Conference on Language Resources and Evaluation Workshop on Linguistics Coreference*, pages 563–566.

P. Brown, S. Della Pietra, V. Della Pietra, and R. Mercer. 1993. The mathematics of statistical machine translation: Parameter estimation. *Computational Linguistics*, 19(2).

Donna K. Byron. 2002. Resolving pronominal reference to abstract entities. In *Proceedings of the 40th Annual Meeting of the Association for Computational Linguistics (ACL2002)*, pages 80–87, Philadelphia, PA, USA, July 6–12.

Claire Cardie and Kiri Wagstaff. 1999. Noun phrase coreference as clustering. In *In Proceedings of EMNLP*, pages 82–89.

Eugene Charniak and Mark Johnson. 2005. Coarse-to-fine n-best parsing and MaxEnt discriminative reranking. In *Proc. of the 2005 Meeting of the Assoc. for Computational Linguistics (ACL)*, pages 173–180.

Colin Cherry and Shane Bergsma. 2005. An Expectation Maximization approach to pronoun resolution. In *Proceedings of the Ninth Conference on Computational Natural Language Learning (CoNLL-2005)*, pages 88–95, Ann Arbor, Michigan, June. Association for Computational Linguistics.

Michael Collins and Yorav Singer. 1999. Unsupervised models for named entity classification. In *Proceedings of the Joint SIGDAT Conference on Empirical Methods in Natural Language Processing and Very Large Corpora (EMNLP 99)*.

Niyu Ge, John Hale, and Eugene Charniak. 1998. A statistical approach to anaphora resolution. In *Proceedings of the Sixth Workshop on Very Large Corpora*, pages 161–171, Orlando, Florida. Harcourt Brace.

Aria Haghighi and Dan Klein. 2007. Unsupervised coreference resolution in a nonparametric Bayesian model. In *Proceedings of the 45th Annual Meeting of the Association for Computational Linguistics*, pages 848–855. Association for Computational Linguistics.

Andrew Kehler, Douglas Appelt, Lara Taylor, and Aleksandr Simma. 2004a. Competitive self-trained pronoun interpretation. In Daniel Marcu Susan Dumais and Salim Roukos, editors, *HLT-NAACL 2004: Short Papers*, pages 33–36, Boston, Massachusetts, USA, May 2 - May 7. Association for Computational Linguistics.

Andrew Kehler, Douglas E. Appelt, Lara Taylor, and Aleksandr Simma. 2004b. The (non)utility of predicate-argument frequencies for pronoun interpretation. In *Proceedings of the 2004 Human Language Technology Conference of the North American Chapter of the Association for Computational Linguistics*, pages 289–296.

Shalom Lappin and Herber J. Leass. 1994. An algorithm for pronouminal anaphora resolution. *Computational Linguistics*, 20(4):535–561.

Min-Yen Kan Long Qiu and Tat-Seng Chua. 2004. A public reference implementation of the RAP anaphora resolution algorithm. In *Proceedings of the Fourth International Conference on Language Resources and Evaluation*, volume I, pages 291–294.

David McClosky, Eugene Charniak, and MarkJohnson. 2008. *BLLIP North American News Text, Complete*. Linguistic Data Consortium. LDC2008T13.

Bernard Merialdo. 1991. Tagging text with a probabilistic model. In *International Conference on Speech and Signal Processing*, volume 2, pages 801–818.

Ruslan Mitkov, Richard Evans, and Constantin Orăsan. 2002. A new, fully automatic version of Mitkov's knowledge-poor pronoun resolution method. In *Proceedings of the Third International Conference on Intelligent Text Processing and Computational Linguistics (CICLing-2002)*, Mexico City, Mexico, February, 17 – 23.

Thomas Morton, Joern Kottmann, Jason Baldridge, and Gann Bierner. 2005. Opennlp: A java-based nlp toolkit. http://opennlp.sourceforge.net.

Massimo Poesio and Mijail A. Kabadjov. 2004. A general-purpos, of-the-shelf anaphora resolution module: implementataion and preliminary evaluation. In *Proceedings of the 2004 international Conference on Language Evaluation and Resources*, pages 663,668.

Massimo Poesio and Renata Vieira. 1998. A corpus-based investigation of definite description use. *Computational Linguistics*, 24(2):183–216.

Wee Meng Soon, Hwee Tou Ng, and Daniel Chung Yong Lim. 2001. A machine learning approach to coreference resolution of noun phrases. *Computational Linguistics*, 27(4):521–544.

Joel R. Tetreault. 2001. A corpus-based evaluation of centering and pronoun resolution. *Computational Linguistics*, 27(4):507–520.

Yannick Versley, Simone Ponzetto, Massimo Poesio, Vladimir Eidelman, Alan Jern, Jason Smith, Xiaofeng Yang, and Alessandro Moschitti. 2008. Bart: A modular toolkit for coreference resolution. In *Companion Volume of the Proceedings of the 46th Annual Meeting of the Association for Computational Linguistics*, pages 9–12.

Marilyn A. Walker. 1989. Evaluating discourse processing algorithms. In *ACL*, pages 251–261.

Xiaofeng Yang, Jian Su, Guodong Zhou, and Chew Lim Tan. 2004. Improving pronoun resolution by incorporating coreferential information of candidates. In *Proceedings of the 42nd Annual Meeting of the Association for Computational Linguistics (ACL2004)*, pages 127–134, Barcelona, Spain, July 21–26.

Xiaofeng Yang, Jian Su, and Chew Lim Tan. 2006. Kernel-based pronoun resolution with structured syntactic knowledge. In *Proceedings of the 21st International Conference on Computational Linguistics and 44th Annual Meeting of the Association for Computational Linguistics*, pages 41–48, Sydney, Australia, July. Association for Computational Linguistics.

Web augmentation of language models for continuous speech recognition of SMS text messages

Mathias Creutz[1], **Sami Virpioja**[1,2] and **Anna Kovaleva**[1]
[1]Nokia Research Center, Helsinki, Finland
[2]Adaptive Informatics Research Centre, Helsinki University of Technology, Espoo, Finland
mathias.creutz@nokia.com, sami.virpioja@tkk.fi, annakov@gmx.de

Abstract

In this paper, we present an efficient query selection algorithm for the retrieval of web text data to augment a statistical language model (LM). The number of retrieved relevant documents is optimized with respect to the number of queries submitted.

The querying scheme is applied in the domain of SMS text messages. Continuous speech recognition experiments are conducted on three languages: English, Spanish, and French. The web data is utilized for augmenting in-domain LMs in general and for adapting the LMs to a user-specific vocabulary. Word error rate reductions of up to 6.6 % (in LM augmentation) and 26.0 % (in LM adaptation) are obtained in setups, where the size of the web mixture LM is limited to the size of the baseline in-domain LM.

1 Introduction

An automatic speech recognition (ASR) system consists of acoustic models of speech sounds and of a statistical language model (LM). The LM learns the probabilities of word sequences from text corpora available for training. The performance of the model depends on the amount and style of the text. The more text there is, the better the model is, in general. It is also important that the model be trained on text that matches the style of language used in the ASR application. Well matching, in-domain, text may be both difficult and expensive to obtain in the large quantities that are needed.

A popular solution is to utilize the World Wide Web as a source of additional text for LM training. A small in-domain set is used as seed data, and more data of the same kind is retrieved from the web. A decade ago, Berger and Miller (1998) proposed a just-in-time LM that updated the current LM by retrieving data from the web using recent recognition hypotheses as queries submitted to a search engine. Perplexity reductions of up to 10 % were reported.[1] Many other works have followed. Zhu and Rosenfeld (2001) retrieved page and phrase counts from the web in order to update the probabilities of infrequent trigrams that occur in N-best lists. Word error rate (WER) reductions of about 3 % were obtained on TREC-7 data.

In more recent work, the focus has turned to the collection of text rather than n-gram statistics based on page counts. More effort has been put into the selection of query strings. Bulyko et al. (2003; 2007) first extend their baseline vocabulary with words from a small in-domain training corpus. They then use n-grams with these new words in their web queries in order to retrieve text of a certain genre. For instance, they succeed in obtaining conversational style phrases, such as "we were friends but we don't actually have a relationship." In a number of experiments, word error rate reductions of 2-3 % are obtained on English data, and 6 % on Mandarin. The same method for web data collection is applied by Çetin and Stolcke (2005) in meeting and lecture transcription tasks. The web sources reduce perplexity by 10 % and 4.3 %, respectively, and word error rates by 3.5 % and 2.2 %, respectively.

Sarikaya et al. (2005) chunk the in-domain text into "n-gram islands" consisting of only content words and excluding frequently occurring stop words. An island such as "stock fund portfolio" is then extended by adding context, producing "my stock fund portfolio", for instance. Multiple islands are combined using *and* and *or* operations to form web queries. Significant word error reductions between 10 and 20 % are obtained; however, the in-domain data set is very small, 1700 phrases,

[1]All reported percentage differences are *relative* unless explicitly stated otherwise.

Proceedings of the 12th Conference of the European Chapter of the ACL, pages 157–165,
Athens, Greece, 30 March – 3 April 2009. ©2009 Association for Computational Linguistics

which makes (any) new data a much needed addition.

Similarly, Misu and Kawahara (2006) obtain very good word error reductions (20 %) in spoken dialogue systems for software support and sightseeing guidance. Nouns that have high tf/idf scores in the in-domain documents are used in the web queries. The existing in-domain data sets poorly match the speaking style of the task and therefore existing dialogue corpora of different domains are included, which improves the performance considerably.

Wan and Hain (2006) select query strings by comparing the n-gram counts within an in-domain topic model to the corresponding counts in an out-of-domain background model. Topic-specific n-grams are used as queries, and perplexity reductions of 5.4 % are obtained.

It is customary to postprocess and filter the downloaded web texts. Sentence boundaries are detected using some heuristics. Text chunks with a high out-of-vocabulary (OOV) rate are discarded. Additionally, the chunks are often ranked according to their similarity with the in-domain data, and the lowest ranked chunks are discarded. As a similarity measure, the *perplexity* of the sentence according to the in-domain LM can be used; for instance, Bulyko et al. (2007). Another measure for ranking is *relative perplexity* (Weilhammer et al., 2006), where the in-domain perplexity is divided by the perplexity given by an LM trained on the web data. Also the BLEU score familiar from the field of machine translation has been used (Sarikaya et al., 2005).

Some criticism has been raised by Sethy et al. (2007), who claim that sentence ranking has an inherent bias towards the center of the in-domain distribution. They propose a data selection algorithm that selects a sentence from the web set, if adding the sentence to the already selected set reduces the relative entropy with respect to the in-domain data distribution. The algorithm appears efficient in producing a rather small subset (1/11) of the web data, while degrading the WER only marginally.

The current paper describes a new method for query selection and its applications in LM augmentation and adaptation using web data. The language models are part of a continuous speech recognition system that enables users to use speech as an input modality on mobile devices, such as mobile phones. The particular domain of interest is personal communication: The user dictates a message that is automatically transcribed into text and sent to a recipient as an SMS text message. Memory consumption and computational speed are crucial factors in mobile applications. While most studies ignore the sizes of the LMs when comparing models, we aim at improving the LM *without increasing its size* when web data is added.

Another aspect that is typically overlooked is that the collection of web data costs time and computational resources. This applies to the querying, downloading and postprocessing of the data. The query selection scheme proposed in this paper is *economical* in the sense that it strives to download as much relevant text from the web as possible using as few queries as possible avoiding overlap between the set of pages found by different queries.

2 Query selection and web data retrieval

Our query selection scheme involves multiple steps. The assumption is that a batch of queries will be created. These queries are submitted to a search engine and the matching documents are downloaded. This procedure is repeated for multiple query batches.

In particular, our scheme attempts to maximize the number of retrieved relevant documents, when two restrictions apply: (1) queries are not "free": each query costs some time or money; for instance, the number of queries submitted within a particular period of time is limited, and (2) the number of documents retrieved for a particular query is limited to a particular number of "top hits".

2.1 N-gram selection and prospection querying

Some text reflecting the target domain must be available. A set of the most frequent n-grams occurring in the text is selected, from unigrams up to five-grams. Some of these n-grams are characteristic of the domain of interest (such as "Hogwarts School of Witchcraft and Wizardry"), others are just frequent in general ("but they did not say"); we do not know yet which ones.

All n-grams are submitted as queries to the web search engine. Exact matches of the n-grams are required; different inflections or matches of the words individually are not accepted.

The search engine returns the total number of hits $h(q_s)$ for each query q_s as well as the URLs of a predefined maximum number of "top hit" web pages. The top hit pages are downloaded and post-processed into plain text, from which duplicate paragraphs and paragraphs with a high OOV rate are removed.

N-gram language models are then trained separately on the in-domain text and the the filtered web text. If the amount of web text is very large, only a subset is used, which consists of the parts of the web data that are the most similar to the in-domain text. As a similarity measure, relative perplexity is used. The LM trained on web data is called a *background LM* to distinguish it from the *in-domain LM*.

2.2 Focused querying

Next, the querying is made more specific and targeted on the domain of interest. New queries are created that consist of n-gram pairs, requiring that a document contain two n-grams ("but they did not say"+"Hogwarts School of Witchcraft and Wizardry").[2]

If all possible n-gram pairs are formed from the n-grams selected in Section 2.1, the number of pairs is very large, and we cannot afford using them all as queries. Typical approaches for query selection include the following: (i) select pairs that include n-grams that are relatively more frequent in the in-domain text than in the background text, (ii) use some extra source of knowledge for selecting the best pairs.

2.2.1 Extra linguistic knowledge

We first tested the second (ii) query selection approach by incorporating some simple linguistic knowledge: In an experiment on English, queries were obtained by combining a highly frequent n-gram with a slightly less frequent n-gram that had to contain a first- or second-person pronoun (I, you, we, me, us, my, your, our). Such n-grams were thought to capture direct speech, which is characteristic for the desired genre of personal communication. (Similar techniques are reported in the literature cited in Section 1.)

Although successful for English, this scheme is more difficult to apply to other languages, where person is conveyed as verbal suffixes rather than single words. Linguistic knowledge is needed for every language, and it turns out that many of the queries are "wasted", because they are too specific and return only few (if any) documents.

[2]Higher order tuples could be used as well, but we have only tested n-gram pairs.

2.2.2 Statistical approach

The other proposed query selection technique (i) allows for an automatic identification of the n-grams that are characteristic of the in-domain genre. If the relative frequency of an n-gram is higher in the in-domain data than in the background data, then the n-gram is potentially valuable. However, as in the linguistic approach, there is no guarantee that queries are not wasted, since the identified n-gram may be very rare on the Internet. Pairing it with some other n-gram (which may also be rare) often results in very few hits.

To get out the most of the queries, we propose a query selection algorithm that attempts to optimize the relevance of the query to the target domain, but also takes into account the expected amount of data retrieved by the query. Thus, the potential queries are ranked according to the *expected number of retrieved relevant documents*. Only the highest ranked pairs, which are likely to produce the highest number of relevant web pages, are used as queries.

We denote queries that consist of two n-grams s and t by $q_{s\wedge t}$. The expected number of retrieved relevant documents for the query $q_{s\wedge t}$ is $r(q_{s\wedge t})$:

$$r(q_{s\wedge t}) = n(q_{s\wedge t}) \cdot \rho(q_{s\wedge t} \mid Q), \qquad (1)$$

where $n(q_{s\wedge t})$ is the expected number of retrieved documents for the query, and $\rho(q_{s\wedge t} \mid Q)$ is the expected proportion of relevant documents within all documents retrieved by the query. The expected proportion of relevant documents is a value between zero and one, and as explained below, it is dependent on all past queries, the query history Q.

Expected number of retrieved documents $n(q_{s\wedge t})$. From the prospection querying phase (Section 2.1), we know the numbers of hits for the single n-grams s and t, separately: $h(q_s)$ and $h(q_t)$. We make the operational, but overly simplifying, assumption that the n-grams occur evenly distributed over the web collection, independently of each other. The expected size of the intersection $q_{s\wedge t}$ is then:

$$\hat{h}(q_{s\wedge t}) = \frac{h(q_s) \cdot h(q_t)}{N}, \qquad (2)$$

where N is the size of the web collection that our n-gram selection covers (total number of documents). N is not known, but different estimates can be used, for instance, $N = \max_{\forall q_s} h(q_s)$, where it is assumed that the most frequent n-gram occurs in every document in the collection (probably an underestimate of the actual value).

Ideally, the expected number of retrieved documents equals the expected number of hits, but since the search engine returns a limited maximum number of "top hit" pages, M, we get:

$$n(q_{s \wedge t}) = \min(\hat{h}(q_{s \wedge t}), M). \quad (3)$$

Expected proportion of relevant documents $\rho(q_{s \wedge t} \mid Q)$. As in the case of $n(q_{s \wedge t})$, an independence assumption can be applied in the derivation of the expected proportion of relevant documents for the combined query $q_{s \wedge t}$: We simply put together the chances of obtaining relevant documents by the single n-gram queries q_s and q_t individually. The union equals:

$$\rho(q_{s \wedge t} \mid Q) = 1 - \big(1 - \rho(q_s \mid Q)\big) \cdot \big(1 - \rho(q_t \mid Q)\big). \quad (4)$$

However, we do not know the values for $\rho(q_s \mid Q)$ and $\rho(q_t \mid Q)$. As mentioned earlier, it is straightforward to obtain a relevance *ranking* for a set of n-grams: For each n-gram s, the LM probability is computed using both the in-domain and the background LM. The in-domain probability is divided by the background probability and the n-grams are sorted, highest relative probability first. The first n-gram is much more prominent in the in-domain than the background data, and we wish to obtain more text with this crucial n-gram. The opposite is true for the last n-gram.

We need to transform the ranking into $\rho(\cdot)$ values between zero and one. There is no absolute division into relevant and irrelevant documents from the point of view of LM training. We use a probabilistic query ranking scheme, such that we define that of all documents containing an x % relevant n-gram, x % are relevant. When the n-grams have been ranked into a presumed order of relevance, we decide that the most relevant n-gram is 100 % relevant and the least relevant n-gram is 0 % relevant; finally, we scale the relevances of the other n-grams according to rank.

When scoring the remaining n-grams, linear scaling is avoided, because the majority of the n-grams are irrelevant or neutral with respect to our domain of interest, and many of them would obtain fairly high relevance values. Instead, we fix the relevance value of the "most domain-neutral" n-gram (the one with the relative probability value closest to one); we might assume that only 5 % of all documents containing this n-gram are indeed relevant. We then fit a polynomial curve through the three points with known values (0, 0.05, and 1) to get the missing $\rho(\cdot)$ values for all q_s.

Decay factor $\delta(s \mid Q)$. We noticed that if constant relevance values are used, the top ranked queries will consist of a rather small set of top ranked n-grams that are paired with each other in all possible combinations. However, it is likely that each time an n-gram is used in a query, the need for finding more occurrences of this particular n-gram decreases. Therefore, we introduced a decay factor $\delta(s \mid Q)$, by which the initial $\rho(\cdot)$ value, written $\rho_0(q_s)$, is multiplied:

$$\rho(q_s \mid Q) = \rho_0(q_s) \cdot \delta(s \mid Q), \quad (5)$$

The decay is exponential:

$$\delta(s \mid Q) = (1 - \epsilon)^{\sum_{\forall s \in Q} 1}. \quad (6)$$

ϵ is a small value between zero and one (for instance 0.05), and $\sum_{\forall s \in Q} 1$ is the number of times the n-gram s has occurred in past queries.

Overlap with previous queries. Some queries are likely to retrieve the same set of documents as other queries. This occurs if two queries share one n-gram and there is strong correlation between the second n-grams (for instance, "we wish you"+"Merry Christmas" vs. "we wish you"+ "and a Happy New Year"). In principle, when assessing the relevance of a query, one should estimate the overlap of that query with all past queries. We have tested an approximate solution that allows for fast computing. However, the real effect of this addition was insignificant, and a further description is omitted in this paper.

Optimal order of the queries. We want to maximize the expected number of retrieved relevant documents while keeping the number of submitted queries as low as possible. Therefore we sort the queries best first and submit as many queries we can afford from the top of the list. However, the relevance of a query is dependent on the sequence of past queries (because of the decay factor). Finding the optimal order of the queries takes $O(n^2)$ operations, if n is the total number of queries.

A faster solution is to apply an iterative algorithm: All queries are put in some initial order. For each query, its $r(q_{s \wedge t})$ value is computed according to Equation 1. The queries are then rearranged into the order defined by the new $r(\cdot)$ values, best first. These two steps are repeated until convergence.

Repeated focused querying. Focused querying can be run multiple times. Some ten thousands of the top ranked queries are submitted to the search engine and the documents matching the queries are downloaded. A new background LM is trained using the new web data, and a new round of focused querying can take place.

2.2.3 Comparison of the linguistic and statistical focused querying schemes

On one language (German), the statical focused querying algorithm (Section 2.2.2) was shown to retrieve 50 % more unique web pages and 70 % more words than the linguistic scheme (Section 2.2.1) for the same number of queries. Also results from language modeling and speech recognition experiments favored statistical querying.

2.3 Web collections obtained

For the speech recognition experiments described in the current paper, we have collected web texts for three languages: US English, European Spanish, and Canadian French.

As in-domain data we used 230,000 English text messages (4 million words), 65,000 Spanish messages (2 million words), and 60,000 French messages (1 million words). These text messages were obtained in data collection projects involving thousand of participants, who used a web interface to enter messages according to different scenarios of personal communication situations.[3] A few example messages are shown in Figure 1.

The queries were submitted to Yahoo!'s web search engine. The web pages that were retrieved by the queries were filtered and cleaned and divided into chunks consisting of single paragraphs. For English, we obtained 210 million paragraphs and 13 billion words, for Spanish 160 million paragraphs and 12 billion words, and for French 44 million paragraphs and 3 billion words.

[3]Real messages sent from mobile phones would be the best data, but are hard to get because of privacy protection. The postprocessing of authentic messages would, however, require proper handling of artifacts resulting from the limited input capacities on keypads of mobile devices, such as specific acronyms: *i'll c u l8er*. In our setup, we did not have to face such issues.

I hope you have a long and happy marriage. Congratulations!
Remember to pick up Billy at practice at five o'clock!
Hey Eric, how was the trip with the kids over winter vacation? Did you go to Texas?

Figure 1: Example text messages (US English).

The linguistic focused querying method was applied in the US English task (because the statistical method did not yet exist). The Spanish and Canadian French web collections were obtained using statistical querying. Since the French set was smaller than the other sets ("only" 3 billion words), web crawling was performed, such that those web sites that had provided us with the most valuable data (measured by relative perplexity) were downloaded entirely. As a result, the number of paragraphs increased to 110 million and the number of words to 8 billion.

3 Speech Recognition Experiments

We have trained language models on the in-domain data together with web data, and these models have been used in speech recognition experiments. Two kinds of experiments have been performed: (1) the in-domain LM is augmented with web data, and (2) the LM is adapted to a user-specific vocabulary utilizing web data as an additional data source.

One hundred native speakers for each language were recorded reading held-out subsets of the in-domain text data. The speech data was partitioned into training and test sets, such that around one fourth of the speakers were reserved for testing.

We use a continuous speech recognizer optimized for low memory footprint and fast recognition (Olsen et al., 2008). The recognizer runs on a server (Core2 2.33 GHz) in about one fourth of real time. The LM probabilities are quantized and precompiled together with the speaker-independent acoustic models (intra-word triphones) into a finite state transducer (FST).

3.1 Language model augmentation

Each paragraph in the web data is treated as a potential text message and scored according to its similarity to the in-domain data. Relative perplexity is used as the similarity measure. The paragraphs are sorted, lowest relative perplexity first,

US English				
FST size [MB]	10	20	40	70
In-domain	42.7	40.1	39.1	–
Web mixture	42.0	37.6	35.7	33.8
Ppl reduction [%]	1.6	6.2	8.7	13.6

European Spanish				
FST size [MB]	10	20	25	40
In-domain	68.0	64.6	64.3	–
Web mixture	63.9	58.4	55.0	52.1
Ppl reduction [%]	6.0	9.6	14.5	19.0

Canadian French				
FST size [MB]	10	20	25	50
In-domain	57.6	–	–	–
Web mixture	51.7	47.9	45.9	44.6
Ppl reduction [%]	10.2	16.8	20.3	22.6

Table 1: *Perplexities.*

US English				
FST size [MB]	10	20	40	70
In-domain	17.9	17.5	17.3	–
Web mixture	17.5	16.7	16.4	15.8
WER reduction	2.2	4.4	5.2	8.4

European Spanish				
FST size [MB]	10	20	25	40
In-domain	18.9	18.7	18.6	–
Web mixture	18.7	17.9	17.4	16.8
WER reduction	1.4	4.1	6.6	9.7

Canadian French				
FST size [MB]	10	20	25	50
In-domain	22.6	–	–	–
Web mixture	22.1	21.7	21.3	20.9
WER reduction	2.3	4.1	5.8	7.5

Table 2: *Word error rates* [%].

In the tables, the perplexity and word error rate reductions of the web mixtures are computed with respect to the in-domain models of the same size, if such models exist; otherwise the comparison is made to the largest in-domain model available.

and the highest ranked paragraphs are used as LM training data. The optimal size of the set depends on the test, but the largest chosen set contains 15 million paragraphs and 500 million words.

Separate LMs are trained on the in-domain data and web data. The two LMs are then linearly interpolated into a mixture model. Roughly the same interpolation weights (0.5) are obtained for the LMs, when the optimal value is chosen based on a held-out in-domain development test set.

3.1.1 Test set perplexities

In Table 1, the prediction abilities of the in-domain and web mixture language models are compared. As an evaluation measure we use perplexity calculated on test sets consisting of in-domain text. The comparison is performed on FSTs of different sizes. The FSTs contain the acoustic models, language model and lexicon, but the LM makes up for most of the size. The availability of data varies for the different languages, and therefore the FST sizes are not exactly the same across languages.

The LMs have been created using the SRI LM toolkit (Stolcke, 2002). Good-Turing smoothing with Katz backoff (Katz, 1987) has been used, and the different model sizes are obtained by pruning down the full models using entropy-based pruning (Stolcke, 1998). N-gram orders up to five have been tested: 5-grams always work best on the mixture models, whereas the best in-domain models are 4- or 5-grams.

For every language and model size, the web mixture model performs better than the corresponding in-domain model. The perplexity reductions obtained increase with the size of the model. Since it is possible to create larger mixture models than in-domain models, there are no in-domain results for the largest model sizes.

Especially if large models can be afforded, the perplexity reductions are considerable. The largest improvements are observed for French (between 10.2 % and 22.6 % relative). This is not surprising, as the French in-domain set is the smallest, which leaves much room for improvement.

3.1.2 Word error rates

Speech recognition results for the different LMs are given in Table 2. The results are consistent in the sense that the web mixture models outperform the in-domain models, and augmentation helps more with larger models. The largest word error rate reduction is observed for the largest Spanish model (9.7 % relative). All WER reductions are statistically significant (one-sided Wilcoxon signed-rank test; level 0.05) except the 10 MB Spanish setup.

Although the observed word error rate reductions are mostly smaller than the corresponding perplexity reductions, the results are actually very good, when we consider the fact that considerable reductions in perplexity may typically translate into meager word error reductions; see, for instance, Rosenfeld (2000), Goodman (2001). This suggests that the web texts are very welcome complementary data that improve on the robustness of the recognition.

3.1.3 Modified Kneser-Ney smoothing

In the above experiments, Good-Turing (GT) smoothing with Katz backoff was used, although modified Kneser-Ney (KN) interpolation has been shown to outperform other smoothing methods (Chen and Goodman, 1999). However, as demonstrated by Siivola et al. (2007), KN smoothing is not compatible with simple pruning methods such as entropy-based pruning. In order to make a meaningful comparison, we used the revised Kneser pruning and Kneser-Ney growing techniques proposed by Siivola et al. (2007). For the three languages, we built KN models that resulted in FSTs of the same sizes as the largest GT in-domain models. The perplexities decreased 4–8%, but in speech recognition, the improvements were mostly negligible: the error rates were 17.0 for English, 18.7 for Spanish, and 22.5 for French.

For English, we also created web mixture models with KN smoothing. The error rates were 16.5, 15.9 and 15.7 for the 20 MB, 40 MB and 70 MB models, respectively. Thus, Kneser-Ney outperformed Good-Turing, but the improvements were small, and a statistically significant difference was measured only for the 40 MB LMs. This was expected, as it has been observed before that very simple smoothing techniques can perform well on large data sets, such as web data (Brants et al., 2007).

For the purpose of demonstrating the usefulness of our web data retrieval system, we concluded that there was no significant difference between GT and KN smoothing in our current setup.

3.2 Language model adaptation

In the second set of experiments we envisage a system that adapts to the user's own vocabulary. Some words that the user needs may not be included in the built-in vocabulary of the device, such as names in the user's contact list, names of places or words related to some specific hobby or other focus of interest.

Two adaptation techniques have been tested: (1) *Unigram adaptation* is a simple technique, in which user-specific words (for instance, names from the contact list) are added to the vocabulary. No context information is available, and thus only unigram probabilities are created for these words. (2) In *message adaptation*, the LM is augmented selectively with paragraphs of web data that contain user-specific words. Now, higher order n-grams can be estimated, since the words occur within passages of running text. This idea is not new: information retrieval has been suggested as a solution by Bigi et al. (2004) among others.

In our message adaptation, we have not created web queries dynamically on demand. Instead, we used the large web collections described in Section 2.3, from which we selected paragraphs containing user-specific words. We have tested both adaptation by pooling (adding the paragraphs to the original training data), and adaptation by interpolation (using the new data to train a separate LM, which is interpolated with the original LM). One million words from the web data were selected for each language. The adaptation was thought to take place off-line on a server.

3.2.1 Data sets

For each language, the adaptation takes place on two baseline models, which are the in-domain and web mixture LMs of Section 3.1; however, the amount of in-domain training data is reduced slightly (as explained below).

In order to evaluate the success of the adaptation, a simulated user-specific test set is created. This set is obtained by selecting a subset of a larger potential test set. Words that occur both in the training set and the potential test set and that are infrequent in the training set are chosen as the user-specific vocabulary. For Spanish and French, a training set frequency threshold of one is used, resulting in 606 and 275 user-specific words, respectively. For English the threshold is 5, which results in 99 words. All messages in the potential test set containing any of these words are selected into the user-specific test set. Any message containing user-specific words is removed from the in-domain training set. In this manner, we obtain a test set with a certain over-representation of a specific vocabulary, without biasing the word frequency distribution of the training set to any noticeable degree.

For comparison, performance is additionally computed on a generic in-domain test set, as be-

US English, 23 MB models				
Model	WER (reduction)			
	user-specific		in-domain	
In-domain	29.1	(–)	17.9	(–)
+unigram adapt.	*24.4*	(16.3)	*17.1*	(4.7)
+message adapt.	*21.6*	(26.0)	16.8	(6.0)
Web mixture	25.7	(11.8)	16.9	(5.9)
+unigram adapt.	*23.1*	(20.6)	*16.3*	(8.8)
+message adapt.	*22.2*	(23.8)	16.4	(8.5)

European Spanish, 23 MB models				
Model	WER (reduction)			
	user-specific		in-domain	
In-domain	25.3	(–)	18.6	(–)
+unigram adapt.	*23.4*	(7.7)	18.5	(0.3)
+message adapt.	*21.7*	(14.4)	*18.0*	(3.2)
Web mixture	21.9	(13.7)	17.5	(5.8)
+unigram adapt.	*21.5*	(15.3)	17.7	(5.0)
+message adapt.	*21.2*	(16.5)	17.7	(4.7)

Canadian French, 21 MB models				
Model	WER (reduction)			
	user-specific		in-domain	
In-domain	30.3	(–)	22.6	(–)
+unigram adapt.	*28.3*	(6.4)	22.5	(0.4)
+message adapt.	*26.6*	(12.1)	22.2	(1.8)
Web mixture	26.7	(11.8)	21.4	(5.1)
+unigram adapt.	*26.0*	(14.3)	21.4	(5.4)
+message adapt.	26.0	(14.2)	21.6	(4.3)

Table 3: *Adaptation, word error rates* [%]. Six models have been evaluated on two types of test sets: a user-specific test set with a higher number of user-specific words and a generic in-domain test set. The numbers in brackets are relative WER reductions [%] compared to the in-domain model. WER values for the unigram adaptation are rendered in italics, if the improvement obtained is statistically significant compared to the corresponding non-adapted model. WER values for the message adaptation are in italics, if there is a statistically significant reduction with respect to unigram adaptation.

fore. User-specific and generic development test sets are used for the estimation of optimal interpolation weights.

3.2.2 Results

The adaptation experiments are summarized in Table 3. Only medium sized FSTs (21–23 MB) have been tested. The two baseline models have been adapted using the simple unigram reweighting scheme and using selective web message augmentation. For the in-domain baseline, pooling works the best, that is, adding the web messages to the original in-domain training set. For the web mixture baseline, a mixture model is the only option; that is, one more layer of interpolation is added.

In the adaptation of the in-domain LMs, message selection is almost twice as effective as unigram adaptation for all data sets. Also the performance on the generic in-domain test set is slightly improved, because more training data is available.

Except for English, the best results on the user-specific test sets are produced by the adaptation of the web mixture models. The benefit of using message adaptation instead of simple unigram adaptation is smaller when we have a web mixture model as a baseline rather than an in-domain-only LM.

On the generic test sets, the adaptation of the web mixture makes a difference only for English. Since there were practically no singleton words in the English in-domain data, the user-specific vocabulary consists of words occurring at most five times. Thus, the English user-specific words are more frequent than their Spanish and French equivalents, which shows in larger WER reductions for English in all types of adaptation.

4 Discussion and conclusion

Mobile applications need to run in small memory, but not much attention is usually paid to memory consumption in related LM work. We have shown that LM augmentation using web data can be successful, even when the resulting mixture model is not allowed to grow any larger than the initial in-domain model. Yet, the benefit of the web data is larger, the larger model can be used.

The largest WER reductions were observed in the adaptation to a user-specific vocabulary. This can be compared to Misu and Kawahara (2006), who obtained similar accuracy improvements with clever selection of web data, when there was initially no in-domain data available with both the correct topic and speaking style.

We used relative perplexity ranking to filter the downloaded web data. More elaborate algorithms could be exploited, such as the one proposed by Sethy et al. (2007). Initially, we have experimented along those lines, but it did not pay off; maybe future refinements will be more successful.

References

Adam Berger and Robert Miller. 1998. Just-in-time language modeling. In *In ICASSP-98*, pages 705–708.

Brigitte Bigi, Yan Huang, and Renato De Mori. 2004. Vocabulary and language model adaptation using information retrieval. In *Proc. Interspeech 2004 – ICSLP*, pages 1361–1364, Jeju Island, Korea.

Thorsten Brants, Ashok C. Popat, Peng Xu, Franz J. Och, and Jeffrey Dean. 2007. Large language models in machine translation. In *Proceedings of the 2007 Joint Conference on Empirical Methods in Natural Language Processing and Computational Natural Language Learning (EMNLP-CoNLL)*, pages 858–867.

Ivan Bulyko, Mari Ostendorf, and Andreas Stolcke. 2003. Getting more mileage from web text sources for conversational speech language modeling using class-dependent mixtures. In *NAACL '03: Proceedings of the 2003 Conference of the North American Chapter of the Association for Computational Linguistics on Human Language Technology*, pages 7–9, Morristown, NJ, USA. Association for Computational Linguistics.

Ivan Bulyko, Mari Ostendorf, Manhung Siu, Tim Ng, Andreas Stolcke, and Özgür Çetin. 2007. Web resources for language modeling in conversational speech recognition. *ACM Trans. Speech Lang. Process.*, 5(1):1–25.

Özgür Çetin and Andreas Stolcke. 2005. Language modeling in the ICSI-SRI spring 2005 meeting speech recognition evaluation system. Technical Report 05-006, International Computer Science Institute, Berkeley, CA, USA, July.

S. F. Chen and J. Goodman. 1999. An empirical study of smoothing techniques for language modeling. *Computer Speech and Language*, 13:359–394.

Joshua T. Goodman. 2001. A bit of progress in language modeling. *Computer Speech and Language*, 15:403–434.

Slava M. Katz. 1987. Estimation of probabilities from sparse data for the language model component of a speech recognizer. *IEEE Transactions on Acoustics, Speech and Signal Processing*, ASSP-35(3):400–401, March.

Teruhisa Misu and Tatsuya Kawahara. 2006. A bootstrapping approach for developing language model of new spoken dialogue systems by selecting web texts. In *Proc. INTERSPEECH '06*, pages 9–13, Pittsburgh, PA, USA, September, 17–21.

Jesper Olsen, Yang Cao, Guohong Ding, and Xinxing Yang. 2008. A decoder for large vocabulary continuous short message dictation on embedded devices. In *Proc. ICASSP 2008*, Las Vegas, Nevada.

Ronald Rosenfeld. 2000. Two decades of language modeling: Where do we go from here? *Proceedings of the IEEE*, 88(8):1270–1278.

Ruhi Sarikaya, Augustin Gravano, and Yuqing Gao. 2005. Rapid language model development using external resources for new spoken dialog domains. In *Proc. IEEE International Conference on Acoustics, Speech, and Signal Processing (ICASSP '05)*, volume I, pages 573–576.

Abhinav Sethy, Shrikanth Narayanan, and Bhuvana Ramabhadran. 2007. Data driven approach for language model adaptation using stepwise relative entropy minimization. In *Proc. IEEE International Conference on Acoustics, Speech, and Signal Processing (ICASSP '07)*, volume IV, pages 177–180.

Vesa Siivola, Teemu Hirsimäki, and Sami Virpioja. 2007. On growing and pruning Kneser-Ney smoothed n-gram models. *IEEE Transactions on Audio, Speech and Language Processing*, 15(5):1617–1624.

A. Stolcke. 1998. Entropy-based pruning of backoff language models. In *Proc. DARPA BNTU Workshop*, pages 270–274, Lansdowne, VA, USA.

A. Stolcke. 2002. SRILM – an extensible language modeling toolkit. In *Proc. ICSLP*, pages 901–904. `http://www.speech.sri.com/projects/srilm/`.

Vincent Wan and Thomas Hain. 2006. Strategies for language model web-data collection. In *Proc. IEEE International Conference on Acoustics, Speech, and Signal Processing (ICASSP '06)*, volume I, pages 1069–1072.

Karl Weilhammer, Matthew N. Stuttle, and Steve Young. 2006. Bootstrapping language models for dialogue systems. In *Proc. INTERSPEECH 2006 - ICSLP Ninth International Conference on Spoken Language Processing*, Pittsburgh, PA, USA, September 17–21.

Xiaojin Zhu and R. Rosenfeld. 2001. Improving trigram language modeling with the world wide web. In *Proc. IEEE International Conference on Acoustics, Speech, and Signal Processing (ICASSP '01)*., volume 1, pages 533–536.

An Alignment Algorithm using Belief Propagation and a Structure-Based Distortion Model

Fabien Cromières
Graduate school of informatics
Kyoto University
Kyoto, Japan
fabien@nlp.kuee.kyoto-u.ac.jp

Sadao Kurohashi
Graduate school of informatics
Kyoto University
Kyoto, Japan
kuro@i.kyoto-u.ac.jp

Abstract

In this paper, we first demonstrate the interest of the Loopy Belief Propagation algorithm to train and use a simple alignment model where the expected marginal values needed for an efficient EM-training are not easily computable. We then improve this model with a distortion model based on structure conservation.

1 Introduction and Related Work

Automatic word alignment of parallel corpora is an important step for data-oriented Machine translation (whether Statistical or Example-Based) as well as for automatic lexicon acquisition. Many algorithms have been proposed in the last twenty years to tackle this problem. One of the most successfull alignment procedure so far seems to be the so-called "IBM model 4" described in (Brown et al., 1993). It involves a very complex distortion model (here and in subsequent usages "distortion" will be a generic term for the reordering of the words occurring in the translation process) with many parameters that make it very complex to train.

By contrast, the first alignment model we are going to propose is fairly simple. But this simplicity will allow us to try and experiment different ideas for making a better use of the sentence structures in the alignment process. This model (and even more so its subsequents variations), although simple, do not have a computationally efficient procedure for an exact EM-based training. However, we will give some theoretical and empirical evidences that Loopy Belief Propagation can give us a good approximation procedure.

Although we do not have the space to review the many alignment systems that have already been proposed, we will shortly refer to works that share some similarities with our approach. In particular, the first alignment model we will present has already been described in (Melamed, 2000). We differ however in the training and decoding procedure we propose. The problem of making use of syntactic trees for alignment (and translation), which is the object of our second alignment model has already received some attention, notably by (Yamada and Knight, 2001) and (Gildea, 2003) .

2 Factor Graphs and Belief Propagation

In this paper, we will make several use of Factor Graphs. A Factor Graph is a graphical model, much like a Bayesian Network. The three most common types of graphical models (Factor Graphs, Bayesian Network and Markov Network) share the same purpose: intuitively, they allow to represent the dependencies among random variables; mathematically, they represent a factorization of the joint probability of these variables.

Formally, a factor graph is a bipartite graph with 2 kinds of nodes. On one side, the Variable Nodes (abbreviated as V-Node from here on), and on the other side, the Factor Nodes (abbreviated as F-Node). If a Factor Graph represents a given joint distribution, there will be one V-Node for every random variable in this joint distribution. Each F-Node is associated with a function of the V-Nodes to which it is connected (more precisely, a function of the values of the random variables associated with the V-Nodes, but for brevity, we will frequently mix the notions of V-Node, Random Variables and their values). The joint distribution is then the product of these functions (and of a normalizing constant). Therefore, each F-Node actually represent a factor in the factorization of the joint distribution.

As a short example, let us consider a problem classically used to introduce Bayesian Network. We want to model the joint probability of the Weather(W) being sunny or rainy, the Sprinkle(S) being on or off, and the Lawn(L) being wet or dry. Figure 1 show the dependencies of

Proceedings of the 12th Conference of the European Chapter of the ACL, pages 166–174,
Athens, Greece, 30 March – 3 April 2009.

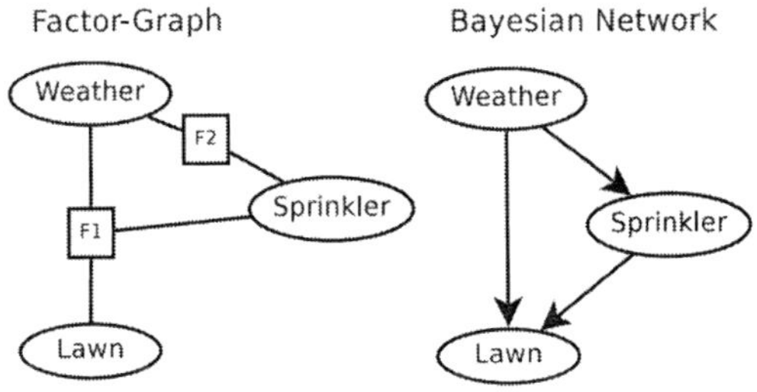

Figure 1: A classical example

the variables represented with a Factor Graph and with a Bayesian Network. Mathematically, the Bayesian Network imply that the joint probability has the following factorization: $P(W, L, S) = P(W) \cdot P(S|W) \cdot P(L|W, S)$. The Factor Graph imply there exist two functions φ_1 and φ_2 as well as a normalization constant C such that we have the factorization: $P(W, L, S) = C \cdot \varphi_2(W, S) \cdot \varphi_1(L, W, S)$. If we set $C = 1$, $\varphi_2(W, S) = P(W) \cdot P(S|W)$ and $\varphi_1(L, W, S) = P(L|W, S)$, the Factor Graph express exactly the same factorization as the Bayesian Network.

A reason to use Graphical Models is that we can use with them an algorithm called Belief Propagation (abbreviated as BP from here on) (Pearl, 1988). The BP algorithm comes in two flavors: sum-product BP and max-product BP. Each one respectively solve two problems that arise often (and are often intractable) in the use of a probabilistic model: "what are the marginal probabilities of each individual variable?" and "what is the set of values with the highest probability?". More precisely, the BP algorithm will give the correct answer to these questions if the graph representing the distribution is a forest. If it is not the case, the BP algorithm is not even guaranteed to converge. It has been shown, however, that the BP algorithm do converge in many practical cases, and that the results it produces are often surprisingly good approximations (see, for example, (Murphy et al., 1999) or (Weiss and Freeman, 2001)).

(Yedidia et al., 2003) gives a very good presentation of the sum-product BP algorithm, as well as some theoretical justifications for its success. We will just give an outline of the algorithm. The BP algorithm is a message-passing algorithm. Messages are sent during several iterations until convergence. At each iteration, each V-Node sends to its neighboring F-Nodes a message representing an estimation of its own marginal values. The message sent by the V-Node V_i to the F-Node F_j estimating the marginal probability of V_i to take the value x is :

$$m_{Vi \to Fj}(x) = \prod_{Fk \in N(Vi) \setminus Fj} m_{Fk \to Vi}(x)$$

(N(Vi) represent the set of the neighbours of V_i)

Also, every F-Node send a message to its neighboring V-Nodes that represent its estimates of the marginal values of the V-Node:

$$m_{Fj \to Vi}(x) = \sum_{v_1, \ldots, v_n} \varphi_j(v_1, .., x, .., v_n) \cdot$$

$$\cdot \prod_{Vk \in N(Fj) \setminus Vi} m_{Vk \to Fj}(v_k)$$

At any point, the *belief* of a V-Node Vi is given by

$$b_i(x) = \prod_{Fk \in N(Vi)} m_{Fk \to Vi}(x)$$

, b_i being normalized so that $\sum_x b_i(x) = 1$. The belief $b_i(x)$ is expected to converge to the marginal probability (or an approximation of it) of V_i taking the value x .

An interesting point to note is that each message can be "scaled" (that is, multiplied by a constant) by any factor at any point without changing the result of the algorithm. This is very useful both for preventing overflow and underflow during computation, and also sometimes for simplifying the algorithm (we will use this in section 3.2). Also, damping schemes such as the ones proposed in (Murphy et al., 1999) or (Heskes, 2003) are useful for decreasing the cases of non-convergence.

As for the max-product BP, it is best explained as "sum-product BP where each sum is replaced by a maximization".

3 The monolink model

We are now going to present a simple alignment model that will serve both to illustrate the efficiency of the BP algorithm and as basis for further improvement. As previously mentioned, this model is mostly identical to one already proposed in (Melamed, 2000). The training and decoding procedures we propose are however different.

3.1 Description

Following the usual convention, we will designate the two sides of a sentence pair as *French* and *English*. A sentence pair will be noted (e, f). e_i represents the word at position i in e.

In this first simple model, we will pay little attention to the structure of the sentence pair we want to align. Actually, each sentence will be reduced to a bag of words.

Intuitively, the two sides of a sentence pair express the same set of meanings. What we want to do in the alignment process is find the parts of the sentences that originate from the same meaning. We will suppose here that each meaning generate at most one word on each side, and we will name *concept* the pair of words generated by a meaning. It is possible for a meaning to be expressed in only one side of the sentence pair. In that case, we will have a *"one-sided" concept* consisting of only one word. In this view, a sentence pair appears "superficially" as a pair of bag of words, but the bag of words are themselves the visible part of an underlying bag of concepts.

We propose a simple generative model to describe the generation of a sentence pair (or rather, its underlying bag of concepts):

- First, an integer n, representing the number of concepts of the sentence is drawn from a distribution P_{size}
- Then, n concepts are drawn independently from a distribution $P_{concept}$

The probability of a bag of concepts $\mathcal{C}$ is then:

$$P(\mathcal{C}) = P_{size}(|\mathcal{C}|) \prod_{(w_1,w_2)\in\mathcal{C}} P_{concept}((w_1, w_2))$$

We can alternatively represent a bag of concepts as a pair of sentence (e, f), plus an alignment a. a is a set of links, a link being represented as a pair of positions in each side of the sentence pair (the special position -1 indicating the empty side of a one-sided concept). This alternative representation has the advantage of better separating what is observed (the sentence pair) and what is hidden (the alignment). It is not a strictly equivalent representation (it also contains information about the word positions) but this will not be relevant here. The joint distribution of e,f and a is then:

$$P(e, f, a) = P_{size}(|a|) \prod_{(i,j)\in a} P_{concept}(e_i, f_j) \quad (1)$$

This model only take into consideration one-to-one alignments. Therefore, from now on, we will call this model "monolink". Considering only one-to-one alignments can be seen as a limitation compared to others models that can often produce at least one-to-many alignments, but on the good side, this allow the monolink model to be nicely symmetric. Additionally, as already argued in (Melamed, 2000), there are ways to determine the boundaries of some multi-words phrases (Melamed, 2002), allowing to treat several words as a single token. Alternatively, a procedure similar to the one described in (Cromieres, 2006), where substrings instead of single words are aligned (thus considering every segmentation possible) could be used.

With the monolink model, we want to do two things: first, we want to find out good values for the distributions P_{size} and $P_{concept}$. Then we want to be able to find the most likely alignment a given the sentence pair (e, f).

We will consider P_{size} to be a uniform distribution over the integers up to a sufficiently big value (since it is not possible to have a uniform distribution over an infinite discrete set). We will not need to determine the exact value of P_{size} . The assumption that it is uniform is actually enough to "remove" it of the computations that follow.

In order to determine the $P_{concept}$ distribution, we can use an EM procedure. It is easy to show that, at every iteration, the EM procedure will require to set $P_{concept}(w_e, w_f)$ proportional to the sum of the expected counts of the concept (w_e, w_f) over the training corpus. This, in turn, mean we have to compute the conditional expectation:

$$E((i,j) \in a|e, f) = \sum_{a|(i,j)\in a} P(a|e, f)$$

for every sentence pair (e, f). This computation require a sum over all the possible alignments, whose numbers grow exponentially with the size of the sentences. As noted in (Melamed, 2000), it does not seem possible to compute this expectation efficiently with dynamic programming tricks like the one used in the IBM models 1 and 2 (as a passing remark, these "tricks" can actually be seen as instances of the BP algorithm).

We propose to solve this problem by applying the BP algorithm to a Factor Graph representing the conditional distribution $P(a|e, f)$. Given a sentence pair (e, f), we build this graph as follows.

We create a V-node V_i^e for every position i in the English sentence. This V-Node can take for

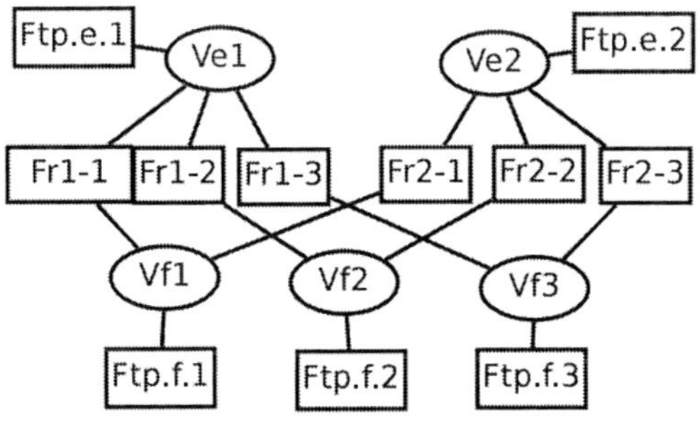

Figure 2: A Factor Graph for the monolink model in the case of a 2-words English sentence and a 3-words french sentence (F_{ij}^{rec} nodes are noted Fri-j)

value any position in the french sentence, or the special position -1 (meaning this position is not aligned, corresponding to a one-sided concept). We create symmetrically a V-node V_j^f for every position in the french sentence.

We have to enforce a "reciprocal love" condition: if a V-Node at position i choose a position j on the opposite side, the opposite V-Node at position j must choose the position i. This is done by adding a F-Node $F_{i,j}^{rec}$ between every opposite node V_i^e and V_j^f, associated with the function:

$$\varphi_{i,j}^{rec}(k,l) = \begin{cases} 1 & \text{if } (i = l \text{ and } j = k) \\ & \text{or } (i \neq l \text{ and } j \neq k) \\ 0 & \text{else} \end{cases}$$

We then connect a "translation probability" F-Node $F_i^{tp.e}$ to every V-Node V_i^e associated with the function:

$$\varphi_i^{tp.e}(j) = \begin{cases} \sqrt{P_{concept}(e_i, f_j)} & \text{if } j \neq -1 \\ P_{concept}(e_i, \emptyset) & \text{if } j = -1 \end{cases}$$

We add symmetrically on the French side F-Nodes $F_j^{tp.f}$ to the V-Nodes V_j^f.

It should be fairly easy to see that such a Factor Graph represents $P(a|e,f)$. See figure 2 for an example.

Using the sum-product BP, the beliefs of every V-Node V_i^e to take the value j and of every node V_j^f to take the value i should converge to the marginal expectation $E((i,j) \in a|e,f)$ (or rather, a hopefully good approximation of it).

We can also use max-product BP on the same graph to decode the most likely alignment. In the monolink case, decoding is actually an instance of the "assignment problem", for which efficient algorithms are known. However this will not be the case for the more complex model of the next section. Actually, (Bayati et al., 2005) has recently proved that max-product BP always give the optimal solution to the assignment problem.

3.2 Efficient BP iterations

Applying naively the BP algorithm would lead us to a complexity of $O(|e|^2 \cdot |f|^2)$ per BP iteration. While this is not intractable, it could turn out to be a bit slow. Fortunately, we found it is possible to reduce this complexity to $O(|e| \cdot |f|)$ by making two useful observations.

Let us note m_{ij}^e the resulting message from V_i^e to V_j^f (that is the message sent by $F_{i,j}^{rec}$ to V_j^f after it received its own message from V_i^e). $m_{ij}^e(x)$ has the same value for every x different from i: $m_{ij}^e(x \neq i) = \sum_{k \neq j} \frac{b_i^e(k)}{m_{ji}^f(k)}$. We can divide all the messages m_{ij}^e by $m_{ij}^e(x \neq i)$, so that $m_{ij}^e(x) = 1$ except if $x = i$; and the same can be done for the messages coming from the French side m_{ij}^f. It follows that $m_{ij}^e(x \neq i) = \sum_{k \neq j} b_i^e(k) = 1 - b_i^e(j)$ if the b_i^e are kept normalized. Therefore, at every step, we only need to compute $m_{ij}^e(j)$, not $m_{ij}^e(x \neq j)$.

Hence the following algorithm ($m_{ij}^e(j)$ will be here abbreviated to m_{ij}^e since it is the only value of the message we need to compute). We describe the process for computing the English-side messages and beliefs (m_{ij}^e and b_i^e) , but the process must also be done symmetrically for the French-side messages and beliefs (m_{ij}^f and b_i^f) at every iteration.

0- Initialize all messages and beliefs with: $m_{ij}^{e(0)} = 1$ and $b_i^{e(0)}(j) = \varphi_i^{tp.e}(j)$

Until convergence (or for a set number of iteration):

1- Compute the messages m_{ij}^e: $m_{ij}^{e(t+1)} = b_i^{e(t)}(j)/((1 - b_i^{e(t)}(j)) \cdot m_{ji}^{f(t)})$

2- Compute the beliefs $b_i^e(j)$:$b_i(j)^{e(t+1)} = \varphi_i^{tp.e}(j) \cdot m_{ji}^{f(t+1)}$

3- And then normalize the $b_i(j)^{e(t+1)}$ so that $\sum_j b_i(j)^{e(t+1)} = 1$.

A similar algorithm can be found for the max-product BP.

3.3 Experimental Results

We evaluated the monolink algorithm with two languages pairs: French-English and Japanese-English.

For the English-French Pair, we used 200,000 sentence pairs extracted from the Hansard corpus (Germann, 2001). Evaluation was done with the scripts and gold standard provided during the workshop HLT-NAACL 2003[1] (Mihalcea and Pedersen, 2003). Null links are not considered for the evaluation.

For the English-Japanese evaluation, we used 100,000 sentence pairs extracted from a corpus of English/Japanese news. We used 1000 sentence pairs extracted from pre-aligned data(Utiyama and Isahara, 2003) as a gold standard. We segmented all the Japanese data with the automatic segmenter Juman (Kurohashi and Nagao, 1994). There is a caveat to this evaluation, though. The reason is that the segmentation and alignment scheme used in our gold standard is not very fine-grained: mostly, big chunks of the Japanese sentence covering several words are aligned to big chunks of the English sentence. For the evaluation, we had to consider that when two chunks are aligned, there is a link between every pair of words belonging to each chunk. A consequence is that our gold standard will contain a lot more links than it should, some of them not relevants. This means that the recall will be largely underestimated and the precision will be overestimated.

For the BP/EM training, we used 10 BP iterations for each sentences, and 5 global EM iterations. By using a damping scheme for the BP algorithm, we never observed a problem of non-convergence (such problems do commonly appears without damping). With our python/C implementation, training time approximated 1 hour. But with a better implementation, it should be possible to reduce this time to something comparable to the model 1 training time with Giza++.

For the decoding, although the max-product BP should be the algorithm of choice, we found we could obtain slightly better results (by between 1 and 2 AER points) by using the sum-product BP, choosing links with high beliefs, and cutting-off links with very small beliefs (the cut-off was chosen roughly by manually looking at a few aligned sentences not used in the evaluation, so as not to create too much bias).

Due to space constraints, all of the results of this section and the next one are summarized in two tables (tables 1 and 2) at the end of this paper.

In order to compare the efficiency of the BP training procedure to a more simple one, we reimplemented the Competitive Link Algorithm (abbreviated as CLA from here on) that is used in (Melamed, 2000) to train an identical model. This algorithm starts with some relatively good estimates found by computing correlation score (we used the G-test score) between words based on their number of co-occurrences. A greedy Viterbi training is then applied to improve this initial guess. In contrast, our BP/EM training do not need to compute correlation scores and start the training with uniform parameters.

We only evaluated the CLA on the French/English pair. The first iteration of CLA did improve alignment quality, but subsequent ones decreased it. The reported score for CLA is therefore the one obtained during the best iteration. The BP/EM training demonstrate a clear superiority over the CLA here, since it produce almost 7 points of AER improvement over CLA.

In order to have a comparison with a well-known and state-of-the-art system, we also used the GIZA++ program (Och and Ney, 1999) to align the same data. We tried alignments in both direction and provide the results for the direction that gave the best results. The settings used were the ones used by the training scripts of the Moses system[2], which we assumed to be fairly optimal. We tried alignment with the default Moses settings (5 iterations of model 1, 5 of Hmm, 3 of model 3, 3 of model 4) and also tried with increased number of iterations for each model (up to 10 per model).

We are aware that the score we obtained for model 4 in English-French is slightly worse than what is usually reported for a similar size of training data. At the time of this paper, we did not have the time to investigate if it is a problem of non-optimal settings in GIZA++, or if the training data we used was "difficult to learn from" (it is common to extract sentences of moderate length for the training data but we didn't, and some sentences of our training corpus do have more than 200 words; also, we did not use any kind of pre-processing). In any case, Giza++ is compared here with an algorithm trained on the same data and with no possibilities for fine-tuning; therefore the comparison should be fair.

The comparison show that performance-wise, the monolink algorithm is between the model 2 and the model 3 for English/French. Considering

[1] http://www.cs.unt.edu/ rada/wpt/

[2] http://www.statmt.org/moses/

our model has the same number of parameters as the model 1 (namely, the word translation probabilities, or concept probabilities in our model), these are pretty good results. Overall, the monolink model tend to give better precision and worse recall than the Giza++ models, which was to be expected given the different type of alignments produced (1-to-1 and 1-to-many).

For English/Japanese, monolink is at just about the level of model 1, but model 1,2 and 3 have very close performances for this language pair (interestingly, this is different from the English/French pair). Incidentally, these performances are very poor. Recall was expected to be low, due to the previously mentioned problem with the gold standard. But precision was expected to be better. It could be the algorithms are confused by the very fine-grained segmentation produced by Juman.

4 Adding distortion through structure

4.1 Description

While the simple monolink model gives interesting results, it is somehow limited in that it do not use any model of distortion. We will now try to add a distortion model; however, rather than directly modeling the movement of the positions of the words, as is the case in the IBM models, we will try to design a distortion model based on the structures of the sentences. In particular, we are interested in using the trees produced by syntactic parsers.

The intuition we want to use is that, much like there is a kind of "lexical conservation" in the translation process, meaning that a word on one side has usually an equivalent on the other side, there should also be a kind of "structure conservation", with most structures on one side having an equivalent on the other.

Before going further, we should precise the idea of "structure" we are going to use. As we said, our prime (but not only) interest will be to make use of the syntactic trees of the sentences to be aligned. However these kind of trees come in very different shapes depending on the language and the type of parser used (dependency, constituents,...). This is why we decided the only information we would keep from a syntactic tree is the set of its sub-nodes. More specifically, for every sub-node, we will only consider the set of positions it cover in the underlying sentence. We will call such a set of positions a P-set. This simplification will allow

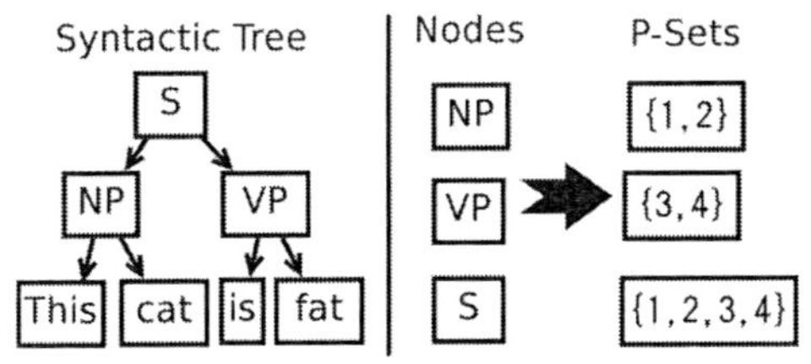

Figure 3: A small syntactic tree and the 3 P-Sets it generates

us to process dependency trees, constituents trees and other structures in a uniformized way. Figure 3 gives an example of a constituents tree and the P-sets it generates.

According to our intuition about the "conservation of structure", some (not all) of the P-sets on one side should have an equivalent on the other side. We can model this in a way similar to how we represented equivalence between words with *concepts*. We postulate that, in addition to a bag of concepts, sentence pairs are underlaid by a set of *P-concepts*. *P-concepts* being actually pairs of P-sets (a P-set for each side of the sentence pair). We also allow the existence of one-sided P-concepts.

In the previous model, sentence pairs where just bag of words underlaid by a or bag of concepts, and there was no modeling of the position of the words. P-concepts bring a notion of word position to the model. Intuitively, there should be coherency between P-concepts and concepts. This coherence will come from a *compatibility constraint*: if a sentence contains a two-sided P-concept (PS_e, PS_f), and if a word w_e covered by PS_e come from a two-sided concept (w_e, w_f), then w_f must be covered by PS_f.

Let us describe the model more formally. In the view of this model, a sentence pair is fully described by: e and f (the sentences themselves), a (the word alignment giving us the underlying bag of concept), s^e and s^f (the sets of P-sets on each side of the sentence) and a_s (the P-set alignment that give us the underlying set of P-concepts). e,f,s^e,s^f are considered to be observed (even if we will need parsing tools to observe s^e and s^f); a and a_s are hidden. The probability of a sentence pair is given by the joint probability of these variables :$P(e, f, s^e, s^f, a, a_s)$. By making some simple independence assumptions, we can write:

$$P(a, a_s, e, f, s^e, s^f) = P_{ml}(a, e, f) \cdot \\ \cdot P(s^e, s^f | e, f) \cdot P(a_s | a, s^e, s^f)$$

$P_{ml}(a, e, f)$ is taken to be identical to the monolink model (see equation (1)). We are not interested in $P(s^e, s^f|e, f)$ (parsers will deal with it for us). In our model, $P(a_s|a, s^e, s^f)$ will be equal to:

$$P(a_s|a, s^e, s^f) = C \cdot \prod_{(i,j)\in a_s} P_{pc}(s^e_i, s^f_j) \cdot$$
$$\cdot\, comp(a, a_s, s^e, s^f)$$

where $comp(a, a_s, s^e, s^f)$ is equal to 1 if the *compatibility constraint* is verified, and 0 else. C is a normalizing constant. P_{pc} describe the probability of each P-concept.

Although it would be possible to learn parameters for the distribution P_{pc} depending on the characteristics of each P-concepts, we want to keep our model simple. Therefore, P_{pc} will have only two different values. One for the one-sided P-concepts, and one for the two-sided ones. Considering the constraint of normalization, we then have actually one parameter: $\alpha = \frac{P_{pc}(1-sided)}{P_{pc}(2-sided)}$. Although it would be possible to learn the parameter α during the EM-training, we choose to set it at a preset value. Intuitively, we should have $0 < \alpha < 1$, because if α is greater than 1, then the one-sided P-concepts will be favored by the model, which is not what we want. Some empirical experiments showed that all values of α in the range [0.5,0.9] were giving good results, which lead to think that α can be set mostly independently from the training corpus.

We still need to train the concepts probabilities (used in $P_{ml}(a, e, f)$), and to be able to decode the most probable alignments. This is why we are again going to represent $P(a, a_s|e, f, s_e, s_f)$ as a Factor Graph.

This Factor Graph will contain two instances of the monolink Factor Graph as subgraph: one for a, the other for a_s (see figure 4). More precisely, we create again a V-Node for every position on each side of the sentence pair. We will call these V-Nodes "Word V-Nodes", to differentiate them from the new "P-set V-Nodes". We will create a "P-set V-Node" $V^{ps.e}_i$ for every P-set in s_e, and a "P-set V-Node" $V^{ps.f}_j$ for every P-set in s_j. We inter-connect all of the Word V-Nodes so that we have a subgraph identical to the Factor Graph used in the monolink case. We also create a "monolink subgraph" for the P-set V-Nodes.

We now have 2 disconnected subgraphs. However, we need to add F-Nodes between them to enforce the *compatibility constraint* between a_s and

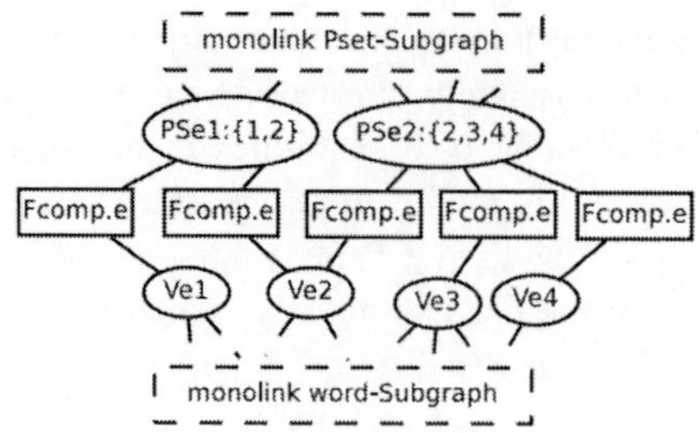

Figure 4: A part of a Factor Graph showing the connections between P-set V-Nodes and Word V-Nodes on the English side.The V-Nodes are connected to the French side through the 2 monolink subgraphs

a. On the English side, for every P-set V-Node V^{pse}_k, and for every position i that the corresponding P-set cover, we add a F-Node $F^{comp.e}_{k,i}$ between V^{pse}_k and V^e_i, associated with the function:

$$\varphi^{comp.e}_{k,i}(l, j) = \begin{cases} 1 & \text{if } j \in s^f_l \text{ or} \\ & j = -1 \text{ or } l = -1 \\ 0 & \text{else} \end{cases}$$

We proceed symmetrically on the French side.

Messages inside each monolink subgraph can still be computed with the efficient procedure described in section 3.2. We do not have the space to describe in details the messages sent between P-set V-Nodes and Word V-Nodes, but they are easily computed from the principles of the BP algorithm. Let $N_E = \sum_{ps\in s^e} |ps|$ and $N_F = \sum_{ps\in s^f} |ps|$. Then the complexity of one BP iteration will be $O(N_G \cdot N_D + |e| \cdot |f|)$.

An interesting aspect of this model is that it is flexible towards enforcing the respect of the structures by the alignment, since not every P-set need to have an equivalent in the opposite sentence. (Gildea, 2003) has shown that too strict an enforcement can easily degrade alignment quality and that good balance was difficult to find.

Another interesting aspect is the fact that we have a somehow "parameterless" distortion model. There is only one real-valued parameter to control the distortion: α. And even this parameter is actually pre-set before any training on real data. The distortion is therefore totally controlled by the two sets of P-sets on each side of the sentence.

Finally, although we introduced the P-sets as being generated from a syntactic tree, they do not need to. In particular, we found interesting to use P-sets consisting of every pair of adjacent positions in a sentence. For example, with a sentence of length 5, we generate the P-sets $\{1,2\}$,$\{2,3\}$,$\{3,4\}$ and $\{4,5\}$. The underlying intuition is that "adjacency" is often preserved in translation (we can see this as another case of "conservation of structure"). Practically, using P-sets of adjacent positions create a distortion model where permutation of words are not penalized, but gaps are penalized.

4.2 Experimental Results

The evaluation setting is the same as in the previous section. We created syntactic trees for every sentences. For English,we used the Dan Bikel implementation of the Collins parser (Collins, 2003). For French, the SYGMART parser (Chauché, 1984) and for Japanese, the KNP parser (Kurohashi and Nagao, 1994).

The line *SDM:Parsing* (SDM standing for "Structure-based Distortion Monolink") shows the results obtained by using P-sets from the trees produced by these parsers. The line *SDM:Adjacency* shows results obtained by using adjacent positions P-sets ,as described at the end of the previous section (therefore, *SDM:Adjacency* do not use any parser).

Several interesting observations can be made from the results. First, our structure-based distortion model did improve the results of the monolink model. There are however some surprising results. In particular, *SDM:Adjacency* produced surprisingly good results. It comes close to the results of the IBM model 4 in both language pairs, while it actually uses exactly the same parameters as model 1. The fact that an assumption as simple as "allow permutations, penalize gaps" can produce results almost on par with the complicated distortion model of model 4 might be an indication that this model is unnecessarily complex for languages with similar structure.Another surprising result is the fact that *SDM:Adjacency* gives better results for the English-French language pair than *SDM:Parsing*, while we expected that information provided by parsers would have been more relevant for the distortion model. It might be an indication that the structure of English and French is so close that knowing it provide only moderate information for word reordering. The contrast with the English-Japanese pair is, in this respect, very interesting. For this language pair, *SDM:Adjacency* did provide a strong improvement, but significantly less so than *SDM:Parsing*. This tend to show that for language pairs that have very different structures, the information provided by syntactic tree is much more relevant.

Algorithm	AER	P	R
Monolink	0.197	0.881	0.731
SDM:Parsing	0.166	0.882	0.813
SDM:Adjacency	0.135	**0.887**	0.851
CLA	0.26	0.819	0.665
GIZA++ /Model 1	0.281	0.667	0.805
GIZA++ /Model 2	0.205	0.754	0.863
GIZA++ /Model 3	0.162	0.806	0.890
GIZA++ /Model 4	**0.121**	0.849	**0.927**

Table 1: Results for English/French

Algorithm	F	P	R
Monolink	0.263	0.594	0.169
SDM:Parsing	0.291	**0.662**	0.186
SDM:Adjacency	0.279	0.636	0.179
GIZA++ /Model 1	0.263	0.555	0.172
GIZA++ /Model 2	0.268	0.566	0.176
GIZA++ /Model 3	0.267	0.589	0.173
GIZA++ /Model 4	**0.299**	0.658	**0.193**

Table 2: Results for Japanese/English.

5 Conclusion and Future Work

We will summarize what we think are the 4 more interesti ng contributions of this paper. BP algorithm has been shown to be useful and flexible for training and decoding complex alignment models. An original mostly non-parametrical distortion model based on a simplified structure of the sentences has been described. Adjacence constraints have been shown to produce very efficient distortion model. Empirical performances differences in the task of aligning Japanese and English to French hint that considering different paradigms depending on language pairs could be an improvement on the "one-size-fits-all" approach generally used in Statistical alignment and translation.

Several interesting improvement could also be made on the model we presented. Especially, a more elaborated P_{pc}, that would take into account the nature of the nodes (NP, VP, head,..) to parametrize the P-set alignment probability, and would use the EM-algorithm to learn those parameters.

References

M. Bayati, D. Shah, and M. Sharma. 2005. Maximum weight matching via max-product belief propagation. *Information Theory, 2005. ISIT 2005. Proceedings. International Symposium on*, pages 1763–1767.

Peter E Brown, Vincent J. Della Pietra, Stephen A. Della Pietra, and Robert L. Mercer, 1993. *The mathematics of statistical machine translation: parameter estimation*, volume 19, pages 263–311.

J. Chauché. 1984. *Un outil multidimensionnel de lanalyse du discours. Coling84.* Stanford University, California.

M. Collins. 2003. Head-driven statistical models for natural language parsing. *Computational Linguistics.*

Fabien Cromieres. 2006. Sub-sentential alignment using substring co-occurrence counts. In *Proceedings of ACL*. The Association for Computer Linguistics.

U. Germann. 2001. Aligned hansards of the 36th parliament of canada. *http://www.isi.edu/naturallanguage/download/hansard/.*

D. Gildea. 2003. Loosely tree-based alignment for machine translation. *Proceedings of ACL*, 3.

T. Heskes. 2003. Stable fixed points of loopy belief propagation are minima of the bethe free energy. *Advances in Neural Information Processing Systems 15: Proceedings of the 2002 Conference.*

S. Kurohashi and M. Nagao. 1994. A syntactic analysis method of long japanese sentences based on the detection of conjunctive structures. *Computational Linguistics*, 20(4):507–534.

I. D. Melamed. 2000. Models of translational equivalence among words. *Computational Linguistics*, 26(2):221–249.

I. Melamed. 2002. *Empirical Methods for Exploiting Parallel Texts.* The MIT Press.

Rada Mihalcea and Ted Pedersen. 2003. An evaluation exercise for word alignment. In Rada Mihalcea and Ted Pedersen, editors, *HLT-NAACL 2003 Workshop: Building and Using Parallel Texts: Data Driven Machine Translation and Beyond*, pages 1–10, Edmonton, Alberta, Canada, May 31. Association for Computational Linguistics.

Kevin P Murphy, Yair Weiss, and Michael I Jordan. 1999. Loopy belief propagation for approximate inference: An empirical study. *In Proceedings of Uncertainty in AI*, pages 467—475.

Franz Josef Och and Hermann Ney. 1999. Improved alignment models for statistical machine translation. *University of Maryland, College Park, MD*, pages 20—28.

J. Pearl. 1988. *Probabilistic Reasoning in Intelligent Systems: Networks of Plausible Inference.* Morgan Kaufmann Publishers.

M. Utiyama and H. Isahara. 2003. Reliable measures for aligning japanese-english news articles and sentences. *Proceedings of the 41st Annual Meeting on Association for Computational Linguistics-Volume 1*, pages 72–79.

Y. Weiss and W. T. Freeman. 2001. On the optimality of solutions of the max-product belief propagation algorithm in arbitrary graphs. *IEEE Trans. on Information Theory*, 47(2):736–744.

K. Yamada and K. Knight. 2001. A syntax-based statistical translation model. *Proceedings of ACL.*

Jonathan S. Yedidia, William T. Freeman, and Yair Weiss, 2003. *Understanding belief propagation and its generalizations*, pages 239–269. Morgan Kaufmann Publishers Inc., San Francisco, CA, USA.

Translation and Extension of Concepts Across Languages

Dmitry Davidov
ICNC
The Hebrew University of Jerusalem
dmitry@alice.nc.huji.ac.il

Ari Rappoport
Institute of Computer Science
The Hebrew University of Jerusalem
arir@cs.huji.ac.il

Abstract

We present a method which, given a few words defining a concept in some language, retrieves, disambiguates and extends corresponding terms that define a similar concept in another specified language. This can be very useful for cross-lingual information retrieval and the preparation of multi-lingual lexical resources. We automatically obtain term translations from multilingual dictionaries and disambiguate them using web counts. We then retrieve web snippets with co-occurring translations, and discover additional concept terms from these snippets. Our term discovery is based on co-appearance of similar words in symmetric patterns. We evaluate our method on a set of language pairs involving 45 languages, including combinations of very dissimilar ones such as Russian, Chinese, and Hebrew for various concepts. We assess the quality of the retrieved sets using both human judgments and automatically comparing the obtained categories to corresponding English WordNet synsets.

1 Introduction

Numerous NLP tasks utilize lexical databases that incorporate concepts (or word categories): sets of terms that share a significant aspect of their meanings (e.g., terms denoting types of food, tool names, etc). These sets are useful by themselves for improvement of thesauri and dictionaries, and they are also utilized in various applications including textual entailment and question answering. Manual development of lexical databases is labor intensive, error prone, and susceptible to arbitrary human decisions. While databases like WordNet (WN) are invaluable for NLP, for some applications any offline resource would not be extensive enough. Frequently, an application requires data on some very specific topic or on very recent news-related events. In these cases even huge and ever-growing resources like Wikipedia may provide insufficient coverage. Hence applications turn to Web-based on-demand queries to obtain the desired data.

The majority of web pages are written in English and a few other salient languages, hence most of the web-based information retrieval studies are done on these languages. However, due to the substantial growth of the multilingual web[1], queries can be performed and the required information can be found in less common languages, while the query language frequently does not match the language of available information.

Thus, if we are looking for information about some lexical category where terms are given in a relatively uncommon language such as Hebrew, it is likely to find more detailed information and more category instances in a salient language such as English. To obtain such information, we need to discover a word list that represents the desired category in English. This list can be used, for instance, in subsequent focused search in order to obtain pages relevant for the given category. Thus given a few Hebrew words as a description for some category, it can be useful to obtain a similar (and probably more extended) set of English words representing the same category.

In addition, when exploring some lexical category in a common language such as English, it is

[1]http://www.internetworldstats.com/stats7.htm

Proceedings of the 12th Conference of the European Chapter of the ACL, pages 175–183,
Athens, Greece, 30 March – 3 April 2009.

frequently desired to consider available resources from different countries. Such resources are likely to be written in languages different from English. In order to obtain such resources, as before, it would be beneficial, given a concept definition in English, to obtain word lists denoting the same concept in different languages. In both cases a concept as a set of words should be translated as a whole from one language to another.

In this paper we present an algorithm that given a concept defined as a set of words in some source language discovers and extends a similar set in some specified target language. Our approach comprises three main stages. First, given a few terms, we obtain sets of their translations to the target language from multilingual dictionaries, and use web counts to select the appropriate word senses. Next, we retrieve search engine snippets with the translated terms and extract symmetric patterns that connect these terms. Finally, we use these patterns to *extend* the translated concept, by obtaining more terms from the snippets.

We performed thorough evaluation for various concepts involving 45 languages. The obtained categories were manually verified with two human judges and, when appropriate, automatically compared to corresponding English WN synsets. In all tested cases we discovered dozens of concept terms with state-of-the-art precision.

Our major contribution is a novel framework for concept translation across languages. This framework utilizes web queries together with dictionaries for translation, disambiguation and extension of given terms. While our framework relies on the existence of multilingual dictionaries, we show that even with basic 1000 word dictionaries we achieve good performance. Modest time and data requirements allow the incorporation of our method in practical applications.

In Section 2 we discuss related work, Section 3 details the algorithm, Section 4 describes the evaluation protocol and Section 5 presents our results.

2 Related work

Substantial efforts have been recently made to manually construct and interconnect WN-like databases for different languages (Pease et al., 2008; Charoenporn et al., 2007). Some studies (e.g., (Amasyali, 2005)) use semi-automated methods based on language-specific heuristics and dictionaries.

At the same time, much work has been done on automatic lexical acquisition, and in particular, on the acquisition of concepts. The two main algorithmic approaches are pattern-based discovery, and clustering of context feature vectors. The latter represents word contexts as vectors in some space and use similarity measures and automatic clustering in that space (Deerwester et al., 1990). Pereira (1993), Curran (2002) and Lin (1998) use syntactic features in the vector definition. (Pantel and Lin, 2002) improves on the latter by clustering by committee. Caraballo (1999) uses conjunction and appositive annotations in the vector representation. While a great effort has focused on improving the computational complexity of these methods (Gorman and Curran, 2006), they still remain data and computation intensive.

The current major algorithmic approach for concept acquisition is to use lexico-syntactic patterns. Patterns have been shown to produce more accurate results than feature vectors, at a lower computational cost on large corpora (Pantel et al., 2004). Since (Hearst, 1992), who used a manually prepared set of initial lexical patterns in order to acquire relationships, numerous pattern-based methods have been proposed for the discovery of concepts from seeds (Pantel et al., 2004; Davidov et al., 2007; Pasca et al., 2006). Most of these studies were done for English, while some show the applicability of their method to some other languages including Russian, Greek, Czech and French.

Many papers directly target specific applications, and build lexical resources as a side effect. Named Entity Recognition can be viewed as an instance of the concept acquisition problem where the desired categories contain words that are names of entities of a particular kind, as done in (Freitag, 2004) using co-clustering and in (Etzioni et al., 2005) using predefined pattern types. Many Information Extraction papers discover relationships between words using syntactic patterns (Riloff and Jones, 1999).

Unlike in the majority of recent studies where the acquisition framework is designed with specific languages in mind, in our task the algorithm should be able to deal well with a wide variety of target languages without any significant manual adaptations. While some of the proposed frameworks could potentially be language-independent, little research has been done to confirm it yet.

There are a few obstacles that may hinder applying common pattern-based methods to other languages. Many studies utilize parsing or POS tagging, which frequently depends on the availability and quality of language-specific tools. Most studies specify seed patterns in advance, and it is not clear whether translated patterns can work well on different languages. Also, the absence of clear word segmentation in some languages (e.g., Chinese) can make many methods inapplicable.

A few recently proposed concept acquisition methods require only a handful of seed words (Davidov et al., 2007; Pasca and Van Durme, 2008). While these studies avoid some of the obstacles above, it still remains unconfirmed whether such methods are indeed language-independent. In the concept extension part of our algorithm we adapt our concept acquisition framework (Davidov and Rappoport, 2006; Davidov et al., 2007; Davidov and Rappoport, 2008a; Davidov and Rappoport, 2008b) to suit diverse languages, including ones without explicit word segmentation. In our evaluation we confirm the applicability of the adapted methods to 45 languages.

Our study is related to cross-language information retrieval (CLIR/CLEF) frameworks. Both deal with information extracted from a set of languages. However, the majority of CLIR studies pursue different targets. One of the main CLIR goals is the retrieval of *documents* based on explicit queries, when the document language is not the query language (Volk and Buitelaar, 2002). These frameworks usually develop language-specific tools and algorithms including parsers, taggers and morphology analyzers in order to integrate multilingual *queries* and *documents* (Jagarlamudi and Kumaran, 2007). Our goal is to develop and evaluate a *language-independent* method for the translation and extension of *lexical categories*. While our goals are different from CLIR, CLIR systems can greatly benefit from our framework, since our translated categories can be directly utilized for subsequent document retrieval.

Another field indirectly related to our research is Machine Translation (MT). Many MT tasks require automated creation or improvement of dictionaries (Koehn and Knight, 2001). However, MT mainly deals with translation and disambiguation of words at the sentence or document level, while we translate whole concepts defined independently of contexts. Our primary target is not translation of given words, but the discovery and extension of a concept in a target language when the concept definition is given in some different source language.

3 Cross-lingual Concept Translation Framework

Our framework has three main stages: (1) given a set of words in a source language as definition for some concept, we automatically translate them to the target language with multilingual dictionaries, disambiguating translations using web counts; (2) we retrieve from the web snippets where these translations co-appear; (3) we apply a pattern-based concept extension algorithm for discovering additional terms from the retrieved data.

3.1 Concept words and sense selection

We start from a set of words denoting a category in a source language. Thus we may use words like *(apple, banana, ...)* as the definition of fruits or *(bear, wolf, fox, ...)* as the definition of wild animals[2]. Each of these words can be ambiguous. Multilingual dictionaries usually provide many translations, one or more for each sense. We need to select the appropriate translation for each term. In practice, some or even most of the category terms may be absent in available dictionaries. In these cases, we attempt to extract "chain" translations, i.e., if we cannot find Source→Target translation, we can still find some indirect Source→Intermediate1→Intermediate2→Target paths. Such translations are generally much more ambiguous, hence we allow up to two intermediate languages in a chain. We collect all possible translations at the chains having minimal length, and skip category terms for whom this process results in no translations.

Then we use the conjecture that terms of the same concept tend to co-appear more frequently than ones belonging to different concepts[3]. Thus,

[2]In order to reduce noise, we limit the length (in words) of multiword expressions considered as terms. To calculate this limit for a language we randomly take 100 terms from the appropriate dictionary and set a limit as $Lim_{mwe} = round(avg(length(w)))$ where $length(w)$ is the number of words in term w. For languages like Chinese without inherent word segmentation, $length(w)$ is the number of characters in w. While for many languages $Lim_{mwe} = 1$, some languages like Vietnamese usually require two words or more to express terms.

[3]Our results in this paper support this conjecture.

we select a translation of a term co-appearing most frequently with some translation of a different term of the same concept. We estimate how well translations of different terms are connected to each other. Let $C = \{C_i\}$ be the given seed words for some concept. Let $Tr(C_i, n)$ be the n-th available translation of word C_i and $Cnt(s)$ denote the web count of string s obtained by a search engine. Then we select translation $Tr(C_i)$ according to:

$$F(w_1, w_2) = \frac{Cnt(\text{"}w_1 * w_2\text{"}) \times Cnt(\text{"}w_2 * w_1\text{"})}{Cnt(w_1) \times Cnt(w_2)}$$

$$Tr(C_i) = \underset{s_i}{argmax} \left(\max_{\substack{s_j \\ j \neq i}} (F(Tr(C_i, s_i), Tr(C_j, s_j))) \right)$$

We utilize the $Yahoo!$ "x * y" wildcard that allows to count only co-appearances where x and y are separated by a single word. As a result, we obtain a set of disambiguated term translations. The number of queries in this stage depends on the ambiguity of concept terms translation to the target language. Unlike many existing disambiguation methods based on statistics obtained from parallel corpora, we take a rather simplistic query-based approach. This approach is powerful (as shown in our evaluation) and only relies on a few web queries in a language independent manner.

3.2 Web mining for translation contexts

We need to restrict web mining to specific target languages. This restriction is straightforward if the alphabet or term translations are language-specific or if the search API supports restriction to this language[4]. In case where there are no such natural restrictions, we attempt to detect and add to our queries a few language-specific frequent words. Using our dictionaries, we find 1–3 of the 15 most frequent words in a desired language that are unique to that language, and we 'and' them with the queries to ensure selection of the proper language. While some languages as Esperanto do not satisfy any of these requirements, more than 60 languages do.

For each pair A, B of disambiguated term translations, we construct and execute the following 2 queries: {"A * B", "B * A"}[5]. When we have 3 or more terms we also add {A B C ...}-like conjunction queries which include 3–5 terms. For languages with $Lim_{mwe} > 1$, we also construct queries with several "*" wildcards between terms. For each query we collect snippets containing text fragments of web pages. Such snippets frequently include the search terms. Since $Yahoo!$ allows retrieval of up to the 1000 first results (100 in each query), we collect several thousands snippets. For most of the target languages and categories, only a few dozen queries (20 on the average) are required to obtain sufficient data. Thus the relevant data can be downloaded in seconds. This makes our approach practical for on-demand retrieval tasks.

3.3 Pattern-based extension of concept terms

First we extract from the retrieved snippets contexts where translated terms co-appear, and detect patterns where they co-appear symmetrically. Then we use the detected patterns to discover additional concept terms. In order to define word boundaries, for each target language we manually specify boundary characters such as punctuation/space symbols. This data, along with dictionaries, is the only language-specific data in our framework.

3.3.1 Meta-patterns

Following (Davidov et al., 2007) we seek symmetric patterns to retrieve concept terms. We use two meta-pattern types. First, a *Two-Slot* pattern type constructed as follows:

$$[Prefix]\ C_1\ [Infix]\ C_2\ [Postfix]$$

C_i are slots for concept terms. We allow up to Lim_{mwe} space-separated[6] words to be in a single slot. Infix may contain punctuation, spaces, and up to $Lim_{mwe} \times 4$ words. Prefix and Postfix are limited to contain punctuation characters and/or Lim_{mwe} words.

Terms of the same concept frequently co-appear in lists. To utilize this, we introduce two additional *List* pattern types[7]:

$$[Prefix]\ C_1[Infix]\ (C_i[Infix])\text{+} \quad (1)$$

$$[Infix]\ (C_i[Infix])\text{+}\ C_n\ [Postfix] \quad (2)$$

As in (Widdows and Dorow, 2002; Davidov and Rappoport, 2006), we define a pattern graph. Nodes correspond to terms and patterns to edges. If term pair (w_1, w_2) appears in pattern P, we add nodes N_{w_1}, N_{w_2} to the graph and a directed edge $E_P(N_{w_1}, N_{w_2})$ between them.

[4]Yahoo! allows restrictions for 42 languages.

[5]These are Yahoo! queries where enclosing words in "" means searching for an exact phrase and "*" means a wildcard for exactly one arbitrary word.

[6]As before, for languages without explicit space-based word separation Lim_{mwe} limits the number of characters instead.

[7]$(X)+$ means one or more instances of X.

3.3.2 Symmetric patterns

We consider only symmetric patterns. We define a symmetric pattern as a pattern where some category terms C_i, C_j appear both in left-to-right and right-to-left order. For example, if we consider the terms $\{apple, pineapple\}$ we select a List pattern "$(one\ C_i,)+\ and\ C_n$." if we find both "one *apple*, one *pineapple*, one guava and orange." and "one watermelon, one *pineapple* and *apple*.". If no such patterns are found, we turn to a weaker definition, considering as symmetric those patterns where the same terms appear in the corpus in at least two different slots. Thus, we select a pattern "for C_1 and C_2" if we see both "for *apple* and guava," and "for orange and *apple*,".

3.3.3 Retrieving concept terms

We collect terms in two stages. First, we obtain "high-quality" core terms and then we retrieve potentially more noisy ones. In the first stage we collect all terms[8] that are bidirectionally connected to at least two different original translations, and call them *core* concept terms C_{core}. We also add the original ones as core terms. Then we detect the rest of the terms C_{rest} that appear with more different C_{core} terms than with 'out' (non-core) terms as follows:

$G_{in}(c)=\{w\in C_{core}|E(N_w, N_c) \vee E(N_c, N_w)\}$

$G_{out}(c)=\{w\notin C_{core}|E(N_w, N_c) \vee E(N_c, N_w)\}$

$C_{rest}=\{c|\ |G_{in}(c)|>|G_{out}(c)|\ \}$

where $E(N_a, N_b)$ correspond to existence of a graph edge denoting that translated terms a and b co-appear in a pattern in this order. Our final term set is the union of C_{core} and C_{rest}.

For the sake of simplicity, unlike in the majority of current research, we do not attempt to discover more patterns/instances iteratively by re-examining the data or re-querying the web. If we have enough data, we use windowing to improve result quality. If we obtain more than 400 snippets for some concept, we randomly divide the data into equal parts, each containing up to 400 snippets. We apply our algorithm independently to each part and select only the words that appear in more than one part.

4 Experimental Setup

We describe here the languages, concepts and dictionaries we used in our experiments.

[8]We do not consider as terms the 50 most frequent words.

4.1 Languages and categories

One of the main goals in this research is to verify that the proposed basic method can be applied to different languages unmodified. We examined a wide variety of languages and concepts. Table 3 shows a list of 45 languages used in our experiments, including west European languages, Slavic languages, Semitic languages, and diverse Asian languages.

Our concept set was based on English WN synsets, while concept definitions for evaluation were based on WN glosses. For automated evaluation we selected as categories 150 synsets/subtrees with at least 10 single-word terms in them. For manual evaluation we used a subset of 24 of these categories. In this subset we tried to select generic categories, such that no domain expert knowledge was required to check their correctness.

Ten of these categories were equal to ones used in (Widdows and Dorow, 2002; Davidov and Rappoport, 2006), which allowed us to indirectly compare to recent work. Table 1 shows these 10 concepts along with the sample terms. While the number of tested categories is still modest, it provides a good indication for the quality of our approach.

Concept	Sample terms
Musical instruments	guitar, flute, piano
Vehicles/transport	train, bus, car
Academic subjects	physics, chemistry, psychology
Body parts	hand, leg, shoulder
Food	egg, butter, bread
Clothes	pants, skirt, jacket
Tools	hammer, screwdriver, wrench
Places	park, castle, garden
Crimes	murder, theft, fraud
Diseases	rubella, measles, jaundice

Table 1: 10 of the selected categories with sample terms.

4.2 Multilingual dictionaries

We developed a set of tools for automatic access to several dictionaries. We used Wikipedia cross-language links as our main source (60%) for offline translation. These links include translation of Wikipedia terms into dozens of languages. The main advantage of using Wikipedia is its wide coverage of concepts and languages. However, one problem in using it is that it frequently encodes too specific senses and misses common ones. Thus *bear* is translated as *family Ursidae* missing its common "wild animal" sense. To overcome these difficulties, we also used Wiktionary and complemented these offline resources with a few automated queries to several (20) online dictionaries. We start with Wikipedia definitions, then if not found, Wiktionary, and then we turn to online dictionaries.

5 Evaluation and Results

While there are numerous concept acquisition studies, no framework has been developed so far to evaluate this type of cross-lingual concept discovery, limiting our ability to perform a meaningful comparison to previous work. Fair estimation of translated concept quality is a challenging task. For most languages there are no widely accepted concept databases. Moreover, the contents of the same concept may vary across languages. Fortunately, when English is taken as a target language, the English WN allows an automated evaluation of concepts. We conducted evaluation in three different settings, mostly relying on human judges and utilizing the English WN where possible.

1. English as source language. We applied our algorithm on a subset of 24 categories using each of the 45 languages as a target language. Evaluation is done by two judges[9].

2. English as target language. All other languages served as source languages. In this case human subjects manually provided input terms for 150 concept definitions in each of the target languages using 150 selected English WN glosses. For each gloss they were requested to provide at least 2 terms. Then we ran the algorithm on these term lists. Since the obtained results were English words, we performed both manual evaluation of the 24 categories and automated comparison to the original WN data.

3. Language pairs. We created 10 different non-English language pairs for the 24 concepts. Concept definitions were the same as in (2) and manual evaluation followed the same protocol as in (1).

The absence of exhaustive term lists makes recall estimation problematic. In all cases we assess the quality of the discovered lists in terms of precision (P) and length of retrieved lists (T).

[9]For 19 of the languages, at least one judge was a native speaker. For other languages at least one of the subjects was fluent with this language.

5.1 Manual evaluation

Each discovered concept was evaluated by two judges. All judges were fluent English speakers and for each target language, at least one was a fluent speaker of this language. They were given one-line English descriptions of each category and the full lists obtained by our algorithm for each of the 24 concepts. Table 2 shows the lists obtained by our algorithm for the category described as *Relatives* (e.g., grandmother) for several language pairs including Hebrew→French and Chinese→Czech. We mixed "noise" words into each list of terms[10]. These words were automatically and randomly extracted from the same text. Subjects were required to select all words fitting the provided description. They were unaware of algorithm details and desired results. They were instructed to accept common abbreviations, alternative spellings or misspellings like yelow∈color and to accept a term as belonging to a category if at least one of its senses belongs to it, like orange∈color and orange∈fruit. They were asked to reject terms related or associated but not belonging to the target category, like tasty∉food, or that are too general, like animal∉dogs.

The first 4 columns of Table 3 show averaged results of manual evaluation for 24 categories. In the first two columns English is used as a source language and in the next pair of columns English is used as the target. In addition we display in parentheses the amount of terms added during the extension stage. We can see that for all languages, average precision (% of correct terms in concept) is above 80, and frequently above 90, and the average number of extracted terms is above 30. Internal concept quality is in line with values observed on similarly evaluated tasks for recent concept acquisition studies in English. As a baseline, only 3% of the inserted 20-40% noise words were incorrectly labeled by judges. Due to space limitation we do not show the full per-concept behavior; all medians for P and T were close to the average.

We can also observe that the majority ($>60\%$) of target language terms were obtained during the extension stage. Thus, even when considering translation from a rich language such as English (where given concepts frequently contain dozens of terms), most of the discovered target language terms are not discovered through translation but

[10]To reduce annotator bias, we used a different number of noise words, adding 20–40% of the original number of words.

English→Portuguese: afilhada,afilhado,amigo,avó,avô,bisavó,bisavô, bisneta,bisneto,cônjuge,cunhada,cunhado,companheiro, descendente,enteado,filha,filho,irmã,irmão,irmãos,irmãs, madrasta,madrinha,mãe,marido,mulher,namorada, namorado,neta,neto,noivo,padrasto,pai,papai,parente, prima,primo,sogra,sogro,sobrinha,sobrinho,tia,tio,vizinho
Hebrew→French: amant,ami,amie,amis,arrière-grand-mère, arrière-grand-père,beau-frère,beau-parent,beau-père,bebe, belle-fille,belle-mère,belle-soeur,bèbè,compagnon, concubin,conjoint,cousin,cousine,demi-frère,demi-soeur, épouse,époux,enfant,enfants,famille,femme,fille,fils,foyer, frère,garcon,grand-mère,grand-parent,grand-père, grands-parents,maman,mari,mère,neveu,nièce,oncle, papa,parent,père,petit-enfant,petit-fils,soeur,tante
English→Spanish: abuela,abuelo,amante,amiga,amigo,confidente,bisabuelo, cuñada,cuñado,cónyuge,esposa,esposo,espíritu,familia, familiar,hermana,hermano,hija,hijo,hijos,madre,marido, mujer,nieta,nieto,niño, novia,padre,papá,primo,sobrina, sobrino,suegra,suegro,tía,tío,tutor, viuda,viudo
Chinese→Czech: babička,bratr,brácha,chlapec,dcera,děda,dědeček,druh, kamarád,kamarádka,mama,manžel,manželka,matka, muž,otec,podnajemnik,přítelkyně, sestra,starši,strýc, strýček, syn,ségra,tchán,tchyně,teta,vnuk,vnučka,žena

Table 2: Sample of results for the Relatives concept. Note that precision is not 100% (e.g. the Portuguese set includes 'friend' and 'neighbor').

during the subsequent concept extension. In fact, brief examination shows that less than half of source language terms successfully pass translation and disambiguation stage. However, more than 80% of terms which were skipped due to lack of available translations were re-discovered in the target language during the extension stage, along with the discovery of new correct terms not existing in the given source definition.

The first two columns of Table 4 show similar results for non-English language pairs. We can see that these results are only slightly inferior to the ones involving English.

5.2 WordNet based evaluation

We applied our algorithm on 150 concepts with English used as the target language. Since we want to consider common misspellings and morphological combinations of correct terms as hits, we used a basic speller and stemmer to resolve typos and drop some English endings. The WN columns in Table 3 display P and T values for this evaluation. In most cases we obtain $> 85\%$ precision. While these results (P=87,T=17) are lower than in manual evaluation, the task is much harder due to the large number (and hence sparseness) of the utilized 150 WN categories and the incomplete nature of WN data. For the 10 categories of Table 1 used in previous work, we have obtained (P=92,T=41) which outperforms the seed-based concept acquisition of (Widdows and Dorow, 2002; Davidov and Rappoport, 2006) (P=90,T=35) on the same concepts. However, it should be noted that our task setting is substantially different since we utilize more seeds and they come from languages different from English.

5.3 Effect of dictionary size and source category size

The first stage in our framework heavily relies on the existence and quality of dictionaries, whose coverage may be insufficient. In order to check the effect of dictionary coverage on our task, we re-evaluated 10 language pairs using reduced dictionaries containing only the 1000 most frequent words. The last columns in Table 4 show evaluation results for such reduced dictionaries. Surprisingly, while we see a difference in coverage and precision, this difference is below 8%, thus even basic 1000-word dictionaries may be useful for some applications.

This may suggest that only a few correct translations are required for successful discovery of the corresponding category. Hence, even a small dictionary containing translations of the most frequent terms could be enough. In order to test this hypothesis, we re-evaluated the 10 language pairs using full dictionaries while reducing the initial concept definition to the 3 most frequent words. The results of this experiment are shown at columns 3–4 of Table 4. We can see that for most language pairs, 3 seeds were sufficient to achieve equally good results, and providing more extensive concept definitions had little effect on performance.

5.4 Variance analysis

We obtained high precision. However, we also observed high variance in the number of terms between different language pairs for the same concept. There are many possible reasons for this outcome. Below we briefly discuss some of them; detailed analysis of inter-language and inter-concept variance is a major target for future work.

Web coverage of languages is not uniform (Paolillo et al., 2005); e.g. Georgian has much less web hits than English. Indeed, we observed a correlation between reported web coverage and the number of retrieved terms. Concept coverage and

Language	English as source		English as target			
	Manual		Manual		WN	
	T[xx]	P	T[xx]	P	T	P
Arabic	29 [12]	90	41 [35]	91	17	87
Armenian	27 [21]	93	40 [32]	92	15	86
Afrikaans	40 [29]	89	51 [28]	86	19	85
Bengali	23 [18]	95	42 [34]	93	18	88
Belorussian	23 [15]	91	43 [30]	93	17	87
Bulgarian	46 [36]	85	58 [33]	87	19	83
Catalan	45 [29]	81	56 [46]	88	21	86
Chinese	47 [34]	87	56 [22]	90	22	89
Croatian	46 [26]	90	57 [35]	92	16	89
Czech	58 [40]	89	65 [39]	94	23	88
Danish	48 [35]	94	59 [38]	97	17	90
Dutch	41 [28]	92	60 [36]	94	20	88
Estonian	35 [21]	96	47 [24]	96	16	90
Finnish	34 [21]	88	47 [29]	90	19	85
French	56 [30]	89	61 [31]	93	17	87
Georgian	22 [15]	95	39 [31]	96	16	90
German	54 [32]	91	62 [34]	92	21	83
Greek	27 [16]	93	44 [30]	95	17	91
Hebrew	38 [28]	93	45 [32]	93	18	92
Hindi	30 [10]	92	46 [28]	93	16	86
Hungarian	43 [27]	90	44 [28]	93	15	87
Italian	45 [26]	89	51 [29]	88	16	81
Icelandic	27 [21]	90	39 [27]	92	15	85
Indonesian	33 [25]	96	49 [25]	95	15	90
Japanese	40 [16]	89	50 [22]	91	20	83
Kazakh	22 [14]	96	43 [36]	97	16	92
Korean	33 [15]	88	46 [29]	89	16	85
Latvian	41 [30]	92	55 [46]	90	19	83
Lithuanian	36 [26]	94	44 [35]	95	16	89
Norwegian	37 [25]	89	46 [29]	93	15	85
Persian	17 [6]	98	40 [29]	96	15	92
Polish	38 [25]	89	55 [36]	92	17	96
Portuguese	55 [34]	87	64 [33]	90	21	85
Romanian	46 [29]	93	56 [25]	96	15	91
Russian	58 [40]	91	65 [35]	92	22	84
Serbian	19 [11]	93	36 [30]	95	17	90
Slovak	32 [20]	89	56 [39]	90	15	87
Slovenian	28 [16]	94	43 [36]	95	18	89
Spanish	53 [37]	90	66 [32]	91	23	85
Swedish	52 [33]	89	62 [39]	93	16	87
Thai	26 [13]	95	41 [34]	97	16	92
Turkish	42 [33]	92	50 [25]	93	16	88
Ukrainian	47 [33]	88	54 [28]	88	16	83
Vietnamese	26 [8]	84	48 [25]	89	15	82
Urdu	27 [14]	84	42 [36]	88	14	82
Average	38 [24]	91	50 [32]	92	17	87

Table 3: Concept translation and extension results. The first column shows the 45 tested languages. **Bold** are languages evaluated with at least one native speaker. P: precision, T: number of retrieved terms. "[xx]": number of terms added during the concept extension stage. Columns 1-4 show results for manual evaluation on 24 concepts. Columns 5-6 show automated WN-based evaluation on 150 concepts. For columns 1-2 the input category is given in English, in other columns English served as the target language.

content is also different for each language. Thus, concepts involving fantasy creatures were found to have little coverage in Arabic and Hindi, and wide coverage in European languages. For vehicles, Snowmobile was detected in Finnish and Swedish while Rickshaw appears in Hindi.

Language pair Source-Target	Regular data		Reduced seed		Reduced dict.	
	T[xx]	P	T	P	T	P
Hebrew-French	43[28]	89	39	90	35	87
Arabic-Hebrew	31[24]	90	25	94	29	82
Chinese-Czech	35[29]	85	33	84	25	75
Hindi-Russian	45[33]	89	45	87	38	84
Danish-Turkish	28[20]	88	24	88	24	80
Russian-Arabic	28[18]	87	19	91	22	86
Hebrew-Russian	45[31]	92	44	89	35	84
Thai-Hebrew	28[25]	90	26	92	23	78
Finnish-Arabic	21[11]	90	14	92	16	84
Greek-Russian	48[36]	89	47	87	35	81
Average	35[26]	89	32	89	28	82

Table 4: Results for non-English pairs. P: precision, T: number of terms. "[xx]": number of terms added in the extension stage. Columns 1-2 show results for normal experiment settings, 3-4 show data for experiments where the 3 most frequent terms were used as concept definitions, 5-6 describe results for experiment with 1000-word dictionaries.

Morphology was completely neglected in this research. To co-appear in a text, terms frequently have to be in a certain form different from that shown in dictionaries. Even in English, plurals like *spoons, forks* co-appear more than *spoon, fork*. Hence dictionaries that include morphology may greatly improve the quality of our framework. We have conducted initial experiments with promising results in this direction, but we do not report them here due to space limitations.

6 Conclusions

We proposed a framework that when given a set of terms for a category in some source language uses dictionaries and the web to retrieve a similar category in a desired target language. We showed that the same pattern-based method can successfully extend dozens of different concepts for many languages with high precision. We observed that even when we have very few ambiguous translations available, the target language concept can be discovered in a fast and precise manner without relying on any language-specific preprocessing, databases or parallel corpora. The average concept total processing time, including all web requests, was below 2 minutes[11]. The short running time and the absence of language-specific requirements allow processing queries within minutes and makes it possible to apply our method to on-demand cross-language concept mining.

[11] We used a single PC with ADSL internet connection.

References

M. Fatih Amasyali, 2005. Automatic Construction of Turkish WordNet. *Signal Processing and Communications Applications Conference.*

Sharon Caraballo, 1999. Automatic Construction of a Hypernym-Labeled Noun Hierarchy from Text. *ACL '99.*

Thatsanee Charoenporn, Virach Sornlertlamvanich, Chumpol Mokarat, Hitoshi Isahara, 2008. Semi-Automatic Compilation of Asian WordNet. *Proceedings of the 14th NLP-2008, University of Tokyo, Komaba Campus, Japan.*

James R. Curran, Marc Moens, 2002. Improvements in Automatic Thesaurus Extraction. *SIGLEX '02*, 59–66.

Dmitry Davidov, Ari Rappoport, 2006. Efficient Unsupervised Discovery of Word Categories Using Symmetric Patterns and High Frequency Words. *COLING-ACL '06.*

Dmitry Davidov, Ari Rappoport, Moshe Koppel, 2007. Fully Unsupervised Discovery of Concept-Specific Relationships by Web Mining. *ACL '07.*

Dmitry Davidov, Ari Rappoport, 2008a. Unsupervised Discovery of Generic Relationships Using Pattern Clusters and its Evaluation by Automatically Generated SAT Analogy Questions. *ACL '08.*

Dmitry Davidov, Ari Rappoport, 2008b. Classification of Semantic Relationships between Nominals Using Pattern Clusters. *ACL '08.*

Scott Deerwester, Susan Dumais, George Furnas, Thomas Landauer, Richard Harshman, 1990. Indexing by Latent Semantic Analysis. *Journal of the American Society for Info. Science*, 41(6):391–407.

Beate Dorow, Dominic Widdows, Katarina Ling, Jean-Pierre Eckmann, Danilo Sergi, Elisha Moses, 2005. Using Curvature and Markov Clustering in Graphs for Lexical Acquisition and Word Sense Discrimination. *MEANING '05.*

Oren Etzioni, Michael Cafarella, Doug Downey, S. Kok, Ana-Maria Popescu, Tal Shaked, Stephen Soderland, Daniel S. Weld, Alexander Yates, 2005. Unsupervised Named-Entity Extraction from the Web: An Experimental Study. *Artificial Intelligence, 165(1):91134.*

Dayne Freitag, 2004. Trained Named Entity Recognition Using Distributional lusters. *EMNLP '04.*

James Gorman , James R. Curran, 2006. Scaling Distributional Similarity to Large Corpora *COLING-ACL '06.*

Marti Hearst, 1992. Automatic Acquisition of Hyponyms from Large Text Corpora. *COLING '92.*

Jagadeesh Jagarlamudi, A Kumaran, 2007. Cross-Lingual Information Retrieval System for Indian Languages *Working Notes for the CLEF 2007 Workshop.*

Philipp Koehn, Kevin Knight, 2001. Knowledge Sources for Word-Level Translation Models. *EMNLP '01.*

Dekang Lin, 1998. Automatic Retrieval and Clustering of Similar Words. *COLING '98.*

Margaret Matlin, 2005. *Cognition, 6th edition.* John Wiley & Sons.

Patrick Pantel, Dekang Lin, 2002. Discovering Word Senses from Text. *SIGKDD '02.*

Patrick Pantel, Deepak Ravichandran, Eduard Hovy, 2004. Towards Terascale Knowledge Acquisition. *COLING '04.*

John Paolillo, Daniel Pimienta, Daniel Prado, et al., 2005. Measuring Linguistic Diversity on the Internet. *UNESCO Institute for Statistics Montreal, Canada.*

Marius Pasca, Dekang Lin, Jeffrey Bigham, Andrei Lifchits, Alpa Jain, 2006. Names and Similarities on the Web: Fact Extraction in the Fast Lane. *COLING-ACL '06.*

Marius Pasca, Benjamin Van Durme, 2008. Weakly-Supervised Acquisition of Open-Domain Classes and Class Attributes from Web Documents and Query Logs. *ACL '08.*

Adam Pease, Christiane Fellbaum, Piek Vossen, 2008. Building the Global WordNet Grid. *CIL18.*

Fernando Pereira, Naftali Tishby, Lillian Lee, 1993. Distributional Clustering of English Words. *ACL '93.*

Ellen Riloff, Rosie Jones, 1999. Learning Dictionaries for Information Extraction by Multi-Level Bootstrapping. *AAAI '99.*

Martin Volk, Paul Buitelaar, 2002. A Systematic Evaluation of Concept-Based Cross-Language Information Retrieval in the Medical Domain. *In: Proc. of 3rd Dutch-Belgian Information Retrieval Workshop.* Leuven.

Dominic Widdows, Beate Dorow, 2002. A Graph Model for Unsupervised Lexical Acquisition. *COLING '02.*

Learning to Interpret Utterances Using Dialogue History

David DeVault
Institute for Creative Technologies
University of Southern California
Marina del Rey, CA 90292
devault@ict.usc.edu

Matthew Stone
Department of Computer Science
Rutgers University
Piscataway, NJ 08845-8019
Matthew.Stone@rutgers.edu

Abstract

We describe a methodology for learning a disambiguation model for deep pragmatic interpretations in the context of situated task-oriented dialogue. The system accumulates training examples for ambiguity resolution by tracking the fates of alternative interpretations across dialogue, including subsequent clarificatory episodes initiated by the system itself. We illustrate with a case study building maximum entropy models over abductive interpretations in a referential communication task. The resulting model correctly resolves 81% of ambiguities left unresolved by an initial handcrafted baseline. A key innovation is that our method draws exclusively on a system's own skills and experience and requires no human annotation.

1 Introduction

In dialogue, the basic problem of interpretation is to identify the contribution a speaker is making to the conversation. There is much to recognize: the domain objects and properties the speaker is referring to; the kind of action that the speaker is performing; the presuppositions and implicatures that relate that action to the ongoing task. Nevertheless, since the seminal work of Hobbs et al. (1993), it has been possible to conceptualize pragmatic interpretation as a unified reasoning process that selects a representation of the speaker's contribution that is most preferred according to a background model of how speakers tend to behave.

In principle, the problem of pragmatic interpretation is qualitatively no different from the many problems that have been tackled successfully by data-driven models in NLP. However, while researchers have shown that it is sometimes possible to annotate corpora that capture *features* of interpretation, to provide empirical support for theories, as in (Eugenio et al., 2000), or to build classifiers that assist in dialogue reasoning, as in (Jordan and Walker, 2005), it is rarely feasible to fully annotate the interpretations themselves. The distinctions that must be encoded are subtle, theoretically-loaded and task-specific—and they are not always signaled unambiguously by the speaker. See (Poesio and Vieira, 1998; Poesio and Artstein, 2005), for example, for an overview of problems of vagueness, underspecification and ambiguity in reference annotation.

As an alternative to annotation, we argue here that dialogue systems can and should prepare their own training data by inference from underspecified models, which provide sets of candidate meanings, and from skilled engagement with their interlocutors, who know which meanings are right. Our specific approach is based on *contribution tracking* (DeVault, 2008), a framework which casts linguistic inference in situated, task-oriented dialogue in probabilistic terms. In contribution tracking, ambiguous utterances may result in alternative possible contexts. As subsequent utterances are interpreted in those contexts, ambiguities may ramify, cascade, or disappear, giving new insight into the pattern of activity that the interlocutor is engaged in. For example, consider what happens if the system initiates clarification. The interlocutor's answer may indicate not only what they mean now but also what they must have meant earlier when they used the original ambiguous utterance.

Contribution tracking allows a system to accumulate training examples for ambiguity resolution by tracking the fates of alternative interpretations across dialogue. The system can use these examples to improve its models of pragmatic interpretation. To demonstrate the feasibility of this approach in realistic situations, we present a system that tracks contributions to a referential communication task using an abductive interpretation

Proceedings of the 12th Conference of the European Chapter of the ACL, pages 184–192,
Athens, Greece, 30 March – 3 April 2009.

model: see Section 2. A user study with this system, described in Section 3, shows that this system can, in the course of interacting with its users, discover the correct interpretations of many potentially ambiguous utterances. The system thereby automatically acquires a body of training data in its native representations. We use this data to build a maximum entropy model of pragmatic interpretation in our referential communication task. After training, we correctly resolve 81% of the ambiguities left open in our handcrafted baseline.

2 Contribution tracking

We continue a tradition of research that uses simple referential communication tasks to explore the organization and processing of human–computer and mediated human–human conversation, including recently (DeVault and Stone, 2007; Gergle et al., 2007; Healey and Mills, 2006; Schlangen and Fernández, 2007). Our specific task is a two-player object-identification game adapted from the experiments of Clark and Wilkes-Gibbs (1986) and Brennan and Clark (1996); see Section 2.1. To play this game, our agent, COREF, interprets utterances as performing sequences of task-specific problem-solving acts using a combination of grammar-based constraint inference and abductive plan recognition; see Section 2.2. Crucially, COREF's capabilities also include the ambiguity management skills described in Section 2.3, including policies for asking and answering clarification questions.

2.1 A referential communication task

The game plays out in a special-purpose graphical interface, which can support either human–human or human–agent interactions. Two players work together to create a specific configuration of objects, or a *scene*, by adding objects into the scene one at a time. Their interfaces display the same set of candidate objects (geometric objects that differ in shape, color and pattern), but their locations are shuffled. The shuffling undermines the use of spatial expressions such as "the object at bottom left". Figures 1 and 2 illustrate the different views.[1]

[1]Note that in a human–human game, there are literally two versions of the graphical interface on the separate computers the human participants are using. In a human–agent interaction, COREF does not literally use the graphical interface, but the information that COREF is provided is limited to the information the graphical interface would provide to a human participant. For example, COREF is not aware of the locations of objects on its partner's screen.

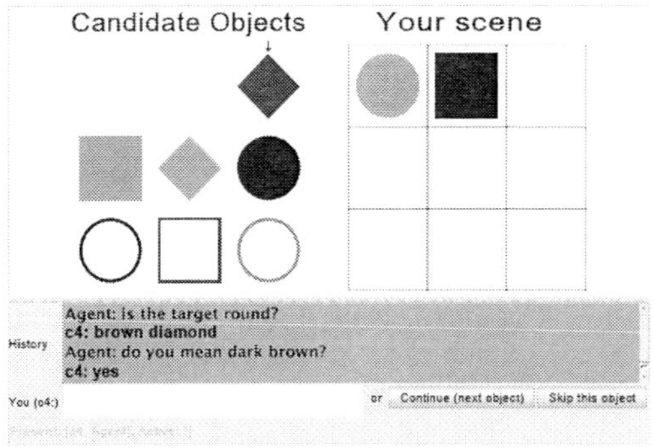

Figure 1: A human user plays an object identification game with COREF. The figure shows the perspective of the user (denoted c4). The user is playing the role of director, and trying to identify the diamond at upper right (indicated to the user by the blue arrow) to COREF.

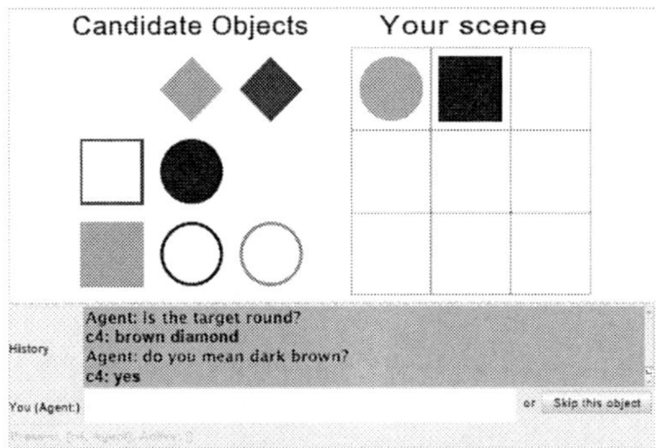

Figure 2: The conversation of Figure 1 from COREF's perspective. COREF is playing the role of matcher, and trying to determine which object the user wants COREF to identify.

As in the experiments of Clark and Wilkes-Gibbs (1986) and Brennan and Clark (1996), one of the players, who plays the role of *director*, instructs the other player, who plays the role of *matcher*, which object is to be added next to the scene. As the game proceeds, the next target object is automatically determined by the interface and privately indicated to the director with a blue arrow, as shown in Figure 1. (Note that the corresponding matcher's perspective, shown in Figure 2, does not include the blue arrow.) The director's job is then to get the matcher to click on (their version of) this target object.

To achieve agreement about the target, the two players can exchange text through an instant-messaging modality. (This is the only communication channel.) Each player's interface provides a real-time indication that their partner is "Active" while their partner is composing an utterance, but the interface does not show in real-time what is being typed. Once the `Enter` key is pressed, the utterance appears to both players at the bottom of a scrollable display which provides full access to all the previous utterances in the dialogue.

When the matcher clicks on an object they believe is the target, their version of that object is privately moved into their scene. The director has no visible indication that the matcher has clicked on an object. However, the director needs to click the `Continue (next object)` button (see Figure 1) in order to move the current target into the *director's* scene, and move on to the next target object. This means that the players need to discuss not just what the target object is, but also whether the matcher has added it, so that they can coordinate on the right moment to move on to the next object. If this coordination succeeds, then after the director and matcher have completed a series of objects, they will have created the exact same scene in their separate interfaces.

2.2 Interpreting user utterances

COREF treats interpretation broadly as a problem of abductive intention recognition (Hobbs et al., 1993).[2] We give a brief sketch here to highlight the content of COREF's representations, the sources of information that COREF uses to construct them, and the demands they place on disambiguation. See DeVault (2008) for full details.

COREF's utterance interpretations take the form of action sequences that it believes would constitute coherent contributions to the dialogue task in the current context. Interpretations are constructed abductively in that the initial actions in the sequence need not be directly tied to observable events; they may be *tacit* in the terminology of Thomason et al. (2006). Examples of such tacit actions include clicking an object, initiating a clarification, or abandoning a previous question. As a concrete example, consider utterance (1b) from the dialogue of Figure 1, repeated here as (1):

(1)	a.	COREF:	is the target round?
	b.	`c4`:	brown diamond
	c.	COREF:	do you mean dark brown?
	d.	`c4`:	yes

[2]In fact, the same reasoning interprets utterances, button presses and the other actions COREF observes!

In interpreting (1b), COREF hypothesizes that the user has tacitly abandoned the agent's question in (1a). In fact, COREF identifies two possible interpretations for (1b):

$i_{2,1}$= ⟨ `c4:tacitAbandonTasks[2]`,
`c4:addcr[t7,rhombus(t7)]`,
`c4:setPrag[inFocus(t7)]`,
`c4:addcr[t7,saddlebrown(t7)]`⟩

$i_{2,2}$= ⟨ `c4:tacitAbandonTasks[2]`,
`c4:addcr[t7,rhombus(t7)]`,
`c4:setPrag[inFocus(t7)]`,
`c4:addcr[t7,sandybrown(t7)]`⟩

Both interpretations begin by assuming that user `c4` has tacitly abandoned the previous question, and then further analyze the utterance as performing three additional dialogue acts. When a dialogue act is preceded by tacit actions in an interpretation, the speaker of the utterance *implicates* that the earlier tacit actions have taken place (DeVault, 2008). These implicatures are an important part of the interlocutors' coordination in COREF's dialogues, but they are a major obstacle to annotating interpretations by hand.

Action sequences such as $i_{2,1}$ and $i_{2,2}$ are coherent only when they match the state of the ongoing referential communication game and the semantic and pragmatic status of information in the dialogue. COREF tracks these connections by maintaining a probability distribution over a set of dialogue states, each of which represents a possible thread that resolves the ambiguities in the dialogue history. For performance reasons, COREF entertains up to three alternative threads of interpretation; COREF strategically drops down to the single most probable thread at the moment each object is completed. Each dialogue state represents the stack of processes underway in the referential communication game; constituent activities include problem-solving interactions such as identifying an object, information-seeking interactions such as question–answer pairs, and grounding processes such as acknowledgment and clarification. Dialogue states also represent pragmatic information including recent utterances and referents which are salient or in focus.

COREF abductively recognizes the intention I of an actor in three steps. First, for each dialogue state s_k, COREF builds a *horizon graph* of possible tacit action sequences that could be assumed coherently, given the pending tasks (DeVault, 2008).

Second, COREF uses the horizon graph and other resources to solve any constraints associated with the observed action. This step instantiates any free parameters associated with the action to contextually relevant values. For utterances, the relevant constraints are identified by parsing the utterance using a hand-built, lexicalized tree-adjoining grammar. In interpreting (1b), the parse yields an ambiguity in the dialogue act associated with the word "brown", which may mean either of the two shades of brown in Figure 1, which COREF distinguishes using its `saddlebrown` and `sandybrown` concepts.

Once COREF has identified a set of interpretations $\{i_{t,1}, ..., i_{t,n}\}$ for an utterance o at time t, the last step is to assign a probability to each. In general, we conceive of this following Hobbs et al. (1993): the agent should weigh the different assumptions that went into constructing each interpretation.[3] Ultimately, this process should be made sensitive to the rich range of factors that are available from COREF's deep representation of the dialogue state and the input utterance—this is our project in this paper. However, in our initial implemented prototype, COREF assigned these probabilities using a simple hand-built model considering only N_{T}, the number of tacit actions abductively assumed to occur in an interpretation:

$$P(I = i_{t,j} | o, S_t = s_k) \propto \frac{1}{N_{\mathrm{T}}(i_{t,j}) + 1} \quad (1)$$

In effect, this is a "null hypothesis" that assigns relatively uniform weights to different abductive hypotheses.

2.3 Interactive disambiguation

COREF uses its probabilistic model of context in order to tolerate ambiguity as it moves forward with its dialogues and to resolve ambiguity over time. We have put particular effort into COREF's skills with three kinds of ambiguity: word-sense ambiguities, where COREF finds multiple resolutions for the domain concept evoked by the use of a lexical item, as in the interaction (1) of Figure 1; referential ambiguities, where COREF takes a noun phrase to be compatible with multiple objects from the display; and speech act ambiguities, where alternative interpretations communicate or implicate different kinds of contributions to the ongoing task.

The resolution of ambiguity may involve some combination of asking questions of the user, aggregating information provided by the user across multiple turns of dialogue, and strategically dropping threads of interpretation. For example, COREF represents the context resulting from (1b) in terms of two states: one from interpretation $i_{2,1}$ and one from $i_{2,2}$. COREF asks a clarification question (1c); the user's explicit answer *yes* allows COREF to discard one of the possible states and allocate all its probability mass to the other one.

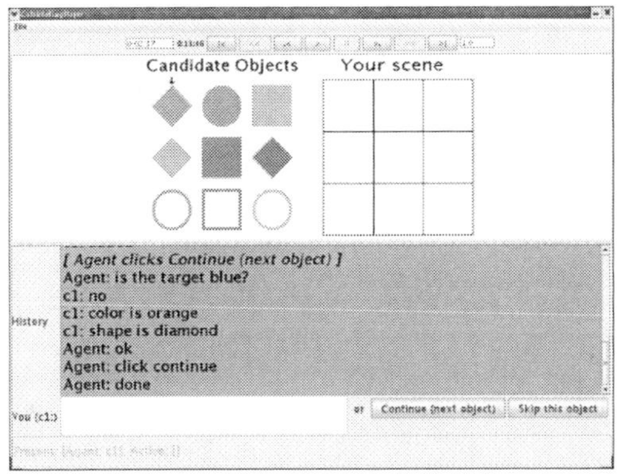

Figure 3: A human user plays the director role in an object identification game with COREF. The figure shows the perspective of the user.

The dialogue in (2) shows an alternative case.

(2) a. `c1`: color is orange
b. `c1`: shape is diamond
c. COREF: ok

The example is taken from the setting shown in Figure 3. In this case, COREF finds two colors on the screen it thinks the user could intend to evoke with the word *orange*; the peachy orange of the diamond and circle on the top row and the brighter orange of the solid and empty squares in the middle column. COREF responds to the ambiguity by introducing two states which track the alternative colors. Immediately COREF gets an additional description from the user, and adds the constraint that the object is a diamond. As there is no bright orange diamond, there is no way to interpret the user's utterance in the bright orange state; COREF discards this state and allocates all its probability mass to the other one.

3 Inferring the fates of interpretations

Our approach is based on the observation that COREF's contribution tracking can be viewed as assigning a *fate* to every dialogue state it entertains as part of some thread of interpretation. In

[3] Though note that Hobbs et al. do not explicitly construe their weights in terms of probabilities.

particular, if we consider the agent's contribution tracking retrospectively, every dialogue state can be assigned a fate of *correct* or *incorrect*, where a state is viewed as correct if it or some of its descendants eventually capture all the probability mass that COREF is distributing across the viable surviving states, and incorrect otherwise.

In general, there are two ways that a state can end up with fate *incorrect*. One way is that the state and all of its descendants are eventually denied any probability mass due to a failure to interpret a subsequent utterance or action as a coherent contribution from any of those states. In this case, we say that the incorrect state was *eliminated*. The second way a state can end up incorrect is if COREF makes a strategic decision to drop the state, or all of its surviving descendants, at a time when the state or its descendants were assigned nonzero probability mass. In this case we say that the incorrect state was *dropped*. Meanwhile, because COREF drops all states but one after each object is completed, there is a single hypothesized state at each time t whose descendants will ultimately capture all of COREF's probability mass. Thus, for each time t, COREF will retrospectively classify exactly one state as correct.

Of course, we really want to classify interpretations. Because we seek to estimate $P(I = i_{t,j}|o, S_t = s_k)$, which conditions the probability assigned to $I = i_{t,j}$ on the correctness of state s_k, we consider only those interpretations arising in states that are retrospectively identified as correct. For each such interpretation, we start from the state where that interpretation is adopted and trace forward to a correct state or to its last surviving descendant. We classify the interpretation the same way as that final state, either *correct*, *eliminated*, or *dropped*.

We harvested a training set using this methodology from the transcripts of a previous evaluation experiment designed to exercise COREF's ambiguity management skills. The data comes from 20 subjects—most of them undergraduates participating for course credit—who interacted with COREF over the web in three rounds of the referential communication each. The number of objects increased from 4 to 9 to 16 across rounds; the roles of director and matcher alternated in each round, with the initial role assigned at random.

Of the 3275 sensory events that COREF interpreted in these dialogues, from the (retrospectively) correct state, COREF hypothesized 0 interpretations for 345 events, 1 interpretation for 2612 events, and more than one interpretation for 318 events. The overall distribution in the number of interpretations hypothesized from the correct state is given in Figure 4.

N	Percentage	N	Percentage
0	10.53	5	0.21
1	79.76	6	0.12
2	7.79	7	0.09
3	0.85	8	0.06
4	0.58	9	0.0

Figure 4: Distribution of degree of ambiguity in training set. The table lists percentage of events that had a specific number N of candidate interpretations constructed from the correct state.

4 Learning pragmatic interpretation

We capture the fate of each interpretation $i_{t,j}$ in a discrete variable F whose value is *correct*, *eliminated*, or *dropped*. We also represent each intention $i_{t,j}$, observation o, and state s_k in terms of features. We seek to learn a function

$$P(F = \mathit{correct} \mid \mathrm{features}(i_{t,j}), \mathrm{features}(o), \mathrm{features}(s_k))$$

from a set of training examples $E = \{e_1, ..., e_n\}$ where, for $l = 1..n$, we have:

$$e_l = (F = \mathrm{fate}(i_{t,j}), \mathrm{features}(i_{t,j}), \mathrm{features}(o), \mathrm{features}(s_k)).$$

We chose to train maximum entropy models (Berger et al., 1996). Our learning framework is described in Section 4.1; the results in Section 4.2.

4.1 Learning setup

We defined a range of potentially useful features, which we list in Figures 5, 6, and 7. These features formalize pragmatic distinctions that plausibly provide evidence of the correct interpretation for a user utterance or action. You might annotate any of these features by hand, but computing them automatically lets us easily explore a much larger range of possibilities. To allow these various kinds of features (integer-valued, binary-valued, and string-valued) to interface to the maximum entropy model, these features were converted into a much broader class of indicator features taking on a value of either 0.0 or 1.0.

feature set	description
NumTacitActions	The number of tacit actions in $i_{t,j}$.
TaskActions	These features represent the action type (function symbol) of each action a_k in $i_{t,j} = \langle A_1 : a_1, A_2 : a_2, ..., A_n : a_n \rangle$, as a string.
ActorDoesTaskAction	For each $A_k : a_k$ in $i_{t,j} = \langle A_1 : a_1, A_2 : a_2, ..., A_n : a_n \rangle$, a feature indicates that A_k (represented as string "Agent" or "User") has performed action a_k (represented as a string action type, as in the TaskActions features).
Presuppositions	If o is an utterance, we include a string representation of each presupposition assigned to o by $i_{t,j}$. The predicate/argument structure is captured in the string, but any gensym identifiers within the string (e.g. `target12`) are replaced with exemplars for that identifier type (e.g. `target`).
Assertions	If o is an utterance, we include a string representation of each dialogue act assigned to o by $i_{t,j}$. Gensym identifiers are filtered as in the Presuppositions features.
Syntax	If o is an utterance, we include a string representation of the bracketed phrase structure of the syntactic analysis assigned to o by $i_{t,j}$. This includes the categories of all non-terminals in the structure.
FlexiTaskIntentionActors	Given $i_{t,j} = \langle A_1 : a_1, A_2 : a_2, ..., A_n : a_n \rangle$, we include a single string feature capturing the actor sequence $\langle A_1, A_2, ..., A_n \rangle$ in $i_{t,j}$ (e.g. "User, Agent, Agent").

Figure 5: The interpretation features, features($i_{t,j}$), available for selection in our learned model.

feature set	description
Words	If o is an utterance, we include features that indicate the presence of each word that occurs in the utterance.

Figure 6: The observation features, features(o), available for selection in our learned model.

feature set	description
NumTasksUnderway	The number of tasks underway in s_k.
TasksUnderway	The name, stack depth, and current task state for each task underway in s_k.
NumRemainingReferents	The number of objects yet to be identified in s_k.
TabulatedFacts	String features representing each proposition in the conversational record in s_k (with filtered gensym identifiers).
CurrentTargetConstraints	String features for each positive and negative constraint on the current target in s_k (with filtered gensym identifiers). E.g. "`positive: squareFigureObject(target)`" or "`negative: solidFigureObject(target)`".
UsefulProperties	String features for each property instantiated in the experiment interface in s_k. E.g. "`squareFigureObject`", "`solidFigureObject`", etc.

Figure 7: The dialogue state features, features(s_k), available for selection in our learned model.

We used the MALLET maximum entropy classifier (McCallum, 2002) as an off-the-shelf, trainable maximum entropy model. Each run involved two steps. First, we applied MALLET's feature selection algorithm, which incrementally selects features (as well as conjunctions of features) that maximize an exponential gain function which represents the value of the feature in predicting interpretation fates. Based on manual experimentation, we chose to have MALLET select about 300 features for each learned model. In the second step, the selected features were used to train the model to estimate probabilities. We used MALLET's implementation of Limited-Memory BFGS (Nocedal, 1980).

4.2 Evaluation

We are generally interested in whether COREF's experience with previous subjects can be leveraged to improve its interactions with new subjects. Therefore, to evaluate our approach, while making maximal use of our available data set, we performed a hold-one-subject-out cross-validation using our 20 human subjects $H = \{h_1, ..., h_{20}\}$. That is, for each subject h_i, we trained a model on the training examples associated with subjects $H \setminus \{h_i\}$, and then tested the model on the examples associated with subject h_i.

To quantify the performance of the learned model in comparison to our baseline, we adapt the mean reciprocal rank statistic commonly used for evaluation in information retrieval (Vorhees, 1999). We expect that a system will use the probabilities calculated by a disambiguation model to decide which interpretations to pursue and how to follow them up through the most efficient interaction. What matters is not the absolute probability of the correct interpretation but its rank with respect to competing interpretations. Thus, we consider each utterance as a query; the disambiguation model produces a ranked list of responses for this query (candidate interpretations), ordered by probability. We find the rank r of the correct interpretation in this list and measure the outcome of the query as $\frac{1}{r}$. Because of its weak assumptions, our baseline disambiguation model actually leaves many ties. So in fact we must compute an *expected* reciprocal rank (ERR) statistic that averages $\frac{1}{r}$ over all ways of ordering the correct interpretation against competitors of equal probability.

Figure 8 shows a histogram of ERR across

ERR range	Hand-built model	Learned models
1	20.75%	81.76%
$[\frac{1}{2}, 1)$	74.21%	16.35%
$[\frac{1}{3}, \frac{1}{2})$	3.46%	1.26%
$[0, \frac{1}{3})$	1.57%	0.63%
mean(ERR)	0.77	0.92
var(ERR)	0.02	0.03

Figure 8: For the 318 ambiguous sensory events, the distribution of the expected reciprocal of rank of the correct interpretation, for the initial, hand-built model and the learned models in aggregate.

the ambiguous utterances from the corpus. The learned models correctly resolve almost 82%, while the baseline model correctly resolves about 21%. In fact, the learned models get much of this improvement by learning weights to break the ties in our baseline model. The overall performance measure for a disambiguation model is the mean expected reciprocal rank across all examples in the corpus. The learned model improves this metric to 0.92 from a baseline of 0.77. The difference is unambiguously significant (Wilcoxon rank sum test $W = 23743.5, p < 10^{-15}$).

4.3 Selected features

Feature selection during training identified a variety of syntactic, semantic, and pragmatic features as useful in disambiguating correct interpretations. Selections were made from every feature set in Figures 5, 6, and 7. It was often possible to identify relevant features as playing a role in successful disambiguation by the learned models. For example, the learned model trained on $H \setminus \{\texttt{c4}\}$ delivered the following probabilities for the two interpretations COREF found for `c4`'s utterance (1b):

$$P(I = i_{2,1}|o, S_2 = s_{8923}) = \quad 0.665$$
$$P(I = i_{2,2}|o, S_2 = s_{8923}) = \quad 0.335$$

The correct interpretation, $i_{2,1}$, hypothesizes that the user means `saddlebrown`, the darker of the two shades of brown in the display. Among the features selected in this model is a Presuppositions feature (see Figure 5) which is present just in case the word 'brown' is interpreted as meaning `saddlebrown` rather than some other shade. This feature allows the learned model to prefer to interpret `c4`'s use of 'brown' as meaning this darker shade of brown, based on the observed linguistic behavior of other users.

5 Results in context

Our work adds to a body of research learning deep models of language from evidence implicit in an agent's interactions with its environment. It shares much of its motivation with co-training (Blum and Mitchell, 1998) in improving initial models by leveraging additional data that is easy to obtain. However, as the examples of Section 2.3 illustrate, COREF's interactions with its users offer substantially more information about interpretation than the raw text generally used for co-training. Closer in spirit is AI research on learning vocabulary items by connecting user vocabulary to the agent's perceptual representations at the time of utterance (Oates et al., 2000; Roy and Pentland, 2002; Cohen et al., 2002; Yu and Ballard, 2004; Steels and Belpaeme, 2005). Our framework augments this information about utterance context with additional evidence about meaning from linguistic interaction. In general, dialogue coherence is an important source of evidence for all aspects of language, for both human language learning (Saxton et al., 2005) as well as machine models. For example, Bohus et al. (2008) use users' confirmations of their spoken requests in a multi-modal interface to tune the system's ASR rankings for recognizing subsequent utterances.

Our work to date has a number of limitations. First, although 318 ambiguous interpretations did occur, this user study provided a relatively small number of ambiguous interpretations, in machine learning terms; and most (80.2%) of those that did occur were 2-way ambiguities. A richer domain would require both more data and a generative approach to model-building and search.

Second, this learning experiment has been performed after the fact, and we have not yet investigated the performance of the learned model in a follow-up experiment in which COREF uses the learned model in interactions with its users.

A third limitation lies in the detection of 'correct' interpretations. Our scheme sometimes conflates the user's actual intentions with COREF's subsequent assumptions about them. If COREF decides to strategically drop the user's *actual intended interpretation*, our scheme may mark another interpretation as 'correct'. Alternative approaches may do better at harvesting meaningful examples of correct and incorrect interpretations from an agent's dialogue experience. Our approach also depends on having clear evidence about what an interlocutor has said and whether the system has interpreted it correctly—evidence that is often unavailable with spoken input or information-seeking tasks. Thus, even when spoken language interfaces use probabilistic inference for dialogue management (Williams and Young, 2007), new techniques may be needed to mine their experience for correct interpretations.

6 Conclusion

We have implemented a system COREF that makes productive use of its dialogue experience by learning to rank new interpretations based on features it has historically associated with correct utterance interpretations. We present these results as a proof-of-concept that contribution tracking provides a source of information that an agent can use to improve its statistical interpretation process. Further work is required to scale these techniques to richer dialogue systems, and to understand the best architecture for extracting evidence from an agent's interpretive experience and modeling that evidence for future language use. Nevertheless, we believe that these results showcase how judicious system-building efforts can lead to dialogue capabilities that defuse some of the bottlenecks to learning rich pragmatic interpretation. In particular, a focus on improving our agents' basic abilities to tolerate and resolve ambiguities as a dialogue proceeds may prove to be a valuable technique for improving the overall dialogue competence of the agents we build.

Acknowledgments

This work was sponsored in part by NSF CCF-0541185 and HSD-0624191, and by the U.S. Army Research, Development, and Engineering Command (RDECOM). Statements and opinions expressed do not necessarily reflect the position or the policy of the Government, and no official endorsement should be inferred. Thanks to our reviewers, Rich Thomason, David Traum and Jason Williams.

References

Adam L. Berger, Stephen Della Pietra, and Vincent J. Della Pietra. 1996. A maximum entropy approach to natural language processing. *Computational Linguistics*, 22(1):39–71.

Avrim Blum and Tom Mitchell. 1998. Combining labeled and unlabeled data with co-training. In *Proceedings of the 11th Annual Conference on Computational Learning Theory*, pages 92–100.

Dan Bohus, Xiao Li, Patrick Nguyen, and Geoffrey Zweig. 2008. Learning n-best correction models from implicit user feedback in a multi-modal local search application. In *The 9th SIGdial Workshop on Discourse and Dialogue*.

Susan E. Brennan and Herbert H. Clark. 1996. Conceptual pacts and lexical choice in conversation. *Journal of Experimental Psychology*, 22(6):1482–1493.

Herbert H. Clark and Deanna Wilkes-Gibbs. 1986. Referring as a collaborative process. In Philip R. Cohen, Jerry Morgan, and Martha E. Pollack, editors, *Intentions in Communication*, pages 463–493. MIT Press, Cambridge, Massachusetts, 1990.

Paul R. Cohen, Tim Oates, Carole R. Beal, and Niall Adams. 2002. Contentful mental states for robot baby. In *Eighteenth national conference on Artificial intelligence*, pages 126–131, Menlo Park, CA, USA. American Association for Artificial Intelligence.

David DeVault and Matthew Stone. 2007. Managing ambiguities across utterances in dialogue. In *Proceedings of the 11th Workshop on the Semantics and Pragmatics of Dialogue (Decalog 2007)*, pages 49–56.

David DeVault. 2008. *Contribution Tracking: Participating in Task-Oriented Dialogue under Uncertainty*. Ph.D. thesis, Department of Computer Science, Rutgers, The State University of New Jersey, New Brunswick, NJ.

Barbara Di Eugenio, Pamela W. Jordan, Richmond H. Thomason, and Johanna D. Moore. 2000. The agreement process: An empirical investigation of human-human computer-mediated collaborative dialogue. *International Journal of Human-Computer Studies*, 53:1017–1076.

Darren Gergle, Carolyn P. Rosé, and Robert E. Kraut. 2007. Modeling the impact of shared visual information on collaborative reference. In *CHI 2007 Proceedings*, pages 1543–1552.

Patrick G. T. Healey and Greg J. Mills. 2006. Participation, precedence and co-ordination in dialogue. In *Proceedings of Cognitive Science*, pages 1470–1475.

Jerry R. Hobbs, Mark Stickel, Douglas Appelt, and Paul Martin. 1993. Interpretation as abduction. *Artificial Intelligence*, 63:69–142.

Pamela W. Jordan and Marilyn A. Walker. 2005. Learning content selection rules for generating object descriptions in dialogue. *JAIR*, 24:157–194.

Andrew McCallum. 2002. MALLET: A MAchine learning for LanguagE toolkit. http://mallet.cs.umass.edu.

Jorge Nocedal. 1980. Updating quasi-newton matrices with limited storage. *Mathematics of Computation*, 35(151):773–782.

Tim Oates, Zachary Eyler-Walker, and Paul R. Cohen. 2000. Toward natural language interfaces for robotic agents. In *Proc. Agents*, pages 227–228.

Massimo Poesio and Ron Artstein. 2005. Annotating (anaphoric) ambiguity. In *Proceedings of the Corpus Linguistics Conference*.

Massimo Poesio and Renata Vieira. 1998. A corpus-based investigation of definite description use. *Computational Linguistics*, 24(2):183–216.

Deb Roy and Alex Pentland. 2002. Learning words from sights and sounds: A computational model. *Cognitive Science*, 26(1):113–146.

Matthew Saxton, Carmel Houston-Price, and Natasha Dawson. 2005. The prompt hypothesis: clarification requests as corrective input for grammatical errors. *Applied Psycholinguistics*, 26(3):393–414.

David Schlangen and Raquel Fernández. 2007. Speaking through a noisy channel: Experiments on inducing clarification behaviour in human–human dialogue. In *Proceedings of Interspeech 2007*.

Luc Steels and Tony Belpaeme. 2005. Coordinating perceptually grounded categories through language. a case study for colour. *Behavioral and Brain Sciences*, 28(4):469–529.

Richmond H. Thomason, Matthew Stone, and David DeVault. 2006. Enlightened update: A computational architecture for presupposition and other pragmatic phenomena. For the Ohio State Pragmatics Initiative, 2006, available at http://www.research.rutgers.edu/~ddevault/.

Ellen M. Vorhees. 1999. The TREC-8 question answering track report. In *Proceedings of the 8th Text Retrieval Conference*, pages 77–82.

Jason Williams and Steve Young. 2007. Partially observable markov decision processes for spoken dialog systems. *Computer Speech and Language*, 21(2):393–422.

Chen Yu and Dana H. Ballard. 2004. A multimodal learning interface for grounding spoken language in sensory perceptions. *ACM Transactions on Applied Perception*, 1:57–80.

Correcting Dependency Annotation Errors

Markus Dickinson
Indiana University
Bloomington, IN, USA
md7@indiana.edu

Abstract

Building on work detecting errors in dependency annotation, we set out to correct local dependency errors. To do this, we outline the properties of annotation errors that make the task challenging and their existence problematic for learning. For the task, we define a feature-based model that explicitly accounts for non-relations between words, and then use ambiguities from one model to constrain a second, more relaxed model. In this way, we are successfully able to correct many errors, in a way which is potentially applicable to dependency parsing more generally.

1 Introduction and Motivation

Annotation error detection has been explored for part-of-speech (POS), syntactic constituency, semantic role, and syntactic dependency annotation (see Boyd et al., 2008, and references therein). Such work is extremely useful, given the harmfulness of annotation errors for training, including the learning of noise (e.g., Hogan, 2007; Habash et al., 2007), and for evaluation (e.g., Padro and Marquez, 1998). But little work has been done to show the full impact of errors, or what types of cases are the most damaging, important since noise can sometimes be overcome (cf. Osborne, 2002). Likewise, it is not clear how to learn from consistently misannotated data; studies often only note the presence of errors or eliminate them from evaluation (e.g., Hogan, 2007), and a previous attempt at correction was limited to POS annotation (Dickinson, 2006). By moving from annotation error detection to error correction, we can more fully elucidate ways in which noise can be overcome and ways it cannot.

We thus explore annotation error correction and its feasibility for dependency annotation, a form of annotation that provides argument relations among words and is useful for training and testing dependency parsers (e.g., Nivre, 2006; McDonald and Pereira, 2006). A recent innovation in dependency parsing, relevant here, is to use the predictions made by one model to refine another (Nivre and McDonald, 2008; Torres Martins et al., 2008). This general notion can be employed here, as different models of the data have different predictions about whch parts are erroneous and can highlight the contributions of different features. Using differences that complement one another, we can begin to sort accurate from inaccurate patterns, by integrating models in such a way as to learn the true patterns and not the errors. Although we focus on dependency annotation, the methods are potentially applicable for different types of annotation, given that they are based on the similar data representations (see sections 2.1 and 3.2).

In order to examine the effects of errors and to refine one model with another's information, we need to isolate the problematic cases. The data representation must therefore be such that it clearly allows for the specific identification of errors between words. Thus, we explore relatively simple models of the data, emphasizing small substructures (see section 3.2). This simple modeling is not always rich enough for full dependency parsing, but different models can reveal conflicting information and are generally useful as part of a larger system. Graph-based models of dependency parsing (e.g., McDonald et al., 2006), for example, rely on breaking parsing down into decisions about smaller substructures, and focusing on pairs of words has been used for domain adaptation (Chen et al., 2008) and in memory-based parsing (Canisius et al., 2006). Exploring annotation error correction in this way can provide insights into more general uses of the annotation, just as previous work on correction for POS annotation (Dickinson, 2006) led to a way to improve POS

Proceedings of the 12th Conference of the European Chapter of the ACL, pages 193–201,
Athens, Greece, 30 March – 3 April 2009. ©2009 Association for Computational Linguistics

tagging (Dickinson, 2007).

After describing previous work on error detection and correction in section 2, we outline in section 3 how we model the data, focusing on individual relations between pairs of words. In section 4, we illustrate the difficulties of error correction and show how simple combinations of local features perform poorly. Based on the idea that ambiguities from strict, lexical models can constrain more general POS models, we see improvement in error correction in section 5.

2 Background

2.1 Error detection

We base our method of error correction on a form of error detection for dependency annotation (Boyd et al., 2008). The variation n-gram approach was developed for constituency-based treebanks (Dickinson and Meurers, 2003, 2005) and it detects strings which occur multiple times in the corpus with varying annotation, the so-called *variation nuclei*. For example, the variation nucleus *next Tuesday* occurs three times in the Wall Street Journal portion of the Penn Treebank (Taylor et al., 2003), twice labeled as NP and once as PP (Dickinson and Meurers, 2003).

Every variation detected in the annotation of a nucleus is classified as either an annotation error or as a genuine ambiguity. The basic heuristic for detecting errors requires one word of recurring context on each side of the nucleus. The nucleus with its repeated surrounding context is referred to as a *variation n-gram*. While the original proposal expanded the context as far as possible given the repeated n-gram, using only the immediately surrounding words as context is sufficient for detecting errors with high precision (Boyd et al., 2008). This "shortest" context heuristic receives some support from research on first language acquisition (Mintz, 2006) and unsupervised grammar induction (Klein and Manning, 2002).

The approach can detect both bracketing and labeling errors in constituency annotation, and we already saw a labeling error for *next Tuesday*. As an example of a bracketing error, the variation nucleus *last month* occurs within the NP *its biggest jolt last month* once with the label NP and once as a non-constituent, which in the algorithm is handled through a special label NIL.

The method for detecting annotation errors can be extended to discontinuous constituency annotation (Dickinson and Meurers, 2005), making it applicable to dependency annotation, where words in a relation can be arbitrarily far apart. Specifically, Boyd et al. (2008) adapt the method by treating dependency pairs as variation nuclei, and they include NIL elements for pairs of words not annotated as a relation. The method is successful at detecting annotation errors in corpora for three different languages, with precisions of 93% for Swedish, 60% for Czech, and 48% for German.[1]

2.2 Error correction

Correcting POS annotation errors can be done by applying a POS tagger and altering the input POS tags (Dickinson, 2006). Namely, ambiguity class information (e.g., IN/RB/RP) is added to each corpus position for training, creating complex ambiguity tags, such as <IN/RB/RP,IN>. While this results in successful correction, it is not clear how it applies to annotation which is not positional and uses NIL labels. However, ambiguity class information is relevant when there is a choice between labels; we return to this in section 5.

3 Modeling the data

3.1 The data

For our data set, we use the written portion (sections P and G) of the Swedish Talbanken05 treebank (Nivre et al., 2006), a reconstruction of the Talbanken76 corpus (Einarsson, 1976) The written data of Talbanken05 consists of 11,431 sentences with 197,123 tokens, annotated using 69 types of dependency relations.

This is a small sample, but it matches the data used for error detection, which results in 634 shortest non-fringe variation n-grams, corresponding to 2490 tokens. From a subset of 210 nuclei (917 tokens), hand-evaluation reveals error detection precision to be 93% (195/210), with 274 (of the 917) corpus positions in need of correction (Boyd et al., 2008). This means that 643 positions do not need to be corrected, setting a baseline of 70.1% (643/917) for error correction.[2] Following Dickinson (2006), we train our models on the entire corpus, explicitly including NIL relations (see

[1] The German experiment uses a more relaxed heuristic; precision is likely higher with the shortest context heuristic.

[2] Detection and correction precision are different measurements: for detection, it is the percentage of variation nuclei types where at least one is incorrect; for correction, it is the percentage of corpus tokens with the true (corrected) label.

section 3.2); we train on the original annotation, but not the corrections.

3.2 Individual relations

Annotation error correction involves overcoming noise in the corpus, in order to learn the true patterns underlying the data. This is a slightly different goal from that of general dependency parsing methods, which often integrate a variety of features in making decisions about dependency relations (cf., e.g., Nivre, 2006; McDonald and Pereira, 2006). Instead of maximizing a feature model to improve parsing, we isolate individual pieces of information (e.g., context POS tags), thereby being able to pinpoint, for example, when non-local information is needed for particular types of relations and pointing to cases where pieces of information conflict (cf. also McDonald and Nivre, 2007).

To support this isolation of information, we use dependency pairs as the basic unit of analysis and assign a dependency label to each word pair. Following Boyd et al. (2008), we add *L* or *R* to the label to indicate which word is the head, the left (L) or the right (R). This is tantamount to handling pairs of words as single entries in a "lexicon" and provides a natural way to talk of ambiguities. Breaking the representation down into strings whch receive a label also makes the method applicable to other annotation types (e.g., Dickinson and Meurers, 2005).

A major issue in generating a lexicon is how to handle pairs of words which are not dependencies. We follow Boyd et al. (2008) and generate NIL labels for those pairs of words which also occur as a true labeled relation. In other words, only word pairs which can be relations can also be NILs. For every sentence, then, when we produce feature lists (see section 3.3), we produce them for all word pairs that are related or could potentially be related, but not those which have never been observed as a dependency pair. This selection of NIL items works because there are no unknown words. We use the method in Dickinson and Meurers (2005) to efficiently calculate the NIL tokens.

Focusing on word pairs and not attempting to build a a whole dependency graph allows us to explore the relations between different kinds of features, and it has the potential benefit of not relying on possibly erroneous sister relations. From the perspective of error correction, we cannot assume that information from the other relations in the sentence is reliable.[3] This representation also fits nicely with previous work, both in error detection (see section 2.1) and in dependency parsing (e.g., Canisius et al., 2006; Chen et al., 2008). Most directly, Canisius et al. (2006) integrate such a representation into a memory-based dependency parser, treating each pair individually, with words and POS tags as features.

3.3 Method of learning

We employ memory-based learning (MBL) for correction. MBL stores all corpus instances as vectors of features, and given a new instance, the task of the classifier is to find the most similar cases in memory to deduce the best class. Given the previous discussion of the goals of correcting errors, what seems to be needed is a way to find patterns which do not fully generalize because of noise appearing in very similar cases in the corpus. As Zavrel et al. (1997, p. 137) state about the advantages of MBL:

> Because language-processing tasks typically can only be described as a complex interaction of regularities, subregularities and (families of) exceptions, storing all empirical data as potentially useful in analogical extrapolation works better than extracting the main regularities and forgetting the individual examples (Daelemans, 1996).

By storing all corpus examples, as MBL does, both correct and incorrect data is maintained, allowing us to pinpoint the effect of errors on training. For our experiments, we use TiMBL, version 6.1 (Daelemans et al., 2007), with the default settings. We use the default overlap metric, as this maintains a direct connection to majority-based correction. We could run TiMBL with different values of k, as this should lead to better feature integration. However, this is difficult to explore without development data, and initial experiments with higher k values were not promising (see section 4.2).

To fully correct every error, one could also experiment with a real dependency parser in the future, in order to look beyond the immediate context and to account for interactions between rela-

[3] We use POS information, which is also prone to errors, but on a different level of annotation. Still, this has its problems, as discussed in section 4.1.

tions. The approach to correction pursued here, however, isolates problems for assigning dependency structures, highlighting the effectiveness of different features within the same local domain. Initial experiments with a dependency parser were again not promising (see section 4.2).

3.4 Integrating features

When using features for individual relations, we have different options for integrating them. On the one hand, one can simply additively combine features into a larger vector for training, as described in section 4.2. On the other hand, one can use one set of features to constrain another set, as described in section 5. Pulling apart the features commonly employed in dependency parsing can help indicate the contributions each has on the classification.

This general idea is akin to the notion of classifier stacking, and in the realm of dependency parsing, Nivre and McDonald (2008) successfully stack classifiers to improve parsing by "allow[ing] a model to learn relative to the predictions of the other" (p. 951). The output from one classifier is used as a feature in the next one (see also Torres Martins et al., 2008). Nivre and McDonald (2008) use different kinds of learning paradigms, but the general idea can be carried over to a situation using the same learning mechanism. Instead of focusing on what one learning algorithm informs another about, we ask what one set of more or less informative features can inform another set about, as described in section 5.1.

4 Performing error correction

4.1 Challenges

The task of automatic error correction in some sense seems straightforward, in that there are no unknown words. Furthermore, we are looking at identical recurring words, which should for the most part have consistent annotation. But it is precisely this similarity of local contexts that makes the correction task challenging.

Given that variations contain sets of corpus positions with differing labels, it is tempting to take the error detection output and use a heuristic of "majority rules" for the correction cases, i.e., correct the cases to the majority label. When using only information from the word sequence, this runs into problems quickly, however, in that there are many non-majority labels which are correct. Some of these non-majority cases pattern in uniform ways and are thus more correctable; others are less tractable in being corrected, as they behave in non-uniform and often non-local ways. Exploring the differences will highlight what can and cannot be easily corrected, underscoring the difficulties in training from erroneous annotation.

Uniform non-majority cases The first problem with correction to the majority label is an issue of coverage: a large number of variations are ties between two different labels. Out of 634 shortest non-fringe variation nuclei, 342 (53.94%) have no majority label; for the corresponding 2490 tokens, 749 (30.08%) have no majority tag.

The variation *är väg* ('is way'), for example, appears twice with the same local context shown in (1),[4] once incorrectly labeled as OO-L (other object [head on the left]) and once correctly as SP-L (subjective predicative complement). To distinguish these two, more information is necessary than the exact sequence of words. In this case, for example, looking at the POS categories of the nuclei could potentially lead to accurate correction: AV NN is SP-L 1032 times and OO-L 32 times (AV = the verb "vara" (be), NN = other noun). While some ties might require non-local information, we can see that local—but more general—information could accurately break this tie.

(1) kärlekens <u>väg</u> **är/AV** <u>en</u> <u>lång</u> **väg/NN** <u>och</u>
love's way is a long way and
...
...

Secondly, in a surprising number of cases where there is a majority tag (122 out of the 917 tokens we have a correction for), a non-majority label is actually correct. For the example in (2), the string *institution kvarleva* ('institution remnant') varies between CC-L (sister of first conjunct in binary branching analysis of coordination) and AN-L (apposition).[5] CC-L appears 5 times and AN-L 3 times, but the CC-L cases are incorrect and need to be changed to AN-L.

(2) en <u>föråldrad</u> **institution/NN** <u>,/IK</u> <u>en/EN</u>
an obsolete institution , a
kvarleva/NN <u>från</u> 1800-talets
remnant from the 1800s

[4] We put variation nuclei in bold and underline the immediately surrounding context.

[5] Note that CC is a category introduced in the conversion from the 1976 to the 2005 corpus.

Other cases with a non-majority label have other problems. In example (3), for instance, the string *under hägnet* ('under protection') varies in this context between HD-L (other head, 3 cases) and PA-L (complement of preposition, 5 cases), where the PA-L cases need to be corrected to HD-L. Both of these categories are new, so part of the issue here could be in the consistency of the conversion.

(3) fria liv **under/PR hägnet/ID|NN**
free life under the protection
av/ID|PR ett en gång givet löfte
of a one time given promise

The additional problem is that there are other, correlated errors in the analysis, as shown in figure 1. In the case of the correct HD analysis, both *hägnet* and *av* are POS-annotated as ID (part of idiom (multi-word unit)) and are HD dependents of *under*, indicating that the three words make up an idiom. The PA analysis is a non-idiomatic analysis, with *hägnet* as NN.

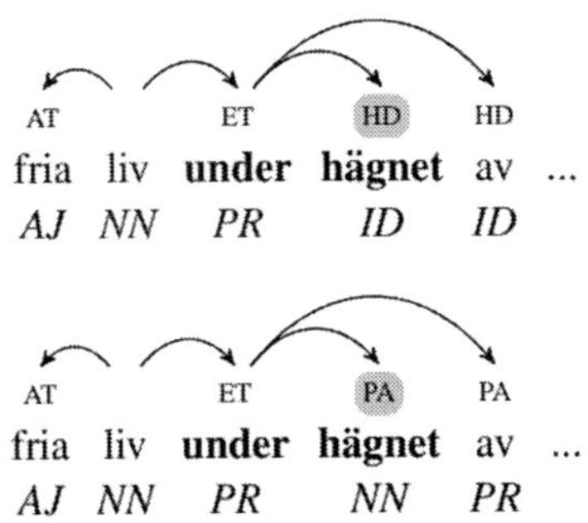

Figure 1: Erroneous POS & dependency variation

Significantly, *hägnet* only appears 10 times in the corpus, all with *under* as its head, 5 times HD-L and 5 times PA-L. We will not focus explicitly on correcting these types of cases, but the example serves to emphasize the necessity of correction at all levels of annotation.

Non-uniform non-majority cases All of the above cases have in common that whatever change is needed, it needs to be done for all positions in a variation. But this is not sound, as error detection precision is not 100%. Thus, there are variations which clearly must not change.

For example, in (4), there is legitimate variation between PA-L (4a) and HD-L (4b), stemming from the fact that one case is non-idiomatic, and the other is idiomatic, despite having identical local context. In these examples, at least the POS labels are different. Note, though, that in (4) we need to trust the POS labels to overcome the similarity of text, and in (3) we need to distrust them.[6]

(4) a. **Med/PR** andra **ord/NN** en
with other words an
ändamålsenlig ...
appropriate

b. **Med/AB** andra **ord/ID** en form av
with other words a form of
prostitution .
prostitution

Without non-local information, some legitimate variations are virtually irresolvable. Consider (5), for instance: here, we find variation between SS-R (other subject), as in (5a), and FS-R (dummy subject), as in (5b). Crucially, the POS tags are the same, and the context is the same. What differentiates these cases is that *går* has a different set of dependents in the two sentences, as shown in figure 2; to use this information would require us to trust the rest of the dependency structure or to use a dependency parser which accurately derives the structural differences.

(5) a. **Det/PO går/VV** bara inte ihop .
it goes just not together
'It just doesn't add up.'

b. **Det/PO går/VV** bara inte att hålla
it goes just not to hold
ihop ...
together ...

4.2 Using local information

While some variations require non-local information, we have seen that some cases are correctable simply with different kinds of local information (cf. (1)). In this paper, we will not attempt to directly cover non-local cases or cases with POS annotation problems, instead trying to improve the integration of different pieces of local information.

In our experiments, we trained simple models of the original corpus using TiMBL (see section 3.3) and then tested on the same corpus. The models we use include words (W) and/or tags (T) for nucleus and/or context positions, where context here

[6] Rerunning the experiments in the paper by first running a POS tagger showed slight degradations in precision.

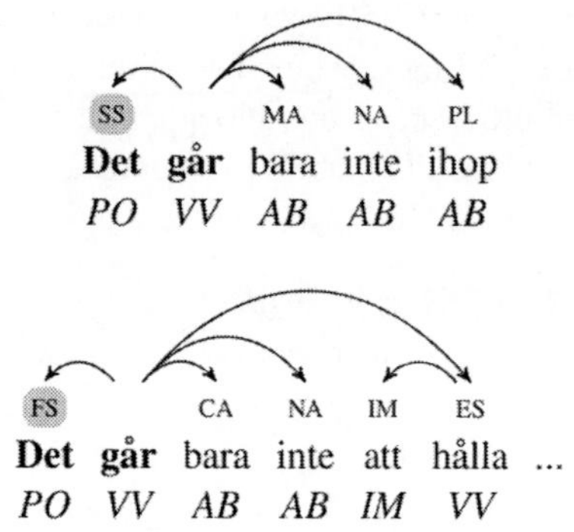

Figure 2: Correct dependency variation

refers only to the immediately surrounding words. These are outlined in table 1, for different models of the nucleus (*Nuc.*) and the context (*Con.*). For instance, the model 6 representation of example (6) (=(1)) consists of all the underlined words and tags.

(6) kärlekens väg/NN **är/AV** en/EN lång/AJ **väg/NN** och/++ man gör oklokt ...

In table 1, we report the precision figures for different models on the 917 positions we have corrections for. We report the correction precision for positions the classifier changed the label of (*Changed*), and the overall correction precision (*Overall*). We also report the precision TiMBL has for the whole corpus, with respect to the original tags (instead of the corrected tags).

#	Nuc.	Con.	TiMBL	Changed	Overall
1	W	-	86.6%	34.0%	62.5%
2	W, T	-	88.1%	35.9%	64.8%
3	W	W	99.8%	50.3%	72.7%
4	W	W, T	99.9%	52.6%	**73.5%**
5	W, T	W	99.9%	50.8%	72.4%
6	W, T	W, T	99.9%	51.2%	72.6%
7	T	-	73.4%	20.1%	49.5%
8	T	T	92.7%	50.2%	73.2%

Table 1: The models tested

We can draw a few conclusions from these results. First, all models using contexual information perform essentially the same—approximately 50% on changed positions and 73% overall. When not generalizing to new data, simply adding features (i.e., words or tags) to the model is less important than the sheer presence of context. This is true even for some higher values of k: model 6, for example, has only 73.2% and 72.1% overall precision for $k = 2$ and $k = 3$, respectively.

Secondly, these results confirm that the task is difficult, even for a corpus with relatively high error detection precision (see section 2.1). Despite high similarity of context (e.g., model 6), the best results are only around 73%, and this is given a baseline (no changes) of 70%. While a more expansive set of features would help, there are other problems here, as the method appears to be overtraining. There is no question that we are learning the "correct" patterns, i.e., 99.9% similarity to the benchmark in the best cases. The problem is that, for error correction, we have to overcome noise in the data. Training and testing with the dependency parser MaltParser (Nivre et al., 2007, default settings) is no better, with 72.1% overall precision (despite a labeled attachment score of 98.3%).

Recall in this light that there are variations for which the non-majority label is the correct one; attempting to get a non-majority label correct using a strict lexical model does not work. To be able not to learn the erroneous patterns requires a more general model. Interestingly, a more general model—e.g., treating the corpus as a sequence of tags (model 8)—results in equally good correction, without being a good overall fit to the corpus data (only 92.7%). This model, too, learns noise, as it misses cases that the lexical models get correct. Simply combining the features does not help (cf. model 6); what we need is to use information from both stricter and looser models in a way that allows general patterns to emerge without overgeneralizing.

5 Model combination

Given the discussion in section 4.1 surrounding examples (1)-(5), it is clear that the information needed for correction is sometimes within the immediate context, although that information is needed, however, is often different. Consider the more general models, 7 and 8, which only use POS tag information. While sometimes this general information is effective, at times it is dramatically incorrect. For example, for (7), the original (incorrect) relation between *finna* and *erbjuda* is CC-L; the model 7 classifier selects OO-L as the correct tag; model 8 selects NIL; and the correct label is +F-L (coordination at main clause level).

(7) försöker **finna/VV** ett lämpligt arbete i
try to find a suitable job in
öppna marknaden eller **erbjuda/VV** andra
open market or to offer other
arbetsmöjligheter .
work possibilities

The original variation for the nucleus *finna erbjuda* ('find offer') is between CC-L and +F-L, but when represented as the POS tags VV VV (other verb), there are 42 possible labels, with OO-L being the most frequent. This allows for too much confusion. If model 7 had more restrictions on the set of allowable tags, it could make a more sensible choice and, in this case, select the correct label.

5.1 Using ambiguity classes

Previous error correction work (Dickinson, 2006) used ambiguity classes for POS annotation, and this is precisely the type of information we need to constrain the label to one which we know is relevant to the current case. Here, we investigate ambiguity class information derived from one model integrated into another model.

There are at least two main ways we can use ambiguity classes in our models. The first is what we have just been describing: an ambiguity class can serve as a constraint on the set of possible outcomes for the system. If the correct label is in the ambiguity class (as it usually is for error correction), this constraining can do no worse than the original model. The other way to use an ambiguity class is as a feature in the model. The success of this approach depends on whether or not each ambiguity class patterns in its own way, i.e., defines a sub-regularity within a feature set.

5.2 Experiment details

We consider two different feature models, those containing only tags (models 7 and 8), and add to these ambiguity classes derived from two other models, those containing only words (models 1 and 3). To correct the labels, we need models which do not strictly adhere to the corpus, and the tag-based models are best at this (see the *TiMBL* results in table 1). The ambiguity classes, however, must be fairly constrained, and the word-based models do this best (cf. example (7)).

5.2.1 Ambiguity classes as constraints

As described in section 5.1, we can use ambiguity classes to constrain the output of a model. Specifically, we take models 7 and 8 and constrain each selected tag to be one which is within the ambiguity class of a lexical model, either 1 or 3. That is, if the TiMBL-determined label is not in the ambiguity class, we select the most likely tag of the ones which are. If no majority label can be decided from this restricted set, we fall back to the TiMBL-selected tag. In (7), for instance, if we use model 7, the TiMBL tag is OO-L, but model 3's ambiguity class restricts this to either CC-L or +F-L. For the representation VV VV, the label CC-L appears 315 times and +F-L 544 times, so +F-L is correctly selected.[7]

The results are given in table 2, which can be compared to the the original models 7 and 8 in table 1, i.e., total precisions of 49.5% and 73.2%, respectively. With these simple constraints, model 8 now outperforms any other model (75.5%), and model 7 begins to approach all the models that use contextual information (68.8%).

#	AC	Changed	Total
7	1	28.5% (114/400)	57.4% (526/917)
7	3	45.9% (138/301)	68.8% (631/917)
8	1	54.0% (142/263)	74.8% (686/917)
8	3	56.7% (144/254)	75.5% (692/917)

Table 2: Constraining TiMBL with ACs

5.2.2 Ambiguity classes as features

Ambiguity classes from one model can also be used as features for another (see section 5.1); in this case, ambiguity class information from lexical models (1 and 3) is used as a feature for POS tag models (7 and 8). The results are given in table 3, where we can see dramatically improved performance from the original models (cf. table 1) and generally improved performance over using ambiguity classes as constraints (cf. table 2).

#	AC	Changed	Total
7	1	33.2% (122/368)	61.9% (568/917)
7	3	50.2% (131/261)	72.1% (661/917)
8	1	59.0% (148/251)	**76.4%** (701/917)
8	3	55.1% (130/236)	73.6% (675/917)

Table 3: TiMBL with ACs as features

If we compare the two results for model 7 (61.9% vs. 72.1%) and then the two results for model 8 (76.4% vs. 73.6%), we observe that the

[7]Even if CC-L had been selected here, the choice is significantly better than OO-L.

better use of ambiguity classes integrates contextual and non-contextual features. Model 7 (POS, no context) with model 3 ambiguity classes (lexical, with context) is better than using ambiguity classes derived from a non-contextual model. For model 8, on the other hand, which uses contextual POS features, using the ambiguity class without context (model 1) does better. In some ways, this combination of model 8 with model 1 ambiguity classes makes the most sense: ambiguity classes are derived from a lexicon, and for dependency annotation, a lexicon can be treated as a set of pairs of words. It is also noteworthy that model 7, despite not using context directly, achieves comparable results to all the previous models using context, once appropriate ambiguity classes are employed.

5.2.3 Both methods

Given that the results of ambiguity classes as features are better than that of constraining, we can now easily combine both methodologies, by constraining the output from section 5.2.2 with the ambiguity class tags. The results are given in table 4; as we can see, all results are a slight improvement over using ambiguity classes as features without constraining the output (table 3). Using only local context, the best model here is 3.2% points better than the best original model, representing an improvement in correction.

#	AC	Changed	Total
7	1	33.5% (123/367)	62.2% (570/917)
7	3	55.8% (139/249)	74.1% (679/917)
8	1	59.6% (149/250)	**76.7%** (703/917)
8	3	57.1% (133/233)	74.3% (681/917)

Table 4: TiMBL w/ ACs as features & constraints

6 Summary and Outlook

After outlining the challenges of error correction, we have shown how to integrate information from different models of dependency annotation in order to perform annotation error correction. By using ambiguity classes from lexical models, both as features and as constraints on the final output, we saw improvements in POS models that were able to overcome noise, without using non-local information.

A first step in further validating these methods is to correct other dependency corpora; this is limited, of course, by the amount of corpora with corrected data available. Secondly, because this work is based on features and using ambiguity classes, it can in principle be applied to other types of annotation, e.g., syntactic constituency annotation and semantic role annotation. In this light, it is interesting to note the connection to annotation error detection: the work here is in some sense an extension of the variation n-gram method. Whether it can be employed as an error detection system on its own requires future work.

Another way in which this work can be extended is to explore how these representations and integration of features can be used for dependency parsing. There are several issues to work out, however, in making insights from this work more general. First, it is not clear that pairs of words are sufficiently general to treat them as a lexicon, when one is parsing new data. Secondly, we have explicit representations for word pairs not annotated as a dependency relation (i.e., NILs), and these are constrained by looking at those which are the same words as real relations. Again, one would have to determine which pairs of words need NIL representations in new data.

Acknowledgements

Thanks to Yvonne Samuelsson for help with the Swedish examples; to Joakim Nivre, Mattias Nilsson, and Eva Pettersson for the evaluation data for Talbanken05; and to the three anonymous reviewers for their insightful comments.

References

Boyd, Adriane, Markus Dickinson and Detmar Meurers (2008). On Detecting Errors in Dependency Treebanks. *Research on Language and Computation* 6(2), 113–137.

Canisius, Sander, Toine Bogers, Antal van den Bosch, Jeroen Geertzen and Erik Tjong Kim Sang (2006). Dependency parsing by inference over high-recall dependency predictions. In *Proceedings of CoNLL-X*. New York.

Chen, Wenliang, Youzheng Wu and Hitoshi Isahara (2008). Learning Reliable Information for Dependency Parsing Adaptation. In *Proceedings of Coling 2008*. Manchester.

Daelemans, Walter (1996). Abstraction Considered Harmful: Lazy Learning of Language Processing. In *Proceedings of the 6th Belgian-Dutch Conference on Machine Learning*. Maastricht, The Netherlands.

Daelemans, Walter, Jakub Zavrel, Ko Van der Sloot and Antal Van den Bosch (2007). *TiMBL: Tilburg Memory Based Learner, version 6.1, Reference Guide*. Tech. rep., ILK Research Group. ILK Research Group Technical Report Series no. 07-07.

Dickinson, Markus (2006). From Detecting Errors to Automatically Correcting Them. In *Proceedings of EACL-06*. Trento, Italy.

Dickinson, Markus (2007). Determining Ambiguity Classes for Part-of-Speech Tagging. In *Proceedings of RANLP-07*. Borovets, Bulgaria.

Dickinson, Markus and W. Detmar Meurers (2003). Detecting Inconsistencies in Treebanks. In *Proceedings of TLT-03*. Växjö, Sweden.

Dickinson, Markus and W. Detmar Meurers (2005). Detecting Errors in Discontinuous Structural Annotation. In *Proceedings of ACL-05*.

Einarsson, Jan (1976). *Talbankens skriftspr⌀akskonkordans*. Tech. rep., Lund University, Dept. of Scandinavian Languages.

Habash, Nizar, Ryan Gabbard, Owen Rambow, Seth Kulick and Mitch Marcus (2007). Determining Case in Arabic: Learning Complex Linguistic Behavior Requires Complex Linguistic Features. In *Proceedings of EMNLP-07*.

Hogan, Deirdre (2007). Coordinate Noun Phrase Disambiguation in a Generative Parsing Model. In *Proceedings of ACL-07*. Prague.

Klein, Dan and Christopher D. Manning (2002). A Generative Constituent-Context Model for Improved Grammar Induction. In *Proceedings of ACL-02*. Philadelphia, PA.

McDonald, Ryan, Kevin Lerman and Fernando Pereira (2006). Multilingual Dependency Analysis with a Two-Stage Discriminative Parser. In *Proceedings of CoNLL-X*. New York City.

McDonald, Ryan and Joakim Nivre (2007). Characterizing the Errors of Data-Driven Dependency Parsing Models. In *Proceedings of EMNLP-CoNLL-07*. Prague, pp. 122–131.

McDonald, Ryan and Fernando Pereira (2006). Online learning of approximate dependency parsing algorithms. In *Proceedings of EACL-06*. Trento.

Mintz, Toben H. (2006). Finding the verbs: distributional cues to categories available to young learners. In K. Hirsh-Pasek and R. M. Golinkoff (eds.), *Action Meets Word: How Children Learn Verbs*, New York: Oxford University Press, pp. 31–63.

Nivre, Joakim (2006). *Inductive Dependency Parsing*. Berlin: Springer.

Nivre, Joakim, Johan Hall, Jens Nilsson, Atanas Chanev, Gulsen Eryigit, Sandra Kubler, Svetoslav Marinov and Erwin Marsi (2007). MaltParser: A language-independent system for data-driven dependency parsing. *Natural Language Engineering* 13(2), 95–135.

Nivre, Joakim and Ryan McDonald (2008). Integrating Graph-Based and Transition-Based Dependency Parsers. In *Proceedings of ACL-08: HLT*. Columbus, OH.

Nivre, Joakim, Jens Nilsson and Johan Hall (2006). Talbanken05: A Swedish Treebank with Phrase Structure and Dependency Annotation. In *Proceedings of LREC-06*. Genoa, Italy.

Osborne, Miles (2002). Shallow Parsing using Noisy and Non-Stationary Training Material. In *JMLR Special Issue on Machine Learning Approaches to Shallow Parsing*, vol. 2, pp. 695–719.

Padro, Lluis and Lluis Marquez (1998). On the Evaluation and Comparison of Taggers: the Effect of Noise in Testing Corpora. In *Proceedings of ACL-COLING-98*. San Francisco, CA.

Taylor, Ann, Mitchell Marcus and Beatrice Santorini (2003). The Penn Treebank: An Overview. In Anne Abeillé (ed.), *Treebanks: Building and using syntactically annotated corpora*, Dordrecht: Kluwer, chap. 1, pp. 5–22.

Torres Martins, André Filipe, Dipanjan Das, Noah A. Smith and Eric P. Xing (2008). Stacking Dependency Parsers. In *Proceedings of EMNLP-08*. Honolulu, Hawaii, pp. 157–166.

Zavrel, Jakub, Walter Daelemans and Jorn Veenstra (1997). Resolving PP attachment Ambiguities with Memory-Based Learning. In *Proceedings of CoNLL-97*. Madrid.

Re-Ranking Models For Spoken Language Understanding

Marco Dinarelli
University of Trento
Italy
dinarelli@disi.unitn.it

Alessandro Moschitti
University of Trento
Italy
moschitti@disi.unitn.it

Giuseppe Riccardi
University of Trento
Italy
riccardi@disi.unitn.it

Abstract

Spoken Language Understanding aims at mapping a natural language spoken sentence into a semantic representation. In the last decade two main approaches have been pursued: generative and discriminative models. The former is more robust to overfitting whereas the latter is more robust to many irrelevant features. Additionally, the way in which these approaches encode prior knowledge is very different and their relative performance changes based on the task. In this paper we describe a machine learning framework where both models are used: a generative model produces a list of ranked hypotheses whereas a discriminative model based on structure kernels and Support Vector Machines, re-ranks such list. We tested our approach on the MEDIA corpus (human-machine dialogs) and on a new corpus (human-machine and human-human dialogs) produced in the European LUNA project. The results show a large improvement on the state-of-the-art in concept segmentation and labeling.

1 Introduction

In Spoken Dialog Systems, the Language Understanding module performs the task of translating a spoken sentence into its meaning representation based on semantic constituents. These are the units for meaning representation and are often referred to as concepts. Concepts are instantiated by sequences of words, therefore a Spoken Language Understanding (SLU) module finds the association between words and concepts.

In the last decade two major approaches have been proposed to find this correlation: (i) generative models, whose parameters refer to the joint probability of concepts and constituents; and (ii) discriminative models, which learn a classification function to map words into concepts based on geometric and statistical properties. An example of generative model is the Hidden Vector State model (HVS) (He and Young, 2005). This approach extends the discrete Markov model encoding the context of each state as a vector. State transitions are performed as stack shift operations followed by a push of a preterminal semantic category label. In this way the model can capture semantic hierarchical structures without the use of tree-structured data. Another simpler but effective generative model is the one based on Finite State Transducers. It performs SLU as a translation process from words to concepts using Finite State Transducers (FST). An example of discriminative model used for SLU is the one based on Support Vector Machines (SVMs) (Vapnik, 1995), as shown in (Raymond and Riccardi, 2007). In this approach, data are mapped into a vector space and SLU is performed as a classification problem using Maximal Margin Classifiers (Shawe-Taylor and Cristianini, 2004).

Generative models have the advantage to be more robust to overfitting on training data, while discriminative models are more robust to irrelevant features. Both approaches, used separately, have shown a good performance (Raymond and Riccardi, 2007), but they have very different characteristics and the way they encode prior knowledge is very different, thus designing models able to take into account characteristics of both approaches are particularly promising.

In this paper we propose a method for SLU based on generative and discriminative models: the former uses FSTs to generate a list of SLU hypotheses, which are re-ranked by SVMs. These exploit all possible word/concept subsequences (with gaps) of the spoken sentence as features (*i.e.* all possible n-grams). Gaps allow for the encod-

Proceedings of the 12th Conference of the European Chapter of the ACL, pages 202–210,
Athens, Greece, 30 March – 3 April 2009. ©2009 Association for Computational Linguistics

ing of long distance dependencies between words in relatively small n-grams. Given the huge size of this feature space, we adopted kernel methods and in particular sequence kernels (Shawe-Taylor and Cristianini, 2004) and tree kernels (Raymond and Riccardi, 2007; Moschitti and Bejan, 2004; Moschitti, 2006) to implicitly encode n-grams and other structural information in SVMs.

We experimented with different approaches for training the discriminative models and two different corpora: the well-known MEDIA corpus (Bonneau-Maynard et al., 2005) and a new corpus acquired in the European project LUNA[1] (Raymond et al., 2007). The results show a great improvement with respect to both the FST-based model and the SVM model alone, which are the current state-of-the-art for concept classification on such corpora. The rest of the paper is organized as follows: Sections 2 and 3 show the generative and discriminative models, respectively. The experiments and results are reported in Section 4 whereas the conclusions are drawn in Section 5.

2 Generative approach for concept classification

In the context of Spoken Language Understanding (SLU), concept classification is the task of associating the best sequence of concepts to a given sentence, *i.e.* word sequence. A concept is a class containing all the words carrying out the same semantic meaning with respect to the application domain. In SLU, concepts are used as semantic units and are represented with concept tags. The association between words and concepts is learned from an annotated corpus.

The Generative model used in our work for concept classification is the same used in (Raymond and Riccardi, 2007). Given a sequence of words as input, a translation process based on FST is performed to output a sequence of concept tags. The translation process involves three steps: (1) the mapping of words into classes (2) the mapping of classes into concepts and (3) the selection of the best concept sequence.

The first step is used to improve the generalization power of the model. The word classes at this level can be both domain-dependent, *e.g.* "Hotel" in MEDIA or "Software" in the LUNA corpus, or domain-independent, *e.g.* numbers, dates, months etc. The class of a word not belonging to any class is the word itself.

In the second step, classes are mapped into concepts. The mapping is not one-to-one: a class may be associated with more than one concept, *i.e.* more than one SLU hypothesis can be generated.

In the third step, the best or the m-best hypotheses are selected among those produced in the previous step. They are chosen according to the maximum probability evaluated by the Conceptual Language Model, described in the next section.

2.1 Stochastic Conceptual Language Model (SCLM)

An SCLM is an n-gram language model built on semantic tags. Using the same notation proposed in (Moschitti et al., 2007) and (Raymond and Riccardi, 2007), our SCLM trains joint probability $P(W, C)$ of word and concept sequences from an annotated corpus:

$$P(W, C) = \prod_{i=1}^{k} P(w_i, c_i | h_i),$$

where $W = w_1..w_k$, $C = c_1..c_k$ and $h_i = w_{i-1}c_{i-1}..w_1c_1$. Since we use a 3-gram conceptual language model, the history h_i is $\{w_{i-1}c_{i-1}, w_{i-2}c_{i-2}\}$.

All the steps of the translation process described here and above are implemented as Finite State Transducers (FST) using the AT&T FSM/GRM tools and the SRILM (Stolcke, 2002) tools. In particular the SCLM is trained using SRILM tools and then converted to an FST. This allows the use of a wide set of stochastic language models (both back-off and interpolated models with several discounting techniques like Good-Turing, Witten-Bell, Natural, Kneser-Ney, Unchanged Kneser-Ney etc). We represent the combination of all the translation steps as a transducer λ_{SLU} (Raymond and Riccardi, 2007) in terms of FST operations:

$$\lambda_{SLU} = \lambda_W \circ \lambda_{W2C} \circ \lambda_{SLM},$$

where λ_W is the transducer representation of the input sentence, λ_{W2C} is the transducer mapping words to classes and λ_{SLM} is the Semantic Language Model (SLM) described above. The best SLU hypothesis is given by

$$C = project_C(bestpath_1(\lambda_{SLU})),$$

where $bestpath_n$ (in this case n is 1 for the 1-best hypothesis) performs a Viterbi search on the FST

[1]Contract n. 33549

and outputs the n-best hypotheses and $project_C$ performs a projection of the FST on the output labels, in this case the concepts.

2.2 Generation of m-best concept labeling

Using the FSTs described above, we can generate m best hypotheses ranked by the joint probability of the SCLM.

After an analysis of the m-best hypotheses of our SLU model, we noticed that many times the hypothesis ranked first by the SCLM is not the closest to the correct concept sequence, *i.e.* its error rate using the Levenshtein alignment with the manual annotation of the corpus is not the lowest among the m hypotheses. This means that re-ranking the m-best hypotheses in a convenient way could improve the SLU performance. The best choice in this case is a discriminative model, since it allows for the use of informative features, which, in turn, can model easily feature dependencies (also if they are infrequent in the training set).

3 Discriminative re-ranking

Our discriminative re-ranking is based on SVMs or a perceptron trained with pairs of conceptually annotated sentences. The classifiers learn to select which annotation has an error rate lower than the others so that the m-best annotations can be sorted based on their correctness.

3.1 SVMs and Kernel Methods

Kernel Methods refer to a large class of learning algorithms based on inner product vector spaces, among which Support Vector Machines (SVMs) are one of the most well known algorithms. SVMs and perceptron learn a hyperplane $H(\vec{x}) = \vec{w}\vec{x} + b = 0$, where $\vec{x}$ is the feature vector representation of a classifying object o, $\vec{w} \in \mathbb{R}^n$ (a vector space) and $b \in \mathbb{R}$ are parameters (Vapnik, 1995). The classifying object o is mapped into $\vec{x}$ by a feature function ϕ. The kernel trick allows us to rewrite the decision hyperplane as $\sum_{i=1..l} y_i\alpha_i\phi(o_i)\phi(o) + b = 0$, where y_i is equal to 1 for positive and -1 for negative examples, $\alpha_i \in \mathbb{R}^+$, $o_i \forall i \in \{1..l\}$ are the training instances and the product $K(o_i, o) = \langle\phi(o_i)\phi(o)\rangle$ is the kernel function associated with the mapping ϕ. Note that we do not need to apply the mapping ϕ, we can use $K(o_i, o)$ directly (Shawe-Taylor and Cristianini, 2004). For example, next section shows a kernel function that counts the number of word sequences in common between two sentences, in the space of n-grams (for any n).

3.2 String Kernels

The String Kernels that we consider count the number of substrings containing gaps shared by two sequences, *i.e.* some of the symbols of the original string are skipped. Gaps modify the weight associated with the target substrings as shown in the following.

Let Σ be a finite alphabet, $\Sigma^* = \bigcup_{n=0}^{\infty} \Sigma^n$ is the set of all strings. Given a string $s \in \Sigma^*$, $|s|$ denotes the length of the strings and s_i its compounding symbols, i.e $s = s_1..s_{|s|}$, whereas $s[i : j]$ selects the substring $s_i s_{i+1}..s_{j-1}s_j$ from the i-th to the j-th character. u is a subsequence of s if there is a sequence of indexes $\vec{I} = (i_1, ..., i_{|u|})$, with $1 \leq i_1 < ... < i_{|u|} \leq |s|$, such that $u = s_{i_1}..s_{i_{|u|}}$ or $u = s[\vec{I}]$ for short. $d(\vec{I})$ is the distance between the first and last character of the subsequence u in s, *i.e.* $d(\vec{I}) = i_{|u|} - i_1 + 1$. Finally, given s_1, $s_2 \in \Sigma^*$, $s_1 s_2$ indicates their concatenation.

The set of all substrings of a text corpus forms a feature space denoted by $\mathcal{F} = \{u_1, u_2, ..\} \subset \Sigma^*$. To map a string s in $\mathbb{R}^\infty$ space, we can use the following functions: $\phi_u(s) = \sum_{\vec{I}:u=s[\vec{I}]} \lambda^{d(\vec{I})}$ for some $\lambda \leq 1$. These functions count the number of occurrences of u in the string s and assign them a weight $\lambda^{d(\vec{I})}$ proportional to their lengths. Hence, the inner product of the feature vectors for two strings s_1 and s_2 returns the sum of all common subsequences weighted according to their frequency of occurrences and lengths, *i.e.*

$$SK(s_1, s_2) = \sum_{u\in\Sigma^*} \phi_u(s_1) \cdot \phi_u(s_2) = \sum_{u\in\Sigma^*} \sum_{\vec{I_1}:u=s_1[\vec{I_1}]} \lambda^{d(\vec{I_1})}$$

$$\sum_{\vec{I_2}:u=s_2[\vec{I_2}]} \lambda^{d(\vec{I_2})} = \sum_{u\in\Sigma^*} \sum_{\vec{I_1}:u=s_1[\vec{I_1}]} \sum_{\vec{I_2}:u=s_2[\vec{I_2}]} \lambda^{d(\vec{I_1})+d(\vec{I_2})},$$

where $d(.)$ counts the number of characters in the substrings as well as the gaps that were skipped in the original string. It is worth noting that:

(a) longer subsequences receive lower weights;

(b) some characters can be omitted, *i.e.* gaps; and

(c) gaps determine a weight since the exponent of λ is the number of characters and gaps between the first and last character.

Characters in the sequences can be substituted with any set of symbols. In our study we preferred to use words so that we can obtain word sequences. For example, given the sentence: *How may I help you ?* sample substrings, extracted by the Sequence Kernel (SK), are: *How help you ?*, *How help ?*, *help you*, *may help you*, etc.

3.3 Tree kernels

Tree kernels represent trees in terms of their substructures (fragments). The kernel function detects if a tree subpart (common to both trees) belongs to the feature space that we intend to generate. For such purpose, the desired fragments need to be described. We consider two important characterizations: the syntactic tree (STF) and the partial tree (PTF) fragments.

3.3.1 Tree Fragment Types

An STF is a general subtree whose leaves can be non-terminal symbols. For example, Figure 1(a) shows 10 STFs (out of 17) of the subtree rooted in `VP` (of the left tree). The STFs satisfy the constraint that grammatical rules cannot be broken. For example, `[VP [V NP]]` is an STF, which has two non-terminal symbols, `V` and `NP`, as leaves whereas `[VP [V]]` is not an STF. If we relax the constraint over the STFs, we obtain more general substructures called *partial trees fragments* (PTFs). These can be generated by the application of partial production rules of the grammar, consequently `[VP [V]]` and `[VP [NP]]` are valid PTFs. Figure 1(b) shows that the number of PTFs derived from the same tree as before is still higher (*i.e.* 30 PTs).

3.4 Counting Shared SubTrees

The main idea of tree kernels is to compute the number of common substructures between two trees T_1 and T_2 without explicitly considering the whole fragment space. To evaluate the above kernels between two T_1 and T_2, we need to define a set $\mathcal{F} = \{f_1, f_2, \ldots, f_{|\mathcal{F}|}\}$, *i.e.* a tree fragment space and an indicator function $I_i(n)$, equal to 1 if the target f_i is rooted at node n and equal to 0 otherwise. A tree-kernel function over T_1 and T_2 is $TK(T_1, T_2) = \sum_{n_1 \in N_{T_1}} \sum_{n_2 \in N_{T_2}} \Delta(n_1, n_2)$, where N_{T_1} and N_{T_2} are the sets of the T_1's and T_2's nodes, respectively and $\Delta(n_1, n_2) = \sum_{i=1}^{|\mathcal{F}|} I_i(n_1) I_i(n_2)$. The latter is equal to the number of common fragments rooted in the n_1 and n_2 nodes. In the following sections we report the equation for the efficient evaluation of Δ for ST and PT kernels.

3.5 Syntactic Tree Kernels (STK)

The Δ function depends on the type of fragments that we consider as *basic* features. For example, to evaluate the fragments of type STF, it can be defined as:

1. if the productions at n_1 and n_2 are different then $\Delta(n_1, n_2) = 0$;
2. if the productions at n_1 and n_2 are the same, and n_1 and n_2 have only leaf children (*i.e.* they are pre-terminals symbols) then $\Delta(n_1, n_2) = 1$;
3. if the productions at n_1 and n_2 are the same, and n_1 and n_2 are not pre-terminals then

$$\Delta(n_1, n_2) = \prod_{j=1}^{nc(n_1)} (\sigma + \Delta(c_{n_1}^j, c_{n_2}^j)) \quad (1)$$

where $\sigma \in \{0, 1\}$, $nc(n_1)$ is the number of children of n_1 and c_n^j is the j-th child of the node n. Note that, since the productions are the same, $nc(n_1) = nc(n_2)$. $\Delta(n_1, n_2)$ evaluates the number of STFs common to n_1 and n_2 as proved in (Collins and Duffy, 2002).

Moreover, a decay factor λ can be added by modifying steps (2) and (3) as follows[2]:

2. $\Delta(n_1, n_2) = \lambda$,
3. $\Delta(n_1, n_2) = \lambda \prod_{j=1}^{nc(n_1)} (\sigma + \Delta(c_{n_1}^j, c_{n_2}^j))$.

The computational complexity of Eq. 1 is $O(|N_{T_1}| \times |N_{T_2}|)$ but as shown in (Moschitti, 2006), the average running time tends to be linear, *i.e.* $O(|N_{T_1}| + |N_{T_2}|)$, for natural language syntactic trees.

3.6 The Partial Tree Kernel (PTK)

PTFs have been defined in (Moschitti, 2006). Their computation is carried out by the following Δ function:

1. if the node labels of n_1 and n_2 are different then $\Delta(n_1, n_2) = 0$;
2. else $\Delta(n_1, n_2) =$
$1 + \sum_{\vec{I}_1, \vec{I}_2, l(\vec{I}_1) = l(\vec{I}_2)} \prod_{j=1}^{l(\vec{I}_1)} \Delta(c_{n_1}(\vec{I}_{1j}), c_{n_2}(\vec{I}_{2j}))$

[2] To have a similarity score between 0 and 1, we also apply the normalization in the kernel space, *i.e.*: $K'(T_1, T_2) = \frac{TK(T_1, T_2)}{\sqrt{TK(T_1, T_1) \times TK(T_2, T_2)}}$.

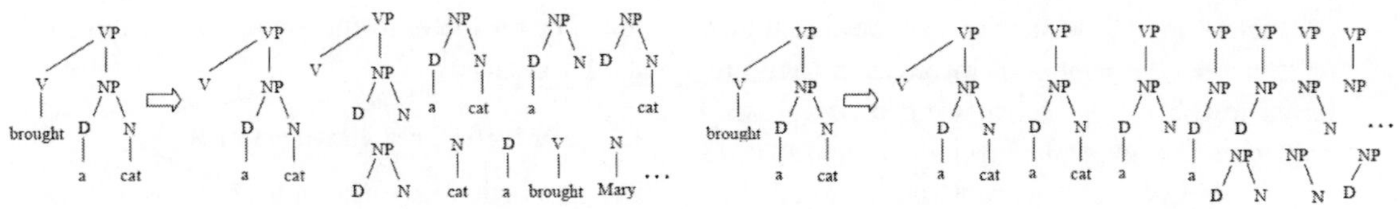

(a) Syntactic Tree fragments (STF) (b) Partial Tree fragments (PTF)

Figure 1: Examples of different classes of tree fragments.

where $\vec{I_1} = \langle h_1, h_2, h_3, ..\rangle$ and $\vec{I_2} = \langle k_1, k_2, k_3, ..\rangle$ are index sequences associated with the ordered child sequences c_{n_1} of n_1 and c_{n_2} of n_2, respectively, $\vec{I}_{1j}$ and $\vec{I}_{2j}$ point to the j-th child in the corresponding sequence, and, again, $l(\cdot)$ returns the sequence length, *i.e.* the number of children.

Furthermore, we add two decay factors: μ for the depth of the tree and λ for the length of the child subsequences with respect to the original sequence, *i.e.* we account for gaps. It follows that $\Delta(n_1, n_2) =$

$$\mu\Big(\lambda^2 + \sum_{\vec{I_1},\vec{I_2},l(\vec{I_1})=l(\vec{I_2})} \lambda^{d(\vec{I_1})+d(\vec{I_2})} \prod_{j=1}^{l(\vec{I_1})} \Delta(c_{n_1}(\vec{I}_{1j}), c_{n_2}(\vec{I}_{2j}))\Big), \quad (2)$$

where $d(\vec{I_1}) = \vec{I}_{1l(\vec{I_1})} - \vec{I}_{11}$ and $d(\vec{I_2}) = \vec{I}_{2l(\vec{I_2})} - \vec{I}_{21}$. This way, we penalize both larger trees and child subsequences with gaps. Eq. 2 is more general than Eq. 1. Indeed, if we only consider the contribution of the longest child sequence from node pairs that have the same children, we implement the STK kernel.

3.7 Re-ranking models using sequences

The FST generates the m most likely concept annotations. These are used to build annotation pairs, $\langle s^i, s^j\rangle$, which are positive instances if s^i has a lower concept annotation error than s^j, with respect to the manual annotation in the corpus. Thus, a trained binary classifier can decide if s^i is more accurate than s^j. Each candidate annotation s^i is described by a word sequence where each word is followed by its concept annotation. For example, given the sentence:

ho (I have) un (a) problema (problem) con (with) la (the) scheda di rete (network card) ora (now)

a pair of annotations $\langle s^i, s^j\rangle$ could be

s^i: *ho **NULL** un **NULL** problema **PROBLEM-B** con **NULL** la **NULL** scheda **HW-B** di **HW-I** rete **HW-I** ora **RELATIVETIME-B***

s^j: *ho **NULL** un **NULL** problema **ACTION-B** con **NULL** la **NULL** scheda **HW-B** di **HW-B** rete **HW-B** ora **RELATIVETIME-B***

where **NULL**, **ACTION**, **RELATIVETIME**, and **HW** are the assigned concepts whereas **B** and **I** are the usual begin and internal tags for concept subparts. The second annotation is less accurate than the first since *problema* is annotated as an action and *"scheda di rete"* is split in three different concepts.

Given the above data, the sequence kernel is used to evaluate the number of common n-grams between s^i and s^j. Since the string kernel skips some elements of the target sequences, the counted n-grams include: concept sequences, word sequences and any subsequence of words and concepts at any distance in the sentence.

Such counts are used in our re-ranking function as follows: let e_i be the pair $\langle s_i^1, s_i^2\rangle$ we evaluate the kernel:

$$\begin{aligned} K_R(e_1, e_2) &= SK(s_1^1, s_2^1) + SK(s_1^2, s_2^2) \quad (3) \\ &- SK(s_1^1, s_2^2) - SK(s_1^2, s_2^1) \end{aligned}$$

This schema, consisting in summing four different kernels, has been already applied in (Collins and Duffy, 2002) for syntactic parsing re-ranking, where the basic kernel was a tree kernel instead of SK and in (Moschitti et al., 2006), where, to re-rank Semantic Role Labeling annotations, a tree kernel was used on a semantic tree similar to the one introduced in the next section.

3.8 Re-ranking models using trees

Since the aim in concept annotation re-ranking is to exploit innovative and effective source of information, we can use the power of tree kernels to generate correlation between concepts and word structures.

Fig. 2 describes the structural association between the concept and the word level. This kind of trees allows us to engineer new kernels and consequently new features (Moschitti et al., 2008),

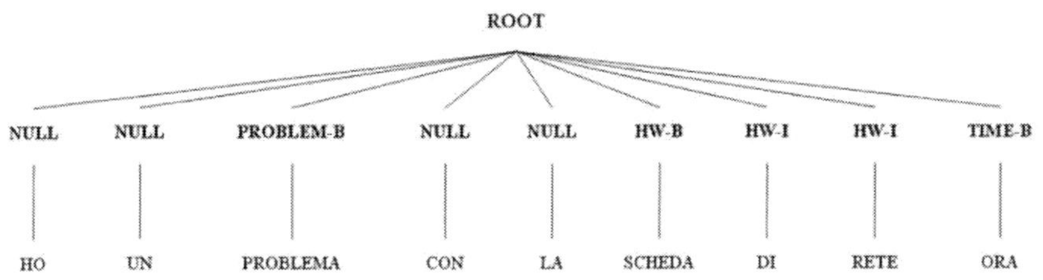

Figure 2: An example of the semantic tree used for STK or PTK

Corpus LUNA	Train set		Test set	
	words	concepts	words	concepts
Dialogs WOZ	183		67	
Dialogs HH	180		-	
Turns WOZ	1.019		373	
Turns HH	6.999		-	
Tokens WOZ	8.512	2.887	2.888	984
Tokens WOZ	62.639	17.423	-	-
Vocab. WOZ	1.172	34	-	-
Vocab. HH	4.692	49	-	-
OOV rate	-	-	3.2%	0.1%

Table 1: Statistics on the LUNA corpus

Corpus Media	Train set		Test set	
	words	concepts	words	concepts
Turns	12,922		3,518	
# of tokens	94,912	43,078	26,676	12,022
Vocabulary	5,307	80	-	-
OOV rate	-	-	0.01%	0.0%

Table 2: Statistics on the MEDIA corpus

e.g. their subparts extracted by STK or PTK, like the tree fragments in figures 1(a) and 1(b). These can be used in SVMs to learn the classification of words in concepts.

More specifically, in our approach, we use tree fragments to establish the order of correctness between two alternative annotations. Therefore, given two trees associated with two annotations, a re-ranker based on tree kernel, K_R, can be built in the same way of the sequence-based kernel by substituting SK in Eq. 3 with STK or PTK.

4 Experiments

In this section, we describe the corpora, parameters, models and results of our experiments of word chunking and concept classification. Our baseline relates to the error rate of systems based on only FST and SVMs. The re-ranking models are built on the FST output. Different ways of producing training data for the re-ranking models determine different results.

4.1 Corpora

We used two different speech corpora:

The corpus LUNA, produced in the homonymous European project is the first Italian corpus of spontaneous speech on spoken dialog: it is based on the help-desk conversation in the domain of software/hardware repairing (Raymond et al., 2007). The data are organized in transcriptions and annotations of speech based on a new multi-level protocol. Data acquisition is still in progress. Currently, 250 dialogs acquired with a WOZ approach and 180 Human-Human (HH) dialogs are available. Statistics on LUNA corpus are reported in Table 1.

The corpus MEDIA was collected within the French project MEDIA-EVALDA (Bonneau-Maynard et al., 2005) for development and evaluation of spoken understanding models and linguistic studies. The corpus is composed of 1257 dialogs, from 250 different speakers, acquired with a Wizard of Oz (WOZ) approach in the context of hotel room reservations and tourist information. Statistics on transcribed and conceptually annotated data are reported in Table 2.

4.2 Experimental setup

We defined two different training sets in the LUNA corpus: one using only the WOZ training dialogs and one merging them with the HH dialogs. Given the small size of LUNA corpus, we did not carried out parameterization on a development set but we used default or a priori parameters.

We experimented with LUNA WOZ and six re-rankers obtained with the combination of SVMs and perceptron (PCT) with three different types of kernels: Syntactic Tree Kernel (STK), Partial Tree kernels (PTK) and the String Kernel (SK) described in Section 3.3.

Given the high number and the cost of these experiments, we ran only one model, *i.e.* the one

Corpus	LUNA WOZ+HH		MEDIA
Approach (STK)	MT	ST	MT
FST	18.2	18.2	12.6
SVM	23.4	23.4	13.7
RR-A	**15.6**	17.0	**11.6**
RR-B	16.2	16.5	11.8
RR-C	16.1	16.4	11.7

Table 3: Results of experiments (CER) using FST and SVMs with the Sytntactic Tree Kernel (STK) on two different corpora: LUNA WOZ + HH, and MEDIA.

WOZ	Monolithic Training					
	SVM			PCT		
	STK	PTK	SK	STK	PTK	SK
RR-A	**18.5**	19.3	19.1	24.2	28.3	23.3
RR-B	**18.5**	19.3	19.0	29.4	23.7	20.3
RR-C	**18.5**	19.3	19.1	31.5	30.0	20.2

Table 4: Results of experiments, in terms of Concept Error Rate (CER), on the LUNA WOZ corpus using Monolithic Training approach. The baseline with FST and SVMs used separately are **23.2%** and **26.7%** respectively.

WOZ	Split Training					
	SVM			PCT		
	STK	PTK	SK	STK	PTK	SK
RR-A	20.0	18.0	**16.1**	28.4	29.8	27.8
RR-B	19.0	19.0	19.0	26.3	30.0	25.6
RR-C	19.0	18.4	16.6	27.1	26.2	30.3

Table 5: Results of experiments, in terms of Concept Error Rate (CER), on the LUNA WOZ corpus using Split Training approach. The baseline with FST and SVMs used separately are **23.2%** and **26.7%** respectively.

based on SVMs and STK[3] , on the largest datasets, *i.e.* WOZ merged with HH dialogs and Media. We trained all the SCLMs used in our experiments with the SRILM toolkit (Stolcke, 2002) and we used an interpolated model for probability estimation with the Kneser-Ney discount (Chen and Goodman, 1998). We then converted the model in an FST as described in Section 2.1.

The model used to obtain the SVM baseline for concept classification was trained using YamCHA (Kudo and Matsumoto, 2001). For the re-ranking models based on structure kernels, SVMs or perceptron, we used the SVM-Light-TK toolkit (available at dit.unitn.it/moschitti). For λ (see Section 3.2), cost-factor and trade-off parameters, we used, 0.4, 1 and 1, respectively.

4.3 Training approaches

The FST model generates the m-best annotations, *i.e.* the data used to train the re-ranker based on SVMs and perceptron. Different training approaches can be carried out based on the use of the corpus and the method to generate the m-best. We apply two different methods for training: **Monolithic Training** and **Split Training**.

In the former, FSTs are learned with the whole training set. The m-best hypotheses generated by such models are then used to train the re-ranker classifier. In Split Training, the training data are divided in two parts to avoid bias in the FST generation step. More in detail, we train FSTs on part 1 and generate the m-best hypotheses using part 2. Then, we re-apply these procedures inverting part 1 with part 2. Finally, we train the re-ranker on the merged m-best data. At the classification time, we generate the m-best of the test set using the FST trained on all training data.

[3]The number of parameters, models and training approaches make the exhaustive experimentation expensive in terms of processing time, which approximately requires 2 or 3 months.

Regarding the generation of the training instances $\langle s^i, s^j \rangle$, we set m to 10 and we choose one of the 10-best hypotheses as the second element of the pair, s_j, thus generating 10 different pairs.

The first element instead can be selected according to three different approaches:

(A): s_i is the manual annotation taken from the corpus;

(B) s_i is the most accurate annotation, in terms of the edit distance from the manual annotation, among the 10-best hypotheses of the FST model;

(C) as above but s_i is selected among the 100-best hypotheses. The pairs are also inverted to generate negative examples.

4.4 Re-ranking results

All the results of our experiments, expressed in terms of concept error rate (CER), are reported in Table 3, 4 and 5.

In Table 3, the corpora, *i.e.* LUNA (WOZ+HH) and Media, and the training approaches, *i.e.* Monolithic Training (MT) and Split Training (ST), are reported in the first and second row. Column 1 shows the concept classification model used, *i.e.* the baselines FST and SVMs, and the re-ranking models (RR) applied to FST. A, B and C refer to the three approaches for generating training instances described above. As already mentioned for these large datasets, SVMs only use STK.

We note that our re-rankers relevantly improve our baselines, *i.e.* the FST and SVM concept classifiers on both corpora. For example, SVM re-ranker using STK, MT and RR-A improves FST concept classifier of 23.2-15.6 = 7.6 points.

Moreover, the monolithic training seems the most appropriate to train the re-rankers whereas approach A is the best in producing training instances for the re-rankers. This is not surprising since method A considers the manual annotation as a referent gold standard and it always allows comparing candidate annotations with the perfect one.

Tables 4 and 5 have a similar structure of Table 3 but they only show experiments on LUNA WOZ corpus with respect to the monolithic and split training approach, respectively. In these tables, we also report the result for SVMs and perceptron (PCT) using STK, PTK and SK. We note that:

First, the small size of WOZ training set (only 1,019 turns) impacts on the accuracy of the systems, *e.g.* FST and SVMs, which achieved a CER of 18.2% and 23.4%, respectively, using also HH dialogs, with only the WOZ data, they obtain 23.2% and 26.7%, respectively.

Second, the perceptron algorithm appears to be ineffective for re-ranking. This is mainly due to the reduced size of the WOZ data, which clearly prevents an on line algorithm like PCT to adequately refine its model by observing many examples[4].

Third, the kernels which produce higher number of substructures, *i.e.* PTK and SK, improves the kernel less rich in terms of features, *i.e.* STK. For example, using split training and approach A, STK is improved by 20.0-16.1=3.9. This is an interesting result since it shows that (a) richer structures do produce better ranking models and (b) kernel methods give a remarkable help in feature design.

Next, although the training data is small, the re-rankers based on kernels appear to be very effective. This may also alleviate the burden of annotating a lot of data.

Finally, the experiments of MEDIA show a not so high improvement using re-rankers. This is due to: (a) the baseline, *i.e.* the FST model is very accurate since MEDIA is a large corpus thus the re-ranker can only *"correct"* small number of errors; and (b) we could only experiment with the less expensive but also less accurate models, *i.e.* monolithic training and STK.

[4]We use only one iteration of the algorithm.

Media also offers the possibility to compare with the state-of-the-art, which our re-rankers seem to improve. However, we need to consider that many Media corpus versions exist and this makes such comparisons not completely reliable. Future work on the paper research line appears to be very interesting: the assessment of our best models on Media and WOZ+HH as well as other corpora is required. More importantly, the structures that we have proposed for re-ranking are just two of the many possibilities to encode both word/concept statistical distributions and linguistic knowledge encoded in syntactic/semantic parse trees.

5 Conclusions

In this paper, we propose discriminative re-ranking of concept annotation to capitalize from the benefits of generative and discriminative approaches. Our generative approach is the state-of-the-art in concept classification since we used the same FST model used in (Raymond and Riccardi, 2007). We could improve it by 1% point in MEDIA and 7.6 points (until 30% of relative improvement) on LUNA, where the more limited availability of annotated data leaves a larger room for improvement.

It should be noted that to design the re-ranking model, we only used two different structures, *i.e.* one sequence and one tree. Kernel methods show that combinations of feature vectors, sequence kernels and other structural kernels, *e.g.* on shallow or deep syntactic parse trees, appear to be a promising research line (Moschitti, 2008). Also, the approach used in (Zanzotto and Moschitti, 2006) to define cross pair relations may be exploited to carry out a more effective pair re-ranking. Finally, the experimentation with automatic speech transcriptions is interesting to test the robustness of our models to transcription errors.

Acknowledgments

This work has been partially supported by the European Commission - LUNA project, contract n. 33549.

References

H. Bonneau-Maynard, S. Rosset, C. Ayache, A. Kuhn, and D. Mostefa. 2005. Semantic annotation of the french media dialog corpus. In *Proceedings of Interspeech2005*, Lisbon, Portugal.

S. F. Chen and J. Goodman. 1998. An empirical study of smoothing techniques for language modeling. In *Technical Report of Computer Science Group*, Harvard, USA.

M. Collins and N. Duffy. 2002. New Ranking Algorithms for Parsing and Tagging: Kernels over Discrete structures, and the voted perceptron. In *ACL02*, pages 263–270.

Y. He and S. Young. 2005. Semantic processing using the hidden vector state model. *Computer Speech and Language*, 19:85–106.

T. Kudo and Y. Matsumoto. 2001. Chunking with support vector machines. In *Proceedings of NAACL2001*, Pittsburg, USA.

A. Moschitti and C. Bejan. 2004. A semantic kernel for predicate argument classification. In *CoNLL-2004*, Boston, MA, USA.

A. Moschitti, D. Pighin, and R. Basili. 2006. Semantic role labeling via tree kernel joint inference. In *Proceedings of CoNLL-X*, New York City.

A. Moschitti, G. Riccardi, and C. Raymond. 2007. Spoken language understanding with kernels for syntactic/semantic structures. In *Proceedings of ASRU2007*, Kyoto, Japan.

A. Moschitti, D. Pighin, and R. Basili. 2008. Tree kernels for semantic role labeling. *Computational Linguistics*, 34(2):193–224.

A. Moschitti. 2006. Efficient Convolution Kernels for Dependency and Constituent Syntactic Trees. In *Proceedings of ECML 2006*, pages 318–329, Berlin, Germany.

A. Moschitti. 2008. Kernel methods, syntax and semantics for relational text categorization. In *CIKM '08: Proceeding of the 17th ACM conference on Information and knowledge management*, pages 253–262, New York, NY, USA. ACM.

C. Raymond and G. Riccardi. 2007. Generative and discriminative algorithms for spoken language understanding. In *Proceedings of Interspeech2007*, Antwerp,Belgium.

C. Raymond, G. Riccardi, K. J. Rodrigez, and J. Wisniewska. 2007. The luna corpus: an annotation scheme for a multi-domain multi-lingual dialogue corpus. In *Proceedings of Decalog2007*, Trento, Italy.

J. Shawe-Taylor and N. Cristianini. 2004. *Kernel Methods for Pattern Analysis*. Cambridge University Press.

A. Stolcke. 2002. Srilm: an extensible language modeling toolkit. In *Proceedings of SLP2002*, Denver, USA.

V. Vapnik. 1995. *The Nature of Statistical Learning Theory*. Springer.

F. M. Zanzotto and A. Moschitti. 2006. Automatic learning of textual entailments with cross-pair similarities. In *Proceedings of the 21st Coling and 44th ACL*, pages 401–408, Sydney, Australia, July.

Inference Rules and their Application to Recognizing Textual Entailment

Georgiana Dinu
Saarland University
Campus, D-66123 Saarbrücken
dinu@coli.uni-sb.de

Rui Wang
Saarland University
Campus, D-66123 Saarbrücken
rwang@coli.uni-sb.de

Abstract

In this paper, we explore ways of improving an inference rule collection and its application to the task of recognizing textual entailment. For this purpose, we start with an automatically acquired collection and we propose methods to refine it and obtain more rules using a hand-crafted lexical resource. Following this, we derive a dependency-based structure representation from texts, which aims to provide a proper base for the inference rule application. The evaluation of our approach on the recognizing textual entailment data shows promising results on precision and the error analysis suggests possible improvements.

1 Introduction

Textual inference plays an important role in many natural language processing (NLP) tasks. In recent years, the recognizing textual entailment (RTE) (Dagan et al., 2006) challenge, which focuses on detecting semantic inference, has attracted a lot of attention. Given a text **T** (several sentences) and a hypothesis **H** (one sentence), the goal is to detect if **H** can be inferred from **T**.

Studies such as (Clark et al., 2007) attest that lexical substitution (e.g. synonyms, antonyms) or simple syntactic variation account for the entailment only in a small number of pairs. Thus, one essential issue is to identify more complex expressions which, in appropriate contexts, convey the same (or similar) meaning. However, more generally, we are also interested in pairs of expressions in which only a uni-directional inference relation holds[1].

A typical example is the following RTE pair in which *accelerate to* in **H** is used as an alternative formulation for *reach speed of* in **T**.

T: *The high-speed train, scheduled for a trial run on Tuesday, is able to* ***reach*** *a maximum* ***speed of*** *up to 430 kilometers per hour, or 119 meters per second.*

H: *The train* ***accelerates*** *to 430 kilometers per hour.*

One way to deal with textual inference is through rule representation, for example *X wrote Y* $\approx$ *X is author of Y*. However, manually building collections of inference rules is time-consuming and it is unlikely that humans can exhaustively enumerate all the rules encoding the knowledge needed in reasoning with natural language. Instead, an alternative is to acquire these rules automatically from large corpora. Given such a rule collection, the next step to focus on is how to successfully use it in NLP applications. This paper tackles both aspects, acquiring inference rules and using them for the task of recognizing textual entailment.

For the first aspect, we extend and refine an existing collection of inference rules acquired based on the *Distributional Hypothesis* (DH). One of the main advantages of using the DH is that the only input needed is a large corpus of (parsed) text[2]. For the extension and refinement, a hand-crafted lexical resource is used for augmenting the original inference rule collection and exclude some of the incorrect rules.

For the second aspect, we focus on applying these rules to the RTE task. In particular, we use a structure representation derived from the dependency parse trees of **T** and **H**, which aims to capture the essential information they convey.

The rest of the paper is organized as follows: Section 2 introduces the inference rule collection

[1] We will use the term inference rule to stand for such concept; the two expressions can be actual paraphrases if the relation is bi-directional

[2] Another line of work on acquiring paraphrases uses comparable corpora, for instance (Barzilay and McKeown, 2001), (Pang et al., 2003)

Proceedings of the 12th Conference of the European Chapter of the ACL, pages 211–219,
Athens, Greece, 30 March – 3 April 2009.

we use, based on the Discovery of Inference Rules from Text (henceforth DIRT) algorithm and discusses previous work on applying it to the RTE task. Section 3 focuses on the rule collection itself and on the methods in which we use an external lexical resource to extend and refine it. Section 4 discusses the application of the rules for the RTE data, describing the structure representation we use to identify the appropriate context for the rule application. The experimental results will be presented in Section 5, followed by an error analysis and discussions in Section 6. Finally Section 7 will conclude the paper and point out future work directions.

2 Background

A number of automatically acquired inference rule/paraphrase collections are available, such as (Szpektor et al., 2004), (Sekine, 2005). In our work we use the DIRT collection because it is the largest one available and it has a relatively good accuracy (in the 50% range for top generated paraphrases, (Szpektor et al., 2007)). In this section, we describe the DIRT algorithm for acquiring inference rules. Following that, we will overview the RTE systems which take DIRT as an external knowledge resource.

2.1 Discovery of Inference Rules from Text

The DIRT algorithm has been introduced by (Lin and Pantel, 2001) and it is based on what is called the *Extended Distributional Hypothesis*. The original DH states that *words* occurring in similar contexts have similar meaning, whereas the extended version hypothesizes that *phrases* occurring in similar contexts are similar.

An inference rule in DIRT is a pair of binary relations $\langle\ pattern_1(X,Y),\ pattern_2(X,Y)\ \rangle$ which stand in an inference relation. $pattern_1$ and $pattern_2$ are chains in dependency trees[3] while X and Y are placeholders for nouns at the end of this chain. The two patterns will constitute a candidate paraphrase if the sets of X and Y values exhibit relevant overlap. In the following example, the two patterns are *prevent* and *provide protection against*.

$$\mathbf{X} \xleftarrow{subj} prevent \xrightarrow{obj} \mathbf{Y}$$

$$\mathbf{X} \xleftarrow{subj} provide \xrightarrow{obj} protection \xrightarrow{mod} against \xrightarrow{pcomp} \mathbf{Y}$$

[3]obtained with the Minipar parser (Lin, 1998)

X put emphasis on Y
≈ *X pay attention to Y*
≈ *X attach importance to Y*
≈ *X increase spending on Y*
≈ *X place emphasis on Y*
≈ *Y priority of X*
≈ *X focus on Y*

Table 1: Example of DIRT algorithm output. Most confident paraphrases of *X put emphasis on Y*

Such rules can be informally defined (Szpektor et al., 2007) as directional relations between two text patterns with variables. The left-hand-side pattern is assumed to entail the right-hand-side pattern in certain contexts, under the same variable instantiation. The definition relaxes the intuition of inference, as we only require the entailment to hold in *some* and not *all* contexts, motivated by the fact that such inferences occur often in natural text.

The algorithm does not extract directional inference rules, it can only identify candidate paraphrases; many of the rules are however unidirectional. Besides syntactic rewriting or lexical rules, rules in which the patterns are rather complex phrases are also extracted. Some of the rules encode lexical relations which can also be found in resources such as WordNet while others are lexical-syntactic variations that are unlikely to occur in hand-crafted resources (Lin and Pantel, 2001). Table 1 gives a few examples of rules present in DIRT[4].

Current work on inference rules focuses on making such resources more precise. (Basili et al., 2007) and (Szpektor et al., 2008) propose attaching selectional preferences to inference rules. These are semantic classes which correspond to the anchor values of an inference rule and have the role of making precise the context in which the rule can be applied [5]. This aspect is very important and we plan to address it in our future work. However in this paper we investigate the first and more basic issue: how to successfully use rules in their current form.

[4]For simplification, in the rest of the paper we will omit giving the dependency relations in a pattern.

[5]For example *X won Y* entails *X played Y* only when *Y* refers to some sort of competition, but not if *Y* refers to a musical instrument.

2.2 Related Work

Intuitively such inference rules should be effective for recognizing textual entailment. However, only a small number of systems have used DIRT as a resource in the RTE-3 challenge, and the experimental results have not fully shown it has an important contribution.

In (Clark et al., 2007)'s approach, semantic parsing to clause representation is performed and true entailment is decided only if every clause in the semantic representation of **T** semantically matches some clause in **H**. The only variation allowed consists of rewritings derived from WordNet and DIRT. Given the preliminary stage of this system, the overall results show very low improvement over a random classification baseline.

(Bar-Haim et al., 2007) implement a proof system using rules for generic linguistic structures, lexical-based rules, and lexical-syntactic rules (these obtained with a DIRT-like algorithm on the first CD of the Reuters RCV1 corpus). The entailment considers not only the strict notion of proof but also an approximate one. Given premise p and hypothesis h, the lexical-syntactic component marks all lexical noun alignments. For every pair of alignment, the paths between the two nouns are extracted, and the DIRT algorithm is applied to obtain a similarity score. If the score is above a threshold the rule is applied. However these lexical-syntactic rules are only used in about 3% of the attempted proofs and in most cases there is no lexical variation.

(Iftene and Balahur-Dobrescu, 2007) use DIRT in a more relaxed manner. A DIRT rule is employed in the system if at least one of the anchors match in **T** and **H**, i.e. they use them as unary rules. However, the detailed analysis of the system that they provide shows that the DIRT component is the least relevant one (adding 0.4% of precision).

In (Marsi et al., 2007), the focus is on the usefulness of DIRT. In their system a paraphrase substitution step is added on top of a system based on a tree alignment algorithm. The basic paraphrase substitution method follows three steps. Initially, the two patterns of a rule are matched in **T** and **H** (instantiations of the anchors X, Y do not have to match). The text tree is transformed by applying the paraphrase substitution. Following this, the transformed text tree and hypothesis trees are aligned. The coverage (proportion of aligned content words) is computed and if above some threshold, entailment is true. The paraphrase component adds 1.0% to development set results and only 0.5% to test sets, but a more detailed analysis on the results of the interaction with the other system components is not given.

X write Y →X author Y
X, founded in Y →X, opened in Y
X launch Y → X produce Y
X represent Z → X work for Y
death relieved X → X died
X faces menace from Y ↔ X endangered by Y
X, peace agreement for Y   *→ X is formulated to end war in Y*

Table 2: Example of inference rules needed in RTE

3 Extending and refining DIRT

Based on observations of using the inference rule collection on the real data, we discover that 1) some of the needed rules still lack even in a very large collection such as DIRT and 2) some systematic errors in the collection can be excluded. On both aspects, we use WordNet as additional lexical resource.

Missing Rules

A closer look into the RTE data reveals that DIRT lacks many of the rules that entailment pairs require.

Table 2 lists a selection of such rules. The first rows contain rules which are structurally very simple. These, however, are missing from DIRT and most of them also from other hand-crafted resources such as WordNet (i.e. there is no short path connecting the two verbs). This is to be expected as they are rules which hold in specific contexts, but difficult to be captured by a sense distinction of the lexical items involved.

The more complex rules are even more difficult to capture with a DIRT-like algorithm. Some of these do not occur frequently enough even in large amounts of text to permit acquiring them via the DH.

Combining WordNet and DIRT

In order to address the issue of missing rules, we investigate the effects of combining DIRT with an exact hand-coded lexical resource in order to create new rules.

For this we extended the DIRT rules by adding

X face threat of Y	
	≈ *X at risk of Y*
face	
	≈ *confront, front, look, face up*
threat	
	≈ *menace, terror, scourge*
risk	
	≈ *danger, hazard, jeopardy, endangerment, peril*

Table 3: Lexical variations creating new rules based on DIRT rule *X face threat of Y* → *X at risk of Y*

rules in which any of the lexical items involved in the patterns can be replaced by WordNet synonyms. In the example above, we consider the DIRT rule *X face threat of Y* → *X, at risk of Y* (Table 3).

Of course at this moment due to the lack of sense disambiguation, our method introduces lots of rules that are not correct. As one can see, expressions such as *front scourge* do not make any sense, therefore any rules containing this will be incorrect. However some of the new rules created in this example, such as *X face threat of Y* ≈ *X, at danger of Y* are reasonable ones and the rules which are incorrect often contain patterns that are very unlikely to occur in natural text.

The idea behind this is that a combination of various lexical resources is needed in order to cover the vast variety of phrases which humans can judge to be in an inference relation.

The method just described allows us to identify the first four rules listed in Table 2. We also acquire the rule *X face menace of Y* ≈ *X endangered by Y* (via *X face threat of Y* ≈ *X threatened by Y*, $menace \approx threat$, $threaten \approx endanger$).

Our extension is application-oriented therefore it is not intended to be evaluated as an independent rule collection, but in an application scenario such as RTE (Section 6).

In our experiments we also made a step towards removing the most systematic errors present in DIRT. DH algorithms have the main disadvantage that not only phrases with the same meaning are extracted but also phrases with opposite meaning.

In order to overcome this problem and since such errors are relatively easy to detect, we applied a filter to the DIRT rules. This eliminates inference rules which contain WordNet antonyms. For such a rule to be eliminated the two patterns have to be identical (with respect to edge labels and content words) except from the antonymous words; an example of a rule eliminated this way is *X **have** confidence in Y* ≈ *X **lack** confidence in Y*.

As pointed out by (Szpektor et al., 2007) a thorough evaluation of a rule collection is not a trivial task; however due to our methodology we can assume that the percentage of rules eliminated this way that are indeed contradictions gets close to 100%.

4 Applying DIRT on RTE

In this section we point out two issues that are encountered when applying inference rules for textual entailment. The first issue is concerned with correctly identifying the pairs in which the knowledge encoded in these rules is needed. Following this, another non-trivial task is to determine the way this knowledge interacts with the rest of information conveyed in an entailment pair. In order to further investigate these issues, we apply the rule collection on a dependency-based representation of text and hypothesis, namely Tree Skeleton.

4.1 Observations

A straightforward experiment can reveal the number of pairs in the RTE data which contain rules present in DIRT. For all the experiments in this paper, we use the DIRT collection provided by (Lin and Pantel, 2001), derived from the DIRT algorithm applied on 1GB of news text. The results we report here use only the most confident rules amounting to more than 4 million rules (top 40 following (Lin and Pantel, 2001)).[6]

Following the definition of an entailment rule, we identify RTE pairs in which $pattern_1(w1, w2)$ and $pattern_2(w1, w2)$ are matched one in **T** and the other one in **H** and $\langle pattern_1(X, Y), pattern2(X, Y)\rangle$ is an inference rule. The pair bellow is an example of this.

T: *The sale was made to pay Yukos US$ 27.5 billion tax bill, Yuganskneftegaz was originally sold for US$ 9.4 billion to a little known company **Baikalfinansgroup** which was later **bought by** the Russian state-owned oil company **Rosneft**.*

H: ***Baikalfinansgroup** was **sold to Rosneft**.*

[6] Another set of experiments showed that for this particular task, using the entire collection instead of a subset gave similar results.

On average, only 2% of the pairs in the RTE data is subject to the application of such inference rules. Out of these, approximately 50% are lexical rules (one verb entailing the other). Out of these lexical rules, around 50% are present in WordNet in a synonym, hypernym or sister relation. At a manual analysis, close to 80% of these are correct rules; this is higher than the estimated accuracy of DIRT, probably due to the bias of the data which consists of pairs which are entailment candidates.

However, given the small number of inference rules identified this way, we performed another analysis. This aims at determining an upper bound of the number of pairs featuring entailment phrases present in a collection. Given DIRT and the RTE data, we compute in how many pairs the two patterns of a paraphrase can be matched irrespective of their anchor values. An example is the following pair,

T: *Libya's case against Britain and the US* ***concerns*** *the dispute over their demand for extradition of Libyans charged with blowing up a Pan Am jet over Lockerbie in 1988.*

H: *One case* ***involved*** *the extradition of Libyan suspects in the Pan Am Lockerbie bombing.*

This is a case in which the rule is correct and the entailment is positive. In order to determine this, a system will have to know that *Libya's case against Britain and the US* in **T** entails *one case* in **H**. Similarly, in this context, *the dispute over their demand for extradition of Libyans charged with blowing up a Pan Am jet over Lockerbie in 1988* in **T** can be replaced with *the extradition of Libyan suspects in the Pan Am Lockerbie bombing* preserving the meaning.

Altogether in around 20% of the pairs, patterns of a rule can be found this way, many times with more than one rule found in a pair. However, in many of these pairs, finding the patterns of an inference rule does not imply that the rule is truly present in that pair.

Considering a system is capable of correctly identifying the cases in which an inference rule is needed, subsequent issues arise from the way these fragments of text interact with the surrounding context. Assuming we have a correct rule present in an entailment pair, the cases in which the pair is still not a positive case of entailment can be summarized as follows:

- The entailment rule is present in parts of the text which are not relevant to the entailment value of the pair.
- The rule is relevant, however the sentences in which the patterns are embedded block the entailment (e.g. through negative markers, modifiers, embedding verbs not preserving entailment)[7]
- The rule is correct in a limited number of contexts, but the current context is not the correct one.

To sum up, making use of the knowledge encoded with such rules is not a trivial task. If rules are used strictly in concordance with their definition, their utility is limited to a very small number of entailment pairs. For this reason, 1) instead of forcing the anchor values to be identical as most previous work, we allow more flexible rule matching (similar to (Marsi et al., 2007)) and 2) furthermore, we control the rule application process using a text representation based on dependency structure.

4.2 Tree Skeleton

The Tree Skeleton (TS) structure was proposed by (Wang and Neumann, 2007), and can be viewed as an extended version of the predicate-argument structure. Since it contains not only the predicate and its arguments, but also the dependency paths in-between, it captures the essential part of the sentence.

Following their algorithm, we first preprocess the data using a dependency parser[8] and then select overlapping topic words (i.e. nouns) in **T** and **H**. By doing so, we use fuzzy match at the substring level instead of full match. Starting with these nouns, we traverse the dependency tree to identify the lowest common ancestor node (named as *root node*). This sub-tree without the inner yield is defined as a Tree Skeleton. Figure 1 shows the TS of **T** of the following positive example,

T *For their discovery of ulcer-causing bacteria, Australian doctors Robin Warren and Barry Marshall have received the 2005 Nobel Prize in Physiology or Medicine.*

H *Robin Warren was awarded a Nobel Prize.*

Notice that, in order to match the inference rules with two anchors, the number of the dependency

[7] See (Nairn et al., 2006) for a detailed analysis of these aspects.

[8] Here we also use Minipar for the reason of consistence

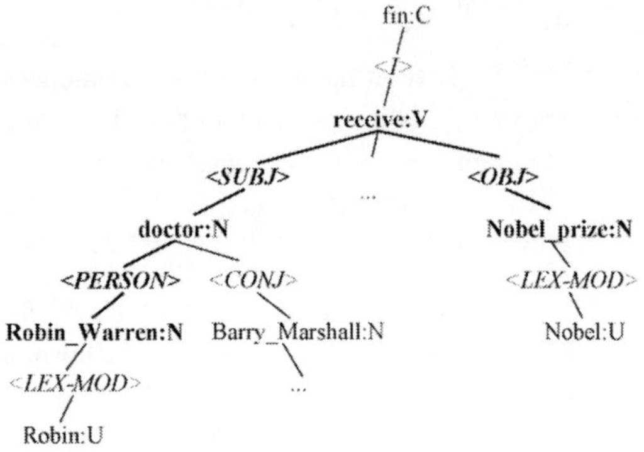

Figure 1: Dependency structure of text. Tree skeleton in bold

paths contained in a TS should also be two. In practice, among all the 800 T-H pairs of the RTE-2 test set, we successfully extracted tree skeletons in 296 text pairs, i.e., 37% of the test data is covered by this step and results on other data sets are similar.

Applying DIRT on a TS

Dependency representations like the tree skeleton have been explored by many researchers, e.g. (Zanzotto and Moschitti, 2006) have utilized a tree kernel method to calculate the similarity between T and H, and (Wang and Neumann, 2007) chose subsequence kernel to reduce the computational complexity. However, the focus of this paper is to evaluate the application of inference rules on RTE, instead of exploring methods of tackling the task itself. Therefore, we performed a straightforward matching algorithm to apply the inference rules on top of the tree skeleton structure. Given tree skeletons of **T** and **H**, we check if the two left dependency paths, the two right ones or the two root nodes contain the patterns of a rule.

In the example above, the rule $X \xleftarrow{obj} receive \xrightarrow{subj} Y \approx X \xleftarrow{obj2} award \xrightarrow{obj1} Y$ satisfies this criterion, as it is matched at the root nodes. Notice that the rule is correct only in restricted contexts, in which the object of *receive* is something which is conferred on the basis of merit. However in this pair, the context is indeed the correct one.

5 Experiments

Our experiments consist in predicting positive entailment in a very straightforward rule-based manner (Table 4 summarizes the results using three different rule collections). For each collection we select the RTE pairs in which we find a tree skeleton and match an inference rule. The first number in our table entries represents how many of such pairs we have identified, out the 1600 of development and test pairs. For these pairs we simply predict positive entailment and the second entry represents what percentage of these pairs are indeed positive entailment. Our work does not focus on building a complete RTE system; however, we also combine our method with a bag of words baseline to see the effects on the whole data set.

5.1 Results on a subset of the data

In the first two columns (Dirt$_{TS}$ and Dirt+WN$_{TS}$) we consider DIRT in its original state and DIRT with rules generated with WordNet as described in Section 3; all precisions are higher than 67%[9]. After adding WordNet, approximately in twice as many pairs, tree skeletons and rules are matched, while the precision is not harmed. This may indicate that our method of adding rules does not decrease precision of an RTE system.

In the third column we report the results of using a set of rules containing only the trivial identity ones (Id$_{TS}$). For our current system, this can be seen as a *precision* upper bound for all the other collections, in concordance with the fact that identical rules are nothing but inference rules of highest possible confidence. The fourth column (Dirt+Id+WN$_{TS}$) contains what can be considered our best setting. In this setting considerably more pairs are covered using a collection containing DIRT and identity rules with WordNet extension.

Although the precision results with this setting are encouraging (65% for RTE2 data and 72% for RTE3 data), the coverage is still low, 8% for RTE2 and 6% for RTE3. This aspect together with an error analysis we performed are the focus of Section 7.

The last column (Dirt+Id+WN) gives the precision we obtain if we simply decide a pair is true entailment if we have an inference rule matched in it (irrespective of the values of the anchors or of the existence of tree skeletons). As expected, only identifying the patterns of a rule in a pair irrespective of tree skeletons does not give any indication of the entailment value of the pair.

[9]The RTE task is considered to be difficult. The average accuracy of the systems in the RTE-3 challenge is around 61% (Giampiccolo et al., 2007)

RTE Set	Dirt_{TS}	Dirt + WN_{TS}	Id_{TS}	Dirt + Id + WN_{TS}	Dirt + Id + WN
RTE2	49/69.38	94/67.02	45/66.66	130/65.38	673/50.07
RTE3	42/69.04	70/70.00	29/79.31	93/72.05	661/55.06

Table 4: Coverage/precision with various rule collections

RTE Set	BoW	Main
RTE2 (85 pairs)	51.76%	60.00%
RTE3 (64 pairs)	54.68%	62.50%

Table 5: Precision on the covered RTE data

RTE Set (800 pairs)	BoW	Main & BoW
RTE2	56.87%	57.75%
RTE3	61.12%	61.75%

Table 6: Precision on full RTE data

5.2 Results on the entire data

At last, we also integrate our method with a bag of words baseline, which calculates the ratio of overlapping words in **T** and **H**. For the pairs that our method covers, we overrule the baseline's decision. The results are shown in Table 6 (Main stands for the Dirt + Id + WN_{TS} configuration). On the full data set, the improvement is still small due to the low coverage of our method, however on the pairs that are covered by our method (Table 5), there is a significant improvement over the overlap baseline.

6 Discussion

In this section we take a closer look at the data in order to better understand how does our method of combining tree skeletons and inference rules work. We will first perform error analysis on what we have considered our best setting so far. Following this, we analyze data to identify the main reasons which cause the low coverage.

For error analysis we consider the pairs incorrectly classified in the RTE3 test data set, consisting of a total of 25 pairs. We classify the errors into three main categories: rule application errors, inference rule errors, and other errors (Table 7).

In the first category, the tree skeleton fails to match the corresponding anchors of the inference rules. For instance, if someone founded *the Institute of Mathematics (Instituto di Matematica) at the University of Milan*, it does not follow that they founded *The University of Milan*. The *Institute of Mathematics* should be aligned with the *University of Milan*, which should avoid applying the inference rule for this pair.

A rather small portion of the errors (16%) are caused by incorrect inference rules. Out of these, two are correct in some contexts but not in the entailment pairs in which they are found. For example, the following rule *X generate Y* $\approx$ *X earn Y* is used incorrectly, however in the restricted context of *money* or *income*, the two verbs have similar meaning. An example of an incorrect rule is *X issue Y* $\approx$ *X hit Y* since it is difficult to find a context in which this holds.

The last category contains all the other errors. In all these cases, the additional information conveyed by the text or the hypothesis which cannot be captured by our current approach, affects the entailment. For example *an imitation diamond* is not a *diamond*, and *more than 1,000 members of the Russian and foreign media* does not entail *more than 1,000 members from Russia*; these are not trivial, since lexical semantics and fine-grained analysis of the restrictors are needed.

For the second part of our analysis we discuss the coverage issue, based on an analysis of uncovered pairs. A main factor in failing to detect pairs in which entailment rules should be applied is the fact that the tree skeleton does not find the corresponding lexical items of two rule patterns.

Issues will occur even if the tree skeleton structure is modified to align all the corresponding fragments together. Consider cases such as *threaten to boycott* and *boycott* or similar constructions with other embedding verbs such as *manage, forget, attempt*. Our method can detect if the two embedded verbs convey a similar meaning, however not how the embedding verbs affect the implication.

Independent of the shortcomings of our tree skeleton structure, a second factor in failing to detect true entailment still lies in lack of rules. For instance, the last two examples in Table 2 are entailment pair fragments which can be formulated as inference rules, but it is not straightforward to acquire them via the DH.

Source of error	% pairs
Incorrect rule application	32%
Incorrect inference rules	16%
Other errors	52%

Table 7: Error analysis

7 Conclusion

Throughout the paper we have identified important issues encountered in using inference rules for textual entailment and proposed methods to solve them. We explored the possibility of combining a collection obtained in a statistical, unsupervised manner, DIRT, with a hand-crafted lexical resource in order to make inference rules have a larger contribution to applications. We also investigated ways of effectively applying these rules. The experiment results show that although coverage is still not satisfying, the precision is promising. Therefore our method has the potential to be successfully integrated in a larger entailment detection framework.

The error analysis points out several possible future directions. The tree skeleton representation we used needs to be enhanced in order to capture more accurately the relevant fragments of the text. A different issue remains the fact that a lot of rules we could use for textual entailment detection are still lacking. A proper study of the limitations of the DH as well as a classification of the knowledge we want to encode as inference rules would be a step forward towards solving this problem.

Furthermore, although all the inference rules we used aim at recognizing positive entailment cases, it is natural to use them for detecting negative cases of entailment as well. In general, we can identify pairs in which the patterns of an inference rule are present but the anchors are mismatched, or they are not the correct hypernym/hyponym relation. This can be the base of a principled method for detecting structural contradictions (de Marneffe et al., 2008).

8 Acknowledgments

We thank Dekang Lin and Patrick Pantel for providing the DIRT collection and to Grzegorz Chrupała, Alexander Koller, Manfred Pinkal and Stefan Thater for very useful discussions. Georgiana Dinu and Rui Wang are funded by the IRTG and PIRE PhD scholarship programs.

References

Roy Bar-Haim, Ido Dagan, Iddo Greental, Idan Szpektor, and Moshe Friedman. 2007. Semantic inference at the lexical-syntactic level for textual entailment recognition. In *Proceedings of the ACL-PASCAL Workshop on Textual Entailment and Paraphrasing*, pages 131–136, Prague, June. Association for Computational Linguistics.

Regina Barzilay and Kathleen R. McKeown. 2001. Extracting paraphrases from a parallel corpus. In *Proceedings of 39th Annual Meeting of the Association for Computational Linguistics*, pages 50–57, Toulouse, France, July. Association for Computational Linguistics.

Roberto Basili, Diego De Cao, Paolo Marocco, and Marco Pennacchiotti. 2007. Learning selectional preferences for entailment or paraphrasing rules. In *In Proceedings of RANLP*, Borovets, Bulgaria.

Peter Clark, Phil Harrison, John Thompson, William Murray, Jerry Hobbs, and Christiane Fellbaum. 2007. On the role of lexical and world knowledge in rte3. In *Proceedings of the ACL-PASCAL Workshop on Textual Entailment and Paraphrasing*, pages 54–59, Prague, June. Association for Computational Linguistics.

Ido Dagan, Oren Glickman, and Bernardo Magnini. 2006. The pascal recognising textual entailment challenge. In *Lecture Notes in Computer Science, Vol. 3944, Springer*, pages 177–190. Quionero-Candela, J.; Dagan, I.; Magnini, B.; d'Alch-Buc, F. Machine Learning Challenges.

Marie-Catherine de Marneffe, Anna N. Rafferty, and Christopher D. Manning. 2008. Finding contradictions in text. In *Proceedings of ACL-08: HLT*, pages 1039–1047, Columbus, Ohio, June. Association for Computational Linguistics.

Danilo Giampiccolo, Bernardo Magnini, Ido Dagan, and Bill Dolan. 2007. The third pascal recognizing textual entailment challenge. In *Proceedings of the ACL-PASCAL Workshop on Textual Entailment and Paraphrasing*, pages 1–9, Prague, June. Association for Computational Linguistics.

Adrian Iftene and Alexandra Balahur-Dobrescu. 2007. Hypothesis transformation and semantic variability rules used in recognizing textual entailment. In *Proceedings of the ACL-PASCAL Workshop on Textual Entailment and Paraphrasing*, pages 125–130, Prague, June. Association for Computational Linguistics.

Dekang Lin and Patrick Pantel. 2001. Dirt. discovery of inference rules from text. In *KDD '01: Proceedings of the seventh ACM SIGKDD international conference on Knowledge discovery and data mining*, pages 323–328, New York, NY, USA. ACM.

Dekang Lin. 1998. Dependency-based evaluation of minipar. In *Proc. Workshop on the Evaluation of Parsing Systems*, Granada.

Erwin Marsi, Emiel Krahmer, and Wauter Bosma. 2007. Dependency-based paraphrasing for recognizing textual entailment. In *Proceedings of the ACL-PASCAL Workshop on Textual Entailment and Paraphrasing*, pages 83–88, Prague, June. Association for Computational Linguistics.

Rowan Nairn, Cleo Condoravdi, and Lauri Karttunen. 2006. Computing relative polarity for textual inference. In *Proceedings of ICoS-5 (Inference in Computational Semantics*, Buxton, UK.

Bo Pang, Kevin Knight, and Daniel Marcu. 2003. Syntax-based alignment of multiple translations: Extracting paraphrases and generating new sentences. In *HLT-NAACL*, pages 102–109.

Satoshi Sekine. 2005. Automatic paraphrase discovery based on context and keywords between NE pairs. In *Proceedings of International Workshop on Paraphrase*, pages 80–87, Jeju Island, Korea.

Idan Szpektor, Hristo Tanev, Ido Dagan, and Bonaventura Coppola. 2004. Scaling web-based acquisition of entailment relations. In *In Proceedings of EMNLP*, pages 41–48.

Idan Szpektor, Eyal Shnarch, and Ido Dagan. 2007. Instance-based evaluation of entailment rule acquisition. In *Proceedings of the 45th Annual Meeting of the Association of Computational Linguistics*, pages 456–463, Prague, Czech Republic, June. Association for Computational Linguistics.

Idan Szpektor, Ido Dagan, Roy Bar-Haim, and Jacob Goldberger. 2008. Contextual preferences. In *Proceedings of ACL-08: HLT*, pages 683–691, Columbus, Ohio, June. Association for Computational Linguistics.

Rui Wang and Günter Neumann. 2007. Recognizing textual entailment using sentence similarity based on dependency tree skeletons. In *Proceedings of the ACL-PASCAL Workshop on Textual Entailment and Paraphrasing*, pages 36–41, Prague, June. Association for Computational Linguistics.

Fabio Massimo Zanzotto and Alessandro Moschitti. 2006. Automatic learning of textual entailments with cross-pair similarities. In *ACL-44: Proceedings of the 21st International Conference on Computational Linguistics and the 44th annual meeting of the Association for Computational Linguistics*, pages 401–408, Morristown, NJ, USA. Association for Computational Linguistics.

Semi-Supervised Semantic Role Labeling

Hagen Fürstenau
Dept. of Computational Linguistics
Saarland University
Saarbrücken, Germany
hagenf@coli.uni-saarland.de

Mirella Lapata
School of Informatics
University of Edinburgh
Edinburgh, UK
mlap@inf.ed.ac.uk

Abstract

Large scale annotated corpora are prerequisite to developing high-performance semantic role labeling systems. Unfortunately, such corpora are expensive to produce, limited in size, and may not be representative. Our work aims to reduce the annotation effort involved in creating resources for semantic role labeling via semi-supervised learning. Our algorithm augments a small number of manually labeled instances with unlabeled examples whose roles are inferred automatically via annotation projection. We formulate the projection task as a generalization of the linear assignment problem. We seek to find a role assignment in the unlabeled data such that the argument similarity between the labeled and unlabeled instances is maximized. Experimental results on semantic role labeling show that the automatic annotations produced by our method improve performance over using hand-labeled instances alone.

1 Introduction

Recent years have seen a growing interest in the task of automatically identifying and labeling the semantic roles conveyed by sentential constituents (Gildea and Jurafsky, 2002). This is partly due to its relevance for applications ranging from information extraction (Surdeanu et al., 2003; Moschitti et al., 2003) to question answering (Shen and Lapata, 2007), paraphrase identification (Padó and Erk, 2005), and the modeling of textual entailment relations (Tatu and Moldovan, 2005). Resources like FrameNet (Fillmore et al., 2003) and PropBank (Palmer et al., 2005) have also facilitated the development of semantic role labeling methods by providing high-quality annotations for use in training. Semantic role labelers are commonly developed using a supervised learning paradigm[1] where a classifier learns to predict role labels based on features extracted from annotated training data.

Examples of the annotations provided in FrameNet are given in (1). Here, the meaning of predicates (usually verbs, nouns, or adjectives) is conveyed by *frames*, schematic representations of situations. Semantic roles (or *frame elements*) are defined for each frame and correspond to salient entities present in the situation evoked by the predicate (or *frame evoking element*). Predicates with similar semantics instantiate the same frame and are attested with the same roles. In our example, the frame *Cause_harm* has three core semantic roles, *Agent*, *Victim*, and *Body_part* and can be instantiated with verbs such as *punch*, *crush*, *slap*, and *injure*. The frame may also be attested with non-core (peripheral) roles that are more generic and often shared across frames (see the roles *Degree*, *Reason*, and *Means*, in (1c) and (1d)).

(1) a. [Lee]$_{Agent}$ punched [John]$_{Victim}$ [in the eye]$_{Body\_part}$.
b. [A falling rock]$_{Cause}$ crushed [my ankle]$_{Body\_part}$.
c. [She]$_{Agent}$ slapped [him]$_{Victim}$ [hard]$_{Degree}$ [for his change of mood]$_{Reason}$.
d. [Rachel]$_{Agent}$ injured [her friend]$_{Victim}$ [by closing the car door on his left hand]$_{Means}$.

The English FrameNet (version 1.3) contains 502 frames covering 5,866 lexical entries. It also comes with a set of manually annotated example sentences, taken mostly from the British National Corpus. These annotations are often used

[1] The approaches are too numerous to list; we refer the interested reader to the proceedings of the SemEval-2007 shared task (Baker et al., 2007) for an overview of the state-of-the-art.

Proceedings of the 12th Conference of the European Chapter of the ACL, pages 220–228,
Athens, Greece, 30 March – 3 April 2009.

as training data for semantic role labeling systems. However, the applicability of these systems is limited to those words for which labeled data exists, and their accuracy is strongly correlated with the amount of labeled data available. Despite the substantial annotation effort involved in the creation of FrameNet (spanning approximately twelve years), the number of annotated instances varies greatly across lexical items. For instance, FrameNet contains annotations for 2,113 verbs; of these 12.3% have five or less annotated examples. The average number of annotations per verb is 29.2. Labeled data is thus scarce for individual predicates within FrameNet's target domain and would presumably be even scarcer across domains. The problem is more severe for languages other than English, where training data on the scale of FrameNet is virtually non-existent. Although FrameNets are being constructed for German, Spanish, and Japanese, these resources are substantially smaller than their English counterpart and of limited value for modeling purposes.

One simple solution, albeit expensive and time-consuming, is to manually create more annotations. A better alternative may be to begin with an initial small set of labeled examples and augment it with unlabeled data sufficiently similar to the original labeled set. Suppose we have manual annotations for sentence (1a). We shall try and find in an unlabeled corpus other sentences that are both structurally and semantically similar. For instance, we may think that *Bill will punch me in the face* and *I punched her hard in the head* resemble our initial sentence and are thus good examples to add to our database. Now, in order to use these new sentences as training data we must somehow infer their semantic roles. We can probably guess that constituents in the same syntactic position must have the same semantic role, especially if they refer to the same concept (e.g., "body parts") and thus label *in the face* and *in the head* with the role *Body_part*. Analogously, *Bill* and *I* would be labeled as *Agent* and *me* and *her* as *Victim*.

In this paper we formalize the method sketched above in order to expand a small number of FrameNet-style semantic role annotations with large amounts of unlabeled data. We adopt a learning strategy where annotations are projected from labeled onto unlabeled instances via maximizing a similarity function measuring syntactic and semantic compatibility. We formalize the annotation projection problem as a generalization of the linear assignment problem and solve it efficiently using the simplex algorithm. We evaluate our algorithm by comparing the performance of a semantic role labeler trained on the annotations produced by our method and on a smaller dataset consisting solely of hand-labeled instances. Results in several experimental settings show that the automatic annotations, despite being noisy, bring significant performance improvements.

2 Related Work

The lack of annotated data presents an obstacle to developing many natural language applications, especially when these are not in English. It is therefore not surprising that previous efforts to reduce the need for semantic role annotation have focused primarily on non-English languages.

Annotation projection is a popular framework for transferring frame semantic annotations from one language to another by exploiting the translational and structural equivalences present in parallel corpora. The idea here is to leverage the existing English FrameNet and rely on word or constituent alignments to automatically create an annotated corpus in a new language. Padó and Lapata (2006) transfer semantic role annotations from English onto German and Johansson and Nugues (2006) from English onto Swedish. A different strategy is presented in Fung and Chen (2004), where English FrameNet entries are mapped to concepts listed in HowNet, an on-line ontology for Chinese, without consulting a parallel corpus. Then, Chinese sentences with predicates instantiating these concepts are found in a monolingual corpus and their arguments are labeled with FrameNet roles.

Other work attempts to alleviate the data requirements for semantic role labeling either by relying on unsupervised learning or by extending existing resources through the use of unlabeled data. Swier and Stevenson (2004) present an unsupervised method for labeling the arguments of verbs with their semantic roles. Given a verb instance, their method first selects a frame from VerbNet, a semantic role resource akin to FrameNet and PropBank, and labels each argument slot with sets of possible roles. The algorithm proceeds iteratively by first making initial unambiguous role assignments, and then successively updating a probability model on which future assignments are based. Being unsupervised, their approach requires no manual effort other than creating the frame dictionary. Unfortunately, existing resources do not have exhaustive coverage and a large number of verbs may be assigned no semantic role information since they are not in the dictionary in the first place. Pennacchiotti et al. (2008) address precisely this problem by augmenting FrameNet with new lexical units if they are similar to an existing frame (their notion of similarity combines distributional and WordNet-based measures). In a similar vein, Gordon and Swanson (2007) attempt to increase the coverage of PropBank. Their approach leverages existing annotations to handle novel verbs. Rather than annotating new sentences that contain novel verbs, they find syntactically similar verbs and use their annotations as surrogate training data.

Our own work aims to reduce but not entirely eliminate the annotation effort involved in creating training data for semantic role labeling. We thus assume that a small number of manual annotations is initially available. Our algorithm augments these with unlabeled examples whose roles are inferred automatically. We apply our method in a monolingual setting, and thus do not project annotations between languages but within the same language. In contrast to Pennacchiotti et al. (2008) and Gordon and Swanson (2007), we do not aim to handle novel verbs, although this would be a natural extension of our method. Given a verb and a few labeled instances exemplifying its roles, we wish to find more instances of the same verb in an unlabeled corpus so as to improve the performance of a hypothetical semantic role labeler without having to annotate more data manually. Although the use of semi-supervised learning is widespread in many natural language tasks, ranging from parsing to word sense disambiguation, its application to FrameNet-style semantic role labeling is, to our knowledge, novel.

3 Semi-Supervised Learning Method

Our method assumes that we have access to a small *seed* corpus that has been manually annotated. This represents a relatively typical situation where some annotation has taken place but not on a scale that is sufficient for high-performance supervised learning. For each sentence in the seed corpus we select a number of similar sentences

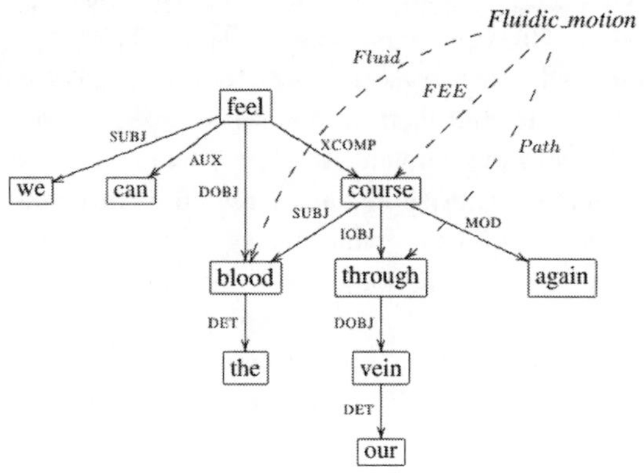

Figure 1: Labeled dependency graph with semantic role annotations for the frame evoking element (FEE) *course* in the sentence *We can feel the blood coursing through our veins again.* The frame is *Fluidic_motion*, and its roles are *Fluid* and *Path*. Directed edges (without dashes) represent dependency relations between words, edge labels denote types of grammatical relations (e.g., SUBJ, AUX).

from an unlabeled *expansion* corpus. These are automatically annotated by projecting relevant semantic role information from the labeled sentence. The similarity between two sentences is operationalized by measuring whether their arguments have a similar structure and whether they express related meanings. The seed corpus is then enlarged with the k most similar unlabeled sentences to form the expanded corpus. In what follows we describe in more detail how we measure similarity and project annotations.

3.1 Extracting Predicate-Argument Structures

Our method operates over labeled dependency graphs. We show an example in Figure 1 for the sentence *We can feel the blood coursing through our veins again.* We represent verbs (i.e., frame evoking elements) in the seed and unlabeled corpora by their predicate-argument structure. Specifically, we record the direct dependents of the predicate *course* (e.g., *blood* or *again* in Figure 1) and their grammatical roles (e.g., SUBJ, MOD). Prepositional nodes are collapsed, i.e., we record the preposition's object and a composite grammatical role (like IOBJ_THROUGH, where IOBJ stands for "prepositional object" and THROUGH for the preposition itself). In addition to direct dependents, we also

Lemma	GramRole	SemRole
blood	SUBJ	*Fluid*
vein	IOBJ_THROUGH	*Path*
again	MOD	—

Table 1: Predicate-argument structure for the verb *course* in Figure 1.

consider nodes coordinated with the predicate as arguments. Finally, for each argument node we record the semantic roles it carries, if any. All surface word forms are lemmatized. An example of the argument structure information we obtain for the predicate *course* (see Figure 1) is shown in Table 1.

We obtain information about grammatical roles from the output of RASP (Briscoe et al., 2006), a broad-coverage dependency parser. However, there is nothing inherent in our method that restricts us to this particular parser. Any other parser with broadly similar dependency output could serve our purposes.

3.2 Measuring Similarity

For each frame evoking verb in the seed corpus our method creates a labeled predicate-argument representation. It also extracts all sentences from the unlabeled corpus containing the same verb. Not all of these sentences will be suitable instances for adding to our training data. For example, the same verb may evoke a different frame with different roles and argument structure. We therefore must select sentences which resemble the seed annotations. Our hypothesis is that verbs appearing in similar syntactic and semantic contexts will behave similarly in the way they relate to their arguments.

Estimating the similarity between two predicate argument structures amounts to finding the highest-scoring alignment between them. More formally, given a labeled predicate-argument structure p^l with m arguments and an unlabeled predicate-argument structure p^u with n arguments, we consider (and score) all possible alignments between these arguments. A (partial) alignment can be viewed as an injective function $\sigma : M_\sigma \rightarrow \{1, \ldots, n\}$ where $M_\sigma \subset \{1, \ldots, m\}$. In other words, an argument i of p^l is aligned to argument $\sigma(i)$ of p^u if $i \in M_\sigma$. Note that this allows for unaligned arguments on both sides.

We score each alignment σ using a similarity function $\text{sim}(\sigma)$ defined as:

$$\sum_{i \in M_\sigma} \left(A \cdot \text{syn}(g_i^l, g_{\sigma(i)}^u) + \text{sem}(w_i^l, w_{\sigma(i)}^u) - B \right)$$

where $\text{syn}(g_i^l, g_{\sigma(i)}^u)$ denotes the syntactic similarity between grammatical roles g_i^l and $g_{\sigma(i)}^u$ and $\text{sem}(w_i^l, w_{\sigma(i)}^u)$ the semantic similarity between head words w_i^l and $w_{\sigma(i)}^u$.

Our goal is to find an alignment such that the similarity function is maximized: $\sigma^* := \arg\max_\sigma \text{sim}(\sigma)$. This optimization problem is a generalized version of the linear assignment problem (Dantzig, 1963). It can be straightforwardly expressed as a linear programming problem by associating each alignment σ with a set of binary indicator variables x_{ij}:

$$x_{ij} := \begin{cases} 1 & \text{if } i \in M_\sigma \wedge \sigma(i) = j \\ 0 & \text{otherwise} \end{cases}$$

The similarity objective function then becomes:

$$\sum_{i=1}^{m} \sum_{j=1}^{n} \left(A \cdot \text{syn}(g_i^l, g_j^u) + \text{sem}(w_i^l, w_j^u) - B \right) x_{ij}$$

subject to the following constraints ensuring that σ is an injective function on some M_σ:

$$\sum_{j=1}^{n} x_{ij} \leq 1 \quad \text{for all } i = 1, \ldots, m$$

$$\sum_{i=1}^{m} x_{ij} \leq 1 \quad \text{for all } j = 1, \ldots, n$$

Figure 2 graphically illustrates the alignment projection problem. Here, we wish to project semantic role information from the seed *blood coursing through our veins again* onto the unlabeled sentence *Adrenalin was still coursing through her veins*. The predicate *course* has three arguments in the labeled sentence and four in the unlabeled sentence (represented as rectangles in the figure). There are 73 possible alignments in this example. In general, for any m and n arguments, where $m \leq n$, the number of alignments is $\sum_{k=0}^{m} \frac{m!n!}{(m-k)!(n-k)!k!}$. Each alignment is scored by taking the sum of the similarity scores of the individual alignment pairs (e.g., between *blood* and *be*, *vein* and *still*). In this example, the highest scoring alignment is between *blood* and *adrenalin*, *vein* and *vein*, and *again* and *still*, whereas *be* is left unaligned (see the non-dotted edges in Figure 2). Note that only *vein* and *blood* carry semantic roles (i.e., *Fluid* and *Path*) which are projected onto *adrenalin* and *vein*, respectively.

Finding the best alignment crucially depends on estimating the syntactic and semantic similarity between arguments. We define the syntactic measure on the grammatical relations produced by RASP. Specifically, we set $\text{syn}(g^l_i, g^u_{\sigma(i)})$ to 1 if the relations are identical, to $a \leq 1$ if the relations are of the same type but different subtype[2] and to 0 otherwise. To avoid systematic errors, syntactic similarity is also set to 0 if the predicates differ in voice. We measure the semantic similarity $\text{sem}(w^l_i, w^u_{\sigma(i)})$ with a semantic space model. The meaning of each word is represented by a vector of its co-occurrences with neighboring words. The cosine of the angle of the vectors representing w^l and w^u quantifies their similarity (Section 4 describes the specific model we used in our experiments in more detail).

The parameter A counterbalances the importance of syntactic and semantic information, while the parameter B can be interpreted as the lowest similarity value for which an alignment between two arguments is possible. An optimal alignment σ^* cannot link arguments i_0 of p^l and j_0 of p^u, if $A \cdot \text{syn}(g^l_{i_0}, g^u_{j_0}) + \text{sem}(w^l_{i_0}, w^u_{j_0}) < B$ (i.e., either $i_0 \notin M_{\sigma^*}$ or $\sigma^*(i_0) \neq j_0$). This is because for an alignment σ with $\sigma(i_0) = j_0$ we can construct a better alignment σ_0, which is identical to σ on all $i \neq i_0$, but leaves i_0 unaligned (i.e., $i_0 \notin M_{\sigma_0}$). By eliminating a negative term from the scoring function, it follows that $\text{sim}(\sigma_0) > \text{sim}(\sigma)$. Therefore, an alignment σ satisfying $\sigma(i_0) = j_0$ cannot be optimal and conversely the optimal alignment σ^* can never link two arguments with each other if the sum of their weighted syntactic and semantic similarity scores is below B.

3.3 Projecting Annotations

Once we obtain the best alignment σ^* between p^l and p^u, we can simply transfer the role of each role-bearing argument i of p^l to the aligned argument $\sigma^*(i)$ of p^u, resulting in a labeling of p^u.

To increase the accuracy of our method we discard projections if they fail to transfer all roles of the labeled to the unlabeled dependency graph.

[2]This concerns fine-grained distinctions made by the parser, e.g., the underlying grammatical roles in passive constructions.

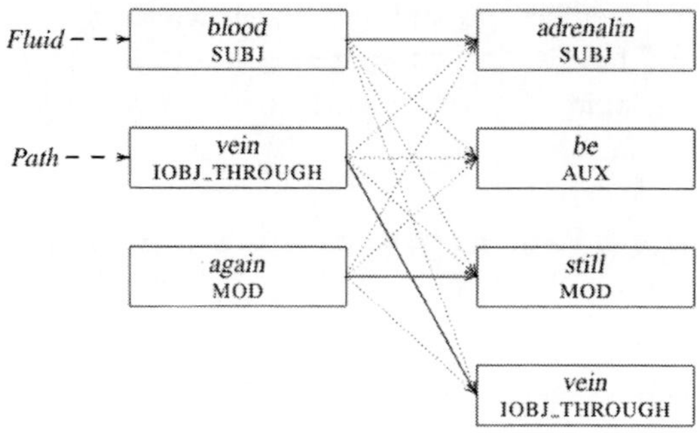

Figure 2: Alignments between the argument structures representing the clauses *blood coursing through our veins again* and *Adrenalin was still coursing through her veins*; non-dotted lines illustrate the highest scoring alignment.

This can either be the case if p^l does not cover all roles annotated on the graph (i.e., there are role-bearing nodes which we do not recognize as arguments of the frame evoking verb) or if there are unaligned role-bearing arguments (i.e., $i \notin M_{\sigma^*}$ for a role-bearing argument i of p^l).

The remaining projections form our expansion corpus. For each seed instance we select the k most similar neighbors to add to our training data. The parameter k controls the trade-off between annotation confidence and expansion size.

4 Experimental Setup

In this section we discuss our experimental setup for assessing the usefulness of the method presented above. We give details on our training procedure and parameter estimation, describe the semantic labeler we used in our experiments and explain how its output was evaluated.

Corpora Our seed corpus was taken from FrameNet. The latter contains approximately 2,000 verb entries out of which we randomly selected a sample of 100. We next extracted all annotated sentences for each of these verbs. These sentences formed our gold standard corpus, 20% of which was reserved as test data. We used the remaining 80% as seeds for training purposes. We generated seed corpora of various sizes by randomly reducing the number of annotation instances per verb to a maximum of n. An additional (non-overlapping) random sample of 100 verbs was used as development set for tuning the parameters for our method. We gathered unlabeled sentences from the BNC.

The seed and unlabeled corpora were parsed with RASP (Briscoe et al., 2006). The FrameNet annotations in the seed corpus were converted into dependency graphs (see Figure 1) using the method described in Fürstenau (2008). Briefly, the method works by matching nodes in the dependency graph with role bearing substrings in FrameNet. It first finds the node in the graph which most closely matches the frame evoking element in FrameNet. Next, individual graph nodes are compared against labeled substrings in FrameNet to transfer all roles onto their closest matching graph nodes.

Parameter Estimation The similarity function described in Section 3.2 has three free parameters. These are the weight A which determines the relative importance of syntactic and semantic information, the parameter B which determines when two arguments cannot be aligned and the syntactic score a for almost identical grammatical roles. We optimized these parameters on the development set using Powell's direction set method (Brent, 1973) with F_1 as our loss function. The optimal values for A, B and a were 1.76, 0.41 and 0.67, respectively.

Our similarity function is further parametrized in using a semantic space model to compute the similarity between two words. Considerable latitude is allowed in specifying the parameters of vector-based models. These involve the definition of the linguistic context over which co-occurrences are collected, the number of components used (e.g., the k most frequent words in a corpus), and their values (e.g., as raw co-occurrence frequencies or ratios of probabilities).

We created a vector-based model from a lemmatized version of the BNC. Following previous work (Bullinaria and Levy, 2007), we optimized the parameters of our model on a word-based semantic similarity task. The task involves examining the degree of linear relationship between the human judgments for two individual words and vector-based similarity values. We experimented with a variety of dimensions (ranging from 50 to 500,000), vector component definitions (e.g., pointwise mutual information or log likelihood ratio) and similarity measures (e.g., cosine or confusion probability). We used WordSim353, a benchmark dataset (Finkelstein et al., 2002), consisting of relatedness judgments (on a scale of 0 to 10) for 353 word pairs.

We obtained best results with a model using a context window of five words on either side of the target word, the cosine measure, and 2,000 vector dimensions. The latter were the most common context words (excluding a stop list of function words). Their values were set to the ratio of the probability of the context word given the target word to the probability of the context word overall. This configuration gave high correlations with the WordSim353 similarity judgments using the cosine measure.

Solving the Linear Program A variety of algorithms have been developed for solving the linear assignment problem efficiently. In our study, we used the simplex algorithm (Dantzig, 1963). We generate and solve an LP of every unlabeled sentence we wish to annotate.

Semantic role labeler We evaluated our method on a semantic role labeling task. Specifically, we compared the performance of a generic semantic role labeler trained on the seed corpus and a larger corpus expanded with annotations produced by our method. Our semantic role labeler followed closely the implementation of Johansson and Nugues (2008). We extracted features from dependency parses corresponding to those routinely used in the semantic role labeling literature (see Baker et al. (2007) for an overview). SVM classifiers were trained to identify the arguments and label them with appropriate roles. For the latter we performed multi-class classification following the one-versus-one method[3] (Friedman, 1996). For the experiments reported in this paper we used the LIBLINEAR library (Fan et al., 2008). The misclassification penalty C was set to 0.1.

To evaluate against the test set, we linearized the resulting dependency graphs in order to obtain labeled role bracketings like those in example (1) and measured labeled precision, labeled recall and labeled F_1. (Since our focus is on role labeling and not frame prediction, we let our role labeler make use of gold standard frame annotations, i.e., labeling of frame evoking elements with frame names.)

5 Results

The evaluation of our method was motivated by three questions: (1) How do different training set sizes affect semantic role labeling performance?

[3]Given n classes the one-versus-one method builds $n(n-1)/2$ classifiers.

TrainSet	Size	Prec (%)	Rec (%)	F_1 (%)
0-NN	849	35.5	42.0	38.5
1-NN	1205	36.4	43.3	39.5
2-NN	1549	38.1	44.1	40.9*
3-NN	1883	37.9	43.7	40.6*
4-NN	2204	38.0	43.9	40.7*
5-NN	2514	37.4	43.9	40.4*
self train	1609	34.0	41.0	37.1

Table 2: Semantic role labeling performance using different amounts of training data; the seeds are expanded with their k nearest neighbors; *: F_1 is significantly different from 0-NN ($p < 0.05$).

Training size varies depending on the number of unlabeled sentences added to the seed corpus. The quality of these sentences also varies depending on their similarity to the seed sentences. So, we would like to assess whether there is a trade-off between annotation quality and training size. (2) How does the size of the seed corpus influence role labeling performance? Here, we are interested to find out what is the least amount of manual annotation possible for our method to have some positive impact. (3) And finally, what are the annotation savings our method brings?

Table 2 shows the performance of our semantic role labeler when trained on corpora of different sizes. The seed corpus was reduced to at most 10 instances per verb. Each row in the table corresponds to adding the k nearest neighbors of these instances to the training data. When trained solely on the seed corpus the semantic role labeler yields a (labeled) F_1 of 38.5%, (labeled) recall is 42.0% and (labeled) precision is 35.5% (see row 0-NN in the table). All subsequent expansions yield improved precision and recall. In all cases except $k = 1$ the improvement is statistically significant ($p < 0.05$). We performed significance testing on F_1 using stratified shuffling (Noreen, 1989), an instance of assumption-free approximative randomization testing. As can be seen, the optimal trade-off between the size of the training corpus and annotation quality is reached with two nearest neighbors. This corresponds roughly to doubling the number of training instances. (Due to the restrictions mentioned in Section 3.3 a 2-NN expansion does not triple the number of instances.)

We also compared our results against a self-training procedure (see last row in Table 2). Here, we randomly selected unlabeled sentences corresponding in number to a 2-NN expansion, labeled them with our role labeler, added them to the training set, and retrained. Self-training resulted in performance inferior to the baseline of adding no unlabeled data at all (see the first row in Table 2). Performance decreased even more with the addition of more self-labeled instances. These results indicate that the similarity function is crucial to the success of our method.

An example of the annotations our method produces is given below. Sentence (2a) is the seed. Sentences (2b)–(2e) are its most similar neighbors. The sentences are presented in decreasing order of similarity.

(2)
a. [He]$_{Theme}$ stared and came [slowly]$_{Manner}$ [towards me]$_{Goal}$.
b. [He]$_{Theme}$ had heard the shooting and come [rapidly]$_{Manner}$ [back towards the house]$_{Goal}$.
c. Without answering, [she]$_{Theme}$ left the room and came [slowly]$_{Manner}$ [down the stairs]$_{Goal}$.
d. [Then]$_{Manner}$ [he]$_{Theme}$ won't come [to Salisbury]$_{Goal}$.
e. Does [he]$_{Theme}$ always come round [in the morning]$_{Goal}$ [then]$_{Manner}$?

As we can see, sentences (2b) and (2c) accurately identify the semantic roles of the verb *come* evoking the frame *Arriving*. In (2b) *He* is labeled as *Theme*, *rapidly* as *Manner*, and *towards the house* as *Goal*. Analogously, in (2c) *she* is the *Theme*, *slowly* is *Manner* and *down the stairs* is *Goal*. The quality of the annotations decreases with less similar instances. In (2d) *then* is marked erroneously as *Manner*, whereas in (2e) only the *Theme* role is identified correctly.

To answer our second question, we varied the size of the training corpus by varying the number of seeds per verb. For these experiments we fixed $k = 2$. Table 3 shows the performance of the semantic role labeler when the seed corpus has one annotation per verb, five annotations per verb, and so on. (The results for 10 annotations are repeated from Table 2). With 1, 5 or 10 instances per verb our method significantly improves labeling performance. We observe improvements in F_1 of 1.5%, 2.1%, and 2.4% respectively when adding the 2 most similar neighbors to these training corpora. Our method also improves F_1 when a 20 seeds

TrainSet	Size	Prec (%)	Rec (%)	F_1 (%)
$\leq$ 1 seed	95	24.9	31.3	27.7
+ 2-NN	170	26.4	32.6	29.2*
$\leq$ 5 seeds	450	29.7	38.4	33.5
+ 2-NN	844	31.8	40.4	35.6*
$\leq$ 10 seeds	849	35.5	42.0	38.5
+ 2-NN	1549	38.1	44.1	40.9*
$\leq$ 20 seeds	1414	38.7	46.1	42.1
+ 2-NN	2600	40.5	46.7	43.4
all seeds	2323	38.3	47.0	42.2
+ 2-NN	4387	39.5	46.7	42.8

Table 3: Semantic role labeling performance using different numbers of seed instances per verb in the training corpus; the seeds are expanded with their $k = 2$ nearest neighbors; *: F_1 is significantly different from seed corpus ($p < 0.05$).

corpus or all available seeds are used, however the difference is not statistically significant.

The results in Table 3 also allow us to draw some conclusions regarding the relative quality of manual and automatic annotation. Expanding a seed corpus with 10 instances per verb improves F_1 from 38.5% to 40.9%. We can compare this to the labeler's performance when trained solely on the 20 seeds corpus (without any expansion). The latter has approximately the same size as the expanded 10 seeds corpus. Interestingly, F_1 on this exclusively hand-annotated corpus is only 1.2% better than on the expanded corpus. So, using our expansion method on a 10 seeds corpus performs almost as well as using twice as many manual annotations. Even in the case of the 5 seeds corpus, where there is limited information for our method to expand from, we achieve an improvement from 33.5% to 35.6%, compared to 38.5% for manual annotation of about the same number of instances. In sum, while additional manual annotation is naturally more effective for improving the quality of the training data, we can achieve substantial proportions of these improvements by automatic expansion alone. This is a promising result suggesting that it is possible to reduce annotation costs without drastically sacrificing quality.

6 Conclusions

This paper presents a novel method for reducing the annotation effort involved in creating resources for semantic role labeling. Our strategy is to expand a manually annotated corpus by projecting semantic role information from labeled onto unlabeled instances. We formulate the projection problem as an instance of the linear assignment problem. We seek to find role assignments that maximize the similarity between labeled and unlabeled instances. Similarity is measured in terms of structural and semantic compatibility between argument structures.

Our method improves semantic role labeling performance in several experimental conditions. It is especially effective when a small number of annotations is available for each verb. This is typically the case when creating frame semantic corpora for new languages or new domains. Our experiments show that expanding such corpora with our method can yield almost the same relative improvement as using exclusively manual annotation.

In the future we plan to extend our method in order to handle novel verbs that are not attested in the seed corpus. Another direction concerns the systematic modeling of diathesis alternations (Levin, 1993). These are currently only captured implicitly by our method (when the semantic similarity overrides syntactic dissimilarity). Ideally, we would like to be able to systematically identify changes in the realization of the argument structure of a given predicate. Although our study focused solely on FrameNet annotations, we believe it can be adapted to related annotation schemes, such as PropBank. An interesting question is whether the improvements obtained by our method carry over to other role labeling frameworks.

Acknowledgments The authors acknowledge the support of DFG (IRTG 715) and EPSRC (grant GR/T04540/01). We are grateful to Richard Johansson for his help with the re-implementation of his semantic role labeler.

References

Collin F. Baker, Michael Ellsworth, and Katrin Erk. 2007. SemEval-2007 Task 19: Frame Semantic Structure Extraction. In *Proceedings of the 4th International Workshop on Semantic Evaluations*, pages 99–104, Prague, Czech Republic.

R. P. Brent. 1973. *Algorithms for Minimization without Derivatives*. Prentice-Hall, Englewood Cliffs, NJ.

Ted Briscoe, John Carroll, and Rebecca Watson. 2006. The Second Release of the RASP System. In *Proceedings of the COLING/ACL 2006 Interactive Presentation Sessions*, pages 77–80, Sydney, Australia.

J. A. Bullinaria and J. P. Levy. 2007. Extracting semantic representations from word co-occurrence statistics: A computational study. *Behavior Research Methods*, 39:510–526.

George B. Dantzig. 1963. *Linear Programming and Extensions*. Princeton University Press, Princeton, NJ, USA.

R.-E. Fan, K.-W. Chang, C.-J. Hsieh, X.-R. Wang, and C.-J. Lin. 2008. LIBLINEAR: A library for large linear classification. *Journal of Machine Learning Research*, 9:1871–1874.

Charles J. Fillmore, Christopher R. Johnson, and Miriam R. L. Petruck. 2003. Background to FrameNet. *International Journal of Lexicography*, 16:235–250.

Lev Finkelstein, Evgeniy Gabrilovich, Yossi Matias, Ehud Rivlin, Zach Solan, Gadi Wolfman, and Eytan Ruppin. 2002. Placing search in context: The concept revisited. *ACM Transactions on Information Systems*, 20(1):116–131.

Jerome H. Friedman. 1996. Another approach to polychotomous classification. Technical report, Department of Statistics, Stanford University.

Pascale Fung and Benfeng Chen. 2004. BiFrameNet: Bilingual frame semantics resources construction by cross-lingual induction. In *Proceedings of the 20th International Conference on Computational Linguistics*, pages 931–935, Geneva, Switzerland.

Hagen Fürstenau. 2008. Enriching frame semantic resources with dependency graphs. In *Proceedings of the 6th Language Resources and Evaluation Conference*, Marrakech, Morocco.

Daniel Gildea and Dan Jurafsky. 2002. Automatic labeling of semantic roles. *Computational Linguistics*, 28:3:245–288.

Andrew Gordon and Reid Swanson. 2007. Generalizing semantic role annotations across syntactically similar verbs. In *Proceedings of the 45th Annual Meeting of the Association of Computational Linguistics*, pages 192–199, Prague, Czech Republic.

Richard Johansson and Pierre Nugues. 2006. A FrameNet-based semantic role labeler for Swedish. In *Proceedings of the COLING/ACL 2006 Main Conference Poster Sessions*, pages 436–443, Sydney, Australia.

Richard Johansson and Pierre Nugues. 2008. The effect of syntactic representation on semantic role labeling. In *Proceedings of the 22nd International Conference on Computational Linguistics*, pages 393–400, Manchester, UK.

Beth Levin. 1993. *English Verb Classes and Alternations: A Preliminary Investigation*. University of Chicago Press.

Alessandro Moschitti, Paul Morarescu, and Sanda Harabagiu. 2003. Open-domain information extraction via automatic semantic labeling. In *Proceedings of FLAIRS 2003*, pages 397–401, St. Augustine, FL.

E. Noreen. 1989. *Computer-intensive Methods for Testing Hypotheses: An Introduction*. John Wiley and Sons Inc.

Sebastian Padó and Katrin Erk. 2005. To cause or not to cause: Cross-lingual semantic matching for paraphrase modelling. In *Proceedings of the EUROLAN Workshop on Cross-Linguistic Knowledge Induction*, pages 23–30, Cluj-Napoca, Romania.

Sebastian Padó and Mirella Lapata. 2006. Optimal constituent alignment with edge covers for semantic projection. In *Proceedings of the 21st International Conference on Computational Linguistics and 44th Annual Meeting of the Association for Computational Linguistics*, pages 1161–1168, Sydney, Australia.

Martha Palmer, Dan Gildea, and Paul Kingsbury. 2005. The Proposition Bank: An annotated corpus of semantic roles. *Computational Linguistics*, 31(1):71–106.

Marco Pennacchiotti, Diego De Cao, Roberto Basili, Danilo Croce, and Michael Roth. 2008. Automatic induction of FrameNet lexical units. In *Proceedings of the Conference on Empirical Methods in Natural Language Processing*, pages 457–465, Honolulu, Hawaii.

Dan Shen and Mirella Lapata. 2007. Using semantic roles to improve question answering. In *Proceedings of the joint Conference on Empirical Methods in Natural Language Processing and Conference on Computational Natural Language Learning*, pages 12–21, Prague, Czech Republic.

Mihai Surdeanu, Sanda Harabagiu, John Williams, and Paul Aarseth. 2003. Using predicate-argument structures for information extraction. In *Proceedings of the 41st Annual Meeting of the Association for Computational Linguistics*, pages 8–15, Sapporo, Japan.

Robert S. Swier and Suzanne Stevenson. 2004. Unsupervised semantic role labelling. In *Proceedings of the Conference on Empirical Methods in Natural Language Processing*, pages 95–102. Bacelona, Spain.

Marta Tatu and Dan Moldovan. 2005. A semantic approach to recognizing textual entailment. In *Proceedings of the joint Human Language Technology Conference and Conference on Empirical Methods in Natural Language Processing*, pages 371–378, Vancouver, BC.

Cognitively Motivated Features for Readability Assessment

Lijun Feng
The City University of New York,
Graduate Center
New York, NY, USA
lijun7.feng@gmail.com

Noémie Elhadad
Columbia University
New York, NY, USA
noemie@dbmi.columbia.edu

Matt Huenerfauth
The City University of New York,
Queens College & Graduate Center
New York, NY, USA
matt@cs.qc.cuny.edu

Abstract

We investigate linguistic features that correlate with the readability of texts for adults with intellectual disabilities (ID). Based on a corpus of texts (including some experimentally measured for comprehension by adults with ID), we analyze the significance of novel discourse-level features related to the cognitive factors underlying our users' literacy challenges. We develop and evaluate a tool for automatically rating the readability of texts for these users. Our experiments show that our discourse-level, cognitively-motivated features improve automatic readability assessment.

1 Introduction

Assessing the degree of readability of a text has been a field of research as early as the 1920's. Dale and Chall define readability as "the sum total (including all the interactions) of all those elements within a given piece of printed material that affect the success a group of readers have with it. The success is the extent to which they understand it, read it at optimal speed, and find it interesting" (Dale and Chall, 1949). It has long been acknowledged that readability is a function of text characteristics, but also of the readers themselves. The literacy skills of the readers, their motivations, background knowledge, and other internal characteristics play an important role in determining whether a text is readable for a particular group of people. In our work, we investigate how to assess the readability of a text for people with intellectual disabilities (ID).

Previous work in automatic readability assessment has focused on generic features of a text at the lexical and syntactic level. While such features are essential, we argue that audience-specific features that model the cognitive characteristics of a user group can improve the accuracy of a readability assessment tool. The contributions of this paper are: (1) we present a corpus of texts with readability judgments from adults with ID; (2) we propose a set of cognitively-motivated features which operate at the discourse level; (3) we evaluate the utility of these features in predicting readability for adults with ID.

Our framework is to create tools that benefit people with intellectual disabilities (ID), specifically those classified in the "mild level" of mental retardation, IQ scores 55-70. About 3% of the U.S. population has intelligence test scores of 70 or lower (U.S. Census Bureau, 2000). People with ID face challenges in reading literacy. They are better at decoding words (sounding them out) than at comprehending their meaning (Drew & Hardman, 2004), and most read below their mental age-level (Katims, 2000). Our research addresses two literacy impairments that distinguish people with ID from other low-literacy adults: limitations in (1) working memory and (2) discourse representation. People with ID have problems remembering and inferring information from text (Fowler, 1998). They have a slower speed of semantic encoding and thus units are lost from the working memory before they are processed (Perfetti & Lesgold, 1977; Hickson-Bilsky, 1985). People with ID also have trouble building cohesive representations of discourse (Hickson-Bilsky, 1985). As less information is integrated into the mental representation of the current discourse, less is comprehended.

Adults with ID are limited in their choice of reading material. Most texts that they can readily understand are targeted at the level of readability of children. However, the topics of these texts often fail to match their interests since they are meant for younger readers. Because of the mismatch between their literacy and their interests, users may not read for pleasure and therefore miss valuable reading-skills practice time. In a feasibility study we conducted with adults

Proceedings of the 12th Conference of the European Chapter of the ACL, pages 229–237,
Athens, Greece, 30 March – 3 April 2009. ©2009 Association for Computational Linguistics

with ID, we asked participants what they enjoyed learning or reading about. The majority of our subjects mentioned enjoying watching the news, in particular local news. Many mentioned they were interested in information that would be relevant to their daily lives. While for some genres, human editors can prepare texts for these users, this is not practical for news sources that are frequently updated and specific to a limited geographic area (like local news). Our goal is to create an automatic metric to predict the readability of local news articles for adults with ID. Because of the low levels of written literacy among our target users, we intend to focus on comprehension of texts displayed on a computer screen and read aloud by text-to-speech software; although some users may depend on the text-to-speech software, we use the term *readability*.

This paper is organized as follows. Section 2 presents related work on readability assessment. Section 3 states our research hypotheses and describes our methodology. Section 4 focuses on the data sets used in our experiments, while section 5 describes the feature set we used for readability assessment along with a corpus-based analysis of each feature. Section 6 describes a readability assessment tool and reports on evaluation. Section 7 discusses the implications of the work and proposes direction for future work.

2 Related Work on Readability Metrics

Many readability metrics have been established as a function of shallow features of texts, such as the number of syllables per word and number of words per sentence (Flesch, 1948; McLaughlin, 1969; Kincaid et al., 1975). These so-called traditional readability metrics are still used today in many settings and domains, in part because they are very easy to compute. Their results, however, are not always representative of the complexity of a text (Davison and Kantor, 1982). They can easily misrepresent the complexity of technical texts, or reveal themselves un-adapted to a set of readers with particular reading difficulties. Other formulas rely on lexical information; e.g., the New Dale-Chall readability formula consults a static, manually-built list of "easy" words to determine whether a text contains unfamiliar words (Chall and Dale, 1995).

Researchers in computational linguistics have investigated the use of statistical language models (unigram in particular) to capture the range of vocabulary from one grade level to another (Si and Callan, 2001; Collins-Thompson and Callan, 2004). These metrics predicted readability better than traditional formulas when tested against a corpus of web pages. The use of syntactic features was also investigated (Schwarm and Ostendorf, 2005; Heilman et al., 2007; Petersen and Ostendorf, 2009) in the assessment of text readability for English as a Second Language readers. While lexical features alone outperform syntactic features in classifying texts according to their reading levels, combining the lexical and syntactic features yields the best results.

Several elegant metrics that focus solely on the syntax of a text have also been developed. The Yngve (1960) measure, for instance, focuses on the depth of embedding of nodes in the parse tree; others use the ratio of terminal to non-terminal nodes in the parse tree of a sentence (Miller and Chomsky, 1963; Frazier, 1985). These metrics have been used to analyze the writing of potential Alzheimer's patients to detect mild cognitive impairments (Roark, Mitchell, and Hollingshead, 2007), thereby indicating that cognitively motivated features of text are valuable when creating tools for specific populations.

Barzilay and Lapata (2008) presented early work in investigating the use of discourse to distinguish abridged from original encyclopedia articles. Their focus, however, is on style detection rather than readability assessment *per se*. Coh-Metrix is a tool for automatically calculating text coherence based on features such as repetition of lexical items across sentences and latent semantic analysis (McNamara et al., 2006). The tool is based on comprehension data collected from children and college students.

Our research differs from related work in that we seek to produce an automatic readability metric that is tailored to the literacy skills of adults with ID. Because of the specific cognitive characteristics of these users, it is an open question whether existing readability metrics and features are useful for assessing readability for adults with ID. Many of these earlier metrics have focused on the task of assigning texts to particular elementary school grade levels. Traditional grade levels may not be the ideal way to score texts to indicate how readable they are for adults with ID. Other related work has used models of vocabulary (Collins-Thompson and Callan, 2004). Since we would like to use our tool to give adults with ID access to local news stories, we choose to keep our metric topic-independent.

Another difference between our approach and previous approaches is that we have designed the features used by our readability metric based on the cognitive aspects of our target users. For example, these users are better at decoding words than at comprehending text meaning (Drew & Hardman, 2004); so, shallow features like "syllable count per word" or unigram models of word frequency (based on texts designed for children) may be less important indicators of reading difficulty. A critical challenge for our users is to create a cohesive representation of discourse. Due to their impairments in semantic encoding speed, our users may have particular difficulty with texts that place a significant burden on working memory (items fall out of memory before they can be semantically encoded).

While we focus on readability of texts, other projects have automatically generated texts for people with aphasia (Carroll et al., 1999) or low reading skills (Williams and Reiter, 2005).

3 Research Hypothesis and Methods

We hypothesize that the complexity of a text for adults with ID is related to the number of entities referred to in the text overall. If a paragraph or a text refers to too many entities at once, the reader has to work harder at mapping each entity to a semantic representation and deciding how each entity is related to others. On the other hand, when a text refers to few entities, less work is required both for semantic encoding and for integrating the entities into a cohesive mental representation. Section 5.2 discusses some novel discourse-level features (based on the "entity density" of a text) that we believe will correlate to comprehension by adults with ID.

To test our hypothesis, we used the following methodology. We collected four corpora (as described in Section 4). Three of them (Britannica, LiteracyNet and WeeklyReader) have been examined in previous work on readability. The fourth (LocalNews) is novel and results from a user study we conducted with adults with ID. We then analyzed how significant each feature is on our Britannica and LiteracyNet corpora. Finally, we combined the significant features into a linear regression model and experimented with several feature combinations. We evaluated our model on the WeeklyReader and LocalNews corpora.

4 Corpora and Readability Judgments

To study how certain linguistic features indicate the readability of a text, we collected a corpus of English text at different levels of readability. An ideal corpus for our research would contain texts that have been written specifically for our audience of adults with intellectual disabilities – in particular if such texts were paired with alternate versions of each text written for a general audience. We are not aware of such texts available electronically, and so we have instead mostly collected texts written for an audience of children. The texts come from online and commercial sources, and some have been analyzed previously by text simplification researchers (Petersen and Ostendorf, 2009). Our corpus also contains some novel texts produced as part of an experimental study involving adults with ID.

4.1 Paired and Graded Generic Corpora: Britannica, LiteracyNet, and Weekly Reader

The first section of our corpus (which we refer to as Britannica) has 228 articles from the Encyclopedia Britannica, originally collected by (Barzilay and Elhadad, 2003). This consists of 114 articles in two forms: original articles written for adults and corresponding articles rewritten for an audience of children. While the texts are paired, the content of the texts is not identical: some details are omitted from the child version, and additional background is sometimes inserted. The resulting corpus is comparable in content.

Because we are particularly interested in making local news articles accessible to adults with ID, we collected a second paired corpus, which we refer to as LiteracyNet, consisting of 115 news articles made available through (Western/Pacific Literacy Network / LiteracyNet, 2008). The collection of local CNN stories is available in an original and simplified/abridged form (230 total news articles) designed for use in literacy education.

The third corpus we collected (Weekly Reader) was obtained from the Weekly Reader corporation (Weekly Reader, 2008). It contains articles for students in elementary school. Each text is labeled with its target grade level (grade 2: 174 articles, grade 3: 289 articles, grade 4: 428 articles, grade 5: 542 articles). Overall, the corpus has 1433 articles. (U.S. elementary school grades 2 to 5 generally are for children ages 7 to 10.)

The corpora discussed above are similar to those used by Petersen and Ostendorf (2009). While the focus of our research is adults with ID, most of the texts discussed in this section have been simplified or written by human authors to be readable for children. Despite the texts being intended for a different audience than the focus of our research, we still believe these texts to be of value. It is rare to encounter electronically available corpora in which an original and a simplified version of a text is paired (as in the Britannica and LiteracyNet corpora) or texts labeled as being at specific levels of readability (as in the Weekly Reader corpus).

4.2 Readability-Specific Corpus: LocalNews

The final section of our corpus contains local news articles that are labeled with comprehension scores. These texts were produced for a feasibility study involving adults with ID. Each text was read by adults with ID, who then answered comprehension questions to measure their understanding of the texts. Unlike the previous corpora, LocalNews is novel and was not investigated by previous research in readability.

After obtaining university approval for our experimental protocol and informed consent process, we conducted a study with 14 adults with mild intellectual disabilities who participate in daytime educational programs in the New York area. Participants were presented with ten articles collected from various local New York based news websites. Some subjects saw the original form of an article and others saw a simplified form (edited by a human author); no subject saw both versions. The texts were presented in random order using software that displayed the text on the screen, read it aloud using text-to-speech software, and highlighted each word as it was read. Afterward, subjects were asked aloud multiple-choice comprehension questions. We defined the readability score of a story as the percentage of correct answers averaged across the subjects who read that particular story.

A human editor performed the text simplification with the goal of making the text more readable for adults with mild ID. The editor made the following types of changes to the original news stories: breaking apart complex sentences, unembedding information in complex prepositional phrases and reintegrating it as separate sentences, replacing infrequent vocabulary items with more common/colloquial equivalents, omitting sentences and phrases from the story that mention entities and phrases extraneous to the main theme of the article. For instance, the original sentence "*They're installing an induction loop system in cabs that would allow passengers with hearing aids to tune in specifically to the driver's voice.*" was transformed into "*They're installing a system in cabs. It would allow passengers with hearing aids to listen to the driver's voice.*"

This corpus of local news articles that have been human edited and scored for comprehension by adults with ID is small in size (20 news articles), but we consider it a valuable resource. Unlike the texts that have been simplified for children (the rest of our corpus), these texts have been rated for readability by actual adults with ID. Furthermore, comprehension scores are derived from actual reader comprehension tests, rather than self-perceived comprehension. Because of the small size of this part of our corpus, however, we primarily use it for evaluation purposes (not for training the readability models).

5 Linguistic Features and Readability

We now describe the set of features we investigated for assessing readability automatically. Table 1 contains a list of the features – including a short code name for each feature which may be used throughout this paper. We have begun by implementing the simple features used by the Flesh-Kincaid and FOG metrics: average number of words per sentence, average number of syllables per word, and percentage of words in the document with 3+ syllables.

5.1 Basic Features Used in Earlier Work

We have also implemented features inspired by earlier research on readability. Petersen and Ostendorf (2009) included features calculated from parsing the sentences in their corpus using the Charniak parser (Charniak, 2000): average parse tree height, average number of noun phrases per sentence, average number of verb phrases per sentence, and average number of SBARs per sentence. We have implemented versions of most of these parse-tree-related features for our project. We also parse the sentences in our corpus using Charniak's parser and calculate the following features listed in Table 1: aNP, aN, aVP, aAdj, aSBr, aPP, nNP, nN, nVP, nAdj, nSBr, and nPP.

5.2 Novel Cognitively-Motivated Features

Because of the special reading characteristics of our target users, we have designed a set of cognitively motivated features to predict readability of texts for adults with ID. We have discussed how working memory limits the semantic encoding of new information by these users; so, our features indicate the number of entities in a text that the reader must keep in mind while reading each sentence and throughout the entire document. It is our hypothesis that this "entity density" of a

Code	Feature
aWPS	average number of words per sentence
aSPW	average number of syllables per word
%3+S	% of words in document with 3+ syllables
aNP	avg. num. NPs per sentence
aN	avg. num. common+proper nouns per sentence
aVP	avg. num. VPs per sentence
aAdj	avg. num. Adjectives per sentence
aSBr	avg. num. SBARs per sentence
aPP	avg. num. prepositional phrases per sentence
nNP	total number of NPs per sentence
nN	total num. of common+proper nouns in document
nVP	total number of VPs in the document
nAdj	total number of Adjectives in the document
nSBr	total number of SBARs in the document
nPP	total num. of prepositional phrases in document
nEM	number of entity mentions in document
nUE	number of unique entities in document
aEM	avg. num. entity mentions per sentence
aUE	avg. num. unique entities per sentence
nLC	number of lexical chains in document
nLC2	num. lex. chains, span > half document length
aLCL	average lexical chain length
aLCS	average lexical chain span
aLCw	avg. num. lexical chains active at each word
aLCn	avg. num. lexical chains active at each NP

Table 1: Implemented Features

text plays an important role in the difficulty of that text for readers with intellectual disabilities.

The first set of features incorporates the LingPipe named entity detection software (Alias-i, 2008), which detects three types of entities: person, location, and organization. We also use the part-of-speech tagger in LingPipe to identify the common nouns in the document, and we find the union of the common nouns and the named entity noun phrases in the text. The union of these two sets is our definition of "entity" for this set of features. We count both the total number of "entity mentions" in a text (each token appearance of an entity) and the total number of unique entities (exact-string-match duplicates only counted once). Table 1 lists these features: nEM, nUE, aEM, and aUE. We count the totals per document to capture how many entities the reader must keep track of while reading the document. We also expect sentences with more entities to be more difficult for our users to semantically encode due to working memory limitations; so, we also count the averages per sentence to capture how many entities the reader must keep in mind to understand each sentence.

To measure the working memory burden of a text, we'd like to capture the number of discourse entities that a reader must keep in mind. However, the "unique entities" identified by the named entity recognition tool may not be a perfect representation of this – several unique entities may actually refer to the same real-world entity under discussion. To better model how multiple noun phrases in a text refer to the same entity or concept, we have also built features using lexical chains (Galley and McKeown, 2003). Lexical chains link nouns in a document connected by relations like synonymy or hyponomy; chains can indicate concepts that recur throughout a text. A lexical chain has both a length (number of noun phrases it includes) and a span (number of words in the document between the first noun phrase at the beginning of the chain and the last noun phrase that is part of the chain). We calculate the number of lexical chains in the document (nLC) and those with a span greater than half the document length (nLC2). We believe these features may indicate the number of entities/concepts that a reader must keep in mind during a document and the subset of very important entities/concepts that are the main topic of the document. The average length and average span of the lexical chains in a document (aLCL and aLCS) may also indicate how many of the chains in the document are short-lived, which may mean that they are ancillary entities/concepts, not the main topics.

The final two features in Table 1 (aLCw and aLCe) use the concept of an "active" chain. At a particular location in a text, we define a lexical chain to be "active" if the span (between the first and last noun in the lexical chain) includes the current location. We expect these features may indicate the total number of concepts that the reader needs to keep in mind during a specific moment in time when reading a text. Measuring the average number of concepts that the reader of a text must keep in mind may suggest the working memory burden of the text over time. We were unsure if individual words or individual noun-phrases in the document should be used as the basic unit of "time" for the purpose of averaging the number of active lexical chains; so, we included both features.

5.3 Testing the Significance of Features

To select which features to include in our automatic readability assessment tool (in Section 6), we analyzed the documents in our paired corpora (Britannica and LiteracyNet). Because they contain a complex and a simplified version of each article, we can examine differences in readability while holding the topic and genre constant. We calculated the value of each feature for each document, and we used a paired t-test to determine if the difference between the complex and simple documents was significant for that corpus.

Table 2 contains the results of this feature selection process; the columns in the table indicate the values for the following corpora: Britannica complex, Britannica simple, LiteracyNet complex, and LiteracyNet simple. An asterisk appears in the "Sig" column if the difference between the feature values for the complex vs. simple documents is statistically significant for that corpus (significance level: $p<0.00001$).

The only two features which did not show a significant difference ($p>0.01$) between the complex and simple versions of the articles were: average lexical chain length (aLCL) and number of lexical chains with span greater than half the document length (nLC2). The lack of significance for aLCL may be explained by the vast majority of lexical chains containing few members; complex articles contained more of these chains – but their chains did not contain more members. In the case of nLC2, over 80% of the articles in each category contained no lexical chains whose span was greater than half the document length. The rarity of a lexical chain spanning the majority of a document may have led to there being no significant difference between complex/simple.

Feature	Brit. Com.	Brit. Simp.	Sig	LitN. Com.	LitN. Simp.	Sig
aWPS	20.13	14.37	*	17.97	12.95	*
aSPW	1.708	1.655	*	1.501	1.455	*
%3+S	0.196	0.177	*	0.12	0.101	*
aNP	8.363	6.018	*	6.519	4.691	*
aN	7.024	5.215	*	5.319	3.929	*
aVP	2.334	1.868	*	3.806	2.964	*
aAdj	1.95	1.281	*	1.214	0.876	*
aSBr	0.266	0.205	*	0.793	0.523	*
aPP	2.858	1.936	*	1.791	1.22	*
nNP	798	219.2	*	150.2	102.9	*
nN	668.4	190.4	*	121.4	85.75	*
nVP	242.8	69.19	*	88.2	65.52	*
nAdj	205	47.32	*	28.11	19.04	*
nSBr	31.33	7.623	*	18.16	11.43	*
nPP	284.7	70.75	*	41.06	26.79	*
nEM	624.2	172.7	*	115.2	82.83	*
nUE	355	117	*	81.56	54.94	*
aEM	6.441	4.745	*	5.035	3.789	*
aUE	4.579	3.305	*	3.581	2.55	*
nLC	59.21	17.57	*	12.43	8.617	*
nLC2	0.175	0.211		0.191	0.226	
aLCL	3.009	3.022		2.817	2.847	
aLCS	357	246.1	*	271.9	202.9	*
aLCw	1.803	1.358	*	1.407	1.091	*
aLCn	1.852	1.42	*	1.53	1.201	*

Table 2: Feature Values of Paired Corpora

6 A Readability Assessment Tool

After testing the significance of features using paired corpora, we used linear regression and our graded corpus (Weekly Reader) to build a readability assessment tool. To evaluate the tool's usefulness for adults with ID, we test the correlation of its scores with the LocalNews corpus.

6.1 Versions of Our Model

We began our evaluation by implementing three versions of our automatic readability assessment tool. The first version uses only those features studied by previous researchers (aWPS, aSPW, %3+S, aNP, aN, aVP, aAdj, aSBr, aPP, nNP, nN, nVP, nAdj, nSBr, nPP). The second version uses only our novel cognitively motivated features (section 5.2). The third version uses the union of both sets of features. By building three versions of the tool, we can compare the relative impact of our novel cognitively-motivated features. For all versions, we have only included those features that showed a significant difference between the complex and simple articles in our paired corpora (as discussed in section 5.3).

6.2 Learning Technique and Training Data

Early work on automatic readability analysis framed the problem as a classification task: creating multiple classifiers for labeling a text as being one of several elementary school grade levels (Collins-Thompson and Callan, 2004). Because we are focusing on a unique user group with special reading challenges, we do not know *a priori* what level of text difficulty is ideal for our users. We would not know where to draw category boundaries for classification. We also prefer that our assessment tool assign numerical difficulty scores to texts. Thus, after creating this tool, we can conduct further reading comprehension experiments with adults with ID to determine what threshold (for readability scores assigned by our tool) is appropriate for our users.

To select features for our model, we used our paired corpora (Britannica and LiteracyNet) to measure the significance of each feature. Now that we are training a model, we make use of our *graded* corpus (articles from Weekly Reader). This corpus contains articles that have each been labeled with an elementary school grade level for which it was written. We divide this corpus – using 80% of articles as training data and 20% as testing data. We model the grade level of the articles using linear regression; our model is implemented using R (R Development Core Team, 2008).

6.3 Evaluation of Our Readability Tool

We conducted two rounds of training and evaluation of our three regression models. We also compare our models to a baseline readability assessment tool: the popular Flesh-Kincaid Grade Level index (Kincaid et al., 1975).

In the first round of evaluation, we trained and tested our regression models on the Weekly Reader corpus. This round of evaluation helped to determine whether our feature-set and regression technique were successfully modeling those aspects of the texts that were relevant to their grade level. Our results from this round of evaluation are presented in the form of average error scores. (For each article in the Weekly Reader testing data, we calculate the difference between the output score of the model and the correct grade-level for that article.) Table 3 presents the average error results for the baseline system and our three regression models. We can see that the model trained on the shallow and parse-related features out-performs the model trained only on our novel features; however, the best model overall is the one is trained on all of the features. This model predicts the grade level of Weekly Reader articles to within roughly 0.565 grade levels on average.

Readability Model (or baseline)	Average Error
Baseline: Flesh-Kincaid Index	2.569
Basic Features Only	0.6032
Cognitively Motivated Features Only	0.6110
Basic + Cognitively-Motiv. Features	0.5650

Table 3: Predicting Grade Level of Weekly Reader

In our second round of evaluation, we trained the regression model on the Weekly Reader corpus, but we tested it against the LocalNews corpus. We measured the correlation between our regression models' output and the comprehension scores of adults with ID on each text. For this reason, we do not calculate the "average error"; instead, we simply measure the correlation between the models' output and the comprehension scores. (We expect negative correlations because comprehension scores should increase as the predicted grade level of the text goes down.)

Table 4 presents the correlations for our three models and the baseline system in the form of Pearson's R-values. We see a surprising result: the model trained only on the cognitively-motivated features is more tightly correlated with the comprehension scores of the adults with ID. While the model trained on all features was better at assigning grade levels to Weekly Reader articles, when we tested it on the local news articles from our user-study, it was not the top-performing model. This result suggests that the shallow and parse-related features of texts designed for children (the Weekly Reader articles, our training data) are not the best predictors of text readability for adults with ID.

Readability Model (or baseline)	Pearson's R
Baseline: Flesh-Kincaid Index	-0.270
Basic Features Only	-0.283
Cognitively Motivated Features Only	-0.352
Basic + Cognitively-Motiv. Features	-0.342

Table 4: Correlation to User-Study Comprehension

7 Discussion

Based on the cognitive and literacy skills of adults with ID, we designed novel features that were useful in assessing the readability of texts for these users. The results of our study have supported our hypothesis that the complexity of a text for adults with ID is related to the number of entities referred to in the text. These "entity density" features enabled us to build models that were better at predicting text readability for adults with intellectual disabilities.

This study has also demonstrated the value of collecting readability judgments from target users when designing a readability assessment tool. The results in Table 4 suggest that models trained on corpora containing texts designed for children may not always lead to accurate models of the readability of texts for other groups of low-literacy users. Using features targeting specific aspects of literacy impairment have allowed us to make better use of children's texts when designing a model for adults with ID.

7.1 Future Work

In order to study more features and models of readability, we will require more testing data for tracking progress of our readability regression models. Our current study has illustrated the usefulness of texts that have been evaluated by adults with ID, and we therefore plan to increase the size of this corpus in future work. In addition to using this corpus for evaluation, we may want to use it to *train* our regression models. For this study, we trained on Weekly Reader text labeled with elementary school grade levels, but this is not ideal. Texts designed for children may differ from those that are best for adults with ID, and "grade levels" may not be the best way to rank/rate text readability for these users. While our user-study comprehension-test corpus is currently too small for training, we intend to grow the size of this corpus in future work.

We also plan on refining our cognitively motivated features for measuring the difficulty of a text for our users. Currently, we use lexical chain software to link noun phrases in a document that may refer to similar entities/concepts. In future work, we plan to use co-reference resolution software to model how multiple "entity mentions" may refer to a single discourse entity.

For comparison purposes, we plan to implement other features that have been used in earlier readability assessment systems. For example, Petersen and Ostendorf (2009) created lists of the most common words from the Weekly Reader articles, and they used the percentage of words in a document not on this list as a feature.

The overall goal of our research is to develop a software system that can automatically simplify the reading level of local news articles and present them in an accessible way to adults with ID. Our automatic readability assessment tool will be a component in this future text simplification system. We have therefore preferred to include features in our tool that focus on aspects of the text that can be modified during a simplification process. In future work, we will study how to use our readability assessment tool to guide how a text revision system decides to modify a text to increase its readability for these users.

7.2 Summary of Contributions

We have contributed to research on automatic readability assessment by designing a new method for assessing the complexity of a text at the level of discourse. Our novel "entity density" features are based on named entity and lexical chain software, and they are inspired by the cognitive underpinnings of the literacy challenges of adults with ID – specifically, the role of slow semantic encoding and working memory limitations. We have demonstrated the usefulness of these novel features in modeling the grade level of elementary school texts and in correlating to readability judgments from adults with ID.

Another contribution of our work is the collection of an initial corpus of texts of local news stories that have been manually simplified by a human editor. Both the original and the simplified versions of these stories have been evaluated by adults with intellectual disabilities. We have used these comprehension scores in the evaluation phase of this study, and we have suggested how constructing a larger corpus of such articles could be useful for training readability tools.

More broadly, this project has demonstrated how focusing on a specific user population, analyzing their cognitive skills, and involving them in a user-study has led to new insights in modeling text readability. As Dale and Chall's definition (1949) originally argued, characteristics of the reader are central to the issue of readability. We believe our user-focused research paradigm may be used to drive further advances in readability assessment for other groups of users.

Acknowledgements

We thank the Weekly Reader Corporation for making its corpus available for our research. We are grateful to Martin Jansche for his assistance with the statistical data analysis and regression.

References

Alias-i. 2008. LingPipe 3.6.0. http://alias-i.com/lingpipe (accessed October 1, 2008)

Barzilay, R., Elhadad, N., 2003. Sentence alignment for monolingual comparable corpora. In *Proc EMNLP*, pp. 25-32.

Barzilay R., Lapata, M., 2008. Modeling Local Coherence: An Entity-based Approach. *Computational Linguistics*. 34(1):1-34.

Carroll, J., Minnen, G., Pearce, D., Canning, Y., Devlin, S., Tait, J. 1999. Simplifying text for language-impaired readers. In *Proc. EACL Poster*, p. 269.

Chall, J.S., Dale, E., 1995. *Readability Revisited: The New Dale-Chall Readability Formula*. Brookline Books, Cambridge, MA.

Charniak, E. 2000. A maximum-entropy-inspired parser. In *Proc. NAACL*, pp. 132-139.

Collins-Thompson, K., and Callan, J. 2004. A language modeling approach to predicting reading difficulty. In *Proc. NAACL*, pp. 193-200.

Dale, E. and J. S. Chall. 1949. The concept of readability. *Elementary English* 26(23).

Davison, A., and Kantor, R. 1982. On the failure of readability formulas to define readable texts: A case study from adaptations. *Reading Research Quarterly*, 17(2):187-209.

Drew, C.J., and Hardman, M.L. 2004. *Mental retardation: A lifespan approach to people with intellectual disabilities (8th ed.)*. Columbus, OH: Merrill.

Flesch, R. 1948. A new readability yardstick. *Journal of Applied Psychology*, 32:221-233.

Fowler, A.E. 1998. Language in mental retardation. In Burack, Hodapp, and Zigler (Eds.), *Handbook of Mental Retardation and Development*. Cambridge, UK: Cambridge Univ. Press, pp. 290-333.

Frazier, L. 1985. *Natural Language Parsing: Psychological, Computational, and Theoretical Perspectives*, chapter Syntactic complexity, pp. 129-189. Cambridge University Press.

Galley, M., McKeown, K. 2003. Improving Word Sense Disambiguation in Lexical Chaining. In *Proc. IJCAI*, pp. 1486-1488.

Gunning, R. 1952. *The Technique* of *Clear Writing*. McGraw-Hill.

Heilman, M., Collins-Thompson, K., Callan, J., and Eskenazi, M. 2007. Combining lexical and grammatical features to improve readability measures for first and second language texts. In *Proc. NAACL*, pp. 460-467.

Hickson-Bilsky, L. 1985. Comprehension and mental retardation. *International Review of Research in Mental Retardation*, 13: 215-246.

Katims, D.S. 2000. Literacy instruction for people with mental retardation: Historical highlights and contemporary analysis. *Education and Training in Mental Retardation and Developmental Disabilities*, 35(1): 3-15.

Kincaid, J. P., Fishburne, R. P., Rogers, R. L., and Chissom, B. S. 1975. Derivation of new readability formulas for Navy enlisted personnel, Research Branch Report 8-75, Millington, TN.

Kincaid, J., Fishburne, R., Rodgers, R., and Chisson, B. 1975. Derivation of new readability formulas for navy enlisted personnel. Technical report, Research Branch Report 8-75, U.S. Naval Air Station.

McLaughlin, G.H. 1969. SMOG grading - a new readability formula. *Journal of Reading*, 12(8):639-646.

McNamara, D.S., Ozuru, Y., Graesser, A.C., & Louwerse, M. (2006) Validating Coh-Metrix., In *Proc. Conference of the Cognitive Science Society*, pp. 573.

Miller, G., and Chomsky, N. 1963. *Handbook of Mathematical Psychology*, chapter Finatary models of language users, pp. 419-491. Wiley.

Perfetti, C., and Lesgold, A. 1977. Cognitive Processes in Comprehension, chapter Discourse Comprehension and sources of individual differences. Erlbaum.

Petersen, S.E., Ostendorf, M. 2009. A machine learning approach to reading level assessment. *Computer Speech and Language*, 23: 89-106.

R Development Core Team. 2008. *R: A Language and Environment for Statistical Computing*. Vienna, Austria: R Foundation for Statistical Computing. http://www.R-project.org

Roark, B., Mitchell, M., and Hollingshead, K. 2007. Syntactic complexity measures for detecting mild cognitive impairment. In *Proc. ACL Workshop on Biological, Translational, and Clinical Language Processing (BioNLP'07)*, pp. 1-8.

Schwarm, S., and Ostendorf, M. 2005. Reading level assessment using support vector machines and statistical language models. In *Proc. ACL*, pp. 523-530.

Si, L., and Callan, J. 2001. A statistical model for scientific readability. In *Proc. CIKM*, pp. 574-576.

Stenner, A.J. 1996. Measuring reading comprehension with the Lexile framework. 4th North American Conference on Adolescent/Adult Literacy.

U.S. Census Bureau. 2000. *Projections of the total resident population by five-year age groups* and *sex, with special age categories: Middle series 2025-2045*. Washington: U.S. Census Bureau, Populations Projections Program, Population Division.

Weekly Reader, 2008. http://www.weeklyreader.com (Accessed Oct., 2008).

Western/Pacific Literacy Network / Literacyworks, 2008. CNN SF learning resources. http://literacynet.org/cnnsf/ (Accessed Oct., 2008).

Williams, S., Reiter, E. 2005. Generating readable texts for readers with low basic skills. In *Proc. European Workshop on Natural Language Generation*, pp. 140-147.

Yngve, V. 1960. A model and a hypothesis for language structure. *American Philosophical Society*, 104: 446-466.

Effects of Word Confusion Networks on Voice Search

Junlan Feng, Srinivas Bangalore
AT&T Labs-Research
Florham Park, NJ, USA
junlan,srini@research.att.com

Abstract

Mobile voice-enabled search is emerging as one of the most popular applications abetted by the exponential growth in the number of mobile devices. The automatic speech recognition (ASR) output of the voice query is parsed into several fields. Search is then performed on a text corpus or a database. In order to improve the robustness of the query parser to noise in the ASR output, in this paper, we investigate two different methods to query parsing. Both methods exploit multiple hypotheses from ASR, in the form of word confusion networks, in order to achieve tighter coupling between ASR and query parsing and improved accuracy of the query parser. We also investigate the results of this improvement on search accuracy. Word confusion-network based query parsing outperforms ASR 1-best based query-parsing by 2.7% absolute and the search performance improves by 1.8% absolute on one of our data sets.

1 Introduction

Local search specializes in serving geographically constrained search queries on a structured database of local business listings. Most text-based local search engines provide two text fields: the "SearchTerm" (e.g. *Best Chinese Restaurant*) and the "LocationTerm" (e.g. a city, state, street address, neighborhood etc.). Most voice-enabled local search dialog systems mimic this two-field approach and employ a two-turn dialog strategy. The dialog system solicits from the user a LocationTerm in the first turn followed by a SearchTerm in the second turn (Wang et al., 2008).

Although the two-field interface has been widely accepted, it has several limitations for *mobile* voice search. First, most mobile devices are location-aware which obviates the need to specify the LocationTerm. Second, it's not always straightforward for users to be aware of the distinction between these two fields. It is common for users to specify location information in the SearchTerm field. For example, "restaurants near Manhattan" for SearchTerm and "NY NY" for LocationTerm. For voice-based search, it is more natural for users to specify queries in a single utterance[1]. Finally, many queries often contain other constraints (assuming LocationTerm is a constraint) such as *that deliver* in *restaurants that deliver* or *open 24 hours* in *night clubs open 24 hours*. It would be very cumbersome to enumerate each constraint as a different text field or a dialog turn. An interface that allows for specifying constraints in a natural language utterance would be most convenient.

In this paper, we introduce a voice-based search system that allows users to specify search requests in a single natural language utterance. The output of ASR is then parsed by a query parser into three fields: LocationTerm, SearchTerm, and Filler. We use a local search engine, *http://www.yellowpages.com/*, which accepts the SearchTerm and LocationTerm as two query fields and returns the search results from a business listings database. We present two methods for parsing the voice query into different fields with particular emphasis on exploiting the ASR output beyond the 1-best hypothesis. We demonstrate that by parsing word confusion networks, the accuracy of the query parser can be improved. We further investigate the effect of this improvement on the search task and demonstrate the benefit of tighter coupling of ASR and the query parser on search accuracy.

The paper outline is as follows. In Section 2, we discuss some of the related threads of research relevant for our task. In Section 3, we motivate the need for a query parsing module in voice-based search systems. We present two different query parsing models in Section 4 and Section 5 and discuss experimental results in Section 6. We summarize our results in Section 7.

[1]Based on the returned results, the query may be refined in subsequent turns of a dialog.

Proceedings of the 12th Conference of the European Chapter of the ACL, pages 238–245,
Athens, Greece, 30 March – 3 April 2009.

2 Related Work

The role of query parsing can be considered as similar to spoken language understanding (SLU) in dialog applications. However, voice-based search systems currently do not have SLU as a separate module, instead the words in the ASR 1-best output are directly used for search. Most voice-based search applications apply a conventional vector space model (VSM) used in information retrieval systems for search. In (Yu et al., 2007), the authors enhanced the VSM by deemphasizing term frequency in Listing Names and using character level instead of word level uni/bi-gram terms to improve robustness to ASR errors. While this approach improves recall it does not improve precision. In other work (Natarajan et al., 2002), the authors proposed a two-state hidden Markov model approach for query understanding and speech recognition in the same step (Natarajan et al., 2002).

There are two other threads of research literature relevant to our work. Named entity (NE) extraction attempts to identify entities of interest in speech or text. Typical entities include locations, persons, organizations, dates, times monetary amounts and percentages (Kubala et al., 1998). Most approaches for NE tasks rely on machine learning approaches using annotated data. These algorithms include a hidden Markov model, support vector machines, maximum entropy, and conditional random fields. With the goal of improving robustness to ASR errors, (Favre et al., 2005) described a finite-state machine based approach to take as input ASR n-best strings and extract the NEs. Although our task of query segmentation has similarity with NE tasks, it is arguable whether the SearchTerm is a well-defined entity, since a user can provide varied expressions as they would for a general web search. Also, it is not clear how the current best performing NE methods based on maximum entropy or conditional random fields models can be extended to apply on weighted lattices produced by ASR.

The other related literature is natural language interface to databases (NLIDBs), which had been well-studied during 1960s-1980s (Androutsopoulos, 1995). In this research, the aim is to map a natural language query into a structured query that could be used to access a database. However, most of the literature pertains to textual queries, not spoken queries. Although in its full generality the task of NLIDB is significantly more ambitious than our current task, some of the challenging problems (e.g. modifier attachment in queries) can also be seen in our task as well.

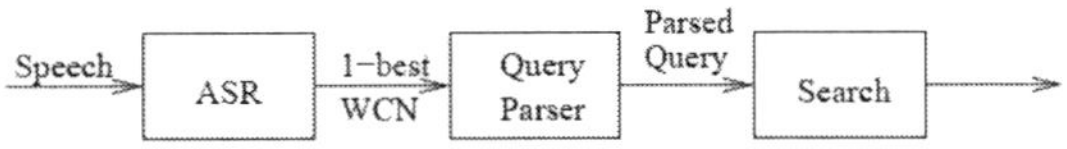

Figure 1: Architecture of a voice-based search system

3 Voice-based Search System Architecture

Figure 1 illustrates the architecture of our voice-based search system. As expected the ASR and Search components perform speech recognition and search tasks. In addition to ASR and Search, we also integrate a query parsing module between ASR and Search for a number of reasons.

First, as can be expected the ASR 1-best output is typically error-prone especially when a user query originates from a noisy environment. However, ASR word confusion networks which compactly encode multiple word hypotheses with their probabilities have the potential to alleviate the errors in a 1-best output. Our motivation to introduce the understanding module is to rescore the ASR output for the purpose of maximizing search performance. In this paper, we show promising results using richer ASR output beyond 1-best hypothesis.

Second, as mentioned earlier, the query parser not only provides the search engine "what" and "where" information, but also segments the query to phrases of other concepts. For the example we used earlier, we segment *night club open 24 hours* into *night club* and *open 24 hours*. Query segmentation has been considered as a key step to achieving higher retrieval accuracy (Tan and Peng, 2008).

Lastly, we prefer to reuse an existing local search engine *http://www.yellowpages.com/*, in which many text normalization, task specific tuning, business rules, and scalability issues have been well addressed. Given that, we need a module to translate ASR output to the query syntax that the local search engine supports.

In the next section, we present our proposed approaches of how we parse ASR output including ASR 1-best string and lattices in a scalable framework.

4 Text Indexing and Search-based Parser (PARIS)

As we discussed above, there are many potential approaches such as those for NE extraction we can explore for parsing a query. In the context of voice local search, users expect overall system response time to be similar to that of web search. Consequently, the relatively long ASR latency leaves no room for a slow parser. On the other hand, the parser needs to be tightly synchronized with changes in the listing database, which is updated at least once a day. Hence, the parser's training process also needs to be quick to accomodate these changes. In this section, we propose a probabilistic query parsing approach called PARIS (parsing using indexing and search). We start by presenting a model for parsing ASR 1-best and extend the approach to consider ASR lattices.

4.1 Query Parsing on ASR 1-best output

4.1.1 The Problem

We formulate the query parsing task as follows. A 1-best ASR output is a sequence of words: $Q = q_1, q_2, \ldots, q_n$. The parsing task is to segment Q into a sequence of concepts. Each concept can possibly span multiple words. Let $S = s_1, s_2, \ldots, s_k, \ldots, s_m$ be one of the possible segmentations comprising of m segments, where $s_k = q_j^i = q_i, \ldots q_j, 1 \leq i \leq j \leq n+1$. The corresponding concept sequence is represented as $C = c_1, c_2, \ldots, c_k, \ldots, c_m$.

For a given Q, we are interested in searching for the best segmentation and concept sequence (S^*, C^*) as defined by Equation 1, which is rewritten using Bayes rule as Equation 2. The prior probability $P(C)$ is approximated using an h-gram model on the concept sequence as shown in Equation 3. We model the segment sequence generation probability $P(S|C)$ as shown in Equation 4, using independence assumptions. Finally, the query terms corresponding to a segment and concept are generated using Equations 5 and 6.

$$(S^*, C^*) = \underset{S,C}{argmax}\ P(S, C) \quad (1)$$

$$= \underset{S,C}{argmax}\ P(C) * P(S|C) \quad (2)$$

$$P(C) = P(c_1) * \prod_{i}^{m} P(c_i|c_{i-1}^{i-h+1}) \quad (3)$$

$$P(S|C) = \prod_{k=1}^{m} P(s_k \mid c_k) \quad (4)$$

$$P(s_k|c_k) = P(q_j^i|c_k) \quad (5)$$

$$P(q_j^i|c_k) = P_{c_k}(q_i) * \prod_{l=i+1}^{j} P_{c_k}(q_l \mid q_{l-1}^{l-k+1}) \quad (6)$$

To train this model, we only have access to text query logs from two distinct fields (SearchTerm, LocationTerm) and the business listing database. We built a SearchTerm corpus by including valid queries that users typed to the SearchTerm field and all the unique business listing names in the listing database. Valid queries are those queries for which the search engine returns at least one business listing result or a business category. Similarly, we built a corpus for LocationTerm by concatenating valid LocationTerm queries and unique addresses including street address, city, state, and zip-code in the listing database. We also built a small corpus for Filler, which contains common carrier phrases and stop words. The generation probabilities as defined in 6 can be learned from these three corpora.

In the following section, we describe a scalable way of implementation using standard text indexer and searcher.

4.1.2 Probabilistic Parsing using Text Search

We use Apache-Lucene (Hatcher and Gospodnetic, 2004), a standard text indexing and search engines for query parsing. Lucene is an open-source full-featured text search engine library. Both Lucene indexing and search are efficient enough for our tasks. It takes a few milliseconds to return results for a common query. Indexing millions of search logs and listings can be done in minutes. Reusing text search engines allows a seamless integration between query parsing and search.

We changed the `tf.idf` based document-term relevancy metric in Lucene to reflect $P(q_j^i|c_k)$ using $Relevancy$ as defined below.

$$P(q_j^i|c_k) = Relevancy(q_j^i, d_k) = \frac{tf(q_j^i, d_k) + \sigma}{N} \quad (7)$$

where d_k is a corpus of examples we collected for the concept c_k; $tf(q_j^i, d_k)$ is referred as the term frequency, the frequency of q_j^i in d_k; N is the number of entries in d_k; σ is an empirically determined smoothing factor.

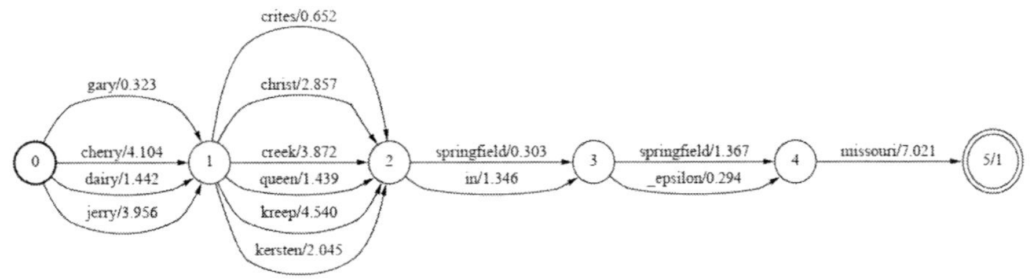

Figure 2: An example confusion network for "Gary crities Springfield Missouri"

Inputs:

- A set of K concepts:$C = c_1, c_2, \ldots, c_K$, in this paper, $K = 3$, $c_1 = SearchTerm$, $c_2 = LocationTerm$, $c_3 = Filler$
- Each concept c_k associates with a text corpus: d_k. Corpora are indexed using Lucene Indexing.
- A given query: $Q = q_1, q_2, \ldots, q_n$
- A given maximum number of words in a query segment: Ng

Parsing:

- Enumerate possible segments in Q up to Ng words long: $q_j^i = q_i, q_{i+1}, \ldots, q_j$, $j >= i$, $|j - i| < Ng$
- Obtain $P(q_j^i|c_k))$ for each pair of c_k and q_j^i using Lucene Search
- Boost $P(q_j^i|c_k))$ based on the position of q_j^i in the query $P(q_j^i|c_k) = P(q_j^i|c_k) * boost_{c_k}(i, j, n)$
- Search for the best segment sequence and concept sequence using Viterbi search

Fig.3. Parsing procedure using Text Indexer and Searcher

$$p_{c_k}(q_j^i) = \frac{tf(q_i^i \sim dis(i,j), d_k) + \sigma}{N * shift} \quad (8)$$

When $tf(q_j^i, d_k)$ is zero for all concepts, we loosen the phrase search to be proximity search, which searches words in q_j^i within a specific distance. For instance, "burlington west virginia" $\sim$ 5 will find entries that include these three words within 5 words of each other. $tf(q_j^i, d_k)$ is discounted for proximity search. For a given q_j^i, we allow a distance of $dis(i,j) = (j - i + shift)$ words. *shift* is a parameter that is set empirically. The discounting formula is given in 8.

Figure 3 shows the procedure we use for parsing. It enumerates possible segments q_j^i of a given Q. It then obtains $P(q_j^i|c_k)$ using Lucene Search. We boost $p_{c_k}(q_j^i))$ based on the position of q_j^i in Q. In our case, we simply set: $boost_{c_k}(i, j, n) = 3$ if $j = n$ and $c_k = LocationTerm$. Otherwise, $boost_{c_k}(i, j, n) = 1$. The algorithm searches for the best segmentation using the Viterbi algorithm. Out-of-vocabulary words are assigned to c_3 (Filler).

4.2 Query Parsing on ASR Lattices

Word confusion networks (WCNs) is a compact lattice format (Mangu et al., 2000). It aligns a speech lattice with its top-1 hypothesis, yielding a "sausage"-like approximation of lattices. It has been used in applications such as word spotting and spoken document retrieval. In the following, we present our use of WCNs for query parsing task.

Figure 2 shows a pruned WCN example. For each word position, there are multiple alternatives and their associated negative log posterior probabilities. The 1-best path is "Gary Crites Springfield Missouri". The reference is "Dairy Queen in Springfield Missouri". ASR misrecognized "Dairy Queen" as "Gary Crities". However, the correct words "Dairy Queen" do appear in the lattice, though with lower probability. The challenge is to select the correct words from the lattice by considering both ASR posterior probabilities and parser probabilities.

The hypotheses in WCNs have to be reranked

by the Query Parser to prefer those that have meaningful concepts. Clearly, each business name in the listing database corresponds to a single concept. However, the long queries from query logs tend to contain multiple concepts. For example, a frequent query is "night club for 18 and up". We know "night club" is the main subject. And "18 and up" is a constraint. Without matching "night club", any match with "18 and up" is meaningless. The data fortunately can tell us which words are more likely to be a subject. We rarely see "18 and up" as a complete query. Given these observations, we propose calculating the probability of a query term to be a subject. "Subject" here specifically means a complete query or a listing name. For the example shown in Figure 2, we observe the negative log probability for "Dairy Queen" to be a subject is 9.3. "Gary Crites" gets 15.3. We refer to this probability as subject likelihood. Given a candidate query term $s = w_1, w_2, ..w_m$, we represent the subject likelihood as $P_{sb}(s)$. In our experiments, we estimate P_{sb} using relative frequency normorlized by the length of s. We use the following formula to combine it with posterior probabilities in WCNs $P_{cf}(s)$:

$$P(s) = P_{cf}(s) * P_{sb}(s)^{\lambda}$$
$$P_{cf}(s) = \prod_{j=1,\ldots,nw} P_{cf}(w_i)$$

where λ is used to flatten ASR posterior probabilities and nw is the number of words in s. In our experiments, λ is set to 0.5. We then re-rank ASR outputs based on $P(s)$. We will report experimental results with this approach. "Subject" is only related to SearchTerm. Considering this, we parse the ASR 1-best out first and keep the Location terms extracted as they are. Only word alternatives corresponding to the search terms are used for reranking. This also improves speed, since we make the confusion network lattice much smaller. In our initial investigations, such an approach yields promising results as illustrated in the experiment section.

Another capability that the parser does for both ASR 1-best and lattices is spelling correction. It corrects words such as *restaurants* to *restaurants*. ASR produces spelling errors because the language model is trained on query logs. We need to make more efforts to clean up the query log database, though progresses had been made.

5 Finite-state Transducer-based Parser

In this section, we present an alternate method for parsing which can transparently scale to take as input word lattices from ASR. We encode the problem of parsing as a weighted finite-state transducer (FST). This encoding allows us to apply the parser on ASR 1-best as well as ASR WCNs using the composition operation of FSTs.

We formulate the parsing problem as associating with each token of the input a label indicating whether that token belongs to one of a business listing (*bl*), city/state (*cs*) or neither (*null*). Thus, given a word sequence ($W = w_1, \ldots, w_n$) output from ASR, we search of the most likely label sequence ($T = t_1, \ldots, t_n$), as shown in Equation 9. We use the joint probability $P(W, T)$ and approximate it using an k-gram model as shown in Equations 10,11.

$$T^* = \underset{T}{argmax}\ P(T|W) \quad (9)$$
$$= \underset{T}{argmax}\ P(W,T) \quad (10)$$
$$= \underset{T}{argmax} \prod_{i}^{n} P(w_i, t_i \mid w_{i-1}^{i-k+1}, t_{i-1}^{i-k+1}) \quad (11)$$

A k-gram model can be encoded as a weighted finite-state acceptor (FSA) (Allauzen et al., 2004). The states of the FSA correspond to the k-gram histories, the transition labels to the pair (w_i, t_i) and the weights on the arcs are $-log(P(w_i, t_i \mid w_{i-1}^{i-k+1}, t_{i-1}^{i-k+1}))$. The FSA also encodes back-off arcs for purposes of smoothing with lower order k-grams. An annotated corpus of words and labels is used to estimate the weights of the FSA. A sample corpus is shown in Table 1.

1. pizza_bl hut_bl new_cs york_cs new_cs york_cs
2. home_bl depot_bl around_null san_cs francisco_cs
3. please_null show_null me_null indian_bl restaurants_bl in_null chicago_cs
4. pediatricians_bl open_null on_null sundays_null
5. hyatt_bl regency_bl in_null honolulu_cs hawaii_cs

Table 1: A Sample set of annotated sentences

The FSA on the joint alphabet is converted into an FST. The paired symbols (w_i, t_i) are reinterpreted as consisting of an input symbol w_i and output symbol t_i. The resulting FST (M) is used to parse the 1-best ASR (represented as FSTs (I)), using composition of FSTs and a search for the lowest weight path as shown in Equation 12. The output symbol sequence (π_2) from the lowest weight path is T^*.

$$T^* = \pi_2(Bestpath(I \circ M)) \quad (12)$$

Equation 12 shows a method for parsing the 1-best ASR output using the FST. However, a similar method can be applied for parsing WCNs. The WCN arcs are associated with a posterior weight that needs to be scaled suitably to be comparable to the weights encoded in M. We represent the result of scaling the weights in WCN by a factor of λ as WCN^λ. The value of the scaling factor is determined empirically. Thus the process of parsing a WCN is represented by Equation 13.

$$T^* = \pi_2(Bestpath(WCN^\lambda \circ M)) \quad (13)$$

6 Experiments

We have access to text query logs consisting of 18 million queries to the two text fields: SearchTerm and LocationTerm. In addition to these logs, we have access to 11 million unique business listing names and their addresses. We use the combined data to train the parameters of the two parsing models as discussed in the previous sections. We tested our approaches on three data sets, which in total include 2686 speech queries. These queries were collected from users using mobile devices from different time periods. Labelers transcribed and annotated the test data using SearchTerm and LocationTerm tags.

Data Sets	Number of Speech Queries	WACC
Test1	1484	70.1%
Test2	544	82.9%
Test3	658	77.3%

Table 2: ASR Performance on three Data Sets

We use an ASR with a trigram-based language model trained on the query logs. Table 2 shows the ASR word accuracies on the three data sets. The accuracy is the lowest on Test1, in which many users were non-native English speakers and a large percentage of queries are not intended for local search.

We measure the parsing performance in terms of extraction accuracy on the two non-filler slots: SearchTerm and LocationTerm. Extraction accuracy computes the percentage of the test set where the string identified by the parser for a slot is exactly the same as the annotated string for that slot.

Table 3 reports parsing performance using the PARIS approach for the two slots. The "Transcription" columns present the parser's performances on human transcriptions (i.e. word accuracy=100%) of the speech. As expected, the parser's performance heavily relies on ASR word accuracy. We achieved lower parsing performance on Test1 compared to other test sets due to lower ASR accuracy on this test set. The promising aspect is that we consistently improved SearchTerm extraction accuracy when using WCN as input. The performance under "Oracle path" column shows the upper bound for the parser using the oracle path[2] from the WCN. We pruned the WCN by keeping only those arcs that are within $cthresh$ of the lowest cost arc between two states. $Cthresh = 4$ is used in our experiments. For Test2, the upper bound improvement is 7.6% (82.5%-74.9%) absolute. Our proposed approach using pruned WCN achieved 2.7% improvement, which is 35% of the maximum potential gain. We observed smaller improvements on Test1 and Test3. Our approach did not take advantage of WCN for LocationTerm extraction, hence we obtained the same performance with WCNs as using ASR 1-best.

In Table 4, we report the parsing performance for the FST-based approach. We note that the FST-based parser on a WCN also improves the SearchTerm and LocationTerm extraction accuracy over ASR 1-best, an improvement of about 1.5%. The accuracies on the oracle path and the transcription are slightly lower with the FST-based parser than with the PARIS approach. The performance gap, however, is bigger on ASR 1-best. The main reason is PARIS has embedded a module for spelling correction that is not included in the FST approach. For instance, it corrects *nieman* to *neiman*. These improvements from spelling correction don't contribute much to search perfor-

[2]Oracle text string is the path in the WCN that is closest to the reference string in terms of Levenshtein edit distance

Data Sets	SearchTerm Extraction Accuracy				LocationTerm Extraction Accuracy			
Input	ASR 1-best	WCN	Oracle Path 4	Transcription	ASR 1best	WCN	Oracle Path 4	Transcription
Test1	60.0%	**60.7%**	67.9%	94.1%	80.6%	80.6%	85.2%	97.5%
Test2	74.9%	**77.6%**	82.5%	98.6%	89.0%	89.0%	92.8%	98.7%
Test3	64.7%	**65.7%**	71.5%	96.7%	88.8%	88.8%	90.5%	97.4%

Table 3: Parsing performance using the PARIS approach

Data Sets	SearchTerm Extraction Accuracy				LocationTerm Extraction Accuracy			
Input	ASR 1-best	WCN	Oracle Path 4	Transcription	ASR 1best	WCN	Oracle Path 4	Transcription
Test1	56.9%	**57.4%**	65.6%	92.2%	79.8%	79.8%	83.8%	95.1%
Test2	69.5%	**71.0%**	81.9%	98.0%	89.4%	89.4%	92.7%	98.5%
Test3	59.2%	**60.6%**	69.3%	96.1%	87.1%	87.1%	89.3%	97.3%

Table 4: Parsing performance using the FST approach

mance as we will see below, since the search engine is quite robust to spelling errors. ASR generates spelling errors because the language model is trained using query logs, where misspellings are frequent.

We evaluated the impact of parsing performance on search accuracy. In order to measure search accuracy, we need to first collect a reference set of search results for our test utterances. For this purpose, we submitted the human annotated two-field data to the search engine (*http://www.yellowpages.com/*) and extracted the top 5 results from the returned pages. The returned search results are either business categories such as "Chinese Restaurant" or business listings including business names and addresses. We considered these results as the reference search results for our test utterances.

In order to evaluate our voice search system, we submitted the two fields resulting from the query parser on the ASR output (1-best/WCN) to the search engine. We extracted the top 5 results from the returned pages and we computed the Precision, Recall and F1 scores between this set of results and the reference search set. Precision is the ratio of relevant results among the top 5 results the voice search system returns. Recall refers to the ratio of relevant results to the reference search result set. F1 combines precision and recall as: (2 * Recall * Precision) / (Recall + Precision) (van Rijsbergen, 1979).

In Table 5 and Table 6, we report the search performance using PARIS and FST approaches. The overall improvement in search performance is not as large as the improvement in the slot accuracies between using ASR 1-best and WCNs. On Test1, we obtained higher recall but lower precision with WCN resulting in a slight decrease in F1 score. For both approaches, we observed that using WCNs consistently improves recall but not precision. Although this might be counterintuitive, given that WCNs improve the slot accuracy overall. One possible explanation is that we have observed errors made by the parser using WCNs are more "severe" in terms of their relationship to the original queries. For example, in one particular

Data Sets		Precision	Recall	F1
ASR	Test1	71.8%	66.4%	68.8%
1-best	Test2	80.7%	76.5%	78.5%
	Test3	72.9%	68.8%	70.8%
WCN	Test1	70.8%	67.2%	69.0%
	Test2	81.6%	79.0%	80.3%
	Test3	73.0%	69.1%	71.0%

Table 5: Search performances using the PARIS approach

Data Sets		Precision	Recall	F1
ASR	Test1	71.6%	64.3%	67.8%
1-best	Test2	79.6%	76.0%	77.7%
	Test3	72.9%	67.2%	70.0%
WCN	Test1	70.5%	64.7%	67.5%
	Test2	80.3%	77.3%	78.8%
	Test3	72.9%	68.1%	70.3%

Table 6: Search performances using the FST approach

case, the annotated SearchTerm is "book stores", for which the ASR 1-best-based parser returned "books" (due to ASR error) as the SearchTerm, while the WCN-based parser identified "banks" as the SearchTerm. As a result, the returned results from the search engine using the 1-best-based parser were more relevant compared to the results returned by the WCN-based parser.

There are few directions that this observation suggests. First, the weights on WCNs may need to be scaled suitably to optimize the search performance as opposed to the slot accuracy performance. Second, there is a need for tighter coupling between the parsing and search components as the eventual goal for models of voice search is to improve search accuracy and not just the slot accuracy. We plan to investigate such questions in future work.

7 Summary

This paper describes two methods for query parsing. The task is to parse ASR output including 1-best and lattices into database or search fields. In our experiments, these fields are SearchTerm and LocationTerm for local search. Our first method, referred to as PARIS, takes advantage of a generic search engine (for text indexing and search) for parsing. All probabilities needed are retrieved on-the-fly. We used keyword search, phrase search and proximity search. The second approach, referred to as FST-based parser, which encodes the problem of parsing as a weighted finite-state transduction (FST). Both PARIS and FST successfully exploit multiple hypotheses and posterior probabilities from ASR encoded as word confusion networks and demonstrate improved accuracy. These results show the benefits of tightly coupling ASR and the query parser. Furthermore, we evaluated the effects of this improvement on search performance. We observed that the search accuracy improves using word confusion networks. However, the improvement on search is less than the improvement we obtained on parsing performance. Some improvements the parser achieves do not contribute to search. This suggests the need of coupling the search module and the query parser as well.

The two methods, namely PARIS and FST, achieved comparable performances on search. One advantage with PARIS is the fast training process, which takes minutes to index millions of query logs and listing entries. For the same amount of data, FST needs a number of hours to train. The other advantage is PARIS can easily use proximity search to loosen the constrain of N-gram models, which is hard to be implemented using FST. FST, on the other hand, does better smoothing on learning probabilities. It can also more directly exploit ASR lattices, which essentially are represented as FST too. For future work, we are interested in ways of harnessing the benefits of the both these approaches.

References

C. Allauzen, M. Mohri, M. Riley, and B. Roark. 2004. A generalized construction of speech recognition transducers. In *ICASSP*, pages 761–764.

I. Androutsopoulos. 1995. Natural language interfaces to databases - an introduction. *Journal of Natural Language Engineering*, 1:29–81.

B. Favre, F. Bechet, and P. Nocera. 2005. Robust named entity extraction from large spoken archives. In *Proceeding of HLT 2005*.

E. Hatcher and O. Gospodnetic. 2004. *Lucene in Action (In Action series)*. Manning Publications Co., Greenwich, CT, USA.

F. Kubala, R. Schwartz, R. Stone, and R. Weischedel. 1998. Named entity extraction from speech. In *in Proceedings of DARPA Broadcast News Transcription and Understanding Workshop*, pages 287–292.

L. Mangu, E. Brill, and A. Stolcke. 2000. Finding consensus in speech recognition: Word error minimization and other applications of confusion networks. *Computation and Language*, 14(4):273–400, October.

P. Natarajan, R. Prasad, R.M. Schwartz, and J. Makhoul. 2002. A scalable architecture for directory assistance automation. In *ICASSP 2002*.

B. Tan and F. Peng. 2008. Unsupervised query segmentation using generative language models and wikipedia. In *Proceedings of WWW-2008*.

C.V. van Rijsbergen. 1979. *Information Retrieval*. Boston. Butterworth, London.

Y. Wang, D. Yu, Y. Ju, and A. Alex. 2008. An introduction to voice search. *Signal Processing Magzine*, 25(3):29–38.

D. Yu, Y.C. Ju, Y.Y. Wang, G. Zweig, and A. Acero. 2007. Automated directory assistance system - from theory to practice. In *Interspeech*.

Company-Oriented Extractive Summarization of Financial News*

Katja Filippova†, **Mihai Surdeanu**‡, **Massimiliano Ciaramita**‡, **Hugo Zaragoza**‡
†EML Research gGmbH
Schloss-Wolfsbrunnenweg 33
69118 Heidelberg, Germany
‡Yahoo! Research
Avinguda Diagonal 177
08018 Barcelona, Spain
filippova@eml-research.de, {mihais,massi,hugoz}@yahoo-inc.com

Abstract

The paper presents a multi-document summarization system which builds company-specific summaries from a collection of financial news such that the extracted sentences contain novel and relevant information about the corresponding organization. The user's familiarity with the company's profile is assumed. The goal of such summaries is to provide information useful for the short-term trading of the corresponding company, i.e., to facilitate the inference from news to stock price movement in the next day. We introduce a novel query (i.e., company name) expansion method and a simple unsupervized algorithm for sentence ranking. The system shows promising results in comparison with a competitive baseline.

1 Introduction

Automatic text summarization has been a field of active research in recent years. While most methods are extractive, the implementation details differ considerably depending on *the goals* of a summarization system. Indeed, the intended use of the summaries may help significantly to adapt a particular summarization approach to a specific task whereas the broadly defined goal of preserving relevant, although generic, information may turn out to be of little use.

In this paper we present a system whose goal is to extract sentences from a collection of financial news to inform about important events concerning companies, e.g., to support trading (i.e., buy or sell) the corresponding symbol on the next day, or managing a portfolio. For example, a company's announcement of surpassing its earnings' estimate is likely to have a positive short-term effect on its stock price, whereas an announcement of job cuts is likely to have the reverse effect. We demonstrate how existing methods can be extended to achieve precisely this goal.

In a way, the described task can be classified as query-oriented multi-document summarization because we are mainly interested in information *related* to the company and its sector. However, there are also important differences between the two tasks.

- The name of the company is not a query, e.g., as it is specified in the context of the DUC competitions[1], and requires an extension. Initially, a query consists exclusively of the "*symbol*", i.e., the abbreviation of the name of a company as it is listed on the stock market. For example, *WPO* is the abbreviation used on the stock market to refer to *The Washington Post*–a large media and education company. Such symbols are rarely encountered in the news and cannot be used to find all the related information.

- The summary has to provide *novel* information related to the company and should avoid general facts about it which the user is supposed to know. This point makes the task related to update summarization where one has to provide the user with new information

*This work was done during the first author's internship at Yahoo! Research. Mihai Surdeanu is currently affiliated with Stanford University (mihais@stanford.edu). Massimiliano Ciaramita is currently at Google (massi@google.com).

[1]http://duc.nist.gov; since 2008 TAC: http://www.nist.gov/tac.

Proceedings of the 12th Conference of the European Chapter of the ACL, pages 246–254,
Athens, Greece, 30 March – 3 April 2009.

given some background knowledge[2]. In our case, general facts about the company are assumed to be known by the user. Given *WPO*, we want to distinguish between *The Washington Post is owned by The Washington Post Company, a diversified education and media company* and *The Post recently went through its third round of job cuts and reported an 11% decline in print advertising revenues for its first quarter*, the former being an example of background information whereas the latter is what we would like to appear in the summary. Thus, the similarity to the query alone is not the decisive parameter in computing sentence relevance.

- While the summaries must be specific for a given organization, important but general financial events that drive the overall market must be included in the summary. For example, the recent subprime mortgage crisis affected the entire economy regardless of the sector.

Our system proceeds in the three steps illustrated in Figure 1. First, the company symbol is expanded with terms relevant for the company, either directly – e.g., *iPod* is directly related to Apple Inc. – or indirectly – i.e., using information about the industry or sector the company operates in. We detail our symbol expansion algorithm in Section 3. Second, this information is used to rank sentences based on their relatedness to the expanded query and their overall importance (Section 4). Finally, the most relevant sentences are re-ranked based on the degree of novelty they carry (Section 5).

The paper makes the following contributions. First, we present a new query expansion technique which is useful in the context of company-dependent news summarization as it helps identify sentences important to the company. Second, we introduce a simple and efficient method for sentence ranking which foregrounds novel information of interest. Our system performs well in terms of the ROUGE score (Lin & Hovy, 2003) compared with a competitive baseline (Section 6).

2 Data

The data we work with is a collection of financial news consolidated and distributed by Yahoo! Finance[3] from various sources[4]. Each story is labeled as being relevant for a company – i.e., it appears in the company's RSS feed – if the story mentions either the company itself or the sector the company belongs to. Altogether the corpus contains 88,974 news articles from a period of about 5 months (148 days). Some articles are labeled as being relevant for several companies. The total number of *(company name, news collection)* pairs is 46,444.

The corpus is cleaned of HTML tags, embedded graphics and unrelated information (e.g., ads, frames) with a set of manually devised rules. The filtering is not perfect but removes most of the noise. Each article is passed through a language processing pipeline (described in (Atserias et al., 2008)). Sentence boundaries are identified by means of simple heuristics. The text is tokenized according to Penn TreeBank style and each token lemmatized using Wordnet's morphological functions. Part of speech tags and named entities (*LOC, PER, ORG, MISC*) are identified by means of a publicly available named-entity tagger[5] (Ciaramita & Altun, 2006, SuperSense). Apart from that, all sentences which are shorter than 5 tokens and contain neither nouns nor verbs are sorted out. We apply the latter filter as we are interested in textual information only. Numeric information contained, e.g., in tables can be easily and more reliably obtained from the indices tables available online.

3 Query Expansion

In company-oriented summarization query expansion is crucial because, by default, our query contains only the *symbol*, that is the abbreviation of the name of the company. Unfortunately, existing query expansion techniques which utilize such knowledge sources as WordNet or Wikipedia are not useful for symbol expansion. WordNet does not include organizations in any systematic way. Wikipedia covers many companies but it is unclear how it can be used for expansion.

[2]See the DUC 2007 and 2008 update tracks.

[3]http://finance.yahoo.com

[4]http://biz.yahoo.com, http://www.seekingalpha.com, http://www.marketwatch.com, http://www.reuters.com, http://www.fool.com, http://www.thestreet.com, http://online.wsj.com, http://www.forbes.com, http://www.cnbc.com, http://us.ft.com, http://www.minyanville.com

[5]http://sourceforge.net/projects/supersensetag

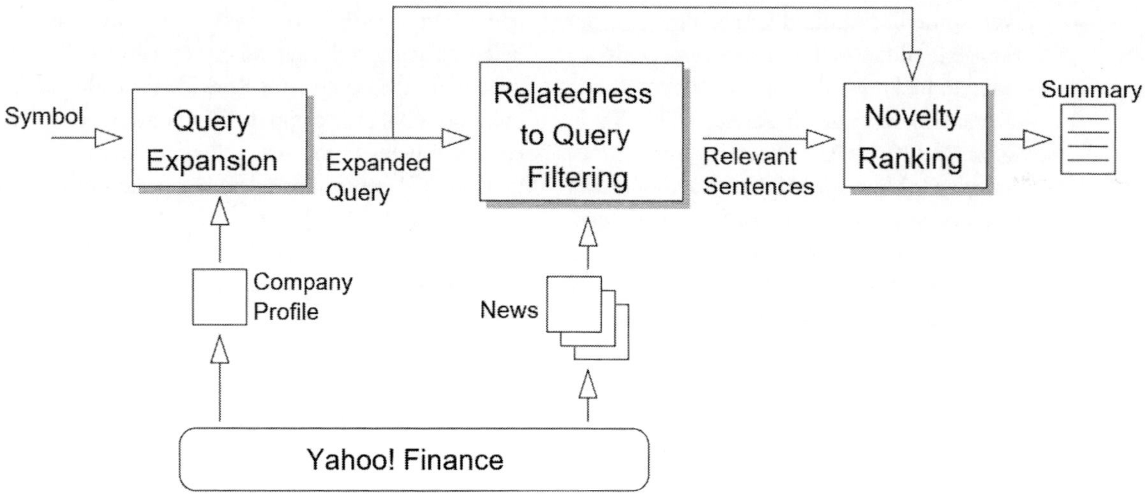

Figure 1: System architecture

Intuitively, a good expansion method should provide us with a list of products, or properties, of the company, the field it operates in, the typical customers, etc. Such information is normally found on the profile page of a company at Yahoo! Finance[6]. There, so called "business summaries" provide succinct and financially relevant information about the company. Thus, we use business summaries as follows. For every company symbol in our collection, we download its business summary, split it into tokens, remove all words but nouns and verbs which we then lemmatize. Since words like *company* are fairly uninformative in the context of our task, we do not want to include them in the expanded query. To filter out such words, we compute the company-dependent TF*IDF score for every word on the collection of all business summaries:

$$\text{score}(w) = \text{tf}_{w,c} \times \log\left(\frac{N}{\text{cf}_w}\right) \quad (1)$$

where c is the business summary of a company, $\text{tf}_{w,c}$ is the frequency of w in c, N is the total number of business summaries we have, cf_w is the number of summaries that contain w. This formula penalizes words occurring in most summaries (e.g., *company, produce, offer, operate, found, headquarter, management*). At the moment of running the experiments, N was about 3,000, slightly less than the total number of symbols because some companies do not have a business summary on Yahoo! Finance. It is important to point out that companies without a business summary are usually small and are seldom mentioned in news articles: for example, these companies had relevant news articles in only 5% of the days monitored in this work.

Table 1 gives the ten high scoring words for three companies (Apple Inc. – the computer and software manufacture, Delta Air Lines – the airline, and DaVita – dyalisis services). Table 1 shows that this approach succeeds in expanding the symbol with terms directly related to the company, e.g., *ipod* for Apple, but also with more general information like the industry or the company operates in, e.g., *software* and *computer* for Apple. All words whose TF*IDF score is above a certain threshold θ are included in the expanded query (θ was tuned to a value of 5.0 on the development set).

4 Relatedness to Query

Once the expanded query is generated, it can be used for sentence ranking. We chose the system of Otterbacher et al. (2005) as a a starting point for our approach and also as a competitive baseline because it has been successfully tested in a similar setting–it has been applied to multi-document query-focused summarization of news documents.

Given a graph $G = (S, E)$, where S is the set of all sentences from all input documents, and E is the set of edges representing normalized sentence similarities, Otterbacher et al. (2005) rank all sen-

[6] `http://finance.yahoo.com/q/pr?s=AAPL` where the trading symbol of any company can be used instead of AAPL.

AAPL	DAL	DVA
apple	air	dialysis
music	flight	davita
mac	delta	esrd
software	lines	kidney
ipod	schedule	inpatient
computer	destination	outpatient
peripheral	passenger	patient
movie	cargo	hospital
player	atlanta	disease
desktop	fleet	service

Table 1: Top 10 scoring words for three companies

tence nodes based on the inter-sentence relations as well as the relevance to the query q. Sentence ranks are found iteratively over the set of graph nodes with the following formula:

$$r(s,q) = \lambda \frac{\text{rel}(s|q)}{\sum_{t \in S} \text{rel}(t|q)} + (1-\lambda) \sum_{t \in S} \frac{\text{sim}(s,t)}{\sum_{v \in S} \text{sim}(v,t)} r(t,q) \quad (2)$$

The first term represents the importance of a sentence defined in respect to the query, whereas the second term infers the importance of the sentence from its relation to other sentences in the collection. $\lambda \in (0,1)$ determines the relative importance of the two terms and is found empirically. Another parameter whose value is determined experimentally is the sentence similarity threshold τ, which determines the inclusion of a sentence in G. Otterbacher et al. (2005) report 0.2 and 0.95 to be the optimal values for τ and λ respectively. These values turned out to produce the best results also on our development set and were used in all our experiments. Similarity between sentences is defined as the cosine of their vector representations:

$$\text{sim}(s,t) = \frac{\sum_{w \in s \cap t} \text{weight}(w)^2}{\sqrt{\sum_{w \in s} \text{weight}(w)^2} \times \sqrt{\sum_{w \in t} \text{weight}(w)^2}} \quad (3)$$

$$\text{weight}(w) = \text{tf}_{w,s} \text{idf}_{w,S} \quad (4)$$

$$\text{idf}_{w,S} = \log \left(\frac{|S|+1}{0.5 + \text{sf}_w} \right) \quad (5)$$

where $\text{tf}_{w,s}$ is the frequency of w in sentence s, $|S|$ is the total number of sentences in the documents from which sentences are to be extracted, and sf_w is the number of sentences which contain the word w (all words in the documents as well as in the query are stemmed and stopwords are removed from them). Relevance to the query is defined in Equation (6) which has been previously used for sentence retrieval (Allan et al., 2003):

$$\text{rel}(s|q) = \sum_{w \in q} \log(\text{tf}_{w,s} + 1) \times \log(\text{tf}_{w,q} + 1) \times \text{idf}_{w,S} \quad (6)$$

where $\text{tf}_{w,x}$ stands for the number of times w appears in x, be it a sentence (s) or the query (q). If a sentence shares no words other than stopwords with the query, the relevance becomes zero. Note that without the relevance to the query part Equation 2 takes only inter-sentence similarity into account and computes the weighted PageRank (Brin & Page, 1998).

In defining the relevance to the query, in Equation (6), words which do not appear in too many sentences in the document collection weigh more. Indeed, if a word from the query is contained in many sentences, it should not count much. But it is also true that not all words from the query are equally important. As it has been mentioned in Section 3, words like *product* or *offer* appear in many business summaries and are equally related to any company. To penalize such words, when computing the relevance to the query, we multiply the relevance score of a given word w with the inverted document frequency of w on the corpus of business summaries Q – $\text{idf}_{w,Q}$:

$$\text{idf}_{w,Q} = \log \left(\frac{|Q|}{\text{qf}_w} \right) \quad (7)$$

We also replace $\text{tf}_{w,s}$ with the indicator function $s(w)$ since it has been reported to be more adequate for sentences, in particular for sentence alignment (Nelken & Shieber, 2006):

$$s(w) = \begin{cases} 1 & \text{if } s \text{ contains } w \\ 0 & \text{otherwise} \end{cases} \quad (8)$$

Thus, the modified formula we use to compute sentence ranks is as follows:

$$\text{rel}(s|q) = \sum_{w \in q} s(w) \times \log(\text{tf}_{w,q} + 1) \times \text{idf}_{w,S} \times \text{idf}_{w,Q} \quad (9)$$

We call these two ranking algorithms that use the formula in (2) OTTERBACHER and QUERY WEIGHTS, the difference being the way the relevance to the query is computed: (6) or (9). We use the OTTERBACHER algorithm as a baseline in the experiments reported in Section 6.

5 Novelty Bias

Apart from being related to the query, a good summary should provide the user with novel information. According to Equation (2), if there are, say, two sentences which are highly similar to the query and which share some words, they are likely to get a very high score. Experimenting with the development set, we observed that sentences about the company, such as e.g., *DaVita, Inc. is a leading provider of kidney care in the United States, providing dialysis services and education for patients with chronic kidney failure and end stage renal disease*, are ranked high although they do not contribute new information. However, a non-zero similarity to the query is indeed a good filter of the information related to the company and to its sector and can be used as a prerequisite of a sentence to be included in the summary. These observations motivate our proposal for a ranking method which aims at providing relevant *and* novel information at the same time.

Here, we explore two alternative approaches to add the novelty bias to the system:

- The first approach bypasses the relatedness to query step introduced in Section 4 completely. Instead, this method merges the discovery of query relatedness and novelty into a single algorithm, which uses a sentence graph that contains edges *only* between sentences related to the query, (i.e., sentences for which $rel(s|q) > 0$). All edges connecting sentences which are unrelated to the query are skipped in this graph. In this way we limit the novelty ranking process to a subset of sentences related to the query.

- The second approach models the problem in a re-ranking architecture: we take the top ranked sentences after the relatedness-to-query filtering component (Section 4) and re-rank them using the novelty formula introduced below.

The main difference between the two approaches is that the former uses relatedness-to-query and novelty information but ignores the overall importance of a sentence as given by the PageRank algorithm in Section 4, while the latter combines all these aspects –i.e., importance of sentences, relatedness to query, and novelty– using the re-ranking architecture.

To amend the problem of general information ranked inappropriately high, we modify the word-weighting formula (4) so that it implements a novelty bias, thus becoming dependent on the query. A straightforward way to define the novelty weight of a word would be to draw a line between the "known" words, i.e., words appearing in the business summary, and the rest. In this approach all the words from the business summary are equally related to the company and get the weight of 0:

$$\text{weight}(w) = \begin{cases} 0 & \text{if } Q \text{ contains } w \\ \text{tf}_{w,s}\text{idf}_{w,S} & \text{otherwise} \end{cases} \tag{10}$$

We call this weighting scheme SIMPLE. As an alternative, we also introduce a more elaborate weighting procedure which incorporates the relatedness-to-query (or rather distance from query) in the word weight formula. Intuitively, the more related to the query a word is (e.g., *DaVita*, the name of the company), the more familiar to the user it is and the smaller its novelty contribution is. If a word does not appear in the query at all, its weight becomes equal to the usual $\text{tf}_{w,s}\text{idf}_{w,S}$:

$$\text{weight}(w) = \left(1 - \frac{\text{tf}_{w,q} \times \text{idf}_{w,Q}}{\sum_{w_i \in q} \text{tf}_{w_i,q} \times \text{idf}_{w_i,Q}}\right) \times \text{tf}_{w,s}\text{idf}_{w,S} \tag{11}$$

The overall novelty ranking formula is based on the query-dependent PageRank introduced in Equation (2). However, since we already incorporate the relatedness to the query in these two settings, we focus only on related sentences and thus may drop the relatedness to the query part from (2):

$$\text{r'}(s,q) = \lambda + (1-\lambda) \sum_{t \in S} \frac{\text{sim}(s,t,q)}{\sum_{u \in S} \text{sim}(t,u,q)} \tag{12}$$

We set λ to the same value as in OTTERBACHER. We deliberately set the sentence similarity threshold τ to a very low value (0.05) to prevent the graph from becoming exceedingly bushy. Note that this novelty-ranking formula can be equally applied in both scenarios introduced at the beginning of this section. In the first scenario, S stands for the set of nodes in the graph that contains only sentences related to the query. In the second scenario, S contains the highest ranking sentences detected by the relatedness-to-query component (Section 4).

5.1 Redundancy Filter

Some sentences are repeated several times in the collection. Such repetitions, which should be avoided in the summary, can be filtered out either before or after the sentence ranking. We apply a simple repetition check when incrementally adding ranked sentences to the summary. If a sentence to be added is almost identical to the one already included in the summary, we skip it. Identity check is done by counting the percentage of non-stop word lemmas in common between two sentences. 95% is taken as the threshold.

We do not filter repetitions *before* the ranking has taken place because often such repetitions carry important and relevant information. The redundancy filter is applied to all the systems described as they are equally prone to include repetitions.

6 Evaluation

We randomly selected 23 company stock names, and constructed a document collection for each containing all the news provided in the Yahoo! Finance news feed for that company in a period of two days (the time period was chosen randomly). The average length of a news collection is about 600 tokens. When selecting the company names, we took care of not picking those which have only a few news articles for that period of time. This resulted into 9.4 news articles per collection on average. From each of these, three human annotators independently selected up to ten sentences. All annotators had average to good understanding of the financial domain. The annotators were asked to choose the sentences which could best help them decide whether to buy, sell or retain stock for the company the following day and present them in the order of decreasing importance. The annotators compared their summaries of the first four collections and clarified the procedure before proceeding with the other ones. These four collections were then later used as a development set.

All summaries – manually as well as automatically generated – were cut to the first 250 words which made the summaries 10 words shorter on average. We evaluated the performance automatically in terms of ROUGE-2 (Lin & Hovy, 2003) using the parameters and following the methodology from the DUC events. The results are presented in Table 2. We also report the 95% confidence intervals in brackets. As in DUC, we used

METHOD	ROUGE-2
Otterbacher	0.255 (0.226 - 0.285)
Query Weights	0.289 (0.254 - 0.324)
Novelty Bias (simple)	**0.315** (0.287 - 0.342)
Novelty Bias	0.302 (0.277 - 0.329)
Manual	0.472 (0.415 - 0.531)

Table 2: Results of the four extraction methods and human annotators

jackknife for each *(query, summary)* pair and computed a macro-average to make human and automatic results comparable (Dang, 2005). The scores computed on summaries produced by humans are given in the bottom line (MANUAL) and serve as upper bound and also as an indicator for the inter-annotator agreement.

6.1 Discussion

From Table 2 follows that the modifications we applied to the baseline are sensible and indeed bring an improvement. QUERY WEIGHTS performs better than OTTERBACHER and is in turn outperformed by the algorithms biased to novel information (the two NOVELTY systems). The overlap between the confidence intervals of the baseline and the simple version of the novelty algorithm is minimal (0.002).

It is remarkable that the achieved improvement is due to a more balanced relatedness to the query ranking (9), as well as to the novelty bias reranking. The fact that the simpler novelty weighting formula (10) produced better results than the more elaborated one (11) requires a deeper analysis and a larger test set to explain the difference. Our conjecture so far is that the SIMPLE approach allows for a better combination of both novelty and relatedness to query. Since the more complex novelty ranking formula penalizes terms related to the query (Equation (11)), it favors a scenario where novelty is boosted in detriment of relatedness to query, which is not always realistic.

It is important to note that, compared with the baseline, we did not do any parameter tuning for λ and the inter-sentence similarity threshold. The improvement between the system of Otterbacher et al. (2005) and our best model is statistically significant.

6.2 System Combination

Recall from Section 5 that the motivation for promoting novel information came from the fact that sentences with background information about the company obtained very high scores: they were related but not novel. The sentences ranked by OTTERBACHER or QUERY WEIGHTS required a re-ranking to include related *and* novel sentences in the summary. We checked whether novelty re-ranking brings an improvement if added on top of a system which does not have a novelty bias (baseline or QUERY WEIGHTS) and compared it with the setting where we simply limit the novelty ranking to all the sentences related to the query (NOVELTY SIMPLE and NOVELTY). In the similarity graph, we left only edges between the first 30 sentences from the ranked list produced by one of the two algorithms described in Section 4 (OTTERBACHER or QUERY WEIGHTS). Then we ranked the sentences biased to novel information the same way as described in Section 5. The results are presented in Table 3. What we evaluate here is whether a combination of two methods performs better than the simple heuristics of discarding edges between sentences unrelated to the query.

METHOD	ROUGE-2
Otterbacher + Novelty simple	**0.280** (0.254 - 0.306)
Otterbacher + Novelty	**0.273** (0.245 - 0.301)
Query Weights + Novelty simple	0.275 (0.247 - 0.302)
Query Weights + Novelty	0.265 (0.242 - 0.289)

Table 3: Results of the combinations of the four methods

From the four possible combinations, there is an improvement over the baseline only (0.255 vs. 0.280 resp. 0.273). None of the combinations performs better than the simple novelty bias algorithm on a subset of edges. This experiment suggests that, at least in the scenario investigated here (short-term monitoring of publicly-traded companies), novelty is more important than relatedness to query. Hence, the simple novelty bias algorithm, which emphasizes novelty and incorporates relatedness to query only through a loose constraint ($rel(s|q) > 0$) performs better than complex models, which are more constrained by the relatedness to query.

7 Related Work

Summarization has been extensively investigated in recent years and to date there exists a multitude of very different systems. Here, we review those that come closest to ours in respect to the task and that concern extractive multi-document query-oriented summarization. We also mention some work on using textual news data for stock indices prediction which we are aware of.

Stock market prediction: Wüthrich et al. (1998) were among the first who introduced an automatic stock indices prediction system which relies on textual information only. The system generates weighted rules each of which returns the probability of the stock going up, down or remaining steady. The only information used in the rules is the presence or absence of certain keyphrases provided by a human expert who *"judged them to be influential factors potentially moving stock markets"*. In this approach, training data is required to measure the usefulness of the keyphrases for each of the three classes. More recently, Lerman et al. (2008) introduced a forecasting system for prediction markets that combines news analysis with a price trend analysis model. This approach was shown to be successful for the forecasting of public opinion about political candidates in such prediction markets. Our approach can be seen as a complement to both these approaches, necessary especially for financial markets where the news typically cover many events, only some related to the company of interest.

Unsupervized summarization systems extract sentences whose relevance can be inferred from the inter-sentence relations in the document collection. In (Radev et al., 2000), the centroid of the collection, i.e., the words with the highest TF*IDF, is considered and the sentences which contain more words from the centroid are extracted. Mihalcea & Tarau (2004) explore several methods developed for ranking documents in information retrieval for the single-document summarization task. Similarly, Erkan & Radev (2004) apply in-degree and PageRank to build a summary from a collection of related documents. They show that their method, called LexRank, achieves good results. In (Otterbacher et al., 2005; Erkan, 2006) the ranking function of LexRank is extended to become applicable to query-focused summarization. The rank of a sentence is determined not just by its relation to other sentences in the document collection but also by its relevance to the query. Relevance to the query is defined as the word-based similarity between query and sentence.

Query expansion has been used for improving information retrieval (IR) or question answering (QA) systems with mixed results. One of the problems is that the queries are expanded word by word, ignoring the context and as a result the extensions often become inadequate[7]. However, Riezler et al. (2007) take the entire query into account when adding new words by utilizing techniques used in statistical machine translation.

Query expansion for summarization has not yet been explored as extensively as in IR or QA. Nastase (2008) uses Wikipedia and WordNet for query expansion and proposes that a concept can be expanded by adding the text of all hyperlinks from the first paragraph of the Wikipedia article about this concept. The automatic evaluation demonstrates that extracting relevant concepts from Wikipedia leads to better performance compared with WordNet: both expansion systems outperform the no-expansion version in terms of the ROUGE score. Although this method proved helpful on the DUC data, it seems less appropriate for expanding company names. For small companies there are short articles with only a few links; the first paragraphs of the articles about larger companies often include interesting rather than relevant information. For example, the text preceding the contents box in the article about Apple Inc. (AAPL) states that *"Fortune magazine named Apple the most admired company in the United States"*[8]. The link to the article about the Fortune magazine can be hardly considered relevant for the expansion of AAPL. Wikipedia category information, which has been successfully used in some NLP tasks (Ponzetto & Strube, 2006, inter alia), is too general and does not help discriminate between two companies from the same sector.

Our work suggests that query expansion is needed for summarization in the financial domain. In addition to previous work, we also show that another key factor for success in this task is detecting and modeling the novelty of the target content.

[7]E.g., see the proceedings of TREC 9, TREC 10: `http://trec.nist.gov`.

[8]Checked on September 17, 2008.

8 Conclusions

In this paper we presented a multi-document company-oriented summarization algorithm which extracts sentences that are both relevant for the given organization and novel to the user. The system is expected to be useful in the context of stock market monitoring and forecasting, that is, to help the trader predict the move of the stock price for the given company. We presented a novel query expansion method which works particularly well in the context of company-oriented summarization. Our sentence ranking method is unsupervized and requires little parameter tuning. An automatic evaluation against a competitive baseline showed supportive results, indicating that the ranking algorithm is able to select relevant sentences and promote novel information at the same time.

In the future, we plan to experiment with positional features which have proven useful for generic summarization. We also plan to test the system extrinsically. For example, it would be of interest to see if a classifier may predict the move of stock prices based on a set of features extracted from company-oriented summaries.

Acknowledgments: We would like to thank the anonymous reviewers for their helpful feedback.

References

Allan, James, Courtney Wade & Alvaro Bolivar (2003). Retrieval and novelty detection at the sentence level. In *Proceedings of the 26th Annual International ACM SIGIR Conference on Research and Development in Information Retrieval* Toronto, On., Canada, 28 July – 1 August 2003, pp. 314–321.

Atserias, Jordi, Hugo Zaragoza, Massimiliano Ciaramita & Giuseppe Attardi (2008). Semantically annotated snapshot of the English Wikipedia. In *Proceedings of the 6th International Conference on Language Resources and Evaluation,* Marrakech, Morocco, 26 May – 1 June 2008.

Brin, Sergey & Lawrence Page (1998). The anatomy of a large-scale hypertextual web search engine. *Computer Networks and ISDN Systems*, 30(1–7):107–117.

Ciaramita, Massimiliano & Yasemin Altun (2006). Broad-coverage sense disambiguation and information extraction with a supersense sequence tagger. In *Proceedings of the 2006 Conference on Empirical Methods in Natural Language Processing,* Sydney, Australia, 22–23 July 2006, pp. 594–602.

Dang, Hoa Trang (2005). Overview of DUC 2005. In *Proceedings of the 2005 Document Understanding Conference held at the Human Language Technology Conference and Conference on Empirical Methods in Natural Language Processing,* Vancouver, B.C., Canada, 9–10 October 2005.

Erkan, Güneş (2006). Using biased random walks for focused summarization. In *Proceedings of the 2006 Document Understanding Conference held at the Human Language Technology Conference of the North American Chapter of the Association for Computational Linguistics,,* New York, N.Y., 8–9 June 2006.

Erkan, Güneş & Dragomir R. Radev (2004). LexRank: Graph-based lexical centrality as salience in text summarization. *Journal of Artificial Intelligence Research,* 22:457–479.

Lerman, Kevin, Ari Gilder, Mark Dredze & Fernando Pereira (2008). Reading the markets: Forecasting public opinion of political candidates by news analysis. In *Proceedings of the 22st International Conference on Computational Linguistics,* Manchester, UK, 18–22 August 2008, pp. 473–480.

Lin, Chin-Yew & Eduard H. Hovy (2003). Automatic evaluation of summaries using N-gram co-occurrence statistics. In *Proceedings of the Human Language Technology Conference of the North American Chapter of the Association for Computational Linguistics,* Edmonton, Alberta, Canada, 27 May –1 June 2003, pp. 150–157.

Mihalcea, Rada & Paul Tarau (2004). Textrank: Bringing order into texts. In *Proceedings of the 2004 Conference on Empirical Methods in Natural Language Processing,* Barcelona, Spain, 25–26 July 2004, pp. 404–411.

Nastase, Vivi (2008). Topic-driven multi-document summarization with encyclopedic knowledge and activation spreading. In *Proceedings of the 2008 Conference on Empirical Methods in Natural Language Processing,* Honolulu, Hawaii, 25–27 October 2008. To appear.

Nelken, Rani & Stuart M. Shieber (2006). Towards robust context-sensitive sentence alignment for monolingual corpora. In *Proceedings of the 11th Conference of the European Chapter of the Association for Computational Linguistics,* Trento, Italy, 3–7 April 2006, pp. 161–168.

Otterbacher, Jahna, Güneş Erkan & Dragomir Radev (2005). Using random walks for question-focused sentence retrieval. In *Proceedings of the Human Language Technology Conference and the 2005 Conference on Empirical Methods in Natural Language Processing,* Vancouver, B.C., Canada, 6–8 October 2005, pp. 915–922.

Ponzetto, Simone Paolo & Michael Strube (2006). Exploiting semantic role labeling, WordNet and Wikipedia for coreference resolution. In *Proceedings of the Human Language Technology Conference of the North American Chapter of the Association for Computational Linguistics,* New York, N.Y., 4–9 June 2006, pp. 192–199.

Radev, Dragomir R., Hongyan Jing & Malgorzata Budzikowska (2000). Centroid-based summarization of mutliple documents: Sentence extraction, utility-based evaluation, and user studies. In *Proceedings of the Workshop on Automatic Summarization at ANLP/NAACL 2000,* Seattle, Wash., 30 April 2000, pp. 21–30.

Riezler, Stefan, Alexander Vasserman, Ioannis Tsochantaridis, Vibhu Mittal & Yi Liu (2007). Statistical machine translation for query expansion in answer retrieval. In *Proceedings of the 45th Annual Meeting of the Association for Computational Linguistics,* Prague, Czech Republic, 23–30 June 2007, pp. 464–471.

Wüthrich, B, D. Permunetilleke, S. Leung, V. Cho, J. Zhang & W. Lam (1998). Daily prediction of major stock indices from textual WWW data. In *In Proceedings of the 4th International Conference on Knowledge Discovery and Data Mining - KDD-98,* pp. 364–368.

Reconstructing false start errors in spontaneous speech text

Erin Fitzgerald
Johns Hopkins University
Baltimore, MD, USA
erinf@jhu.edu

Keith Hall
Google, Inc.
Zurich, Switzerland
kbhall@google.com

Frederick Jelinek
Johns Hopkins University
Baltimore, MD, USA
jelinek@jhu.edu

Abstract

This paper presents a conditional random field-based approach for identifying speaker-produced disfluencies (i.e. if and where they occur) in spontaneous speech transcripts. We emphasize false start regions, which are often missed in current disfluency identification approaches as they lack lexical or structural similarity to the speech immediately following. We find that combining lexical, syntactic, and language model-related features with the output of a state-of-the-art disfluency identification system improves overall word-level identification of these and other errors. Improvements are reinforced under a stricter evaluation metric requiring exact matches between cleaned sentences annotator-produced reconstructions, and altogether show promise for general reconstruction efforts.

1 Introduction

The output of an automatic speech recognition (ASR) system is often not what is required for subsequent processing, in part because speakers themselves often make mistakes (e.g. stuttering, self-correcting, or using filler words). A cleaner speech transcript would allow for more accurate language processing as needed for natural language processing tasks such as machine translation and conversation summarization which often assume a grammatical sentence as input.

A system would accomplish reconstruction of its spontaneous speech input if its output were to represent, in flawless, fluent, and content-preserving text, the message that the speaker intended to convey. Such a system could also be applied not only to spontaneous English speech, but to correct common mistakes made by non-native speakers (Lee and Seneff, 2006), and possibly extended to non-English speaker errors.

A key motivation for this work is the hope that a cleaner, reconstructed speech transcript will allow for simpler and more accurate human and natural language processing, as needed for applications like machine translation, question answering, text summarization, and paraphrasing which often assume a grammatical sentence as input. This benefit has been directly demonstrated for statistical machine translation (SMT). Rao et al. (2007) gave evidence that simple disfluency removal from transcripts can improve BLEU (a standard SMT evaluation metric) up to 8% for sentences with disfluencies. The presence of disfluencies were found to hurt SMT in two ways: making utterances longer without adding semantic content (and sometimes adding false content) and exacerbating the data mismatch between the spontaneous input and the clean text training data.

While full speech reconstruction would likely require a range of string transformations and potentially deep syntactic and semantic analysis of the errorful text (Fitzgerald, 2009), in this work we will first attempt to resolve less complex errors, corrected by deletion alone, in a given manually-transcribed utterance.

We build on efforts from (Johnson et al., 2004), aiming to improve overall recall – especially of false start or non-copy errors – while concurrently maintaining or improving precision.

1.1 Error classes in spontaneous speech

Common simple disfluencies in sentence-like utterances (SUs) include *filler words* (i.e. "um", "ah", and discourse markers like "you know"), as well as speaker edits consisting of a *reparandum*, an *interruption point (IP)*, an optional *interregnum* (like "I mean"), and a *repair* region (Shriberg, 1994), as seen in Figure 1.

Proceedings of the 12th Conference of the European Chapter of the ACL, pages 255–263,
Athens, Greece, 30 March – 3 April 2009.

$$\underbrace{[\text{that's}]}_{\text{reparandum}} \overset{\text{IP}}{\widehat{+}} \underbrace{\{\text{uh}\}}_{\text{interregnum}} \underbrace{\text{that's}}_{\text{repair}} \text{ a relief}$$

Figure 1: Typical edit region structure. In these and other examples, reparandum regions are in brackets ('[', ']'), interregna are in braces ('{', '}'), and interruption points are marked by '+'.

These reparanda, or *edit regions*, can be classified into three main groups:

1. In a **repetition** (above), the repair phrase is approximately identical to the reparandum.

2. In a **revision**, the repair phrase alters reparandum words to correct the previously stated thought.

   EX1: but [when he] + {i mean} when she put it that way

   EX2: it helps people [that are going to quit] + that would be quitting anyway

3. In a **restart fragment** (also called a false start), an utterance is aborted and then restarted with a new train of thought.

   EX3: and [i think he's] + he tells me he's glad he has one of those

   EX4: [amazon was incorporated by] {uh} well i only knew two people there

In *simple cleanup* (a precursor to full speech reconstruction), all detected filler words are deleted, and the reparanda and interregna are deleted while the repair region is left intact. This is a strong initial step for speech reconstruction, though more complex and less deterministic changes are often required for generating fluent and grammatical speech text.

In some cases, such as the repetitions mentioned above, simple cleanup is adequate for reconstruction. However, simply deleting the identified reparandum regions is not always optimal. We would like to consider preserving these fragments (for false starts in particular) if

1. the fragment contains content words, and

2. its information content is distinct from that in surrounding utterances.

In the first restart fragment example (EX3 in Section 1.1), the reparandum introduces no new active verbs or new content, and thus can be safely deleted. The second example (EX4) however demonstrates a case when the reparandum may be considered to have unique and preservable content of its own. Future work should address how to most appropriately reconstruct speech in this and similar cases; this initial work will for risk information loss as we identify and delete these reparandum regions.

1.2 Related Work

Stochastic approaches for simple disfluency detection use features such as lexical form, acoustic cues, and rule-based knowledge. Most state-of-the-art methods for edit region detection such as (Johnson and Charniak, 2004; Zhang and Weng, 2005; Liu et al., 2004; Honal and Schultz, 2005) model speech disfluencies as a noisy channel model. In a noisy channel model we assume that an unknown but fluent string F has passed through a disfluency-adding channel to produce the observed disfluent string D, and we then aim to recover the most likely input string $\hat{F}$, defined as

$$\begin{aligned} \hat{F} &= \text{argmax}_F P(F|D) \\ &= \text{argmax}_F P(D|F)P(F) \end{aligned}$$

where $P(F)$ represents a language model defining a probability distribution over fluent "source" strings F, and $P(D|F)$ is the channel model defining a conditional probability distribution of observed sentences D which may contain the types of construction errors described in the previous subsection. The final output is a word-level tagging of the error condition of each word in the sequence, as seen in line 2 of Figure 2.

The Johnson and Charniak (2004) approach, referred to in this document as JC04, combines the noisy channel paradigm with a tree-adjoining grammar (TAG) to capture approximately repeated elements. The TAG approach models the crossed word dependencies observed when the reparandum incorporates the same or very similar words in roughly the same word order, which JC04 refer to as a *rough copy*. Our version of this system does not use external features such as prosodic classes, as they use in Johnson et al. (2004), but otherwise appears to produce comparable results to those reported.

While much progress has been made in simple disfluency detection in the last decade, even top-performing systems continue to be ineffective at identifying words in reparanda. To better understand these problems and identify areas

Label	% of words	Precision	Recall	F-score
Fillers	5.6%	64%	59%	61%
Edit (reparandum)	7.8%	85%	68%	75%

Table 1: Disfluency detection performance on the SSR test subcorpus using JC04 system.

Label	% of edits	Recall
Rough copy (RC) edits	58.8%	84.8%
Non-copy (NC) edits	41.2%	43.2%
Total edits	100.0%	67.6%

Table 2: Deeper analysis of edit detection performance on the SSR test subcorpus using JC04 system.

```
1 he  that  's  uh that 's a relief
2 E    E     E  FL  -   - -    -
3 NC   RC   RC  FL  -   - -    -
```

Figure 2: Example of word class and refined word class labels, where - denotes a non-error, FL denotes a filler, E generally denotes reparanda, and RC and NC indicate rough copy and non-copy speaker errors, respectively.

for improvement, we used the top-performing[1] JC04 noisy channel TAG edit detector to produce edit detection analyses on the test segment of the Spontaneous Speech Reconstruction (SSR) corpus (Fitzgerald and Jelinek, 2008). Table 1 demonstrates the performance of this system for detecting filled pause fillers, discourse marker fillers, and edit words. The results of a more granular analysis compared to a hand-refined reference (as shown in line 3 of Figure 2) are shown in Table 2. The reader will recall that precision P is defined as $P = \frac{|\text{correct}|}{|\text{correct}|+|\text{false}|}$ and recall $R = \frac{|\text{correct}|}{|\text{correct}|+|\text{miss}|}$. We denote the harmonic mean of P and R as F-score F and calculate it $F = \frac{2}{1/P+1/R}$.

As expected given the assumptions of the TAG approach, JC04 identifies repetitions and most revisions in the SSR data, but less successfully labels false starts and other speaker self-interruptions which do not have a cross-serial correlations. These non-copy errors (with a recall of only 43.2%), are hurting the overall edit detection recall score. Precision (and thus F-score) cannot be calculated for the experiment in Table 2; since the JC04 does not explicitly label edits as rough copies or non-copies, we have no way of knowing whether words falsely labeled as edits would have been considered as false RCs or false NCs. This will unfortunately hinder us from using JC04 as a direct baseline comparison in our work targeting false starts; however, we consider these results to be further motivation for the work.

Surveying these results, we conclude that there is still much room for improvement in the field of simple disfluency identification, especially the cases of detecting non-copy reparandum and learning how and where to implement non-deletion reconstruction changes.

2 Approach

2.1 Data

We conducted our experiments on the recently released Spontaneous Speech Reconstruction (SSR) corpus (Fitzgerald and Jelinek, 2008), a medium-sized set of disfluency annotations atop Fisher conversational telephone speech (CTS) data (Cieri et al., 2004). Advantages of the SSR data include

- aligned parallel original and cleaned sentences
- several levels of error annotations, allowing for a coarse-to-fine reconstruction approach
- multiple annotations per sentence reflecting the occasional ambiguity of corrections

As reconstructions are sometimes non-deterministic (illustrated in EX6 in Section 1.1), the SSR provides two manual reconstructions for each utterance in the data. We use these dual annotations to learn complementary approaches in training and to allow for more accurate evaluation.

The SSR corpus does not explicitly label all reparandum-like regions, as defined in Section 1.1, but only those which annotators selected to delete.

[1] As determined in the RT04 EARS Metadata Extraction Task

Thus, for these experiments we must implicitly attempt to replicate annotator decisions regarding whether or not to delete reparandum regions when labeling them as such. Fortunately, we expect this to have a negligible effect here as we will emphasize utterances which do not require more complex reconstructions in this work.

The Spontaneous Speech Reconstruction corpus is partitioned into three subcorpora: 17,162 training sentences (119,693 words), 2,191 sentences (14,861 words) in the development set, and 2,288 sentences (15,382 words) in the test set. Approximately 17% of the total utterances contain a reparandum-type error.

The output of the JC04 model ((Johnson and Charniak, 2004) is included as a feature and used as an approximate baseline in the following experiments. The training of the TAG model within this system requires a very specific data format, so this system is trained not with SSR but with Switchboard (SWBD) (Godfrey et al., 1992) data as described in (Johnson and Charniak, 2004). Key differences in these corpora, besides the form of their annotations, include:

- SSR aims to correct speech output, while SWBD edit annotation aims to identify reparandum structures specifically. Thus, as mentioned, SSR only marks those reparanda which annotators believe must be deleted to generate a grammatical and content-preserving reconstruction.
- SSR considers some phenomena such as leading conjunctions ("and i did" → "i did") to be fillers, while SWBD does not.
- SSR includes more complex error identification and correction, though these effects should be negligible in the experimental setup presented herein.

While we hope to adapt the trained JC04 model to SSR data in the future, for now these difference in task, evaluation, and training data will prevent direct comparison between JC04 and our results.

2.2 Conditional random fields

Conditional random fields (Lafferty et al., 2001), or CRFs, are undirected graphical models whose prediction of a hidden variable sequence Y is globally conditioned on a given observation sequence X, as shown in Figure 3. Each observed

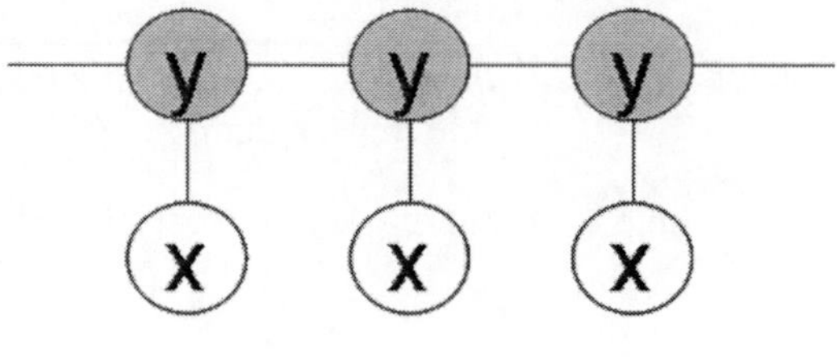

Figure 3: Illustration of a conditional random field. For this work, **x** represents observable inputs for each word as described in Section 3.1 and **y** represents the error class of each word (Section 3.2).

state $x_i \in X$ is composed of the corresponding word w_i and a set of additional features F_i, detailed in Section 3.1.

The conditional probability of this model can be represented as

$$p_\Lambda(Y|X) = \frac{1}{Z_\lambda(X)} \exp(\sum_k \lambda_k F_k(X,Y)) \quad (1)$$

where $Z_\lambda(X)$ is a global normalization factor and $\Lambda = (\lambda_1 \ldots \lambda_K)$ are model parameters related to each feature function $F_k(X,Y)$.

CRFs have been widely applied to tasks in natural language processing, especially those involving tagging words with labels such as part-of-speech tagging and shallow parsing (Sha and Pereira, 2003), as well as sentence boundary detection (Liu et al., 2005; Liu et al., 2004). These models have the advantage that they model sequential context (like hidden Markov models (HMMs)) but are discriminative rather than generative and have a less restricted feature set. Additionally, as compared to HMMs, CRFs offer conditional (versus joint) likelihood, and directly maximizes posterior label probabilities $P(E|O)$.

We used the GRMM package (Sutton, 2006) to implement our CRF models, each using a zero-mean Gaussian prior to reduce over-fitting our model. No feature reduction is employed, except where indicated.

3 Word-Level ID Experiments

3.1 Feature functions

We aim to train our CRF model with sets of features with orthogonal analyses of the errorful text, integrating knowledge from multiple sources. While we anticipate that repetitions and other rough copies will be identified primarily by lexical and local context features, this will not necessarily help for false starts with little or no lexical overlap between reparandum and repair. To catch these errors, we add both language model features (trained with the SRILM toolkit (Stolcke, 2002) on SWBD data with `EDITED` reparandum nodes removed), and syntactic features to our model. We also included the output of the JC04 system – which had generally high precision on the SSR data – in the hopes of building on these results.

Altogether, the following features F were extracted for each observation x_i.

- **Lexical features**, including
  - the lexical item and part-of-speech (POS) for tokens t_i and t_{i+1},
  - distance from previous token to the next matching word/POS,
  - whether previous token is partial word and the distance to the next word with same start, and
  - the token's (normalized) position within the sentence.
- **JC04-edit**: whether previous, next, or current word is identified by the JC04 system as an edit and/or a filler (fillers are classified as described in (Johnson et al., 2004)).
- **Language model features**: the unigram log probability of the next word (or POS) token $p(t)$, the token log probability conditioned on its multi-token history h $(p(t|h))$[2], and the log ratio of the two $(log\frac{p(t|h)}{p(t)})$ to serve as an approximation for mutual information between the token and its history, as defined below.

$$I(t;h) = \sum_{h,t} p(h,t) \log \frac{p(h,t)}{p(h)p(t)} = \sum_{h,t} p(h,t) \left[\log \frac{p(t|h)}{p(t)} \right]$$

  This aims to capture unexpected n-grams produced by the juxtaposition of the reparandum and the repair. The mutual information feature aims to identify when common words are seen in uncommon context (or, alternatively, penalize rare n-grams normalized for rare words).

- **Non-terminal (NT) ancestors**: Given an automatically produced parse of the utterance (using the Charniak (1999) parser trained on Switchboard (SWBD) (Godfrey et al., 1992) CTS data), we determined for each word all NT phrases just completed (if any), all NT phrases about to start to its right (if any), and all NT constituents for which the word is included.

  (Ferreira and Bailey, 2004) and others have found that false starts and repeats tend to end at certain points of phrases, which we also found to be generally true for the annotated data.

Note that the syntactic and POS features we used are extracted from the output of an automatic parser. While we do not expect the parser to always be accurate, especially when parsing errorful text, we hope that the parser will at least be consistent in the types of structures it assigns to particular error phenomena. We use these features in the hope of taking advantage of that consistency.

3.2 Experimental setup

In these experiments, we attempt to label the following word-boundary classes as annotated in SSR corpus:

- fillers (`FL`), including filled pauses and discourse markers (~5.6% of words)
- rough copy (`RC`) edit (reparandum incorporates the same or very similar words in roughly the same word order, including repetitions and some revisions) (~4.6% of words)
- non-copy (`NC`) edit (a speaker error where the reparandum has no lexical or structural relationship to the repair region following, as seen in restart fragments and some revisions) (~3.2% of words)

Other labels annotated in the SSR corpus (such as insertions and word reorderings), have been ignored for these error tagging experiments.

We approach our training of CRFs in several ways, detailed in Table 3. In half of our experiments (#1, 3, and 4), we trained a single model to predict all three annotated classes (as defined at the beginning of Section 3.3), and in the other half (#2, 5, and 6), we trained the model to predict `NC`s only, `NC`s and `FL`s, `RC`s only, or `RC`s and `FL`s (as `FL`s often serve as interregnum, we predict that these will be a valuable cue for other edits).

[2] In our model, word historys h encompassed the previous two words (a 3-gram model) and POS history encompassed the previous four POS labels (a 5-gram model)

Setup	Train data	Test data	Classes trained per model
#1	Full train	Full test	FL + RC + NC
#2	Full train	Full test	{RC,NC}, FL+{RC,NC}
#3	Errorful SUs	Errorful SUs	FL + RC + NC
#4	Errorful SUs	Full test	FL + RC + NC
#5	Errorful SUs	Errorful SUs	{RC,NC}, FL+{RC,NC}
#6	Errorful SUs	Full test	{RC,NC}, FL+{RC,NC}

Table 3: Overview of experimental setups for word-level error predictions.

We varied the subcorpus utterances used in training. In some experiments (#1 and 2) we trained with the entire training set[3], including sentences without speaker errors, and in others (#3-6) we trained only on those sentences containing the relevant deletion errors (and no additionally complex errors) to produce a densely errorful training set. Likewise, in some experiments we produced output only for those test sentences which we knew to contain simple errors (#3 and 5). This was meant to emulate the ideal condition where we could perfectly predict which sentences contain errors before identifying where exactly those errors occurred.

The JC04-edit feature was included to help us build on previous efforts for error classification. To confirm that the model is not simply replicating these results and is indeed learning on its own with the other features detailed, we also trained models without this JC04-edit feature.

3.3 Evaluation of word-level experiments

3.3.1 Word class evaluation

We first evaluate edit detection accuracy on a per-word basis. To evaluate our progress identifying word-level error classes, we calculate precision, recall and F-scores for each labeled class c in each experimental scenario. As usual, these metrics are calculated as ratios of correct, false, and missed predictions. However, to take advantage of the double reconstruction annotations provided in SSR (and more importantly, in recognition of the occasional ambiguities of reconstruction) we modified these calculations slightly as shown below.

$$\begin{aligned} \text{corr}(c) &= \sum_{i:c_{w_i}=c} \delta(c_{w_i} = c_{g_1,i} \text{ or } c_{w_i} = c_{g_2,i}) \\ \text{false}(c) &= \sum_{i:c_{w_i}=c} \delta(c_{w_i} \neq c_{g_1,i} \text{ and } c_{w_i} \neq c_{g_2,i}) \\ \text{miss}(c) &= \sum_{i:c_{g_1,i}=c} \delta(c_{w_i} \neq c_{g_1,i}) \end{aligned}$$

where c_{w_i} is the hypothesized class for w_i and $c_{g_1,i}$ and $c_{g_2,i}$ are the two reference classes.

Setup	Class labeled	FL	RC	NC
Train and test on all SUs in the subcorpus				
#1	FL+RC+NC	**71.0**	80.3	47.4
#2	NC	-	-	42.5
#2	NC+FL	70.8	-	**47.5**
#2	RC	-	84.2	-
#2	RC+FL	67.8	**84.7**	-
Train and test on errorful SUs				
#3	FL+RC+NC	91.6	84.1	52.2
#4	FL+RC+NC	44.1	69.3	31.6
#5	NC	-	-	73.8
#6	*w/ full test*	-	-	39.2
#5	NC+FL	90.7	-	69.8
#6	*w/ full test*	50.1	-	38.5
#5	RC	-	88.7	-
#6	*w/ full test*	-	75.0	-
#5	RC+FL	92.3	87.4	-
#6	*w/ full test*	62.3	73.9	-

Table 4: Word-level error prediction F_1-score results: Data variation. The first column identifies which data setup was used for each experiment (Table 3). The highest performing result for each class in the first set of experiments has been highlighted.

Analysis: Experimental results can be seen in Tables 4 and 5. Table 4 shows the impact of

[3] Using both annotated SSR reference reconstructions for each utterance

Features	FL	RC	NC
JC04 only	56.6	69.9-81.9	1.6-21.0
lexical only	56.5	72.7	33.4
LM only	0.0	15.0	0.0
NT bounds only	44.1	35.9	11.5
All but JC04	58.5	79.3	33.1
All but lexical	66.9	76.0	19.6
All but LM	67.9	83.1	41.0
All but NT bounds	61.8	79.4	33.6
All	**71.0**	**80.3**	**47.4**

Table 5: Word-level error prediction F-score results: Feature variation. All models were trained with experimental setup #1 and with the set of features identified.

training models for individual features and of constraining training data to contain only those utterances known to contain errors. It also demonstrates the potential impact on error classification after prefiltering test data to those SUs with errors. Table 5 demonstrates the contribution of each group of features to our CRF models.

Our results demonstrate the impact of varying our training data and the number of label classes trained for. We see in Table 4 from setup #5 experiments that training and testing on error-containing utterances led to a dramatic improvement in F_1-score. On the other hand, our results for experiments using setup #6 (where training data was filtered to contain errorful data but test data was fully preserved) are consistently worse than those of either setup #2 (where both train and test data was untouched) or setup #5 (where both train and test data were prefiltered). The output appears to suffer from sample bias, as the prior of an error occurring in training is much higher than in testing. This demonstrates that a densely errorful training set alone cannot improve our results when testing data conditions do not match training data conditions. However, efforts to identify errorful sentences before determining where errors occur in those sentences may be worthwhile in preventing false positives in error-less utterances.

We next consider the impact of the four feature groups on our prediction results. The CRF model appears competitive even without the advantage of building on JC04 results, as seen in Table 5[4]. Interestingly and encouragingly, the NT bounds features which indicate the linguistic phrase structures beginning and ending at each word according to an automatic parse were also found to be highly contribututive for both fillers and non-copy identification. We believe that further pursuit of syntactic features, especially those which can take advantage of the context-free weakness of statistical parsers like (Charniak, 1999) will be promising in future research.

It was unexpected that NC classification would be so sensitive to the loss of lexical features while RC labeling was generally resilient to the dropping of any feature group. We hypothesize that for rough copies, the information lost from the removal of the lexical items might have been compensated for by the JC04 features as JC04 performed most strongly on this error type. This should be further investigated in the future.

3.3.2 Strict evaluation: SU matching

Depending on the downstream task of speech reconstruction, it could be imperative not only to identify many of the errors in a given spoken utterance, but indeed to identify *all* errors (and only those errors), yielding the precise cleaned sentence that a human annotator might provide.

In these experiments we apply *simple cleanup* (as described in Section 1.1) to both JC04 output and the predicted output for each experimental setup in Table 3, deleting words when their right boundary class is a filled pause, rough copy or non-copy.

Taking advantage of the dual annotations for each sentence in the SSR corpus, we can report both single-reference and double-reference evaluation. Thus, we judge that if a hypothesized cleaned sentence exactly matches *either* reference sentence cleaned in the same manner, we count the cleaned utterance as correct and otherwise assign no credit.

Analysis: We see the outcome of this set of experiments in Table 6. While the unfiltered test sets of JC04-1, setup #1 and setup #2 appear to have much higher sentence-level cleanup accuracy than the other experiments, we recall that this is natural also due to the fact that the majority of these sentences should not be cleaned at all, besides

[4] JC04 results are shown as a range for the reasons given in Section 1.2: since JC04 does not on its own predict whether an "edit" is a rough copy or non-copy, it is impossible to calculate precision and thus F_1 score precisely. Instead, here we show the resultant F_1 for the best case and worst case precision range.

Setup	Classes deleted	# SUs	# SUs which match gold	% accuracy
Baseline	only filled pauses	2288	1800	78.7%
JC04-1	E+FL	2288	1858	81.2%
CRF-#1	RC, NC, and FL	2288	1922	84.0%
CRF-#2	$\bigcup$ {RC,NC}	2288	1901	83.1%
Baseline	only filled pauses	281	5	1.8%
JC04-2	E+FL	281	126	44.8%
CRF-#3	RC, NC, and FL	281	156	55.5%
CRF-#5	$\bigcup$ {RC,NC}	281	132	47.0%

Table 6: Word-level error predictions: exact SU match results. JC04-2 was run only on test sentences known to contain some error to match the conditions of Setup #3 and #5 (from Table 3). For the baselines, we delete only filled pause filler words like "eh" and "um".

occasional minor filled pause deletions. Looking specifically on cleanup results for sentences known to contain at least one error, we see, once again, that our system outperforms our baseline JC04 system at this task.

4 Discussion

Our first goal in this work was to focus on an area of disfluency detection currently weak in other state-of-the-art speaker error detection systems – false starts – while producing comparable classification on repetition and revision speaker errors. Secondly, we attempted to quantify how far deleting identified edits (both RC and NC) and filled pauses could bring us to full reconstruction of these sentences.

We've shown in Section 3 that by training and testing on data prefiltered to include only utterances with errors, we can dramatically improve our results, not only by improving identification of errors but presumably by reducing the risk of falsely predicting errors. We would like to further investigate to understand how well we can automatically identify errorful spoken utterances in a corpus.

5 Future Work

This work has shown both achievable and demonstrably feasible improvements in the area of identifying and cleaning simple speaker errors. We believe that improved sentence-level identification of errorful utterances will help to improve our word-level error identification and overall reconstruction accuracy; we will continue to research these areas in the future. We intend to build on these efforts, adding prosodic and other features to our CRF and maximum entropy models,

In addition, as we improve the word-level classification of rough copies and non-copies, we will begin to move forward to better identify more complex speaker errors such as missing arguments, misordered or redundant phrases. We will also work to apply these results directly to the output of a speech recognition system instead of to transcripts alone.

Acknowledgments

The authors thank our anonymous reviewers for their valuable comments. Support for this work was provided by NSF PIRE Grant No. OISE-0530118. Any opinions, findings, conclusions, or recommendations expressed in this material are those of the authors and do not necessarily reflect the views of the supporting agency.

References

J. Kathryn Bock. 1982. Toward a cognitive psychology of syntax: Information processing contributions to sentence formulation. *Psychological Review*, 89(1):1–47, January.

Eugene Charniak. 1999. A maximum-entropy-inspired parser. In *Meeting of the North American Association for Computational Linguistics*.

Christopher Cieri, Stephanie Strassel, Mohamed Maamouri, Shudong Huang, James Fiumara, David Graff, Kevin Walker, and Mark Liberman. 2004. Linguistic resource creation and distribution for EARS. In *Rich Transcription Fall Workshop*.

Fernanda Ferreira and Karl G. D. Bailey. 2004. Disfluencies and human language comprehension. *Trends in Cognitive Science*, 8(5):231–237, May.

Erin Fitzgerald and Frederick Jelinek. 2008. Linguistic resources for reconstructing spontaneous speech text. In *Proceedings of the Language Resources and Evaluation Conference*, May.

Erin Fitzgerald. 2009. *Reconstructing Spontaneous Speech*. Ph.D. thesis, The Johns Hopkins University.

John J. Godfrey, Edward C. Holliman, and Jane McDaniel. 1992. SWITCHBOARD: Telephone speech corpus for research and development. In *Proceedings of the IEEE International Conference on Acoustics, Speech, and Signal Processing*, pages 517–520, San Francisco.

Matthias Honal and Tanja Schultz. 2005. Automatic disfluency removal on recognized spontaneous speech – rapid adaptation to speaker-dependent disfluenices. In *Proceedings of the IEEE International Conference on Acoustics, Speech, and Signal Processing*.

Mark Johnson and Eugene Charniak. 2004. A TAG-based noisy channel model of speech repairs. In *Proceedings of the Annual Meeting of the Association for Computational Linguistics*.

Mark Johnson, Eugene Charniak, and Matthew Lease. 2004. An improved model for recognizing disfluencies in conversational speech. In *Rich Transcription Fall Workshop*.

John Lafferty, Andrew McCallum, and Fernando Pereira. 2001. Conditional random fields: Probabilistic models for segmenting and labeling sequence data. In *Proc. 18th International Conf. on Machine Learning*, pages 282–289. Morgan Kaufmann, San Francisco, CA.

John Lee and Stephanie Seneff. 2006. Automatic grammar correction for second-language learners. In *Proceedings of the International Conference on Spoken Language Processing*.

Yang Liu, Elizabeth Shriberg, Andreas Stolcke, Barbara Peskin, and Mary Harper. 2004. The ICSI/UW RT04 structural metadata extraction system. In *Rich Transcription Fall Workshop*.

Yang Liu, Andreas Stolcke, Elizabeth Shriberg, and Mary Harper. 2005. Using conditional random fields for sentence boundary detection in speech. In *Proceedings of the Annual Meeting of the Association for Computational Linguistics*, pages 451–458, Ann Arbor, MI.

Sharath Rao, Ian Lane, and Tanja Schultz. 2007. Improving spoken language translation by automatic disfluency removal: Evidence from conversational speech transcripts. In *Machine Translation Summit XI*, Copenhagen, Denmark, October.

Fei Sha and Fernando Pereira. 2003. Shallow parsing with conditional random fields. In *HLT-NAACL*.

Elizabeth Shriberg. 1994. *Preliminaries to a Theory of Speech Disfluencies*. Ph.D. thesis, University of California, Berkeley.

Andreas Stolcke. 2002. SRILM - an extensible language modeling toolkit. In *Proceedings of the IEEE International Conference on Acoustics, Speech, and Signal Processing*, Denver, CO, September.

Charles Sutton. 2006. GRMM: A graphical models toolkit. http://mallet.cs.umass.edu.

Qi Zhang and Fuliang Weng. 2005. Exploring features for identifying edited regions in disfluent sentences. In *Proceedings of the International Workshop on Parsing Techniques*, pages 179–185.

TBL-Improved Non-Deterministic Segmentation and POS Tagging for a Chinese Parser

Martin Forst & Ji Fang
Intelligent Systems Laboratory
Palo Alto Research Center
Palo Alto, CA 94304, USA
{mforst | fang}@parc.com

Abstract

Although a lot of progress has been made recently in word segmentation and POS tagging for Chinese, the output of current state-of-the-art systems is too inaccurate to allow for syntactic analysis based on it. We present an experiment in improving the output of an off-the-shelf module that performs segmentation and tagging, the tokenizer-tagger from Beijing University (PKU). Our approach is based on transformation-based learning (TBL). Unlike in other TBL-based approaches to the problem, however, both obligatory and optional transformation rules are learned, so that the final system can output multiple segmentation and POS tagging analyses for a given input. By allowing for a small amount of ambiguity in the output of the tokenizer-tagger, we achieve a very considerable improvement in accuracy. Compared to the PKU tokenizer-tagger, we improve segmentation F-score from 94.18% to 96.74%, tagged word F-score from 84.63% to 92.44%, segmented sentence accuracy from 47.15% to 65.06% and tagged sentence accuracy from 14.07% to 31.47%.

1 Introduction

Word segmentation and tagging are the necessary initial steps for almost any language processing system, and Chinese parsers are no exception. However, automatic Chinese word segmentation and tagging has been recognized as a very difficult task (Sproat and Emerson, 2003), for the following reasons:

First, Chinese text provides few cues for word boundaries (Xia, 2000; Wu, 2003) and part-of-speech (POS) information. With the exception of punctuation marks, Chinese does not have word delimiters such as the whitespace used in English text, and unlike other languages without whitespaces such as Japanese, Chinese lacks morphological inflections that could provide cues for word boundaries and POS information. In fact, the lack of word boundary marks and morphological inflection contributes not only to mistakes in machine processing of Chinese; it has also been identified as a factor for parsing miscues in Chinese children's reading behavior (Chang et al., 1992).

Second, in addition to the two problems described above, segmentation and tagging also suffer from the fact that the notion of a word is very unclear in Chinese (Xu, 1997; Packard, 2000; Hsu, 2002). While the word is an intuitive and salient notion in English, it is by no means a clear notion in Chinese. Instead, for historical reasons, the intuitive and clear notion in Chinese language and culture is the character rather than the word. Classical Chinese is in general monosyllabic, with each syllable corresponding to an independent morpheme that can be visually rendered with a written character. In other words, characters did represent the basic syntactic unit in Classical Chinese, and thus became the sociologically intuitive notion. However, although colloquial Chinese quickly evolved throughout Chinese history to be disyllabic or multi-syllabic, monosyllabic Classical Chinese has been considered more elegant and proper and was commonly used in written text until the early 20th century in China. Even in Modern Chinese written text, Classical Chinese elements are not rare. Consequently, even if a morpheme represented by a character is no

Proceedings of the 12th Conference of the European Chapter of the ACL, pages 264–272,
Athens, Greece, 30 March – 3 April 2009.

longer used independently in Modern colloquial Chinese, it might still appear to be a free morpheme in modern written text, because it contains Classical Chinese elements. This fact leads to a phenomenon in which Chinese speakers have difficulty differentiating whether a character represents a bound or free morpheme, which in turn affects their judgment regarding where the word boundaries should be. As pointed out by Hoosain (Hoosain, 1992), the varying knowledge of Classical Chinese among native Chinese speakers in fact affects their judgments about what is or is not a word. In summary, due to the influence of Classical Chinese, the notion of a word and the boundary between a bound and free morpheme is very unclear for Chinese speakers, which in turn leads to a fuzzy perception of where word boundaries should be.

Consequently, automatic segmentation and tagging in Chinese faces a serious challenge from prevalent ambiguities. For example [1], the string "有意见" can be segmented as (1a) or (1b), depending on the context.

(1) a. 有 意见
yǒu yìjian
have disagreement

b. 有意 见
yǒuyì jiàn
have the intention meet

The contrast shown in (2) illustrates that even a string that is not ambiguous in terms of segmentation can still be ambiguous in terms of tagging.

(2) a. 白/a 花/n
bái huā
white flower

b. 白/d 花/v
bái huā
in vain spend
'spend (money, time, energy etc.) in vain'

Even Chinese speakers cannot resolve such ambiguities without using further information from a bigger context, which suggests that resolving segmentation and tagging ambiguities probably should not be a task or goal at the word level. Instead, we should preserve such ambiguities in this level and leave them to be resolved in a later stage, when more information is available.

[1](1) and (2) are cited from (Fang and King, 2007)

To summarize, the word as a notion and hence word boundaries are very unclear; segmentation and tagging are prevalently ambiguous in Chinese. These facts suggest that Chinese segmentation and part-of-speech identification are probably inherently non-deterministic at the word level. However most of the current segmentation and/or tagging systems output a single result.

While a deterministic approach to Chinese segmentation and POS tagging might be appropriate and necessary for certain tasks or applications, it has been shown to suffer from a problem of low accuracy. As pointed out by Yu (Yu et al., 2004), although the segmentation and tagging accuracy for certain types of text can reach as high as 95%, the accuracy for open domain text is only slightly higher than 80%. Furthermore, Chinese segmentation (SIGHAN) bakeoff results also show that the performance of the Chinese segmentation systems has not improved a whole lot since 2003. This fact also indicates that deterministic approaches to Chinese segmentation have hit a bottleneck in terms of accuracy.

The system for which we improved the output of the Beijing tokenizer-tagger is a hand-crafted Chinese grammar. For such a system, as probably for any parsing system that presupposes segmented (and tagged) input, the accuracy of the segmentation and POS tagging analyses is critical. However, as described in detail in the following section, even current state-of-art systems cannot provide satisfactory results for our application. Based on the experiments presented in section 3, we believe that a proper amount of non-deterministic results can significantly improve the Chinese segmentation and tagging accuracy, which in turn improves the performance of the grammar.

2 Background

The improved tokenizer-tagger we developed is part of a larger system, namely a deep Chinese grammar (Fang and King, 2007). The system is hybrid in that it uses probability estimates for parse pruning (and it is planned to use trained weights for parse ranking), but the "core" grammar is rule-based. It is written within the framework of Lexical Functional Grammar (LFG) and implemented on the XLE system (Crouch et al., 2006; Maxwell and Kaplan, 1996). The input to our system is a raw Chinese string such as (3).

(3)

小王 走 了 。
xiǎowáng zǒu le .
XiaoWang leave ASP[2] .
'XiaoWang left.'

The output of the Chinese LFG consists of a Constituent Structure (c-structure) and a Functional Structure (f-structure) for each sentence. While c-structure represents phrasal structure and linear word order, f-structure represents various functional relations between parts of sentences. For example, (4) and (5) are the c-structure and f-structure that the grammar produces for (3). Both c-structure and f-structure information are carried in syntactic rules in the grammar.

(4) c-structure of (3)

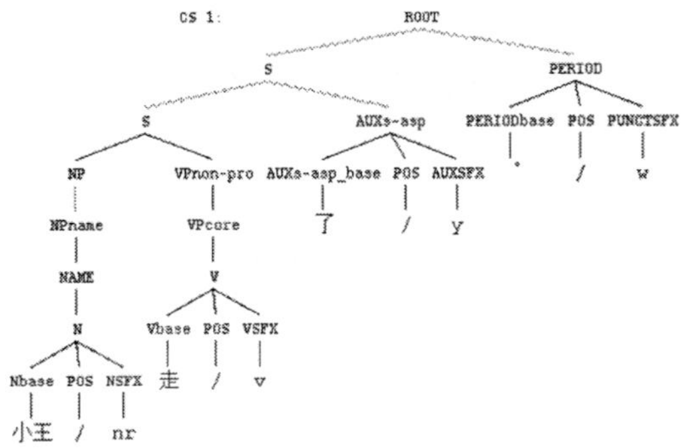

(5) f-structure of (3)

```
  [PRED       '走<[1:小王]>'                          ]
  |           [PRED  '小王'                  ]        |
  |SUBJ       |NTYPE [NSYN proper]           |        |
  |          1[ANIM +, NUM sg, PERS 3        ]        |
  |TNS-ASP    [ASPECT [SENT-ASPECT perfect]]          |
26[CLAUSE-TYPE decl, VTYPE main                       ]
```

To parse a sentence, the Chinese LFG minimally requires three components: a tokenizer-tagger, a lexicon, and syntactic rules. The tokenizer-tagger that is currently used in the grammar is developed by Beijing University (PKU)[3] and is incorporated as a library transducer (Crouch et al., 2006).

Because the grammar's syntactic rules are applied based upon the results produced by the tokenizer-tagger, the performance of the latter is critical to overall quality of the system's output. However, even though PKU's tokenizer-tagger is one of the state-of-art systems, its performance is not satisfactory for the Chinese LFG. This becomes clear from a small-scale evaluation in which the system was tested on a set of 101 gold sentences chosen from the Chinese Treebank 5 (CTB5) (Xue et al., 2002; Xue et al., 2005). These 101 sentences are 10-20 words long and all of them are chosen from Xinhua sources [4]. Based on the deterministic segmentation and tagging results produced by PKU's tokenizer-tagger, the Chinese LFG can only parse 80 out of the 101 sentences. Among the 80 sentences that are parsed, 66 received full parses and 14 received fragmented parses. Among the 21 completely failed sentences, 20 sentences failed due to segmentation and tagging mistakes.

This simple test shows that in order for the deep Chinese grammar to be practically useful, the performance of the tokenizer-tagger must be improved. One way to improve the segmentation and tagging accuracy is to allow non-deterministic segmentation and tagging for Chinese for the reasons stated in Section 1. Therefore, our goal is to find a way to transform PKU's tokenizer-tagger into a system that produces a proper amount of non-deterministic segmentation and tagging results, one that can significantly improve the system's accuracy without a substantial sacrifice in terms of efficiency. Our approach is described in the following section.

3 FST[5] Rules for the Improvement of Segmentation and Tagging Output

For grammars of other languages implemented on the XLE grammar development platform, the input is usually preprocessed by a cascade of generally non-deterministic finite state transducers that perform tokenization, morphological analysis etc. Since word segmentation and POS tagging are such hard problems in Chinese, this traditional setup is not an option for the Chinese grammar. However, finite state rules seem a quite natural approach to improving in XLE the output of a sep-

[2] ASP stands for aspect marker.

[3] http://www.icl.pku.edu.cn/icl_res/

[4] The reason why only sentences from Xinhua sources were chosen is because the version of PKU's tokenizer-tagger that was integrated into the system was not designed to handle data from Hong Kong and Taiwan.

[5] We use the abbreviation "FST" for "finite-state transducer". *fst* is used to refer to the finite-state tool called *fst*, which was developed by Beesley and Karttunen (2003).

arate segmentation and POS tagging module like PKU's tokenizer-tagger.

3.1 Hand-Crafted FST Rules for Concept Proving

Although the grammar developer had identified PKU's tokenizer-tagger as the most suitable for the preprocessing of Chinese raw text that is to be parsed with the Chinese LFG, she noticed in the process of development that (i) certain segmentation and/or tagging decisions taken by the tokenizer-tagger systematically go counter her morphosyntactic judgment and that (ii) the tokenizer-tagger (as any software of its kind) makes mistakes. She therefore decided to develop a set of finite-state rules that transform the output of the module; a set of mostly obligatory rewrite rules adapts the POS-tagged word sequence to the grammar's standard, and another set of mostly optional rules tries to offer alternative segment and tag sequences for sequences that are frequently processed erroneously by PKU's tokenizer-tagger.

Given the absence of data segmented and tagged according to the standard the LFG grammar developer desired, the technique of hand-crafting FST rules to postprocess the output of PKU's tokenizer-tagger worked surprisingly well. Recall that based on the deterministic segmentation and tagging results produced by PKU's tokenizer-tagger, our system can only parse 80 out of the 101 sentences, and among the 21 completely failed sentences, 20 sentences failed due to segmentation and tagging mistakes. In contrast, after the application of the hand-crafted FST rules for post-processing, 100 out of the 101 sentences can be parsed. However, this approach involved a lot of manual development work (about 3-4 person months) and has reached a stage where it is difficult to systematically work on further improvements.

3.2 Machine-Learned FST Rules

Since there are large amounts of training data that are close to the segmentation and tagging standard the grammar developer wants to use, the idea of inducing FST rules rather than hand-crafting them comes quite naturally. The easiest way to do this is to apply transformation-based learning (TBL) to the combined problem of Chinese segmentation and POS tagging, since the cascade of transformational rules learned in a TBL training run can straightforwardly be translated into a cascade of FST rules.

3.2.1 Transformation-Based Learning and μ-TBL

TBL is a machine learning approach that has been employed to solve a number of problems in natural language processing; most famously, it has been used for part-of-speech tagging (Brill, 1995). TBL is a supervised learning approach, since it relies on gold-annotated training data. In addition, it relies on a set of templates of transformational rules; learning consists in finding a sequence of instantiations of these templates that minimizes the number of errors in a more or less naive base-line output with respect to the gold-annotated training data.

The first attempts to employ TBL to solve the problem of Chinese word segmentation go back to Palmer (1997) and Hockenmaier and Brew (1998). In more recent work, TBL was used for the adaption of the output of a statistical "general purpose" segmenter to standards that vary depending on the application that requires sentence segmentation (Gao et al., 2004). TBL approaches to the combined problem of segmenting and POS-tagging Chinese sentences are reported in Florian and Ngai (2001) and Fung et al. (2004).

Several implementations of the TBL approach are freely available on the web, the most well-known being the so-called Brill tagger, fnTBL, which allows for multi-dimensional TBL, and μ-TBL (Lager, 1999). Among these, we chose μ-TBL for our experiments because (like fnTBL) it is completely flexible as to whether a sample is a word, a character or anything else and (unlike fnTBL) it allows for the induction of optional rules. Probably due to its flexibility, μ-TBL has been used (albeit on a small scale for the most part) for tasks as diverse as POS tagging, map tasks, and machine translation.

3.2.2 Experiment Set-up

We started out with a corpus of thirty gold-segmented and -tagged daily editions of the Xinhua Daily, which were provided by the Institute of Computational Linguistics at Beijing University. Three daily editions, which comprise 5,054 sentences with 129,377 words and 213,936 characters, were set aside for testing purposes; the remaining 27 editions were used for training. With the idea of learning both obligatory and optional transformational rules in mind, we then split the training data into two roughly equally sized subsets. All the data were broken into sentences using a very simple method: The end of a paragraph was always considered a sentence boundary. Within paragraphs, sentence-final punctuation marks such as periods (which are unambiguous in Chinese), question marks and exclamation marks, potentially followed by a closing parenthesis, bracket or quote mark, were considered sentence boundaries.

We then had to come up with a way of casting the problem of combined segmentation and POS tagging as a TBL problem. Following a strategy widely used in Chinese word segmentation, we did this by regarding the problem as a character tagging problem. However, since we intended to learn rules that deal with segmentation and POS tagging simultaneously, we could not adopt the BIO-coding approach.[6] Also, since the TBL-induced transformational rules were to be converted into FST rules, we had to keep our character tagging scheme one-dimensional, unlike Florian and Ngai (2001), who used a multi-dimensional TBL approach to solve the problem of combined segmentation and POS tagging.

The character tagging scheme that we finally chose is illustrated in (6), where a. and b. show the character tags that we used for the analyses in (1a) and (1b) respectively. The scheme consists in tagging the last character of a word with the part-of-speech of the entire word; all non-final characters are tagged with '-'. The main advantages of this character tagging scheme are that it expresses both word boundaries and parts-of-speech and that, at the same time, it is always consistent; inconsistencies between BIO tags indicating word boundaries and part-of-speech tags, which Florian and Ngai (2001), for example, have to resolve, can simply not arise.

(6)

	有	意	见
a.	v	-	n
b.	-	v	v

Both of the training data subsets were tagged according to our character tagging scheme and converted to the data format expected by μ-TBL. The first training data subset was used for learning obligatory resegmentation and retagging rules. The corresponding rule templates, which define the space of possible rules to be explored, are given in Figure 1. The training parameters of μ-TBL, which are an accuracy threshold and a score threshold, were set to 0.75 and 5 respectively; this means that a potential rule was only retained if at least 75% of the samples to which it would have applied were actually modified in the sense of the gold standard and not in some other way and that the learning process was terminated when no more rule could be found that applied to at least 5 samples in the first training data subset. With these training parameters, 3,319 obligatory rules were learned by μ-TBL.

Once the obligatory rules had been learned on the first training data subset, they were applied to the second training data subset. Then, optional rules were learned on this second training data subset. The rule templates used for optional rules are very similar to the ones used for obligatory rules; a few templates of optional rules are given in Figure 2. The difference between obligatory rules and optional rules is that the former replace one character tag by another, whereas the latter add character tags. They hence introduce ambiguity, which is why we call them optional rules. Like in the learning of the obligatory rules, the accuracy threshold used was 0.75; the score theshold was set to 7 because the training software seemed to hit a bug below that threshold. 753 optional rules were learned. We did not experiment with the adjustment of the training parameters on a separate held-out set.

Finally, the rule sets learned were converted into the *fst* (Beesley and Karttunen, 2003) notation for transformational rules, so that they could be tested and used in the FST cascade used for preprocessing the input of the Chinese LFG. For evaluation, the converted rules were applied to our test data set of 5,054 sentences. A few example rules learned by μ-TBL with the set-up described above are given in Figure 3; we show them both in μ-TBL notation and in *fst* notation.

3.2.3 Results

The results achieved by PKU's tokenizer-tagger on its own and in combination with the transformational rules learned in our experiments are given in Table 1. We compare the output of PKU's

[6] In this character tagging approach to word segmentation, characters are tagged as the beginning of a word (B), inside (or at the end) of a multi-character word (I) or a word of their own (O). Their are numerous variations of this approach.

```
tag:m> - <- wd:'一'@[0] & wd:'个'@[1] &
            tag:q@[1,2,3,4] & {\+q=(-)}.
tag:r>n <- wd:'我'@[-1] & wd:'国'@[0].
tag:add nr <- tag:(-)@[0] & wd:'铸'@[1].
...
```

```
"/" m WS @-> 0 || 一 _ 个 [ ( TAG )
                       CHAR ]^{0,3} "/" q WS
"/" r WS @-> "/" n TB || 我 ( TAG ) 国 _
[..] (@->) "/" n r TB || CHAR _ 铸
...
```

Figure 3: Sample rules learned in our experiments in μ-TBL notation on the left and in *fst* notation on the right[8]

```
tag:A>B <- ch:C@[0].
tag:A>B <- ch:C@[1].
tag:A>B <- ch:C@[-1] & ch:D@[0].
tag:A>B <- ch:C@[0] & ch:D@[1].
tag:A>B <- ch:C@[1] & ch:D@[2].
tag:A>B <- ch:C@[-2] & ch:D@[-1] &
           ch:E@[0].
tag:A>B <- ch:C@[-1] & ch:D@[0] &
           ch:E@[1].
tag:A>B <- ch:C@[0] & ch:D@[1] & ch:E@[2].
tag:A>B <- ch:C@[1] & ch:D@[2] & ch:E@[3].
tag:A>B <- tag:C@[-1].
tag:A>B <- tag:C@[1].
tag:A>B <- tag:C@[1] & tag:D@[2].
tag:A>B <- tag:C@[-2] & tag:D@[-1].
tag:A>B <- tag:C@[-1] & tag:D@[1].
tag:A>B <- tag:C@[1] & tag:D@[2].
tag:A>B <- tag:C@[1] & tag:D@[2] &
           tag:E@[3].
tag:A>B <- tag:C@[-1] & ch:W@[0].
tag:A>B <- tag:C@[1] & ch:W@[0].
tag:A>B <- tag:C@[1] & tag:D@[2] &
           ch:W@[0].
tag:A>B <- tag:C@[-2] & tag:D@[-1] &
           ch:W@[0].
tag:A>B <- tag:C@[-1] & tag:D@[1] &
           ch:W@[0].
tag:A>B <- tag:C@[1] & tag:D@[2] &
           ch:W@[0].
tag:A>B <- tag:C@[1] & tag:D@[2] &
           tag:E@[3] & ch:W@[0].
tag:A>B <- tag:C@[-1] & ch:W@[1].
tag:A>B <- tag:C@[1] & ch:W@[1].
tag:A>B <- tag:C@[1] & tag:D@[2] &
           ch:W@[1].
tag:A>B <- tag:C@[-2] & tag:D@[-1] &
           ch:W@[1].
tag:A>B <- tag:C@[-1] & ch:D@[0] &
           ch:E@[1].
tag:A>B <- tag:C@[-1] & tag:D@[1] &
           ch:W@[1].
tag:A>B <- tag:C@[1] & tag:D@[2] &
           ch:W@[1].
tag:A>B <- tag:C@[1] & tag:D@[2] &
           tag:E@[3] & ch:W@[1].
tag:A>B <- tag:C@[1,2,3,4] & {\+C='-'}.
tag:A>B <- ch:C@[0] & tag:D@[1,2,3,4] &
           {\+D='-'}.
tag:A>B <- tag:C@[-1] & ch:D@[0] &
           tag:E@[1,2,3,4] & {\+E='-'}.
tag:A>B <- ch:C@[0] & ch:D@[1] &
           tag:E@[1,2,3,4] & {\+E='-'}.
```

Figure 1: Templates of obligatory rules used in our experiments

```
tag:add B <- tag:A@[0] & ch:C@[0].
tag:add B <- tag:A@[0] & ch:C@[1].
tag:add B <- tag:A@[0] & ch:C@[-1] &
             ch:D@[0].
...
```

Figure 2: Sample templates of optional rules used in our experiments

tokenizer-tagger run in the mode where it returns only the most probable tag for each word (PKU one tag), of PKU's tokenizer-tagger run in the mode where it returns all possible tags for a given word (PKU all tags), of PKU's tokenizer-tagger in one-tag mode augmented with the obligatory transformational rules learned on the first part of our training data (PKU one tag + deterministic rule set), and of PKU's tokenizer-tagger augmented with both the obligatory and optional rules learned on the first and second parts of our training data respectively (PKU one tag + non-deterministic rule set). We give results in terms of character tag accuracy and ambiguity according to our character tagging scheme. Then we provide evaluation figures for the word level. Finally, we give results referring to the sentence level in order to make clear how serious a problem Chinese segmentation and POS tagging still are for parsers, which obviously operate at the sentence level.

These results show that simply switching from the one-tag mode of PKU's tokenizer-tagger to its all-tags mode is not a solution. First of all, since the tokenizer-tagger always produces only one segmentation regardless of the mode it is used in, segmentation accuracy would stay completely unaffected by this change, which is particularly serious because there is no way for the grammar to recover from segmentation errors and the tokenizer-tagger produces an entirely correct segmentation only for 47.15% of the sentences. Second, the improved tagging accuracy would come at a very heavy price in terms of ambiguity; the median number of combined segmentation and POS tagging analyses per sentence would be 1,440.

In contrast, machine-learned transformation rules are an effective means to improve the output of PKU's tokenizer-tagger. Applying only the obligatory rules that were learned already improves segmented sentence accuracy from 47.15% to 63.14% and tagged sentence accuracy from 14.07% to 27.21%, and this at no cost in terms of ambiguity. Adding the optional rules that were learned and hence making the rule set used for post-processing the output of PKU's tokenizer-tagger non-deterministic makes it possible to improve segmented sentence accuracy and tagged sentence accuracy further to 65.06% and 31.47% respectively, i.e. tagged sentence accuracy is more than doubled with respect to the baseline. While this last improvement does come at a price in terms of ambiguity, the ambiguity resulting from the application of the non-deterministic rule set is very low in comparison to the ambiguity of the output of PKU's tokenizer-tagger in all-tags mode; the median number of analyses per sentences only increases to 2. Finally, it should be noted that the transformational rules provide entirely correct segmentation and POS tagging analyses not only for more sentences, but also for longer sentences. They increase the average length of a correctly segmented sentence from 18.22 words to 21.94 words and the average length of a correctly segmented and POS-tagged sentence from 9.58 words to 16.33 words.

4 Comparison to related work and Discussion

Comparing our results to other results in the literature is not an easy task because segmentation and POS tagging standards vary, and our test data have not been used for a final evaluation before. Nevertheless, there are of course systems that perform word segmentation and POS tagging for Chinese and have been evaluated on data similar to our test data.

Published results also vary as to the evaluation measures used, in particular when it comes to combined word segmentation and POS tagging. For word segmentation considered separately, the consensus is to use the (segmentation) F-score (SF). The quality of systems that perform both segmentation and POS tagging is often expressed in terms of (character) tag accuracy (TA), but this obviously depends on the character tagging scheme adopted. An alternative measure is POS tagging F-score (TF), which is the geometric mean of precision and recall of correctly segmented and POS-tagged words. Evaluation measures for the sentence level have not been given in any publication that we are aware of, probably because segmenters and POS taggers are rarely considered as pre-processing modules for parsers, but also because the figures for measures like sentence accuracy are strikingly low.

For systems that perform only word segmentation, we find the following results in the literature: (Gao et al., 2004), who use TBL to adapt a "general purpose" segmenter to varying standards, report an SF of 95.5% on PKU data and an SF of 90.4% on CTB data. (Tseng et al., 2005) achieve an SF of 95.0%, 95.3% and 86.3% on PKU data from the Sighan Bakeoff 2005, PKU data from the Sighan Bakeoff 2003 and CTB data from the Sighan Bakeoff 2003 respectively. Finally, (Zhang et al., 2006) report an SF of 94.8% on PKU data.

For systems that perform both word segmentation and POS tagging, the following results were published: Florian and Ngai (2001) report an SF of 93.55% and a TA of 88.86% on CTB data. Ng and Low (2004) report an SF of 95.2% and a TA of 91.9% on CTB data. Finally, Zhang and Clark (2008) achieve an SF of 95.90% and a TF of 91.34% by 10-fold cross validation using CTB data.

Last but not least, there are parsers that operate on characters rather than words and who perform segmentation and POS tagging as part of the parsing process. Among these, we would like to mention Luo (2003), who reports an SF 96.0% on Chinese Treebank (CTB) data, and (Fung et al., 2004), who achieve "a word segmentation precision/recall performance of 93/94%". Both the SF and the TF results achieved by our "PKU one tag + non-deterministic rule set" setup, whose output is slightly ambiguous, compare favorably with all the results mentioned, and even the results achieved by our "PKU one tag + deterministic rule set" setup are competitive.

5 Conclusions and Future Work

The idea of carrying some ambiguity from one processing step into the next in order not to prune good solutions is not new. E.g., Prins and van Noord (2003) use a probabilistic part-of-speech tagger that keeps multiple tags in certain cases for a hand-crafted HPSG-inspired parser for Dutch,

	PKU one tag	PKU all tags	PKU one tag + det. rule set	PKU one tag + non-det. rule set
Character tag accuracy (in %)	89.98	92.79	94.69	95.27
Avg. number of tags per char.	1.00	1.39	1.00	1.03
Avg. number of words per sent.	26.26	26.26	25.77	25.75
Segmented word precision (in %)	93.00	93.00	96.18	96.46
Segmented word recall (in %)	95.39	95.39	96.84	97.02
Segmented word F-score (in %)	94.18	94.18	96.51	96.74
Tagged word precision (in %)	83.57	87.87	91.27	92.17
Tagged word recall (in %)	85.72	90.23	91.89	92.71
Tagged word F-score (in %)	84.63	89.03	91.58	92.44
Segmented sentence accuracy (in %)	47.15	47.15	63.14	65.06
Avg. nmb. of words per correctly segm. sent.	18.22	18.22	21.69	21.94
Tagged sentence accuracy (in %)	14.07	21.09	27.21	31.47
Avg. number of analyses per sent.	1.00	4.61e18	1.00	12.84
Median nmb. of analyses per sent.	1	1,440	1	2
Avg. nmb. of words per corr. tagged sent.	9.58	13.20	15.11	16.33

Table 1: Evaluation figures achieved by four different systems on the 5,054 sentences of our test set

and Curran et al. (2006) show the benefits of using a multi-tagger rather than a single-tagger for an induced CCG for English. However, to our knowledge, this idea has not made its way into the field of Chinese parsing so far. Chinese parsing systems either pass on a single segmentation and POS tagging analysis to the parser proper or they are character-based, i.e. segmentation and tagging are part of the parsing process. Although several treebank-induced character-based parsers for Chinese have achieved promising results, this approach is impractical in the development of a hand-crafted deep grammar like the Chinese LFG. We therefore believe that the development of a "multi-tokenizer-tagger" is the way to go for this sort of system (and all systems that can handle a certain amount of ambiguity that may or may not be resolved at later processing stages). Our results show that we have made an important first step in this direction.

As to future work, we hope to resolve the problem of not having a gold standard that is segmented and tagged exactly according to the guidelines established by the Chinese LFG developer by semi-automatically applying the hand-crafted transformational rules that were developed to the PKU gold standard. We will then induce obligatory and optional FST rules from this "grammar-compliant" gold standard and hope that these will be able to replace the hand-crafted transformation rules currently used in the grammar. Finally, we plan to carry out more training runs; in particular, we intend to experiment with lower accuracy (and score) thresholds for optional rules. The idea is to find the optimal balance between ambiguity, which can probably be higher than with our current set of induced rules without affecting efficiency too adversely, and accuracy, which still needs further improvement, as can easily be seen from the sentence accuracy figures.

References

Kenneth R. Beesley and Lauri Karttunen. 2003. *Finite State Morphology*. CSLI Publications, Stanford, CA.

Eric Brill. 1995. Transformation-based error-driven learning and natural language processing: a case study in part-of-speech tagging. *Computational Linguistics*, 21(4):543–565.

J.M Chang, D.L. Hung, and O.J.L. Tzeng. 1992. Miscue analysis of chinese children's reading behavior at the entry level. *Journal of Chinese Linguistics*, 20(1).

Dick Crouch, Mary Dalrymple, Ron Kaplan, Tracy Holloway King, John Maxwell, and Paula Newman. 2006. XLE documentation. http://www2.parc.com/isl/groups/nltt/xle/doc/.

James R. Curran, Stephen Clark, and David Vadas. 2006. Multi-Tagging for Lexicalized-Grammar Parsing. In *In Proceedings of COLING/ACL-06*, pages 697–704, Sydney, Australia.

Ji Fang and Tracy Holloway King. 2007. An lfg chinese grammar for machine use. In Tracy Holloway

King and Emily M. Bender, editors, *Proceedings of the GEAF 2007 Workshop*. CSLI Studies in Computational Linguistics ONLINE.

Radu Florian and Grace Ngai. 2001. Multidimensional transformation-based learning. In *CoNLL '01: Proceedings of the 2001 workshop on Computational Natural Language Learning*, pages 1–8, Morristown, NJ, USA. Association for Computational Linguistics.

Pascale Fung, Grace Ngai, Yongsheng Yang, and Benfeng Chen. 2004. A maximum-entropy Chinese parser augmented by transformation-based learning. *ACM Transactions on Asian Language Information Processing (TALIP)*, 3(2):159–168.

Jianfeng Gao, Andi Wu, Mu Li, Chang-Ning Huang, Hongqiao Li, Xinsong Xia, and Haowei Qin. 2004. Adaptive Chinese word segmentation. In *ACL '04: Proceedings of the 42nd Annual Meeting on Association for Computational Linguistics*, page 462, Morristown, NJ, USA. Association for Computational Linguistics.

Julia Hockenmaier and Chris Brew. 1998. Error-Driven Segmentation of Chinese. *International Journal of the Chinese and Oriental Languages Information Processing Society*, 8(1):69?–84.

R. Hoosain. 1992. Psychological reality of the word in chinese. In H.-C. Chen and O.J.L. Tzeng, editors, *Language Processing in Chinese*. North-Holland and Elsevier, Amsterdam.

Kylie Hsu. 2002. *Selected Issues in Mandarin Chinese Word Structure Analysis*. The Edwin Mellen Press, Lewiston, New York, USA.

Torbjörn Lager. 1999. The μ-TBL System: Logic Programming Tools for Transformation-Based Learning. In *Proceedings of the Third International Workshop on Computational Natural Language Learning (CoNLL'99)*, Bergen.

Xiaoqiang Luo. 2003. A Maximum Entropy Chinese Character-Based Parser. In Michael Collins and Mark Steedman, editors, *Proceedings of the 2003 Conference on Empirical Methods in Natural Language Processing*, pages 192–199.

John Maxwell and Ron Kaplan. 1996. An efficient parser for LFG. In *Proceedings of the First LFG Conference*. CSLI Publications.

Hwee Tou Ng and Jin Kiat Low. 2004. Chinese Part-of-Speech Tagging: One-at-a-Time or All-at-Once? Word-Based or Character-Based? . In Dekang Lin and Dekai Wu, editors, *Proceedings of EMNLP 2004*, pages 277–284, Barcelona, Spain, July. Association for Computational Linguistics.

Jerome L. Packard. 2000. *The Morphology of Chinese*. Cambridge University Press, Cambridge, UK.

David D. Palmer. 1997. A trainable rule-based algorithm for word segmentation. In *Proceedings of the 35th annual meeting on Association for Computational Linguistics*, pages 321–328, Morristown, NJ, USA. Association for Computational Linguistics.

Robbert Prins and Gertjan van Noord. 2003. Reinforcing parser preferences through tagging. *Traitement Automatique des Langues*, 44(3):121–139.

Richard Sproat and Thomas Emerson. 2003. The first international chinese word segmentation bakeoff. In *Proceedings of the Second SIGHAN Workshop on Chinese Language Processing*, pages 133–143.

Huihsin Tseng, Pichuan Chang, Galen Andrew, Daniel Jurafsky, and Christopher Manning. 2005. A Conditional Random Field Word Segmenter for SIGHAN Bakeoff 2005. In *Proceedings of Fourth SIGHAN Workshop on Chinese Language Processing*.

A.D. Wu. 2003. Customizable segmentation of morphologically derived words in chinese. *International Journal of Computational Linguistics and Chinese Language Processing*, 8(1):1–28.

Fei Xia. 2000. The segmentation guidelines for the penn chinese treebank (3.0). Technical report, University of Pennsylvania.

Nianwen Xue, Fu-Dong Chiou, and Martha Palmer. 2002. Building a large-scale annotated Chinese corpus. In *Proceedings of the 19th. International Conference on Computational Linguistics*.

Nianwen Xue, Fei Xia, Fu-Dong Chiou, and Martha Palmer. 2005. The Penn Chinese treebank: Phrase structure annotation of a large corpus. *Natural Language Engineering*, pages 207–238.

Tongqiang Xu（徐通锵）. 1997. *On Language*（语言论）. Dongbei Normal University Publishing, Changchun, China.

Shiwen Yu（俞士汶）, Baobao Chang （常宝宝）, and Weidong Zhan （詹卫东）. 2004. *An Introduction of Computational Linguistics* （计算语言学概论）. Shangwu Yinshuguan Press, Beijing, China.

Yue Zhang and Stephen Clark. 2008. Joint Word Segmentation and POS Tagging Using a Single Perceptron. In *Proceedings of ACL-08*, Columbus, OH.

Ruiqiang Zhang, Genichiro Kikui, and Eiichiro Sumita. 2006. Subword-based tagging for confidence-dependent Chinese word segmentation. In *Proceedings of the COLING/ACL on Main conference poster sessions*, pages 961–968, Morristown, NJ, USA. Association for Computational Linguistics.

Who is "You"? Combining Linguistic and Gaze Features to Resolve Second-Person References in Dialogue*

Matthew Frampton[1], *Raquel Fernández*[1], *Patrick Ehlen*[1], *Mario Christoudias*[2], *Trevor Darrell*[2] and *Stanley Peters*[1]

[1]Center for the Study of Language and Information, Stanford University
{frampton, raquelfr, ehlen, peters}@stanford.edu

[2]International Computer Science Institute, University of California at Berkeley
cmch@icsi.berkeley.edu, trevor@eecs.berkeley.edu

Abstract

We explore the problem of resolving the second person English pronoun *you* in multi-party dialogue, using a combination of linguistic and visual features. First, we distinguish generic and referential uses, then we classify the referential uses as either plural or singular, and finally, for the latter cases, we identify the addressee. In our first set of experiments, the linguistic and visual features are derived from manual transcriptions and annotations, but in the second set, they are generated through entirely automatic means. Results show that a multimodal system is often preferable to a unimodal one.

1 Introduction

The English pronoun *you* is the second most frequent word in unrestricted conversation (after *I* and right before *it*).[1] Despite this, with the exception of Gupta et al. (2007b; 2007a), its resolution has received very little attention in the literature. This is perhaps not surprising since the vast amount of work on anaphora and reference resolution has focused on text or discourse - mediums where second-person deixis is perhaps not as prominent as it is in dialogue. For spoken dialogue pronoun resolution modules however, resolving *you* is an essential task that has an important impact on the capabilities of dialogue summarization systems.

Besides being important for computational implementations, resolving *you* is also an interesting and challenging research problem. As for third person pronouns such as *it*, some uses of *you* are not strictly referential. These include discourse marker uses such as *you know* in example (1), and generic uses like (2), where *you* does not refer to the addressee as it does in (3).

(1) It's not just, you know, noises like something hitting.

(2) Often, you need to know specific button sequences to get certain functionalities done.

(3) I think it's good. You've done a good review.

However, unlike *it*, *you* is ambiguous between singular and plural interpretations - an issue that is particularly problematic in multi-party conversations. While *you* clearly has a plural referent in (4), in (3) the number of its referent is ambiguous.[2]

(4) I don't know if you guys have any questions.

When an utterance contains a singular referential *you*, resolving the *you* amounts to identifying the individual to whom the utterance is addressed. This is trivial in two-person dialogue since the current listener is always the addressee, but in conversations with multiple participants, it is a complex problem where different kinds of linguistic and visual information play important roles (Jovanovic, 2007). One of the issues we investigate here is

*We thank the anonymous EACL reviewers, and Surabhi Gupta, John Niekrasz and David Demirdjian for their comments and technical assistance. This work was supported by the CALO project (DARPA grant NBCH-D-03-0010).

[1]See e.g. http://www.kilgarriff.co.uk/BNC_lists/

[2]In contrast, the referential use of the pronoun *it* (as well as that of some demonstratives) is ambiguous between NP interpretations and discourse-deictic ones (Webber, 1991).

Proceedings of the 12th Conference of the European Chapter of the ACL, pages 273–281,
Athens, Greece, 30 March – 3 April 2009.

how this applies to the more concrete problem of resolving the second person pronoun *you*.

We approach this issue as a three-step problem. Using the AMI Meeting Corpus (McCowan et al., 2005) of multi-party dialogues, we first discriminate between referential and generic uses of *you*. Then, within the referential uses, we distinguish between singular and plural, and finally, we resolve the singular referential instances by identifying the intended addressee. We use multimodal features: initially, we extract discourse features from manual transcriptions and use visual information derived from manual annotations, but then we move to a fully automatic approach, using 1-best transcriptions produced by an automatic speech recognizer (ASR) and visual features automatically extracted from raw video.

In the next section of this paper, we give a brief overview of related work. We describe our data in Section 3, and explain how we extract visual and linguistic features in Sections 4 and 5 respectively. Section 6 then presents our experiments with manual transcriptions and annotations, while Section 7, those with automatically extracted information. We end with conclusions in Section 8.

2 Related Work

2.1 Reference Resolution in Dialogue

Although the vast majority of work on reference resolution has been with monologic text, some recent research has dealt with the more complex scenario of spoken dialogue (Strube and Müller, 2003; Byron, 2004; Arstein and Poesio, 2006; Müller, 2007). There has been work on the identification of non-referential uses of the pronoun *it*: Müller (2006) uses a set of shallow features automatically extracted from manual transcripts of two-party dialogue in order to train a rule-based classifier, and achieves an F-score of 69%.

The only existing work on the resolution of *you* that we are aware of is Gupta et al. (2007b; 2007a). In line with our approach, the authors first disambiguate between generic and referential *you*, and then attempt to resolve the reference of the referential cases. Generic uses of *you* account for 47% of their data set, and for the generic *vs.* referential disambiguation, they achieve an accuracy of 84% on two-party conversations and 75% on multi-party dialogue. For the reference resolution task, they achieve 47%, which is 10 points over a baseline that always classifies the next speaker as the addressee. These results are achieved without visual information, using manual transcripts, and a combination of surface features and manually tagged dialogue acts.

2.2 Addressee Detection

Resolving the referential instances of *you* amounts to determining the addressee(s) of the utterance containing the pronoun. Recent years have seen an increasing amount of research on automatic addressee detection. Much of this work focuses on communication between humans and computational agents (such as robots or ubiquitous computing systems) that interact with users who may be engaged in other activities, including interaction with other humans. In these situations, it is important for a system to be able to recognize when it is being addressed by a user. Bakx et al. (2003) and Turnhout et al. (2005) studied this issue in the context of mixed human-human and human-computer interaction using facial orientation and utterance length as clues for addressee detection, while Katzenmaier et al. (2004) investigated whether the degree to which a user utterance fits the language model of a conversational robot can be useful in detecting system-addressed utterances. This research exploits the fact that humans tend to speak differently to systems than to other humans.

Our research is closer to that of Jovanovic et al. (2006a; 2007), who studied addressing in human-human multi-party dialogue. Jovanovic and colleagues focus on addressee identification in face-to-face meetings with four participants. They use a Bayesian Network classifier trained on several multimodal features (including visual features such as gaze direction, discourse features such as the speaker and dialogue act of preceding utterances, and utterance features such as lexical clues and utterance duration). Using a combination of features from various resources was found to improve performance (the best system achieves an accuracy of 77% on a portion of the AMI Meeting Corpus). Although this result is very encouraging, it is achieved with the use of manually produced information - in particular, manual transcriptions, dialogue acts and annotations of visual focus of attention. One of the issues we aim to investigate here is how automatically extracted multimodal information can help in detecting the addressee(s) of *you*-utterances.

Generic	Referential	Ref_Sing.	Ref_Pl.
49.14%	50.86%	67.92%	32.08%

Table 1: Distribution of *you* interpretations

L_1	L_2	L_3
35.17%	30.34%	34.49%

Table 2: Distribution of addressees for singular *you*

3 Data

Our experiments are performed using the AMI Meeting Corpus (McCowan et al., 2005), a collection of scenario-driven meetings among four participants, manually transcribed and annotated with several different types of information (including dialogue acts, topics, visual focus of attention, and addressee). We use a sub-corpus of 948 utterances containing *you*, and these were extracted from 10 different meetings. The *you*-utterances are annotated as either *discourse marker*, *generic* or *referential*.

We excluded the *discourse marker* cases, which account for only 8% of the data, and of the *referential* cases, selected those with an AMI addressee annotation.[3] The addressee of a dialogue act can be `unknown`, a single meeting participant, two participants, or the whole audience (three participants in the AMI corpus). Since there are very few instances of two-participant addressee, we distinguish only between singular and plural addressees. The resulting distribution of classes is shown in Table 1.[4]

We approach the reference resolution task as a two-step process, first discriminating between plural and singular references, and then resolving the reference of the singular cases. The latter task requires a classification scheme for distinguishing between the three potential addressees (listeners) for the given *you*-utterance.

In their four-way classification scheme, Gupta et al. (2007a) label potential addressees in terms of the order in which they speak after the *you*-utterance. That is, for a given *you*-utterance, the potential addressee who speaks next is labeled 1, the potential addressee who speaks after that is 2, and the remaining participant is 3. Label 4 is used for group addressing. However, this results in a very skewed class distribution because the next speaker is the intended addressee 41% of the time, and 38% of instances are plural - the remaining two classes therefore make up a small percentage of the data.

We were able to obtain a much less skewed class distribution by identifying the potential addressees in terms of their position in relation to the current speaker. The meeting setting includes a rectangular table with two participants seated at each of its opposite longer sides. Thus, for a given *you*-utterance, we label listeners as either L_1, L_2 or L_3 depending on whether they are sitting opposite, diagonally or laterally from the speaker. Table 2 shows the resulting class distribution for our dataset. Such a labelling scheme is more similar to Jovanovic (2007), where participants are identified by their seating position.

4 Visual Information

4.1 Features from Manual Annotations

We derived per-utterance visual features from the Focus Of Attention (FOA) annotations provided by the AMI corpus. These annotations track meeting participants' head orientation and eye gaze during a meeting.[5] Our first step was to use the FOA annotations in order to compute what we refer to as Gaze Duration Proportion (GDP) values for each of the utterances of interest - a measure similar to the "Degree of Mean Duration of Gaze" described by (Takemae et al., 2004). Here a GDP value denotes the proportion of time in utterance u for which subject i is looking at target j:

$$GDP_u(i,j) = \sum_j T(i,j)/T_u$$

were T_u is the length of utterance u in milliseconds, and $T(i,j)$, the amount of that time that i spends looking at j. The gazer i can only refer to one of the four meeting participants, but the target j can also refer to the white-board/projector screen present in the meeting room. For each utterance then, all of the possible values of i and j are used to construct a matrix of GDP values. From this matrix, we then construct "Highest GDP" features for each of the meeting participants: such

[3]Addressee annotations are not provided for some dialogue act types - see (Jovanovic et al., 2006b).

[4]Note that the percentages of the referential singular and referential plural are relative to the total of referential instances.

[5]A description of the FOA labeling scheme is available from the AMI Meeting Corpus website `http://corpus.amiproject.org/documentations/guidelines-1/`

For each participant Pi
– target for whole utterance
– target for first third of utterance
– target for second third of utterance
– target for third third of utterance
– target for -/+ 2 secs from *you* start time
– ratio 2nd hyp. target / 1st hyp. target
– ratio 3rd hyp. target / 1st hyp. target
– participant in mutual gaze with speaker

Table 3: Visual Features

features record the target with the highest GDP value and so indicate whom/what the meeting participant spent most time looking at during the utterance.

We also generated a number of additional features for each individual. These include firstly, three features which record the candidate "gazee" with the highest GDP during each third of the utterance, and which therefore account for gaze transitions. So as to focus more closely on where participants are looking around the time when *you* is uttered, another feature records the candidate with the highest GDP -/+ 2 seconds from the start time of the *you*. Two further features give some indication of the amount of looking around that the speaker does during an utterance - we hypothesized that participants (especially the speaker) might look around more in utterances with plural addressees. The first is the ratio of the second highest GDP to the highest, and the second is the ratio of the third highest to the highest. Finally, there is a highest GDP *mutual gaze* feature for the speaker, indicating with which other individual, the speaker spent most time engaged in a mutual gaze.

Hence this gives a total of 29 features: seven features for each of the four participants, plus one mutual gaze feature. They are summarized in Table 3. These visual features are different to those used by Jovanovic (2007) (see Section 2). Jovanovic's features record the number of times that each participant looks at each other participant during the utterance, and in addition, the gaze direction of the current speaker. Hence, they are not highest GDP values, they do not include a mutual gaze feature and they do not record whether participants look at the white-board/projector screen.

4.2 Automatic Features from Raw Video

To perform automatic visual feature extraction, a six degree-of-freedom head tracker was run over each subject's video sequence for the utterances containing *you*. For each utterance, this gave 4 sequences, one per subject, of the subject's 3D head orientation and location at each video frame along with 3D head rotational velocities. From these measurements we computed two types of visual information: participant gaze and mutual gaze.

The 3D head orientation and location of each subject along with camera calibration information was used to compute participant gaze information for each video frame of each sequence in the form of a gaze probability matrix. More precisely, camera calibration is first used to estimate the 3D head orientation and location of all subjects in the same world coordinate system.

The gaze probability matrix is a 4×5 matrix where entry i, j stores the probability that subject i is looking at subject j for each of the four subjects and the last column corresponds to the white-board/projector screen (i.e., entry i, j where $j = 5$ is the probability that subject i is looking at the screen). Gaze probability $G(i, j)$ is defined as

$$G(i,j) = G_0 e^{-\alpha_{i,j}{}^2/\gamma^2}$$

where $\alpha_{i,j}$ is the angular difference between the gaze of subject i and the direction defined by the location of subjects i and j. G_0 is a normalization factor such that $\sum_j G(i,j) = 1$ and γ is a user-defined constant (in our experiments, we chose $\gamma = 15$ degrees).

Using the gaze probability matrix, a 4×1 per-frame mutual gaze vector was computed that for entry i stores the probability that the speaker and subject i are looking at one another.

In order to create features equivalent to those described in Section 4.1, we first collapse the frame-level probability matrix into a matrix of binary values. We convert the probability for each frame into a binary judgement of whether subject i is looking at target j:

$$H(i,j) = \beta G(i,j)$$

β is a binary value to evaluate $G(i,j) > \theta$, where θ is a high-pass thresholding value - or "gaze probability threshold" (GPT) - between 0 and 1.

Once we have a frame-level matrix of binary values, for each subject i, we compute GDP values for the time periods of interest, and in each case, choose the target with the highest GDP as the candidate. Hence, we compute a candidate target for the utterance overall, for each third of the utterance, and for the period -/+ 2 seconds from the *you* start time, and in addition, we compute a candidate participant for mutual gaze with the speaker for the utterance overall.

We sought to use the GPT threshold which produces automatic visual features that agree best with the features derived from the FOA annotations. Hence we experimented with different GPT values in increments of 0.1, and compared the resulting features to the manual features using the *kappa* statistic. A threshold of 0.6 gave the best *kappa* scores, which ranged from 20% to 44%.[6]

5 Linguistic Information

Our set of discourse features is a simplified version of those employed by Galley et al. (2004) and Gupta et al. (2007a). It contains three main types (summarized in Table 4):

— *Sentential features* (1 to 13) encode structural, durational, lexical and shallow syntactic patterns of the *you*-utterance. Feature 13 is extracted using the AMI "Named Entity" annotations and indicates whether a particular participant is mentioned in the *you*-utterance. Apart from this feature, all other sentential features are automatically extracted, and besides 1, 8, 9, and 10, they are all binary.

— *Backward Looking (BL)/Forward Looking (FL) features* (14 to 22) are mostly extracted from utterance pairs, namely the *you*-utterance and the BL/FL (previous/next) utterance by each listener L_i (potential addressee). We also include a few extra features which are not computed in terms of utterance pairs. These indicate the number of participants that speak during the previous and next 5 utterances, and the BL and FL speaker order. All of these features are computed automatically.

— *Dialogue Act (DA) features* (23 to 24) use the manual AMI dialogue act annotations to represent the conversational function of the *you*-utterance and the BL/FL utterance by each potential addressee. Along with the sentential feature based on the AMI Named Entity annotations, these are the only discourse features which are not computed automatically. [7]

(1) # of *you* pronouns
(2) you (say|said|tell|told| mention(ed)|mean(t)| sound(ed))
(3) `auxiliary` you
(4) `wh-word` you
(5) you guys
(6) if you
(7) you know
(8) # of words in *you*-utterance
(9) duration of *you*-utterance
(10) speech rate of *you*-utterance
(11) 1st person
(12) general case
(13) person Named Entity tag

(14) # of utterances between *you*- and BL/FL utt.
(15) # of speakers between *you*- and BL/FL utt.
(16) overlap between *you*- and BL/FL utt. (binary)
(17) duration of overlap between *you*- and BL/FL utt.
(18) time separation between *you*- and BL/FL utt.
(19) ratio of words in *you*- that are in BL/FL utt.
(20) # of participants that speak during prev. 5 utt.
(21) # of participants that speak during next 5 utt.
(22) speaker order BL/FL

(23) dialogue act of the *you*-utterance
(24) dialogue act of the BL/FL utterance

Table 4: Discourse Features

6 First Set of Experiments & Results

In this section we report our experiments and results when using manual transcriptions and annotations. In Section 7 we will present the results obtained using ASR output and automatically extracted visual information. All experiments (here and in the next section) are performed using a Bayesian Network classifier with 10-fold cross-validation.[8] In each task, we give raw overall accuracy results and then F-scores for each of the classes. We computed measures of *information gain* in order to assess the predictive power of the various features, and did some experimentation with Correlation-based Feature Selection (CFS) (Hall, 2000).

6.1 Generic *vs.* Referential Uses of *You*

We first address the task of distinguishing between generic and referential uses of *you*.

Baseline. A majority class baseline that classifies all instances of *you* as referential yields an accuracy of 50.86% (see Table 1).

Results. A summary of the results is given in Table 5. Using discourse features only we achieve an accuracy of 77.77%, while using multimodal

[6] The fact that our gaze estimator is getting any useful agreement with respect to these annotations is encouraging and suggests that an improved tracker and/or one that adapts to the user more effectively could work very well.

[7] Since we use the manual transcripts of the meetings, the transcribed words and the segmentation into utterances or dialogue acts are of course not given automatically. A fully automatic approach would involve using ASR output instead of manual transcriptions— something which we attempt in Section 7.

[8] We use the the BayesNet classifier implemented in the Weka toolkit `http://www.cs.waikato.ac.nz/ml/weka/`.

Features	Acc	F1-Gen	F1-Ref
Baseline	50.86	0	67.4
Discourse	77.77	78.8	76.6
Visual	60.32	64.2	55.5
MM	79.02	80.2	77.7
Dis w/o FL	78.34	79.1	77.5
MM w/o FL	78.22	79.0	77.4
Dis w/o DA	69.44	71.5	67.0
MM w/o DA	72.75	74.4	70.9

Table 5: Generic *vs.* referential uses

(MM) yields 79.02%, but this increase is not statistically significant.

In spite of this, visual features do help to distinguish between generic and referential uses - note that the visual features alone are able to beat the baseline ($p < .005$). The listeners' gaze is more predictive than the speaker's: if listeners look mostly at the white-board/projector screen instead of another participant, then the *you* is more likely to be referential. More will be said on this in Section 6.2.1 in the analysis of the results for the singular *vs.* plural referential task.

We found sentential features of the *you*-utterance to be amongst the best predictors, especially those that refer to surface lexical properties, such as features 1, 11, 12 and 13 in Table 4. Dialogue act features provide useful information as well. As pointed out by Gupta et al. (2007b; 2007a), a *you* pronoun within a question (e.g. an utterance tagged as `elicit-assess` or `elicit-inform`) is more likely to be referential. Eliminating information about dialogue acts (w/o DA) brings down performance ($p < .005$), although accuracy remains well above the baseline ($p < .001$). Note that the small changes in performance when FL information is taken out (w/o FL) are not statistically significant.

6.2 Reference Resolution

We now turn to the referential instances of *you*, which can be resolved by determining the addressee(s) of the given utterance.

6.2.1 Singular *vs.* Plural Reference

We start by trying to discriminate singular *vs.* plural interpretations. For this, we use a two-way classification scheme that distinguishes between individual and group addressing. To our knowledge, this is the first attempt at this task using linguistic information.[9]

[9]But see e.g. (Takemae et al., 2004) for an approach that uses manually extracted visual-only clues with similar aims.

Baseline. A majority class baseline that considers all instances of *you* as referring to an individual addressee gives 67.92% accuracy (see Table 1).

Results. A summary of the results is shown in Table 6. There is no statistically significant difference between the baseline and the results obtained when visual features are used alone (67.92% *vs.* 66.28%). However, we found that visual information did contribute to identifying some instances of plural addressing, as shown by the F-score for that class. Furthermore, the visual features helped to improve results when combined with discourse information: using multimodal (MM) features produces higher results than the discourse-only feature set ($p < .005$), and increases from 74.24% to 77.05% with CFS.

As in the generic *vs.* referential task, the white-board/projector screen value for the listeners' gaze features seems to have discriminative power - when listeners' gaze features take this value, it is often indicative of a plural rather than a singular *you*. It seems then, that in our data-set, the speaker often uses the white-board/projector screen when addressing the group, and hence draws the listeners' gaze in this direction. We should also note that the ratio features which we thought might be useful here (see Section 4.1) did not prove so.

Amongst the most useful discourse features are those that encode similarity relations between the *you*-utterance and an utterance by a potential addressee. Utterances by individual addressees tend to be more lexically cohesive with the *you*-utterance and so if features such as feature 19 in Table 4 indicate a low level of lexical similarity, then this increases the likelihood of plural addressing. Sentential features that refer to surface lexical patterns (features 6, 7, 11 and 12) also contribute to improved results, as does feature 21 (number of speakers during the next five utterances) - fewer speaker changes correlates with plural addressing.

Information about dialogue acts also plays a role in distinguishing between singular and plural interpretations. Questions tend to be addressed to individual participants, while statements show a stronger correlation with plural addressees. When no DA features are used (w/o DA), the drop in performance for the multimodal classifier to 71.19% is statistically significant ($p < .05$). As for the generic *vs.* referential task, FL information does not have a significant effect on performance.

Features	Acc	F1-Sing.	F1-Pl.
Baseline	67.92	80.9	0
Discourse	71.19	78.9	54.6
Visual	66.28	74.8	48.9
MM*	77.05	83.3	63.2
Dis w/o FL	72.13	80.1	53.7
MM w/o FL	72.60	79.7	58.1
Dis w/o DA	68.38	78.5	40.5
MM w/o DA	71.19	78.8	55.3

Table 6: Singular *vs.* plural reference; * = with Correlation-based Feature Selection (CFS).

Features	Acc	F1-L_1	F1-L_2	F1-L_3
MC baseline	35.17	52.0	0	0
Discourse	60.69	59.1	60.0	62.7
Visual	65.52	69.1	63.5	64.0
MM*	80.34	80.0	82.4	79.0
Dis w/o FL	52.41	50.7	51.8	54.5
MM w/o FL	66.55	68.7	62.7	67.6
Dis w/o DA	61.03	58.5	59.9	64.2
MM w/o DA	73.10	72.4	69.5	72.0

Table 7: Addressee detection for singular references; * = with Correlation-based Feature Selection (CFS).

6.2.2 Detection of Individual Addressees

We now turn to resolving the singular referential uses of *you*. Here we must detect the individual addressee of the utterance that contains the pronoun.

Baselines. Given the distribution shown in Table 2, a majority class baseline yields an accuracy of 35.17%. An off-line system that has access to future context could implement a next-speaker baseline that always considers the next speaker to be the intended addressee, so yielding a high raw accuracy of 71.03%. A previous-speaker baseline that does not require access to future context achieves 35% raw accuracy.

Results. Table 7 shows a summary of the results, and these all outperform the majority class (MC) and previous-speaker baselines. When all discourse features are available, adding visual information does improve performance (74.48% *vs.* 60.69%, $p < .005$), and with CFS, this increases further to 80.34% ($p < .005$). Using discourse or visual features alone gives scores that are below the next-speaker baseline (60.69% and 65.52% *vs.* 71.03%). Taking all forward-looking (FL) information away reduces performance ($p < .05$), but the small increase in accuracy caused by taking away dialogue act information is not statistically significant.

When we investigated individual feature contribution, we found that the most predictive features were the FL and backward-looking (BL) speaker order, and the speaker's visual features (including mutual gaze). Whomever the speaker spent most time looking at or engaged in a mutual gaze with was more likely to be the addressee. All of the visual features had some degree of predictive power apart from the ratio features. Of the other BL/FL discourse features, features 14, 18 and 19 (see Table 4) were more predictive. These indicate that utterances spoken by the intended addressee are often adjacent to the *you*-utterance and lexically similar.

7 A Fully Automatic Approach

In this section we describe experiments which use features derived from ASR transcriptions and automatically-extracted visual information. We used SRI's Decipher (Stolcke et al., 2008)[10] in order to generate ASR transcriptions, and applied the head-tracker described in Section 4.2 to the relevant portions of video in order to extract the visual information. Recall that the Named Entity features (feature 13) and the DA features used in our previous experiments had been manually annotated, and hence are not used here. We again divide the problem into the same three separate tasks: we first discriminate between generic and referential uses of *you*, then singular *vs.* plural referential uses, and finally we resolve the addressee for singular uses. As before, all experiments are performed using a Bayesian Network classifier and 10-fold cross validation.

7.1 Results

For each of the three tasks, Figure 7 compares the accuracy results obtained using the fully-automatic approach with those reported in Section 6. The figure shows results for the majority class baselines (MCBs), and with discourse-only (Dis), and multimodal (MM) feature sets. Note that the data set for the automatic approach is smaller, and that the majority class baselines have changed slightly. This is because of differences in the utterance segmentation, and also because not all of the video sections around the *you* utterances were processed by the head-tracker.

In all three tasks we are able to significantly outperform the majority class baseline, but the visual features only produce a significant improve-

[10]Stolcke et al. (2008) report a word error rate of 26.9% on AMI meetings.

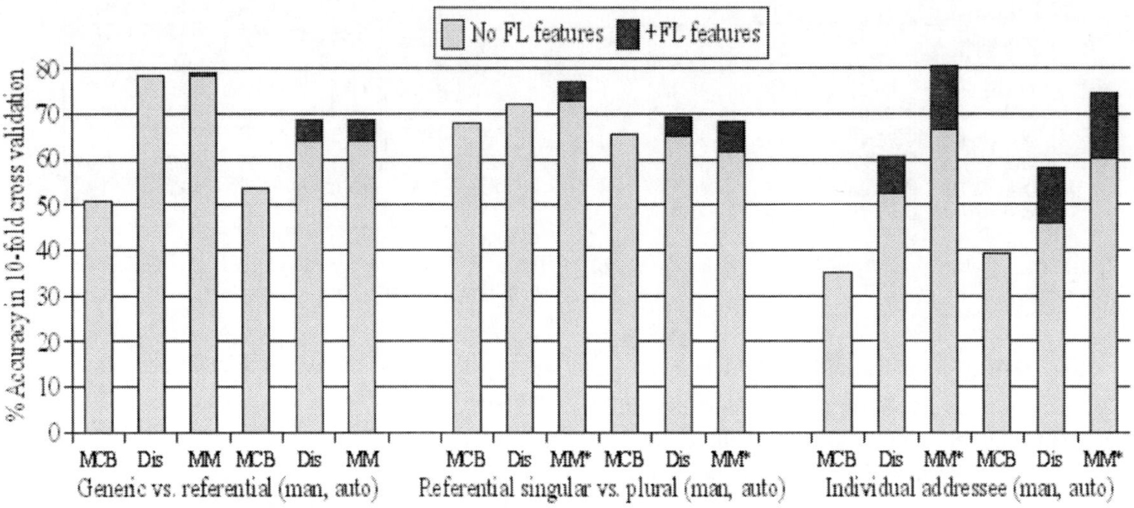

Figure 1: Results for the manual and automatic systems; MCB = majority class baseline, Dis = discourse features, MM = multimodal, * = with Correlation-based Feature Selection (CFS), FL = forward-looking, man = manual, auto = automatic.

ment in the individual addressee resolution task. For the generic *vs.* referential task, the discourse and multimodal classifiers both outperform the majority class baseline ($p < .001$), achieving accuracy scores of 68.71% and 68.48% respectively. In contrast to when using manual transcriptions and annotations (see Section 6.1), removing forward-looking (FL) information reduces performance ($p < .05$). For the referential singular *vs.* plural task, the discourse and multimodal with CFS classifier improve over the majority class baseline ($p < .05$). Multimodal with CFS does not improve over the discourse classifier - indeed without feature selection, the addition of visual features causes a drop in performance ($p < .05$). Here, taking away FL information does not cause a significant reduction in performance. Finally, in the individual addressee resolution task, the discourse, visual (60.78%) and multimodal classifiers all outperform the majority class baseline ($p < .005$, $p < .001$ and $p < .001$ respectively). Here the addition of visual features causes the multimodal classifier to outperform the discourse classifier in raw accuracy by nearly ten percentage points (67.32% *vs.* 58.17%, $p < .05$), and with CFS, the score increases further to 74.51% ($p < .05$). Taking away FL information does cause a significant drop in performance ($p < .05$).

8 Conclusions

We have investigated the automatic resolution of the second person English pronoun *you* in multi-party dialogue, using a combination of linguistic and visual features. We conducted a first set of experiments where our features were derived from manual transcriptions and annotations, and then a second set where they were generated by entirely automatic means. To our knowledge, this is the first attempt at tackling this problem using automatically extracted multimodal information.

Our experiments showed that visual information can be highly predictive in resolving the addressee of singular referential uses of *you*. Visual features significantly improved the performance of both our manual and automatic systems, and the latter achieved an encouraging 75% accuracy. We also found that our visual features had predictive power for distinguishing between generic and referential uses of *you*, and between referential singulars and plurals. Indeed, for the latter task, they significantly improved the manual system's performance. The listeners' gaze features were useful here: in our data set it was apparently the case that the speaker would often use the whiteboard/projector screen when addressing the group, thus drawing the listeners' gaze in this direction.

Future work will involve expanding our dataset, and investigating new potentially predictive features. In the slightly longer term, we plan to integrate the resulting system into a meeting assistant whose purpose is to automatically extract useful information from multi-party meetings.

References

Ron Arstein and Massimo Poesio. 2006. Identifying reference to abstract objects in dialogue. In *Proceedings of the 10th Workshop on the Semantics and Pragmatics of Dialogue (Brandial'06)*, pages 56–63, Potsdam, Germany.

Ilse Bakx, Koen van Turnhout, and Jacques Terken. 2003. Facial orientation during multi-party interaction with information kiosks. In *Proceedings of INTERACT*, Zurich, Switzerland.

Donna Byron. 2004. *Resolving pronominal reference to abstract entities*. Ph.D. thesis, University of Rochester, Department of Computer Science.

Michel Galley, Kathleen McKeown, Julia Hirschberg, and Elizabeth Shriberg. 2004. Identifying agreement and disagreement in conversational speech: Use of Bayesian networks to model pragmatic dependencies. In *Proceedings of the 42nd Annual Meeting of the Association for Computational Linguistics (ACL)*.

Surabhi Gupta, John Niekrasz, Matthew Purver, and Daniel Jurafsky. 2007a. Resolving "you" in multi-party dialog. In *Proceedings of the 8th SIGdial Workshop on Discourse and Dialogue*, Antwerp, Belgium, September.

Surabhi Gupta, Matthew Purver, and Daniel Jurafsky. 2007b. Disambiguating between generic and referential "you" in dialog. In *Proceedings of the 45th Annual Meeting of the Association for Computational Linguistics (ACL)*.

Mark Hall. 2000. *Correlation-based Feature Selection for Machine Learning*. Ph.D. thesis, University of Waikato.

Natasa Jovanovic, Rieks op den Akker, and Anton Nijholt. 2006a. Addressee identification in face-to-face meetings. In *Proceedings of the 11th Conference of the European Chapter of the ACL (EACL)*, pages 169–176, Trento, Italy.

Natasa Jovanovic, Rieks op den Akker, and Anton Nijholt. 2006b. A corpus for studying addressing behaviour in multi-party dialogues. *Language Resources and Evaluation*, 40(1):5–23. ISSN=1574-020X.

Natasa Jovanovic. 2007. *To Whom It May Concern - Addressee Identification in Face-to-Face Meetings*. Ph.D. thesis, University of Twente, Enschede, The Netherlands.

Michael Katzenmaier, Rainer Stiefelhagen, and Tanja Schultz. 2004. Identifying the addressee in human-human-robot interactions based on head pose and speech. In *Proceedings of the 6th International Conference on Multimodal Interfaces*, pages 144–151, State College, Pennsylvania.

Iain McCowan, Jean Carletta, W. Kraaij, S. Ashby, S. Bourban, M. Flynn, M. Guillemot, T. Hain, J. Kadlec, V. Karaiskos, M. Kronenthal, G. Lathoud, M. Lincoln, A. Lisowska, W. Post, D. Reidsma, and P. Wellner. 2005. The AMI Meeting Corpus. In *Proceedings of Measuring Behavior, the 5th International Conference on Methods and Techniques in Behavioral Research*, Wageningen, Netherlands.

Christoph Müller. 2006. Automatic detection of non-referential *It* in spoken multi-party dialog. In *Proceedings of the 11th Conference of the European Chapter of the Association for Computational Linguistics (EACL)*, pages 49–56, Trento, Italy.

Christoph Müller. 2007. Resolving it, this, and that in unrestricted multi-party dialog. In *Proceedings of the 45th Annual Meeting of the Association for Computational Linguistics*, pages 816–823, Prague, Czech Republic.

Andreas Stolcke, Xavier Anguera, Kofi Boakye, Özgür Çetin, Adam Janin, Matthew Magimai-Doss, Chuck Wooters, and Jing Zheng. 2008. The icsi-sri spring 2007 meeting and lecture recognition system. In *Proceedings of CLEAR 2007 and RT2007*. Springer Lecture Notes on Computer Science.

Michael Strube and Christoph Müller. 2003. A machine learning approach to pronoun resolution in spoken dialogue. In *Proceedings of ACL'03*, pages 168–175.

Yoshinao Takemae, Kazuhiro Otsuka, and Naoki Mukawa. 2004. An analysis of speakers' gaze behaviour for automatic addressee identification in multiparty conversation and its application to video editing. In *Proceedings of IEEE Workshop on Robot and Human Interactive Communication*, pages 581–586.

Koen van Turnhout, Jacques Terken, Ilse Bakx, and Berry Eggen. 2005. Identifying the intended addressee in mixed human-humand and human-computer interaction from non-verbal features. In *Proceedings of ICMI*, Trento, Italy.

Bonnie Webber. 1991. Structure and ostension in the interpretation of discourse deixi. *Language and Cognitive Processes*, 6(2):107–135.

Rich bitext projection features for parse reranking

Alexander Fraser **Renjing Wang** **Hinrich Schütze**
Institute for Natural Language Processing
University of Stuttgart
{fraser,wangrg}@ims.uni-stuttgart.de

Abstract

Many different types of features have been shown to improve accuracy in parse reranking. A class of features that thus far has not been considered is based on a projection of the syntactic structure of a translation of the text to be parsed. The intuition for using this type of *bitext projection feature* is that ambiguous structures in one language often correspond to unambiguous structures in another. We show that reranking based on bitext projection features increases parsing accuracy significantly.

1 Introduction

Parallel text or *bitext* is an important knowledge source for solving many problems such as machine translation, cross-language information retrieval, and the projection of linguistic resources from one language to another. In this paper, we show that bitext-based features are effective in addressing another NLP problem, increasing the accuracy of statistical parsing. We pursue this approach for a number of reasons. First, one limiting factor for syntactic approaches to statistical machine translation is parse quality (Quirk and Corston-Oliver, 2006). Improved parses of bitext should result in improved machine translation. Second, as more and more texts are available in several languages, it will be increasingly the case that a text to be parsed is itself part of a bitext. Third, we hope that the improved parses of bitext will serve as higher quality training data for improving monolingual parsing using a process similar to self-training (McClosky et al., 2006).

It is well known that different languages encode different types of grammatical information (agreement, case, tense etc.) and that what can be left unspecified in one language must be made explicit in another. This information can be used for syntactic disambiguation. However, it is surprisingly hard to do this well. We use parses and alignments that are automatically generated and hence imperfect. German parse quality is considered to be worse than English parse quality, and the annotation style is different, e.g., NP structure in German is flatter.

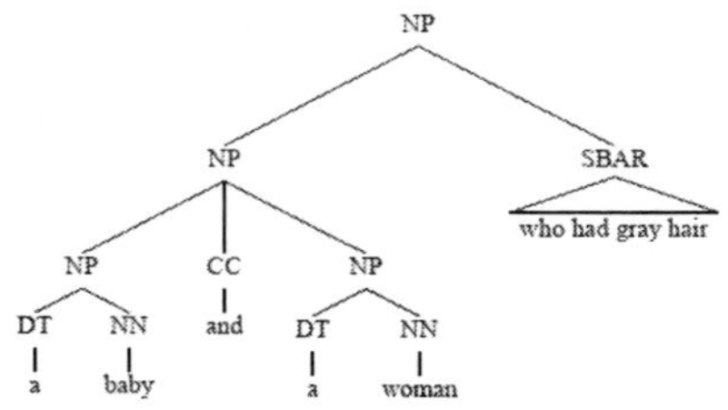

Figure 1: English parse with high attachment

We conduct our research in the framework of N-best parse reranking, but apply it to bitext and add only features based on *syntactic projection* from German to English. We test the idea that, generally, English parses with more isomorphism with respect to the projected German parse are better. The system takes as input (i) English sentences with a list of automatically generated syntactic parses, (ii) a translation of the English sentences into German, (iii) an automatically generated parse of the German translation, and (iv) an automatically generated word alignment. We achieve a significant improvement of 0.66 F_1 (absolute) on test data.

The paper is organized as follows. Section 2 outlines our approach and section 3 introduces the model. Section 4 describes training and section 5 presents the data and experimental results. In section 6, we discuss previous work. Section 7 analyzes our results and section 8 concludes.

Proceedings of the 12th Conference of the European Chapter of the ACL, pages 282–290,
Athens, Greece, 30 March – 3 April 2009.

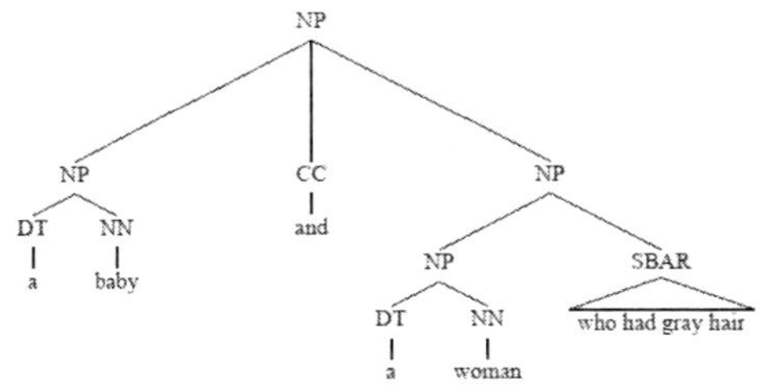

Figure 2: English parse with low attachment

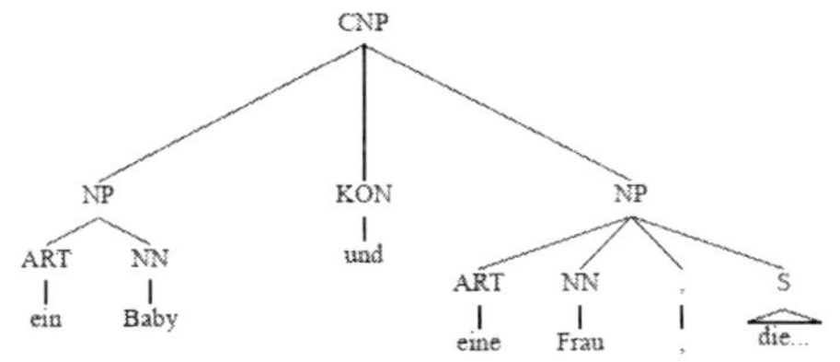

Figure 3: German parse with low attachment

2 Approach

Consider the English sentence "He saw a baby and a woman who had gray hair". Suppose that the baseline parser generates two parses, containing the NPs shown in figures 1 and 2, respectively, and that the semantically more plausible second parse in figure 2 is correct. How can we determine that the second parse should be favored? Since we are parsing bitext, we can observe the German translation which is "Er sah ein Baby und eine Frau, die graue Haare hatte" (glossed: "he saw a baby and a woman, who gray hair had"). The singular verb in the subordinate clause ("hatte": "had") indicates that the subordinate S must be attached low to "woman" ("Frau") as shown in figure 3.

We follow Collins' (2000) approach to discriminative reranking (see also (Riezler et al., 2002)). Given a new sentence to parse, we first select the best N parse trees according to a generative model. Then we use new features to learn discriminatively how to rerank the parses in this N-best list. We use features derived using projections of the 1-best German parse onto the hypothesized English parse under consideration.

In more detail, we take the 100 best English parses from the BitPar parser (Schmid, 2004) and rerank them. We have a good chance of finding the optimal parse among the 100-best[1]. An automatically generated word alignment determines translational correspondence between German and English. We use features which measure *syntactic divergence* between the German and English trees to try to rank the English trees which have less divergence higher. Our test set is 3718 sentences from the English Penn treebank (Marcus et al., 1993) which were translated into German. We hold out these sentences, and train BitPar on the remaining Penn treebank training sentences. The average F_1 parsing accuracy of BitPar on this test set is 87.89%, which is our baseline[2]. We implement features based on projecting the German parse to each of the English 100-best parses in turn via the word alignment. By performing cross-validation and measuring test performance within each fold, we compare our new system with the baseline on the 3718 sentence set. The overall test accuracy we reach is 88.55%, a statistically significant improvement over baseline of 0.66.

Given a word alignment of the bitext, the system performs the following steps for each English sentence to be parsed:
(i) run BitPar trained on English to generate 100-best parses for the English sentence
(ii) run BitPar trained on German to generate the 1-best parse for the German sentence
(iii) calculate feature function values which measure different kinds of syntactic divergence
(iv) apply a model that combines the feature function values to score each of the 100-best parses
(v) pick the best parse according to the model

3 Model

We use a log-linear model to choose the best English parse. The feature functions are functions on the hypothesized English parse e, the German parse g, and the word alignment a, and they assign a score (varying between 0 and infinity) that measures *syntactic divergence*. The alignment of a sentence pair is a function that, for each English word, returns a set of German words that the English word is aligned with as shown here for the sentence pair from section 2:

Er sah ein Baby und eine Frau , die graue Haare hatte

He{1} saw{2} a{3} baby{4} and{5} a{6} woman{7} who{9} had{12} gray{10} hair{11}

Feature function values are calculated either by taking the negative log of a probability, or by using a heuristic function which scales in a similar fash-

[1]Using an oracle to select the best parse results in an F_1 of 95.90, an improvement of 8.01 absolute over the baseline.

[2]The test set is very challenging, containing English sentences of up to 99 tokens.

ion[3]. The form of the log-linear model is shown in eq. 1. There are M feature functions $h_1, \ldots, h_M$. The vector λ is used to control the contribution of each feature function.

$$p_\lambda(e|g,a) = \frac{exp(-\sum_i \lambda_i h_i(e,g,a))}{\sum_{e'} exp(-\sum_i \lambda_i h_i(e',g,a))} \quad (1)$$

Given a vector of weights λ, the best English parse $\hat{e}$ can be found by solving eq. 2. The model is trained by finding the weight vector λ which maximizes accuracy (see section 4).

$$\hat{e} = \underset{e}{\mathrm{argmax}}\, p_\lambda(e|g,a) = \underset{e}{\mathrm{argmin}}\, exp(\sum_i \lambda_i h_i(e,g,a)) \quad (2)$$

3.1 Feature Functions

The basic idea behind our feature functions is that any constituent in a sentence should play approximately the same syntactic role and have a similar span as the corresponding constituent in a translation. If there is an obvious disagreement, it is probably caused by wrong attachment or other syntactic mistakes in parsing. Sometimes in translation the syntactic role of a given semantic constitutent changes; we assume that our model penalizes all hypothesized parses equally in this case. For the initial experiments, we used a set of 34 probabilistic and heuristic feature functions.

BitParLogProb (the only monolingual feature) is the negative log probability assigned by BitPar to the English parse. If we set $\lambda_1 = 1$ and $\lambda_i = 0$ for all $i \neq 1$ and evaluate eq. 2, we will select the parse ranked best by BitPar.

In order to define our feature functions, we first introduce auxiliary functions operating on individual word positions or sets of word positions. Alignment functions take an alignment a as an argument. In the descriptions of these functions we omit a as it is held constant for a sentence pair (i.e., an English sentence and its German translation).

$f(i)$ returns the set of word positions of German words aligned with an English word at position i.

$f'(i)$ returns the leftmost word position of the German words aligned with an English word at position i, or zero if the English word is unaligned.

$f^{-1}(i)$ returns the set of positions of English words aligned with a German word at position i.

$f'^{-1}(i)$ returns the leftmost word position of the English words aligned with a German word at position i, or zero if the German word is unaligned.

We overload the above functions to allow the argument i to be a set, in which case union is used, for example, $f(i) = \cup_{j \in i} f(j)$. Positions in a tree are denoted with integers. First, the POS tags are numbered from 1 to the length of the sentence (i.e., the same as the word positions). Constituents higher in the tree are also indexed using consecutive integers. We refer to the constituent that has been assigned index i in the tree t as "constituent i in tree t" or simply as "constituent i". The following functions have the English and German trees as an implicit argument; it should be obvious from the argument to the function whether the index i refers to the German tree or the English tree. When we say "constituents", we include nodes on the POS level of the tree. Our syntactic trees are annotated with a syntactic head for each constituent. Finally, the tag at position 0 is NULL.

mid2sib(i) returns 0 if i is 0, returns 1 if i has exactly two siblings, one on the left of i and one on the right, and otherwise returns 0.

head(i) returns the index of the head of i. The head of a POS tag is its own position.

tag(i) returns the tag of i.

left(i) returns the index of the leftmost sibling of i.

right(i) returns the index of the rightmost sibling.

up(i) returns the index of i's parent.

$\Delta(i)$ returns the set of word positions covered by i. If i is a set, Δ returns all word positions between the leftmost position covered by any constituent in the set and the rightmost position covered by any constituent in the set (inclusive).

$n(A)$ returns the size of the set A.

$c(A)$ returns the number of characters (including punctuation and excluding spaces) covered by the constituents in set A.

$[\![\pi]\!]$ is 1 if π is true, and 0 otherwise.

l and m are the lengths in words of the English and German sentences, respectively.

3.1.1 Count Feature Functions

Feature **CrdBin** counts binary events involving the heads of coordinated phrases. If in the English parse we have a coordination where the English CC is aligned only with a German KON, and both have two siblings, then the value contributed to **CrdBin** is 1 (indicating a constraint violation) un-

[3]For example, a probability of 1 is a feature value of 0, while a low probability is a feature value which is $\gg 0$.

less the head of the English left conjunct is aligned with the head of the German left conjunct and likewise the right conjuncts are aligned. Eq. 3 calculates the value of **CrdBin**.

$$\sum_{i=1}^{l} [\![(\text{tag}(i) = \text{CC}]\!][\![(n(f(i)) = 1]\!] \quad \text{mid2sib}(i)$$
$$\text{mid2sib}(f'(i)) \quad [\![\text{tag}(f'(i)) = \text{KON-CD}]\!]$$
$$[\![[\text{head}(\text{left}(f'(i))) \neq f'(\text{head}(\text{left}(i)))] \text{ OR}$$
$$[\text{head}(\text{right}(f'(i))) \neq f'(\text{head}(\text{right}(i)))]]\!] \quad (3)$$

Feature **Q** simply captures a mismatch between questions and statements. If an English sentence is parsed as a question but the parallel German sentence is not, or vice versa, the feature value is 1; otherwise the value is 0.

3.1.2 Span Projection Feature Functions

Span projection features calculate the percentage difference between a constituent's span and the span of its projection. Span size is measured in characters or words. To project a constituent in a parse, we use the word alignment to project all word positions covered by the constituent and then look for the smallest covering constituent in the parse of the parallel sentence.

CrdPrj is a feature that measures the divergence in the size of coordination constituents and their projections. If we have a constituent (XP1 CC XP2) in English that is projected to a German coordination, we expect the English and German left conjuncts to span a similar percentage of their respective sentences, as should the right conjuncts. The feature computes a character-based percentage difference as shown in eq. 4.

$$\sum_{i=1}^{l} [\![\text{tag}(i) = \text{CC}]\!][\![n(f(i)) = 1]\!] \quad (4)$$
$$[\![\text{tag}(f'(i)) = \text{KON-CD}]\!]$$
$$\text{mid2sib}(i)\text{mid2sib}(f'(i))$$
$$(|\frac{c(\Delta(\text{left}(i)))}{r} - \frac{c(\Delta(\text{left}(f'(i))))}{s}|$$
$$+|\frac{c(\Delta(\text{right}(i)))}{r} - \frac{c(\Delta(\text{right}(f'(i))))}{s}|)$$

r and s are the lengths in characters of the English and German sentences, respectively. In the English parse in figure 1, the left conjunct has 5 characters and the right conjunct has 6, while in figure 2 the left conjunct has 5 characters and the right conjunct has 20. In the German parse (figure 3) the left conjunct has 7 characters and the right conjunct has 27. Finally, $r = 33$ and $s = 42$. Thus, the value of **CrdPrj** is 0.48 for the first hypothesized parse and 0.05 for the second, which captures the higher divergence of the first English parse from the German parse.

POSParentPrj is based on computing the span difference between all the parent constituents of POS tags in a German parse and their respective coverage in the corresponding hypothesized parse. The feature value is the sum of all the differences. POSPar(i) is true if i immediately dominates a POS tag. The projection direction is from German to English, and the feature computes a percentage difference which is character-based. The value of the feature is calculated in eq. 5, where M is the number of constituents (including POS tags) in the German tree.

$$\sum_{i=1}^{M} [\![\text{POSPar}(i)]\!] |\frac{c(\Delta(i))}{s} - \frac{c(\Delta(f^{-1}(\Delta(i))))}{r}| \quad (5)$$

The right conjunct in figure 3 is a POSParent that corresponds to the coordination NP in figure 1, contributing a score of 0.21, and to the right conjunct in figure 2, contributing a score of 0.04. For the two parses of the full sentences containing the NPs in figure 1 and figure 2, we sum over 7 POSParents and get a value of 0.27 for parse 1 and 0.11 for parse 2. The lower value for parse 2 correctly captures the fact that the first English parse has higher divergence than the second due to incorrect high attachment.

AbovePOSPrj is similar to **POSParentPrj**, but it is word-based and the projection direction is from English to German. Unlike **POSParentPrj** the feature value is calculated over all constituents above the POS level in the English tree.

Another span projection feature function is **DTNNPrj**, which projects English constituents of the form (NP(DT)(NN)). DTNN(i) is true if i is an NP immediately dominating only DT and NN. The feature computes a percentage difference which is word-based, shown in eq. 6.

$$\sum_{i=1}^{L} [\![\text{DTNN}(i)]\!] |\frac{n(\Delta(i))}{l} - \frac{n(\Delta(f(\Delta(i))))}{m}| \quad (6)$$

L is the number of constituents in the English tree. This feature is designed to disprefer parses where constituents starting with "DT NN", e.g., (NP (DT NN NN NN)), are incorrectly split into two NPs, e.g., (NP (DT NN)) and (NP (NN NN)). This feature fires in this case, and projects the (NP (DT NN)) into German. If the German projection is a surprisingly large number of words (as should be the case if the German also consists of a determiner followed by several nouns) then the penalty paid by this feature is large. This feature is important as (NP (DT NN)) is a very common construction.

3.1.3 Probabilistic Feature Functions

We use Europarl (Koehn, 2005), from which we extract a parallel corpus of approximately 1.22 million sentence pairs, to estimate the probabilistic feature functions described in this section.

For the **PDepth** feature, we estimate English parse depth probability conditioned on German parse depth from Europarl by calculating a simple probability distribution over the 1-best parse pairs for each parallel sentence. A very deep German parse is unlikely to correspond to a flat English parse and we can penalize such a parse using **PDepth**. The index i refers to a sentence pair in Europarl, as does j. Let l_i and m_i be the depths of the top BitPar ranked parses of the English and German sentences, respectively. We calculate the probability of observing an English tree of depth l' given German tree of depth m' as the maximum likelihood estimate, shown in eq. 7, where $\delta(z, z') = 1$ if $z = z'$ and 0 otherwise. To avoid noisy feature values due to outliers and parse errors, we bound the value of **PDepth** at 5 as shown in eq. 8[4].

$$p(l'|m') = \frac{\sum_i \delta(l', l_i)\delta(m', m_i)}{\sum_j \delta(m', m_j)} \qquad (7)$$

$$\min(5, -\log_{10}(p(l'|m'))) \qquad (8)$$

The full parse of the sentence containing the English high attachment has a parse depth of 8 while the full parse of the sentence containing the English low attachment has a depth of 9. Their feature values given the German parse depth of 6 are $-\log_{10}(0.12) = 0.93$ and $-\log_{10}(0.14) = 0.84$. The wrong parse is assigned a higher feature value indicating its higher divergence.

The feature **PTagEParentGPOSGParent** measures tagging inconsistency based on estimating the probability that for an English word at position i, the parent of its POS tag has a particular label. The feature value is calculated in eq. 10.

$$q(i, j) = p(\text{tag}(\text{up}(i))|\text{tag}(j), \text{tag}(\text{up}(j))) \qquad (9)$$

$$\sum_{i=1}^{l} \min(5, \frac{\sum_{j \in f(i)} -\log_{10}(q(i, j))}{n(f(i))}) \qquad (10)$$

Consider (S(NP(NN fruit))(VP(V flies))) and (NP(NN fruit)(NNS flies)) with the translation (NP(NNS Fruchtfliegen)). Assume that "fruit" and "flies" are aligned with the German compound noun "Fruchtfliegen". In the incorrect English parse the parent of the POS of "fruit" is NP and the parent of the POS of "flies" is VP, while in the correct parse the parent of the POS of "fruit" is NP and the parent of the POS of "flies" is NP. In the German parse the compound noun is POS-tagged as an NNS and the parent is an NP. The probabilities considered for the two English parses are $p(\text{NP}|\text{NNS}, \text{NP})$ for "fruit" in both parses, $p(\text{VP}|\text{NNS}, \text{NP})$ for "flies" in the incorrect parse, and $p(\text{NP}|\text{NNS}, \text{NP})$ for "flies" in the correct parse. A German NNS in an NP has a higher probability of being aligned with a word in an English NP than with a word in an English VP, so the second parse will be preferred.

As with the **PDepth** feature, we use relative frequency to estimate this feature. When an English word is aligned with two words, estimation is more complex. We heuristically give each English and German pair one count. The value calculated by the feature function is the geometric mean[5] of the pairwise probabilities, see eq. 10.

3.1.4 Other Features

Our best system uses the nine features we have described in detail so far. In addition, we implemented the following 25 other features, which did not improve performance (see section 7): (i) 7 "ptag" features similar to **PTagEParentGPOSGParent** but predicting and conditioning on different combinations of tags (POS tag, parent of POS, grandparent of POS)

(ii) 10 "prj" features similar to **POSParentPrj** measuring different combinations of character and word percentage differences at the POS parent and

[4]Throughout this paper, assume $\log(0) = -\infty$.

[5]Each English word has the same weight regardless of whether it was aligned with one or with more German words.

POS grandparent levels, projecting from both English and German

(iii) 3 variants of the **DTNN** feature function

(iv) A **NPPP** feature function, similar to the **DTNN** feature function but trying to counteract a bias towards (NP (NP) (PP)) units

(v) A feature function which penalizes aligning clausal units to non-clausal units

(vi) The BitPar rank

4 Training

Log-linear models are often trained using the Maximum Entropy criterion, but we train our model directly to maximize F_1. We score F_1 by comparing hypothesized parses for the discriminative training set with the gold standard. To try to find the optimal λ vector, we perform direct accuracy maximization, meaning that we search for the λ vector which directly optimizes F_1 on the training set.

Och (2003) has described an efficient exact one-dimensional accuracy maximization technique for a similar search problem in machine translation. The technique involves calculating an explicit representation of the piecewise constant function $g_m(x)$ which evaluates the accuracy of the hypotheses which would be picked by eq. 2 from a set of hypotheses if we hold all weights constant, except for the weight λ_m, which is set to x. This is calculated in one pass over the data.

The algorithm for training is initialized with a choice for λ and is described in figure 4. The function $F_1(\lambda)$ returns F_1 of the parses selected using λ. Due to space we do not describe step 8 in detail (see (Och, 2003)). In step 9 the algorithm performs approximate normalization, where feature weights are forced towards zero. The implementation of step 9 is straight-forward given the M explicit functions $g_m(x)$ created in step 8.

1: **Algorithm** TRAIN(λ)
2: **repeat**
3: add λ to the set s
4: let t be a set of 1000 randomly generated vectors
5: let $\lambda = \text{argmax}_{\rho \in (s \cup t)} F_1(\rho)$
6: let $\lambda' = \lambda$
7: **repeat**
8: repeatedly run one-dimensional error minimization step (updating a single scalar of the vector λ) until no further error reduction
9: adjust each scalar of λ in turn towards 0 such that there is no increase in error (if possible)
10: **until** no scalar in λ changes in last two steps (8 and 9)
11: **until** $\lambda = \lambda'$
12: return λ

Figure 4: Sketch of the training algorithm

5 Data and Experiments

We used the subset of the Wall Street Journal investigated in (Atterer and Schütze, 2007) for our experiments, which consists of all sentences that have at least one prepositional phrase attachment ambiguity. This difficult subset of sentences seems particularly interesting when investigating the potential of information in bitext for improving parsing performance. The first 500 sentences of this set were translated from English to German by a graduate student and an additional 3218 sentences by a translation bureau. We withheld these 3718 English sentences (and an additional 1000 reserved sentences) when we trained BitPar on the Penn treebank.

Parses. We use the BitPar parser (Schmid, 2004) which is based on a bit-vector implementation (cf. (Graham et al., 1980)) of the Cocke-Younger-Kasami algorithm (Kasami, 1965; Younger, 1967). It computes a compact parse forest for all possible analyses. As all possible analyses are computed, any number of best parses can be extracted. In contrast, other treebank parsers use sophisticated search strategies to find the most probable analysis without examining the set of all possible analyses (Charniak et al., 1998; Klein and Manning, 2003). BitPar is particularly useful for N-best parsing as the N-best parses can be computed efficiently.

For the 3718 sentences in the translated set, we created 100-best English parses and 1-best German parses. The German parser was trained on the TIGER treebank. For the Europarl corpus, we created 1-best parses for both languages.

Word Alignment. We use a word alignment of the translated sentences from the Penn treebank, as well as a word alignment of the Europarl corpus. We align these two data sets together with data from the JRC Acquis (Steinberger et al., 2006) to try to obtain better quality alignments (it is well known that alignment quality improves as the amount of data increases (Fraser and Marcu, 2007)). We aligned approximately 3.08 million sentence pairs. We tried to obtain better alignment quality as alignment quality is a problem in many cases where syntactic projection would otherwise work well (Fossum and Knight, 2008).

	System	Train	+base	Test	+base
1	Baseline	87.89		87.89	
2	Contrastive (5 trials/fold)	88.70	0.82	88.45	0.56
3	Contrastive (greedy selection)	88.82	0.93	88.55	0.66

Table 1: Average F_1 of 7-way cross-validation

To generate the alignments, we used Model 4 (Brown et al., 1993), as implemented in GIZA++ (Och and Ney, 2003). As is standard practice, we trained Model 4 with English as the source language, and then trained Model 4 with German as the source language, resulting in two Viterbi alignments. These were combined using the *Grow Diag Final And* symmetrization heuristic (Koehn et al., 2003).

Experiments. We perform 7-way cross-validation on 3718 sentences. In each fold of the cross-validation, the training set is 3186 sentences, while the test set is 532 sentences. Our results are shown in table 1. In row 1, we take the hypothesis ranked best by BitPar. In row 2, we train using the algorithm outlined in section 4. To cancel out any effect caused by a particularly effective or ineffective starting λ value, we perform 5 trials each time. Columns 3 and 5 report the improvement over the baseline on train and test respectively. We reach an improvement of 0.56 over the baseline using the algorithm as described in section 4.

Our initial experiments used many highly correlated features. For our next experiment we use greedy feature selection. We start with a λ vector that is zero for all features, and then run the error minimization without the random generation of vectors (figure 4, line 4). This means that we add one feature at a time. This greedy algorithm winds up producing a vector with many zero weights. In row 3 of table 1, we used the greedy feature selection algorithm and trained using F_1, resulting in a performance of 0.66 over the baseline which is our best result. We performed a planned one-tailed paired t-test on the F_1 scores of the parses selected by the baseline and this system for the 3718 sentences (parses were taken from the test portion of each fold). We found that there is a significant difference with the baseline ($t(3717) = 6.42$, $p < .01$). We believe that using the full set of 34 features (many of which are very similar to one another) made the training problem harder without improving the fit to the training data, and that greedy feature selection helps with this (see also section 7).

6 Previous Work

As we mentioned in section 2, work on parse reranking is relevant, but a vital difference is that we use features based only on *syntactic projection* of the two languages in a bitext. For an overview of different types of features that have been used in parse reranking see Charniak and Johnson (2005). Like Collins (2000) we use cross-validation to train our model, but we have access to much less data (3718 sentences total, which is less than 1/10 of the data Collins used). We use rich feature functions which were designed by hand to specifically address problems in English parses which can be disambiguated using the German translation.

Syntactic projection has been used to bootstrap treebanks in resource poor languages. Some examples of projection of syntactic parses from English to a resource poor language for which no parser is available are the works of Yarowsky and Ngai (2001), Hwa et al. (2005) and Goyal and Chatterjee (2006). Our work differs from theirs in that we are performing a parse reranking task in English using knowledge gained from German parses, and parsing accuracy is generally thought to be worse in German than in English.

Hopkins and Kuhn (2006) conducted research with goals similar to ours. They showed how to build a powerful generative model which flexibly incorporates features from parallel text in four languages, but were not able to show an improvement in parsing performance. After the submission of our paper for review, two papers outlining relevant work were published. Burkett and Klein (2008) describe a system for simultaneously improving Chinese and English parses of a Chinese/English bitext. This work is complementary to ours. The system is trained using gold standard trees in both Chinese and English, in contrast with our system which only has access to gold standard trees in English. Their system uses a tree alignment which varies within training, but this does not appear to make a large difference in performance. They use coarsely defined features which are language independent. We use several features similar to their two best performing sets of features, but in contrast with their work, we also define features which are specifically aimed at English disambiguation problems that we have observed can be resolved using German parses. They use an in-domain Chinese parser and out-of-domain English parser, while for us the English parser is in-domain and the German parser is out-of-domain, both of which make improving the English parse more difficult. Their Maximum Entropy training is more appropriate for their numerous coarse features, while we use Minimum Error Rate Training, which is much faster. Finally, we are projecting from a single German parse which is a more difficult problem. Fossum and Knight (2008) outline a system for using Chinese/English word alignments to determine ambiguous English PP-attachments. They first use an oracle to choose PP-attachment decisions which are ambiguous in the English side of a Chinese/English bitext, and then build a classifier which uses information from a word alignment to make PP-attachment decisions. No Chinese syntactic information is required. We use automatically generated German parses to improve English syntactic parsing, and have not been able to find a similar phenomenon for which only a word alignment would suffice.

7 Analysis

We looked at the weights assigned during the cross-validation performed to obtain our best result. The weights of many of the 34 features we defined were frequently set to zero. We sorted the features by the number of times the relevant λ scalar was zero (i.e., the number of folds of the cross-validation for which they were zero; the greedy feature selection is deterministic and so we do not run multiple trials). We then reran the same greedy feature selection algorithm as was used in table 1, row 3, but this time using only the top 9 feature values, which were the features which were active on 4 or more folds[6]. The result was an improvement on train of 0.84 and an improvement on test of 0.73. This test result may be slightly overfit, but the result supports the inference that these 9 feature functions are the most important. We chose these feature functions to be described in detail in section 3. We observed that the variants of the similar features **POSParentPrj** and **AbovePOSPrj** projected in opposite directions and measured character and word differences, respectively, and this complementarity seems to help.

[6] We saw that many features canceled one another out on different folds. For instance either the word-based or the character-based version of **DTNN** was active in each fold, but never at the same time as one another.

We also tried to see if our results depended strongly on the log-linear model and training algorithm, by using the SVM-Light ranker (Joachims, 2002). In order to make the experiment tractable, we limited ourselves to the 8-best parses (rather than 100-best). Our training algorithm and model was 0.74 better than the baseline on train and 0.47 better on test, while SVM-Light was 0.54 better than baseline on train and 0.49 better on test (using linear kernels). We believe that the results are not unduly influenced by the training algorithm.

8 Conclusion

We have shown that rich bitext projection features can improve parsing accuracy. This confirms the hypothesis that the divergence in what information different languages encode grammatically can be exploited for syntactic disambiguation. Improved parsing due to bitext projection features should be helpful in syntactic analysis of bitexts (by way of mutual syntactic disambiguation) and in computing syntactic analyses of texts that have translations in other languages available.

Acknowledgments

This work was supported in part by Deutsche Forschungsgemeinschaft Grant SFB 732. We would like to thank Helmut Schmid for support of BitPar and for his many helpful comments on our work. We would also like to thank the anonymous reviewers.

References

Michaela Atterer and Hinrich Schütze. 2007. Prepositional phrase attachment without oracles. *Computational Linguistics*, 33(4).

Peter F. Brown, Stephen A. Della Pietra, Vincent J. Della Pietra, and R. L. Mercer. 1993. The mathematics of statistical machine translation: parameter estimation. *Computational Linguistics*, 19(2).

David Burkett and Dan Klein. 2008. Two languages are better than one (for syntactic parsing). In *EMNLP*.

Eugene Charniak and Mark Johnson. 2005. Coarse-to-fine n-best parsing and MaxEnt discriminative reranking. In *ACL*.

Eugene Charniak, Sharon Goldwater, and Mark Johnson. 1998. Edge-based best-first chart parsing. In *Proceedings of the Sixth Workshop on Very Large Corpora*.

Michael Collins. 2000. Discriminative reranking for natural language parsing. In *ICML*.

Victoria Fossum and Kevin Knight. 2008. Using bilingual Chinese-English word alignments to resolve PP-attachment ambiguity in English. In *AMTA*.

Alexander Fraser and Daniel Marcu. 2007. Measuring word alignment quality for statistical machine translation. *Computational Linguistics*, 33(3).

Shailly Goyal and Niladri Chatterjee. 2006. Parsing aligned parallel corpus by projecting syntactic relations from annotated source corpus. In *Proceedings of the COLING/ACL main conference poster sessions*.

Susan L. Graham, Michael A. Harrison, and Walter L. Ruzzo. 1980. An improved context-free recognizer. *ACM Transactions on Programming Languages and Systems*, 2(3).

Mark Hopkins and Jonas Kuhn. 2006. A framework for incorporating alignment information in parsing. In *Proceedings of the EACL 2006 Workshop on Cross-Language Knowledge Induction*.

Rebecca Hwa, Philip Resnik, Amy Weinberg, Clara Cabezas, and Okan Kolak. 2005. Bootstrapping parsers via syntactic projection across parallel texts. *Nat. Lang. Eng.*, 11(3).

Thorsten Joachims. 2002. Optimizing search engines using clickthrough data. In *Proceedings of the Eighth ACM SIGKDD*.

Takao Kasami. 1965. An efficient recognition and syntax analysis algorithm for context-free languages. Technical Report AFCRL-65-7558, Air Force Cambridge Research Laboratory.

Dan Klein and Christopher Manning. 2003. A* parsing: fast exact viterbi parse selection. In *HLT-NAACL*.

Philipp Koehn, Franz J. Och, and Daniel Marcu. 2003. Statistical phrase-based translation. In *HLT-NAACL*.

Philipp Koehn. 2005. Europarl: a parallel corpus for statistical machine translation. In *MT Summit X*.

Mitchell P. Marcus, Beatrice Santorini, and Mary Ann Marcinkiewicz. 1993. Building a large annotated corpus of English: the Penn treebank. *Computational Linguistics*, 19(2).

David McClosky, Eugene Charniak, and Mark Johnson. 2006. Effective self-training for parsing. In *HLT-NAACL*.

Franz J. Och and Hermann Ney. 2003. A systematic comparison of various statistical alignment models. *Computational Linguistics*, 29(1).

Franz J. Och. 2003. Minimum error rate training in statistical machine translation. In *ACL*.

Chris Quirk and Simon Corston-Oliver. 2006. The impact of parse quality on syntactically-informed statistical machine translation. In *EMNLP*.

Stefan Riezler, Tracy H. King, Ronald M. Kaplan, Richard S. Crouch, John T. Maxwell III, and Mark Johnson. 2002. Parsing the Wall Street Journal using a lexical-functional grammar and discriminative estimation techniques. In *ACL*.

Helmut Schmid. 2004. Efficient parsing of highly ambiguous context-free grammars with bit vectors. In *COLING*.

Ralf Steinberger, Bruno Pouliquen, Anna Widiger, Camelia Ignat, Tomaz Erjavec, Dan Tufis, and Daniel Varga. 2006. The JRC-Acquis: a multilingual aligned parallel corpus with 20+ languages. In *LREC*.

David Yarowsky and Grace Ngai. 2001. Inducing multilingual POS taggers and NP bracketers via robust projection across aligned corpora. In *NAACL*.

Daniel H. Younger. 1967. Recognition of context-free languages in time n^3. *Information and Control*, 10.

Parsing Mildly Non-projective Dependency Structures*

Carlos Gómez-Rodríguez
Departamento de Computación
Universidade da Coruña, Spain
cgomezr@udc.es

David Weir and John Carroll
Department of Informatics
University of Sussex, United Kingdom
{davidw,johnca}@sussex.ac.uk

Abstract

We present parsing algorithms for various mildly non-projective dependency formalisms. In particular, algorithms are presented for: all well-nested structures of gap degree at most 1, with the same complexity as the best existing parsers for constituency formalisms of equivalent generative power; all well-nested structures with gap degree bounded by any constant k; and a new class of structures with gap degree up to k that includes some ill-nested structures. The third case includes all the gap degree k structures in a number of dependency treebanks.

1 Introduction

Dependency parsers analyse a sentence in terms of a set of directed links (dependencies) expressing the head-modifier and head-complement relationships which form the basis of predicate argument structure. We take dependency structures to be directed trees, where each node corresponds to a word and the root of the tree marks the syntactic head of the sentence. For reasons of efficiency, many practical implementations of dependency parsing are restricted to *projective* structures, in which the subtree rooted at each word covers a contiguous substring of the sentence. However, while free word order languages such as Czech do not satisfy this constraint, parsing without the projectivity constraint is computationally complex. Although it is possible to parse non-projective structures in quadratic time under a model in which each dependency decision is independent of all the others (McDonald et al., 2005), the problem is intractable in the absence of this assumption (McDonald and Satta, 2007).

Nivre and Nilsson (2005) observe that most non-projective dependency structures appearing in practice are "close" to being projective, since they contain only a small proportion of non-projective arcs. This has led to the study of classes of dependency structures that lie between projective and unrestricted non-projective structures (Kuhlmann and Nivre, 2006; Havelka, 2007). Kuhlmann (2007) investigates several such classes, based on well-nestedness and gap degree constraints (Bodirsky et al., 2005), relating them to lexicalised constituency grammar formalisms. Specifically, he shows that: linear context-free rewriting systems (LCFRS) with fan-out k (Vijay-Shanker et al., 1987; Satta, 1992) induce the set of dependency structures with gap degree at most $k-1$; coupled context-free grammars in which the maximal rank of a nonterminal is k (Hotz and Pitsch, 1996) induce the set of well-nested dependency structures with gap degree at most $k-1$; and LTAGs (Joshi and Schabes, 1997) induce the set of well-nested dependency structures with gap degree at most 1.

These results establish that there must be polynomial-time dependency parsing algorithms for well-nested structures with bounded gap degree, since such parsers exist for their corresponding lexicalised constituency-based formalisms. However, since most of the non-projective structures in treebanks are well-nested and have a small gap degree (Kuhlmann and Nivre, 2006), developing efficient dependency parsing strategies for these sets of structures has considerable practical interest, since we would be able to parse directly with dependencies in a data-driven manner, rather than indirectly by constructing intermediate constituency grammars and extracting dependencies from constituency parses.

We address this problem with the following contributions: (1) we define a parsing algorithm

*Partially supported by MEC and FEDER (HUM2007-66607-C04) and Xunta de Galicia (PGIDIT07SIN005206PR, INCITE08E1R104022ES, INCITE08ENA305025ES, INCITE08PXIB302179PR, Rede Galega de Proc. da Linguaxe e RI, Bolsas para Estadías INCITE – FSE cofinanced).

Proceedings of the 12th Conference of the European Chapter of the ACL, pages 291–299,
Athens, Greece, 30 March – 3 April 2009. ©2009 Association for Computational Linguistics

for well-nested dependency structures of gap degree 1, and prove its correctness. The parser runs in time $O(n^7)$, the same complexity as the best existing algorithms for LTAG (Eisner and Satta, 2000), and can be optimised to $O(n^6)$ in the non-lexicalised case; (2) we generalise the previous algorithm to any well-nested dependency structure with gap degree at most k in time $O(n^{5+2k})$; (3) we generalise the previous parsers to be able to analyse not only well-nested structures, but also ill-nested structures with gap degree at most k satisfying certain constraints[1], in time $O(n^{4+3k})$; and (4) we characterise the set of structures covered by this parser, which we call *mildly ill-nested* structures, and show that it includes all the trees present in a number of dependency treebanks.

2 Preliminaries

A *dependency graph* for a string $w_1 \dots w_n$ is a graph $G = (V, E)$, where $V = \{w_1, \dots, w_n\}$ and $E \subseteq V \times V$. We write the edge (w_i, w_j) as $w_i \rightarrow w_j$, meaning that the word w_i is a syntactic *dependent* (or a *child*) of w_j or, conversely, that w_j is the *governor* (*parent*) of w_i. We write $w_i \rightarrow^\star w_j$ to denote that there exists a (possibly empty) path from w_i to w_j. The *projection* of a node w_i, denoted $\lfloor w_i \rfloor$, is the set of reflexive-transitive dependents of w_i, that is: $\lfloor w_i \rfloor = \{w_j \in V \mid w_j \rightarrow^\star w_i\}$. An *interval* (with endpoints i and j) is a set of the form $[i, j] = \{w_k \mid i \leq k \leq j\}$.

A dependency graph is said to be a *tree* if it is: (1) acyclic: $w_j \in \lfloor w_i \rfloor$ implies $w_i \rightarrow w_j \notin E$; and (2) each node has exactly one parent, except for one node which we call the *root* or *head*. A graph verifying these conditions and having a vertex set $V \subseteq \{w_1, \dots, w_n\}$ is a *partial dependency tree*. Given a dependency tree $T = (V, E)$ and a node $u \in V$, the *subtree* induced by the node u is the graph $T_u = (\lfloor u \rfloor, E_u)$ where $E_u = \{w_i \rightarrow w_j \in E \mid w_j \in \lfloor u \rfloor\}$.

2.1 Properties of dependency trees

We now define the concepts of gap degree and well-nestedness (Kuhlmann and Nivre, 2006). Let T be a (possibly partial) dependency tree for $w_1 \dots w_n$: We say that T is **projective** if $\lfloor w_i \rfloor$ is an interval for every word w_i. Thus every node in the dependency structure must dominate a contiguous substring in the sentence. The **gap degree** of a particular node w_k in T is the minimum $g \in \mathbb{N}$ such that $\lfloor w_k \rfloor$ can be written as the union of $g+1$ intervals; that is, the number of discontinuities in $\lfloor w_k \rfloor$. The gap degree of the dependency tree T is the maximum among the gap degrees of its nodes. Note that T has gap degree 0 if and only if T is projective. The subtrees induced by nodes w_p and w_q are **interleaved** if $\lfloor w_p \rfloor \cap \lfloor w_q \rfloor = \emptyset$ and there are nodes $w_i, w_j \in \lfloor w_p \rfloor$ and $w_k, w_l \in \lfloor w_q \rfloor$ such that $i < k < j < l$. A dependency tree T is **well-nested** if it does not contain two interleaved subtrees. A tree that is not well-nested is said to be **ill-nested**. Note that projective trees are always well-nested, but well-nested trees are not always projective.

2.2 Dependency parsing schemata

The framework of parsing schemata (Sikkel, 1997) provides a uniform way to describe, analyse and compare parsing algorithms. Parsing schemata were initially defined for constituency-based grammatical formalisms, but Gómez-Rodríguez et al. (2008a) define a variant of the framework for dependency-based parsers. We use these *dependency parsing schemata* to define parsers and prove their correctness. Due to space constraints, we only provide brief outlines of the main concepts behind dependency parsing schemata.

The parsing schema approach considers parsing as deduction, generating intermediate results called *items*. An initial set of items is obtained from the input sentence, and the parsing process involves *deduction steps* which produce new items from existing ones. Each item contains information about the sentence's structure, and a successful parsing process produces at least one *final item* providing a full dependency analysis for the sentence or guaranteeing its existence. In a dependency parsing schema, items are defined as sets of partial dependency trees[2]. To define a parser by means of a schema, we must define an item set and provide a set of deduction steps that operate on it. Given an item set $\mathcal{I}$, the set of *final items* for strings of length n is the set of items in $\mathcal{I}$ that contain a full dependency tree for some arbitrary string of length n. A final item containing a dependency tree for a particular string $w_1 \dots w_n$ is said to be a *correct final item* for that string. These

[1] Parsing unrestricted ill-nested structures, even when the gap degree is bounded, is NP-complete: these structures are equivalent to LCFRS for which the recognition problem is NP-complete (Satta, 1992).

[2] The formalism allows items to contain forests, and the dependency structures inside items are defined in a notation with terminal and preterminal nodes, but these are not needed here.

concepts can be used to prove the correctness of a parser: for each input string, a parsing schema's deduction steps allow us to infer a set of items, called *valid items* for that string. A schema is said to be *sound* if all valid final items it produces for any arbitrary string are correct for that string. A schema is said to be *complete* if all correct final items are valid. A *correct* parsing schema is one which is both sound and complete.

In constituency-based parsing schemata, deduction steps usually have grammar rules as side conditions. In the case of dependency parsers it is also possible to use grammars (Eisner and Satta, 1999), but many algorithms use a data-driven approach instead, making individual decisions about which dependencies to create by using probabilistic models (Eisner, 1996) or classifiers (Yamada and Matsumoto, 2003). To represent these algorithms as deduction systems, we use the notion of *D-rules* (Covington, 1990). D-rules take the form $a \rightarrow b$, which says that word b can have a as a dependent. Deduction steps in non-grammar-based parsers can be tied to the D-rules associated with the links they create. In this way, we obtain a representation of the underlying logic of the parser while abstracting away from control structures (the particular model used to create the decisions associated with D-rules). Furthermore, the choice points in the parsing process and the information we can use to make decisions are made explicit in the steps linked to D-rules.

3 The *WG*$_1$ parser

3.1 Parsing schema for *WG*$_1$

We define *WG*$_1$, a parser for well-nested dependency structures of gap degree ≤ 1, as follows:

The item set is $\mathcal{I}_{WG1} = \mathcal{I}_1 \cup \mathcal{I}_2$, with

$$\mathcal{I}_1 = \{[i, j, h, \diamond, \diamond] \mid i, j, h \in \mathbb{N}, 1 \leq h \leq n, 1 \leq i \leq j \leq n, h \neq j, h \neq i-1\},$$

where each item of the form $[i, j, h, \diamond, \diamond]$ represents the set of all well-nested partial dependency trees[3] with gap degree at most 1, rooted at w_h, and such that $\lfloor w_h \rfloor = \{w_h\} \cup [i, j]$, and

$$\mathcal{I}_2 = \{[i, j, h, l, r] \mid i, j, h, l, r \in \mathbb{N}, 1 \leq h \leq n, 1 \leq i < l \leq r < j \leq n, h \neq j, h \neq i-1, h \neq l-1, h \neq r\}$$

where each item of the form $[i, j, h, l, r]$ represents the set of all well-nested partial dependency trees rooted at w_h such that $\lfloor w_h \rfloor = \{w_h\} \cup ([i, j] \setminus [l, r])$, and all the nodes (except possibly h) have gap degree at most 1. We call items of this form *gapped items*, and the interval $[l, r]$ the *gap* of the item. Note that the constraints $h \neq j, h \neq i+1, h \neq l-1, h \neq r$ are added to items to avoid redundancy in the item set. Since the result of the expression $\{w_h\} \cup ([i, j] \setminus [l, r])$ for a given head can be the same for different sets of values of i, j, l, r, we restrict these values so that we cannot get two different items representing the same dependency structures. Items ι violating these constraints always have an alternative representation that does not violate them, that we can express with a normalising function $nm(\iota)$ as follows:

$nm([i, j, j, l, r]) = [i, j-1, j, l, r]$ (if $r \leq j-1$ or $r = \diamond$),
or $[i, l-1, j, \diamond, \diamond]$ (if $r = j-1$).
$nm([i, j, l-1, l, r]) = [i, j, l-1, l-1, r]$(if $l > i+1$),
or $[r+1, j, l-1, \diamond, \diamond]$ (if $l = i+1$).
$nm([i, j, i-1, l, r]) = [i-1, j, i-1, l, r]$.
$nm([i, j, r, l, r]) = [i, j, r, l, r-1]$ (if $l < r$),
or $[i, j, r, \diamond, \diamond]$ (if $l = r$).

$nm([i, j, h, l, r]) = [i, j, h, l, r]$ for all other items.

When defining the deduction steps for this and other parsers, we assume that they always produce normalised items. For clarity, we do not explicitly write this in the deduction steps, writing ι instead of $nm(\iota)$ as antecedents and consequents of steps.

The set of initial items is defined as the set

$$\mathcal{H} = \{[h, h, h, \diamond, \diamond] \mid h \in \mathbb{N}, 1 \leq h \leq n\},$$

where each item $[h, h, h, \diamond, \diamond]$ represents the set containing the trivial partial dependency tree consisting of a single node w_h and no links. This same set of hypotheses can be used for all the parsers, so we do not make it explicit for subsequent schemata. Note that initial items are separate from the item set $\mathcal{I}_{WG1}$ and not subject to its constraints, so they do not require normalisation.

The set of final items for strings of length n in *WG*$_1$ is defined as the set

$$\mathcal{F} = \{[1, n, h, \diamond, \diamond] \mid h \in \mathbb{N}, 1 \leq h \leq n\},$$

which is the set of items in $\mathcal{I}_{WG1}$ containing dependency trees for the complete input string (from position 1 to n), with their head at any word w_h.

The deduction steps of the parser can be seen in Figure 1A.

The *WG*$_1$ parser proceeds bottom-up, by building dependency subtrees and joining them to form larger subtrees, until it finds a complete dependency tree for the input sentence. The logic of

[3] In this and subsequent schemata, we use D-rules to express parsing decisions, so partial dependency trees are assumed to be taken from the set of trees licensed by a set of D-rules.

A. WG_1 parser:

Link Ungapped: $$\frac{[h1, h1, h1, \diamond, \diamond] \quad [i2, j2, h2, \diamond, \diamond]}{[i2, j2, h1, \diamond, \diamond]} \; w_{h2} \to w_{h1}$$
such that $w_{h2} \in [i2, j2] \wedge w_{h1} \notin [i2, j2]$,

Link Gapped: $$\frac{[h1, h1, h1, \diamond, \diamond] \quad [i2, j2, h2, l2, r2]}{[i2, j2, h1, l2, r2]} \; w_{h2} \to w_{h1}$$
such that $w_{h2} \in [i2, j2] \setminus [l2, r2] \wedge w_{h1} \notin [i2, j2] \setminus [l2, r2]$,

Combine Ungapped: $$\frac{[i, j, h, \diamond, \diamond] \quad [j+1, k, h, \diamond, \diamond]}{[i, k, h, \diamond, \diamond]}$$

Combine Opening Gap: $$\frac{[i, j, h, \diamond, \diamond] \quad [k, l, h, \diamond, \diamond]}{[i, l, h, j+1, k-1]}$$
such that $j < k - 1$,

Combine Keeping Gap Left: $$\frac{[i, j, h, l, r] \quad [j+1, k, h, \diamond, \diamond]}{[i, k, h, l, r]}$$

Combine Keeping Gap Right: $$\frac{[i, j, h, \diamond, \diamond] \quad [j+1, k, h, l, r]}{[i, k, h, l, r]}$$

Combine Closing Gap: $$\frac{[i, j, h, l, r] \quad [l, r, h, \diamond, \diamond]}{[i, j, h, \diamond, \diamond]}$$

Combine Shrinking Gap Left: $$\frac{[i, j, h, l, r] \quad [l, k, h, \diamond, \diamond]}{[i, j, h, k+1, r]}$$

Combine Shrinking Gap Right: $$\frac{[i, j, h, l, r] \quad [k, r, h, \diamond, \diamond]}{[i, j, h, l, k-1]}$$

Combine Shrinking Gap Centre: $$\frac{[i, j, h, l, r] \quad [l, r, h, l2, r2]}{[i, j, h, l2, r2]}$$

B. WG_K parser:

Link: $$\frac{[h1, h1, h1, []] \quad [i2, j2, h2, [(l_1, r_1), \ldots, (l_g, r_g)]]}{[i2, j2, h1, [(l_1, r_1), \ldots, (l_g, r_g)]]} \; w_{h2} \to w_{h1}$$
such that $w_{h2} \in [i2, j2] \setminus \bigcup_{p=1}^{g} [l_p, r_p]$
$\wedge w_{h1} \notin [i2, j2] \setminus \bigcup_{p=1}^{g} [l_p, r_p]$.

Combine Opening Gap: $$\frac{[i, l_q - 1, h, [(l_1, r_1), \ldots, (l_{q-1}, r_{q-1})]] \quad [r_q + 1, m, h, [(l_{q+1}, r_{q+1}), \ldots, (l_g, r_g)]]}{[i, m, h, [(l_1, r_1), \ldots, (l_g, r_g)]]}$$
such that $g \leq k$ and $l_q \leq r_q$,

Combine Keeping Gaps: $$\frac{[i, j, h, [(l_1, r_1), \ldots, (l_q, r_q)]] \quad [j+1, m, h, [(l_{q+1}, r_{q+1}), \ldots, (l_g, r_g)]]}{[i, m, h, [(l_1, r_1), \ldots, (l_g, r_g)]]}$$
such that $g \leq k$,

Combine Shrinking Gap Right: $$\frac{[i, j, h, [(l_1, r_1), \ldots, (l_{q-1}, r_{q-1}), (l_q, r'), (l_s, r_s), \ldots, (l_g, r_g)]] \quad [r_q + 1, r', h, [(l_{q+1}, r_{q+1}), \ldots, (l_{s-1}, r_{s-1})]]}{[i, j, h, [(l_1, r_1), \ldots, (l_g, r_g)]]}$$
such that $g \leq k$

Combine Shrinking Gap Left: $$\frac{[i, j, h, [(l_1, r_1), \ldots, (l_q, r_q), (l', r_s), (l_{s+1}, r_{s+1}), \ldots, (l_g, r_g)]] \quad [l', l_s - 1, h, [(l_{q+1}, r_{q+1}), \ldots, (l_{s-1}, r_{s-1})]]}{[i, j, h, [(l_1, r_1), \ldots, (l_g, r_g)]]}$$
such that $g \leq k$

Combine Shrinking Gap Centre: $$\frac{[i, j, h, [(l_1, r_1), \ldots, (l_q, r_q), (l', r'), (l_s, r_s), \ldots, (l_g, r_g)]] \quad [l', r', h, [(l_{q+1}, r_{q+1}), \ldots, (l_{s-1}, r_{s-1})]]}{[i, j, h, [(l_1, r_1), \ldots, (l_g, r_g)]]}$$
such that $g \leq k$

C. Additional steps to turn WG_1 into MG_1:

Combine Interleaving: $$\frac{[i, j, h, l, r] \quad [l, k, h, r+1, j]}{[i, k, h, \diamond, \diamond]}$$

Combine Interleaving Gap C: $$\frac{[i, j, h, l, r] \quad [l, k, h, m, j]}{[i, k, h, m, r]}$$
such that $m < r + 1$,

Combine Interleaving Gap L: $$\frac{[i, j, h, l, r] \quad [l, k, h, r+1, u]}{[i, k, h, j+1, u]}$$
such that $u > j$,

Combine Interleaving Gap R: $$\frac{[i, j, h, l, r] \quad [k, m, h, r+1, j]}{[i, m, h, l, k-1]}$$
such that $k > l$.

D. General form of the MG_k Combine step:

$$\frac{[i_{a_1}, i_{a_p+1} - 1, h, [(i_{a_1+1}, i_{a_2} - 1), \ldots, (i_{a_{p-1}+1}, i_{a_p} - 1)]] \quad [i_{b_1}, i_{b_q+1} - 1, h, [(i_{b_1+1}, i_{b_2} - 1), \ldots, (i_{b_{q-1}+1}, i_{b_q} - 1)]]}{[i_{min(a_1, b_1)}, i_{max(a_p+1, b_q+1)} - 1, h, [(i_{g_1}, i_{g_1+1} - 1), \ldots, (i_{g_r}, i_{g_r+1} - 1)]]}$$

for each string of length n with a's located at positions $a_1 \ldots a_p (1 \leq a_1 < \ldots < a_p \leq n)$, b's at positions $b_1 \ldots b_q (1 \leq b_1 < \ldots < b_q \leq n)$, and g's at positions $g_1 \ldots g_r (2 \leq g_1 < \ldots < g_r \leq n - 1)$, such that $1 \leq p \leq k, 1 \leq q \leq k, 0 \leq r \leq k - 1$, $p + q + r = n$, and the string does not contain more than one consecutive appearance of the same symbol.

Figure 1: Deduction steps for the parsers defined in the paper.

the parser can be understood by considering how it infers the item corresponding to the subtree induced by a particular node, given the items for the subtrees induced by the direct dependents of that node. Suppose that, in a complete dependency analysis for a sentence $w_1 \ldots w_n$, the word w_h has $w_{d_1} \ldots w_{d_p}$ as direct dependents (i.e. we have dependency links $w_{d_1} \to w_h, \ldots, w_{d_p} \to w_h$). Then, the item corresponding to the subtree induced by w_h is obtained from the ones corresponding to the subtrees induced by $w_{d_1} \ldots w_{d_p}$ by: (1) applying the *Link Ungapped* or *Link Gapped* step to each of the items corresponding to the subtrees induced by the direct dependents, and to the hypothesis $[h, h, h, \diamond, \diamond]$. This allows us to infer p items representing the result of linking each of the dependent subtrees to the new head w_h; (2) applying the various *Combine* steps to join all of the items obtained in the previous step into a single item. The *Combine* steps perform a union operation between subtrees. Therefore, the result is a dependency tree containing all the dependent subtrees, and with all of them linked to h: this is the subtree induced by w_h. This process is applied repeatedly to build larger subtrees, until, if the parsing process is successful, a final item is found containing a dependency tree for the complete sentence.

3.2 Proving correctness

The parsing schemata formalism can be used to prove the correctness of a parsing schema. To prove that WG_1 is correct, we need to prove its soundness and completeness.[4] Soundness is proven by checking that valid items always contain well-nested trees. Completeness is proven by induction, taking initial items as the base case and showing that an item containing a correct subtree for a string can always be obtained from items corresponding to smaller subtrees. In order to prove this induction step, we use the concept of **order annotations** (Kuhlmann, 2007; Kuhlmann and Möhl, 2007), which are strings that lexicalise the precedence relation between the nodes of a dependency tree. Given a correct subtree, we divide the proof into cases according to the order annotation of its head and we find that, for every possible form of this order annotation, we can find a sequence of *Combine* steps to infer the relevant item from smaller correct items.

3.3 Computational complexity

The time complexity of WG_1 is $O(n^7)$, as the step *Combine Shrinking Gap Centre* works with 7 free string positions. This complexity with respect to the length of the input is as expected for this set of structures, since Kuhlmann (2007) shows that they are equivalent to LTAG, and the best existing parsers for this formalism also perform in $O(n^7)$ (Eisner and Satta, 2000). Note that the *Combine* step which is the bottleneck only uses the 7 indexes, and not any other entities like D-rules, so its $O(n^7)$ complexity does not have any additional factors due to grammar size or other variables. The space complexity of WG_1 is $O(n^5)$ for recognition, due to the 5 indexes in items, and $O(n^7)$ for full parsing.

[4] Due to space constraints, correctness proofs for the parsers are not given here. Full proofs are provided in the extended version of this paper, see (Gómez-Rodríguez et al., 2008b).

It is possible to build a variant of this parser with time complexity $O(n^6)$, as with parsers for unlexicalised TAG, if we work with unlexicalised D-rules specifying the possibility of dependencies between pairs of categories instead of pairs of words. In order to do this, we expand the item set with unlexicalised items of the form $[i, j, C, l, r]$, where C is a category, apart from the existing items $[i, j, h, l, r]$. Steps in the parser are duplicated, to work both with lexicalised and unlexicalised items, except for the *Link* steps, which always work with a lexicalised item and an unlexicalised hypothesis to produce an unlexicalised item, and the *Combine Shrinking Gap* steps, which can work only with unlexicalised items. Steps are added to obtain lexicalised items from their unlexicalised equivalents by binding the head to particular string positions. Finally, we need certain variants of the *Combine Shrinking Gap* steps that take 2 unlexicalised antecedents and produce a lexicalised consequent; an example is the following:

$$\textit{Combine Shrinking Gap Centre L:}\ \frac{[i, j, C, l, r] \quad [l+1, r, C, l2, r2]}{[i, j, l, l2, r2]}$$

such that $cat(w_l) = C$

Although this version of the algorithm reduces time complexity with respect to the length of the input to $O(n^6)$, it also adds a factor related to the number of categories, as well as constant factors due to using more kinds of items and steps than the original WG_1 algorithm. This, together with the advantages of lexicalised dependency parsing, may mean that the original WG_1 algorithm is more practical than this version.

4 The WG_k parser

The WG_1 parsing schema can be generalised to obtain a parser for all well-nested dependency structures with gap degree bounded by a constant $k (k \geq 1)$, which we call WG_k parser. In order to do this, we extend the item set so that it can contain items with up to k gaps, and modify the deduction steps to work with these multi-gapped items.

4.1 Parsing schema for WG_k

The item set $\mathcal{I}_{WGk}$ is the set of all $[i, j, h, [(l_1, r_1), \ldots, (l_g, r_g)]]$ where $i, j, h, g \in \mathbb{N}$, $0 \leq g \leq k$, $1 \leq h \leq n$, $1 \leq i \leq j \leq n$, $h \neq j$, $h \neq i-1$; and for each $p \in \{1, 2, \ldots, g\}$: $l_p, r_p \in \mathbb{N}$, $i < l_p \leq r_p < j$, $r_p < l_{p+1} - 1$, $h \neq l_p - 1$, $h \neq r_p$.

An item $[i, j, h, [(l_1, r_1), \ldots, (l_g, r_g)]]$ represents the set of all well-nested partial dependency trees rooted at w_h such that $\lfloor w_h \rfloor = \{w_h\} \cup ([i,j] \setminus \bigcup_{p=1}^{g} [l_p, r_p])$, where each interval $[l_p, r_p]$ is called a gap. The constraints $h \neq j, h \neq i+1, h \neq l_p - 1, h \neq r_p$ are added to avoid redundancy, and normalisation is defined as in WG_1. The set of final items is defined as the set $\mathcal{F} = \{[1, n, h, []] \mid h \in \mathbb{N}, 1 \leq h \leq n\}$. Note that this set is the same as in WG_1, as these are the items that we denoted $[1, n, h, \diamond, \diamond]$ in the previous parser.

The deduction steps can be seen in Figure 1B. As expected, the WG_1 parser corresponds to WG_k when we make $k = 1$. WG_k works in the same way as WG_1, except for the fact that *Combine* steps can create items with more than one gap[5]. The correctness proof is also analogous to that of WG_1, but we must take into account that the set of possible order annotations is larger when $k > 1$, so more cases arise in the completeness proof.

4.2 Computational complexity

The WG_k parser runs in time $O(n^{5+2k})$: as in the case of WG_1, the deduction step with most free variables is *Combine Shrinking Gap Centre*, and in this case it has $5 + 2k$ free indexes. Again, this complexity result is in line with what could be expected from previous research in constituency parsing: Kuhlmann (2007) shows that the set of well-nested dependency structures with gap degree at most k is closely related to coupled context-free grammars in which the maximal rank of a nonterminal is $k + 1$; and the constituency parser defined by Hotz and Pitsch (1996) for these grammars also adds an n^2 factor for each unit increment of k. Note that a small value of k should be enough to cover the vast majority of the non-projective sentences found in natural language treebanks. For example, the Prague Dependency Treebank contains no structures with gap degree greater than 4. Therefore, a WG_4 parser would be able to analyse all the well-nested structures in this treebank, which represent 99.89% of the total. Increasing k beyond 4 would not produce further improvements in coverage.

5 Parsing ill-nested structures

The WG_k parser analyses dependency structures with bounded gap degree as long as they are well-nested. This covers the vast majority of the structures that occur in natural-language treebanks (Kuhlmann and Nivre, 2006), but there is still a significant minority of sentences that contain ill-nested structures. Unfortunately, the general problem of parsing ill-nested structures is NP-complete, even when the gap degree is bounded: this set of structures is closely related to LCFRS with bounded fan-out and unbounded production length, and parsing in this formalism has been proven to be NP-complete (Satta, 1992). The reason for this high complexity is the problem of *unrestricted crossing configurations*, appearing when dependency subtrees are allowed to interleave in every possible way. However, just as it has been noted that most non-projective structures appearing in practice are only "slightly" non-projective (Nivre and Nilsson, 2005), we characterise a sense in which the structures appearing in treebanks can be viewed as being only "slightly" ill-nested. In this section, we generalise the algorithms WG_1 and WG_k to parse a proper superset of the set of well-nested structures in polynomial time; and give a characterisation of this new set of structures, which includes all the structures in several dependency treebanks.

5.1 The MG_1 and MG_k parsers

The WG_k parser presented previously is based on a bottom-up process, where *Link* steps are used to link completed subtrees to a head, and *Combine* steps are used to join subtrees governed by a common head to obtain a larger structure. As WG_k is a parser for well-nested structures of gap degree up to k, its *Combine* steps correspond to all the ways in which we can join two sets of sibling subtrees meeting these constraints, and having a common head, into another. Thus, this parser does not use *Combine* steps that produce interleaved subtrees, since these would generate items corresponding to ill-nested structures.

We obtain a polynomial parser for a wider set of structures of gap degree at most k, including some ill-nested ones, by having *Combine* steps representing every way in which two sets of sibling subtrees of gap degree at most k with a common head can be joined into another, including those producing interleaved subtrees, like the steps for gap degree 1 shown in Figure 1C. Note that this does not mean that we can build every possible ill-nested structure: some structures with complex crossed configurations have gap degree k, but cannot be built by combining two structures of that gap degree. More specifically, our algorithm will be able

[5]In all the parsers in this paper, *Combine* steps may be applied in different orders to produce the same result, causing spurious ambiguity. In WG_1 and WG_k, this can be avoided when implementing the schemata, by adding flags to items so as to impose a particular order.

to parse a dependency structure (well-nested or not) if there exists a *binarisation* of that structure that has gap degree at most k. The parser implicitly works by finding such a binarisation, since *Combine* steps are always applied to two items and no intermediate item generated by them can exceed gap degree k (not counting the position of the head in the projection).

More formally, let T be a dependency structure for the string $w_1 \dots w_n$. A **binarisation** of T is a dependency tree T' over a set of nodes, each of which may be unlabelled or labelled with a word in $\{w_1 \dots w_n\}$, such that the following conditions hold: (1) each node has at most two children, and (2) $w_i \rightarrow w_j$ in T if and only if $w_i \rightarrow^{\star} w_j$ in T'. A dependency structure is **mildly ill-nested** for gap degree k if it has at least one binarisation of gap degree $\leq k$. Otherwise, we say that it is **strongly ill-nested** for gap degree k. It is easy to prove that the set of mildly ill-nested structures for gap degree k includes all well-nested structures with gap degree up to k.

We define MG_1, a parser for mildly ill-nested structures for gap degree 1, as follows: (1) the item set is the same as that of WG_1, except that items can now contain any mildly ill-nested structures for gap degree 1, instead of being restricted to well-nested structures; and (2) deduction steps are the same as in WG_1, plus the additional steps shown in Figure 1C. These extra *Combine* steps allow the parser to combine interleaved subtrees with simple crossing configurations. The MG_1 parser still runs in $O(n^7)$, as these new steps do not use more than 7 string positions.

The proof of correctness for this parser is similar to that of WG_1. Again, we use the concept of order annotations. The set of mildly ill-nested structures for gap degree k can be defined as those that only contain annotations meeting certain constraints. The soundness proof involves showing that *Combine* steps always generate items containing trees with such annotations. Completeness is proven by induction, by showing that if a subtree is mildly ill-nested for gap degree k, an item for it can be obtained from items for smaller subtrees by applying *Combine* and *Link* steps. In the cases where *Combine* steps have to be applied, the order in which they may be used to produce a subtree can be obtained from its head's order annotation.

To generalise this algorithm to mildly ill-nested structures for gap degree k, we need to add a *Combine* step for every possible way of joining two structures of gap degree at most k into another. This can be done systematically by considering a set of strings over an alphabet of three symbols: a and b to represent intervals of words in the projection of each of the structures, and g to represent intervals that are not in the projection of either structure, and will correspond to gaps in the joined structure. The legal combinations of structures for gap degree k will correspond to strings where symbols a and b each appear at most $k+1$ times, g appears at most k times and is not the first or last symbol, and there is no more than one consecutive appearance of any symbol. Given a string of this form, the corresponding *Combine* step is given by the expression in Figure 1D. As a particular example, the *Combine Interleaving Gap C* step in Figure 1C is obtained from the string $abgab$.

Thus, we define the parsing schema for MG_k, a parser for mildly ill-nested structures for gap degree k, as the schema where (1) the item set is like that of WG_k, except that items can now contain any mildly ill-nested structures for gap degree k, instead of being restricted to well-nested structures; and (2) the set of deduction steps consists of a *Link* step as the one in WG_k, plus a set of *Combine* steps obtained as expressed in Figure 1D.

As the string used to generate a *Combine* step can have length at most $3k+2$, and the resulting step contains an index for each symbol of the string plus two extra indexes, the MG_k parser has complexity $O(n^{3k+4})$. Note that the item and deduction step sets of an MG_k parser are always supersets of those of WG_k. In particular, the steps for WG_k are those obtained from strings that do not contain $abab$ or $baba$ as a scattered substring.

5.2 Mildly ill-nested dependency structures

The MG_k algorithm defined in the previous section can parse any mildly ill-nested structure for a given gap degree k in polynomial time. We have characterised the set of mildly ill-nested structures for gap degree k as those having a binarisation of gap degree $\leq k$. Since a binarisation of a dependency structure cannot have lower gap degree than the original structure, this set only contains structures with gap degree at most k. Furthermore, by the relation between MG_k and WG_k, we know that it contains all the well-nested structures with gap degree up to k.

Figure 2 shows an example of a structure that has gap degree 1, but is strongly ill-nested for gap degree 1. This is one of the smallest possible such structures: by generating all the possible trees up to 10 nodes (without counting a dummy root node

Language	Structures								
	Total	Nonprojective							
		Total	By gap degree				By nestedness		
			Gap degree 1	Gap degree 2	Gap degree 3	Gap deg. > 3	Well-Nested	Mildly Ill-Nested	Strongly Ill-Nested
Arabic	2995	205	189	13	2	1	204	1	0
Czech	87889	20353	19989	359	4	1	20257	96	0
Danish	5430	864	854	10	0	0	856	8	0
Dutch	13349	4865	4425	427	13	0	4850	15	0
Latin	3473	1743	1543	188	10	2	1552	191	0
Portuguese	9071	1718	1302	351	51	14	1711	7	0
Slovene	1998	555	443	81	21	10	550	5	0
Swedish	11042	1079	1048	19	7	5	1008	71	0
Turkish	5583	685	656	29	0	0	665	20	0

Table 1: Counts of dependency trees classified by gap degree, and mild and strong ill-nestedness (for their gap degree); appearing in treebanks for Arabic (Hajič et al., 2004), Czech (Hajič et al., 2006), Danish (Kromann, 2003), Dutch (van der Beek et al., 2002), Latin (Bamman and Crane, 2006), Portuguese (Afonso et al., 2002), Slovene (Džeroski et al., 2006), Swedish (Nilsson et al., 2005) and Turkish (Oflazer et al., 2003; Atalay et al., 2003).

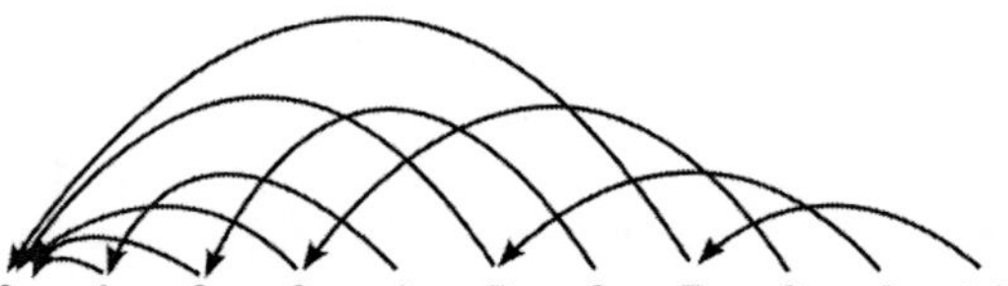

Figure 2: One of the smallest strongly ill-nested structures. This dependency structure has gap degree 1, but is only mildly ill-nested for gap degree ≥ 2.

located at position 0), it can be shown that all the structures of any gap degree k with length smaller than 10 are well-nested or only mildly ill-nested for that gap degree k.

Even if a structure T is strongly ill-nested for a given gap degree, there is always some $m \in \mathbb{N}$ such that T is mildly ill-nested for m (since every dependency structure can be binarised, and binarisations have finite gap degree). For example, the structure in Figure 2 is mildly ill-nested for gap degree 2. Therefore, MG_k parsers have the property of being able to parse any possible dependency structure as long as we make k large enough.

In practice, structures like the one in Figure 2 do not seem to appear in dependency treebanks. We have analysed treebanks for nine different languages, obtaining the data presented in Table 1. None of these treebanks contain structures that are strongly ill-nested for their gap degree. Therefore, in any of these treebanks, the MG_k parser can parse every sentence with gap degree at most k.

6 Conclusions and future work

We have defined a parsing algorithm for well-nested dependency structures with bounded gap degree. In terms of computational complexity, this algorithm is comparable to the best parsers for related constituency-based formalisms: when the gap degree is at most 1, it runs in $O(n^7)$, like the fastest known parsers for LTAG, and can be made $O(n^6)$ if we use unlexicalised dependencies. When the gap degree is greater than 1, the time complexity goes up by a factor of n^2 for each extra unit of gap degree, as in parsers for coupled context-free grammars. Most of the non-projective sentences appearing in treebanks are well-nested and have a small gap degree, so this algorithm directly parses the vast majority of the non-projective constructions present in natural languages, without requiring the construction of a constituency grammar as an intermediate step.

Additionally, we have defined a set of structures for any gap degree k which we call mildly ill-nested. This set includes ill-nested structures verifying certain conditions, and can be parsed in $O(n^{3k+4})$ with a variant of the parser for well-nested structures. The practical interest of mildly ill-nested structures can be seen in the data obtained from several dependency treebanks, showing that all of the ill-nested structures in them are mildly ill-nested for their corresponding gap degree. Therefore, our $O(n^{3k+4})$ parser can analyse all the gap degree k structures in these treebanks.

The set of mildly ill-nested structures for gap degree k is defined as the set of structures that have a binarisation of gap degree at most k. This definition is directly related to the way the MG_k parser works, since it implicitly finds such a binarisation. An interesting line of future work would be to find an equivalent characterisation of mildly ill-nested structures which is more grammar-oriented and would provide a more linguistic insight into these structures. Another research direction, which we are currently working on, is exploring how variants of the MG_k parser's strategy can be applied to the problem of binarising LCFRS (Gómez-Rodríguez et al., 2009).

References

Susana Afonso, Eckhard Bick, Renato Haber, and Diana Santos. 2002. "Floresta sintá(c)tica": a treebank for Portuguese. In *Proc. of LREC 2002*, pages 1968–1703, Las Palmas, Spain.

Nart B. Atalay, Kemal Oflazer, and Bilge Say. 2002. The annotation process in the Turkish treebank. In *Proc. of EACL Workshop on Linguistically Interpreted Corpora - LINC*, Budapest, Hungary.

David Bamman and Gregory Crane. 2006. The design and use of a Latin dependency treebank. In *Proc. of 5th Workshop on Treebanks and Linguistic Theories (TLT2006)*, pages 67–78.

Manuel Bodirsky, Marco Kuhlmann, and Mathias Möhl. 2005. Well-nested drawings as models of syntactic structure. Technical Report, Saarland University. Electronic version available at: `http://www.ps.uni-sb.de/Papers/`.

Michael A. Covington. 1990. A dependency parser for variable-word-order languages. Technical Report AI-1990-01, Athens, GA.

Sašo Džeroski, Tomaž Erjavec, Nina Ledinek, Petr Pajas, Zdeněk Žabokrtský, and Andreja Žele. 2006. Towards a Slovene dependency treebank. In *Proc. of LREC 2006*, pages 1388–1391, Genoa, Italy.

Jason Eisner and Giorgio Satta. 1999. Efficient parsing for bilexical context-free grammars and head automaton grammars. In *Proc. of ACL-99*, pages 457–464, Morristown, NJ. ACL.

Jason Eisner and Giorgio Satta. 2000. A faster parsing algorithm for lexicalized tree-adjoining grammars. In *Proc. of 5th Workshop on Tree-Adjoining Grammars and Related Formalisms (TAG+5)*, pages 14–19, Paris.

Jason Eisner. 1996. Three new probabilistic models for dependency parsing: An exploration. In *Proc. of COLING-96*, pages 340–345, Copenhagen.

Carlos Gómez-Rodríguez, John Carroll, and David Weir. 2008a. A deductive approach to dependency parsing. In *Proc. of ACL'08:HLT*, pages 968–976, Columbus, Ohio. ACL.

Carlos Gómez-Rodríguez, David Weir, and John Carroll. 2008b. Parsing mildly non-projective dependency structures. Technical Report CSRP 600, Department of Informatics, University of Sussex.

Carlos Gómez-Rodríguez, Marco Kuhlmann, Giorgio Satta, and David Weir. 2009. Optimal reduction of rule length in linear context-free rewriting systems. In *Proc. of NAACL'09:HLT* (to appear).

Jan Hajič, Otakar Smrž, Petr Zemánek, Jan Šnaidauf, and Emanuel Beška. 2004. Prague Arabic dependency treebank: Development in data and tools. In *Proc. of NEMLAR International Conference on Arabic Language Resources and Tools*, pages 110–117.

Jan Hajič, Jarmila Panevová, Eva Hajičová, Jarmila Panevová, Petr Sgall, Petr Pajas, Jan Štěpánek, Jiří Havelka, and Marie Mikulová. 2006. Prague dependency treebank 2.0. CDROM CAT: LDC2006T01, ISBN 1-58563-370-4.

Jiří Havelka. 2007. Beyond projectivity: Multilingual evaluation of constraints and measures on non-projective structures. In *Proc. of ACL 2007*, Prague, Czech Republic. ACL.

Günter Hotz and Gisela Pitsch. 1996. On parsing coupled-context-free languages. *Theor. Comput. Sci.*, 161(1-2):205–233. Elsevier, Essex, UK.

Aravind K. Joshi and Yves Schabes. 1997. Tree-adjoining grammars. In *Handbook of formal languages*, pages 69–124. Springer-Verlag, Berlin/Heidelberg/NY.

Matthias T. Kromann. 2003. The Danish dependency treebank and the underlying linguistic theory. In *Proc. of the 2nd Workshop on Treebanks and Linguistic Theories (TLT2003)*.

Marco Kuhlmann and Mathias Möhl. 2007. Mildly context-sensitive dependency languages. In *Proc. of ACL 2007*, Prague, Czech Republic. ACL.

Marco Kuhlmann and Joakim Nivre. 2006. Mildly non-projective dependency structures. In *Proc. of COLING/ACL main conference poster sessions*, pages 507–514, Morristown, NJ, USA. ACL.

Marco Kuhlmann. 2007. *Dependency Structures and Lexicalized Grammars*. Doctoral dissertation, Saarland University, Saarbrücken, Germany.

Ryan McDonald and Giorgio Satta. 2007. On the complexity of non-projective data-driven dependency parsing. In *IWPT 2007: Proc. of the 10th Conference on Parsing Technologies*. ACL.

Ryan McDonald, Fernando Pereira, Kiril Ribarov, and Jan Hajič. 2005. Non-projective dependency parsing using spanning tree algorithms. In *Proc. of HLT/EMNLP 2005*, pages 523–530, Morristown, NJ, USA. ACL.

Jens Nilsson, Johan Hall, and Joakim Nivre. 2005. MAMBA meets TIGER: Reconstructing a Swedish treebank from antiquity. In *Proc. of NODALIDA 2005 Special Session on Treebanks*, pages 119–132.

Joakim Nivre and Jens Nilsson. 2005. Pseudo-projective dependency parsing. In *Proc. of ACL'05*, pages 99–106, Morristown, NJ, USA. ACL.

Kemal Oflazer, Bilge Say, Dilek Zeynep Hakkani-Tür and Gökhan Tür. 2003. Building a Turkish treebank. In A. Abeille, ed., *Building and Exploiting Syntactically-annotated Corpora*. Kluwer, Dordrecht.

Giorgio Satta. 1992. Recognition of linear context-free rewriting systems. In *Proc. of ACL-92*, pages 89–95, Morristown, NJ. ACL.

Klaas Sikkel. 1997. *Parsing Schemata — A Framework for Specification and Analysis of Parsing Algorithms*. Springer-Verlag, Berlin/Heidelberg/NY.

L. van der Beek, G. Bouma, R. Malouf, and G. van Noord. 2002. The Alpino dependency treebank. In *Computational Linguistics in the Netherlands (CLIN)*, Twente University.

K. Vijay-Shanker, David J. Weir, and Aravind K. Joshi. 1987. Characterizing structural descriptions produced by various grammatical formalisms. In *Proc. of ACL-87*, pages 104–111, Morristown, NJ. ACL.

Hiroyasu Yamada and Yuji Matsumoto. 2003. Statistical dependency analysis with support vector machines. In *Proc. of 8th International Workshop on Parsing Technologies (IWPT 2003)*, pages 195–206.

Structural, Transitive and Latent Models for Biographic Fact Extraction

Nikesh Garera and **David Yarowsky**
Department of Computer Science, Johns Hopkins University
Human Language Technology Center of Excellence
Baltimore MD, USA
{ngarera,yarowsky}@cs.jhu.edu

Abstract

This paper presents six novel approaches to biographic fact extraction that model structural, transitive and latent properties of biographical data. The ensemble of these proposed models substantially outperforms standard pattern-based biographic fact extraction methods and performance is further improved by modeling inter-attribute correlations and distributions over functions of attributes, achieving an average extraction accuracy of 80% over seven types of biographic attributes.

1 Introduction

Extracting biographic facts such as "Birthdate", "Occupation", "Nationality", etc. is a critical step for advancing the state of the art in information processing and retrieval. An important aspect of web search is to be able to narrow down search results by distinguishing among people with the same name leading to multiple efforts focusing on web person name disambiguation in the literature (Mann and Yarowsky, 2003; Artiles et al., 2007, Cucerzan, 2007). While biographic facts are certainly useful for disambiguating person names, they also allow for automatic extraction of encyclopedic knowledge that has been limited to manual efforts such as Britannica, Wikipedia, etc. Such encyploedic knowledge can advance vertical search engines such as http://www.spock.com that are focused on people searches where one can get an enhanced search interface for searching by various biographic attributes. Biographic facts are also useful for powerful query mechanisms such as finding what attributes are common between two people (Auer and Lehmann, 2007).

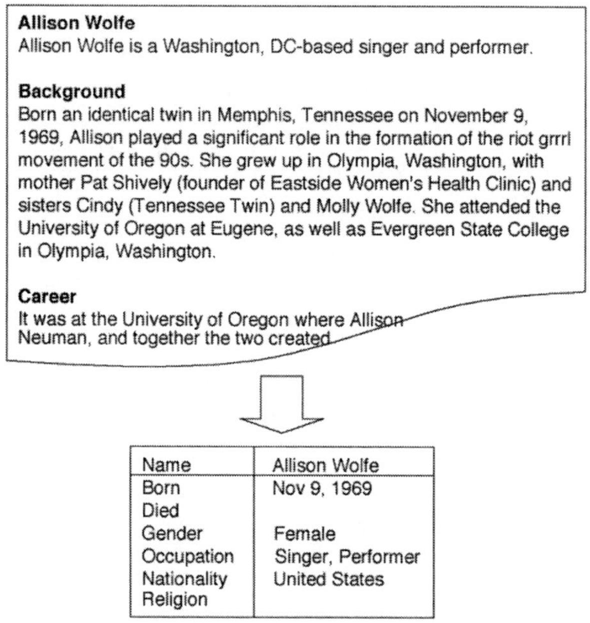

Figure 1: Goal: extracting attribute-value biographic fact pairs from biographic free-text

While there are a large quantity of biographic texts available online, there are only a few biographic fact databases available[1], and most of them have been created manually, are incomplete and are available primarily in English.

This work presents multiple novel approaches for automatically extracting biographic facts such as "Birthdate", "Occupation", "Nationality", and "Religion", making use of diverse sources of information present in biographies.
In particular, we have proposed and evaluated the following 6 distinct original approaches to this

[1]E.g.: http://www.nndb.com, http://www.biography.com, Infoboxes in Wikipedia

Proceedings of the 12th Conference of the European Chapter of the ACL, pages 300–308,
Athens, Greece, 30 March – 3 April 2009. ©2009 Association for Computational Linguistics

task with large collective empirical gains:

1. An improvement to the Ravichandran and Hovy (2002) algorithm based on *Partially Untethered Contextual Pattern Models*

2. Learning a *position-based* model using absolute and relative positions and sequential order of hypotheses that satisfy the domain model. For example, "Deathdate" very often appears after "Birthdate" in a biography.

3. Using *transitive models over attributes* via co-occurring entities. For example, other people mentioned person's biography page tend to have similar attributes such as occupation (See Figure 4).

4. Using *latent wide-document-context models* to detect attributes that may not be mentioned directly in the article (e.g. the words *"song, hits, album, recorded,.."* all collectively indicate the occupation of *singer* or *musician* in the article.

5. Using *inter-attribute correlations*, for filtering unlikely biographic attribute combinations. For example, a tuple consisting of < "Nationality" = India, "Religion" = Hindu > has a higher probability than a tuple consisting of < "Nationality" = France, "Religion" = Hindu >.

6. Learning *distributions over functions of attributes*, for example, using an age distribution to filter tuples containing improbable <deathyear>-<birthyear> lifespan values.

We propose and evaluate techniques for exploiting all of the above classes of information in the next sections.

2 Related Work

The literature for biography extraction falls into two major classes. The first one deals with identifying and extracting *biographical sentences* and treats the problem as a summarization task (Cowie et al., 2000, Schiffman et al., 2001, Zhou et al., 2004). The second and more closely related class deals with extracting specific *facts* such as *"birthplace", "occupation", etc.* For this task, the primary theme of work in the literature has been to treat the task as a general semantic-class learning problem where one starts with a few seeds of the semantic relationship of interest and learns contextual patterns such as "<NAME> was born in <Birthplace>" or "<NAME> (born <Birthdate>)" (Hearst, 1992; Riloff, 1996; Thelen and Riloff, 2002; Agichtein and Gravano, 2000; Ravichandran and Hovy, 2002; Mann and Yarowsky, 2003; Jijkoun et al., 2004; Mann and Yarowsky, 2005; Alfonseca et al., 2006; Pasca et al., 2006). There has also been some work on extracting biographic facts directly from Wikipedia pages. Culotta et al. (2006) deal with learning contextual patterns for extracting family relationships from Wikipedia. Ruiz-Casado et al. (2006) learn contextual patterns for biographic facts and apply them to Wikipedia pages.

While the pattern-learning approach extends well for a few biography classes, some of the biographic facts like "Gender" and "Religion" do not have consistent contextual patterns, and only a few of the explicit biographic attributes such as "Birthdate", "Deathdate", "Birthplace" and "Occupation" have been shown to work well in the pattern-learning framework (Mann and Yarowsky, 2005; Alfonesca, 2006; Pasca et al., 2006).

Secondly, there is a general lack of work that attempts to utilize the typical information sequencing within biographic texts for fact extraction, and we show how the information structure of biographies can be used to improve upon pattern based models. Furthermore, we also present additional novel models of attribute correlation and age distribution that aid the extraction process.

3 Approach

We first implement the standard pattern-based approach for extracting biographic facts from the raw prose in Wikipedia people pages. We then present an array of novel techniques exploiting different classes of information including partially-tethered contextual patterns, relative attribute position and sequence, transitive attributes of co-occurring entities, broad-context topical profiles, inter-attribute correlations and likely human age distributions. For illustrative purposes, we motivate each technique using one or two attributes but in practice they can be applied to a wide range of attributes and empirical results in Table 4 show that they give consistent performance gains across multiple attributes.

4 Contextual Pattern-Based Model

A standard model for extracting biographic facts is to learn templatic contextual patterns such as <NAME> "was born in" <Birthplace>. Such templatic patterns can be learned using seed examples of the attribute in question and, there has been a plethora of work in the seed-based bootstrapping literature which addresses this problem (Ravichandran and Hovy, 2002; Thelen and Riloff, 2002; Mann and Yarowsky, 2005; Alfonseca et al., 2006; Pasca et al., 2006)

Thus for our baseline we implemented a standard Ravichandran and Hovy (2002) pattern learning model using 100 seed[2] examples from an online biographic database called NNDB (http://www.nndb.com) for each of the biographic attributes: "Birthdate", "Birthplace", "Deathdate", "Gender", "Nationality", "Occupation" and "Religion". Given the seed pairs, patterns for each attribute were learned by searching for seed *<Name,Attribute Value>* pairs in the Wikipedia page and extracting the left, middle and right contexts as various contextual patterns[3].

While the biographic text was obtained from Wikipedia articles, all of the 7 attribute values used as seed and test person names could not be obtained from Wikipedia due to incomplete and unnormalized (for attribute value format) infoboxes. Hence, the values for training/evaluation were extracted from NNDB which provides a cleaner set of gold truth, and is similar to an approach utilizing trained annotators for marking up and extracting the factual information in a standard format. For consistency, only the people names whose articles occur in Wikipedia where selected as part of seed and test sets.

Given the attribute values of the seed names and their text articles, the probability of a relationship r(Attribute Name), given the surrounding context "A_1 p A_2 q A_3", where p and q are <NAME> and <Attrib Val> respectively, is given using the rote extractor model probability as in (Ravichandran and Hovy, 2002; Mann and Yarowsky 2005):

$$P(r(p,q)|A_1pA_2qA_3) = \frac{\sum_{x,y\in r} c(A_1xA_2yA_3)}{\sum_{x,z} c(A_1xA_2zA_3)}$$

Thus, the probability for each contextual pattern is based on how often it correctly predicts a relationship in the seed set. And, each extracted attribute value q using the given pattern can thus be ranked according to the above probability. We tested this approach for extracting values for each of the seven attributes on a test set of 100 held-out names and report Precision, Pseudo-recall and F-score for each attribute which are computed in the standard way as follows, for say Attribute "Birthplace (bplace)":

$$\text{Precision}_{\text{bplace}} = \frac{\text{\# people with bplace correctly extracted}}{\text{\# of people with bplace extracted}}$$

$$\text{Pseudo-rec}_{\text{bplace}} = \frac{\text{\# people with bplace correctly extracted}}{\text{\# of people with bplace in test set}}$$

$$\text{F-score}_{\text{bplace}} = \frac{2\cdot\text{Precision}_{\text{bplace}}\cdot\text{Pseudo-rec}_{\text{bplace}}}{\text{Precision}_{\text{bplace}} + \text{Pseudo-rec}_{\text{bplace}}}$$

Since the true values of each attribute are obtained from a cleaner and normalized person-database (NNDB), not all the attribute values maybe present in the Wikipedia article for a given name. Thus, we also compute accuracy on the subset of names for which the value of a given attribute is also explictly stated in the article. This is denoted as:

$$\text{Acc}_{\text{truth pres}} = \frac{\text{\# people with bplace correctly extracted}}{\text{\# of people with true bplace stated in article}}$$

We further applied a domain model for each attribute to filter noisy targets extracted from lexical patterns. Our domain models of attributes include lists of acceptable values (such as lists of places, occupations and religions) and structural constraints such as possible date formats for "Birthdate" and "Deathdate". The rows with subscript "$RH02$"in Table 4 shows the performance of this Ravichandran and Hovy (2002) model with additional attribute domain modeling for each attribute, and Table 3 shows the average performance across all attributes.

5 Partially Untethered Templatic Contextual Patterns

The pattern-learning literature for fact extraction often consists of patterns with a "hook" and "target" (Mann and Yarowsky, 2005). For example, in the pattern "<Name> *was born in* <Birthplace>", "<NAME>" is the hook and "<Birthplace>" is the target. The disadvantage of this approach is that the intervening dually-tethered patterns can be quite long and highly variable, such as "<NAME> *was highly influ-*

[2]The seed examples were chosen randomly, with a bias against duplicate attribute values to increase training diversity. Both the seed and test names and data will be made available online to the research community for replication and extension.

[3]We implemented a noisy model of coreference resolution by resolving any gender-correct pronoun used in the Wikipedia page to the title person name of the article. Gender is also extracted automatically as a biographic attribute.

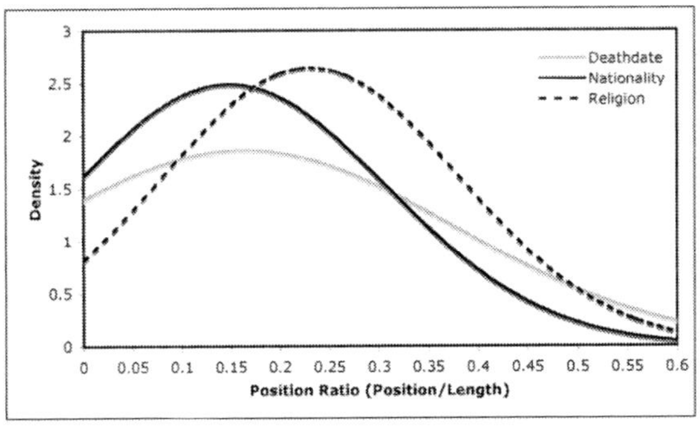

Figure 2: Distribution of the observed document mentions of Deathdate, Nationality and Religion.

ential in his role as <Occupation>". We overcome this problem by modeling partially untethered variable-length ngram patterns adjacent to only the *target*, with the only constraint being that the hook entity appear somewhere in the sentence[4]. Examples of these new contextual ngram features include "*his role as* <Occupation>" and '*role as* <Occupation>". The pattern probability model here is essentially the same as in Ravichandran and Hovy, 2002 and just the pattern representation is changed. The rows with subscript "$RH02_{\text{imp}}$" in tables 4 and 3 show performance gains using this improved templatic-pattern-based model, yielding an absolute 21% gain in accuracy.

6 Document-Position-Based Model

One of the properties of biographic genres is that primary biographic attributes[5] tend to appear in characteristic positions, often toward the beginning of the article. Thus, the absolute position (in percentage) can be modeled explicitly using a Gaussian parametric model as follows for choosing the best candidate value v^* for a given attribute A:

$$v^* = argmax_{v \in domain(A)} f(posn_v|A)$$

where,

$$f(posn_v|A)$$
$$= \mathcal{N}(posn_v; \hat{\mu_A}, \hat{\sigma_A^2})$$
$$= \frac{1}{\hat{\sigma_A}\sqrt{2\pi}} e^{-(posn_v - \hat{\mu_A})^2/2\hat{\sigma_A}^2}$$

[4]This constraint is particularly viable in biographic text, which tends to focus on the properties of a single individual.

[5]We use the hyperlinked phrases as potential values for all attributes except "Gender". For "Gender" we used pronouns as potential values ranked according to the their distance from the beginning of the page.

In the above equation, $posn_v$ is the absolute position ratio (position/length) and $\hat{\mu_A}, \hat{\sigma_A}^2$ are the sample mean and variance based on the sample of correct position ratios of attribute values in biographies with attribute A. Figure 2, for example, shows the positional distribution of the seed attribute values for deathdate, nationality and religion in Wikipedia articles, fit to a Gaussian distribution. Combining this empirically derived position model with a domain model[6] of acceptable attribute values is effective enough to serve as a stand-alone model.

Attribute	Best rank in seed set	P(Rank)
Birthplace	1	0.61
Birthdate	1	0.98
Deathdate	2	0.58
Gender	1	1.0
Occupation	1	0.70
Nationality	1	0.83
Religion	1	0.80

Table 1: Majority rank of the correct attribute value in the Wikipedia pages of the seed names used for learning relative ordering among attributes satisfying the domain model

6.1 Learning Relative Ordering in the Position-Based Model

In practice, for attributes such as birthdate, the first text pattern satisfying the domain model is often the correct answer for biographical articles. Deathdate also tends to occur near the beginning of the article, but almost always some point after the birthdate. This motivates a second, sequence-based position model based on the rank of the attribute values among other values in the domain of the attribute, as follows:

$$v^* = argmax_{v \in domain(A)} P(rank_v|A)$$

where $P(rank_v|A)$ is the fraction of biographies having attribute a with the correct value occuring at rank $rank_v$, where rank is measured according to the relative order in which the values belonging to the attribute domain occur from the beginning

[6]The domain model is the same as used in Section 4 and remains constant across all the models developed in this paper

of the article. We use the seed set to learn the relative positions between attributes, that is, in the Wikipedia pages of seed names what is the rank of the correct attribute.

Table 1 shows the most frequent rank of the correct attribute value and Figure 3 shows the distribution of the correct ranks for a sample of attributes. We can see that 61% of the time the first location mentioned in a biography is the individuals's birthplace, while 58% of the time the 2nd date in the article is the deathdate. Thus, "Deathdate" often appears as the second date in a Wikipedia page as expected. These empirical distributions for the correct rank provide a direct vehicle for scoring hypotheses, and the rows with "$rel.posn$" as the subscript in Table 4 shows the improvement in performance using the learned relative ordering. Averaging across different attributes, table 3 shows an absolute 11% average gain in accuracy of the position-sequence-based models relative to the improved Ravichandran and Hovy results achieved here.

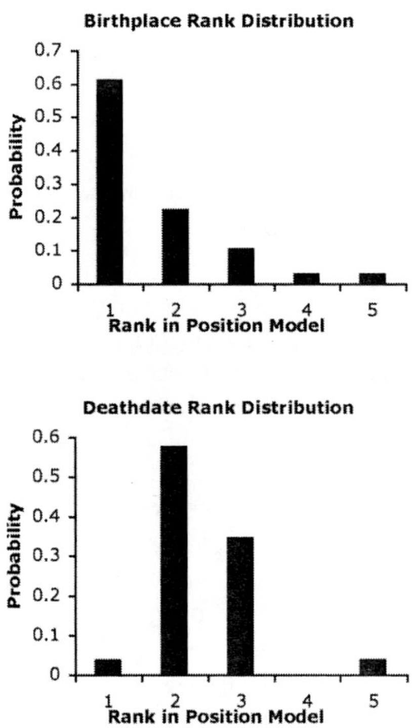

Figure 3: Empirical distribution of the relative position of the correct (seed) answers among all text phrases satisfying the domain model for "birthplace" and "death date".

7 Implicit Models

Some of the biographic attributes such as "Nationality", "Occupation" and "Religion" can be extracted successfully even when the answer is not directly mentioned in the biographic article. We present two such models for doing so in the following subsections:

7.1 Extracting Attributes Transitively using Neighboring Person-Names

Attributes such as "Occupation" are transitive in nature, that is, the people names appearing close to the target name will tend to have the same occupation as the target name. Based on this intution, we implemented a transitive model that predicts occupation based on consensus voting via the extracted occupations of neighboring names[7] as follows:

$$v^* = argmax_{v \in domain(A)} P(v|A, \mathcal{S}_{\text{neighbors}})$$

where,

$$P(v|A, \mathcal{S}_{\text{neighbors}}) = \frac{\text{\# neighboring names with attrib value } v}{\text{\# of neighboring names in the article}}$$

The set of neighboring names is represented as $\mathcal{S}_{\text{neighbors}}$ and the best candidate value for an attribute A is chosen based on the the fraction of neighboring names having the same value for the respective attribute. We rank candidates according to this probability and the row labeled "trans" in Table 4 shows that this model helps in subsantially improving the recall of "Occupation" and "Religion", yielding a 7% and 3% average improvement in F-measure respectively, on top of the position model described in Section 6.

7.2 Latent Model based on Document-Wide Context Profiles

In addition to modeling cross-entity attribute transitively, attributes such as "Occupation" can also be modeled successfully using a document-wide context or topic model. For example, the distribution of words occuring in a biography

[7]We only use the neighboring names whose attribute value can be obtained from an encylopedic database. Furthermore, since we are dealing with biographic pages that talk about a single person, all other person-names mentioned in the article whose attributes are present in an encyclopedia were considered for consensus voting

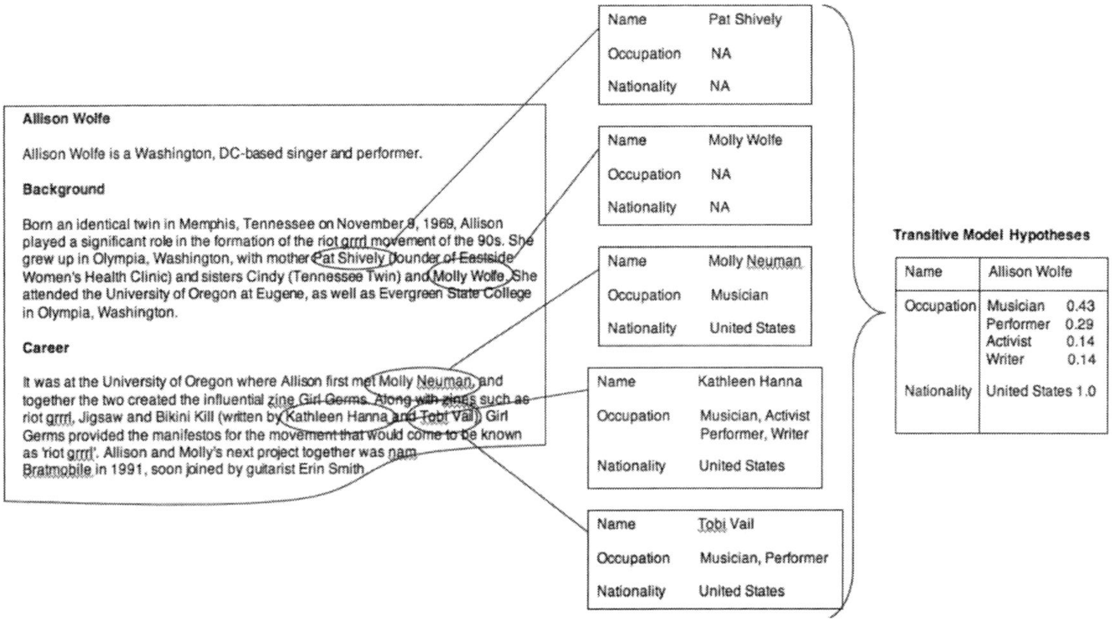

Figure 4: Illustration of modeling "occupation" and "nationality" transitively via consensus from attributes of neighboring names

of a politician would be different from that of a scientist. Thus, even if the occupation is not explicitly mentioned in the article, one can infer it using a bag-of-words topic profile learned from the seed examples.

Given a value v, for an attribute A, (for example v = "Politician" and A = "Occupation"), we learn a centroid weight vector:

$C_v = [w_{1,v}, w_{2,v}, ..., w_{n,v}]$ where,

$$w_{t,v} = \frac{1}{N}\, tf_{t,v} \cdot log\frac{|A|}{|t \in A|}$$

$tf_{t,v}$ is the frequency of word t in the articles of People having attribute $A = v$

$|A|$ is the total number of values of attribute A

$|t \in A|$ is the total number of values of attribute A, such that the articles of people having one of those values contain the term t

N is the total number of People in the seed set

Given a biography article of a test name and an attribute in question, we compute a similar word weight vector $C' = [w'_1, w'_2, ..., w'_n]$ for the test name and measure its cosine similarity to the centroid vector of each value of the given attribute. Thus, the best value a^* is chosen as:

$$v^* = argmax_v \frac{w'_1 \cdot w_{1,v} + w'_2 \cdot w_{2,v} + ... + w'_n \cdot w_{n,v}}{\sqrt{w'^2_1 + w'^2_2 + ... + w'^2_n}\ \sqrt{w^2_{1,v} + w^2_{2,v} + ... + w^2_{n,v}}}$$

Tables 3 and 4 show performance using the latent document-wide-context model. We see that this model by itself gives the top performance on "Occupation", outperforming the best alternative model by 9% absolute accuracy, indicating the usefulness of implicit attribute modeling via broad-context word frequencies.

This latent model can be further extended using the multilingual nature of Wikipedia. We take the corresponding German pages of the training names and model the German word distributions characterizing each seed occupation. Table 4 shows that English attribute classification can be successful using only the words in a parallel German article. For some attributes, the performance of latent model modeled via cross-language (noted as latentCL) is close to that of English suggesting potential future work by exploiting this multilingual dimension.

It is interesting to note that both the transitive model and the latent wide-context model do not rely on the actual "Occupation" being explicitly mentioned in the article, they still outperform ex-

Occupation	Weight Vector
	English
Physicist	<magnetic:32.7, electromagnetic:18.2, wire: 18.2, electricity: 17.7, optical:14.5, discovered:11.2>
Singer	<song:40, hits:30.5, hit:29.6, reggae:23.6, album:17.1, francis:15.2, music:13.8, recorded:13.6, ...>
Politician	<humphrey:367.4, soviet: 97.4, votes: 70.6, senate: 64.7, democratic: 57.2, kennedy: 55.9, ...>
Painter	<mural:40.0, diego:14.7, paint:14.5, fresco:10.9. paintings:10.9, museum of modern art:8.83, ...>
Auto racing	<renault:76.3, championship:32.7. schumacher:32.7, race:30.4, pole:29.1, driver:28.1 >
	German
Physicist	<faraday:25.4, chemie:7.3, vorlesungsserie:7.2, 1846:5.8, entdeckt:4.5, rotation:3.6 ...>
Singer	<song:16.22, jamaikanischen:11.77, platz:7.3, hit: 6.7, soloünstler:4.5, album:4.1, widmet:4.0, ...>
Politician	<konservativen:26.5, wahlkreis:26.5, romano:21.8, stimmen:18.6, gewählt:18.4, ...>
Painter	<rivera:32.7, malerin:7.6, wandgemälde:7.3, kunst:6.75, 1940:5.8, maler:5.1, auftrag:4.5, ...>
Auto racing	<team:29.4,mclaren:18.1,teamkollegen:18.1,sieg:11.7, meisterschaft:10.9, gegner:10.9, ...>

Table 2: Sample of occupation weight vectors in English and German learned using the latent model.

plicit pattern-based and position-based models. This implicit modeling also helps in improving the recall of less-often directly mentioned attributes such as a person's "Religion".

8 Model Combination

While the pattern-based, position-based, transitive and latent models are all stand-alone models, they can complement each other in combination as they provide relatively orthogonal sources of information. To combine these models, we perform a simple backoff-based combination for each attribute based on stand-alone model performance, and the rows with subscript "*combined*" in Tables 3 and 4 shows an average 14% absolute performance gain of the combined model relative to the improved Ravichandran and Hovy 2002 model.

9 Further Extensions: Reducing False Positives

Since the position-and-domain-based models will almost always posit an answer, one of the problems is the high number of false positives yielded by these algorithms. The following subsections introduce further extensions using interesting properties of biographic attributes to reduce the effect of false positives.

9.1 Using Inter-Attribute Correlations

One of the ways to filter false positives is by filtering empirically incompatible inter-attribute pairings. The motivation here is that the attributes are *not independent* of each other when modeled for the same individual. For example, P(Religion=Hindu | Nationality=India) is higher than P(Religion=Hindu | Nationality=France) and

Model	F_{score}	Acc truth pres
Ravichandran and Hovy, 2002	0.37	0.43
Improved RH02 Model	0.54	0.64
Position-Based Model	0.53	0.75
$\text{Combined}_{\text{above 3+trans+latent+cl}}$	0.59	0.78
Combined + Age Dist + Corr	**0.62** (+24%)	**0.80** (+37%)

Table 3: Average Performance of different models across all biographic attributes

similarly we can find positive and negative correlations among other attribute pairings. For implementation, we consider all possible 3-tuples of ("Nationality", "Birthplace", "Religion")[8] and search on NNDB for the presence of the tuple for any individual in the database (excluding the test data of course). As an agressive but effective filter, we filter the tuples for which no name in NNDB was found containing the candidate 3-tuples. The rows with label "combined+corr" in Table 4 and Table 3 shows substantial performaance gains using inter-attribute correlations, such as the 7% absolute average gain for Birthplace over the Section 8 combined models, and a 3% absolute gain for Nationality and Religion.

9.2 Using Age Distribution

Another way to filter out false positives is to consider distributions on meta-attributes, for example: while age is not explicitly extracted, we can use the fact that age is a function of two extracted attributes (<Deathyear>-<Birthyear>) and use the age distribution to filter out false positives for

[8]The test of joint-presence between these three attributes were used since they are strongly correlated

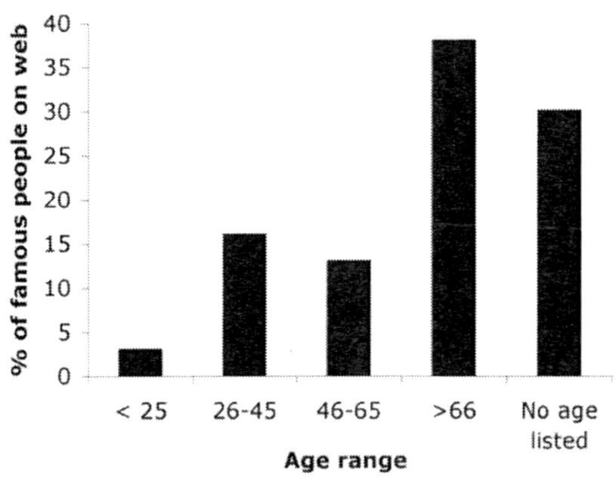

Figure 5: Age distribution of famous people on the web (from www.spock.com)

<Birthdate> and <Deathdate>. Based on the age distribution for famous people[9] on the web shown in Figure 5, we can bias against unusual candidate lifespans and filter out completely those outside the range of 25-100, as most of the probability mass is concentrated in this range. Rows with subscript "$comb + age\ dist$" in Table 4 shows the performance gains using this feature, yielding an average 5% absolute accuracy gain for Birthdate.

10 Conclusion

This paper has shown six successful novel approaches to biographic fact extraction using structural, transitive and latent properties of biographic data. We first showed an improvement to the standard Ravichandran and Hovy (2002) model utilizing untethered contextual pattern models, followed by a document position and sequence-based approach to attribute modeling.

Next we showed transitive models exploiting the tendency for individuals occurring together in an article to have related attribute values. We also showed how latent models of wide document context, both monolingually and translingually, can capture facts that are not stated directly in a text.

Each of these models provide substantial performance gain, and further performance gain is achived via classifier combination. We also showed how inter-attribution correlations can be modeled to filter unlikely attribute combinations, and how models of functions over attributes, such as deathdate-birthdate distributions, can further constrain the candidate space. These approaches collectively achieve 80% average accuracy on a test set of 7 biographic attribute types, yielding a 37% absolute accuracy gain relative to a standard algorithm on the same data.

[9]Since all the seed and test examples were used from nndb.com, we use the age distribution of famous people on the web: http://blog.spock.com/2008/02/08/age-distribution-of-people-on-the-web/

Attribute	Prec	P-Rec	F_{score}	Acc truth pres
Birthdate$_{RH02}$	0.86	0.38	0.53	0.88
Birthdate$_{RH02_{imp}}$	0.52	0.52	0.52	0.67
Birthdate$_{rel.\ posn}$	0.42	0.40	0.41	0.93
Birthdate$_{combined}$	0.58	0.58	0.58	0.95
Birthdate$_{comb+age\ dist}$	0.63	0.60	**0.61**	**1.00**
Deathdate$_{RH02}$	0.80	0.19	0.30	0.36
Deathdate$_{RH02_{imp}}$	0.50	0.49	0.49	0.59
Deathdate$_{rel.\ posn}$	0.46	0.44	0.45	**0.86**
Deathdate$_{combined}$	0.49	0.49	0.49	**0.86**
Deathdate$_{comb+age\ dist}$	0.51	0.49	**0.50**	**0.86**
Birthplace$_{RH02}$	0.42	0.38	0.40	0.42
Birthplace$_{RH02_{imp}}$	0.41	0.41	0.41	0.45
Birthplace$_{rel.\ posn}$	0.47	0.41	0.44	0.48
Birthplace$_{combined}$	0.44	0.44	0.44	0.48
Birthplace$_{combined+corr}$	0.53	0.50	**0.51**	**0.55**
Occupation$_{RH02}$	0.54	0.18	0.27	0.26
Occupation$_{RH02_{imp}}$	0.38	0.34	0.36	0.48
Occupation$_{rel.\ posn}$	0.48	0.35	0.40	0.50
Occupation$_{trans}$	0.49	0.46	0.47	0.50
Occupation$_{latent}$	0.48	0.48	**0.48**	**0.59**
Occupation$_{latentCL}$	0.48	0.48	0.48	0.54
Occupation$_{combined}$	0.48	0.48	**0.48**	**0.59**
Nationality$_{RH02}$	0.40	0.25	0.31	0.27
Nationality$_{RH02_{imp}}$	0.75	0.75	0.75	0.81
Nationality$_{rel.\ posn}$	0.73	0.72	0.71	0.78
Nationality$_{trans}$	0.51	0.48	0.49	0.49
Nationality$_{latent}$	0.56	0.56	0.56	0.56
Nationality$_{latentCL}$	0.55	0.48	0.51	0.48
Nationality$_{combined}$	0.75	0.75	0.75	0.81
Nationality$_{comb+corr}$	0.77	0.77	**0.77**	**0.84**
Gender$_{RH02}$	0.76	0.76	0.76	0.76
Gender$_{RH02_{imp}}$	0.99	0.99	0.99	0.99
Gender$_{rel.\ posn}$	1.00	1.00	**1.00**	**1.00**
Gender$_{trans}$	0.79	0.75	0.77	0.75
Gender$_{latent}$	0.82	0.82	0.82	0.82
Gender$_{latentCL}$	0.83	0.72	0.77	0.72
Gender$_{combined}$	1.00	1.00	**1.00**	**1.00**
Religion$_{RH02}$	0.02	0.02	0.04	0.06
Religion$_{RH02_{imp}}$	0.55	0.18	0.27	0.45
Religion$_{rel.\ posn}$	0.49	0.24	0.32	0.73
Religion$_{trans}$	0.38	0.33	0.35	0.48
Religion$_{latent}$	0.36	0.36	0.36	0.45
Religion$_{latentCL}$	0.30	0.26	0.28	0.22
Religion$_{combined}$	0.41	0.41	0.41	0.76
Religion$_{combined+corr}$	0.44	0.44	**0.44**	**0.79**

Table 4: Attribute-wise performance comparison of all the models across several biographic attributes.

References

E. Agichtein and L. Gravano. 2000. Snowball: extracting relations from large plain-text collections. *Proceedings of ICDL*, pages 85–94.

E. Alfonseca, P. Castells, M. Okumura, and M. Ruiz-Casado. 2006. A rote extractor with edit distance-based generalisation and multi-corpora precision calculation. *Proceedings of COLING-ACL*, pages 9–16.

J. Artiles, J. Gonzalo, and S. Sekine. 2007. The semeval-2007 weps evaluation: Establishing a benchmark for the web people search task. In *Proceedings of SemEval*, pages 64–69.

S. Auer and J. Lehmann. 2007. What have Innsbruck and Leipzig in common? Extracting Semantics from Wiki Content. *Proceedings of ESWC*, pages 503–517.

A. Bagga and B. Baldwin. 1998. Entity-Based Cross-Document Coreferencing Using the Vector Space Model. *Proceedings of COLING-ACL*, pages 79–85.

R. Bunescu and M. Pasca. 2006. Using encyclopedic knowledge for named entity disambiguation. *Proceedings of EACL*, pages 3–7.

J. Cowie, S. Nirenburg, and H. Molina-Salgado. 2000. Generating personal profiles. *The International Conference On MT And Multilingual NLP.*

S. Cucerzan. 2007. Large-scale named entity disambiguation based on wikipedia data. *Proceedings of EMNLP-CoNLL*, pages 708–716.

A. Culotta, A. McCallum, and J. Betz. 2006. Integrating probabilistic extraction models and data mining to discover relations and patterns in text. *Proceedings of HLT-NAACL*, pages 296–303.

E. Filatova and J. Prager. 2005. Tell me what you do and I'll tell you what you are: Learning occupation-related activities for biographies. *Proceedings of HLT-EMNLP*, pages 113–120.

M. Hearst. 1992. Automatic acquisition of hyponyms from large text corpora. In *Proceedings of COLING*, pages 539–545.

V. Jijkoun, M. de Rijke, and J. Mur. 2004. Information extraction for question answering: improving recall through syntactic patterns. *Proceedings of COLING*, page 1284.

G.S. Mann and D. Yarowsky. 2003. Unsupervised personal name disambiguation. In *Proceedings of CoNLL*, pages 33–40.

G.S. Mann and D. Yarowsky. 2005. Multi-field information extraction and cross-document fusion. In *Proceedings of ACL*, pages 483–490.

A. Nenkova and K. McKeown. 2003. References to named entities: a corpus study. *Proceedings of HLT-NAACL companion volume*, pages 70–72.

M. Pasca, D. Lin, J. Bigham, A. Lifchits, and A. Jain. 2006. Organizing and searching the World Wide Web of Facts Step one: The One-Million Fact Extraction Challenge. *Proceedings of AAAI*, pages 1400–1405.

D. Ravichandran and E. Hovy. 2002. Learning surface text patterns for a question answering system. *Proceedings of ACL*, pages 41–47.

Y. Ravin and Z. Kazi. 1999. Is Hillary Rodham Clinton the President? Disambiguating Names across Documents. *Proceedings of ACL.*

M. Remy. 2002. Wikipedia: The Free Encyclopedia. *Online Information Review Year*, 26(6).

E. Riloff. 1996. Automatically Generating Extraction Patterns from Untagged Text. *Proceedings of AAAI*, pages 1044–1049.

M. Ruiz-Casado, E. Alfonseca, and P. Castells. 2005. Automatic extraction of semantic relationships for wordnet by means of pattern learning from wikipedia. *Proceedings of NLDB 2005.*

M. Ruiz-Casado, E. Alfonseca, and P. Castells. 2006. From Wikipedia to semantic relationships: a semi-automated annotation approach. *Proceedings of ESWC.*

B. Schiffman, I. Mani, and K.J. Concepcion. 2001. Producing biographical summaries: combining linguistic knowledge with corpus statistics. *Proceedings of ACL*, pages 458–465.

M. Thelen and E. Riloff. 2002. A bootstrapping method for learning semantic lexicons using extraction pattern contexts. In *Proceedings of EMNLP*, pages 14–21.

N. Wacholder, Y. Ravin, and M. Choi. 1997. Disambiguation of proper names in text. *Proceedings of ANLP*, pages 202–208.

C. Walker, S. Strassel, J. Medero, and K. Maeda. 2006. Ace 2005 multilingual training corpus. *Linguistic Data Consortium.*

R. Weischedel, J. Xu, and A. Licuanan. 2004. A Hybrid Approach to Answering Biographical Questions. *New Directions In Question Answering*, pages 59–70.

M. Wick, A. Culotta, and A. McCallum. 2006. Learning field compatibilities to extract database records from unstructured text. In *Proceedings of EMNLP*, pages 603–611.

L. Zhou, M. Ticrea, and E. Hovy. 2004. Multidocument biography summarization. *Proceedings of EMNLP*, pages 434–441.

Semitic Morphological Analysis and Generation Using Finite State Transducers with Feature Structures

Michael Gasser
Indiana University, School of Informatics
Bloomington, Indiana, USA
gasser@indiana.edu

Abstract

This paper presents an application of finite state transducers weighted with feature structure descriptions, following Amtrup (2003), to the morphology of the Semitic language Tigrinya. It is shown that feature-structure weights provide an efficient way of handling the templatic morphology that characterizes Semitic verb stems as well as the long-distance dependencies characterizing the complex Tigrinya verb morphotactics. A relatively complete computational implementation of Tigrinya verb morphology is described.

1 Introduction

1.1 Finite state morphology

Morphological analysis is the segmentation of words into their component morphemes and the assignment of grammatical morphemes to grammatical categories and lexical morphemes to lexemes. For example, the English noun *parties* could be analyzed as *party*+PLURAL. **Morphological generation** is the reverse process. Both processes relate a **surface** level to a **lexical** level. The relationship between these levels has concerned many phonologists and morphologists over the years, and traditional descriptions, since the pioneering work of Chomsky and Halle (1968), have characterized it in terms of a series of ordered content-sensitive rewrite rules, which apply in the generation, but not the analysis, direction.

Within computational morphology, a very significant advance came with the demonstration that phonological rules could be implemented as **finite state transducers** (Johnson, 1972; Kaplan and Kay, 1994) (FSTs) and that the rule ordering could be dispensed with using FSTs that relate the surface and lexical levels directly (Koskenniemi, 1983). Because of the invertibility of FSTs, "two-level" phonology and morphology permitted the creation of systems of FSTs that implemented both analysis (surface input, lexical output) and generation (lexical input, surface output).

In addition to inversion, FSTs are closed under **composition**. A second important advance in computational morphology was the recognition by Karttunen et al. (1992) that a cascade of composed FSTs could implement the two-level model. This made possible quite complex finite state systems, including ordered **alternation rules** representing context-sensitive variation in the phonological or orthographic shape of morphemes, the **morphotactics** characterizing the possible sequences of morphemes (in canonical form) for a given word class, and one or more **sublexicons**. For example, to handle written English nouns, we could create a cascade of FSTs covering the rules that insert an *e* in words like *bushes* and *parties* and relate lexical *y* to surface *i* in words like *buggies* and *parties* and an FST that represents the possible sequences of morphemes in English nouns, including all of the noun stems in the English lexicon. The key feature of such systems is that, even though the FSTs making up the cascade must be composed in a particular order, the result of composition is a single FST relating surface and lexical levels directly, as in two-level morphology.

1.2 FSTs for non-concatenative morphology

These ideas have revolutionized computational morphology, making languages with complex word structure, such as Finnish and Turkish, far more amenable to analysis by traditional computational techniques. However, finite state morphology is inherently biased to view morphemes as sequences of characters or phones and words as concatenations of morphemes. This presents problems in the case of **non-concatenative morphology**: discontinuous morphemes (circumfix-

Proceedings of the 12th Conference of the European Chapter of the ACL, pages 309–317,
Athens, Greece, 30 March – 3 April 2009.

ation); infixation, which breaks up a morpheme by inserting another within it; reduplication, by which part or all of some morpheme is copied; and the **template morphology** (also called stem-pattern morphology, intercalation, and interdigitation) that characterizes Semitic languages, and which is the focus of much of this paper. The stem of a Semitic verb consists of a **root**, essentially a sequence of consonants, and a **pattern**, a sort of template which inserts other segments between the root consonants and possibly copies certain of them (see Tigrinya examples in the next section).

Researchers within the finite state framework have proposed a number of ways to deal with Semitic template morphology. One approach is to make use of separate tapes for root and pattern at the lexical level (Kiraz, 2000). A transition in such a system relates a single surface character to multiple lexical characters, one for each of the distinct sublexica.

Another approach is to have the transducers at the lexical level relate an upper abstract characterization of a stem to a lower string that directly represents the merging of a particular root and pattern. This lower string can then be compiled into an FST that yields a surface expression (Beesley and Karttunen, 2003). Given the extra **compile-and-replace** operation, this resulting system maps directly between abstract lexical expressions and surface strings. In addition to Arabic, this approach has been applied to a portion of the verb morphology system of the Ethio-Semitic language Amharic (Amsalu and Demeke, 2006), which is characterized by all of the same sorts of complexity as Tigrinya.

A third approach makes use of a finite set of registers that the FST can write to and read from (Cohen-Sygal and Wintner, 2006). Because it can remember relevant previous states, a "finite-state registered transducer" for template morphology can keep the root and pattern separate as it processes a stem.

This paper proposes an approach which is closest to this last framework, one that starts with familiar extension to FSTs, weights on the transitions. The next section gives an overview of Tigrinya verb morphology. The following section discusses weighted FSTs, in particular, with weights consisting of feature structure descriptions. Then I describe a system that applies this approach to Tigrinya verb morphology.

2 Tigrinya Verb Morphology

Tigrinya is an Ethio-Semitic language spoken by 5-6 million people in northern Ethiopia and central Eritrea. There has been almost no computational work on the language, and there are effectively no corpora or digitized dictionaries containing roots. For a language with the morphological complexity of Tigrinya, a crucial early step in computational linguistic work must be the development of morphological analyzers and generators.

2.1 The stem

A Tigrinya verb (Leslau, 1941 is a standard reference for Tigrinya grammar) consists of a stem and one or more prefixes and suffixes. Most of the complexity resides in the stem, which can be described in terms of three dimensions: **root** (the only strictly lexical component of the verb), **tense-aspect-mood** (TAM), and **derivational category**. Table 1 illustrates the possible combinations of TAM and derivational category for a single root.[1]

A Tigrinya verb root consists of a sequence of three, four, or five consonants. In addition, as in other Ethio-Semitic languages, certain roots include inherent vowels and/or gemination (lengthening) of particular consonants. Thus among the three-consonant roots, there are three subclasses: *CCC*, *CaCC*, *CC_C*. As we have seen, the stem of a Semitic verb can be viewed as the result of the insertion of pattern vowels between root consonants and the copying of root consonants in particular positions. For Tigrinya, each combination of root class, TAM, and derivational category is characterized by a particular pattern.

With respect to TAM, there are four possibilities, as shown in Table 1, conventionally referred to in English as PERFECTIVE, IMPERFECTIVE, JUSSIVE-IMPERATIVE, and GERUNDIVE. Word-forms within these four TAM categories combine with auxiliaries to yield the full range of possbilities in the complex Tigrinya tense-aspect-mood system. Since auxiliaries are written as separate words or separated from the main verbs by an apostrophe, they will not be discussed further.

Within each of the TAM categories, a Tigrinya verb root can appear in up to eight different deriva-

[1] I use *i* for the high central vowel of Tigrinya, *ɛ* for the mid central vowel, *q* for the velar ejective, a dot under a character to represent other ejectives, a right quote to represent a glottal stop, a left quote to represent the voiced pharyngeal fricative, and _ to represent gemination. Other symbols are conventional International Phonetic Alphabet.

	simple	pas/refl	caus	freqv	recip1	caus-rec1	recip2	caus-rec2
perf	*fɛlɛṭ*	*tɛfɛl(ɛ)ṭ*	*aflɛṭ*	*fɛlalɛṭ*	*tɛfalɛṭ*	*af_alɛṭ*	*tɛfɛlalɛṭ*	*af_ɛlalɛṭ*
imprf	*fɛl(_ɨ)ṭ*	*fɨl_ɛṭ*	*af(ɨ)l(_)ɨṭ*	*fɛlalṭ*	*f_alɛṭ*	*af_alṭ*	*f_ɛlalɛṭ*	*af_ɛlalṭ*
jus/impv	*flɛṭ*	*tɛfɛlɛṭ*	*aflɨṭ*	*fɛlalṭ*	*tɛfalɛṭ*	*af_alṭ*	*tɛfɛlalɛṭ*	*af_ɛlalṭ*
ger	*fɛliṭ*	*tɛfɛliṭ*	*afliṭ*	*fɛlaliṭ*	*tɛfaliṭ*	*af_aliṭ*	*tɛfɛlaliṭ*	*af_ɛlaliṭ*

Table 1: Stems based on the Tigrinya root $\sqrt{}$*flṭ*.

tional categories, which can can be characterized in terms of four binary features, each with particular morphological consequences. These features will be referred to in this paper as "ps" ("passive"), "tr" ("transitive"), "it" ("iterative"), and "rc" ("reciprocal"). The eight possible combinations of these features (see Table 1 for examples) are SIMPLE [-ps,-tr,-it,-rc], PASSIVE/REFLEXIVE [+ps,-tr,-it,-rc], TRANSITIVE/CAUSATIVE: [-ps,+tr,-it,-rc], FREQUENTATIVE [-ps,-tr,+it,-rc], RECIPROCAL 1 [+ps,-tr,-it,+rc], CAUSATIVE RECIPROCAL 1 [-ps,+tr,-it,+rc], RECIPROCAL 2 [+ps,-tr,+it,-rc], CAUSATIVE RECIPROCAL 2 [-ps,+tr,+it,-rc]. Notice that the [+ps,+it] and [+tr,+it] combinations are roughly equivalent semantically to the [+ps,+rc] and [+tr,+rc] combinations, though this is not true for all verb roots.

2.2 Affixes

The affixes closest to the stem represent **subject agreement**; there are ten combinations of person, number, and gender in the Tigrinya pronominal and verb-agreement system. For imperfective and jussive verbs, as in the corresponding TAM categories in other Semitic languages, subject agreement takes the form of prefixes and sometimes also suffixes, for example, *yiflɛṭ* 'that he know', *yiflɛṭu* 'that they (mas.) know'. In the perfective, imperative, and gerundive, subject agreement is expressed by suffixes alone, for example, *fɛlɛṭki* 'you (sg., fem.) knew', *fɛlɛṭu* 'they (mas.) knew!'.

Following the subject agreement suffix (if there is one), a transitive Tigrinya verb may also include an **object suffix** (or object agreement marker), again in one of the same set of ten possible combinations of person, number, and gender. There are two sets of object suffixes, a plain set representing direct objects and a prepositional set representing various sorts of dative, benefactive, locative, and instrumental complements, for example, *yifɛlṭɛn_i* 'he knows me', *yifɛlṭɛl_ɛy* 'he knows for me'.

Preceding the subject prefix of an imperfective or jussive verb or the stem of a perfective, imperative, or gerundive verb, there may be the prefix indicating **negative polarity**, *ay-*. Non-finite negative verbs also require the suffix *-n*: *yifɛlṭɛn_i* 'he knows me'; *ay_ifɛlṭɛn_in* 'he doesn't know me'.

Preceding the negative prefix (if there is one), an imperfective or perfective verb may also include the prefix marking **relativization**, *(z)i-*, for example, *zifɛlṭɛn_i* '(he) who knows me'. The relativizer can in turn be preceded by one of a set of seven **prepositions**, for example, *kabzifɛlṭɛn_i* 'from him who knows me'. Finally, in the perfective, imperfective, and gerundive, there is the possibility of one or the other of several **conjunctive prefixes** at the beginning of the verb (without the relativizer), for example, *kifɛlṭɛn_i* 'so that he knows me' and one of several **conjunctive suffixes** at the end of the verb, for example, *yifɛlṭɛn_in* 'and he knows me'.

Given up to 32 possible stem templates (combinations of four tense-aspect-mood and eight derivational categories) and the various possible combinations of agreement, polarity, relativization, preposition, and conjunction affixes, a Tigrinya verb root can appear in well over 100,000 different wordforms.

2.3 Complexity

Tigrinya shares with other Semitic languages complex variations in the stem patterns when the root contains glottal or pharyngeal consonants or semivowels. These and a range of other regular language-specific morphophonemic processes can be captured in alternation rules. As in other Semitic languages, reduplication also plays a role in some of the stem patterns (as seen in Table 1). Furthermore, the second consonant of the most important conjugation class, as well as the consonant of most of the object suffixes, geminates in certain environments and not others (Buckley, 2000), a process that depends on syllable weight.

The morphotactics of the Tigrinya verb is replete with dependencies which span the verb stem: (1) the negative circumfix *ay-n*, (2) absence of the negative suffix *-n* following a subordinating prefix, (3) constraints on combinations of subject agreement prefixes and suffixes in the imperfective and jussive, (4) constraints on combinations of subject agreement affixes and object suffixes.

There is also considerable ambiguity in the system. For example, the second person and third person feminine plural imperfective and jussive subject suffix is identical to one allomorph of the third person feminine singular object suffix (*yifɛlṭa*) 'he knows her; they (fem.) know'). Tigrinya is written in the Ge'ez (Ethiopic) syllabary, which fails to mark gemination and to distinguish between syllable final consonants and consonants followed by the vowel *ɨ*. This introduces further ambiguity.

In sum, the complexity of Tigrinya verbs presents a challenge to any computational morphology framework. In the next section I consider an augmentation to finite state morphology offering clear advantages for this language.

3 FSTs with Feature Structures

A **weighted FST** (Mohri et al., 2000) is a finite state transducer whose transitions are augmented with weights. The weights must be elements of a **semiring**, an algebraic structure with an "addition" operation, a "multiplication" operation, identity elements for each operation, and the constraint that multiplication distributes over addition. Weights on a path of transitions through a transducer are "multiplied", and the weights associated with alternate paths through a transducer are "added". Weighted FSTs are closed under the same operations as unweighted FSTs; in particular, they can be composed. Weighted FSTs are familiar in speech processing, where the semiring elements usually represent probabilities, with "multiplication" and "addition" in their usual senses.

Amtrup (2003) recognized the advantages that would accrue to morphological analyzers and generators if they could accommodate structured representations. One familiar approach to representing linguistic structure is **feature structures** (FSs) (Carpenter, 1992; Copestake, 2002). A feature structure consists of a set of attribute-value pairs, for which values are either atomic properties, such as FALSE or FEMININE, or feature structures. For example, we might represent the morphological structure of the Tigrinya noun *gɛzay* 'my house' as [lex=*gɛza*, num=sing, poss=[pers=1, num=sg]]. The basic operation over FSs is **unification**. Loosely speaking, two FSs unify if their attribute-values pairs are compatible; the resulting unification combines the features of the FSs. For example, the two FSs [lex=*gɛza*, num=sg] and [poss=[pers=1, num=sg]] unify to yield the FS [lex=*gɛza*, num=sg, poss=[pers=1, num=sg]]. The distinguished FS TOP unifies with any other FS.

Amtrup shows that sets of FSs constitute a semiring, with pairwise unification as the multiplication operator, set union as the addition operator, TOP as the identity element for multiplication, and the empty set as the identity element for addition. Thus FSTs can be weighted with FSs. In an FST with FS weights, traversing a path through the network for a given input string yields an FS set, in addition to the usual output string. The FS set is the result of repeated unification of the FS sets on the arcs in the path, starting with an initial input FS set. A path through the network fails not only if the current input character fails to match the input character on the arc, but also if the current accumulated FS set fails to unify with the FS set on an arc.

Using examples from Persian, Amtrup demonstrates two advantages of FSTs weighted with FS sets. First, long-distance dependencies within words present notorious problems for finite state techniques. For generation, the usual approach is to overgenerate and then filter out the illegal strings below, but this may result in a much larger network because of the duplication of state descriptions. Using FSs, enforcing long-distance constraints is straightforward. Weights on the relevant transitions early in the word specify values for features that must agree with similar feature specifications on transitions later in the word (see the Tigrinya examples in the next section). Second, many NLP applications, such a machine translation, work with the sort of structured representations that are elegantly handled by FS descriptions. Thus it is often desirable to have the output of a morphological analyzer exhibit this richness, in contrast to the string representations that are the output of an unweighted finite state analyzer.

4 Weighted FSTs for Tigrinya Verbs

4.1 Long-distance dependencies

As we have seen, Tigrinya verbs exhibit various sorts of long-distance dependencies. The circumfix that marks the negative of non-subordinate verbs, *ay...n*, is one example. Figure 1 shows how this constraint can be handled naturally using an FST weighted with FS sets. In place of the separate negative and affirmative subnetworks that would have to span the entire FST in the absence of weighted arcs, we have simply the negative and affirmative branches at the beginning and end of the weighted FST. In the analysis direction, this FST will accept forms such as *ay_ifɛlṭun* 'they don't know' and *yifɛlṭu* 'they know' and reject forms such as *ay_ifɛlṭu*. In the generation direction, the FST will correctly generate a form such as *ay_ifɛlṭun* given a initial FS that includes the feature [pol=neg].

4.2 Stems: root and derivational pattern

Now consider the source of most of the complexity of the Tigrinya verb, the stem. The stem may be thought of as conveying three types of information: lexical (the root of the verb), derivational, and TAM. However, unlike the former two types, the TAM category of the verb is redundantly coded for by the combination of subject agreement affixes. Thus, analysis of a stem should return at least the root and the derivational category, and generation should start with a root and a derivational category and return a stem. We can represent each root as a sequence of consonants, separated in some cases by the vowel *a* or the gemination character (_). Given a particular derivational pattern and a TAM category, extracting the root from the stem is a straightforward matter with an FST. For example, for the imperfective passive, the *CC_C* root pattern appears in the template *CiC_ɛC*, and the root is what is left if the two vowels in the stem are skipped over.

However, we want to extract both the derivational pattern and the root, and the problem for finite state methods, as discussed in Section 1.2, is that both are spread throughout the stem. The analyzer needs to alternate between recording elements of the root and clues about the derivational pattern as it traverses the stem, and the generator needs to alternate between outputting characters that represent root elements and characters that depend on the derivational pattern as it produces the stem. The process is complicated further because some stem characters, such as the gemination character, may be either lexical (that is, a root element) or derivational, and others may provide information about both components. For example, a stem with four consonants and *a* separating the second and third consonants represents the frequentative of a three-consonant root if the third and fourth consonants are identical (e.g., *fɛlalɛṭ* 'knew repeatedly', root: *flṭ*) and a four-consonant root (*CCaCC* root pattern) in the simple derivational category if they are not (e.g., *kɛlakɛl* 'prevented', root *klakl*).

As discussed in Section 1.2, one of the familiar approaches to this problem, that of Beesley and Karttunen (2003), precompiles all of the combinations of roots and derivational patterns into stems. The problem with this approach for Tigrinya is that we do not have anything like a complete list of roots; that is, we expect many stems to be novel and will need to be able to analyze them on the fly. The other two approaches discussed in 1.2, that of Kiraz (2000) and that of Cohen-Sygal & Wintner (2006), are closer to what is proposed here. Each has an explicit mechanism for keeping the root and pattern distinct: separate tapes in the case of Kiraz (2000) and separate memory registers in the case of Cohen-Sygal & Wintner (2006).

The present approach also divides the work of processing the root and the derivational patterns between two components of the system. However, instead of the additional overhead required for implementing a multi-tape system or registers, this system makes use of the FSTs weighted with FSs that are already motivated for other aspects of morphology, as argued above. In this approach, the lexical aspects of morphology are handled by the ordinary input-output character correspondences, and the grammatical aspects of morphology, in particular the derivational patterns, are handled by the FS weights on the FST arcs and the unification that takes place as accumulated weights are matched against the weights on FST arcs.

As explained in Section 2, we can represent the eight possible derivational categories for a Tigrinya verb stem in terms of four binary features (ps, tr, rc, it). Each of these features is reflected more or less directly in the stem form (though differently for different root classes and for different TAM categories). However, they are sometimes distributed across the stem: different parts of a stem may be constrained by the presence of a particular feature. For example, the feature +ps (abbreviating [ps=True]) causes the gemination of the stem-initial consonant under various circum-

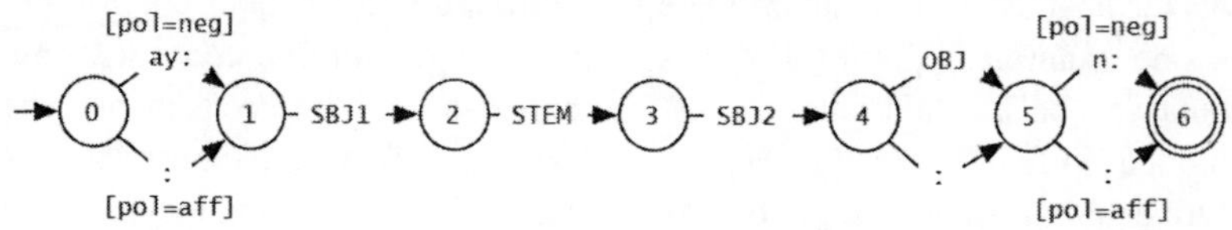

Figure 1: Handling Tigrinya (non-subordinate, imperfective) negation using feature structure weights. Arcs with uppercase labels represents subnetworks that are not spelled out in the figure.

stances and also controls the final vowel in the stem in the imperfective, and the feature +tr is marked by the vowel *a* before the first root consonant and, in the imperfective, by the nature of the vowel that follows the first root consonant (*ε* where we would otherwise expect *ɨ*, *ɨ* where we would otherwise expect *ε*.) That is, as with the verb affixes, there are long-distance dependencies within the verb stem.

Figure 2 illustrates this division of labor for the portion of the stem FST that covers the *CC_C* root pattern for the imperfective. This FST (including the subnetwork not shown that is responsible for the reduplicated portion of the +it patterns) handles all eight possible derivational categories. For the root √*fṣm* 'finish', the stems are [-ps,-tr,-rc,-it]: *fiṣ_ɨm*, [+ps,-tr,-rc,-it]: *fiṣ_εm*, [-ps,+tr,-rc,-it]: *afεṣ_ɨm*, [-ps,-tr,-rc,+it]: *fεṣaṣ_ɨm*, [+ps,-tr,+rc,-it]: *f_aṣ_εm*, [-ps,+tr,+rc,-it]: *af_aṣ_ɨm*, [+ps,-tr,-rc,+it]: *f_εṣaṣ_εm*, [-ps,+tr,-rc,+it]: *af_εṣaṣ_ɨm*. What is notable is the relatively small number of states that are required; among the consonant and vowel positions in the stems, all but the first are shared among the various derivational categories.

Of course the full stem FST, applying to all combinations of the eight root classes, the eight derivational categories, and the four TAM categories, is much larger, but the FS weights still permit a good deal of sharing, including sharing across the root classes and across the TAM categories.

4.3 Architecture

The full verb morphology processing system (see Figure 3) consists of analysis and generation FSTs for both orthographic and phonemically represented words, four FSTs in all. Eleven FSTs are composed to yield the phonemic analysis FST (denoted by the dashed border in Figure 3), and two additional FSTs are composed onto this FST to yield the orthographic FST (denoted by the large solid rectangle). The generation FSTs are created by inverting the analysis FSTs. Only the orthographic FSTs are discussed in the remainder of this paper.

At the most abstract (lexical) end is the heart of the system, the morphotactic FST, and the heart of this FST is the stem FST described above. The stem FST is composed from six FSTs, including three that handle the morphotactics of the stem, one that handles root constraints, and two that handle phonological processes that apply only to the stem. A prefix FST and a suffix FST are then concatenated onto the composed stem FST to create the full verb morphotactic FST. Within the whole FST, it is only the morphotactic FSTs (the yellow rectangles in Figure 3) that have FS weights.[2]

In the analysis direction, the morphotactic FST takes as input words in an abstract canonical form and an initial weight of TOP; that is, at this point in analysis, no grammatical information has been extracted. The output of the morphotactic FST is either the empty list if the form is unanalyzable, or one or more analyses, each consisting of a root string and a fully specified grammatical description in the form of an FS. For example, given the form *'aytɨfɨl_eṭun*, the morphotactic FST would output the root *flṭ* and the FS [tam=imprf, der=[+ps,-tr,-rc,-it], sbj=[+2p,+plr,-fem], +neg, obj=nil, -rel] (see Figure 3). That is, this word represents the imperfective, negative, non-relativized passive of the verb root √*flṭ* ('know') with second person plural masculine subject and no object: 'you (plr., mas.) are not known'. The system has no actual lexicon, so it outputs all roots that are compatible with the input, even if such roots do not exist in the language. In the generation direction, the opposite happens. In this case, the input root can be any legal sequence of characters that matches one of the eight

[2]The reduplication that characterizes [+it] stems and the "anti-reduplication" that prevents sequences of identical root consonants in some positions are handled with separate transitions for each consonant pair.

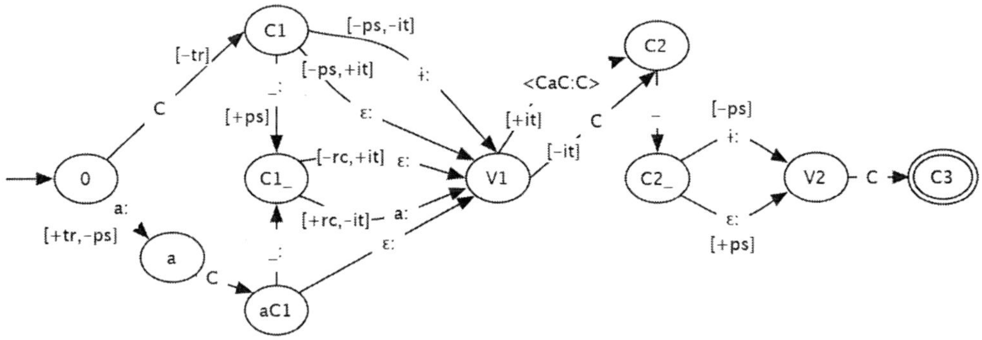

Figure 2: FST for imperfective verb stems of root type *CC_C*. <CaC:C> indicates a subnetwork, not shown, which handles the reduplicated portion of +it stems, for example, *feṣaṣ_ɨm*.

root patterns (there are some constraints on what can constitute a root), though not necessarily an actual root in the language.

The highest FST below the morphotactic FST handles one case of allomorphy: the two allomorphs of the relativization prefix. Below this are nine FSTs handling phonology; for example, one of these converts the sequence *aɨ* to *ε*. At the bottom end of the cascade are two orthographic FSTs which are required when the input to analysis or the output of generation is in standard Tigrinya orthography. One of these is responsible for the insertion of the vowel *ɨ* and for consonant gemination (neither of which is indicated in the orthography); the other inserts a glottal stop before a word-initial vowel.

The full orthographic FST consists of 22,313 states and 118,927 arcs. The system handles verbs in all of the root classes discussed by Leslau (1941), including those with laryngeals and semivowels in different root positions and the three common irregular verbs, and all grammatical combinations of subject, object, negation, relativization, preposition, and conjunction affixes.

For the orthographic version of the analyzer, a word is entered in Ge'ez script (UTF-8 encoding). The program romanizes the input using the SERA transcription conventions (Firdyiwek and Yaqob, 1997), which represent Ge'ez characters with the ASCII character set, before handing it to the orthographic analysis FST. For each possible analysis, the output consists of a (romanized) root and a FS set. Where a set contains more than one FS, the interpretation is that any of the FS elements constitutes a possible analysis. Input to the generator consists of a romanized root and a single feature

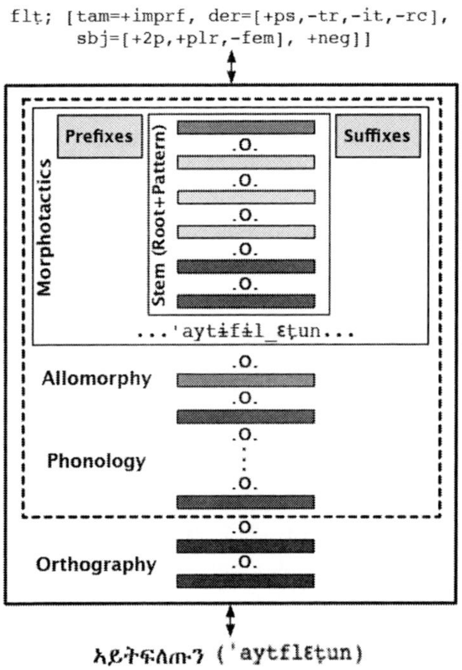

Figure 3: Architecture of the system. Rectangles represent FSTs, ".o."composition.

structure. The output of the orthographic generation FST is an orthographic representation, using SERA conventions, of each possible form that is compatible with the input root and FS. These forms are then converted to Ge'ez orthography.

The analyzer and generator are publicly accessible on the Internet at `www.cs.indiana.edu/cgi-pub/gasser/L3/morpho/Ti/v`.

4.4 Evaluation

Systematic evaluation of the system is difficult since no Tigrinya corpora are currently available. One resource that is useful, however, is the Tigrinya word list compiled by Biniam Gebremichael, available on the Internet at www.cs.ru.nl/ biniam/geez/crawl.php. Biniam extracted 227,984 distinct wordforms from Tigrinya texts by crawling the Internet. As a first step toward evaluating the morphological analyzer, the orthographic analyzer was run on 400 wordforms selected randomly from the list compiled by Biniam, and the results were evaluated by a human reader.

Of the 400 wordforms, 329 were unambiguously verbs. The program correctly analyzed 308 of these. The 21 errors included irregular verbs and orthographic/phonological variants that had not been built into the FST; these will be straightforward to add. Fifty other words were not verbs. The program again responded appropriately, given its knowledge, either rejecting the word or analyzing it as a verb based on a non-existent root. Thirteen other words appeared to be verb forms containing a simple typographical error, and I was unable to identify the remaining eight words. For the latter two categories, the program again responded by rejecting the word or treating it as a verb based on a non-existent root.

To test the morphological generator, the program was run on roots belonging to all 21 of the major classes discussed by Leslau (1941), including those with glottal or pharyngeal consonants or semivowels in different positions within the roots. For each of these classes, the program was asked to generate all possible derivational patterns (in the third person singular masculine form). In addition, for a smaller set of four root classes in the simple derivational pattern, the program was tested on all relevant combinations of the subject and object affixes[3] and, for the imperfective and perfective, on 13 combinations of the relativization, negation, prepositional, and conjunctive affixes. For each of the 272 tests, the generation FST succeeded in outputting the correct form (and in some cases a phonemic and/or orthographic alternative).

In conclusion, the orthographic morphological analyzer and generator provide good coverage of Tigrinya verbs. One weakness of the present system results from its lack of a root dictionary. The analyzer produces as many as 15 different analyses of words, when in many cases only one contains a root that exists in the language. The number could be reduced somewhat by a more extensive filter on possible root segment sequences; however, root internal phonotactics is an area that has not been extensively studied for Tigrinya. In any case, once a Tigrinya root dictionary becomes available, it will be straightforward to compose a lexical FST onto the existing FSTs that will reject all but acceptable roots. Even a relatively small root dictionary should also permit inferences about possible root segment sequences in the language, enabling the construction of a stricter filter for roots that are not yet contained in the dictionary.

5 Conclusion

Progress in all applications for a language such as Tigrinya is held back when verb morphology is not dealt with adequately. Tigrinya morphology is complex in two senses. First, like other Semitic languages, it relies on template morphology, presenting unusual challenges to any computational framework. This paper presents a new answer to these challenges, one which has the potential to integrate morphological processing into other knowledge-based applications through the inclusion of the powerful and flexible feature structure framework. This approach should extend to other Semitic languages, such as Arabic, Hebrew, and Amharic. Second, Tigrinya verbs are simply very elaborate. In addition to the stems resulting from the intercalation of eight root classes, eight derivational patterns and four TAM categories, there are up to four prefix slots and four suffix slots; various sorts of prefix-suffix dependencies; and a range of interacting phonological processes, including those sensitive to syllable structure, as well as segmental context. Just putting together all of these constraints in a way that works is significant. Since the motivation for this project is primarily practical rather than theoretical, the main achievement of the paper is the demonstration that, with some effort, a system can be built that actually handles Tigrinya verbs in great detail. Future work will focus on fine-tuning the verb FST, developing an FST for nouns, and applying this same approach to other Semitic languages.

[3]With respect to their morphophonological behavior, the subject affixes and object suffixes each group into four categories.

References

Saba Amsalu and Girma A. Demeke. 2006. Non-concatenative finite-state morphotactics of Amharic simple verbs. *ELRC Working Papers*, 2(3).

Jan Amtrup. 2003. Morphology in machine translation systems: Efficient integration of finite state transducers and feature structure descriptions. *Machine Translation*, 18:213–235.

Kenneth R. Beesley and Lauri Karttunen. 2003. *Finite State Morphology*. CSLI Publications, Stanford, CA, USA.

Eugene Buckley. 2000. Alignment and weight in the Tigrinya verb stem. In Vicki Carstens and Frederick Parkinson, editors, *Advances in African Linguistics*, pages 165–176. Africa World Press, Lawrenceville, NJ, USA.

Bob Carpenter. 1992. *The Logic of Typed Feature Structures*. Cambridge University Press, Cambridge.

Noam Chomsky and Morris Halle. 1968. *The Sound Pattern of English*. Harper and Row, New York.

Yael Cohen-Sygal and Shuly Wintner. 2006. Finite-state registered automata for non-concatenative morphology. *Computational Linguistics*, 32:49–82.

Ann Copestake. 2002. *Implementing Typed Feature Structure Grammars*. CSLI Publications, Stanford, CA, USA.

Yitna Firdyiwek and Daniel Yaqob. 1997. The system for Ethiopic representation in ascii. URL: citeseer.ist.psu.edu/56365.html.

C. Douglas Johnson. 1972. *Formal Aspects of Phonological Description*. Mouton, The Hague.

Ronald M. Kaplan and Martin Kay. 1994. Regular models of phonological rule systems. *Computational Linguistics*, 20:331–378.

Lauri Karttunen, Ronald M. Kaplan, and Annie Zaenen. 1992. Two-level morphology with composition. In *Proceedings of the International Conference on Computational Linguistics*, volume 14, pages 141–148.

George A. Kiraz. 2000. Multitiered nonlinear morphology using multitape finite automata: a case study on Syriac and Arabic. *Computational Linguistics*, 26(1):77–105.

Kimmo Koskenniemi. 1983. Two-level morphology: a general computational model for word-form recognition and production. Technical Report Publication No. 11, Department of General Linguistics, University of Helsinki.

Wolf Leslau. 1941. *Documents Tigrigna: Grammaire et Textes*. Libraire C. Klincksieck, Paris.

Mehryar Mohri, Fernando Pereira, and Michael Riley. 2000. Weighted finite-state transducers in speech recognition. In *Proceedings of ISCA ITRW on Automatic Speech Recognition: Challenges for the Millenium*, pages 97–106, Paris.

Cube Summing, Approximate Inference with Non-Local Features, and Dynamic Programming without Semirings

Kevin Gimpel and **Noah A. Smith**
Language Technologies Institute
Carnegie Mellon University
Pittsburgh, PA 15213, USA
{kgimpel,nasmith}@cs.cmu.edu

Abstract

We introduce *cube summing*, a technique that permits dynamic programming algorithms for summing over structures (like the forward and inside algorithms) to be extended with non-local features that violate the classical structural independence assumptions. It is inspired by cube pruning (Chiang, 2007; Huang and Chiang, 2007) in its computation of non-local features dynamically using scored k-best lists, but also maintains additional residual quantities used in calculating approximate marginals. When restricted to local features, cube summing reduces to a novel semiring (*k-best+residual*) that generalizes many of the semirings of Goodman (1999). When non-local features are included, cube summing does not reduce to any semiring, but is compatible with generic techniques for solving dynamic programming equations.

1 Introduction

Probabilistic NLP researchers frequently make independence assumptions to keep inference algorithms tractable. Doing so limits the *features* that are available to our models, requiring features to be structurally local. Yet many problems in NLP—machine translation, parsing, named-entity recognition, and others—have benefited from the addition of *non-local* features that break classical independence assumptions. Doing so has required algorithms for *approximate* inference.

Recently *cube pruning* (Chiang, 2007; Huang and Chiang, 2007) was proposed as a way to leverage existing dynamic programming algorithms that find optimal-scoring derivations or structures when only local features are involved. Cube pruning permits approximate decoding with non-local features, but leaves open the question of how the feature weights or probabilities are learned. Meanwhile, some learning algorithms, like maximum likelihood for conditional log-linear models (Lafferty et al., 2001), unsupervised models (Pereira and Schabes, 1992), and models with hidden variables (Koo and Collins, 2005; Wang et al., 2007; Blunsom et al., 2008), require *summing* over the scores of many structures to calculate marginals.

We first review the semiring-weighted logic programming view of dynamic programming algorithms (Shieber et al., 1995) and identify an intuitive property of a program called *proof locality* that follows from feature locality in the underlying probability model (§2). We then provide an analysis of cube pruning as an approximation to the intractable problem of exact optimization over structures with non-local features and show how the use of non-local features with k-best lists breaks certain semiring properties (§3). The primary contribution of this paper is a novel technique—*cube summing*—for approximate summing over discrete structures with non-local features, which we relate to cube pruning (§4). We discuss implementation (§5) and show that cube summing becomes exact and expressible as a semiring when restricted to local features; this semiring generalizes many commonly-used semirings in dynamic programming (§6).

2 Background

In this section, we discuss dynamic programming algorithms as semiring-weighted logic programs. We then review the definition of semirings and important examples. We discuss the relationship between locally-factored structure scores and proofs in logic programs.

2.1 Dynamic Programming

Many algorithms in NLP involve dynamic programming (e.g., the Viterbi, forward-backward,

Proceedings of the 12th Conference of the European Chapter of the ACL, pages 318–326,
Athens, Greece, 30 March – 3 April 2009. ©2009 Association for Computational Linguistics

probabilistic Earley's, and minimum edit distance algorithms). Dynamic programming (DP) involves solving certain kinds of recursive equations with shared substructure and a topological ordering of the variables.

Shieber et al. (1995) showed a connection between DP (specifically, as used in parsing) and *logic programming*, and Goodman (1999) augmented such logic programs with semiring weights, giving an algebraic explanation for the intuitive connections among classes of algorithms with the same logical structure. For example, in Goodman's framework, the forward algorithm and the Viterbi algorithm are comprised of the same logic program with different semirings. Goodman defined other semirings, including ones we will use here. This formal framework was the basis for the Dyna programming language, which permits a declarative specification of the logic program and compiles it into an efficient, agenda-based, bottom-up procedure (Eisner et al., 2005).

For our purposes, a DP consists of a set of recursive equations over a set of indexed variables. For example, the probabilistic CKY algorithm (run on sentence $w_1 w_2 \ldots w_n$) is written as

$$
\begin{aligned}
C_{X,i-1,i} &= p_{X \to w_i} \qquad (1)\\
C_{X,i,k} &= \max_{Y,Z \in \mathcal{N}; j \in \{i+1,\ldots,k-1\}} \\
&\qquad p_{X \to Y Z} \times C_{Y,i,j} \times C_{Z,j,k} \\
goal &= C_{\mathbf{S},0,n}
\end{aligned}
$$

where $\mathcal{N}$ is the nonterminal set and $\mathbf{S} \in \mathcal{N}$ is the start symbol. Each $C_{X,i,j}$ variable corresponds to the chart value (probability of the most likely subtree) of an X-constituent spanning the substring $w_{i+1} \ldots w_j$. *goal* is a special variable of greatest interest, though solving for *goal* correctly may (in general, but not in this example) require solving for all the other values. We will use the term "index" to refer to the subscript values on variables (X, i, j on $C_{X,i,j}$).

Where convenient, we will make use of Shieber et al.'s logic programming view of dynamic programming. In this view, each variable (e.g., $C_{X,i,j}$ in Eq. 1) corresponds to the value of a "theorem," the constants in the equations (e.g., $p_{X \to Y Z}$ in Eq. 1) correspond to the values of "axioms," and the DP defines quantities corresponding to weighted "proofs" of the *goal* theorem (e.g., finding the maximum-valued proof, or aggregating proof values). The value of a proof is a combination of the values of the axioms it starts with. Semirings define these values and define two operators over them, called "aggregation" (max in Eq. 1) and "combination" ($\times$ in Eq. 1).

Goodman and Eisner et al. assumed that the values of the variables are in a semiring, and that the equations are defined solely in terms of the two semiring operations. We will often refer to the "probability" of a proof, by which we mean a non-negative $\mathbb{R}$-valued score defined by the semantics of the dynamic program variables; it may not be a normalized probability.

2.2 Semirings

A *semiring* is a tuple $\langle A, \oplus, \otimes, \mathbf{0}, \mathbf{1} \rangle$, in which A is a set, $\oplus : A \times A \to A$ is the aggregation operation, $\otimes : A \times A \to A$ is the combination operation, $\mathbf{0}$ is the additive identity element ($\forall a \in A, a \oplus \mathbf{0} = a$), and $\mathbf{1}$ is the multiplicative identity element ($\forall a \in A, a \otimes \mathbf{1} = a$). A semiring requires $\oplus$ to be associative and commutative, and $\otimes$ to be associative and to distribute over $\oplus$. Finally, we require $a \otimes \mathbf{0} = \mathbf{0} \otimes a = \mathbf{0}$ for all $a \in A$.[1] Examples include the inside semiring, $\langle \mathbb{R}_{\geq 0}, +, \times, 0, 1 \rangle$, and the Viterbi semiring, $\langle \mathbb{R}_{\geq 0}, \max, \times, 0, 1 \rangle$. The former sums the probabilities of all proofs of each theorem. The latter (used in Eq. 1) calculates the probability of the most probable proof of each theorem. Two more examples follow.

Viterbi proof semiring. We typically need to recover the steps in the most probable proof in addition to its probability. This is often done using backpointers, but can also be accomplished by representing the most probable proof for each theorem in its entirety as part of the semiring value (Goodman, 1999). For generality, we define a proof as a string that is constructed from strings associated with axioms, but the particular form of a proof is problem-dependent. The "Viterbi proof" semiring includes the probability of the most probable proof and the proof itself. Letting $\mathcal{L} \subseteq \Sigma^*$ be the proof language on some symbol set Σ, this semiring is defined on the set $\mathbb{R}_{\geq 0} \times \mathcal{L}$ with $\mathbf{0}$ element $\langle 0, \epsilon \rangle$ and $\mathbf{1}$ element $\langle 1, \epsilon \rangle$. For two values $\langle u_1, U_1 \rangle$ and $\langle u_2, U_2 \rangle$, the aggregation operator returns $\langle \max(u_1, u_2), U_{\operatorname{argmax}_{i \in \{1,2\}} u_i} \rangle$.

[1] When cycles are permitted, i.e., where the value of one variable depends on itself, infinite sums can be involved. We must ensure that these infinite sums are well defined under the semiring. So-called *complete semirings* satisfy additional conditions to handle infinite sums, but for simplicity we will restrict our attention to DPs that do not involve cycles.

Semiring	A	Aggregation ($\oplus$)	Combination ($\otimes$)	$\mathbf{0}$	$\mathbf{1}$
inside	$\mathbb{R}_{\geq 0}$	$u_1 + u_2$	$u_1 u_2$	0	1
Viterbi	$\mathbb{R}_{\geq 0}$	$\max(u_1, u_2)$	$u_1 u_2$	0	1
Viterbi proof	$\mathbb{R}_{\geq 0} \times \mathcal{L}$	$\langle \max(u_1, u_2), U_{\text{argmax}_{i \in \{1,2\}} u_i} \rangle$	$\langle u_1 u_2, U_1.U_2 \rangle$	$\langle 0, \epsilon \rangle$	$\langle 1, \epsilon \rangle$
k-best proof	$(\mathbb{R}_{\geq 0} \times \mathcal{L})^{\leq k}$	$\max\text{-}k(\mathbf{u}_1 \cup \mathbf{u}_2)$	$\max\text{-}k(\mathbf{u}_1 \star \mathbf{u}_2)$	$\emptyset$	$\{\langle 1, \epsilon \rangle\}$

Table 1: Commonly used semirings. An element in the Viterbi proof semiring is denoted $\langle u_1, U_1 \rangle$, where u_1 is the probability of proof U_1. The max-k function returns a sorted list of the top-k proofs from a set. The $\star$ function performs a cross-product on two k-best proof lists (Eq. 2).

The combination operator returns $\langle u_1 u_2, U_1.U_2 \rangle$, where $U_1.U_2$ denotes the string concatenation of U_1 and U_2.[2]

k-best proof semiring. The "k-best proof" semiring computes the values and proof strings of the k most-probable proofs for each theorem. The set is $(\mathbb{R}_{\geq 0} \times \mathcal{L})^{\leq k}$, i.e., sequences (up to length k) of sorted probability/proof pairs. The aggregation operator $\oplus$ uses max-k, which chooses the k highest-scoring proofs from its argument (a set of scored proofs) and sorts them in decreasing order. To define the combination operator $\otimes$, we require a cross-product that pairs probabilities and proofs from two k-best lists. We call this $\star$, defined on two semiring values $\mathbf{u} = \langle \langle u_1, U_1 \rangle, ..., \langle u_k, U_k \rangle \rangle$ and $\mathbf{v} = \langle \langle v_1, V_1 \rangle, ..., \langle v_k, V_k \rangle \rangle$ by:

$$\mathbf{u} \star \mathbf{v} = \{\langle u_i v_j, U_i.V_j \rangle \mid i, j \in \{1, ..., k\}\} \quad (2)$$

Then, $\mathbf{u} \otimes \mathbf{v} = \max\text{-}k(\mathbf{u} \star \mathbf{v})$. This is similar to the k-best semiring defined by Goodman (1999).

These semirings are summarized in Table 1.

2.3 Features and Inference

Let $\mathcal{X}$ be the space of inputs to our logic program, i.e., $x \in \mathcal{X}$ is a set of axioms. Let $\mathcal{L}$ denote the proof language and let $\mathcal{Y} \subseteq \mathcal{L}$ denote the set of proof strings that constitute full proofs, i.e., proofs of the special *goal* theorem. We assume an exponential probabilistic model such that

$$p(y \mid x) \propto \prod_{m=1}^{M} \lambda_m^{h_m(x,y)} \quad (3)$$

where each $\lambda_m \geq 0$ is a parameter of the model and each h_m is a *feature function*. There is a bijection between $\mathcal{Y}$ and the space of discrete structures that our model predicts.

Given such a model, DP is helpful for solving two kinds of inference problems. The first problem, *decoding*, is to find the highest scoring proof $\hat{y} \in \mathcal{Y}$ for a given input $x \in \mathcal{X}$:

$$\hat{y}(x) = \text{argmax}_{y \in \mathcal{Y}} \prod_{m=1}^{M} \lambda_m^{h_m(x,y)} \quad (4)$$

The second is the *summing* problem, which marginalizes the proof probabilities (without normalization):

$$s(x) = \sum_{y \in \mathcal{Y}} \prod_{m=1}^{M} \lambda_m^{h_m(x,y)} \quad (5)$$

As defined, the feature functions h_m can depend on arbitrary parts of the input axiom set x and the entire output proof y.

2.4 Proof and Feature Locality

An important characteristic of problems suited for DP is that the *global* calculation (i.e., the value of *goal*) depend only on *local* factored parts. In DP equations, this means that each equation connects a relatively small number of indexed variables related through a relatively small number of indices. In the logic programming formulation, it means that each step of the proof depends only on the theorems being used at that step, *not* the full proofs of those theorems. We call this property *proof locality*. In the statistical modeling view of Eq. 3, classical DP requires that the probability model make strong Markovian conditional independence assumptions (e.g., in HMMs, $S_{t-1} \perp S_{t+1} \mid S_t$); in exponential families over discrete structures, this corresponds to *feature locality*.

For a particular proof y of *goal* consisting of t intermediate theorems, we define a set of proof strings $\ell_i \in \mathcal{L}$ for $i \in \{1, ..., t\}$, where ℓ_i corresponds to the proof of the ith theorem.[3] We can break the computation of feature function h_m into a summation over terms corresponding to each ℓ_i:

$$h_m(x, y) = \sum_{i=1}^{t} f_m(x, \ell_i) \quad (6)$$

This is simply a way of noting that feature functions "fire" incrementally at specific points in the

[2]We assume for simplicity that the best proof will never be a tie among more than one proof. Goodman (1999) handles this situation more carefully, though our version is more likely to be used in practice for both the Viterbi proof and k-best proof semirings.

[3]The theorem indexing scheme might be based on a topological ordering given by the proof structure, but is not important for our purposes.

proof, normally at the first opportunity. *Any* feature function can be expressed this way. For local features, we can go farther; we define a function $top(\ell)$ that returns the proof string corresponding to the antecedents and consequent of the *last* inference step in ℓ. Local features have the property:

$$h_m^{loc}(x, y) = \sum_{i=1}^{t} f_m(x, top(\ell_i)) \quad (7)$$

Local features only have access to the most recent deductive proof step (though they may "fire" repeatedly in the proof), while non-local features have access to the entire proof up to a given theorem. For both kinds of features, the "f" terms are used within the DP formulation. When taking an inference step to prove theorem i, the value $\prod_{m=1}^{M} \lambda_m^{f_m(x,\ell_i)}$ is combined into the calculation of that theorem's value, along with the values of the antecedents. Note that typically only a small number of f_m are nonzero for theorem i.

When non-local h_m/f_m that depend on arbitrary parts of the proof are involved, the decoding and summing inference problems are NP-hard (they instantiate probabilistic inference in a fully connected graphical model). Sometimes, it is possible to achieve proof locality by adding more indices to the DP variables (for example, consider modifying the bigram HMM Viterbi algorithm for trigram HMMs). This increases the number of variables and hence computational cost. In general, it leads to exponential-time inference in the worst case.

There have been many algorithms proposed for approximately solving instances of these decoding and summing problems with non-local features. Some stem from work on graphical models, including loopy belief propagation (Sutton and McCallum, 2004; Smith and Eisner, 2008), Gibbs sampling (Finkel et al., 2005), sequential Monte Carlo methods such as particle filtering (Levy et al., 2008), and variational inference (Jordan et al., 1999; MacKay, 1997; Kurihara and Sato, 2006). Also relevant are stacked learning (Cohen and Carvalho, 2005), interpretable as approximation of non-local feature values (Martins et al., 2008), and M-estimation (Smith et al., 2007), which allows training without inference. Several other approaches used frequently in NLP are approximate methods for decoding only. These include beam search (Lowerre, 1976), cube pruning, which we discuss in §3, integer linear programming (Roth and Yih, 2004), in which arbitrary features can act as constraints on y, and approximate solutions like McDonald and Pereira (2006), in which an exact solution to a related decoding problem is found and then modified to fit the problem of interest.

3 Approximate Decoding

Cube pruning (Chiang, 2007; Huang and Chiang, 2007) is an approximate technique for decoding (Eq. 4); it is used widely in machine translation. Given proof locality, it is essentially an efficient implementation of the k-best proof semiring. Cube pruning goes farther in that it permits non-local features to weigh in on the proof probabilities, at the expense of making the k-best operation approximate. We describe the two approximations cube pruning makes, then propose *cube decoding*, which removes the second approximation. Cube decoding cannot be represented as a semiring; we propose a more general algebraic structure that accommodates it.

3.1 Approximations in Cube Pruning

Cube pruning is an approximate solution to the decoding problem (Eq. 4) in two ways.

Approximation 1: $k < \infty$. Cube pruning uses a finite k for the k-best lists stored in each value. If $k = \infty$, the algorithm performs exact decoding with non-local features (at obviously formidable expense in combinatorial problems).

Approximation 2: lazy computation. Cube pruning exploits the fact that $k < \infty$ to use lazy computation. When combining the k-best proof lists of d theorems' values, cube pruning does not enumerate all k^d proofs, apply non-local features to all of them, and then return the top k. Instead, cube pruning uses a more efficient but approximate solution that only calculates the non-local factors on $O(k)$ proofs to obtain the approximate top k. This trick is only approximate if non-local features are involved.

Approximation 2 makes it impossible to formulate cube pruning using separate aggregation and combination operations, as the use of lazy computation causes these two operations to effectively be performed simultaneously. To more directly relate our summing algorithm (§4) to cube pruning, we suggest a modified version of cube pruning that does not use lazy computation. We call this algorithm *cube decoding*. This algorithm can be written down in terms of separate aggregation and combination operations, though we will show it is not a semiring.

3.2 Cube Decoding

We formally describe cube decoding, show that it does not instantiate a semiring, then describe a more general algebraic structure that it does instantiate.

Consider the set $\mathcal{G}$ of non-local feature functions that map $\mathcal{X} \times \mathcal{L} \to \mathbb{R}_{\geq 0}$.[4] Our definitions in §2.2 for the k-best proof semiring can be expanded to accommodate these functions within the semiring value. Recall that values in the k-best proof semiring fall in $A_k = (\mathbb{R}_{\geq 0} \times \mathcal{L})^{\leq k}$. For cube decoding, we use a different set A_{cd} defined as

$$A_{cd} = \underbrace{(\mathbb{R}_{\geq 0} \times \mathcal{L})^{\leq k}}_{A_k} \times \mathcal{G} \times \{0, 1\}$$

where the binary variable indicates whether the value contains a k-best list (0, which we call an "ordinary" value) or a non-local feature function in $\mathcal{G}$ (1, which we call a "function" value). We denote a value $\mathbf{u} \in A_{cd}$ by

$$\mathbf{u} = \langle \underbrace{\langle\langle u_1, U_1\rangle, \langle u_2, U_2\rangle, ..., \langle u_k, U_k\rangle\rangle}_{\bar{\mathbf{u}}}, g_u, u_s\rangle$$

where each $u_i \in \mathbb{R}_{\geq 0}$ is a probability and each $U_i \in \mathcal{L}$ is a proof string.

We use $\oplus_k$ and $\otimes_k$ to denote the k-best proof semiring's operators, defined in §2.2. We let g_0 be such that $g_0(\ell)$ is undefined for all $\ell \in \mathcal{L}$. For two values $\mathbf{u} = \langle \bar{\mathbf{u}}, g_u, u_s\rangle, \mathbf{v} = \langle \bar{\mathbf{v}}, g_v, v_s\rangle \in A_{cd}$, cube decoding's aggregation operator is:

$$\mathbf{u} \oplus_{cd} \mathbf{v} = \langle \bar{\mathbf{u}} \oplus_k \bar{\mathbf{v}}, g_0, 0\rangle \text{ if } \neg u_s \wedge \neg v_s \quad (8)$$

Under standard models, only ordinary values will be operands of $\oplus_{cd}$, so $\oplus_{cd}$ is undefined when $u_s \vee v_s$. We define the combination operator $\otimes_{cd}$:

$$\mathbf{u} \otimes_{cd} \mathbf{v} = \quad (9)$$
$$\begin{cases} \langle \bar{\mathbf{u}} \otimes_k \bar{\mathbf{v}}, g_0, 0\rangle & \text{if } \neg u_s \wedge \neg v_s, \\ \langle \text{max-}k(exec(g_v, \bar{\mathbf{u}})), g_0, 0\rangle & \text{if } \neg u_s \wedge v_s, \\ \langle \text{max-}k(exec(g_u, \bar{\mathbf{v}})), g_0, 0\rangle & \text{if } u_s \wedge \neg v_s, \\ \langle\langle\rangle, \lambda z.(g_u(z) \times g_v(z)), 1\rangle & \text{if } u_s \wedge v_s. \end{cases}$$

where $exec(g, \bar{\mathbf{u}})$ executes the function g upon each proof in the proof list $\bar{\mathbf{u}}$, modifies the scores in place by multiplying in the function result, and returns the modified proof list:

$$\begin{aligned} g' &= \lambda\ell.g(x, \ell) \\ exec(g, \bar{\mathbf{u}}) &= \langle\langle u_1 g'(U_1), U_1\rangle, \langle u_2 g'(U_2), U_2\rangle, \\ &\quad ..., \langle u_k g'(U_k), U_k\rangle\rangle \end{aligned}$$

Here, max-k is simply used to re-sort the k-best proof list following function evaluation.

The semiring properties fail to hold when introducing non-local features in this way. In particular, $\otimes_{cd}$ is not associative when $1 < k < \infty$. For example, consider the probabilistic CKY algorithm as above, but using the cube decoding semiring with the non-local feature functions collectively known as "*NGramTree*" features (Huang, 2008) that score the string of terminals and nonterminals along the path from word j to word $j + 1$ when two constituents $C_{Y,i,j}$ and $C_{Z,j,k}$ are combined. The semiring value associated with such a feature is $\mathbf{u} = \langle\langle\rangle, NGramTree_\pi(), 1\rangle$ (for a specific path π), and we rewrite Eq. 1 as follows (where ranges for summation are omitted for space):

$$C_{X,i,k} = \bigoplus\nolimits_{cd} p_{X \to YZ} \otimes_{cd} C_{Y,i,j} \otimes_{cd} C_{Z,j,k} \otimes_{cd} \mathbf{u}$$

The combination operator is not associative since the following will give different answers:[5]

$$(p_{X \to YZ} \otimes_{cd} C_{Y,i,j}) \otimes_{cd} (C_{Z,j,k} \otimes_{cd} \mathbf{u}) \quad (10)$$
$$((p_{X \to YZ} \otimes_{cd} C_{Y,i,j}) \otimes_{cd} C_{Z,j,k}) \otimes_{cd} \mathbf{u} \quad (11)$$

In Eq. 10, the non-local feature function is executed on the k-best proof list for Z, while in Eq. 11, $NGramTree_\pi$ is called on the k-best proof list for the X constructed from Y and Z. Furthermore, neither of the above gives the desired result, since we actually wish to expand the full set of k^2 proofs of X and then apply $NGramTree_\pi$ to each of them (or a higher-dimensional "cube" if more operands are present) before selecting the k-best. The binary operations above retain only the top k proofs of X in Eq. 11 before applying $NGramTree_\pi$ to each of them. We actually would like to redefine combination so that it can operate on *arbitrarily-sized sets* of values.

We can understand cube decoding through an algebraic structure with two operations $\oplus$ and $\otimes$, where $\otimes$ need not be associative and need not distribute over $\oplus$, and furthermore where $\oplus$ and $\otimes$ are

[4] In our setting, $g_m(x, \ell)$ will most commonly be defined as $\lambda_m^{f_m(x,\ell)}$ in the notation of §2.3. But functions in $\mathcal{G}$ could also be used to implement, e.g., hard constraints or other non-local score factors.

[5] Distributivity of combination over aggregation fails for related reasons. We omit a full discussion due to space.

defined on arbitrarily many operands. We will refer here to such a structure as a *generalized semiring*.[6] To define $\otimes_{cd}$ on a set of operands with N' ordinary operands and N function operands, we first compute the full $O(k^{N'})$ cross-product of the ordinary operands, then apply each of the N functions from the remaining operands in turn upon the full N'-dimensional "cube," finally calling $\max\text{-}k$ on the result.

4 Cube Summing

We present an approximate solution to the summing problem when non-local features are involved, which we call *cube summing*. It is an extension of cube decoding, and so we will describe it as a generalized semiring. The key addition is to maintain in each value, in addition to the k-best list of proofs from A_k, a scalar corresponding to the *residual* probability (possibly unnormalized) of all proofs not among the k-best.[7] The k-best proofs are still used for dynamically computing non-local features but the aggregation and combination operations are redefined to update the residual as appropriate.

We define the set A_{cs} for cube summing as

$$A_{cs} = \mathbb{R}_{\geq 0} \times (\mathbb{R}_{\geq 0} \times \mathcal{L})^{\leq k} \times \mathcal{G} \times \{0, 1\}$$

A value $\mathbf{u} \in A_{cs}$ is defined as

$$\mathbf{u} = \langle u_0, \underbrace{\langle \langle u_1, U_1 \rangle, \langle u_2, U_2 \rangle, ..., \langle u_k, U_k \rangle \rangle}_{\bar{\mathbf{u}}}, g_u, u_s \rangle$$

For a proof list $\bar{\mathbf{u}}$, we use $\|\bar{\mathbf{u}}\|$ to denote the sum of all proof scores, $\sum_{i:\langle u_i, U_i \rangle \in \bar{\mathbf{u}}} u_i$.

The aggregation operator over operands $\{\mathbf{u}_i\}_{i=1}^N$, all such that $u_{is} = 0$,[8] is defined by:

$$\bigoplus_{i=1}^N \mathbf{u}_i = \left\langle \sum_{i=1}^N u_{i0} + \left\| Res\left(\bigcup_{i=1}^N \bar{\mathbf{u}}_i\right)\right\|, \max\text{-}k\left(\bigcup_{i=1}^N \bar{\mathbf{u}}_i\right), g_0, 0 \right\rangle \tag{12}$$

where Res returns the "residual" set of scored proofs *not* in the k-best among its arguments, possibly the empty set.

For a set of $N+N'$ operands $\{\mathbf{v}_i\}_{i=1}^N \cup \{\mathbf{w}_j\}_{j=1}^{N'}$ such that $v_{is} = 1$ (non-local feature functions) and $w_{js} = 1$ (ordinary values), the combination operator $\otimes$ is shown in Eq. 13 Fig. 1. Note that the case where $N' = 0$ is not needed in this application; an ordinary value will always be included in combination.

In the special case of two ordinary operands (where $u_s = v_s = 0$), Eq. 13 reduces to

$$\mathbf{u} \otimes \mathbf{v} = \langle u_0 v_0 + u_0 \|\bar{\mathbf{v}}\| + v_0 \|\bar{\mathbf{u}}\| + \|Res(\bar{\mathbf{u}} \star \bar{\mathbf{v}})\|, \max\text{-}k(\bar{\mathbf{u}} \star \bar{\mathbf{v}}), g_0, 0 \rangle \tag{14}$$

We define $\mathbf{0}$ as $\langle 0, \langle\rangle, g_0, 0 \rangle$; an appropriate definition for the combination identity element is less straightforward and of little practical importance; we leave it to future work.

If we use this generalized semiring to solve a DP and achieve *goal* value of $\mathbf{u}$, the approximate sum of all proof probabilities is given by $u_0 + \|\bar{\mathbf{u}}\|$. If all features are local, the approach is exact. With non-local features, the k-best list may not contain the k-best proofs, and the residual score, while including all possible proofs, may not include all of the non-local features in all of those proofs' probabilities.

5 Implementation

We have so far viewed dynamic programming algorithms in terms of their declarative specifications as semiring-weighted logic programs. Solvers have been proposed by Goodman (1999), by Klein and Manning (2001) using a hypergraph representation, and by Eisner et al. (2005). Because Goodman's and Eisner et al.'s algorithms assume semirings, adapting them for cube summing is non-trivial.[9]

To generalize Goodman's algorithm, we suggest using the directed-graph data structure known variously as an *arithmetic circuit* or *computation graph*.[10] Arithmetic circuits have recently drawn interest in the graphical model community as a

[6] Algebraic structures are typically defined with binary operators only, so we were unable to find a suitable term for this structure in the literature.

[7] Blunsom and Osborne (2008) described a related approach to approximate summing using the chart computed during cube pruning, but did not keep track of the residual terms as we do here.

[8] We assume that operands $\mathbf{u}_i$ to $\oplus_{cs}$ will never be such that $u_{is} = 1$ (non-local feature functions). This is reasonable in the widely used log-linear model setting we have adopted, where weights λ_m are factors in a proof's product score.

[9] The bottom-up agenda algorithm in Eisner et al. (2005) might possibly be generalized so that associativity, distributivity, and binary operators are not required (John Blatz, p.c.).

[10] This data structure is not specific to any particular set of operations. We have also used it successfully with the inside semiring.

$$\bigotimes_{i=1}^{N} \mathbf{v}_i \otimes \bigotimes_{j=1}^{N'} \mathbf{w}_j = \Bigg\langle \Bigg(\sum_{B\in\mathcal{P}(S)} \prod_{b\in B} w_{b0} \prod_{c\in S\setminus B} \|\bar{\mathbf{w}}_c\| \Bigg) + \left\|Res(exec(g_{v_1},\ldots exec(g_{v_N}, \bar{\mathbf{w}}_1 \star\cdots\star \bar{\mathbf{w}}_{N'})\ldots))\right\|, \; \text{max-}k(exec(g_{v_1},\ldots exec(g_{v_N},\bar{\mathbf{w}}_1\star\cdots\star\bar{\mathbf{w}}_{N'})\ldots)), g_0, 0\Bigg\rangle \tag{13}$$

Figure 1: Combination operation for cube summing, where $S = \{1, 2, \ldots, N'\}$ and $\mathcal{P}(S)$ is the power set of S excluding $\emptyset$.

tool for performing probabilistic inference (Darwiche, 2003). In the directed graph, there are vertices corresponding to axioms (these are sinks in the graph), $\oplus$ vertices corresponding to theorems, and $\otimes$ vertices corresponding to summands in the dynamic programming equations. Directed edges point from each node to the nodes it depends on; $\oplus$ vertices depend on $\otimes$ vertices, which depend on $\oplus$ and axiom vertices.

Arithmetic circuits are amenable to automatic differentiation in the reverse mode (Griewank and Corliss, 1991), commonly used in backpropagation algorithms. Importantly, this permits us to calculate the *exact* gradient of the *approximate* summation with respect to axiom values, following Eisner et al. (2005). This is desirable when carrying out the optimization problems involved in parameter estimation. Another differentiation technique, implemented within the semiring, is given by Eisner (2002).

Cube pruning is based on the k-best algorithms of Huang and Chiang (2005), which save time over generic semiring implementations through lazy computation in both the aggregation and combination operations. Their techniques are not as clearly applicable here, because our goal is to sum over *all proofs* instead of only finding a small subset of them. If computing non-local features is a computational bottleneck, they can be computed only for the $O(k)$ proofs considered when choosing the best k as in cube pruning. Then, the computational requirements for approximate summing are nearly equivalent to cube pruning, but the approximation is less accurate.

6 Semirings Old and New

We now consider interesting special cases and variations of cube summing.

6.1 The k-best+residual Semiring

When restricted to local features, cube pruning and cube summing can be seen as proper semirings. Cube pruning reduces to an implementation of the k-best semiring (Goodman, 1998), and cube summing reduces to a novel semiring we call the *k-best+residual* semiring. Binary instantiations of $\otimes$ and $\oplus$ can be iteratively reapplied to give the equivalent formulations in Eqs. 12 and 13. We define $\mathbf{0}$ as $\langle 0, \langle\rangle\rangle$ and $\mathbf{1}$ as $\langle 1, \langle 1, \epsilon\rangle\rangle$. The $\oplus$ operator is easily shown to be commutative. That $\oplus$ is associative follows from associativity of max-k, shown by Goodman (1998). Showing that $\otimes$ is associative and that $\otimes$ distributes over $\oplus$ are less straightforward; proof sketches are provided in Appendix A. The k-best+residual semiring generalizes many semirings previously introduced in the literature; see Fig. 2.

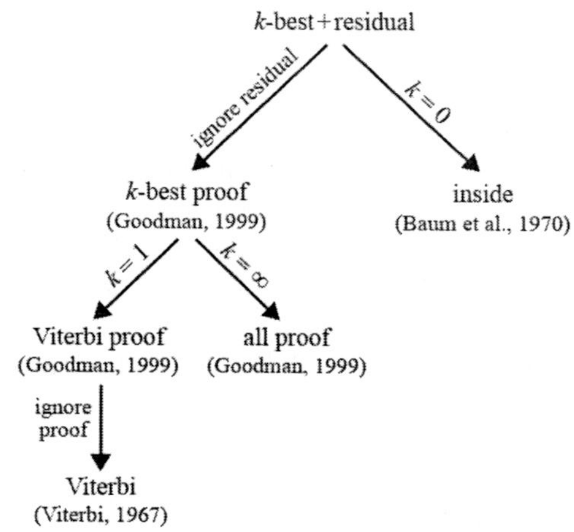

Figure 2: Semirings generalized by k-best+residual.

6.2 Variations

Once we relax requirements about associativity and distributivity and permit aggregation and combination operators to operate on sets, several extensions to cube summing become possible. First, when computing approximate summations with non-local features, we may not always be interested in the *best* proofs for each item. Since the purpose of summing is often to calculate statistics under a model distribution, we may wish instead to *sample* from that distribution. We can replace the $\max\text{-}k$ function with a sample-k function that samples k proofs from the scored list in its argument, possibly using the scores or possibly uniformly at random. This breaks associativity of $\oplus$. We conjecture that this approach can be used to simulate particle filtering for structured models.

Another variation is to vary k for different theorems. This might be used to simulate beam search, or to reserve computation for theorems closer to *goal*, which have more proofs.

7 Conclusion

This paper has drawn a connection between cube pruning, a popular technique for approximately solving decoding problems, and the semiring-weighted logic programming view of dynamic programming. We have introduced a generalization called cube summing, to be used for solving summing problems, and have argued that cube pruning and cube summing are both semirings that can be used generically, as long as the underlying probability models only include local features. *With* non-local features, cube pruning and cube summing can be used for approximate decoding and summing, respectively, and although they no longer correspond to semirings, generic algorithms can still be used.

Acknowledgments

We thank three anonymous EACL reviewers, John Blatz, Pedro Domingos, Jason Eisner, Joshua Goodman, and members of the ARK group for helpful comments and feedback that improved this paper. This research was supported by NSF IIS-0836431 and an IBM faculty award.

A k-best+residual is a Semiring

In showing that k-best+residual is a semiring, we will restrict our attention to the computation of the residuals. The computation over proof lists is identical to that performed in the k-best proof semiring, which was shown to be a semiring by Goodman (1998). We sketch the proofs that $\otimes$ is associative and that $\otimes$ distributes over $\oplus$; associativity of $\oplus$ is straightforward.

For a proof list $\bar{\mathbf{a}}$, $\|\bar{\mathbf{a}}\|$ denotes the sum of proof scores, $\sum_{i:\langle a_i, A_i\rangle \in \bar{\mathbf{a}}} a_i$. Note that:

$$\|Res(\bar{\mathbf{a}})\| + \|\max\text{-}k(\bar{\mathbf{a}})\| = \|\bar{\mathbf{a}}\| \tag{15}$$

$$\|\bar{\mathbf{a}} \star \bar{\mathbf{b}}\| = \|\bar{\mathbf{a}}\| \, \|\bar{\mathbf{b}}\| \tag{16}$$

Associativity. Given three semiring values $\mathbf{u}$, $\mathbf{v}$, and $\mathbf{w}$, we need to show that $(\mathbf{u}\otimes\mathbf{v})\otimes\mathbf{w} = \mathbf{u}\otimes(\mathbf{v}\otimes\mathbf{w})$. After expanding the expressions for the residuals using Eq. 14, there are 10 terms on each side, five of which are identical and cancel out immediately. Three more cancel using Eq. 15, leaving:

$$\begin{aligned}\text{LHS} &= \|Res(\bar{\mathbf{u}} \star \bar{\mathbf{v}})\| \, \|\bar{\mathbf{w}}\| + \|Res(\max\text{-}k(\bar{\mathbf{u}} \star \bar{\mathbf{v}}) \star \bar{\mathbf{w}})\| \\ \text{RHS} &= \|\bar{\mathbf{u}}\| \, \|Res(\bar{\mathbf{v}} \star \bar{\mathbf{w}})\| + \|Res(\bar{\mathbf{u}} \star \max\text{-}k(\bar{\mathbf{v}} \star \bar{\mathbf{w}}))\|\end{aligned}$$

If LHS = RHS, associativity holds. Using Eq. 15 again, we can rewrite the second term in LHS to obtain

$$\begin{aligned}\text{LHS} = {} & \|Res(\bar{\mathbf{u}} \star \bar{\mathbf{v}})\| \, \|\bar{\mathbf{w}}\| + \|\max\text{-}k(\bar{\mathbf{u}} \star \bar{\mathbf{v}}) \star \bar{\mathbf{w}}\| \\ & - \|\max\text{-}k(\max\text{-}k(\bar{\mathbf{u}} \star \bar{\mathbf{v}}) \star \bar{\mathbf{w}})\|\end{aligned}$$

Using Eq. 16 and pulling out the common term $\|\bar{\mathbf{w}}\|$, we have

$$\begin{aligned}\text{LHS} = {} & (\|Res(\bar{\mathbf{u}} \star \bar{\mathbf{v}})\| + \|\max\text{-}k(\bar{\mathbf{u}} \star \bar{\mathbf{v}})\|) \, \|\bar{\mathbf{w}}\| \\ & - \|\max\text{-}k(\max\text{-}k(\bar{\mathbf{u}} \star \bar{\mathbf{v}}) \star \bar{\mathbf{w}})\| \\ = {} & \|(\bar{\mathbf{u}} \star \bar{\mathbf{v}}) \star \bar{\mathbf{w}}\| - \|\max\text{-}k(\max\text{-}k(\bar{\mathbf{u}} \star \bar{\mathbf{v}}) \star \bar{\mathbf{w}})\| \\ = {} & \|(\bar{\mathbf{u}} \star \bar{\mathbf{v}}) \star \bar{\mathbf{w}}\| - \|\max\text{-}k((\bar{\mathbf{u}} \star \bar{\mathbf{v}}) \star \bar{\mathbf{w}})\|\end{aligned}$$

The resulting expression is intuitive: the residual of $(\mathbf{u}\otimes\mathbf{v})\otimes\mathbf{w}$ is the difference between the sum of all proof scores and the sum of the k-best. RHS can be transformed into this same expression with a similar line of reasoning (and using associativity of $\star$). Therefore, LHS = RHS and $\otimes$ is associative.

Distributivity. To prove that $\otimes$ distributes over $\oplus$, we must show left-distributivity, i.e., that $\mathbf{u}\otimes(\mathbf{v}\oplus\mathbf{w}) = (\mathbf{u}\otimes\mathbf{v})\oplus(\mathbf{u}\otimes\mathbf{w})$, and right-distributivity. We show left-distributivity here. As above, we expand the expressions, finding 8 terms on the LHS and 9 on the RHS. Six on each side cancel, leaving:

$$\begin{aligned}\text{LHS} &= \|Res(\bar{\mathbf{v}} \cup \bar{\mathbf{w}})\| \, \|\bar{\mathbf{u}}\| + \|Res(\bar{\mathbf{u}} \star \max\text{-}k(\bar{\mathbf{v}} \cup \bar{\mathbf{w}}))\| \\ \text{RHS} &= \|Res(\bar{\mathbf{u}} \star \bar{\mathbf{v}})\| + \|Res(\bar{\mathbf{u}} \star \bar{\mathbf{w}})\| \\ & \quad + \|Res(\max\text{-}k(\bar{\mathbf{u}} \star \bar{\mathbf{v}}) \cup \max\text{-}k(\bar{\mathbf{u}} \star \bar{\mathbf{w}}))\|\end{aligned}$$

We can rewrite LHS as:

$$\begin{aligned}\text{LHS} = {} & \|Res(\bar{\mathbf{v}} \cup \bar{\mathbf{w}})\| \, \|\bar{\mathbf{u}}\| + \|\bar{\mathbf{u}} \star \max\text{-}k(\bar{\mathbf{v}} \cup \bar{\mathbf{w}})\| \\ & - \|\max\text{-}k(\bar{\mathbf{u}} \star \max\text{-}k(\bar{\mathbf{v}} \cup \bar{\mathbf{w}}))\| \\ = {} & \|\bar{\mathbf{u}}\| \, (\|Res(\bar{\mathbf{v}} \cup \bar{\mathbf{w}})\| + \|\max\text{-}k(\bar{\mathbf{v}} \cup \bar{\mathbf{w}})\|) \\ & - \|\max\text{-}k(\bar{\mathbf{u}} \star \max\text{-}k(\bar{\mathbf{v}} \cup \bar{\mathbf{w}}))\| \\ = {} & \|\bar{\mathbf{u}}\| \, \|\bar{\mathbf{v}} \cup \bar{\mathbf{w}}\| - \|\max\text{-}k(\bar{\mathbf{u}} \star (\bar{\mathbf{v}} \cup \bar{\mathbf{w}}))\| \\ = {} & \|\bar{\mathbf{u}}\| \, \|\bar{\mathbf{v}} \cup \bar{\mathbf{w}}\| - \|\max\text{-}k((\bar{\mathbf{u}} \star \bar{\mathbf{v}}) \cup (\bar{\mathbf{u}} \star \bar{\mathbf{w}}))\|\end{aligned}$$

where the last line follows because $\star$ distributes over $\cup$ (Goodman, 1998). We now work with the RHS:

$$\begin{aligned}\text{RHS} = {} & \|Res(\bar{\mathbf{u}} \star \bar{\mathbf{v}})\| + \|Res(\bar{\mathbf{u}} \star \bar{\mathbf{w}})\| \\ & + \|Res(\max\text{-}k(\bar{\mathbf{u}} \star \bar{\mathbf{v}}) \cup \max\text{-}k(\bar{\mathbf{u}} \star \bar{\mathbf{w}}))\| \\ = {} & \|Res(\bar{\mathbf{u}} \star \bar{\mathbf{v}})\| + \|Res(\bar{\mathbf{u}} \star \bar{\mathbf{w}})\| \\ & + \|\max\text{-}k(\bar{\mathbf{u}} \star \bar{\mathbf{v}}) \cup \max\text{-}k(\bar{\mathbf{u}} \star \bar{\mathbf{w}})\| \\ & - \|\max\text{-}k(\max\text{-}k(\bar{\mathbf{u}} \star \bar{\mathbf{v}}) \cup \max\text{-}k(\bar{\mathbf{u}} \star \bar{\mathbf{w}}))\|\end{aligned}$$

Since $\max\text{-}k(\bar{\mathbf{u}} \star \bar{\mathbf{v}})$ and $\max\text{-}k(\bar{\mathbf{u}} \star \bar{\mathbf{w}})$ are disjoint (we assume no duplicates; i.e., two different theorems cannot have exactly the same proof), the third term becomes $\|\max\text{-}k(\bar{\mathbf{u}} \star \bar{\mathbf{v}})\| + \|\max\text{-}k(\bar{\mathbf{u}} \star \bar{\mathbf{w}})\|$ and we have

$$\begin{aligned} = {} & \|\bar{\mathbf{u}} \star \bar{\mathbf{v}}\| + \|\bar{\mathbf{u}} \star \bar{\mathbf{w}}\| \\ & - \|\max\text{-}k(\max\text{-}k(\bar{\mathbf{u}} \star \bar{\mathbf{v}}) \cup \max\text{-}k(\bar{\mathbf{u}} \star \bar{\mathbf{w}}))\| \\ = {} & \|\bar{\mathbf{u}}\| \, \|\bar{\mathbf{v}}\| + \|\bar{\mathbf{u}}\| \, \|\bar{\mathbf{w}}\| \\ & - \|\max\text{-}k((\bar{\mathbf{u}} \star \bar{\mathbf{v}}) \cup (\bar{\mathbf{u}} \star \bar{\mathbf{w}}))\| \\ = {} & \|\bar{\mathbf{u}}\| \, \|\bar{\mathbf{v}} \cup \bar{\mathbf{w}}\| - \|\max\text{-}k((\bar{\mathbf{u}} \star \bar{\mathbf{v}}) \cup (\bar{\mathbf{u}} \star \bar{\mathbf{w}}))\| .\end{aligned}$$

References

L. E. Baum, T. Petrie, G. Soules, and N. Weiss. 1970. A maximization technique occurring in the statistical analysis of probabilistic functions of Markov chains. *Annals of Mathematical Statistics*, 41(1).

P. Blunsom and M. Osborne. 2008. Probabilistic inference for machine translation. In *Proc. of EMNLP*.

P. Blunsom, T. Cohn, and M. Osborne. 2008. A discriminative latent variable model for statistical machine translation. In *Proc. of ACL*.

D. Chiang. 2007. Hierarchical phrase-based translation. *Computational Linguistics*, 33(2):201–228.

W. W. Cohen and V. Carvalho. 2005. Stacked sequential learning. In *Proc. of IJCAI*.

A. Darwiche. 2003. A differential approach to inference in Bayesian networks. *Journal of the ACM*, 50(3).

J. Eisner, E. Goldlust, and N. A. Smith. 2005. Compiling Comp Ling: Practical weighted dynamic programming and the Dyna language. In *Proc. of HLT-EMNLP*.

J. Eisner. 2002. Parameter estimation for probabilistic finite-state transducers. In *Proc. of ACL*.

J. R. Finkel, T. Grenager, and C. D. Manning. 2005. Incorporating non-local information into information extraction systems by gibbs sampling. In *Proc. of ACL*.

J. Goodman. 1998. *Parsing inside-out*. Ph.D. thesis, Harvard University.

J. Goodman. 1999. Semiring parsing. *Computational Linguistics*, 25(4):573–605.

A. Griewank and G. Corliss. 1991. *Automatic Differentiation of Algorithms*. SIAM.

L. Huang and D. Chiang. 2005. Better k-best parsing. In *Proc. of IWPT*.

L. Huang and D. Chiang. 2007. Forest rescoring: Faster decoding with integrated language models. In *Proc. of ACL*.

L. Huang. 2008. Forest reranking: Discriminative parsing with non-local features. In *Proc. of ACL*.

M. I. Jordan, Z. Ghahramani, T. Jaakkola, and L. Saul. 1999. An introduction to variational methods for graphical models. *Machine Learning*, 37(2).

D. Klein and C. Manning. 2001. Parsing and hypergraphs. In *Proc. of IWPT*.

T. Koo and M. Collins. 2005. Hidden-variable models for discriminative reranking. In *Proc. of EMNLP*.

K. Kurihara and T. Sato. 2006. Variational Bayesian grammar induction for natural language. In *Proc. of ICGI*.

J. Lafferty, A. McCallum, and F. Pereira. 2001. Conditional random fields: Probabilistic models for segmenting and labeling sequence data. In *Proc. of ICML*.

R. Levy, F. Reali, and T. Griffiths. 2008. Modeling the effects of memory on human online sentence processing with particle filters. In *Advances in NIPS*.

B. T. Lowerre. 1976. *The Harpy Speech Recognition System*. Ph.D. thesis, Carnegie Mellon University.

D. J. C. MacKay. 1997. Ensemble learning for hidden Markov models. Technical report, Cavendish Laboratory, Cambridge.

A. F. T. Martins, D. Das, N. A. Smith, and E. P. Xing. 2008. Stacking dependency parsers. In *Proc. of EMNLP*.

R. McDonald and F. Pereira. 2006. Online learning of approximate dependency parsing algorithms. In *Proc. of EACL*.

F. C. N. Pereira and Y. Schabes. 1992. Inside-outside reestimation from partially bracketed corpora. In *Proc. of ACL*, pages 128–135.

D. Roth and W. Yih. 2004. A linear programming formulation for global inference in natural language tasks. In *Proc. of CoNLL*.

S. Shieber, Y. Schabes, and F. Pereira. 1995. Principles and implementation of deductive parsing. *Journal of Logic Programming*, 24(1-2):3–36.

D. A. Smith and J. Eisner. 2008. Dependency parsing by belief propagation. In *Proc. of EMNLP*.

N. A. Smith, D. L. Vail, and J. D. Lafferty. 2007. Computationally efficient M-estimation of log-linear structure models. In *Proc. of ACL*.

C. Sutton and A. McCallum. 2004. Collective segmentation and labeling of distant entities in information extraction. In *Proc. of ICML Workshop on Statistical Relational Learning and Its Connections to Other Fields*.

A. J. Viterbi. 1967. Error bounds for convolutional codes and an asymptotically optimal decoding algorithm. *IEEE Transactions on Information Processing*, 13(2).

M. Wang, N. A. Smith, and T. Mitamura. 2007. What is the Jeopardy model? a quasi-synchronous grammar for QA. In *Proc. of EMNLP-CoNLL*.

Enhancing Unlexicalized Parsing Performance using a Wide Coverage Lexicon, Fuzzy Tag-set Mapping, and EM-HMM-based Lexical Probabilities

Yoav Goldberg[1*] **Reut Tsarfaty**[2†] **Meni Adler**[1‡] **Michael Elhadad**[1]

[1]Department of Computer Science, Ben Gurion University of the Negev
{yoavg|adlerm|elhadad}@cs.bgu.ac.il

[2]Institute for Logic, Language and Computation, University of Amsterdam
R.Tsarfaty@uva.nl

Abstract

We present a framework for interfacing a PCFG parser with lexical information from an external resource following a different tagging scheme than the treebank. This is achieved by defining a stochastic mapping layer between the two resources. Lexical probabilities for rare events are estimated in a semi-supervised manner from a lexicon and large unannotated corpora. We show that this solution greatly enhances the performance of an unlexicalized Hebrew PCFG parser, resulting in state-of-the-art Hebrew parsing results both when a segmentation oracle is assumed, and in a real-word parsing scenario of parsing unsegmented tokens.

1 Introduction

The intuition behind unlexicalized parsers is that the lexicon is mostly separated from the syntax: specific lexical items are mostly irrelevant for accurate parsing, and can be mediated through the use of POS tags and morphological hints. This same intuition also resonates in highly lexicalized formalism such as CCG: while the lexicon categories are very fine grained and syntactic in nature, once the lexical category for a lexical item is determined, the specific lexical form is not taken into any further consideration.

Despite this apparent separation between the lexical and the syntactic levels, both are usually estimated solely from a single treebank. Thus, while PCFGs can be accurate, they suffer from vocabulary coverage problems: treebanks are small and lexicons induced from them are limited.

The reason for this treebank-centric view in PCFG learning is 3-fold: the English treebank is fairly large and English morphology is fairly simple, so that in English, the treebank does provide mostly adequate lexical coverage[1]; Lexicons enumerate analyses, but don't provide probabilities for them; and, most importantly, the treebank and the external lexicon are likely to follow different annotation schemas, reflecting different linguistic perspectives.

On a different vein of research, current POS tagging technology deals with much larger quantities of training data than treebanks can provide, and lexicon-based unsupervised approaches to POS tagging are practically unlimited in the amount of training data they can use. POS taggers rely on richer knowledge than lexical estimates derived from the treebank, have evolved sophisticated strategies to handle OOV and can provide distributions $p(t|w, context)$ instead of "best tag" only.

Can these two worlds be combined? We propose that parsing performance can be greatly improved by using a wide coverage lexicon to suggest analyses for unknown tokens, and estimating the respective lexical probabilities using a semi-supervised technique, based on the training procedure of a lexicon-based HMM POS tagger. For many resources, this approach can be taken only on the proviso that the annotation schemes of the two resources can be aligned.

We take Modern Hebrew parsing as our case study. Hebrew is a Semitic language with rich

*Supported by the Lynn and William Frankel Center for Computer Sciences, Ben Gurion University

†Funded by the Dutch Science Foundation (NWO), grant number 017.001.271.

‡Post-doctoral fellow, Deutsche Telekom labs at Ben Gurion University

[1]This is not the case with other languages, and also not true for English when adaptation scenarios are considered.

Proceedings of the 12th Conference of the European Chapter of the ACL, pages 327–335,
Athens, Greece, 30 March – 3 April 2009. ©2009 Association for Computational Linguistics

morphological structure. This rich structure yields a large number of distinct word forms, resulting in a high OOV rate (Adler et al., 2008a). This poses a serious problem for estimating lexical probabilities from small annotated corpora, such as the Hebrew treebank (Sima'an et al., 2001).

Hebrew has a wide coverage lexicon / morphological-analyzer (henceforth, *KC Analyzer*) available[2], but its tagset is different than the one used by the Hebrew Treebank. These are not mere technical differences, but derive from different perspectives on the data. The Hebrew TB tagset is syntactic in nature, while the KC tagset is lexicographic. This difference in perspective yields different performance for parsers induced from tagged data, and a simple mapping between the two schemes is impossible to define (Sec. 2).

A naive approach for combining the use of the two resources would be to manually re-tag the Treebank with the KC tagset, but we show this approach harms our parser's performance. Instead, we propose a novel, *layered* approach (Sec. 2.1), in which syntactic (TB) tags are viewed as contextual refinements of the lexicon (KC) tags, and conversely, KC tags are viewed as lexical clustering of the syntactic ones. This layered representation allows us to easily integrate the syntactic and the lexicon-based tagsets, without explicitly requiring the Treebank to be re-tagged.

Hebrew parsing is further complicated by the fact that common prepositions, conjunctions and articles are prefixed to the following word and pronominal elements often appear as suffixes. The segmentation of prefixes and suffixes can be ambiguous and must be determined in a specific context only. Thus, *the leaves of the syntactic parse trees do not correspond to space-delimited tokens*, and the yield of the tree is not known in advance.

We show that enhancing the parser with external lexical information is greatly beneficial, both in an artificial scenario where the token segmentation is assumed to be known (Sec. 4), and in a more realistic one in which parsing and segmentation are handled jointly by the parser (Goldberg and Tsarfaty, 2008) (Sec. 5). External lexical information enhances *unlexicalized* parsing performance by as much as 6.67 F-points, an error reduction of 20% over a Treebank-only parser. Our results are not only the best published results for parsing Hebrew, but also on par with state-of-the-art *lexicalized* Arabic parsing results assuming gold-standard fine-grained Part-of-Speech (Maamouri et al., 2008).[3]

2 A Tale of Two Resources

Modern Hebrew has 2 major linguistic resources: the Hebrew Treebank (*TB*), and a wide coverage Lexicon-based morphological analyzer developed and maintained by the Knowledge Center for Processing Hebrew (*KC Analyzer*).

The Hebrew Treebank consists of sentences manually annotated with constituent-based syntactic information. The most recent version (V2) (Guthmann et al., 2009) has 6,219 sentences, and covers 28,349 unique tokens and 17,731 unique segments[4].

The KC Analyzer assigns morphological analyses (prefixes, suffixes, POS, gender, person, etc.) to Hebrew tokens. It is based on a lexicon of roughly 25,000 word lemmas and their inflection patterns. From these, 562,439 unique word forms are derived. These are then prefixed (subject to constraints) by 73 prepositional prefixes.

It is interesting to note that even with these numbers, the Lexicon's coverage is far from complete. Roughly 1,500 unique tokens from the Hebrew Treebank cannot be assigned any analysis by the KC Lexicon, and Adler et al.(2008a) report that roughly 4.5% of the tokens in a 42M tokens corpus of news text are unknown to the Lexicon. For roughly 400 unique cases in the Treebank, the Lexicon provides some analyses, but not a correct one. This goes to emphasize the productive nature of Hebrew morphology, and stress that robust lexical probability estimates cannot be derived from an annotated resource as small as the Treebank.

Lexical vs. Syntactic POS Tags The analyses produced by the KC Analyzer are not compatible with the Hebrew TB.

The KC tagset (Adler et al., 2008b; Netzer et al., 2007; Adler, 2007) takes a lexical approach to POS tagging ("a word can assume only POS tags that would be assigned to it in a dictionary"), while the TB takes a syntactic one ("if the word in this particular positions functions as an Adverb, tag it as an Adverb, even though it is listed in the dictionary only as a Noun"). We present 2 cases that emphasize the difference: **Adjectives:** the Treebank

[2]http://mila.cs.technion.ac.il/hebrew/resources/lexicons/

[3]Our method is orthogonal to lexicalization and can be used in addition to it if one so wishes.

[4]In these counts, all numbers are conflated to one canonical form

treats any word in an adjectivial position as an Adjective. This includes also demonstrative pronouns ילד זה (**this** boy). However, from the KC point of view, the fact that a pronoun can be used to modify a noun does not mean it should appear in a dictionary as an adjective. **The MOD tag:** similarly, the TB has a special POS-tag for words that perform syntactic modification. These are mostly adverbs, but almost any Adjective can, in some circumstances, belong to that class as well. This category is highly syntactic, and does not conform to the lexicon based approach.

In addition, many adverbs and prepositions in Hebrew are lexicalized instances of a preposition followed by a noun (e.g., ברכות, "in+softness", *softly*). These can admit both the lexicalized and the compositional analyses. Indeed, many words admit the lexicalized analyses in one of the resource but not in the other (e.g., לטובת "for+benefit" is Prep in the TB but only Prep+Noun in the KC, while for מצד "from+side" it is the other way around).

2.1 A Unified Resource

While the syntactic POS tags annotation of the TB is very useful for assigning the correct tree structure when the correct POS tag is known, there are clear benefits to an annotation scheme that can be easily backed by a dictionary.

We created a unified resource, in which every word occurrence in the Hebrew treebank is assigned a KC-based analysis. This was done in a semi-automatic manner – for most cases the mapping could be defined deterministically. The rest (less than a thousand instances) were manually assigned. Some Treebank tokens had no analyses in the KC lexicon, and some others did not have a correct analysis. These were marked as "UNKNOWN" and "MISSING" respectively.[5]

The result is a Treebank which is morphologically annotated according to two different schemas. On average, each of the 257 TB tags is mapped to 2.46 of the 273 KC tags.[6] While this resource can serve as a basis for many linguistically motivated inquiries, the rest of this paper is devoted to using it for constructing a better parser.

Tagsets Comparison In (Adler et al., 2008b), we hypothesized that due to its syntax-based nature, the Treebank morphological tagset is more suitable than the KC one for syntax related tasks. Is this really the case? To verify it, we simulate a scenario in which the complete gold morphological information is available. We train 2 PCFG grammars, one on each tagged version of the Treebank, and test them on the subset of the development set in which every token is completely covered by the KC Analyzer (351 sentences).[7] The input to the parser is the yields and disambiguated pre-terminals of the trees to be parsed. The parsing results are presented in Table 1. Note that this scenario does not reflect actual parsing performance, as the gold information is never available in practice, and surface forms are highly ambiguous.

Tagging Scheme	Precision	Recall
TB / syntactic	82.94	83.59
KC / dictionary	81.39	81.20

Table 1: evalb results for parsing with Oracle morphological information, for the two tagsets

With gold morphological information, the TB tagging scheme is more informative for the parser.

The syntax-oriented annotation scheme of the TB is more informative for parsing than the lexicographic KC scheme. Hence, we would like our parser to use this TB tagset whenever possible, and the KC tagset only for rare or unseen words.

A Layered Representation It seems that learning a treebank PCFG assuming such a different tagset would require a treebank tagged with the alternative annotation scheme. Rather than assuming the existence of such an alternative resource, we present here a novel approach in which we view the different tagsets as corresponding to different aspects of the morphosyntactic representation of pre-terminals in the parse trees. Each of these layers captures subtleties and regularities in the data, none of which we would want to (and sometimes, cannot) reduce to the other. We, therefore, propose to retain both tagsets and learn a *fuzzy mapping* between them.

In practice, we propose an integrated representation of the tree in which the bottommost layer represents the yield of the tree, the surface forms

[5]Another solution would be to add these missing cases to the KC Lexicon. In our view this act is harmful: we don't want our Lexicon to artificially overfit our annotated corpora.

[6]A "tag" in this context means the complete morphological information available for a morpheme in the Treebank: its part of speech, inflectional features and possessive suffixes, but not prefixes or nominative and accusative suffixes, which are taken to be separate morphemes.

[7]For details of the train/dev splits as well as the grammar, see Section 4.2.

are tagged with dictionary-based KC POS tags, and syntactic TB POS tags are in turn mapped onto the KC ones (see Figure 1).

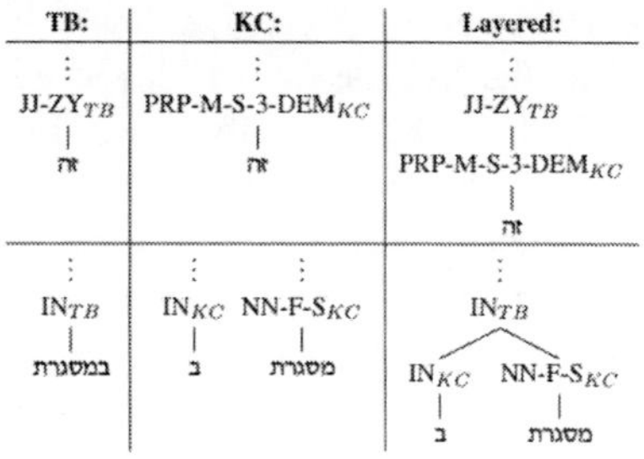

Figure 1: Syntactic (TB), Lexical (KC) and Layered representations

This representation helps to retain the information both for the syntactic and the morphological POS tagsets, and can be seen as capturing the interaction between the morphological and syntactic aspects, allowing for a seamless integration of the two levels of representation. We refer to this intermediate layer of representation as a *morphosyntactic-transfer layer* and we formally depict it as $p(t_{KC}|t_{TB})$.

This layered representation naturally gives rise to a generative model in which a phrase level constituent first generates a syntactic POS tag (t_{TB}), and this in turn generates the lexical POS tag(s) (t_{KC}). The KC tag then ultimately generates the terminal symbols (w). We assume that a morphological analyzer assigns all possible analyses to a given terminal symbol. Our terminal symbols are, therefore, pairs: $\langle w, t\rangle$, and our lexical rules are of the form $t \rightarrow \langle w, t\rangle$. This gives rise to the following equivalence:

$$p(\langle w, t_{KC}\rangle | t_{TB}) = p(t_{KC}|t_{TB})p(\langle w, t_{KC}\rangle | t_{KC})$$

In Sections (4, 5) we use this layered generative process to enable a smooth integration of a PCFG treebank-learned grammar, an external wide-coverage lexicon, and lexical probabilities learned in a semi-supervised manner.

3 Semi-supervised Lexical Probability Estimations

A PCFG parser requires lexical probabilities of the form $p(w|t)$ (Charniak et al., 1996). Such information is not readily available in the lexicon. However, it can be estimated from the lexicon and large *unannotated* corpora, by using the well-known Baum-Welch (EM) algorithm to learn a trigram HMM tagging model of the form $p(t_1, \ldots, t_n, w_1, \ldots, w_n) = argmax \prod p(t_i|t_{i-1}, t_{i-2})p(w_i|t_i)$, and taking the emission probabilities $p(w|t)$ of that model.

In Hebrew, things are more complicated, as each emission w is not a space delimited token, but rather a smaller unit (a morphological segment, henceforth a *segment*). Adler and Elhadad (2006) present a lattice-based modification of the Baum-Welch algorithm to handle this segmentation ambiguity.

Traditionally, such unsupervised EM-trained HMM taggers are thought to be inaccurate, but (Goldberg et al., 2008) showed that by feeding the EM process with sufficiently good initial probabilities, accurate taggers ($> 91\%$ accuracy) can be learned for both English and Hebrew, based on a (possibly incomplete) lexicon and large amount of raw text. They also present a method for automatically obtaining these initial probabilities.

As stated in Section 2, the KC Analyzer (Hebrew Lexicon) coverage is incomplete. Adler et al.(2008a) use the lexicon to learn a Maximum Entropy model for predicting possible analyses for unknown tokens based on their orthography, thus extending the lexicon to cover (even if noisily) any unknown token. In what follows, we use *KC Analyzer* to refer to this extended version.

Finally, these 3 works are combined to create a state-of-the-art POS-tagger and morphological disambiguator for Hebrew (Adler, 2007): initial lexical probabilities are computed based on the MaxEnt-extended KC Lexicon, and are then fed to the modified Baum-Welch algorithm, which is used to fit a morpheme-based tagging model over a very large corpora. Note that the emission probabilities $P(W|T)$ of that model cover all the morphemes seen in the unannotated training corpus, even those not covered by the KC Analyzer.[8]

We hypothesize that such emission probabilities are good estimators for the morpheme-based $P(T \rightarrow W)$ lexical probabilities needed by a PCFG parser. To test this hypothesis, we use it to estimate $p(t_{KC} \rightarrow w)$ in some of our models.

4 Parsing with a Segmentation Oracle

We now turn to describing our first set of experiments, in which we assume the correct segmen-

[8] $P(W|T)$ is defined also for words not seen during training, based on the initial probabilities calculation procedure. For details, see (Adler, 2007).

tation for each input sentence is known. This is a strong assumption, as the segmentation stage is ambiguous, and segmentation information provides very useful morphological hints that greatly constrain the search space of the parser. However, the setting is simpler to understand than the one in which the parser performs both segmentation and POS tagging, and the results show some interesting trends. Moreover, some recent studies on parsing Hebrew, as well as all studies on parsing Arabic, make this oracle assumption. As such, the results serve as an interesting comparison. Note that in real-world parsing situations, the parser is faced with a stream of ambiguous unsegmented tokens, making results in this setting not indicative of real-world parsing performance.

4.1 The Models

The main question we address is the incorporation of an external lexical resource into the parsing process. This is challenging as different resources follow different tagging schemes. One way around it is re-tagging the treebank according to the new tagging scheme. This will serve as a baseline in our experiment. The alternative method uses the Layered Representation described above (Sec. 2.1). We compare the performance of the two approaches, and also compare them against the performance of the original treebank without external information.

We follow the intuition that external lexical resources are needed only when the information contained in the treebank is too sparse. Therefore, we use treebank-derived estimates for reliable events, and resort to the external resources only in the cases of rare or OOV words, for which the treebank distribution is not reliable.

Grammar and Notation For all our experiments, we use the same grammar, and change only the way lexical probabilities are implemented. The grammar is an unlexicalized treebank-estimated PCFG with linguistically motivated state-splits.[9]

In what follows, a lexical event is a word segment which is assigned a single POS thereby functioning as a leaf in a syntactic parse tree. A *rare (lexical) event* is an event occurring less than K times in the training data, and a *reliable (lexical) event* is one occurring at least K times in the training data. We use *OOV* to denote lexical events appearing 0 times in the training data. $count(\cdot)$ is a counting function over the training data, $rare$ stands for any rare event, and w_{rare} is a specific rare event. $KCA(\cdot)$ is the KC Analyzer function, mapping a lexical event to a set of possible tags (analyses) according to the lexicon.

[9]Details of the grammar: all functional information is removed from the non-terminals, finite and non-finite verbs, as well as possessive and other PPs are distinguished, definiteness structure of constituents is marked, and parent annotation is employed. It is the same grammar as described in (Goldberg and Tsarfaty, 2008).

Lexical Models

All our models use relative frequency estimated probabilities for reliable lexical events: $p(t \rightarrow w|t) = \frac{count(w,t)}{count(t)}$. They differ only in their treatment of rare (including OOV) events.

In our **Baseline**, no external resource is used. We smooth for rare and OOV events using a per-tag probability distribution over rare segments, which we estimate using relative frequency over rare segments in the training data: $p(w_{rare}|t) = \frac{count(rare,t)}{count(t)}$. This is the way lexical probabilities in treebank grammars are usually estimated.

We experiment with two flavours of lexical models. In the first, **LexFilter**, the KC Analyzer is consulted for rare events. We estimate rare events using the same per-tag distribution as in the baseline, but use the KC Analyzer to filter out any incompatible cases, that is, we force to 0 the probability of any analysis not supported by the lexicon:

$$p(w_{rare}|t) = \begin{cases} \frac{count(rare,t)}{count(t)} & t \in KCA(w_{rare}) \\ 0 & t \notin KCA(w_{rare}) \end{cases}$$

Our second flavour of lexical models, **LexProbs**, the KC Analyzer is consulted to propose analyses for rare events, and the probability of an analysis is estimated via the HMM emission function described in Section 3, which we denote B: $p(w_{rare}|t) = B(w_{rare}, t)$

In both **LexFilter** and **LexProbs**, we resort to the relative frequency estimation in case the event is not covered in the KC Analyzer.

Tagset Representations

In this work, we are comparing 3 different representations: *TB*, which is the original Treebank, *KC* which is the Treebank converted to use the KC Analyzer tagset, and *Layered*, which is the layered representation described above.

The details of the lexical models vary according to the representation we choose to work with.
For the *TB* setting, our lexical rules are of the form

$t_{tb} \rightarrow w$. Only the **Baseline** models are relevant here, as the tagset is not compatible with that of the external lexicon.

For the *KC* setting, our lexical rules are of the form $t_{kc} \rightarrow w$, and their probabilities are estimated as described above. Note that this setting requires our trees to be tagged with the new (KC) tagset, and parsed sentences are also tagged with this tagset.

For the *Layered* setting, we use lexical rules of the form $t_{tb} \rightarrow w$. Reliable events are estimated as usual, via relative frequency over the original treebank. For rare events, we estimate $p(t_{tb} \rightarrow w|t_{tb}) = p(t_{tb} \rightarrow t_{kc}|t_{tb})p(t_{kc} \rightarrow w|t_{kc})$, where the transfer probabilities $p(t_{tb} \rightarrow t_{kc})$ are estimated via relative frequencies over the layered trees, and the emission probabilities are estimated either based on other rare events (**LexFilter**) or based on the semi-supervised method described in Section 3 (**LexProbs**).

The layered setting has several advantages: First, the resulting trees are all tagged with the original TB tagset. Second, the training procedure does not require a treebank tagged with the KC tagset: Instead of learning the transfer layer from the treebank we could alternatively base our counts on a different parallel resource, estimate it from unannotated data using EM, define it heuristically, or use any other estimation procedure.

4.2 Experiments

We perform all our experiments on Version 2 of the Hebrew Treebank, and follow the train/test/dev split introduced in (Tsarfaty and Sima'an, 2007): section 1 is used for development, sections 2-12 for training, and section 13 is the test set, which we do not use in this work. All the reported results are on the development set.[10] After removal of empty sentences, we have 5241 sentences for training, and 483 for testing. Due to some changes in the Treebank[11], our results are not directly comparable to earlier works. However, our baseline models are very similar to the models presented in, e.g. (Goldberg and Tsarfaty, 2008).

In order to compare the performance of the model on the various tagset representations (TB tags, KC tags, Layered), we remove from the test set 51 sentences in which at least one token is marked as not having any correct segmentation in the KC Analyzer. This introduces a slight bias in favor of the KC-tags setting, and makes the test somewhat easier for all the models. However, it allows for a relatively fair comparison between the various models.[12]

Results and Discussion

Results are presented in Table 2.[13]

	Baseline			
	rare: < 2		rare: < 10	
	Prec	Rec	Prec	Rec
TB	72.80	71.70	67.66	64.92
KC	72.23	70.30	67.22	64.31
	LexFilter			
	rare: < 2		rare: < 10	
	Prec	Rec	Prec	Rec
KC	77.18	76.31	77.34	76.20
Layered	76.69	76.40	76.66	75.74
	LexProbs			
	rare: < 2		rare: < 10	
	Prec	Rec	Prec	Rec
KC	77.29	76.65	77.22	76.36
Layered	76.81	76.49	76.85	76.08

Table 2: evalb results for parsing with a segmentation Oracle.

As expected, all the results are much lower than those with gold fine-grained POS (Table 1).

When not using any external knowledge (**Baseline**), the TB tagset performs slightly better than the converted treebank (KC). Note, however, that the difference is less pronounced than in the gold morphology case. When varying the rare words threshold from 2 to 10, performance drops considerably. Without external knowledge, the parser is facing difficulties coping with unseen events.

The incorporation of an external lexical knowledge in the form of pruning illegal tag assignments for unseen words based on the KC lexicon (**LexFilter**) substantially improves the results (~ 72 to ~ 77). The additional lexical knowledge clearly improves the parser. Moreover, varying the rare words threshold in this setting hardly affects the parser performance: the external lexicon suffices to guide the parser in the right direction. Keeping the rare words threshold high is desirable, as it reduces overfitting to the treebank vocabulary.

We expected the addition of the semi-supervised $p(t \rightarrow w)$ distribution (**LexProbs**) to improve the parser, but found it to have an insignificant effect. The correct segmentation seems

[10]This work is part of an ongoing work on a parser, and the test set is reserved for final evaluation of the entire system.

[11]Normalization of numbers and percents, correcting of some incorrect trees, etc.

[12]We are forced to remove these sentences because of the artificial setting in which the correct segmentation is given. In the no-oracle setting (Sec. 5), we do include these sentences.

[13]The layered trees have an extra layer of bracketing ($t_{TB} \rightarrow t_{KC}$). We remove this layer prior to evaluation.

to remove enough ambiguity as to let the parser base its decisions on the generic tag distribution for rare events.

In all the settings with a Segmentation Oracle, there is no significant difference between the KC and the Layered representation. We prefer the layered representation as it provides more flexibility, does not require trees tagged with the KC tagset, and produces parse trees with the original TB POS tags at the leaves.

5 Parsing without a Segmentation Oracle

When parsing real world data, correct token segmentation is not known in advance. For methodological reasons, this issue has either been set-aside (Tsarfaty and Sima'an, 2007), or dealt with in a pipeline model in which a morphological disambiguator is run prior to parsing to determine the correct segmentation. However, Tsarfaty (2006) argues that there is a strong interaction between syntax and morphological segmentation, and that the two tasks should be modeled jointly, and not in a pipeline model. Several studies followed this line, (Cohen and Smith, 2007) the most recent of which is Goldberg and Tsarfaty (2008), who presented a model based on unweighted lattice parsing for performing the joint task.

This model uses a morphological analyzer to construct a lattice over all possible morphological analyses of an input sentence. The arcs of the lattice are $\langle w, t \rangle$ pairs, and a lattice parser is used to build a parse over the lattice. The Viterbi parse over the lattice chooses a lattice path, which induces a segmentation over the input sentence. Thus, parsing and segmentation are performed jointly.

Lexical rules in the model are defined over the lattice arcs ($t \rightarrow \langle w, t \rangle | t$), and smoothed probabilities for them are estimated from the treebank via relative frequency over terminal/preterminal pairs. The lattice paths themselves are unweighted, reflecting the intuition that all morphological analyses are a-priori equally likely, and that their perspective strengths should come from the segments they contain and their interaction with the syntax.

Goldberg and Tsarfaty (2008) use a data-driven morphological analyzer derived from the treebank. Their better models incorporated some external lexical knowledge by use of an Hebrew spell checker to prune some illegal segmentations.

In what follows, we use the layered representation to adapt this joint model to use as its morphological analyzer the wide coverage KC Analyzer in enhancement of a data-driven one. Then, we further enhance the model with the semi-supervised lexical probabilities described in Sec 3.

5.1 Model

The model of Goldberg and Tsarfaty (2008) uses a morphological analyzer to constructs a lattice for each input token. Then, the sentence lattice is built by concatenating the individual token lattices. The morphological analyzer used in that work is data driven based on treebank observations, and employs some well crafted heuristics for OOV tokens (for details, see the original paper). Here, we use instead a morphological analyzer which uses the KC Lexicon for rare and OOV tokens.

We begin by adapting the rare vs. reliable events distinction from Section 4 to cover unsegmented tokens. We define a *reliable token* to be a token from the training corpus, which each of its possible segments according to the training corpus was seen in the training corpus at least K times.[14] All other tokens are considered to be rare.

Our morphological analyzer works as follows:
For reliable tokens, it returns the set of analyses seen for this token in the treebank (each analysis is a sequence of pairs of the form $\langle w, t_{TB} \rangle$).
For rare tokens, it returns the set of analyses returned by the KC analyzer (here, analyses are sequences of pairs of the form $\langle w, t_{KC} \rangle$).

The lattice arcs, then, can take two possible forms, either $\langle w, t_{TB} \rangle$ or $\langle w, t_{KC} \rangle$.
Lexical rules of the form $t_{TB} \rightarrow \langle w, t_{TB} \rangle$ are reliable, and their probabilities estimated via relative frequency over events seen in training.
Lexical rules of the form $t_{TB} \rightarrow \langle w, t_{KC} \rangle$ are estimated in accordance with the transfer layer introduced above: $p(t_{TB} \rightarrow \langle w, t_{KC} \rangle) = p(t_{KC}|t_{TB})p(\langle w, t_{KC} \rangle | t_{KC})$.

The remaining question is how to estimate $p(\langle w, t_{KC} \rangle | t_{KC})$. Here, we use either the **LexFilter** (estimated over all rare events) or **LexProbs** (estimated via the semisupervised emission probabilities)models, as defined in Section 4.1 above.

5.2 Experiments

As our **Baseline**, we take the best model of (Goldberg and Tsarfaty, 2008), run against the current

[14] Note that this is more inclusive than requiring that the token itself is seen in the training corpus at least K times, as some segments may be shared by several tokens.

version of the Treebank.[15] This model uses the same grammar as described in Section 4.1 above, and use some external information in the form of a spell-checker wordlist. We compare this Baseline with the **LexFilter** and **LexProbs** models over the Layered representation.

We use the same test/train splits as described in Section 4. Contrary to the Oracle segmentation setting, here we evaluate against all sentences, including those containing tokens for which the KC Analyzer does not contain any correct analyses.

Due to token segmentation ambiguity, the resulting parse yields may be different than the gold ones, and evalb can not be used. Instead, we use the evaluation measure of (Tsarfaty, 2006), also used in (Goldberg and Tsarfaty, 2008), which is an adaptation of parseval to use characters instead of space-delimited tokens as its basic units.

Results and Discussion

Results are presented in Table 3.

	rare: < 2		rare: < 10	
	Prec	Rec	Prec	Rec
Baseline	67.71	66.35	—	—
LexFilter	68.25	69.45	57.72	59.17
LexProbs	73.40	73.99	70.09	73.01

Table 3: Parsing results for the joint parsing+seg task, with varying external knowledge

The results are expectedly lower than with the segmentation Oracle, as the joint task is much harder, but the external lexical information greatly benefits the parser also in the joint setting. While significant, the improvement from the **Baseline** to **LexFilter** is quite small, which is due to the Baseline's own rather strong illegal analyses filtering heuristic. However, unlike the oracle segmentation case, here the semisupervised lexical probabilities (**LexProbs**) have a major effect on the parser performance ($\sim$ 69 to $\sim$ 73.5 F-score), an overall improvement of $\sim$ 6.6 F-points over the Baseline, which is the previous state-of-the art for this joint task. This supports our intuition that rare lexical events are better estimated using a large unannotated corpus, and not using a generic treebank distribution, or sparse treebank based counts, and that lexical probabilities have a crucial role in resolving segmentation ambiguities.

[15] While we use the same software as (Goldberg and Tsarfaty, 2008), the results reported here are significantly lower. This is due to differences in annotation scheme between V1 and V2 of the Hebrew TB

The parsers with the extended lexicon were unable to assign a parse to about 10 of the 483 test sentences. We count them as having 0-Fscore in the table results.[16] The Baseline parser could not assign a parse to more than twice that many sentences, suggesting its lexical pruning heuristic is quite harsh. In fact, the unparsed sentences amount to most of the difference between the **Baseline** and **LexFilter** parsers.

Here, changing the rare tokens threshold has a significant effect on parsing accuracy, which suggests that the segmentation for rare tokens is highly consistent within the corpus. When an unknown token is encountered, a clear bias should be taken toward segmentations that were previously seen in the same corpus. Given that that effect is remedied to some extent by introducing the semi-supervised lexical probabilities, we believe that segmentation accuracy for unseen tokens can be further improved, perhaps using resources such as (Gabay et al., 2008), and techniques for incorporating some document, as opposed to sentence level information, into the parsing process.

6 Conclusions

We present a framework for interfacing a parser with an external lexicon following a different annotation scheme. Unlike other studies (Yang Huang et al., 2005; Szolovits, 2003) in which such interfacing is achieved by a restricted heuristic mapping, we propose a novel, stochastic approach, based on a layered representation. We show that using an external lexicon for dealing with rare lexical events greatly benefits a PCFG parser for Hebrew, and that results can be further improved by the incorporation of lexical probabilities estimated in a semi-supervised manner using a wide-coverage lexicon and a large unannotated corpus. In the future, we plan to integrate this framework with a parsing model that is specifically crafted to cope with morphologically rich, free-word order languages, as proposed in (Tsarfaty and Sima'an, 2008).

Apart from Hebrew, our method is applicable in any setting in which there exist a small treebank and a wide-coverage lexical resource. For example parsing Arabic using the Arabic Treebank and the Buckwalter analyzer, or parsing English biomedical text using a biomedical treebank and the UMLS Specialist Lexicon.

[16] When discarding these sentences from the test set, result on the better LexProbs model leap to 74.95P/75.56R.

References

M. Adler and M. Elhadad. 2006. An unsupervised morpheme-based hmm for hebrew morphological disambiguation. In *Proc. of COLING/ACL2006*.

Meni Adler, Yoav Goldberg, David Gabay, and Michael Elhadad. 2008a. Unsupervised lexicon-based resolution of unknown words for full morphological analysis. In *Proc. of ACL 2008*.

Meni Adler, Yael Netzer, David Gabay, Yoav Goldberg, and Michael Elhadad. 2008b. Tagging a hebrew corpus: The case of participles. In *Proc. of LREC 2008*.

Meni Adler. 2007. *Hebrew Morphological Disambiguation: An Unsupervised Stochastic Word-based Approach*. Ph.D. thesis, Ben-Gurion University of the Negev, Beer-Sheva, Israel.

Eugene Charniak, Glenn Carroll, John Adcock, Anthony Cassandra, Yoshihiko Gotoh, Jeremy Katz, Michael Littman, and John McCann. 1996. Taggers for parsers. *Artif. Intell.*, 85(1-2):45–57.

Shay B. Cohen and Noah A. Smith. 2007. Joint morphological and syntactic disambiguation. In *Proceedings of EMNLP-CoNLL-07*, pages 208–217.

David Gabay, Ziv Ben Eliahu, and Michael Elhadad. 2008. Using wikipedia links to construct word segmentation corpora. In *Proc. of the WIKIAI-08 Workshop, AAAI-2008 Conference*.

Yoav Goldberg and Reut Tsarfaty. 2008. A single generative model for joint morphological segmentation and syntactic parsing. In *Proc. of ACL 2008*.

Yoav Goldberg, Meni Adler, and Michael Elhadad. 2008. Em can find pretty good hmm pos-taggers (when given a good start). In *Proc. of ACL 2008*.

Noemie Guthmann, Yuval Krymolowski, Adi Milea, and Yoad Winter. 2009. Automatic annotation of morpho-syntactic dependencies in a modern hebrew treebank. In *Proc. of TLT*.

Mohamed Maamouri, Ann Bies, and Seth Kulick. 2008. Enhanced annotation and parsing of the arabic treebank. In *INFOS 2008, Cairo, Egypt, March 27-29, 2008*.

Yael Netzer, Meni Adler, David Gabay, and Michael Elhadad. 2007. Can you tag the modal? you should! In *ACL07 Workshop on Computational Approaches to Semitic Languages*, Prague, Czech.

K. Sima'an, A. Itai, Y. Winter, A. Altman, and N. Nativ. 2001. Building a tree-bank of modern hebrew text. *Traitement Automatique des Langues*, 42(2).

P. Szolovits. 2003. Adding a medical lexicon to an english parser. In *Proc. AMIA 2003 Annual Symposium*.

Reut Tsarfaty and Khalil Sima'an. 2007. Three-dimensional parametrization for parsing morphologically rich languages. In *Proc. of IWPT 2007*.

Reut Tsarfaty and Khalil Sima'an. 2008. Relational-realizational parsing. In *Proc. of CoLING*, pages 889–896, Manchester, UK, August. Coling 2008.

Reut Tsarfaty. 2006. Integrated Morphological and Syntactic Disambiguation for Modern Hebrew. In *Proceedings of ACL-SRW-06*.

MS Yang Huang, MD Henry J. Lowe, PhD Dan Klein, and MS Russell J. Cucina, MD. 2005. Improved identification of noun phrases in clinical radiology reports using a high-performance statistical natural language parser augmented with the umls specialist lexicon. *J Am Med Inform Assoc*, 12(3), May.

Person Identification from Text and Speech Genre Samples

Jade Goldstein-Stewart
U.S. Department of Defense
jadeg@acm.org

Ransom Winder
The MITRE Corporation
Hanover, MD, USA
rwinder@mitre.org

Roberta Evans Sabin
Loyola University
Baltimore, MD, USA
res@loyola.edu

Abstract

In this paper, we describe experiments conducted on identifying a person using a novel unique correlated corpus of text and audio samples of the person's communication in six genres. The text samples include essays, emails, blogs, and chat. Audio samples were collected from individual interviews and group discussions and then transcribed to text. For each genre, samples were collected for six topics. We show that we can identify the communicant with an accuracy of 71% for six fold cross validation using an average of 22,000 words per individual across the six genres. For person identification in a particular genre (train on five genres, test on one), an average accuracy of 82% is achieved. For identification from topics (train on five topics, test on one), an average accuracy of 94% is achieved. We also report results on identifying a person's communication in a genre using text genres only as well as audio genres only.

1 Introduction

Can one identify a person from samples of his/her communication? What common patterns of communication can be used to identify people? Are such patterns consistent across varying genres?

People tend to be interested in subjects and topics that they discuss with friends, family, colleagues and acquaintances. They can communicate with these people textually via email, text messages and chat rooms. They can also communicate via verbal conversations. Other forms of communication could include blogs or even formal writings such as essays or scientific articles. People communicating in these different "genres" may have different stylistic patterns and we are interested in whether or not we could identify people from their communications in different genres.

The attempt to identify authorship of written text has a long history that predates electronic computing. The idea that features such as average word length and average sentence length could allow an author to be identified dates to Mendenhall (1887). Mosteller and Wallace (1964) used function words in a groundbreaking study that identified authors of *The Federalist Papers*. Since then many attempts at authorship attribution have used function words and other features, such as word class frequencies and measures derived from syntactic analysis, often combined using multivariable statistical techniques.

Recently, McCarthy (2006) was able to differentiate three authors' works, and Hill and Provost (2003), using a feature of co-citations, showed that they could successfully identify scientific articles by the same person, achieving 85% accuracy when the person has authored over 100 papers. Levitan and Argamon (2006) and McCombe (2002) further investigated authorship identification of *The Federalist Papers* (three authors).

The genre of the text may affect the authorship identification task. The attempt to characterize genres dates to Biber (1988) who selected 67 linguistic features and analyzed samples of 23 spoken and written genres. He determined six factors that could be used to identify written text. Since his study, new "cybergenres" have evolved, including email, blogs, chat, and text messaging. Efforts have been made to characterize the linguistic features of these genres (Baron, 2003; Crystal, 2001; Herring, 2001; Shepherd and Watters, 1999; Yates, 1996). The task is complicated by the great diversity that can be exhibited within even a single genre. Email can be business-related, personal, or spam; the style

Proceedings of the 12th Conference of the European Chapter of the ACL, pages 336–344,
Athens, Greece, 30 March – 3 April 2009.

can be tremendously affected by demographic factors, including gender and age of the sender. The context of communication influences language style (Thomson and Murachver, 2001; Coupland, et al., 1988). Some people use abbreviations to ease the efficiency of communication in informal genres – items that one would not find in a formal essay. Informal writing may also contain emoticons (e.g., ":-)" or "☺") to convey mood.

Successes have been achieved in categorizing web page decriptions (Calvo, et al., 2004) and genre determination (Goldstein-Stewart, et al., 2007; Santini 2007). Genders of authors have been successfully identified within the British National Corpus (Koppel, et al., 2002). In authorship identification, recent research has focused on identifying authors within a particular genre: email collections, news stories, scientific papers, listserv forums, and computer programs (de Vel, et al., 2001; Krsul and Spafford, 1997; Madigan, et al., 2005; McCombe, 2002). In the KDD Cup 2003 Competitive Task, systems attempted to identify successfully scientific articles authored by the same person. The best system (Hill and Provost, 2003) was able to identify successfully scientific articles by the same person 45% of the time; for authors with over 100 papers, 85% accuracy was achieved.

Are there common features of communication of an individual across and within genres? Undoubtedly, the lack of corpora has been an impediment to answering this question, as gathering personal communication samples faces considerable privacy and accessibility hurdles. To our knowledge, all previous studies have focused on individual communications in one or possibly two genres.

To analyze, compare, and contrast the communication of individuals across and within different modalities, we collected a corpus consisting of communication samples of 21 people in six genres on six topics. We believe this corpus is the first attempt to create such a correlated corpus.

From this corpus, we are able to perform experiments on person identification. Specifically, this means recognizing which individual of a set of people composed a document or spoke an utterance which was transcribed. We believe using text and transcribed speech in this manner is a novel research area. In particular, the following types of experiments can be performed:

- Identification of person in a novel genre (using five genres as training)
- Identification of person in a novel topic (using five topics as training)
- Identification of person in written genres, after training on the two spoken genres
- Identification of person in spoken genres, after training on the written genres
- Identification of person in written genres, after training on the other written genres

In this paper, we discuss the formation and statistics of this corpus and report results for identifying individual people using techniques that utilize several different feature sets.

2 Corpus Collection

Our interest was in the research question: can a person be identified from their writing and audio samples? Since we hypothesize that people communicate about items of interest to them across various genres, we decided to test this theory. Email and chat were chosen as textual genres (Table 1), since text messages, although very common, were not easy to collect. We also collected blogs and essays as samples of textual genres. For audio genres, to simulate conversational speech as much as possible, we collected data from interviews and discussion groups that consisted of sets of subjects participating in the study. Genres labeled "peer give and take" allowed subjects to interact.

Such a collection of genres allows us to examine both conversational and non-conversational genres, both written and spoken modalities, and both formal and informal writing with the aim of contrasting and comparing computer-mediated and non-computer-mediated genres as well as informal and formal genres.

Genre	Computer-mediated	Peer Give and Take	Mode	Conversational	Audience
Email	yes	no	text	yes	addressee
Essay	No	no	text	no	unspec
Interview	No	no	speech	yes	interviewer
Blog	yes	yes	text	no	world
Chat	yes	yes	text	yes	group
Discussion	No	yes	speech	yes	group

Table 1. Genres

In order to ensure that the students could produce enough data, we chose six topics that were controversial and politically and/or socially relevant for college students from among whom the subjects would be drawn. These six topics were chosen from a pilot study consisting of twelve topics, in which we analyzed the amount of information that people tended to "volunteer" on the topics as well as their thoughts about being able to write/speak on such a topic. The six topics are listed in Table 2.

Topic	Question
Church	Do you feel the Catholic Church needs to change its ways to adapt to life in the 21st Century?
Gay Marriage	While some states have legalized gay marriage, others are still opposed to it. Do you think either side is right or wrong?
Privacy Rights	Recently, school officials prevented a school shooting because one of the shooters posted a myspace bulletin. Do you think this was an invasion of privacy?
Legalization of Marijuana	The city of Denver has decided to legalize small amounts of marijuana for persons over 21. How do you feel about this?
War in Iraq	The controversial war in Iraq has made news headlines almost every day since it began. How do you feel about the war?
Gender Discrimination	Do you feel that gender discrimination is still an issue in the present-day United States?

Table 2. Topics

The corpus was created in three phases (Goldstein-Stewart, 2008). In Phase I, emails, essays and interviews were collected. In Phase II, blogs and chat and discussion groups were created and samples collected. For blogs, subjects blogged over a period of time and could read and/or comment on other subjects' blogs in their own blog. A graduate research assistant acted as interviewer and discussion and chat group moderator.

Of the 24 subjects who completed Phase I, 7 decided not to continue into Phase II. Seven additional students were recruited for Phase II. In Phase III, these replacement students were then asked to provide samples for the Phase I genres. Four students fully complied, resulting in a corpus with a full set of samples for 21 subjects, 11 women and 10 men.

All audio recordings, interviews and discussions, were transcribed. Interviewer/moderator comments were removed and, for each discussion, four individual files, one for each participant's contribution, were produced.

Our data is somewhat homogeneous: it samples only undergraduate university students and was collected in controlled settings. But we believe that controlling the topics, genres, and demographics of subjects allows the elimination of many variables that effect communicative style and aids the identification of common features.

3 Corpus Statistics

3.1 Word Count

The mean word counts for the 21 students per genre and per topic are shown in Figures 1 and 2, respectively. Figure 1 shows that the students produced more content in the directly interactive genres – interview and discussion (the spoken genres) as well as chat (a written genre).

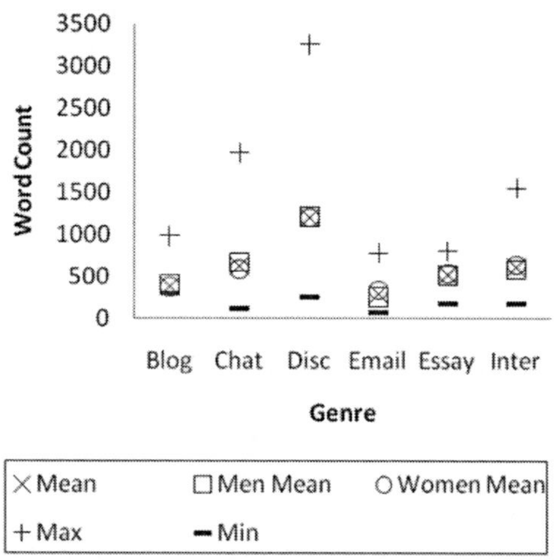

Figure 1. Mean word counts for gender and genre

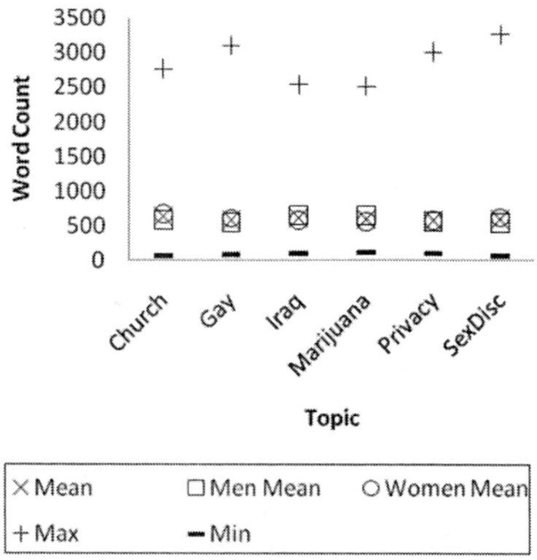

Figure 2. Mean word counts for gender and topic

The email genre had the lowest mean word count, perhaps indicating that it is a genre intended for succinct messaging.

3.2 Word Usage By Individuals

We performed an analysis of the word usage of individuals. Among the top 20 most frequently occurring words, the most frequent word used by all males was "the". For the 11 females, six most frequently used "the", four used "I", and one used "like". Among abbreviations, 13 individuals used "lol". Abbreviations were mainly used in chat. Other abbreviations were used to varying degrees such as the abbreviation "u". Emoticons were used by five participants.

4 Classification

4.1 Features

Frequencies of words in word categories were determined using Linguistic Inquiry and Word Count (LIWC). LIWC2001 analyzes text and produces 88 output variables, among them word count and average words per sentence. All others are percentages, including percentage of words that are parts of speech or belong to given dictionaries (Pennebaker, et al., 2001). Default dictionaries contain categories of words that indicate basic emotional and cognitive dimensions and were used here. LIWC was designed for both text and speech and has categories, such negations, numbers, social words, and emotion. Refer to LIWC (www.liwc.net) for a full description of categories. Here the 88 LIWC features are denoted feature set L.

From the original 24 participants' documents and the new 7 participants' documents from Phase II, we aggregated all samples from all genres and computed the top 100 words for males and for females, including stop words. Six words differed between males and females. Of these top words, the 64 words with counts that varied by 10% or more between male and female usage were selected. Excluded from this list were 5 words that appeared frequently but were highly topic-specific: "catholic", "church", "marijuana", "marriage", and "school."

Most of these words appeared on a large stop word list (www.webconfs.com/stop-words.php). Non-stop word terms included the word "feel", which was used more frequently by females than males, as well as the terms "yea" and "lot" (used more commonly by women) and "uh" (used more commonly by men). Some stop words were used more by males ("some", "any"), others by females ("I", "and"). Since this set mainly consists of stop words, we refer to it as the functional word features or set F.

The third feature set (T) consisted of the five topic specific words excluded from F.

The fourth feature set (S) consisted of the stop word list of 659 words mentioned above.

The fifth feature set (I) we consider informal features. It contains nine common words not in set S: "feel", "lot", "uh", "women", "people", "men", "gonna", "yea" and "yeah". This set also contains the abbreviations and emotional expressions "lol", "ur", "tru", "wat", and "haha". Some of the expressions could be characteristic of particular individuals. For example the term "wat" was consistently used by one individual in the informal chat genre.

Another feature set (E) was built around the emoticons that appeared in the corpus. These included ":)", ":(", ":-(", ";)", ":-/", and ">:o)".

For our results, we use eight feature set combinations: 1. All 88 LIWC features (denoted L); 2. LIWC and functional word features, (L+F); 3. LIWC plus all functional word features and the topic words (L+F+T); 4. LIWC plus all functional word features and emoticons (L+F+E); 5. LIWC plus all stop word features (L+S); 6. LIWC plus all stop word and informal features (L+S+I); 7. LIWC supplemented by informal, topic, and stop word features, (L+S+I+T). Note that, when combined, sets S and I cover set F.

4.2 Classifiers

Classification of all samples was performed using four classifiers of the Weka workbench, version 3.5 (Witten and Frank, 2005). All were used with default settings except the Random Forest classifier (Breiman, 2001), which used 100 trees. We collected classification results for Naïve-Bayes, J48 (decision tree), SMO (support vector machine) (Cortes and Vapnik, 1995; Platt, 1998) and RF (Random Forests) methods.

5 Person Identification Results

5.1 Cross Validation Across Genres

To identify a person as the author of a text, six fold cross validation was used. All 756 samples were divided into 126 "documents," each consisting of all six samples of a person's expression in a single genre, regardless of topic. There is a baseline of approximately 5% accuracy if randomly guessing the person. Table 3 shows the accuracy results of classification using combinations of the feature sets and classifiers.

The results show that SMO is by far the best classifier of the four and, thus, we used only this classifier on subsequent experiments. L+S performed better alone than when adding the informal features – a surprising result.

Table 4 shows a comparison of results using feature sets L+F and L+F+T. The five topic words appear to grant a benefit in the best trained case (SMO).

Table 5 shows a comparison of results using feature sets L+F and L+F+E, and this shows that the inclusion of the individual emoticon features does provide a benefit, which is interesting considering that these are relatively few and are typically concentrated in the chat documents.

Feature	SMO	RF100	J48	NB
L	52	30	15	17
L+F	60	44	21	25
L+S	71	42	19	33
L+S+I	71	39	17	33
L+S+I+T	71	40	17	33

Table 3. Person identification accuracy (%) using six fold cross validation

Feature	SMO	RF100	J48	NB
L+F	60	44	21	25
L+F+T	67	40	21	25

Table 4. Accuracy (%) using six fold cross validation with and without topic word features (T)

Feature	SMO	RF100	J48	NB
L+F	60	44	21	25
L+F+E	65	41	21	25

Table 5. Accuracy (%) using six fold cross validation with and without emoticon features (E)

5.2 Predict Communicant in One Genre Given Information on Other Genres

The next set of experiments we performed was to identify a person based on knowledge of the person's communication in other genres. We first train on five genres, and we then test on one – a "hold out" or test genre.

Again, as in six fold cross validation, a total of 126 "documents" were used: for each genre, 21 samples were constructed, each the concatenation of all text produced by an individual in that genre, across all topics. Table 6 shows the results of this experiment. The result of 100% for L+F, L+F+T, and L+F+E in email was surprising, especially since the word counts for email were the lowest. The lack of difference in L+F and L+F+E results is not surprising since the emoticon features appear only in chat documents, with one exception of a single emoticon in a blog document (":-/"), which did not appear in any chat documents. So there was no emoticon feature that appeared across different genres.

SMO	HOLD OUT (TEST GENRE)						
Features	A	B	C	D	E	S	I
L	**60**	76	52	43	76	81	29
L+F	**75**	81	57	48	**100**	90	71
L+F+T	**76**	86	62	52	**100**	86	71
L+F+E	**75**	81	57	48	**100**	90	71
L+S	**82**	81	67	67	86	90	**100**
L+S+I	**79**	86	52	57	86	90	**100**
L+S+I+T	**81**	86	52	67	90	90	**100**

Table 6. Person identification accuracy (%) training with SMO on 5 genres and testing on 1. A=Average over all genres, B=Blog, C=Chat, D=Discussion, E=Email, S=Essay, I=Interview

Train	Test	L+F	L+F+T
CDSI	Email	67	95
BDSI	Email	71	52
BCSI	Email	76	100
BCDI	Email	57	90
BCDS	Email	57	81

Table 7. Accuracy (%) using SMO for predicting email author after training on 4 other genres. B=Blog, C=Chat, D=Discussion, S=Essay, I=Interview

We attempted to determine which genres were most influential in identifying email authorship, by reducing the number of genres in its training set. Results are reported in Table 7. The difference between the two sets, which differ only in five topic specific word features, is more marked here. The lack of these features causes accuracy to drop far more rapidly as the training set is reduced. It also appears that the chat genre is important when identifying the email genre when topical features are included. This is probably not just due to the volume of data since discussion groups also have a great deal of data. We need to investigate further the reason for such a high performance on the email genre.

The results in Table 6 are also interesting for the case of L+S (which has more stop words than L+F). With this feature set, classification for the interview genre improved significantly, while that of email decreased. This may indicate that the set of stop words may be very genre specific – a hypothesis we will test in future work. If this in indeed the case, perhaps certain different sets of stop words may be important for identifying certain genres, genders and individual authorship. Previous results indicate that the usage of certain stop words as features assists with identifying gender (Sabin, et al., 2008).

Table 6 also shows that, using the informal words (feature set I) decreased performance in two genres: chat (the genre in which the abbreviations are mostly used) and discussion. We plan to run further experiments to investigate this. The sections that follow will typically show the results achieved with L+F and L+S features.

Train\Test	B	C	D	E	S	I
Blog	100	14	14	76	57	5
Chat	24	100	29	38	19	10
Discussion	10	5	100	5	10	29
Email	43	10	5	100	48	0
Essay	67	5	5	33	100	5
Interview	5	5	5	5	5	100

Table 8. Accuracy (%) using SMO for predicting person between genres after training on one genre using L+F features

Table 8 displays the accuracies when the L+F feature set of single genre is used for training a model tested on one genre. This generally suggests the contribution of each genre when all are used in training. When the training and testing sets are the same, 100% accuracy is achieved. Examining this chart, the highest accuracies are achieved when training and test sets are textual. Excluding models trained and tested on the same genre, the average accuracy for training and testing within written genres is 36% while the average accuracy for training and testing within spoken genres is 17%. Even lower are average accuracies of the models trained on spoken and tested on textual genres (9%) and the models trained on textual and tested on spoken genres (6%). This indicates that the accuracies that feature the same mode (textual or spoken) in training and testing tend to be higher.

Of particular interest here is further examination of the surprising results of testing on email with the L+F feature set. Of these tests, a model trained on blogs achieved the highest score, perhaps due to a greater stylistic similarity to email than the other genres. This is also the highest score in the chart apart from cases where train and test genres were the same. Training on chat and essay genres shows some improvement over the baseline, but models trained with the two spoken genres do not rise above baseline accuracy when tested on the textual email genre.

5.3 Predict Communicant in One Topic Given Information on Five Topics

This set of experiments was designed to determine if there was no training data provided for a certain topic, yet there were samples of communication for an individual across genres for other topics, could an author be determined?

SMO	HOLD OUT (TEST TOPIC)						
Features	**Avg**	Ch	Gay	Iraq	Mar	Pri	Sex
L+F	**87**	81	95	86	95	100	67
L+F+T	**65**	76	71	86	29	62	67
L+F+E	**87**	81	95	86	95	95	67
L+S	**94**	95	95	81	100	100	95

Table 9. Person identification accuracy (%) training with SMO on 5 topics and testing on 1. Avg = Average over all topics: Ch=Catholic Church, Gay=Gay Marriage, Iraq=Iraq War, Mar=Marijuana Legalization, Pri=Privacy Rights, Sex=Sex Discrimination

Again a total of 126 "documents" were used: for each topic, 21 samples were constructed, each the concatenation of all text produced by an individual on that topic, across all genres. One topic was withheld and 105 documents (on the other 5 topics) were used for training. Table 9 shows that overall the L+S feature set performed better than either the L+F or L+F+T sets. The most noticeable differences are the drops in the accuracy when the five topic words are added, particularly on the topics of marijuana and privacy rights. For L+F+T, if "marijuana" is withheld from the topic word features when the marijuana topic is the test set, the accuracy rises to 90%. Similarly, if "school" is withheld from the topic word features when the privacy rights topic is the test set, the accuracy rises to 100%. This indicates the topic words are detrimental to determining the communicant, and this appears to be supported by the lack of an accuracy drop in the testing on the Iraq and sexual discrimination topics, both of which featured the fewest uses of the five topic words. That the results rise when using the L+S features shows that more features that are independent of the topic tend to help distinguish the person (as only the Iraq set experienced a small drop using these features in training and testing, while the others either increased or remained the same). The similarity here of the results using L+F features when compared to L+F+E is likely due to the small number of emoticons observed in the corpus (16 total examples).

5.4 Predict Communicant in a Speech Genre Given Information on the Other

One interesting experiment used one speech genre for training, and the other speech genre for testing. The results (Table 10) show that the additional stop words (S compared to F) make a positive difference in both sets. We hypothesize that the increased performance of training with discussion data and testing on interview data is due to the larger amount of training data available in discussions. We will test this in future work.

Train	Test	L+F	L+S
Inter	Disc	5	19
Disc	Inter	29	48

Table 10. Person identification accuracy (%) training and testing SMO on spoken genres

5.5 Predict Authorship in a Textual Genre Given Information on Speech Genres

Train	Test	L+F	L+S
Disc+Inter	Blog	19	24
Disc+Inter	Chat	5	14
Disc+Inter	Email	5	10
Disc+Inter	Essay	10	29

Table 11. Person identification accuracy (%) training SMO on spoken genres and testing on textual genres

Table 11 shows the results of training on speech data only and predicting the author of the text genre. Again, the speech genres alone do not do well at determining the individual author of the text genre. The best score was 29% for essays.

5.6 Predict Authorship in a Textual Genre Given Information on Other Textual Genres

Table 12 shows the results of training on text data only and predicting authorship for one of the four text genres. Recognizing the authors in chat is the most difficult, which is not surprising since the blogs, essays and emails are more similar to each other than the chat genre, which uses abbreviations and more informal language as well as being immediately interactive.

Train	Test	L+F	L+S
C+E+S	Blog	76	86
B+E+S	Chat	10	19
B+C+S	Email	90	81
B+C+E	Essay	90	86

Table 12. Person identification accuracy (%) training and testing SMO on textual genres

5.7 Predict Communicant in a Speech Genre Given Information on Textual Genres

Training on text and classifying speech-based samples by author showed poor results. Similar to the results for speech genres, using the text genres alone to determine the individual in the speech genre results in a maximum score of 29% for the interview genre (Table 13).

Train	Test	L+F	L+S
B+C+E+S	Discussion	14	23
B+C+E+S	Interview	14	29

Table 13. Person identification accuracy (%) training SMO on textual genres and testing on speech genres

5.8 Error Analysis

Results for different training and test sets vary considerably. A key factor in determining which sets can successfully be used to train other sets seems to be the mode, that is, whether or not a set is textual or spoken, as the lowest accuracies tend to be found between genres of different modes. This suggests that how people write and how they speak may be somewhat distinct.

Typically, more data samples in the training tends to increase the accuracy of the tests, but more features does not guarantee the same result. An examination of the feature sets revealed further explanations for this apart from any inherent difficulties in recognizing authors between sets. For many tests, there is a tendency for the same person to be chosen for classification, indicating a bias to that person in the training data. This is typically caused by features that have mostly, but not all, zero values in training samples, but have many non-zero values in testing. The most striking examples of this are described in 5.3, where the removal of certain topic-related features was found to dramatically increase the accruacy. Targetted removal of other features that have the same biasing effect could increase accuracy.

While Weka normalizes the incoming features for SMO, it was also discovered that a simple initial normalization of the feature sets by dividing by the maximum or standardization by subtracting the mean and dividing by the standard deviation of the feature sets could increase the accuracy across the different tests.

6 Conclusion

In this paper, we have described a novel unique corpus consisting of samples of communication of 21 individuals in six genres across six topics as well as experiments conducted to identify a person's samples within the corpus. We have shown that we can identify individuals with reasonably high accuracy for several cases: (1) when we have samples of their communication across genres (71%), (2) when we have samples of their communication in specific genres other than the one being tested (81%), and (3) when they are communicating on a new topic (94%).

For predicting a person's communication in one text genre using other text genres only, we were able to achieve a good accuracy for all genres (above 76%) except chat. We believe this is because chat, due to its "real-time communication" nature is quite different from the other text genres of emails, essays and blogs.

Identifying a person in one speech genre after training with the other speech genre had lower accuracies (less than 48%). Since these results differed significantly, we hypothesize this is due to the amount of data available for training – a hypothesis we plan to test in the future.

Future plans also include further investigation of some of the suprising results mentioned in this paper as well investigation of stop word lists particular to communicative genres. We also plan to investigate if it is easier to identify those participants who have produced more data (higher total word count) as well as perform a systematic study the effects of the number of words gathered on person identificaton.

In addition, we plan to investigate the efficacy of using other features besides those available in LIWC, stopwords and emoticons in person identification. These include spelling errors, readability measures, complexity measures, suffixes, and content analysis measures.

References

Naomi S. Baron. 2003. Why email looks like speech. In J. Aitchison and D. M. Lewis, editors, *New Media Language*. Routledge, London, UK.

Douglas Biber. 1988. *Variation across speech and writing*. Cambridge University Press, Cambridge, UK.

Leo Breiman. 2001. Random forests. Technical Report for Version 3, University of California, Berkeley, CA.

Rafael A. Calvo, Jae-Moon Lee, and Xiaobo Li. 2004. Managing content with automatic document classification. *Journal of Digital Information*, 5(2).

Corinna Cortes and Vladimir Vapnik. 1995. Support vector networks. *Machine Learning*, 20(3):273-297.

Nikolas Coupland, Justine Coupland, Howard Giles, and Karen L. Henwood. 1988. Accommodating the elderly: Invoking and extending a theory, *Language in Society*, 17(1):1-41.

David Crystal. 2001. *Language and the Internet*. Cambridge University Press, Cambridge, UK.

Olivier de Vel, Alison Anderson, Malcolm Corney, George Mohay. 2001. Mining e-mail content for author identification forensics, In *SIGMOD: Special Section on Data Mining for Intrusion Detection and Threat Analysis*.

Jade Goldstein-Stewart, Gary Ciany, and Jaime Carbonell. 2007. Genre identification and goal-focused summarization, In *Proceedings of the ACM 16th Conference on Information and Knowledge Management (CIKM) 2007*, pages 889-892.

Jade Goldstein-Stewart, Kerri A. Goodwin, Roberta E. Sabin, and Ransom K. Winder. 2008. Creating and using a correlated corpora to glean communicative commonalities. In *LREC2008 Proceedings*, Marrakech, Morocco.

Susan Herring. 2001. Gender and power in online communication. Center for Social Informatics, Working Paper, WP-01-05.

Susan Herring. 1996. Two variants of an electronic message schema. In Susan Herring, editor, *Computer-Mediated Communication: Linguistic, Social and Cross-Cultural Perspectives*. John Benjamins, Amsterdam, pages 81-106.

Shawndra Hill and Foster Provost. 2003. The myth of the double-blind review? Author identification using only citations. *SIGKDD Explorations*. 5(2):179-184.

Moshe Koppel, Shlomo Argamon, and Anat Rachel Shimoni. 2002. Automatically categorizing written texts by author gender. *Literary and Linguistic Computation*. 17(4):401-412.

Ivan Krsul and Eugene H. Spafford. 1997. Authorship analysis: Identifying the author of a program. *Computers and Security* 16(3):233-257.

Shlomo Levitan and Shlomo Argamon. 2006. Fixing the federalist: correcting results and evaluating editions for automated attribution. In *Digital Humanities*, pages 323-328, Paris.

LIWC, Linguistic Inquiry and Word Count. http://www.liwc.net/

David Madigan, Alexander Genkin, David Lewis, Shlomo Argamon, Dmitriy Fradkin, and Li Ye. 2005. Author identification on the large scale. *Proc. of the Meeting of the Classification Society of North America*.

Philip M. McCarthy, Gwyneth A. Lewis, David F. Dufty, and Danielle S. McNamara. 2006. Analyzing writing styles with Coh-Metrix, In *Proceedings of AI Research Society International Conference (FLAIRS)*, pages 764-769.

Niamh McCombe. 2002. Methods of author identification, Final Year Project, Trinity College, Ireland.

Thomas C. Mendenhall. 1887. The characteristic curves of composition. *Science*, 9(214):237-249.

Frederick Mosteller and David L. Wallace. 1964. *Inference and Disputed Authorship: The Federalist*. Addison-Wesley, Boston.

James W. Pennebaker, Martha E. Francis, and Roger J. Booth. 2001. *Linguistic Inquiry and Word Count (LIWC): LIWC2001*. Lawrence Erlbaum Associates, Mahwah, NJ.

John C. Platt. 1998. Using sparseness and analytic QP to speed training of support vector machines. In M. S. Kearns, S. A. Solla, and D. A. Cohn, editors, *Advances in Neural Information Processing Systems 11*. MIT Press, Cambridge, Mass.

Roberta E. Sabin, Kerri A. Goodwin, Jade Goldstein-Stewart, and Joseph A. Pereira. 2008. Gender differences across correlated corpora: preliminary results. *FLAIRS Conference 2008*, Florida, pages 207-212.

Marina Santini. 2007. *Automatic Identification of Genre in Web Pages*. Ph.D., thesis, University of Brighton, Brighton, UK.

Michael Shepherd and Carolyn Watters. 1999. The functionality attribute of cybergenres. In *Proceedings of the 32nd Hawaii International Conf. on System Sciences (HICSS1999)*, Maui, HI.

Rob Thomson and Tamar Murachver. 2001. Predicting gender from electronic discourse. *British Journal of Social Psychology*. 40(2):193-208.

Ian Witten and Eibe Frank. 2005. *Data Mining: Practical Machine Learning Tools and Techniques (Second Edition)*. Morgan Kaufmann, San Francisco, CA.

Simeon J. Yates. 1996. Oral and written linguistic aspects of computer conferencing: a corpus based study. In Susan Herring, editor, *Computer-mediated Communication: Linguistic, Social, and Cross-Cultural Perspectives*. John Benjamins, Amsterdam, pages 29-46.

End-to-End Evaluation in Simultaneous Translation

Olivier Hamon[1,2], Christian Fügen[3], Djamel Mostefa[1], Victoria Arranz[1], Muntsin Kolss[3], Alex Waibel[3,4] and Khalid Choukri[1]
[1]Evaluations and Language Resources Distribution Agency (ELDA), Paris, France
[2] LIPN (UMR 7030) – Université Paris 13 & CNRS, Villetaneuse, France
[3] Univerität Karlsruhe (TH), Germany
[4] Carnegie Mellon University, Pittsburgh, USA
{hamon|mostefa|arranz|choukri}@elda.org,
{fuegen|kolss|waibel}@ira.uka.de

Abstract

This paper presents the end-to-end evaluation of an automatic simultaneous translation system, built with state-of-the-art components. It shows whether, and for which situations, such a system might be advantageous when compared to a human interpreter. Using speeches in English translated into Spanish, we present the evaluation procedure and we discuss the results both for the recognition and translation components as well as for the overall system. Even if the translation process remains the Achilles' heel of the system, the results show that the system can keep at least half of the information, becoming potentially useful for final users.

1 Introduction

Anyone speaking at least two different languages knows that translation and especially simultaneous interpretation are very challenging tasks. A human translator has to cope with the special nature of different languages, comprising phenomena like terminology, compound words, idioms, dialect terms or neologisms, unexplained acronyms or abbreviations, proper names, as well as stylistic and punctuation differences. Further, translation or interpretation are not a word-by-word rendition of what was said or written in a source language. Instead, the meaning and intention of a given sentence have to be reexpressed in a natural and fluent way in another language.

Most professional full-time conference interpreters work for international organizations like the United Nations, the European Union, or the African Union, whereas the world's largest employer of translators and interpreters is currently the European Commission. In 2006, the European Parliament spent about 300 million Euros, 30% of its budget, on the interpretation and translation of the parliament speeches and EU documents. Generally, about 1.1 billion Euros are spent per year on the translating and interpreting services within the European Union, which is around 1% of the total EU-Budget (Volker Steinbiss, 2006).

This paper presents the end-to-end evaluation of an automatic simultaneous translation system, built with state-of-the-art components. It shows whether, and in which cases, such a system might be advantageous compared to human interpreters.

2 Challenges in Human Interpretation

According to Al-Khanji et al. (2000), researchers in the field of psychology, linguistics and interpretation seem to agree that simultaneous interpretation (SI) is a highly demanding cognitive task involving a basic psycholinguistic process. This process requires the interpreter to monitor, store and retrieve the input of the source language in a continuous manner in order to produce the oral rendition of this input in the target language. It is clear that this type of difficult linguistic and cognitive operation will force even professional interpreters to elaborate lexical or synthetic search strategies.

Fatigue and *stress* have a negative effect on the interpreter, leading to a decrease in simultaneous interpretation quality. In a study by Moser-Mercer et al. (1998), in which professional speakers were asked to work until they could no longer provide acceptable quality, it was shown that (1) during the first 20 minutes the frequency of errors rose steadily, (2) the interpreters, however, seemed to be unaware of this decline in quality, (3) after 60 minutes, all subjects made a total of 32.5 meaning errors, and (4) in the category of nonsense the number of errors almost doubled after 30 minutes on the task.

Since the audience is only able to evaluate the simultaneously interpreted discourse by its form,

Proceedings of the 12th Conference of the European Chapter of the ACL, pages 345–353,
Athens, Greece, 30 March – 3 April 2009.

the *fluency* of an interpretation is of utmost importance. According to a study by Kopczynski (1994), *fluency* and *style* were third on a list of priorities (after content and terminology) of elements rated by speakers and attendees as contributing to quality. Following the overview in (Yagi, 2000), an interpretation should be as natural and as authentic as possible, which means that artificial pauses in the middle of a sentence, hesitations, and false-starts should be avoided, and tempo and intensity of the speaker's voice should be imitated.

Another point to mention is the time span between a source language chunk and its target language chunk, which is often referred to as *ear-voice-span*. Following the summary in (Yagi, 2000), the ear-voice-span is variable in duration depending on some source and target language variables, like speech delivery rate, information density, redundancy, word order, syntactic characteristics, etc. Short delays are usually preferred for several reasons. For example, the audience is irritated when the delay is too large and is soon asking whether there is a problem with the interpretation.

3 Automatic Simultaneous Translation

Given the explanations above on human interpretation, one has to weigh two factors when considering the use of simultaneous translation systems: *translation quality* and *cost*.

The major disadvantage of an automatic system compared to human interpretation is its translation quality, as we will see in the following sections. Current state-of-the-art systems may reach satisfactory quality for people not understanding the lecturer at all, but are still worse than human interpretation. Nevertheless, an automatic system may have considerable advantages.

One such advantage is its considerable short-term memory: storing long sequences of words is not a problem for a computer system. Therefore, compensatory strategies are not necessary, regardless of the speaking rate of the speaker. However, depending on the system's translation speed, latency may increase. While it is possible for humans to compress the length of an utterance without changing its meaning (summarization), it is still a challenging task for automatic systems.

Human simultaneous interpretation is quite expensive, especially due to the fact that usually two interpreters are necessary. In addition, human interpreters require preparation time to become familiar with the topic. Moreover, simultaneous interpretation requires a soundproof booth with audio equipment, which adds an overall cost that is unacceptable for all but the most elaborate multilingual events. On the other hand, a simultaneous translation system also needs time and effort for preparation and adaptation towards the target application, language and domain. However, once adapted, it can be easily re-used in the same domain, language, etc. Another advantage is that the transcript of a speech or lecture is produced for free by using an automatic system in the source and target languages.

3.1 The Simultaneous Translation System

Figure 1 shows a schematic overview of the simultaneous translation system developed at Universität Karlsruhe (TH) (Fügen et al., 2006b). The speech of the lecturer is recorded with the help of a close-talk microphone and processed by the speech recognition component (ASR). The partial hypotheses produced by the ASR module are collected in the resegmentation component, for merging and re-splitting at appropriate "semantic" boundaries. The resegmented hypotheses are then transferred to one or more machine translation components (MT), at least one per language pair. Different output technologies may be used for presenting the translations to the audience. For a detailed description of the components as well as the client-server framework used for connecting the components please refer to (Fügen et al., 2006b; Fügen et al., 2006a; Kolss et al., 2006; Fügen and Kolss, 2007; Fügen et al., 2001).

3.2 End-to-End Evaluation

The evaluation in speech-to-speech translation jeopardises many concepts and implies a lot of subjectivity. Three components are involved and an overall system may grow the difficulty of estimating the output quality. However, two criteria are mainly accepted in the community: measuring the information preservation and determining how much of the translation is understandable.

Several end-to-end evaluations in speech-to-speech translation have been carried out in the last few years, in projects such as JANUS (Gates et al., 1996), Verbmobil (Nübel, 1997) or TC-STAR (Hamon et al., 2007). Those projects use the main criteria depicted above, and protocols differ in terms of data preparation, rating, procedure, etc.

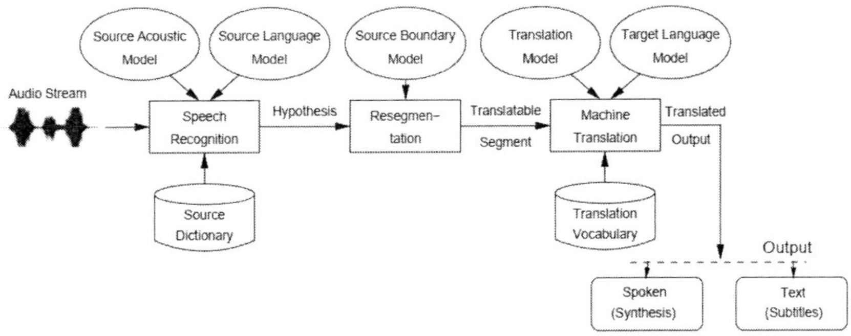

Figure 1: Schematic overview and information flow of the simultaneous translation system. The main components of the system are represented by cornered boxes and the models used for theses components by ellipses. The different output forms are represented by rounded boxes.

To our opinion, to evaluate the performance of a complete speech-to-speech translation system, we need to compare the source speech used as input to the translated output speech in the target language. To that aim, we reused a large part of the evaluation protocol from the TC-STAR project(Hamon et al., 2007).

4 Evaluation Tasks

The evaluation is carried out on the simultaneously translated speech of a single speaker's talks and lectures in the field of speech processing, given in English, and translated into Spanish.

4.1 Data used

Two data sets were selected from the talks and lectures. Each set contained three excerpts, no longer than 6 minutes each and focusing on different topics. The former set deals with speech recognition and the latter with the descriptions of European speech research projects, both from the same speaker. This represents around 7,200 English words. The excerpts were manually transcribed to produce the reference for the ASR evaluation. Then, these transcriptions were manually translated into Spanish by two different translators. Two reference translations were thus available for the spoken language translation (SLT) evaluation. Finally, one human interpretation was produced from the excerpts as reference for the end-to-end evaluation. It should be noted that for the translation system, speech synthesis was used to produce the spoken output.

4.2 Evaluation Protocol

The system is evaluated as a whole (black box evaluation) and component by component (glass box evaluation):

ASR evaluation. The ASR module is evaluated by computing the Word Error Rate (WER) in case insensitive mode.

SLT evaluation. For the SLT evaluation, the automatically translated text from the ASR output is compared with two manual reference translations by means of automatic and human metrics. Two automatic metrics are used: BLEU (Papineni et al., 2001) and mWER (Niessen et al., 2000).

For the human evaluation, each segment is evaluated in relation to *adequacy* and *fluency* (White and O'Connell, 1994). For the evaluation of adequacy, the target segment is compared to a reference segment. For the evaluation of fluency, the quality of the language is evaluated. The two types of evaluation are done independently, but each evaluator did both evaluations (first that of fluency, then that of adequacy) for a certain number of segments. For the evaluation of fluency, evaluators had to answer the question: "Is the text written in good Spanish?". For the evaluation of adequacy, evaluators had to answer the question: "How much of the meaning expressed in the reference translation is also expressed in the target translation?".

For both evaluations, a five-point scale is proposed to the evaluators, where only extreme values are explicitly defined. Three evaluations are carried out per segment, done by three different evaluators, and segments are divided randomly, because evaluators must not recreate a "story" and thus be influenced by the context. The total number of judges was 10, with around 100 segments per judge. Furthermore, the same number of judges was recruited for both categories: experts, from the domain with a knowledge of the technology, and non-experts, without that knowledge.

End-to-End evaluation. The End-to-End evaluation consists in comparing the speech in the source language to the output speech in the target language. Two important aspects should be taken into account when assessing the quality of a speech-to-speech system.

First, the information preservation is measured by using "comprehension questionnaires". Questions are created from the source texts (the English excerpts), then questions and answers are translated into Spanish by professional translators. These questions are asked to human judges after they have listened to the output speech in the target language (Spanish). At a second stage, the answers are analysed: for each answer a Spanish validator gives a score according to a binary scale (the information is either correct or incorrect). This allows us to measure the *information preservation*. Three types of questions are used in order to diversify the difficulty of the questions and test the system at different levels: simple Factual (70%), yes/no (20%) and list (10%) questions. For instance, questions were: *What is the larynx responsible for?*, *Have all sites participating in CHIL built a CHIL room?*, *Which types of knowledge sources are used by the decoder?*, respectively.

The second important aspect of a speech-to-speech system is the quality of the speech output (hereafter *quality evaluation*). For assessing the quality of the speech output one question is asked to the judges at the end of each comprehension questionnaire: "Rate the overall quality of this audio sample", and values go from 1 ("1: Very bad, unusable") to 5 ("It is very useful"). Both automatic system and interpreter outputs were evaluated with the same methodology.

Human judges are real users and native Spanish speakers, experts and non-experts, but different from those of the SLT evaluation. Twenty judges were involved (12 excerpts, 10 evaluations per excerpt and 6 evaluations per judge) and each judge evaluated both automatic and human excerpts on a 50/50 percent basis.

5 Components Results

5.1 Automatic Speech Recognition

The ASR output has been evaluated using the manual transcriptions of the excerpts. The overall Word Error Rate (WER) is 11.9%. Table 1 shows the WER level for each excerpt.

Excerpts	WER [%]
L043-1	14.5
L043-2	14.5
L043-3	9.6
T036-1	11.3
T036-2	11.7
T036-3	9.2
Overall	11.9

Table 1: Evaluation results for ASR.

T036 excerpts seem to be easier to recognize automatically than *L043* ones, probably due to the more general language of the former.

5.2 Machine Translation

5.2.1 Human Evaluation

Each segment within the human evaluation is evaluated 4 times, each by a different judge. This aims at having a significant number of judgments and measuring the consistency of the human evaluations. The consistency is measured by computing the Cohen's Kappa coefficient (Cohen, 1960).

Results show a substantial agreement for fluency (kappa of 0.64) and a moderate agreement for adequacy (0.52).The overall results of the human evaluation are presented in Table 2. Regarding both experts' and non-experts' details, agreement is very similar (0.30 and 0.28, respectively).

	All judges	Experts	Non experts
Fluency	3.13	2.84	3.42
Adequacy	3.26	3.21	3.31

Table 2: Average rating of human evaluations [1<5].

Both fluency and adequacy results are over the mean. They are lower for experts than for non-experts. This may be due to the fact that experts are more familiar with the domain and therefore more demanding than non experts. Regarding the detailed evaluation per judge, scores are generally lower for non-experts than for experts.

5.2.2 Automatic Evaluation

Scores are computed using case-sensitive metrics. Table 3 shows the detailed results per excerpt.

Excerpts	BLEU [%]	mWER [%]
L043-1	25.62	58.46
L043-2	22.60	62.47
L043-3	28.73	62.64
T036-1	34.46	55.13
T036-2	29.41	59.91
T036-3	35.17	50.77
Overall	28.94	58.66

Table 3: Automatic Evaluation results for SLT.

Scores are rather low, with a mWER of 58.66%, meaning that more than half of the translation is correct. According to the scoring, the *T036* excerpts seem to be easier to translate than the *L043* ones, the latter being of a more technical nature.

6 End-to-End Results

6.1 Evaluators Agreement

In this study, ten judges carried out the evaluation for each excerpt. In order to observe the inter-judges agreement, the global Fleiss's Kappa coefficient was computed, which allows to measure the agreement between m judges with r criteria of judgment. This coefficient shows a global agreement between all the judges, which goes beyond Cohen's Kappa coefficient. However, a low coefficient requires a more detailed analysis, for instance, by using Kappa for each pair of judges. Indeed, this allows to see how deviant judges are from the typical judge behaviour. For m judges, n evaluations and r criteria, the global Kappa is defined as follows:

$$\kappa = 1 - \frac{nm^2 - \sum_{i=1}^{n}\sum_{j=1}^{r} X_{ij}^2}{nm(m-1)\sum_{j=1}^{r} P_j(1-P_j)}$$

where:

$$P_j = \frac{\sum_{i=1}^{n} X_{ij}}{nm}$$

and: X_{ij} is the number of judgments for the ith evaluation and the jth criteria.

Regarding quality evaluation ($n = 6$, $m = 10$, $r = 5$), Kappa values are low for both human interpreters ($\kappa = 0.07$) and the automatic system ($\kappa = 0.01$), meaning that judges agree poorly (Landis and Koch, 1977). This is explained by the extreme subjectivity of the evaluation and the small number of evaluated excerpts. Looking at each pair of judges and the Kappa coefficients themselves, there is no real agreement, since most of the Kappa values are around zero. However, some judge pairs show fair agreement, and some others show moderate or substantial agreement. It is observed, though, that some criteria are not frequently selected by the judges, which limits the statistical significance of the Kappa coefficient.

The limitations are not the same for the comprehension evaluation ($n = 60$, $m = 10$, $r = 2$), since the criteria are binary (i.e. *true* or *false*). Regarding the evaluated excerpts, Kappa values are 0.28 for the automatic system and 0.30 for the interpreter. According to Landis and Koch (1977), those values mean that judges agree fairly. In order to go further, the Kappa coefficients were computed for each pair of judges. Results were slightly better for the interpreter than for the automatic system. Most of them were between 0.20 and 0.40, implying a fair agreement. Some judges agreed moderately.

Furthermore, it was also observed that for the 120 available questions, 20 had been answered correctly by all the judges (16 for the interpreter evaluation and 4 for the automatic system one) and 6 had been answered wrongly by all judges (1 for the former and 5 for the latter). That shows a trend where the interpreter comprehension would be easier than that of the automatic system, or at least where the judgements are less questionable.

6.2 Quality Evaluation

Table 4 compares the quality evaluation results of the interpreter to those of the automatic system.

Samples	Interpreter	Automatic system
L043-1	3.1	1.6
L043-2	2.9	2.3
L043-3	2.4	2.1
T036-1	3.6	3.1
T036-2	2.7	2.5
T036-3	3.5	2.5
Mean	3.03	2.35

Table 4: Quality evaluation results for the interpreter and the automatic system [1<5].

As can be seen, with a mean score of 3.03 even for **the interpreter**, the excerpts were difficult to interpret and translate. This is particularly so for

L043, which is more technical than *T036*. The *L043-3* excerpt is particularly technical, with formulae and algorithm descriptions, and even a complex description of the human articulatory system. In fact, *L043* provides a typical presentation with an introduction, followed by a deeper description of the topic. This increasing complexity is reflected on the quality scores of the three excerpts, going from 3.1 to 2.4.

T036 is more fluent due to the less technical nature of the speech and the more general vocabulary used. However, the *T036-2* and *T036-3* excerpts get a lower quality score, due to the description of data collections or institutions, and thus the use of named entities. The interpreter does not seem to be at ease with them and is mispronouncing some of them, such as "Grenoble" pronounced like in English instead of in Spanish. The interpreter seems to be influenced by the speaker, as can also be seen in his use of the neologism "el cenario" ("the scenario") instead of "el escenario". Likewise, "Karlsruhe" is pronounced three times differently, showing some inconsistency of the interpreter.

The general trend in quality errors is similar to those of previous evaluations: lengthening words ("seeeeñales"), hesitations, pauses between syllables and catching breath ("caracterís...ticas"), careless mistakes ("probibilidad" instead of "probabilidad"), self-correction of wrong interpreting ("reconocien-/reconocimiento"), etc.

An important issue concerns gender and number agreement. Those errors are explained by the presence of morphological gender in Spanish, like in "estos señales" instead of "estas señales" ("these signals") together with the speaker's speed of speech. The speaker seems to start by default with a masculine determiner (which has no gender in English), adjusting the gender afterward depending on the noun following. A quick translation may also be the cause for this kind of errors, like "del señal acustico" ("of the acoustic signal") with a masculine determiner, a feminine substantive and ending in a masculine adjective. Some translation errors are also present, for instance "computerizar" instead of "calcular" ("compute").

The errors made by the interpreter help to understand how difficult oral translation is. This should be taken into account for the evaluation of the automatic system.

The **automatic system results**, like those of the interpreter, are higher for *T036* than for *L043*. However, scores are lower, especially for the *L043-1* excerpt. This seems to be due to the type of lexicon used by the speaker for this excerpt, more medical, since the speaker describes the articulatory system. Moreover, his description is sometimes metaphorical and uses a rather colloquial register. Therefore, while the interpreter finds it easier to deal with these excerpts (known vocabulary among others) and *L043-3* seems to be more complicated (domain-specific, technical aspect), the automatic system finds it more complicated with the former and less with the latter. In other words, the interpreter has to "understand" what is said in *L043-3*, contrary to the automatic system, in order to translate.

Scores are higher for the *T036* excerpts. Indeed, there is a high lexical repetition, a large number of named entities, and the quality of the excerpt is very training-dependant. However, the system runs into trouble to process foreign names, which are very often not understandable. Differences between *T036-1* and the other *T036* excerpts are mainly due to the change in topic. While the former deals with a general vocabulary (i.e. description of projects), the other two excerpts describe the data collection, the evaluation metrics, etc., thus increasing the complexity of translation.

Generally speaking, quality scores of the automatic system are mainly due to the translation component, and to a lesser extent to the recognition component. Many English words are not translated ("bush", "keyboards", "squeaking", etc.), and word ordering is not always correct. This is the case for the sentence "how we solve it", translated into "cómo nos resolvers lo" instead of "cómo lo resolvemos". Funnily enough, the problems of gender ("maravillosos aplicaciones" - masc. vs fem.) and number ("pueden realmente ser aplicado" - plu. vs sing.) the interpreter has, are also found for the automatic system. Moreover, the translation of compound nouns often shows wrong word ordering, in particular when they are long, i.e. up to three words (e.g. "reconocimiento de habla sistemas" for "speech recognition system" instead of "sistemas de reconocimiento de habla").

Finally, some error combinations result in fully non-understandable sentences, such as:

> "usted tramo se en emacs es squeaking ruido y dries todos demencial"

where the following errors take place:

- *tramo*: this translation of "stretch" results from the choice of a substantive instead of a verb, giving rise to two choices due to the lexical ambiguity: "estiramiento" and "tramo", which is more a *linear distance* than a *stretch* in that context;
- *se*: the pronoun "it" becomes the reflexive "se" instead of the personal pronoun "lo";
- *emacs*: the recognition module transcribed the couple of words "it makes" into "emacs", not translated by the translation module;
- *squeaking*: the word is not translated by the translation module;
- *dries*: again, two successive errors are made: the word "drives" is transcribed into "dries" by the recognition module, which is then left untranslated.

The TTS component also contributes to decreasing the output quality. The prosody module finds it hard to make the sentences sound natural. Pauses between words are not very frequent, but they do not sound natural (i.e. like catching breath) and they are not placed at specific points, as it would be done by a human. For instance, the prosody module does not link the noun and its determiner (e.g. "otros aplicaciones"). Finally, a not user-friendly aspect of the TTS component is the repetition of the same words always pronounced in the same manner, what is quite disturbing for the listener.

6.3 Comprehension Evaluation

Tables 5 and 6 present the results of the comprehension evaluation, for the interpreter and for the automatic system, respectively. They provide the following information:

identifiers of the excerpt: Source data are the same for the interpreter and the automatic system, namely the English speech;

subj. E2E: The subjective results of the end-to-end evaluation are done by the same assessors who did the quality evaluation. This shows the percentage of good answers;

fair E2E: The objective verification of the answers. The audio files are validated to check whether they contain the answers to the questions or not (as the questions were created from the English source). This shows the maximum percentage of answers an evaluator managed to find from either the interpreter (speaker audio) or the automatic system output (TTS) in Spanish. For instance, information in English could have been missed by the interpreter because he/she felt that this information was meaningless and could be discarded. We consider those results as an objective evaluation.

SLT, ASR: Verification of the answers in each component of the end-to-end process. In order to determine where the information for the automatic system is lost, files from each component (recognised files for ASR, translated files for SLT, and synthesised files for TTS in the "fair E2E" column) are checked.

Excerpts	subj. E2E	fair E2E
L043-1	69	90
L043-2	75	80
L043-3	72	60
T036-1	80	100
T036-2	73	80
T036-3	76	100
Mean	74	85

Table 5: Comprehension evaluation results for the interpreter [%].

Regarding Table 5, **the interpreter** loses 15% of the information (i.e. 15% of the answers were incorrect or not present in the interpreter's translation) and judges correctly answered 74% of the questions. Five documents get above 80% of correct results, while judges find almost above 70% of the answers for the six documents.

Regarding **the automatic system** results (Table 6), the information rate found by judges is just above 50% since, by extension, more than half the questions were correctly answered. The lowest excerpt, *L043-1*, gets a rate of 25%, the highest, *T036-1*, a rate of 76%, which is in agreement with the observation for the quality evaluation. Information loss can be found in each component, especially for the SLT module (35% of the information is lost here). It should be noticed that the TTS module made also errors which prevented judges

Excerpts	subj. E2E	fair E2E	SLT	ASR
L043-1	25	30	30	70
L043-2	62	70	80	70
L043-3	43	40	60	100
T036-1	76	80	90	100
T036-2	61	70	60	80
T036-3	47	60	70	80
Mean	52	58	65	83

Table 6: Comprehension evaluation results for the automatic system [%].

from answering related questions. Moreover, the ASR module loses 17% of the information. Those results are certainly due to the specific vocabulary used in this experiment.

So as to *objectively compare* the interpreter with the automatic system, we selected the questions for which the answers were included in the interpreter files (i.e. those in the "fair E2E" column of Table 5). The goal was to compare the overall quality of the speech-to-speech translation to interpreters' quality, without the noise factor of the information missing. The assumption is that the interpreter translates the "important information" and skips the useless parts of the original speech. This experiment is to measure the level of this information that is preserved by the automatic system. So a new subset of results was obtained, on the information kept by the interpreter. The same study was repeated for the three components and the results are shown in Tables 7 and 8.

Excerpts	subj. E2E	fair E2E	SLT	ASR
L043-1	27	33	33	78
L043-2	65	75	88	75
L043-3	37	67	83	100
T036-1	76	80	90	100
T036-2	69	88	75	100
T036-3	47	60	70	80
Mean	53	60	70	80

Table 7: Evaluation results for the automatic system restricted to the questions for which answers can be found in the interpreter speech [%].

Comparing the automatic system to the interpreter, the automatic system keeps 40% of the information where the interpreter translates the documents correctly. Those results confirm that ASR loses a lot of information (20%), while SLT loses 10% further, and so does the TTS. Judges are quite close to the objective validation and found most of the answers they could possibly do.

Excerpts	subj. E2E
L043-1	66
L043-2	90
L043-3	88
T036-1	80
T036-2	81
T036-3	76
Mean	80

Table 8: Evaluation results for interpreter, restricted to the questions for which answers can be found in the interpreter speech [%].

Subjective results for the restricted evaluation are similar to the previous results, on the full data (80% vs 74% of the information found by the judges). Performance is good for the interpreter: 98% of the information correctly translated by the automatic system is also correctly interpreted by the human. Although we can not compare the performance of the restricted automatic system to that of the restricted interpreter (since data sets of questions are different), it seems that of the interpreter is better. However, the loss due to subjective evaluation seems to be higher for the interpreter than for the automatic system.

7 Conclusions

Regarding the SLT evaluation, the results achieved with the simultaneous translation system are still rather low compared to the results achieved with offline systems for translating European parliament speeches in TC-STAR. However, the offline systems had almost no latency constraints, and parliament speeches are much easier to recognize and translate when compared to the more spontaneous talks and lectures focused in this paper. This clearly shows the difficulty of the whole task. However, the human end-to-end evaluation of the system in which the system is compared with human interpretation shows that the current translation quality allows for understanding of at least half of the content, and therefore, may be already quite helpful for people not understanding the language of the lecturer at all.

References

Rajai Al-Khanji, Said El-Shiyab, and Riyadh Hussein. 2000. On the Use of Compensatory Strategies in Simultaneous Interpretation. *Meta : Journal des traducteurs*, 45(3):544–557.

Jacob Cohen. 1960. A coefficient of agreement for nominal scales. In *Educational and Psychological Measurement*, volume 20, pages 37–46.

Christian Fügen and Muntsin Kolss. 2007. The influence of utterance chunking on machine translation performance. In *Proc. of the European Conference on Speech Communication and Technology (INTERSPEECH)*, Antwerp, Belgium, August. ISCA.

Christian Fügen, Martin Westphal, Mike Schneider, Tanja Schultz, and Alex Waibel. 2001. LingWear: A Mobile Tourist Information System. In *Proc. of the Human Language Technology Conf. (HLT)*, San Diego, California, March. NIST.

Christian Fügen, Shajith Ikbal, Florian Kraft, Kenichi Kumatani, Kornel Laskowski, John W. McDonough, Mari Ostendorf, Sebastian Stüker, and Matthias Wölfel. 2006a. The isl rt-06s speech-to-text system. In Steve Renals, Samy Bengio, and Jonathan Fiskus, editors, *Machine Learning for Multimodal Interaction: Third International Workshop, MLMI 2006, Bethesda, MD, USA*, volume 4299 of *Lecture Notes in Computer Science*, pages 407–418. Springer Verlag Berlin/ Heidelberg.

Christian Fügen, Muntsin Kolss, Matthias Paulik, and Alex Waibel. 2006b. Open Domain Speech Translation: From Seminars and Speeches to Lectures. In *TC-Star Speech to Speech Translation Workshop*, Barcelona, Spain, June.

Donna Gates, Alon Lavie, Lori Levin, Alex. Waibel, Marsal Gavalda, Laura Mayfield, and Monika Woszcyna. 1996. End-to-end evaluation in janus: A speech-to-speech translation system. In *Proceedings of the 6th ECAI*, Budapest.

Olivier Hamon, Djamel Mostefa, and Khalid Choukri. 2007. End-to-end evaluation of a speech-to-speech translation system in tc-star. In *Proceedings of the MT Summit XI*, Copenhagen, Denmark, September.

Muntsin Kolss, Bing Zhao, Stephan Vogel, Ashish Venugopal, and Ying Zhang. 2006. The ISL Statistical Machine Translation System for the TC-STAR Spring 2006 Evaluations. In *TC-Star Workshop on Speech-to-Speech Translation*, Barcelona, Spain, December.

Andrzej Kopczynski, 1994. *Bridging the Gap: Empirical Research in Simultaneous Interpretation*, chapter Quality in Conference Interpreting: Some Pragmatic Problems, pages 87–100. John Benjamins, Amsterdam/ Philadelphia.

J. Richard Landis and Gary G. Koch. 1977. The measurement of observer agreement for categorical data. In Biometrics, *Vol. 33, No. 1 (Mar., 1977), pp. 159-174.*

Barbara Moser-Mercer, Alexander Kunzli, and Marina Korac. 1998. Prolonged turns in interpreting: Effects on quality, physiological and psychological stress (pilot study). *Interpreting: International journal of research and practice in interpreting*, 3(1):47–64.

Sonja Niessen, Franz Josef Och, Gregor Leusch, and Hermann Ney. 2000. An evaluation tool for machine translation: Fast evaluation for mt research. In *Proceedings of the 2nd International Conference on Language Resources and Evaluation*, Athens, Greece.

Rita Nübel. 1997. End-to-end Evaluation in Verbmobil I. In *Proceedings of the MT Summit VI*, San Diego.

Kishore Papineni, Salim Roukos, Todd Ward, and Wei-Jing Zhu. 2001. Bleu: a method for automatic evaluation of machine translation. Technical Report RC22176 (W0109-022), Research Report, Computer Science IBM Research Division, T.J.Watson Research Center.

Accipio Consulting Volker Steinbiss. 2006. Sprachtechnologien für Europa. `www.tc-star.org/pubblicazioni/D17_HLT_DE.pdf`.

John S. White and Theresa A. O'Connell. 1994. Evaluation in the arpa machine translation program: 1993 methodology. In *HLT '94: Proceedings of the workshop on Human Language Technology*, pages 135–140, Morristown, NJ, USA. Association for Computational Linguistics.

Sane M. Yagi. 2000. Studying Style in Simultaneous Interpretation. *Meta : Journal des traducteurs*, 45(3):520–547.

Learning-Based Named Entity Recognition for Morphologically-Rich, Resource-Scarce Languages

Kazi Saidul Hasan and **Md. Altaf ur Rahman** and **Vincent Ng**
Human Language Technology Research Institute
University of Texas at Dallas
Richardson, TX 75083-0688
{saidul,altaf,vince}@hlt.utdallas.edu

Abstract

Named entity recognition for morphologically rich, case-insensitive languages, including the majority of semitic languages, Iranian languages, and Indian languages, is inherently more difficult than its English counterpart. Worse still, progress on machine learning approaches to named entity recognition for many of these languages is currently hampered by the scarcity of annotated data and the lack of an accurate part-of-speech tagger. While it is possible to rely on manually-constructed gazetteers to combat data scarcity, this gazetteer-centric approach has the potential weakness of creating irreproducible results, since these name lists are not publicly available in general. Motivated in part by this concern, we present a learning-based named entity recognizer that does not rely on manually-constructed gazetteers, using Bengali as our representative resource-scarce, morphologically-rich language. Our recognizer achieves a relative improvement of 7.5% in F-measure over a baseline recognizer. Improvements arise from (1) using induced affixes, (2) extracting information from online lexical databases, and (3) jointly modeling part-of-speech tagging and named entity recognition.

1 Introduction

While research in natural language processing has gained a lot of momentum in the past several decades, much of this research effort has been focusing on only a handful of politically-important languages such as English, Chinese, and Arabic. On the other hand, being the fifth most spoken language[1] with more than 200 million native speakers residing mostly in Bangladesh and the Indian state of West Bengal, Bengali has far less electronic resources than the aforementioned languages. In fact, a major obstacle to the automatic processing of Bengali is the scarcity of annotated corpora.

One potential solution to the problem of data scarcity is to hand-annotate a small amount of data with the desired linguistic information and then develop bootstrapping algorithms for combining this small amount of labeled data with a large amount of unlabeled data. In fact, co-training (Blum and Mitchell, 1998) has been successfully applied to English named entity recognition (NER) (Collins & Singer [henceforth C&S] (1999)). In C&S's approach, consecutive words tagged as proper nouns are first identified as potential NEs, and each such NE is then labeled by combining the outputs of two co-trained classifiers. Unfortunately, there are practical difficulties in applying this technique to Bengali NER. First, one of C&S's co-trained classifiers uses features based on capitalization, but Bengali is case-insensitive. Second, C&S identify potential NEs based on proper nouns, but unlike English, (1) proper noun identification for Bengali is non-trivial, due to the lack of capitalization; and (2) there does not exist an accurate Bengali part-of-speech (POS) tagger for providing such information, owing to the scarcity of annotated data for training the tagger.

In other words, Bengali NER is complicated not only by the scarcity of annotated data, but also by the lack of an accurate POS tagger. One could imagine building a Bengali POS tagger using un-

[1] See http://en.wikipedia.org/wiki/Bengali_language.

Proceedings of the 12th Conference of the European Chapter of the ACL, pages 354–362,
Athens, Greece, 30 March – 3 April 2009. ©2009 Association for Computational Linguistics

supervised induction techniques that have been successfully developed for English (e.g., Schütze (1995), Clark (2003)), including the recently-proposed prototype-driven approach (Haghighi and Klein, 2006) and Bayesian approach (Goldwater and Griffiths, 2007). The majority of these approaches operate by clustering distributionally similar words, but they are unlikely to work well for Bengali for two reasons. First, Bengali is a relatively free word order language, and hence the distributional information collected for Bengali words may not be as reliable as that for English words. Second, many closed-class words that typically appear in the distributional representation of an English word (e.g., prepositions and particles such as "in" and "to") are realized as inflections in Bengali, and the absence of these informative words implies that the context vector may no longer capture sufficient information for accurately clustering the Bengali words.

In view of the above problems, many learning-based Bengali NE recognizers have relied heavily on manually-constructed name lists for identifying persons, organizations, and locations. There are at least two weaknesses associated with this gazetteer-centric approach. First, these name lists are typically not publicly available, making it difficult to reproduce the results of these NE recognizers. Second, it is not clear how comprehensive these lists are. Relying on comprehensive lists that comprise a large portion of the names in the test set essentially reduces the NER problem to a dictionary-lookup problem, which is arguably not very interesting from a research perspective.

In addition, many existing learning-based Bengali NE recognizers have several common weaknesses. First, they use as features *pseudo-affixes*, which are created by extracting the first n and the last n characters of a word (where $1 \leq n \leq 4$) (e.g., Dandapat et al. (2007)). While affixes encode essential grammatical information in Bengali due to its morphological richness, this extraction method is arguably too ad-hoc and does not cover many useful affixes. Second, they typically adopt a *pipelined* NER architecture, performing POS tagging prior to NER and encoding the resulting not-so-accurate POS information as a feature. In other words, errors in POS tagging are propagated to the NE recognizer via the POS feature, thus limiting its performance.

Motivated in part by these weaknesses, we investigate how to improve a learning-based NE recognizer that does *not* rely on manually-constructed gazetteers. Specifically, we investigate two learning architectures for our NER system. The first one is the aforementioned pipelined architecture in which the NE recognizer uses as features the output of a POS tagger that is trained independently of the recognizer. Unlike existing Bengali POS and NE taggers, however, we examine two new knowledge sources for training these taggers: (1) affixes induced from an unannotated corpus and (2) semantic class information extracted from Wikipedia. In the second architecture, we *jointly* learn the POS tagging and the NER tasks, allowing features for one task to be accessible to the other task during learning. The goal is to examine whether any benefits can be obtained via joint modeling, which could address the error propagation problem with the pipelined architecture.

While we focus on Bengali NER in this paper, none of the proposed techniques are language-specific. In fact, we believe that these techniques are of relevance and interest to the EACL community because they can be equally applicable to the numerous resource-scarce European and Middle Eastern languages that share similar linguistic and extra-linguistic properties as Bengali. For instance, the majority of semitic languages and Iranian languages are, like Bengali, morphologically productive; and many East European languages such as Czech and Polish resemble Bengali in terms of not only their morphological richness, but also their relatively free word order.

The rest of the paper is organized as follows. In Section 2, we briefly describe the related work. Sections 3 and 4 show how we induce affixes from an unannotated corpus and extract semantic class information from Wikipedia. In Sections 5 and 6, we train and evaluate a POS tagger and an NE recognizer independently, augmenting the feature set typically used for these two tasks with our new knowledge sources. Finally, we describe and evaluate our joint model in Section 7.

2 Related Work

Cucerzan and Yarowsky (1999) exploit morphological and contextual patterns to propose a language-independent solution to NER. They use affixes based on the paradigm that named entities corresponding to a particular class have similar morphological structure. Their bootstrapping approach is tested on Romanian, English, Greek, Turkish, and Hindi. The recall for Hindi is the lowest (27.84%) among the five languages, suggesting that the lack of case information can significantly complicate the NER task.

To investigate the role of gazetteers in NER, Mikheev et al. (1999) combine grammar rules with maximum entropy models and vary the gazetteer size. Experimental results show that (1) the F-scores for NE classes like person and organization are still high without gazetteers, ranging from 85% to 92%; and (2) a small list of country names can improve the low F-score for locations substantially. It is worth noting that their recognizer requires that the input data contain POS tags and simple semantic tags, whereas ours automatically acquires such linguistic information. In addition, their approach uses part of the dataset to extend the gazetteer. Therefore, the resulting gazetteer list is specific to a particular domain; on the other hand, our approach does not generate a domain-specific list, since it makes use of Wikipedia articles.

Kozareva (2006) generates gazetteer lists for person and location names from unlabeled data using common patterns and a graph exploration algorithm. The location pattern is essentially a preposition followed by capitalized context words. However, this approach is inadequate for a morphologically-rich language like Bengali, since prepositions are often realized as inflections.

3 Affix Induction

Since Bengali is morphologically productive, a lot of grammatical information about Bengali words is expressed via affixes. Hence, these affixes could serve as useful features for training POS and NE taggers. In this section, we show how to induce affixes from an unannotated corpus.

We rely on a simple idea proposed by Keshava and Pitler (2006) for inducing affixes. Assume that (1) V is a vocabulary (i.e., a set of distinct words) extracted from a large, unannotated corpus, (2) α and β are two character sequences, and (3) $\alpha\beta$ is the concatenation of α and β. If $\alpha\beta$ and α are found in V, we extract β as a suffix. Similarly, if $\alpha\beta$ and β are found in V, we extract α as a prefix.

In principle, we can use all of the induced affixes as features for training a POS tagger and an NE recognizer. However, we choose to use only those features that survive our feature selection process (to be described below), for the following reasons. First, the number of induced affixes is large, and using only a subset of them as features could make the training process more efficient. Second, the above affix induction method is arguably overly simplistic and hence many of the induced affixes could be spurious.

Our feature selection process is fairly simple: we (1) score each affix by multiplying its *frequency* (i.e., the number of distinct words in V to which each affix attaches) and its *length*[2], and (2) select only those whose score is above a certain threshold. In our experiments, we set this threshold to 50, and generate our vocabulary of 140K words from five years of articles taken from the Bengali newspaper *Prothom Alo*. This enables us to induce 979 prefixes and 975 suffixes.

4 Semantic Class Induction from Wikipedia

Wikipedia has recently been used as a knowledge source for various language processing tasks, including taxonomy construction (Ponzetto and Strube, 2007a), coreference resolution (Ponzetto and Strube, 2007b), and English NER (e.g., Bunescu and Paşca (2006), Cucerzan (2007), Kazama and Torisawa (2007), Watanabe et al. (2007)). Unlike previous work on using Wikipedia for NER, our goal here is to (1) generate a list of phrases and tokens that are potentially named entities from the 16914 articles in the Bengali Wikipedia[3] and (2) heuristically annotate each of them with one of four classes, namely, PER (person), ORG (organization), LOC (location), or OTHERS (i.e., anything other than PER, ORG and LOC).

4.1 Generating an Annotated List of Phrases

We employ the steps below to generate our annotated list.

Generating and annotating the titles Recall that each Wikipedia article has been optionally assigned to one or more categories by its creator and/or editors. We use these categories to help annotate the title of an article. Specifically, if an article has a category whose name starts with "Born on" or "Death on," we label the corresponding title with PER. Similarly, if it has a category whose name starts with "Cities of" or "Countries of," we

[2] The dependence on frequency and length is motivated by the observation that less frequent and shorter affixes are more likely to be erroneous (see Goldsmith (2001)).

[3] See http://bn.wikipedia.org. In our experiments, we used the Bengali Wikipedia dump obtained on October 22, 2007.

NE Class	Keywords
PER	"born," "died," "one," "famous"
LOC	"city," "area," "population," "located," "part of"
ORG	"establish," "situate," "publish"

Table 1: Keywords for each named entity class

label the title as LOC. If an article does not belong to one of the four categories above, we label its title with the help of a small set of seed keywords shown in Table 1. Specifically, for each of the three NE classes shown on the left of Table 1, we compute a weighted sum of its keywords: a keyword that appears in the first paragraph has a weight of 3, a keyword that appears elsewhere in the article has a weight of 1, and a keyword that does not appear in the article has a weight of 0. The rationale behind using different weights is simple: the first paragraph is typically a brief exposition of the title, so it should in principle contain words that correlate more closely with the title than words appearing in the rest of the article. We then label the title with the class that has the largest weighted sum. Note, however, that we ignore any article that contains fewer than two keywords, since we do not have reliable evidence for labeling its title as one of the NE classes. We put all these annotated titles into a *title list*.

Getting more location names To get more location names, we search for the character sequences "birth place:" and "death place:" in each article, extracting the phrase following any of these sequences and label it as LOC. We put all such labeled locations into the title list.

Generating and annotating the tokens in the titles Next, we extract the word tokens from each title in the title list and label each token with an NE class. The reason for doing this is to improve generalization: if "Dhaka University" is labeled as ORG in the title list, then it is desirable to also label the token "University" as ORG, because this could help identify an unseen phrase that contains the term "University" as an organization. Our token labeling method is fairly simple. First, we generate the tokens from each title in the title list, assigning to each token the same NE label as that of the title from which it is generated. For instance, from the title "Anna Frank," "Anna" will be labeled as PER; and from "Anna University," " Anna" will be labeled as LOC. To resolve such ambiguities (i.e., assigning different labels to the same token), we keep a count of how many times "Anna" is labeled with each NE class, and set its final label to be the most frequent NE class. We put all these annotated tokens into a *token list*. If the title list and the token list have an element in common, we remove the element from the token list, since we have a higher confidence in the labels of the titles.

Merging the lists Finally, we append the token list to the title list. The resulting title list contains 4885 PERs, 15176 LOCs, and 188 ORGs.

4.2 Applying the Annotated List to a Text

We can now use the title list to annotate a text. Specifically, we process each word w in the text in a left-to-right manner, using the following steps:

1. Check whether w has been labeled. If so, we skip this word and process the next one.
2. Check whether w appears in the Samsad Bengali-English Dictionary[4]. If so, we assume that w is more likely to be used as a non-named entity, thus leaving the word unlabeled and processing the next word instead.
3. Find the longest unlabeled word sequence[5] that begins with w and appears in the title list. If no such sequence exists, we leave w unlabeled and process the next word. Otherwise, we label it with the NE tag given by the title list. To exemplify, consider a text that starts with the sentence "Smith College is in Massachusetts." When processing "Smith," "Smith College" is the longest sequence that starts with "Smith" and appears in the title list (as an ORG). As a result, we label *all* occurrences of "Smith College" in the text as an ORG. (Note that without using the longest match heuristic, "Smith" would likely be mislabeled as PER.) In addition, we take the last word of the ORG (which in this case is "College") and annotate each of its occurrence in the rest of the text as ORG.[6]

These automatic annotations will then be used to derive a set of WIKI features for training our POS tagger and NE recognizer. Hence, unlike existing Bengali NE recognizers, our "gazetteers" are induced rather than manually created.

[4]See http://dsal.uchicago.edu/dictionaries/biswasbengali/.

[5]This is a sequence in which each word is unlabeled.

[6]However, if we have a PER match (e.g., "Anna Frank") or a LOC match (e.g., "Las Vegas"), we take *each* word in the matched phrase and label each of its occurrence in the rest of the text with the same NE tag.

Current word	w_i
Previous word	w_{i-1}
2nd previous word	w_{i-2}
Next word	w_{i+1}
2nd next word	w_{i+2}
Current pseudo-affixes	pf_i (prefix), sf_i (suffix)
Current induced affixes	pi_i (prefix), si_i (suffix)
Previous induced affixes	pi_{i-1} (prefix), si_{i-1} (suffix)
Induced affix bigrams	$pi_{i-1}pi_i$ (prefix), $si_{i-1}si_i$ (suffix)
Current Wiki tag	$wiki_i$
Previous Wiki tag	$wiki_{i-1}$
Wiki bigram	$wiki_{i-1}wiki_i$
Word bigrams	$w_{i-2}w_{i-1}$, $w_{i-1}w_i$, w_iw_{i+1}, $w_{i+1}w_{i+2}$
Word trigrams	$w_{i-2}w_{i-1}w_i$
Current number	q_i

Table 2: Feature templates for the POS tagging experiments

5 Part-of-Speech Tagging

In this section, we will show how we train and evaluate our POS tagger. As mentioned before, we hypothesize that introducing our two knowledge sources into the feature set for the tagger could improve its performance: using the induced affixes could improve the extraction of grammatical information from the words, and using the Wikipedia-induced list, which in principle should comprise mostly of names, could help improve the identification of proper nouns.

Corpus Our corpus is composed of 77942 words and is annotated with one of 26 POS tags in the tagset defined by IIIT Hyderabad[7]. Using this corpus, we perform 5-fold cross-validation (CV) experiments in our evaluation. It is worth noting that this dataset has a high unknown word rate of 15% (averaged over the five folds), which is due to the small size of the dataset. While this rate is comparable to another Bengali POS dataset described in Dandapat et al. (2007), it is much higher than the 2.6% unknown word rate in the test set for Ratnaparkhi's (1996) English POS tagging experiments.

Creating training instances Following previous work on POS tagging, we create one training instance for each word in the training set. The class value of an instance is the POS tag of the corresponding word. Each instance is represented by a set of linguistic features, as described next.

Features Our feature set consists of (1) *baseline* features motivated by those used in Dandapat *et al.*'s (2007) Bengali POS tagger and Singh *et al.*'s (2006) Hindi POS tagger, as well as (2) features derived from our induced affixes and the Wikipedia-induced list. More specifically, the baseline feature set has (1) word unigrams, bigrams and trigrams; (2) pseudo-affix features that are created by taking the first three characters and the last three characters of the current word; and (3) a binary feature that determines whether the current word is a number. As far as our new features are concerned, we create one induced prefix feature and one induced suffix feature from both the current word and the previous word, as well as two bigrams involving induced prefixes and induced suffixes. We also create three WIKI features, including the Wikipedia-induced NE tag of the current word and that of the previous word, as well as the combination of these two tags. Note that the Wikipedia-induced tag of a word can be obtained by annotating the test sentence under consideration using the list generated from the Bengali Wikipedia (see Section 4). To make the description of these features more concrete, we show the feature templates in Table 2.

Learning algorithm We used CRF++[8], a C++ implementation of conditional random fields (Lafferty et al., 2001), as our learning algorithm for training a POS tagging model.

Evaluating the model To evaluate the resulting POS tagger, we generate test instances in the same way as the training instances. 5-fold CV results of the POS tagger are shown in Table 3. Each row consists of three numbers: the overall accuracy, as well as the accuracies on the seen and the unseen words. Row 1 shows the accuracy when the baseline feature set is used; row 2 shows the accuracy when the baseline feature set is augmented with our two induced affix features; and the last row shows the results when both the induced affix and the WIKI features are incorporated into the baseline feature set. Perhaps not surprisingly, (1) adding more features improves performance, and (2) accuracies on the seen words are substantially better than those on the unseen words. In fact, adding the induced affixes to the baseline feature set yields a 7.8% reduction in relative error in overall accuracy. We also applied a two-tailed paired t-test ($p < 0.01$), first to the overall accura-

[7]A detailed description of these POS tags can be found in http://shiva.iiit.ac.in/SPSAL2007/iiit_tagset_guidelines.pdf, and are omitted here due to space limitations. This tagset and the Penn Treebank tagset differ in that (1) nouns do not have a number feature; (2) verbs do not have a tense feature; and (3) adjectives and adverbs are not subcategorized.

[8]Available from http://crfpp.sourceforge.net

Experiment	Overall	Seen	Unseen
Baseline	89.83	92.96	72.08
Baseline+Induced Affixes	90.57	93.39	74.64
Baseline+Induced Affixes+Wiki	**90.80**	93.50	75.58

Table 3: 5-fold cross-validation accuracies for POS tagging

Predicted Tag	Correct Tag	% of Error
NN	NNP	22.7
NN	JJ	9.6
JJ	NN	7.4
NNP	NN	5.0
NN	VM	4.9

Table 4: Most frequent errors for POS tagging

cies in rows 1 and 2, and then to the overall accuracies in rows 2 and 3. Both pairs of numbers are statistically significantly different from each other, meaning that incorporating the two induced affix features and then the WIKI features both yields significant improvements.

Error analysis To better understand the results, we examined the errors made by the tagger. The most frequent errors are shown in Table 4. From the table, we see that the largest source of errors arises from mislabeling proper nouns as common nouns. This should be expected, as proper noun identification is difficult due to the lack of capitalization information. Unfortunately, failure to identify proper nouns could severely limit the recall of an NE recognizer. Also, adjectives and common nouns are difficult to distinguish, since these two syntactic categories are morphologically and distributionally similar to each other. Finally, many errors appear to involve mislabeling a word as a common noun. The reason is that there is a larger percentage of common nouns (almost 30%) in the training set than other POS tags, thus causing the model to prefer tagging a word as a common noun.

6 Named Entity Recognition

In this section, we show how to train and evaluate our NE recognizer. The recognizer adopts a traditional architecture, assuming that POS tagging is performed prior to NER. In other words, the NE recognizer will use the POS acquired in Section 5 as one of its features. As in Section 5, we will focus on examining how our knowledge sources (the induced affixes and the WIKI features) impact the performance of our recognizer.

Corpus The corpus we used for NER evaluation is the same as the one described in the previous section. Specifically, in addition to POS information, each sentence in the corpus is annotated with NE information. We focus on recognizing the three major NE types in this paper, namely persons (PER), organizations (ORG), and locations (LOC). There are 1721 PERs, 104 ORGs, and 686 LOCs in the corpus. As far as evaluation is concerned, we conduct 5-fold CV experiments, dividing the corpus into the same five folds as in POS tagging.

POS of current word	t_i
POS of previous word	t_{i-1}
POS of 2nd previous word	t_{i-2}
POS of next word	t_{i+1}
POS of 2nd next word	t_{i+2}
POS bigrams	$t_{i-2}t_{i-1}$, $t_{i-1}t_i$, t_it_{i+1}, $t_{i+1}t_{i+2}$
First word	fw_i

Table 5: Additional feature templates for the NER experiments

Creating training instances We view NE recognition as a sequence labeling problem. In other words, we combine NE identification and classification into one step, labeling each word in a test text with its NE tag. Any word that does not belong to one of our three NE tags will be labeled as OTHERS. We adopt the IOB convention, preceding an NE tag with a B if the word is the first word of an NE and an I otherwise. Now, to train the NE recognizer, we create one training instance from each word in a training text. The class value of an instance is the NE tag of the corresponding word, or OTHERS if the word is not part of an NE. Each instance is represented by a set of linguistic features, as described next.

Features Our feature set consists of (1) *baseline* features motivated by those used in Ekbal *et al.*'s (2008) Bengali NE recognizer, as well as (2) features derived from our induced affixes and the Wikipedia-induced list. More specifically, the baseline feature set has (1) word unigrams; (2) pseudo-affix features that are created by taking the first three characters and the last three characters of the current word; (3) a binary feature that determines whether the current word is the first word of a sentence; and (4) a set of POS-related features, including the POS of the current word and its surrounding words, as well as POS bigrams formed from the current and surrounding words. Our induced affixes and WIKI features are incorporated into the baseline NE feature set in the same manner as in POS tagging. In essence, the feature tem-

Experiment	R	P	F
Baseline	60.97	74.46	67.05
Person	66.18	74.06	69.90
Organization	29.81	44.93	35.84
Location	52.62	80.40	63.61
Baseline+Induced Affixes	60.45	73.30	66.26
Person	65.70	72.61	69.02
Organization	31.73	46.48	37.71
Location	51.46	80.05	62.64
Baseline+Induced Affixes+Wiki	63.24	75.19	**68.70**
Person	66.47	75.16	70.55
Organization	30.77	43.84	36.16
Location	60.06	79.69	68.50

Table 6: 5-fold cross-validation results for NER

plates employed by the NE recognizer are the top 12 templates in Table 2 and those in Table 5.

Learning algorithm We again use CRF++ as our sequence learner for acquiring the recognizer.

Evaluating the model To evaluate the resulting NE tagger, we generate test instances in the same way as the training instances. To score the output of the recognizer, we use the CoNLL-2000 scoring program[9], which reports performance in terms of recall (R), precision (P), and F-measure (F). All NE results shown in Table 6 are averages of the 5-fold CV experiments. The first block of the Table 6 shows the overall results when the baseline feature set is used; in addition, we also show results for each of the three NE tags. As we can see, the baseline achieves an F-measure of 67.05. The second block shows the results when the baseline feature set is augmented with our two induced affix features. Somewhat unexpectedly, F-measure drops by 0.8% in comparison to the baseline. Additional experiments are needed to determine the reason. Finally, when the WIKI features are incorporated into the augmented feature set, the system achieves an F-measure of 68.70 (see the third block), representing a statistically significant increase of 1.6% in F-measure over the baseline. As we can see, improvements stem primarily from dramatic gains in recall for locations.

Discussions Several points deserve mentioning. First, the model performs poorly on the ORGs, owing to the small number of organization names in the corpus. Worse still, the recall drops after adding the WIKI features. We examined the list of induced ORG names and found that it is fairly noisy. This can be attributed in part to the difficulty in forming a set of seed words that can extract ORGs with high precision (e.g., the ORG seed "situate" extracted many LOCs). Second, using the WIKI features does not help recalling the PERs. A closer examination of the corpus reveals the reason: many sentences describe fictitious characters, whereas Wikipedia would be most useful for articles that describe famous people. Overall, while the WIKI features provide our recognizer with a small, but significant, improvement, the usefulness of the Bengali Wikipedia is currently limited by its small size. Nevertheless, we believe the Bengali Wikipedia will become a useful resource for language processing as its size increases.

[9]http://www.cnts.ua.ac.be/conll2000/chunking/conlleval.txt

7 A Joint Model for POS Tagging and NER

The NE recognizer described thus far has adopted a pipelined architecture, and hence its performance could be limited by the errors of the POS tagger. In fact, as discussed before, the major source of errors made by our POS tagger concerns the confusion between proper nouns and common nouns, and this type of error, when propagated to the NE recognizer, could severely limit its recall. Also, there is strong empirical support for this argument: the NE recognizers, when given access to the correct POS tags, have F-scores ranging from 76-79%, which are 10% higher on average than those with POS tags that were automatically computed. Consequently, we hypothesize that modeling POS tagging and NER jointly would yield better performance than learning the two tasks separately. In fact, many approaches have been developed to jointly model POS tagging and noun phrase chunking, including transformation-based learning (Ngai and Florian, 2001), factorial HMMs (Duh, 2005), and dynamic CRFs (Sutton et al., 2007). Some of these approaches are fairly sophisticated and also require intensive computations during inference. For instance, when jointly modeling POS tagging and chunking, Sutton et al. (2007) reduce the number of POS tags from 45 to 5 when training a factorial dynamic CRF on a small dataset (with only 209 sentences) in order to reduce training and inference time.

In contrast, we propose a relatively simple model for jointly learning Bengali POS tagging and NER, by exploiting the limited dependencies between the two tasks. Specifically, we make the observation that most of the Bengali words that are part of an NE are also proper nouns. In fact, based on statistics collected from our evaluation corpus (see Sections 5 and 6), this observation is correct

Experiment	R	P	F
Baseline	54.76	81.70	65.57
Baseline+Induced Affixes	56.79	88.96	69.32
Baseline+Induced Affixes+Wiki	61.73	86.35	**71.99**

Table 7: 5-fold cross-validation joint modeling results for NER

97.3% of the time. Note, however, that this observation does not hold for English, since many prepositions and determiners are part of an NE. On the other hand, this observation largely holds for Bengali because prepositions and determiners are typically realized as noun suffixes.

This limited dependency between the POS tags and the NE tags allows us to develop a simple model for jointly learning the two tasks. More specifically, we will use CRF++ to learn the joint model. Training and test instances are generated as described in the previous two subsections (i.e., one instance per word). The feature set will consist of the union of the features that were used to train the POS tagger and the NE tagger independently, minus the POS-related features that were used in the NE tagger. The class value of an instance is computed as follows. If a word is not a proper noun, its class is simply its POS tag. Otherwise, its class is its NE tag, which can be PER, ORG, LOC, or OTHERS. In other words, our joint model exploits the observation that we made earlier in the section by assuming that only proper nouns can be part of a named entity. This allows us to train a joint model without substantially increasing the number of classes.

We again evaluate our joint model using 5-fold CV experiments. The NE results of the model are shown in Table 7. The rows here can be interpreted in the same manner as those in Table 6. Comparing these three experiments with their counterparts in Table 6, we can see that, except for the baseline, jointly modeling offers a significant improvement of 3.3% in overall F-measure.[10] In particular, the joint model benefits significantly from our two knowledge sources, achieving an F-measure of 71.99% when both of them are incorporated.

Finally, to better understand the value of the induced affix features in the joint model as well as the pipelined model described in Section 6, we conducted an ablation experiment, in which we incorporated only the WIKI features into the baseline feature set. With pipelined modeling, the F-measure for NER is 68.87%, which is similar to the case where both induced affixes and the WIKI features are used. With joint modeling, however, the F-measure for NER is 70.87%, which is 1% lower than the best joint modeling score. These results provide suggestive evidence that the induced affix features play a significant role in the improved performance of the joint model.

8 Conclusions

We have explored two types of linguistic features, namely the induced affix features and the Wikipedia-related features, to improve a Bengali POS tagger and NE recognizer. Our experimental results have demonstrated that (1) both types of features significantly improve a baseline POS tagger and (2) the Wikipedia-related features significantly improve a baseline NE recognizer. Moreover, by exploiting the limited dependencies between Bengali POS tags and NE tags, we proposed a new model for jointly learning the two tasks, which not only avoids the error-propagation problem present in the pipelined system architecture, but also yields statistically significant improvements over the NE recognizer that is trained independently of the POS tagger. When applied in combination, our three extensions contributed to a relative improvement of 7.5% in F-measure over the baseline NE recognizer. Most importantly, we believe that these extensions are of relevance and interest to the EACL community because many European and Middle Eastern languages resemble Bengali in terms of not only their morphological richness but also their scarcity of annotated corpora. We plan to empirically verify our belief in future work.

Acknowledgments

We thank the three anonymous reviewers for their invaluable comments on the paper. We also thank CRBLP, BRAC University, Bangladesh, for providing us with Bengali resources. This work was supported in part by NSF Grant IIS-0812261.

[10]The POS tagging results are not shown due to space limitations. Overall, the POS accuracies drop insignificantly as a result of joint modeling, for the following reason. Recall from Section 5 that the major source of POS tagging errors arises from the mislabeling of many proper nouns as common nouns, due primarily to the large number of common nouns in the corpus. The joint model aggravates this problem by subcategorizing the proper nouns into different NE classes, causing the tagger to have an even stronger bias towards labeling a proper noun as a common noun than before. Nevertheless, as seen from the results in Tables 6 and 7, such a bias has yielded an increase in NER precision.

References

Avrim Blum and Tom Mitchell. 1998. Combining labeled and unlabeled data with co-training. In *Proceedings of COLT*, pages 92–100.

Razvan Bunescu and Marius Paşca. 2006. Using encyclopedic knowledge for named entity disambiguation. In *Proceedings of EACL*, pages 9–16.

Alexander Clark. 2003. Combining distributional and morphological information for part-of-speech induction. In *Proceedings of EACL*, pages 59–66.

Michael Collins and Yoram Singer. 1999. Unsupervised models for named entity classification. In *Proceedings of EMNLP/VLC*, pages 100–110.

Silviu Cucerzan and David Yarowsky. 1999. Language independent named entity recognition combining morphological and contextual evidence. In *Proceedings of EMNLP/VLC*, pages 90–99.

Silviu Cucerzan. 2007. Large-scale named entity disambiguation based on Wikipedia data. In *Proceedings of EMNLP-CoNLL*, pages 708–716.

Sandipan Dandapat, Sudeshna Sarkar, and Anupam Basu. 2007. Automatic part-of-speech tagging for Bengali: An approach for morphologically rich languages in a poor resource scenario. In *Proceedings of the ACL Companion Volume*, pages 221–224.

Kevin Duh. 2005. Jointly labeling multiple sequences: A factorial HMM approach. In *Proceedings of the ACL Student Research Workshop*, pages 19–24.

Asif Ekbal, Rejwanul Haque, and Sivaji Bandyopadhyay. 2008. Named entity recognition in Bengali: A conditional random field approach. In *Proceedings of IJCNLP*, pages 589–594.

John Goldsmith. 2001. Unsupervised learning of the morphology of a natural language. *Computational Linguistics*, 27(2):153–198.

Sharon Goldwater and Thomas L. Griffiths. 2007. A fully Bayesian approach to unsupervised part-of-speech tagging. In *Proceedings of the ACL*, pages 744–751.

Aria Haghighi and Dan Klein. 2006. Prototype-driven learning for sequence models. In *Proceedings of HLT-NAACL*, pages 320–327.

Jun'ichi Kazama and Kentaro Torisawa. 2007. Exploiting Wikipedia as external knowledge for named entity recognition. In *Proceedings of EMNLP-CoNLL*, pages 698–707.

Samarth Keshava and Emily Pitler. 2006. A simpler, intuitive approach to morpheme induction. In *PASCAL Challenge Workshop on Unsupervised Segmentation of Words into Morphemes*.

Zornitsa Kozareva. 2006. Bootstrapping named entity recognition with automatically generated gazetteer lists. In *Proceedings of the EACL Student Research Workshop*, pages 15–22.

John D. Lafferty, Andrew McCallum, and Fernando C. N. Pereira. 2001. Conditional random fields: Probabilistic models for segmenting and labeling sequence data. In *Proceedings of ICML*, pages 282–289.

Andrei Mikheev, Marc Moens, and Claire Grover. 1999. Named entity recognition without gazetteers. In *Proceedings of EACL*, pages 1–8.

Grace Ngai and Radu Florian. 2001. Transformation based learning in the fast lane. In *Proceedings of NAACL*, pages 40–47.

Simone Paolo Ponzetto and Michael Strube. 2007a. Deriving a large scale taxonomy from wikipedia. In *Proceedings of AAAI*, pages 1440–1445.

Simone Paolo Ponzetto and Michael Strube. 2007b. Knowledge derived from Wikipedia for computing semantic relatedness. *Journal of Artificial Intelligence Research*, 30:181–212.

Adwait Ratnaparkhi. 1996. A maximum entropy model for part-of-speech tagging. In *Proceedings of EMNLP*, pages 133–142.

Hinrich Schütze. 1995. Distributional part-of-speech tagging. In *Proceedings of EACL*, pages 141–148.

Smriti Singh, Kuhoo Gupta, Manish Shrivastava, and Pushpak Bhattacharyya. 2006. Morphological richness offsets resource demand — Experiences in constructing a POS tagger for Hindi. In *Proceedings of the COLING/ACL 2006 Main Conference Poster Sessions*, pages 779–786.

Charles Sutton, Andrew McCallum, and Khashayar Rohanimanesh. 2007. Dynamic conditional random fields: Factorized probabilistic models for labeling and segmenting sequence data. *Journal of Machine Learning Research*, 8:693–723.

Yotaro Watanabe, Masayuki Asahara, and Yuji Matsumoto. 2007. A graph-based approach to named entity categorization in Wikipedia using conditional random fields. In *Proceedings of EMNLP-CoNLL*, pages 649–657.

Weakly Supervised Part-of-Speech Tagging for Morphologically-Rich, Resource-Scarce Languages

Kazi Saidul Hasan and **Vincent Ng**
Human Language Technology Research Institute
University of Texas at Dallas
Richardson, TX 75083-0688
{saidul,vince}@hlt.utdallas.edu

Abstract

This paper examines unsupervised approaches to part-of-speech (POS) tagging for morphologically-rich, resource-scarce languages, with an emphasis on Goldwater and Griffiths's (2007) fully-Bayesian approach originally developed for English POS tagging. We argue that existing unsupervised POS taggers unrealistically assume as input a perfect POS lexicon, and consequently, we propose a weakly supervised fully-Bayesian approach to POS tagging, which relaxes the unrealistic assumption by automatically acquiring the lexicon from a small amount of POS-tagged data. Since such relaxation comes at the expense of a drop in tagging accuracy, we propose two extensions to the Bayesian framework and demonstrate that they are effective in improving a fully-Bayesian POS tagger for Bengali, our representative morphologically-rich, resource-scarce language.

1 Introduction

Unsupervised POS tagging requires neither manual encoding of tagging heuristics nor the availability of data labeled with POS information. Rather, an unsupervised POS tagger operates by only assuming as input a POS lexicon, which consists of a list of possible POS tags for each word. As we can see from the partial POS lexicon for English in Figure 1, "the" is *unambiguous* with respect to POS tagging, since it can only be a determiner (DT), whereas "sting" is *ambiguous*, since it can be a common noun (NN), a proper noun (NNP) or a verb (VB). In other words, the lexicon imposes constraints on the possible POS tags of each word, and such constraints are then used by an unsupervised tagger to label a new sentence. Conceivably, tagging accuracy decreases with the increase in ambiguity: unambiguous words such as "the" will always be tagged correctly; on the other hand, *unseen* words (or words not present in the POS lexicon) are among the most ambiguous words, since they are not constrained at all and therefore can receive any of the POS tags. Hence, unsupervised POS tagging can present significant challenges to natural language processing researchers, especially when a large fraction of the words are ambiguous. Nevertheless, the development of unsupervised taggers potentially allows POS tagging technologies to be applied to a substantially larger number of natural languages, most of which are resource-scarce and, in particular, have little or no POS-tagged data.

Word	POS tag(s)
...	...
running	NN, JJ
sting	NN, NNP, VB
the	DT
...	...

Figure 1: A partial lexicon for English

The most common approach to unsupervised POS tagging to date has been to train a hidden Markov model (HMM) in an unsupervised manner to maximize the likelihood of an unannotated corpus, using a special instance of the expectation-maximization (EM) algorithm (Dempster et al., 1977) known as Baum-Welch (Baum, 1972). More recently, a fully-Bayesian approach to unsupervised POS tagging has been developed by Goldwater and Griffiths (2007) [henceforth G&G] as a viable alternative to the traditional maximum-likelihood-based HMM approach. While unsupervised POS taggers adopting both approaches have

Proceedings of the 12th Conference of the European Chapter of the ACL, pages 363–371,
Athens, Greece, 30 March – 3 April 2009.

demonstrated promising results, it is important to note that they are typically evaluated by assuming the availability of a *perfect* POS lexicon. This assumption, however, is fairly unrealistic in practice, as a perfect POS lexicon can only be constructed by having a linguist manually label each word in a language with its possible POS tags.[1] In other words, the labor-intensive POS lexicon construction process renders unsupervised POS taggers a lot less unsupervised than they appear. To make these unsupervised taggers practical, one could attempt to automatically construct a POS lexicon, a task commonly known as *POS induction*. However, POS induction is by no means an easy task, and it is not clear how well unsupervised POS taggers work when used in combination with an automatically constructed POS lexicon.

The goals of this paper are three-fold. First, motivated by the successes of unsupervised approaches to English POS tagging, we aim to investigate whether such approaches, especially G&G's fully-Bayesian approach, can deliver similar performance for Bengali, our representative resource-scarce language. Second, to relax the unrealistic assumption of employing a perfect lexicon as in existing unsupervised POS taggers, we propose a *weakly supervised* fully-Bayesian approach to POS tagging, where we automatically construct a POS lexicon from a small amount of POS-tagged data. Hence, unlike a perfect POS lexicon, our automatically constructed lexicon is necessarily *incomplete*, yielding a large number of words that are completely ambiguous. The high ambiguity rate inherent in our weakly supervised approach substantially complicates the POS tagging process. Consequently, our third goal of this paper is to propose two potentially performance-enhancing extensions to G&G's Bayesian POS tagging approach, which exploit morphology and techniques successfully used in supervised POS tagging.

The rest of the paper is organized as follows. Section 2 presents related work on unsupervised approaches to POS tagging. Section 3 gives an introduction to G&G's fully-Bayesian approach to unsupervised POS tagging. In Section 4, we describe our two extensions to G&G's approach. Section 5 presents experimental results on Bengali POS tagging, focusing on evaluating the effectiveness of our two extensions in improving G&G's approach. Finally, we conclude in Section 6.

2 Related Work

With the notable exception of Synder et al.'s (2008; 2009) recent work on unsupervised multilingual POS tagging, existing approaches to unsupervised POS tagging have been developed and tested primarily on English data. For instance, Merialdo (1994) uses maximum likelihood estimation to train a trigram HMM. Schütze (1995) and Clark (2000) apply syntactic clustering and dimensionality reduction in a knowledge-free setting to obtain meaningful clusters. Haghighi and Klein (2006) develop a prototype-driven approach, which requires just a few prototype examples for each POS tag and exploits these labeled words to constrain the labels of their distributionally similar words. Smith and Eisner (2005) train an unsupervised POS tagger using contrastive estimation, which seeks to move probability mass to a positive example *e* from its neighbors (i.e., negative examples are created by perturbing *e*). Wang and Schuurmans (2005) improve an unsupervised HMM-based tagger by constraining the learned structure to maintain appropriate marginal tag probabilities and using word similarities to smooth the lexical parameters.

As mentioned before, Goldwater and Griffiths (2007) have recently proposed an unsupervised fully-Bayesian POS tagging framework that operates by integrating over the possible parameter values instead of fixing a set of parameter values for unsupervised sequence learning. Importantly, this Bayesian approach facilitates the incorporation of sparse priors that result in a more practical distribution of tokens to lexical categories (Johnson, 2007). Similar to Goldwater and Griffiths (2007) and Johnson (2007), Toutanova and Johnson (2007) also use Bayesian inference for POS tagging. However, their work departs from existing Bayesian approaches to POS tagging in that they (1) introduce a new sparse prior on the distribution over tags for each word, (2) extend the Latent Dirichlet Allocation model, and (3) explicitly model ambiguity class. While their tagging model, like Goldwater and Griffiths's, assumes as input an incomplete POS lexicon and a large unlabeled corpus, they consider their approach "semi-supervised" simply because of the human knowledge involved in constructing the POS lexicon.

[1]When evaluating an unsupervised POS tagger, researchers typically construct a *pseudo-perfect* POS lexicon by collecting the possible POS tags of a word directly from the corpus on which the tagger is to be evaluated.

3 A Fully Bayesian Approach

3.1 Motivation

As mentioned in the introduction, the most common approach to unsupervised POS tagging is to train an HMM on an unannotated corpus using the Baum-Welch algorithm so that the likelihood of the corpus is maximized. To understand what the HMM parameters are, let us revisit how an HMM simultaneously generates an output sequence $\mathbf{w} = (w_0, w_1, ..., w_n)$ and the associated hidden state sequence $\mathbf{t} = (t_0, t_1, ..., t_n)$. In the context of POS tagging, each state of the HMM corresponds to a POS tag, the output sequence **w** is the given word sequence, and the hidden state sequence **t** is the associated POS tag sequence. To generate **w** and **t**, the HMM begins by guessing a state t_0 and then emitting w_0 from t_0 according to a state-specific output distribution over word tokens. After that, we move to the next state t_1, the choice of which is based on t_0's transition distribution, and emit w_1 according to t_1's output distribution. This generation process repeats until the end of the word sequence is reached. In other words, the parameters of an HMM, θ, are composed of a set of state-specific (1) output distributions (over word tokens) and (2) transition distributions, both of which can be learned using the EM algorithm. Once learning is complete, we can use the resulting set of parameters to find the most likely hidden state sequence given a word sequence using the Viterbi algorithm.

Nevertheless, EM sometimes fails to find good parameter values.[2] The reason is that EM tries to assign roughly the same number of word tokens to each of the hidden states (Johnson, 2007). In practice, however, the distribution of word tokens to POS tags is highly skewed (i.e., some POS categories are more populated with tokens than others). This motivates a fully-Bayesian approach, which, rather than committing to a particular set of parameter values as in an EM-based approach, integrates over all possible values of θ and, most importantly, allows the use of priors to favor the learning of the skewed distributions, through the use of the term $P(\theta|\mathbf{w})$ in the following equation:

$$P(\mathbf{t}|\mathbf{w}) = \int P(\mathbf{t}|\mathbf{w}, \theta)P(\theta|\mathbf{w})d\theta \qquad (1)$$

The question, then, is: which priors on θ would allow the acquisition of skewed distributions? To answer this question, recall that in POS tagging, θ is composed of a set of tag transition distributions and output distributions. Each such distribution is a multinomial (i.e., each trial produces exactly one of some finite number of possible outcomes). For a multinomial with K outcomes, a K-dimensional Dirichlet distribution, which is conjugate to the multinomial, is a natural choice of prior. For simplicity, we assume that a distribution in θ is drawn from a symmetric Dirichlet with a certain hyperparameter (see Teh et al. (2006) for details).

The value of a hyperparameter, α, affects the skewness of the resulting distribution, as it assigns different probabilities to different distributions. For instance, when $\alpha < 1$, higher probabilities are assigned to *sparse* multinomials (i.e., multinomials in which only a few entries are nonzero). Intuitively, the tag transition distributions and the output distributions in an HMM-based POS tagger are sparse multinomials. As a result, it is logical to choose a Dirichlet prior with $\alpha < 1$. By integrating over all possible parameter values, the probability that i-th outcome, y_i, takes the value k, given the previous $i-1$ outcomes $\mathbf{y}_{-i} = (y_1, y_2, ..., y_{i-1})$, is

$$P(k|\mathbf{y}_{-i}, \alpha) = \int P(k|\theta)P(\theta|\mathbf{y}_{-i}, \alpha)d\theta \qquad (2)$$

$$= \frac{n_k + \alpha}{i - 1 + K\alpha} \qquad (3)$$

where n_k is the frequency of k in $\mathbf{y}_{-i}$. See MacKay and Peto (1995) for the derivation.

3.2 Model

Our baseline POS tagging model is a standard trigram HMM with tag transition distributions and output distributions, each of which is a sparse multinomial that is learned by applying a symmetric Dirichlet prior:

$$\begin{aligned} t_i \mid t_{i-1}, t_{i-2}, \tau^{(t_{i-1}, t_{i-2})} &\sim \text{Mult}(\tau^{(t_{i-1}, t_{i-2})}) \\ w_i \mid t_i, \omega^{(t_i)} &\sim \text{Mult}(\omega^{(t_i)}) \\ \tau^{(t_{i-1}, t_{i-2})} \mid \alpha &\sim \text{Dirichlet}(\alpha) \\ \omega^{(t_i)} \mid \beta &\sim \text{Dirichlet}(\beta) \end{aligned}$$

where w_i and t_i denote the i-th word and tag. With a tagset of size T (including a special tag used as sentence delimiter), each of the tag transition distributions has T components. For the output symbols, each of the $\omega^{(t_i)}$ has W_{t_i} components, where W_{t_i} denotes the number of word types that can be emitted from the state corresponding to t_i.

[2]When given good parameter initializations, however, EM can find good parameter values for an HMM-based POS tagger. See Goldberg et al. (2008) for details.

From the closed form in Equation 3, given previous outcomes, we can compute the tag transition and output probabilities of the model as follows:

$$P(t_i|\mathbf{t}_{-i},\alpha) = \frac{n_{(t_{i-2},t_{i-1},t_i)} + \alpha}{n_{(t_{i-2},t_{i-1})} + T\alpha} \quad (4)$$

$$P(w_i|t_i,\mathbf{t}_{-i},\mathbf{w}_{-i},\beta) = \frac{n_{(t_i,w_i)} + \beta}{n_{t_i} + W_{t_i}\beta} \quad (5)$$

where $n_{(t_{i-2},t_{i-1},t_i)}$ and $n_{(t_i,w_i)}$ are the frequencies of observing the tag trigram (t_{i-2},t_{i-1},t_i) and the tag-word pair (t_i,w_i), respectively. These counts are taken from the $i-1$ tags and words generated previously. The inference procedure described next exploits the property that trigrams (and outputs) are *exchangeable*; that is, the probability of a set of trigrams (and outputs) does not depend on the order in which it was generated.

3.3 Inference Procedure

We perform inference using Gibbs sampling (Geman and Geman, 1984), using the following posterior distribution to generate samples:

$$P(\mathbf{t}|\mathbf{w},\alpha,\beta) \propto P(\mathbf{w}|\mathbf{t},\beta)P(\mathbf{t}|\alpha)$$

Starting with a random assignment of a POS tag to each word (subject to the constraints in the POS lexicon), we resample each POS tag, t_i, according to the conditional distribution shown in Figure 2. Note that the current counts of other trigrams and outputs can be used as "previous" observations due to the property of exchangeability.

Following G&G, we use simulated annealing to find the MAP tag sequence. The temperature decreases by a factor of $\exp(\frac{\log(\frac{\theta_2}{\theta_1})}{N-1})$ after each iteration, where θ_1 is the initial temperature and θ_2 is the temperature after N sampling iterations.

4 Two Extensions

In this section, we present two extensions to G&G's fully-Bayesian framework to unsupervised POS tagging, namely, induced suffix emission and discriminative prediction.

4.1 Induced Suffix Emission

For morphologically-rich languages like Bengali, a lot of grammatical information (e.g., POS) is expressed via suffixes. In fact, several approaches to unsupervised POS induction for morphologically-rich languages have exploited the observation that some suffixes can only be associated with a small number of POS tags (e.g., Clark (2003), Dasgupta and Ng (2007)). To exploit suffixes in HMM-based POS tagging, one can (1) convert the word-based POS lexicon to a *suffix-based POS lexicon*, which lists the possible POS tags for each suffix; and then (2) have the HMM emit suffixes rather than words, subject to the constraints in the suffix-based POS lexicon. Such a suffix-based HMM, however, may suffer from over-generalization. To prevent over-generalization and at the same time exploit suffixes, we propose as our first extension to G&G's framework a hybrid approach to word/suffix emission: a word is emitted if it is present in the word-based POS lexicon; otherwise, its suffix is emitted. In other words, our approach imposes suffix-based constraints on the tagging of words that are unseen w.r.t. the word-based POS lexicon. Below we show how to induce the suffix of a word and create the suffix-based POS lexicon.

Inducing suffixes To induce suffixes, we rely on Keshava and Pitler's (2006) method. Assume that (1) V is a vocabulary (i.e., a set of distinct words) extracted from a large, unannotated corpus, (2) C_1 and C_2 are two character sequences, and (3) C_1C_2 is the concatenation of C_1 and C_2. If C_1C_2 and C_1 are found in V, we extract C_2 as a suffix.

However, this unsupervised suffix induction method is arguably overly simplistic and hence many of the induced affixes could be spurious. To identify suffixes that are likely to be correct, we employ a simple procedure: we (1) score each suffix by multiplying its *frequency* (i.e., the number of distinct words in V to which each suffix attaches) and its *length*[3], and (2) select only those whose score is above a certain threshold. In our experiments, we set this threshold to 50, and generate our vocabulary from five years of articles taken from the Bengali newspaper *Prothom Alo*. This enables us to induce 975 suffixes.

Constructing a suffix-based POS lexicon Next, we construct a suffix-based POS lexicon. For each word w in the original word-based POS lexicon, we (1) use the induced suffix list obtained in the previous step to identify the longest-matching suffix of w, and then (2) assign all the POS tags associated with w to this suffix.

Incorporating suffix-based output distributions Finally, we extend our trigram model by introduc-

[3]The dependence on frequency and length is motivated by the observation that less frequent and shorter affixes are more likely to be erroneous (see Goldsmith (2001)).

$$P(t_i|\mathbf{t}_{-i}, \mathbf{w}, \alpha, \beta) \propto \frac{n_{(t_i,w_i)} + \beta}{n_{t_i} + W_{t_i}\beta} \cdot \frac{n_{(t_{i-2},t_{i-1},t_i)} + \alpha}{n_{(t_{i-2},t_{i-1})} + T\alpha} \cdot \frac{n_{(t_{i-1},t_i,t_{i+1})} + I(t_{i-2} = t_{i-1} = t_i = t_{i+1}) + \alpha}{n_{(t_{i-1},t_i)} + I(t_{i-2} = t_{i-1} = t_i) + T\alpha} \cdot \frac{n_{(t_i,t_{i+1},t_{i+2})} + I(t_{i-2} = t_i = t_{i+2}, t_{i-1} = t_{i+1}) + I(t_{i-1} = t_i = t_{i+1} = t_{i+2}) + \alpha}{n_{(t_i,t_{i+1})} + I(t_{i-2} = t_i, t_{i-1} = t_{i+1}) + I(t_{i-1} = t_i = t_{i+1}) + T\alpha}$$

Figure 2: The sampling distribution for t_i (taken directly from Goldwater and Griffiths (2007)). All n_x values are computed from the current values of all tags except for t_i. Here, $I(arg)$ is a function that returns 1 if arg is true and 0 otherwise, and $\mathbf{t}_{-i}$ refers to the current values of all tags except for t_i.

ing a state-specific probability distribution over induced suffixes. Specifically, if the current word is present in the word-based POS lexicon, or if we cannot find any suffix for the word using the induced suffix list, then we emit the word. Otherwise, we emit its suffix according to a suffix-based output distribution, which is drawn from a symmetric Dirichlet with hyperparameter γ:

$$\begin{aligned} s_i \mid t_i, \sigma^{(t_i)} &\sim \text{Mult}(\sigma^{(t_i)}) \\ \sigma^{(t_i)} \mid \gamma &\sim \text{Dirichlet}(\gamma) \end{aligned}$$

where s_i denotes the induced suffix of the i-th word. The distribution, $\sigma^{(t_i)}$, has S_{t_i} components, where S_{t_i} denotes the number of induced suffixes that can be emitted from the state corresponding to t_i. We compute the induced suffix emission probabilities of the model as follows:

$$P(s_i|t_i, \mathbf{t}_{-i}, \mathbf{s}_{-i}, \gamma) = \frac{n_{(t_i,s_i)} + \gamma}{n_{t_i} + S_{t_i}\gamma} \quad (6)$$

where $n_{(t_i,s_i)}$ is the frequency of observing the tag-suffix pair (t_i, s_i).

This extension requires that we slightly modify the inference procedure. Specifically, if the current word is unseen (w.r.t. the word-based POS lexicon) and has a suffix (according to the induced suffix list), then we sample from a distribution that is almost identical to the one shown in Figure 2, except that we replace the first fraction (i.e., the fraction involving the emission counts) with the one shown in Equation (6). Otherwise, we simply sample from the distribution in Figure 2.

4.2 Discriminative Prediction

As mentioned in the introduction, the (word-based) POS lexicons used in existing approaches to unsupervised POS tagging were created somewhat unrealistically by collecting the possible POS tags of a word directly from the corpus on which the tagger is to be evaluated. To make the lexicon formation process more realistic, we propose a *weakly supervised* approach to Bayesian POS tagging, in which we *automatically* create the word-based POS lexicon from a small set of POS-tagged sentences that is disjoint from the test data. Adopting a weakly supervised approach has an additional advantage: the presence of POS-tagged sentences makes it possible to exploit techniques developed for supervised POS tagging, which is the idea behind discriminative prediction, our second extension to G&G's framework.

Given a small set of POS-tagged sentences L, discriminative prediction uses the statistics collected from L to predict the POS of a word in a discriminative fashion whenever possible. More specifically, discriminative prediction relies on two simple ideas typically exploited by supervised POS tagging algorithms: (1) if the target word (i.e., the word whose POS tag is to be predicted) appears in L, we can label the word with its POS tag in L; and (2) if the target word does not appear in L but its context does, we can use its context to predict its POS tag. In bigram and trigram POS taggers, the context of a word is represented using the preceding one or two words. Nevertheless, since L is typically small in a weakly supervised setting, it is common for a target word not to satisfy any of the two conditions above. Hence, if it is not possible to predict a target word in a discriminative fashion (due to the limited size of L), we resort to the sampling equation in Figure 2.

To incorporate the above discriminative decision steps into G&G's fully-Bayesian framework for POS tagging, the algorithm estimates three types of probability distributions from L. First, to capture context, it computes (1) a distribution over the POS tags following a word bigram, (w_{i-2}, w_{i-1}), that appears in L [henceforth $D_1(w_{i-2}, w_{i-1})$] and (2) a distribution over the POS tags following a word unigram, w_{i-1}, that appears in L [henceforth $D_2(w_{i-1})$]. Then, to cap-

Algorithm 1 Algorithm for incorporating discriminative prediction

Input: w_i: current word
w_{i-1}: previous word
w_{i-2}: second previous word
L: a set of POS-tagged sentences
Output: Predicted tag, t_i
1: **if** $w_i \in L$ **then**
2: $t_i \leftarrow$ Tag drawn from the distribution of w_i's candidate tags
3: **else if** $(w_{i-2}, w_{i-1}) \in L$ **then**
4: $t_i \leftarrow$ Tag drawn from the distribution of the POS tags following the word bigram (w_{i-2}, w_{i-1})
5: **else if** $w_{i-1} \in L$ **then**
6: $t_i \leftarrow$ Tag drawn from the distribution of the POS tags following the word unigram w_{i-1}
7: **else**
8: $t_i \leftarrow$ Tag obtained using the sampling equation
9: **end if**

ture the fact that a word can have more than one POS tag, it also estimates a distribution over POS tags for each word w_i that appears in L [henceforth $D_3(w_i)$].

Implemented as a set of if-else clauses, the algorithm uses these three types of distributions to tag a target word, w_i, in a discriminative manner. First, it checks whether w_i appears in L (line 1). If so, it tags w_i according to $D_3(w_i)$. Otherwise, it attempts to label w_i based on its context. Specifically, if (w_{i-2}, w_{i-1}), the word bigram preceding w_i, appears in L (line 3), then w_i is tagged according to $D_1(w_{i-2}, w_{i-1})$. Otherwise, it backs off to a unigram distribution: if w_{i-1}, the word preceding w_i, appears in L (line 5), then w_i is tagged according to $D_2(w_{i-1})$. Finally, if it is not possible to tag the word discriminatively (i.e., if all the above cases fail), it resorts to the sampling equation (lines 7–8). We apply simulated annealing to all four cases in this iterative tagging procedure.

5 Evaluation

5.1 Experimental Setup

Corpus Our evaluation corpus is the one used in the shared task of the IJCNLP-08 Workshop on NER for South and South East Asian Languages.[4] Specifically, we use the portion of the Bengali dataset that is manually POS-tagged. IIIT Hyderabad's POS tagset[5], which consists of 26 tags specifically developed for Indian languages, has been used to annotate the data. The corpus is composed of a training set and a test set with approximately 50K and 30K tokens, respectively. Importantly, all our POS tagging results will be reported using only the test set; the training set will be used for lexicon construction, as we will see shortly.

Tagset We collapse the set of 26 POS tags into 15 tags. Specifically, while we retain the tags corresponding to the major POS categories, we merge some of the infrequent tags designed to capture Indian language specific structure (e.g., reduplication, echo words) into a category called OTHERS.

Hyperparameter settings Recall that our tagger consists of three types of distributions — tag transition distributions, word-based output distributions, and suffix-based output distributions — drawn from a symmetric Dirichlet with α, β, and γ as the underlying hyperparameters, respectively. We automatically determine the values of these hyperparameters by (1) randomly initializing them and (2) resampling their values by using a Metropolis-Hastings update (Gilks et al., 1996) at the end of each sampling iteration. Details of this update process can be found in G&G.

Inference Inference is performed by running a Gibbs sampler for 5000 iterations. The initial temperature is set to 2.0, which is gradually lowered to 0.08 over the iterations. Owing to the randomness involved in hyperparameter initialization, all reported results are averaged over three runs.

Lexicon construction methods To better understand the role of a POS lexicon in tagging performance, we evaluate each POS tagging model by employing lexicons constructed by three methods.

The first lexicon construction method, arguably the most unrealistic among the three, follows that of G&G: for each word, w, in the *test* set, we (1) collect from each occurrence of w in the training set *and* the test set its POS tag, and then (2) insert w and all the POS tags collected for w into the POS lexicon. This method is unrealistic because (1) in practice, a human needs to list all possible POS tags for each word in order to construct this lexicon, thus rendering the resulting tagger considerably less unsupervised than it appears; and (2) constructing the lexicon using the dataset on which the tagger is to be evaluated implies that there is no *unseen* word w.r.t. the lexicon, thus unrealistically simplifies the POS tagging task. To make the method more realistic, G&G also create a set of *relaxed* lexicons. Each of these lexicons includes the tags for only the words that appear at least d times in the test corpus, where d ranges

[4]The corpus is available from http://ltrc.iiit.ac.in/ner-ssea-08/index.cgi?topic=5.

[5]http://shiva.iiit.ac.in/SPSAL2007/iiit_tagset_guidelines.pdf

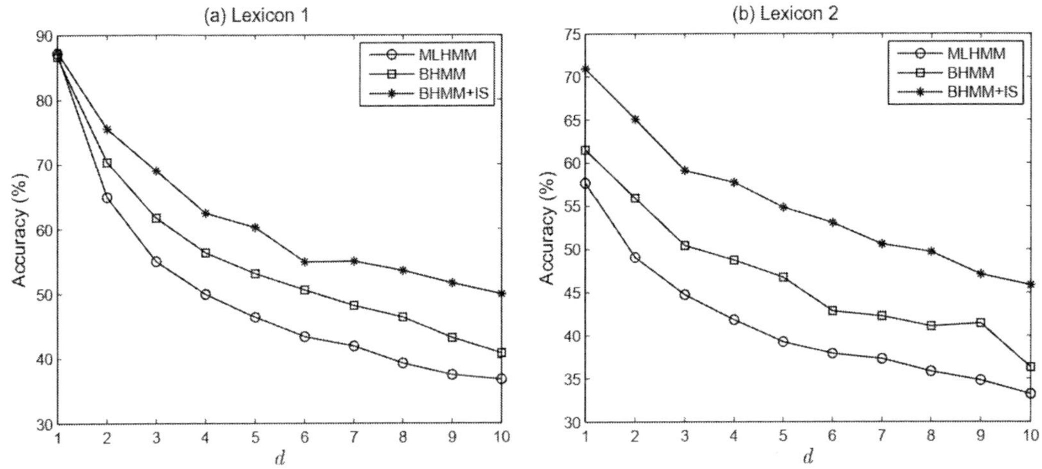

Figure 3: Accuracies of POS tagging models using (a) Lexicon 1 and (b) Lexicon 2

from 1 to 10 in our experiments. Any unseen (i.e., out-of-dictionary) word is ambiguous among the 15 possible tags. Not surprisingly, both ambiguity and the unseen word rate increase with d. For instance, the ambiguous token rate increases from 40.0% with 1.7 tags/token (d=1) to 77.7% with 8.1 tags/token (d=10). Similarly, the unseen word rate increases from 16% (d=2) to 46% (d=10). We will refer to this set of tag dictionaries as *Lexicon 1*.

The second method generates a set of relaxed lexicons, *Lexicon 2*, in essentially the same way as the first method, except that these lexicons include only the words that appear at least d times in the training data. Importantly, the words that appear solely in the test data are not included in any of these relaxed POS lexicons. This makes Lexicon 2 a bit more realistic than Lexicon 1 in terms of the way they are constructed. As a result, in comparison to Lexicon 1, Lexicon 2 has a considerably higher ambiguous token rate and unseen word rate: its ambiguous token rate ranges from 64.3% with 5.3 tags/token (d=1) to 80.5% with 8.6 tags/token (d=10), and its unseen word rate ranges from 25% (d=1) to 50% (d=10).

The third method, arguably the most realistic among the three, is motivated by our proposed weakly supervised approach. In this method, we (1) form ten different datasets from the (labeled) training data of sizes 5K words, 10K words, ..., 50K words, and then (2) create one POS lexicon from each dataset L by listing, for each word w in L, all the tags associated with w in L. This set of tag dictionaries, which we will refer to as *Lexicon 3*, has an ambiguous token rate that ranges from 57.7% with 5.1 tags/token (50K) to 61.5% with 8.1 tags/token (5K), and an unseen word rate that ranges from 25% (50K) to 50% (5K).

5.2 Results and Discussion

5.2.1 Baseline Systems

We use as our first baseline system G&G's Bayesian POS tagging model, as our goal is to evaluate the effectiveness of our two extensions in improving their model. To further gauge the performance of G&G's model, we employ another baseline commonly used in POS tagging experiments, which is an unsupervised trigram HMM trained by running EM to convergence.

As mentioned previously, we evaluate each tagging model by employing the three POS lexicons described in the previous subsection. Figure 3(a) shows how the tagging accuracy varies with d when Lexicon 1 is used. Perhaps not surprisingly, the trigram HMM (MLHMM) and G&G's Bayesian model (BHMM) achieve almost identical accuracies when d=1 (i.e., the complete lexicon with a zero unseen word rate). As d increases, both ambiguity and the unseen word rate increase; as a result, the tagging accuracy decreases. Also, consistent with G&G's results, BHMM outperforms MLHMM by a large margin (4–7%).

Similar performance trends can be observed when Lexicon 2 is used (see Figure 3(b)). However, both baselines achieve comparatively lower tagging accuracies, as a result of the higher unseen word rate associated with Lexicon 2.

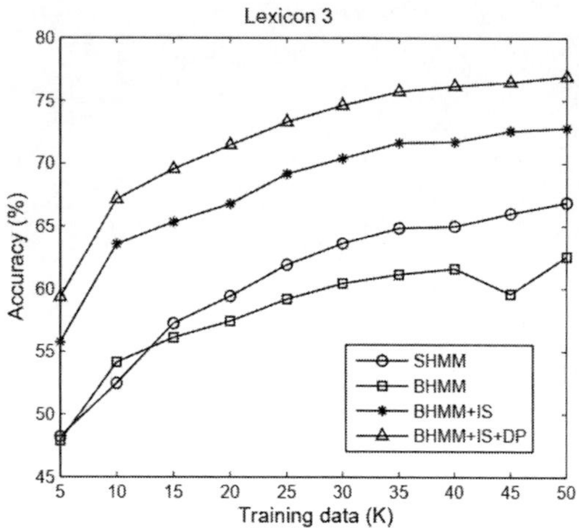

Figure 4: Accuracies of the POS tagging models using Lexicon 3

Results using Lexicon 3 are shown in Figure 4. Owing to the availability of POS-tagged sentences, we replace MLHMM with its *supervised* counterpart that is trained on the available labeled data, yielding the SHMM baseline. The accuracies of SHMM range from 48% to 67%, outperforming BHMM as the amount of labeled data increases.

5.2.2 Adding Induced Suffix Emission

Next, we augment BHMM with our first extension, induced suffix emission, yielding BHMM+IS. For Lexicon 1, BHMM+IS achieves the same accuracy as the two baselines when d=1. The reason is simple: as all the test words are in the POS lexicon, the tagger never emits an induced suffix. More importantly, BHMM+IS beats BHMM and MLHMM by 4–9% and 10–14%, respectively. Similar trends are observed for Lexicon 2, where BHMM+IS outperforms BHMM and MLHMM by a larger margin of 5–10% and 12–16%, respectively. For Lexicon 3, BHMM+IS outperforms SHMM, the stronger baseline, by 6–11%. Overall, these results suggest that induced suffix emission is a strong performance-enhancing extension to G&G's approach.

5.2.3 Adding Discriminative Prediction

Finally, we augment BHMM+IS with discriminative prediction, yielding BHMM+IS+DP. Since this extension requires labeled data, it can only be applied in combination with Lexicon 3. As seen in Figure 4, BHMM+IS+DP outperforms SHMM by 10–14%. Its discriminative nature proves to be strong as it even beats BHMM+IS by 3–4%.

Predicted Tag	Correct Tag	% of Error
NN	NNP	8.4
NN	JJ	6.9
VM	VAUX	5.9

Table 1: Most frequent POS tagging errors for BHMM+IS+DP on the 50K-word training set

5.2.4 Error Analysis

Table 1 lists the most common types of errors made by the best-performing tagging model, BHMM+IS+DP (50K-word labeled data). As we can see, common nouns and proper nouns (row 1) are difficult to distinguish, due in part to the case insensitivity of Bengali. Also, it is difficult to distinguish Bengali common nouns and adjectives (row 2), as they are distributionally similar to each other. The confusion between main verbs [VM] and auxiliary verbs [VAUX] (row 3) arises from the fact that certain Bengali verbs can serve as both a main verb and an auxiliary verb, depending on the role the verb plays in the verb sequence.

6 Conclusions

While Goldwater and Griffiths's fully-Bayesian approach and the traditional maximum-likelihood parameter-based approach to unsupervised POS tagging have offered promising results for English, we argued in this paper that such results were obtained under the unrealistic assumption that a perfect POS lexicon is available, which renders these taggers less unsupervised than they appear. As a result, we investigated a weakly supervised fully-Bayesian approach to POS tagging, which relaxes the unrealistic assumption by automatically acquiring the lexicon from a small amount of POS-tagged data. Since such relaxation comes at the expense of a drop in tagging accuracy, we proposed two performance-enhancing extensions to the Bayesian framework, namely, induced suffix emission and discriminative prediction, which effectively exploit morphology and techniques from supervised POS tagging, respectively.

Acknowledgments

We thank the three anonymous reviewers and Sajib Dasgupta for their comments. We also thank CRBLP, BRAC University, Bangladesh, for providing us with Bengali resources and Taufiq Hasan Al Banna for his MATLAB code. This work was supported in part by NSF Grant IIS-0812261.

References

Leonard E. Baum. 1972. An equality and associated maximization technique in statistical estimation for probabilistic functions of Markov processes. *Inequalities*, 3:1–8.

Alexander Clark. 2000. Inducing syntactic categories by context distribution clustering. In *Proceedings of CoNLL: Short Papers*, pages 91–94.

Alexander Clark. 2003. Combining distributional and morphological information for part-of-speech induction. In *Proceedings of the EACL*, pages 59–66.

Sajib Dasgupta and Vincent Ng. 2007. Unsupervised part-of-speech acquisition for resource-scarce languages. In *Proceedings of EMNLP-CoNLL*, pages 218–227.

Arthur P. Dempster, Nan M. Laird, and Donald B. Rubin. 1977. Maximum likelihood from incomplete data via the EM algorithm. *Journal of the Royal Statistical Society. Series B (Methodological)*, 39:1–38.

Stuart Geman and Donald Geman. 1984. Stochastic relaxation, Gibbs distributions, and the Bayesian restoration of images. *IEEE Transactions on Pattern Analysis and Machine Intelligence*, 6:721–741.

Walter R. Gilks, Sylvia Richardson, and David J. Spiegelhalter (editors). 1996. *Markov Chain Monte Carlo in Practice.* Chapman & Hall, Suffolk.

Yoav Goldberg, Meni Adler, and Michael Elhadad. 2008. EM can find pretty good HMM POS-taggers (when given a good start). In *Proceedings of ACL-08:HLT*, pages 746–754.

John Goldsmith. 2001. Unsupervised learning of the morphology of a natural language. *Computational Linguistics*, 27(2):153–198.

Sharon Goldwater and Thomas L. Griffiths. 2007. A fully Bayesian approach to unsupervised part-of-speech tagging. In *Proceedings of the ACL*, pages 744–751.

Aria Haghighi and Dan Klein. 2006. Prototype-driven learning for sequence models. In *Proceedings of HLT-NAACL*, pages 320–327.

Mark Johnson. 2007. Why doesn't EM find good HMM POS-taggers? In *Proceedings of EMNLP-CoNLL*, pages 296–305.

Samarth Keshava and Emily Pitler. 2006. A simpler, intuitive approach to morpheme induction. In *PASCAL Challenge Workshop on Unsupervised Segmentation of Words into Morphemes*.

David J. C. MacKay and Linda C. Bauman Peto. 1995. A hierarchical Dirichlet language model. *Natural Language Engineering*, 1:289–307.

Bernard Merialdo. 1994. Tagging English text with a probabilistic model. *Computational Linguistics*, 20(2):155–172.

Hinrich Schütze. 1995. Distributional part-of-speech tagging. In *Proceedings of EACL*, pages 141–148.

Noah A. Smith and Jason Eisner. 2005. Contrastive estimation: Training log-linear models on unlabeled data. In *Proceedings of the ACL*, pages 354–362.

Benjamin Snyder, Tahira Naseem, Jacob Eisenstein, and Regina Barzilay. 2008. Unsupervised multilingual learning for POS tagging. In *Proceedings of EMNLP*, pages 1041–1050.

Benjamin Snyder, Tahira Naseem, Jacob Eisenstein, and Regina Barzilay. 2009. Adding more languages improves unsupervised multilingual tagging. In *Proceedings of NAACL-HLT*.

Yee Whye Teh, Michael Jordan, Matthew Beal, and David Blei. 2006. Hierarchical Dirichlet processes. *Journal of the American Statistical Association*, 101(476):1527–1554.

Kristina Toutanova and Mark Johnson. 2007. A Bayesian LDA-based model for semi-supervised part-of-speech tagging. In *Proceedings of NIPS*.

Qin Iris Wang and Dale Schuurmans. 2005. Improved estimation for unsupervised part-of-speech tagging. In *Proceedings of the 2005 IEEE International Conference on Natural Language Processing and Knowledge Engineering (IEEE NLP-KE)*, pages 219–224.

Improving Mid-Range Reordering using Templates of Factors

Hieu Hoang
School of Informatics
University of Edinburgh
h.hoang@sms.ed.ac.uk

Philipp Koehn
School of Informatics
University of Edinburgh
pkoehn@inf.ed.ac.uk

Abstract

We extend the factored translation model (Koehn and Hoang, 2007) to allow translations of longer phrases composed of factors such as POS and morphological tags to act as templates for the selection and reordering of surface phrase translation. We also reintroduce the use of alignment information within the decoder, which forms an integral part of decoding in the Alignment Template System (Och, 2002), into phrase-based decoding.

Results show an increase in translation performance of up to 1.0% BLEU for out-of-domain French–English translation. We also show how this method compares and relates to lexicalized reordering.

1 Introduction

One of the major issues in statistical machine translation is reordering due to systematic word-ordering differences between languages. Often reordering is best explained by linguistic categories, such as part-of-speech tags. In fact, prior work has examined the use of part-of-speech tags in pre-reordering schemes, Tomas and Casacuberta (2003).

Re-ordering can also be viewed as composing of a number of related problems which can be explained or solved by a variety of linguistic phenomena. Firstly, differences between phrase ordering account for much of the long-range reordering. Syntax-based and hierarchical models such as (Chiang, 2005) attempts to address this problem. Shorter range re-ordering, such as intra-phrasal word re-ordering, can often be predicted from the underlying property of the words and its context, the most obvious property being POS tags.

In this paper, we tackle the issue of shorter-range re-ordering in phrase-based decoding by presenting an extension of the factored translation which directly models the translation of non-surface factors such as POS tags. We shall call this extension the *factored template model*. We use the fact that factors such as POS-tags are less sparse than surface words to obtain longer phrase translations. These translations are used to inform the re-ordering of surface phrases.

Despite the ability of phrase-based systems to use multi-word phrases, the majority of phrases used during decoding are one word phrases, which we will show in later sections. Using word translations negates the implicit capability of phrases to re-order words. We show that the proposed extension increases the number of multi-word phrases used during decoding, capturing the implicit ordering with the phrase translation, leading to overall better sentence translation. In our tests, we obtained 1.0% increase in absolute for French-English translation, and 0.8% increase for German-English translation, trained on News Commentary corpora [1].

We will begin by recounting the phrase-based and factored model in Section 2 and describe the language model and lexicalized re-ordering model and the advantages and disadvantages of using these models to influence re-ordering. The proposed model is described in Section 4.

2 Background

Let us first provide some background on phrase-based and factored translation, as well as the use of part-of-speech tags in reordering.

2.1 Phrase-Based Models

Phrase-based statistical machine translation has emerged as the dominant paradigm in machine translation research. We model the translation of a given source language sentence **s** into a target language sentence **t** with a probability distribution $p(\mathbf{t}|\mathbf{s})$. The goal of translation is to find the best translation according to the model

$$\mathbf{t}_{\text{BEST}} = \text{argmax}_{\mathbf{t}}\ p(\mathbf{t}|\mathbf{s}) \quad (1)$$

The argmax function defines the search objective of the decoder. We estimate $p(\mathbf{t}|\mathbf{s})$ by decom-

[1] http://www.statmt.org/wmt07/shared-task.html

Proceedings of the 12th Conference of the European Chapter of the ACL, pages 372–379,
Athens, Greece, 30 March – 3 April 2009. ©2009 Association for Computational Linguistics

posing it into component models

$$p(\mathbf{t}|\mathbf{s}) = \frac{1}{Z} \prod_m h'_m(\mathbf{t},\mathbf{s})^{\lambda_m} \tag{2}$$

where $h'_m(\mathbf{t},\mathbf{s})$ is the feature function for component m and λ_m is the weight given to component m. Z is a normalization factor which is ignored in practice. Components are translation model scoring functions, language model, reordering models and other features.

The problem is typically presented in log-space, which simplifies computations, but otherwise does not change the problem due to the monotonicity of the log function ($h_m = \log h'_m$)

$$\log p(\mathbf{t}|\mathbf{s}) = \sum_m \lambda_m \, h_m(\mathbf{t},\mathbf{s}) \tag{3}$$

Phrase-based models (Koehn et al., 2003) are limited to the mapping of small contiguous chunks of text. In these models, the source sentence $\mathbf{s}$ is segmented into a number of phrases $\bar{s}_k$, which are translated one-to-one into target phrases $\bar{t}_k$. The translation feature functions $h_{\text{TM}}(\mathbf{t},\mathbf{s})$ are computed as sum of phrase translation feature functions $\bar{h}_{\text{TM}}(\bar{t}_k, \bar{s}_k)$:

$$h_{\text{TM}}(\mathbf{t},\mathbf{s}) = \sum_k \bar{h}_{\text{TM}}(\bar{t}_k, \bar{s}_k) \tag{4}$$

where $\bar{t}_k$ and $\bar{s}_k$ are the phrases that make up the target and source sentence. Note that typically multiple feature functions for one translation table are used (such as forward and backward probabilities and lexical backoff).

2.2 Reordering in Phrase Models

Phrase-based systems implicitly perform short-range reordering by translating multi-word phrases where the component words may be reordered relative to each other. However, multi-word phrases have to have been seen and learnt from the training corpus. This works better when the parallel corpus is large and the training corpus and input are from the same domain. Otherwise, the ability to apply multi-word phrases is lessened due to data sparsity, and therefore most used phrases are only 1 or 2 words long.

A popular model for phrasal reordering is lexicalized reordering (Tillmann, 2004) which introduces a probability distribution for each phrase pair that indicates the likelihood of being translated monotone, swapped, or placed discontinuous to its previous phrase. However, whether a phrase is reordered may depend on its neighboring phrases, which this model does not take into account. For example, the French phrase *noir* would be reordered if preceded by a noun when translating into English, as in as in *chat noir*, but would remain in the same relative position when preceded by a conjunction such as *rouge et noir*.

The use of language models on the decoding output also has a significant effect on reordering by preferring hypotheses which are more fluent. However, there are a number of disadvantages with this low-order Markov model over consecutive surface words. Firstly, the model has no information about the source and may prefer orderings of target words that are unlikely given the source. Secondly, data sparsity may be a problem, even if language models are trained on a large amount of monolingual data which is easier to obtain than parallel data. When the test set is out-of-domain or rare words are involved, it is likely that the language model backs off to lower order n-grams, thus further reducing the context window.

2.3 POS-Based Reordering

This paper will look at the use of POS tags to condition reordering of phrases which are closely positioned in the source and target, such as intra-clausal reordering, however, we do not explicit segment along clausal boundaries. By mid-range reordering we mean a maximum distortion of about 5 or 6 words.

The phrase-based translation model is generally believed to perform short-range reordering adequately. It outperforms more complex models such as hierarchical translation when the most of the reordering in a particular language pair is reasonably short (Anonymous, 2008), as is the case with Arabic–English. However, phrase-based models can fail to reorder words or phrases which would seem obvious if it had access to the POS tags of the individual words. For example, a translation from French to English will usually correctly reorder the French phrase with POS tags NOUN ADJECTIVE if the surface forms exists in the phrase table or language model, e.g.,

Union Européenne $\rightarrow$ *European Union*

However, phrase-based models may not reorder even these small two-word phrases if the phrase is not in the training data or involves rare words. This situation worsens for longer phrases where the likelihood of the phrase being previously unseen is higher. The following example has a source POS pattern NOUN ADJECTIVE CONJUNCTION ADJECTIVE but is incorrectly ordered as the surface phrase does not occur in training,

difficultés économiques et socials
$\rightarrow$ *economic and social difficulties*

However, even if the training data does not contain this particular phrase, it contains many similar phrases with the same underlying POS tags. For example, the correct translation of the corresponding POS tags of the above translation

NOUN ADJ CONJ ADJ
$\rightarrow$ ADJ CONJ ADJ NOUN

is typically observed many times in the training corpus.

The alignment information in the training corpus shows exactly how the individual words in this phrase should be distorted, along with the POS tag of the target words. The challenge addressed by this paper is to integrate POS tag phrase translations and alignment information into a phrase-based decoder in order to improve reordering.

2.4 Factor Model Decomposition

Factored translation models (Koehn and Hoang, 2007) extend the phrase-based model by integrating word level factors into the decoding process. Words are represented by vectors of factors, not simple tokens. Factors are user-definable and do not have any specific meaning within the model. Typically, factors are obtained from linguistic tools such as taggers and parsers.

The factored decoding process can be decomposed into multiple steps to fully translate the input. Formally, this decomposes Equation 4 further into sub-component models (also called translation steps)

$$\bar{h}_{\text{TM}}(\bar{t}, \bar{s}) = \sum_i \bar{h}^i_{\text{TM}}(\bar{t}, \bar{s}) \tag{5}$$

with an translation feature function $\bar{h}^i_{\text{TM}}$ for each translation step for each factor (or sets of factors). There may be also generation models which create target factors from other target factors but we exclude this in our presentation for the sake of clarity.

Decomposition is a convenient and flexible method for integrating word level factors into phrase-based decoding, allowing source and target sentences to be augmented with factors, while at the same time controlling data sparsity. However, decomposition also implies certain independence assumptions which may not be justified. Various internal experiments show that decomposition may decrease performance and that better results can often be achieved by simply translating all factors jointly. While we can gain benefit from adding factor information into phrase-based decoding, our experience also shows the shortcomings of decomposing phrase translation.

3 Related Work

Efforts have been made to integrate syntactic information into the decoding process to improve reordering.

Collins et al. (2005) reorder the source sentence using a sequence of six manually-crafted rules, given the syntactic parse tree of the source sentence. While the transformation rules are specific to the German parser that was used, they could be adapted to other languages and parsers. Xia and McCord (2004) automatically create rewrite rules which reorder the source sentence. Zhang and Zens (2007) take a slightly different approach by using chunk level tags to reorder the source sentence, creating a confusion network to represent the possible reorderings of the source sentence. All these approaches seek to improve reordering by making the ordering of the source sentence similar to the target sentence.

Costa-jussà and Fonollosa (2006) use a two stage process to reorder translation in an n-gram based decoder. The first stage uses word classes of source words to reorder the source sentence into a string of word classes which can be translated monotonically to the target sentences in the second stage.

The Alignment Template System (Och, 2002) performs reordering by translating word classes with their corresponding alignment information, then translates each surface word to be consistent with the alignment. Tomas and Casacuberta (2003) extend ATS by using POS tags instead of automatically induced word classes.

Note the limitation of the existing work of POS-driven reordering in phrase-based models: the reordering model is separated from the translation model and the two steps are pipelined, with passing the 1-best reordering or at most a lattice to the translation stage. The ATS models do provide an integrated approach, but their lexical translation is limited to the word level.

In contrast to prior work, we present a integrated approach that allows POS-based reordering and phrase translation. It is also open to the use of any other factors, such as driving reordering with automatic word classes.

Our proposed solution is similar to structural templates described in Phillips (2007) which was applied to an example-based MT system.

4 Translation Using Templates of Factors

A major motivation for the introduction of factors into machine translation is to generalize phrase translation over longer segments using less sparse factors than is possible with surface forms. (Koehn and Hoang, 2007) describes various strategies for the decomposition of the decoding into multiple translation models using the Moses decoder. We shall focus on POS-tags as an example of a less-sparsed factor.

Decomposing the translation by separately decoding the POS tags and surface forms is be the obvious option, which also has a probabilistic interpretation. However, this combined factors into target words which don't exist naturally and bring down translation quality. Therefore, the decoding is constrained by decomposing into two translation models; a model with POS-tag phrase pairs only and one which jointly translates POS-tags and surface forms. This can be expressed using feature-functions

$$\bar{h}_{\text{TM}}(\bar{t}, \bar{s}) = \bar{h}^{pos}_{\text{TM}}(\bar{t}, \bar{s})\bar{h}^{surface}_{\text{TM}}(\bar{t}, \bar{s}) \quad (6)$$

Source segment must be decoded by both translation models but only phrase pairs where the overlapping factors are the same are used. As an additional constraint, the alignment information is retained in the translation model from the training data for every phrase pair, and both translation models must produce consistent alignments. This is expressed formally in Equation 7 to 9.

An alignment is a relationship which maps a source word at position i to a target word at position j:

$$a : i \rightarrow j \quad (7)$$

Each word at each position can be aligned to multiple words, therefore, we alter the alignment relation to express this explicitly:

$$a : i \rightarrow j \quad (8)$$

where J is the set of positions, $j \epsilon J$, that I is aligned to in the other language. Phrase pairs for each translation model are used only if they can satisfy condition 9 for each position of every source word covered.

$$\forall a, b \epsilon T \quad \forall p : J^p_a J^p_b \neq \emptyset \quad (9)$$

where J^p_a is the alignment information for translation model, a, at word position, p and T is the set of translation models.

4.1 Training

The training procedure is identical to the factored phrase-based training described in (Koehn and Hoang, 2007). The phrase model retains the word alignment information found during training. Where multiple alignment exists in the training data for a particular phrase pair, the most frequent is used, in a similar manner to the calculation of the lexicalized probabilities.

Words positions which remain unaligned are artificially aligned to every word in the other language in the phrase translation during decoding to allow the decoder to cover the position.

4.2 Decoding

The beam search decoding algorithm is unchanged from traditional phrase-based and factored decoding. However, the creation of translation options is extended to include the use of factored templates. Translation options are the intermediate representation between the phrase pairs from the translation models and the hypotheses in the stack decoder which cover specific source spans of a sentence and are applied to hypotheses to create new hypotheses.

In phrase-based decoding, a translation option strictly contains one phrase pair. In factored decoding, strictly one phrase pair from each translation model is used to create a translation options. This is possible only when the segmentation is identical for both source and target span of each phrase pair in each translation model. However, this constraint limits the ability to use long POS-tag phrase pairs in conjunction with shorter surface phrase pairs.

The factored template approach extend factored decoding by constructing translation options from a single phrase pair from the POS-tag translation model, but allowing multiple phrase pairs from other translation models. A simplified stack decoder is used to compose phrases from the other translation models. This so called intra-phrase decoder is constrained to creating phrases which adheres to the constraint described in Section 4. The intra-phrase decoder uses the same feature functions as the main beam decoder but uses a larger stack size due to the difficulty of creating completed phrases which satisfy the constraint. Every source position must be covered by every translation model.

The intra-phrase decoder is used for each contiguous span in the input sentence to produce translation options which are then applied as usual by the main decoder.

5 Experiments

We performed our experiments on the news commentary corpus[2] which contains 60,000 parallel sentences for German–English and 43,000 sentences for French–English. Tuning was done on a 2000 sentence subset of the Europarl corpus (Koehn, 2005) and tested on a 2000 sentence Europarl subset for out-of-domain, and a 1064 news commentary sentences for in-domain.

The training corpus is aligned using Giza++ (Och and Ney, 2003). To create POS tag translation models, the surface forms on both source and target language training data are replaced with POS tags before phrases are extracted. The taggers used were the Brill Tagger (Brill, 1995) for English, the Treetagger for French (Schmid, 1994), and the LoPar Tagger (Schmidt and Schulte im Walde, 2000) for German. The training script supplied with the Moses toolkit (Koehn et al., 2007) was used, extended to enable alignment information of each phrase pair. The vanilla Moses MERT tuning script was used throughout.

Results are also presented for models trained on the larger Europarl corpora[3].

5.1 German–English

We use as a baseline the traditional, non-factored phrase model which obtained a BLEU score of 14.6% on the out-of-domain test set and 18.2% on the in-domain test set (see Table 1, line 1).

POS tags for both source and target languages were augmented to the training corpus and used in the decoding and an additional trigram language model was used on the target POS tags. This increased translation performance (line 2). This model has the same input and output factors, and the same language models, as the factored model we will present shortly and it therefore offers a fairer comparison of the factored template model than the non-factored baseline.

#	Model	out-domain	in-domain
1	Unfactored	14.6	18.2
2	Joint factors	15.0	18.8
3	Factored template	15.3	18.8

Table 1: German–English results, in %BLEU

#	Model	out-domain	in-domain
1	Unfactored	19.6	23.1
2	Joint factors	19.8	23.0
3	Factored template	20.6	24.1

Table 2: French–English results

The factored template model (line 3) outperforms the baseline on both sets and the joint factor model on the out-of-domain set.

However, we believe the language pair German–English is not particularly suited for the factored template approach as many of the short-range ordering properties of German and English are similar. For example, ADJECTIVE NOUN phrases are ordered the same in both languages.

5.2 French–English

Repeating the same experiments for French–English produces bigger gains for the factored template model. See Table 4 for details. Using the factored template model produces the best result, with gains of 1.0 %BLEU over the unfactored baseline on both test sets. It also outperforms the joint factor model.

5.3 Maximum Size of Templates

Typical phrase-based model implementation use a maximum phrase length of 7 but such long phrases are rarely used. Long templates over POS may be more valuable. The factored template models were retrained with increased maximum phrase length but this made no difference or negatively impacted translation performance, Figure 1.

However, using larger phrase lengths over 5 words does not increase translation performance,

[2] http://www.statmt.org/wmt07/shared-task.html
[3] http://www.statmt.org/europarl/

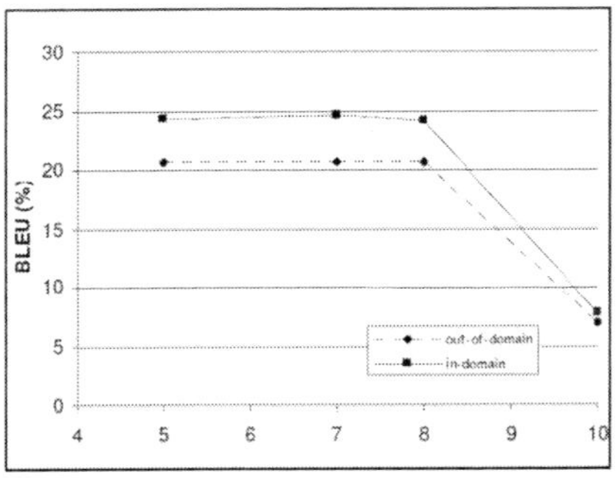

Figure 1: Varying max phrase length

as had been expected. Translation is largely unaffected until the maximum phrase length reaches 10 when performance drops dramatically. This results suggested that the model is limited to mid-range reordering.

6 Lexicalized Reordering Models

There has been considerable effort to improve reordering in phrase-based systems. One of the most well known is the lexicalized reordering model (Tillmann, 2004).

The model uses the same word alignment that is used for phrase table construction to calculate the probability that a phrase is reordered, relative to the previous and next source phrase.

6.1 Smoothing

Tillmann (2004) proposes a block orientation model, where phrase translation and reordering orientation is predicted by the same probability distribution $p(o, \bar{s}|\bar{t})$. The variant of this implemented in Moses uses a separate phrase translation model $p(\bar{s}|\bar{t})$ and lexicalized reordering model $p(o|\bar{s}, \bar{t})$

The parameters for the lexicalized reordering model are calculated using maximum likelihood with a smoothing value α

$$p(o|\bar{s}, \bar{t}) = \frac{\text{count}(o, \bar{s}, \bar{t}) + \alpha}{\sum_{o'}(\text{count}(o, \bar{s}, \bar{t}) + \alpha)} \qquad (10)$$

where the predicted orientation o is either monotonic, swap or discontinuous.

The effect of smoothing lexical reordering tables on translation is negligible for both surface forms and POS tags, except when smoothing is disabled (α=0). Then, performance decreases markedly, see Figure 2 for details. Note that the

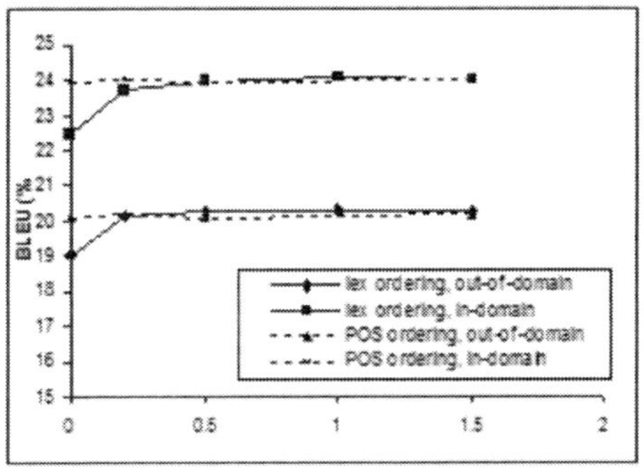

Figure 2: Effect of smoothing on lexicalized reordering

#	Model	out-domain	in-domain
1	Unfactored	19.6	23.1
1a	+ word LR	20.2	24.0
2	Joint factors	19.8	23.0
2a	+ POS LR	20.1	24.0
2b	+ POS LR + word LR	20.3	24.1
3	Factored template	20.6	24.1
3a	+ POS LR	20.6	24.3

Table 3: Extending the models with lexicalized reordering (LR)

un-smoothed setting is closer to the block orientation model by Tillmann (2004).

6.2 Factors and Lexicalized Reordering

The model can easily be extended to take advantage of the factored approach available in Moses. In addition to the lexicalized reordering model trained on surface forms (see line 1a in Table 3), we also conducted various experiments with the lexicalized reordering model for comparison.

In the joint factored model, we have both surface forms and POS tags available to train the lexicalized reordering models on. The lexicalized reordering model can be trained on the surface form, the POS tags, jointly on both factors, or independent models can be trained on each factor. It can be seen from Table 3 that generalizing the reordering model on POS tags (line 2a) improves performance, compared to the non-lexicalized reordering model (line 2). However, this performance does not improve over the lexicalized reordering model on surface forms (line 1a). The surface and POS tag models complement each other to give an overall better BLEU score (line 2b).

In the factored template model, we add a POS-based lexicalized reordering model on the level of the templates (line 3a). This gives overall the best performance. However, the use of lexicalized reordering models in the factored template model only shows improvements in the in-domain test set.

Lexicalized reordering model on POS tags in factored models underperforms factored template model as the latter includes a larger context of the source and target POS tag sequence, while the former is limited to the extent of the surface word phrase.

7 Analysis

A simple POS sequence that phrase-based systems often fail to reorder is the French–English

NOUN ADJ → ADJ NOUN

We analyzed a random sample of such phrases from the out-of-domain corpus. The baseline system correctly reorders 58% of translations. Adding a lexicalized reordering model or the factored template significantly improves the reordering to above 70% (Figure 3).

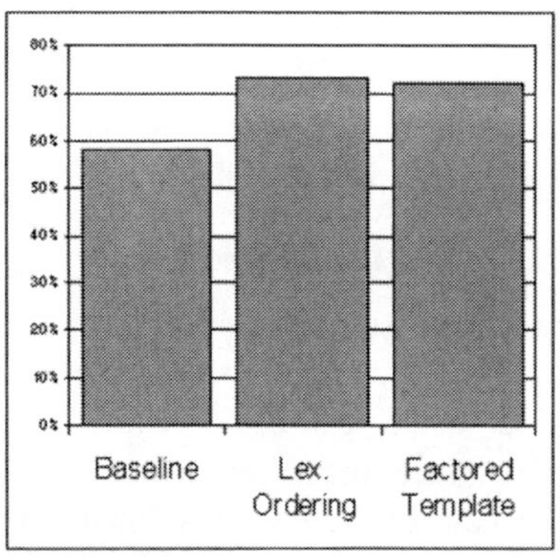

Figure 3: Percentage of correctly ordered NOUN ADJ phrases (100 samples)

A more challenging phrase to translate, such as

NOUN ADJ CONJ ADJ → ADJ CONJ ADJ NOUN

was judge in the same way and the results show the variance between the lexicalized reordering and factored template model (Figure 4).

The factored template model successfully uses POS tag templates to enable longer phrases to be used in decoding. It can be seen from Figure 5, that the majority of input sentence is decoded word-by-word even in a phrase-based system. However, the factored template configura-

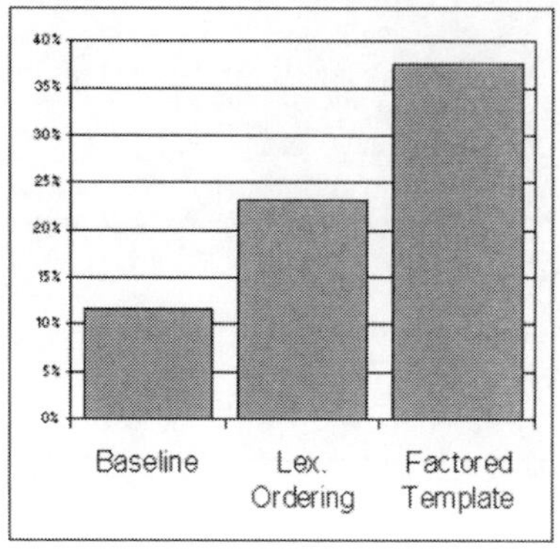

Figure 4: Percentage of correctly ordered NOUN ADJ CONJ ADJ phrases (69 samples)

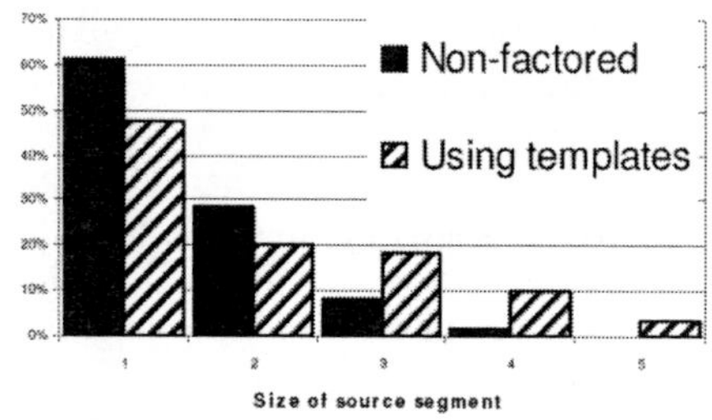

Figure 5: Length of source segmentation when decoding out-of-domain test set

tion contains more longer phrases which enhances mid-range reordering.

8 Larger training corpora

It is informative to compare the relative performance of the factored template model when trained with more data. We therefore used the Europarl corpora to train and tuning the models for French to English translation. The BLEU scores are shown below, showing no significant advantage to adding POS tags or using the factored template model. This result is similar to many others which have shown that the large amounts of additional data negates the improvements from better models.

#	Model	out-domain	in-domain
1	Unfactored	31.8	32.2
2	Joint factors	31.6	32.0
3	Factored template	31.7	32.2

Table 4: French–English results, trained on Europarl corpus

9 Conclusion

We have shown the limitations of the current factored decoding model which restrict the use of long phrase translations of less-sparsed factors. This negates the effectiveness of decomposing the translation process, dragging down translation quality.

An extension to the factored model was implemented which showed that using POS tag translations to create templates for surface word translations can create longer phrase translation and lead to higher performance, dependent on language pair.

For French–English translation, we obtained a 1.0% BLEU increase on the out-of-domain and in-domain test sets, over the non-factored baseline. The increase was also 0.4%/0.3% when using a lexicalized reordering model in both cases.

In future work, we would like to apply the factored template model to reorder longer phrases. We believe that this approach has the potential for longer range reordering which has not yet been realized in this paper. It also has some similarity to example-based machine translation (Nagao, 1984) which we would like to draw experience from.

We would also be interested in applying this to other language pairs and using factor types other than POS tags, such as syntactic chunk labels or automatically clustered word classes.

Acknowledgments

This work was supported by the EuroMatrix project funded by the European Commission (6th Framework Programme) and made use of the resources provided by the Edinburgh Compute and Data Facility (`http://www.ecdf.ed.ac.uk/`). The ECDF is partially supported by the eDIKT initiative (`http://www.edikt.org.uk/`).

References

Anonymous (2008). Understanding reordering in statistical machine translation. In *(submitted for publucation)*.

Brill, E. (1995). Transformation-based error-driven learning and natural language processing: A case study in part of speech tagging. *Computational Linguistics*, 21(4).

Chiang, D. (2005). A hierarchical phrase-based model for statistical machine translation. In *Proceedings of the 43rd Annual Meeting of the Association for Computational Linguistics (ACL'05)*, pages 263–270, Ann Arbor, Michigan. Association for Computational Linguistics.

Collins, M., Koehn, P., and Kucerova, I. (2005). Clause restructuring for statistical machine translation. In *Proceedings of the 43rd Annual Meeting of the Association for Computational Linguistics (ACL'05)*, pages 531–540, Ann Arbor, Michigan. Association for Computational Linguistics.

Costa-jussà, M. R. and Fonollosa, J. A. R. (2006). Statistical machine reordering. In *Proceedings of the 2006 Conference on Empirical Methods in Natural Language Processing*, pages 70–76, Sydney, Australia. Association for Computational Linguistics.

Koehn, P. (2005). Europarl: A parallel corpus for statistical machine translation. In *Proceedings of the Tenth Machine Translation Summit (MT Summit X)*, Phuket, Thailand.

Koehn, P. and Hoang, H. (2007). Factored translation models. In *Proceedings of the 2007 Joint Conference on Empirical Methods in Natural Language Processing and Computational Natural Language Learning (EMNLP-CoNLL)*, pages 868–876.

Koehn, P., Hoang, H., Birch, A., Callison-Burch, C., Federico, M., Bertoldi, N., Cowan, B., Shen, W., Moran, C., Zens, R., Dyer, C., Bojar, O., Constantin, A., and Herbst, E. (2007). Moses: Open source toolkit for statistical machine translation. In *Proceedings of the 45th Annual Meeting of the Association for Computational Linguistics Companion Volume Proceedings of the Demo and Poster Sessions*, pages 177–180, Prague, Czech Republic. Association for Computational Linguistics.

Koehn, P., Och, F. J., and Marcu, D. (2003). Statistical phrase based translation. In *Proceedings of the Joint Conference on Human Language Technologies and the Annual Meeting of the North American Chapter of the Association of Computational Linguistics (HLT-NAACL)*.

Nagao, M. (1984). A framework of a mechanical translation between japanese and english by analogy principle. In *Proceedings of Artificial and Human Intelligence*.

Och, F. J. (2002). *Statistical Machine Translation: From Single-Word Models to Alignment Templates*. PhD thesis, RWTH Aachen, Germany.

Och, F. J. and Ney, H. (2003). A systematic comparison of various statistical alignment models. *Computational Linguistics*, 29(1):19–52.

Phillips, A. B. (2007). Sub-phrasal matching and structural templates in example-based mt. In *Theoretical and Methodological Issues in Machine Translation*, Prague, Czech Republic.

Schmid, H. (1994). Probabilistic part-of-speech tagger using decision trees. In *International Conference on New methods in Language Processing*.

Schmidt, H. and Schulte im Walde, S. (2000). Robust German noun chunking with a probabilistic context-free grammar. In *Proceedings of the International Conference on Computational Linguistics (COLING)*.

Tillmann, C. (2004). A unigram orientation model for statistical machine translation. In *Proceedings of the Joint Conference on Human Language Technologies and the Annual Meeting of the North American Chapter of the Association of Computational Linguistics (HLT-NAACL)*.

Tomas, J. and Casacuberta, F. (2003). Combining phrase-based and template-based alignment models in statistical translation. In *IbPRIA*.

Xia, F. and McCord, M. (2004). Improving a statistical MT system with automatically learned rewrite patterns. In *Proceedings of Coling 2004*, pages 508–514, Geneva, Switzerland. COLING.

Zhang, Y. and Zens, R. (2007). Improved chunk-level reordering for statistical machine translation. In *International Workshop on Spoken Language Translation*.

Rule Filtering by Pattern for Efficient Hierarchical Translation

Gonzalo Iglesias* Adrià de Gispert‡ Eduardo R. Banga* William Byrne‡
* University of Vigo. Dept. of Signal Processing and Communications. Vigo, Spain
{giglesia,erbanga}@gts.tsc.uvigo.es
‡ University of Cambridge. Dept. of Engineering. CB2 1PZ Cambridge, U.K.
{ad465,wjb31}@eng.cam.ac.uk

Abstract

We describe refinements to hierarchical translation search procedures intended to reduce both search errors and memory usage through modifications to hypothesis expansion in cube pruning and reductions in the size of the rule sets used in translation. Rules are put into syntactic classes based on the number of non-terminals and the pattern, and various filtering strategies are then applied to assess the impact on translation speed and quality. Results are reported on the 2008 NIST Arabic-to-English evaluation task.

1 Introduction

Hierarchical phrase-based translation (Chiang, 2005) has emerged as one of the dominant current approaches to statistical machine translation. Hiero translation systems incorporate many of the strengths of phrase-based translation systems, such as feature-based translation and strong target language models, while also allowing flexible translation and movement based on hierarchical rules extracted from aligned parallel text. The approach has been widely adopted and reported to be competitive with other large-scale data driven approaches, e.g. (Zollmann et al., 2008).

Large-scale hierarchical SMT involves automatic rule extraction from aligned parallel text, model parameter estimation, and the use of cube pruning k-best list generation in hierarchical translation. The number of hierarchical rules extracted far exceeds the number of phrase translations typically found in aligned text. While this may lead to improved translation quality, there is also the risk of lengthened translation times and increased memory usage, along with possible search errors due to the pruning procedures needed in search.

We describe several techniques to reduce memory usage and search errors in hierarchical translation. Memory usage can be reduced in cube pruning (Chiang, 2007) through smart memoization, and spreading neighborhood exploration can be used to reduce search errors. However, search errors can still remain even when implementing simple phrase-based translation. We describe a 'shallow' search through hierarchical rules which greatly speeds translation without any effect on quality. We then describe techniques to analyze and reduce the set of hierarchical rules. We do this based on the structural properties of rules and develop strategies to identify and remove redundant or harmful rules. We identify groupings of rules based on non-terminals and their patterns and assess the impact on translation quality and computational requirements for each given rule group. We find that with appropriate filtering strategies rule sets can be greatly reduced in size without impact on translation performance.

1.1 Related Work

The search and rule pruning techniques described in the following sections add to a growing literature of refinements to the hierarchical phrase-based SMT systems originally described by Chiang (2005; 2007). Subsequent work has addressed improvements and extensions to the search procedure itself, the extraction of the hierarchical rules needed for translation, and has also reported contrastive experiments with other SMT architectures.

Hiero Search Refinements Huang and Chiang (2007) offer several refinements to cube pruning to improve translation speed. Venugopal et al. (2007) introduce a Hiero variant with relaxed constraints for hypothesis recombination during parsing; speed and results are comparable to those of cube pruning, as described by Chiang (2007). Li and Khudanpur (2008) report significant improvements in translation speed by taking unseen n-grams into account within cube pruning to minimize language model requests. Dyer et al. (2008)

Proceedings of the 12th Conference of the European Chapter of the ACL, pages 380–388,
Athens, Greece, 30 March – 3 April 2009.

extend the translation of source sentences to translation of input lattices following Chappelier et al. (1999).

Extensions to Hiero Blunsom et al. (2008) discuss procedures to combine discriminative latent models with hierarchical SMT. The Syntax-Augmented Machine Translation system (Zollmann and Venugopal, 2006) incorporates target language syntactic constituents in addition to the synchronous grammars used in translation. Shen at al. (2008) make use of target dependency trees and a target dependency language model during decoding. Marton and Resnik (2008) exploit shallow correspondences of hierarchical rules with source syntactic constituents extracted from parallel text, an approach also investigated by Chiang (2005). Zhang and Gildea (2006) propose binarization for synchronous grammars as a means to control search complexity arising from more complex, syntactic, hierarchical rules sets.

Hierarchical rule extraction Zhang et al. (2008) describe a linear algorithm, a modified version of shift-reduce, to extract phrase pairs organized into a tree from which hierarchical rules can be directly extracted. Lopez (2007) extracts rules on-the-fly from the training bitext during decoding, searching efficiently for rule patterns using suffix arrays.

Analysis and Contrastive Experiments Zollman et al. (2008) compare phrase-based, hierarchical and syntax-augmented decoders for translation of Arabic, Chinese, and Urdu into English, and they find that attempts to expedite translation by simple schemes which discard rules also degrade translation performance. Lopez (2008) explores whether lexical reordering or the phrase discontiguity inherent in hierarchical rules explains improvements over phrase-based systems. Hierarchical translation has also been used to great effect in combination with other translation architectures (e.g. (Sim et al., 2007; Rosti et al., 2007)).

1.2 Outline

The paper proceeds as follows. Section 2 describes memoization and spreading neighborhood exploration in cube pruning intended to reduce memory usage and search errors, respectively. A detailed comparison with a simple phrase-based system is presented. Section 3 describes pattern-based rule filtering and various procedures to select rule sets for use in translation with an aim to improving translation quality while minimizing rule set size. Finally, Section 4 concludes.

2 Two Refinements in Cube Pruning

Chiang (2007) introduced cube pruning to apply language models in pruning during the generation of k-best translation hypotheses via the application of hierarchical rules in the CYK algorithm. In the implementation of Hiero described here, there is the parser itself, for which we use a variant of the CYK algorithm closely related to CYK+ (Chappelier and Rajman, 1998); it employs hypothesis recombination, without pruning, while maintaining back pointers. Before k-best list generation with cube pruning, we apply a *smart memoization* procedure intended to reduce memory consumption during k-best list expansion. Within the cube pruning algorithm we use *spreading neighborhood exploration* to improve robustness in the face of search errors.

2.1 Smart Memoization

Each cell in the chart built by the CYK algorithm contains all possible derivations of a span of the source sentence being translated. After the parsing stage is completed, it is possible to make a very efficient sweep through the backpointers of the CYK grid to count how many times each cell will be accessed by the k-best generation algorithm. When k-best list generation is running, the number of times each cell is visited is logged so that, as each cell is visited for the last time, the k-best list associated with each cell is deleted. This continues until the one k-best list remaining at the top of the chart spans the entire sentence. Memory reductions are substantial for longer sentences: for the longest sentence in the tuning set described later (105 words in length), smart memoization reduces memory usage during the cube pruning stage from 2.1GB to 0.7GB. For average length sentences of approx. 30 words, memory reductions of 30% are typical.

2.2 Spreading Neighborhood Exploration

In generation of a k-best list of translations for a source sentence span, every derivation is transformed into a cube containing the possible translations arising from that derivation, along with their translation and language model scores (Chiang, 2007). These derivations may contain non-terminals which must be expanded based on hypotheses generated by lower cells, which them-

HIERO MJ1	HIERO	HIERO SHALLOW
$X \rightarrow \langle V_2V_1,V_1V_2 \rangle$	$X \rightarrow \langle \gamma,\alpha \rangle$	$X \rightarrow \langle \gamma_s,\alpha_s \rangle$
$X \rightarrow \langle V,V \rangle$	$\gamma,\alpha \in (\{X\} \cup \mathbf{T})^+$	$X \rightarrow \langle V,V \rangle$
$V \rightarrow \langle s,t \rangle$		$V \rightarrow \langle s,t \rangle$
$s,t \in \mathbf{T}^+$		$s,t \in \mathbf{T}^+;\ \gamma_s,\alpha_s \in (\{V\} \cup \mathbf{T})^+$

Table 1: Hierarchical grammars (not including glue rules). $\mathbf{T}$ is the set of terminals.

selves may contain non-terminals. For efficiency each cube maintains a queue of hypotheses, called here the *frontier queue*, ranked by translation and language model score; it is from these frontier queues that hypotheses are removed to create the k-best list for each cell. When a hypothesis is extracted from a frontier queue, that queue is updated by searching through the neighborhood of the extracted item to find novel hypotheses to add; if no novel hypotheses are found, that queue necessarily shrinks. This shrinkage can lead to search errors. We therefore require that, when a hypothesis is removed, new candidates must be added by exploring a neighborhood which spreads from the last extracted hypothesis. Each axis of the cube is searched (here, to a depth of 20) until a novel hypothesis is found. In this way, up to three new candidates are added for each entry extracted from a frontier queue.

Chiang (2007) describes an initialization procedure in which these frontier queues are seeded with a single candidate per axis; we initialize each frontier queue to a depth of $b^{N_{nt}+1}$, where N_{nt} is the number of non-terminals in the derivation and b is a search parameter set throughout to 10. By starting with deep frontier queues and by forcing them to grow during search we attempt to avoid search errors by ensuring that the universe of items within the frontier queues does not decrease as the k-best lists are filled.

2.3 A Study of Hiero Search Errors in Phrase-Based Translation

Experiments reported in this paper are based on the NIST MT08 Arabic-to-English translation task. Alignments are generated over all allowed parallel data, (~150M words per language). Features extracted from the alignments and used in translation are in common use: target language model, source-to-target and target-to-source phrase translation models, word and rule penalties, number of usages of the glue rule, source-to-target and target-to-source lexical models, and three rule

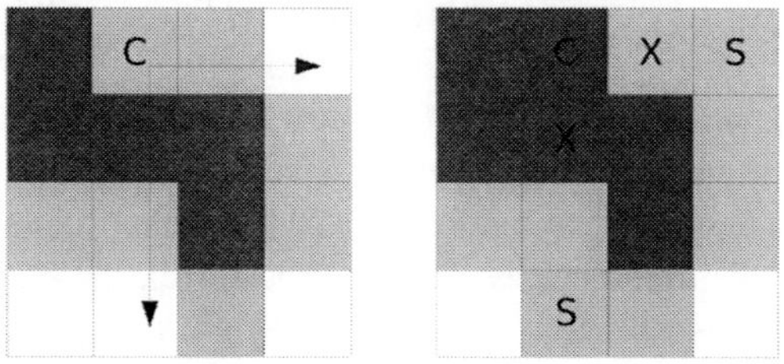

Figure 1: Spreading neighborhood exploration within a cube, just before and after extraction of the item C. Grey squares represent the frontier queue; black squares are candidates already extracted. Chiang (2007) would only consider adding items X to the frontier queue, so the queue would shrink. Spreading neighborhood exploration adds candidates S to the frontier queue.

count features inspired by Bender et al. (2007). MET (Och, 2003) iterative parameter estimation under IBM BLEU is performed on the development set. The English language used model is a 4-gram estimated over the parallel text and a 965 million word subset of monolingual data from the English Gigaword Third Edition. In addition to the MT08 set itself, we use a development set *mt02-05-tune* formed from the odd numbered sentences of the NIST MT02 through MT05 evaluation sets; the even numbered sentences form the validation set *mt02-05-test*. The *mt02-05-tune* set has 2,075 sentences.

We first compare the cube pruning decoder to the TTM (Kumar et al., 2006), a phrase-based SMT system implemented with Weighted Finite-State Tansducers (Allauzen et al., 2007). The system implements either a monotone phrase order translation, or an MJ1 (maximum phrase jump of 1) reordering model (Kumar and Byrne, 2005). Relative to the complex movement and translation allowed by Hiero and other models, MJ1 is clearly inferior (Dreyer et al., 2007); MJ1 was developed with efficiency in mind so as to run with a minimum of search errors in translation and to be easily and exactly realized via WFSTs. Even for the large models used in an evaluation task, the TTM system is reported to run largely without pruning (Blackwood et al., 2008).

The Hiero decoder can easily be made to implement MJ1 reordering by allowing only a restricted set of reordering rules in addition to the usual glue rule, as shown in left-hand column of Table 1, where **T** is the set of terminals. Constraining Hiero in this way makes it possible to compare its performance to the exact WFST TTM implementation and to identify any search errors made by Hiero.

Table 2 shows the lowercased IBM BLEU scores obtained by the systems for *mt02-05-tune* with monotone and reordered search, and with MET-optimised parameters for MJ1 reordering. For Hiero, an N-best list depth of 10,000 is used throughout. In the monotone case, all phrase-based systems perform similarly although Hiero does make search errors. For simple MJ1 reordering, the basic Hiero search procedure makes many search errors and these lead to degradations in BLEU. Spreading neighborhood expansion reduces the search errors and improves BLEU score significantly but search errors remain a problem. Search errors are even more apparent after MET. This is not surprising, given that *mt02-05-tune* is the set over which MET is run: MET drives up the likelihood of good hypotheses at the expense of poor hypotheses, but search errors often increase due to the expanded dynamic range of the hypothesis scores.

Our aim in these experiments was to demonstrate that spreading neighborhood exploration can aid in avoiding search errors. We emphasize that we are not proposing that Hiero should be used to implement reordering models such as MJ1 which were created for completely different search procedures (e.g. WFST composition). However these experiments do suggest that search errors may be an issue, particularly as the search space grows to include the complex long-range movement allowed by the hierarchical rules. We next study various filtering procedures to reduce hierarchical rule sets to find a balance between translation speed, memory usage, and performance.

	Monotone		MJ1		MJ1+MET	
	BLEU	SE	BLEU	SE	BLEU	SE
a	44.7	-	47.2	-	49.1	-
b	44.5	342	46.7	555	48.4	822
c	44.7	77	47.1	191	48.9	360

Table 2: Phrase-based TTM and Hiero performance on *mt02-05-tune* for TTM (a), Hiero (b), Hiero with spreading neighborhood exploration (c). SE is the number of Hiero hypotheses with search errors.

3 Rule Filtering by Pattern

Hierarchical rules $X \rightarrow \langle\gamma,\alpha\rangle$ are composed of sequences of terminals and non-terminals, which we call *elements*. In the source, a maximum of two non-adjacent non-terminals is allowed (Chiang, 2007). Leaving aside rules without non-terminals (i.e. phrase pairs as used in phrase-based translation), rules can be classed by their number of non-terminals, N_{nt}, and their number of elements, N_e. There are 5 possible classes: $N_{nt}.N_e$= $1.2, 1.3, 2.3, 2.4, 2.5$.

During rule extraction we search each class separately to control memory usage. Furthermore, we extract from alignments only those rules which are relevant to our given test set; for computation of backward translation probabilities we log general counts of target-side rules but discard unneeded rules. Even with this restriction, our initial ruleset for *mt02-05-tune* exceeds 175M rules, of which only 0.62M are simple phrase pairs.

The question is whether all these rules are needed for translation. If the rule set can be reduced without reducing translation quality, both memory efficiency and translation speed can be increased. Previously published approaches to reducing the rule set include: enforcing a minimum span of two words per non-terminal (Lopez, 2008), which would reduce our set to 115M rules; or a minimum count (mincount) threshold (Zollmann et al., 2008), which would reduce our set to 78M (mincount=2) or 57M (mincount=3) rules. Shen et al. (2008) describe the result of filtering rules by insisting that target-side rules are well-formed dependency trees. This reduces their rule set from 140M to 26M rules. This filtering leads to a degradation in translation performance (see Table 2 of Shen et al. (2008)), which they counter by adding a dependency LM in translation. As another reference point, Chiang (2007) reports Chinese-to-English translation experiments based on 5.5M rules.

Zollmann et al. (2008) report that filtering rules

en masse leads to degradation in translation performance. Rather than apply a coarse filtering, such as a mincount for all rules, we follow a more syntactic approach and further classify our rules according to their *pattern* and apply different filters to each pattern depending on its value in translation. The premise is that some patterns are more important than others.

3.1 Rule Patterns

Class $N_{nt}.N_e$	Rule Pattern $\langle$source , target$\rangle$	Types
1.2	$\langle wX_1 , wX_1\rangle$	1185028
	$\langle wX_1 , wX_1w\rangle$	153130
	$\langle wX_1 , X_1w\rangle$	97889
1.3	$\langle wX_1w , wX_1w\rangle$	32903522
	$\langle wX_1w , wX_1\rangle$	989540
2.3	$\langle X_1wX_2 , X_1wX_2\rangle$	1554656
	$\langle X_2wX_1 , X_1wX_2\rangle$	39163
2.4	$\langle wX_1wX_2 , wX_1wX_2\rangle$	26901823
	$\langle X_1wX_2w , X_1wX_2w\rangle$	26053969
	$\langle wX_1wX_2 , wX_1wX_2w\rangle$	2534510
	$\langle wX_2wX_1 , wX_1wX_2\rangle$	349176
	$\langle X_2wX_1w , X_1wX_2w\rangle$	259459
2.5	$\langle wX_1wX_2w , wX_1wX_2w\rangle$	61704299
	$\langle wX_1wX_2w , wX_1X_2w\rangle$	3149516
	$\langle wX_1wX_2w , X_1wX_2w\rangle$	2330797
	$\langle wX_2wX_1w , wX_1wX_2w\rangle$	275810
	$\langle wX_2wX_1w , wX_1X_2w\rangle$	205801

Table 3: Hierarchical rule patterns classed by number of non-terminals, N_{nt}, number of elements N_e, source and target patterns, and types in the rule set extracted for *mt02-05-tune*.

Given a rule set, we define *source patterns* and *target patterns* by replacing every sequence of non-terminals by a single symbol 'w' (indicating word, i.e. terminal string, $w \in T^+$). Each hierarchical rule has a unique source and target pattern which together define the *rule pattern*.

By ignoring the identity and the number of adjacent terminals, the rule pattern represents a natural generalization of any rule, capturing its structure and the type of reordering it encodes. In total, there are 66 possible rule patterns. Table 3 presents a few examples extracted for *mt02-05-tune*, showing that some patterns are much more diverse than others. For example, patterns with two non-terminals (N_{nt}=2) are richer than patterns with N_{nt}=1, as they cover many more distinct rules. Additionally, patterns with two non-terminals which also have a monotonic relationship between source and target non-terminals are much more diverse than their reordered counterparts.

Some examples of extracted rules and their corresponding pattern follow, where Arabic is shown in Buckwalter encoding.

Pattern $\langle wX_1 , wX_1w\rangle$:
  $\langle$w+ qAl X_1 , the X_1said$\rangle$
Pattern $\langle wX_1w , wX_1\rangle$:
  $\langle$fy X_1kAnwn Al>wl , on december $X_1\rangle$
Pattern $\langle wX_1wX_2 , wX_1wX_2w\rangle$:
  $\langle$Hl X_1lAzmp X_2 , a X_1solution to the X_2crisis$\rangle$

3.2 Building an Initial Rule Set

We describe a greedy approach to building a rule set in which rules belonging to a pattern are added to the rule set guided by the improvements they yield on *mt02-05-tune* relative to the monotone Hiero system described in the previous section. We find that certain patterns seem not to contribute to any improvement. This is particularly significant as these patterns often encompass large numbers of rules, as with patterns with matching source and target patterns. For instance, we found no improvement when adding the pattern $\langle X_1w,X_1w\rangle$, of which there were 1.2M instances (Table 3). Since concatenation is already possible under the general glue rule, rules with this pattern are redundant. By contrast, the much less frequent reordered counterpart, i.e. the $\langle wX_1,X_1w\rangle$ pattern (0.01M instances), provides substantial gains. The situation is analogous for rules with two non-terminals (N_{nt}=2).

Based on exploratory analyses (not reported here, for space) an initial rule set was built by excluding patterns reported in Table 4. In total, 171.5M rules are excluded, for a remaining set of 4.2M rules, 3.5M of which are hierarchical. We acknowledge that adding rules in this way, by greedy search, is less than ideal and inevitably raises questions with respect to generality and repeatability. However in our experience this is a robust approach, mainly because the initial translation system runs very fast; it is possible to run many exploratory experiments in a short time.

	Excluded Rules	Types
a	$\langle X_1w,X_1w\rangle$, $\langle wX_1,wX_1\rangle$	2332604
b	$\langle X_1wX_2,*\rangle$	2121594
c	$\langle X_1wX_2w,X_1wX_2w\rangle$, $\langle wX_1wX_2,wX_1wX_2\rangle$	52955792
d	$\langle wX_1wX_2w,*\rangle$	69437146
e	$N_{nt}.N_e$= 1.3 w mincount=5	32394578
f	$N_{nt}.N_e$= 2.3 w mincount=5	166969
g	$N_{nt}.N_e$= 2.4 w mincount=10	11465410
h	$N_{nt}.N_e$= 2.5 w mincount=5	688804

Table 4: Rules excluded from the initial rule set.

3.3 Shallow versus Fully Hierarchical Translation

In measuring the effectiveness of rules in translation, we also investigate whether a 'fully hierarchical' search is needed or whether a shallow search is also effective. In constrast to full Hiero, in the shallow search, only phrases are allowed to be substituted into non-terminals. The rules used in each case can be expressed as shown in the 2nd and 3rd columns of Table 1. Shallow search can be considered (loosely) to be a form of rule filtering.

As can be seen in Table 5 there is no impact on BLEU, while translation speed increases by a factor of 7. Of course, these results are specific to this Arabic-to-English translation task, and need not be expected to carry over to other language pairs, such as Chinese-to-English translation. However, the impact of this search simplification is easy to measure, and the gains can be significant enough, that it may be worth investigation even for languages with complex long distance movement.

mt02-05-	*-tune*		*-test*
System	**Time**	**BLEU**	**BLEU**
HIERO	14.0	52.1	51.5
HIERO - shallow	2.0	52.1	51.4

Table 5: Translation performance and time (in seconds per word) for full vs. shallow Hiero.

3.4 Individual Rule Filters

We now filter rules individually (not by class) according to their number of translations. For each fixed $\gamma \notin \mathrm{T}^+$ (i.e. with at least 1 non-terminal), we define the following filters over rules $X \rightarrow \langle\gamma,\alpha\rangle$:

- **Number of translations (NT).** We keep the **NT** most frequent α, i.e. each γ is allowed to have at most **NT** rules.
- **Number of reordered translations (NRT).** We keep the **NRT** most frequent α with monotonic non-terminals and the **NRT** most frequent α with reordered non-terminals.
- **Count percentage (CP).** We keep the most frequent α until their aggregated number of counts reaches a certain percentage **CP** of the total counts of $X \rightarrow \langle\gamma,*\rangle$. Some γ's are allowed to have more α's than others, depending on their count distribution.

Results applying these filters with various thresholds are given in Table 6, including number of rules and decoding time. As shown, all filters achieve at least a 50% speed-up in decoding time by discarding 15% to 25% of the baseline rules. Remarkably, performance is unaffected when applying the simple **NT** and **NRT** filters with a threshold of 20 translations. Finally, the **CM** filter behaves slightly worse for thresholds of 90% for the same decoding time. For this reason, we select **NRT**=20 as our general filter.

mt02-05-	*-tune*			*-test*
Filter	**Time**	**Rules**	**BLEU**	**BLEU**
baseline	2.0	4.20	52.1	51.4
NT=10	0.8	3.25	52.0	51.3
NT=15	0.8	3.43	52.0	51.3
NT=20	0.8	3.56	52.1	51.4
NRT=10	0.9	3.29	52.0	51.3
NRT=15	1.0	3.48	52.0	51.4
NRT=20	1.0	3.59	52.1	51.4
CP=50	0.7	2.56	51.4	50.9
CP=90	1.0	3.60	52.0	51.3

Table 6: Impact of general rule filters on translation (IBM BLEU), time (in seconds per word) and number of rules (in millions).

3.5 Pattern-based Rule Filters

In this section we first reconsider whether reintroducing the monotonic rules (originally excluded as described in rows 'b', 'c', 'd' in Table 4) affects performance. Results are given in the upper rows of Table 7. For all classes, we find that reintroducing these rules increases the total number of rules

mt02-05-		*-tune*			*-test*
$N_{nt}.N_e$	Filter	**Time**	**Rules**	**BLEU**	**BLEU**
baseline **NRT**=20		1.0	3.59	52.1	51.4
2.3	+monotone	1.1	4.08	51.5	51.1
2.4	+monotone	2.0	11.52	51.6	51.0
2.5	+monotone	1.8	6.66	51.7	51.2
1.3	mincount=3	1.0	5.61	52.1	51.3
2.3	mincount=1	1.2	3.70	52.1	51.4
2.4	mincount=5	1.8	4.62	52.0	51.3
2.4	mincount=15	1.0	3.37	52.0	51.4
2.5	mincount=1	1.1	4.27	52.2	51.5
1.2	mincount=5	1.0	3.51	51.8	51.3
1.2	mincount=10	1.0	3.50	51.7	51.2

Table 7: Effect of pattern-based rule filters. Time in seconds per word. Rules in millions.

substantially, despite the NRT=20 filter, but leads to degradation in translation performance.

We next reconsider the mincount threshold values for $N_{nt}.N_e$ classes 1.3, 2.3, 2.4 and 2.5 originally described in Table 4 (rows 'e' to 'h'). Results under various mincount cutoffs for each class are given in Table 7 (middle five rows). For classes 2.3 and 2.5, the mincount cutoff can be reduced to 1 (i.e. all rules are kept) with slight translation improvements. In contrast, reducing the cutoff for classes 1.3 and 2.4 to 3 and 5, respectively, adds many more rules with no increase in performance. We also find that increasing the cutoff to 15 for class 2.4 yields the same results with a smaller rule set. Finally, we consider further filtering applied to class 1.2 with mincount 5 and 10 (final two rows in Table 7). The number of rules is largely unchanged, but translation performance drops consistently as more rules are removed.

Based on these experiments, we conclude that it is better to apply separate mincount thresholds to the classes to obtain optimal performance with a minimum size rule set.

3.6 Large Language Models and Evaluation

Finally, in this section we report results of our shallow hierarchical system with the 2.5 mincount=1 configuration from Table 7, after including the following N-best list rescoring steps.

- *Large-LM rescoring*. We build sentence-specific zero-cutoff stupid-backoff (Brants et al., 2007) 5-gram language models, estimated using ~4.7B words of English newswire text, and apply them to rescore each 10000-best list.
- *Minimum Bayes Risk (MBR)*. We then rescore the first 1000-best hypotheses with MBR, taking the negative sentence level BLEU score as the loss function to minimise (Kumar and Byrne, 2004).

Table 8 shows results for *mt02-05-tune*, *mt02-05-test*, the NIST subsets from the MT06 evaluation (*mt06-nist-nw* for newswire data and *mt06-nist-ng* for newsgroup) and *mt08*, as measured by lowercased IBM BLEU and TER (Snover et al., 2006). Mixed case NIST BLEU for this system on *mt08* is 42.5. This is directly comparable to official MT08 evaluation results[1].

4 Conclusions

This paper focuses on efficient large-scale hierarchical translation while maintaining good translation quality. Smart memoization and spreading neighborhood exploration during cube pruning are described and shown to reduce memory consumption and Hiero search errors using a simple phrase-based system as a contrast.

We then define a general classification of hierarchical rules, based on their number of non-terminals, elements and their patterns, for refined extraction and filtering.

For a large-scale Arabic-to-English task, we show that shallow hierarchical decoding is as good

[1]Full MT08 results are available at http://www.nist.gov/speech/tests/mt/2008/. It is worth noting that many of the top entries make use of system combination; the results reported here are for single system translation.

	mt02-05-tune	*mt02-05-test*	*mt06-nist-nw*	*mt06-nist-ng*	*mt08*
HIERO+MET	52.2 / 41.6	51.5 / 42.2	48.4 / 43.6	35.3 / 53.2	42.5 / 48.6
+rescoring	53.2 / 40.8	52.6 / 41.4	49.4 / 42.9	36.6 / 53.5	43.4 / 48.1

Table 8: Arabic-to-English translation results (lower-cased IBM BLEU / TER) with large language models and MBR decoding.

as fully hierarchical search and that decoding time is dramatically decreased. In addition, we describe individual rule filters based on the distribution of translations with further time reductions at no cost in translation scores. This is in direct contrast to recent reported results in which other filtering strategies lead to degraded performance (Shen et al., 2008; Zollmann et al., 2008).

We find that certain patterns are of much greater value in translation than others and that separate minimum count filters should be applied accordingly. Some patterns were found to be redundant or harmful, in particular those with two monotonic non-terminals. Moreover, we show that the value of a pattern is not directly related to the number of rules it encompasses, which can lead to discarding large numbers of rules as well as to dramatic speed improvements.

Although reported experiments are only for Arabic-to-English translation, we believe the approach will prove to be general. Pattern relevance will vary for other language pairs, but we expect filtering strategies to be equally worth pursuing.

Acknowledgments

This work was supported in part by the GALE program of the Defense Advanced Research Projects Agency, Contract No. HR0011- 06-C-0022. G. Iglesias supported by Spanish Government research grant BES-2007-15956 (project TEC2006-13694-C03-03).

References

Cyril Allauzen, Michael Riley, Johan Schalkwyk, Wojciech Skut, and Mehryar Mohri. 2007. OpenFst: A general and efficient weighted finite-state transducer library. In *Proceedings of CIAA*, pages 11–23.

Oliver Bender, Evgeny Matusov, Stefan Hahn, Sasa Hasan, Shahram Khadivi, and Hermann Ney. 2007. The RWTH Arabic-to-English spoken language translation system. In *Proceedings of ASRU*, pages 396–401.

Graeme Blackwood, Adrià de Gispert, Jamie Brunning, and William Byrne. 2008. Large-scale statistical machine translation with weighted finite state transducers. In *Proceedings of FSMNLP*, pages 27–35.

Phil Blunsom, Trevor Cohn, and Miles Osborne. 2008. A discriminative latent variable model for statistical machine translation. In *Proceedings of ACL-HLT*, pages 200–208.

Thorsten Brants, Ashok C. Popat, Peng Xu, Franz J. Och, and Jeffrey Dean. 2007. Large language models in machine translation. In *Proceedings of EMNLP-ACL*, pages 858–867.

Jean-Cédric Chappelier and Martin Rajman. 1998. A generalized CYK algorithm for parsing stochastic CFG. In *Proceedings of TAPD*, pages 133–137.

Jean-Cédric Chappelier, Martin Rajman, Ramón Aragüés, and Antoine Rozenknop. 1999. Lattice parsing for speech recognition. In *Proceedings of TALN*, pages 95–104.

David Chiang. 2005. A hierarchical phrase-based model for statistical machine translation. In *Proceedings of ACL*, pages 263–270.

David Chiang. 2007. Hierarchical phrase-based translation. *Computational Linguistics*, 33(2):201–228.

Markus Dreyer, Keith Hall, and Sanjeev Khudanpur. 2007. Comparing reordering constraints for SMT using efficient BLEU oracle computation. In *Proceedings of SSST, NAACL-HLT 2007 / AMTA Workshop on Syntax and Structure in Statistical Translation*.

Christopher Dyer, Smaranda Muresan, and Philip Resnik. 2008. Generalizing word lattice translation. In *Proceedings of ACL-HLT*, pages 1012–1020.

Liang Huang and David Chiang. 2007. Forest rescoring: Faster decoding with integrated language models. In *Proceedings of ACL*, pages 144–151.

Shankar Kumar and William Byrne. 2004. Minimum Bayes-risk decoding for statistical machine translation. In *Proceedings of HLT-NAACL*, pages 169–176.

Shankar Kumar and William Byrne. 2005. Local phrase reordering models for statistical machine translation. In *Proceedings of HLT-EMNLP*, pages 161–168.

Shankar Kumar, Yonggang Deng, and William Byrne. 2006. A weighted finite state transducer translation template model for statistical machine translation. *Natural Language Engineering*, 12(1):35–75.

Zhifei Li and Sanjeev Khudanpur. 2008. A scalable decoder for parsing-based machine translation with equivalent language model state maintenance. In *Proceedings of the ACL-HLT Second Workshop on Syntax and Structure in Statistical Translation*, pages 10–18.

Adam Lopez. 2007. Hierarchical phrase-based translation with suffix arrays. In *Proceedings of EMNLP-CONLL*, pages 976–985.

Adam Lopez. 2008. Tera-scale translation models via pattern matching. In *Proceedings of COLING*, pages 505–512.

Yuval Marton and Philip Resnik. 2008. Soft syntactic constraints for hierarchical phrased-based translation. In *Proceedings of ACL-HLT*, pages 1003–1011.

Franz J. Och. 2003. Minimum error rate training in statistical machine translation. In *Proceedings of ACL*, pages 160–167.

Antti-Veikko Rosti, Necip Fazil Ayan, Bing Xiang, Spyros Matsoukas, Richard Schwartz, and Bonnie Dorr. 2007. Combining outputs from multiple machine translation systems. In *Proceedings of HLT-NAACL*, pages 228–235.

Libin Shen, Jinxi Xu, and Ralph Weischedel. 2008. A new string-to-dependency machine translation algorithm with a target dependency language model. In *Proceedings of ACL-HLT*, pages 577–585.

Khe Chai Sim, William Byrne, Mark Gales, Hichem Sahbi, and Phil Woodland. 2007. Consensus network decoding for statistical machine translation system combination. In *Proceedings of ICASSP*, volume 4, pages 105–108.

Matthew Snover, Bonnie J. Dorr, Richard Schwartz, Linnea Micciulla, and John Makhoul. 2006. A study of translation edit rate with targeted human annotation. In *Proceedings of AMTA*, pages 223–231.

Ashish Venugopal, Andreas Zollmann, and Vogel Stephan. 2007. An efficient two-pass approach to synchronous-CFG driven statistical MT. In *Proceedings of HLT-NAACL*, pages 500–507.

Hao Zhang and Daniel Gildea. 2006. Synchronous binarization for machine translation. In *Proceedings of HLT-NAACL*, pages 256–263.

Hao Zhang, Daniel Gildea, and David Chiang. 2008. Extracting synchronous grammar rules from word-level alignments in linear time. In *Proceedings of COLING*, pages 1081–1088.

Andreas Zollmann and Ashish Venugopal. 2006. Syntax augmented machine translation via chart parsing. In *Proceedings of NAACL Workshop on Statistical Machine Translation*, pages 138–141.

Andreas Zollmann, Ashish Venugopal, Franz Och, and Jay Ponte. 2008. A systematic comparison of phrase-based, hierarchical and syntax-augmented statistical MT. In *Proceedings of COLING*, pages 1145–1152.

An Empirical Study on Class-based Word Sense Disambiguation*

Rubén Izquierdo & Armando Suárez
Deparment of Software and Computing Systems
University of Alicante. Spain
{ruben,armando}@dlsi.ua.es

German Rigau
IXA NLP Group.
EHU. Donostia, Spain
german.rigau@ehu.es

Abstract

As empirically demonstrated by the last SensEval exercises, assigning the appropriate meaning to words in context has resisted all attempts to be successfully addressed. One possible reason could be the use of inappropriate set of meanings. In fact, WordNet has been used as a de-facto standard repository of meanings. However, to our knowledge, the meanings represented by WordNet have been only used for WSD at a very fine-grained sense level or at a very coarse-grained class level. We suspect that selecting the appropriate level of abstraction could be on between both levels. We use a very simple method for deriving a small set of appropriate meanings using basic structural properties of WordNet. We also empirically demonstrate that this automatically derived set of meanings groups senses into an adequate level of abstraction in order to perform class-based Word Sense Disambiguation, allowing accuracy figures over 80%.

1 Introduction

Word Sense Disambiguation (WSD) is an intermediate Natural Language Processing (NLP) task which consists in assigning the correct semantic interpretation to ambiguous words in context. One of the most successful approaches in the last years is the *supervised learning from examples*, in which statistical or Machine Learning classification models are induced from semantically annotated corpora (Màrquez et al., 2006). Generally, supervised systems have obtained better results than the unsupervised ones, as shown by experimental work and international evaluation exercises such as Senseval[1]. These annotated corpora are usually manually tagged by lexicographers with word senses taken from a particular lexical semantic resource –most commonly WordNet[2] (WN) (Fellbaum, 1998).

WN has been widely criticized for being a sense repository that often provides too fine–grained sense distinctions for higher level applications like Machine Translation or Question & Answering. In fact, WSD at this level of granularity has resisted all attempts of inferring robust broad-coverage models. It seems that many word–sense distinctions are too subtle to be captured by automatic systems with the current small volumes of word–sense annotated examples. Possibly, building class-based classifiers would allow to avoid the data sparseness problem of the word-based approach. Recently, using WN as a sense repository, the organizers of the English all-words task at SensEval-3 reported an inter-annotation agreement of 72.5% (Snyder and Palmer, 2004). Interestingly, this result is difficult to outperform by state-of-the-art sense-based WSD systems.

Thus, some research has been focused on deriving different word-sense groupings to overcome the fine–grained distinctions of WN (Hearst and Schütze, 1993), (Peters et al., 1998), (Mihalcea and Moldovan, 2001), (Agirre and LopezDeLaCalle, 2003), (Navigli, 2006) and (Snow et al., 2007). That is, they provide methods for grouping senses of the same **word**, thus producing coarser word sense groupings for better disambiguation.

Wikipedia[3] has been also recently used to overcome some problems of automatic learning methods: excessively fine–grained definition of meanings, lack of annotated data and strong domain dependence of existing annotated corpora. In this way, Wikipedia provides a new very large source of annotated data, constantly expanded (Mihalcea, 2007).

*This paper has been supported by the European Union under the projects QALL-ME (FP6 IST-033860) and KYOTO (FP7 ICT-211423), and the Spanish Government under the project Text-Mess (TIN2006-15265-C06-01) and KNOW (TIN2006-15049-C03-01)

[1] http://www.senseval.org
[2] http://wordnet.princeton.edu
[3] http://www.wikipedia.org

Proceedings of the 12th Conference of the European Chapter of the ACL, pages 389–397,
Athens, Greece, 30 March – 3 April 2009. ©2009 Association for Computational Linguistics

In contrast, some research have been focused on using predefined sets of sense-groupings for learning class-based classifiers for WSD (Segond et al., 1997), (Ciaramita and Johnson, 2003), (Villarejo et al., 2005), (Curran, 2005) and (Ciaramita and Altun, 2006). That is, grouping senses of different words into the same explicit and comprehensive semantic class.

Most of the later approaches used the original Lexicographical Files of WN (more recently called SuperSenses) as very coarse–grained sense distinctions. However, not so much attention has been paid on learning class-based classifiers from other available sense–groupings such as WordNet Domains (Magnini and Cavaglià, 2000), SUMO labels (Niles and Pease, 2001), EuroWordNet Base Concepts (Vossen et al., 1998), Top Concept Ontology labels (Alvez et al., 2008) or Basic Level Concepts (Izquierdo et al., 2007). Obviously, these resources relate senses at some level of abstraction using different semantic criteria and properties that could be of interest for WSD. Possibly, their combination could improve the overall results since they offer different semantic perspectives of the data. Furthermore, to our knowledge, to date no comparative evaluation has been performed on SensEval data exploring different levels of abstraction. In fact, (Villarejo et al., 2005) studied the performance of class–based WSD comparing only SuperSenses and SUMO by 10–fold cross–validation on SemCor, but they did not provide results for SensEval2 nor SensEval3.

This paper empirically explores on the supervised WSD task the performance of different levels of abstraction provided by WordNet Domains (Magnini and Cavaglià, 2000), SUMO labels (Niles and Pease, 2001) and Basic Level Concepts (Izquierdo et al., 2007). We refer to this approach as class–based WSD since the classifiers are created at a class level instead of at a sense level. Class-based WSD clusters senses of different words into the same explicit and comprehensive grouping. Only those cases belonging to the same semantic class are grouped to train the classifier. For example, the coarser word grouping obtained in (Snow et al., 2007) only has one remaining sense for "church". Using a set of Base Level Concepts (Izquierdo et al., 2007), the three senses of "church" are still represented by *faith.n#3*, *building.n#1* and *religious_ceremony.n#1*.

The contribution of this work is threefold. We empirically demonstrate that a) Basic Level Concepts group senses into an adequate level of abstraction in order to perform supervised class–based WSD, b) that these semantic classes can be successfully used as semantic features to boost the performance of these classifiers and c) that the class-based approach to WSD reduces dramatically the required amount of training examples to obtain competitive classifiers.

After this introduction, section 2 presents the sense-groupings used in this study. In section 3 the approach followed to build the class–based system is explained. Experiments and results are shown in section 4. Finally some conclusions are drawn in section 5.

2 Semantic Classes

WordNet (Fellbaum, 1998) synsets are organized in forty five Lexicographer Files, more recetly called **SuperSenses**, based on open syntactic categories (nouns, verbs, adjectives and adverbs) and logical groupings, such as person, phenomenon, feeling, location, etc. There are 26 basic categories for nouns, 15 for verbs, 3 for adjectives and 1 for adverbs.

WordNet Domains[4] (Magnini and Cavaglià, 2000) is a hierarchy of 165 Domain Labels which have been used to label all WN synsets. Information brought by Domain Labels is complementary to what is already in WN. First of all a Domain Labels may include synsets of different syntactic categories: for instance MEDICINE groups together senses from nouns, such as doctor and hospital, and from Verbs such as to operate. Second, a Domain Label may also contain senses from different WordNet subhierarchies. For example, SPORT contains senses such as athlete, deriving from life form, game equipment, from physical object, sport from act, and playing field, from location.

SUMO[5] (Niles and Pease, 2001) was created as part of the IEEE Standard Upper Ontology Working Group. The goal of this Working Group is to develop a standard upper ontology to promote data interoperability, information search and retrieval, automated inference, and natural language processing. SUMO consists of a set of concepts, relations, and axioms that formalize an upper ontology. For these experiments, we used the complete WN1.6 mapping with 1,019 SUMO labels.

[4] http://wndomains.itc.it/

[5] http://www.ontologyportal.org/

Basic Level Concepts[6] (BLC) (Izquierdo et al., 2007) are small sets of meanings representing the whole nominal and verbal part of WN. BLC can be obtained by a very simple method that uses basic structural WN properties. In fact, the algorithm only considers the relative number of relations of each synset along the hypernymy chain. The process follows a bottom-up approach using the chain of hypernymy relations. For each synset in WN, the process selects as its BLC the first local maximum according to the relative number of relations. The local maximum is the synset in the hypernymy chain having more relations than its immediate hyponym and immediate hypernym. For synsets having multiple hypernyms, the path having the local maximum with higher number of relations is selected. Usually, this process finishes having a number of preliminary BLC. Obviously, while ascending through this chain, more synsets are subsumed by each concept. The process finishes checking if the number of concepts subsumed by the preliminary list of BLC is higher than a certain threshold. For those BLC not representing enough concepts according to the threshold, the process selects the next local maximum following the hypernymy hierarchy. Thus, depending on the type of relations considered to be counted and the threshold established, different sets of BLC can be easily obtained for each WN version.

In this paper, we empirically explore the performance of the different levels of abstraction provided by Basic Level Concepts (BLC) (Izquierdo et al., 2007).

Table 1 presents the total number of BLC and its average depth for WN1.6, varying the threshold and the type of relations considered (all relations or only hyponymy).

Thres.	Rel.	PoS	#BLC	Av. depth.
0	all	Noun	3,094	7.09
		Verb	1,256	3.32
	hypo	Noun	2,490	7.09
		Verb	1,041	3.31
20	all	Noun	558	5.81
		Verb	673	1.25
	hypo	Noun	558	5.80
		Verb	672	1.21
50	all	Noun	253	5.21
		Verb	633	1.13
	hypo	Noun	248	5.21
		Verb	633	1.10

Table 1: BLC for WN1.6 using all or hyponym relations

[6]http://adimen.si.ehu.es/web/BLC

Classifier	Examples	# of examples
church.n#2 *(sense approach)*	church.n#2	58
building, edifice *(class approach)*	church.n#2	58
	building.n#1	48
	hotel.n#1	39
	hospital.n#1	20
	barn.n#1	17
	......	......
		TOTAL= 371 examples

Table 2: Examples and number of them in Semcor, for sense approach and for class approach

3 Class-based WSD

We followed a supervised machine learning approach to develop a set of class-based WSD taggers. Our systems use an implementation of a Support Vector Machine algorithm to train the classifiers (one per class) on semantic annotated corpora for acquiring positive and negative examples of each class and on the definition of a set of features for representing these examples. The system decides and selects among the possible semantic classes defined for a word. In the sense approach, one classifier is generated for each word sense, and the classifiers choose between the possible senses for the word. The examples to train a single classifier for a concrete word are all the examples of this word sense. In the semantic–class approach, one classifier is generated for each semantic class. So, when we want to label a word, our program obtains the set of possible semantic classes for this word, and then launch each of the semantic classifiers related with these semantic categories. The most likely category is selected for the word. In this approach, contrary to the word sense approach, to train a classifier we can use all examples of all words belonging to the class represented by the classifier. In table 2 an example for a sense of "church" is shown. We think that this approach has several advantages. First, semantic classes reduce the average polysemy degree of words (some word senses are grouped together within the same class). Moreover, the well known problem of acquisition bottleneck in supervised machine learning algorithms is attenuated, because the number of examples for each classifier is increased.

3.1 The learning algorithm: SVM

Support Vector Machines (SVM) have been proven to be robust and very competitive in many NLP tasks, and in WSD in particular (Màrquez et al., 2006). For these experiments, we used SVM-Light (Joachims, 1998). SVM are used to learn an hyperplane that separates the positive from the negative examples with the maximum margin. It means that the hyperplane is located in an intermediate position between positive and negative examples, trying to keep the maximum distance to the closest positive example, and to the closest negative example. In some cases, it is not possible to get a hyperplane that divides the space linearly, or it is better to allow some errors to obtain a more efficient hyperplane. This is known as "soft-margin SVM", and requires the estimation of a parameter (C), that represent the trade-off allowed between training errors and the margin. We have set this value to 0.01, which has been proved as a good value for SVM in WSD tasks.

When classifying an example, we obtain the value of the output function for each SVM classifier corresponding to each semantic class for the word example. Our system simply selects the class with the greater value.

3.2 Corpora

Three semantic annotated corpora have been used for training and testing. SemCor has been used for training while the corpora from the English all-words tasks of SensEval-2 and SensEval-3 has been used for testing. We also considered SemEval-2007 coarse–grained task corpus for testing, but this dataset was discarded because this corpus is also annotated with clusters of word senses.

SemCor (Miller et al., 1993) is a subset of the Brown Corpus plus the novel *The Red Badge of Courage*, and it has been developed by the same group that created WordNet. It contains 253 texts and around 700,000 running words, and more than 200,000 are also lemmatized and sense-tagged according to Princeton WordNet 1.6.

SensEval-2[7] English all-words corpus (hereinafter SE2) (Palmer et al., 2001) consists on 5,000 words of text from three WSJ articles representing different domains from the Penn TreeBank II. The sense inventory used for tagging is WordNet 1.7. Finally, **SensEval-3**[8] English all-words corpus (hereinafter SE3) (Snyder and Palmer, 2004), is made up of 5,000 words, extracted from two WSJ articles and one excerpt from the Brown Corpus. Sense repository of WordNet 1.7.1 was used to tag 2,041 words with their proper senses.

3.3 Feature types

We have defined a set of features to represent the examples according to previous works in WSD and the nature of class-based WSD. Features widely used in the literature as in (Yarowsky, 1994) have been selected. These features are pieces of information that occur in the context of the target word, and can be organized as:

Local features: bigrams and trigrams that contain the target word, including part-of-speech (PoS), lemmas or word-forms.

Topical features: word–forms or lemmas appearing in windows around the target word.

In particular, our systems use the following **basic features**:

Word–forms and lemmas in a window of 10 words around the target word

PoS: the concatenation of the preceding/following three/five PoS

Bigrams and trigrams formed by lemmas and word-forms and obtained in a window of 5 words. We use of all tokens regardless their PoS to build bi/trigrams. The target word is replaced by *X* in these features to increase the generalization of them for the semantic classifiers

Moreover, we also defined a set of **Semantic Features** to explode different semantic resources in order to enrich the set of basic features:

Most frequent semantic class calculated over SemCor, the most frequent semantic class for the target word.

Monosemous semantic classes semantic classes of the monosemous words arround the target word in a window of size 5. Several types of semantic classes have been considered to create these features. In particular, two different sets of BLC (BLC20 and BLC50[9]), SuperSenses, WordNet Domains (WND) and SUMO.

In order to increase the generalization capabilities of the classifiers we filter out irrelevant features. We measure the relevance of a feature[10]. *f* for a class *c* in terms of the frequency of *f*. For each class *c*, and for each feature *f* of that class, we calculate the frequency of the feature within the class (the number of times that it occurs in examples

[7] http://www.sle.sharp.co.uk/senseval2

[8] http://www.senseval.org/senseval3

[9] We have selected these set since they represent different levels of abstraction. Remember that 20 and 50 refer to the threshold of minimum number of synsets that a possible BLC must subsume to be considered as a proper BLC. These BLC sets were built using all kind of relations.

[10] That is, the value of the feature, for example a *feature type* can be **word-form**, and a *feature* of that type can be "houses"

of the class), and also obtain the total frequency of the feature, for all the classes. We divide both values (classFreq / totalFreq) and if the result is not greater than a certain threshold t, the feature is removed from the feature list of the class c[11]. In this way, we ensure that the features selected for a class are more frequently related with that class than with others. We set this threshold t to 0.25, obtained empirically with very preliminary versions of the classifiers on SensEval3 test.

4 Experiments and Results

To analyze the influence of each feature type in the class-based WSD, we designed a large set of experiments. An experiment is defined by two sets of semantic classes. First, the semantic class type for selecting the examples used to build the classifiers (determining the abstraction level of the system). In this case, we tested: sense[12], BLC20, BLC50, WordNet Domains (WND), SUMO and SuperSense (SS). Second, the semantic class type used for building the semantic features. In this case, we tested: BLC20, BLC50, SuperSense, WND and SUMO. Combining them, we generated the set of experiments described later.

Test	pos	Sense	BLC20	BLC50	WND	SUMO	SS
SE2	N	4.02	3.45	3.34	2.66	3.33	2.73
	V	9.82	7.11	6.94	2.69	5.94	4.06
SE3	N	4.93	4.08	3.92	3.05	3.94	3.06
	V	10.95	8.64	8.46	2.49	7.60	4.08

Table 3: Average polysemy on SE2 and SE3

Table 3 presents the average polysemy on SE2 and SE3 of the different semantic classes.

4.1 Baselines

The most frequent classes (MFC) of each word calculated over SemCor are considered to be the baselines of our systems. Ties between classes on a specific word are solved obtaining the global frequency in SemCor of each of these tied classes, and selecting the more frequent class over the whole training corpus. When there are no occurrences of a word of the test corpus in SemCor (we are not able to calculate the most frequent class of the word), we obtain again the global frequency for each of its possible semantic classes (obtained from WN) over SemCor, and we select the most frequent.

4.2 Results

Tables 4 and 5 present the F1 measures (harmonic mean of recall and precision) for nouns and verbs respectively when training our systems on SemCor and testing on SE2 and SE3. Those results showing a statistically significant[13] positive difference when compared with the baseline are in marked bold. Column labeled as "Class" refers to the target set of semantic classes for the classifiers, that is, the desired semantic level for each example. Column labeled as "Sem. Feat." indicates the class of the semantic features used to train the classifiers. For example, class BLC20 combined with Semantic Feature BLC20 means that this set of classes were used both to label the test examples and to define the semantic features. In order to compare their contribution we also performed a "basicFeat" test without including semantic features.

As expected according to most literature in WSD, the performances of the MFC baselines are very high. In particular, those corresponding to nouns (ranging from 70% to 80%). While nominal baselines seem to perform similarly in both SE2 and SE3, verbal baselines appear to be consistently much lower for SE2 than for SE3. In SE2, verbal baselines range from 44% to 68% while in SE3 verbal baselines range from 52% to 79%. An exception is the results for verbs considering WND: the results are very high due to the low polysemy for verbs according to WND. As expected, when increasing the level of abstraction (from senses to SuperSenses) the results also increase. Finally, it also seems that SE2 task is more difficult than SE3 since the MFC baselines are lower.

As expected, the results of the systems increase while augmenting the level of abstraction (from senses to SuperSenses), and almost in every case, the baseline results are reached or outperformed. This is very relevant since the baseline results are very high.

Regarding nouns, a very different behaviour is observed for SE2 and SE3. While for SE3 none of the system presents a significant improvement over the baselines, for SE2 a significant improvement is obtained by using several types of seman-

[11] Depending on the experiment, around 30% of the original features are removed by this filter.

[12] We included this evaluation for comparison purposes since the current system have been designed for class-based evaluation only.

[13] Using the McNemar's test.

tic features. In particular, when using WordNet Domains but also BLC20. In general, BLC20 semantic features seem to be better than BLC50 and SuperSenses.

Regarding verbs, the system obtains significant improvements over the baselines using different types of semantic features both in SE2 and SE3. In particular, when using again WordNet Domains as semantic features.

In general, the results obtained by BLC20 are not so much different to the results of BLC50 (in a few cases, this difference is greater than 2 points). For instance, for nouns, if we consider the number of classes within BLC20 (558 classes), BLC50 (253 classes) and SuperSense (24 classes), BLC classifiers obtain high performance rates while maintaining much higher expressive power than SuperSenses. In fact, using SuperSenses (40 classes for nouns and verbs) we can obtain a very accurate semantic tagger with performances close to 80%. Even better, we can use BLC20 for tagging nouns (558 semantic classes and F1 over 75%) and SuperSenses for verbs (14 semantic classes and F1 around 75%).

Obviously, the classifiers using WordNet Domains as target grouping obtain very high performances due to its reduced average polysemy. However, when used as semantic features it seems to improve the results in most of the cases.

In addition, we obtain very competitive classifiers at a sense level.

4.3 Learning curves

We also performed a set of experiments for measuring the behaviour of the class-based WSD system when gradually increasing the number of training examples. These experiments have been carried for nouns and verbs, but only noun results are shown since in both cases, the trend is very similar but more clear for nouns.

The training corpus has been divided in portions of 5% of the total number of files. That is, complete files are added to the training corpus of each incremental test. The files were randomly selected to generate portions of 5%, 10%, 15%, etc. of the SemCor corpus[14]. Then, we train the system on each of the training portions and we test the system on SE2 and SE3. Finally, we also compare the

Class	Sem. Feat.	SensEval2		SensEval3	
		Poly	All	Poly	All
Sense	baseline	59.66	70.02	64.45	72.30
	basicFeat	61.13	71.20	65.45	73.15
	BLC20	61.93	71.79	65.45	73.15
	BLC50	61.79	71.69	65.30	73.04
	SS	61.00	71.10	64.86	72.70
	WND	61.13	71.20	65.45	73.15
	SUMO	61.66	71.59	65.45	73.15
BLC20	baseline	65.92	75.71	67.98	76.29
	basicFeat	65.65	75.52	64.64	73.82
	BLC20	**68.70**	**77.69**	68.29	76.52
	BLC50	**68.83**	**77.79**	67.22	75.73
	SS	65.12	75.14	64.64	73.82
	WND	**68.97**	**77.88**	65.25	74.24
	SUMO	68.57	77.60	64.49	73.71
BLC50	baseline	67.20	76.65	68.01	76.74
	basicFeat	64.28	74.57	66.77	75.84
	BLC20	**69.72**	**78.45**	68.16	76.85
	BLC50	67.20	76.65	68.01	76.74
	SS	65.60	75.52	65.07	74.61
	WND	**70.39**	**78.92**	65.38	74.83
	SUMO	**71.31**	**79.58**	66.31	75.51
WND	baseline	78.97	86.11	76.74	83.8
	basicFeat	70.96	80.81	67.85	77.64
	BLC20	72.53	81.85	72.37	80.79
	BLC50	73.25	82.33	71.41	80.11
	SS	74.39	83.08	68.82	78.31
	WND	78.83	86.01	76.58	83.71
	SUMO	75.11	83.55	73.02	81.24
SUMO	baseline	66.40	76.09	71.96	79.55
	basicFeat	68.53	77.60	68.10	76.74
	BLC20	65.60	75.52	68.10	76.74
	BLC50	65.60	75.52	68.72	77.19
	SS	68.39	77.50	68.41	76.97
	WND	**68.92**	**77.88**	69.03	77.42
	SUMO	68.92	77.88	70.88	78.76
SS	baseline	70.48	80.41	72.59	81.50
	basicFeat	69.77	79.94	69.60	79.48
	BLC20	71.47	81.07	72.43	81.39
	BLC50	70.20	80.22	72.92	81.73
	SS	70.34	80.32	65.12	76.46
	WND	**73.59**	**82.47**	70.10	79.82
	SUMO	70.62	80.51	71.93	81.05

Table 4: Results for nouns

resulting system with the baseline computed over the same training portion.

Figures 1 and 2 present the learning curves over SE2 and SE3, respectively, of a class-based WSD system based on BLC20 using the basic features and the semantic features built with WordNet Domains.

Surprisingly, in SE2 the system only improves the F1 measure around 2% while increasing the training corpus from 25% to 100% of SemCor. In SE3, the system again only improves the F1 measure around 3% while increasing the training corpus from 30% to 100% of SemCor. That is, most of the knowledge required for the class-based WSD system seems to be already present on a small part of SemCor.

Figures 3 and 4 present the learning curves over SE2 and SE3, respectively, of a class-based WSD system based on SuperSenses using the basic features and the semantic features built with WordNet Domains.

Again, in SE2 the system only improves the F1

[14]Each portion contains also the same files than the previous portion. For example, all files in the 25% portion are also contained in the 30% portion.

Class	Sem. Feat.	SensEval2		SensEval3	
		Poly	All	Poly	All
Sense	baseline	41.20	44.75	49.78	52.88
	basicFeat	42.01	45.53	**54.19**	**57.02**
	BLC20	41.59	45.14	**53.74**	**56.61**
	BLC50	42.01	45.53	**53.6**	**56.47**
	SS	41.80	45.34	**53.89**	**56.75**
	WND	42.01	45.53	**53.89**	**56.75**
	SUMO	42.22	45.73	**54.19**	**57.02**
BLC20	baseline	50.21	55.13	54.87	58.82
	basicFeat	52.36	57.06	**57.27**	**61.10**
	BLC20	52.15	56.87	56.07	59.92
	BLC50	51.07	55.90	**56.82**	**60.60**
	SS	51.50	56.29	**57.57**	**61.29**
	WND	**54.08**	**58.61**	57.12	60.88
	SUMO	52.36	57.06	**57.42**	**61.15**
BLC50	baseline	49.78	54.93	55.96	60.06
	basicFeat	**53.23**	**58.03**	58.07	61.97
	BLC20	**52.59**	**57.45**	57.32	61.29
	BLC50	51.72	56.67	57.01	61.01
	SS	52.59	57.45	57.92	61.83
	WND	**55.17**	**59.77**	**58.52**	**62.38**
	SUMO	52.16	57.06	57.92	61.83
WND	baseline	84.80	90.33	84.96	92.20
	basicFeat	84.50	90.14	78.63	88.92
	BLC20	84.50	90.14	81.53	90.42
	BLC50	84.50	90.14	81.00	90.15
	SS	83.89	89.75	78.36	88.78
	WND	85.11	90.52	84.96	92.20
	SUMO	85.11	90.52	80.47	89.88
SUMO	baseline	54.24	60.35	59.69	64.71
	basicFeat	56.25	62.09	61.41	66.21
	BLC20	55.13	61.12	61.25	66.07
	BLC50	56.25	62.09	61.72	66.48
	SS	53.79	59.96	59.69	64.71
	WND	55.58	61.51	61.56	66.35
	SUMO	54.69	60.74	60.00	64.98
SS	baseline	62.79	68.47	76.24	79.07
	basicFeat	**66.89**	**71.95**	75.47	78.39
	BLC20	63.70	69.25	74.69	77.70
	BLC50	63.70	69.25	74.69	77.70
	SS	63.70	69.25	74.84	77.84
	WND	**66.67**	**71.76**	77.02	79.75
	SUMO	64.84	70.21	74.69	77.70

Table 5: Results for verbs

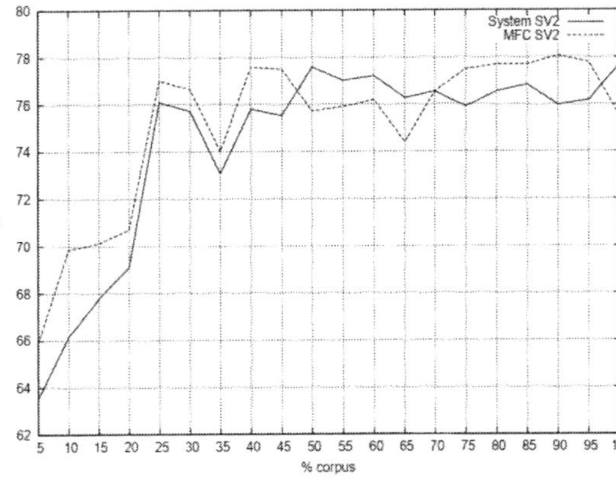

Figure 1: Learning curve of BLC20 on SE2

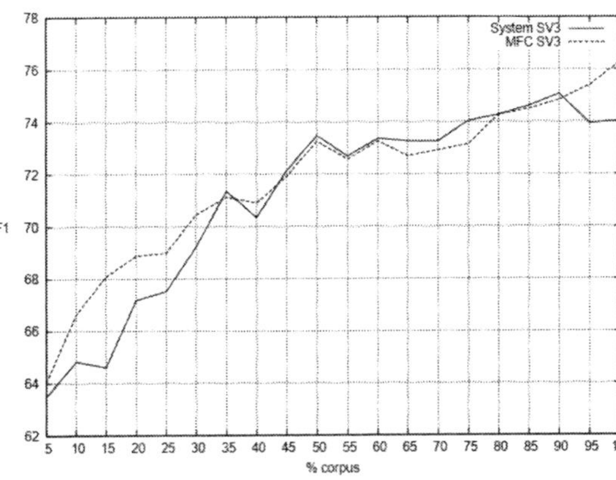

Figure 2: Learning curve of BLC20 on SE3

measure around 2% while increasing the training corpus from 25% to 100% of SemCor. In SE3, the system again only improves the F1 measure around 2% while increasing the training corpus from 30% to 100% of SemCor. That is, with only 25% of the whole corpus, the class-based WSD system reaches a F1 close to the performance using all corpus. This evaluation seems to indicate that the class-based approach to WSD reduces dramatically the required amount of training examples.

In both cases, when using BLC20 or SuperSenses as semantic classes for tagging, the behaviour of the system is similar to MFC baseline. This is very interesting since the MFC obtains high results due to the way it is defined, since the MFC over the total corpus is assigned if there are no occurrences of the word in the training corpus. Without this definition, there would be a large number of words in the test set with no occurrences when using small training portions. In these cases, the recall of the baselines (and in turn F1) would be much lower.

5 Conclusions and discussion

We explored on the WSD task the performance of different levels of abstraction and sense groupings. We empirically demonstrated that Base Level Concepts are able to group word senses into an adequate medium level of abstraction to perform supervised class–based disambiguation. We also demonstrated that the semantic classes provide a rich information about polysemous words and can be successfully used as semantic features. Finally we confirm the fact that the class–based approach reduces dramatically the required amount of training examples, opening the way to solve the well known acquisition bottleneck problem for supervised machine learning algorithms.

In general, the results obtained by BLC20 are not very different to the results of BLC50. Thus, we can select a medium level of abstraction, without having a significant decrease of the perfor-

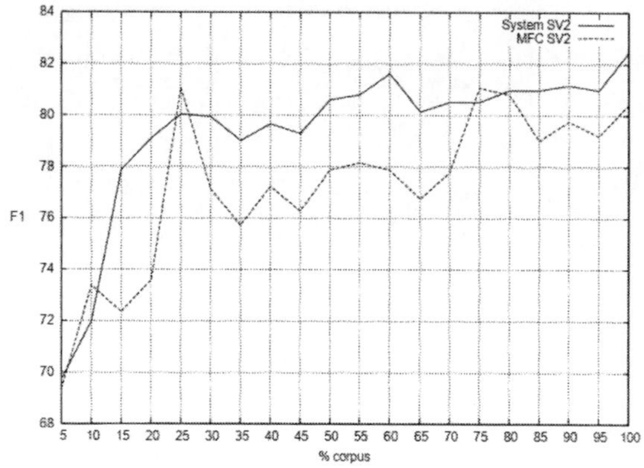

Figure 3: Learning curve of SuperSense on SE2

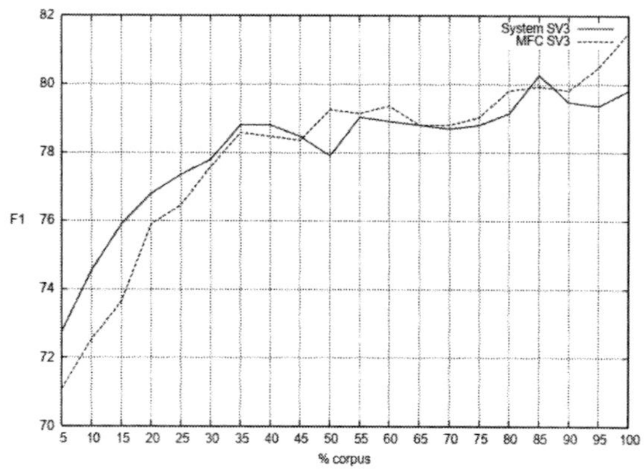

Figure 4: Learning curve of SuperSense on SE3

mance. Considering the number of classes, BLC classifiers obtain high performance rates while maintaining much higher expressive power than SuperSenses. However, using SuperSenses (46 classes) we can obtain a very accurate semantic tagger with performances around 80%. Even better, we can use BLC20 for tagging nouns (558 semantic classes and F1 over 75%) and SuperSenses for verbs (14 semantic classes and F1 around 75%).

As BLC are defined by a simple and fully automatic method, they can provide a user–defined level of abstraction that can be more suitable for certain NLP tasks.

Moreover, the traditional set of features used for sense-based classifiers do not seem to be the most adequate or representative for the class-based approach. We have enriched the usual set of features, by adding semantic information from the monosemous words of the context and the MFC of the target word. With this new enriched set of features, we can generate robust and competitive class-based classifiers.

To our knowledge, the best results for class–based WSD are those reported by (Ciaramita and Altun, 2006). This system performs a sequence tagging using a perceptron–trained HMM, using SuperSenses, training on SemCor and testing on SensEval3. The system achieves an F1–score of 70.54, obtaining a significant improvement from a baseline system which scores only 64.09. In this case, the first sense baseline is the SuperSense of the most frequent synset for a word, according to the WN sense ranking. Although this result is achieved for the all words SensEval3 task, including adjectives, we can compare both results since in SE2 and SE3 adjectives obtain very high performance figures. Using SuperSenses, adjectives only have three classes (WN Lexicographic Files 00, 01 and 44) and more than 80% of them belong to class 00. This yields to really very high performances for adjectives which usually are over 90%.

As we have seen, supervised WSD systems are very dependent of the corpora used to train and test the system. We plan to extend our system by selecting new corpora to train or test. For instance, by using the sense annotated glosses from WordNet.

References

E. Agirre and O. LopezDeLaCalle. 2003. Clustering wordnet word senses. In *Proceedings of RANLP'03*, Borovets, Bulgaria.

J. Alvez, J. Atserias, J. Carrera, S. Climent, E. Laparra, A. Oliver, and G. Rigau G. 2008. Complete and consistent annotation of wordnet using the top concept ontology. In *6th International Conference on Language Resources and Evaluation LREC*, Marrakesh, Morroco.

M. Ciaramita and Y. Altun. 2006. Broad-coverage sense disambiguation and information extraction with a supersense sequence tagger. In *Proceedings of the Conference on Empirical Methods in Natural Language Processing (EMNLP'06)*, pages 594–602, Sydney, Australia. ACL.

M. Ciaramita and M. Johnson. 2003. Supersense tagging of unknown nouns in wordnet. In *Proceedings of the Conference on Empirical methods in natural language processing (EMNLP'03)*, pages 168–175. ACL.

J. Curran. 2005. Supersense tagging of unknown nouns using semantic similarity. In *Proceedings of the 43rd Annual Meeting on Association for Computational Linguistics (ACL'05)*, pages 26–33. ACL.

C. Fellbaum, editor. 1998. *WordNet. An Electronic Lexical Database*. The MIT Press.

M. Hearst and H. Schütze. 1993. Customizing a lexicon to better suit a computational task. In *Proceedingns of the ACL SIGLEX Workshop on Lexical Acquisition*, Stuttgart, Germany.

R. Izquierdo, A. Suarez, and G. Rigau. 2007. Exploring the automatic selection of basic level concepts. In Galia Angelova et al., editor, *International Conference Recent Advances in Natural Language Processing*, pages 298–302, Borovets, Bulgaria.

T. Joachims. 1998. Text categorization with support vector machines: learning with many relevant features. In Claire Nédellec and Céline Rouveirol, editors, *Proceedings of ECML-98, 10th European Conference on Machine Learning*, number 1398, pages 137–142, Chemnitz, DE. Springer Verlag, Heidelberg, DE.

B. Magnini and G. Cavaglià. 2000. Integrating subject field codes into wordnet. In *Proceedings of LREC*, Athens. Greece.

Ll. Màrquez, G. Escudero, D. Martínez, and G. Rigau. 2006. Supervised corpus-based methods for wsd. In *E. Agirre and P. Edmonds (Eds.) Word Sense Disambiguation: Algorithms and applications.*, volume 33 of *Text, Speech and Language Technology*. Springer.

R. Mihalcea and D. Moldovan. 2001. Automatic generation of coarse grained wordnet. In *Proceding of the NAACL workshop on WordNet and Other Lexical Resources: Applications, Extensions and Customizations*, Pittsburg, USA.

R. Mihalcea. 2007. Using wikipedia for automatic word sense disambiguation. In *Proceedings of NAACL HLT 2007*.

G. Miller, C. Leacock, R. Tengi, and R. Bunker. 1993. A Semantic Concordance. In *Proceedings of the ARPA Workshop on Human Language Technology*.

R. Navigli. 2006. Meaningful clustering of senses helps boost word sense disambiguation performance. In *ACL-44: Proceedings of the 21st International Conference on Computational Linguistics and the 44th annual meeting of the Association for Computational Linguistics*, pages 105–112, Morristown, NJ, USA. Association for Computational Linguistics.

I. Niles and A. Pease. 2001. Towards a standard upper ontology. In *Proceedings of the 2nd International Conference on Formal Ontology in Information Systems (FOIS-2001)*, pages 17–19. Chris Welty and Barry Smith, eds.

M. Palmer, C. Fellbaum, S. Cotton, L. Delfs, and H. Trang Dang. 2001. English tasks: All-words and verb lexical sample. In *Proceedings of the SENSEVAL-2 Workshop. In conjunction with ACL'2001/EACL'2001*, Toulouse, France.

W. Peters, I. Peters, and P. Vossen. 1998. Automatic sense clustering in eurowordnet. In *First International Conference on Language Resources and Evaluation (LREC'98)*, Granada, Spain.

F. Segond, A. Schiller, G. Greffenstette, and J. Chanod. 1997. An experiment in semantic tagging using hidden markov model tagging. In *ACL Workshop on Automatic Information Extraction and Building of Lexical Semantic Resources for NLP Applications*, pages 78–81. ACL, New Brunswick, New Jersey.

R. Snow, Prakash S., Jurafsky D., and Ng A. 2007. Learning to merge word senses. In *Proceedings of Joint Conference on Empirical Methods in Natural Language Processing and Computational Natural Language Learning (EMNLP-CoNLL)*, pages 1005–1014.

B. Snyder and M. Palmer. 2004. The english all-words task. In Rada Mihalcea and Phil Edmonds, editors, *Senseval-3: Third International Workshop on the Evaluation of Systems for the Semantic Analysis of Text*, pages 41–43, Barcelona, Spain, July. Association for Computational Linguistics.

L. Villarejo, L. Màrquez, and G. Rigau. 2005. Exploring the construction of semantic class classifiers for wsd. In *Proceedings of the 21th Annual Meeting of Sociedad Espaola para el Procesamiento del Lenguaje Natural SEPLN'05*, pages 195–202, Granada, Spain, September. ISSN 1136-5948.

P. Vossen, L. Bloksma, H. Rodriguez, S. Climent, N. Calzolari, A. Roventini, F. Bertagna, A. Alonge, and W. Peters. 1998. The eurowordnet base concepts and top ontology. Technical report, Paris, France, France.

D. Yarowsky. 1994. Decision lists for lexical ambiguity resolution: Application to accent restoration in spanish and french. In *Proceedings of the 32nd Annual Meeting of the Association for Computational Linguistics (ACL'94)*.

Generating a Non-English Subjectivity Lexicon: Relations That Matter

Valentin Jijkoun and Katja Hofmann
ISLA, University of Amsterdam
Amsterdam, The Netherlands
{jijkoun,k.hofmann}@uva.nl

Abstract

We describe a method for creating a non-English subjectivity lexicon based on an English lexicon, an online translation service and a general purpose thesaurus: Wordnet. We use a PageRank-like algorithm to bootstrap from the translation of the English lexicon and rank the words in the thesaurus by polarity using the network of lexical relations in Wordnet. We apply our method to the Dutch language. The best results are achieved when using synonymy and antonymy relations only, and ranking positive and negative words simultaneously. Our method achieves an accuracy of 0.82 at the top 3,000 negative words, and 0.62 at the top 3,000 positive words.

1 Introduction

One of the key tasks in subjectivity analysis is the automatic detection of subjective (as opposed to objective, factual) statements in written documents (Mihalcea and Liu, 2006). This task is essential for applications such as online marketing research, where companies want to know what customers say about the companies, their products, specific products' features, and whether comments made are positive or negative. Another application is in political research, where public opinion could be assessed by analyzing user-generated online data (blogs, discussion forums, etc.).

Most current methods for subjectivity identification rely on *subjectivity lexicons*, which list words that are usually associated with positive or negative sentiments or opinions (i.e., words with *polarity*). Such a lexicon can be used, e.g., to classify individual sentences or phrases as subjective or not, and as bearing positive or negative sentiments (Pang et al., 2002; Kim and Hovy, 2004; Wilson et al., 2005a). For English, manually created subjectivity lexicons have been available for a while, but for many other languages such resources are still missing.

We describe a language-independent method for automatically bootstrapping a subjectivity lexicon, and apply and evaluate it for the Dutch language. The method starts with an English lexicon of positive and negative words, automatically translated into the target language (Dutch in our case). A PageRank-like algorithm is applied to the Dutch wordnet in order to filter and expand the set of words obtained through translation. The Dutch lexicon is then created from the resulting ranking of the wordnet nodes. Our method has several benefits:

- It is applicable to any language for which a wordnet and an automatic translation service or a machine-readable dictionary (from English) are available. For example, the EuroWordnet project (Vossen, 1998), e.g., provides wordnets for 7 languages, and free online translation services such as the one we have used in this paper are available for many other languages as well.

- The method ranks all (or almost all) entries of a wordnet by polarity (positive or negative), which makes it possible to experiment with different settings of the precision/coverage threshold in applications that use the lexicon.

We apply our method to the most recent version of Cornetto (Vossen et al., 2007), an extension of the Dutch WordNet, and we experiment with various parameters of the algorithm, in order to arrive at a good setting for porting the method to other languages. Specifically, we evaluate the quality of the resulting Dutch subjectivity lexicon using different subsets of wordnet relations and information in the glosses (definitions). We also examine

Proceedings of the 12th Conference of the European Chapter of the ACL, pages 398–405,
Athens, Greece, 30 March – 3 April 2009.

the effect of the number of iterations on the performance of our method. We find that best performance is achieved when using only synonymy and antonymy relations and, moreover, the algorithm converges after about 10 iterations.

The remainder of the paper is organized as follows. We summarize related work in section 2, present our method in section 3 and describe the manual assessment of the lexicon in section 4. We discuss experimental results in section 5 and conclude in section 6.

2 Related work

Creating subjectivity lexicons for languages other than English has only recently attracted attention of the research community. (Mihalcea et al., 2007) describes experiments with subjectivity classification for Romanian. The authors start with an English subjectivity lexicon with 6,856 entries, OpinionFinder (Wiebe and Riloff, 2005), and automatically translate it into Romanian using two bilingual dictionaries, obtaining a Romanian lexicon with 4,983 entries. A manual evaluation of a sample of 123 entries of this lexicon showed that 50% of the entries do indicate subjectivity.

In (Banea et al., 2008) a different approach based on boostrapping was explored for Romanian. The method starts with a small seed set of 60 words, which is iteratively (1) expanded by adding synonyms from an online Romanian dictionary, and (2) filtered by removing words which are not similar (at a preset threshold) to the original seed, according to an LSA-based similarity measure computed on a half-million word corpus of Romanian. The lexicon obtained after 5 iterations of the method was used for sentence-level sentiment classification, indicating an 18% improvement over the lexicon of (Mihalcea et al., 2007).

Both these approaches produce unordered sets of positive and negative words. Our method, on the other hand, assigns polarity scores to words and produces a ranking of words by polarity, which provides a more flexible experimental framework for applications that will use the lexicon.

Esuli and Sebastiani (Esuli and Sebastiani, 2007) apply an algorithm based on PageRank to rank synsets in English WordNet according to positive and negativite sentiments. The authors view WordNet as a graph where nodes are synsets and synsets are linked with the synsets of terms used in their glosses (definitions). The algorithm is initialized with positivity/negativity scores provided in SentiWordNet (Esuli and Sebastiani, 2006), an English sentiment lexicon. The weights are then distributed through the graph using an the algorithm similar to PageRank. Authors conclude that larger initial seed sets result in a better ranking produced by the method. The algorithm is always run twice, once for positivity scores, and once for negativity scores; this is different in our approach, which ranks words from negative to positive in one run. See section 5.4 for a more detailed comparison between the existing approaches outlined above and our approach.

3 Approach

Our approach extends the techniques used in (Esuli and Sebastiani, 2007; Banea et al., 2008) for mining English and Romanian subjectivity lexicons.

3.1 Boostrapping algorithm

We hypothesize that concepts (synsets) that are closely related in a wordnet have similar meaning and thus similar polarity. To determine relatedness between concepts, we view a wordnet as a graph of lexical relations between words and synsets:

- nodes correspond to lexical units (words) and synsets; and
- directed arcs correspond to relations between synsets (hyponymy, meronymy, etc.) and between synsets and words they contain; in one of our experiments, following (Esuli and Sebastiani, 2007), we also include relations between synsets and all words that occur in their glosses (definitions).

Nodes and arcs of such a graph are assigned weights, which are then propagated through the graph by iteratively applying a PageRank-like algorithm.

Initially, weights are assigned to nodes and arcs in the graph using translations from an English polarity lexicon as follows:

- words that are translations of the positive words from the English lexicon are assigned a weight of 1, words that are translations of the negative words are initialized to -1; in general, weight of a word indicates its polarity;

- All arcs are assigned a weight of 1, except for antonymy relations which are assigned a weight of -1; the intuition behind the arc weights is simple: arcs with weight 1 would usually connect synsets of the same (or similar) polarity, while arcs with weight -1 would connect synsets with opposite polarities.

We use the following notation. Our algorithm is iterative and $k = 0, 1, \ldots$ denotes an iteration. Let a_i^k be the weight of the node i at the k-th iteration. Let w_{jm} be the weight of the arc that connects node j with node m; we assume the weight is 0 if the arc does not exist. Finally, α is a damping factor of the PageRank algorithm, set to 0.8. This factor balances the impact of the initial weight of a node with the impact of weight received through connections to other nodes.

The algorithm proceeds by updating the weights of nodes iteratively as follows:

$$a_i^{k+1} = \alpha \cdot \sum_j \frac{a_j^k \cdot w_{ji}}{\sum_m |w_{jm}|} + (1 - \alpha) \cdot a_i^0$$

Furthermore, at each iterarion, all weights a_i^{k+1} are normalized by $\max_j |a_j^{k+1}|$.

The equation above is a straightforward extension of the PageRank method for the case when arcs of the graph are weighted. Nodes propagate their polarity mass to neighbours through outgoing arcs. The mass transferred depends on the weight of the arcs. Note that for arcs with negative weight (in our case, antonymy relation), the polarity of transferred mass is inverted: i.e., synsets with negative polarity will enforce positive polarity in their antonyms.

We iterate the algorithm and read off the resulting weight of the word nodes. We assume words with the lowest resulting weight to have negative polarity, and word nodes with the highest weight positive polarity. The output of the algorithm is a list of words ordered by polarity score.

3.2 Resources used

We use an English subjectivity lexicon of OpinionFinder (Wilson et al., 2005b) as the starting point of our method. The lexicon contains 2,718 English words with positive polarity and 4,910 words with negative polarity. We use a free online translation service[1] to translate positive and negative polarity words into Dutch, resulting in 974 and 1,523 Dutch words, respectively. We assumed that a word was translated into Dutch successfully if the translation occurred in the Dutch wordnet (therefore, the result of the translation is smaller than the original English lexicon).

The Dutch wordnet we used in our experiments is the most recent version of Cornetto (Vossen et al., 2007). This wordnet contains 103,734 lexical units (words), 70,192 synsets, and 157,679 relations between synsets.

4 Manual assessments

To assess the quality of our method we re-used assessments made for earlier work on comparing two resources in terms of their usefulness for automatically generating subjectivity lexicons (Jijkoun and Hofmann, 2008). In this setting, the goal was to compare two versions of the Dutch Wordnet: the first from 2001 and the other from 2008. We applied the method described in section 3 to both resources and generated two subjectivity rankings. From each ranking, we selected the 2000 words ranked as most negative and the 1500 words ranked as most positive, respectively. More negative than positive words were chosen to reflect the original distribution of positive vs. negative words. In addition, we selected words for assessment from the remaining parts of the ranked lists, randomly sampling chunks of 3000 words at intervals of 10000 words with a sampling rate of 10%. The selection was made in this way because we were mostly interested in negative and positive words, i.e., the words near either end of the rankings.

4.1 Assessment procedure

Human annotators were presented with a list of words in random order, for each word its part-of-speech tag was indicated. Annotators were asked to identify positive and negative words in this list, i.e., words that indicate positive (negative) emotions, evaluations, or positions.

Annotators were asked to classify each word on the list into one of five classes:

++ the word is positive in most contexts (*strongly positive*)

\+ the word is positive in some contexts (*weakly positive*)

0 the word is hardly ever positive or negative (*neutral*)

[1] `http://translate.google.com`

– the a word is negative in some contexts (*weakly negative*)

–– the word is negative in most contexts (*strongly negative*)

Cases where assessors were unable to assign a word to one of the classes, were separately marked as such.

For the purpose of this study we were only interested in identifying subjective words without considering subjectivity strength. Furthermore, a pilot study showed assessments of the strength of subjectivity to be a much harder task (54% inter-annotator agreement) than distinguishing between positive, neutral and negative words only (72% agreement). We therefore collapsed the classes of strongly and weakly subjective words for evaluation. These results for three classes are reported and used in the remainder of this paper.

4.2 Annotators

The data were annotated by two undergraduate university students, both native speakers of Dutch. Annotators were recruited through a university mailing list. Assessment took a total of 32 working hours (annotating at approximately 450-500 words per hour) which were distributed over a total of 8 annotation sessions.

4.3 Inter-annotator Agreement

In total, 9,089 unique words were assessed, of which 6,680 words were assessed by both annotators. For 205 words, one or both assessors could not assign an appropriate class; these words were excluded from the subsequent study, leaving us with 6,475 words with double assessments.

Table 1 shows the number of assessed words and inter-annotator agreement overall and per part-of-speech. Overall agreement is 69% (Cohen's κ=0.52). The highest agreement is for adjectives, at 76% (κ=0.62) . This is the same level of agreement as reported in (Kim and Hovy, 2004) for English. Agreement is lowest for verbs (55%, κ=0.29) and adverbs (56%, κ=0.18), which is slightly less than the 62% agreement on verbs reported by Kim and Hovy. Overall we judge agreement to be reasonable.

Table 2 shows the confusion matrix between the two assessors. We see that one assessor judged more words as subjective overall, and that more words are judged as negative than positive (this can be explained by our sampling method described above).

POS	Count	% agreement	κ
noun	3670	70%	0.51
adjective	1697	76%	0.62
adverb	25	56%	0.18
verb	1083	55%	0.29
overall	6475	69%	0.52

Table 1: Inter-annotator agreement per part-of-speech.

	–	0	+	Total
–	1803	137	39	1979
0	1011	1857	649	3517
+	81	108	790	979
Total	2895	2102	1478	6475

Table 2: Contingency table for all words assessed by two annotators.

5 Experiments and results

We evaluated several versions of the method of section 3 in order to find the best setting.

Our **baseline** is a ranking of all words in the wordnet with the weight -1 assigned to the translations of English negative polarity words, 1 assigned to the translations of positive words, and 0 assigned to the remaining words. This corresponds to simply translating the English subjectivity lexicon.

In the run **all.100** we applied our method to all words, synsets and relations from the Dutch Wordnet to create a graph with 153,386 nodes (70,192 synsets, 83,194 words) and 362,868 directed arcs (103,734 word-to-synset, 103,734 synset-to-word, 155,400 synset-to-synset relations). We used 100 iterations of the PageRank algorihm for this run (and all runs below, unless indicated otherwise).

In the run **syn.100** we only used synset-to-word, word-to-synset relations and 2,850 near-synonymy relations between synsets. We added 1,459 near-antonym relations to the graph to produce the run **syn+ant.100**. In the run **syn+hyp.100** we added 66,993 hyponymy and 66,993 hyperonymy relations to those used in run syn.100.

We also experimented with the information provided in the definitions (glosses) of synset. The glosses were available for 68,122 of the 70,192 synsets. Following (Esuli and Sebastiani, 2007), we assumed that there is a semantic relationship between a synset and each word used in its gloss. Thus, the run **gloss.100** uses a graph with 70,192 synsets, 83,194 words and 350,855 directed arcs from synsets to lemmas of all words in their glosses. To create these arcs, glosses were lemmatized and lemmas not found in the wordnet were ignored.

To see if the information in the glosses can complement the wordnet relations, we also generated a hybrid run **syn+ant+gloss.100** that used arcs derived from word-to-synset, synset-to-word, synonymy, antonymy relations and glosses.

Finally, we experimented with the number of iterations of PageRank in two setting: using all wordnet relations and using only synonyms and antonyms.

5.1 Evaluation measures

We used several measures to evaluate the quality of the word rankings produced by our method.

We consider the evaluation of a ranking parallel to the evaluation for a binary classification problem, where words are classified as positive (resp. negative) if the assigned score exceeds a certain threshold value. We can select a specific threshold and classify all words exceeding this score as positive. There will be a certain amount of correctly classified words (true positives), and some incorrectly classified words (false positives). As we move the threshold to include a larger portion of the ranking, both the number of true positives and the number of false positives increase.

We can visualize the quality of rankings by plotting their *ROC curves*, which show the relation between true positive rate (portion of the data correctly labeled as positive instances) and false positive rate (portion of the data incorrectly labeled as positive instances) at all possible threshold settings.

To compare rankings, we compute the *area under the ROC curve (AUC)*, a measure frequently used to evaluate the performance of ranking classifiers. The AUC value corresponds to the probability that a randomly drawn positive instance will be ranked higher than a randomly drawn negative instance. Thus, an AUC of 0.5 corresponds to random performance, a value of 1.0 corresponds to perfect performance. When evaluating word rankings, we compute AUC^- and AUC^+ as evaluation measures for the tasks of identifying words with negative (resp., positive) polarity.

Run	τ_k	D_k	AUC^-	AUC^+
baseline	0.395	0.303	0.701	0.733
syn.10	0.641	0.180	0.829	0.837
gloss.100	0.637	0.181	0.829	0.835
all.100	0.565	0.218	0.792	0.787
syn.100	0.645	0.177	0.831	0.839
syn+ant.100	**0.650**	**0.175**	**0.833**	**0.841**
syn+ant+gloss.100	0.643	0.178	0.831	0.838
syn+hyp.100	0.594	0.203	0.807	0.810

Table 3: Evaluation results

Other measures commonly used to evaluate rankings are Kendall's rank correlation, or Kendall's tau coefficient, and Kendall's distance (Fagin et al., 2004; Esuli and Sebastiani, 2007). When comparing rankings, Kendall's measures look at the number of pairs of ranked items that agree or disagree with the ordering in the gold standard. The measures can deal with partially ordered sets (i.e., rankings with ties): only pairs that are ordered in the gold standard are used. Let $T = \{(a_i, b_i)\}_i$ denote the set of pairs ordered in the gold standard, i.e., $a_i \prec_g b_i$. Let $C = \{(a,b) \in T \mid a \prec_r b\}$ be the set of concordant pairs, i.e., pairs ordered the same way in the gold standard and in the ranking. Let $D = \{(a,b) \in T \mid b \prec_r a\}$ be the set of discordant pairs and $U = T \setminus (C \cup D)$ the set of pairs ordered in the gold standard, but tied in the ranking. Kendall's rank correlation coefficient τ_k and Kendall's distance D_k are defined as follows:

$$\tau_k = \frac{|C| - |D|}{|T|} \qquad D_k = \frac{|D| + p \cdot |U|}{|T|}$$

where p is a penalization factor for ties, which we set to 0.5, following (Esuli and Sebastiani, 2007).

The value of τ_k ranges from -1 (perfect disagreement) to 1 (perfect agreement), with 0 indicating an almost random ranking. The value of D_k ranges from 0 (perfect agreement) to 1 (perfect disagreement).

When applying Kendall's measures we assume that the gold standard defines a partial order: for two words a and b, $a \prec_g b$ holds when $a \in N_g, b \in U_g \cup P_g$ or when $a \in U_g, b \in P_g$; here N_g, U_g, P_g are sets of words judged as negative, neutral and positive, respectively, by human assessors.

5.2 Types of wordnet relations

The results in Table 3 indicate that the method performs best when only synonymy and antonymy

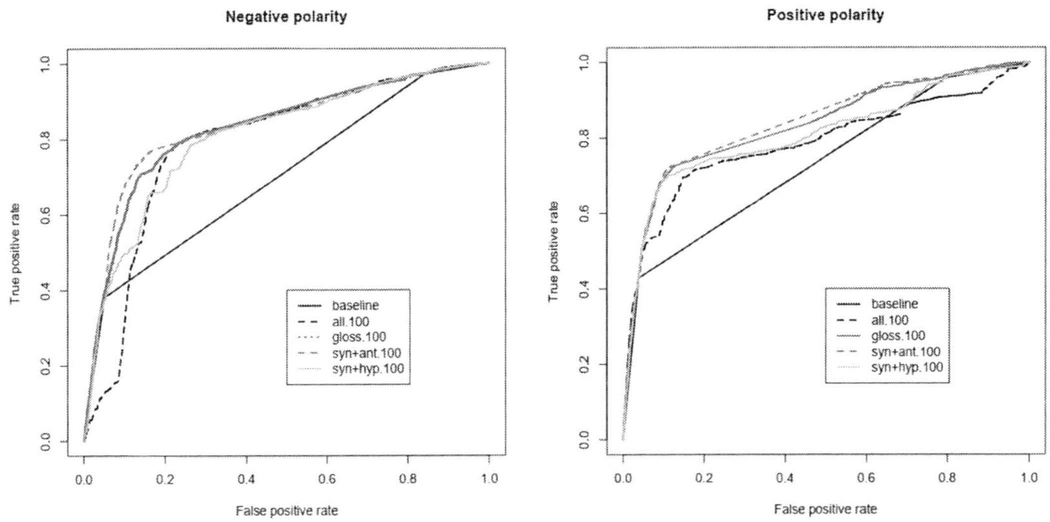

Figure 1: ROC curves showing the impact of using different sets of relations for negative and positive polarity. Graphs were generated using ROCR (Sing et al., 2005).

relations are considered for ranking. Adding hyponyms and hyperonyms, or adding relations between synsets and words in their glosses substantially decrease the performance, according to all four evaluation measures. With all relations, the performance degrades even further. Our hypothesis is that with many relations the polarity mass of the seed words is distributed too broadly. This is supported by the drop in the performance early in the ranking at the "negative" side of runs with all relations and with hyponyms (Figure 1, left). Another possible explanation can be that words with many incoming arcs (but without strong connections to the seed words) get substantial weights, thereby decreasing the quality of the ranking.

Antonymy relations also prove useful, as using them in addition to synonyms results in a small improvement. This justifies our modification of the PageRank algorithm, when we allow negative node and arc weights.

In the best setting (syn+ant.100), our method achieves an accuracy of 0.82 at top 3,000 negative words, and 0.62 at top 3,000 positive words (estimated from manual assessments of a sample, see section 4). Moreover, Figure 1 indicates that the accuracy of the seed set (i.e., the baseline translations of the English lexicon) is maintained at the positive and negative ends of the ranking for most variants of the method.

5.3 The number of iterations

In Figure 2 we plot how the AUC^{-} measure changes when the number of PageRank iterations increases (for positive polarity; the plots are almost identical for negative polarity). Although the absolute maximum of AUC is achieved at 110 iteration (60 iterations for positive polarity), the AUC clearly converges after 20 iterations. We conclude that after 20 iterations all useful information has been propagated through the graph. Moreover, our version of PageRank reaches a stable weight distribution and, at the same time, produces the best ranking.

5.4 Comparison to previous work

Although the values in the evaluation results are, obviously, language-dependent, we tried to replicate the methods used in the literature for Romanian and English (section 2), to the degree possible.

Our **baseline** replicates the method of (Mihalcea et al., 2007): i.e., a simple translation of the English lexicon into the target language. The run **syn.10** is similar to the iterative method used in (Banea et al., 2008), except that we do not perform a corpus-based filtering. We run PageRank for 10 iterations, so that polarity is propagated from the seed words to all their 5-step-synonymy neighbours. Table 3 indicates that increasing the number of iterations in the method of (Banea et

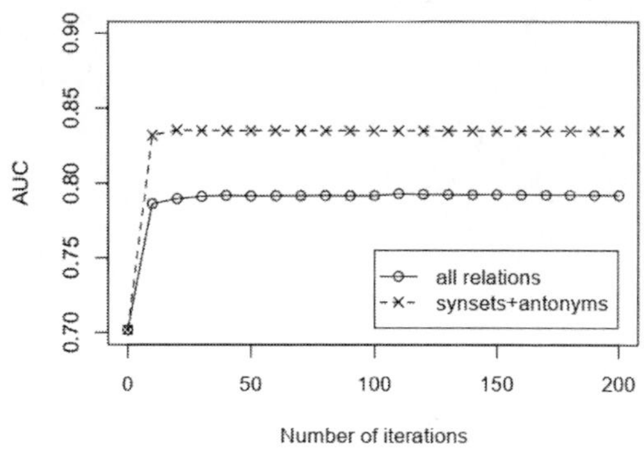

Figure 2: The number of iterations and the ranking quality (AUC), for positive polarity. Rankings for negative polarity behave similarly.

al., 2008) might help to generate a better subjectivity lexicon.

The run **gloss.100** is similar to the PageRank-based method of (Esuli and Sebastiani, 2007). The main difference is that Esuli and Sebastiani used the extended English WordNet, where words in all glosses are manually assigned to their correct synsets: the PageRank method then uses relations between synsets and *synsets of words in their glosses*. Since such a resource is not available for our target language (Dutch), we used relations between synsets and *words in their glosses*, instead. With this simplification, the PageRank method using glosses produces worse results than the method using synonyms. Further experiments with the extended English WordNet are necessary to investigate whether this decrease can be attributed to the lack of disambiguation for glosses.

An important difference between our method and (Esuli and Sebastiani, 2007) is that the latter produces two independent rankings: one for positive and one for negative words. To evaluate the effect of this choice, we generated runs **gloss.100.N** and **gloss.100.P** that used only negative (resp., only positive) seed words. We compare these runs with the run **gloss.100** (that starts with both positive and negative seeds) in Table 4. To allow a fair comparison of the generated rankings, the evaluation measures in this case are calculated separately for two binary classification problems: words with negative polarity versus all words, and words with positive polarity versus all.

The results in Table 4 clearly indicate that in-

Run	τ_k^-	D_k^-	AUC^-
gloss.100	**0.669**	**0.166**	**0.829**
gloss.100.N	0.562	0.219	0.782
	τ_k^+	D_k^+	AUC^+
gloss.100	**0.665**	**0.167**	**0.835**
gloss.100.P	0.580	0.210	0.795

Table 4: Comparison of separate and simultaneous rankings of negative and positive words.

formation about words of one polarity class helps to identify words of the other polarity: negative words are unlikely to be also positive, and vice versa. This supports our design choice: ranking words from negative to positive in one run of the method.

6 Conclusion

We have presented a PageRank-like algorithm that bootstraps a subjectivity lexicon from a list of initial seed examples (automatic translations of words in an English subjectivity lexicon). The algorithm views a wordnet as a graph where words and concepts are connected by relations such as synonymy, hyponymy, meronymy etc. We initialize the algorithm by assigning high weights to positive seed examples and low weights to negative seed examples. These weights are then propagated through the wordnet graph via the relations. After a number of iterations words are ranked according to their weight. We assume that words with lower weights are likely negative and words with high weights are likely positive.

We evaluated several variants of the method for the Dutch language, using the most recent version of Cornetto, an extension of Dutch WordNet. The evaluation was based on the manual assessment of 9,089 words (with inter-annotator agreement 69%, κ=0.52). Best results were achieved when the method used only synonymy and antonymy relations, and was ranking positive and negative words simultaneously. In this setting, the method achieves an accuracy of 0.82 at the top 3,000 negative words, and 0.62 at the top 3,000 positive words.

Our method is language-independent and can easily be applied to other languages for which wordnets exist. We plan to make the implementation of the method publicly available.

An additional important outcome of our experiments is the first (to our knowledge) manually annotated sentiment lexicon for the Dutch language.

The lexicon contains 2,836 negative polarity and 1,628 positive polarity words. The lexicon will be made publicly available as well. Our future work will focus on using the lexicon for sentence- and phrase-level sentiment extraction for Dutch.

Acknowledgments

This work was supported by projects DuO-MAn and Cornetto, carried out within the STEVIN programme which is funded by the Dutch and Flemish Governments (`http://www.stevin-tst.org`), and by the Netherlands Organization for Scientific Research (NWO) under project number 612.061.814.

References

Carmen Banea, Rada Mihalcea, and Janyce Wiebe. 2008. A bootstrapping method for building subjectivity lexicons for languages with scarce resources. In *LREC*.

Andrea Esuli and Fabrizio Sebastiani. 2006. Sentiwordnet: A publicly available lexical resource for opinion mining. In *Proceedings of LREC 2006*, pages 417–422.

Andrea Esuli and Fabrizio Sebastiani. 2007. Pageranking wordnet synsets: An application to opinion mining. In *Proceedings of the 45th Annual Meeting of the Association of Computational Linguistics*, pages 424—431.

Ronald Fagin, Ravi Kumar, Mohammad Mahdian, D. Sivakumar, and Erik Vee. 2004. Comparing and aggregating rankings with ties. In *PODS '04: Proceedings of the twenty-third ACM SIGMOD-SIGACT-SIGART symposium on Principles of database systems*, pages 47–58, New York, NY, USA. ACM.

Valentin Jijkoun and Katja Hofmann. 2008. Task-based Evaluation Report: Building a Dutch Subjectivity Lexicon. Technical report. Technical report, University of Amsterdam. `http://ilps.science.uva.nl/biblio/cornetto-subjectivity-lexicon`.

Soo-Min Kim and Eduard Hovy. 2004. Determining the sentiment of opinions. In *Proceedings of the 20th International Conference on Computational Linguistics (COLING)*.

R. Mihalcea and H. Liu. 2006. A corpus-based approach to finding happiness. In *Proceedings of the AAAI Spring Symposium on Computational Approaches to Weblogs*.

Rada Mihalcea, Carmen Banea, and Janyce Wiebe. 2007. Learning multilingual subjective language via cross-lingual projections. In *Proceedings of the 45th Annual Meeting of the Association of Computational Linguistics*, pages 976–983, Prague, Czech Republic, June. Association for Computational Linguistics.

Bo Pang, Lillian Lee, and Shivakumar Vaithyanathan. 2002. Thumbs up? sentiment classification using machine learning techniques. In *Proceedings of the Conference on Empirical Methods in Natural Language Processing (EMNLP 2002)*, pages 79–86.

T. Sing, O. Sander, N. Beerenwinkel, and T. Lengauer. 2005. ROCR: visualizing classifier performance in R. *Bioinformatics*, 21(20):3940–3941.

P. Vossen, K. Hofman, M. De Rijke, E. Tjong Kim Sang, and K. Deschacht. 2007. The cornetto database: Architecture and user-scenarios. In *Proceedings of 7th Dutch-Belgian Information Retrieval Workshop DIR2007*.

Piek Vossen, editor. 1998. *EuroWordNet: a multilingual database with lexical semantic networks*. Kluwer Academic Publishers, Norwell, MA, USA.

Janyce Wiebe and Ellen Riloff. 2005. Creating subjective and objective sentence classifiers from unannotated texts. In *Proceeding of CICLing-05, International Conference on Intelligent Text Processing and Computational Linguistics*, volume 3406 of *Lecture Notes in Computer Science*, pages 475–486. Springer-Verlag.

Theresa Wilson, Janyce Wiebe, and Paul Hoffmann. 2005a. Recognizing contextual polarity in phrase-level sentiment analysis. In *Proceedings of Human Language Technology Conference and Conference on Empirical Methods in Natural Language Processing (HLT/EMNLP 2005)*, pages 347–354.

Theresa Wilson, Janyce Wiebe, and Paul Hoffmann. 2005b. Recognizing contextual polarity in phrase-level sentiment analysis. In *Proceedings of HLTEMNLP 2005*.

Parsing Coordinations

Sandra Kübler
Indiana University
skuebler@indiana.edu

Erhard Hinrichs
Universität Tübingen
eh@sfs.uni-tuebingen.de

Wolfgang Maier
Unversität Tübingen
wo.maier@uni-tuebingen.de

Eva Klett
Universität Tübingen
eklett@sfs.uni-tuebingen.de

Abstract

The present paper is concerned with statistical parsing of constituent structures in German. The paper presents four experiments that aim at improving parsing performance of coordinate structure: 1) reranking the n-best parses of a PCFG parser, 2) enriching the input to a PCFG parser by gold scopes for any conjunct, 3) reranking the parser output for all possible scopes for conjuncts that are permissible with regard to clause structure. Experiment 4 reranks a combination of parses from experiments 1 and 3.

The experiments presented show that n-best parsing combined with reranking improves results by a large margin. Providing the parser with different scope possibilities and reranking the resulting parses results in an increase in F-score from 69.76 for the baseline to 74.69. While the F-score is similar to the one of the first experiment (n-best parsing and reranking), the first experiment results in higher recall (75.48% vs. 73.69%) and the third one in higher precision (75.43% vs. 73.26%). Combining the two methods results in the best result with an F-score of 76.69.

1 Introduction

The present paper is concerned with statistical parsing of constituent structures in German. German is a language with relatively flexible phrasal ordering, especially of verbal complements and adjuncts. This makes processing complex cases of coordination particularly challenging and error-prone. The paper presents four experiments that aim at improving parsing performance of coordinate structures: the first experiment involves reranking of n-best parses produced by a PCFG parser, the second experiment enriches the input to a PCFG parser by offering gold pre-bracketings for any coordinate structures that occur in the sentence. In the third experiment, the reranker is given all possible pre-bracketed candidate structures for coordinated constituents that are permissible with regard to clause macro- and microstructure. The parsed candidates are then reranked. The final experiment combines the parses from the first and the third experiment and reranks them. Improvements in this final experiment corroborate our hypothesis that forcing the parser to work with pre-bracketed conjuncts provides parsing alternatives that are not present in the n-best parses.

Coordinate structures have been a central issue in both computational and theoretical linguistics for quite some time. Coordination is one of those phenomena where the simple cases can be accounted for by straightforward empirical generalizations and computational techniques. More specifically, it is the observation that coordination involves two or more constituents of the same categories. However, there are a significant number of more complex cases of coordination that defy this generalization and that make the parsing task of detecting the right scope of individual conjuncts and correctly delineating the correct scope of the coordinate structure as a whole difficult. (1) shows some classical examples of this kind from English.

(1) a. Sandy is a Republican and proud of it.
b. Bob voted, but Sandy did not.
c. Bob supports him and Sandy me.

In (1a), unlike categories (NP and adjective) are conjoined. (1b) and (1c) are instances of ellipsis (VP ellipsis and gapping). Yet another difficult set of examples present cases of non-constituent conjunction, as in (2), where the direct and indirect object of a ditransitive verb are conjoined.

(2) Bob gave a book to Sam and a record to Jo.

Proceedings of the 12th Conference of the European Chapter of the ACL, pages 406–414,
Athens, Greece, 30 March – 3 April 2009. ©2009 Association for Computational Linguistics

2 Coordination in German

The above phenomena have direct analogues in German.[1] Due to the flexible ordering of phrases, their variability is even higher. For example, due to constituent fronting to clause-initial position in German verb-second main clauses, cases of non-constituent conjunction can involve any two NPs (including the subject) of a ditransitive verb to the exclusion of the third NP complement that appears in clause-initial position. In addition, German exhibits cases of asymmetric coordination first discussed by Höhle (1983; 1990; 1991) and illustrated in (3).[2]

(3) In den Wald ging ein Jäger und
Into the woods went a hunter and
schoss einen Hasen.
shot a hare.

Such cases of subject gap coordination are frequently found in text corpora (cf. (4) below) and involve conjunction of a full verb-second clause with a VP whose subject is identical to the subject in the first conjunct.

3 Experimental Setup and Baseline

3.1 The Treebank

The data source used for the experiments is the Tübingen Treebank of Written German (TüBa-D/Z) (Telljohann et al., 2005). TüBa-D/Z uses the newspaper 'die tageszeitung' (taz) as its data source, version 3 comprises approximately 27 000 sentences. The treebank annotation scheme distinguishes four levels of syntactic constituency: the lexical level, the phrasal level, the level of topological fields, and the clausal level. The primary ordering principle of a clause is the inventory of topological fields (VF, LK, MF, VC, and NF), which characterize the word order regularities among different clause types of German. TüBa-D/Z annotation relies on a context-free backbone (i.e. proper trees without crossing branches) of phrase structure combined with edge labels that specify the grammatical function of the phrase in question. Conjuncts are generally marked with the function label KONJ. Figure 1 shows the annotation that sentence (4) received in the treebank. Syntactic categories are displayed as nodes, grammatical functions as edge labels in gray (e.g. OA: direct object, PRED: predicate). This is an example of a subject-gap coordination, in which both conjuncts (FKONJ) share the subject (ON) that is realized in the first conjunct.

(4) Damit hat sich der Bevölkerungs-
So has itself the decline in
rückgang zwar abgeschwächt, ist
population though lessened, is
aber noch doppelt so groß wie 1996.
however still double so big as 1996.
'For this reason, although the decline in population has lessened, it is still twice as big as in 1996.'

The syntactic annotation scheme of the TüBa-D/Z is described in more detail in Telljohann et al. (2004; 2005).

All experiments reported here are based on a data split of 90% training data and 10% test data.

3.2 The Parsers and the Reranker

Two parsers were used to investigate the influence of scope information on parser performance on coordinate structures: BitPar (Schmid, 2004) and LoPar (Schmid, 2000). BitPar is an efficient implementation of an Earley style parser that uses bit vectors. However, BitPar cannot handle pre-bracketed input. For this reason, we used LoPar for the experiments where such input was required. LoPar, as it is used here, is a pure PCFG parser, which allows the input to be partially bracketed. We are aware that the results that can be obtained by pure PCFG parsers are not state of the art as reported in the shared task of the ACL 2008 Workshop on Parsing German (Kübler, 2008). While BitPar reaches an F-score of 69.76 (see next section), the best performing parser (Petrov and Klein, 2008) reaches an F-score of 83.97 on TüBa-D/Z (but with a different split of training and test data). However, our experiments require certain features in the parsers, namely the capability to provide n-best analyses and to parse pre-bracketed input. To our knowledge, the parsers that took part in the shared task do not provide these features. Should they become available, the methods presented here could be applied to such parsers. We see no reason why our

[1] To avoid having to gloss German examples, they were illustrated for English.

[2] Yet, another case of such asymmetric coordination discussed by Höhle involves cases of conjunction of different clause types: [$_{V-final}$ *Wenn du nach Hause kommst*] und [$_{V-2nd}$ *da warten Polizeibeamte vor der Tür.* 'If you come home and there are policemen waiting in front of the door].'

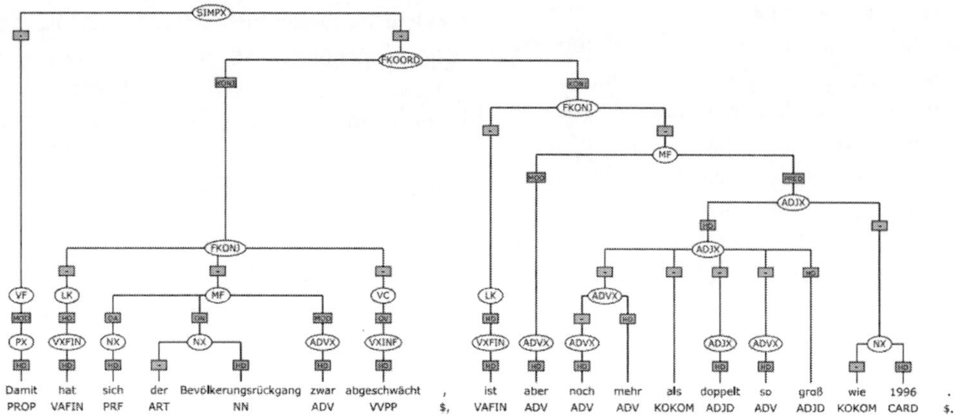

Figure 1: A tree with coordination.

methods should not be able to improve the results of these parsers further.

Since we are interested in parsing coordinations, all experiments are conducted with gold POS tags, so as to abstract away from POS tagging errors. Although the treebank contains morphological information, this type of information is not used in the experiments presented here.

The reranking experiments were conducted using the reranker by Collins and Koo (2005). This reranker uses a set of candidate parses for a sentence and reranks them based on a set of features that are extracted from the trees. The reranker uses a boosting method based on the approach by Freund et al. (1998). We used a similar feature set to the one Collins and Koo used; the following types of features were included: rules, bigrams, grandparent rules, grandparent bigrams, lexical bigrams, two-level rules, two-level bigrams, trigrams, head-modifiers, PPs, and distance for head-modifier relations, as well as all feature types involving rules extended by closed class lexicalization. For a more detailed description of the rules, the interested reader is referred to Collins and Koo (2005). For coordination, these features give a wider context than the original parser has and should thus result in improvements for this phenomenon.

3.3 The Baseline

When trained on 90% of the approximately 27,000 sentences of the TüBa-D/Z treebank, BitPar reaches an F-Score of 69.73 (precision: 68.63%, recall: 70.93%) on the full test set of 2611 sentences. These results as well as all further results presented here are labeled results, including grammatical functions. Since German has a relatively free word order, it is impossible to deduce the grammatical function of a noun phrase from the configuration of the sentence. Consequently, an evaluation based solely on syntactic constituent labels would be meaningless (cf. (Kübler, 2008) for a discussion of this point). The inclusion of grammatical labels in the trees, makes the parsing process significantly more complex.

Looking at sentences with coordination (i.e. sentences that contain a conjunction which is not in sentence-initial position), we find that 34.9% of the 2611 test sentences contain coordinations. An evaluation of only sentences with coordination shows that there is a noticeable difference: the F-score reaches 67.28 (precision: 66.36%, recall: 68.23%) as compared to 69.73 for the full test set.

The example of a wrong parse shown below illustrates why parsing of complex coordinations is so hard. Complex coordinations can take up a considerable part of the input string and accordingly of the overall sentence structure. Such global phenomena are particularly hard for pure PCFG parsing, due to the independence assumption inherent in the statistical models for PCFGs.

Sentence (4) has the following Viterbi parse:

```
(VROOT
  (SIMPX
    (VF
      (SIMPX-OS
        (VF (PX-MOD (PROP-HD Damit)))
        (LK
          (VXFIN-HD (VAFIN-HD hat)))
        (MF
```

```
        (NX-OA (PRF-HD sich))
        (NX-ON (ART der)
          (NN-HD Bevölkerungsrückgang))
        (ADVX-MOD (ADV-HD zwar)))
      (VC (VXINF-OV
          (VVPP-HD abgeschwächt))))
  ($, ,)
  (LK
    (VXFIN-HD (VAFIN-HD ist)))
  (MF
    (ADVX-MOD (ADV-HD aber))
    (ADVX-MOD (ADV-HD noch))
    (ADJX-PRED
      (ADJX-HD (ADVX (ADV-HD mehr))
        (ADJX (KOKOM als)
          (ADJD-HD doppelt))
        (ADVX (ADV-HD so))
        (ADJD-HD groß))
      (NX (KOKOM wie)
        (CARD-HD 1996)))))
($. .))
```

The parse shows that the parser did not recognize the coordination. Instead, the first conjunct including the fronted constituent, `Damit hat sich der Bevölkerungsrückgang zwar abgeschwächt`, is treated as a fronted subordinate clause.

4 Experiment 1: n-Best Parsing and Reranking

The first hypothesis for improving coordination parsing is based on the assumption that the correct parse may not be the most probable one in Viterbi parsing but may be recovered by n-best parsing and reranking, a technique that has become standard in the last few years. If this hypothesis holds, we should find the correct parse among the n-best parses. In order to test this hypothesis, we conducted an experiment with BitPar (Schmid, 2004). We parsed the test sentences in a 50-best setting.

A closer look at the 50-best parses shows that of the 2611 sentences, 195 (7.5%) were assigned the correct parse as the best parse. For 325 more sentences (12.4%), the correct parse could be found under the 50 best analyses. What is more, in 90.2% of these 520 sentences, for which the correct parse was among the 50 best parses, the best parse was among the first 10 parses. Additionally, only in 4 cases were the correct analyses among the 40-best to 50-best parses, an indication that increasing n may not result in improving the results significantly. These findings resulted in the decision not to conduct experiments with higher n.

That the 50 best analyses contain valuable information can be seen from an evaluation in which an oracle chooses from the 50 parses. In this case, we reach an F-score of 80.28. However, this F-score is also the upper limit for improvement that can be achieved by reranking the 50-best parses.

For reranking, the features of Collins and Koo (2005) were extended in the following way: Since the German treebank used for our experiments includes grammatical function information on almost all levels in the tree, all feature types were also included with grammatical functions attached: All nodes except the root node of the subtree in question were annotated with their grammatical information. Thus, for the noun phrase (NX) rule with grandparent prepositional phrase (PX) PX_{GP} NX $\rightarrow$ `ART ADJX NN`, we add an additional rule PX_{GP} `NX-HD` $\rightarrow$ `ART ADJX NN-HD`.

After pruning all features that occurred in the training data with a frequency lower than 5, the extractions produced more than 5 mio. different features. The reranker was optimized on the training data, the 50-best parses were produced in a 5-fold cross-validation setting. A non-exhaustive search for the best value for the α parameter showed that Collins and Koo's value of 0.0025 produced the best results. The row for exp. 1 in Table 1 shows the results of this experiment. The evaluation of the full data set shows an improvement of 4.77 points in the F-score, which reached 74.53. This is a relative reduction in error rate of 18.73%, which is slightly higher that the error rate reduction reported by Collins and Koo for the Penn Treebank (13%). However, the results for Collins and Koo's original parses were higher, and they did not evaluate on grammatical functions.

The evaluation of coordination sentences shows that such sentences profit from reranking to the same degree. These results prove that while coordination structures profit from reranking, they do not profit more than other phenomena. We thus conclude that reranking is no cure-all for solving the problem of accurate coordination parsing.

5 Experiment 2: Gold Scope

The results of experiment 1 lead to the conclusion that reranking the n-best parses can only result in restricted improvements on coordinations. The fact that the correct parse often cannot be found in the 50-best analyses suggests that the different possible scopes of a coordination are so different in their probability distribution that not all of the possible scopes are present in the 50-best analyses.

		all sentences			coord. sentences		
		precision	recall	F-score	precision	recall	F-score
	baseline:	68.63	70.93	69.76	66.36	68.23	67.28
exp. 1:	50-best reranking:	73.26	75.84	74.53	70.67	72.72	71.68
exp. 2:	with gold scope:	76.12	72.87	74.46	75.78	72.22	73.96
exp. 3:	automatic scope:	75.43	73.96	74.69	72.88	71.42	72.14
exp. 4:	comb. 1 and 3:	76.15	77.23	76.69	73.79	74.73	74.26

Table 1: The results of parsing all sentences and coordinated sentences only

If this hypothesis holds, forcing the parser to consider the different scope readings should increase the accuracy of coordination parsing. In order to force the parser to use the different scope readings, we first extract these scope readings, and then for each of these scope readings generate a new sentence with partial bracketing that represents the corresponding scope (see below for an example). LoPar is equipped to parse partially-bracketed input. Given input sentences with partial brackets, the parser restricts analyses to such cases that do not contradict the brackets in the input.

(5) Was stimmt, weil sie
Which is correct, because they
unterhaltsam sind, aber auch falsche
entertaining are, but also wrong
Assoziationen weckt.
associations wakes.

'Which is correct because they are entertaining, but also triggers wrong associations.'

In order to test the validity of this hypothesis, we conducted an experiment with coordination scopes extracted from the treebank trees. These scopes were translated into partial brackets that were included in the input sentences. For the sentence in (5) from the treebank (sic), the input for LoPar would be the following:

```
Was/PWS stimmt/VVFIN ,/$, weil/
KOUS ( sie/PPER unterhalt-
sam/ADJD sind/VAFIN ) ,/$,
aber/KON ( auch/ADV falsche/ADJA
Assoziationen/NN weckt/VVFIN )
```

The round parentheses delineate the conjuncts. LoPar was then forced to parse sentences containing coordination with the correct scope for the coordination. The results for this experiment are shown in Table 1 as exp. 2.

The introduction of partial brackets that delimit the scope of the coordination improve overall results on the full test set by 4.7 percent points, a rather significant improvement when we consider that only approximately one third of the test sentences were modified. The evaluation of the set of sentences that contain coordination shows that here, the difference is even higher: 6.7 percent points. It is also worth noticing that provided with scope information, the parser parses such sentences with the same accuracy as other sentences. The difference in F-scores between all sentences and only sentences with coordination in this experiment is much lower (0.5 percent points) than for all other experiments (2.5–3.0 percent points).

When comparing the results of experiment 1 (n-best parsing) with the present one, it is evident that the F-scores are very similar: 74.53 for the 50-best reranking setting, and 74.46 for the one where we provided the gold scope. However, a comparison of precision and recall shows that there are differences: 50-best reranking results in higher recall, providing gold scope for coordinations in higher precision. The lower recall in the latter experiment indicates that the provided brackets in some cases are not covered by the grammar. This is corroborated by the fact that in n-best parsing, only 1 sentence could not be parsed; but in parsing with gold scope, 8 sentences could not be parsed.

6 Experiment 3: Extracting Scope

The previous experiment has shown that providing the scope of a coordination drastically improves results for sentences with coordination as well as for the complete test set (although to a lower degree). The question that remains to be answered is whether automatically generated possible scopes can provide enough information for the reranker to improve results.

The first question that needs to be answered is how to find the possible scopes for a coordination. One possibility is to access the parse forest of a chart parser such as LoPar and extract information about all the possible scope analyses that the parser found. If the same parser is used for this step and for the final parse, we can be certain that only scopes are extracted that are compatible with the grammar of the final parser. However, parse forests are generally stored in a highly packed format so that an exhaustive search of the structures is very inefficient and proved impossible with present day computing power.

(6) "Es gibt zwar ein paar
"There are indeed a few
Niederflurbusse, aber das reicht ja
low-floor buses, but that suffices *part.*
nicht", sagt er.
not", says he.
'"There are indeed a few low-floor buses, but that isn't enough", he says.

Another solution consists of generating all possible scopes around the coordination. Thus, for the sentence in (6), the conjunction is *aber*. The shortest possible left conjunct is *Niederflurbusse*, the next one *paar Niederflurbusse*, etc. Clearly, many of these possibilities, such as the last example, are nonsensical, especially when the proposed conjunct crosses into or out of base phrase boundaries. Another type of boundary that should not be crossed is a clause boundary. Since the conjunction is part of the subordinated clause in the present example, the right conjunct cannot extend beyond the end of the clause, i.e. beyond *nicht*.

For this reason, we used KaRoPars (Müller and Ule, 2002), a partial parser for German, to parse the sentences. From the partial parses, we extracted base phrases and clauses. For (6), the relevant bracketing provided by KaRoPars is the following:

```
( " Es gibt zwar { ein paar
Niederflurbusse } , ) aber ( das
reicht ja nicht ) " , sagt er .
```

The round parentheses mark clause boundaries, the curly braces the one base phrase that is longer than one word. In the creation of possible conjuncts, only such conjuncts are listed that do not cross base phrase or clause boundaries. In order to avoid unreasonably high numbers of pre-bracketed versions, we also use higher level phrases, such as coordinated noun phrases. KaRoPars groups such higher level phrases only in contexts that allow a reliable decision. While a small percentage of such decisions is wrong, the heuristic used turns out to be reliable and efficient.

For each scope, a partially bracketed version of the input sentence is created, in which only the brackets for the suggested conjuncts are inserted. Each pre-bracketed version of the sentence is parsed with LoPar. Then all versions for one sentence are reranked. The reranker was trained on the data from experiment 1 (n-best parsing). The results of the reranker show that our restrictions based on the partial parser may have been too restrictive. Only 375 sentences had more than one pre-bracketed version, and only 328 sentence resulted in more than one parse. Only the latter set could then profit from reranking.

The results of this experiment are shown in Table 1 as exp. 3. They show that extracting possible scopes for conjuncts from a partial parse is possible. The difference in F-score between this experiment and the baseline reaches 5.93 percent points. The F-score is also minimally higher than the F-score for experiment 2 (gold scope), and recall is increased by approximately 1 percent point (even though only 12.5% of the sentences were reranked). This can be attributed to two factors: First, we provide different scope possibilities. This means that if the correct scope is not covered by the grammar, the parser may still be able to parse the next closest possibility instead of failing completely. Second, reranking is not specifically geared towards improving coordinated structures. Thus, it is possible that a parse is reranked higher because of some other feature. It is, however, not the case that the improvement results completely from reranking. This can be deduced from two points: First, while the F-score for experiment 1 (50-best analyses plus reranking) and the present experiment are very close (74.53 vs. 74.69), there are again differences in precision and recall: In experiment 1, recall is higher, and in the present experiment precision. Second, a look at the evaluation on only sentences with coordination shows that the F-score for the present experiment is higher than the one for experiment 1 (72.14 vs. 71.68). Additionally, precision for the present experiment is more than 2 percent points higher.

7 Experiment 4: Combining n-Best Parses and Extracted Scope Parses

As described above, the results for reranking the 50-best analyses and for reranking the versions with automatically extracted scope readings are very close. This raises the question whether the two methods produce similar improvements in the parse trees. One indicator that this is not the case can be found in the differences in precision and recall. Another possibility of verifying our assumption that the improvements do not overlap lies in the combination of the 50-best parses with the parses resulting from the automatically extracted scopes. This increases the number of parses between which the reranker can choose. In effect, this means a combination of the methods of experiments 1 (n-best) and 3 (automatic scope). Consequently, if the results from this experiment are very close to the results from experiment 1 (n-best), we can conclude that adding the parses with automatic scope readings does not add new information. If, however, adding these parses improves results, we can conclude that new information was present in the parses with automatic scope that was not covered in the 50-best parses. Note that the combination of the two types of input for the reranker should not be regarded as a parser ensemble but rather as a resampling of the n-best search space since both parsers use the same grammar, parsing model, and probability model. The only difference is that LoPar can accept partially bracketed input, and BitPar can list the n-best analyses.

The results of this experiment are shown in Table 1 as exp. 4. For all sentences, both precision and recall are higher than for experiment 1 and 3, resulting in an F-score of 76.69. This is more than 2 percent points higher than for the 50-best parses. This is a very clear indication that the parses contributed by the automatically extracted scopes provide parses that were not present in the 50 best parses from experiment 1 (n-best). The same trend can be seen in the evaluation of the sentences containing coordination: Here, the improvement in F-score is higher than for the whole set, a clear indication that this method is suitable for improving coordination parsing. A comparison of the results of the present experiment and experiment 3 (with automatic scope only) shows that the gain in precision is rather small, but the combination clearly improves recall, from 73.96% to 77.23%. We can conclude that adding the 50 best parses remedies the lacking coverage that was the problem of experiment 3. More generally, experiment 4 suggests that for the notoriously difficult problem of parsing coordination structures, a hybrid approach that combines parse selection of n best analyses with pre-bracketed scope in the input results in a considerable reduction in error rate compared to each of these methods used in isolation.

8 Related Work

Parsing of coordinate structures for English has received considerable attention in computational linguistics. Collins (1999), among many other authors, reports in the error analysis of his WSJ parsing results that coordination is one of the most frequent cases of incorrect parses, particularly if the conjuncts involved are complex. He manages to reduce errors for simple cases of NP coordination by introducing a special phrasal category of base NPs. In the experiments presented above, no explicit distinction is made between simple and complex cases of coordination, and no transformations are performed on the treebank annotations used for training.

Our experiment 1, reranking 50-best parses, is similar to the approaches of Charniak and Johnson (2005) and of Hogan (2007). However, it differs from their experiments in two crucial ways: 1) Compared to Charniak and Johnson, who use 1.1 mio. features, our feature set is appr. five times larger (more than 5 mio. features), with the same threshold of at least five occurrences in the training set. 2) Both Hogan and Charniak and Johnson use special features for coordinate structures, such as a Boolean feature for marking parallelism (Charniak and Johnson) or for distinguishing between coordination of base NPs and coordination of complex conjuncts (Hogan), while our approach refrains from such special-purpose features.

Our experiments using scope information are similar to the approaches of Kurohashi and Nagao (1994) and Agarwal and Bogges (1992) in that they try to identify coordinate structure bracketings. However, the techniques used by Agarwal and Bogges and in the present paper are quite different. Agarwal and Bogges and Kurohashi and Nagao rely on shallow parsing techniques to detect parallelism of conjuncts while we use a partial parser only for suggesting possible scopes of conjuncts. Both of these approaches are limited to coordinate structures with two conjuncts only, while our approach has no such limitation. Moreover, the goal of Agarwal and Bogges is quite different from ours. Their goal is robust detection of coordinate structures only (with the intended application of term extraction), while our goal is to improve the performance of a parser that assigns a complete sentence structure to an input sentence.

Finally, our approach at present is restricted to purely syntactic structural properties. This is in contrast to approaches that incorporate semantic information. Hogan (2007) uses bi-lexical head-head co-occurrences in order to identify nominal heads of conjuncts more reliably than by syntactic information alone. Chantree et al. (2005) resolve attachment ambiguities in coordinate structures, as in (7a) and (7b), by using word frequency information obtained from generic corpora as an effective estimate of the semantic compatibility of a modifier vis-à-vis the candidate heads.

(7) a. Project managers and designers
  b. Old shoes and boots

We view the work by Hogan and by Chantree et al. as largely complementary to, but at the same time as quite compatible with our approach. We must leave the integration of structural syntactic and lexical semantic information to future research.

9 Conclusion and Future Work

We have presented a study on improving the treatment of coordinated structures in PCFG parsing. While we presented experiments for German, the methods are applicable for any language. We have chosen German because it is a language with relatively flexible phrasal ordering (cf. Section 2) which makes parsing coordinations particularly challenging. The experiments presented show that n-best parsing combined with reranking improves results by a large margin. However, the number of cases in which the correct parse is present in the n-best parses is rather low. This led us to the assumption that the n-best analyses often do not cover the whole range of different scope possibilities but rather present minor variations of parses with few differences in coordination scope. The experiments in which the parser was forced to assume predefined scopes show that the scope information is important for parsing quality. Providing the parser with different scope possibilities and reranking the resulting parses results in an increase in F-score from 69.76 for the baseline to 74.69. One of the major challenges for this approach lies in extracting a list of possible conjuncts. Forcing the parser to parse all possible sequences results in a prohibitively large number of possibilities, especially for sentences with 3 or more conjunctions. For this reason, we used chunks above base phases, such as coordinated noun chunks, to restrict the space. However, an inspection of the lists of bracketed versions of the sentences shows that the definition of base phrases is one of the areas that must be refined. As mentioned above, the partial parser groups sequences of "NP KON NP" into a single base phrase. This may be correct in many cases, but there are exceptions such as (8).

(8) Die 31jährige Gewerkschaftsmitarbei-
The 31-year-old union staff member
terin und ausgebildete Industriekauffrau
and trained industrial clerk
aus Oldenburg bereitet nun ihre
from Oldenburg is preparing now her
erste eigene CD vor.
first own CD *part.*.

For (8), the partial parser groups *Die 31jährige Gewerkschaftsmitarbeiterin und ausgebildete Industriekauffrau* as one noun chunk. Since our proposed conjuncts cannot cross these boundaries, the correct second conjunct, *ausgebildete Industriekauffrau aus Oldenburg*, cannot be suggested. However, if we remove these chunk boundaries, the number of possible conjuncts increases dramatically, and parsing times become prohibitive. As a consequence, we will need to find a good balance between these two needs. Our plan is to increase flexibility very selectively, for example by enabling the use of wider scopes in cases where the conjunction is preceded and followed by base noun phrases. For the future, we are planning to repeat experiment 3 (automatic scope) with different phrasal boundaries extracted from the partial parser. It will be interesting to see if improvements in this experiment will still improve results in experiment 4 (combining 50-best parses with exp. 3).

Another area of improvement is the list of features used for reranking. At present, we use a feature set that is similar to the one used by Collins and Koo (2005). However, this feature set does not contain any coordination specific features. We are planning to extend the feature set by features on structural parallelism as well as on lexical similarity of the conjunct heads.

References

Rajeev Agarwal and Lois Boggess. 1992. A simple but useful approach to conjunct identification. In *Proceedings of the 30th Annual Meeting of the Association for Computational Linguistics (ACL-92)*, pages 15–21, Newark, DE.

Francis Chantree, Adam Kilgarriff, Anne de Roeck, and Alistair Willis. 2005. Disambiguating coordinations using word distribution information. In *Proceedings of Recent Advances in NLP (RANLP 2005)*, pages 144–151, Borovets, Bulgaria.

Eugene Charniak and Mark Johnson. 2005. Coarse-to-fine n-best parsing and MaxEnt discriminative reranking. In *Proceedings of the 43rd Annual Meeting of the Association for Computational Linguistics (ACL'05)*, pages 173–180, Ann Arbor, MI.

Michael Collins and Terry Koo. 2005. Discriminative reranking for natural language parsing. *Computational Linguistics*, 31(1):25–69.

Michael Collins. 1999. *Head-Driven Statistical Models for Natural Language Parsing*. Ph.D. thesis, University of Pennsylvania.

Anette Frank. 2002. A (discourse) functional analysis of asymmetric coordination. In *Proceedings of the LFG-02 Conference*, Athens, Greece.

Yoav Freund, Ray Iyer, Robert Shapire, and Yoram Singer. 1998. An efficient boosting algorithm for combining preferences. In *Proceedings of the 15th International Conference on Machine Learning*, Madison, WI.

Deirdre Hogan. 2007. Coordinate noun phrase disambiguation in a generative parsing model. In *Proceedings of the 45th Annual Meeting of the Association of Computational Linguistics*, pages 680–687, Prague, Czech Republic.

Tilman Höhle. 1983. Subjektlücken in Koordinationen. Universität Tübingen.

Tilman Höhle. 1990. Assumptions about asymmetric coordination in German. In Joan Mascaró and Marina Nespor, editors, *Grammar in Progress. Glow Essays for Henk van Riemsdijk*, pages 221–235. Foris, Dordrecht.

Tilman Höhle. 1991. On reconstruction and coordination. In Hubert Haider and Klaus Netter, editors, *Representation and Derivation in the Theory of Grammar*, volume 22 of *Studies in Natural Language and Linguistic Theory*, pages 139–197. Kluwer, Dordrecht.

Andreas Kathol. 1990. Linearization vs. phrase structure in German coordination constructions. *Cognitive Linguistics*, 10(4):303–342.

Sandra Kübler. 2008. The PaGe 2008 shared task on parsing German. In *Proceedings of the ACL Workshop on Parsing German*, pages 55–63, Columbus, Ohio.

Sadao Kurohashi and Makoto Nagao. 1994. A syntactic analysis method of long Japanese sentences based on the detection of conjunctive structures. *Computational Linguistics*, 20(4):507–534.

Frank Henrik Müller and Tylman Ule. 2002. Annotating topological fields and chunks–and revising POS tags at the same time. In *Proceedings of the 19th International Conference on Computational Linguistics, COLING'02*, pages 695–701, Taipei, Taiwan.

Slav Petrov and Dan Klein. 2008. Parsing German with latent variable grammars. In *Proceedings of the ACL Workshop on Parsing German*, pages 33–39, Columbus, Ohio.

Helmut Schmid. 2000. LoPar: Design and implementation. Technical report, Universität Stuttgart.

Helmut Schmid. 2004. Efficient parsing of highly ambiguous context-free grammars with bit vectors. In *Proceedings of the 20th International Conference on Computational Linguistics (COLING 2004)*, Geneva, Switzerland.

Heike Telljohann, Erhard Hinrichs, and Sandra Kübler. 2004. The TüBa-D/Z treebank: Annotating German with a context-free backbone. In *Proceedings of the Fourth International Conference on Language Resources and Evaluation (LREC 2004)*, pages 2229–2235, Lisbon, Portugal.

Heike Telljohann, Erhard W. Hinrichs, Sandra Kübler, and Heike Zinsmeister, 2005. *Stylebook for the Tübingen Treebank of Written German (TüBa-D/Z)*. Seminar für Sprachwissenschaft, Universität Tübingen, Tübingen, Germany.

Dieter Wunderlich. 1988. Some problems of coordination in German. In Uwe Reyle and Christian Rohrer, editors, *Natural Language Parsing and Linguistic Theories*, Studies in Linguistics and Philosophy, pages 289–316. Reidel, Dordrecht.

Automatic Single-Document Key Fact Extraction from Newswire Articles

Itamar Kastner
Department of Computer Science
Queen Mary, University of London, UK
itk1@dcs.qmul.ac.uk

Christof Monz
ISLA, University of Amsterdam
Amsterdam, The Netherlands
christof@science.uva.nl

Abstract

This paper addresses the problem of extracting the most important facts from a news article. Our approach uses syntactic, semantic, and general statistical features to identify the most important sentences in a document. The importance of the individual features is estimated using generalized iterative scaling methods trained on an annotated newswire corpus. The performance of our approach is evaluated against 300 unseen news articles and shows that use of these features results in statistically significant improvements over a provenly robust baseline, as measured using metrics such as precision, recall and ROUGE.

1 Introduction

The increasing amount of information that is available to both professional users (such as journalists, financial analysts and intelligence analysts) and lay users has called for methods condensing information, in order to make the most important content stand out. Several methods have been proposed over the last two decades, among which keyword extraction and summarization are the most prominent ones. Keyword extraction aims to identify the most relevant words or phrases in a document, e.g., (Witten et al., 1999), while summarization aims to provide a short (commonly 100 words), coherent full-text summary of the document, e.g., (McKeown et al., 1999). Key fact extraction falls in between key word extraction and summarization. Here, the challenge is to identify the most relevant facts in a document, but not necessarily in a coherent full-text form as is done in summarization.

Evidence of the usefulness of key fact extraction is CNN's web site which since 2006 has most of its news articles preceded by a list of story highlights, see Figure 1. The advantage of the news highlights as opposed to full-text summaries is that they are much 'easier on the eye' and are better suited for quick skimming.

So far, only CNN.com offers this service and we are interested in finding out to what extent it can be automated and thus applied to any newswire source. Although these highlights could be easily generated by the respective journalists, many news organization shy away from introducing an additional manual stage into the workflow, where pushback times of minutes are considered unacceptable in an extremely competitive news business which competes in terms of seconds rather than minutes. Automating highlight generation can help eliminate those delays.

Journalistic training emphasizes that news articles should contain the most important information in the beginning, while less important information, such as background or additional details, appears further down in the article. This is also the main reason why most summarization systems applied to news articles do not outperform a simple baseline that just uses the first 100 words of an article (Svore et al., 2007; Nenkova, 2005).

On the other hand, most of CNN's story highlights are *not* taken from the beginning of the articles. In fact, more than 50% of the highlights stem from sentences that are not among the first 100 words of the articles. This makes identifying story highlights a much more challenging task than single-document summarization in the news domain.

In order to automate story highlight identification we automatically extract syntactic, semantic,

Proceedings of the 12th Conference of the European Chapter of the ACL, pages 415–423,
Athens, Greece, 30 March – 3 April 2009. ©2009 Association for Computational Linguistics

WORLD

Pope 'deeply sorry' for Muslim fury

STORY HIGHLIGHTS

- Pope says he is "deeply sorry" for reaction to his comments on Islam
- Italian police raise alert level around Vatican, papal summer residence
- Thousands protest at pope's comments; churches in West Bank fire-bombed
- Pope appeared to endorse view early Muslims spread religion by violence

Adjust font size:

CASTEL GANDOLFO, Rome (CNN) -- Pope Benedict XVI has said he is "deeply sorry" for the reaction to his comments on Islam and said a quote he used from a medieval text about holy wars did not reflect his personal thoughts.

The pope's speech in Germany last week -- in which he appeared to endorse a Christian view, contested by most Muslims, that early Muslims spread their religion by violence -- has sparked protests around the world.

"I am deeply sorry for the reactions in some countries to a few passages of my address at the University of Regensburg, which were considered offensive to the sensibility of Muslims," the pope said in his regular Sunday blessing, the Angelus, at his summer residence at Castel Gandolfo, southeast of Rome.

"This was a quote from a medieval text which does not express in any way my personal thoughts."

Figure 1: CNN.com screen shot of a story excerpt with highlights.

and purely statistical features from the document. The weights of the features are estimated using machine learning techniques, trained on an annotated corpus. In this paper, we focus on identifying the relevant sentences in the news article from which the highlights were generated. The system we have implemented is named AURUM: AUtomatic Retrieval of Unique information with Machine learning. A full system would also contain a sentence compression step (Knight and Marcu, 2000), but since both steps are largely independent of each other, existing sentence compression or simplification techniques can be applied to the sentences identified by our approach.

The remainder of this paper is organized as follows: The next section describes the relevant work done to date in keyfact extraction and automatic summarization. Section 3 lays out our features and explains how they were learned and estimated. Section 4 presents the experimental setup and our results, and Section 5 concludes with a short discussion.

2 Related Work

As mentioned above, the problem of identifying story highlight lies somewhere between keyword extraction and single-document summarization.

The KEA keyphrase extraction system (Witten et al., 1999) mainly relies on purely statistical features such as term frequencies, using the *tf.idf* measure from Information Retrieval,[1] as well as on a term's position in the text. In addition to *tf.idf* scores, Hulth (2004) uses part-of-speech tags and NP chunks and complements this with machine learning; the latter has been used to good results in similar cases (Turney, 2000; Neto et al., 2002). The B&C system (Barker and Cornacchia, 2000), also used linguistic methods to a very limited extent, identifying NP heads.

INFORMATIONFINDER (Krulwich and Burkey, 1996) requires user feedback to train the system, whereby a user notes whether a given document is of interest to them and specifies their own keywords which are then learned by the system.

Over the last few years, numerous single- as well as multi-document summarization approaches have been developed. In this paper we will focus mainly on single-document summarization as it is more relevant to the issue we aim to address and traditionally proves harder to accomplish. A good example of a powerful approach is a method named Maximum Marginal Relevance which extracts a sentence for the summary only if it is different than previously selected ones, thereby striving to reduce redundancy (Carbonell and Goldstein, 1998).

More recently, the work of Svore et al. (2007) is closely related to our approach as it has also exploited the CNN Story Highlights, although their focus was on summarization and using ROUGE as an evaluation and training measure. Their approach also heavily relies on additional data resources, mainly indexed Wikipedia articles and Microsoft Live query logs, which are not readily available.

Linguistic features are today used mostly in summarization systems, and include the standard features sentence length, n-gram frequency, sentence position, proper noun identification, similarity to title, *tf.idf*, and so-called 'bonus'/'stigma' words (Neto et al., 2002; Leite et al., 2007; Pollock and Zamora, 1975; Goldstein et al., 1999). On the other hand, for most of these systems, simple statistical features and *tf.idf* still turn out to be the most important features.

Attempts to integrate discourse models have also been made (Thione et al., 2004), hand in hand with some of Marcu's (1995) earlier work.

[1] $tf(t, d)$ = frequency of term t in document d.
$idf(t, N)$ = inverse frequency of documents d containing term t in corpus N, $log(\frac{|N|}{|d_t|})$

Regarding syntax, it seems to be used mainly in sentence compression or trimming. The algorithm used by Dorr et al. (2003) removes subordinate clauses, to name one example. While our approach does not use syntactical features as such, it is worth noting these possible enhancements.

3 Approach

In this section we describe which features were used and how the data was annotated to facilitate feature extraction and estimation.

3.1 Training Data

In order to determine the features used for predicting which sentences are the sources for story highlights, we gathered statistics from 1,200 CNN newswire articles. An additional 300 articles were set aside to serve as a test set later on. The articles were taken from a wide range of topics: politics, business, sport, health, world affairs, weather, entertainment and technology. Only articles with story highlights were considered.

For each article we extracted a number of n-gram statistics, where $n \in \{1, 2, 3\}$.

n-gram score. We observed the frequency and probability of unigrams, bigrams and trigrams appearing in both the article body and the highlights of a given story. An important phrase (of length $n \leq 3$) in the article would likely be used again in the highlights. These phrases were ranked and scored according to the probability of their appearing in a given text and its highlights.

Trigger phrases. These are phrases which cause adjacent words to appear in the highlights. Over the entire set, such phrases become significant. We specified a limit of 2 words to the left and 4 words to the right of a phrase. For example, the word *according* caused other words in the same sentence to appear in the highlights nearly 25% of the time. Consider the highlight/sentence pair in Table 1:

highlight:	61 percent of those polled now say it was not worth invading Iraq, poll says
Text:	Now, 61 percent of those surveyed say it was not worth invading Iraq, according to the poll.

Table 1: Example highlight with source sentence.

The word *according* receives a score of 3 since {*invading, Iraq, poll*} are all in the highlight. It should be noted that the trigram {*invading Iraq according*} would receive an identical score, since {*not, worth, poll*} are in the highlights as well.

Spawned phrases. Conversely, spawned phrases occur frequently in the highlights and in close proximity to trigger phrases. Continuing the example in Table 1, {*invading, Iraq, poll, not, worth*} are all considered to be spawned phrases.

Of course, simply using the identities of words neglects the issue of lexical paraphrasing, e.g., involving synonyms, which we address to some extent by using WordNet and other features described in this Section. Table 2 gives an example involving paraphrasing.

highlight:	Sources say men were planning to shoot soldiers at Army base
Text:	The federal government has charged five alleged Islamic radicals with plotting to kill U.S. soldiers at Fort Dix in New Jersey.

Table 2: An example of paraphrasing between a highlight and its source sentence.

Other approaches have tried to select linguistic features which could be useful (Chuang and Yang, 2000), but these gather them under one heading rather than treating them as separate features. The identification of common verbs has been used both as a positive (Turney, 2000) and as a negative feature (Goldstein et al., 1999) in some systems, whereas we score such terms according to a scale. Turney also uses a 'final adjective' measure. Use of a thesaurus has also shown to improve results in automatic summarization, even in multi-document environments (McKeown et al., 1999) and other languages such as Portuguese (Leite et al., 2007).

3.2 Feature Selection

By manually inspecting the training data, the linguistic features were selected. AURUM has two types of features: *sentence features*, such as the position of the sentence or the existence of a negation word, receive the same value for the entire sentence. On the other hand, *word features* are evaluated for each of the words in the sentence, normalized over the number of words in the sentence.

Our features resemble those suggested by previous works in keyphrase extraction and automatic summarization, but map more closely to the journalistic characteristics of the corpus, as explained in the following.

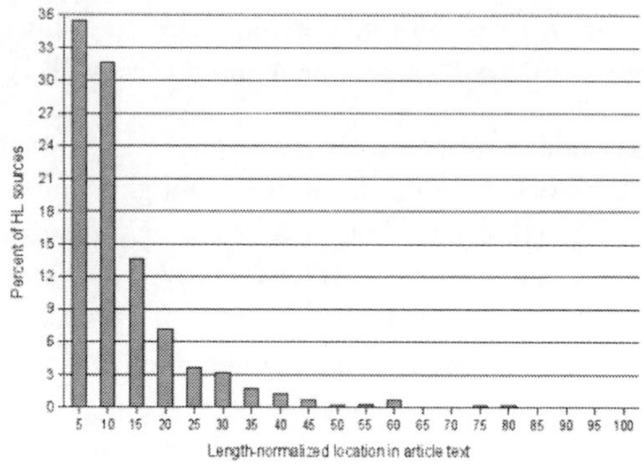

Figure 2: Positions of sentences from which highlights (HLs) were generated.

3.2.1 Sentence Features

These are the features which apply once for each sentence.

Position of the sentence in the text. Intuitively, facts of greater importance will be placed at the beginning of the text, and this is supported by the data, as can be seen in Figure 2. Only half of the highlights stem from sentences in the first fifth of the article. Nevertheless, selecting sentences from only the first few lines is not a sure-fire approach. Table 3 presents an article in which none of the first four sentences were in the highlights. While the baseline found no sentences, AURUM's performance was better.

The sentence positions score is defined as $p_i = 1 - (\log i / \log N)$, where i is the position of the sentence in the article and N the total number of sentences in the article.

Numbers or dates. This is especially evident in news reports mentioning figures of casualties, opinion poll results, or financial news.

Source attribution. Phrasings such as *according to a source* or *officials say.*

Negations. Negations are often used for introducing new or contradictory information: "*Kelly is due in a Chicago courtroom Friday for yet another status hearing,* ***but*** *there's still no trial date in sight.*[2]" We selected a number of typical negation phrases to this end.

Causal adverbs. Manually compiled list of phrases, including *in order to, hoping for* and *because.*

Temporal adverbs. Manually compiled list of phrases, such as *after less than, for two weeks* and *Thursday.*

Mention of the news agency's name. Journalistic scoops and other exclusive nuggets of information often recall the agency's name, especially when there is an element of self-advertisement involved, as in "*...The debates are being held by CNN, WMUR and the New Hampshire Union Leader.*" It is interesting to note that an opposite approach has previously been taken (Goldstein et al., 1999), albeit involving a different corpus.

Story Highlights:
- Memorial Day marked by parades, cookouts, ceremonies
- AAA: 38 million Americans expected to travel at least 50 miles during weekend
- President Bush gives speech at Arlington National Cemetery
- Gulf Coast once again packed with people celebrating holiday weekend

First sentences of article:
1. Veterans and active soldiers unfurled a 90-by-100-foot U. S. flag as the nation's top commander in the Middle East spoke to a Memorial Day crowd gathered in Central Park on Monday.
2. Navy Adm. William Fallon, commander of U. S. Central Command, said America should remember those whom the holiday honors.
3. "Their sacrifice has enabled us to enjoy the things that we, I think in many cases, take for granted," Fallon said.
4. Across the nation, flags snapped in the wind over decorated gravestones as relatives and friends paid tribute to their fallen soldiers.

Sentences the Highlights were derived from:
5. Millions more kicked off summer with trips to beaches or their backyard grills.
6. **AAA estimated 38 million Americans would travel 50 miles or more during the weekend – up 1.7 percent from last year – even with gas averaging $3.20 a gallon for self-service regular.**
7. In the nation's capital, thousands of motorcycles driven by military veterans and their loved ones roared through Washington to the Vietnam Veterans Memorial.
9. President Bush spoke at nearby Arlington National Cemetery, honoring U. S. troops who have fought and died for freedom and expressing his resolve to succeed in the war in Iraq.
21. Elsewhere, Alabama's Gulf Coast was once again packed with holiday-goers after the damage from hurricanes Ivan and Katrina in 2004 and 2005 kept the tourists away.

Table 3: Sentence selection outside the first four sentences (correctly identified sentence by AURUM in **boldface**).

[2]This sentence was included in the highlights

3.2.2 Word Features

These features are tested on each word in the sentence.

'Bonus' words. A list of phrases similar to *sensational, badly, ironically, historic*, identified from the training data. This is akin to 'bonus'/'stigma' words (Neto et al., 2002; Leite et al., 2007; Pollock and Zamora, 1975; Goldstein et al., 1999).

Verb classes. After exploring the training data we manually compiled two classes of verbs, each containing 15-20 inflected and uninflected lexemes, `talkVerbs` and `actionVerbs`. `talkVerbs` include verbs such as {*report, mention, accuse*} and `actionVerbs` refer to verbs such as {*provoke, spend, use*}. Both lists also contain the WordNet synonyms of each word in the list (Fellbaum, 1998).

Proper nouns. Proper nouns and other parts of speech were identified running Charniak's parser (Charniak, 2000) on the news articles.

3.2.3 Sentence Scoring

The overall score of a sentence is computed as the weighted linear combination of the sentence and word scores. The score $\sigma(s)$ of sentence s is defined as follows:

$$\sigma(s) = w_{pos}p_{pos(s)} + \sum_{k=1}^{n} w_k f_k + \sum_{j=1}^{|s|}\sum_{k=1}^{m} w_k g_{jk}$$

Each of the sentences s in the article was tested against the position feature $p_{pos(s)}$ and against each of the sentence features f_k, see Section 3.2.1, where $pos(s)$ returns the position of sentence s. Each word j of sentence s is tested against all applicable word features g_{jk}, see Section 3.2.2. A weight (w_{pos} and w_k) is associated with each feature. How to estimate the weights is discussed next.

3.3 Parameter Estimation

There are various optimization methods that allow one to estimate the weights of features, including generalized iterative scaling and quasi-Newton methods (Malouf, 2002). We opted for generalized iterative scaling as it is commonly used for other NLP tasks and off-the-shelf implementations exist. Here we used YASMET.[3]

[3]A maximum entropy toolkit by Franz Josef Och, `http://www.fjoch.com/YASMET.html`

We used a development set of 240 news articles to train YASMET. As YASMET is a supervised optimizer, we had to generate annotated data on which it was to be trained. For each document in the development set, we labeled each sentence as to whether a story highlight was generated from it. For instance, in the article presented in Figure 3, sentences 5, 6, 7, 9 and 21 were marked as highlight sources, whereas all other sentences in the document were not.[4]

When annotating, all sentences that were directly relevant to the highlights were marked, with preference given to those appearing earlier in the story or containing more precise information. At this point it is worth noting that while the overlap between different editors is unknown, the highlights were originally written by a number of different people, ensuring enough variation in the data and helping to avoid over-fitting to a specific editor.

4 Experiments and Results

The CNN corpus was divided into a training set and a development and test set. As we had only 300 manually annotated news articles and we wanted to maximize the number of documents usable for parameter estimation, we applied cross-folding, which is commonly used for situations with limited data. The dev/test set was randomly partitioned into five folds. Four of the five folds were used as development data (i.e. for parameter estimation with YASMET), while the remaining fold was used for testing. The procedure was repeated five times, each time with four folds used for development and a separate one for testing. Cross-folding is safe to use as long as there are no dependencies between the folds, which is safe to assume here.

Some statistics on our training and development/test data can be found in Table 4.

Corpus subset	`Dev/Test`	`Train`
Documents	300	1220
Avg. sentences per article	33.26	31.02
Avg. sentence length	20.62	20.50
Avg. number of highlights	3.71	3.67
Avg. number of highlight sources	4.32	-
Avg. highlight length in words	10.26	10.28

Table 4: Characteristics of the evaluation corpus.

[4]The annotated data set is available at: `http://www.science.uva.nl/~christof/data/hl/`.

Most summarization evaluation campaigns, such as NIST's Document Understanding Conferences (DUC), impose a maximum length on summaries (e.g., 75 characters for the headline generation task or 100 words for the summarization task). When identifying sentences from which story highlights are generated, the situation is slightly different, as the number of story highlights is not fixed. On the other hand, most stories have between three and four highlights, and on average between four and five sentences per story from which the highlights were generated. This variation led to us to carry out two sets of experiments: In the first experiment (`fixed`), the number of highlight sources is fixed and our system always returns exactly four highlight sources. In the second experiment (`thresh`), our system can return between three and six highlight sources, depending on whether a sentence score passes a given threshold. The threshold θ was used to allocate sentences s_i of article a to the highlight list HL by first finding the highest-scoring sentence for that article $\sigma(s_h)$. The threshold score was thus $\theta * \sigma(s_h)$ and sentences were judged accordingly. The algorithm used is given in Figure 3.

```
initialize HL, s_h
sort s_i in s by σ(s_i)
set s_h = s_0
for each sentence s_i in article a:
   if |HL| < 3
      include s_i
   else if (θ * σ(s_h) ≤ σ(s_i)) && (|HL| ≤ 5)
      include s_i
   else
      discard s_i
return HL
```

Figure 3: Procedure for selecting highlight sources.

All scores were compared to a baseline, which simply returns the first n sentences of a news article. $n = 4$ in the `fixed` experiment. For the `thresh` experiment, the baseline always selected the same number of sentences as `AURUM-thresh`, but from the beginning of the article. Although this is a very simple baseline, it is worth reiterating that it is also a very competitive baseline, which most single-document summarization systems fail to beat due to the nature of news articles.

Since we are mainly interested in determining to what extent our system is able to correctly identify the highlight sources, we chose precision and recall as evaluation metrics. Precision is the percentage of all returned highlight sources which are correct:

$$\text{Precision} = \frac{|R \cap T|}{|R|}$$

where R is the set of returned highlight sources and T is the set of manually identified true sources in the test set. Recall is defined as the percentage of all true highlight sources that have been correctly identified by the system:

$$\text{Recall} = \frac{|R \cap T|}{|T|}$$

Precision and recall can be combined by using the F-measure, which is the harmonic mean of the two:

$$\text{F-measure} = \frac{2(precision * recall)}{precision + recall}$$

Table 5 shows the results for both experiments (`fixed` and `thresh`) as an average over the folds. To determine whether the observed differences between two approaches are statistically significant and not just caused by chance, we applied statistical significance testing. As we did not want to make the assumption that the score differences are normally distributed, we used the bootstrap method, a powerful non-parametric inference test (Efron, 1979). Improvements at a confidence level of more than 95% are marked with "*".

We can see that our approach consistently outperforms the baseline, and most of the improvements—in particular the F-measure scores—are statistically significant at the 0.95 level. As to be expected, `AURUM-fixed` achieves higher precision gains, while `AURUM-thresh` achieves higher recall gains. In addition, for 83.3 percent of the documents, our system's F-measure score is higher than or equal to that of the baseline.

Figure 4 shows how far down in the documents our system was able to correctly identify highlight sources. Although the distribution is still heavily skewed towards extracting sentences from the beginning of the document, it is so to a lesser extent than just using positional information as a prior; see Figure 2.

In a third set of experiments we measured the n-gram overlap between the sentences we have identified as highlight sources and the actual story highlights in the ground truth. To this end we use

System	Recall	Precision	F-Measure	Extracted
Baseline-fixed	40.69	44.14	42.35	240
AURUM-fixed	41.88 (+2.96%*)	**45.40** (+2.85%)	43.57 (+2.88%*)	240
Baseline-thresh	42.91	41.82	42.36	269
AURUM-thresh	**44.49 (+3.73%*)**	43.30 (**+3.53%**)	**43.88 (+3.59%*)**	269

Table 5: Evaluation scores for the four extraction systems.

System	ROUGE-1	ROUGE-2
Baseline-fixed	47.73	15.98
AURUM-fixed	49.20 (**+3.09%***)	16.53 (**+3.63%***)
Baseline-thresh	55.11	19.31
AURUM-thresh	**56.73** (+2.96%*)	**19.66** (+1.87%)

Table 6: ROUGE scores for AURUM-fixed, returning 4 sentences, and AURUM-thresh, returning between 3 and 6 sentences.

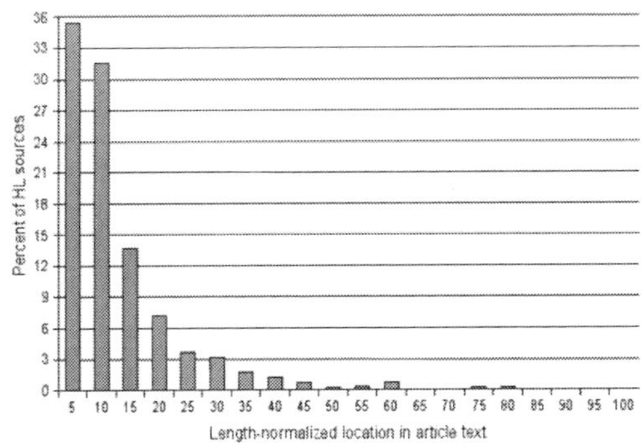

Figure 4: Position of correctly extracted sources by AURUM-thresh.

ROUGE (Lin, 2004), a recall-oriented evaluation package for automatic summarization. ROUGE operates essentially by comparing n-gram co-occurrences between a *candidate* summary and a number of *reference* summaries, and comparing that number in turn to the total number of n-grams in the reference summaries:

ROUGE-n =

$$\frac{\sum_{S \in References} \sum_{ngram_n \in S} Match(ngram_n)}{\sum_{S \in References} \sum_{ngram_n \in S} Count(ngram_n)}$$

Where n is the length of the n-gram, with lengths of 1 and 2 words most commonly used in current evaluations. ROUGE has become the standard tool for evaluating automatic summaries, though it is not the optimal system for this experiment. This is due to the fact that it is geared towards a different task—as ours is not automatic summarization per se—and that ROUGE works best judging between a number of candidate and model summaries. The ROUGE scores are shown in Table 6.

Similar to the precision and recall scores, our approach consistently outperforms the baseline, with all but one difference being statistically significant. Furthermore, in 76.2 percent of the documents, our system's ROUGE-1 score is higher than or equal to that of the baseline, and likewise for 85.2 percent of ROUGE-2 scores. Our ROUGE scores and their improvements over the baseline are comparable to the results of Svore et al. (2007), who optimized their approach towards ROUGE and gained significant improvements from using third-party data resources, both of which our approach does not require.[5]

Table 7 shows the unique sentences extracted by every system, which are the number of sentences one system extracted correctly while the other did not; this is thus an intuitive measure of how much two systems differ. Essentially, a system could simply pick the first two sentences of each article and might thus achieve higher precision scores, since it is less likely to return 'wrong' sentences. However, if the scores are similar but there is a difference in the number of unique sentences extracted, this means a system has gone beyond the first 4 sentences and extracted others from deeper down inside the text.

To get a better understanding of the importance of the individual features we examined the weights as determined by YASMET. Table 8 contains example output from the development sets, with feature selection determined implicitly by the weights the MaxEnt model assigns, where non-discriminative features receive a low weight.

[5] Since the test data of (Svore et al., 2007) is not publicly available we were unable to carry out a more detailed comparison.

Clearly, sentence position is of highest importance, while trigram 'trigger' phrases were quite important as well. Simple bigrams continued to be a good indicator of data value, as is often the case. Proper nouns proved to be a valuable pointer to new information, but mention of the news agency's name had less of an impact than originally thought. Other particularly significant features included temporal adjectives, superlatives and all n-gram measures.

System	Unique highlight sources	Baseline
AURUM-fixed	11.8	7.2
AURUM-thresh	**14.2**	7.6

Table 7: Unique recall scores for the systems.

Feature	Weight	Feature	Weight
Sentence pos.	10.23	Superlative	4.15
Proper noun	5.18	Temporal adj.	1.75
Trigger 3-gram	3.70	1-gram score	2.74
Spawn 2-gram	3.73	3-gram score	3.75
CNN mention	1.30	Trigger 2-gram	3.74

Table 8: Typical weights learned from the data.

5 Conclusions

A system for extracting essential facts from a news article has been outlined here. Finding the data nuggets deeper down is a cross between keyphrase extraction and automatic summarization, a task which requires more elaborate features and parameters.

Our approach emphasizes a wide variety of features, including many linguistic features. These features range from the standard (n-gram frequency), through the essential (sentence position), to the semantic (spawned phrases, verb classes and types of adverbs).

Our experimental results show that a combination of statistical and linguistic features can lead to competitive performance. Our approach not only outperformed a notoriously difficult baseline but also achieved similar performance to the approach of (Svore et al., 2007), without requiring their third-party data resources.

On top of the statistically significant improvements of our approach over the baseline, we see value in the fact that it does not settle for sentences from the beginning of the articles.

Most single-document automatic summarization systems use other features, ranging from discourse structure to lexical chains. Considering Marcu's conclusion (2003) that different approaches should be combined in order to create a good summarization system (aided by machine learning), there seems to be room yet to use basic linguistic cues. Seeing as how our linguistic features—which are predominantly semantic—aid in this task, it is quite possible that further integration will aid in both automatic summarization and keyphrase extraction tasks.

References

Ken Barker and Nadia Cornacchia. 2000. Using noun phrase heads to extract document keyphrases. In *Proceedings of the 13th Conference of the CSCSI, AI 2000*, volume 1882 of *Lecture Notes in Artificial Intelligence*, pages 40–52.

Jaime G. Carbonell and Jade Goldstein. 1998. The use of MMR, diversity-based reranking for reordering documents and producing summaries. In *Proceedings of SIGIR 1998*, pages 335–336.

Eugene Charniak. 2000. A maximum-entropy-inspired parser. In *Proceedings of the First Conference of the North American Chapter of the Association for Computational Linguistics*, pages 132–139.

Wesley T. Chuang and Jihoon Yang. 2000. Extracting sentence segments for text summarization: A machine learning approach. In *Proceedings of the 23rd ACM SIGIR*, pages 152–159.

Bonnie Dorr, David Zajic, and Richard Schwartz. 2003. Hedge Trimmer: A parse-and-trim approach to headline generation. In *Proceedings of the HLT-NAACL 03 Summarization Workshop*, pages 1–8.

Brad Efron. 1979. Bootstrap methods: Another look at the jackknife. *Annals of Statistics*, 7(1):1–26.

Christiane Fellbaum, editor. 1998. *WordNet: An Electronic Lexical Database*. MIT Press.

Jade Goldstein, Mark Kantrowitz, Vibhu Mittal, and Jaime Carbonell. 1999. Summarizing text documents: Sentence selection and evaluation metrics. In *Proceedings of the 22nd annual international ACM SIGIR on Research and Development in IR*, pages 121–128.

Anette Hulth. 2004. *Combining Machine Learning and Natural Language Processing for Automatic Keyword Extraction*. Ph.D. thesis, Department of Computer and Systems Sciences, Stockholm University.

Kevin Knight and Daniel Marcu. 2000. Statistics-based summarization—step one: Sentence compression. In *Proceedings of AAAI 2000*, pages 703–710.

Bruce Krulwich and Chad Burkey. 1996. Learning user information interests through the extraction of semantically significant phrases. In M. Hearst and H. Hirsh, editors, *AAAI 1996 Spring Symposium on Machine Learning in Information Access*.

Daniel S. Leite, Lucia H.M. Rino, Thiago A.S. Pardo, and Maria das Graças V. Nunes. 2007. Extractive automatic summarization: Does more linguistic knowledge make a difference? In *TextGraphs-2: Graph-Based Algorithms for Natural Language Processing*, pages 17–24, Rochester, New York, USA. Association for Computational Linguistics.

Chin-Yew Lin. 2004. ROUGE: a package for automatic evaluation of summaries. In *Proceedings of the Workshop on Text Summarization Branches Out (WAS 2004)*, Barcelona, Spain.

Robert Malouf. 2002. A comparison of algorithms for maximum entropy parameter estimation. In *Proceedings of the Sixth Conference on Natural Language Learning (CoNLL-2002)*, pages 49–55.

Daniel Marcu. 1995. Discourse trees are good indicators of importance in text. In Inderjeet Mani and Mark T. Maybury, editors, *Advances in Automatic Text Summarization*, pages 123–136, Cambridge, MA. MIT Press.

Daniel Marcu. 2003. Automatic abstracting. In *Encyclopedia of Library and Information Science*, pages 245–256.

Kathleen McKeown, Judith Klavans, Vasileios Hatzivassiloglou, Regina Barzilay, and Eleazar Eskin. 1999. Towards multidocument summarization by reformulation: Progress and prospects. In *Proceeding of the 16th national conference of the American Association for Artificial Intelligence (AAAI-1999)*, pages 453–460.

Ani Nenkova. 2005. Automatic text summarization of newswire: Lessons learned from the document understanding conference. In *20th National Conference on Artificial Intelligence (AAAI 2005)*.

J. Larocca Neto, A.A. Freitas, and C.A.A Kaestner. 2002. Automatic text summarization using a machine learning approach. In *XVI Brazilian Symp. on Artificial Intelligence*, volume 2057 of *Lecture Notes in Artificial Intelligence*, pages 205–215.

J. J. Pollock and Antonio Zamora. 1975. Automatic abstracting research at chemical abstracts service. *Journal of Chemical Information and Computer Sciences*, 15(4).

Krysta M. Svore, Lucy Vanderwende, and Christopher J.C. Burges. 2007. Enhancing single-document summarization by combining RankNet and third-party sources. In *Proceedings of the 2007 Joint Conference on Empirical Methods in Natural Language Processing and Computational Natural Language Learning (EMNLP-CoNLL)*, pages 448–457.

Gian Lorenzo Thione, Martin van den Berg, Livia Polanyi, and Chris Culy. 2004. Hybrid text summarization: Combining external relevance measures with structural analysis. In *Proceedings of the ACL-04*, pages 51–55.

Peter D. Turney. 2000. Learning algorithms for keyphrase extraction. *Information Retrieval*, 2(4):303–336.

Ian H. Witten, Gordon W. Paynter, Eibe Frank, Carl Gutwin, and Craig G. Nevill-Manning. 1999. Kea: Practical automatic keyphrase extraction. In *Proceedings of the ACM Conference on Digital Libraries (DL-99)*.

N-gram-based Statistical Machine Translation versus Syntax Augmented Machine Translation: comparison and system combination

Maxim Khalilov and **José A.R. Fonollosa**
Universitat Politècnica de Catalunya
Campus Nord UPC, 08034
Barcelona, Spain
{khalilov,adrian}@talp.upc.edu

Abstract

In this paper we compare and contrast two approaches to Machine Translation (MT): the CMU-UKA Syntax Augmented Machine Translation system (SAMT) and UPC-TALP N-gram-based Statistical Machine Translation (SMT). SAMT is a hierarchical syntax-driven translation system underlain by a phrase-based model and a target part parse tree. In N-gram-based SMT, the translation process is based on bilingual units related to word-to-word alignment and statistical modeling of the bilingual context following a maximum-entropy framework. We provide a step-by-step comparison of the systems and report results in terms of automatic evaluation metrics and required computational resources for a smaller Arabic-to-English translation task ($1.5M$ tokens in the training corpus). Human error analysis clarifies advantages and disadvantages of the systems under consideration. Finally, we combine the output of both systems to yield significant improvements in translation quality.

1 Introduction

There is an ongoing controversy regarding whether or not information about the syntax of language can benefit MT or contribute to a hybrid system.

Classical IBM word-based models were recently augmented with a phrase translation capability, as shown in Koehn et al. (2003), or in more recent implementation, the MOSES MT system[1] (Koehn et al., 2007). In parallel to the phrase-based approach, the N-gram-based approach appeared (Mariño et al., 2006). It stemms from the Finite-State Transducers paradigm, and is extended to the log-linear modeling framework, as shown in (Mariño et al., 2006). A system following this approach deals with bilingual units, called tuples, which are composed of one or more words from the source language and zero or more words from the target one. The N-gram-based systems allow for linguistically motivated word reordering by implementing word order monotonization.

Prior to the SMT revolution, a major part of MT systems was developed using rule-based algorithms; however, starting from the 1990's, syntax-driven systems based on phrase hierarchy have gained popularity. A representative sample of modern syntax-based systems includes models based on bilingual synchronous grammar (Melamed, 2004), parse tree-to-string translation models (Yamada and Knight, 2001) and non-isomorphic tree-to-tree mappings (Eisner, 2003).

The orthodox phrase-based model was enhanced in Chiang (2005), where a hierarchical phrase model allowing for multiple generalizations within each phrase was introduced. The open-source toolkit SAMT[2] (Zollmann and Venugopal, 2006) is a further evolution of this approach, in which syntactic categories extracted from the target side parse tree are directly assigned to the hierarchically structured phrases.

Several publications discovering similarities and differences between distinct translation models have been written over the last few years. In Crego et al. (2005b), the N-gram-based system is contrasted with a state-of-the-art phrase-based framework, while in DeNeefe et al. (2007), the authors seek to estimate the advantages, weakest points and possible overlap between syntax-based MT and phrase-based SMT. In Zollmann et al. (2008) the comparison of phrase-based , "Chiang's style" hirearchical system and SAMT is pro-

[1] www.statmt.org/moses/

[2] www.cs.cmu.edu/~zollmann/samt

Proceedings of the 12th Conference of the European Chapter of the ACL, pages 424–432,
Athens, Greece, 30 March – 3 April 2009.

vided.

In this study, we intend to compare the differences and similarities of the statistical N-gram-based SMT approach and the SAMT system. The comparison is performed on a small Arabic-to-English translation task from the news domain.

2 SAMT system

A criticism of phrase-based models is data sparseness. This problem is even more serious when the source, the target, or both languages are inflectional and rich in morphology. Moreover, phrase-based models are unable to cope with global reordering because the distortion model is based on movement distance, which may face computational resource limitations (Och and Ney, 2004).

This problem was successfully addressed when the MT system based on generalized hierarchically structured phrases was introduced and discussed in Chiang (2005). It operates with only two markers (a substantial phrase category and "a glue marker"). Moreover, a recent work (Zollmann and Venugopal, 2006) reports significant improvement in terms of translation quality if complete or partial syntactic categories (derived from the target side parse tree) are assigned to the phrases.

2.1 Modeling

A formalism for Syntax Augmented Translation is probabilistic synchronous context-free grammar (PSynCFG), which is defined in terms of source and target terminal sets and a set of non-terminals:

$$X \longrightarrow \langle \gamma, \alpha, \sim, \omega \rangle$$

where X is a non-terminal, γ is a sequence of source-side terminals and non-terminals, α is a sequence of target-side terminals and non-terminals, $\sim$ is a one-to-one mapping from non-terminal tokens space in γ to non-terminal space in α, and ω is a non-negative weight assigned to the rule.

The non-terminal set is generated from the syntactic categories corresponding to the target-side Penn Treebank set, a set of glue rules and a special marker representing the "Chiang-style" rules, which do not span the parse tree. Consequently, all lexical mapping rules are covered by the phrases mapping table.

2.2 Rules annotation, generalization and pruning

The SAMT system is based on a purely lexical phrase table, which is identified as shown in Koehn et al. (2003), and word alignment, which is generated by the *grow-diag-final-and* method (expanding the alignment by adding directly neighboring alignment points and alignment points in the diagonal neighborhood) (Och and Ney, 2003).

Meanwhile, the target of the training corpus is parsed with Charniak's parser (Charniak, 2000), and each phrase is annotated with the constituent that spans the target side of the rules. The set of non-terminals is extended by means of conditional and additive categories according to Combinatory Categorical Grammar (CCG) (Steedman, 1999). Under this approach, new rules can be formed. For example, *RB+VB*, can represent an additive constituent consisting of two synthetically generated adjacent categories [3], i.e., an adverb and a verb. Furthermore, *DT\NP* can indicate an incomplete noun phrase with a missing determiner to the left.

The rule recursive generalization procedure coincides with the one proposed in Chiang (2005), but violates the restrictions introduced for single-category grammar; for example, rules that contain adjacent generalized elements are not discarded.

Thus, each rule

$$N \longrightarrow f_1 \dots f_m / e_1 \dots e_n$$

can be extended by another existing rule

$$M \longrightarrow f_i \dots f_u / e_j \dots e_v$$

where $1 \leq i < u \leq m$ and $1 \leq j < v \leq n$, to obtain a new rule

$$N \longrightarrow f_1 \dots f_{i-1} M_k f_{u+1} \dots f_m / \\ e_1 \dots e_{j-1} M_k e_{v+1} \dots e_n$$

where k is an index for the non-terminal M that indicates a one-to-one correspondence between the new M tokens on the two sides.

Figure 1 shows an example of initial rules extraction, which can be further extended using the hierarchical model, as shown in Figure 2 (consequently involving more general elements in rule description).

Rules pruning is necessary because the set of generalized rules can be huge. Pruning is performed according to the relative frequency and the nature of the rules: non-lexical rules that have been seen only once are discarded; source-conditioned rules with a relative frequency of appearance below a threshold are also eliminated.

[3]Adjacent generalized elements are not allowed in Chiang's work because of over-generation. However, over-generation is not an issue within the SAMT framework due to restrictions introduced by target-side syntax

Rules that do not contain non-terminals are not pruned.

2.3 Decoding and feature functions

The decoding process is accomplished using a top-down log-linear model. The source sentence is decoded and enriched with the PSynCFG in such a way that translation quality is represented by a set of feature functions for each rule, i.e.:

- rule *conditional probabilities*, given *a source, a target or a left-hand-side category*;
- *lexical weights features*, as described in Koehn et al. (2003);
- *counters* of target words and rule applications;
- *binary features* reflecting *rule context* (purely lexical and purely abstract, among others);
- rule *rareness* and *unbalancedness* penalties.

The decoding process can be represented as a search through the space of neg log probability of the target language terminals. The set of feature functions is combined with a finite-state target-side n-gram language model (LM), which is used to derive the target language sequence during a parsing decoding. The feature weights are optimized according to the highest BLEU score. For more details refer to Zollmann and Venugopal (2006).

3 UPC n-gram SMT system

A description of the UPC-TALP N-gram translation system can be found in Mariño et al. (2006).

SMT is based on the principle of translating a source sentence (f) into a sentence in the target language (e). The problem is formulated in terms of source and target languages; it is defined according to equation (1) and can be reformulated as selecting a translation with the highest probability from a set of target sentences (2):

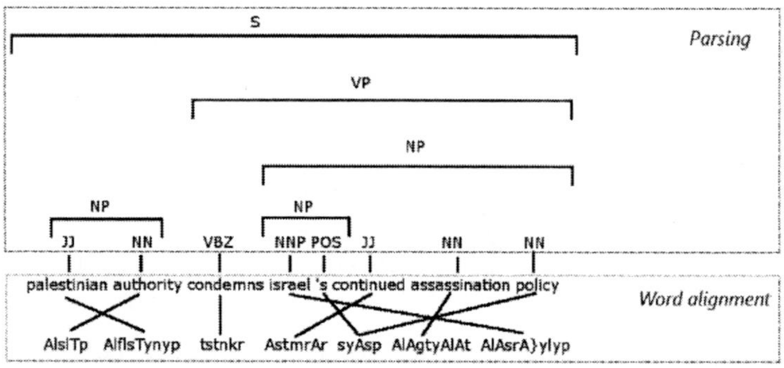

TUPLES (unfolded):
palestinian# AlflsTynyp
authority#AlsTp
condemns#tstnkr
's continued assassination policy#AstmrAr syAsp AlAgtyAlAt
israel# AlAsrA}ylyp

SAMT (example of initial rules):
JJ -> palestinian, AlflsTynyp
NN -> authority, AlsITp
VBZ -> condemns, tstnkr
...
NP -> palestinian authority, AlsITp AlflsTynyp
VBZ+NP -> condemns israel 's continued assassination policy, tsnkr AstmrAr syAsp AlAgtyAlAt AlAsrA}ylyp
VBZ/VP -> israel 's continued assassination policy, AstmrAr syAsp AlAgtyAlAt AlAsrA}ylyp

Figure 1: Example of SAMT and N-gram elements extraction.

SAMT generalized rules (example)

VBZ+NP -> VBZ Israel 's continued assassination policy, VBZ AstmAr syAsp AlAgtyAlAt AlAsrA\}ylyp
VBZ+NP -> VBZ NNP 's continued assassination policy, VBZ AstmAr syAsp AlAgtyAlAt NNP

Figure 2: Example of SAMT generalized rules.

$$\hat{e}_1^I = \arg\max_{e_1^I} \left\{ p(e_1^I \mid f_1^J) \right\} = \quad (1)$$

$$= \arg\max_{e_1^I} \left\{ p(f_1^J \mid e_1^I) \cdot p(e_1^I) \right\} \quad (2)$$

where I and J represent the number of words in the target and source languages, respectively.

Modern state-of-the-art SMT systems operate with the bilingual units extracted from the parallel corpus based on word-to-word alignment. They are enhanced by the *maximum entropy approach* and the posterior probability is calculated as a *log-linear combination* of a set of feature functions (Och and Ney, 2002). Using this technique, the additional models are combined to determine the translation hypothesis, as shown in (3):

$$\hat{e}_1^I = \arg\max_{e_1^I} \left\{ \sum_{m=1}^{M} \lambda_m h_m(e_1^I, f_1^J) \right\} \quad (3)$$

where the feature functions h_m refer to the system models and the set of λ_m refers to the weights corresponding to these models.

3.1 N-gram-based translation system

The N-gram approach to SMT is considered to be an alternative to the *phrase-based* translation, where a given source word sequence is decomposed into monolingual phrases that are then translated one by one (Marcu and Wong, 2002).

The N-gram-based approach regards translation as a stochastic process that maximizes the joint probability $p(f, e)$, leading to a decomposition based on bilingual n-grams. The core part of the system constructed in this way is a translation model (TM), which is based on bilingual units, called tuples, that are extracted from a word alignment (performed with GIZA++ tool[4]) according to certain constraints. A bilingual TM actually constitutes an n-gram LM of tuples, which approximates the joint probability between the languages under consideration and can be seen here as a LM, where the language is composed of tuples.

3.2 Additional features

The N-gram translation system implements a log-linear combination of five additional models:

- *an n-gram target LM;*
- *a target LM of Part-of-Speech tags;*
- *a word penalty model* that is used to compensate for the system's preference for short output sentences;
- *source-to-target and target-to-source lexicon models* as shown in Och and Ney (2004)).

3.3 Extended word reordering

An extended monotone distortion model based on the automatically learned reordering rules was implemented as described in Crego and Mariño (2006). Based on the word-to-word alignment, tuples were extracted by an *unfolding* technique. As a result, the tuples were broken into smaller tuples, and these were sequenced in the order of the target words. An example of unfolding tuple extraction, contrasted with the SAMT chunk-based rules construction, is presented in Figure 1.

The reordering strategy is additionally supported by a 4-gram LM of reordered source POS tags. In training, POS tags are reordered according to the extracted reordering patterns and word-to-word links. The resulting sequence of source POS tags is used to train the n-gram LM.

3.4 Decoding and optimization

The open-source MARIE[5] decoder was used as a search engine for the translation system. Details can be found in Crego et al. (2005a). The decoder implements a beam-search algorithm with pruning capabilities. All the additional feature models were taken into account during the decoding process. Given the development set and references, the log-linear combination of weights was adjusted using a *simplex* optimization method and an n-best re-ranking as described in *http://www.statmt.org/jhuws/*.

4 Experiments

4.1 Evaluation framework

As training corpus, we used the $50K$ first-lines extraction from the Arabic-English corpus that was provided to the NIST'08[6] evaluation campaign and belongs to the news domain. The corpus statistics can be found in Table 1. The development and test sets were provided with 4 reference translations, belong to the same domain and contain 663 and 500 sentences, respectively.

[4] http://code.google.com/p/giza-pp/

[5] http://gps-tsc.upc.es/veu/soft/soft/marie/

[6] www.nist.gov/speech/tests/mt/2008/

	Arabic	English
Sentences	50 K	50 K
Words	1.41 M	1.57 K
Average sentence length	28.15	31.22
Vocabulary	51.10 K	31.51 K

Table 1: Basic statistics of the training corpus.

Evaluation conditions were case-insensitive and sensitive to tokenization. The word alignment is automatically computed by using GIZA++ (Och and Ney, 2004) in both directions, which are made symmetric by using the *grow-diag-final-and* operation.

The experiments were done on a dual-processor Pentium IV Intel Xeon Quad Core X5355 2.66 GHz machine with 24 G of RAM. All computational times and memory size results are approximated.

4.2 Arabic data preprocessing

Arabic is a VSO (SVO in some cases) pro-drop language with rich templatic morphology, where words are made up of roots and affixes and clitics agglutinate to words. For preprocessing, a similar approach to that shown in Habash and Sadat (2006) was employed, and the MADA+TOKAN system for disambiguation and tokenization was used. For disambiguation, only diacritic unigram statistics were employed. For tokenization, the D3 scheme with -TAGBIES option was used. The scheme splits the following set of clitics: w+, f+, b+, k+, l+, Al+ and pronominal clitics. The -TAGBIES option produces Bies POS tags on all taggable tokens.

4.3 SAMT experiments

The SAMT guideline was used to perform the experiments and is available on-line: *http://www.cs.cmu.edu/~zollmann/samt/*.

Moses MT script was used to create the $grow - diag - final$ word alignment and extract purely lexical phrases, which are then used to induce the SAMT grammar. The target side (English) of the training corpus was parsed with the Charniak's parser (Charniak, 2000).

Rule extraction and filtering procedures were restricted to the concatenation of the development and test sets, allowing for rules with a maximal length of 12 elements in the source side and with a zero minimum occurrence criterion for both non-lexical and purely lexical rules.

Moses-style phrases extracted with a phrase-based system were $4.8M$, while a number of generalized rules representing the hierarchical model grew dramatically to $22.9M$. $10.8M$ of them were pruned out on the filtering step.

The vocabulary of the English Penn Treebank elementary non-terminals is 72, while a number of generalized elements, including additive and truncated categories, is $35.7K$.

The $FastTranslateChart$ beam-search decoder was used as an engine of MER training aiming to tune the feature weight coefficients and produce final n-best and 1-best translations by combining the intensive search with a standard 4-gram LM as shown in Venugopal et al. (2007). The iteration limit was set to 10 with 1000-best list and the highest BLEU score as optimization criteria. We did not use completely abstract rules (without any source-side lexical utterance), since these rules significantly slow down the decoding process ($noAllowAbstractRules$ option).

Table 2 shows a summary of computational time and RAM needed at each step of the translation.

Step	Time	Memory
Parsing	1.5h	80Mb
Rules extraction	10h	3.5Gb
Filtering&merging	3h	4.0Gb
Weights tuning	40h	3Gb
Testing	2h	3Gb

Table 2: SAMT: Computational resources.

Evaluation scores including results of system combination (see subsection 4.6) are reported in Table 3.

4.4 N-gram system experiments

The core model of the N-gram-based system is a 4-gram LM of bilingual units containing: 184.345 1-grams[7], 552.838 2-grams, 179.466 3-grams and 176.221 4-grams.

Along with this model, an N-gram SMT system implements a log-linear combination of a *5-gram target LM* estimated on the English portion of the parallel corpus, as well as supporting *4-gram source and target models of POS tags. Bies*

[7]This number also corresponds to the bilingual model vocabulary.

	BLEU	NIST	mPER	mWER	METEOR
SAMT	43.20	9.26	36.89	49.45	58.50
N-gram-based SMT	46.39	10.06	32.98	48.47	62.36
System combination	48.00	10.15	33.20	47.54	62.27
MOSES Factored System	44.73	9.62	33.92	47.23	59.84
Oracle	61.90	11.41	28.84	41.52	66.19

Table 3: Test set evaluation results

POS tags were used for the Arabic portion, as shown in subsection 4.2; a TnT tool was used for English POS tagging (Brants, 2000).

The number of non-unique initially extracted tuples is $1.1M$, which were pruned according to the maximum number of translation options per tuple on the source side (30). Tuples with a NULL on the source side were attached to either the previous or the next unit (Mariño et al., 2006). The feature models weights were optimized according to the same optimization criteria as in the SAMT experiments (the highest BLEU score).

Stage-by-stage RAM and time requirements are presented in Table 4, while translation quality evaluation results can be found in Table 3.

Step	Time	Memory
Models estimation	0.2h	1.9Gb
Reordering	1h	—
Weights tuning	15h	120Mb
Testing	2h	120Mb

Table 4: Tuple-based SMT: Computational resources.

4.5 Statistical significance

A statistical significance test based on a bootstrap resampling method, as shown in Koehn (2004), was performed. For the 98% confidence interval and 1000 set resamples, translations generated by SAMT and N-gram system are significantly different according to BLEU (43.20$\pm$1.69 for SAMT vs. 46.42 ± 1.61 for tuple-based system).

4.6 System combination

Many MT systems generate very different translations of similar quality, even if the models involved into translation process are analogous. Thus, the outputs of syntax-driven and purely statistical MT systems were combined at the sentence level using 1000-best lists of the most probable translations produced by the both systems.

For system combination, we followed a Minimum Bayes-risk algorithm, as introduced in Kumar and Byrne (2004). Table 3 shows the results of the system combination experiments on the test set, which are contrasted with the *oracle* translation results, performed as a selection of the translations with the highest BLEU score from the union of two 1000-best lists generated by SAMT and N-gram SMT.

We also analyzed the percentage contribution of each system to the system combination: 55-60% of best translations come from the $tuples$-based system 1000-best list, both for system combination and oracle experiments on the test set.

4.7 Phrase-based reference system

In order to understand the obtained results compared to the state-of-the-art SMT, a reference phrase-based factored SMT system was trained and tested on the same data using the MOSES toolkit. *Surface* forms of words (factor "0"), *POS* (factor "1") and canonical forms of the words (*lemmata*) (factor "2") were used as English factors, and *surface* forms and *POS* were the Arabic factors.

Word alignment was performed according to the *grow-diag-final* algorithm with the GIZA++ tool, a *msd-bidirectional-fe* conditional reordering model was trained; the system had access to the target-side 4-gram LMs of words and POS. The *0-0,1+0-1,2+0-1* scheme was used on the translation step and *1,2-0,1+1-0,1* to create generation tables. A detailed description of the model training can be found on the MOSES tutorial web-page[8]. The results may be seen in Table 3.

5 Error analysis

To understand the strong and weak points of both systems under consideration, a human analysis of

[8]http://www.statmt.org/moses/

the typical translation errors generated by each system was performed following the framework proposed in Vilar et al. (2006) and contrasting the systems output with four reference translations. Human evaluation of translation output is a time-consuming process, thus a set of 100 randomly chosen sentences was picked out from the corresponding system output and was considered as a representative sample of the automatically generated translation of the test corpus. According to the proposed error topology, some classes of errors can overlap (for example, an unknown word can lead to a reordering problem), but it allows finding the most prominent source of errors in a reliable way (Vilar et al., 2006; Povovic et al., 2006). Table 5 presents the comparative statistics of errors generated by the SAMT and the N-gram-based SMT systems. The average length of the generated translations is 32.09 words for the SAMT translation and 35.30 for the N-gram-based system.

Apart from unknown words, the most important sources of errors of the SAMT system are missing content words and extra words generated by the translation system, causing 17.22 % and 10.60 % of errors, respectively. A high number of missing content words is a serious problem affecting the translation accuracy. In some cases, the system is able to construct a grammatically correct translation, but omitting an important content word leads to a significant reduction in translation accuracy:

SAMT translation: *the ministers of arab environment for the closure of the Israeli dymwnp reactor .*
Ref 1: *arab environment ministers demand the closure of the Israeli daemona nuclear reactor .*
Ref 2: *arab environment ministers demand the closure of Israeli dimona reactor .*
Ref 3: *arab environment ministers call for Israeli nuclear reactor at dimona to be shut down .*
Ref 4: *arab environmental ministers call for the shutdown of the Israeli dimona reactor .*

Extra words embedded into the correctly translated phrases are a well-known problem of MT systems based on hierarchical models operating on the small corpora. For example, in many cases the Arabic expression `AlbHr Almyt` is translated into English as `dead sea side` and not as `dead sea`, since the bilingual instances contain only the whole English phrase, like following:

```
AlbHr Almyt#the dead sea side#@NP
```

The N-gram-based system handles missing words more correctly – only 9.40 % of the errors come from the missing content

Type	Sub-type	SAMT	N-gram
Missing words		**152 (25.17 %)**	**92 (15.44 %)**
	Content words	104 (17.22 %)	56 (9.40 %)
	Filler words	48 (7.95 %)	36 (6.04 %)
Word order		**96 (15.89 %)**	**140 (23.49 %)**
	Local word order	20 (3.31 %)	68 (11.41 %)
	Local phrase order	20 (3.31 %)	20 (3.36 %)
	Long range word order	32 (5.30 %)	48 (8.05 %)
	Long range phrase order	24 (3.97 %)	4 (0.67 %)
Incorrect words		**164 (27.15 %)**	**204 (34.23 %)**
	Sense: wrong lexical choice	24 (3.97 %)	60 (10.07 %)
	Sense: incorrect disambiguation	16 (2.65 %)	8 (1.34 %)
	Incorrect form	24 (3.97 %)	56 (9.40 %)
	Extra words	64 (10.60 %)	56 (9.40 %)
	Style	28 (4.64 %)	20 (3.36 %)
	Idioms	4 (0.07 %)	4 (0.67 %)
Unknown words		**132 (21.85 %)**	**104 (17.45 %)**
Punctuation		**60 (9.93 %)**	**56 (9.40 %)**
Total		**604**	**596**

Table 5: Human made error statistics for a representative test set.

words; however, it does not handle local and long-term reordering, thus the main problem is phrase reordering (11.41 % and 8.05 % of errors). In the example below, the underlined block (Circumstantial Complement: `from local officials in the tourism sector`) is embedded between the verb and the direct object, while in correct translation it must be placed in the end of the sentence.

N-gram translation: *the winner received from local officials in the tourism sector three gold medals .*
Ref 1: *the winner received three gold medals from local officials from the tourism sector .*
Ref 2: *the winner received three gold medals from the local tourism officials .*
Ref 3: *the winner received his prize of 3 gold medals from local officials in the tourist industry .*
Ref 4: *the winner received three gold medals from local officials in the tourist sector .*

Along with inserting extra words and wrong lexical choice, another prominent source of incorrect translation, generated by the N-gram system, is an erroneous grammatical form selection, i.e., a situation when the system is able to find the correct translation but cannot choose the correct form. For example, `arab environment minister call for closing dymwnp Israeli reactor,` where the verb-preposition combination `call for` was correctly translated on the stem level, but the system was not able to generate a third person conjugation `calls for`. In spite of the fact that English is a language with nearly no inflection, 9.40 % of errors stem from poor word form modeling. This is an example of the weakest point of the SMT systems having access to a small training material; the decoder does not use syntactic information about the subject of the sentence (singular) and makes a choice only concerning the tuple probability.

The difference in total number of errors is negligible, however a subjective evaluation of the systems output shows that the translation generated by the N-gram system is more understandable than the SAMT one, since more content words are translated correctly and the meaning of the sentence is still preserved.

6 Discussion and conclusions

In this study two systems are compared: the UPC-TALP N-gram-based and the CMU-UKA SAMT systems, originating from the ideas of Finite-State Transducers and hierarchical phrase translation, respectively. The comparison was created to be as fair as possible, using the same training material and the same tools on the preprocessing, word-to-word alignment and language modeling steps. The obtained results were also contrasted with the state-of-the-art phrase-based SMT.

Analyzing the automatic evaluation scores, the N-gram-based approach shows good performance for the small Arabic-to-English task and significantly outperforms the SAMT system. The results shown by the modern phrase-based SMT (factored MOSES) lie between the two systems under consideration. Considering memory size and computational time, the tuple-based system has obtained significantly better results than SAMT, primarily because of its smaller search space.

Interesting results were obtained for the PER and WER metrics: according to the PER, the UPC-TALP system outperforms the SAMT by 10%, while the WER improvement hardly achieves a 2% difference. The N-gram-based SMT can translate the context better, but produces more reordering errors than SAMT. This may be explained by the fact that Arabic and English are languages with high disparity in word order, and the N-gram system deals worse with long-distance reordering because it attempts to use shorter units. However, by means of introducing the word context into the TM, short-distance bilingual dependencies can be captured effectively.

The main conclusion that can be made from the human evaluation analysis is that the systems commit a comparable number of errors, but they are distributed dissimilarly. In case of the SAMT system, the frequent errors are caused by missing or incorrectly inserted extra words, while the N-gram-based system suffers from reordering problems and wrong words/word form choice

Significant improvement in translation quality was achieved by combining the outputs of the two systems based on different translating principles.

7 Acknowledgments

This work has been funded by the Spanish Government under grant TEC2006-13964-C03 (AVIVAVOZ project).

References

T. Brants. 2000. TnT – a statistical part-of-speech tagger. In *Proceedings of the 6th Applied Natural Language Processing (ANLP-2000)*.

E. Charniak. 2000. A maximum entropy-inspired parser. In *Proceedings of NAACL 2000*, pages 132–139.

D. Chiang. 2005. A hierarchical phrase-based model for statistical machine translation. In *Proceedings of ACL 2005*, pages 263–270.

J. M. Crego and J. B. Mariño. 2006. Improving statistical MT by coupling reordering and decoding. *Machine Translation*, 20(3):199–215.

J. M. Crego, J. Mariño, and A. de Gispert. 2005a. An Ngram-based Statistical Machine Translation Decoder. In *Proceedings of INTERSPEECH05*, pages 3185–3188.

J.M. Crego, M.R. Costa-jussà, J.B. Mariño, and J.A.R. Fonollosa. 2005b. Ngram-based versus phrase-based statistical machine translation. In *Proc. of the IWSLT 2005*, pages 177–184.

S. DeNeefe, K. Knight, W. Wang, and D. Marcu. 2007. What can syntax-based MT learn from phrase-based MT? In *Proceedings of EMNLP-CoNLL 2007*, pages 755–763.

J. Eisner. 2003. Learning non-isomorphic tree mappings for machine translation. In *Proceedings of ACL 2003 (companion volume)*, pages 205–208.

N. Habash and F. Sadat. 2006. Arabic preprocessing schemes for statistical machine translation. In *Proceedings of HLT/NAACL 2006*, pages 49–52.

Ph. Koehn, F.J. Och, and D. Marcu. 2003. Statistical phrase-based machine translation. In *Proceedings of HLT-NAACL 2003*, pages 48–54.

Ph. Koehn, H. Hoang, A. Birch, C. Callison-Burch, M. Federico, N. Bertoldi, B. Cowan, W. Shen, C. Moran, R. Zens, C. Dyer, O. Bojar, A. Constantin, and E. Herbst. 2007. Moses: open-source toolkit for statistical machine translation. In *Proceedings of ACL 2007*, pages 177–180.

P. Koehn. 2004. Statistical significance tests for machine translation evaluation. In *Proceedings of EMNLP 2004*, pages 388–395.

S. Kumar and W. Byrne. 2004. Minimum bayes-risk decoding for statistical machine translation. In *Proceedings of HLT/NAACL 2004*.

D. Marcu and W. Wong. 2002. A Phrase-based, Joint Probability Model for Statistical Machine Translation. In *Proceedings of EMNLP02*, pages 133–139.

J. B. Mariño, R. E. Banchs, J. M. Crego, A. de Gispert, P. Lambert, J. A. R. Fonollosa, and M. R. Costa-jussà. 2006. N-gram based machine translation. *Computational Linguistics*, 32(4):527–549, December.

I.D. Melamed. 2004. Statistical machine translation by parsing. In *Proceedings of ACL 2004*, pages 111–114.

F. J. Och and H. Ney. 2002. Discriminative Training and Maximum Entropy Models for Statistical Machine Translation. In *Proceedings of ACL 2002*, pages 295–302.

F. Och and H. Ney. 2003. A systematic comparison of various statistical alignment models. *Computational Linguistics*, 29(1):19–51.

F. Och and H. Ney. 2004. The alignment template approach to statistical machine translation. *Computational Linguistics*, 30(4):417–449.

M. Povovic, A. de Gispert, D. Gupta, P. Lambert, J.B. Mariño, M. Federico, H. Ney, and R. Banchs. 2006. Morpho-syntactic information for automatic error analysis of statistic machine translation output. In *In Proceeding of the HLT-NAACL Workshop on Statistical Machine Translation*, pages 1–6.

M. Steedman. 1999. Alternative quantifier scope in ccg. In *Proceedings of ACL 1999*, pages 301–308.

A. Venugopal, A. Zollmann, and S. Vogel. 2007. An Efficient Two-Pass Approach to Synchronous-CFG Driven Statistical MT. In *Proceedings of HLT/NAACL 2007*, pages 500–507.

D. Vilar, J. Xu, L. F. D'Haro, and H. Ney. 2006. Error Analysis of Machine Translation Output. In *Proceedings of LREC'06*, pages 697–702.

K. Yamada and K. Knight. 2001. A syntax-based statistical translation model. In *Proceedings of ACL 2001*, pages 523–530.

A. Zollmann and A. Venugopal. 2006. Syntax augmented machine translation via chart parsing. In *Proceedings of NAACL 2006*.

A. Zollmann, A. Venugopal, F. Och, and J. Ponte. 2008. Systematic comparison of Phrase-based, Hierarchical and Syntax-Augmented Statistical mt. In *Proceedings of Coling 2008*, pages 1145–1152.

Lightly Supervised Transliteration for Machine Translation

Amit Kirschenbaum
Department of Computer Science
University of Haifa
31905 Haifa, Israel
akirsche@cs.haifa.ac.il

Shuly Wintner
Department of Computer Science
University of Haifa
31905 Haifa, Israel
shuly@cs.haifa.ac.il

Abstract

We present a Hebrew to English transliteration method in the context of a machine translation system. Our method uses machine learning to determine which terms are to be transliterated rather than translated. The training corpus for this purpose includes only positive examples, acquired semi-automatically. Our classifier reduces more than 38% of the errors made by a baseline method. The identified terms are then transliterated. We present an SMT-based transliteration model trained with a parallel corpus extracted from Wikipedia using a fairly simple method which requires minimal knowledge. The correct result is produced in more than 76% of the cases, and in 92% of the instances it is one of the top-5 results. We also demonstrate a small improvement in the performance of a Hebrew-to-English MT system that uses our transliteration module.

1 Introduction

Transliteration is the process of converting terms written in one language into their approximate spelling or phonetic equivalents in another language. Transliteration is defined for a pair of languages, a *source* language and a *target* language. The two languages may differ in their script systems and phonetic inventories. This paper addresses transliteration from Hebrew to English as part of a machine translation system.

Transliteration of terms from Hebrew into English is a hard task, for the most part because of the differences in the phonological and orthographic systems of the two languages. On the one hand, there are cases where a Hebrew letter can be pronounced in multiple ways. For example, Hebrew ב can be pronounced either as [b] or as [v]. On the other hand, two different Hebrew sounds can be mapped into the same English letter. For example, both ת and ט are in most cases mapped to [t]. A major difficulty stems from the fact that in the Hebrew orthography (like Arabic), words are represented as sequences of consonants where vowels are only partially and very inconsistently represented. Even letters that are considered as representing vowels may sometimes represent consonants, specifically ו [v]/[o]/[u] and י [y]/[i]. As a result, the mapping between Hebrew orthography and phonology is highly ambiguous.

Transliteration has acquired a growing interest recently, particularly in the field of Machine Translation (MT). It handles those terms where no translation would suffice or even exist. Failing to recognize such terms would result in poor performance of the translation system. In the context of an MT system, one has to first identify which terms should be transliterated rather than translated, and then produce a proper transliteration for these terms. We address both tasks in this work.

Identification of Terms To-be Transliterated (TTT) must not be confused with recognition of Named Entities (NE) (Hermjakob et al., 2008). On the one hand, many NEs should be translated rather than transliterated, for example:[1]

m$rd	hm$p@im
misrad	*hamishpatim*
ministry-of	the-sentences
'Ministry of Justice'	

[1]To facilitate readability, examples are presented with interlinear gloss, including an ASCII representation of Hebrew orthography followed by a broad phonemic transcription, a word-for-word gloss in English where relevant, and the corresponding free text in English. The following table presents the ASCII encoding of Hebrew used in this paper:

א	ב	ג	ד	ה	ו	ז	ח	ט	י	כ
a	b	g	d	h	w	z	x	@	i	k
ל	מ	נ	ס	ע	פ	צ	ק	ר	ש	ת
l	m	n	s	&	p	c	q	r	$	t

Proceedings of the 12th Conference of the European Chapter of the ACL, pages 433–441,
Athens, Greece, 30 March – 3 April 2009. ©2009 Association for Computational Linguistics

him	htikwn
hayam	*hatichon*
the-sea	the-central
'the Mediterranean Sea'	

On the other hand, there are terms that are not NEs, such as borrowed words or culturally specific terms that are transliterated rather than translated, as shown by the following examples:

aqzis@ncializm	@lit
eqzistentzializm	*talit*
'Existentialism'	'Tallit'

As these examples show, transliteration cannot be considered the default strategy to handle NEs in MT and translation does not necessarily apply for all other cases.

Candidacy for either transliteration or translation is not necessarily determined by orthographic features. In contrast to English (and many other languages), proper names in Hebrew are not capitalized. As a result, the following homographs may be interpreted as either a proper name, a noun, or a verb:

alwn	alwn	alwn
alon	*alun*	*alon*
'oak'	'I will sleep'	'Alon' (name)

One usually distinguishes between two types of transliteration (Knight and Graehl, 1997): *Forward transliteration*, where an originally Hebrew term is to be transliterated to English; and *Backward transliteration*, in which a foreign term that has already been transliterated into Hebrew is to be recovered. Forward transliteration may result in several acceptable alternatives. This is mainly due to phonetic gaps between the languages and lack of standards for expressing Hebrew phonemes in English. For example, the Hebrew term *cdiq* may be transliterated as *Tzadik, Tsadik, Tsaddiq*, etc. On the other hand, backward transliteration is restrictive. There is usually only one acceptable way to express the transliterated term. So, for example, the name *wiliam* can be transliterated only to *William* and not, for example, to *Viliem*, even though the Hebrew character *w* may stand for the consonant [v] and the character *a* may be vowelized as [e].

We approach the task of transliteration in the context of Machine Translation in two phases. First, we describe a lightly-supervised classifier that can identify TTTs in the text (section 4). The identified terms are then transliterated (section 5) using a transliteration model based on Statistical Machine Translation (SMT). The two modules are combined and integrated in a Hebrew to English MT system (section 6).

The main contribution of this work is the actual transliteration module, which has already been integrated in a Hebrew to English MT system. The accuracy of the transliteration is comparable with state-of-the-art results for other language pairs, where much more training material is available. More generally, we believe that the method we describe here can be easily adapted to other language pairs, especially those for which few resources are available. Specifically, we did not have access to a significant parallel corpus, and most of the resources we used are readily available for many other languages.

2 Previous Work

In this section we sketch some related works, focusing on transliteration from Hebrew and Arabic, and on the context of machine translation.

Arbabi et al. (1994) present a hybrid algorithm for romanization of Arabic names using neural networks and a knowledge based system. The program applies vowelization rules, based on Arabic morphology and stemming from the knowledge base, to unvowelized names. This stage, termed the *broad* approach, exhaustively yields all valid vowelizations of the input. To solve this overgeneration, the *narrow* approach is then used. In this approach, the program uses a neural network to filter unreliable names, that is, names whose vowelizations are not in actual use. The vowelized names are converted into a standard phonetic representation which in turn is used to produce various spellings in languages which use Roman alphabet. The broad approach covers close to 80% of the names given to it, though with some extraneous vowelization. The narrow approach covers over 45% of the names presented to it with higher precision than the broad approach.

This approach requires a vast linguistic knowledge in order to create the knowledge base of vowelization rules. In addition, these rules are applicable only to names that adhere to the Arabic morphology.

Stalls and Knight (1998) propose a method for back transliteration of names that originate in English and occur in Arabic texts. The method uses a sequence of probabilistic models to convert names written in Arabic into the English script. First, an Arabic name is passed through a phonemic model producing a network of possible English sound sequences, where the probability of each sound is location dependent. Next, phonetic sequences are transformed into English phrases. Finally, each possible result is scored according to a unigram word model. This method translates correctly about 32% of the tested names. Those not translated are frequently not foreign names.

This method uses a pronunciation dictionary and is therefore restricted to transliterating only words of known pronunciation. Both of the above methods perform only unidirectional transliteration, that is, either forward- or backward- transliteration, while our work handles both.

Al-Onaizan and Knight (2002) describe a system which combines a phonetic based model with a spelling model for transliteration. The spelling based model directly maps sequences of English letters into sequences of Arabic letters without the need of English pronunciation. The method uses a translation model based on IBM Model 1 (Brown et al., 1993), in which translation candidates of a phrase are generated by combining translations and transliterations of the phrase components, and matching the result against a large corpus. The system's overall accuracy is about 72% for top-1 results and 84% for top-20 results.

This method is restricted to transliterating NEs, and performs best for person names. As noted above, the TTT problem is not identical to the NER problem. In addition, the method requires a list of transliteration pairs from which the transliteration model could be learned.

Yoon et al. (2007) use phonetic distinctive features and phonology-based pseudo features to learn both language-specific and language-universal transliteration characteristics. Distinctive features are the characteristics that define the set of phonemic segments (consonants, vowels) in a given language. Pseudo features capture sound change patterns that involve the position in the syllable. Distinctive features and pseudo features are extracted from source- and target-language training data to train a linear classifier. The classifier computes compatibility scores between English source words and target-language words. When several target-language strings are transliteration candidates for a source word, the one with the highest score is selected as the transliteration. The method was evaluated using parallel corpora of English with each of four target languages. NEs were extracted from the English side and were compared with all the words in the target language to find proper transliterations. The baseline presented for the case of transliteration from English to Arabic achieves Mean Reciprocal Rank (MRR) of 0.66 and this method improves its results by 7%. This technique involves knowledge about phonological characteristics, such as elision of consonants based on their position in the word, which requires expert knowledge of the language. In addition, conversion of terms into a phonemic representation poses hurdles in representing short vowels in Arabic and will have similar behavior in Hebrew. Moreover, English to Arabic transliteration is easier than Arabic to English, because in the former, vowels should be deleted whereas in the latter they should be generated.

Matthews (2007) presents a model for transliteration from Arabic to English based on SMT. The parallel corpus from which the translation model is acquired contains approximately 2500 pairs, which are part of a bilingual person names corpus (LDC2005G02). This biases the model toward transliterating person names. The language model presented for that method consisted of 10K entries of names which is, again, not complete. This model also uses different settings for maximum phrase length in the translation model and different n-gram order for the language model. It achieves an accuracy of 43% when transliterating from Arabic to English.

Goldwasser and Roth (2008) introduce a discriminative method for identifying NE transliteration pairs in English-Hebrew. Given a word pair (w_s, w_t), where w_s is an English NE, the system determines whether w_t, a string in Hebrew, is its transliteration. The classification is based on pairwise features: sets of substrings are extracted from each of the words, and substrings from the two sets are then coupled to form the features. The accuracy of correctly identifying transliteration pairs in top-1 and top-5 was 52% and 88%, respectively. Whereas this approach *selects* most suitable transliteration out of a list of candidates, our approach *generates* a list of possible transliterations ranked by their accuracy.

Despite the importance of identifying TTTs, this task has only been addressed recently. Goldberg and Elhadad (2008) present a loosely supervised method for non contextual identification of transliterated foreign words in Hebrew texts. The method is a Naive-Bayes classifier which learns from noisy data. Such data are acquired by over-generation of transliterations for a set of words in a foreign script, using mappings from the phonemic representation of words to the Hebrew script. Precision and recall obtained are 80% and 82%, respectively. However, although foreign words are indeed often TTTs, many originally Hebrew words should sometimes be transliterated. As explained in section 4, there are words in Hebrew that may be subject to either translation or transliteration, depending on the context. A non-contextual approach would not suffice for our task.

Hermjakob et al. (2008) describe a method for identifying NEs that should be transliterated in Arabic texts. The method first tries to find a matching English word for each Arabic word in a parallel corpus, and tag the Arabic words as either names or non-names based on a matching algorithm. This algorithm uses a scoring model which assigns manually-crafted costs to pairs of Arabic and English substrings, allowing for context restrictions. A number of language specific heuristics, such as considering only capitalized words as candidates and using lists of stop words, are used to enhance the algorithm's accuracy. The tagged Arabic corpus is then divided: One part is used to collect statistics about the distribution of name/non-name patterns among tokens, bigrams and trigrams. The rest of the tagged corpus is used for training using an averaged perceptron. The precision of the identification task is 92.1% and its recall is 95.9%. This work also presents a novel transliteration model, which is integrated into a machine translation system. Its accuracy, measured by the percentage of correctly translated names, is 89.7%.

Our work is very similar in its goals and the overall framework, but in contrast to Hermjakob et al. (2008) we use much less supervision, and in particular, we do not use a parallel corpus. We also do not use manually-crafted weights for (hundreds of) bilingual pairs of strings. More generally, our transliteration model is much more language-pair neutral.

3 Resources and Methodology

Our work consists of of two sub-tasks: Identifying TTTs and then transliterating them. Specifically, we use the following resources for this work: For the identification task we use a large un-annotated corpus of articles from Hebrew press and web-forums (Itai and Wintner, 2008) consisting of 16 million tokens. The corpus is POS-tagged (Bar-Haim et al., 2008). We bootstrap a training corpus for one-class SVM (section 4.2) using a list of rare Hebrew character n-grams (section 4.1) to generate a set of positive, high-precision examples for TTTs in the tagged corpus. POS tags for the positive examples and their surrounding tokens are used as features for the one-class SVM (section 4.2).

For the transliteration itself we use a list that maps Hebrew consonants to their English counterparts to extract a list of Hebrew-English translation pairs from Wikipedia (section 5.2). To learn the transliteration model we utilize Moses (section 5) which is also used for decoding. Decoding also relies on a target language model, which is trained by applying SRILM to Web 1T corpus (section 5.1).

Importantly, the resources we use for this work are readily available for a large number of languages and can be easily obtained. None of these require any special expertise in linguistics. Crucially, no parallel corpus was used.

4 What to transliterate

The task in this phase, then, is to determine for each token in a given text whether it should be translated or transliterated. We developed a set of guidelines to determine which words are to be transliterated. For example, person names are always transliterated, although many of them have homographs that can be translated. Foreign words, which retain the sound patterns of their original language with no semantic translation involved, are also (back-)transliterated. On the other hand, names of countries may be subject to translation or transliteration, as demonstrated in the following examples:

crpt	sprd	qwngw
tsarfat	*sfarad*	*kongo*
'France'	'Spain'	'Congo'

We use information obtained from POS tagging (Bar-Haim et al., 2008) to address the problem of identifying TTTs. Each token is assigned a POS and is additionally marked if it was not found in a lexicon (Itai et al., 2006). As a baseline, we tag for transliteration Out Of Vocabulary (OOV) tokens.

Our evaluation metric is tagging accuracy, that is, the percentage of correctly tagged tokens.

4.1 Rule-based tagging

Many of the TTTs do appear in the lexicon, though, and their number will grow with the availability of more language resources. As noted above, some TTTs can be identified based on their surface forms; these words are mainly loan words. For example, the word *brwdqsting* (broadcasting) contains several sequences of graphemes that are not frequent in Hebrew (e.g., *ng* in a word-final position).

We manually generated a list of such features to serve as tagging rules. To create this list we used a few dozens of character bigrams, about a dozen trigrams and a couple of unigrams and four-grams, that are highly unlikely to occur in words of Hebrew origin. Rules associate n-grams with scores and these scores are summed when applying the rules to tokens. A typical rule is of the form: if $\sigma_1\sigma_2$ are the final characters of w, add c to the score of w, where w is a word in Hebrew, σ_1 and σ_2 are Hebrew characters, and c is an positive integer. A word is tagged for transliteration if the sum of the scores associated with its substrings is higher than a predefined threshold.

We apply these rules to a large Hebrew corpus and create an initial set of instances of terms that, with high probability, should be be transliterated rather than translated. Of course, many TTTs, especially those whose surface forms are typical of Hebrew, will be missed when using this tagging technique. Our solution is to learn the *contexts* in which TTTs tend to occur, and contrast these contexts with those for translated terms. The underlying assumption is that the former contexts are *syntactically* determined, and are independent of the actual surface form of the term (and of whether or not it occurs in the lexicon). Since the result of the rule-based tagging is considered as examples of TTTs, this automatically-annotated corpus can be used to extract such contexts.

4.2 Training with one class classifier

The above process provides us with 40279 examples of TTTs out of a total of more than 16 million tokens. These examples, however, are only positive examples. In order to learn from the incomplete data we utilized a One Class Classifier. Classification problems generally involve two or more classes of objects. A function separating these classes is to be learned and used by the classifier. *One class* classification utilizes only target class objects to learn a function that distinguishes them from any other objects.

SVM (Support Vector Machine) (Vapnik, 1995) is a classification technique which finds a linear separating hyperplane with maximal margins between data instances of two classes. The separating hyperplane is found for a mapping of data instances into a higher dimension, using a kernel function. Schölkopf et al. (2000) introduce an adaptation of the SVM methodology to the problem of one-class classification. We used one-class SVM as implemented in LIBSVM (Chang and Lin, 2001). The features selected to represent each TTT were its POS and the POS of the token preceding it in the sentence. The kernel function which yielded the best results on this problem was a sigmoid with standard parameters.

4.3 Results

To evaluate the TTT identification model we created a gold standard, tagged according to the guidelines described above, by a single lexicographer. The testing corpus consists of 25 sentences from the same sources as the training corpus and contains 518 tokens, of which 98 are TTTs. We experimented with two different baselines: the naïve baseline always decides to translate; a slightly better baseline consults the lexicon, and tags as TTT any token that does not occur in the lexicon. We measure our performance in error rate reduction of tagging accuracy, compared with the latter baseline.

Our initial approach consisted of consulting only the decision of the one-class SVM. However, since there are TTTs that can be easily identified using features obtained from their surface form, our method also examines each token using surface-form features, as described in section 4.1. If a token has no surface features that identify it as a TTT, we take the decision of the one-class SVM. Table 1 presents different configurations we experimented with, and their results. The first two columns present the two baselines we used, as explained above. The third column (OCS) shows the results based only on decisions made by the One Class SVM. The penultimate column shows the results obtained by our method combining the SVM with surface-based features. The final column presents the Error Rate Reduction (ERR) achieved when using our method, compared to the baseline of transliterating OOV words. As can be observed, our method increases classification accuracy: more than 38% of the errors over the baseline are reduced.

Naïve	Baseline	OCS	Our	ERR
79.9	84.23	88.04	90.26	38.24

Table 1: TTT identification results (% of the instances identified correctly)

The importance of the recognition process is demonstrated in the following example. The underlined phrase was recognized correctly by our method.

kbwdw	habwd	$l	bn	ari
kvodo	*heavud*	*shel*	*ben*	*ari*
His-honor	the-lost	of	Ben	Ari

'Ben Ari's lost honor '

Both the word *ben* and the word *ari* have literal meanings in Hebrew (*son* and *lion*, respectively), and their combination might be interpreted as a phrase since it is formed as a Hebrew noun construct. Recognizing them as transliteration candidates is crucial for improving the performance of MT systems.

5 How to transliterate

Once a token is classified as a TTT, it is sent to the transliteration module. Our approach handles the transliteration task as a case of phrase-based SMT, based on the noisy channel model. According to this model, when translating a string f in the source language into the target language, a string $\hat{e}$ is chosen out of all target language strings e if it has the maximal probability given f (Brown et al., 1993):

$$\begin{aligned}\hat{e} &= \arg\max_{e} \{Pr(e|f)\} \\ &= \arg\max_{e} \{Pr(f|e) \cdot Pr(e)\}\end{aligned}$$

where $Pr(f|e)$ is the translation model and $Pr(e)$ is the target language model. In phrase-based translation, f is divided into phrases $\bar{f}_1 \ldots \bar{f}_I$, and each source phrase $\bar{f}_i$ is translated into target phrase $\bar{e}_i$ according to a phrase translation model. Target phrases may then be reordered using a distortion model.

We use SMT for transliteration; this approach views transliteration pairs as aligned sentences and characters are viewed as words. In the case of phrase-based SMT, phrases are sequences of characters. We used Moses (Koehn et al., 2007), a phrase-based SMT toolkit, for training the translation model (and later for decoding). In order to extract phrases, bidirectional word level alignments are first created, both source to target and target to source. Alignments are merged heuristically if they are consistent, in order to extract phrases.

5.1 Target language model

We created an English target language model from unigrams of Web 1T (Brants and Franz, 2006). The unigrams are viewed as character n-grams to fit into the SMT system. We used SRILM (Stolcke, 2002) with a modified Kneser-Ney smoothing, to generate a language model of order 5.

5.2 Hebrew-English translation model

No parallel corpus of Hebrew-English transliteration pairs is available, and compiling one manually is time-consuming and labor-intensive. Instead, we extracted a parallel list of Hebrew and English terms from Wikipedia and automatically generated such a corpus. The terms are parallel titles of Wikipedia articles and thus can safely be assumed to denote the same entity. In many cases these titles are transliterations of one another. From this list we extracted transliteration pairs according to similarity of consonants in parallel English and Hebrew entries.

The similarity measure is based only on consonants since vowels are often not represented at all in Hebrew. We constructed a table relating Hebrew and English consonants, based on common knowledge patterns that relate sound to spelling in both languages. Sound patterns that are not part of the phoneme inventory of Hebrew but are nonetheless represented in Hebrew orthography were also included in the table. Every entry in the mapping table consists of a Hebrew letter and a possible Latin letter or letter sequences that might match it. A typical entry is the following:

$:SH|S|CH

such that SH, S or CH are possible candidates for matching the Hebrew letter $.

Both Hebrew and English titles in Wikipedia may be composed of several words. However, words composing the entries in each of the languages may be ordered differently. Therefore, every word in Hebrew is compared with every word in English, assuming that titles are short enough. The example in Table 2 presents an aligned pair of multi-lingual Wikipedia entries with high similarity of consonants. This is therefore considered as a transliteration pair. In contrast, the title *empty set* which is translated to *hqbwch hriqh* shows a low similarity of consonants. This pair is not selected for the training corpus.

g r a	t	e f u l	d e a d
g r	i i @	p w l	d d

Table 2: Titles of Wikipedia entries

Out of 41914 Hebrew and English terms retrieved from Wikipedia, more than 20000 were determined as transliteration pairs. Out of this set, 500 were randomly chosen to serve as a test set, 500 others were chosen to serve as a development set, and the rest are the training set. Minimum error rate training was done on the development set to optimize translation performance obtained by the training phase.[2] For decoding, we prohibited Moses form performing character reordering (distortion). While reordering may be needed for translation, we want to ensure the monotone nature of transliteration.

5.3 Results

We applied Moses to the test set to get a list of top-n transliteration options for each entry in the set. The results obtained by Moses were further re-ranked to take into account their frequency as reflected in the unigrams of Web 1T (Brants and Franz, 2006). The re-ranking method first normalizes the scores of Moses' results to the range of $[0, 1]$. The respective frequencies of these results in Web1T corpus are also normalized to this range. The score s of each transliteration option is a linear combination of these two elements: $s = \alpha s_M + (1 - \alpha)s_W$, where s_M is the normalized score obtained for the transliteration option by Moses, and s_W is its normalized frequency. α is empirically set to 0.75. Table 3 summarizes the proportion of the terms transliterated correctly across top-n results as achieved by Moses, and their improvement after re-ranking.

We further experimented with two methods for reducing the list of transliteration options to the most prominent ones by taking a *variable* number of candidates rather than a fixed number. This is

[2]We used `moses-mert.pl` in the Moses package.

Results	Top-1	Top-2	Top-5	Top-10
Moses	68.4	81.6	90.2	93.6
Re-ranked	76.6	86.6	92.6	93.6

Table 3: Transliteration results (% of the instances transliterated correctly)

important for limiting the search space of MT systems. The first method (var1) measures the ratio between the scores of each two consecutive options and generates the option that scored lower only if this ratio exceeds a predefined threshold. We found that the best setting for the threshold is 0.75, resulting in an accuracy of 88.6% and an average of 2.32 results per token. Our second method (var2) views the score as a probability mass, and generates all the results whose combined probabilities are at most p. We found that the best value for p is 0.5, resulting in an accuracy of 87.4% and 1.92 results per token on average. Both methods outperform the top-2 accuracy.

Table 4 presents a few examples from the test set that were correctly transliterated by our method. Some incorrect transliterations are demonstrated in Table 5.

Source	Transliteration
np$	nefesh
hlmsbrgr	hellmesberger
smb@iwn	sambation
hiprbwlh	hyperbola
$prd	shepard
ba$h	bachet
xt$pswt	hatshepsut
brgnch	berganza
ali$r	elissar
g'wbani	giovanni

Table 4: Transliteration examples generated correctly from the test set

6 Integration with machine translation

We have integrated our system as a module in a Machine Translation system, based on Lavie et al. (2004a). The system consults the TTT classifier described in section 4 for each token, before translating it. If the classifier determines that the token should be transliterated, then the transliteration procedure described in section 5 is applied to the token to produce the transliteration results.

Source	Transliteration	Target
rbindrnt	rbindrant	rabindranath
aswirh	asuira	essaouira
kmpi@	champit	chamaephyte
bwdlr	bodler	baudelaire
lwrh	laura	lorre
hwlis	ollies	hollies
wnwm	onom	venom

Table 5: Incorrect transliteration examples

We provide an external evaluation in the form of BLEU (Papineni et al., 2001) and Meteor (Lavie et al., 2004b) scores for SMT with and without the transliteration module.

When integrating our method in the MT system we use the best transliteration options as obtained when using the re-ranking procedure described in section 5.3. The translation results for all conditions are presented in Table 6, compared to the basic MT system where no transliteration takes place. Using the transliteration module yields a statistically significant improvement in METEOR scores ($p < 0.05$). METEOR scores are most relevant since they reflect improvement in recall. The MT system cannot yet take into consideration the weights of the transliteration options. Translation results are expected to improve once these weights are taken into account.

System	BLEU	METEOR
Base	9.35	35.33127
Top-1	9.85	38.37584
Top-10	9.18	37.95336
var1	8.72	37.28186
var2	8.71	37.11948

Table 6: Integration of transliteration module in MT system

7 Conclusions

We presented a new method for transliteration in the context of Machine Translation. This method identifies, for a given text, tokens that should be transliterated rather than translated, and applies a transliteration procedure to the identified words. The method uses only positive examples for learning which words to transliterate and achieves over 38% error rate reduction when compared to the baseline. In contrast to previous studies this method does not use any parallel corpora for learning the features which define the transliterated terms. The simple transliteration scheme is accurate and requires minimal resources which are general and easy to obtain. The correct transliteration is generated in more than 76% of the cases, and in 92% of the instances it is one of the top-5 results.

We believe that some simple extensions could further improve the accuracy of the transliteration module, and these are the focus of current and future research. First, we would like to use available gazetteers, such as lists of place and person names available from the US census bureau, `http://world-gazetteer.com/` or `http://geonames.org`. Then, we consider utilizing the bigram and trigram parts of Web 1T (Brants and Franz, 2006), to improve the TTT identifier with respect to identifying multi-token expressions which should be transliterated. In addition, we would like to take into account the weights of the different transliteration options when deciding which to select in the translation. Finally, we are interested in applying this module to different language pairs, especially ones with limited resources.

Acknowledgments

We wish to thank Gennadi Lembersky for his help in integrating our work into the MT system, as well as to Erik Peterson and Alon Lavie for providing the code for extracting bilingual article titles from Wikipedia. We thank Google Inc. and the LDC for making the Web 1T corpus available to us. Dan Roth provided good advice in early stages of this work. This research was supported by THE ISRAEL SCIENCE FOUNDATION (grant No. 137/06); by the Israel Internet Association; by the Knowledge Center for Processing Hebrew; and by the Caesarea Rothschild Institute for Interdisciplinary Application of Computer Science at the University of Haifa.

References

Yaser Al-Onaizan and Kevin Knight. 2002. Translating named entities using monolingual and bilingual resources. In *ACL '02: Proceedings of the 40th Annual Meeting on Association for Computational Linguistics*, pages 400–408, Morristown, NJ, USA. Association for Computational Linguistics.

Mansur Arbabi, Scott M. Fischthal, Vincent C. Cheng,

and Elizabeth Bart. 1994. Algorithms for arabic name transliteration. *IBM Journal of Research and Development*, 38(2):183–194.

Roy Bar-Haim, Khalil Sima'an, and Yoad Winter. 2008. Part-of-speech tagging of Modern Hebrew text. *Natural Language Engineering*, 14(2):223–251.

Thorsten Brants and Alex Franz. 2006. Web 1T 5-gram version 1.1. Technical report, Google Reseach.

Peter F. Brown, Stephen Della Pietra, Vincent J. Della Pietra, and Robert L. Mercer. 1993. The mathematic of statistical machine translation: Parameter estimation. *Computational Linguistics*, 19(2):263–311.

Chih-Chung Chang and Chih-Jen Lin, 2001. *LIBSVM: a library for support vector machines.* Software available at `http://www.csie.ntu.edu.tw/~cjlin/libsvm`.

Yoav Goldberg and Michael Elhadad. 2008. Identification of transliterated foreign words in hebrew script. In *CICLing*, pages 466–477.

Dan Goldwasser and Dan Roth. 2008. Active sample selection for named entity transliteration. In *Proceedings of ACL-08: HLT, Short Papers*, pages 53–56, Columbus, Ohio, June. Association for Computational Linguistics.

Ulf Hermjakob, Kevin Knight, and Hal Daumé III. 2008. Name translation in statistical machine translation - learning when to transliterate. In *Proceedings of ACL-08: HLT*, pages 389–397, Columbus, Ohio, June. Association for Computational Linguistics.

Alon Itai and Shuly Wintner. 2008. Language resources for Hebrew. *Language Resources and Evaluation*, 42(1):75–98, March.

Alon Itai, Shuly Wintner, and Shlomo Yona. 2006. A computational lexicon of contemporary hebrew. In *Proceedings of the 5th International Conference on Language Resources and Evaluation (LREC-2006)*, pages 19–22, Genoa, Italy.

Kevin Knight and Jonathan Graehl. 1997. Machine transliteration. In *Proceedings of the 35th Annual Meeting of the Association for Computational Linguistics*, pages 128–135, Madrid, Spain. Association for Computational Linguistics.

Philipp Koehn, Hieu Hoang, Alexandra Birch, Chris Callison-Burch, Marcello Federico, Nicola Bertoldi, Brooke Cowan, Wade Shen, Christine Moran, Richard Zens, Chris Dyer, Ondrej Bojar, Alexandra Constantin, and Evan Herbst. 2007. Moses: Open source toolkit for statistical machine translation. In *Proceedings of the 45th Annual Meeting of the Association for Computational Linguistics Companion Volume Proceedings of the Demo and Poster Sessions*, pages 177–180, Prague, Czech Republic, June. Association for Computational Linguistics.

Alon Lavie, Erik Peterson, Katharina Probst, Shuly Wintner, and Yaniv Eytani. 2004a. Rapid prototyping of a transfer-based Hebrew-to-English machine translation system. In *Proceedings of the 10th International Conference on Theoretical and Methodological Issues in Machine Translation*, pages 1–10, Baltimore, MD, October.

Alon Lavie, Kenji Sagae, and Shyamsundar Jayaraman. 2004b. The significance of recall in automatic metrics for mt evaluation. In Robert E. Frederking and Kathryn Taylor, editors, *AMTA*, volume 3265 of *Lecture Notes in Computer Science*, pages 134–143. Springer.

David Matthews. 2007. Machine transliteration of proper names. Master's thesis, School of Informatics, University of Edinburgh.

Kishore Papineni, Salim Roukos, Todd Ward, and Wei-Jing Zhu. 2001. BLEU: a method for automatic evaluation of machine translation. In *ACL '02: Proceedings of the 40th Annual Meeting on Association for Computational Linguistics*, pages 311–318, Morristown, NJ, USA. Association for Computational Linguistics.

Bernhard Schölkopf, Alex J. Smola, Robert Williamson, and Peter Bartlett. 2000. New support vector algorithms. *Neural Computation*, 12:1207–1245.

Bonnie Glover Stalls and Kevin Knight. 1998. Translating names and technical terms in Arabic text. In *Proceedings of the COLING/ACL Workshop on Computational Approaches to Semitic Languages*, pages 34–41.

Andreas Stolcke. 2002. SRILM - an extensible language modeling toolkit. In *Proceedings International Conference on Spoken Language Processing (ICSLP 2002)*, pages 901–904.

Vladimir N. Vapnik. 1995. *The nature of statistical learning theory.* Springer-Verlag New York, Inc., New York, NY, USA.

Su-Youn Yoon, Kyoung-Young Kim, and Richard Sproat. 2007. Multilingual transliteration using feature based phonetic method. In *Proceedings of the 45th Annual Meeting of the Association of Computational Linguistics*, pages 112–119, Prague, Czech Republic, June. Association for Computational Linguistics.

Optimization in Coreference Resolution Is Not Needed: A Nearly-Optimal Algorithm with Intensional Constraints

Manfred Klenner & Étienne Ailloud
Computational Linguistics
Zurich University, Switzerland
{klenner, ailloud}@cl.uzh.ch

Abstract

We show how global constraints such as transitivity can be treated intensionally in a Zero-One Integer Linear Programming (ILP) framework which is geared to find the optimal and coherent partition of coreference sets given a number of candidate pairs and their weights delivered by a pairwise classifier (used as reliable clustering seed pairs). In order to find out whether ILP optimization, which is NP-complete, actually is the best we can do, we compared the first consistent solution generated by our adaptation of an efficient Zero-One algorithm with the optimal solution. The first consistent solution, which often can be found very fast, is already as good as the optimal solution; optimization is thus not needed.

1 Introduction

One of the main advantages of Integer Linear Programming (ILP) applied to NLP problems is that prescriptive linguistic knowledge can be used to pose global restrictions on the set of desirable solutions. ILP tries to find an optimal solution while adhering to the global constraints. One of the central global constraints in the field of coreference resolution evolves from the interplay of intra-sentential binding constraints and the transitivity of the anaphoric relation. Consider the following sentence taken from the Internet: 'He told him that he deeply admired him'. 'He' and 'him' are exclusive (i.e. they could never be coreferent) within their clauses (the main and the subordinate clause, respectively). A pairwise classifier could learn this given appropriate features or, alternatively, binding constraints could act as a hard filter preventing such pairs from being generated at all. But in either case, since pairwise classification is trapped in its local perspective, nothing can prevent the classifier to resolve the 'he' and 'him' from the subordinate clause in two independently carried out steps to the same antecedent from the main clause. It is transitivity that prohibits such an assignment: if two elements are both coreferent to a common third element, then the two are (transitively given) coreferent as well. If they are known to be exclusive, such an assignment is disallowed. But transitivity is beyond the scope of pairwise classification—it is a global phenomena. The solution is to take ILP as a clustering device, where the probabilities of the pairwise classifier are interpreted as weights and transitivity and other restrictions are acting as global constraints.

Unfortunately, in an ILP program every constraint has to be extensionalized (i.e. all instantiations of the constraint are to be generated). Capturing transitivity for e.g. 150 noun phrases (about 30 sentences) already produces 1,500,000 equations (cf. Section 4). Solving such ILP programs is far too slow for real applications (let alone its brute force character).

A closer look at existing ILP approaches to NLP reveals that they are of a special kind, namely Zero-One ILP with unweighted constraints. Although still NP-complete there exist a number of algorithms such as the Balas algorithm (Balas, 1965) that efficiently explore the search space and reduce thereby run time complexity in the mean. We have adapted Balas' algorithm to the special needs of coreference resolution. First and foremost, this results in an optimization algorithm that treats global constraints intensionally, i.e. that generates instantiations of a constraint only on demand. Thus, transitivity can be captured for even the longest texts. But more important, we found out empirically that 'full optimization' is not really needed. The first consistent solution, which often can be found very fast, is already as good—in terms of F-measure values—as the optimal solution. This is good news, since it reduces runtime and at same time maintains the empirical results.

We first introduce Zero-One ILP, discuss our baseline model and give an ILP formalization of coreference resolution. Then we go into the details of our Balas adaptation and provide empirical evidence for our central claim—that optimization search can already be stopped (without qual-

Proceedings of the 12th Conference of the European Chapter of the ACL, pages 442–450,
Athens, Greece, 30 March – 3 April 2009. ©2009 Association for Computational Linguistics

ity loss) when the first consistent solution has been found.

2 Zero-One Integer Linear Programming (ILP)

The algorithm in (Balas, 1965) solves Zero-One Integer Linear Programming (ILP), where a weighted linear function (the *objective function*) of binary variables $F(x_1,\ldots,x_n) = w_1x_1 + \ldots + w_nx_n$ is to be minimized under the regiment of linear inequalities $a_1x_1 + \ldots + a_nx_n \geq A$.[1] Unlike its real-valued counterpart, Zero-One ILP is NP-complete (cf., say, (Papadimitriou and Steiglitz, 1998)), but branch-and-bound algorithms with efficient heuristics exist, as the Balas Algorithm: Balas (1965) proposes an approach where the objective function's addends are sorted according to the magnitude of the weights: $0 \leq w_1 \leq \ldots \leq w_n$. This preliminary ordering induces the following functioning principles for the algorithm (see (Chinneck, 2004, Chap. 13) for more details):

1. It seeks to minimize F, so that a solution with as few 1s as possible is preferred.

2. If, during exploration of solutions, constraints force an x_i to be set to 1, then it should bear as small an index as possible.

The Balas algorithm follows a depth-first search while checking feasibility (i.e., through the constraints) of the branches partially explored: Upon branching, the algorithm *bounds* the cost of setting the current variable x_N to 1 by the costs accumulated so far: $w_1x_1 + \ldots + w_{N-1}x_{N-1} + w_N$ is now the lowest cost this branch may yield. If, on the contrary, x_N is set to 0, a violated $\geq$-constraint may only be satisfied via an x_i set to 1 ($i > N$), so the cheapest change to ameliorate the partial solution is to set the right-next variable to 1: $w_1x_1 + \ldots + w_{N-1}x_{N-1} + w_{N+1}$ would be the cheapest through this branch.

If setting all weights past the branching variable to 0 yields a cheaper solution than the so far minimal solution obtained, then it is worthwile exploring this branch, and the algorithms goes on to the next weighted variable, until it reaches a feasible solution; otherwise it backtracks to the last unexplored branching. The complexity thus remains exponential in the worst case, but the initial ordering of weights is a clever guide.

[1]Maximization and coping with $\leq$-constraints are also accessible via simple transformations.

3 Our Baseline Model

The memory-based learner TiMBL (Daelemans et al., 2004) is used as a (pairwise) classifier. TiMBL stores all training examples, learns feature weights and classifies test instances according to the majority class of the k-nearest (i.e. most similar) neighbors. We have experimented with various features; Table 1 lists the set we have finally used (Soon et al. (2001) and Ng and Cardie (2002) more thoroughly discuss different features and their benefits):

- distance in sentences and markables
- part of speech of the head of the markables
- the grammatical functions
- parallelism of grammatical functions
- do the heads match or not
- where is the pronoun (if any): left or right
- word form if POS is pronoun
- salience of the non-pronominal phrases
- semantic class of noun phrase heads

Table 1: Features for Pairwise Classification

As a gold standard the TüBa-D/Z (Telljohann et al., 2005; Naumann, 2006) coreference corpus is used. The TüBa is a treebank (1,100 German newspaper texts, 25,000 sentences) augmented with coreference annotations[2]. In total, there are 13,818 anaphoric, 1,031 cataphoric and 12,752 coreferential relations. There are 3,295 relative pronouns, 8,929 personal pronouns, 2,987 reflexive pronouns, and 3,921 possessive pronouns.

There are some rather long texts in the TüBa corpus. Which pair generation algorithm is reasonable? Should we pair every markable (even from the beginning of the text) with every other succeeding markable? This is linguistically implausible. Pronouns are acting as a kind of local variables. A 'he' at the beginning of a text and a second distant 'he' at the end of the text hardly tend to corefer, except if there is a long chain of coreference 'renewals' that lead somehow from the first 'he' to the second 'he'. But the plain 'he'-'he' pair does not reliably indicate coreference.

A smaller window seems to be appropriate. We have experimented with various window sizes and found that a size of 3 sentences worked best. Candidate pairs are generated only within that

[2]Recently, a new version of the TüBa was released with 35,000 sentences with coreference annotations.

window, which is moved sentence-wise over the whole text.

4 Our Constraint-Based Model

The output of the TiMBL classifier is the input to the optimization step, it provides the set of variables and their weights. In order to utilize TiMBL's classification results as weights in a minimization task, we have defined a measure called *classification costs* (see Fig. 1).

$$w_{ij} = \frac{|\, neg_{ij} \,|}{|\, neg_{ij} \cup pos_{ij} \,|}$$

Figure 1: Score for Classification Costs

$|\, neg_{ij} \,|$ ($|\, pos_{ij} \,|$) denotes the number of instances similar (according to TiMBL's metric) to $\langle i, j \rangle$ that are negative (positive) examples. If no negative instances are found, a safe positive classification decision is proposed at zero cost. Accordingly, the cost of a decision without any positive instances is high, namely one. If both sets are non-empty, the ratio of the negative instances to the total of all instances is taken. For example, if TiMBL finds 10 positive and 5 negative examples similar to the yet unclassified new example $\langle i, j \rangle$ the cost of a positive classification is 5/15 while a negative classification costs 10/15.

We introduce our model in an ILP style. In section 6 we discuss our Balas adaptation which allows us to define constraints intensionally.

The objective function is:

$$min: \sum_{\langle i,j \rangle \in O_{0.5}} w_{ij} \cdot c_{ij} + (1 - w_{ij}) \cdot c_{ji} \quad (1)$$

$O_{0.5}$ is the set of pairs $\langle i, j \rangle$ that have received a weight ≤ 0.5 according to our weight function (see Fig. 1). Any binary variable c_{ij} combines the ith markable (of the text) with the jth markable ($i < j$) within a fixed window[3].

c_{ji} represents the (complementary) decision that i and j are not coreferent. The weight of this decision is $(1 - w_{ij})$. Please note that every optimization model of coreference resolution must include both variables[4]. Otherwise optimization would completely ignore the classification decisions of the pairwise classifier (i.e., that ≤ 0.5 suggests coreference). For example, the choice not to set $c_{ij} = 1$ at costs $w_{ij} \leq 0.5$ must be sanctioned by instantiating its inverse variable $c_{ji} = 1$ and adding $(1 - w_{ij})$ to the objective function's value. Otherwise minimization would turn—in the worst case—everything to be non-coreferent, while maximization would preferentially set everything to be actually coreferent (as long as no constraints are violated, of course).[5]

The first constraint then is:

$$c_{ij} + c_{ji} = 1, \ \forall \langle i, j \rangle \in O_{0.5} \quad (2)$$

A pair $\langle i, j \rangle$ is either coreferent or not.

Transitivity is captured by (see (Finkel and Manning, 2008) for an alternative but equivalent formalization):

$$\begin{aligned} c_{ij} + c_{jk} &\leq c_{ik} + 1, \ \forall i,j,k \ (i < j < k) \\ c_{ik} + c_{jk} &\leq c_{ij} + 1, \ \forall i,j,k \ (i < j < k) \\ c_{ij} + c_{ik} &\leq c_{jk} + 1, \ \forall i,j,k \ (i < j < k) \end{aligned} \quad (3)$$

In order to take full advantage of ILP's reasoning capacities, three equations are needed given three markables. The extensionalization of transitivity thus produces $\frac{n!}{3!(n-3)!} \cdot 3$ equations for n markables. Note that transitivity—as a global constraint—ought to spread over the whole candidate set, not just within in the window.

Transitivity without further constraints is pointless.[6] What we really can gain from transitivity is consistency at the linguistic level, namely (globally) adhering to exclusiveness constraints (cf. the example in the introduction). We have defined two predicates that replace the traditional c-command (which requires full syntactical analysis) and approximate it: *clause_bound* and *np_bound*.

Two mentions are *clause-bound* if they occur in the same subclause, none of them being a reflexive or a possessive pronoun, and they do not form an apposition. There are only 16 cases in our data set where this predicate produces false negatives (e.g. in clauses with predicative verbs: 'He$_i$ is still prime minister$_i$'). We currently regard this shortcoming as noise.

[3] As already discussed, the window is realized as part of the vector generation component, so $O_{0.5}$ automatically only captures pairs within the window.

[4] Even if an anaphoricity classifier is used.

[5] The need for optimization or other numerical preference mechanisms originates from the fact that coreference resolution is underconstrained—due to the lack of a deeper text understanding.

[6] Although it might lead to a reordering of coreference sets by better 'balancing the weights'.

Two markables that are clause-bound (in the sense defined above) are exclusive, i.e.

$$c_{ij} = 0, \ \forall i, j \ (clause\_bound(i, j)). \qquad (4)$$

A possessive pronoun is exclusive to all markables in the noun phrase it is contained in (e.g. $c_{ij} = 0$ given a noun phrase "[her$_i$ manager$_j$]"), but might get coindexed with markables outside of such a local context ("Anne$_i$ talks to her$_i$ manager"). We define a predicate *np_bound* that is true of two markables, if they occur in the same noun phrase. In general, two markables that *np-bind* each other are exclusive:

$$c_{ij} = 0, \ \forall i, j \ (np\_bound(i, j)) \qquad (5)$$

5 Representing ILP Constraints Intensionally

Existing ILP-based approaches to NLP (e.g. (Punyakanok et al., 2004; Althaus et al., 2004; Marciniak and Strube, 2005)) belong to the class of Zero-One ILP: only binary variables are needed. This has been seldom remarked (but see (Althaus et al., 2004)) and generic (out-of-the-box) ILP implementations are used. Moreover, these models form a very restricted variant of Zero-One ILP: the constraints come without any weights. The reason for this lies in the logical nature of NLP constraints. For example in the case of coreference, we have the following types of constraints:

1. exclusivity of two instantiations (e.g. either coreferent or not, equation 2)
2. dependencies among three instantiations (transitivity: if two are coreferent then so the third, equation 3)
3. the prohibition of pair instantiation (binding constraints, equations 4 and 5)
4. enforcement of at least one instantiation of a markable in some pair (equation 6 below).

We call the last type of constraints 'boundness enforcement constraints'. Only two classes of pronouns strictly belong to this class: relative (POS label 'PRELS') and possessive pronouns (POS label 'PPOSAT')[7]. The corresponding ILP constraint is, e.g. for possessive pronouns:

$$\sum_i c_{ij} \geq 1, \ \forall j \ s.t. \ pos(j) = \text{'PPOSAT'} \qquad (6)$$

[7]In rare cases, even reflexive pronouns are (correctly) used non-anaphorically, and, more surprisingly, 15% of the personal pronouns in the TüBa are used non-anaphorically.

Note that boundness enforcement constraints lead to exponential time in the worst case. Given that such a constraint holds on a pair with the highest costs of all pairs (thus being the last element of the Balas ordered list with n elements): in order to prove whether it can be bound (set to one), 2^n (binary) variable flips need to be checked in the worst case. All other constraints can be satisfied by setting some $c_{ij} = 0$ (i.e. non-coreferent) which does not affect already taken or (any) yet to be taken assignments. Although exponential in the worst case, the integration of constraint (6) has slowed down CPU time only slightly in our experiments.

A closer look at these constraints reveals that most of them can be treated intensionally in an efficient manner. This is a big advantage, since now transitivity can be captured even for long texts (which is infeasible for most generic ILP models).

To intensionally capture transitivity, we only need to explicitly maintain the evolving coreference sets. If a new markable is about to enter a set (e.g. if it is related to another markable that is already member of the set) it is verified that it is compatible with all members of the set.

A markable i is *compatible* with a coreference set if, for all members j of the set, $\langle i, j \rangle$ does not violate binding constraints, agrees morphologically and semantically. Morphological agreement depends on the POS tags of a pair. Two personal pronouns must agree in person, number and gender. In German, a possessive pronoun must only agree in person with its antecedent. Two nouns might even have different grammatical gender, so no morphological agreement is checked here.

Checking binding for the *clause_bound* constraint is simple: each markable has a subclause ID attached (extracted from the TüBa). If two markables (except reflexive or possessive pronouns) share an ID they are exclusive. Possessive pronouns must not be np-bound. All members of the noun phrase containing the possessive pronoun are exclusive to it.

Note that such a representation of constraints is intensional since we need not enumerate all exclusive pairs as an ILP approach would have to. We simply check (on demand) the identity of IDs.

There is also no need to explicitly maintain constraint (2), either, which states that a pair is either coreferent or not. In the case that a pair cannot be set to 1 (representing coreference), it is set to 0; i.e. c_{ij} and c_{ji} are represented by the same index position p of a Balas solution v (cf. Section 6); no extensional modelling is necessary.

Although our special-purpose Balas adaptation no longer constitutes a general framework that can be fed with each and every Zero-One ILP formalization around, the algorithm is simple enough to justify this. Even if one uses an ILP translator such as Zimpl[8], writing a program for a concrete ILP problem quickly becomes comparably complex.

6 A Variant of the Balas Algorithm

Our algorithm proceeds as follows: we generate the first consistent solution according to the Balas algorithm (Balas-First, henceforth). The result is a vector v of dimension n, where n is the size of $O_{0.5}$. The dimensions take binary values: a value 1 at position p represents the decision that the pth pair c_{ij} from the (Balas-ordered) objective function is coreferent (0 indicates non-coreference). One minor difference to the original Balas algorithm is that the primary choice of our algorithm is to set a variable to 1, not to 0—thus favoring coreference. However, in our case, 1 is the cheapest solution (with cost $w_{ij} \leq 0.5$). Setting a variable to zero has cost $1 - w_{ij}$ which is more expensive in any case. But aside from this assignment convention, the principal idea is preserved, namely that the assignment is guided by lowest cost decisions.

The search for less expensive solutions is done a bit differently from the original. The Balas algorithm takes profit from weighted constraints. As discussed in Section 5, constraints in existing ILP models for NLP are unweighted. Another difference is that in the case of coreference resolution both decisions have costs: setting a variable to 1 (w_{ij}) and setting it to 0 ($1 - w_{ij}$). This is the key to our cost function that guides the search.

Let us first make some properties of the search space explicit. First of all, given no constraints were violated, the optimal solution would be the one with all pairs from $O_{0.5}$ set to 1 (since any 0 would add a suboptimal weight, namely $1 - w_{ij}$). Now we can see that any less expensive solution than Balas-First must be longer than Balas-First, where the length (1-length, henceforth) of a Balas solution is defined as the number of dimensions with value 1. A shorter solution would turn at least a single 1 into 0, which leads to a higher objective function value.

[8]`http://zimpl.zib.de/`

Any solution with the same 1-length is more expensive since it requires swapping a 1 to 0 at one position and a 0 to 1 at a farther position. The permutation of 1/0s from Balas-First is induced by the weights and the constraints. A 0 at position q is forced by (a constraint together with) some (or more) 1 at position p ($p < q$). Thus, we can only swap a 0 to 1 if we swap at least one preceding 1 to 0. The costs of swapping a preceding 1 to 0 are higher than the gain from swapping the 0 to 1 (as a consequence of the Balas ordering). So no solution with the same 1-length can be less expensive than Balas-First.

We then have to search for solutions with higher 1-length. In Section 7 we will argue that this actually goes in the wrong direction.

Any longer solution must swap—for every 1 swapped to 0—at least two 0s to 1. Otherwise the costs are higher than the gain. We can utilize this for a reduction of the search space.

Let p be a position index of Balas-First (v), where the value of the dimension at p is 1 and there exist at least two 0s with position indices $q > p$.

Consider $v = \langle 1,0,1,1,0,0 \rangle$. Positions 1, 3 and 4 are such positions (identifying the following parts of v resp.: $\langle 1,0,1,1,0,0 \rangle, \langle 1,1,0,0 \rangle$ and $\langle 1,0,0 \rangle$).

We define a projection $c(p)$ that returns the weight w_{ij} of the pth pair c_{ij} from the Balas ordering. $v(p)$ is the value of dimension p in v (0 or 1). The cost of swapping 1 at position p to 0 is the difference between the cost of c_{ji} ($1 - c(p)$) and c_{ij} ($c(p)$): $costs(p) = 1 - 2 \cdot c(p)$.

We define the potential gain $pg(p)$ of swapping a 1 at position p to 0 and every succeeding 0 to 1 by:

$$pg(p) = costs(p) - \sum_{q>p \text{ s.t. } v(q)=0} 1 - 2 \cdot c(q) \quad (7)$$

For example, let $v = \langle 1,0,1,1,0,0 \rangle$, $p = 4$, $c(4) = 0.2$ and (the two 0s) $c(5) = 0.3$, $c(6) = 0.35$. $costs(4) = 1 - 0.4 = 0.6$ and $pg(4) = 0.6 - (0.4+0.3) = -0.1$. Even if all 0s (after position 4) can be swapped to 1, the objective function value is lower that before, namely by 0.1. Thus, we need not consider this branch.

In general, each time a 0 is turned into 1, the potential gain is preserved, but if we have to turn another 1 to 0 (due to a constraint), or if a 0 cannot be swapped to 1, the potential gain is decremented by a certain cost factor. If the potential gain is exhausted that way, we can stop searching.

7 Is Optimization Really Needed? Empirical Evidence

The first observation we made when running our algorithm was that in more than 90% of all cases, Balas-First already constitutes the optimal solution. That is, the time-consuming search for a less expensive solution ended without further success.

As discussed in Section 6, any less expensive solution must be longer (1-length) than Balas-First. But can longer solutions be better (in terms of F-measure scores) than shorter ones? They might: if the 1-length re-assignment of variables removes as much false positives as possible and raises instead as much of the true positives as can be found in $O_{0.5}$. Such a solution might have a better F-measure score. But what about its objective function value? Is it less expensive than Balas-First?

We have designed an experiment with all (true) coreferent pairs from $O_{0.5}$ (as indicated by the gold standard) set to 1. Note that this is just another kind of constraints: the enforcement of coreference (this time extensionally given).

The result was surprising: The objective function values that our algorithm finds under these constraints were in any case higher than Balas-First without that constraint.

Fig. 2 illustrates this schematically (Fig. 4 below justifies the curve's shape). The curve represents a function mapping objective values to F-measure scores. Note that it is not monotonically decreasing (from lower objective values to higher ones)—as one would expect (less expensive = higher F-measure). The vertical line labelled b identifies Balas-First. Starting with Balas-First, optimization searches to the left, i.e. searching for smaller objective function values. The horizontal line labelled m shows the local maximum of that search region (the arrow from left points to it). But unfortunately, the global maximum (the arrow from right), i.e. the 1-length solution with all (true) coreferent pairs set to 1, lies to the right-hand side of Balas-First.

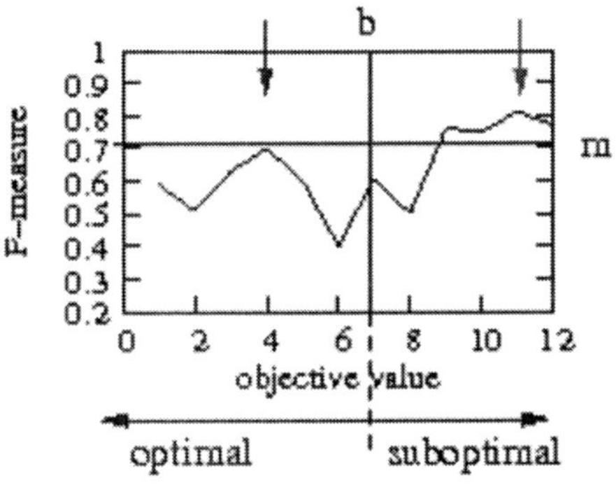

Figure 2: The best solution is 'less optimal'

This indicates that, in our experimental conditions, optimization efforts can never reach the global maximum, but it also indicates that searching for less expensive solutions nevertheless might lead (at least) to a local maximum. However, if it is true that the goal function is not monotonic, there is no guarantee that the optimal solution actually constitutes the local maximum, i.e. the best solution in terms of F-measure scores.

Unfortunately, we cannot prove mathematically any hypotheses about the optimal values and their behavior. However, we can compare the optimal value's F-measure scores to the Balas-First F-measure scores empirically. Two experiments were designed to explore this. In the first experiment, we computed for each text the difference between the F-measure value of the optimal solution and the F-measure value of Balas-First. It is positive if the optimal solution has higher F-measure score than Balas-First and negative otherwise. This was done for each text (99) that has more than one objective function value (remember that in more than 90% of texts Balas-First was already the optimal solution).

Fig. 3 shows the results. The horizontal line is separating gain from loss. Points above it indicate that the optimal solution has a better F-measure score, points below indicate a loss in percentage

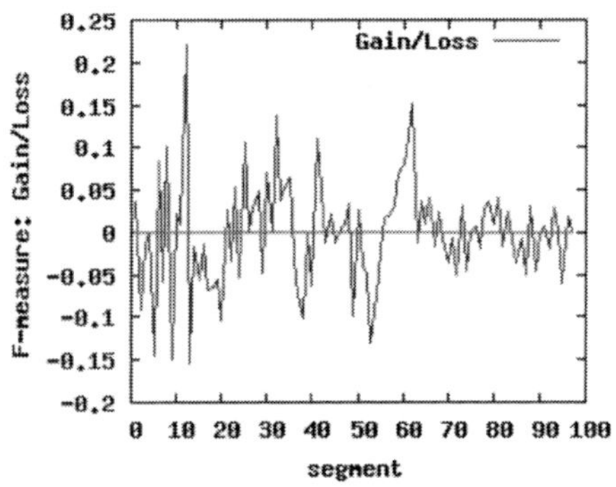

Figure 3: Balas-First or Optimal Solution

(for readability, we have drawn a curve). Taking the mean of loss and gain across all texts, we found that the optimal solution shows no significant F-measure difference with the Balas-First solution: the optimal solution even slightly worsens the F-measure compared to Balas-First by -0.086%.

The second experiment was meant to explore the curve shape of the goal function that maps an objective function value to a F-measure value. This is shown in Fig. 4. The values of that function are empirically given, i.e. they are produced by our algorithm. The x-axis shows the mean of the nth objective function value better than Balas-First. The y-value of the nth x-value thus marks the effect (positive or negative) in F-measure scores while proceeding to find the optimal solution. As can be seen from the figure, the function (at least empirically) is rather erratic. In other words, searching for the optimal solution beyond Balas-First does not seem to lead reliably (and monotonically) to better F-measure values.

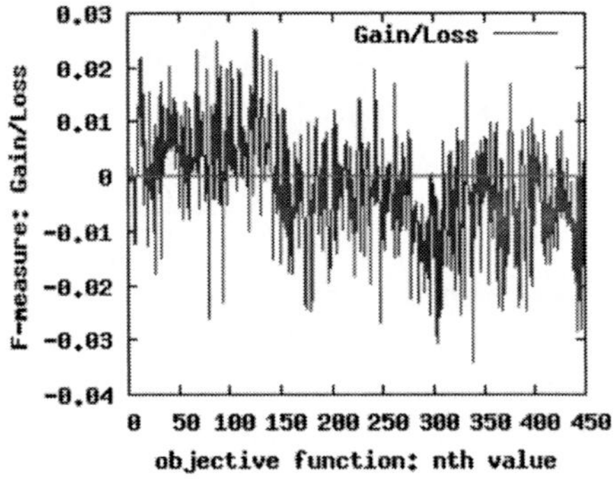

Figure 4: 1st Compared to Balas-nth Value

In the next section, we show that Balas-First as the first optimization step actually is a significant improvement over the classifier output. So we are not saying that we should dispense with optimization efforts completely.

8 Does Balas-First help? Empirical Evidence

Besides the empirical fact that Balas-First slightly outperforms the optimal solution, we must demonstrate that Balas-First actually improves the baseline. Our experiments are based on a five-fold cross-validation setting (1100 texts from the TüBa coreference corpus). Each experiment was carried out in two variants. One where all markables have been taken as input—an application-oriented setting, and one where only markables that represent true mentions have been taken (cf. (Luo et al., 2004; Ponzetto and Strube, 2006) for other approaches with an evaluation based on true mentions only). The assumption is that if only true mentions are considered, the effects of a model can be better measured.

We have used the Entity-Constrained Measure (ECM), introduced in (Luo et al., 2004; Luo, 2005). As argued in (Klenner and Ailloud, 2008), it is more appropriate to evaluate the quality of coreference sets than the MUC score.[9]

To obtain the baseline, we merged all pairs that TiMBL classified as coreferent into coreference sets. Table 2 shows the results.

	all mentions		true mentions	
	Timbl	B-First	Timbl	B-First
F	61.83	64.27	71.47	78.90
P	66.52	72.05	73.81	84.10
R	57.76	58.00	69.28	74.31

Table 2: Balas-First (B-First) vs. Baseline

In the 'all mentions setting', 2.4% F-measure improvement was achieved, with 'true mentions' it is 7.43%. These improvements clearly demonstrate that Balas-First is superior to the results based on the classifier output.

But is the specific order proposed by the Balas algorithm itself useful? Since we have dispensed with 'full optimization', why not dispense with the Balas ordering as well? Since the ordering of the pairs does not affect the rest of our algorithm we have been able to compare the Balas order to the more natural linear order. Note that all constraints are applied in the linear variant as well, so the only difference is the ordering. Linear ordering over pairs is established by sorting according to the index of the first pair element (the i from c_{ij}).

	all mentions		true mentions	
	linear	B-First	linear	B-First
F	62.83	64.27	76.08	78.90
P	70.39	72.05	81.40	84.10
R	56.73	58.00	71.41	74.31

Table 3: Balas Order vs. Linear Order

Our experiments (cf. Table 3) indicate that the

[9] Various authors have remarked on the shortcomings of the MUC evaluation scheme (Bagga and Baldwin, 1998; Luo, 2005; Nicolae and Nicolae, 2006).

Balas ordering does affect the empirical results. The F-measure improvement is 1.44% ('all mentions') and 2.82% ('true mentions').

The search for Balas-First remains, in general, NP-complete. However, constraint models without boundness enforcement constraints (cf. Section 5) pose no computational burden, they can be solved in quadratic time. In the presence of boundness enforcement constraints, exponential time is required in the worst case. In our experiments, boundness enforcement constraints have proved to be unproblematic. Most of the time, the classifier has assigned low costs to candidate pairs containing a relative or a possessive pronoun, which means that they get instantiated rather soon (although this is not guaranteed).

9 Related Work

The focus of our paper lies on the evaluation of the benefits optimization could have for coreference resolution. Accordingly, we restrict our discussion to methodologically related approaches (i.e. ILP approaches). Readers interested in other work on anaphora resolution for German on the basis of the TüBa coreference corpus should consider (Hinrichs et al., 2005) (pronominal anaphora) and (Versley, 2006) (nominal anaphora).

Common to all ILP approaches (incl. ours) is that they apply ILP on the output of pairwise machine-learning. Denis and Baldridge (2007; 2008) have an ILP model to jointly determine anaphoricity and coreference, but take neither transitivity nor exclusivity into account. So no complexity problems arise in their approach. The model from (Finkel and Manning, 2008) utilizes transitivity, but not exclusivity. The benefits of transitivity are thus restricted to an optimal balancing of the weights (e.g. given two positively classified pairs, the transitively given third pair in some cases is negative, ILP globally resolves these cases to the optimal solution). The authors do not mention complexity problems with extensionalizing transitivity. Klenner (2007) utilizes both transitivity and exclusivity. To overcome the overhead of transitivity extensionalization, he proposes a fixed transitivity window. This, however, is bound to produce transitivity gaps, so the benefits of complete transitivity propagation are lost.

Another attempt to overcome the problem of complexity with ILP models is described in (Riedel and Clarke, 2006) (dependency parsing). Here an incremental—or better, cascaded—ILP model is proposed, where at each cascade only those constraints are added that have been violated in the preceding one. The search stops with the first consistent solution (as we suggest in the present paper). However, it is difficult to quantify the number of cascades needed to come to it and moreover, the full ILP machinery is being used (so again, constraints need to be extensionalized).

To the best of our knowledge, our work is the first that studies the proper utility of ILP optimization for NLP, while offering an intensional alternative to ILP constraints.

10 Conclusion and Future Work

In this paper, we have argued that ILP for NLP reduces to Zero-One ILP with unweighted constraints. We have proposed such a Zero-One ILP model that combines exclusivity, transitivity and boundness enforcement constraints in an intensional model driven by best-first inference.

We furthermore claim and empirically demonstrate for the domain of coreference resolution that NLP approaches can take advantage from that new perspective. The pitfall of ILP, namely the need to extensionalize each and every constraint, can be avoided. The solution is an easy to carry out reimplementation of a Zero-One algorithm such as Balas', where (most) constraints can be treated intensionally. Moreover, we have found empirical evidence that 'full optimization' is not needed. The first found consistent solution is as good as the optimal one. Depending on the constraint model this can reduce the costs from exponential time to polynomial time.

Optimization efforts, however, are not superfluous, as we have showed. The first consistent solution found with our Balas reimplementation improves the baseline significantly. Also, the Balas ordering itself has proven superior over other orders, e.g. linear order.

In the future, we will experiment with more complex constraint models in the area of coreference resolution. But we will also consider other domains in order to find out whether our results actually are widely applicable.

Acknowledgement The work described herein is partly funded by the Swiss National Science Foundation (grant 105211-118108). We would like to thank the anonymous reviewers for their helpful comments.

References

E. Althaus, N. Karamanis, and A. Koller. 2004. Computing locally coherent discourses. In *Proc. of the ACL.*

A. Bagga and B. Baldwin. 1998. Algorithms for scoring coreference chains. In *Proceedings of the Linguistic Coreference Workshop at The First International Conference on Language Resources and Evaluation (LREC98)*, pages 563–566.

E. Balas. 1965. An additive algorithm for solving linear programs with zero-one variables. *Operations Research*, 13(4):517–546.

J.W. Chinneck. 2004. Practical optimization: a gentle introduction. Electronic document: `http://www.sce.carleton.ca/faculty/chinneck/po.html`.

W. Daelemans, J. Zavrel, K. van der Sloot, and A. van den Bosch. 2004. TiMBL: Tilburg Memory-Based Learner.

P. Denis and J. Baldridge. 2007. Joint determination of anaphoricity and coreference resolution using integer programming. *Proceedings of NAACL HLT*, pages 236–243.

P. Denis and J. Baldridge. 2008. Specialized models and ranking for coreference resolution. In *Proceedings of the Empirical Methods in Natural Language Processing (EMNLP 2008)*, Hawaii, USA. To appear.

J.R. Finkel and C.D. Manning. 2008. Enforcing transitivity in coreference resolution. Association for Computational Linguistics.

E. Hinrichs, K. Filippova, and H. Wunsch. 2005. A data-driven approach to pronominal anaphora resolution in German. In Proc. of RANLP '05.

M. Klenner and É. Ailloud. 2008. Enhancing coreference clustering. In C. Johansson, editor, *Proc. of the Second Workshop on Anaphora Resolution (WAR II)*, volume 2 of *NEALT Proceedings Series*, pages 31–40, Bergen, Norway.

M. Klenner. 2007. Enforcing consistency on coreference sets. In *Recent Advances in Natural Language Processing (RANLP)*, pages 323–328, September.

X. Luo, A. Ittycheriah, H. Jing, N. Kambhatla, and S. Roukos. 2004. A mention-synchronous coreference resolution algorithm based on the Bell tree. *Proceedings of the 42nd Annual Meeting on Association for Computational Linguistics.*

X. Luo. 2005. On coreference resolution performance metrics. In *Proceedings of the conference on Human Language Technology and Empirical Methods in Natural Language Processing*, pages 25–32. Association for Computational Linguistics Morristown, NJ, USA.

T. Marciniak and M. Strube. 2005. Beyond the pipeline: Discrete optimization in NLP. In *Proc. of the CoNLL.*

K. Naumann. 2006. Manual for the annotation of indocument referential relations. Electronic document: `http://www.sfs.uni-tuebingen.de/de_tuebadz.shtml`.

V. Ng and C. Cardie. 2002. Improving machine learning approaches to coreference resolution. In Proc. of the ACL.

C. Nicolae and G. Nicolae. 2006. Best Cut: A graph algorithm for coreference resolution. In *Proceedings of the 2006 Conference on Empirical Methods in Natural Language Processing*, pages 275–283. Association for Computational Linguistics.

C.H. Papadimitriou and K. Steiglitz. 1998. *Combinatorial Optimization: Algorithms and Complexity.* Dover Publications.

S.P. Ponzetto and M. Strube. 2006. Exploiting semantic role labeling, WordNet and Wikipedia for coreference resolution. In *Proc. of HLT-NAACL*, volume 6, pages 192–199.

V. Punyakanok, D. Roth, W. Yih, and D. Zimak. 2004. Semantic role labeling via integer linear programming inference. In *Proc. of the COLING.*

S. Riedel and J. Clarke. 2006. Incremental integer linear programming for non-projective dependency parsing. In *Proc. of the EMNLP.*

W.M. Soon, H.T. Ng, and D.C.Y. Lim. 2001. A machine learning approach to coreference resolution of noun phrases. *Computational Linguistics*, 27(4):521–544.

H. Telljohann, E.W. Hinrichs, S. Kübler, and H. Zinsmeister. 2005. Stylebook for the Tübingen treebank of written German (TüBa-D/Z). *Seminar fur Sprachwissenschaft, Universität Tübingen, Tübingen, Germany.*

Y. Versley. 2006. A constraint-based approach to noun phrase coreference resolution in German newspaper text. In Konferenz zur Verarbeitung Natürlicher Sprache (KONVENS).

A Logic of Semantic Representations for Shallow Parsing

Alexander Koller
Saarland University
Saarbrücken, Germany
koller@mmci.uni-saarland.de

Alex Lascarides
University of Edinburgh
Edinburgh, UK
alex@inf.ed.ac.uk

Abstract

One way to construct semantic representations in a robust manner is to enhance shallow language processors with semantic components. Here, we provide a model theory for a semantic formalism that is designed for this, namely Robust Minimal Recursion Semantics (RMRS). We show that RMRS supports a notion of entailment that allows it to form the basis for comparing the semantic output of different parses of varying depth.

1 Introduction

Representing semantics as a logical form that supports automated inference and model construction is vital for deeper language engineering tasks, such as dialogue systems. Logical forms can be obtained from hand-crafted deep grammars (Butt et al., 1999; Copestake and Flickinger, 2000) but this lacks robustness: not all words and constructions are covered and by design ill-formed phrases fail to parse. There has thus been a trend recently towards robust wide-coverage semantic construction (e.g., (Bos et al., 2004; Zettlemoyer and Collins, 2007)). But there are certain semantic phenomena that these robust approaches don't capture reliably, including quantifier scope, optional arguments, and long-distance dependencies (for instance, Clark et al. (2004) report that the parser used by Bos et al. (2004) yields 63% accuracy on object extraction; e.g., *the man that I met...*). Forcing a robust parser to make a decision about these phenomena can therefore be error-prone. Depending on the application, it may be preferable to give the parser the option to leave a semantic decision open when it's not sufficiently informed—i.e., to compute a partial semantic representation and to complete it later, using information extraneous to the parser.

In this paper, we focus on an approach to semantic representation that supports this strategy: Robust Minimal Recursion Semantics (RMRS, Copestake (2007a)). RMRS is designed to support underspecification of lexical information, scope, and predicate-argument structure. It is an emerging standard for representing partial semantics, and has been applied in several implemented systems. For instance, Copestake (2003) and Frank (2004) use it to specify semantic components to shallow parsers ranging in depth from POS taggers to chunk parsers and intermediate parsers such as RASP (Briscoe et al., 2006). MRS analyses (Copestake et al., 2005) derived from deep grammars, such as the English Resource Grammar (ERG, (Copestake and Flickinger, 2000)) are special cases of RMRS. But RMRS, unlike MRS and related formalisms like dominance constraints (Egg et al., 2001), is able to express semantic information in the absence of full predicate argument structure and lexical subcategorisation.

The key contribution we make is to cast RMRS, for the first time, as a logic with a well-defined model theory. Previously, no such model theory existed, and so RMRS had to be used in a somewhat ad-hoc manner that left open exactly what any given RMRS representation actually *means*. This has hindered practical progress, both in terms of understanding the relationship of RMRS to other frameworks such as MRS and predicate logic and in terms of the development of efficient algorithms. As one application of our formalisation, we use entailment to propose a novel way of characterising consistency of RMRS analyses across different parsers.

Section 2 introduces RMRS informally and illustrates why it is necessary and useful for representing semantic information across deep and shallow language processors. Section 3 defines the syntax and model-theory of RMRS. We finish in Section 4 by pointing out some avenues for future research.

Proceedings of the 12th Conference of the European Chapter of the ACL, pages 451–459,
Athens, Greece, 30 March – 3 April 2009. ©2009 Association for Computational Linguistics

2 Deep and shallow semantic construction

Consider the following (toy) sentence:

(1) Every fat cat chased some dog.

It exhibits several kinds of ambiguity, including a quantifier scope ambiguity and lexical ambiguities—e.g., the nouns "cat" and "dog" have 8 and 7 WordNet senses respectively. Simplifying slightly by ignoring tense information, two of its readings are shown as logical forms below; these can be represented as trees as shown in Fig. 1.

(2) $\_\mathsf{every\_q\_1}(x, \_\mathsf{fat\_j\_1}(e', x) \wedge \_\mathsf{cat\_n\_1}(x),$
$\_\mathsf{some\_q\_1}(y, \_\mathsf{dog\_n\_1}(y),$
$\_\mathsf{chase\_v\_1}(e, x, y)))$

(3) $\_\mathsf{some\_q\_1}(y, \_\mathsf{dog\_n\_2}(y),$
$\_\mathsf{every\_q\_1}(x, \_\mathsf{fat\_j\_1}(e', x) \wedge \_\mathsf{cat\_n\_2}(x),$
$\_\mathsf{chase\_v\_1}(e, x, y)))$

Now imagine trying to extract semantic information from the output of a part-of-speech (POS) tagger by using the word lemmas as lexical predicate symbols. Such a semantic representation is highly partial. It will use predicate symbols such as _cat_n, which might resolve to the predicate symbols _cat_n_1 or _cat_n_2 in the complete semantic representation. (Notice the different fonts for the ambiguous and unambiguous predicate symbols.) But most underspecification formalisms (e.g., MRS (Copestake et al., 2005) and CLLS (Egg et al., 2001)) are unable to represent semantic information that is as partial as what we get from a POS tagger because they cannot underspecify predicate-argument structure. RMRS (Copestake, 2007a) is designed to address this problem. In RMRS, the information we get from the POS tagger is as follows:

(4) $l_1 : a_1 : \_\mathrm{every\_q}(x_1),$
$l_{41} : a_{41} : \_\mathrm{fat\_j}(e'),$
$l_{42} : a_{42} : \_\mathrm{cat\_n}(x_3)$
$l_5 : a_5 : \_\mathrm{chase\_v}(e),$
$l_6 : a_6 : \_\mathrm{some\_q}(x_6),$
$l_9 : a_9 : \_\mathrm{dog\_n}(x_7)$

This RMRS expresses only that certain predications are present in the semantic representation—it doesn't say anything about semantic scope, about most arguments of the predicates (e.g., _chase_v(e) doesn't say who chases whom), or about the coindexation of variables (_every_q binds the variable x_1, whereas _cat_n speaks about x_3), and it maintains the lexical ambiguities. Technically, it consists of six *elementary predications* (EPs), one for each word lemma in the sentence; each of them is prefixed by a *label* and an *anchor*, which are essentially variables that refer to nodes in the trees in Fig. 1. We can say that the two trees *satisfy* this RMRS because it is possible to map the labels and anchors in (4) into nodes in each tree and variable names like x_1 and x_3 into variable names in the tree in such a way that the predications of the nodes that labels and anchors denote are consistent with those in the EPs of (4)—e.g., l_1 and a_1 can map to the root of the first tree in Fig. 1, x_1 to x, and the root label _every_q_1 is consistent with the EP predicate _every_q.

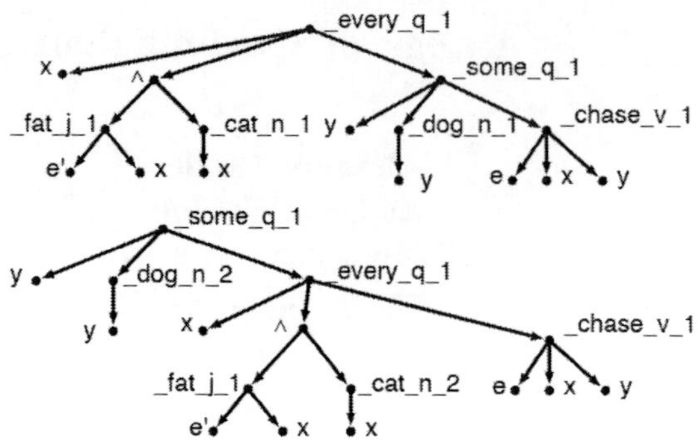

Figure 1: Semantic representations (2) and (3) as trees.

There are of course many other trees (and thus, fully specific semantic representations such as (2)) that are described equally well by the RMRS (4); this is not surprising, given that the semantic output from the POS tagger is so incomplete. If we have information about subjects and objects from a chunk parser like Cass (Abney, 1996), we can represent it in a more detailed RMRS:

(5) $l_1 : a_1 : \_\mathrm{every\_q}(x_1),$
$l_{41} : a_{41} : \_\mathrm{fat\_j}(e'),$
$l_{42} : a_{42} : \_\mathrm{cat\_n}(x_3)$
$l_5 : a_5 : \_\mathrm{chase\_v}(e),$
$\mathsf{ARG}_1(a_5, x_4), \mathsf{ARG}_2(a_5, x_5)$
$l_6 : a_6 : \_\mathrm{some\_q}(x_6),$
$l_9 : a_9 : \_\mathrm{dog\_n}(x_7)$
$x_3 = x_4, x_5 = x_7$

This introduces two new types of atoms. $x_3 = x_4$ means that x_3 and x_4 map to the same variable in any fully specific logical form; e.g., both to the variable x in Fig. 1. $\mathsf{ARG}_i(a, z)$ (and $\mathsf{ARG}_i(a, h)$)

express that the i-th child (counting from 0) of the node to which the anchor a refers is the variable name that z denotes (or the node that the *hole* h denotes). So unlike earlier underspecification formalisms, RMRS can specify the predicate of an atom separately from its arguments; this is necessary for supporting parsers where information about lexical subcategorisation is absent. If we also allow atoms of the form $\mathsf{ARG}_{\{2,3\}}(a, x)$ to express uncertainty as to whether x is the second or third child of the anchor a, then RMRS can even specify the arguments to a predicate while underspecifying their position. This is useful for specifying arguments to _give_v when a parser doesn't handle unbounded dependencies and is faced with *Which bone did you give the dog?* vs. *To which dog did you give the bone?*

Finally, the RMRS (6) is a notational variant of the MRS derived by the ERG, a wide-coverage deep grammar:

(6) $l_1 : a_1$:_every_q_1(x_1),
$\quad\mathsf{RSTR}(a_1, h_2), \mathsf{BODY}(a_1, h_3)$
$l_{41} : a_{41}$:_fat_j_1(e'), $\mathsf{ARG}_1(a_{41}, x_2)$
$l_{42} : a_{42}$:_cat_n_1(x_3)
$l_5 : a_5$:_chase_v_1(e),
$\quad\mathsf{ARG}_1(a_5, x_4), \mathsf{ARG}_2(a_5, x_5)$
$l_6 : a_6$:_some_q_1(x_6),
$\quad\mathsf{RSTR}(a_6, h_7), \mathsf{BODY}(a_6, h_8)$
$l_9 : a_9$:_dog_n_1(x_7)
$h_2 =_q l_{42}, l_{41} = l_{42}, h_7 =_q l_9$
$x_1 = x_2, x_2 = x_3, x_3 = x_4,$
$x_5 = x_6, x_5 = x_7$

RSTR and BODY are conventional names for the ARG_1 and ARG_2 of a quantifier predicate symbol. Atoms like $h_2 =_q l_{42}$ ("qeq") specify a certain kind of "outscopes" relationship between the hole and the label, and are used here to underspecify the scope of the two quantifiers. Notice that the labels of the EPs for "fat" and "cat" are stipulated to be equal in (6), whereas the anchors are not. In the tree, it is the anchors that are mapped to the nodes with the labels _fat_j_1 and _cat_n_1; the label is mapped to the conjunction node just above them. In other words, the role of the anchor in an EP is to connect a predicate to its arguments, while the role of the label is to connect the EP to the surrounding formula. Representing conjunction with label sharing stems from MRS and provides compact representations.

Finally, (6) uses predicate symbols like _dog_n_1 that are meant to be more specific than symbols like _dog_n which the earlier RMRSs used. This reflects the fact that the deep grammar performs some lexical disambiguation that the chunker and POS tagger don't. The fact that the former symbol should be more specific than the latter can be represented using SPEC atoms like _dog_n_1 $\sqsubseteq$ _dog_n. Note that even a deep grammar will not fully disambiguate to semantic predicate symbols, such as WordNet senses, and so _dog_n_1 can still be consistent with multiple symbols like _dog_n_1 and _dog_n_2 in the semantic representation. However, unlike the output of a POS tagger, an RMRS symbol that's output by a deep grammar is consistent with symbols that all have the *same* arity, because a deep grammar fully determines lexical subcategorisation.

In summary, RMRS allows us to represent in a uniform way the (partial) semantics that can be extracted from a wide range of NLP tools. This is useful for hybrid systems which exploit shallower analyses when deeper parsing fails, or which try to match deeply parsed queries against shallow parses of large corpora; and in fact, RMRS is gaining popularity as a practical interchange format for exactly these purposes (Copestake, 2003). However, RMRS is still relatively ad-hoc in that its formal semantics is not defined; we don't know, formally, what an RMRS *means* in terms of semantic representations like (2) and (3), and this hinders our ability to design efficient algorithms for processing RMRS. The purpose of this paper is to lay the groundwork for fixing this problem.

3 Robust Minimal Recursion Semantics

We will now make the basic ideas from Section 2 precise. We will first define the syntax of the RMRS language; this is a notational variant of earlier definitions in the literature. We will then define a model theory for our version of RMRS, and conclude this section by carrying over the notion of *solved forms* from CLLS (Egg et al., 2001).

3.1 RMRS Syntax

We define RMRS syntax in the style of CLLS (Egg et al., 2001). We assume an infinite set of *node variables* $\mathsf{NVar} = \{X, Y, X_1, \ldots\}$, used as labels, anchors, and holes; the distinction between these will come from their position in the formulas. We also assume an infinite set of *base variables* BVar, consisting of individual variables $\{x, x_1, y, \ldots\}$ and event variables $\{e_1, \ldots\}$, and a vocabulary of *predicate symbols* Pred $= \{P, Q, P_1, \ldots\}$. RMRS formulas are defined as follows.

Definition 1. *An* RMRS *is a finite set* φ *of atoms of one of the following forms;* $S \subseteq \mathbb{N}$ *is a set of numbers that is either finite or* $\mathbb{N}$ *itself (throughout the paper, we assume* $0 \in \mathbb{N}$*).*

$$\begin{array}{rcl} A & ::= & X{:}Y{:}P \\ & | & \mathsf{ARG}_S(X, v) \\ & | & \mathsf{ARG}_S(X, Y) \\ & | & X \lhd^* Y \\ & | & v_1 = v_2 \mid v_1 \neq v_2 \\ & | & X = Y \mid X \neq Y \\ & | & P \sqsubseteq Q \end{array}$$

A node variable X *is called a* label *iff* φ *contains an atom of the form* $X{:}Y{:}P$ *or* $Y \lhd^* X$*; it is an* anchor *iff* φ *contains an atom of the form* $Y{:}X{:}P$ *or* $\mathsf{ARG}_S(X, i)$*; and it is a* hole *iff* φ *contains an atom of the form* $\mathsf{ARG}_S(Y, X)$ *or* $X \lhd^* Y$.

Def. 1 combines similarities to earlier presentations of RMRS (Copestake, 2003; Copestake, 2007b) and to CLLS/dominance constraints (Egg et al., 2001). For the most part, our syntax generalises that of older versions of RMRS: We use $\mathsf{ARG}_{\{i\}}$ (with a singleton set S) instead of ARG_i and $\mathsf{ARG}_{\mathbb{N}}$ instead of ARG_n, and the EP $l{:}a{:}P(v)$ (as in Section 2) is an abbreviation of $\{l{:}a{:}P, \mathsf{ARG}_{\{0\}}(a, v)\}$. Similarly, we don't assume that labels, anchors, and holes are syntactically different objects; they receive their function from their positions in the formula. One major difference is that we use dominance ($\lhd^*$) rather than qeq; see Section 3.4 for a discussion. Compared to dominance constraints, the primary difference is that we now have a mechanism for representing lexical ambiguity, and we can specify a predicate and its arguments separately.

3.2 Model Theory

The model theory formalises the relationship between an RMRS and the fully specific, alternative logical forms that it describes, expressed in the base language. We represent such a logical form as a tree τ, such as the ones in Fig. 1, and we can then define satisfaction of formulas in the usual way, by taking the tree as a model structure that interprets all predicate symbols specified above.

In this paper, we assume for simplicity that the base language is as in MRS; essentially, τ becomes the structure tree of a formula of predicate logic. We assume that Σ is a ranked signature consisting of the symbols of predicate logic: a unary constructor $\neg$ and binary constructors $\wedge$, $\rightarrow$, etc.; a set of 3-place quantifier symbols such as _every_q_1 and _some_q_1 (with the children being the bound variable, the restrictor, and the scope); and constructors of various arities for the predicate symbols; e.g., _chase_v_1 is of arity 3. Other base languages may require a different signature Σ and/or a different mapping between formulas and trees; the only strict requirement we make is that the signature contains a binary constructor $\wedge$ to represent conjunction. We write Σ_i and $\Sigma_{\geq i}$ for the set of all constructors in Σ with arity i and at least i, respectively. We will follow the typographical convention that non-logical symbols in Σ are written in sans-serif, as opposed to the RMRS predicate symbols like _cat_n and _cat_n_1.

The models of RMRS are then defined to be finite constructor trees (see also (Egg et al., 2001)):

Definition 2. *A* finite constructor tree τ *is a function* $\tau : D \rightarrow \Sigma$ *such that* D *is a* tree domain *(i.e., a subset of* $\mathbb{N}^*$ *which is closed under prefix and left sibling) and the number of children of each node* $u \in D$ *is equal to the arity of* $\tau(u)$.

We write $D(\tau)$ for the tree domain of a constructor tree τ, and further define the following relations between nodes in a finite constructor tree:

Definition 3. $u \lhd^* v$ (dominance) *iff* u *is a prefix of* v*, i.e. the node* u *is equal to or above the node* v *in the tree.* $u \lhd^*_\wedge v$ *iff* $u \lhd^* v$*, and all symbols on the path from* u *to* v *(not including* v*) are* $\wedge$.

The *satisfaction* relation between an RMRS φ and a finite constructor tree τ is defined in terms of several assignment functions. First, a node variable assignment function α : NVar $\rightarrow D(\tau)$ maps the node variables in an RMRS to the nodes of τ. Second, a base language assignment function g : BVar $\rightarrow \Sigma_0$ maps the base variables to nullary constructors representing variables in the base language. Finally, a function σ from Pred to the power set of $\Sigma_{\geq 1}$ maps each RMRS predicate symbol to a set of constructors from Σ. As we'll see shortly, this function allows an RMRS to underspecify lexical ambiguities.

Definition 4. *Satisfaction of atoms is defined as*

follows:

$\tau, \alpha, g, \sigma \models X{:}Y{:}P$ *iff*
$\quad \tau(\alpha(Y)) \in \sigma(P)$ *and* $\alpha(X) \lhd^*_\wedge \alpha(Y)$
$\tau, \alpha, g, \sigma \models \mathsf{ARG}_S(X, a)$ *iff exists* $i \in S$ *s.t.*
$\quad \alpha(X) \cdot i \in D(\tau)$ *and* $\tau(\alpha(X) \cdot i) = g(a)$
$\tau, \alpha, g, \sigma \models \mathsf{ARG}_S(X, Y)$ *iff exists* $i \in S$ *s.t.*
$\quad \alpha(X) \cdot i \in D(\tau), \alpha(X) \cdot i = \alpha(Y)$
$\tau, \alpha, g, \sigma \models X \lhd^* Y$ *iff* $\alpha(X) \lhd^* \alpha(Y)$
$\tau, \alpha, g, \sigma \models X =/\neq Y$ *iff* $\alpha(X) =/\neq \alpha(Y)$
$\tau, \alpha, g, \sigma \models v_1 =/\neq v_2$ *iff* $g(v_1) =/\neq g(v_2)$
$\tau, \alpha, g, \sigma \models P \sqsubseteq Q$ *iff* $\sigma(P) \subseteq \sigma(Q)$

A 4-tuple τ, α, g, σ *satisfies an* RMRS φ *(written* $\tau, \alpha, g, \sigma \models \varphi$*) iff it satisfies all of its elements.*

Notice that one RMRS may be satisfied by multiple trees; we can take the RMRS to be a partial description of each of these trees. In particular, RMRSs may represent semantic scope ambiguities and/or missing information about semantic dependencies, lexical subcategorisation and lexical senses. For $j = \{1, 2\}$, suppose that $\tau_j, \alpha_j, g_j, \sigma \models \varphi$. Then φ exhibits a semantic scope ambiguity if there are variables $Y, Y' \in \mathsf{NVar}$ such that $\alpha_1(Y) \lhd^* \alpha_1(Y')$ and $\alpha_2(Y') \lhd^* \alpha_2(Y)$. It exhibits missing information about semantic dependencies if there are base-language variables $v, v' \in \mathsf{BVar}$ such that $g_1(v) = g_1(v')$ and $g_2(v) \neq g_2(v')$. It exhibits missing lexical subcategorisation information if there is a $Y \in \mathsf{NVar}$ such that $\tau_1(\alpha_1(Y))$ is a constructor of a different type from $\tau_2(\alpha_2(Y))$ (i.e., the constructors are of a different arity or they differ in whether their arguments are scopal vs. non-scopal). And it exhibits missing lexical sense information if $\tau_1(\alpha_1(Y))$ and $\tau_2(\alpha_2(Y))$ are different base-language constructors, but of the same type.

Let's look again at the RMRS (4). This is satisfied by the trees in Fig. 1 (among others) together with some particular α, g, and σ. For instance, consider the left-hand side tree in Fig. 1. The RMRS (4) satisfies this tree with an assignment function α that maps the variables l_1 and a_1 to the root node, l_{41} and l_{42} to its second child (labeled with "$\wedge$"), a_{41} to the first child of *that* node (i.e. the node 21, labelled with "fat") and a_{42} to the node 22, and so forth. g will map x_1 and x_3 to x, and x_6 and x_7 to y, and so on. And σ will map each RMRS predicate symbol (which represents a word) to the set of its fully resolved meanings, e.g. _cat_n to a set containing _cat_n_1

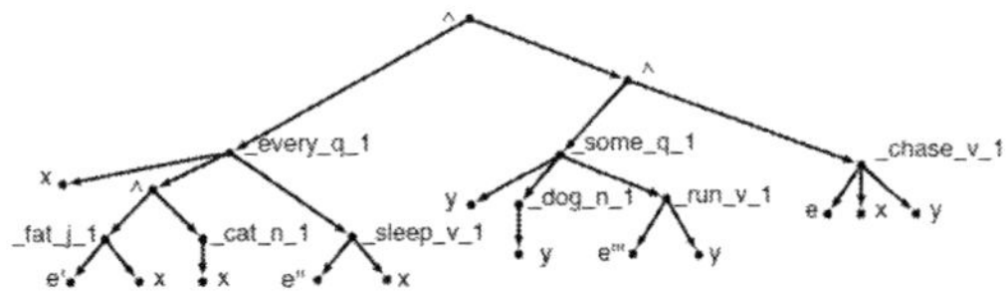

Figure 2: Another tree which satisfies (6).

and possibly others. It is then easy to verify that every single atom in the RMRS is satisfied—most interestingly, the EPs $l_{41}{:}a_{41}{:}\_\text{fat\_j}(e')$ and $l_{42}{:}a_{42}{:}\_\text{cat\_n}(x_3)$ are satisfied because $\alpha(l_{41}) \lhd^*_\wedge \alpha(a_{41})$ and $\alpha(l_{42}) \lhd^*_\wedge \alpha(a_{42})$.

Truth, validity and entailment can now be defined in terms of satisfiability in the usual way:

Definition 5. truth: $\tau \models \varphi$ *iff* $\exists \alpha, g, \sigma$ *such that* $\tau, \alpha, g, \sigma \models \varphi$

validity: $\models \varphi$ *iff* $\forall \tau, \tau \models \varphi$.

entailment: $\varphi \models \varphi'$ *iff* $\forall \tau$, *if* $\tau \models \varphi$ *then* $\tau \models \varphi'$.

3.3 Solved Forms

One aspect in which our definition of RMRS is like dominance constraints and unlike MRS is that any satisfiable RMRS has an infinite number of models which only differ in the areas that the RMRS didn't "talk about". Reading (6) as an MRS or as an RMRS of the previous literature, this formula is an instruction to build a semantic representation out of the pieces for "every fat cat", "some dog", and "chased"; a semantic representation as in Fig. 2 would *not* be taken as described by this RMRS. However, under the semantics we proposed above, this tree is a correct model of (6) because all atoms are still satisfied; the RMRS didn't say anything about "sleep" or "run", but it couldn't enforce that the tree shouldn't contain those subformulas either.

In the context of robust semantic processing, this is a desirable feature, because it means that when we enrich an RMRS obtained from a shallow processor with more semantic information—such as the relation symbols introduced by syntactic constructions such as appositives, noun-noun compounds and free adjuncts—we don't change the set of models; we only *restrict* the set of models further and further towards the semantic representation we are trying to reconstruct. Furthermore, it has been shown in the literature that a dominance-constraint style semantics for underspecified representations gives us more room to manoeuvre when developing efficient solvers than an MRS-style semantics (Althaus et al., 2003).

However, enumerating an infinite number of models is of course infeasible. For this reason, we will now transfer the concept of *solved forms* from dominance constraints to RMRS. An RMRS in solved form is guaranteed to be satisfiable, and thus each solved form represents an infinite class of models. However, each satisfiable RMRS has only a finite number of solved forms which partition the space of possible models into classes such that models within a class differ only in 'irrelevant' details. A solver can then enumerate the solved forms rather than all models.

Intuitively, an RMRS in solved form is fully specified with respect to the predicate-argument structure, all variable equalities and inequalities and scope ambiguities have been resolved, and only lexical sense ambiguities remain. This is made precise below.

Definition 6. *An RMRS φ is* in solved form *iff:*

1. *every variable in φ is either a hole, a label or an anchor (but not two of these);*
2. *φ doesn't contain equality, inequality, and SPEC ($\sqsubseteq$) atoms;*
3. *if $\mathsf{ARG}_S(Y,i)$ is in φ, then $|S| = 1$;*
4. *for any label Y and index set S, there are no two atoms $\mathsf{ARG}_S(Y,i)$ and $\mathsf{ARG}_S(Y,i')$ in φ;*
5. *if Y is an anchor in some* EP *$X{:}Y{:}P$ and k is the maximum number such that $\mathsf{ARG}_{\{k\}}(X,i)$ is in φ for any i, then there is a constructor $p \in \sigma(P)$ whose arity is at least k;*
6. *no label occurs on the right-hand side of two different $\triangleleft^*$ atoms.*

Because solved forms are so restricted, we can 'read off' at least one model from each solved form:

Proposition 1. *Every* RMRS *in solved form is satisfiable.*

Proof (sketch; see also (Duchier and Niehren, 2000)). For each EP, we choose to label the anchor with the constructor p of sufficiently high arity whose existence we assumed; we determine the edges between an anchor and its children from the uniquely determined ARG atoms; plugging labels into holes is straightforward because no label is dominated by more than one hole; and spaces between the labels and anchors are filled with conjunctions. □

We can now define the solved forms *of* an RMRS φ; these finitely many RMRSs in solved form partition the space of models of φ into classes of models with trivial differences.

Definition 7. *The* syntactic dominance relation *$D(\varphi)$ in an* RMRS *φ is the reflexive, transitive closure of the binary relation*

$$\{(X,Y) \mid \varphi \text{ contains } X \triangleleft^* Y \text{ or } ARG_S(X,Y) \text{ for some } S\}$$

An RMRS φ' is a solved form of *the RMRS φ iff φ' is in solved form and there is a substitution s that maps the node and base variables of φ to the node and base variables of φ' such that*

1. *φ' contains the* EP *$X'{:}Y'{:}P$ iff there are variables X, Y such that $X{:}Y{:}P$ is in φ, $X' = s(X)$, and $Y' = s(Y)$;*
2. *for every atom $\mathsf{ARG}_S(X,i)$ in φ, there is exactly one atom $\mathsf{ARG}_{S'}(X',i')$ in φ' with $X' = s(X)$, $i' = s(i)$, and $S' \subseteq S$;*
3. *$D(\varphi') \supseteq s(D(\varphi))$.*

Proposition 2. *For every tuple $(\tau, \alpha, g, \sigma)$ that satisfies some* RMRS *φ, there is a solved form φ' of φ such that $(\tau, \alpha, g, \sigma)$ also satisfies φ'.*

Proof. We construct the substitution s from α and g. Then we add all dominance atoms that are satisfied by α and restrict the ARG atoms to those child indices that are actually used in τ. The result is in solved form because τ is a tree; it is a solved form of φ by construction. □

Proposition 3. *Every* RMRS *φ has only a finite number of solved forms, up to renaming of variables.*

Proof. Up to renaming of variables, there is only a finite number of substitutions on the node and base variables of φ. Let s be such a substitution. This fixes the set of EPs of any solved form of φ that is based on s uniquely. There is only a finite set of choices for the subsets S' in condition 2 of Def. 7, and there is only a finite set of choices of new dominance atoms that satisfy condition 3. Therefore, the set of solved forms of φ is finite. □

Let's look at an example for all these definitions. All the RMRSs presented in Section 2 (replacing $=_q$ by $\lhd^*$) are in solved form; this is least obvious for (6), but becomes clear once we notice that no label is on the right-hand side of two dominance atoms. However, the model constructed in the proof of Prop. 1 looks a bit like Fig. 2; both models are problematic in several ways and in particular contain an unbound variable y even though they also contains a quantifier that binds y. If we restrict the class of models to those in which such variables are bound (as Copestake et al. (2005) do), we can enforce that the quantifiers outscope their bound variables without changing models of the RMRS further—i.e., we add the atoms $h_3 \lhd^* l_5$ and $h_8 \lhd^* l_5$. Fig. 2 is no longer a model for the extended RMRS, which in turn is no longer in solved form because the label l_5 is on the right-hand side of two dominance atoms. Instead, it has the following two solved forms:

(7) $l_1{:}a_1{:}\_\text{every\_q\_1}(x_1)$,
$\mathsf{RSTR}(a_1, h_2)$, $\mathsf{BODY}(a_1, h_3)$,
$l_{41}{:}a_{41}{:}\_\text{fat\_j\_1}(e')$, $\mathsf{ARG}_1(a_{41}, x_1)$,
$l_{41}{:}a_{42}{:}\_\text{cat\_n\_1}(x_1)$,
$l_6{:}a_6{:}\_\text{some\_q\_1}(x_6)$,
$\mathsf{RSTR}(a_6, h_7)$, $\mathsf{BODY}(a_6, h_8)$,
$l_9{:}a_9{:}\_\text{dog\_n\_1}(x_6)$,
$l_5{:}a_5{:}\_\text{chase\_v\_1}(e)$,
$\mathsf{ARG}_1(a_5, x_1)$, $\mathsf{ARG}_2(a_5, x_6)$,
$h_2 \lhd^* l_{41}$, $h_3 \lhd^* l_6$, $h_7 \lhd^* l_9$, $h_8 \lhd^* l_5$

(8) $l_1{:}a_1{:}\_\text{every\_q\_1}(x_1)$,
$\mathsf{RSTR}(a_1, h_2)$, $\mathsf{BODY}(a_1, h_3)$,
$l_{41}{:}a_{41}{:}\_\text{fat\_j\_1}(e')$, $\mathsf{ARG}_1(a_{41}, x_1)$,
$l_{41}{:}a_{42}{:}\_\text{cat\_n\_1}(x_1)$,
$l_6{:}a_6{:}\_\text{some\_q\_1}(x_6)$,
$\mathsf{RSTR}(a_6, h_7)$, $\mathsf{BODY}(a_6, h_8)$,
$l_9{:}a_9{:}\_\text{dog\_n\_1}(x_6)$,
$l_5{:}a_5{:}\_\text{chase\_v\_1}(e)$,
$\mathsf{ARG}_1(a_5, x_1)$, $\mathsf{ARG}_2(a_5, x_6)$,
$h_2 \lhd^* l_{41}$, $h_3 \lhd^* l_5$, $h_7 \lhd^* l_9$, $h_8 \lhd^* l_1$

Notice that we have eliminated all equalities by unifying the variable names, and we have fixed the relative scope of the two quantifiers. Each of these solved forms now stands for a separate class of models; for instance, the first model in Fig. 1 is a model of (7), whereas the second is a model of (8).

3.4 Extensions

So far we have based the syntax and semantics of RMRS on the dominance relation from Egg et al. (2001) rather than the qeq relation from Copestake et al. (2005). This is partly because dominance is the weaker relation: If a dependency parser links a determiner to a noun and this noun to a verb, then we can use dominance but not qeq to represent that the predicate introduced by the verb is outscoped by the quantifier introduced by the determiner (see earlier discussion). However, it is very straightforward to extend the syntax and semantics of the language to include the qeq relation. This extension adds a new atom $X =_q Y$ to Def. 1, and τ, α, g, σ will satisfy $X =_q Y$ iff $\alpha(X) \lhd^* \alpha(Y)$, each node on the path is a quantifier, and each step in the path goes to the rightmost child. All the above propositions about solved forms still hold if "dominance" is replaced with "qeq".

Furthermore, grammar developers such as those in the DELPH-IN community typically adopt conventions that restrict them to a fragment of the language from Def. 1 (once qeq is added to it), or they restrict attention to only a subset of the models (e.g., ones with correctly bound variables, or ones which don't contain extra material like Fig. 2). Our formalism provides a general framework into which all these various fragments fit, and it's a matter of future work to explore these fragments further.

Another feature of the existing RMRS literature is that each term of an RMRS is equipped with a *sort*. In particular, individual variables x, event variables e and holes h are arranged together with their subsorts (e.g., e_{past}) and supersorts (e.g., sort i abstracts over x and e) into a sort hierarchy $\mathcal{S}$. For simplicity we defined RMRS without sorts, but it is straightforward to add them. For this, one assumes that the signature Σ is sorted, i.e. assigns a sort $s_1 \times \ldots s_n \rightarrow s$ to each constructor, where n is the constructor's arity (possibly zero) and $s, s_1, \ldots, s_n \in \mathcal{S}$ are atomic sorts. We restrict the models of RMRS to trees that are *well-sorted* in the usual sense, i.e. those in which we can infer a sort for each subtree, and require that the variable assignment functions likewise respect the sorts. If we then modify Def. 6 such that the constructor p of sufficiently high arity is also consistent with the sorts of the known arguments—i.e., if p has sort $s_1 \times \ldots \times s_n \rightarrow s$ and the RMRS contains an atom $\mathsf{ARG}_{\{k\}}(Y, i)$ and i is of sort s', then s' is a subsort of s_k—all the above propositions about solved forms remain true.

4 Future work

The above definitions serve an important theoretical purpose: they formally underpin the use of RMRS in practical systems. Next to the peace of mind that comes with the use of a well-understood formalism, we hope that the work reported here will serve as a starting point for future research.

One direction to pursue from this paper is the development of efficient solvers for RMRS. As a first step, it would be interesting to define a practically useful fragment of RMRS with polynomial-time satisfiability. Our definition is sufficiently close to that of dominance constraints that we expect that it should be feasible to carry over the definition of *normal dominance constraints* (Althaus et al., 2003) to RMRS; neither the lexical ambiguity of the node labels nor the separate specification of predicates and arguments should make satisfiability harder.

Furthermore, the above definition of RMRS provides new concepts which can help us phrase questions of practical grammar engineering in well-defined formal terms. For instance, one crucial issue in developing a hybrid system that combines or compares the outputs of deep and shallow processors is to determine whether the RMRSs produced by the two systems are compatible. In the new formal terms, we can characterise compatibility of a more detailed RMRS φ (perhaps from a deep grammar) and a less detailed RMRS φ' simply as *entailment* $\varphi \models \varphi'$. If entailment holds, this tells us that all claims that φ' makes about the semantic content of a sentence are consistent with the claims that φ makes.

At this point, we cannot provide an efficient algorithm for testing entailment of RMRS. However, we propose the following novel syntactic characterisation as a starting point for research along those lines. We call an RMRS φ' an *extension* of the RMRS φ if φ' contains all the EPs of φ and $D(\varphi') \supseteq D(\varphi)$.

Proposition 4. *Let φ, φ' be two RMRSs. Then $\varphi \models \varphi'$ iff for every solved form S of φ, there is a solved form S' of φ' such that S is an extension of S'.*

Proof (sketch). "$\Leftarrow$" follows from Props. 1 and 2.

"$\Rightarrow$": We construct a solved form for φ' by choosing a solved form for φ and appropriate substitutions for mapping the variables of φ and φ' onto each other, and removing all atoms using variables that don't occur in φ'. The hard part is the proof that the result is a solved form of φ'; this step involves proving that if $\varphi \models \varphi'$ with the same variable assignments, then all EPs in φ' also occur in φ. □

5 Conclusion

In this paper, we motivated and defined RMRS—a semantic framework that has been used to represent, compare, and combine semantic information computed from deep and shallow parsers. RMRS is designed to be maximally flexible on the type of semantic information that can be left underspecified, so that the semantic output of a shallow parser needn't over-determine or under-determine the semantics that can be extracted from the shallow syntactic analysis. Our key contribution was to lay the formal foundations for a formalism that is emerging as a standard in robust semantic processing.

Although we have not directly provided new tools for modelling or processing language, we believe that a cleanly defined model theory for RMRS is a crucial prerequisite for the future development of such tools; this strategy was highly successful for dominance constraints (Althaus et al., 2003). We hope that future research will build upon this paper to develop efficient algorithms and implementations for solving RMRSs, performing inferences that enrich RMRSs from shallow analyses with deeper information, and checking consistency of RMRSs that were obtained from different parsers.

Acknowledgments. We thank Ann Copestake, Dan Flickinger, and Stefan Thater for extremely fruitful discussions and the reviewers for their comments. The work of Alexander Koller was funded by a DFG Research Fellowship and the Cluster of Excellence "Multimodal Computing and Interaction".

References

S. Abney. 1996. Partial parsing via finite-state cascades. In John Carroll, editor, *Workshop on Robust Parsing (ESSLLI-96)*, pages 8–15, Prague.

E. Althaus, D. Duchier, A. Koller, K. Mehlhorn, J. Niehren, and S. Thiel. 2003. An efficient graph algorithm for dominance constraints. *J. Algorithms*, 48:194–219.

J. Bos, S. Clark, M. Steedman, J. Curran, and J. Hockenmaier. 2004. Wide coverage semantic representations from a CCG parser. In *Proceedings of the International Conference on Computational Linguistics (COLING 2004)*, Geneva, Switzerland.

E.J. Briscoe, J. Carroll, and R. Watson. 2006. The second release of the rasp system. In *Proceedings of the COLING/ACL 2006 Interaction Presentation Sessions*, Sydney, Australia.

M. Butt, T. Holloway King, M. Niño, and F. Segond. 1999. *A Grammar Writer's Cookbook*. CSLI Publications.

S. Clark, M. Steedman, and J. Curran. 2004. Object extraction and question parsing using CCG. In *Proceedings from the Conference on Empirical Methods in Natural Language Processing (EMNLP)*, pages 111–118, Barcelona.

A. Copestake and D. Flickinger. 2000. An open-source grammar development environment and english grammar using HPSG. In *Proceedings of the Second Conference on Language Resources and Evaluation (*LREC 2000*)*, pages 591–600, Athens.

A. Copestake, D. Flickinger, I. Sag, and C. Pollard. 2005. Minimal recursion semantics: An introduction. *Research on Language and Computation*, 3(2–3):281–332.

A. Copestake. 2003. Report on the design of RMRS. Technical Report EU Deliverable for Project number IST-2001-37836, WP1a, Computer Laboratory, University of Cambridge.

A. Copestake. 2007a. Applying robust semantics. In *Proceedings of the 10th Conference of the Pacific Assocation for Computational Linguistics (PACLING)*, pages 1–12, Melbourne. Invited talk.

A. Copestake. 2007b. Semantic composition with (robust) minimal recursion semantics. In *ACL-07 workshop on Deep Linguistic Processing*, pages 73–80, Prague.

D. Duchier and J. Niehren. 2000. Dominance constraints with set operators. In *In Proceedings of the First International Conference on Computational Logic (CL2000), LNCS*, pages 326–341. Springer.

M. Egg, A. Koller, and J. Niehren. 2001. The constraint language for lambda structures. *Journal of Logic, Language, and Information*, 10:457–485.

A. Frank. 2004. Constraint-based RMRS construction from shallow grammars. In *Proceedings of the International Conference in Computational Linguistics (COLING 2004)*, Geneva, Switzerland.

L. Zettlemoyer and M. Collins. 2007. Online learning of relaxed CCG grammars for parsing to logical form. In *Proceedings of the 2007 Joint Conference on Empirical Methods in Natural Language Processing and Computational Natural Language Learning (EMNLP-CoNLL)*, pages 678–687.

Dependency trees and the strong generative capacity of CCG

Alexander Koller
Saarland University
Saarbrücken, Germany
koller@mmci.uni-saarland.de

Marco Kuhlmann
Uppsala University
Uppsala, Sweden
marco.kuhlmann@lingfil.uu.se

Abstract

We propose a novel algorithm for extracting dependencies from the derivations of a large fragment of CCG. Unlike earlier proposals, our dependency structures are always tree-shaped. We then use these dependency trees to compare the strong generative capacities of CCG and TAG and obtain surprising results: Both formalisms generate the same languages of derivation trees – but the mechanisms they use to bring the words in these trees into a linear order are incomparable.

1 Introduction

Combinatory Categorial Grammar (CCG; Steedman (2001)) is an increasingly popular grammar formalism. Next to being theoretically well-motivated due to its links to combinatory logic and categorial grammar, it is distinguished by the availability of efficient open-source parsers (Clark and Curran, 2007), annotated corpora (Hockenmaier and Steedman, 2007; Hockenmaier, 2006), and mechanisms for wide-coverage semantic construction (Bos et al., 2004).

However, there are limits to our understanding of the formal properties of CCG and its relation to other grammar formalisms. In particular, while it is well-known that CCG belongs to a family of mildly context-sensitive formalisms that all generate the same string languages (Vijay-Shanker and Weir, 1994), there are few results about the *strong* generative capacity of CCG. This makes it difficult to gauge the similarities and differences between CCG and other formalisms in how they model linguistic phenomena such as scrambling and relative clauses (Hockenmaier and Young, 2008), and hampers the transfer of algorithms from one formalism to another.

In this paper, we propose a new method for deriving a dependency tree from a CCG derivation tree for PF-CCG, a large fragment of CCG. We then explore the strong generative capacity of PF-CCG in terms of dependency trees. In particular, we cast new light on the relationship between CCG and other mildly context-sensitive formalisms such as Tree-Adjoining Grammar (TAG; Joshi and Schabes (1997)) and Linear Context-Free Rewrite Systems (LCFRS; Vijay-Shanker et al. (1987)). We show that if we only look at valencies and ignore word order, then the dependency trees induced by a PF-CCG grammar form a regular tree language, just as for TAG and LCFRS. To our knowledge, this is the first time that the regularity of CCG's derivational structures has been exposed. However, if we take the word order into account, then the classes of PF-CCG-induced and TAG-induced dependency trees are incomparable; in particular, CCG-induced dependency trees can be unboundedly non-projective in a way that TAG-induced dependency trees cannot.

The fact that all our dependency structures are *trees* brings our approach in line with the emerging mainstream in dependency parsing (McDonald et al., 2005; Nivre et al., 2007) and TAG derivation trees. The price we pay for restricting ourselves to trees is that we derive fewer dependencies than the more powerful approach by Clark et al. (2002). Indeed, we do not claim that our dependencies are linguistically meaningful beyond recording the way in which syntactic valencies are filled. However, we show that our dependency trees are still informative enough to reconstruct the semantic representations.

The paper is structured as follows. In Section 2, we introduce CCG and the fragment PF-CCG that we consider in this paper, and compare our contribution to earlier research. In Section 3, we then show how to read off a dependency tree from a CCG derivation. Finally, we explore the strong generative capacity of CCG in Section 4 and conclude with ideas for future work.

Proceedings of the 12th Conference of the European Chapter of the ACL, pages 460–468,
Athens, Greece, 30 March – 3 April 2009.

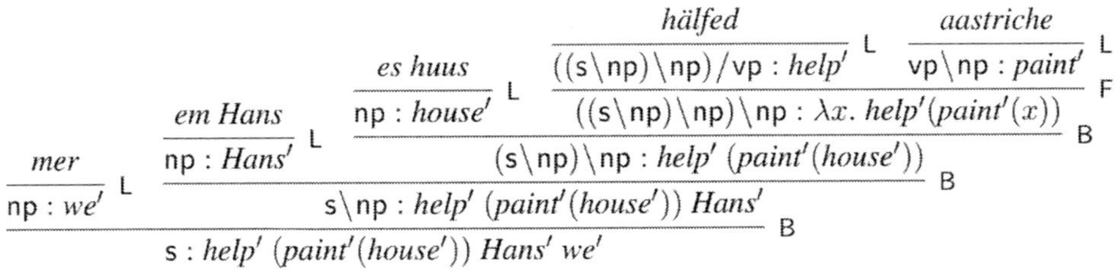

Figure 1: A PF-CCG derivation

2 Combinatory Categorial Grammars

We start by introducing the Combinatory Categorial Grammar (CCG) formalism. Then we introduce the fragment of CCG that we consider in this paper, and discuss some related work.

2.1 CCG

Combinatory Categorial Grammar (Steedman, 2001) is a grammar formalism that assigns *categories* to substrings of an input sentence. There are *atomic* categories such as s and np; and if A and B are categories, then $A\backslash B$ and A/B are *functional* categories representing a constituent that will have category A once it is combined with another constituent of type B to the left or right, respectively. Each word is assigned a category by the lexicon; adjacent substrings can then be combined by *combinatory rules*. As an example, Steedman and Baldridge's (2009) analysis of Shieber's (1985) Swiss German subordinate clause *(das) mer em Hans es huus hälfed aastriiche* ('(that) we help Hans paint the house') is shown in Figure 1.

Intuitively, the arguments of a functional category can be thought of as the syntactic valencies of the lexicon entry, or as arguments of a function that maps categories to categories. The core combinatory mechanism underlying CCG is the composition and application of these functions. In their most general forms, the combinatory rules of (forward and backward) application and composition can be written as in Figure 2. The symbol | stands for an arbitrary (forward or backward) slash; it is understood that the slash before each B_i above the line is the same as below. The rules derive statements about triples $w \vdash A : f$, expressing that the substring w can be assigned the category A and the semantic representation f; an entire string counts as grammatical if it can be assigned the start category s. In parallel to the combination of substrings by the combinatory rules, their semantic representations are combined by functional composition.

We have presented the composition rules of CCG in their most general form. In the literature, the special cases for $n = 0$ are called forward and backward *application*; the cases for $n > 0$ where the slash before B_n is the same as the slash before B are called *composition of degree* n; and the cases where $n > 0$ and the slashes have different directions are called *crossed composition of degree* n. For instance, the F application that combines *hälfed* and *aastriche* in Figure 1 is a forward crossed composition of degree 1.

2.2 PF-CCG

In addition to the composition rules introduced above, CCG also allows rules of substitution and type-raising. Substitution is used to handle syntactic phenomena such as parasitic gaps; type-raising allows a constituent to serve syntactically as a functor, while being used semantically as an argument. Furthermore, it is possible in CCG to restrict the instances of the rule schemata in Figure 2—for instance, to say that the application rule may only be used for the case $A =$ s. We call a CCG grammar *pure* if it does not use substitution, type-raising, or restricted rule schemata. Finally, the argument categories of a CCG category may themselves be functional categories; for instance, the category of a VP modifier like *passionately* is (s\np)\(s\np). We call a category that is either atomic or only has atomic arguments a *first-order category*, and call a CCG grammar *first-order* if all categories that its lexicon assigns to words are first-order.

In this paper, we only consider CCG grammars that are pure and first-order. This fragment, which we call PF-CCG, is less expressive than full CCG, but it significantly simplifies the definitions in Section 3. At the same time, many real-world CCG grammars do not use the substitution rule, and type-raising can be compiled into the grammar in the sense that for any CCG grammar, there is an equivalent CCG grammar that does not use type-raising and assigns the same semantic representations to

$$\frac{(a, A, f) \text{ is a lexical entry}}{a \vdash A : f} \; \mathsf{L}$$

$$\frac{v \vdash A/B : \lambda x.\, f(x) \qquad w \vdash B \mid B_n \mid \ldots \mid B_1 : \lambda y_1, \ldots, y_n.\, g(y_1, \ldots, y_n)}{vw \vdash A \mid B_n \mid \ldots \mid B_1 : \lambda y_1, \ldots, y_n.\, f(g(y_1, \ldots, y_n))} \; \mathsf{F}$$

$$\frac{v \vdash B \mid B_n \mid \ldots \mid B_1 : \lambda y_1, \ldots, y_n.\, g(y_1, \ldots, y_n) \qquad w \vdash A \backslash B : \lambda x.\, f(x)}{vw \vdash A \mid B_n \mid \ldots \mid B_1 : \lambda y_1, \ldots, y_n.\, f(g(y_1, \ldots, y_n))} \; \mathsf{B}$$

Figure 2: The generalized combinatory rules of CCG

each string. On the other hand, the restriction to first-order grammars is indeed a limitation in practice. We take the work reported here as a first step towards a full dependency-tree analysis of CCG, and discuss ideas for generalization in the conclusion.

2.3 Related work

The main objective of this paper is the definition of a novel way in which dependency trees can be extracted from CCG derivations. This is similar to Clark et al. (2002), who aim at capturing 'deep' dependencies, and encode these into annotated lexical categories. For instance, they write $(\mathsf{np}_i\backslash\mathsf{np}_i)/(\mathsf{s}\backslash\mathsf{np}_i)$ for subject relative pronouns to express that the relative pronoun, the trace of the relative clause, and the modified noun phrase are all semantically the same. This means that the relative pronoun has multiple parents; in general, their dependency structures are not necessarily trees. By contrast, we aim to extract only dependency *trees*, and achieve this by recording only the fillers of syntactic valencies, rather than the semantic dependencies: the relative pronoun gets two dependents and one parent (the verb whose argument the modified np is), just as the category specifies. So Clark et al.'s and our dependency approach represent two alternatives of dealing with the tradeoff between simple and expressive dependency structures.

Our paper differs from the well-known results of Vijay-Shanker and Weir (1994) in that they establish the *weak* equivalence of different grammar formalisms, while we focus on comparing the derivational structures. Hockenmaier and Young (2008) present linguistic motivations for comparing the strong generative capacities of CCG and TAG, and the beginnings of a formal comparison between CCG and spinal TAG in terms of Linear Indexed Grammars.

3 Induction of dependency trees

We now explain how to extract a dependency tree from a PF-CCG derivation. The basic idea is to associate, with every step of the derivation, a corresponding operation on dependency trees, in much the same way as derivation steps can be associated with operations on semantic representations.

3.1 Dependency trees

When talking about a dependency tree, it is usually convenient to specify its tree structure and the linear order of its nodes separately. The tree structure encodes the valency structure of the sentence (immediate dominance), whereas the linear precedence of the words is captured by the linear order.

For the purposes of this paper, we represent a *dependency tree* as a pair $d = (t, s)$, where t is a ground term over some suitable alphabet, and s is a linearization of the nodes (term addresses) of t, where by a linearization of a set S we mean a list of elements of S in which each element occurs exactly once (see also Kuhlmann and Möhl (2007)). As examples, consider

$$(f(a, b), [1, \varepsilon, 2]) \quad \text{and} \quad (f(g(a)), [1 \cdot 1, \varepsilon, 1])\,.$$

These expressions represent the dependency trees

$d_1 =$ 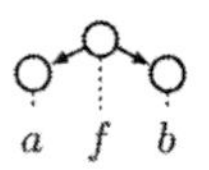

and $d_2 =$ 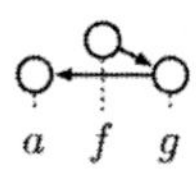

.

Notice that it is because of the separate specification of the tree and the order that dependency trees can become non-projective; d_2 is an example.

A *partial dependency tree* is a pair (t, s) where t is a term that may contain variables, and s is a linearization of those nodes of t that are not labelled with variables. We restrict ourselves to terms in which each variable appears exactly once, and will also prefix partial dependency trees with λ-binders to order the variables.

$$\frac{e = (a, A \mid A_m \cdots \mid A_1) \text{ is a lexical entry}}{a \vdash A \mid A_m \cdots \mid A_1 : \lambda x_1, \ldots, x_m.\ (e(x_1, \ldots, x_m), [\varepsilon])}\ \mathsf{L}$$

$$\frac{v \vdash A \mid A_m \cdots \mid A_1 / B : \lambda x, x_1, \ldots, x_m.\ d \qquad w \vdash B \mid B_n \cdots \mid B_1 : \lambda y_1, \ldots, y_n.\ d'}{vw \vdash A \mid A_m \cdots \mid A_1 \mid B_n \cdots \mid B_1 : \lambda y_1, \ldots, y_n, x_1, \ldots, x_m.\ d[\,x := d'\,]_F}\ \mathsf{F}$$

$$\frac{w \vdash B \mid B_n \cdots \mid B_1 : \lambda y_1, \ldots, y_n.\ d' \qquad v \vdash A \mid A_m \cdots \mid A_1 \backslash B : \lambda x, x_1, \ldots, x_m.\ d}{wv \vdash A \mid A_m \cdots \mid A_1 \mid B_n \cdots \mid B_1 : \lambda y_1, \ldots, y_n, x_1, \ldots, x_m.\ d[\,x := d'\,]_B}\ \mathsf{B}$$

Figure 3: Computing dependency trees in CCG derivations

3.2 Operations on dependency trees

Let t be a term, and let x be a variable in t. The result of the substitution of the term t' into t for x is denoted by $t[\,x := t'\,]$. We extend this operation to dependency trees as follows. Given a list of addresses s, let xs be the list of addresses obtained from s by prefixing every address with the address of the (unique) node that is labelled with x in t. Then the operations of *forward and backward concatenation* are defined as

$$\begin{aligned}(t, s)[\,x := (t', s')\,]_F &= (t[\,x := t'\,], s \cdot xs'),\\ (t, s)[\,x := (t', s')\,]_B &= (t[\,x := t'\,], xs' \cdot s).\end{aligned}$$

The concatenation operations combine two given dependency trees (t, s) and (t', s') into a new tree by substituting t' into t for some variable x of t, and adding the (appropriately prefixed) list s' of nodes of t' either before or after the list s of nodes of t. Using these two operations, the dependency trees d_1 and d_2 from above can be written as follows. Let $d_a = (a, [\varepsilon])$ and $d_b = (b, [\varepsilon])$.

$$\begin{aligned}d_1 &= (f(x, y), [\varepsilon])[\,x := d_a\,]_F[\,y := d_b\,]_F\\ d_2 &= (f(x), [\varepsilon])[\,x := (g(y), [\varepsilon])\,]_F[\,y := d_a\,]_B\end{aligned}$$

Here is an alternative graphical notation for the composition of d_2:

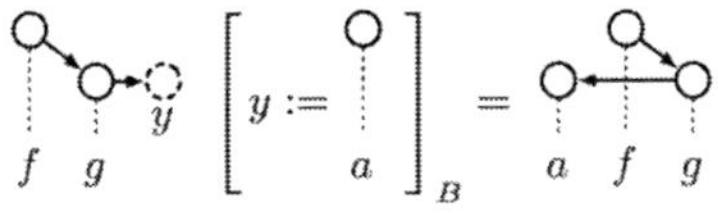

In this notation, nodes that are not marked with variables are positioned (indicated by the dotted projection lines), while the (dashed) variable nodes dangle unpositioned.

3.3 Dependency trees for CCG derivations

To encode CCG derivations as dependency trees, we annotate each composition rule of PF-CCG with instructions for combining the partial dependency trees for the substrings into a partial dependency tree for the larger string. Essentially, we now combine partial dependency trees using forward and backward concatenation rather than combining semantic representations by functional composition and application. From now on, we assume that the node labels in the dependency trees are CCG lexicon entries, and represent these by just the word in them.

The modified rules are shown in Figure 3. They derive statements about triples $w \vdash A : p$, where w is a substring, A is a category, and p is a lambda expression over a partial dependency tree. Each variable of p corresponds to an argument category in A, and vice versa. Rule L covers the base case: the dependency tree for a lexical entry e is a tree with one node for the item itself, labelled with e, and one node for each of its syntactic arguments, labelled with a variable. Rule F captures forward composition: given two dependency trees d and d', the new dependency tree is obtained by forward concatenation, binding the outermost variable in d. Rule B is the rule for backward composition. The result of translating a complete PF-CCG derivation δ in this way is always a dependency tree without variables; we call it $d(\delta)$.

As an example, Figure 4 shows the construction for the derivation in Figure 1. The induced dependency tree looks like this:

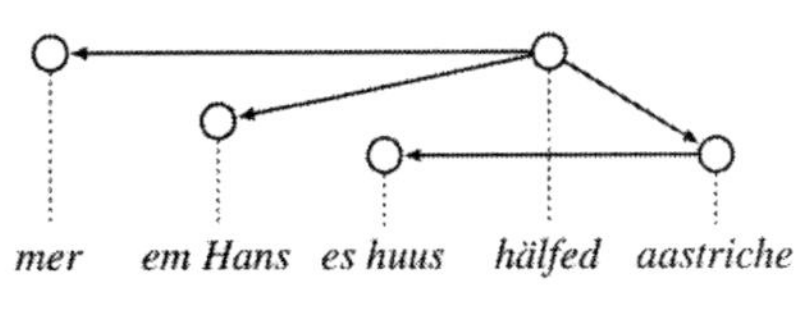

For instance, the partial dependency tree for the lexicon entry of *aastriiche* contains two nodes: the root (with address ε) is labelled with the lexicon entry, and its child (address 1) is labelled with the

$$\dfrac{\textit{hälfed}}{\lambda x,y,z.\ (\textit{hälfed}(x,y,z),[\varepsilon])}\ \mathsf{L} \qquad \dfrac{\textit{aastriiche}}{\lambda w.\ (\textit{aastriiche}(w),[\varepsilon])}\ \mathsf{L}$$

$$\dfrac{\lambda x,y,z.\ (\textit{hälfed}(x,y,z),[\varepsilon]) \quad \lambda w.\ (\textit{aastriiche}(w),[\varepsilon])}{\lambda w,y,z.\ (\textit{hälfed}(\textit{aastriiche}(w),y,z),[\varepsilon,1])}\ \mathsf{F}$$

$$\dfrac{\dfrac{\textit{es huus}}{(\textit{huus},[\varepsilon])}\ \mathsf{L} \quad \lambda w,y,z.\ (\textit{hälfed}(\textit{aastriiche}(w),y,z),[\varepsilon,1])}{\lambda y,z.\ (\textit{hälfed}(\textit{aastriiche}(\textit{huus}),y,z),[11,\varepsilon,1])}\ \mathsf{B}$$

$$\dfrac{\dfrac{\textit{em Hans}}{(\textit{Hans},[\varepsilon])}\ \mathsf{L} \quad \lambda y,z.\ (\textit{hälfed}(\textit{aastriiche}(\textit{huus}),y,z),[11,\varepsilon,1])}{\lambda z.\ (\textit{hälfed}(\textit{aastriiche}(\textit{huus}),\textit{Hans},z),[2,11,\varepsilon,1])}\ \mathsf{B}$$

$$\dfrac{\dfrac{\textit{mer}}{(\textit{mer},[\varepsilon])}\ \mathsf{L} \quad \lambda z.\ (\textit{hälfed}(\textit{aastriiche}(\textit{huus}),\textit{Hans},z),[2,11,\varepsilon,1])}{(\textit{hälfed}(\textit{aastriiche}(\textit{huus}),\textit{Hans},\textit{mer}),[3,2,11,\varepsilon,1])}\ \mathsf{B}$$

Figure 4: Computing a dependency tree for the derivation in Figure 1

variable x. This tree is inserted into the tree from *hälfed* by forward concatenation. The variable w is passed on into the new dependency tree, and later filled by backward concatenation to *huus*. Passing the argument slot of *aastriiche* to *hälfed* to be filled on its left creates a non-projectivity; it corresponds to a crossed composition in CCG terms. Notice that the categories derived in Figure 1 mirror the functional structure of the partial dependency trees at each step of the derivation.

3.4 Semantic equivalence

The mapping from derivations to dependency trees loses some information: different derivations may induce the same dependency tree. This is illustrated by Figure 5, which provides two possible derivations for the phrase *big white rabbit*, both of which induce the same dependency tree. Especially in light of the fact that our dependency trees will typically contain fewer dependencies than the DAGs derived by Clark et al. (2002), one could ask whether dependency trees are an appropriate way of representing the structure of a CCG derivation.

However, at the end of the day, the most important information that can be extracted from a CCG derivation is the semantic representation it computes; and it is possible to reconstruct the semantic representation of a derivation δ from $d(\delta)$ alone. If we forget the word order information in the dependency trees, the rules F and B in Figure 3 are merely η-expanded versions of the semantic construction rules in Figure 2. This means that $d(\delta)$ records everything we need to know about constructing the semantic representation: We can traverse it bottom-up and apply the lexical semantic representation of each node to those of its subterms. So while the dependency trees obliterate some information in the CCG derivations (particularly its associative structure), they are indeed appropriate representations because they record all syntactic valencies and encode enough information to recompute the semantics.

4 Strong generative capacity

Now that we know how to see PF-CCG derivations as dependency trees, we can ask what sets of such trees can be generated by PF-CCG grammars. This is the question about the strong generative capacity of PF-CCG, measured in terms of dependency trees (Miller, 2000). In this section, we give a partial answer to this question: We show that the sets of PF-CCG-induced *valency trees* (dependency trees without their linear order) form regular tree languages, but that the sets of dependency trees themselves are irregular. This is in contrast to other prominent mildly context-sensitive grammar formalisms such as Tree Adjoining Grammar (TAG; Joshi and Schabes (1997)) and Linear Context-Free Rewrite Systems (LCFRS; Vijay-Shanker et al. (1987)), in which both languages are regular.

4.1 CCG term languages

Formally, we define the language of all dependency trees generated by a PF-CCG grammar G as the set

$$L_D(G) = \{\, d(\delta) \mid \delta \text{ is a derivation of } G \,\}\,.$$

Furthermore, we define the set of *valency trees* to be the set of just the term parts of each $d(\delta)$:

$$L_V(G) = \{\, t \mid (t,s) \in L_D(G) \,\}\,.$$

By our previous assumption, the node labels of a valency tree are CCG lexicon entries.

We will now show that the valency tree languages of PF-CCG grammars are *regular tree languages* (Gécseg and Steinby, 1997). Regular tree languages are sets of trees that can be generated by *regular tree grammars*. Formally, a regular tree grammar (RTG) is a construct $\Gamma = (N, \Sigma, S, P)$, where N is an alphabet of non-terminal symbols, Σ is an alphabet of ranked term constructors called terminal symbols, $S \in N$ is a distinguished start symbol, and P is a finite set of production rules of the form $A \to \gamma$, where $A \in N$ and γ is a term over Σ and N, where the nonterminals can be used

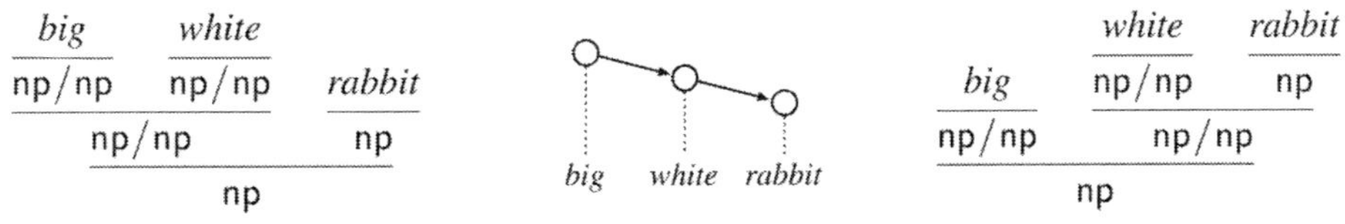

Figure 5: Different derivations may induce the same dependency tree

as constants. The grammar Γ generates trees from the start symbol by successively expanding occurrences of nonterminals using production rules. For instance, the grammar that contains the productions $S \to f(A, A)$, $A \to g(A)$, and $A \to a$ generates the tree language $\{\, f(g^m(a), g^n(a)) \mid m, n \geq 0 \,\}$.

We now construct an RTG $\Gamma(G)$ that generates the set of valency trees of a PF-CCG G. For the terminal alphabet, we choose the lexicon entries: If $e = (a, A \mid B_1 \ldots \mid B_n, f)$ is a lexicon entry of G, we take e as an n-ary term constructor. We also take the atomic categories of G as our nonterminal symbols; the start category s of G counts as the start symbol. Finally, we encode each lexicon entry as a production rule: The lexicon entry e above encodes to the rule $A \to e(B_n, \ldots, B_1)$.

Let us look at our running example to see how this works. Representing the lexicon entries as just the words for brevity, we can write the valency tree corresponding to the CCG derivation in Figure 4 as $t_0 = \textit{hälfed}(\textit{aastriiche}(\textit{huus}), \textit{Hans}, \textit{mer})$; here *hälfed* is a ternary constructor, *aastriiche* is unary, and all others are constants. Taking the lexical categories into account, we obtain the RTG with

$$\begin{aligned} \mathsf{s} &\to \textit{hälfed}(\mathsf{vp}, \mathsf{np}, \mathsf{np}) \\ \mathsf{vp} &\to \textit{aastriiche}(\mathsf{np}) \\ \mathsf{np} &\to \textit{huus} \mid \textit{Hans} \mid \textit{mer} \end{aligned}$$

This grammar indeed generates t_0, and all other valency trees induced by the sample grammar.

More generally, $L_V(G) \subseteq L(\Gamma(G))$ because the construction rules in Figure 3 ensure that if a node v becomes the i-th child of a node u in the term, then the result category of v's lexicon entry equals the i-th argument category of u's lexicon entry. This guarantees that the i-th nonterminal child introduced by the production for u can be expanded by the production for v. The converse inclusion can be shown by reconstructing, for each valency tree t, a CCG derivation δ that induces t. This construction can be done by arranging the nodes in t into an order that allows us to combine every parent in t with its children using only forward and backward application. The CCG derivation we obtain for the example is shown in Figure 6; it is a derivation for the sentence *das mer em Hans hälfed es huus aastriiche*, using the same lexicon entries. Together, this shows that $L(\Gamma(G)) = L_V(G)$. Thus:

Theorem 1 *The sets of valency trees generated by PF-CCG are regular tree languages.* □

By this result, CCG falls in line with context-free grammars, TAG, and LCFRS, whose sets of derivational structures are all regular (Vijay-Shanker et al., 1987). To our knowledge, this is the first time the regular structure of CCG derivations has been exposed. It is important to note that while CCG derivations themselves can be seen as trees as well, they do *not* always form regular tree languages (Vijay-Shanker et al., 1987). Consider for instance the CCG grammar from Vijay-Shanker and Weir's (1994) Example 2.4, which generates the string language $a^n b^n c^n d^n$; Figure 7 shows the derivation of $aabbccdd$. If we follow this derivation bottom-up, starting at the first c, the intermediate categories collect an increasingly long tail of $\backslash a$ arguments; for longer words from the language, this tail becomes as long as the number of cs in the string. The infinite set of categories this produces translates into the need for an infinite nonterminal alphabet in an RTG, which is of course not allowed.

4.2 Comparison with TAG

If we now compare PF-CCG to its most prominent mildly context-sensitive cousin, TAG, the regularity result above paints a suggestive picture: A PF-CCG valency tree assigns a lexicon entry to each word and says which other lexicon entry fills each syntactic valency. In this respect, it is the analogue of a TAG derivation tree (in which the lexicon entries are elementary trees), and we just saw that PF-CCG and TAG generate the same tree languages. On the other hand, CCG and TAG are weakly equivalent (Vijay-Shanker and Weir, 1994), i.e. they generate the same linear word orders. So one could expect that CCG and TAG also induce the same dependency trees. Interestingly, this is not the case.

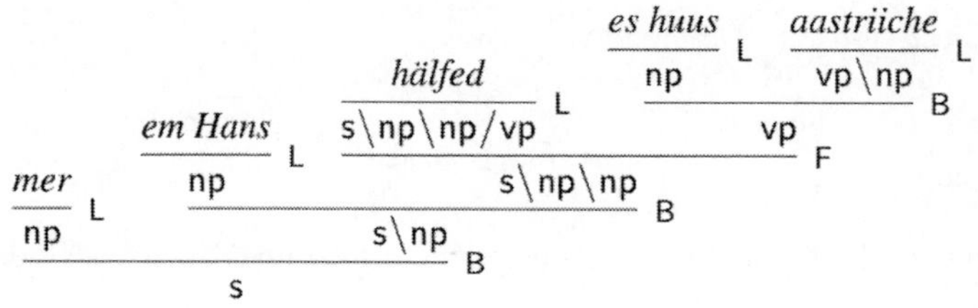

Figure 6: CCG derivation reconstructed from the dependency tree from Figure 4 using only applications

We know from the literature that those dependency trees that can be constructed from TAG derivation trees are exactly those that are well-nested and have a block-degree of at most 2 (Kuhlmann and Möhl, 2007). The block-degree of a node u in a dependency tree is the number of 'blocks' into which the subtree below u is separated by intervening nodes that are not below u, and the block-degree of a dependency tree is the maximum block-degree of its nodes. So for instance, the dependency tree on the right-hand side of Figure 8 has block-degree two. It is also well-nested, and can therefore be induced by TAG derivations.

Things are different for the dependency trees that can be induced by PF-CCG. Consider the left-hand dependency tree in Figure 8, which is induced by a PF-CCG derivation built from words with the lexical categories a / a, b \ a, b \ b, and a. While this dependency tree is well-nested, it has block-degree *three*: The subtree below the leftmost node consists of three parts. More generally, we can insert more words with the categories a / a and b \ b in the middle of the sentence to obtain dependency trees with arbitrarily high block-degrees from this grammar. This means that unlike for TAG-induced dependency trees, there is no upper bound on the block-degree of dependency trees induced by PF-CCG—as a consequence, there are CCG dependency trees that cannot be induced by TAG.

On the other hand, there are also dependency trees that can be induced by TAG, but not by PF-CCG. The tree on the right-hand side of Figure 8 is an example. We have already argued that this tree can be induced by a TAG. However, it contains no two adjacent nodes that are connected by an edge; and every nontrivial PF-CCG derivation must combine two adjacent words at least at one point during the derivation. Therefore, the tree cannot be induced by a PF-CCG grammar. Furthermore, it is known that all dependency languages that can be generated by TAG or even, more generally, by LCRFS, are regular in the sense of Kuhlmann and Möhl (2007). One crucial property of regular dependency languages is that they have a bounded block-degree; but as we have seen, there are PF-CCG dependency languages with unbounded block-degree. Therefore there are PF-CCG dependency languages that are not regular. Hence:

Theorem 2 *The sets of dependency trees generated by PF-CCG and TAG are incomparable.* □

We believe that these results will generalize to full CCG. While we have not yet worked out the induction of dependency trees from full CCG, the basic rule that CCG combines adjacent substrings should still hold; therefore, every CCG-induced dependency tree will contain at least one edge between adjacent nodes. We are thus left with a very surprising result: TAG and CCG both generate the same string languages and the same sets of valency trees, but they use incomparable mechanisms for linearizing valency trees into sentences.

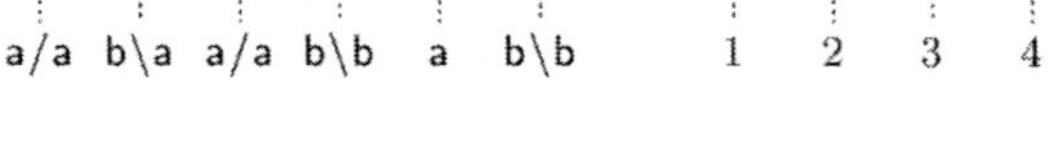

Figure 8: The divergence between CCG and TAG

4.3 A note on weak generative capacity

As a final aside, we note that the construction for extracting purely applicative derivations from the terms described by the RTG has interesting consequences for the weak generative capacity of PF-CCG. In particular, it has the corollary that for any PF-CCG derivation δ over a string w, there is a permutation of w that can be accepted by a PF-CCG derivation that uses only application—that is, every string language L that can be generated by a PF-CCG grammar has a context-free sublanguage L' such that all words in L are permutations of words in L'.

This means that many string languages that we commonly associate with CCG cannot be generated

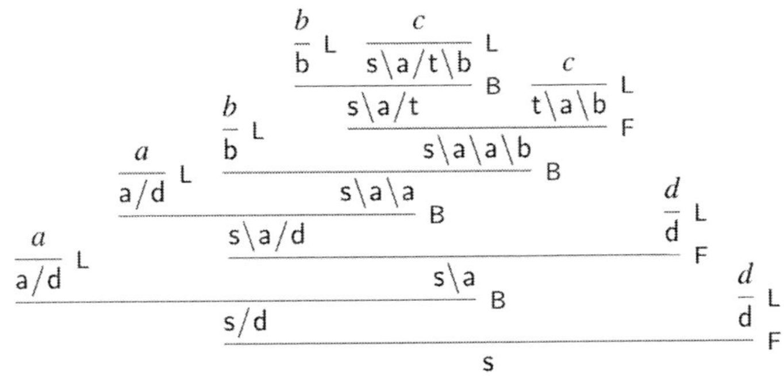

Figure 7: The CCG derivation of *aabbccdd* using Example 2.4 in Vijay-Shanker and Weir (1994)

by PF-CCG. One such language is $a^n b^n c^n d^n$. This language is not itself context-free, and therefore any PF-CCG grammar whose language contains it also contains permutations in which the order of the symbols is mixed up. The culprit for this among the restrictions that distinguish PF-CCG from full CCG seems to be that PF-CCG grammars must allow all instances of the application rules. This would mean that the ability of CCG to generate non-context-free languages (also linguistically relevant ones) hinges crucially on its ability to restrict the allowable instances of rule schemata, for instance, using slash types (Baldridge and Kruijff, 2003).

5 Conclusion

In this paper, we have shown how to read derivations of PF-CCG as dependency trees. Unlike previous proposals, our view on CCG dependencies is in line with the mainstream dependency parsing literature, which assumes tree-shaped dependency structures; while our dependency trees are less informative than the CCG derivations themselves, they contain sufficient information to reconstruct the semantic representation. We used our new dependency view to compare the strong generative capacity of PF-CCG with other mildly context-sensitive grammar formalisms. It turns out that the valency trees generated by a PF-CCG grammar form regular tree languages, as in TAG and LCFRS; however, unlike these formalisms, the sets of dependency trees including word order are *not* regular, and in particular can be more non-projective than the other formalisms permit. Finally, we found new formal evidence for the importance of restricting rule schemata for describing non-context-free languages in CCG.

All these results were technically restricted to the fragment of PF-CCG, and one focus of future work will be to extend them to as large a fragment of CCG as possible. In particular, we plan to extend the lambda notation used in Figure 3 to cover type-raising and higher-order categories. We would then be set to compare the behavior of wide-coverage statistical parsers for CCG with statistical dependency parsers.

We anticipate that our results about the strong generative capacity of PF-CCG will be useful to transfer algorithms and linguistic insights between formalisms. For instance, the CRISP generation algorithm (Koller and Stone, 2007), while specified for TAG, could be generalized to arbitrary grammar formalisms that use regular tree languages—given our results, to CCG in particular. On the other hand, we find it striking that CCG and TAG generate the same string languages from the same tree languages by incomparable mechanisms for ordering the words in the tree. Indeed, the exact characterization of the class of CCG-inducable dependency languages is an open issue. This also has consequences for parsing complexity: We can understand why TAG and LCFRS can be parsed in polynomial time from the bounded block-degree of their dependency trees (Kuhlmann and Möhl, 2007), but CCG can be parsed in polynomial time (Vijay-Shanker and Weir, 1990) without being restricted in this way. This constitutes a most interesting avenue of future research that is opened up by our results.

Acknowledgments. We thank Mark Steedman, Jason Baldridge, and Julia Hockenmaier for valuable discussions about CCG, and the reviewers for their comments. The work of Alexander Koller was funded by a DFG Research Fellowship and the Cluster of Excellence "Multimodal Computing and Interaction". The work of Marco Kuhlmann was funded by the Swedish Research Council.

References

Jason Baldridge and Geert-Jan M. Kruijff. 2003. Multi-modal Combinatory Categorial Grammar. In *Proceedings of the Tenth EACL*, Budapest, Hungary.

Johan Bos, Stephen Clark, Mark Steedman, James R. Curran, and Julia Hockenmaier. 2004. Wide-coverage semantic representations from a CCG parser. In *Proceedings of the 20th COLING*, Geneva, Switzerland.

Stephen Clark and James Curran. 2007. Wide-coverage efficient statistical parsing with CCG and log-linear models. *Computational Linguistics*, 33(4).

Stephen Clark, Julia Hockenmaier, and Mark Steedman. 2002. Building deep dependency structures with a wide-coverage CCG parser. In *Proceedings of the 40th ACL*, Philadelphia, USA.

Ferenc Gécseg and Magnus Steinby. 1997. Tree languages. In Rozenberg and Salomaa (Rozenberg and Salomaa, 1997), pages 1–68.

Julia Hockenmaier and Mark Steedman. 2007. CCG-bank: a corpus of CCG derivations and dependency structures extracted from the Penn Treebank. *Computational Linguistics*, 33(3):355–396.

Julia Hockenmaier and Peter Young. 2008. Non-local scrambling: the equivalence of TAG and CCG revisited. In *Proceedings of TAG+9*, Tübingen, Germany.

Julia Hockenmaier. 2006. Creating a CCGbank and a wide-coverage CCG lexicon for German. In *Proceedings of COLING/ACL*, Sydney, Australia.

Aravind K. Joshi and Yves Schabes. 1997. Tree-Adjoining Grammars. In Rozenberg and Salomaa (Rozenberg and Salomaa, 1997), pages 69–123.

Alexander Koller and Matthew Stone. 2007. Sentence generation as planning. In *Proceedings of the 45th ACL*, Prague, Czech Republic.

Marco Kuhlmann and Mathias Möhl. 2007. Mildly context-sensitive dependency languages. In *Proceedings of the 45th ACL*, Prague, Czech Republic.

Ryan McDonald, Fernando Pereira, Kiril Ribarov, and Jan Hajic. 2005. Non-projective dependency parsing using spanning tree algorithms. In *Proceedings of HLT/EMNLP*.

Philip H. Miller. 2000. *Strong Generative Capacity: The Semantics of Linguistic Formalism*. University of Chicago Press.

Joakim Nivre, Johan Hall, Jens Nilsson, Atanas Chanev, Gülsen Eryigit, Sandra Kübler, Svetoslav Marinov, and Erwin Marsi. 2007. MaltParser: A language-independent system for data-driven dependency parsing. *Natural Language Engineering*, 13(2):95–135.

Grzegorz Rozenberg and Arto Salomaa, editors. 1997. *Handbook of Formal Languages*. Springer.

Stuart Shieber. 1985. Evidence against the context-freeness of natural language. *Linguistics and Philosophy*, 8:333–343.

Mark Steedman and Jason Baldridge. 2009. Combinatory categorial grammar. In R. Borsley and K. Borjars, editors, *Non-Transformational Syntax*. Blackwell. To appear.

Mark Steedman. 2001. *The Syntactic Process*. MIT Press.

K. Vijay-Shanker and David Weir. 1990. Polynomial time parsing of combinatory categorial grammars. In *Proceedings of the 28th ACL*, Pittsburgh, USA.

K. Vijay-Shanker and David J. Weir. 1994. The equivalence of four extensions of context-free grammars. *Mathematical Systems Theory*, 27(6):511–546.

K. Vijay-Shanker, David J. Weir, and Aravind K. Joshi. 1987. Characterizing structural descriptions produced by various grammatical formalisms. In *Proceedings of the 25th ACL*, Stanford, CA, USA.

Lattice Parsing to Integrate Speech Recognition and Rule-Based Machine Translation

Selçuk Köprü
AppTek, Inc.
METU Technopolis
Ankara, Turkey
skopru@apptek.com

Adnan Yazıcı
Department of Computer Engineering
Middle East Technical University
Ankara, Turkey
yazici@metu.edu.tr

Abstract

In this paper, we present a novel approach to integrate speech recognition and rule-based machine translation by lattice parsing. The presented approach is hybrid in two senses. First, it combines structural and statistical methods for language modeling task. Second, it employs a chart parser which utilizes manually created syntax rules in addition to scores obtained after statistical processing during speech recognition. The employed chart parser is a unification-based active chart parser. It can parse word graphs by using a mixed strategy instead of being bottom-up or top-down only. The results are reported based on word error rate on the NIST HUB-1 word-lattices. The presented approach is implemented and compared with other syntactic language modeling techniques.

1 Introduction

The integration of speech and language technologies plays an important role in speech to text translation. This paper describes a unification-based active chart parser and how it is utilized for language modeling in speech recognition or speech translation. The fundamental idea behind the proposed solution is to combine the strengths of unification-based chart parsing and statistical language modeling. In the solution, all sentence hypotheses, which are represented in word-lattice format at the end of automatic speech recognition (ASR), are parsed simultaneously. The chart is initialized with the lattice and it is processed until the first sentence hypothesis is selected by the parser. The parser also utilizes the scores assigned to words during the speech recognition process. This leads to a hybrid solution.

An important benefit of this approach is that it allows one to make use of the available grammars and parsers for language modeling task. So as to be used for this task, syntactic analyzer components developed for a rule-based machine translation (RBMT) system are modified. In speech translation (ST), this approach leads to a perfect integration of the ASR and RBMT components. Language modeling effort in ASR and syntactic analysis effort in RBMT are overlapped and merged into a single task. Its advantages are twofold. First, this allows us to avoid unnecessary duplication of similar jobs. Secondly, by using the available components, we avoid the difficulty of building a syntactic language model all from the beginning.

There are two basic methods that are being used to integrate ASR and rule-based MT systems: First-best method and the N-best list method. Both techniques are motivated from a software engineering perspective. In the First-best approach (Figure 1.a), the ASR module sends a single recognized text to the MT component to translate. Any ambiguity existing in the recognition process is resolved inside the ASR. In contrast to the First-best approach, in the N-best List approach (Figure 1.b); the ASR outputs N possible recognition hypotheses to be evaluated by the MT component. The MT picks the first hypothesis and translates it if it is grammatically correct. Otherwise, it moves to the second hypothesis and so on. If none of the available hypotheses are syntactically correct, then it translates the first one.

We propose a new method to couple ASR and rule-based MT system as an alternative to the ap-

Proceedings of the 12th Conference of the European Chapter of the ACL, pages 469–477,
Athens, Greece, 30 March – 3 April 2009.

proaches mentioned above. Figure 1 represents the two currently in-use coupling methods followed by the new approach we introduce (Figure 1.c). In the newly proposed technique, which we call the N-best word graph approach, the ASR module outputs a word graph containing all N-best hypotheses. The MT component parses the word graph, thus, all possible hypotheses at one time.

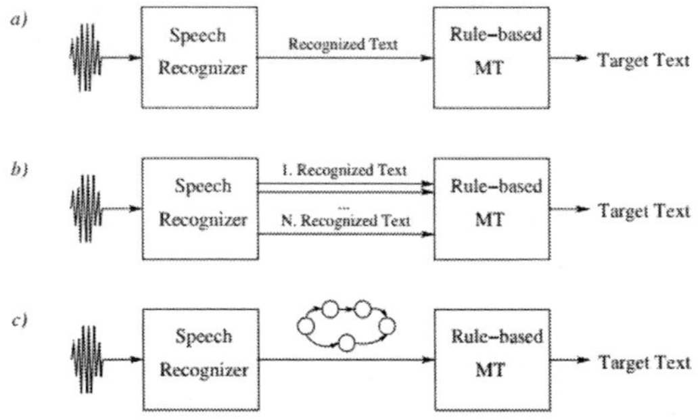

Figure 1: ASR and rule-based MT coupling: a) First-best b) N-best list c) N-best word graph.

While integrating the SR system with the rule-based MT system, this study uses word graphs and chart parsing with new extensions. Parsing of word lattices has been a topic of research over the past decade. The idea of chart parsing the word graph in SR systems has been previously used in different studies in order to resolve ambiguity. Tomita (1986) introduced the concept of word-lattice parsing for the purpose of speech recognition and used an LR parser. Next, Paeseler (1988) used a chart parser to process word-lattices. However, to the best of our knowledge, the specific method for chart parsing a word graph introduced in this paper has not been previously used for coupling purposes.

Recent studies point out the importance of utilizing word graphs in speech tasks (Dyer et al., 2008). Previous work on language modeling can be classified according to whether a system uses purely statistical methods or whether it uses them in combination with syntactic methods. In this paper, the focus is on systems that contain syntactic approaches. In general, these language modeling approaches try to parse the ASR output in word-lattice format in order to choose the most probable hypothesis. Chow and Roukos (1989) used a unification-based CYK parser for the purpose of speech understanding. Chien et al. (1990) and Weber (1994) utilized probabilistic context free grammars in conjunction with unification grammars to chart-parse a word-lattice. There are various differences between the work of Chien et al. (1990) and Weber (1994) and the work presented in this paper. First, in the previously mentioned studies, the chart is populated with the same word graph that comes from the speech recognizer without any pruning, whereas in our approach the word graph is reduced to an acceptable size. Otherwise, the efficiency becomes a big challenge because the search space introduced by a chart with over thousands of initial edges can easily be beyond current practical limits. Another important difference in our approach is the modification of the chart parsing algorithm to eliminate spurious parses.

Ney (1991) deals with the use of probabilistic CYK parser for continous speech recognition task. Stolcke (1995) summarizes extensively their approach to utilize probabilistic Earley parsing. Chappelier et al. (1999) gives an overview of different approaches to integrate linguistic models into speech recognition systems. They also research various techniques of producing sets of hypotheses that contain more "semantic" variability than the commonly used ones. Some of the recent studies about structural language modeling extract a list of N-best hypotheses using an N-gram and then apply structural methods to decide on the best hypothesis (Chelba, 2000; Roark, 2001). This contrasts with the approach presented in this study where, instead of a single sentence, the word-lattice is parsed. Parsing all sentence hypotheses simultaneously enables a reduction in the number of edges produced during the parsing process. This is because the shared word hypotheses are processed only once compared to the N-best list approach, where the shared words are processed each time they occur in a hypothesis. Similar to the current work, other studies parse the whole word-lattice without extracting a list (Hall, 2005). A significant distinction between the work of Hall (2005) and our study is the parsing algorithm. In contrast to our chart parsing approach augmented by unification based feature structures, Charniak parser is used in Hall (2005)'s along with PCFG.

The rest of the paper is organized as follows: In the following section, an overview of the proposed language model is presented. Next, in Section 3, the parsing process of the word-lattice is described in detail. Section 4 describes the experiments and reports the obtained results. Finally, Section 5 concludes the paper.

2 Hybrid language modeling

The general architecture of the system is depicted in Figure 2. The HTK toolkit (Woodland, 2000) word-lattice file format is used as the default file format in the proposed solution. The word-lattice output from ASR is converted into a finite state machine (FSM). This conversion enables us to benefit from standard theory and algorithms on FSMs. In the converted FSM, non-determinism is removed and it is minimized by eliminating redundant nodes and arcs. Next, the chart is initialized with the deterministic and minimal FSM. Finally, this chart is used in the structural analysis.

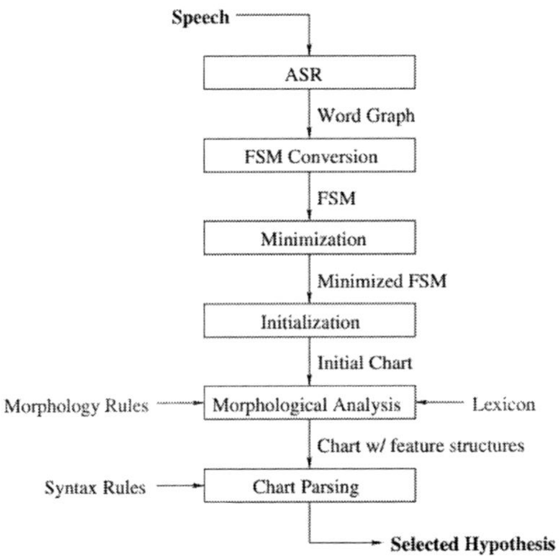

Figure 2: The hybrid language model architecture.

Structural analysis of the word-lattice is accomplished in two consecutive tasks. First, morphological analysis is performed on the word level and any information carried by the word is extracted to be used in the following stages. Second, syntactic analysis is performed on the sentence level. The syntactic analyzer consists of a chart parser in which the rules modeling the language grammar are augmented with functional expressions.

3 Word Graph Processing

The word graphs produced by an ASR are beyond the limits of a unification-based chart parser. A small-sized lattice from the NIST HUB-1 data set (Pallett et al., 1994) can easily contain a couple of hundred states and more than one thousand arcs. The largest lattice in the same data set has 25 000 states and almost 1 million arcs. No unification-based chart parser is capable of coping with an input of this size. It is unpractical and unreasonable to parse the lattice in the same form as it is output from the ASR. Instead, the word graph is pruned to a reasonable size so that it can be parsed according to acceptable time and memory limitations.

3.1 Word graph to FSM conversion

The pruning process starts by converting the time-state lattice to a finite state machine. This way, algorithms and data structures for FSMs are utilized in the following processing steps. Each word in the time-state lattice corresponds to a state node in the new FSM. The time slot information is also dropped in the recently built automata. The links between the words in the lattice are mapped as the FSM arcs.

In the original representation, the word labels in the time-state lattices are on the nodes, and the acoustic scores and the statistical language model scores are on the arcs. Similarly, the words are also on the nodes. This representation does not fit into the chart definition where the words are on the arcs. Therefore, the FSM is converted to an arc labeled FSM. The conversion is accomplished by moving back the word label on a state to the incoming arcs. The weights on the arcs represent the negative logarithms of probabilities. In order to find the weight of a path in the FSM, all weights on the arcs existing on that path are added up.

The resulting FSM contains redundant arcs that are inherited from the word graph. Many arcs correspond to the same word with a different score. The FSM is *nondeterministic* because, at a given state, there are different alternative arcs with the same word label. Before parsing the converted FSM, it is essential to find an equivalent finite automata that is *deterministic* and that has as few nodes as possible. This way, the work necessary during parsing is reduced and efficient processing is ensured.

The *minimization* process serves to shrink down the FSM to an equivalent automata with a suitable size for parsing. However, it is usually the case that the size is not small enough to meet the time and memory limitations in parsing. N-best list selection can be regarded as the last step in constricting the size. A subset of possible hypotheses is selected among many that are contained in the *mini-*

mized FSM. The selection mechanism favors only the best hypotheses according to the scores present in the FSM arcs.

3.2 Chart parsing

The parsing engine implemented for this work is an active chart parser similar to the one described in Kay (1986). The language grammar that is processed by the parser can be designed top-down, bottom-up or in a combined manner. It employs an *agenda* to store the edges prior to inserting to the chart. Edges are defined to be either *complete* or *incomplete*. Incomplete edges describe the rule state where one or more syntactic categories are expected to be matched. An incomplete edge becomes complete if all syntactic categories on the right-hand-side of the rule are matched.

Parsing starts from the rules that are associated to the lexical entries. This corresponds to the bottom-up parsing strategy. Moreover, parsing also starts from the rules that build the final symbol in the grammar. This corresponds to the top-down parsing strategy. Bottom-up rules and top-down rules differ in that the former contains a non-terminal that is marked as the *trigger* or *central element* on the left-hand-side of the rule. This central element is the starting point for the execution of the bottom-up rule. After the central element is matched, the extension continues in a bidirectional manner to complete the missing constituents. Bottom-up incomplete edges are described with *double-dotted* rules to keep track of the beginning and end of the matched fragment.

The anticipated edges are first inserted into the agenda. Edges popped out from the agenda are processed with the *fundamental rule* of chart parsing. The agenda allows the reorganization of the edge processing order. After the application of the fundamental rule, new edges are predicted according to either bottom-up or top-down parsing strategy. This strategy is determined by how the current edge has been created.

3.3 Chart initialization

The chart initialization procedure creates from an input FSM, which is derived from the ASR word lattice, a valid chart that can be parsed in an active chart parser. The initialization starts with filling in the *distance* value for each node. The *distance* of a node in the FSM is defined as the number of nodes on the *longest* path from the start state to the current state. After the *distance* value is set for all nodes in the FSM, an *edge* is created for each arc. The *edge* structure contains the *start* and *end* values in addition to the *weight* and *label* data fields. These position values represent the edge location relative to the beginning of the chart. The starting and ending node information for the arc is also copied to the edge. This node information is later utilized in chart parsing to eliminate spurious parses. The number of edges in the chart equals to the number of edges in the input FSM at the end of initialization.

Consider the simple FSM $\mathcal{F}_1$ depicted in Figure 3, the corresponding two-dimensional chart and the related hypotheses. The chart is populated with the converted word graph before parsing begins. Words in the same column can be regarded as a single lexical entry with different senses (e.g., '*boy*' and '*boycott*' in column 2). Words spanning more than one column can be regarded as idiomatic entries (e.g. '*escalated*' from column 3 to 5). Merged cells in the chart (e.g., '*the*' and '*yesterday*' at columns 1 and 6, respectively) are shared in both sentence hypotheses.

$\mathcal{F}_1$:

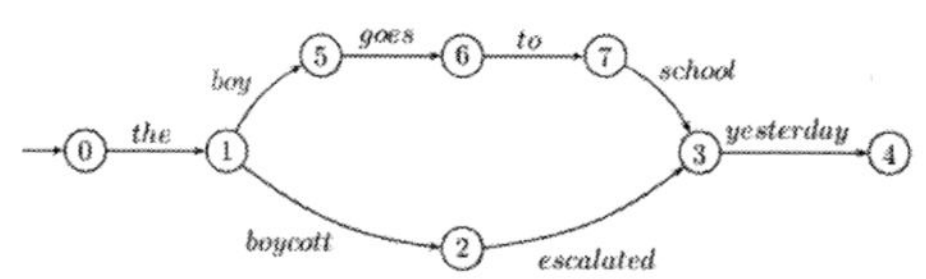

Chart:

0 1	2	3	4	5	6
$_0$ *the* $_1$	$_1$ *boy* $_5$	$_5$ *goes* $_6$	$_6$ *to* $_7$	$_7$ *school* $_3$	$_3$ *yesterday* $_4$
	$_1$ *boycott* $_2$	$_2$ *escalated* $_3$			

Hypotheses:

- *The boy goes to school yesterday*
- *The boycott escalated yesterday*

Figure 3: Sample FSM $\mathcal{F}_4$, the corresponding chart and the hypotheses.

3.4 Extended Chart Parsing

In a standard active chart parser, the chart depicted in Figure 3 could produce some spurious parses. For example, both of the complete edges in the initial chart at location [1-2] (i.e. '*boy*' and '*boycott*) can be combined with the word '*goes*', although '*boycott goes*' is not allowed in the original word graph. We have eliminated these kinds of spurious parses by making use of the *arcstart* and *arcfinish* values. These labels indicate the starting and ending node identifiers of the path spanned by the edge in subject. The application of this idea is illustrated in Figure 4. Different from the original implementation of the fundamental rule, the procedure has the additional parameters to define starting and ending node identifiers. Before creating a new incomplete edge, it is checked whether the node identifiers match or not.

When we consider the chart given in Figure 3, '$_1$ *boycott* $_2$' and '$_5$ *goes* $_6$' cannot be combined according to the new *fundamental rule* in a parse tree because the ending node id, i.e. 2, of the former does not match the starting node id, i.e. 5, of the latter. In another example, '$_0$ *the* $_1$' can be combined with both '$_1$ *boy* $_5$' and '$_1$ *boycott* $_2$' because their respective node identifiers match. After the two edges, '*boycott*' and '*escalated*', are combined and a new edge is generated, the starting node identifiers for the entire edge will be as in '$_1$ *boycott escalated* $_3$'.

The utilization of the node identifiers enables the two-dimensional modeling of a word graph in a chart. This extension to chart parsing makes the current approach word-graph based rather than confusion-network based. Parse trees that conflict with the input word graph are blocked and all the processing resources are dedicated to proper edges. The chart parsing algorithm is listed in Figure 4.

```
input: grammar, word-graph
output: chart

algorithm CHART-PARSE(grammar, word-graph)
   INITIALIZE (chart, agenda, word-graph)
   while agenda is not empty
      edge ← POP (agenda)
      PROCESS-EDGE (edge)
   end while
end algorithm

procedure PROCESS-EDGE (A → B • α • C, [j, k], [n_s, n_e])
   PUSH (chart, A → B • α • C, [j, k], [n_s, n_e])
   FUNDAMENTAL-RULE (A → B • α • C, [j, k], [n_s, n_e])
   PREDICT (A → B • α • C, [j, k], [n_s, n_e])
end procedure

procedure FUNDAMENTAL-RULE (A → B • α • C, [j, k], [n_s, n_e])
   if B = βD       // edge is incomplete
      for each (D → •δ•, [i, j], [n_r, n_s]) in chart
         PUSH (agenda, (A → β • Dα • C, [i, k], [n_r, n_e]) )
      end for
   end if
   if C = Dγ       // edge is incomplete
      for each (D → •δ•, [k, l], [n_e, n_f]) in chart
         PUSH (agenda, (A → B • αD•γ, [j, l], [n_s, n_f]) )
      end for
   end if
   if B is null and C is null // edge is complete
      for each (D → βA • γ • δ, [k, l], [n_e, n_f]) in chart
         PUSH (agenda, (D → β • Aγ • δ, [j, l], [n_s, n_f]) )
      end for
      for each (D → β • γ • Aδ, [i, j], [n_r, n_s]) in chart
         PUSH (agenda, (D → β • γA • δ, [i, k], [n_r, n_e]) )
      end for
   end if
end procedure

procedure PREDICT (A → B • α • C, [j, k], [n_s, n_e])
   if B is null and C is null // edge is complete
      for each D → βAγ in grammar where A is trigger
         PUSH (agenda, (D → β • A • γ, [j, k], [n_s, n_e]) )
      end for
   else
      if B = βD // edge is incomplete
         for each D → γ in grammar
            PUSH (agenda, (D → γ•, [j, j], [n_s, n_s]) )
         end for
      end if
      if C = Dγ // edge is incomplete
         for each D → γ in grammar
            PUSH (agenda, (D → •γ, [k, k], [n_e, n_e]) )
         end for
      end if
   end if
end procedure
```

Figure 4: Extended chart parsing algorithm used to parse word graphs. Fundamental rule and predict procedures are updated to handle word graphs in a bidirectional manner.

3.5 Unification-based chart parsing

The grammar rules are implemented using *Lexical Functional Grammar* (LFG) paradigm. The primary data structure to represent the features and values is a directed acyclic graph (dag). The system also includes an expressive Boolean formalism, used to represent functional equations to access, inspect or modify features or feature sets in the dag. Complex feature structures (e.g. lists, sets, strings, and conglomerate lists) can be associated with lexical entries and grammatical categories using inheritance operations. Unification is used as the fundamental mechanism to integrate information from lexical entries into larger grammatical constituents.

The constituent structure (c-structure) represents the composition of syntactic constituents for a phrase. It is the term used for parse tree in LFG. The functional structure (f-structure) is the representation of grammatical functions in LFG. Attribute-value-matrices are used to describe f-structures. A sample c-structure and the corresponding f-structures in English are shown in Figure 5. For simplicity, many details and feature values are not given. The dag containing the information originated from the lexicon and the information extracted from morphological analysis is shown on the leaf levels of the parse tree in Figure 5. The final dag corresponding to the root node is built during the parsing process in cascaded unification operations specified in the grammar rules.

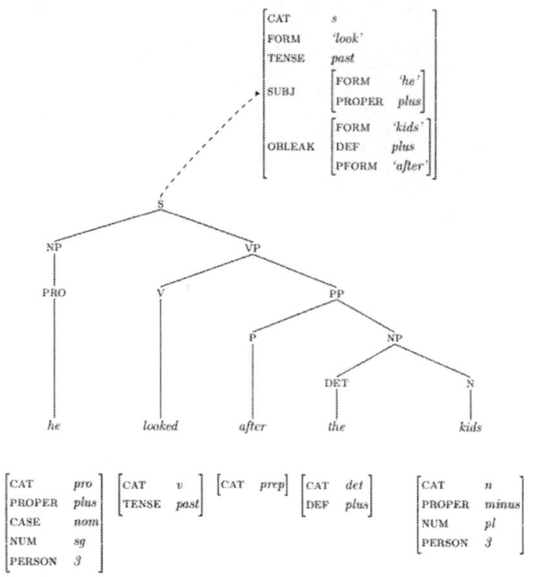

Figure 5: The c-structure and the associated f-structures.

3.6 Parse evaluation and recovery

After all rules are executed and no more edges are left in the agenda, the chart parsing process ends and parse evaluation begins. The chart is searched for complete edges with the final symbol of the grammar (e.g. SBAR) as their category. Any such edge spanning the entire input represents the full parse. If there is no such edge then the parse recovery process takes control.

If the input sentence is ambiguous, then, at the end of parsing, there will multiple parse trees in the chart that span the entire input. Similarly, a grammar built with insufficient constraints can lead to multiple parse trees. In this case, all possible edges are evaluated for *completeness* and *coherence* (Bresnan, 1982) starting from the edge with the highest weight. A parse tree is *complete* if all the functional roles (SUBJ, OBJ, SCOMP etc.) governed by the verb are actually present in the c-structure; it is *coherent* if all the functional roles present are actually governed by the verb. The parse tree that is evaluated as *complete* and *coherent* and has the highest weight is selected for further processing.

In general, a parsing process is said to be successful if a parse tree can be built according to the input sentence. The building of the parse tree fails when the sentence is ungrammatical. For the goal of MT, however, a parse tree is required for the transfer stage and the generation stage even if the input is not grammatical. Therefore, for any input sentence, a corresponding parse tree is built at the end of parsing.

If parsing fails, i.e. if all rules are exhausted and no successful parse tree has been produced, then the system tries to recover from the failure by creating a tree like structure. Appropriate complete edges in the chart are used for this purpose. The idea is to piece together all partial parses for the input sentence, so that the number of constituent edges is minimum and the score of the final tree is maximum. While selecting the constituents, overlapping edges are not chosen.

The recovery process functions as follows:

- The whole chart is traversed and a complete edge is inserted into a candidate list if it has the highest score for that start-end position. If two edges have the same score, then the farthest one to the leaf level is preferred.
- The candidate list is traversed and a combination with the minimum number of constituents is selected. The edges with the widest span get into the winning combination.
- The c-structures and f-structures of the edges in the winning combination are joined into a whole c-structure and f-structure which represent the final parse tree for the input.

4 Experiments

The experiments carried out in this paper are run on word graphs based on 1993 benchmark tests for the ARPA spoken language program (Pallett et al., 1994). In the large-vocabulary continuous speech recognition (CSR) tests reported by Pallett et al. (1994), Wall Street Journal-based CSR corpus material was made use of. Those tests intended to measure basic speaker-independent performance on a 64K-word read-speech test set which consists of 213 utterances. Each of the 10 different speakers provided 20 to 23 utterances. An acoustic model and a trigram language model is trained using Wall Street Journal data by Chelba (2000) who also generated the 213 word graphs used in the current experiments. The word graphs, referred as HUB-1 data set, contain both the acoustic scores and the trigram language model scores. Previously, the same data set was used in other studies (Chelba, 2000; Roark, 2001; Hall, 2005) for language modeling task in ASR.

4.1 N-best list pruning

The 213 word graphs in the HUB-1 data set are pruned as described in Section 3 in order to prepare them for chart parsing. AT&T toolkit (Mohri et al., 1998) is used for determinization and minimization of the word graphs and for n-best path extraction. Prior to feeding in the word graphs to the FSM tools, the acoustic model and the trigram language model in the original lattices are combined into a single score using Equation 1, where $\mathcal{S}$ represents the combined score of an arc, $\mathcal{A}$ is the acoustic model (AM) score, $\mathcal{L}$ is the language model (LM) score, α is the AM scale factor and β is the LM scale factor.

$$\mathcal{S} \;=\; \alpha\mathcal{A}+\beta\mathcal{L} \qquad (1)$$

Figure 6 depicts the word error rates for the first-best hypotheses obtained heuristically by using $\alpha = 1$ and β values from 1 to 25. The lowest WER (13.32) is achieved when α is set to 1 and β to 15. This result is close with the findings from Hall (2005) who reported to use 16 as the LM scale factor for the same data set. WER score for LM-only was 26.8 where in comparison the AM-only score was 29.64. The results imply that the language model has more predicting power over the acoustic model in the HUB-1 lattices. For the rest of the experiments, we used 1 and 15 as the acoustic model and language model scale factors, respectively.

4.2 Word graph accuracy

Using the scale factors found in the previous section we built N-best word graphs for different N values. In order to measure the word graph accuracy we constructed the FSM for reference hypotheses, $\mathcal{F}_{Ref}$, and we took the intersection of all the word graphs with the reference FSM. Table 1 lists the word graph accuracy rate for different N values. For example, an accuracy rate of 30.98 denotes that 66 word graphs out of 213 contain the correct sentences. The accuracy rate for the original word graphs in the data set (last row in Table 1) is 66.67 which indicates that only 142 out of 213 contain the reference sentence. That is, in 71 of the instances, the reference sentence is not included in the untouched word graph. The accurate rates express the maximum sentence error rate (SER) that can be achieved for the data set.

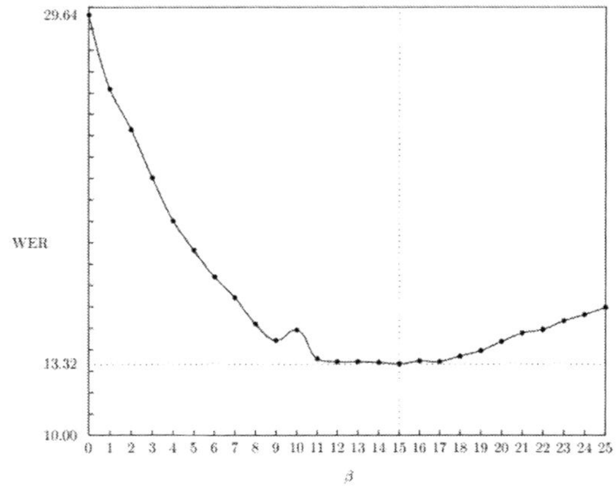

Figure 6: WER for HUB-1 first-best hypotheses obtained using different language-model scaling factors and $\alpha = 1$. The unsteadiness of the WER for $\beta = 10$ needs further investigation.

Table 1: Word graph accuracy for different N values in the data set with 213 word graphs.

N	Accuracy	N	Accuracy
1	30.98	60	59.15
10	51.17	70	59.15
20	56.34	80	59.15
30	58.22	90	60.10
40	59.15	100	60.10
50	59.15	*full*	66.67

4.3 Linguistic Resources

The English grammar used in the chart parser contained 20 morphology analysis rules and 225 syntax analysis rules. All the rules and the unification constraints are implemented in LFG formalism. The number of rules to model the language grammar is quite few compared to probabilistic CFGs which contain more than 10 000 rules. The monolingual analysis lexicon consists of 40 000 lexical entries.

4.4 Chart parsing experiment

We conducted experiments to compare the performance for N-best list parsing and N-best word graph parsing. Compared to the N-best list approach, in N-best word graph parsing approach, the shared edges are processed only once for all hypotheses. This saves a lot on the number of

Table 2: Number of complete and incomplete edges generated for the NIST HUB-1 data set using different approaches.

Approach	Hypotheses	Complete edges	Incomplete edges
N-best list	4869	798 K	12.125 M
	1	164	2490
N-best word graph	4869	150.8 K	1.662 M
	1	31	341

complete and incomplete edges generated during parsing. Hence, the overall processing time required to analyze the hypotheses are reduced. In an N-best list approach, where each hypothesis is processed separately in the analyzer, there are different charts and different parsing instances for each sentence hypothesis. Shared words in different sentences are parsed repeatedly and same edges will be created at each instance.

Table 2 represents the number of complete and incomplete edges generated for the NIST HUB-1 data set. For each hypothesis, 164 complete edges and 2490 incomplete edges are generated on the average in the N-best list approach. In the N-best word graph approach, the average number of complete edges and incomplete edges reduced to 31 and 341, respectively. The decrease is 81.1% in complete edges and 86.3% in incomplete edges for the NIST HUB-1 data set. The profit introduced in the number of edges by using the N-best word graph approach is immense.

4.5 Language modeling experiment

In order to compare this approach to previous language modeling approaches we used the same data set. Table 3 lists the WER for the NIST HUB-1 data set for different approaches including ours. The N-best word graph approach presented in this paper scored 12.6 WER and still needs some improvements. The English analysis grammar that was used in the experiments was designed to parse typed text containing punctuation information. The speech data, however, does not contain any punctuation. Therefore, the grammar has to be adjusted accordingly to improve the WER. Another common source of error in parsing is because of unnormalized text.

Table 3: WER taken from Hall and Johnson (2003) for various language models on HUB-1 lattices in addition to our approach presented in the fifth row.

Model	WER
Charniak Parser (Charniak, 2001)	11.8
Attention Shifting (Hall and Johnson, 2004)	11.9
PCFG (Hall, 2005)	12.0
A* decoding (Xu et al., 2002)	12.3
N-best word graph *(this study)*	**12.6**
PCFG (Roark, 2001)	12.7
PCFG (Hall and Johnson, 2004)	13.0
40m-word trigram (Hall and Johnson, 2003)	13.7
PCFG (Hall and Johnson, 2003)	15.5

5 Conclusions

The primary aim of this research was to propose a new and efficient method for integrating an SR system with an MT system employing a chart parser. The main idea is to populate the initial chart parser with the word graph that comes out of the SR component.

This paper presents an attempt to blend statistical SR systems with rule-based MT systems. The goal of the final assembly of these two components was to achieve an enhanced Speech Translation (ST) system. Specifically, we propose to parse the word graph generated by the SR module inside the rule-based parser. This approach can be generalized to any MT system employing chart parsing in its analysis stage. In addition to utilizing rule-based MT in ST, this study used word graphs and chart parsing with new extensions.

For further improvement of the overall system, our future studies include the following: 1. Adjusting the English syntax analysis rules to handle spoken text which does not include any punctuation. 2. Normalization of the word arcs in the input lattice to match words in the analysis lexicon.

Acknowledgments

Thanks to Jude Miller and Mirna Miller for providing the Arabic reference translations. We also thank Brian Roark and Keith Hall for providing the test data, and Nagendra Goel, Cem Bozşahin, Ayşenur Birtürk and Tolga Çiloğlu for their valuable comments.

References

J. Bresnan. 1982. Control and complementation. In J. Bresnan, editor, *The Mental Representation of Grammatical Relations*, pages 282–390. MIT Press, Cambridge, MA.

J.-C. Chappelier, M. Rajman, R. Aragues, and A. Rozenknop. 1999. Lattice parsing for speech recognition. In *TALN'99*, pages 95–104.

Eugene Charniak. 2001. Immediate-head parsing for language models. In *Proceedings of the 39th Annual Meeting on Association for Computational Linguistics*. Association for Computational Linguistics.

Ciprian Chelba. 2000. *Exploiting Syntactic Structure for Natural Language Modeling*. Ph.D. thesis, Johns Hopkins University.

Lee-Feng Chien, K. J. Chen, and Lin-Shan Lee. 1990. An augmented chart data structure with efficient word lattice parsing scheme in speech recognition applications. In *Proceedings of the 13th conference on Computational linguistics*, pages 60–65, Morristown, NJ, USA. Association for Computational Linguistics.

Lee-Feng Chien, K. J. Chen, and Lin-Shan Lee. 1993. A best-first language processing model integrating the unification grammar and markov language model for speech recognition applications. *IEEE Transactions on Speech and Audio Processing*, 1(2):221–240.

Yen-Lu Chow and Salim Roukos. 1989. Speech understanding using a unification grammar. In *ICAASP'89: Proc. of the International Conference on Acoustics, Speech, and Signal Processing*, pages 727–730. IEEE.

Christopher Dyer, Smaranda Muresan, and Philip Resnik. 2008. Generalizing word lattice translation. In *Proceedings of ACL-08: HLT*, pages 1012–1020, Columbus, Ohio, June. Association for Computational Linguistics.

Keith Hall and Mark Johnson. 2003. Language modelling using efficient best-first bottom-up parsing. In *ASR'03: IEEE Workshop on Automatic Speech Recognition and Understanding*, pages 507–512. IEEE.

Keith Hall and Mark Johnson. 2004. Attention shifting for parsing speech. In *ACL '04: Proceedings of the 42nd Annual Meeting on Association for Computational Linguistics*, page 40, Morristown, NJ, USA. Association for Computational Linguistics.

Keith Hall. 2005. *Best-First Word Lattice Parsing: Techniques for Integrated Syntax Language Modeling*. Ph.D. thesis, Brown University.

Martin Kay. 1986. Algorithm schemata and data structures in syntactic processing. *Readings in natural language processing*, pages 35–70.

C. D. Manning and H. Schütze. 2000. *Foundations of Statistical Natural Language Processing*. The MIT Press.

Mehryar Mohri, Fernando C. N. Pereira, and Michael Riley. 1998. A rational design for a weighted finite-state transducer library. In *WIA '97: Revised Papers from the Second International Workshop on Implementing Automata*, pages 144–158, London, UK. Springer-Verlag.

Hermann Ney. 1991. Dynamic programming parsing for context-free grammars in continuous speech recognition. *IEEE Transactions on Signal Processing*, 39(2):336–340.

A. Paeseler. 1988. Modification of Earley's algorithm for speech recognition. In *Proceedings of the NATO Advanced Study Institute on Recent advances in speech understanding and dialog systems*, pages 465–472, New York, NY, USA. Springer-Verlag New York, Inc.

David S. Pallett, Jonathan G. Fiscus, William M. Fisher, John S. Garofolo, Bruce A. Lund, and Mark A. Przybocki. 1994. In *HLT '94: Proceedings of the workshop on Human Language Technology*, pages 49–74, Morristown, NJ, USA. Association for Computational Linguistics.

Brian Roark. 2001. Probabilistic top-down parsing and language modeling. *Computational Linguistics*, 27(2):249–276.

Andreas Stolcke. 1995. An efficient probabilistic context-free parsing algorithm that computes prefix probabilities. *Computational Linguistics*, 21(2):165–201.

Masaru Tomita. 1986. An efficient word lattice parsing algorithm for continuous speech recognition. *Acoustics, Speech, and Signal Processing, IEEE International Conference on ICASSP '86.*, 11:1569–1572.

Hans Weber. 1994. Time synchronous chart parsing of speech integrating unification grammars with statistics. In *Proceedings of the Eighth Twente Workshop on Language Technology*, pages 107–119.

Phil Woodland. 2000. *HTK Speech Recognition Toolkit*. Cambridge University Engineering Department, `http://htk.eng.cam.ac.uk`.

Peng Xu, Ciprian Chelba, and Frederick Jelinek. 2002. A study on richer syntactic dependencies for structured language modeling. In *ACL '02: Proceedings of the 40th Annual Meeting on Association for Computational Linguistics*, pages 191–198. Association for Computational Linguistics.

Treebank Grammar Techniques for Non-Projective Dependency Parsing

Marco Kuhlmann
Uppsala University
Uppsala, Sweden
marco.kuhlmann@lingfil.uu.se

Giorgio Satta
University of Padua
Padova, Italy
satta@dei.unipd.it

Abstract

An open problem in dependency parsing is the accurate and efficient treatment of non-projective structures. We propose to attack this problem using chart-parsing algorithms developed for mildly context-sensitive grammar formalisms. In this paper, we provide two key tools for this approach. First, we show how to reduce non-projective dependency parsing to parsing with Linear Context-Free Rewriting Systems (LCFRS), by presenting a technique for extracting LCFRS from dependency treebanks. For efficient parsing, the extracted grammars need to be transformed in order to minimize the number of nonterminal symbols per production. Our second contribution is an algorithm that computes this transformation for a large, empirically relevant class of grammars.

1 Introduction

Dependency parsing is the task of predicting the most probable dependency structure for a given sentence. One of the key choices in dependency parsing is about the class of candidate structures for this prediction. Many parsers are confined to *projective* structures, in which the yield of a syntactic head is required to be continuous. A major benefit of this choice is computational efficiency: an exhaustive search over all projective structures can be done in cubic, greedy parsing in linear time (Eisner, 1996; Nivre, 2003). A major drawback of the restriction to projective dependency structures is a potential loss in accuracy. For example, around 23% of the analyses in the Prague Dependency Treebank of Czech (Hajič et al., 2001) are non-projective, and for German and Dutch treebanks, the proportion of non-projective structures is even higher (Havelka, 2007).

The problem of non-projective dependency parsing under the joint requirement of accuracy and efficiency has only recently been addressed in the literature. Some authors propose to solve it by techniques for recovering non-projectivity from the output of a projective parser in a post-processing step (Hall and Novák, 2005; Nivre and Nilsson, 2005), others extend projective parsers by heuristics that allow at least certain non-projective constructions to be parsed (Attardi, 2006; Nivre, 2007). McDonald et al. (2005) formulate dependency parsing as the search for the most probable spanning tree over the *full* set of all possible dependencies. However, this approach is limited to probability models with strong independence assumptions. Exhaustive non-projective dependency parsing with more powerful models is intractable (McDonald and Satta, 2007), and one has to resort to approximation algorithms (McDonald and Pereira, 2006).

In this paper, we propose to attack non-projective dependency parsing in a principled way, using polynomial chart-parsing algorithms developed for mildly context-sensitive grammar formalisms. This proposal is motivated by the observation that most dependency structures required for the analysis of natural language are very nearly projective, differing only minimally from the best projective approximation (Kuhlmann and Nivre, 2006), and by the close link between such 'mildly non-projective' dependency structures on the one hand, and grammar formalisms with mildly context-sensitive generative capacity on the other (Kuhlmann and Möhl, 2007). Furthermore, as pointed out by McDonald and Satta (2007), chart-parsing algorithms are amenable to augmentation by non-local information such as arity constraints and Markovization, and therefore should allow for more predictive statistical models than those used by current systems for non-projective dependency parsing. Hence, mildly non-projective dependency parsing promises to be both efficient and accurate.

Proceedings of the 12th Conference of the European Chapter of the ACL, pages 478–486,
Athens, Greece, 30 March – 3 April 2009.

Contributions In this paper, we contribute two key tools for making the mildly context-sensitive approach to accurate and efficient non-projective dependency parsing work.

First, we extend the standard technique for extracting context-free grammars from phrase-structure treebanks (Charniak, 1996) to mildly context-sensitive grammars and dependency treebanks. More specifically, we show how to extract, from a given dependency treebank, a lexicalized Linear Context-Free Rewriting System (LCFRS) whose derivations capture the dependency analyses in the treebank in the same way as the derivations of a context-free treebank grammar capture phrase-structure analyses. Our technique works for arbitrary, even non-projective dependency treebanks, and essentially reduces non-projective dependency to parsing with LCFRS. This problem can be solved using standard chart-parsing techniques.

Our extraction technique yields a grammar whose parsing complexity is polynomial in the length of the sentence, but exponential in both a measure of the non-projectivity of the treebank and the maximal number of dependents per word, reflected as the *rank* of the extracted LCFRS. While the number of highly non-projective dependency structures is negligible for practical applications (Kuhlmann and Nivre, 2006), the rank cannot easily be bounded. Therefore, we present an algorithm that transforms the extracted grammar into a normal form that has rank 2, and thus can be parsed more efficiently. This contribution is important even independently of the extraction procedure: While it is known that a rank-2 normal form of LCFRS does not exist in the general case (Rambow and Satta, 1999), our algorithm succeeds for a large and empirically relevant class of grammars.

2 Preliminaries

We start by introducing dependency trees and Linear Context-Free Rewriting Systems (LCFRS). Throughout the paper, for positive integers i and j, we write $[i, j]$ for the **interval** $\{ k \mid i \leq k \leq j \}$, and use $[n]$ as a shorthand for $[1, n]$.

2.1 Dependency Trees

Dependency parsing is the task to assign dependency structures to a given sentence w. For the purposes of this paper, dependency structures are edge-labelled trees. More formally, let w be a sentence, understood as a sequence of tokens over some given alphabet T, and let L be an alphabet of edge labels. A **dependency tree** for w is a construct $D = (w, E, \lambda)$, where E forms a rooted tree (in the standard graph-theoretic sense) on the set $[|w|]$, and λ is a total function that assigns every edge in E a label in L. Each node of D represents a (position of a) token in w.

Example 1 Figure 2 shows a dependency tree for the sentence *A hearing is scheduled on the issue today*, which consists of 8 tokens and the edges $\{ (2,1), (2,5), (3,2), (3,4), (4,8), (5,7), (7,6) \}$. The edges are labelled with syntactic functions such as sbj for 'subject'. The root node is marked by a dotted line. □

Let u be a node of a dependency tree D. A node u' is a **descendant** of u, if there is a (possibly empty) path from u to u'. A **block** of u is a maximal interval of descendants of u. The number of blocks of u is called the **block-degree** of u. The block-degree of a dependency tree is the maximum among the block-degrees of its nodes. A dependency tree is **projective**, if its block-degree is 1.

Example 2 The tree shown in Figure 2 is not projective: both node 2 (*hearing*) and node 4 (*scheduled*) have block-degree 2. Their blocks are $\{ 2 \}, \{ 5, 6, 7 \}$ and $\{ 4 \}, \{ 8 \}$, respectively.

2.2 LCFRS

Linear Context-Free Rewriting Systems (LCFRS) have been introduced as a generalization of several mildly context-sensitive grammar formalisms. Here we use the standard definition of LCFRS (Vijay-Shanker et al., 1987) and only fix our notation; for a more thorough discussion of this formalism, we refer to the literature.

Let G be an LCFRS. Recall that each nonterminal symbol A of G comes with a positive integer called the **fan-out** of A, and that a production p of G has the form

$$A \to g(A_1, \ldots, A_r)\,;\; g(\vec{x}_1, \ldots, \vec{x}_r) = \vec{\alpha}\,,$$

where $A, A_1, \ldots, A_r$ are nonterminals with fan-out $f, f_1, \ldots, f_r$, respectively, g is a function symbol, and the equation to the right of the semicolon specifies the semantics of g. For each $i \in [r]$, $\vec{x}_i$ is an f_i-tuple of variables, and $\vec{\alpha} = \langle \alpha_1, \ldots, \alpha_f \rangle$ is a tuple of strings over the variables on the left-hand side of the equation and the alphabet of terminal symbols in which each variable appears exactly once. The production p is said to have **rank** r, **fan-out** f, and **length** $|\alpha_1| + \cdots + |\alpha_f| + (f - 1)$.

3 Grammar Extraction

We now explain how to extract an LCFRS from a dependency treebank, in very much the same way as a context-free grammar can be extracted from a phrase-structure treebank (Charniak, 1996).

3.1 Dependency Treebank Grammars

A simple way to induce a context-free grammar from a phrase-structure treebank is to read off the productions of the grammar from the trees. We will specify a procedure for extracting, from a given dependency treebank, a lexicalized LCFRS G that is **adequate** in the sense that for every analysis D of a sentence w in the treebank, there is a derivation tree of G that is isomorphic to D, meaning that it becomes equal to D after a suitable renaming and relabelling of nodes, and has w as its derived string. Here, a **derivation tree** of an LCFRS G is an ordered tree such that each node u is labelled with a production p of G, the number of children of u equals the rank r of p, and for each $i \in [r]$, the ith child of u is labelled with a production that has as its left-hand side the ith nonterminal on the right-hand side of p.

The basic idea behind our extraction procedure is that, in order to represent the compositional structure of a possibly non-projective dependency tree, one needs to represent the decomposition and relative order not of subtrees, but of blocks of subtrees (Kuhlmann and Möhl, 2007). We introduce some terminology. A **component** of a node u in a dependency tree is either a block B of some child u' of u, or the singleton interval that contains u; this interval will represent the position in the string that is occupied by the lexical item corresponding to u. We say that u' **contributes** B, and that u contributes $[u, u]$ to u. Notice that the number of components that u' contributes to its parent u equals the block-degree of u'. Our goal is to construct for u a production of an LCFRS that specifies how each block of u decomposes into components, and how these components are ordered relative to one another. These productions will make an adequate LCFRS, in the sense defined above.

3.2 Annotating the Components

The core of our extraction procedure is an efficient algorithm that annotates each node u of a given dependency tree with the list of its components, sorted by their left endpoints. It is helpful to think of this algorithm as of two independent parts, one that annotates each node u with the list of the left endpoints of its components (ANNOTATE-L) and one that annotates the corresponding right endpoints (ANNOTATE-R). The list of components can then be obtained by zipping the two lists of endpoints together in linear time.

Function ANNOTATE-L(D)
for each u of D, from left to right **do**
    if u is the first node of D **then**
        $b :=$ the root node of D
    else
        $b :=$ the lca of u and its predecessor
    for each u' on the path $b \cdots u$ **do**
        left$[u']$:= left$[u'] \cdot u$

Figure 1: Annotation with components

Figure 1 shows pseudocode for ANNOTATE-L; the pseudocode for ANNOTATE-R is symmetric. We do a single left-to-right sweep over the nodes of the input tree D. In each step, we annotate all nodes u' that have the current node u as the left endpoint of one of their components. Since the sweep is from left to right, this will get us the left endpoints of u' in the desired order. The nodes that we annotate are the nodes u' on the path between u and the **least common ancestor (lca)** b of u and its predecessor, or the path from the root node to u, in case that u is the leftmost node of D.

Example 3 For the dependency tree in Figure 2, ANNOTATE-L constructs the following lists left$[u]$ of left endpoints, for $u = 1, \dots, 8$:

$$1,\ 1\cdot 2\cdot 5,\ 1\cdot 3\cdot 4\cdot 5\cdot 8,\ 4\cdot 8,\ 5\cdot 6,\ 6,\ 6\cdot 7,\ 8$$

The following Lemma establishes the correctness of the algorithm:

Lemma 1 *Let D be a dependency tree, and let u and u' be nodes of D. Let b be the least common ancestor of u and its predecessor, or the root node in case that u is the leftmost node of D. Then u is the left endpoint of a component of u' if and only if u' lies on the path from b to u.* □

PROOF It is clear that u' must be an ancestor of u. If u is the leftmost node of D, then u is the left endpoint of the leftmost component of all of its ancestors. Now suppose that u is not the leftmost node of D, and let $\hat{u}$ be the predecessor of u. Distinguish three cases: If u' is not an ancestor of $\hat{u}$, then $\hat{u}$ does not belong to any component of u'; therefore, u is the left endpoint of a component of u'. If u' is an ancestor of $\hat{u}$ but $u' \neq b$, then $\hat{u}$ and u belong to the same component of u'; therefore, u is not the left endpoint of this component. Finally, if $u' = b$, then $\hat{u}$ and u belong to different components of u'; therefore, u is the left endpoint of the component it belongs to. ■

We now turn to an analysis of the runtime of the algorithm. Let n be the number of components of D. It is not hard to imagine an algorithm that performs the annotation task in time $O(n \log n)$: such an algorithm could construct the components for a given node u by essentially merging the list of components of the children of u into a new sorted list. In contrast, our algorithm takes time $O(n)$. The crucial part of the analysis is the assignment in line 6, which computes the least common ancestor of u and its predecessor. Using markers for the path from the root node to u, it is straightforward to implement this assignment in time $O(|\pi|)$, where π is the path $b \cdots u$. Now notice that, by our correctness argument, line 8 of the algorithm is executed exactly n times. Therefore, the sum over the lengths of all the paths π, and hence the amortized time of computing all the least common ancestors in line 6, is $O(n)$. This runtime complexity is optimal for the task we are solving.

3.3 Extraction Procedure

We now describe how to extend the annotation algorithm into a procedure that extracts an LCFRS from a given dependency tree D. The basic idea is to transform the list of components of each node u of D into a production p. This transformation will only rename and relabel nodes, and therefore yield an adequate derivation tree. For the construction of the production, we actually need an extended version of the annotation algorithm, in which each component is annotated with the node that contributed it. This extension is straightforward, and does not affect the linear runtime complexity.

Let D be a dependency tree for a sentence w. Consider a single node u of D, and assume that u has r children, and that the block-degree of u is f. We construct for u a production p with rank r and fan-out f. For convenience, let us order the children of u, say by their leftmost descendants, and let us write u_i for the ith child of u according to this order, and f_i for the block-degree of u_i, $i \in [r]$. The production p has the form

$$L \to g(L_1, \ldots, L_r) \; ; \; g(\vec{x}_1, \ldots, \vec{x}_r) = \vec{\alpha} \, ,$$

where L is the label of the incoming edge of u (or the special label root in case that u is the root node of D) and for each $i \in [r]$: L_i is the label of the incoming edge of u_i; $\vec{x}_i$ is a f_i-tuple of variables of the form $x_{i,j}$, where $j \in [f_i]$; and $\vec{\alpha}$ is an f-tuple that is constructed in a single left-to-right sweep over the list of components computed for u as follows. Let $k \in [f_i]$ be a pointer to a current segment of $\vec{\alpha}$; initially, $k = 1$. If the current component is not adjacent (as an interval) to the previous component, we increase k by one. If the current component is contributed by the child u_i, $i \in [r]$, we add the variable $x_{i,j}$ to α_k, where j is the number of times we have seen a component contributed by u_i during the sweep. Notice that $j \in [f_i]$. If the current component is the (unique) component contributed by u, we add the token corresponding to u to α_k. In this way, we obtain a complete specification of how the blocks of u (represented by the segments of the tuple $\vec{\alpha}$) decompose into the components of u, and of the relative order of the components. As an example, Figure 2 shows the productions extracted from the tree above.

3.4 Parsing the Extracted Grammar

Once we have extracted the grammar for a dependency treebank, we can apply any parsing algorithm for LCFRS to non-projective dependency parsing. The generic chart-parsing algorithm for LCFRS runs in time $O(|P| \cdot |w|^{f(r+1)})$, where P is the set of productions of the input grammar G, w is the input string, r is the maximal rank, and f is the maximal fan-out of a production in G (Seki et al., 1991). For a grammar G extracted by our technique, the number f equals the maximal block-degree per node. Hence, without any further modification, we obtain a parsing algorithm that is polynomial in the length of the sentence, but exponential in both the block-degree and the rank. This is clearly unacceptable in practical systems. The relative frequency of analyses with a block-degree ≥ 2 is almost negligible (Havelka, 2007); the bigger obstacle in applying the treebank grammar is the rank of the resulting LCFRS. Therefore, in the remainder of the paper, we present an algorithm that can transform the productions of the input grammar G into an equivalent set of productions with rank at most 2, while preserving the fan-out. This transformation, if it succeeds, yields a parsing algorithm that runs in time $O(|P| \cdot r \cdot |w|^{3f})$.

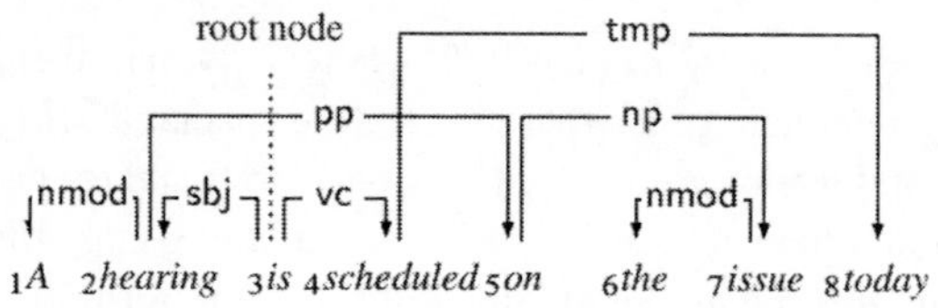

$\mathsf{nmod} \to g_1$	$g_1 = \langle A \rangle$
$\mathsf{sbj} \to g_2(\mathsf{nmod}, \mathsf{pp})$	$g_2(\langle x_{1,1} \rangle, \langle x_{2,1} \rangle) = \langle x_{1,1}\ \textit{hearing},\ x_{2,1} \rangle$
$\mathsf{root} \to g_3(\mathsf{sbj}, \mathsf{vc})$	$g_3(\langle x_{1,1}, x_{1,2} \rangle, \langle x_{2,1}, x_{2,2} \rangle) = \langle x_{1,1}\ \textit{is}\ x_{2,1}\ x_{1,2}\ x_{2,2} \rangle$
$\mathsf{vc} \to g_4(\mathsf{tmp})$	$g_4(\langle x_{1,1} \rangle) = \langle \textit{scheduled},\ x_{1,1} \rangle$
$\mathsf{pp} \to g_5(\mathsf{np})$	$g_5(\langle x_{1,1} \rangle) = \langle \textit{on}\ x_{1,1} \rangle$
$\mathsf{nmod} \to g_6$	$g_6 = \langle \textit{the} \rangle$
$\mathsf{np} \to g_7(\mathsf{nmod})$	$g_7(\langle x_{1,1} \rangle) = \langle x_{1,1}\ \textit{issue} \rangle$
$\mathsf{tmp} \to g_8$	$g_8 = \langle \textit{today} \rangle$

Figure 2: A dependency tree, and the LCFRS extracted for it

4 Adjacency

In this section we discuss a method for factorizing an LCFRS into productions of rank 2. Before starting, we get rid of the 'easy' cases. A production p is **connected** if any two strings α_i, α_j in p's definition share at least one variable referring to the same nonterminal. It is not difficult to see that, when p is *not* connected, we can always split it into new productions of lower rank. Therefore, throughout this section we assume that LCFRS only have connected productions. We can split p into its connected components using standard methods for finding the strongly connected components of an undirected graph. This can be implemented in time $O(r \cdot f)$, where r and f are the rank and the fan-out of p, respectively.

4.1 Adjacency Graphs

Let p be a production with length n and fan-out f, associated with function a g. The set of **positions** of p is the set $[n]$. Informally, each position represents a variable or a lexical element in one of the components of the definition of g, or else a 'gap' between two of these components. (Recall that n also accounts for the $f - 1$ gaps in the body of g.)

Example 4 The set of positions of the production for *hearing* in Figure 2 is [4]: 1 for variable x_1, 2 for *hearing*, 3 for the gap, and 4 for y_1. □

Let $i_1, j_1, i_2, j_2 \in [n]$. An interval $[i_1, j_1]$ is **adjacent** to an interval $[i_2, j_2]$ if either $j_1 = i_2 - 1$ (left-adjacent) or $i_1 = j_2 + 1$ (right-adjacent). A multi-interval, or **m-interval** for short, is a set v of pairwise disjoint intervals such that no interval in v is adjacent to any other interval in v. The **fan-out** of v, written $f(v)$, is defined as $|v|$.

We use m-intervals to represent the nonterminals and the lexical element heading p. The ith nonterminal on the right-hand side of p is represented by the m-interval obtained by collecting all the positions of p that represent a variable from the ith argument of g. The head of p is represented by the m-interval containing the associated position. Note that all these m-intervals are pairwise disjoint.

Example 5 Consider the production for *is* in Figure 2. The set of positions is [5]. The first nonterminal is represented by the m-interval $\{[1,1],[4,4]\}$, the second nonterminal by $\{[3,3],[5,5]\}$, and the lexical head by $\{[2,2]\}$. □

For disjoint m-intervals v_1, v_2, we say that v_1 is **adjacent** to v_2, denoted by $v_1 \to v_2$, if for every interval $I_1 \in v_1$, there is an interval $I_2 \in v_2$ such that I_1 is adjacent to I_2. Adjacency is not symmetric: if $v_1 = \{[1,1],[4,4]\}$ and $v_2 = \{[2,2]\}$, then $v_2 \to v_1$, but not vice versa.

Let V be some collection of pairwise disjoint m-intervals representing p as above. The **adjacency graph** associated with p is the graph $G = (V, \to_G)$ whose vertices are the m-intervals in V, and whose edges $\to_G$ are defined by restricting the adjacency relation $\to$ to the set V.

For m-intervals $v_1, v_2 \in V$, the **merger** of v_1 and v_2, denoted by $v_1 \oplus v_2$, is the (uniquely determined) m-interval whose span is the union of the spans of v_1 and v_2. As an example, if $v_1 = \{[1,1],[3,3]\}$ and $v_2 = \{[2,2]\}$, then $v_1 \oplus v_2 = \{[1,3]\}$. Notice that the way in which we defined m-intervals ensures that a merging operation collapses all adjacent intervals. The proof of the following lemma is straightforward and omitted for space reasons:

1: **Function** FACTORIZE($G = (V, \rightarrow_G)$)
2: $R := \emptyset$;
3: **while** $\rightarrow_G \neq \emptyset$ **do**
4: **choose** $(v_1, v_2) \in \rightarrow_G$;
5: $R := R \cup \{ (v_1, v_2) \}$;
6: $V := V - \{ v_1, v_2 \} \cup \{ v_1 \oplus v_2 \}$;
7: $\rightarrow_G := \{ (v, v') \mid v, v' \in V,\ v \rightarrow v' \}$;
8: **if** $|V| = 1$ **then**
9: output R and accept;
10: **else**
11: reject;

Figure 3: Factorization algorithm

Lemma 2 *If* $v_1 \rightarrow v_2$, *then* $f(v_1 \oplus v_2) \leq f(v_2)$.

4.2 The Adjacency Algorithm

Let $G = (V, \rightarrow_G)$ be some adjacency graph, and let $v_1 \rightarrow_G v_2$. We can **derive** a new adjacency graph from G by merging v_1 and v_2. The resulting graph G' has vertices $V' = V - \{ v_1, v_2 \} \cup \{ v_1 \oplus v_2 \}$ and set of edges $\rightarrow_{G'}$ obtained by restricting the adjacency relation $\rightarrow$ to V'. We denote the derive relation as $G \Rightarrow_{(v_1,v_2)} G'$.

Informally, if G represents some LCFRS production p and v_1, v_2 represent nonterminals A_1, A_2, then G' represents a production p' obtained from p by replacing A_1, A_2 with a fresh nonterminal A. A new production p'' can also be constructed, expanding A into A_1, A_2, so that p', p'' together will be equivalent to p. Furthermore, p' has a rank smaller than the rank of p and, from Lemma 2, A does not increase the overall fan-out of the grammar.

In order to simplify the notation, we adopt the following convention. Let $G \Rightarrow_{(v_1,v_2)} G'$ and let $v \rightarrow_G v_1$, $v \neq v_2$. If $v \rightarrow_{G'} v_1 \oplus v_2$, then edges (v, v_1) and $(v, v_1 \oplus v_2)$ will be identified, and we say that G' **inherits** $(v, v_1 \oplus v_2)$ from G. If $v \not\rightarrow_{G'} v_1 \oplus v_2$, then we say that (v, v_1) does not **survive** the derive step. This convention is used for all edges incident upon v_1 or v_2.

Our factorization algorithm is reported in Figure 3. We start from an adjacency graph representing some LCFRS production that needs to be factorized. We arbitrarily choose an edge e of the graph, and push it into a set R, in order to keep a record of the candidate factorization. We then merge the two m-intervals incident to e, and we recompute the adjacency relation for the new set of vertices. We iterate until the resulting graph has an empty edge set. If the final graph has one one vertex, then we have managed to factorize our production into a set of productions with rank at most two that can be computed from R.

Example 6 Let $V = \{ v_1, v_2, v_3 \}$ with $v_1 = \{ [4,4] \}$, $v_2 = \{ [1,1], [3,3] \}$, and $v_3 = \{ [2,2], [5,5] \}$. Then $\rightarrow_G = \{ (v_1, v_2) \}$. After merging v_1, v_2 we have a new graph G with $V = \{ v_1 \oplus v_2, v_3 \}$ and $\rightarrow_G = \{ (v_1 \oplus v_2, v_3) \}$. We finally merge $v_1 \oplus v_2, v_3$ resulting in a new graph G with $V = \{ v_1 \oplus v_2 \oplus v_3 \}$ and $\rightarrow_G = \emptyset$. We then accept and stop. □

4.3 Mathematical Properties

We have already argued that, if the algorithm accepts, then a binary factorization that does not increase the fan-out of the grammar can be built from R. We still need to prove that the algorithm answers consistently on a given input, despite of possibly different choices of edges at line 4. We do this through several intermediate results.

A **derivation** for an adjacency graph G is a sequence of edges $d = \langle e_1, \ldots, e_n \rangle$, $n \geq 1$, such that $G = G_0$ and $G_{i-1} \Rightarrow_{e_i} G_i$ for every i with $1 \leq i \leq n$. For short, we write $G_0 \Rightarrow_d G_n$. Two derivations for G are **competing** if one is a permutation of the other.

Lemma 3 *If* $G \Rightarrow_{d_1} G_1$ *and* $G \Rightarrow_{d_2} G_2$ *with* d_1 *and* d_2 *competing derivations, then* $G_1 = G_2$.

PROOF We claim that the statement of the lemma holds for $|d_1| = 2$. To see this, let $G \Rightarrow_{e_1} G'_1 \Rightarrow_{e_2} G_1$ and $G \Rightarrow_{e_2} G'_2 \Rightarrow_{e_1} G_2$ be valid derivations. We observe that G_1 and G_2 have the same set of vertices. Since the edges of G_1 and G_2 are defined by restricting the adjacency relation to their set of vertices, our claim immediately follows.

The statement of the lemma then follows from the above claim and from the fact that we can always obtain the sequence d_2 starting from d_1 by repeatedly switching consecutive edges. ■

We now consider derivations for the same adjacency graph that are not competing, and show that they always lead to isomorphic adjacency graphs. Two graphs are **isomorphic** if they become equal after some suitable renaming of the vertices.

Lemma 4 *The out-degree of* G *is bounded by* 2.

PROOF Assume $v \rightarrow_G v_1$ and $v \rightarrow_G v_2$, with $v_1 \neq v_2$, and let $I \in v$. I must be adjacent to some interval $I_1 \in v_1$. Without loss of generality, assume that I is left-adjacent to I_1. I must also be adjacent to some interval $I_2 \in v_2$. Since v_1 and v_2

are disjoint, I must be right-adjacent to I_2. This implies that I cannot be adjacent to an interval in any other m-interval v' of G. ■

A vertex v of G such that $v \rightarrow_G v_1$ and $v \rightarrow_G v_2$ is called a **bifurcation**.

Example 7 Assume $v = \{[2,2]\}$, $v_1 = \{[3,3],[5,5]\}$, $v_2 = \{[1,1]\}$ with $v \rightarrow_G v_1$ and $v \rightarrow_G v_2$. The m-interval $v \oplus v_1 = \{[2,3],[5,5]\}$ is no longer adjacent to v_2. □

The example above shows that, when choosing one of the two outgoing edges in a bifurcation for merging, the other edge might not survive. Thus, such a choice might lead to distinguishable derivations that are not competing (one derivation has an edge that is not present in the other). As we will see (in the proof of Theorem 1), bifurcations are the only cases in which edges might not survive a merging.

Lemma 5 *Let v be a bifurcation of G with outgoing edges e_1, e_2, and let $G \Rightarrow_{e_1} G_1$, $G \Rightarrow_{e_2} G_2$. Then G_1 and G_2 are isomorphic.*

PROOF (SKETCH) Assume e_1 has the form $v \rightarrow_G v_1$ and e_2 has the form $v \rightarrow_G v_2$. Let also V_S be the set of vertices shared by G_1 and G_2. We show that the statement holds under the isomorphism mapping $v \oplus v_1$ and v_2 in G_1 to v_1 and $v \oplus v_2$ in G_2, respectively.

When restricted to V_S, the graphs G_1 and G_2 are equal. Let us then consider edges from G_1 and G_2 involving exactly one vertex in V_S. We show that, for $v' \in V_S$, $v' \rightarrow_{G_1} v \oplus v_1$ if and only if $v' \rightarrow_{G_2} v_1$. Consider an arbitrary interval $I' \in v'$. If $v' \rightarrow_{G_1} v \oplus v_1$, then I' must be adjacent to some interval $I_1 \in v \oplus v_1$. If $I_1 \in v_1$ we are done. Otherwise, I_1 must be the concatenation of two intervals I_{1v} and I_{1v_1} with $I_{1v} \in v$ and $I_{1v_1} \in v_1$. Since $v \rightarrow_{G_2} v_2$, I_{1v} is also adjacent to some interval in v_2. However, v' and v_2 are disjoint. Thus I' must be adjacent to $I_{1v_1} \in v_1$. Conversely, if $v' \rightarrow_{G_2} v_1$, then I' must be adjacent to some interval $I_1 \in v_1$. Because v' and v are disjoint, I' must also be adjacent to some interval in $v \oplus v_1$.

Using very similar arguments, we can conclude that G_1 and G_2 are isomorphic when restricted to edges with at most one vertex in V_S.

Finally, we need to consider edges from G_1 and G_2 that are not incident upon vertices in V_S. We show that $v \oplus v_1 \rightarrow_{G_1} v_2$ only if $v_1 \rightarrow_{G_2} v \oplus v_2$; a similar argument can be used to prove the converse. Consider an arbitrary interval $I_1 \in v \oplus v_1$. If $v \oplus v_1 \rightarrow_{G_1} v_2$, then I_1 must be adjacent to some interval $I_2 \in v_2$. If $I_1 \in v_1$ we are done. Otherwise, I_1 must be the concatenation of two adjacent intervals I_{1v} and I_{1v_1} with $I_{1v} \in v$ and $I_{1v_1} \in v_1$. Since I_{1v} is also adjacent to some interval $I_2' \in v_2$ (here I_2' might as well be I_2), we conclude that $I_{1v_1} \in v_1$ is adjacent to the concatenation of I_{1v} and I_2', which is indeed an interval in $v \oplus v_2$. Note that our case distinction is exhaustive. We thus conclude that $v_1 \rightarrow_{G_2} v \oplus v_2$.

A symmetrical argument can be used to show that $v_2 \rightarrow_{G_1} v \oplus v_1$ if and only if $v \oplus v_2 \rightarrow_{G_2} v_1$, which concludes our proof. ■

Theorem 1 *Let d_1 and d_2 be derivations for G, describing two different computations c_1 and c_2 of the algorithm of Figure 3 on input G. Computation c_1 is accepting if and only if c_2 is accepting.*

PROOF First, we prove the claim that if e is not an edge outgoing from a bifurcation vertex, then in the derive relation $G \Rightarrow_e G'$ all of the edges of G but e and its reverse are inherited by G'. Let us write e in the form $v_1 \rightarrow_G v_2$. Obviously, any edge of G not incident upon v_1 or v_2 will be inherited by G'. If $v \rightarrow_G v_2$ for some m-interval $v \neq v_1$, then every interval $I \in v$ is adjacent to some interval in v_2. Since v and v_1 are disjoint, I will also be adjacent to some interval in $v_1 \oplus v_2$. Thus we have $v \rightarrow_{G'} v_1 \oplus v_2$. A similar argument shows that $v \rightarrow_G v_1$ implies $v \rightarrow_{G'} v_1 \oplus v_2$.

If $v_2 \rightarrow_G v$ for some $v \neq v_1$, then every interval $I \in v_2$ is adjacent to some interval in v. From $v_1 \rightarrow_G v_2$ we also have that each interval $I_{12} \in v_1 \oplus v_2$ is either an interval in v_2 or else the concatenation of exactly two intervals $I_1 \in v_1$ and $I_2 \in v_2$. (The interval I_2 cannot be adjacent to more than an interval in v_1, because $v_2 \rightarrow_G v$). In both cases I_{12} is adjacent to some interval in v, and hence $v_1 \oplus v_2 \rightarrow_{G'} v$. This concludes the proof of our claim.

Let d_1, d_2 be as in the statement of the theorem, with $G \Rightarrow_{d_1} G_1$ and $G \Rightarrow_{d_2} G_2$. If d_1 and d_2 are competing, then the theorem follows from Lemma 3. Otherwise, assume that d_1 and d_2 are not competing. From our claim above, some bifurcation vertices must appear in these derivations. Let us reorder the edges in d_1 in such a way that edges outgoing from a bifurcation vertex are processed last and in some canonical order. The resulting derivation has the form dd_1', where d_1' involves the processing of all bifurcation vertices. We can also reorder edges in d_2 to obtain dd_2', where d_2' involves the processing of all bifurcation

not context-free	102 687	100.00%
not binarizable	24	0.02%
not well-nested	622	0.61%

Table 1: Properties of productions extracted from the CoNLL 2006 data (3 794 605 productions)

vertices in exactly the same order as in d_1', but with possibly different choices for the outgoing edges.

Let $G \Rightarrow_d G_d \Rightarrow_{d_1'} G_1'$ and $G \Rightarrow_d G_d \Rightarrow_{d_2'} G_2'$. Derivations dd_1' and d_1 are competing. Thus, by Lemma 3, we have $G_1' = G_1$. Similarly, we can conclude that $G_2' = G_2$. Since bifurcation vertices in d_1' and in d_2' are processed in the same canonical order, from repeated applications of Lemma 5 we have that G_1' and G_2' are isomorphic. We then conclude that G_1 and G_2 are isomorphic as well. The statement of the theorem follows immediately. ■

We now turn to a computational analysis of the algorithm of Figure 3. Let G be the representation of an LCFRS production p with rank r. G has r vertices and, following Lemma 4, $O(r)$ edges. Let v be an m-interval of G with fan-out f_v. The incoming and outgoing edges for v can be detected in time $O(f_v)$ by inspecting the $2 \cdot f_v$ endpoints of v. Thus we can compute G in time $O(|p|)$.

The number of iterations of the while cycle in the algorithm is bounded by r, since at each iteration one vertex of G is removed. Consider now an iteration in which m-intervals v_1 and v_2 have been chosen for merging, with $v_1 \rightarrow_G v_2$. (These m-intervals might be associated with nonterminals in the right-hand side of p, or else might have been obtained as the result of previous merging operations.) Again, we can compute the incoming and outgoing edges of $v_1 \oplus v_2$ in time proportional to the number of endpoints of such an m-interval. By Lemma 2, this number is bounded by $O(f)$, f the fan-out of the grammar. We thus conclude that a run of the algorithm on G takes time $O(r \cdot f)$.

5 Discussion

We have shown how to extract mildly context-sensitive grammars from dependency treebanks, and presented an efficient algorithm that attempts to convert these grammars into an efficiently parseable binary form. Due to previous results (Rambow and Satta, 1999), we know that this is not always possible. However, our algorithm may fail even in cases where a binarization exists—our notion of adjacency is not strong enough to capture all binarizable cases. This raises the question about the practical relevance of our technique.

In order to get at least a preliminary answer to this question, we extracted LCFRS productions from the data used in the 2006 CoNLL shared task on data-driven dependency parsing (Buchholz and Marsi, 2006), and evaluated how large a portion of these productions could be binarized using our algorithm. The results are given in Table 1. Since it is easy to see that our algorithm always succeeds on context-free productions (productions where each nonterminal has fan-out 1), we evaluated our algorithm on the 102 687 productions with a higher fan-out. Out of these, only 24 (0.02%) could *not* be binarized using our technique. We take this number as an indicator for the usefulness of our result.

It is interesting to compare our approach with techniques for **well-nested** dependency trees (Kuhlmann and Nivre, 2006). Well-nestedness is a property that implies the binarizability of the extracted grammar; however, the classes of well-nested trees and those whose corresponding productions can be binarized using our algorithm are incomparable—in particular, there are well-nested productions that cannot be binarized in our framework. Nevertheless, the coverage of our technique is actually higher than that of an approach that relies on well-nestedness, at least on the CoNLL 2006 data (see again Table 1).

We see our results as promising first steps in a thorough exploration of the connections between non-projective and mildly context-sensitive parsing. The obvious next step is the evaluation of our technique in the context of an actual parser.

As a final remark, we would like to point out that an alternative technique for efficient non-projective dependency parsing, developed by Gómez Rodríguez et al. independently of this work, is presented elsewhere in this volume.

Acknowledgements We would like to thank Ryan McDonald, Joakim Nivre, and the anonymous reviewers for useful comments on drafts of this paper, and Carlos Gómez Rodríguez and David J. Weir for making a preliminary version of their paper available to us. The work of the first author was funded by the Swedish Research Council. The second author was partially supported by MIUR under project PRIN No. 2007TJNZRE_002.

References

Giuseppe Attardi. 2006. Experiments with a multilanguage non-projective dependency parser. In *Tenth Conference on Computational Natural Language Learning (CoNLL)*, pages 166–170, New York, USA.

Sabine Buchholz and Erwin Marsi. 2006. CoNLL-X shared task on multilingual dependency parsing. In *Tenth Conference on Computational Natural Language Learning (CoNLL)*, pages 149–164, New York, USA.

Eugene Charniak. 1996. Tree-bank grammars. In *13th National Conference on Artificial Intelligence*, pages 1031–1036, Portland, Oregon, USA.

Jason Eisner. 1996. Three new probabilistic models for dependency parsing: An exploration. In *16th International Conference on Computational Linguistics (COLING)*, pages 340–345, Copenhagen, Denmark.

Carlos Gómez-Rodríguez, David J. Weir, and John Carroll. 2009. Parsing mildly non-projective dependency structures. In *Twelfth Conference of the European Chapter of the Association for Computational Linguistics (EACL)*, Athens, Greece.

Jan Hajič, Barbora Vidova Hladka, Jarmila Panevová, Eva Hajičová, Petr Sgall, and Petr Pajas. 2001. Prague Dependency Treebank 1.0. Linguistic Data Consortium, 2001T10.

Keith Hall and Václav Novák. 2005. Corrective modelling for non-projective dependency grammar. In *Ninth International Workshop on Parsing Technologies (IWPT)*, pages 42–52, Vancouver, Canada.

Jiří Havelka. 2007. Beyond projectivity: Multilingual evaluation of constraints and measures on non-projective structures. In *45th Annual Meeting of the Association for Computational Linguistics (ACL)*, pages 608–615, Prague, Czech Republic.

Marco Kuhlmann and Mathias Möhl. 2007. Mildly context-sensitive dependency languages. In *45th Annual Meeting of the Association for Computational Linguistics (ACL)*, pages 160–167, Prague, Czech Republic.

Marco Kuhlmann and Joakim Nivre. 2006. Mildly non-projective dependency structures. In *21st International Conference on Computational Linguistics and 44th Annual Meeting of the Association for Computational Linguistics (COLING-ACL), Main Conference Poster Sessions*, pages 507–514, Sydney, Australia.

Ryan McDonald and Fernando Pereira. 2006. Online learning of approximate dependency parsing algorithms. In *Eleventh Conference of the European Chapter of the Association for Computational Linguistics (EACL)*, pages 81–88, Trento, Italy.

Ryan McDonald and Giorgio Satta. 2007. On the complexity of non-projective data-driven dependency parsing. In *Tenth International Conference on Parsing Technologies (IWPT)*, pages 121–132, Prague, Czech Republic.

Ryan McDonald, Fernando Pereira, Kiril Ribarov, and Jan Hajič. 2005. Non-projective dependency parsing using spanning tree algorithms. In *Human Language Technology Conference (HLT) and Conference on Empirical Methods in Natural Language Processing (EMNLP)*, pages 523–530, Vancouver, Canada.

Joakim Nivre and Jens Nilsson. 2005. Pseudo-projective dependency parsing. In *43rd Annual Meeting of the Association for Computational Linguistics (ACL)*, pages 99–106, Ann Arbor, USA.

Joakim Nivre. 2003. An efficient algorithm for projective dependency parsing. In *Eighth International Workshop on Parsing Technologies (IWPT)*, pages 149–160, Nancy, France.

Joakim Nivre. 2007. Incremental non-projective dependency parsing. In *Human Language Technologies: The Conference of the North American Chapter of the Association for Computational Linguistics (HLT-NAACL)*, pages 396–403, Rochester, NY, USA.

Owen Rambow and Giorgio Satta. 1999. Independent parallelism in finite copying parallel rewriting systems. *Theoretical Computer Science*, 223(1–2):87–120.

Hiroyuki Seki, Takashi Matsumura, Mamoru Fujii, and Tadao Kasami. 1991. On Multiple Context-Free Grammars. *Theoretical Computer Science*, 88(2):191–229.

K. Vijay-Shanker, David J. Weir, and Aravind K. Joshi. 1987. Characterizing structural descriptions produced by various grammatical formalisms. In *25th Annual Meeting of the Association for Computational Linguistics (ACL)*, pages 104–111, Stanford, CA, USA.

Improvements in Analogical Learning: Application to Translating multi-Terms of the Medical Domain

Philippe Langlais
DIRO
Univ. of Montreal, Canada
felipe@iro.umontreal.ca

François Yvon and Pierre Zweigenbaum
LIMSI-CNRS
Univ. Paris-Sud XI, France
{yvon,pz}@limsi.fr

Abstract

Handling terminology is an important matter in a translation workflow. However, current Machine Translation (MT) systems do not yet propose anything proactive upon tools which assist in managing terminological databases. In this work, we investigate several enhancements to analogical learning and test our implementation on translating medical terms. We show that the analogical engine works equally well when translating from and into a morphologically rich language, or when dealing with language pairs written in different scripts. Combining it with a phrase-based statistical engine leads to significant improvements.

1 Introduction

If machine translation is to meet commercial needs, it must offer a sensible approach to translating terms. Currently, MT systems offer at best database management tools which allow a human (typically a translator, a terminologist or even the vendor of the system) to specify bilingual terminological entries. More advanced tools are meant to identify inconsistencies in terminological translations and might prove useful in controlled-language situations (Itagaki et al., 2007).

One approach to translate terms consists in using a domain-specific parallel corpus with standard alignment techniques (Brown et al., 1993) to *mine* new translations. Massive amounts of parallel data are certainly available in several pairs of languages for domains such as parliament debates or the like. However, having at our disposal a domain-specific (*e.g.* computer science) bitext with an adequate coverage is another issue. One might argue that domain-specific comparable (or perhaps unrelated) corpora are easier to acquire, in which case context-vector techniques (Rapp, 1995; Fung and McKeown, 1997) can be used to *identify* the translation of terms. We certainly agree with that point of view to a certain extent, but as discussed by Morin et al. (2007), for many specific domains and pairs of languages, such resources simply do not exist. Furthermore, the task of translation identification is more difficult and error-prone.

Analogical learning has recently regained some interest in the NLP community. Lepage and Denoual (2005) proposed a machine translation system entirely based on the concept of *formal analogy*, that is, analogy on forms. Stroppa and Yvon (2005) applied analogical learning to several morphological tasks also involving analogies on words. Langlais and Patry (2007) applied it to the task of translating unknown words in several European languages, an idea investigated as well by Denoual (2007) for a Japanese to English translation task.

In this study, we improve the state-of-the-art of analogical learning by (i) proposing a simple yet effective implementation of an analogical solver; (ii) proposing an efficient solution to the search issue embedded in analogical learning, (iii) investigating whether a classifier can be trained to recognize bad candidates produced by analogical learning. We evaluate our analogical engine on the task of translating terms of the medical domain; a domain well-known for its tendency to create new words, many of which being complex lexical constructions. Our experiments involve five language pairs, including languages with very different morphological systems.

Proceedings of the 12th Conference of the European Chapter of the ACL, pages 487–495,
Athens, Greece, 30 March – 3 April 2009. ©2009 Association for Computational Linguistics

In the remainder of this paper, we first present in Section 2 the principle of analogical learning. Practical issues in analogical learning are discussed in Section 3 along with our solutions. In Section 4, we report on experiments we conducted with our analogical device. We conclude this study and discuss future work in Section 5.

2 Analogical Learning

2.1 Definitions

A *proportional analogy*, or analogy for short, is a relation between four items noted $[x : y = z : t]$ which reads as "x is to y as z is to t". Among proportional analogies, we distinguish *formal analogies*, that is, those we can identify at a graphemic level, such as [*adrenergic beta-agonists*, *adrenergic beta-antagonists*, *adrenergic alpha-agonists*, *adrenergic alpha-antagonists*].

Formal analogies can be defined in terms of factorizations[1]. Let x be a string over an alphabet Σ, a *factorization* of x, noted f_X, is a sequence of n *factors* $f_X = (f_X^1, \ldots, f_X^n)$, such that $x = f_X^1 \odot f_X^2 \odot \ldots \odot f_X^n$, where $\odot$ denotes the concatenation operator. After (Stroppa and Yvon, 2005) we thus define a formal analogy as:

Definition 1 $\forall (x, y, z, t) \in {\Sigma^\star}^4$, $[x : y = z : t]$ ***iff*** *there exist factorizations* $(f_X, f_Y, f_Z, f_t) \in ({\Sigma^\star}^d)^4$ *of* (x, y, z, t) *such that,* $\forall i \in [1, d]$, $(f_Y^i, f_Z^i) \in \left\{(f_X^i, f_t^i), (f_t^i, f_X^i)\right\}$. *The smallest d for which this definition holds is called the degree of the analogy.*

Intuitively, this definition states that (x, y, z, t) are made up of a common set of alternating substrings. It is routine to check that it captures the exemplar analogy introduced above, based on the following set of factorizations:

$$\begin{array}{lcl} f_X & \equiv & (\text{adrenergic bet, a-agonists}) \\ f_Y & \equiv & (\text{adrenergic bet, a-antagonists}) \\ f_Z & \equiv & (\text{adrenergic alph, a-agonists}) \\ f_t & \equiv & (\text{adrenergic alph, a-antagonists}) \end{array}$$

As no smaller factorization can be found, the degree of this analogy is 2. In the sequel, we call an *analogical equation* an analogy where one item (usually the fourth) is missing and we note it $[x : y = z : ?]$.

[1]Factorizations of strings correspond to segmentations. We keep the former term, to emphasize the genericity of the definition, which remains valid for other algebraic structures, for which factorization and segmentation are no longer synonymous.

2.2 Analogical Inference

Let $\mathcal{L} = \{(i, o) \,|\, i \in \mathcal{I}, o \in \mathcal{O}\}$ be a learning set of observations, where $\mathcal{I}$ ($\mathcal{O}$) is the set of possible forms of the input (output) linguistic system under study. We denote $I(u)$ ($O(u)$) the projection of u into the input (output) space; that is, if $u = (i, o)$, then $I(u) \equiv i$ and $O(u) \equiv o$. For an incomplete observation $u = (i, ?)$, the inference procedure is:

1. building $\mathcal{E}_\mathcal{I}(u) = \{(x, y, z) \in \mathcal{L}^3 \mid [I(x) : I(y) = I(z) : I(u)]\}$, the set of input triplets that define an analogy with $I(u)$.
2. building $\mathcal{E}_\mathcal{O}(u) = \{o \in \mathcal{O} \mid \exists (x, y, z) \in \mathcal{E}_\mathcal{I}(u) \text{ s.t. } [O(x) : O(y) = O(z) : o]\}$ the set of solutions to the equations obtained by projecting the triplets of $\mathcal{E}_\mathcal{I}(u)$ into the output space.
3. selecting candidates among $\mathcal{E}_\mathcal{O}(u)$.

In the sequel, we distinguish the *generator* which implements the first two steps, from the *selector* which implements step 3.

To give an example, assume $\mathcal{L}$ contains the following entries: *(beeta-agonistit, adrenergic beta-agonists)*, *(beetasalpaajat, adrenergic beta-antagonists)* and *(alfa-agonistit, adrenergic alpha-agonists)*. We might translate the Finnish term *alfasalpaajat* into the English term *adrenergic alpha-antagonists* by 1) identifying the input triplet: *(beeta-agonistit, beetasalpaajat, alfa-agonistit)*; 2) projecting it into the equation [*adrenergic beta-agonists* : *adrenergic beta-antagonists* = *adrenergic alpha-agonists* : ?]; and solving it: *adrenergic alpha-antagonists* is one of its solutions.

During inference, analogies are recognized independently in the input and the output space, and nothing pre-establishes which subpart of one input form corresponds to which subpart of the output one. This "knowledge" is passively captured thanks to the inductive bias of the learning strategy (an analogy in the input space corresponds to one in the output space). Also worth mentioning, this procedure does not rely on any pre-defined notion of word. This might come at an advantage for languages that are hard to segment (Lepage and Lardilleux, 2007).

3 Practical issues

Each step of analogical learning, that is, *searching* for input triplets, *solving* output equations and *selecting* good candidates involves some practical issues. Since searching for input triplets might involve the need for solving (input) equations, we discuss the solver first.

3.1 The solver

Lepage (1998) proposed an algorithm for solving an analogical equation $[x : y = z : ?]$. An alignment between x and y and between x and z is first computed (by edit-distance) as illustrated in Figure 1. Then, the three strings are synchronized using x as a backbone of the synchronization. The algorithm can be seen as a deterministic finite-state machine where a state is defined by the two edit-operations being visited in the two tables. This is schematized by the two cursors in the figure. Two actions are allowed: `copy` one symbol from y or z into the solution and `move` one or both cursors.

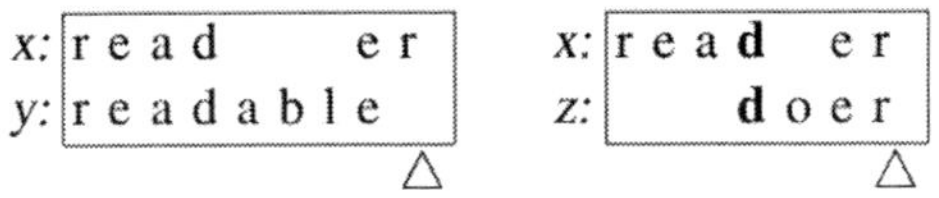

Figure 1: Illustration of the synchronization done by the solver described in (Lepage, 1998).

There are two things to realize with this algorithm. First, since several (minimal-cost) alignments can be found between two strings, several synchronizations are typically carried out while solving an equation, leading to (possibly many) different solutions. Indeed, in adverse situations, an exponential number of synchronizations will have to be computed. Second, the algorithm fails to deliver an expected form in a rather frequent situation where two identical symbols align fortuitously in two strings. This is for instance the case in our running example where the symbol *d* in *doer* aligns to the one in *reader*, which puzzles the synchronization. Indeed, *dabloe* is the only form proposed to [*reader* : *readable* = *doer* : ?], while the expected one is *doable*. The algorithm would have no problem, however, to produce the form *writable* out of the equation [*reader* : *readable* = *writer* : ?].

Yvon et al. (2004) proposed an analogical solver which is not exposed to the latter problem. It consists in building a finite state transducer which generates the solutions to $[x : y = z : ?]$ while recognizing the form x.

Theorem 1 *t is a solution to $[x : y = z : ?]$ iff t belongs to $\{y \circ z\} \backslash x$.*

shuffle and *complement* are two rational operations. The *shuffle* of two strings w and v, noted $w \circ v$, is the regular language containing the strings obtained by selecting (without replacement) alternatively in w and v, sequences of characters in a left-to-right manner. For instance, *spondyondontilalgiatis* and *ondspondonylaltitisgia* are two strings belonging to *spondylalgia* $\circ$ *ondontitis*). The *complementary set* of w with respect to v, noted $w \backslash v$, is the set of strings formed by removing from w, in a left-to-right manner, the symbols in v. For instance, *spondylitis* and *spydoniltis* are belonging to *spondyondontilalgiatis* $\backslash$ *ondontalgia*. Our implementation of the two rational operations are sketched in Algorithm 1.

Because the shuffle of two strings may contain an exponential number of elements with respect to the length of those strings, building such an automaton may face combinatorial problems. Our solution simply consists in randomly sampling strings in the shuffle set. Our solver, depicted in Algorithm 2, is thus controlled by a sampling size s, the impact of which is illustrated in Table 1. By increasing s, the solver generates more (mostly spurious) solutions, but also increases the relative frequency with which the expected output is generated. In practice, provided a large enough sampling size,[2] the expected form very often appears among the most frequent ones.

s	*nb*	(solution,frequency)		
10	11	(doable,7)	(dabloe,3)	(adbloe,3)
10^2	22	(doable,28)	(dabloe,21)	(abldoe,21)
10^3	29	(doable,333)	(dabloe,196)	(abldoe,164)

Table 1: The 3-most frequent solutions generated by our solver, for different sampling sizes s, for the equation [*reader* : *readable* = *doer* : ?]. *nb* indicates the number of (different) solutions generated. According to our definition, there are 32 distinct solutions to this equation. Note that our solver has no problem producing *doable*.

3.2 Searching for input triplets

A brute-force approach to identifying the input triplets that define an analogy with the incomplete observation $u = (t, ?)$ consists in enumerating triplets in the input space and checking for an

[2] We used s = 2 000 in this study.

```
function shuffle(y,z)
  Input: ⟨y, z⟩ two forms
  Output: a random word in y ∘ z
  if y = ϵ then
    return z
  else
    n ← rand(1,|y|)
    return y[1:n] . shuffle(z,y[n+1:])

function complementary(m,x,r,s)
  Input: m ∈ y ∘ z, x
  Output: the set m \ x
  if (m = ϵ) then
    if (x = ϵ) then
      s ← s ∪ r
  else
    complementary(m[2:],x,r.m[1],s)
    if m[1] = x[1] then
      complementary(m[2:],x[2:],r,s)
```

Algorithm 1: Simulation of the two rational operations required by the solver. $x[a{:}b]$ denotes the sequence of symbols x starting from index a to index b inclusive. $x[a{:}]$ denotes the suffix of x starting at index a.

analogical relation with t. This amounts to check $o(|\mathcal{I}|^3)$ analogies, which is manageable for toy problems only. Instead, Langlais and Patry (2007) proposed to solve analogical equations $[y : x = t : ?]$ for some pairs $\langle x, y\rangle$ belonging to the neighborhood[3] of $I(u)$, denoted $\mathcal{N}(t)$. Those solutions that belong to the input space are the z-forms retained;

$$\mathcal{E}_{\mathcal{I}}(u) = \{\ \langle x,y,z\rangle\ :\ \ x \in \mathcal{N}(t)\ ,\ y \in \mathcal{N}(x),\ z \in [y : x = t : ?] \cap \mathcal{I}\ \}$$

This strategy (hereafter named LP) directly follows from a symmetrical property of an analogy ($[x : y = z : t] \Leftrightarrow [y : x = t : z]$), and reduces the search procedure to the resolution of a number of analogical equations which is quadratic with the number of pairs $\langle x, y\rangle$ sampled.

We found this strategy to be of little use for input spaces larger than a few tens of thousands forms. To solve this problem, we exploit a property on symbol counts that an analogical relation must fulfill (Lepage, 1998):

$$[x : y = z : t] \Rightarrow |x|_c + |t|_c = |y|_c + |z|_c \quad \forall c \in \mathcal{A}$$

[3]The authors proposed to sample x and y among the closest forms in terms of edit-distance to I(u).

```
function solver(⟨x, y, z⟩, s)
  Input: ⟨x, y, z⟩, a triplet, s the sampling size
  Output: a set of solutions to [x : y = z : ?]
  sol ← ϕ
  for i ← 1 to s do
    ⟨a, b⟩ ← odd(rand(0, 1))? ⟨z, y⟩ : ⟨y, z⟩
    m ← shuffle(a,b)
    c ← complementary(m,x,ϵ,{})
    sol ← sol ∪ c
  return sol
```

Algorithm 2: A Stroppa&Yvon flavored solver. $\mathtt{rand}(a, b)$ returns a random integer between a and b (included). The ternary operator `?:` is to be understood as in the C language.

where $\mathcal{A}$ is the alphabet on which the forms are built, and $|x|_c$ stands for the number of occurrences of symbol c in x.

Our search strategy (named TC) begins by selecting an x-form in the input space. This enforces a set of necessary constraints on the counts of characters that any two forms y and z must satisfy for $[x : y = z : t]$ to be true. By considering all forms x in turn,[4] we collect a set of candidate triplets for t. A verification of those that define with t an analogy must then be carried out. Formally, we built:

$$\mathcal{E}_{\mathcal{I}}(u) = \{\ \langle x,y,z\rangle\ :\ \ x \in \mathcal{I},\ \langle y,z\rangle \in \mathcal{C}(\langle x,t\rangle),\ [x : y = z : t]\ \}$$

where $\mathcal{C}(\langle x,t\rangle)$ denotes the set of pairs $\langle y,z\rangle$ which satisfy the count property.

This strategy will only work if (i) the number of quadruplets to check is much smaller than the number of triplets we can form in the input space (which happens to be the case in practice), and if (ii) we can efficiently identify the pairs $\langle y,z\rangle$ that satisfy a set of constraints on character counts. To this end, we proposed in (Langlais and Yvon, 2008) to organize the input space into a data structure which supports efficient runtime retrieval.

3.3 The selector

Step 3 of analogical learning consists in selecting one or several solutions from the set of candidate forms produced by the generator. We trained in a supervised manner a binary classifier to distinguish good translation candidates (as defined by

[4]Anagram forms do not have to be considered separately.

a reference) from spurious ones. We applied to this end the *voted-perceptron* algorithm described by Freund and Schapire (1999). Online voted-perceptrons have been reported to work well in a number of NLP tasks (Collins, 2002; Liang et al., 2006). Training such a classifier is mainly a matter of feature engineering. An *example* e is a pair of source-target analogical relations $(r, \hat{r})$ identified by the generator, and which elects $\hat{t}$ as a translation for the term t:

$$e \equiv (r, \hat{r}) \equiv ([x : y = z : t], [\hat{x} : \hat{y} = \hat{z} : \hat{t}])$$

where $\hat{x}$, $\hat{y}$, and $\hat{z}$ are respectively the projections of the source terms x, y and z. We investigated many features including (i) the degree of r and $\hat{r}$, (ii) the frequency with which a form is generated,[5] (iii) length ratios between t and $\hat{t}$, (iv) likelihoods scores (min, max, avg.) computed by a character-based n-gram model trained on a large general corpus (without overlap to DEV or TRAIN), etc.

4 Experiments

4.1 Calibrating the engine

We compared the two aforementioned searching strategies on a task of identifying triplets in an input space of French words for 1 000 randomly selected test words. We considered input spaces of various sizes. The results are reported in Table 2. TC clearly outperforms LP by systematically identifying more triplets in much less time. For the largest input space of 84 000 forms, TC could identify an average of 746 triplets for 946 test words in 1.2 seconds, while the best compromise we could settle with LP allows the identification of 56 triplets on average for 889 words in 6.3 seconds on average. Note that in this experiment, LP was calibrated for each input space so that the best compromise between recall ($\%s$) and speed could be found. Reducing the size of the neighborhood in LP improves computation time, but significantly affects recall. In the following, we only consider the TC search strategy.

4.2 Experimental Protocol

Datasets The data we used in this study comes from the Medical Subject Headings (MeSH) thesaurus. This thesaurus is used by the US National Library of Medicine to index the biomedical scientific literature in the MEDLINE database.[6] Its preferred terms are called "Main Headings". We collected pairs of source and target Main Headings (TTY = 'MH') with the same MeSH identifiers (SDUI).

	s	$\%s$	(s)	s	$\%s$	(s)	s	$\%s$	(s)
TC	34	83.1	0.2	261	94.1	0.5	746	96.4	1.2
LP	17	71.7	7.4	46	85.0	7.6	56	88.9	6.3
$\|\mathcal{I}\|$	20 000			50 000			84 076		

Table 2: Average number s of input analogies found over 1 000 test words as a function of the size of the input space. $\%s$ stands for the percentage of source forms for which (at least) one source triplet is found; and (s) indicates the average time (counted in seconds) to treat one form.

We considered five language pairs with three relatively close European languages (English-French, English-Spanish and English-Swedish), a more distant one (English-Finnish) and one pair involving different scripts (English-Russian).[7]

The material was split in three randomly selected parts, so that the development and test material contain exactly 1 000 terms each. The characteristics of this material are reported in Table 3. For the Finnish-English and Swedish-English language pairs, the ratio of uni-terms in the Foreign language ($u_f\%$) is twice the ratio of uni-terms in the English counterpart. This is simply due to the agglutinative nature of these two languages. For instance, according to MeSH, the English multi-term *speech articulation tests* corresponds to the Finnish uni-term *ääntämiskokeet* and to the Swedish one *artikulationstester.* The ratio of out-of-vocabulary forms (space-separated words unseen in TRAIN) in the TEST material is rather high: between 36% and 68% for all Foreign-to-English translation directions, but Finnish-to-English, where surprisingly, only 6% of the word forms are unknown.

Evaluation metrics For each experimental condition, we compute the following measures:

Coverage the fraction of input words for which the system can generate translations. If N_t words receive translations among N, coverage is N_t/N.

[5] A form $\hat{t}$ may be generated thanks to many examples.

[6] The MeSH thesaurus and its translations are included in the UMLS Metathesaurus.

[7] Russian MeSH is normally written in Cyrillic, but some terms are simply English terms written in uppercase Latin script (e.g., *ACHROMOBACTER* for English *Achromobacter*). We removed those terms.

f	TRAIN nb	$u_f\%$	$u_e\%$	TEST nb	DEV $u_f\%$	$u_f\%$	TEST oov%
FI	19 787	63.7	33.7	1 000	64.2	64.0	5.7
FR	17 230	29.8	29.3	1 000	30.8	28.3	36.3
RU	21 407	38.6	38.6	1 000	38.5	40.2	44.4
SP	19 021	31.1	31.1	1 000	31.7	33.3	36.6
SW	17 090	67.9	32.5	1 000	67.4	67.9	68.4

Table 3: Main characteristics of our datasets. nb indicates the number of pairs of terms in a bitext, $u_f\%$ ($u_e\%$) stands for the percentage of uniterms in the *Foreign* (English) part. oov% indicates the percentage of out-of-vocabulary forms (space-separated forms of TEST unseen in TRAIN).

	Cov	P_1	R_1	P_{100}	R_{100}	R_∞
→ FI	**47.1**	*31.6*	14.9	*57.7*	27.2	31.9
FR	41.2	35.4	*14.6*	60.4	24.9	*26.5*
RU	46.2	40.5	18.7	69.9	32.3	34.8
SP	47.0	41.5	19.5	69.1	**32.5**	**35.9**
SW	42.8	36.0	15.4	66.8	28.6	31.9
← FI	44.8	36.6	16.4	66.7	29.9	33.2
FR	*38.5*	47.0	18.1	69.9	*26.9*	29.4
RU	42.1	**49.4**	**20.8**	70.3	29.6	32.3
SP	42.6	47.7	20.3	**75.1**	32.0	33.7
SW	44.6	40.8	18.2	69.5	31.0	32.9

Table 4: Main characteristics of the generator, as a function of the translation directions (TEST).

Precision among the N_t words for which the system proposes an answer, precision is the proportion of those for which a correct translation is output. Depending on the number of output translations k that one is willing to examine, a correct translation will be output for N_k input words. Precision at rank k is thus defined as $P_k = N_k/N_t$.

Recall is the proportion of the N input words for which a correct translation is output. Recall at rank k is defined as $R_k = N_k/N$.

In all our experiments, candidate translations are sorted in decreasing order of frequency with which they were generated.

4.3 The generator

The performances of the generator on the 10 translation sessions are reported in Table 4. The coverage of the generator varies between 38.5% (French-to-English) and 47.1% (English-to-Finnish), which is rather low. In most cases, the silence of the generator is due to a failure to identify analogies in the input space (step 1). The last column of Table 4 reports the maximum recall we can obtain if we consider all the candidates output by the generator. The relative accuracy of the generator, expressed by the ratio of R_∞ to cov, ranges from 64.3% (English-French) to 79.1% (Spanish-to-English), for an average value of 73.8% over all translation directions. This roughly means that one fourth of the test terms with at least one solution do not contain the reference.

Overall, we conclude that analogical learning offers comparable performances for all translation directions, although some fluctuations are observed. We do not observe that the approach is affected by language pairs which do not share the same script (Russian/English). The best (worse) case (as far as R_∞ is concerned) corresponds to translating into Spanish (French).

Admittedly, the largest recall and R_∞ values reported in Table 4 are disappointing. Clearly, for analogical learning to work efficiently, enough linguistic phenomena must be attested in the TRAIN material. To illustrate this, we collected for the Spanish-English language pair a set of medical terms from the Medical Drug Regulatory Activities thesaurus (MedDRA) which contains roughly three times more terms than the Spanish-English material used in this study. This extra material allows to raise the coverage to 73.4% (Spanish to English) and 79.7% (English to Spanish), an absolute improvement of more than 30%.

4.4 The selector

We trained our classifiers on the several millions of *examples* generated while translating the development material. Since we considered numerous feature representations in this study, this implies saving many huge datafiles on disk. In order to save some space, we decided to remove forms that were generated less than 3 times.[8] Each classifier was trained using 20 epochs.

It is important to note that we face a very unbalanced task. For instance, for the English to Finnish task, the generator produces no less than 2.7 millions of examples, among which only 4 150 are positive ones. Clearly, classifying all the examples as negative will achieve a very high classification accuracy, but will be of no practical use. Therefore, we measure the ability of a classifier to iden-

[8] Averaged over all translation directions, this incurs an absolute reduction of the coverage of 3.4%.

	FI→EN		FR→EN		RU→EN		SP→EN		SW→EN	
	p	r	p	r	p	r	p	r	p	r
`argmax-f1`	41.3	56.7	46.7	63.9	48.1	65.6	49.2	63.4	43.2	61.0
`s-best`	53.6	61.3	57.5	68.4	61.9	66.7	64.3	70.0	53.1	64.4

Table 5: Precision (p) and recall (r) of some classifiers on the TEST material.

tify the few positive *forms* among the set of candidates. We measure *precision* as the percentage of forms selected by the classifier that are sanctioned by the reference lexicon, and *recall* as the percentage of forms selected by the classifier over the total number of sanctioned forms that the classifier could possibly select. (Recall that the generator often fails to produce oracle forms.)

The performance measured on the TEST material of the best classifier we monitored on DEV are reported in Table 5 for the Foreign-to-English translation directions (we made consistent observations on the reverse directions). For comparison purposes, we implemented a baseline classifier (lines `argmax-f1`) which selects the most-frequent candidate form. This is the selector used as a default in several studies on analogical learning (Lepage and Denoual, 2005; Stroppa and Yvon, 2005). The baseline identifies between 56.7% to 65.6% of the sanctioned forms, at precision rates ranging from 41.3% to 49.2%. We observe for all translation directions that the best classifier we trained systematically outperforms this baseline, both in terms of precision and recall.

4.4.1 The overall system

Table 6 shows the overall performance of the analogical translation device in terms of precision, recall and coverage rates as defined in Section 4.2. Overall, our best configuration (the one embedding the `s-best` classifier) translates between 19.3% and 22.5% of the test material, with a precision ranging from 50.4% to 63.2%. This is better than the variant which always proposes the most frequent generated form (`argmax-f1`). Allowing more answers increases both precision and recall. If we allow up to 10 candidates per source term, the analogical translator translates one fourth of the terms (26.1%) with a precision of 70.9%, averaged over all translation directions. The `oracle` variant, which looks at the reference for selecting the good candidates produced by the generator, gives an upper bound of the performance that could be obtained with our approach: less than a third of the source terms can be translated correctly. Recall however that increasing the TRAIN material leads to drastic improvements in coverage.

4.5 Comparison with a PB-SMT engine

To put these figures in perspective, we measured the performance of a phrase-based statistical MT (PB-SMT) engine trained to handle the same translation task. We trained a phrase table on TRAIN, using the standard approach.[9] However, because of the small training size, and the rather huge OOV rate of the translation tasks we address, we did not train translation models on word-tokens, but at the character level. Therefore a phrase is indeed a sequence of characters. This idea has been successively investigated in a Catalan-to-Spanish translation task by Vilar et al. (2007). We tuned the 8 coefficients of the so-called log-linear combination maximized at decoding time on the first 200 pairs of terms of the DEV corpora. On the DEV set, BLEU scores[10] range from 67.2 (English-to-Finnish) to 77.0 (Russian-to-English).

Table 7 reports the precision and recall of both translation engines. Note that because the SMT engine always propose a translation, its precision equals its recall. First, we observe that the precision of the SMT engine is not high (between 17% and 31%), which demonstrates the difficulty of the task. The analogical device does better for all translation directions (see Table 6), but at a much lower recall, remaining silent more than half of the time. This suggests that combining both systems could be advantageous. To verify this, we ran a straightforward combination: whenever the analogical device produces a translation, we pick it; otherwise, the statistical output is considered. The gains of the resulting system over the SMT alone are reported in column ΔB. Averaged over

[9] We used the scripts distributed by Philipp Koehn to train the phrase-table, and `Pharaoh` (Koehn, 2004) for producing the translations.

[10] We computed BLEU scores at the character level.

	k	FI→EN		FR→EN		RU→EN		SP→EN		SW→EN	
		P_k	R_k	P_k	R_k	P_k	R_k	P_k	R_k	P_k	R_k
`argmax-f`	1	41.3	17.3	46.7	16.8	47.8	18.6	48.7	19.2	43.4	18.1
	10	61.6	25.8	62.8	22.6	61.7	24.0	69.3	27.3	62.1	25.9
`s-best`	1	53.5	20.8	56.9	19.3	58.5	20.3	63.2	22.5	50.4	21
	10	69.4	27.0	69.0	23.4	71.8	24.9	78.4	27.9	65.7	27.4
oracle	1	100	30.5	100	26.3	100	28.5	100	30.6	100	29.5

Table 6: Precision and recall at rank 1 and 10 for the Foreign-to-English translation tasks (TEST).

all translation directions, BLEU scores increase on TEST from 66.2 to 71.5, that is, an absolute improvement of 5.3 points.

	→ EN		← EN	
	P_{smt}	ΔB	P_{smt}	ΔB
FI	20.2	+7.4	21.6	+6.4
FR	19.9	+5.3	17.0	+6.0
RU	24.1	+3.1	28.0	+6.4
SP	22.1	+4.9	26.4	+5.5
SW	25.9	+4.2	31.6	+3.2

Table 7: Translation performances on TEST. P_{smt} stands for the precision and recall of the SMT engine. ΔB indicates the absolute gain in BLEU score of the combined system.

We noticed a tendency of the statistical engine to produce literal translations; a default the analogical device does not show. For instance, the Spanish term *instituciones de atención ambulatoria* is translated word for word by `Pharaoh` into *institutions, atention ambulatory* while analogical learning produces *ambulatory care facilities*. We also noticed that analogical learning sometimes produces wrong translations based on morphological regularities that are applied blindly. This is, for instance, the case in a Russian/English example where *mouthal manifestations* is produced, instead of *oral manifestations*.

5 Discussion and future work

In this study, we proposed solutions to practical issues involved in analogical learning. A simple yet effective implementation of a solver is described. A search strategy is proposed which outperforms the one described in (Langlais and Patry, 2007). Also, we showed that a classifier trained to select good candidate translations outperforms the *most-frequently-generated* heuristic used in several works on analogical learning.

Our analogical device was used to translate medical terms in different language pairs. The approach rates comparably across the 10 translation directions we considered. In particular, we do not see a drop in performance when translating into a morphology rich language (such as Finnish), or when translating into languages with different scripts. Averaged over all translation directions, the best variant could translate in first position 21% of the terms with a precision of 57%, while at best, one could translate 30% of the terms with a perfect precision. We show that the analogical translations are of better quality than those produced by a phrase-based engine trained at the character level, albeit with much lower recall. A straightforward combination of both approaches led an improvement of 5.3 BLEU points over the SMT alone. Better SMT performance could be obtained with a system based on morphemes, see for instance (Toutanova et al., 2008). However, since lists of morphemes specific to the medical domain do not exist for all the languages pairs we considered here, unsupervised methods for acquiring morphemes would be necessary, which is left as a future work. In any case, this comparison is meaningful, since both the SMT and the analogical device work at the character level.

This work opens up several avenues. First, we will test our approach on terminologies from different domains, varying the size of the training material. Second, analyzing the segmentation induced by analogical learning would be interesting. Third, we need to address the problem of combining the translations produced by analogy into a front-end statistical translation engine. Last, there is no reason to constrain ourselves to translating terminology only. We targeted this task in the first place, because terminology typically plugs translation systems, but we think that analogical learning could be useful for translating infrequent entities.

References

P. F. Brown, S. A. Della Pietra, V. J. Della Pietra, and R. L. Mercer. 1993. The mathematics of statistical machine translation: Parameter estimation. *Computational Linguistics*, 19(2):263–311.

M. Collins. 2002. Discriminative training methods for hidden markov models: theory and experiments with perceptron algorithms. In *EMNLP*, pages 1–8, Morristown, NJ, USA.

E. Denoual. 2007. Analogical translation of unknown words in a statistical machine translation framework. In *MT Summit, XI*, pages 10–14, Copenhagen.

Y. Freund and R. E. Schapire. 1999. Large margin classification using the perceptron algorithm. *Mach. Learn.*, 37(3):277–296.

P. Fung and K. McKeown. 1997. Finding terminology translations from non-parallel corpora. In *5th Annual Workshop on Very Large Corpora*, pages 192–202, Hong Kong.

M. Itagaki, T. Aikawa, and X. He. 2007. Automatic validation of terminology translation consistency with statistical method. In *MT Summit XI*, pages 269–274, Copenhagen, Denmark.

P. Koehn. 2004. Pharaoh: A beam search decoder for phrase-based statistical machine translation models. In *AMTA*, pages 115–124, Washington, DC, USA.

P. Langlais and A. Patry. 2007. Translating unknown words by analogical learning. In *EMNLP-CoNLL*, pages 877–886, Prague, Czech Republic.

P. Langlais and F. Yvon. 2008. Scaling up analogical learning. In *22nd International Conference on Computational Linguistics (COLING 2008)*, pages 51–54, Manchester, United Kingdom.

Y. Lepage and E. Denoual. 2005. ALEPH: an EBMT system based on the preservation of proportionnal analogies between sentences across languages. In *International Workshop on Statistical Language Translation (IWSLT)*, Pittsburgh, PA, October.

Y. Lepage and A. Lardilleux. 2007. The GREYC Machine Translation System for the IWSLT 2007 Evaluation Campaign. In *IWLST*, pages 49–53, Trento, Italy.

Y. Lepage. 1998. Solving analogies on words: an algorithm. In *COLING-ACL*, pages 728–734, Montreal, Canada.

P. Liang, A. Bouchard-Côté, D. Klein, and B. Taskar. 2006. An end-to-end discriminative approach to machine translation. In *21st COLING and 44th ACL*, pages 761–768, Sydney, Australia.

E. Morin, B. Daille, K. Takeuchi, and K. Kageura. 2007. Bilingual terminology mining - using brain, not brawn comparable corpora. In *45th ACL*, pages 664–671, Prague, Czech Republic.

R. Rapp. 1995. Identifying word translation in non-parallel texts. In *33rd ACL*, pages 320–322, Cambridge,Massachusetts, USA.

N. Stroppa and F. Yvon. 2005. An analogical learner for morphological analysis. In *9th CoNLL*, pages 120–127, Ann Arbor, MI.

K Toutanova, H. Suzuki, and A. Ruopp. 2008. Applying morphology generation models to machine translation. In *ACL-8 HLT*, pages 514–522, Colombus, Ohio, USA.

D. Vilar, J. Peter, and H. Ney. 2007. Can we translate letters? In *Proceedings of the Second Workshop on Statistical Machine Translation*, pages 33–39, Prague, Czech Republic, June.

F. Yvon, N. Stroppa, A. Delhay, and L. Miclet. 2004. Solving analogical equations on words. Technical Report D005, École Nationale Supérieure des Télécommunications, Paris, France, July.

Language-independent bilingual terminology extraction from a multilingual parallel corpus

Els Lefever[1,2], Lieve Macken[1,2] and Veronique Hoste[1,2]

[1]LT3
School of Translation Studies
University College Ghent
Groot-Brittanniëlaan 45
9000 Gent, Belgium

[2]Department of Applied Mathematics
and Computer Science
Ghent University
Krijgslaan281-S9
9000 Gent, Belgium

{Els.Lefever, Lieve.Macken, Veronique.Hoste}@hogent.be

Abstract

We present a language-pair independent terminology extraction module that is based on a sub-sentential alignment system that links linguistically motivated phrases in parallel texts. Statistical filters are applied on the bilingual list of candidate terms that is extracted from the alignment output.

We compare the performance of both the alignment and terminology extraction module for three different language pairs (French-English, French-Italian and French-Dutch) and highlight language-pair specific problems (e.g. different compounding strategy in French and Dutch).

Comparisons with standard terminology extraction programs show an improvement of up to 20% for bilingual terminology extraction and competitive results (85% to 90% accuracy) for monolingual terminology extraction, and reveal that the linguistically based alignment module is particularly well suited for the extraction of complex multiword terms.

1 Introduction

Automatic Term Recognition (ATR) systems are usually categorized into two main families. On the one hand, the linguistically-based or rule-based approaches use linguistic information such as PoS tags, chunk information, etc. to filter out stop words and restrict candidate terms to predefined syntactic patterns (Ananiadou, 1994), (Dagan and Church, 1994). On the other hand, the statistical corpus-based approaches select n-gram sequences as candidate terms that are filtered by means of statistical measures. More recent ATR systems use hybrid approaches that combine both linguistic and statistical information (Frantzi and Ananiadou, 1999).

Most bilingual terminology extraction systems first identify candidate terms in the source language based on predefined source patterns, and then select translation candidates for these terms in the target language (Kupiec, 1993).

We present an alternative approach that generates candidate terms directly from the aligned words and phrases in our parallel corpus. In a second step, we use frequency information of a general purpose corpus and the n-gram frequencies of the automotive corpus to determine the term specificity. Our approach is more flexible in the sense that we do not first generate candidate terms based on language-dependent predefined PoS patterns (e.g. for French, N N, N Prep N, and N Adj are typical patterns), but immediately link linguistically motivated phrases in our parallel corpus based on lexical correspondences and syntactic similarity.

This article reports on the term extraction experiments for 3 language pairs, i.e. French-Dutch, French-English and French-Italian. The focus was on the extraction of automative lexicons.

The remainder of this paper is organized as follows: Section 2 describes the corpus. In Section 3 we present our linguistically-based sub-sentential alignment system and in Section 4 we describe how we generate and filter our list of candidate terms. We compare the performance of our system with both bilingual and monolingual state-of-the-art terminology extraction systems. Section 5 concludes this paper.

Proceedings of the 12th Conference of the European Chapter of the ACL, pages 496–504,
Athens, Greece, 30 March – 3 April 2009. ©2009 Association for Computational Linguistics

2 Corpus

The focus of this research project was on the automatic extraction of 20 bilingual automative lexicons. All work was carried out in the framework of a customer project for a major French automotive company. The final goal of the project is to improve vocabulary consistency in technical texts across the 20 languages in the customer's portfolio. The French database contains about 400,000 entries (i.e. sentences and parts of sentences with an average length of 9 words) and the translation percentage of the database into 19 languages depends on the target market.

For the development of the alignment and terminology extraction module, we created three parallel corpora (Italian, English, Dutch) with French as a central language. Figures about the size of each parallel corpus can be found in table 1.

	Target Lang.	# Sentence pairs	# words
French	Italian	364,221	6,408,693
French	English	363,651	7,305,151
French	Dutch	364,311	7,100,585

Table 1: Number of sentence pairs and total number of words in the three parallel corpora

2.1 Preprocessing

We PoS-tagged and lemmatized the French, English and Italian corpora with the freely available TreeTagger tool (Schmid, 1994) and we used TadPole (Van den Bosch et al., 2007) to annotate the Dutch corpus.

In a next step, chunk information was added by a rule-based language-independent chunker (Macken et al., 2008) that contains distituency rules, which implies that chunk boundaries are added between two PoS codes that cannot occur in the same constituent.

2.2 Test and development corpus

As we presume that sentence length has an impact on the alignment performance, and thus on term extraction, we created three test sets with varying sentence lengths. We distinguished short sentences (2-7 words), medium-length sentences (8-19 words) and long sentences (> 19 words). Each test corpus contains approximately 9,000 words; the number of sentence pairs per test set can be found in table 2. We also created a development corpus with sentences of varying length to debug the linguistic processing and the alignment module as well as to define the thresholds for the statistical filtering of the candidate terms (see 4.1).

	# Words	# Sentence pairs
Short (< 8 words)	+- 9,000	823
Medium (8-19 words)	+- 9,000	386
Long (> 19 words)	+- 9,000	180
Development corpus	+-5,000	393

Table 2: Number of words and sentence pairs in the test and development corpora

3 Sub-sentential alignment module

As the basis for our terminology extraction system, we used the sub-sentential alignment system of (Macken and Daelemans, 2009) that links linguistically motivated phrases in parallel texts based on lexical correspondences and syntactic similarity. In the first phase of this system, *anchor chunks* are linked, i.e. chunks that can be linked with a very high precision. We think these anchor chunks offer a valid and language-independent alternative to identify candidate terms based on predefined PoS patterns. As the automotive corpus contains rather literal translations, we expect that a high percentage of anchor chunks can be retrieved.

Although the architecture of the sub-sentential alignment system is language-independent, some language-specific resources are used. First, a bilingual lexicon to generate the lexical correspondences and second, tools to generate additional linguistic information (PoS tagger, lemmatizer and a chunker). The sub-sentential alignment system takes as input sentence-aligned texts, together with the additional linguistic annotations for the source and the target texts.

The source and target sentences are divided into chunks based on PoS information, and lexical correspondences are retrieved from a bilingual dictionary. In order to extract bilingual dictionaries from the three parallel corpora, we used the Perl implementation of IBM Model One that is part of the Microsoft Bilingual Sentence Aligner (Moore, 2002).

In order to link chunks based on lexical clues and chunk similarity, the following steps are taken for each sentence pair:

1. Creation of the lexical link matrix

2. Linking chunks based on lexical correspondences and chunk similarity

3. Linking remaining chunks

3.1 Lexical Link Matrix

For each source and target word, all translations for the word form and the lemma are retrieved from the bilingual dictionary. In the process of building the lexical link matrix, function words are neglected. For all content words, a lexical link is created if a source word occurs in the set of possible translations of a target word, or if a target word occurs in the set of possible translations of the source words. Identical strings in source and target language are also linked.

3.2 Linking Anchor chunks

Candidate anchor chunks are selected based on the information available in the lexical link matrix. The candidate target chunk is built by concatenating all target chunks from a *begin index* until an *end index*. The begin index points to the first target chunk with a lexical link to the source chunk under consideration. The end index points to the last target chunk with a lexical link to the source chunk under consideration. This way, 1:1 and 1:n candidate target chunks are built. The process of selecting candidate chunks as described above, is performed a second time starting from the target sentence. This way, additional n:1 candidates are constructed. For each selected candidate pair, a *similarity test* is performed. Chunks are considered to be similar if at least a certain percentage of words of source and target chunk(s) are either linked by means of a lexical link or can be linked on the basis of corresponding part-of-speech codes. The percentage of words that have to be linked was empirically set at 85%.

3.3 Linking Remaining Chunks

In a second step, chunks consisting of one function word – mostly punctuation marks and conjunctions – are linked based on corresponding part-of-speech codes if their left or right neighbour on the diagonal is an anchor chunk. Corresponding final punctuation marks are also linked.

In a final step, additional candidates are constructed by selecting non-anchor chunks in the source and target sentence that have corresponding left and right anchor chunks as neigbours. The anchor chunks of the first step are used as contextual information to link n:m chunks or chunks for which no lexical link was found in the lexical link matrix.

In Figure 1, the chunks [Fr: gradient] – [En: gradient] and the final punctuation mark have been retrieved in the first step as anchor chunk. In the last step, the n:m chunk [Fr: de remontée pédale d' embrayage] – [En: of rising of the clutch pedal] is selected as candidate anchor chunk because it is enclosed within anchor chunks.

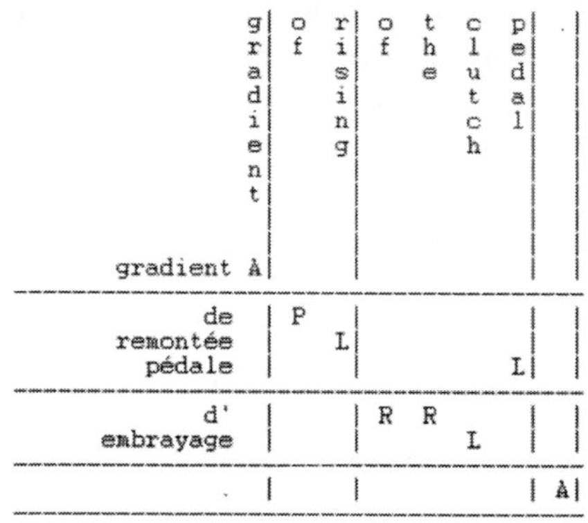

Figure 1: n:m candidate chunk: 'A' stands for anchor chunks, 'L' for lexical links, 'P' for words linked on the basis of corresponding PoS codes and 'R' for words linked by language-dependent rules.

As the contextual clues (the left and right neigbours of the additional candidate chunks are anchor chunks) provide some extra indication that the chunks can be linked, the similarity test for the final candidates was somewhat relaxed: the percentage of words that have to be linked was lowered to 0.80 and a more relaxed PoS matching function was used.

3.4 Evaluation

To test our alignment module, we manually indicated all translational correspondences in the three test corpora. We used the evaluation methodology of Och and Ney (2003) to evaluate the system's performance. They distinguished *sure* alignments (S) and *possible* alignments (P) and introduced the following redefined precision and recall measures (where A refers to the set of alignments):

$$precision = \frac{|A \cap P|}{|A|}, recall = \frac{|A \cap S|}{|S|} \quad (1)$$

and the alignment error rate (AER):

$$AER(S, P; A) = 1 - \frac{|A \cap P| + |A \cap S|}{|A| + |S|} \quad (2)$$

Table 3 shows the alignment results for the three language pairs. (Macken et al., 2008) showed that the results for French-English were competitive to state-of-the-art alignment systems.

	SHORT			MEDIUM			LONG		
	p	r	e	p	r	e	p	r	e
Italian	.99	.93	.04	.95	.89	.08	.95	.89	.07
English	.97	.91	.06	.95	.85	.10	.92	.85	.12
Dutch	.96	.83	.11	.87	.73	.20	.87	.67	.24

Table 3: Precision (p), recall (r) and alignment error rate (e) for our sub-sentential alignment system evaluated on French-Italian, French-English and French-Dutch

As expected, the results show that the alignment quality is closely related to the similarity between languages. As shown in example (1), Italian and French are syntactically almost identical – and hence easier to align, English and French are still close but show some differences (e.g different compounding strategy and word order) and French and Dutch present a very different language structure (e.g. in Dutch the different compound parts are not separated by spaces, *separable verbs*, i.e. verbs with prefixes that are stripped off, occur frequently (*losmaken* as an infinitive versus *maak los* in the conjugated forms) and a different word order is adopted).

(1) Fr: déclipper le renvoi de ceinture de sécurité.
(En: unclip the mounting of the belt of safety)
It: sganciare il dispositivo di riavvolgimento della cintura di sicurezza.
(En: unclip the mounting of the belt of satefy)
En: unclip the seat belt mounting.
Du: maak de oprolautomaat van de autogordel los.
(En: clip the mounting of the seat-belt un)

We tried to improve the low recall for French-Dutch by adding a decompounding module to our alignment system. In case the target word does not have a lexical correspondence in the source sentence, we decompose the Dutch word into its meaningful parts and look for translations of the compound parts. This implies that, without decompounding, in example 2 only the correspondences *doublure – binnenpaneel*, *arc – dakversteviging* and *arrière – achter* will be found. By decomposing the compound into its meaningful parts (binnenpaneel = binnen + paneel, dakversteviging = dak + versteviging) and retrieving the lexical links for the compound parts, we were able to link the missing correspondence: *pavillon – dakversteviging*.

(2) Fr: doublure arc pavillon arrière.
(En: rear roof arch lining)
Du: binnenpaneel dakversteviging achter.

We experimented with the decompounding module of (Vandeghinste, 2008), which is based on the Celex lexical database (Baayen et al., 1993). The module, however, did not adapt well to the highly technical automotive domain, which is reflected by its low recall and the low confidence values for many technical terms. In order to adapt the module to the automotive domain, we implemented a domain-dependent extension to the decompounding module on the basis of the development corpus. This was done by first running the decompounding module on the Dutch sentences to construct a list with possible *compound heads*, being valid compound parts in Dutch. This list was updated by inspecting the decompounding results on the development corpus. While decomposing, we go from right to left and strip off the longest valid part that occurs in our preconstructed list with compound parts and we repeat this process on the remaining part of the word until we reach the beginning of the word.

Table 4 shows the impact of the decompounding module, which is more prominent for short and medium sentences than for long sentences. A superficial error analysis revealed that long sentences combine a lot of other French – Dutch alignment difficulties next to the decompounding problem (e.g. different word order and separable verbs).

	SHORT			MEDIUM			LONG		
	p	r	e	p	r	e	p	r	e
Dutch									
no_dec	.95	.76	.16	.88	.67	.24	.88	.64	.26
dec	.96	.83	.11	.87	.73	.20	.87	.67	.24

Table 4: Precision (p), recall (r) and alignment error rate (e) for French-Dutch without and with decompounding information

4 Term extraction module

As described in Section 1, we generate candidate terms from the aligned phrases. We believe these anchor chunks offer a more flexible approach because the method is language-pair independent and is not restricted to a predefined set of PoS patterns to identify valid candidate terms. In a second step, we use a general-purpose corpus and the n-gram frequency of the automotive corpus to determine the specificity of the candidate terms.

The candidate terms are generated in several steps, as illustrated below for example (3).

(3) Fr: Tableau de commande de climatisation automatique

En: Automatic air conditioning control panel

1. Selection of all anchor chunks (minimal chunks that could be linked together) and lexical links within the anchor chunks:

tableau de commande	control panel
climatisation	air conditioning
commande	control
tableau	panel

2. combine each NP + PP chunk:

commande de climatisation automatique	automatic air conditioning control
tableau de commande de climatisation automatique	automatic air conditioning control panel

3. strip off the adjectives from the anchor chunks:

commande de climatisation	air conditioning control
tableau de commande de climatisation	air conditioning control panel

4.1 Filtering candidate terms

To filter our candidate terms, we keep following criteria in mind:

- each entry in the extracted lexicon should refer to an object or action that is relevant for the domain (notion of *termhood* that is used to express "the degree to which a linguistic unit is related to domain-specific context" (Kageura and Umino, 1996))
- multiword terms should present a high degree of cohesiveness (notion of *unithood* that expresses the "degree of strength or stability of syntagmatic combinations or collocations" (Kageura and Umino, 1996))
- all term pairs should contain valid translation pairs (translation quality is also taken into consideration)

To measure the termhood criterion and to filter out general vocabulary words, we applied Log-Likelihood filters on the French single-word terms. In order to filter on low unithood values, we calculated the Mutual Expectation Measure for the multiword terms in both source and target language.

4.1.1 Log-Likelihood Measure

The Log-Likehood measure (LL) should allow us to detect single word terms that are *distinctive* enough to be kept in our bilingual lexicon (Daille, 1995). This metric considers word frequencies weighted over two different corpora (in our case a technical automotive corpus and the more general purpose corpus "Le Monde"[1]), in order to assign high LL-values to words having much higher or lower frequencies than expected. We implemented the formula for both the expected values and the Log-Likelihood values as described by (Rayson and Garside, 2000).

Manual inspection of the Log-Likelihood figures confirmed our hypothesis that more domain-specific terms in our corpus were assigned high LL-values. We experimentally defined the threshold for Log-Likelihood values corresponding to distinctive terms on our development corpus. Example (4) shows some translation pairs which are filtered out by applying the LL threshold.

(4) Fr: cependant – En: however – It: tuttavia – Du: echter

Fr: choix – En: choice – It: scelta – Du: keuze

Fr: continuer – En: continue – It: continuare – Du: verdergaan

Fr: cadre – En: frame – It: cornice – Du: frame (erroneous filtering)

Fr: allégement – En: lightening – It: alleggerire – Du: verlichten (erroneous filtering)

4.1.2 Mutual Expectation Measure

The Mutual Expectation measure as described by Dias and Kaalep (2003) is used to measure the degree of cohesiveness between words in a text. This way, candidate multiword terms whose components do not occur together more often than expected by chance get filtered out. In a first step, we have calculated all n-gram frequencies (up to 8-grams) for our four automotive corpora and then used these frequencies to derive the Normalised

[1] http://catalog.elra.info/product_info.php?products_id=438

Expectation (NE) values for all multiword entries, as specified by the formula of Dias and Kaalep:

$$NE = \frac{prob(n - gram)}{\frac{1}{n}\sum prob(n - 1 - grams)} \quad (3)$$

The Normalised Expectation value expresses the cost, in terms of cohesiveness, of the possible loss of one word in an n-gram. The higher the frequency of the n-1-grams, the smaller the NE, and the smaller the chance that it is a valid multiword expression. The final Mutual Expectation (ME) value is then obtained by multiplying the NE values by the n-gram frequency. This way, the Mutual Expectation between n words in a multiword expression is based on the Normalised Expectation and the relative frequency of the n-gram in the corpus.

We calculated Mutual Expectation values for all candidate multiword term pairs and filtered out incomplete or erroneous terms having ME values below an experimentally set threshold (being below 0.005 for both source and target multiword or below 0.0002 for one of the two multiwords in the translation pair). The following incomplete candidate terms in example (5) were filtered out by applying the ME filter:

(5) Fr: fermeture embout - En: end closing - It: chiusura terminale - Du: afsluiting deel (should be: Fr: fermeture embout de brancard - En: chassis member end closing panel - It: chiusura terminale del longherone - Du: afsluiting voorste deel van langsbalk)

4.2 Evaluation

The terminology extraction module was tested on all sentences from the three test corpora. The output was manually labeled and the annotators were asked to judge both the *translational quality* of the entry (both languages should refer to the same referential unit) as well as the *relevance* of the term in an automotive context. Three labels were used: OK (valid entry), NOK (not a valid entry) and MAYBE (in case the annotator was not sure about the relevance of the term).

First, the impact of the statistical filtering was measured on the bilingual term extraction. Secondly, we compared the output of our system with the output of a commercial bilingual terminology extraction module and with the output of a set of standard monolingual term extraction modules.

Since the annotators labeled system output, the reported scores all refer to precision scores. In future work, we will develop a gold standard corpus which will enable us to also calculate recall scores.

4.2.1 Impact of filtering

Table 5 shows the difference in performance for both single and multiword terms with and without filtering. Single-word filtering seems to have a bigger impact on the results than multiword filtering. This can be explained by the fact that our candidate multiword terms are generated from anchor chunks (chunks aligned with a very high precision) that already answer to strict syntactical constraints. The annotators also mentioned the difficulty of judging the relevance of single word terms for the automotive domain (no clear distinction between technical and common vocabulary).

	Not Filtered			Filtered		
	OK	NOK	MAY	OK	NOK	MAY
FR-EN						
Sing_w	82%	17%	1%	86.5%	12%	1.5%
Mult_w	81%	16.5%	2.5%	83%	14.5%	2.5%
FR-IT						
Sing_w	80.5%	19%	0.5%	84.5%	15%	0.5%
Mult_w	69%	30%	1.0%	72%	27%	1.0%
FR-DU						
Sing_w	72%	25%	3%	75%	22%	3%
Mult_w	83%	15%	2%	84%	14%	2%

Table 5: Impact of statistical filters on Single and Multiword terminology extraction

4.2.2 Comparison with bilingual terminology extraction

We compared the three filtered bilingual lexicons (French versus English-Italian-Dutch) with the output of a commercial state-of-the-art terminology extraction program SDL MultiTerm Extract[2]. MultiTerm is a statistically based system that first generates a list of candidate terms in the source language (French in our case) and then looks for translations of these terms in the target language. We ran MultiTerm with its default settings (default noise-silence threshold, default stopword list, etc.) on a large portion of our parallel corpus that also contains all test sentences[3]. We ran our system (where term extraction happens on a sentence per sentence basis) on the three test sets.

[2] www.translationzone.com/en/products/sdlmultitermextract

[3] 70,000 sentences seemed to be the maximum size of the corpus that could be easily processed within MultiTerm Extract.

Table 6 shows that even after applying statistical filters, our term extraction module retains a much higher number of candidate terms than MultiTerm.

	# Extracted terms	# Terms after filtering	MultiTerm
FR-EN	4052	3386	1831
FR-IT	4381	3601	1704
FR-DU	3285	2662	1637

Table 6: Number of terms before and after applying Log-Likelihood and ME filters

Table 7 lists the results of both systems and shows the differences in performance for single and multiword terms. Following observations can be made:

- The performance of both systems is comparable for the extraction of single word terms, but our system clearly outperforms MultiTerm when it comes to the extraction of more complex multiword terms.

- Although the alignment results for French-Italian were very good, we do not achieve comparable results for Italian multiword extraction. This can be due to the fact that the syntactic structure is very similar in both languages. As a result, smaller syntactic chunks are linked. However one can argue that, just because of the syntactic resemblance of both languages, the need for complex multiword terms is less prominent in closely related languages as translators can just paste smaller noun phrases together in the same order in both languages. If we take the following example for instance:

  déposer – l' embout – de brancard
  togliere – il terminale – del sottoporta

  we can recompose the larger compound *l'embout de brancard* or *il terminale del sottoporta* by translating the smaller parts in the same order (*l'embout – il terminale* and *de brancard – del sottoporta*

- Despite the worse alignment results for Dutch, we achieve good accuracy results on the multiword term extraction. Part of that can be explained by the fact that French and Dutch use a different compounding strategy: whereas French compounds are created by concatenating prepositional phrases, Dutch usually tends to concatenate noun phrases (even without inserting spaces between the different compound parts). This way we can extract larger Dutch chunks that correspond to several French chunks, for instance:

  Fr: feu régulateur – de pression carburant.
  Du: brandstofdrukregelaar.

	ANCHOR CHUNK APPROACH			MULTITERM		
	OK	NOK	MAY	OK	NOK	MAY
FR-EN						
Sing_w	86.5%	12%	1.5%	77%	21%	2%
Mult_w	83%	14.5%	2.5%	47%	51%	2%
Total	84.5%	13.5%	2 %	64%	34%	2%
FR-IT						
Sing_w	84.5%	15%	0.5%	85%	14%	1%
Mult_w	72%	27%	1.0%	65%	34%	1%
Total	77.5%	22%	1%	76.5%	22.5%	1%
FR-DU						
Sing_w	75%	22%	3%	64.5%	33%	2.5%
Mult_w	84%	14%	2%	49.5%	49.5%	1%
Total	79.5%	20%	2.5%	58%	40%	2%

Table 7: Precision figures for our term extraction system and for SDL MultiTerm Extract

4.2.3 Comparison with monolingual terminology extraction

In order to have insights in the performance of our terminology extraction module, without considering the validity of the bilingual terminology pairs, we contrasted our extracted English terms with state-of-the art monolingual terminology systems. As we want to include both single words and multiword terms in our technical automotive lexicon, we only considered ATR systems which extract both categories. We used the implementation for these systems from (Zhang et al., 2008) which is freely available at[1].

We compared our system against 5 other ATR systems:

1. Baseline system (Simple Term Frequency)

2. Weirdness algorithm (Ahmad et al., 2007) which compares term frequencies in the target and reference corpora

3. C-value (Frantzi and Ananiadou, 1999) which uses term frequencies as well as unit-hood filters (to measure the collocation strength of units)

[1]http://www.dcs.shef.ac.uk/~ziqizhang/resources/tools/

4. Glossex (Kozakov et al., 2004) which uses term frequency information from both the target and reference corpora and compares term frequencies with frequencies of the multiword components

5. TermExtractor (Sclano and Velardi, 2007) which is comparable to Glossex but introduces the "domain consensus" which "simulates the consensus that a term must gain in a community before being considered a relevant domain term"

For all of the above algorithms, the input automotive corpus is PoS tagged and linguistic filters (selecting nouns and noun phrases) are applied to extract candidate terms. In a second step, stopwords are removed and the same set of extracted candidate terms (1105 single words and 1341 multiwords) is ranked differently by each algorithm. To compare the performance of the ranking algorithms, we selected the top terms (300 single and multiword terms) produced by all algorithms and compared these with our top candidate terms that are ranked by descending Log-likelihood (calculated on the BNC corpus) and Mutual Expectation values. Our filtered list of unique English automotive terms contains 1279 single words and 1879 multiwords in total. About 10% of the terms do not overlap between the two term lists. All candidate terms have been manually labeled by linguists. Table 8 shows the results of this comparison.

	SINGLE WORD TERMS			MULTIWORD TERMS		
	OK	NOK	MAY	OK	NOK	MAY
Baseline	80%	19.5%	0.5%	84.5%	14.5%	1%
Weirdness	95.5%	3.5%	1%	96%	2.5%	1.5%
C-value	80%	19.5%	0.5%	94%	5%	1%
Glossex	94.5%	4.5%	1%	85.5%	14%	0.5%
TermExtr.	85%	15%	0%	79%	20%	1%
AC approach	85.5%	14.5%	0%	90%	8%	2%

Table 8: Results for monolingual Term Extraction on the English part of the automotive corpus

Although our term extraction module has been tailored towards bilingual term extraction, the results look competitive to monolingual state-of-the-art ATR systems. If we compare these results with our bilingual term extraction results, we can observe that we gain more in performance for multiwords than for single words, which might mean that the filtering and ranking based on the Mutual Expectation works better than the Log-Likelihood ranking.

An error analysis of the results leads to the following insights:

- All systems suffer from partial retrieval of complex multiwords (e.g. ATR *management ecu* instead of *engine management ecu*, AC approach *chassis leg end piece closure* instead of *chassis leg end piece closure panel*).

- We manage to extract nice sets of multiwords that can be associated with a given concept, which could be nice for automatic ontology population (e.g. AC approach *gearbox casing, gearbox casing earth, gearbox casing earth cable, gearbox control, gearbox control cables, gearbox cover, gearbox ecu, gearbox ecu initialisation procedure, gearbox fixing, gearbox lower fixings, gearbox oil, gearbox oil cooler protective plug*).

- Sometimes smaller compounds are not extracted because they belong to the same syntactic chunk (E.g we extract *passenger compartment assembly, passenger compartment safety, passenger compartment side panel,* etc. but not *passenger compartment* as such).

5 Conclusions and further work

We presented a bilingual terminology extraction module that starts from sub-sentential alignments in parallel corpora and applied it on three different parallel corpora that are part of the same automotive corpus. Comparisons with standard terminology extraction programs show an improvement of up to 20% for bilingual terminology extraction and competitive results (85% to 90% accuracy) for monolingual terminology extraction. In the near future we want to experiment with other filtering techniques, especially to measure the domain distinctiveness of terms and work on a gold standard for measuring recall next to accuracy. We will also investigate our approach on languages which are more distant from each other (e.g. French – Swedish).

Acknowledgments

We would like to thank PSA Peugeot Citroën for funding this project.

References

K. Ahmad, L. Gillam, and L. Tostevin. 2007. University of surrey participation in trec8: Weirdness indexing for logical document extrapolation and rerieval (wilder). In *Proceedings of the Eight Text REtrieval Conference (TREC-8)*.

S. Ananiadou. 1994. A methodology for automatic term recognition. In *Proceedings of the 15th conference on computational linguistics*, pages 1034–1038.

R.H. Baayen, R. Piepenbrock, and H. van Rijn. 1993. The celex lexical database on cd-rom.

I. Dagan and K. Church. 1994. Termight: identifying and translating technical terminology. In *Proceedings of Applied Language Processing*, pages 34–40.

B. Daille. 1995. Study and implementation of combined techniques for automatic extraction of terminology. In J. Klavans and P. Resnik, editors, *The Balancing Act: Combining Symbolic and Statistical Approaches to Language*, pages 49–66. MIT Press, Cambridge, Massachusetts; London, England.

G. Dias and H. Kaalep. 2003. Automatic extraction of multiword units for estonian: Phrasal verbs. *Languages in Development*, 41:81–91.

K.T. Frantzi and S. Ananiadou. 1999. the c-value/nc-value domain independent method for multiword term extraction. *journal of Natural Language Processing*, 6(3):145–180.

K. Kageura and B. Umino. 1996. Methods of automatic term recognition: a review. *Terminology*, 3(2):259–289.

L. Kozakov, Y. Park, T.-H Fin, Y. Drissi, Y.N. Doganata, and T. Confino. 2004. Glossary extraction and knowledge in large organisations via semantic web technologies. In *Proceedings of the 6th International Semantic Web Conference and he 2nd Asian Semantic Web Conference (Se-mantic Web Challenge Track)*.

J. Kupiec. 1993. An algorithm for finding noun phrase correspondences in bilingual corpora. In *Proceedings of the 31st Annual Meeting of the Association for Computational Linguistics*.

L. Macken and W. Daelemans. 2009. Aligning linguistically motivated phrases. In van Halteren H. Verberne, S. and P.-A. Coppen, editors, *Selected Papers from the 18th Computational Linguistics in the Netherlands Meeting*, pages 37–52, Nijmegen, The Netherlands.

L. Macken, E. Lefever, and V. Hoste. 2008. Linguistically-based sub-sentential alignment for terminology extraction from a bilingual automotive corpus. In *Proceedings of the 22nd International Conference on Computational Linguistics (Coling 2008)*, pages 529–536, Manchester, United Kingdom.

R. C. Moore. 2002. Fast and accurate sentence alignment of bilingual corpora. In *Proceedings of the 5th Conference of the Association for Machine Translation in the Americas*, Machine Translation: from research to real users, pages 135–244, Tiburon, California.

F. J. Och and H. Ney. 2003. A systematic comparison of various statistical alignment models. *Computational Linguistics*, 29(1):19–51.

P. Rayson and R. Garside. 2000. Comparing corpora using frequency profiling. In *Proceedings of the workshop on Comparing Corpora, 38th annual meeting of the Association for Computational Linguistics (ACL 2000)*, pages 1–6.

H. Schmid. 1994. Probabilistic part-of-speech tagging using decision trees. In *International Conference on New Methods in Language Processing*, Manchester, UK.

F. Sclano and P. Velardi. 2007. Termextractor: a web application to learn the shared terminology of emergent web communities. In *Proceedings of the 3rd International Conference on Interoperability for Enterprise Software and Applications (I-ESA 2007)*.

A. Van den Bosch, G.J. Busser, W. Daelemans, and S. Canisius. 2007. An efficient memory-based morphosyntactic tagger and parser for dutch. In *Selected Papers of the 17th Computational Linguistics in the Netherlands Meeting*, pages 99–114, Leuven, Belgium.

V. Vandeghinste. 2008. *A Hybrid Modular Machine Translation System. LoRe-MT: Low Resources Machine Translation.* Ph.D. thesis, Centre for Computational Linguistics, KULeuven.

Z. Zhang, J. Iria, C. Brewster, and F. Ciravegna. 2008. A comparative evaluation of term recognition algorithms. In *Proceedings of the sixth international conference of Language Resources and Evaluation (LREC 2008)*.

User Simulations for context-sensitive speech recognition in Spoken Dialogue Systems

Oliver Lemon
Edinburgh University
olemon@inf.ed.ac.uk

Ioannis Konstas
University of Glasgow
konstas@dcs.gla.ac.uk

Abstract

We use a machine learner trained on a combination of acoustic and contextual features to predict the accuracy of incoming n-best automatic speech recognition (ASR) hypotheses to a spoken dialogue system (SDS). Our novel approach is to use a simple statistical User Simulation (US) for this task, which measures the likelihood that the user would say each hypothesis in the current context. Such US models are now common in machine learning approaches to SDS, are trained on real dialogue data, and are related to theories of "alignment" in psycholinguistics. We use a US to predict the user's next dialogue move and thereby re-rank n-best hypotheses of a speech recognizer for a corpus of 2564 user utterances. The method achieved a significant relative reduction of Word Error Rate (WER) of 5% (this is 44% of the possible WER improvement on this data), and 62% of the possible semantic improvement (Dialogue Move Accuracy), compared to the baseline policy of selecting the topmost ASR hypothesis. The majority of the improvement is attributable to the User Simulation feature, as shown by Information Gain analysis.

1 Introduction

A crucial problem in the design of spoken dialogue systems (SDS) is to decide for incoming recognition hypotheses whether a system should *accept* (consider correctly recognized), *reject* (assume misrecognition), or *ignore* (classify as noise or speech not directed to the system) them.

Obviously, incorrect decisions at this point can have serious negative effects on system usability and user satisfaction. On the one hand, accepting misrecognized hypotheses leads to misunderstandings and unintended system behaviors which are usually difficult to recover from. On the other hand, users might get frustrated with a system that behaves too cautiously and rejects or ignores too many utterances. Thus an important feature in dialogue system engineering is the tradeoff between avoiding task failure (due to misrecognitions) and promoting overall dialogue efficiency, flow, and naturalness.

In this paper, we investigate the use of machine learning trained on a combination of acoustic features and features computed from dialogue context to predict the quality of incoming n-best recognition hypotheses to a SDS. These predictions are then used to select a "best" hypothesis and to decide on appropriate system reactions. We evaluate this approach in comparison with a baseline system that works in the standard way: always choosing the topmost hypothesis in the n-best list. In such systems, complex repair strategies are required when the top hypothesis is incorrect.

The main novelty of this work is that we explore the use of predictions from simple statistical User Simulations to re-rank n-best lists of ASR hypotheses. These User Simulations are now commonly used in statistical learning approaches to dialogue management (Williams and Young, 2003; Schatzmann et al., 2006; Young, 2006; Young et al., 2007; Schatzmann et al., 2007), but they have not been used for context-sensitive ASR before.

In our model, the system's "belief" $b(h)$ in a recognition hypothesis h is factored in two parts: the observation probability $P(o|h)$ (approximated by the ASR confidence score) and the User Simulation probability $P(h|us, C)$ of the hypothesis:

$$b(h) = P(o|h).P(h|us, C) \qquad (1)$$

where us is the state of the User Simulation in context C. The context is simply a window of di-

Proceedings of the 12th Conference of the European Chapter of the ACL, pages 505–513,
Athens, Greece, 30 March – 3 April 2009.

alogue acts in the dialogue history, that the US is sensitive to (see section 3).

The paper is organized as follows. After a short relation to previous work, we describe the data (Section 5) and derive baseline results (Section 6). Section 3 describes the User Simulations that we use for re-ranking hypotheses. Section 7 describes our learning experiments for classifying and selecting from n-best recognition hypotheses and Section 9 reports our results.

2 Relation to Previous Work

In psycholinguistics, the idea that human dialogue participants simulate each other to some extent is gaining currency. (Pickering and Garrod, 2007) write:

> "if B overtly imitates A, then A's comprehension of B's utterance is facilitated by A's memory for A's previous utterance."

We explore aspects of this idea in a computational manner. Similar work in the area of spoken dialogue systems is described below.

(Litman et al., 2000) use acoustic-prosodic information extracted from speech waveforms, together with information derived from their speech recognizer, to automatically predict misrecognized turns in a corpus of train-timetable information dialogues. In our experiments, we also use recognizer confidence scores and a limited number of acoustic-prosodic features (e.g. amplitude in the speech signal) for hypothesis classification, but we also use User Simulation predictions.

(Walker et al., 2000) use a combination of features from the speech recognizer, natural language understanding, and dialogue manager/discourse history to classify hypotheses as correct, partially correct, or misrecognized. Our work is related to these experiments in that we also combine confidence scores and higher-level features for classification. However, both (Litman et al., 2000) and (Walker et al., 2000) consider only single-best recognition results and thus use their classifiers as "filters" to decide whether the best recognition hypothesis for a user utterance is correct or not. We go a step further in that we classify n-best hypotheses and then select among the alternatives. We also explore the use of more dialogue and task-oriented features (e.g. the dialogue move type of a recognition hypothesis) for classification.

(Gabsdil and Lemon, 2004) similarly perform reordering of n-best lists by combining acoustic and pragmatic features. Their study shows that dialogue features such as the previous system question and whether a hypothesis is the correct answer to a particular question contributed more to classification accuracy than the other attributes.

(Jonson, 2006) classifies recognition hypotheses with labels denoting acceptance, clarification, confirmation and rejection. These labels were learned in a similar way to (Gabsdil and Lemon, 2004) and correspond to varying levels of confidence, being essentially potential directives to the dialogue manager. Apart from standard features Jonson includes attributes that account for the whole n-best list, i.e. standard deviation of confidence scores.

As well as the use of a User Simulation, the main difference between our approach and work on hypothesis reordering (e.g. (Chotimongkol and Rudnicky, 2001)) is that we make a decision regarding whether a dialogue system should accept, clarify, reject, or ignore a user utterance. Like (Gabsdil and Lemon, 2004; Jonson, 2006), our approach is more generally applicable than preceding research, since we frame our methodology in the *Information State Update* (ISU) approach to dialogue management (Traum et al., 1999) and therefore expect it to be applicable to a range of related multimodal dialogue systems.

3 User Simulations

What makes this study different from the previous work in the area of post-processing of the ASR hypotheses is the incorporation of a User Simulation output as an additional feature. The history of a dialogue between a user and a dialogue system plays an important role as to what the user might be expected to say next. As a result, most of the studies mentioned in the previous section make various efforts to capture history by including relevant features directly in their classifiers.

Various statistical User Simulations have been trained on corpora of dialogue data in order to simulate real user behaviour (Schatzmann et al., 2006; Young, 2006; Georgila et al., 2006; Young et al., 2007; Schatzmann et al., 2007). We developed a simple n-gram User Simulation, using n-grams of dialogue moves. It treats a dialogue as a sequence of lists of consecutive user and system turns in a high level semantic representation, i.e.

$< SpeechAct >, < Task >$ pairs, for example $< provide\_info >, < music\_genre(punk) >$. It takes as input the $n-1$ most recent lists of $< SpeechAct >, < Task >$ pairs in the dialogue history, and uses the statistics in the training set to compute a distribution over the possible next user actions. If no n-grams match the current history, the model can back-off to n-grams of lower order. We use this model to assess the likelihood of each candidate ASR hypothesis. Intuitively, this is the likelihood that the user really would say the hypothesis in the current dialogue situation. The benefit of using n-gram models is that they are fast and simple to train even on large corpora.

The main hypothesis that we investigate is that by using the User Simulation model to predict the next user utterance, we can effectively increase the performance of the speech recogniser module.

4 Evaluation metrics

To evaluate performance we use Dialogue Move Accuracy (DMA), a strict variant of Concept Error Rate (CER) as defined by (Boros et al., 1996), which takes into account the semantic aspects of the difference between the classified utterance and the true transcription. CER is similar to WER, since it takes into account deletions, insertions and substitutions on the semantic (rather than the word) level of the utterance. DMA is stricter than CER in the sense that it does not allow for partial matches in the semantic representation. In other words, if the classified utterance corresponds to the same semantic representation as the transcribed then we have 100% DMA, otherwise 0%.

Sentence Accuracy (SA) is the alignment of a single hypothesis in the n-best list with the true transcription. Similarly to DMA, it accounts for perfect alignment between the hypothesis and the transcription, i.e. if they match perfectly we have 100% SA, otherwise 0%.

5 Data Collection

For our experiments, we use data collected in a user study with the Town-Info spoken dialogue system, using the HTK speech recognizer (Young, 2007). In this study 18 subjects had to solve 10 search/browsing tasks with the system, resulting in 180 complete dialogues and 2564 utterances (average 14.24 user utterances per dialogue).

For each utterance we have a series of files of 60-best lists produced by the speech recogniser, namely the transcription hypotheses on a sentence level along with the acoustic model score and the equivalent transcriptions on a word level, with information such as the duration of each recognised frame and the confidence score of the acoustic and language model of each word.

5.1 Labeling

We transcribed all user utterances and parsed the transcriptions offline using a natural language understanding component (a robust Keyword Parser) in order to get a gold-standard labeling of the data.

We devised four labels with decreasing order of confidence: 'opt' (optimal), 'pos' (positive), 'neg' (negative), 'ign' (ignore). These are automatically generated using two different modules: a keyword parser that computes the $< SpeechAct >< Task >$ pair as described in the previous section and a Levenshtein Distance calculator, for the computation of the DMA and WER of each hypothesis respectively. The reason for opting for a more abstract level, namely the semantics of the hypotheses rather than individual word recognition, is that in SDS it is usually sufficient to rely on the meaning of message that is being conveyed by the user rather than the precise words that they used.

Similar to (Gabsdil and Lemon, 2004; Jonson, 2006) we ascribe to each utterance either of the 'opt', 'pos', 'neg', 'ign' labels according to the following schema:

- **opt**: The hypothesis is perfectly aligned and semantically identical to the transcription
- **pos**: The hypothesis is not entirely aligned (WER < 50) but is semantically identical to the transcription
- **neg**: The hypothesis is semantically identical to the transcription but does not align well (WER > 50) or is semantically different to the transcription
- **ign**: The hypothesis was not addressed to the system (crosstalk), or the user laughed, coughed, etc.

The 50% value for the WER as a threshold for the distinction between the 'pos' and 'neg' category is adopted from (Gabsdil, 2003), based on the fact that WER is affected by concept accuracy (Boros et al., 1996). In other words, if a hypothesis is erroneous as far as its transcript is concerned

Transcript: I'd like to find a bar please	
I WOULD LIKE TO FIND A BAR PLEASE	pos
I LIKE TO FIND A FOUR PLEASE	neg
I'D LIKE TO FIND A BAR PLEASE	opt
WOULD LIKE TO FIND THE OR PLEASE	ign

Table 1: Example hypothesis labelling

then it is highly likely that it does not convey the correct message from a semantic point of view. We always label conceptually equivalent hypotheses to a particular transcription as potential candidate dialogue strategy moves, and total misrecognitions as rejections. In table 5.1 we show examples of the four labels. Note that in the case of silence, we give an 'opt' to the empty hypothesis.

6 The Baseline and Oracle Systems

The baseline for our experiments is the behavior of the Town-Info spoken dialogue system that was used to collect the experimental data. We evaluate the performance of the baseline system by analyzing the dialogue logs from the user study.

As an oracle for the system we defined the choice of either the first 'opt' in the n-best list, or if this does not exist the first 'pos' in the list. In this way it is guaranteed that we always get as output a perfect match to the true transcript as far as its Dialogue Move is concerned, provided there exists a perfect match somewhere in the list.

6.1 Baseline and Oracle Results

Table 2 summarizes the evaluation of the baseline and oracle systems. We note that the Baseline system already performs quite well on this data, when we consider that in about 20% of n-best lists there is no semantically correct hypothesis.

	Baseline	Oracle
WER	47.72%	42.16%
DMA	75.05%	80.20%
SA	40.48%	45.27%

Table 2: Baseline and Oracle results (statistically significant at $p < 0.001$)

7 Classifying and Selecting N-best Recognition Hypotheses

We use a threshold (50%) on a hypothesis' WER as an indicator for whether hypotheses should be clarified or rejected. This is adopted from (Gabsdil, 2003), based on the fact that WER correlates with concept accuracy (CA, (Boros et al., 1996)).

7.1 Classification: Feature Groups

We represent recognition hypotheses as 13-dimensional feature vectors for automatic classification. The feature vectors combine recognizer confidence scores, low-level acoustic information, and information from the User Simulation.

All the features used by the system are extracted by the dialogue logs, the n-best lists per utterance and per word and the audio files. The majority of the features chosen are based on their success in previous systems as described in the literature (see section 2). The novel feature here is the User Simulation score which may make redundant most of the dialogue features used in other studies.

In order to measure the usefulness of each candidate feature and thus choose the most important we use the metrics of Information Gain and Gain Ratio (see table 3 in section 8.1) on the whole training set, i.e. 93240 hypotheses.

In total 13 attributes were extracted, that can be grouped into 4 main categories; those that concern the current hypothesis to be classified, those that concern low-level statistics of the audio files, those that concern the whole n-best list, and finally the User Simulation feature.

- Current Hypothesis Features (CHF) (6): acoustic score, overall model confidence score, minimum word confidence score, grammar parsability, hypothesis length and hypothesis duration.
- Acoustic Features (AF) (3): minimum, maximum and RMS amplitude
- List Features (LF) (3): n-best rank, deviation of confidence scores in the list, match with most frequent Dialogue Move
- User Simulation (US) (1): User Simulation confidence score

The **Current Hypothesis features (CHF)** were extracted from the n-best list files that contained the hypotheses' transcription along with overall acoustic score per utterance and from the equivalent files that contained the transcription of each word along with the start of frame, end of frame and confidence score:

Acoustic score is the negative log likelihood ascribed by the speech recogniser to the whole hypothesis, being the sum of the individual word acoustic scores. Intuitively this is considered to be helpful since it depicts the confidence of the statistical model only for each word and is also adopted in previous studies. Incorrect alignments shall tend to adapt less well to the model and thus have low log likelihood.

Overall model confidence score is the average of the individual word confidence scores.

Minimum word confidence score is also computed by the individual word transcriptions and accounts for the confidence score of the word which the speech recogniser is least certain of. It is expected to help our classifier distinguish between poor overall hypothesis recognitions since a high overall confidence score can sometimes be misleading.

Grammar Parsability is the negative log likelihood of the transcript for the current hypothesis as produced by the Stanford Parser, a wide-coverage Probabilistic Context-Free Grammar (PCFG) (Klein and Manning, 2003) [1]. This feature seems helpful since we expect that a highly ungrammatical hypothesis is likely not to match with the true transcription semantically.

Hypothesis duration is the length of the hypothesis in milliseconds as extracted from the n-best list files with transcriptions per word that include the start and the end time of the recognised frame. The reason for the inclusion of this feature is that it can help distinguish between short utterances such as yes/no answers, medium-sized utterances of normal answers and long utterances caused by crosstalk.

Hypothesis length is the number of words in a hypothesis and is considered to help in a similar way as the above feature.

The **Acoustic Features (AF)** were extracted directly from the wave files using SoX: Minimum, maximum and RMS amplitude are straightforward features common in the previous studies mentioned in section 2.

The **List Features (LF)** were calculated based on the n-best list files with transcriptions per utterance and per word and take into account the whole list:

N-best rank is the position of the hypothesis in the list and could be useful in the sense that 'opt' and 'pos' may be found in the upper part of the list rather than the bottom.

Deviation of confidence scores in the list is the deviation of the overall model confidence score of the hypothesis from the mean confidence score in the list. This feature is extracted in the hope that it will indicate potential clusters of confidence scores in particular positions in the list, i.e. group hypotheses that deviate in a specific fashion from the mean and thus indicating them being classified with the same label.

Match with most frequent Dialogue Move is the only boolean feature and indicates whether the Dialogue Move of the current hypothesis, i.e. the pair of $< SpeechAct >< Task >$ coincides with the most frequent one. The trend in n-best lists is to have a majority of utterances that belong to one or two labels and only one hypothesis belonging to the 'opt' category and/or a few to the 'pos' category. As a result, the idea behind this feature is to extract such potential outliers which are the desired goal for the re-ranker.

Finally, the **User Simulation score** is given as an output from the User Simulation model and adapted for the purposes of this study (see section 3 for more details). The model is operating with 5-grams. Its input is given by two different sources: the history of the dialogue, namely the 4 previous Dialogue Moves, is taken from the dialogue log and the current hypothesis' semantic parse which is generated on the fly by the same keyword parser used in the automatic labelling.

User Simulation score is the probability that the current hypothesis' Dialogue Move has really been said by the user given the 4 previous Dialogue Moves. The potential advantages of this feature have been discussed in section 3.

7.2 Learner and Selection Procedure

We use the memory based learner TiMBL (Daelemans et al., 2002) to predict the class of each of the 60-best recognition hypotheses for a given utterance.

TiMBL was trained using different parameter combinations mainly choosing between number of k-nearest neighbours (1 to 5) and distance metrics (Weighted Overlap and Modified Value Difference Metric). In a second step, we decide which (if any) of the classified hypotheses we actually want to pick as the best result and how the user utterance should be classified as a whole.

[1] http://nlp.stanford.edu/software/lex-parser.shtml

1. Scan the list of classified n-best recognition hypotheses top-down. Return the first result that is classified as 'opt'.

2. If 1. fails, scan the list of classified n-best recognition hypotheses top-down. Return the first result that is classified as 'pos'.

3. If 2. fails, count the number of negs and igns in the classified recognition hypotheses. If the number of negs is larger or equal than the number of igns then return the first 'neg'.

4. Else return the first 'ign' utterance.

8 Experiments

Experiments were conducted in two layers: the first layer concerns only the classifier, i.e. the ability of the system to correctly classify each hypothesis to either of the four labels 'opt', 'pos', 'neg', 'ign' and the second layer the re-ranker, i.e. the ability of the system to boost the speech recogniser's accuracy.

All results are drawn from the TiMBL classifier trained with the Weighted Overlap metric and k = 1 nearest neighbours settings. Both layers are trained on 75% of the same Town-Info Corpus of 126 dialogues containing 60-best lists for 1554 user utterances or a total of 93240 hypotheses. The first layer was tested against a separate Town-Info Corpus of 58 dialogues containing 510 user utterances or a total of 30600 hypotheses, while the second was tested on the whole training set with 10-fold cross-validation.

Using this corpus, a series of experiments was carried out using different sets of features in order to both determine and illustrate the increasing performance of the classifier. These sets were determined not only by the literature but also by the Information Gain measures that were calculated on the training set using WEKA, as shown in table 3.

8.1 Information Gain

Quite surprisingly, we note that the rank given by the Information Gain measure coincides perfectly with the logical grouping of the attributes that was initially performed (see table 3).

As a result, we chose to use this grouping for the final 4 feature sets on which the classifier experiments were performed, in the following order:

Experiment 1: List Features (LF)

InfoGain	Attribute
1.0324	userSimulationScore
0.9038	rmsAmp
0.8280	minAmp
0.8087	maxAmp
0.4861	parsability
0.3975	acousScore
0.3773	hypothesisDuration
0.2545	hypothesisLength
0.1627	avgConfScore
0.1085	minWordConfidence
0.0511	nBestRank
0.0447	standardDeviation
0.0408	matchesFrequentDM

Table 3: Information Gain

Experiment 2: List Features + Current Hypothesis Features (LF+CHF)
Experiment 3: List Features + Current Hypothesis Features + Acoustic Features (LF+CHF+AF)
Experiment 4: List Features + Current Hypothesis Features + Acoustic Features + User Simulation (LF+CHF+AF+US)

Note that the User Simulation score is a very strong feature, scoring first in the Information Gain rank, validating our central hypothesis.

The testing of the classifier using each of the above feature sets was performed on the remaining 25% of the Town-Info corpus comprising of 58 dialogues, consisting of 510 utterances and taking the 60-best lists resulting in a total of 30600 vectors. In each experiment we measured Precision, Recall, F-measure per class and total Accuracy of the classifier .

For the second layer, we used a trained instance of the TiMBL classifier on the 4th feature set (List Features + Current Hypothesis Features + Acoustic Features + User Simulation) and performed reranking using the algorithm presented in section 7.2 on the same training set used in the first layer using 10-fold cross validation.

9 Results and Evaluation

We performed two series of experiments in two layers: the first corresponds to the training of the classifier alone and the second to the system as a whole measuring the re-ranker's output.

Feature set (opt)	Precision	Recall	F1
LF	42.5%	58.4%	49.2%
LF+CHF	62.4%	65.7%	64.0%
LF+CHF+AF	55.6%	61.6%	58.4%
LF+CHF+AF+US	70.5%	73.7%	72.1%

Table 4: Results for the 'opt' category

Feature set (pos)	Precision	Recall	F1
LF	25.2%	1.7%	3.2%
LF+CHF	51.2%	57.4%	54.1%
LF+CHF+AF	51.5%	54.6%	53.0%
LF+CHF+AF+US	64.8%	61.8%	63.3%

Table 5: Results for the 'pos' category

Feature set (ign)	Precision	Recall	F1
LF	19.6%	1.3%	2.5%
LF+CHF	63.5%	48.7%	55.2%
LF+CHF+AF	59.3%	48.9%	53.6%
LF+CHF+AF+US	99.9%	99.9%	99.9%

Table 7: Results for the 'ign' category

Feature set	F1	Accuracy
Baseline	-	51.1%
LF	37.3%	53.1%
LF+CHF	64.1%	64.8%
LF+CHF+AF	62.6%	63.4%
LF+CHF+AF+US	86.0%	84.9%

Table 8: F1-Measure and Accuracy for the four attribute sets

9.1 First Layer: Classifier Experiments

In these series of experiments we measure precision, recall and F1-measure for each of the four labels and overall F1-measure and accuracy of the classifier. In order to have a better view of the classifier's performance we have also included the confusion matrix for the final experiment with all 13 attributes. Tables 4 -7 show per class and per attribute set measures, while Table 8 shows a collective view of the results for the four sets of attributes and the baseline being the majority class label 'neg'. Table 9 shows the confusion matrix for the final experiment.

In tables 4 - 8 we generally notice an increase in precision, recall and F1-measure as we progressively add more attributes to the system with the exception of the addition of the Acoustic Features which seem to impair the classifier's performance. We also make note of the fact that in the case of the 4th attribute set the classifier can distinguish very well the 'neg' and 'ign' categories with 86.3% and 99.9% F1-measure respectively. Most importantly, we observe a remarkable boost in F1-measure and accuracy with the addition of the User Simulation score. We find a 37.36% relative increase in F1-measure and 34.02% increase in the accuracy compared to the 3rd experiment, which contains all but the User Simulation score attribute and a 66.20% relative increase of the accuracy compared to the Baseline. In table 7 we make note of a rather low recall measure for the 'ign' category in the case of the LF experiment, suggesting that the list features do not add extra value to the classifier, partially validating the Information Gain measure (Table 3).

Taking a closer look at the 4th experiment with all 13 features we notice in table 9 that most errors occur between the 'pos' and 'neg' category. In fact, for the 'neg' category the False Positive Rate (FPR) is 18.17% and for the 'pos' 8.9%, all in all a lot larger than for the other categories.

9.2 Second Layer: Re-ranker Experiments

In these experiments we measure WER, DMA and SA for the system as a whole. In order to make sure that the improvement noted was really attributed to the classifier we computed the p-values for each of these measures using the Wilcoxon signed rank test for WER and McNemar chi-square test for the DMA and SA measures.

In table 10 we note that the classifier scores

Feature set (neg)	Precision	Recall	F1
LF	54.2%	96.4%	69.4%
LF+CHF	70.7%	75.0%	72.8%
LF+CHF+AF	69.5%	73.4%	71.4%
LF+CHF+AF+US	85.6%	87.0%	86.3%

Table 6: Results for the 'neg' category

	opt	pos	neg	ign
opt	232	37	46	0
pos	47	4405	2682	8
neg	45	2045	13498	0
ign	5	0	0	7550

Table 9: Confusion Matrix for LF+CHF+AF+US

	Baseline	Classifier	Oracle
WER	47.72%	45.27% **	42.16%***
DMA	75.05%	78.22% *	80.20% ***
SA	40.48%	42.26%	45.27%***

Table 10: Baseline, Classifier, and Oracle results (*** = $p < 0.001$, ** = $p < 0.01$, * = $p < 0.05$)

Label	Precision	Recall	F1
opt	74.0%	64.1%	68.7%
pos	76.3%	46.2%	57.6%
neg	81.9%	94.4%	87.7%
ign	99.9%	99.9%	99.9%

Table 11: Precision, Recall and F1: high-level features

45.27% WER making a notable relative reduction of 5.13% compared to the baseline and 78.22% DMA incurring a relative improvement of 4.22%. The classifier scored 42.26% on SA but it was not considered significant compared to the baseline ($0.05 < p < 0.10$). Comparing the classifier's performance with the Oracle it achieves a 44.06% of the possible WER improvement on this data, 61.55% for the DMA measure and 37.16% for the SA measure.

Finally, we also notice that the Oracle has a 80.20% for the DMA, which means that 19.80% of the n-best lists did not include at all a hypothesis that matched semantically to the true transcript.

10 Experiment with high-level features

We trained a Memory Based Classifier based only on the higher level features of merely the User Simulation score and the Grammar Parsability (US + GP). The idea behind this choice is to try and find a combination of features that ignores low level characteristics of the user's utterances as well as features that heavily rely on the speech recogniser and thus by default are not considered to be very trustworthy.

Quite surprisingly, the results taken from an experiment with just the User Simulation score and the Grammar Parsability are very promising and comparable with those acquired from the 4th experiment with all 13 attributes. Table 11 shows the precision, recall and F1-measure per label and table 12 illustrates the classifier's performance in comparison with the 4th experiment.

Table 12 shows that there is a somewhat considerable decrease in the recall and a corresponding increase in the precision of the 'pos' and 'opt' categories compared to the LF + CHF + AF + US attribute set, which account for lower F1-measures. However, all in all the US + GP set manages to classify correctly 207 more vectors and quite interestingly commits far fewer ties and manages to resolve more compared to the full 13 attribute set.

Feature set	F1	Accuracy	Ties
LF+CHF+AF+US	86.0%	84.9%	4993
US+GP	85.7%	85.6%	115

Table 12: F1, Accuracy and number of ties correctly resolved for LF+CHF+AF+US and US+GP feature sets

11 Conclusion

We used a combination of acoustic features and features computed from dialogue context to predict the quality of incoming recognition hypotheses to an SDS. In particular we use a score computed from a simple statistical User Simulation, which measures the likelihood that the user really said each hypothesis. The approach is novel in combining User Simulations, machine learning, and n-best processing for spoken dialogue systems. We employed a User Simulation model, trained on real dialogue data, to predict the user's next dialogue move. This prediction was used to re-rank n-best hypotheses of a speech recognizer for a corpus of 2564 user utterances. The results, obtained using TiMBL and an n-gram User Simulation, show a significant relative reduction of Word Error Rate of 5% (this is 44% of the possible WER improvement on this data), and 62% of the possible Dialogue Move Accuracy improvement, compared to the baseline policy of selecting the topmost ASR hypothesis. The majority of the improvement is attributable to the User Simulation feature. Clearly, this improvement would result in better dialogue system performance overall.

Acknowledgments

We thank Helen Hastie and Kallirroi Georgila. The research leading to these results has received funding from the EPSRC (project no. EP/E019501/1) and from the European Community's Seventh Framework Programme (FP7/2007-2013) under grant agreement no. 216594 (CLASSiC project www.classic-project.org)

References

M. Boros, W. Eckert, F. Gallwitz, G. Görz, G. Hanrieder, and H. Niemann. 1996. Towards understanding spontaneous speech: Word accuracy vs. concept accuracy. In *Proceedings ICSLP '96*, volume 2, pages 1009–1012, Philadelphia, PA.

Ananlada Chotimongkol and Alexander I. Rudnicky. 2001. N-best Speech Hypotheses Reordering Using Linear Regression. In *Proceedings of EuroSpeech 2001*, pages 1829–1832.

Walter Daelemans, Jakub Zavrel, Ko van der Sloot, and Antal van den Bosch. 2002. TIMBL: Tilburg Memory Based Learner, version 4.2, Reference Guide. In *ILK Technical Report 02-01*.

Malte Gabsdil and Oliver Lemon. 2004. Combining acoustic and pragmatic features to predict recognition performance in spoken dialogue systems. In *Proceedings of ACL-04*, pages 344–351.

Malte Gabsdil. 2003. Classifying Recognition Results for Spoken Dialogue Systems. In *Proceedings of the Student Research Workshop at ACL-03*.

Kallirroi Georgila, James Henderson, and Oliver Lemon. 2006. User simulation for spoken dialogue systems: Learning and evaluation. In *Proceedings of Interspeech/ICSLP*, pages 1065–1068.

R. Jonson. 2006. Dialogue Context-Based Re-ranking of ASR Hypotheses. In *Proceedings IEEE 2006 Workshop on Spoken Language Technology*.

D. Klein and C. Manning. 2003. Fast exact inference with a factored model for natural language parsing. *Journal of Advances in Neural Information Processing Systems*, 15(2).

Diane J. Litman, Julia Hirschberg, and Marc Swerts. 2000. Predicting Automatic Speech Recognition Performance Using Prosodic Cues. In *Proceedings of NAACL*.

M. Pickering and S. Garrod. 2007. Do people use language production to make predictions during comprehension? *Journal of Trends in Cognitive Sciences*, 11(3).

J Schatzmann, K Weilhammer, M N Stuttle, and S J Young. 2006. A Survey of Statistical User Simulation Techniques for Reinforcement-Learning of Dialogue Management Strategies. *Knowledge Engineering Review*, 21:97–126.

J. Schatzmann, B. Thomson, K. Weilhammer, H. Ye, and S. Young. 2007. Agenda-based User Simulation for Bootstrapping a POMDP Dialogue System. In *Proceedings of HLT/NAACL*.

David Traum, Johan Bos, Robin Cooper, Staffan Larsson, Ian Lewin, Colin Matheson, and Massimo Poesio. 1999. A Model of Dialogue Moves and Information State Revision. Technical Report D2.1, Trindi Project.

Marilyn Walker, Jerry Wright, and Irene Langkilde. 2000. Using Natural Language Processing and Discourse Features to Identify Understanding Errors in a Spoken Dialogue System. In *Proceedings of ICML-2000*.

Jason Williams and Steve Young. 2003. Using wizard-of-oz simulations to bootstrap reinforcement-learning-based dialog management systems. In *Proc. 4th SIGdial workshop*.

SJ Young, J Schatzmann, K Weilhammer, and H Ye. 2007. The Hidden Information State Approach to Dialog Management. In *ICASSP 2007*.

SJ Young. 2006. Using POMDPs for Dialog Management. In *IEEE/ACL Workshop on Spoken Language Technology (SLT 2006)*, Aruba.

Steve Young. 2007. ATK: An Application Toolkit for HTK, Version 1.6. Technical report, Cambridge University Engineering Department.

Sentiment Summarization: Evaluating and Learning User Preferences

Kevin Lerman
Columbia University
New York, NY
klerman@cs.columbia.edu

Sasha Blair-Goldensohn
Google, Inc.
New York, NY
sasha@google.com

Ryan McDonald
Google, Inc.
New York, NY
ryanmcd@google.com

Abstract

We present the results of a large-scale, end-to-end human evaluation of various sentiment summarization models. The evaluation shows that users have a strong preference for summarizers that model sentiment over non-sentiment baselines, but have no broad overall preference between any of the sentiment-based models. However, an analysis of the human judgments suggests that there are identifiable situations where one summarizer is generally preferred over the others. We exploit this fact to build a new summarizer by training a ranking SVM model over the set of human preference judgments that were collected during the evaluation, which results in a 30% relative reduction in error over the previous best summarizer.

1 Introduction

The growth of the Internet as a commerce medium, and particularly the Web 2.0 phenomenon of user-generated content, have resulted in the proliferation of massive numbers of product, service and merchant reviews. While this means that users have plenty of information on which to base their purchasing decisions, in practice this is often too much information for a user to absorb. To alleviate this information overload, research on systems that automatically aggregate and summarize opinions have been gaining interest (Hu and Liu, 2004a; Hu and Liu, 2004b; Gamon et al., 2005; Popescu and Etzioni, 2005; Carenini et al., 2005; Carenini et al., 2006; Zhuang et al., 2006; Blair-Goldensohn et al., 2008).

Evaluating these systems has been a challenge, however, due to the number of human judgments required to draw meaningful conclusions. Often systems are evaluated piecemeal, selecting pieces that can be evaluated easily and automatically (Blair-Goldensohn et al., 2008). While this technique produces meaningful evaluations of the selected components, other components remain untested, and the overall effectiveness of the entire system as a whole remains unknown. When systems are evaluated end-to-end by human judges, the studies are often small, consisting of only a handful of judges and data points (Carenini et al., 2006). Furthermore, automated summarization metrics like ROUGE (Lin and Hovy, 2003) are non-trivial to adapt to this domain as they require human curated outputs.

We present the results of a large-scale, end-to-end human evaluation of three sentiment summarization models applied to user reviews of consumer products. The evaluation shows that there is no significant difference in rater preference between any of the sentiment summarizers, but that raters do prefer sentiment summarizers over non-sentiment baselines. This indicates that even simple sentiment summarizers provide users utility. An analysis of the rater judgments also indicates that there are identifiable situations where one sentiment summarizer is generally preferred over the others. We attempt to learn these preferences by training a ranking SVM that exploits the set of preference judgments collected during the evaluation. Experiments show that the ranking SVM summarizer's cross-validation error decreases by as much as 30% over the previous best model.

Human evaluations of text summarization have been undertaken in the past. McKeown et al. (2005) presented a task-driven evaluation in the news domain in order to understand the utility of different systems. Also in the news domain, the Document Understanding Conference[1] has run a number of multi-document and query-driven summarization shared-tasks that have used a wide

[1] http://duc.nist.gov/

Proceedings of the 12th Conference of the European Chapter of the ACL, pages 514–522,
Athens, Greece, 30 March – 3 April 2009. ©2009 Association for Computational Linguistics

iPod Shuffle: 4/5 stars

"In final analysis the iPod Shuffle is a decent player that offers a sleek compact form factor an excessively simple user interface and a low price" ... "It's not good for carrying a lot of music but for a little bit of music you can quickly grab and go with this nice little toy" ... "Mine came in a nice bright orange color that makes it easy to locate."

Figure 1: An example summary.

range of automatic and human-based evaluation criteria. This year, the new Text Analysis Conference[2] is running a shared-task that contains an opinion component. The goal of that evaluation is to summarize answers to opinion questions about entities mentioned in blogs.

Our work most closely resembles the evaluations in Carenini et al. (2006, 2008). Carenini et al. (2006) had raters evaluate extractive and abstractive summarization systems. Mirroring our results, they show that both extractive and abstractive summarization outperform a baseline, but that overall, humans have no preference between the two. Again mirroring our results, their analysis indicates that even though there is no overall difference, there are situations where one system generally outperforms the other. In particular, Carenini and Cheung (2008) show that an entity's *controversiality*, e.g., mid-range star rating, is correlated with which summary has highest value.

The study presented here differs from Carenini et al. in many respects: First, our evaluation is over different extractive summarization systems in an attempt to understand what model properties are correlated with human preference irrespective of presentation; Secondly, our evaluation is on a larger scale including hundreds of judgments by hundreds of raters; Finally, we take a major next step and show that it is possible to automatically learn significantly improved models by leveraging data collected in a large-scale evaluation.

2 Sentiment Summarization

A standard setting for sentiment summarization assumes a set of documents $D = \{d_1, \ldots, d_m\}$ that contain opinions about some entity of interest. The goal of the system is to generate a summary S of that entity that is representative of the average opinion and speaks to its important aspects. An example summary is given in figure 1. For simplicity we assume that all opinions in D are about the entity being summarized. When this assumption fails, one can parse opinions at a finer-level (Jindal and Liu, 2006; Stoyanov and Cardie, 2008)

In this study, we look at an extractive summarization setting where S is built by extracting representative bits of text from the set D, subject to pre-specified length constraints. Specifically, assume each document d_i is segmented into candidate text excerpts. For ease of discussion we will assume all excerpts are sentences, but in practice they can be phrases or multi-sentence groups. Viewed this way, D is a set of candidate sentences for our summary, $D = \{s_1, \ldots, s_n\}$, and summarization becomes the following optimization:

$$\arg\max_{S \subseteq D} \mathcal{L}(S) \quad \text{s.t.: } \textsc{length}(S) \leq K \qquad (1)$$

where $\mathcal{L}$ is some score over possible summaries, $\textsc{length}(S)$ is the length of the summary and K is the pre-specified length constraint. The definition of $\mathcal{L}$ will be the subject of much of this section and it is precisely different forms of $\mathcal{L}$ that will be compared in our evaluation. The nature of LENGTH is specific to the particular use case.

Solving equation 1 is typically NP-hard, even under relatively strong independence assumptions between the sentences selected for the summary (McDonald, 2007). In cases where solving $\mathcal{L}$ is non-trivial we use an approximate hill climbing technique. First we randomly initialize the summary S to length $\sim K$. Then we greedily insert/delete/swap sentences in and out of the summary to maximize $\mathcal{L}(S)$ while maintaining the bound on length. We run this procedure until no operation leads to a higher scoring summary. In all our experiments convergence was quick, even when employing random restarts.

Alternate formulations of sentiment summarization are possible, including aspect-based summarization (Hu and Liu, 2004a), abstractive summarization (Carenini et al., 2006) or related tasks such as opinion attribution (Choi et al., 2005). We choose a purely extractive formulation as it makes it easier to develop baselines and allows raters to compare summaries with a simple, consistent presentation format.

2.1 Definitions

Before delving into the details of the summarization models we must first define some useful functions. The first is the sentiment polarity function that maps a lexical item t, e.g., word or short phrase, to a real-valued score,

$$\textsc{lex-sent}(t) \in [-1, 1]$$

[2] http://www.nist.gov/tac/

The LEX-SENT function maps items with positive polarity to higher values and items with negative polarity to lower values. To build this function we constructed large sentiment lexicons by seeding a semantic word graph induced from WordNet with positive and negative examples and then propagating this score out across the graph with a decaying confidence. This method is common among sentiment analysis systems (Hu and Liu, 2004a; Kim and Hovy, 2004; Blair-Goldensohn et al., 2008). In particular, we use the lexicons that were created and evaluated by Blair-Goldensohn et al. (2008).

Next we define sentiment intensity,

$$\text{INTENSITY}(s) = \sum_{t \in s} |\text{LEX-SENT}(t)|$$

which simply measures the magnitude of sentiment in a sentence. INTENSITY can be viewed as a measure of subjectiveness irrespective of polarity.

A central function in all our systems is a sentences normalized sentiment,

$$\text{SENT}(s) = \frac{\sum_{t \in s} \text{LEX-SENT}(t)}{\alpha + \text{INTENSITY}(s)}$$

This function measures the (signed) ratio of lexical sentiment to intensity in a sentence. Sentences that only contain lexical items of the same polarity will have high absolute normalized sentiment, whereas sentences with mixed polarity items or no polarity items will have a normalized sentiment near zero. We include the constant α in the denominator so that SENT gives higher absolute scores to sentences containing many strong sentiment items of the same polarity over sentences with a small number of weak items of the same polarity.

Most sentiment summarizers assume that as input, a system is given an overall rating of the entity it is attempting to summarize, $R \in [-1, 1]$, where a higher rating indicates a more favorable opinion. This rating may be obtained directly from user provided information (e.g., star ratings) or automatically derived by averaging the SENT function over all sentences in D. Using R, we can define a mismatch function between the sentiment of a summary and the known sentiment of the entity,

$$\text{MISMATCH}(S) = (R - \frac{1}{|S|} \sum_{s_i \in S} \text{SENT}(s_i))^2$$

Summaries with a higher mismatch are those whose sentiment disagrees most with R.

Another key input many sentiment summarizers assume is a list of salient entity aspects, which are specific properties of an entity that people tend to rate when expressing their opinion. For example, aspects of a digital camera could include picture quality, battery life, size, color, value, etc. Finding such aspects is a challenging research problem that has been addressed in a number of ways (Hu and Liu, 2004b; Gamon et al., 2005; Carenini et al., 2005; Zhuang et al., 2006; Branavan et al., 2008; Blair-Goldensohn et al., 2008; Titov and McDonald, 2008b; Titov and McDonald, 2008a). We denote the set of aspects for an entity as A and each aspect as $a \in A$. Furthermore, we assume that given A it is possible to determine whether some sentence $s \in D$ mentions an aspect in A. For our experiments we use a hybrid supervised-unsupervised method for finding aspects as described and evaluated in Blair-Goldensohn et al. (2008).

Having defined what an aspect is, we next define a summary diversity function over aspects,

$$\text{DIVERSITY}(S) = \sum_{a \in A} \text{COVERAGE}(a)$$

where $\text{COVERAGE}(a) \in \mathbb{R}$ is a function that weights how well the aspect is covered in the summary and is proportional to the importance of the aspect as some aspects are more important to cover than others, e.g., "picture quality" versus "strap" for digital cameras. The diversity function rewards summaries that cover many important aspects and plays the redundancy reducing role that is common in most extractive summarization frameworks (Goldstein et al., 2000).

2.2 Systems

For our evaluation we developed three extractive sentiment summarization systems. Each system models increasingly complex objectives.

2.2.1 Sentiment Match (SM)

The first system that we look at attempts to extract sentences so that the average sentiment of the summary is as close as possible to the entity level sentiment R, which was previously defined in section 2.1. In this case $\mathcal{L}$ can be simply defined as,

$$\mathcal{L}(S) = -\text{MISMATCH}(S)$$

Thus, the model prefers summaries with average sentiment as close as possible to the average sentiment across all the reviews.

There is an obvious problem with this model. For entities that have a mediocre rating, i.e., $R \approx 0$, the model could prefer a summary that only contains sentences with no opinion whatsoever. There are two ways to alleviate this problem. The first is to include the INTENSITY function into $\mathcal{L}$,

$$\mathcal{L}(S) = \alpha \cdot \text{INTENSITY}(S) - \beta \cdot \text{MISMATCH}(S)$$

Where the coefficients allow one to trade-off sentiment intensity versus sentiment mismatch.

The second method, and the one we chose based on initial experiments, was to address the problem at inference time. This is done by prohibiting the algorithm from including a given positive or negative sentence in the summary if another more positive/negative sentence is not included. Thus the summary is forced to consist of only the most positive and most negative sentences, the exact mix being dependent upon the overall star rating.

2.2.2 Sentiment Match + Aspect Coverage (SMAC)

The SM model extracts sentences for the summary without regard to the content of each sentence relative to the others in the summary. This is in contrast to standard summarization models that look to promote sentence diversity in order to cover as many important topics as possible (Goldstein et al., 2000). The sentiment match + aspect coverage system (SMAC) attempts to model diversity by building a summary that trades-off maximally covering important aspects with matching the overall sentiment of the entity. The model does this through the following linear score,

$$\mathcal{L}(S) = \alpha \cdot \text{INTENSITY}(S) - \beta \cdot \text{MISMATCH}(S) + \gamma \cdot \text{DIVERSITY}(S)$$

This score function rewards summaries for being highly subjective (INTENSITY), reflecting the overall product rating (MISMATCH), and covering a variety of product aspects (DIVERSITY). The coefficients were set by inspection.

This system has its roots in *event-based summarization* (Filatova and Hatzivassiloglou, 2004) for the news domain. In that work an optimization problem was developed that attempted to maximize summary informativeness while covering as many (weighted) sub-events as possible.

2.2.3 Sentiment-Aspect Match (SAM)

Because the SMAC model only utilizes an entity's overall sentiment when calculating MISMATCH, it is susceptible to degenerate solutions. Consider a product with aspects A and B, where reviewers overwhelmingly like A and dislike B, resulting in an overall SENT close to zero. If the SMAC model finds a very negative sentence describing A and a very positive sentence describing B, it will assign that summary a high score, as the summary has high intensity, has little overall mismatch, and covers both aspects. However, in actuality, the summary is entirely misleading.

To address this issue, we constructed the sentiment-aspect match model (SAM), which not only attempts to cover important aspects, but cover them with appropriate sentiment. There are many ways one might design a model to do this, including linear combinations of functions similar to the SMAC model. However, we decided to employ a probabilistic approach as it provided performance benefits based on development data experiments. Under the SAM model, each sentence is treated as a bag of aspects and their corresponding mentions' sentiments. For a given sentence s, we define A_s as the set of aspects mentioned within it. For a given aspect $a \in A_s$, we denote $\text{SENT}(a_s)$ as the sentiment associated with the textual mention of a in s. The probability of a sentence is defined as,

$$p(s) = p(a^1, \ldots, a^n, \text{SENT}(a_s^1), \ldots, \text{SENT}(a_s^n))$$

which can be re-written as,

$$\prod_{a \in A_s} p(a, \text{SENT}(a_s)) = \prod_{a \in A_s} p(a)p(\text{SENT}(a_s)|a)$$

if we assume aspect mentions are generated independently of one another. Thus we need to estimate both $p(a)$ and $p(\text{SENT}(a_s)|a)$. The probability of seeing an aspect, $p(a)$, is simply set to the maximum likelihood estimates over the data set D. Furthermore, we assume that $p(\text{SENT}(a_s)|a)$ is normal about the mean sentiment for the aspect μ_a with a constant standard deviation, σ_a. The mean and standard deviation are estimated straight-forwardly using the data set D. Note that the number of parameters our system must estimate is very small. For every possible aspect $a \in A$ we need three values: $p(a)$, μ_a, and σ_a. Since $|A|$ is typically small – on the order of 5-10 – it is not difficult to estimate these models even from small sets of data.

Having constructed this model, one logical approach to summarization would be to select sentences for the summary that have highest probability under the model trained on D. We found, however, that this produced very redundant summaries – if one aspect is particularly prevalent in a product's reviews, this approach will select all sentences about that aspect, and discuss nothing else. To combat this we developed a technique that scores the summary as a whole, rather than by individual components. First, denote $\text{SAM}(D)$ as the previously described model learned over the set of entity documents D. Next, denote $\text{SAM}(S)$ as an identical model, but learned over a candidate summary S, i.e., given a summary S, compute $p(a)$, m_a, and σ_a for all $a \in A$ using only the sentences from S. We can then measure the difference between these models using KL-divergence:

$$\mathcal{L}(S) = -\text{KL}(\text{SAM}(D), \text{SAM}(S))$$

In our case we have $1 + |A|$ distributions – $p(a)$, and $p(\cdot|a)$ for all $a \in A$ – so we just sum the KL-divergence of each. The key property of the SAM system is that it naturally builds summaries where important aspects are discussed with appropriate sentiment, since it is precisely these aspects that will contribute the most to the KL-divergence. It is important to note that the short length of a candidate summary S can make estimates in $\text{SAM}(S)$ rather crude. But we only care about finding the "best" of a set of crude models, not about finding one that is "good" in absolute terms. Between the few parameters we must learn and the specific way we use these models, we generally get models useful for our purposes.

Alternatively we could have simply incorporated the DIVERSITY measure into the objective function or used an inference algorithm that specifically accounts for redundancy, e.g., maximal marginal relevance (Goldstein et al., 2000). However, we found that this solution was well grounded and required no tuning of coefficients.

Initial experiments indicated that the SAM system, as described above, frequently returned sentences with low intensity when important aspects had luke-warm sentiment. To combat this we removed low intensity sentences from consideration, which had the effect of encouraging important luke-warm aspects to mentioned multiple times in order to balance the overall sentiment.

Though the particulars of this model are unique, fundamentally it is closest to the work of Hu and Liu (2004a) and Carenini et al. (2006).

3 Experiments

We evaluated summary performance for reviews of consumer electronics. In this setting an entity to be summarized is one particular product, D is a set of user reviews about that product, and R is the normalized aggregate star ratings left by users. We gathered reviews for 165 electronics products from several online review aggregators. The products covered a variety of electronics, such as MP3 players, digital cameras, printers, wireless routers, and video game systems. Each product had a minimum of four reviews and up to a maximum of nearly 3000. The mean number of reviews per product was 148, and the median was 70. We ran each of our algorithms over the review corpus and generated summaries for each product with $K = 650$. All summaries were roughly equal length to avoid length-based rater bias[3]. In total we ran four experiments for a combined number of 1980 rater judgments (plus additional judgments during the development phase of this study).

Our initial set of experiments were over the three opinion-based summarization systems: SM, SMAC, and SAM. We ran three experiments comparing SMAC to SM, SAM to SM, and SAM to SMAC. In each experiment two summaries of the same product were placed side-by-side in a random order. Raters were also shown an overall rating, R, for each product (these ratings are often provided in a form such as "3.5 of 5 stars"). The two summaries on either side were shown below this information with links to the full text of the reviews for the raters to explore.

Raters were asked to express their preference for one summary over the other. For two summaries S_A and S_B they could answer,

1. No preference
2. Strongly preferred S_A (or S_B)
3. Preferred S_A (or S_B)
4. Slightly preferred S_A (or S_B)

Raters were free to choose any rating, but were specifically instructed that their rating should account for a summaries representativeness of the overall set of reviews. Raters were also asked to provide a brief comment justifying their rating. Over 100 raters participated in each study, and each comparison was evaluated by three raters with no rater making more than five judgments.

[3]In particular our systems each extracted four text excerpts of roughly 160-165 characters.

Comparison (A v B)	Agreement (%)	No Preference (%)	Preferred A (%)	Preferred B (%)	Mean Numeric
SM v SMAC	65.4	6.0	52.0	42.0	0.01
SAM v SM	69.3	16.8	46.0	37.2	0.01
SAM v SMAC†	73.9	11.5	51.6	36.9	0.08
SMAC v LT†	64.1	4.1	70.4	25.5	0.24

Table 1: Results of side-by-side experiments. *Agreement* is the percentage of items for which all raters agreed on a positive/negative/no-preference rating. *No Preference* is the percentage of agreement items in which the raters had no preference. *Preferred A/B* is the percentage of agreement items in which the raters preferred either A or B respectively. *Mean Numeric* is the average of the numeric ratings (converted from discreet preference decisions) indicating on average the raters preferred system A over B on a scale of -1 to 1. Positive scores indicate a preference for system A. † significant at a 95% confidence interval for the mean numeric score.

We chose to have raters leave pairwise preferences, rather than evaluate each candidate summary in isolation, because raters can make a preference decisions more quickly than a valuation judgment, which allowed for collection of more data points. Furthermore, there is evidence that rater agreement is much higher in preference decisions than in value judgments (Ariely et al., 2008).

Results are shown in the first three rows of table 1. The first column of the table indicates the experiment that was run. The second column indicates the percentage of judgments for which the raters were in agreement. Agreement here is a *weak agreement*, where three raters are defined to be in agreement if they all gave a no preference rating, or if there was a preference rating, but no two preferences conflicted. The next three columns indicate the percentage of judgments for each preference category, grouped here into three coarse assignments. The final column indicates a numeric average for the experiment. This was calculated by converting users ratings to a scale of 1 (strongly preferred S_A) to -1 (strongly preferred S_B) at 0.33 intervals. Table 1 shows only results for items in which the raters had agreement in order to draw reliable conclusions, though the results change little when all items are taken into account.

Ultimately, the results indicate that none of the sentiment summarizers are strongly preferred over any other. Only the SAM v SMAC model has a difference that can be considered statistically significant. In terms of order we might conclude that SAM is the most preferred, followed by SM, followed by SMAC. However, the slight differences make any such conclusions tenuous at best. This leads one to wonder whether raters even require any complex modeling when summarizing opinions. To test this we took the lowest scoring model overall, SMAC, and compared it to a leading text baseline (LT) that simply selects the first sentence from a ranked list of reviews until the length constraint is violated. The results are given in the last row of 1. Here there is a clear distinction as raters preferred SMAC to LT, indicating that they did find usefulness in systems that modeled aspects and sentiment. However, there are still 25.5% of agreement items where the raters did choose a simple leading text baseline.

4 Analysis

Looking more closely at the results we observed that, even though raters did not strongly prefer any one sentiment-aware summarizer over another overall, they mostly did express preferences between systems on individual pairs of comparisons. For example, in the SAM vs SM experiment, only 16.8% of the comparisons yielded a "no preference" judgment from all three raters – by far the highest percentage of any experiment. This left 83.2% "slight preference" or higher judgments.

With this in mind we began examining the comments left by raters throughout all our experiments, including a set of additional experiments used during development of the systems. We observed several trends: 1) Raters tended to prefer summaries with lists, e.g., pros-cons lists; 2) Raters often did not like text without sentiment, hence the dislike of the leading text system where there is no guarantee that the first sentence will have any sentiment; 3) Raters disliked overly general comments, e.g., "The product was good". These statements carry no additional information over a product's overall star rating; 4) Raters did recognize (and strongly disliked) when the overall sentiment of the summary was inconsistent with the star rating; 5) Raters tended to prefer different systems depending on what the star rating was. In particular, the SMAC system was generally preferred for products with neutral overall ratings, whereas the SAM system is preferred for products with ratings at the extremes. We hypothesize that SAM's low performance on neutral rated products is because the system suffers from the dual imperatives of selecting high intensity snippets and of selecting snippets that individually reflect particular sentiment polarities. When the desired sentiment polarity is neutral, it is difficult to find a snippet with lots of sentiment, whose overall polarity is still neutral, thus SAM may either ignore that aspect or include multiple mentions of that aspect at the expense of others; 6) Raters also preferred summaries with grammatically fluent text, which benefitted the leading text baseline.

These observations suggest that we could build a new system that takes into account all these factors (weighted accordingly) or we could build a rule-based meta-classifier that selects a single summary from the four systems described in this paper based on the global characteristics of each. The problem with the former is that it will require hand-tuning of coefficients for many different signals that are all, for the most part, weakly correlated to summary quality. The problem with the latter is inefficiency, i.e., it will require the maintenance and output of all four systems. In the next section we explore an alternate method that leverages the data gathered in the evaluation to automatically learn a new model. This approach is beneficial as it will allow any coefficients to be automatically tuned and will result in a single model that can be used to build new summaries.

5 Summarization with Ranking SVMs

Besides allowing us to assess the relative performance of our summarizers, our evaluation produced several hundred points of empirical data indicating which among two summaries raters prefer. In this section we explore how to build improved summarizers with this data by learning preference ranking SVMs, which are designed to learn relative to a set of preference judgments (Joachims, 2002).

A ranking SVM typically assumes as input a set of queries and associated partial ordering on the items returned by the query. The training data is defined as pairs of points, $\mathcal{T} = \{(x_i^k, x_j^k)_t\}_{t=1}^{|\mathcal{T}|}$, where each pair indicates that the ith item is preferred over the jth item for the kth query. Each input point $x_i^k \in \mathbb{R}^m$ is a feature vector representing the properties of that particular item relative to the query. The goal is to learn a scoring function $s(x_i^k) \in \mathbb{R}$ such that $s(x_i^k) > s(x_j^k)$ if $(x_i^k, x_j^k) \in \mathcal{T}$. In other words, a ranking SVM learns a scoring function whose induced ranking over data points respects all preferences in the training data. The most straight-forward scoring function, and the one used here, is a linear classifier, $s(x_i^k) = w \cdot x_i^k$, making the goal of learning to find an appropriate weight vector $w \in \mathbb{R}^m$.

In its simplest form, the ranking SVM optimization problem can be written as the following quadratic programming problem,

$$\min \frac{1}{2}||w||^2 \quad \text{s.t.: } \forall (x_i^k, x_j^k) \in \mathcal{T},$$
$$s(x_i^k) - s(x_j^k) \geq \text{PREF}(x_i^k, x_j^k)$$

where $\text{PREF}(x_i^k, x_j^k) \in \mathbb{R}$ is a function indicating to what degree item x_i^k is preferred over x_j^k (and serves as the margin of the classifier). This optimization is well studied and can be solved with a wide variety of techniques. In our experiments we used the SVM-light software package[4].

Our summarization evaluation provides us with precisely a large collection of preference points over different summaries for different product queries. Thus, we naturally have a training set $\mathcal{T}$ where each query is analogous to a specific product of interest and training points are two possible summarizations produced by two different systems with corresponding rater preferences. Assuming an appropriate choice of feature representation it is straight-forward to then train the model on our data using standard techniques for SVMs.

To train and test the model we compiled 1906 pairs of summary comparisons, each judged by three different raters. These pairs were extracted from the four experiments described in section 3 as well as the additional experiments we ran during development. For each pair of summaries (S_i^k, S_j^k) (for some product query indexed by k), we recorded how many raters preferred each of the items as v_i^k and v_j^k respectively, i.e., v_i^k is the number of the three raters who preferred summary S_i over S_j for product k. Note that $v_i^k + v_j^k$ does not necessarily equal 3 since some raters expressed no preference between them. We set the loss function $\text{PREF}(S_i^k, S_j^k) = v_i^k - v_j^k$, which in some cases

[4]http://svmlight.joachims.org/

could be zero, but never negative since the pairs are ordered. Note that this training set includes all data points, even those in which raters disagreed. This is important as the model can still learn from these points as the margin function PREF encodes the fact that these judgments are less certain.

We used a variety of features for a candidate summary: how much capitalization, punctuation, pros-cons, and (unique) aspects a summary had; the overall intensity, sentiment, min sentence sentiment, and max sentence sentiment in the summary; the overall rating R of the product; and conjunctions of these. Note that none of these features encode which system produced the summary or which experiment it was drawn from. This is important, as it allows the model to be used as standalone scoring function, i.e., we can set $\mathcal{L}$ to the learned linear classifier $s(S)$. Alternatively we could have included features like *what system was the summary produced from*. This would have helped the model learn things like the SMAC system is typically preferred for products with mid-range overall ratings. Such a model could only be used to rank the outputs of other summarizers and cannot be used standalone.

We evaluated the trained model by measuring its accuracy on predicting a single preference prediction, i.e., given pairs of summaries (S_i^k, S_j^k), how accurate is the model at predicting that S_i is preferred to S_j for product query k? We measured 10-fold cross-validation accuracy on the subset of the data for which the raters were in agreement. We measure accuracy for both weak agreement cases (at least one rater indicated a preference and the other two raters were in agreement or had no preference) and strong agreement cases (all three raters indicated the same preference). We ignored pairs in which all three raters made a no preference judgment as both summaries can can be considered equally valid. Furthermore, we ignored pairs in which two raters indicated conflicting preferences as there is no gold standard for such cases.

Results are given in table 2. We compare the ranking SVM summarizer to a baseline system that always selects the overall-better-performing summarization system from the experiment that the given datapoint was drawn from, e.g., for all the data points drawn from the SAM versus SMAC experiment, the baseline always chooses the SAM summary as its preference. Note that in most experiments the two systems emerged in a statistical tie, so this baseline performs only slightly better than chance. Table 2 clearly shows that the ranking SVM can predict preference accuracy much better than chance, and much better than that obtained by using only one summarizer (a reduction in error of 30% for strong agreement cases).

	Preference Prediction Accuracy	
	Weak Agr.	Strong Agr.
Baseline	54.3%	56.9%
Ranking SVM	61.8%	69.9%

Table 2: Accuracies for learned summarizers.

We can thus conclude that the data gathered in human preference evaluation experiments, such as the one presented here, have a beneficial secondary use as training data for constructing a new and more accurate summarizer. This raises an interesting line of future research: can we iterate this process to build even better summarizers? That is, can we use this trained summarizer (and variants of it) to generate more examples for raters to judge, and then use that data to learn even more powerful summarizers, which in turn could be used to generate even more training judgments, etc. This could be accomplished using Mechanical Turk[5] or another framework for gathering large quantities of cheap annotations.

6 Conclusions

We have presented the results of a large-scale evaluation of different sentiment summarization algorithms. In doing so, we explored different ways of using sentiment and aspect information. Our results indicated that humans prefer sentiment informed summaries over a simple baseline. This shows the usefulness of modeling sentiment and aspects when summarizing opinions. However, the evaluations also show no strong preference between different sentiment summarizers. A detailed analysis of the results led us to take the next step in this line of research – leveraging preference data gathered in human evaluations to automatically learn new summarization models. These new learned models show large improvements in preference prediction accuracy over the previous single best model.

Acknowledgements: The authors would like to thank Kerry Hannan, Raj Krishnan, Kristen Parton and Leo Velikovich for insightful discussions.

[5]http://www.mturk.com

References

D. Ariely, G. Loewenstein, and D. Prelec. 2008. Coherent arbitrariness: Stable demand curves without stable preferences. *The Quarterly Journal of Economics*, 118:73105.

S. Blair-Goldensohn, K. Hannan, R. McDonald, T. Neylon, G.A. Reis, and J. Reynar. 2008. Building a sentiment summarizer for local service reviews. In *WWW Workshop on NLP in the Information Explosion Era*.

S.R.K. Branavan, H. Chen, J. Eisenstein, and R. Barzilay. 2008. Learning document-level semantic properties from free-text annotations. In *Proceedings of the Annual Conference of the Association for Computational Linguistics (ACL)*.

G. Carenini and J. Cheung. 2008. Extractive vs. nlg-based abstractive summarization of evaluative text: The effect of corpus controversiality. In *International Conference on Natural Language Generation (INLG)*.

G. Carenini, R.T. Ng, and E. Zwart. 2005. Extracting knowledge from evaluative text. In *Proceedings of the International Conference on Knowledge Capture*.

G. Carenini, R. Ng, and A. Pauls. 2006. Multi-document summarization of evaluative text. In *Proceedings of the Conference of the European Chapter of the Association for Computational Linguistics (EACL)*.

Y. Choi, C. Cardie, E. Riloff, and S. Patwardhan. 2005. Identifying sources of opinions with conditional random fields and extraction patterns. In *Proceedings the Joint Conference on Human Language Technology and Empirical Methods in Natural Language Processing (HLT-EMNLP)*.

E. Filatova and V. Hatzivassiloglou. 2004. A formal model for information selection in multi-sentence text extraction. In *Proceedings of the International Conference on Computational Linguistics (COLING)*.

M. Gamon, A. Aue, S. Corston-Oliver, and E. Ringger. 2005. Pulse: Mining customer opinions from free text. In *Proceedings of the 6th International Symposium on Intelligent Data Analysis (IDA)*.

J. Goldstein, V. Mittal, J. Carbonell, and M. Kantrowitz. 2000. Multi-document summarization by sentence extraction. *In Proceedings of the ANLP/NAACL Workshop on Automatic Summarization*.

M. Hu and B. Liu. 2004a. Mining and summarizing customer reviews. In *Proceedings of the International Conference on Knowledge Discovery and Data Mining (KDD)*.

M. Hu and B. Liu. 2004b. Mining opinion features in customer reviews. In *Proceedings of National Conference on Artificial Intelligence (AAAI)*.

N. Jindal and B. Liu. 2006. Mining comprative sentences and relations. In *Proceedings of 21st National Conference on Artificial Intelligence (AAAI)*.

T. Joachims. 2002. Optimizing search engines using clickthrough data. In *Proceedings of the ACM Conference on Knowledge Discovery and Data Mining (KDD)*.

S.M. Kim and E. Hovy. 2004. Determining the sentiment of opinions. In *Proceedings of Conference on Computational Linguistics (COLING)*.

C.Y. Lin and E. Hovy. 2003. Automatic evaluation of summaries using n-gram cooccurrence statistics. In *Proceedings of the Conference on Human Language Technologies and the North American Chapter of the Association for Computational Linguistics (HLT-NAACL)*.

R. McDonald. 2007. A Study of Global Inference Algorithms in Multi-document Summarization. In *Proceedings of the European Conference on Information Retrieval (ECIR)*.

K. McKeown, R.J. Passonneau, D.K. Elson, A. Nenkova, and J. Hirschberg. 2005. Do Summaries Help? A Task-Based Evaluation of Multi-Document Summarization. In *Proceedings of the ACM SIGIR Conference on Research and Development in Information Retrieval*.

A.M. Popescu and O. Etzioni. 2005. Extracting product features and opinions from reviews. In *Proceedings of the Conference on Empirical Methods in Natural Language Processing (EMNLP)*.

V. Stoyanov and C. Cardie. 2008. Topic identification for fine-grained opinion analysis. In *Proceedings of the Conference on Computational Linguistics (COLING)*.

I. Titov and R. McDonald. 2008a. A joint model of text and aspect ratings. In *Proceedings of the Annual Conference of the Association for Computational Linguistics (ACL)*.

I. Titov and R. McDonald. 2008b. Modeling online reviews with multi-grain topic models. In *Proceedings of the Annual World Wide Web Conference (WWW)*.

L. Zhuang, F. Jing, and X.Y. Zhu. 2006. Movie review mining and summarization. In *Proceedings of the International Conference on Information and Knowledge Management (CIKM)*.

Correcting a PoS-tagged corpus using three complementary methods

Hrafn Loftsson
School of Computer Science
Reykjavik University
Reykjavik, Iceland
hrafn@ru.is

Abstract

The quality of the part-of-speech (PoS) annotation in a corpus is crucial for the development of PoS taggers. In this paper, we experiment with three complementary methods for automatically detecting errors in the PoS annotation for the Icelandic Frequency Dictionary corpus. The first two methods are language independent and we argue that the third method can be adapted to other morphologically complex languages. Once possible errors have been detected, we examine each error candidate and hand-correct the corresponding PoS tag if necessary. Overall, based on the three methods, we hand-correct the PoS tagging of 1,334 tokens (0.23% of the tokens) in the corpus. Furthermore, we re-evaluate existing state-of-the-art PoS taggers on Icelandic text using the corrected corpus.

1 Introduction

Part-of-speech (PoS) tagged corpora are valuable resources for developing PoS taggers, i.e. programs which automatically tag each word in running text with morphosyntactic information. Corpora in various languages, such as the English *Penn Treebank* corpus (Marcus et al., 1993), the Swedish *Stockholm-Umeå* corpus (Ejerhed et al., 1992), and the *Icelandic Frequency Dictionary* (IFD) corpus (Pind et al., 1991), have been used to train (in the case of data-driven methods) and develop (in the case of linguistic rule-based methods) different taggers, and to evaluate their accuracy, e.g. (van Halteren et al., 2001; Megyesi, 2001; Loftsson, 2006). Consequently, the quality of the PoS annotation in a corpus (the gold standard annotation) is crucial.

Many corpora are annotated semi-automatically. First, a PoS tagger is run on the corpus text, and, then, the text is hand-corrected by humans. Despite human post-editing, (large) tagged corpora are almost certain to contain errors, because humans make mistakes. Thus, it is important to apply known methods and/or develop new methods for automatically detecting tagging errors in corpora. Once an error has been detected it can be corrected by humans or an automatic method.

In this paper, we experiment with three different methods of PoS error detection using the IFD corpus. First, we use the *variation n-gram* method proposed by Dickinson and Meurers (2003). Secondly, we run five different taggers on the corpus and examine those cases where all the taggers agree on a tag, but, at the same time, disagree with the gold standard annotation. Lastly, we use *IceParser* (Loftsson and Rögnvaldsson, 2007) to generate shallow parses of sentences in the corpus and then develop various patterns, based on feature agreement, for finding candidates for annotation errors.

Once error candidates have been detected by each method, we examine the candidates manually and correct the errors. Overall, based on these methods, we hand-correct the PoS tagging of 1,334 tokens or 0.23% of the tokens in the IFD corpus. We are not aware of previous corpus error detection/correction work applying the last two methods above. Note that the first two methods are completely language-independent, and the third method can be tailored to the language at hand, assuming the existence of a shallow parser.

Our results show that the three methods are complementary. A large ratio of the tokens that get hand-corrected based on each method is uniquely corrected by that method[1].

[1]To be precise, when we say that an error is corrected by a method, we mean that the method detected the error candidate which was then found to be a true error by the separate error correction phase.

Proceedings of the 12th Conference of the European Chapter of the ACL, pages 523–531,
Athens, Greece, 30 March – 3 April 2009.

After hand-correcting the corpus, we retrain and re-evaluate two of the best three performing taggers on Icelandic text, which results in up to 0.18% higher accuracy than reported previously.

The remainder of this paper is organised as follows. In Section 2 we describe related work, with regard to error detection and PoS tagging of Icelandic text. Our three methods of error detection are described in Section 3 and results are provided in Section 4. We re-evaluate taggers in Section 5 and we conclude with a summary in Section 6.

2 Related work

2.1 Error detection

The field of automatic error detection/correction in corpora has gained increased interest during the last few years. Most work in this field has focused on finding elements in corpora that violate consistency, i.e. finding inconsistent tagging of a word across comparable occurrences.

The variation n-gram algorithm is of this nature. This method finds identical strings (n-grams of words) in a corpus that are annotated differently. The difference in PoS tags between the strings is called a *variation* and the word(s) exhibiting the variation is called a *variation nucleus* (Dickinson and Meurers, 2003). A particular variation is thus a possible candidate for an error. The variation might be due to an error in the annotation or it might exhibit different (correct) tagging because of different contexts. Intuitively, the more similar the context of a variation, the more likely it is for the variation to be an error.

When Dickinson and Meurers applied their variation n-gram algorithm to the Wall Street Journal (WSJ) corpus of about 1.3 million words, it produced variations up to length $n = 224$. Note that a variation n-gram of length n contains two variation n-grams of length $n - 1$, obtained by removing either the first or the last word. Moreover, each variation n-gram contains at least two different annotations of the same string. Therefore, it is not straightforward to compute the precision (the ratio of correctly detected errors to all error candidates) of this method. However, by ignoring variation n-grams of length ≤ 5, Dickinson and Meurers found that 2436 of the 2495 distinct variation nuclei (each nucleus is only counted for the longest n-gram it appears in) were true errors, i.e. 97.6%. This resulted in 4417 tag corrections, i.e. about 0.34% of the tokens in the whole corpus were found to be incorrectly tagged[2].

Intuitively, the variation n-gram method is most suitable for corpora containing specific genres, e.g. business news like the WSJ, or very large balanced corpora, because in both types of corpora one can expect the length of the variations to be quite large. Furthermore, this method may not be suitable for corpora tagged with a large fine-grained tagset, because in such cases a large ratio of the variation n-grams may actually reflect true ambiguity rather than inconsistent tagging.

Another example of a method, based on finding inconsistent tagging of a word across comparable occurrences, is the one by Nakagawa and Matsumoto (2002). They use support vector machines (SVMs) to find elements in a corpus that violate consistency. The SVMs assign a weight to each training example in a corpus – a large weight is assigned to examples that are hard for the SVMs to classify. The hard examples are thus candidates for errors in the corpus. The result was a remarkable 99.5% precision when examples from the WSJ corpus were extracted with a large weight greater than or equal to a threshold value. However, the disadvantage with this approach is that a model of SVMs needs to be trained for each PoS tag, which makes it unfeasible for large tagsets.

A set of invalid n-grams can be used to search for annotation errors. The algorithm proposed by Květŏn and Oliva (2002) starts from a known set of invalid bigrams, *[first,second]*, and incrementally constructs a set of *allowed inner tags* appearing between the tags *first* and *second*. This set is then used to generate the complement, *impossible inner tags* (the set of all tags excluding the set *allowed inner tags*). Now, any n-gram consisting of the tag *first*, followed by any number of tags from the set *impossible inner tags*, finally followed by the tag *second*, is a candidate for an annotation error in a corpus. When this method was applied on the NEGRA corpus (containing 350,000 tokens) it resulted in the hand-correction of 2,661 tokens or 0.8% of the corpus. The main problem with this approach is that is presupposes a set of invalid bigrams (e.g. constructed by a linguist). For a large tagset, for example the Icelandic one (see Section 2.2), constructing this set is a very hard task. Moreover, this method fails to detect annotation errors where a particular n-gram tag sequence

[2] In a more recent work, Dickinson (2008) has developed a method for increasing the recall (the ratio of correctly detected errors to all errors in the corpus).

is valid but erroneous in the given context.

PoS taggers have also been used to point to possible errors in corpora. If the output of a tagger does not agree with the gold standard then either the tagger is incorrect or the gold standard is incorrectly annotated. A human can then look at the disagreements and correct the gold standard where necessary. van Halteren (2000) trained a tagger on the written texts of the British National Corpus sampler CD (about 1 million words). In a random sample of 660 disagreements, the tagger was correct and the gold standard incorrect in 84 cases, i.e. the precision of this error detection method was 12.7%. A natural extension of this method is to use more than one tagger to point to disagreements.

2.2 PoS tagging Icelandic

The IFD corpus is a balanced corpus, consisting of 590,297 tokens. The corpus was semi-automatically tagged using a tagger based on linguistic rules and probabilities (Briem, 1989). The main Icelandic tagset, constructed in the compilation of the corpus, is large (700 possible tags) compared to related languages. In this tagset, each character in a tag has a particular function. The first character denotes the *word class*. For each word class there is a predefined number of additional characters (at most six), which describe morphological features, like *gender*, *number* and *case* for nouns; *degree* and *declension* for adjectives; *voice*, *mood* and *tense* for verbs, etc. To illustrate, consider the word "*hestarnir*" ('(the) horses'). The corresponding tag is "*nkfng*", denoting noun (*n*), masculine (*k*), plural (*f*), nominative (*n*), and suffixed definite article (*g*).

The large tagset mirrors the morphological complexity of the Icelandic language. This, in turn, is the main reason for a relatively low tagging accuracy obtained by PoS taggers on Icelandic text, so far. The state-of-the art tagging accuracy, measured against the IFD corpus, is 92.06%, obtained by applying a bidirectional PoS tagging method (Dredze and Wallenberg, 2008). We have developed a linguistic rule-based tagger, *IceTagger*, achieving about 91.6% tagging accuracy (Loftsson, 2008). Evaluation has shown that the well known statistical tagger, *TnT* (Brants, 2000), obtains about 90.4% accuracy (Helgadóttir, 2005; Loftsson, 2008). Finally, an accuracy of about 93.5% has been achieved by using a tagger combination method using five taggers (Loftsson, 2006).

3 Three methods for error detection

In this section, we describe the three methods we used to detect (and correct) annotation errors in the IFD corpus. Each method returns a set of error candidates, which we then manually inspect and correct the corresponding tag if necessary.

3.1 Variation n-grams

We used the Decca software (`http://decca.osu.edu/`) to find the variation n-grams in the corpus. The length of the longest variation n-gram was short, i.e. it consisted of only 20 words. The longest variation that contained a true tagging error was 15 words long. As an example of a tagging error found by this method, consider the two occurrences of the 4-gram variation "henni datt í hug" (meaning 'she got an idea'):

1) henni/fpveþ datt/sfg3eþ í/a**þ** hug/nke**þ**
2) henni/fpveþ datt/sfg3eþ í/a**o** hug/nke**o**

In the first occurrence, the substring "í hug" (the variation nucleus) is incorrectly tagged as a preposition governing the dative case ("aþ"), and a noun in masculine, singular, dative ("nkeþ"). In the latter occurrence, the same substring is correctly tagged as a preposition governing the accusative case ("ao"), and a noun in masculine, singular, accusative ("nkeo"). In both cases, note the agreement in case between the preposition and the noun.

As discussed earlier, the longer variation n-grams are more likely to contain true errors than the shorter ones. Therefore, we manually inspected all the variations of length ≥ 5 produced by this method (752 in total), but only "browsed through" the variations of length 4 (like the one above; 2070 variations) and of length 3 (7563 variations).

3.2 Using five taggers

Instead of using a single tagger to tag the text in the IFD corpus, and compare the output of the taggers to the gold standard (as described in Section 2.1), we decided to use five taggers. It is well known that a combined tagger usually obtains higher accuracy than individual taggers in the combination pool. For example, by using simple voting (in which each tagger "votes" for a tag and the tag with the highest number of votes is selected by the combined tagger), the tagging accuracy can increase significantly (van Halteren et al., 2001; Loftsson, 2006). Moreover, if all the taggers in the pool agree on a vote, one would expect the tagging accuracy for the respective words to be high. Indeed, we have previously shown that when five taggers all agree on a tag in the IFD corpus, the corresponding accuracy is 98.9% (Loftsson, 2007b). For the remaining 1.1% tokens, one would expect that the five taggers are actually correct in some of the cases, but the gold standard incorrectly annotated. In general, both the precision and the recall should be higher when relying on five agreeing taggers as compared to using only a single tagger.

Thus, we used the five taggers, MBL (Daelemans et al., 1996), MXPOST (Ratnaparkhi, 1996), fnTBL (Ngai and Florian, 2001), TnT, and IceTagger[3], in the same manner as described in (Loftsson, 2006), but with the following minor changes. We extended the dictionaries of the TnT tagger and IceTagger by using data from a full-form morphological database of inflections (Bjarnadóttir, 2005). The accuracy of the two taggers increases substantially (because the ratio of unknown words drops dramatically) and, in turn, the corresponding accuracy when all the taggers agree increases from 98.9% to 99.1%. Therefore, we only needed to inspect about 0.9% of the tokens in the corpus.

The following example from the IFD corpus shows a disagreement found between the five taggers and the gold standard: "fjölskylda spákonunnar í gamla húsinu" ('family (the) fortune-teller's in (the) old house').

3) fjölskylda/nven spákonunnar/nveeg í/a**o** gamla/lhe**þ**vf húsinu/nhe**þ**g

In this case, the disagreement lies in the tagging of the preposition "í". All the five taggers suggest the correct tag "aþ" for the preposition (because case agreement is needed between the preposition and the following adjective/noun).

3.3 Shallow parsing

In a morphologically complex language like Icelandic, feature agreement, for example inside noun phrases or between a preposition and a noun phrase, plays an important role. Therefore, of the total number of possible errors existing in an Icelandic corpus, feature agreement errors are likely to be prevalent. A constituent parser is of great help in finding such error candidates, because it annotates phrases which are needed by the error detection mechanism. We used IceParser, a shallow parser for parsing Icelandic text, for this purpose.

The input to IceParser is PoS tagged text, using the IFD tagset. It produces annotation of both constituent structure and syntactic functions. To illustrate, consider the output of IceParser when parsing the input from 3) above:

4) {*SUBJ [NP fjölskylda nven NP] {*QUAL [NP spákonunnar nveeg NP] *QUAL} *SUBJ} [PP í ao [NP [AP gamla lheþvf AP] húsinu nheþg NP] PP]

The constituent labels seen here are: *PP*=a preposition phrase, *AP*=an adjective phrase, and *NP*=a noun phrase. The syntactic functions are **SUBJ*=a subject, and **QUAL*=a genitive qualifier.

This (not so shallow) output makes it relatively easy to find error candidates. Recall from example 3) that the accusative preposition tag "ao", associated with the word "í", is incorrect (the correct tag is the dative "aþ"). Since a preposition governs the case of the following noun phrase, the case of the adjective "gamla" and the noun "húsinu" should match the case of the preposition. Finding such error candidates is thus just a matter of writing regular expression patterns, one for each type of error.

Furthermore, IceParser makes it even simpler to write such patterns than it might seem when examining the output in 4). IceParser is designed as a sequence of finite-state transducers. The output of one transducer is used as the input to the next transducer in the sequence. One of these transducers marks the case of noun phrases, and another one the case of adjective phrases. This is carried out to simplify the annotation of syntactic functions in the transducers that follow, but is removed from the final output (Loftsson and Rögnvaldsson, 2007). Let us illustrate again:

5) {*SUBJ [NP**n** fjölskylda nven NP] {*QUAL [NP**g** spákonunnar nveeg NP] *QUAL} *SUBJ}

[3] The first four taggers are data-driven, but IceTagger is a linguistic rule-based tagger.

[PP í ao [NP**d** [AP**d** gamla lheþvf AP] húsinu nheþg NP] PP]

In 5), an intermediate output is shown from one of the transducers of IceParser, for the sentence from 4). Note that letters have been appended to some of the phrase labels. This letter denotes the case of the corresponding phrase, e.g. "n"=nominative, "a"=accusative, "d"=dative, and "g"=genitive.

The case letter attached to the phrase labels can thus be used when searching for specific types of errors. Consider, for example, the pattern *PrepAccError* (slightly simplified) which is used for detecting the error shown in 5) (some details are left out)[4]:

```
PrepTagAcc = ao{WhiteSpace}+
PrepAcc = {Word}{PrepTagAcc}

PrepAccError =
  "[PP"{PrepAcc}("[NP"[nde]~"NP]")
```

This pattern searches for a string starting with "[PP" followed by a preposition governing the accusative case ({PrepAcc}), followed by a substring starting with a noun phrase "[NP", marked as either nominative, dative or genitive case ("[nde]"), and ending with "NP]".

We have designed three kinds of patterns, one for PP errors as shown above, one for disagreement errors inside NPs, and one for specific VP (verb phrase) errors.

The NP patterns are more complicated than the PP patterns, and due to lack of space we are not able to describe them here in detail. Briefly, we extract noun phrases and use string processing to compare the gender, number and case features in nouns to, for example, the previous adjective or pronoun. If a disagreement is found, we print out the corresponding noun phrase. To illustrate, consider the sentence "í þessum landshluta voru fjölmörg einkasjúkrahús" ('in this part-of-the-country were numerous private-hospitals'), annotated by IceParser in the following way:

6) [PP í aþ [NP þessum fa**kfþ** landshluta n**keþ** NP] PP] [VPb voru sfg3fþ VPb] {*SUBJ< [NP [AP fjölmörg lhfnsf AP] einkasjúkrahús nhfn NP] *SUBJ<}

[4]For writing regular expression patterns, we used the lexical analyser generator tool JFlex, `http://jflex.de/`.

In this example, there is a disagreement error in number between the demonstrative pronoun "þessum" and the following noun "landshluta". The second "f" letter in the tag "fakfþ" for "þessum" denotes plural and the letter "e" in the tag "nkeþ" for "landshluta" denotes singular.

Our VP patterns mainly search for disagreements (in person and number) between a subject and the following verb[5]. Consider, for example, the sentence "ég les meira um vísindin" ('I read more about (the) science'), annotated by IceParser in the following manner:

7) {*SUBJ> [NP ég fp**1**en NP] *SUBJ>} [VP les sfg**3**en VP] {*OBJ< [AP meira lheovm AP] *OBJ<} [PP um ao [NP vísindin nhfog NP] PP]

The subject "ég" is here correctly tagged as personal pronoun, first person, ("fp1en"), but the verb "les" is incorrectly tagged as third person ("sfg3en").

By applying these pattern searches to the output of IceParser for the whole IFD corpus, we needed to examine 1,489 error candidates, or 0.25% of the corpus. Since shallow parsers have been developed for various languages, this error detection method may be tailored to other morphologically complex languages.

Notice that the above search patterns could potentially be used in a grammar checking component for Icelandic text. In that case, input text would be PoS tagged with any available tagger, shallow parsed with IceParser, and then the above patterns used to find these specific types of feature agreement error candidates.

4 Results

Table 1 shows the results of applying the three error detection methods on the IFD corpus. The column "Error candidates" shows the number of PoS tagging error candidates detected by each method. The column "Errors corrected" shows the number of tokens actually corrected, i.e. how many of the error candidates were true errors. The column "Precision" shows the ratio of correctly detected errors to all error candidates. The column "Ratio of corpus" shows the ratio of tokens corrected to all tokens in the IFD corpus. The column

[5]Additionally, one VP pattern searches for a substring containing the infinitive marker (the word "að" ('to')), immediately followed by a verb which is not tagged as an infinitive verb.

Method	Sub-type	Error candidates	Errors corrected	Precision (%)	Ratio of corpus (%)	Uniqueness rate (%)	Feature agreement (%)
variation n-gram			254		0.04	65.0	4.7
5 taggers		5317	883	16.6	0.15	78.0	24.8
shallow parsing	All	1489	448	30.1	0.08	60.0	80.2
	PP	511	226	44.2	0.04	51.3	70.4
	NP	740	160	21.6	0.03	70.0	95.0
	VP	238	62	26.1	0.01	61.3	77.1
Total distinct errors			1334		0.23		

Table 1: Results for the three error detection methods

"Uniqueness rate" shows how large a ratio of the errors corrected by a method were not found by any other method. Finally, the column "Feature agreement" shows the ratio of errors that were feature agreement errors.

As discussed in Section 2.1, it is not straightforward to compute the precision of the variation n-gram method, and we did not attempt to do so. However, we can, using our experience from examining the variations, claim that the precision is substantially lower than the 96.7% precision obtained by Dickinson and Meurers (2003). We had, indeed, expected low precision when using the variation n-gram on the IFD corpus, because this corpus and the underlying tagset is not as suitable for the method as the WSJ corpus (again, see the discussion in Section 2.1). Note that as a result of applying the variation n-gram method, only 0.04% of the tokens in the IFD corpus were found to be incorrectly tagged. This ratio is 8.5 times lower than the ratio obtained by Dickinson and Meurers when applying the same method on the WSJ corpus. On the other hand, the variation n-gram method nicely complements the other methods, because 65.0% of the 254 hand-corrected errors were uniquely corrected on the basis of this method.

Table 1 shows that most errors were detected by applying the "5 taggers" method – 0.15% of the tokens in the corpus were found to be incorrectly annotated on the basis of this method. The precision of the method is 16.6%. Recall that by using a single tagger for error detection, van Halteren (2000) obtained a precision of 12.7%. One might have expected more difference in precision by using five taggers vs. a single tagger, but note that the languages used in the two experiments, as well as the tagsets, are totally different. Therefore, the comparison in precision may not be viable. Moreover, it has been shown that tagging Icelandic text, using the IFD tagset, is a hard task (see Section 2.2). Hence, even though five agreeing taggers disagree with the gold standard, in a large majority of the disagreements (83.4% in our case) the taggers are indeed wrong.

Consider, for example, the simple sentence "þá getur það enginn" ('then can it nobody', meaning 'then nobody can do-it'), which exemplifies the free word order in Icelandic. Here the subject is "enginn" and the object is "það". Therefore, the correct tagging (which is the one in the corpus) is "þá/aa getur/sfg3en það/fpheo enginn/foken", in which "það" is tagged with the accusative case (the last letter in the tag "fpheo"). However, all the five taggers make the mistake of tagging "það" with the nominative case ("fphen"), i.e. assuming it is the subject of the sentence.

The uniqueness ratio for the 5-taggers method is high or 78.0%, i.e. a large number of the errors corrected based on this method were not found (corrected) by any of the other methods. However, bear in mind, that this method produces most error candidates.

The error detection method based on shallow parsing resulted in about twice as many errors corrected than by applying the variation n-gram method. Even though the precision of this method as a whole (the subtype marked "All" in Table 1) is considerably higher than when applying the 5-taggers methods (30.1% vs. 16.6%), we did expect higher precision. Most of the false positives (error candidates which turned out not to be errors) are due to incorrect phrase annotation in IceParser. A common incorrect phrase annotation is one which includes a genitive qualifier. To illustrate, consider the following sentence "sumir farþeganna voru á heimleið" ('some of-the-passengers were on-their-way home'), matched by one of the NP error patterns:

8) {*QUAL [NP sumir fo**kfn** farþeganna **nkfe**g NP] *QUAL} [VPb voru sfg3fþ VPb] [PP á aþ [NP heimleið nveþ NP] PP]

Here "sumir farþeganna" is annotated as a single noun phrase, but should be annotated as two noun phrases "[NP sumir fokfn NP]" and "[NP farþeganna nkfeg NP]", where the second one is the genitive qualifier of the first one. If this was correctly annotated by IceParser, the NP error pattern would not detect any feature agreement error for this sentence, because no match is carried out across phrases.

The last column in Table 1 shows the ratio of feature agreement errors, which are errors resulting from mismatch in gender/person, number or case between two words (e.g., see examples 6) and 7) above). Examples of errors not resulting from feature agreement are: a tag denoting the incorrect word class, and a tag of a an object containing an incorrect case (verbs govern the case of their objects).

Recall from Section 3.3 that rules were written to search for feature agreement errors in the output of IceParser. Therefore, a high ratio of the total errors corrected by the shallow parsing method (80.2%) are indeed due to feature agreement mismatches. 95.0% and 70.4% of the NP errors and the PP errors are feature agreement errors, respectively. The reason for a lower ratio in the PP errors is the fact that in some cases the proposed preposition should actually have been tagged as an adverb (the proposed tag therefore denotes an incorrect word class). In the case of the 5-taggers method, 24.8% of the errors corrected are due to feature agreement errors but only 4.7% in the case of the variation n-gram method.

The large difference between the three methods with regard to the ratio of feature agreement errors, as well as the uniqueness ratio discussed above, supports our claim that the methods are indeed complementary, i.e. a large ratio of the tokens that get hand-corrected based on each method is uniquely corrected by that method.

Overall, we were able to correct 1,334 distinct errors, or 0.23% of the IFD corpus, by applying the three methods (see the last row of Table 1). Compared to related work, this ratio is, for example, lower than the one obtained by applying the variation n-gram method on the WSJ corpus (0.34%). The exact ratio is, however, not of prime importance because the methods have been applied to different languages, different corpora and different tagsets. Rather, our work shows that using a single method which has worked well for an English corpus (the variation n-gram method) does not work particularly well for an Icelandic corpus but adding two other complementary methods helps in finding errors missed by the first method.

5 Re-evaluation of taggers

Earlier work on evaluation of tagging accuracy for Icelandic text has used the original IFD corpus (without any error correction attempts). Since we were able to correct several errors in the corpus, we were confident that the tagging accuracy published hitherto had been underestimated.

To verify this, we used IceTagger and TnT, two of the three best performing taggers on Icelandic text. Additionally, we used a changed version of TnT, which utilises functionality from IceMorphy, the morphological analyser of IceTagger, and a changed version of IceTagger which uses a hidden Markov Model (HMM) to disambiguate words which can not be further disambiguated by applying rules (Loftsson, 2007b). In tables 2 and 3 below, *Ice* denotes IceTagger, *Ice** denotes IceTagger+HMM, and *TnT** denotes TnT+IceMorphy.

We ran 10-fold cross-validation, using the exact same data-splits as used in (Loftsson, 2006), both before error correction (i.e. on the original corpus) and after the error correction (i.e. on the corrected corpus). Note that in these two steps we did not retrain the TnT tagger, i.e. it still used the language model derived from the original uncorrected corpus.

Using the original corpus, the average tagging accuracy results (using the first nine splits), for unknown words, known words, and all words, are shown in Table 2[6]. The average unknown word ratio is 6.8%.

Then we repeated the evaluation, now using the corrected corpus. The results are shown in Table 3. By comparing the tagging accuracy for all words in tables 2 and 3, it can be seen that the accuracy had be underestimated by 0.13-0.18 percentage points. The taggers TnT* and Ice* benefit the most from the corpus error correction – their

[6]The accuracy figures shown in Table 2 are comparable to the results in (Loftsson, 2006).

Words	TnT	TnT*	Ice	Ice*
Unknown	71.82	72.98	75.30	75.63
Known	91.82	92.60	92.78	93.01
All	90.45	91.25	91.59	91.83

Table 2: Average tagging accuracy (%) using the original IFD corpus

Words	TnT	TnT*	Ice	Ice*
Unknown	71.88	73.03	75.36	75.70
Known	91.96	92.75	92.95	93.20
All	90.58	91.43	91.76	92.01

Table 3: Average tagging accuracy (%) using the corrected IFD corpus

accuracy for all words increases by 0.18 percentage points. Recall that we hand-corrected 0.23% of the tokens in the corpus, and therefore TnT* and Ice* correctly annotate 78.3% (0.18/0.23) of the corrected tokens.

Since the TnT tagger is a data-driven tagger, it is interesting to see whether the corrected corpus changes the language model (to the better) of the tagger. In other words, does retraining using the corrected corpus produce better results than using the language model generated from the original corpus? The answer is yes, as can be seen by comparing the accuracy figures for TnT and TnT* in tables 3 and 4. The tagging accuracy for all words increases by 0.10 and 0.07 percentage points for TnT and TnT*, respectively.

The re-evaluation of the above taggers, with or without retraining, clearly indicates that the quality of the PoS annotation in the IFD corpus has significant effect on the accuracy of the taggers.

6 Conclusion

The work described in this paper consisted of two stages. In the first stage, we used three error detection methods to hand-correct PoS errors in an Icelandic corpus. The first two methods are language independent, and we argued that the third method can be adapted to other morphologically complex languages.

As we expected, the application of the first method used, the variation n-gram method, did result in relatively few errors being detected and corrected (i.e. 254 errors). By adding two new methods, the first based on the agreement of five taggers, and the second based on shallow parsing, we were able to detect and correct 1,334 errors in

Words	TnT	TnT*
Unknown	71.97	73.10
Known	92.06	92.85
All	90.68	91.50

Table 4: Average tagging accuracy (%) of TnT after retraining using the corrected IFD corpus

total, or 0.23% of the tokens in the corpus. Our analysis shows that the three methods are complementary, i.e. a large ratio of the tokens that get hand-corrected based on each method is uniquely corrected by that method.

An interesting side effect of the first stage is the fact that by inspecting the error candidates resulting from the shallow parsing method, we have noticed a number of systematic errors made by IceParser which should, in our opinion, be relatively easy to fix. Moreover, we noted that our regular expression search patterns, for finding feature agreement errors in the output of IceParser, could potentially be used in a grammar checking tool for Icelandic.

In the second stage, we re-evaluated and retrained two PoS taggers for Icelandic based on the corrected corpus. The results of the second stage clearly indicate that the quality of the PoS annotation in the IFD corpus has a significant effect on the accuracy of the taggers.

It is, of course, difficult to estimate the recall of our methods, i.e. how many of the true errors in the corpus we actually hand-corrected. In future work, one could try to increase the recall by a variant of the 5-taggers method. Instead of demanding that all five taggers agree on a tag before comparing the result to the gold standard, one could inspect those cases in which four out of the five taggers agree. The problem, however, with that approach is that the number of cases that need to be inspected grows substantially. By demanding that all the five taggers agree on the tag, we needed to inspect 5,317 error candidates. By relaxing the conditions to four votes out of five, we would need to inspect an additional 9,120 error candidates.

Acknowledgements

Thanks to the Árni Magnússon Institute for Icelandic Studies for providing access to the IFD corpus and the morphological database of inflections, and to all the developers of the software used in this research for sharing their work.

References

Kristín Bjarnadóttir. 2005. Modern Icelandic Inflections. In H. Holmboe, editor, *Nordisk Sprogteknologi 2005*, pages 49–50. Museum Tusculanums Forlag, Copenhagen.

Thorsten Brants. 2000. TnT: A statistical part-of-speech tagger. In *Proceedings of the 6th Conference on Applied Natural Language Processing*, Seattle, WA, USA.

Stefán Briem. 1989. Automatisk morfologisk analyse af islandsk tekst. In *Papers from the Seventh Scandinavian Conference of Computational Linguistics*, Reykjavik, Iceland.

Walter Daelemans, Jakub Zavrel, Peter Berck, and Steven Gillis. 1996. MBT: a Memory-Based Part of Speech Tagger-Generator. In *Proceedings of the 4th Workshop on Very Large Corpora*, Copenhagen, Denmark.

Markus Dickinson and W. Detmar Meurers. 2003. Detecting Errors in Part-of-Speech Annotation. In *Proceedings of the 11th Conference of the European Chapter of the Association for Computational Linguistics*, Budapest, Hungary.

Markus Dickinson. 2008. Representations for category disambiguation. In *Proceedings of the 22nd International Conference on Computational Linguistics (COLING-08)*, Manchester, UK.

Mark Dredze and Joel Wallenberg. 2008. Icelandic Data Driven Part of Speech Tagging. In *Proceedings of the 46th Annual Meeting of the Association for Computational Linguistics: Human Language Technologies*, Columbus, OH, USA.

Eva Ejerhed, Gunnel Källgren, Ola Wennstedt, and Magnus Åström. 1992. *The Linguistic Annotation System of the Stockholm-Umeå Project*. Department of General Linguistics, University of Umeå.

Sigrún Helgadóttir. 2005. Testing Data-Driven Learning Algorithms for PoS Tagging of Icelandic. In H. Holmboe, editor, *Nordisk Sprogteknologi 2004*, pages 257–265. Museum Tusculanums Forlag, Copenhagen.

Pavel Květõn and Karel Oliva. 2002. Achieving an Almost Correct PoS-Tagged Corpus. In P. Sojka, I. Kopeček, and K. Pala, editors, *Proceedings of the 5th International Conference on TEXT, SPEECH and DIALOGUE*, Brno, Czech Republic.

Hrafn Loftsson and Eiríkur Rögnvaldsson. 2007. IceParser: An Incremental Finite-State Parser for Icelandic. In *Proceedings of the 16th Nordic Conference of Computational Linguistics (NoDaLiDa 2007)*, Tartu, Estonia.

Hrafn Loftsson. 2006. Tagging Icelandic text: an experiment with integrations and combinations of taggers. *Language Resources and Evaluation*, 40(2):175–181.

Hrafn Loftsson. 2007b. *Tagging and Parsing Icelandic Text*. Ph.D. thesis, University of Sheffield, Sheffield, UK.

Hrafn Loftsson. 2008. Tagging Icelandic text: A linguistic rule-based approach. *Nordic Journal of Linguistics*, 31(1):47–72.

Mitchell P. Marcus, Beatrice Santorini, and Mary A. Marcinkiewicz. 1993. Building a Large Annotated Corpus of English: The Penn Treebank. *Computational Linguistics*, 19(2):313–330.

Beáta Megyesi. 2001. Comparing Data-Driven Learning Algorithms for PoS Tagging of Swedish. In *Proceedings of the Conference on Empirical Methods in Natural Language Processing (EMNLP 2001)*, Pittsburgh, PA, USA.

Tetsuji Nakagawa and Yuji Matsumoto. 2002. Detecting errors in corpora using support vector machines. In *Proceedings of the 19th International Conference on Computational Linguistics*, Taipei, Taiwan.

Grace Ngai and Radu Florian. 2001. Transformation-Based Learning in the Fast Lane. In *Proceedings of the 2nd Conference of the North American Chapter of the ACL*, Pittsburgh, PA, USA.

Jörgen Pind, Friðrik Magnússon, and Stefán Briem. 1991. *Íslensk orðtíðnibók [The Icelandic Frequency Dictionary]*. The Institute of Lexicography, University of Iceland, Reykjavik.

Adwait Ratnaparkhi. 1996. A Maximum Entropy Model for Part-Of-Speech Tagging. In *Proceedings of the Conference on Empirical Methods in Natural Language Processing*, Philadelphia, PA, USA.

Hans van Halteren, Jakub Zavrel, and Walter Daelemans. 2001. Improving Accuracy in Wordclass Tagging through Combination of Machine Learning Systems. *Computational Linguistics*, 27(2):199–230.

Hans van Halteren. 2000. The Detection of Inconsistency in Manually Tagged Text. In A. Abeillé, T. Brants, and H. Uszkoreit, editors, *Proceedings of the 2nd Workshop on Linguistically Interpreted Corpora*, Luxembourg.

Translation as Weighted Deduction

Adam Lopez
University of Edinburgh
10 Crichton Street
Edinburgh, EH8 9AB
United Kingdom
alopez@inf.ed.ac.uk

Abstract

We present a unified view of many translation algorithms that synthesizes work on deductive parsing, semiring parsing, and efficient approximate search algorithms. This gives rise to clean analyses and compact descriptions that can serve as the basis for modular implementations. We illustrate this with several examples, showing how to build search spaces for several disparate phrase-based search strategies, integrate non-local features, and devise novel models. Although the framework is drawn from parsing and applied to translation, it is applicable to many dynamic programming problems arising in natural language processing and other areas.

1 Introduction

Implementing a large-scale translation system is a major engineering effort requiring substantial time and resources, and understanding the tradeoffs involved in model and algorithm design decisions is important for success. As the space of systems described in the literature becomes more crowded, identifying their common elements and isolating their differences becomes crucial to this understanding. In this work, we present a common framework for model manipulation and analysis that accomplishes this, and use it to derive surprising conclusions about phrase-based models.

Most translation algorithms do the same thing: dynamic programming search over a space of weighted rules (§2). Fortunately, we need not search far for modular descriptions of dynamic programming algorithms. Deductive logic (Pereira and Warren, 1983), extended with semirings (Goodman, 1999), is an established formalism used in parsing. It is occasionally used to describe formally syntactic translation models, but these treatments tend to be brief (Chiang, 2007; Venugopal et al., 2007; Dyer et al., 2008; Melamed, 2004). We apply weighted deduction much more thoroughly, first extending it to phrase-based models and showing that the set of search strategies used by these models have surprisingly different implications for model and search error (§3, §4). We then show how it can be used to analyze common translation problems such as non-local parameterizations (§5), alignment, and novel model design (§6). Finally, we show that it leads to a simple analysis of cube pruning (Chiang, 2007), an important approximate search algorithm (§7).

2 Translation Models

A translation model consists of two distinct elements: an *unweighted* ruleset, and a parameterization (Lopez, 2008). A **ruleset** licenses the steps by which a source string $f_1...f_I$ may be rewritten as a target string $e_1...e_J$, thereby defining the finite set of all possible rewritings of a source string. A **parameterization** defines a weight function over every sequence of rule applications.

In a phrase-based model, the ruleset is simply the unweighted phrase table, where each phrase pair $f_i...f_{i'}/e_j...e_{j'}$ states that phrase $f_i...f_{i'}$ in the source is rewritten as $e_j...e_{j'}$ in the the target.

The model operates by iteratively applying rewrites to the source sentence until each source word has been consumed by exactly one rule. We call a sequence of rule applications a **derivation**. A target string $e_1...e_J$ yielded by a derivation D is obtained by concatenating the target phrases of the rules in the order in which they were applied. We define $Y(D)$ to be the target string yielded by D.

Proceedings of the 12th Conference of the European Chapter of the ACL, pages 532–540,
Athens, Greece, 30 March – 3 April 2009. ©2009 Association for Computational Linguistics

Now consider the Viterbi approximation to a noisy channel parameterization of this model, $P(f|D) \cdot P(D)$.[1] We define $P(f|D)$ in the standard way.

$$P(f|D) = \prod_{f_i...f_{i'}/e_j...e_{j'} \in D} p(f_i...f_{i'}|e_j...e_{j'}) \tag{1}$$

Note that in the channel model, we can replace any rule application with any other rule containing the same source phrase without affecting the partial score of the rest of the derivation. We call this a **local** parameterization.

Now we define a standard n-gram model $P(D)$.

$$P(D) = \prod_{e_j \in Y(D)} p(e_j|e_{j-n+1}...e_{j-1}) \tag{2}$$

This parameterization differs from the channel model in an important way. If we replace a single rule in the derivation, the partial score of the rest of derivation is also affected, because the terms $e_{j-n+1}...e_j$ may come from more than one rule. In other words, this parameterization encodes a dependency between the steps in a derivation. We call this a **non-local** parameterization.

3 Translation As Deduction

For the first part of the discussion that follows, we consider deductive logics purely over unweighted rulesets. As a way to introduce deductive logic, we consider the CKY algorithm for context-free parsing, a common example that we will revisit in §6.2. It is also relevant since it can form the basis of a decoder for inversion transduction grammar (Wu, 1996). In the discussion that follows, we use A, B, and C to denote arbitrary nonterminal symbols, S to denote the start nonterminal symbol, and a to denote a terminal symbol. CKY works on grammars in Chomsky normal form: all rules are either binary as in $A \rightarrow BC$, or unary as in $A \rightarrow a$.

The number of possible binary-branching parses of a sentence is defined by the Catalan number, an exponential combinatoric function (Church and Patil, 1982), so dynamic programming is crucial for efficiency. CKY computes all parses in cubic time by reusing subparses. To parse a sentence $a_1...a_K$, we compute a set of **items** in the form $[A, k, k']$, where A is a nonterminal category, k and k' are both integers in the range $[0, n]$. This item represents the fact that there is some parse of span $a_{k+1}...a_{k'}$ rooted at A (span indices are on the spaces between words). CKY works by creating items over successively longer spans. First it creates items $[A, k-1, k]$ for any rule $A \rightarrow a$ such that $a = a_k$. It then considers spans of increasing length, creating items $[A, k, k']$ whenever it finds two items $[B, k, k'']$ and $[C, k'', k']$ for some grammar rule $A \rightarrow BC$ and some midpoint k''. Its goal is an item $[S, 0, K]$, indicating that there is a parse of $a_1...a_K$ rooted at S.

A CKY logic describes its actions as **inference rules**, equivalent to Horn clauses. The inference rule is a list of **antecedents**, items and rules that must all be true for the inference to occur; and a single **consequent** that is inferred. To denote the creation of item $[A, k, k']$ based on existence of rule $A \rightarrow BC$ and items $[B, k, k'']$ and $[C, k'', k']$, we write an inference rule with antecedents on the top line and consequent on the second line, following Goodman (1999) and Shieber et al. (1995).

$$\frac{R(A \rightarrow BC) \;\; [B, k, k''] \;\; [C, k'', k']}{[A, k, k']}$$

We now give the complete Logic CKY.

$$\textbf{item form: } [A, k, k'] \quad \textbf{goal: } [S, 0, K]$$

$$\textbf{rules: } \begin{cases} \dfrac{R(A \rightarrow a_k)}{[A, k-1, k]} \\[2ex] \dfrac{R(A \rightarrow BC) \;\; [B, k, k''] \;\; [C, k'', k']}{[A, k, k']} \end{cases} \tag{Logic CKY}$$

A benefit of this declarative description is that complexity can be determined by inspection (McAllester, 1999). We elaborate on complexity in §7, but for now it suffices to point out that the number of possible items and possible deductions depends on the product of the domains of the free variables. For example, the number of possible CKY items for a grammar with G nonterminals is $O(GK^2)$, because k and k' are both in range $[0, K]$. Likewise, the number of possible inference rules that can fire is $O(G^3K^3)$.

3.1 A Simple Deductive Decoder

For our first example of a translation logic we consider a simple case: monotone decoding (Mariño et al., 2006; Zens and Ney, 2004). Here, rewrite rules are applied strictly from left to right on the source sentence. Despite its simplicity, the search

[1]The true noisy channel parameterization $p(f|e) \cdot p(e)$ would require a marginalization over D, and is intractable for most models.

space can be very large—in the limit there could be a translation for every possible segmentation of the sentence, so there are exponentially many possible derivations. Fortunately, we know that monotone decoding can easily be cast as a dynamic programming problem. For any position i in the source sentence $f_1...f_I$, we can freely combine any partial derivation covering $f_1...f_i$ on its left with any partial derivation covering $f_{i+1}...f_I$ on its right to yield a complete derivation.

In our deductive program for monotone decoding, an item simply encodes the index of the rightmost word that has been rewritten.

item form: $[i]$ **goal:** $[I]$ **rule:** $$\frac{[i] \;\; R(f_{i+1}...f_{i'}/e_j...e_{j'})}{[i']}$$

(Logic MONOTONE)

This is the algorithm of Zens and Ney (2004). With a maximum phrase length of m, i' will range over $[i+1, \min(i+m, I)]$, giving a complexity of $O(Im)$. In the limit it is $O(I^2)$.

3.2 More Complex Decoders

Now we consider phrase-based decoders with more permissive reordering. In the limit we allow arbitrary reordering, so our item must contain a coverage vector. Let V be a binary vector of length I; that is, $V \in \{0,1\}^I$. Le 0^m be a vector of m 0's. For example, bit vector 00000 will be abbreviated 0^5 and bit vector 000110 will be abbreviated $0^3 1^2 0^1$. Finally, we will need bitwise AND ($\wedge$) and OR ($\vee$). Note that we impose an additional requirement that is not an item in the deductive system as a **side condition** (we elaborate on the significance of this in §4).

item form: $[\{0,1\}^I]$ **goal:** $[1^I]$

rule:

$$\frac{[V] \;\; R(f_{i+1}...f_{i'}/e_j...e_{j'})}{[V \vee 0^i 1^{i'-i} 0^{I-i'}]} \quad V \wedge 0^i 1^{i'-i} 0^{I-i'} = 0^I$$

(Logic PHRASE-BASED)

The runtime complexity is exponential, $O(I^2 2^I)$. Practical decoding strategies are more restrictive, implementing what is frequently called a *distortion limit* or *reordering limit*. We found that these terms are inexact, used to describe a variety of quite different strategies.[2] Since we did not feel that the relationship between these various strategies was obvious or well-known, we give logics for several of them and a brief analysis of the implications. Each strategy uses a parameter d, generically called the distortion limit or reordering limit.

The **Maximum Distortion d strategy** (MDd) requires that the first word of a phrase chosen for translation be within d words of the the last word of the most recently translated phrase (Figure 1).[3] The effect of this strategy is that, up to the last word covered in a partial derivation, there must be a covered word in every d words. Its complexity is $O(I^3 2^d)$.

MDd can produce partial derivations that cannot be completed by any allowed sequence of jumps. To prevent this, the **Window Length d strategy** (WLd) enforces a tighter restriction that the last word of a phrase chosen for translation cannot be more than d words from the leftmost untranslated word in the source (Figure 1).[4] For this logic we use a bitwise shift operator ($\ll$), and a predicate (α_1) that counts the number of leading ones in a bit array.[5] Its runtime is exponential in parameter d, but *linear* in sentence length, $O(d^2 2^d I)$.

The **First d Uncovered Words strategy** (FdUW) is described by Tillman and Ney (2003) and Zens and Ney (2004), who call it the *IBM Constraint*.[6] It requires at least one of the leftmost d uncovered words to be covered by a new phrase. Items in this strategy contain the index i of the rightmost covered word and a vector $U \in [1, I]^d$ of the d leftmost uncovered words (Figure 1). Its complexity is $O(dI\binom{I}{d+1})$, which is roughly exponential in d.

There are additional variants, such as the **Maximum Jump d strategy** (MJd), a polynomial-time strategy described by Kumar and Byrne (2005), and possibly others. We lack space to describe all of them, but simply depicting the strategies as logics permits us to make some simple analyses.

First, it should be clear that these reordering strategies define overlapping but not identical search spaces: for most values of d it is impossible to find d' such that any of the other strategies would be identical (except for degenerate cases

[2] Costa-jussà and Fonollosa (2006) refer to the reordering limit and distortion limit as two distinct strategies.

[3] Moore and Quirk (2007) give a nice description of MDd.

[4] We do not know if WLd is documented anywhere, but from inspection it is used in Moses (Koehn et al., 2007). This was confirmed by Philipp Koehn and Hieu Hoang (p.c.).

[5] When a phrase covers the first uncovered word in the source sentence, the new first uncovered word may be further along in the sentence (if the phrase completely filled a gap), or just past the end of the phrase (otherwise).

[6] We could not identify this strategy in the IBM patents.

$$(1)\quad \begin{array}{c}\textbf{item form: } [i, \{0,1\}^I] \\ \textbf{goal: } [i \in [I-d, I], 1^I]\end{array} \quad \textbf{rule: } \frac{[i'', V] \;\; R(f_{i+1}...f_{i'}/e_j...e_{j'})}{[i', V \vee 0^i 1^{i'-i} 0^{I-i'}]} \; V \wedge 0^i 1^{i'-i} 0^{I-i'} = 0^I, |i - i''| \leq d$$

$$\begin{array}{c}(2) \\ \textbf{item form: } [i, \{0,1\}^d] \\ \textbf{goal: } [I, 0^d]\end{array} \quad \textbf{rules: } \begin{cases} \dfrac{[i, C] \;\; R(f_{i+1}...f_{i'}/e_j...e_{j'})}{[i'', C \ll i'' - i]} & \begin{array}{c} C \wedge 1^{i'-i} 0^{d-i'+i} = 0^d, i' - i \leq d, \\ \alpha_1(C \vee 1^{i'-i} 0^{d-i'+i}) = i'' - i \end{array} \\ \dfrac{[i, C] \;\; R(f_{i'}...f_{i''}/e_j...e_{j'})}{[i, C \vee 0^{i'-i} 1^{i''-i'} 0^{d-i''+i}]} & C \wedge 0^{i'-i} 1^{i''-i'} 0^{d-i''+i} = 0^d, i'' - i \leq d \end{cases}$$

$$(3)\quad \textbf{item form: } [i, [1, I+d]^d] \quad \textbf{goal: } [I, [I+1, I+d]]$$

$$\textbf{rules: } \begin{cases} \dfrac{[i, U] \;\; R(f_{i'}...f_{i''}/e_j...e_{j'})}{[i'', U - [i', i''] \vee [i'', i'' + d - |U - [i', i'']|]]} \; i' > i, f_{i+1} \in U \\ \dfrac{[i, U] \;\; R(f_{i'}...f_{i''}/e_j...e_{j'})}{[i, U - [i', i''] \vee [\max(U \vee i) + 1, \max(U \vee i) + 1 + d - |U - [i', i'']|]]} \; i' < i, [f_{i'}, f_{i''}] \subset U \end{cases}$$

Figure 1: Logics (1) MDd, (2) WLd, and (3) FdUW. Note that the goal item of MDd (1) requires that the last word of the last phrase translated be within d words of the end of the source sentence.

$d = 0$ and $d = I$). This has important ramifications for scientific studies: results reported for one strategy may not hold for others, and in cases where the strategy is not clearly described it may be impossible to replicate results. Furthermore, it should be clear that the strategy can have significant impact on decoding speed and pruning strategies (§7). For example, MDd is more complex than WLd, and we expect implementations of the former to require more pruning and suffer from more search errors, while the latter would suffer from more model errors since its space of possible reorderings is smaller.

We emphasize that many other translation models can be described this way. Logics for the IBM Models (Brown et al., 1993) would be similar to our logics for phrase-based models. Syntax-based translation logics are similar to parsing logics; a few examples already appear in the literature (Chiang, 2007; Venugopal et al., 2007; Dyer et al., 2008; Melamed, 2004). For simplicity, we will use the MONOTONE logic for the remainder of our examples, but all of them generalize to more complex logics.

4 Adding Local Parameterizations via Semiring-Weighted Deduction

So far we have focused solely on unweighted logics, which correspond to search using only rule-sets. Now we turn our focus to parameterizations. As a first step, we consider only local parameterizations, which make computing the score of a derivation quite simple. We are given a set of inferences in the following form (interpreting side conditions $\mathcal{B}_1...\mathcal{B}_M$ as boolean constraints).

$$\frac{\mathcal{A}_1...\mathcal{A}_L}{\mathcal{C}} \; \mathcal{B}_1...\mathcal{B}_M$$

Now suppose we want to find the highest-scoring derivation. Each antecedent item $\mathcal{A}_\ell$ has a probability $p(\mathcal{A}_\ell)$: if $\mathcal{A}_\ell$ is a rule, then the probability is given, otherwise its probability is computed recursively in the same way that we now compute $p(\mathcal{C})$. Since $\mathcal{C}$ can be the consequent of multiple deductions, we take the max of its current value (initially 0) and the result of the new deduction.

$$p(\mathcal{C}) = \max(p(\mathcal{C}), (p(\mathcal{A}_1) \times ... \times p(\mathcal{A}_L))) \quad (3)$$

If for every $\mathcal{A}_\ell$ that is an item, we replace $p(\mathcal{A}_\ell)$ recursively with this expression, we end up with a maximization over a product of rule probabilities. Applying this to logic MONOTONE, the result will be a maximization (over all possible derivations D) of the algebraic expression in Equation 1.

We might also want to calculate the total probability of all possible derivations, which is useful for parameter estimation (Blunsom et al., 2008). We can do this using the following equation.

$$p(\mathcal{C}) = p(\mathcal{C}) + (p(\mathcal{A}_1) \times ... \times p(\mathcal{A}_L)) \quad (4)$$

Equations 3 and 4 are quite similar. This suggests a useful generalization: semiring-weighted deduction (Goodman, 1999).[7] A **semiring** $\langle \mathbb{A}, \otimes, \oplus \rangle$ consists of a domain $\mathbb{A}$, a multiplicative operator $\otimes$ and an additive operator $\oplus$.[8] In Equation 3 we use the Viterbi semiring $\langle [0,1], \times, \max \rangle$, while in Equation 4 we use the inside semiring $\langle [0,1], \times, + \rangle$. The general form of Equations 3 and 4 can be written for weights $w \in \mathbb{A}$.

$$w(\mathcal{C}) \oplus= w(\mathcal{A}_1) \otimes ... \otimes w(\mathcal{A}_\ell) \quad (5)$$

Many quantities can be computed simply by using the appropriate semiring. Goodman (1999) describes semirings for the Viterbi derivation, k-best Viterbi derivations, derivation forest, and number of paths.[9] Eisner (2002) describes the *expectation semiring* for parameter learning. Gimpel and Smith (2009) describe *approximation semirings* for approximate summing in (usually intractable) models. In parsing, the boolean semiring $\langle \{\top, \bot\}, \cap, \cup \rangle$ is used to determine grammaticality of an input string. In translation it is relevant for alignment (§6.1).

5 Adding Non-Local Parameterizations with the PRODUCT Transform

A problem arises with the semiring-weighted deductive formalism when we add non-local parameterizations such as an n-gram model (Equation 2). Suppose we have a derivation $D = (d_1, ..., d_M)$, where each d_m is a rule application. We can view the language model as a function on D.

$$P(D) = f(d_1, ..., d_m, ..., d_M) \quad (6)$$

The problem is that replacing d_m with a lower-scoring rule d'_m may actually improve f due to the language model dependency. This means that f is *nonmonotonic*—it does not display the *optimal substructure* property on partial derivations, which is required for dynamic programming (Cormen et al., 2001). The logics still work for some semirings (e.g. boolean), but not others. Therefore, non-local parameterizations break semiring-weighted deduction, because we can no longer use the same logic under all semirings. We need new logics; for this we will use a logic programming transform called the PRODUCT transform (Cohen et al., 2008).

We first define a logic for the non-local parameterization. The logic for an n-gram language model generates sequence $e_1...e_Q$ by generating each new word given the past $n-1$ words.[10]

item form: $[e_q, ..., e_{q+n-2}]$ **goal:** $[e_{Q-n+2}, ..., e_Q]$

rule: $$\frac{[e_q, ..., e_{q+n-2}] R(e_q, ..., e_{q+n-1})}{[e_{q+1}, ..., e_{q+n-1}]}$$

(Logic NGRAM)

Now we want to combine NGRAM and MONOTONE. To make things easier, we modify MONOTONE to encode the idea that once a source phrase has been recognized, its target words are generated one at a time. We will use u_e and v_e to denote (possibly empty) sequences in $e_j...e'_j$. Borrowing the notation of Earley (1970), we encode progress using a dotted phrase $u_e \bullet v_e$.

item form: $[i, u_e \bullet v_e]$ **goal:** $[I, u_e \bullet v_e]$

rules:

$$\frac{[i, u_e \bullet] \quad R(f_{i+1}...f_{i'}/e_j v_e)}{[i', e_j \bullet v_e]} \qquad \frac{[i, u_e \bullet e_j v_e]}{[i, u_e e_j \bullet v_e]}$$

(Logic MONOTONE-GENERATE)

We combine NGRAM and MONOTONE-GENERATE using the PRODUCT transform, which takes two logics as input and essentially does the following.[11]

1. Create a new item type from the cross-product of item types in the input logics.
2. Create inference rules for the new item type from the cross-product of all inference rules in the input logics.
3. Constrain the new logic as needed. This is done by hand, but quite simple, as we will show by example.

The first two steps give us logic MONOTONE-GENERATE $\circ$ NGRAM (Figure 2). This is close to what we want, but not quite done. The constraint we want to apply is that each word written by logic MONOTONE-GENERATE is equal to the word generated by logic NGRAM. We accomplish this by unifying variables e_q and e_{n-i} in the inference rules, giving us logic MONOTONE-GENERATE + NGRAM (Figure 2).

[7] General weighted deduction subsumes semiring-weighted deduction (Eisner et al., 2005; Eisner and Blatz, 2006; Nederhof, 2003), but semiring-weighted deduction covers all translation models we are aware of, so it is a good first step in applying weighted deduction to translation.

[8] See Goodman (1999) for additional conditions on semirings used in this framework.

[9] Eisner and Blatz (2006) give an alternate strategy for the best derivation.

[10] We ignore start and stop probabilities for simplicity.

[11] The description of Cohen et al. (2008) is much more complete and includes several examples.

(1)

item form: $[i, u_e \bullet v_e, e_q, ..., e_{q+n-2}]$

goal: $[I, u_e\bullet, e_{Q-n+2}, ..., e_Q]$

rules:

$$\frac{[i, u_e\bullet, e_q, ..., e_{q+n-2}] \;\; R(f_i...f_{i'}/e_j u_e) \;\; R(e_q, ..., e_{q+n-1})}{[i', e_j \bullet u_e, e_{q+1}, ..., e_{q+n-1}]}$$

$$\frac{[i, u_e \bullet e_j v_e, e_q, ..., e_{q+n-2}] \;\; R(e_q, ..., e_{q+n-1})}{[i, u_e e_j \bullet v_e, e_{q+1}, ..., e_{q+n-1}]}$$

---

(2)

item form: $[i, u_e \bullet v_e, e_j, ..., e_{j+n-2}]$

goal: $[I, u_e\bullet, e_{J-n+2}, ..., e_J]$

rules:

$$\frac{[i, u_e\bullet, e_{j-n+1}, ..., e_{j-1}] \;\; R(f_i...f_{i'}/e_j v_e) \;\; R(e_{j-n+2}...e_j)}{[i', e_j \bullet v_e, e_{j-n+2}, ..., e_j]}$$

$$\frac{[i, u_e \bullet e_{i+n-1} v_e, e_i, ..., e_{i+n-2}] \;\; R(e_{j-n+2}...e_j)}{[i+1, u_e e_j \bullet v_e, e_{j-n+2}, ..., e_j]}$$

---

(3) **item form:** $[i, u_e \bullet v_e, e_i, ..., e_{n-i-2}]$ **goal:** $[I, u_e\bullet, e_{I-n+2}, ..., e_I]$

rule: $$\frac{[i, e_{j-n+1}, ..., e_{j-1}] \;\; R(f_i...f_{i'}/e_j...e_{j'})R(e_{j-n+1}, ..., e_j)...R(e_{j'-n+1}...e_{j'})}{[i', e_{j'-n+2}...e_{j'}]}$$

Figure 2: Logics (1) MONOTONE-GENERATE ∘ NGRAM, (2) MONOTONE-GENERATE + NGRAM and (3) MONOTONE-GENERATE + NGRAM SINGLE-SHOT.

This logic restores the optimal subproblem property and we can apply semiring-weighted deduction. Efficient algorithms are given in §7, but a brief comment is in order about the new logic. In most descriptions of phrase-based decoding, the n-gram language model is applied all at once. MONOTONE-GENERATE+NGRAM applies the n-gram language model one word at a time. This illuminates a space of search strategies that are to our knowledge unexplored. If a four-word phrase were proposed as an extension of a partial hypothesis in a typical decoder implementation using a five-word language model, all four n-grams will be applied even though the first n-gram might have a very low score. Viewing each n-gram application as producing a new state may yield new strategies for approximate search.

We can derive the more familiar logic by applying a different transform: *unfolding* (Eisner and Blatz, 2006). The idea is to replace an item with the sequence of antecedents used to produce it (similar to function inlining). This gives us MONOTONE-GENERATE+NGRAM SINGLE-SHOT (Figure 2).

We call the ruleset-based logic the **minimal logic** and the logic enhanced with non-local parameterization the **complete logic**. Note that the set of variables in the complete logic is a superset of the set of variables in the minimal logic. We can view the minimal logic as a projection of the complete logic into a smaller dimensional space. It is important to note that complete logic is substantially more complex than the minimal logic, by a factor of $O(|V_E|^n)$ for a target vocabulary of V_E. Thus, the complexity of non-local parameterizations often makes search spaces large regardless of the complexity of the minimal logic.

6 Other Uses of the PRODUCT Transform

The PRODUCT transform can also implement alignment and help derive new models.

6.1 Alignment

In the alignment problem (sometimes called *constrained decoding* or *forced decoding*), we are given a reference target sentence $r_1, ..., r_J$, and we require the translation model to generate only derivations that produce that sentence. Alignment is often used in training both generative and discriminative models (Brown et al., 1993; Blunsom et al., 2008; Liang et al., 2006). Our approach to alignment is similar to the one for language modeling. First, we implement a logic requiring an input to be identical to the reference.

$$\textbf{item form: } [j] \quad \textbf{goal: } [J] \qquad \textbf{rule: } \frac{[j]}{[j+1]} \; e_{j+1} = r_{j+1}$$

(Logic RECOGNIZE)

The logic only reaches its goal if the input is identical to the reference. In fact, partial derivations must produce a prefix of the reference. When we combine this logic with MONOTONE-GENERATE, we obtain a logic that only succeeds if the translation logic generates the reference.

$$\textbf{item form: } [i, j, u_e \bullet v_e] \quad \textbf{goal: } [I, j, u_e \bullet]$$

$$\textbf{rules: } \begin{cases} \dfrac{[i, j, u_e \bullet] \quad R(f_i...f_{i'}/e_j...e_{j'})}{[i', j, \bullet e_j...e_{j'}]} \\ \dfrac{[i, j, u_e \bullet e_j v_e]}{[i, j+1, u_e e_j \bullet v_e]} \; e_{j+1} = r_{j+1} \end{cases}$$

(Logic MONOTONE-ALIGN)

Under the boolean semiring, this (minimal) logic decides if a training example is reachable by the model, which is required by some discriminative training regimens (Liang et al., 2006; Blunsom et al., 2008). We can also compute the Viterbi derivation or the sum over all derivations of a training example, needed for some parameter estimation methods. Cohen et al. (2008) derive an alignment logic for ITG from the product of two CKY logics.

6.2 Translation Model Design

A motivation for many syntax-based translation models is to use target-side syntax as a language model (Charniak et al., 2003). Och et al. (2004) showed that simply parsing the N-best outputs of a phrase-based model did not work; to obtain the full power of a language model, we need to integrate it into the search process. Most approaches to this problem focus on synchronous grammars, but it is possible to integrate the target-side language model with a phrase-based translation model. As an exercise, we integrate CKY with the output of logic MONOTONE-GENERATE. The constraint is that the indices of the CKY items unify with the *items* of the translation logic, which form a word lattice. Note that this logic retains the rules in the basic MONOTONE logic, which are not depicted (Figure 3).

The result is a lattice parser on the output of the translation model. Lattice parsing is not new to translation (Dyer et al., 2008), but to our knowledge it has not been used in this way. Viewing translation as deduction is helpful for the design and construction of novel models.

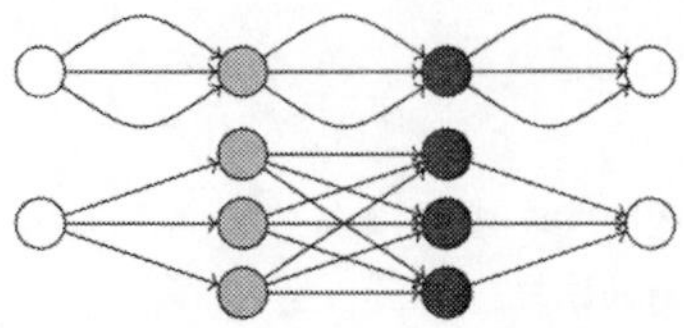

Figure 4: Example graphs corresponding to a simple minimal (1) and complete (2) logic, with corresponding nodes in the same color. The state-splitting induced by non-local features produces in a large number of arcs which must be evaluated, which can be reduced by cube pruning.

7 Algorithms

Most translation logics are too expensive to exhaustively search. However, the logics conveniently specify the full search space, which forms a hypergraph (Klein and Manning, 2001).[12] The equivalence is useful for complexity analysis: items correspond to nodes and deductions correspond to hyperarcs. These equivalences make it easy to compute algorithmic bounds.

Cube pruning (Chiang, 2007) is an approximate search technique for syntax-based translation models with integrated language models. It operates on two objects: a $-LM$ graph containing no language model state, and a $+LM$ hypergraph containing state. The idea is to generate a fixed number of nodes in the $+LM$ for each node in the $-LM$ graph, using a clever enumeration strategy. We can view cube pruning as arising from the interaction between a minimal logic and the state splits induced by non-local features. Figure 4 shows how the added state information can dramatically increase the number of deductions that must be evaluated. Cube pruning works by considering the most promising states paired with the most promising extensions. In this way, it easily fits any search space constructed using the technique of §5. Note that the efficiency of cube pruning is limited by the minimal logic.

Stack decoding is a search heuristic that simplifies the complexity of searching a minimal logic. Each item is associated with a stack whose signa-

[12] Specifically a B-hypergraph, equivalent to an and-or graph (Gallo et al., 1993) or context-free grammar (Nederhof, 2003). In the degenerate case, this is simply a graph, as is the case with most phrase-based models.

$$\textbf{item forms: } [i, u_e \bullet v_e], [A, i, u_e \bullet v_e, i', u'_e \bullet v'_e] \quad \textbf{goal: } [S, 0, \bullet, I, u_e \bullet]$$

rules:

$$\frac{[i, u_e \bullet] \;\; R(f_{i+1}...f_{i'}/e_j v_e) \;\; R(A \rightarrow e_j)}{[A, i, u_e \bullet, i', e_j \bullet v_e]} \qquad \frac{[i, u_e \bullet e_j v_e] \;\; R(A \rightarrow e_j)}{[A, i, u_e \bullet e_j v_e, i, u_e e_j \bullet v_e]}$$

$$\frac{[B, i, u_e \bullet v_e, i'', u''_e \bullet v''_e] \;\; [C, i'', u''_e \bullet v''_e, i', u'_e \bullet v'_e] \;\; R(A \rightarrow BC)}{[A, i, u_e \bullet v_e, i', u'_e \bullet v'_e]}$$

Figure 3: Logic MONOTONE-GENERATE + CKY

ture is a projection of the item signature (or a predicate on the item signatures)—multiple items are associated to the same stack. The strength of the pruning (and resulting complexity improvements) depending on how much the projection reduces the search space. In many phrase-based implementations the stack signature is just the number of words translated, but other strategies are possible (Tillman and Ney, 2003).

It is worth noting that logic FdUW (§3.2), depends on stack pruning for speed. Because the number of stacks is linear in the length of the input, so is the number of unpruned nodes in the search graph. In contrast, the complexity of logic WLd is naturally linear in input length. As mentioned in §3.2, this implies a wide divergence in the model and search errors of these logics, which to our knowledge has not been investigated.

8 Related Work

We are not the first to observe that phrase-based models can be represented as logic programs (Eisner et al., 2005; Eisner and Blatz, 2006), but to our knowledge we are the first to provide explicit logics for them.[13] We also showed that deductive logic is a useful analytical tool to tackle a variety of problems in translation algorithm design.

Our work is strongly influenced by Goodman (1999) and Eisner et al. (2005). They describe many issues not mentioned here, including conditions on semirings, termination conditions, and strategies for cyclic search graphs. However, while their weighted deductive formalism is general, they focus on concerns relevant to parsing, such as boolean semirings and cyclicity. Our work focuses on concerns common for translation, including a general view of non-local parameterizations and cube pruning.

[13] Huang and Chiang (2007) give an informal example, but do not elaborate on it.

9 Conclusions and Future Work

We have described a general framework that synthesizes and extends deductive parsing and semiring parsing, and adapts it to translation. Our goal has been to show that logics make an attractive shorthand for description, analysis, and construction of translation models. For instance, we have shown that it is quite easy to mechanically construct search spaces using non-local features, and to create exotic models. We showed that different flavors of phrase-based models should suffer from quite different types of error, a problem that to our knowledge was heretofore unknown. However, we have only scratched the surface, and we believe it is possibly to unify a wide variety of translation algorithms. For example, we believe that cube pruning can be described as an agenda discipline in chart parsing (Kay, 1986).

Although the work presented here is abstract, our motivation is practical. Isolating the errors in translation systems is a difficult task which can be made easier by describing and analyzing models in a modular way (Auli et al., 2009). Furthermore, building large-scale translation systems from scratch should be unnecessary if existing systems were built using modular logics and algorithms. We aim to build such systems.

Acknowledgments

This work developed from discussions with Phil Blunsom, Chris Callison-Burch, Chris Dyer, Hieu Hoang, Martin Kay, Philipp Koehn, Josh Schroeder, and Lane Schwartz. Many thanks go to Chris Dyer, Josh Schroeder, the three anonymous EACL reviewers, and one anonymous NAACL reviewer for very helpful comments on earlier drafts. This research was supported by the Euromatrix Project funded by the European Commission (6th Framework Programme).

References

M. Auli, A. Lopez, P. Koehn, and H. Hoang. 2009. A systematic analysis of translation model search spaces. In *Proc. of WMT*, Mar.

P. Blunsom, T. Cohn, and M. Osborne. 2008. A discriminative latent variable model for statistical machine translation. In *Proc. of ACL:HLT*.

P. F. Brown, S. A. D. Pietra, V. J. D. Pietra, and R. L. Mercer. 1993. The mathematics of statistical machine translation: Parameter estimation. *Computational Linguistics*, 19(2):263–311, Jun.

E. Charniak, K. Knight, and K. Yamada. 2003. Syntax-based language models for statistical machine translation. In *Proceedings of MT Summit*, Sept.

D. Chiang. 2007. Hierarchical phrase-based translation. *Computational Linguistics*, 33(2):201–228.

K. Church and R. Patil. 1982. Coping with syntactic ambiguity or how to put the block in the box on the table. *Computational Linguistics*, 8(3–4):139–149, Jul.

S. B. Cohen, R. J. Simmons, and N. A. Smith. 2008. Dynamic programming algorithms as products of weighted logic programs. In *Proc. of ICLP*.

T. H. Cormen, C. D. Leiserson, R. L. Rivest, and C. Stein. 2001. *Introduction to Algorithms*. MIT Press, 2nd edition.

M. R. Costa-jussà and J. A. R. Fonollosa. 2006. Statistical machine reordering. In *Proc. of EMNLP*, pages 70–76, Jul.

C. J. Dyer, S. Muresan, and P. Resnik. 2008. Generalizing word lattice translation. In *Proc. of ACL:HLT*, pages 1012–1020.

J. Earley. 1970. An efficient context-free parsing algorithm. *Communications of the ACM*, 13(2):94–102, Feb.

J. Eisner and J. Blatz. 2006. Program transformations for optimization of parsing algorithms and other weighted logic programs. In *Proc. of Formal Grammar*, pages 45–85.

J. Eisner, E. Goldlust, and N. A. Smith. 2005. Compiling comp ling: Weighted dynamic programming and the Dyna language. In *Proc. of HLT-EMNLP*, pages 281–290.

J. Eisner. 2002. Parameter estimation for probabilistic finite-state transducers. In *Proc. of ACL*, pages 1–8, Jul.

G. Gallo, G. Longo, and S. Pallottino. 1993. Directed hypergraphs and applications. *Discrete Applied Mathematics*, 42(2), Apr.

K. Gimpel and N. A. Smith. 2009. Approximation semirings: Dynamic programming with non-local features. In *Proc. of EACL*, Mar.

J. Goodman. 1999. Semiring parsing. *Computational Linguistics*, 25(4):573–605, Dec.

L. Huang and D. Chiang. 2007. Forest rescoring: Faster decoding with integrated language models. In *Proc. of ACL*, pages 144–151, Jun.

M. Kay. 1986. Algorithm schemata and data structures in syntactic processing. In B. J. Grosz, K. S. Jones, and B. L. Webber, editors, *Readings in Natural Language Processing*, pages 35–70. Morgan Kaufmann.

D. Klein and C. Manning. 2001. Parsing and hypergraphs. In *Proc. of IWPT*.

P. Koehn, H. Hoang, A. Birch, C. Callison-Burch, M. Federico, N. Bertoldi, B. Cowan, W. Shen, C. Moran, R. Zens, C. Dyer, O. Bojar, A. Constantin, and E. Herbst. 2007. Moses: Open source toolkit for statistical machine translation. In *Proc. of ACL Demo and Poster Sessions*, pages 177–180, Jun.

S. Kumar and W. Byrne. 2005. Local phrase reordering models for statistical machine translation. In *Proc. of HLT-EMNLP*, pages 161–168.

P. Liang, A. Bouchard-Côté, B. Taskar, and D. Klein. 2006. An end-to-end discriminative approach to machine translation. In *Proc. of ACL-COLING*, pages 761–768, Jul.

A. Lopez. 2008. Statistical machine translation. *ACM Computing Surveys*, 40(3), Aug.

J. B. Mariño, R. E. Banchs, J. M. Crego, A. de Gispert, P. Lambert, J. A. R. Fonollosa, and M. R. Costa-jussà. 2006. N-gram based statistical machine translation. *Computational Linguistics*, 32(4):527–549, Dec.

D. McAllester. 1999. On the complexity analysis of static analyses. In *Proc. of Static Analysis Symposium*, volume 1694/1999 of *LNCS*. Springer Verlag.

I. D. Melamed. 2004. Statistical machine translation by parsing. In *Proc. of ACL*, pages 654–661, Jul.

R. C. Moore and C. Quirk. 2007. Faster beam-search decoding for phrasal statistical machine translation. In *Proc. of MT Summit*.

M.-J. Nederhof. 2003. Weighted deductive parsing and Knuth's algorithm. *Computational Linguistics*, 29(1):135–143, Mar.

F. J. Och, D. Gildea, S. Khudanpur, A. Sarkar, K. Yamada, A. Fraser, S. Kumar, L. Shen, D. Smith, K. Eng, V. Jain, Z. Jin, and D. Radev. 2004. A smorgasbord of features for statistical machine translation. In *Proc. of HLT-NAACL*, pages 161–168, May.

F. C. N. Pereira and D. H. D. Warren. 1983. Parsing as deduction. In *Proc. of ACL*, pages 137–144.

S. M. Shieber, Y. Schabes, and F. C. N. Pereira. 1995. Principles and implementation of deductive parsing. *Journal of Logic Programming*, 24(1–2):3–36, Jul.

C. Tillman and H. Ney. 2003. Word reordering and a dynamic programming beam search algorithm for statistical machine translation. *Computational Linguistics*, 29(1):98–133, Mar.

A. Venugopal, A. Zollmann, and S. Vogel. 2007. An efficient two-pass approach to synchronous-CFG driven statistical MT. In *Proc. of HLT-NAACL*.

D. Wu. 1996. A polynomial-time algorithm for statistical machine translation. In *Proc. of ACL*, pages 152–158, Jun.

R. Zens and H. Ney. 2004. Improvements in phrase-based statistical machine translation. In *Proc. of HLT-NAACL*, pages 257–264, May.

Performance Confidence Estimation for Automatic Summarization

Annie Louis
University of Pennsylvania
lannie@seas.upenn.edu

Ani Nenkova
University of Pennsylvania
nenkova@seas.upenn.edu

Abstract

We address the task of automatically predicting if summarization system performance will be good or bad based on features derived directly from either single- or multi-document inputs. Our labelled corpus for the task is composed of data from large scale evaluations completed over the span of several years. The variation of data between years allows for a comprehensive analysis of the robustness of features, but poses a challenge for building a combined corpus which can be used for training and testing. Still, we find that the problem can be mitigated by appropriately normalizing for differences within each year. We examine different formulations of the classification task which considerably influence performance. The best results are 84% prediction accuracy for single- and 74% for multi-document summarization.

1 Introduction

The input to a summarization system significantly affects the quality of the summary that can be produced for it, by either a person or an automatic method. Some inputs are *difficult* and summaries produced by any approach will tend to be *poor*, while other inputs are *easy* and systems will exhibit *good* performance. User satisfaction with the summaries can be improved, for example by automatically flagging summaries for which a system expects to perform poorly. In such cases the user can ignore the summary and avoid the frustration of reading poor quality text.

(Brandow et al., 1995) describes an intelligent summarizer system that could identify documents which would be difficult to summarize based on structural properties. Documents containing question/answer sessions, speeches, tables and embedded lists were identified based on patterns and these features were used to determine whether an acceptable summary can be produced. If not, the inputs were flagged as unsuitable for automatic summarization. In our work, we provide deeper insight into how other characteristics of the text itself and properties of document clusters can be used to identify difficult inputs.

The task of predicting the confidence in system performance for a given input is in fact relevant not only for summarization, but in general for all applications aimed at facilitating information access. In question answering for example, a system may be configured not to answer questions for which the confidence of producing a correct answer is low, and in this way increase the overall accuracy of the system whenever it does produce an answer (Brill et al., 2002; Dredze and Czuba, 2007).

Similarly in machine translation, some sentences might contain difficult to translate phrases, that is, portions of the input are likely to lead to garbled output if automatic translation is attempted. Automatically identifying such phrases has the potential of improving MT as shown by an oracle study (Mohit and Hwa, 2007). More recent work (Birch et al., 2008) has shown that properties of reordering, source and target language complexity and relatedness can be used to predict translation quality. In information retrieval, the problem of predicting system performance has generated considerable interest and has led to notably good results (Cronen-Townsend et al., 2002; Yom-Tov et al., 2005; Carmel et al., 2006).

Proceedings of the 12th Conference of the European Chapter of the ACL, pages 541–548,
Athens, Greece, 30 March – 3 April 2009.

2 Task definition

In summarization, researchers have recognized that some inputs might be more successfully handled by a particular subsystem (McKeown et al., 2001), but little work has been done to qualify the general characteristics of inputs that lead to suboptimal performance of systems. Only recently the issue has drawn attention: (Nenkova and Louis, 2008) present an initial analysis of the factors that influence system performance in content selection. This study was based on results from the Document Understanding Conference (DUC) evaluations (Over et al., 2007) of multi-document summarization of news. They showed that input, system identity and length of the target summary were all significant factors affecting summary quality. Longer summaries were consistently better than shorter ones for the same input, so improvements can be easy in applications where varying target size is possible. Indeed, varying summary size is desirable in many situations (Kaisser et al., 2008).

The most predictive factor of summary quality was input identity, prompting a closer investigation of input properties that are indicative of deterioration in performance. For example, summaries of articles describing different opinions about an issue or of articles describing multiple distinct events of the same type were of overall poor quality, while summaries of more focused inputs, dealing with descriptions of a single event, subject or person (biographical), were on average better.

A number of features were defined, capturing aspects of how focused on a single topic a given input is. Analysis of the predictive power of the features was done using only one year of DUC evaluations. Data from later evaluations was used to train and test a logistic regression classifier for prediction of expected system performance. The task could be performed with accuracy of 61.45%, significantly above chance levels.

The results also indicated that special care needs to be taken when pooling data from different evaluations into a single dataset. Feature selection performed on data from one year was not useful for prediction on data from other years, and actually led to worse performance than using all features. Moreover, directly indicating which evaluation the data came from was the most predictive feature when testing on data from more than one year.

In the work described here, we show how the approach for predicting performance confidence can be improved considerably by paying special attention to the way data from different years is combined, as well as by adopting alternative task formulations (pairwise comparisons of inputs instead of binary class prediction), and utilizing more representative examples for good and bad performance. We also extend the analysis to single document summarization, for which predicting system performance turns out to be much more accurate than for multi-document summarization. We address three key questions.

What features are predictive of performance on a given input? In Section 4, we discuss four classes of features capturing properties of the input, related to input size, information-theoretic properties of the distribution of words in the input, presence of descriptive (topic) words and similarity between the documents in multi-document inputs. Rather than using a single year of evaluations for the analysis, we report correlation with expected system performance for all years and tasks, showing that in fact the power of these features varies considerably across years (Section 5).

How to combine data from different years? The available data spans several years of summarization evaluations. Between years, systems change, as well as number of systems and average input difficulty. All of these changes impact system performance and make data from different years difficult to analyze when taken together. Still, one would want to combine all of the available evaluations in order to have more data for developing machine learning models. In Section 6 we demonstrate that this indeed can be achieved, by normalizing within each year by the highest observed performance and only then combining the data.

How to define input difficulty? There are several possible definitions of "input difficulty" or "good performance". All the data can be split in two binary classes of "good" and "bad" performance respectively, or only representative examples in which there is a clear difference in performance can be used. In Section 7 we show that these alternatives can dramatically influence prediction accuracy: using representative examples improves accuracy by more than 10%. Formulating the task as ranking of two inputs, predicting which one is more difficult, also turns out to be helpful, offering more data even within the same year of evaluation.

3 Data

We use the data from single- and multi-document evaluations performed as part of the Document Understanding Conferences (Over et al., 2007) from 2001 to 2004.[1] Generic multi-document summarization was evaluated in all of these years, single document summaries were evaluated only in 2001 and 2002. We use the 100-word summaries from both tasks.

In the years 2002-2004, systems were evaluated respectively on 59, 37 and 100 (50 for generic summarization and 50 biographical) multi-document inputs. There were 149 inputs for single document summarization in 2001 and 283 inputs in 2002. Combining the datasets from the different years yields a collection of 432 observations for single-document summarization, and 196 for multi-document summarization.

Input difficulty, or equivalently expected confidence of system performance, was defined empirically, based on actual content selection evaluations of system summaries. More specifically, expected performance for each input was defined as the average coverage score of all participating systems evaluated on that input. In this way, the performance confidence is not specific to any given system, but instead reflects what can be expected from automatic summarizers in general.

The coverage score was manually computed by NIST evaluators. It measures content selection by estimating overlap between a human model and a system summary. The scale for the coverage score was different in 2001 compared to other years: 0 to 4 scale, switching to a 0 to 1 scale later.

4 Features

For our experiments we use the features proposed, motivated and described in detail by (Nenkova and Louis, 2008). Four broad classes of easily computable features were used to capture aspects of the input predictive of system performance.

Input size-related Number of sentences in the input, number of tokens, vocabulary size, percentage of words used only once, type-token ratio.

Information-theoretic measures Entropy of the input word distribution and KL divergence between the input and a large document collection.

[1]Evaluations from later years did not include generic summarization, but introduced new tasks such as topic-focused and update summarization.

Log-likelihood ratio for words in the input Number of topic signature words (Lin and Hovy, 2000; Conroy et al., 2006) and percentage of signature words in the vocabulary.

Document similarity in the input set These features apply to multi-document summarization only. Pairwise similarity of documents within an input were computed using tf.idf weighted vector representations of the documents, either using all words or using only topic signature words. In both settings, minimum, maximum and average cosine similarity was computed, resulting in six similarity features.

Multi-document summaries from DUC 2001 were used for feature selection. The 29 sets for that year were divided according to the average coverage score of the evaluated systems. Sets with coverage below the average were deemed to be the ones that will elicit poor performance and the rest were considered examples of sets for which systems perform well. T-tests were used to select features that were significantly different between the two classes. Six features were selected: vocabulary size, entropy, KL divergence, percentage of topic signatures in the vocabulary, and average cosine and topic signature similarity.

5 Correlations with performance

The Pearson correlations between features of the input and average system performance for each year is shown in Tables 1 and 2 for multi- and single-document summarization respectively. The last two columns show correlations for the combined data from different evaluation years. For the last column in both tables, the scores in each year were first normalized by the highest score that year. Features that were significantly correlated with expected performance at confidence level of 0.95 are marked with (*). Overall, better performance is associated with smaller inputs, lower entropy, higher KL divergence and more signature terms, as well as with higher document similarity for multi-document summarization.

Several important observations can be made from the correlation numbers in the two tables.

Cross-year variation There is a large variation in the strength of correlation between performance and various features. For example, KL divergence is significantly correlated with performance for most years, with correlation of 0.4618 for the generic summaries in 2004, but the correlation was

features	2001	2002	2003	2004G	2004B	All(UN)	All(N)
tokens	-0.2813	-0.2235	-0.3834*	-0.4286*	-0.1596	-0.2415*	-0.2610*
sentences	-0.2511	-0.1906	-0.3474*	-0.4197*	-0.1489	-0.2311*	-0.2753*
vocabulary	-0.3611*	-0.3026*	-0.3257*	-0.4286*	-0.2239	-0.2568*	-0.3171*
per-once	-0.0026	-0.0375	0.1925	0.2687	0.2081	0.2175*	0.1813*
type/token	-0.0276	-0.0160	0.1324	0.0389	-0.1537	-0.0327	-0.0993
entropy	-0.4256*	-0.2936*	-0.1865	-0.3776*	-0.1954	-0.2283*	-0.2761*
KL divergence	0.3663*	0.1809	0.3220*	0.4618*	0.2359	0.2296*	0.2879*
avg cosine	0.2244	0.2351	0.1409	0.1635	0.2602	0.1894*	0.2483*
min cosine	0.0308	0.2085	-0.5330*	-0.1766	0.1839	-0.0337	-0.0494
max cosine	0.1337	0.0305	0.2499	0.1044	-0.0882	0.0918	0.1982*
num sign	-0.1880	-0.0773	-0.1799	-0.0149	0.1412	-0.0248	0.0084
% sign. terms	0.3277	0.1645	0.1429	0.3174*	0.3071*	0.1952*	0.2609*
avg topic	0.2860	0.3678*	0.0826	0.0321	0.1215	0.1745*	0.2021*
min topic	0.0414	0.0673	-0.0167	-0.0025	-0.0405	-0.0177	-0.0469
max topic	0.2416	0.0489	0.1815	0.0134	0.0965	0.1252	0.2082*

Table 1: Correlations between input features and average system performance for multi-document inputs of DUC 2001-2003, 2004G (generic task), 2004B (biographical task), All data (2002-2004) - UNnormalized and Normalized coverage scores. P-values smaller than 0.05 are marked by *.

not significant (0.1809) for 2002 data. Similarly, the average similarity of topic signature vectors is significant in 2002, but has correlations close to zero in the following two years. This shows that no feature exhibits robust predictive power, especially when there are relatively few datapoints. In light of this finding, developing additional features and combining data to obtain a larger collection of samples are important for future progress.

Normalization Because of the variation from year to year, normalizing performance scores is beneficial and leads to higher correlation for almost all features. On average, correlations increase by 0.05 for all features. Two of the features, maximum cosine similarity and max topic word similarity, become significant only in the normalized data. As we will see in the next section, prediction accuracy is also considerably improved when scores are normalized before pooling the data from different years together.

Single- vs. multi-document task The correlations between performance and input features are higher in single-document summarization than in multi-document. For example, in the normalized data KL divergence has correlation of 0.28 for multi-document summarization but 0.40 for single document. The number of signature terms is highly correlated with performance in single-document summarization (-0.25) but there is practically no correlation for multi-document summaries. Consequently, we can expect that the performance prediction will be more accurate for single-document summarization.

features	2001	2002	All(N)
tokens	-0.3784*	-0.2434*	-0.3819*
sentences	-0.3999*	-0.2262*	-0.3705*
vocabulary	-0.4410*	-0.2706*	-0.4196*
per-once	-0.0718	0.0087	0.0496
type/token	0.1006	0.0952	0.1785
entropy	-0.5326*	-0.2329*	-0.3789*
KL divergence	0.5332*	0.2676*	0.4035*
num sign	-0.2212*	-0.1127	-0.2519*
% sign	0.3278*	0.1573*	0.2042*

Table 2: Correlations between input features and average system performance for single doc. inputs of DUC'01, '02, All ('01+'02) N-normalized. P-values smaller than 0.05 are marked by *.

6 Classification experiments

In this section we explore how the alternative task formulations influence success of predicting system performance. Obviously, the two classes of interest for the prediction will be "good performance" and "poor performance". But separating the real valued coverage scores for inputs into these two classes can be done in different ways. All the data can be used and the definition of "good" or "bad" can be determined in relation to the average performance on all inputs. Or only the best and worst sets can be used as representative examples. We explore the consequences of adopting either of these options.

For the first set of experiments, we divide all inputs based on the mean value of the average system scores as in (Nenkova and Louis, 2008). All multi-document results reported in this paper are based on the use of the six significant features discussed in Section 4. DUC 2002, 2003 and 2004 data was used for 10-fold cross validation. We experimented with three classifiers available in R—logistic regression (LogR), decision tree (DTree) and support vector machines (SVM). SVM and decision tree classifiers are libraries under CRAN packages e1071 and rpart.[2] Since our development set was very small (only 29 inputs), we did not perform any parameter tuning.

There is nearly equal number of inputs on either side of the average system performance and the random baseline performance in this case would give 50% accuracy.

6.1 Multi-document task

The classification accuracy for the multi-document inputs is reported in Table 3. The partitioning into classes was done based on the average performance (87 easy sets and 109 difficult sets).

As expected, normalization considerably improves results. The absolute largest improvement of 10% is for the logistic regression classifier. For this classifier, prediction accuracy for the non-normalized data is 54% while for the normalized data, it is 64%. Logistic regression gives the best overall classification accuracy on the normalized data compared to SVM classifier that does best on the unnormalized data (56% accuracy). Normalization also improves precision and recall for the SVM and logistic regression classifiers.

The differences in accuracies obtained by the classifiers is also noticable and we discuss these further in Section 7.

6.2 Single document task

We now turn to the task of predicting summarization performance for single document inputs. As we saw in section 5, the features are stronger predictors for summarization performance in the single-document task. In addition, there is more data from evaluations of single document summarizers. Stronger features and more training data can both help achieve higher prediction accuracies. In this section, we separate out the two factors and demonstrate that indeed the features are much more predictive for single document summarization than for multidocument.

In order to understand the effect of having more training data, we did not divide the single document inputs into a separate development set to use for feature selection. Instead, all the features

[2]http://cran.r-project.org/web/packages/

classifier	accuracy	P	R	F
DTree	66.744	66.846	67.382	67.113
LogR	67.907	67.089	69.806	68.421
SVM	69.069	66.277	80.317	72.625

Table 4: Single document input classification Precision (P), Recall (R),and F score (F) for difficult inputs on DUC'01 and '02 (total 432 examples) divided into 2 classes based on the average coverage score (217 difficult and 215 easy inputs).

discussed in Section 4 except the six cosine and topic signature similarity measures are used. The coverage score ranges in DUC 2001 and 2002 are different. They are normalized by the maximum score within the year, then combined and partitioned in two classes with respect to the average coverage score. In this way, the 432 observations are split into almost equal halves, 215 good performance examples and 217 bad performance. Table 4 shows the accuracy, precision and recall of the classifiers on single-document inputs.

From the results in Table 4 it is evident that all three classifiers achieve accuracies higher than those for multi-document summarization. The improvement is largest for decision tree classification, nearly 15%. The SVM classifier has the highest accuracy for single document summarization inputs, (69%), which is 7% absolute improvement over the performance of the SVM classifier for the multi-document task. The smallest improvement of 4% is for the logistic regression classifier which is the one with highest accuracy for the multi-document task

Improved accuracy could be attributed to the fact that almost double the amount of data is available for the single-document summarization experiments. To test if this was the main reason for improvement, we repeated the single-document experiments using a random sample of 196 inputs, the same amount of data as for the multi-document case. Even with reduced data, single-document inputs are more easily classifiable as difficult or easy compared to multi-document, as shown in Tables 3 and 5. The SVM classifier is still the best for single-document summarization and its accuracy is the same with reduced data as with all data. With less data, the performance of the logistic regression and decision tree classifiers degrades more and is closer to the numbers for multi-document inputs.

Classifier	N/UN	Acc	Pdiff	Rdiff	Peasy	Reasy	Fdiff	Feasy
DTree	UN	51.579	56.580	56.999	46.790	45.591	55.383	44.199
	N	52.105	56.474	57.786	46.909	45.440	55.709	44.298
LogR	UN	54.211	56.877	71.273	50.135	34.074	62.145	39.159
	N	63.684	63.974	79.536	63.714	45.980	69.815	51.652
SVM	UN	55.789	57.416	73.943	50.206	32.753	63.784	38.407
	N	62.632	61.905	81.714	61.286	38.829	69.873	47.063

Table 3: Multi-document input classification results on **UN**normalized and **N**ormalized data from DUC 2002 to 2004. Both Normalized and UNormalized data contain 109 difficult and 87 easy inputs. Since the split is not balanced, the accuracy of classification as well as the Precision (P), Recall (R) and F score (F) are reported for both classes of easy and diff(icult) inputs.

classifier	accuracy	P	R	F
DTree	53.684	54.613	53.662	51.661
LogR	61.579	63.335	60.400	60.155
SVM	69.474	66.339	85.835	73.551

Table 5: Single-document-input classification Precision (P), Recall (R), and F score (F) for difficult inputs on a random sample of 196 observations (99 difficult/97 easy) from DUC'01 and '02.

7 Learning with representative examples

In the experiments in the previous section, we used the average coverage score to split inputs into two classes of expected performance. Poor performance was assigned to the inputs for which the average system coverage score was lower than the average for all inputs. Good performance was assigned to those with higher than average coverage score. The best results for this formulation of the prediction task is 64% accuracy for multi-document classification (logistic regression classifier; 196 datapoints) and 69% for single-document (SVM classifier; 432 and 196 datapoints).

However, inputs with coverage scores close to the average may not be representative of either class. Moreover, inputs for which performance was very similar would end up in different classes. We can refine the dataset by using only those observations that are highly representative of the category they belong to, removing inputs for which system performance was close to the average. It is desirable to be able to classify mediocre inputs as a separate category. Further studies are necessary to come up with better categorization of inputs rather than two strict classes of difficult and easy. For now, we examine the strength of our features in distinguishing the extreme types by training and testing only on inputs that are representative of these classes.

We test this hypothesis by starting with 196 multi-document inputs and performing the 10-fold cross validation using only 80%, 60% and 50% of the data, incrementally throwing away observations around the mean. For example, the 80% model was learnt on 156 observations, taking the extreme 78 observations on each side into the difficult and easy categories. For the single document case, we performed the same tests starting with a random sample of 196 observations as 100% data.[3] All classifiers were trained and tested on the same division of folds during cross validation and compared using a paired t-test to determine the significance of differences if any. Results are shown in Table 6. In parentheses after the accuracy of a given classifier, we indicate the classifiers that are significantly better than it.

Classifiers trained and tested using only representative examples perform more reliably. The SVM classifier is the best one for the single-document setting and in most cases significantly outperforms logistic regression and decision tree classifiers on accuracy and recall. In the multi-document setting, SVM provides better overall recall than logistic regression. However, with respect to accuracy, SVM and logistic regression classifiers are indistinguishable. The decision tree classifier performs worse.

For multi-document classification, the F score drops initially when data is reduced to only 80%. But when using only half of the data, accuracy of prediction reaches 74%, amounting to 10% absolute improvement compared to the scenario in which all available data is used. In the single-document case, accuracy for the SVM classifier increases consistently, reaching accuracy of 84%.

8 Pairwise ranking approach

The task we addressed in previous sections was to classify inputs into ones for which we expect good

[3] We use the same amount of data as is available for multi-document so that the results can be directly comparable.

		Single document classification				Multi-document classification			
Data	CL	Acc	P	R	F	Acc	P	R	F
100%	DTree	53.684 (S)	54.613	53.662 (S)	51.661	52.105 (S,L)	56.474	57.786 (S,L)	55.709
	LogR	61.579 (S)	63.335	60.400 (S)	60.155	63.684	63.974	79.536	69.815
	SVM	69.474	66.339	85.835	73.551	62.632	61.905	81.714	69.873
80%	DTree	62.000 (S)	62.917 (S)	67.089 (S)	62.969	53.333	57.517	55.004 (S)	51.817
	LogR	68.000	68.829	69.324 (S)	67.686	58.667	60.401	59.298 (S)	57.988
	SVM	71.333	70.009	86.551	75.577	62.000	61.492	71.075	63.905
60%	DTree	68.182 (S)	72.750	60.607 (S)	64.025	57.273 (S)	63.000	58.262 (S)	54.882
	LogR	70.909	73.381	69.250	69.861	67.273	68.357	70.167	65.973
	SVM	76.364	73.365	82.857	76.959	66.364	68.619	75.738	67.726
50%	DTree	70.000 (S)	69.238	67.905 (S)	66.299	65.000	60.381 (L)	70.809	64.479
	LogR	76.000 (S)	76.083	72.500 (S)	72.919	74.000	72.905	70.381 (S)	70.965
	SVM	84.000	83.476	89.000	84.379	72.000	67.667	79.143	71.963

Table 6: Performance of multiple classifiers on extreme observations from single and multi-document data (100% data = 196 data points in both cases divided into 2 classes on the basis of average coverge score). Reported precision (P), recall (R) and F score (F) are for difficult inputs. Experiments on extremes use equal number of examples from each class - baseline performance is 50%. Systems whose performance is significantly better than the specified numbers are shown in brackets (S-SVM, D-Decision Tree, L-Logistic Regression).

performance and ones for which poor system performance is expected. In this section, we evaluate a different approach to input difficulty classification. Given a pair of inputs, can we identify the one on which systems will perform better? This ranking task is easier than requiring a strict decision on whether performance will be good or not.

Ranking approaches are widely used in text planning and sentence ordering (Walker et al., 2001; Karamanis, 2003) to select the text with best structure among a set of possible candidates. Under the summarization framework, (Barzilay and Lapata, 2008) ranked different summaries for the same input according to their coherence. Similarly, ranking alternative document clusters on the same topic to choose the best input will prove an added advantage to summarizer systems. When summarization is used as part of an information access interface, the clustering of related documents that form the input to a system is done automatically. Currently, the clustering of documents is completely independent of the need for subsequent summarization of the resulting clusters. Techniques for predicting summarizer performance can be used to inform clustering so that the clusters most suitable for summarization can be chosen. Also, when sample inputs for which summaries were deemed to be good are available, these can be used as a standard with which new inputs can be compared.

For the pairwise comparison task, the features are the difference in feature values between the two inputs A and B that form a pair. The difference in average system scores of inputs A and B in the pair is used to determine the input for which performance was better. Every pair could give two training examples, one positive and one negative depending on the direction in which the differences are computed. We choose one example from every pair, maintaining an equal number of positive and negative instances.

The idea of using representative examples can be applied for the pairwise formulation of the task as well—the larger the difference in system performance is, the better example the pair represents. Very small score differences are not as indicative of performance on one input being better than the other. Hence the experiments were duplicated on 80%, 60% and 40% of the data where the retained examples were the ones with biggest difference between the system performance on the two sets (as indicated by the average coverage score). The range of score differences in each year are indicated in the Table 7.

All scores are normalized by the maximum score within the year. Therefore the smallest and largest possible differences are 0 and 1 respectively. The entries corresponding to the years 2002, 2003 and 2004 show the SVM classification results when inputs were paired only with those within the same year. Next inputs of all years were paired with no restrictions. We report the classification accuracies on a random sample of these examples equal in size to the number of datapoints in the 2004 examples.

Using only representative examples leads to

Amt	Data	Min score diff	Points	Acc.
All	2002	0.00028	1710	65.79
	2003	0.00037	666	73.94
	2004	0.00023	4948	70.71
	2002-2004	0.00005	4948	68.85
80%	2002	0.05037	1368	68.39
	2003	0.08771	532	78.87
	2004	0.05226	3958	73.36
	2002-2004	0.02376	3958	70.68
60%	2002	0.10518	1026	73.04
	2003	0.17431	400	82.50
	2004	0.11244	2968	77.41
	2002-2004	0.04844	2968	71.39
40%	2002	0.16662	684	76.03
	2003	0.27083	266	87.31
	2004	0.18258	1980	79.34
	2002-2004	0.07489	1980	74.95

Maximum score difference 2002 (0.8768), 2003 (0.8969), 2004 (0.8482), 2002-2004 (0.8768)

Table 7: Accuracy of SVM classification of multidocument input pairs. When inputs are paired irrespective of year (2002-2004), datapoints equal in number to that in 2004 were chosen at random.

consistently better results than using all the data. The best classification accuracy is 76%, 87% and 79% for comparisons within the same year and 74% for comparisons across years. It is important to observe that when inputs are compared without any regard to the year, the classifier performance is worse than when both inputs in the pair are taken from the same evaluation year, presenting additional evidence of the cross-year variation discussed in Section 5. A possible explanation is that system improvements in later years might cause better scores to be obtained on inputs which were difficult previously.

9 Conclusions

We presented a study of predicting expected summarization performance on a given input. We demonstrated that prediction of summarization system performance can be done with high accuracy. Normalization and use of representative examples of difficult and easy inputs both prove beneficial for the task. We also find that performance predictions for single-document summarization can be done more accurately than for multi-document summarization. The best classifier for single-document classification are SVMs, and the best for multi-document—logistic regression and SVM. We also record good prediction performance on pairwise comparisons which can prove useful in a variety of situations.

References

R. Barzilay and M. Lapata. 2008. Modeling local coherence: An entity-based approach. *CL*, 34(1):1–34.

A. Birch, M. Osborne, and P. Koehn. 2008. Predicting success in machine translation. In *Proceedings of EMNLP*, pages 745–754.

R. Brandow, K. Mitze, and L. F. Rau. 1995. Automatic condensation of electronic publications by sentence selection. *Inf. Process. Manage.*, 31(5):675–685.

E. Brill, S. Dumais, and M. Banko. 2002. An analysis of the askmsr question-answering system. In *Proceedings of EMNLP*.

D. Carmel, E. Yom-Tov, A. Darlow, and D. Pelleg. 2006. What makes a query difficult? In *Proceedings of SIGIR*, pages 390–397.

J. Conroy, J. Schlesinger, and D. O'Leary. 2006. Topic-focused multi-document summarization using an approximate oracle score. In *Proceedings of ACL*.

S. Cronen-Townsend, Y. Zhou, and W. B. Croft. 2002. Predicting query performance. In *Proceedings of SIGIR*, pages 299–306.

M. Dredze and K. Czuba. 2007. Learning to admit you're wrong: Statistical tools for evaluating web qa. In *NIPS Workshop on Machine Learning for Web Search*.

M. Kaisser, M. A. Hearst, and J. B. Lowe. 2008. Improving search results quality by customizing summary lengths. In *Proceedings of ACL: HLT*, pages 701–709.

N. Karamanis. 2003. *Entity Coherence for Descriptive Text Structuring*. Ph.D. thesis, University of Edinburgh.

C. Lin and E. Hovy. 2000. The automated acquisition of topic signatures for text summarization. In *Proceedings of COLING*, pages 495–501.

K. McKeown, R. Barzilay, D. Evans, V. Hatzivassiloglou, B. Schiffman, and S. Teufel. 2001. Columbia multi-document summarization: Approach and evaluation. In *Proceedings of DUC*.

B. Mohit and R. Hwa. 2007. Localization of difficult-to-translate phrases. In *Proceedings of ACL Workshop on Statistical Machine Translations*.

A. Nenkova and A. Louis. 2008. Can you summarize this? identifying correlates of input difficulty for multi-document summarization. In *Proceedings of ACL: HLT*, pages 825–833.

P. Over, H. Dang, and D. Harman. 2007. Duc in context. *Inf. Process. Manage.*, 43(6):1506–1520.

M. Walker, O. Rambow, and M. Rogati. 2001. Spot: a trainable sentence planner. In *Proceedings of NAACL*, pages 1–8.

E. Yom-Tov, S. Fine, D. Carmel, and A. Darlow. 2005. Learning to estimate query difficulty: including applications to missing content detection and distributed information retrieval. In *Proceedings of SIGIR*, pages 512–519.

Bilingually Motivated Domain-Adapted Word Segmentation for Statistical Machine Translation

Yanjun Ma **Andy Way**
National Centre for Language Technology
School of Computing
Dublin City University
Dublin 9, Ireland
{yma, away}@computing.dcu.ie

Abstract

We introduce a word segmentation approach to languages where word boundaries are not orthographically marked, with application to Phrase-Based Statistical Machine Translation (PB-SMT). Instead of using manually segmented *monolingual* domain-specific corpora to train segmenters, we make use of bilingual corpora and statistical word alignment techniques. First of all, our approach is adapted for the specific translation task at hand by taking the corresponding source (target) language into account. Secondly, this approach does not rely on manually segmented training data so that it can be automatically adapted for different domains. We evaluate the performance of our segmentation approach on PB-SMT tasks from two domains and demonstrate that our approach scores consistently among the best results across different data conditions.

1 Introduction

State-of-the-art Statistical Machine Translation (SMT) requires a certain amount of bilingual corpora as training data in order to achieve competitive results. The only assumption of most current statistical models (Brown et al., 1993; Vogel et al., 1996; Deng and Byrne, 2005) is that the aligned sentences in such corpora should be segmented into sequences of tokens that are meant to be words. Therefore, for languages where word boundaries are not orthographically marked, tools which segment a sentence into words are required. However, this segmentation is normally performed as a preprocessing step using various word segmenters. Moreover, most of these segmenters are usually trained on a manually segmented domain-specific corpus, which is not adapted for the specific translation task at hand given that the manual segmentation is performed in a *monolingual* context. Consequently, such segmenters cannot produce consistently good results when used across different domains.

A substantial amount of research has been carried out to address the problems of word segmentation. However, most research focuses on combining various segmenters either in SMT training or decoding (Dyer et al., 2008; Zhang et al., 2008). One important yet often neglected fact is that the optimal segmentation of the source (target) language is dependent on the target (source) language itself, its domain and its genre. Segmentation considered to be "good" from a *monolingual* point of view may be unadapted for training alignment models or PB-SMT decoding (Ma et al., 2007). The resulting segmentation will consequently influence the performance of an SMT system.

In this paper, we propose a bilingually motivated automatically domain-adapted approach for SMT. We utilise a small bilingual corpus with the relevant language segmented into basic writing units (e.g. characters for Chinese or kana for Japanese). Our approach consists of using the output from an existing statistical word aligner to obtain a set of candidate "words". We evaluate the reliability of these candidates using simple metrics based on co-occurrence frequencies, similar to those used in associative approaches to word alignment (Melamed, 2000). We then modify the segmentation of the respective sentences in the parallel corpus according to these candidate words; these modified sentences are then given back to the word aligner, which produces new alignments. We evaluate the validity of our approach by measuring the influence of the segmentation process on Chinese-to-English Machine Translation (MT) tasks in two different domains.

The remainder of this paper is organised as fol-

Proceedings of the 12th Conference of the European Chapter of the ACL, pages 549–557,
Athens, Greece, 30 March – 3 April 2009. ©2009 Association for Computational Linguistics

lows. In section 2, we study the influence of word segmentation on PB-SMT across different domains. Section 3 describes the working mechanism of our bilingually motivated word segmentation approach. In section 4, we illustrate the adaptation of our decoder to this segmentation scheme. The experiments conducted in two different domains are reported in Section 5 and 6. We discuss related work in section 7. Section 8 concludes and gives avenues for future work.

2 The Influence of Word Segmentation on SMT: A Pilot Investigation

The *monolingual* word segmentation step in traditional SMT systems has a substantial impact on the performance of such systems. A considerable amount of recent research has focused on the influence of word segmentation on SMT (Ma et al., 2007; Chang et al., 2008; Zhang et al., 2008); however, most explorations focused on the impact of various segmentation guidelines and the mechanisms of the segmenters themselves. A current research interest concerns consistency of performance across different domains. From our experiments, we show that monolingual segmenters cannot produce consistently good results when applied to a new domain.

Our pilot investigation into the influence of word segmentation on SMT involves three off-the-shelf Chinese word segmenters including ICTCLAS (ICT) Olympic version[1], LDC segmenter[2] and Stanford segmenter version 2006-05-11[3]. Both ICTCLAS and Stanford segmenters utilise machine learning techniques, with Hidden Markov Models for ICT (Zhang et al., 2003) and conditional random fields for the Stanford segmenter (Tseng et al., 2005). Both segmentation models were trained on news domain data with named entity recognition functionality. The LDC segmenter is dictionary-based with word frequency information to help disambiguation, both of which are collected from data in the news domain. We used Chinese character-based and manual segmentations as contrastive segmentations. The experiments were carried out on a range of data sizes from news and dialogue domains using a state-of-the-art Phrase-Based SMT (PB-SMT) system—Moses (Koehn et al., 2007). The performance of PB-SMT system is measured with BLEU score (Papineni et al., 2002).

We firstly measure the influence of word segmentation on in-domain data with respect to the three above mentioned segmenters, namely UN data from the NIST 2006 evaluation campaign. As can be seen from Table 1, using monolingual segmenters achieves consistently better SMT performance than character-based segmentation (CS) on different data sizes, which means character-based segmentation is not good enough for this domain where the vocabulary tends to be large. We can also observe that the ICT and Stanford segmenter consistently outperform the LDC segmenter. Even using 3M sentence pairs for training, the differences between them are still statistically significant ($p < 0.05$) using approximate randomisation (Noreen, 1989) for significance testing.

	40K	160K	640K	3M
CS	8.33	12.47	14.40	17.80
ICT	10.17	14.85	**17.20**	20.50
LDC	9.37	13.88	15.86	19.59
Stanford	**10.45**	**15.26**	16.94	**20.64**

Table 1: Word segmentation on NIST data sets

However, when tested on out-of-domain data, i.e. IWSLT data in the dialogue domain, the results seem to be more difficult to predict. We trained the system on different sizes of data and evaluated the system on two test sets: IWSLT 2006 and 2007. From Table 2, we can see that on the IWSLT 2006 test sets, LDC achieves consistently good results and the Stanford segmenter is the worst.[4] Furthermore, the character-based segmentation also achieves competitive results. On IWSLT 2007, all monolingual segmenters outperform character-based segmentation and the LDC segmenter is only slightly better than the other segmenters.

From the experiments reported above, we can reach the following conclusions. First of all, character-based segmentation cannot achieve state-of-the-art results in most experimental SMT settings. This also motivates the necessity to work on better segmentation strategies. Second, monolingual segmenters cannot achieve consis-

[1]http://ictclas.org/index.html

[2]http://www.ldc.upenn.edu/Projects/Chinese

[3]http://nlp.stanford.edu/software/segmenter.shtml

[4]Interestingly, the developers themselves also note the sensitivity of the Stanford segmenter and incorporate external lexical information to address such problems (Chang et al., 2008).

		40K	160K
IWSLT06	CS	19.31	23.06
	Manual	19.94	-
	ICT	20.34	23.36
	LDC	**20.37**	**24.34**
	Stanford	18.25	21.40
IWSLT07	CS	29.59	30.25
	Manual	**33.85**	-
	ICT	31.18	33.38
	LDC	31.74	**33.44**
	Stanford	30.97	33.41

Table 2: Word segmentation on IWSLT data sets

tently good results when used in another domain. In the following sections, we propose a bilingually motivated segmentation approach which can be automatically derived from a small representative data set and the experiments show that we can consistently obtain state-of-the-art results in different domains.

3 Bilingually Motivated Word Segmentation

3.1 Notation

While in this paper, we focus on Chinese–English, the method proposed is applicable to other language pairs. The notation, however, assumes Chinese–English MT. Given a Chinese sentence c_1^J consisting of J characters $\{c_1, \ldots, c_J\}$ and an English sentence e_1^I consisting of I words $\{e_1, \ldots, e_I\}$, $A_{C \rightarrow E}$ will denote a Chinese-to-English word alignment between c_1^J and e_1^I. Since we are primarily interested in 1-to-n alignments, $A_{C \rightarrow E}$ can be represented as a set of pairs $a_i = \langle C_i, e_i \rangle$ denoting a link between one single English word e_i and a few Chinese characters C_i.The set C_i is empty if the word e_i is not aligned to any character in c_1^J.

3.2 Candidate Extraction

In the following, we assume the availability of an automatic word aligner that can output alignments $A_{C \rightarrow E}$ for any sentence pair (c_1^J, e_1^I) in a parallel corpus. We also assume that $A_{C \rightarrow E}$ contain 1-to-n alignments. Our method for Chinese word segmentation is as follows: whenever a single English word is aligned with several consecutive Chinese characters, they are considered candidates for grouping. Formally, given an alignment $A_{C \rightarrow E}$ between c_1^J and e_1^I, if $a_i = \langle C_i, e_i \rangle \in A_{C \rightarrow E}$, with $C_i = \{c_{i_1}, \ldots, c_{i_m}\}$ and $\forall k \in [\![1, m-1]\!]$, $i_{k+1} - i_k = 1$, then the alignment a_i between e_i and the sequence of words C_i is considered a candidate word. Some examples of such 1-to-n alignments between Chinese and English we can derive automatically are displayed in Figure 1.[5]

may	可 能	favorite	最 喜 欢
may	可 以	interesting	有 意 思
food	食 物	miami	迈 阿 密
food	食 品	last	最 后 一
july	七 月	block	个 街 区

Figure 1: Example of 1-to-n word alignments between English words and Chinese characters

3.3 Candidate Reliability Estimation

Of course, the process described above is error-prone, especially on a small amount of training data. If we want to change the input segmentation to give to the word aligner, we need to make sure that we are not making harmful modifications. We thus additionally evaluate the reliability of the candidates we extract and filter them before inclusion in our bilingual dictionary. To perform this filtering, we use two simple statistical measures. In the following, $a_i = \langle C_i, e_i \rangle$ denotes a candidate.

The first measure we consider is co-occurrence frequency ($COOC(C_i, e_i)$), i.e. the number of times C_i and e_i co-occur in the bilingual corpus. This very simple measure is frequently used in associative approaches (Melamed, 2000). The second measure is the alignment confidence (Ma et al., 2007), defined as

$$AC(a_i) = \frac{C(a_i)}{COOC(C_i, e_i)},$$

where $C(a_i)$ denotes the number of alignments proposed by the word aligner that are identical to a_i. In other words, $AC(a_i)$ measures how often the aligner aligns C_i and e_i when they co-occur. We also impose that $|C_i| \leq k$, where k is a fixed integer that may depend on the language pair (between 3 and 5 in practice). The rationale behind this is that it is very rare to get reliable alignments between one word and k consecutive words when k is high.

[5]While in this paper we are primarily concerned with languages where the word boundaries are not orthographically marked, this approach, however, can also be applied to languages marked with word boundaries to construct *bilingually* motivated "words".

The candidates are included in our bilingual dictionary if and only if their measures are above some fixed thresholds t_{COOC} and t_{AC}, which allow for the control of the size of the dictionary and the quality of its contents. Some other measures (including the Dice coefficient) could be considered; however, it has to be noted that we are more interested here in the filtering than in the discovery of alignments *per se*, since our method builds upon an existing aligner. Moreover, we will see that even these simple measures can lead to an improvement in the alignment process in an MT context.

3.4 Bootstrapped word segmentation

Once the candidates are extracted, we perform word segmentation using the bilingual dictionaries constructed using the method described above; this provides us with an updated training corpus, in which some character sequences have been replaced by a single token. This update is totally naive: if an entry $a_i = \langle C_i, e_i \rangle$ is present in the dictionary and matches one sentence pair (c_1^J, e_1^I) (i.e. C_i and e_i are respectively contained in c_1^J and e_1^I), then we replace the sequence of characters C_i with a single token which becomes a new lexical unit.[6] Note that this replacement occurs even if no alignment was found between C_i and e_i for the pair (c_1^J, e_1^I). This is motivated by the fact that the filtering described above is quite conservative; we trust the entry a_i to be correct.

This process can be applied several times: once we have grouped some characters together, they become the new basic unit to consider, and we can re-run the same method to get additional groupings. However, we have not seen in practice much benefit from running it more than twice (few new candidates are extracted after two iterations).

4 Word Lattice Decoding

4.1 Word Lattices

In the decoding stage, the various segmentation alternatives can be encoded into a compact representation of word lattices. A word lattice $G = \langle V, E \rangle$ is a directed acyclic graph that formally is a weighted finite state automaton. In the case of word segmentation, each edge is a candidate word associated with its weights. A straightforward estimation of the weights is to distribute the probability mass for each node uniformly to each outgoing edge. The single node having no outgoing edges is designated the "end node". An example of word lattices for a Chinese sentence is shown in Figure 2.

4.2 Word Lattice Generation

Previous research on generating word lattices relies on multiple *monolingual* segmenters (Xu et al., 2005; Dyer et al., 2008). One advantage of our approach is that the bilingually motivated segmentation process facilitates word lattice generation without relying on other segmenters. As described in section 3.4, the update of the training corpus based on the constructed *bilingual* dictionary requires that the sentence pair meets the bilingual constraints. Such a segmentation process in the training stage facilitates the utilisation of word lattice decoding.

4.3 Phrase-Based Word Lattice Decoding

Given a Chinese input sentence c_1^J consisting of J characters, the traditional approach is to determine the best word segmentation and perform decoding afterwards. In such a case, we first seek a single best segmentation:

$$\hat{f}_1^K = \arg\max_{f_1^K, K}\{Pr(f_1^K|c_1^J)\}$$

Then in the decoding stage, we seek:

$$\hat{e}_1^I = \arg\max_{e_1^I, I}\{Pr(e_1^I|\hat{f}_1^K)\}$$

In such a scenario, some segmentations which are potentially optimal for the translation may be lost. This motivates the need for word lattice decoding. The search process can be rewritten as:

$$\begin{aligned}
\hat{e}_1^I &= \arg\max_{e_1^I, I}\{\max_{f_1^K, K} Pr(e_1^I, f_1^K|c_1^J)\} \\
&= \arg\max_{e_1^I, I}\{\max_{f_1^K, K} Pr(e_1^I) Pr(f_1^K|e_1^I, c_1^J)\} \\
&= \arg\max_{e_1^I, I}\{\max_{f_1^K, K} Pr(e_1^I) Pr(f_1^K|e_1^I) Pr(f_1^K|c_1^J)\}
\end{aligned}$$

Given the fact that the number of segmentations f_1^K grows exponentially with respect to the number of characters K, it is impractical to firstly enumerate all possible f_1^K and then to decode. However, it is possible to enumerate all the alternative segmentations for a substring of c_1^J, making the utilisation of word lattices tractable in PB-SMT.

[6] In case of overlap between several groups of words to replace, we select the one with the highest confidence (according to t_{AC}).

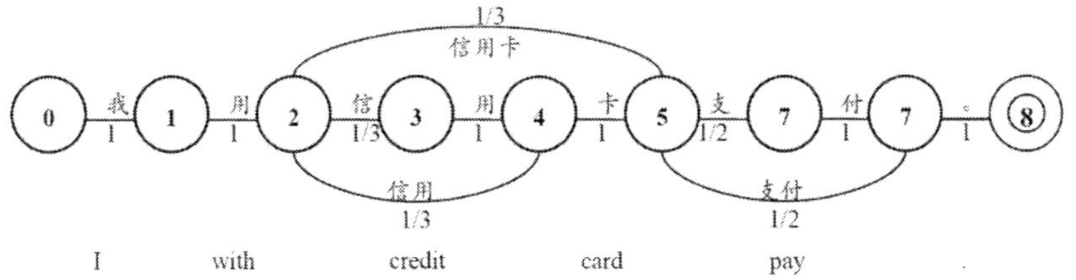

Figure 2: Example of a word lattice

5 Experimental Setting

5.1 Evaluation

The intrinsic quality of word segmentation is normally evaluated against a manually segmented gold-standard corpus using F-score. While this approach can give a direct evaluation of the quality of the word segmentation, it is faced with several limitations. First of all, it is really difficult to build a reliable and objective gold-standard given the fact that there is only 70% agreement between native speakers on this task (Sproat et al., 1996). Second, an increase in F-score does not necessarily imply an improvement in translation quality. It has been shown that F-score has a very weak correlation with SMT translation quality in terms of BLEU score (Zhang et al., 2008). Consequently, we chose to extrinsically evaluate the performance of our approach via the Chinese–English translation task, i.e. we measure the influence of the segmentation process on the final translation output. The quality of the translation output is mainly evaluated using BLEU, with NIST (Doddington, 2002) and METEOR (Banerjee and Lavie, 2005) as complementary metrics.

5.2 Data

The data we used in our experiments are from two different domains, namely news and travel dialogues. For the news domain, we trained our system using a portion of UN data for NIST 2006 evaluation campaign. The system was developed on LDC Multiple-Translation Chinese (MTC) Corpus and tested on MTC part 2, which was also used as a test set for NIST 2002 evaluation campaign.

For the dialogue data, we used the Chinese–English datasets provided within the IWSLT 2007 evaluation campaign. Specifically, we used the standard training data, to which we added devset1 and devset2. Devset4 was used to tune the parameters and the performance of the system was tested on both IWSLT 2006 and 2007 test sets. We used both test sets because they are quite different in terms of sentence length and vocabulary size. To test the scalability of our approach, we used HIT corpus provided within IWSLT 2008 evaluation campaign. The various statistics for the corpora are shown in Table 3.

5.3 Baseline System

We conducted experiments using different segmenters with a standard log-linear PB-SMT model: GIZA++ implementation of IBM word alignment model 4 (Och and Ney, 2003), the refinement and phrase-extraction heuristics described in (Koehn et al., 2003), minimum-error-rate training (Och, 2003), a 5-gram language model with Kneser-Ney smoothing trained with SRILM (Stolcke, 2002) on the English side of the training data, and Moses (Koehn et al., 2007; Dyer et al., 2008) to translate both single best segmentation and word lattices.

6 Experiments

6.1 Results

The initial word alignments are obtained using the baseline configuration described above by segmenting the Chinese sentences into characters. From these we build a bilingual 1-to-n dictionary, and the training corpus is updated by grouping the characters in the dictionaries into a single word, using the method presented in section 3.4. As previously mentioned, this process can be repeated several times. We then extract aligned phrases using the same procedure as for the baseline system; the only difference is the basic unit we are considering. Once the phrases are extracted, we perform the estimation of weights for the features of the log-linear model. We then use a simple dictionary-based maximum matching algorithm to obtain a single-best segmentation for the Chinese sentences in the development set so that

		Train		Dev.		Eval.	
		Zh	**En**	**Zh**	**En**	**Zh**	**En**
Dialogue	Sentences	40,958		489 (7 ref.)		489 (6 ref.)/489 (7 ref.)	
	Running words	488,303	385,065	8,141	46,904	8,793/4,377	51,500/23,181
	Vocabulary size	2,742	9,718	835	1,786	936/772	2,016/1,339
News	Sentences	40,000		993 (9 ref.)		878 (4 ref.)	
	Running words	1,412,395	956,023	41,466	267,222	38,700	105,530
	Vocabulary size	6057	20,068	1,983	10,665	1,907	7,388

Table 3: Corpus statistics for Chinese (Zh) character segmentation and English (En)

minimum-error-rate training can be performed.[7] Finally, in the decoding stage, we use the same segmentation algorithm to obtain the single-best segmentation on the test set, and word lattices can also be generated using the bilingual dictionary. The various parameters of the method (k, t_{COOC}, t_{AC}, cf. section 3) were optimised on the development set. One iteration of character grouping on the NIST task was found to be enough; the optimal set of values was found to be $k = 3$, $t_{AC} = 0.0$ and $t_{COOC} = 0$, meaning that all the entries in the bilingually dictionary are kept. On IWSLT data, we found that two iterations of character grouping were needed: the optimal set of values was found to be $k = 3$, $t_{AC} = 0.3$, $t_{COOC} = 8$ for the first iteration, and $t_{AC} = 0.2$, $t_{COOC} = 15$ for the second.

As can be seen from Table 4, our bilingually motivated segmenter (BS) achieved statistically significantly better results than character-based segmentation when enhanced with word lattice decoding.[8] Compared to the best in-domain segmenter, namely the Stanford segmenter on this particular task, our approach is inferior according to BLEU and NIST. We firstly attribute this to the small amount of training data, from which a high quality bilingual dictionary cannot be obtained due to data sparseness problems. We also attribute this to the vast amount of named entity terms in the test sets, which is extremely difficult for our approach.[9] We expect to see better results when a larger amount of data is used and the segmenter is enhanced with a named entity recogniser. On IWSLT data (cf. Tables 5 and 6), our approach yielded a consistently good performance on both translation tasks compared to the best in-domain segmenter—the LDC segmenter. Moreover, the good performance is confirmed by all three evaluation measures.

	BLEU	NIST	METEOR
CS	8.43	4.6272	0.3778
Stanford	**10.45**	**5.0675**	0.3699
BS-SingleBest	7.98	4.4374	0.3510
BS-WordLattice	9.04	4.6667	**0.3834**

Table 4: BS on NIST task

	BLEU	NIST	METEOR
CS	0.1931	6.1816	0.4998
LDC	0.2037	6.2089	0.4984
BS-SingleBest	0.1865	5.7816	0.4602
BS-WordLattice	**0.2041**	**6.2874**	**0.5124**

Table 5: BS on IWSLT 2006 task

	BLEU	NIST	METEOR
CS	0.2959	6.1216	0.5216
LDC	**0.3174**	6.2464	0.5403
BS-SingleBest	0.3023	6.0476	0.5125
BS-WordLattice	0.3171	**6.3518**	**0.5603**

Table 6: BS on IWSLT 2007 task

6.2 Parameter Search Graph

The reliability estimation process is computationally intensive. However, this can be easily parallelised. From our experiments, we observed that the translation results are very sensitive to the parameters and this search process is essential to achieve good results. Figure 3 is the search graph on the IWSLT data set in the first iteration step. From this graph, we can see that filtering of the bilingual dictionary is essential in order to achieve better performance.

[7] In order to save computational time, we used the same set of parameters obtained above to decode both the single-best segmentation and the word lattice.

[8] Note the BLEU scores are particularly low due to the number of references used (4 references), in addition to the small amount of training data available.

[9] As we previously point out, both ICT and Stanford segmenters are equipped with named entity recognition functionality. This may risk causing data sparseness problems on small training data. However, this is beneficial in the translation process compared to character-based segmentation.

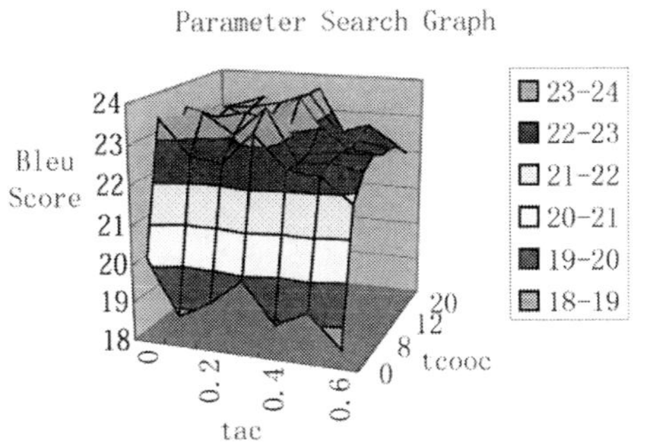

Figure 3: The search graph on development set of IWSLT task

6.3 Vocabulary Size

Our bilingually motivated segmentation approach has to overcome another challenge in order to produce competitive results, i.e. data sparseness. Given that our segmentation is based on bilingual dictionaries, the segmentation process can significantly increase the size of the vocabulary, which could potentially lead to a data sparseness problem when the size of the training data is small. Tables 7 and 8 list the statistics of the Chinese side of the training data, including the total vocabulary (Voc), number of character vocabulary (Char.voc) in Voc, and the running words (Run.words) when different word segmentations were used. From Table 7, we can see that our approach suffered from data sparseness on the NIST task, i.e. a large vocabulary was generated, of which a considerable amount of characters still remain as separate words. On the IWSLT task, since the dictionary generation process is more conservative, we maintained a reasonable vocabulary size, which contributed to the final good performance.

	Voc.	Char.voc	Run. Words
CS	6,057	6,057	1,412,395
ICT	16,775	1,703	870,181
LDC	16,100	2,106	881,861
Stanford	22,433	1,701	880,301
BS	**18,111**	**2,803**	**927,182**

Table 7: Vocabulary size of NIST task (40K)

6.4 Scalability

The experimental results reported above are based on a small training corpus containing roughly 40,000 sentence pairs. We are particularly interested in the performance of our segmentation approach when it is scaled up to larger amounts of data. Given that the optimisation of the bilingual dictionary is computationally intensive, it is impractical to directly extract candidate words and estimate their reliability. As an alternative, we can use the obtained bilingual dictionary optimised on the small corpus to perform segmentation on the larger corpus. We expect competitive results when the small corpus is a representative sample of the larger corpus and large enough to produce reliable bilingual dictionaries without suffering severely from data sparseness.

	Voc.	Char.voc	Run. Words
CS	2,742	2,742	488,303
ICT	11,441	1,629	358,504
LDC	9,293	1,963	364,253
Stanford	18,676	981	348,251
BS	**3,828**	**2,740**	**402,845**

Table 8: Vocabulary size of IWSLT task (40K)

As we can see from Table 9, our segmentation approach achieved consistent results on both IWSLT 2006 and 2007 test sets. On the NIST task (cf. Table 10), our approach outperforms the basic character-based segmentation; however, it is still inferior compared to the other in-domain monolingual segmenters due to the low quality of the bilingual dictionary induced (cf. section 6.1).

	IWSLT06	IWSLT07
CS	23.06	30.25
ICT	23.36	33.38
LDC	**24.34**	**33.44**
Stanford	21.40	33.41
BS-SingleBest	22.45	30.76
BS-WordLattice	24.18	32.99

Table 9: Scale-up to 160K on IWSLT data sets

	160K	640K
CS	12.47	14.40
ICT	14.85	**17.20**
LDC	13.88	15.86
Stanford	**15.26**	16.94
BS-SingleBest	12.58	14.11
BS-WordLattice	13.74	15.33

Table 10: Scalability of BS on NIST task

6.5 Using different word aligners

The above experiments rely on GIZA++ to perform word alignment. We next show that our approach is not dependent on the word aligner given that we have a conservative reliability estimation procedure. Table 11 shows the results obtained on the IWSLT data set using the MTTK alignment tool (Deng and Byrne, 2005; Deng and Byrne, 2006).

	IWSLT06	IWSLT07
CS	21.04	31.41
ICT	20.48	31.11
LDC	20.79	30.51
Stanford	17.84	29.35
BS-SingleBest	19.22	29.75
BS-WordLattice	**21.76**	**31.75**

Table 11: BS on IWSLT data sets using MTTK

7 Related Work

(Xu et al., 2004) were the first to question the use of word segmentation in SMT and showed that the segmentation proposed by word alignments can be used in SMT to achieve competitive results compared to using monolingual segmenters. Our approach differs from theirs in two aspects. Firstly, (Xu et al., 2004) use word aligners to reconstruct a (monolingual) Chinese dictionary and reuse this dictionary to segment Chinese sentences as other monolingual segmenters. Our approach features the use of a bilingual dictionary and conducts a different segmentation. In addition, we add a process which optimises the bilingual dictionary according to translation quality. (Ma et al., 2007) proposed an approach to improve word alignment by optimising the segmentation of both source and target languages. However, the reported experiments still rely on some monolingual segmenters and the issue of scalability is not addressed. Our research focuses on avoiding the use of monolingual segmenters in order to improve the robustness of segmenters across different domains.

(Xu et al., 2005) were the first to propose the use of word lattice decoding in PB-SMT, in order to address the problems of segmentation. (Dyer et al., 2008) extended this approach to hierarchical SMT systems and other language pairs. However, both of these methods require some monolingual segmentation in order to generate word lattices. Our approach facilitates word lattice generation given that our segmentation is driven by the bilingual dictionary.

8 Conclusions and Future Work

In this paper, we introduced a bilingually motivated word segmentation approach for SMT. The assumption behind this motivation is that the language to be segmented can be tokenised into basic writing units. Firstly, we extract 1-to-n word alignments using statistical word aligners to construct a bilingual dictionary in which each entry indicates a correspondence between one English word and n Chinese characters. This dictionary is then filtered using a few simple association measures and the final bilingual dictionary is deployed for word segmentation. To overcome the segmentation problem in the decoding stage, we deployed word lattice decoding.

We evaluated our approach on translation tasks from two different domains and demonstrate that our approach is (i) not as sensitive as monolingual segmenters, and (ii) that the SMT system using our word segmentation can achieve state-of-the-art performance. Moreover, our approach can easily be scaled up to larger data sets and achieves competitive results if the small data used is a representative sample.

As for future work, firstly we plan to integrate some named entity recognisers into our approach. We also plan to try our approach in more domains and on other language pairs (e.g. Japanese–English). Finally, we intend to explore the correlation between vocabulary size and the amount of training data needed in order to achieve good results using our approach.

Acknowledgments

This work is supported by Science Foundation Ireland (O5/IN/1732) and the Irish Centre for High-End Computing.[10] We would like to thank the reviewers for their insightful comments.

References

Satanjeev Banerjee and Alon Lavie. 2005. METEOR: An automatic metric for MT evaluation with improved correlation with human judgments. In *Proceedings of the ACL Workshop on Intrinsic and Extrinsic Evaluation Measures for Machine Translation and/or Summarization*, pages 65–72, Ann Arbor, MI.

[10]http://www.ichec.ie/

Peter F. Brown, Stephen A. Della Pietra, Vincent J. Della Pietra, and Robert L. Mercer. 1993. The mathematics of statistical machine translation: Parameter estimation. *Computational Linguistics*, 19(2):263–311.

Pi-Chuan Chang, Michel Galley, and Christopher D. Manning. 2008. Optimizing Chinese word segmentation for machine translation performance. In *Proceedings of the Third Workshop on Statistical Machine Translation*, pages 224–232, Columbus, OH.

Yonggang Deng and William Byrne. 2005. HMM word and phrase alignment for statistical machine translation. In *Proceedings of Human Language Technology Conference and Conference on Empirical Methods in Natural Language Processing*, pages 169–176, Vancouver, BC, Canada.

Yonggang Deng and William Byrne. 2006. MTTK: An alignment toolkit for statistical machine translation. In *Proceedings of the Human Language Technology Conference of the NAACL*, pages 265–268, New York City, NY.

George Doddington. 2002. Automatic evaluation of machine translation quality using n-gram co-occurrence statistics. In *Proceedings of the second international conference on Human Language Technology Research*, pages 138–145, San Francisco, CA.

Christopher Dyer, Smaranda Muresan, and Philip Resnik. 2008. Generalizing word lattice translation. In *Proceedings of the 46th Annual Meeting of the Association for Computational Linguistics: Human Language Technologies*, pages 1012–1020, Columbus, OH.

Philipp Koehn, Franz Och, and Daniel Marcu. 2003. Statistical phrase-based translation. In *Proceedings of Human Language Technology Conference and Conference on Empirical Methods in Natural Language Processing*, pages 48–54, Edmonton, AL, Canada.

Philipp Koehn, Hieu Hoang, Alexandra Birch, Chris Callison-Burch, Marcello Federico, Nicola Bertoldi, Brooke Cowan, Wade Shen, Christine Moran, Richard Zens, Chris Dyer, Ondrej Bojar, Alexandra Constantin, and Evan Herbst. 2007. Moses: Open source toolkit for statistical machine translation. In *Proceedings of the 45th Annual Meeting of the Association for Computational Linguistics Companion Volume Proceedings of the Demo and Poster Sessions*, pages 177–180, Prague, Czech Republic.

Yanjun Ma, Nicolas Stroppa, and Andy Way. 2007. Bootstrapping word alignment via word packing. In *Proceedings of the 45th Annual Meeting of the Association of Computational Linguistics*, pages 304–311, Prague, Czech Republic.

I. Dan Melamed. 2000. Models of translational equivalence among words. *Computational Linguistics*, 26(2):221–249.

Eric W. Noreen. 1989. *Computer-Intensive Methods for Testing Hypotheses: An Introduction*. Wiley-Interscience, New York, NY.

Franz Och and Hermann Ney. 2003. A systematic comparison of various statistical alignment models. *Computational Linguistics*, 29(1):19–51.

Franz Och. 2003. Minimum error rate training in statistical machine translation. In *Proceedings of the 41st Annual Meeting of the Association for Computational Linguistics*, pages 160–167, Sapporo, Japan.

Kishore Papineni, Salim Roukos, Todd Ward, and Wei-Jing Zhu. 2002. BLEU: a method for automatic evaluation of machine translation. In *Proceedings of the 40th Annual Meeting of the Association for Computational Linguistics*, pages 311–318, Philadelphia, PA.

Richard W Sproat, Chilin Shih, William Gale, and Nancy Chang. 1996. A stochastic finite-state word-segmentation algorithm for Chinese. *Computational Linguistics*, 22(3):377–404.

Andrea Stolcke. 2002. SRILM – An extensible language modeling toolkit. In *Proceedings of the International Conference on Spoken Language Processing*, pages 901–904, Denver, CO.

Huihsin Tseng, Pichuan Chang, Galen Andrew, Daniel Jurafsky, and Christopher Manning. 2005. A conditional random field word segmenter for sighan bakeoff 2005. In *Proceedings of Fourth SIGHAN Workshop on Chinese Language Processing*, pages 168–171, Jeju Island, Republic of Korea.

Stefan Vogel, Hermann Ney, and Christoph Tillmann. 1996. HMM-based word alignment in statistical translation. In *Proceedings of the 16th International Conference on Computational Linguistics*, pages 836–841, Copenhagen, Denmark.

Jia Xu, Richard Zens, and Hermann Ney. 2004. Do we need Chinese word segmentation for statistical machine translation? In *ACL SIGHAN Workshop 2004*, pages 122–128, Barcelona, Spain.

Jia Xu, Evgeny Matusov, Richard Zens, and Hermann Ney. 2005. Integrated Chinese word segmentation in statistical machine translation. In *Proceedings of the International Workshop on Spoken Language Translation*, pages 141–147, Pittsburgh, PA.

Huaping Zhang, Hongkui Yu, Deyi Xiong, and Qun Liu. 2003. HHMM-based Chinese lexical analyzer ICTCLAS. In *Proceedings of Second SIGHAN Workshop on Chinese Language Processing*, pages 184–187, Sappora, Japan.

Ruiqiang Zhang, Keiji Yasuda, and Eiichiro Sumita. 2008. Improved statistical machine translation by multiple Chinese word segmentation. In *Proceedings of the Third Workshop on Statistical Machine Translation*, pages 216–223, Columbus, OH.

Evaluating the Inferential Utility of Lexical-Semantic Resources

Shachar Mirkin, Ido Dagan, Eyal Shnarch
Computer Science Department, Bar-Ilan University
Ramat-Gan 52900, Israel
{mirkins,dagan,shey}@cs.biu.ac.il

Abstract

Lexical-semantic resources are used extensively for applied semantic inference, yet a clear quantitative picture of their current utility and limitations is largely missing. We propose system- and application-independent evaluation and analysis methodologies for resources' performance, and systematically apply them to seven prominent resources. Our findings identify the currently limited recall of available resources, and indicate the potential to improve performance by examining non-standard relation types and by distilling the output of distributional methods. Further, our results stress the need to include auxiliary information regarding the lexical and logical contexts in which a lexical inference is valid, as well as its prior validity likelihood.

1 Introduction

Lexical information plays a major role in semantic inference, as the meaning of one term is often inferred form another. Lexical-semantic resources, which provide the needed knowledge for lexical inference, are commonly utilized by applied inference systems (Giampiccolo et al., 2007) and applications such as Information Retrieval and Question Answering (Shah and Croft, 2004; Pasca and Harabagiu, 2001). Beyond WordNet (Fellbaum, 1998), a wide range of resources has been developed and utilized, including extensions to WordNet (Moldovan and Rus, 2001; Snow et al., 2006) and resources based on automatic distributional similarity methods (Lin, 1998; Pantel and Lin, 2002). Recently, Wikipedia is emerging as a source for extracting semantic relationships (Suchanek et al., 2007; Kazama and Torisawa, 2007).

As of today, only a partial comparative picture is available regarding the actual utility and limitations of available resources for lexical-semantic inference. Works that do provide quantitative information regarding resources utility have focused on few particular resources (Kouylekov and Magnini, 2006; Roth and Sammons, 2007) and evaluated their impact on a specific system. Most often, works which utilized lexical resources do not provide information about their isolated contribution; rather, they only report overall performance for systems in which lexical resources serve as components.

Our paper provides a step towards clarifying this picture. We propose a system- and application-independent evaluation methodology that isolates resources' performance, and systematically apply it to seven prominent lexical-semantic resources. The evaluation and analysis methodology is specified within the Textual Entailment framework, which has become popular in recent years for modeling practical semantic inference in a generic manner (Dagan and Glickman, 2004). To that end, we assume certain definitions that extend the textual entailment paradigm to the lexical level.

The findings of our work provide useful insights and suggested directions for two research communities: developers of applied inference systems and researchers addressing lexical acquisition and resource construction. Beyond the quantitative mapping of resources' performance, our analysis points at issues concerning their effective utilization and major characteristics. Even more importantly, the results highlight current gaps in existing resources and point at directions towards filling them. We show that the coverage of most resources is quite limited, where a substantial part of recall is attributable to semantic relations that are typically not available to inference systems. Notably, distributional acquisition methods

Proceedings of the 12th Conference of the European Chapter of the ACL, pages 558–566,
Athens, Greece, 30 March – 3 April 2009.

are shown to provide many useful relationships which are missing from other resources, but these are embedded amongst many irrelevant ones. Additionally, the results highlight the need to represent and inference over various aspects of contextual information, which affect the applicability of lexical inferences. We suggest that these gaps should be addressed by future research.

2 Sub-sentential Textual Entailment

Textual entailment captures the relation between a *text* t and a textual statement (termed *hypothesis*) h, such that a person reading t would infer that h is most likely correct (Dagan et al., 2005).

The entailment relation has been defined insofar in terms of truth values, assuming that h is a complete sentence (proposition). However, there are major aspects of inference that apply to the sub-sentential level. First, in certain applications, the target hypotheses are often sub-sentential. For example, search queries in IR, which play the hypothesis role from an entailment perspective, typically consist of a single term, like *drug legalization*. Such sub-sentential hypotheses are not regarded naturally in terms of truth values and therefore do not fit well within the scope of the textual entailment definition. Second, many entailment models apply a compositional process, through which they try to infer each sub-part of the hypothesis from some parts of the text (Giampiccolo et al., 2007).

Although inferences over sub-sentential elements are being applied in practice, so far there are no standard definitions for entailment at sub-sentential levels. To that end, and as a prerequisite of our evaluation methodology and our analysis, we first establish two relevant definitions for sub-sentential entailment relations: (a) entailment of a sub-sentential hypothesis by a text, and (b) entailment of one lexical element by another.

2.1 Entailment of Sub-sentential Hypotheses

We first seek a definition that would capture the entailment relationship between a text and a sub-sentential hypothesis. A similar goal was addressed in (Glickman et al., 2006), who defined the notion of *lexical reference* to model the fact that in order to entail a hypothesis, the text has to entail each non-compositional lexical element within it. We suggest that a slight adaptation of their definition is suitable to capture the notion of entailment for any sub-sentential hypotheses, including compositional ones:

Definition 1 *A sub-sentential hypothesis h is entailed by a text t if there is an explicit or implied reference in t to a possible meaning of h.*

For example, the sentence *"crude steel output is likely to fall in 2000"* entails the sub-sentential hypotheses *production*, *steel production* and *steel output decrease*.

Glickman et al., achieving good inter-annotator agreement, empirically found that almost all non-compositional terms in an entailed sentential hypothesis are indeed referenced in the entailing text. This finding suggests that the above definition is consistent with the original definition of textual entailment for sentential hypotheses and can thus model compositional entailment inferences.

We use this definition in our annotation methodology described in Section 3.

2.2 Entailment between Lexical Elements

In the majority of cases, the reference to an "atomic" (non-compositional) lexical element e in h stems from a particular lexical element e' in t, as in the example above where the word *output* implies the meaning of *production*.

To identify this relationship, an entailment system needs a knowledge resource that would specify that the meaning of e' implies the meaning of e, at least in some contexts. We thus suggest the following definition to capture this relationship between e' and e:

Definition 2 *A lexical element e' entails another lexical element e, denoted e'⇒e, if there exist some natural (non-anecdotal) texts containing e' which entail e, such that the reference to the meaning of e can be implied solely from the meaning of e' in the text.*

(Entailment of e by a text follows Definition 1).

We refer to this relation in this paper as *lexical entailment*[1], and call $e' \Rightarrow e$ a *lexical entailment rule*. e' is referred to as the rule's left hand side (*LHS*) and e as its right hand side (*RHS*).

Currently there are no knowledge resources designed specifically for lexical entailment modeling. Hence, the types of relationships they capture do not fully coincide with entailment inference needs. Thus, the definition suggests a specification for the rules that should be provided by

[1] Section 6 discusses other definitions of lexical entailment

a lexical entailment resource, following an operative rationale: a rule $e' \Rightarrow e$ should be included in an entailment knowledge resource if it would be needed, as part of a compositional process, to infer the meaning of e from some natural texts. Based on this definition, we perform an analysis of the relationships included in lexical-semantic resources, as described in Section 5.

A rule need not apply in all contexts, as long as it is appropriate for some texts. Two contextual aspects affect rule applicability. First is the "lexical context" specifying the meanings of the text's words. A rules is applicable in a certain context only when the intended sense of its LHS term matches the sense of that term in the text. For example, the application of the rule *lay* ⇒ *produce* is valid only in contexts where the producer is poultry and the products are eggs. This is a well known issue observed, for instance, by Voorhees (1994).

A second contextual factor requiring validation is the "logical context". The logical context determines the monotonicity of the LHS and is induced by logical operators such as negation and (explicit or implicit) quantifiers. For example, the rule *mammal* ⇒ *whale* may not be valid in most cases, but is applicable in universally quantified texts like "*mammals are warm-blooded*". This issue has been rarely addressed in applied inference systems (de Marneffe et al., 2006). The above mentioned rules both comply with Definition 2 and should therefore be included in a lexical entailment resource.

3 Evaluating Entailment Resources

Our evaluation goal is to assess the utility of lexical-semantic resources as sources for entailment rules. An inference system applies a rule by inferring the rule's RHS from texts that match its LHS. Thus, the utility of a resource depends on the performance of its rule applications rather than on the proportion of correct rules it contains. A rule, whether correct or incorrect, has insignificant effect on the resource's utility if it rarely matches texts in real application settings. Additionally, correct rules might produce incorrect applications when applied in inappropriate contexts. Therefore, we use an *instance-based* evaluation methodology, which simulates rule applications by collecting texts that contain rules' LHS and manually assessing the correctness of their applications.

Systems typically handle lexical context either implicitly or explicitly. Implicit context validation occurs when the different terms of a composite hypothesis disambiguate each other. For example, the rule *waterside* ⇒ *bank* is unlikely to be applied when trying to infer the hypothesis *bank loans*, since texts that match *waterside* are unlikely to contain also the meaning of *loan*. Explicit methods, such as word-sense disambiguation or sense matching, validate each rule application according to the broader context in the text. Few systems also address logical context validation by handling quantifiers and negation. As we aim for a system-independent comparison of resources, and explicit approaches are not standardized yet within inference systems, our evaluation uses only implicit context validation.

3.1 Evaluation Methodology

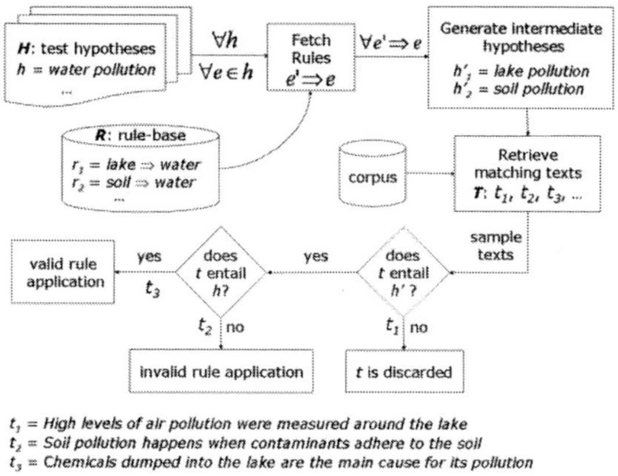

Figure 1: Evaluation methodology flow chart

The input for our evaluation methodology is a lexical-semantic resource R, which contains lexical entailment rules. We evaluate R's utility by testing how useful it is for inferring a sample of test hypotheses H from a corpus. Each hypothesis in H contains more than one lexical element in order to provide implicit context validation for rule applications, e.g. h: *water pollution*.

We next describe the steps of our evaluation methodology, as illustrated in Figure 1. We refer to the examples in the figure when needed:

1) Fetch rules: For each $h \in H$ and each lexical element $e \in h$ (e.g. *water*), we fetch all rules $e' \Rightarrow e$ in R that might be applied to entail e (e.g. *lake* ⇒ *water*).

2) Generate intermediate hypotheses h': For each rule r: $e' \Rightarrow e$, we generate an intermediate hypothesis h' by replacing e in h with e' (e.g.

h'_1: *lake pollution*). From a text t entailing h', h can be further entailed by the single application of r. We thus simulate the process by which an entailment system would infer h from t using r.

3) Retrieve matching texts: For each h' we retrieve from a corpus all texts that contain the lemmatized words of h' (not necessarily as a single phrase). These texts may entail h'. We discard texts that also match h since entailing h from them might not require the application of any rule from the evaluated resource. In our example, the retrieved texts contain *lake* and *pollution* but do not contain *water*.

4) Annotation: A sample of the retrieved texts is presented to human annotators. The annotators are asked to answer the following two questions for each text, simulating the typical inference process of an entailment system:

a) Does t entail h'? If t does not entail h' then the text would not provide a useful example for the application of r. For instance, t_1 (in Figure 1) does not entail h'_1 and thus we cannot deduce h from it by applying the rule r. Such texts are discarded from further evaluation.

b) Does t entail h? If t is annotated as entailing h', an entailment system would then infer h from h' by applying r. If h is not entailed from t even though h' is, the rule application is considered invalid. For instance, t_2 does not entail h even though it entails h'_2. Indeed, the application of r_2: **soil ⇒ water* [2], from which h'_2 was constructed, yields incorrect inference. If the answer is 'yes', as in the case of t_3, the application of r for t is considered valid.

The above process yields a sample of annotated rule applications for each test hypothesis, from which we can measure resources performance, as described in Section 5.

4 Experimental Setting

4.1 Dataset and Annotation

Current available state-of-the-art lexical-semantic resources mainly deal with nouns. Therefore, we used nominal hypotheses for our experiment[3].

We chose TREC 1-8 (excluding 4) as our test corpus and randomly sampled 25 ad-hoc queries of two-word compounds as our hypotheses. We did not use longer hypotheses to ensure that enough texts containing the intermediate hypotheses are found in the corpus. For annotation simplicity, we retrieved single sentences as our texts.

For each rule applied for an hypothesis h, we sampled 10 sentences from the sentences retrieved for that rule. As a baseline, we also sampled 10 sentences for each original hypothesis h in which both words of h are found. In total, 1550 unique sentences were sampled and annotated by two annotators.

To assess the validity of our evaluation methodology, the annotators first judged a sample of 220 sentences. The Kappa scores for inter-annotator agreement were 0.74 and 0.64 for judging h' and h, respectively. These figures correspond to substantial agreement (Landis and Koch, 1997) and are comparable with related semantic annotations (Szpektor et al., 2007; Bhagat et al., 2007).

4.2 Lexical-Semantic Resources

We evaluated the following resources:

WordNet (WN^d): There is no clear agreement regarding which set of WordNet relations is useful for entailment inference. We therefore took a conservative approach using only synonymy and hyponymy rules, which typically comply with the lexical entailment relation and are commonly used by textual entailment systems, e.g. (Herrera et al., 2005; Bos and Markert, 2006). Given a term e, we created a rule $e' \Rightarrow e$ for each e' amongst the synonyms or direct hyponyms for all senses of e in WordNet 3.0.

Snow ($Snow^{30k}$): Snow et al. (2006) presented a probabilistic model for taxonomy induction which considers as features paths in parse trees between related taxonomy nodes. They show that the best performing taxonomy was the one adding 30,000 hyponyms to WordNet. We created an entailment rule for each new hyponym added to WordNet by their algorithm[4].

LCC's extended WordNet ($XWN^{\star}$): In (Moldovan and Rus, 2001) WordNet glosses were transformed into logical form axioms. From this representation we created a rule $e' \Rightarrow e$ for each e' in the gloss which was tagged as referring to the same entity as e.

CBC: A knowledgebase of labeled clusters generated by the statistical clustering and labeling algorithms in (Pantel and Lin, 2002; Pantel and

[2] The asterisk marks an incorrect rule.

[3] We suggest that the definitions and methodologies can be applied for other parts of speech as well.

[4] Available at http://ai.stanford.edu/-rion/swn

Ravichandran, 2004)[5]. Given a cluster label e, an entailment rule $e' \Rightarrow e$ is created for each member e' of the cluster.

Lin Dependency Similarity (*Lin-dep*): A distributional word similarity resource based on syntactic-dependency features (Lin, 1998). Given a term e and its list of similar terms, we construct for each e' in the list the rule $e' \Rightarrow e$. This resource was previously used in textual entailment engines, e.g. (Roth and Sammons, 2007).

Lin Proximity Similarity (*Lin-prox*): A knowledgebase of terms with their cooccurrence-based distributionally similar terms. Rules are created from this resource as from the previous one[6].

Wikipedia first sentence (*WikiFS*): Kazama and Torisawa (2007) used Wikipedia as an external knowledge to improve Named Entity Recognition. Using the first step of their algorithm, we extracted from the first sentence of each page a noun that appears in a *is-a* pattern referring to the title. For each such pair we constructed a rule *title* $\Rightarrow$ *noun* (e.g. *Michelle Pfeiffer* $\Rightarrow$ *actress*).

The above resources represent various methods for detecting semantic relatedness between words: Manually and semi-automatically constructed (WN^d and $XWN^\star$, respectively), automatically constructed based on a lexical-syntactic pattern (*WikiFS*), distributional methods (*Lin-dep* and *Lin-prox*) and combinations of pattern-based and distributional methods (*CBC* and $Snow^{30k}$).

5 Results and Analysis

The results and analysis described in this section reveal new aspects concerning the utility of resources for lexical entailment, and experimentally quantify several intuitively-accepted notions regarding these resources and the lexical entailment relation. Overall, our findings highlight where efforts in developing future resources and inference systems should be invested.

5.1 Resources Performance

Each resource was evaluated using two measures - *Precision* and *Recall-share*, macro averaged over all hypotheses. The results achieved for each resource are summarized in Table 1.

[5]Kindly provided to us by Patrick Pantel.

[6]Lin's resources were downloaded from: http://www.cs.ualberta.ca/-lindek/demos.htm

Resource	Precision (%)	Recall-share (%)
$Snow^{30k}$	56	8
WN^d	55	24
$XWN^\star$	51	9
WikiFS	45	7
CBC	33	9
Lin-dep	28	45
Lin-prox	24	36

Table 1: Lexical resources performance

5.1.1 Precision

The *Precision* of a resource R is the percentage of valid rule applications for the resource. It is estimated by the percentage of texts entailing h from those that entail h': $\frac{count_R(entailing\ h{=}yes)}{count_R(entailing\ h'{=}yes)}$.

Not surprisingly, resources such as WN^d, $XWN^\star$ or *WikiFS* achieved relatively high precision scores, due to their accurate construction methods. In contrast, Lin's distributional resources are not designed to include lexical entailment relationships. They provide pairs of contextually similar words, of which many have non-entailing relationships, such as co-hyponyms[7] (e.g. **doctor* $\Rightarrow$ *journalist*) or topically-related words, such as **radiotherapy* $\Rightarrow$ *outpatient*. Hence their relatively low precision.

One visible outcome is the large gap between the perceived high accuracy of resources constructed by accurate methods, most notably WN^d, and their performance in practice. This finding emphasizes the need for instance-based evaluations, which capture the "real" contribution of a resource. To better understand the reasons for this gap we further assessed the three factors that contribute to incorrect applications: incorrect rules, lexical context and logical context (see Section 2.2). This analysis is presented in Table 2.

From Table 2 we see that the gap for accurate resources is mainly caused by applications of correct rules in inappropriate contexts. More interestingly, the information in the table allows us to asses the lexical "context-sensitivity" of resources. When considering only the COR-LEX rules to recalculate resources precision, we find that *Lin-dep* achieves precision of 71% ($\frac{15\%}{15\%+6\%}$), while WN^d yields only 56% ($\frac{55\%}{55\%+44\%}$). This result indicates that correct *Lin-dep* rules are less sensitive to lexical context, meaning that their prior likelihoods to

[7]a.k.a. *sister terms* or *coordinate terms*

(%)	Invalid Rule Applications				Valid Rule Applications			
	INCOR	COR-LOG	COR-LEX	Total	INCOR	COR-LOG	COR-LEX	Total (P)
WN^d	1	0	44	45	0	0	55	55
WikiFS	13	0	42	55	3	0	42	45
XWN*	19	0	30	49	0	0	51	51
Snow^{30k}	23	0	21	44	0	0	56	56
CBC	51	12	4	67	14	0	19	33
Lin-prox	59	4	13	76	8	3	13	24
Lin-dep	61	5	6	72	9	4	15	28

Table 2: The distribution of invalid and valid rule applications by rule types: incorrect rules (INCOR), correct rules requiring "logical context" validation (COR-LOG), and correct rules requiring "lexical context" matching (COR-LEX). The numbers of each resource's valid applications add up to the resource's precision.

be correct are higher. This is explained by the fact that *Lin-dep*'s rules are calculated across multiple contexts and therefore capture the more frequent usages of words. WordNet, on the other hand, includes many anecdotal rules whose application is rare, and thus is very sensitive to context. Similarly, *WikiFS* turns out to be very context-sensitive. This resource contains many rules for polysemous proper nouns that are scarce in their proper noun sense, e.g. *Captive* $\Rightarrow$ *computer game*. *Snow*^{30k}, when applied with the same calculation, reaches 73%, which explains how it achieved a comparable result to *WN*^{d}, even though it contains many incorrect rules in comparison to *WN*^{d}.

5.1.2 Recall

Absolute recall cannot be measured since the total number of texts in the corpus that entail each hypothesis is unknown. Instead, we measure *recall-share*, the contribution of each resource to recall relative to matching only the words of the original hypothesis without any rules. We denote by $yield(h)$ the number of texts that match h directly and are annotated as entailing h. This figure is estimated by the number of sampled texts annotated as entailing h multiplied by the sampling proportion. In the same fashion, for each resource R, we estimate the number of texts entailing h obtained through entailment rules of the resource R, denoted $yield_R(h)$. Recall-share of R for h is the proportion of the yield obtained by the resource's rules relative to the overall yield with and without the rules from R: $\frac{yield_R(h)}{yield(h)+yield_R(h)}$.

From Table 1 we see that along with their relatively low precision, Lin's resources' recall greatly surpasses that of any other resource, including WordNet[8]. The rest of the resources are even inferior to *WN*^{d} in that respect, indicating their limited utility for inference systems.

As expected, synonyms and hyponyms in WordNet contributed a noticeable portion to recall in all resources. Additional correct rules correspond to hyponyms and synonyms missing from WordNet, many of them proper names and some slang expressions. These rules were mainly provided by *WikiFS* and *Snow*^{30k}, significantly supplementing WordNet, whose *HasInstance* relation is quite partial. However, there are other interesting types of entailment relations contributing to recall. These are discussed in Sections 5.2 and 5.3. Examples for various rule types are found in Table 3.

5.1.3 Valid Applications of Incorrect Rules

We observed that many entailing sentences were retrieved by inherently incorrect rules in the distributional resources. Analysis of these rules reveals they were matched in entailing texts when the LHS has noticeable statistical correlation with another term in the text that does entail the RHS. For example, for the hypothesis *wildlife extinction*, the rule **species* $\Rightarrow$ *extinction* yielded valid applications in contexts about *threatened* or *endangered species*. Has the resource included a rule between the entailing term in the text and the RHS, the entailing text would have been matched without needing the incorrect rule.

These correlations accounted for nearly a third of Lin resources' recall. Nonetheless, in principle, we suggest that such rules, which do not conform with Definition 2, should not be included in a lexical entailment resource, since they also cause invalid rule applications, while the entailing texts they retrieve will hopefully be matched by addi-

[8] A preliminary experiment we conducted showed that recall does not dramatically improve when using the entire hyponymy subtree from WordNet.

Type	Correct Rules	
HYPO	*Shevardnadze* ⇒ *official*	$Snow^{30k}$
ANT	*efficacy* ⇒ *ineffectiveness*	*Lin-dep*
HOLO	*government* ⇒ *official*	*Lin-prox*
HYPER	*arms* ⇒ *gun*	*Lin-prox*
-	*childbirth* ⇒ *motherhood*	*Lin-dep*
-	*mortgage* ⇒ *bank*	*Lin-prox*
-	*Captive* ⇒ *computer*	*WikiFS*
-	*negligence* ⇒ *failure*	*CBC*
-	*beatification* ⇒ *pope*	*XWN**

Type	Incorrect Rules	
CO-HYP	*alcohol* ⇒ *cigarette*	*CBC*
-	*radiotherapy* ⇒ *outpatient*	*Lin-dep*
-	*teen-ager* ⇒ *gun*	$Snow^{30k}$
-	*basic* ⇒ *paper*	*WikiFS*
-	*species* ⇒ *extinction*	*Lin-prox*

Table 3: Examples of lexical resources rules by types. HYPO: hyponymy, HYPER: hypernymy (class entailment of its members), HOLO: holonymy, ANT: antonymy, CO-HYP: co-hyponymy. The non-categorized relations do not correspond to any WordNet relation.

tional correct rules in a more comprehensive resource.

5.2 Non-standard Entailment Relations

An important finding of our analysis is that some less standard entailment relationships have a considerable impact on recall (see Table 3). These rules, which comply with Definition 2 but do not conform to any WordNet relation type, were mainly contributed by Lin's distributional resources and to a smaller degree are also included in *XWN**. In *Lin-dep*, for example, they accounted for approximately a third of the recall.

Among the finer grained relations we identified in this set are topical entailment (e.g. *IBM* as the company entailing the topic *computers*), consequential relationships (*pregnancy* ⇒ *motherhood*) and an entailment of inherent arguments by a predicate, or of essential participants by a scenario description, e.g. *beatification* ⇒ *pope*. A comprehensive typology of these relationships requires further investigation, as well as the identification and development of additional resources from which they can be extracted.

As opposed to hyponymy and synonymy rules, these rules are typically non-substitutable, i.e. the RHS of the rule is unlikely to have the exact same role in the text as the LHS. Many inference systems perform rule-based transformations, substituting the LHS by the RHS. This finding suggests that different methods may be required to utilize such rules for inference.

5.3 Logical Context

WordNet relations other than synonyms and hyponyms, including antonyms, holonyms and hypernyms (see Table 3), contributed a noticeable share of valid rule applications for some resources. Following common practice, these relations are missing by construction from the other resources.

As shown in Table 2 (COR-LOG columns), such relations accounted for a seventh of *Lin-dep*'s valid rule applications, as much as was the contribution of hyponyms and synonyms to this resource's recall. Yet, using these rules resulted with more erroneous applications than correct ones. As discussed in Section 2.2, the rules induced by these relations do conform with our lexical entailment definition. However, a valid application of these rules requires certain logical conditions to occur, which is not the common case. We thus suggest that such rules are included in lexical entailment resources, as long as they are marked properly by their types, allowing inference systems to utilize them only when appropriate mechanisms for handling logical context are in place.

5.4 Rules Priors

In Section 5.1.1 we observed that some resources are highly sensitive to context. Hence, when considering the validity of a rule's application, two factors should be regarded: the actual context in which the rule is to be applied, as well as the rule's prior likelihood to be valid in an arbitrary context. Somewhat indicative, yet mostly indirect, information about rules' priors is contained in some resources. This includes sense ranks in WordNet, SemCor statistics (Miller et al., 1993), and similarity scores and rankings in Lin's resources. Inference systems often incorporated this information, typically as top-*k* or threshold-based filters (Pantel and Lin, 2003; Roth and Sammons, 2007). By empirically assessing the effect of several such filters in our setting, we found that this type of data is indeed informative in the sense that precision increases as the threshold rises. Yet, no specific filters were found to improve results in terms of F1 score (where recall is measured relatively to the yield of the unfiltered resource) due to a significant drop in relative recall. For example, *Lin-*

prox loses more than 40% of its recall when only the top-50 rules for each hypothesis are exploited, and using only the first sense of WN^d costs the resource over 60% of its recall. We thus suggest a better strategy might be to combine the prior information with context matching scores in order to obtain overall likelihood scores for rule applications, as in (Szpektor et al., 2008). Furthermore, resources should include explicit information regarding the prior likelihoods of of their rules.

5.5 Operative Conclusions

Our findings highlight the currently limited recall of available resources for lexical inference. The higher recall of Lin's resources indicates that many more entailment relationships can be acquired, particularly when considering distributional evidence. Yet, available distributional acquisition methods are not geared for lexical entailment. This suggests the need to develop acquisition methods for dedicated and more extensive knowledge resources that would subsume the correct rules found by current distributional methods. Furthermore, substantially better recall may be obtained by acquiring non-standard lexical entailment relationships, as discussed in Section 5.2, for which a comprehensive typology is still needed. At the same time, transformation-based inference systems would need to handle these kinds of rules, which are usually non-substitutable. Our results also quantify and stress earlier findings regarding the severe degradation in precision when rules are applied in inappropriate contexts. This highlights the need for resources to provide explicit information about the suitable lexical and logical contexts in which an entailment rule is applicable. In parallel, methods should be developed to utilize such contextual information within inference systems. Additional auxiliary information needed in lexical resources is the prior likelihood for a given rule to be correct in an arbitrary context.

6 Related Work

Several prior works defined lexical entailment. WordNet's lexical entailment is a relationship between verbs only, defined for propositions (Fellbaum, 1998). Geffet and Dagan (2004) defined *substitutable lexical entailment* as a relation between substitutable terms. We find this definition too restrictive as non-substitutable rules may also be useful for entailment inference. Examples are *breastfeeding* ⇒ *baby* and *hospital* ⇒ *medical*. Hence, Definition 2 is more broadly applicable for defining the desired contents of lexical entailment resources. We empirically observed that the rules satisfying their definition are a proper subset of the rules covered by our definition. Dagan and Glickman (2004) referred to entailment at the subsentential level by assigning truth values to subpropositional text fragments through their existential meaning. We find this criterion too permissive. For instance, the existence of *country* implies the existence of its *flag*. Yet, the meaning of *flag* is typically not implied by *country*.

Previous works assessing rule application via human annotation include (Pantel et al., 2007; Szpektor et al., 2007), which evaluate acquisition methods for lexical-syntactic rules. They posed an additional question to the annotators asking them to filter out invalid contexts. In our methodology implicit context matching for the full hypothesis was applied instead. Other related instance-based evaluations (Giuliano and Gliozzo, 2007; Connor and Roth, 2007) performed lexical substitutions, but did not handle the non-substitutable cases.

7 Conclusions

This paper provides several methodological and empirical contributions. We presented a novel evaluation methodology for the utility of lexical-semantic resources for semantic inference. To that end we proposed definitions for entailment at subsentential levels, addressing a gap in the textual entailment framework. Our evaluation and analysis provide a first quantitative comparative assessment of the isolated utility of a range of prominent potential resources for entailment rules. We have shown various factors affecting rule applicability and resources performance, while providing operative suggestions to address them in future inference systems and resources.

Acknowledgments

The authors would like to thank Naomi Frankel and Iddo Greental for their excellent annotation work, as well as Roy Bar-Haim and Idan Szpektor for helpful discussion and advice. This work was partially supported by the Negev Consortium of the Israeli Ministry of Industry, Trade and Labor, the PASCAL-2 Network of Excellence of the European Community FP7-ICT-2007-1-216886 and the Israel Science Foundation grant 1095/05.

References

Rahul Bhagat, Patrick Pantel, and Eduard Hovy. 2007. LEDIR: An unsupervised algorithm for learning directionality of inference rules. In *Proceedings of EMNLP-CoNLL*.

J. Bos and K. Markert. 2006. When logical inference helps determining textual entailment (and when it doesn't). In *Proceedings of the Second PASCAL RTE Challenge*.

Michael Connor and Dan Roth. 2007. Context sensitive paraphrasing with a global unsupervised classifier. In *Proceedings of ECML*.

Ido Dagan and Oren Glickman. 2004. Probabilistic textual entailment: Generic applied modeling of language variability. In *PASCAL Workshop on Learning Methods for Text Understanding and Mining*.

Ido Dagan, Oren Glickman, and Bernardo Magnini. 2005. The pascal recognising textual entailment challenge. In Joaquin Quinonero Candela, Ido Dagan, Bernardo Magnini, and Florence d'Alché Buc, editors, *MLCW*, Lecture Notes in Computer Science.

Marie-Catherine de Marneffe, Bill MacCartney, Trond Grenager, Daniel Cer, Anna Rafferty, and Christopher D. Manning. 2006. Learning to distinguish valid textual entailments. In *Proceedings of the Second PASCAL RTE Challenge*.

Christiane Fellbaum, editor. 1998. *WordNet: An Electronic Lexical Database (Language, Speech, and Communication)*. The MIT Press.

Maayan Geffet and Ido Dagan. 2004. Feature vector quality and distributional similarity. In *Proceedings of COLING*.

Danilo Giampiccolo, Bernardo Magnini, Ido Dagan, and Bill Dolan. 2007. The third pascal recognizing textual entailment challenge. In *Proceedings of ACL-WTEP Workshop*.

Claudio Giuliano and Alfio Gliozzo. 2007. Instance based lexical entailment for ontology population. In *Proceedings of EMNLP-CoNLL*.

Oren Glickman, Eyal Shnarch, and Ido Dagan. 2006. Lexical reference: a semantic matching subtask. In *Proceedings of EMNLP*.

Jesús Herrera, Anselmo Peñas, and Felisa Verdejo. 2005. Textual entailment recognition based on dependency analysis and wordnet. In *Proceedings of the First PASCAL RTE Challenge*.

Jun'ichi Kazama and Kentaro Torisawa. 2007. Exploiting Wikipedia as external knowledge for named entity recognition. In *Proceedings of EMNLP-CoNLL*.

Milen Kouylekov and Bernardo Magnini. 2006. Building a large-scale repository of textual entailment rules. In *Proceedings of LREC*.

J. R. Landis and G. G. Koch. 1997. The measurements of observer agreement for categorical data. In *Biometrics*, pages 33:159–174.

Dekang Lin. 1998. Automatic retrieval and clustering of similar words. In *Proceedings of COLING-ACL*.

George A. Miller, Claudia Leacock, Randee Tengi, and Ross T. Bunker. 1993. A semantic concordance. In *Proceedings of HLT*.

Dan Moldovan and Vasile Rus. 2001. Logic form transformation of wordnet and its applicability to question answering. In *Proceedings of ACL*.

Patrick Pantel and Dekang Lin. 2002. Discovering word senses from text. In *Proceedings of ACM SIGKDD*.

Patrick Pantel and Dekang Lin. 2003. Automatically discovering word senses. In *Proceedings of NAACL*.

Patrick Pantel and Deepak Ravichandran. 2004. Automatically labeling semantic classes. In *Proceedings of HLT-NAACL*.

Patrick Pantel, Rahul Bhagat, Bonaventura Coppola, Timothy Chklovski, and Eduard Hovy. 2007. ISP: Learning inferential selectional preferences. In *Proceedings of HLT*.

Marius Pasca and Sanda M. Harabagiu. 2001. The informative role of wordnet in open-domain question answering. In *Proceedings of NAACL Workshop on WordNet and Other Lexical Resources*.

Dan Roth and Mark Sammons. 2007. Semantic and logical inference model for textual entailment. In *Proceedings of ACL-WTEP Workshop*.

Chirag Shah and Bruce W. Croft. 2004. Evaluating high accuracy retrieval techniques. In *Proceedings of SIGIR*.

Rion Snow, Daniel Jurafsky, and Andrew Y. Ng. 2006. Semantic taxonomy induction from heterogenous evidence. In *Proceedings of COLING-ACL*.

Fabian M. Suchanek, Gjergji Kasneci, and Gerhard Weikum. 2007. Yago: A core of semantic knowledge - unifying wordnet and wikipedia. In *Proceedings of WWW*.

Idan Szpektor, Eyal Shnarch, and Ido Dagan. 2007. Instance-based evaluation of entailment rule acquisition. In *Proceedings of ACL*.

Idan Szpektor, Ido Dagan, Roy Bar-Haim, and Jacob Goldberger. 2008. Contextual preferences. In *Proceedings of ACL*.

Ellen M. Voorhees. 1994. Query expansion using lexical-semantic relations. In *Proceedings of SIGIR*.

Text-to-text Semantic Similarity for Automatic Short Answer Grading

Michael Mohler and **Rada Mihalcea**
Department of Computer Science
University of North Texas
mgm0038@unt.edu, rada@cs.unt.edu

Abstract

In this paper, we explore unsupervised techniques for the task of automatic short answer grading. We compare a number of knowledge-based and corpus-based measures of text similarity, evaluate the effect of domain and size on the corpus-based measures, and also introduce a novel technique to improve the performance of the system by integrating automatic feedback from the student answers. Overall, our system significantly and consistently outperforms other unsupervised methods for short answer grading that have been proposed in the past.

1 Introduction

One of the most important aspects of the learning process is the assessment of the knowledge acquired by the learner. In a typical examination setting (e.g., an exam, assignment or quiz), this assessment implies an instructor or a grader who provides students with feedback on their answers to questions that are related to the subject matter. There are, however, certain scenarios, such as the large number of worldwide sites with limited teacher availability, or the individual or group study sessions done outside of class, in which an instructor is not available and yet students need an assessment of their knowledge of the subject. In these instances, we often have to turn to computer-assisted assessment.

While some forms of computer-assisted assessment do not require sophisticated text understanding (e.g., multiple choice or true/false questions can be easily graded by a system if the correct solution is available), there are also student answers that consist of free text which require an analysis of the text in the answer. Research to date has concentrated on two main subtasks of computer-assisted assessment: the grading of essays, which is done mainly by checking the style, grammaticality, and coherence of the essay (cf. (Higgins et al., 2004)), and the assessment of short student answers (e.g., (Leacock and Chodorow, 2003; Pulman and Sukkarieh, 2005)), which is the focus of this paper.

An automatic short answer grading system is one which automatically assigns a grade to an answer provided by a student through a comparison with one or more correct answers. It is important to note that this is different from the related task of paraphrase detection, since a requirement in student answer grading is to provide a grade on a certain scale rather than a binary yes/no decision.

In this paper, we explore and evaluate a set of unsupervised techniques for automatic short answer grading. Unlike previous work, which has either required the availability of manually crafted patterns (Sukkarieh et al., 2004; Mitchell et al., 2002), or large training data sets to bootstrap such patterns (Pulman and Sukkarieh, 2005), we attempt to devise an unsupervised method that requires no human intervention. We address the grading problem from a text similarity perspective and examine the usefulness of various text-to-text semantic similarity measures for automatically grading short student answers.

Specifically, in this paper we seek answers to the following questions. First, given a number of corpus-based and knowledge-based methods as previously proposed in the past for word and text semantic similarity, what are the measures that work best for the task of short answer grading? Second, given a corpus-based measure of similarity, what is the impact of the domain and the size of the corpus on the accuracy of the measure? Finally, can we use the student answers themselves to improve the quality of the grading system?

2 Related Work

There are a number of approaches that have been proposed in the past for automatic short answer grading. Several state-of-the-art short answer graders (Sukkarieh et al., 2004; Mitchell et al., 2002) require manually crafted patterns which, if matched, indicate that a question has been answered correctly. If an annotated corpus is avail-

Proceedings of the 12th Conference of the European Chapter of the ACL, pages 567–575,
Athens, Greece, 30 March – 3 April 2009. ©2009 Association for Computational Linguistics

able, these patterns can be supplemented by learning additional patterns semi-automatically. The Oxford-UCLES system (Sukkarieh et al., 2004) bootstraps patterns by starting with a set of keywords and synonyms and searching through windows of a text for new patterns. A later implementation of the Oxford-UCLES system (Pulman and Sukkarieh, 2005) compares several machine learning techniques, including inductive logic programming, decision tree learning, and Bayesian learning, to the earlier pattern matching approach with encouraging results.

C-Rater (Leacock and Chodorow, 2003) matches the syntactical features of a student response (subject, object, and verb) to that of a set of correct responses. The method specifically disregards the bag-of-words approach to take into account the difference between "dog bites man" and "man bites dog" while trying to detect changes in voice ("the man was bitten by a dog").

Another short answer grading system, AutoTutor (Wiemer-Hastings et al., 1999), has been designed as an immersive tutoring environment with a graphical "talking head" and speech recognition to improve the overall experience for students. AutoTutor eschews the pattern-based approach entirely in favor of a bag-of-words LSA approach (Landauer and Dumais, 1997). Later work on AutoTutor (Wiemer-Hastings et al., 2005; Malatesta et al., 2002) seeks to expand upon the original bag-of-words approach which becomes less useful as causality and word order become more important.

These methods are often supplemented with some light preprocessing, e.g., spelling correction, punctuation correction, pronoun resolution, lemmatization and tagging. Likewise, in order to facilitate their goals of providing feedback to the student more robust than a simple "correct" or "incorrect," several systems break the gold-standard answers into constituent concepts that must individually be matched for the answer to be considered fully correct (Callear et al., 2001). In this way the system can determine which parts of an answer a student understands and which parts he or she is struggling with.

Automatic short answer grading is closely related to the task of text similarity. While more general than short answer grading, text similarity is essentially the problem of detecting and comparing the features of two texts. One of the earliest approaches to text similarity is the vector-space model (Salton et al., 1997) with a term frequency / inverse document frequency (*tf.idf*) weighting. This model, along with the more sophisticated LSA semantic alternative (Landauer and Dumais, 1997), has been found to work well for tasks such as information retrieval and text classification.

Another approach (Hatzivassiloglou et al., 1999) has been to use a machine learning algorithm in which features are based on combinations of simple features (e.g., a pair of nouns appear within 5 words from one another in both texts). This method also attempts to account for synonymy, word ordering, text length, and word classes.

Another line of work attempts to extrapolate text similarity from the arguably simpler problem of word similarity. (Mihalcea et al., 2006) explores the efficacy of applying WordNet-based word-to-word similarity measures (Pedersen et al., 2004) to the comparison of texts and found them generally comparable to corpus-based measures such as LSA.

An interesting study has been performed at the University of Adelaide (Lee et al., 2005), comparing simpler word and n-gram feature vectors to LSA and exploring the types of vector similarity metrics (e.g., binary vs. count vectors, Jaccard vs. cosine vs. overlap distance measure, etc.). In this case, LSA was shown to perform better than the word and n-gram vectors and performed best at around 100 dimensions with binary vectors weighted according to an entropy measure, though the difference in measures was often subtle.

SELSA (Kanejiya et al., 2003) is a system that attempts to add context to LSA by supplementing the feature vectors with some simple syntactical features, namely the part-of-speech of the previous word. Their results indicate that SELSA does not perform as well as LSA in the best case, but it has a wider threshold window than LSA in which the system can be used advantageously.

Finally, explicit semantic analysis (ESA) (Gabrilovich and Markovitch, 2007) uses Wikipedia as a source of knowledge for text similarity. It creates for each text a feature vector where each feature maps to a Wikipedia article. Their preliminary experiments indicated that ESA was able to significantly outperform LSA on some text similarity tasks.

3 Data Set

In order to evaluate the methods for short answer grading, we have created a data set of questions from introductory computer science assignments with answers provided by a class of undergraduate students. The assignments were administered as part of a Data Structures course at the University of North Texas. For each assignment, the student answers were collected via the WebCT online learning environment.

The evaluations reported in this paper are carried out on the answers submitted for three of the assignments in this class. Each assignment consisted of seven short-answer questions.[1] Thirty students were enrolled in the class and submitted answers to these assignments. Thus, the data set we work with consists of a total of 630 student answers (3 assignments x 7 questions/assignment x 30 student answers/question).

The answers were independently graded by two human judges, using an integer scale from 0 (completely incorrect) to 5 (perfect answer). Both human judges were graduate computer science students; one was the teaching assistant in the Data Structures class, while the other is one of the authors of this paper. Table 1 shows two question-answer pairs with three sample student answers each. The grades assigned by the two human judges are also included.

The evaluations are run using Pearson's correlation coefficient measured against the average of the human-assigned grades on a per-question and a per-assignment basis. In the per-question setting, every question and the corresponding student answer is considered as an independent data point in the correlation, and thus the emphasis is placed on the correctness of the grade assigned to each answer. In the per-assignment setting, each data point is an assignment-student pair created by totaling the scores given to the student for each question in the assignment. In this setting, the emphasis is placed on the overall grade a student receives for the assignment rather than on the grade received for each independent question.

The correlation between the two human judges is measured using both settings. In the per-question setting, the two annotators correlated at (r=0.6443). For the per-assignment setting, the correlation was (r=0.7228).

A deeper look into the scores given by the two annotators indicates the underlying subjectivity in grading short answer assignments. Of the 630 grades given, only 358 (56.8%) were exactly agreed upon by the annotators. Even more striking, a full 107 grades (17.0%) differed by more than one point on the five point scale, and 19 grades (3.0%) differed by 4 points or more. [2] Furthermore, on the occasions when the annotators disagreed, the same annotator gave the higher grade 79.8% of the time.

Over the course of this work, much attention was given to our choice of correlation metric. Previous work in text similarity and short-answer grading seems split on the use of Pearson's and Spearman's metric. It was not initially clear that the underlying assumptions necessary for the proper use of Pearson's metric (e.g. normal distribution, interval measurement level, linear correlation model) would be met in our experimental setup. We considered both Spearman's and several less often used metrics (e.g. Kendall's tau, Goodman-Kruskal's gamma), but in the end, we have decided to follow previous work using Pearson's so that our scores can be more easily compared.[3]

4 Automatic Short Answer Grading

Our experiments are centered around the use of measures of similarity for automatic short answer grading. In particular, we carry out three sets of experiments, seeking answers to the following three research questions.

First, *what are the measures of semantic similarity that work best for the task of short answer grading?* To answer this question, we run several comparative evaluations covering a number of knowledge-based and corpus-based measures of semantic similarity. While previous work has considered such comparisons for the related task of paraphrase identification (Mihalcea et al., 2006), to our knowledge no comprehensive evaluation has been carried out for the task of short answer grading which includes all the similarity measures proposed to date.

Second, *to what extent do the domain and the size of the data used to train the corpus-based measures of similarity influence the accuracy of the measures?* To address this question, we run a set of experiments which vary the size and domain of the corpus used to train the LSA and the ESA metrics, and we measure their effect on the accuracy of short answer grading.

Finally, *given a measure of similarity, can we integrate the answers with the highest scores and improve the accuracy of the measure?* We use a technique similar to the pseudo-relevance feedback method used in information retrieval (Rocchio, 1971) and augment the correct answer with

[1] In addition, the assignments had several programming exercises which have not been considered in any of our experiments.

[2] An example should suffice to explain this discrepancy in annotator scoring: *Question: What does a function signature include? Answer: The name of the function and the types of the parameters. Student: input parameters and return type. Scores: 1, 5.* This example suggests that the graders were not always consistent in comparing student answers to the instructor answer. Additionally, the instructor answer may be insufficient to account for correct student answers, as "return type" does seem to be a valid component of a "function signature" according to some literature on the web.

[3] Consider this an open call for discussion in the NLP community regarding the proper usage of correlation metrics with the ultimate goal of consistency within the community.

Sample questions, correct answers, and student answers	Grade
Question: What is the role of a prototype program in problem solving? *Correct answer: To simulate the behavior of portions of the desired software product.*	
Student answer 1: A prototype program is used in problem solving to collect data for the problem.	1, 2
Student answer 2: It simulates the behavior of portions of the desired software product.	5, 5
Student answer 3: To find problem and errors in a program before it is finalized.	2, 2
Question: What are the main advantages associated with object-oriented programming? *Correct answer: Abstraction and reusability.*	
Student answer 1: They make it easier to reuse and adapt previously written code and they separate complex programs into smaller, easier to understand classes.	5, 4
Student answer 2: Object oriented programming allows programmers to use an object with classes that can be changed and manipulated while not affecting the entire object at once.	1, 1
Student answer 3: Reusable components, Extensibility, Maintainability, it reduces large problems into smaller more manageable problems.	4, 4

Table 1: Two sample questions with short answers provided by students and the grades assigned by the two human judges

the student answers receiving the best score according to a similarity measure.

In all the experiments, the evaluations are run on the data set described in the previous section. The results are compared against a simple baseline that assigns a grade based on a measurement of the cosine similarity between the weighted vector-space representations of the correct answer and the candidate student answer. The Pearson correlation for this model, using an inverse document frequency derived from the British National Corpus (BNC), is r=0.3647 for the per-question evaluation and r=0.4897 for the per-assignment evaluation.

5 Text-to-text Semantic Similarity

We run our comparative evaluations using eight knowledge-based measures of semantic similarity (shortest path, Leacock & Chodorow, Lesk, Wu & Palmer, Resnik, Lin, Jiang & Conrath, Hirst & St. Onge), and two corpus-based measures (LSA and ESA). For the knowledge-based measures, we derive a text-to-text similarity metric by using the methodology proposed in (Mihalcea et al., 2006): for each open-class word in one of the input texts, we use the maximum semantic similarity that can be obtained by pairing it up with individual open-class words in the second input text. More formally, for each word W of part-of-speech class C in the instructor answer, we find $maxsim(W, C)$:

$$maxsim(W, C) = \max SIM_x(W, w_i)$$

where w_i is a word in the student answer of class C and the SIM_x function is one of the functions described below. All the word-to-word similarity scores obtained in this way are summed up and normalized with the length of the two input texts. We provide below a short description for each of these similarity metrics.

5.1 Knowledge-Based Measures

The **shortest path** similarity is determined as:

$$Sim_{path} = \frac{1}{length} \quad (1)$$

where $length$ is the length of the shortest path between two concepts using node-counting (including the end nodes).

The **Leacock & Chodorow** (Leacock and Chodorow, 1998) similarity is determined as:

$$Sim_{lch} = -\log \frac{length}{2 * D} \quad (2)$$

where $length$ is the length of the shortest path between two concepts using node-counting, and D is the maximum depth of the taxonomy.

The **Lesk** similarity of two concepts is defined as a function of the overlap between the corresponding definitions, as provided by a dictionary. It is based on an algorithm proposed by Lesk (1986) as a solution for word sense disambiguation.

The **Wu & Palmer** (Wu and Palmer, 1994) similarity metric measures the depth of two given concepts in the WordNet taxonomy, and the depth of the least common subsumer (LCS), and combines these figures into a similarity score:

$$Sim_{wup} = \frac{2 * depth(LCS)}{depth(concept_1) + depth(concept_2)} \quad (3)$$

The measure introduced by **Resnik** (Resnik, 1995) returns the information content (IC) of the LCS of two concepts:

$$Sim_{res} = IC(LCS) \quad (4)$$

where IC is defined as:

$$IC(c) = -\log P(c) \quad (5)$$

and $P(c)$ is the probability of encountering an instance of concept c in a large corpus.

The measure introduced by **Lin** (Lin, 1998) builds on Resnik's measure of similarity, and adds a normalization factor consisting of the information content of the two input concepts:

$$Sim_{lin} = \frac{2 * IC(LCS)}{IC(concept_1) + IC(concept_2)} \quad (6)$$

We also consider the **Jiang & Conrath** (Jiang and Conrath, 1997) measure of similarity:

$$Sim_{jnc} = \frac{1}{IC(concept_1) + IC(concept_2) - 2 * IC(LCS)} \quad (7)$$

Finally, we consider the **Hirst & St. Onge** (Hirst and St-Onge, 1998) measure of similarity, which determines the similarity strength of a pair of synsets by detecting lexical chains between the pair in a text using the WordNet hierarchy.

5.2 Corpus-Based Measures

Corpus-based measures differ from knowledge-based methods in that they do not require any encoded understanding of either the vocabulary or the grammar of a text's language. In many of the scenarios where CAA would be advantageous, robust language-specific resources (e.g. WordNet) may not be available. Thus, state-of-the-art corpus-based measures may be the only available approach to CAA in languages with scarce resources.

One corpus-based measure of semantic similarity is latent semantic analysis (LSA) proposed by Landauer (Landauer and Dumais, 1997). In LSA, term co-occurrences in a corpus are captured by means of a dimensionality reduction operated by a singular value decomposition (SVD) on the term-by-document matrix **T** representing the corpus. For the experiments reported in this section, we run the SVD operation on several corpora including the BNC (**LSA BNC**) and the entire English Wikipedia (**LSA Wikipedia**).[4]

Explicit semantic analysis (ESA) (Gabrilovich and Markovitch, 2007) is a variation on the standard vectorial model in which the dimensions of the vector are directly equivalent to abstract concepts. Each article in Wikipedia represents a concept in the ESA vector. The relatedness of a term to a concept is defined as the tf*idf score for the term within the Wikipedia article, and the relatedness between two words is the cosine of the two concept vectors in a high-dimensional space. We refer to this method as **ESA Wikipedia**.

[4]Throughout this paper, the references to the Wikipedia corpus refer to a version downloaded in September 2007.

5.3 Implementation

For the knowledge-based measures, we use the WordNet-based implementation of the word-to-word similarity metrics, as available in the WordNet::Similarity package (Patwardhan et al., 2003). For latent semantic analysis, we use the InfoMap package.[5] For ESA, we use our own implementation of the ESA algorithm as described in (Gabrilovich and Markovitch, 2006). Note that all the word similarity measures are normalized so that they fall within a 0–1 range. The normalization is done by dividing the similarity score provided by a given measure with the maximum possible score for that measure.

Table 2 shows the results obtained with each of these measures on our evaluation data set.

Measure	Correlation
Knowledge-based measures	
Shortest path	0.4413
Leacock & Chodorow	0.2231
Lesk	0.3630
Wu & Palmer	0.3366
Resnik	0.2520
Lin	0.3916
Jiang & Conrath	0.4499
Hirst & St-Onge	0.1961
Corpus-based measures	
LSA BNC	0.4071
LSA Wikipedia	0.4286
ESA Wikipedia	0.4681
Baseline	
tf*idf	0.3647

Table 2: Comparison of knowledge-based and corpus-based measures of similarity for short answer grading

6 The Role of Domain and Size

One of the key considerations when applying corpus-based techniques is the extent to which size and subject matter affect the overall performance of the system. In particular, based on the underlying processes involved, the LSA and ESA corpus-based methods are expected to be especially sensitive to changes in domain and size. Building the language models depends on the relatedness of the words in the training data which suggests that, for instance, in a computer science domain the terms "object" and "oriented" will be more closely related than in a more general text. Similarly, a large amount of training data will lead to less sparse

[5]http://infomap-nlp.sourceforge.net/

vector spaces, which in turn is expected to affect the performance of the corpus-based methods.

With this in mind, we developed two training corpora for use with the corpus-based measures that covered the computer science domain. The first corpus (**LSA slides**) consists of several online lecture notes associated with the class textbook, specifically covering topics that are used as questions in our sample. The second domain-specific corpus is a subset of Wikipedia (**LSA Wikipedia CS**) consisting of articles that contain any of the following words: computer, computing, computation, algorithm, recursive, or recursion.

The performance on the domain-specific corpora is compared with the one observed on the open-domain corpora mentioned in the previous section, namely **LSA Wikipedia** and **ESA Wikipedia**. In addition, for the purpose of running a comparison with the LSA slides corpus, we also created a random subset of the LSA Wikipedia corpus approximately matching the size of the LSA slides corpus. We refer to this corpus as **LSA Wikipedia (small)**.

Table 3 shows an overview of the various corpora used in the experiments, along with the Pearson correlation observed on our data set.

Measure - Corpus	Size	Correlation
Training on generic corpora		
LSA BNC	566.7MB	0.4071
LSA Wikipedia	1.8GB	0.4286
LSA Wikipedia (small)	0.3MB	0.3518
ESA Wikipedia	1.8GB	0.4681
Training on domain-specific corpora		
LSA Wikipedia CS	77.1MB	0.4628
LSA slides	0.3MB	0.4146
ESA Wikipedia CS	77.1MB	0.4385

Table 3: Corpus-based measures trained on corpora from different domains and of different sizes

Assuming a corpus of comparable size, we expect a measure trained on a domain-specific corpus to outperform one that relies on a generic one. Indeed, by comparing the results obtained with LSA slides to those obtained with LSA Wikipedia (small), we see that by using the in-domain computer science slides we obtain a correlation of r=0.4146, which is higher than the correlation of r=0.3518 obtained with a corpus of the same size but open-domain. The effect of the domain is even more pronounced when we compare the performance obtained with LSA Wikipedia CS (r=0.4628) with the one obtained with the full LSA Wikipedia (r=0.4286).[6] The smaller, domain-specific corpus performs better, despite the fact that the generic corpus is 23 times larger and is a superset of the smaller corpus. This suggests that for LSA the quality of the texts is vastly more important than their quantity.

When using the domain-specific subset of Wikipedia, we observe decreased performance with ESA compared to the full Wikipedia space. We suggest that for ESA the high-dimensionality of the concept space[7] is paramount, since many relations between generic words may be lost to ESA that can be detected latently using LSA.

In tandem with our exploration of the effects of domain-specific data, we also look at the effect of size on the overall performance. The main intuitive trends are there, i.e., the performance obtained with the large LSA-Wikipedia is better than the one that can be obtained with LSA Wikipedia (small). Similarly, in the domain-specific space, the LSA Wikipedia CS corpus leads to better performance than the smaller LSA slides data set. However, an analysis carried out at a finer grained scale, in which we calculate the performance obtained with LSA when trained on 5%, 10%, ..., 100% fractions of the full LSA Wikipedia corpus, does not reveal a close correlation between size and performance, which suggests that further analysis is needed to determine the exact effect of corpus size on performance.

7 Relevance Feedback based on Student Answers

The automatic grading of student answers implies a measure of similarity between the answers provided by the students and the correct answer provided by the instructor. Since we only have one correct answer, some student answers may be wrongly graded because of little or no similarity with the correct answer that we have.

To address this problem, we introduce a novel technique that feeds back from the student answers themselves in a way similar to the pseudo-relevance feedback used in information retrieval (Rocchio, 1971). In this way, the paraphrasing that is usually observed across student answers will enhance the vocabulary of the correct answer, while at the same time maintaining the correctness of the gold-standard answer.

Briefly, given a metric that provides similarity scores between the student answers and the correct answer, scores are ranked from most similar

[6]The difference was found significant using a paired t-test ($p<0.001$).

[7]In ESA, all the articles in Wikipedia are used as dimensions, which leads to about 1.75 million dimensions in the ESA Wikipedia corpus, compared to only 55,000 dimensions in the ESA Wikipedia CS corpus.

to least. The words of the top N ranked answers are then added to the gold standard answer. The remaining answers are then rescored according the the new gold standard vector. In practice, we hold the scores from the first run (i.e., with no feedback) constant for the top N highest-scoring answers, and the second-run scores for the remaining answers are multiplied by the first-run score of the Nth highest-scoring answer. In this way, we keep the original scores for the top N highest-scoring answers (and thus prevent them from becoming artificially high), and at the same time, we guarantee that none of the lower-scored answers will get a new score higher than the best answers.

The effects of relevance feedback are shown in Figure 9, which plots the Pearson correlation between automatic and human grading (Y axis) versus the number of student answers that are used for relevance feedback (X axis).

Overall, an improvement of up to 0.047 on the 0-1 Pearson scale can be obtained by using this technique, with a maximum improvement observed after about 4-6 iterations on average. After an initial number of high-scored answers, it is likely that the correctness of the answers degrades, and thus the decrease in performance observed after an initial number of iterations. Our results indicate that the LSA and WordNet similarity metrics respond more favorably to feedback than the ESA metric. It is possible that supplementing the bag-of-words in ESA (with e.g. synonyms and phrasal differences) does not drastically alter the resultant concept vector, and thus the overall effect is smaller.

8 Discussion

Our experiments show that several knowledge-based and corpus-based measures of similarity perform comparably when used for the task of short answer grading. However, since the corpus-based measures can be improved by accounting for domain and corpus size, the highest performance can be obtained with a corpus-based measure (LSA) trained on a domain-specific corpus. Further improvements were also obtained by integrating the highest-scored student answers through a relevance feedback technique.

Table 4 summarizes the results of our experiments. In addition to the per-question evaluations that were reported throughout the paper, we also report the per-assignment evaluation, which reflects a cumulative score for a student on a single assignment, as described in Section 3.

Overall, in both the per-question and per-assignment evaluations, we obtained the best performance by using an LSA measure trained on a medium size domain-specific corpus obtained from Wikipedia, with relevance feedback from the four highest-scoring student answers. This method improves significantly over the tf*idf baseline and also over the LSA trained on BNC model, which has been used extensively in previous work. The differences were found to be significant using a paired t-test (p<0.001).

Measure	Correlation per-quest.	Correlation per-assign.
Baselines		
tf*idf	0.3647	0.4897
LSA BNC	0.4071	0.6465
Relevance Feedback based on Student Answers		
WordNet shortest path	0.4887	0.6344
LSA Wikipedia CS	**0.5099**	**0.6735**
ESA Wikipedia full	0.4893	0.6498
Annotator agreement	0.6443	0.7228

Table 4: Summary of results obtained with various similarity measures, with relevance feedback based on six student answers. We also list the tf*idf and the LSA trained on BNC baselines (no feedback), as well as the annotator agreement upper bound.

To gain further insights, we made an additional analysis where we determined the ability of our system to make a binary accept/reject decision. In this evaluation, we map the 0-5 human grading of the data set to an accept/reject annotation by using a threshold of 2.5. Every answer with a grade higher than 2.5 is labeled as "accept," while every answer below 2.5 is labeled as "reject." Next, we use our best system (LSA trained on domain-specific data with relevance feedback), and run a ten-fold cross-validation on the data set. Specifically, for each fold, the system uses the remaining nine folds to automatically identify a threshold to maximize the matching with the gold standard. The threshold identified in this way is used to automatically annotate the test fold with "accept"/"reject" labels. The ten-fold cross validation resulted in an accuracy of 92%, indicating the ability of the system to automatically make a binary accept/reject decision.

9 Conclusions

In this paper, we explored unsupervised techniques for automatic short answer grading.

We believe the paper made three important contributions. First, while there are a number of word and text similarity measures that have been proposed in the past, to our knowledge no previous work has considered a comprehensive evalu-

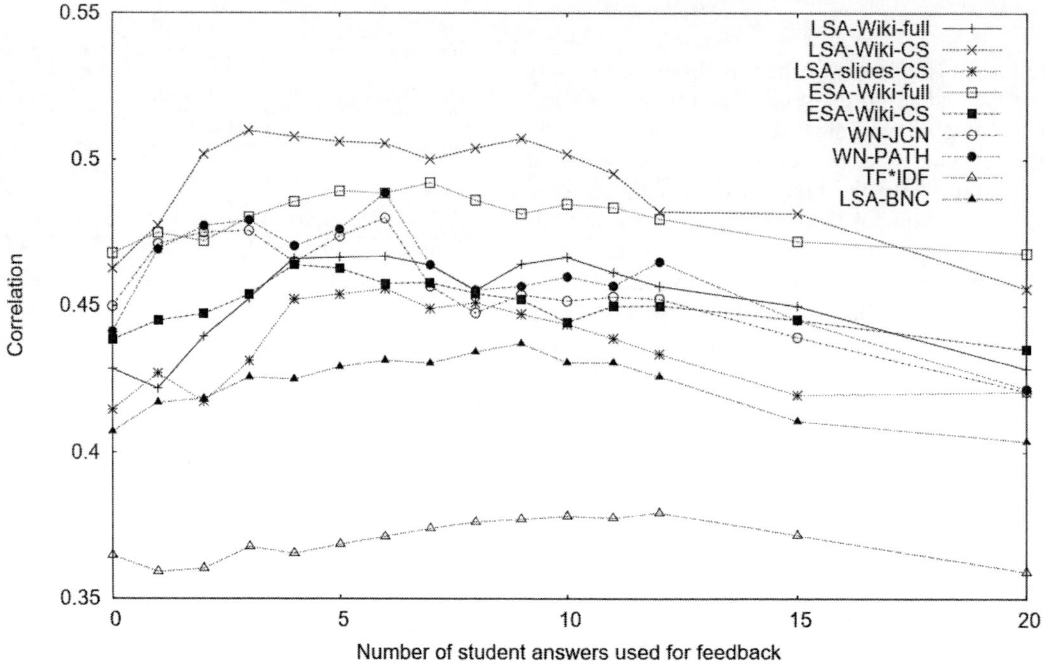

Figure 1: Effect of relevance feedback on performance

ation of all the measures for the task of short answer grading. We filled this gap by running comparative evaluations of several knowledge-based and corpus-based measures on a data set of short student answers. Our results indicate that when used in their original form, the results obtained with the best knowledge-based (WordNet shortest path and Jiang & Conrath) and corpus-based measures (LSA and ESA) have comparable performance. The benefit of the corpus-based approaches over knowledge-based approaches lies in their language independence and the relative ease in creating a large domain-sensitive corpus versus a language knowledge base (e.g., WordNet).

Second, we analysed the effect of domain and corpus size on the effectiveness of the corpus-based measures. We found that significant improvements can be obtained for the LSA measure when using a medium size domain-specific corpus built from Wikipedia. In fact, when using LSA, our results indicate that the corpus domain may be significantly more important than corpus size once a certain threshold size has been reached.

Finally, we introduced a novel technique for integrating feedback from the student answers themselves into the grading system. Using a method similar to the pseudo-relevance feedback technique used in information retrieval, we were able to improve the quality of our system by a few percentage points.

Overall, our best system consists of an LSA measure trained on a domain-specific corpus built on Wikipedia with feedback from student answers, which was found to bring a significant absolute improvement on the 0-1 Pearson scale of 0.14 over the tf*idf baseline and 0.10 over the LSA BNC model that has been used in the past.

In future work, we intend to expand our analysis of both the gold-standard answer and the student answers beyond the bag-of-words paradigm by considering basic logical features in the text (i.e., AND, OR, NOT) as well as the existence of shallow grammatical features such as predicate-argument structure(Moschitti et al., 2007) as well as semantic classes for words. Furthermore, it may be advantageous to expand upon the existing measures by applying machine learning techniques to create a hybrid decision system that would exploit the advantages of each measure.

The data set introduced in this paper, along with the human-assigned grades, can be downloaded from http://lit.csci.unt.edu/index.php/Downloads.

Acknowledgments

This work was partially supported by a National Science Foundation CAREER award #0747340. The authors are grateful to Samer Hassan for making available his implementation of the ESA algorithm.

References

D. Callear, J. Jerrams-Smith, and V. Soh. 2001. CAA of Short Non-MCQ Answers. *Proceedings of the 5th International Computer Assisted Assessment conference*.

E. Gabrilovich and S. Markovitch. 2006. Overcoming the brittleness bottleneck using Wikipedia: Enhancing text categorization with encyclopedic knowledge. In *Proceedings of the National Conference on Artificial Intelligence (AAAI)*, Boston.

E. Gabrilovich and S. Markovitch. 2007. Computing Semantic Relatedness using Wikipedia-based Explicit Semantic Analysis. *Proceedings of the 20th International Joint Conference on Artificial Intelligence*, pages 6–12.

V. Hatzivassiloglou, J. Klavans, and E. Eskin. 1999. Detecting text similarity over short passages: Exploring linguistic feature combinations via machine learning. *Proceedings of the Joint SIGDAT Conference on Empirical Methods in Natural Language Processing and Very Large Corpora*.

D. Higgins, J. Burstein, D. Marcu, and C. Gentile. 2004. Evaluating multiple aspects of coherence in student essays. In *Proceedings of the annual meeting of the North American Chapter of the Association for Computational Linguistics*, Boston, MA.

G. Hirst and D. St-Onge, 1998. *Lexical chains as representations of contexts for the detection and correction of malaproprisms*. The MIT Press.

J. Jiang and D. Conrath. 1997. Semantic similarity based on corpus statistics and lexical taxonomy. In *Proceedings of the International Conference on Research in Computational Linguistics*, Taiwan.

D. Kanejiya, A. Kumar, and S. Prasad. 2003. Automatic evaluation of students' answers using syntactically enhanced LSA. *Proceedings of the HLT-NAACL 03 workshop on Building educational applications using natural language processing-Volume 2*, pages 53–60.

T.K. Landauer and S.T. Dumais. 1997. A solution to plato's problem: The latent semantic analysis theory of acquisition, induction, and representation of knowledge. *Psychological Review*, 104.

C. Leacock and M. Chodorow. 1998. Combining local context and WordNet sense similarity for word sense identification. In *WordNet, An Electronic Lexical Database*. The MIT Press.

C. Leacock and M. Chodorow. 2003. C-rater: Automated Scoring of Short-Answer Questions. *Computers and the Humanities*, 37(4):389–405.

M.D. Lee, B. Pincombe, and M. Welsh. 2005. An empirical evaluation of models of text document similarity. *Proceedings of the 27th Annual Conference of the Cognitive Science Society*, pages 1254–1259.

M.E. Lesk. 1986. Automatic sense disambiguation using machine readable dictionaries: How to tell a pine cone from an ice cream cone. In *Proceedings of the SIGDOC Conference 1986*, Toronto, June.

D. Lin. 1998. An information-theoretic definition of similarity. In *Proceedings of the 15th International Conference on Machine Learning*, Madison, WI.

K.I. Malatesta, P. Wiemer-Hastings, and J. Robertson. 2002. Beyond the Short Answer Question with Research Methods Tutor. In *Proceedings of the Intelligent Tutoring Systems Conference*.

R. Mihalcea, C. Corley, and C. Strapparava. 2006. Corpus-based and knowledge-based approaches to text semantic similarity. In *Proceedings of the American Association for Artificial Intelligence (AAAI 2006)*, Boston.

T. Mitchell, T. Russell, P. Broomhead, and N. Aldridge. 2002. Towards robust computerised marking of free-text responses. *Proceedings of the 6th International Computer Assisted Assessment (CAA) Conference*.

Alessandro Moschitti, Silvia Quarteroni, Roberto Basili, and Suresh Manandhar. 2007. Exploiting syntactic and shallow semantic kernels for question/answer classification. In *Proceedings of the 45th Conference of the Association for Computational Linguistics*.

S. Patwardhan, S. Banerjee, and T. Pedersen. 2003. Using measures of semantic relatedness for word sense disambiguation. In *Proceedings of the Fourth International Conference on Intelligent Text Processing and Computational Linguistics*, Mexico City, February.

T. Pedersen, S. Patwardhan, and J. Michelizzi. 2004. WordNet:: Similarity-Measuring the Relatedness of Concepts. *Proceedings of the National Conference on Artificial Intelligence*, pages 1024–1025.

S.G. Pulman and J.Z. Sukkarieh. 2005. Automatic Short Answer Marking. *ACL WS Bldg Ed Apps using NLP*.

P. Resnik. 1995. Using information content to evaluate semantic similarity. In *Proceedings of the 14th International Joint Conference on Artificial Intelligence*, Montreal, Canada.

J. Rocchio, 1971. *Relevance feedback in information retrieval*. Prentice Hall, Ing. Englewood Cliffs, New Jersey.

G. Salton, A. Wong, and C.S. Yang. 1997. A vector space model for automatic indexing. In *Readings in Information Retrieval*, pages 273–280. Morgan Kaufmann Publishers, San Francisco, CA.

J.Z. Sukkarieh, S.G. Pulman, and N. Raikes. 2004. Auto-Marking 2: An Update on the UCLES-Oxford University research into using Computational Linguistics to Score Short, Free Text Responses. *International Association of Educational Assessment, Philadephia*.

P. Wiemer-Hastings, K. Wiemer-Hastings, and A. Graesser. 1999. Improving an intelligent tutor's comprehension of students with Latent Semantic Analysis. *Artificial Intelligence in Education*, pages 535–542.

P. Wiemer-Hastings, E. Arnott, and D. Allbritton. 2005. Initial results and mixed directions for research methods tutor. In *AIED2005 - Supplementary Proceedings of the 12th International Conference on Artificial Intelligence in Education*, Amsterdam.

Z. Wu and M. Palmer. 1994. Verb semantics and lexical selection. In *Proceedings of the 32nd Annual Meeting of the Association for Computational Linguistics*, Las Cruces, New Mexico.

Syntactic and Semantic Kernels for Short Text Pair Categorization

Alessandro Moschitti
Department of Computer Science and Engineering
University of Trento
Via Sommarive 14
38100 POVO (TN) - Italy
moschitti@disi.unitn.it

Abstract

Automatic detection of general relations between short texts is a complex task that cannot be carried out only relying on language models and bag-of-words. Therefore, learning methods to exploit syntax and semantics are required. In this paper, we present a new kernel for the representation of shallow semantic information along with a comprehensive study on kernel methods for the exploitation of syntactic/semantic structures for short text pair categorization. Our experiments with Support Vector Machines on question/answer classification show that our kernels can be used to greatly improve system accuracy.

1 Introduction

Previous work on Text Categorization (TC) has shown that advanced linguistic processing for document representation is often ineffective for this task, e.g. (Lewis, 1992; Furnkranz et al., 1998; Allan, 2000; Moschitti and Basili, 2004). In contrast, work in question answering suggests that syntactic and semantic structures help in solving TC (Voorhees, 2004; Hickl et al., 2006). From these studies, it emerges that when the categorization task is linguistically *complex*, syntax and semantics may play a relevant role. In this perspective, the study of the automatic detection of relationships between short texts is particularly interesting. Typical examples of such relations are given in (Giampiccolo et al., 2007) or those holding between question and answer, e.g. (Hovy et al., 2002; Punyakanok et al., 2004; Lin and Katz, 2003), i.e. if a text fragment correctly responds to a question.

In Question Answering, the latter problem is mostly tackled by using different heuristics and classifiers, which aim at extracting the best answers (Chen et al., 2006; Collins-Thompson et al., 2004). However, for definitional questions, a more effective approach would be to test if a *correct relationship* between the answer and the query holds. This, in turns, depends on the structure of the two text fragments. Designing language models to capture such relation is too complex since probabilistic models suffer from (i) computational complexity issues, e.g. for the processing of large bayesian networks, (ii) problems in effectively estimating and smoothing probabilities and (iii) high sensitiveness to irrelevant features and processing errors. In contrast, discriminative models such as Support Vector Machines (SVMs) have theoretically been shown to be robust to noise and irrelevant features (Vapnik, 1995). Thus, partially correct linguistic structures may still provide a relevant contribution since only the relevant information would be taken into account. Moreover, such a learning approach supports the use of kernel methods which allow for an efficient and effective representation of structured data.

SVMs and Kernel Methods have recently been applied to natural language tasks with promising results, e.g. (Collins and Duffy, 2002; Kudo and Matsumoto, 2003; Cumby and Roth, 2003; Shen et al., 2003; Moschitti and Bejan, 2004; Culotta and Sorensen, 2004; Kudo et al., 2005; Toutanova et al., 2004; Kazama and Torisawa, 2005; Zhang et al., 2006; Moschitti et al., 2006). In particular, in question classification, tree kernels, e.g. (Zhang and Lee, 2003), have shown accuracy comparable to the best models, e.g. (Li and Roth, 2005).

Moreover, (Shen and Lapata, 2007; Moschitti et al., 2007; Surdeanu et al., 2008; Chali and Joty,

Proceedings of the 12th Conference of the European Chapter of the ACL, pages 576–584,
Athens, Greece, 30 March – 3 April 2009.

2008) have shown that shallow semantic information in the form of Predicate Argument Structures (PASs) (Jackendoff, 1990; Johnson and Fillmore, 2000) improves the automatic detection of correct answers to a target question. In particular, in (Moschitti et al., 2007) kernels for the processing of PASs (in PropBank[1] format (Kingsbury and Palmer, 2002)) extracted from question/answer pairs were proposed. However, the relatively high kernel computational complexity and the limited improvement on bag-of-words (BOW) produced by this approach do not make the use of such technique practical for real world applications.

In this paper, we carry out a complete study on the use of syntactic/semantic structures for relational learning from questions and answers. We designed sequence kernels for words and Part of Speech Tags which capture basic lexical semantics and basic syntactic information. Then, we design a novel shallow semantic kernel which is far more efficient and also more accurate than the one proposed in (Moschitti et al., 2007).

The extensive experiments carried out on two different corpora of questions and answers, derived from Web documents and the TREC corpus, show that:

- Kernels based on PAS, POS-tag sequences and syntactic parse trees improve the BOW approach on both datasets. On the TREC data the improvement is interestingly high, e.g. about 61%, making its application worthwhile.
- The new kernel for processing PASs is more efficient and effective than previous models so that it can be practically used in systems for short text pair categorization, e.g. question/answer classification.

In the remainder of this paper, Section 2 presents well-known kernel functions for structural information whereas Section 3 describes our new shallow semantic kernel. Section 4 reports on our experiments with the above models and, finally, a conclusion is drawn in Section 5.

2 String and Tree Kernels

Feature design, especially for modeling syntactic and semantic structures, is one of the most difficult aspects in defining a learning system as it requires efficient feature extraction from learning objects. Kernel methods are an interesting representation approach as they allow for the use of all object substructures as features. In this perspective, String Kernel (SK) proposed in (Shawe-Taylor and Cristianini, 2004) and the Syntactic Tree Kernel (STK) (Collins and Duffy, 2002) allow for modeling structured data in high dimensional spaces.

2.1 String Kernels

The String Kernels that we consider count the number of substrings containing gaps shared by two sequences, i.e. some of the symbols of the original string are skipped. Gaps modify the weight associated with the target substrings as shown in the following.

Let Σ be a finite alphabet, $\Sigma^* = \bigcup_{n=0}^{\infty} \Sigma^n$ is the set of all strings. Given a string $s \in \Sigma^*$, $|s|$ denotes the length of the strings and s_i its compounding symbols, i.e $s = s_1..s_{|s|}$, whereas $s[i:j]$ selects the substring $s_i s_{i+1}..s_{j-1}s_j$ from the i-th to the j-th character. u is a subsequence of s if there is a sequence of indexes $\vec{I} = (i_1, ..., i_{|u|})$, with $1 \le i_1 < ... < i_{|u|} \le |s|$, such that $u = s_{i_1}..s_{i_{|u|}}$ or $u = s[\vec{I}]$ for short. $d(\vec{I})$ is the distance between the first and last character of the subsequence u in s, i.e. $d(\vec{I}) = i_{|u|} - i_1 + 1$. Finally, given s_1, s_2 $\in \Sigma^*$, $s_1 s_2$ indicates their concatenation.

The set of all substrings of a text corpus forms a feature space denoted by $\mathcal{F} = \{u_1, u_2, ..\} \subset \Sigma^*$. To map a string s in $\mathbb{R}^\infty$ space, we can use the following functions: $\phi_u(s) = \sum_{\vec{I}:u=s[\vec{I}]} \lambda^{d(\vec{I})}$ for some $\lambda \le 1$. These functions count the number of occurrences of u in the string s and assign them a weight $\lambda^{d(\vec{I})}$ proportional to their lengths. Hence, the inner product of the feature vectors for two strings s_1 and s_2 returns the sum of all common subsequences weighted according to their frequency of occurrences and lengths, i.e.

$$SK(s_1, s_2) = \sum_{u\in\Sigma^*} \phi_u(s_1)\cdot\phi_u(s_2) = \sum_{u\in\Sigma^*} \sum_{\vec{I}_1:u=s_1[\vec{I}_1]} \lambda^{d(\vec{I}_1)}$$

$$\sum_{\vec{I}_2:u=t[\vec{I}_2]} \lambda^{d(\vec{I}_2)} = \sum_{u\in\Sigma^*} \sum_{\vec{I}_1:u=s_1[\vec{I}_1]} \sum_{\vec{I}_2:u=t[\vec{I}_2]} \lambda^{d(\vec{I}_1)+d(\vec{I}_2)},$$

where $d(.)$ counts the number of characters in the substrings as well as the gaps that were skipped in the original string.

2.2 Syntactic Tree Kernel (STK)

Tree kernels compute the number of common substructures between two trees T_1 and T_2 without explicitly considering the whole fragment space. Let $\mathcal{F} = \{f_1, f_2, \ldots, f_{|\mathcal{F}|}\}$ be the set of tree

[1]www.cis.upenn.edu/~ace

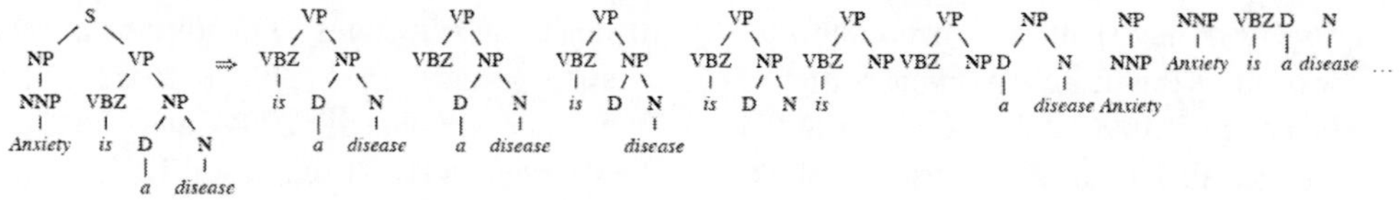

Figure 1: A tree for the sentence "Anxiety is a disease" with some of its syntactic tree fragments.

fragments and $\chi_i(n)$ be an indicator function, equal to 1 if the target f_i is rooted at node n and equal to 0 otherwise. A tree kernel function over T_1 and T_2 is defined as $TK(T_1, T_2) = \sum_{n_1 \in N_{T_1}} \sum_{n_2 \in N_{T_2}} \Delta(n_1, n_2)$, where N_{T_1} and N_{T_2} are the sets of nodes in T_1 and T_2, respectively and $\Delta(n_1, n_2) = \sum_{i=1}^{|\mathcal{F}|} \chi_i(n_1)\chi_i(n_2)$.

Δ function counts the number of subtrees rooted in n_1 and n_2 and can be evaluated as follows (Collins and Duffy, 2002):
1. if the productions at n_1 and n_2 are different then $\Delta(n_1, n_2) = 0$;
2. if the productions at n_1 and n_2 are the same, and n_1 and n_2 have only leaf children (i.e. they are pre-terminal symbols) then $\Delta(n_1, n_2) = \lambda$;
3. if the productions at n_1 and n_2 are the same, and n_1 and n_2 are not pre-terminals then $\Delta(n_1, n_2) = \lambda \prod_{j=1}^{l(n_1)} (1 + \Delta(c_{n_1}(j), c_{n_2}(j)))$, where $l(n_1)$ is the number of children of n_1, $c_n(j)$ is the j-th child of node n and λ is a decay factor penalizing larger structures.

Figure 1 shows some fragments of the subtree on the left part. These satisfy the constraint that grammatical rules cannot be broken. For example, *[VP [VBZ NP]]* is a valid fragment which has two non-terminal symbols, *VBZ* and *NP*, as leaves whereas *[VP [VBZ]]* is not a valid feature.

3 Shallow Semantic Kernels

The extraction of semantic representations from text is a very complex task. For it, traditionally used models are based on lexical similarity and tends to neglect lexical dependencies. Recently, work such as (Shen and Lapata, 2007; Surdeanu et al., 2008; Moschitti et al., 2007; Moschitti and Quarteroni, 2008; Chali and Joty, 2008), uses PAS to consider such dependencies but only the latter three researches attempt to completely exploit PAS with Shallow Semantic Tree Kernels (SSTKs). Unfortunately, these kernels result computational expensive for real world applications. In the remainder of this section, we present our new kernel for PASs and compare it with the previous SSTK.

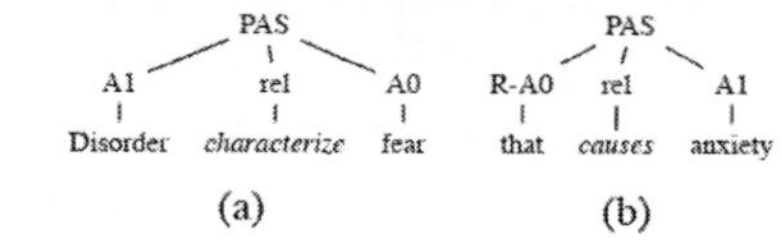

Figure 2: Predicate Argument Structure trees associated with the sentence: "Panic disorder is characterized by unexpected and intense fear that causes anxiety.".

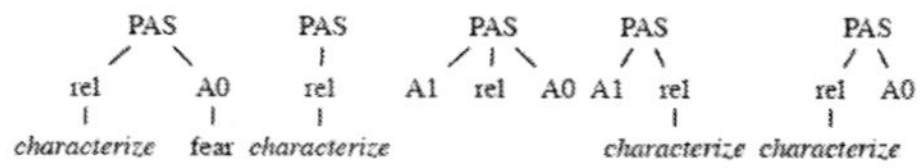

Figure 3: Some of the tree substructures useful to capture shallow semantic properties.

3.1 Shallow Semantic Structures

Shallow approaches to semantic processing are making large strides in the direction of efficiently and effectively deriving tacit semantic information from text. Large data resources annotated with levels of semantic information, such as in the FrameNet (Johnson and Fillmore, 2000) and PropBank (PB) (Kingsbury and Palmer, 2002) projects, make it possible to design systems for the automatic extraction of predicate argument structures (PASs) (Carreras and Màrquez, 2005). PB-based systems produce sentence annotations like:
[$_{A1}$ Panic disorder] is [$_{rel}$ characterized] [$_{A0}$ by unexpected and intense fear] [$_{R-A0}$ that] [$_{rel}$causes] [$_{A1}$ anxiety].
A tree representation of the above semantic information is given by the two PAS trees in Figure 2, where the argument words are replaced by the head word to reduce data sparseness. Hence, the semantic similarity between sentences can be measured in terms of the number of substructures between the two trees. The required substructures violate the STK constraint (about breaking production rules), i.e. since we need any set of nodes linked by edges of the initial tree. For example, interesting semantic fragments of Figure 2.a are shown in Figure 3.

Unfortunately, STK applied to PAS trees cannot generate such fragments. To overcome this problem, a Shallow Semantic Tree Kernel (SSTK) was designed in (Moschitti et al., 2007).

3.2 Shallow Semantic Tree Kernel (SSTK)

SSTK is obtained by applying two different steps: first, the PAS tree is transformed by adding a layer of SLOT nodes as many as the number of possible argument types, where each slot is assigned to an argument following a fixed ordering (e.g. *rel*, *A0*, *A1*, *A2*, ...). For example, if an A1 is found in the sentence annotation it will be always positioned under the third slot. This is needed to "artificially" allow SSTK to generate structures containing subsets of arguments. For example, the tree in Figure 2.a is transformed into the first tree of Fig. 4, where "null" just states that there is no corresponding argument type.

Second, to discard fragments only containing slot nodes, in the STK algorithm, a new step 0 is added and the step 3 is modified (see Sec. 2.2):

0. if n_1 (or n_2) is a pre-terminal node and its child label is *null*, $\Delta(n_1, n_2) = 0$;

3. $\Delta(n_1, n_2) = \prod_{j=1}^{l(n_1)} (1 + \Delta(c_{n_1}(j), c_{n_2}(j))) - 1$.

For example, Fig. 4 shows the fragments generated by SSTK. The comparison with the ideal fragments in Fig. 3 shows that SSTK well approximates the semantic features needed for the PAS representation. The computational complexity of SSTK is $O(n^2)$, where n is the number of the PAS nodes (leaves excluded). Considering that the tree including all the PB arguments contains 52 slot nodes, the computation becomes very expensive. To overcome this drawback, in the next section, we propose a new kernel to efficiently process PAS trees with no addition of slot nodes.

3.3 Semantic Role Kernel (SRK)

The idea of SRK is to produce all child subsequences of a PAS tree, which correspond to sequences of predicate arguments. For this purpose, we can use a string kernel (SK) (see Section 2.1) for which efficient algorithms have been developed. Once a sequence of arguments is output by SK, for each argument, we account for the potential matches of its children, i.e. the head of the argument (or more in general the argument word sequence).

More formally, given two sequences of argument nodes, s_1 and s_2, in two PAS trees and considering the string kernel in Sec 2.1, the SRK(s_1, s_2) is defined as:

$$\sum_{\substack{\vec{I}_1:u=s_1[\vec{I}_1]\\ \vec{I}_2:u=s_2[\vec{I}_2]}} \prod_{l=1..|u|} (1 + \sigma(s_1[\vec{I}_{1l}], s_2[\vec{I}_{2l}]))\lambda^{d(\vec{I}_1)+d(\vec{I}_2)}, \quad (1)$$

where u is any subsequence of argument nodes, $\vec{I}_l$ is the index of the l-th argument node, $s[\vec{I}_l]$ is the corresponding argument node in the sequence s and $\sigma(s_1[\vec{I}_{1l}], s_2[\vec{I}_{2l}])$ is 1 if the heads of the arguments are identical, otherwise is 0.

Proposition 1 *SRK computes the number of all possible tree substructures shared by the two evaluating PAS trees, where the considered substructures of a tree T are constituted by any set of nodes (at least two) linked by edges of T.*

Proof The PAS trees only contain three node levels and, according to the proposition's thesis, substructures contain at least two nodes. The number of substructures shared by two trees, T_1 and T_2, constituted by the root node (PAS) and the subsequences of argument nodes is evaluated by $\sum_{\vec{I}_1:u=s_1[\vec{I}_1], \vec{I}_2:u=s_2[\vec{I}_2]} \lambda^{d(\vec{I}_1)+d(\vec{I}_2)}$ (when $\lambda = 1$). Given a node in a shared subsequence u, its child (i.e. the head word) can be both in T_1 and T_2, originating two different shared structures (with or without such head node). The matches on the heads (for each shared node of u) are combined together generating different substructures. Thus the number of substructures originating from u is the product, $\prod_{l=1..|u|}(1+\sigma(s_1[\vec{I}_{1l}], s_2[\vec{I}_{2l}]))$. This number multiplied by all shared subsequences leads to Eq. 1. □

We can efficiently compute SRK by following a similar approach to the string kernel evaluation in (Shawe-Taylor and Cristianini, 2004) by defining the following dynamic matrix:

$$D_p(k, l) = \sum_{i=1}^{k} \sum_{r=1}^{l} \lambda^{k-i+l-r} \times \gamma_{p-1}(s_1[1:i], s_2[1:r]), \quad (2)$$

where $\gamma_p(s_1, s_2)$ counts the number of shared substructures of exactly p argument nodes between s_1 and s_2 and again, $s[1:i]$ indicates the sequence portion from argument 1 to i. The above matrix is then used to evaluate $\gamma_p(s_1 a, s_2 b) =$

$$\begin{cases} \lambda^2(1 + \sigma(h(a), h(b)))D_p(|s_1|, |s_2|) & \text{if } a = b; \\ 0 & \textit{otherwise}. \end{cases} \quad (3)$$

where $s_1 a$ and $s_2 b$ indicate the concatenation of the sequences s and t with the argument nodes, a and b, respectively and $\sigma(h(a), h(b))$ is 1 if the children of a and b are identical (e.g. same head). The interesting property is that:

$$\begin{aligned} D_p(k, l) &= \gamma_{p-1}(s_1[1:k], s_2[1:l]) + \lambda D_p(k, l-1) \\ &+ \lambda D_p(k-1, l) - \lambda^2 D_p(k-1, l-1). \end{aligned} \quad (4)$$

To obtain the final kernel, we need to consider all possible subsequence lengths. Let m be the minimum between $|s_1|$ and $|s_2|$,

$$SRK(s_1, s_2) = \sum_{p=1}^{m} \gamma_p(s_1, s_2).$$

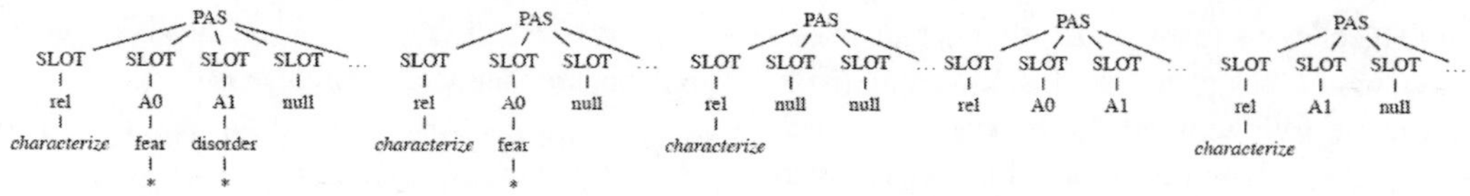

Figure 4: Fragments of Fig. 2.a produced by the SSTK (similar to those of Fig. 3).

Regarding the processing time, if ρ is the maximum number of arguments in a predicate structure, the worst case computational complexity of SRK is $O(\rho^3)$.

3.4 SRK vs. SSTK

A comparison between SSTK and SRK suggests the following points: first, although the computational complexity of SRK is larger than the one of SSTK, we will show in the experiment section that the running time (for both training and testing) is much lower. The worse case is not really informative since as shown in (Moschitti, 2006), we can design fast algorithm with a linear average running time (we use such algorithm for SSTK).

Second, although SRK uses trees with only three levels, in Eq.1, the function σ (defined to give 1 or 0 if the heads match or not) can be substituted by any kernel function. Thus, σ can recursively be an SRK (and evaluate Nested PASs (Moschitti et al., 2007)) or any other potential kernel (over the arguments). The very interesting aspect is that the efficient algorithm that we provide (Eqs 2, 3 and 4) can be accordingly modified to efficiently evaluate new kernels obtained with the σ substitution[2].

Third, the interesting difference between SRK and SSTK (in addition to efficiency) is that SSTK requires an ordered sequence of arguments to evaluate the number of argument subgroups (arguments are sorted before running the kernel). This means that the natural order is lost. SRK instead is based on subsequence kernels so it naturally takes into account the order which is very important: without it, syntactic/semantic properties of predicates cannot be captured, e.g. passive and active forms have the same argument order for SSTK.

Finally, SRK gives a weight to the predicate substructures by considering their length, which also includes gaps, e.g. the sequence (A0, A1) is more similar to (A0, A1) than (A0, A-LOC, A1), in turn, the latter produces a heavier match than (A0, A-LOC, A2, A1) (please see Section 2.1). This is another important property for modeling shallow semantics similarity.

[2]For space reasons we cannot discuss it here.

4 Experiments

Our experiments aim at studying the impact of our kernels applied to syntactic/semantic structures for the detection of relations between short texts. In particular, we first show that our SRK is far more efficient and effective than SSTK. Then, we study the impact of the above kernels as well as sequence kernels based on words and Part of Speech Tags and tree kernels for the classification of question/answer text pairs.

4.1 Experimental Setup

The task used to test our kernels is the classification of the correctness of $\langle q, a \rangle$ pairs, where a is an answer for the query q. The text pair kernel operates by comparing the content of questions and the content of answers in a separate fashion. Thus, given two pairs $p_1 = \langle q_1, a_1 \rangle$ and $p_2 = \langle q_2, a_2 \rangle$, a kernel function is defined as $K(p_1, p_2) = \sum_\tau K_\tau(q_1, q_2) + \sum_\tau K_\tau(a_1, a_2)$, where τ varies across different kernel functions described hereafter.

As a basic kernel machine, we used our SVM-Light-TK toolkit, available at `disi.unitn.it/moschitti` (which is based on SVM-Light (Joachims, 1999) software). In it, we implemented: the String Kernel (SK), the Syntactic Tree Kernel (STK), the Shallow Semantic Tree Kernel (SSTK) and the Semantic Role Kernel (SRK) described in sections 2 and 3. Each kernel is associated with the above linguistic objects: (i) the linear kernel is used with the bag-of-words (BOW) or the bag-of-POS-tags (POS) features. (ii) SK is used with word sequences (i.e. the Word Sequence Kernel, WSK) and POS sequences (i.e. the POS Sequence Kernel, PSK). (iii) STK is used with syntactic parse trees automatically derived with Charniak's parser; (iv) SSTK and SRK are applied to two different PAS trees (see Section 3.1), automatically derived with our SRL system.

It is worth noting that, since answers often con-

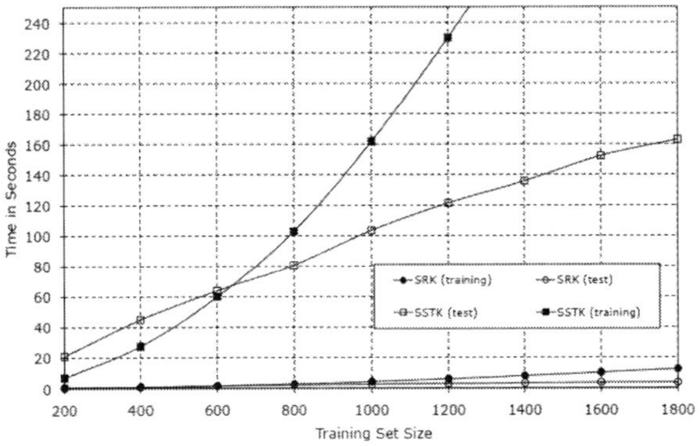

Figure 5: Efficiency of SRK and SSTK

tain more than one PAS, we applied SRK or SSTK to all pairs $P_1 \times P_2$ and sum the obtained contribution, where P_1 and P_2 are the set of PASs of the first and second answer[3]. Although different kernels can be used for questions and for answers, we used (and summed together) the same kernels except for those based on PASs, which are only used on answers.

4.1.1 Datasets

To train and test our text QA classifiers, we adopted the two datasets of question/answer pairs available at `disi.unitn.it/~silviaq`, containing answers to only definitional questions. The datasets are based on the 138 TREC 2001 test questions labeled as "description" in (Li and Roth, 2005). Each question is paired with all the top 20 answer paragraphs extracted by two basic QA systems: one trained with the web documents and the other trained with the AQUAINT data used in TREC'07.

The WEB corpus (Moschitti et al., 2007) of QA pairs contains 1,309 sentences, 416 of which are positive[4] answers whereas the TREC corpus contains 2,256 sentences, 261 of which are positive.

4.1.2 Measures and Parameterization

The accuracy of the classifiers is provided by the average F1 over 5 different samples using 5-fold cross-validation whereas each plot refers to a single fold. We carried out some preliminary experiments of the basic kernels on a validation set and we noted that the F1 was maximized by using the default cost parameters (option -c of SVM-Light), $\lambda = 0.04$ (see Section 2). The trade-off parameter varied according to different kernels on WEB data (so it needed an ad-hoc estimation) whereas a value of 10 was optimal for any kernel on the TREC corpus.

4.2 Shallow Semantic Kernel Efficiency

Section 2 has illustrated that SRK is applied to more compact PAS trees than SSTK, which runs on large structures containing as many slots as the number of possible predicate argument types. This impacts on the memory occupancy as well as on the kernel computation speed. To empirically verify our analytical findings (Section 3.3), we divided the training (TREC) data in 9 bins of increasing size (200 instances between two contiguous bins) and we measured the learning and test time[5] for each bin. Figure 5 shows that in both the classification and learning phases, SRK is much faster than SSTK. With all training data, SSTK employs 487.15 seconds whereas SRK only uses 12.46 seconds, i.e. it is about 40 times faster, making the experimentation of SVMs with large datasets feasible. It is worth noting that to implement SSTK we used the fast version of STK and that, although the PAS trees are smaller than syntactic trees, they may still contain more than half million of substructures (when they are formed by seven arguments).

4.3 Results for Question/Answer Classification

In these experiments, we tested different kernels and some of their most promising combinations, which are simply obtained by adding the different kernel contributions[6] (this yields the joint feature space of the individual kernels).

Table 1 shows the average F1 $\pm$ the standard deviation[7] over 5-folds on Web (and TREC) data of SVMs using different kernels. We note that: (a) BOW achieves very high accuracy, comparable to the one produced by STK, i.e. 65.3 vs 65.1; (b) the BOW+STK combination achieves 66.0, im-

[3]More formally, let P_t and $P_{t'}$ be the sets of PASs extracted from text fragments t and t'; the resulting kernel will be $K_{all}(P_t, P_{t'}) = \sum_{p \in P_t} \sum_{p' \in P_{t'}} SRK(p, p')$.

[4]For instance, given the question "What are invertebrates?", the sentence "At least 99% of all animal species are invertebrates, comprising ..." was labeled "-1", while "Invertebrates are animals without backbones." was labeled "+1".

[5]Processing time in seconds of a Mac-Book Pro 2.4 Ghz.

[6]All adding kernels are normalized to have a similarity score between 0 and 1, i.e. $K'(X_1, X_2) = \frac{K(X_1,X_2)}{\sqrt{K(X_1,X_1) \times K(X_2,X_2)}}$.

[7]The Std. Dev. of the difference between two classifier F1s is much lower making statistically significant almost all our system ranking in terms of performance.

BOW	POS	PSK	WSK	STK	SSTK	SRK	BOW+POS	BOW+STK	PSK+STK	WSK+STK	STK+SSTK	STK+SRK
WEB Corpus												
65.3±2.9	56.8±0.8	62.5±2.3	65.7±6.0	65.1±3.9	52.9±1.7	50.8±1.2	63.7±1.6	66.0±2.7	65.3±2.4	66.6±3.0	(+WSK) 68.0±2.7	(+WSK) **68.2**±4.3
TREC Corpus												
24.2±5.0	26.5±7.9	31.6±6.8	14.0±4.2	33.1±3.8	21.8±3.7	23.6±4.7	31.9±7.1	30.3±4.1	36.4±7.0	23.7±3.9	(+PSK) 37.2±6.9	(+PSK) **39.1**±7.3

Table 1: F1 ± Std. Dev. of the question/answer classifier according to several kernels on the WEB and TREC corpora.

proving both BOW and STK; (c) WSK (65.7) improves BOW and it is enhanced by WSK+STK (66.6), demonstrating that word sequences and STKs are very relevant for this task; and finally, WSK+STK+SSTK is slightly improved by WSK+STK+SRK, 68.0% vs 68.2% (not significantly) and both improve on WSK+STK.

The above findings are interesting as the syntactic information provided by STK and the semantic information brought by WSK and SRK improve on BOW. The high accuracy of BOW is surprising if we consider that at classification time, instances of the training models (e.g. support vectors) are compared with different test examples since questions cannot be shared between training and test set[8]. Therefore the answer words should be different and useless to generalize rules for answer classification. However, error analysis reveals that although questions are not shared between training and test set, there are common words in the answers due to typical Web page patterns which indicate if a retrieved passage is an incorrect answer, e.g. `Learn more about X`.

Although the ability to detect these patterns is beneficial for a QA system as it improves its overall accuracy, it is slightly misleading for the study that we are carrying out. Thus, we experimented with the TREC corpus which does not contain Web extra-linguistic texts and it is more complex from a QA task viewpoint (it is more difficult to find a correct answer).

Table 1 also shows the classification results on the TREC dataset. A comparative analysis suggests that: (a) the F1 of all models is much lower than for the Web dataset; (b) BOW shows the lowest accuracy (24.2) and also the accuracy of its combination with STK (30.3) is lower than the one of STK alone (33.1); (c) PSK (31.6) improves POS (26.5) information and PSK+STK (36.4) improves on PSK and STK; and (d) PAS adds further information as the best model is PSK+STK+SRK, which improves BOW from 24.2 to 39.1, i.e. 61%. Finally, it is worth noting that SRK provides a higher improvement (39.1-36.4) than SSTK (37.2-36.4).

4.4 Precision/Recall Curves

To better study the benefit of the proposed linguistic structures, we also plotted the Precision/Recall curves (one fold for each corpus). Figure 6 shows the curve of some interesting kernels applied to the Web dataset. As expected, BOW shows the lowest curves, although, its relevant contribution is evident. STK improves BOW since it provides a better model generalization by exploiting syntactic structures. Also, WSK can generate a more accurate model than BOW since it uses n-grams (with gaps) and when it is summed to STK, a very accurate model is obtained[9]. Finally, WSK+STK+SRK improves all the models showing the potentiality of PASs.

Such curves show that there is no superior model. This is caused by the high contribution of BOW, which de-emphasize all the other models's result. In this perspective, the results on TREC are more interesting as shown by Figure 7 since the contribution of BOW is very low making the difference in accuracy with the other linguistic models more evident. PSK+STK+SRK, which encodes the most advanced syntactic and semantic information, shows a very high curve which outperforms all the others.

The analysis of the above results suggests that: first as expected, BOW does not prove very relevant to capture the relations between short texts from examples. In the QA classification, while BOW is useful to establish the initial ranking by measuring the similarity between question and answer, it is almost irrelevant to capture typical rules suggesting if a description is valid or not. Indeed, since test questions are not in the training set, their words as well as those of candidate answers will be different, penalizing BOW models. In these

[8] Sharing questions between test and training sets would be an error from a machine learning viewpoint as we cannot expect new questions to be identical to those in the training set.

[9] Some of the kernels have been removed from the figures so that the plots result more visible.

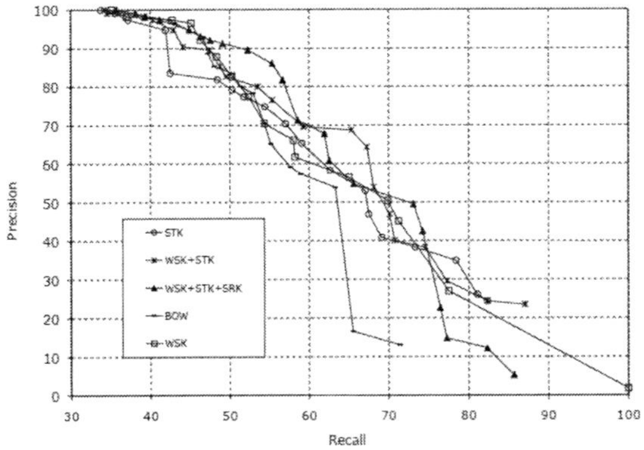

Figure 6: Precision/Recall curves of some kernel combinations on the WEB dataset.

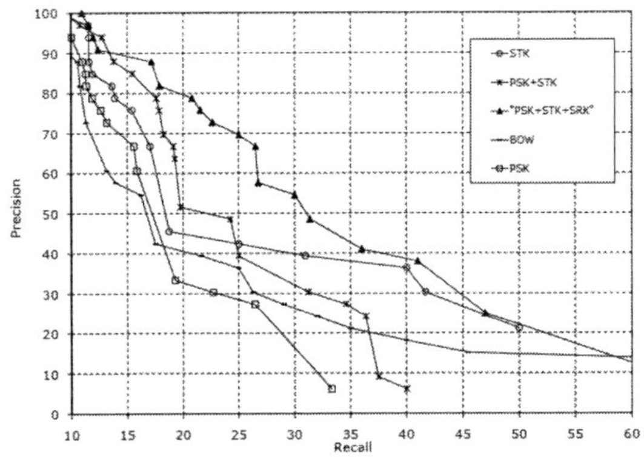

Figure 7: Precision/Recall curves of some kernel combinations on the TREC dataset.

conditions, we need to rely on syntactic structures which at least allow for detecting well formed descriptions.

Second, the results show that STK is important to detect typical description patterns but also POS sequences provide additional information since they are less sparse than tree fragments. Such patterns improve on the bag of POS-tags by about 6% (see POS vs PSK). This is a relevant result considering that in standard text classification bigrams or trigrams are usually ineffective.

Third, although PSK+STK generates a very rich feature set, SRK significantly improves the classification F1 by about 3%, suggesting that shallow semantics can be very useful to detect if an answer is well formed and is related to a question. Error analysis revealed that PAS can provide patterns like:

```
- A0(X) R-A0(that) rel(result) A1(Y)
- A1(X) rel(characterize) A0(Y),
```

where X and Y need not necessarily be matched.

Finally, the best model, PSK+STK+SRK, improves on BOW by 61%. This is strong evidence that complex natural language tasks require advanced linguistic information that should be exploited by powerful algorithms such as SVMs and using effective feature engineering techniques such as kernel methods.

5 Conclusion

In this paper, we have studied several types of syntactic/semantic information: bag-of-words (BOW), bag-of-POS tags, syntactic parse trees and predicate argument structures (PASs), for the design of short text pair classifiers. Our learning framework is constituted by Support Vector Machines (SVMs) and kernel methods applied to automatically generated syntactic and semantic structures.

In particular, we designed (i) a new Semantic Role Kernel (SRK) based on a very fast algorithm; (ii) a new sequence kernel over POS tags to encode shallow syntactic information; (iii) many kernel combinations (to our knowledge no previous work uses so many different kernels) which allow for the study of the role of several linguistic levels in a well defined statistical framework.

The results on two different question/answer classification corpora suggest that (a) SRK for processing PASs is more efficient and effective than previous models, (b) kernels based on PAS, POS-tag sequences and syntactic parse trees improve on BOW on both datasets and (c) on the TREC data the improvement is remarkably high, e.g. about 61%.

Promising future work concerns the definition of a kernel on the entire argument information (e.g. by means of lexical similarity between all the words of two arguments) and the design of a *discourse kernel* to exploit the relational information gathered from different sentence pairs. A closer relationship between questions and answers can be exploited with models presented in (Moschitti and Zanzotto, 2007; Zanzotto and Moschitti, 2006). Also the use of PAS derived from FrameNet and PropBank (Giuglea and Moschitti, 2006) appears to be an interesting research line.

Acknowledgments

I would like to thank Silvia Quarteroni for her work on extracting linguistic structures. This work has been partially supported by the European Commission - LUNA project, contract n. 33549.

References

J. Allan. 2000. Natural Language Processing for Information Retrieval. In *NAACL/ANLP (tutorial notes)*.

X. Carreras and L. Màrquez. 2005. Introduction to the CoNLL-2005 shared task: SRL. In *CoNLL-2005*.

Y. Chali and S. Joty. 2008. Improving the performance of the random walk model for answering complex questions. In *Proceedings of ACL-08: HLT, Short Papers*, Columbus, Ohio.

Y. Chen, M. Zhou, and S. Wang. 2006. Reranking answers from definitional QA using language models. In *ACL'06*.

M. Collins and N. Duffy. 2002. New ranking algorithms for parsing and tagging: Kernels over discrete structures, and the voted perceptron. In *ACL'02*.

K. Collins-Thompson, J. Callan, E. Terra, and C. L.A. Clarke. 2004. The effect of document retrieval quality on factoid QA performance. In *SIGIR'04*.

Aron Culotta and Jeffrey Sorensen. 2004. Dependency Tree Kernels for Relation Extraction. In *ACL04*, Barcelona, Spain.

C. Cumby and D. Roth. 2003. Kernel Methods for Relational Learning. In *Proceedings of ICML 2003*, Washington, DC, USA.

J. Furnkranz, T. Mitchell, and E. Rilof. 1998. A case study in using linguistic phrases for text categorization on the www. In *Working Notes of the AAAI/ICML, Workshop on Learning for Text Categorization*.

D. Giampiccolo, B. Magnini, I. Dagan, and B. Dolan. 2007. The third pascal recognizing textual entailment challenge. In *Proceedings of the ACL-PASCAL Workshop*, Prague.

A.-M. Giuglea and A. Moschitti. 2006. Semantic role labeling via framenet, verbnet and propbank. In *Proceedings of ACL 2006*, Sydney, Australia.

A. Hickl, J. Williams, J. Bensley, K. Roberts, Y. Shi, and B. Rink. 2006. Question answering with lccs chaucer at trec 2006. In *Proceedings of TREC'06*.

E. Hovy, U. Hermjakob, C.-Y. Lin, and D. Ravichandran. 2002. Using knowledge to facilitate factoid answer pinpointing. In *Proceedings of Coling*, Morristown, NJ, USA.

R. Jackendoff. 1990. *Semantic Structures*. MIT Press.

T. Joachims. 1999. Making large-scale SVM learning practical. In B. Schölkopf, C. Burges, and A. Smola, editors, *Advances in Kernel Methods*.

C. R. Johnson and C. J. Fillmore. 2000. The framenet tagset for frame-semantic and syntactic coding of predicate-argument structures. In *ANLP-NAACL'00*, pages 56–62.

J. Kazama and K. Torisawa. 2005. Speeding up Training with Tree Kernels for Node Relation Labeling. In *Proceedings of EMNLP 2005*, pages 137–144, Toronto, Canada.

P. Kingsbury and M. Palmer. 2002. From Treebank to PropBank. In *LREC'02*.

T. Kudo and Y. Matsumoto. 2003. Fast Methods for Kernel-Based Text Analysis. In Erhard Hinrichs and Dan Roth, editors, *Proceedings of ACL*.

T. Kudo, J. Suzuki, and H Isozaki. 2005. Boosting-based parse reranking with subtree features. In *Proceedings of ACL'05*, US.

D. D. Lewis. 1992. An evaluation of phrasal and clustered representations on a text categorization task. In *Proceedings of SIGIR-92*.

X. Li and D. Roth. 2005. Learning question classifiers: the role of semantic information. *JNLE*.

J. Lin and B. Katz. 2003. Question answering from the web using knowledge annotation and knowledge mining techniques. In *CIKM '03*.

A. Moschitti and R. Basili. 2004. Complex linguistic features for text classification: A comprehensive study. In *ECIR, Sunderland, UK*.

A. Moschitti and C. Bejan. 2004. A semantic kernel for predicate argument classification. In *CoNLL-2004*, Boston, MA, USA.

A. Moschitti and S. Quarteroni. 2008. Kernels on linguistic structures for answer extraction. In *Proceedings of ACL-08: HLT, Short Papers*, Columbus, Ohio.

A. Moschitti and F. Zanzotto. 2007. Fast and effective kernels for relational learning from texts. In Zoubin Ghahramani, editor, *Proceedings of ICML 2007*.

A. Moschitti, D. Pighin, and R. Basili. 2006. Semantic role labeling via tree kernel joint inference. In *Proceedings of CoNLL-X*, New York City.

A. Moschitti, S. Quarteroni, R. Basili, and S. Manandhar. 2007. Exploiting syntactic and shallow semantic kernels for question/answer classification. In *ACL'07*, Prague, Czech Republic.

A. Moschitti. 2006. Making Tree Kernels Practical for Natural Language Learning. In *Proceedings of EACL2006*.

V. Punyakanok, D. Roth, and W. Yih. 2004. Mapping dependencies trees: An application to question answering. In *Proceedings of AI&Math 2004*.

J. Shawe-Taylor and N. Cristianini. 2004. *Kernel Methods for Pattern Analysis*. Cambridge University Press.

D. Shen and M. Lapata. 2007. Using semantic roles to improve question answering. In *Proceedings of EMNLP-CoNLL*.

L. Shen, A. Sarkar, and A. k. Joshi. 2003. Using LTAG Based Features in Parse Reranking. In *EMNLP*, Sapporo, Japan.

M. Surdeanu, M. Ciaramita, and H. Zaragoza. 2008. Learning to rank answers on large online QA collections. In *Proceedings of ACL-08: HLT*, Columbus, Ohio.

K. Toutanova, P. Markova, and C. Manning. 2004. The Leaf Path Projection View of Parse Trees: Exploring String Kernels for HPSG Parse Selection. In *Proceedings of EMNLP 2004*, Barcelona, Spain.

V. Vapnik. 1995. *The Nature of Statistical Learning Theory*. Springer.

E. M. Voorhees. 2004. Overview of the trec 2001 question answering track. In *Proceedings of the Thirteenth Text REtreival Conference (TREC 2004)*.

F. M. Zanzotto and A. Moschitti. 2006. Automatic learning of textual entailments with cross-pair similarities. In *Proceedings of the 21st Coling and 44th ACL*, Sydney, Australia.

D. Zhang and W. Lee. 2003. Question classification using support vector machines. In *SIGIR'03*, Toronto, Canada. ACM.

M. Zhang, J. Zhang, and J. Su. 2006. Exploring Syntactic Features for Relation Extraction using a Convolution tree kernel. In *Proceedings of NAACL*, New York City, USA.

Discovering Global Patterns in Linguistic Networks through Spectral Analysis: A Case Study of the Consonant Inventories

Animesh Mukherjee*
Indian Institute of Technology, Kharagpur
animeshm@cse.iitkgp.ernet.in

Monojit Choudhury and **Ravi Kannan**
Microsoft Research India
{monojitc,kannan}@microsoft.com

Abstract

Recent research has shown that language and the socio-cognitive phenomena associated with it can be aptly modeled and visualized through networks of linguistic entities. However, most of the existing works on linguistic networks focus only on the local properties of the networks. This study is an attempt to analyze the structure of languages via a purely structural technique, namely spectral analysis, which is ideally suited for discovering the global correlations in a network. Application of this technique to PhoNet, the co-occurrence network of consonants, not only reveals several natural linguistic principles governing the structure of the consonant inventories, but is also able to quantify their relative importance. We believe that this powerful technique can be successfully applied, in general, to study the structure of natural languages.

1 Introduction

Language and the associated socio-cognitive phenomena can be modeled as networks, where the nodes correspond to linguistic entities and the edges denote the pairwise interaction or relationship between these entities. The study of linguistic networks has been quite popular in the recent times and has provided us with several interesting insights into the nature of language (see Choudhury and Mukherjee (to appear) for an extensive survey). Examples include study of the WordNet (Sigman and Cecchi, 2002), syntactic dependency network of words (Ferrer-i-Cancho, 2005) and network of co-occurrence of consonants in sound inventories (Mukherjee et al., 2008; Mukherjee et al., 2007).

Most of the existing studies on linguistic networks, however, focus only on the local structural properties such as the degree and clustering coefficient of the nodes, and shortest paths between pairs of nodes. On the other hand, although it is a well known fact that the *spectrum* of a network can provide important information about its global structure, the use of this powerful mathematical machinery to infer global patterns in linguistic networks is rarely found in the literature. Note that spectral analysis, however, has been successfully employed in the domains of biological and social networks (Farkas et al., 2001; Gkantsidis et al., 2003; Banerjee and Jost, 2007). In the context of linguistic networks, (Belkin and Goldsmith, 2002) is the only work we are aware of that analyzes the eigenvectors to obtain a two dimensional visualize of the network. Nevertheless, the work does not study the spectrum of the graph.

The aim of the present work is to demonstrate the use of spectral analysis for discovering the global patterns in linguistic networks. These patterns, in turn, are then interpreted in the light of existing linguistic theories to gather deeper insights into the nature of the underlying linguistic phenomena. We apply this rather generic technique to find the principles that are responsible for shaping the consonant inventories, which is a well researched problem in phonology since 1931 (Trubetzkoy, 1931; Lindblom and Maddieson, 1988; Boersma, 1998; Clements, 2008). The analysis is carried out on a network defined in (Mukherjee et al., 2007), where the consonants are the nodes and there is an edge between two nodes u and v if the consonants corresponding to them co-occur in a language. The number of times they co-occur across languages define the weight of the edge. We explain the results obtained from the spectral analysis of the network post-facto using three linguistic principles. The method also automatically reveals the quantitative importance of each of these

*This research has been conducted during the author's internship at Microsoft Research India.

Proceedings of the 12th Conference of the European Chapter of the ACL, pages 585–593,
Athens, Greece, 30 March – 3 April 2009.

principles.

It is worth mentioning here that earlier researchers have also noted the importance of the aforementioned principles. However, what was not known was how much importance one should associate with each of these principles. We also note that the technique of spectral analysis neither explicitly nor implicitly assumes that these principles exist or are important, but deduces them automatically. Thus, we believe that spectral analysis is a promising approach that is well suited to the discovery of linguistic principles underlying a set of observations represented as a network of entities. The fact that the principles "discovered" in this study are already well established results adds to the credibility of the method. Spectral analysis of large linguistic networks in the future can possibly reveal hitherto unknown universal principles.

The rest of the paper is organized as follows. Sec. 2 introduces the technique of spectral analysis of networks and illustrates some of its applications. The problem of consonant inventories and how it can be modeled and studied within the framework of linguistic networks are described in Sec. 3. Sec. 4 presents the spectral analysis of the consonant co-occurrence network, the observations and interpretations. Sec. 5 concludes by summarizing the work and the contributions and listing out future research directions.

2 A Primer to Spectral Analysis

Spectral analysis[1] is a powerful tool capable of revealing the global structural patterns underlying an enormous and complicated environment of interacting entities. Essentially, it refers to the systematic study of the eigenvalues and the eigenvectors of the adjacency matrix of the network of these interacting entities. Here we shall briefly review the basic concepts involved in spectral analysis and describe some of its applications (see (Chung, 1994; Kannan and Vempala, 2008) for details).

A network or a graph consisting of n nodes (labeled as 1 through n) can be represented by a $n \times n$ square matrix $\mathbf{A}$, where the entry a_{ij} represents the weight of the edge from node i to node j. $\mathbf{A}$, which is known as the *adjacency matrix*, is symmetric for an undirected graph and have binary entries for an unweighted graph. λ is an eigenvalue of $\mathbf{A}$ if there is an n-dimensional vector $\mathbf{x}$ such that

$$\mathbf{Ax} = \lambda\mathbf{x}$$

Any real symmetric matrix $\mathbf{A}$ has n (possibly non-distinct) eigenvalues $\lambda_0 \leq \lambda_1 \leq \ldots \leq \lambda_{n-1}$, and corresponding n eigenvectors that are mutually orthogonal. The *spectrum* of a graph is the set of the distinct eigenvalues of the graph and their corresponding multiplicities. It is usually represented as a plot with the eigenvalues in x-axis and their multiplicities plotted in the y-axis.

The spectrum of real and random graphs display several interesting properties. Banerjee and Jost (2007) report the spectrum of several biological networks that are significantly different from the spectrum of artificially generated graphs[2]. Spectral analysis is also closely related to *Principal Component Analysis* and Multidimensional Scaling. If the first few (say d) eigenvalues of a matrix are much higher than the rest of the eigenvalues, then it can be concluded that the rows of the matrix can be approximately represented as linear combinations of d orthogonal vectors. This further implies that the corresponding graph has a few motifs (subgraphs) that are repeated a large number of time to obtain the global structure of the graph (Banerjee and Jost, to appear).

Spectral properties are representative of an n-dimensional average behavior of the underlying system, thereby providing considerable insight into its global organization. For example, the principal eigenvector (i.e., the eigenvector corresponding to the largest eigenvalue) is the direction in which the sum of the square of the projections of the row vectors of the matrix is maximum. In fact, the principal eigenvector of a graph is used to compute the centrality of the nodes, which is also known as *PageRank* in the context of WWW. Similarly, the second eigen vector component is used for graph clustering.

In the next two sections we describe how spectral analysis can be applied to discover the organizing principles underneath the structure of consonant inventories.

[1]The term spectral analysis is also used in the context of signal processing, where it refers to the study of the frequency spectrum of a signal.

[2]Banerjee and Jost (2007) report the spectrum of the graph's Laplacian matrix rather than the adjacency matrix. It is increasingly popular these days to analyze the spectral properties of the graph's Laplacian matrix. However, for reasons explained later, here we will be conduct spectral analysis of the adjacency matrix rather than its Laplacian.

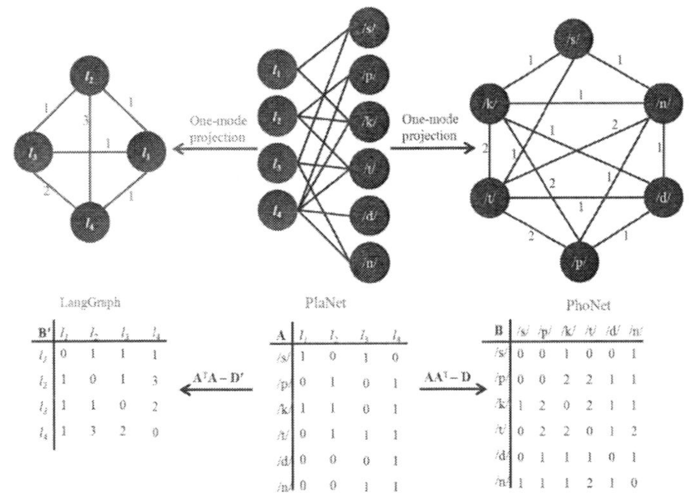

Figure 1: Illustration of the nodes and edges of PlaNet and PhoNet along with their respective adjacency matrix representations.

3 Consonant Co-occurrence Network

The most basic unit of human languages are the speech sounds. The repertoire of sounds that make up the sound inventory of a language are not chosen arbitrarily even though the speakers are capable of producing and perceiving a plethora of them. In contrast, these inventories show exceptionally regular patterns across the languages of the world, which is in fact, a common point of consensus in phonology. Right from the beginning of the 20th century, there have been a large number of linguistically motivated attempts (Trubetzkoy, 1969; Lindblom and Maddieson, 1988; Boersma, 1998; Clements, 2008) to explain the formation of these patterns across the consonant inventories. More recently, Mukherjee and his colleagues (Choudhury et al., 2006; Mukherjee et al., 2007; Mukherjee et al., 2008) studied this problem in the framework of complex networks. Since here we shall conduct a spectral analysis of the network defined in Mukherjee et al. (2007), we briefly survey the models and the important results of their work.

Choudhury et al. (2006) introduced a bipartite network model for the consonant inventories. Formally, a set of consonant inventories is represented as a graph $G = \langle V_L, V_C, E_{lc} \rangle$, where the nodes in one partition correspond to the languages (V_L) and that in the other partition correspond to the consonants (V_C). There is an edge (v_l, v_c) between a language node $v_l \in V_L$ (representing the language l) and a consonant node $v_c \in V_C$ (representing the consonant c) iff the consonant c is present in the inventory of the language l. This network is called the **P**honeme-**La**nguage **Net**work or **PlaNet** and represent the connections between the language and the consonant nodes through a 0-1 matrix $\mathbf{A}$ as shown by a hypothetical example in Fig. 1. Further, in (Mukherjee et al., 2007), the authors define the **Pho**neme-Phoneme **Net**work or **PhoNet** as the one-mode projection of PlaNet onto the consonant nodes, i.e., a network $G = \langle V_C, E_{cc'} \rangle$, where the nodes are the consonants and two nodes v_c and $v_{c'}$ are linked by an edge with weight equal to the number of languages in which both c and c' occur together. In other words, PhoNet can be expressed as a matrix $\mathbf{B}$ (see Fig. 1) such that $\mathbf{B} = \mathbf{A}\mathbf{A}^{\mathrm{T}} - \mathbf{D}$ where $\mathbf{D}$ is a diagonal matrix with its entries corresponding to the frequency of occurrence of the consonants. Similarly, we can also construct the one-mode projection of PlaNet onto the language nodes (which we shall refer to as the Language-Language Graph or LangGraph) can be expressed as $\mathbf{B}' = \mathbf{A}^{\mathrm{T}}\mathbf{A} - \mathbf{D}'$, where $\mathbf{D}'$ is a diagonal matrix with its entries corresponding to the size of the consonant inventories for each language.

The matrix $\mathbf{A}$ and hence, $\mathbf{B}$ and $\mathbf{B}'$ have been constructed from the UCLA Phonological Segment Inventory Database (UPSID) (Maddieson, 1984) that hosts the consonant inventories of 317 languages with a total of 541 consonants found across them. Note that, UPSID uses articulatory features to describe the consonants and assumes these features to be binary-valued, which in turn implies that every consonant can be represented by a binary vector. Later on, we shall use this representation for our experiments.

By construction, we have $|V_L| = 317$, $|V_C| = 541$, $|E_{lc}| = 7022$, and $|E_{cc'}| = 30412$. Consequently, the order of the matrix $\mathbf{A}$ is 541×317 and that of the matrix $\mathbf{B}'$ is 541×541. It has been found that the degree distribution of both PlaNet and PhoNet roughly indicate a power-law behavior with exponential cut-offs towards the tail (Choudhury et al., 2006; Mukherjee et al., 2007). Furthermore, PhoNet is also characterized by a very high clustering coefficient. The topological properties of the two networks and the generative model explaining the emergence of these properties are summarized in (Mukherjee et al., 2008). However, all the above properties are useful in characterizing the local patterns of the network and provide very little insight about its global structure.

4 Spectral Analysis of PhoNet

In this section we describe the procedure and results of the spectral analysis of PhoNet. We begin with computation of the spectrum of PhoNet. After the analysis of the spectrum, we systematically investigate the top few eigenvectors of PhoNet and attempt to characterize their linguistic significance. In the process, we also analyze the corresponding eigenvectors of LanGraph that helps us in characterizing the properties of languages.

4.1 Spectrum of PhoNet

Using a simple Matlab script we compute the spectrum (i.e., the list of eignevalues along with their multiplicities) of the matrix $\mathbf{B}$ corresponding to PhoNet. Fig. 2(a) shows the spectral plot, which has been obtained through *binning*[3] with a fixed bin size of 20. In order to have a better visualization of the spectrum, in Figs. 2(b) and (c) we further plot the top 50 (absolute) eigenvalues from the two ends of the spectrum versus the index representing their sorted order in doubly-logarithmic scale. Some of the important observations that one can make from these results are as follows.

First, the major bulk of the eigenvalues are concentrated at around 0. This indicates that though the order of $\mathbf{B}$ is 541×541, its numerical rank is quite low. Second, there are at least a few very large eigenvalues that dominate the entire spectrum. In fact, 89% of the spectrum, or the square of the Frobenius norm, is occupied by the principal (i.e., the topmost) eigenvalue, 92% is occupied by the first and the second eigenvalues taken together, while 93% is occupied by the first three taken together. The individual contribution of the other eigenvalues to the spectrum is significantly lower than that of the top three. Third, the eigenvalues on either ends of the spectrum tend to decay gradually, mostly indicating a power-law behavior. The power-law exponents at the positive and the negative ends are -1.33 (the R^2 value of the fit is 0.98) and -0.88 ($R^2 \sim 0.92$) respectively.

The numerically low rank of PhoNet suggests that there are certain prototypical structures that frequently repeat themselves across the consonant inventories, thereby, increasing the number of 0 eigenvalues to a large extent. In other words, all the rows of the matrix $\mathbf{B}$ (i.e., the inventories) can be expressed as the linear combination of a few independent row vectors, also known as *factors*.

Furthermore, the fact that the principal eigenvalue constitutes 89% of the Frobenius norm of the spectrum implies that there exist one very strong organizing principle which should be able to explain the basic structure of the inventories to a very good extent. Since the second and third eigenvalues are also significantly larger than the rest of the eigenvalues, one should expect two other organizing principles, which along with the basic principle, should be able to explain, (almost) completely, the structure of the inventories. In order to "discover" these principles, we now focus our attention to the first three eigenvectors of PhoNet.

4.2 The First Eigenvector of PhoNet

Fig. 2(d) shows the first eigenvector component for each consonant node versus its frequency of occurrence across the language inventories (i.e., its degree in PlaNet). The figure clearly indicates that the two are highly correlated ($r = 0.99$), which in turn means that 89% of the spectrum and hence, the organization of the consonant inventories, can be explained to a large extent by the occurrence frequency of the consonants. The question arises: Does this tell us something special about the structure of PhoNet or is it always the case for any symmetric matrix that the principal eigenvector will

[3] Binning is the process of dividing the entire range of a variable into smaller intervals and counting the number of observations within each bin or interval. In fixed binning, all the intervals are of the same size.

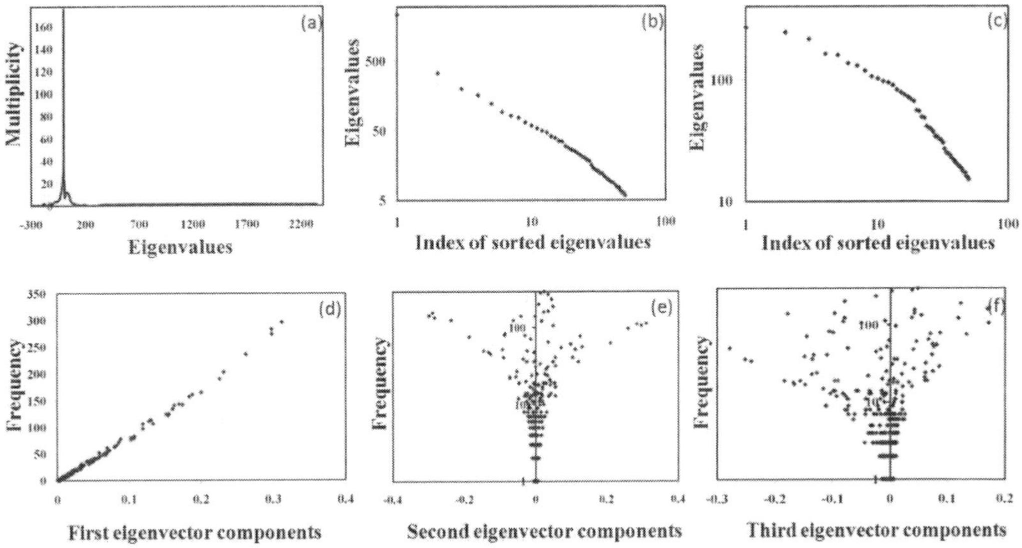

Figure 2: Eigenvalues and eigenvectors of **B**. (a) Binned distribution of the eigenvalues (bin size = 20) versus their multiplicities. (b) the top 50 (absolute) eigenvalues from the positive end of the spectrum and their ranks. (c) Same as (b) for the negative end of the spectrum. (d), (e) and (f) respectively represents the first, second and the third eigenvector components versus the occurrence frequency of the consonants.

be highly correlated with the frequency? We assert that the former is true, and indeed, the high correlation between the principal eigenvector and the frequency indicates high "proportionate co-occurrence" - a term which we will explain.

To see this, consider the following $2n \times 2n$ matrix $\mathbf{X}$

$$\mathbf{X} = \begin{pmatrix} 0 & M_1 & 0 & 0 & 0 & \dots \\ M_1 & 0 & 0 & 0 & 0 & \dots \\ 0 & 0 & 0 & M_2 & 0 & \dots \\ 0 & 0 & M_2 & 0 & 0 & \dots \\ \vdots & \vdots & \vdots & \vdots & \vdots & \ddots \end{pmatrix}$$

where $X_{i,i+1} = X_{i+1,i} = M_{(i+1)/2}$ for all odd i and 0 elsewhere. Also, $M_1 > M_2 > \ldots > M_n \geq 1$. Essentially, this matrix represents a graph which is a collection of n disconnected edges, each having weights M_1, M_2, and so on. It is easy to see that the principal eigenvector of this matrix is $(1/\sqrt{2}, 1/\sqrt{2}, 0, 0, \ldots, 0)^\top$, which of course is very different from the frequency vector: $(M_1, M_1, M_2, M_2, \ldots, M_n, M_n)^\top$.

At the other extreme, consider an $n \times n$ matrix $\mathbf{X}$ with $X_{i,j} = Cf_i f_j$ for some vector $\mathbf{f} = (f_1, f_2, \ldots f_n)^\top$ that represents the frequency of the nodes and a normalization constant C. This is what we refer to as "proportionate co-occurrence" because the extent of co-occurrence between the nodes i and j (which is $X_{i,j}$ or the weight of the edge between i and j) is exactly proportionate to the frequencies of the two nodes. The principal eigenvector in this case is $\mathbf{f}$ itself, and thus, correlates perfectly with the frequencies. Unlike this hypothetical matrix $\mathbf{X}$, PhoNet has all 0 entries in the diagonal. Nevertheless, this perturbation, which is equivalent to subtracting f_i^2 from the ith diagonal, seems to be sufficiently small to preserve the "proportionate co-occurrence" behavior of the adjacency matrix thereby resulting into a high correlation between the principal eigenvector component and the frequencies.

On the other hand, to construct the Laplacian matrix, we would have subtracted $f_i \sum_{j=1}^{n} f_j$ from the ith diagonal entry, which is a much larger quantity than f_i^2. In fact, this operation would have completely destroyed the correlation between the frequency and the principal eigenvector component because the eigenvector corresponding to the smallest[4] eigenvalue of the Laplacian matrix is $[1, 1, \ldots, 1]^\top$.

Since the first eigenvector of **B** is perfectly cor-

[4]The role played by the top eigenvalues and eigenvectors in the spectral analysis of the adjacency matrix is comparable to that of the smallest eigenvalues and the corresponding eigenvectors of the Laplacian matrix (Chung, 1994)

related with the frequency of occurrence of the consonants across languages it is reasonable to argue that there is a universally observed innate preference towards certain consonants. This preference is often described through the linguistic concept of *markedness*, which in the context of phonology tells us that the substantive conditions that underlie the human capacity of speech production and perception renders certain consonants more favorable to be included in the inventory than some other consonants (Clements, 2008). We observe that markedness plays a very important role in shaping the global structure of the consonant inventories. In fact, if we arrange the consonants in a non-increasing order of the first eigenvector components (which is equivalent to increasing order of statistical markedness), and compare the set of consonants present in an inventory of size s with that of the first s entries from this hierarchy, we find that the two are, on an average, more than 50% similar. This figure is surprisingly high because, in spite of the fact that $\forall_s\ s \ll \frac{541}{2}$, on an average $\frac{s}{2}$ consonants in an inventory are drawn from the first s entries of the markedness hierarchy (a small set), whereas the rest $\frac{s}{2}$ are drawn from the remaining $(541 - s)$ entries (a much larger set).

The high degree of proportionate co-occurrence in PhoNet implied by this high correlation between the principal eigenvector and frequency further indicates that the innate preference towards certain phonemes is independent of the presence of other phonemes in the inventory of a language.

4.3 The Second Eigenvector of PhoNet

Fig. 2(e) shows the second eigenvector component for each node versus their occurrence frequency. It is evident from the figure that the consonants have been clustered into three groups. Those that have a very low or a very high frequency club around 0 whereas, the medium frequency zone has clearly split into two parts. In order to investigate the basis for this split we carry out the following experiment.

Experiment I

(i) Remove all consonants whose frequency of occurrence across the inventories is very low (< 5).

(ii) Denote the absolute maximum value of the positive component of the second eigenvector as MAX_+ and the absolute maximum value of the negative component as MAX_-. If the absolute value of a positive component is less than 15% of MAX_+ then assign a *neutral* class to the corresponding consonant; else assign it a *positive* class. Denote the set of consonants in the *positive* class by C_+. Similarly, if the absolute value of a negative component is less than 15% of MAX_- then assign a *neutral* class to the corresponding consonant; else assign it a *negative* class. Denote the set of consonants in the *negative* class by C_-.

(iii) Using the above training set of the classified consonants (represented as boolean feature vectors) learn a decision tree (C4.5 algorithm (Quinlan, 1993)) to determine the features that are responsible for the split of the medium frequency zone into the *negative* and the *positive* classes.

Fig. 3(a) shows the decision rules learnt from the above training set. It is clear from these rules that the split into C_- and C_+ has taken place mainly based on whether the consonants have the combined "dental_alveolar" feature (*negative* class) or the "dental" and the "alveolar" features separately (*positive* class). Such a combined feature is often termed *ambiguous* and its presence in a particular consonant c of a language l indicates that the speakers of l are unable to make a distinction as to whether c is articulated with the tongue against the upper teeth or the alveolar ridge. In contrast, if the features are present separately then the speakers are capable of making this distinction. In fact, through the following experiment, we find that the consonant inventories of almost all the languages in UPSID get classified based on whether they preserve this distinction or not.

Experiment II

(i) Construct $\mathbf{B}' = \mathbf{A}^T\mathbf{A} - \mathbf{D}'$ (i.e., the adjacency matrix of LangGraph).

(ii) Compute the second eigenvector of $\mathbf{B}'$. Once again, the positive and the negative components split the languages into two distinct groups L_+ and L_- respectively.

(iii) For each language $l \in L_+$ count the number of consonants in C_+ that occur in l. Sum up the counts for all the languages in L_+ and normalize this sum by $|L_+||C_+|$. Similarly, perform the same step for the pairs (L_+,C_-), (L_-,C_+) and (L_-,C_-).

From the above experiment, the values obtained for the pairs (i) (L_+,C_+), (L_+,C_-) are 0.35, 0.08 respectively, and (ii) (L_-,C_+), (L_-,C_-) are 0.07, 0.32 respectively. This immediately implies that almost all the languages in L_+ preserve the dental/alveolar distinction while those in L_- do not.

Rules from second eigenvector: (a)

Rule 1: *if* alveolar = *true* AND voiced = *false*
→ class = *positive*
OR
Rule 2: *if* aspirated = *false* AND dental = *true* AND plosive = *true*
→ class = *positive*
OR
Rule 3: *if* aspirated = *false* AND palatal = *true* AND plosive = *true*
→ class = *positive*

Rule 1: *if* dental_alveolar = *true* AND long = *false* AND laryngealized = *false* AND palatalized = *false*
→ class = *negative*

Rules from third eigenvector: (b)

Rule 1: *if* alveolar = *false* AND aspirated = *false* AND labialized = *false* AND long = *false* AND palatalized = *false* AND palato_alveolar = *false* AND plosive = *true* AND uvular = *false* AND voiceless = *true*
→ class *positive*
OR
Rule 2: *if* labialized = *false* AND laryngealized = *false* AND palatalized = *false* AND plosive = *true* AND prenasalized = *false* AND uvular = *false* AND voiced = *true*
→ class *positive*
OR
Rule 3: *if* labialized = *false* AND labial_velar = *false* AND laryngealized = *false* AND long = *false* AND nasal = *true* AND palatalized = *false* AND voiceless = *false*
→ class *positive*
OR
Rule 4: *if* approximant = *true* AND retroflex = *true*
→ class *positive*

Rule 1: *if* alveolar = *true* AND voiceless = *true*
→ class *negative*
OR
Rule 2: *if* ejective = *true*
→ class *negative*
OR
Rule 3: *if* labialized = *true*
→ class *negative*
OR
Rule 4: *if* plosive = *true* AND uvular = *true*
→ class *negative*
OR
Rule 5: *if* aspirated = *true* AND dental = *false* AND retroflex = *false*
→ class *negative*
OR
Rule 6: *if* laryngealized = *true*
→ class *negative*
OR
Rule 7: *if* lateral = *true* AND voiceless = *true*
→ class *negative*
OR
Rule 8: if glottal = *true*
→ class *negative*

Figure 3: Decision rules obtained from the study of (a) the second, and (b) the third eigenvectors. The classification errors for both (a) and (b) are less than 15%.

4.4 The Third Eigenvector of PhoNet

We next investigate the relationship between the third eigenvector components of **B** and the occurrence frequency of the consonants (Fig. 2(f)). The consonants are once again found to get clustered into three groups, though not as clearly as in the previous case. Therefore, in order to determine the basis of the split, we repeat experiments I and II. Fig. 3(b) clearly indicates that in this case the consonants in C_+ lack the complex features that are considered difficult for articulation. On the other hand, the consonants in C_- are mostly composed of such complex features. The values obtained for the pairs (i) (L_+,C_+), (L_+,C_-) are 0.34, 0.06 respectively, and (ii) (L_-,C_+), (L_-,C_-) are 0.19, 0.18 respectively. This implies that while there is a prevalence of the consonants from C_+ in the languages of L_+, the consonants from C_- are almost absent. However, there is an equal prevalence of the consonants from C_+ and C_- in the languages of L_-. Therefore, it can be argued that the presence of the consonants from C_- in a language can (phonologically) imply the presence of the consonants from C_+, but not vice versa. We do not find any such aforementioned pattern for the fourth and the higher eigenvector components.

4.5 Control Experiment

As a control experiment we generated a set of random inventories and carried out the experiments I and II on the adjacency matrix, $\mathbf{B_R}$, of the random version of PhoNet. We construct these inventories as follows. Let the frequency of occurrence for each consonant c in UPSID be denoted by f_c. Let there be 317 bins each corresponding to a language in UPSID. f_c bins are then chosen uniformly at random and the consonant c is packed into these bins. Thus the consonant inventories of the 317 languages corresponding to the bins are generated. Note that this method of inventory construction leads to proportionate co-occurrence. Consequently, the first eigenvector components of $\mathbf{B_R}$ are highly correlated to the occurrence frequency of the consonants. However, the plots of the second and the third eigenvector components versus the occurrence frequency of the consonants indicate absolutely no pattern thereby, resulting in a large number of decision rules and very high classification errors (upto 50%).

5 Discussion and Conclusion

Are there any linguistic inferences that can be drawn from the results obtained through the study of the spectral plot and the eigenvectors of PhoNet? In fact, one can correlate several phonological theories to the aforementioned observations, which have been construed by the past researchers through very specific studies.

One of the most important problems in defining a feature-based classificatory system is to decide when a sound in one language is different from a similar sound in another language. According to Ladefoged (2005) "two sounds in different languages should be considered as distinct if we can point to a third language in which the same two sounds distinguish words". The dental versus alveolar distinction that we find to be highly instrumental in splitting the world's languages into two different groups (i.e., L_+ and L_- obtained from the analysis of the second eigenvectors of $\mathbf{B}$ and $\mathbf{B}'$) also has a strong classificatory basis. It may well be the case that certain categories of sounds like the dental and the alveolar sibilants are not sufficiently distinct to constitute a reliable linguistic contrast (see (Ladefoged, 2005) for reference). Nevertheless, by allowing the possibility for the dental versus alveolar distinction, one does not increase the complexity or introduce any redundancy in the classificatory system. This is because, such a distinction is prevalent in many other sounds, some of which are (a) nasals in Tamil (Shanmugam, 1972) and Malayalam (Shanmugam, 1972; Ladefoged and Maddieson, 1996), (b) laterals in Albanian (Ladefoged and Maddieson, 1996), and (c) stops in certain dialectal variations of Swahili (Hayward et al., 1989). Therefore, it is sensible to conclude that the two distinct groups L_+ and L_- induced by our algorithm are true representatives of two important linguistic typologies.

The results obtained from the analysis of the third eigenvectors of $\mathbf{B}$ and $\mathbf{B}'$ indicate that implicational universals also play a crucial role in determining linguistic typologies. The two typologies that are predominant in this case consist of (a) languages using only those sounds that have simple features (e.g., plosives), and (b) languages using sounds with complex features (e.g., lateral, ejectives, and fricatives) that automatically imply the presence of the sounds having simple features. The distinction between the simple and complex phonological features is a very common hypothesis underlying the implicational hierarchy and the corresponding typological classification (Clements, 2008). In this context, Locke and Pearson (1992) remark that "Infants heavily favor stop consonants over fricatives, and there are languages that have stops and no fricatives but no languages that exemplify the reverse pattern. [Such] 'phonologically universal' patterns, which cut across languages and speakers are, in fact, the phonetic properties of Homo sapiens." (as quoted in (Vallee et al., 2002)).

Therefore, it turns out that the methodology presented here essentially facilitates the induction of linguistic typologies. Indeed, spectral analysis derives, in a unified way, the importance of these principles and at the same time quantifies their applicability in explaining the structural patterns observed across the inventories. In this context, there are at least two other novelties of this work. The first novelty is in the systematic study of the spectral plots (i.e., the distribution of the eigenvalues), which is in general rare for linguistic networks, although there have been quite a number of such studies in the domain of biological and social networks (Farkas et al., 2001; Gkantsidis et al., 2003; Banerjee and Jost, 2007). The second novelty is in the fact that there is not much work in the complex network literature that investigates the nature of the eigenvectors and their interactions to infer the organizing principles of the system represented through the network.

To summarize, spectral analysis of the complex network of speech sounds is able to provide a holistic as well as quantitative explanation of the organizing principles of the sound inventories. This scheme for typology induction is not dependent on the specific data set used as long as it is representative of the real world. Thus, we believe that the scheme introduced here can be applied as a generic technique for typological classifications of phonological, syntactic and semantic networks; each of these are equally interesting from the perspective of understanding the structure and evolution of human language, and are topics of future research.

Acknowledgement

We would like to thank Kalika Bali for her valuable inputs towards the linguistic analysis.

References

A. Banerjee and J. Jost. 2007. Spectral plots and the representation and interpretation of biological data. *Theory in Biosciences*, 126(1):15–21.

A. Banerjee and J. Jost. to appear. Graph spectra as a systematic tool in computational biology. *Discrete Applied Mathematics*.

M. Belkin and J. Goldsmith. 2002. Using eigenvectors of the bigram graph to infer morpheme identity. In *Proceedings of the ACL-02 Workshop on Morphological and Phonological Learning*, pages 41–47. Association for Computational Linguistics.

P. Boersma. 1998. *Functional Phonology*. The Hague: Holland Academic Graphics.

M. Choudhury and A. Mukherjee. to appear. The structure and dynamics of linguistic networks. In N. Ganguly, A. Deutsch, and A. Mukherjee, editors, *Dynamics on and of Complex Networks: Applications to Biology, Computer Science, Economics, and the Social Sciences*. Birkhauser.

M. Choudhury, A. Mukherjee, A. Basu, and N. Ganguly. 2006. Analysis and synthesis of the distribution of consonants over languages: A complex network approach. In *COLING-ACL'06*, pages 128–135.

F. R. K. Chung. 1994. *Spectral Graph Theory*. Number 2 in CBMS Regional Conference Series in Mathematics. American Mathematical Society.

G. N. Clements. 2008. The role of features in speech sound inventories. In E. Raimy and C. Cairns, editors, *Contemporary Views on Architecture and Representations in Phonological Theory*. Cambridge, MA: MIT Press.

E. J. Farkas, I. Derenyi, A. -L. Barabási, and T. Vicseck. 2001. Real-world graphs: Beyond the semicircle law. *Phy. Rev. E*, 64:026704.

R. Ferrer-i-Cancho. 2005. The structure of syntactic dependency networks: Insights from recent advances in network theory. In Levickij V. and Altmman G., editors, *Problems of quantitative linguistics*, pages 60–75.

C. Gkantsidis, M. Mihail, and E. Zegura. 2003. Spectral analysis of internet topologies. In *INFOCOM'03*, pages 364–374.

K. M. Hayward, Y. A. Omar, and M. Goesche. 1989. Dental and alveolar stops in Kimvita Swahili: An electropalatographic study. *African Languages and Cultures*, 2(1):51–72.

R. Kannan and S. Vempala. 2008. *Spectral Algorithms*. Course Lecture Notes: http://www.cc.gatech.edu/~vempala/spectral/spectral.pdf.

P. Ladefoged and I. Maddieson. 1996. *Sounds of the Worlds Languages*. Oxford: Blackwell.

P. Ladefoged. 2005. Features and parameters for different purposes. In *Working Papers in Phonetics*, volume 104, pages 1–13. Dept. of Linguistics, UCLA.

B. Lindblom and I. Maddieson. 1988. Phonetic universals in consonant systems. In M. Hyman and C. N. Li, editors, *Language, Speech, and Mind*, pages 62–78.

J. L. Locke and D. M. Pearson. 1992. Vocal learning and the emergence of phonological capacity. A neurobiological approach. In *Phonological development. Models, Research, Implications*, pages 91–129. York Press.

I. Maddieson. 1984. *Patterns of Sounds*. Cambridge University Press.

A. Mukherjee, M. Choudhury, A. Basu, and N. Ganguly. 2007. Modeling the co-occurrence principles of the consonant inventories: A complex network approach. *Int. Jour. of Mod. Phys. C*, 18(2):281–295.

A. Mukherjee, M. Choudhury, A. Basu, and N. Ganguly. 2008. Modeling the structure and dynamics of the consonant inventories: A complex network approach. In *COLING-08*, pages 601–608.

J. R. Quinlan. 1993. *C4.5: Programs for Machine Learning*. Morgan Kaufmann.

S. V. Shanmugam. 1972. Dental and alveolar nasals in Dravidian. In *Bulletin of the School of Oriental and African Studies*, volume 35, pages 74–84. University of London.

M. Sigman and G. A. Cecchi. 2002. Global organization of the wordnet lexicon. *Proceedings of the National Academy of Science*, 99(3):1742–1747.

N. Trubetzkoy. 1931. Die phonologischen systeme. *TCLP*, 4:96–116.

N. Trubetzkoy. 1969. *Principles of Phonology*. University of California Press, Berkeley.

N. Vallee, L J Boe, J. L. Schwartz, P. Badin, and C. Abry. 2002. The weight of phonetic substance in the structure of sound inventories. *ZASPiL*, 28:145–168.

Using Cycles and Quasi-Cycles to Disambiguate Dictionary Glosses

Roberto Navigli
Dipartimento di Informatica
Sapienza - Università di Roma
Via Salaria, 113 - 00198 Roma Italy
navigli@di.uniroma1.it

Abstract

We present a novel graph-based algorithm for the automated disambiguation of glosses in lexical knowledge resources. A dictionary graph is built starting from senses (vertices) and explicit or implicit relations in the dictionary (edges). The approach is based on the identification of edge sequences which constitute cycles in the dictionary graph (possibly with one edge reversed) and relate a source to a target word sense. Experiments are performed on the disambiguation of ambiguous words in the glosses of WordNet and two machine-readable dictionaries.

1 Introduction

In the last two decades, we have witnessed an increasing availability of wide-coverage lexical knowledge resources in electronic format, most notably thesauri (such as Roget's Thesaurus (Roget, 1911), the Macquarie Thesaurus (Bernard, 1986), etc.), machine-readable dictionaries (e.g., the Longman Dictionary of Contemporary English (Proctor, 1978)), computational lexicons (e.g. WordNet (Fellbaum, 1998)), etc.

The information contained in such resources comprises (depending on their kind) sense inventories, paradigmatic relations (e.g. $flesh_n^3$ is a kind of *plant tissue*$_n^1$),[1] text definitions (e.g. $flesh_n^3$ is defined as "a soft moist part of a fruit"), usage examples, and so on.

Unfortunately, not all the semantics are made explicit within lexical resources. Even WordNet, the most widespread computational lexicon of English, provides explanatory information in the form of textual glosses, i.e. strings of text which explain the meaning of concepts in terms of possibly ambiguous words.

Moreover, while computational lexicons like WordNet contain semantically explicit information such as, among others, *hypernymy* and *meronymy* relations, most thesauri, glossaries, and machine-readable dictionaries are often just electronic transcriptions of their paper counterparts. As a result, for each entry (e.g. a word sense or thesaurus entry) they mostly provide implicit information in the form of free text.

The production of semantically richer lexical resources can help alleviate the knowledge acquisition bottleneck and potentially enable advanced Natural Language Processing applications (Cuadros and Rigau, 2006). However, in order to reduce the high cost of manual annotation (Edmonds, 2000), and to avoid the repetition of this effort for each knowledge resource, this task must be supported by wide-coverage automated techniques which do not rely on the specific resource at hand.

In this paper, we aim to make explicit large quantities of semantic information implicitly contained in the glosses of existing wide-coverage lexical knowledge resources (specifically, machine-readable dictionaries and computational lexicons). To this end, we present a method for Gloss Word Sense Disambiguation (WSD), called the Cycles and Quasi-Cycles (CQC) algorithm. The algorithm is based on a novel notion of cycles in the dictionary graph (possibly with one edge reversed) which support a disambiguation choice. First, a dictionary graph is built from the input lexical knowledge resource. Next, the method explicitly disambiguates the information associated with sense entries (i.e. gloss words) by associating senses for which the richest sets of paths can be found in the dictionary graph.

In Section 2, we provide basic definitions, present the gloss disambiguation algorithm, and il-

[1] We denote as w_p^i the ith sense in a reference dictionary of a word w with part of speech p.

Proceedings of the 12th Conference of the European Chapter of the ACL, pages 594–602,
Athens, Greece, 30 March – 3 April 2009.

lustrate the approach with an example. In Section 3, we present a set of experiments performed on a variety of lexical knowledge resources, namely WordNet and two machine-readable dictionaries. Results are discussed in Section 4, and related work is presented in Section 5. We give our conclusions in Section 6.

2 Approach

2.1 Definitions

Given a dictionary D, we define a **dictionary graph** as a directed graph $G = (V, E)$ whose vertices V are the word senses in the sense inventory of D and whose set of unlabeled edges E is obtained as follows:

i) Initially, $E := \emptyset$;

ii) For each sense $s \in V$, and for each lexico-semantic relation in D connecting sense s to $s' \in V$, we perform: $E := E \cup \{(s, s')\}$;

iii) For each sense $s \in V$, let $gloss(s)$ be the set of content words in its part-of-speech tagged gloss. Then for each content word w' in $gloss(s)$ and for each sense s' of w', we add the corresponding edge to the dictionary graph, i.e.: $E := E \cup \{(s, s')\}$.

For instance, consider WordNet as our input dictionary D. As a result of step (ii), given the semantic relation "$sport^1_n$ is a hypernym of $racing^1_n$", the edge ($racing^1_n$, $sport^1_n$) is added to E (similarly, an inverse edge is added due to the hyponymy relation holding between $sport^1_n$ and $racing^1_n$). During step (iii), the gloss of $racing^1_n$ "the sport of engaging in contests of speed" is part-of-speech tagged, obtaining the following set of content words: { $sport_n$, $engage_v$, $contest_n$, $speed_n$ }. The following edges are then added to E: { ($racing^1_n$, $sport^1_n$), ($racing^1_n$, $sport^2_n$), ..., ($racing^1_n$, $sport^6_n$), ..., ($racing^1_n$, $speed^1_n$), ..., ($racing^1_n$, $speed^5_n$) }. The above steps are performed for all the senses in V.

We now recall the definition of **graph cycle**. A cycle in a graph G is a sequence of edges of G that forms a path $v_1 \rightarrow v_2 \rightarrow \cdots \rightarrow v_n$ ($v_i \in V$) such that the first vertex of the path corresponds to the last, i.e. $v_1 = v_n$ (Cormen et al., 1990, p. 88). For example, the cycle in Figure 1(a) is given by the path $racing^1_n \rightarrow contest^1_n \rightarrow race^3_n \rightarrow run^3_n \rightarrow racing^1_n$ in the WordNet dictionary graph. In fact

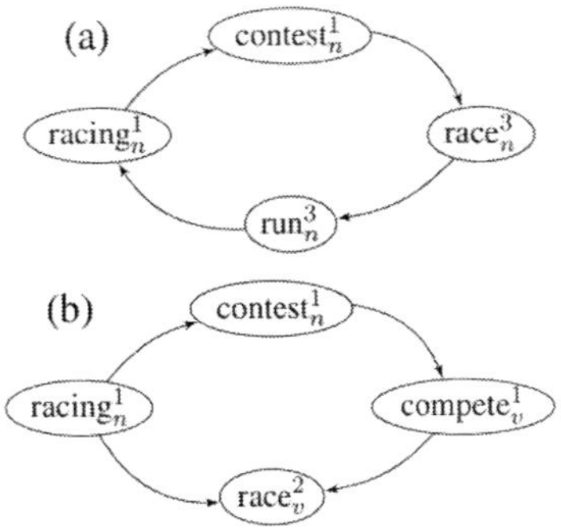

Figure 1: An example of cycle (a) and quasi-cycle (b) in WordNet.

$contest_n$ occurs in the gloss of $racing^1_n$, $race^3_n$ is a hyponym of $contest^1_n$, and so on.

We further provide the definition of **quasi-cycle** as a sequence of edges in which the reversal of the orientation of a single edge creates a cycle (Bohman and Thoma, 2000). For instance, the quasi-cycle in Figure 1(b) is given by the path $racing^1_n \rightarrow contest^1_n \rightarrow compete^1_v \rightarrow race^2_v \leftarrow racing^1_n$. In fact, the reversal of the edge ($racing^1_n$, $race^2_v$) creates a cycle.

Finally, we call a path a (quasi-)cycle if it is either a cycle or a quasi-cycle. Further, we say that a path is (quasi-)cyclic if it forms a (quasi-)cycle in the graph.

2.2 The CQC Algorithm

Given a dictionary graph $G = (V, E)$ built as described in the previous section, our objective is to disambiguate dictionary glosses with the support of (quasi-)cycles. (Quasi-)cyclic paths are intuitively better than unconstrained paths as each sense choice s is reinforced by the very fact of s being reachable from itself through a sequence of other senses.

Let $a(s)$ be the set of ambiguous words to be disambiguated in the part-of-speech tagged gloss of sense s. Given a word $w' \in a(s)$, our aim is to disambiguate w' according to the sense inventory of D, i.e. to assign it the right sense chosen from its set of senses $Senses(w')$. To this end, we propose the use of a graph-based algorithm which searches the dictionary graph and collects the following kinds of (quasi-)cyclic paths:

i) $s \rightarrow s' \rightarrow s_1 \rightarrow \cdots \rightarrow s_{n-2} \rightarrow s$ (cycle)

ii) $s \rightarrow s' \rightarrow s_1 \rightarrow \cdots \rightarrow s_{n-2} \leftarrow s$ (quasi-cycle)

	CQC-Algorithm(s, w')
1	**for each** sense $s' \in Senses(w')$
2	$\quad CQC(s') :=$ DFS(s', s)
3	$All\_CQC := \bigcup_{s' \in Senses(w')} CQC(s')$
4	**for each** sense $s' \in Senses(w')$
5	$\quad score(s') := 0$
6	$\quad$ **for each** path $c \in CQC(s')$
7	$\quad\quad l := length(c)$
8	$\quad\quad v := \omega(l) \cdot \frac{1}{NumCQC(All\_CQC, l)}$
9	$\quad\quad score(s') := score(s') + v$
10	**return** $\underset{s' \in Senses(w')}{\text{argmax}}\ score(s')$

Table 1: The Cycles and Quasi-Cycles (CQC) algorithm in pseudocode.

where s is our source sense, s' is a candidate sense of $w' \in gloss(s)$, s_i is a sense in V, and n is the length of the path (given by the number of its edges). We note that both kinds of paths start and end with the same vertex s, and that we restrict quasi-cycles to those whose inverted edge departs from s. To avoid any redundancy, we require that no vertex is repeated in the path aside from the start/end vertex (i.e. $s \neq s' \neq s_i \neq s_j$ for any $i, j \in \{1, \ldots, n-2\}$).

The Cycles and Quasi-Cycles (CQC) algorithm, reported in pseudo-code in Table 1, takes as input a source sense s and a target word w' (in our setting[2] $w' \in a(s)$). It consists of two main phases.

During steps 1-3, cycles and quasi-cycles are sought for each sense of w'. This step is performed with a depth-first search (DFS, cf. (Cormen et al., 1990, pp. 477–479)) up to a depth δ. To this end, we first define $next(s) = \{s'' : (s, s'') \in E\}$, that is the set of senses which can be directly reached from sense s. The DFS starts from a sense $s' \in Senses(w')$, and recursively explores the senses in $next(s')$ until sense s or a sense in $next(s)$ is encountered, obtaining a cycle or a quasi-cycle, respectively. For each sense s' of w' the DFS returns the full set $CQC(s')$ of (quasi-)cyclic paths collected. Note that the DFS recursively keeps track of previously visited senses, so as to discard (quasi-)cycles including the same sense twice. Finally, in step 3, *All_CQC* is set to store the cycles and quasi-cycles for all the senses of w'.

[2]Note that potentially w' can be any word of interest. The very same algorithm can be applied to determine semantic similarity or to disambiguate collocations.

The second phase (steps 4-10) computes a score for each sense s' of w' based on the paths collected for s' during the first phase. Let c be such a path, and let l be its length, i.e. the number of edges in the path. Then the contribution of c to the score of s' is given by a function of its length $\omega(l)$, which associates with l a number between 0 and 1. This contribution is normalized by a factor given by $NumCQC(All\_CQC, l)$, which calculates the overall number of paths of length l. In this work, we will employ the function $\omega(l) = 1/e^l$, which weighs a path with the inverse of the exponential of its length (so as to exponentially decrease the contribution of longer paths)[3]. Steps 4-9 are repeated for each candidate sense of w'. Finally, step 10 returns the highest-scoring sense of w'.

As a result of the systematic application of the CQC algorithm to the dictionary graph $G = (V, E)$ associated with a dictionary D, a graph $\hat{G} = (V, \hat{E})$ is output, where V is again the sense inventory of D, and $\hat{E} \subseteq E$, such that each edge $(s, s') \in \hat{E}$ either represents an unambiguous relation in E (i.e. it was either a lexico-semantic relation in D or a relation between s and a monosemous word occurring in its gloss) or is the result of an execution of the CQC algorithm with input s and $w' \in a(s)$.

2.3 An Example

Consider the following example: WordNet defines the third sense of $flesh_n$ as "a soft moist part of a fruit". As a result of part-of-speech tagging, we obtain:

$$gloss(flesh_n^3) = \{soft_a, moist_a, part_n, fruit_n\}$$

Let us assume we aim to disambiguate the noun *fruit*. Our call to the CQC algorithm in Table 1 is then *CQC-Algorithm*($flesh_n^3$, $fruit_n$).

As a result of the first two steps of the algorithm, a set of cycles and quasi-cycles for each sense of $fruit_n$ is collected, based on a DFS starting from the respective senses of our target word (we assume $\delta = 5$). In Figure 2, we show some of the (quasi-)cycles collected for senses #1 and #3 of $fruit_n$, respectively defined as "the ripened reproductive body of a seed plant" and "an amount of a product" (we neglect sense #2 as the length and number of its paths is not dissimilar from that of sense #3).

[3]Other weight functions, such as $\omega(l) = 1$ (which weighs each path independent of its length) proved to perform worse.

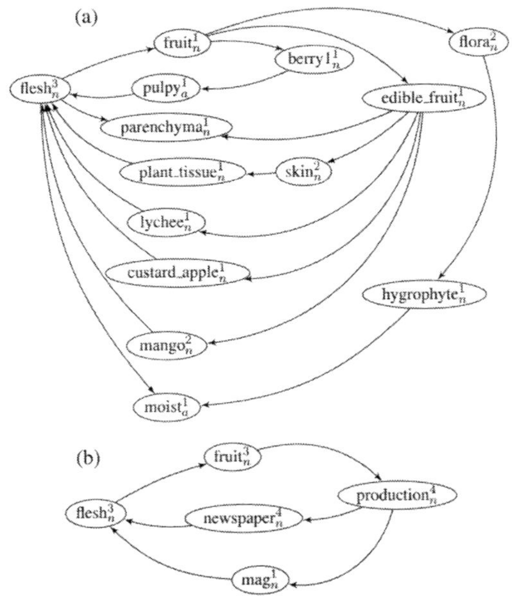

Figure 2: Some cycles and quasi-cycles connecting *flesh*^3_n to *fruit*^1_n (a), and *fruit*^3_n (b).

During the second phase of the algorithm, and for each sense of *fruit*$_n$, the contribution of each (quasi-)cycle is calculated (steps 6-9 of the algorithm). For example, for sense *fruit*^1_n in Figure 2(a), 5 (quasi-)cycles of length 4 and 2 of length 5 were returned by DFS(*fruit*^1_n, *flesh*^3_n). As a result, the following score is calculated:[4]

$$\begin{aligned} score(fruit^1_n) &= \frac{5}{e^4} \cdot \frac{1}{NumCQC(all\_chains,4)} \\ &\quad + \frac{2}{e^5} \cdot \frac{1}{NumCQC(all\_chains,5)} \\ &= \frac{5}{e^4 \cdot 7} + \frac{2}{e^5 \cdot 2} \\ &= 0.013 + 0.006 = 0.019 \end{aligned}$$

whereas for *fruit*^3_n (see Figure 2(b)) we get:

$$\begin{aligned} score(fruit^3_n) &= \frac{2}{e^4} \cdot \frac{1}{NumCQC(all\_chains,4)} \\ &= \frac{2}{e^4 \cdot 7} = 0.005 \end{aligned}$$

where $NumCQC(All\_CQC, l)$ is the total number of cycles and quasi-cycles of length l over all the senses of *fruit*$_n$ (according to Figure 2, this amounts to 7 paths for $l = 4$ and 2 paths for $l = 5$).

Finally, the sense with the highest score (i.e. *fruit*^1_n) is returned.

3 Experiments

To test and compare the performance of our algorithm, we performed a set of experiments on a variety of resources. First, we summarize the resources (Section 3.1) and algorithms (Section 3.2) that we adopted. In Section 3.3 we report our experimental results.

3.1 Resources

The following resources were used in our experiments:

- **WordNet** (Fellbaum, 1998), the most widespread computational lexicon of English. It encodes concepts as synsets, and provides textual glosses and lexico-semantic relations between synsets. Its latest version (3.0) contains around 155,000 lemmas, and over 200,000 word senses;

- **Macquarie Concise Dictionary** (Yallop, 2006), a machine-readable dictionary of (Australian) English, which includes around 50,000 lemmas and almost 120,000 word senses, for which it provides textual glosses and examples;

- **Ragazzini/Biagi Concise** (Ragazzini and Biagi, 2006), a bilingual English-Italian dictionary, containing over 90,000 lemmas and 150,000 word senses. The dictionary provides Italian translations for each English word sense, and vice versa.

We used TreeTagger (Schmid, 1997) to part-of-speech tag the glosses in the three resources.

3.2 Algorithms

Hereafter we briefly summarize the algorithms that we applied in our experiments:

- **CQC**: we applied the CQC algorithm as described in Section 2.2;

- **Cycles**, which applies the CQC algorithm but searches for cycles only (i.e. quasi-cycles are not collected);

- An adaptation of the **Lesk algorithm** (Lesk, 1986), which, given a source sense s of word w and a word w' occurring in the gloss of s, determines the right sense of w' as that which maximizes the (normalized) overlap between each sense s' of w' and s:

$$\operatorname*{argmax}_{s' \in Senses(w')} \frac{|next^*(s) \cap next^*(s')|}{\max\{|next^*(s)|, |next^*(s')|\}}$$

[4]Note that, for the sake of simplicity, we are calculating our scores based on the paths shown in Figure 2. However, we tried to respect the proportion of paths collected by the algorithm for the two senses.

where we define $next^*(s) = words(s) \cup next(s)$, and $words(s)$ is the set of lexicalizations of sense s (e.g. the synonyms in the synset s). When WordNet is our reference resource, we employ an extension of the Lesk algorithm, namely Extended Gloss Overlap (Banerjee and Pedersen, 2003), which extends the sense definition with words from the definitions of related senses (such as hypernyms, hyponyms, etc.). We use the same set of relations available in the authors' implementation of the algorithm.

We also compared the performance of the above algorithms with two standard baselines, namely the First Sense Baseline (abbreviated as FS BL) and the Random Baseline (Random BL).

3.3 Results

Our experiments concerned the disambiguation of the gloss words in three datasets, one for each resource, namely WordNet, Macquarie Concise, and Ragazzini/Biagi. In all datasets, given a sense s, our set $a(s)$ is given by the set of part-of-speech-tagged ambiguous content words in the gloss of sense s from our reference dictionary.

WordNet. When using WordNet as a reference resource, given a sense s whose gloss we aim to disambiguate, the dictionary graph includes not only edges connecting s to senses of gloss words (step (iii) of the graph construction procedure, cf. Section 2.1), but also those obtained from any of the WordNet lexico-semantics relations (step (ii)).

For WordNet gloss disambiguation, we employed the dataset used in the Senseval-3 Gloss WSD task (Litkowski, 2004), which contains 15,179 content words from 9,257 glosses[5]. We compared the performance of CQC, Cycles, Lesk, and the two baselines. To get full coverage and high performance, we learned a threshold for each system below which they recur to the FS heuristic. The threshold and maximum path length were tuned on a small in-house manually-annotated dataset of 100 glosses. The results are shown in Table 2. We also included in the table the performance of the best-ranking system in the Senseval-3 Gloss WSD task, namely the TALP system (Castillo et al., 2004).

Algorithm	Prec./Recall
CQC	64.25
Cycles	63.74
Lesk	51.75
TALP	68.60/68.30
FS BL	55.44
Random BL	26.29

Table 2: Gloss WSD performance on WordNet.

CQC outperforms all other proposed approaches, obtaining a 64.25% precision and recall. We note that Cycles also gets high performance, compared to Lesk and the baselines. Also, compared to CQC, the difference is not statistically significant. However, we observe that, if we do not recur to the first sense as a backoff strategy, we get a much lower recall for Cycles (P = 65.39, R = 26.70 for CQC, P = 72.03, R = 16.39 for Cycles).

CQC performs about 4 points below the TALP system. As also discussed later, we believe this result is relevant, given that our approach does not rely on additional knowledge resources, as TALP does (though both algorithms recur to the FS backoff strategy).

Finally, we observe that the FS baseline has lower performance than in typical all-words disambiguation settings (usually above 60% accuracy). We believe that this is due to the absence of monosemous words from the test set, and to the possibly different distribution of senses in the dataset.

Macquarie Concise. Automatically disambiguating glosses in a computational lexicon such as WordNet is certainly useful. However, disambiguating a machine-readable dictionary is an even more ambitious task. In fact, while computational lexicons typically encode some explicit semantic relations which can be used as an aid to the disambiguation task, machine-readable dictionaries only rarely provide sense-tagged information (often in the form of references to other word senses). As a result, in this latter setting the dictionary graph typically contains only edges obtained from the gloss words of sense s (step (iii), Section 2.1).

To experiment with machine-readable dictionaries, we employed the Macquarie Concise Dic-

[5]Recently, Princeton University released a richer corpus of disambiguated glosses, namely the "Princeton WordNet Gloss Corpus" (http://wordnet.princeton.edu). However, in order to allow for a comparison with the state of the art (see below), we decided to adopt the Senseval-3 dataset.

Algorithm	Prec./Recall
CQC	77.13
Cycles	67.63
Lesk	30.16
FS BL	51.48
Random BL	23.28

Table 3: Gloss WSD performance on Macquarie Concise.

Algorithm	Prec./Recall
CQC	89.34
Cycles	85.40
Lesk	63.89
FS BL	73.15
Random BL	51.69

Table 4: Gloss WSD performance on Ragazzini/Biagi.

tionary (Yallop, 2006). A dataset was prepared by randomly selecting 1,000 word senses from the dictionary and annotating the content words in their glosses according to the dictionary sense inventory. Overall, 2,678 words were sense tagged.

The results are shown in Table 3. CQC obtains an accuracy of 77.13% (in case of ties, a random choice is made, thus leading to the same precision and recall), Cycles achieves an accuracy of almost 10% less than CQC (the difference is statistically significant; $p < 0.01$). The FS baseline, here, is based on the first sense listed in the Macquarie sense inventory, which – in contrast to WordNet – does not depend on the occurrence frequency of senses in a semantically-annotated corpus. However, we note that the FS baseline is not very different from that of the WordNet experiment.

We observe that the Lesk performance is very low on this dataset (around 7 points above the Random BL), due to the impossibility of using the Extended Gloss Overlap approach (semantic relations are not available in the Macquarie Concise) and to the low number of matches between source and target entries.

Ragazzini/Biagi. Finally, we performed an experiment on the Ragazzini/Biagi English-Italian machine-readable dictionary. In this experiment, disambiguating a word w' in the gloss of a sense s from one section (e.g. Italian-English) equals to selecting a word sense s' of w' listed in the other section of the dictionary (e.g. English-Italian). For example, given the English entry $race^1_n$, translated as "$corsa_n$, $gara_n$", our objective is to assign the right Italian sense from the Italian-English section to $corsa_n$ and $gara_n$.

To apply the CQC algorithm, a simple adaptation is needed, so as to allow (quasi-)cycles to connect word senses from the two distinct sections. The algorithm must seek cyclic and quasi-cyclic paths, respectively of the kind:

i) $s \to s' \to s_1 \to \cdots \to s_{n-2} \to s$

ii) $s \to s' \to s_1 \to \cdots \to s_{n-2} \leftarrow s$

where n is the path length, s and s' are senses respectively from the source (e.g. Italian/English) and the target (e.g. English/Italian) section of the dictionary, s_i is a sense from the target section for $i \leq k$ and from the source section for $i > k$, for some k such that $0 \leq k \leq n-2$. In other words, the DFS can jump at any time from the target section to the source section. After the jump, the depth search continues in the source section, in the hope to reach s. For example, the following is a cycle with $k = 1$:

$$race^1_n \to corsa^2_n \to gara^2_n \to race^1_n$$

where the edge between $corsa^2_n$ and $gara^2_n$ is due to the occurrence of $gara_n$ in the gloss of $corsa^2_n$ as a domain label for that sense.

To perform this experiment, we randomly selected 250 entries from each section (500 overall), including a total number of 1,069 translations that we manually sense tagged. In Table 4 we report the results of CQC, Cycles and Lesk on this task. Overall, the figures are higher than in previous experiments, thanks to a lower average degree of polysemy of the resource, which also impacts positively on the FS baseline. However, given a random baseline of 51.69%, the performance of CQC, over 89% precision and recall, is significantly higher. Cycles obtains around 4 points less than CQC (the difference is statistically significant; $p < 0.01$). The performance of Lesk (63.89%) is also much higher than in our previous experiments, thanks to the higher chance of finding a 1:1 correspondence between the two sections. However, we observed that this does not always hold, as also supported by the better results of CQC.

4 Discussion

The experiments presented in the previous section are inherently heterogeneous, due to the different nature of the resources adopted (a computational lexicon, a monolingual and a bilingual machine-readable dictionary). Our aim was to show the flexibility of our approach in tagging gloss words with senses from the same dictionary.

We show the average polysemy of the three datasets in Table 5. Notice that none of the datasets included monosemous items, so our experiments cannot be compared to typical all-words disambiguation tasks, where monosemous words are part of the test set.

Given that words in the Macquarie dataset have a higher average polysemy than in the WordNet dataset, one might wonder why disambiguating glosses from a computational lexicon such as WordNet is more difficult than performing a similar task on a machine-readable dictionary such as the Macquarie Concise Dictionary, which does not provide any explicit semantic hint. We believe there are at least two reasons for this outcome: the first specifically concerns the Senseval-3 Gloss WSD dataset, which does not reflect the distribution of genus-differentiae terms in dictionary glosses: less than 10% of the items were hypernyms, thus making the task harder. As for the second reason, we believe that the Macquarie Concise provides more clear-cut definitions, thus making sense assignments relatively easier.

An analytical comparison of the results of Cycles and CQC show that, especially for machine-readable dictionaries, employing both cycles and quasi-cycles is highly beneficial, as additional support is provided by the latter patterns. Our results on WordNet prove to be more difficult to analyze, because of the need of employing the first sense heuristic to get full coverage. Also, the maximum path length used for WordNet was different ($\delta = 3$ according to our tuning, compared to $\delta = 4$ for Macquarie and Ragazzini/Biagi). However, quasi-cycles are shown to provide over 10% improvement in terms of recall (at the price of a decrease in precision of 6.6 points).

Further, we note that the performance of the CQC algorithm dramatically improves as the maximum score (i.e. the score which leads to a sense assignment) increases. As a result, users can tune the disambiguation performance based on their specific needs (coverage, precision, etc.). For instance, WordNet Gloss WSD can perform up to 85.7% precision and 10.1% recall if we require the score to be ≥ 0.2 and do not use the FS baseline as a backoff strategy. Similarly, we can reach up to 93.8% prec., 20.0% recall for Macquarie Concise (score ≥ 0.12) and even 95.2% prec., 70.6% recall (score ≥ 0.1) for Ragazzini/Biagi.

	WN	Mac	R/B
Polysemy	6.68	7.97	3.16

Table 5: Average polysemy of the three datasets.

5 Related Work

Word Sense Disambiguation is a large research field (see (Navigli, 2009) for an up-to-date overview). However, in this paper we focused on a specific kind of WSD, namely the disambiguation of dictionary definitions. Seminal works on the topic date back to the late 1970s, with the development of models for the identification of taxonomies from lexical resources (Litkowski, 1978; Amsler, 1980). Subsequent works focused on the identification of genus terms (Chodorow et al., 1985) and, more in general, on the extraction of explicit information from machine-readable dictionaries (see, e.g., (Nakamura and Nagao, 1988; Ide and Véronis, 1993)). Kozima and Furugori (1993) provide an approach to the construction of ambiguous semantic networks from glosses in the Longman Dictionary of Contemporary English (LDOCE). In this direction, it is worth citing the work of Vanderwende (1996) and Richardson et al. (1998), who describe the construction of MindNet, a lexical knowledge base obtained from the automated extraction of lexico-semantic information from two machine-readable dictionaries. As a result, weighted relation paths are produced to infer the semantic similarity between pairs of words.

Several heuristics have been presented for the disambiguation of the genus of a dictionary definition (Wilks et al., 1996; Rigau et al., 1997). More recently, a set of heuristic techniques has been proposed to semantically annotate WordNet glosses, leading to the release of the eXtended WordNet (Harabagiu et al., 1999; Moldovan and Novischi, 2004). Among the methods, the cross reference heuristic is the closest technique to our notion of cycles and quasi-cycles. Given a pair of words w and w', this heuristic is based on the occurrence of

w in the gloss of a sense s' of w' and, vice versa, of w' in the gloss of a sense s of w. In other words, a graph cycle $s \rightarrow s' \rightarrow s$ of length 2 is sought.

Based on the eXtended WordNet, a gloss disambiguation task was organized at Senseval-3 (Litkowski, 2004). Interestingly, the best performing systems, namely the TALP system (Castillo et al., 2004), and SSI (Navigli and Velardi, 2005), are knowledge-based and rely on rich knowledge resources: respectively, the Multilingual Central Repository (Atserias et al., 2004), and a proprietary lexical knowledge base.

In contrast, the approach presented in this paper performs the disambiguation of ambiguous words by exploiting only the reference dictionary itself. Furthermore, as we showed in Section 3.3, our method does not rely on WordNet, and can be applied to any lexical knowledge resource, including bilingual dictionaries.

Finally, methods in the literature more focused on a specific disambiguation task include statistical methods for the attachment of hyponyms under the most likely hypernym in the WordNet taxonomy (Snow et al., 2006), structural approaches based on semantic clusters and distance metrics (Pennacchiotti and Pantel, 2006), supervised machine learning methods for the disambiguation of meronymy relations (Girju et al., 2003), etc.

6 Conclusions

In this paper we presented a novel approach to disambiguate the glosses of computational lexicons and machine-readable dictionaries, with the aim of alleviating the knowledge acquisition bottleneck. The method is based on the identification of cycles and quasi-cycles, i.e. circular edge sequences (possibly with one edge reversed) relating a source to a target word sense.

The strength of the approach lies in its weakly supervised nature: (quasi-)cycles rely exclusively on the structure of the input lexical resources. No additional resource (such as labeled corpora or external knowledge bases) is required, assuming we do not resort to the FS baseline. As a result, the approach can be applied to obtain a semantic network from the disambiguation of virtually any lexical resource available in machine-readable format for which a sense inventory is provided.

The utility of gloss disambiguation is even greater in bilingual dictionaries, as idiosyncrasies such as missing or redundant translations can be discovered, thus helping lexicographers improve the resources[6]. An adaptation similar to that described for disambiguating the Ragazzini/Biagi can be employed for mapping pairs of lexical resources (e.g. FrameNet (Baker et al., 1998) to WordNet), thus contributing to the beneficial knowledge integration process. Following this direction, we are planning to further experiment on the mapping of FrameNet, VerbNet (Kipper et al., 2000), and other lexical resources.

The graphs output by the CQC algorithm for our datasets are available from `http://lcl.uniroma1.it/cqc`. We are scheduling the release of a software package which includes our implementation of the CQC algorithm and allows its application to any resource for which a standard interface can be written.

Finally, starting from the work of Budanitsky and Hirst (2006), we plan to experiment with the CQC algorithm when employed as a semantic similarity measure, and compare it with the most successful existing approaches. Although in this paper we focused on the disambiguation of dictionary glosses, the same approach can be applied for disambiguating collocations according to a dictionary of choice, thus providing a way to further enrich lexical resources with external knowledge.

Acknowledgments

The author is grateful to Ken Litkowski and the anonymous reviewers for their useful comments. He also wishes to thank Zanichelli and Macquarie for kindly making their dictionaries available for research purposes.

References

Robert A. Amsler. 1980. *The structure of the Merriam-Webster pocket dictionary, Ph.D. Thesis.* University of Texas, Austin, TX, USA.

Jordi Atserias, Luís Villarejo, German Rigau, Eneko Agirre, John Carroll, Bernardo Magnini, and Piek Vossen. 2004. The meaning multilingual central repository. In *Proceedings of GWC 2004*, pages 23–30, Brno, Czech Republic.

Collin F. Baker, Charles J. Fillmore, and John B. Lowe. 1998. The berkeley framenet project. In *Proceedings of COLING-ACL 1998*, pages 86–90, Montreal, Canada.

[6]This is indeed an ongoing line of research in collaboration with the Zanichelli dictionary publisher.

Satanjeev Banerjee and Ted Pedersen. 2003. Extended gloss overlaps as a measure of semantic relatedness. In *Proceedings of IJCAI 2003*, pages 805–810, Acapulco, Mexico.

John Bernard, editor. 1986. *Macquarie Thesaurus*. Macquarie, Sydney, Australia.

Tom Bohman and Lubos Thoma. 2000. A note on sparse random graphs and cover graphs. *The Electronic Journal of Combinatorics*, 7:1–9.

Alexander Budanitsky and Graeme Hirst. 2006. Evaluating wordnet-based measures of semantic distance. *Computational Linguistics*, 32(1):13–47.

Mauro Castillo, Francis Real, Jordi Asterias, and German Rigau. 2004. The talp systems for disambiguating wordnet glosses. In *Proceedings of ACL 2004 SENSEVAL-3 Workshop*, pages 93–96, Barcelona, Spain.

Martin Chodorow, Roy Byrd, and George Heidorn. 1985. Extracting semantic hierarchies from a large on-line dictionary. In *Proceedings of ACL 1985*, pages 299–304, Chicago, IL, USA.

Thomas H. Cormen, Charles E. Leiserson, and Ronald L. Rivest. 1990. *Introduction to algorithms*. MIT Press, Cambridge, MA.

Montse Cuadros and German Rigau. 2006. Quality assessment of large scale knowledge resources. In *Proceedings of EMNLP 2006*, pages 534–541, Sydney, Australia.

Philip Edmonds. 2000. Designing a task for SENSEVAL-2. Technical note.

Christiane Fellbaum, editor. 1998. *WordNet: An Electronic Database*. MIT Press, Cambridge, MA.

Roxana Girju, Adriana Badulescu, and Dan Moldovan. 2003. Learning semantic constraints for the automatic discovery of part-whole relations. In *Proceedings of NAACL 2003*, pages 1–8, Edmonton, Canada.

Sanda Harabagiu, George Miller, and Dan Moldovan. 1999. Wordnet 2 - a morphologically and semantically enhanced resource. In *Proceedings of SIGLEX-99*, pages 1–8, Maryland, USA.

Nancy Ide and Jean Véronis. 1993. Extracting knowledge bases from machine-readable dictionaries: Have we wasted our time? In *Proceedings of Workshop on Knowledge Bases and Knowledge Structures*, pages 257–266, Tokyo, Japan.

Karin Kipper, Hoa Trang Dang, and Martha Palmer. 2000. Class-based construction of a verb lexicon. In *Proceedings of AAAI 2000*, pages 691–696, Austin, TX, USA.

Hideki Kozima and Teiji Furugori. 1993. Similarity between words computed by spreading activation on an english dictionary. In *Proceedings of ACL 1993*, pages 232–239, Utrecht, The Netherlands.

Michael Lesk. 1986. Automatic sense disambiguation using machine readable dictionaries: How to tell a pine cone from an ice cream cone. In *Proceedings of the 5th SIGDOC*, pages 24–26, New York, NY.

Kenneth C. Litkowski. 1978. Models of the semantic structure of dictionaries. *American Journal of Computational Linguistics*, (81):25–74.

Kenneth C. Litkowski. 2004. Senseval-3 task: Word-sense disambiguation of wordnet glosses. In *Proceedings of ACL 2004 SENSEVAL-3 Workshop*, pages 13–16, Barcelona, Spain.

Dan Moldovan and Adrian Novischi. 2004. Word sense disambiguation of wordnet glosses. *Computer Speech & Language*, 18:301–317.

Jun-Ichi Nakamura and Makoto Nagao. 1988. Extraction of semantic information from an ordinary english dictionary and its evaluation. In *Proceedings of COLING 1988*, pages 459–464, Budapest, Hungary.

Roberto Navigli and Paola Velardi. 2005. Structural semantic interconnections: a knowledge-based approach to word sense disambiguation. *IEEE Transactions of Pattern Analysis and Machine Intelligence (TPAMI)*, 27(7):1075–1088.

Roberto Navigli. 2009. Word sense disambiguation: a survey. *ACM Computing Surveys*, 41(2):1–69.

Marco Pennacchiotti and Patrick Pantel. 2006. Ontologizing semantic relations. In *Proceedings of COLING-ACL 2006*, pages 793–800, Sydney, Australia.

Paul Proctor, editor. 1978. *Longman Dictionary of Contemporary English*. Longman Group, UK.

Giuseppe Ragazzini and Adele Biagi, editors. 2006. *Il Ragazzini-Biagi, 4th Edition*. Zanichelli, Italy.

Stephen D. Richardson, William B. Dolan, and Lucy Vanderwende. 1998. Mindnet: acquiring and structuring semantic information from text. In *Proceedings of COLING 1998*, pages 1098–1102, Montreal, Quebec, Canada.

German Rigau, Jordi Atserias, and Eneko Agirre. 1997. Combining unsupervised lexical knowledge methods for word sense disambiguation. In *Proceedings of ACL/EACL 1997*, pages 48–55, Madrid, Spain.

Peter M. Roget. 1911. *Roget's International Thesaurus (1st edition)*. Cromwell, New York, USA.

Helmut Schmid. 1997. Probabilistic part-of-speech tagging using decision trees. In Daniel Jones and Harold Somers, editors, *New Methods in Language Processing*, Studies in Computational Linguistics, pages 154–164. UCL Press, London, UK.

Rion Snow, Daniel Jurafsky, and Andrew Y. Ng. 2006. Semantic taxonomy induction from heterogenous evidence. In *Proceedings of COLING-ACL 2006*, pages 801–808, Sydney, Australia.

Lucy Vanderwende. 1996. *The analysis of noun sequences using semantic information extracted from on-line dictionaries, Ph.D. Thesis*. Georgetown University, Washington, USA.

Yorick Wilks, Brian Slator, and Louise Guthrie, editors. 1996. *Electric words: Dictionaries, computers and meanings*. MIT Press, Cambridge, MA.

Colin Yallop, editor. 2006. *The Macquarie Concise Dictionary 4th Edition*. Macquarie Library Pty Ltd, Sydney, Australia.

Deterministic shift-reduce parsing for unification-based grammars by using default unification

Takashi Ninomiya
Information Technology Center
University of Tokyo, Japan
ninomi@r.dl.itc.u-tokyo.ac.jp

Takuya Matsuzaki
Department of Computer Science
University of Tokyo, Japan
matuzaki@is.s.u-tokyo.ac.jp

Nobuyuki Shimizu
Information Technology Center
University of Tokyo, Japan
shimizu@r.dl.itc.u-tokyo.ac.jp

Hiroshi Nakagawa
Information Technology Center
University of Tokyo, Japan
nakagawa@dl.itc.u-tokyo.ac.jp

Abstract

Many parsing techniques including parameter estimation assume the use of a packed parse forest for efficient and accurate parsing. However, they have several inherent problems deriving from the restriction of locality in the packed parse forest. Deterministic parsing is one of solutions that can achieve simple and fast parsing without the mechanisms of the packed parse forest by accurately choosing search paths. We propose (i) deterministic shift-reduce parsing for unification-based grammars, and (ii) best-first shift-reduce parsing with beam thresholding for unification-based grammars. Deterministic parsing cannot simply be applied to unification-based grammar parsing, which often fails because of its hard constraints. Therefore, it is developed by using default unification, which almost always succeeds in unification by overwriting inconsistent constraints in grammars.

1 Introduction

Over the last few decades, probabilistic unification-based grammar parsing has been investigated intensively. Previous studies (Abney, 1997; Johnson et al., 1999; Kaplan et al., 2004; Malouf and van Noord, 2004; Miyao and Tsujii, 2005; Riezler et al., 2000) defined a probabilistic model of unification-based grammars, including head-driven phrase structure grammar (HPSG), lexical functional grammar (LFG) and combinatory categorial grammar (CCG), as a maximum entropy model (Berger et al., 1996). Geman and Johnson (Geman and Johnson, 2002) and Miyao and Tsujii (Miyao and Tsujii, 2002) proposed a feature forest, which is a dynamic programming algorithm for estimating the probabilities of all possible parse candidates. A feature forest can estimate the model parameters without unpacking the parse forest, i.e., the chart and its edges.

Feature forests have been used successfully for probabilistic HPSG and CCG (Clark and Curran, 2004b; Miyao and Tsujii, 2005), and its parsing is empirically known to be fast and accurate, especially with supertagging (Clark and Curran, 2004a; Ninomiya et al., 2007; Ninomiya et al., 2006). Both estimation and parsing with the packed parse forest, however, have several inherent problems deriving from the restriction of locality. First, feature functions can be defined only for local structures, which limit the parser's performance. This is because parsers segment parse trees into constituents and factor equivalent constituents into a single constituent (edge) in a chart to avoid the same calculation. This also means that the semantic structures must be segmented. This is a crucial problem when we think of designing semantic structures other than predicate argument structures, e.g., synchronous grammars for machine translation. The size of the constituents will be exponential if the semantic structures are not segmented. Lastly, we need delayed evaluation for evaluating feature functions. The application of feature functions must be delayed until all the values in the

Proceedings of the 12th Conference of the European Chapter of the ACL, pages 603–611,
Athens, Greece, 30 March – 3 April 2009.

segmented constituents are instantiated. This is because values in parse trees can propagate anywhere throughout the parse tree by unification. For example, values may propagate from the root node to terminal nodes, and the final form of the terminal nodes is unknown until the parser finishes constructing the whole parse tree. Consequently, the design of grammars, semantic structures, and feature functions becomes complex. To solve the problem of locality, several approaches, such as reranking (Charniak and Johnson, 2005), shift-reduce parsing (Yamada and Matsumoto, 2003), search optimization learning (Daumé and Marcu, 2005) and sampling methods (Malouf and van Noord, 2004; Nakagawa, 2007), were studied.

In this paper, we investigate shift-reduce parsing approach for unification-based grammars without the mechanisms of the packed parse forest. Shift-reduce parsing for CFG and dependency parsing have recently been studied (Nivre and Scholz, 2004; Ratnaparkhi, 1997; Sagae and Lavie, 2005, 2006; Yamada and Matsumoto, 2003), through approaches based essentially on deterministic parsing. These techniques, however, cannot simply be applied to unification-based grammar parsing because it can fail as a result of its hard constraints in the grammar. Therefore, in this study, we propose deterministic parsing for unification-based grammars by using default unification, which almost always succeeds in unification by overwriting inconsistent constraints in the grammars. We further pursue best-first shift-reduce parsing for unification-based grammars.

Sections 2 and 3 explain unification-based grammars and default unification, respectively. Shift-reduce parsing for unification-based grammars is presented in Section 4. Section 5 discusses our experiments, and Section 6 concludes the paper.

2 Unification-based grammars

A unification-based grammar is defined as a pair consisting of a set of lexical entries and a set of phrase-structure rules. The lexical entries express word-specific characteristics, while the phrase-structure rules describe constructions of constituents in parse trees. Both the phrase-structure rules and the lexical entries are represented by feature structures (Carpenter, 1992), and constraints in the grammar are forced by unification. Among the phrase-structure rules, a binary rule is a partial function: $\mathcal{F} \times \mathcal{F} \rightarrow \mathcal{F}$, where $\mathcal{F}$ is the set of all possible feature structures. The binary rule takes two partial parse trees as daughters and returns a larger partial parse tree that consists of the daughters and their mother. A unary rule is a partial function: $\mathcal{F} \rightarrow \mathcal{F}$, which corresponds to a unary branch.

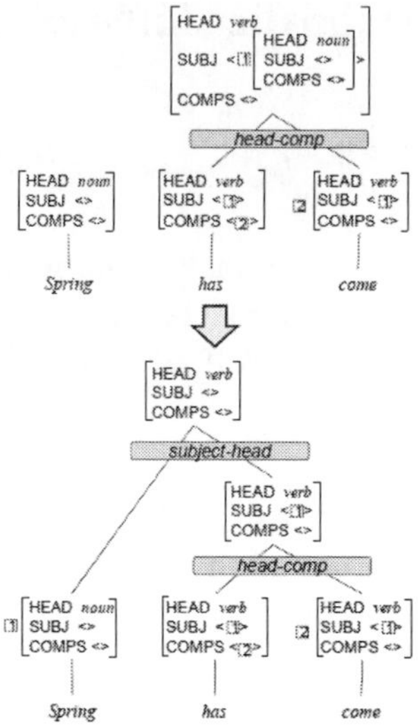

Figure 1: Example of HPSG parsing.

In the experiments, we used an HPSG (Pollard and Sag, 1994), which is one of the sophisticated unification-based grammars in linguistics. Generally, an HPSG has a small number of phrase-structure rules and a large number of lexical entries. Figure 1 shows an example of HPSG parsing of the sentence, "Spring has come." The upper part of the figure shows a partial parse tree for "has come," which is obtained by unifying each of the lexical entries for "has" and "come" with a daughter feature structure of the head-complement rule. Larger partial parse trees are obtained by repeatedly applying phrase-structure rules to lexical/phrasal partial parse trees. Finally, the parse result is output as a parse tree that dominates the sentence.

3 Default unification

Default unification was originally investigated in a series of studies of lexical semantics, in order to deal with default inheritance in a lexicon. It is also desirable, however, for robust processing, because (i) it almost always succeeds and (ii) a feature structure is relaxed such that the amount of information is maximized (Ninomiya et al., 2002). In our experiments, we tested a simplified version of Copestake's default unification. Before explaining it, we first explain Carpenter's two definitions of default unification (Carpenter, 1993).

(Credulous Default Unification)

$$F \overset{<}{\sqcup}_c G = \left\{ F \sqcup G' \middle| \begin{array}{c} G' \sqsubseteq G \text{ is maximal such} \\ \text{that } F \sqcup G' \text{is defined} \end{array} \right\}$$

(Skeptical Default Unification)

$$F \overset{<}{\sqcup}_s G = \sqcap (F \overset{<}{\sqcup}_c G)$$

F is called a strict feature structure, whose information must not be lost, and G is called a default feature structure, whose information can be lost but as little as possible so that F and G can be unified.

Credulous default unification is greedy, in that it tries to maximize the amount of information from the default feature structure, but it results in a set of feature structures. Skeptical default unification simply generalizes the set of feature structures resulting from credulous default unification. Skeptical default unification thus leads to a unique result so that the default information that can be found in every result of credulous default unification remains. The following is an example of skeptical default unification:

$$[\text{F}: \mathbf{a}] \overset{<}{\sqcup}_s \begin{bmatrix} \text{F}: \boxed{1}\,\mathbf{b} \\ \text{G}: \boxed{1} \\ \text{H}: \mathbf{c} \end{bmatrix} = \sqcap \left\{ \begin{bmatrix} \text{F}: \mathbf{a} \\ \text{G}: \mathbf{b} \\ \text{H}: \mathbf{c} \end{bmatrix}, \begin{bmatrix} \text{F}: \boxed{1}\,\mathbf{a} \\ \text{G}: \boxed{1} \\ \text{H}: \mathbf{c} \end{bmatrix} \right\} = \begin{bmatrix} \text{F}: \mathbf{a} \\ \text{G}: \bot \\ \text{H}: \mathbf{c} \end{bmatrix}.$$

Copestake mentioned that the problem with Carpenter's default unification is its time complexity (Copestake, 1993). Carpenter's default unification takes exponential time to find the optimal answer, because it requires checking the unifiability of the power set of constraints in a default feature structure. Copestake thus proposed another definition of default unification, as follows. Let $PV(G)$ be a function that returns a set of path values in G, and let $PE(G)$ be a function that returns a set of path equations, i.e., information about structure sharing in G.

(Copestake's default unification)

$$F \overset{<}{\sqcup}_a G = H \sqcup \bigsqcup \left\{ F \middle| \begin{array}{c} F \in PV(G) \text{and there is no } F' \in PV(G) \\ \text{such that } H \sqcup F' \text{is defined and} \\ H \sqcup F \sqcup F' \text{is not defined} \end{array} \right\},$$

where $H = F \sqcup \bigsqcup PE(G)$.

Copestake's default unification works efficiently because all path equations in the default feature structure are unified with the strict feature structures, and because the unifiability of path values is checked one by one for each node in the result of unifying the path equations. The implementation is almost the same as that of normal unification, but each node of a feature structure has a set of values marked as "strict" or "default." When types are involved, however, it is not easy to find unifiable path values in the default feature structure. Therefore, we implemented a more simply typed version of Corpestake's default unification.

```
procedure forced_unification(p, q)
  queue := {⟨p, q⟩};
  while( queue is not empty )
    ⟨p, q⟩ := shift(queue);
    p := deref(p); q := deref(q);
    if p ≠ q
      θ(p) := θ(p) ∪ θ(q);
      θ(q) := ptr(p);
      forall f ∈ feat(p)∪ feat(q)
        if f ∈ feat(p) ∧ f ∈ feat(q)
          queue := queue ∪ ⟨δ(f, p), δ(f, q)⟩;
        if f ∉ feat(p) ∧ f ∈ feat(q)
          δ(f, p) := δ(f, q);
procedure mark(p, m)
  p := deref(p);
  if p has not been visited
    θ(p) := {⟨θ(p), m⟩};
    forall f ∈ feat(p)
      mark(δ(f, p), m);
procedure collapse_defaults(p)
  p := deref(p);
  if p has not been visited
    ts := ⊥; td := ⊥;
    forall ⟨t, strict⟩ ∈ θ(p)
      ts := ts ⊔ t;
    forall ⟨t, default⟩ ∈ θ(p)
      td := td ⊔ t;
    if ts is not defined
      return false;
    if ts ⊔ td is defined
      θ(p) := ts ⊔ td;
    else
      θ(p) := ts;
    forall f ∈ feat(p)
      collapse_defaults(δ(f, p));
procedure default_unification(p, q)
  mark(p, strict);
  mark(q, default);
  forced_unification(p, q);
  collapse_defaults(p);
```

θ(p) is (i) a single type, (ii) a pointer, or (iii) a set of pairs of types and markers in the feature structure node p.
A marker indicates that the types in a feature structure node originally belong to the strict feature structures or the default feature structures.
A pointer indicates that the node has been unified with other nodes and it points the unified node. A function deref traverses pointer nodes until it reaches to non-pointer node.
δ(f, p) returns a feature structure node which is reached by following a feature f from p.

Figure 2: Algorithm for the simply typed version of Corpestake's default unification.

Figure 2 shows the algorithm by which we implemented the simply typed version. First, each node is marked as "strict" if it belongs to a strict feature structure and as "default" otherwise. The marked strict and default feature structures

Common features: Sw(i), Sp(i), Shw(i), Shp(i), Snw(i), Snp(i), Ssy(i), Shsy(i), Snsy(i), wi-1, wi,wi+1, pi-2, pi-1, pi, pi+1, pi+2, pi+3
Binary reduce features: d, c, spl, syl, hwl, hpl, hll, spr, syr, hwr, hpr, hlr
Unary reduce features: sy, hw, hp, hl

Sw(i) ... head word of i-th item from the top of the stack
Sp(i) ... head POS of i-th item from the top of the stack
Shw(i) ... head word of the head daughter of i-th item from the top of the stack
Shp(i) ... head POS of the head daughter of i-th item from the top of the stack
Snw(i) ... head word of the non-head daughter of i-th item from the top of the stack
Snp(i) ... head POS of the non-head daughter of i-th item from the top of the stack
Ssy(i) ... symbol of phrase category of the i-th item from the top of the stack
Shsy(i) ... symbol of phrase category of the head daughter of the i-th item from the top of the stack
Snsy(i) ... symbol of phrase category of the non-head daughter of the i-th item from the top of the stack
d ... distance between head words of daughters
c ... whether a comma exists between daughters and/or inside daughter phrases
sp ... the number of words dominated by the phrase
sy ... symbol of phrase category
hw ... head word
hp ... head POS
hl ... head lexical entry

Figure 3: Feature templates.

Shift Features
[Sw(0)] [Sw(1)] [Sw(2)] [Sw(3)] [Sp(0)] [Sp(1)] [Sp(2)] [Sp(3)] [Shw(0)] [Shw(1)] [Shp(0)] [Shp(1)] [Snw(0)] [Snw(1)] [Snp(0)] [Snp(1)] [Ssy(0)] [Ssy(1)] [Shsy(0)] [Shsy(1)] [Snsy(0)] [Snsy(1)] [d] [wi-1] [wi] [wi+1] [pi-2] [pi-1] [pi] [pi+1] [pi+2] [pi+3] [wi-1, wi] [wi, wi+1] [pi-1, wi] [pi, wi] [pi+1, wi] [pi, pi+1, pi+2, pi+3] [pi-2, pi-1, pi] [pi-1, pi, pi+1] [pi, pi+1, pi+2] [pi-2, pi-1] [pi-1, pi] [pi, pi+1] [pi+1, pi+2]

Binary Reduce Features
[Sw(0)] [Sw(1)] [Sw(2)] [Sw(3)] [Sp(0)] [Sp(1)] [Sp(2)] [Sp(3)] [Shw(0)] [Shw(1)] [Shp(0)] [Shp(1)] [Snw(0)] [Snw(1)] [Snp(0)] [Snp(1)] [Ssy(0)] [Ssy(1)] [Shsy(0)] [Shsy(1)] [Snsy(0)] [Snsy(1)] [d] [wi-1] [wi] [wi+1] [pi-2] [pi-1] [pi] [pi+1] [pi+2] [pi+3] [d,c,hw,hp,hl] [d,c,hw,hp] [d, c, hw, hl] [d, c, sy, hw] [c, sp, hw, hp, hl] [c, sp, hw, hp] [c, sp, hw,hl] [c, sp, sy, hw] [d, c, hp, hl] [d, c, hp] [d, c, hl] [d, c, sy] [c, sp, hp, hl] [c, sp, hp] [c, sp, hl] [c, sp, sy]

Unary Reduce Features
[Sw(0)] [Sw(1)] [Sw(2)] [Sw(3)] [Sp(0)] [Sp(1)] [Sp(2)] [Sp(3)] [Shw(0)] [Shw(1)] [Shp(0)] [Shp(1)] [Snw(0)] [Snw(1)] [Snp(0)] [Snp(1)] [Ssy(0)] [Ssy(1)] [Shsy(0)] [Shsy(1)] [Snsy(0)] [Snsy(1)] [d] [wi-1] [wi] [wi+1] [pi-2] [pi-1] [pi] [pi+1] [pi+2] [pi+3] [hw, hp, hl] [hw, hp] [hw, hl] [sy, hw] [hp, hl] [hp] [hl] [sy]

Figure 4: Combinations of feature templates.

are unified, whereas the types in the feature structure nodes are not unified but merged as a set of types. Then, all types marked as "strict" are unified into one type for each node. If this fails, the default unification also returns unification failure as its result. Finally, each node is assigned a single type, which is the result of type unification for all types marked as both "default" and "strict" if it succeeds or all types marked only as "strict" otherwise.

4 Shift-reduce parsing for unification-based grammars

Non-deterministic shift-reduce parsing for unification-based grammars has been studied by Briscoe and Carroll (Briscoe and Carroll, 1993). Their algorithm works non-deterministically with the mechanism of the packed parse forest, and hence it has the problem of locality in the packed parse forest. This section explains our shift-reduce parsing algorithms, which are based on deterministic shift-reduce CFG parsing (Sagae and Lavie, 2005) and best-first shift-reduce CFG parsing (Sagae and Lavie, 2006). Sagae's parser selects the most probable shift/reduce actions and non-terminal symbols without assuming explicit CFG rules. Therefore, his parser can proceed deterministically without failure. However, in the case of unification-based grammars, a deterministic parser can fail as a result of its hard constraints in the grammar. We propose two new shift-reduce parsing approaches for unification-based grammars: deterministic shift-reduce parsing and shift-reduce parsing by backtracking and beam search. The major difference between our algorithm and Sagae's algorithm is that we use default unification. First, we explain the deterministic shift-reduce parsing algorithm, and then we explain the shift-reduce parsing with backtracking and beam search.

4.1 Deterministic shift-reduce parsing for unification-based grammars

The deterministic shift-reduce parsing algorithm for unification-based grammars mainly comprises two data structures: a stack S, and a queue W. Items in S are partial parse trees, including a lexical entry and a parse tree that dominates the whole input sentence. Items in W are words and POSs in the input sentence. The algorithm defines two types of parser actions, shift and reduce, as follows.

- Shift: A shift action removes the first item (a word and a POS) from W. Then, one lexical entry is selected from among the candidate lexical entries for the item. Finally, the selected lexical entry is put on the top of the stack.

- Binary Reduce: A binary reduce action removes two items from the top of the stack. Then, partial parse trees are derived by applying binary rules to the first removed item and the second removed item as a right daughter and left daughter, respectively. Among the candidate partial parse trees, one is selected and put on the top of the stack.
- Unary Reduce: A unary reduce action removes one item from the top of the stack. Then, partial parse trees are derived by applying unary rules to the removed item. Among the candidate partial parse trees, one is selected and put on the top of the stack.

Parsing fails if there is no candidate for selection (i.e., a dead end). Parsing is considered successfully finished when W is empty and S has only one item which satisfies the sentential condition: the category is verb and the subcategorization frame is empty. Parsing is considered a non-sentential success when W is empty and S has only one item but it does not satisfy the sentential condition.

In our experiments, we used a maximum entropy classifier to choose the parser's action. Figure 3 lists the feature templates for the classifier, and Figure 4 lists the combinations of feature templates. Many of these features were taken from those listed in (Ninomiya et al., 2007), (Miyao and Tsujii, 2005) and (Sagae and Lavie, 2005), including global features defined over the information in the stack, which cannot be used in parsing with the packed parse forest. The features for selecting shift actions are the same as the features used in the supertagger (Ninomiya et al., 2007). Our shift-reduce parsers can be regarded as an extension of the supertagger.

The deterministic parsing can fail because of its grammar's hard constraints. So, we use default unification, which almost always succeeds in unification. We assume that a head daughter (or, an important daughter) is determined for each binary rule in the unification-based grammar. Default unification is used in the binary rule application in the same way as used in Ninomiya's offline robust parsing (Ninomiya et al., 2002), in which a binary rule unified with the head daughter is the strict feature structure and the non-head daughter is the default feature structure, i.e., $(R \sqcup H) \overset{<}{\sqcup} NH$, where R is a binary rule, H is a head daughter and NH is a non-head daughter. In the experiments, we used the simply typed version of Copestake's default unification in the binary rule application[1]. Note that default unification was always used instead of normal unification in both training and evaluation in the case of the parsers using default unification. Although Copestake's default unification almost always succeeds, the binary rule application can fail if the binary rule cannot be unified with the head daughter, or inconsistency is caused by path equations in the default feature structures. If the rule application fails for all the binary rules, backtracking or beam search can be used for its recovery as explained in Section 4.2. In the experiments, we had no failure in the binary rule application with default unification.

4.2 Shift-reduce parsing by backtracking and beam-search

Another approach for recovering from the parsing failure is backtracking. When parsing fails or ends with non-sentential success, the parser's state goes back to some old state (backtracking), and it chooses the second best action and tries parsing again. The old state is selected so as to minimize the difference in the probabilities for selecting the best candidate and the second best candidate. We define a maximum number of backtracking steps while parsing a sentence. Backtracking repeats until parsing finishes with sentential success or reaches the maximum number of backtracking steps. If parsing fails to find a parse tree, the best continuous partial parse trees are output for evaluation.

From the viewpoint of search algorithms, parsing with backtracking is a sort of depth-first search algorithms. Another possibility is to use the best-first search algorithm. The best-first parser has a state priority queue, and each state consists of a tree stack and a word queue, which are the same stack and queue explained in the shift-reduce parsing algorithm. Parsing proceeds by applying shift-reduce actions to the best state in the state queue. First, the best state is re-

[1] We also implemented Ninomiya's default unification, which can weaken path equation constraints. In the preliminary experiments, we tested binary rule application given as $(R \sqcup H) \overset{<}{\sqcup} NH$ with Copestake's default unification, $(R \sqcup H) \overset{<}{\sqcup} NH$ with Ninomiya's default unification, and $(H \sqcup NH) \overset{<}{\sqcup} R$ with Ninomiya's default unification. However, there was no significant difference of F-score among these three methods. So, in the main experiments, we only tested $(R \sqcup H) \overset{<}{\sqcup} NH$ with Copestake's default unification because this method is simple and stable.

		Section 23 (Gold POS)								
		LP (%)	LR (%)	LF (%)	Avg. Time (ms)	# of backtrack	Avg. # of states	# of dead end	# of non-sentential success	# of sentential success
Previous studies	(Miyao and Tsujii, 2005)	87.26	86.50	86.88	604	-	-	-	-	-
	(Ninomiya et al., 2007)	89.78	89.28	89.53	234	-	-	-	-	-
Ours	det	76.45	82.00	79.13	122	0	-	867	35	1514
	det+du	87.78	87.45	87.61	256	0	-	0	117	2299
	back40	81.93	85.31	83.59	519	18986	-	386	23	2007
	back10 + du	87.79	87.46	87.62	267	574	-	0	45	2371
	beam(7.4)	86.17	87.77	86.96	510	-	226	369	30	2017
	beam(20.1)+du	88.67	88.79	88.48	457	-	205	0	16	2400
	beam(403.4)	89.98	89.92	89.95	10246	-	2822	71	14	2331

		Section 23 (Auto POS)								
		LP (%)	LR (%)	LF (%)	Avg. Time (ms)	# of backtrack	Avg. # of states	# of dead end	# of non sentential success	# of sentential success
Previous studies	(Miyao and Tsujii, 2005)	84.96	84.25	84.60	674	-	-	-	-	-
	(Ninomiya et al., 2007)	87.28	87.05	87.17	260	-	-	-	-	-
	(Matsuzaki et al., 2007)	86.93	86.47	86.70	30	-	-	-	-	-
	(Sagae et al., 2007)	88.50	88.00	88.20	-	-	-	-	-	-
Ours	det	74.13	80.02	76.96	127	0	-	909	31	1476
	det+du	85.93	85.72	85.82	252	0	-	0	124	2292
	back40	78.71	82.86	80.73	568	21068	-	438	27	1951
	back10 + du	85.96	85.75	85.85	270	589	-	0	46	2370
	beam(7.4)	83.84	85.82	84.82	544	-	234	421	33	1962
	beam(20.1)+du	86.59	86.36	86.48	550	-	222	0	21	2395
	beam(403.4)	87.70	87.86	87.78	16822	-	4553	89	16	2311

Table 1: Experimental results for Section 23.

moved from the state queue, and then shift-reduce actions are applied to the state. The newly generated states as results of the shift-reduce actions are put on the queue. This process repeats until it generates a state satisfying the sentential condition. We define the probability of a parsing state as the product of the probabilities of selecting actions that have been taken to reach the state. We regard the state probability as the objective function in the best-first search algorithm, i.e., the state with the highest probabilities is always chosen in the algorithm. However, the best-first algorithm with this objective function searches like the breadth-first search, and hence, parsing is very slow or cannot be processed in a reasonable time. So, we introduce beam thresholding to the best-first algorithm. The search space is pruned by only adding a new state to the state queue if its probability is greater than 1/b of the probability of the best state in the states that has had the same number of shift-reduce actions. In what follows, we call this algorithm beam search parsing.

In the experiments, we tested both backtracking and beam search with/without default unification. Note that, the beam search parsing for unification-based grammars is very slow compared to the shift-reduce CFG parsing with beam search. This is because we have to copy parse trees, which consist of a large feature structures, in every step of searching to keep many states on the state queue. In the case of backtracking, copying is not necessary.

5 Experiments

We evaluated the speed and accuracy of parsing with Enju 2.3β, an HPSG for English (Miyao and Tsujii, 2005). The lexicon for the grammar was extracted from Sections 02-21 of the Penn Treebank (39,832 sentences). The grammar consisted of 2,302 lexical entries for 11,187 words. Two probabilistic classifiers for selecting shift-reduce actions were trained using the same portion of the treebank. One is trained using normal unification, and the other is trained using default unification.

We measured the accuracy of the predicate argument relation output of the parser. A predicate-argument relation is defined as a tuple $\langle \sigma, w_h, a, w_a \rangle$, where σ is the predicate type (e.g.,

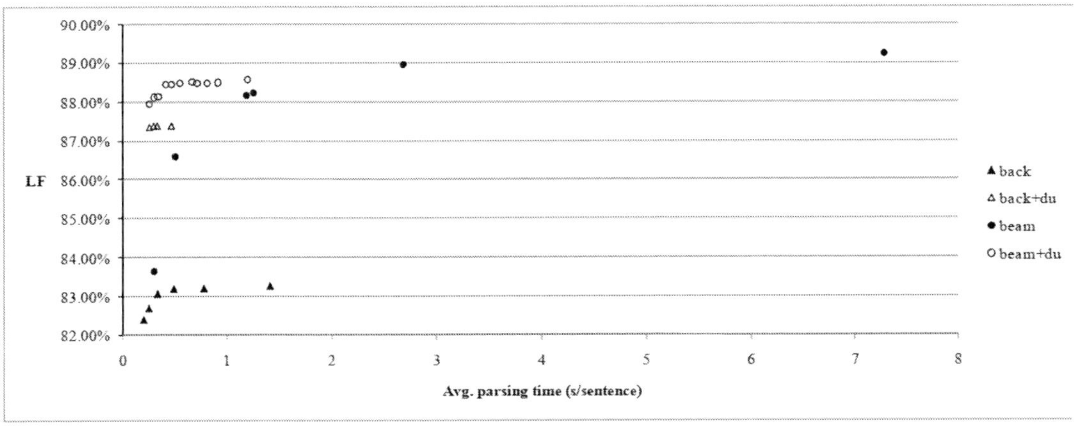

Figure 5: The relation between LF and the average parsing time (Section 22, Gold POS).

adjective, intransitive verb), w_h is the head word of the predicate, a is the argument label (MOD-ARG, ARG1, ..., ARG4), and w_a is the head word of the argument. The labeled precision (LP) / labeled recall (LR) is the ratio of tuples correctly identified by the parser, and the labeled F-score (LF) is the harmonic mean of the LP and LR. This evaluation scheme was the same one used in previous evaluations of lexicalized grammars (Clark and Curran, 2004b; Hockenmaier, 2003; Miyao and Tsujii, 2005). The experiments were conducted on an Intel Xeon 5160 server with 3.0-GHz CPUs. Section 22 of the Penn Treebank was used as the development set, and the performance was evaluated using sentences of ≤ 100 words in Section 23. The LP, LR, and LF were evaluated for Section 23.

Table 1 lists the results of parsing for Section 23. In the table, "Avg. time" is the average parsing time for the tested sentences. "# of backtrack" is the total number of backtracking steps that occurred during parsing. "Avg. # of states" is the average number of states for the tested sentences. "# of dead end" is the number of sentences for which parsing failed. "# of non-sentential success" is the number of sentences for which parsing succeeded but did not generate a parse tree satisfying the sentential condition. "det" means the deterministic shift-reduce parsing proposed in this paper. "back$n$" means shift-reduce parsing with backtracking at most n times for each sentence. "du" indicates that default unification was used. "beam$b$" means best-first shift-reduce parsing with beam threshold b. The upper half of the table gives the results obtained using gold POSs, while the lower half gives the results obtained using an automatic POS tagger. The maximum number of backtracking steps and the beam threshold were determined by observing the performance for the development set (Section 22) such that the LF was maximized with a parsing time of less than 500 ms/sentence (except "beam(403.4)"). The performance of "beam(403.4)" was evaluated to see the limit of the performance of the beam-search parsing.

Deterministic parsing without default unification achieved accuracy with an LF of around 79.1% (Section 23, gold POS). With backtracking, the LF increased to 83.6%. Figure 5 shows the relation between LF and parsing time for the development set (Section 22, gold POS). As seen in the figure, the LF increased as the parsing time increased. The increase in LF for deterministic parsing without default unification, however, seems to have saturated around 83.3%. Table 1 also shows that deterministic parsing with default unification achieved higher accuracy, with an LF of around 87.6% (Section 23, gold POS), without backtracking. Default unification is effective: it ran faster and achieved higher accuracy than deterministic parsing with normal unification. The beam-search parsing without default unification achieved high accuracy, with an LF of around 87.0%, but is still worse than deterministic parsing with default unification. However, with default unification, it achieved the best performance, with an LF of around 88.5%, in the settings of parsing time less than 500ms/sentence for Section 22.

For comparison with previous studies using the packed parse forest, the performances of Miyao's parser, Ninomiya's parser, Matsuzaki's parser and Sagae's parser are also listed in Table 1. Miyao's parser is based on a probabilistic model estimated only by a feature forest. Ninomiya's parser is a mixture of the feature forest

Path	Strict type	Default type	Freq
SYNSEM:LOCAL:CAT:HEAD:MOD:	cons	nil	434
SYNSEM:LOCAL:CAT:HEAD:MOD:hd:CAT:HEAD:MOD:	cons	nil	237
SYNSEM:LOCAL:CAT:VAL:SUBJ:	nil	cons	231
SYNSEM:LOCAL:CAT:HEAD:MOD:hd:CAT:VAL:SUBJ:	nil	cons	125
SYNSEM:LOCAL:CAT:HEAD:	verb	noun	110
SYNSEM:LOCAL:CAT:VAL:SPR:hd:LOCAL:CAT:VAL:SPEC:hd:LOCAL:CAT: HEAD:MOD:	cons	nil	101
SYNSEM:LOCAL:CAT:HEAD:MOD:hd:CAT:VAL:SPR:hd:LOCAL:CAT:VAL:SPEC: hd:LOCAL:CAT:HEAD:MOD:	cons	nil	96
SYNSEM:LOCAL:CAT:HEAD:MOD:	nil	cons	92
SYNSEM:LOCAL:CAT:HEAD:MOD:hd:CAT:HEAD:	verb	noun	91
SYNSEM:LOCAL:CAT:VAL:SUBJ:	cons	nil	79
SYNSEM:LOCAL:CAT:HEAD:	noun	verbal	77
SYNSEM:LOCAL:CAT:HEAD:MOD:hd:CAT:HEAD:	noun	verbal	77
SYNSEM:LOCAL:CAT:HEAD:	nominal	verb	75
SYNSEM:LOCAL:CAT:VAL:CONJ:hd:LOCAL:CAT:HEAD:MOD:	cons	nil	74
SYNSEM:LOCAL:CAT:VAL:CONJ:tl:hd:LOCAL:CAT:HEAD:MOD:	cons	nil	69
SYNSEM:LOCAL:CAT:VAL:CONJ:tl:hd:LOCAL:CAT:VAL:SUBJ:	nil	cons	64
SYNSEM:LOCAL:CAT:VAL:CONJ:hd:LOCAL:CAT:VAL:SUBJ:	nil	cons	64
SYNSEM:LOCAL:CAT:VAL:COMPS:hd:LOCAL:CAT:HEAD:	nominal	verb	63
SYNSEM:LOCAL:CAT:HEAD:MOD:hd:CAT:VAL:SUBJ:	cons	nil	63
...	...	...	...
Total			10,598

Table 2: Path values overwritten by default unification in Section 22.

and an HPSG supertagger. Matsuzaki's parser uses an HPSG supertagger and CFG filtering. Sagae's parser is a hybrid parser with a shallow dependency parser. Though parsing without the packed parse forest is disadvantageous to the parsing with the packed parse forest in terms of search space complexity, our model achieved higher accuracy than Miyao's parser.

"beam(403.4)" in Table 1 and "beam" in Figure 5 show possibilities of beam-search parsing. "beam(403.4)" was very slow, but the accuracy was higher than any other parsers except Sagae's parser.

Table 2 shows the behaviors of default unification for "det+du." The table shows the 20 most frequent path values that were overwritten by default unification in Section 22. In most of the cases, the overwritten path values were in the selection features, i.e., subcategorization frames (COMPS:, SUBJ:, SPR:, CONJ:) and modifiee specification (MOD:). The column of 'Default type' indicates the default types which were overwritten by the strict types in the column of 'Strict type,' and the last column is the frequency of overwriting. 'cons' means a non-empty list, and 'nil' means an empty list. In most of the cases, modifiee and subcategorization frames were changed from empty to non-empty and vice versa. From the table, overwriting of head information was also observed, e.g., 'noun' was changed to 'verb.'

6 Conclusion and Future Work

We have presented shift-reduce parsing approach for unification-based grammars, based on deterministic shift-reduce parsing. First, we presented deterministic parsing for unification-based grammars. Deterministic parsing was difficult in the framework of unification-based grammar parsing, which often fails because of its hard constraints. We introduced default unification to avoid the parsing failure. Our experimental results have demonstrated the effectiveness of deterministic parsing with default unification. The experiments revealed that deterministic parsing with default unification achieved high accuracy, with a labeled F-score (LF) of 87.6% for Section 23 of the Penn Treebank with gold POSs. Second, we also presented the best-first parsing with beam search for unification-based grammars. The best-first parsing with beam search achieved the best accuracy, with an LF of 87.0%, in the settings without default unification. Default unification further increased LF from 87.0% to 88.5%. By widening the beam width, the best-first parsing achieved an LF of 90.0%.

References

Abney, Steven P. 1997. Stochastic Attribute-Value Grammars. Computational Linguistics, 23(4), 597-618.

Berger, Adam, Stephen Della Pietra, and Vincent Della Pietra. 1996. A Maximum Entropy Approach to Natural Language Processing. Computational Linguistics, 22(1), 39-71.

Briscoe, Ted and John Carroll. 1993. Generalized probabilistic LR-Parsing of natural language (corpora) with unification-based grammars. Computational Linguistics, 19(1), 25-59.

Carpenter, Bob. 1992. The Logic of Typed Feature Structures: Cambridge University Press.

Carpenter, Bob. 1993. Skeptical and Credulous Default Unification with Applications to Templates and Inheritance. In Inheritance, Defaults, and the Lexicon. Cambridge: Cambridge University Press.

Charniak, Eugene and Mark Johnson. 2005. Coarse-to-Fine n-Best Parsing and MaxEnt Discriminative Reranking. In proc. of ACL'05, pp. 173-180.

Clark, Stephen and James R. Curran. 2004a. The importance of supertagging for wide-coverage CCG parsing. In proc. of COLING-04, pp. 282-288.

Clark, Stephen and James R. Curran. 2004b. Parsing the WSJ using CCG and log-linear models. In proc. of ACL'04, pp. 104-111.

Copestake, Ann. 1993. Defaults in Lexical Representation. In Inheritance, Defaults, and the Lexicon. Cambridge: Cambridge University Press.

Daumé, Hal III and Daniel Marcu. 2005. Learning as Search Optimization: Approximate Large Margin Methods for Structured Prediction. In proc. of ICML 2005.

Geman, Stuart and Mark Johnson. 2002. Dynamic programming for parsing and estimation of stochastic unification-based grammars. In proc. of ACL'02, pp. 279-286.

Hockenmaier, Julia. 2003. Parsing with Generative Models of Predicate-Argument Structure. In proc. of ACL'03, pp. 359-366.

Johnson, Mark, Stuart Geman, Stephen Canon, Zhiyi Chi, and Stefan Riezler. 1999. Estimators for Stochastic ``Unification-Based'' Grammars. In proc. of ACL '99, pp. 535-541.

Kaplan, R. M., S. Riezler, T. H. King, J. T. Maxwell III, and A. Vasserman. 2004. Speed and accuracy in shallow and deep stochastic parsing. In proc. of HLT/NAACL'04.

Malouf, Robert and Gertjan van Noord. 2004. Wide Coverage Parsing with Stochastic Attribute Value Grammars. In proc. of IJCNLP-04 Workshop ``Beyond Shallow Analyses''.

Matsuzaki, Takuya, Yusuke Miyao, and Jun'ichi Tsujii. 2007. Efficient HPSG Parsing with Supertagging and CFG-filtering. In proc. of IJCAI 2007, pp. 1671-1676.

Miyao, Yusuke and Jun'ichi Tsujii. 2002. Maximum Entropy Estimation for Feature Forests. In proc. of HLT 2002, pp. 292-297.

Miyao, Yusuke and Jun'ichi Tsujii. 2005. Probabilistic disambiguation models for wide-coverage HPSG parsing. In proc. of ACL'05, pp. 83-90.

Nakagawa, Tetsuji. 2007. Multilingual dependency parsing using global features. In proc. of the CoNLL Shared Task Session of EMNLP-CoNLL 2007, pp. 915-932.

Ninomiya, Takashi, Takuya Matsuzaki, Yusuke Miyao, and Jun'ichi Tsujii. 2007. A log-linear model with an n-gram reference distribution for accurate HPSG parsing. In proc. of IWPT 2007, pp. 60-68.

Ninomiya, Takashi, Takuya Matsuzaki, Yoshimasa Tsuruoka, Yusuke Miyao, and Jun'ichi Tsujii. 2006. Extremely Lexicalized Models for Accurate and Fast HPSG Parsing. In proc. of EMNLP 2006, pp. 155-163.

Ninomiya, Takashi, Yusuke Miyao, and Jun'ichi Tsujii. 2002. Lenient Default Unification for Robust Processing within Unification Based Grammar Formalisms. In proc. of COLING 2002, pp. 744-750.

Nivre, Joakim and Mario Scholz. 2004. Deterministic dependency parsing of English text. In proc. of COLING 2004, pp. 64-70.

Pollard, Carl and Ivan A. Sag. 1994. Head-Driven Phrase Structure Grammar: University of Chicago Press.

Ratnaparkhi, Adwait. 1997. A linear observed time statistical parser based on maximum entropy models. In proc. of EMNLP'97.

Riezler, Stefan, Detlef Prescher, Jonas Kuhn, and Mark Johnson. 2000. Lexicalized Stochastic Modeling of Constraint-Based Grammars using Log-Linear Measures and EM Training. In proc. of ACL'00, pp. 480-487.

Sagae, Kenji and Alon Lavie. 2005. A classifier-based parser with linear run-time complexity. In proc. of IWPT 2005.

Sagae, Kenji and Alon Lavie. 2006. A best-first probabilistic shift-reduce parser. In proc. of COLING/ACL on Main conference poster sessions, pp. 691-698.

Sagae, Kenji, Yusuke Miyao, and Jun'ichi Tsujii. 2007. HPSG parsing with shallow dependency constraints. In proc. of ACL 2007, pp. 624-631.

Yamada, Hiroyasu and Yuji Matsumoto. 2003. Statistical Dependency Analysis with Support Vector Machines. In proc. of IWPT-2003.

Analysing Wikipedia and Gold-Standard Corpora for NER Training

Joel Nothman and **Tara Murphy** and **James R. Curran**
School of Information Technologies
University of Sydney
NSW 2006, Australia
{jnot4610,tm,james}@it.usyd.edu.au

Abstract

Named entity recognition (NER) for English typically involves one of three gold standards: MUC, CoNLL, or BBN, all created by costly manual annotation. Recent work has used Wikipedia to automatically create a massive corpus of named entity annotated text.

We present the first comprehensive cross-corpus evaluation of NER. We identify the causes of poor cross-corpus performance and demonstrate ways of making them more compatible. Using our process, we develop a Wikipedia corpus which outperforms gold standard corpora on cross-corpus evaluation by up to 11%.

1 Introduction

Named Entity Recognition (NER), the task of identifying and classifying the names of people, organisations and other entities within text, is central to many NLP systems. NER developed from information extraction in the Message Understanding Conferences (MUC) of the 1990s. By MUC 6 and 7, NER had become a distinct task: tagging proper names, and temporal and numerical expressions (Chinchor, 1998).

Statistical machine learning systems have proven successful for NER. These learn patterns associated with individual entity classes, making use of many contextual, orthographic, linguistic and external knowledge features. However, they rely heavily on large annotated training corpora. This need for costly expert annotation hinders the creation of more task-adaptable, high-performance named entity recognisers.

In acquiring new sources for annotated corpora, we require an analysis of training data as a variable in NER. This paper compares the three main gold-standard corpora. We found that tagging models built on each corpus perform relatively poorly when tested on the others. We therefore present three methods for analysing internal and inter-corpus inconsistencies. Our analysis demonstrates that seemingly minor variations in the text itself, starting right from tokenisation can have a huge impact on practical NER performance.

We take this experience and apply it to a corpus created automatically using Wikipedia. This corpus was created following the method of Nothman et al. (2008). By training the C&C tagger (Curran and Clark, 2003) on the gold-standard corpora and our new Wikipedia-derived training data, we evaluate the usefulness of the latter and explore the nature of the training corpus as a variable in NER.

Our Wikipedia-derived corpora exceed the performance of non-corresponding training and test sets by up to 11% F-score, and can be engineered to automatically produce models consistent with various NE-annotation schema. We show that it is possible to automatically create large, free, named entity-annotated corpora for general or domain specific tasks.

2 NER and annotated corpora

Research into NER has rarely considered the impact of training corpora. The CoNLL evaluations focused on machine learning methods (Tjong Kim Sang, 2002; Tjong Kim Sang and De Meulder, 2003) while more recent work has often involved the use of external knowledge. Since many tagging systems utilise gazetteers of known entities, some research has focused on their automatic extraction from the web (Etzioni et al., 2005) or Wikipedia (Toral et al., 2008), although Mikheev et al. (1999) and others have shown that larger NE lists do not necessarily correspond to increased NER performance. Nadeau et al. (2006) use such lists in an unsupervised NE recogniser, outperforming some entrants of the MUC Named Entity Task. Unlike statistical approaches which learn

Proceedings of the 12th Conference of the European Chapter of the ACL, pages 612–620,
Athens, Greece, 30 March – 3 April 2009. ©2009 Association for Computational Linguistics

patterns associated with a particular type of entity, these unsupervised approaches are limited to identifying common entities present in lists or those caught by hand-built rules.

External knowledge has also been used to augment supervised NER approaches. Kazama and Torisawa (2007) improve their F-score by 3% by including a Wikipedia-based feature in their machine learner. Such approaches are limited by the gold-standard data already available.

Less common is the automatic creation of training data. An et al. (2003) extracted sentences containing listed entities from the web, and produced a 1.8 million word Korean corpus that gave similar results to manually-annotated training data. Richman and Schone (2008) used a method similar to Nothman et al. (2008) in order to derive NE-annotated corpora in languages other than English. They classify Wikipedia articles in foreign languages by transferring knowledge from English Wikipedia via inter-language links. With these classifications they automatically annotate entire articles for NER training, and suggest that their results with a 340k-word Spanish corpus are comparable to 20k-40k words of gold-standard training data when using MUC-style evaluation metrics.

2.1 Gold-standard corpora

We evaluate our Wikipedia-derived corpora against three sets of manually-annotated data from (a) the MUC-7 Named Entity Task (MUC, 2001); (b) the English CoNLL-03 Shared Task (Tjong Kim Sang and De Meulder, 2003); (c) the BBN Pronoun Coreference and Entity Type Corpus (Weischedel and Brunstein, 2005). We consider only the generic newswire NER task, although domain-specific annotated corpora have been developed for applications such as bio-text mining (Kim et al., 2003).

Stylistic and genre differences between the source texts affect compatibility for NER evaluation e.g., the CoNLL corpus formats headlines in all-caps, and includes non-sentential data such as tables of sports scores.

Each corpus uses a different set of entity labels. MUC marks locations (LOC), organisations (ORG) and personal names (PER), in addition to numerical and time information. The CoNLL NER shared tasks (Tjong Kim Sang, 2002; Tjong Kim Sang and De Meulder, 2003) mark PER, ORG and LOC entities, as well as a broad miscellaneous class

Corpus	# tags	Number of tokens		
		TRAIN	DEV	TEST
MUC-7	3	83601	18655	60436
CoNLL-03	4	203621	51362	46435
BBN	54	901894	142218	129654

Table 1: Gold-standard NE-annotated corpora

(MISC; e.g. events, artworks and nationalities). BBN annotates the entire Penn Treebank corpus with 105 fine-grained tags (Brunstein, 2002): 54 corresponding to CoNLL entities; 21 for numerical and time data; and 30 for other classes. For our evaluation, BBN's tags were reduced to the equivalent CoNLL tags, with extra tags in the BBN and MUC data removed. Since no MISC tags are marked in MUC, they need to be removed from CoNLL, BBN and Wikipedia data for comparison.

We transformed all three corpora into a common format and annotated them with part-of-speech tags using the Penn Treebank-trained C&C POS tagger. We altered the default MUC tokenisation to attach periods to abbreviations when sentence-internal. While standard training (TRAIN), development (DEV) and final test (TEST) set divisions were available for CoNLL and MUC, the BBN corpus was split at our discretion: sections 03–21 for TRAIN, 00–02 for DEV and 22-24 for TEST. Corpus sizes are compared in Table 1.

2.2 Evaluating NER performance

One challenge for NER research is establishing an appropriate evaluation metric (Nadeau and Sekine, 2007). In particular, entities may be correctly delimited but mis-classified, or entity boundaries may be mismatched.

MUC (Chinchor, 1998) awarded equal score for matching *type*, where an entity's *class* is identified with at least one boundary matching, and *text*, where an entity's boundaries are precisely delimited, irrespective of the classification. This equal weighting is unrealistic, as some boundary errors are highly significant, while others are arbitrary.

CoNLL awarded exact (*type* and *text*) phrasal matches, ignoring boundary issues entirely and providing a lower-bound measure of NER performance. Manning (2006) argues that CoNLL-style evaluation is biased towards systems which leave entities with ambiguous boundaries untagged, since boundary errors amount simultaneously to false positives and false negatives. In both MUC and CoNLL, micro-averaged precision, recall and F_1 score summarise the results.

Tsai et al. (2006) compares a number of methods for relaxing boundary requirements: matching only the left or right boundary, any tag overlap, per-token measures, or more semantically-driven matching. ACE evaluations instead use a customizable evaluation metric with weights specified for different types of error (NIST-ACE, 2008).

3 Corpus and error analysis approaches

To evaluate the performance impact of a corpus we may analyse (a) the annotations themselves; or (b) the model built on those annotations and its performance. A corpus can be considered in isolation or by comparison with other corpora. We use three methods to explore intra- and inter-corpus consistency in MUC, CoNLL, and BBN in Section 4.

3.1 N-gram tag variation

Dickinson and Meurers (2003) present a clever method for finding inconsistencies within POS annotated corpora, which we apply to NER corpora. Their approach finds all n-grams in a corpus which appear multiple times, albeit with variant tags for some sub-sequence, the *nucleus* (see e.g. Table 3). To remove valid ambiguity, they suggest using (a) a minimum n-gram length; (b) a minimum margin of invariant terms around the nucleus.

For example, the BBN TRAIN corpus includes eight occurrences of the 6-gram the San Francisco Bay area ,. Six instances of area are tagged as non-entities, but two instances are tagged as part of the LOC that precedes it. The other five tokens in this n-gram are consistently labelled.

3.2 Entity type frequency

An intuitive approach to finding discrepancies between corpora is to compare the distribution of entities within each corpus. To make this manageable, instances need to be grouped by more than their class labels. We used the following groups:

POS sequences: Types of candidate entities may often be distinguished by their POS tags, e.g. nationalities are often JJ or NNPS.

Wordtypes: Collins (2002) proposed *wordtypes* where all uppercase characters map to A, lowercase to a, and digits to 0. Adjacent characters in the same orthographic class were collapsed. However, we distinguish single from multiple characters by duplication. e.g. USS Nimitz (CVN-68) has wordtype AA Aaa (AA-00).

Wordtype with functions: We also map content words to wordtypes only—function words are retained, e.g. Bank of New England Corp. maps to Aaa of Aaa Aaa Aaa..

No approach provides sufficient discrimination alone: wordtype patterns are able to distinguish within common POS tags and vice versa. Each method can be further simplified by merging repeated tokens, NNP NNP becoming NNP.

By calculating the distribution of entities over these groupings, we can find anomalies between corpora. For instance, 4% of MUC's and 5.9% of BBN's PER entities have wordtype Aaa A. Aaa, e.g. David S. Black, while CoNLL has only 0.05% of PERs like this. Instead, CoNLL has many names of form A. Aaa, e.g. S. Waugh, while BBN and MUC have none. We can therefore predict incompatibilities between systems trained on BBN and evaluated on CoNLL or vice-versa.

3.3 Tag sequence confusion

A confusion matrix between predicted and correct classes is an effective method of error analysis. For phrasal sequence tagging, this can be applied to either exact boundary matches or on a per-token basis, ignoring entity bounds. We instead compile two matrices: C/P comparing correct entity classes against predicted tag sequences; and P/C comparing predicted classes to correct tag sequences.

C/P equates oversized boundaries to correct matches, and tabulates cases of undersized boundaries. For example, if [ORG Johnson and Johnson] is tagged [PER Johnson] and [PER Johnson], it is marked in matrix coordinates (ORG, PER O PER). P/C emphasises oversized boundaries: if gold-standard Mr. [PER Ross] is tagged PER, it is counted as confusion between PER and O PER. To further distinguish classes of error, the entity type groupings from Section 3.2 are also used.

This analysis is useful for both tagger evaluation and cross-corpus evaluation, e.g. BBN versus CoNLL on a BBN test set. This involves finding confusion matrix entries where BBN and CoNLL's performance differs significantly, identifying common errors related to difficult instances in the test corpus as well as errors in the NER model.

4 Comparing gold-standard corpora

We trained the C&C NER tagger (Curran and Clark, 2003) to build separate models for each gold-standard corpus. The C&C tagger utilises a number

TRAIN	With MISC		Without MISC		
	CoNLL	BBN	MUC	CoNLL	BBN
MUC	—	—	*73.5*	55.5	67.5
CoNLL	*81.2*	62.3	65.9	*82.1*	62.4
BBN	54.7	*86.7*	77.9	53.9	*88.4*

Table 2: Gold standard F-scores (exact-match)

of orthographic, contextual and in-document features, as well as gazetteers for personal names. Table 2 shows that each training set performs much better on corresponding (same corpus) test sets (italics) than on test sets from other sources, also identified by (Ciaramita and Altun, 2005). NER research typically deals with small improvements ($\sim$1% F-score). The 12-32% mismatch between training and test corpora suggests that an appropriate training corpus is a much greater concern. The exception is BBN on MUC, due to differing TEST and DEV subject matter. Here we analyse the variation within and between the gold standards.

Table 3 lists some n-gram tag variations for BBN and CoNLL (TRAIN + DEV). These include cases of schematic variations (e.g. the period in Co .) and tagging errors. Some n-grams have three variants, e.g. the Standard & Poor 's 500 which appears untagged, as the [ORG Standard & Poor] 's 500, or the [ORG Standard & Poor 's] 500. MUC is too small for this method. CoNLL only provides only a few examples, echoing BBN in the ambiguities of trailing periods and leading determiners or modifiers.

Wordtype distributions were also used to compare the three gold standards. We investigated all wordtypes which occur with at least twice the frequency in one corpus as in another, if that wordtype was sufficiently frequent. Among the differences recovered from this analysis are:

- CoNLL has an over-representation of uppercase words due to all-caps headlines.
- Since BBN also annotates common nouns, some have been mistakenly labelled as proper-noun entities.
- BBN tags text like Munich-based as LOC; CoNLL tags it as MISC; MUC separates the hyphen as a token.
- CoNLL is biased to sports and has many event names in the form of 1990 World Cup.
- BBN separates organisation names from their products as in [ORG Commodore] [MISC 64].
- CoNLL has few references to abbreviated US states.
- CoNLL marks conjunctions of people (e.g. Ruth and Edwin Brooks) as a single PER entity.
- CoNLL text has Co Ltd instead of Co. Ltd.

We analysed the tag sequence confusion when training with each corpus and testing on BBN DEV. While full confusion matrices are too large for this paper, Table 4 shows some examples where the

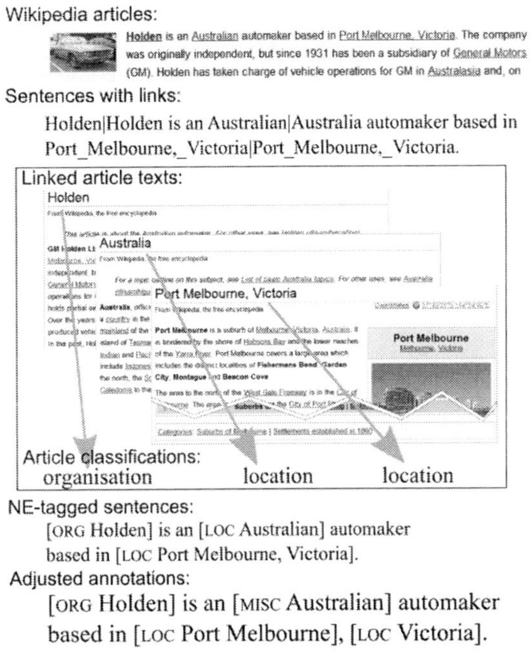

Figure 1: Deriving training data from Wikipedia

NER models disagree. MUC fails to correctly tag U.K. and U.S.. U.K. only appears once in MUC, and U.S. appears 22 times as ORG and 77 times as LOC. CoNLL has only three instances of Mr., so it often mis-labels Mr. as part of a PER entity. The MUC model also has trouble recognising ORG names ending with corporate abbreviations, and may fail to identify abbreviated US state names.

Our analysis demonstrates that seemingly minor orthographic variations in the text, tokenisation and annotation schemes can have a huge impact on practical NER performance.

5 From Wikipedia to NE-annotated text

Wikipedia is a collaborative, multilingual, online encyclopedia which includes over 2.3 million articles in English alone. Our baseline approach detailed in Nothman et al. (2008) exploits the hyperlinking between articles to derive a NE corpus.

Since $\sim$74% of Wikipedia articles describe topics covering entity classes, many of Wikipedia's links correspond to entity annotations in gold-standard NE corpora. We derive a NE-annotated corpus by the following steps:

1. Classify all articles into entity classes
2. Split Wikipedia articles into sentences
3. Label NEs according to link targets
4. Select sentences for inclusion in a corpus

N-gram	Tag	#	Tag	#
Co .	-	52	ORG	111
Smith Barney , Harris Upham & Co.	-	1	ORG	9
the **Contra** rebels	MISC	1	ORG	2
in the **West** is	-	1	LOC	1
that **the** Constitution	MISC	2	-	1
Chancellor of the **Exchequer** Nigel Lawson	-	11	ORG	2
the **world** 's	-	80	LOC	1
1993 BellSouth Classic	-	1	MISC	1
Atlanta Games	LOC	1	MISC	1
Justice Minister	-	1	ORG	1
GOLF - GERMAN OPEN	-	2	LOC	1

Table 3: Examples of n-gram tag variations in BBN (top) and CoNLL (bottom). Nucleus is in bold.

Tag sequence Correct	Tag sequence Pred.	Grouping	# if trained on MUC	# if trained on CoNLL	# if trained on BBN	Example
LOC	LOC	A.A.	101	349	343	U.K.
- PER	PER	Aa. Aaa	9	242	0	Mr. Watson
-	LOC	Aa.	16	109	0	Mr.
ORG	ORG	Aaa Aaa.	118	214	218	Campeau Corp.
LOC	-	Aaa.	20	0	3	Calif.

Table 4: Tag sequence confusion on BBN DEV when training on gold-standard corpora (no MISC)

In Figure 1, a sentence introducing Holden as an Australian car maker based in Port Melbourne has links to separate articles about each entity. Cues in the linked article about Holden indicate that it is an organisation, and the article on Port Melbourne is likewise classified as a location. The original sentence can then be automatically annotated with these facts. We thus extract millions of sentences from Wikipedia to form a new NER corpus.

We classify each article in a bootstrapping process using its category head nouns, definitional nouns from opening sentences, and title capitalisation. Each article is classified as one of: unknown; a member of a NE category (LOC, ORG, PER, MISC, as per CoNLL); a disambiguation page (these list possible referent articles for a given title); or a non-entity (NON). This classifier classifier achieves 89% F-score.

A sentence is selected for our corpus when all of its capitalised words are linked to articles with a known class. Exceptions are made for common titlecase words, e.g. I, Mr., June, and sentence-initial words. We also infer additional links — variant titles are collected for each Wikipedia topic and are marked up in articles which link to them — which Nothman et al. (2008) found increases coverage.

Transforming links into annotations that conform to a gold standard is far from trivial. Link boundaries need to be adjusted, e.g. to remove excess punctuation. Adjectival forms of entities (e.g. American, Islamic) generally link to nominal articles. However, they are treated by CoNLL and our BBN mapping as MISC. POS tagging the corpus and relabelling entities ending with JJ as MISC solves this heuristically. Although they are capitalised in English, personal titles (e.g. Prime Minister) are not typically considered entities. Initially we assume that all links immediately preceding PER entities are titles and delete their entity classification.

N-gram	Tag	#	Tag	#
of **Batman** 's	MISC	2	PER	5
in **the** Netherlands	-	58	LOC	4
Chicago , Illinois	-	8	LOC	3
the **American** and	LOC	1	MISC	2

Table 5: N-gram variations in the Wiki baseline

6 Improving Wikipedia performance

The baseline system described above achieves only 58.9% and 62.3% on the CoNLL and BBN TEST sets (exact-match scoring) with 3.5-million training tokens. We apply methods proposed in Section 3 to to identify and minimise Wikipedia errors on the BBN DEV corpus.

We begin by considering Wikipedia's internal consistency using n-gram tag variation (Table 5). The breadth of Wikipedia leads to greater genuine ambiguity, e.g. Batman (a character or a comic strip). It also shares gold-standard inconsistencies like leading modifiers. Variations in American and Chicago, Illinois indicate errors in adjectival entity labels and in correcting link boundaries.

Some errors identified with tag sequence confusion are listed in Table 6. These correspond to re-

Tag sequence		Grouping	# if trained on		Example
Correct	Pred.		BBN	Wiki	
LOC	LOC	Aaa.	103	14	Calif.
LOC - LOC	ORG	Aaa , Aaa.	0	15	Norwalk , Conn.
LOC	LOC	Aaa-aa	23	0	Texas-based
- PER	PER	Aa. Aaa	4	208	Mr. Yamamoto
- PER	PER	Aaa Aaa	1	49	Judge Keenan
-	PER	Aaa	7	58	President
MISC	MISC	A.	25	1	R.
MISC	LOC	NNPS	0	39	Soviets

Table 6: Tag sequence confusion on BBN DEV with training on BBN and the Wikipedia baseline

sults of an entity type frequency analysis and motivate many of our Wikipedia extensions presented below. In particular, personal titles are tagged as PER rather than unlabelled; plural nationalities are tagged LOC, not MISC; LOCs hyphenated to following words are not identified; nor are abbreviated US state names. Using R. to abbreviate Republican in BBN is also a high-frequency error.

6.1 Inference from disambiguation pages

Our baseline system infers extra links using a set of alternative titles identified for each article. We extract the alternatives from the article and redirect titles, the text of all links to the article, and the first and last word of the article title if it is labelled PER.

Our extension is to extract additional inferred titles from Wikipedia's disambiguation pages. Most disambiguation pages are structured as lists of articles that are often referred to by the title D being disambiguated. For each link with target A that appears at the start of a list item on D's page, D and its redirect aliases are added to the list of alternative titles for A.

Our new source of alternative titles includes acronyms and abbreviations (AMP links to AMP Limited and Ampere), and given or family names (Howard links to Howard Dean and John Howard).

6.2 Personal titles

Personal titles (e.g. Brig. Gen., Prime Minister-elect) are capitalised in English. Titles are sometimes linked in Wikipedia, but the target articles, e.g. U.S. President, are in Wikipedia categories like Presidents of the United States, causing their incorrect classification as PER.

Our initial implementation assumed that links immediately preceding PER entity links are titles. While this feature improved performance, it only captured one context for personal titles and failed to handle instances where the title was only a portion of the link text, such as Australian *Prime Minister-elect* or *Prime Minister* of Australia.

To handle titles more comprehensively, we compiled a list of the terms most frequently linked immediately prior to PER links. These were manually filtered, removing LOC or ORG mentions and complemented with abbreviated titles extracted from BBN, producing a list of 384 base title forms, 11 prefixes (e.g. Vice) and 3 suffixes (e.g. -elect). Using these gazetteers, titles are stripped of erroneous NE tags.

6.3 Adjectival forms

In English, capitalisation is retained in adjectival entity forms, such as American or Islamic. While these are not exactly entities, both CoNLL and BBN annotate them as MISC. Our baseline approach POS tagged the corpus and marked all adjectival entities as MISC. This missed instances where nationalities are used nominally, e.g. five Italians.

We extracted 339 frequent LOC and ORG references with POS tag JJ. Words from this list (e.g. Italian) are relabelled MISC, irrespective of POS tag or pluralisation (e.g. Italian/JJ, Italian/NNP, Italian/NNPS). This unfiltered list includes some errors from POS tagging, e.g. First, Emmy; and others where MISC is rarely the appropriate tag, e.g. the Democrats (an ORG).

6.4 Miscellaneous changes

Entity-word aliases Longest-string matching for inferred links often adds redundant words, e.g. both Australian and Australian people are redirects to Australia. We therefore exclude from inference titles of form X Y where X is an alias of the same article and Y is lowercase.

State abbreviations A gold standard may use stylistic forms which are rare in Wikipedia. For instance, the Wall Street Journal (BBN) uses US state abbreviations, while Wikipedia nearly always refers to states in full. We boosted performance by substituting a random selection of US state names in Wikipedia with their abbreviations.

TRAIN	With MISC		No MISC		
	CoN.	BBN	MUC	CoN.	BBN
MUC	—	—	*82.3*	54.9	69.3
CoNLL	*85.9*	61.9	69.9	*86.9*	60.2
BBN	59.4	*86.5*	80.2	59.0	*88.0*
WP0 – no inf.	62.8	69.7	69.7	64.7	70.0
WP1	67.2	73.4	75.3	67.7	73.6
WP2	**69.0**	**74.0**	76.6	69.4	**75.1**
WP3	68.9	73.5	**77.2**	**69.5**	73.7
WP4 – all inf.	66.2	72.3	75.6	67.3	73.3

Table 7: Exact-match DEV F-scores

TRAIN	With MISC		No MISC		
	CoN.	BBN	MUC	CoN.	BBN
MUC	—	—	*89.0*	68.2	79.2
CoNLL	*91.0*	75.1	81.4	*90.9*	72.6
BBN	72.7	*91.1*	87.6	71.8	*91.5*
WP0 – no inf.	71.0	79.3	76.3	71.1	78.7
WP1	74.9	82.3	81.4	73.1	81.0
WP2	76.1	**82.7**	81.6	74.5	**81.9**
WP3	**76.3**	82.2	**81.9**	**74.7**	80.7
WP4 – all inf.	74.3	81.4	80.9	73.1	80.7

Table 8: MUC-style DEV F-scores

Removing rare cases We explicitly removed sentences containing title abbreviations (e.g. Mr.) appearing in non-PER entities such as movie titles. Compared to newswire, these forms as personal titles are rare in Wikipedia, so their appearance in entities causes tagging errors. We used a similar approach to personal names including of, which also act as noise.

Fixing tokenization Hyphenation is a problem in tokenisation: should London-based be one token, two, or three? Both BBN and CoNLL treat it as one token, but BBN labels it a LOC and CoNLL a MISC. Our baseline had split hyphenated portions from entities. Fixing this to match the BBN approach improved performance significantly.

7 Experiments

We evaluated our annotation process by building separate NER models learned from Wikipedia-derived and gold-standard data. Our results are given as micro-averaged precision, recall and F-scores both in terms of MUC-style and CoNLL-style (exact-match) scoring. We evaluated all experiments with and without the MISC category.

Wikipedia's articles are freely available for download.[1] We have used data from the 2008 May 22 dump of English Wikipedia which includes 2.3 million articles. Splitting this into sentences and tokenising produced 32 million sentences each containing an average of 24 tokens.

Our experiments were performed with a Wikipedia corpus of 3.5 million tokens. Although we had up to 294 million tokens available, we were limited by the RAM required by the C&C tagger training software.

8 Results

Tables 7 and 8 show F-scores on the MUC, CoNLL, and BBN development sets for CoNLL-style exact

[1]http://download.wikimedia.org/

Training corpus	DEV (MUC-style F)		
	MUC	CoNLL	BBN
Corresponding TRAIN	89.0	91.0	91.1
TRAIN + WP2	90.6	91.7	91.2

Table 9: Wikipedia as additional training data

TRAIN	With MISC		No MISC		
	CoN.	BBN	MUC	CoN.	BBN
MUC	—	—	*73.5*	55.5	67.5
CoNLL	*81.2*	62.3	65.9	*82.1*	62.4
BBN	54.7	*86.7*	77.9	53.9	*88.4*
WP2	60.9	69.3	76.9	61.5	69.9

Table 10: Exact-match TEST results for WP2

TRAIN	With MISC		No MISC		
	CoN.	BBN	MUC	CoN.	BBN
MUC	—	—	*81.0*	68.5	77.6
CoNLL	*87.8*	75.0	76.2	*87.9*	74.1
BBN	69.3	*91.1*	83.6	68.5	*91.9*
WP2	70.2	79.1	81.3	68.6	77.3

Table 11: MUC-eval TEST results for WP2

match and MUC-style evaluations (which are typically a few percent higher). The cross-corpus gold standard experiments on the DEV sets are shown first in both tables. As in Table 2, the performance drops significantly when the training and test corpus are from different sources. The corresponding TEST set scores are given in Tables 9 and 10.

The second group of experiments in these tables show the performance of Wikipedia corpora with increasing levels of link inference (described in Section 6.1). Links inferred upon matching article titles (WP1) and disambiguation titles (WP2) consistently increase F-score by ~5%, while surnames for PER entities (WP3) and all link texts (WP4) tend to introduce error. A key result of our work is that the performance of non-corresponding gold standards is often significantly exceeded by our Wikipedia training data.

Our third group of experiments combined our Wikipedia corpora with gold-standard data to improve performance beyond traditional train-test pairs. Table 9 shows that this approach may lead

Token	Corr.	Pred.	Count	Why?
.	ORG	-	90	Inconsistencies in BBN
House	ORG	LOC	56	Article White House is a LOC due to classification bootstrapping
Wall	-	LOC	33	Wall Street is ambiguously a location and a concept
Gulf	ORG	LOC	29	Georgia Gulf is common in BBN, but Gulf indicates LOC
,	ORG	-	26	A difficult NER ambiguity in e.g. Robertson , Stephens & Co.
's	ORG	-	25	Unusually high frequency of ORGs ending 's in BBN
Senate	ORG	LOC	20	Classification bootstrapping identifies Senate as a house, i.e. LOC
S&P	-	MISC	20	Rare in Wikipedia, and inconsistently labelled in BBN
D.	MISC	PER	14	BBN uses D. to abbreviate Democrat

Table 12: Tokens in BBN DEV that our Wikipedia model frequently mis-tagged

Class	By exact phrase			By token		
	P	R	F	P	R	F
LOC	66.7	87.9	75.9	64.4	89.8	75.0
MISC	48.8	58.7	53.3	46.5	61.6	53.0
ORG	76.9	56.5	65.1	88.9	68.1	77.1
PER	67.3	91.4	77.5	70.5	93.6	80.5
All	68.6	69.9	69.3	80.9	75.3	78.0

Table 13: Category results for WP2 on BBN TEST

to small F-score increases.

Our per-class Wikipedia results are shown in Table 13. LOC and PER entities are relatively easy to identify, although a low precision for PER suggests that many other entities have been marked erroneously as people, unlike the high precision and low recall of ORG. As an ill-defined category, with uncertain mapping between BBN and CoNLL classes, MISC precision is unsurprisingly low. We also show results evaluating the correct labelling of each token, where Nothman et al. (2008) had reported results 13% higher than phrasal matching, reflecting a failure to correctly identify entity boundaries. We have reduced this difference to 9%. A BBN-trained model gives only 5% difference between phrasal and token F-score.

Among common tagging errors, we identified: tags continuing over additional words as in New York-based Loews Corp. all being marked as a single ORG; nationalities marked as LOC rather than MISC; White House a LOC rather than ORG, as with many sports teams; single-word ORG entities marked as PER; titles such as Dr. included in PER tags; mis-labelling un-tagged title-case terms and tagged lowercase terms in the gold-standard.

The corpus analysis methods described in Section 3 show greater similarity between our Wikipedia-derived corpus and BBN after implementing our extensions. There is nonetheless much scope for further analysis and improvement. Notably, the most commonly mis-tagged tokens in BBN (see Table 12) relate more often to individual entities and stylistic differences than to a generalisable class of errors.

9 Conclusion

We have demonstrated the enormous variability in performance between using NER models trained and tested on the same corpus versus tested on other gold standards. This variability arises from not only mismatched annotation schemes but also stylistic conventions, tokenisation, and missing frequent lexical items. Therefore, NER corpora must be carefully matched to the target text for reasonable performance. We demonstrate three approaches for gauging corpus and annotation mismatch, and apply them to MUC, CoNLL and BBN, and our automatically-derived Wikipedia corpora.

There is much room for improving the results of our Wikipedia-based NE annotations. In particular, a more careful approach to link inference may further reduce incorrect boundaries of tagged entities. We plan to increase the largest training set the C&C tagger can support so that we can fully exploit the enormous Wikipedia corpus.

However, we have shown that Wikipedia can be used a source of free annotated data for training NER systems. Although such corpora need to be engineered specifically to a desired application, Wikipedia's breadth may permit the production of large corpora even within specific domains. Our results indicate that Wikipedia data can perform better (up to 11% for CoNLL on MUC) than training data that is not matched to the evaluation, and hence is widely applicable. Transforming Wikipedia into training data thus provides a free and high-yield alternative to the laborious manual annotation required for NER.

Acknowledgments

We would like to thank the Language Technology Research Group and the anonymous reviewers for their feedback. This project was supported by Australian Research Council Discovery Project DP0665973 and Nothman was supported by a University of Sydney Honours Scholarship.

References

Joohui An, Seungwoo Lee, and Gary Geunbae Lee. 2003. Automatic acquisition of named entity tagged corpus from world wide web. In *The Companion Volume to the Proceedings of 41st Annual Meeting of the Association for Computational Linguistics*, pages 165–168.

Ada Brunstein. 2002. Annotation guidelines for answer types. LDC2005T33.

Nancy Chinchor. 1998. Overview of MUC-7. In *Proc. of the 7th Message Understanding Conference*.

Massimiliano Ciaramita and Yasemin Altun. 2005. Named-entity recognition in novel domains with external lexical knowledge. In *Proceedings of the NIPS Workshop on Advances in Structured Learning for Text and Speech Processing*.

Michael Collins. 2002. Ranking algorithms for named-entity extraction: boosting and the voted perceptron. In *Proceedings of the 40th Annual Meeting on Association for Computational Linguistics*, pages 489–496, Morristown, NJ, USA.

James R. Curran and Stephen Clark. 2003. Language independent NER using a maximum entropy tagger. In *Proceedings of the 7th Conference on Natural Language Learning*, pages 164–167.

Markus Dickinson and W. Detmar Meurers. 2003. Detecting errors in part-of-speech annotation. In *Proceedings of the 10th Conference of the European Chapter of the Association for Computational Linguistics*, pages 107–114, Budapest, Hungary.

Oren Etzioni, Michael Cafarella, Doug Downey, Ana-Maria Popescu, Tal Shaked, Stephen Soderland, Daniel S. Weld, and Alexander Yates. 2005. Unsupervised named-entity extraction from the web: An experimental study. *Artificial Intelligence*, 165(1):91–134.

Jun'ichi Kazama and Kentaro Torisawa. 2007. Exploiting Wikipedia as external knowledge for named entity recognition. In *Proceedings of the 2007 Joint Conference on Empirical Methods in Natural Language Processing and Computational Natural Language Learning*, pages 698–707.

Jin-Dong Kim, Tomoko Ohta, Yuka Tateisi, and Jun'ichi Tsujii. 2003. GENIA corpus—a semantically annotated corpus for bio-textmining. *Bioinformatics*, 19(suppl. 1):i180–i182.

Christopher Manning. 2006. Doing named entity recognition? Don't optimize for F_1. In *NLPers Blog*, 25 August. `http://nlpers.blogspot.com`.

Andrei Mikheev, Marc Moens, and Claire Grover. 1999. Named entity recognition without gazetteers. In *Proceedings of the 9th Conference of the European Chapter of the Association for Computational Linguistics*, pages 1–8, Bergen, Norway.

2001. *Message Understanding Conference (MUC) 7*. Linguistic Data Consortium, Philadelphia.

David Nadeau and Satoshi Sekine. 2007. A survey of named entity recognition and classification. *Lingvisticae Investigationes*, 30:3–26.

David Nadeau, Peter D. Turney, and Stan Matwin. 2006. Unsupervised named-entity recognition: Generating gazetteers and resolving ambiguity. In *Proceedings of the 19th Canadian Conference on Artificial Intelligence*, volume 4013 of *LNCS*, pages 266–277.

NIST-ACE. 2008. Automatic content extraction 2008 evaluation plan (ACE08). NIST, April 7.

Joel Nothman, James R. Curran, and Tara Murphy. 2008. Transforming Wikipedia into named entity training data. In *Proceedings of the Australian Language Technology Workshop*, pages 124–132, Hobart.

Alexander E. Richman and Patrick Schone. 2008. Mining wiki resources for multilingual named entity recognition. In *46th Annual Meeting of the Association for Computational Linguistics: Human Language Technologies*, pages 1–9, Columbus, Ohio.

Erik F. Tjong Kim Sang and Fien De Meulder. 2003. Introduction to the CoNLL-2003 shared task: Language-independent named entity recognition. In *Proceedings of the 7th Conference on Natural Language Learning*, pages 142–147.

Erik F. Tjong Kim Sang. 2002. Introduction to the CoNLL-2002 shared task: language-independent named entity recognition. In *Proceedings of the 6th Conference on Natural Language Learning*, pages 1–4.

Antonio Toral, Rafael Muñoz, and Monica Monachini. 2008. Named entity WordNet. In *Proceedings of the 6th International Language Resources and Evaluation Conference*.

Richard Tzong-Han Tsai, Shih-Hung Wu, Wen-Chi Chou, Yu-Chun Lin, Ding He, Jieh Hsiang, Ting-Yi Sung, and Wen-Lian Hsu. 2006. Various criteria in the evaluation of biomedical named entity recognition. *BMC Bioinformatics*, 7:96–100.

Ralph Weischedel and Ada Brunstein. 2005. *BBN Pronoun Coreference and Entity Type Corpus*. Linguistic Data Consortium, Philadelphia.

Using lexical and relational similarity to classify semantic relations

Diarmuid Ó Séaghdha
Computer Laboratory
University of Cambridge
15 JJ Thomson Avenue
Cambridge CB3 0FD
United Kingdom
do242@cl.cam.ac.uk

Ann Copestake
Computer Laboratory
University of Cambridge
15 JJ Thomson Avenue
Cambridge CB3 0FD
United Kingdom
aac10@cl.cam.ac.uk

Abstract

Many methods are available for computing semantic similarity between individual words, but certain NLP tasks require the comparison of word pairs. This paper presents a kernel-based framework for application to relational reasoning tasks of this kind. The model presented here combines information about two distinct types of word pair similarity: lexical similarity and relational similarity. We present an efficient and flexible technique for implementing relational similarity and show the effectiveness of combining lexical and relational models by demonstrating state-of-the-art results on a compound noun interpretation task.

1 Introduction

The problem of modelling semantic similarity between words has long attracted the interest of researchers in Natural Language Processing and has been shown to be important for numerous applications. For some tasks, however, it is more appropriate to consider the problem of modelling similarity between pairs of words. This is the case when dealing with tasks involving *relational* or *analogical reasoning*. In such tasks, the challenge is to compare pairs of words on the basis of the semantic relation(s) holding between the members of each pair. For example, the noun pairs (*steel,knife*) and (*paper,cup*) are similar because in both cases the relation N_2 *is made of* N_1 frequently holds between their members. Analogical tasks are distinct from (but not unrelated to) other kinds of "relation extraction" tasks where each data item is tied to a specific sentence context (e.g., Girju et al. (2007)).

One such relational reasoning task is the problem of compound noun interpretation, which has received a great deal of attention in recent years (Girju et al., 2005; Turney, 2006; Butnariu and Veale, 2008). In English (and other languages), the process of producing new lexical items through compounding is very frequent and very productive. Furthermore, the noun-noun relation expressed by a given compound is not explicit in its surface form: a *steel knife* may be a *knife made from steel* but a *kitchen knife* is most likely to be a *knife used in a kitchen*, not a *knife made from a kitchen*. The assumption made by similarity-based interpretation methods is that the likely meaning of a novel compound can be predicted by comparing it to previously seen compounds whose meanings are known. This is a natural framework for computational techniques; there is also empirical evidence for similarity-based interpretation in human compound processing (Ryder, 1994; Devereux and Costello, 2007).

This paper presents an approach to relational reasoning based on combining information about two kinds of similarity between word pairs: *lexical similarity* and *relational similarity*. The assumptions underlying these two models of similarity are sketched in Section 2. In Section 3 we describe how these models can be implemented for statistical machine learning with kernel methods. We present a new flexible and efficient kernel-based framework for classification with relational similarity. In Sections 4 and 5 we apply our methods to a compound interpretation task and demonstrate that combining models of lexical and relational similarity can give state-of-the-art results on a compound noun interpretation task, surpassing the performance attained by either model taken alone. We then discuss previous research on relational similarity, and show that some previously proposed models can be implemented in our framework as special cases. Given the good performance achieved for compound interpretation, it seems likely that the methods presented in this pa-

Proceedings of the 12th Conference of the European Chapter of the ACL, pages 621–629,
Athens, Greece, 30 March – 3 April 2009. ©2009 Association for Computational Linguistics

per can also be applied successfully to other relational reasoning tasks; we suggest some directions for future research in Section 7.

2 Two models of word pair similarity

While there is a long tradition of NLP research on methods for calculating semantic similarity between words, calculating similarity between pairs (or n-tuples) of words is a less well-understood problem. In fact, the problem has rarely been stated explicitly, though it is implicitly addressed by most work on compound noun interpretation and semantic relation extraction. This section describes two complementary approaches for using distributional information extracted from corpora to calculate noun pair similarity.

The first model of pair similarity is based on standard methods for computing semantic similarity between individual words. According to this *lexical similarity* model, word pairs (w_1, w_2) and (w_3, w_4) are judged similar if w_1 is similar to w_3 and w_2 is similar to w_4. Given a measure $wsim$ of word-word similarity, a measure of pair similarity $psim$ can be derived as a linear combination of pairwise lexical similarities:

$$psim((w_1, w_2), (w_3, w_4)) = \alpha[wsim(w_1, w_3)] + \beta[wsim(w_2, w_4)] \quad (1)$$

A great number of methods for lexical semantic similarity have been proposed in the NLP literature. The most common paradigm for corpus-based methods, and the one adopted here, is based on the *distributional hypothesis*: that two words are semantically similar if they have similar patterns of co-occurrence with other words in some set of contexts. Curran (2004) gives a comprehensive overview of distributional methods.

The second model of pair similarity rests on the assumption that when the members of a word pair are mentioned in the same context, that context is likely to yield information about the relations holding between the words' referents. For example, the members of the pair $(bear, forest)$ may tend to co-occur in contexts containing patterns such as w_1 *lives in the* w_2 and *in the* w_2,*... a* w_1, suggesting that a *LOCATED_IN* or *LIVES_IN* relation frequently holds between bears and forests. If the contexts in which *fish* and *reef* co-occur are similar to those found for *bear* and *forest*, this is evidence that the same semantic relation tends to hold between the members of each pair. A *relational distributional hypothesis* therefore states that two word pairs are semantically similar if their members appear together in similar contexts.

The distinction between lexical and relational similarity for word pair comparison is recognised by Turney (2006) (he calls the former *attributional similarity*), though the methods he presents focus on relational similarity. Ó Séaghdha and Copestake's (2007) classification of information sources for noun compound interpretation also includes a description of lexical and relational similarity. Approaches to compound noun interpretation have tended to use either lexical or relational similarity, though rarely both (see Section 6 below).

3 Kernel methods for pair similarity

3.1 Kernel methods

The kernel framework for machine learning is a natural choice for similarity-based classification (Shawe-Taylor and Cristianini, 2004). The central concept in this framework is the *kernel function*, which can be viewed as a measure of similarity between data items. Valid kernels must satisfy the mathematical condition of *positive semi-definiteness*; this is equivalent to requiring that the kernel function equate to an inner product in some vector space. The kernel can be expressed in terms of a mapping function ϕ from the input space $\mathcal{X}$ to a feature space $\mathcal{F}$:

$$k(\mathbf{x}_i, \mathbf{x}_j) = \langle \phi(\mathbf{x}_i), \phi(\mathbf{x}_j) \rangle_{\mathcal{F}} \quad (2)$$

where $\langle \cdot, \cdot \rangle_{\mathcal{F}}$ is the inner product associated with $\mathcal{F}$. $\mathcal{X}$ and $\mathcal{F}$ need not have the same dimensionality or be of the same type. $\mathcal{F}$ is by definition an inner product space, but the elements of $\mathcal{X}$ need not even be vectorial, so long as a suitable mapping function ϕ can be found. Furthermore, it is often possible to calculate kernel values without explicitly representing the elements of $\mathcal{F}$; this allows the use of implicit feature spaces with a very high or even infinite dimensionality.

Kernel functions have received significant attention in recent years, most notably due to the successful application of Support Vector Machines (Cortes and Vapnik, 1995) to many problems. The SVM algorithm learns a decision boundary between two data classes that maximises the minimum distance or *margin* from the training points in each class to the boundary. The geometry of the space in which this boundary is set depends on the kernel function used to compare data items. By tailoring the choice of kernel to the task at hand, the user can use prior knowledge and intuition to improve classification performance.

One useful property of kernels is that any sum or linear combination of kernel functions is itself a valid kernel. Theoretical analyses (Cristianini et al., 2001; Joachims et al., 2001) and empirical investigations (e.g., Gliozzo et al. (2005)) have shown that combining kernels in this way can have a beneficial effect when the component kernels capture different "views" of the data while individually attaining similar levels of discriminative performance. In the experiments described below, we make use of this insight to integrate lexical and relational information for semantic classification of compound nouns.

3.2 Lexical kernels

Ó Séaghdha and Copestake (2008) demonstrate how standard techniques for distributional similarity can be implemented in a kernel framework. In particular, kernels for comparing probability distributions can be derived from standard probabilistic distance measures through simple transformations. These distributional kernels are suited to a data representation where each word w is identified with the a vector of conditional probabilities $(P(c_1|w), \dots, P(c_{|C|}|w))$ that defines a distribution over other terms c co-occurring with w. For example, the following positive semi-definite kernel between words can be derived from the well-known Jensen-Shannon divergence:

$$k_{jsd}(w_1, w_2) = \\ -\sum_c [P(c|w_1)\log_2(\frac{P(c|w_1)}{P(c|w_1)+P(c|w_2)}) \\ + P(c|w_2)\log_2(\frac{P(c|w_2)}{P(c|w_1)+P(c|w_2)})] \quad (3)$$

A straightforward method of extending this model to word pairs is to represent each pair (w_1, w_2) as the concatenation of the co-occurrence probability vectors for w_1 and w_2. Taking k_{jsd} as a measure of word similarity and introducing parameters α and β to scale the contributions of w_1 and w_2 respectively, we retrieve the lexical model of pair similarity defined above in (1). Without prior knowledge of the relative importance of each pair constituent, it is natural to set both scaling parameters to 0.5, and this is done in the experiments below.

3.3 String embedding functions

The necessary starting point for our implementation of relational similarity is a means of comparing contexts. Contexts can be represented in a variety of ways, from unordered bags of words to rich syntactic structures. The context representation adopted here is based on *strings*, which preserve useful information about the order of words in the context yet can be processed and compared quite efficiently. *String kernels* are a family of kernels that compare strings $\mathbf{s}$, $\mathbf{t}$ by mapping them into feature vectors $\phi_{String}(\mathbf{s})$, $\phi_{String}(\mathbf{t})$ whose non-zero elements index the subsequences contained in each string.

A *string* is defined as a finite sequence $\mathbf{s} = (s_1, \dots, s_l)$ of symbols belonging to an alphabet Σ. Σ^l is the set of all strings of length l, and Σ^* is set of all strings or the *language*. A subsequence $\mathbf{u}$ of $\mathbf{s}$ is defined by a sequence of indices $\mathbf{i} = (i_1, \dots, i_{|\mathbf{u}|})$ such that $1 \leq i_1 < \dots < i_{|\mathbf{u}|} \leq |\mathbf{s}|$, where $|\mathbf{s}|$ is the length of $\mathbf{s}$. $len(\mathbf{i}) = i_{|\mathbf{u}|} - i_1 + 1$ is the length of the subsequence in $\mathbf{s}$. An *embedding* $\phi_{String} : \Sigma^* \rightarrow \mathbb{R}^{|\Sigma|^l}$ is a function that maps a string s onto a vector of positive "counts" that correspond to subsequences contained in $\mathbf{s}$.

One example of an embedding function is a *gap-weighted embedding*, defined as

$$\phi_{gap_l}(\mathbf{s}) = [\sum_{\mathbf{i}:\mathbf{s}[\mathbf{i}]=\mathbf{u}} \lambda^{len(\mathbf{i})}]_{\mathbf{u}\in\Sigma^l} \quad (4)$$

λ is a decay parameter between 0 and 1; the smaller its value, the more the influence of a discontinuous subsequence is reduced. When $l = 1$ this corresponds to a "bag-of-words" embedding. Gap-weighted string kernels implicitly compute the similarity between two strings $\mathbf{s}$, $\mathbf{t}$ as an inner product $\langle\phi(\mathbf{s}), \phi(\mathbf{t})\rangle$. Lodhi et al. (2002) present an efficient dynamic programming algorithm that evaluates this kernel in $O(l|s||t|)$ time without explicitly representing the feature vectors $\phi(\mathbf{s})$, $\phi(\mathbf{t})$.

An alternative embedding is that used by Turney (2008) in his PairClass system (see Section 6). For the PairClass embedding ϕ_{PC}, an n-word context

$$[0-1 \text{ words}]\ N_{1|2}\ [0-3 \text{ words}]\ N_{1|2}\ [0-1 \text{ words}]$$

containing target words N_1, N_2 is mapped onto the 2^{n-2} patterns produced by substituting zero or more of the context words with a wildcard $*$. Unlike the patterns used by the gap-weighted embedding these are not truly discontinuous, as each wildcard must match exactly one word.

3.4 Kernels on sets

String kernels afford a way of comparing individual contexts. In order to compute the relational similarity of two pairs, however, we do not want to associate each pair with a single context but rather with the set of contexts in which they appear together. In this section, we use string embeddings to define kernels on sets of strings.

One natural way of defining a kernel over sets is to take the average of the pairwise basic kernel values between members of the two sets A and B. Let k_0 be a kernel on a set $\mathcal{X}$, and let $A, B \subseteq \mathcal{X}$ be sets of cardinality $|A|$ and $|B|$ respectively. The *averaged kernel* is defined as

$$k_{ave}(A, B) = \frac{1}{|A||B|} \sum_{a \in A} \sum_{b \in B} k_0(a, b) \quad (5)$$

This kernel was introduced by Gärtner et al. (2002) in the context of multiple instance learning. It was first used for computing relational similarity by Ó Séaghdha and Copestake (2007). The efficiency of the kernel computation is dominated by the $|A| \times |B|$ basic kernel calculations. When each basic kernel calculation $k_0(a, b)$ has significant complexity, as is the case with string kernels, calculating k_{ave} can be slow.

A second perspective views each set as corresponding to a probability distribution, and takes the members of that set as observed samples from that distribution. In this way a kernel on distributions can be cast as a kernel on sets. In the case of sets whose members are strings, a string embedding ϕ_{String} can be used to estimate a probability distribution over subsequences for each set by taking the normalised sum of the feature mappings of its members:

$$\phi_{Set}(A) = \frac{1}{Z} \sum_{\mathbf{s} \in A} \phi_{String}(\mathbf{s}) \quad (6)$$

where Z is a normalisation factor. Different choices of ϕ_{String} yield different relational similarity models. In this paper we primarily use the gap-weighted embedding ϕ_{gap_l}; we also discuss the PairClass embedding ϕ_{PC} for comparison.

Once the embedding ϕ_{Set} has been calculated, any suitable inner product can be applied to the resulting vectors, e.g. the linear kernel (dot product) or the Jensen-Shannon kernel defined in (3). In the latter case, which we term k_{jsd} below, the natural choice for normalisation is the sum of the entries in $\sum_{\mathbf{s} \in A} \phi_{String}(\mathbf{s})$, ensuring that $\phi_{Set}(A)$ has unit L_1 norm and defines a probability distribution. Furthermore, scaling $\phi_{Set}(A)$ by $\frac{1}{|A|}$, applying L_2 vector normalisation and applying the linear kernel retrieves the averaged set kernel $k_{ave}(A, B)$ as a special case of the distributional framework for sets of strings.

Instead of requiring $|A||B|$ basic kernel evaluations for each pair of sets, distributional set kernels only require the embedding $\phi_{Set}(A)$ to be computed once for each set and then a single vector inner product for each pair of sets. This is generally far more efficient than the kernel averaging method. The significant drawback is that representing the feature vector for each set demands a large amount of memory; for the gap-weighted embedding with subsequence length l, each vector potentially contains up to $|A|\binom{|\mathbf{s}_{max}|}{l}$ entries, where $\mathbf{s}_{max}$ is the longest string in A. In practice, however, the vector length will be lower due to subsequences occurring more than once and many strings being shorter than $\mathbf{s}_{max}$.

One way to reduce the memory load is to reduce the lengths of the strings used, either by retaining just the part of each string expected to be informative or by discarding all strings longer than an acceptable maximum. The PairClass embedding function implicitly restricts the contexts considered by only applying to strings where no more than three words occur between the targets, and by ignoring all non-intervening words except single ones adjacent to the targets. A further technique is to trade off time efficiency for space efficiency by computing the set kernel matrix in a blockwise fashion. To do this, the input data is divided into blocks of roughly equal size – the size that is relevant here is the sum of the cardinalities of the sets in a given block. Larger block sizes b therefore allow faster computation, but they require more memory. In the experiments described below, b was set to 5,000 for embeddings of length $l = 1$ and $l = 2$, and to 3,000 for $l = 3$.

4 Experimental setup for compound noun interpretation

4.1 Dataset

The dataset used in our experiments is Ó Séaghdha and Copestake's (2007) set of 1,443 compound nouns extracted from the British National Corpus (BNC).[1] Each compound is annotated with one of

[1] The data are available from `http://www.cl.cam.ac.uk/~do242/resources.html`.

six semantic relations: *BE, HAVE, IN, AGENT, INSTRUMENT* and *ABOUT*. For example, *air disaster* is labelled *IN* (*a disaster in the air*) and *freight train* is labelled *INSTRUMENT* (*a train that carries freight*). The best previous classification result on this dataset was reported by Ó Séaghdha and Copestake (2008), who achieved 61.0% accuracy and 58.8% F-score with a purely lexical model of compound similarity.

4.2 General Methodology

All experiments were run using the LIBSVM Support Vector Machine library.[2] The one-versus-all method was used to decompose the multiclass task into six binary classification tasks. Performance was evaluated using five-fold cross-validation. For each fold the SVM cost parameter was optimised in the range $(2^{-6}, 2^{-4}, \ldots, 2^{12})$ through cross-validation on the training set.

All kernel matrices were precomputed on near-identical machines with 2.4 Ghz 64-bit processors and 8Gb of memory. The kernel matrix computation is trivial to parallelise, as each cell is independent. Spreading the computational load across multiple processors is a simple way to reduce the real time cost of the procedure.

4.3 Lexical features

Our implementation of the lexical similarity model uses the same feature set as Ó Séaghdha and Copestake (2008). Two corpora were used to extract co-occurrence information: the written component of the BNC (Burnard, 1995) and the Google Web 1T 5-Gram Corpus (Brants and Franz, 2006). For each noun appearing as a compound constituent in the dataset, we estimate a co-occurrence distribution based on the nouns in coordinative constructions. Conjunctions are identified in the BNC by first parsing the corpus with RASP (Briscoe et al., 2006) and extracting instances of the `conj` grammatical relation. As the 5-Gram corpus does not contain full sentences it cannot be parsed, so regular expressions were used to extract coordinations. In each corpus, the set of co-occurring terms is restricted to the 10,000 most frequent conjuncts in that corpus so that each constituent distribution is represented with a 10,000-dimensional vector. The probability vector for the compound is created by appending the two constituent vectors, each scaled by 0.5 to weight both constituents equally and ensure that the new vector sums to 1. To perform classification with these features we use the Jensen-Shannon kernel (3).[3]

4.4 Relational features

To extract data for computing relational similarity, we searched a large corpus for sentences in which both constituents of a compound co-occur. The corpora used here are the written BNC, containing 90 million words of British English balanced across genre and text type, and the English Gigaword Corpus, 2nd Edition (Graff et al., 2005), containing 2.3 billion words of newswire text. Extraction from the Gigaword Corpus was performed at the paragraph level as the corpus is not annotated for sentence boundaries, and a dictionary of plural forms and American English variants was used to expand the coverage of the corpus trawl.

The extracted contexts were split into sentences, tagged and lemmatised with RASP. Duplicate sentences were discarded, as were sentences in which the compound head and modifier were more than 10 words apart. Punctuation and tokens containing non-alphanumeric characters were removed. The compound modifier and head were replaced with placeholder tokens `M:n` and `H:n` in each sentence to ensure that the classifier would learn from relational information only and not from lexical information about the constituents. Finally, all tokens more than five words to the left of the leftmost constituent or more than five words to the right of the rightmost constituent were discarded; this has the effect of speeding up the kernel computations and should also focus the classifier on the most informative parts of the context sentences. Examples of the context strings extracted for the modifier-head pair (*history,book*) are *the:a 1957:m pulitizer:n prize-winning:j H:n describe:v event:n in:i american:j M:n when:c elect:v official:n take:v principle:v* and *he:p read:v constantly:r usually:r H:n about:i american:j M:n or:c biography:n*.

This extraction procedure resulted in a corpus of 1,472,798 strings. There was significant variation in the number of context strings extracted for each compound: 288 compounds were associated with 1,000 or more sentences, while 191 were as-

[2] `http://www.csie.ntu.edu.tw/~cjlin/libsvm`

[3] Ó Séaghdha and Copestake (2008) achieve their single best result with a different kernel (the *Jensen-Shannon RBF kernel*), but the kernel used here (the *Jensen-Shannon linear kernel*) generally achieves equivalent performance and presents one fewer parameter to optimise.

	k_{jsd}		k_{ave}	
Length	Acc	F	Acc	F
1	47.9	45.8	43.6	40.4
2	51.7	49.5	49.7	48.3
3	50.7	48.4	50.1	48.6
Σ_{12}	51.5	49.6	48.3	46.8
Σ_{23}	**52.1**	**49.9**	50.9	49.5
Σ_{123}	51.3	49.0	50.5	49.1
ϕ_{PC}	44.9	43.3	40.9	40.0

Table 1: Results for combinations of embedding functions and set kernels

sociated with 10 or fewer and no sentences were found for 45 constituent pairs. The largest context sets were predominantly associated with political or economic topics (e.g., *government official*, *oil price*), reflecting the journalistic sources of the Gigaword sentences.

Our implementation of relational similarity applies the two set kernels k_{ave} and k_{jsd} defined in Section 3.4 to these context sets. For each kernel we tested gap-weighted embedding functions with subsequence length values l in the range $1, 2, 3$, as well as summed kernels for all combinations of values in this range. The decay parameter λ for the subsequence feature embedding was set to 0.5 throughout, in line with previous recommendations (e.g., Cancedda et al. (2003)). To investigate the effects of varying set sizes, we ran experiments with context sets of maximal cardinality $q \in \{50, 250, 1000\}$. These sets were randomly sampled for each compound; for compounds associated with fewer strings than the maximal cardinality, all associated strings were used. For $q = 50$ we average results over five runs in order to reduce sampling variation. We also report some results with the PairClass embedding ϕ_{PC}. The restricted representative power of this embedding brings greater efficiency and we were able to use $q = 5,000$; for all but 22 compounds, this allowed the use of all contexts for which the ϕ_{PC} embedding was defined.

5 Results

Table 1 presents results for classification with relational set kernels, using $q = 1,000$ for the gap-weighted embedding. In general, there is little difference between the performance of k_{jsd} and k_{ave} with ϕ_{gap_l}; the only statistically significant differences (at $p < 0.05$, using paired t-tests) are between the kernels $k_{l=1}$ with subsequence length $l = 1$ and the summed kernels $k_{\Sigma_{12}} = k_{l=1} + k_{l=2}$. The best performance of 52.1% accuracy, 49.9% F-score is obtained with the Jensen-Shannon kernel k_{jsd} computed on the summed feature embeddings of length 2 and 3. This is significantly lower than the performance achieved by Ó Séaghdha and Copestake (2008) with their lexical similarity model, but it is well above the majority class baseline (21.3%). Results for the PairClass embedding are much lower than for the gap-weighted embedding; the superiority of ϕ_{gap_l} is statistically significant in all cases except $l = 1$.

Results for combinations of lexical co-occurrence kernels and (gap-weighted) relational set kernels are given in Table 2. With the exception of some combinations of the length-1 set kernel, these results are clearly better than the best results obtained with either the lexical or the relational model taken alone. The best result is obtained by the combining the lexical kernel computed on BNC conjunction features with the summed Jensen-Shannon set kernel $k_{\Sigma_{23}}$; this combination achieves 63.1% accuracy and 61.6% F-score, a statistically significant improvement (at the $p < 0.01$ level) over the lexical kernel alone and the best result yet reported for this dataset. Also, the benefit of combining set kernels of different subsequence lengths l is evident; of the 12 combinations presented Table 2 that include summed set kernels, nine lead to statistically significant improvements over the corresponding lexical kernels taken alone (the remaining three are also close to significance).

Our experiments also show that the distributional implementation of set kernels (6) is much more efficient than the averaging implementation (5). The time behaviour of the two methods with increasing set cardinality q and subsequence length l is illustrated in Figure 1. At the largest tested values of q and l (1,000 and 3, respectively), the averaging method takes over 33 days of CPU time, while the distributional method takes just over one day. In theory, k_{ave} scales quadratically as q increases; this was not observed because for many constituent pairs there are not enough context strings available to keep adding as q grows large, but the dependence is certainly superlinear. The time taken by k_{jsd} is theoretically linear in q, but again scales less dramatically in practice. On the other hand k_{ave} is linear in l, while k_{jsd} scales exponentially. This exponential dependence may

	k_{jsd}				k_{ave}			
	BNC		5-Gram		BNC		5-Gram	
Length	Acc	F	Acc	F	Acc	F	Acc	F
1	60.6	58.6	60.3	58.1	59.5	57.6	59.1	56.5
2	61.9*	60.4*	62.6	60.8	62.0	60.5*	61.3	59.1
3	62.5*	60.8*	61.7	59.9	62.8*	61.2**	62.3**	60.8**
Σ_{12}	62.6*	61.0**	62.3*	60.6*	62.0*	60.3*	61.5	59.2
Σ_{23}	**63.1****	**61.6****	62.3*	60.5*	62.2*	60.7*	62.0	60.3
Σ_{123}	62.9**	61.3**	62.6	60.8*	61.9*	60.4*	62.4*	60.6*
No Set	59.9	57.8	60.2	58.1	59.9	57.8	60.2	58.1

Table 2: Results for set kernel and lexical kernel combination. */** indicate significant improvement at the 0.05/0.01 level over the corresponding lexical kernel alone, estimated by paired t-tests.

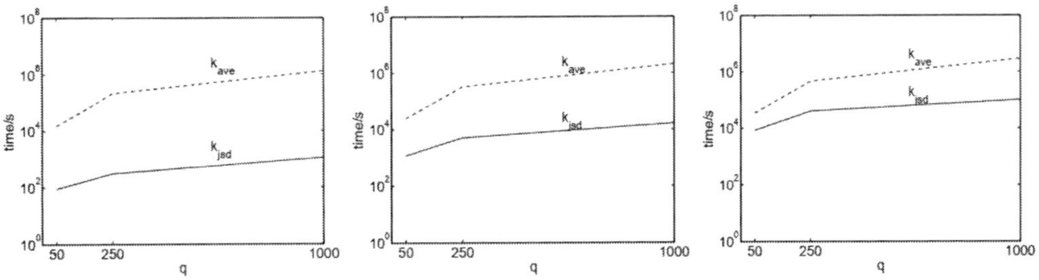

(a) $l = 1$ (b) $l = 2$ (c) $l = 3$

Figure 1: Timing results (in seconds, log-scaled) for averaged and Jensen-Shannon set kernels

seem worrying, but in practice only short subsequence lengths are used with string kernels. In situations where set sizes are small but long subsequence features are desired, the averaging approach may be more appropriate. However, it seems likely that many applications will be similar to the task considered here, where short subsequences are sufficient and it is desirable to use as much data as possible to represent each set. We note that calculating the PairClass embedding, which counts far fewer patterns, took just 1h21m. For optimal efficiency, it seems best to use a gap-weighted embedding with small set cardinality; averaged across five runs k_{jsd} with $q = 50$ and $l = \Sigma_{123}$ took 26m to calculate and still achieved 47.6% Accuracy, 45.1% F-score.

6 Related work

Turney et al. (2003) suggest combining various information sources for solving SAT analogy problems. However, previous work on compound interpretation has generally used either lexical similarity or relational similarity but not both in combination. Previously proposed lexical models include the WordNet-based methods of Kim and Baldwin (2005) and Girju et al. (2005), and the distributional model of Ó Séaghdha and Copestake (2008). The idea of using relational similarity to understand compounds goes back at least as far as Lebowitz' (1988) RESEARCHER system, which processed patent abstracts in an incremental fashion and associated an unseen compound with the relation expressed in a context where the constituents previously occurred.

Turney (2006) describes a method (*Latent Relational Analysis*) that extracts subsequence patterns for noun pairs from a large corpus, using query expansion to increase the recall of the search and feature selection and dimensionality reduction to reduce the complexity of the feature space. LRA performs well on analogical tasks including compound interpretation, but has very substantial resource requirements. Turney (2008) has recently proposed a simpler SVM-based algorithm for analogical classification called *PairClass*. While it does not adopt a set-based or distributional model of relational similarity, we have noted above that PairClass implicitly uses a feature representation similar to the one presented above as (6) by extracting subsequence patterns from observed co-occurrences of word pair members. Indeed, PairClass can be viewed as a special case of our framework; the differences from the model we have used consist in the use of a different embedding function ϕ_{PC} and a more restricted notion of context, a frequency cutoff to eliminate less common subsequences and the Gaussian kernel to compare vectors. While we cannot compare methods directly as we do not possess the large corpus of 5×10^{10} words used by Turney, we have tested the impact of each of these modifications on our model.[4] None improve performance with our set kernels, but the only statistically significant effect is that of changing the embedding model as reported in section Section 5. Implementing the full PairClass algorithm on our corpus yields 46.2% accuracy, 44.9% F-score, which is again significantly worse than all results for the gap-weighted model with $l > 1$.

In NLP, there has not been widespread use of set representations for data items, and hence set classification techniques have received little attention. Notable exceptions include Rosario and Hearst (2005) and Bunescu and Mooney (2007), who tackle relation classification and extraction tasks by considering the set of contexts in which the members of a candidate relation argument pair co-occur. While this gives a set representation for each pair, both sets of authors apply classification methods at the level of individual set members rather than directly comparing sets. There is also a close connection between the multinomial probability model we have proposed and the pervasive *bag of words* (or *bag of n-grams*) representation. Distributional kernels based on a gap-weighted feature embedding extend these models by using bags of discontinuous n-grams and down-weighting gappy subsequences.

A number of set kernels other than those discussed here have been proposed in the machine learning literature, though none of these proposals have explicitly addressed the problem of comparing sets of strings or other structured objects, and many are suitable only for comparing sets of small cardinality. Kondor and Jebara (2003) take a distributional approach similar to ours, fitting multivariate normal distributions to the feature space mappings of sets A and B and comparing the mappings with the Bhattacharrya vector inner product. The model described above in (6) implicitly fits multinomial distributions in the feature space $\mathcal{F}$; this seems more intuitive for string kernel embeddings that map strings onto vectors of positive-valued "counts". Experiments with Kondor and Jebara's Bhattacharrya kernel indicate that it can in fact come close to the performances reported in Section 5 but has significantly greater computational requirements due to the need to perform costly matrix manipulations.

[4]Turney (p.c.) reports that the full PairClass model achieves 50.0% accuracy, 49.3% F-score.

7 Conclusion and future directions

In this paper we have presented a combined model of lexical and relational similarity for relational reasoning tasks. We have developed an efficient and flexible kernel-based framework for comparing sets of contexts using the feature embedding associated with a string kernel.[5] By choosing a particular embedding function and a particular inner product on subsequence vectors, the previously proposed set-averaging and PairClass algorithms for relational similarity can be retrieved as special cases. Applying our methods to the task of compound noun interpretation, we have shown that combining lexical and relational similarity is a very effective approach that surpasses either similarity model taken individually.

Turney (2008) argues that many NLP tasks can be formulated in terms of analogical reasoning, and he applies his PairClass algorithm to a number of problems including SAT verbal analogy tests, synonym/antonym classification and distinction between semantically similar and semantically associated words. Our future research plans include investigating the application of our combined similarity model to analogical tasks other than compound noun interpretation. A second promising direction is to investigate relational models for unsupervised semantic analysis of noun compounds. The range of semantic relations that can be expressed by compounds is the subject of some controversy (Ryder, 1994), and unsupervised learning methods offer a data-driven means of discovering relational classes.

Acknowledgements

We are grateful to Peter Turney, Andreas Vlachos and the anonymous EACL reviewers for their helpful comments. This work was supported in part by EPSRC grant EP/C010035/1.

[5]The treatment presented here has used a string representation of context, but the method could be extended to other structural representations for which substructure embeddings exist, such as syntactic trees (Collins and Duffy, 2001).

References

Thorsten Brants and Alex Franz, 2006. *Web 1T 5-gram Corpus Version 1.1*. Linguistic Data Consortium.

Ted Briscoe, John Carroll, and Rebecca Watson. 2006. The second release of the RASP system. In *Proceedings of the ACL-06 Interactive Presentation Sessions*.

Razvan C. Bunescu and Raymond J. Mooney. 2007. Learning to extract relations from the Web using minimal supervision. In *Proceedings of the 45th Annual Meeting of the Association for Computational Linguistics (ACL-07)*.

Lou Burnard, 1995. *Users' Guide for the British National Corpus*. British National Corpus Consortium.

Cristina Butnariu and Tony Veale. 2008. A concept-centered approach to noun-compound interpretation. In *Proceedings of the 22nd International Conference on Computational Linguistics (COLING-08)*.

Nicola Cancedda, Eric Gaussier, Cyril Goutte, and Jean-Michel Renders. 2003. Word-sequence kernels. *Journal of Machine Learning Research*, 3:1059–1082.

Michael Collins and Nigel Duffy. 2001. Convolution kernels for natural language. In *Proceedings of the 15th Conference on Neural Information Processing Systems (NIPS-01)*.

Corinna Cortes and Vladimir Vapnik. 1995. Support vector networks. *Machine Learning*, 20(3):273–297.

Nello Cristianini, Jaz Kandola, Andre Elisseeff, and John Shawe-Taylor. 2001. On kernel target alignment. Technical Report NC-TR-01-087, NeuroCOLT.

James Curran. 2004. *From Distributional to Semantic Similarity*. Ph.D. thesis, School of Informatics, University of Edinburgh.

Barry Devereux and Fintan Costello. 2007. Learning to interpret novel noun-noun compounds: Evidence from a category learning experiment. In *Proceedings of the ACL-07 Workshop on Cognitive Aspects of Computational Language Acquisition*.

Thomas Gärtner, Peter A. Flach, Adam Kowalczyk, and Alex J. Smola. 2002. Multi-instance kernels. In *Proceedings of the 19th International Conference on Machine Learning (ICML-02)*.

Roxana Girju, Dan Moldovan, Marta Tatu, and Daniel Antohe. 2005. On the semantics of noun compounds. *Computer Speech and Language*, 19(4):479–496.

Roxana Girju, Preslav Nakov, Vivi Nastase, Stan Szpakowicz, Peter Turney, and Deniz Yuret. 2007. SemEval-2007 Task 04: Classification of semantic relations between nominals. In *Proceedings of the 4th International Workshop on Semantic Evaluations (SemEval-07)*.

Alfio Gliozzo, Claudio Giuliano, and Carlo Strapparava. 2005. Domain kernels for word sense disambiguation. In *Proceedings of the 43rd Annual Meeting of the Association for Computational Linguistics (ACL-05)*.

David Graff, Junbo Kong, Ke Chen, and Kazuaki Maeda, 2005. *English Gigaword Corpus, 2nd Edition*. Linguistic Data Consortium.

Thorsten Joachims, Nello Cristianini, and John Shawe-Taylor. 2001. Composite kernels for hypertext categorisation. In *Proceedings of the 18th International Conference on Machine Learning (ICML-01)*.

Su Nam Kim and Timothy Baldwin. 2005. Automatic interpretation of noun compounds using WordNet similarity. In *Proceedings of the 2nd International Joint Conference on Natural Language Processing (IJCNLP-05)*.

Risi Kondor and Tony Jebara. 2003. A kernel between sets of vectors. In *Proceedings of the 20th International Conference on Machine Learning (ICML-03)*.

Michael Lebowitz. 1988. The use of memory in text processing. *Communications of the ACM*, 31(12):1483–1502.

Huma Lodhi, Craig Saunders, John Shawe-Taylor, Nello Cristianini, and Christopher J. C. H. Watkins. 2002. Text classification using string kernels. *Journal of Machine Learning Research*, 2:419–444.

Diarmuid Ó Séaghdha and Ann Copestake. 2007. Co-occurrence contexts for noun compound interpretation. In *Proceedings of the ACL-07 Workshop on A Broader Perspective on Multiword Expressions*.

Diarmuid Ó Séaghdha and Ann Copestake. 2008. Semantic classification with distributional kernels. In *Proceedings of the 22nd International Conference on Computational Linguistics (COLING-08)*.

Barbara Rosario and Marti A. Hearst. 2005. Multi-way relation classification: Application to protein-protein interactions. In *Proceedings of the 2005 Human Language Technology Conference and Conference on Empirical Methods in Natural Language Processing (HLT-EMNLP-05)*.

Mary Ellen Ryder. 1994. *Ordered Chaos: The Interpretation of English Noun-Noun Compounds*. University of California Press, Berkeley, CA.

John Shawe-Taylor and Nello Cristianini. 2004. *Kernel Methods for Pattern Analysis*. Cambridge University Press, Cambridge.

Peter D. Turney, Michael L. Littman, Jeffrey Bigham, and Victor Shnayder. 2003. Combining independent modules to solve multiple-choice synonym and analogy problems. In *Proceedings of the 2003 International Conference on Recent Advances in Natural Language Processing (RANLP-03)*.

Peter D. Turney. 2006. Similarity of semantic relations. *Computational Linguistics*, 32(3):379–416.

Peter D. Turney. 2008. A uniform approach to analogies, synonyms, antonyms, and associations. In *Proceedings of the 22nd International Conference on Computational Linguistics (COLING-08)*.

Empirical evaluations of animacy annotation

Lilja Øvrelid
Department of Linguistics
University of Potsdam
Germany
lilja@ling.uni-potsdam.de

Abstract

This article presents empirical evaluations of aspects of annotation for the linguistic property of animacy in Swedish, ranging from manual human annotation, automatic classification and, finally, an external evaluation in the task of syntactic parsing. We show that a treatment of animacy as a lexical semantic property of noun types enables generalization over distributional properties of these nouns which proves beneficial in automatic classification and furthermore gives significant improvements in terms of parsing accuracy for Swedish, compared to a state-of-the-art baseline parser with gold standard animacy information.

1 Introduction

The property of animacy influences linguistic phenomena in a range of different languages, such as case marking (Aissen, 2003) and argument realization (Bresnan et al., 2005; de Swart et al., 2008), and has been shown to constitute an important factor in the production and comprehension of syntactic structure (Branigan et al., 2008; Weckerly and Kutas, 1999).[1] In computational linguistic work, animacy has been shown to provide important information in anaphora resolution (Orăsan and Evans, 2007), argument disambiguation (Dell'Orletta et al., 2005) and syntactic parsing in general (Øvrelid and Nivre, 2007).

The dimension of animacy roughly distinguishes between entities which are alive and entities which are not, however, other distinctions are also relevant and the animacy dimension is often viewed as a continuum ranging from humans to inanimate objects. Following Silverstein (1976) several animacy hierarchies have been proposed in typological studies, focusing on the *linguistic* category of animacy, i.e., the distinctions which are relevant for linguistic phenomena. An example of an animacy hierarchy, taken from (Aissen, 2003), is provided in (1):

(1) Human > Animate > Inanimate

Clearly, non-human animates, like animals, are not less animate than humans in a biological sense, however, humans and animals show differing linguistic behaviour.

Empirical studies of animacy require human annotation efforts, and, in particular, a well-defined annotation task. However, annotation studies of animacy differ distinctly in their treatment of animacy as a type or token-level phenomenon, as well as in terms of granularity of categories. The use of the annotated data as a computational resource furthermore poses requirements on the annotation which do not necessarily agree with more theoretical considerations. Methods for the induction of animacy information for use in practical applications require the resolution of issues of level of representation, as well as granularity.

This article addresses these issues through empirical and experimental evaluation. We present an in-depth study of a manually annotated data set which indicates that animacy may be treated as a lexical semantic property at the type level. We then evaluate this proposal through supervised machine learning of animacy information and focus on an in-depth error analysis of the resulting classifier, addressing issues of granularity of the animacy dimension. Finally, the automatically an-

[1]Parts of the research reported in this paper has been supported by the *Deutsche Forschungsgemeinschaft* (DFG, *Sonderforschungsbereich 632*, project D4).

Proceedings of the 12th Conference of the European Chapter of the ACL, pages 630–638, notated data set is employed in order to train a syntactic parser and we investigate the effect of the animacy information and contrast the automatically acquired features with gold standard ones.

The rest of the article is structured as follows. In section 2, we briefly discuss annotation schemes for animacy, the annotation strategies and categories proposed there. We go on to describe annotation for the binary distinction of 'human reference' found in a Swedish dependency treebank in section 3 and we perform an evaluation of the consistency of the human annotation in terms of linguistic level. In section 4, we present experiments in lexical acquisition of animacy based on morphosyntactic features extracted from a considerably larger corpus. Section 5 presents experiments with the acquired animacy information applied in the data-driven dependency parsing of Swedish. Finally, section 6 concludes the article and provides some suggestions for future research.

2 Animacy annotation

Annotation for animacy is not a common component of corpora or treebanks. However, following from the theoretical interest in the property of animacy, there have been some initiatives directed at animacy annotation of corpus data.

Corpus studies of animacy (Yamamoto, 1999; Dahl and Fraurud, 1996) have made use of annotated data, however they differ in the extent to which the annotation has been explicitly formulated as an annotation scheme. The annotation study presented in Zaenen et. al. (2004) makes use of a coding manual designed for a project studying genitive modification (Garretson et al., 2004) and presents an explicit annotation scheme for animacy, illustrated by figure 1. The main class distinction for animacy is three-way, distinguishing Human, Other animate and Inanimate, with subclasses under two of the main classes. The 'Other animate' class further distinguishes Organizations and Animals. Within the group of inanimates, further distinctions are made between concrete and non-concrete inanimate, as well as time and place nominals.[2]

The annotation scheme described in Zaenen et. al. (2004) annotates the markables according to the animacy of their referent in the particular context. Animacy is thus treated as a token level property, however, has also been proposed as a lexical semantic property of nouns (Yamamoto, 1999). The indirect encoding of animacy in lexical resources, such as WordNet (Fellbaum, 1998) can also be seen as treating animacy as a type-level property. We may thus distinguish between a purely *type level* annotation strategy and a purely *token level* one. Type level properties hold for lexemes and are context-independent, i.e., independent of the particular linguistic context, whereas token-level properties are determined in context and hold for referring expressions, rather than lexemes.

3 Human reference in Swedish

Talbanken05 is a Swedish treebank which was created in the 1970's and which has recently been converted to dependency format (Nivre et al., 2006b) and made freely available. The written sections of the treebank consist of professional prose and student essays and amount to 197,123 running tokens, spread over 11,431 sentences. Figure 2 shows the labeled dependency graph of example (2), taken from Talbanken05.

(2) *Samma erfarenhet gjorde engelsmännen*
same experience made englishmen-DEF
'The same experience, the Englishmen had'

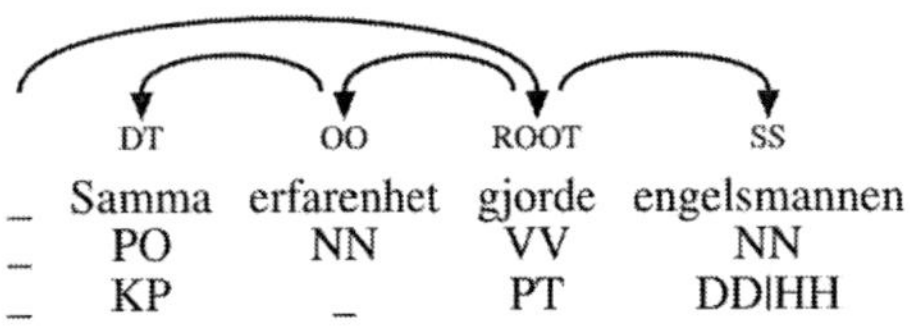

Figure 2: Dependency representation of example (2) from Talbanken05.

In addition to information on part-of-speech, dependency head and relation, and various morphosyntactic properties such as definiteness, the annotation expresses a distinction for nominal elements between reference to human and non-human. The annotation manual (Teleman, 1974) states that a markable should be tagged as human (HH) if it may be replaced by the interrogative pronoun *vem* 'who' and be referred to by the personal pronouns *han* 'he' or *hon* 'she'.

There are clear similarities between the annotation for human reference found in Talbanken05 and the annotation scheme for animacy discussed

[2] The fact that the study focuses on genitival modification has clearly influenced the categories distinguished, as these are all distinctions which have been claimed to influence the choice of genitive construction. For instance, temporal nouns are frequent in genitive constructions, unlike the other inanimate nouns.

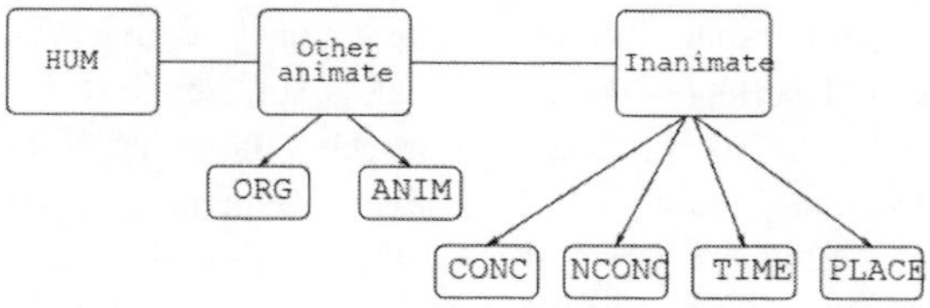

Figure 1: Animacy classification scheme (Zaenen et al., 2004).

above. The human/non-human contrast forms the central distinction in the animacy dimension and, in this respect, the annotation schemes do not conflict. If we compare the annotation found in Talbanken05 with the annotation proposed in Zaenen et. al. (2004), we find that the schemes differ primarily in the granularity of classes distinguished. The main source of variation in class distinctions consists in the annotation of collective nouns, including organizations, as well as animals.

3.1 Level of annotation

We distinguished above between type and token level annotation strategies, where a type level annotation strategy entails that an element consistently be assigned to only one class. A token level strategy, in contrast, does not impose this restriction on the annotation and class assignment may vary depending on the specific context. Garretson et. al (2004) propose a token level annotation strategy and state that "when coding for animacy [...] we are not considering the nominal per se (e.g., the word 'church'), but rather the entity that is the referent of that nominal (e.g. some particular thing in the real world)". This indicates that for all possible markables, a referent should be determinable.

The brief instruction with respect to annotation for human reference in the annotation manual for Talbanken05 (Teleman, 1974, 223) gives leeway for interpretation in the annotation and does not clearly state that it should be based on token level reference in context. It may thus be interesting to examine the extent to which this manual annotation is consistent across lexemes or whether we observe variation. We manually examine the intersection of the two classes of noun lemmas in the written sections of Talbanken, i.e., the set of nouns which have been assigned both classes by the annotators. It contains 82 noun lemmas, which corresponds to only 1.1% of the total number of noun lemmas in the treebank (7554 lemmas all together). After a manual inspection of the intersective elements along with their linguistic contexts, we may group the nouns which were assigned to both classes, into the following categories:that 'HH' is the tag for

Abstract nouns Nouns with underspecified or vague type level properties with respect to animacy, such as quantifying nouns, e.g. *hälft* 'half', *miljon* 'million', as well as nouns which may be employed with varying animacy, e.g. *element* 'element', *part* 'party', as in (3) and (4):

(3) ... *också den andra* **parten**$_{HH}$ *står utanför*
... also the other party-DEF stands outside
'... also the other party is left outside'

(4) *I ett förhållande är aldrig bägge* **parter_** *lika starka*
in a relationship are never both parties same strong
'In a relationship, both parties are never equally strong'

We also find that nouns which denote abstract concepts regarding humans show variable annotation, e.g. *individ* 'individual', *adressat* 'addressee', *medlem* 'member', *kandidat* 'candidate', *representant* 'representative', *auktoritet* 'authority'

Reference shifting contexts These are nouns whose type level animacy is clear but which are employed in a specific context which shifts their reference. Examples include metonymic usage of nouns, as in (5) and nouns occurring in dereferencing constructions, such as predicative constructions (6), titles (7) and idioms (8):

(5) ... **daghemmens**$_{HH}$ *otillräckliga resurser*
... kindergarten-DEF.GEN inadequate resources
'... the kindergarten's inadequate resources'

(6) ... *för att bli en bra* **soldat_**
... for to become a good soldier
'... in order to become a good soldier'

(7) ... *menar* **biskop_** *Hellsten*
... thinks bishop Hellsten
'thinks bishop Hellsten'

(8) *ta* **studenten_**
take student-DEF
'graduate from highschool (lit. take the student)'

It is interesting to note that the main variation in annotation stems precisely from difficulties in determining reference, either due to bleak type level properties such as for the abstract nouns, or due to properties of the context, as in the reference shifting constructions. The small amount of variation in the human annotation for animacy clearly supports a type-level approach to animacy, however, underline the influence of the linguistic context on the conception of animacy, as noted in the literature (Zaenen et al., 2004; Rosenbach, 2008).

4 Lexical acquisition of animacy

Even though knowledge about the animacy of a noun clearly has some interesting implications, little work has been done within the field of lexical acquisition in order to automatically acquire animacy information. Orăsan and Evans (2007) make use of hyponym-relations taken from the WordNet resource in order to classify animate referents. However, such a method is clearly restricted to languages for which large scale lexical resources, such as the WordNet, are available. The task of animacy classification bears some resemblance to the task of named entity recognition (NER) which usually makes reference to a 'person' class. However, whereas most NER systems make extensive use of orthographic, morphological or contextual clues (titles, suffixes) and gazetteers, animacy for nouns is not signaled overtly in the same way.

Following a strategy in line with work on verb classification (Merlo and Stevenson, 2001; Stevenson and Joanis, 2003), we set out to classify common noun *lemmas* based on their morphosyntactic distribution in a considerably larger corpus. This is thus equivalent to treatment of animacy as a lexical semantic property and the classification strategy is based on generalization of morphosyntactic behaviour of common nouns over large quantities of data. Due to the small size of the Talbanken05 treebank and the small amount of variation, this strategy was pursued for the acquisition of animacy information.

In the animacy classification of common nouns we exploit well-documented correlations between morphosyntactic realization and semantic properties of nouns. For instance, animate nouns tend to be realized as agentive subjects, inanimate nouns do not (Dahl and Fraurud, 1996). Animate nouns make good 'possessors', whereas inanimate nouns are more likely 'possessees' (Rosenbach, 2008). Table 1 presents an overview of the animacy data

Class	Types	Tokens covered
Animate	644	6010
Inanimate	6910	34822
Total	7554	40832

Table 1: The animacy data set from Talbanken05; number of noun lemmas (Types) and tokens in each class.

for common nouns in Talbanken05. It is clear that the data is highly skewed towards the non-human class, which accounts for 91.5% of the type instances. For classification we organize the data into *accumulated frequency bins*, which include all nouns with frequencies above a certain threshold. We here approximate the class of 'animate' to 'human' and the class of 'inanimate' to 'non-human'. Intersective elements, see section 3.1, are assigned to their majority class.[3]

4.1 Features for animacy classification

We define a feature space, which makes use of distributional data regarding the general syntactic properties of a noun, as well as various morphological properties. It is clear that in order for a syntactic environment to be relevant for animacy classification it must be, at least potentially, nominal. We define the *nominal potential* of a dependency relation as the frequency with which it is realized by a nominal element (noun or pronoun) and determine empirically a threshold of .10. The syntactic and morphological features in the feature space are presented below:

Syntactic features A feature for each dependency relation with nominal potential: (transitive) subject (SUBJ), object (OBJ), prepositional complement (PA), root (ROOT)[4], apposition (APP), conjunct (CC), determiner (DET), predicative (PRD), complement of comparative subjunction (UK). We also include a feature for the head of a genitive modifier, the so-called 'possessee', (GENHD).

Morphological features A feature for each morphological distinction relevant for a noun

[3] When there is no majority class, i.e. in the case of ties, the noun is removed from the data set. 12 lemmas were consequently removed.

[4] Nominal elements may be assigned the root relation of the dependency graph in sentence fragments which do not contain a finite verb.

in Swedish: gender (NEU/UTR), number (SIN/PLU), definiteness (DEF/IND), case (NOM/GEN). Also, the part-of-speech tags distinguish dates (DAT) and quantifying nouns (SET), e.g. *del, rad* 'part, row', so these are also included as features.

For extraction of distributional data for the set of Swedish nouns we make use of the Swedish Parole corpus of 21.5M tokens.[5] To facilitate feature extraction, we part-of-speech tag the corpus and parse it with MaltParser[6], which assigns a dependency analysis.[7]

4.2 Experimental methodology

For machine learning, we make use of the Tilburg Memory-Based Learner (TiMBL) (Daelemans et al., 2004).[8] Memory-based learning is a supervised machine learning method characterized by a lazy learning algorithm which postpones learning until classification time, using the k-nearest neighbor algorithm for the classification of unseen instances. For animacy classification, the TiMBL parameters are optimized on a subset of the full data set.[9]

For training and testing of the classifiers, we make use of leave-one-out cross-validation. The baseline represents assignment of the majority class (inanimate) to all nouns in the data set. Due to the skewed distribution of classes, as noted above, the baseline accuracy is very high, usually around 90%.Clearly, however, the class-based measures of precision and recall, as well as the combined F-score measure are more informative for these results. The baseline F-score for the animate class is thus 0, and a main goal is to improve on the rate of true positives for animates, while limiting the trade-off in terms of performance for the majority class of inanimates, which start out with F-scores approaching 100. For calculation of the statistical significance of differences in the performance of classifiers tested on the same data set, McNemar's test (Dietterich, 1998) is employed.

Bin	Instances	Baseline	MBL	SVM
>1000	291	89.3	97.3	95.2
>500	597	88.9	97.3	97.1
>100	1668	90.5	96.8	96.9
>50	2278	90.6	96.1	96.0
>10	3786	90.8	95.4	95.1
>0	5481	91.3	93.9	93.7

Table 2: Accuracy for MBL and SVM classifiers on Talbanken05 nouns in accumulated frequency bins by Parole frequency.

4.3 Results

Column four (MBL) in table 2 shows the accuracy obtained with all features in the general feature space. We observe a clear improvement on all data sets ($p<.0001$), compared to the respective baselines. As we recall, the data sets are successively larger, hence it seems fair to conclude that the size of the data set partially counteracts the lower frequency of the test nouns. It is not surprising, however, that a method based on distributional features suffers when the absolute frequencies approach 1. We obtain results for animacy classification, ranging from 97.3% accuracy to 93.9% depending on the sparsity of the data. With an absolute frequency threshold of 10, we obtain an accuracy of 95.4%, which constitutes a 50% reduction of error rate.

Table 3 presents the experimental results relative to class. We find that classification of the inanimate class is quite stable throughout the experiments, whereas the classification of the minority class of animate nouns suffers from sparse data. It is an important point, however, that it is largely recall for the animate class which goes down with increased sparseness, whereas precision remains quite stable. All of these properties are clearly advantageous in the application to realistic data sets, where a more conservative classifier is to be preferred.

4.4 Error analysis

The human reference annotation of the Talbanken05 nouns distinguishes only the classes corresponding to 'human' and 'inanimate' along the

[5]Parole is freely available at http://spraakbanken.gu.se

[6]http://www.maltparser.org

[7]For part-of-speech tagging, we employ the MaltTagger – a HMM part-of-speech tagger for Swedish (Hall, 2003). For parsing, we employ MaltParser (Nivre et al., 2006a), a language-independent system for data-driven dependency parsing , with the pretrained model for Swedish, which has been trained on the tags output by the tagger.

[8]http://ilk.uvt.nl/software.html

[9]For parameter optimization we employ the paramsearch tool, supplied with TiMBL, see http://ilk.uvt.nl/software.html. Paramsearch implements a hill climbing search for the optimal settings on iteratively larger parts of the supplied data. We performed parameter optimization on 20% of the total data set, where we balanced the data with respect to frequency. The resulting settings are $k = 11$, GainRatio feature weighting and Inverse Linear (IL) class voting weights.

	Animate			Inanimate		
	Precision	Recall	Fscore	Precision	Recall	Fscore
>1000	89.7	83.9	86.7	98.1	98.8	98.5
>500	89.1	86.4	87.7	98.3	98.7	98.5
>100	87.7	76.6	81.8	97.6	98.9	98.2
>50	85.8	70.2	77.2	97.0	98.9	97.9
>10	81.9	64.0	71.8	96.4	98.6	97.5
>0	75.7	44.9	56.4	94.9	98.6	96.7

Table 3: Precision, recall and F-scores for the two classes in MBL-experiments with a general feature space.

>10 nouns		
(a)	(b)	← classified as
222	125	(a) class animate
49	3390	(b) class inanimate

Table 4: Confusion matrix for the MBL-classifier with a general feature space on the >10 data set on Talbanken05 nouns.

animacy dimension. An interesting question is whether the errors show evidence of the gradience in categories discussed earlier and explicitly expressed in the annotation scheme by Zaenen et.al. (2004) in figure 1. If so, we would expect erroneously classified inanimate nouns to contain nouns of intermediate animacy, such as animals and organizations.

The error analysis examines the performance of the MBL-classifier employing all features on the > 10 data set in order to abstract away from the most serious effects of data sparseness. Table 4 shows a confusion matrix for the classification of the nouns. If we examine the errors for the inanimate class we indeed find evidence of gradience within this category. The errors contain a group of nouns referring to animals and other living beings (bacteria, algae), as listed in (9), as well as one noun referring to an "intelligent machine", included in the intermediate animacy category in Zaenen et al. (2004). Collective nouns with human reference and organizations are also found among the errors, listed in (11). We also find some nouns among the errors with human denotation, listed in (12). These are nouns which typically occur in dereferencing contexts, such as titles, e.g. *herr* 'mister', *biskop* 'bishop' and which were annotated as non-human referring by the human annotators.[10] Finally, a group of abstract, human-denoting nouns are also found among the errors, as listed in (13). In summary, we find that nouns with gradient animacy properties account for 53.1% of the errors for the inanimate class.

(9) Animals/living beings:
alg 'algae', *apa* 'monkey', *bakterie* 'bacteria', *björn* 'bear', *djur* 'animal', *fågel* 'bird', *fladdermöss* 'bat', *myra* 'ant', *mås* 'seagull', *parasit* 'parasite'

(10) Intelligent machines:
robot 'robot'

(11) Collective nouns, organizations:
myndighet 'authority', *nation* 'nation', *företagsledning* 'corporate-board', *personal* 'personell', *stiftelse* 'foundation', *idrottsklubb* 'sport-club'

(12) Human-denoting nouns:
biskop 'bishop', *herr* 'mister', *nationalist* 'nationalist', *tolk* 'interpreter'

(13) Abstract, human nouns:
förlorare 'loser', *huvudpart* 'main-party', *konkurrent* 'competitor', *majoritet* 'majority', *värd* 'host'

It is interesting to note that both the human and automatic annotation showed difficulties in ascertaining class for a group of abstract, human-denoting nouns, like *individ* 'individual', *motståndare* 'opponent', *kandidat* 'candidate', *representant* 'representative'. These were all assigned to the animate majority class during extraction, but were misclassified as inanimate during classification.

4.5 SVM classifiers

In order to evaluate whether the classification method generalizes to a different machine learning algorithm, we design an identical set of experiments to the ones presented above, but where classification is performed with Support Vector Machines (SVMs) instead of MBL. We use the LIBSVM package (Chang and Lin, 2001) with a RBF kernel ($C = 8.0, \gamma = 0.5$).[11]

[10] In fact, both of these showed variable annotation in the treebank and were assigned their majority class – inanimate – in the extraction of training data.

[11] As in the MBL-experiment, parameter optimization, i.e., choice of kernel function, C and γ values, is performed on 20% of the total data set with the `easy.py` tool, supplied with LIBSVM.

As column 5 (SVM) in table 2 shows, the classification results are very similar to the results obtained with MBL.[12] We furthermore find a very similar set of errors, and in particular, we find that 51.0 % of the errors for the inanimate class are nouns with the gradient animacy properties presented in (9)-(13) above.

5 Parsing with animacy information

As an external evaluation of our animacy classifier, we apply the induced information to the task of syntactic parsing. Seeing that we have a treebank with gold standard syntactic information and gold standard as well as induced animacy information, it should be possible to study the direct effect of the added animacy information in the assignment of syntactic structure.

5.1 Experimental methodology

We use the freely available MaltParser system, which is a language-independent system for data-driven dependency parsing (Nivre, 2006; Nivre et al., 2006c). A set of parsers are trained on Talbanken05, both with and without additional animacy information, the origin of which is either the manual annotation described in section 3 or the automatic animacy classifier described in section 4.2- 4.4 (MBL). The common nouns in the treebank are classified for animacy using leave-one-out training and testing. This ensures that the training and test instances are disjoint at all times. Moreover, the fact that the distributional data is taken from a separate data set ensures non-circularity since we are not basing the classification on gold standard parses.

All parsing experiments are performed using 10-fold cross-validation for training and testing on the entire written part of Talbanken05. Overall parsing accuracy will be reported using the standard metrics of *labeled attachment score* (LAS) and *unlabeled attachment score* (UAS).[13] Statistical significance is checked using Dan Bikel's randomized parsing evaluation comparator.[14] As our baseline, we use the settings optimized for Swedish in the CoNLL-X shared task (Buchholz and Marsi, 2006), where this parser was the best performing parser for Swedish.

	Gold standard		Automatic	
	UAS	LAS	UAS	LAS
Baseline	89.87	84.92	89.87	84.92
Anim	89.81	84.94	89.87	**84.99**

Table 5: Overall results in experiments with automatic features compared to gold standard features, expressed as unlabeled and labeled attachment scores.

5.2 Results

The addition of automatically assigned animacy information for common nouns (Anim) causes a small, but significant improvement in overall results (p<.04) compared to the baseline, *as well as* the corresponding gold standard experiment (p<.04). In the gold standard experiment, the results are not significantly better than the baseline and the main, overall, improvement from the gold standard animacy information reported in Øvrelid and Nivre (2007) and Øvrelid (2008) stems largely from the animacy annotation of pronouns.[15] This indicates that the animacy information for common nouns, which has been automatically acquired from a considerably larger corpus, captures distributional distinctions which are important for the general effect of animacy and furthermore that the differences from the gold standard annotation prove beneficial for the results.

We see from Table 5, that the improvement in overall parse results is mainly in terms of dependency labeling, reflected in the LAS score. A closer error analysis shows that the performance of the two parsers employing gold and automatic animacy information is very similar with respect to dependency relations and we observe an improved analysis for subjects, (direct and indirect) objects and subject predicatives with only minor variations. This in itself is remarkable, since the covered set of animate instances is notably smaller in the automatically annotated data set. We furthermore find that the main difference between the gold standard and automatic Anim-experiments

[12] The SVM-classifiers generally show slightly lower results, however, only performance on the >1000 data set is significantly lower (p<.05).

[13] LAS and UAS report the percentage of tokens that are assigned the correct head *with* (labeled) or *without* (unlabeled) the correct dependency label.

[14] http://www.cis.upenn.edu/~dbikel/software.html

[15] Recall that the Talbanken05 treebank contains animacy information for all nominal elements – pronouns, proper and common nouns. When the totality of this information is added the overall parse results are significantly improved (p<.0002) (Øvrelid and Nivre, 2007; Øvrelid, 2008).

does not reside in the analysis of syntactic arguments, but rather of non-arguments. One relation for which performance deteriorates with the added information in the gold Anim-experiment is the nominal postmodifier relation (ET) which is employed for relative clauses and nominal PP-attachment. With the automatically assigned feature, in contrast, we observe an improvement in the performance for the ET relation, compared to the gold standard experiment, from a F-score in the latter of 76.14 to 76.40 in the former. Since this is a quite common relation, with a frequency of 5% in the treebank as a whole, the improvement has a clear effect on the results.

The parser's analysis of postnominal modification is influenced by the differences in the added animacy annotation for the nominal head, as well as the internal dependent. If we examine the corrected errors in the automatic experiment, compared to the gold standard experiment, we find elements with differing annotation. Preferences with respect to the animacy of prepositional complements vary. In (14), the automatic annotation of the noun *djur* 'animal' as animate results in correct assignment of the ET relation to the preposition *hos* 'among', as well as correct nominal, as opposed to verbal, attachment. This preposition is one of the few with a preference for animate complements in the treebank. In contrast, the example in (15) illustrates an error where the automatic classification of *barn* 'children' as inanimate causes a correct analysis of the head preposition *om* 'about'.[16]

(14) ...*samhällsbildningar* *hos* *olika* **djur**
...societies among different animals
'... social organizations among different animals'

(15) *Föräldrar* *har* *vårdnaden* *om* *sina* **barn**
parents have custody-DEF of their children
'Parents have the custody of their children'

A more thorough analysis of the different factors involved in PP-attachment is a complex task which is clearly beyond the scope of the present study. We may note, however, that the distinctions induced by the animacy classifier based purely on linguistic evidence proves useful for the analysis of both arguments and non-arguments.

[16]Recall that the classification is based purely on linguistic evidence and in this respect children largely pattern with the inanimate nouns. A child is probably more like a physical object in the sense that it is something one possesses and otherwise reacts *to*, rather than being an agent that acts upon its surroundings.

6 Conclusion

This article has dealt with an empirical evaluation of animacy annotation in Swedish, where the main focus has been on the use of such annotation for computational purposes.

We have seen that human annotation for animacy shows little variation at the type-level for a binary animacy distinction. Following from this observation, we have shown how a type-level induction strategy based on morphosyntactic distributional features enables automatic animacy classification for noun lemmas which furthermore generalizes to different machine learning algorithms (MBL, SVM). We obtain results for animacy classification, ranging from 97.3% accuracy to 93.9% depending on the sparsity of the data. With an absolute frequency threshold of 10, we obtain an accuracy of 95.4%, which constitutes a 50% reduction of error rate. A detailed error analysis revealed some interesting results and we saw that more than half of the errors performed by the animacy classifier for the large class of inanimate nouns actually included elements which have been assigned an intermediate animacy status in theoretical work, such as animals and collective nouns.

The application of animacy annotation in the task of syntactic parsing provided a test bed for the applicability of the annotation, where we could contrast the manually assigned classes with the automatically acquired ones. The results showed that the automatically acquired information gives a slight, but significant improvement of overall parse results where the gold standard annotation does not, despite a considerably lower coverage. This is a suprising result which highlights important properties of the annotation. First of all, the automatic annotation is completely consistent at the type level. Second, the automatic animacy classifier captures important distributional properties of the nouns, exemplified by the case of nominal postmodifiers in PP-attachment. The automatic annotation thus captures a purely linguistic notion of animacy and abstracts over contextual influence in particular instances.

Animacy has been shown to be an important property in a range of languages, hence animacy classification of other languages constitutes an interesting line of work for the future, where empirical evaluations may point to similarities and differences in the linguistic expression of animacy.

References

Judith Aissen. 2003. Differential Object Marking: Iconicity vs. economy. *Natural Language and Linguistic Theory*, 21(3):435–483.

Holly P. Branigan, Martin J. Pickering, and Mikihiro Tanaka. 2008. Contributions of animacy to grammatical function assignment and word order production. *Lingua*, 118(2):172–189.

Joan Bresnan, Anna Cueni, Tatiana Nikitina, and Harald Baayen. 2005. Predicting the dative alternation. In Gosse Bouma, Irene Kraemer, and Joost Zwarts, editors, *Cognitive foundations of interpretation*, pages 69–94. Royal Netherlands Academy of Science, Amsterdam.

Sabine Buchholz and Erwin Marsi. 2006. CoNLL-X shared task on multilingual dependency parsing. In *Proceedings of the Tenth Conference on Computational Natural Language Learning (CoNLL-X)*, pages 149–164.

Chih-Chung Chang and Chih-Jen Lin. 2001. LIBSVM: A library for support vector machines. Software available at http://www.csie.ntu.edu.tw/~cjlin/libsvm.

Walter Daelemans, Jakub Zavrel, Ko Van der Sloot, and Antal Van den Bosch. 2004. TiMBL: Tilburg Memory Based Learner, version 5.1, Reference Guide. Technical report, ILK Technical Report Series 04-02.

Östen Dahl and Kari Fraurud. 1996. Animacy in grammar and discourse. In Thorstein Fretheim and Jeanette K. Gundel, editors, *Reference and referent accessibility*, pages 47–65. John Benjamins, Amsterdam.

Peter de Swart, Monique Lamers, and Sander Lestrade. 2008. Animacy, argument structure and argument encoding: Introduction to the special issue on animacy. *Lingua*, 118(2):131–140.

Felice Dell'Orletta, Alessandro Lenci, Simonetta Montemagni, and Vito Pirrelli. 2005. Climbing the path to grammar: A maximum entropy model of subject/object learning. In *Proceedings of the 2nd Workshop on Psychocomputational Models of Human Language Acquisition*, pages 72–81.

Thomas G. Dietterich. 1998. Approximate statistical test for comparing supervised classification learning algorithms. *Neural Computation*, 10(7):1895–1923.

Christiane Fellbaum, editor. 1998. *WordNet: an electronic lexical database*. MIT Press, Cambridge, MA.

Gregory Garretson, M. Catherine O'Connor, Barbora Skarabela, and Marjorie Hogan, 2004. *Optimal Typology of Determiner Phrases Coding Manual*. Boston University, version 3.2 edition. Downloaded from http://people.bu.edu/depot/coding_manual.html on 02/15/2006.

Johan Hall. 2003. A probabilistic part-of-speech tagger with suffix probabilities. Master's thesis, Växjö University, Sweden.

Paola Merlo and Suzanne Stevenson. 2001. Automatic verb classification based on statistical distributions of argument structure. *Computational Linguistics*, 27(3):373–408.

Joakim Nivre, Johan Hall, and Jens Nilsson. 2006a. Maltparser: A data-driven parser-generator for dependency parsing. In *Proceedings of the Fifth International Conference on Language Resources and Evaluation (LREC)*, pages 2216–2219.

Joakim Nivre, Jens Nilsson, and Johan Hall. 2006b. Talbanken05: A Swedish treebank with phrase structure and dependency annotation. In *Proceedings of the fifth International Conference on Language Resources and Evaluation (LREC)*, pages 1392–1395.

Joakim Nivre, Jens Nilsson, Johan Hall, Gülşen Eryiğit, and Svetoslav Marinov. 2006c. Labeled pseudo-projective dependency parsing with Support Vector Machines. In *Proceedings of the Conference on Computational Natural Language Learning (CoNLL)*.

Joakim Nivre. 2006. *Inductive Dependency Parsing*. Springer, Dordrecht.

Constantin Orăsan and Richard Evans. 2007. NP animacy resolution for anaphora resolution. *Journal of Artificial Intelligence Research*, 29:79–103.

Lilja Øvrelid and Joakim Nivre. 2007. When word order and part-of-speech tags are not enough – Swedish dependency parsing with rich linguistic features. In *Proceedings of the International Conference on Recent Advances in Natural Language Processing (RANLP)*, pages 447–451.

Lilja Øvrelid. 2008. Linguistic features in data-driven dependency parsing. In *Proceedings of the Conference on Computational Natural Language Learning (CoNLL 2008)*.

Anette Rosenbach. 2008. Animacy and grammatical variation - findings from English genitive variation. *Lingua*, 118(2):151–171.

Michael Silverstein. 1976. Hierarchy of features and ergativity. In Robert M.W. Dixon, editor, *Grammatical categories in Australian Languages*, pages 112–171. Australian Institute of Aboriginal Studies, Canberra.

Suzanne Stevenson and Eric Joanis. 2003. Semi-supervised verb class discovery using noisy features. In *Proceedings of the Conference on Computational Natural Language Learning (CoNLL)*, pages 71–78.

Ulf Teleman. 1974. *Manual för grammatisk beskrivning av talad och skriven svenska*. Studentlitteratur, Lund.

J. Weckerly and M. Kutas. 1999. An electrophysiological analysis of animacy effects in the processing of object relative sentences. *Psychophysiology*, 36:559–570.

Mutsumi Yamamoto. 1999. *Animacy and Reference: A cognitive approach to corpus linguistics*. John Benjamins, Amsterdam.

Annie Zaenen, Jean Carletta, Gregory Garretson, Joan Bresnan, Andrew Koontz-Garboden, Tatiana Nikitina, M. Catherine O'Connor, and Tom Wasow. 2004. Animacy encoding in English: why and how. In Donna Byron and Bonnie Webber, editors, *Proceedings of the ACL Workshop on Discourse Annotation*.

Outclassing Wikipedia in Open-Domain Information Extraction: Weakly-Supervised Acquisition of Attributes over Conceptual Hierarchies

Marius Paşca
Google Inc.
Mountain View, California 94043
mars@google.com

Abstract

A set of labeled classes of instances is extracted from text and linked into an existing conceptual hierarchy. Besides a significant increase in the coverage of the class labels assigned to individual instances, the resulting resource of labeled classes is more effective than similar data derived from the manually-created Wikipedia, in the task of attribute extraction over conceptual hierarchies.

1 Introduction

Motivation: Sharing basic intuitions and long-term goals with other tasks within the area of Web-based information extraction (Banko and Etzioni, 2008; Davidov and Rappoport, 2008), the task of acquiring class attributes relies on unstructured text available on the Web, as a data source for extracting generally-useful knowledge. In the case of attribute extraction, the knowledge to be extracted consists in quantifiable properties of various classes (e.g., *top speed*, *body style* and *gas mileage* for the class of *sports cars*).

Existing work on large-scale attribute extraction focuses on producing ranked lists of attributes, for target classes of instances available in the form of flat sets of instances (e.g., *ferrari modena*, *porsche carrera gt*) sharing the same class label (e.g., *sports cars*). Independently of how the input target classes are populated with instances (manually (Paşca, 2007) or automatically (Paşca and Van Durme, 2008)), and what type of textual data source is used for extracting attributes (Web documents or query logs), the extraction of attributes operates at a lexical rather than semantic level. Indeed, the class labels of the target classes may be not more than text surface strings (e.g., *sports cars*) or even artificially-created labels (e.g., *CartoonChar* in lieu of *cartoon characters*). Moreover, although it is commonly accepted that *sports cars* are also *cars*, which in turn are also *motor vehicles*, the presence of *sports cars* among the input target classes does not lead to any attributes being extracted for *cars* and *motor vehicles*, unless the latter two class labels are also present explicitly among the input target classes.

Contributions: The contributions of this paper are threefold. First, we investigate the role of classes of instances acquired automatically from unstructured text, in the task of attribute extraction over concepts from existing conceptual hierarchies. For this purpose, ranked lists of attributes are acquired from query logs for various concepts, after linking a set of more than 4,500 open-domain, automatically-acquired classes containing a total of around 250,000 instances into conceptual hierarchies available in WordNet (Fellbaum, 1998). In comparison, previous work extracts attributes for either manually-specified classes of instances (Paşca, 2007), or for classes of instances derived automatically but considered as flat rather than hierarchical classes, and manually associated to existing semantic concepts (Paşca and Van Durme, 2008). Second, we expand the set of classes of instances acquired from text, thus increasing their usefulness in attribute extraction in particular and information extraction in general. To this effect, additional class labels (e.g., *motor vehicles*) are identified for existing instances (e.g., *ferrari modena*) of existing class labels (e.g., *sports cars*), by exploiting IsA relations available within the conceptual hierarchy (e.g., *sports cars* are also *motor vehicles*). Third, we show that large-scale, automatically-derived classes of in-

Proceedings of the 12th Conference of the European Chapter of the ACL, pages 639–647,
Athens, Greece, 30 March – 3 April 2009. ©2009 Association for Computational Linguistics

stances can have as much as, or even bigger, practical impact in open-domain information extraction tasks than similar data from large-scale, high-coverage, manually-compiled resources. Specifically, evaluation results indicate that the accuracy of the extracted lists of attributes is higher by 8% at rank 10, 13% at rank 30 and 18% at rank 50, when using the automatically-extracted classes of instances rather than the comparatively more numerous and a-priori more reliable, human-generated, collaboratively-vetted classes of instances available within Wikipedia (Remy, 2002).

2 Attribute Extraction over Hierarchies

Extraction of Flat Labeled Classes: Unstructured text from a combination of Web documents and query logs represents the source for deriving a flat set of labeled classes of instances, which are necessary as input for attribute extraction experiments. The labeled classes are acquired in three stages:

1) extraction of a noisy pool of pairs of a class label and a potential class instance, by applying a few Is-A extraction patterns, selected from (Hearst, 1992), to Web documents:

(*fruits, apple*), (*fruits, corn*), (*fruits, mango*), (*fruits, orange*), (*foods, broccoli*), (*crops, lettuce*), (*flowers, rose*);

2) extraction of unlabeled clusters of distributionally similar phrases, by clustering vectors of contextual features collected around the occurrences of the phrases within Web documents (Lin and Pantel, 2002):

{*lettuce, broccoli, corn, ..*},

{*carrot, mango, apple, orange, rose, ..*};

3) merging and filtering of the raw pairs and unlabeled clusters into smaller, more accurate sets of class instances associated with class labels, in an attempt to use unlabeled clusters to filter noisy raw pairs instead of merely using clusters to generalize class labels across raw pairs (Paşca and Van Durme, 2008):

fruits={*apple, mango, orange, ..*}.

To increase precision, the vocabulary of class instances is confined to the set of queries that are most frequently submitted to a general-purpose Web search engine. After merging, the resulting pairs of an instance and a class label are arranged into instance sets (e.g., {*ferrari modena, porsche carrera gt*}), each associated with a class label (e.g., *sports cars*).

Linking Labeled Classes into Hierarchies: Manually-constructed language resources such as WordNet provide reliable, wide-coverage upper-level conceptual hierarchies, by grouping together phrases with the same meaning (e.g., {*analgesic, painkiller, pain pill*}) into sets of synonyms (synsets), and organizing the synsets into conceptual hierarchies (e.g., *painkillers* are a subconcept, or a hyponym, of *drugs*) (Fellbaum, 1998). To determine the points of insertion of automatically-extracted labeled classes into hand-built WordNet hierarchies, the class labels are looked up in WordNet using built-in morphological normalization routines. When a class label (e.g., *age-related diseases*) is not found in WordNet, it is looked up again after iteratively removing its leading words (e.g., *related diseases*, and *diseases*) until a potential point of insertion is found where one or more senses exist in WordNet for the class label.

An efficient heuristic for sense selection is to uniformly choose the first (that is, most frequent) sense of the class label in WordNet, as point of insertion. Due to its simplicity, the heuristic is bound to make errors whenever the correct sense is not the first one, thus incorrectly linking *academic journals* under the sense of *journals* as personal diaries rather than periodicals, and *active volcanoes* under the sense of *volcanoes* as fissures in the earth, rather than mountains formed by volcanic material. Nevertheless, choosing the first sense is attractive for three reasons. First, WordNet senses are often too fine-grained, making the task of choosing the correct sense difficult even for humans (Palmer et al., 2007). Second, choosing the first sense from WordNet is sometimes better than more intelligent disambiguation techniques (Pradhan et al., 2007). Third, previous experimental results on linking Wikipedia classes to WordNet concepts confirm that first-sense selection is more effective in practice than other techniques (Suchanek et al., 2007). Thus, a class label and its associated instances are inserted under the first WordNet sense available for the class label. For example, *silicon valley companies* and its associated instances (*apple*, *hewlett packard* etc.) are inserted under the first of the 9 senses of *companies* in WordNet, which corresponds to companies as institutions created to conduct business.

In order to trade off coverage for higher precision, the heuristic can be restricted to link a class label under the first WordNet sense available, as before, but only when no other senses are available at the point of insertion beyond the first sense. With the modified heuristic, the class label *internet search engines* is linked under the first and only sense of *search engines* in WordNet, but *silicon valley companies* is no longer linked under the first of the 9 senses of *companies*.

Extraction of Attributes for Hierarchy Concepts: The labeled classes of instances linked to conceptual hierarchies constitute the input to the acquisition of attributes of hierarchy concepts, by mining a collection of Web search queries. The attributes capture properties that are relevant to the concept. The extraction of attributes exploits the sets of class instances rather than the associated class labels. More precisely, for each hierarchy concept for which attributes must be extracted, the instances associated to all class labels linked under the subhierarchy rooted at the concept are collected as a union set of instances, thus exploiting the transitivity of IsA relations. This step is equivalent to propagating the instances upwards, from their class labels to higher-level WordNet concepts under which the class labels are linked, up to the root of the hierarchy. The resulting sets of instances constitute the input to the acquisition of attributes, which consists of four stages:

1) identification of a noisy pool of candidate attributes, as remainders of queries that also contain one of the class instances. In the case of the concept *movies*, whose instances include *jay and silent bob strike back* and *kill bill*, the query *"cast jay and silent bob strike back"* produces the candidate attribute *cast*;

2) construction of internal vector representations for each candidate attribute, based on queries (e.g., *"cast selection for kill bill"*) that contain a candidate attribute (*cast*) and a class instance (*kill bill*). These vectors consist of counts tied to the frequency with which an attribute occurs with a given "templatized" query. The latter replaces specific attributes and instances from the query with common placeholders, e.g., *"X for Y"*;

3) construction of a reference internal vector representation for a small set of seed attributes provided as input. A reference vector is the normalized sum of the individual vectors corresponding to the seed attributes;

4) ranking of candidate attributes with respect to each concept, by computing the similarity between their individual vector representations and the reference vector of the seed attributes.

The result of the four stages, which are described in more detail in (Paşca, 2007), is a ranked list of attributes (e.g., [*opening song, cast, characters,...*]) for each concept (e.g., *movies*).

3 Experimental Setting

Textual Data Sources: The acquisition of open-domain knowledge relies on unstructured text available within a combination of Web documents maintained by, and search queries submitted to the Google search engine. The textual data source for extracting labeled classes of instances consists of around 100 million documents in English, as available in a Web repository snapshot from 2006. Conversely, the acquisition of open-domain attributes relies on a random sample of fully-anonymized queries in English submitted by Web users in 2006. The sample contains about 50 million unique queries. Each query is accompanied by its frequency of occurrence in the logs. Other sources of similar data are available publicly for research purposes (Gao et al., 2007).

Parameters for Extracting Labeled Classes: When applied to the available document collection, the method for extracting open-domain classes of instances from unstructured text introduced in (Paşca and Van Durme, 2008) produces 4,583 class labels associated to 258,699 unique instances, for a total of 869,118 pairs of a class instance and an associated class label. All collected instances occur among to the top five million queries with the highest frequency within the input query logs. The data is further filtered by discarding labeled classes with fewer than 25 instances. The classes, examples of which are shown in Table 1, are linked under conceptual hierarchies available within WordNet 3.0, which contains a total of 117,798 English noun phrases grouped in 82,115 concepts (or synsets).

Parameters for Extracting Attributes: For each target concept from the hierarchy, given the union of all instances associated to class labels linked to the target concept or one of its subconcepts, and given a set of five seed attributes (e.g., {*quality, speed, number of users, market share, reliability*} for *search engines*), the method described in (Paşca, 2007) extracts ranked lists of attributes from the input query logs. Internally, the ranking of attributes uses Jensen-Shannon (Lee, 1999) to compute similarity scores between internal rep-

Class Label	Class Size	Class Instances
accounting systems	40	flexcube, myob, oracle financials, peachtree accounting, sybiz
antimicrobials	97	azithromycin, chloramphenicol, fusidic acid, quinolones, sulfa drugs
civilizations	197	ancient greece, chaldeans, etruscans, inca, indians, roman republic
elementary particles	33	axions, electrons, gravitons, leptons, muons, neutrons, positrons
farm animals	61	angora goats, burros, cattle, cows, donkeys, draft horses, mule, oxen
forages	27	alsike clover, rye grass, tall fescue, sericea lespedeza, birdsfoot trefoil
ideologies	179	egalitarianism, laissez-faire capitalism, participatory democracy
social events	436	academic conferences, afternoon teas, block parties, masquerade balls

Table 1: Examples of instances within labeled classes extracted from unstructured text, used as input for attribute extraction experiments

resentations of seed attributes, on one hand, and each of the newly acquired attributes, on the other hand. Depending on the experiments, the amount of supervision is thus limited to either 5 seed attributes for each target concept, or to 5 seed attributes (*population*, *area*, *president*, *flag* and *climate*) provided for only one of the extracted labeled classes, namely *european countries*.

Description	Source of Hierarchy and Instances			
	N	Y	E_s	E_a
Include instances from WordNet?	√	√	-	-
Include instances from elsewhere?	-	√	√	√
#Instances ($\times 10^3$)	14.3	1,296.5	108.0	257.0
#Class labels	945	30,338	1,315	4,517
#Pairs of a class label and instance ($\times 10^3$)	17.4	2,839.8	191.0	859.0

Table 2: Source of class instances for various experimental runs

Experimental Runs: The experiments consist of four different runs, which correspond to different choices for the source of conceptual hierarchies and class instances linked to those hierarchies, as illustrated in Table 2. In the first run, denoted N, the class instances are those available within the latest version of WordNet (3.0) itself via HasInstance relations. The second run, Y, corresponds to an extension of WordNet based on the manually-compiled classes of instances from categories in Wikipedia, as available in the 2007-w50-5 version of Yago (Suchanek et al., 2007). Therefore, run Y has the advantage of the fact that Wikipedia categories are a rich source of useful and accurate knowledge (Nastase and Strube, 2008), which explains their previous use as a source for evaluation gold standards (Blohm et al., 2007). The last two runs from Table 2, E_s and E_a, correspond to the set of open-domain labeled classes acquired from unstructured text. In both E_s and E_a, class labels are linked to the first sense available at the point of insertion in WordNet. In E_s, the class labels are linked only if no other senses are available at the point of insertion beyond the first sense, thus promoting higher linkage precision at the expense of fewer links. For example, since the phrases *impressionists*, *sports cars* and *painters* have 1, 1 and 4 senses available in WordNet respectively, the class labels *french impressionists* and *sports cars* are linked to the respective WordNet concepts, whereas the class label *painters* is not. Comparatively, in E_a, the class labels are uniformly linked to the first sense available in WordNet, regardless of whether other senses may or may not be available. Thus, E_a trades off potentially lower precision for the benefit of higher linkage recall, and results in more of the class labels and their associated instances extracted from text to be linked to WordNet than in the case of run E_s.

4 Evaluation

4.1 Evaluation of Labeled Classes

Coverage of Class Instances: In run N, the input class instances are the component phrases of synsets encoded via HasInstance relations under other synsets in WordNet. For example, the synset corresponding to {*search engine*}, defined as *"a computer program that retrieves documents or files or data from a database or from a computer network"*, has 3 HasInstance instances in WordNet, namely *Ask Jeeves*, *Google* and *Yahoo*. Table 3 illustrates the coverage of the class instances extracted from unstructured text and linked to WordNet in runs E_s and E_a respectively, relative to all 945 WordNet synsets that contain HasInstance instances. Note that the coverage scores are conservative assessments of actual coverage, since a run (i.e., E_s or E_a) receives credit for a WordNet instance only if the run contains an instance that is a full-length, case-insensitive match (e.g., *ask*

	Concept	HasInstance Instances within WordNet		Cvg	
Synset	Offset	Examples	Count	E_s	E_a
{existentialist, existentialist, philosopher, existential philosopher}	10071557	Albert Camus, Beauvoir, Camus, Heidegger, Jean-Paul Sartre	8	1.00	1.00
{search engine}	06578654	Ask Jeeves, Google, Yahoo	3	1.00	1.00
{university}	04511002	Brown, Brown University, Carnegie Mellon University	44	0.61	0.77
{continent}	09254614	Africa, Antarctic continent, Europe, Eurasia, Gondwanaland, Laurasia	13	0.54	0.54
{microscopist}	10313872	Anton van Leeuwenhoek, Anton van Leuwenhoek, Swammerdam	6	0.00	0.00
Average over all 945 WordNet concepts that have HasInstance instance(s)			18.71	0.21	0.40

Table 3: Coverage of class instances extracted from text and linked to WordNet (used as input in runs E_s and E_a respectively), measured as the fraction of WordNet HasInstance instances (used as input in run N) that occur among the class instances (Cvg=coverage)

jeeves) of the WordNet instance. On average, the coverage scores for class instances of runs E_s and E_a relative to run N are 0.21 and 0.40 respectively, as shown in the last row in Table 3. Comparatively, the equivalent instance coverage for run Y, which already includes most of the WordNet instances by design (cf. (Suchanek et al., 2007)), is 0.59.

Relative Coverage of Class Labels: The linking of class labels to WordNet concepts allows for the expansion of the set of classes of instances acquired from text, thus increasing its usefulness in attribute extraction in particular and information extraction in general. To this effect, additional class labels are identified for existing instances, in the form of component phrases of the synsets that are superconcepts (or hypernyms, in WordNet terminology) of the synset under which the class label of the instance is linked in WordNet. For example, since the class label *sports cars* is linked under the WordNet synset {*sports car, sport car*}, and the latter has the synset {*motor vehicle, automotive vehicle*} among its hypernyms, the phrases *motor vehicles* and *automotive vehicles* are collected as new class labels [1] and associated to existing instances of *sports cars* from the original set, such as *ferrari modena*. No phrases are collected from a selected set of 10 top-level WordNet synsets, including {*entity*} and {*object, physical object*}, which are deemed too general to be useful as class labels. As illustrated in Table 4, a collected pair of a new class label and an existing instance either does not have any impact, if the pair already occurs in the original set of labeled classes; or expands existing classes, if the class label already occurs in the original set of labeled classes but not in association to the instance; or creates new classes of instances, if the class label is not part of the original set. The latter two cases aggregate to increases in coverage, relative to the pairs from the original sets of labeled classes, of 53% for E_s and 304% for E_a.

Already in original labeled classes:	
painters	alfred sisley
european countries	austria
Expansion of existing labeled classes:	
animals	avocet
animals	northern oriole
scientists	howard gardner
scientists	phil zimbardo
Creation of new labeled classes:	
automotive vehicles	acura nsx
automotive vehicles	detomaso pantera
creative persons	aaron copland
creative persons	yoshitomo nara

Table 4: Examples of additional class labels collected from WordNet, for existing instances of the original labeled classes extracted from text

4.2 Evaluation of Attributes

Target Hierarchy Concepts: The performance of attribute extraction is assessed over a set of 25 target concepts also used for evaluation in (Paşca, 2008). The set of 25 target concepts includes: *Actor, Award, Battle, CelestialBody, ChemicalElement, City, Company, Country, Currency, DigitalCamera, Disease, Drug, FictionalCharacter, Flower, Food, Holiday, Mountain, Movie, NationalPark, Painter, Religion, River, SearchEngine, Treaty, Wine*. Each target concept represents exactly one WordNet concept (synset). For instance,

[1]For consistency with the original labeled classes, new class labels collected from WordNet are converted from singular (e.g., *motor vehicle*) to plural (e.g., *motor vehicles*).

one of the target concepts, denoted *Country*, corresponds to a synset situated at the internal offset 08544813 in WordNet 3.0, which groups together the synonymous phrases *country*, *state* and *land* and associates them with the definition *"the territory occupied by a nation"*. The target concepts exhibit variation with respect to their depths within WordNet conceptual hierarchies, ranging from a minimum of 5 (e.g., for *Food*) to a maximum of 11 (for *Flower*), with a mean depth of 8 over the 25 concepts.

Evaluation Procedure: The measurement of recall requires knowledge of the complete set of items (in our case, attributes) to be extracted. Unfortunately, this number is often unavailable in information extraction tasks in general (Hasegawa et al., 2004), and attribute extraction in particular. Indeed, the manual enumeration of all attributes of each target concept, to measure recall, is unfeasible. Therefore, the evaluation focuses on the assessment of attribute accuracy.

To remove any bias towards higher-ranked attributes during the assessment of class attributes, the ranked lists of attributes produced by each run to be evaluated are sorted alphabetically into a merged list. Each attribute of the merged list is manually assigned a correctness label within its respective class. In accordance with previously introduced methodology, an attribute is *vital* if it must be present in an ideal list of attributes of the class (e.g., *side effects* for *Drug*); *okay* if it provides useful but non-essential information; and *wrong* if it is incorrect (Paşca, 2007).

To compute the precision score over a ranked list of attributes, the correctness labels are converted to numeric values (*vital* to 1, *okay* to 0.5 and *wrong* to 0). Precision at some rank N in the list is thus measured as the sum of the assigned values of the first N attributes, divided by N.

Attribute Accuracy: Figure 1 plots the precision at ranks 1 through 50 for the ranked lists of attributes extracted by various runs as an average over the 25 target concepts, along two dimensions. In the leftmost graphs, each of the 25 target concepts counts towards the computation of precision scores of a given run, regardless of whether any attributes were extracted or not for the target concept. In the rightmost graphs, only target concepts for which some attributes were extracted are included in the precision scores of a given run. Thus, the leftmost graphs properly penalize a run

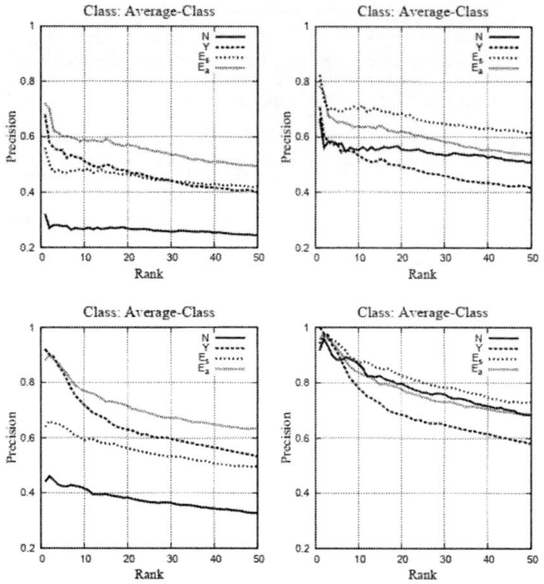

Figure 1: Accuracy of the attributes extracted for various runs, as an average over the entire set of 25 target concepts (left graphs) and as an average over (variable) subsets of the 25 target concepts for which some attributes were extracted in each run (right graphs). Seed attributes are provided as input for only one target concept (top graphs), or for each target concept (bottom graphs)

for failing to extract any attributes for some target concepts, whereas the rightmost graphs do not include any such penalties. On the other dimension, in the graphs at the top of Figure 1, seed attributes are provided only for one class (namely, *european countries*), for a total of 5 attributes over all classes. In the graphs at the bottom of the figure, there are 5 seed attributes for each of the 25 target concepts in the graphs at the bottom of Figure 1, for a total of 5×25=125 attributes.

Several conclusions can be drawn after inspecting the results. First, providing more supervision, in the form of seed attributes for all concepts rather than for only one concept, translates into higher attribute accuracy for all runs, as shown by the graphs at the top vs. graphs at the bottom of Figure 1. Second, in the leftmost graphs, run N has the lowest precision scores, which is in line with the relatively small number of instances available in the original WordNet, as confirmed by the counts from Table 2. Third, in the leftmost graphs, the more restrictive run E_s has lower precision scores across all ranks than its less restrictive counterpart E_a. In other words, adding more

Class	Precision											
	@10				@30				@50			
	N	Y	E_s	E_a	N	Y	E_s	E_a	N	Y	E_s	E_a
Actor	1.00	1.00	1.00	1.00	0.78	0.85	0.98	0.95	0.62	0.84	0.95	0.96
Award	0.00	0.50	0.95	0.85	0.00	0.35	0.80	0.73	0.00	0.29	0.70	0.69
Battle	0.80	0.90	0.00	0.90	0.76	0.80	0.00	0.80	0.74	0.72	0.00	0.73
CelestialBody	1.00	1.00	1.00	0.40	1.00	1.00	0.93	0.16	0.98	0.89	0.91	0.12
ChemicalElement	0.00	0.65	0.80	0.80	0.00	0.45	0.83	0.63	0.00	0.48	0.84	0.51
City	1.00	1.00	0.00	1.00	0.86	0.80	0.00	0.83	0.78	0.70	0.00	0.76
Company	0.00	1.00	0.90	1.00	0.00	0.90	0.93	0.88	0.00	0.77	0.82	0.80
Country	1.00	0.90	1.00	1.00	0.98	0.81	0.96	0.96	0.97	0.76	0.98	0.97
Currency	0.00	0.90	0.00	0.90	0.00	0.53	0.00	0.83	0.00	0.36	0.00	0.87
DigitalCamera	0.00	0.20	0.85	0.85	0.00	0.10	0.85	0.85	0.00	0.10	0.82	0.82
Disease	0.00	0.60	0.75	0.75	0.00	0.76	0.83	0.83	0.00	0.63	0.87	0.86
Drug	0.00	1.00	1.00	1.00	0.00	0.91	1.00	1.00	0.00	0.88	0.96	0.96
FictionalCharacter	0.80	0.70	0.00	0.55	0.65	0.48	0.00	0.38	0.42	0.41	0.00	0.34
Flower	0.00	0.65	0.00	0.70	0.00	0.26	0.00	0.55	0.00	0.16	0.00	0.53
Food	0.00	0.80	0.90	1.00	0.00	0.65	0.71	0.96	0.00	0.53	0.59	0.96
Holiday	0.00	0.60	0.80	0.80	0.00	0.50	0.48	0.48	0.00	0.37	0.41	0.41
Mountain	1.00	0.75	0.00	0.90	0.96	0.61	0.00	0.86	0.77	0.58	0.00	0.74
Movie	0.00	1.00	1.00	1.00	0.00	0.90	0.80	0.78	0.00	0.85	0.75	0.74
NationalPark	0.90	0.80	0.00	0.00	0.85	0.76	0.00	0.00	0.82	0.75	0.00	0.00
Painter	1.00	1.00	1.00	1.00	0.96	0.93	0.88	0.96	0.92	0.89	0.76	0.93
Religion	0.00	0.00	1.00	1.00	0.00	0.00	1.00	1.00	0.00	0.00	0.92	0.97
River	1.00	0.80	0.00	0.00	0.70	0.60	0.00	0.00	0.61	0.58	0.00	0.00
SearchEngine	0.40	0.00	0.25	0.25	0.23	0.00	0.35	0.35	0.32	0.00	0.43	0.43
Treaty	0.50	0.90	0.80	0.80	0.33	0.65	0.53	0.53	0.26	0.59	0.42	0.42
Wine	0.00	0.30	0.80	0.80	0.00	0.26	0.43	0.45	0.00	0.20	0.28	0.29
Average (over 25)	0.41	0.71	0.59	**0.77**	0.36	0.59	0.53	**0.67**	0.32	0.53	0.49	**0.63**
Average (over non-empty)	0.86	0.78	**0.87**	0.83	0.75	0.64	**0.78**	0.73	0.68	0.57	**0.73**	0.68

Table 5: Comparative accuracy of the attributes extracted by various runs, for individual concepts, as an average over the entire set of 25 target concepts, and as an average over (variable) subsets of the 25 target concepts for which some attributes were extracted in each run. Seed attributes are provided as input for each target concept

restrictions may improve precision but hurts recall of class instances, which results in lower average precision scores for the attributes. Fourth, in the leftmost graphs, the runs using the automatically-extracted labeled classes (E_s and E_a) not only outperform N, but one of them (E_a) also outperforms Y. This is the most important result. It shows that large-scale, automatically-derived classes of instances can have as much as, or even bigger, practical impact in attribute extraction than similar data from larger (cf. Table 2), manually-compiled, collaboratively created and maintained resources such as Wikipedia. Concretely, in the graph on the bottom left of Figure 1, the precision scores at ranks 10, 30 and 50 are 0.71, 0.59 and 0.53 for run Y, but 0.77, 0.67 and 0.63 for run E_a. The scores correspond to attribute accuracy improvements of 8% at rank 10, 13% at rank 30, and 18% at rank 50 for run E_a over run Y. In fact, in the rightmost graphs, that is, without taking into account target concepts without any extracted attributes, the precision scores of both E_s and E_a are higher than for run Y across most, if not all, ranks from 1 through 50. In this case, it is E_1 that produces the most accurate attributes, in a task-based demonstration that the more cautious linking of class labels to WordNet concepts in E_s vs. E_a leads to less coverage but higher precision of the linked labeled classes, which translates into extracted attributes of higher accuracy but for fewer target concepts.

Analysis: The curves plotted in the two graphs at the bottom of Figure 1 are computed as averages over precision scores for individual target concepts, which are shown in detail in Table 5. Precision scores of 0.00 correspond to runs for which no attributes are acquired from query logs, because no instances are available in the subhierarchy rooted at the respective concepts. For example, precision scores for run N are 0.00 for *Award* and *DigitalCamera*, among others concepts in Table 5, due to the lack of any HasInstance instances in WordNet for the respective concepts. The number of target concepts for which some attributes are extracted is 12 for run N, 23 for Y, 17 for E_s

and 23 for E_a. Thus, both run N and run E_s exhibit rather binary behavior across individual classes, in that they tend to either not retrieve any attributes or retrieve attributes of relatively higher quality than the other runs, causing E_s and N to have the worst precision scores in the last but one row of Table 5, but the best precision scores in the last row of Table 5.

The individual scores shown for E_s and E_a in Table 5 concur with the conclusion drawn earlier from the graphs in Figure 1, that Run E_s has lower precision than E_a as an average over all target concepts. Notable exceptions are the scores obtained for the concepts *CelestialBody* and *ChemicalElement*, where E_s significantly outperforms E_a in Table 5. This is due to confusing instances (e.g., *kobe bryant*) being associated with class labels (e.g., *nba stars*) that are incorrectly linked under the target concepts (e.g., *Star*, which is a subconcept of *CelestialBody* in WordNet) in E_a, but not linked at all and thus not causing confusion in E_s.

Run Y performs better than E_a for 5 of the 25 individual concepts, including *NationalPark*, for which no instances of *national parks* or related class labels are available in run E_a; and *River*, for which relevant instances in the labeled classes in E_a, but they are associated to the class label *river systems*, which is incorrectly linked to the WordNet concept *systems* rather than to *rivers*. However, run E_a outperforms Y on 12 individual concepts (e.g., *Award*, *DigitalCamera* and *Disease*), and also as an average over all classes (last two rows in Table 5).

5 Related Work

Previous work on the automatic acquisition of attributes for open-domain classes from text requires the manual enumeration of sets of instances and seed attributes, for each class for which attributes are to be extracted. In contrast, the current method operates on automatically-extracted classes. The experiments reported in (Paşca and Van Durme, 2008) also exploit automatically-extracted classes for the purpose of attribute extraction. However, they operate on flat classes, as opposed to concepts organized hierarchically. Furthermore, they require manual mappings from extracted class labels into a selected set of evaluation classes (e.g., by mapping *river systems* to *River*, *football clubs* to *SoccerClub*, and *parks* to *NationalPark*), whereas the current method maps class labels to concepts automatically, by linking class labels and their associated instances to concepts. Manually-encoded attributes available within Wikipedia articles are used in (Wu and Weld, 2008) in order to derive other attributes from unstructured text within Web documents. Comparatively, the current method extracts attributes from query logs rather than Web documents, using labeled classes extracted automatically rather than available in manually-created resources, and requiring minimal supervision in the form of only 5 seed attributes provided for only one concept, rather than thousands of attributes available in millions of manually-created Wikipedia articles. To our knowledge, there is only one previous study (Paşca, 2008) that directly addresses the problem of extracting attributes over conceptual hierarchies. However, that study uses labeled classes extracted from text with a different method; extracts attributes for labeled classes and propagates them upwards in the hierarchy, in order to compute attributes of hierarchy concepts from attributes of their subconcepts; and does not consider resources similar to Wikipedia, as sources of input labeled classes for attribute extraction.

6 Conclusion

This paper introduces an extraction framework for exploiting labeled classes of instances to acquire open-domain attributes from unstructured text available within search query logs. The linking of the labeled classes into existing conceptual hierarchies allows for the extraction of attributes over hierarchy concepts, without a-priori restrictions to specific domains of interest and with little supervision. Experimental results show that the extracted attributes are more accurate when using automatically-derived labeled classes, rather than classes of instances derived from manually-created resources such as Wikipedia. Current work investigates the impact of the semantic distribution of the classes of instances on the overall accuracy of attributes; the potential benefits of using more compact conceptual hierarchies (Snow et al., 2007) on attribute accuracy; and the organization of labeled classes of instances into conceptual hierarchies, as an alternative to inserting them into existing conceptual hierarchies created manually from scratch or automatically by filtering manually-generated relations among classes from Wikipedia (Ponzetto and Strube, 2007).

References

M. Banko and O. Etzioni. 2008. The tradeoffs between open and traditional relation extraction. In *Proceedings of the 46th Annual Meeting of the Association for Computational Linguistics (ACL-08)*, pages 28–36, Columbus, Ohio.

S. Blohm, P. Cimiano, and E. Stemle. 2007. Harvesting relations from the web - quantifiying the impact of filtering functions. In *Proceedings of the 22nd National Conference on Artificial Intelligence (AAAI-07)*, pages 1316–1321, Vancouver, British Columbia.

D. Davidov and A. Rappoport. 2008. Classification of semantic relationships between nominals using pattern clusters. In *Proceedings of the 46th Annual Meeting of the Association for Computational Linguistics (ACL-08)*, pages 227–235, Columbus, Ohio.

C. Fellbaum, editor. 1998. *WordNet: An Electronic Lexical Database and Some of its Applications*. MIT Press.

W. Gao, C. Niu, J. Nie, M. Zhou, J. Hu, K. Wong, and H. Hon. 2007. Cross-lingual query suggestion using query logs of different languages. In *Proceedings of the 30th ACM Conference on Research and Development in Information Retrieval (SIGIR-07)*, pages 463–470, Amsterdam, The Netherlands.

T. Hasegawa, S. Sekine, and R. Grishman. 2004. Discovering relations among named entities from large corpora. In *Proceedings of the 42nd Annual Meeting of the Association for Computational Linguistics (ACL-04)*, pages 415–422, Barcelona, Spain.

M. Hearst. 1992. Automatic acquisition of hyponyms from large text corpora. In *Proceedings of the 14th International Conference on Computational Linguistics (COLING-92)*, pages 539–545, Nantes, France.

L. Lee. 1999. Measures of distributional similarity. In *Proceedings of the 37th Annual Meeting of the Association of Computational Linguistics (ACL-99)*, pages 25–32, College Park, Maryland.

D. Lin and P. Pantel. 2002. Concept discovery from text. In *Proceedings of the 19th International Conference on Computational linguistics (COLING-02)*, pages 1–7.

V. Nastase and M. Strube. 2008. Decoding Wikipedia categories for knowledge acquisition. In *Proceedings of the 23rd National Conference on Artificial Intelligence (AAAI-08)*, pages 1219–1224, Chicago, Illinois.

M. Paşca and B. Van Durme. 2008. Weakly-supervised acquisition of open-domain classes and class attributes from web documents and query logs. In *Proceedings of the 46th Annual Meeting of the Association for Computational Linguistics (ACL-08)*, pages 19–27, Columbus, Ohio.

M. Paşca. 2007. Organizing and searching the World Wide Web of facts - step two: Harnessing the wisdom of the crowds. In *Proceedings of the 16th World Wide Web Conference (WWW-07)*, pages 101–110, Banff, Canada.

M. Paşca. 2008. Turning Web text and search queries into factual knowledge: Hierarchical class attribute extraction. In *Proceedings of the 23rd National Conference on Artificial Intelligence (AAAI-08)*, pages 1225–1230, Chicago, Illinois.

M. Palmer, H. Dang, and C. Fellbaum. 2007. Making fine-grained and coarse-grained sense distinctions, both manually and automatically. *Natural Language Engineering*, 13(2):137–163.

S. Ponzetto and M. Strube. 2007. Deriving a large scale taxonomy from Wikipedia. In *Proceedings of the 22nd National Conference on Artificial Intelligence (AAAI-07)*, pages 1440–1447, Vancouver, British Columbia.

S. Pradhan, E. Loper, D. Dligach, and M. Palmer. 2007. SemEval-2007 Task-17: English lexical sample, SRL and all words. In *Proceedings of the 4th Workshop on Semantic Evaluations (SemEval-07)*, pages 87–92, Prague, Czech Republic.

M. Remy. 2002. Wikipedia: The free encyclopedia. *Online Information Review*, 26(6):434.

R. Snow, S. Prakash, D. Jurafsky, and A. Ng. 2007. Learning to merge word senses. In *Proceedings of the 2007 Conference on Empirical Methods in Natural Language Processing (EMNLP-07)*, pages 1005–1014, Prague, Czech Republic.

F. Suchanek, G. Kasneci, and G. Weikum. 2007. Yago: a core of semantic knowledge unifying WordNet and Wikipedia. In *Proceedings of the 16th World Wide Web Conference (WWW-07)*, pages 697–706, Banff, Canada.

F. Wu and D. Weld. 2008. Automatically refining the Wikipedia infobox ontology. In *Proceedings of the 17th World Wide Web Conference (WWW-08)*, pages 635–644, Beijing, China.

Predicting Strong Associations on the Basis of Corpus Data

Yves Peirsman
Research Foundation – Flanders &
QLVL, University of Leuven
Leuven, Belgium
yves.peirsman@arts.kuleuven.be

Dirk Geeraerts
QLVL, University of Leuven
Leuven, Belgium
dirk.geeraerts@arts.kuleuven.be

Abstract

Current approaches to the prediction of associations rely on just one type of information, generally taking the form of either word space models or collocation measures. At the moment, it is an open question how these approaches compare to one another. In this paper, we will investigate the performance of these two types of models and that of a new approach based on compounding. The best single predictor is the log-likelihood ratio, followed closely by the document-based word space model. We will show, however, that an ensemble method that combines these two best approaches with the compounding algorithm achieves an increase in performance of almost 30% over the current state of the art.

1 Introduction

Associations are words that immediately come to mind when people hear or read a given cue word. For instance, a word like *pepper* calls up *salt*, and *wave* calls up *sea*. Aitchinson (2003) and Schulte im Walde and Melinger (2005) show that such associations can be motivated by a number of factors, from semantic similarity to collocation. Current computational models of association, however, tend to focus on one of these, by using either collocation measures (Michelbacher et al., 2007) or word space models (Sahlgren, 2006; Peirsman et al., 2008). To this day, two general problems remain. First, the literature lacks a comprehensive comparison between these general types of models. Second, we are still looking for an approach that combines several sources of information, so as to correctly predict a larger variety of associations.

Most computational models of semantic relations aim to model semantic similarity in particular (Landauer and Dumais, 1997; Lin, 1998; Padó and Lapata, 2007). In Natural Language Processing, these models have applications in fields like query expansion, thesaurus extraction, information retrieval, etc. Similarly, in Cognitive Science, such models have helped explain neural activation (Mitchell et al., 2008), sentence and discourse comprehension (Burgess et al., 1998; Foltz, 1996; Landauer and Dumais, 1997) and priming patterns (Lowe and McDonald, 2000), to name just a few examples. However, there are a number of applications and research fields that will surely benefit from models that target the more general phenomenon of association. For instance, automatically predicted associations may prove useful in models of *information scent*, which seek to explain the paths that users follow in their search for relevant information on the web (Chi et al., 2001). After all, if the visitor of a web shop clicks on *music* to find the prices of iPods, this behaviour is motivated by an associative relation different from similarity. Other possible applications lie in the field of models of text coherence (Landauer and Dumais, 1997) and automated essay grading (Kakkonen et al., 2005). In addition, all research in Cognitive Science that we have referred to above could benefit from computational models of association in order to study the effects of association in comparison to those of similarity.

Our article is structured as follows. In section 2, we will discuss the phenomenon of association and introduce the variety of relations that it is motivated by. Parallel to these relations, section 3 presents the three basic types of approaches that we use to predict strong associations. Section 4 will first compare the results of these three approaches, for a total of 43 models. Section 5 will then show how these results can be improved by the combination of several models in an ensemble. Finally, section 6 wraps up with conclusions and an outlook for future research.

Proceedings of the 12th Conference of the European Chapter of the ACL, pages 648–656,
Athens, Greece, 30 March – 3 April 2009.

cue	association
amfibie ('amphibian')	kikker ('frog')
peper ('pepper')	zout ('salt')
roodborstje ('robin')	vogel ('bird')
granaat ('grenade')	oorlog ('war')
helikopter ('helicopter')	vliegen ('to fly')
werk ('job')	geld ('money')
acteur ('actor')	film ('film')
cello ('cello')	muziek ('music')
kruk ('stool')	bar ('bar')

Table 1: Examples of cues and their strongest association.

2 Associations

There are several reasons why a word may be associated to its cue. According to Aitchinson (2003), the four major types of associations are, in order of frequency, co-ordination (co-hyponyms like *pepper* and *salt*), collocation (like *salt* and *water*), superordination (*insect* as a hypernym of *butterfly*) and synonymy (like *starved* and *hungry*). As a result, a computational model that is able to predict associations accurately has to deal with a wide range of semantic relations. Past systems, however, generally use only one type of information (Wettler et al., 2005; Sahlgren, 2006; Michelbacher et al., 2007; Peirsman et al., 2008; Wandmacher et al., 2008), which suggests that they are relatively restricted in the number of associations they will find.

In this article, we will focus on a set of Dutch cue words and their single strongest association, collected from a large psycholinguistic experiment. Table 1 gives a few examples of such cue–association pairs. It illustrates the different types of linguistic phenomena that an association may be motivated by. The first three word pairs are based on similarity. In this case, strong associations can be hyponyms (as in *amphibian–frog*), co-hyponyms (as in *pepper–salt*) or hypernyms of their cue (as in *robin–bird*). The next three pairs represent semantic links where no relation of similarity plays a role. Instead, the associations seem to be motivated by a topical relation to their cue, which is possibly reflected by their frequent co-occurrence in a corpus. The final three word pairs suggest that morphological factors might play a role, too. Often, a cue and its association form the building blocks of a compound, and it is possible that one part of a compound calls up the other. The examples show that the process of compounding can go in either direction: the compound may consist of cue plus association (as in *cellomuziek* 'cello music'), or of association plus cue (as in *filmacteur* 'film actor'). While it is not clear if it is the compounds themselves that motivate the association, or whether it is just the topical relation between their two parts, they might still be able to help identify strong associations.

3 Approaches

Motivated by the three types of cue–association pairs that we identified in Table 1, we study three sources of information (two types of distributional information, and one type of morphological information) that may provide corpus-based evidence for strong associatedness: collocation measures, word space models and compounding.

3.1 Collocation measures

Probably the most straightforward way to predict strong associations is to assume that a cue and its strong association often co-occur in text. As a result, we can use collocation measures like point-wise mutual information (Church and Hanks, 1989) or the log-likelihood ratio (Dunning, 1993) to predict the strong association for a given cue. **Point-wise mutual information** (PMI) tells us if two words w_1 and w_2 occur together more or less often than expected on the basis of their individual frequencies and the independence assumption:

$$PMI(w_1, w_2) = \log_2 \frac{P(w_1, w_2)}{P(w_1) * P(w_2)}$$

The **log-likelihood ratio** compares the likelihoods L of the independence hypothesis (i.e., $p = P(w_2|w_1) = P(w_2|\neg w_1)$) and the dependence hypothesis (i.e., $p_1 = P(w_2|w_1) \neq P(w_2|\neg w_1) = p_2$), under the assumption that the words in a text are binomially distributed:

$$\log \lambda = \log \frac{L(P(w_2|w_1); p) * L(P(w_2|\neg w_1); p)}{L(P(w_2|w_1); p_1) * L(P(w_2|\neg w_1); p_2)}$$

3.2 Word Space Models

A respectable proportion (in our data about 18%) of the strong associations are motivated by semantic similarity to their cue. They can be synonyms, hyponyms, hypernyms, co-hyponyms or antonyms. Collocation measures, however, are not specifically targeted towards the discovery of semantic similarity. Instead, they model similarity mainly as a side effect of collocation. Therefore we also investigated a large set of computational models that were specifically developed for the discovery of semantic similarity. These so-called word space models or distributional models of lexical semantics are motivated by the distributional hypothesis, which claims that semantically similar words appear in similar contexts. As a result, they model each word in terms of its contexts in a corpus, as a so-called *context vector*. Distributional similarity is then operationalized as the similarity between two such context vectors. These models will thus look for possible associations by searching words with a context vector similar to the given cue.

Crucial in the implementation of word space models is their definition of context. In the current literature, there are basically three popular approaches. **Document-based models** use some sort of textual entity as features (Landauer and Dumais, 1997; Sahlgren, 2006). Their context vectors note what documents, paragraphs, articles or similar stretches of text a target word appears in. Without dimensionality reduction, in these models two words will be distributionally similar if they often occur together in the same paragraph, for instance. This approach still bears some similarity to the collocation measures above, since it relies on the direct co-occurrence of two words in text. Second, **syntax-based** models focus on the syntactic relationships in which a word takes part (Lin, 1998). Here two words will be similar when they often appear in the same syntactic roles, like `subject of fly`. Third, **word-based models** simply use as features the words that appear in the context of the target, without considering the syntactic relations between them. Context is thus defined as the set of n words around the target (Sahlgren, 2006). Obviously, the choice of context size will again have a major influence on the behaviour of the model. Syntax-based and word-based models differ from collocation measures and document-based models in that they do not search for words that co-occur directly. Instead, they look for words that often occur together with the same context words or syntactic relations. Even though all these models were originally developed to model semantic similarity relations, syntax-based models have been shown to favour such relations more than word-based and document-based models, which might capture more associative relationships (Sahlgren, 2006; Van der Plas, 2008).

3.3 Compounding

As we have argued before, one characteristic of cues and their strong associations is that they can sometimes be combined into a compound. Therefore we developed a third approach which discovers for every cue the words in the corpus that in combination with it lead to an existing compound. Since in Dutch compounds are generally written as one word, this is relatively easy. We attached each candidate association to the cue (both in the combination cue+association and association+cue), following a number of simple morphological rules for compounding. We then determined if any of these hypothetical compounds occurred in the corpus. The possible associations that led to an observed compound were then ranked according to the frequency of that compound.[1] Note that, for languages where compounds are often spelled as two words, like English, our approach will have to recognize multiword units to deal with this issue.

3.4 Previous research

In previous research, most attention has gone out to the first two of our models. Sahlgren (2006) tries to find associations with word space models. He argues that document-based models are better suited to the discovery of associations than word-based ones. In addition, Sahlgren (2006) as well as Peirsman et al. (2008) show that in word-based models, large context sizes are more effective than small ones. This supports Wandmacher et al.'s (2008) model of associations, which uses a context size of 75 words to the left and right of the target. However, Peirsman et al. (2008) find that word-based distributional models are clearly outperformed by simple collocation measures, particularly the log-likelihood ratio. Such collocation measures are also used by Michelbacher et al. (2007) in their classification of asymmetric associations. They show the chi-square metric to be a robust classifier of associations as either symmetric or asymmetric, while a measure based on conditional probabilities is particularly suited to model

[1] If both compounds cue+association and association+cue occurred in the corpus, their frequencies were summed.

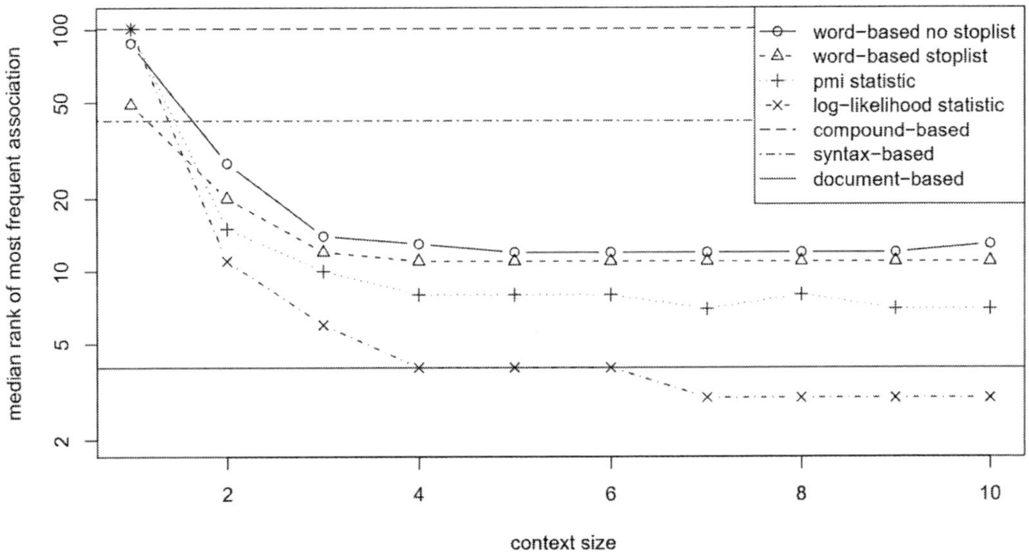

Figure 1: Median rank of the strong associations.

the magnitude of asymmetry. In a similar vein, Wettler et al. (2005) successfully predict associations on the basis of co-occurrence in text, in the framework of associationist learning theory. Despite this wealth of systems, it is an open question how their results compare to each other. Moreover, a model that combines several of these systems might outperform any basic approach.

4 Experiments

Our experiments were inspired by the association prediction task at the ESSLLI-2008 workshop on distributional models. We will first present this precise setup and then go into the results and their implications.

4.1 Setup

Our data was the Twente Nieuws Corpus (TwNC), which contains 300 million words of Dutch newspaper articles. This corpus was compiled at the University of Twente and subsequently parsed by the Alpino parser at the University of Groningen (van Noord, 2006). The newspaper articles in the corpus served as the contextual features for the document-based system; the dependency triples output by Alpino were used as input for the syntax-based approach. These syntactic features of the type `subject of fly` covered eight syntactic relations — subject, direct object, prepositional complement, adverbial prepositional phrase, adjective modification, PP postmodification, apposition and coordination. Finally, the collocation measures and word-based distributional models took into account context sizes ranging from one to ten words to the left and right of the target.

Because of its many parameters, the precise implementation of the word space models deserves a bit more attention. In all cases, we used the context vectors in their full dimensionality. While this is somewhat of an exception in the literature, it has been argued that the full dimensionality leads to the best results for word-based models at least (Bullinaria and Levy, 2007). For the syntax-based and word-based approaches, we only took into account features that occurred at least two times together with the target. For the word-based models, we experimented with the use of a stoplist, which allowed us to exclude semantically "empty" words as features. The simple co-occurrence frequencies in the context vectors were replaced by the pointwise mutual information between the target and the feature (Bullinaria and Levy, 2007; Van der Plas, 2008). The similarity between two vectors was operationalized as the cosine of the angle be-

	similar			related, not similar		
models	mean	med	rank1	mean	med	rank1
pmi context 10	16.4	4	23%	25.2	9	10%
log-likelihood ratio context 10	12.8	2	41%	18.0	3	31%
syntax-based	16.3	4	22%	61.9	70	2%
word-based context 10 stoplist	10.7	3	27%	36.9	17	12%
document-based	10.1	3	26%	20.2	4	26%
compounding	80.7	101	5%	51.9	26	12%

Table 2: Performance of the models on semantically similar cue-association pairs and related but not similar pairs.

med = median; rank1 = number of associations at rank 1

tween them. This measure is more or less standard in the literature and leads to state-of-the-art results (Schütze, 1998; Padó and Lapata, 2007; Bullinaria and Levy, 2007). While the cosine is a symmetric measure, however, association strength is asymmetric. For example, *snelheid* ('speed') triggered *auto* ('car') no fewer than 55 times in the experiment, whereas *auto* evoked *snelheid* a mere 3 times. Like Michelbacher et al. (2007), we solve this problem by focusing not on the similarity score itself, but on the rank of the association in the list of nearest neighbours to the cue. We thus expect that *auto* will have a much higher rank in the list of nearest neighbours to *snelheid* than vice versa.

Our Gold Standard was based on a large-scale psycholinguistic experiment conducted at the University of Leuven (De Deyne and Storms, 2008). In this experiment, participants were asked to list three different associations for all cue words they were presented with. Each of the 1425 cues was given to at least 82 participants, resulting in a total of 381,909 responses. From this set, we took only noun cues with a single strong association. This means we found the most frequent association to each cue, and only included the pair in the test set if the association occurred at least 1.5 times more often than the second most frequent one. This resulted in a final test set of 593 cue-association pairs. Next we brought together all the associations in a set of candidate associations, and complemented it with 1000 random words from the corpus with a frequency of at least 200. From these candidate words, we had each model select the 100 highest scoring ones (the nearest neighbours). Performance was then expressed as the median and mean rank of the strongest association in this list. Associations absent from the list automatically received a rank of 101. Thus, the lower the rank, the better the performance of the system. While there are obviously many more ways of assembling a test set and scoring the several systems, we found these all gave very similar results to the ones reported here.

4.2 Results and discussion

The median ranks of the strong associations for all models are plotted in Figure 1. The means show the same pattern, but give a less clear indication of the number of associations that were suggested in the top n most likely candidates. The most successful approach is the log-likelihood ratio (median 3 with a context size of 10, mean 16.6), followed by the document-based model (median 4, mean 18.4) and point-wise mutual information (median 7 with a context size of 10, mean 23.1). Next in line are the word-based distributional models with and without a stoplist (highest medians at 11 and 12, highest means at 30.9 and 33.3, respectively), and then the syntax-based word space model (median 42, mean 51.1). The worst performance is recorded for the compounding approach (median 101, mean 56.7). Overall, corpus-based approaches that rely on direct co-occurrence thus seem most appropriate for the prediction of strong associations to a cue. This is probably a result of two factors. First, collocation itself is an important motivation for human associations (Aitchinson, 2003). Second, while collocation approaches in themselves do not target semantic similarity, semantically similar associations are often also collocates to their cues. This is particularly the case for co-hyponyms, like *pepper* and *salt*, which score very high both in terms of collocation and in terms of similarity.

Let us discuss the results of all models in a bit

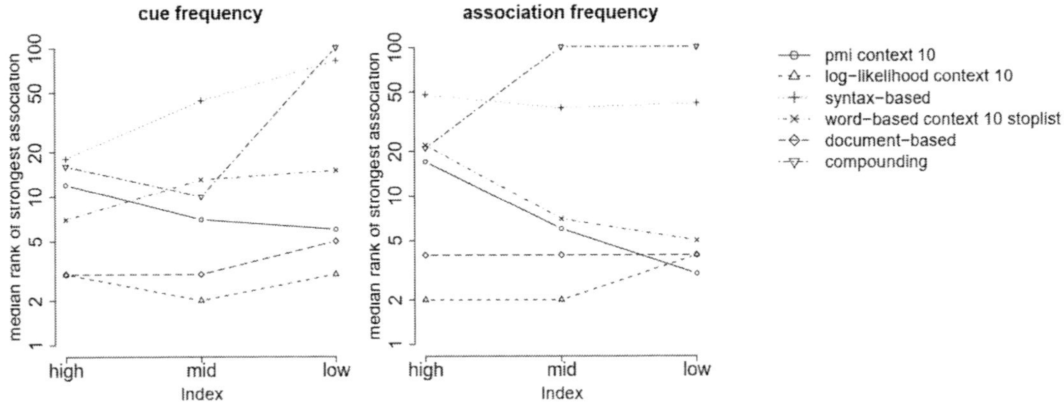

Figure 2: Performance of the models in three cue and association frequency bands.

more detail. A first factor of interest is the difference between associations that are similar to their cue and those which are related but not similar. Most of our models show a crucial difference in performance with respect to these two classes. The most important results are given in Table 2. The log-likelihood ratio gives the highest number of associations at rank 1 for both classes. Particularly surprising is its strong performance with respect to semantic similarity, since this relation is only a side effect of collocation. In fact, the log-likelihood ratio scores better at predicting semantically similar associations than related but not similar associations. Its performance moreover lies relatively close to that of the word space models, which were specifically developed to model semantic similarity. This underpins the observation that even associations that are semantically similar to their cues are still highly motivated by direct co-occurrence in text. Interestingly, only the compounding approach has a clear preference for associations that are related to their cue, but not similar.

A second factor that influences the performance of the models is frequency. In order to test its precise impact, we split up the cues and their associations in three frequency bands of comparable size. For the cues, we constructed a band for words with a frequency of less than 500 in the corpus (low), between 500 and 2,500 (mid) and more than 2,500 (high). For the associations, we had bands for words with a frequency of less than 7,500 (low), between 7,500 and 20,000 (mid) and more than 20,000 (high). Figure 2 shows the performance of the most important models in these frequency bands. With respect to cue frequency, the word space models and compounding approach suffer most from low frequencies and hence, data sparseness. The log-likelihood ratio is much more robust, while point-wise mutual information even performs better with low-frequency cues, although it does not yet reach the performance of the document-based system or the log-likelihood ratio. With respect to association frequency, the picture is different. Here the word-based distributional models and PMI perform better with low-frequency associations. The document-based approach is largely insensitive to association frequency, while the log-likelihood ratio suffers slightly from low frequencies. The performance of the compounding approach decreases most. What is particularly interesting about this plot is that it points towards an important difference between the log-likelihood ratio and point-wise mutual information. In its search for nearest neighbours to a given cue word, the log-likelihood ratio favours frequent words. This is an advantageous feature in the prediction of strong associations, since people tend to give frequent words as associations. PMI, like the syntax-based and word-based models, lacks this characteristic. It therefore fails to discover mid- and high-frequency associations in particular.

Finally, despite the similarity in results between the log-likelihood ratio and the document-based word space model, there exists substantial variation in the associations that they predict successfully. Table 3 gives an overview of the top ten associations that are predicted better by one model than the other, according to the difference be-

model	cue–association pairs
document-based model	*cue–billiards, amphibian–frog, fair–doughnut ball, sperm whale–sea, map–trip, avocado–green, carnivore–meat, one-wheeler–circus, wallet–money, pinecone–wood*
log-likelihood ratio	*top–toy, oven–hot, sorbet–ice cream, rhubarb–sour, poppy–red, knot–rope, pepper–red, strawberry–red, massage–oil, raspberry–red*

Table 3: A comparison of the document-based model and the log-likelihood ratio on the basis of the cue–target pairs with the largest difference in log ranks between the two approaches.

tween the models in the logarithm of the rank of the association. The log-likelihood ratio seems to be biased towards "characteristics" of the target. For instance, it finds the strong associative relation between *poppy, pepper, strawberry, raspberry* and their shared colour *red* much better than the document-based model, just like it finds the relatedness between *oven* and *hot* and *rhubarb* and *sour*. The document-based model recovers more associations that display a strong topical connection with their cue word. This is thanks to its reliance on direct co-occurrence within a large context, which makes it less sensitive to semantic similarity than word-based models. It also appears to have less of a bias toward frequent words than the log-likelihood ratio. Note, for instance, the presence of *doughnut ball* (or *smoutebol* in Dutch) as the third nearest neighbour to *fair*, despite the fact it occurs only once (!) in the corpus. This complementarity between our two most successful approaches suggests that a combination of the two may lead to even better results. We therefore investigated the benefits of a committee-based or ensemble approach.

5 Ensemble-based prediction of strong associations

Given the varied nature of cue–association relations, it could be beneficial to develop a model that relies on more than one type of information. Ensemble methods have already proved their effectiveness in the related area of automatic thesaurus extraction (Curran, 2002), where semantic similarity is the target relation. Curran (2002) explored three ways of combining multiple ordered sets of words: (1) **mean**, taking the mean rank of each word over the ensemble; (2) **harmonic**, taking the harmonic mean; (3) **mixture**, calculating the mean similarity score for each word. We will study only the first two of these approaches, as the different metrics of our models cannot simply be combined in a mean relatedness score. More particularly, we will experiment with ensembles taking the (harmonic) mean of the natural logarithm of the ranks, since we found these to perform better than those working with the original ranks.[2]

Table 4 compares the results of the most important ensembles with that of the single best approach, the log-likelihood ratio with a context size of 10. By combining the two best approaches from the previous section, the log-likelihood ratio and the document-based model, we already achieve a substantial increase in performance. The mean rank of the association goes from 3 to 2, the mean from 16.6 to 13.1 and the number of strong associations with rank 1 climbs from 194 to 223. This is a statistically significant increase (one-tailed paired Wilcoxon test, $W = 30866$, $p = .0002$). Adding another word space model to the ensemble, either a word-based or syntax-based model, brings down performance. However, the addition of the compound model does lead to a clear gain in performance. This ensemble finds the strongest association at a median rank of 2, and a mean of 11.8. In total, 249 strong associations (out of a total 593) are presented as the best candidate by the model — an increase of 28.4% compared to the log-likelihood ratio. Hence, despite its poor performance as a simple model, the compound-based approach can still give useful information about the strong association of a cue word when combined with other models. Based on the original ranks, the increase from the previous ensemble is not statistically significant ($W = 23929$, $p = .31$). If we consider differences at the start of the neighbour list more important and compare the logarithms of the ranks, however, the increase becomes significant ($W = 29787.5$, $p = 0.0008$). Its precise impact should thus further be investigated.

[2] In the case of the harmonic mean, we actually take the logarithm of rank+1, in order to avoid division by zero.

	mean			harmonic mean		
systems	med	mean	rank1	med	mean	rank1
$loglik_{10}$ (baseline)	3	16.6	194			
$loglik_{10}$ + doc	2	13.1	223	3	13.4	211
$loglik_{10}$ + doc + $word_{10}$	3	13.8	182	3	14.2	187
$loglik_{10}$ + doc + syn	3	14.4	179	4	14.7	184
$loglik_{10}$ + doc + comp	**2**	**11.8**	**249**	2	12.2	221

Table 4: Results of ensemble methods.

$loglik_{10}$ = log-likelihood ratio with context size 10;
doc = document-based model;
$word_{10}$ = word-based model with context size 10 and a stoplist;
syn = syntax-based model;
comp = compound-based model;
med = median; rank1 = number of associations at rank 1

Let us finally take a look at the types of strong associations that still tend to receive a low rank in this ensemble system. The first group consists of adjectives that refer to an inherent characteristic of the cue word that is rarely mentioned in text. This is the case for *tennis ball–yellow*, *cheese–yellow*, *grapefruit–bitter*. The second type brings together polysemous cues whose strongest association relates to a different sense than that represented by its corpus-based nearest neighbour. This applies to Dutch *kant*, which is polysemous between *side* and *lace*. Its strongest association, *Bruges*, is clearly related to the latter meaning, but its corpus-based neighbours *ball* and *water* suggest the former. The third type reflects human encyclopaedic knowledge that is less central to the semantics of the cue word. Examples are *police–blue*, *love–red*, or *triangle–maths*. In many of these cases, it appears that the failure of the model to recover the strong associations results from corpus limitations rather than from the model itself.

6 Conclusions and future research

In this paper, we explored three types of basic approaches to the prediction of strong associations to a given cue. Collocation measures like the log-likelihood ratio simply recover those words that strongly collocate with the cue. Word space models look for words that appear in similar contexts, defined as documents, context words or syntactic relations. The compounding approach, finally, searches for words that combine with the target to form a compound. The log-likelihood ratio with a large context size emerged as the best predictor of strong association, followed closely by the document-based word space model. Moreover, we showed that an ensemble method combining the log-likelihood ratio, the document-based word space model and the compounding approach, outperformed any of the basic methods by almost 30%.

In a number of ways, this paper is only a first step towards the successful modelling of cue–association relations. First, the newspaper corpus that served as our data has some restrictions, particularly with respect to diversity of genres. It would be interesting to investigate to what degree a more general corpus — a web corpus, for instance — would be able to accurately predict a wider range of associations. Second, the models themselves might benefit from some additional features. For instance, we are curious to find out what the influence of dimensionality reduction would be, particularly for document-based word space models. Finally, we would like to extend our test set from strong associations to more associations for a given target, in order to investigate how well the discussed models predict relative association strength.

References

Jean Aitchinson. 2003. *Words in the Mind. An Introduction to the Mental Lexicon.* Blackwell, Oxford.

John A. Bullinaria and Joseph P. Levy. 2007. Extracting semantic representations from word co-occurrence statistics: A computational study. *Behaviour Research Methods*, 39:510–526.

Curt Burgess, Kay Livesay, and Kevin Lund. 1998. Explorations in context space: Words, sentences, discourse. *Discourse Processes*, 25:211–257.

Ed H. Chi, Peter Pirolli, Kim Chen, and James Pitkow. 2001. Using information scent to model user information needs and actions on the web. In *Proceedings of the ACM Conference on Human Factors and Computing Systems (CHI 2001)*, pages 490–497.

Kenneth Ward Church and Patrick Hanks. 1989. Word association norms, mutual information and lexicography. In *Proceedings of ACL-27*, pages 76–83.

James R. Curran. 2002. Ensemble methods for automatic thesaurus extraction. In *Proceedings of the Conference on Empirical Methods in Natural Language Processing (EMNLP-2002)*, pages 222–229.

Simon De Deyne and Gert Storms. 2008. Word associations: Norms for 1,424 Dutch words in a continuous task. *Behaviour Research Methods*, 40:198–205.

Ted Dunning. 1993. Accurate methods for the statistics of surprise and coincidence. *Computational Linguistics*, 19:61–74.

Peter W. Foltz. 1996. Latent Semantic Analysis for text-based research. *Behaviour Research Methods, Instruments, and Computers*, 29:197–202.

Tuomo Kakkonen, Niko Myller, Jari Timonen, and Erkki Sutinen. 2005. Automatic essay grading with probabilistic latent semantic analysis. In *Proceedings of the 2nd Workshop on Building Educational Applications Using NLP*, pages 29–36.

Thomas K. Landauer and Susan T. Dumais. 1997. A solution to Plato's problem: The Latent Semantic Analysis theory of acquisition, induction and representation of knowledge. *Psychological Review*, 104(2):211–240.

Dekang Lin. 1998. Automatic retrieval and clustering of similar words. In *Proceedings of COLING-ACL98*, pages 768–774, Montreal, Canada.

Will Lowe and Scott McDonald. 2000. The direct route: Mediated priming in semantic space. In *Proceedings of COGSCI 2000*, pages 675–680. Lawrence Erlbaum Associates.

Lukas Michelbacher, Stefan Evert, and Hinrich Schütze. 2007. Asymmetric association measures. In *Proceedings of the International Conference on Recent Advances in Natural Language Processing (RANLP-07)*.

Tom M. Mitchell, Svetlana V. Shinkareva, Andrew Carlson, Kai-Min Chang, Vicente L. Malva, Robert A. Mason, and Marcel Adam Just. 2008. Predicting human brain activity associated with the meanings of nouns. *Science*, 320:1191–1195.

Sebastian Padó and Mirella Lapata. 2007. Dependency-based construction of semantic space models. *Computational Linguistics*, 33(2):161–199.

Yves Peirsman, Kris Heylen, and Dirk Geeraerts. 2008. Size matters. Tight and loose context definitions in English word space models. In *Proceedings of the ESSLLI Workshop on Distributional Lexical Semantics*, pages 9–16.

Magnus Sahlgren. 2006. *The Word-Space Model. Using Distributional Analysis to Represent Syntagmatic and Paradigmatic Relations Between Words in High-dimensional Vector Spaces.* Ph.D. thesis, Stockholm University, Stockholm, Sweden.

Sabine Schulte im Walde and Alissa Melinger. 2005. Identifying semantic relations and functional properties of human verb associations. In *Proceedings of the conference on Human Language Technology and Empirical Methods in Natural Language Processing*, pages 612–619.

Hinrich Schütze. 1998. Automatic word sense discrimination. *Computational Linguistics*, 24(1):97–124.

Lonneke Van der Plas. 2008. *Automatic Lexico-Semantic Acquisition for Question Answering.* Ph.D. thesis, University of Groningen, Groningen, The Netherlands.

Gertjan van Noord. 2006. At last parsing is now operational. In Piet Mertens, Cédrick Fairon, Anne Dister, and Patrick Watrin, editors, *Verbum Ex Machina. Actes de la 13e Conférence sur le Traitement Automatique des Langues Naturelles (TALN)*, pages 20–42.

Tonio Wandmacher, Ekaterina Ovchinnikova, and Theodore Alexandrov. 2008. Does Latent Semantic Analysis reflect human associations? In *Proceedings of the ESSLLI Workshop on Distributional Lexical Semantics*, pages 63–70.

Manfred Wettler, Reinhard Rapp, and Peter Sedlmeier. 2005. Free word associations correspond to contiguities between words in texts. *Journal of Quantitative Linguistics*, 12(2/3):111–122.

Measuring frame relatedness

Marco Pennacchiotti
Yahoo! Inc.
Santa Clara, CA 95054
pennac@yahoo-inc.com

Michael Wirth
Computational Linguistics
Saarland University, Germany
miwirth@coli.uni-sb.de

Abstract

In this paper we introduce the notion of "frame relatedness", i.e. relatedness among prototypical situations as represented in the FrameNet database. We first demonstrate the cognitive plausibility of that notion through an annotation experiment, and then propose different types of computational measures to automatically assess relatedness. Results show that our measures provide good performance on the task of ranking pairs of frames.

1 Introduction

Measuring relatedness among linguistic entities is a crucial topic in NLP. Automatically assessing the degree of similarity or relatedness between two words or two expressions, is of great help in a variety of tasks, such as Question Answering, Recognizing Textual Entailment (RTE), Information Extraction and discourse processing. Since the very beginning of computational linguistics, many studies have been devoted to the definition and the implementation of automatic measures for word relatedness (e.g. (Rubenstein and Goodenough, 1965; Resnik, 1995; Lin, 1998; Budanitsky and Hirst, 2006; Mohammad and Hirst, 2006)). More recently, relatedness between lexical-syntactic patterns has also been studied (Lin and Pantel, 2001; Szpektor et al., 2004), to support advanced tasks such as paraphrasing and RTE. Unfortunately, no attention has been paid so far to the definition of relatedness at the more abstract *situational level* – i.e. relatedness between two prototypical actions, events or state-of-affairs, taken out of context (e.g. the situations of *Killing* and *Death*). A prominent definition of "prototypical situation" is given in frame semantics (Fillmore, 1985), where a situation is modelled as a conceptual structure (a *frame*) constituted by the predicates that can evoke the situation, and the semantic roles expressing the situation's participants.

As measures of word relatedness help in discovering if two word occurrences express related concepts, so measures of **frame relatedness** should help to discover if two large text fragments are related or talk about similar situations. Such measures would be valuable in many tasks. For example, consider the following fragment, in the context of discourse processing:

"In the 1950s the Shah initiated Iran 's nuclear research program and developed an ambitious plan to produce 23,000MW from nuclear power. The program was stopped by the Islamic Revolution in 1979, but it was revived later in the decade, when strategic interests began to drive the nuclear program."

The underlined words evoke highly related frames, namely ACTIVITY_START, ACTIVITY_STOP and CAUSE_TO_RESUME. This could suggest to link the three textual fragments associated to the words, into a single coherent discourse unit, where the semantic roles of the different fragments can be easily mapped as co-referential (e.g. "Iran's nuclear research program" - "The program" - "it"). Frame relatedness can also help in RTE. Consider for example the following entailment pair:

Text : "An avalanche has struck a popular skiing resort in Austria, killing at least 11 people."

Hypothesis : "Humans died in an avalanche."

The frames KILLING and DEATH, respectively evoked by *killing* and *died*, are highly related and can then be mapped. Leveraging this mapping, an RTE system could easily discover that the Text entails the Hypothesis, by verifying that the fillers of the mapped semantic roles of the two frames are semantically equivalent.

Proceedings of the 12th Conference of the European Chapter of the ACL, pages 657–665,
Athens, Greece, 30 March – 3 April 2009. ©2009 Association for Computational Linguistics

In this paper we investigate the notion of relatedness in the context of frame semantics, and propose different types of automatic measures to compute relatedness between frames. Our main contributions can be summarized as follows: (1) We empirically show that the notion of frame relatedness is intuitive and principled from a cognitive perspective: to support this claim, we report agreement results over a pool of human annotators on the task of ranking frame pairs on relatedness; (2) We propose a variety of measures for computing frame relatedness, inspired by different approaches and by existing measures for word relatedness; (3) We show that our measures offer good performance, thus opening the path to the use of frame relatedness as a practical tool for NLP, and showing that measures for word relatedness can be successfully adapted to frames. The paper is organized as follows. In Section 2 we summarize related work. In Section 3 we describe the experiment of humans ranking frame pairs, and discuss the results. In Section 4 and 5 we respectively introduce our relatedness measures, and test them over a manual gold standard. In Section 6 we draw final conclusions and outline future work.

2 Related Work

Much research in NLP has studied similarity and relatedness between words. Rubenstein and Goodenough (1965) were the first to propose a procedure to assess human agreement on ranking pairs of words on relatedness. Their experiment was later replicated by Resnik (1995) and Charles (2000). All these studies reported good levels of agreements among annotators, suggesting that the notion of word relatedness is cognitively principled. In our experiment in Section 3.2 we apply the same procedure to assess agreement on ranking frames.

Measures for estimating word relatedness have been systematically proposed since the early 90's, and are today widely used in NLP for various tasks. Most measures can be classified either as corpus-based or ontology-based. *Corpus-based measures* compute relatedness looking at the distributional properties of the two words: words that tend to co-occur in the same contexts or having similar distributional profiles, are deemed to be highly related. A complete survey on these measures is reported in (Mohammad and Hirst, 2006). *Ontology-based measures* estimate relatedness by studying the path connecting the two words in an ontology or a hierarchical lexicon (e.g. WordNet). The basic idea is that closer words are more related than distant ones. Budanitsky and Hirst (2006) provide an extensive survey of these measures.

Budanitsky and Hirst (2006) also point out an important distinction, between *relatedness* and *similarity*. Two words are related if any type of relation stands between them, e.g. antonymy or meronymy; they are similar when related through an *is-a* like hierarchy. Similarity is then a special case of relatedness. Following Budanitsky and Hirst (2006), we consider two frames as *similar* if they are linked via *is-a* like relations (e.g. GETTING and COMMERCE_BUY), while as *related* if any relation stands between them (e.g. causation between KILLING and DEATH). In this paper, we focus our attention solely on the notion of frame relatedness.

3 Defining frame relatedness

In this section we check if the notion of frame relatedness is intuitive and principled from a cognitive perspective. In Section 3.1 we first introduce the basic concepts or frame semantics; in Section 3.2 we report the agreement results obtained by human annotators, on the task of ranking a dataset of frame pairs according to relatedness.

3.1 Frame Semantics and FrameNet

Frame semantics (Fillmore, 1985) seeks to describe the meaning of a sentence as it is actually understood by characterizing the background knowledge necessary to understand the sentence. Background knowledge is represented in the form of *frames*, conceptual structures modelling prototypical situations. Linguistically, a frame is a semantic class containing predicates called *lexical units* (LU), that can *evoke* the described situation (see example in Table 1). Each frame comes with its own set of semantic roles, called *frame elements* (FE). These are the participants and props in the abstract situation described. Roles are local to individual frames, thus avoiding the commitment to a small set of universal roles, whose specification has turned out to be unfeasible in the past.

The Berkeley FrameNet project (Baker et al., 1998) has been developing a frame-semantic lexicon for the core vocabulary of English since 1997. The current FrameNet release contains about 800 frames and 10,000 lexical units. Part of FrameNet

	Frame: STATEMENT	
	This frame contains verbs and nouns that communicate the act of a SPEAKER to address a MESSAGE to some ADDRESSEE using language. A number of the words can be used performatively, such as *declare* and *insist*.	
FEs	SPEAKER	**Evelyn** said she wanted to leave.
	MESSAGE	Evelyn announced **that she wanted to leave.**
	ADDRESSEE	Evelyn spoke **to me** about her past.
	TOPIC	Evelyn's statement **about her past**
	MEDIUM	Evelyn preached to me **over the phone**.
LUs	acknowledge.v, acknowledgment.n, add.v, address.v, admission.n, admit.v, affirm.v, affirmation.n, allegation.n, allege.v, announce.v, ...	

Table 1: Example frame from FrameNet.

is also a corpus of annotated example sentences from the British National Corpus, currently containing 135,000 sentences.

In FrameNet, asymmetric frame relations can relate two frames, forming a complex hierarchy (Ruppenhofer et al., 2005): *Inheritance*: anything true in the semantics of the parent frame, must also be true for the other (e.g. KILLING – EXECUTION). *Uses*: a part of the situation evoked by one frame refers to the other. *Subframe*: one frame describes a subpart of a complex situation described in the other (e.g. CRIMINAL-PROCESS – SENTENCING). *Causative_of* : the action in one frame causes the event described in the other (e.g. KILLING – DEATH). *Inchoative_of*: the event in one frame ends in the state described in the other (e.g. DEATH – DEAD_OR_ALIVE). *Precedes*: one frame temporally proceeds the other (e.g. FALL_ASLEEP – SLEEP). *Perspective_on*: one frame describes a specific point-of-view on a neutral frame.

The first two are *is-a* like relations, while the others are non-hierarchical.

3.2 Manually ranking related frames

We asked a pool of human annotators to manually rank a set of frame pairs according to their relatedness. The goal was twofolds. First, we wanted to check how intuitive the notion of frame relatedness is, by computing inter-annotator agreement, and by comparing the agreement results to those obtained by Rubenstein and Goodenough (1965) for word relatedness. Second, we planned to use the produced dataset as a gold standard for testing the relatedness measures, as described in Section 5. In the rest of the section we describe the annotation process in detail.

Dataset creation. We created two different datasets, a *simple* and a *controlled set*, each containing 155 pairs. Frame pairs in the *simple set* were randomly selected from the FrameNet database. Frame pairs in the *controlled set* were either composed of two frames belonging to the same scenario[1], or being so that one frame is one edge from the scenario of the other. This ensured that all pairs in the controlled set contained semantically related frames. Indeed, we use the controlled set to check if human agreement and automatic measure accuracy get better when considering only highly related frames.

Human ranking agreement. A preliminary annotation phase involved a group of 15 annotators consisting of graduate students and researchers, native or nearly native speakers of English. For each set, each annotator was given 15 frame pairs from the original 155 set: 5 of these where shared with all other annotators. This setting has three advantages: (1) The set is small enough to obtain a reliable annotation in a short time; (2) We can compute the agreement among the 15 annotators over the shared pairs; (3) We can check the reliability of the final gold standard created in the second phase (see following section) by comparing to the annotations. Each annotator was asked to order a shuffled deck of 15 cards, each one describing a pair of frames. The card contained the following information about the two frames: names; definitions; the lists of core FEs; a frame annotated sentence for each frame, randomly chosen from the FrameNet database. Similarly to Rubenstein and Goodenough (1965) we gave the annotators the following instructions: (i) After looking through the whole deck, order the pairs according to amount of relatedness; (ii) You may assign the same rank to pairs having the same degree of relatedness (i.e. ties are allowed).

We checked the agreement among the 15 annotators in ranking the 5 shared pairs by using the Kendall's τ correlation coefficient (Kendall, 1938). Kendall's τ can be interpreted as the difference between the probability that in the dataset two variables are in the same order versus the probability that they are in different orders (see (Lapata, 2006) for details). The average corre-

[1]A scenario frame is a "hub" frame describing a general topic; specific frames modelling situations related to the topic are linked to it (e.g. COMMERCE_BUY and COMMERCIAL_TRANSACTION are linked to COMMERCE_SCENARIO). FrameNet contains 16 scenarios.

lation[2] among annotators on the simple and controlled sets was $\tau = 0.600$ and $\tau = 0.547$.

Gold standard ranking. The final dataset was created by two expert annotators, jointly working to rank the 155 pairs collected in the data creation phase. We computed the rank correlation agreement between this annotation and the 15 annotation produced in the first stage. We obtained an average Kendall's $\tau = 0.530$ and $\tau = 0.566$ respectively on the simple and controlled sets (Standard deviations from the average are $StdDev = 0.146$ and $StdDev = 0.173$). These results are all statistically significant at the 99% level, indicating that the notion of "frame relatedness" is intuitive and principled for humans, and that the final datasets are reliable enough to be used as gold standard for our experiments. Table 2 reports the first and last 5 ranked frame pairs for the two datasets.

We compared the correlation results obtained above on "frame relatedness", to those derived from previous works on "word relatedness". This comparison should indicate if ranking related frames (i.e. situations) is more or less complex and intuitive than ranking words.[3] As for words, we computed the average Kendall's τ among three different annotation efforts (namely, (Rubenstein and Goodenough, 1965; Resnik, 1995; Charles, 2000)) carried out over a same dataset of 28 word pairs originally created by Rubenstein and Goodenough. Note that the annotation schema followed in the three works is the same as ours. We obtained a Kendall's $\tau = 0.775$, which is statistically significant at the 99% level. As expected, the correlation for word relatedness is higher than for frames: Humans find it easier to compare two words than two complex situations, as the former are less complex linguistic entities than the latter.

4 Measures for frame relatedness

Manually computing relatedness between all possible frame pairs in FrameNet is an unfeasible task. The on-going FrameNet project and automatic methods for FrameNet expansion (e.g. (Pennacchiotti et al., 2008)) are expected to produce an ever growing set of frames. The definition of automatic measures for frame relatedness is thus a key issue. In this section we propose different types of such measures.

4.1 WordNet-based measures

WordNet-based measures estimate relatedness by leveraging the WordNet hierarchy. The hypothesis is that two frames whose sets of LUs are close in WordNet are likely to be related. We assume that LUs are sense-tagged, i.e. we know which WordNet senses of a LU map to a given frame. For example, among the 25 senses of the LU *charge.v*, only the sense *charge.v#3* ("demand payment") maps to the frame COMMERCE_COLLECT.

Given a frame F, we define S_F as the set of all WordNet senses that map to any frame's LU (e.g. for COMMERCE_COLLECT, S_F contains *charge.v#3*, *collect.v#4*, *bill.v#1*). A generic WordNet-based measure is then defined as follows:

$$wn(F_1, F_2) = \frac{\sum_{s_1 \in S_{F_1}} \sum_{s_2 \in S_{F_2}} wn\_rel(s1, s2)}{|S_{F_1}| \cdot |S_{F_2}|} \quad (1)$$

where $wn\_rel(s1, s2)$ is a sense function estimating the relatedness between two senses in WordNet. Since we focus on frame relatedness, we are interested in assigning high scores to pairs of senses which are related by any type of relations in WordNet (i.e. not limited to *is-a*). We therefore adopt as function wn_rel the Hirst-St.Onge measure (Hirst and St.Onge, 1998) as it accounts for different relations. We also experiment with the Jiang and Conrath's (Jiang and Conrath, 1997) measure which relies only on the *is-a* hierarchy, but proved to be the best WordNet-based measure in the task of ranking words (Budanitsky and Hirst, 2006). We call the frame relatedness measures using the two functions respectively as $wn\_hso(F_1, F_2)$ and $wn\_jcn(F_1, F_2)$.

4.2 Corpus-based measures

Corpus-based measures compute relatedness looking at the distributional properties of the two frames over a corpus. The intuition is that related frames should occur in the same or similar contexts.

[2] Average correlation is computed by averaging the τ obtained on each pair of annotators, as suggested in (Siegel and Castellan, 1988); note that the obtained value corresponds to the Kendall u correlation coefficient. Ties are properly treated with the correction factor described in (Siegel and Castellan, 1988).

[3] The comparison should be taken only as indicative, as words can be ambiguous while frames are not. A more principled comparison should involve word senses, not words.

SIMPLE SET	CONTROLLED SET
Measure volume - Measure mass (1)	Knot creation - Rope manipulation (1,5)
Communication manner - Statement (2)	Shoot projectiles - Use firearm (1,5)
Giving - Sent items (3)	Scouring - Scrutiny (3)
Abundance - Measure linear extent (4)	Ambient temperature - Temperature (4)
Remembering information - Reporting (5)	Fleeing - Escaping (5)
...	...
Research - Immobilization (126)	Reason - Taking time (142)
Resurrection - Strictness (126)	Rejuvenation - Physical artworks (142)
Social event - Word relations (126)	Revenge - Bungling (142)
Social event - Rope manipulation (126)	Security - Likelihood (142)
Sole instance - Chatting (126)	Sidereal appearance - Aggregate (142)

Table 2: Human gold standard ranking: first and last 5 ranked pairs (in brackets ranks allowing ties).

4.2.1 Co-occurrence measures

Given two frames F_1 and F_2, the **co-occurrence measure** computes relatedness as the pointwise mutual information (pmi) between them:

$$pmi(F_1, F_2) = log_2 \frac{P(F_1, F_2)}{P(F_1)P(F_2)} \qquad (2)$$

Given a corpus C consisting of a set of documents $c \in C$, we estimate pmi as the number of contexts in the corpus (either documents or sentences)[4] in which the two frames co-occur:

$$cr\_occ(F_1, F_2) = log_2 \frac{|C_{F_1,F_2}|}{|C_{F_1}||C_{F_2}|} \qquad (3)$$

where C_{F_i} is the set of documents in which F_i occurs, and C_{F_1,F_2} is the set of documents in which F_1 and F_2 co-occur. A frame F_i is said to occur in a document if at least one of its LUs l_{F_i} occurs in the document, i.e.:

$$C_{F_i} = \{c \in C : \exists l_{F_i} \text{ in } c\} \qquad (4)$$

$$C_{F_1,F_2} = \{c \in C : \exists l_{F_1} \text{ and } \exists l_{F_2} \text{ in } c\} \qquad (5)$$

A limitation of the above measure is that it does not treat ambiguity. If a word is a LU of a frame F , but it occurs in a document with a sense $s \notin S_F$, it still counts as a frame occurrence. For example, consider the word *charge.v*, whose third sense *charge.v#3* maps in FrameNet to COMMERCE_COLLECT. In the sentence: *"Tripp Isenhour was charged with killing a hawk on purpose"*, *charge.v* co-occurs with *kill.v*, which in FrameNet maps to KILLING. The sentence would then result as a co-occurrence of the two above frames. Unfortunately this is not the case, as the sentence's sense *charge.v#2* does not map to the frame. Ideally, one could solve the problem by using a sense-tagged corpus where senses' occurrences are mapped to frames. While sense-to-frame mappings exist (e.g. mapping between frames and WordNet senses in (Shi and Mihalcea, 2005)), sense-tagged corpora large enough for distributional studies are not yet available (e.g., the SemCor WordNet-tagged corpus (Miller et al., 1993) consists of only 700,000 words).

We therefore circumvent the problem, by implementing pmi in a **weighted co-occurrence measure**, which gives lower weights to co-occurrences of ambiguous words:

$$cr\_wgt(F_1, F_2) = log_2 \frac{\sum_{c \in C_{F_1,F_2}} w_{F_1}(c) \cdot w_{F_2}(c)}{\sum_{c \in C_{F_1}} w_{F_1}(c) \cdot \sum_{c \in C_{F_2}} w_{F_2}(c)} \qquad (6)$$

The weighting function $w_F(c)$ estimates the probability that the document c contains a LU of the frame F in the correct sense. Formally, given the set of senses S_l of a LU (e.g. *charge.v#1...charge.v#24*), we define S_{l_F} as the set of senses mapping to the frame (e.g. *charge.v#3* for COMMERCE_COLLECT). The weighting function is then:

$$w_F(c) = \arg\max_{l_F \in L_F \text{ in } c} P(S_{l_F}|l_F) \qquad (7)$$

where L_F is the set of LUs of F. We estimate $P(S_{l_F}|l_F)$ by counting sense occurrences of l_F over the SemCor corpus:

$$P(S_{l_F}|l_F) = \frac{|S_{l_F}|}{|S_l|} \qquad (8)$$

In other terms, a frame receives a high weight in a document when the document contains a LU whose most frequent senses are those mapped to the frame.[5] For example, in the sentence: *"Tripp Isenhour was charged with killing a hawk on purpose."*, $w_F(c) = 0.17$, as *charge.v#3* is not very frequent in SemCor.

[4]For sake of simplicity in the rest of the section we refer to documents, but the same holds for sentences.

[5]In Eq.8 we use Lidstone smoothing (Lidstone, 1920) to account for unseen senses in SemCor. Also, if a LU does not occur in SemCor, an equal probability (corresponding to the inverse of the number of word's senses) is given to all senses.

4.2.2 Distributional measure

The previous measures promote (i.e. give a higher rank to) frames co-occurring in the *same* contexts. The distributional measure promotes frames occurring in *similar* contexts. The distributional hypothesis (Harris, 1964) has been widely and successfully used in NLP to compute relatedness among words (Lin, 1998), lexical patterns (Lin and Pantel, 2001), and other entities. The underlying intuition is that target entities occurring in similar contexts are likely to be semantically related. In our setting, we consider either documents and sentences as valid contexts.

Each frame F is modelled by a distributional vector $\vec{F}$, whose dimensions are documents. The value of each dimension expresses the association ratio $A(F, c)$ between a document c and the frame. We say that a document is highly associated to a frame when most of the FrameNet LUs it contains, map to the given frame in the correct senses:

$$A(F,c) = \frac{\sum\limits_{l \in L_F \text{ in } c} P(S_{l_F}|l_F)}{\sum\limits_{F_i \in \mathcal{F}} \sum\limits_{l \in F_i \text{ in } c} P(S_{l_{F_i}}|l_{F_i})} \quad (9)$$

where $\mathcal{F}$ is the set of all FrameNet frames, and $P(S_{l_F}|l_F)$ is as in Eq. 8. We then compute relatedness between two frames using cosine similarity:

$$cr\_dist(F_1, F_2) = \frac{\vec{F_1} \cdot \vec{F_2}}{|\vec{F_1}| * |\vec{F_2}|} \quad (10)$$

When we use sentences as contexts we refer to $cr\_dist\_sent(F_1, F_2)$, otherwise to $cr\_dist\_doc(F_1, F_2)$

4.3 Hierarchy-based measures

A third family or relatedness measures leverages the FrameNet hierarchy. The hierarchy forms a directed graph of 795 nodes (frames), 1136 edges, 86 roots, 7 islands and 26 independent components. Similarly to measures for word relatedness, we here compute frame relatedness leveraging graph-based measures over the FrameNet hierarchy. The intuition is that the closer in the hierarchy two frames are, the more related they are[6]. We here experiment with the Hirst-St.Onge and the Wu and Palmer (Wu and Palmer, 1994) measures, as they are pure taxonomic measures, i.e. they do not require any corpus statistics.

[6]The *Pathfinder Through FrameNet* tool gives a practical proof of this intuition: `http://fnps.coli.uni-saarland.de/pathsearch`.

WU and Palmer: this measure calculates relatedness by considering the depths of the two frames in the hierarchy, along with the depth of their least common subsumer (LCS):

$$hr\_wu(F_1, F_2) = \frac{2 \cdot dp(LCS)}{ln(F_1, LCS) + ln(F_2, LCS) + 2 \cdot dp(LCS)} \quad (11)$$

where ln is the length of the path connecting two frames, and dp is the length of the path between a frame and a root. If a path does not exist, then $hr\_wu(F_1, F_2) = 0$.

Hirst-St.Onge: two frames are semantically close if they are connected in the FrameNet hierarchy through a "not too long path which does not change direction too often":

$$hr\_hso(F_1, F_2) = M - \text{ path length } - k \cdot d \quad (12)$$

where M and and k are constants, and d is the number of changes of direction in the path. If a path does not exist, $hr\_hso(F_1, F_2) = 0$. For both measures we consider as valid edges all relations.

The FrameNet hierarchy also provides for each relation a partial or complete FE mapping between the two linked frames (for example the role *Victim* of KILLING maps to the role *Protagonist* of DEATH). We leverage this property implementing a **FE overlap measure**, which given the set of FEs of the two frames, FE_1 and FE_2 , computes relatedness as the percentage of mapped FEs:

$$hr\_fe(F_1, F_2) = \frac{|FE_1 \cap FE_2|}{max(|FE_1|, |FE_2|)} \quad (13)$$

The intuition is that FE overlap between frames is a more fine grained and accurate predictor of relatedness wrt. simple frame relation measures as those above – i.e. two frames are highly related not only if they describe connected situations, but also if they share many participants.

5 Experiments

We evaluate the relatedness measures by comparing their rankings over the two datasets described in Section 3.2, using the manual gold standard annotation as reference. As evaluation metrics we use Kendall's τ. As baselines, we adopt a *definition overlap measure* that counts the percentage of overlapping content words in the definition of the two frames;[7] and a *LU overlap baseline*

[7]We use stems of nouns, verbs and adjectives.

Measure	*Simple Set*	*Controlled Set*
wn_jcn	0.114	0.141
wn_hso	0.106	0.141
cr_occ_sent	0.239	0.340
cr_wgt_sent	**0.281**	**0.349**
cr_occ_doc	0.143	0.227
cr_wgt_doc	0.173	0.240
cr_dist_doc	0.152	0.240
hr_wu	0.139	0.286
hr_hso	0.134	0.296
hr_fe	0.252	0.326
def overlap baseline	*0.056*	*0.210*
LU overlap baseline	*0.080*	*0.253*
human upper bound	*0.530*	*0.566*

Table 3: Kendall's τ correlation results for different measures over the two dataset.

that counts the percentage of overlapping LUs between the two frames. We also defined as *upper-bound* the human agreement over the gold standard. As regards distributional measures, statistics are drawn from the TREC-2002 Vol.2 corpus, consisting of about 110 million words, organized in 230,401 news documents and 5,433,048 sentences[8]. LUs probabilities in Eq. 8 are estimate over the SemCor 2.0 corpus, consisting of 700,000 running words, sense-tagged with WordNet 2.0 senses.[9]. WordNet-based measures are computed using WordNet 2.0 and implemented as in (Patwardhan et al., 2003). Mappings between WordNet senses and FrameNet verbal LUs are taken from Shi and Mihalcea (2005); as mappings for nouns and adjectives are not available, for the WordNet-based measures we use the first sense heuristic.

Note that some of the measures we adopt need some degree of supervision. The WordNet-based and the *cr_wgt* measures rely on a WordNet-FrameNet mapping, which has to be created manually or by some reliable automatic technique. Hierarchy-based measures instead rely on the FrameNet hierarchy that is also a manual artifact.

5.1 Experimental Results

Table 3 reports the correlation results over the two datasets. Table 4 reports the best 10 ranks produced by some of the best performing measures. Results show that all measures are positively correlated with the human gold standard, with a level of significance beyond the $p < 0.01$ level , but the wn_jcn measure which is at $p < 0.05$. All measures, but the WordNet-based ones, significantly outperform the *definition overlap* baseline on both datasets, and most of them also beat the more informed *LU overlap* baseline.[10] It is interesting to notice that the two best performing measures, namely *cr_wgt_sent* and *hr_fe*, use respectively a distributional and a hierarchy-based strategy, suggesting that both approaches are valuable. WordNet-based measures are less effective, performing close or below the baselines.

Results obtained on the simple set are in general lower than those on the controlled set, suggesting that it is easier to discriminate among pairs of connected frames than random ones. A possible explanation is that when frames are connected, all measures can rely on meaningful evidence for most of the pairs, while this is not always the case for random pairs. For example, corpus-based measures tend to suffer the problem of data sparseness much more on the simple set, because many of the pairs are so loosely related that statistical information cannot significantly emerge from the corpus.

WordNet-based measures. The low performance of these measures is mainly due to the fact that they fail to predict relatedness for many pairs, e.g. *wn_hso* assigns zero to 137 and 119 pairs, respectively on the simple and controlled sets. This is mostly caused by the limited set of relations of the WordNet database. Most importantly in our case, WordNet misses the *situational relation* (Hirst and St.Onge, 1998), which typically relates words participating in the same situation (e.g. *child care - school*). This is exactly the relation that would help in mapping frames' LUs. Another problem relates to adjectives and adverbs: WordNet measures cannot be trustfully applied to these part-of-speech, as they are not hierarchically organized. Unfortunately, 18% of FrameNet LUs are either adjectives or adverbs, meaning that such amount of useful information is lost. Finally, WordNet has in general an incomplete lexical coverage: Shi and Mihalcea (2005) show that 7% of FrameNet verbal LUs do not have a mapping in WordNet.

Corpus-based measures. Table 3 shows that co-occurrence measures are effective when using

[8]For computational limitations we could not afford experimenting the *cr_dist_sent* measure, as the number and size of the vectors was too big.

[9]We did not use directly the SemCor for drawing distributional statistics, because of its small size.

[10]The average level of correlation obtained by our measures is comparable to that obtained in other complex information-ordering tasks, e.g. measuring compositionality of verb-noun collations (Venkatapathy and Joshi, 2005)

WN_JCN	CR_WGT_SENT	HR_FE
Ambient temperature - Temperature (4)	Change of phase - Cause change of phase (7)	Shoot projectiles - Use firearm (1,5)
Run risk - Endangering (27)	Knot creation - Rope manipulation (1,5)	Intentionally affect - Rope manipulation (37,5)
Run risk - Safe situation (51)	Ambient temperature - Temperature (4)	Knot creation - Rope manipulation (1,5)
Knot creation - Rope manipulation (1,5)	Shoot projectiles - Use firearm (1,5)	Ambient temperature - Temperature (4)
Endangering - Safe situation (62)	Hit target - Use firearm (18)	Hit target - Intentionally affect (91,5)
Shoot projectiles - Use firearm (1,5)	Run risk - Safe situation (51)	Safe situation - Security (28)
Scouring - Scrutiny (3)	Safe situation - Security (28)	Suspicion - Criminal investigation (40)
Reliance - Contingency (109)	Cause impact - Hit target (10)	Age - Speed (113)
Safe situation - Security (28)	Rape - Arson (22)	Motion noise - Motion directional (55)
Change of phase - Cause change of phase (7)	Suspicion - Robbery (98)	Body movement - Motion (45)

Table 4: First 10 ranked frame pairs for different relatedness measure on the Controlled Set; in brackets, the rank in the gold standard (full list available at *(suppressed)*).

sentences as contexts, while correlation decreases by about 10 points using documents as contexts. This suggest that sentences are suitable contextual units to model situational relatedness, while documents (i.e. news) may be so large to include unrelated situations. It is interesting to notice that corpus-based measures promote frame pairs which are in a non-hierarchical relation, more than other measures do. For example the pair CHANGE OF PHASE - CAUSE CHANGE OF PHASE score first, and RAPE - ARSON score ninth, while the other measures tend to rank them much lower. By contrast, the two frames SCOURING - INSPECTING which are siblings in the FrameNet hierarchy and rank 17th in the gold standard, are ranked only 126th by *cr_wgt_sent*. This is due to the fact that hierarchically related frames are substitutional – i.e. they tend not to co-occur in the same documents; while otherwise related frames are mostly in syntagmatic relation. As for *cr_dist_doc*, it performs in line with *cr_wgt_doc*, but their ranks differ; *cr_dist_doc* promotes more hierarchical relations: distributional methods capture both paradigmatically and syntagmatically related entities.

Hierarchy-based measures. As results show, the FrameNet hierarchy is a good indicator of relatedness, especially when considering FE mappings. Hierarchy-based measures promote frame pairs related by diverse relations, with a slight predominance of *is-a* like ones (indeed, the FrameNet hierarchy contains roughly twice as many is-a relations as other ones). These measures are slightly penalized by the low coverage of the FrameNet hierarchy. For example, they assign zero to CHANGE OF PHASE - ALTERED PHASE, as an inchoative link connecting the frames is missing.

Correlation between measures. We computed the Kendall's τ among the experimented measures, to investigate if they model relatedness in different or similar ways. As expected, measures of the same type are highly correlated (e.g. *hr_fe* and *hr_wu* have $\tau = 0.52$), while those of different types seem complementary, showing negative or non-significant correlation (e.g. *cr_wgt_sent* has $\tau = -0.034$ with *hr_wu*, and $\tau = 0.078$ with *wn_jcn*). The *LU overlap baseline* shows significant correlation only with *hr_wu* ($\tau = 0.284$), suggesting that in the FrameNet hierarchy frames correlated by some relation do share LUs.

Comparison to word relatedness. The best performing measures score about 0.200 points below the human upper bound, indicating that ranking frames is much easier for humans than for machines. A direct comparison to the word ranking task, suggests that ranking frames is harder than words, not only for humans (as reported in Section 3.2), but also for machines: Budanitsky and Hirst (2006) show that measures for ranking words get much closer to the human upper-bound than our measures do, confirming that frame relatedness is a fairly complex notion to model.

6 Conclusions

We empirically defined a notion of frame relatedness. Experiments suggest that this notion is cognitively principled, and can be safely used in NLP tasks. We introduced a variety of measures for automatically estimating relatedness. Results show that our measures have good performance, all statistically significant at the 99% level, though improvements are expected by using other evidence. As future work, we will build up and refine these basic measures, and investigate more complex ones. We will also use our measures in applications, to check their effectiveness in supporting various tasks, e.g. in mapping frames across Text and Hypothesis in RTE, in linking related frames in discourse, or in inducing frames for LU which are not in FrameNet (Baker et al., 2007).

References

Collin F. Baker, Charles J. Fillmore, and John B. Lowe. 1998. The Berkeley FrameNet project. In *Proceedings of COLING-ACL*, Montreal, Canada.

Collin Baker, Michael Ellsworth, and Katrin Erk. 2007. SemEval-2007 Task 19: Frame Semantic Structure Extraction. In *Proceedings of the Fourth International Workshop on Semantic Evaluations (SemEval-2007)*, pages 99–104, Prague, Czech Republic, June.

Alexander Budanitsky and Graeme Hirst. 2006. Evaluating WordNet-based measures of lexical semantic relatedness. *Computational Linguistics*, 32(1):13–47.

Walter Charles. 2000. Contextual correlates of meaning. *Applied Psycholinguistics*, (21):502–524.

C. J. Fillmore. 1985. Frames and the Semantics of Understanding. *Quaderni di Semantica*, IV(2).

Zellig Harris. 1964. Distributional structure. In Jerrold J. Katz and Jerry A. Fodor, editors, *The Philosophy of Linguistics*, New York. Oxford University Press.

Graeme Hirst and David St.Onge, 1998. *Lexical chains as representations of context for the detection and correction of malapropisms*, pages 305–332. MIT press.

Jay J. Jiang and David W. Conrath. 1997. Semantic similarity based on corpus statistics and lexical taxonomy. In *Proceedings of International Conference on Research in Computational Linguistics (ROCLING X)*, Taiwan.

Maurice Kendall. 1938. A new measure of rank correlation. *Biometrika*, (30):81–93.

Mirella Lapata. 2006. Automatic evaluation of information ordering: Kendall's tau. *Computational Linguistics*, 32(4):471–484.

G.J. Lidstone. 1920. Note on the general case of the Bayes-Laplace formula for inductive or a posteriori probabilities. *Transactions of the Faculty of Actuaries*, 8:182–192.

Dekang Lin and Patrick Pantel. 2001. DIRT-discovery of inference rules from text. In *Proceedings of KDD-01*, San Francisco, CA.

Dekang Lin. 1998. Automatic retrieval and clustering of similar word. In *Proceedings of COLING-ACL*, Montreal, Canada.

G. A. Miller, C. Leacock, T. Randee, and Bunker R. 1993. A Semantic Concordance. In *In Proceedings of the 3rd DARPA Workshop on Human Language Technology*, Plainsboro, New Jersey.

Saif Mohammad and Graeme Hirst. 2006. Distributional measures of concept-distance. a task-oriented evaluation. In *Proceedings of EMNLP-2006*, Sydney,Australia.

S. Patwardhan, S. Banerjee, and T. Pedersen. 2003. Using measures of semantic relatedness for word sense disambiguation. In *Proceedings of Fourth International Conference on Intelligent Text Processing and Computational Linguistics*, Mexico City, Mexico.

Marco Pennacchiotti, Diego De Cao, Paolo Marocco, and Roberto Basili. 2008. Towards a vector space model for framenet-like resources. In *Proceedings of LREC*, Marrakech, Marocco.

Philip Resnik. 1995. Using information content to evaluate semantic similarity. In *Proceedings of the 14th International Joint Conference on Artificial Intelligence*, Montreal, Canada.

H. Rubenstein and J.B. Goodenough. 1965. Contextual correlates of synonymy. *Communications of the ACM*, 8(10):627–633.

Josef Ruppenhofer, Michael Ellsworth, Miriam R. L. Petruck, and Christopher R. Johnson. 2005. FrameNet II: Extended Theory and Practice. In *ICSI Technical Report*.

Lei Shi and Rada Mihalcea. 2005. Putting Pieces Together: Combining FrameNet, VerbNet and WordNet for Robust Semantic Parsing. In *In Proceedings of Cicling*, Mexico.

S. Siegel and N. J. Castellan. 1988. *Nonparametric Statistics for the Behavioral Sciences*. McGraw-Hill.

Idan Szpektor, Hristo Tanev, Ido Dagan, and Bonaventura Coppola. 2004. Scaling web-based acquisition of entailment relations. In *Proceedings of the 2004 Conference on Empirical Methods in Natural Language Processing*, Barcellona, Spain.

Sriram Venkatapathy and Aravind K. Joshi. 2005. Measuring the relative compositionality of verb noun (V-N) collocations by integrating features. In *Proceedings of HLT/EMNLP*, Vancouver, Canad.

Z. Wu and M. Palmer. 1994. Verb semantics and lexical selection. In *32nd Annual Meeting of the Association for Computational Linguistics*, pages 133–138, Las Cruces, New Mexico.

Flexible Answer Typing with Discriminative Preference Ranking

Christopher Pinchak[†] **Dekang Lin**[‡] **Davood Rafiei**[†]

[†]**Department of Computing Science**
University of Alberta
Edmonton, Alberta, Canada
{pinchak,drafiei}@cs.ualberta.ca

[‡]**Google Inc.**
1600 Amphitheatre Parkway
Mountain View, CA, USA
lindek@google.com

Abstract

An important part of question answering is ensuring a candidate answer is plausible as a response. We present a flexible approach based on discriminative preference ranking to determine which of a set of candidate answers are appropriate. Discriminative methods provide superior performance while at the same time allow the flexibility of adding new and diverse features. Experimental results on a set of focused What ...? and Which ...? questions show that our learned preference ranking methods perform better than alternative solutions to the task of answer typing. A gain of almost 0.2 in MRR for both the first appropriate and first correct answers is observed along with an increase in precision over the entire range of recall.

1 Introduction

Question answering (QA) systems have received a great deal of attention because they provide both a natural means of querying via questions and because they return short, concise answers. These two advantages simplify the task of finding information relevant to a topic of interest. Questions convey more than simply a natural language query; an implicit expectation of answer type is provided along with the question words. The discovery and exploitation of this implicit expected type is called *answer typing*.

We introduce an answer typing method that is sufficiently flexible to use a wide variety of features while at the same time providing a high level of performance. Our answer typing method avoids the use of pre-determined classes that are often lacking for unanticipated answer types. Because answer typing is only part of the QA task, a flexible answer typing model ensures that answer typing can be easily and usefully incorporated into a complete QA system. A discriminative preference ranking model with a preference for appropriate answers is trained and applied to unseen questions. In terms of Mean Reciprocal Rank (MRR), we observe improvements over existing systems of around 0.2 both in terms of the correct answer and in terms of appropriate responses. This increase in MRR brings the performance of our model to near the level of a full QA system on a subset of questions, despite the fact that we rely on answer typing features alone.

The amount of information given about the expected answer can vary by question. If the question contains a *question focus*, which we define to be the head noun following the *wh*-word such as *city* in "What *city* hosted the 1988 Winter Olympics?", some of the typing information is explicitly stated. In this instance, the answer is required to be a city. However, there is often additional information available about the type. In our example, the answer must plausibly host a Winter Olympic Games. The focus, along with the additional information, give strong clues about what are appropriate as responses.

We define an *appropriate* candidate answer as one that a user, who does not necessarily know the correct answer, would identify as a plausible answer to a given question. For most questions, there exist plausible responses that are not correct answers to the question. For our above question, the city of Vancouver is plausible even though it is not correct. For the purposes of this paper, we assume correct answers are a subset of appropriate candidates. Because answer typing is only intended to be a component of a full QA system, we rely on other components to help establish the true correctness of a candidate answer.

The remainder of the paper is organized as follows. Section 2 presents the application of discriminative preference rank learning to answer typing. Section 3 introduces the models we use

Proceedings of the 12th Conference of the European Chapter of the ACL, pages 666–674,
Athens, Greece, 30 March – 3 April 2009. ©2009 Association for Computational Linguistics

for learning appropriate answer preferences. Sections 4 and 5 discuss our experiments and their results, respectively. Section 6 presents prior work on answer typing and the use of discriminative methods in QA. Finally, concluding remarks and ideas for future work are presented in Section 7.

2 Preference Ranking

Preference ranking naturally lends itself to any problem in which the relative ordering between examples is more important than labels or values assigned to those examples. The classic example application of preference ranking (Joachims, 2002) is that of information retrieval results ranking. Generally, information retrieval results are presented in some ordering such that those higher on the list are either more relevant to the query or would be of greater interest to the user.

In a preference ranking task we have a set of candidates $c_1, c_2, ..., c_n$, and a ranking r such that the relation $c_i <_r c_j$ holds if and only if candidate c_i should be ranked higher than c_j, for $1 \leq i, j \leq n$ and $i \neq j$. The ranking r can form a total ordering, as in information retrieval, or a partial ordering in which we have both $c_i \not<_r c_j$ and $c_j \not<_r c_i$. Partial orderings are useful for our task of answer typing because they can be used to specify candidates that are of an equivalent rank.

Given some $c_i <_r c_j$, preference ranking only considers the difference between the feature representations of c_i and c_j ($\Phi(c_i)$ and $\Phi(c_j)$, respectively) as evidence. We want to learn some weight vector $\vec{w}$ such that $\vec{w} \cdot \Phi(c_i) > \vec{w} \cdot \Phi(c_j)$ holds for all pairs c_i and c_j that have the relation $c_i <_r c_j$. In other words, we want $\vec{w} \cdot (\Phi(c_i) - \Phi(c_j)) > 0$ and we can use some margin in the place of 0. In the context of Support Vector Machines (Joachims, 2002), we are trying to minimize the function:

$$V(\vec{w}, \vec{\xi}) = \frac{1}{2}\vec{w} \cdot \vec{w} + C \sum \xi_{i,j} \qquad (1)$$

subject to the constraints:

$$\forall (c_i <_r c_j) : \vec{w} \cdot (\Phi(c_i) - \Phi(c_j)) \geq 1 - \xi_{i,j} \quad (2)$$
$$\forall i, j : \xi_{i,j} \geq 0 \qquad (3)$$

The margin incorporates slack variables $\xi_{i,j}$ for problems that are not linearly separable. This ranking task is analogous to the SVM classification task on the pairwise difference vectors $(\Phi(c_i) - \Phi(c_j))$, known as *rank constraints*. Unlike classification, no explicit negative evidence is required as $\vec{w} \cdot (\Phi(c_i) - \Phi(c_j)) = (-1)\vec{w} \cdot (\Phi(c_j) - \Phi(c_i))$. It is also important to note that no rank constraints are generated for candidates for which no order relation exists under the ranking r.

Support Vector Machines (SVMs) have previously been used for preference ranking in the context of information retrieval (Joachims, 2002). We adopt the same framework for answer typing by preference ranking. The SVM^{light} package (Joachims, 1999) implements the preference ranking of Joachims (2002) and is used here for learning answer types.

2.1 Application to Answer Typing

Assigning meaningful scores for answer typing is a difficult task. For example, given the question "What city hosted the 1988 Winter Olympics?" and the candidates New York, Calgary, and the word blue, how can we identify New York and Calgary as appropriate and the word blue as inappropriate? Scoring answer candidates is complicated by the fact that a gold standard for appropriateness scores does not exist. Therefore, we have no *a priori* notion that New York is better than the word blue by some amount v. Because of this, we approach the problem of answer typing as one of preference ranking in which the relative appropriateness is more important than the absolute scores.

Preference ranking stands in contrast to *classification*, in which a candidate is classified as appropriate or inappropriate depending on the values in its feature representation. Unfortunately, simple classification does not work well in the face of a large imbalance in positive and negative examples. In answer typing we typically have far more inappropriate candidates than appropriate candidates, and this is especially true for the experiments described in Section 4. This is indeed a problem for our system, as neither re-weighting nor attempting to balance the set of examples with the use of random negative examples were shown to give better performance on development data. This is not to say that *some* means of balancing the data would not provide comparable or superior performance, but rather that such a weighting or sampling scheme is not obvious.

An additional benefit of preference ranking over classification is that preference ranking models the *better-than* relationship between candidates. Typically a set of candidate answers are all related to a question in some way, and we wish to know which of the candidates are better than others. In contrast, binary classification simply deals with the *is/is-not* relationship and will have difficulty when two responses with similar feature values are classified differently. With preference ranking, violations of some rank constraints will affect the resulting order of candidates, but sufficient ordering information may still be present to correctly identify appropriate candidates.

To apply preference ranking to answer typing, we learn a model over a set of questions $q_1, ..., q_n$. Each question q_i has a list of appropriate candidate answers $a_{(i,1)}, ..., a_{(i,u)}$ and a list of inappropriate candidate answers $b_{(i,1)}, ..., b_{(i,v)}$. The partial ordering r is simply the set

$$\forall i, j, k : \{a_{(i,j)} <_r b_{(i,k)}\} \tag{4}$$

This means that rank constraints are only generated for candidate answers $a_{(i,j)}$ and $b_{(i,k)}$ for question q_i and not between candidates $a_{(i,j)}$ and $b_{(l,k)}$ where $i \neq l$. For example, the candidate answers for the question "What city hosted the 1988 Winter Olympics?" are not compared with those for "What colour is the sky?" because our partial ordering r does not attempt to rank candidates for one question in relation to candidates for another. Moreover, no rank constraints are generated between $a_{(i,j)}$ and $a_{(i,k)}$ nor $b_{(i,j)}$ and $b_{(i,k)}$ because the partial ordering does not include orderings between two candidates of the same class. Given two appropriate candidates to the question "What city hosted the 1988 Winter Olympics?", New York and Calgary, rank constraints will not be created for the pair (New York, Calgary).

3 Methods

We begin with the work of Pinchak and Lin (2006) in which *question contexts* (dependency tree paths involving the *wh*-word) are extracted from the question and matched against those found in a corpus of text. The basic idea is that words that are appropriate as answers will appear in place of the *wh*-word in these contexts when found in the corpus. For example, the question "What city hosted the 1988 Winter Olympics?" will have as one of the question contexts "X hosted Olympics." We then consult a corpus to discover what replacements for X were actually mentioned and smooth the resulting distribution.

We use the model of Pinchak and Lin (2006) to produce features for our discriminative model.

Table 1: Feature templates

Pattern	Description
$E(t, c)$	Estimated count of term t in context c
$C(t, c)$	Observed count of term t in context c
$\sum_{t'} C(t', c)$	Count of all terms appearing in context c
$\sum_{c'} C(t, c')$	Count of term t in all contexts
$S(t)$	Count of the times t occurs in the candidate list

These features are mostly based on question contexts, and are briefly summarized in Table 1. Following Pinchak and Lin (2006), all of our features are derived from a limited corpus (AQUAINT); large-scale text resources are not required for our model to perform well. By restricting ourselves to relatively small corpora, we believe that our approach will easily transfer to other domains or languages (provided parsing resources are available).

To address the sparseness of question contexts, we remove lexical elements from question context paths. This removal is performed after feature values are obtained for the fully lexicalized path; the removal of lexical elements simply allows many similar paths to share a single learned weight. For example, the term Calgary in context $X \leftarrow$ *subject* $\leftarrow$ host $\rightarrow$ *object* $\rightarrow$ Olympics (X hosted Olympics) is used to obtain a feature value v that is assigned to a feature such as $C(\text{Calgary}, X \leftarrow subject \leftarrow * \rightarrow object \rightarrow *) = v$. Removal of lexical elements results in a space of 73 possible question contexts. To facilitate learning, all counts are log values and feature vectors are normalized to unit length.

The estimated count of term t in context c, $E(t, c)$, is a component of the model of Pinchak and Lin (2006) and is calculated according to:

$$E(t, c) = \sum_{\chi} \Pr(\chi|t) C(\chi, c) \tag{5}$$

Essentially, this equation computes an expected count for term t in question c by observing how likely t is to be part of a cluster χ ($\Pr(\chi|t)$) and then observing how often terms of cluster χ occur in context c ($C(\chi, c)$). Although the model of Pinchak and Lin (2006) is significantly more complex, we use their core idea of cluster-based smoothing to decide how often a term t will occur in a context c, regardless of whether or not t was actually observed in c within our corpus. The Pinchak and Lin (2006) system is unable to assign individual weights to different question contexts, even though not all question contexts are equally important. For example, the Pinchak and Lin (2006) model is forced to consider a question focus context (such as "X is a city") to be of equal importance to non-focus contexts (such as "X host Olympics"). However, we have observed that it is more important that candidate X is a city than it hosted an Olympics in this instance. Appropriate answers are required to be cities even though not all cities have hosted Olympics. We wish to address this problem with the use of discriminative methods.

The observed count features of term t in context c, $C(t, c)$, are included to allow for combination with the estimated values from the model of Pinchak and Lin (2006). Because Pinchak and Lin (2006) make use of cluster-based smoothing, errors may occur. By including the observed counts of term t in context c, we hope to allow for the use of more accurate statistics whenever they are available, and for the smoothed counts in cases for which they are not.

Finally, we include the frequency of a term t in the list of candidates, $S(t)$. The idea here is that the correct and/or appropriate answers are likely to be repeated many times in a list of candidate answers. Terms that are strongly associated with the question and appear often in results are likely to be what the question is looking for.

Both the $C(t, c)$ and $S(t)$ features are extensions to the Pinchak and Lin (2006) model and can be incorporated into the Pinchak and Lin (2006) model with varying degrees of difficulty. The value of $S(t)$ in particular is highly dependent on the means used to obtain the candidate list, and the distribution of words over the candidate list is often very different from the distribution of words in the corpus. Because this feature value comes from a different source than our other features, it would be difficult to use in a non-discriminative model.

Correct answers to our set of questions are obtained from the TREC 2002-2006 results (Voorhees, 2002). For appropriateness labels we turn to human annotators. Two annotators were instructed to label a candidate as appropriate if that candidate was believable as an answer, even if that candidate was not correct. For a question such as "What city hosted the 1988 Winter Olympics?", all cities should be labeled as appropriate even though only Calgary is correct. This task comes with a moderate degree of difficulty, especially when dealing with questions for which appropriate answers are less obvious (such as "What kind of a community is a Kibbutz?"). We observed an inter-annotator (kappa) agreement of 0.73, which indicates substantial agreement. This value of kappa conveys the difficulty that even human annotators have when trying to decide which candidates are appropriate for a given question. Because of this value of kappa, we adopt strict gold standard appropriateness labels that are the intersection of the two annotators' labels (i.e., a candidate is only appropriate if both annotators label it as such, otherwise it is inappropriate).

We introduce four different models for the ranking of appropriate answers, each of which makes use of appropriateness labels in different ways:

Correctness Model: Although appropriateness and correctness are not equivalent, this model deals with distinguishing correct from incorrect candidates in the hopes that the resulting model will be able to perform well on finding both correct and appropriate answers. For learning, correct answers are placed at a rank above that of incorrect candidates, regardless of whether or not those candidates are appropriate. This represents the strictest definition of appropriateness and requires no human annotation.

Appropriateness Model: The correctness model assumes only correct answers are appropriate. In reality, this is seldom the case. For example, documents or snipppets returned for the question "What country did Catherine the Great rule?" will contain not only Russia (the correct answer), but also Germany (the nationality of her parents) and Poland (her modern-day birthplace). To better address this overly strict definition of appropriateness, we rank all candidates labeled as appropriate above those labeled as inappropriate, without regards to correctness. Because we want to learn a model for appropriateness, training on appropriateness rather than correctness information should produce a model closer to what we desire.

Combined Model: Discriminative preference ranking is not limited to only two ranks. We combine the ideas of correctness and appropriateness together to form a three-rank combined model. This model places correct answers above appropriate-but-incorrect candidates, which are in turn placed above inappropriate-and-incorrect candidates.

Reduced Model: Both the appropriateness model and the combined model incorporate a large number of rank constraints. We can reduce the number of rank constraints generated by simply removing all appropriate, but incorrect, candidates from consideration and otherwise following the correctness model. The main difference is that some appropriate candidates are no longer assigned a low rank. By removing appropriate, but incorrect, candidates from the generation of rank constraints, we no longer rank correct answers above appropriate candidates.

4 Experiments

To compare with the prior approach of Pinchak and Lin (2006), we use a set of *what* and *which* questions with question focus (questions with a noun phrase following the *wh*-word). These are a subset of the more general *what*, *which*, and *who* questions dealt with by Pinchak and Lin (2006). Although our model can accommodate a wide range of *what*, *which*, *when*, and *who* questions, the focused *what* and *which* questions are an easily identifiable subclass that are rarely definitional or otherwise complex in terms of the desired answer. We take the set of focused *what* and *which* questions from TREC 2002-2006 (Voorhees, 2002) comprising a total of 385 questions and performed 9-fold cross-validation, with one dedicated development partition (the tenth partition). The development partition was used to tune the regularization parameter of the SVM used for testing.

Candidates are obtained by submitting the question as-is to the Google search engine and chunking the top 20 snippets returned, resulting in an average of 140 candidates per question. Google snippets create a better confusion set than simply random words for appropriate and inappropriate candidates; many of the terms found in Google snippets are related in some way to the question. To ensure a correct answer is present (where possible), we append the list of correct answers to the list of candidates.

As a measure of performance, we adopt Mean Reciprocal Rank (MRR) for both correct and appropriate answers, as well as precision-recall for appropriate answers. MRR is useful as a measure of overall QA system performance (Voorhees, 2002), but is based only on the top correct or appropriate answer encountered in a ranked list. For this reason, we also show the precision-recall curve to better understand how our models perform.

We compare our models with three alternative approaches, the simplest of which is *random*. For random, the candidate answers are randomly shuffled and performance is averaged over a number of runs (100). The *snippet frequency* approach orders candidates based on their frequency of occurrence in the Google snippets, and is simply the $S(t)$ feature of our discriminative models in isolation. We remove terms comprised solely of question words from all approaches to prevent question words (which tend to be very frequent in the snippets) from being selected as answers. The last of our alternative systems is an implementation of the work of Pinchak and Lin (2006) in which the output probabilities of their model are used to rank candidates.

4.1 Results

Figures 1 and 2 show the MRR results and precision-recall curve of our correctness model against the alternative approaches. In comparison to these alternative systems, we show two versions of our correctness model. The first uses a linear kernel and is able to outperform the alternative approaches. The second uses a radial basis function (RBF) kernel and exhibits performance superior to that of the linear kernel. This suggests a degree of non-linearity present in the data that cannot be captured by the linear kernel alone. Both the training and running times of the RBF kernel are considerably larger than that of the linear kernel. The accuracy gain of the RBF kernel must therefore be weighed against the increased time required to use the model.

Figures 3 and 4 give the MRR results and precision-recall curves for our additional models in comparison with that of the correctness model. Although losses in MRR and precision are observed for both the appropriate and combined model using the RBF kernel, the linear kernel versions of these models show slight performance gains.

Figure 1: MRR results for the correctness model

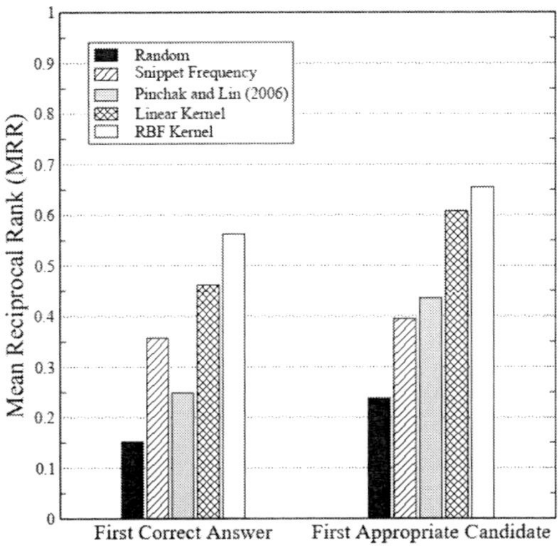

Figure 2: Precision-recall of appropriate candidates under the correctness model

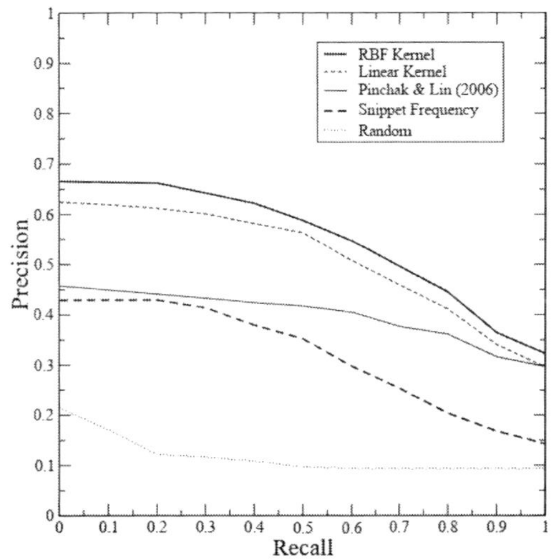

5 Discussion of Results

The results of our correctness model, found in Figures 1 and 2 show considerable gains over our alternative systems, including that of Pinchak and Lin (2006). The Pinchak and Lin (2006) system was specifically designed with answer typing in mind, although it makes use of a brittle generative model that does not account for ranking of answer candidates nor for the variable strength of various question contexts. These results show that our discriminative preference ranking approach creates a better model of both correctness and appropriateness via weighting of contexts, preference rank learning, and with the incorporation of additional related features (Table 1). The last feature, snippet frequency, is not particularly strong on its own, but can be easily incorporated into our discriminative model. The ability to add a wide variety of potentially helpful features is one of the strengths of discriminative techniques in general.

By moving away from simply correct answers in the correctness model and incorporating labeled appropriate examples in various ways, we are able to further improve upon the performance of our approach. Training on appropriateness labels instead of correct answers results in a loss in MRR for the first correct answer, but a gain in MRR for the first appropriate candidate. Unfortunately, this does not carry over to the entire range of precision over recall. For the linear kernel, our three additional models (appropriateness, combined, and reduced) show consistent improvements over the correctness model, but with the RBF kernel only the reduced model produces a meaningful change.

The precision-recall curves of Figures 2 and 4 show remarkable consistency across the full range of recall, despite the fact that candidates exist for which feature values cannot easily be obtained. Due to tagging and chunking errors, ill-formed candidates may exist that are judged appropriate by the annotators. For example, "explorer Hernando Soto" is a candidate marked appropriate by both annotators to the question "What Spanish explorer discovered the Mississippi River?" However, our context database does not include the phrase "explorer Hernando Soto" meaning that only a few features will have non-zero values. Despite these occasional problems, our models are able to rank most correct and appropriate candidates high in a ranked list.

Finally, we examine the effects of training set size on MRR. The learning curve for a single partitioning under the correctness model is presented in Figure 5. Although the model trained with the RBF kernel exhibits some degree of instability below 100 training questions, both the linear and RBF models gain little benefit from additional training questions beyond 100. This may be due to the fact that the most common unlexicalized question contexts have been observed in the first

Figure 3: MRR results (RBF kernel)

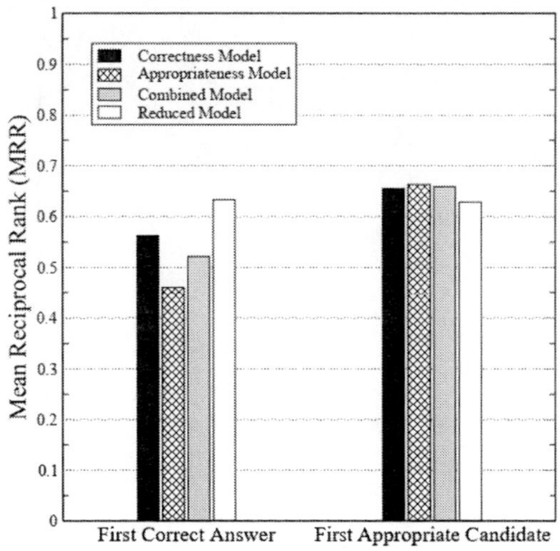

Figure 4: Precision-recall of appropriate (RBF kernel)

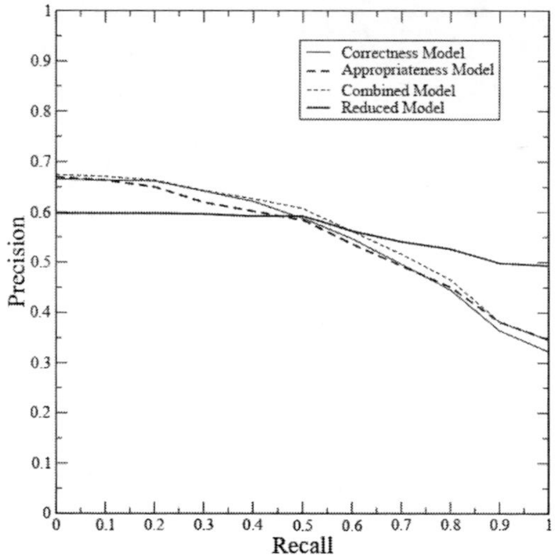

100 training examples and so therefore additional questions simply repeat the same information. Requiring only a relatively small number of training examples means that an effective model can be learned with relatively little input in the form of question-answer pairs or annotated candidate lists.

6 Prior Work

The expected answer type can be captured in a number of possible ways. By far the most common is the assignment of one or more predefined types to a question during a question analysis phase. Although the vast majority of the approaches to answer type detection make use of rules (either partly or wholly) (Harabagiu et al., 2005; Sun et al., 2005; Wu et al., 2005; Mollá and Gardiner, 2004), a few notable learned methods for answer type detection exist.

One of the first attempts at learning a model for answer type detection was made by Ittycheriah et al. (2000; 2001) who learn a maximum entropy classifier over the Message Understanding Conference (MUC) types. Those same MUC types are then assigned by a named-entity tagger to identify appropriate candidate answers. Because of the potential for unanticipated types, Ittycheriah et al. (2000; 2001) include a *Phrase* type as a catch-all class that is used when no other class is appropriate. Although the classifier and named-entity tagger are shown to be among the components with the lowest error rate in their QA system, it is not clear how much benefit is obtained from using a relatively coarse-grained set of classes.

The approach of Li and Roth (2002) is similar in that it uses learning for answer type detection. They make use of multi-class learning with a Sparse Network of Winnows (SNoW) and a two-layer class hierarchy comprising a total of fifty possible answer types. These finer-grained classes are of more use when computing a notion of appropriateness, although one major drawback is that no entity tagger is discussed that can identify these types in text. Li and Roth (2002) also rely on a rigid set of classes and so run the risk of encountering a new question of an unseen type.

Pinchak and Lin (2006) present an alternative in which the probability of a term being appropriate to a question is computed directly. Instead of assigning an answer type to a question, the question is broken down into a number of possibly overlapping contexts. A candidate is then evaluated as to how likely it is to appear in these contexts. Unfortunately, Pinchak and Lin (2006) use a brittle generative model when combining question contexts that assumes all contexts are equally important. This assumption was dealt with by Pinchak and Lin (2006) by discarding all non-focus contexts with a focus context is present, but this is not an ideal solution.

Learning methods are abundant in QA research

Figure 5: Learning curve for MRR of the first correct answer under the correctness model

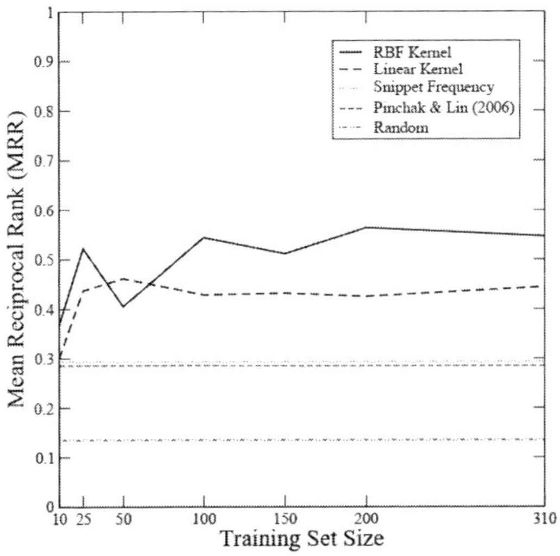

and have been applied in a number of different ways. Ittycheriah et al. (2000) created an entire QA system based on maximum entropy components in addition to the question classifier discussed above. Ittycheriah et al. (2000) were able to obtain reasonable performance from learned components alone, although future versions of the system use non-learned components in addition to learned components (Prager et al., 2003). The JAVELIN I system (Nyberg et al., 2005) uses a SVM during the answer/information extraction phase. Although learning is applied in many QA tasks, very few QA systems rely solely on learning. Compositional approaches, in which multiple distinct QA techniques are combined, also show promise for improving QA performance. Echihabi et al. (2003) use three separate answer extraction agents and combine the output scores with a maximum entropy re-ranker.

Surdeanu et al. (2008) explore preference ranking for advice or "how to" questions in which a unique correct answer is preferred over all other candidates. Their focus is on complex-answer questions in addition to the use of a collection of user-generated answers rather than answer typing. However, their use of preference ranking mirrors the techniques we describe here in which the relative difference between two candidates at different ranks is more important than the individual candidates.

7 Conclusions and Future Work

We have introduced a means of flexible answer typing with discriminative preference rank learning. Although answer typing does not represent a complete QA system, it is an important component to ensure that those candidates selected as answers are indeed appropriate to the question being asked. By casting the problem of evaluating appropriateness as one of preference ranking, we allow for the learning of what differentiates an appropriate candidate from an inappropriate one.

Experimental results on focused *what* and *which* questions show that a discriminatively trained preference rank model is able to outperform alternative approaches designed for the same task. This increase in performance comes from both the flexibility to easily combine a number of weighted features and because comparisons only need to be made between appropriate and inappropriate candidates. A preference ranking model can be trained from a relatively small set of example questions, meaning that only a small number of question/answer pairs or annotated candidate lists are required.

The power of an answer typing system lies in its ability to identify, in terms of some given query, appropriate candidates. Applying the flexible model described here to a domain other than question answering could allow for a more focused set of results. One straight-forward application is to apply our model to the process of information or document retrieval itself. Ensuring that there are terms present in the document appropriate to the query could allow for the intelligent expansion of the query. In a related vein, queries are occasionally comprised of natural language text fragments that can be treated similarly to questions. Rarely are users searching for simple mentions of the query in pages; we wish to provide them with something more useful. Our model achieves the goal of finding those appropriate related concepts.

Acknowledgments

We would like to thank Debra Shiau for her assistance annotating training and test data and the anonymous reviewers for their insightful comments. We would also like to thank the Alberta Informatics Circle of Research Excellence and the Alberta Ingenuity Fund for their support in developing this work.

References

A. Echihabi, U. Hermjakob, E. Hovy, D. Marcu, E. Melz, and D. Ravichandran. 2003. Multiple-Engine Question Answering in TextMap. In *Proceedings of the Twelfth Text REtrieval Conference (TREC-2003)*, Gaithersburg, Maryland.

S. Harabagiu, D. Moldovan, C. Clark, M. Bowden, A. Hickl, and P. Wang. 2005. Employing Two Question Answering Systems in TREC-2005. In *Proceedings of the Fourteenth Text REtrieval Conference (TREC-2005)*, Gaithersburg, Maryland.

A. Ittycheriah, M. Franz, W-J. Zhu, A. Ratnaparkhi, and R. Mammone. 2000. IBM's Statistical Question Answering System. In *Proceedings of the 9th Text REtrieval Conference (TREC-9)*, Gaithersburg, Maryland.

A. Ittycheriah, M. Franz, and S. Roukos. 2001. IBM's Statistical Question Answering System – TREC-10. In *Proceedings of the 10th Text REtrieval Conference (TREC-10)*, Gaithersburg, Maryland.

T. Joachims. 1999. Making Large-Scale SVM Learning Practical. In B. Schölkopf, C. Burges, and A. Smola, editors, *Advances in Kernel Methods - Support Vector Learning*. MIT-Press.

T. Joachims. 2002. Optimizing Search Engines Using Clickthrough Data. In *Proceedings of the ACM Conference on Knowledge Discovery and Data Mining (KDD)*. ACM.

X. Li and D. Roth. 2002. Learning Question Classifiers. In *Proceedings of the International Conference on Computational Linguistics (COLING 2002)*, pages 556–562.

D. Mollá and M. Gardiner. 2004. AnswerFinder - Question Answering by Combining Lexical, Syntactic and Semantic Information. In *Proceedings of the Australian Language Technology Workshop (ALTW 2004*, pages 9–16, Sydney, December.

E. Nyberg, R. Frederking, T. Mitamura, M. Bilotti, K. Hannan, L. Hiyakumoto, J. Ko, F. Lin, L. Lita, V. Pedro, and A. Schlaikjer. 2005. JAVELIN I and II Systems at TREC 2005. In *Proceedings of the Fourteenth Text REtrieval Conference (TREC-2005)*, Gaithersburg, Maryland.

C. Pinchak and D. Lin. 2006. A Probabilistic Answer Type Model. In *Proceedings of the Eleventh Conference of the European Chapter of the Association for Computational Linguistics (EACL 2006)*, Trento, Italy, April.

J. Prager, J. Chu-Carroll, K. Czuba, C. Welty, A. Ittycheriah, and R. Mahindru. 2003. IBM's PIQUANT in TREC2003. In *Proceedings of the Twelfth Text REtrieval Conference (TREC-2003)*, Gaithersburg, Maryland.

R. Sun, J. Jiang, Y.F. Tan, H. Cui, T-S. Chua, and M-Y. Kan. 2005. Using Syntactic and Semantic Relation Analysis in Question Answering. In *Proceedings of the Fourteenth Text REtrieval Conference (TREC-2005)*, Gaithersburg, Maryland.

M. Surdeanu, M. Ciaramita, and H. Zaragoza. 2008. Learning to rank answers on large online QA collections. In *Proceedings of the 46th Annual Meeting for the Association for Computational Linguistics: Human Language Technologies (ACL-08: HLT)*, pages 719–727, Columbus, Ohio, June. Association for Computational Linguistics.

E.M. Voorhees. 2002. Overview of the TREC 2002 Question Answering Track. In *Proceedings of TREC 2002*, Gaithersburg, Maryland.

M. Wu, M. Duan, S. Shaikh, S. Small, and T. Strzalkowski. 2005. ILQUA – An IE-Driven Question Answering System. In *Proceedings of the Fourteenth Text REtrieval Conference (TREC-2005)*, Gaithersburg, Maryland.

Semi-Supervised Polarity Lexicon Induction

Delip Rao*
Department of Computer Science
Johns Hopkins University
Baltimore, MD
delip@cs.jhu.edu

Deepak Ravichandran
Google Inc.
1600 Amphitheatre Parkway
Mountain View, CA
deepakr@google.com

Abstract

We present an extensive study on the problem of detecting polarity of words. We consider the polarity of a word to be either positive or negative. For example, words such as *good, beautiful*, and *wonderful* are considered as positive words; whereas words such as *bad, ugly*, and *sad* are considered negative words. We treat polarity detection as a semi-supervised label propagation problem in a graph. In the graph, each node represents a word whose polarity is to be determined. Each weighted edge encodes a relation that exists between two words. Each node (word) can have two labels: positive or negative. We study this framework in two different resource availability scenarios using WordNet and OpenOffice thesaurus when WordNet is not available. We report our results on three different languages: English, French, and Hindi. Our results indicate that label propagation improves significantly over the baseline and other semi-supervised learning methods like Mincuts and Randomized Mincuts for this task.

1 Introduction

Opinionated texts are characterized by words or phrases that communicate positive or negative sentiment. Consider the following example of two movie reviews[1] shown in Figure 1. The positive review is peppered with words such as *enjoyable, likeable, decent, breathtakingly* and the negative comment uses words like *ear-shattering, humorless, unbearable*. These terms and prior knowledge of their polarity could be used as features in a supervised classification framework to determine the sentiment of the opinionated text (E.g., (Esuli and Sebastiani, 2006)). Thus lexicons indicating polarity of such words are indispensable resources not only in automatic sentiment analysis but also in other natural language understanding tasks like textual entailment. This motivation was seen in the *General Enquirer* effort by Stone et al. (1966) and several others who manually construct such lexicons for the English language.[2] While it is possible to manually build these resources for a language, the ensuing effort is onerous. This motivates the need for automatic language-agnostic methods for building sentiment lexicons. The importance of this problem has warranted several efforts in the past, some of which will be reviewed here.

Figure 1: Movie Reviews with positive (left) and negative (right) sentiment.

We demonstrate the application of graph-based semi-supervised learning for induction of polarity lexicons. We try several graph-based semi-

*Work done as a summer intern at Google Inc.

[1]Source: *Live Free or Die Hard*, rottentomatoes.com

[2]The *General Inquirer* tries to classify English words along several dimensions, including polarity.

Proceedings of the 12th Conference of the European Chapter of the ACL, pages 675–682,
Athens, Greece, 30 March – 3 April 2009. ©2009 Association for Computational Linguistics

supervised learning methods like Mincuts, Randomized Mincuts, and Label Propagation. In particular, we define a graph with nodes consisting of the words or phrases to be classified either as positive or negative. The edges between the nodes encode some notion of similarity. In a transductive fashion, a few of these nodes are labeled using seed examples and the labels for the remaining nodes are derived using these seeds. We explore natural word-graph sources like WordNet and exploit different relations within WordNet like synonymy and hypernymy. Our method is not just confined to WordNet; any source listing synonyms could be used. To demonstrate this, we show the use of OpenOffice thesaurus – a free resource available in several languages.[3]

We begin by discussing some related work in Section 2 and briefly describe the learning methods we use, in Section 3. Section 4 details our evaluation methodology along with detailed experiments for English. In Section 5 we demonstrate results in French and Hindi, as an example of how the method could be easily applied to other languages as well.

2 Related Work

The literature on sentiment polarity lexicon induction can be broadly classified into two categories, those based on corpora and the ones using WordNet.

2.1 Corpora based approaches

One of the earliest work on learning polarity of terms was by Hatzivassiloglou and McKeown (1997) who deduce polarity by exploiting constraints on conjoined adjectives in the Wall Street Journal corpus. For example, the conjunction "and" links adjectives of the same polarity while "but" links adjectives of opposite polarity. However the applicability of this method for other important classes of sentiment terms like nouns and verbs is yet to be demonstrated. Further they assume linguistic features specific to English.

Wiebe (2000) uses Lin (1998a) style distributionally similar adjectives in a cluster-and-label process to generate sentiment lexicon of adjectives.

In a different work, Riloff et al. (2003) use manually derived pattern templates to extract subjective nouns by bootstrapping.

[3]http://www.openoffice.org

Another corpora based method due to Turney and Littman (2003) tries to measure the semantic orientation $O(t)$ for a term t by

$$O(t) = \sum_{t_i \in S^+} PMI(t, t_i) - \sum_{t_j \in S^-} PMI(t, t_j)$$

where S^+ and S^- are minimal sets of polar terms that contain prototypical positive and negative terms respectively, and $PMI(t, t_i)$ is the pointwise mutual information (Lin, 1998b) between the terms t and t_i. While this method is general enough to be applied to several languages our aim was to develop methods that exploit more structured sources like WordNet to leverage benefits from the rich network structure.

Kaji and Kitsuregawa (2007) outline a method of building sentiment lexicons for Japanese using structural cues from HTML documents. Apart from being very specific to Japanese, excessive dependence on HTML structure makes their method brittle.

2.2 WordNet based approaches

These approaches use lexical relations defined in WordNet to derive sentiment lexicons. A simple but high-precision method proposed by Kim and Hovy (2006) is to add all synonyms of a polar word with the same polarity and its antonyms with reverse polarity. As demonstrated later, the method suffers from low recall and is unsuitable in situations when the seed polar words are too few – not uncommon in low resource languages.

In line with Turney's work, Kamps et. al. (2004) try to determine sentiments of adjectives in WordNet by measuring relative distance of the term from exemplars, such as "good" and "bad". The polarity orientation of a term t is measured as follows

$$O(t) = \frac{d(t, \mathsf{good}) - d(t, \mathsf{bad})}{d(\mathsf{good}, \mathsf{bad})}$$

where $d(.)$ is a WordNet based relatedness measure (Pedersen et al., 2004). Again they report results for adjectives alone.

Another relevant example is the recent work by Mihalcea et. al. (2007) on multilingual sentiment analysis using cross-lingual projections. This is achieved by using bridge resources like dictionaries and parallel corpora to build sentence subjectivity classifiers for the target language (Romanian). An interesting result from their work is that only a small fraction of the lexicon entries preserve their polarities under translation.

The primary contributions of this paper are :

- An application of graph-based semi-supervised learning methods for inducing sentiment lexicons from WordNet and other thesauri. The label propagation method naturally allows combining several relations from WordNet.

- Our approach works on all classes of words and not just adjectives

- Though we report results for English, Hindi, and French, our methods can be easily replicated for other languages where WordNet is available.[4] In the absence of WordNet, any thesaurus listing synonyms could be used. We present one such result using the OpenOffice thesaurus – a freely available multilingual resource scarcely used in NLP literature.

3 Graph based semi-supervised learning

Most natural language data has some structure that could be exploited even in the absence of fully annotated data. For instance, documents are similar in the terms they contain, words could be synonyms of each other, and so on. Such information can be readily encoded as a graph where the presence of an edge between two nodes would indicate a relationship between the two nodes and, optionally, the weight on the edge could encode strength of the relationship. This additional information aids learning when very few annotated examples are present. We review three well known graph based semi-supervised learning methods – mincuts, randomized mincuts, and label propagation – that we use in induction of polarity lexicons.

3.1 Mincuts

A mincut of a weighted graph $G(V, E)$ is a partitioning the vertices V into V_1 and V_2 such that sum of the edge weights of all edges between V_1 and V_2 is minimal (Figure 2).

Mincuts for semi-supervised learning proposed by Blum and Chawla (2001) tries to classify datapoints by partitioning the similarity graph such that it minimizes the number of similar points being labeled differently. Mincuts have been used

[4]As of this writing, WordNet is available for more than 40 world languages (http://www.globalwordnet.org)

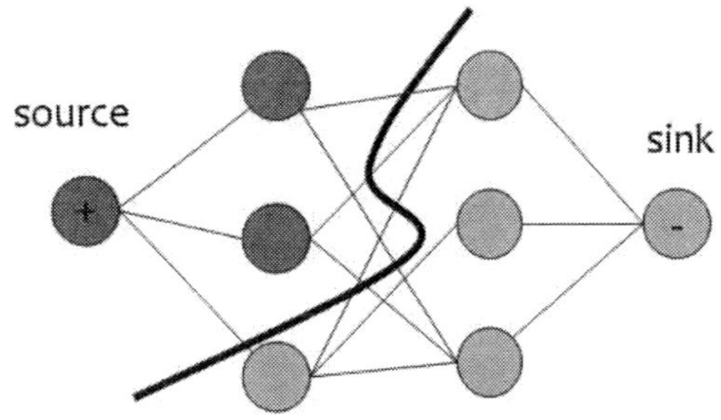

Figure 2: Semi-supervised classification using mincuts

in semi-supervised learning for various tasks, including document level sentiment analysis (Pang and Lee, 2004). We explore the use of mincuts for the task of sentiment lexicon learning.

3.2 Randomized Mincuts

An improvement to the basic mincut algorithm was proposed by Blum et. al. (2004). The deterministic mincut algorithm, solved using max-flow, produces only one of the several possible mincuts. Some of these cuts could be skewed thereby negatively effecting the results. As an extreme example consider the graph in Figure 3a. Let the nodes with degree one be labeled as positive and negative respectively, and for the purpose of illustration let all edges be of the same weight. The graph in Figure 3a. can be partitioned in four equal cost cuts – two of which are shown in (b) and (c). The min-

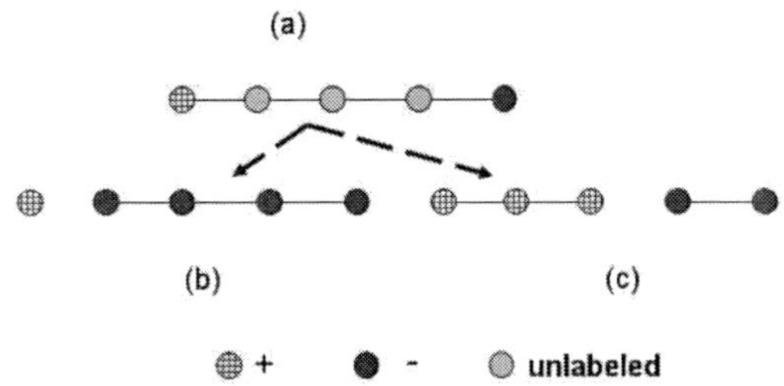

Figure 3: Problem with mincuts

cut algorithm, depending on the implementation, will return only one of the extreme cuts (as in (b)) while the desired classification might be as shown in Figure 3c.

The randomized mincut approach tries to address this problem by randomly perturbing the adjacency matrix by adding random noise.[5] Mincut is then performed on this perturbed graph. This is

[5]We use a Gaussian noise $\mathcal{N}(0, 1)$.

repeated several times and unbalanced partitions are discarded. Finally the remaining partitions are used to deduce the final classification by majority voting. In the unlikely event of the voting resulting in a tie, we refrain from making a decision thus favoring precision over recall.

3.3 Label propagation

Another semi-supervised learning method we use is label propagation by Zhu and Ghahramani (2002). The label propagation algorithm is a transductive learning framework which uses a few examples, or seeds, to label a large number of unlabeled examples. In addition to the seed examples, the algorithm also uses a relation between the examples. This relation should have two requirements:

1. It should be transitive.
2. It should encode some notion of relatedness between the examples.

To name a few, examples of such relations include, synonymy, hypernymy, and similarity in some metric space. This relation between the examples can be easily encoded as a graph. Thus every node in the graph is an example and the edge represents the relation. Also associated with each node, is a probability distribution over the labels for the node. For the seed nodes, this distribution is known and kept fixed. The aim is to derive the distributions for the remaining nodes.

Consider a graph $G(V, E, W)$ with vertices V, edges E, and an $n \times n$ edge weight matrix $W = [w_{ij}]$, where $n = |V|$. The label propagation algorithm minimizes a quadratic energy function

$$\mathcal{E} = \frac{1}{2} \sum_{(i,j) \in E} w_{ij}(y_i - y_j)^2$$

where y_i and y_j are the labels assigned to the nodes i and j respectively.[6] Thus, to derive the labels at y_i, we set $\frac{\partial}{\partial y_i}\mathcal{E} = 0$ to obtain the following update equation

$$y_i = \frac{\sum_{(i,j)\in E} w_{ij} y_j}{\sum_{(i,j)\in E} w_{ij}}$$

In practice, we use the following iterative algorithm as noted by Zhu and Ghahramani (2002). A $n \times n$ stochastic transition matrix T is derived by row-normalizing W as follows:

$$T_{ij} = P(j \rightarrow i) = \frac{w_{ij}}{\sum_{k=1}^{n} w_{kj}}$$

where T_{ij} can be viewed as the transition probability from node j to node i. The algorithm proceeds as follows:

1. Assign a $n \times C$ matrix Y with the initial assignment of labels, where C is the number of classes.
2. Propagate labels for all nodes by computing $Y = TY$
3. Row-normalize Y such that each row adds up to one.
4. Clamp the seed examples in Y to their original values
5. Repeat 2-5 until Y converges.

There are several points to be noted. First, we add a special label "DEFAULT" to existing set of labels and set $P(\texttt{DEFAULT} \mid node = u) = 1$ for all unlabeled nodes u. For all the seed nodes s with class label L we define $P(\texttt{L} \mid node = s) = 1$. This ensures nodes that cannot be labeled at all[7] will retain $P(\texttt{DEFAULT}) = 1$ thereby leading to a quick convergence. Second, the algorithm produces a probability distribution over the labels for all unlabeled points. This makes this method specially suitable for classifier combination approaches. For this paper, we simply select the most likely label as the predicted label for the point. Third, the algorithm eventually converges. For details on the proof for convergence we refer the reader to Zhu and Ghahramani (2002).

4 Evaluation and Experiments

We use the General Inquirer (GI)[8] data for evaluation. General Inquirer is lexicon of English words hand-labeled with categorical information along several dimensions. One such dimension is called valence, with 1915 words labeled "Positiv" (sic) and 2291 words labeled "Negativ" for words with positive and negative sentiments respectively. Since we want to evaluate the performance of the

[6]For binary classification $y_k \in \{-1, +1\}$.

[7]As an example of such a situation, consider a disconnected component of unlabeled nodes with no seed in it.

[8]http://www.wjh.harvard.edu/~inquirer/

algorithms alone and not the recall issues in using WordNet, we only consider words from GI that also occur in WordNet. This leaves us the distribution of words as enumerated in Table 1.

PoS type	No. of Positives	No. of Negatives
Nouns	517	579
Verbs	319	562
Adjectives	547	438

Table 1: English evaluation data from General Inquirer

All experiments reported in Sections 4.1 to 4.5 use the data described above with a 50-50 split so that the first half is used as seeds and the second half is used for test. Note that all the experiments described below did not involve any parameter tuning thus obviating the need for a separate development test set. The effect of number of seeds on learning is described in Section 4.6.

4.1 Kim-Hovy method and improvements

Kim and Hovy (2006) enrich their sentiment lexicon from WordNet as follows. Synonyms of a positive word are positive while antonyms are treated as negative. This basic version suffers from a very poor recall as shown in the Figure 4 for adjectives (see iteration 1). The recall can be improved for a slight trade-off in precision if we re-run the above algorithm on the output produced at the previous level. This could be repeated iteratively until there is no noticeable change in precision/recall. We consider this as the best possible F1-score produced by the Kim-Hovy method. The classwise F1 for this method is shown in Table 2. We use these scores as our baseline.

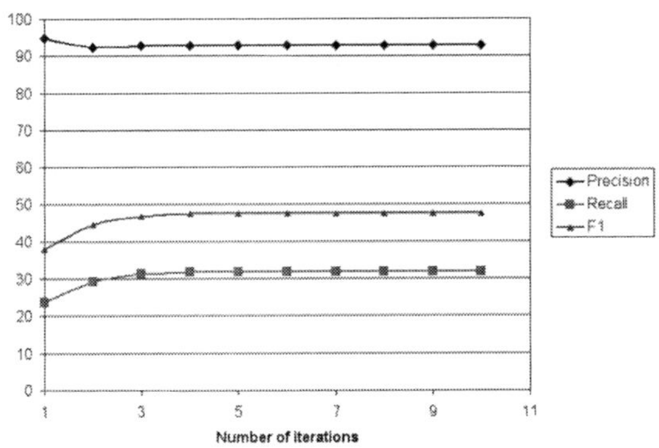

Figure 4: Kim-Hovy method

PoS type	P	R	F1
Nouns	92.59	21.43	34.80
Verbs	87.89	38.31	53.36
Adjectives	92.95	31.71	47.28

Table 2: Precision/Recall/F1-scores for Kim-Hovy method

4.2 Using prototypes

We now consider measuring semantic orientation from WordNet using prototypical examples such as "good" and "bad" similar to Kamps et al. (2004). Kamps et. al., report results only for adjectives though their method could be used for other part-of-speech types. The results for using prototypes are listed in Table 3. Note that the seed data was fully unused except for the examples "good" and "bad". We still test on the same test data as earlier for comparing results. Also note that the recall need not be 100 in this case as we refrain from making a decision when $d(t, \text{good}) = d(t, \text{bad})$.

PoS type	P	R	F1
Nouns	48.03	99.82	64.86
Verbs	58.12	100.00	73.51
Adjectives	57.35	99.59	72.78

Table 3: Precision/Recall/F1-scores for prototype method

4.3 Using mincuts and randomized mincuts

We now report results for mincuts and randomized mincuts algorithm using the WordNet synonym graph. As seen in Table 4, we only observed a marginal improvement (for verbs) over mincuts by using randomized mincuts.

But the overall improvement of using graph-based semi-supervised learning methods over the Kim-Hovy and Prototype methods is quite significant.

4.4 Using label propagation

We extract the synonym graph from WordNet with an edge between two nodes being defined iff one is a synonym of the other. When label propagation is performed on this graph results in Table 5 are observed. The results presented in Tables 2-5 need deeper inspection. The iterated Kim-Hovy method suffers from poor recall. However both mincut methods and the prototype method by

	P	R	F1
Nouns			
Mincut	68.25	100.00	81.13
RandMincut	68.32	99.09	80.08
Verbs			
Mincut	72.34	100.00	83.95
RandMincut	73.06	99.02	84.19
Adjectives			
Mincut	73.78	100.00	84.91
RandMincut	73.58	100.00	84.78

Table 4: Precision/Recall/F1-scores using mincuts and randomized mincuts

PoS type	P	R	F1
Nouns	82.55	58.58	58.53
Verbs	81.00	85.94	83.40
Adjectives	84.76	64.02	72.95

Table 5: Precision/Recall/F1-scores for Label Propogation

Kamps et. al., have high recall as they end up classifying every node as either positive or negative. Note that the recall for randomized mincut is not 100 as we do not make a classification decision when there is a tie in majority voting (refer Section 3.2). Observe that the label propagation method performs significantly better than previous graph based methods in precision. The reason for lower recall is attributed to the lack of connectivity between plausibly related nodes, thereby not facilitating the "spread" of labels from the labeled seed nodes to the unlabeled nodes. We address this problem by adding additional edges to the synonym graph in the next section.

4.5 Incorporating hypernyms

The main reason for low recall in label propagation is that the WordNet synonym graph is highly disconnected. Even nodes which are logically related have paths missing between them. For example the positive nouns *compliment* and *laud* belong to different synonym subgraphs without a path between them. But incorporating the hypernym edges the two are connected by the noun *praise*. So, we incorporated hypernyms of every node to improve connectivity. Performing label propagation on this combined graph gives much better results (Table 6) with much higher recall and even slightly better precision. In Table 6., we do not report results for adjectives as WordNet does not define hypernyms for adjectives. A natural question to ask is if we can use other WordNet relations too. We will defer this until section 6.

PoS type	P	R	F1
Nouns	83.88	99.64	91.08
Verbs	85.49	100.00	92.18
Adjectives	N/A	N/A	N/A

Table 6: Effect of adding hypernyms

4.6 Effect of number of seeds

The results reported in Sections 4.1 to 4.5 fixed the number of seeds. We now investigate the performance of the various methods on the number of seeds used. In particular, we are interested in performance under conditions when the number of seeds are few – which is the motivation for using semi-supervised learning in the first place. Figure 5 presents our results for English. Observe that Label Propagation performs much better than our baseline even when the number of seeds is as low as ten. Thus label propagation is especially suited when annotation data is extremely sparse.

One reason for mincuts performing badly with few seeds is because they generate degenrate cuts.

5 Adapting to other languages

In order to demonstrate the ease of adaptability of our method for other languages, we used the Hindi WordNet[9] to derive the adjective synonym graph. We selected 489 adjectives at random from a list of 10656 adjectives and this list was annotated by two native speakers of the language. The annotated list was then split 50-50 into seed and test sets. Label propagation was performed using the seed list and evaluated on the test list. The results are listed in Table 7.

Hindi	P	R	F1
	90.99	95.10	93.00

Table 7: Evaluation on Hindi dataset

WordNet might not be freely available for all languages or may not exist. In such cases building graph from an existing thesaurus might also suffice. As an example, we consider French. Although the French WordNet is available[10], we

[9] http://www.cfilt.iitb.ac.in/wordnet/webhwn/

[10] http://www.illc.uva.nl/EuroWordNet/consortium-ewn.html

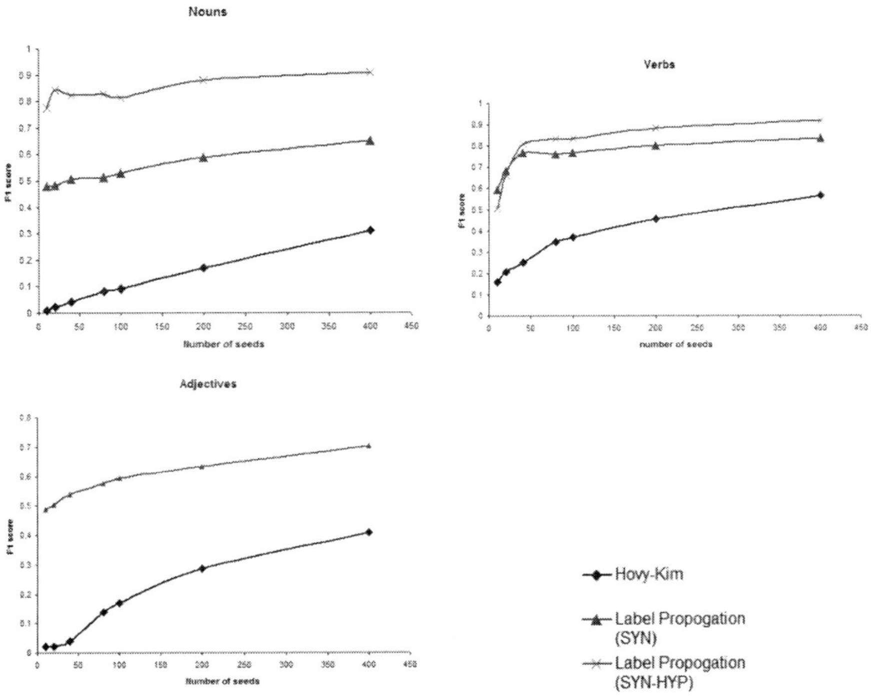

Figure 5: Effect of number of seeds on the F-score for Nouns, Verbs, and Adjectives. The X-axis is number of seeds and the Y-axis is the F-score.

found the cost prohibitive to obtain it. Observe that if we are using only the synonymy relation in WordNet then any thesaurus can be used instead. To demonstrate this, we consider the OpenOffice thesaurus for French, that is freely available. The synonym graph of French adjectives has 9707 vertices and 1.6M edges. We manually annotated a list of 316 adjectives and derived seed and test sets using a 50-50 split. The results of label propagation on such a graph is shown in Table 8.

French	P	R	F1
	73.65	93.67	82.46

Table 8: Evaluation on French dataset

The reason for better results in Hindi compared to French can be attributed to (1) higher inter-annotator agreement ($\kappa = 0.7$) in Hindi compared that in French ($\kappa = 0.55$).[11] (2) The Hindi experiment, like English, used WordNet while the French experiment was performed on graphs derived from the OpenOffice thesaurus due lack of freely available French WordNet.

[11]We do not have κ scores for English dataset derived from the Harvard Inquirer project.

6 Conclusions and Future Work

This paper demonstrated the utility of graph-based semi-supervised learning framework for building sentiment lexicons in a variety of resource availability situations. We explored how the structure of WordNet could be leveraged to derive polarity lexicons. The paper combines, for the first time, relationships like synonymy and hypernymy to improve label propagation results. All of our methods are independent of language as shown in the French and Hindi cases. We demonstrated applicability of our approach on alternative thesaurus-derived graphs when WordNet is not freely available, as in the case of French.

Although our current work uses WordNet and other thesauri, in resource poor situations when only monolingual raw text is available we can perform label propagation on nearest neighbor graphs derived directly from raw text using distributional similarity methods. This is work in progress.

We are also currently working on the possibility of including WordNet relations other than synonymy and hypernymy. One relation that is interesting and useful is antonymy. Antonym edges cannot be added in a straight-forward way to the graph for label propagation as antonymy encodes negative similarity (or dissimilarity) and the dissimilarity relation is not transitive.

References

[Blum and Chawla2001] Avrim Blum and Shuchi Chawla. 2001. Learning from labeled and unlabeled data using graph mincuts. In *Proc. 18th International Conf. on Machine Learning*, pages 19–26.

[Blum et al.2004] Blum, Lafferty, Rwebangira, and Reddy. 2004. Semi-supervised learning using randomized mincuts. In *Proceedings of the ICML*.

[Esuli and Sebastiani2006] Andrea Esuli and Fabrizio Sebastiani. 2006. Determining term subjectivity and term orientation for opinion mining. In *Proceedings of the 11th Conference of the European Chapter of the Association for Computational Linguistics*, pages 193–200.

[Hatzivassiloglou and McKeown1997] Vasileios Hatzivassiloglou and Kathleen McKeown. 1997. Predicting the semantic orientation of adjectives. In *Proceedings of the ACL*, pages 174–181.

[Kaji and Kitsuregawa2007] Nobuhiro Kaji and Masaru Kitsuregawa. 2007. Building lexicon for sentiment analysis from massive collection of HTML documents. In *Proceedings of the Joint Conference on Empirical Methods in Natural Language Processing and Computational Natural Language Learning (EMNLP-CoNLL)*, pages 1075–1083.

[Kamps et al.2004] Jaap Kamps, Maarten Marx, R. ort. Mokken, and Maarten de Rijke. 2004. Using WordNet to measure semantic orientation of adjectives. In *Proceedings of LREC-04, 4th International Conference on Language Resources and Evaluation*, volume IV.

[Kim and Hovy2006] Soo-Min Kim and Eduard H. Hovy. 2006. Identifying and analyzing judgment opinions. In *Proceedings of the HLT-NAACL*.

[Lin1998a] Dekang Lin. 1998a. Automatic retrieval and clustering of similar words. In *Proceedings of COLING*, pages 768–774.

[Lin1998b] Dekang Lin. 1998b. An information-theoretic definition of similarity. In *Proceedings of the 15th International Conference in Machine Learning*, pages 296–304.

[Mihalcea et al.2007] Rada Mihalcea, Carmen Banea, and Janyce Wiebe. 2007. Learning multilingual subjective language via cross-lingual projections. In *Proceedings of the 45th Annual Meeting of the Association of Computational Linguistics*, pages 976–983.

[Pang and Lee2004] Bo Pang and Lillian Lee. 2004. A sentimental education: Sentiment analysis using subjectivity summarization based on minimum cuts. In *Proceedings of the ACL*, pages 271–278.

[Pedersen et al.2004] Ted Pedersen, Siddharth Patwardhan, and Jason Michelizzi. 2004. Wordnet::similarity - measuring the relatedness of concepts. In *Proceeding of the HLT-NAACL*.

[Riloff et al.2003] Ellen Riloff, Janyce Wiebe, and Theresa Wilson. 2003. Learning subjective nouns using extraction pattern bootstrapping. In *Proceedings of the 7th Conference on Natural Language Learning*, pages 25–32.

[Stone et al.1966] Philip J. Stone, Dexter C. Dunphy, Marshall S. Smith, and Daniel M. Ogilvie. 1966. *The General Inquirer: A Computer Approach to Content Analysis*. MIT Press.

[Turney and Littman2003] Peter D. Turney and Michael L. Littman. 2003. Measuring praise and criticism: Inference of semantic orientation from association. *ACM Transactions on Information Systems*, 21(4):315–346.

[Wiebe2000] Janyce M. Wiebe. 2000. Learning subjective adjectives from corpora. In *Proceedings of the 2000 National Conference on Artificial Intelligence*. AAAI.

[Zhu and Ghahramani2002] Xiaojin Zhu and Zoubin Ghahramani. 2002. Learning from labeled and unlabeled data with label propagation. Technical Report CMU-CALD-02-107, Carnegie Mellon University.

Natural Language Generation as Planning Under Uncertainty for Spoken Dialogue Systems

Verena Rieser
School of Informatics
University of Edinburgh
vrieser@inf.ed.ac.uk

Oliver Lemon
School of Informatics
University of Edinburgh
olemon@inf.ed.ac.uk

Abstract

We present and evaluate a new model for Natural Language Generation (NLG) in Spoken Dialogue Systems, based on statistical planning, given noisy feedback from the current generation context (e.g. a user and a surface realiser). We study its use in a standard NLG problem: how to present information (in this case a set of search results) to users, given the complex trade-offs between utterance length, amount of information conveyed, and cognitive load. We set these trade-offs by analysing existing MATCH data. We then train a NLG policy using Reinforcement Learning (RL), which adapts its behaviour to noisy feedback from the current generation context. This policy is compared to several baselines derived from previous work in this area. The learned policy significantly outperforms all the prior approaches.

1 Introduction

Natural language allows us to achieve the same communicative goal ("what to say") using many different expressions ("how to say it"). In a Spoken Dialogue System (SDS), an abstract communicative goal (CG) can be generated in many different ways. For example, the CG to present database results to the user can be realized as a summary (Polifroni and Walker, 2008; Demberg and Moore, 2006), or by comparing items (Walker et al., 2004), or by picking one item and recommending it to the user (Young et al., 2007).

Previous work has shown that it is useful to adapt the generated output to certain features of the dialogue context, for example user preferences, e.g. (Walker et al., 2004; Demberg and Moore, 2006), user knowledge, e.g. (Janarthanam and Lemon, 2008), or predicted TTS quality, e.g. (Nakatsu and White, 2006).

In extending this previous work we treat NLG as a statistical sequential planning problem, analogously to current statistical approaches to Dialogue Management (DM), e.g. (Singh et al., 2002; Henderson et al., 2008; Rieser and Lemon, 2008a) and "conversation as action under uncertainty" (Paek and Horvitz, 2000). In NLG we have similar trade-offs and unpredictability as in DM, and in some systems the content planning and DM tasks are overlapping. Clearly, very long system utterances with many actions in them are to be avoided, because users may become confused or impatient, but each individual NLG action will convey some (potentially) useful information to the user. There is therefore an optimization problem to be solved. Moreover, the user judgements or next (most likely) action after each NLG action are unpredictable, and the behaviour of the surface realizer may also be variable (see Section 6.2).

NLG could therefore fruitfully be approached as a sequential statistical planning task, where there are trade-offs and decisions to make, such as whether to choose another NLG action (and which one to choose) or to instead stop generating. Reinforcement Learning (RL) allows us to optimize such trade-offs in the presence of uncertainty, i.e. the chances of achieving a better state, while engaging in the risk of choosing another action.

In this paper we present and evaluate a new model for NLG in Spoken Dialogue Systems as planning under uncertainty. In Section 2 we argue for applying RL to NLG problems and explain the overall framework. In Section 3 we discuss challenges for NLG for Information Presentation. In Section 4 we present results from our analysis of the MATCH corpus (Walker et al., 2004). In Section 5 we present a detailed example of our proposed NLG method. In Section 6 we report on experimental results using this framework for exploring Information Presentation policies. In Section 7 we conclude and discuss future directions.

Proceedings of the 12th Conference of the European Chapter of the ACL, pages 683–691,
Athens, Greece, 30 March – 3 April 2009. ©2009 Association for Computational Linguistics

2 NLG as planning under uncertainty

We adopt the general framework of NLG as planning under uncertainty (see (Lemon, 2008) for the initial version of this approach). Some aspects of NLG have been treated as planning, e.g. (Koller and Stone, 2007; Koller and Petrick, 2008), but never before as statistical planning.

NLG actions take place in a stochastic environment, for example consisting of a user, a realizer, and a TTS system, where the individual NLG actions have uncertain effects on the environment. For example, presenting differing numbers of attributes to the user, and making the user more or less likely to choose an item, as shown by (Rieser and Lemon, 2008b) for multimodal interaction.

Most SDS employ fixed template-based generation. Our goal, however, is to employ a stochastic realizer for SDS, see for example (Stent et al., 2004). This will introduce additional noise, which higher level NLG decisions will need to react to. In our framework, the NLG component must achieve a high-level Communicative Goal from the Dialogue Manager (e.g. to present a number of items) through planning a sequence of lower-level generation steps or actions, for example first to summarize all the items and then to recommend the highest ranking one. Each such action has unpredictable effects due to the stochastic realizer. For example the realizer might employ 6 attributes when recommending item i_4, but it might use only 2 (e.g. price and cuisine for restaurants), depending on its own processing constraints (see e.g. the realizer used to collect the MATCH project data). Likewise, the user may be likely to choose an item after hearing a summary, or they may wish to hear more. Generating appropriate language in context (e.g. attributes presented so far) thus has the following important features in general:

- NLG is *goal driven* behaviour
- NLG must plan a *sequence* of actions
- each action *changes* the environment state or context
- the effect of each action is *uncertain*.

These facts make it clear that the problem of planning how to generate an utterance falls naturally into the class of statistical planning problems, rather than rule-based approaches such as (Moore et al., 2004; Walker et al., 2004), or supervised learning as explored in previous work, such as classifier learning and re-ranking, e.g. (Stent et al., 2004; Oh and Rudnicky, 2002). Supervised approaches involve the ranking of a set of completed plans/utterances and as such cannot adapt online to the context or the user. Reinforcement Learning (RL) provides a principled, data-driven optimisation framework for our type of planning problem (Sutton and Barto, 1998).

3 The Information Presentation Problem

We will tackle the well-studied problem of Information Presentation in NLG to show the benefits of this approach. The task here is to find the best way to present a set of search results to a user (e.g. some restaurants meeting a certain set of constraints). This is a task common to much prior work in NLG, e.g. (Walker et al., 2004; Demberg and Moore, 2006; Polifroni and Walker, 2008).

In this problem, there there are many decisions available for exploration. For instance, which presentation strategy to apply (*NLG strategy selection*), how many attributes of each item to present (*attribute selection*), how to rank the items and attributes according to different models of user preferences (*attribute ordering*), how many (specific) items to tell them about (*conciseness*), how many sentences to use when doing so (*syntactic planning*), and which words to use (*lexical choice*) etc. All these parameters (and potentially many more) can be varied, and ideally, jointly optimised based on user judgements.

We had two corpora available to study some of the regions of this decision space. We utilise the MATCH corpus (Walker et al., 2004) to extract an evaluation function (also known as "reward function") for RL. Furthermore, we utilise the SPaRKy corpus (Stent et al., 2004) to build a high quality stochastic realizer. Both corpora contain data from "overhearer" experiments targeted to Information Presentation in dialogues in the restaurant domain. While we are ultimately interested in how hearers *engaged* in dialogues judge different Information Presentations, results from overhearers are still directly relevant to the task.

4 MATCH corpus analysis

The MATCH project made two data sets available, see (Stent et al., 2002) and (Whittaker et al., 2003), which we combine to define an evaluation function for different Information Presentation strategies.

strategy	example	$av.\#attr$	$av.\#sentence$
SUMMARY	*"The 4 restaurants differ in food quality, and cost."* ($\#attr = 2, \#sentence = 1$)	2.07±.63	1.56±.5
COMPARE	*"Among the selected restaurants, the following offer exceptional overall value. Aureole's price is 71 dollars. It has superb food quality, superb service and superb decor. Daniel's price is 82 dollars. It has superb food quality, superb service and superb decor."* ($\#attr = 4, \#sentence = 5$)	3.2±1.5	5.5±3.11
RECOMMEND	*"Le Madeleine has the best overall value among the selected restaurants. Le Madeleine's price is 40 dollars and It has very good food quality. It's in Midtown West. "* ($\#attr = 3, \#sentence = 3$)	2.4±.7	3.5±.53

Table 1: NLG strategies present in the MATCH corpus with average no. attributes and sentences as found in the data.

The first data set, see (Stent et al., 2002), comprises 1024 ratings by 16 subjects (where we only use the speech-based half, $n = 512$) on the following presentation strategies: RECOMMEND, COMPARE, SUMMARY. These strategies are realized using templates as in Table 2, and varying numbers of attributes. In this study the users rate the individual presentation strategies as significantly different ($F(2) = 1361, p < .001$). We find that SUMMARY is rated significantly worse ($p = .05$ with Bonferroni correction) than RECOMMEND and COMPARE, which are rated as equally good.

This suggests that one should never generate a SUMMARY. However, SUMMARY has different qualities from COMPARE and RECOMMEND, as it gives users a general overview of the domain, and probably helps the user to feel more confident when choosing an item, especially when they are unfamiliar with the domain, as shown by (Polifroni and Walker, 2008).

In order to further describe the strategies, we extracted different surface features as present in the data (e.g. number of attributes realised, number of sentences, number of words, number of database items talked about, etc.) and performed a stepwise linear regression to find the features which were important to the overhearers (following the PARADISE framework (Walker et al., 2000)). We discovered a trade-off between the *length* of the utterance ($\#sentence$) and the number of attributes realised ($\#attr$), i.e. its *informativeness*, where overhearers like to hear as many attributes as possible in the most concise way, as indicated by the regression model shown in Equation 1 ($R^2 = .34$). [1]

$$score = .775 \times \#attr + (-.301) \times \#sentence; \quad (1)$$

The second MATCH data set, see (Whittaker et al., 2003), comprises 1224 ratings by 17 subjects on the NLG strategies RECOMMEND and COMPARE. The strategies realise varying numbers of attributes according to different "conciseness" values: `concise` (1 or 2 attributes), `average` (3 or 4), and `verbose` (4,5, or 6). Overhearers rate all conciseness levels as significantly different ($F(2) = 198.3, p < .001$), with `verbose` rated highest and `concise` rated lowest, supporting our findings in the first data set. However, the relation between number of attributes and user ratings is not strictly linear: ratings drop for $\#attr = 6$. This suggests that there is an upper limit on how many attributes users like to hear. We expect this to be especially true for real users engaged in actual dialogue interaction, see (Winterboer et al., 2007). We therefore include "cognitive load" as a variable when training the policy (see Section 6).

In addition to the trade-off between *length* and *informativeness* for single NLG strategies, we are interested whether this trade-off will also hold for generating *sequences* of NLG actions. (Whittaker et al., 2002), for example, generate a *combined strategy* where first a SUMMARY is used to describe the retrieved subset and then they RECOMMEND one specific item/restaurant. For example *"The 4 restaurants are all French, but differ in*

[1] For comparison: (Walker et al., 2000) report on R^2 between .4 and .5 on a slightly lager data set.

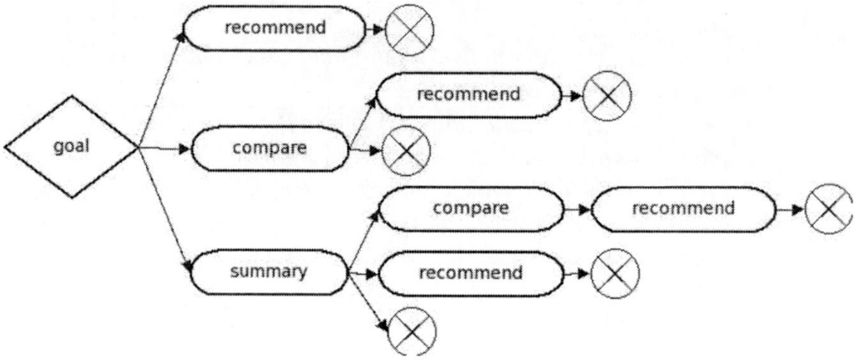

Figure 1: Possible NLG policies (X=stop generation)

food quality, and cost. Le Madeleine has the best overall value among the selected restaurants. Le Madeleine's price is 40 dollars and It has very good food quality. It's in Midtown West."

We therefore extend the set of possible strategies present in the data for exploration: we allow ordered combinations of the strategies, assuming that only COMPARE or RECOMMEND can follow a SUMMARY, and that only RECOMMEND can follow COMPARE, resulting in 7 possible actions:

1. RECOMMEND
2. COMPARE
3. SUMMARY
4. COMPARE+RECOMMEND
5. SUMMARY+RECOMMEND
6. SUMMARY+COMPARE
7. SUMMARY+COMPARE+RECOMMEND

We then analytically solved the regression model in Equation 1 for the 7 possible strategies using average values from the MATCH data. This is solved by a system of linear inequalities. According to this model, the best ranking strategy is to do all the presentation strategies in one sequence, i.e. SUMMARY+COMPARE+RECOMMEND. However, this analytic solution assumes a "one-shot" generation strategy where there is no intermediate feedback from the environment: users are simply static overhearers (they cannot "barge-in" for example), there is no variation in the behaviour of the surface realizer, i.e. one would use fixed templates as in MATCH, and the user has unlimited cognitive capabilities. These assumptions are not realistic, and must be relaxed. In the next Section we describe a worked through example of the overall framework.

5 Method: the RL-NLG model

For the reasons discussed above, we treat the NLG module as a statistical planner, operating in a stochastic environment, and optimise it using Reinforcement Learning. The input to the module is a Communicative Goal supplied by the Dialogue Manager. The CG consists of a Dialogue Act to be generated, for example `present_items`(i_1, i_2, i_5, i_8), and a System Goal (`SysGoal`) which is the desired user reaction, e.g. to make the user choose one of the presented items (`user_choose_one_of`(i_1, i_2, i_5, i_8)). The RL-NLG module must plan a sequence of lower-level NLG actions that achieve the goal (at lowest cost) in the current context. The context consists of a user (who may remain silent, supply more constraints, choose an item, or quit), and variation from the sentence realizer described above.

Now let us walk-through one simple utterance plan as carried out by this model, as shown in Table 2. Here, we start with the CG `present_items`(i_1, i_2, i_5, i_8) & `user_choose_one_of`(i_1, i_2, i_5, i_8) from the system's DM. This initialises the NLG state ($init$). The policy chooses the action SUMMARY and this transitions us to state $s1$, where we observe that 4 attributes and 1 sentence have been generated, and the user is predicted to remain silent. In this state, the current NLG policy is to RECOMMEND the top ranked item (i_5, for this user), which takes us to state $s2$, where 8 attributes have been generated in a total of 4 sentences, and the user chooses an item. The policy holds that in states like $s2$ the

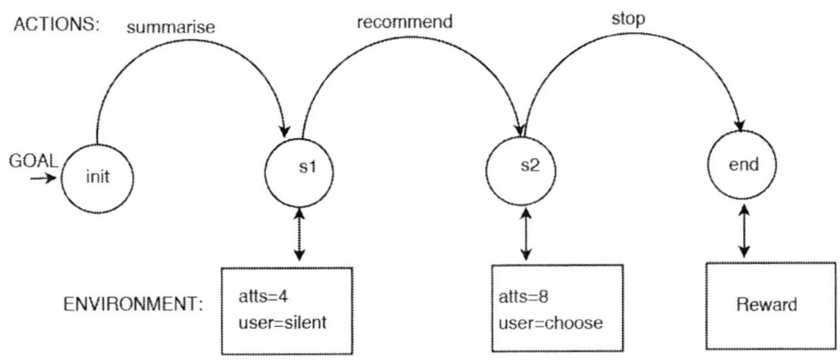

Figure 2: Example RL-NLG action sequence for Table 4

State	Action	State change/effect
init	SysGoal: `present_items` (i_1, i_2, i_5, i_8) & `user_choose_one_of` (i_1, i_2, i_5, i_8)	initialise state
s1	RL-NLG: SUMMARY(i_1, i_2, i_5, i_8)	att=4, sent=1, user=silent
s2	RL-NLG: RECOMMEND(i_5)	att=8, sent=4, user=choose(i_5)
end	RL-NLG: stop	calculate Reward

Table 2: Example utterance planning sequence for Figure 2

best thing to do is "stop" and pass the turn to the user. This takes us to the state *end*, where the total reward of this action sequence is computed (see Section 6.3), and used to update the NLG policy in each of the visited state-action pairs via back-propagation.

6 Experiments

We now report on a proof-of-concept study where we train our policy in a simulated learning environment based on the results from the MATCH corpus analysis in Section 4. Simulation-based RL allows to explore unseen actions which are not in the data, and thus less initial data is needed (Rieser and Lemon, 2008b). Note, that we cannot directly learn from the MATCH data, as therefore we would need data from an interactive dialogue. We are currently collecting such data in a Wizard-of-Oz experiment.

6.1 User simulation

User simulations are commonly used to train strategies for Dialogue Management, see for example (Young et al., 2007). A user simulation for NLG is very similar, in that it is a predictive model of the most likely next user act. However, this user act does not actually change the overall dialogue state (e.g. by filling slots) but it only changes the generator state. In other words, the NLG user simulation tells us what the user is most likely to do next, *if we were to stop generating now.* It also tells us the probability whether the user chooses to "barge-in" after a system NLG action (by either choosing an item or providing more information).

The user simulation for this study is a simple bi-gram model, which relates the number of attributes presented to the next likely user actions, see Table 3. The user can either follow the goal provided by the DM (`SysGoal`), for example choosing an item. The user can also do something else (`userElse`), e.g. providing another constraint, or the user can quit (`userQuit`).

For simplification, we discretise the number of attributes into `concise-average-verbose`, reflecting the conciseness values from the MATCH data, as described in Section 4. In addition, we assume that the user's cognitive abilities are limited ("cognitive load"), based on the results from the second MATCH data set in Section 4. Once the number of attributes is more than the "magic number 7" (reflecting psychological results on short-term memory) (Baddeley, 2001)) the user is more likely to become confused and quit.

The probabilities in Table 3 are currently manually set heuristics. We are currently conducting a Wizard-of-Oz study in order to learn these probabilities (and other user parameters) from real data.

	SysGoal	userElse	userQuit
concise	20.0	60.0	20.0
average	60.0	20.0	20.0
verbose	20.0	20.0	60.0

Table 3: NLG bi-gram user simulation

6.2 Realizer model

The sequential NLG model assumes a realizer, which updates the context after each generation step (i.e. after each single action). We estimate the realiser's parameters from the mean values we found in the MATCH data (see Table 1). For this study we first (randomly) vary the number of attributes, whereas the number of sentences is fixed (see Table 4). In current work we replace the realizer model with an implemented generator that replicates the variation found in the SPaRKy realizer (Stent et al., 2004).

	$\#attr$	$\#sentence$
SUMMARY	1 or 2	2
COMPARE	3 or 4	6
RECOMMEND	2 or 3	3

Table 4: Realizer parameters

6.3 Reward function

The reward function defines the final goal of the utterance generation sequence. In this experiment the reward is a function of the various data-driven trade-offs as identified in the data analysis in Section 4: utterance length and number of provided attributes, as weighted by the regression model in Equation 1, as well as the next predicted user action. Since we currently only have overhearer data, we manually estimate the reward for the next most likely user act, to supplement the data-driven model. If in the *end* state the next most likely user act is `userQuit`, the learner gets a penalty of -100, `userElse` receives 0 reward, and `SysGoal` gains $+100$ reward. Again, these hand coded scores need to be refined by a more targeted data collection, but the other components of the reward function are data-driven.

Note that RL learns to "make compromises" with respect to the different trade-offs. For example, the user is less likely to choose an item if there are more than 7 attributes, but the realizer can generate 9 attributes. However, in some contexts it might be desirable to generate all 9 attributes, e.g. if the generated utterance is short. Threshold-based approaches, in contrast, cannot (easily) reason with respect to the current content.

6.4 State and Action Space

We now formulate the problem as a Markov Decision Process (MDP), relating states to actions. Each state-action pair is associated with a *transition probability*, which is the probability of moving from state s at time t to state s' at time $t+1$ after having performed action a when in state s. This transition probability is computed by the environment model (i.e. user and realizer), and explicitly captures noise/uncertainty in the environment. This is a major difference to other non-statistical planning approaches. Each transition is also associated with a reinforcement signal (or reward) r_{t+1} describing how good the result of action a was when performed in state s.

The state space comprises 9 binary features representing the number of attributes, 2 binary features representing the predicted user's next action to follow the system goal or quit, as well as a discrete feature reflecting the number of sentences generated so far, as shown in Figure 3. This results in $2^{11} \times 6 = 12,288$ distinct generation states. We trained the policy using the well known SARSA algorithm, using linear function approximation (Sutton and Barto, 1998). The policy was trained for 3600 simulated NLG sequences.

In future work we plan to learn lower level decisions, such as lexical adaptation based on the vocabulary used by the user.

6.5 Baselines

We derive the baseline policies from Information Presentation strategies as deployed by current dialogue systems. In total we utilise 7 different baselines (B1-B7), which correspond to single branches in our policy space (see Figure 1):

B1: RECOMMEND only, e.g. (Young et al., 2007)

B2: COMPARE only, e.g. (Henderson et al., 2008)

B3: SUMMARY only, e.g. (Polifroni and Walker, 2008)

B4: SUMMARY followed by RECOMMEND, e.g. (Whittaker et al., 2002)

B5: Randomly choosing between COMPARE and RECOMMEND, e.g. (Walker et al., 2007)

$$
\left[action: \begin{bmatrix} \text{SUMMARY} \\ \text{COMPARE} \\ \text{RECOMMEND} \\ \texttt{end} \end{bmatrix} state: \begin{bmatrix} \texttt{attributes |1|-|9|:} \{\texttt{0,1}\} \\ \texttt{sentence:} \{\texttt{1-11}\} \\ \texttt{userGoal:} \{\texttt{0,1}\} \\ \texttt{userQuit:} \{\texttt{0,1}\} \end{bmatrix} \right]
$$

Figure 3: State-Action space for RL-NLG

B6: Randomly choosing between all 7 outputs

B7: Always generating whole sequence, i.e. SUMMARY+COMPARE+RECOMMEND, as suggested by the analytic solution (see Section 4).

6.6 Results

We analyse the test runs (n=200) using an ANOVA with a PostHoc T-Test (with Bonferroni correction). RL significantly ($p < .001$) outperforms all baselines in terms of final reward, see Table 5. RL is the only policy which significantly improves the next most likely user action by adapting to features in the current context. In contrast to conventional approaches, RL learns to 'control' its environment according to the estimated transition probabilities and the associated rewards.

The learnt policy can be described as follows: It either starts with SUMMARY or COMPARE after the *init* state, i.e. it learnt to never start with a RECOMMEND. It stops generating after COMPARE if the `userGoal` is (probably) reached (e.g. the user is most likely to choose an item in the next turn, which depends on the number of attributes generated), otherwise it goes on and generates a RECOMMEND. If it starts with SUMMARY, it always generates a COMPARE afterwards. Again, it stops if the `userGoal` is (probably) reached, otherwise it generates the full sequence (which corresponds to the analytic solution B7).

The analytic solution B7 performs second best, and significantly outperforms all the other baselines ($p < .01$). Still, it is significantly worse ($p < .001$) than the learnt policy as this 'one-shot-strategy' cannot robustly and dynamically adopt to noise or changes in the environment.

In general, generating sequences of NLG actions rates higher than generating single actions only: B4 and B6 rate directly after RL and B7, while B1, B2, B3, B5 are all equally bad given our data-driven definition of reward and environment. Furthermore, the simulated environment allows us to replicate the results in the MATCH corpus (see Section 4) when only comparing single strategies: SUMMARY performs significantly worse, while RECOMMEND and COMPARE perform equally well.

policy	reward	($\pm$*std*)
B1	99.1	($\pm$129.6)
B2	90.9	($\pm$142.2)
B3	65.5	($\pm$137.3)
B4	176.0	($\pm$154.1)
B5	95.9	($\pm$144.9)
B6	168.8	($\pm$165.3)
B7	229.3	($\pm$157.1)
RL	310.8	($\pm$136.1)

Table 5: Evaluation Results ($p < .001$)

7 Conclusion

We presented and evaluated a new model for Natural Language Generation (NLG) in Spoken Dialogue Systems, based on statistical planning. After motivating and presenting the model, we studied its use in Information Presentation.

We derived a data-driven model predicting users' judgements to different information presentation actions (reward function), via a regression analysis on MATCH data. We used this regression model to set weights in a reward function for Reinforcement Learning, and so optimize a context-adaptive presentation policy. The learnt policy was compared to several baselines derived from previous work in this area, where the learnt policy significantly outperforms all the baselines.

There are many possible extensions to this model, e.g. using the same techniques to jointly optimise choosing the number of attributes, aggregation, word choice, referring expressions, and so on, in a hierarchical manner.

We are currently collecting data in targeted Wizard-of-Oz experiments, to derive a fully data-driven training environment and test the learnt policy with real users, following (Rieser and Lemon, 2008b). The trained NLG strategy will also be integrated in an end-to-end statistical system within the CLASSiC project (`www.classic-project.org`).

Acknowledgments

The research leading to these results has received funding from the European Community's Seventh Framework Programme (FP7/2007-2013) under grant agreement no. 216594 (CLASSiC project project: `www.classic-project.org`) and from the EPSRC project no. EP/E019501/1.

References

A. Baddeley. 2001. Working memory and language: an overview. *Journal of Communication Disorder*, 36(3):189–208.

Vera Demberg and Johanna D. Moore. 2006. Information presentation in spoken dialogue systems. In *Proceedings of EACL.*

James Henderson, Oliver Lemon, and Kallirroi Georgila. 2008. Hybrid reinforcement / supervised learning of dialogue policies from fixed datasets. *Computational Linguistics (to appear).*

Srinivasan Janarthanam and Oliver Lemon. 2008. User simulations for online adaptation and knowledge-alignment in Troubleshooting dialogue systems. In *Proc. of SEMdial.*

Alexander Koller and Ronald Petrick. 2008. Experiences with planning for natural language generation. In *ICAPS.*

Alexander Koller and Matthew Stone. 2007. Sentence generation as planning. In *Proceedings of ACL.*

Oliver Lemon. 2008. Adaptive Natural Language Generation in Dialogue using Reinforcement Learning. In *Proceedings of SEMdial.*

Johanna Moore, Mary Ellen Foster, Oliver Lemon, and Michael White. 2004. Generating tailored, comparative descriptions in spoken dialogue. In *Proc. FLAIRS.*

Crystal Nakatsu and Michael White. 2006. Learning to say it well: Reranking realizations by predicted synthesis quality. In *Proceedings of ACL.*

Alice Oh and Alexander Rudnicky. 2002. Stochastic natural language generation for spoken dialog systems. *Computer, Speech & Language*, 16(3/4):387–407.

Tim Paek and Eric Horvitz. 2000. Conversation as action under uncertainty. In *Proc. of the 16th Conference on Uncertainty in Artificial Intelligence.*

Joseph Polifroni and Marilyn Walker. 2008. Intensional Summaries as Cooperative Responses in Dialogue Automation and Evaluation. In *Proceedings of ACL.*

Verena Rieser and Oliver Lemon. 2008a. Does this list contain what you were searching for? Learning adaptive dialogue strategies for Interactive Question Answering. *J. Natural Language Engineering*, 15(1):55–72.

Verena Rieser and Oliver Lemon. 2008b. Learning Effective Multimodal Dialogue Strategies from Wizard-of-Oz data: Bootstrapping and Evaluation. In *Proceedings of ACL.*

S. Singh, D. Litman, M. Kearns, and M. Walker. 2002. Optimizing dialogue management with Reinforcement Learning: Experiments with the NJFun system. *JAIR*, 16:105–133.

Amanda Stent, Marilyn Walker, Steve Whittaker, and Preetam Maloor. 2002. User-tailored generation for spoken dialogue: an experiment. In *In Proc. of ICSLP.*

Amanda Stent, Rashmi Prasad, and Marilyn Walker. 2004. Trainable sentence planning for complex information presentation in spoken dialog systems. In *Association for Computational Linguistics.*

R. Sutton and A. Barto. 1998. *Reinforcement Learning.* MIT Press.

Marilyn A. Walker, Candace A. Kamm, and Diane J. Litman. 2000. Towards developing general models of usability with PARADISE. *Natural Language Engineering*, 6(3).

Marilyn Walker, S. Whittaker, A. Stent, P. Maloor, J. Moore, M. Johnston, and G. Vasireddy. 2004. User tailored generation in the match multimodal dialogue system. *Cognitive Science*, 28:811–840.

Marilyn Walker, Amanda Stent, François Mairesse, and Rashmi Prasad. 2007. Individual and domain adaptation in sentence planning for dialogue. *Journal of Artificial Intelligence Research (JAIR)*, 30:413–456.

Steve Whittaker, Marilyn Walker, and Johanna Moore. 2002. Fish or Fowl: A Wizard of Oz evaluation of dialogue strategies in the restaurant domain. In *Proc. of the International Conference on Language Resources and Evaluation (LREC).*

Stephen Whittaker, Marilyn Walker, and Preetam Maloor. 2003. Should i tell all? an experiment on conciseness in spoken dialogue. In *Proc. European Conference on Speech Processing (EUROSPEECH).*

Andi Winterboer, Jiang Hu, Johanna D. Moore, and Clifford Nass. 2007. The influence of user tailoring and cognitive load on user performance in spoken dialogue systems. In *Proc. of the 10th International Conference of Spoken Language Processing (Interspeech/ICSLP)*.

SJ Young, J Schatzmann, K Weilhammer, and H Ye. 2007. The Hidden Information State Approach to Dialog Management. In *ICASSP 2007*.

Tagging Urdu Text with Parts of Speech: A Tagger Comparison

Hassan Sajjad
Universität Stuttgart
Stuttgart. Germany
sajjad@ims.uni-stuttgart.de

Helmut Schmid
Universität Stuttgart
Stuttgart, Germany
schmid@ims.uni-stuttgart.de

Abstract

In this paper, four state-of-art probabilistic taggers i.e. TnT tagger, TreeTagger, RF tagger and SVM tool, are applied to the Urdu language. For the purpose of the experiment, a syntactic tagset is proposed. A training corpus of 100,000 tokens is used to train the models. Using the lexicon extracted from the training corpus, SVM tool shows the best accuracy of 94.15%. After providing a separate lexicon of 70,568 types, SVM tool again shows the best accuracy of 95.66%.

1 Urdu Language

Urdu belongs to the Indo-Aryan language family. It is the national language of Pakistan and is one of the official languages of India. The majority of the speakers of Urdu spread over the area of South Asia, South Africa and the United Kingdom[1].

Urdu is a free order language with general word order SOV. It shares its phonological, morphological and syntactic structures with Hindi. Some linguists considered them as two different dialects of one language (Bhatia and Koul, 2000). However, Urdu is written in Perso-arabic script and inherits most of the vocabulary from Arabic and Persian. On the other hand, Hindi is written in Devanagari script and inherits vocabulary from Sanskrit.

Urdu is a morphologically rich language. Forms of the verb, as well as case, gender, and number are expressed by the morphology. Urdu represents case with a separate character after the head noun of the noun phrase. Due to their separate occurrence and their place of occurrence, they are sometimes considered as postpositions. Considering them as case markers, Urdu has nominative, ergative, accusative, dative, instrumental, genitive and locative cases (Butt, 1995: pg 10). The Urdu verb phrase contains a main verb, a light verb describing the aspect, and a tense verb describing the tense of the phrase (Hardie, 2003; Hardie, 2003a).

2 Urdu Tagset

There are various questions that need to be answered during the design of a tagset. The granularity of the tagset is the first problem in this regard. A tagset may consist either of general parts of speech only or it may consist of additional morpho-syntactic categories such as number, gender and case. In order to facilitate the tagger training and to reduce the lexical and syntactic ambiguity, we decided to concentrate on the syntactic categories of the language. Purely syntactic categories lead to a smaller number of tags which also improves the accuracy of manual tagging[2] (Marcus *et al.*, 1993).

Urdu is influenced from Arabic, and can be considered as having three main parts of speech, namely noun, verb and particle (Platts, 1909; Javed, 1981; Haq, 1987). However, some grammarians proposed ten main parts of speech for Urdu (Schmidt, 1999). The work of Urdu grammar writers provides a full overview of all the features of the language. However, in the perspective of the tagset, their analysis is lacking the computational grounds. The semantic, morphological and syntactic categories are mixed in their distribution of parts of speech. For example, Haq (1987) divides the common nouns into situational (smile, sadness, darkness), locative (park, office, morning, evening), instrumental (knife, sword) and collective nouns (army, data).

In 2003, Hardie proposed the first computational part of speech tagset for Urdu (Hardie,

[1] http://www.ethnologue.com/14/show_language.asp?code=URD

[2] A part of speech tagger for Indian languages, available at http://shiva.iiit.ac.in/SPSAL2007 /iiit_tagset_guidelines.pdf

Proceedings of the 12th Conference of the European Chapter of the ACL, pages 692–700,
Athens, Greece, 30 March – 3 April 2009.

2003a). It is a morpho-syntactic tagset based on the EAGLES guidelines. The tagset contains 350 different tags with information about number, gender, case, etc. (van Halteren, 2005). The EAGLES guidelines are based on three levels, major word classes, recommended attributes and optional attributes. Major word classes include thirteen tags: noun, verb, adjective, pronoun/determiner, article, adverb, adposition, conjunction, numeral, interjection, unassigned, residual and punctuation. The recommended attributes include number, gender, case, finiteness, voice, etc.[3] In this paper, we will focus on purely syntactic distributions thus will not go into the details of the recommended attributes of the EAGLES guidelines. Considering the EAGLES guidelines and the tagset of Hardie in comparison with the general parts of speech of Urdu, there are no articles in Urdu. Due to the phrase level and semantic differences, pronoun and demonstrative are separate parts of speech in Urdu. In the Hardie tagset, the possessive pronouns like میرا /mera/ (my), تمہارا /tumhara/ (your), ہمارا /humara/ (our) are assigned to the category of possessive adjective. Most of the Urdu grammarians consider them as pronouns (Platts, 1909; Javed, 1981; Haq, 1987). However, all these possessive pronouns require a noun in their noun phrase, thus show a similar behavior as demonstratives. The locative and temporal adverbs (یہاں /yahan/ (here), وہاں /wahan/ (there), اب /ab/ (now), etc.) and, the locative and temporal nouns (صبح /subah/ (morning), شام /sham/ (evening), گھر /gher/ (home)) appear in a very similar syntactic context. In order to keep the structure of pronoun and noun consistent, locative and temporal adverbs are treated as pronouns. The tense and aspect of a verb in Urdu is represented by a sequence of auxiliaries. Consider the example[4]:

ہے	رہا	جا	کرتا	کام	جان
Hai	raha	Ja	kerta	kam	Jan
Is	Doing		Kept	Work	John
John is kept on doing work					

"Table 1: The aspect of the verb کرتا /kerta/ (doing) is represented by two separate words جا /ja/ and رہا /raha/ and the last word of the sentence ہے /hai/ (is) shows the tense of the verb."

[3] The details on the EAGLES guidelines can be found at: http://www.ilc.cnr.it/EAGLES/browse.html

[4] Urdu is written in right to left direction.

The above considerations lead to the following tagset design for Urdu. The general parts of speech are noun, pronoun, demonstrative, verb, adjective, adverb, conjunction, particle, number and punctuation. The further refinement of the tagset is based on syntactic properties. The morphologically motivated features of the language are not encoded in the tagset. For example, an Urdu verb has 60 forms which are morphologically derived from its root form. All these forms are annotated with the same category i.e. verb.

During manual tagging, some words are hard for the linguist to disambiguate reliably. In order to keep the training data consistent, such words are assigned a separate tag. For instance, the semantic marker سے /se/ gets a separate tag due to its various confusing usages such as locative and instrumental (Platts, 1909).

The tagset used in the experiments reported in this paper contains 42 tags including three special tags. Nouns are divided into noun (NN) and proper name (PN). Demonstratives are divided into personal (PD), KAF (KD), adverbial (AD) and relative demonstratives (RD). All four categories of demonstratives are ambiguous with four categories of pronouns. Pronouns are divided into six types i.e. personal (PP), reflexive (RP), relative (REP), adverbial (AP), KAF (KP) and adverbial KAF (AKP) pronouns. Based on phrase level differences, genitive reflexive (GR) and genitive (G) are kept separate from pronouns. The verb phrase is divided into verb, aspectual auxiliaries and tense auxiliaries. Numerals are divided into cardinal (CA), ordinal (OR), fractional (FR) and multiplicative (MUL). Conjunctions are divided into coordinating (CC) and subordinating (SC) conjunctions. All semantic markers except سے /se/ are kept in one category. Adjective (ADJ), adverb (ADV), quantifier (Q), measuring unit (U), intensifier (I), interjection (INT), negation (NEG) and question words (QW) are handled as separate categories. Adjectival particle (A), KER (KER), SE (SE) and WALA (WALA) are ambiguous entities which are annotated with separate tags. A complete list of the tags with the examples is given in appendix A. The examples of the weird categories such as WALA, KAF pronoun, KAF demonstratives, etc. are given in appendix B.

3 Tagging Methodologies

The work on automatic part of speech tagging started in early 1960s. Klein and Simmons

(1963) rule based POS tagger can be considered as the first automatic tagging system. In the rule based approach, after assigning each word its potential tags, a list of hand written disambiguation rules are used to reduce the number of tags to one (Klein and Simmons, 1963; Green and Rubin, 1971; Hindle, 1989; Chanod and Tapanainen 1994). A rule based model has the disadvantage of requiring lots of linguistic efforts to write rules for the language.

Data-driven approaches resolve this problem by automatically extracting the information from an already tagged corpus. Ambiguity between the tags is resolved by selecting the most likely tag for a word (Bahl and Mercer, 1976; Church, 1988; Brill, 1992). Brill's transformation based tagger uses lexical rules to assign each word the most frequent tag and then applies contextual rules over and over again to get a high accuracy. However, Brill's tagger requires training on a large number of rules which reduces the efficiency of machine learning process. Statistical approaches usually achieve an accuracy of 96%-97% (Hardie, 2003: 295). However, statistical taggers require a large training corpus to avoid data sparseness. The problem of low frequencies can be resolved by applying different methods such as smoothing, decision trees, etc. In the next section, an overview of the statistical taggers is provided which are evaluated on the Urdu tagset.

3.1 Probabilistic Disambiguation

The Hidden Markov model is the most widely used method for statistical part of speech tagging. Each tag is considered as a state. States are connected by transition probabilities which represent the cost of moving from one state to another. The probability of a word having a particular tag is called lexical probability. Both, the transitional and the lexical probabilities are used to select the tag of a particular word.

As a standard HMM tagger, The TnT tagger is used for the experiments. The TnT tagger is a trigram HMM tagger in which the transition probability depends on two preceding tags. The performance of the tagger was tested on NEGRA corpus and Penn Treebank corpus. The average accuracy of the tagger is 96% to 97% (Brants, 2000).

The second order Markov model used by the TnT tagger requires large amounts of tagged data to get reasonable frequencies of POS trigrams. The TnT tagger smooths the probability with linear interpolation to handle the problem of data sparseness. The Tags of unknown words are predicted based on the word suffix. The longest ending string of an unknown word having one or more occurrences in the training corpus is considered as a suffix. The tag probabilities of a suffix are evaluated from all the words in the training corpus (Brants, 2000).

In 1994, Schmid proposed a probabilistic part of speech tagger very similar to a HMM based tagger. The transition probabilities are calculated by decision trees. The decision tree merges infrequent trigrams with similar contexts until the trigram frequencies are large enough to get reliable estimates of the transition probabilities. The TreeTagger uses an unknown word POS guesser similar to that of the TnT tagger. The TreeTagger was trained on 2 million words of the Penn-Treebank corpus and was evaluated on 100,000 words. Its accuracy is compared against a trigram tagger built on the same data. The TreeTagger showed an accuracy of 96.06% (Schmid, 1994a).

In 2004, Giménez and Màrquez proposed a part of speech tagger (SVM tool) based on support vector machines and reported accuracy higher than all state-of-art taggers. The aim of the development was to have a simple, efficient, robust tagger with high accuracy. The support vector machine does a binary classification of the data. It constructs an N-dimensional hyperplane that separates the data into positive and negative classes. Each data element is considered as a vector. Those vectors which are close to the separating hyperplane are called support vectors[5].

A support vector machine has to be trained for each tag. The complexity is controlled by introducing a lexicon extracted from the training data. Each word tag pair in the training corpus is considered as a positive case for that tag class and all other tags in the lexicon are considered negative cases for that word. This feature avoids generating useless cases for the comparison of classes.

The SVM tool was evaluated on the English Penn Treebank. Experiments were conducted using both polynomial and linear kernels. When using n-gram features, the linear kernel showed a significant improvement in speed and accuracy. Unknown words are considered as the most ambiguous words by assigning them all open class POS tags. The disambiguation of unknowns uses features such as prefixes, suffixes,

[5] Andrew Moore: http://www.autonlab.org/tutorials/svm.html

upper case, lower case, word length, etc. On the Penn Treebank corpus, SVM tool showed an accuracy of 97.16% (Giménez and Màrquez, 2004).

In 2008, Schmid and Florian proposed a probabilistic POS tagger for fine grained tagsets. The basic idea is to consider POS tags as sets of attributes. The context probability of a tag is the product of the probabilities of its attributes. The probability of an attribute given the previous tags is estimated with a decision tree. The decision tree uses different context features for the prediction of different attributes (Schmid and Laws, 2008).

The RF tagger is well suited for languages with a rich morphology and a large fine grained tagset. The RF tagger was evaluated on the German Tiger Treebank and Czech Academic corpus which contain 700 and 1200 POS tags, respectively. The RF tagger achieved a higher accuracy than TnT and SVMTool.

Urdu is a morphologically rich language. Training a tagger on a large fine grained tagset requires a large training corpus. Therefore, the tagset which we are using for these experiments is only based on syntactic distributions. However, it is always interesting to evaluate new disambiguation ideas like RF tagger on different languages.

4 Experiments

A corpus of approx 110,000 tokens was taken from a news corpus (www.jang.com.pk). In the filtering phase, diacritics were removed from the text and normalization was applied to keep the Unicode of the characters consistent. The problem of space insertion and space deletion was manually solved and space is defined as the word boundary. The data was randomly divided into two parts, 90% training corpus and 10% test corpus. A part of the training set was also used as held out data to optimize the parameters of the taggers. The statistics of the training corpus and test corpus are shown in table 2 and table 3. The optimized parameters of the TreeTagger are context size 2, with minimum information gain for decision tree 0.1 and information gain at leaf node 1.4. For TnT, a default trigram tagger is used with suffix length of 10, sparse data mode 4 with lambda1 0.03 and lambda2 0.4. The RF tagger uses a context length of 4 with threshold of suffix tree pruning 1.5. The SVM tool is trained at right to left direction with model 4. Model 4 improves the detection of unknown words by artificially marking some known words as unknown words and then learning the model.

	Training corpus	Test corpus
Tokens	100,000	9000
Types	7514	1931
Unknown Tokens	--	754
Unknown Types	--	444

"Table 2: Statistics of training and test data."

Tag	Total	Unknown	Tag	Total	Unknown
NN	2537	458	PN	459	101
P	1216	0	AA	379	0
VB	971	81	TA	285	0
ADJ	510	68	ADV	158	21

"Table 3: Eight most frequent tags in the test corpus."

In the first experiment, no external lexicon was provided. The types from the training corpus were used as the lexicon by the tagger. SVM tool showed the best accuracy for both known and unknown words. Table 4 shows the accuracies of all the taggers. The baseline result where each word is annotated with its most frequent tag, irrespective of the context, is 88.0%.

TnT tagger	TreeTagger	RF tagger	SVM tagger
93.40%	93.02%	93.28%	94.15%
Known			
95.78%	95.60%	95.68%	96.15%
Unknown			
68.44%	65.92%	68.08%	73.21%

"Table 4: Accuracies of the taggers without using any external lexicon. SVM tool shows the best result for both known and unknown words."

The taggers show poor accuracy while detecting proper names. In most of the cases, proper name is confused with adjective and noun. This is because in Urdu, there is no clear distinction between noun and proper name. Also, the usage of an adjective as a proper name is a frequent phenomenon in Urdu. The accuracies of open class tags are shown in table 5. The detailed discussion on the results of the taggers is done after providing an external lexicon to the taggers.

Tag	TnT tagger	Tree-Tagger	RF tagger	SVM tagger
VB	93.20%	91.86%	92.68%	94.23%
NN	94.12%	96.21%	93.89%	96.45%
PN	73.20%	66.88%	72.77%	68.62%
ADV	75.94%	72.78%	74.68%	72.15%
ADJ	85.67%	80.78%	86.5%	85.88%

"Table 5: Accuracies of open class tags without having an external lexicon"

In the second stage of the experiment, a large lexicon consisting of 70,568 types was provided[6]. After adding the lexicon, there are 112 unknown tokens and 81 unknown types in the test corpus[7]. SVM tool again showed the best accuracy of 95.66%. Table 6 shows the accuracy of the taggers. The results of open class words significantly improve due to the smaller number of unknown words in the test corpus. The total accuracy of open class tags and their accuracy on unknown words are given in table 7 and table 8 respectively.

TnT tagger	Tree-Tagger	RF tagger	SVM tool
94.91%	95.17%	95.26%	95.66%
Known			
95.42%	95.65%	95.66%	96.11%
Unknown			
56.25%	58.04%	64.60%	61.61%

"Table 6: Accuracies of the taggers after adding the lexicon. SVM tool shows the best accuracy for known word disambiguation. RF tagger shows the best accuracy for unknown words."

Tag	TnT tagger	Tree-Tagger	RF tagger	SVM tool
VB	95.88%	95.88%	96.58%	96.80%
NN	94.64%	95.85%	94.79%	96.64%
PN	86.92%	79.73%	84.96%	81.70%
ADV	82.28%	79.11%	81.64%	81.01%
ADJ	91.59%	89.82%	92.37%	88.26%

"Table 7: Accuracies of open class tags after adding an external lexicon."

[6] Additional lexicon is taken from CRULP, Lahore, Pakistan (www.crulp.org).

[7] The lexicon was added by using the default settings provided by each tagger. No probability distribution information was given with the lexicon.

Tag	TnT tagger	Tree-Tagger	RF tagger	SVM tool
VB	28.57%	0.00%	42.86%	42.86%
NN	74.47%	95.74%	80.85%	80.85%
PN	68.18%	54.54%	63.63%	50.00%
ADV	8.33%	0.00%	8.33%	0.00%
ADJ	30.00%	20.00%	70.00%	80.00%

"Table 8: Accuracies of open class tags on unknown words. The number of unknown words with tag VB and ADJ are less than 10 in this experiment."

The results of the taggers are analyzed by finding the most frequently confused pairs for all the taggers. It includes both the known and unknown words. Only those pairs are added in the table which have an occurrence of more than 10. Table 9 shows the results.

Confused pair		TnT tagger	Tree-Tagger	RF tagger	SVM tool
NN	ADJ	85	87	87	95
NN	PN	118	140	129	109
NN	ADV	12	15	13	15
NN	VB	14	17	12	12
VB	TA	12	0	0	0
KER	P	14	14	14	0
ADV	ADJ	11	14	13	11
PD	PP	26	26	30	14

"Table 9: Most frequently confused tag pairs with total number of occurrences."

5 Discussion

The output of table 9 can be analyzed in many ways e.g. ambiguous tags, unknown words, open class tags, close class tags, etc. In the close class tags, the most frequent errors are between demonstrative and pronoun, and between KER tag and semantic marker (P). The difference between demonstrative and pronoun is at the phrase level. Demonstratives are followed by a noun which belongs to the same noun phrase whereas pronouns form a noun phrase by itself. Taggers analyze the language in a flat structure and are unable to handle the phrase level differences. It is interesting to see that the SVM tool shows a clear improvement in detecting the phrase level differences over the other taggers. It might be due to the SVM tool ability to look not only at the neighboring tags but at the neighboring words as well.

(a)

گے	گائیں	گانا	لوگ	وہ
Gay	gayain	Gana	log	Voh
TA	VB	NN	NN	PD
Will	sing	Song	people	Those
Those people will sing a song.				

(b)

گے	گائیں	گانا	وہ
Gay	Gayain	gana	Voh
TA	VB	NN	PP
Will	Sing	Song	those
Those will sing a song.			

"Table 10: The word وہ /voh/ is occurring both as pronoun and demonstrative. In both of the cases, it is followed by a noun. But looking at the phrases, demonstrative وہ has the noun inside the noun phrase."

The second most frequent error among the closed class tags is the distinction between the KER tag کے /kay/ and the semantic marker کے /kay/. The KER tag always takes a verb before it and the semantic marker always takes a noun before it. The ambiguity arises when a verbal noun occurs. In the tagset, verbal nouns are handled as verb. Syntactically, verbal nouns occur at the place of a noun and can also take a semantic marker after them. This decreases the accuracy in two ways; the wrong disambiguation of KER tag and the wrong disambiguation of unknown verbal nouns. Due to the small amount of training data, unknown words are frequent in the test corpus. Whenever an unknown word occurs at the place of a noun, the most probable tag for that word will be noun which is wrong in our case. Table 11 shows an example of such a scenario.

(a)

بعد	کے	کرنے	کام
baad	Kay	kernay	kam
NN	P	VB	NN
after	--	doing	work
After doing work			

(b)

کے	کر	کام
kay	ker	kam
KER	VB	NN
--	Doing	work
(After) doing work		

"Table 11: (a) Verbal noun with semantic marker, (b) syntactic structure of KER tag."[8]

All the taggers other than the SVM tool have difficulties to disambiguate between KER tags and semantic markers.

(a)

دو	خوراک	کو	لوگوں	ضرورتمند
do	khoraak	Ko	log	zarorat-mand
VB	NN	P	NN	ADJ
give	food	To	people	needy
Give food to the needy people				

(b)

دو	خوراک	کو	ضرورتمند
do	khoraak	ko	zaroratmand
VB	NN	P	NN
give	food	To	needy
Give food to the needy			

"Table 12: (a) Occurrence of adjective with noun, (b) dropping of main noun from the noun phrase. In that case, adjective becomes the noun."

Coming to open class tags, the most frequent errors are between noun and the other open class tags in the noun phrase like proper noun, adjective and adverb. In Urdu, there is no clear distinction between noun and proper noun. The phenomenon of dropping of words is also frequent in Urdu. If a noun in a noun phrase is dropped, the adjective becomes a noun in that phrase (see table 12). The ambiguity between noun and verb is due to verbal nouns as explained above (see table 11).

6 Conclusion

In this paper, probabilistic part of speech tagging technologies are tested on the Urdu language. The main goal of this work is to investigate whether general disambiguation techniques and standard POS taggers can be used for the tagging of Urdu. The results of the taggers clearly answer this question positively. With the small training corpus, all the taggers showed accuracies around 95%. The SVM tool shows the best accuracy in

[8] One possible solution to this problem could be to introduce a separate tag for verbal nouns which will certainly remove the ambiguity between the KER tag and the semantic marker and reduce the ambiguity between verb and noun.

disambiguating the known words and the RF tagger shows the best accuracy in detecting the tags of unknown words.

Appendices

Appendix A. Urdu part of speech tagset

Following is the complete list of the tags of Urdu. There are some occurrences in which two Urdu words are mapped to the same translation of English. There are two reasons for that, either the Urdu words have different case or there is no significant meaning difference between the two words which can be described by different English translations.

Tag	Example
Personal demonstrative (PD)	ہم (we) ، تم (you) ، آپ (you[9])، یہ (this)، وہ (that)، اس (that)
Relative demonstrative (RD)	جو (that) ، جن(that)، جنہوں(that)
Kaf demonstrative (KD)	کن(whose) ، کوئی (someone)
Adverbial demonstrative (AD)	اب (now) ، تب (then) ، ادھر (here) ، یہاں (here)
Noun (NN)	جہاز (ship) ، زمین (earth) ، لڑکا (boy) ، اوپر (above)، اندر (inside) ، سمیت (with) ، طرح (like)
Proper noun (PN)	جرمنی (Germany) ، پاکستان (Pakistan)
Personal pronoun (PP)	میں(I) ، ہم (we) ، تم(you) ، آپ (you) ، یہ (he) ، وہ (he)، اس(he)
Reflexive pronoun (RP)	خود (myself) ، آپ (myself)
Relative pronoun (REP)	جو(that)، جن(that)، جنہوں(that)
Adverbial pronoun (AD)	اب (now) ، تب (then) ، ادھر (here) ، یہاں (here)
Kaf pronoun (KP)	کون (who) ، کوئی (someone)، ، کن (which)
Adverbial kaf pro (AKP)	کدھر (where) ، کب (when)، کیسا (how)
Genitive reflexive (GR)	اپنا (my)
Genitives (G)	میرا (my) ، تمھارا (your) ، ہمارا (our) ، تیرا (your)
Verb (VB)	لکھنا (write) ، کھاتا (eat) ، جاتا (go) ، کرنا (do)
Aspectual auxiliary (AA)	رہا، کرنا، چکہ[10]
Tense auxiliary (TA)	ہے (is) ، ہیں (are) ، تھا (was)، تھے (were)
Adjective (ADJ)	ظالم (cruel) ، خوبصورت (beautiful)، کمزور (weak)
Adverb (ADV)	بہت (very) ، نہایت (very) ، بڑا (very)
Quantifier (Q)	کچھ (some) ،تمام (all) ، اتنے (this much) ، کل (total)
Cardinal (CA)	ایک(one) ، دو (two) ، تین (three)
Ordinal (OR)	پہلا (first) ، دوسرا (second)، آخری (last)
Fractional (FR)	چوتھائی(one fourth) ، ڈھائی (two and a half)
Multiplicative (MUL)	گنا(times) ، دگنا (two times)
Measuring unit (U)	کلو (kilo)
Coordinating (CC)	اور (and) ,یا (or)
Subordinating (SC)	کہ (that),کیونکہ (because)
Intensifier (I)	ہی، بھی، تو
Adjectival particle	سا (like)
KER	کے، کر
Pre-title (PRT)	حضرت(Mr.) ، میاں(Mr.)
Post-title (POT)	جی ، صاحب(Mr.)
Case marker (P)	کا ، کو ، کی ، کے ، نے، میں، تک تلک ، پر،
SE (SE)	سے
WALA (WALA)	والا، والی، والے
Negation (NEG)	[نہ ، نہیں(not/no)]
Interjection (INT)	واہ (hurrah), سبحان اللہ، اچھا(Good)
Question word (QW)	کیا (what) ، کیوں (why)
Sentence marker (SM)	'.', '?'
Phrase marker (PM)	',', ';'
DATE	2007, 1999
Expression (Exp): Any word or symbol which is not handled in the tagset will be catered under expression. It can be mathematical symbols, digits, etc.	

"Table 13: Tagset of Urdu"

[9] Polite form of you which is used while talking with the elders and with the strangers

[10] They always occur with a verb and can not be translated standalone.

Appendix B. Examples of WALA, Noun with locative behavior, KAF pronoun and KAF demonstrative and multiplicative.

WALA والا:

Attributive	Demonstrative	Occupation
عزت والا Respectable	یہ والا This one	دودھ والا Milk man

Manner	Possession	Time
آہستہ والا The one with the manner "slow"	کانٹوں والا پھول Flower with thorns	صبح والا اخبار Morning newspaper

Place	Doer	--
باہر والا جوتا Shoes which is bought from some other country	پڑھنے والا The one whose study	-- --

"Table 14: Examples of tag WALA"

Noun with locative behavior:

Adverb	Noun
نیچے والی دکان Down shop	نیچے سے آنا Coming from downstairs

Postposition	Noun
میز کے نیچے Under the table	نیچے جاتا Goes down

"Table 15: Examples of noun with locative behavior

Multiplicative:

وہ مجھ سے دگنا (دوگنا) موٹا ہے۔ He is two times fatter than me.

"Table 16: Example of Multiplicative

KAF pronoun and KAF demonstrative:

KAF pronoun
کن لوگوں کو آم اچھے لگتے ہیں ؟ Which people like mangoes?

KAF Demonstrative
کن کو آم اچھے لگتے ہیں ؟ Which one like mangoes?

Adverbial KAF pronoun
وہ کدھر گیا ہے ؟ Where did he go?

"Table 17: Examples of KAF pronoun and KAF demonstrative

References

Bahl, L. R. and Mercer, R. L. 1976. Part of speech assignment by a statistical decision algorithm, *IEEE International Symposium on Information Theory*, pp. 88-89.

Bhatia, TK and Koul, A. 2000. Colloquial Urdu. London: Routledge.

Brants, Thorsten. 2000. TnT – a statistical part-of-speech tagger. In *Proceedings of the Sixth Applied Natural Language Processing Conference ANLP-2000* Seattle, WA.

Brill, E. 1992. A simple rule-based part of speech tagger, Department of Computer Science, University of Pennsylvania.

Butt, M. 1995. The structure of complex predicates in Urdu. CSLI, Stanford.

Chanod, Jean-Pierre and Tapananinen, Pasi 1994. Statistical and constraint-Based taggers for French, Technical report MLTT-016, RXRC Grenoble.

Church, K. W. 1988. A stochastic parts program and noun phrase parser for unrestricted test, In the proceedings of *2nd conference on Applied Natural Language Processing*, pp. 136-143.

Giménez and Màrquez. 2004. SVMTool: A general POS tagger generator based on support vector machines. In *Proceedings of the IV International Conference on Language Resources and Evaluation (LREC' 04)*, Lisbon, Portugal.

Green, B. and Rubin, G. 1971. Automated grammatical tagging of English, Department of Linguistics, Brown University.

Haq, M. Abdul. 1987. صرف و نحو اردو, Amjuman-e-Taraqqi Urdu (Hind).

Hardie, A. 2003. Developing a tag-set for automated part-of-speech tagging in Urdu. In *Archer, D, Rayson, P, Wilson, A, and McEnery, T (eds.)* Proceedings of *the Corpus Linguistics 2003 conference. UCREL Technical Papers Volume 16.* Department of Linguistics, Lancaster University, UK.

Hardie, A. 2003a. The computational analysis of morphosyntactic categories in Urdu, PhD thesis, Lancaster University.

Hindle, D. 1989. Acquiring disambiguation rules from text, Proceedings of *27th annual meeting of Association for Computational Linguistics.*

van Halteren, H, 2005. Syntactic Word Class Tagging, Springer.

Javed, Ismat. 1981. اردو قواعد نئی, Taraqqi Urdu Bureau, New Delhi.

Klein, S. and Simmons, R.F. 1963. A computational approach to grammatical coding of English words, JACM 10: pp. 334-347.

Marcus, M. P., Santorini, B. and Marcinkiewicz, M. A. 1993. Building a large annotated corpus of English: the Penn Treebank Computational Linguistics 19, pp. 313-330

Platts, John T 1909. A grammar of the Hindustani or Urdu language, London.

Schmid, H. 1994. Probabilistic part-of-speech tagging using decision tree, Institut für Maschinelle Sprachverarbeitung, Universität Stuttgart, Germany.

Schmid, H. 1994a. Part-of-speech tagging with neural networks, In the Proceedings of *International Conference on Computational Linguistics*, pp. 172-176, Kyoto, Japan.

Schmid, H. and Laws, F. 2008. Estimation of conditional Probabilities with Decision Trees and an Application to Fine-Grained POS tagging, *COLING 2008*, Manchester, Great Britain.

Schmidt, RL 1999. Urdu: an essential grammar, London: Routledge.

Unsupervised Methods for Head Assignments

Federico Sangati, Willem Zuidema
Institute for Logic, Language and Computation
University of Amsterdam, the Netherlands
{f.sangati,zuidema}@uva.nl

Abstract

We present several algorithms for assigning heads in phrase structure trees, based on different linguistic intuitions on the role of heads in natural language syntax. Starting point of our approach is the observation that a head-annotated treebank defines a unique lexicalized tree substitution grammar. This allows us to go back and forth between the two representations, and define objective functions for the unsupervised learning of head assignments in terms of features of the implicit lexicalized tree grammars. We evaluate algorithms based on the match with gold standard head-annotations, and the comparative parsing accuracy of the lexicalized grammars they give rise to. On the first task, we approach the accuracy of hand-designed heuristics for English and inter-annotation-standard agreement for German. On the second task, the implied lexicalized grammars score 4% points higher on parsing accuracy than lexicalized grammars derived by commonly used heuristics.

1 Introduction

The *head* of a phrasal constituent is a central concept in most current grammatical theories and many syntax-based NLP techniques. The term is used to mark, for any nonterminal node in a syntactic tree, the specific daughter node that fulfills a special role; however, theories and applications differ widely in what that special role is supposed to be. In descriptive grammatical theories, the role of the head can range from the determinant of agreement or the locus of inflections, to the governor that selects the morphological form of its sister nodes or the constituent that is distributionally equivalent to its parent (Corbett et al., 2006).

In computational linguistics, heads mainly serve to select the lexical content on which the probability of a production should depend (Charniak, 1997; Collins, 1999). With the increased popularity of dependency parsing, head annotations have also become a crucial level of syntactic information for transforming constituency treebanks to dependency structures (Nivre et al., 2007) or richer syntactic representations (e.g., Hockenmaier and Steedman, 2007).

For the WSJ-section of the Penn Treebank, a set of heuristic rules for assigning heads has emerged from the work of (Magerman, 1995) and (Collins, 1999) that has been employed in a wide variety of studies and proven extremely useful, even in rather different applications from what the rules were originally intended for. However, the rules are specific to English and the treebank's syntactic annotation, and do not offer much insights into how headedness can be learned in principle or in practice. Moreover, the rules are heuristic and might still leave room for improvement with respect to recovering linguistic head assignment even on the Penn WSJ corpus; in fact, we find that the head-assignments according to the Magerman-Collins rules correspond only in 85% of the cases to dependencies such as annotated in PARC 700 Dependency Bank (see section 5).

Automatic methods for identifying heads are therefore of interest, both for practical and more fundamental linguistic reasons. In this paper we investigate possible ways of finding heads based on lexicalized tree structures that can be extracted from an available treebank. The starting point of our approach is the observation that a head-annotated treebank (obeying the constraint that every nonterminal node has exactly one daughter marked as head) defines a unique lexicalized tree substitution grammar (obeying the constraint that every elementary tree has exactly one lexical anchor). This allows us to go back and forth between

Proceedings of the 12th Conference of the European Chapter of the ACL, pages 701–709,
Athens, Greece, 30 March – 3 April 2009. ©2009 Association for Computational Linguistics

the two representations, and define objective functions for the unsupervised learning of head assignments in terms of features of the implicit Lexicalized Tree Substitution Grammars.

Using this grammar formalism (LTSGs) we will investigate which objective functions we should optimize for recovering heads. Should we try to reduce uncertainty about the grammatical frames that can be associated with a particular lexical item? Or should we assume that linguistic head assignments are based on the occurrence frequencies of the productive units they imply?

We present two new algorithms for unsupervised recovering of heads – entropy minimization and a greedy technique we call "familiarity maximization" – that can be seen as ways to operationalize these last two linguistic intuitions. Both algorithms are *unsupervised*, in the sense that they are trained on data without head annotations, but both take labeled phrase-structure trees as input.

Our work fits well with several recent approaches aimed at completely unsupervised learning of the key aspects of syntactic structure: lexical categories (Schütze, 1993), phrase-structure (Klein and Manning, 2002; Seginer, 2007), phrasal categories (Borensztajn and Zuidema, 2007; Reichart and Rappoport, 2008) and dependencies (Klein and Manning, 2004).

For the specific task addressed in this paper – assigning heads in treebanks – we only know of one earlier paper: Chiang and Bikel (2002). These authors investigated a technique for identifying heads in constituency trees based on maximizing likelihood, using EM, under a Tree Insertion Grammar (TIG)model[1]. In this approach, headedness in some sense becomes a *state-split*, allowing for grammars that more closely match empirical distributions over trees. The authors report somewhat disappointing results, however: the automatically induced head-annotations do not lead to significantly more accurate parsers than simple leftmost or rightmost head assignment schemes[2].

In section 2 we define the grammar model we will use. In section 3 we describe the head-assignment algorithms. In section 4, 5 and 6 we then describe our evaluations of these algorithms.

[1]The space over the possible head assignments that these authors consider – essentially regular expressions over CFG rules – is more restricted than in the current work where we consider a larger "domain of locality".

[2]However, the authors' approach of using EM for inducing latent information in treebanks has led to extremely accurate constituency parsers, that neither make use of nor produce headedness information; see (Petrov et al., 2006)

2 Lexicalized Tree Grammars

In this section we define Lexicalised Tree Substitution Grammars (LTSGs) and show how they can be read off unambiguously from a head-annotated treebank. LTSGs are best defined as a restriction of the more general Probabilistic Tree Substitution Grammars, which we describe first.

2.1 Tree Substitution Grammars

A tree substitution grammar (TSG) is a 4-tuple $\langle V_n, V_t, S, T\rangle$ where V_n is the set of nonterminals; V_t is the set of of terminals; $S \in V_n$ is the start symbol; and T is the set of elementary trees, having root and internal nodes in V_n and leaf nodes in $V_n \cup V_t$. Two elementary trees α and β can be combined by means of the substitution operation $\alpha \circ \beta$ to produce a new tree, only if the root of β has the same label of the leftmost nonterminal leaf of α. The combined tree corresponds to α with the leftmost nonterminal leaf replaced with β. When the tree resulting from a series of substitution operations is a complete parse tree, i.e. the root is the start symbol and all leaf nodes are terminals, we define the sequence of the elementary trees used as a *complete derivation*.

A probabilistic TSG defines a probabilistic space over the set of elementary trees: for every $\tau \in T$, $P(\tau) \in [0, 1]$ and $\sum_{\tau':r(\tau')=r(\tau)} P(\tau') = 1$, where $r(\tau)$ returns the root node of τ. Assuming subsequent substitutions are stochastically independent, we define the probability of a derivation as the product of the probability of its elementary trees. If a derivation d consists of n elementary trees $\tau_1 \circ \tau_2 \circ \ldots \circ \tau_n$, we have:

$$P(d) = \prod_{i=1}^{n} P(\tau_i) \tag{1}$$

Depending on the set T of elementary trees, we might have different derivations producing the same parse tree. For any given parse tree t, we define $\delta(t)$ as the set of its derivations licensed by the grammar. Since any derivation $d \in \delta(t)$ is a possible way to construct the parse tree, we will compute the probability of a parse tree as the sum of the probabilities of its derivations:

$$P(t) = \sum_{d \in \delta(t)} \prod_{\tau \in d} P(\tau) \tag{2}$$

Lexicalized Tree Substitution Grammars are defined as TSGs with the following contraint on the set of elementary trees T: every τ in T must have at least one terminal (the *lexical anchor*) among its leaf nodes. In this paper, we are only concerned with single-anchored LTSGs, in which all elementary trees have *exactly* one lexical anchor. Like TSGs, LTSGs have a weak generative capacity that is context-free; but whereas PTSGs are both probabilistically and in terms of strong generative capacity richer than PCFGs (Bod, 1998), LTSG are more restricted (Joshi and Schabes, 1991). This limits the usefulness of LTSGs for modeling the full complexity of natural language syntax; however, computationally, LTSGs have many advantages over richer formalisms and for the current purposes represent a useful compromise between linguistic adequacy and computational complexity.

2.2 Extracting LTSGs from a head-annotated corpus

In this section we will describe a method for assigning to each word token that occurs in the corpus a unique elementary tree. This method depends on the annotation of heads in the treebank, such as for instance provided for the Penn Treebank by the Magerman-Collins head-percolation rules. We adopt the same constraint as used in this scheme, that each nonterminal node in every parse tree must have exactly one of its children annotated as head. Our method is similar to (Chiang, 2000), but is even simpler in ignoring the distinction between arguments and adjuncts (and thus the sister-adjunction operation). Figure 1 shows an example parse tree enriched with head-annotation: the suffix -H indicates that the specific node is the head of the production above it.

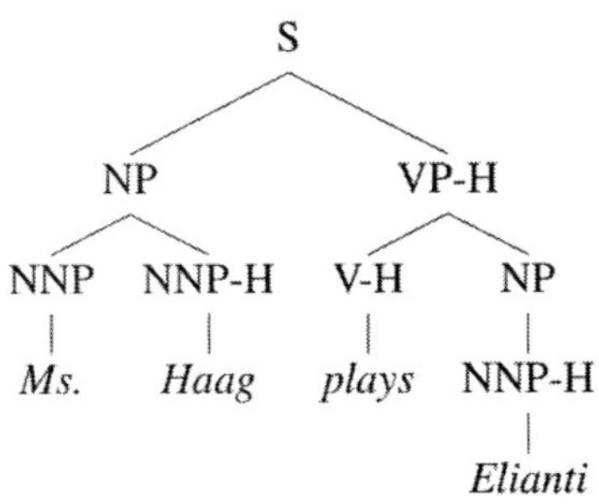

Figure 1: Parse tree of the sentence *"Ms. Haag plays Elianti"* annotated with head markers.

Once a parse tree is annotated with head markers in such a manner, we will be able to extract for every leaf its *spine*. Starting from each lexical production we need to move upwards towards the root on a path of head-marked nodes until we find the first internal node which is not marked as head or until we reach the root of the tree. In the example above, the verb of the sentence *"plays"* is connected through head-marked nodes to the root of the tree. In this way we can extract the 4 spines from the parse tree in figure 1, as shown in figure 2.

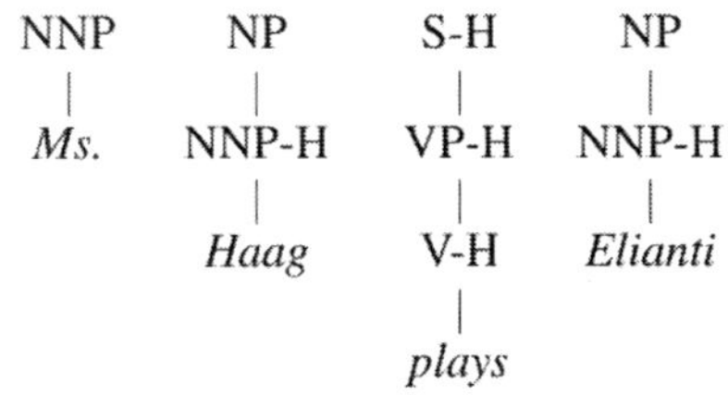

Figure 2: The lexical spines of the tree in fig. 1.

It is easy to show that this procedure yields a unique spine for each of its leaves, when applied to a parse tree where all nonterminals have a single head-daughter and all terminals are generated by a unary production. Having identified the spines, we convert them to elementary trees, by completing every internal node with the other daughter nodes not on the spine. In this way we have defined a way to obtain a derivation of any parse tree composed of lexical elementary trees. The 4 elementary trees completed from the previous paths are in figure 3 with the substitution sites marked with ⇓.

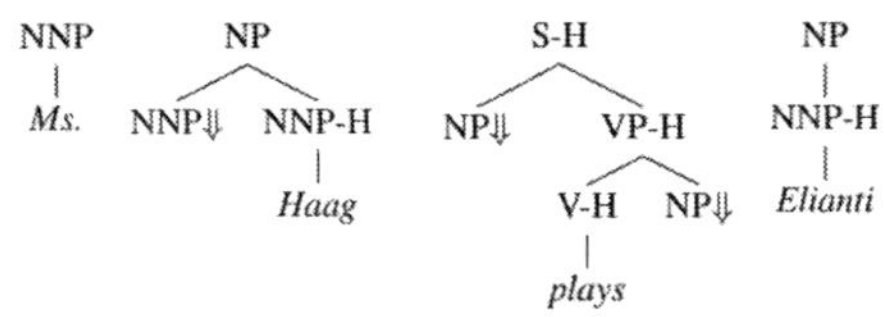

Figure 3: The extracted elementary trees.

3 Head Assignment Algorithms

We investigate two novel approaches to automatically assign head dependencies to a training corpus where the heads are not annotated: *entropy minimization* and *familiarity maximization*. The baselines for our experiments will be given by the Magerman and Collins scheme together with the random, the leftmost daughter, and the rightmost daughter-based assignments.

3.1 Baselines

The Magerman-Collins scheme, and very similar versions, are well-known and described in detail elsewhere (Magerman, 1995; Collins, 1999; Yamada and Matsumoto, 2003); here we just mention that it is based on a number of heuristic rules that only use the labels of nonterminal nodes and the ordering of daughter nodes. For instance if the root label of a parse tree is S, the head-percolation scheme will choose to assign the head marker to the first daughter from the left, labeled with TO. If no such label is present, it will look for the first IN. If no IN is found, it will look for the first VP, and so on. We used the freely available software "Treep" (Chiang and Bikel, 2002) to annotate the Penn WSJ treebank with heads.

We consider three other baselines, that are applicable to other treebanks and other languages as well: RANDOM, where, for every node in the treebank, we choose a random daughter to be marked as head; LEFT, where the leftmost daughter is marked; and RIGHT, where the rightmost daughter is marked.

3.2 Minimizing Entropy

In this section we will describe an entropy based algorithm, which aims at learning the simplest grammar fitting the data. Specifically, we take a "supertagging" perspective (Bangalore and Joshi, 1999) and aim at reducing the uncertainty about which elementary tree (supertag) to assign to a given lexical item. We achieve this by minimizing an objective function based on the general definition of entropy in information theory.

The entropy measure that we are going to describe is calculated from the bag of lexicalized elementary trees T extracted from a given training corpus of head annotated parse trees. We define T_l as a discrete stochastic variable, taking as values the elements from the set of all the elementary trees having l as lexical anchor $\{\tau_{l_1}, \tau_{l_2}, \ldots, \tau_{l_n}\}$. T_l thus takes n possible values with specific probabilities; its entropy is then defined as:

$$H(T_l) = -\sum_{i=1}^{n} p(\tau_{l_i}) \log_2 p(\tau_{l_i}) \qquad (3)$$

The most intuitive way to assign probabilities to each elementary tree is considering its relative frequency in T. If $f(\tau)$ is the frequency of the fragment τ and $f(l)$ is the total frequency of fragments with l as anchor we will have:

$$p(\tau_{l_j}) = \frac{f(\tau_{l_j})}{f(lex(\tau_{l_j}))} = \frac{f(\tau_{l_j})}{\sum_{i=1}^{n} f(\tau_{l_i}))} \qquad (4)$$

We will then calculate the entropy $H(T)$ of our bag of elementary trees by summing the entropy of each single discrete stochastic variable T_l for each choice of l:

$$H(T) = \sum_{l=1}^{|\mathscr{L}|} H(T_l) \qquad (5)$$

In order to minimize the entropy, we apply a *hill-climbing* strategy. The algorithm starts from an already annotated tree-bank (for instance using the RANDOM annotator) and iteratively tries out a random change in the annotation of each parse tree. Only if the change reduces the entropy of the entire grammar it is kept. These steps are repeated until no further modification which could reduce the entropy is possible. Since the entropy measure is defined as the sum of the function $p(\tau)\log_2 p(\tau)$ of each fragment τ, we do not need to re-calculate the entropy of the entire grammar, when modifying the annotation of a single parse tree. In fact:

$$\begin{aligned} H(T) &= -\sum_{l=1}^{|\mathscr{L}|}\sum_{i=1}^{n} p(\tau_{l_i}) \log_2 p(\tau_{l_i}) \\ &= -\sum_{j=1}^{|T|} p(\tau_j) \log_2 p(\tau_j) \end{aligned} \qquad (6)$$

For each input parse tree under consideration, the algorithm selects a non-terminal node and tries to change the head annotation from its current head-daughter to a different one. As an example, considering the parse tree of figure 1 and the internal node NP (the leftmost one), we try to annotate its leftmost daughter as the new head. When considering the changes that this modification brings on the set of the elementary trees T, we understand that there are only 4 elementary trees affected, as shown in figure 4.

After making the change in the head annotation, we just need to decrease the frequencies of the *old trees* by one unit, and increase the ones of the *new trees* by one unit. The change in the entropy of our grammar can therefore be computed by calculating the change in the partial entropy of these four

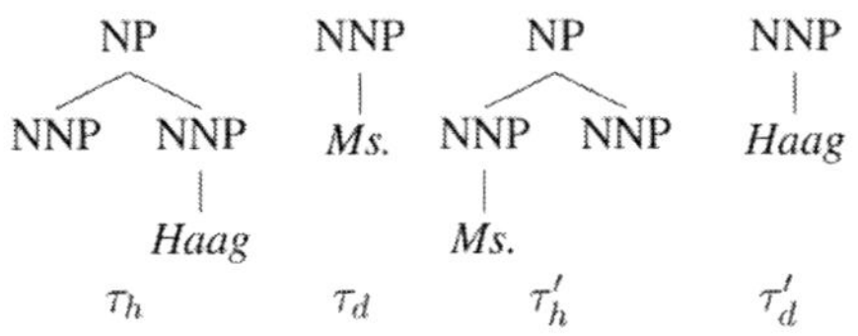

Figure 4: Lexical trees considered in the ENTROPY algorithm when changing the head assingnment from the second NNP to the first NNP of the leftmost NP node of figure 1. τ_h is the *old head tree*; τ_d the *old dependent tree*; τ'_d the *new dependent tree*; τ'_h the *new head tree*.

elementary trees before and after the change. If such change results in a lower entropy of the grammar, the new annotation is kept, otherwise we go back to the previous annotation. Although there is no guarantee our algorithm finds the global minimum, it is very efficient and succeeds in drastically minimize the entropy from a random annotated corpus.

3.3 Maximizing Familiarity

The main intuition behind our second method is that we like to assign heads to a tree t in such a way that the elementary trees that we can extract from t are frequently observed in other trees as well. That is, we like to use elementary trees which are general enough to occur in many possible constructions.

We start with building the bag of all one-anchor lexicalized elementary trees from the training corpus, consistent with *any* annotation of the heads. This operation is reminiscent of the extraction of all subtrees in Data-Oriented Parsing (Bod, 1998). Fortunately, and unlike DOP, the number of possible lexicalised elementary trees is not exponential in sentence length n, but polynomial: it is always smaller than n^2 if the tree is binary branching.

Next, for each node in the treebank, we need to select a specific lexical anchor, among the ones it dominates, and annotate the nodes in the spine with head annotations. Our algorithm selects the lexical anchor which maximizes the frequency of the implied elementary tree in the bag of elementary trees. In figure 5, algorithm 1 (right) gives the pseudo-code for the algorithm, and the tree (left) shows an example of its usage.

3.4 Spine and POS-tag reductions

The two algorithms described in the previous two sections are also evaluated when performing two possible generalization operations on the elementary trees, which can be applied both alone or in combination:

- in the *spine reduction*, lexicalized trees are transformed to their respective spines. This allows to merge elementary trees that are slightly differing in argument structures.
- in the *POStag reduction*, every lexical item of every elementary tree is replaced by its POStag category. This allows for merging elementary trees with the same internal structure but differing in lexical production.

4 Implementation details

4.1 Using CFGs for TSG parsing

When evaluating parsing accuracy of a given LTSG, we use a CKY PCFG parser. We will briefly describe how to set up an LTSG parser using the CFG formalism. Every elementary tree in the LTSG should be treated by our parser as a unique block which cannot be further decomposed. But to feed it to a CFG-parser, we need to break it down into trees of depth 1. In order to keep the integrity of every elementary tree we will assign to its internal node a unique label. We will achieve this by adding "@i" to each i-th internal node encountered in T.

Finally, we read off a PCFG from the elementary trees, assigning to each PCFG rule a weight proportional to the weight of the elementary tree it is extracted from. In this way the PCFG is equivalent to the original LTSG: it will produce exactly the same derivation trees with the same probabilities, although we would have to sum over (exponentially) many derivations to obtain the correct probabilities of a parse tree (*derived tree*). We approximate parse probability by computing the n-best derivations and summing over the ones that yield the same parse tree (by removing the "@i"-labels). We then take the parse tree with highest probability as best parse of the input sentence.

4.2 Unknown words and smoothing

We use a simple strategy to deal with unknown words occurring in the test set. We replace all the words in the training corpus occurring once, and all the unknown words in the test set, with a special *UNKNOWN* tag. Moreover we replace all the numbers in the training and test set with a special *NUMBER* tag.

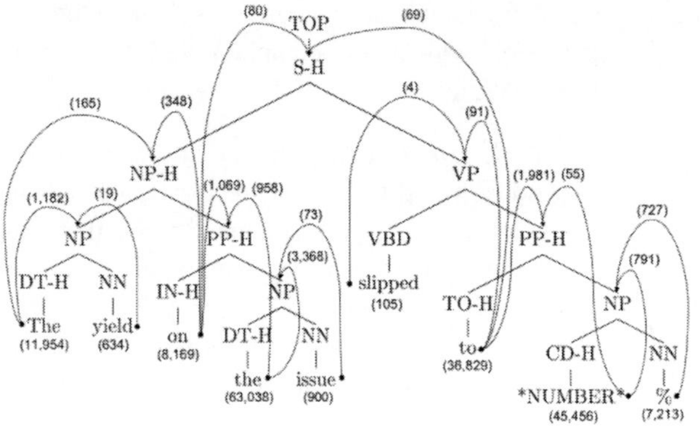

Algorithm 1: $MaximizeFamiliarity(N)$

Input: a non-terminal node N of a parsetree.
begin
  $L = null$; $MAX = -1$;
  foreach *leaf l under N* **do**
    τ_l^N = lex. tree rooted in N and anchored in l;
    F = frequency of τ_l^N;
    if $F > MAX$ **then**
      $L = l$; $MAX = F$;
  Mark all nodes in the path from N to L with heads;
  foreach *substitution site* N_i *of* τ_L^N **do**
    $MaximizeFamiliarity(N_i)$;
end

Figure 5: Left: example of a parse tree in an instantiation of the "Familiarity" algorithm. Each arrow, connecting a word to an internal node, represents the elementary tree anchored in that word and rooted in that internal node. Numbers in parentheses give the frequencies of these trees in the bag of subtrees collected from WSJ20. The number below each leaf gives the total frequency of the elementary trees anchored in that lexical item. Right: pseudo-code of the "Familiarity" algorithm.

Even with unknown words treated in this way, the lexicalized elementary trees that are extracted from the training data are often too specific to parse all sentences in the test set. A simple strategy to ensure full coverage is to smooth with the treebank PCFG. Specifically, we add to our grammars all CFG rules that can be extracted from the training corpus and give them a small weight proportional to their frequency[3]. This in general will ensure coverage, i.e. that all the sentences in the test set can be successfully parsed, but still prioritizing lexicalized trees over CFG rules[4].

4.3 Corpora

The evaluations of the different models were carried out on the Penn Wall Street Journal corpus (Marcus et al., 1993) for English, and the Tiger treebank (Brants et al., 2002) for German. As gold standard head annotations corpora, we used the Parc 700 Dependency Bank (King et al., 2003) and the Tiger Dependency Bank (Forst et al., 2004), which contain independent reannotations of extracts of the WSJ and Tiger treebanks.

5 Results

We evaluate the head annotations our algorithms find in two ways. First, we compare the head annotations to gold standard manual annotations of heads. Second, we evaluate constituency parsing performance using an LTSG parser (trained on the various LTSGs), and a state-of-the-art parser (Bikel, 2004).

5.1 Gold standard head annotations

Table 1 reports the performance of different algorithms against gold standard head annotations of the WSJ and the Tiger treebank. These annotations were obtained by converting the dependency structures of the PARC corpus (700 sentences from section 23) and the Tiger Dependency Bank (2000 sentences), into head annotations[5]. Since the algorithm doesn't guarantee that the recovered head annotations always follow the one-head-per-node constraint, when evaluating the accuracy of head annotations of different algorithms, we exclude the cases in which in the gold corpus no head or multiple heads are assigned to the daughters of an internal node[6], as well as cases in which an internal node has a single daughter.

In the evaluation against gold standard dependencies for the PARC and Tiger dependency banks, we find that the FAMILIARITY algorithm when run with POStags and Spine conversion obtains around 74% recall for English and 69% for German. The different scores of the RANDOM assignment for the two languages can be explained

[3] In our implementation, each CFG rule frequency is divided by a factor 100.

[4] In this paper, we prefer these simple heuristics over more elaborate techniques, as our goal is to compare the merits of the different head-assignment algorithms.

[5] This procedure is not reported here for reasons of space, but it is available for other researchers (together with the extracted head assignments) at `http://staff.science.uva.nl/~fsangati`.

[6] After the conversion, the percentage of incorrect heads in PARC 700 is around 9%; in Tiger DB it is around 43%.

by their different branching factors: trees in the German treebank are typically more flat than those in the English WSJ corpus. However, note that other settings of our two annotation algorithms do not always obtain better results than random.

When focusing on the Tiger results, we observe that the RIGHT head assignment recall is much better than the LEFT one. This result is in line with a classification of German as a predominantly head-final language (in contrast to English). More surprisingly, we find a relatively low recall of the head annotation in the Tiger treebank, when compared to a gold standard of dependencies for the same sentences as given by the Tiger dependency bank. Detailed analysis of the differences in head assigments between the two approaches is left for future work; for now, we note that our best performing algorithm approaches the inter-annotation-scheme agreement within only 10 percentage points[7].

5.2 Constituency Parsing results

Table 2 reports the parsing performances of our LTSG parser on different LTSGs extracted from the WSJ treebank, using our two heuristics together with the 4 baseline strategies (plus the result of a standard treebank PCFG). The parsing results are computed on WSJ20 (WSJ sentences up to length 20), using sections 02-21 for training and section 22 for testing.

We find that all but one of the head-assignment algorithms lead to LTSGs that without any fine-tuning perform better than the treebank PCFG. On this metric, our best performing algorithm scores 4 percentage points higher than the Magerman-Collins annotation scheme (a 19% error reduction). The poor results with the RIGHT assignment, in contrast with the good results with the LEFT baseline (performing even better than the Magerman-Collins assignments), are in line with the linguistic tradition of listing English as a predominantly head-initial language. A surprising result is that the RANDOM-assignment gives the best performing LTSG among the baselines. Note, however, that this strategy leads to much wieldier grammars; with many more elementary trees than for instance the left-head assignment, the RANDOM strategy is apparently better equipped to parse novel sentences. Both the FAMILIARITY and the ENTROPY strategy are at the level of the random-head assignment, but do in fact lead to much more compact grammars.

We have also used the same head-enriched treebank as input to a state-of-the-art constituency parser[8] (Bikel, 2004), using the same training and test set. Results, shown in table 3, confirm that the differences in parsing success due to different head-assignments are relatively minor, and that even RANDOM performs well. Surprisingly, our best FAMILIARITY algorithm performs as well as the Collins-Magerman scheme.

	LFS	UFS	|T|
PCFG	78.23	82.12	-
RANDOM	**82.70**	**85.54**	**64k**
LEFT	80.05	83.21	46k
Magerman-Collins	79.01	82.67	54k
RIGHT	73.04	77.90	49k
FAMILIARITY	**84.44**	**87.22**	**42k**
ENTROPY-POStags	82.81	85.80	64k
FAMILIARITY-Spine	82.67	85.35	47k
ENTROPY-POStags-Spine	82.64	85.55	64k

Table 2: Parsing accuracy on WSJ20 of the LTSGs extracted from various head assignments, when computing the most probable derivations for every sentence in the test set. The Labeled F-Score (LFS) and unlabeled F-Score (UFS) results are reported. The final column gives the total number of extracted elementary trees (in thousands).

	LFS	UFS
Magerman-Collins	**86.20**	**88.35**
RANDOM	84.58	86.97
RIGHT	81.62	84.41
LEFT	81.13	83.95
FAMILIARITY-POStags	**86.27**	**88.32**
FAMILIARITY-POStags-Spine	85.45	87.71
FAMILIARITY-Spine	84.41	86.83
FAMILIARITY	84.28	86.53

Table 3: Evaluation on WSJ20 of various head assignments on Bikel's parser.

[7]We have also used the various head-assignments to convert the treebank trees to dependency structures, and used these in turn to train a dependency parser (Nivre et al., 2005). Results from these experiments confirm the ordering of the various *unsupervised* head-assignment algorithms. Our best results, with the FAMILIARITY algorithm, give us an Unlabeled Attachment Score (UAS) of slightly over 50% against a gold standard obtained by applying the Collins-Magerman rules to the test set. This is much higher than the three baselines, but still considerably worse than results based on *supervised* head-assignments.

[8]Although we had to change a small part of the code, since the parser was not able to extract heads from an enriched treebank, but it was only compatible with rule-based assignments. For this reason, results are reported only as a base of comparison.

Gold = PARC 700	% correct
Magerman-Collins	**84.51**
LEFT	47.63
RANDOM	43.96
RIGHT	40.70
FAMILIARITY-POStags-Spine	**74.05**
FAMILIARITY-POStags	51.10
ENTROPY-POStags-Spine	43.23
FAMILIARITY-Spine	39.68
FAMILIARITY	37.40

Gold = Tiger DB	% correct
Tiger TB Head Assignment†	**77.39**
RIGHT	52.59
RANDOM	38.66
LEFT	18.64
FAMILIARITY-POStags-Spine	**68.88**
FAMILIARITY-POStags	41.74
ENTROPY-POStags-Spine	37.99
FAMILIARITY	26.08
FAMILIARITY-Spine	22.21

Table 1: Percentage of correct head assignments against gold standard in Penn WSJ and Tiger.
† The Tiger treebank already comes with built-in head labels, but not for all categories. In this case the score is computed only for the internal nodes that conform to the one head per node constraint.

6 Conclusions

In this paper we have described an empirical investigation into possible ways of enriching corpora with head information, based on different linguistic intuitions about the role of heads in natural language syntax. We have described two novel algorithms, based on entropy minimization and familiarity maximization, and several variants of these algorithms including POS-tag and spine reduction.

Evaluation of head assignments is difficult, as no widely agreed upon gold standard annotations exist. This is illustrated by the disparities between the (widely used) Magerman-Collins scheme and the Tiger-corpus head annotations on the one hand, and the "gold standard" dependencies according to the corresponding Dependency Banks on the other. We have therefore not only evaluated our algorithms against such gold standards, but also tested the parsing accuracies of the implicit lexicalized grammars (using three different parsers). Although the ordering of the algorithms on performance on these various evaluations is different, we find that the best performing strategies in all cases and for two different languages are with variants of the "familiarity" algorithm.

Interestingly, we find that the parsing results are consistently better for the algorithms that keep the full lexicalized elementary trees, whereas the best matches with gold standard annotations are obtained by versions that apply the POStag and spine reductions. Given the uncertainty about the gold standards, the possibility remains that this reflects biases towards the most general headedness-rules in the annotation practice rather than a linguistically real phenomenon.

Unsupervised head assignment algorithms can be used for the many applications in NLP where information on headedness is needed to convert constituency trees into dependency trees, or to extract head-lexicalised grammars from a constituency treebank. Of course, it remains to be seen which algorithm performs best in any of these specific applications. Nevertheless, we conclude that among currently available approaches, i.e., our two algorithms and the EM-based approach of (Chiang and Bikel, 2002), "familiarity maximization" is the most promising approach for automatic assignments of heads in treebanks.

From a linguistic point of view, our work can be seen as investigating ways in which distributional information can be used to determine headedness in phrase-structure trees. We have shown that lexicalized tree grammars provide a promising methodology for linking alternative head assignments to alternative dependency structures (needed for deeper grammatical structure, including e.g., argument structure), as well as to alternative derivations of the same sentences (i.e. the set of lexicalized elementary trees need to derive the given parse tree). In future work, we aim to extend these results by moving to more expressive grammatical formalisms (e.g., tree adjoining grammar) and by distinguishing adjuncts from arguments.

Acknowledgments We gratefully acknowledge funding by the Netherlands Organization for Scientific Research (NWO): FS is funded through a Vici-grant "Integrating Cognition" (277.70.006) to Rens Bod and WZ through a Veni-grant "Discovering Grammar" (639.021.612). We thank Rens Bod, Yoav Seginer, Reut Tsarfaty and three anonymous reviewers for helpful comments, Thomas By for providing us with his dependency bank and Joakim Nivre and Dan Bikel for help in adapting their parsers to work with our data.

References

S. Bangalore and A.K. Joshi. 1999. Supertagging: An approach to almost parsing. *Computational Linguistics*, 25(2):237–265.

D.M. Bikel. 2004. Intricacies of Collins' Parsing Model. *Computational Linguistics*, 30(4):479–511.

R. Bod. 1998. *Beyond Grammar: An experience-based theory of language*. CSLI, Stanford, CA.

G. Borensztajn, and W. Zuidema. 2007. Bayesian Model Merging for Unsupervised Constituent Labeling and Grammar Induction. Technical Report, ILLC.

S. Brants, S. Dipper, S. Hansen, W. Lezius, and G. Smith. 2002. The TIGER treebank. In *Proceedings of the Workshop on Treebanks and Linguistic Theories*, Sozopol.

T. By. 2007. Some notes on the PARC 700 dependency bank. *Natural Language Engineering*, 13(3):261–282.

E. Charniak. 1997. Statistical parsing with a context-free grammar and word statistics. In *Proceedings of the fourteenth national conference on artificial intelligence*, Menlo Park. AAAI Press/MIT Press.

D. Chiang and D.M. Bikel. 2002. Recovering latent information in treebanks. *Proceedings of the 19th international conference on Computational linguistics-Volume 1*, pages 1–7.

D. Chiang. 2000. Statistical parsing with an automatically-extracted tree adjoining grammar. In *Proceedings of the 38th Annual Meeting of the ACL.*

M. Collins. 1999. *Head-Driven Statistical Models for Natural Language Parsing*. Ph.D. thesis, University of Pennsylvania.

G. Corbett, N. Fraser, and S. McGlashan, editors. 2006. *Heads in Grammatical Theory*. Cambridge University Press.

M. Forst, N. Bertomeu, B. Crysmann, F. Fouvry, S. Hansen-Schirra, and V. Kordoni. 2004. Towards a dependency-based gold standard for German parsers.

J. Hockenmaier and M. Steedman. 2007. CCGbank: A corpus of ccg derivations and dependency structures extracted from the penn treebank. *Comput. Linguist.*, 33(3):355–396.

A.K. Joshi and Y. Schabes. 1991. Tree-adjoining grammars and lexicalized grammars. Technical report, Department of Computer & Information Science, University of Pennsylvania.

T. King, R. Crouch, S. Riezler, M. Dalrymple, and R. Kaplan. 2003. The PARC 700 dependency bank.

D. Klein and C.D. Manning. 2002. A generative constituent-context model for improved grammar induction. In *Proceedings of the 40th Annual Meeting of the ACL.*

D. Klein and C.D. Manning. 2004. Corpus-based induction of syntactic structure: models of dependency and constituency. In *Proceedings of the 42nd Annual Meeting of the ACL.*

D.M. Magerman. 1995. Statistical decision-tree models for parsing. In *Proceedings of the 33rd Annual Meeting of the ACL.*

M.P. Marcus, B. Santorini, and M.A. Marcinkiewicz. 1993. Building a large annotated corpus of English: The Penn Treebank. *Computational Linguistics*, 19(2).

J. Nivre and J. Hall. 2005. MaltParser: A Language-Independent System for Data-Driven Dependency Parsing. In Proceedings of the Fourth Workshop on Treebanks and Linguistic Theories (TLT2005), pages 137–148.

J. Nivre, J. Hall, S. Kübler, R. McDonald, J. Nilsson,S. Riedel, and D. Yuret. 2007. The conll 2007 shared task on dependency parsing. In *Proc. of the CoNLL 2007 Shared Task.*, June.

J. Nivre. 2007. Inductive Dependency Parsing. *Computational Linguistics*, 33(2).

S. Petrov, L. Barrett, R. Thibaux, and D. Klein. 2006. Learning accurate, compact, and interpretable tree annotation. In *Proceedings ACL-COLING'06*, pages 443–440.

R. Reichart and A. Rappoport. 2008. Unsupervised Induction of Labeled Parse Trees by Clustering with Syntactic Features. In *Proceedings Coling*.

H. Schütze. 1993. Part-of-speech induction from scratch. In *Proceedings of the 31st annual meeting of the ACL.*

Y. Seginer 2007. *Learning Syntactic Structure*. Ph.D. thesis, University of Amsterdam.

H. Yamada, and Y. Matsumoto. 2003. Statistical Dependency Analysis with Support Vector Machines. In *Proceedings of the Eighth International Workshop on Parsing Technologies*. Nancy, France.

A General, Abstract Model of Incremental Dialogue Processing

David Schlangen
Department of Linguistics
University of Potsdam, Germany
das@ling.uni-potsdam.de

Gabriel Skantze*
Dept. of Speech, Music and Hearing
KTH, Stockholm, Sweden
gabriel@speech.kth.se

Abstract

We present a general model and conceptual framework for specifying architectures for incremental processing in dialogue systems, in particular with respect to the topology of the network of modules that make up the system, the way information flows through this network, how information increments are 'packaged', and how these increments are processed by the modules. This model enables the precise specification of incremental systems and hence facilitates detailed comparisons between systems, as well as giving guidance on designing new systems.

1 Introduction

Dialogue processing is, by its very nature, *incremental*. No dialogue agent (artificial or natural) processes whole dialogues, if only for the simple reason that dialogues are *created* incrementally, by participants taking turns. At this level, most current implemented dialogue systems are incremental: they process user utterances as a whole and produce their response utterances as a whole.

Incremental processing, as the term is commonly used, means more than this, however, namely that processing starts before the input is complete (e.g., (Kilger and Finkler, 1995)). Incremental systems hence are those where "Each processing component will be triggered into activity by a minimal amount of its characteristic input" (Levelt, 1989). If we assume that the characteristic input of a dialogue system is the utterance (see (Traum and Heeman, 1997) for an attempt to define this unit), we would expect an incremental system to work on units smaller than utterances.

Our aim in the work presented here is to describe and give names to the options available to designers of incremental systems. We define some abstract data types, some abstract methods that are applicable to them, and a range of possible constraints on processing modules. The notions introduced here allow the (abstract) specification of a wide range of different systems, from non-incremental pipelines to fully incremental, asynchronous, parallel, predictive systems, thus making it possible to be explicit about similarities and differences between systems. We believe that this will be of great use in the future development of such systems, in that it makes clear the choices and trade-offs one can make. While we sketch our work on one such system, our main focus here is on the conceptual framework. What we are *not* doing here is to argue for one particular 'best architecture'—what this is depends on the particular aims of an implementation/model and on more low-level technical considerations (e.g., availability of processing modules).[1]

In the next section, we give some examples of differences in system architectures that we want to capture, with respect to the topology of the network of modules that make up the system, the way information flows through this network and how the modules process information, in particular how they deal with incrementality. In Section 3, we present the abstract model that underlies the system specifications, of which we give an example in Section 4. We close with a brief discussion of related work.

2 Motivating Examples

Figure 1 shows three examples of *module networks*, representations of systems in terms of their component modules and the connections between them. Modules are represented by boxes, and connections by arrows indicating the path and the di-

*The work reported here was done while the second author was at the University of Potsdam.

[1]As we are also not trying to *prove* properties of the specified systems here, the formalisations we give are not supported by a formal semantics here.

Proceedings of the 12th Conference of the European Chapter of the ACL, pages 710–718,
Athens, Greece, 30 March – 3 April 2009. ©2009 Association for Computational Linguistics

rection of information flow. Arrows not coming from or going to modules represent the global input(s) and output(s) to and from the system.

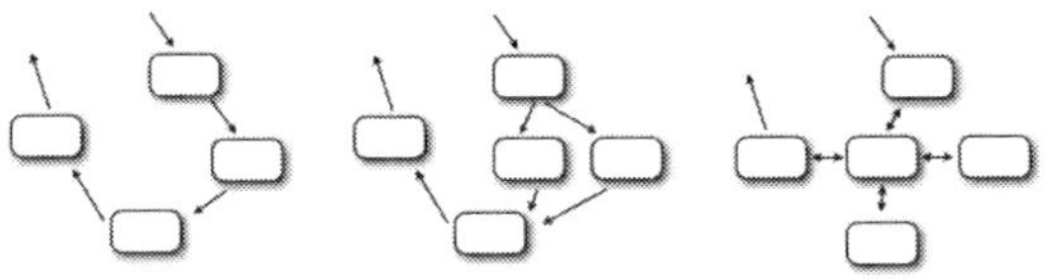

Figure 1: Module Network Topologies

One of our aims here is to facilitate exact and concise description of the differences between module networks such as in the example. Informally, the network on the left can be described as a simple pipeline with no parallel paths, the one in the middle as a pipeline enhanced with a parallel path, and the one on the right as a star-architecture; we want to be able to describe exactly the constraints that define each type of network.

A second desideratum is to be able to specify how information flows in the system and between the modules, again in an abstract way, without saying much about the information itself (as the nature of the information depends on details of the actual modules). The directed edges in Figure 1 indicate the direction of information flow (i.e., whose output is whose input); as an additional element, we can visualise *parallel* information streams between modules as in Figure 2 (left), where multiple hypotheses about the same input increments are passed on. (This isn't meant to imply that there are three actual communications channels active. As described below, we will encode the parallelism directly on the increments.)

One way such parallelism may occur in an incremental dialogue system is illustrated in Figure 2 (right), where for some stretches of an input signal (a sound wave), alternative hypotheses are entertained (note that the boxes here do *not* represent modules, but rather bits of incremental information). We can view these alternative hypotheses about the same original signal as being parallel to each other (with respect to the input they are grounded in).

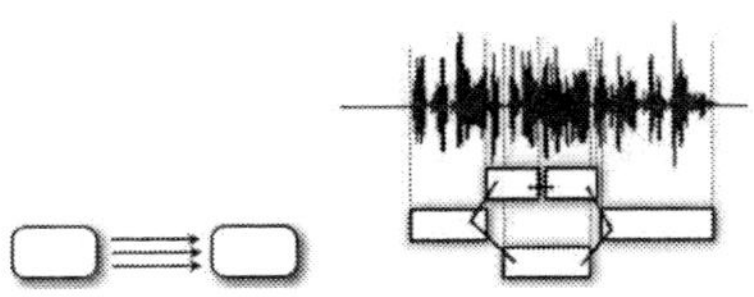

Figure 2: Parallel Information Streams (left) and Alternative Hypotheses (right)

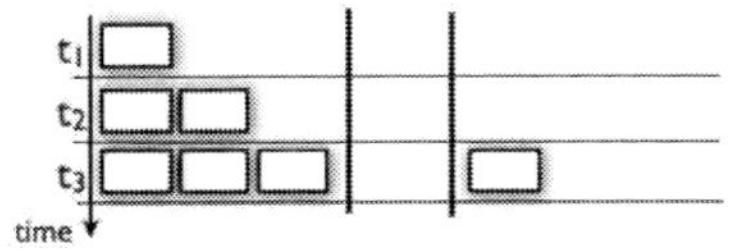

Figure 3: Incremental Input mapped to (less) incremental output

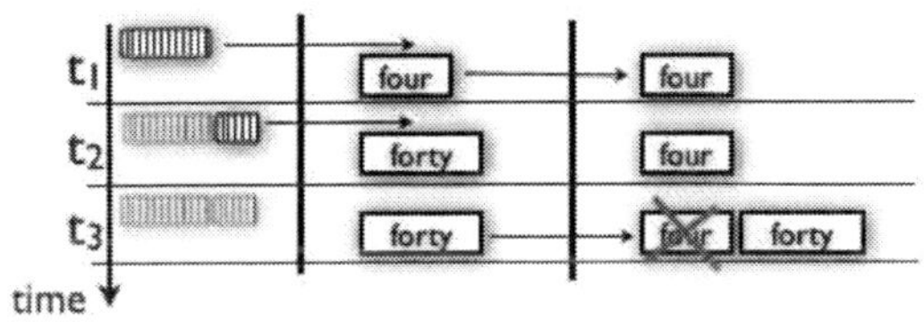

Figure 4: Example of Hypothesis Revision

We also want to be able to specify the ways incremental bits of input ("minimal amounts of characteristic input") can relate to incremental bits of output. Figure 3 shows one possible configuration, where over time incremental bits of input (shown in the left column) accumulate before one bit of output (in the right column) is produced. (As for example in a parser that waits until it can compute a major phrase out of the words that are its input.) Describing the range of possible module behaviours with respect to such input/output relations is another important element of the abstract model presented here.

It is in the nature of incremental processing, where output is generated on the basis of incomplete input, that such output may have to be revised once more information becomes available. Figure 4 illustrates such a case. At time-step t_1, the available frames of acoustic features lead the processor, an automatic speech recogniser, to hypothesize that the word "four" has been spoken. This hypothesis is passed on as output. However, at time-point t_2, as additional acoustic frames have come in, it becomes clear that "forty" is a better hypothesis about the previous frames together with the new ones. It is now not enough to just output the new hypothesis: it is possible that later modules have already started to work with the hypothesis "four", so the changed status of this hypothesis has to be communicated as well. This is shown at time-step t_3. Defining such operations and the conditions under which they are necessary is the final aim of our model.

3 The Model

3.1 Overview

We model a dialogue processing system in an abstract way as a collection of connected processing modules, where information is passed between the modules along these connections. The third component beside the modules and their connections is the basic unit of information that is communicated between the modules, which we call the *incremental unit* (IU). We will only characterise those properties of IUs that are needed for our purpose of specifying different system types and basic operations needed for incremental processing; we will not say anything about the actual, module specific *payload* of these units.

The processing module itself is modelled as consisting of a *Left Buffer* (LB), the *Processor* proper, and a *Right Buffer* (RB). When talking about operations of the Processor, we will sometimes use *Left Buffer-Incremental Unit* (LB-IU) for units in LB and *Right Buffer-Incremental Unit* (RB-IU) for units in RB.

This setup is illustrated in Figure 4 above. IUs in LB (here, acoustic frames as input to an ASR) are *consumed* by the processor (i.e., is processed), which creates an internal result, in the case shown here, this internal result is *posted* as an RB-IU only after a series of LB-IUs have accumulated. In our descriptions below, we will abstract away from the time processing takes and describe Processors as relations between (sets of) LBs and RBs.

We begin our description of the model with the specification of network topologies.

3.2 Network Topology

Connections between modules are expressed through *connectedness axioms* which simply state that IUs in one module's right buffer are also in another buffer's left buffer. (Again, in an implemented system communication between modules will take time, but we abstract away from this here.) This connection can also be partial or filtered. For example, $\forall x(x \in RB_1 \wedge NP(x) \leftrightarrow x \in LB_2)$ expresses that all and only NPs in module one's right buffer appear in module two's left buffer. If desired, a given RB can be connected to more than one LB, and more than one RB can feed into the same LB (see the middle example in Figure 1). Together, the set of these axioms define the network topology of a concrete system. Different topology types can then be defined through constraints on module sets and their connections. I.e., a pipeline system is one in which it cannot happen that an IU is in more than one right buffer and more than one left buffer.

Note that we are assuming token identity here, and not for example copying of data structures. That is, we assume that it indeed is the *same* IU that is in the left and right buffers of connected modules. This allows a special form of bi-directionality to be implemented, namely one where processors are allowed to make changes to IUs in their buffers, and where these changes automatically percolate through the network. This is different to and independent of the bi-directionality that can be expressed through connectedness axioms.

3.3 Incremental Units

So far, all we have said about IUs is that they are holding a 'minimal amount of characteristic input' (or, of course, a minimal amount of characteristic *output*, which is to be some other module's input). Communicating just these minimal information bits is enough only for the simplest kind of system that we consider, a pipeline with only a single stream of information and no revision. If more advanced features are desired, there needs to be more structure to the IUs. In this section we define what we see as the most complete version of IUs, which makes possible operations like hypothesis revision, prediction, and parallel hypothesis processing. (These operations will be explained in the next section.) If in a particular system some of these operations aren't required, some of the structure on IUs can be simplified.

Informally, the representational desiderata are as follows. First, we want to be able to represent relations between IUs produced by the same processor. For example, in the output of an ASR, two word-hypothesis IUs may stand in a *successor* relation, meaning that word 2 is what the ASR takes to be the continuation of the utterance begun with word 1. In a different situation, word 2 may be an alternative hypothesis about the same stretch of signal as word 1, and here a different relation would hold. The incremental outputs of a parser may be related in yet another way, through dominance: For example, a newly built IU_3, representing a VP, may want to express that it links via a dominance relation to IU_1, a V, and IU_2, an NP, which were both posted earlier. What is common to all relations of this type is that they relate IUs coming from the same processor(s); we will in this case say that the IUs are *on the same level*. Information about these *same level links* will be useful for the consumers of IUs. For example, a parsing module consuming ASR-output IUs will need to do different things depending on whether an incoming IU continues an utterance or forms an alternative hypothesis to a string that was already parsed.

The second relation between IUs that we want to capture cuts across levels, by linking RB-IUs to those LB-IUs that were used by the processor to produce them. For this we will say that the RB-IU is *grounded* in LB-IU(s). This relation then tracks the flow of information through the modules; following its transitive closure one can go back from the highest level IU, which is output by the system, to the input IU or set of input IUs on which it is ultimately grounded. The network spanned by this relation will be useful in implementing the revision process mentioned above when discussing Figure 4, where the doubt about a hypothesis must spread to all hypotheses grounded in it.

Apart from these relations, we want IUs to carry three other types of information: a confidence score representing the confidence its producer had in it being accurate; a field recording whether revisions of the IU are still to be expected or not; and another field recording whether the IU has already been processed by consumers, and if so, by whom.

Formally, we define IUs as tuples $\mathcal{IU} = \langle \mathcal{I}, \mathcal{L}, \mathcal{G}, \mathcal{T}, \mathcal{C}, \mathcal{S}, \mathcal{P} \rangle$, where

- $\mathcal{I}$ is an identifier, which has to be unique for each IU over the lifetime of a system. (That is, at no point in the system's life can there be two or more IUs with the same ID.)
- $\mathcal{L}$ is the *same level link*, holding a statement about how, if at all, the given IU relates to other IUs at the same level, that is, to IUs produced by the same processor. If an IU is not linked to any other IU, this slot holds the special value $\top$.
  The definition demands that the same level links of all IUs belonging to the same larger unit form a graph; the type of the graph will depend on the purposes of the sending and consuming module(s). For a one-best output of an ASR it might be enough for the graph to be a chain, whereas an n-best output might be better represented as a tree (with all first words linked to $\top$) or even a lattice (as in Figure 2 (right)); the output of a parser might require trees (possibly underspecified).
- $\mathcal{G}$ is the *grounded in* field, holding an ordered list of IDs pointing to those IUs out of which the current IU was built. For example, an IU holding a (partial) parse might be grounded in a set of word hypothesis IUs, and these in turn might be grounded in sets of IUs holding acoustic features. While the *same level link* always points to IUs on the same level, the *grounded in* link always points to IUs from a previous level.[2] The transitive closure of this relation hence links system output IUs to a set of system input IUs. For convenience, we may define a predicate *supports(x,y)* for cases where y is grounded in x; and hence the closure of this relation links input-IUs to the output that is (eventually) built on them.
  This is also the hook for the mechanism that realises the revision process described above with Figure 4: if a module decides to revoke one of its hypotheses, it sets its confidence value (see below) to 0; on noticing this event, all consuming modules can then check whether they have produced RB-IUs that link to this LB-IU, and do the same for them. In this way, information about revision will automatically percolate through the module network.
  Finally, an empty *grounded in* field can also be used to trigger *prediction*: if an RB-IU has an empty *grounded in* field, this can be understood as a directive to the processor to find evidence for this IU (i.e., to prove it), using the information in its left buffer.
- $\mathcal{T}$ is the *confidence* (or trust) slot, through which the generating processor can pass on its confidence in its hypothesis. This then can have an influence on decisions of the consuming processor. For example, if there are parallel hypotheses of different quality (confidence), a processor may decide to process

[2] The link to the previous level may be indirect. E.g., for an IU holding a phrase that is built out of previously built phrases (and not words), this link may be expressed by pointing to the same level link, meaning something like "I'm grounded in whatever the IUs are grounded in that I link to on the same level link, and also in the act of combination that is expressed in that same level link".

(and produce output for) the best first.

A special value (e.g., 0, or -1) can be defined to flag hypotheses that are being revoked by a processor, as described above.

- $\mathcal{C}$ is the *committed* field, holding a Boolean value that indicates whether the producing module has committed to the IU or not, that is, whether it guarantees that it will never revoke the IU. See below for a discussion of how such a decision may be made, and how it travels through the module network.
- $\mathcal{S}$ is the *seen* field. In this field consuming processors can record whether they have "looked at"—that is, attempted to process—the IU. In the simplest case, the positive fact can be represented simply by adding the processor ID to the list; in more complicated setups one may want to offer status information like "is being processed by module ID" or "no use has been found for IU by module ID". This allows processors both to keep track of which LB-IUs they have already looked at (and hence, to more easily identify new material that may have entered their LB) and to recognise which of its RB-IUs have been of use to later modules, information which can then be used for example to make decisions on which hypothesis to expand next.
- $\mathcal{P}$ finally is the actual *payload*, the module-specific unit of 'characteristic input', which is what is processed by the processor in order to produce RB-IUs.

It will also be useful later to talk about the *completeness* of an IU (or of sets of IUs). This we define informally as its relation to (the type of) what would count as a *maximal* input or output of the module. For example, for an ASR module, such maximally complete input may be the recording of the whole utterance, for the parser maximal output may be a parse of type sentence (as opposed to one of type NP, for example).[3] This allows us to see non-incremental systems as a special case of incremental systems, namely those with only maximally complete IUs, which are always committed.

[3]This definition will only be used for abstractly classifying modules. Practically, it is of course rarely possible to know how complete or incomplete the already seen part of an ongoing input is. Investigating how a dialogue system can better predict completion of an utterance is in fact one of the aims of the project in which this framework was developed.

3.4 Modules

3.4.1 Operations

We describe in this section operations that the processors may perform on IUs. We leave open how processors are triggered into action, we simply assume that on receiving new LB-IUs or noticing changes to LB or RB-IUs, they will eventually perform these operations. Again, we describe here the complete set of operations; systems may differ in which subset of the functions they implement.

purge LB-IUs that are revoked by their producer (by having their confidence score set to the special value) must be purged from the internal state of the processor (so that they will not be used in future updates) and all RB-IUs grounded in them must be revoked as well.

Some reasons for revoking hypotheses have already been mentioned. For example, a speech recogniser might decide that a previously output word hypothesis is not valid anymore (i.e., is not anymore among the n-best that are passed on). Or, a parser might decide in the light of new evidence that a certain structure it has built is a dead end, and withdraw support for it. In all these cases, *all* 'later' hypotheses that build on this IU (i.e., all hypotheses that are in the transitive closure of this IU's *support* relation) must be purged. If all modules implement the purge operation, this revision information will be guaranteed to travel through the network.

update New LB-IUs are integrated into the internal state, and eventually new RB-IUs are built based on them (not necessarily in the same frequency as new LB-IUs are received; see Figure 3 above, and discussion below). The fields of the new RB-IUs (e.g., the *same level links* and the *grounded in* pointers) are filled appropriately. This is in some sense the basic operation of a processor, and must be implemented in all useful systems.

We can distinguish two implementation strategies for dealing with updates: a) all state is thrown away and results are computed again for the whole input set. The result must then be compared with the previous result to determine what the new output increment is. b) The new information is integrated into internal state, and only the new output increment is produced. For our purposes here, we can abstract away from these differences and assume that only actual increments are communicated. (Practically, it might be an advantage to keep using an existing processor and just wrap it into a module that computes increments by differences.)

We can also distinguish between modules along another dimension, namely based on which types of updates are allowed. To do so, we must first define the notion of a 'right edge' of a set of IUs. This is easiest to explain for strings, where the right edge simply is the end of the string, or for a lattice, where it is the (set of) smallest element(s). A similar notion may be defined for trees as well (compare the 'right frontier constraint' of Polanyi (1988)). If now a processor only expects IUs that extend the right frontier, we can follow Wirén (1992) in saying that it is only *left-to-right incremental*. Within what Wirén (1992) calls *fully incremental*, we can make more distinctions, namely according to whether revisions (as described above) and/or *insertions* are allowed. The latter can easily be integrated into our framework, by allowing *same-level links* to be changed to fit new IUs into existing graphs.

Processors can take *supports* information into account when deciding on their update order. A processor might for example decide to first try to use the new information (in its LB) to extend structures that have already proven useful to later modules (that is, that support new IUs). For example, a parser might decide to follow an interpretation path that is deemed more likely by a contextual processing module (which has grounded hypotheses in the partial path). This may result in better use of resources—the downside of such a strategy of course is that modules can be garden-pathed.[4]

Update may also work towards a goal. As mentioned above, putting ungrounded IUs in a module's RB can be understood as a request to the module to try to find evidence for it. For example, the dialogue manager might decide based on the dialogue context that a certain type of dialogue act is likely to follow. By requesting the dialogue act recognition module to find evidence for this hypothesis, it can direct processing resources towards this task. (The dialogue recognition module then can in turn decide on which evidence it would like to see, and ask lower modules to prove this. Ideally, this could filter down to the interface module, the ASR, and guide its hypothesis forming. Technically, something like this is probably easier to realise by other means.)

[4]It depends on the goals behind building the model whether this is considered a downside or desired behaviour.

We finally note that in certain setups it may be necessary to consume different types of IUs in one module. As explained above, we allow more than one module to feed into another modules LB. An example where something like this could be useful is in the processing of multi-modal information, where information about both words spoken and gestures performed may be needed to compute an interpretation.

commit There are three ways in which a processor may have to deal with commits. First, it can decide for itself to commit RB-IUs. For example, a parser may decide to commit to a previously built structure if it failed to integrate into it a certain number of new words, thus assuming that the previous structure is complete. Second, a processor may notice that a previous module has committed to IUs in its LB. This might be used by the processor to remove internal state kept for potential revisions. Eventually, this commitment of previous modules might lead the processor to also commit to its output, thus triggering a chain of commitments.

Interestingly, it can also make sense to let commits flow from right to left. For example, if the system has committed to a certain interpretation by making a publicly observable action (e.g., an utterance, or a multi-modal action), this can be represented as a commit on IUs. This information would then travel down the processing network; leading to the potential for a clash between a revoke message coming from the left and the commit directive from the right. In such a case, where the justification for an action is revoked when the action has already been performed, self-correction behaviours can be executed.[5]

3.4.2 Characterising Module Behaviour

It is also useful to be able to abstractly describe the relation between LB-IUs and RB-IUs in a module or a collection of modules. We do this here along the dimensions *update frequency*, *connectedness* and *completeness*.

Update Frequency The first dimension we consider here is that of how the update frequency of LB-IUs relates to that of (connected) RB-IUs.

We write *f:in=out* for modules that guarantee that every new LB-IU will lead to a new RB-IU

[5]In future work, we will explore in more detail if and how through the implementation of a self-monitoring cycle and *commits* and *revokes* the various types of dysfluencies described for example by Levelt (1989) can be modelled.

(that is grounded in the LB-IU). In such a setup, the consuming module lags behind the sending module only for exactly the time it needs to process the input. Following Nivre (2004), we can call this *strict incrementality*.

f:in≥out describes modules that potentially collect a certain amount of LB-IUs before producing an RB-IU based on them. This situation has been depicted in Figure 3 above.

f:in≤out characterises modules that update RB *more* often than their LB is updated. This could happen in modules that produce endogenic information like clock signals, or that produce continuously improving hypotheses over the same input (see below), or modules that 'expand' their input, like a TTS that produces audio frames.

Connectedness We may also want to distinguish between modules that produce 'island' hypotheses that are, at least when initially posted, not connected via *same level links* to previously output IUs, and those that guarantee that this is not the case. For example, to achieve an *f:in=out* behaviour, a parser may output hypotheses that are not connected to previous hypotheses, in which case we may call the hypotheses 'unconnected'. Conversely, to guarantee connectedness, a parsing module might need to accumulate input, resulting in an *f:in≥out* behaviour.[6]

Completeness Building on the notion of completeness of (sets of) IUs introduced above, we can also characterise modules according to how the completeness of LB and RB relates.

In a *c:in=out*-type module, the most complete RB-IU (or set of RB-IUs) is only as complete as the most complete (set of) LB-IU(s). That is, the module does not speculate about completions, nor does it lag behind. (This may technically be difficult to realise, and practically not very relevant.)

More interesting is the difference between the following types: In a *c:in≥out*-type module, the most complete RB-IU potentially lags behind the most complete LB-IU. This will typically be the case in *f:in≥out* modules. *c:in≤out*-type modules finally potentially produce output that is *more* complete than their input, i.e., they *predict* continuations. An extreme case would be a module that always predicts complete output, given partial input. Such a module may be useful in cases where modules have to be used later in the processing chain that can only handle complete input (that is, are non-incremental); we may call such a system *prefix-based predictive, semi-incremental*.

With these categories in hand, we can make further distinctions within what Dean and Boddy (1988) call *anytime algorithms*. Such algorithms are defined as a) producing output at any time, which however b) improves in quality as the algorithm is given more time. Incremental modules by definition implement a reduced form of a): they may not produce an output at any time, but they do produce output at more times than non-incremental modules. This output then also improves over time, fulfilling condition b), since more input becomes available and either the guesses the module made (if it is a *c:out≥in* module) will improve or the completeness in general increases (as more complete RB-IUs are produced). Processing modules, however, can also be anytime algorithms in a more restricted sense, namely if they continuously produce new and improved output even for a constant set of LB-IUs, i.e. without changes on the input side. (Which would bring them towards the *f:out≥in* behaviour.)

3.5 System Specification

Combining all these elements, we can finally define a system specification as the following:

- A list of modules that are part of the system.
- For each of those a description in terms of which operations from Section 3.4.1 the module implements, and a characterisation of its behaviour in the terms of Section 3.4.2.
- A set of axioms describing the connections between module buffers (and hence the network topology), as explained in Section 3.2.
- Specifications of the format of the IUs that are produced by each module, in terms of the definition of slots in Section 3.3.

4 Example Specification

We have built a fully incremental dialogue system, called NUMBERS (for more details see Skantze and Schlangen (2009)), that can engage in dialogues in a simple domain, number dictation. The system can not only be described in the terms explained here, but it also directly instantiates some of the data types described here.

[6]The notion of *connectedness* is adapted from Sturt and Lombardo (2005), who provide evidence that the human parser strives for connectedness.

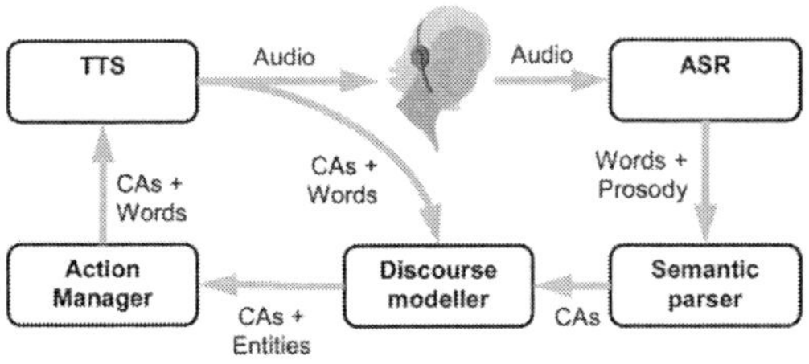

Figure 5: The NUMBERS System Architecture (CA = communicative act)

The module network topology of the system is shown in Figure 5. This is pretty much a standard dialogue system layout, with the exception that prosodic analysis is done in the ASR and that dialogue management is divided into a discourse modelling module and an action manager. As can be seen in the figure, there is also a self-monitoring feedback loop—the system's actions are sent from the TTS to the discourse modeller. The system has two modules that interface with the environment (i.e., are system boundaries): the ASR and the TTS.

A single hypothesis chain connects the modules (that is, no two same level links point to the same IU). Modules pass messages between them that can be seen as XML-encodings of IU-tokens. Information strictly flows from LB to RB. All IU slots except seen ($\mathcal{S}$) are realised. The purge and commit operations are fully implemented. In the ASR, revision occurs as already described above with Figure 4, and word-hypothesis IUs are committed (and the speech recognition search space is cleared) after 2 seconds of silence are detected. (Note that later modules work with all IUs from the moment that they are sent, and do not have to wait for them being committed.) The parser may revoke its hypotheses if the ASR revokes the words it produces, but also if it recovers from a "garden path", having built and closed off a larger structure too early. As a heuristic, the parser waits until a syntactic construct is followed by three words that are not part of it until it commits. For each new discourse model increment, the action manager may produce new communicative acts (CAs), and possibly revoke previous ones that have become obsolete. When the system has spoken a CA, this CA becomes committed, which is recorded by the discourse modeller.

No hypothesis testing is done (that is, no ungrounded information is put on RBs). All modules have a $f{:}in \geq out$; $c{:}in \geq out$ characteristic.

The system achieves a very high degree of responsiveness—by using incremental ASR and prosodic analysis for turn-taking decisions, it can react in around 200ms when suitable places for backchannels are detected, which should be compared to a typical minimum latency of 750ms in common systems where only a simple silence threshold is used.

5 Related Work, Future Work

The model described here is inspired partially by Young et al. (1989)'s token passing architecture; our model can be seen as a (substantial) generalisation of the idea of passing smaller information bits around, out of the domain of ASR and into the system as a whole. Some of the characterisations of the behaviour of incremental modules were inspired by Kilger and Finkler (1995), but again we generalised the definitions to fit all kinds of incremental modules, not just generation.

While there recently have been a number of papers about incremental systems (e.g., (DeVault and Stone, 2003; Aist et al., 2006; Brick and Scheutz, 2007)), none of those offer general considerations about architectures. (Despite its title, (Aist et al., 2006) also only describes one particular setup.)

In future work, we will give descriptions of these systems in the terms developed here. We are also currently exploring how more cognitively motivated models such as that of generation by Levelt (1989) can be specified in our model. A further direction for extension is the implementation of modality fusion as IU-processing. Lastly, we are now starting to work on connecting the model for incremental processing and grounding of interpretations in previous processing results described here with models of dialogue-level grounding in the information-state update tradition (Larsson and Traum, 2000). The first point of contact here will be the investigation of self-corrections, as a phenomenon that connects sub-utterance processing and discourse-level processing (Ginzburg et al., 2007).

Acknowledgments This work was funded by a grant in the DFG Emmy Noether Programme. Thanks to Timo Baumann and Michaela Atterer for discussion of the ideas reported here, and to the anonymous reviewers for their very detailed and helpful comments.

References

G.S. Aist, J. Allen, E. Campana, L. Galescu, C.A. Gomez Gallo, S. Stoness, M. Swift, and M Tanenhaus. 2006. Software architectures for incremental understanding of human speech. In *Proceedings of the International Conference on Spoken Language Processing (ICSLP)*, Pittsburgh, PA, USA, September.

Timothy Brick and Matthias Scheutz. 2007. Incremental natural language processing for HRI. In *Proceedings of the Second ACM IEEE International Conference on Human-Robot Interaction*, pages 263–270, Washington, DC, USA.

Thomas Dean and Mark Boddy. 1988. An analysis of time-dependent planning. In *Proceedings of AAAI-88*, pages 49–54. AAAI.

David DeVault and Matthew Stone. 2003. Domain inference in incremental interpretation. In *Proceedings of ICOS 4: Workshop on Inference in Computational Semantics*, Nancy, France, September. INRIA Lorraine.

Jonathan Ginzburg, Raquel Fernández, and David Schlangen. 2007. Unifying self- and other-repair. In *Proceeding of DECALOG, the 11th International Workshop on the Semantics and Pragmatics of Dialogue (SemDial07)*, Trento, Italy, June.

Anne Kilger and Wolfgang Finkler. 1995. Incremental generation for real-time applications. Technical Report RR-95-11, DFKI, Saarbrücken, Germany.

Staffan Larsson and David Traum. 2000. Information state and dialogue management in the TRINDI dialogue move engine toolkit. *Natural Language Engineering*, pages 323–340.

Willem J.M. Levelt. 1989. *Speaking*. MIT Press, Cambridge, USA.

Joakim Nivre. 2004. Incrementality in deterministic dependency parsing. pages 50–57, Barcelona, Spain, July.

Livia Polanyi. 1988. A formal model of the structure of discourse. *Journal of Pragmatics*, 12:601–638.

Gabriel Skantze and David Schlangen. 2009. Incremental dialogue processing in a micro-domain. In *Proceedings of the 12th Conference of the European Chapter of the Association for Computational Linguistics (EACL 2009)*, Athens, Greece, April.

Patrick Sturt and Vincenzo Lombardo. 2005. Processing coordinated structures: Incrementality and connectedness. *Cognitive Science*, 29:291–305.

D. Traum and P. Heeman. 1997. Utterance units in spoken dialogue. In E. Maier, M. Mast, and S. LuperFoy, editors, *Dialogue Processing in Spoken Language Systems*, Lecture Notes in Artificial Intelligence. Springer-Verlag.

Mats Wirén. 1992. *Studies in Incremental Natural Language Analysis*. Ph.D. thesis, Linköping University, Linköping, Sweden.

S.J. Young, N.H. Russell, and J.H.S. Thornton. 1989. Token passing: a conceptual model for connected speech recognition systems. Technical report CUED/FINFENG/TR 38, Cambridge University Engineering Department.

Word Lattices for Multi-Source Translation

Josh Schroeder, Trevor Cohn, and Philipp Koehn
School of Informatics
University of Edinburgh
10 Crichton Street, Edinburgh EH8 9AB
Scotland, United Kingdom
{jschroe1, tcohn, pkoehn}@inf.ed.ac.uk

Abstract

Multi-source statistical machine translation is the process of generating a single translation from multiple inputs. Previous work has focused primarily on selecting from potential outputs of separate translation systems, and solely on multi-parallel corpora and test sets. We demonstrate how multi-source translation can be adapted for multiple monolingual inputs. We also examine different approaches to dealing with multiple sources, including consensus decoding, and we present a novel method of input combination to generate lattices for multi-source translation within a single translation model.

1 Introduction

Multi-source statistical machine translation was first formally defined by Och and Ney (2001) as the process of translating multiple meaning-equivalent source language texts into a single target language. Multi-source translation is of particular use when translating a document that has already been translated into several languages, either by humans or machines, and needs to be further translated into other target languages. This situation occurs often in large multi-lingual organisations such as the United Nations and the European Parliament, which must translate their proceedings into the languages of the member institutions. It is also common in multi-national companies, which need to translate product and marketing documentation for their different markets. Clearly, any existing translations for a document can help automatic translation into other languages. These different versions of the input can resolve deficiencies and ambiguities (e.g., syntactic and semantic ambiguity) present in a single input, resulting in higher quality translation output.

In this paper, we present three models of multi-source translation, with increasing degrees of sophistication, which we compare empirically on a number of different corpora. We generalize the definition of multi-source translation to include any translation case with multiple inputs and a single output, allowing for, e.g., multiple paraphrased inputs in a single language. Our methods include simple *output selection*, which treats the multi-source translation task as many independent translation steps followed by selection of one of their outputs (Och and Ney, 2001), and *output combination*, which uses consensus decoding to construct a string from n-gram fragments of the translation outputs (Bangalore et al., 2001). We also present a novel method, *input combination*, in which we compile the input texts into a compact lattice, over which we perform a single decoding pass. We show that as we add additional inputs, the simplest output selection method performs quite poorly relative to a single input translation system, while the latter two methods are able to make better use of the additional inputs.

The paper is structured as follows. §2 presents the three methods for multi-source translation in detail: output selection, output combination, and our novel lattice-based method for input combination. We report experiments applying these techniques to three different corpora, with both monolingual inputs (§3) and multilingual inputs (§4). We finish in §5 by analyzing the benefits and drawbacks of these approaches.

2 Approaches to Multi-Source Translation

We now present three ways to combine multiple inputs into a single output translation, in the context of related work for each technique.

Proceedings of the 12th Conference of the European Chapter of the ACL, pages 719–727,
Athens, Greece, 30 March – 3 April 2009.

2.1 Output Selection

The most straightforward approach to multi-source translation, proposed by Och and Ney (2001), is to independently translate each of the N source languages and then select a single translation from the outputs. Given N sources $\mathbf{s}_1^N = \mathbf{s}_1, \ldots, \mathbf{s}_N$, first translate each with a separate translation system, $p_1, \ldots, p_N$, to obtain N target translations, $\mathbf{t}_1^N = \mathbf{t}_1, \ldots, \mathbf{t}_N$. Och and Ney present two approaches for selecting a single target from these outputs.

The first, PROD, finds the maximiser of the product, $\arg\max_{\mathbf{t}\in\mathbf{t}_1^N} p(\mathbf{t}) \prod_{n=1}^{N} p_n(\mathbf{s}_n|\mathbf{t})$, where $p(\mathbf{t})$ is the language model probability. For reasons of tractability, the maximisation is performed only over targets generated by the translation systems, $\mathbf{t}_1^N$, not the full space of all translations. The PROD method requires each model to provide a model score for each $\mathbf{t}_n$ generated by the other models. However, this is often impossible due to the models' highly divergent output spaces (Schwartz, 2008), and therefore the technique cannot be easily applied.

The second approach, MAX, solves $\arg\max_{\mathbf{t}\in\mathbf{t}_1^N} \max_{n=1}^{N} p(\mathbf{t}) p_n(\mathbf{s}_n|\mathbf{t})$, which is much easier to calculate. As with PROD, the translation models' outputs are used for the candidate translations. While different models may have different score ranges, Och and Ney (2001) state that there is little benefit in weighting these scores to normalise the output range. In their experiments, they show that MAX used on pairs or triples of language inputs can outperform a model with single language input, but that performance degrades as more languages are added.

These methods limit the explored space to a full translation output of one of the inputs, and therefore cannot make good use of the full diversity of the translations. In this paper we present MAX scores as a baseline for output selection, and approximate an oracle using the BLEU metric as an upper bound for the output selection technique.

2.2 Output Combination

Consensus decoding as a form of system combination is typically used to integrate the outputs of multiple translation systems into a single synthetic output that seeks to combine the best fragments from each component system. Multi-source translation can be treated as a special case of consensus decoding. Indeed, several authors have seen

the	ϵ	dog	barked	very	loudly
a	big	dog	barked	ϵ	loudly
sub	*insert*	–	*shift*	*delete*	–

Table 1: Example minimum TER edit script.

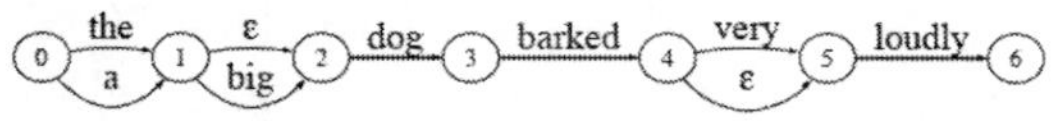

Figure 1: Conversion of TER script from Table 1 to a confusion network.

improvements in translation quality by performing multi-source translation using generic system combination techniques (Matusov et al., 2006; Paulik et al., 2007).

One class of approaches to consensus decoding focuses on construction of a confusion network or lattice[1] from translation outputs, from which new sentences can be created using different reorderings or combinations of translation fragments (e.g., Bangalore et al. (2001); Rosti et al. (2007b)). These methods differ in the types of lattices used, their means of creation, and scoring method used to extract the best consensus output from the lattice. The system used in this paper is a variant of the one proposed in Rosti et al. (2007a), which we now describe in detail.

The first step in forming a lattice is to align the inputs. Consensus decoding systems often use the script of edit operations that minimises the translation edit rate (TER; Snover et al. (2006)). TER is a word-based measure of edit distance which also allows n-gram shifts when calculating the best match between a hypothesis and reference. Because TER describes the correspondence between the hypothesis and reference as a sequence of insertions, substitutions, deletions, and shifts, the edit script it produces can be used to create a confusion network.

Consider a reference of "The dog barked very loudly" and a hypothesis "A big dog loudly barked." The TER alignment is shown in Table 1, along with the edit operations. Note that the matching "barked" tokens are labelled *shift*, as one needs to be shifted for this match to occur. Using the shifted hypothesis, we can form a confusion

[1]Different authors refer to "lattices," "confusion networks," "word sausages," etc. to describe these data structures, and specific terminology varies from author to author. We define a lattice as a weighted directed acyclic graph, and a confusion network as a special case where each node n in the ordered graph has word arcs only to node $n+1$.

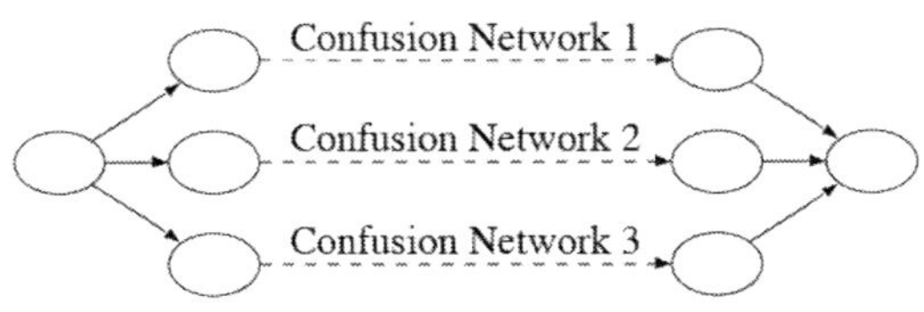

Figure 2: Structure of a lattice of confusion networks for consensus decoding.

network as in Figure 1. Additional sentences can be added by aligning them to the reference as well. Each link is weighted by the number of component sentences sharing that particular word at the given location.

Similar to Rosti et al. (2007a), we let each hypothesis take a turn as the "reference" for TER, using it as a skeleton for a confusion network. We then form a lattice of confusion networks (Figure 2), assigning a prior weight to each confusion network based on the average TER of the selected skeleton with the other hypotheses. This allows each system to set the word order for a component confusion network, but at the cost of a more complex lattice structure.

We can score paths $\mathcal{P}$ through these lattices with the assistance of a language model. Formally, the path score is given by:

$$w(\mathcal{P}) = \nu \log p_{LM}(t(\mathcal{P})) + \sum_{d\in\mathcal{P}} \left[\sum_{n=1}^{N} \lambda_n \log p_n(d|\mathbf{s}_n) + \mu\delta(d,\epsilon) + \xi(1-\delta(d,\epsilon)) \right]$$

where p_{LM} is the language model probability of the target string specified by the lattice path, $t(\mathcal{P})$, $p_n(d|s_n)$ is the proportion of system n's k-best outputs that use arc d in path $\mathcal{P}$, and the last two terms count the number of epsilon and non-epsilon transitions in the path. The model parameters are $\lambda_1, \ldots, \lambda_n, \nu, \mu, \xi$, which are trained using Powell's search to maximise the BLEU score for the highest scoring path, $\arg\max_{\mathcal{P}} w(\mathcal{P})$.

2.3 Input Combination

Loosely defined, *input combination* refers to finding a compact single representation of N translation inputs. The hope is that the new input preserves as many of the salient differences between the inputs as possible, while eliminating redundant information. Lattices are well suited to this task.

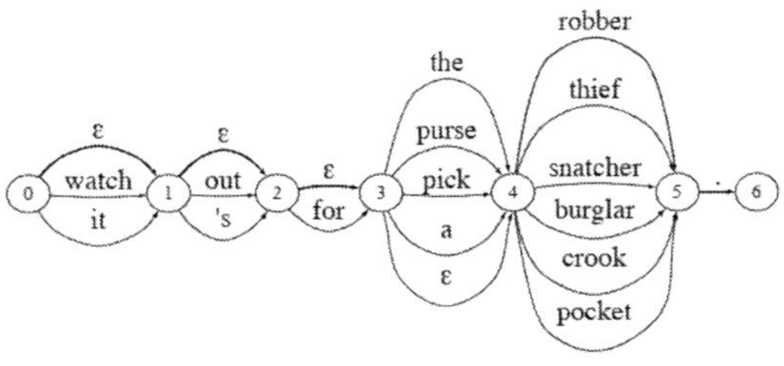

Figure 3: A monolingual confusion network. Thicker lines indicate higher probability word arcs.

When translating speech recognition output, previous work has shown that representing the ambiguity in the recognized text via confusion networks leads to better translations than simply translating the single best hypothesis of the speech recognition system (Bertoldi et al., 2007). The application of input lattices to other forms of input ambiguity has been limited to encoding input reorderings, word segmentation, or morphological segmentation, all showing improvements in translation quality (Costa-jussà et al., 2007; Xu et al., 2005; Dyer et al., 2008). However, these applications encode the ambiguity arising from a single input, while in this work we combine distinct inputs into a more compact and expressive single input format.

When given many monolingual inputs, we can apply TER and construct a confusion network as in Section 2.2.[2] In this application of confusion networks, arc weights are calculated by summing votes from each input for a given word, and normalizing all arcs leaving a node to sum to 1.

Figure 3 shows an example of a TER-derived input from IWSLT data. Because the decoder will handle reordering, we select the input with the lowest average TER against the other inputs to serve as the skeleton system, and do not create a lattice with multiple skeletons.

The problem becomes more complex when we consider cases of multi-lingual multi-source translation. We cannot easily apply TER across languages because there is no clear notion of an exact match between words. Matusov et al. (2006) propose using a statistical word alignment algorithm as a more robust way of aligning (monolingual) outputs into a confusion network for system com-

[2]Barzilay and Lee (2003) construct lattices over paraphrases using an iterative pairwise multiple sequence alignment (MSA) algorithm. Unlike our approach, MSA does not allow reordering of inputs.

bination. We take a similar approach for multi-lingual lattice generation.

Our process consists of four steps: (i) Align words for each of the $N(N-1)$ pairs of inputs; (ii) choose an input (or many inputs) to be the lattice skeleton; (iii) extract all *minimal consistent alignments* between the skeleton and the other inputs; and (iv) add links to the lattice for each aligned phrase pair.

A multi-parallel corpus such as Europarl (Koehn, 2005) is ideally suited for training this setup, as training data is available for each pair of input languages needed by the word aligner. We used the GIZA++ word alignment tool (Och and Ney, 2003) for aligning inputs, trained on a portion of the Europarl training data for each pair.

We select a skeleton input based on which single-language translation system performs the best when translating a development set. For our Europarl test condition, this was French.

We define a *minimal consistent alignment* (MCA) as a member of the set of multi-word alignment pairs that can be extracted from a many-to-many word alignment between skeleton sentence $\mathbf{x}$ and non-skeleton sentence $\mathbf{y}$ with the following restrictions: (i) no word in $\mathbf{x}$ or $\mathbf{y}$ is used more than once in the set of MCAs; (ii) words and phrases selected from $\mathbf{y}$ cannot be aligned to *null*; and (iii) no smaller MCA can be decomposed from a given pair. This definition is similar to that of *minimal translation units* as described in Quirk and Menezes (2006), although they allow *null* words on either side.

Different word alignment approaches will result in different sets of MCAs. For input lattices, we want sets of MCAs with as many aligned words as possible, while minimising the average number of words in each pair in the set. Experiments with GIZA++ on the Europarl data showed that the "grow-diag-final-and" word alignment symmetrization heuristic had the best balance between coverage and pair length: over 85% of skeleton words were part of a non-*null* minimal pair, and the average length of each pair was roughly 1.5 words. This indicates that our lattices will preserve most of the input space while collapsing easily alignable sub-segments.

Once a set of phrase alignments has been found, we construct a lattice over the skeleton sentence $\mathbf{x}$. For each additional input $\mathbf{y}_n$ we add a set of links and nodes for each word in $\mathbf{x}$ to any relevant

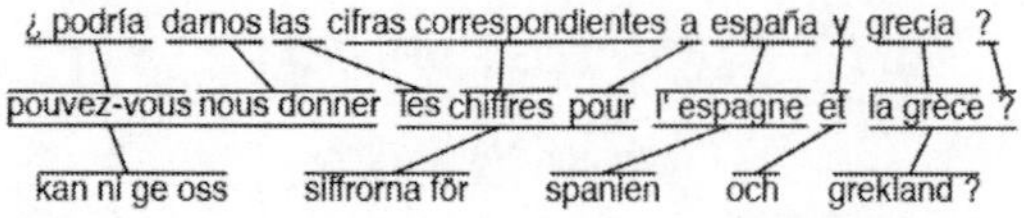

Figure 4: A multi-lingual alignment between French, Spanish and Swedish, showing the minimal consistent alignments. The lattice generated by this alignment is shown in Figure 5.

words in $\mathbf{y}_n$, rejoining at the last word in $\mathbf{x}$ that is covered by the pair. Figures 4 and 5 show an example of the alignments and lattice generated by using a French skeleton with Spanish and Swedish sentences.

Once a lattice is created, we can submit it to a phrase-based decoder in place of text input. The decoder traverses lattice nodes in a manner similar to how words are traversed in text translation. Instead of one input word represented by each location in the coverage vector as in text input, with lattices there are a set of possible input word arcs, each with its own translation possibilities. The concept of compatible coverage vectors for the locations of translated words becomes the notion of reachability between frontier nodes in the lattice (Dyer et al., 2008).

It is possible to construct multi-skeleton lattices by connecting up a set of N lattices, each built around a different skeleton $\mathbf{x}_n$, in much the same manner as multiple confusion networks can be connected to form a lattice in output combination. With sufficient diversity in the input ordering of each skeleton, the decoder need not perform reordering. Because of the size and complexity of these multi-skeleton lattices, we attempt only monotonic decoding. In this scenario, as in consensus decoding, we hope to exploit the additional word order information provided by the alternative skeletons.

3 Experiments: Monolingual Input

We start our experimental evaluation by translating multiple monolingual inputs into a foreign language. This is a best-case scenario for testing and analytic purposes because we have a single translation model from one source language to one target language. While translating from multiple monolingual inputs is not a common use for machine translation, it could be useful in situations where we have a number of paraphrases of the input text, e.g., cross-language information retrieval and summarization.

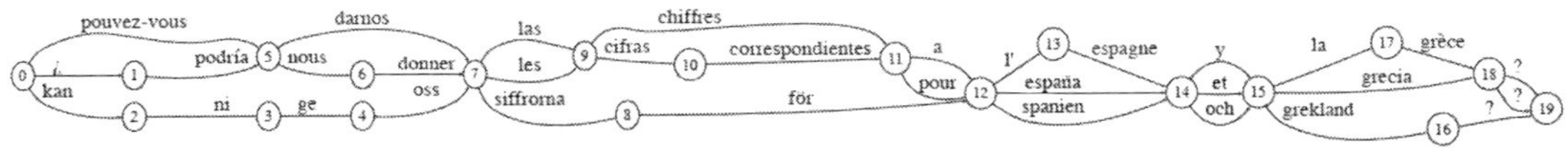

Figure 5: A multi-lingual lattice input for French, Spanish, and Swedish from Europarl dev2006.

Data sets for this condition are readily available in the form of test sets created for machine translation evaluation, which contains multiple target references for each source sentence. By flipping these test sets around, we create multiple monolingual inputs (the original references) and a single reference output (the original source text). We examine two datasets: the BTEC Italian-English corpus (Takezawa et al., 2002), and the Multiple Translation Chinese to English (MTC) corpora,[3] as used in past years' NIST MT evaluations.

All of our translation experiments use the Moses decoder (Koehn et al., 2007), and are evaluated using BLEU-4. Moses is a phrase-based decoder with features for lexicalized reordering, distance-based reordering, phrase and word translation probabilities, phrase and word counts, and an n-gram language model.

3.1 English to Italian

We use the portion of the BTEC data made available for the Italian-English translation task at IWSLT 2007, consisting of approximately 24,000 sentences. We also use the Europarl English-Italian parallel corpus to supplement our training data with approximately 1.2 million out-of-domain sentences. We train a 5-gram language model over both training corpora using SRILM (Stolcke, 2002) with Kneser-Ney smoothing and linear interpolation, the interpolation weight chosen to minimise perplexity on the Italian side of the development tuning set.

For multiple translation data, we use IWSLT test sets devset1-3 which have sixteen English translations for each Italian sentence. The Italian version of the BTEC corpus was created after the original Japanese-English version, and only the first English translation was used to generate the Italian data. The other fifteen versions of each English sentence were generated as paraphrases of the primary English translation. We explore translation conditions using only the fifteen paraphrased inputs ("Para." in Table 2), as well as using all sixteen English inputs ("All").

[3] LDC2002T01, LDC2003T17, LDC2004T07 and LDC2006T04.

	All	Para.
BEST	40.06	24.02
ORACLE	51.64	47.27
MAX	29.32	23.94
SYSCOMB	**32.89**	**30.39**
CN INPUT	31.86	27.62

Table 2: BLEU scores on the BTEC test set for translating English inputs into Italian.

We tune our translation models on devset1, system combination on devset2 and report results on devset3 for each condition.

When tuning the single input "Para." and "All" baselines, we include all relevant copies of the 506 lines of devset1 English data, and repeat the Italian reference fifteen or sixteen times on the target side, resulting in a total of 7,590 and 8,096 sentence pairs respectively.

The results for devset3 are shown in Table 2. For comparison, we show the BEST score any input produced, as well as an approximated ORACLE output selection generated by choosing the best BLEU-scoring output for each sentence using a greedy search. Our output combination method, SYSCOMB, uses no system-specific weights to distinguish the inputs. For SYSCOMB and MAX, we translated all versions of the English input separately, and we use the top ten distinct hypotheses from each input sentence for n-best input to SYSCOMB.

For input combination, CN INPUT, we used the TER-based monolingual input lattice approach described in Section 2.3, choosing as a skeleton the input with the lowest average TER score when compared with the other inputs (assessed separately for each sentence). Each input was given equal probability in the confusion network links.

Note that the quality of output from translating the primary English input is much higher than from translating any of the paraphrases. The primary input sentence scores a BLEU of 40.06, while the highest scoring paraphrased input manages only a 24.02. When we look at "Para." the difference in the scores when using a single input

(BEST) versus all the inputs (SYSCOMB and CN INPUT) is striking – clearly there is considerable information in the other inputs which can radically improve the translation output. Removing the primary input from ORACLE reinforces this observation: the score drops by only 4.37 BLEU despite the nearly 16 BLEU drop for the single best input.

Interestingly, the output selection technique, MAX, performs at a similar level to the combination techniques when we include the primary input, but degrades when given only the lower quality translations of paraphrased input under condition "Para." In previous work on multi-lingual output selection, the MAX score degraded after two or three outputs were combined, but even without the primary reference it maintains a score near the best single paraphrased input when combining fifteen outputs. One possible explanation for this is that the inputs are all being translated with the same translation model, so comparing their scores can give a more accurate ranking of their relative translation quality according to the model. The input combination method, CN INPUT, performs better than MAX and only slightly worse than the output combination approach.

3.2 English to Chinese

We can add an extra dimension to monolingual multi-source translation by considering inputs of differing quality. A multi-source translation system can exploit features indicating the origin of the input to improve output quality. For these experiments, we use the MTC English-Chinese corpus, parts 1–4. This data was translated from Chinese into English by four teams of annotators, denoted E01–E04. This allows us to examine the results for translating the same team's work over multiple years.

We train on the news domain portion of the official NIST data[4] (excluding the UN and Hong Kong data) for both the translation model and the 5-gram Chinese language model.

While we still have a single translation model, all of our inputs are now of a traceable origin and are known to have quality differences when judged by human evaluators. With this information we can tune one of two ways: We can create a set of all input systems and replicate the reference as we did for English to Italian translation ("All tuned"),

Team	Tuning	Part 3	Part 4
E01	All	**16.18**	15.52
E01	Self	16.02	**15.63**
E02	All	**14.29**	14.00
E02	Self	13.88	**14.05**
E03	All	14.99	**15.06**
E03	Self	**15.10**	14.94
E04	All	14.03	**12.65**
E04	Self	14.03	12.59

Table 3: BLEU scores using single inputs from each different team on the MTC. Bold indicates the better score between All and Self tuning.

Approach	Tuning	Part 3	Part 4
MAX	All	**15.06**	**15.08**
MAX	Self	14.97	13.75
SYSCOMB	All	16.82	16.24
SYSCOMB	Self	**16.87**	**16.45**

Table 4: BLEU scores for multi-source translations of MTC test sets. Better score for each output-based multi-source method is shown in bold.

or we can tune each input using only the version of the tuning data generated by the same translation team ("Self tuned").[5] For example, we can tune a system with the MTC Part 2 data provided by translation team E01, and then decode E01's translations of parts 3 and 4 with the weights obtained in tuning. The results for each system are shown in Table 3. Despite the different tuning conditions, there is no clear advantage to tuning to all inputs versus tuning to each input separately – on average we see a 0.06 BLEU score advantage by using "All" weights.

With four different inputs to our multi-source translation system, and two ways of weighting the features for each input, how can we best utilize these systems in output selection and combination? We perform system combination and MAX selection and obtain the scores shown in Table 4. The consensus decoding approach uses system-specific features as described in Section 2.2 to distinguish between E01-E04.

As with English to Italian, output combination performs the best of the multi-source techniques. MAX performs better with translations generated by "All" weights than with "Self", and the con-

[4] http://www.nist.gov/speech/tests/mt/2008

[5] Note that in the "Self tuned" setting we have only a quarter as much tuning data as for "All tuned".

Input Language	test2006	test2007
French (FR)	29.72	30.21
Spanish (ES)	29.55	29.62
Swedish (SV)	29.33	29.44
Portuguese (PT)	28.75	28.79
Danish (DA)	27.20	27.48
Greek (EL)	26.93	26.78
Italian (IT)	26.82	26.51
German (DE)	24.04	24.41
Dutch (NL)	23.79	24.28
Finnish (FI)	18.96	18.85

Table 5: BLEU scores for individual translation systems into English trained on Europarl, from best to worst.

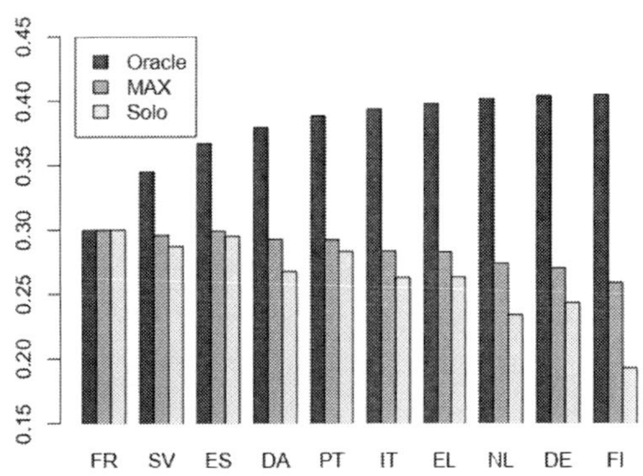

Figure 6: Performance for multilingual multi-source translation (test2005) as each language input is added, showing Oracle target selection, MAX score, or just a single language input (Solo).

verse is true for SYSCOMB. Given the robust performance of MAX when translation scores originated from the same translation model in English to Italian, it is not surprising that it favors the case where all the outputs are scored by the same model ("All tuned"). On the other hand, diversity amongst the system outputs has been shown to be important to the performance of system combination techniques (Macherey and Och, 2007). This may give an indication as to why the "Self tuned" data produced higher scores in consensus decoding – the outputs will be more highly divergent due to their different tuning conditions.

4 Experiments: Multilingual Input

Multilingual cases are the traditional realm of multi-source translation. We no longer have directly comparable translation models; instead each input language has a separate set of rules for translating to the output language. However, the availability of (and demand for) multi-parallel corpora makes this form of multi-source translation of great practical use.

4.1 Lattice Inputs

As described in Section 2.3, lattices can be used to provide a compact format for translating multilingual inputs to a multi-source translation system. We trim all non-skeleton node paths to a maximum length of four to reduce complexity when decoding. Such long paths are mostly a result of errors in the original word alignments, and therefore pruning these links is largely innocuous.

We train on the Europarl corpus and use the in-domain test sets provided for previous years' Workshops on Statistical Machine Translation. Because of the computational complexity of dealing with so many models, we train on only the first 100,000 sentences of each parallel corpus. Single system baseline scores for each language are shown in Table 5.

Besides comparing the different multi-source translation methods discussed above, in this task we also want to examine what happens when we use different numbers of input languages. To determine the best order to add languages, we performed a greedy search over oracle BLEU scores for test set test2005. We started with the best scoring single system, French to English, and in each iteration picked one additional system that would maximise BLEU if we always selected the translation system output closest to the reference. The results are shown in Figure 6.

The oracle selection order differs from the order of the best performing systems, which could be due to the high scoring systems having very similar output while lower scoring systems exhibit greater diversity. Interestingly, the order of the languages chosen iterates between the Roman and Germanic language families and includes Greek early on. This supports our claim that diversity is important. Note though that Finnish, which is also in a separate language family, is selected last, most likely due to difficulties in word alignment and translation stemming from its morphological complexity (Birch et al., 2008). This finding might also carry over to phrase-table triangulation (Cohn and Lapata, 2007), where multi-parallel data is used in training to augment a standard translation

Approach	test2006	test2007
French Only	29.72	30.21
French + Swedish		
MAX	29.86	30.13
LATTICE	29.33	29.97
MULTILATTICE	29.55	29.88
SYSCOMB	31.32	31.77
French + Swedish + Spanish		
MAX	30.18	30.33
LATTICE	29.98	30.45
MULTILATTICE	30.50	30.50
SYSCOMB	33.77	33.87
6 Languages		
MAX	28.37	28.33
LATTICE	30.22	30.91
MULTILATTICE	30.59	30.59
SYSCOMB	35.47	36.03

Table 6: BLEU scores for multi-source translation systems into English trained on Europarl. Single source French decoding is shown as a baseline.

system.

We choose to evaluate translation performance at three combination levels: two languages (French and Swedish), three languages (+Spanish), and six languages (+Danish, Portuguese, Italian). For each combination we apply MAX, SYSCOMB, French skeleton lattice input translation LATTICE, and monotone decoding over multiple skeleton lattices, MULTILATTICE. Results are shown in Table 6.

To enable the decoder used in LATTICE and MULTILATTICE to learn weights for different sources, we add a feature to the phrase table for each of the languages being translated. This feature takes as its value the number of words on the source side of the phrase. By weighting this feature up or down for each language, the decoder can prefer word links from specific languages.

As seen in previous work in multi-source translation, MAX output selection performs well with two or three languages but degrades as more languages are added to the input. Conversely, our lattice input method shows upward trends: LATTICE is comparable with MAX on three inputs and scores increase in the six language case.

Given the higher scores for output combination over input combination, what differences can we observe between the systems? Both systems have features that indicate the contributions of each input language to the final output. With input combination, we are forced by the decoder to take the maximum scoring path through the lattice, but in output combination we have the aggregate vote of word confidences generated by each system. If we could combine word arc scores across inputs, as in output combination, we might get a more robust solution for taking advantage of the available similarities on the target side of the translation. This points to a direction for future research.

Other differences between the systems may explain the score gap between our input and output combination approaches. Consensus decoding allows you to mix and match fragments that aren't necessarily stored as fragments in the phrase table. Another difference is the richer space of reorderings in TER-based lattices, due to the ability of the metric to handle long-distance alignments.

5 Conclusion

We analyzed three approaches for dealing with multi-source translation. While MAX is mostly a poor performer, the upper bound of output selection is stunning. The very positive results for output system combination across all data conditions are quite promising. Output combination achieves these results while the using the limited expressive power of n-best inputs. The potential of using a more expressive format – such as lattices that represent the joint search space of multiple models – is high. Our first attempts at adapting lattices to multi-source translation input show promise for future development. We have only scratched the surface of methods for constructing input lattices, and plan to actively continue research into improving these methods.

Acknowledgments

Thanks to Chris Callison-Burch for many insightful discussions, and to Chris Dyer for his implementation of lattice decoding in Moses.

This work was supported by the EuroMatrix project funded by the European Commission (6th Framework Programme), and has made use of the resources provided by the Edinburgh Compute and Data Facility (http://www.ecdf.ed.ac.uk/), which is partially supported by the eDIKT initiative (http://www.edikt.org). We also acknowledge the support of the EPSRC (grant GR/T04557/01).

References

Srinivas Bangalore, German Bordel, and Giuseppe Riccardi. 2001. Computing consensus translation from multiple machine translation systems. In *Proceedings of ASRU*, pages 351–354, Trento, Italy, December.

Regina Barzilay and Lillian Lee. 2003. Learning to paraphrase: An unsupervised approach using multiple-sequence alignment. In *Proceedings of NAACL: HLT*, pages 16–23, Edmonton, Canada, May.

Nicola Bertoldi, Richard Zens, and Marcello Federico. 2007. Speech translation by confusion network decoding. In *Proceedings of IEEE ICASSP*, pages 1297–1300, Honolulu, Hawaii, USA, April.

Alexandra Birch, Miles Osborne, and Philipp Koehn. 2008. Predicting success in machine translation. In *Proceedings of EMNLP*, pages 745–754, Honolulu, Hawaii, USA, October.

Trevor Cohn and Mirella Lapata. 2007. Machine translation by triangulation: Making effective use of multi-parallel corpora. In *Proceedings of ACL*, pages 728–735, Prague, Czech Republic, June.

Marta Ruiz Costa-jussà, Josep M. Crego, Patrik Lambert, Maxim Khalilov, José A. R. Fonollosa, José B. Mario, and Rafael E. Banchs. 2007. Ngram-based statistical machine translation enhanced with multiple weighted reordering hypotheses. In *Proceedings of the Second Workshop on Statistical Machine Translation*, pages 167–170, Prague, Czech Republic, June.

Christopher J. Dyer, Smaranda Muresan, and Philip Resnik. 2008. Generalizing word lattice translation. In *Proceedings of ACL: HLT*, pages 1012–1020, Columbus, Ohio, USA, June.

Philipp Koehn, Hieu Hoang, Alexandra Birch, Chris Callison-Burch, Marcello Federico, Nicola Bertoldi, Brooke Cowan, Wade Shen, Christine Moran, Richard Zens, Christopher J. Dyer, Ondřej Bojar, Alexandra Constantin, and Evan Herbst. 2007. Moses: Open source toolkit for statistical machine translation. In *Proceedings of ACL: Demo and Poster Sessions*, pages 177–180, Prague, Czech Republic, June.

Philipp Koehn. 2005. Europarl: A parallel corpus for statistical machine translation. In *Proceedings of MT Summit X*, pages 79–86, Phuket, Thailand, September.

Wolfgang Macherey and Franz J. Och. 2007. An empirical study on computing consensus translations from multiple machine translation systems. In *Proceedings of EMNLP-CoNLL*, pages 986–995, Prague, Czech Republic, June.

Evgeny Matusov, Nicola Ueffing, and Hermann Ney. 2006. Computing consensus translation for multiple machine translation systems using enhanced hypothesis alignment. In *Proceedings of EACL*, pages 33–40, Trento, Italy, April.

Franz Josef Och and Hermann Ney. 2001. Statistical multi-source translation. In *Proceedings of MT Summit VIII*, pages 253–258, Santiago de Compostela, Spain, September.

Franz Josef Och and Hermann Ney. 2003. A systematic comparison of various statistical alignment models. *Computational Linguistics*, 29(1):19–52.

Matthias Paulik, Kay Rottmann, Jan Niehues, Almut Silja Hildebrand, and Stephan Vogel. 2007. The ISL phrase-based MT system for the 2007 ACL workshop on statistical machine translation. In *Proceedings of the Second Workshop on Statistical Machine Translation*, pages 197–202, Prague, Czech Republic, June.

Chris Quirk and Arul Menezes. 2006. Do we need phrases? Challenging the conventional wisdom in statistical machine translation. In *Proceedings of ACL: HLT, Main Conference*, pages 9–16, New York, New York, USA, June.

Antti-Veikko I. Rosti, Spyros Matsoukas, and Richard Schwartz. 2007a. Improved word-level system combination for machine translation. In *Proceedings of ACL*, pages 312–319, Prague, Czech Republic, June.

Antti-Veikko I. Rosti, Bing Xiang, Spyros Matsoukas, Richard Schwartz, Necip Fazil Ayan, and Bonnie J. Dorr. 2007b. Combining output from multiple machine translation systems. In *Proceedings of NAACL: HLT*, pages 228–235, Rochester, New York, USA, April.

Lane Schwartz. 2008. Multi-source translation methods. In *Proceedings of AMTA*, pages 279–288, Waikiki, Hawaii, USA, October.

Matthew Snover, Bonnie J. Dorr, Richard Schwartz, Linnea Micciulla, and John Makhoul. 2006. A study of translation edit rate with targeted human annotation. In *Proceedings of AMTA*, pages 223–231, Boston, Massachusetts, USA, August.

Andreas Stolcke. 2002. SRILM - an extensible language modeling toolkit. In *Proceedings of ICSLP*, pages 901–904, Denver, Colorado, USA, October.

Toshiyuki Takezawa, Eiichiro Sumita, Fumiaki Sugaya, Hirofumi Yamamoto, and Seiichi Yamamoto. 2002. Toward a broad-coverage bilingual corpus for speech translation of travel conversations in the real world. In *Proceedings of LREC*, pages 147–152, Las Palmas, Canary Islands, Spain, May.

Jia Xu, Evgeny Matusov, Richard Zens, and Hermann Ney. 2005. Integrated Chinese word segmentation in statistical machine translation. In *Proceedings of IWSLT*, Pittsburgh, Pennsylvania, USA, October.

Frequency Matters: Pitch Accents and Information Status

Katrin Schweitzer, Michael Walsh, Bernd Möbius,
Arndt Riester, Antje Schweitzer, Hinrich Schütze
University of Stuttgart
Stuttgart, Germany
<firstname>.<surname>@ims.uni-stuttgart.de

Abstract

This paper presents the results of a series of experiments which examine the impact of two information status categories (*given* and *new*) and frequency of occurrence on pitch accent realisations. More specifically the experiments explore within-type similarity of pitch accent productions and the effect information status and frequency of occurrence have on these productions. The results indicate a significant influence of both pitch accent type and information status category on the degree of within-type variability, in line with exemplar-theoretic expectations.

1 Introduction

It seems both intuitive and likely that prosody should have a significant role to play in marking information status in speech. While there are well established expectations concerning typical associations between categories of information status and categories of pitch accent, e.g. rising L∗H accents are often a marker for givenness, there is nevertheless some variability here (Baumann, 2006). Furthermore, little research has focused on how pitch accent tokens of the same type are realised nor have the effects of information status and frequency of occurrence been considered.

From the perspective of speech technology, the tasks of automatically inferring and assigning information status clearly have significant importance for speech synthesis and speech understanding systems.

The research presented in this paper examines a number of questions concerning the relationship between two information status categories (*new* and *given*), and how tokens of associated pitch accent types are realised. Furthermore the effect of frequency of occurrence is also examined from an exemplar-theoretic perspective.

The questions directly addressed in this paper are as follows:

1. How are different tokens of a pitch accent type realised?
   Does frequency of occurrence of the pitch accent type play a role?
2. What effect does information status have on realisations of a pitch accent type?
   Does frequency of occurrence of the information status category play a role?
3. Does frequency of occurrence in pitch accents *and* in information status play a role, i.e. is there a combined effect?

In examining the realisation of pitch accent tokens, their degree of similarity is the characteristic under investigation. Similarity is calculated by determining the cosine of the angle between pairs of pitch accent vector representations (see section 6).

The results in this study are examined from an exemplar-theoretic perspective (see section 3). The expectations within that framework are based upon two different aspects. Firstly, it is expected that, since all exemplars are stored, exemplars of a type that occur often, offer the speaker a wider selection of exemplars to choose from during production (Schweitzer and Möbius, 2004), i.e. the realisations are expected to be more variable than those of a rare type. However, another aspect of Exemplar Theory has to be considered, namely entrenchment (Pierrehumbert, 2001; Bybee, 2006). The central idea here is that frequently occurring behaviours undergo processes of entrenchment, they become in some sense routine. Therefore realisations of a very frequent type are expected to be realised similar to each other. Thus, similarity and variability are expressions of the same characteristic: the higher the degree of similarity of pitch accent tokens, the lower their realisation variability.

Proceedings of the 12th Conference of the European Chapter of the ACL, pages 728–736,
Athens, Greece, 30 March – 3 April 2009.

The structure of this paper is as follows: Section 2 briefly examines previous work on the interaction of information status categories and pitch accents. Section 3 provides a short introduction to Exemplar Theory. In this study similarity of pitch accent realisations on syllables, annotated with the information status categories of the words they belong to, is examined using the parametric intonation model (Möhler, 1998) which is outlined in Section 4. Section 5 discusses the corpus employed. Section 6 introduces a general methodology which is used in the experiments in Sections 7, 8 and 9. Section 10 then presents some discussion, conclusions and opportunities for future research.

2 Information Status and Intonation

It is commonly assumed that pitch accents are the main correlate of information status[1] in speech (Halliday, 1967). Generally, accenting is said to signal novelty while deaccenting signals given information (Brown, 1983), although there is counter evidence: various studies note given information being accented (Yule, 1980; Bard and Aylett, 1999). Terken and Hirschberg (1994) point out that new information can also be deaccented.

As for the question of which pitch accent type (in terms of ToBI categories (Silverman et al., 1992)) is typically assigned to different degrees of givenness, Pierrehumbert and Hirschberg (1990) find H∗ to be the standard novelty accent for English, a finding which has also been confirmed by Baumann (2006) and Schweitzer et al. (2008) for German. Given information on the other hand, if accented at all, is found to carry L∗ accent in English (Pierrehumbert and Hirschberg, 1990). Baumann (2006) finds deaccentuation to be the most preferred realisation for givenness in his experimental phonetics studies on German. However, Baumann (2006) points out that H+L∗ has also been found as a marker of givenness in a German corpus study. Previous findings on the corpus used in the present study found L∗H being the typical marker for givenness (Schweitzer et al., 2008).

Leaving the phonological level and examining correlates of information status in acoustic detail, Kohler (1991) reports that in a falling accent, an early peak indicates established facts, while a medial peak is used to mark novelty. In a recent study Kügler and Féry (2008) found givenness to lower the high tones of prenuclear pitch accents and to cancel them out postnuclearly. These findings among others (Kügler and Féry, 2008) motivate an examination of the acoustic detail of pitch accent shape across different information status categories.

The experiments presented here go one step further, however, in that they also investigate potential exemplar-theoretic effects.

3 Exemplar Theory

Exemplar Theory is concerned with the idea that the acquisition of language is significantly facilitated by repeated exposure to concrete language input, and it has successfully accounted for a number of language phenomena, including diachronic language change and frequency of occurrence effects (Bybee, 2006), the emergence of grammatical knowledge (Abbot-Smith and Tomasello, 2006), syllable duration variability (Schweitzer and Möbius, 2004; Walsh et al., 2007), entrenchment and lenition (Pierrehumbert, 2001), among others. Central to Exemplar Theory are the notions of exemplar storage, frequency of occurrence, recency of occurrence, and similarity. There is an increasing body of evidence which indicates that significant storage of language input exemplars, rich in detail, takes place in memory (Johnson, 1997; Croot and Rastle, 2004; Whiteside and Varley, 1998). These stored exemplars are then employed in the categorisation of new input percepts. Similarly, production is facilitated by accessing these stored exemplars. Computational models of the exemplar memory also argue that it is in a constant state of flux with new inputs updating it and old unused exemplars gradually fading away (Pierrehumbert, 2001).

Up to now, virtually no exemplar-theoretic research has examined pitch accent prosody (but see Marsi et al. (2003) for memory-based prediction of pitch accents and prosodic boundaries, and Walsh et al. (2008)(discussed below)) and to the authors' knowledge this paper represents the first attempt to examine the relationship between pitch accent prosody and information status from an exemplar-theoretic perspective. Given the considerable weight of evidence for the influence of frequency of occurrence effects in a variety of other linguistic domains it seems reasonable to explore such effects on pitch accent and information sta-

[1] The term *information status* is used in (Prince, 1992) for the first time. Before that the terms *givenness*, *novelty* or *information structure* were used for these concepts.

tus realisations. For example, what effect might givenness have on a frequently/infrequently occurring pitch accent? Does novelty produce a similar result?

The search for possible frequency of occurrence effects takes place with respect to pitch accent shapes captured by the parametric intonation model discussed next.

4 The Parametric Representation of Intonation Events - PaIntE

The model approximates stretches of F_0 by employing a phonetically motivated model function (Möhler, 1998). This function consists of the sum of two sigmoids (rising and falling) with a fixed time delay which is selected so that the peak does not fall below 96% of the function's range. The resulting function has six parameters which describe the contour and were employed in the analysis: parameters a1 and a2 express the gradient of the accent's rise and fall, parameter b describes the accent's temporal alignment (which has been shown to be crucial in the description of an accent's shape (van Santen and Möbius, 2000)), c1 and c2 model the ranges of the rising and falling amplitude of the accent's contour, respectively, and parameter d expresses the peak height of the accent.[2] These six parameters are thus appropriate to describe different pitch accent shapes.

For the annotation of intonation the GToBI(S) annotation scheme (Mayer, 1995) was used. In earlier versions of PaIntE, the approximation of the F_0-contour for H∗L and H∗ was carried out on the accented and post–accented syllables. However, for these accents the beginning of the rise is likely to start at the preaccented syllable. In the current version of PaIntE the window used for the approximation of the F_0-contour for H∗L and H∗ accents has been extended to the preaccented syllable, so that the parameters are calculated over the span of the accented syllables and its immediate neighbours (unless it is followed by a boundary tone which causes the window to end at the end of the accented syllable).

5 Corpus

The experiments that follow (sections 7, 9 and 8), were carried out on German pitch accents from the IMS Radio News Corpus (Rapp, 1998). This corpus was automatically segmented and manually labelled according to GToBI(S) (Mayer, 1995). In the corpus, 1233 syllables are associated with an L∗H accent, 704 with an H∗L accent and 162 with an H∗ accent.

The corpus contains data from three speakers, two female and a male one, but the majority of the data is produced by the male speaker (888 L∗H accents, 527 H∗L accents and 152 H∗ accents). In order to maximise the number of tokens, all three speakers were combined. Of the analysed data, 77.92% come from the male speaker. However, it is not necessarily the case that the same percentage of the variability also comes from this speaker: Both, PaIntE and z-scoring (cf. section 6) normalise across speakers, so the contribution from each individual speaker is unclear.

The textual transcription of the corpus was annotated with respect to information status using the annotation scheme proposed by Riester (2008). In this taxonomy information status categories reflect the default contexts in which presuppositions are resolved, which include e. g. discourse context, environment context or encyclopaedic context.

The annotations are based solely on the written text and follow strict semantic criteria. Given that textual information alone (i.e. without prosodic or speech related information) is not necessarily sufficient to unambiguously determine the information status associated with a particular word, there are therefore cases where words have multiple annotations, reflecting underspecification of information status. However, it is important to note that in all the experiments reported here, only unambiguous cases are considered.

The rich annotation scheme employed in the corpus makes establishing inter-annotator agreement a time-consuming task which is currently underway. Nevertheless, the annotation process was set up in a way to ensure a maximal smoothing of uncertainties. Texts were independently labelled by two annotators. Subsequently, a third, more experienced annotator compared the two results and, in the case of discrepancies, took a final decision.

In the present study the categories *given* and *new* are examined. These categories do not represent a binary distinction but are two extremes from a set of clearly distinguished categories. For the most part they correspond to the categories *textually given* and *brand-new* that are used in Bau-

[2] Further information and illustrations concerning the mechanics of the PaIntE model can be found in Möhler and Conkie (1998).

mann (2006), but their scope is more tightly constrained. The information status annotations are mapped to the phonetically transcribed speech signals, from which individual syllable tokens bearing information status are derived.

Syllables for which one of the PaIntE-parameters was identified as an outlier, were removed. Outliers were defined such that the upper 2.5 percentile as well as the lower 2.5 percentile of the data were excluded. This led to a reduced number of pitch accent tokens: 1021 L*H accents, 571 H*L accents and 134 H* accents. Thus, there is a continuum of frequency of occurrence, high to low, from L*H to H*.

With respect to information status, 102 L*H accents, 87 H*L accents and 21 H* accents were unambiguously labelled as *new*. For givenness the number of tokens is: 114 L*H accents, 44 H*L accents and 10 H* accents.

6 General Methodology

In the experiments the general methodology for calculation of similarity detailed in this section was employed.

For tokens of the pitch accent types L*H, H*L and H*, each token was modelled using the full set of PaIntE parameters. Thus, each token was represented in terms of a 6-dimensional vector.

For each of the pitch accent types the following steps were carried out:

- For each 6-dimensional pitch accent category token calculate the z-score value for each dimension. The z-score value represents the number of standard deviations the value is away from the mean value for that dimension and allows comparison of values from different normal distributions. The z-score is given by:

$$z - score_{dim} = \frac{value_{dim} - mean_{dim}}{sdev_{dim}} \quad (1)$$

  Hence, at this point each pitch accent is represented by a 6-dimensional vector where each dimension value is a z-score.

- For each token z-scored vector calculate how similar it is to every other z-scored vector within the same pitch accent category, and, in Experiment 2 and 3, with the same information status value (e.g. new), using the cosine of the angle between the vectors. This is given by:

$$cos(\vec{i}, \vec{j}) = \frac{\vec{i} \bullet \vec{j}}{\| \vec{i} \| \| \vec{j} \|} \quad (2)$$

  where *i* and *j* are vectors of the same pitch accent category and • represents the dot product.

  Each comparison between vectors yields a similarity score in the range [-1,1], where -1 represents high dissimilarity and 1 represents high similarity.

The experiments that follow examine distributions of token similarity. In order to establish whether distributions differ significantly two different levels of significance were employed, depending on the number of pairwise comparisons performed.

When comparing two distributions (i.e. performing one test), the significance level was set to $\alpha = 0.05$. In those cases where multiple tests were carried out (Experiment 1 and Experiment 3), the level of significance was adjusted (Bonferroni correction) according to the following formula:

$$\alpha = 1 - (1 - \alpha_1)^{\frac{1}{n}} \quad (3)$$

where α_1 represents the target significance level (set to 0.05) and n represents the number of tests being performed. The Bonferroni correction is often discussed controversially. The main criticism concerns the increased likelihood of type II errors that lead to non-significance of actually significant findings (Pernegger, 1998). Although this conservative adjustment was applied, the statistical tests in this study resulted in significant p-values indicating the robustness of the findings.

7 Experiment 1: Examining frequency of occurrence effects in pitch accents

In accordance with the general methodology set out in section 6, the PaIntE vectors of pitch accent tokens of types L*H, H*L, and H* were all z-scored and, within each type, every token was compared for similarity against every other token of the same type, using the cosine of the angle between their vectors. In essence, this experiment illustrates how similarly pitch accents of the same type are realised.

Figure 1 depicts the results of the analysis. It shows the density plot for each distribution of cosine-similarity comparison values, whereby the

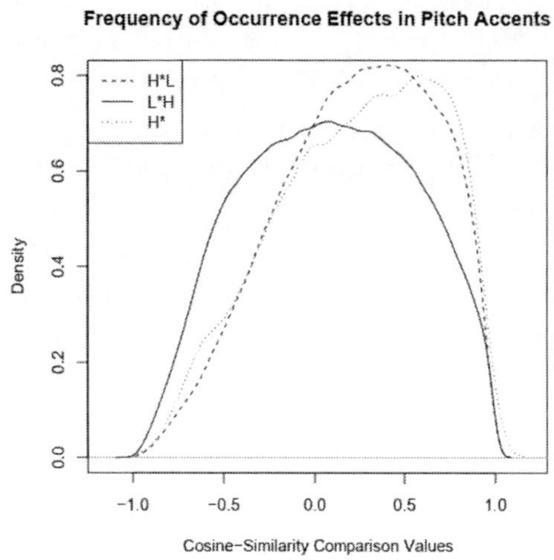

Figure 1: *Density plots for similarity within pitch accent types. All distributions differ significantly from each other. There is a trend towards greater similarity from high-frequency* L∗H *to low-frequency* H∗.

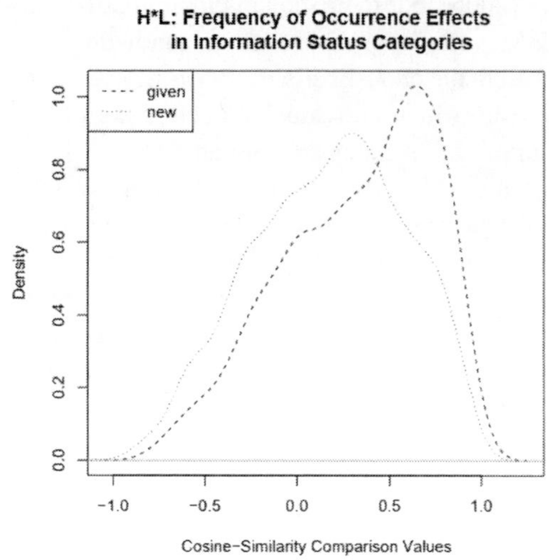

Figure 2: *Density plots for similarity of* H∗L *tokens. Tokens of the low-frequency information status category* given *display greater similarity to each other than those of the high-frequency information status category* new.

distributions can be compared directly – irrespective of the different number of data points.

An initial observation is that L∗H tokens tend to be realised fairly variably, the main portion of the distribution is centred around zero. Tokens of H∗L tend to be produced more similarly (i.e. the distribution is centred around a higher similarity value), and tokens of H∗ more similarly again. These three distributions were tested against each other for significance using the Kolmogorov-Smirnov test ($\alpha = 0.017$), yielding p-values of $p \ll 0.001$. Thus there are significant differences between these distributions.

What is particularly noteworthy is that a *decrease* in frequency of occurrence across pitch accent types co-occurs significantly with an *increase* in within-type token similarity.

While the differences between the graphed distributions do not appear to be highly marked the frequency of occurrence effect is nevertheless in keeping with exemplar-theoretic expectations as posited by Bybee (2006) and Schweitzer and Möbius (2004), that is, the high frequency of occurrence entails a large number of stored exemplars, giving the speaker the choice from among a large number of production targets. This wider choice leads to a broader range of chosen targets for different productions and thus to more variable realisations of tokens of the same type.

Walsh et al. (2008) also reported significant differences between these distributions, however, there did not appear to be a clear frequency of occurrence effect. The results in the present study differ from their results because the distributions centre around different ranges of the similarity scale clearly indicating that each accent type behaves differently in terms of similarity/variability between the tokens of the respective type. The differences between the two findings can be ascribed to the augmented PaIntE model (section 4).

Given the results from this experiment, the next experiment seeks to establish what relationship, if any, exists between information status and pitch accent production variability.

8 Experiment 2: Examining frequency of occurrence effects in information status categories

This experiment was carried out in the same manner as Experiment 1 above with the exception that in this experiment a subset of the corpus was employed: only syllables that were unambiguously labelled with either the information status category *new* or the category *given* were included in the analyses. The experiment aims to investigate the effect of information status on the similarity/variability of tokens of different pitch accent types. For each pitch accent type, tokens that were labelled with the information status category *new*

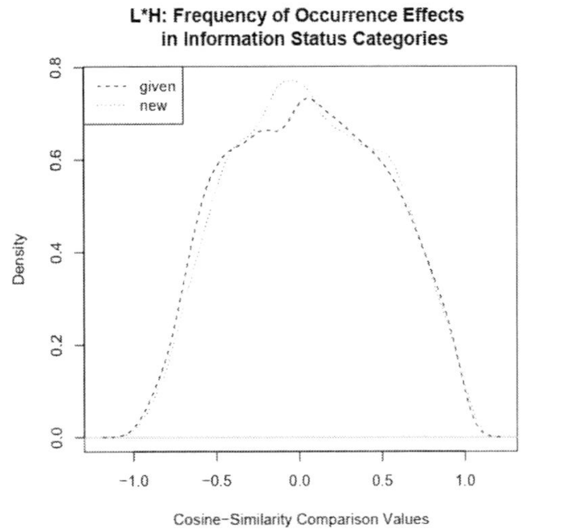

Figure 3: *Density plots for similarity of* L∗H *tokens. The curves differ significantly, a trend towards greater similarity is not observable. The number of tokens for both information status categories is comparable.*

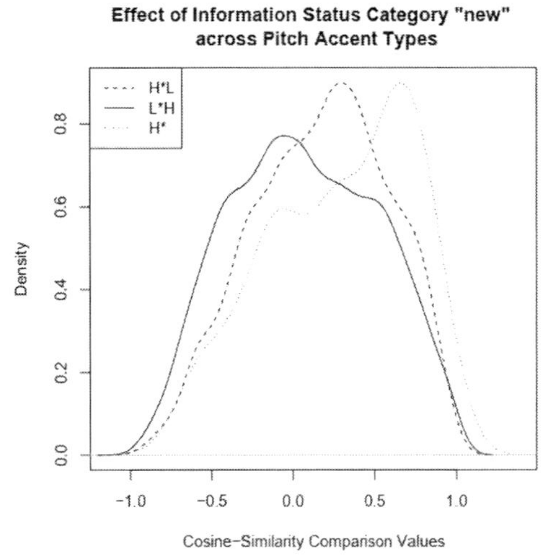

Figure 4: *Density plots for similarity of* new *tokens across three pitch accent types. In comparison to fig. 1 the trend towards greater similarity from high-frequency* L∗H *to low-frequency* H∗ *is even more pronounced.*

were compared to tokens labelled as *given*. Again, a pairwise Kolmogorov-Smirnov test was applied for each comparison ($\alpha = 0.05$). Figure 2 depicts the results for H∗L accents. The K-S test yielded a highly significant difference between the two distributions ($p \ll 0.001$), reflecting the clearly visible difference between the two curves. It is noteworthy here that for H∗L the information status category *new* is more frequent than the category *given*. Indeed, approximately twice as many are labelled as *new* than those labelled *given*. Figure 2 illustrates that *new* H∗L accents are realised more variably than *given* ones. That is, again, an increase in frequency of occurrence co-occurs with an increase in similarity, this time at the level of information status.

Figure 3 depicts the difference in similarity/variability for L∗H between *new* tokens and *given* tokens. It is clearly visible that the two curves do not differ as much as those under the H∗L condition. Both curves centre around zero reflecting the fact that for both types the tokens are variable. Although the Kolmogorov-Smirnov test indicates significance ($\alpha = 0.05, p = 0.044$), the nature of the impact that information status has in this case is unclear.

Here again an effect of frequency of occurrence might be the reason for this result. The high frequency of L∗H accents in general results in a relative high frequency of *given* L∗H tokens. So the token number for both types is similar (102 *new* L∗H tokens vs. 114 *given* L∗H tokens), there is high frequency in both cases, hence variability.

These results, particularly in the case of H∗L (fig. 2) indicate that information status affects pitch accent realisation. The next experiment compares the effect across different pitch accent types.

9 Experiment 3: Examining the effect of information status across pitch accent types

This experiment was carried out in the same manner as Experiments 1 and 2 above. For each pitch accent type, figure 4 depicts within-type pitch accent similarity for tokens unambiguously labelled as *new*.

As with Experiments 1 and 2, frequency of occurrence once more appears to play a significant role. Again, all Kolmogorov-Smirnov tests yielded significant results ($p < 0.017$ in all cases). Indeed, the difference between the distributions of L∗H, H∗L, and H∗ similarity plots appears to be considerably more prominent than in Experiment 1 (see fig. 1). This indicates that under the condition of *novelty* the frequency of occurrence effect is more pronounced. In other words, there is a considerably more noticeable difference across the distributions of L∗H, H∗L and H∗, when nov-

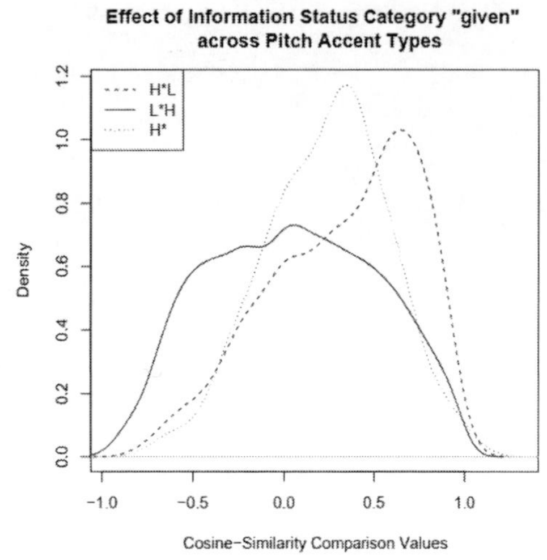

Figure 5: *Density plots for similarity of* given *tokens across three pitch accent types. Mid-frequency* H∗L *displays greater similarity than high-frequency* L∗H. *For lowest frequency* H∗ *(only 10 tokens) the trend cannot be observed.*

elty is considered: novelty compounds the frequency of occurrence effect.

Figure 5 illustrates results of the same analysis methodology but applied to tokens of pitch accents unambiguously labelled as *given*. Once again there is a considerable difference between the distributions of L∗H and H∗L tokens ($p < 0.017$). And again, this difference reflects a more pronounced frequency of occurrence effect for *given* tokens than for all accents pooled (as described in Experiment 1): the information status category *given* compounds the frequency of occurrence effect for L∗H and H∗L.

For H∗ the result is not as clear as for the two more frequent accents. The comparison between H∗ and L∗H results in a significant difference ($p < 0.017$) whereas the comparison between H∗ and H∗L is slightly above the conservative significance level ($p = 0.0186$). Moreover, the distribution is centred between the distributions for L∗H and H∗L and it is thus not clear how to interpret this result with respect to a possible frequency of occurrence effect. However, having only ten instances of *given* H∗, the explanatory power of these comparisons is questionable.

10 Discussion

The experiments discussed above yield a number of interesting results with implications for research in prosody, information status, the interaction between the two domains, and for exemplar theory.

Returning to the first question posed at the outset in section 1, it is quite clear from Experiment 1 that a certain amount of variability exists when different tokens of the same pitch accent type are produced. It is also clear, from the same experiment, that the frequency of occurrence of the pitch accent type does indeed play a role: with an increase in frequency comes an increase in variability. This result is in line with the exemplar-theoretic view that since all exemplars are stored, exemplars of a type that occur often are more variable because they offer the speaker a wider selection of exemplars to choose from during production (Schweitzer and Möbius, 2004). However, with respect to entrenchment (Pierrehumbert, 2001; Bybee, 2006), i.e. the idea that frequently occurring behaviours undergo processes of entrenchment, in Experiment 1 one might expect to see greater similarity in the realisations of L∗H. However, it is important to note that while tokens of L∗H are not particularly similar to each other (the bulk of the distribution is around zero (see figure 1)), they are not too dissimilar either. That is, they rest at the midpoint of the similarity continuum produced by cosine calculation, in quite a normal looking distribution. This is not at odds with the idea of entrenchment. As productions of a pitch accent type become more frequent, the distribution of similarity spreads from the right side of the graph (where infrequent and highly similar H∗ tokens lie) leftwards (through H∗L) to the point where the L∗H distribution is found. Beyond this point tokens are excessively different.

The second question posed in section 1, and addressed in Experiment 2, sought to ascertain the impact, if any, information status has on pitch accent realisation. Distributions of *given* and *new* H∗L similarity scores differed significantly, as did distributions of *given* and *new* L∗H similarity scores, indicating that information status affects realisation. In other words, for both pitch accent types, *given* and *new* tokens behave differently. Concerning the frequency of occurrence of the information status categories, certainly in the case of H∗L the higher frequency *new* tokens exhibited more variability. In the case of L∗H similar numbers of *new* and *given* tokens, possibly due to the high frequency of L∗H in general,

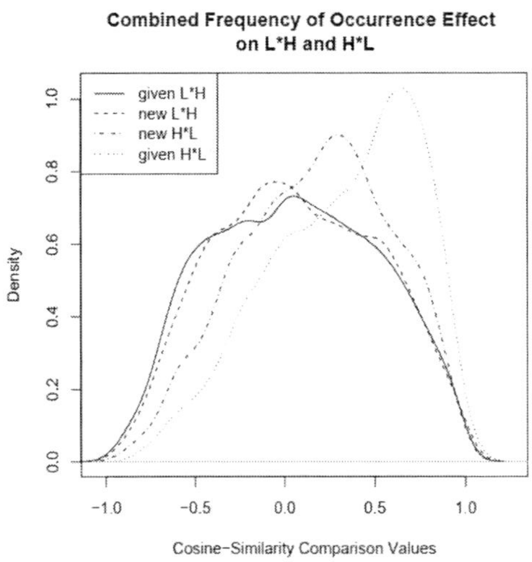

Figure 6: *Density plots for similarity of combinations of information status categories* given *and* new *with pitch accent types* L∗H *and* H∗L. *The distributions show a clear trend towards greater similarity form high-frequency* "given L∗H" *and* "new L∗H" *to mid-frequency* "new H∗L" *and low-frequency* "given H∗L".

led to visually similar yet significantly different distributions. Once again sensitivity to frequency of occurrence seems to be present, in line with exemplar-theoretic predictions.

The final question concerns the possibility of a combined effect of pitch accent frequency of occurrence and information status frequency of occurrence. Figures 4 and 5 depict a clear compounding effect of both information status categories across the different pitch accent types (and their inherent frequencies) when compared to figure 1. Interestingly, the less frequently occurring *given* appears to have a greater impact, particularly on high frequency L∗H.

Figure 6 displays all possible combinations of L∗H, H∗L, *given* and *new*. H∗ is omitted in this graph because of the small number of tokens (10 *given*, 21 *new*) and the resulting lack of explanatory power. It is evident that an overall frequency of occurrence effect can be observed: "*given* L∗H" and "*new* L∗H", which have a similar number of instances (114 vs. 102 tokens) both centre around zero and are thus the most leftward skewed curves in the graph. The distribution of "*new* H∗L" (87 tokens) shows a trend towards the right hand side of the graph and thus represents greater similarity of the tokens. The distribution of similarity values for the least frequent combination of pitch accent and information status, "*given* H∗L" (44 tokens), centres between 0.5 and 1.0 and is thus the most rightward curve in the graph, reflecting the highest similarity between the tokens.

These results highlight an intricate relationship between pitch accent production and information status. The information status of the word influences not only the type and shape of the pitch accent (Pierrehumbert and Hirschberg, 1990; Baumann, 2006; Kügler and Féry, 2008; Schweitzer et al., 2008) but also the similarity of tokens within a pitch accent type. Moreover, this effect is well explainable within the framework of Exemplar Theory as it is subject to frequency of occurrence: tokens of rare types are produced more similar to each other than tokens of frequent types.

In the context of speech technology, unfortunately the high variability in highly frequent pitch accents has a negative consequence, as the correlation between a certain pitch accent or a certain information status category and the F_0 contour is not a one-to-one relationship. However, forewarned is forearmed and perhaps a finer grained contextual analysis might yield more context specific solutions.

11 Future Work

The methodology outlined in section 6 gives a lucid insight into the levels of similarity found in pitch accent realisations. Further insights, however, could be gleaned from a fine-grained examination of the PaIntE parameters. For example, which parameters differ and under what conditions when examining highly variable tokens? Information status evidently plays a role in pitch accent production but the contexts in which this takes place have yet to be examined. In addition, the role of information *structure* (focus-background, contrast) also needs to be investigated. A further line of research worth pursuing concerns the impact of information status on the temporal structure of spoken utterances and possible compounding with frequency of occurrence effects.

References

Kirsten Abbot-Smith and Michael Tomasello. 2006. Exemplar-learning and schematization in a usage-based account of syntactic acquisition. *The Linguistic Review*, 23(3):275–290.

Ellen G. Bard and M. P. Aylett. 1999. The dissociation of deaccenting, givenness, and syntactic role in spontaneous speech. In *Proceedings of ICPhS (San Francisco)*, volume 3, pages 1753–1756.

Stefan Baumann. 2006. *The Intonation of Givenness – Evidence from German.*, volume 508 of *Linguistische Arbeiten*. Niemeyer, Tübingen. Ph.D. thesis, Saarland University.

Gillian Brown. 1983. Prosodic structure and the given/new distinction. In Anne Cutler and D. Robert Ladd, editors, *Prosody: Models and Measurements*, pages 67–77. Springer, New York.

Joan Bybee. 2006. From usage to grammar: The mind's response to repetition. *Language*, 84:529–551.

Karen Croot and Kathleen Rastle. 2004. Is there a syllabary containing stored articulatory plans for speech production in English? In *Proceedings of the 10th Australian International Conference on Speech Science and Technology (Sydney)*, pages 376–381.

Michael A. K. Halliday. 1967. *Intonation and Grammar in British English*. Mouton, The Hague.

Keith Johnson. 1997. Speech perception without speaker normalization: An exemplar model. In K. Johnson and J. W. Mullennix, editors, *Talker Variability in Speech Processing*, pages 145–165. Academic Press, San Diego.

Klaus J. Kohler. 1991. Studies in german intonation. *AIPUK (Univ. Kiel)*, 25.

Frank Kügler and Caroline Féry. 2008. Pitch accent scaling on given, new and focused constituents in german. *Journal of Phonetics*.

Erwin Marsi, Martin Reynaert, Antal van den Bosch, Walter Daelemans, and Véronique Hoste. 2003. Learning to predict pitch accents and prosodic boundaries in dutch. In *Proceedings of the ACL-2003 Conference (Sapporo, Japan)*, pages 489–496.

Jörg Mayer. 1995. Transcribing German Intonation – The Stuttgart System. Technical report, Universität Stuttgart. http://www.ims.uni-stuttgart.de/phonetik/joerg/labman/STGTsystem.html.

Gregor Möhler and Alistair Conkie. 1998. Parametric modeling of intonation using vector quantization. In *Third Intern. Workshop on Speech Synth (Jenolan Caves)*, pages 311–316.

Gregor Möhler. 1998. Describing intonation with a parametric model. In *Proceedings ICSLP*, volume 7, pages 2851–2854.

T. V. Pernegger. 1998. What's wrong with Bonferroni adjustment. *British Medical Journal*, 316:1236–1238.

Janet Pierrehumbert and Julia Hirschberg. 1990. The meaning of intonational contours in the interpretation of discourse. In P. R. Cohen, J. Morgan, and M. E. Pollack, editors, *Intentions in Communication*, pages 271–311. MIT Press, Cambridge.

Janet Pierrehumbert. 2001. Exemplar dynamics: Word frequency, lenition and contrast. In Joan Bybee and Paul Hopper, editors, *Frequency and the Emergence of Linguistic Structure*, pages 137–157. Amsterdam.

Ellen F. Prince. 1992. The ZPG Letter: Subjects, Definiteness and Information Status. In W. C. Mann and S. A. Thompson, editors, *Discourse Description: Diverse Linguistic Analyses of a Fund-Raising Text*, pages 295–325. Amsterdam.

Stefan Rapp. 1998. *Automatisierte Erstellung von Korpora für die Prosodieforschung*. Ph.D. thesis, IMS, Universität Stuttgart. AIMS 4 (1).

Arndt Riester. 2008. A Semantic Explication of Information Status and the Underspecification of the Recipients' Knowledge. In Atle Grønn, editor, *Proceedings of Sinn und Bedeutung 12*, Oslo.

Antje Schweitzer and Bernd Möbius. 2004. Exemplar-based production of prosody: Evidence from segment and syllable durations. In *Speech Prosody 2004 (Nara, Japan)*, pages 459–462.

Katrin Schweitzer, Arndt Riester, Hans Kamp, and Grzegorz Dogil. 2008. Phonological and acoustic specification of information status - a semantic and phonetic analysis. Poster at "Experimental and Theoretical Advances in Prosody", Cornell University.

Kim Silverman, Mary Backman, John Pitrelli, Mari Ostendorf, Colin Wightman, Patti Price, Janet Pierrehumbert, and Julia Hirschberg. 1992. Tobi: A standard for Labeling English Prosody. In *Proceedings of ICSLP (Banff, Kanada)*, volume 2, pages 867–870, Banff, Canada.

Jacques Terken and Julia Hirschberg. 1994. Deaccentuation of words representing 'given' information: effects of persistence of grammatical function and surface position. *Language and Speech*, 37:125–145.

Jan P. H. van Santen and Bernd Möbius. 2000. A quantitative model of F0 generation and alignment. In A. Botinis, editor, *Intonation—Analysis, Modelling and Technology*, pages 269–288. Kluwer.

Michael Walsh, Hinrich Schütze, Bernd Möbius, and Antje Schweitzer. 2007. An exemplar-theoretic account of syllable frequency effects. In *Proceedings of ICPhS (Saarbrücken)*, pages 481–484.

Michael Walsh, Katrin Schweitzer, Bernd Möbius, and Hinrich Schütze. 2008. Examining pitch-accent variability from an exemplar-theoretic perspective. In *Proceedings of Interspeech 2008 (Brisbane)*.

Sandra P. Whiteside and Rosemary A. Varley. 1998. Dual-route phonetic encoding: Some acoustic evidence. In *Proceedings of ICSLP (Sydney)*, volume 7, pages 3155–3158.

George Yule. 1980. Intonation and Givenness in Spoken Discourse. *Studies in Language*, pages 271–286.

Using Non-lexical Features to Identify Effective Indexing Terms for Biomedical Illustrations

Matthew Simpson, Dina Demner-Fushman, Charles Sneiderman, Sameer K. Antani, George R. Thoma
Lister Hill National Center for Biomedical Communications
National Library of Medicine, NIH, Bethesda, MD, USA
{simpsonmatt, ddemner, csneiderman, santani, gthoma}@mail.nih.gov

Abstract

Automatic image annotation is an attractive approach for enabling convenient access to images found in a variety of documents. Since image captions and relevant discussions found in the text can be useful for summarizing the content of images, it is also possible that this text can be used to generate salient indexing terms. Unfortunately, this problem is generally domain-specific because indexing terms that are useful in one domain can be ineffective in others. Thus, we present a supervised machine learning approach to image annotation utilizing *non-lexical* features[1] extracted from image-related text to select useful terms. We apply this approach to several subdomains of the biomedical sciences and show that we are able to reduce the number of ineffective indexing terms.

1 Introduction

Authors of biomedical publications often utilize images and other illustrations to convey information essential to the article and to support and reinforce textual content. These images are useful in support of clinical decisions, in rich document summaries, and for instructional purposes. The task of delivering these images, and the publications in which they are contained, to biomedical clinicians and researchers in an accessible way is an information retrieval problem.

Current research in the biomedical domain (e.g., Antani et al., 2008; Florea et al., 2007), has investigated hybrid approaches to image retrieval, combining elements of content-based image retrieval (CBIR) and annotation-based image retrieval (ABIR). ABIR, compared to the image-only approach of CBIR, offers a practical advantage in that queries can be more naturally specified by a human user (Inoue, 2004). However, manually annotating biomedical images is a laborious and subjective task that often leads to noisy results.

Automatic image annotation is a more robust approach to ABIR than manual annotation. Unfortunately, automatically selecting the most appropriate indexing terms is an especially challenging problem for biomedical images because of the domain-specific nature of these images and the many vocabularies used in the biomedical sciences. For example, the term "sweat gland adenocarcinoma" could be a useful indexing term for an image found in a dermatology publication, but it is less likely to have much relevance in describing an image from a cardiology publication. On the other hand, the term "mitral annular calcification" may be of great relevance for cardiology images, but of little relevance for dermatology ones.

Our problem may be summarized as follows: Given an image, its caption, its discussion in the article text (henceforth the image *mention*), and a list of potential indexing terms, select the terms that are most effective at describing the content of the image. For example, assume the image shown in Figure 1, obtained from the article "Metastatic Hidradenocarcinoma: Efficacy of Capecitabine" by Thomas et al. (2006) in *Archives of Dermatology*, has the following potential indexing terms,

- Histopathology finding
- Reviewed
- Confirmation
- Diagnosis aspect
- Diagnosis
- Eccrine
- Sweat gland adenocarcinoma
- Lesion

which have been extracted from the image mention. While most of these do not uniquely identify

[1] Non-lexical features describe attributes of image-related text but not the text *itself*, e.g., unlike a bag-of-words model.

Proceedings of the 12th Conference of the European Chapter of the ACL, pages 737–744,
Athens, Greece, 30 March – 3 April 2009. ©2009 Association for Computational Linguistics

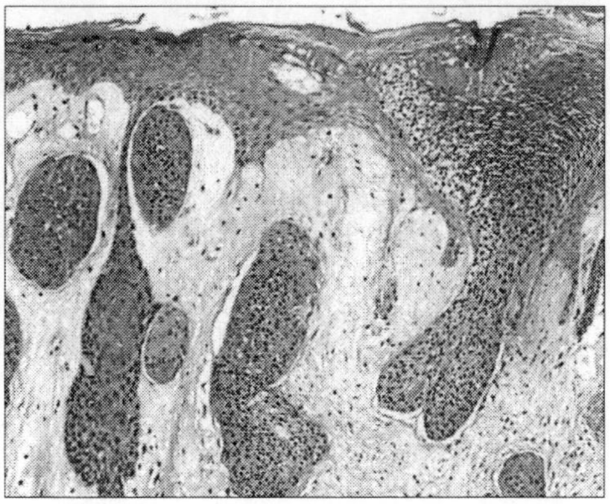

Caption: Figure 1. On recurrence, histologic features of porocarcinoma with an intraepidermal spread of neoplastic clusters (hematoxylin-eosin, original magnification x100).

Mention: Histopathologic findings were reviewed and confirmed a diagnosis of eccrine hidradenocarcinoma for all lesions excised (Figure 1).

Figure 1: Example Image. We index an image with concepts generated from its caption and discussion in the document text (mention). This image is from "Metastatic Hidradenocarcinoma: Efficacy of Capecitabine" by Thomas et al. (2006) and is reprinted with permission from the authors.

the image, we would like to automatically select "sweat gland adenocarcinoma" and "eccrine" for indexing because they clearly describe the content and purpose of the image—supporting a diagnosis of hidradenocarinoma, an invasive cancer of sweat glands. Note that effective indexing terms need not be exact lexical matches of the text. Even though "diagnosis" is an exact match, its meaning is too broad in this context to be a useful term.

In a machine learning approach to image annotation, training data based on lexical features alone is not sufficient for finding salient indexing terms. Indeed, we must classify terms that are not encountered while training. Therefore, we hypothesize that non-lexical features, which have been successfully used for speech and genre classification tasks, among others (see Section 5 for related work), may be useful in classifying text associated with images. While this approach is broad enough to apply to any retrieval task, given the goals of our ongoing research, we restrict ourselves to studying its feasibility in the biomedical domain.

In order to achieve this, we make use of the previously developed MetaMap (Aronson, 2001) tool, which maps text to concepts contained in the Unified Medical Language System® (UMLS) Metathesaurus® (Lindberg et al., 1993). The UMLS is a compendium of several controlled vocabularies in the biomedical sciences that provides a semantic mapping relating concepts from the various vocabularies (Section 2). We then use a supervised machine learning approach, described in Section 3, to classify the UMLS concepts as useful indexing terms based on their non-lexical features, gleaned from the article text and MetaMap output.

Experimental results, presented in Section 4, indicate that ineffective indexing terms can be reduced using this classification technique. We conclude that ABIR approaches to biomedical image retrieval as well as hybrid CBIR/ABIR approaches, which rely on both image content and annotations, can benefit from an automatic annotation process utilizing non-lexical features to aid in the selection of useful indexing terms.

2 Image Retrieval: Recent Work

Automatic image annotation is a broad topic, and the automatic annotation of biomedical images, specifically, has been a frequent component of the ImageCLEF[2] cross-language image retrieval workshop. In this section, we describe previous work in biomedical image retrieval that forms the basis of our approach. Refer to Section 5 for work related to our method in general.

Demner-Fushman et al. (2007) developed a machine learning approach to identify images from biomedical publications that are relevant to clinical decision support. In this work, the authors utilized both image and textual features to classify images based on their usefulness in evidence-based medicine. In contrast, our work is focused on selecting useful biomedical image indexing terms; however, we utilize the methods developed in their work to extract images and their related captions and mentions.

Authors of biomedical publications often assemble multiple images into a single multi-panel figure. Antani et al. (2008) developed a unique two-phase approach for detecting and segmenting these figures. The authors rely on cues from captions to inform an image analysis algorithm that determines panel edge information. We make use of this approach to uniquely associate caption and mention text with a single image.

[2]http://imageclef.org/

Our current work most directly stems from the results of a term extraction and image annotation evaluation performed by Demner-Fushman et al. (2008). In this study, the authors utilized MetaMap to extract potential indexing terms (UMLS concepts) from image captions and mentions. They then asked a group of five physicians and one medical imaging specialist (four of whom are trained in medical informatics) to manually classify each concept as being "useful for indexing" its associated images or ineffective for this purpose. The reviewers also had the opportunity to identify additional indexing terms that were not automatically extracted by MetaMap.

In total, the reviewers evaluated 4006 concepts (3,281 of which were unique), associated with 186 images from 109 different biomedical articles. Each reviewer was given 50 randomly chosen images from the 2006–2007 issues of *Archives of Facial Plastic Surgery*[3] and *Cardiovascular Ultrasound*[4]. Since MetaMap did not automatically extract all of the useful indexing terms, this selection process exhibited high recall averaging 0.64 but a low precision of 0.11. Indeed, assuming all the extracted terms were selected for indexing, this results in an average F_1-score of only 0.182 for the classification problem. Our work is aimed at improving this baseline classification by reducing the number of ineffective terms selected for indexing.

3 Term Selection Method

A pictorial representation of our term extraction and selection process is shown in Figure 2. We rely on the previously described methods to extract images and their corresponding captions and mentions, and the MetaMap tool to map this text to UMLS concepts. These concepts are potential indexing terms for the associated image.

We derive term features from various textual items, such as the preferred name of the UMLS concept, the MetaMap output for the concept, the text that generated the concept, the article containing the image, and the document collection containing the article. These are all described in more detail in Section 3.2. Once the feature vectors are built, we automatically classify the term as either being useful for indexing the image or not.

To select useful indexing terms, we trained a binary classifier, described in Section 3.3, in a supervised learning scenario with data obtained from the previous study by Demner-Fushman et al. (2008). We obtained our evaluation data from the 2006 *Archives of Dermatology*[5] journal. Note that our training and evaluation data represent distinct subdomains of the biomedical sciences.

In order to reduce noise in the classification of our evaluation data, we asked two of the reviewers who participated in the initial study to manually classify our extracted terms as they did for our training data. In doing so, they each evaluated an identical set of 1539 potential indexing terms relating to 50 randomly chosen images from 31 different articles. We measured the performance of our classifier in terms of how well it performed against this manual evaluation. These results, as well as a discussion pertaining to the inter-annotator agreement of the two reviewers, are presented in Section 4.

Since our general approach is not specific to the biomedical domain, it could equally be applied in

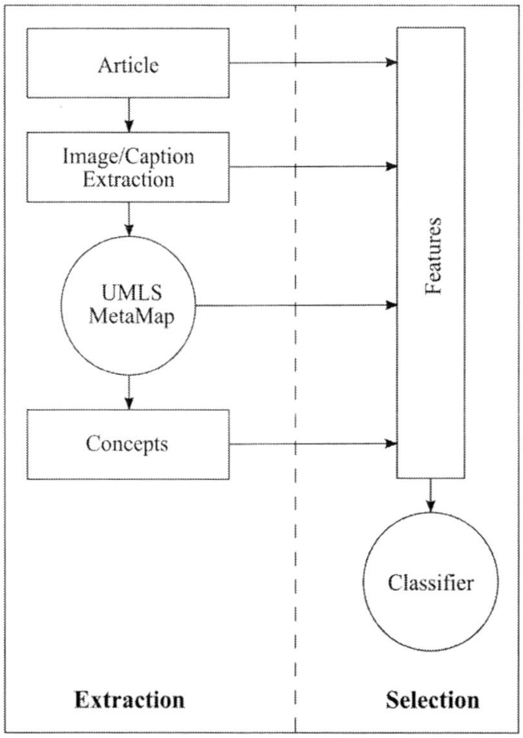

Figure 2: Term Extraction and Selection. We gather features for the extracted terms and use them to train a classifier that selects the terms that are useful for indexing the associated images.

[3]http://archfaci.ama-assn.org/

[4]http://www.cardiovascularultrasound.com/

[5]http://archderm.ama-assn.org/

any domain with an existing ontology. For example, the UMLS and MetaMap can be replaced by the Art and Architecture Thesaurus[6] and an equivalent mapping tool to annotate images related to art and art history (Klavans et al., 2008).

3.1 Terminology

To describe our features, we adopt the following terminology.

- A *collection* contains all the articles from a given publication for a specified number of years. For example, the 2006–2007 issues of *Cardiovascular Ultrasound* represent a single collection.
- A *document* is a specific biomedical article from a particular collection and contains images and their captions and mentions.
- A *phrase* is the portion of text that MetaMap maps to UMLS concepts. For example, from the caption in Figure 1, the noun phrase "histologic features" maps to four UMLS concepts: "Histologic," "Characteristics," "Protein Domain" and "Array Feature."
- A *mapping* is an assignment of a phrase to a particular set of UMLS concepts. Each phrase can have more than one mapping.

3.2 Features

Using this terminology, we define the following features used to classify potential indexing terms. We refer to these as *non-lexical* features because they generally characterize UMLS concepts, going beyond the surface representation of words and lexemes appearing in the article text.

F.1 *CUI (nominal):* The Concept Unique Identifier (CUI) assigned to the concept in the UMLS Metathesaurus. We choose the concept identifier as a feature because some frequently mapped concepts are consistently ineffective for indexing the images in our training and evaluation data. For example, the CUI for "Original," another term mapped from the caption shown in Figure 1, is "C0205313." Our results indicate that "C0205313," which occurs 19 times in our evaluation data, *never* identifies a useful indexing term.

F.2 *Semantic Type (nominal):* The concept's semantic categorization. There are currently 132 different semantic types[7] in the UMLS Metathesaurus. For example, The semantic type of "Original" is "Idea or Concept."

F.3 *Presence in Caption (nominal):* **true** if the phrase that generated the concept is located in the image caption; **false** if the phrase is located in the image mention.

F.4 *MeSH Ratio (real):* The ratio of words c_i in the concept c that are also contained in the Medical Subject Headings (MeSH terms)[8] $\mathcal{M}$ assigned to the document to the total number of words in the concept.

$$\mathrm{R}^{(m)} = \frac{|\{c_i : c_i \in \mathcal{M}\}|}{|c|} \tag{1}$$

MeSH is a controlled vocabulary created by the US National Library of Medicine (NLM) to index biomedical articles. For example, "Adenoma, Sweat" is one MeSH term assigned to "Metastatic Hidradenocarcinoma: Efficacy of Capecitabine" (Thomas et al., 2006), the article containing the image from Figure 1.

F.5 *Abstract Ratio (real):* The ratio of words c_i in the concept c that are also in the document's abstract $\mathcal{A}$ to the total number of words in the concept.

$$\mathrm{R}^{(a)} = \frac{|\{c_i : c_i \in \mathcal{A}\}|}{|c|} \tag{2}$$

F.6 *Title Ratio (real):* The ratio of words c_i in the concept c that are also in the document's title $\mathcal{T}$ to the total number of words in the concept.

$$\mathrm{R}^{(t)} = \frac{|\{c_i : c_i \in \mathcal{T}\}|}{|c|} \tag{3}$$

F.7 *Parts-of-Speech Ratio (real):* The ratio of words p_i in the phrase p that have been tagged as having part of speech s to the total number of words in the phrase.

$$\mathrm{R}^{(s)} = \frac{|\{p_i : \text{TAG}(p_i) = s\}|}{|p|} \tag{4}$$

This feature is computed for noun, verb, adjective and adverb part-of-speech tags. We

[6] http://www.getty.edu/research/conducting_research/vocabularies/aat/

[7] http://www.nlm.nih.gov/research/umls/META3_current_semantic_types.html

[8] http://www.nlm.nih.gov/mesh/

obtain tagging information from the output of MetaMap.

F.8 *Concept Ambiguity (real):* The ratio of the number of mappings m_i of phrase p that contain concept c to the total number of mappings for the phrase:

$$A = \frac{|\{m_i^p : c \in m_i^p\}|}{|m^p|} \quad (5)$$

F.9 *Tf-idf (real):* The frequency of term t_i (*i.e.*, the phrase that generated the concept) times its inverse document frequency:

$$\text{tfidf}_{i,j} = \text{tf}_{i,j} \times \text{idf}_i \quad (6)$$

The term frequency $\text{tf}_{i,j}$ of term t_i in document d_j is given by

$$\text{tf}_{i,j} = \frac{n_{i,j}}{\sum_{k=1}^{|\mathcal{D}|} n_{k,j}} \quad (7)$$

where $n_{i,j}$ is the number of occurrences of t_i in d_j, and the denominator is the number of occurrences of all terms in d_j. The inverse document frequency idf_i of t_i is given by

$$\text{idf}_i = \log \frac{|\mathcal{D}|}{|\{d_j : t_i \in d_j\}|} \quad (8)$$

where $|\mathcal{D}|$ is the total number of documents in the collection, and the denominator is the total number of documents that contain t_i (see Salton and Buckley, 1988).

F.10 *Document Location (real):* The location in the document of the phrase that generated the concept. This feature is continuous on $[0, 1]$ with 0 representing the beginning of the document and 1 representing the end.

F.11 *Concept Length (real):* The length of the concept, measured in number of characters.

For the purpose of computing F.9 and F.10, we indexed each collection with the Terrier[9] information retrieval platform. Terrier was configured to use a block indexing scheme with a Tf-idf weighting model. Computation of all other features is straightforward.

3.3 Classifier

We explored these feature vectors using various classification approaches available in the RapidMiner[10] tool. Unlike many similar text and image classification problems, we were unable to achieve results with a Support Vector Machine (SVM) learner (libSVMLearner) using the Radial Base Function (RBF). Common cost and width parameters were used, yet the SVM classified all terms as ineffective. Identical results were observed using a Naïve Bayes (NB) learner.

For these reasons, we chose to use the Averaged One-Dependence Estimator (AODE) learner (Webb et al., 2005) available in RapidMiner. AODE is capable of achieving highly accurate classification results with the quick training time usually associated with NB. Because this learner does not handle continuous attributes, we preprocessed our features with equal frequency discretization. The AODE learner was trained in a ten-fold cross validation of our training data.

4 Results

Results relating to specific aspects of our work (annotation, features and classification) are presented below.

4.1 Inter-Annotator Agreement

Two independent reviewers manually classified the extracted terms from our evaluation data as useful for indexing their associated images or not. The inter-annotator agreement between reviewers A and B is shown in the first row of Table 1. Although both reviewers are physicians trained in medical informatics, their initial agreement is only moderate, with $\kappa = 0.519$. This illustrates the subjective nature of manual ABIR and, in general, the difficultly in reliably classifying potential indexing terms for biomedical images.

Annotator	Pr(a)	Pr(e)	κ
A/B	0.847	0.682	0.519
A/Standard	0.975	0.601	0.938
B/Standard	0.872	0.690	0.586

Table 1: Inter-annotator Agreement. The probability of agreement Pr(a), expected probability of chance agreement Pr(e), and the associated Cohen's kappa coefficient κ are given for each reviewer combination.

After their initial classification, the two reviewers were instructed to collaboratively reevaluate the subset of extracted terms upon which they disagreed (roughly 15% of the terms) and create a

[9] http://ir.dcs.gla.ac.uk/terrier/
[10] http://rapid-i.com/

Feature		Gain	χ^2
F.1	CUI	0.003	13.331
F.2	Semantic Type	0.015	68.232
F.3	Presence in Caption	0.008	35.303
F.4	MeSH Ratio	0.043	285.701
F.5	Abstract Ratio	0.023	114.373
F.6	Title Ratio	0.021	132.651
F.7	Noun Ratio	0.053	287.494
	Verb Ratio	0.009	26.723
	Adjective Ratio	0.021	96.572
	Adverb Ratio	0.002	5.271
F.8	Concept Ambiguity	0.008	33.824
F.9	Tf-idf	0.004	21.489
F.10	Document Location	0.002	12.245
F.11	Phrase Length	0.021	102.759

Table 2: Feature Comparison. The information gain and chi-square statistic is shown for each feature. A higher score indicates greater influence on term effectiveness.

gold standard evaluation. The second and third rows of Table 1 suggest the resulting evaluation strongly favors reviewer A's initial classification compared to that of reviewer B.

Since the reviewers of the *training* data each classified terms from different sets of randomly selected images, it is impossible to calculate their inter-annotator agreement.

4.2 Effectiveness of Features

The effectiveness of individual features in describing the potential indexing terms is shown in Table 2. We used two measures, both of which indicate a similar trend, to calculate feature effectiveness: Information gain (Kullback-Leibler divergence) and the chi-square statistic.

Under both measures, the MeSH ratio (F.4) is one of the most effective features. This makes intuitive sense because MeSH terms are assigned to articles by specially trained NLM professionals. Given the large size of the MeSH vocabulary, it is not unreasonable to assume that an article's MeSH terms could be descriptive, at a coarse granularity, of the images it contains. Also, the subjectivity of the reviewers' initial data calls into question the usefulness of our training data. It may be that MeSH terms, consistently assigned to all documents in a particular collection, are a more reliable determiner of the usefulness of potential indexing terms. Furthermore, the study by Demner-Fushman et al. (2008) found that, on average, roughly 25% of the additional (useful) terms the reviewers added to the set of extracted terms were also found in the MeSH terms assigned to the document containing the particular image.

The abstract and title ratios (F.6 and F.5) also had a significant effect on the classification outcome. Similar to the argument for MeSH terms, as these constructs are a coarse summary of the contents of an article, it is not unreasonable to assume they summarize the images contained therein.

Finally, the noun ratio (F.7) was a particularly effective feature, and the length of the UMLS concept (F.11) was moderately effective. Interestingly, tf-idf and document location (F.9 and F.10), both features computed using standard information retrieval techniques, are among the least effective features.

4.3 Classification

While the AODE learner performed reasonably well for this task, the difficulty encountered when training the SVM learner may be explained as follows. The initial inter-annotator agreement of the evaluation data suggests that it is likely that our training data contained contradictory or mislabeled observations, preventing the construction of a maximal-margin hyperplane required by the SVM. An SVM implementation utilizing soft margins (Cortes and Vapnik, 1995) would likely achieve better results on our data, although at the expense of greater training time. The success of the AODE learner in this case is probably due to its resilience to mislabeled observations.

Annotator	Precision	Recall	F_1-score
A	0.258	0.442	0.326
B	0.200	0.225	0.212
Combined	0.326	0.224	0.266
Standard	0.453	0.229	0.304
Standard[a]	0.492	0.231	0.314
Training	0.502	0.332	0.400

Table 3: Classification Results. The classifier's precision and recall, as well as the corresponding F_1-score, are given for the responses of each reviewer.

[a]For comparison, the classifier was also trained using the subset of training data containing responses from reviewers A and B only.

Classification results are shown in Table 3. The precision and recall of the classification scheme is shown for the manual classification by reviewers A and B in the first and second rows. The third row contains the results obtained from combining the results of the two reviewers, and the fourth row shows the classification results compared to the gold standard obtained after discovering the initial inter-annotator agreement.

We hypothesized that the training data labels may have been highly sensitive to the subjectivity of the reviewers. Therefore, we retrained the learner with only those observations made by reviewers A and B (of the five total reviewers) and again compared the classification results with the gold standard. Not surprisingly, the F_1-score of this classification (shown in the fifth row) is somewhat improved compared to that obtained when utilizing the full training set.

The last row in Table 3 shows the results of classifying the training data. That is, it shows the results of classifying one tenth of the data after a ten-fold cross validation and can be considered an upper bound for the performance of this classifier on our evaluation data. Notice that the associated F_1-score for this experiment is only marginally better than that of the unseen data. This implies that it is possible to use training data from particular subdomains of the biomedical sciences (cardiology and plastic surgery) to classify potential indexing terms in other subdomains (dermatology).

Overall, the classifier performed best when verified with reviewer A, with an F_1-score of 0.326. Although this is relatively low for a classification task, these results improve upon the baseline classification scheme (all extracted terms are useful for indexing) with an F_1-score of 0.182 (Demner-Fushman et al., 2008). Thus, non-lexical features can be leveraged, albeit to a small degree with our current features and classifier, in automatically selecting useful image indexing terms. In future work, we intend to explore additional features and alternative tools for mapping text to the UMLS.

5 Related Work

Non-lexical features have been successful in many contexts, particularly in the areas of genre classification and text and speech summarization.

Genre classification, unlike text classification, discriminates between document *style* instead of *topic*. Dewdney et al. (2001) show that non-lexical features, such as parts of speech and line-spacing, can be successfully used to classify genres, and Ferizis and Bailey (2006) demonstrate that accurate classification of Internet documents is possible even without the expensive part-of-speech tagging of similar methods. Recall that the noun ratio (F.7) was among the most effective of our features.

Finn and Kushmerick (2006) describe a study in which they classified documents from various domains as "subjective" or "objective." They, too, found that part-of-speech statistics as well as general text statistics (e.g., average sentence length) are more effective than the traditional bag-of-words representation when classifying documents from multiple domains. This supports the notion that we can use non-lexical features to classify potential indexing terms in one biomedical subdomain using training data from another.

Maskey and Hirschberg (2005) found that prosodic features (see Ward, 2004) combined with structural features are sufficient to summarize spoken news broadcasts. Prosodic features relate to intonational variation and are associated with particularly important items, whereas structural features are associated with the organization of a typical broadcast: headlines, followed by a description of the stories, etc.

Finally, Schilder and Kondadadi (2008) describe non-lexical word-frequency features, similar to our *ratio* features (F.4–F.7), which are used with a regression SVM to efficiently generate query-based multi-document summaries.

6 Conclusion

Images convey essential information in biomedical publications. However, automatically extracting and selecting useful indexing terms from the article text is a difficult task given the domain-specific nature of biomedical images and vocabularies. In this work, we use the manual classification results of a previous study to train a binary classifier to automatically decide whether a potential indexing term is useful for this purpose or not. We use non-lexical features generated for each term with the most effective including whether the term appears in the MeSH terms assigned to the article and whether it is found in the article's title and caption. While our specific retrieval task relates to the biomedical domain, our results indicate that ABIR approaches to image retrieval in *any* domain can benefit from an automatic annotation process utilizing non-lexical features to aid in the selection of indexing terms or the reduction of ineffective terms from a set of potential ones.

References

Sameer Antani, Dina Demner-Fushman, Jiang Li, Balaji V. Srinivasan, and George R. Thoma. 2008. Exploring use of images in clinical articles for decision support in evidence-based medicine. In *Proc. of SPIE-IS&T Electronic Imaging*, pages 1–10.

Alan R. Aronson. 2001. Effective mapping of biomedical text to the UMLS metathesaurus: The MetaMap program. In *Proc. of the Annual Symp. of the American Medical Informatics Association (AMIA)*, pages 17–21.

Corinna Cortes and Vladimir Vapnik. 1995. Support-vector networks. *Machine Learning*, 20(3):273–297.

Dina Demner-Fushman, Sameer Antani, Matthew Simpson, and George Thoma. 2008. Combining medical domain ontological knowledge and low-level image features for multimedia indexing. In *Proc. of the Language Resources for Content-Based Image Retrieval Workshop (OntoImage)*, pages 18–23.

Dina Demner-Fushman, Sameer K. Antani, and George R. Thoma. 2007. Automatically finding images for clinical decision support. In *Proc. of the Intl. Workshop on Data Mining in Medicine (DM-Med)*, pages 139–144.

Nigel Dewdney, Carol VanEss-Dykema, and Richard MacMillan. 2001. The form is the substance: Classification of genres in text. In *Proc. of the Workshop on Human Language Technology and Knowledge Management*, pages 1–8.

George Ferizis and Peter Bailey. 2006. Towards practical genre classification of web documents. In *Proc. of the Intl. Conference on the World Wide Web (WWW)*, pages 1013–1014.

Aidan Finn and Nicholas Kushmerick. 2006. Learning to classify documents according to genre. *Journal of the American Society for Information Science and Technology (JASIST)*, 57(11):1506–1518.

F. Florea, V. Buzuloiu, A. Rogozan, A. Bensrhair, and S. Darmoni. 2007. Automatic image annotation: Combining the content and context of medical images. In *Intl. Symp. on Signals, Circuits and Systems (ISSCS)*, pages 1–4.

Masashi Inoue. 2004. On the need for annotation-based image retrieval. In *Proc. of the Workshop on Information Retrieval in Context (IRiX)*, pages 44–46.

Judith Klavans, Carolyn Sheffield, Eileen Abels, Joan Beaudoin, Laura Jenemann, Tom Lipincott, Jimmy Lin, Rebecca Passonneau, Tandeep Sidhu, Dagobert Soergel, and Tae Yano. 2008. Computational linguistics for metadata building: Aggregating text processing technologies for enhanced image access. In *Proc. of the Language Resources for Content-Based Image Retrieval Workshop (OntoImage)*, pages 42–47.

D.A. Lindberg, B.L. Humphreys, and A.T. McCray. 1993. The unified medical language system. *Methods of Information in Medicine*, 32(4):281–291.

Sameer Maskey and Julia Hirschberg. 2005. Comparing lexical, acoustic/prosodic, structural and discourse features for speech summarization. In *Proc. of the European Conference on Speech Communication and Technology (EUROSPEECH)*, pages 621–624.

Gerard Salton and Christopher Buckley. 1988. Term-weighting approaches in automatic text retrieval. *Information Processing & Management*, 24(5):513–523.

Frank Schilder and Ravikumar Kondadadi. 2008. FastSum: Fast and accurate query-based multi-document summarization. In *Proc. of the Workshop on Human Language Technology and Knowledge Management*, pages 205–208.

Jouary Thomas, Kaiafa Anastasia, Lipinski Philippe, Vergier Béatrice, Lepreux Sébastien, Delaunay Michèle, and TaïebAlain. 2006. Metastatic hidradenocarcinoma: Efficacy of capecitabine. *Archives of Dermatology*, 142(10):1366–1367.

Nigel Ward. 2004. Pragmatic functions of prosodic features in non-lexical utterances. In *Proc. of the Intl. Conference on Speech Prosody*, pages 325–328.

Geoffrey I. Webb, Janice R. Boughton, and Zhihai Wang. 2005. Not so naïve bayes: Aggregating one-dependence estimators. *Machine Learning*, 58(1):5–24.

Incremental Dialogue Processing in a Micro-Domain

Gabriel Skantze[1]
Dept. of Speech, Music and Hearing
KTH, Stockholm, Sweden
gabriel@speech.kth.se

David Schlangen
Department of Linguistics
University of Potsdam, Germany
das@ling.uni-potsdam.de

Abstract

This paper describes a fully incremental dialogue system that can engage in dialogues in a simple domain, number dictation. Because it uses incremental speech recognition and prosodic analysis, the system can give rapid feedback as the user is speaking, with a very short latency of around 200ms. Because it uses incremental speech synthesis and self-monitoring, the system can react to feedback from the user as the system is speaking. A comparative evaluation shows that naïve users preferred this system over a non-incremental version, and that it was perceived as more human-like.

1 Introduction

A traditional simplifying assumption for spoken dialogue systems is that the dialogue proceeds with strict turn-taking between user and system. The minimal unit of processing in such systems is the *utterance*, which is processed in whole by each module of the system before it is handed on to the next. When the system is speaking an utterance, it assumes that the user will wait for it to end before responding. (Some systems accept barge-ins, but then treat the interrupted utterance as basically unsaid.)

Obviously, this is not how natural human-human dialogue proceeds. Humans understand and produce language *incrementally* – they use multiple knowledge sources to determine when it is appropriate to speak, they give and receive backchannels in the middle of utterances, they start to speak before knowing exactly what to say, and they incrementally monitor the listener's reactions to what they say (Clark, 1996).

This paper presents a dialogue system, called NUMBERS, in which all components operate incrementally. We had two aims: First, to explore technical questions such as how the components of a modularized dialogue system should be arranged and made to interoperate to support incremental processing, and which requirements incremental processing puts on dialogue system components (e.g., speech recognition, prosodic analysis, parsing, discourse modelling, action selection and speech synthesis). Second, to investigate whether incremental processing can help us to better model certain aspects of human behaviour in dialogue systems – especially turn-taking and feedback – and whether this improves the user's experience of using such a system.

2 Incremental dialogue processing

All dialogue systems are 'incremental', in some sense – they proceed in steps through the exchange of 'utterances'. However, incremental processing typically means more than this; a common requirement is that processing starts before the input is complete and that the first output increments are produced as soon as possible (e.g., Kilger & Finkler, 1995). Incremental modules hence are those where "Each processing component will be triggered into activity by a minimal amount of its characteristic input" (Levelt, 1989). If we assume that the 'characteristic input' of a dialogue system is the utterance, this principle demands that 'minimal amounts' of an utterance already trigger activity. It should be noted though, that there is a trade-off between responsiveness and output quality, and that an incremental process therefore should produce output only as soon as it is possible to reach a desired output quality criterion.

2.1 Motivations & related work

The claim that humans do not understand and produce speech in utterance-sized chunks, but

[1] The work reported in this paper was done while the first author was at the University of Potsdam.

Proceedings of the 12th Conference of the European Chapter of the ACL, pages 745–753,
Athens, Greece, 30 March – 3 April 2009.

rather incrementally, can be supported by an impressive amount of psycholinguistic literature on the subject (e.g., Tanenhaus & Brown-Schmidt, 2008; Levelt, 1989). However, when it comes to spoken dialogue systems, the dominant minimal unit of processing has been the utterance. Moreover, traditional systems follow a very strict sequential processing order of utterances – interpretation, dialogue management, generation – and there is most often no monitoring of whether (parts of) the generated message is successfully delivered.

Allen et al. (2001) discuss some of the shortcomings of these assumptions when modelling more conversational human-like dialogue. First, they fail to account for the frequently found mid-utterance reactions and feedback (in the form of acknowledgements, repetition of fragments or clarification requests). Second, people often seem to start to speak before knowing exactly what to say next (possibly to grab the turn), thus producing the utterance incrementally. Third, when a speaker is interrupted or receives feedback in the middle of an utterance, he is able to continue the utterance from the point where he was interrupted.

Since a non-incremental system needs to process the whole user utterance using one module at a time, it cannot utilise any higher level information for deciding when the user's turn or utterance is finished, and typically has to rely only on silence detection and a time-out. Silence, however, is not a good indicator: sometimes there is silence but no turn-change is intended (e.g., hesitations), sometimes there isn't silence, but the turn changes (Sacks et al., 1974). Speakers appear to use other knowledge sources, such as prosody, syntax and semantics to detect or even project the end of the utterance. Attempts have been made to incorporate such knowledge sources for turn-taking decisions in spoken dialogue systems (e.g., Ferrer et al., 2002; Raux & Eskenazi, 2008). To do so, incremental dialogue processing is clearly needed.

Incremental processing can also lead to better use of resources, since later modules can start to work on partial results and do not have to wait until earlier modules have completed processing the whole utterance. For example, while the speech recogniser starts to identify words, the parser can already add these to the chart. Later modules can also assist in the processing and for example resolve ambiguities as they come up. Stoness et al. (2004) shows how a reference resolution module can help an incremental parser with NP suitability judgements. Similarly, Aist et al. (2006) shows how a VP advisor could help an incremental parser.

On the output side, an incremental dialogue system could *monitor* what is actually happening to the utterance it produces. As discussed by Raux & Eskenazi (2007), most dialogue managers operate asynchronously from the output components, which may lead to problems if the dialogue manager produces several actions and the user responds to one of them. If the input components do not have any information about the timing of the system output, they cannot relate them to the user's response. This is even more problematic if the user reacts (for example with a backchannel) in the middle of system utterances. The system must then relate the user's response to the parts of its planned output it has managed to realise, but also be able to stop speaking and possibly continue the interrupted utterance appropriately. A solution for handling mid-utterance responses from the user is proposed by Dohsaka & Shimazu (1997). For incremental generation and synthesis, the output components must also cope with the problem of revision (discussed in more detail below), which may for example lead to the need for the generation of speech repairs, as discussed by Kilger & Finkler (1995).

As the survey above shows, a number of studies have been done on incrementality in different areas of language processing. There are, however, to our knowledge no studies on how the various components could or should be integrated into a complete, fully incremental dialogue system, and how such a system might be perceived by naïve users, compared to a non-incremental system. This we provide here.

2.2 A general, abstract model

The NUMBERS system presented in this paper can be seen as a specific instance (with some simplifying assumptions) of a more general, abstract model that we have developed (Schlangen & Skantze, 2009). We will here only briefly describe the parts of the general model that are relevant for the exposition of our system.

We model the dialogue processing system as a collection of connected processing *modules*. The smallest unit of information that is communicated along the connections is called the *incremental unit* (IU), the unit of the "minimal amount of characteristic input". Depending on what the module does, IUs may be audio frames, words, syntactic phrases, communicative acts, etc. The processing module itself is modelled as consisting of a *Left Buffer* (LB), the *Processor* proper, and a *Right Buffer* (RB). An example of two connected modules is shown in Figure 1. As IU_1 enters the LB of module A, it may be *consumed* by the processor. The processor may then produce new IUs, which are posted on the RB (IU_2 in the example). As the example shows, the modules in the system are connected so that an IU posted on the RB in one module may be consumed in the LB of another module. One RB may of course be connected to many other LB's, and vice versa, allowing a range of different network topologies.

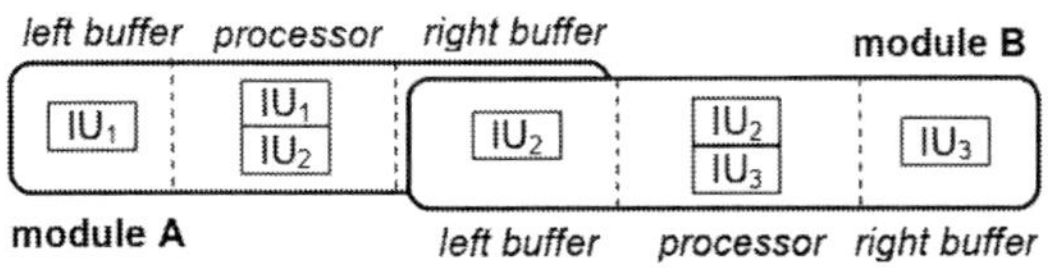

Figure 1: Two connected modules.

In the NUMBERS system, information is only allowed to flow from left to right, which means that the LB may be regarded as the input buffer and the RB as the output buffer. However, in the general model, information may flow in both directions.

A more concrete example is shown in Figure 2, which illustrates a module that does incremental speech recognition. The IUs consumed from the LB are audio frames, and the IUs posted in the RB are the words that are recognised.

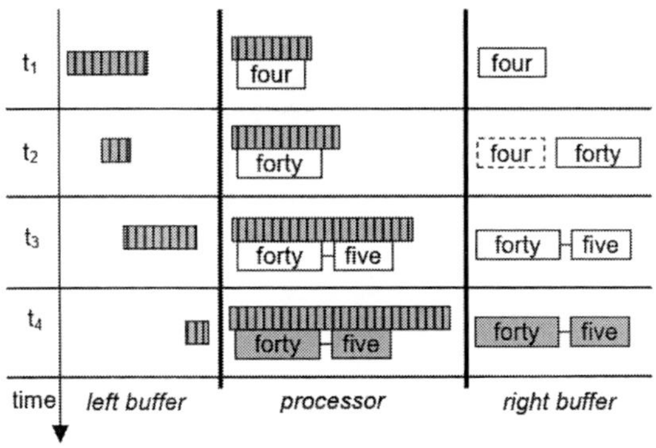

Figure 2: Speech recognition as an example of incremental processing.

We identify three different generic module operations on IUs: *update*, *purge* and *commit*. First, as an IU is added to the LB, the processor needs to **update** its internal state. In the example above, the speech recogniser has to continuously add incoming audio frames to its internal state, and as soon as the recogniser receives enough audio frames to decide that the word "four" is a good-enough candidate, the IU holding this word will be put on the RB (time-point t_1). If a processor only expects IUs that extend the rightmost IU currently produced, we can follow Wirén (1992) in saying that it is only *left-to-right incremental*. A *fully incremental* system (which we aim at here), on the other hand, also allows insertions and/or revisions.

An example of *revision* is illustrated at time-point t_2 in Figure 2. As more audio frames are consumed by the recogniser, the word "four" is no longer the best candidate for this stretch of audio. Thus, the module must now revoke the IU holding the word "four" (marked with a dotted outline) and add a new IU for the word "forty". All other modules consuming these IUs must now **purge** them from their own states and possibly revoke other IUs. By allowing revision, a module may produce tentative results and thus make the system more responsive.

As more audio frames are consumed in the example above, a new word "five" is identified and added to the RB (time-point t_3). At time-point t_4, no more words are identified, and the module may decide to **commit** to the IUs that it has produced (marked with a darker shade). A committed IU is guaranteed to not being revoked later, and can hence potentially be removed from the processing window of later modules, freeing up resources.

3 Number dictation: a micro-domain

Building a fully incremental system with a behaviour more closely resembling that of human dialogue participants raises a series of new challenges. Therefore, in order to make the task more feasible, we have chosen a very limited domain – what might be called a *micro-domain* (cf. Edlund et al., 2008): the dictation of number sequences. In this scenario, the user dictates a sequence of numbers (such as a telephone number or a credit card number) to the dialogue system. This is a very common situation in commercial telephone-based dialogue systems, which however operate in a non-incremental manner: The user is first asked to read out the whole number sequence, which the system then confirms. Should the recognition be incorrect, the user has to repeat the whole sequence again. In an incremental version of this scenario, the system might give continuous feedback (such as acknowledgements and clarification requests) as the user is reading the sequence. When the system repeats the sequence, the user is also given the opportunity to give feedback and make corrections at any time. Obviously, such a dialogue will result in many more speaker-shifts, which in turn increases the need for the rapid turn-taking. Thus, while the number dictation task might appear simple at a first glance (very limited vocabulary, simple syntax and semantics), there are several issues – not typically considered in most dialogue systems – which an incremental and more human-like dialogue system must address.

To explore dialogue phenomena in this domain, we gave 8 pairs of subjects the task of dictating number sequences to each other. The subjects were sitting in different rooms and used headsets to communicate. To induce more feedback behaviour, noise was randomly inserted in the utterances from the information giver (as in the setting used by Schlangen & Fernández (2007)). The subjects were all speaking German (their native tongue). The recorded dialogues were then transcribed and annotated. The observed dialogue strategies directly influenced the design of our system (see below). Table 1 shows an example of a dialogue between a user and the system and illustrates some of the phenomena we intended to model.

U.01	two five three -
S.02	*okay*
U.03	one forty, five -
S.04	*sorry, do you mean one and then forty and then five?*
U.05	no, one forty five
S.06	*okay, one forty five*
U.07	yeah, and six eight four -
S.08	*okay*
U.09	seven twelve nine.
S.10	*so, from the start, two five three -*
U.11	yeah
S.12	*one forty five -*
S.13	*six six four -*
U.14	no, six eight four
S.15	*okay, six eight four -*
S.16	*and then seven twelve nine.*
U.17	that's right

Table 1: An example dialogue between a user and the NUMBERS system.

Just like in this example, a common strategy for the subjects was to first let the information giver read the number sequence and then switch roles and let the information follower repeat it. Instead of reading out the whole number sequence at once, subjects tended to package pieces of information into what Clark (1996) refers to as *installments* (in this case small groups of numbers). After each installment, the other speaker may react by giving an acknowledgement (as in S.02) a clarification request (as in S.04), a correction (as in U.14), or do nothing (as after S.12).

As there are a lot of speaker shifts, there needs to be a mechanism for rapid turn taking. In the example above, the system must recognize that the last digit in U.01, U.03, U.05 and U.07 ends an installment and calls for a reaction, while the last digit in U.09 ends the whole sequence. One information source that has been observed to be useful for this is prosody (Koiso et al., 1998). When analysing the recorded dialogues, it seemed like mid-sequence installments most often ended with a prolonged duration and a rising pitch, while end-sequence installments most often ended with a shorter duration and a falling pitch. How prosody is used by the NUMBERS system for this classification is described in section 4.2.

4 The NUMBERS system components

The NUMBERS system has been implemented using the HIGGINS spoken dialogue system framework (Skantze, 2007). All modules have been adapted and extended to allow incremental processing. It took us roughly 6 months to implement the changes described here to a fully working baseline system. Figure 3 shows the architecture of the system[2].

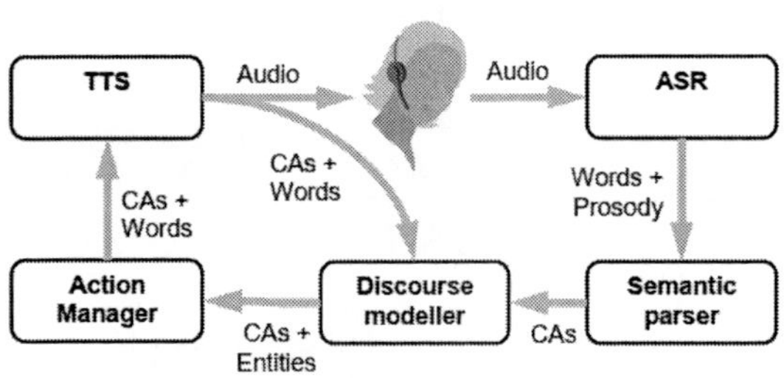

Figure 3: The system architecture.
CA = communicative act.

This is pretty much a standard dialogue system layout, with some exceptions that will be discussed below. Most notably perhaps is that dialogue management is divided into a discourse modelling module and an action manager. As can

[2] A video showing an example run of the system has been uploaded to
http://www.youtube.com/watch?v=_rDkb1K1si8

be seen in the figure, the discourse modeller also receives information about what the system itself says. The modules run asynchronously in separate processes and communicate by sending XML messages containing the IUs over sockets.

We will now characterize each system module by what kind of IUs they consume and produce, as well as the criteria for committing to an IU.

4.1 Speech recognition

The automatic speech recognition module (ASR) is based on the Sphinx 4 system (Lamere et al., 2003). The Sphinx system is capable of incremental processing, but we have added support for producing incremental results that are compatible with the HIGGINS framework. We have also added prosodic analysis to the system, as described in 4.2. For the NUMBERS domain, we use a very limited context-free grammar accepting number words as well as some expressions for feedback and meta-communication.

An illustration of the module buffers is shown in Figure 2 above. The module consumes audio frames (each 100 msec) from the LB and produces words with prosodic features in the RB. The RB is updated every time the sequence of top word hypotheses in the processing windows changes. After 2 seconds of silence has been detected, the words produced so far are committed and the speech recognition search space is cleared. Note that this does not mean that other components have to wait for this amount of silence to pass before starting to process or that the system cannot respond until then – incremental results are produced as soon as the ASR determines that a word has ended.

4.2 Prosodic analysis

We implemented a simple form of prosodic analysis as a data processor in the Sphinx frontend. Incremental F0-extraction is done by first finding pitch candidates (on the semitone scale) for each audio frame using the SMDSF algorithm (Liu et al., 2005). An optimal path between the candidates is searched for, using dynamic programming (maximising candidate confidence scores and minimising F0 shifts). After this, median smoothing is applied, using a window of 5 audio frames.

In order for this sequence of F0 values to be useful, it needs to be parameterized. To find out whether pitch and duration could be used for the distinction between mid-sequence installments and end-sequence installments, we did a machine learning experiment on the installment-ending digits in our collected data. There were roughly an equal amount of both types, giving a majority class baseline of 50.9%.

As features we calculated a delta pitch parameter for each word by computing the sum of all F0 shifts (negative or positive) in the pitch sequence. (Shifts larger than a certain threshold (100 cents) were excluded from the summarization, in order to sort out artefacts.) A duration parameter was derived by calculating the sum of the phoneme lengths in the word, divided by the sum of the average lengths of these phonemes in the whole data set. Both of these parameters were tested as predictors separately and in combination, using the Weka Data Mining Software (Witten & Frank, 2005). The best results were obtained with a J.48 decision tree, and are shown in Table 2.

Baseline	50.9%
Pitch	81.2%
Duration	62.4%
Duration + Pitch	80.8%

Table 2: The results of the installment classification (accuracy).

As the table shows, the best predictor was simply to compare the delta pitch parameter against an optimal threshold. While the performance of 80.8% is significantly above baseline, it could certainly be better. We do not know yet whether the sub-optimal performance is due to the fact that the speakers did not always use these prosodic cues, or whether there is room for improvement in the pitch extraction and parameterization.

Every time the RB of the ASR is updated, the delta pitch parameter is computed for each word and the derived threshold is used to determine a pitch slope class (rising/falling) for the word. (Note that there is no class for a flat pitch. This class is not really needed here, since the digits within installments are followed by no or only very short pauses.) The strategy followed by the system then is this: when a digit with a rising pitch is detected, the system *plans* to immediately give a mid-sequence reaction utterance, and does so if indeed no more words are received. If a digit with a falling pitch is detected, the system plans an end-of-sequence utterance, but waits a little bit longer before producing it, to see if there really are no more words coming in. In other words, the system bases its turn-taking decisions on a combination of ASR, prosody and silence-thresholds, where the length of the threshold differs for different prosodic signals, and where reactions are planned already during the silence. (This is in contrast to Raux & Eskenazi (2008), where context-dependent thresholds are used as well, but only simple end-pointing is performed.)

The use of prosodic analysis in combination with incremental processing allows the NUMBERS system to give feedback after mid-sequence installments in about 200 ms. This should be compared with most dialogue systems which first use a silence threshold of about 750-1500 msec, after which each module must process the utterance.

4.3 Semantic parsing

For semantic parsing, the incremental processing in the HIGGINS module PICKERING (Skantze & Edlund, 2004) has been extended. PICKERING is based on a modified chart parser which adds automatic relaxations to the CFG rules for robustness, and produces semantic interpretations in the form of concept trees. It can also use features that are attached to incoming words, such as prosody and timestamps. For example, the number groups in U.03 and U.05 in Table 1 render different parses due to the pause lengths between the words.

The task of PICKERING in the NUMBERS domain is very limited. Essentially, it identifies communicative acts (CAs), such as number installments. The only slightly more complex parsing is that of larger numbers such as "twenty four". There are also cases of "syntactic ambiguity", as illustrated in U.03 in the dialogue example above ("forty five" as "45" or "40 5"). In the NUMBERS system, only 1-best hypotheses are communicated between the modules, but PICKERING can still assign a lower parsing confidence score to an ambiguous interpretation, which triggers a clarification request in S.04.

Figure 4 show a very simple example of the incremental processing in PICKERING. The LB contains words with prosodic features produced by the ASR (compare with Figure 2 above). The RB consists of the CAs that are identified. Each time a word is added to the chart, PICKERING continues to build the chart and then searches for an optimal sequence of CAs in the chart, allowing non-matching words in between. To handle revision, a copy of the chart is saved after each word has been added.

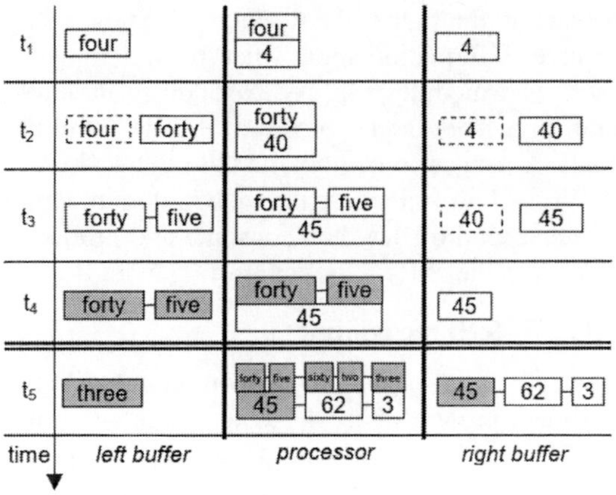

Figure 4: Incremental parsing. There is a jump in time between *t4* and *t5*.

As can be seen at time-point t_4, even if all words that a CA is based on are committed, the parser does not automatically commit the CA. This is because later words may still cause a revision of the complex output IU that has been built. As a heuristic, PICKERING instead waits until a CA is followed by three words that are not part of it until it commits, as shown at time-point t_5. After a CA has been committed, the words involved may be cleared from the chart. This way, PICKERING parses a "moving window" of words.

4.4 Discourse modelling

For discourse modelling, the HIGGINS module GALATEA (Skantze, 2008) has been extended to operate incrementally. The task of GALATEA is to interpret utterances in their context by transforming ellipses into full propositions, indentify discourse entities, resolve anaphora and keep track of the grounding status of concepts (their confidence score and when they have been grounded in the discourse). As can be seen in Figure 3, GALATEA models both utterances from the user as well as the system. This makes it possible for the system to monitor its own utterances and relate them to the user's utterances, by using timestamps produced by the ASR and the speech synthesiser.

In the LB GALATEA consumes CAs from both the user (partially committed, as seen in Figure 4) and the system (always committed, see 4.6). In the RB GALATEA produces an incremental discourse model. This model contains a list of resolved communicative acts and list of resolved discourse entities. This model is then consulted by an action manager which decides what the system should do next. The discourse model is committed up to the point of the earliest non-committed incoming CA. In the NUMBERS domain, the discourse entities are the number installments.

4.5 Action management

Based on the discourse model (from the LB), the action manager (AM) generates system actions (CAs) in semantic form (for GALATEA) with an attached surface form (for the TTS), and puts them on the RB. (In future extensions of the system, we will add an additional generation module that generates the surface form from the semantic form.) In the NUMBERS system, possible system actions are acknowledgements, clarification requests and repetitions of the number sequence. The choice of actions to perform is based on the grounding status of the concepts (which is represented in the discourse model). For example, if the system has already clarified the first part of the number sequence due to an ambiguity, it does not need to repeat this part of the sequence again.

The AM also attaches a desired timing to the produced CA, relative to the end time of last user utterance. For example, if a number group with a final rising pitch is detected, the AM may tell the TTS to execute the CA immediately after the user has stopped speaking. If there is a falling pitch, it may tell the TTS to wait until 500 msec of silence has been detected from the user before executing the action. If the discourse model gets updated during this time, the AM may revoke previous CAs and replace them with new ones.

4.6 Speech synthesis

A diphone MBROLA text-to-speech synthesiser (TTS) is used in the system (Dutoit et al., 1996), and a wrapper for handling incremental processing has been implemented. The TTS consumes words linked to CAs from the LB, as produced by the AM. As described above, each CA has a timestamp. The TTS places them on a queue, and prepares to synthesise and start sending the audio to the speakers. When the system utterance has been played, the corresponding semantic concepts for the CA are sent to GALATEA. If the TTS is interrupted, the semantic fragments of the CA that corresponds to the words that were spoken are sent. This way, GALATEA can monitor what the system actually says and provide the AM with this information. Since the TTS only sends (parts of) the CAs that have actually been spoken, these are always marked as committed.

There is a direct link from the ASR to the TTS as well (not shown in Figure 3), informing the TTS of start-of-speech and end-of-speech events. As soon as a start-of-speech event is detected, the TTS stops speaking. If the TTS does not receive any new CAs from the AM as a consequence of what the user said, it automatically resumes from the point of interruption. (This implements a "reactive behaviour" in the sense of (Brooks, 1991), which is outside of the control of the AM.)

An example of this is shown in Table 1. After U.09, the AM decides to repeat the whole number sequence and sends a series of CAs to the TTS for doing this. After S.10, the user gives feedback in the form of an acknowledgement (U.11). This causes the TTS to make a pause. When GALATEA receives the user feedback, it uses the time-stamps to find out that the feedback is related to the number group in S.10 and the grounding status for this group is boosted. When the AM receives the updated discourse model, it decides that this does not call for any revision to the already planned series of actions. Since the TTS does not receive any revisions, it resumes the repetition of the number sequence in S.12.

The TTS module is fully incremental in that it can stop and resume speaking in the middle of an utterance, revise planned output, and can inform other components of what (parts of utterances) has been spoken. However, the actual text-to-speech processing is done before the utterance starts and not yet incrementally as the utterance is spoken, which could further improve the efficiency of the system. This is a topic for future research, together with the generation of hidden and overt repair as discussed by Kilger & Finkler (1995).

5 Evaluation

It is difficult to evaluate complete dialogue systems such as the one presented here, since there are so many different components involved (but see Möller et al. (2007) for methods used). In our case, we're interested in the benefits of a specific aspect, though, namely incrementality. No evaluation is needed to confirm that an incremental system such as this allows more flexible turn-taking and that it can potentially respond faster – this is so by design. However, we also want this behaviour to result in an improved user experience. To test whether we have achieved this, we implemented for comparison a non-incremental version of the system, very much like a standard number dictation dialogue in a commercial application. In this version, the user is asked to read out the whole number sequence in one go. After a certain amount of silence, the system confirms the whole sequence and asks a yes/no question whether it was correct. If not, the user has to repeat the whole sequence.

Eight subjects were given the task of using the two versions of the system to dictate number sequences (in English) to the system. (The subjects were native speakers of German with a good command of English.) Half of the subjects used the incremental version first and the other half started with the non-incremental version. They were asked to dictate eight number sequences to each version, resulting in 128 dialogues. For each sequence, they were given a time limit of 1 minute. After each sequence, they were asked whether they had succeeded in dictating the sequence or not, as well as to mark their agreement (on a scale from 0-6) with statements concerning how well they had been understood by the system, how responsive the system was, if the system behaved as expected, and how human-like the conversational partner was. After using both versions of the system, they were also asked whether they preferred one of the versions and to what extent (1 or 2 points, which gives a maximum score of 16 to any version, when totalling all subjects).

There was no significant difference between the two versions with regard to how many of the tasks were completed successfully. However, the incremental version was clearly preferred in the overall judgement (9 points versus 1). Only one of the more specific questions yielded any significant difference between the versions: the incremental version was judged to be more human-like for the successful dialogues (5,2 on average vs. 4,5; Wilcoxon signed rank test; $p<0.05$).

The results from the evaluation are in line with what could be expected. A non-incremental system can be very efficient if the system understands the number sequence the first time, and the ASR vocabulary is in this case very limited, which explains why the success-rate was the same for both systems. However, the incremental version was experienced as more pleasant and human-like. One explanation for the better rating of the incremental version is that the acknowledgements encouraged the subjects to package the digits into installments, which helped the system to better read back the sequence using the same installments.

6 Conclusions and future work

To sum up, we have presented a dialogue system that through the use of novel techniques (incremental prosodic analysis, reactive connection between ASR and TTS, fully incremental architecture) achieves an unprecedented level of reactiveness (from a minimum latency of 750ms, as typically used in dialogue systems, down to one of 200ms), and is consequently evaluated as more natural than more typical setups by human users. While the domain we've used is relatively simple, there are no principled reasons why the techniques introduced here should not scale up.

In future user studies, we will explore which factors contribute to the improved experience of using an incremental system. Such factors may include improved responsiveness, better installment packaging, and more elaborate feedback. It would also be interesting to find out when rapid responses are more important (e.g. acknowledgements), and when they may be less important (e.g., answers to task-related questions).

We are currently investigating the transfer of the prosodic analysis to utterances in a larger domain, where similarly instructions by the user can be given in installments. But even within the currently used micro-domain, there are interesting issues still to be explored. In future versions of the system, we will let the modules pass parallel hypotheses and also improve the incremental generation and synthesis. Since the vocabulary is very limited, it would also be possible to use a limited domain synthesis (Black & Lenzo, 2000), and explore how the nuances of different backchannels might affect the dialogue. Another challenge that can be researched within this micro-domain is how to use the prosodic analysis for other tasks, such as distinguishing correction from dictation (for example if U.14 in Table 1 would not begin with a "no"). In general, we think that this paper shows that narrowing down the domain while shifting the focus to the modelling of more low-level, conversational dialogue phenomena is a fruitful path.

Acknowledgements

This work was funded by a DFG grant in the Emmy Noether programme. We would also like to thank Timo Baumann and Michaela Atterer for their contributions to the project, as well as Anna Iwanow and Angelika Adam for collecting and transcribing the data used in this paper.

References

Aist, G., Allen, J. F., Campana, E., Galescu, L., Gómez Gallo, C. A., Stoness, S. C., Swift, M., & Tanenhaus, M. (2006). Software Architectures for Incremental Understanding of Human Speech. In *Proceedings of Interspeech* (pp. 1922-1925). Pittsburgh PA, USA.

Allen, J. F., Ferguson, G., & Stent, A. (2001). An architecture for more realistic conversational systems. In *Proceedings of the 6th international conference on Intelligent user interfaces* (pp. 1-8).

Black, A., & Lenzo, K. (2000). Limited domain synthesis. In *Proceedings of ICSLP* (pp. 410-415). Beijing, China.

Brooks, R. A. (1991). Intelligence without representation. *Artificial Intelligence, 47*, 139-159.

Clark, H. H. (1996). *Using language*. Cambridge, UK: Cambridge University Press.

Dohsaka, K., & Shimazu, A. (1997). System architecture for spoken utterance production in collaborative dialogue. In *Working Notes of IJCAI 1997 Workshop on Collaboration, Cooperation and Conflict in Dialogue Systems*.

Dutoit, T., Pagel, V., Pierret, N., Bataille, F., & Vreken, O. v. d. (1996). The MBROLA project: Towards a set of high-quality speech synthesizers free of use for non-commercial purposes. In *Proceedings of ICSLIP '96* (pp. 1393-1396).

Edlund, J., Gustafson, J., Heldner, M., & Hjalmarsson, A. (2008). Towards human-like spoken dialogue systems. *Speech Communication, 50*(8-9), 630-645.

Ferrer, L., Shriberg, E., & Stolcke, A. (2002). Is the speaker done yet? Faster and more accurate end-of utterance detection using prosody. In *Proceedings of ICSLP* (pp. 2061-2064).

Kilger, A., & Finkler, W. (1995). *Incremental Generation for Real-Time Applications*. Technical Report RR-95-11, German Research Center for Artificial Intelligence.

Koiso, H., Horiuchi, Y., Tutiya, S., Ichikawa, A., & Den, Y. (1998). An analysis of turn-taking and backchannels based on prosodic and syntactic features in Japanese Map Task dialogs. *Language and Speech, 41*, 295-321.

Lamere, P., Kwok, P., Gouvea, E., Raj, B., Singh, R., Walker, W., Warmuth, M., & Wolf, P. (2003). The CMU SPHINX-4 speech recognition system.. In *Proceedings of the IEEE Intl. Conf. on Acoustics, Speech and Signal Processing*. Hong Kong.

Levelt, W. J. M. (1989). *Speaking: From Intention to Articulation*. Cambridge, Mass., USA: MIT Press.

Liu, J., Zheng, T. F., Deng, J., & Wu, W. (2005). Real-time pitch tracking based on combined SMDSF. In *Proceedings of Interspeech* (pp. 301-304). Lisbon, Portugal.

Möller, S., Smeele, P., Boland, H., & Krebber, J. (2007). Evaluating spoken dialogue systems according to de-facto standards: A case study. *Computer Speech & Language, 21*(1), 26-53.

Raux, A., & Eskenazi, M. (2007). A multi-Layer architecture for semi-synchronous event-driven dialogue Management. In *ASRU 2007*. Kyoto, Japan..

Raux, A., & Eskenazi, M. (2008). Optimizing endpointing thresholds using dialogue features in a spoken dialogue system. In *Proceedings of SIGdial 2008*. Columbus, OH, USA.

Sacks, H., Schwegloff, E., & Jefferson, G. (1974). A simplest systematics for the organization of turn-taking for conversation. *Language, 50*, 696-735.

Schlangen, D., & Fernández, R. (2007). Speaking through a noisy channel: experiments on inducing clarification behaviour in human-human dialogue. In *Proceedings of Interspeech 2007*. Antwerp, Belgium.

Schlangen, D., & Skantze, G. (2009). A general, abstract model of incremental dialogue processing. In *Proceedings of the 12th Conference of the European Chapter of the Association for Computational Linguistics (EACL-09)*. Athens, Greece.

Skantze, G., & Edlund, J. (2004). Robust interpretation in the Higgins spoken dialogue system. In *Proceedings of ISCA Tutorial and Research Workshop (ITRW) on Robustness Issues in Conversational Interaction*. Norwich, UK.

Skantze, G. (2007). *Error Handling in Spoken Dialogue Systems - Managing Uncertainty, Grounding and Miscommunication*. Doctoral dissertation, KTH, Department of Speech, Music and Hearing.

Skantze, G. (2008). Galatea: A discourse modeller supporting concept-level error handling in spoken dialogue systems. In Dybkjær, L., & Minker, W. (Eds.), *Recent Trends in Discourse and Dialogue*. Springer.

Stoness, S. C., Tetreault, J., & Allen, J. (2004). Incremental parsing with reference interaction. In *Proceedings of the ACL Workshop on Incremental Parsing* (pp. 18-25).

Tanenhaus, M. K., & Brown-Schmidt, S. (2008). Language processing in the natural world. In Moore, B. C. M., Tyler, L. K., & Marslen-Wilson, W. D. (Eds.), *The perception of speech: from sound to meaning* (pp. 1105-1122).

Wirén, M. (1992). *Studies in Incremental Natural Language Analysis*. Doctoral dissertation, Linköping University, Linköping, Sweden.

Witten, I. H., & Frank, E. (2005). *Data Mining: Practical machine learning tools and techniques*. San Francisco: Morgan Kaufmann.

Unsupervised Recognition of Literal and Non-Literal Use of Idiomatic Expressions

Caroline Sporleder and **Linlin Li**
Saarland University
Postfach 15 11 50
66041 Saarbrücken, Germany
{csporled, linlin}@coli.uni-saarland.de

Abstract

We propose an unsupervised method for distinguishing literal and non-literal usages of idiomatic expressions. Our method determines how well a literal interpretation is linked to the overall cohesive structure of the discourse. If strong links can be found, the expression is classified as literal, otherwise as idiomatic. We show that this method can help to tell apart literal and non-literal usages, even for idioms which occur in canonical form.

1 Introduction

Texts frequently contain expressions whose meaning is not strictly literal, such as metaphors or idioms. Non-literal expressions pose a major challenge to natural language processing as they often exhibit lexical and syntactic idiosyncrasies. For example, idioms can violate selectional restrictions (as in *push one's luck* under the assumption that only concrete things can normally be pushed), disobey typical subcategorisation constraints (e.g., *in line* without a determiner before *line*), or change the default assignments of semantic roles to syntactic categories (e.g., in *break sth with X* the argument *X* would typically be an instrument but for the idiom *break the ice* it is more likely to fill a patient role, as in *break the ice with Russia*).

To avoid erroneous analyses, a natural language processing system should recognise if an expression is used non-literally. While there has been a lot of work on recognising idioms (see Section 2), most previous approaches have focused on a *type-based classification*, dividing expressions into "idiom" or "not an idiom" irrespective of their actual use in a discourse context. However, while some expressions, such as *by and large*, always have a non-compositional, idiomatic meaning, many idioms, such as *break the ice* or *spill the beans*, share their linguistic form with perfectly literal expressions (see examples (1) and (2), respectively). For some expressions, such as *drop the ball*, the literal usage can even dominate in some domains. Hence, whether a potentially ambiguous expression has literal or non-literal meaning has to be inferred from the discourse context.

(1) Dad had to break the ice on the chicken troughs so that they could get water.

(2) Somehow I always end up spilling the beans all over the floor and looking foolish when the clerk comes to sweep them up.

Type-based idiom classification thus only addresses part of the problem. While it can automatically compile lists of *potentially* idiomatic expressions, it does not say anything about the idiomaticity of an expression in a particular context. In this paper, we propose a novel, cohesion-based approach for detecting non-literal usages (*token-based idiom classification*). Our approach is unsupervised and similar in spirit to Hirst and St-Onge's (1998) method for detecting malapropisms. Like them, we rely on the presence or absence of cohesive links between the words in a text. However, unlike Hirst and St-Onge we do not require a hand-crafted resource like WordNet or Roget's Thesaurus; our approach is knowledge-lean.

2 Related Work

Most studies on idiom classification focus on type-based classification; few researchers have worked on token-based approaches. Type-based methods frequently exploit the fact that idioms have

Proceedings of the 12th Conference of the European Chapter of the ACL, pages 754–762,
Athens, Greece, 30 March – 3 April 2009. ©2009 Association for Computational Linguistics

a number of properties which differentiate them from other expressions. Apart from not having a (strictly) compositional meaning, they also exhibit some degree of syntactic and lexical fixedness. For example, some idioms do not allow internal modifiers (**shoot the long breeze*) or passivisation (**the bucket was kicked*). They also typically only allow very limited lexical variation (**kick the vessel, *strike the bucket*).

Many approaches for identifying idioms focus on one of these two aspects. For instance, measures that compute the association strength between the elements of an expression have been employed to determine its degree of compositionality (Lin, 1999; Fazly and Stevenson, 2006) (see also Villavicencio et al. (2007) for an overview and a comparison of different measures). Other approaches use Latent Semantic Analysis (LSA) to determine the similarity between a potential idiom and its components (Baldwin et al., 2003). Low similarity is supposed to indicate low compositionality. Bannard (2007) proposes to identify idiomatic expressions by looking at their syntactic fixedness, i.e., how likely they are to take modifiers or be passivised, and comparing this to what would be expected based on the observed behaviour of the component words. Fazly and Stevenson (2006) combine information about syntactic and lexical fixedness (i.e., estimated degree of compositionality) into one measure.

The few token-based approaches include a study by Katz and Giesbrecht (2006), who devise a supervised method in which they compute the meaning vectors for the literal and non-literal usages of a given expression in the training data. An unseen test instance of the same expression is then labelled by performing a nearest neighbour classification. They report an average accuracy of 72%, though their evaluation is fairly small scale, using only one expression and 67 instances. Birke and Sarkar (2006) model literal vs. non-literal classification as a word sense disambiguation task and use a clustering algorithm which compares test instances to two automatically constructed seed sets (one with literal and one with non-literal expressions), assigning the label of the closest set. While the seed sets are created without immediate human intervention they do rely on manually created resources such as databases of known idioms.

Cook et al. (2007) and Fazly et al. (To appear) propose an alternative method which crucially relies on the concept of *canonical form* (CForm). It is assumed that for each idiom there is a fixed form (or a small set of those) corresponding to the syntactic pattern(s) in which the idiom normally occurs (Riehemann, 2001).[1] The canonical form allows for inflectional variation of the head verb but not for other variations (such as nominal inflection, choice of determiner etc.). It has been observed that if an expression is used idiomatically, it typically occurs in its canonical form. For example, Riehemann (2001, p. 34) found that for decomposable idioms 75% of the occurrences are in canonical form, rising to 97% for non-decomposable idioms.[2] Cook et al. exploit this behaviour and propose an unsupervised method in which an expression is classified as idiomatic if it occurs in canonical form and literal otherwise. Canonical forms are determined automatically using a statistical, frequency-based measure. The authors report an average accuracy of 72% for their classifier.

3 Using Lexical Cohesion to Identify Idiomatic Expressions

3.1 Lexical Cohesion

In this paper we exploit lexical cohesion to detect idiomatic expressions. *Lexical cohesion* is a property exhibited by coherent texts: concepts referred to in individual sentences are typically related to other concepts mentioned elsewhere (Halliday and Hasan, 1976). Such sequences of semantically related concepts are called *lexical chains*. Given a suitable measure of semantic relatedness, such chains can be computed automatically and have been used successfully in a number of NLP applications, starting with Hirst and St-Onge's (1998) seminal work on detecting real-word spelling errors. Their approach is based on the insight that misspelled words do not "fit" their context, i.e., they do not normally participate in lexical chains. Content words which do not belong to any lexical chain but which are orthographically close to words which do, are therefore good candidates for spelling errors.

Idioms behave similarly to spelling errors in that they typically also do not exhibit a high de-

[1]This is also the form in which an idiom is usually listed in a dictionary.

[2]Decomposable idioms are expressions such as *spill the beans* which have a composite meaning whose parts can be mapped to the words of the expression (e.g., *spill*→'reveal', *beans*→'secret').

gree of lexical cohesion with their context, at least not if one assumes a *literal meaning* for their component words. Hence if the component words of a potentially idiomatic expression do not participate in any lexical chain, it is likely that the expression is indeed used idiomatically, otherwise it is probably used literally. For instance, in example (3), where the expression *play with fire* is used in a literal sense, the word *fire* does participate in a chain (shown in bold face) that also includes the words *grilling*, *dry-heat*, *cooking*, and *coals*, while for the non-literal usage in example (4) there are no chains which include *fire*.[3]

(3) **Grilling** outdoors is much more than just another **dry-heat cooking** method. It's the chance to play with **fire**, satisfying a primal urge to stir around in **coals**.

(4) And PLO chairman Yasser Arafat has accused Israel of playing with fire by supporting HAMAS in its infancy.

Unfortunately, there are also a few cases in which a cohesion-based approach fails. Sometimes an expression is used literally but does not feature prominently enough in the discourse to participate in a chain, as in example (5) where the main focus of the discourse is on the use of morphine and not on children playing with fire.[4] The opposite case also exists: sometimes idiomatic usages do exhibit lexical cohesion on the component word level. This situation is often a consequence of a deliberate "play with words", e.g. the use of several related idioms or metaphors (see example (6)). However, we found that both cases are relatively rare. For instance, in a study of 75 literal usages of various expressions, we only discovered seven instances in which no relevant chain could be found, including some cases where the context was too short to establish the cohesive structure (e.g., because the expression occurred in a headline).

(5) Chinamasa compared McGown's attitude to morphine to a child's attitude to playing with fire – a lack of concern over the risks involved.

(6) Saying that the Americans were "playing with **fire**" the official press speculated that the "**gunpowder** barrel" which is Taiwan might well "**explode**" if Washington and Taipei do not put a stop to their "**incendiary** gesticulations."

[3]Idioms may, of course, link to the surrounding discourse with their *idiomatic meaning*, i.e., for *play with fire* one may expect other words in the discourse which are related to the concept "danger".

[4]Though one could argue that there is a chain linking *child* and *play* which points to the literal usage here.

3.2 Modelling Semantic Relatedness

While a cohesion-based approach to token-based idiom classification should be intuitively successful, its practical usefulness depends crucially on the availability of a suitable method for computing semantic relatedness. This is currently an area of active research. There are two main approaches. Methods based on manually built lexical knowledge bases, such as WordNet, model semantic relatedness by computing the shortest path between two concepts in the knowledge base and/or by looking at word overlap in the glosses (see Budanitsky and Hirst (2006) for an overview). Distributional approaches, on the other hand, rely on text corpora, and model relatedness by comparing the contexts in which two words occur, assuming that related words occur in similar context (e.g., Hindle (1990), Lin (1998), Mohammad and Hirst (2006)). More recently, there has also been research on using Wikipedia and related resources for modelling semantic relatedness (Ponzetto and Strube, 2007; Zesch et al., 2008).

All approaches have advantages and disadvantages. WordNet-based approaches, for instance, typically have a low coverage and only work for so-called "classical relations" like hypernymy, antonymy etc. Distributional approaches usually conflate different word senses and may therefore lead to unintuitive results. For our task, we need to model a wide range of semantic relations (Morris and Hirst, 2004), for example, relations based on some kind of functional or situational association, as between *fire* and *coal* in (3) or between *ice* and *water* in example (1). Likewise we also need to model relations between non-nouns, for instance between *spill* and *sweep up* in example (2). Some relations also require world-knowledge, as in example (7), where the literal usage of *drop the ball* is not only indicated by the presence of *goalkeeper* but also by knowing that Wayne Rooney and Kevin Campbell are both football players.

(7) When **Rooney** collided with the **goalkeeper**, causing him to drop the **ball**, **Kevin Campbell** followed in.

We thus decided against a WordNet-based measure of semantic relatedness, opting instead for a distributional approach, *Normalized Google Distance* (NGD, see Cilibrasi and Vitanyi (2007)), which computes relatedness on the basis of page counts returned by a search engine. NGD is a measure of association that quantifies the strength of a relationship between two words. It is defined as follows:

$$NGD(x,y) = \frac{max\{log\ f(x), log\ f(y)\} - log\ f(x,y)}{log\ M - min\{log\ f(x), log\ f(y)\}} \tag{8}$$

where x and y are the two words whose association strength is computed (e.g., *fire* and *coal*), $f(x)$ is the page count returned by the search engine for the term x (and likewise for $f(y)$ and y), $f(x, y)$ is the page count returned when querying for "x AND y" (i.e., the number of pages that contain both, x and y), and M is the number of web pages indexed by the search engine. The basic idea is that the more often two terms occur together relative to their overall occurrence the more closely they are related. For most pairs of search terms the NGD falls between 0 and 1, though in a small number of cases NGD can exceed 1 (see Cilibrasi and Vitanyi (2007) for a detailed discussion of the mathematical properties of NGD).

Using web counts rather than bi-gram counts from a corpus as the basis for computing semantic relatedness was motivated by the fact that the web is a significantly larger database than any compiled corpus, which makes it much more likely that we can find information about the concepts we are looking for (thus alleviating data sparseness). The information is also more up-to-date, which is important for modelling the kind of world knowledge about named entities we need to resolve examples like (7). Furthermore, it has been shown that web counts can be used as reliable proxies for corpus-based counts and often lead to better statistical models (Zhu and Rosenfeld, 2001; Lapata and Keller, 2005).

To obtain the web counts we used Yahoo rather than Google because we found Yahoo gave us more stable counts over time. Both the Yahoo and the Google API seemed to have problems with very high frequency words, so we excluded those cases. Effectively, this amounted to filtering out function words. As it is difficult to obtain reliable figures for the number of pages indexed by a search engine, we approximated this number (M in formula (8) above) by setting it to the number of hits obtained for the word *the*, assuming that this word occurs in virtually all English language pages (Lapata and Keller, 2005). When generating the queries we made sure that we queried for all combinations of inflected forms (for example "fire AND coal" would be expanded to "fire AND coal", "fires AND coal", "fire AND coals", and "fires AND coals"). The inflected forms were generated by the *morph* tools developed at the University of Sussex (Minnen et al., 2001).[5]

3.3 Cohesion-based Classifiers

We implemented two cohesion-based classifiers: the first one computes the **lexical chains** for the input text and classifies an expression as literal or non-literal depending on whether its component words participate in any of the chains, the second classifier builds a **cohesion graph** and determines how this graph changes when the expression is inserted or left out.

Chain-based classifier Various methods for building lexical chains have been proposed in the literature (Hirst and St-Onge, 1998; Barzilay and Elhadad, 1997; Silber and McCoy, 2002) but the basic idea is as follows: the content words of the text are considered in sequence and for each word it is determined whether it is similar enough to (the words in) one of the existing chains to be placed in that chain, if not it is placed in a chain of its own. Depending on the chain building algorithm used, a word is placed in a chain if it is related to *one* other word in the chain or to *all* of them. The latter strategy is more conservative and tends to lead to shorter but more reliable chains and it is the method we adopted here.[6] Note that the chaining algorithm has a free parameter, namely a threshold which has to be surpassed to consider two words related (*relatedness threshold*).

On the basis of the computed chains, the classifier has to decide whether the target expression is used literally or not. A simple strategy would classify an expression as literal whenever one or more of its component words participates in *any* chain. However, as the chains are potentially noisy, this may not be the best strategy. We therefore also evaluate the strength of the chain(s) in which the expression participates. If a component word of the expression participates in a long chain (and is related to all words in the chain, as we require)

[5]The tools are available at: `http://www.informatics.susx.ac.uk/research/groups/nlp/carroll/morph.html`.

[6]If a WordNet-based relatedness measure is used, the chaining algorithm has to perform word sense disambiguation as well. As we use a distributional relatedness measure which conflates different senses anyway, we do not have to disambiguate here.

then this is good evidence that the expression is indeed used in a literal sense. For instance, in (3) the word *fire* belongs to the relatively long chain *grilling – dry-heat – cooking – fire – coals*, providing strong evidence of literal usage of *play with fire*. To determine the strength of the evidence in favour of a literal interpretation, we take the longest chain in which any of the component words of the idiom participate[7] and check whether this is above a predefined threshold (the *classification threshold*). Both the relatedness threshold and the classification threshold are set empirically by optimising on a manually annotated development set (see Section 4.2).

Graph-based classifier The chain-based classifier has two parameters which need to be optimised on labelled data, making this method weakly supervised. To overcome this drawback, we designed a second classifier which does not have free parameters and is thus fully unsupervised. This classifier relies on *cohesion graphs*. The vertices of such a cohesion graph correspond to the (content) word tokens in the text, each pair of vertices is connected by an edge and the edges are weighted by the semantic relatedness (i.e., the inverse NGD) between the two words. The cohesion graph for example (1) is shown in Figure 1 (for expository reasons, edge weights are excluded from the figure). Once we have built the cohesion graph we compute its connectivity (defined as the average edge weight) and compare it to the connectivity of the graph that results from removing the (component words of the) target expression. For instance in Figure 1, we would compare the connectivity of the graph as it is shown to the connectivity that results from removing the dashed edges. If removing the idiom words from the graph leads to a higher connectivity, we assume that the idiom is used non-literally, otherwise we assume it is used literally. In Figure 1, for example, most edges would have a relatively low weight, indicating a weak relation between the words they link. The edge between *ice* and *water*, however, would have a higher weight. Removing *ice* from the graph would therefore lead to a decreased connectivity and the classifier would predict that *break the ice* is used in the literal sense in example (1). Effectively, we replace the explicit thresholds of the lexical chain method by an *implicit threshold* (i.e., change in connectivity), which does not have to be optimised.

[7]Note, that it is not only the noun that can participate in a chain. In example (2), the word *spill* can be linked to *sweep up* to provide evidence of literal usage.

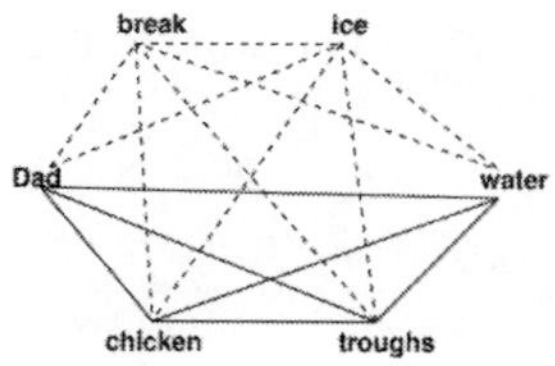

Figure 1: Cohesion graph for example (1)

4 Evaluating the Cohesion-Based Approach

We tested our two cohesion-based classifiers as well as a supervised classifier on a manually annotated data set. Section 4.2 gives details of the experiments and results. We start, however, by describing the data used in the experiments.

4.1 Data

We chose 17 idioms from the *Oxford Dictionary of Idiomatic English* (Cowie et al., 1997) and other idiom lists found on the internet. The idioms were more or less selected randomly, subject to two constraints: First, because the focus of the present study is on distinguishing literal and non-literal usage, we chose expressions for which we assumed that the literal meaning was not too infrequent. We thus disregarded expressions like *play the second fiddle* or *sail under false colours*. Second, in line with many previous approaches to idiom classification (Fazly et al., To appear; Cook et al., 2007; Katz and Giesbrecht, 2006), we focused mainly on expressions of the form V+NP or V+PP as this is a fairly large group and many of these expressions can be used literally as well, making them an ideal test set for our purpose. However, our approach also works for expressions which match a different syntactic pattern and to test the generality of our method we included a couple of these in the data set (e.g., *get one's feet wet*). For the same reason, we also included some expressions for which we could not find a literal use in the corpus (e.g., *back the wrong horse*).

For each of the 17 expressions shown in Table 1, we extracted all occurrences found in the Gigaword corpus that were in canonical form (the forms listed in the table plus inflectional variations of the head verb).[8] Hence, for *rock the boat* we would extract *rocked the boat* and *rocking the boat* but not *rock a boat*, *rock the boats* or *rock the ship*. The motivation for this was two-fold. First, as was discussed in Section 2, the vast majority of idiomatic usages are in canonical form. This is especially true for non-decomposable idioms (most of our 17 idioms), where only around 3% of the idiomatic usages are not in canonical form. Second, we wanted to test whether our approach would be able to detect literal usages in the set of canonical form expressions as this is precisely the set of expressions that would be classified as idiomatic by the unsupervised CForm classifier (Cook et al. (2007), Fazly et al. (To appear)). While expressions in the canonical form are more likely to be used idiomatically, it is still possible to find literal usages as in examples (1) and (2). For some expressions, such as *drop the ball* the literal usage even outweighs the non-literal usage. These literal usages would be mis-classified by the CForm classifier.

In principle, though, our approach is very general and would also work on expressions that are not in canonical form and expressions whose idiomatic status is unclear, i.e., we do not necessarily require a predefined set of idioms but could run the classifiers on any V+NP or V+PP chunk.

For each extracted example, we included five paragraphs of context (the current paragraph plus the two preceding and following ones).[9] This was the context used by the classifiers. The examples were then labelled as "literal" or "non-literal" by an experienced annotator. If the distinction could not be made reliably, e.g., because the context was not long enough to disambiguate, the annotator was allowed to annotate "?". These cases were excluded from the data sets. To estimate the reliability of our annotation, a randomly selected sample (300 instances) was annotated independently by a second annotator. The annotations deviated in eight cases from the original, amounting to an inter-annotator agreement of over 97% and a kappa score of 0.7 (Cohen, 1960). All deviations were cases in which one of the annotators chose "?", often because there was not sufficient context and the annotation decision had to be made on the basis of world knowledge.

[8]The extraction was done via manually built regular expressions.

[9]Note that paragraphs tend to be rather short in newswire. For other genres it may be sufficient to extract one paragraph.

expression	literal	non-literal	all
back the wrong horse	0	25	25
bite off more than one can chew	2	142	144
bite one's tongue	16	150	166
blow one's own trumpet	0	9	9
bounce off the wall*	39	7	46
break the ice	20	521	541
drop the ball*	688	215	903
get one's feet wet	17	140	157
pass the buck	7	255	262
play with fire	34	532	566
pull the trigger*	11	4	15
rock the boat	8	470	478
set in stone	9	272	281
spill the beans	3	172	175
sweep under the carpet	0	9	9
swim against the tide	1	125	126
tear one's hair out	7	54	61
all	862	3102	3964

Table 1: Idiom statistics (* indicates expressions for which the literal usage is more common than the non-literal one)

4.2 Experimental Set-Up and Results

For the lexical chain classifier we ran two experiments. In the first, we used the data for one expression (*break the ice*) as a development set for optimising the two parameters (the relatedness threshold and the classification threshold). To find good thresholds, a simple hill-climbing search was implemented during which we increased the relatedness threshold in steps of 0.02 and the classification threshold (governing the minimum chain length needed) in steps of 1. We optimised the F-Score for the literal class, though we found that the selected parameters varied only minimally when optimising for accuracy. We then used the parameter values determined in this way and applied the classifier to the remainder of the data.

The results obtained in this way depend to some extent on the data set used for the parameter setting.[10] To control this factor, we also ran another experiment in which we used an oracle to set the parameters (i.e., the parameters were optimised for the complete set). While this is not a realistic scenario as it assumes that the labels of the test data are known during parameter setting, it does provide an *upper bound* for the lexical chain method.

For comparison, we also implemented an **informed baseline classifier**, which employs a simple model of cohesion, classifying expressions as

[10]We also ran the experiment for different development sets and found that there was a relatively high degree of variation in the parameters selected and in the results obtained with those settings.

literal if the noun inside the expression (e.g., *ice* for *break the ice*) is repeated elsewhere in the context, and non-literal otherwise. One would expect this classifier to have a high precision for literal expressions but a low recall.

Finally, we implemented a **supervised classifier**. Supervised classifiers have been used before for this task, notably by Katz and Giesbrecht (2006). Our approach is slightly different: instead of creating meaning vectors we look at the word overlap[11] of a test instance with the literal and non-literal instances in the training set (for the same expression) and then assign the label of the closest set.

That such an approach might be promising becomes clear when one looks at some examples of literal and non-literal usage. For instance, non-literal examples of *break the ice* occur frequently with words such as *diplomacy, relations, dialogue* etc. Effectively these words form lexical chains with the *idiomatic* meaning of *break the ice*. They are absent for literal usages. A supervised classifier can learn which terms are indicative of which usage. Note that this information is expression-specific, i.e., it is not possible to train a classifier for *play with fire* on labelled examples for *break the ice*. This makes the supervised approach quite expensive in terms of annotation effort as data has to be labelled for each expression. Nonetheless, it is instructive to see how well one could do with this approach. In the experiments, we ran the supervised classifier in leave-one-out mode on each expression for which we had literal examples.

Table 2 shows the results for the five classifiers discussed above: the informed baseline classifier (Rep), the cohesion graph (Graph), the lexical chain classifier with the parameters optimised on *break the ice* (LC), the lexical chain classifier with the parameters set by an oracle (LC-O), and the supervised classifier (Super). The table also shows the accuracy that would be obtained by a CForm classifier (Cook et al., 2007; Fazly et al., To appear) with gold standard canonical forms. This classifier would label all examples in our data set as "non-literal" (it is thus equivalent to a majority class baseline). Since the majority of examples is indeed used idiomatically, this classifier achieves a relatively high accuracy. However, accuracy is not the best evaluation measure here because we are interested in detecting literal usages among the canonical forms. Therefore, we also computed the precision (P_l), recall (R_l), and F-score (F_l) for the literal class.

	CForm	Rep	Graph	LC	LC-O	Super
Acc	78.25	79.06	79.61	80.50	80.42	95.69
P_l	-	70.00	52.21	62.26	53.89	84.62
R_l	-	5.96	67.87	26.21	69.03	96.45
F_l	-	10.98	59.02	36.90	60.53	90.15

Table 2: Accuracy, literal precision (P_l), recall (R_l), and F-Score (F_l) for the classifiers

It can be seen that all classifiers obtain a relatively high accuracy but vary in precision, recall and F-Score. For the CForm classifier, precision, recall, and F-Score are undefined as it does not label any examples as "literal". As expected the baseline classifier, which looks for repetitions of the component words of the target expression, has a relatively high precision, showing that the expression is typically used in the literal sense if part of it is repeated in the context. The recall, though, is very low, indicating that lexical repetition is not a sufficient signal for literal usage.

The graph-based classifier and the globally optimised lexical chain classifier (LC-O) outperform the other two unsupervised classifiers (CForm and Rep), with an F-Score of around 60%. For both classifiers recall is higher than precision. Note, however, that this is an upper bound for the lexical chain classifier that would not be obtained in a realistic scenario. An example of the values that can be expected in a realistic setting (with parameter optimisation on a development set that is separate from the test set) is shown in column five (LC). Here the F-Score is much lower due to lower recall. This classifier is too conservative when creating the chains and deciding how to interpret the chain structure; it thus only rarely outputs the literal class. The reason for this conservatism may be that literal usages of *break the ice* (the development data) tend to have very strong chains, hence when optimising the parameters for this data set, it pays to be conservative. It is positive to note that the (unsupervised) graph-based classifier performs just as well as the (weakly supervised) chain-based classifier does under optimal circumstances. This means that one can by-pass the parameter setting and the need to label development data by employing the graph-based method.

Finally, as expected, the supervised classifier

[11] We used the Dice coefficient as implemented in Ted Pedersen's Text::Similarity module: `http://www.d.umn.edu/~tpederse/text-similarity.html`.

outperforms all other classifiers. It does so by a large margin, which is surprising given that it is based on relatively simplistic model. This shows that the context in which an expression occurs can really provide vital cues about its idiomaticity. Note that our results are noticeably higher than those reported by Cook et al. (2007), Fazly et al. (To appear) and Katz and Giesbrecht (2006) for similar supervised classifiers. We believe that this may be partly explained by the size of our data set which is significantly larger than the ones used in these studies.

To assess how well our cohesion-based approach works for different idioms, we also computed the accuracy of the graph-based classifier for each expression individually (Table 3). We report accuracy here rather than literal F-Score as the latter is often undefined for the individual data sets (either because all examples of an expression are non-literal or because the classifier only predicts non-literal usages). It can be seen that the performance of the classifier is generally relatively stable, with accuracies above 50% for most idioms.[12] In particular, the classifier performs well on both, expressions with a dominant non-literal meaning and those with a dominant literal meaning; it is not biased towards the non-literal class. For expressions with a dominant literal meaning like *drop the ball*, it correctly classifies more items as "literal" (530 items, 472 of which are correct) than as "non-literal" (373 items, 157 correct).

expression	Accuracy
back the wrong horse	68.00
bite off more than one can chew	79.17
bite one's tongue	37.35
blow one's own trumpet	11.11
bounce off the wall*	47.82
break the ice	85.03
drop the ball*	69.66
get one's feet wet	64.33
pass the buck	82.44
play with fire	82.33
pull the trigger*	60.00
rock the boat	98.95
set in stone	85.41
spill the beans	83.43
sweep under the carpet	88.89
swim against the tide	93.65
tear one's hair out	49.18

Table 3: Accuracies of the graph-based classifier on each of the expressions (* indicates a dominant literal usage)

5 Conclusion

In this paper, we described a novel method for token-based idiom classification. Our approach is based on the observation that literally used expressions typically exhibit cohesive ties with the surrounding discourse, while idiomatic expressions do not. Hence idiomatic expressions can be detected by the absence of such ties. We propose two methods that exploit this behaviour, one based on lexical chains, the other based on cohesion graphs.

We showed that a cohesion-based approach is well suited for distinguishing literal and non-literal usages, even for expressions in canonical form which tend to be largely idiomatic and would all be classified as non-literal by the previously proposed CForm classifier. Moreover, our findings suggest that the graph-based method performs nearly as well as the best performance to be expected for the chain-based method. This means that the task can be addressed in a completely unsupervised way.

While our results are encouraging they are still below the results obtained by a basic supervised classifier. In future work we would like to explore whether better performance can be achieved by adopting a bootstrapping strategy, in which we use the examples about which the unsupervised classifier is most confident (i.e., those with the largest difference in connectivity in either direction) as input for a second stage supervised classifier.

Another potential improvement has to do with the way in which the cohesion graph is computed. Currently the graph includes all content words in the context. This means that the graph is relatively big and removing the potential idiom often does not have a big effect on the connectivity; all changes in connectivity are fairly close to zero. In future, we want to explore intelligent strategies for pruning the graph (e.g., by including a smaller context). We believe that this might result in more reliable classifications.

Acknowledgments

This work was funded by the German Research Foundation DFG (under grant PI 154/9-3 and the MMCI Cluster of Excellence). Thanks to Anna Mündelein for her help with preparing the data and to Marco Pennacchiotti and Josef Ruppenhofer, for feedback and comments.

[12] Note that the data set for the worst performing idiom, *blow one's own trumpet* only contained 9 instances. Hence, the low performance for this idiom may well be accidental.

References

Timothy Baldwin, Colin Bannard, Takaaki Tanaka, and Dominic Widdows. 2003. An empirical model of multiword expression decomposability. In *Proceedings of the ACL 2003 workshop on Multiword expressions: analysis, acquisition and treatment*, pages 89–96.

Colin Bannard. 2007. A measure of syntactic flexibility for automatically identifying multiword expressions in corpora. In *Proceedings of the ACL-07 Workshop on A Broader Perspective on Multiword Expressions*, pages 1–8.

Regina Barzilay and Michael Elhadad. 1997. Using lexical chains for text summarization. In *Proceedings of the ACL-97 Intelligent Scalable Text Summarization Workshop (ISTS-97)*.

Julia Birke and Anoop Sarkar. 2006. A clustering approach for the nearly unsupervised recognition of nonliteral language. In *Proceedings of EACL-06*, pages 329–336.

Alexander Budanitsky and Graeme Hirst. 2006. Evaluating WordNet-based measures of semantic distance. *Computational Linguistics*, 32(1):13–47.

Rudi L. Cilibrasi and Paul M.B. Vitanyi. 2007. The Google similarity distance. *IEEE Trans. Knowledge and Data Engineering*, 19(3):370–383.

Jacob Cohen. 1960. A coefficient of agreement for nominal scales. *Educational and Psychological Measurements*, 20:37–46.

Paul Cook, Afsaneh Fazly, and Suzanne Stevenson. 2007. Pulling their weight: Exploiting syntactic forms for the automatic identification of idiomatic expressions in context. In *Proceedings of the ACL-07 Workshop on A Broader Perspective on Multiword Expressions*, pages 41–48.

A.P. Cowie, R. Mackin, and I.R. McCaig. 1997. *Oxford dictionary of English idioms*. Oxford University Press.

Afsaneh Fazly and Suzanne Stevenson. 2006. Automatically constructing a lexicon of verb phrase idiomatic combinations. In *Proceedings of EACL-06*.

Afsaneh Fazly, Paul Cook, and Suzanne Stevenson. To appear. Unsupervised type and token identification of idiomatic expressions. *Computational Linguistics*.

M.A.K. Halliday and R. Hasan. 1976. *Cohesion in English*. Longman House, New York.

Donald Hindle. 1990. Noun classification from predicate-argument structures. In *Proceedings of ACL-90*, pages 268–275.

Graeme Hirst and David St-Onge. 1998. Lexical chains as representations of context for the detection and correction of malapropisms. In Christiane Fellbaum, editor, *WordNet: An electronic lexical database*, pages 305–332. The MIT Press.

Graham Katz and Eugenie Giesbrecht. 2006. Automatic identification of non-compositional multiword expressions using latent semantic analysis. In *Proceedings of the ACL/COLING-06 Workshop on Multiword Expressions: Identifying and Exploiting Underlying Properties*, pages 12–19.

Mirella Lapata and Frank Keller. 2005. Web-based models for natural language processing. *ACM Transactions on Speech and Language Processing*, 2:1–31.

Dekang Lin. 1998. Automatic retrieval and clustering of similar words. In *Proceedings of ACL-98*, pages 768–774.

Dekang Lin. 1999. Automatic identification of non-compositional phrases. In *Proceedings of ACL-99*, pages 317–324.

Guido Minnen, John Carroll, and Darren Pearce. 2001. Applied morphological processing of English. *Natural Language Engineering*, 7(3):207–223.

Saif Mohammad and Graeme Hirst. 2006. Distributional measures of concept-distance: A task-oriented evaluation. In *Proceedings of EMNLP-06*.

Jane Morris and Graeme Hirst. 2004. Non-classical lexical semantic relations. In *HLT-NAACL-04 Workshop on Computational Lexical Semantics*, pages 46–51.

Simone Paolo Ponzetto and Michael Strube. 2007. Knowledge derived from Wikipedia for computing semantic relatedness. *Journal of Artificial Intelligence Research*, 30:181–212.

Susanne Riehemann. 2001. *A Constructional Approach to Idioms and Word Formation*. Ph.D. thesis, Stanford University.

H. Gregory Silber and Kathleen F. McCoy. 2002. Efficiently computed lexical chains as an intermediate representation for automatic text summarization. *Computational Linguistics*, 28(4):487–496.

Aline Villavicencio, Valia Kordoni, Yi Zhang, Marco Idiart, and Carlos Ramisch. 2007. Validation and evaluation of automatically acquired multiword expressions for grammar engineering. In *Proceedings of EMNLP-07*, pages 1034–1043.

Torsten Zesch, Christof Müller, and Iryna Gurevych. 2008. Using wiktionary for computing semantic relatedness. In *Proceedings of AAAI-08*, pages 861–867.

Xiaojin Zhu and Ronald Rosenfeld. 2001. Improving trigram language modeling with the world wide web. In *Proceedings of ICASSP-01*.

Semi-supervised Training for the Averaged Perceptron POS Tagger

Drahomíra "johanka" Spoustová Jan Hajič Jan Raab Miroslav Spousta
Institute of Formal and Applied Linguistics
Faculty of Mathematics and Physics,
Charles University Prague, Czech Republic
{johanka,hajic,raab,spousta}@
ufal.mff.cuni.cz

Abstract

This paper describes POS tagging experiments with semi-supervised training as an extension to the (supervised) averaged perceptron algorithm, first introduced for this task by (Collins, 2002). Experiments with an iterative training on standard-sized supervised (manually annotated) dataset (10^6 tokens) combined with a relatively modest (in the order of 10^8 tokens) unsupervised (plain) data in a bagging-like fashion showed significant improvement of the POS classification task on typologically different languages, yielding better than state-of-the-art results for English and Czech (4.12 % and 4.86 % relative error reduction, respectively; absolute accuracies being 97.44 % and 95.89 %).

1 Introduction

Since 2002, we have seen a renewed interest in improving POS tagging results for English, and an inflow of results (initial or improved) for many other languages. For English, after a relatively big jump achieved by (Collins, 2002), we have seen two significant improvements: (Toutanova et al., 2003) and (Shen et al., 2007) pushed the results by a significant amount each time.[1]

Even though an improvement in POS tagging might be a questionable enterprise (given that its effects on other tasks, such as parsing or other NLP problems are less than clear—at least for English), it is still an interesting problem. Moreover, the "ideal"[2] situation of having a single algorithm (and its implementation) for many (if not all) languages has not been reached yet. We have chosen Collins' perceptron algorithm because of its simplicity, short training times, and an apparent room for improvement with (substantially) growing data sizes (see Figure 1). However, it is clear that there is usually little chance to get (substantially) more manually annotated data. Thus, we have been examining the effect of adding a large monolingual corpus to Collins' perceptron, appropriately extended, for two typologically different languages: English and Czech. It is clear however that the features (feature templates) that the taggers use are still language-dependent.

One of the goals is also to have a fast implementation for tagging large amounts of data quickly. We have experimented with various classifier combination methods, such as those described in (Brill and Wu, 1998) or (van Halteren et al., 2001), and got improved results, as expected. However, we view this only as a side effect (yet, a positive one)—our goal was to stay on the turf of single taggers, which are both the common ground for competing on tagger accuracy today and also significantly faster at runtime.[3] Nevertheless, we have found that it is advantageous to use them to (pre-)tag the large amounts of plain text data dur-

[1] In our final comparison, we have also included the results of (Giménez and Màrquez, 2004), because it has surpassed (Collins, 2002) as well and we have used this tagger in the data preparation phase. See more details below. Most recently, (Suzuki and Isozaki, 2008) published their Semi-supervised sequential labelling method, whose results on POS tagging seem to be optically better than (Shen et al., 2007), but no significance tests were given and the tool is not available for download, i.e. for repeating the results and significance testing. Thus, we compare our results only to the tools listed above.

[2] We mean easy to use for further research on problems requiring POS tagging, especially multilingual ones.

[3] And much easier to (re)implement as libraries in prototype systems, which is often difficult if not impossible with other people's code.

Proceedings of the 12th Conference of the European Chapter of the ACL, pages 763–771,
Athens, Greece, 30 March – 3 April 2009. ©2009 Association for Computational Linguistics

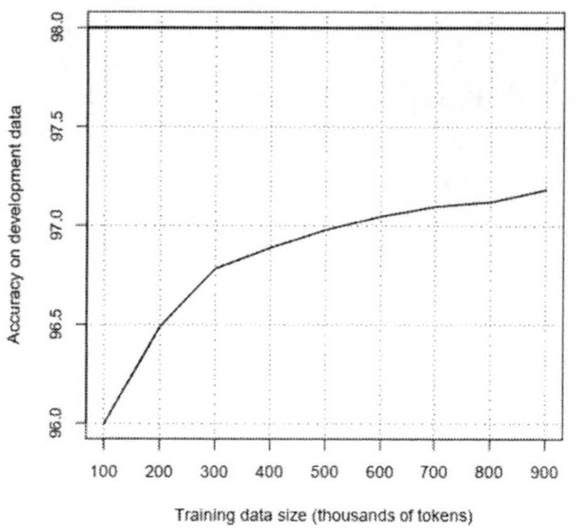

Figure 1: Accuracy of the original averaged perceptron, supervised training on PTB/WSJ (English)

ing the training phase.

Apart from feeding the perceptron by various mixtures of manually tagged ("supervised") and auto-tagged ("unsupervised")[4] data, we have also used various feature templates extensively; for example, we use lexicalization (with the added twist of lemmatization, useful especially for Czech, an inflectionally rich language), "manual" tag classification into large classes (again, useful especially for Czech to avoid the huge, still-to-be-overcome data sparseness for such a language[5]), and sub-lexical features mainly targeted at OOV words. Inspired i.a. by (Toutanova et al., 2003) and (Hajič and Vidová-Hladká, 1998), we also use "lookahead" features (however, we still remain in the left-to-right HMM world – in this respect our solution is closer to the older work of (Hajič and Vidová-Hladká, 1998) than to (Toutanova et al., 2003), who uses bidirectional dependencies to include the right-hand side *disambiguated* tags, which we cannot.)

To summarize, we can describe our system as follows: it is based on (Votrubec, 2006)'s implementation of (Collins, 2002), which has been fed at each iteration by a different dataset consisting of the supervised and unsupervised part: precisely, by a concatenation of the manually tagged training data (WSJ portion of the PTB 3 for English, morphologically disambiguated data from PDT 2.0 for Czech) and a chunk of automatically tagged unsupervised data. The "parameters" of the training process (feature templates, the size of the unsupervised chunks added to the trainer at each iteration, number of iterations, the combination of taggers that should be used in the auto-tagging of the unsupervised chunk, etc.) have been determined empirically in a number of experiments on a development data set. We should also note that as a result of these development-data-based optimizations, no feature pruning has been employed (see Section 4 for details); adding (even lexical) features from the auto-tagged data did not give significant accuracy improvements (and only made the training very slow).

The final taggers have surpassed the current state-of-the-art taggers by significant margins (we have achieved 4.12 % relative error reduction for English and 4.86 % for Czech over the best previously published results, single or combined), using a single tagger. However, the best English tagger combining some of the previous state-of-the-art ones is still "optically" better (yet not significantly—see Section 6).

2 The perceptron algorithm

We have used the Morče[6] tagger (Votrubec, 2006) as a main component in our experiments. It is a reimplementation of the averaged perceptron described in (Collins, 2002), which uses such features that it behaves like an HMM tagger and thus the standard Viterbi decoding is possible. Collins' `GEN(x)` set (a set of possible tags at any given position) is generated, in our case, using a morphological analyzer for the given language (essen-

[4]For brevity, we will use the terms "supervised" and "unsupervised" data for "manually annotated" and "(automatically annotated) plain (raw) text" data, respectively, even though these adjectives are meant to describe the *process* of learning, not the data themselves.

[5]As (Hajič, 2004) writes, Czech has 4400 plausible tags, of which we have observed almost 2000 in the 100M corpus we have used in our experiments. However, only 1100 of them have been found in the manually annotated PDT 2.0 corpus (the corpus on which we have based the supervised experiments). The situation with word forms (tokens) is even worse: Czech has about 20M different word forms, and the OOV rate based on the 1.5M PDT 2.0 data and measured against the 100M raw corpus is almost 10 %.

[6]The name "Morče" stands for "MORfologie ČEštiny" ("Czech morphology", see (Votrubec, 2006)), since it has been originally developed for Czech. We keep this name in this paper as the generic name of the averaged perceptron tagger for the English-language experiments as well. We have used the version available at `http://ufal.mff.cuni.cz/morce/`.

tially, a dictionary that returns all possible tags[7] for an input word form). The transition and output scores for the candidate tags are based on a large number of binary-valued features and their weights, which are determined during iterative training by the averaged perceptron algorithm.

The binary features describe the tag being predicted and its context. They can be derived from any information we already have about the text at the point of decision (respecting the HMM-based overall setting). Every feature can be true or false in a given context, so we can consider the true features at the current position to be the description of a tag and its context.

For every feature, the perceptron keeps its weight coefficient, which is (in its basic version) an integer number, (possibly) changed at every training sentence. After its final update, this integer value is stored with the feature to be later retrieved and used at runtime. Then, the task of the perceptron algorithm is to sum up all the coefficients of true features in a given context. The result is passed to the Viterbi algorithm as a transition and output weight for the current state.[8] We can express it as

$$w(C,T) = \sum_{i=1}^{n} \alpha_i.\phi_i(C,T) \quad (1)$$

where $w(C,T)$ is the transition weight for tag T in context C, n is the number of features, α_i is the weight coefficient of the ith feature and $\phi_i(C,T)$ is the evaluation of the ith feature for context C and tag T. In the averaged perceptron, the values of every coefficient are added up at each update, which happens (possibly) at each training sentence, and their arithmetic average is used instead.[9] This trick makes the algorithm more resistant to weight oscillations during training (or, more precisely, at the end of it) and as a result, it substantially improves its performance.[10]

[7] And lemmas, which are then used in some of the features. A (high recall, low precision) "guesser" is used for OOV words.

[8] Which identifies unambiguously the corresponding tag.

[9] Implementation note: care must be taken to avoid integer overflows, which (at 100 iterations through millions of sentences) can happen for 32bit integers easily.

[10] Our experiments have shown that using averaging helps tremendously, confirming both the theoretical and practical results of (Collins, 2002). On Czech, using the best feature set, the difference on the development data set is 95.96 % vs. 95.02 %. Therefore, all the results presented in the following text use averaging.

The supervised training described in (Collins, 2002) uses manually annotated data for the estimation of the weight coefficients α. The training algorithm is very simple—only integer numbers (counts and their sums for the averaging) are updated for each feature at each sentence with imperfect match(es) found against the gold standard. Therefore, it can be relatively quickly retrained and thus many different feature sets and other training parameters, such as the number of iterations, feature thresholds etc. can be considered and tested. As a result of this tuning, our (fully supervised) version of the Morče tagger gives the best accuracy among all single taggers for Czech and also very good results for English, being beaten only by the tagger (Shen et al., 2007) (by 0.10 % absolute) and (not significantly) by (Toutanova et al., 2003).

3 The data

3.1 The "supervised" data

For English, we use the same data division of Penn Treebank (PTB) `parsed` section (Marcus et al., 1994) as all of (Collins, 2002), (Toutanova et al., 2003), (Giménez and Màrquez, 2004) and (Shen et al., 2007) do; for details, see Table 1.

data set	*tokens*	*sentences*
train (0-18)	912,344	38,220
dev-test (19-21)	131,768	5,528
eval-test (22-24)	129,654	5,463

Table 1: English supervised data set — WSJ part of Penn Treebank 3

For Czech, we use the current standard Prague Dependency Treebank (PDT 2.0) data sets (Hajič et al., 2006); for details, see Table 2.

data set	*tokens*	*sentences*
train	1,539,241	91,049
dev-test	201,651	11,880
eval-test	219,765	13,136

Table 2: Czech supervised data set — Prague Dependency Treebank 2.0

3.2 The "unsupervised" data

For English, we have processed the North American News Text corpus (Graff, 1995) (without the

WSJ section) with the Stanford segmenter and tokenizer (Toutanova et al., 2003). For Czech, we have used the SYN2005 part of Czech National Corpus (CNC, 2005) (with the original segmentation and tokenization).

3.3 GEN(x): The morphological analyzers

For English, we perform a very simple morphological analysis, which reduces the full PTB tagset to a small list of tags for each token on input. The resulting list is larger than such a list derived solely from the PTB/WSJ, but much smaller than a full list of tags found in the PTB/WSJ.[11] The English morphological analyzer is thus (empirically) optimized for precision while keeping as high recall as possible (it still overgenerates). It consists of a small dictionary of exceptions and a small set of general rules, thus covering also a lot of OOV tokens.[12]

For Czech, the separate morphological analyzer (Hajič, 2004) usually precedes the tagger. We use the version from April 2006 (the same as (Spoustová et al., 2007), who reported the best previous result on Czech tagging).

4 The perceptron feature sets

The averaged perceptron's accuracy is determined (to a large extent) by the set of features used. A feature set is based on feature templates, i.e. general patterns, which are filled in with concrete values from the training data. Czech and English are morphosyntactically very different languages, therefore each of them needs a different set of feature templates. We have empirically tested hundreds of feature templates on both languages, taken over from previous works for direct comparison, inspired by them, or based on a combination of previous experience, error analysis and linguistic intuition.

In the following sections, we present the best performing set of feature templates as determined on the development data set using only the supervised training setting; our feature templates have thus not been influenced nor extended by the unsupervised data.[13]

[11] The full list of tags, as used by (Shen et al., 2007), also makes the underlying Viterbi algorithm unbearably slow.

[12] The English morphology tool is also downloadable as a separate module on the paper's accompanying website.

[13] Another set of experiments has shown that there is not, perhaps surprisingly, a significant gain in doing so.

4.1 English feature templates

The best feature set for English consists of 30 feature templates. All templates predict the current tag as a whole. A detailed description of the English feature templates can be found in Table 3.

Context predicting whole tag	
Tags	Previous tag Previous two tags First letter of previous tag
Word forms	Current word form Previous word form Previous two word forms Following word form Following two word forms Last but one word form
Current word affixes	Prefixes of length 1-9 Suffixes of length 1-9
Current word features	Contains number Contains dash Contains upper case letter

Table 3: Feature templates for English

A total of 1,953,463 features has been extracted from the supervised training data using the templates from Table 3.

4.2 Czech feature templates

The best feature set for Czech consists of 63 feature templates. 26 of them predict current tag as a whole, whereas the rest predicts only some parts of the current tag separately (e.g., detailed POS, gender, case) to avoid data sparseness. Such a feature is true, in an identical context, for several different tags belonging to the same class (e.g., sharing a locative case). The individual grammatical categories used for such classing have been chosen on both linguistic grounds (POS, detailed fine-grained POS) and also such categories have been used which contribute most to the elimination of the tagger errors (based on an extensive error analysis of previous results, the detailed description of which can be found in (Votrubec, 2006)).

Several features can look ahead (to the right of the current position) - apart from the obvious word form, which is unambiguous, we have used (in case of ambiguity) a random tag and lemma of the first position to the right from the current position which might be occupied with a verb (based on dictionary and the associated morphological guesser restrictions).

A total of 8,440,467 features has been extracted from the supervised training data set. A detailed description is included in the distribution downloadable from the Morče website.

5 The (un)supervised training setup

We have extended the averaged perceptron setup in the following way: the training algorithm is fed, in each iteration, by a concatenation of the supervised data (the manually tagged corpus) and the automatically pre-tagged unsupervised data, different for each iteration (in this order). In other words, the training algorithm proper does not change at all: it is the data and their selection (including the selection of the way they are automatically tagged) that makes all the difference.

The following "parameters" of the (unsupervised part of the) data selection had to be determined experimentally:

- the tagging process for tagging the selected data
- the selection mechanism (sequential or random with/without replacement)
- the size to use for each iteration
- and the use and order of concatenation with the manually tagged data.

We have experimented with various settings to arrive at the best performing configuration, described below. In each subsection, we compare the result of our „winning" configuration with results of the experiments which have the selected attributes omitted or changed; everything is measured on the development data set.

5.1 Tagging the plain data

In order to simulate the labeled training events, we have tagged the unsupervised data simply by a combination of the best available taggers. For practical reasons (to avoid prohibitive training times), we have tagged all the data in advance, i.e. no re-tagging is performed between iterations.

The setup for the combination is as follows (the idea is simplified from (Spoustová et al., 2007) where it has been used in a more complex setting):

1. run N different taggers independently;
2. join the results on each position in the data from the previous step — each token thus ends up with between 1 and N tags, a union of the tags output by the taggers at that position;
3. do final disambiguation (by a single tagger[14]).

Tagger	*Accuracy*
Morče	97.21
Shen	97.33
Combination	97.44

Table 4: Dependence on the tagger(s) used to tag the additional plain text data (English)[16]

Table 4 illustrates why it is advantageous to go through this (still)[16] complicated setup against a single-tagger bootstrapping mechanism, which always uses the same tagger for tagging the unsupervised data.

For both English and Czech, the selection of taggers, the best combination and the best overall setup has been optimized on the development data set. A bit surprisingly, the final setup is very similar for both languages (two taggers to tag the data in Step 1, and a third one to finish it up).

For English, we use three state-of-the-art taggers: the taggers of (Toutanova et al., 2003) and (Shen et al., 2007) in Step 1, and the SVM tagger (Giménez and Màrquez, 2004) in Step 3. We run the taggers with the parameters which were shown to be the best in the corresponding papers. The SVM tagger needed to be adapted to accept the (reduced) list of possible tags.[17]

For Czech, we use the Feature-based tagger (Hajič, 2004) and the Morče tagger (with the new feature set as described in section 4) in Step 1, and an HMM tagger (Krbec, 2005) in Step 3. This combination outperforms the results in (Spoustová et al., 2007) by a small margin.

5.2 Selection mechanism for the plain data

We have found that it is better to feed the training with different chunks of the unsupervised data at each iteration. We have then experimented with

[14]This tagger (possibly different from any of the N taggers from Step 1) runs as usual, but it is given a minimal list of (at most N) tags that come from Step 2 only.

[15]"Accuracy" means accuracy of the semi-supervised method using this tagger for pre-tagging the unsupervised data, not the accuracy of the tagger itself.

[16]In fact, we have experimented with other tagger combinations and configurations as well—with the TnT (Brants, 2000), MaxEnt (Ratnaparkhi, 1996) and TreeTagger (Schmid, 1994), with or without the Morče tagger in the pack; see below for the winning combination.

[17]This patch is available on the paper's website (see Section 7).

three methods of unsupervised data selection, i.e. generating the unsupervised data chunks for each training iteration from the „pool" of sentences. These methods are: simple sequential chopping, randomized data selection with replacement and randomized selection without replacement. Table 5 demonstrates that there is practically no difference in the results. Thus, we use the sequential chopping mechanism, mainly for its simplicity.

Method of data selection	*English*	*Czech*
Sequential chopping	97.44	96.21
Random without replacement	97.44	96.20
Random with replacement	97.44	96.21

Table 5: Unsupervised data selection

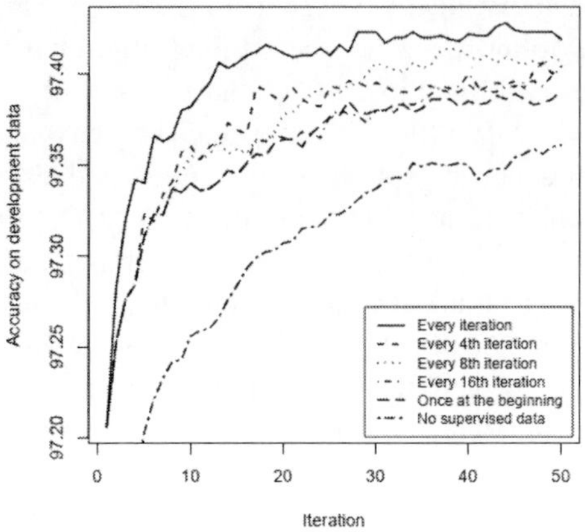

Figure 2: Dependence on the inclusion of the supervised training data (English)

	English	*Czech*
No supervised data	97.37	95.88
Once at the beginning	97.40	96.00
Every training iteration	97.44	96.21

Table 6: Dependence on the inclusion of the supervised training data

5.3 Joining the data

We have experimented with various sizes of the unsupervised parts (from 500k tokens to 5M) and also with various numbers of iterations. The best results (on the development data set) have been achieved with the unsupervised chunks containing approx. 4 million tokens for English and 1 million tokens for Czech. Each training process consists of (at most) 100 iterations (Czech) or 50 iterations (English); therefore, for the 50 (100) iterations we needed only about 200,000,000 (100,000,000) tokens of raw texts. The best development data set results have been (with the current setup) achieved on the 44th (English) and 33th (Czech) iteration.

The development data set has been also used to determine the best way to "merge" the manually labeled data (the PTB/WSJ and the PDT 2.0 training data) and the unsupervised parts of the data. Given the properties of the perceptron algorithm, it is not too surprising that the best solution is to put (the full size of) the manually labeled data first, followed by the (four) million-token chunk of the automatically tagged data (different data in each chunk but of the same size for each iteration). It corresponds to the situation when the trainer is periodically "returned to the right track" by giving it the gold standard data time to time.

Figure 2 (English) and especially Figure 3 (Czech) demonstrate the perceptron behavior in cases where the supervised data precede the unsupervised data only in selected iterations. A subset of these development results is also present in Table 6.

5.4 The morphological analyzers and the perceptron feature templates

The whole experiment can be performed with the original perceptron feature set described in (Collins, 2002) instead of the feature set described in this article. The results are compared in Table 7 (for English only).

Also, for English it is not necessary to use our morphological analyzer described in section 3.3 (other variants are to use the list of tags derived solely from the WSJ training data or to give each token the full list of tags found in WSJ). It is practically impossible to perform the unsupervised training with the full list of tags (it would take several years instead of several days with the default setup), thus we compare only the results with morphological analyzer to the results with the list of tags derived from the training data, see Table 8.

It can be expected (some approximated experiments were performed) that the results with the full list of tags would be very similar to the results with the morphological analyzer, i.e. the morphological analyzer is used mainly for technical reasons. Our expectations are based mainly (but not

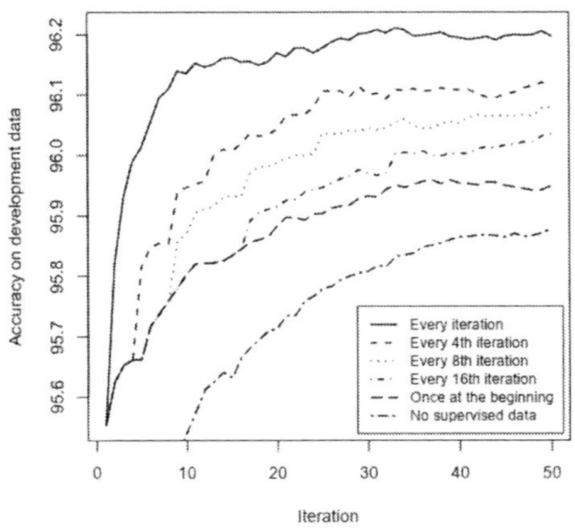

Figure 3: Dependence on the inclusion of the supervised training data (Czech)

only) on the supervised training results, where the performance of the taggers using the morphological analyzer output and using the full list of tags are nearly the same, see Table 9.

Feature set	*Accuracy*
Collins'	97.38
Our's	97.44

Table 7: Dependence on the feature set used by the perceptron algorithm (English)

GEN(x)	*Accuracy*
List of tags derived from train	97.13
Our morphological analyzer	97.44

Table 8: Dependence on the GEN(x)

6 Results

In Tables 10 and 11, the main results (on the eval-test data sets) are summarized. The state-of-the art taggers are using feature sets discribed in the corresponding articles ((Collins, 2002), (Giménez and Màrquez, 2004), (Toutanova et al., 2003) and (Shen et al., 2007)), Morče supervised and Morče semi-supervised are using feature set desribed in section 4.

For significance tests, we have used the paired Wilcoxon signed rank test as implemented in the R package (R Development Core Team, 2008)

GEN(x)	*Accuracy*
List of tags derived from train	95.89
Our morphological analyzer	97.17
Full tagset	97.15

Table 9: Supervised training results: dependence on the GEN(x)

Tagger	accuracy
Collins	97.07 %
SVM	97.16 %
Stanford	97.24 %
Shen	97.33 %
Morče supervised	97.23 %
combination	97.48 %
Morče semi-supervised	**97.44 %**

Table 10: Evaluation of the English taggers

Tagger	accuracy
Feature-based	94.04 %
HMM	94.82 %
Morče supervised	95.67 %
combination	95.70 %
Morče semi-supervised	**95.89 %**

Table 11: Evaluation of the Czech taggers

in `wilcox.test()`, dividing the data into 100 chunks (data pairs).

6.1 English

The combination of the three existing English taggers seems to be best, but it is not significantly better than our semi-supervised approach.

The combination is significantly better than (Shen et al., 2007) at a very high level, but more importantly, Shen's results (currently representing the replicable state-of-the-art in POS tagging) have been significantly surpassed also by the semi-supervised Morče (at the 99 % confidence level).

In addition, the semi-supervised Morče performs (on single CPU and development data set) 77 times faster than the combination and 23 times faster than (Shen et al., 2007).

6.2 Czech

The best results (Table 11) are statistically significantly better than the previous results: the semi-supervised Morče is significantly better than both the combination and the supervised (original) variant at a very high level.

7 Download

We decided to publish our system for wide use under the name COMPOST (Common POS Tagger). All the programs, patches and data files are available at the website http://ufal.mff.cuni.cz/compost under either the original data provider license, or under the usual GNU General Public License, unless they are available from the widely-known and easily obtainable sources (such as the LDC, in which case pointers are provided on the download website).

The Compost website also contains easy-to-run Linux binaries of the best English and Czech single taggers (based on the Morče technology) as described in Section 6.

8 Conclusion and Future Work

We have shown that the "right"[18] mixture of supervised and unsupervised (auto-tagged) data can significantly improve tagging accuracy of the averaged perceptron on two typologically different languages (English and Czech), achieving the best known accuracy to date.

To determine what is the contribution of the individual "dimensions" of the system setting, as described in Sect. 5, we have performed experiments fixing all but one of the dimensions, and compared their contribution (or rather, their loss when compared to the best "mix" overall). For English, we found that excluding the state-of-the-art-tagger (in fact, a carefully selected combination of taggers yielding significantly higher quality than any of them has) drops the resulting accuracy the most (0.2 absolute). Significant yet smaller drop (less than 0.1 percent) appears when the manually tagged portion of the data is not used or used only once (or infrequently) in the input to the perceptron's learner. The difference in using various feature templates (yet all largely similar to what state-of-the-art taggers currently use) is not significant. Similarly, the way the unsupervised data is selected plays no role, either; this differs from the bagging technique (Breiman, 1996) where it *is* significant. For Czech, the drop in accuracy appears in all dimensions, except the unsupervised data selection one. We have used novel features inspired by previous work but not used in the standard perceptron setting yet (linguistically motivated tag classes in features, lookahead features). Interestingly, the resulting tagger is better than even a combination of the previous state-of-the-art taggers (for English, this comparison is inconclusive).

We are working now on parallelization of the perceptron training, which seems to be possible (based i.a. on small-scale preliminary experiments with only a handful of parallel processes and specific data sharing arrangements among them). This would further speed up the training phase, not just as a nice bonus per se, but it would also allow for a semi-automated feature template selection, avoiding the (still manual) feature template preparation for individual languages. This would in turn facilitate one of our goals to (publicly) provide single-implementation, easy-to-maintain state-of-the-art tagging tools for as many languages as possible (we are currently preparing Dutch, Slovak and several other languages).[19]

Another area of possible future work is more principled tag classing for languages with large tagsets (in the order of 10^3), and/or adding syntactically-motivated features; it has helped Czech tagging accuracy even when only the "introspectively" defined classes have been added. It is an open question if a similar approach helps English as well (certain grammatical categories can be generalized from the current WSJ tagset as well, such as number, degree of comparison, 3rd person present tense).

Finally, it would be nice to merge some of the approaches by (Toutanova et al., 2003) and (Shen et al., 2007) with the ideas of semi-supervised learning introduced here, since they seem orthogonal in at least some aspects (e.g., to replace the rudimentary lookahead features with full bidirectionality).

Acknowledgments

The research described here was supported by the projects *MSM0021620838* and *LC536* of *Ministry of Education, Youth and Sports* of the Czech Republic, *GA405/09/0278* of the Grant Agency of the Czech Republic and *1ET101120503* of Academy of Sciences of the Czech Republic.

[18] As empirically determined on the development data set.

[19] Available soon also on the website.

References

Thorsten Brants. 2000. TnT - a Statistical Part-of-Speech Tagger. In *Proceedings of the 6th Applied Natural Language Processing Conference*, pages 224–231, Seattle, WA. ACL.

Leo Breiman. 1996. Bagging predictors. *Mach. Learn.*, 24(2):123–140.

Eric Brill and Jun Wu. 1998. Classifier Combination for Improved Lexical Disambiguation. In *Proceedings of the 17th international conference on Computational linguistics*, pages 191–195, Montreal, Quebec, Canada. Association for Computational Linguistics.

CNC, 2005. *Czech National Corpus – SYN2005*. Institute of Czech National Corpus, Faculty of Arts, Charles University, Prague, Czech Republic.

Michael Collins. 2002. Discriminative Training Methods for Hidden Markov Models: Theory and Experiments with Perceptron Algorithms. In *EMNLP '02: Proceedings of the ACL-02 conference on Empirical methods in natural language processing*, volume 10, pages 1–8, Philadelphia, PA.

Jesús Giménez and Lluís Màrquez. 2004. SVMTool: A General POS Tagger Generator Based on Support Vector Machines. In *Proceedings of the 4th International Conference on Language Resources and Evaluation*, pages 43–46, Lisbon, Portugal.

David Graff, 1995. *North American News Text Corpus*. Linguistic Data Consortium, Cat. LDC95T21, Philadelphia, PA.

Jan Hajič and Barbora Vidová-Hladká. 1998. Tagging Inflective Languages: Prediction of Morphological Categories for a Rich, Structured Tagset. In *Proceedings of the 17th international conference on Computational linguistics*, pages 483–490. Montreal, Quebec, Canada.

Jan Hajič. 2004. *Disambiguation of Rich Inflection (Computational Morphology of Czech)*. Nakladatelství Karolinum, Prague.

Jan Hajič, Eva Hajičová, Jarmila Panevová, Petr Sgall, Petr Pajas, Jan Štěpánek, Jiří Havelka, and Marie Mikulová. 2006. Prague Dependency Treebank v2.0, CDROM, LDC Cat. No. LDC2006T01. Linguistic Data Consortium, Philadelphia, PA.

Pavel Krbec. 2005. *Language Modelling for Speech Recognition of Czech*. Ph.D. thesis, UK MFF, Prague, Malostranské náměstí 25, 118 00 Praha 1.

Mitchell P. Marcus, Mary Ann Marcinkiewicz, and Beatrice Santorini. 1994. Building a large annotated corpus of English: The Penn Treebank. *Computational Linguistics*, 19(2):313–330.

R Development Core Team, 2008. *R: A Language and Environment for Statistical Computing*. R Foundation for Statistical Computing, Vienna, Austria. ISBN 3-900051-07-0.

Adwait Ratnaparkhi. 1996. A maximum entropy model for part-of-speech tagging. In *Proceedings of the 1st EMNLP*, pages 133–142, New Brunswick, NJ. ACL.

Helmut Schmid. 1994. Probabilistic part-of-speech tagging using decision trees. In *Proceedings of the International Conference on New Methods in Language Processing*, page 9pp., Manchester, GB.

Libin Shen, Giorgio Satta, and Aravind K. Joshi. 2007. Guided Learning for Bidirectional Sequence Classification. In *Proceedings of the 45th Annual Meeting of the Association of Computational Linguistics*, pages 760–767, Prague, Czech Republic, June. Association for Computational Linguistics.

Drahomíra "johanka" Spoustová, Jan Hajič, Jan Votrubec, Pavel Krbec, and Pavel Květoň. 2007. The Best of Two Worlds: Cooperation of Statistical and Rule-Based Taggers for Czech. In *Proceedings of the Workshop on Balto-Slavonic Natural Language Processing 2007*, pages 67–74, Prague, Czech Republic, June. Association for Computational Linguistics.

Jun Suzuki and Hideki Isozaki. 2008. Semi-supervised sequential labeling and segmentation using giga-word scale unlabeled data. In *Proceedings of ACL-08: HLT*, pages 665–673, Columbus, Ohio, June. Association for Computational Linguistics.

Kristina Toutanova, Dan Klein, Christopher D. Manning, and Yoram Singer. 2003. Feature-Rich Part-of-Speech Tagging with a Cyclic Dependency Network. In *NAACL '03: Proceedings of the 2003 Conference of the North American Chapter of the Association for Computational Linguistics on Human Language Technology*, pages 173–180, Edmonton, Canada. Association for Computational Linguistics.

Hans van Halteren, Walter Daelemans, and Jakub Zavrel. 2001. Improving accuracy in word class tagging through the combination of machine learning systems. *Computational Linguistics*, 27(2):199–229.

Jan Votrubec. 2006. Morphological Tagging Based on Averaged Perceptron. In *WDS'06 Proceedings of Contributed Papers*, pages 191–195, Prague, Czech Republic. Matfyzpress, Charles University.

Sequential Labeling with Latent Variables: An Exact Inference Algorithm and Its Efficient Approximation

Xu Sun[†] **Jun'ichi Tsujii**[†‡§]
[†]Department of Computer Science, University of Tokyo, Japan
[‡]School of Computer Science, University of Manchester, UK
[§]National Centre for Text Mining, Manchester, UK
{sunxu, tsujii}@is.s.u-tokyo.ac.jp

Abstract

Latent conditional models have become popular recently in both natural language processing and vision processing communities. However, establishing an effective and efficient inference method on latent conditional models remains a question. In this paper, we describe the latent-dynamic inference (LDI), which is able to produce the optimal label sequence on latent conditional models by using efficient search strategy and dynamic programming. Furthermore, we describe a straightforward solution on approximating the LDI, and show that the approximated LDI performs as well as the exact LDI, while the speed is much faster. Our experiments demonstrate that the proposed inference algorithm outperforms existing inference methods on a variety of natural language processing tasks.

1 Introduction

When data have distinct sub-structures, models exploiting latent variables are advantageous in learning (Matsuzaki et al., 2005; Petrov and Klein, 2007; Blunsom et al., 2008). Actually, discriminative probabilistic latent variable models (DPLVMs) have recently become popular choices for performing a variety of tasks with sub-structures, e.g., vision recognition (Morency et al., 2007), syntactic parsing (Petrov and Klein, 2008), and syntactic chunking (Sun et al., 2008). Morency et al. (2007) demonstrated that DPLVM models could efficiently learn sub-structures of natural problems, and outperform several widely-used conventional models, e.g., support vector machines (SVMs), conditional random fields (CRFs) and hidden Markov models (HMMs). Petrov and Klein (2008) reported on a syntactic parsing task that DPLVM models can learn more compact and accurate grammars than the conventional techniques without latent variables. The effectiveness of DPLVMs was also shown on a syntactic chunking task by Sun et al. (2008).

DPLVMs outperform conventional learning models, as described in the aforementioned publications. However, inferences on the latent conditional models are remaining problems. In conventional models such as CRFs, the optimal label path can be efficiently obtained by the dynamic programming. However, for latent conditional models such as DPLVMs, the inference is not straightforward because of the inclusion of latent variables.

In this paper, we propose a new inference algorithm, latent dynamic inference (LDI), by systematically combining an efficient search strategy with the dynamic programming. The LDI is an exact inference method producing the most probable label sequence. In addition, we also propose an approximated LDI algorithm for faster speed. We show that the approximated LDI performs as well as the exact one. We will also discuss a post-processing method for the LDI algorithm: the minimum bayesian risk reranking.

The subsequent section describes an overview of DPLVM models. We discuss the probability distribution of DPLVM models, and present the LDI inference in Section 3. Finally, we report experimental results and begin our discussions in Section 4 and Section 5.

Proceedings of the 12th Conference of the European Chapter of the ACL, pages 772–780,
Athens, Greece, 30 March – 3 April 2009.

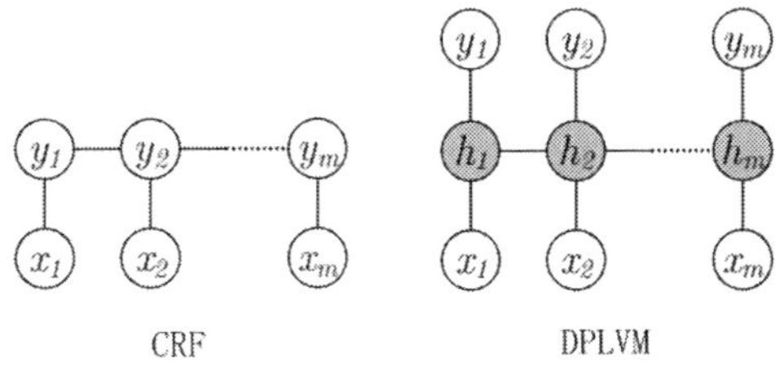

Figure 1: Comparison between CRF models and DPLVM models on the training stage. x represents the observation sequence, y represents labels and h represents the latent variables assigned to the labels. Note that only the white circles are observed variables. Also, only the links with the current observations are shown, but for both models, long range dependencies are possible.

2 Discriminative Probabilistic Latent Variable Models

Given the training data, the task is to learn a mapping between a sequence of observations $\mathbf{x} = x_1, x_2, \ldots, x_m$ and a sequence of labels $\mathbf{y} = y_1, y_2, \ldots, y_m$. Each y_j is a class label for the j'th token of a word sequence, and is a member of a set $\mathbf{Y}$ of possible class labels. For each sequence, the model also assumes a sequence of latent variables $\mathrm{h} = h_1, h_2, \ldots, h_m$, which is unobservable in training examples.

The DPLVM model is defined as follows (Morency et al., 2007):

$$P(\mathbf{y}|\mathbf{x}, \mathbf{\Theta}) = \sum_{\mathbf{h}} P(\mathbf{y}|\mathbf{h}, \mathbf{x}, \mathbf{\Theta}) P(\mathbf{h}|\mathbf{x}, \mathbf{\Theta}), \quad (1)$$

where $\mathbf{\Theta}$ represents the parameter vector of the model. DPLVM models can be seen as a natural extension of CRF models, and CRF models can be seen as a special case of DPLVMs that employ only one latent variable for each label.

To make the training and inference efficient, the model is restricted to have disjointed sets of latent variables associated with each class label. Each h_j is a member in a set $\mathbf{H}_{y_j}$ of possible latent variables for the class label y_j. $\mathbf{H}$ is defined as the set of all possible latent variables, i.e., the union of all $\mathbf{H}_{y_j}$ sets. Since sequences which have any $h_j \notin \mathbf{H}_{y_j}$ will by definition have $P(\mathbf{y}|h_j, \mathbf{x}, \mathbf{\Theta}) = 0$, the model can be further defined as:

$$P(\mathbf{y}|\mathbf{x}, \mathbf{\Theta}) = \sum_{\mathbf{h} \in \mathbf{H}_{y_1} \times \ldots \times \mathbf{H}_{y_m}} P(\mathbf{h}|\mathbf{x}, \mathbf{\Theta}), \quad (2)$$

where $P(\mathbf{h}|\mathbf{x}, \mathbf{\Theta})$ is defined by the usual conditional random field formulation:

$$P(\mathbf{h}|\mathbf{x}, \mathbf{\Theta}) = \frac{\exp \mathbf{\Theta} \cdot \mathbf{f}(\mathbf{h}, \mathbf{x})}{\sum_{\forall \mathbf{h}} \exp \mathbf{\Theta} \cdot \mathbf{f}(\mathbf{h}, \mathbf{x})}, \quad (3)$$

in which $\mathbf{f}(\mathbf{h}, \mathbf{x})$ is a feature vector. Given a training set consisting of n labeled sequences, $(\mathbf{x}_i, \mathbf{y}_i)$, for $i = 1 \ldots n$, parameter estimation is performed by optimizing the objective function,

$$L(\mathbf{\Theta}) = \sum_{i=1}^{n} \log P(\mathbf{y}_i|\mathbf{x}_i, \mathbf{\Theta}) - R(\mathbf{\Theta}). \quad (4)$$

The first term of this equation represents a conditional log-likelihood of a training data. The second term is a regularizer that is used for reducing overfitting in parameter estimation.

3 Latent-Dynamic Inference

On latent conditional models, marginalizing latent paths exactly for producing the optimal label path is a computationally expensive problem. Nevertheless, we had an interesting observation on DPLVM models that they normally had a highly concentrated probability mass, i.e., the major probability are distributed on top-n ranked latent paths.

Figure 2 shows the probability distribution of a DPLVM model using a L_2 regularizer with the variance $\sigma^2 = 1.0$. As can be seen, the probability distribution is highly concentrated, e.g., 90% of the probability is distributed on top-800 latent paths.

Based on this observation, we propose an inference algorithm for DPLVMs by efficiently combining search and dynamic programming.

3.1 LDI Inference

In the inference stage, given a test sequence $\mathbf{x}$, we want to find the most probable label sequence, $\mathbf{y}^*$:

$$\mathbf{y}^* = \mathrm{argmax}_{\mathbf{y}} P(\mathbf{y}|\mathbf{x}, \mathbf{\Theta}^*). \quad (5)$$

For latent conditional models like DPLVMs, the $\mathbf{y}^*$ cannot directly be produced by the Viterbi algorithm because of the incorporation of latent variables.

In this section, we describe an exact inference algorithm, the latent-dynamic inference (LDI), for producing the optimal label sequence $\mathbf{y}^*$ on DPLVMs (see Figure 3). In short, the algorithm

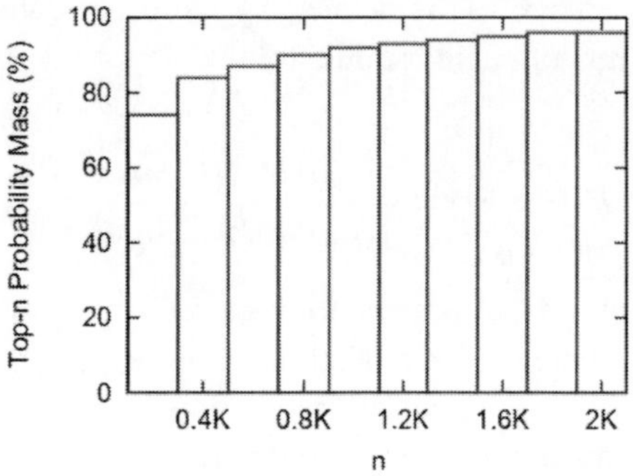

Figure 2: The probability mass distribution of latent conditional models on a NP-chunking task. The horizontal line represents the n of top-n latent paths. The vertical line represents the probability mass of the top-n latent paths.

generates the best latent paths in the order of their probabilities. Then it maps each of these to its associated label paths and uses a method to compute their exact probabilities. It can continue to generate the next best latent path and the associated label path until there is not enough probability mass left to beat the best label path.

In detail, an A^* search algorithm[1] (Hart et al., 1968) with a Viterbi heuristic function is adopted to produce top-n latent paths, $\mathbf{h}_1, \mathbf{h}_2, \ldots \mathbf{h}_n$. In addition, a forward-backward-style algorithm is used to compute the exact probabilities of their corresponding label paths, $\mathbf{y}_1, \mathbf{y}_2, \ldots \mathbf{y}_n$. The model then tries to determine the optimal label path based on the top-n statistics, without enumerating the remaining low-probability paths, which could be exponentially enormous.

The optimal label path y^* is ready when the following "exact-condition" is achieved:

$$P(\mathbf{y}_1|\mathbf{x},\Theta) - (1 - \sum_{\mathbf{y}_k \in \mathbf{LP}_n} P(\mathbf{y}_k|\mathbf{x},\Theta)) \geq 0, \quad (6)$$

where $\mathbf{y}_1$ is the most probable label sequence in current stage. It is straightforward to prove that $\mathbf{y}^* = \mathbf{y}_1$, and further search is unnecessary. This is because the remaining probability mass, $1 - \sum_{\mathbf{y}_k \in \mathbf{LP}_n} P(\mathbf{y}_k|\mathbf{x},\Theta)$, cannot beat the current optimal label path in this case.

[1] A^* search and its variants, like beam-search, are widely used in statistical machine translation. Compared to other search techniques, an interesting point of A^* search is that it can produce top-n results one-by-one in an efficient manner.

Definition:
$\text{Proj}(\mathbf{h}) = \mathbf{y} \iff h_j \in \mathbf{H}_{y_j}$ *for* $j = 1 \ldots m$;
$P(\mathbf{h}) = P(\mathbf{h}|\mathbf{x},\Theta)$;
$P(\mathbf{y}) = P(\mathbf{y}|\mathbf{x},\Theta)$.
Input:
weight vector Θ, *and feature vector* $F(\mathbf{h},\mathbf{x})$.
Initialization:
$\text{Gap} = -1$; $n = 0$; $P(\mathbf{y}^*) = 0$; $\mathbf{LP}_0 = \emptyset$.
Algorithm:

while $\text{Gap} < 0$ **do**
  $n = n + 1$
  $\mathbf{h}_n = \text{HeapPop}[\Theta, F(\mathbf{h},\mathbf{x})]$
  $\mathbf{y}_n = \text{Proj}(\mathbf{h}_n)$
  if $\mathbf{y}_n \notin \mathbf{LP}_{n-1}$ **then**
    $P(\mathbf{y}_n) = \text{DynamicProg} \sum_{\mathbf{h}:\text{Proj}(\mathbf{h})=\mathbf{y}_n} P(\mathbf{h})$
    $\mathbf{LP}_n = \mathbf{LP}_{n-1} \cup \{\mathbf{y}_n\}$
    if $P(\mathbf{y}_n) > P(\mathbf{y}^*)$ **then**
      $\mathbf{y}^* = \mathbf{y}_n$
    $\text{Gap} = P(\mathbf{y}^*) - (1 - \sum_{\mathbf{y}_k \in \mathbf{LP}_n} P(\mathbf{y}_k))$
  else
    $\mathbf{LP}_n = \mathbf{LP}_{n-1}$

Output:
the most probable label sequence $\mathbf{y}^*$.

Figure 3: The exact LDI inference for latent conditional models. In the algorithm, HeapPop means popping the next hypothesis from the A^* heap; By the definition of the A^* search, this hypothesis (on the top of the heap) should be the latent path with maximum probability in current stage.

3.2 Implementation Issues

We have presented the framework of the LDI inference. Here, we describe the details on implementing its two important components: designing the heuristic function, and an efficient method to compute the probabilities of label path.

As described, the A^* search can produce top-n results one-by-one using a heuristic function (the backward term). In the implementation, we use the Viterbi algorithm (Viterbi, 1967) to compute the admissible heuristic function for the forward-style A^* search:

$$\text{Heu}_i(h_j) = \max_{\mathbf{h}'_i = h_j \wedge \mathbf{h}' \in \mathbf{HP}_i^{|\mathbf{h}|}} P'(\mathbf{h}'|\mathbf{x},\Theta^*), \quad (7)$$

where $\mathbf{h}'_i = h_j$ represents a partial latent path started from the latent variable h_j. $\mathbf{HP}_i^{|\mathbf{h}|}$ represents all possible partial latent paths from the position i to the ending position, $|\mathbf{h}|$. As described in the Viterbi algorithm, the backward term, $\text{Heu}_i(h_j)$, can be efficiently computed by using dynamic programming to reuse the terms (e.g., $\text{Heu}_{i+1}(h_j)$) in previous steps. Because this Viterbi heuristic is quite good in practice, this way we can produce the exact top-n latent paths efficiently (see efficiency comparisons in Section 5), even though the original problem is NP-hard.

The probability of a label path, $P(\mathbf{y}_n)$ in Figure 3, can be efficiently computed by a forward-backward algorithm with a restriction on the target label path:

$$P(\mathbf{y}|\mathbf{x}, \mathbf{\Theta}) = \sum_{\mathbf{h} \in \mathbf{H}_{y_1} \times \ldots \times \mathbf{H}_{y_m}} P(\mathbf{h}|\mathbf{x}, \mathbf{\Theta}). \quad (8)$$

3.3 An Approximated Version of the LDI

By simply setting a threshold value on the search step, n, we can approximate the LDI, i.e., LDI-Approximation (LDI-A). This is a quite straightforward method for approximating the LDI. In fact, we have also tried other methods for approximation. Intuitively, one alternative method is to design an approximated "exact condition" by using a factor, α, to estimate the distribution of the remaining probability:

$$P(\mathbf{y}_1|\mathbf{x}, \mathbf{\Theta}) - \alpha(1 - \sum_{\mathbf{y}_k \in \mathbf{LP}_n} P(\mathbf{y}_k|\mathbf{x}, \mathbf{\Theta})) \geq 0. \quad (9)$$

For example, if we believe that at most 50% of the unknown probability, $1 - \sum_{\mathbf{y}_k \in \mathbf{LP}_n} P(\mathbf{y}_k|\mathbf{x}, \mathbf{\Theta})$, can be distributed on a single label path, we can set $\alpha = 0.5$ to make a loose condition to stop the inference. At first glance, this seems to be quite natural. However, when we compared this alternative method with the aforementioned approximation on search steps, we found that it worked worse than the latter, in terms of performance and speed. Therefore, we focus on the approximation on search steps in this paper.

3.4 Comparison with Existing Inference Methods

In Matsuzaki et al. (2005), the Best Hidden Path inference (BHP) was used:

$$\mathbf{y}_{BHP} = \underset{\mathbf{y}}{\operatorname{argmax}}\, P(\mathbf{h_y}|\mathbf{x}, \mathbf{\Theta}^*), \quad (10)$$

where $\mathbf{h_y} \in \mathbf{H}_{y_1} \times \ldots \times \mathbf{H}_{y_m}$. In other words, the Best Hidden Path is the label sequence which is directly projected from the optimal latent path $\mathbf{h}^*$. The BHP inference can be seen as a special case of the LDI, which replaces the marginalization-operation over latent paths with the max-operation.

In Morency et al. (2007), $\mathbf{y}^*$ is estimated by the Best Point-wise Marginal Path (BMP) inference. To estimate the label y_j of token j, the marginal probabilities $P(\mathbf{h}_j = a|\mathbf{x}, \mathbf{\Theta})$ are computed for all possible latent variables $a \in \mathbf{H}$. Then the marginal probabilities are summed up according to the disjoint sets of latent variables $\mathbf{H}_{y_j}$ and the optimal label is estimated by the marginal probabilities at each position i:

$$\mathbf{y}_{BMP}(i) = \underset{\mathbf{y}_i \in \mathbf{Y}}{\operatorname{argmax}}\, P(\mathbf{y}_i|\mathbf{x}, \mathbf{\Theta}^*), \quad (11)$$

where

$$P(\mathbf{y}_i = a|\mathbf{x}, \mathbf{\Theta}) = \frac{\sum_{\mathbf{h} \in \mathbf{H}_a} P(\mathbf{h}|\mathbf{x}, \mathbf{\Theta})}{\sum_{\mathbf{h}} P(\mathbf{h}|\mathbf{x}, \mathbf{\Theta})}. \quad (12)$$

Although the motivation is similar, the exact LDI (LDI-E) inference described in this paper is a different algorithm compared to the BLP inference (Sun et al., 2008). For example, during the search, the LDI-E is able to compute the exact probability of a label path by using a restricted version of the forward-backward algorithm, also, the exact condition is different accordingly. Moreover, in this paper, we more focus on how to approximate the LDI inference with high performance.

The LDI-E produces $\mathbf{y}^*$ while the LDI-A, the BHP and the BMP perform estimation on $\mathbf{y}^*$. We will compare them via experiments in Section 4.

4 Experiments

In this section, we choose Bio-NER and NP-chunking tasks for experiments. First, we describe the implementations and settings.

We implemented DPLVMs by extending the HCRF library developed by Morency et al. (2007). We added a Limited-Memory BFGS optimizer (L-BFGS) (Nocedal and Wright, 1999), and re-implemented the code on training and inference for higher efficiency. To reduce overfitting, we employed a Gaussian prior (Chen and Rosenfeld, 1999). We varied the the variance of the Gaussian prior (with values 10^k, k from -3 to 3), and we found that $\sigma^2 = 1.0$ is optimal for DPLVMs on the development data, and used it throughout the experiments in this section.

The training stage was kept the same as Morency et al. (2007). In other words, there is no need to change the conventional parameter estimation method on DPLVM models for adapting the various inference algorithms in this paper. For more information on training DPLVMs, refer to Morency et al. (2007) and Petrov and Klein (2008).

Since the CRF model is one of the most successful models in sequential labeling tasks (Lafferty et al., 2001; Sha and Pereira, 2003), in this paper, we choosed CRFs as a baseline model for the comparison. Note that the feature sets were kept the same in DPLVMs and CRFs. Also, the optimizer and fine tuning strategy were kept the same.

4.1 BioNLP/NLPBA-2004 Shared Task (Bio-NER)

Our first experiment used the data from the BioNLP/NLPBA-2004 shared task. It is a biomedical named-entity recognition task on the GENIA corpus (Kim et al., 2004). Named entity recognition aims to identify and classify technical terms in a given domain (here, molecular biology) that refer to concepts of interest to domain experts. The training set consists of 2,000 abstracts from MEDLINE; and the evaluation set consists of 404 abstracts from MEDLINE. We divided the original training set into 1,800 abstracts for the training data and 200 abstracts for the development data.

The task adopts the `BIO` encoding scheme, i.e., `B-x` for words beginning an entity `x`, `I-x` for words continuing an entity `x`, and `O` for words being outside of all entities. The Bio-NER task contains 5 different named entities with 11 `BIO` encoding labels.

The standard evaluation metrics for this task are precision p (the fraction of output entities matching the reference entities), recall r (the fraction of reference entities returned), and the F-measure given by $F = 2pr/(p+r)$.

Following Okanohara et al. (2006), we used word features, POS features and orthography features (prefix, postfix, uppercase/lowercase, etc.), as listed in Table 1. However, their globally dependent features, like preceding-entity features, were not used in our system. Also, to speed up the training, features that appeared rarely in the training data were removed. For DPLVM models, we tuned the number of latent variables per label from 2 to 5 on preliminary experiments, and used the number 4.

Word Features:
$\{w_{i-2},\ w_{i-1},\ w_i,\ w_{i+1},\ w_{i+2},\ w_{i-1}w_i,\ w_iw_{i+1}\}$
$\times\{h_i,\ h_{i-1}h_i\}$
POS Features:
$\{t_{i-2},\ t_{i-1},\ t_i,\ t_{i+1},\ t_{i+2},\ t_{i-2}t_{i-1},\ t_{i-1}t_i,\ t_it_{i+1},\ t_{i+1}t_{i+2},\ t_{i-2}t_{i-1}t_i,\ t_{i-1}t_it_{i+1},\ t_it_{i+1}t_{i+2}\}$
$\times\{h_i,\ h_{i-1}h_i\}$
Orth. Features:
$\{o_{i-2}, o_{i-1}, o_i, o_{i+1}, o_{i+2}, o_{i-2}o_{i-1}, o_{i-1}o_i, o_io_{i+1}, o_{i+1}o_{i+2}\}$
$\times\{h_i,\ h_{i-1}h_i\}$

Table 1: Feature templates used in the Bio-NER experiments. w_i is the current word, t_i is the current POS tag, o_i is the orthography mode of the current word, and h_i is the current latent variable (for the case of latent models) or the current label (for the case of conventional models). No globally dependent features were used; also, no external resources were used.

Word Features:
$\{w_{i-2},\ w_{i-1},\ w_i,\ w_{i+1},\ w_{i+2},\ w_{i-1}w_i,\ w_iw_{i+1}\}$
$\times\{h_i,\ h_{i-1}h_i\}$

Table 2: Feature templates used in the NP-chunking experiments. w_i and h_i are defined following Table 1.

Two sets of experiments were performed. First, on the development data, the value of n (the search step, see Figure 3 for its definition) was varied in the LDI inference; the corresponding F-measure, exactitude (the fraction of sentences that achieved the *exact condition*, Eq. 6), #latent-path (number of latent paths that have been searched), and inference-time were measured. Second, the n tuned on the development data was employed for the LDI on the test data, and experimental comparisons with the existing inference methods, the BHP and the BMP, were made.

4.2 NP-Chunking Task

On the Bio-NER task, we have studied the LDI on a relatively rich feature-set, including word features, POS features and orthographic features. However, in practice, there are many tasks with

Models	S.A.	Pre.	Rec.	F_1	Time
LDI-A	40.64	68.34	66.50	**67.41**	0.4K s
LDI-E	40.76	68.36	66.45	67.39	4K s
BMP	39.10	65.85	66.49	66.16	0.3K s
BHP	39.93	67.60	65.46	66.51	0.1K s
CRF	37.44	63.69	64.66	64.17	0.1K s

Table 3: On the test data of the Bio-NER task, experimental comparisons among various inference algorithms on DPLVMs, and the performance of CRFs. S.A. signifies *sentence accuracy*. As can be seen, at a much lower cost, the LDI-A (A signifies *approximation*) performed slightly better than the LDI-E (E signifies *exact*).

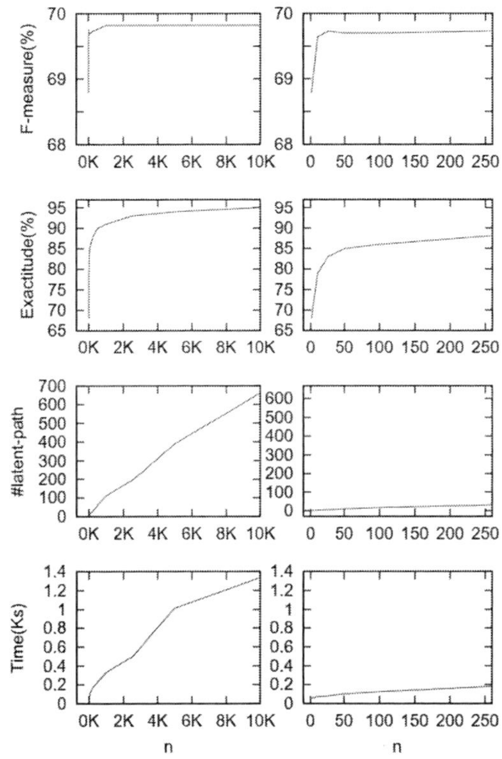

Figure 4: (Left) F-measure, exactitude, #latent-path (averaged number of latent paths being searched), and inference time of the DPLVM-LDI model, against the parameter n, on the development dataset of the Bio-NER task. (Right) Enlargement of the beginning portion of the left figures. As can be seen, the curve of the F-measure approached its plateau when n went to 30, with a high exactitude and a low inference time.

only poor features available. For example, in POS-tagging task and Chinese/Japanese word segmentation task, there are only word features available. For this reason, it is necessary to check the performance of the LDI on poor feature-set. We chose another popular task, the NP-chunking, for this study. Here, we used only poor feature-set, i.e., feature templates that depend only on words (see Table 2 for details), taking into account $200K$ features. No external resources were used.

The NP-chunking data was extracted from the training/test data of the CoNLL-2000 shallow-parsing shared task (Sang and Buchholz, 2000). In this task, the non-recursive cores of noun phrases called base NPs are identified. The training set consists of 8,936 sentences, and the test set consists of 2,012 sentences. Our preliminary experiments in this task suggested the use of 5 latent variables for each label on latent models.

5 Results and Discussions

5.1 Bio-NER

Figure 4 shows the F-measure, exactitude, #latent-path and inference inference time of the DPLVM-LDI model, against the parameter n (the search step, see Table 3), on the development dataset. As can be seen, there was a dramatic climbing curve on the F-measure, from 68.78% to 69.73%, when we increased the number of the search step from 1 to 30. When $n = 30$, the F-measure has already reached its plateau, with the exactitude of 83.0%, and the inference time of 80 seconds. In other words, the F-measure approached its plateau when n went to 30, with a high exactitude and a low inference time.

Our significance test based on McNemar's test (Gillick and Cox, 1989) shows that the LDI with $n = 30$ was significantly more accurate ($P < 0.01$) than the BHP inference, while the inference time was at a comparable level. Further growth of n after the beginning point of the plateau increases the inference time linearly (roughly), but achieved only very marginal improvement on F-measure. This suggests that the LDI inference can be approximated aggressively by stopping the inference within a small number of search steps, n. This can achieve high efficiency, without an obvious degradation on the performance.

Table 3 shows the experimental comparisons among the LDI-Approximation, the LDI-Exact (here, *exact* means the n is big enough, e.g., $n = 10K$), the BMP, and the BHP on DPLVM mod-

Models	S.A.	Pre.	Rec.	F_1	Time
LDI-A	60.98	91.76	90.59	**91.17**	42 s
LDI-E	60.88	91.72	90.61	91.16	1K s
BHP	59.34	91.54	90.30	90.91	25 s
CRF	58.37	90.92	90.33	90.63	18 s

Table 4: Experimental comparisons among different inference algorithms on DPLVMs, and the performance of CRFs using the same feature set on the word features.

els. The baseline was the CRF model with the same feature set. On the LDI-A, the parameter n tuned on the development data was employed, i.e., $n = 30$.

To our surprise, the LDI-A performed slightly better than the LDI-E even though the performance difference was marginal. We expected that LDI-A would perform worse than the LDI-E because LDI-A uses the aggressive approximation for faster speed. We have not found the exact cause of this interesting phenomenon, but removing latent paths with low probabilities may resemble the strategy of pruning features with low frequency in the training phase. Further analysis is required in the future.

The LDI-A significantly outperformed the BHP and the BMP, with a comparable inference time. Also, all models of DPLVMs significantly outperformed CRFs.

5.2 NP-Chunking

As can be seen in Figure 5, compared to Figure 4 of the Bio-NER task, very similar curves were observed in the NP-chunking task. It is interesting because the tasks are different, and their feature sets are very different.

The F-measure reached its plateau when n was around 30, with a fast inference speed. This echoes the experimental results on the Bio-NER task. Moreover, as can be seen in Table 4, at a much lower cost on inference time, the LDI-A performed as well as the LDI-E. The LDI-A outperforms the BHP inference. All the DPLVM models outperformed CRFs. The experimental results demonstrate that the LDI also works well on poor feature-set.

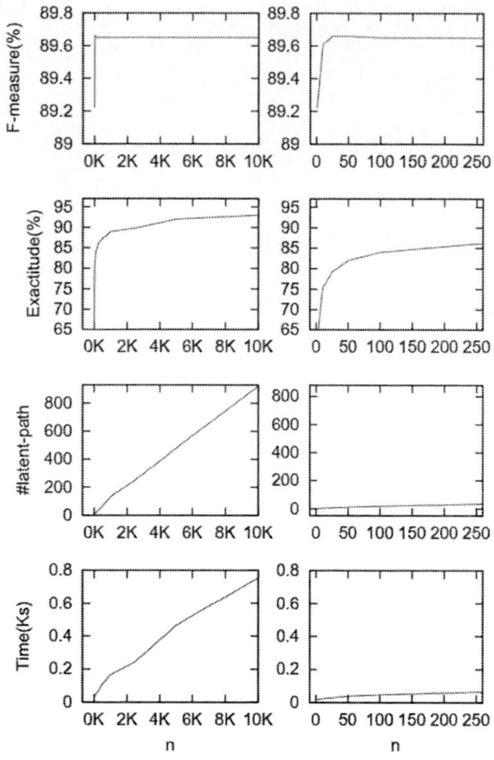

Figure 5: (Left) F-measure, exactitude, #latent-path, and inference time of the DPLVM-LDI model against the parameter n on the NP-chunking development dataset. (Right) Enlargement of the beginning portion of the left figures. The curves echo the results on the Bio-NER task.

5.3 Post-Processing of the LDI: Minimum Bayesian Risk Reranking

Although the label sequence produced by the LDI inference is indeed the optimal label sequence by means of probability, in practice, it may be beneficial to use some post-processing methods to adapt the LDI towards factual evaluation metrics. For example, in practice, many natural language processing tasks are evaluated by F-measures based on chunks (e.g., named entities).

We further describe in this section the MBR reranking method for the LDI. Here MBR reranking can be seen as a natural extension of the LDI for adapting it to various evaluation criterions, *EVAL*:

$$\mathbf{y}_{MBR} = \underset{\mathbf{y}}{\operatorname{argmax}} \sum_{\mathbf{y}' \in \mathbf{LP}_n} P(\mathbf{y}') f_{EVAL}(\mathbf{y}|\mathbf{y}'). \quad (13)$$

The intuition behind our MBR reranking is the

Models	Pre.	Rec.	F_1	Time
LDI-A	91.76	90.59	91.17	42 s
LDI-A + MBR	92.22	90.40	**91.30**	61 s

Table 5: The effect of MBR reranking on the NP-chunking task. As can be seen, MBR-reranking improved the performance of the LDI.

"voting" by those results (label paths) produced by the LDI inference. Each label path is a voter, and it gives another one a "score" (the score depending on the reference $\mathbf{y}'$ and the evaluation metric $EVAL$, i.e., $f_{EVAL}(\mathbf{y}|\mathbf{y}')$) with a "confidence" (the probability of this voter, i.e., $P(\mathbf{y}')$). Finally, the label path with the highest value, combining scores and confidences, will be the optimal result. For more details of the MBR technique, refer to Goel & Byrne (2000) and Kumar & Byrne (2002).

An advantage of the LDI over the BHP and the BMP is that the LDI can efficiently produce the probabilities of the label sequences in $\mathbf{LP}_n$. Such probabilities can be used directly for performing the MBR reranking. We will show that it is easy to employ the MBR reranking for the LDI, because the necessary statistics (e.g., the probabilities of the label paths, $\mathbf{y}_1, \mathbf{y}_2, \dots \mathbf{y}_n$) are already produced. In other words, by using LDI inference, a set of possible label sequences has been collected with associated probabilities. Although the cardinality of the set may be small, it accounts for most of the probability mass by the definition of the LDI. Eq.13 can be directly applied on this set to perform reranking.

In contrast, the BHP and the BMP inference are unable to provide such information for the reranking. For this reason, we can only report the results of the reranking for the LDI.

As can be seen in Table 5, MBR-reranking improved the performance of the LDI on the NP-chunking task with a poor feature set. The presented MBR reranking algorithm is a general solution for various evaluation criterions. We can see that the different evaluation criterion, *EVAL*, shares the common framework in Eq. 13. In practice, it is only necessary to re-implement the component of $f_{EVAL}(\mathbf{y}, \mathbf{y}')$ for a different evaluation criterion. In this paper, the evaluation criterion is the F-measure.

6 Conclusions and Future Work

In this paper, we propose an inference method, the LDI, which is able to decode the optimal label sequence on latent conditional models. We study the properties of the LDI, and showed that it can be approximated aggressively for high efficiency, with no loss in the performance. On the two NLP tasks, the LDI-A outperformed the existing inference methods on latent conditional models, and its inference time was comparable to that of the existing inference methods.

We also briefly present a post-processing method, i.e., MBR reranking, upon the LDI algorithm for various evaluation purposes. It demonstrates encouraging improvement on the NP-chunking tasks. In the future, we plan to perform further experiments to make a more detailed study on combining the LDI inference and the MBR reranking.

The LDI inference algorithm is not necessarily limited in linear-chain structure. It could be extended to other latent conditional models with tree structure (e.g., syntactic parsing with latent variables), as long as it allows efficient combination of search and dynamic-programming. This could also be a future work.

Acknowledgments

We thank Xia Zhou, Yusuke Miyao, Takuya Matsuzaki, Naoaki Okazaki and Galen Andrew for enlightening discussions, as well as the anonymous reviewers who gave very helpful comments. The first author was partially supported by University of Tokyo Fellowship (UT-Fellowship). This work was partially supported by Grant-in-Aid for Specially Promoted Research (MEXT, Japan).

References

Phillip Blunsom, Trevor Cohn, and Miles Osborne. 2008. A discriminative latent variable model for statistical machine translation. *Proceedings of ACL'08.*

Stanley F. Chen and Ronald Rosenfeld. 1999. A gaussian prior for smoothing maximum entropy models. *Technical Report CMU-CS-99-108, CMU.*

L. Gillick and S. Cox. 1989. Some statistical issues in the comparison of speech recognition algorithms. *International Conference on Acoustics Speech and Signal Processing*, v1:532–535.

V. Goel and W. Byrne. 2000. Minimum bayes-risk automatic speech recognition. *Computer Speech and Language*, 14(2):115–135.

P.E. Hart, N.J. Nilsson, and B. Raphael. 1968. A formal basis for the heuristic determination of minimum cost path. *IEEE Trans. On System Science and Cybernetics*, SSC-4(2):100–107.

Jin-Dong Kim, Tomoko Ohta, Yoshimasa Tsuruoka, and Yuka Tateisi. 2004. Introduction to the bio-entity recognition task at JNLPBA. *Proceedings of JNLPBA'04*, pages 70–75.

S. Kumar and W. Byrne. 2002. Minimum bayes-risk alignment of bilingual texts. *Proceedings of EMNLP'02*.

John Lafferty, Andrew McCallum, and Fernando Pereira. 2001. Conditional random fields: Probabilistic models for segmenting and labeling sequence data. *Proceedings of ICML'01*, pages 282–289.

Takuya Matsuzaki, Yusuke Miyao, and Jun'ichi Tsujii. 2005. Probabilistic CFG with latent annotations. *Proceedings of ACL'05*.

Louis-Philippe Morency, Ariadna Quattoni, and Trevor Darrell. 2007. Latent-dynamic discriminative models for continuous gesture recognition. *Proceedings of CVPR'07*, pages 1–8.

Jorge Nocedal and Stephen J. Wright. 1999. Numerical optimization. *Springer*.

Daisuke Okanohara, Yusuke Miyao, Yoshimasa Tsuruoka, and Jun'chi Tsujii. 2006. Improving the scalability of semi-markov conditional random fields for named entity recognition. *Proceedings of ACL'06*.

Slav Petrov and Dan Klein. 2007. Improved inference for unlexicalized parsing. In *Human Language Technologies 2007: The Conference of the North American Chapter of the Association for Computational Linguistics (HLT-NAACL'07)*, pages 404–411, Rochester, New York, April. Association for Computational Linguistics.

Slav Petrov and Dan Klein. 2008. Discriminative log-linear grammars with latent variables. In J.C. Platt, D. Koller, Y. Singer, and S. Roweis, editors, *Advances in Neural Information Processing Systems 20 (NIPS)*, pages 1153–1160, Cambridge, MA. MIT Press.

Erik Tjong Kim Sang and Sabine Buchholz. 2000. Introduction to the CoNLL-2000 shared task: Chunking. *Proceedings of CoNLL'00*, pages 127–132.

Fei Sha and Fernando Pereira. 2003. Shallow parsing with conditional random fields. *Proceedings of HLT/NAACL'03*.

Xu Sun, Louis-Philippe Morency, Daisuke Okanohara, and Jun'ichi Tsujii. 2008. Modeling latent-dynamic in shallow parsing: A latent conditional model with improved inference. *Proceedings of the 22nd International Conference on Computational Linguistics (COLING'08)*, pages 841–848.

Andrew J. Viterbi. 1967. Error bounds for convolutional codes and an asymptotically optimum decoding algorithm. *IEEE Transactions on Information Theory*, 13(2):260–269.

Text Summarization Model based on Maximum Coverage Problem and its Variant

Hiroya Takamura and **Manabu Okumura**
Precision and Intelligence Laboratory, Tokyo Institute of Technology
4259 Nagatsuta Midori-ku Yokohama, 226-8503
takamura@pi.titech.ac.jp oku@pi.titech.ac.jp

Abstract

We discuss text summarization in terms of maximum coverage problem and its variant. We explore some decoding algorithms including the ones never used in this summarization formulation, such as a greedy algorithm with performance guarantee, a randomized algorithm, and a branch-and-bound method. On the basis of the results of comparative experiments, we also augment the summarization model so that it takes into account the relevance to the document cluster. Through experiments, we showed that the augmented model is superior to the best-performing method of DUC'04 on ROUGE-1 without stopwords.

1 Introduction

Automatic text summarization is one of the tasks that have long been studied in natural language processing. This task is to create a summary, or a short and concise document that describes the content of a given set of documents (Mani, 2001).

One well-known approach to text summarization is the extractive method, which selects some linguistic units (e.g., sentences) from given documents in order to generate a summary. The extractive method has an advantage that the grammaticality is guaranteed at least at the level of the linguistic units. Since the actual generation of linguistic expressions has not achieved the level of the practical use, we focus on the extractive method in this paper, especially the method based on the sentence extraction. Most of the extractive summarization methods rely on sequentially solving binary classification problems of determining whether each sentence should be selected or not. In such sequential methods, however, the viewpoint regarding whether the summary is good as a whole, is not taken into consideration, although a summary conveys information as a whole.

We represent text summarization as an optimization problem and attempt to globally solve the problem. In particular, we represent text summarization as a maximum coverage problem with knapsack constraint (MCKP). One of the advantages of this representation is that MCKP can directly model whether each concept in the given documents is covered by the summary or not, and can dispense with rather counter-intuitive approaches such as giving penalty to each pair of two similar sentences. By formally apprehending the target problem, we can use a lot of knowledge and techniques developed in the combinatorial mathematics, and also analyse results more precisely. In fact, on the basis of the results of the experiments, we augmented the summarization model.

The contributions of this paper are as follows. We are not the first to represent text summarization as MCKP. However, no researchers have exploited the decoding algorithms for solving MCKP in the summarization task. We conduct comprehensive comparative experiments of those algorithms. Specifically, we test the greedy algorithm, the greedy algorithm with performance guarantee, the stack decoding, the linear relaxation problem with randomized decoding, and the branch-and-bound method. On the basis of the experimental results, we then propose an augmented model that takes into account the relevance to the document cluster. We empirically show that the augmented model is superior to the best-performing method of DUC'04 on ROUGE-1 without stopwords.

2 Related Work

Carbonell and Goldstein (2000) used sequential sentence selection in combination with maximal marginal relevance (MMR), which gives penalty to sentences that are similar to the already selected sentences. Schiffman et al.'s method (2002) is also based on sequential sentence selection. Radev et al. (2004), in their method MEAD, used a clustering technique to find the *centroid*, that

Proceedings of the 12th Conference of the European Chapter of the ACL, pages 781–789,
Athens, Greece, 30 March – 3 April 2009.

is, the words with high relevance to the topic of the document cluster. They used the centroid to rank sentences, together with the MMR-like redundancy score. Both relevance and redundancy are taken into consideration, but no global viewpoint is given. In CLASSY, which is the best-performing method in DUC'04, Conroy et al. (2004) scored sentences with the sum of tf-idf scores of words. They also incorporated sentence compression based on syntactic or heuristic rules.

McDonald (2007) formulated text summarization as a knapsack problem and obtained the global solution and its approximate solutions. Its relation to our method will be discussed in Section 6.1. Filatova and Hatzivassiloglou (2004) first formulated text summarization as MCKP. Their decoding method is a greedy one and will be empirically compared with other decoding methods in this paper. Yih et al. (2007) used a slightly-modified stack decoding. The optimization problem they solved was the MCKP with the last sentence truncation. Their stack decoding is one of the decoding methods discussed in this paper. Ye et al. (2007) is another example of coverage-based methods. Shen et al. (2007) regarded summarization as a sequential labelling task and solved it with Conditional Random Fields. Although the model is globally optimized in terms of likelihood, the coverage of concepts is not taken into account.

3 Modeling text summarization

In this paper, we focus on the extractive summarization, which generates a summary by selecting linguistic units (e.g., sentences) in given documents. There are two types of summarization tasks: single-document summarization and multi-document summarization. While single-document summarization is to generate a summary from a single document, multi-document summarization is to generate a summary from multiple documents regarding one topic. Such a set of multiple documents is called *a document cluster*. The method proposed in this paper is applicable to both tasks. In both tasks, documents are split into several linguistic units $D = \{s_1, \cdots, s_{|D|}\}$ in preprocessing. We will select some linguistic units from D to generate a summary. Among other linguistic units that can be used in the method, we use sentences so that the grammaticality at the sentence level is going to be guaranteed.

We introduce *conceptual units* (Filatova and Hatzivassiloglou, 2004), which compose the meaning of a sentence. Sentence s_i is represented by a set of conceptual units $\{e_{i1}, \cdots, e_{i|s_i|}\}$. For example, the sentence "The man bought a book and read it" could be regarded as consisting of two conceptual units "the man bought a book" and "the man read the book". It is not easy, however, to determine the appropriate granularity of conceptual units. A simple way would be to regard the above sentence as consisting of four conceptual units "man", "book", "buy", and "read". There is some work on the definition of conceptual units. Hovy et al. (2006) proposed to use *basic elements*, which are dependency subtrees obtained by trimming dependency trees. Although basic elements were proposed for evaluation of summaries, they can probably be used also for summary generation. However, such novel units have not proved to be useful for summary generation. Since we focus more on algorithms and models in this paper, we simply use words as conceptual units.

The goal of text summarization is to cover as many conceptual units as possible using only a small number of sentences. In other words, the goal is to find a subset $S(\subset D)$ that covers as many conceptual units as possible. In the following, we introduce models for that purpose. We think of the situation that the summary length must be at most K (*cardinality constraint*) and the summary length is measured by the number of words or bytes in the summary.

Let x_i denote a variable which is 1 if sentence s_i is selected, otherwise 0, a_{ij} denote a constant which is 1 if sentence s_i contains word e_j, otherwise 0. We regard word e_j as *covered* when at least one sentence containing e_j is selected as part of the summary. That is, word e_j is covered if and only if $\sum_i a_{ij}x_i \geq 1$. Now our objective is to find the binary assignment on x_i with the best coverage such that the summary length is at most K:

$$\begin{array}{ll} max. & |\{j|\sum_i a_{ij}x_i \geq 1\}| \\ s.t. & \sum_i c_i x_i \leq K;\ \forall i, x_i \in \{0,1\}, \end{array}$$

where c_i is the cost of selecting s_i, i.e., the number of words or bytes in s_i.

For convenience, we rewrite the problem above:

$$\begin{array}{ll} max. & \sum_j z_j \\ s.t. & \sum_i c_i x_i \leq K;\ \forall j, \sum_i a_{ij}x_i \geq z_j; \\ & \forall i, x_i \in \{0,1\};\ \forall j, z_j \in \{0,1\}, \end{array}$$

where z_j is 1 when e_j is covered, 0 otherwise. Notice that this new problem is equivalent to the previous one.

Since not all the words are equally important, we introduce weights w_j on words e_j. Then the objective is restated as maximizing the weighted sum $\sum_j w_j z_j$ such that the summary length is at most K. This problem is called *maximum coverage problem with knapsack constraint (MCKP)*, which is an NP-hard problem (Khuller et al., 1999). We should note that MCKP is different from a knapsack problem. MCKP merely has a constraint of knapsack form. Filatova and Hatzivassiloglou (2004) pointed out that text summarization can be formalized by MCKP.

The performance of the method depends on how to represent words and which words to use. We represent words with their stems. We use only the words that are content words (nouns, verbs, or adjectives) and not in the stopword list used in ROUGE (Lin, 2004).

The weights w_j of words are also an important factor of good performance. We tested two weighting schemes proposed by Yih et al. (2007). The first one is *interpolated weights*, which are interpolated values of the generative word probability in the entire document and that in the beginning part of the document (namely, the first 100 words). Each probability is estimated with the maximum likelihood principle. The second one is *trained weights*. These values are estimated by the logistic regression trained on data instances, which are labeled 1 if the word appears in a summary in the training dataset, 0 otherwise. The feature set for the logistic regression includes the frequency of the word in the document cluster and the position of the word instance and others.

4 Algorithms for solving MCKP

We explain how to solve MCKP. We first explain the greedy algorithm applied to text summarization by Filatova and Hatzivassiloglou (2004). We then introduce a greedy algorithm with performance guarantee. This algorithm has never been applied to text summarization. We next explain the stack decoding used by Yih et al. (2007). We then introduce an approximate method based on linear relaxation and a randomized algorithm, followed by the branch-and-bound method, which provides the exact solution.

Although the algorithms used in this paper themselves are not novel, this work is the first to apply the greedy algorithm with performance guarantee, the randomized algorithm, and the branch-and-bound to solve the MCKP and automatically create a summary. In addition, we conduct a comparative study on summarization algorithms including the above.

There are some other well-known methods for similar problems (e.g., the method of conditional probability (Hromkovič, 2003)). A pipage approach (Ageev and Sviridenko, 2004) has been proposed for MCKP, but we do not use this algorithm, since it requires costly partial enumeration and solutions to many linear relaxation problems.

As in the previous section, D denotes the set of sentences $\{s_1, \cdots, s_{|D|}\}$, and S denotes a subset of D and thus represents a summary.

4.1 Greedy algorithm

Filatova and Hatzivassiloglou (2004) used a greedy algorithm. In this section, W_l denotes the sum of the weights of the words covered by sentence s_l. W'_l denotes the sum of the weights of the words covered by s_l, but not by current summary S. This algorithm sequentially selects sentence s_l with the largest W'_l.

Greedy Algorithm

$U \leftarrow D, S \leftarrow \phi$
while $U \neq \phi$
  $s_i \leftarrow \arg\max_{s_l \in U} W'_l$
  if $c_i + \sum_{s_l \in S} c_l \leq K$ **then** insert s_i into S
  delete s_i in U
end while
output S.

This algorithm has performance guarantee when the problem has a unit cost (i.e., when each sentence has the same length), but no performance guarantee for the general case where costs can have different values.

4.2 Greedy algorithm with performance guarantee

We describe a greedy algorithm with performance guarantee proposed by Khuller et al. (1999), which proves to achieve an approximation factor of $(1 - 1/e)/2$ for MCKP. This algorithm sequentially selects sentence s_l with the largest ratio W'_l/c_l. After the sequential selection, the set of the selected sentences is compared with the single-sentence summary that has the largest value of the objective function. The larger of the two is going to be the output of this new greedy algorithm. Here $score(S)$ is $\sum_j w_j z_j$, the value of the objective function for summary S.

Greedy Algorithm with Performance Guarantee

$U \leftarrow D, S \leftarrow \phi$
while $U \neq \phi$
  $s_i \leftarrow \arg\max_{s_l \in U} W_l'/c_l$
  if $c_i + \sum_{s_l \in S} c_l \leq K$ **then** insert s_i into S
  delete s_i in U
end while
$s_t \leftarrow \arg\max_{s_l} W_l$
if $score(S) \geq W_t$, output S,
otherwise, output $\{s_t\}$.

They also proposed an algorithm with a better performance guarantee, which is not used in this paper because it is costly due to its partial enumeration.

4.3 Stack decoding

Stack decoding is a decoding method proposed by Jelinek (1969). This algorithm requires K priority queues, k-th of which is the queue for summaries of length k. The objective function value is used for the priority measure. A new solution (summary) is generated by adding a sentence to a current solution in k-th queue and inserted into a succeeding queue.[1] The "pop" operation in stack decoding pops the candidate summary with the least priority in the queue. By restricting the size of each queue to a certain constant $stacksize$, we can obtain an approximate solution within a practical computational time.

Stack Decoding

for $k = 0$ **to** $K - 1$
  for each $S \in queues[k]$
    for each $s_l \in D$
      insert s_l into S
      insert S into $queues[k + c_l]$
      pop **if** queue-size exceeds the stacksize
    end for
  end for
end for
return the best solution in $queues[K]$

4.4 Randomized algorithm

Khuller et al. (2006) proposed a randomized algorithm (Hromkovič, 2003) for MCKP. In this algorithm, a relaxation linear problem is generated by replacing the integer constraints $x_i \in \{0, 1\}$ and $z_j \in \{0, 1\}$ with linear constraints $x_i \in [0, 1]$ and $z_j \in [0, 1]$. The optimal solution x_i^* to the relaxation problem is regarded as the probability of sentence s_i being selected as a part of summary: $x_i^* = P(x_i = 1)$. The algorithm randomly selects sentence s_i with probability x_i^*, in order to generate a summary. It has been proved that the expected length of each randomly-generated summary is upper-bounded by K, and the expected value of the objective function is at least the optimal value multiplied by $(1 - 1/e)$ (Khuller et al., 2006). This random generation of a summary is iterated many times, and the summaries that are not longer than K are stored as candidate summaries. Among those many candidate summaries, the one with the highest value of the objective function is going to be the output by this algorithm.

4.5 Branch-and-bound method

The branch-and-bound method (Hromkovič, 2003) is an efficient method for finding the exact solutions to integer problems. Since MCKP is an NP-hard problem, it cannot generally be solved in polynomial time under a reasonable assumption that NP$\neq$P. However, if the size of the problem is limited, sometimes we can obtain the exact solution within a practical time by means of the branch-and-bound method.

4.6 Weakly-constrained algorithms

In evaluation with ROUGE (Lin, 2004), summaries are truncated to a target length K. Yih et al. (2007) used a stack decoding with a slight modification, which allows the last sentence in a summary to be truncated to a target length. Let us call this modified algorithm the *weakly-constrained* stack decoding. The weakly-constrained stack decoding can be implemented simply by replacing $queues[k + c_l]$ with $queues[\min(k + c_l, K)]$. We can also think of weakly-constrained versions of the greedy and randomized algorithms introduced before.

In this paper, we do not adopt weakly-constrained algorithms, because although an advantage of the extractive summarization is the guaranteed grammaticality at the sentence level, the summaries with a truncated sentence will relinquish this advantage. We mentioned the weakly-constrained algorithms in order to explain the relation between the proposed model and the model proposed by Yih et al. (2007).

[1] We should be aware that *stack* in a strict data-structure sense is not used in the algorithm.

5 Experiments and Discussion

5.1 Experimental Setting

We conducted experiments on the dataset of DUC'04 (2004) with settings of task 2, which is a multi-document summarization task. 50 document clusters, each of which consists of 10 documents, are given. One summary is to be generated for each cluster. Following the most relevant previous method (Yih et al., 2007), we set the target length to 100 words. DUC'03 (2003) dataset was used as the training dataset for trained weights. All the documents were segmented into sentences using a script distributed by DUC. Words are stemmed by Porter's stemmer (Porter, 1980). ROUGE version 1.5.5 (Lin, 2004) was used for evaluation.[2] Among others, we focus on ROUGE-1 in the discussion of the result, because ROUGE-1 has proved to have strong correlation with human annotation (Lin, 2004; Lin and Hovy, 2003). Wilcoxon signed rank test for paired samples with significance level 0.05 was used for the significance test of the difference in ROUGE-1. The simplex method and the branch-and-bound method implemented in GLPK (Makhorin, 2006) were used to solve respectively linear and integer programming problems.

The methods that are compared here are the greedy algorithm (*greedy*), the greedy algorithm with performance guarantee (*g-greedy*), the randomized algorithm (*rand*), the stack decoding (*stack*), and the branch-and-bound method (*exact*).

5.2 Results

The experimental results are shown in Tables 1 and 2. The columns 1, 2, and SU4 in the tables respectively refer to ROUGE-1, ROUGE-2, and ROUGE-SU4. In addition, *rand100k* refers to the randomized algorithm with 100,000 randomly-generated solution candidates, and *stack30* refers to *stack* with the stacksize being 30. The right-most column ('time') shows the average computational time required for generating a summary for a document cluster.

Both with interpolated (Table 1) and trained weights (Table 2), *g-greedy* significantly outperformed *greedy*. With interpolated weights, there was no significant difference between *exact* and *g-greedy*, and between *exact* and *stack30*. With trained weights, there was no significant difference between *exact* and the other algorithms except for *greedy* and *rand100k*. The result suggests that approximate fast algorithms can yield results comparable to the exact method in terms of ROUGE-1 score. We will later discuss the results in terms of objective function values and search errors in Table 4.

Table 1: ROUGE of MCKP with interpolated weights. Underlined ROUGE-1 scores are significantly different from the score of *exact*. Computational time was measured in seconds.

	ROUGE			time
	1	2	SU4	(sec)
greedy	<u>0.283</u>	0.083	0.123	<0.01
g-greedy	0.294	0.080	0.121	0.01
rand100k	0.300	0.079	0.119	1.88
stack30	0.304	0.078	0.120	4.53
exact	0.305	0.081	0.121	4.04

Table 2: ROUGE of MCKP with trained weights. Underlined ROUGE-1 scores are significantly different from the score of *exact*. Computational time was measured in seconds.

	ROUGE			time
	1	2	SU4	(sec)
greedy	<u>0.283</u>	0.080	0.121	< 0.01
g-greedy	0.310	0.077	0.118	0.01
rand100k	<u>0.299</u>	0.077	0.117	1.93
stack30	0.309	0.080	0.120	4.23
exact	0.307	0.078	0.119	4.56

We should notice that *stack* outperformed *exact* with interpolated weights. To examine this counter-intuitive point, we changed the stacksize of *stack* with interpolated weights (inter) and trained weights (train) from 10 to 100 and obtained Table 3. This table shows that the ROUGE-1 value does not increase as the stacksize does; ROUGE-1 for *stack* with interpolated weights does not change much with the stacksize, and the peak of ROUGE-1 for trained weights is at the stacksize of 20. Since *stack* with a larger stacksize selects a solution from a larger number of solution candidates, this result is counter-intuitive in the sense that non-global decoding by *stack* has a favorable effect.

We also counted the number of the document clusters for which an approximate algorithm with interpolated weights yielded the same solution as

[2] With options -n 4 -m -2 4 -u -f A -p 0.5 -l 100 -t 0 -d -s.

Table 3: ROUGE of *stack* with various stacksizes

size	10	20	30	50	100
inter	0.304	0.304	0.304	0.304	0.303
train	0.308	0.310	0.309	0.308	0.307

Table 4: Search errors of MCKP with interpolated weights

solution	same	search error		
ROUGE	(=)	=	⇓	⇑
greedy	0	1	35	14
g-greedy	0	5	26	19
rand100k	6	5	25	14
stack30	16	11	8	11

exact ('same solution' column in Table 4). If the approximate algorithm failed to yield the exact solution ('search error' column), we checked whether the search error made ROUGE score unchanged ('=' column), decreased ('⇓' column), or increased ('⇑' column) compared with ROUGE score of *exact*. Table 4 shows that (i) *stack30* is a better optimizer than other approximate algorithms, (ii) when the search error occurs, *stack30* increases ROUGE-1 more often than it decreases ROUGE-1 compared with *exact* in spite of *stack30*'s inaccurate solution, (iii) approximate algorithms sometimes achieved better ROUGE scores. We observed similar phenomena for trained weights, though we skip the details due to space limitation.

These observations on stacksize and search errors suggest that there exists another maximization problem that is more suitable to summarization. We should attempt to find the more suitable maximization problem and solve it using some existing optimization and approximation techniques.

6 Augmentation of the model

On the basis of the experimental results in the previous section, we augment our text summarization model. We first examine the current model more carefully. As mentioned before, we used words as conceptual units because defining those units is hard and still under development by many researchers. Suppose here that a more suitable unit has more detailed information, such as "A did B to C". Then the event "A did D to E" is a completely different unit from "A did B to C". However, when words are used as conceptual units, the two events have a redundant part "A". It can happen that a document is concise as a summary, but redundant on word level. By being to some extent redundant on the word level, a summary can have sentences that are more relevant to the document cluster, as both of the sentences above are relevant to the document cluster if the document cluster is about "A". A summary with high cohesion and coherence would have redundancy to some extent. In this section, we will use this conjecture to augment our model.

6.1 Augmented summarization model

The objective function of MCKP consists of only one term that corresponds to coverage. We add another term $\sum_i(\sum_j w_j a_{ij})x_i$ that corresponds to relevance to the topic of the document cluster. We represent the relevance of sentence s_i by the sum of the weights of words in the sentence $(\sum_j w_j a_{ij})$. We take the summation of the relevance values of the selected sentences:

$$\begin{aligned} max.\quad & (1-\lambda)\sum_j w_j z_j + \lambda\sum_i(\sum_j w_j a_{ij})x_i \\ s.t.\quad & \sum_i c_i x_i \leq K;\ \forall j, \sum_i a_{ij}x_i \geq z_j; \\ & \forall i, x_i \in \{0,1\};\ \forall j, z_j \in \{0,1\}, \end{aligned}$$

where λ is a constant. We call this model *MCKP-Rel*, because the relevance to the document cluster is taken into account.

We discuss the relation to the model proposed by McDonald (2007), whose objective function consists of a relevance term and a negative redundancy term. We believe that MCKP-Rel is more intuitive and suitable for summarization, because coverage in McDonald (2007) is measured by subtracting the redundancy represented with the sum of similarities between two sentences, while MCKP-Rel focuses directly on coverage. Suppose sentence s_1 contains conceptual units A and B, s_2 contains A, and s_3 contains B. The proposed coverage-based methods can capture the fact that s_1 has the same information as $\{s_2, s_3\}$, while similarity-based methods only learn that s_1 is somewhat similar to each of s_2 and s_3. We also empirically showed that our method outperforms McDonald (2007)'s method in experiments on DUC'02, where our method achieved 0.354 ROUGE-1 score with interpolated weights and 0.359 with trained weights when the optimal λ is given, while McDonald (2007)'s method yielded at most 0.348. However, this very point can also

Table 5: ROUGE-1 of MCKP-Rel with interpolated weights. The values in the parentheses are the corresponding values of λ predicted using DUC'03 as development data. Underlined are the values that are significantly different from the corresponding values of MCKP.

	interpolated	trained
greedy	0.287 (0.1)	0.288 (0.8)
g-greedy	0.307 (0.3)	0.320 (0.4)
rand100k	0.310 (0.1)	0.316 (0.5)
stack30	0.324 (0.1)	0.327 (0.3)
exact	0.320 (0.3)	0.329 (0.5)
$exact_{opt}$	0.327 (0.2)	0.329 (0.5)

be a drawback of our method, since our method premises that a sentence is represented as a set of conceptual units. Similarity-based methods are free from such a premise. Taking advantages of both models is left for future work.

The decoding algorithms introduced before are also applicable to MCKP-Rel, because MCKP-Rel can be reduced to MCKP by adding, for each sentence s_i, a dummy conceptual unit which exists only in s_i and has the weight $\sum_j w_j a_{ij}$.

6.2 Experiments of the augmented model

We ran *greedy*, *g-greedy*, *rand*100*k*, *stack*30 and *exact* to solve MCKP-Rel. We experimented on DUC'04 with the same experimental setting as the previous ones.

6.2.1 Experiments with the predicted λ

We determined the value of λ for each method using DUC'03 as development data. Specifically, we conducted experiments on DUC'03 with different λ ($\in \{0.0, 0.1, \cdots, 1.0\}$) and simply selected the one with the highest ROUGE-1 value.

The results with these predicted λ are shown in Table 5. Only ROUGE-1 values are shown. Method $exact_{opt}$ is *exact* with the optimal λ, and can be regarded as the upperbound of MCKP-Rel. To evaluate the appropriateness of models without regard to search quality, we first focused on *exact* and found that MCKP-Rel outperformed MCKP with *exact*. This means that MCKP-Rel model is superior to MCKP model. Among the algorithms, *stack30* and *exact* performed well. All methods except for *greedy* yielded significantly better ROUGE values compared with the corresponding results in Tables 1 and 2.

Figures 1 and 2 show ROUGE-1 for different values of λ. The leftmost part ($\lambda = 0.0$) corresponds to MCKP. We can see from the figures, that MCKP-Rel at the best λ always outperforms MCKP, and that MCKP-Rel tends to degrade for very large λ. This means that excessive weight on relevance has an adversative effect on performance and therefore the coverage is important.

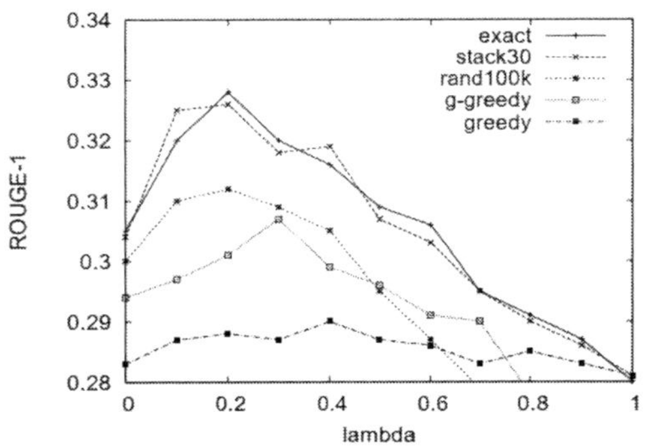

Figure 1: MCKP-Rel with interpolated weights

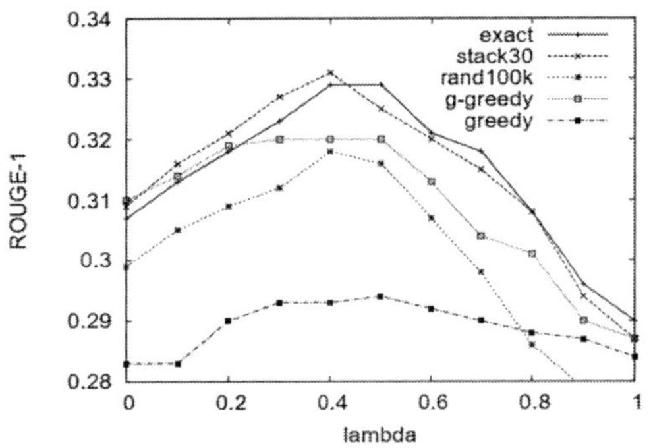

Figure 2: MCKP-Rel with trained weights

6.2.2 Experiments with the optimal λ

In the experiments above, we found that $\lambda = 0.2$ is the optimal value for *exact* with interpolated weights. We suppose that this λ gives the best model, and examined search errors as we did in Section 5.2. We obtained Table 6, which shows that search errors in MCKP-Rel counter-intuitively increase ($\Uparrow$) ROUGE-1 score less often than MCKP did in Table 4. This was the case also for trained weights. This result suggests that MCKP-Rel is more suitable to text summarization than MCKP is. However, *exact* with trained weights at the optimal $\lambda (= 0.4)$ in Figure 2 was outperformed by *stack30*. It suggests that there is still room for future improvement in the model.

Table 6: Search errors of MCKP-Rel with interpolated weights ($\lambda = 0.2$).

solution	same	search error		
ROUGE	(=)	=	$\Downarrow$	$\Uparrow$
greedy	0	2	42	6
g-greedy	1	0	34	15
rand100k	3	6	33	8
stack30	14	13	14	10

6.2.3 Comparison with DUC results

In Section 6.2.1, we empirically showed that the augmented model MCKP-Rel is better than MCKP, whose optimization problem is used also in one of the state-of-the-art methods by Yih et al. (2007). It would also be beneficial to readers to directly compare our method with DUC results. For that purpose, we conducted experiments with the cardinality constraint of DUC'04, i.e., each summary should be 665 bytes long or shorter. Other settings remained unchanged. We compared the MCKP-Rel with *peer65* (Conroy et al., 2004) of DUC'04, which performed best in terms of ROUGE-1 in the competition. Tables 7 and 8 are the ROUGE-1 scores, respectively evaluated without and with stopwords. The latter is the official evaluation measure of DUC'04.

Table 7: ROUGE-1 of MCKP-Rel with byte constraints, evaluated without stopwords. Underlined are the values significantly different from *peer65*.

	interpolated	train
greedy	0.289 (0.1)	0.284 (0.8)
g-greedy	0.297 (0.4)	0.323 (0.3)
rand100k	0.315 (0.2)	0.308 (0.4)
stack30	0.324 (0.2)	0.323 (0.3)
exact	0.325 (0.3)	0.326 (0.5)
exact$_{opt}$	0.325 (0.3)	0.329 (0.4)
peer65	0.309	

In Table 7, MCKP-Rel with *stack*30 and *exact* yielded significantly better ROUGE-1 scores than *peer65*. Although *stack*30 and *exact* yielded greater ROUGE-1 scores than *peer65* also in Table 8, the difference was not significant. Only *greedy* was significantly worse than *peer65*.[3] One possible explanation on the difference between Table 7 and Table 8 is that *peer65* would probably be tuned to the evaluation with stopwords, since it is the official setting of DUC'04.

Table 8: ROUGE-1 of MCKP-Rel with byte constraints, evaluated with stopwords. Underlined are the values significantly different from *peer65*.

	interpolated	train
greedy	0.374 (0.1)	0.377 (0.4)
g-greedy	0.371 (0.0)	0.385 (0.2)
rand100k	0.373 (0.2)	0.366 (0.3)
stack30	0.384 (0.1)	0.386 (0.3)
exact	0.383 (0.3)	0.384 (0.4)
exact$_{opt}$	0.385 (0.1)	0.384 (0.4)
peer65	0.382	

From these results, we can conclude that the MCKP-Rel is at least comparable to the best-performing method, if we choose a powerful decoding method, such as *stack* and *exact*.

7 Conclusion

We regarded text summarization as MCKP. We applied some algorithms to solve the MCKP and conducted comparative experiments. We conducted comparative experiments. We also augmented our model to MCKP-Rel, which takes into consideration the relevance to the document cluster and performs well.

For future work, we will try other conceptual units such as basic elements (Hovy et al., 2006) proposed for summary evaluation. We also plan to include compressed sentences into the set of candidate sentences to be selected as done by Yih et al. (2007). We also plan to design other decoding algorithms for text summarization (e.g., pipage approach (Ageev and Sviridenko, 2004)). As discussed in Section 6.2, integration with similarity-based models is worth consideration. We will incorporate techniques for arranging sentences into an appropriate order, while the current work concerns only selection. Deshpande et al. (2007) proposed a selection and ordering technique, which is applicable only to the unit cost case such as selection and ordering of words for title generation. We plan to refine their model so that it can be applied to general text summarization.

[3] We actually succeeded in greatly improving the ROUGE-1 value of MCKP-Rel evaluated with stopwords by using all the words including stopwords as conceptual units. However, we ignore those results in this paper, because it just trickily uses non-content words to increase the evaluation measure, disregarding the actual quality of summaries.

References

Alexander A. Ageev and Maxim Sviridenko. 2004. Pipage rounding: A new method of constructing algorithms with proven performance guarantee. *Journal of Combinatorial Optimization*, 8(3):307–328.

John M. Conroy, Judith D. Schlesinger, John Goldstein, and Dianne P. O'Leary. 2004. Left-brain/right-brain multi-document summarization. In *Proceedings of the Document Understanding Conference (DUC)*.

Pawan Deshpande, Regina Barzilay, and David Karger. 2007. Randomized decoding for selection-and-ordering problems. In *Proceedings of the Human Language Technologies Conference and the North American Chapter of the Association for Computational Linguistics Annual Meeting (HLT/NAACL)*, pages 444–451.

DUC. 2003. Document Understanding Conference. In *HLT/NAACL Workshop on Text Summarization*.

DUC. 2004. Document Understanding Conference. In *HLT/NAACL Workshop on Text Summarization*.

Elena Filatova and Vasileios Hatzivassiloglou. 2004. A formal model for information selection in multi-sentence text extraction. In *Proceedings of the 20th International Conference on Computational Linguistics (COLING)*, pages 397–403.

Jade Goldstein, Vibhu Mittal, Jaime Carbonell, and Mark Kantrowitz. 2000. Multi-document summarization by sentence extraction. In *Proceedings of ANLP/NAACL Workshop on Automatic Summarization*, pages 40–48.

Eduard Hovy, Chin-Yew Lin, Liang Zhou, and Junichi Fukumoto. 2006. Automated summarization evaluation with basic elements. In *Proceedings of the Fifth International Conference on Language Resources and Evaluation (LREC)*.

Juraj Hromkovič. 2003. *Algorithmics for Hard Problems*. Springer.

Frederick Jelinek. 1969. Fast sequential decoding algorithm using a stack. *IBM Journal of Research and Development*, 13:675–685.

Samir Khuller, Anna Moss, and Joseph S. Naor. 1999. The budgeted maximum coverage problem. *Information Processing Letters*, 70(1):39–45.

Samir Khuller, Louiqa Raschid, and Yao Wu. 2006. LP randomized rounding for maximum coverage problem and minimum set cover with threshold problem. Technical Report CS-TR-4805, The University of Maryland.

Chin-Yew Lin and Eduard Hovy. 2003. Automatic evaluation of summaries using n-gram co-occurrence statistics. In *Proceedings of the 2003 Conference of the North American Chapter of the Association for Computational Linguistics on Human Language Technology (HLT-NAACL'03)*, pages 71–78.

Chin-Yew Lin. 2004. ROUGE: a package for automatic evaluation of summaries. In *Proceedings of the Workshop on Text Summarization Branches Out*, pages 74–81.

Andrew Makhorin, 2006. *Reference Manual of GNU Linear Programming Kit, version 4.9.*

Inderjeet Mani. 2001. *Automatic Summarization*. John Benjamins Publisher.

Ryan McDonald. 2007. A study of global inference algorithms in multi-document summarization. In *Proceedings of the 29th European Conference on Information Retrieval (ECIR)*, pages 557–564.

Martin F. Porter. 1980. An algorithm for suffix stripping. *Program*, 14(3):130–137.

Dragomir R. Radev, Hongyan Jing, Małgorzata Styś, and Daniel Tam. 2004. Centroid-based summarization of multiple documents. *Information Processing Management*, 40(6):919–938.

Barry Schiffman, Ani Nenkova, and Kathleen McKeown. 2002. Experiments in multidocument summarization. In *Proceedings of the Second International Conference on Human Language Technology Research*, pages 52–58.

Dou Shen, Jian-Tao Sun, Hua Li, Qiang Yang, and Zheng Chen. 2007. Document summarization using conditional random fields. In *Proceedings of the 20th International Joint Conference on Artificial Intelligence (IJCAI)*, pages 2862–2867.

Shiren Ye, Tat-Seng Chua, Min-Yen Kan, and Long Qiu. 2007. Document concept lattice for text understanding and summarization. *Information Processing and Management*, 43(6):1643–1662.

Wen-Tau Yih, Joshua Goodman, Lucy Vanderwende, and Hisami Suzuki. 2007. Multi-document summarization by maximizing informative content-words. In *Proceedings of the 20th International Joint Conference on Artificial Intelligence (IJCAI)*, pages 1776–1782.

Fast Full Parsing by Linear-Chain Conditional Random Fields

Yoshimasa Tsuruoka[†‡] **Jun'ichi Tsujii**[†‡*] **Sophia Ananiadou**[†‡]
[†] School of Computer Science, University of Manchester, UK
[‡] National Centre for Text Mining (NaCTeM), UK
[*] Department of Computer Science, University of Tokyo, Japan
{yoshimasa.tsuruoka,j.tsujii,sophia.ananiadou}@manchester.ac.uk

Abstract

This paper presents a chunking-based discriminative approach to full parsing. We convert the task of full parsing into a series of chunking tasks and apply a conditional random field (CRF) model to each level of chunking. The probability of an entire parse tree is computed as the product of the probabilities of individual chunking results. The parsing is performed in a bottom-up manner and the best derivation is efficiently obtained by using a depth-first search algorithm. Experimental results demonstrate that this simple parsing framework produces a fast and reasonably accurate parser.

1 Introduction

Full parsing analyzes the phrase structure of a sentence and provides useful input for many kinds of high-level natural language processing such as summarization (Knight and Marcu, 2000), pronoun resolution (Yang et al., 2006), and information extraction (Miyao et al., 2008). One of the major obstacles that discourage the use of full parsing in large-scale natural language processing applications is its computational cost. For example, the MEDLINE corpus, a collection of abstracts of biomedical papers, consists of 70 million sentences and would require more than two years of processing time if the parser needs one second to process a sentence.

Generative models based on lexicalized PCFGs enjoyed great success as the machine learning framework for full parsing (Collins, 1999; Charniak, 2000), but recently discriminative models attract more attention due to their superior accuracy (Charniak and Johnson, 2005; Huang, 2008) and adaptability to new grammars and languages (Buchholz and Marsi, 2006).

A traditional approach to discriminative full parsing is to convert a full parsing task into a series of classification problems. Ratnaparkhi (1997) performs full parsing in a bottom-up and left-to-right manner and uses a maximum entropy classifier to make decisions to construct individual phrases. Sagae and Lavie (2006) use the shift-reduce parsing framework and a maximum entropy model for local classification to decide parsing actions. These approaches are often called *history-based* approaches.

A more recent approach to discriminative full parsing is to treat the task as a single structured prediction problem. Finkel et al. (2008) incorporated rich local features into a tree CRF model and built a competitive parser. Huang (2008) proposed to use a parse forest to incorporate non-local features. They used a perceptron algorithm to optimize the weights of the features and achieved state-of-the-art accuracy. Petrov and Klein (2008) introduced latent variables in tree CRFs and proposed a caching mechanism to speed up the computation.

In general, the latter whole-sentence approaches give better accuracy than history-based approaches because they can better trade off decisions made in different parts in a parse tree. However, the whole-sentence approaches tend to require a large computational cost both in training and parsing. In contrast, history-based approaches are less computationally intensive and usually produce fast parsers.

In this paper, we present a history-based parser using CRFs, by treating the task of full parsing as a series of chunking problems where it recognizes chunks in a flat input sequence. We use the linear-

Proceedings of the 12th Conference of the European Chapter of the ACL, pages 790–798,
Athens, Greece, 30 March – 3 April 2009. ©2009 Association for Computational Linguistics

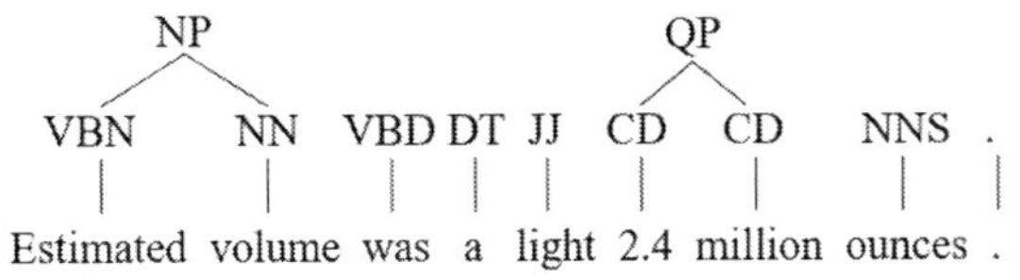

Figure 1: Chunking, the first (base) level.

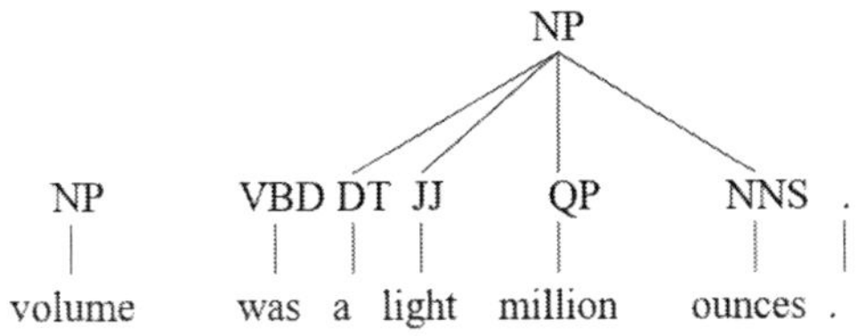

Figure 2: Chunking, the 2nd level.

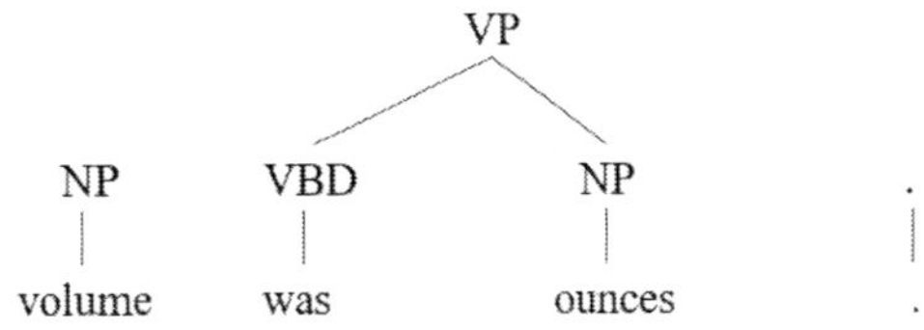

Figure 3: Chunking, the 3rd level.

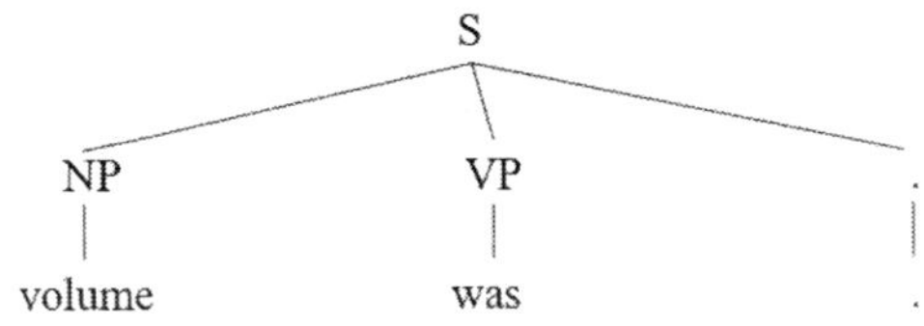

Figure 4: Chunking, the 4th level.

chain CRF model to perform chunking.

Although our parsing model falls into the category of history-based approaches, it is one step closer to the whole-sentence approaches because the parser uses a whole-sequence model (i.e. CRFs) for individual chunking tasks. In other words, our parser could be located somewhere between traditional history-based approaches and whole-sentence approaches. One of our motivations for this work was that our parsing model may achieve a better balance between accuracy and speed than existing parsers.

It is also worth mentioning that our approach is similar in spirit to supertagging for parsing with lexicalized grammar formalisms such as CCG and HPSG (Clark and Curran, 2004; Ninomiya et al., 2006), in which significant speed-ups for parsing time are achieved.

In this paper, we show that our approach is indeed appealing in that the parser runs very fast and gives competitive accuracy. We evaluate our parser on the standard data set for parsing experiments (i.e. the Penn Treebank) and compare it with existing approaches to full parsing.

This paper is organized as follows. Section 2 presents the overall chunk parsing strategy. Section 3 describes the CRF model used to perform individual chunking steps. Section 4 describes the depth-first algorithm for finding the best derivation of a parse tree. The part-of-speech tagger used in the parser is described in section 5. Experimental results on the Penn Treebank corpus are provided in Section 6. Section 7 discusses possible improvements and extensions of our work. Section 8 offers some concluding remarks.

2 Full Parsing by Chunking

This section describes the parsing framework employed in this work.

The parsing process is conceptually very simple. The parser first performs chunking by identifying base phrases, and converts the identified phrases to non-terminal symbols. It then performs chunking for the updated sequence and converts the newly recognized phrases into non-terminal symbols. The parser repeats this process until the whole sequence is chunked as a sentence

Figures 1 to 4 show an example of a parsing process by this framework. In the first (base) level, the chunker identifies two base phrases, (NP Estimated volume) and (QP 2.4 million), and replaces each phrase with its non-terminal symbol and head[1]. In the second level, the chunker identifies a noun phrase, (NP a light million ounces), and converts it into NP. This process is repeated until the whole sentence is chunked at the fourth level. The full parse tree is recovered from the chunking history in a straightforward way.

This idea of converting full parsing into a series of chunking tasks is not new by any means—the history of this kind of approach dates back to 1950s (Joshi and Hopely, 1996). More recently, Brants (1999) used a cascaded Markov model to parse German text. Tjong Kim Sang (2001) used the IOB tagging method to represent chunks and memory-based learning, and achieved an f-score of 80.49 on the WSJ corpus. Tsuruoka and Tsujii (2005) improved upon their approach by using

[1]The head word is identified by using the head-percolation table (Magerman, 1995).

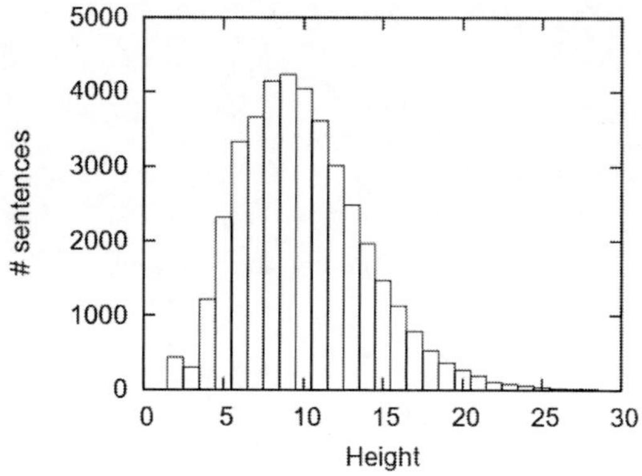

Figure 5: Distribution of tree height in WSJ sections 2-21.

a maximum entropy classifier and achieved an f-score of 85.9. However, there is still a large gap between the accuracy of chunking-based parsers and that of widely-used practical parsers such as Collins parser and Charniak parser (Collins, 1999; Charniak, 2000).

2.1 Heights of Trees

A natural question about this parsing framework is how many levels of chunking are usually needed to parse a sentence. We examined the distribution of the heights of the trees in sections 2-21 of the Wall Street Journal (WSJ) corpus. The result is shown in Figure 5. Most of the sentences have less than 20 levels. The average was 10.0, which means we need to perform, on average, 10 chunking tasks to obtain a full parse tree for a sentence if the parsing is performed in a deterministic manner.

3 Chunking with CRFs

The accuracy of chunk parsing is highly dependent on the accuracy of each level of chunking. This section describes our approach to the chunking task.

A common approach to the chunking problem is to convert the problem into a sequence tagging task by using the "BIO" (B for beginning, I for inside, and O for outside) representation. For example, the chunking process given in Figure 1 is expressed as the following BIO sequences.

B-NP I-NP O O O B-QP I-QP O O

This representation enables us to use the linear-chain CRF model to perform chunking, since the task is simply assigning appropriate labels to a sequence.

3.1 Linear Chain CRFs

A linear chain CRF defines a single log-linear probabilistic distribution over all possible tag sequences $\mathbf{y}$ for the input sequence $\mathbf{x}$:

$$p(\mathbf{y}|\mathbf{x}) = \frac{1}{Z(\mathbf{x})} \exp \sum_{t=1}^{T} \sum_{k=1}^{K} \lambda_k f_k(t, y_t, y_{t-1}, \mathbf{x}),$$

where $f_k(t, y_t, y_{t-1}, \mathbf{x})$ is typically a binary function indicating the presence of feature k, λ_k is the weight of the feature, and $Z(X)$ is a normalization function:

$$Z(\mathbf{x}) = \sum_{y} \exp \sum_{t=1}^{T} \sum_{k=1}^{K} \lambda_k f_k(t, y_t, y_{t-1}, \mathbf{x}).$$

This model allows us to define features on states and edges combined with surface observations.

The weights of the features are determined in such a way that they maximize the conditional log-likelihood of the training data:

$$\mathcal{L}_\lambda = \sum_{i=1}^{N} \log p(\mathbf{y}^{(i)}|\mathbf{x}^{(i)}) + R(\lambda),$$

where $R(\lambda)$ is introduced for the purpose of *regularization* which prevents the model from overfitting the training data. The L1 or L2 norm is commonly used in statistical natural language processing (Gao et al., 2007). We used L1-regularization, which is defined as

$$R(\lambda) = \frac{1}{C} \sum_{k=1}^{K} |\lambda_k|,$$

where C is the meta-parameter that controls the degree of regularization. We used the OWL-QN algorithm (Andrew and Gao, 2007) to obtain the parameters that maximize the L1-regularized conditional log-likelihood.

3.2 Features

Table 1 shows the features used in chunking for the base level. Since the task is basically identical to shallow parsing by CRFs, we follow the feature sets used in the previous work by Sha and Pereira (2003). We use unigrams, bigrams, and trigrams of part-of-speech (POS) tags and words.

The difference between our CRF chunker and that in (Sha and Pereira, 2003) is that we could not use second-order CRF models, hence we could not use trigram features on the BIO states. We

Symbol Unigrams	$s_{-2},\ s_{-1},\ s_0,\ s_{+1},\ s_{+2}$
Symbol Bigrams	$s_{-2}s_{-1},\ s_{-1}s_0,\ s_0s_{+1},\ s_{+1}s_{+2}$
Symbol Trigrams	$s_{-3}s_{-2}s_{-1},\ s_{-2}s_{-1}s_0,\ s_{-1}s_0s_{+1},\ s_0s_{+1}s_{+2},\ s_{+1}s_{+2}s_{+3}$
Word Unigrams	$h_{-2},\ h_{-1},\ h_0,\ h_{+1},\ h_{+2}$
Word Bigrams	$h_{-2}h_{-1},\ h_{-1}h_0,\ h_0h_{+1},\ h_{+1}h_{+2}$
Word Trigrams	$h_{-1}h_0h_{+1}$

Table 1: Feature templates used in the base level chunking. s represents a terminal symbol (i.e. POS tag) and the subscript represents a relative position. h represents a word.

found that using second order CRFs in our task was very difficult because of the computational cost. Recall that the computational cost for CRFs is quadratic to the number of possible states. In our task, we need to consider the states for all non-terminal symbols, whereas their work is only concerned with noun phrases.

Table 2 shows feature templates used in the non-base levels of chunking. In the non-base levels of chunking, we can use a richer set of features than the base-level chunking because the chunker has access to the information about the partial trees that have been already created. In addition to the features listed in Table 1, the chunker looks into the daughters of the current non-terminal symbol and use them as features. It also uses the words and POS tags around the edges of the region covered by the current non-terminal symbol. We also added a special feature to better capture PP-attachment. The chunker looks at the head of the second daughter of the prepositional phrase to incorporate the semantic head of the phrase.

4 Searching for the Best Parse

The probability for an entire parse tree is computed as the product of the probabilities output by the individual CRF chunkers:

$$score = \prod_{i=0}^{h} p(\mathbf{y_i}|\mathbf{x_i}), \qquad (1)$$

where i is the level of chunking and h is the height of the tree. The task of full parsing is then to choose the series of chunking results that maximizes this probability.

It should be noted that there are cases where different derivations (chunking histories) lead to the same parse tree (i.e. phrase structure). Strictly speaking, therefore, what we describe here as the probability of a parse tree is actually the probability of a single derivation. The probabilities of the derivations should then be marginalized over to produce the probability of a parse tree, but in this paper we ignore this effect and simply focus only on the best derivation.

We use a depth-first search algorithm to find the highest probability derivation. Figure 6 shows the algorithm in pseudo-code. The parsing process is implemented with a recursive function. In each level of chunking, the recursive function first invokes a CRF chunker to obtain chunking hypotheses for the given sequence. For each hypothesis whose probability is high enough to have possibility of constituting the best derivation, the function calls itself with the sequence updated by the hypothesis. The parsing process is performed in a bottom up manner and this recursive process terminates if the whole sequence is chunked as a sentence.

To extract multiple chunking hypotheses from the CRF chunker, we use a branch-and-bound algorithm rather than the A* search algorithm, which is perhaps more commonly used in previous studies. We do not give pseudo code, but the basic idea is as follows. It first performs the forward Viterbi algorithm to obtain the best sequence, storing the upper bounds that are used for pruning in branch-and-bound. It then performs a branch-and-bound algorithm in a backward manner to retrieve possible candidate sequences whose probabilities are greater than the given threshold. Unlike A* search, this method is memory efficient because it is performed in a depth-first manner and does not require priority queues for keeping uncompleted hypotheses.

It is straightforward to introduce beam search in this search algorithm—we simply limit the number of hypotheses generated by the CRF chunker. We examine how the width of the beam affects the parsing performance in the experiments.

Symbol Unigrams	s_{-2}, s_{-1}, s_0, s_{+1}, s_{+2}
Symbol Bigrams	$s_{-2}s_{-1}$, $s_{-1}s_0$, s_0s_{+1}, $s_{+1}s_{+2}$
Symbol Trigrams	$s_{-3}s_{-2}s_{-1}$, $s_{-2}s_{-1}s_0$, $s_{-1}s_0s_{+1}$, $s_0s_{+1}s_{+2}$, $s_{+1}s_{+2}s_{+3}$
Head Unigrams	h_{-2}, h_{-1}, h_0, h_{+1}, h_{+2}
Head Bigrams	$h_{-2}h_{-1}$, $h_{-1}h_0$, h_0h_{+1}, $h_{+1}h_{+2}$
Head Trigrams	$h_{-1}h_0h_{+1}$
Symbol & Daughters	s_0d_{01}, ... s_0d_{0m}
Symbol & Word/POS context	s_0w_{j-1}, s_0p_{j-1}, s_0w_{k+1} , s_0p_{k+1}
Symbol & Words on the edges	s_0w_j, s_0w_k
Freshness	whether s_0 has been created in the level just below
PP-attachment	$h_{-1}h_0m_{02}$ (only when s_0 = PP)

Table 2: Feature templates used in the upper level chunking. s represents a non-terminal symbol. h represents a head percolated from the bottom for each symbol. d_{0i} is the ith daughter of s_0. w_j is the first word in the range covered by s_0. w_{j-1} is the word preceding w_j. w_k is the last word in the range covered by s_0. w_{k+1} is the word following w_k. p represents POS tags. m_{02} represents the head of the second daughter of s_0.

Word Unigram	w_{-2}, w_{-1}, w_0, w_{+1}, w_{i+2}
Word Bigram	$w_{-1}w_0$, w_0w_{+1}, $w_{-1}w_{+1}$
Prefix, Suffix	prefixes of w_0 suffixes of w_0 (up to length 10)
Character features	w_0 has a hyphen w_0 has a number w_0 has a capital letter w_0 is all capital
Normalized word	N(w_0)

Table 3: Feature templates used in the POS tagger. w represents a word and the subscript represents a relative position.

5 Part-of-Speech Tagging

We use the CRF model also for POS tagging. The CRF-based POS tagger is incorporated in the parser in exactly the same way as the other layers of chunking. In other words, the POS tagging process is treated like the bottom layer of chunking, so the parser considers multiple probabilistic hypotheses output by the tagger in the search algorithm described in the previous section.

5.1 Features

Table 3 shows the feature templates used in the POS tagger. Most of them are standard features commonly used in POS tagging for English. We used unigrams and bigrams of neighboring words, prefixes and suffixes of the current word, and some characteristics of the word. We also normalized the current word by lowering capital letters and converting all the numerals into '#', and used the normalized word as a feature.

6 Experiments

We ran parsing experiments using the Wall Street Journal corpus. Sections 2-21 were used as the training data. Section 22 was used as the development data, with which we tuned the feature set and parameters for learning and parsing. Section 23 was reserved for the final accuracy report.

The training data for the CRF chunkers were created by converting each parse tree in the training data into a list of chunking sequences like the ones presented in Figures 1 to 4. We trained three CRF models, i.e., the POS tagging model, the base chunking model, and the non-base chunking model. The training took about two days on a single CPU.

We used the *evalb* script provided by Sekine and Collins for evaluating the labeled recall/precision of the parser outputs[2]. All experiments were carried out on a server with 2.2 GHz AMD Opteron processors and 16GB memory.

6.1 Chunking Performance

First, we describe the accuracy of individual chunking processes. Table 4 shows the results for the ten most frequently occurring symbols on the development data. Noun phrases (NP) are the

[2]The script is available at http://nlp.cs.nyu.edu/evalb/. We used the parameter file "COLLINS.prm".

```
procedure PARSESENTENCE(x)
    PARSE(x, 1, 0)

function PARSE(x, p, q)
    if x is chunked as a complete sentence
        return p
    H ← PERFORMCHUNKING(x, q/p)
    for h ∈ H in descending order of their
    probabilities do
        r ← p × h.probability
        if r > q then
            x' ← UPDATESEQUENCE(x, h)
            s ← PARSE(x', r, q)
            if s > q then
                q ← s
    return q

function PERFORMCHUNKING(x, t)
    perform chunking with a CRF chunker and
    return a set of chunking hypotheses whose
    probabilities are greater than t.

function UPDATESEQUENCE(x, h)
    update sequence x according to chunking
    hypothesis h and return the updated
    sequence.
```

Figure 6: Searching for the best parse with a depth-first search algorithm. This pseudo-code illustrates how to find the highest probability parse, but in the real implementation, the function needs to keep track of chunking histories as well as probabilities.

Symbol	# Samples	Recall	Prec.	F-score
NP	317,597	94.79	94.16	94.47
VP	76,281	91.46	91.98	91.72
PP	66,979	92.84	92.61	92.72
S	33,739	91.48	90.64	91.06
ADVP	21,686	84.25	85.86	85.05
ADJP	14,422	77.27	78.46	77.86
QP	14,308	89.43	91.16	90.28
SBAR	11,603	96.42	96.97	96.69
WHNP	8,827	95.54	97.50	96.51
PRT	3,391	95.72	90.52	93.05
:	:	:	:	:
all	579,253	92.63	92.62	92.63

Table 4: Chunking performance (section 22, all sentences).

Beam	Recall	Prec.	F-score	Time (sec)
1	86.72	87.83	87.27	16
2	88.50	88.85	88.67	41
3	88.69	89.08	88.88	61
4	88.72	89.13	88.92	92
5	88.73	89.14	88.93	119
10	88.68	89.19	88.93	179

Table 5: Beam width and parsing performance (section 22, all sentences).

most common symbol and consist of 55% of all phrases. The accuracy of noun phrases recognition was relatively high, but it may be useful to design special features for this particular type of phrase, considering the dominance of noun phrases in the corpus. Although not directly comparable, Sha and Pereira (2003) report almost the same level of accuracy (94.38%) on noun phrase recognition, using a much smaller training set. We attribute their superior performance mainly to the use of second-order features on state transitions. Table 4 also suggests that adverb phrases (ADVP) and adjective phrases (ADJP) are more difficult to recognize than other types of phrases, which coincides with the result reported in (Collins, 1999).

It should be noted that the performance reported in this table was evaluated using the gold standard sequences as the input to the CRF chunkers. In the real parsing process, the chunkers have to use the output from the previous (one level below) chunker, so the quality of the input is not as good as that used in this evaluation.

6.2 Parsing Performance

Next, we present the actual parsing performance. The first set of experiments concerns the relationship between the width of beam and the parsing performance. Table 5 shows the results obtained on the development data. We varied the width of the beam from 1 to 10. The beam width of 1 corresponds to deterministic parsing. Somewhat unexpectedly, the parsing accuracy did not drop significantly even when we reduced the beam width to a very small number such as 2 or 3.

One of the interesting findings was that recall scores were consistently lower than precision scores throughout all experiments. A possible reason is that, since the score of a parse is defined as the product of all chunking probabilities, the parser could prefer a parse tree that consists of a small number of chunk layers. This may stem from the history-based model's inability of properly trading off decisions made by different chunkers.

Overall, the parsing speed was very high. The deterministic version (beam width = 1) parsed 1700 sentences in 16 seconds, which means that the parser needed only 10 msec to parse one sentence. The parsing speed decreases as we increase the beam width.

The parser was also memory efficient. Thanks to L1 regularization, the training process did not result in many non-zero feature weights. The numbers of non-zero weight features were 58,505 (for the base chunker), 263,889 (for the non-base chunker), and 42,201 (for the POS tagger). The parser required only 14MB of memory to run.

There was little accuracy difference between the beam width of 4 and 5, so we adopted the beam width of 4 for the final accuracy report on the test data.

6.3 Comparison with Previous Work

Table 6 shows the performance of our parser on the test data and summarizes the results of previous work. Our parser achieved an f-score of 88.4 on the test data, which is comparable to the accuracy achieved by recent discriminative approaches such as Finkel et al. (2008) and Petrov & Klein (2008), but is not as high as the state-of-the-art accuracy achieved by the parsers that can incorporate global features such as Huang (2008) and Charniak & Johnson (2005). Our parser was more accurate than traditional history-based approaches such as Sagae & Lavie (2006) and Ratnaparkhi (1997), and was significantly better than previous cascaded chunking approaches such as Tsuruoka & Tsujii (2005) and Tjong Kim Sang (2001).

Although the comparison presented in the table is not perfectly fair because of the differences in hardware platforms, the results show that our parsing model is a promising addition to the parsing frameworks for building a fast and accurate parser.

7 Discussion

One of the obvious ways to improve the accuracy of our parser is to improve the accuracy of individual CRF models. As mentioned earlier, we were not able to use second-order features on state transitions, which would have been very useful, due to the problem of computational cost. Incremental feature selection methods such as grafting (Perkins et al., 2003) may help us to incorporate such higher-order features, but the problem of decreased efficiency of dynamic programming in the CRF would probably need to be addressed.

In this work, we treated the chunking problem as a sequence labeling problem by using the BIO representation for the chunks. However, semi-Markov conditional random fields (semi-CRFs) can directly handle the chunking problem by considering all possible combinations of subsequences of arbitrary length (Sarawagi and Cohen, 2004). Semi-CRFs allow one to use a richer set of features than CRFs, so the use of semi-CRFs in our parsing framework should lead to improved accuracy. Moreover, semi-CRFs would allow us to incorporate some useful restrictions in producing chunking hypotheses. For example, we could naturally incorporate the restriction that every chunk has to contain at least one symbol that has just been created in the previous level[3]. It is hard for the normal CRF model to incorporate such restrictions.

Introducing latent variables into the CRF model may be another promising approach. This is the main idea of Petrov and Klein (2008), which significantly improved parsing accuracy.

A totally different approach to improving the accuracy of our parser is to use the idea of "self-training" described in (McClosky et al., 2006). The basic idea is to create a larger set of training data by applying an accurate parser (e.g. reranking parser) to a large amount of raw text. We can then use the automatically created treebank as the additional training data for our parser. This approach suggests that accurate (but slow) parsers and fast (but not-so-accurate) parsers can actually help each other.

Also, since it is not difficult to extend our parser to produce N-best parsing hypotheses, one could build a fast reranking parser by using the parser as the base (hypotheses generating) parser.

8 Conclusion

Although the idea of treating full parsing as a series of chunking problems has a long history, there has not been a competitive parser based on this parsing framework. In this paper, we have demonstrated that the framework actually enables us to

[3]For example, the sequence VBD DT JJ in Figure 2 cannot be a chunk in the current level because it would have been already chunked in the previous level if it were.

	Recall	Precision	F-score	Time (min)
This work (deterministic)	86.3	87.5	86.9	0.5
This work (search, beam width = 4)	88.2	88.7	88.4	1.7
Huang (2008)			91.7	Unk
Finkel et al. (2008)	87.8	88.2	88.0	>250*
Petrov & Klein (2008)			88.3	3*
Sagae & Lavie (2006)	87.8	88.1	87.9	17
Charniak & Johnson (2005)	90.6	91.3	91.0	Unk
Tsuruoka & Tsujii (2005)	85.0	86.8	85.9	2
Collins (1999)	88.1	88.3	88.2	39**
Tjong Kim Sang (2001)	78.7	82.3	80.5	Unk
Charniak (2000)	89.6	89.5	89.5	23**
Ratnaparkhi (1997)	86.3	87.5	86.9	Unk

Table 6: Parsing performance on section 23 (all sentences). * estimated from the parsing time on the training data. ** reported in (Sagae and Lavie, 2006) where Pentium 4 3.2GHz was used to run the parsers.

build a competitive parser if we use CRF models for each level of chunking and a depth-first search algorithm to search for the highest probability parse.

Like other discriminative learning approaches, one of the advantages of our parser is its generality. The design of our parser is very generic, and the features used in our parser are not particularly specific to the Penn Treebank. We expect it to be straightforward to adapt the parser to other projective grammars and languages.

This parsing framework should be useful when one needs to process a large amount of text or when real time processing is required, in which the parsing speed is of top priority. In the deterministic setting, our parser only needed about 10 msec to parse a sentence.

Acknowledgments

This work described in this paper has been funded by the Biotechnology and Biological Sciences Research Council (BBSRC; BB/E004431/1) and the European BOOTStrep project (FP6 - 028099). The research team is hosted by the JISC/BBSRC/EPSRC sponsored National Centre for Text Mining.

References

Galen Andrew and Jianfeng Gao. 2007. Scalable training of L1-regularized log-linear models. In *Proceedings of ICML*, pages 33–40.

Thorsten Brants. 1999. Cascaded markov models. In *Proceedings of EACL*.

Sabine Buchholz and Erwin Marsi. 2006. CoNLL-X shared task on multilingual dependency parsing. In *Proceedings of CoNLL-X*, pages 149–164.

Eugene Charniak and Mark Johnson. 2005. Coarse-to-fine n-best parsing and maxent discriminative reranking. In *Proceedings of ACL*, pages 173–180.

Eugene Charniak. 2000. A maximum-entropy-inspired parser. In *Proceedings of NAACL 2000*, pages 132–139.

Stephen Clark and James R. Curran. 2004. The importance of supertagging for wide-coverage CCG parsing. In *Proceedings of COLING 2004*, pages 282–288.

Michael Collins. 1999. *Head-Driven Statistical Models for Natural Language Parsing*. Ph.D. thesis, University of Pennsylvania.

Jenny Rose Finkel, Alex Kleeman, and Christopher D. Manning. 2008. Efficient, feature-based, conditional random field parsing. In *Proceedings of ACL-08:HLT*, pages 959–967.

Jianfeng Gao, Galen Andrew, Mark Johnson, and Kristina Toutanova. 2007. A comparative study of parameter estimation methods for statistical natural language processing. In *Proceedings of ACL*, pages 824–831.

Liang Huang. 2008. Forest reranking: Discriminative parsing with non-local features. In *Proceedings of ACL-08:HLT*, pages 586–594.

Aravind K. Joshi and Phil Hopely. 1996. A parser from antiquity. *Natural Language Engineering*, 2(4):291–294.

Kevin Knight and Daniel Marcu. 2000. Statistics-based summarization - step one: Sentence compression. In *Proceedings of AAAI/IAAI*, pages 703–710.

David M. Magerman. 1995. Statistical decision-tree models for parsing. In *Proceedings of ACL*, pages 276–283.

David McClosky, Eugene Charniak, and Mark Johnson. 2006. Effective self-training for parsing. In *Proceedings of HLT-NAACL*.

Yusuke Miyao, Rune Saetre, Kenji Sage, Takuya Matsuzaki, and Jun'ichi Tsujii. 2008. Task-oriented evaluation of syntactic parsers and their representations. In *Proceedings of ACL-08:HLT*, pages 46–54.

Takashi Ninomiya, Takuya Matsuzaki, Yoshimasa Tsuruoka, Yusuke Miyao, and Jun'ichi Tsujii. 2006. Extremely lexicalized models for accurate and fast HPSG parsing. In *Proceedings of EMNLP 2006*, pages 155–163.

Simon Perkins, Kevin Lacker, and James Theiler. 2003. Grafting: fast, incremental feature selection by gradient descent in function space. *The Journal of Machine Learning Research*, 3:1333–1356.

Slav Petrov and Dan Klein. 2008. Discriminative log-linear grammars with latent variables. In *Advances in Neural Information Processing Systems 20 (NIPS)*, pages 1153–1160.

Adwait Ratnaparkhi. 1997. A linear observed time statistical parser based on maximum entropy models. In *Proceedings of EMNLP 1997*, pages 1–10.

Kenji Sagae and Alon Lavie. 2006. A best-first probabilistic shift-reduce parser. In *Proceedings of COLING/ACL*, pages 691–698.

Sunita Sarawagi and William W. Cohen. 2004. Semi-markov conditional random fields for information extraction. In *Proceedings of NIPS*.

Fei Sha and Fernando Pereira. 2003. Shallow parsing with conditional random fields. In *Proceedings of HLT-NAACL*.

Erik Tjong Kim Sang. 2001. Transforming a chunker to a parser. In J. Veenstra W. Daelemans, K. Sima'an and J. Zavrel, editors, *Computational Linguistics in the Netherlands 2000*, pages 177–188. Rodopi.

Yoshimasa Tsuruoka and Jun'ichi Tsujii. 2005. Chunk parsing revisited. In *Proceedings of IWPT*, pages 133–140.

Xiaofeng Yang, Jian Su, and Chew Lim Tan. 2006. Kernel-based pronoun resolution with structured syntactic features. In *Proceedings of COLING/ACL*, pages 41–48.

MINT: A Method for Effective and Scalable Mining of Named Entity Transliterations from Large Comparable Corpora

Raghavendra Udupa **K Saravanan** **A Kumaran** **Jagadeesh Jagarlamudi***
Microsoft Research India
Bangalore 560080 INDIA
[raghavu,v-sarak,kumarana,jags}@microsoft.com

Abstract

In this paper, we address the problem of mining transliterations of Named Entities (NEs) from large comparable corpora. We leverage the empirical fact that multilingual news articles with similar news content are rich in Named Entity Transliteration Equivalents (NETEs). Our mining algorithm, MINT, uses a cross-language document similarity model to align multilingual news articles and then mines NETEs from the aligned articles using a transliteration similarity model. We show that our approach is highly effective on 6 different comparable corpora between English and 4 languages from 3 different language families. Furthermore, it performs substantially better than a state-of-the-art competitor.

1 Introduction

Named Entities (NEs) play a critical role in many Natural Language Processing and Information Retrieval (IR) tasks. In Cross-Language Information Retrieval (CLIR) systems, they play an even more important role as the accuracy of their transliterations is shown to correlate highly with the performance of the CLIR systems (Mandl and Womser-Hacker, 2005, Xu and Weischedel, 2005). Traditional methods for transliterations have not proven to be very effective in CLIR. Machine Transliteration systems (AbdulJaleel and Larkey, 2003; Al-Onaizan and Knight, 2002; Virga and Khudanpur, 2003) usually produce incorrect transliterations and translation lexcions such as hand-crafted or statistical dictionaries are too static to have good coverage of NEs[1] occurring in the current news events. Hence, there is a critical need for creating and continually updating multilingual Named Entity transliteration lexicons.

The ubiquitous availability of comparable news corpora in multiple languages suggests a promising alternative to Machine Transliteration, namely, the *mining* of Named Entity Transliteration Equivalents (NETEs) from such corpora. News stories are typically rich in NEs and therefore, comparable news corpora can be expected to contain NETEs (Klementiev and Roth, 2006; Tao et al., 2006). The large quantity and the perpetual availability of news corpora in many of the world's languages, make mining of NETEs a viable alternative to traditional approaches. It is this opportunity that we address in our work.

In this paper, we detail an effective and scalable mining method, called **MINT** (**MI**ning **N**amed-entity **T**ransliteration equivalents), for mining of NETEs from large comparable corpora. MINT addresses several challenges in mining NETEs from large comparable corpora: exhaustiveness (in mining sparse NETEs), computational efficiency (in scaling on corpora size), language independence (in being applicable to many language pairs) and linguistic frugality (in requiring minimal external linguistic resources).

Our contributions are as follows:

- We give empirical evidence for the hypothesis that news articles in different languages with reasonably similar content are rich sources of NETEs (Udupa, et al., 2008).
- We demonstrate that the above insight can be translated into an effective approach for mining NETEs from large comparable corpora even when similar articles are not known a priori.
- We demonstrate MINT's effectiveness on 4 language pairs involving 5 languages (English, Hindi, Kannada, Russian, and Tamil) from 3 different language families, and its scalability on corpora of vastly different sizes (2,000 to 200,000 articles).
- We show that MINT's performance is significantly better than a state of the art method (Klementiev and Roth, 2006).

* Currently with University of Utah.

[1] New NEs are introduced to the vocabulary of a language every day. On an average, 260 and 452 new NEs appeared daily in the XIE and AFE segments of the LDC English Gigaword corpora respectively.

Proceedings of the 12th Conference of the European Chapter of the ACL, pages 799–807,
Athens, Greece, 30 March – 3 April 2009. ©2009 Association for Computational Linguistics

Figure 1. Comparable Corpora

We discuss the motivation behind our approach in Section 2 and present the details in Section 3. In Section 4, we describe the evaluation process and in Section 5, we present the results and analysis. We discuss related work in Section 6.

2 Motivation

MINT is based on the hypothesis that news articles in different languages with similar content contain highly overlapping set of NEs. News articles are typically rich in NEs as news is about events involving people, locations, organizations, etc[2]. It is reasonable to expect that multilingual news articles reporting the same news event mention the same NEs in the respective languages. For instance, consider the English and Hindi news reports from the *New York Times* and the *BBC* on the second oath taking of President Barack Obama (Figure 1). The articles are not parallel but discuss the same event. Naturally, they mention the same NEs (such as Barack Obama, John Roberts, White House) in the respective languages, and hence, are rich sources of NETEs.

Our empirical investigation of comparable corpora confirmed the above insight. A study of 200 pairs of similar news articles published by *The New Indian Express* in 2007 in English and Tamil showed that 87% of the single word NEs in the English articles had at least one transliteration equivalent in the conjugate Tamil articles. The MINT method leverages this empirically backed insight to mine NETEs from such comparable corpora.

However, there are several challenges to the mining process: firstly, vast majority of the NEs in comparable corpora are very sparse; our analysis showed that 80% of the NEs in *The New Indian Express* news corpora appear less than 5 times in the entire corpora. Hence, any mining method that depends mainly on repeated occurrences of the NEs in the corpora is likely to miss vast majority of the NETEs. Secondly, the mining method must restrict the candidate NETEs that need to be examined for match to a reasonably small number, not only to minimize false positives but also to be computationally efficient. Thirdly, the use of linguistic tools and resources must be kept to a minimum as resources are available only in a handful of languages. Finally, it is important to use as little language-specific knowledge as possible in order to make the mining method applicable across a vast majority of languages of the world. The MINT method proposed in this paper addresses all the above issues.

[2] News articles from the BBC corpus had, on an average, 12.9 NEs and new articles from the *The New Indian Express,* about 11.8 NEs.

3 The MINT Mining Method

MINT has two stages. In the first stage, for every document in the source language side, the set of documents in the target language side with similar news content are found using a cross-language document similarity model. In the second stage, the NEs in the source language side are extracted using a Named Entity Recognizer (NER) and, subsequently, for each NE in a source language document, its transliterations are mined from the corresponding target language documents. We present the details of the two stages of MINT in the remainder of this section.

3.1 Finding Similar Document Pairs

The first stage of MINT method (Figure 2) works on the documents from the comparable corpora ($\mathcal{C}_S$, $\mathcal{C}_T$) in languages $\mathcal{S}$ and $\mathcal{T}$ and produces a collection $\mathcal{A}_{S,T}$ of similar article pairs ($\mathcal{D}_S$, $\mathcal{D}_T$). Each article pair ($\mathcal{D}_S$, $\mathcal{D}_T$) in $\mathcal{A}_{S,T}$ consists of an article ($\mathcal{D}_S$) in language $\mathcal{S}$ and an article ($\mathcal{D}_T$) in language $\mathcal{T}$, that have similar content. The cross-language similarity between $\mathcal{D}_S$ and $\mathcal{D}_T$, as measured by the cross-language similarity model $\mathcal{MD}$, is at least $\alpha > 0$.

Cross-language Document Similarity Model: The cross-language document similarity model measures the degree of similarity between a pair of documents in source and target languages. We use the negative KL-divergence between source and target document probability distributions as the similarity measure.

```
Input: Comparable news corpora (C_S, C_T) in languages (S,T)
       Crosslanguage Document Similarity Model MD for (S, T)
       Threshold score α.
Output: Set A_S,T of pairs of similar articles (D_S, D_T) from (C_S, C_T).
A_S,T ← φ;        // Set of Similar articles (D_S, D_T)
for each article D_S in C_S do
  X_S ← φ;     // Set of candidates for D_S.
  for each article d_T in C_T do
    score = CrossLanguageDocumentSimilarity(D_S,d_T,MD);
    if (score ≥ α) then X_S ← X_S ∪ (d_T, score) ;
  end
  D_T = BestScoringCandidate(X_S);
  if (D_T ≠ φ) then A_S,T ← A_S,T ∪ (D_S, D_T) ;
end
CrossLanguageSimilarDocumentPairs
```

Figure 2. Stage 1 of MINT

Given two documents $\mathcal{D}_S$, $\mathcal{D}_T$ in source and target languages respectively, with V_S, V_T denoting the vocabulary of source and target languages, the similarity between the two documents is given by the KL-divergence measure, -KL($\mathcal{D}_S$ || $\mathcal{D}_T$), as:

$$\sum_{w_T \in V_T} p(w_T \mid D_S) \log \frac{p(w_T \mid D_T)}{p(w_T \mid D_S)}$$

where p(w | D) is the likelihood of word w in D. As we are interested in target documents which are similar to a given source document, we can ignore the numerator as it is independent of the target document. Finally, expanding $p(w_T \mid D_s)$ as $\sum_{w_S \in V_S} p(w_S \mid D_S) p(w_T \mid w_S)$ we specify the cross-language similarity score as follows:

Cross-language similarity =

$$\sum_{w_T \in V_T} \sum_{w_S \in V_S} p(w_S \mid D_S) p(w_T \mid w_S) \log p(w_T \mid D_T)$$

3.2 Mining NETEs from Document Pairs

The second stage of the MINT method works on each pair of articles ($\mathcal{D}_S$, $\mathcal{D}_T$) in the collection $\mathcal{A}_{S,T}$ and produces a set $\mathcal{P}_{S,T}$ of NETEs. Each pair (ε_S, ε_T) in $\mathcal{P}_{S,T}$ consists of an NE ε_S in language $\mathcal{S}$, and a token ε_T in language $\mathcal{T}$, that are transliteration equivalents of each other. Furthermore, the transliteration similarity between ε_S and ε_T, as measured by the transliteration similarity model $\mathcal{MT}$, is at least $\beta > 0$. Figure 3 outlines this algorithm.

Discriminative Transliteration Similarity Model:
The transliteration similarity model $\mathcal{MT}$ measures the degree of transliteration equivalence between a source language and a target language term.

```
Input:
   Set A_S,T of similar documents (D_S, D_T) in languages (S,T),
   Transliteration Similarity Model MT for (S, T),
   Threshold score β.
Output: Set P_S,T of NETEs (ε_S, ε_T) from A_S,T;
P_S,T ← φ;
for each pair of articles (D_S, D_T) in A_S,T do
   for each named entity ε_S in D_S do
      Y_S ← φ; // Set of candidates for ε_S.
      for each candidate e_T in D_T do
         score = TransliterationSimilarity(ε_S, e_T, MT) ;
         if (score ≥ β) then Y_S ← Y_S ∪ (e_T, score) ;
      end
      ε_T = BestScoringCandidate(Y_S) ;
      if (ε_T ≠ null) then P_S,T ← P_S,T ∪ (ε_S, ε_T) ;
   end
end
TransliterationEquivalents
```

Figure 3. Stage 2 of MINT

We employ a logistic function as our transliteration similarity model $\mathcal{MT}$, as follows:

$$\text{TransliterationSimilarity}\,(\varepsilon_S, e_T, \mathcal{MT}) = \frac{1}{1+e^{-w^t\cdot\phi(\varepsilon_S, e_T)}}$$

where ϕ (ε_S, e_T) is the feature vector for the pair (ε_S, e_T) and w is the weights vector. Note that the transliteration similarity takes a value in the range [0..1]. The weights vector w is learnt discriminatively over a training corpus of known transliteration equivalents in the given pair of languages.

Features: The features employed by the model capture interesting cross-language associations observed in (ε_S, e_T):

- All unigrams and bigrams from the source and target language strings.
- Pairs of source string n-grams and target string n-grams such that difference in the start positions of the source and target n-grams is at most 2. Here $n \in \{1,2\}$.
- Difference in the lengths of the two strings.

Generative Transliteration Similarity Model: We also experimented with an extension of He's W-HMM model (He, 2007). The transition probability depends on both the jump width and the previous source character as in the W-HMM model. The emission probability depends on the current source character and the previous target character unlike the W-HMM model (Udupa et al., 2009). Instead of using any single alignment of characters in the pair (w_S, w_T), we marginalize over all possible alignments:

$$P(t_1^m \mid s_1^n) = \sum_A \prod_{j=1}^{m} p(a_j \mid a_{j-1}, s_{a_{j-1}})\, p(t_j \mid s_{a_j}, t_{j-1})$$

Here, t_j (and resp. s_i) denotes the jth (and resp. i[th]) character in w_T (and resp. w_S) and $A \equiv a_1^m$ is the hidden alignment between w_T and w_S where t_j is aligned to s_{a_j}, $j = 1, \cdots, m$. We estimate the parameters of the model using the EM algorithm. The transliteration similarity score of a pair (w_S, w_T) is log P(w_T | w_S) appropriately transformed.

4 Experimental Setup

Our empirical investigation consists of experiments in three data environments, with each environment providing answer to specific set of questions, as listed below:

1. **Ideal Environment (IDEAL)**: Given a collection $\mathcal{A}_{S,T}$ of oracle-aligned article pairs ($\mathcal{D}_S$, $\mathcal{D}_T$) in $\mathcal{S}$ and $\mathcal{T}$, how effective is Stage 2 of MINT in mining NETE from $\mathcal{A}_{S,T}$?
2. **Near Ideal Environment** (NEAR-IDEAL): Let $\mathcal{A}_{S,T}$ be a collection of *similar* article pairs ($\mathcal{D}_S$, $\mathcal{D}_T$) in $\mathcal{S}$ and $\mathcal{T}$. Given comparable corpora ($\mathcal{C}_S$, $\mathcal{C}_T$) consisting of only articles from $\mathcal{A}_{S,T}$, but without the knowledge of pairings between the articles,
   a. How effective is Stage 1 of MINT in recovering $\mathcal{A}_{S,T}$ from ($\mathcal{C}_S$, $\mathcal{C}_T$) ?
   b. What is the effect of Stage 1 on the overall effectiveness of MINT?
3. **Real Environment (REAL)**: Given large comparable corpora ($\mathcal{C}_S$, $\mathcal{C}_T$), how effective is MINT, end-to-end?

The IDEAL environment is indeed ideal for MINT since every article in the comparable corpora is paired with exactly one similar article in the other language and the pairing of articles in the comparable corpora is known in advance. We want to emphasize here that such corpora are indeed available in many domains such as technical documents and interlinked multilingual Wikipedia articles. In the IDEAL environment, only Stage 2 of MINT is put to test, as article alignments are given.

In the NEAR-IDEAL data environment, every article in the comparable corpora is known to have exactly one conjugate article in the other language though the pairing itself is not known in advance. In such a setting, MINT needs to discover the article pairing before mining NETEs and therefore, both stages of MINT are put to test. The best performance possible in this environment should ideally be the same as that of IDEAL, and any degradation points to the shortcoming of the Stage 1 of MINT. These two environments quantify the stage-wise performance of the MINT method.

Finally, in the data environment REAL, we test MINT on large comparable corpora, where even the existence of a conjugate article in the target side for a given article in the source side of the comparable corpora is not guaranteed, as in any normal large multilingual news corpora. In this scenario both the stages of MINT are put to test. This is the toughest, and perhaps the typical setting in which MINT would be used.

4.1 Comparable Corpora

In our experiments, the source language is English whereas the 4 target languages are from three different language families (Hindi from the Indo-Aryan family, Russian from the Slavic family, Kannada and Tamil from the Dravidian family). Note that none of the five languages use a common script and hence identification of cognates, spelling variations, suffix transformations, and other techniques commonly used for closely related languages that have a common script are not applicable for mining NETEs. Table 1 summarizes the 6 different comparable corpora that were used for the empirical investigation; 4 for the IDEAL and NEAR-IDEAL environments (in 4 language pairs), and 2 for the REAL environment (in 2 language pairs).

Corpus	Source - Target	Data Environment	Articles (in Thousands)		Words (in Millions)	
			Src	Tgt	Src	Tgt
EK-S	English-Kannada	IDEAL& NEAR-IDEAL	2.90	2.90	0.42	0.34
ET-S	English-Tamil	IDEAL& NEAR-IDEAL	2.90	2.90	0.42	0.32
ER-S	English-Russian	IDEAL& NEAR-IDEAL	2.30	2.30	1.03	0.40
EH-S	English-Hindi	IDEAL& NEAR-IDEAL	11.9	11.9	3.77	3.57
EK-L	English-Kannada	REAL	103.8	111.0	27.5	18.2
ET-L	English-Tamil	REAL	103.8	144.3	27.5	19.4

Table 1: Comparable Corpora

The corpora can be categorized into two separate groups, group S (for *Small*) consisting of EK-S, ET-S, ER-S, and EH-S and group L (for *Large*) consisting of EK-L and ET-L. Corpora in group S are relatively small in size, and contain pairs of articles that have been judged by human annotators as similar. Corpora in group L are two orders of magnitude larger in size than those in group S and contain a large number of articles that may not have conjugates in the target side. In addition the pairings are unknown even for the articles that have conjugates. All comparable corpora had publication dates, except EH-S, which is known to have been published over the same year.

The EK-S, ET-S, EK-L and ET-L corpora are from *The New Indian Express* news paper, whereas the EH-S corpora are from *Web Dunia* and the ER-S corpora are from *BBC/Lenta News Agency* respectively.

4.2 Cross-language Similarity Model

The cross-language document similarity model requires a bilingual dictionary in the appropriate language pair. Therefore, we generated statistical dictionaries for 3 language pairs (from parallel corpora of the following sizes: 11K sentence pairs in English-Kannada, 54K in English-Hindi, and 14K in English-Tamil) using the GIZA++ statistical alignment tool (Och et al., 2003), with 5 iterations each of IBM Model 1 and HMM. We did not have access to an English-Russian parallel corpus and hence could not generate a dictionary for this language pair. Hence, the NEAR-IDEAL experiments were not run for the English-Russian language pair.

Although the coverage of the dictionaries was low, this turned out to be not a serious issue for our cross-language document similarity model as it might have for topic based CLIR (Ballesteros and Croft, 1998). Unlike CLIR, where the query is typically smaller in length compared to the documents, in our case we are dealing with news articles of comparable size in both source and target languages.

When many translations were available for a source word, we considered only the top-4 translations. Further, we smoothed the document probability distributions with collection frequency as described in (Ponte and Croft, 1998).

4.3 Transliteration Similarity Model

The transliteration similarity models for each of the 4 language pairs were produced by learning over a training corpus consisting of about 16,000 single word NETEs, in each pair of languages. The training corpus in English-Hindi, English-Kannada and English-Tamil were hand-crafted by professionals, the English-Russian name pairs were culled from Wikipedia interwiki links and were cleaned heuristically. Equal number of negative samples was used for training the models. To produce the negative samples, we paired each source language NE with a random non-matching target language NE. No language specific features were used and the same feature set was used in each of the 4 language pairs making MINT language neutral.

In all the experiments, our source side language is English, and the Stanford Named Entity Recognizer (Finkel et al, 2005) was used to extract NEs from the source side article. It should be noted here that while the precision of the NER used was consistently high, its recall was low, (~40%) especially in the *New Indian Express* corpus, perhaps due to the differences in the data used for training the NER and the data on which we used it.

4.4 Performance Measures

Our intention is to measure the effectiveness of MINT by comparing its performance with the oracular (human annotator) performance. As transliteration equivalents must exist in the paired articles to be found by MINT, we focus only on those NEs that actually have at least one transliteration equivalent in the conjugate article.

Three performance measures are of interest to us: the fraction of distinct NEs from source language for which we found at least one transliteration in the target side (Recall on distinct NEs), the fraction of distinct NETEs (Recall on distinct NETEs) and the Mean Reciprocal Rank (MRR) of the NETEs mined. Since we are interested in mining not only the highly frequent but also the infrequent NETEs, recall metrics measure how effective our method is in mining NETEs exhaustively. The MRR score indicates how effective our method is in preferring the correct ones among candidates.

To measure the performance of MINT, we created a test bed for each of the language pairs. The test beds are summarized in Table 2.

The test beds consist of pairs of similar articles in each of the language pairs. It should be noted here that as transliteration equivalents must exist in the paired articles to be found by MINT, we focus only on those NEs that actually have at least one transliteration equivalent in the conjugate article.

5 Results & Analysis

In this section, we present qualitative and quantitative performance of the MINT algorithm, in mining NETEs from comparable news corpora. All the results in Sections 5.1 to 5.3 were obtained using the discriminative transliteration similarity model described in Section 3.2. The results using the generative transliteration similarity model are discussed in Section 5.4.

5.1 IDEAL Environment

Our first set of experiments investigated the effectiveness of Stage 2 of MINT, namely the mining of NETEs in an IDEAL environment. As MINT is provided with paired articles in this experiment, all experiments for this environment were run on test beds created from group S corpora (Table 2).

Test Bed	Comparable Corpora	Article Pairs	Distinct NEs	Distinct NETEs
EK-ST	EK-S	200	481	710
ET-ST	ET-S	200	449	672
EH-ST	EH-S	200	347	373
ER-ST	ER-S	100	195	347

Table 2: Test Beds for IDEAL & NEAR-IDEAL

Results in the IDEAL Environment:

The recall measures for distinct NEs and distinct NETEs for the IDEAL environment are reported in Table 3.

Test Bed	Recall (%)	
	Distinct NEs	Distinct NETEs
EK-ST	97.30	95.07
ET-ST	99.11	98.06
EH-ST	98.55	98.66
ER-ST	93.33	85.88

Table 3: Recall of MINT in IDEAL

Note that in the first 3 language pairs MINT was able to mine a transliteration equivalent for almost all the distinct NEs. The performance in English-Russian pair was relatively worse, perhaps due to the noisy training data.

In order to compare the effectiveness of MINT with a state-of-the-art NETE mining approach, we implemented the time series based Co-Ranking algorithm based on (Klementiev and Roth, 2006).

Test Bed	MRR@1		MRR@5	
	MINT	CoRanking	MINT	CoRanking
EK-ST	**0.94**	0.26	**0.95**	0.29
ET-ST	**0.91**	0.26	**0.94**	0.29
EH-ST	0.93	-	0.95	-
ER-ST	**0.80**	0.38	**0.85**	0.43

Table 4: MINT & Co-Ranking in IDEAL

Table 4 shows the MRR results in the IDEAL environment – both for MINT and the Co-Ranking baseline: MINT outperformed Co-Ranking on all the language pairs, despite not using time series similarity in the mining process. The high MRRs (@1 and @5) indicate that in almost all the cases, the top-ranked candidate is a correct NETE. Note that Co-Ranking could not be run on the EH-ST test bed as the articles did not have a date stamp. Co-Ranking is crucially dependent on time series and hence requires date stamps for the articles.

5.2 NEAR-IDEAL Environment

The second set of experiments investigated the effectiveness of Stage 1 of MINT on comparable corpora that are constituted by pairs of similar articles, where the pairing information between the articles is with-held. MINT reconstructed the pairings using the cross-language document similarity model and subsequently mined NETEs. As in previous experiments, we ran our experiments on test beds described in Section 4.4.

Results in the NEAR-IDEAL Environment: There are two parts to this set of experiments. In the first part, we investigated the effectiveness of the cross-language document similarity model described in Section 3.1. Since we know the identity of the conjugate article for every article in the test bed, and articles can be ranked according to the cross-language document similarity score, we simply computed the MRR for the documents identified in each of the test beds, considering only the top-2 results. Further, where available, we made use of the publication date of articles to restrict the number of target articles that are considered in lines 4 and 5 of the MINT algorithm in Figure 2. Table 5 shows the results for two date windows – 3 days and 1 year.

Test Bed	MRR@1		MRR@2	
	3 days	1 year	3 days	1 year
EK-ST	**0.99**	0.91	**0.99**	0.93
ET-ST	**0.96**	0.83	**0.97**	0.87
EH-ST	-	0.81	-	0.82

Table 5: MRR of Stage 1 in NEAR-IDEAL

Subsequently, the output of the Stage 1 was given as the input to the Stage 2 of the MINT method. In Table 6 we report the MRR @1 and @5 for the second stage, for both time windows (3 days & 1 year).

Test Bed	MRR@1		MRR@5	
	3 days	1 year	3 days	1 year
EK-ST	**0.92**	0.87	**0.94**	0.90
ET-ST	**0.88**	0.74	**0.91**	0.78
EH-ST	-	0.82	-	0.87

Table 6: MRR of Stage 2 in NEAR-IDEAL

It is interesting to compare the results of MINT in NEAR-IDEAL data environment (Table 6) with MINT's results in IDEAL environment (Table 4). The drop in MRR@1 is small: ~2% for EK-ST and ~3% for ET-ST. For EH-ST the drop is relatively more (~12%) as may be expected since the time window (3 days) could not be applied for this test bed.

5.3 REAL Environment

The third set of experiments investigated the effectiveness of MINT on large comparable corpora. We ran the experiments on test beds created from group L corpora.

Test-beds for the REAL Environment: The test beds for the REAL environment (Table 7) consisted of only English articles since we do not know in advance whether these articles have any similar articles in the target languages.

Test Bed	Comparable Corpora	Articles	Distinct NEs
EK-LT	EK-L	100	306
ET-LT	ET-L	100	228

Table 7: Test Beds for REAL

Results in the REAL Environment: In real environment, we examined the top 2 articles of returned by Stage 1 of MINT, and mined NETEs from them. We used a date window of 3 in Stage 1. Table 8 summarizes the results for the REAL environment.

Test Bed	MRR	
	@1	@5
EK-LT	0.86	0.88
ET-LT	0.82	0.85

Table 8: MRR of Stage 2 in REAL

We observe that the performance of MINT is impressive, considering the fact that the comparable corpora used in the REAL environment is two orders of magnitude larger than those used in IDEAL and NEAR-IDEAL environments. This implies that MINT is able to effectively mine NETEs whenever the Stage 1 algorithm was able to find a good conjugate for each of the source language articles.

5.4 Generative Transliteration Similarity Model

We employed the extended W-HMM transliteration similarity model in MINT and used it in the IDEAL data environment. Table 9 shows the results.

Test Bed	MRR	
	@1	@5
EK-S	0.85	0.86
ET-S	0.81	0.82
EH-S	0.91	0.93

Table 9: MRR of Stage 2 in IDEAL using generative transliteration similarity model

We see that the results for the generative transliteration similarity model are good but not as good as those for the discriminative transliteration similarity model. As we did not stem either the English NEs or the target language words, the generative model made more mistakes on inflected words compared to the discriminative model.

5.5 Examples of Mined NETEs

Table 10 gives some examples of the NETEs mined from the comparable news corpora.

Language Pair	Source NE	Transliteration
English-Kannada	Woolmer	ವೂಲ್ಮರ್
	Kafeel	ಕಫೀಲ್
	Baghdad	ಬಾಗ್ದಾದ್
English-Tamil	Lloyd	லாயிட்
	Mumbai	மும்பையில்
	Manchester	மான்செஸ்டர்
English-Hindi	Vanhanen	वैनहैनन
	Trinidad	त्रिनिदाद
	Ibuprofen	इबूप्रोफेन
English-Russian	Kreuzberg	Крейцберге
	Gaddafi	Каддафи
	Karadzic	Караджич

Table 10: Examples of Mined NETEs

6 Related Work

CLIR systems have been studied in several works (Ballesteros and Croft, 1998; Kraiij et al, 2003). The limited coverage of dictionaries has been recognized as a problem in CLIR and MT (Demner-Fushman & Oard, 2002; Mandl & Womser-hacker, 2005; Xu &Weischedel, 2005).

In order to address this problem, different kinds of approaches have been taken, from learning transformation rules from dictionaries and applying the rules to find cross-lingual spelling variants (Pirkola et al., 2003), to learning translation lexicon from monolingual and/or comparable corpora (Fung, 1995; Al-Onaizan and Knight, 2002; Koehn and Knight, 2002; Rapp, 1996). While these works have focused on finding translation equivalents of all class of words, we focus specifically on transliteration equivalents of NEs. (Munteanu and Marcu, 2006; Quirk et al., 2007) addresses mining of parallel sentences and fragments from nearly parallel sentences. In contrast, our approach mines NETEs from article pairs that may not even have any parallel or nearly parallel sentences.

NETE discovery from comparable corpora using time series and transliteration model was proposed in (Klementiev and Roth, 2006), and extended for NETE mining for several languages in (Saravanan and Kumaran, 2007). However, such methods miss vast majority of the NETEs due to their dependency on frequency signatures. In addition, (Klementiev and Roth, 2006) may not scale for large corpora, as they examine every word in the target side as a potential transliteration equivalent. NETE mining from comparable corpora using phonetic mappings was proposed in (Tao et al., 2006), but the need for language specific knowledge restricts its applicability across languages. We proposed the idea of mining NETEs from multilingual articles with similar content in (Udupa, et al., 2008). In this work, we extend the approach and provide a detailed description of the empirical studies.

7 Conclusion

In this paper, we showed that MINT, a simple and intuitive technique employing cross-language document similarity and transliteration similarity models, is capable of mining NETEs effectively from large comparable news corpora. Our three stage empirical investigation showed that MINT performed close to optimal on comparable corpora consisting of pairs of similar articles when the pairings are known in advance. MINT induced fairly good pairings and performs exceedingly well even when the pairings are not known in advance. Further, MINT outperformed a state-of-the-art baseline and scaled to large comparable corpora. Finally, we demonstrated the language neutrality of MINT, by mining NETEs from 4 language pairs (between English and one of Russian, Hindi, Kannada or Tamil) from 3 vastly different linguistic families.

As a future work, we plan to use the extended W-HMM model to get features for the discriminative transliteration similarity model. We also want to use a combination of the cross-language document similarity score and the transliteration similarity score for scoring the NETEs. Finally, we would like to use the mined NETEs to improve the performance of the first stage of MINT.

Acknowledgments

We thank Abhijit Bhole for his help and Chris Quirk for valuable comments.

References

AbdulJaleel, N. and Larkey, L.S. 2003. Statistical transliteration for English-Arabic cross language information retrieval. *Proceedings of CIKM 2003.*

Al-Onaizan, Y. and Knight, K. 2002. Translating named entities using monolingual and bilingual resources. *Proceedings of the 40th Annual Meeting of ACL.*

Ballesteros, L. and Croft, B. 1998. Dictionary Methods for Cross-Lingual Information Retrieval. *Proceedings of DEXA'96.*

Chen, H., et al. 1998. Proper Name Translation in Cross-Language Information Retrieval. *Proceedings of the 36th Annual Meeting of the ACL.*

Demner-Fushman, D., and Oard, D. W. 2002. The effect of bilingual term list size on dictionary-based cross-language information retrieval. *Proceedings of the 36th Hawaii International Conference on System Sciences.*

Finkel, J. Trond Grenager, and Christopher Manning. 2005. Incorporating Non-local Information into Information Extraction Systems by Gibbs Sampling. *Proceedings of the 43nd Annual Meeting of the ACL.*

Fung, P. 1995. Compiling bilingual lexicon entries from a non-parallel English-Chinese corpus. *Proceedings of the 3rd Workshop on Very Large Corpora.*

Fung, P. 1995. A pattern matching method for finding noun and proper noun translations from noisy parallel corpora. *Proceedings of ACL 1995.*

He. X. 2007: Using word dependent transition models in HMM based word alignment for statistical machine translation. In *Proceedings of 2nd ACL Workshop on Statistical Machine Translation* .

Hermjakob, U., Knight, K., and Daume, H. 2008. Name translation in statistical machine translation: knowing when to transliterate. *Proceedings ACL 2008.*

Klementiev, A. and Roth, D. 2006. Weakly supervised named entity transliteration and discovery from multilingual comparable corpora. *Proceedings of the 44th Annual Meeting of the ACL.*

Knight, K. and Graehl, J. 1998. Machine Transliteration. *Computational Linguistics.*

Koehn, P. and Knight, K. 2002. Learning a translation lexicon from monolingual corpora. *Proceedings of Unsupervised Lexical Acquisition.*

Kraiij, W., Nie, J-Y. and Simard, M. 2003. Emebdding Web-based Statistical Translation Models in Cross-Language Information Retrieval. *Computational Linguistics.*, 29(3):381-419.

Mandl, T., and Womser-Hacker, C. 2004. How do named entities contribute to retrieval effectiveness? *Proceedings of the 2004 Cross Language Evaluation Forum Campaign 2004.*

Mandl, T., and Womser-Hacker, C. 2005. The Effect of named entities on effectiveness in cross-language information retrieval evaluation. *ACM Symposium on Applied Computing.*

Munteanu, D. and Marcu D. 2006. Extracting parallel sub-sentential fragments from non-parallel corpora. *Proceedings of the ACL 2006.*

Och, F. and Ney, H. 2003. A systematic comparison of various statistical alignment models. *Computational Linguistics.*

Pirkola, A., Toivonen, J., Keskustalo, H., Visala, K. and Jarvelin, K. 2003. Fuzzy translation of cross-lingual spelling variants. *Proceedings of SIGIR 2003.*

Ponte, J. M. and Croft, B. 1998. A Language Modeling Approach to Information Retrieval. *Proceedings of ACM SIGIR 1998.*

Quirk, C., Udupa, R. and Menezes, A. 2007. Generative models of noisy translations with applications to parallel fragments extraction. *Proceedings of the 11th MT Summit.*

Rapp, R. 1996. Automatic identification of word translations from unrelated English and German corpora. *Proceedings of ACL'99*

Saravanan, K. and Kumaran, A. 2007. Some experiments in mining named entity transliteration pairs from comparable corpora. *Proceedings of the 2nd International Workshop on Cross Lingual Information Access.*

Tao, T., Yoon, S., Fister, A., Sproat, R. and Zhai, C. 2006. Unsupervised named entity transliteration using temporal and phonetic correlation. *Proceedings of EMNLP 2006.*

Udupa, R., Saravanan, K., Kumaran, A. and Jagarlamudi, J. 2008. Mining Named Entity Transliteration Equivalents from Comparable Corpora. *Proceedings of the CIKM 2008.*

Udupa, R., Saravanan, K., Bakalov, A. and Bhole, A. 2009. *"They are out there if you know where to look"*: Mining transliterations of OOV terms in cross-language information retrieval. *Proceedings of the ECIR 2009.*

Virga, P. and Khudanpur, S. 2003. Transliteration of proper names in cross-lingual information retrieval. *Proceedings of the ACL Workshop on Multilingual and Mixed Language Named Entity Recognition.*

Xu, J. and Weischedel, R. 2005. Empirical studies on the impact of lexical resources on CLIR performance. *Information Processing and Management.*

Deriving Generalized Knowledge from Corpora using WordNet Abstraction

Benjamin Van Durme, **Phillip Michalak** and **Lenhart K. Schubert**
Department of Computer Science
University of Rochester
Rochester, NY 14627, USA

Abstract

Existing work in the extraction of commonsense knowledge from text has been primarily restricted to factoids that serve as statements about what *may possibly* obtain in the world. We present an approach to deriving stronger, more general claims by abstracting over large sets of factoids. Our goal is to coalesce the observed nominals for a given predicate argument into a few predominant types, obtained as WordNet synsets. The results can be construed as generically quantified sentences restricting the semantic type of an argument position of a predicate.

1 Introduction

Our interest is ultimately in building systems with commonsense reasoning and language understanding abilities. As is widely appreciated, such systems will require large amounts of general world knowledge. Large text corpora are an attractive potential source of such knowledge. However, current natural language understanding (NLU) methods are not general and reliable enough to enable broad assimilation, in a formalized representation, of explicitly stated knowledge in encyclopedias or similar sources. As well, such sources typically do not cover the most obvious facts of the world, such as that ice cream may be delicious and may be coated with chocolate, or that children may play in parks.

Methods currently exist for extracting simple "factoids" like those about ice cream and children just mentioned (see in particular (Schubert, 2002; Schubert and Tong, 2003)), but these are quite weak as general claims, and – being unconditional – are unsuitable for inference chaining. Consider however the fact that when something is said, it is generally said by a person, organization or text source; this a conditional statement dealing with the potential agents of *saying*, and could enable useful inferences. For example, in the sentence, "*The tires were worn and they said I had to replace them*", *they* might be mistakenly identified with *the tires*, without the knowledge that *saying* is something done primarily by persons, organizations or text sources. Similarly, looking into the future one can imagine telling a household robot, "*The cat needs to drink something*", with the expectation that the robot will take into account that if a cat drinks something, it is usually water or milk (whereas people would often have broader options).

The work reported here is aimed at deriving generalizations of the latter sort from large sets of weaker propositions, by examining the hierarchical relations among sets of types that occur in the argument positions of verbal or other predicates. The generalizations we are aiming at are certainly not the only kinds derivable from text corpora (as the extensive literature on finding *isa*-relations, partonomic relations, paraphrase relations, etc. attests), but as just indicated they do seem potentially useful. Also, thanks to their grounding in factoids obtained by open knowledge extraction from large corpora, the propositions obtained are very broad in scope, unlike knowledge extracted in a more targeted way.

In the following we first briefly review the method developed by Schubert and collaborators to abstract factoids from text; we then outline our approach to obtaining strengthened propositions from such sets of factoids. We report positive results, while making only limited use of standard

Proceedings of the 12th Conference of the European Chapter of the ACL, pages 808–816,
Athens, Greece, 30 March – 3 April 2009. ©2009 Association for Computational Linguistics

corpus statistics, concluding that future endeavors exploring knowledge extraction and WordNet should go beyond the heuristics employed in recent work.

2 KNEXT

Schubert (2002) presented an approach to acquiring general world knowledge from text corpora based on parsing sentences and mapping syntactic forms into logical forms (LFs), then gleaning simple propositional factoids from these LFs through abstraction. Logical forms were based on Episodic Logic (Schubert and Hwang, 2000), a formalism designed to accommodate in a straightforward way the semantic phenomena observed in all languages, such as predication, logical compounding, generalized quantification, modification and reification of predicates and propositions, and event reference. An example from Schubert and Tong (2003) of factoids obtained from a sentence in the Brown corpus by their KNEXT system is the following:

Rilly or Glendora had entered her room while she slept, bringing back her washed clothes.

```
A NAMED-ENTITY MAY ENTER A ROOM.
A FEMALE-INDIVIDUAL MAY HAVE A ROOM.
A FEMALE-INDIVIDUAL MAY SLEEP.
A FEMALE-INDIVIDUAL MAY HAVE CLOTHES.
CLOTHES CAN BE WASHED.

((:I (:Q DET NAMED-ENTITY) ENTER[V]
              (:Q THE ROOM[N]))
 (:I (:Q DET FEMALE-INDIVIDUAL) HAVE[V]
              (:Q DET ROOM[N]))
 (:I (:Q DET FEMALE-INDIVIDUAL) SLEEP[V])
 (:I (:Q DET FEMALE-INDIVIDUAL) HAVE[V]
              (:Q DET (:F PLUR CLOTHE[N])))
 (:I (:Q DET (:F PLUR CLOTHE[N])) WASHED[A]))
```

Here the upper-case sentences are automatically generated verbalizations of the abstracted LFs shown beneath them.[1]

The initial development of KNEXT was based on the hand-constructed parse trees in the Penn Treebank version of the Brown corpus, but subsequently Schubert and collaborators refined and extended the system to work with parse trees obtained with statistical parsers (e.g., that of Collins (1997) or Charniak (2000)) applied to larger corpora, such as the British National Corpus (BNC), a 100 million-word, mixed genre collection, along with Web corpora of comparable size (see work of Van Durme et al. (2008) and Van Durme and Schubert (2008) for details). The BNC yielded over 2 factoids per sentence on average, resulting in a total collection of several million. Human judging of the factoids indicates that about 2 out of 3 factoids are perceived as reasonable claims.

The goal in this work, with respect to the example given, would be to derive with the use of a large collection of KNEXT outputs, a general statement such as *If something may sleep, it is probably either an animal or a person.*

3 Resources

3.1 WordNet and Senses

While the community continues to make gains in the automatic construction of reliable, general ontologies, the WordNet sense hierarchy (Fellbaum, 1998) continues to be the resource of choice for many computational linguists requiring an ontology-like structure. In the work discussed here we explore the potential of WordNet as an underlying concept hierarchy on which to base generalization decisions.

The use of WordNet raises the challenge of dealing with multiple semantic concepts associated with the same word, i.e., employing WordNet requires *word sense disambiguation* in order to associate terms observed in text with concepts (*synsets*) within the hierarchy.

In their work on determining selectional preferences, both Resnik (1997) and Li and Abe (1998) relied on uniformly distributing observed frequencies for a given word across all its senses, an approach later followed by Pantel et al. (2007).[2] Others within the knowledge acquisition community have favored taking the first, most dominant sense of each word (e.g., see Suchanek et al. (2007) and Paşca (2008)).

As will be seen, our algorithm does not select word senses prior to generalizing them, but rather as a byproduct of the abstraction process. Moreover, it potentially selects multiple senses of a word deemed equally appropriate in a given context, and in that sense provides *coarse-grained* disambiguation. This also prevents exaggeration of the contribution of a term to the abstraction, as a result of being lexicalized in a particularly fine-grained way.

3.2 Propositional Templates

While the procedure given here is not tied to a particular formalism in representing semantic con-

[1] Keywords like `:i`, `:q`, and `:f` are used to indicate infix predication, unscoped quantification, and function application, but these details need not concern us here.

[2] Personal communication

text, in our experiments we make use of *propositional templates*, based on the verbalizations arising from KNEXT logical forms. Specifically, a proposition F with m argument positions generates m templates, each with one of the arguments replaced by an empty *slot*. Hence, the statement, A MAN MAY GIVE A SPEECH, gives rise to two templates, A MAN MAY GIVE A __, and A __ MAY GIVE A SPEECH. Such templates match statements with identical structure except at the template's slots. Thus, the factoid A POLITICIAN MAY GIVE A SPEECH would match the second template. The slot-fillers from matching factoids (e.g., MAN and POLITICIAN form the input lemmas to our abstraction algorithm described below.

Additional templates are generated by further weakening predicate argument restrictions. Nouns in a template that have not been replaced by a free slot can be replaced with an *wild-card*, indicating that anything may fill its position. While slots accumulate their arguments, these do not, serving simply as relaxed interpretive constraints on the original proposition. For the running example we would have; A __ MAY GIVE A ?, and, A ? MAY GIVE A __, yielding observation sets pertaining to things that may give, and things that may be given.[3]

We have not restricted our focus to two-argument verbal predicates; examples such as A PERSON CAN BE HAPPY WITH A __, and, A __ CAN BE MAGICAL, can be seen in Section 5.

4 Deriving Types

Our method for type derivation assumes access to a word sense taxonomy, providing:

$\mathcal{W}$: set of words, potentially multi-token
$\mathcal{N}$: set of nodes, e.g., word senses, or *synsets*
$\mathcal{P} : \mathcal{N} \rightarrow \{\mathcal{N}^*\}$: parent function
$\mathcal{S} : \mathcal{W} \rightarrow (\mathcal{N}^+)$: sense function
$\mathcal{L} : \mathcal{N} \times \mathcal{N} \rightarrow \mathbb{Q}^{\geq 0}$: path length function

$\mathcal{L}$ is a distance function based on $\mathcal{P}$ that gives the length of the shortest path from a node to a dominating node, with base case: $\mathcal{L}(n, n) = 1$. When appropriate, we write $\mathcal{L}(w, n)$ to stand for the arithmetic mean over $\mathcal{L}(n', n)$ for all senses n'

[3]It is these most general templates that best correlate with existing work in verb argument preference selection; however, a given KNEXT logical form may arise from multiple distinct syntactic constructs.

function SCORE ($n \in \mathcal{N}, \alpha \in \mathbb{R}^+, C \subseteq W \subseteq \mathcal{W}$) :
  $C' \leftarrow \mathcal{D}(n) \setminus C$
  return $\frac{\sum_{w \in C'} \mathcal{L}(w,n)}{|C'|^\alpha}$

function DERIVETYPES ($W \subseteq \mathcal{W}, m \in \mathbb{N}^+, p \in (0, 1]$) :
  $\alpha \leftarrow 1, C \leftarrow \{\}, R \leftarrow \{\}$
  ▷ *while too few words covered*
  while $|C| < p \times |W|$:
    $n' \leftarrow \operatorname{argmin}_{n \in \mathcal{N} \setminus R} \text{SCORE}(n, \alpha, C)$
    $R \leftarrow R \cup \{n'\}$
    $C \leftarrow C \cup \mathcal{D}(n')$
    if $|R| > m$:
      ▷ *cardinality bound exceeded – restart*
      $\alpha \leftarrow \alpha + \delta, C \leftarrow \{\}, R \leftarrow \{\}$
  return R

Figure 1: Algorithm for deriving slot type restrictions, with δ representing a fixed step size.

of w that are dominated by n.[4] In the definition of $\mathcal{S}$, $(\mathcal{N}^+)$ stands for an ordered list of nodes.

We refer to a given predicate argument position for a specified propositional template simply as a *slot*. $W \subseteq \mathcal{W}$ will stand for the set of words found to occupy a given slot (in the corpus employed), and $\mathcal{D} : \mathcal{N} \rightarrow W^*$ is a function mapping a node to the words it (partially) *sense dominates*. That is, for all $n \in \mathcal{N}$ and $w \in W$, if $w \in \mathcal{D}(n)$ then there is at least one sense $n' \in \mathcal{S}(w)$ such that n is an ancestor of n' as determined through use of $\mathcal{P}$. For example, we would expect the word *bank* to be dominated by a node standing for a class such as *company* as well as a separate node standing for, e.g., *location*.

Based on this model we give a greedy search algorithm in Figure 1 for deriving slot type restrictions. The algorithm attempts to find a set of dominating word senses that cover at least one of each of a majority of the words in the given set of observations. The idea is to keep the number of nodes in the dominating set small, while maintaining high coverage and not abstracting too far upward.

For a given slot we start with a set of observed words W, an upper bound m on the number of types allowed in the result R, and a parameter p setting a lower bound on the fraction of items in W that a valid solution must dominate. For example, when $m = 3$ and $p = 0.9$, this says we require the solution to consist of no more than 3 nodes, which together must dominate at least 90% of W.

The search begins with initializing the cover set C, and the result set R as empty, with the variable

[4]E.g., both senses of *female* in WN are dominated by the node for *(organism, being)*, but have different path lengths.

α set to 1. Observe that at any point in the execution of DERIVETYPES, C represents the set of all words from W with at least one sense having as an ancestor a node in R. While C continues to be smaller than the percentage required for a solution, nodes are added to R based on whichever element of $\mathcal{N}$ has the smallest score.

The SCORE function first computes the modified coverage of n, setting C' to be all words in W that are dominated by n that haven't yet been "spoken for" by a previously selected (and thus lower scoring) node. SCORE returns the sum of the path lengths between the elements of the modified set of dominated nodes and n, divided by that set's size, scaled by the exponent α. Note when $\alpha = 1$, SCORE simply returns the average path length of the words dominated by n.

If the size of the result grows beyond the specified threshold, R and C are reset, α is incremented by some step size δ, and the search starts again. As α grows, the function increasingly favors the coverage of a node over the summed path length. Each iteration of DERIVETYPES thus represents a further relaxation of the desire to have the returned nodes be as specific as possible. Eventually, α will be such that the minimum scoring nodes will be found high enough in the tree to cover enough of the observations to satisfy the threshold p, at which point R is returned.

4.1 Non-reliance on Frequency

As can be observed, our approach makes no use of the relative or absolute frequencies of the words in W, even though such frequencies could be added as, e.g., relative weights on length in SCORE. This is a purposeful decision motivated both by practical and theoretical concerns.

Practically, a large portion of the knowledge observed in KNEXT output is infrequently expressed, and yet many tend to be reasonable claims about the world (despite their textual rarity). For example, a template shown in Section 5, A _ MAY WEAR A CRASH_HELMET, was supported by just two sentences in the BNC. However, based on those two observations we were able to conclude that usually *If something wears a crash helmet, it is probably a male person.*

Initially our project began as an application of the closely related MDL approach of Li and Abe (1998), but was hindered by sparse data. We observed that our absolute frequencies were often too low to perform meaningful comparisons of relative frequency, and that different examples in development tended to call for different trade-offs between model cost and coverage. This was due as much to the sometimes idiosyncratic structure of WordNet as it was to lack of evidence.[5]

Theoretically, our goal is distinct from related efforts in acquiring, e.g., verb argument selectional preferences. That work is based on the desire to reproduce distributional statistics underlying the text, and thus relative differences in frequency are the essential characteristic. In this work we aim for general statements about the real world, which in order to gather we rely on text as a limited proxy view. E.g., given 40 hypothetical sentences supporting A MAN MAY EAT A TACO, and just 2 sentences supporting A WOMAN MAY EAT A TACO, we would like to conclude simply that A PERSON MAY EAT A TACO, remaining agnostic as to relative frequency, as we've no reason to view corpus-derived counts as (strongly) tied to the likelihood of corresponding situations in the world; they simply tell us what is generally possible and worth mentioning.

5 Experiments

5.1 Tuning to WordNet

Our method as described thus far is not tied to a particular word sense taxonomy. Experiments reported here relied on the following model adjustments in order to make use of WordNet (version 3.0).

The function $\mathcal{P}$ was set to return the union of a synset's hypernym and instance hypernym relations.

Regarding the function $\mathcal{L}$, WordNet is constructed such that always picking the first sense of a given nominal tends to be correct more often than not (see discussion by McCarthy et al. (2004)). To exploit this structural bias, we employed a modified version of $\mathcal{L}$ that results in a preference for nodes corresponding to the first sense of words to be covered, especially when the number of distinct observations were low (such as earlier, with *crash helmet*):

$$\mathcal{L}(n,n) = \begin{cases} 1 - \frac{1}{|W|} & \exists w \in W : \mathcal{S}(w) = (n, ...) \\ 1 & \text{otherwise} \end{cases}$$

[5] For the given example, this method (along with the constraints of Table 1) led to the overly general type, *living thing*.

word	#	gloss
abstraction	6	a general concept formed by extracting common features from specific examples
attribute	2	an abstraction belonging to or characteristic of an entity
matter	3	that which has mass and occupies space
physical entity	1	an entity that has physical existence
whole	2	an assemblage of parts that is regarded as a single entity

Table 1: ⟨word, sense #⟩ pairs in WordNet 3.0 considered overly general for our purposes.

Propositional Template	Num.
A ___ CAN BE WHISKERED	4
GOVERNORS MAY HAVE ___ -S	4
A ___ CAN BE PREGNANT	28
A PERSON MAY BUY A ___	105
A ___ MAY BARK	6
A COMPANY MAY HAVE A ___	713
A ___ MAY SMOKE	8
A ___ CAN BE TASTY	33
A SONG MAY HAVE A ___	31
A ___ CAN BE SUCCESSFUL	664
___ CAN BE AT A ROAD	20
A ___ CAN BE MAGICAL	96
___ CAN BE FOR A DICTATOR	5
___ MAY FLOAT	5
GUIDELINES CAN BE FOR ___ -S	4
A ___ MAY WEAR A CRASH_HELMET	2
A ___ MAY CRASH	12

Table 2: Development templates, paired with the number of distinct words observed to appear in the given slot.

Note that when $|W| = 1$, then $\mathcal{L}$ returns 0 for the term's first sense, resulting in a score of 0 for that synset. This will be the unique minimum, leading DERIVETYPES to act as the first-sense heuristic when used with single observations.

Parameters were set for our data based on manual experimentation using the templates seen in Table 2. We found acceptable results when using a threshold of $p = 70\%$, and a step size of $\delta = 0.1$. The cardinality bound m was set to 4 when $|W| > 4$, and otherwise $m = 2$.

In addition, we found it desirable to add a few hard restrictions on the maximum level of generality. Nodes corresponding to the word sense pairs given in Table 1 were not allowed as abstraction candidates, nor their ancestors, implemented by giving infinite length to any path that crossed one of these synsets.

5.2 Observations during Development

Our method assumes that if multiple words occurring in the same slot can be subsumed under the same abstract class, then this information should be used to bias sense interpretation of these observed words, even when it means not picking the first sense. In general this bias is crucial to our approach, and tends to select correct senses of the words in an argument set W. But an example where this strategy errs was observed for the template A ___ MAY BARK, which yielded the generalization that *If something barks, then it is probably a person.* This was because there were numerous textual occurrences of various types of people "barking" (speaking loudly and aggressively), and so the occurrences of *dogs* barking, which showed no type variability, were interpreted as involving the unusual sense of *dog* as a slur applied to certain people.

The template, A ___ CAN BE WHISKERED, had observations including both *face* and *head*. This prompted experiments in allowing *part holonym* relations (e.g., a face is part of a head) as part of the definition of $\mathcal{P}$, with the final decision being that such relations lead to less intuitive generalizations rather than more, and thus these relation types were not included. The remaining relation types within WordNet were individually examined via inspection of randomly selected examples from the hierarchy. As with holonyms we decided that using any of these additional relation types would degrade performance.

A shortcoming was noted in WordNet, regarding its ability to represent binary valued attributes, based on the template, A ___ CAN BE PREGNANT. While we were able to successfully generalize to *female person*, there were a number of words observed which unexpectedly fell outside that associated synset. For example, a *queen* and a *duchess* may each be a *female aristocrat*, a *mum* may be a *female parent*,[6] and a *fiancee* has the exclusive interpretation as being synonymous with the gender entailing *bride-to-be*.

6 Experiments

From the entire set of BNC-derived KNEXT propositional templates, evaluations were performed on a set of 21 manually selected examples,

[6]Serving as a good example of distributional preferencing, the primary sense of *mum* is as a flower.

Propositional Template	Num.
A ___ MAY HAVE A BROTHER	28
A ? MAY ATTACK A ___	23
A FISH MAY HAVE A ___	38
A ___ CAN BE FAMOUS	665
A ? MAY ENTERTAIN A ___	8
A ___ MAY HAVE A CURRENCY	18
A MALE MAY BUILD A ___	42
A ___ CAN BE FAST-GROWING	15
A PERSON MAY WRITE A ___	47
A ? MAY WRITE A ___	99
A PERSON MAY TRY TO GET A ___	11
A ? MAY TRY TO GET A ___	17
A ___ MAY FALL_DOWN	5
A PERSON CAN BE HAPPY WITH A ___	36
A ? MAY OBSERVE A ___	38
A MESSAGE MAY UNDERGO A ___	14
A ? MAY WASH A ___	5
A PERSON MAY PAINT A ___	8
A ___ MAY FLY TO A ?	9
A ? MAY FLY TO A ___	4
A ___ CAN BE NERVOUS	131

Table 3: Templates chosen for evaluation.

together representing the sorts of knowledge for which we are most interested in deriving strengthened argument type restrictions. All modification of the system ceased prior to the selection of these templates, and the authors had no knowledge of the underlying words observed for any particular slot. Further, some of the templates were purposefully chosen as potentially problematic, such as, A ? MAY OBSERVE A ___, or A PERSON MAY PAINT A ___. Without additional context, templates such as these were expected to allow for exceptionally broad sorts of arguments.

For these 21 templates, 65 types were derived, giving an average of 3.1 types per slot, and allowing for statements such as seen in Table 4.

One way in which to measure the quality of an argument abstraction is to go back to the underlying observed words, and evaluate the resultant sense(s) implied by the chosen abstraction. We say senses plural, as the majority of KNEXT propositions select senses that are more coarse-grained than WordNet synsets. Thus, we wish to evaluate these more coarse-grained sense disambiguation results entailed by our type abstractions.[7] We performed this evaluation using as comparisons the first-sense, and all-senses heuristics.

The first-sense heuristic can be thought of as striving for maximal specificity at the risk of precluding some admissible senses (reduced recall), while the all-senses heuristic insists on including all admissible senses (perfect recall) at the risk of including inadmissible ones.

Table 5 gives the results of two judges evaluating 314 ⟨word, sense⟩ pairs across the 21 selected templates. These sense pairs correspond to picking one word at random for each abstracted type selected for each template slot. Judges were presented with a sampled word, the originating template, and the glosses for each possible word sense (see Figure 2). Judges did not know ahead of time the subset of senses selected by the system (as entailed by the derived type abstraction). Taking the judges' annotations as the gold standard, we report precision, recall and F-score with a β of 0.5 (favoring precision over recall, owing to our preference for *reliable* knowledge over *more*).

In all cases our method gives precision results comparable or superior to the first-sense heuristic, while at all times giving higher recall. In particular, for the case of Primary type, corresponding to the derived type that accounted for the largest number of observations for the given argument slot, our method shows strong performance across the board, suggesting that our derived abstractions are general enough to pick up multiple acceptable senses for observed words, but not so general as to allow unrelated senses.

We designed an additional test of our method's performance, aimed at determining whether the distinction between admissible senses and inadmissible ones entailed by our type abstractions were in accord with human judgement. To this end, we automatically chose for each template the observed word that had the greatest number of senses not dominated by a derived type

A ___ MAY HAVE A BROTHER

1 WOMAN : an adult female person (as opposed to a man); "the woman kept house while the man hunted"

2 WOMAN : a female person who plays a significant role (wife or mistress or girlfriend) in the life of a particular man; "he was faithful to his woman"

3 WOMAN : a human female employed to do housework; "the char will clean the carpet"; "I have a woman who comes in four hours a day while I write"

***4 WOMAN** : women as a class; "it's an insult to American womanhood"; "woman is the glory of creation"; "the fair sex gathered on the veranda"

Figure 2: Example of a context and senses provided for evaluation, with the fourth sense being judged as inappropriate.

[7]Allowing for multiple fine-grained senses to be judged as appropriate in a given context goes back at least to Sussna (1993); discussed more recently by, e.g., Navigli (2006).

If something is famous, it is probably a $person_1$, an $artifact_1$, or a $communication_2$
If ? writes something, it is probably a $communication_2$
If a person is happy with something, it is probably a $communication_2$, a $work_1$, a $final\_result_1$, or a $state\_of\_affairs_1$
If a fish has something, it is probably a $cognition_1$, a $torso_1$, an $interior_2$, or a $state_2$
If something is fast growing, it is probably a $group_1$ or a $business_3$
If a message undergoes something, it is probably a $message_2$, a $transmission_2$, a $happening_1$, or a $creation_1$
If a male builds something, it is probably a $structure_1$, a $business_3$, or a $group_1$

Table 4: Examples, both good and bad, of resultant statements able to be made post-derivation. Authors manually selected one word from each derived synset, with subscripts referring to sense number. Types are given in order of support, and thus the first are examples of "Primary" in Table 5.

Method	$\bigcup_j$ Prec	$\bigcup_j$ Recall	$\bigcup_j$ $F_{.5}$	$\bigcap_j$ Prec	$\bigcap_j$ Recall	$\bigcap_j$ $F_{.5}$	Type
derived	80.2	39.2	**66.4**	61.5	47.5	**58.1**	All
first	81.5	28.5	59.4	63.1	34.7	54.2	
all	59.2	100.0	64.5	37.6	100.0	42.9	
derived	90.0	50.0	**77.6**	73.3	71.0	**72.8**	Primary
first	85.7	33.3	65.2	66.7	45.2	60.9	
all	69.2	100.0	73.8	39.7	100.0	45.2	

Table 5: Precision, Recall and F-score ($\beta = 0.5$) for coarse grained WSD labels using the methods: derive from corpus data, first-sense heuristic and all-sense heuristic. Results are calculated against both the union $\bigcup_j$ and intersection $\bigcap_j$ of manual judgements, calculated for all derived argument types, as well as Primary derived types exclusively.

THE STATEMENT ABOVE IS A REASONABLY CLEAR, ENTIRELY PLAUSIBLE GENERAL CLAIM AND SEEMS NEITHER TOO SPECIFIC NOR TOO GENERAL OR VAGUE TO BE USEFUL:

1. I agree.
2. I lean towards agreement.
3. I'm not sure.
4. I lean towards disagreement.
5. I disagree.

Figure 3: Instructions for evaluating KNEXT propositions.

	judge 1	judge 2	corr
derived	1.76	2.10	0.60
alternative	3.63	3.54	0.58

Table 6: Average assessed quality for derived and alternative synsets, paired with Pearson correlation values.

restriction. For each of these alternative (non-dominated) senses, we selected the ancestor lying at the same distance towards the root from the given sense as the average distance from the dominated senses to the derived type restriction. In the case where going this far from an alternative sense towards the root would reach a path passing through the derived type and one of its subsumed senses, the distance was cut back until this was no longer the case.

These alternative senses, guaranteed to not be dominated by derived type restrictions, were then presented along with the derived type and the original template to two judges, who were given the same instructions as used by Van Durme and Schubert (2008), which can be found in Figure 3.

Results for this evaluation are found in Table 6, where we see that the automatically derived type restrictions are strongly favored over alternative abstracted types that were possible based on the given word. Achieving even stronger rejection of alternative types would be difficult, since KNEXT templates often provide insufficient context for full disambiguation of all their constituents, and judges were allowed to base their assessments on any interpretation of the verbalization that they could reasonably come up with.

7 Related Work

There is a wealth of existing research focused on learning probabilistic models for selectional restrictions on syntactic arguments. Resnik (1993) used a measure he referred to as *selectional preference strength*, based on the KL-divergence between the probability of a class and that class given a predicate, with variants explored by Ribas (1995). Li and Abe (1998) used a *tree cut* model over WordNet, based on the principle of *Minimum Description Length* (MDL). McCarthy has performed extensive work in the areas of selectional preference and WSD, e.g., (McCarthy, 1997; McCarthy, 2001). Calling the generalization problem a case of engineering in the face of sparse data, Clark and Weir (2002) looked at a number of previous methods, one conclusion being that the approach of Li and Abe appears to over-generalize.

Cao et al. (2008) gave a distributional method for deriving semantic restrictions for FrameNet frames, with the aim of building an Italian FrameNet. While our goals are related, their work can be summarized as taking a pre-existing gold standard, and extending it via distributional similarity measures based on shallow contexts (in this case, n-gram contexts up to length 5). We have presented results on strengthening type restrictions on arbitrary predicate argument structures derived directly from text.

In describing ALICE, a system for *lifelong learning*, Banko and Etzioni (2007) gave a summary of a proposition abstraction algorithm developed independently that is in some ways similar to DERIVETYPES. Beyond differences in node scoring and their use of the first sense heuristic, the approach taken here differs in that it makes no use of relative term frequency, nor contextual information outside a particular propositional template.[8] Further, while we are concerned with general knowledge acquired over diverse texts, ALICE was built as an agent meant for constructing domain-specific theories, evaluated on a 2.5-million-page collection of Web documents pertaining specifically to nutrition.

Minimizing word sense ambiguity by focusing on a specific domain was later seen in the work of Liakata and Pulman (2008), who performed hierarchical clustering using output from their KNEXT-like system first described in (Liakata and Pulman, 2002). Terminal nodes of the resultant structure were used as the basis for inferring semantic type restrictions, reminiscent of the use of CBC clusters (Pantel and Lin, 2002) by Pantel et al. (2007), for typing the arguments of paraphrase rules.

Assigning pre-compiled instances to their first-sense reading in WordNet, Paşca (2008) then generalized *class attributes* extracted for these terms, using as a resource Google search engine query logs.

Katrenko and Adriaans (2008) explored a constrained version of the task considered here. Using manually annotated semantic relation data from SemEval-2007, pre-tagged with correct argument senses, the authors chose the least common subsumer for each argument of each relation considered. Our approach keeps with the intuition of preferring specific over general concepts in WordNet, but allows for the handling of relations automatically discovered, whose arguments are not pre-tagged for sense and tend to be more wide-ranging. We note that the least common subsumer for many of our predicate arguments would in most cases be far too abstract.

8 Conclusion

As the volume of automatically acquired knowledge grows, it becomes more feasible to abstract from existential statements to stronger, more general claims on what usually obtains in the real world. Using a method motivated by that used in deriving selectional preferences for verb arguments, we've shown progress in deriving semantic type restrictions for arbitrary predicate argument positions, with no prior knowledge of sense information, and with no training data other than a handful of examples used to tune a few simple parameters.

In this work we have made no use of relative term counts, nor corpus-wide, distributional frequencies. Despite foregoing these often-used statistics, our methods outperform abstraction based on a strict first-sense heuristic, employed in many related studies.

Future work may include a return to the MDL approach of Li and Abe (1998), but using a frequency model that "corrects" for the biases in texts relative to world knowledge – for example, correcting for the preponderance of people as subjects of textual assertions, even for verbs like *bark, glow*, or *fall*, which we know to be applicable to numerous non-human entities.

Acknowledgements Our thanks to Matthew Post and Mary Swift for their assistance in evaluation, and Daniel Gildea for regular advice. This research was supported in part by NSF grants IIS-0328849 and IIS-0535105, as well as a University of Rochester Provost's Multidisciplinary Award (2008).

[8]Banko and Etzioni abstracted over subsets of pre-clustered terms, built using corpus-wide distributional frequencies

References

Michele Banko and Oren Etzioni. 2007. Strategies for Lifelong Knowledge Extraction from the Web. In *Proceedings of K-CAP*.

BNC Consortium. 2001. The British National Corpus, version 2 (BNC World). Distributed by Oxford University Computing Services.

Diego De Cao, Danilo Croce, Marco Pennacchiotti, and Roberto Basili. 2008. Combining Word Sense and Usage for Modeling Frame Semantics. In *Proceedings of Semantics in Text Processing (STEP)*.

Eugene Charniak. 2000. A Maximum-Entropy-Inspired Parser. In *Proceedings of NAACL*.

Stephen Clark and David Weir. 2002. Class-based probability estimation using a semantic hierarchy. *Computational Linguistics*, 28(2).

Michael Collins. 1997. Three Generative, Lexicalised Models for Statistical Parsing. In *Proceedings of ACL*.

Christiane Fellbaum. 1998. *WordNet: An Electronic Lexical Database*. MIT Press.

Sophia Katrenko and Pieter Adriaans. 2008. Semantic Types of Some Generic Relation Arguments: Detection and Evaluation. In *Proceedings of ACL-HLT*.

Hang Li and Naoki Abe. 1998. Generalizing case frames using a thesaurus and the MDL principle. *Computational Linguistics*, 24(2).

Maria Liakata and Stephen Pulman. 2002. From Trees to Predicate Argument Structures. In *Proceedings of COLING*.

Maria Liakata and Stephen Pulman. 2008. Automatic Fine-Grained Semantic Classification for Domain Adaption. In *Proceedings of Semantics in Text Processing (STEP)*.

Diana McCarthy, Rob Koeling, Julie Weeds, and John Carroll. 2004. Using automatically acquired predominant senses for Word Sense Disambiguation. In *Proceedings of Senseval-3: Third International Workshop on the Evaluation of Systems for the Semantic Analysis of Text*.

Diana McCarthy. 1997. Estimation of a probability distribution over a hierarchical classification. In *The Tenth White House Papers COGS - CSRP 440*.

Diana McCarthy. 2001. *Lexical Acquisition at the Syntax-Semantics Interface: Diathesis Alternations, Subcategorization Frames and Selectional Preferences*. Ph.D. thesis, University of Sussex.

Roberto Navigli. 2006. Meaningful Clustering of Senses Helps Boost Word Sense Disambiguation Performance. In *Proceedings of COLING-ACL*.

Marius Paşca. 2008. Turning Web Text and Search Queries into Factual Knowledge: Hierarchical Class Attribute Extraction. In *Proceedings of AAAI*.

Patrick Pantel and Dekang Lin. 2002. Discovering Word Senses from Text. In *Proceedings of KDD*.

Patrick Pantel, Rahul Bhagat, Bonaventura Coppola, Timothy Chklovski, and Eduard Hovy. 2007. ISP: Learning Inferential Selectional Preferences. In *Proceedings of NAACL-HLT*.

Philip Resnik. 1993. *Selection and Information: A Class-Based Approach to Lexical Relationships*. Ph.D. thesis, University of Pennsylvania.

Philip Resnik. 1997. Selectional preference and sense disambiguation. In *Proceedings of the ACL SIGLEX Workshop on Tagging Text with Lexical Semantics: Why, What, and How?*

Francesc Ribas. 1995. On learning more appropriate Selectional Restrictions. In *Proceedings of EACL*.

Lenhart K. Schubert and Chung Hee Hwang. 2000. Episodic Logic meets Little Red Riding Hood: A comprehensive, natural representation for language understanding. In L. Iwanska and S.C. Shapiro, editors, *Natural Language Processing and Knowledge Representation: Language for Knowledge and Knowledge for Language*. MIT/AAAI Press.

Lenhart K. Schubert and Matthew H. Tong. 2003. Extracting and evaluating general world knowledge from the brown corpus. In *Proceedings of HLT/NAACL Workshop on Text Meaning*, May 31.

Lenhart K. Schubert. 2002. Can we derive general world knowledge from texts? In *Proceedings of HLT*.

Fabian M. Suchanek, Gjergji Kasneci, and Gerhard Weikum. 2007. YAGO: A Core of Semantic Knowledge Unifying WordNet and Wikipedia. In *Proceedings of WWW*.

Michael Sussna. 1993. Word sense disambiguation for free-text indexing using a massive semantic network. In *Proceedings of CIKM*.

Benjamin Van Durme and Lenhart Schubert. 2008. Open Knowledge Extraction through Compositional Language Processing. In *Proceedings of Semantics in Text Processing (STEP)*.

Benjamin Van Durme, Ting Qian, and Lenhart Schubert. 2008. Class-driven Attribute Extraction. In *Proceedings of COLING*.

Learning Efficient Parsing

Gertjan van Noord
University of Groningen
G.J.M.van.noord@rug.nl

Abstract

A corpus-based technique is described to improve the efficiency of wide-coverage high-accuracy parsers. By keeping track of the derivation steps which lead to the best parse for a very large collection of sentences, the parser learns which parse steps can be filtered without significant loss in parsing accuracy, but with an important increase in parsing efficiency. An interesting characteristic of our approach is that it is self-learning, in the sense that it uses unannotated corpora.

1 Introduction

We consider wide-coverage high-accuracy parsing systems such as Alpino, a parser for Dutch which contains a grammar based on HPSG and a maximum entropy disambiguation component trained on a treebank. Even if such parsing systems now obtain satisfactory accuracy for a variety of text types, a drawback concerns the computational properties of such parsers: they typically require lots of memory and are often very slow for longer and very ambiguous sentences.

We present a very simple, fairly general, corpus-based method to improve upon the practical efficiency of such parsers. We use the accurate, slow, parser to parse many (unannotated) input sentences. For each sentence, we keep track of sequences of derivation steps that were required to find the *best* parse of that sentence (i.e., the parse that obtained the best score, highest probability, according to the parser itself).

Given a large set of successful derivation step sequences, we experimented with a variety of simple heuristics to filter unpromising derivation steps. A heuristic that works remarkably well simply states that for a new input sentence, the parser can only consider derivation step sequences in which any sub-sequence of length N has been observed at least once in the training data. Experimental results are provided for various heuristics and amounts of training data.

It is hard to compare fast, accurate, parsers with slow, slightly more accurate parsers. In section 3 we propose both an on-line and an off-line application scenario, introducing a time-out per sentence, which leads to metrics for choosing between parser variants.

In the experimental part we show that, in an on-line scenario, the most successful heuristic leads to a parser that is more accurate than the baseline system, except for unrealistic time-outs per sentence of more than 15 minutes. Furthermore, we show that, in an off-line scenario, the most successful heuristic leads to a parser that is more than four times faster than the base-line variant with the same accuracy.

2 Background: the Alpino parser for Dutch

The experiments are performed using the Alpino parser for Dutch. The Alpino system is a linguistically motivated, wide-coverage grammar and parser for Dutch in the tradition of HPSG. It consists of about 800 grammar rules and a large lexicon of over 300,000 lexemes and various rules to recognize special constructs such as named entities, temporal expressions, etc. Heuristics have been implemented to deal with unknown words and word sequences. Based on the categories assigned to words, and the set of grammar rules compiled from the HPSG grammar, a left-corner parser finds the set of all parses, and stores this set compactly in a packed parse forest. In order to select the best parse from the parse forest, a best-first search algorithm is applied. The algorithm consults a Maximum Entropy disambiguation model to judge the quality of (partial) parses.

Although Alpino is not a dependency grammar

Proceedings of the 12th Conference of the European Chapter of the ACL, pages 817–825,
Athens, Greece, 30 March – 3 April 2009. ©2009 Association for Computational Linguistics

in the traditional sense, dependency structures are generated by the lexicon and grammar rules as the value of a dedicated attribute. The dependency structures are based on CGN (Corpus Gesproken Nederlands, Corpus of Spoken Dutch) (Hoekstra et al., 2003), D-Coi and LASSY (van Noord et al., 2006).

3 Methodology: balancing efficiency and accuracy

3.1 On-line and off-line parsing scenarios

We focus on the speed of parsing, ignoring other computational properties such as memory usage. Problems with respect to parsing are twofold: on the one hand, parsing simply is too slow for many input sentences. On the other hand, the relation between input sentence and expected speed of parsing is typically unknown. For simple parsing systems based on finite-state, context-free or mildly context-sensitive grammars, it is possible to establish an upper-bound of required CPU-time based on the length of an input sentence. For the very powerful constraint-based formalisms considered here, such upper-bounds are not available. In practice, shorter sentences typically can be parsed fairly quickly, whereas longer sentences sometimes can take a very very long time indeed. As a consequence, measures such as number of words parsed per minute, or mean parsing time per sentence are somewhat meaningless. We therefore introduce two slightly different scenarios which include a time-out per sentence.

On-line scenario. In some applications, a parser is applied *on-line*: an actual user is waiting for the response of the system, and if the parser required minutes of CPU-time, the application would not be successful. In such a scenario, we assume that it is possible to determine a maximum amount of CPU-time (a time-out) per sentence, depending on other factors such as speed of the other system components, expected patience of users, etc. If the parser does not finish before the time-out, it is assumed to have not produced anything. In dependency parsing, the parser produces the empty set of dependencies in such cases, and hence such an event has an important negative effect on the accuracy of the system. By studying the relation between different time-outs and accuracy, it is possible to choose the most effective parser variant for a particular application.

Off-line scenario. For other applications, an off-line parsing scenario might be more appropriate. For instance, if we build a question answering system for a medical encyclopedia, and we wish to parse all sentences of that encyclopedia once and for all, then we are not interested in the amount of CPU-time the parser spends on a single sentence, but we want to know how much time it will cost to parse everything.

In such a scenario, it often still is very useful to set a time-out for each sentence, but in this case the time-out can be expected to be (much) higher than in the on-line scenario. In this scenario, we propose to study the relation between mean CPU-time and accuracy – for various settings of the time-out parameter. This allows us to determine, for instance, the mean CPU-time requirements for a given target accuracy level?

3.2 Accuracy: comparing sets of dependencies

Let D_p^i be the number of dependencies produced by the parser for sentence i, D_g^i is the number of dependencies in the treebank parse, and D_o^i is the number of correct dependencies produced by the parser. If no superscript is used, we aggregate over all sentences of the test set, i.e.,:

$$D_p = \sum_i D_p^i \quad D_o = \sum_i D_o^i \quad D_g = \sum_i D_g^i$$

We define precision ($P = D_o/D_p$), ($R = D_o/D_g$) and f-score: $2\mathrm{P} \cdot \mathrm{R}/(\mathrm{P}+\mathrm{R})$.

An alternative similarity score is based on the observation that for a given sentence of n words, a parser would be expected to return (about) n dependencies. In such cases, we can simply use the percentage of correct dependencies as a measure of accuracy. To allow for some discrepancies between the number of expected and returned dependencies, we divide by the maximum (per sentence) of both. This leads to the following definition of *named dependency accuracy*.

$$\text{Acc} = \frac{D_o}{\sum_i \max(D_g^i, D_p^i)}$$

If time-outs are introduced, the difference between f-score and accuracy becomes important. Consider the example in table 1. Here, the parser produces reasonable results for the first three, short, sentences, but for the final, long, sentence no result is produced because of a time-out.

i	D_o^i	D_p^i	D_g^i	prec	rec	f-sc	Acc
1	8	10	11	80	73	76	73
2	8	11	10	76	76	76	73
3	8	9	9	80	80	80	77
4	0	0	30	80	40	53	39

Table 1: Hypothetical result of parser on a test set of four sentences. The columns labeled precision, recall, f-score and accuracy represent aggregates over sentences $1 \ldots i$.

The precision, recall and f-score after the first three sentences is 80%. After the – much longer – fourth sentence, recall drops considerably, but precision remains the same. As a consequence, the f-score is quite a bit higher than 40%: it is over 53%. The accuracy score after three sentences is 77%. Including the fourth sentence leads to a drop in accuracy to 39%.

As this example illustrates, the f-score metric is less sensitive to parse failures than the accuracy score. Also, it appears that the accuracy score is a much better characterization of the success of this parser: after all, the parser only got 24 correct dependencies out of 60 expected dependencies. The f-score measure, on the other hand, can easily be misunderstood to suggest that the parser does a good job for more than 50%.

4 Learning Efficient Parsing

In this section a method is defined for filtering derivation step sequences, based on previous experience of the parser. In a training phase, the parser is fed with thousands of sentences. For each sentence it finds the best parse, and it stores the relevant sequences of derivation steps, that were required to find that best parse. After the training phase, the parser filters those sequences of derivation steps that are unlikely to be useful. By filtering out unlikely derivation step sequences, efficiency is expected to improve. Since certain parses now become impossible, a drop in accuracy is expected as well.

Although the idea of filtering derivation step sequences based on previous experience is fairly general, we define the method in more detail with respect to an actual parsing algorithm: the left-corner parser along the lines of Matsumoto et al. (1983), Pereira and Shieber (1987, section 6.5) and van Noord (1997).

4.1 Left-corner parsing

A left-corner parser is a bottom-up parser with top-down guidance, which is most easily explained as a non-deterministic search procedure. A specification of the left-corner algorithm can be provided in DCG as in figure 2 (Pereira and Shieber, 1987, section 6.5), where the `filter/2` goals should be ignored for the moment. Here, we assume that dictionary look-up is performed by the `word/3` predicate, with the first argument a given word, and the second argument its category; and that rules are accessible via the predicate `rule/3`, where the first argument represents the mother category, and the second argument is the possibly empty list of daughter categories. The third argument of both the `word/3` and `rule/3` predicates are identifiers we need later.

In order to analyze a given sentence as an instance of the top category, we look up the first word of the string, and show that this lexical category is a *left-corner* of the *goal category*. To show that a given category is a left-corner of a given *goal category*, a rule is selected. The left-most daughter node of that rule is identified with the left-corner. The other daughters of the rule are parsed recursively. If this succeeds, it remains to show that the mother node of the rule is a left-corner of the *goal category*. The recursion stops if a left-corner category can be identified with the goal category.

This simple algorithm is improved and extended in a variety of ways, as in Matsumoto et al. (1983) and van Noord (1997), to make it efficient and practical. The extensions include a memoization of the *parse/1* predicate and the construction of a shared parse forest (a compact representation of all parses).

4.2 Left-corner splines

For the left-corner parser, the derivation step sequences that are of interested are left-corner splines. Such a spline consists of a *goal category*, and the rules and lexical entries which were used in the left-corner, in the order from the top to the bottom.

A spline consists of a goal category, followed by a sequence of derivation step names. A derivation step name is typically a rule identifier, but it can also be a lexical type, indicating the lexical category of a word that is the left-corner. A special derivation step name is the reserved symbol

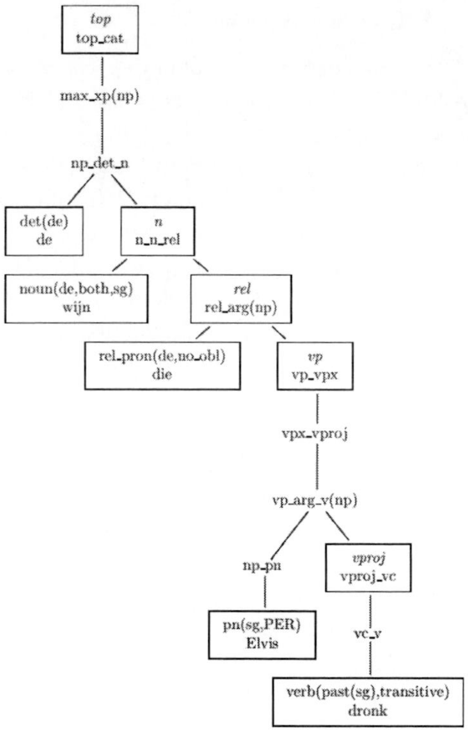


```
(top,[finish,top_cat,max_xp(np),np_det_n,det(de)]).
(n,[finish,n_n_rel,noun(de,both,sg)]).
(rel,[finish,rel_arg(np),rel_pron(de,no_obl)]).
(vp,[finish,vp_vpx,vpx_vproj,vp_arg_v(np),np_pn,pn(sg,PER),]).
(vproj,[finish,vproj_vc,vc_v,verb(past(sg),transitive)]).
```

Figure 1: Annotated derivation tree of the sentence *De wijn die Elvis dronk* (The wine which Elvis drank).

`finish` which is used to indicate that the current category is identified with the goal category (and no further rules are applied). A spline is written $(g, r_n \dots r_1)$ for goal category g and derivation step names $r_1 \dots r_n$. $(g, r_i \dots r_1)$ is a partial spline of $(g, r_n \dots r_i \dots r_1)$.

Consider the annotated derivation tree for the sentence *De wijn die Elvis dronk* (The wine which Elvis drank) in figure 1. Boxed leaf nodes contain the lexical category as well as the corresponding word. Boxed non-leaf nodes contain the goal category (italic) and the rule-name. Non-boxed non-leaf nodes only list the rule name. The first left-corner spline consists of the goal category `top` and the identifiers `finish`, `top_cat`, `max_xp(np)`, `np_det_n`, and the lexical type `det(de)`. All five left-corner splines of the example are listed at the bottom of figure 1.

Left-corner splines of best parses of a large set of sentences constitute the training data for the techniques we develop to learn to parse new sentences more efficiently.

```
parse(Phrase) -->
    leaf(SubPhrase,Id),
    { filter(Phrase,[Id]) },
    lc(SubPhrase,Phrase,[Id]).

leaf(Cat,Id) -->
    [Word], { word(Word,Cat,Id) }.
leaf(Cat,Id) --> { rule(Cat,[],Id) }.

lc(Phrase,Phrase,Spline) -->
    { filter(Phrase,[finish|Spline]) }.
lc(SubPhrase,SuperPhrase,Spline) -->
    rule(Phrase,[SubPhrase|Rest],Id),
    { filter(SuperPhrase,[Id|Spline]) },
    parse_rest(Rest),
    lc(Phrase,SuperPhrase,[Id|Spline]).
```

Figure 2: DCG Specification of a non-deterministic left-corner parser, including spline filtering.

4.3 Filtering left-corner splines

The left-corner parser builds left-corner splines one step at the time. For a given goal, it first selects a potential left-corner, and then continues applying rules from the bottom to the top until the left-corner is identified with the goal category. At every step where the algorithm attempts to extend a left-corner spline, we now introduce a filter. The purpose of this filter is to consider only those partial left-corner splines that look promising - based on the parser's previous experience on the training data. The specification of the left-corner parser given in figure 2 includes calls to this filter.

The purpose of the filter is, that at any time the parser considers extending a left-corner spline $(g, r_{i-1} \dots r_1)$ to $(g, r_i \dots r_1)$, such an extension only is allowed in promising cases. Obviously, there are many ways such a filter could be defined. We identify the following dimensions:

Context size. A filter for $(g, r_i \dots r_1)$ will typically ignore at least some of the derivation step names from the context. We experiment with filters which take into consideration g, r_i, r_{i-1} (*bigram filter*); g, r_i, r_{i-1}, r_{i-2} (*trigram filter*); and $g, r_i, r_{i-1}, r_{i-2}, r_{i-3}$ (*fourgram filter*). A further filter, labeled *prefix filter*, takes the full history into account: $g, r_i \dots r_1$. The prefix filter thus ensures that the parser only considers left-corner splines that are partial splines of splines observed in the training data.

Required evidence. For the various filters, what kind of evidence from the training data do we require in order for the filter to accept this particular derivation step? In initial experiments, we used relative frequencies. For instance, the trigram filter would allow any tuple g, r_{i-2}, r_{i-1}, r_i for some constant threshold τ, provided:

$$\frac{C(g, \dots r_i r_{i-1} r_{i-2} \dots)}{C(g, \dots r_{i-1} r_{i-2} \dots)} > \tau$$

However, we found that filters are more effective (and require much less space – see below), which simply require that every step has been observed often enough in the training data:

$$C(g, \dots r_i r_{i-1} r_{i-2} \dots) > \tau$$

In particular, the case where $\tau = 0$ gave surprisingly good results.

4.4 Comparison with link table

The filter we developed is reminiscent of the *link* predicate of (Pereira and Shieber, 1987). An important difference with the filter developed here is that the *link* predicate removes derivation steps which cannot lead to a successful parse (by an off-line global analysis of the grammar), whereas we filter out derivation steps which *can* lead to a full parse, but which are not expected to lead to a *best* parse. In our implementation, a variant of the *link* predicate is used as well.

4.5 Implementation detail

The definition of the filter predicate depends on our choices with respect to the dimensions identified above. For instance, if we chose the trigram filter as our context size, then the training data can be preprocessed in order to store all goal-trigram-pairs with frequency above the threshold τ. During parsing, if the filter is given the partial spline $(g, r_i r_{i-1} r_{i-2} \dots)$, then a simple table look-up for the tuple $(g, r_{i-2} r_{i-1} r_i)$ is sufficient (this suffices, because each of the preceding trigrams will have been checked earlier). In general, the filter predicate needs access to a table containing a pair of goal category and context, where the context consists of sequences of derivation step names. The table contains items for those pairs that occurred with frequency $> \tau$ in the training data.

To access such tables efficiently, an obvious choice is to use a hash table. The additional storage requirements for such a hash table are considerable. For instance, for the prefix filter four years of newspaper text lead to a table with 941,723 entries - stored as text the data takes 103Mb. To save space, we experimented with a set-up in which only the hash keys are stored, but the original information that the hash key was computed from, is removed. During parsing, in order to check that a given tuple is allowable, we compute its hash key, and check if the hash key is in the table. If so, the computation continues. The drawback of this method is, that in the case a hash collision would have occurred in an ordinary hash table, we now simply assume that the input tuple was in the table. In other words: the filter is potentially too permissive in such cases. In actual practice, we did not observe a difference with respect to accuracy or CPU-time requirements, but the storage costs dropped considerably.

5 Experimental Results

Some of the experiments have been performed with the Alpino Treebank. The Alpino Treebank (van der Beek et al., 2002) consists of manually verified dependency structures for the `cdbl` (newspaper) part of the Eindhoven corpus (den Boogaart, 1975). The treebank contains 7137 sentences. Average sentence length is about 20 tokens.

Some further experiments are performed on the basis of the D-Coi corpus (van Noord et al., 2006). From this corpus, we used the manually verified syntactic annotations of the P-P-H and P-P-L parts. The P-P-H part consists of over 2200 sentences from the Dutch daily newspaper Trouw from 2001. Average sentence length is about 16.5 tokens. The P-P-L part contains 1115 sentences taken from information brochures of Dutch Ministries. Average sentence length is about 18.5 tokens.

For training data, we used newspaper text from the TwNC (*Twente Newspaper*) corpus (Ordelman et al., 2007). We used Volkskrant 2001, NRC 2000, Algemeen Dagblad 1999. In addition, we used Volkskrant 1997 newspaper data extracted from the Volkskrant 1997 CDROM.

5.1 Results on Alpino Treebank

Figure 3 presents results obtained on the Alpino Treebank. In the graphs, the various filters are compared with the baseline variant of the parser. Each of the filters outperforms the default model for all given time-out values. In fact, the base-

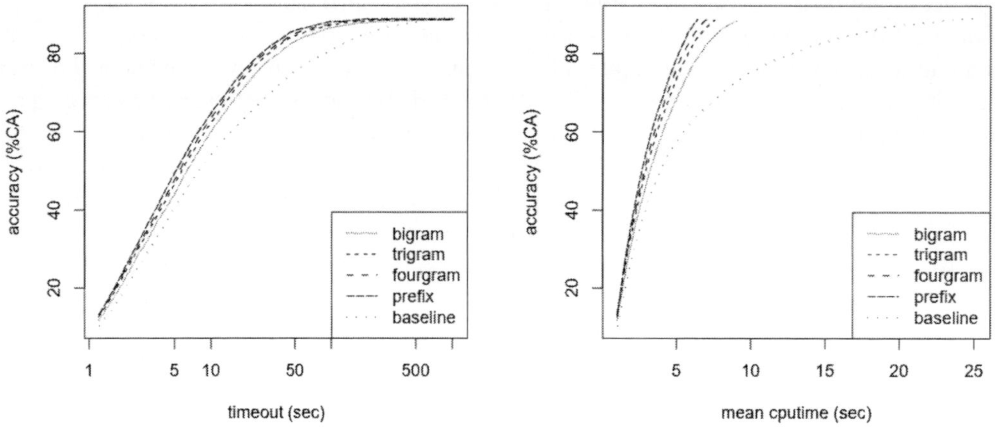

Figure 3: Accuracy versus time-out (on-line scenario), and accuracy versus mean CPU-time (off-line scenario) for various time-outs. The graphs compare the default setting of Alpino with the effect of the various filters based on all available training data. Evaluation on the Alpino treebank.

line parser improves upon the prefix filter only for unrealistic time-outs larger than fifteen minutes of CPU-time. The difference in accuracy for a given time-out value can be considerable: as much as 12% for time-outs around 30 seconds of CPU-time.

If we focus on mean CPU-time (off-line scenario), differences are even more pronounced. Without the filter, an accuracy of about 63% is obtained for a mean CPU-time of 6 seconds. The prefix filtering method obtains accuracy of more than 86% for the same mean CPU-time. For that level of accuracy, the base-line model requires a mean CPU-time of about 25 seconds. In other words, for the same level of accuracy, the prefix filter leads to a parser that is more than four times faster.

5.2 Effect of the amount of training data

In the first two graphs of figure 4 we observe the effect of the amount of training data. As can be expected, increasing the amount of data increases the accuracy, and decreases efficiency (because more derivation steps have been observed, hence fewer derivations are filtered out). Generally, models that take into account larger parts of the history require more data to obtain good accuracy, but they are also faster. For each of the variants, adding more training data after about 40 million words does not lead to much further improvement; the little improvement that is observed, is balanced by a slight increase in parse times too.

It is interesting to note that the accuracy of some of the filters improves slightly upon the baseline parser (without any filtering). This can be explained by the fact that the Alpino parser includes a best-first beam search to select the best parse from the parse forest. Apparently, in some cases the filter throws away candidate parses which would otherwise confuse this heuristic best search procedure.

5.3 Experiment with D-Coi data

In this section, we confirm the experimental results obtained on the Alpino Treebank by performing similar experiments on the D-Coi data. The purpose of this confirmation is twofold. On the one hand, the Alpino Treebank might not be a reliable test set for the Alpino parser, because it has been used quite intensively during the development of various components of the system. On the other hand, we might regard the experiments in the previous section as development experiments from which we learn the best parameters of the approach. The real evaluation of the technique is now performed using only the best method found on the development set, which is the *prefix* filter with $\tau = 0$.

We performed experiments with two parts of the D-Coi corpus. The first data set, P-P-H, contains newspaper data, and is therefore comparable both with the Alpino Treebank, and more importantly, with the training data that we used to develop the filters. In order to check if the success of the filtering methods requires that training data and test data need to be taken from similar texts, we also provide experimental results on a test set consisting of different material: the P-P-L part of the D-Coi corpus, which contains text extracted from information brochures published by Dutch Ministries.

The third and fourth graphs in figure 4 provide results obtained on the P-P-H corpus. The increased efficiency of the prefix filter is slightly less pronounced. This may be due to the smaller mean sentence length of this data set. Still, the prefix filtering method performs much better for a large variety of time-outs. Only for very high, unrealistic, time-outs, the baseline parser obtains better accuracy. The same general trend is observed in the P-P-L data-set. From these results we tentatively conclude that the proposed technique is applicable across text types and domains.

6 Discussion

One may wonder how the technique introduced in this paper relates to techniques in which the disambiguation model is used directly during parsing to eliminate unlikely partial parses. An example in the context of wide coverage unification-based parsing is the beam thresholding technique employed in the Enju HPSG parser for English (Tsuruoka et al., 2004; Ninomiya et al., 2005).

In a beam-search parser, unlikely partial analyses are constructed, and then - based on the probability assigned to these partial analyses - removed from further consideration. One potential advantage of the use of our filters may be, that many of these partial analyses will not even be constructed in the first place, and therefore no time is spent on these alternatives at all.

We have not performed a detailed comparison, because the statistical model employed in Alpino contains some features which refer to arbitrary large parts of a parse. Such non-local features are not allowed in the Enju approach.

A parsing system may also combine both types of techniques. In that case there is room for further experimentation. For instance, during the learning phase, it may be beneficial to allow for a wider beam, to obtain more reliable filters. During testing, the beam can perhaps be smaller than usual, since the filters already rule out many of the competing parses.

The idea that corpora can be used to improve parsing efficiency was an important ingredient of a technique that was called *grammar specialization*. An overview of grammar specialization techniques is given in (Sima'an, 1999). For instance, Rayner and Carter (1996) use explanation-based learning to specialize a given general grammar to a specific domain. They report important efficiency gains (the parser is about three times faster), coupled with a mild reduction of coverage (5% loss).

In contrast to our approach in which no manual annotation is required, Rayner and Carter (1996) report that for each sentence in the training data, the best parse was selected manually from the set of parses generated by the parser. For the experiments described in the paper, this constituted an effort of two and a half person-months. As a consequence, they use only 15.000 training examples (taken from ATIS, so presumably relatively short sentences). In our experiments, we used up to 4 million sentences.

A further difference is related to the pruning strategies. Our pruning strategies are extremely simple. The cutting criteria employed in grammar specialization either require carefully manually tuning, or require more complicated statistical techniques (Samuelsson, 1994); automatically derived cutting criteria, however, perform considerably worse.

A possible improvement of our approach consists of predicting whether for a given input sentence the filter should be used, or whether the sentence appears to be 'easy' enough to allow for a full parse. For instance, one may chose to use the filter only for sentences of a given minimum length. Initial experiments indicate that such a setup may improve somewhat over the results presented here.

Acknowledgments

This research was carried out in part in the context of the STEVIN programme which is funded by the Dutch and Flemish governments (http://taalunieversum.org/taal/technologie/stevin/).

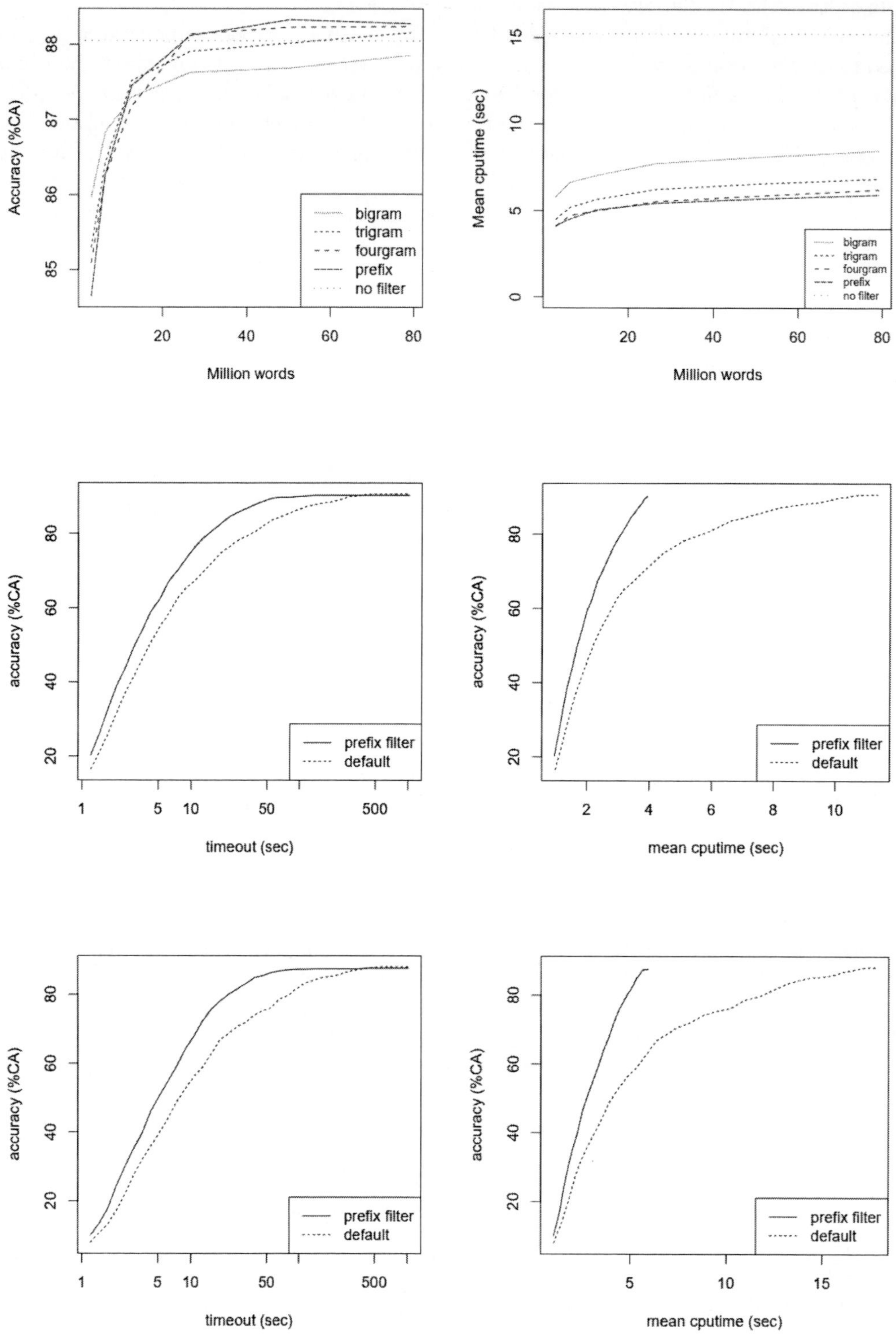

Figure 4: The first two graphs present accuracy (left) and mean CPU-time (right) as a function of the amount of training data used. Evaluation on 10% of the Alpino Treebank. The third and fourth graph present accuracy versus time-out, and accuracy versus mean CPU-time for various time-outs. The graph compares the baseline system with the parser which uses the prefix filter based on all available training data. Evaluation on the D-Coi P-P-H 1-109 data-set (newspaper text). The two last graphs are similar, based on the D-Coi P-P-L data-set (brochures).

References

P. C. Uit den Boogaart. 1975. *Woordfrequenties in geschreven en gesproken Nederlands*. Oosthoek, Scheltema & Holkema, Utrecht. Werkgroep Frequentie-onderzoek van het Nederlands.

Heleen Hoekstra, Michael Moortgat, Bram Renmans, Machteld Schouppe, Ineke Schuurman, and Ton van der Wouden, 2003. *CGN Syntactische Annotatie*, December.

Y. Matsumoto, H. Tanaka, H. Hirakawa, H. Miyoshi, and H. Yasukawa. 1983. BUP: a bottom up parser embedded in Prolog. *New Generation Computing*, 1(2).

Takashi Ninomiya, Yoshimasa Tsuruoka, Yusuke Miyao, and Jun'ichi Tsujii. 2005. Efficacy of beam thresholding, unification filtering and hybrid parsing. In *Proceedings of the International Workshop on Parsing Technologies (IWPT)*.

Roeland Ordelman, Franciska de Jong, Arjan van Hessen, and Hendri Hondorp. 2007. Twnc: a multifaceted Dutch news corpus. *ELRA Newsletter*, 12(3/4):4–7.

Fernando C. N. Pereira and Stuart M. Shieber. 1987. *Prolog and Natural Language Analysis*. Center for the Study of Language and Information Stanford.

Manny Rayner and David Carter. 1996. Fast parsing using pruning and grammar specialization. In *34th Annual Meeting of the Association for Computational Linguistics*, Santa Cruz.

Christer Samuelsson. 1994. Grammar specialization through entropy thresholds. In *32th Annual Meeting of the Association for Computational Linguistics*, New Mexico. ACL.

Khalil Sima'an. 1999. *Learning Efficient Disambiguation*. Ph.D. thesis, University of Utrecht.

Yoshimasa Tsuruoka, Yusuke Miyao, and Jun'ichi Tsujii. 2004. Towards efficient probabilistic hpsg parsing: integrating semantic and syntactic preference to guide the parsing. In *Beyond Shallow Analyses - Formalisms and statistical modeling for deep analyses*, Hainan China. IJCNLP.

Leonoor van der Beek, Gosse Bouma, Robert Malouf, and Gertjan van Noord. 2002. The Alpino dependency treebank. In *Computational Linguistics in the Netherlands*.

Gertjan van Noord, Ineke Schuurman, and Vincent Vandeghinste. 2006. Syntactic annotation of large corpora in STEVIN. In *Proceedings of the 5th International Conference on Language Resources and Evaluation (LREC)*, Genoa, Italy.

Gertjan van Noord. 1997. An efficient implementation of the head corner parser. *Computational Linguistics*, 23(3):425–456. cmp-lg/9701004.

A robust and extensible exemplar-based model of thematic fit

Bram Vandekerckhove[a], Dominiek Sandra[a], Walter Daelemans[b]
[a]Center for Psycholinguistics, [b]Center for Dutch Language and Speech (CNTS)
University of Antwerp
Antwerp, Belgium
{bram.vandekerckhove,dominiek.sandra,walter.daelemans}@ua.ac.be

Abstract

This paper presents a new, exemplar-based model of thematic fit. In contrast to previous models, it does not approximate thematic fit as argument plausibility or 'fit with verb selectional preferences', but directly as semantic role plausibility for a verb-argument pair, through similarity-based generalization from previously seen verb-argument pairs. This makes the model very robust for data sparsity. We argue that the model is easily extensible to a model of semantic role ambiguity resolution during online sentence comprehension.

The model is evaluated on human semantic role plausibility judgments. Its predictions correlate significantly with the human judgments. It rivals two state-of-the-art models of thematic fit and exceeds their performance on previously unseen or low-frequency items.

1 Introduction

Thematic fit (or semantic role plausibility) is the plausibility of a noun phrase referent playing a specific semantic role (like *agent* or *patient*) in the event denoted by a verbal predicate, e.g. the plausibility that a judge sentences someone (which makes the judge the agent of the sentencing event) or that a judge is sentenced him- or herself (which makes the judge the patient). Thematic fit has been an important concept in psycholinguistics as a predictor variable in models of human sentence comprehension, either to discriminate between possible structural analyses during initial processing in constraint-based models (see MacDonald and Seidenberg (2006) for a recent overview), or after initial syntactic processing in modular models (e.g. Frazier (1987)). In fact, thematic fit is at the core of the most-studied of all structural ambiguity phenomena, the ambiguity between a main clause or a reduced relative clause interpretation of an *NP verb-ed* sequence (the MV/RR ambiguity), which is essentially a semantic role ambiguity. If the temporarily ambiguous sentence *The judge sentenced ...* is continued as a main clause (e.g. *The judge sentenced him to 10 years in prison*), the noun phrase *the judge* would be the agent of the verb *sentenced*, while it would be the patient of *sentenced* in a reduced relative clause continuation (e.g. *The judge sentenced to 4 years in prison for indecent exposure could also lose his state pension*). Apart from its importance in psycholinguistics, the concept of thematic fit is also relevant for computational linguistics in general (see Padó et al. (2007) for some examples).

A number of models that try to capture human thematic fit preferences have been developed in recent years (Resnik, 1996; Padó et al., 2006; Padó et al., 2007). These previous approaches rely on the linguistic notion of verb selectional preferences. The plausibility that an argument plays a specific semantic role in the event denoted by a verb—in other words, that a verb, role and argument occur together—is predicted by how well the argument head fits the restrictions that the verb imposes on the argument candidates for the semantic role slot under consideration (e.g. *eat* prefers edible arguments to fill its patient slot). Therefore, what these models capture is actually not semantic role plausibility, but argument plausibility.

The model presented here takes a different approach. Instead of predicting the plausibility of an argument given a verb-role pair (e.g. the plausibility of *judge* given *sentence-patient*), it predicts the plausibility of a semantic role given a verb-argument pair (e.g. the plausibility of *patient* given *sentence-judge*), through similarity-based generalization from previously seen verb-argument pairs. In the context of modeling thematic fit as a con-

Proceedings of the 12th Conference of the European Chapter of the ACL, pages 826–834,
Athens, Greece, 30 March – 3 April 2009.

straint in the resolution of sentence-level ambiguity problems like the MV/RR ambiguity, predicting role fit instead of argument fit seems to be the most straightforward approach. After all, when thematic fit is approached in this way, the model directly captures the semantic role ambiguity that is at stake during the analysis of sentences that are temporarily ambiguous between a main clause and a reduced relative interpretation. This means that our model of thematic fit should be very easy to extend into a full-blown model of the resolution of any sentence-level ambiguity that crucially revolves around a semantic role ambiguity. In addition, the fact that it generalizes from previously seen verb-argument pairs, based on their similarity to the target pair, should make it more robust than previous approaches.

The remainder of the paper is organized as follows: in the next section, we briefly discuss two state-of-the-art thematic fit models, the performance of which will be compared to that of our model. Section 3 introduces three different instantiations of our model. The evaluation of the model and the comparison of its performance with that of the models discussed in Section 2 is presented in Section 4. Section 5 ties everything together with some general conclusions.

2 Previous models

In this section of the paper, we look at two state-of-the-art models of thematic fit, developed by Padó et al. (2006) and Padó et al. (2007). We will not discuss the selectional preferences model of Resnik (1996), but for a comparison between the Resnik model and the Padó models, see Padó et al. (2007).

2.1 Padó et al. (2006)

In their model of thematic fit, Padó et al. (2006) use FrameNet thematic roles (Fillmore et al., 2003) to approximate semantic roles. The thematic fit of a verb-role-argument triple (v, r, a) is given by the joint probability of the role r, the argument headword a, the verb sense v_s, and the grammatical function gf of a:

$$Plausibility_{v,r,a} = P(v_s, r, a, gf) \quad (1)$$

Since computing this joint probability from corpus co-occurrence frequencies is problematic due to an obvious sparse data issue, the term is decomposed into several subterms, including a term $P(a|v_s, gf, r)$ that captures selectional preferences. Good-Turing and class-based smoothing are used to further alleviate the remaining sparse data problem, but because of the fact that the model can only make predictions for verbs that occur in the small FrameNet corpus, for a large number of verbs, it cannot provide any output. For the verbs that do occur in the training corpus, however, the model's predictions correlate very well with human plausibility ratings.

2.2 Padó et al. (2007)

The model of Padó et al. (2007) does not use semantically annotated resources, but approximates the agent and patient relations with the syntactic subject and object relations, respectively. The plausibility of a verb-role-argument triple (v, r, a) is found by calculating the weighted mean semantic similarity of the argument headword a to all headwords that have previously been seen together with the verb-role pair (v, r), as shown in Equation 2. The prediction is that high semantic similarity of a target headword a to seen headwords for a given (v, r) tuple corresponds to high thematic fit of the (v, r, a) tuple, while low similarity implies low thematic fit.

$$Plausibility_{v,r,a} = \sum_{a' \in Seen_r(v)} \frac{w(a') \times sim(a, a')}{|Seen_r(v)|} \quad (2)$$

$w(a')$ is the weighting factor. Padó et al. (2007) used the frequency of the previously seen argument headwords as weights. Similarity between headwords was defined as the cosine between so-called 'dependency vector' representations of these headwords (Padó and Lapata, 2007). These vectors are constructed from the frequency counts with which the target items occur at one end of specific paths in a corpus of syntactic dependency trees. The argument headword vectors Padó et al. (2007) used in their experiments consisted of 2000 features, representing the most frequent $(head, subject)$ and $(head, object)$ pairs in the British National Corpus (BNC). The feature-values of the headword vectors were the log-likelihoods of the headwords occurring at the dependent end of these $(relation, head)$ pairs (so either as subjects or objects of the heads). The model's performance approaches that of the Padó et al. (2006) model on the correlation of its predictions with human ratings, and it attains higher coverage (it can provide plausibility values for a larger proportion of the test items), since the model only requires that the verb occurs with subject and object arguments in the training corpus, and that the target argument headwords occur in the training data frequently enough to attain reliable dependency vectors.

3 Exemplar-based modeling of thematic fit

Exemplar-based models of cognition (also known as Memory-Based Learning or instance/case-based reasoning/learning models) (Fix and Hodges, 1951; Cover and Hart, 1967; Daelemans and van den Bosch, 2005) are classification models that extrapolate their behavior from stored representations of earlier experiences to new situations, based on the similarity of the old and the new situation. These models keep a database of stored exemplars and refer to that database to guide their behavior in new situations. Models can extrapolate from only one similar memory exemplar, a group of similar exemplars (a nearest neighbor set), or even the whole exemplar memory, using some decay function to give less weight to less similar exemplars.

Applied to our model of thematic fit, this means that the model should have a database in which semantic representations of verb-argument pairs are stored together with the semantic roles of the arguments. The plausibility of a semantic role given a new verb-argument pair is then determined by the support for that role among the verb-argument pairs in memory that are semantically most similar to the target pair.

An immediately obvious advantage of this approach should be its potential robustness for data sparsity, since similarity-based smoothing is an intrinsic part of the model. Even if neither the verb nor the argument of a verb-argument pair occur in the exemplar memory, role plausibilities can be predicted, as long as the similarity of the target exemplar's semantic representation with the semantic representations in the exemplar memory can be calculated. An additional advantage of similarity-based smoothing is that it does not involve the estimation of an exponential number of smoothing parameters, as is the case for backed-off smoothing methods (Zavrel and Daelemans, 1997).

For this study, we will implement three different kinds of exemplar-based models. The first model is a basic k-Nearest Neighbor (k-NN) model. In this model, the plausibility rating for a semantic role given a verb-argument pair is simply determined by the (relative) frequency with which that semantic role is assigned to the k verb-argument pairs that are nearest (i.e. most similar) to the target verb-argument pair (these exemplars constitute the nearest neighbor set). The second model adds a decay function to this simple k-NN model, so that not only the role frequency, but also the absolute semantic distance between the target item and the neighbors in the nearest neighbor set determine the plausibility rating. In the third model, a normalization factor ensures that distance of the exemplars in the nearest neighbor set to the target item determines their weight in the calculation of the plausibility rating while factoring out an effect of absolute distance.

The semantic distance between two verb-argument exemplars is determined by the semantic distance between the verbs and between the nouns. In all models described below, the distance between two exemplars i and j (d_{ij}) is given by the sum of the weighted distances (δ) between the semantic representations of the exemplars' nouns (n) and verbs (v):

$$d_{ij} = w_v \times \delta(v_i, v_j) + w_n \times \delta(n_i, n_j) \qquad (3)$$

We are not theoretically committed to any specific semantic representation or similarity metric for the computation of $\delta(v_i, v_j)$ and $\delta(n_i, n_j)$. The only requirement is that they should be able to distinguish nouns that typically occur in the same contexts, but in different roles (like *writer* and *book*), which probably excludes all vector-based approaches that do not take into account syntactic information (see also Padó et al. (2007)).

In the next three sections, each of the three exemplar-based models is discussed in more detail.

3.1 A basic k-NN model

The most basic of all exemplar-based models is a k-NN model in which the preference strength of a class upon presentation of a stimulus is simply the relative frequency of that class among the nearest neighbors of the stimulus. In the context of thematic fit, this means that the preference strength (PS) for a semantic role response J given a verb-argument stimulus i is found by summing the frequencies of all exemplars with semantic role J

Verb	Noun	Role	Rating
sentence	judge	agent	6.9
sentence	judge	patient	1.3
sentence	criminal	agent	1.3
sentence	criminal	patient	6.7

Table 1: Example mean thematic fit ratings from McRae et al. (1998)

among the k nearest neighbors of i (C_J^k) and dividing this by the total number of exemplars in the k-nearest neighbor set, with k (the number of nearest neighbors taken into consideration) being a free parameter:

$$PS(R_J|S_i) = \frac{\sum_{j \in C_J^k} f(j)}{\sum_{l \in C^k} f(l)} \quad (4)$$

We will call this model the k-NN frequency model (henceforth kNNf).

3.2 A distance decay model

The kNNf model uses the similarity between the target exemplar and the memory exemplars only to determine which items belong to the nearest neighbor set. Whether these nearest neighbors are very similar or only slightly similar to the target exemplar, or whether there are some very similar items but also some very dissimilar items among those neighbors does not have any influence on the class's preference strength; only relative frequency within the nearest neighbor set counts.

Only relying on the relative frequency of semantic roles within the nearest neighbor set to predict their plausibilities might indeed be a reasonable approach to modeling thematic fit in a lot of cases. Being a good agent for a given verb often entails being a bad patient for that same verb (or even in general), and the other way around. For example, *judge* is a very plausible agent of the verb *sentence*, while at the same time it is a rather unlikely patient of the same verb, while it is exactly the other way around for *criminal*, as the mean participant ratings (on a 7-point scale) in Table 1 show (these were taken from McRae et al. (1998)). The relative frequencies of the agent and patient roles in the nearest neighbor set could in theory perfectly explain these ratings: a high relative frequency of the agent role among the nearest neighbors of the verb-argument pair $(sentence, judge)$ should correspond to a high rating for the role, and implies low relative frequencies for other roles such as the patient role, which means the patient role should receive a low rating. For $(sentence, criminal)$ this works in exactly the opposite way.

Solely relying on the the relative semantic role frequencies in the nearest neighbor set might not always work, though, since it implies that plausibility ratings for different roles are always completely dependent on and therefore perfectly predictable from each other: high plausibility for a certain semantic role given a verb-argument pair always implies low plausibility for the other roles in the nearest neighbor set, and low plausibility for one semantic role invariably means higher plausibility for the other ones. However, nouns can also be more or less equally good as agents and patients for a given verb—one is hopefully as likely to be helped by a friend as to help a friend oneself—or equally bad—houses only kill in horror movies, and 'to kill a house' can only be made sense of in a metaphorical way. Therefore, we also implement a model that takes distance into account for its plausibility ratings. The basic idea is that a semantic role will receive a lower rating as the nearest neighbors supporting that role become less similar to the target item. The plausibility rating for a semantic role given a verb-argument pair in this model is a joint function of:

1. the frequency with which the role occurs in the set of memory exemplars that are semantically most similar to the target pair
2. the target pairs similarity to those exemplars

We will call this model the Distance Decay model (henceforth DD).

Formally, the preference strength (PS) for a semantic role J (R_J) given a verb-argument tuple i (S_i) is found by summing the distance-weighted frequency of all exemplars with semantic role J in the nearest neighbor set (C_J^k):

$$PS(R_J|S_i) = \sum_{j \in C_J^k} f(j) \times \eta_j \quad (5)$$

The weight of an exemplar j (η_j) is given by an exponential decay function, taken from Shepard (1987), over the distance between that exemplar and the target exemplar i (d_{ij}):

$$\eta_j = \mathrm{e}^{-\alpha \times d_{ij}} \quad (6)$$

In Equation 6, the free parameter α determines the rate of decay over d_{ij}. Higher values of α result in a faster drop in similarity as d_{ij} increases.

3.3 A normalized distance decay model

In Equation 5, we do not include a denominator that sums over the similarity strengths of all exemplars in the nearest neighbor set, because we want to keep the absolute effect of distance into the formula, so as to be able to accurately predict the bad fit of both the agent and patient roles for verb-argument pairs like $(kill, house)$ or the good fit of both agent and patient roles for a pair like $(help, friend)$. To find out whether a non-normalized model is indeed a better predictor of thematic fit than a normalized model, we also run experiments with a normalized version of the model presented in Section 3.2:

$$PS(R_J|T_i) = \frac{\sum_{j \in C_J^k} f(j) \times \eta_j}{\sum_{l \in C^k} f(l) \times \eta_l} \quad (7)$$

Someone familiar with the literature on human categorization behavior might recognize Equation 7; this model is actually simply a Generalized Context Model (GCM) (Nosofsky, 1986), with the 'context' being restricted to the k nearest neighbors of the target item. Therefore, we will refer to this model using the shorthand kGCM.

4 Evaluation

4.1 The task: predicting human plausibility judgments

The model is evaluated by comparing its predictions to thematic fit or semantic role plausibility judgments from two rating experiments with human subjects. In these tasks, participants had to rate the plausibility of verb-role-argument triples on a scale from 1 to 7. They were asked questions like *How common is it for a judge to sentence someone?*, in which *judge* is the agent, or *How common is it for a judge to be sentenced?*, in which *judge* is the patient. The prediction is that model preference strengths of semantic roles given specific verb-argument pairs should correlate positively with participant ratings for the corresponding verb-role-argument triples.

4.2 Training the model

In exemplar-based models, training the model simply amounts to storing exemplars in memory. Our model uses an exemplar memory that consists of 133566 verb-role-noun triples extracted from the Wall Street Journal and Brown parts of the Penn Treebank (Marcus et al., 1993). These were first annotated with semantic roles using a state-of-the-art semantic role labeling system (Koomen et al., 2005).

Semantic roles are approximated by PropBank argument roles (Palmer et al., 2005). These consist of a limited set of numbered roles that are used for all verbs but are defined on a verb-by-verb basis. This contrasts with FrameNet roles, which are sense-specific. Hence PropBank roles provide a shallower level of semantic role annotation. They also do not refer consistently to the same semantic roles over different verbs, although the A0 and A1 roles in the majority of cases do correspond to the agent and patient roles, respectively. The A2 role refers to a third participant involved in the event, but the label can stand for several types of semantic roles, such as *beneficiary* or *recipient*. To create the exemplar memory, all lemmatized verb-noun-role triples that contained the A0, A1, or A2 roles were extracted.

4.3 Testing the model

To obtain the semantic distances between nouns and verbs for the calculation of the distance between exemplars (see Equation 3), we make use of a thesaurus compiled by Lin (1998), which lists the 200 nearest neighbors for a large number of English noun and verb lemmas, together with their similarity values. This resource was created by computing the similarity between word dependency vectors that are composed of frequency counts of $(head, relation, dependent)$ triples (dependency triples) in a 64-million word parsed corpus. To compute these similarities, an information-theoretic similarity metric was used. The basic idea of this metric is that the similarity between two words is the amount of information contained in the commonality between the two words, i.e. the frequency counts of the dependency triples that occur in the descriptions of both words, divided by the amount of information in the descriptions of the words, i.e. the frequency counts of the dependency triples that occur in either of the two words. See Lin (1998) for details. These similarity values were transformed into distances by subtracting them from the maximum similarity value 1.

Gain Ratio is used to determine the weights of

the nouns and verbs in the distance calculation. Gain Ratio is a normalization of Information Gain, an information-theoretic measure that quantifies how informative a feature is in the prediction of a class label; in this case how informative in general nouns or verbs are when one has to predict a semantic role. Based on our exemplar memory, the Gain Ratio values and so the feature weights are 0.0402 for the verbs, and 0.0333 for the nouns.

The model predictions are evaluated against two data sets of human semantic role plausibility ratings for verb-role-noun triples (McRae et al., 1998; Padó et al., 2006). These data sets were chosen because they are the same data sets that were originally used in the evaluation of the two other models discussed in sections 2.1 and 2.2.

The first data set, from McRae et al. (1998), consists of semantic role plausibility ratings for 40 verbs, each coupled with both a good agent and a good patient, which were presented to the raters in both roles. This means there are $40 \times 2 \times 2 = 160$ items in total. We divide this data set in the same 60-item development and 100-item test sets that were used by Padó et al. (2006) and Padó et al. (2007) for the evaluation of their models.

For most of the McRae items, being a good agent for a given verb also entails being a bad patient for that same verb, and the other way around. This leads us to predict that on this data set the kNNf model (see section 3.1) and the kGCM (see section 3.3) should perform no worse than the DD model (see section 3.2).

The second data set is taken from Padó et al. (2006) and consists of 414 verb-role-noun triples. Agent and patient ratings are more evenly distributed, so we predict that a model that exclusively relies on the relative role frequencies in the nearest neighbor sets of these items might not capture as much variability as a model that takes distance into account to weight the exemplars. Therefore, we expect the DD model to do better than the kNNf model on this data set. We randomly divide the data set in a 276-item development set, and a 138-items test set.

Because of the non-normal distribution of the test data, we use Spearman's rank correlation test to measure the correlation strength between the plausibility ratings predicted by the model and the human ratings. To estimate whether the strength with which the predictions of the different models correlate with the human judgments differs significantly between the models, we use an approximate test statistic described in Raghunathan (2003). This test statistic is robust for sample size differences, which is necessary in this case given the fact that the models differ in their coverage. We will refer to this statistic as the Q-statistic.

Experiments on the development sets are run to find optimal values per model for two parameters: k, the number of nearest neighbors that are taken into account for the construction of the nearest neighbor set, and α (for the DD and kGCM models), the rate of decay over distance (see Equation 6).

4.4 Results

4.4.1 McRae data

Results on the McRae test set are summarized in Table 2. The first three rows contain the results for the exemplar-based models. The last two rows show the results of the two previous models for comparison. The values for k and α that were found to be optimal in the experiments on the development set are specified where applicable.

The predictions of all three exemplar-based models correlate significantly with the human ratings, with the DD model doing somewhat better than the kNNf model and the kGCM model, although these differences are not significant ($Q(0.28) = 0.134, p = 2.8 \times 10^{-1}$ and $Q(0.28) = 0.116, p = 2.9 \times 10^{-1}$, respectively). Coverage of the exemplar-based models is very high.

When we compare the results of the exemplar-based models with those of the Padó models, we find that the predictions of the DD model correlate significantly stronger with the human ratings than the predictions of the Padó et al. (2007) model, $Q(0.98) = 4.398$, $p = 3.5 \times 10^{-2}$. The DD model also matches the high performance of the Padó et al. (2006) model. Actually, the correlation strength of the DD predictions with the human ratings is higher, but that difference is not significant, $Q(0.93) = 0.285$, $p = 5.6 \times 10^{-1}$. However, the DD model has a much higher coverage than the model of Padó et al. (2006), $\chi^2(1, N = 100) = 44.5, p = 2.5 \times 10^{-11}$.

4.4.2 Padó data

Table 3 summarizes the results for the Padó data set. We find that the predictions of all three exemplar-based models correlate significantly with the human ratings, and that there are

Model	k	α	Coverage	ρ	p
kNNf	9	-	96%	.407	$p = 3.9 \times 10^{-5}$
DD	11	5	96%	.488	$p = 4.6 \times 10^{-7}$
kGCM	9	21	96%	.397	$p = 6.2 \times 10^{-5}$
Padó et al. (2006)	-	-	56%	.415	$p = 1.5 \times 10^{-3}$
Padó et al. (2007)	-	-	91%	.218	$p = 3.8 \times 10^{-2}$

Table 2: Results for the McRae data.

Model	k	α	Coverage	ρ	p
kNNf	12	-	97%	.521	$p = 1.1 \times 10^{-10}$
DD	8	21	97%	.523	$p = 9.1 \times 10^{-11}$
kGCM	10	25	97%	.512	$p = 2.7 \times 10^{-10}$
Padó et al. (2006)	-	-	96%	.514	$p = 2.9 \times 10^{-10}$
Padó et al. (2007)	-	-	98%	.506	$p = 3.7 \times 10^{-10}$

Table 3: Results for the Padó data.

no significant differences between the three model instantiations. Coverage is again very high.

There are no significant performance differences between the exemplar-based models and the Padó models. Correlation strengths and coverage are more or less the same for all models.

4.5 Discussion

In general, we find that our exemplar-based, semantic role predicting approach attains a very good fit with the human semantic role plausibility ratings from both the McRae and the Padó data set. Moreover, because of the fact that generalization is determined by similarity-based extrapolation from verb-noun pairs, the high correlations of the model's predictions with the human ratings are accompanied by a very high coverage.

As concerns the comparison with the models of Padó et al. (2006) and Padó et al. (2007) on the Padó data, we can be brief: the exemplar-based models' performance matches that of the Padó models, and basically all models perform equally well, both on correlation strength and coverage.

However, there is a striking discrepancy between the performance of the Padó models and the DD model on the McRae data sets. We find that the DD model performs well for both correlation strength *and* coverage, as opposed to the Padó models, both of which score less well on one or the other of these two dimensions. Although the model of Padó et al. (2006) attains a good fit on the McRae data, its coverage is very low. This is especially problematic considering the fact that it is exactly this type of test items that is used in the kind of sentence comprehension experiments for which these thematic fit models should help explain the results. The model of Padó et al. (2007) succeeds in boosting coverage, but at the expense of correlation strength, which is reduced to approximately half the correlation strength attained by the Padó et al. (2006) model.

The model of Padó et al. (2006) requires the test verbs and their senses to be attested in the FrameNet corpus to be able to make its predictions. However, only 64 of the 100 test items in the McRae data set contain verbs that are attested in the FrameNet corpus, 8 of which involve an unattested verb sense. On the other hand, the only requirement for the exemplar-based model to be able to make its predictions is that the similarities between the verbs and the nouns in the target exemplars and the memory exemplars can be computed. In our case, this means that the verbs and nouns need to have entries in the thesaurus we use (see Section 4.3). In the McRae data set, this is the case for all verbs, and for 48 out of the 50 nouns. This explains the large difference in coverage between the DD model and the model of Padó et al. (2006).

Padó et al. (2007) attribute the poorer correlation of their 2007 model with the human ratings in the McRae data set to the much lower frequencies of the nouns in that data set as compared to the frequencies of the nouns in the Padó data set. That is probably also the explanation for the difference in correlation strength between our model and the model of Padó et al. (2007). Both models use similarity-based smoothing to compensate for low-frequency target items, but the generalization problem caused by low frequency nouns is alleviated in our model by the fact that the model not only generalizes over nouns, but also over verbs. Since the model can base its generalizations on verb-noun pairs that contain the noun of the target pair coupled to a verb that is different from the verb in the target pair, the neighbor set that it generalizes from can contain a larger number of exemplars with nouns that are identical to the noun in the target pair. The model of Padó et al. (2007) has no access to nouns that are not coupled to the target verb in the training corpus.

In Section 3, we predicted that the kNNf and the kGCM should perform equally well as the DD model on the McRae data set, because of the balanced nature of that data set (all nouns are either good agents and bad patients, or the other way around), but that the DD model should do better on the less balanced Padó data set. This prediction is not borne out by the results, since the DD model does not perform significantly better on either of the data sets, although on both data sets it achieves the highest correlation strength of all three models. However, what we see is that the performance difference between the DD model on the one hand and the kNNf model and kGCM on the other hand is larger on the McRae data than on the Padó data, which is exactly the opposite of what we predicted. The fact that the differences are not significant makes us hesitant to draw any conclusions from this finding, though.

5 Conclusion

We presented an exemplar-based model of thematic fit that is founded on the idea that semantic role plausibility can be predicted by similarity-based generalization over verb-argument pairs. In contrast to previous models, this model does not implement semantic role plausibility as 'fit with verb selectional preferences', but directly captures the semantic role ambiguity problem comprehenders have to solve when confronted with sentences that contain structural ambiguities like the MV/RR ambiguity, namely deciding which semantic role a noun has in the event denoted by the verb. Therefore, the model should be easily extensible towards a complete model of any sentence-level ambiguity that revolves around a semantic role ambiguity.

We have shown that our model can account very well for human semantic role plausibility judgments, attaining both high correlations with human ratings and high coverage overall, and improving on two state-of-the-art models, the performance of which deteriorates when there is a small overlap between the verbs in the training corpus and in the test data, or when the test nouns have low frequencies in the training corpus. We suggest that this improvement is due to the fact that our model applies similarity-based smoothing over both nouns and verbs. Generally, one can say that the exemplar-based model's architecture makes it very robust for data sparsity.

We also found that a non-normalized version of our model that takes distance into account to weight the memory exemplars seems to perform somewhat better than a simple nearest neighbor model or a normalized distance decay model. However, these performance differences are not statistically significant, and we did not find the predicted advantage of the non-normalized distance decay model on the Padó data set.

In future work, we will test our claim of straightforward extensibility of the model by indeed extending our model to account for reading time patterns in the online processing of sentences exemplifying temporary semantic role ambiguities, more specifically the MV/RR ambiguity. Another avenue for future research is to see how our approach to thematic fit can be used to augment existing semantic role labeling systems.

Acknowledgments

This work was supported by a grant from the Research Foundation – Flanders (FWO). We are grateful to Ken McRae and Ulrike Padó for making their datasets available, Dekang Lin for the thesaurus, and the people of the Cognitive Computation Group at UIUC for their SRL system.

References

Thomas M. Cover and Peter E. Hart. 1967. Nearest neighbor pattern classification. *IEEE Transactions on Information Theory*, 13(1):21–27.

Walter Daelemans and Antal van den Bosch. 2005. *Memory-based language processing*. Cambridge University Press, Cambridge.

Charles J. Fillmore, Christopher R. Johnson, and Miriam R. L. Petruck. 2003. Background to FrameNet. *International Journal of Lexicography*, 16:235–250.

Evelyn Fix and Joseph L. Hodges. 1951. Discriminatory analysis—nonparametric discrimination: consistency properties. Technical Report Project 21-49-004, Report No. 4, USAF School of Aviation Medicine, Randolp Field, TX.

Lyn Frazier. 1987. Sentence processing: A tutorial review. In Max Coltheart, editor, *Attention and Performance XII: The Psychology of Reading*, pages 559–586. Erlbaum, Hillsdale, NJ.

Peter Koomen, Vasin Punyakanok, Dan Roth, and Wen-tau Yih. 2005. Generalized inference with multiple semantic role labeling systems. In Ido Dagan and Daniel Gildea, editors, *Proceedings of the Ninth Conference on Computational Natural Language Learning (CoNLL-2005)*, pages 181–184. Association for Computational Linguistics, Morristown, NJ.

Dekang Lin. 1998. Automatic retrieval and clustering of similar words. In Christian Boitet and Pete Whitelock, editors, *Proceedings of the 17th International Conference on Computational Linguistics*, pages 768–774. Association for Computational Linguistics, Morristown, NJ.

Maryellen C. MacDonald and Mark S. Seidenberg. 2006. Constraint satisfaction accounts of lexical and sentence comprehension. In Matthew J. Traxler and Morton A. Gernsbacher, editors, *Handbook of Psycholinguistics (Second Edition)*, pages 581–611. Academic Press, London.

Mitchell P. Marcus, Mary Ann Marcinkiewicz, and Beatrice Santorini. 1993. Building a large annotated corpus of english: the Penn Treebank. *Computational Linguistics*, 19(2):313–330.

Ken McRae, Michael J. Spivey-Knowlton, and Michael K. Tanenhaus. 1998. Modeling the influence of thematic fit (and other constraints) in on-line sentence comprehension. *Journal of Memory and Language*, 38(3):283–312.

Robert M. Nosofsky. 1986. Attention, similarity, and the identification-categorization relationship. *Journal of Experimental Psychology-General*, 115(1):39–57.

Sebastian Padó and Mirella Lapata. 2007. Dependency-based construction of semantic space models. *Computational Linguistics*, 33(2):161–199.

Ulrike Padó, Frank Keller, and Matthew Crocker. 2006. Combining syntax and thematic fit in a probabilistic model of sentence processing. In Ron Sun and Naomi Miyake, editors, *Proceedings of the 28th Annual Conference of the Cognitive Science Society*, pages 657–662. Cognitive Science Society, Austin, TX.

Sebastian Padó, Ulrike Padó, and Katrin Erk. 2007. Flexible, corpus-based modelling of human plausibility judgements. In Jason Eisner, editor, *Proceedings of the 2007 Joint Conference on Empirical Methods in Natural Language Processing and Computational Natural Language Learning (EMNLP-CoNLL)*, pages 400–409. Association for Computational Linguistics, Morristown, NJ.

Martha Palmer, Daniel Gildea, and Paul Kingsbury. 2005. The Proposition Bank: An annotated corpus of semantic roles. *Computational Linguistics*, 31(1):71–106.

Trivellore Raghunathan. 2003. An approximate test for homogeneity of correlated correlation coefficients. *Quality and Quantity*, 4(1):99–110.

Philip Resnik. 1996. Selectional constraints: an information-theoretic model and its computational realization. *Cognition*, 61(1-2):127–159.

Roger N. Shepard. 1987. Toward a universal law of generalization for psychological science. *Science*, 237(4820):1317–1323.

Jakub Zavrel and Walter Daelemans. 1997. Memory-based learning: Using similarity for smoothing. In Philip R. Cohen and Wolfgang Wahlster, editors, *Proceedings of the 35th Annual Meeting of the Association for Computational Linguistics*, pages 436–443. Association for Computational Linguistics, Morristown, NJ.

Growing Finely-Discriminating Taxonomies from Seeds of Varying Quality and Size

Tony Veale
School of Computer Science
University College Dublin
Ireland
tony.veale@ucd.ie

Guofu Li
School of Computer Science
University College Dublin
Ireland
guofu.li@ucd.ie

Yanfen Hao
School of Computer Science
University College Dublin
Ireland
yanfen.hao@ucd.ie

Abstract

Concept taxonomies offer a powerful means for organizing knowledge, but this organization must allow for many overlapping and fine-grained perspectives if a general-purpose taxonomy is to reflect concepts as they are actually employed and reasoned about in everyday usage. We present here a means of bootstrapping finely-discriminating taxonomies from a variety of different starting points, or seeds, that are acquired from three different sources: WordNet, ConceptNet and the web at large.

1 Introduction

Taxonomies provide a natural and intuitive means of organizing information, from the biological taxonomies of the Linnaean system to the layout of supermarkets and bookstores to the organizational structure of companies. Taxonomies also provide the structural backbone for ontologies in computer science, from common-sense ontologies like Cyc (Lenat and Guha, 1990) and SUMO (Niles and Pease, 2001) to lexical ontologies like WordNet (Miller *et al.*, 1990). Each of these uses is based on the same root-branch-leaf metaphor: the broadest terms with the widest scope occupy the highest positions of a taxonomy, near the root, while specific terms with the most local concerns are located lower in the hierarchy, nearest the leaves. The more interior nodes that a taxonomy possesses, the finer the conceptual distinctions and the more gradated the similarity judgments it can make (e.g., Budanitsky and Hirst, 2006).

General-purpose computational taxonomies are called upon to perform both coarse-grained and fine-grained judgments. In NLP, for instance, the semantics of "eat" requires just enough knowledge to discriminate foods like tofu and cheese from non-foods like wool and steel, while specific applications in the domain of cooking and recipes (e.g., Hammond's (1986) CHEF) require enough discrimination to know that tofu can be replaced with clotted cheese in many recipes because each is a soft, white and bland food.

So while much depends on the domain of usage, it remains an open question as to how many nodes a good taxonomy should possess. Princeton WordNet, for instance, strives for as many nodes as there are word senses in English, yet it also contains a substantial number of composite nodes that are lexicalized not as single words, but as complex phrases. Print dictionaries intended for human consumption aim for some economy of structure, and typically do not include the meaning of phrases that can be understood as straightforward compositions of the meaning of their parts (Hanks, 2004). But WordNet also serves another purpose, as a lexical knowledge-base for computers, not humans, a context in which concerns about space seem quaint. When space is not a issue, there seems no good reason to exclude nodes from a concept taxonomy merely for being composites of other ideas; the real test of entry is whether a given node adds value to a taxonomy, by increasing its level of internal organization through the systematic dissection of overly broad categories into finer, more intuitive and manageable clusters.

In this paper we describe a means by which finely-discriminating taxonomies can be *grown* from a variety of different knowledge *seeds*. These taxonomies comprise composite categories that can be lexicalized as phrases of the form "ADJ NOUN", such as Sharp-Instrument, which represents the set of all instruments that are typically considered sharp, such as knives, scissors, chisels and can-openers. While WordNet already contains an equivalent category, named Edge-

Proceedings of the 12th Conference of the European Chapter of the ACL, pages 835–842,
Athens, Greece, 30 March – 3 April 2009. ©2009 Association for Computational Linguistics

Tool, which it defines with the gloss "any cutting tool with a sharp cutting edge", it provides no structural basis for inferring that any member of this category can be considered *sharp*. For the most part, if two ideas (word senses) belong to the same semantic category X in WordNet, the most we can infer is that both possess the trivial property *X-ness*. Our goal here is to construct taxonomies whose form makes explicit the actual properties that accrue from membership in a category.

Past work on related approaches to taxonomy creation are discussed in section 2, while section 3 describes the different knowledge seeds that serve as the starting point for our bootstrapping process. In section 4 we describe the bootstrapping process in more detail; such processes are prone to noise, so we also discuss how the acquired categorizations are validated and filtered after each bootstrapping cycle. An evaluation of the key ideas is then presented in section 5, to determine which seed yields the highest quality taxonomy once bootstrapping is completed. The paper then concludes with some final remarks in section 6.

2 Related Work

Simple pattern-matching techniques can be surprisingly effective for the extraction of lexico-semantic relations from text when those relations are expressed using relatively stable and unambiguous syntagmatic patterns (Ahlswede and Evens, 1988). For instance, the work of Hearst (1992) typifies this surgical approach to relation extraction, in which a system fishes in a large text for particular word sequences that strongly suggest a semantic relationship such as hypernymy or, in the case of Charniak and Berland (1999), the part-whole relation. Such efforts offer high precision but can exhibit low recall on moderate-sized corpora, and extract just a tiny (but very useful) subset of the semantic content of a text. The *KnowItAll* system of Etzioni *et al.* (2004) employs the same generic patterns as Hearst (e.g., "NPs such as NP1, NP2, …"), and more besides, to extract a whole range of facts that can be exploited for web-based question-answering. Cimiano and Wenderoth (2007) also use a range of Hearst-like patterns to find text sequences in web-text that are indicative of the lexico-semantic properties of words; in particular, these authors use phrases like "to * a new NOUN" and "the purpose of NOUN is to *" to identify the formal (isa), agentive (made by) and telic (used for) roles of nouns.

Snow, Jurafsky and Ng (2004) use supervised learning techniques to acquire those syntagmatic patterns that prove most useful for extracting hypernym relations from text. They train their system using pairs of WordNet terms that exemplify the hypernym relation; these are used to identify specific sentences in corpora that are most likely to express the relation in lexical terms. A binary classifier is then trained on lexico-syntactic features that are extracted from a dependency-structure parse of these sentences. Kashyap *et al.*, (2005) experiment with a bootstrapping approach to growing concept taxonomies in the medical domain. A gold standard taxonomy provides terms that are used to retrieve documents which are then hierarchically clustered; cohesiveness measures are used to yield a taxonomy of terms that can then further drive the retrieval and clustering cycle. Kozareva *et al.* (2008) use a bootstrapping approach that extends the fixed-pattern approach of Hearst (1992) in two intriguing ways. First, they use a doubly-anchored retrieval pattern of the form "$NOUN_{cat}$ such as $NOUN_{example}$ and *" to ground the retrieval relative to a known example of hypernymy, so that any values extracted for the wildcard * are likely to be coordinate terms of $NOUN_{example}$ and even more likely to be good examples of $NOUN_{cat}$. Secondly, they construct a graph of terms that co-occur within this pattern to determine which terms are supported by others, and by how much. These authors also use two kinds of bootstrapping: the first variation, dubbed *reckless*, uses the candidates extracted from the double-anchored pattern (via *) as exemplars ($NOUN_{example}$) for successive retrieval cycles; the second variation first checks whether a candidate is sufficiently supported to be used as an exemplar in future retrieval cycles.

The approach we describe here is most similar to that of Kozareva *et al.* (2008). We too use a double-anchored pattern, but place the anchors in different places to obtain the query patterns "ADJ_{cat} $NOUN_{cat}$ such as *" and "ADJ_{cat} * such as $NOUN_{example}$". As a result, we obtain a finely-discriminating taxonomy based on categories that are explicitly annotated with the properties (ADJ_{cat}) that they bequeath to their members. These categories have an obvious descriptive and organizational utility, but of a kind that one is unlikely to find in conventional resources like WordNet and Wikipedia. Kozareva *et al.* (2008) test their approach on relatively simple and objective categories like *states*, *countries* (both closed sets), *singers* and *fish* (both open, the former more so than the latter), but not on complex categories in which members are tied both to a general category, like *food*, and to a stereotypical property, like *sweet* (Veale and Hao, 2007). By validating membership in these complex categories using WordNet-based heuristics, we can hang these categories and members on specific WordNet senses, and thus enrich WordNet with this additional taxonomic structure.

3 Seeds for Taxonomic Growth

A fine-grained taxonomy can be viewed as a set of triples $T_{ijk} = <C_i, D_j, P_k>$, where C_i denotes a child of the parent term P_k that possesses the discriminating property D_j; in effect, each such triple expresses that C_i is a specialization of the complex taxonym D_j-P_k. Thus, the belief that cola is a carbonated-drink is expressed by the triple *<cola, carbonated, drink>*. From this triple we can identify other categorizations of *cola* (such as *treat* and *refreshment*) via the web query "carbonated * such as cola", or we can identify other similarly fizzy drinks via the query "carbonated drinks such as *". So this web-based bootstrapping of fine-grained category hierarchies requires that we already possess a collection of fine-grained distinctions of a relatively high-quality. We now consider three different starting points for this bootstrapping process, as extracted from three different resources: WordNet, ConceptNet and the web at large.

3.1 WordNet

The noun-sense taxonomy of WordNet makes a number of fine-grained distinctions that prove useful in clustering entities into smaller and more natural groupings. For instance, WordNet differentiates *{feline, felid}* into the sub-categories *{true_cat, cat}* and *{big_cat, cat}*, the former serving to group domesticated cats with other cats of a similar size, the latter serving to cluster cats that are larger, wilder and more exotic. However, such fine-grained distinctions are the exception rather than the norm in WordNet, and not one of the 60+ words of the form *Xess* in WordNet that denote a person (such as hunt*ress*, wait*ress*, Jew*ess*, etc.) express the defining property *female* in explicit taxonomic terms. Nonetheless, the free-text glosses associated with WordNet sense-entries often do state the kind of distinctions we would wish to find expressed as explicit taxonyms. A shallow parse of these glosses thus yields a sizable number of fine-grained distinctions, such as *<lioness, female, lion>*, *<espresso, strong, coffee>* and both *<messiah, awaited, king>* and *<messiah, expected, deliverer>*.

3.2 ConceptNet

Despite its taxonomic organization, WordNet owes much to the centralized and authority-preserving craft of traditional lexicography. ConceptNet (Liu and Singh, 2004), in contrast, is a far less authoritative knowledge-source, one that owes more to the workings of the WWW than to conventional print dictionaries. Comprising factoids culled from the template-structured contributions of thousands of web users, ConceptNet expresses many relationships that accurately reflect a public, common-sense view on a given topic (from vampires to dentists) and many more that are simply bizarre or ill-formed. Looking to the relation that interests us here, the IsA relation, ConceptNet tells us that an *espresso* is a *strong coffee* (correctly, like WordNet) but that a *bagel* is a *Jewish word* (confusing *use* with *mention*). Likewise, we find that *expressionism* is an *artistic style* (correct, though WordNet deems it an *artistic movement*) but that an *explosion* is a *suicide attack* (confusing formal and telic roles). Since we cannot trust the content of ConceptNet directly, lest we bootstrap from a highly unreliable starting point, we use WordNet as a simple filter. While the concise form of ConceptNet contains over 30,000 IsA propositions, we consider as our seed collection only those that define a noun concept (such as "espresso") in terms of a binary compound (e.g., "strong coffee") where the head of the latter (e.g., "coffee") denotes a WordNet hypernym of some sense of the former. This yields triples such as *<Wyoming, great, state>*, *<wreck, serious, accident>* and *<wolf, wild, animal>*.

3.3 Web-derived Stereotypes

Veale and Hao (2007) also use the observations of web-users to acquire common perceptions of oft-mentioned ideas, but do so by harvesting simile expressions of the form "as ADJ as a NOUN" directly from the web. Their approach hinges on the fact that similes exploit stereotypes to draw out the salient properties of a target, thereby allowing rich descriptions of those stereotypes to be easily acquired, e.g., that snowflakes are pure and unique, acrobats are agile and nimble, knifes are sharp and dangerous, viruses are malicious and infectious, and so on. However, because they find that almost 15% of their web-harvested similes are ironic (e.g., "as subtle as a rock", "as bulletproof as a sponge-cake", etc.), they filter irony from these associations by hand, to yield a sizable database of stereotypical attributions that describes over 6000 noun concepts in terms of over 2000 adjectival properties. However, because Veale and Hao's data directly maps stereotypical properties to simile vehicles, it does not provide a parent category for these vehicles. Thus, the seed triples derived from this data are only partially instantiated; for instance, we obtain *<surgeon, skilful, ?>*, *<virus, malicious, ?>* and *<dog, loyal, ?>*. This does not prove to be a serious impediment, however, as the missing field of each triple is quickly identified during the first cycle of bootstrapping.

3.4 Overview of Seed Resources

Neither of these three seeds is an entirely useful knowledge-base in its own right. The WordNet-based seed is clearly a representation of convenience, since it contains only those properties that can be acquired from the glosses that happen to be amenable to a simple shallow-parse. The ConceptNet seed is likewise a small collection of low-hanging fruit, made smaller still by the use of WordNet as a coarse but very necessary noise-filter. And while the simile-derived distinctions obtained from Veale and Hao paint a richly detailed picture of the most frequent objects of comparison, this seed offers no coverage for the majority of concepts that are insufficiently noteworthy to be found in web similes. A quantitative comparison of all three seeds is provided in Table 1 below.

	WordNet	ConceptNet	Simile
# terms in total	12,227	1,133	6512
# triples in total	51,314	1808	16,688
# triples per term	4.12	1.6	2.56
# features	2305	550	1172

Table 1: The size of seed collections yielded from different sources.

We can see that WordNet-derived seed is clearly the largest and apparently the most comprehensive knowledge-source of the three: it contains the most terms (concepts), the most features (discriminating properties of those concepts), and the most triples (which situate those concepts in parent categories that are further specialized by these discriminating features). But size is only weakly suggestive of quality, and as we shall see in the next section, even such dramatic differences in scale can disappear after several cycles of bootstrapping. In section 5 we will then consider which of these seeds yields the highest quality taxonomies after bootstrapping has been applied.

4 Bootstrapping from Seeds

The seeds of the previous section each represent a different starting collection of triples. It is the goal of the bootstrapping process to grow these collections of triples, to capture more of the terms – and more of the distinctions – that a taxonomy is expected to know about. The expansion set of a triple $T_{ijk} = <C_i, D_j, P_k>$ is the set of triples that can be acquired from the web using the following query expansions (* is a search wildcard):

1. "D_j * such as C_i"
2. "D_j P_k such as *"

In the first query, a noun is sought to yield another categorization of C_i, while in the second, other members of the fine-grained category D_j-P_k are sought to accompany C_i. In parsing the text snippets returned by these queries, we also exploit text sequences that match the following patterns:

3. "* and D_j P_k such as *"
4. "* and D_j * such as C_i"

These last two patterns allow us to learn new discriminating features by noting how these discriminators are combined to reinforce each other in some ad-hoc category formulations. For instance, the phrase "cold and refreshing beverages such as lemonade" allows us to acquire the triples *<lemonade, cold, beverage>* and *<lemonade, refreshing, beverage>*. This pattern is necessary if the bootstrapping process is to expand beyond the limited vocabulary of discriminating features (D_j) found in the original seed collections of triples.

We denote the mapping from a triple T to the set of additional triples that can be acquired from the web using the above queries/patterns as *expand(T')*. We currently implement this function using the Google search API. Our experiences with each query suggest that 200 snippets is a good search range for the first query, while 50 is usually more than adequate for the second.

We can now denote the knowledge that is acquired when starting from a given seed collection S after t cycles of bootstrapping as K_t^S. Thus,

$$K_0^S = S$$
$$K_1^S = K_0^S \cup \{T \mid T' \in S \wedge T \in expand(T')\}$$
$$K_{t+1}^S = K_t^S \cup \{T \mid T' \in K_t^S \wedge T \in expand(T')\}$$

Web queries, and the small snippets of text that they return, offer just a keyhole view of language as it is used in real documents. Unsurprisingly, the new triples acquired from the web via *expand(T')* are likely to be very noisy indeed. Following Kozareva *et al.* (2008), we can either indulge in *reckless bootstrapping*, which ignores the question of noise until all bootstrapping is finished, or we can apply a noise filter after each incremental step. The latter approach has the additional advantage of keeping the search-space as small as possible, which is a major consideration when bootstrapping from sizable seeds. We use a simple WordNet-based filter called *near-miss*: a new triple $\langle C_i, D_j, P_k \rangle$ is accepted if WordNet contains a sense of C_i that is a descendant of some sense of P_k (a hit), or a sense of C_i that is a descendant of the direct hypernym of some sense of P_k (a near-miss). This allows the bootstrapping process to acquire structures that are not simply a decorated version of the basic WordNet taxonomy, but to acquire hierarchical relations whose undifferentiated forms are not in WordNet (yet are largely compatible with WordNet). This non-reckless bootstrapping process can be expressed as follows:

$$K_{t+1}^S = K_t^S \cup \left\{T \,\middle|\, T' \in K_t^S \wedge T \in filter_{near-miss}(expand(T'))\right\}$$

Figure 1 and figure 2 below illustrate the rate of growth of triple-sets from each of our three seeds.

Referring again to table 1, we note that while the ConceptNet collection is by far the smallest of the three seeds – more that 7 times smaller than the simile-derived seed, and almost 40 times smaller than the WordNet seed – this difference is size shrinks considerably over the course of five bootstrapping cycles. The WordNet *near-miss* filter ensures that the large body of triples grown from each seed are broadly sound, and that we are not simply generating comparable quantities of nonsense in each case.

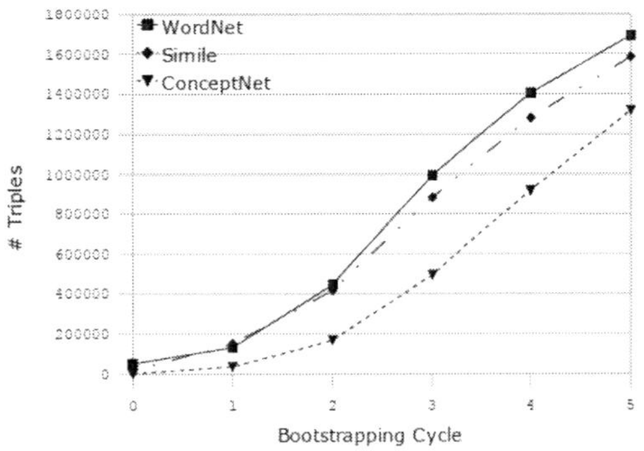

Figure 1: Growth in the number of acquired triples, over 5 cycles of bootstrapping from different seeds.

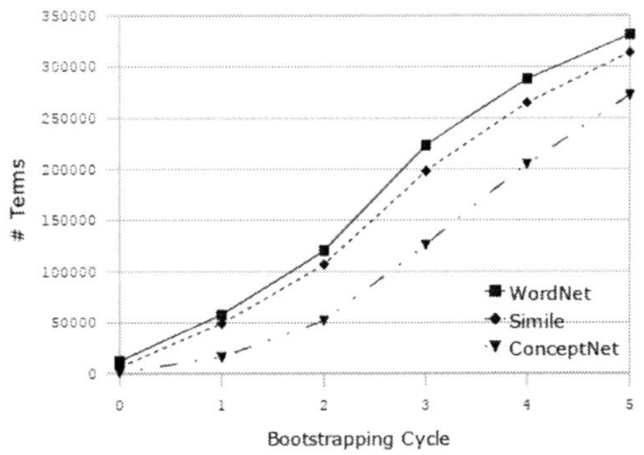

Figure 2: Growth in the number of terms described by the acquired triples, over 5 cycles of bootstrapping from different seeds.

4.1 An Example

Consider *cola*, for which the simile seed has one triple: *<cola, refreshing, beverage>*. After a single cycle of bootstrapping, we find that *cola* can now be described as an *effervescent beverage*, a *sweet beverage*, a *nonalcoholic beverage* and more. After a second cycle, we find it described as a *sugary food*, a *fizzy drink* and a *dark mixer*. After a third cycle, it is found to be a *sensitive beverage*, an *everyday beverage* and a *common drink*. After a fourth cycle, it is also found to be an *irritating food* and an *unhealthy drink*. After the fifth cycle, it is found to be a *stimulating drink*, a *toxic food* and a *corrosive substance*. In all, the single *cola* triple in the simile seed yields 14 triples after 1 cycle, 43 triples after 2 cycles, 72 after 3 cycles, 93 after 4 cycles, and 102 after 5 cycles. During these bootstrapping cycles, the description *refreshing beverage* additionally becomes associated with the terms *champagne*, *lemonade* and *beer*.

5 Empirical Evaluation

The WordNet *near-miss* filter thus ensures that the parent field (P_k) of every triple contains a value that is sensible for the given child concept (C_i), but does not ensure that the discriminating property (D_j) in each triple is equally sensible and apropos. To see whether the bootstrapping process is simply padding the seed taxonomy with large quantities of noise, or whether the acquired D_j values do indeed mark out the implicit essence of the C_i terms they describe, we need an evaluation framework that can quantify the ontological usefulness of these D_j values. For this, we use the experimental setup of Almuhareb and Poesio (2005), who use information extraction from the web to acquire attribute values for different terms/concepts, and who then compare the taxonomy that can be induced by clustering these values with the taxonomic backbone of WordNet.

Almuhareb and Poesio first created a balanced set of 402 nouns from 21 different semantic classes in WordNet. They then acquired attested attribute values for these nouns (such as *hot* for coffee, *red* for car, etc.) using the query "*(a|an|the) * C_i (is|was)*" to find corresponding D_j values for each C_i. Unlike our work, these authors did *not* seek to acquire hypernyms for each C_i during this search, and did not try to link the acquired attribute values to a particular branching point (P_k) in the taxonomy (they did, however, seek matching attributes for these values, such as *Temperature* for *hot*, but that aspect is not relevant here). They acquired 94,989 attribute values in all for the 402 test nouns. These values were then used as features of the corresponding nouns in a clustering experiment, using the CLUTO system of Karypis (2002). By using attribute values as a basis for partitioning the set of 402 nouns into 21 different categories, Almuhareb and Poesio attempted to reconstruct the original 21 WordNet categories from which the nouns were drawn. The more accurate the match to the original WordNet clustering, the more these attribute values can be seen (and used) as a representation of conceptual structure. In their first attempt, they achieved just a 56.7% clustering accuracy against the original human-assigned categories of WordNet. But after using a noise-filter to remove almost half of the web-harvested attribute values, they achieve a higher cluster accuracy of 62.7%. More specifically, Poesio and Almuhareb achieve a cluster purity of 0.627 and a cluster entropy of 0.338 using 51,345 features to describe and cluster the 402 nouns.[1]

We replicate the above experiments using the same 402 nouns, and assess the clustering accuracy (again using WordNet as a gold-standard) after each bootstrapping cycle. Recall that we use only the D_j fields of each triple as features for the clustering process, so the comparison with the WordNet gold-standard is still a fair one. Once again, the goal is to determine how much like the human-crafted WordNet taxonomy is the taxonomy that is clustered automatically from the discriminating words D_j only. The clustering accuracy for all three seeds are shown in Tables 2, 3 and 4.

Cycle	E	P	# Features	Coverage
1st	.327	.629	907	66%
2nd	.253	.712	1,482	77%
3rd	.272	.717	2,114	82%
4th	.312	.640	2,473	83%
5th	.289	.684	2,752	83%

Table 2: Clustering accuracy using the *WordNet* seed collection (E denotes Entropy and P stands for Purity)

Cycle	E	P	# Features	Coverage
1st	.115	.842	363	41%
2nd	.255	.724	787	59%
3rd	.286	.694	1,362	74%
4th	.279	.694	1,853	79%
5th	.299	.673	2,274	82%

Table 3: Clustering accuracy using the *ConceptNet* seed collection

Cycle	E	P	# Features	Coverage
1st	.254	.716	837	59%
2nd	.280	.712	1,338	73%
3rd	.289	.693	1,944	79%
4th	.313	.660	2,312	82%
5th	.157	.843	2,614	82%

Table 4: Clustering accuracy using the *Simile* seed collection

The test-set of 402 nouns contains some low-frequency words, such as *casuarina, cinchona, dodecahedron*, and *concavity*, and Almuhareb and

[1] We use cluster purity as a reflection of clustering accuracy. We express accuracy as a percentage; hence a purity of 0.627 is seen as an accuracy of 62.7%.

Poesio note that one third of their data-set has a low-frequency of between 5-100 occurrences in the British National Corpus. Looking to the coverage column of each table, we thus see that there are words in the Poesio and Almuhareb data set for which no triples can be acquired in 5 cycles of bootstrapping. Interestingly, though each seed is quite different in origin and size (see again Table 1), all reach similar levels of coverage (~82%) after 5 bootstrapping cycles. Test nouns for which all three seeds fail to reach a description include *yesteryear, nonce* (very rare), *salient* (more typically an adjective), *jag, droop, fluting, fete, throb, poundage, stinging, rouble, rupee, riel, drachma, escudo, dinar, dirham, lira, dispensation, hoard, airstream* (not typically a solid compound), *riverside* and *curling*. Figures 3 and 4 summarize the key findings in the above tables: while bootstrapping from all three seeds converges to the same level of coverage, the simile seed clearly produces the highest quality taxonomy.

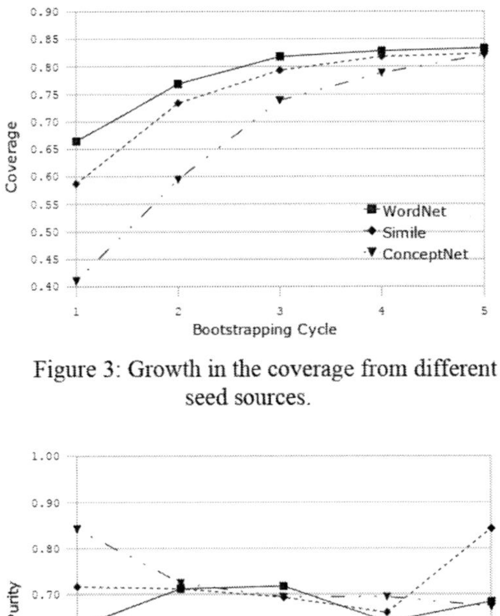

Figure 3: Growth in the coverage from different seed sources.

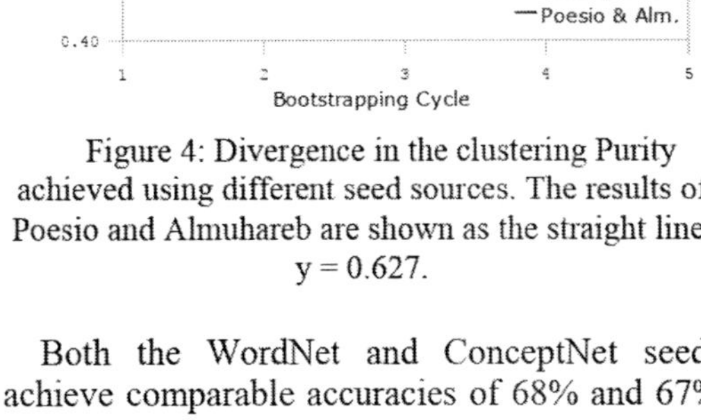

Figure 4: Divergence in the clustering Purity achieved using different seed sources. The results of Poesio and Almuhareb are shown as the straight line: y = 0.627.

Both the WordNet and ConceptNet seeds achieve comparable accuracies of 68% and 67% respectively after 5 cycles of bootstrapping, which compares well with the accuracy of 62.7% achieved by Poesio and Almuhareb. However, the simile seed clearly yields the best accuracy of 84.3%, which also exceeds the accuracy of 66.4% achieved by Poesio and Almuhareb when using both values *and* attributes (such as *Temperature, Color*, etc.) for clustering, or the accuracy of 70.9% they achieve when using attributes alone. Furthermore, bootstrapping from the simile seed yields higher cluster accuracy on the 402-noun data-set than Veale and Hao (2008) themselves achieve with their simile data on the same test-set (69.85%).

But most striking of all is the concision of the representations that are acquired using bootstrapping. The simile seed yields a high cluster accuracy using a pool of just 2,614 fine discriminators, while Poesio and Almuhareb use 51,345 features even after their feature-set has been filtered for noise. Though starting from different initial scales, each seed converges toward a feature-set that is roughly twenty times smaller than that used by Poesio and Almuhareb.

6 Conclusions

These experiments reveal that seed knowledge of different authoritativeness, quality and size will tend to converge toward roughly the same number of finely discriminating properties and toward much the same coverage after 5 or so cycles of bootstrapping. Nonetheless, quality wins out, and the simile-derived seed knowledge shows itself to be a clearly superior basis for reasoning about the structure and organization of conceptual categories. Bootstrapping from the simile seed yields a slightly smaller set of discriminating features than bootstrapping from the WordNet seed, one that is many times smaller than the Poesio and Almuhareb feature set. What matters is that they are the right features to discriminate with.

There appears to be a number of reasons for this significant difference in quality. For one, Veale and Hao (2007) show that similes express highly stereotypical beliefs that strongly influence the affective disposition of a term/concept; negatively perceived concepts are commonly used to exemplify negative properties in similes, while positively perceived concepts are widely used to exemplify positive properties. Veale and Hao (2008) go on to argue that similes offer a very concise snapshot of those widely-held beliefs that are the cornerstone of everyday reasoning, and which should thus be the corner-stone of any general-purpose taxonomy. In addition, beliefs expressed via the "as D_j as C_i" form of similes appear to lend themselves to re-expression via the "D_j P_k such as C_i" form; in each case, a concept C_i is held up as an exemplar of a salient property D_j. Since the "such as" bootstrapping pattern seeks out expressions of prototypicality on the web, a simile-derived seed set is likely the best starting point for this search.

All three seeds appear to suffer the same coverage limitations, topping out at about 82% of the words in the Poesio and Almuhareb data-set. Indeed, after 5 bootstrapping cycles, all three seeds give rise to taxonomies that overlap on 328 words from the 402-noun test-set, accounting for 81.59% of the test-set. In effect then, bootstrapping stumbles over the same core of hard words in each case, no matter the seed that is used. As such, the problem of coverage lies not in the seed collection, but in the queries used to perform the bootstrapping. The same coverage limitations will thus apply to other bootstrapping approaches to knowledge acquisition, such as Kozareva *et al.* (2008), which rely on much the same stock patterns. So while bootstrapping may not be a general solution for acquiring all aspects of a general-purpose taxonomy, it is clearly useful in acquiring large swathes of such a taxonomy if given a sufficiently high-quality seed to start from.

References

Ahlswede, T. and Evans, M. (1988). Parsing vs. Text Processing in the analysis of dictionary definitions. *In Proc. of the 26th* Annual Meeting of the ACL, pp 217-224.

Almuhareb, A. and Poesio, M. (2005). Concept Learning and Categorization from the Web. In *Proc. of the annual meeting of the Cognitive* Science *Society*, Italy, July.

Budanitsky, A. and Hirst, G. (2006). Evaluating WordNet-based Measures of Lexical Semantic Relatedness. *Computational Linguistics,* 32(1):13-47.

Cimiano, P. and Wenderoth, J. (2007). Automatic Acquisition of Ranked Qualia Structures from the Web. *In Proc. of the 45th Annual Meeting of the ACL*, pp 888-895.

Charniak, E. and Berland, M. (1999). Finding parts in very large corpora. *In Proc. of the 37th Annual Meeting of the ACL*, pp 57–64.

Etzioni, O., Kok, S., Soderland, S., Cafarella, M., Popescu, A-M., Weld, D., Downey, D., Shaked, T. and Yates, A. (2004). Web-scale information extraction in KnowItAll (preliminary results). *In Proc. of the 13th WWW Conference*, pp 100–109.

Hammond, K. J. (1986). CHEF : A Model of Case--based Planning. *In Proc. of the 5th National Conference on Artificial Intelligence*, pp 267--271, Philadelphia, Pennsylvania. American Association for Artificial Intelligence.

Hanks, P. (2004). WordNet: What is to be done? In *Proc. of GWC'2004, the 2nd Global WordNet conference*, Masaryk University, Brno.

Hearst, M. (1992). Automatic acquisition of hyponyms from large text corpora. *In Proc. of the 14th Int. Conf. on Computational Linguistics*, pp 539–545.

Kashyap, V. Ramakrishnan, C. and Sheth, T. A. (2005). TaxaMiner: an experimentation framework for automated taxonomy bootstrapping. *Int. Journal of Web and Grid Services* 1(2), pp 240-266.

Karypis, G. (2002). CLUTO: A clustering toolkit. *Technical Report 02-017*, University of Minnesota. http://www-users.cs.umn.edu/~karypis/cluto/.

Kozareva, Z., Riloff, E. and Hovy, E. (2008). Semantic Class Learning from the Web with Hyponym Pattern Linkage Graphs. *In Proc. of the 46th Annual Meeting of the ACL.*

Lenat, D. B. and Guha, R. V. (1990). Building large knowledge-based systems: representation and inference in the Cyc project. NY: Addison-Wesley.

Liu, H. and Singh, P. (2004), ConceptNet: A Practical Commonsense Reasoning Toolkit. *BT Technology Journal*, 22(4):211-226.

Miller, G., Beckwith,R., Fellbaum, C., Gross, D. and Miller, K.J. (1990). Introduction to WordNet: an on-line lexical database. Int. Journal of Lexicography, 3(4):235 – 244.

Niles, I. and Pease, A. (2001). Toward a standard upper ontology. *In Proc. of the 2nd International Conference on Formal Ontology in Information Systems (FOIS-2001).*

Snow, R., Jurafsky, D. and Ng, A. Y. (2004). Learning syntactic patterns for automatic hypernym discovery. *Advances in Neural Information Processing Systems* 17.

Veale, T. and Hao, Y. (2007). Making Lexical Ontologies Functional and Context-Sensitive. *In Proc. of the 45th Annual Meeting of the ACL*, pp 57–64.

Veale, T. and Hao, Y. (2008). A Fluid Knowledge Representation for Understanding and Generating Creative Metaphors. *In Proc. of Coling 2008, The 22nd International Conference on Computational Linguistics*, Manchester.

Feature-based Method for Document Alignment in Comparable News Corpora

Thuy Vu, Ai Ti Aw, Min Zhang
Department of Human Language Technology, Institute for Infocomm Research
1 Fusionopolis Way, #21-01 Connexis, South Tower, Singapore 138632
{tvu, aaiti, mzhang}@i2r.a-star.edu.sg

Abstract

In this paper, we present a feature-based method to align documents with similar content across two sets of bilingual comparable corpora from daily news texts. We evaluate the contribution of each individual feature and investigate the incorporation of these diverse statistical and heuristic features for the task of bilingual document alignment. Experimental results on the English-Chinese and English-Malay comparable news corpora show that our proposed Discrete Fourier Transform-based term frequency distribution feature is very effective. It contributes 4.1% and 8% to performance improvement over Pearson's correlation method on the two comparable corpora. In addition, when more heuristic and statistical features as well as a bilingual dictionary are utilized, our method shows an absolute performance improvement of 23.2% and 15.3% on the two sets of bilingual corpora when comparing with a prior information retrieval-based method.

1 Introduction

The problem of document alignment is described as the task of aligning documents, news articles for instance, across two corpora based on content similarity. The groups of corpora can be in the same or in different languages, depending on the purpose of one's task. In our study, we attempt to align similar documents across comparable corpora which are bilingual, each set written in a different language but having similar content and domain coverage for different communication needs.

Previous works on monolingual document alignment focus on automatic alignment between documents and their presentation slides or between documents and their abstracts. Kan (2007) uses two similarity measures, Cosine and Jaccard, to calculate the candidate alignment score in his SlideSeer system, a digital library software that retrieves documents and their narrated slide presentations. Daumé and Marcu (2004) use a phrase-based HMM model to mine the alignment between documents and their human-written abstracts. The main purpose of this work is to increase the size of the training corpus for a statistical-based summarization system.

The research on similarity calculation for multilingual comparable corpora has attracted more attention than monolingual comparable corpora. However, the purpose and scenario of these works are rather varied. Steinberger et al. (2002) represent document contents using descriptor terms of a multilingual thesaurus EUROVOC[1], and calculate the semantic similarity based on the distance between the two documents' representations. The assignment of descriptors is trained by log-likelihood test and computed by $TFIDF$, Cosine, and Okapi. Similarly, Pouliquen et al. (2004) use a linear combination of three types of knowledge: cognates, geographical place names reference, and map documents based on the EUROVOC. The major limitation of these works is the use of EUROVOC, which is a specific resource workable only for European languages.

Aligning documents across parallel corpora is another area of interest. Patry and Langlais (2005) use three similarity scores, Cosine, Normalized Edit Distance, and Sentence Alignment Score, to compute the similarity between two parallel documents. An Adaboost classifier is trained on a list of scored text pairs labeled as parallel or non-parallel. Then, the learned classifier is used to check the correctness of each alignment candidate. Their method is simple but effective. However, the features used in this method are only suitable for parallel corpora as the measurement is mainly based on structural similarity. One goal of document alignment is for parallel sentence extraction for applications like statistical machine translation. Cheung and Fung (2004) highlight that most

[1] EUROVOC is a multilingual thesaurus covering the fields in which the European Communities are active.

Proceedings of the 12th Conference of the European Chapter of the ACL, pages 843–851,
Athens, Greece, 30 March – 3 April 2009. ©2009 Association for Computational Linguistics

of the current sentence alignment models are applicable for parallel documents, rather than comparable documents. In addition, they argue that document alignment should be done before parallel sentence extraction.

Tao and Zhai (2005) propose a general method to extract comparable bilingual text without using any linguistic resources. The main feature of this method is the frequency correlation of words in different languages. They assume that those words in different languages should have similar frequency correlation if they are actually translations of each other. The association between two documents is then calculated based on this information using Pearson's correlation together with two monolingual features $BM25$, a term frequency normalization (Stephan et al., 1994), and IDF. The main advantages of this approach are that it is purely statistical-based and it is language-independent. However, its performance may be compromised due to the lack of linguistic knowledge, particularly across corpora which are linguistically very different. Recently, Munteanu (2006) introduces a rather simple way to get the group of similar content document in multilingual comparable corpus by using the Lemur IR Toolkit (Ogilvie and Callan, 2001). This method first pushes all the target documents into the database of the Lemur, and then uses a word-by-word translation of each source document as a query to retrieve similar content target documents.

This paper will leverage on previous work, and propose and explore diverse range of features in our system. Our document alignment system consists of three stages: candidate generation, feature extraction and feature combination. We verify our method on two set of bilingual news comparable corpora English-Chinese and English-Malay. Experimental results show that 1) when only using Fourier Transform-based term frequency, our method outperforms our re-implementation of Tao (2005)'s method by 4.1% and 8% for the top 100 alignment candidates and, 2) when using all features, our method significantly outperforms our implementation of Munteanu's (2006) method by 23.2% and 15.3%.

The paper is organized as follows. In section 2, we describe the overall architecture of our system. Section 3 discusses our improved frequency correlation-based feature, while Section 4 describes in detail the document relationship heuristics used in our model. Section 5 reports the experimental results. Finally, we conclude our work in section 6.

2 System Architecture

Fig 1 shows the general architecture of our document alignment system. It consists of three components: candidate generation, feature extraction, and feature combination. Our system works on two sets of monolingual corpora to derive a set of document alignments that are comparable in their content.

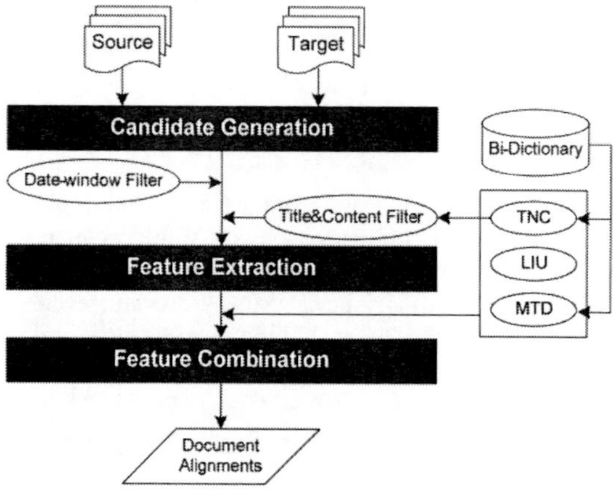

Fig 1. Architecture for Document Alignment Model.

2.1 Candidate Generation

Like many other text processing systems, the system first defines two filtering criteria to prune out "clearly bad" candidates. This will dramatically reduce the search space. We implement the following filers for this purpose:

Date-Window Filter: As mentioned earlier, the data used for the present work are news corpora—a text genre that has very strong links with the time element. The published date of document is available in data, and can easily be used as an indicator to evaluate the relation between two articles in terms of time. Similar to Munteanu's (2006), we aim to constrain the number of candidates by assuming that documents with similar content should have publication dates which are fairly close to each other, even though they reside in two different sets of corpora. By imposing this constraint, both the complexity and the cost in computation can be reduced tremendously as the number of candidates would be significantly reduced. For example, when a 1-day window size is set, this means that for a given source document, the search for its target candidates is set within 3 days of the source document: the same day of publication, the day after, and the day before. With this filter, using the data of one-month in our experiment, a reduction of 90% of all possible alignments can be achieved (section 5.1). Moreover, with our evaluation data, after filtering out document pairs using a 1-day window size, up to 81.6% for English-Chinese and 80.3% for English-Malay of the golden alignments are covered. If the window size is increased to 5, the coverage is 96.6% and 95.6% for two language pairs respectively.

Title-n-Content Filter: previous date window filter constrains the number of candidates based purely on temporal information without exploiting any knowledge of the documents' contents. The number of candidates to be generated is thus dependent on the number of published articles per day, instead of the candidates' potential content similarity. For this reason, we introduce another filter which makes use of document titles to gauge content-wise cross document similarity. As document titles are available in news data, we capitalize on words found in these document titles, favoring alignment candidates where at least one of the title-words in the source document has its translation found in the content of the other target document. This filter can reduce a further 47.9% (English-Chinese) and 26.3% (English-Malay) of the remaining alignment candidates after applying the date-window filter.

2.2 Feature Extraction

The second step extracts all the features for each candidate and computes the score for each individual feature function. In our model, the feature set is composed of the Title-n-Content score (TNC), Linguistic-Independent-Unit score (LIU), and Monolingual Term Distribution similarity (MTD). We will discuss all three features in sections 3 and 4.

2.3 Feature Combination

The final score for each alignment candidate is computed by combining all the feature function scores into a unique score. In literature, there are many methods concerning the estimation of the overall score for a given feature set, which vary from supervised to unsupervised method. Supervised methods such as Support Vector Machine (SVM) and Maximum Entropy (ME) estimate the weight of each feature based on training data which are then used to calculate the final score. However, these supervised learning-based methods may not be applicable to our proposed issue as we are motivated to build a language independent unsupervised system. We simply take a product of all normalized features to obtain one unique score. This is because our features are probabilistically independent. In our implementation, we normalize the scores to make them less sensitive to the absolute value by taking the logarithm $ln(.)$ as follows:

$$norm(x) = \begin{cases} ln(x+T), & x > (e-T) \\ 1, & else \end{cases} \quad (1)$$

$(e-T)$ is a threshold for x to contribute positively to the unique score. In our experiment, we empirically choose T be 2.2, and the threshold for x is 0.51828 (as $e \approx 2.71828$).

3 Monolingual Term Distribution

3.1 Baseline Model

The main feature used in Tao and Zhai (2005) is the frequency distribution similarity or frequency correlation of words in two given corpora. It is assumed that frequency distributions of topically-related words in multilingual comparable corpora are often correlated due to the correlated coverage of the same events.

Let $\mathbf{x} = \{x_1, x_2, \dots, x_n\}$ and $\mathbf{y} = \{y_1, y_2, \dots, y_n\}$ be the frequency distribution vectors of two words x and y in two documents respectively. The frequency correlation of the two words is computed by Pearson's Correlation Coefficient in (2).

$$r(x,y) = \frac{\sum_{i=1}^{n} x_i y_i - \sum_{i=1}^{n} x_i \sum_{i=1}^{n} y_i}{\sqrt{\left(\sum_{i=1}^{n} x_i^2 - \frac{1}{n}\left(\sum_{i=1}^{n} x_i\right)^2\right)\left(\sum_{i=1}^{n} y_i^2 - \frac{1}{n}\left(\sum_{i=1}^{n} y_i\right)^2\right)}} \quad (2)$$

The similarity of two documents is calculated with the addition of two features namely Inverse Document Frequency (IDF) and $BM25$ term frequency normalization shown in the equation (3).

$$s(d_1, d_2) = \sum_{x \in d_1, y \in d_2} IDF(x) \cdot IDF(y) \cdot r(x,y) \cdot BM25(x, d_1) \cdot BM25(y, d_2) \quad (3)$$

Where $BM25(w,d)$ is the word frequency normalization for word w in document d, and $AveDocLen$ is the average length of a document.

$$BM25(w,d) = \frac{k_1 c(w,d)}{c(w,d) + k_1\left(1 - b + b\frac{|d|}{AveDocLen}\right)} \quad (4)$$

It is noted that the key feature used by Tao and Zhai (2005) is the $r(x,y)$ score which depends purely on statistical information. Therefore, our motivation is to propose more features to link the source and target documents more effectively for a better performance.

3.2 Study on Frequency Correlation

We further investigate the frequency correlation of words from comparable sets of corpora comprising three different languages using the above-defined model.

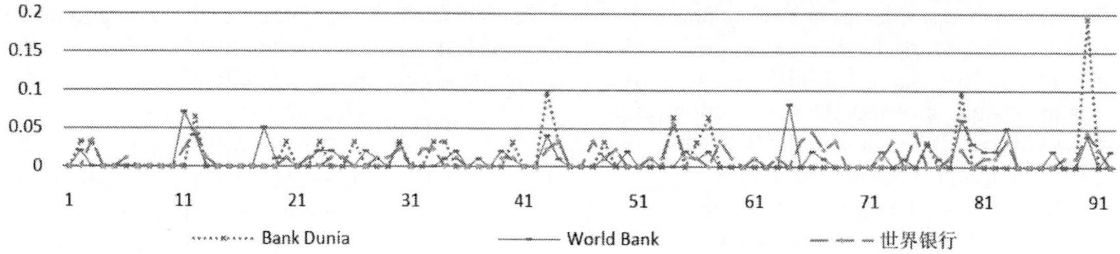

Fig 2. Sample of frequency correlation for "Bank Dunia", "World Bank", and "世界银行".

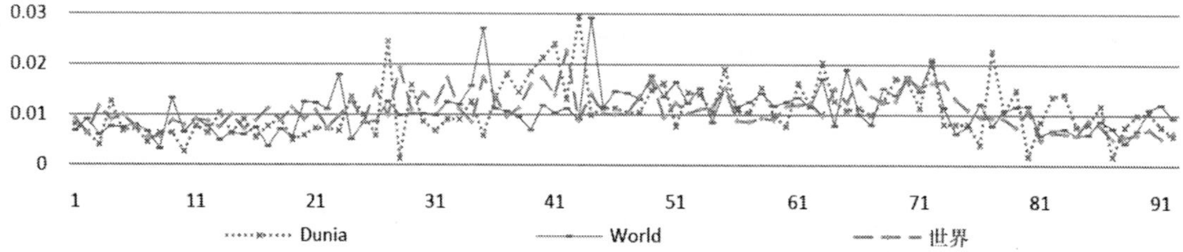

Fig 3. Sample of frequency correlation for "Dunia", "World", and "世界".

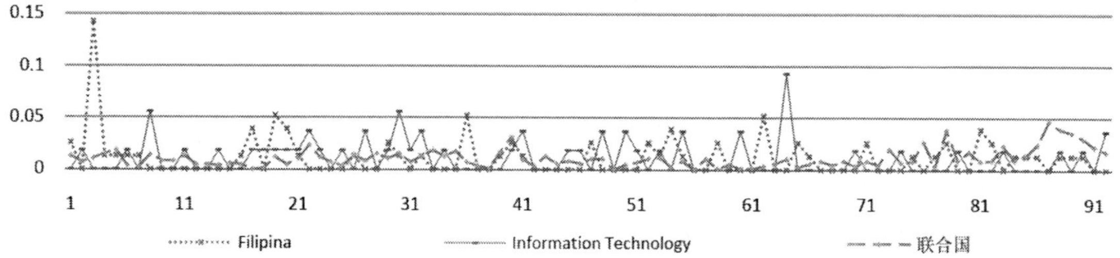

Fig 4. Sample of frequency correlation for "Filipina", "Information Technology", and "联合国".

Using three months - May to July, 2006 – of daily newspaper in Strait Times[2] (in English), Zao Bao[3] (in Chinese), and Berita Harian[4] (in Malay), we conduct the experiments described in the following Fig 2, Fig 3, and Fig 4 showing three different cases of term or word correlation. In these figures, the x-axis denotes time and the y-axis shows the frequency distribution of the term or word.

Multi-word versus Single-word: Fig 2 illustrates that the distributions for multi-word term such as "World Bank", "世界银行(*World Bank* in Chinese)", and "Bank Dunia (*World Bank* in Malay)" in the three language corpora are almost similar because of the discriminative power of that phrase. The phrase has no variance and contains no ambiguity. On the other hand, the distributions for single words may have much less similarity.

Related Common Word: we also investigate the similarity in frequency distribution for related common single words in the case of "World", "世界 (*world* in Chinese)", and "Dunia (*world* in Malay)" as shown in Fig 3. It can be observed that the correlation of these common words is not as strong as that in the multi-word sample illustrated in Fig 2. The reason is that there are many variances of these common words, which usually do not have high discriminative power due to the ambiguities presented within them. Nonetheless, among these variances, there is still a small similar distribution trends that can be detected, which may enable us to discover the associations between them.

Unrelated Common Word: Fig 4 shows the frequency distribution of three unrelated common words over the same three-month period. No correlation in distribution is found among them.

[2] http://www.straitstimes.com/ an English news agency in Singapore. Source © Singapore Press Holdings Ltd.

[3] http://www.zaobao.com/ a Chinese news agency in Singapore. Source © Singapore Press Holdings Ltd.

[4] http://cyberita.asia1.com.sg/ a Malay news agency in Singapore. Source © Singapore Press Holdings Ltd.

3.3 Enhancement from Baseline Model

3.3.1 Monolingual Term Correlation

Due to the inadequacy of the baseline's purely statistical approach, and our studies on the correlations of single, multiple and commonly appearing words, we propose using "term" or "multi-word" instead of "single-word" or "word" to calculate the similarity of term frequency distribution between two documents. This presents us with two main advantages. Firstly, the smaller number of terms compared to the number of words present in any document would imply fewer possible document alignment pairs for the system. This increases the computation speed remarkably. To extract automatically the list of terms in each document, we use the term extraction model from Vu et al. (2008). In corpora used in our experiments, the average ratios of word/term per document are 556/37, 410/28 and 384/28 for English, Chinese, and Malay respectively. The other advantage of using terms is that terms are more distinctive than words as they contain less ambiguity, thus enabling high correlation to be observed when compared with single words.

3.3.2 Bilingual Dictionary Incorporation

In addition to using terms for the computation, we observed from equation (3) that the only mutual feature relating the two documents is the frequency distribution coefficient $r(x,y)$. It is likely that the alignment performance could be enhanced if more features relating the two documents are incorporated.

Following that, we introduce a linguistic feature, $DicScore(x,y)$, to the baseline model to enhance the association between two documents. This feature involves the comparison of the translations of words within a particular term in one language, and the presence of these translations in the corresponding target language term. If more translations obtained from a bilingual dictionary of words within a term are found in the term extracted from the other language's document, it is more likely that the 2 bilingual terms are translations of each other. This feature counts the number of word translation found between the two terms, as described in the following. Let t_1 and t_2 be the term list of d_1 and d_2 respectively, the similarity score in our model is:

$$s_{dic}(d_1,d_2) = \sum_{x\in t_1, y\in t_2} IDF(x)\cdot IDF(y)\cdot r(x,y)\cdot DicScore(x,y)\cdot BM25(x,d_1)\cdot BM25(y,d_2) \quad (5)$$

3.3.3 Distribution Similarity Measurement using Monolingual Term

Finally, we apply the results of time-series research to replace Pearson's correlation which is used in the baseline model, in our calculation of the similarity score of two frequency distributions. A popular technique for time sequence matching is to use Discrete Fourier Transform (DFT) (Agrawal et al, 1993). More recently, Klementiev and Roth (2006) also use F-index (Hetland, 2004), a score using DFT, to calculate the time distribution similarity. In our model, we assume that the frequency chain of a word is a sequence, and calculate DFT score for each chain by the following formula:

$$H_n = \sum_{k=0} h_k . e^{2\pi ikn/N} \quad (6)$$

In time series research, it is proven that only the first few k coefficients of a DFT chain are strong and important for comparison (Agrawal et al, 1993). Our experiments in section 5 show that the best value for k is 7 for both language pairs.

$$R(x,y) = \left(\sqrt{\sum_{i=0}^{k} \left(H_{xi} - H_{yi}\right)^2}\right)^{-1} \quad (7)$$

The $r(x,y)$ in equation (5) is replaced by $R(x,y)$ in equation (8) to calculate the Monolingual Term Distribution (MTD) score.

$$s_{MTD}(d_1,d_2) = \sum_{x\in t_1, y\in t_2} IDF(x)\cdot IDF(y)\cdot R(x,y)\cdot DicScore(x,y)\cdot BM25(x,d_1)\cdot BM25(y,d_2) \quad (8)$$

4 Document Relationship Heuristics

Besides the MTD, we also propose two heuristic-based features that focus directly on the relationship between two multilingual documents, namely the *Title-n-Content* score– TNC , which measures the relationship between the title and content of a document pair, and *Linguistic Independent Unit* score – LIU, which make use of orthographic similarity between unit of words for the different languages.

4.1 Title-n-Content Score (*TNC*)

Besides being a filter for removing bad alignment candidates, TNC is also incorporated as a feature in the computation of document alignment score. In the corpora used, in most documents, "title" does reveal the main topic of a document. The use of words in a news title is typically concise and conveys the essence of the information in the document. Thus, a high TNC score would indicate a high likelihood of similarity between two bilingual documents. Therefore, we use TNC as a quantitative feature in our feature set. Function $TR(w,c)$ checks whether the translation of a word in a document's title is found in the content of its aligned document:

$$TR(w,c) = \begin{cases} 1, & \text{translation of } w \text{ is in } c \\ 0, & \text{else} \end{cases} \quad (9)$$

The TNC score of document d_s and d_t is calculated by the following formula:

$$TNC(d_s,d_t) = \sum_{w_i \in T_s} TR(w_i,c_t) + \sum_{w_j \in T_t} TR(w_j,d_s) \quad (10)$$

Where c_t and c_s are the content of document d_t and d_s; and T_s and T_t are the set of title words of two documents.

In addition, this method speeds up the alignment process without compromising performance when compared with the calculation based only on contents on both sides.

4.2 Linguistic Independent Unit (*LIU*)

Linguistic Independent Unit score (LIU) is defined as the piece of information, which is written in the same way for different languages. The following highlight the number 25, 11, and 50 as linguistic-independent-units for the two sentences.

English: Between Feb ***25*** *and March* ***11*** *this year, she used counterfeit $50 notes* ***10*** *times to pay taxi fares ranging from $2.50 to $4.20.*

*Chinese:*被告使用伪钞的控状，指她从 2 月 **25** 日至 3 月 **11** 日，以 **50** 元面额的伪钞，缴付介于 2 元 5 角至 4 元 2 角的德士费。

5 Experiment and Evaluation

5.1 Experimental Setup

The experiments were conducted on two sets of comparable corpora namely English-Chinese and English-Malay. The data are from three news publications in Singapore: the Strait Times (ST, English), Lian He Zao Bao (ZB, Chinese), and Berita Harian (BH, Malay). Since these languages are from different language families[5], our model can be considered as language independent.

[5] English is in Indo-European; Chinese is in Sino-Tibetan; Malay is in Austronesian family [Wikipedia].

The evaluation is conducted based on a set of manually aligned documents prepared by a group of bilingual students. It is done by carefully reading through each article in the month of June (2006) for both sets of corpora and trying to find articles of similar content in the other language within the given time window. Alignment is based on similarity of content where the same story or event is mentioned. Any two bilingual articles with at least 50% content overlapping are considered as comparable. This set of reference data is cross-validated between annotators. Table 1 shows the statistics of our reference data for document alignment.

Language pair	ST – ZB	ST – BH
Distinct source	396	176
Distinct target	437	175
Total alignments	438	183

Table 1. Statistics on evaluation data.

Note that although there are 438 alignments for ST-ZB, the number of unique ST articles are 396, implying that the mapping is not one-to-one.

5.2 Evaluation Metrics

Evaluation is performed on two levels to reflect performance from two different perspectives. "Macro evaluation" is conducted to assess the correctness of the alignment candidates given their rank among all the alignment candidates. "Micro evaluation" concerns about the correctness of the aligned documents returned for a given source document.

Macro evaluation: we present the performance for macro evaluation using average precision. It is used to evaluate the performance of a ranked list and gives higher score for the list that returns more correct alignment in the top.

Micro evaluation: for micro evaluation, we evaluate the F-Score, calculated from recall and precision, based on the number of correct alignments for the top of alignment candidates for each source document.

5.3 Experiment and Result

First we implement the method of Tao and Zhai (2005) as the baseline. Basically, this method does not depend on any linguistic resources and calculates the similarity between two documents purely by comparing all possible pairs of words. In addition to this, we also implement Munteanu's (2006) method which uses Okapi scoring function from the Lemur Toolkit (Ogilvie and

Callan, 2001) to obtain the similarity score. This approach relies heavily on bilingual dictionaries. To assess performances more fairly, the result from baseline method of Tao and Zhai are compared against the results of the following list of incremental approaches: the baseline **(A)**; the baseline using term instead of word **(B)**; replacing $r(x, y)$ by $R(x, y)$ for DFT feature, with and without bilingual dictionaries in **(C)** and **(D)** respectively; and including LIU and TNC for our final model in **(E)**. Our model is also compared our model with results from the implementation of Munteanu (2006) using Okapi **(F)**, and the results from a combination of our model with Okapi **(G)**. Table 2 and Table 3 show the experimental results for two language pairs English – Chinese (ST-ZB) and English – Malay (ST-BH), respectively. Each row displays the result of each experiment at a certain cut-off among the top returned alignments. The "Top" columns reflect the cut-off threshold.

The first three cases **(A)**, **(B)** and **(C)**, which do not rely on linguistic resources, suggest that our new features lead to better performance improvement over the baseline. It can be seen that the use of term and DFT significantly improves the performance. The improvement indicated by a sharp increase in all cases from **(C)** to **(D)** shows that dictionaries can indeed help DFT features.

Based on the result of **(E)**, our final model significantly outperforms the model of Munteanu **(F)** in both macro and micro evaluation. It is noted that our features rely less heavily on dictionaries as it only makes use of this resource to translate term words and title words of a document while Munteanu (2006) needs to translate entire documents, exclude stopword, and relying on an IR system. It is also observed that the performance of **(G)** shows that although the incorporation of Okapi score in our final model **(E)** improves the average precision performance of ST-ZB slightly, it does not appear to be helpful for our ST-BH data. However, Okapi does help in the F-Measure on both corpora.

Pair		Strait Times – Zao Bao						
Level	Top	A	B	C	D	E	F	G
Ave/Precision Macro	50	0.042	0.083	0.08	0.559	0.430	0.209	0.508
	100	0.042	0.069	0.083	0.438	0.426	0.194	0.479
	200	0.025	0.069	0.110	0.342	0.396	0.153	0.439
	500	0.025	0.054	0.110	0.270	0.351	0.111	0.376
F-Measure Micro	1	0.005	0.007	0.009	0.297	0.315	0.157	0.333
	2	0.006	0.005	0.013	0.277	0.286	0.133	0.308
	5	0.005	0.006	0.009	0.200	0.190	0.096	0.206
	10	0.005	0.005	0.007	0.123	0.119	0.063	0.126
	20	0.006	0.008	0.007	0.073	0.074	0.038	0.076

Table 2. Performance of Strait Times – Zao Bao.

Pair		Strait Times – Berita Harian						
Level	Top	A	B	C	D	E	F	G
Ave/Precision Macro	50	0.000	0.000	0.000	0.514	0.818	0.000	0.782
	100	0.000	0.000	0.080	0.484	0.759	0.052	0.729
	200	0.000	0.008	0.090	0.443	0.687	0.073	0.673
	500	0.005	0.008	0.010	0.383	0.604	0.078	0.591
F-Measure Micro	1	0.000	0.000	0.005	0.399	0.634	0.119	0.650
	2	0.000	0.004	0.010	0.340	0.515	0.128	0.515
	5	0.002	0.005	0.010	0.205	0.270	0.105	0.273
	10	0.004	0.014	0.013	0.130	0.150	0.076	0.150
	20	0.006	0.017	0.017	0.074	0.078	0.043	0.078

Table 3. Performance of Strait Times – Berita Harian.

5.4 Discussion

It can be seen from Table 2 and Table 3 that by exploiting the frequency distribution of terms using Discrete Fourier Transform instead of words on Pearson's Correlation, performance is noticeably improved. Fig 5 shows the incremental improvement of our model for top-200 and top-2 alignments using macro and micro evaluation respectively. The sharp increase can be seen in Fig 5 from point **(C)** onwards.

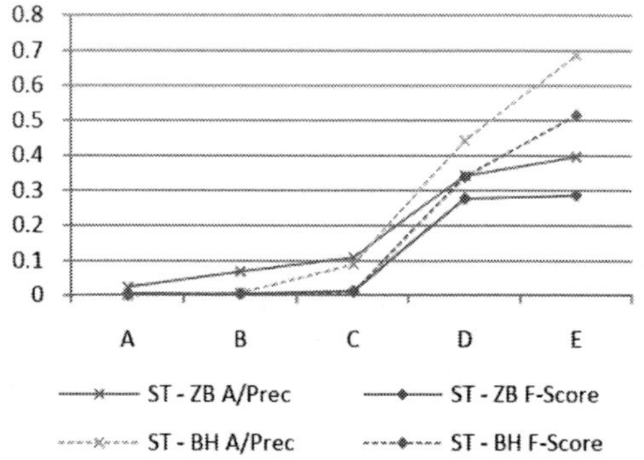

Fig 5. Step-wise improvement at top-200 for macro and top-2 for micro evaluation.

Fig 6 compares the performance of our system with Tao and Zhai (2005) and Munteanu (2006). It is shown that our systems outperform these two systems under the same experimental parameters. Moreover, even without the use of dictionaries, our system's performance on ST-BH data is much better than Munteanu's (2006) on the same data.

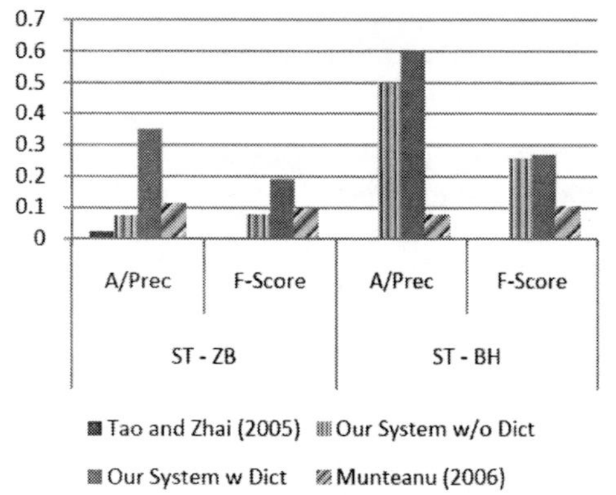

Fig 6. System comparison for ST-ZB and ST-BH at top-500 for macro and top-5 for micro evaluation.

We find that dictionary usage contributes much more to performance improvement in ST-BH compared to that in ST-ZB. We attribute this to the fact that the feature LIU already contributes markedly to the increase in the performance of ST-BH. As a result, it is harder to make further improvements even with the application of bilingual dictionaries.

6 Conclusion and Future Work

In this paper, we propose a feature based model for aligning documents from multilingual comparable corpora. Our feature set is selected based on the need for a method to be adaptable to new language-pairs without relying heavily on linguistic resources, unsupervised learning strategy. Thus, in the proposed method we make use of simple bilingual dictionaries, which are rather inexpensive and easily obtained nowadays. We also explore diverse features, including Monolingual Term Distribution (MTD), Title-and-Content (TNC), and Linguistic Independent Unit (LIU) and measure their contributions in an incremental way. The experiment results show that our system can retrieve similar documents from two comparable corpora much better than using an information retrieval, such as that used by Munteanu (2006). It also performs better than a word correlation-based method such as Tao's (2005).

Besides document alignment as an end, there are many tasks that can directly benefit from comparable corpora with documents that are well-aligned. These include sentence alignment, term alignment, and machine translation, especially statistical machine translation. In the future, we aim to extract other valuable information from comparable corpora which benefits from comparable documents.

Acknowledgements

We would like to thank the anonymous reviewers for their many constructive suggestions for improving this paper. Our thanks also go to Mahani Aljunied for her contributions to the linguistic assessment in our work.

References

Percy Cheung and Pascale Fung. 2004. Sentence Alignment in Parallel, Comparable, and Quasi-comparable Corpora. In *Proceedings of 4th International Conference on Language Resources and Evaluation (LREC)*. Lisbon, Portugal.

Hal Daume III and Daniel Marcu. 2004. A Phrase-Based HMM Approach to Document/Abstract Alignment. In *Proceedings of Empirical Methods in Natural Language Processing (EMNLP)*. Spain.

Min-Yen Kan. 2007. SlideSeer: A Digital Library of Aligned Document and Presentation Pairs. In *Proceedings of the Joint Conference on Digital Libraries (JCDL)*. Vancouver, Canada.

Soto Montalvo, Raquel Martinez, Arantza Casillas, and Victor Fresno. 2006. Multilingual Document Clustering: a Heuristic Approach Based on Cognate Named Entities. In *Proceedings of the 21st International Conference on Computational Linguistics and the 44th Annual Meeting of the ACL*.

Stephen E. Robertson, Steve Walker, Susan Jones, Micheline Hancock-Beaulieu, and Mike Gatford. 1994. Okapi at TREC-3. In *Proceedings of the Third Text REtrieval Conference (TREC 1994)*. Gaithersburg, USA.

Dragos Stefan Munteanu. 2006. Exploiting Comparable Corpora. PhD Thesis. Information Sciences Institute, University of Southern California. USA.

Ogilvie, P., and Callan, J. 2001. Experiments using the Lemur toolkit. In *Proceedings of the 10th Text REtrieval Conference (TREC)*.

Alexandre Patry and Philippe Langlais. 2005. Automatic Identification of Parallel Documents with light or without Linguistics Resources. In *Proceedings of 18th Annual Conference on Artificial Intelligent*.

Bruno Pouliquen, Ralf Steinberger, Camelia Ignat, Emilia Kasper, and Irina Temnikova. 2004. Multilingual and Cross-lingual news topic tracking. In *Proceedings of the 20th International Conference on Computational Linguistics (COLING)*.

Ralf Steinberger, Bruno Pouliquen, and Johan Hagman. 2002. Cross-lingual Document Similarity Calculation Using the Multilingual Thesaurus EUROVOC. *Computational Linguistics and Intelligent Text Processing*.

Tao Tao and ChengXiang Zhai. 2005. Mining Comparable Bilingual Text Corpora for Cross-Language Information Integration. In *Proceedings of the 2005 ACM SIGKDD International Conference on Knowledge Discovery and Data Mining*.

Thuy Vu, Ai Ti Aw and Min Zhang. 2008. Term extraction through unithood and termhood unification. In *Proceedings of the 3rd International Joint Conference on Natural Language Processing (IJCNLP-08)*. Hyderabad, India.

ChengXiang Zhai and John Lafferty. 2001. A study of smoothing methods for language models applied to Ad Hoc information retrieval. In *Proceedings of the 24th annual international ACM SIGIR conference on Research and development in information retrieval*. Louisiana, United States.

R. Agrawal, C. Faloutsos, and A. Swami. 1993. Efficient similarity search in sequence databases. In *Proceedings of the 4th International Conference on Foundations of Data Organization and Algorithms*. Chicago, United States.

Magnus Lie Hetland. 2004. A survey of recent methods for efficient retrieval of similar time sequences. In *Data Mining in Time Series Databases*. World Scientific.

Alexandre Klementiev and Dan Roth. 2006. Weakly Supervised Named Entity Transliteration and Discovery from Multilingual Comparable Corpora. In *Proceedings of the 21st International Conference on Computational Linguistics and the 44th Annual Meeting of the ACL*.

Improving Grammaticality in Statistical Sentence Generation: Introducing a Dependency Spanning Tree Algorithm with an Argument Satisfaction Model

Stephen Wan[†‡] **Mark Dras**[†] **Robert Dale**[†]
[†]Centre for Language Technology
Department of Computing
Macquarie University
Sydney, NSW 2113
swan,madras,rdale@ics.mq.edu.au

Cécile Paris[‡]
[‡]ICT Centre
CSIRO
Sydney, Australia
Cecile.Paris@csiro.au

Abstract

Abstract-like text summarisation requires a means of producing novel summary sentences. In order to improve the grammaticality of the generated sentence, we model a global (sentence) level syntactic structure. We couch statistical sentence generation as a spanning tree problem in order to search for the best dependency tree spanning a set of chosen words. We also introduce a new search algorithm for this task that models argument satisfaction to improve the linguistic validity of the generated tree. We treat the allocation of modifiers to heads as a weighted bipartite graph matching (or assignment) problem, a well studied problem in graph theory. Using BLEU to measure performance on a string regeneration task, we found an improvement, illustrating the benefit of the spanning tree approach armed with an argument satisfaction model.

1 Introduction

Research in statistical novel sentence generation has the potential to extend the current capabilities of automatic text summarisation technology, moving from sentence extraction to abstract-like summarisation. In this paper, we describe a new algorithm that improves upon the grammaticality of statistically generated sentences, evaluated on a string regeneration task, which was first proposed as a surrogate for a grammaticality test by Bangalore et al. (2000). In this task, a system must regenerate the original sentence which has had its word order scrambled.

As an evaluation task, string regeneration reflects the issues that challenge the sentence generation components of machine translation, paraphrase generation, and summarisation systems (Soricut and Marcu, 2005). Our research in summarisation utilises the statistical generation algorithms described in this paper to generate novel summary sentences.

The goal of the string regeneration task is to recover a sentence once its words have been randomly ordered. Similarly, for a text-to-text generation scenario, the goal is to generate a sentence given an unordered list of words, typically using an n-gram language model to select the best word ordering. N-gram language models appear to do well at a *local* level when examining word sequences smaller than n. However, beyond this window size, the sequence is often ungrammatical. This is not surprising as these methods are unable to model grammaticality at the sentence level, unless the size of n is sufficiently large. In practice, the lack of sufficient training data means that n is often smaller than the average sentence length. Even if data exists, increasing the size of n corresponds to a higher degree polynomial complexity search for the best word sequence.

In response, we introduce an algorithm for searching for the best word sequence in a way that attempts to model grammaticality at the sentence level. Mirroring the use of spanning tree algorithms in parsing (McDonald et al., 2005), we present an approach to statistical sentence generation. Given a set of scrambled words, the approach searches for the most probable dependency tree, as defined by some corpus, such that it contains each word of the input set. The tree is then traversed to obtain the final word ordering.

In particular, we present two spanning tree algorithms. We first adapt the Chu-Liu-Edmonds (CLE) algorithm (see Chu and Liu (1965) and Edmonds (1967)), used in McDonald et al. (2005), to include a basic argument model, added to keep track of linear precedence between heads and modifiers. While our adapted version of the CLE algorithm finds an optimal spanning tree, this does

Proceedings of the 12th Conference of the European Chapter of the ACL, pages 852–860,
Athens, Greece, 30 March – 3 April 2009.

not always correspond with a linguistically valid dependency tree, primarily because it does not attempt to ensure that words in the tree have plausible numbers of arguments.

We propose an alternative dependency-spanning tree algorithm which uses a more fine-grained argument model representing argument positions. To find the best modifiers for argument positions, we treat the attachment of edges to the spanning tree as a weighted bipartite graph matching problem (or the *assignment* problem), a standard problem in graph theory.

The remainder of this paper is as follows. Section 2 outlines the graph representation of the spanning tree problem. We describe a standard spanning tree algorithm in Section 3. Section 4 defines a finer-grained argument model and presents a new dependency spanning tree search algorithm. We experiment to determine whether a global dependency structure, as found by our algorithm, improves performance on the string regeneration problem, presenting results in Section 5. Related work is presented in Section 6. Section 7 concludes that an argument model improves the linguistic plausibility of the generated trees, thus improving grammaticality in text generation.

2 A Graph Representation of Dependencies

In couching statistical generation as a spanning tree problem, this work is the generation analog of the parsing work by McDonald et al. (2005). Given a bag of words with no additional constraints, the aim is to produce a dependency tree containing the given words. Informally, as all dependency relations between each pair of words are possible, the set of all possible dependencies can be represented as a graph, as noted by McDonald et al. (2005). Our goal is to find the subset of these edges corresponding to a tree with maximum probability such that each vertex in the graph is visited once, thus including each word once. The resulting tree is a spanning tree, an acyclic graph which spans all vertices. The best tree is the one with an optimal overall score. We use negative log probabilities so that edge weights will correspond to costs. The overall score is the sum of the costs of the edges in the spanning tree, which we want to minimise. Hence, our problem is the minimum spanning tree (MST) problem.

We define a directed graph (digraph) in a standard way, $G = (V, E)$ where V is a set of vertices and $E \subseteq \{(u, v)|u, v \in V\}$ is a set of directed edges. For each sentence $w = w_1 \ldots w_n$, we define the digraph $G_w = (V_w, E_w)$ where $V_w = \{w_0, w_1, \ldots, w_n\}$, with w_0 a dummy root vertex, and $E_w = \{(u, v)|u \in V_w, v \in V_w \setminus \{w_0\}\}$.

The graph is fully connected (except for the root vertex w_0 which is only fully connected outwards) and is a representation of possible dependencies. For an edge (u, v), we refer to u as the head and v as the modifier.

We extend the original formulation of McDonald et al. (2005) by adding a notion of *argument positions* for a word, providing points to attach modifiers. Adopting an approach similar to Johnson (2007), we look at the direction (left or right) of the head with respect to the modifier; we consequently define a set $\mathcal{D} = \{l, r\}$ to represent this. Set $\mathcal{D}$ represents the linear precedence of the words in the dependency relation; consequently, it partially approximates the distinction between syntactic roles like *subject* and *object*.

Each edge has a pair of associated weights, one for each direction, defined by the function $s : E \times \mathcal{D} \rightarrow \mathbb{R}$, based on a probabilistic model of dependency relations. To calculate the edge weights, we adapt the definition of Collins (1996) to use direction rather than relation type (represented in the original as triples of non-terminals). Given a corpus, for some edge $e = (u, v) \in E$ and direction $d \in \mathcal{D}$, we calculate the edge weight as:

$$s((u, v), d) = -log\, prob_{dep}(u, v, d) \quad (1)$$

We define the set of part-of-speech (PoS) tags $\mathcal{P}$ and a function $pos : V \rightarrow \mathcal{P}$, which maps vertices (representing words) to their PoS, to calculate the probability of a dependency relation, defined as:

$$\begin{aligned} &prob_{dep}(u, v, d) \\ &= \frac{cnt((u, pos(u)), (v, pos(v)), d)}{co\text{-}occurs((u, pos(u)), (v, pos(v)))} \end{aligned} \quad (2)$$

where $cnt((u, pos(u)), (v, pos(v)), d)$ is the number of times where $(v, pos(v))$ and $(u, pos(u))$ are seen in a sentence in the training data, and $(v, pos(v))$ modifies $(u, pos(u))$ in direction d. The function $co\text{-}occurs((u, pos(u)), (v, pos(v)))$ returns the number of times that $(v, pos(v))$ and $(u, pos(u))$ are seen in a sentence in the training data. We adopt the same smoothing strategy as Collins (1996), which backs off to PoS for unseen dependency events.

3 Generation via Spanning Trees

3.1 The Chu-Liu Edmonds Algorithm

Given the graph $G_w = (V_w, E_w)$, the Chu-Liu Edmonds (CLE) algorithm finds a rooted directed spanning tree, specified by T_w, which is an acyclic set of edges in E_w minimising $\sum_{e \in T_w, d \in \mathcal{D}} s(e, d)$. The algorithm is presented as Algorithm 1.[1]

There are two stages to the algorithm. The first stage finds the best edge for each vertex, connecting it to another vertex. To do so, all *outgoing* edges of v, that is edges where v is a modifier, are considered, and the one with the best edge weight is chosen, where best is defined as the smallest cost. This minimisation step is used to ensure that each modifier has only one head.

If the chosen edges T_w produce a strongly connected subgraph $G_w^m = (V_w, T_w)$, then this is the MST. If not, a cycle amongst some subset of V_w must be handled in the second stage. Essentially, one edge in the cycle is removed to produce a subtree. This is done by finding the best edge to join some vertex in the cycle to the main tree. This has the effect of finding an alternative head for some word in the cycle. The edge to the original head is discarded (to maintain one head per modifier), turning the cycle into a subtree. When all cycles have been handled, applying a greedy edge selection once more will then yield the MST.

```
/* initialisation */
Discard the edges exiting the w_0 if any.
/* Chu-Liu/Edmonds Algorithm */
begin
    T_w ← (u,v) ∈ E : ∀_{v∈V, d∈D} argmin_{(u,v)} s((u,v), d)
    if M_w = (V_w, T_w) has no cycles then return M_w
    forall C ⊂ T_w : C is a cycle in M_w do
        (e, d) ← argmin_{e*,d*} s(e*, d*) : e ∈ C
        forall c = (v_h, v_m,) ∈ C and d_c ∈ D do
            forall e' = (v_i, v_m) ∈ E and d' ∈ D do
                s(e', d') ← s(e', d') − s(c, d_c) − s(e, d)
            end
        end
        s(e, d) ← s(e, d) + 1
    end
    T_w ← (u,v) ∈ E : ∀_{v∈V, d∈D} argmin_{(u,v)} s((u,v), d)
    return M_w
end
```

Algorithm 1: The pseudo-code for the Chu-Liu Edmonds algorithm with our adaptation to include linear precedence.

3.2 Generating a Word Sequence

Once the tree has been generated, all that remains is to obtain an ordering of words based upon it. Because dependency relations in the tree are either of leftward or rightward direction, it becomes relatively trivial to order child vertices with respect to a parent vertex. The only difficulty lies in finding a relative ordering for the leftward (to the parent) children, and similarly for the rightward (to the parent) children.

We traverse G_w^m using a greedy algorithm to order the siblings using an n-gram language model. Algorithm 2 describes the traversal in pseudo-code. The generated sentence is obtained by calling the algorithm with w_0 and T_w as parameters. The algorithm operates recursively if called on an inner node. If a vertex v is a leaf in the dependency tree, its string realisation *realise*(v) is returned.

We keep track of ordered siblings with two lists, one for each direction. If the sibling set is leftwards, the ordered list, R_l, is initialised to be the singleton set containing a dummy start token with an empty realisation. If the sibling set is rightwards then the ordered list, R_r is initialised to be the realisation of the parent.

For some sibling set $C \subseteq V_w$ to be ordered, the algorithm chooses the next vertex, $v \in C$, to insert into the appropriate ordered list, $R_x, x \in \mathcal{D}$, by maximising the probability of the string of words that would result if the realisation, *realise*(v), were concatenated with R_x.

The probability of the concatenation is calculated based on a window of words around the join. This window length is defined to be $2 \times \text{floor}(n/2)$, for some n, in this case, 4.

If the siblings are leftwards, the window consists of the last $min(n-1, |R_l|)$ previously chosen words concatenated with the first $min(n-1, |realise(v)|)$. If the siblings are rightwards, the window consists of the last $min(n-1, |realise(v)|)$ previously chosen words concatenated with the first $min(n-1, |R_r|)$. The probability of a window of words, $w_0 \ldots w_j$, of length $j+1$ is defined by the following equation:

$$prob_{LMO}(w_0 \ldots w_j) = \prod_{i=0}^{j-k-1} prob_{MLE}(w_{i+k} | w_i \ldots w_{i+k-1}) \quad (3)$$

[1]Adapted from (McDonald et al., 2005) and http://www.ce.rit.edu/~sjyeec/dmst.html . The difference concerns the direction of the edge and the edge weight function. We have also folded the function 'contract' in McDonald et al. (2005) into the main algorithm. Again following that work, we treat the function s as a data structure permitting storage of updated edge weights.

```
/* LMO Algorithm */
input : v, T_w where v ∈ V_w
output: R ⊆ V_w
begin
    if isLeaf(v) then
        return {realise(v)}
    end
    else
        C_l ← getLeftChildren(v, T_w)
        C_r ← getRightChildren(v, T_w)
        R_l ← {start}
        R_r ← {realise(v)}
        while C_l ≠ {} do
            c ← arg max_{c∈C_l} prob_ngram(LMO(c, T_w) ∪ R_l)
            R_l ← realise(c, T_w) ∪ R_l
            C_l ← C_l \ {c}
        end
        while C_r ≠ {} do
            c ← arg max_{c∈C_r} prob_ngram(R_r ∪ LMO(c, T_w))
            R_r ← R_r ∪ realise(c, T_w)
            C_r ← C_r \ {c}
        end
        return R_l ∪ R_r
    end
end
```

Algorithm 2: The Language Model Ordering algorithm for linearising an T_w.

where $k = min(n-1, j-1)$, and,

$$\begin{aligned} prob_{MLE}(w_{i+k}|w_i \ldots w_{i+k-1}) \\ = \frac{cnt(w_i \ldots w_{i+k})}{cnt(w_i \ldots w_{i+k-1})} \end{aligned} \quad (4)$$

where $prob_{MLE}(w_{i+k}|w_i \ldots w_{i+k-1})$ is the maximum likelihood estimate n-gram probability. We refer to this tree linearisation method as the *Language Model Ordering* (LMO).

4 Using an Argument Satisfaction Model

4.1 Assigning Words to Argument Positions

One limitation of using the CLE algorithm for generation is that the resulting tree, though maximal in probability, may not conform to basic linguistic properties of a dependency tree. In particular, it may not have the correct number of arguments for each head word. That is, a word may have too few or too many modifiers.

To address this problem, we can take into account the argument position when assigning a weight to an edge. When attaching an edge connecting a modifier to a head to the spanning tree, we count how many modifiers the head already has. An edge is penalised if it is improbable that the head takes on yet another modifier, say in the example of an attachment to a preposition whose argument position has already been filled.

However, accounting for argument positions makes an edge weight dynamic and dependent on surrounding tree context. This makes the search for an optimal tree an NP-hard problem (McDonald and Satta, 2007) as all possible trees must be considered to find an optimal solution.

Consequently, we must choose a heuristic search algorithm for finding the locally optimum spanning tree. By representing argument positions that can be filled only once, we allow modifiers to compete for argument positions and vice versa. The CLE algorithm only considers this competition in one direction. In line 3 of Algorithm 1, only heads compete for modifiers, and thus the solution will be sub-optimal. In Wan et al. (2007), we showed that introducing a model of argument positions into a greedy spanning tree algorithm had little effect on performance. Thus, to consider both directions of competition, we design a new algorithm for constructing (dependency) spanning trees that casts edge selection as a weighted bipartite graph matching (or assignment) problem.

This problem is to find a weighted alignments between objects of two distinct sets, where an object from one set is uniquely aligned to some object in the other set. The optimal alignment is one where the sum of alignment costs is minimal. The graph of all possible assignments is a weighted bipartite graph. Here, to discuss bipartite graphs, we will extend our notation in a fairly standard way, to write $G^p = (U, V, E^p)$, where U, V are the disjoint sets of vertices and E^p the set of edges.

In our paper, we treat the assignment between attachment positions and words as an assignment problem. The standard polynomial-time solution to the assignment problem is the Kuhn-Munkres (or Hungarian) algorithm (Kuhn, 1955).[2]

4.2 A Dependency-Spanning Tree Algorithm

Our alternative dependency-spanning tree algorithm, presented as Algorithm 3, incrementally adds vertices to a growing spanning tree. At each iteration, the Kuhn-Munkres method assigns words that are as yet unattached to argument positions already available in the tree. We focus on the bipartite graph in Section 4.3.

Let the sentence w have the dependency graph $G_w = (V_w, E_w)$. At some arbitrary iteration of the algorithm (see Figure 1), we have the following:

- $T_w \subseteq E_w$, the set of edges in the spanning tree constructed so far;

[2]GPL code: `http://sites.google.com/site/garybaker/hungarian-algorithm/assignment`

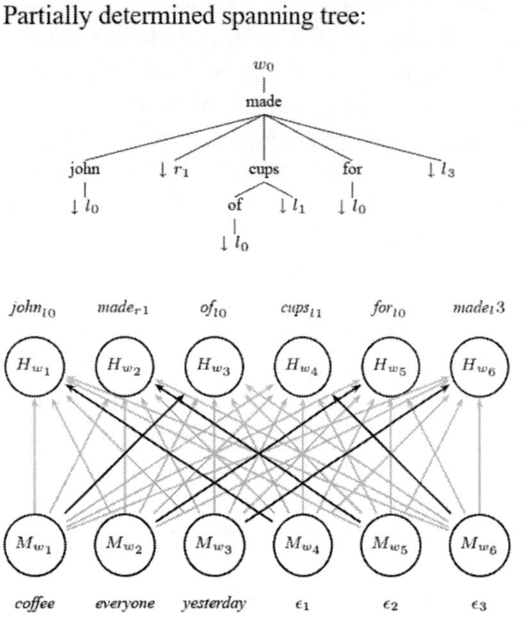

Figure 1: A snapshot of the generation process. Each word in the tree has argument positions to which we can assign remaining words. Padding M_w with ϵ is described in Section 4.3.

- $H_w = \{u, v \mid (u, v) \in T_w\}$, the set of vertices in T_w, or 'attached vertices', and therefore potential heads; and
- $M_w = V_w \backslash H_w$, the set of 'unattached vertices', and therefore potential modifiers.

For the potential heads, we want to define the set of possible attachment positions available in the spanning tree where the potential modifiers can attach. To talk about these attachment positions, we define the set of labels $\mathcal{L} = \{(d, j) | d \in D, j \in \mathbb{N}\}$, an element (d, j) representing an attachment point in direction d, position j. Valid attachment positions must be in sequential order and not missing any intermediate positions (e.g. if position 2 on the right is specified, position 1 must be also): so we define for some $i \in \mathbb{N}$, $0 \le i < N$, a set $A_i \subseteq \mathcal{L}$ such that if the label $(d, j) \in A_i$ then the label $(d, k) \in A_i$ for $0 \le k < j$. Collecting these, we define $A = \{A_i \mid 0 \le i < N\}$.

To map a potential head onto the set of attachment positions, we define a function $q : H_w \to A$. So, given some $v \in H_w$, $q(v) = A_i$ for some $0 \le i < N$. In talking about an individual attachment point $(d, j) \in q(v)$ for potential head v, we use the notation v_{dj}. For example, when referring to the second argument position on the right with respect to v, we use v_{r2}.

```
   /* initialisation */
1  H_w ← {w_0}
2  M_w ← V'
3  U_w ← {w_0R1}
4  U'_w ← {}
5  T_w ← {}
   /* The Assignment-based Algorithm */
6  begin
7      while M_w ≠ {} and U'_w ≠ U_w do
8          U'_w ← U_w
9          foreach ⟨u, (d, j)), v⟩ ∈ Kuhn-Munkres(G^p_w =
           (U_w, M^ε_w, E^p_w)) do
10             T_w ← T_w ∪ {(u, v)}
11             if u ∈ H_w then
12                 U_w ← U_w \ {u}
13             end
14             U_w ← U_w ∪ next(q(u))
15             U_w ← U_w ∪ next(q(m))
16             q(m) ← q(m) \ next(q(m))
17             q(h) ← q(h) \ next(q(h))
18             M_w ← M_w \ {m}
19             H_w ← H_w ∪ {m}
20         end
21     end
22 end
```

Algorithm 3: The Assignment-based Dependency Tree Building algorithm.

For the implementation of the algorithm, we have defined q, to specify attachment points, as follows, given some $v \in H_w$:

$$q(v) = \begin{cases} \{v_{r1}\} & \text{if } v = w_0 \text{, the root} \\ \{v_{l1}\} & \text{if pos}(v) \text{ is a preposition} \\ \mathcal{L} & \text{if pos}(v) \text{ is a verb} \\ \{v_{lj} \mid j \in \mathbb{N}\} & \text{otherwise} \end{cases}$$

Defining q allows one to optionally incorporate linguistic information if desired.

We define the function *next* : $q(v) \to A, v \in H_w$ that returns the position (d, j) with the smallest value of j for direction d. Finally, we write the set of available attachment positions in the spanning tree as $U \subseteq \{(v, l) \mid v \in H_w, l \in q(v)\}$.

4.3 Finding an Assignment

To construct the bipartite graph used for the assignment problem at line 9 of Algorithm 3, given our original dependency graph $G_w = (V_w, E_w)$, and the variables defined from it above in Section 4.2, we do the following. The first set of vertices, of possible heads and their attachment points, is the set U_w. The second set of vertices is the set of possible modifiers augmented by dummy vertices ϵ_i (indicating no modification) such that this set is at least as large as U_w : $M_w^\epsilon = M_w \cup \{\epsilon_0, \ldots, \epsilon_{max(0,|U_w|-|M_w|)}\}$. The bipartite graph is then $G^p_w = (U_w, M^\epsilon_w, E^p_w)$, where $E^p_w = \{(u, v) \mid u \in U_w, v \in M^\epsilon_w\}$.

The weights on the edges of this graph incorporate a model of argument counts. The weight function is of the form $s_{ap} : E^p \rightarrow \mathbb{R}$. We consider some $e \in E^p_w$: $e = (v', v)$ for some $v' \in U_w, v \in M^\epsilon_w$; and $v' = (u, (d, j))$ for some $u \in V_w, d \in \mathcal{D}, j \in \mathbb{N}$. $s(u, M^\epsilon_w)$ is defined to return the maximum cost so that the dummy leaves are only attached as a last resort. We then define:

$$s_{ap}(e) = -log(prob_{dep}(u, v, d) \times prob_{arg}(u, d, j)) \quad (5)$$

where $prob_{dep}(u, v, d)$ is as in equation 2, using the original dependency graph defined in Section 2; and $prob_{arg}(u, d, j)$, an estimate of the probability that a word u with i arguments assigned already can take on more arguments, is defined as:

$$prob_{arg}(u, d, j) = \frac{\sum_{i=j+1}^{\infty} cnt_{arg}(u, d, i)}{cnt(u, d)} \quad (6)$$

where $cnt_{arg}(u, d, i)$ is the number of times word u has been seen with i arguments in direction d; and $cnt(u, d) = \sum_{i \in \mathbb{N}} cnt_{arg}(u, d, i)$. As the probability of argument positions beyond a certain value for i in a given direction will be extremely small, we approximate this sum by calculating the probability density up to a fixed maximum, in this case 7 argument positions, and assume zero probability beyond that.

5 Evaluation

5.1 String Generation Task

The best-performing word ordering algorithm is one that makes fewest grammatical errors. As a surrogate measurement of grammaticality, we use the string regeneration task. Beginning with a human-authored sentence with its word order randomised, the goal is to regenerate the original sentence. Success is indicated by the proportion of the original sentence regenerated, as measured by any string comparison method: in our case, using the BLEU metric (Papineni et al., 2002). One benefit to this evaluation is that content selection, as a factor, is held constant. Specifically, the probability of word selection is uniform for all words.

The string comparison task and its associated metrics like BLEU are not perfect.[3] The evaluation can be seen as being overly strict. It assumes that the *only* grammatical order is that of the original human authored sentence, referred to as the 'gold standard' sentence. Should an approach chance upon an alternative grammatical ordering, it would penalised. However, all algorithms and baselines compared would suffer equally in this respect, and so this will be less problematic when averaging across multiple test cases.

5.2 Data Sets and Training Procedures

The Penn Treebank corpus (PTB) was used to provide a model of dependency relations and argument counts. It contains about 3 million words of text from the Wall Street Journal (WSJ) with human annotations of syntactic structures. Dependency events were sourced from the events file of the Collins parser package, which contains the dependency events found in training sections 2-22 of the corpus. Development was done on section 00 and testing was performed on section 23.

A 4-gram language model (LM) was also obtained from the PTB training data, referred to as PTB-LM. Additionally, a 4-gram language model was obtained from a subsection of the BLLIP'99 Corpus (LDC number: LDC2000T43) containing three years of WSJ data from 1987 to 1989 (Charniak et al., 1999). As in Collins et al. (2004), the 1987 portion of the BLLIP corpus containing 20 million words was also used to create a language model, referred to here as BLLIP-LM. *N*-gram models were smoothed using Katz's method, backing off to smaller values of n.

For this evaluation, tokenisation was based on that provided by the PTB data set. This data set also delimits base noun phrases (noun phrases without nested constituents). Base noun phrases were treated as single tokens, and the rightmost word assumed to be the head. For the algorithms tested, the input set for any test case consisted of the single tokens identified by the PTB tokenisation. Additionally, the heads of base noun phrases were included in this input set. That is, we do not regenerate the base noun phrases.[4]

[3] Alternative grammaticality measures have been developed recently (Mutton et al., 2007). We are currently exploring the use of this and other metrics.

[4] This would correspond to the use of a chunking algorithm or a named-entity recogniser to find noun phrases that could be re-used for sentence generation.

Algorithms	PTB-LM	BLLIP-LM
Viterbi baseline	14.9	18.0
LMO baseline	24.3	26.0
CLE	26.4	26.8
AB	33.6	33.7

Figure 2: String regeneration as measured in BLEU points (maximum 100)

AB: the dow at this point was down about 35 points
CLE: was down about this point 35 points the dow at
LMO: was this point about at down the down 35 points
Viterbi: the down 35 points at was about this point down
Original: at this point, the dow was down about 35 points

Figure 3: Example generated sentences using the BLLIP-LM.

5.3 Algorithms and Baselines

We compare the baselines against the Chu-Liu Edmonds (CLE) algorithm to see if spanning tree algorithms do indeed improve upon conventional language modelling. We also compare the Assignment-based (AB) algorithm against the baselines and CLE to see if, additionally, modelling argument assignments improves the resulting tree and thus the generated word sequence. Two baseline generators based on n-gram language-models were used, representing approaches that optimise word sequences based on the local context of the n-grams.

The first baseline re-uses the *LMO* greedy sequence algorithm on the same set of input words presented to the CLE and AB algorithms. We apply LMO in a rightward manner beginning with a start-of-sentence token. Note that this baseline generator, like the two spanning tree algorithms, will score favourably using BLEU since, minimally, the word order of the base noun phrases will be correct when each is reinserted.

Since the LMO baseline reduces to bigram generation when concatenating single words, we test a second language model baseline which always uses a 4-gram window size. A Viterbi-like generator with a 4-gram model and a beam of 100 is used to generate a sequence. For this baseline, referred to as the *Viterbi* baseline, base noun phrases were separated into their constituent words and included in the input word set.

5.4 Results

The results are presented in Table 2. Significance was measured using the sign test and the sampling method outlined in (Collins et al., 2005). We will examine the results in the PTB-LM column first. The gain of 10 BLEU points by the LMO baseline over the Viterbi baseline shows the performance improvement that can be gained when reinserting the base noun phrases.

The CLE algorithm significantly out-performed the LMO baseline by 2 BLEU points, from which we conclude that incorporating a model for global syntactic structure and treating the search for a dependency tree as a spanning problem helps for novel sentence generation. However, the real improvement can be seen in the performance of the AB system which significantly out-performs all other methods, beating the CLE algorithm by 7 BLEU points, illustrating the benefits of a model for argument counts and of couching tree building as an iterative set of argument assignments.

One might reasonably ask if more n-gram data would narrow the gap between the tree algorithms and the baselines, which encode global and local information respectively. Examining results in the BLLIP-LM column, all approaches improve with the better language model. Unsurprisingly, the improvements are most evident in the baselines which rely heavily on the language model. The margin narrows between the CLE algorithm and the LMO baseline. However, the AB algorithm still out-performs all other approaches by 7 BLEU points, highlighting the benefit in modelling dependency relations. Even with a language model that is one order of magnitude larger than the PTB-LM, the AB still maintains a sizeable lead in performance. Figure 3 presents sample generated strings.

6 Related Work

6.1 Statistical Surface Realisers

The work in this paper is similar to research in statistical surface realisation (for example, Langkilde and Knight (1998); Bangalore and Rambow (2000); Filippova and Strube (2008)). These start with a semantic representation for which a specific rendering, an ordering of words, must be determined, often using language models to govern tree traversal. The task in this paper is different as it is a text-to-text scenario and does not begin with a representation of semantics.

The dependency model and the LMO linearisation algorithm are based heavily on word order statistics. As such, the utility of this approach is limited to human languages with minimal use of inflections, such as English. Approaches for other language types, for example German, have been explored (Filippova and Strube, 2007).

6.2 Text-to-Text Generation

As a text-to-text approach, our work is more similar to work on Information Fusion (Barzilay et al., 1999), a sub-problem in multi-document summarisation. In this work, sentences presenting the same information, for example multiple news articles describing the same event, are merged to form a single summary by aligning repeated words and phrases across sentences.

Other text-to-text approaches for generating novel sentences also aim to recycle sentence fragments where possible, as we do. Work on phrase-based statistical machine translation has been applied to paraphrase generation (Bannard and Callison-Burch, 2005) and multi-sentence alignment in summarisation (Daumé III and Marcu, 2004). These approaches typically use n-gram models to find the best word sequence.

The WIDL formalism (Soricut and Marcu, 2005) was proposed to efficiently encode constraints that restricted possible word sequences, for example dependency information. Though similar, our work here does not explicitly represent the word lattice.

For these text-to-text systems, the order of elements in the generated sentence is heavily based on the original order of words and phrases in the input sentences from which lattices are built. Our approach has the benefit of considering all possible orderings of words, corresponding to a wider range of paraphrases, provided with a suitable dependency model is available.

6.3 Parsing and Semantic Role Labelling

This paper presents work closely related to parsing work by McDonald et al. (2005) which searches for the best parse tree. Our work can be thought of as generating projective dependency trees (that is, without crossing dependencies).

The key difference between parsing and generation is that, in parsing, the word order is fixed, whereas for generation, this must be determined. In this paper, we search across all possible tree structures whilst searching for the best word ordering. As a result, an argument model is needed to identify linguistically plausible spanning trees.

We treated the alignment of modifiers to head words as a bipartite graph matching problem. This is similar to work in semantic role labelling by Padó and Lapata (2006). The alignment of answers to question types as a semantic role labelling task using similar methods was explored by Shen and Lapata (2007).

Our work is also strongly related to that of Wong and Mooney (2007) which constructs symbolic semantic structures via an assignment process in order to provide surface realisers with input. Our approach differs in that we do not begin with a fixed set of semantic labels. Additionally, our end goal is a dependency tree that encodes word precedence order, bypassing the surface realisation stage.

7 Conclusions

In this paper, we presented a new use of spanning tree algorithms for generating sentences from an input set of words, a task common to many text-to-text scenarios. The algorithm finds the best dependency trees in order to ensure that the resulting string has grammaticality modelled at a global (sentence) level. Our algorithm incorporates a model of argument satisfaction which is treated as an assignment problem, using the Kuhn-Munkres assignment algorithm. We found a significant improvement using BLEU to measure improvements on the string regeneration task. We conclude that our new algorithm based on the assignment problem and an argument model finds trees that are linguistically more plausible, thereby improving the grammaticality of the generated word sequence.

References

Srinivas Bangalore and Owen Rambow. 2000. Exploiting a probabilistic hierarchical model for generation. In *Proceedings of the 18th Conference on Computational Linguistics*, Saarbrücken, Germany.

Srinivas Bangalore, Owen Rambow, and Steve Whittaker. 2000. Evaluation metrics for generation. In *Proceedings of the first international conference on Natural language generation*, Morristown, NJ, USA.

Colin Bannard and Chris Callison-Burch. 2005. Paraphrasing with bilingual parallel corpora. In *Proceedings of the 43rd Annual Meeting of the Asso-*

ciation for Computational Linguistics, Ann Arbor, Michigan.

Regina Barzilay, Kathleen R. McKeown, and Michael Elhadad. 1999. Information fusion in the context of multi-document summarization. In *Proceedings of the 37th conference on Association for Computational Linguistics*, Morristown, NJ, USA.

Eugene Charniak, Don Blaheta, Niyu Ge, Keith Hall, John Hale, and Mark Johnson. 1999. Bllip 1987-89 wsj corpus release 1. Technical report, Linguistic Data Consortium.

Y. J. Chu and T. H. Liu. 1965. On the shortest arborescence of a directed graph. *Science Sinica*, v.14:1396–1400.

Christopher Collins, Bob Carpenter, and Gerald Penn. 2004. Head-driven parsing for word lattices. In *Proceedings of the 42nd Annual Meeting on Association for Computational Linguistics*, Morristown, NJ, USA.

Michael Collins, Philipp Koehn, and Ivona Kucerova. 2005. Clause restructuring for statistical machine translation. In *Proceedings of the 43rd Annual Meeting on Association for Computational Linguistics*, Morristown, NJ, USA.

Michael John Collins. 1996. A new statistical parser based on bigram lexical dependencies. In *Proceedings of the Thirty-Fourth Annual Meeting of the Association for Computational Linguistics*, San Francisco.

Hal Daumé III and Daniel Marcu. 2004. A phrase-based hmm approach to document/abstract alignment. In *Proceedings of EMNLP 2004*, Barcelona, Spain..

J. Edmonds. 1967. Optimum branchings. *J. Research of the National Bureau of Standards*, 71B:233–240.

Katja Filippova and Michael Strube. 2007. Generating constituent order in german clauses. In *Proceedings of the 45th Annual Meeting on Association for Computational Linguistics*. Prague, Czech Republic.

Katja Filippova and Michael Strube. 2008. Sentence fusion via dependency graph compression. In *Conference on Empirical Methods in Natural Language Processing*, Waikiki, Honolulu, Hawaii.

Mark Johnson. 2007. Transforming projective bilexical dependency grammars into efficiently-parsable cfgs with unfold-fold. In *Proceedings of the 45th Annual Meeting on Association for Computational Linguistics*. Prague, Czech Republic.

H.W. Kuhn. 1955. The hungarian method for the assignment problem. *Naval Research Logistics Quarterly*, 219552:83–97 83–97.

Irene Langkilde and Kevin Knight. 1998. The practical value of N-grams in derivation. In *Proceedings of the Ninth International Workshop on Natural Language Generation*, New Brunswick, New Jersey.

Ryan McDonald and Giorgio Satta. 2007. On the complexity of non-projective data-driven dependency parsing. In *Proceedings of the Tenth International Conference on Parsing Technologies*, Prague, Czech Republic.

Ryan McDonald, Fernando Pereira, Kiril Ribarov, and Jan Hajic. 2005. Non-projective dependency parsing using spanning tree algorithms. In *Proceedings of the conference on Human Language Technology and Empirical Methods in Natural Language Processing*, Morristown, NJ, USA.

Andrew Mutton, Mark Dras, Stephen Wan, and Robert Dale. 2007. Gleu: Automatic evaluation of sentence-level fluency. In *Proceedings of the 45th Annual Meeting of the Association of Computational Linguistics*, Prague, Czech Republic.

Sebastian Padó and Mirella Lapata. 2006. Optimal constituent alignment with edge covers for semantic projection. In *Proceedings of the 21st International Conference on Computational Linguistics and the 44th annual meeting of the Association for Computational Linguistics*, Morristown, NJ, USA.

Kishore Papineni, Salim Roukos, Todd Ward, and Wei-Jing Zhu. 2002. Bleu: a method for automatic evaluation of machine translation. In *Proceedings of the 40th Annual Meeting of the Association for Computational Linguistics*, Philadelphia, July.

Dan Shen and Mirella Lapata. 2007. Using semantic roles to improve question answering. In *Proceedings of the 2007 Joint Conference on Empirical Methods in Natural Language Processing and Computational Natural Language Learning*, Prague, Czech Republic.

Radu Soricut and Daniel Marcu. 2005. Towards developing generation algorithms for text-to-text applications. In *Proceedings of the 43rd Annual Meeting of the Association for Computational Linguistics*, Ann Arbor, Michigan.

Stephen Wan, Robert Dale, Mark Dras, and Cécile Paris. 2007. Global revision in summarisation: Generating novel sentences with prim's algorithm. In *Proceedings of 10th Conference of the Pacific Association for Computational Linguistic*, Melbourne, Australia.

Yuk Wah Wong and Raymond Mooney. 2007. Generation by inverting a semantic parser that uses statistical machine translation. In *Human Language Technologies 2007: The Conference of the North American Chapter of the Association for Computational Linguistics*, Rochester, New York.

Co-dispersion: A Windowless Approach to Lexical Association

Justin Washtell
University of Leeds
Leeds, UK
washtell@comp.leeds.ac.uk

Abstract

We introduce an alternative approach to extracting word pair associations from corpora, based purely on surface distances in the text. We contrast it with the prevailing window-based co-occurrence model and show it to be more statistically robust and to disclose a broader selection of significant associative relationships - owing largely to the property of scale-independence. In the process we provide insights into the limiting characteristics of window-based methods which complement the sometimes conflicting application-oriented literature in this area.

1 Introduction

The principle of using statistical measures of co-occurrence from corpora as a proxy for word association - by comparing observed frequencies of co-occurrence with expected frequencies - is relatively young. One of the most well known computational studies is that of Church & Hanks (1989). The method by which co-occurrences are counted, now as then, is based on a device which dates back at least to Weaver (1949): the context window. While variations on the specific notion of context have been explored (separation of content and function words, asymmetrical and non-contiguous contexts, the sentence or the document as context) and increasingly sophisticated association measures have been proposed (see Evert, 2007, for a thorough review) the basic principle – that of counting token frequencies within a context region – remains ubiquitous.

Herein we discuss some of the intrinsic limitations of this approach, as are being felt in recent research, and present a principled solution which does not rely on co-occurrence windows at all, but instead on measurements of the surface distance between words.

2 The impact of window size

The issue of how to determine appropriate window size (and shape) has often been glossed over in the literature, with such parameters being determined arbitrarily, or empirically on a per-application basis, and often receiving little more than a cursory mention under the description of method. For reasons that we will discuss however, the issue has been receiving increasing attention. Some have attempted to address it intrinsically (Sahlgren 2006; Schulte im Walde & Melinger, 2008; Hung et al, 2001); others no less earnestly in the interests of specific applications (Lamjiri, 2003; Edmonds, 1997; Wang 2005; Choueka & Lusignan, 1985) (note that this divide is sometimes subtle).

The 2008 Workshop on Distributional Lexical Semantics, held in conjunction with the European Summer School on Logic, Language and Learning (ESSLLI) – hereafter the ESSLLI Workshop - saw this issue (along with other "problem" parameters in distributional lexical semantics) as one of its central themes, and witnessed many different takes upon it. Interestingly, there was little consensus, with some studies appearing on the surface to starkly contradict one-another. It is now generally recognized that window size is, like the choice of corpus or specific association measure, a parameter which can have a potentially profound impact upon the performance of applications which aim to exploit co-occurrence counts.

One widely held (and upheld) intuition - expressed throughout the literature, and echoed by various presenters at the ESSLLI Workshop - is that whereas small windows are well suited to the detection of syntactico-semantic associations, larger windows have the capacity to detect broader "topical" associations. More specifically, we can observe that small windows are unavoidably limited to detecting associations manifest at very close distances in the text. For example, a

Proceedings of the 12th Conference of the European Chapter of the ACL, pages 861–869,
Athens, Greece, 30 March – 3 April 2009.

window size of two words can only ever observe bigrams, and cannot detect associations resulting from larger constructs, however ingrained in the language (e.g. "if ... then", "ne ... pas", "dear ... yours"). This is not the full story however. As, Rapp (2002) observes, choosing a window size involves making a *trade-off* between various qualities. So conversely for example, frequency counts within large windows, though able to detect longer-range associations, are not readily able to distinguish them from bigram style co-occurrences, and so some discriminatory power, and sensitivity to the latter, is lost. Rapp (2002) calls this trade-off "specificity"; equivalent observations were made by Church & Hanks (1989) and Church *et al* (1991), who refer to the tendency for large windows to "wash out", "smear" or "defocus" those associations exhibited at smaller scales.

In the following two sections, we present two important and scarcely discussed facets of this general trade-off related to window size: that of *scale-dependence*, and that concerning the specific way in which the *data sparseness problem* is manifest.

2.1 Scale-dependence

It has been shown that varying the size of the context considered for a word can impact upon the performance of applications (Rapp, 2002; Yarowsky & Florian, 2002), there being no ideal window size for all applications. This is an inescapable symptom of the fact that varying window size fundamentally affects *what* is being measured (both in the raw data sense and linguistically speaking) and so impacts upon the output qualitatively. As Church *et al* (1991) postulated, *"It is probably necessary that the lexicographer adjust the window size to match the scale of phenomena that he is interested in"*.

In the case of inferential lexical semantics, this puts strict limits on the interpretation of association scores derived from co-occurrence counts and, therefore, on higher-level features such as context vectors and similarity measures. As Wang (2005) eloquently observes, with respect to the application of word sense disambiguation, *"window size is an inherent parameter which is necessary for the observer to implement an observation ... [the result] has no meaning if a window size does not accompany"*. More precisely, we can say that window-based co-occurrence counts (and any word-space models we may derive from them) are *scale-dependent*.

It follows that one cannot guarantee there to be an "ideal" window size within even a single application. Distributional lexical semantics often defers to human association norms for evaluation. Schulte im Walde & Melinger (2008) found that the correlation between co-occurrence derived association scores and human association norms were weakly dependent upon the window size used to calculate the former, but that certain associations tended to be represented at certain window sizes, by virtue of the fact that the best *overall* correlation was found by combining evidence from *all* window sizes. By identifying a single window size (whether arbitrary or apparently optimum) and treating other evidence as extraneous, it follows that studies may tend to distance their findings from one another.

As Church *et al* (1991) allude, in certain situations the ability to tune analysis to a specific scale in this way may be desirable (for example, when explicitly searching for statistically significant bigrams, only a 2-token window will do). In other scenarios however, especially where a trade-off in aspects of performance is found between scales, it can clearly be seen as a limitation. And after all, is Church *et al*'s notional lexicographer really interested in those features manifest at a specific scale, or is he interested in a specific *linguistic category* of features? Notwithstanding grammatical notions of scale (the clause, the sentence etc), there is as yet little evidence to suggest how the two are linked.

The existence of these trade-offs has led some authors towards creative solutions: looking for ways of varying window size dynamically in response to some performance measure, or simultaneously exploiting more than one window size in order to maximize the pertinent information captured (Wang, 2005; Quasthoff, 2007; Lamjiri *et a*l, 2003). When the scales at which an association is manifest are the quantity of interest and the subject of systematic study, we have what is known in scale-aware disciplines as *multi-scalar* analysis, of which fractal analysis is a variant. Although a certain amount has been written about the fractal or hierarchical nature of language, approaches to co-occurrence in lexical semantics remain almost exclusively mono-scalar, with the recent work of Quasthoff (2007) being a rare exception.

2.2 Data sparseness

Another facet of the general trade-off identified by Rapp (2002) pertains to how limitations inherent in the combination of data and co-occurrence retrieval method are manifest.

When applying a small window, the number of window positions which can be expected to contain a specific pair of words will tend to be low in comparison to the number of instances of each word type. In some cases, no co-occurrence may be observed at all between certain word pairs, and zero or negative association may be inferred (even though we might reasonably expect such co-occurrences to be feasible within the window, or know that a logical association exists). This is one manifestation of what is commonly referred to as the data sparseness problem, and was discussed by Rapp (2002) as a side-effect of *specificity*. It would of course be inaccurate to suggest that data sparseness itself is a response to window size; a larger window superficially lessens the sparseness problem by inviting more co-occurrences, but encounters the same underlying paucity of information in a different guise: as both the size and overlap between the windows grow, the available information is increasingly diluted both within and amongst the windows, resulting in an over-smoothing of the data. This phenomenon is well illustrated in the extreme case of a single corpus-sized window where - in the absence of any external information - observed and expected co-occurrence frequencies are equivalent, and it is not possible to infer any associations at all.

Addressing the sparseness problem with respect to corpus data has received considerable attention in recent years. It is usually tackled by applying explicit smoothing methods so as to allow the estimation of frequencies of unseen co-occurrences. This may involve applying insights on the statistical limitations of working from a finite sample (add-λ smoothing, Good-Turing smoothing), making inferences from words with similar co-occurrence patterns, or "backing off" to a more general language model based on individual word frequencies, or even another corpus; for example, Keller & Lapata (2003) use the Web. All of these approaches attempt to *mitigate* the data sparseness manifest in the observed co-occurrence frequencies; they do not presume to *reduce* data sparseness by improving the method of observation. Indeed, the general assumption would seem to be that the only way to minimize data sparseness is to use *more data*. However, we will show that, similarly to Wang's (2005) observation concerning windowed measurements in general, apparent data sparseness is as much a manifestation of the observation method as it is of the data itself; there may exist much pertinent information in the corpus which yet remains unexploited.

3 Proximity as association

Comprehensive multi-scalar analyses (such as applied by Quasthoff, 2007; and Schulte im Walde & Melinger, 2008) can be laborious and computationally expensive, and it is not yet clear how to derive simple association scores and suchlike from the dense data they generate (typically a separate set of statistics for each window size examined). There do exist however relatively efficient naturally *scale-independent* tools which are amenable to the detection of linguistically interesting features in text. In some domains the concept of *proximity* (or *distance* – we will use the terms somewhat interchangeably here) has been used as the basis for straightforward alternatives to various frequency-based measures. In biogeography, for example, the dispersion or "clumpiness" of a population of individuals can be accurately estimated by sampling the distances between them (Clark & Evans, 1954): a task more conventionally carried out by "quadrat" sampling, which is directly analogous to the window-based methods typically used to measure dispersion or co-occurrence in a corpus (see Gries, 2008, for an overview of dispersion in a linguistic setting). Such techniques are also been used in archeology. Washtell (2006) found evidence to suggest that distance-based approaches within the geographic domain can be both more accurate and more efficient than their window-based alternatives.

In the present domain, the notion of proximity has been applied by Savický & Hlavácová (2002) and Washtell (2007) - both in Gries (2008) - as an alternative to approaches based on corpus division, for quantifying the dispersion of words within the text. Hardcastle (2005) and Washtell (2007) apply this same concept to measuring word pair associations, the former via a somewhat ad-hoc approach, the latter through an extension of Clark-Evans (1954) dispersion metric to the concept of *co-dispersion*: the tendency of unlike words to gravitate (or be similarly dispersed) in the text. Terra & Clarke (2004) use a very similar approach in order to generate a probabilistic language model, where previously n-gram models have been used,

The allusion to *proximity* as a fundamental indicator of lexical association does in fact permeate the literature. Halliday (1966), for example, in Church *et al* (1991) talked not explicitly of frequencies within windows, but of identifying lexical associates via *"some measure of significant proximity, either a scale or at least a cut-off point"*. For one (possibly practical) reason or another, the "cut-off point" has been adopted and the intuition of proximity has since become entrained within a distinctly frequency-oriented model. By way of example, the notion of proximity has been somewhat more directly courted in some window-based studies through the use of "ramped" or "weighted" windows (Lamjiri et al, 2003; Bullinaria & Levy, 2007), in which co-occurrences appearing towards the extremities of the window are discounted in some way. As with window size however, the specific implementations and resultant performances of this approach have been inconsistent in the literature, with different profiles (even including those where words are discounted towards the *centre* of the window) seeming to prove optimum under varying experimental conditions (compare, for instance, Bullinaria, 2008, and Shaol & Westbury, 2008, from the ESSLLI Workshop).

Performance considerations aside, a problem arising from mixing the metaphors of frequency and distance in this way is that the resultant measures become difficult to interpret; in the present case of association, it is not trivially obvious how one might establish an expected value for a window with a given profile, or apply and interpret conditional probabilities and other well-understood association measures.[1] At the very least, Wang's (2005) observation is exacerbated.

3.1 Co-dispersion

By doing away with the notion of a window entirely and focusing purely upon distance information, Halliday's (1966) intuitions concerning proximity can be more naturally realized. Under the frequency regime, co-occurrence scores correspond directly to probabilities, which are well understood (providing, as Wang, 2005, observes, that a window size is specified as a reference-frame for their interpretation). It happens that similarly intuitive mechanics apply within a purely distance-oriented regime - a fact realised by Clark & Evans (1954), but not exploited by Hardcastle (2005). Co-dispersion, which is derived from the Clark-Evans metric (and more descriptively entitled "co-dispersion by nearest neighbour" - as there exist many ways to measure dispersion), can be generalised as follows:

$$CoDisp_{ab} = \frac{m \cdot n / (\max(freq_a, freq_b) + 1)}{M(dist_{ab_1}, \ldots, dist_{ab_n})}$$

Where, in the denominator, $dist_{abi}$ is the inter-word distance (the number of intervening tokens plus one) between the ith occurrence of word-type a in the corpus, and the nearest preceding or following occurrence of word-type b (if one exists before encountering *(1)* another occurrence of a or *(2)* the edge of the containing document). M is the generalized mean. In the numerator, $freq_i$ is the total number of occurrences of word-type i, n is the number of tokens in the corpus, and m is a constant based on the expected value of the mean (e.g. for the arithmetic mean – as used by Clark & Evans - this is 0.5). Note that the implementation considered here does not distinguish word order; owing to this, and the constraint *(1)*, the measure is symmetric.[2]

Plainly put, co-dispersion calculates the ratio of the mean observed distance to the expected distance between word type pairs in the text; or how much closer the word types occur, on average, than would expected according to chance[3]. In this sense it is conceptually equivalent to Pointwise Mutual Information (PMI) and related association measures which are concerned with gauging how more *frequently* two words occur together (in a window), than would be expected by chance.

Like many of its frequency-oriented cousins, co-dispersion can be used directly as a measure of association, with values in the range $0 >= CoDisp <= \infty$ (with a value of 1 representing no discernible association); and as with these measures, the logarithm can be taken in order to present the values on a scale that more meaningfully represents relative associations (as is the default with PMI). Also as with PMI *et al*, co-dispersion can have a tendency to give inflated estimates where infrequent words are involved. To address this problem, a simple significance-

[1] Existing works do not go into detail on method, so it is possible that this is one source of discrepancies.

[2] This constraint, which was independently adopted by Terra & Clarke (2004), has significant computational advantages as it effectively limits the search distance for frequent words.

[3] The expected distance of an independent word-type pair is assumed to be half the distance between neighbouring occurrences of the more frequent word-type, were it uniformly distributed within the corpus.

corrected measure, more akin to a Z-Score or T-Score (Dennis, 1965; Church *et al*, 1991) can be formed by taking (the root of) the number of word-type occurrences into account (Sackett, 2001). The same principal can be applied to PMI, although in practice more precise significance measures such as Log-Likelihood are favoured.[4]

These similarities aside, co-dispersion has the somewhat abstract distinction of being effectively based on degrees rather than probabilities. Although it is windowless (and therefore, as we will show, scale-independent), it is not without analogous constraints. Just as the concept of mean frequency employed by co-occurrence requires a definition of distance (window size), the concept of distance employed by co-dispersion requires a definition of frequency. In the case presented here, this frequency is 1 (the nearest neighbour). Thus, whereas the assumption with co-occurrence is that the linguistically pertinent words are those that fall within a fixed-sized window of the word of interest, the assumption underpinning co-dispersion is that the relevant information lies (if at all) with the closest neighbouring occurrence of each word type. Among other things, this naturally favours the consideration of nearby function words, whereas (generally less frequent) content words are considered to be of potential relevance at some distance. That this may be a desirable property - or at least a workable constraint - is borne out by the fact that other studies have experienced success by treating these two broad classes of words with separately sized windows (Lamjiri *et al*, 2003).

4 Analyses

4.1 Scale-independence

Table 1 shows a matrix of agreement between word-pair association scores produced by co-occurrence and co-dispersion as applied to the unlemmatised, untagged, Brown Corpus. For co-occurrence, window sizes of ±1, ±3, ±10, ±32, and ±100 words were used (based on to a - somewhat arbitrary - scaling factor of $\sqrt{10}$).

The words used were a cross-section of stimulus-response pairs from human association experiments (Kiss *et al*, 1973), selected to give a uniform spread of association scores, as used in the ESSLLI Workshop shared task. It is not our purpose in the current work to demonstrate competitive correlations with human association norms (which is quite a specific research area) and we are making no cognitive claims here. Their use lends convenience and a (limited) degree of relevance, by allowing us to perform our comparison across a set of word-pairs which are deigned to represent a broad spread of associations according to some independent measure. Nonetheless, correlations with the association norms are presented as this was a straightforward step, and grounds the findings presented here in a more tangible context.

Because the human stimulus-response relationship is generally asymmetric (favouring cases where the stimulus word evokes the response word, but not necessarily vice-versa), the conditional probability of the response word was used, rather than PMI which is symmetric. For the windowless method, co-dispersion was adapted equivalently - by multiplying the resultant association score by the number of word pairings divided by the number of occurrences of the cue word. These association scores were also corrected for statistical significance, as per Sackett (2001). Both of these adjustments were found to improve correlations with human scores across the board, but neither impacts directly upon the comparative analyses performed herein. It is also worth mentioning that many human association reproduction experiments employ higher-order paradigmatic associations, whereas we use only syntagmatic associations.[5] This is appropriate as our focus here is on the information captured at the base level (from which higher order features – paradigmatic associations, semantic categories etc - are invariably derived). It can be seen in the rightmost column of table 1 that, despite the lack of sophistication in our approach, all window sizes and the windowless approach generated statistically significant (if somewhat less than state-of-the-art) correlations with the subset of human association norms used.

Owing to the relatively small size of the corpus, and the removal of stop-words, a large portion of the human stimulus-response pairs used as our basis generated no association (no smoothing was used as we are concerned at this level in raw evidence captured from the corpus). All correlations presented herein therefore consider only those word pairs for which there was *some evidence* under the methods being com-

[4] Although the heuristically derived MI^2 and MI^3 (Daille, 1994) have gained some popularity.

[5] Though interestingly, work done by Wettler *et al* (2005) suggests that paradigmatic associations may not be necessary for cognitive association models.

pared from which to generate a non-zero association score (however statistically insignificant). This number of word pairs, shown in square brackets in the leftmost column of table 1, naturally increases with window size, and is highest for the windowless methods.

Wind'd	±100	±32	±10	±3	±1	Human (r, p)	
±1 [34]	0.18	0.34	0.59	0.81	1	0.35	4.15%
±3 [47]	0.32	0.49	0.70	1		0.41	0.44%
±10 [64]	0.52	0.76	1			0.36	0.31%
±32 [78]	0.83	1				0.50	<0.01%
±100 [89]	1					0.53	<0.01%
W'less [103]	0.46	0.45	0.50	0.55	0.58	0.42	<0.01%

Table 1: Matrix of agreement (*corrected* r^2) between association retrieval methods; and correlations with sample association norms (r, and p-value).

The coefficients of determination (*corrected* r^2 values) in the main part of table 1 show clearly that, as window sizes diverge, their agreement over the apparent association of word pairs in the corpus diminishes - to the point where there is almost as much disagreement as there is agreement between windows whose size differs by a decimal order of magnitude. While relatively small, the fact that there remains a degree of information overlap between the smallest and largest windows in this study (18%), illustrates that some word pairs exhibit associative tendencies which markedly transcend scale. It would follow that single window sizes are particularly impotent where such features are of holistic interest.

The figures in the bottom row of table 1 show, in contrast, that there is a more-or-less constant level of agreement between the windowless and windowed approaches, *regardless* of the window size chosen for the latter.

Figure 1 gives a good two-dimensional schematic approximation of these various relationships (in the style of a Venn diagram). Analysis of partial correlations would give a more accurate picture, but is probably unnecessary in this case as the areas of overlap between methods are large enough to leave marginal room for misrepresentation. It is interesting to observe that co-dispersion *appears* to have a slightly higher affinity for the associations best detected by small windows in this case. Reassuringly nonetheless, the relative correlations with association norms here - and the fact that we see such significant overlap – do indeed suggest that co-dispersion is sensitive to useful information present in each of the various windowed methods. Note that the regions in Figure 1 necessarily have similar areas, as a correlation coefficient describes a symmetric relationship. The diagram therefore says nothing about the *amount* of information captured by each of these methods. It is this issue which we will look at next.

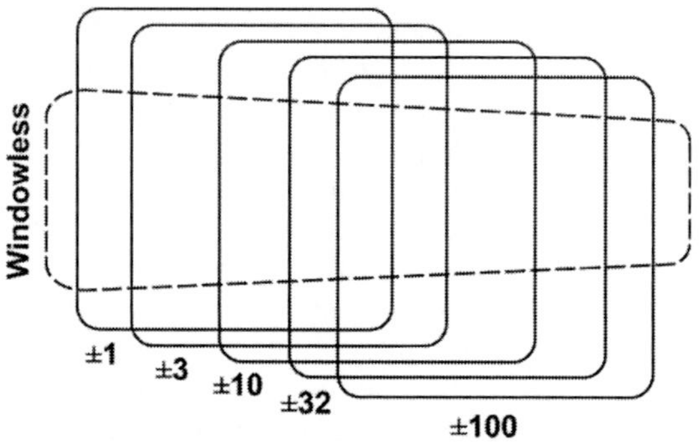

Figure 1: Approximate Venn representation of agreement between windowed and windowless association retrieval methods.

4.2 Statistical power

To paraphrase Kilgariff (2005), language is anything but random. A good language model is one which best captures the non-random structure of language. A good measuring device for any linguistic feature is therefore one which strongly differentiates real language from random data.

The solid lines in figures 2a and 2b give an indication of the relative confidence levels (p-values) attributable to a given association score derived from windowed co-occurrence data. Figure 2a is based on a window size of ±10 words, and 2b ±100 words. The data was generated, Monte Carlo style, from a 1 million word randomly generated corpus. For the sake of statistical convenience and realism, the symbols in the corpus were given a Zipf frequency distribution roughly matching that of words found in the Brown corpus (and most English corpora). Unlike with the previous experiment, *all* possible word pairings were considered. PMI was used for measuring association, owing to its convenience and similarity to co-dispersion, but it should be noted that the specific formulation of the association measure is more-or-less irrelevant in the present context, where we are using *relative* association levels between a real and random corpus as a proxy for how much structural information is captured from the corpus.

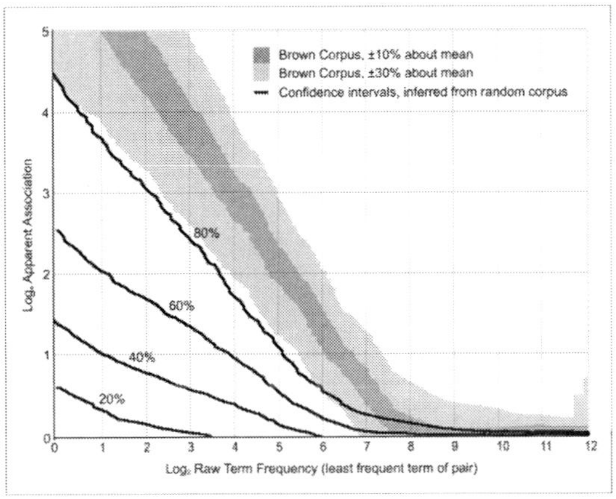

Figure 2a: Co-occurrence significances for a moderate (±10 words) window.

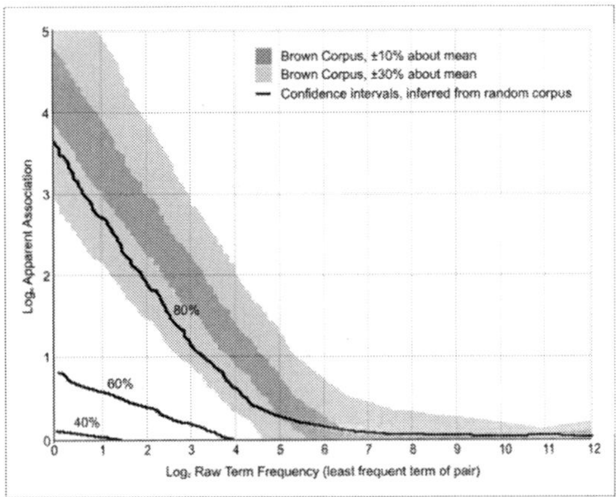

Figure 2b: Co-occurrence significances for a large (±100 words) window.

Precisely put, the figures show the percentage of times a given association score or lower was measured between word types in a corpus which is known to be devoid of any actual syntagmatic association. The closer to the origin these lines, the fewer word instances were required to be present in the random corpus before high levels of apparent association became unlikely, and so the fewer would be required in a real corpus before we could be confident of the import of a measured level of association. Consequently, if word pairs in a real corpus exceed these levels, we say that they show *significant association*.

The shaded regions in figures 2a and 2b show the typical range of apparent association scores found in a *real* corpus – in this case the Brown corpus. The first thing to observe is that both the spread of raw association scores and their significances are relatively constant across word frequencies, up to a frequency threshold which is linked to the window size. This constancy exists in spite of a remarkable variation in the raw association scores, which are increasingly inflated towards the lower frequencies (indeed illustrating the importance of taking statistical significance into account). This observed constancy is intuitive where long-range associations between words prevail: very infrequent words will tend to co-occur within the window less often than moderately frequent words - by simple virtue of their number - yet when they do co-occur, the evidence for association is that much stronger owing to the small size of the window relative to their frequency. Beyond the threshold governed by window size, there can be seen a sharp levelling out in apparent association, accompanied by an attendant drop in overall significance. This is a manifestation of Rapp's *specificity*: as words become much more frequent than window size, the kinds of tight idiomatic co-occurrences and compound forms which would otherwise imply an uncommonly strong association can no longer be detected as such.

A related observation is that, in spite of the lower random baseline exhibited by the larger window size, the actual *significance* of the associations it reports in a real corpus are, for all word frequencies, lower than those reported by the smaller window: i.e. *quantitatively* speaking, larger windows seem to observe less! Evidently, apparent association is as much a function of window size as it is of actual syntagmatic association; it would be very tempting to interpret the association profiles in figures 2a or 2b, in isolation of each other or their baseline plots, as indicating some interesting scale-varying associative structure in the corpus, where in fact they do not.

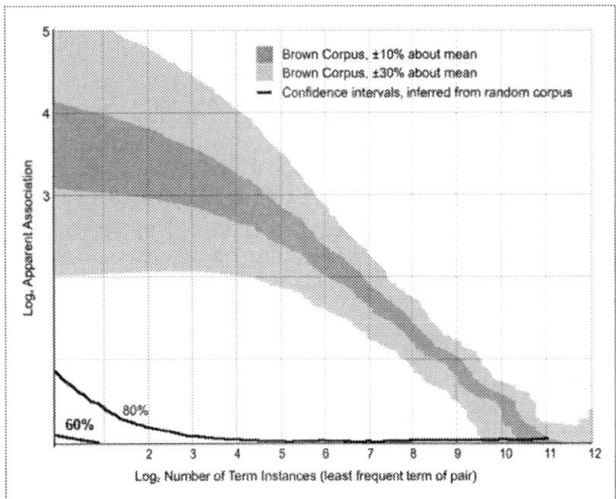

Figure 3: Significances for windowless co-dispersion.

Figure 3 is identical to figures 2a and 2b (the same random and real world corpora were used) but it represents the windowless co-dispersion method presented herein. It can be seen that the random corpus baseline comprises a smooth power curve which gives low initial association levels, rapidly settling towards the expected value of zero as the number of token instances increases. Notably, the bulk of apparent association scores reported from the Brown Corpus are, while not necessarily greater, orders of magnitude more significant than with the windowed examples for all but the most frequent words (ranging well into the 99%+ confidence levels). This gain can only follow from the fact that more information is being taken into account: not only do we now consider relationships that occur at all scales, as previously demonstrated, but we consider the exact distance between word tokens, as opposed to low-range ordinal values linked to window-averaged frequencies. There is no observable threshold effect, and without a window there is no reason to expect one. Accordingly, there is no specificity trade-off: while word pairs interacting at very large distances are captured (as per the largest of windows), very close occurrences are still rewarded appropriately (as per the smallest of window).

5 Conclusions and future direction

We have presented a novel alternative to co-occurrence for measuring lexical association which, while based on similar underlying linguistic intuitions, uses a very different apparatus. We have shown this method to gather more information from the corpus overall, and to be particularly unfettered by issues of scale. While the information gathered is, by definition, linguistically relevant, relevance to a given task (such as reproducing human association norms or performing word-sense disambiguation), or superior performance with small corpora, does not necessarily follow. Further work is to be conducted in applying the method to a range of linguistic tasks, with an initial focus on lexical semantics. In particular, properties of resultant word-space models and similarity measures beg a thorough investigation: while we would expect to gain denser higher-precision vectors, there might prove to be overriding qualitative differences. The relationship to grammatical dependency-based contexts which often out-perform contiguous contexts also begs investigation.

It is also pertinent to explore the more fundamental parameters associated with the windowless approach; the formulation of co-dispersion presented herein is but one interpretation of the specific case of association. In these senses there is much catching-up to do.

At the present time, given the key role of window size in determining the selection and apparent strength of associations under the conventional co-occurrence model - highlighted here and in the works of Church *et al* (1991), Rapp (2002), Wang (2005), and Schulte im Walde & Melinger (2008) - we would urge that this is an issue which window-driven studies continue to conscientiously address; at the very least, scale is a parameter which findings dependent on distributional phenomena must be qualified in light of.

Acknowledgements

Kind thanks go to Reinhard Rapp, Stefan Gries, Katja Markert, Serge Sharoff and Eric Atwell for their helpful feedback and positive support.

References

John A. Bullinaria. 2008. *Semantic Categorization Using Simple Word Co-occurrence Statistics*. In: M. Baroni, S. Evert & A. Lenci (Eds), Proceedings of the ESSLLI Workshop on Distributional Lexical Semantics: 1 - 8

John A. Bullinaria and Joe P. Levy. 2007. *Extracting Semantic Representations from Word Co-occurrence Statistics: A Computational Study*. Behavior Research Methods, 39:510 - 526.

Yaacov Choueka and Serge Lusignan. 1985. *Disambiguation by short contexts*. Computers and the Humanities. 19(3):147 - 157

Kenneth W. Church and Patrick Hanks. 1989. *Word association norms, mutual information, and lexicography*. In Proceedings of the 27th Annual Meeting on Association For Computational Linguistics: 76 - 83

Kenneth W. Church, William A. Gale, Patrick Hanks and Donald Hindle. 1991. *Using statistics in lexical analysis*. In: Lexical Acquisition: Using Online Resources to Build a Lexicon, Lawrence Erlbaum: 115 - 164.

P. J. Clark and F. C. Evans. 1954. *Distance to nearest neighbor as a measure of spatial relationships in populations.*Ecology. 35: 445 - 453.

Béatrice Daille. 1994. *Approche mixte pour l'extraction automatique de terminologie: statistiques lexicales et filtres linguistiques*. PhD thesis, Université Paris.

Sally F. Dennis. 1965. *The construction of a thesaurus automatically from a sample of text*. In Proceedings of the Symposium on Statistical Association Methods For Mechanized Documentation, Washington, DC: 61 - 148.

Philip Edmonds. 1997. *Choosing the word most typical in context using a lexical co-occurrence network*. In Proceedings of the Eighth Conference on European Chapter of the Association For Computational Linguistics: 507 - 509

Stefan Evert. 2007. *Computational Approaches to Collocations: Association Measures*, Institute of Cognitive Science, University of Osnabruck, <http://www.collocations.de>.

Manfred Wettler, Reinhard Rapp and Peter Sedlmeier. 2005. *Free word associations correspond to contiguities between words in texts*. Journal of Quantitative Linguistics, 12:111 - 122.

Michael K. Halliday. 1966 *Lexis as a Linguistic Level*, in Bazell, C., Catford, J., Halliday, M., and Robins, R. (eds.), In Memory of J. R. Firth, Longman, London.

David Hardcastle. 2005. *Using the distributional hypothesis to derive cooccurrence scores from the British National Corpus*. Proceedings of Corpus Linguistics. Birmingham, UK

Kei Yuen Hung, Robert Luk, Daniel Yeung, Korris Chung and Wenhuo Shu. 2001. *Determination of Context Window Size*, International Journal of Computer Processing of Oriental Languages, 14(1): 71 - 80

Stefan Gries. 2008. *Dispersions and Adjusted Frequencies in Corpora*. International Journal of Corpus Linguistics, 13(4)

Frank Keller and Mirella Lapata. 2003. *Using the web to obtain frequencies for unseen bigrams*, Computational Limguistics, 29:459 – 484

Adam Kilgarriff. 2005. Language is never ever ever random. Corpus Linguistics and Linguistic Theory 1: 263 - 276.

George Kiss, Christine Armstrong, Robert Milroy and James Piper. 1973. *An associative thesaurus of English and its computer analysis*. In Aitken, A.J., Bailey, R.W. and Hamilton-Smith, N. (Eds.), The Computer and Literary Studies. Edinburgh University Press.

Abolfazl K. Lamjiri, Osama El Demerdash and Leila Kosseim. 2003. *Simple Features for Statistical Word Sense Disambiguation,* Proceedings of Senseval-3:3rd International Workshop on the Evaluation of Systems for the Semantic Analysis of Text: 133 - 136.

Uwe Quasthoff. 2007. *Fraktale Dimension von Wörtern*. Unpublished manuscript.

Reinhard Rapp. 2002. *The computation of word associations: comparing syntagmatic and paradigmatic approaches*. In Proceedings of the 19th international Conference on Computational Linguistics.

D. L. Sackett. 2001. *Why randomized controlled trials fail but needn't: 2. Failure to employ physiological statistics, or the only formula a clinician-trialist is ever likely to need (or understand!)*. CMAJ, 165(9):1226 - 37.

Magnus Sahlgren. 2006. *The Word-Space Model: using distributional analysis to represent syntagmatic and paradigmatic relations between words in high-dimensional vector space*, PhD Thesis, Stockholm University.

Petr Savický and Jana Hlavácová. 2002. *Measures of word commonness*. Journal of Quantitative Luiguistics, 9(3): 215 – 31.

Cyrus Shaoul, Chris Westbury. 2008. *Performance of HAL-like word space models on semantic clustering*. In: M. Baroni, S. Evert & A. Lenci (Eds), Proceedings of the ESSLLI Workshop on Distributional Lexical Semantics: 1 – 8.

Sabine Schulte im Walde and Alissa Melinger, A. 2008. *An In-Depth Look into the Co-Occurrence Distribution of Semantic Associates*, Italian Journal of Linguistics, Special Issue on From Context to Meaning: Distributional Models of the Lexicon in Linguistics and Cognitive Science.

Egidio Terra and Charles L. A. Clarke. 2004. *Fast Computation of Lexical Affinity Models*, Proceedings of the 20th International Conference on Computational Linguistics, Geneva, Switzerland.

Xiaojie Wang. 2005. *Robust Utilization of Context in Word Sense Disambiguation*, Modeling and Using Context, Lecture Notes in Computer Science, Springer: 529-541.

Justin Washtell. 2006. *Estimating Habitat Area & Related Ecological Metrics: From Theory Towards Best Practice*, BSc Dissertation, University of Leeds.

Justin Washtell. 2007. *Co-Dispersion by Nearest Neighbour: Adapting a Spatial Statistic for the Development of Domain-Independent Language Tools and Metrics*, MSc Thesis, University of Leeds.

Warren Weaver. 1949 *Translation*. Repr. in: Locke, W.N. and Booth, A.D. (eds.) *Machine translation of languages: fourteen essays* (Cambridge, Mass.: Technology Press of the Massachusetts Institute of Technology, 1955), 15-23. Association for Computing Machinery, 28(1):114-133.

David Yarowsky and Radu Florian. 2002. *Evaluating Sense Disambiguation Performance Across Diverse Parameter Spaces*. Journal of Natural Language Engineering, 8(4).

Language ID in the Context of Harvesting Language Data off the Web

Fei Xia
University of Washington
Seattle, WA 98195, USA
fxia@u.washington.edu

William D. Lewis
Microsoft Research
Redmond, WA 98052, USA
wilewis@microsoft.com

Hoifung Poon
University of Washington
Seattle, WA 98195, USA
hoifung@cs.washington.edu

Abstract

As the arm of NLP technologies extends beyond a small core of languages, techniques for working with instances of language data across hundreds to thousands of languages may require revisiting and recalibrating the tried and true methods that are used. Of the NLP techniques that has been treated as "solved" is language identification (language ID) of written text. However, we argue that language ID is far from solved when one considers input spanning not dozens of languages, but rather hundreds to thousands, a number that one approaches when harvesting language data found on the Web. We formulate language ID as a coreference resolution problem and apply it to a Web harvesting task for a specific linguistic data type and achieve a much higher accuracy than long accepted language ID approaches.

1 Introduction

A large number of the world's languages have been documented by linguists; it is now increasingly common to post current research and data to the Web, often in the form of language snippets embedded in scholarly papers. A particularly common format for linguistic data posted to the Web is "interlinearized text", a format used to present language data and analysis relevant to a particular argument or investigation. Since interlinear examples consist of orthographically or phonetically encoded language data aligned with an English translation, the "corpus" of interlinear examples found on the Web, when taken together, constitute a significant multilingual, parallel corpus covering hundreds to thousands of the world's languages. Previous work has discussed methods for harvesting interlinear text off the Web (Lewis, 2006), enriching it via structural projections (Xia and Lewis, 2007), and even making it available to typological analyses (Lewis and Xia, 2008) and search (Xia and Lewis, 2008).

One challenge with harvesting interlinear data off the Web is language identification of the harvested data. There have been extensive studies on language identification (language ID) of written text, and a review of previous research on this topic can be found in (Hughes et al., 2006). In general, a language ID method requires a collection of text for training, something on the order of a thousand or more characters. These methods work well for languages with rich language resources; for instance, Cavnar and Trenkle's N-gram-based algorithm achieved an accuracy as high as 99.8% when tested on newsgroup articles across eight languages (Cavnar and Trenkle, 1994). However, the performance is much worse (with accuracy dropping to as low as 1.66%) if there is very little language data for training and the number of languages being evaluated reaches a few hundred.

In this paper, we treat the language ID of harvested linguistic data as a coreference resolution problem. Our method, although narrowly focused on this very specific data type, makes it possible to collect small snippets of language data across hundreds of languages and use the data for linguistic search and bootstrapping NLP tools.

2 Background

2.1 Interlinear glossed text (IGT)

In linguistics, the practice of presenting language data in interlinear form has a long history, going back at least to the time of the structuralists. Interlinear Glossed Text, or *IGT*, is often used to present data and analysis on a language that the reader may not know much about, and is frequently included in scholarly linguistic documents. The canonical form of an IGT consists

Proceedings of the 12th Conference of the European Chapter of the ACL, pages 870–878,
Athens, Greece, 30 March – 3 April 2009.

of three lines: a line for the language in question (i.e., the *language line*), an English gloss line, and an English translation. Table 1 shows the beginning of a linguistic document (Baker and Stewart, 1996) which contains two IGTs: one in lines 30-32, and the other in lines 34-36. The line numbers are added for the sake of convenience.

1: THE ADJ/VERB DISTINCTION: **EDO** EVIDENCE
2:
3: Mark C. Baker and Osamuyimen **Thompson** Stewart
4: McGill University
....
27: The following shows a similar minimal pair from **Edo**,
28: a **Kwa** language spoken in Nigeria (Agheyisi 1990).
29:
30: (2) a. *Èmèrí mòsé.*
31: Mary be.beautiful(V)
32: 'Mary is beautiful.'
33:
34: b. *Èmèrí *(yé) mòsé.*
35: Mary be.beautiful(A)
36: 'Mary is beautiful (A).'
...

Table 1: A linguistic document that contains IGT: words in boldface are potential language names

2.2 The Online Database of Interlinear text (ODIN)

ODIN, the Online Database of INterlinear text, is a resource built from data harvested from scholarly documents (Lewis, 2006). It was built in three steps: (1) crawling the Web to retrieve documents that may contain IGT, (2) extracting IGT from the retrieved documents, and (3) identifying the language codes of the extracted IGTs. The identified IGTs are then extracted and stored in a database (the ODIN database), which can be easily searched with a GUI interface.[1]

ODIN currently consists about 189,000 IGT instances extracted from three thousand documents, with close to a thousand languages represented. In addition, there are another 130,000 additional IGT-bearing documents that have been crawled and are waiting for further process. Once these additional documents are processed, the database is expected to expand significantly.

ODIN is a valuable resource for linguists, as it can be searched for IGTs that belong to a particular language or a language family, or those that contain a particular linguistic construction (e.g., passive, wh-movement). In addition, there have been some preliminary studies that show the benefits of using the resource for NLP. For instance, our previous work shows that automatically enriched IGT data can be used to answer typological questions (e.g., the canonical word order of a language) with a high accuracy (Lewis and Xia, 2008), and the information could serve as prototypes for prototype learning (Haghighi and Klein, 2006).

[1]http://odin.linguistlist.org

3 The language ID task for ODIN

As the size of ODIN increases dramatically, it is crucial to have a reliable module that automatically identifies the correct language code for each new extracted IGT to be added to ODIN. The current ODIN system uses two language identifiers: one is based on simple heuristics, and the other on Cavnar and Trenkle's algorithm (1994). However, because the task here is very different from a typical language ID task (see below), both algorithms work poorly, with accuracy falling below 55%. The focus of this paper is on building new language identifiers with a much higher accuracy.

3.1 The data set

A small portion of the IGTs in ODIN have been assigned the correct language code semi-automatically. Table 2 shows the size of the data set. We use it for training and testing, and all results reported in the paper are the average of running 10-fold cross validation on the data set unless specified otherwise.

Table 2: The data set for the language ID task

# of IGT-bearing documents	1160
# of IGT instances	15,239
# of words on the language lines	77,063
# of languages	638

3.2 The special properties of the task

The task in hand is very different from a typical language ID task in several respects:

- Large number of languages: The number of languages in our data set is 638 and that of the current ODIN database is close to a thousand. As more data is added to ODIN, the number of languages may reach several thousand as newly added linguistic documents could refer to any of approximately eight thousand living or dead languages.

- The use of language code: When dealing with only a few dozen languages, language names might be sufficient to identify languages. This is not true when dealing with a large number of languages, because some languages have multiple names, and some language names refer to multiple languages (see Section 4.2). To address this problem, we use language codes, since we can (mostly) ensure that each language code maps to exactly one language, and each language maps to exactly one code.

- Unseen languages: In this data set, about 10% of IGT instances in the test data belong to some languages that have never appeared in the training data. We call it the *unseen language problem*. This problem turns out to be the major obstacle to existing language ID methods.

- Extremely limited amount of training data per language: On average, each language in the training data has only 23 IGTs (116 word tokens in the language lines) available, and 45.3% of the languages have no more than 10 word tokens in the training data.

- The length of test instances: The language lines in IGT are often very short. The average length in this data set is 5.1 words. About 0.26% of the language lines in the data set are totally empty due to the errors introduced in the crawling or IGT extraction steps.

- Encoding issues: For languages that do not use Roman scripts in their writing system, the authors of documents often choose to use Romanized scripts (e.g., pinyin for Chinese), making the encoding less informative.

- Multilingual documents: About 40% of documents in the data set contain IGTs from multiple languages. Therefore, the language ID prediction should be made for each individual IGT, not for the whole document.

- Context information: In this task, IGTs are part of a document and there are often various cues in the document (e.g., language names) that could help predict the language ID of specific IGT instances.

Hughes and his colleagues (2006) identified eleven open questions in the domain of language ID that they believed were not adequately addressed in published research to date. Interestingly, our task encounters eight out of the eleven open questions. Because of these properties, existing language ID algorithms do not perform well when applied to the task (see Section 6).

4 Using context information

Various cues in the document can help predict the language ID of IGTs, and they are represented as features in our systems.

4.1 Feature templates

The following feature templates are used in our experiments.

(F1): The nearest language that precedes the current IGT.

(F2): The languages that appear in the neighborhood of the IGT or at the beginning or the end of a document.[2] Another feature checks the most frequent language occurring in the document.

(F3): For each language in the training data, we build three token lists: one for word unigrams, one for morph unigrams and the third for character ngrams ($n \leq 4$). These word lists are compared with the token lists built from the language line of the current IGT.

(F4): Similar to (F3), but the comparison is between the token lists built from the current IGT with the ones built from other IGTs in the same document. If some IGTs in the same document share the same tokens, they are likely to belong to the same language.

Here, all the features are binary: for features in F3 and F4, we use thresholds to turn real-valued features into binary ones. F1-F3 features can be calculated by looking at the documents only, whereas F4 features require knowing the language codes of other IGTs in the same document.

4.2 Language table

To identify language names in a document and map language names to language codes, we need a language table that lists all the (language code,

[2]For the experiments reported here, we use any line within 50 lines of the IGT or the first 50 or the last 50 lines of the document.

language name) pairs. There are three existing language tables: (1) ISO 639-3 maintained by SIL International,[3] (2) the 15th edition of the Ethnologue,[4] and (3) the list of ancient and dead languages maintained by LinguistList.[5] [6] We merged the three tables, as shown in Table 3.

Table 3: Various language name tables

Language table	# of lang codes	# of lang (code, name) pairs
(1) ISO 639-3	7702	9312
(2) Ethnologue v15	7299	42789
(3) LinguistList table	231	232
Merged table	7816	47728

The mapping between language names and language codes is many-to-many. A language code often has several alternate names in addition to the primary name. For instance, the language code *aaa* maps to names such as Alumu, Tesu, Arum, Alumu-Tesu, Alumu, Arum-Cesu, Arum-Chessu, and Arum-Tesu. While most language names map to only one language code, there are exceptions. For instance, the name *Edo* can map to either *bin* or *lew*. Out of 44,071 unique language names in the merged language table, 2625 of them (5.95%) are ambiguous.[7]

To identify language names in a document, we implemented a simple language name detector that scans the document from left to right and finds the longest string that is a language name according to the language table. The language name is then mapped to language codes. If a language name is ambiguous, all the corresponding language codes are considered by later stages. In Table 1, the language names identified by the detector are in boldface. The detector can produce false positive (e.g., *Thompson*) because a language name can have other meanings. Also, the language table is by no means complete and the detector is not able to recognize any language names that are missing from the table.

[3]http://www.sil.org/iso639-3/download.asp

[4]http://www.ethnologue.com/codes/default.asp#using

[5]http://linguistlist.org/forms/langs/GetListOfAncientLgs.html

[6]While ISO 639-3 is supposed to include all the language codes appearing in the other two lists, there is a lag in the adoption of new codes, which means the ISO 639-3 list continues to be somewhat out-of-date with the lists from which it is compiled since these other lists change periodically.

[7]Among the ambiguous names, 1996 names each map to two language codes, 407 map to three codes, 130 map to four codes, and so on. The most ambiguous name is *Miao*, which maps to fourteen language codes.

5 Formulating the language ID task

The language ID task here can be treated as two different learning problems.

5.1 As a classification problem

The language ID task can be treated as a classification problem. A classifier is a function that maps a training/test instance x to a class label y, and y is a member of a pre-defined label set C. For language ID, the training/test instance corresponds to a document (or an IGT in our case), and C is the set of language codes. We call this approach the *classification (CL) approach.*

Most, if not all, of previous language ID methods, fall into this category. They differ with respect to the underlying learning algorithms and the choice of features or similarity functions. When applying a feature-based algorithm (e.g., Maximum entropy) and using the features in Section 4.1, the feature vectors for the two IGTs in Table 1 are shown in Table 4. Each line has the format "*instance_name true_lang_code feat_name1 feat_name2 ...*", where feat_names are the names of features that are present in the instance. Take the first IGT as an example, its true language code is *bin*; the nearest language name (*nearLC*) is *Edo* whose language code is *bin* or *lew*; the languages that appear before the IGT includes Edo (*bin* or *lew*), Thompson (*thp*), and so on. The presence of *LMw1_bin* and *LMm1_bin* means that the overlap between the word/morph lists for *bin* and the ones built from the current IGT is higher than some threshold. The feature vector for the second IGT looks similar, except that it includes a F4 feature *IIw1_bin*, which says that the overlap between the word list built from the other IGTs in the same document with language code *bin* and the word list built from the current IGT is above a threshold. Note that language codes are part of feature names; therefore, a simple feature template such as nearest language (*nearLC*) corresponds to hundreds or even thousands of features (*nearLC_xxx*).

The *CL* approach has several major limitations. First, it cannot handle the *unseen language problem*: if an IGT in the test data belongs to a language that does not appear in the training data, this approach cannot classify it correctly. Second, the lack of parameter tying in this approach makes it unable to generalize between different languages. For instance, if the word *German* appears right before an IGT, the IGT is likely to be German. The

igt1 bin nearLC_bin nearLC_lew prev50_bin prev50_lew prev50_thp ... LMw1_bin LMm1_bin ...
igt2 bin nearLC_bin nearLC_lew prev50_bin prev50_lew prev50_thp ... LMw1_bin LMm1_bin ... IIw1_bin ...

Table 4: Feature vectors for the IGTs in Table 1 when using the *CL* approach (Edo: bin/lew, Thompson: thp, Kwa: etu/fip/kwb)

same is true if the word *German* is replaced by another language name. But this property cannot be leveraged easily by the *CL* approach without modifying the learning algorithm. This results in a proliferation of parameters, making learning harder and more prone to overfitting.

5.2 As a coreference resolution problem

A different way of handling the language ID task is to treat it as a coreference resolution problem: a mention is an IGT or a language name appearing in a document, an entity is a language code, and finding the language code for an IGT is the same as linking a mention (i.e., an IGT) to an entity (i.e., a language code).[8] We call this approach the *CoRef* approach. The major difference between the *CL* approach and the *CoRef* approach is the role of language code: in the former, language code is a class label to be used to tag an IGT; and in the latter, language code is an entity which an IGT can be linked to.

The language ID task shares many similarities with a typical coreference resolution task. For instance, language names are similar to proper nouns in that they are often unambiguous. IGT instances are like pronouns in that they often refer to language names appearing in the neighborhood. Once the language ID task is framed as a *CoRef* problem, all the existing algorithms on *CoRef* can be applied to the task, as discussed below.

5.2.1 Sequence labeling using traditional classifiers

One common approach to the *CoRef* problem processes the mentions sequentially and determine for each mention whether it should start a new entity or be linked to an existing mention (e.g., (Soon et al., 2001; Ng and Cardie, 2002; Luo, 2007)); that is, the approach makes a series of decisions, one decision per (mention, entity) pair. Applying this to the language ID task, the (mention, entity) pair would correspond to an (IGT, lang_code) pair, and each decision would have two possibilities: *Same* when the IGT belongs to the language or *Diff* when the IGT does not. Once the decisions are made for all the pairs, a post-processing procedure would check all the pairs for an IGT and link the IGT to the language code with which the pair has the highest confidence score.

Using the same kinds of features in Section 4.1, the feature vectors for the two IGTs in Table 1 are shown in Table 5. Comparing Table 4 and 5 reveals the differences between the *CL* approach and the *CoRef* approach: the *CoRef* approach has only two class labels (*Same* and *Diff*) where the *CL* approach has hundreds of labels (one for each language code); the *CoRef* approach has much fewer number of features because language code is not part of feature names; the *CoRef* approach has more training instances as each training instance corresponds to an (IGT, lang_code) pair.

igt1-bin	same	nearLC prev50 LMw1 LMm1 ...
igt1-lew	diff	nearLC prev50 ...
igt1-thp	diff	prev50 ...
...		
igt2-bin	same	nearLC prev50 LMw1 LMm1 IIw1 ...
igt2-lew	diff	nearLC prev50 ...
igt2-thp	diff	prev50 ...
...		

Table 5: Feature vectors for the IGTs in Table 1 when using the *CoRef* approach with sequence labeling methods

5.2.2 Joint Inference Using Markov Logic

Recently, joint inference has become a topic of keen interests in both the machine learning and NLP communities (e.g., (Bakir et al., 2007; Sutton et al., 2006; Poon and Domingos, 2007)). There have been increasing interests in formulating coreference resolution in a joint model and conducting joint inference to leverage dependen-

[8] There are minor differences between the language ID and coreference resolution tasks. For instance, each entity in the language ID task must be assigned a language code. This means that ambiguous language names will evoke multiple entities, each with a different language code. These differences are reflected in our algorithms.

cies among the mentions and entities (e.g., (Wellner et al., 2004; Denis and Baldridge, 2007; Poon and Domingos, 2008)). We have built a joint model for language ID in *Markov logic* (Richardson and Domingos, 2006).

Markov logic is a probabilistic extension of first-order logic that makes it possible to compactly specify probability distributions over complex relational domains. A *Markov logic network (MLN)* is a set of weighted first-order clauses. Together with a set of constants, it defines a Markov network with one node per ground atom and one feature per ground clause. The weight of a feature is the weight of the first-order clause that originated it. The probability of a state x in such a network is given by $P(x) = (1/Z)\exp\left(\sum_i w_i f_i(x)\right)$, where Z is a normalization constant, w_i is the weight of the ith clause, $f_i = 1$ if the ith clause is true, and $f_i = 0$ otherwise. Conditional probabilities can be computed using Markov chain Monte Carlo (e.g., MC-SAT (Poon and Domingos, 2006)). The weights can be learned using pseudo-likelihood training with L-BFGS (Richardson and Domingos, 2006). Markov logic is one of the most powerful representations for joint inference with uncertainty, and an implementation of its existing learning and inference algorithms is publicly available in the Alchemy package (Kok et al., 2007).

To use the features defined in Section 4.1, our MLN includes two evidence predicates: the first one is $\texttt{HasFeature(i, l, f)}$ where f is a feature in $F1$-$F3$. The predicate is true iff the IGT-language pair $\texttt{(i, l)}$ has feature f. The second predicate is $\texttt{HasRelation(i1, i2, r)}$ where r is a relation that corresponds to a feature in $F4$; this predicate is true iff relation $\texttt{r}$ holds between two IGTs $\texttt{i1, i2}$. The query predicate is $\texttt{IsSame(i, l)}$, which is true iff IGT $\texttt{i}$ is in language $\texttt{l}$. Table 6 shows the predicates instantiated from the two IGTs in Table 1.

The language ID task can be captured in our MLN with just three formulas:

$$\texttt{IsSame(i, l)}$$

$$\texttt{HasFeature(i, l, +f)} \Rightarrow \texttt{IsSame(i, l)}$$

$$\texttt{HasRelation(i1, i2, +r)} \wedge \texttt{IsSame(i1, l)} \Rightarrow \texttt{IsSame(i2, l)}$$

The first formula captures the default probability that an IGT belongs to a particular language.

IsSame(igt1, bin) HasFeature(igt1, bin, nearLC) HasFeature(igt1, bin, prev50) HasFeature(igt1, bin, LMw1) ... HasFeature(igt1, lew, nearLC) HasFeature(igt1, lew, prev50) ... IsSame(igt2, bin) HasFeature(igt2, bin, nearLC) HasFeature(igt2, bin, prev50) HasFeature(igt2, bin, LMw1) ... HasRelation(igt1, igt2, IIw1) ...

Table 6: The predicates instantiated from the IGTs in Table 1

The second one captures the conditional likelihoods of an IGT being in a language given the features. The third formula says that two IGTs probably belong to the same language if they have a certain relation r.

The plus sign before f and r in the formulas signifies that the MLN will learn a separate weight for each individual feature f and relation r. Note that there is no plus sign before i and l, allowing the MLN to achieve parameter tying by sharing the same weights for different instances or languages.

5.2.3 The advantage of the *Coref* approach

Both methods of the *CoRef* approach address the limitations of the *CL* approach: both can handle the *unseen language problem*, and both do parameter tying in a natural way. Not only does parameter tying reduce the number of parameters, it also makes it possible to accumulate evidence among different languages and different IGTs.

6 Experiments

In this section, we compare the two approaches to the language ID task: the *CL* approach and the *CoRef approach*. In our experiments, we run 10-fold cross validation (90% for training and 10% for testing) on the data set in Table 2 and report the average of language ID accuracy.

The two approaches have different upper bounds. The upper bound of the *CL* approach is the percentage of IGTs in the test data that belong to a *seen* language. The upper bound of the *CoRef* approach is the percentage of IGTs in the test data that belong to a language whose language name appears in the same document. For the data set in Table 2, the upper bounds are 90.33% and

Table 7: The performance of the *CL* approach (# of classes: about 600, # of training instances=13,723)

	Upper bound of *CL* approach	TextCat	MaxEnt classifier using context information			
			F1	F1-F2	F1-F3	F1-F4 (cheating)
# of features	N/A	N/A	769	5492	8226	8793
w/o the language filter	90.33	51.38	49.74	61.55	64.19	66.47
w/ the language filter	*88.95*	60.72	56.69	64.95	67.03	69.20

97.31% respectively. When the training data is much smaller, the upper bound of the *CL* approach would decrease tremendously, whereas the upper bound of the *CoRef* approach remains the same.

6.1 The *CL* approach

As mentioned before, most existing language ID algorithm falls into this category. We chose TextCat,[9] an implementation of Cavnar-Trenkle's algorithm (1994), as an example of these algorithms. In order to take advantage of the context information, we trained several classifiers (e.g., decision tree, Naive Bayes, and maximum entropy) using the Mallet package (McCallum, 2002) and a SVM classifier using the libSVM package (Chang and Lin, 2001).

The result is in Table 7. The first column shows the upper bound of the *CL* approach; the second column is the result of running TextCat;[10] the rest of the table lists the result of running a MaxEnt classifier with different feature sets.[11] F4 features require knowing the language code of other IGTs in the document. In the F1-F4 cheating experiments, the language codes of other IGTs come from the gold standard. We did not implement beam search for this because the difference between the cheating results and the results without F4 features is relatively small and both are much worse than the results in the *CoRef* approach.

In Table 7, the first row shows the number of features; the second row shows the accuracy of the two classifiers; the last row is the accuracy when a post-processing filter is added: the filter takes the ranked language list produced by a classifier, throws away all the languages in the list that do not appear in the document, and then outputs the highest ranked language in the remaining list.

There are several observations. First, applying the post-processing filter improves performance, albeit it also lowers the upper bound of algorithms as the correct language names might not appear in the document. Second, the MaxEnt classifier has hundreds of classes, thousands of features, and millions of model parameters. This will cause severe sparse data and overfitting problems.

6.2 The *CoRef* approach

For the *CoRef* approach, we built two systems as described in Section 5: the first system is a MaxEnt classifier with beam search, and the second one is a MLN for joint inference.[12] The results are in Table 8.[13]

In the first system, the values of F4 features for the test data come from the gold standard in the F1-F4 cheating experiments, and come from beam search in the non-cheating experiments.[14] In the second system, the predicate `HasRelation(i1, i2, r)` instantiated from the test data is treated as evidence in the F1-F4 cheating experiments, and as query in the F1-F4 non-cheating experiments.

The results for the two systems are very similar since they use same kinds of features. However, with Markov logic, it is easy to add predicates and formulas to allow joint inference. Therefore, we believe that Markov logic offers more potential to incorporate arbitrary prior knowledge and leverage further opportunities in joint inference.

Tables 7-8 show that, with the same kind of features and the same amount of training data, the *CoRef* approach has higher upper bound, fewer model parameters, more training instances, and much higher accuracy than the *CL* approach. This study shows that properly formulating a task into a learning problem is very important.

[9] http://odur.let.rug.nl/ vannoord/TextCat/

[10] We varied the lexicon size (m) – an important tuned parameter for the algorithm – from 100 and 800 and observed a minor change to accuracy. The numbers reported here are with lexicon size set to 800.

[11] The MaxEnt classifier slightly outperforms other classifiers with the same feature set.

[12] For learning and inference, we used the existing implementations of pseudo-likelihood training and MC-SAT in Alchemy with default parameters.

[13] No language filter is needed since the approach links an IGT to only the language names appearing in the document.

[14] It turns out that for this task the size of beam does not matter much and simply using the top choice by the MaxEnt classifier for each IGT almost always produces the best results, so that is the setting used for this table and Table 9.

Table 8: The performance of the *CoRef* approach (# of classes=2, # of training instances=511,039)

	Upper bound of CoRef approach	F1	F1-F2	F1-F3	F1-F4 (cheating)	F1-F4 (Non-cheating)
# of features	N/A	2	12	17	22	22
Sequence labeling	*97.31*	54.37	66.32	83.49	90.26	85.10
Markov logic model	*97.31*	54.98	65.94	83.44	90.37	84.70

Table 9: The performance of the *CoRef* approach with less training data (the upper bound of the *Coref* approach remains 97.31%)

% of training data used	F1	F1-F2	F1-F3	F1-F4 (cheating)	F1-F4 (non-cheating)	Upper bound of the *CL* approach
0.1%	54.37	54.84	65.28	81.21	70.15	1.66
0.5%	54.37	62.78	76.74	87.17	80.24	21.15
1.0%	54.37	60.58	76.09	87.24	81.20	28.92
10%	54.37	62.13	77.07	87.20	83.08	54.45

6.3 Experiments with much less data

Table 8 shows that the *CoRef* approach has very few features and a much larger number of training instances; therefore, it is likely that the approach would work well even with much less training data. To test the idea, we trained the model with only a small fraction of the original training data and tested on the same test data. The results with the first system are in Table 9. Notice that the upper bound of the *CoRef* approach remains the same as before. In contrast, the upper bound for the *CL* model is much lower, as shown in the last column of the table. The table shows when there is very little training data, the *CoRef* approach still performs decently, whereas the *CL* approach would totally fail due to the extremely low upper bounds.

6.4 Error analysis

Several factors contribute to the gap between the best *CoRef* system and its upper bound. First, when several language names appear in close range, the surface positions of the language names are often insufficient to determine the prominence of the languages. For instance, in pattern "*Similar to L1, L2* ...", *L*2 is the more prominent than *L*1; whereas in pattern "*L1, a L2 language,* ...", *L*1 is. The system sometimes chooses a wrong language in this case.

Second, the language name detector described in Section 4.2 produces many false negative (due to the incompleteness of the language table) and false positive (due to the fact that language names often have other meanings).

Third, when a language name is ambiguous, choosing the correct language code often requires knowledge that might not even be present in the document. For instance, a language name could refer to a list of related languages spoken in the same region, and assigning a correct language code would require knowledge about the subtle differences among those languages.

7 Conclusion and future work

In this paper we describe a language identification methodology that achieves high accuracy with a very small amount of training data for hundreds of languages, significantly outperforming existing language ID algorithms applied to the task. The gain comes from two sources: by taking advantage of context information in the document, and by formulating the task as a coreference resolution problem.

Our method can be adapted to harvest other kinds of linguistic data from the Web (e.g., lexicon entries, word lists, transcriptions, etc.) and build other ODIN-like resources. Providing a means for rapidly increasing the amount of data in ODIN, while at the same time *automatically* increasing the number of languages, can have a significant positive impact on the linguistic community, a community that already benefits from the existing search facility in ODIN. Likewise, the increased size of the resulting ODIN database could provide sufficient data to bootstrap NLP tools (e.g., POS taggers and parsers) for a large number of low-density languages, greatly benefitting both the fields of linguistics and NLP.

Acknowledgements This work has been supported, in part, by the NSF grants BCS-0748919 and BCS-0720670 and ONR grant N00014-08-1-0670. We would also like to thank three anonymous reviewers for their valuable comments.

References

Mark C. Baker and Osamuyimen Thompson Stewart. 1996. Unaccusativity and the adjective/verb distinction: Edo evidence. In *Proceedings of the Fifth Annual Conference on Document Analysis and Information Retrieval (SDAIR)*, Amherst, Mass.

G. Bakir, T. Hofmann, B. Scholkopf, A. Smola, B. Taskar, and S. Vishwanathan (eds). 2007. *Predicting Structured Data*. MIT Press.

William B. Cavnar and John M. Trenkle. 1994. N-gram-based text categorization. In *Proceedings of SDAIR-94, 3rd Annual Symposium on Document Analysis and Information Retrieval*, pages 161–175, Las Vegas, US.

Chih-Chung Chang and Chih-Jen Lin, 2001. *LIBSVM: a library for support vector machines*. Available at http://www.csie.ntu.edu.tw/ cjlin/libsvm.

Pascal Denis and Jason Baldridge. 2007. Joint determination of anaphoricity and coreference resolution using integer programming. In *Proc. of the Conference on Human Language Technologies (HLT/NAACL 2007)*, pages 236–243, Rochester, New York, April.

Aria Haghighi and Dan Klein. 2006. Prototype-driven grammar induction. In *Proceedings of the 21st International Conference on Computational Linguistics and 44th Annual Meeting of the Association for Computational Linguistics (COLING/ACL 2006)*, pages 881–888, Sydney, Australia, July. Association for Computational Linguistics.

Baden Hughes, Timothy Baldwin, Steven Bird, Jeremy Nicholson, and Andrew MacKinlay. 2006. Reconsidering language identification for written language resources. In *Proceedings of the 5th International Conference on Language Resources and Evaluation (LREC2006)*, pages 485–488, Genoa, Italy.

S. Kok, P. Singla, M. Richardson, P. Domingos, M. Sumner, H Poon, and D. Lowd. 2007. The Alchemy system for statistical relational AI. Technical report, Dept. of CSE, Univ. of Washington.

William Lewis and Fei Xia. 2008. Automatically Identifying Computationally Relevant Typological Features. In *Proc. of the Third International Joint Conference on Natural Language Processing (IJCNLP-2008)*, Hyderabad, India.

William Lewis. 2006. ODIN: A Model for Adapting and Enriching Legacy Infrastructure. In *Proc. of the e-Humanities Workshop, held in cooperation with e-Science 2006: 2nd IEEE International Conference on e-Science and Grid Computing*, Amsterdam.

Xiaoqiang Luo. 2007. Coreference or not: A twin model for coreference resolution. In *Proc. of the Conference on Human Language Technologies (HLT/NAACL 2007)*, pages 73–80, Rochester, New York.

Andrew Kachites McCallum. 2002. Mallet: A machine learning for language toolkit. http://mallet.cs.umass.edu.

Vincent Ng and Claire Cardie. 2002. Improving Machine Learning Approaches to Coreference Resolution. In *Proceedings of the 40th Annual Meeting of the Association for Computational Linguistics (ACL-2002)*, pages 104–111, Philadelphia.

H. Poon and P. Domingos. 2006. Sound and efficient inference with probabilistic and deterministic dependencies. In *Proc. of AAAI-06*.

Hoifung Poon and Pedro Domingos. 2007. Joint inference in information extraction. In *Proceedings of the Twenty-Second National Conference on Artificial Intelligence (AAAI)*, pages 913–918, Vancouver, Canada. AAAI Press.

H. Poon and P. Domingos. 2008. Joint unsupervised coreference resolution with markov logic. In *Proc. of the 13th Conf. on Empirical Methods in Natural Language Processing (EMNLP-2008)*.

M. Richardson and P. Domingos. 2006. Markov logic networks. *Machine Learning*, pages 107–136.

Wee Meng Soon, Hwee Tou Ng, and Daniel Chung Yong Lim. 2001. A machine learning approach to coreference resolution of noun phrases. *Computational Linguistics*, 27(4).

Charles Sutton, Andrew McCallum, and Jeff Bilmes (eds.). 2006. *Proc. of the HLT/NAACL-06 Workshop on Joint Inference for Natural Language Processing*.

B. Wellner, A. McCallum, F. Peng, and M. Hay. 2004. An integrated, conditional model of information extraction and coreference with application to citation matching. In *Proc. of the 20th Conference on Uncertainty in AI (UAI 2004)*.

Fei Xia and William Lewis. 2007. Multilingual structural projection across interlinear text. In *Proc. of the Conference on Human Language Technologies (HLT/NAACL 2007)*, pages 452–459, Rochester, New York.

Fei Xia and William Lewis. 2008. Repurposing Theoretical Linguistic Data for Tool Development and Search. In *Proc. of the Third International Joint Conference on Natural Language Processing (IJCNLP-2008)*, Hyderabad, India.

Character-Level Dependencies in Chinese: Usefulness and Learning

Hai Zhao
Department of Chinese, Translation and Linguistics
City University of Hong Kong
Tat Chee Avenue, Kowloon, Hong Kong, China
haizhao@cityu.edu.hk

Abstract

We investigate the possibility of exploiting character-based dependency for Chinese information processing. As Chinese text is made up of character sequences rather than word sequences, word in Chinese is not so natural a concept as in English, nor is word easy to be defined without argument for such a language. Therefore we propose a character-level dependency scheme to represent primary linguistic relationships within a Chinese sentence. The usefulness of character dependencies are verified through two specialized dependency parsing tasks. The first is to handle trivial character dependencies that are equally transformed from traditional word boundaries. The second furthermore considers the case that annotated internal character dependencies inside a word are involved. Both of these results from character-level dependency parsing are positive. This study provides an alternative way to formularize basic character- and word-level representation for Chinese.

1 Introduction

In many human languages, word can be naturally identified from writing. However, this is not the case for Chinese, for Chinese is born to be written in character[1] sequence rather than word sequence, namely, no natural separators such as blanks exist between words. As word does not appear in a natural way as most European languages[2], it brings the argument about how to determine the word-hood in Chinese. Linguists' views about what is a Chinese word diverge so greatly that multiple word segmentation standards have been proposed for computational linguistics tasks since the first Bakeoff (Bakeoff-1, or Bakeoff-2003)[3] (Sproat and Emerson, 2003).

Up to Bakeoff-4, *seven* word segmentation standards have been proposed. However, this does not effectively solve the open problem what a Chinese word should exactly be but raises another issue: what a segmentation standard should be selected for the successive application. As word often plays a basic role for the further language processing, if it cannot be determined in a unified way, then all successive tasks will be affected more or less.

Motivated by dependency representation for syntactic parsing since (Collins, 1999) that has been drawn more and more interests in recent years, we suggest that character-level dependencies can be adopted to alleviate this difficulty in Chinese processing. If we regard traditional word boundary as a linear representation for neighbored characters, then character-level dependencies can provide a way to represent non-linear relations between non-neighbored characters. To show that character dependencies can be useful, we develop a parsing scheme for the related learning task and demonstrate its effectiveness.

The rest of the paper is organized as follows. The next section shows the drawbacks of the current word boundary representation through some language examples. Section 3 describes a character-level dependency parsing scheme for traditional word segmentation task and reports its evaluation results. Section 4 verifies the usefulness of annotated character dependencies inside a word. Section 5 looks into a few issues concern-

[1]Character here stands for various tokens occurring in a naturally written Chinese text, including Chinese character(hanzi), punctuation, and foreign letters. However, Chinese characters often cover the most part.

[2]Even in European languages, a naive but necessary method to properly define word is to list them all by hand. Thank the first anonymous reviewer who points this fact.

[3]First International Chinese Word Segmentation Bakeoff, available at http://www.sighan.org/bakeoff2003.

Proceedings of the 12th Conference of the European Chapter of the ACL, pages 879–887,
Athens, Greece, 30 March – 3 April 2009. ©2009 Association for Computational Linguistics

ing the role of character dependencies. Section 6 concludes the paper.

2 To Segment or Not: That Is the Question

Though most words can be unambiguously defined in Chinese text, some word boundaries are not so easily determined. We show such three examples as the following.

The first example is from the MSRA segmented corpus of Bakeoff-2 (Bakeoff-2005) (Emerson, 2005):

> 一 / 张 / " / 北京市京剧 O K 联谊会 / 会友 / 入场 / 证 / "
>
> a / piece of / " / Beijing City Beijing Opera OK Sodality / member / entrance / ticket / "

As the guideline of MSRA standard requires any organization's full name as a word, many long words in this form are frequently encountered. Though this type of 'words' may be regarded as an effective unit to some extent, some smaller meaningful constituents can be still identified inside them. Some researchers argue that these should be seen as phrases rather than words. In fact, e.g., a machine translation system will have to segment this type of words into some smaller units for a proper translation.

The second example is from the PKU corpus of Bakeoff-2,

> 中国 / 驻 / 南非 / 大使馆
>
> China / in / South Africa / embassy
>
> (the Chinese embassy in South Africa)

This example demonstrates how researchers can also feel inconvenient if an organization name is segmented into pieces. Though the word '大使馆'(embassy) is right after '南非'(South Africa) in the above phrase, the embassy does not belong to South Africa but China, and it is only located in South Africa.

The third example is an abbreviation that makes use of the characteristics of Chinese characters.

> 星期 / 一 / 三 / 五
>
> Week / one / three / five
>
> (Monday, Wednesday and Friday)

This example shows that there will be in a dilemma to perform segmentation over these characters. If a segmentation position locates before '三'(three) or '五'(five), then this will make them meaningless or losing its original meaning at least because either of these two characters should logically follow the substring '星期' (week) to construct the expected word '星期三'(Wednesday) or '星期五' (Friday). Otherwise, to make all the above five characters as a word will have to ignore all these logical dependent relations among these characters and segment it later for a proper tackling as the above first example.

All these examples suggest that dependencies exist between discontinuous characters, and word boundary representation is insufficient to handle these cases. This motivates us to introduce character dependencies.

3 Character-Level Dependency Parsing

Character dependency is proposed as an alternative to word boundary. The idea itself is extremely simple, character dependencies inside sequence are annotated or formally defined in the similar way that syntactic dependencies over words are usually annotated.

We will initially develop a character-level dependency parsing scheme in this section. Especially, we show character dependencies, even those trivial ones that are equally transformed from pre-defined word boundaries, can be effectively captured in a parsing way.

3.1 Formularization

Using a character-level dependency representation, we first show how a word segmentation task can be transformed into a dependency parsing problem. Since word segmentation is traditionally formularized as an unlabeled character chunking task since (Xue, 2003), only unlabeled dependencies are concerned in the transformation. There are many ways to transform chunks in a sequence into dependency representation. However, for the sake of simplicity, only well-formed and projective output sequences are considered for our processing.

Borrowing the notation from (Nivre and Nilsson, 2005), an unlabeled dependency graph is formally defined as follows:

> An unlabeled dependency graph for a string of cliques (i.e., words and characters) $W =$

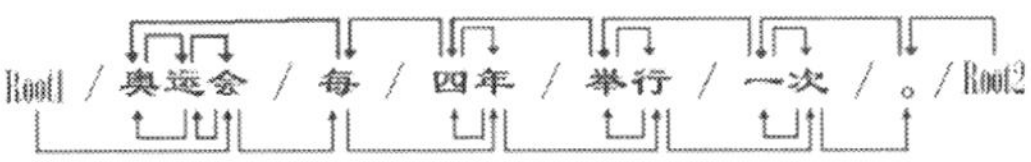

Figure 1: Two character dependency schemes

$w_1 ... w_n$ is an unlabeled directed graph $D = (W, A)$, where

(a) W is the set of ordered nodes, i.e. clique tokens in the input string, ordered by a linear precedence relation $<$,

(b) A is a set of unlabeled arcs (w_i, w_j), where $w_i, w_j \in W$,

If $(w_i, w_j) \in A$, w_i is called the head of w_j and w_j a dependent of w_i. Traditionally, the notation $w_i \rightarrow w_j$ means $(w_i, w_j) \in A$; $w_i \rightarrow^* w_j$ denotes the reflexive and transitive closure of the (unlabeled) arc relation. We assume that the designed dependency structure satisfies the following common constraints in existing literature (Nivre, 2006).

(1) D is weakly connected, that is, the corresponding undirected graph is connected. (CONNECTEDNESS)

(2) The graph D is acyclic, i.e., if $w_i \rightarrow w_j$ then not $w_j \rightarrow^* w_i$. (ACYCLICITY)

(3) There is at most one arc $(w_i, w_j) \in A, \forall w_j \in W$. (SINGLE-HEAD)

(4) An arc $w_i \rightarrow w_k$ is projective iff, for every word w_j occurring between w_i and w_k in the string ($w_i < w_j < w_k$ or $w_i > w_j > w_k$), $w_i \rightarrow^* w_j$. (PROJECTIVITY)

We say that D is well-formed iff it is acyclic and connected, and D is projective iff every arcs in A are projective. Note that the above four conditions entail that the graph D is a single-rooted tree. For an arc $w_i \rightarrow w_j$, if $w_i < w_j$, then it is called right-arc, otherwise left-arc.

Following the above four constraints and considering segmentation characteristics, we may have two character dependency representation schemes as shown in Figure 1 by using a series of trivial dependencies inside or outside a word. Note that we use arc direction to distinguish connected and segmented relation among characters. The scheme with the assistant root node before the sequence in Figure 1 is called Scheme B, and the other Scheme E.

3.2 Shift-reduce Parsing

According to (McDonald and Nivre, 2007), all data-driven models for dependency parsing that have been proposed in recent years can be described as either graph-based or transition-based. Since both dependency schemes that we construct for parsing are well-formed and projective, the latter is chosen as the parsing framework for the sake of efficiency. In detail, a shift-reduce method is adopted as in (Nivre, 2003).

The method is step-wise and a classifier is used to make a parsing decision step by step. In each step, the classifier checks a clique pair [4], namely, *TOP*, the top of a stack that consists of the processed cliques, and, *INPUT*, the first clique in the unprocessed sequence, to determine if a dependent relation should be established between them. Besides two arc-building actions, a shift action and a reduce action are also defined, as follows,

Left-arc: Add an arc from *INPUT* to *TOP* and pop the stack.

Right-arc: Add an arc from *TOP* to *INPUT* and push *INPUT* onto the stack.

Reduce: Pop *TOP* from the stack.

Shift: Push *INPUT* onto the stack.

In this work, we adopt a left-to-right arc-eager parsing model, that means that the parser scans the input sequence from left to right and right dependents are attached to their heads as soon as possible (Hall et al., 2007). In the implementation, as for Scheme E, all four actions are required to pass through an input sequence. However, only three actions, i.e., reduce action will never be used, are needed for Scheme B.

3.3 Learning Model and Features

While memory-based and margin-based learning approaches such as support vector machines are popularly applied to shift-reduce parsing, we apply maximum entropy model as the learning model for efficient training and producing some comparable results. Our implementation of maximum entropy adopts L-BFGS algorithm for parameter optimization as usual. No additional feature selection techniques are used.

With notations defined in Table 1, a feature set as shown in Table 2 is adopted. Here, we explain some terms in Tables 1 and 2.

[4]Here, clique means character or word in a sequence, which depends on what constructs the sequence.

Table 1: Feature Notations

Notation	Meaning
s	The character in the top of stack
s_{-1},...	The first character below the top of stack, etc.
i, i_{+1},...	The first (second) character in the unprocessed sequence, etc.
dprel	Dependent label
h	Head
lm	Leftmost child
rm	Rightmost child
rn	Right nearest child
char	Character form
.	's, i.e., '*s.dprel*' means dependent label of character in the top of stack
+	Feature combination, i.e., '*s.char+i.char*' means both *s.char* and *i.char* work as a feature function.

Table 2: Features for Parsing

Basic	Extension
x.char	itself, its previous two and next two characters, and all bigrams within the five-character window. (x is s or i.)
-	*s.h.char*
-	*s.dprel*
-	*s.rm.dprel*
-	s_{-1}*.cnseq*
-	s_{-1}*.cnseq+s.char*
-	s_{-1}*.curroot.lm.cnseq*
-	s_{-1}*.curroot.lm.cnseq+s.char*
-	s_{-1}*.curroot.lm.cnseq+i.char*
-	s_{-1}*.curroot.lm.cnseq+*s_{-1}*.cnseq*
-	s_{-1}*.curroot.lm.cnseq+s.char+*s_{-1}*.cnseq*
-	s_{-1}*.curroot.lm.cnseq+i.char+*s_{-1}*.cnseq*
-	$s.av_n$+$i.av_n$, $n = 1, 2, 3, 4, 5$
-	$preact_{-1}$
-	$preact_{-2}$
-	$preact_{-2}$+$preact_{-1}$

Since we only considered unlabeled dependency parsing, *dprel* means the arc direction from the head, either left or right. The feature *curroot* returns the root of a partial parsing tree that includes a specified node. The feature *cnseq* returns a substring started from a given character. It checks the direction of the arc that passes the given character and collects all characters with the same arc direction to yield an output substring until the arc direction is changed. Note that all combinational features concerned with this one can be regarded as word-level features.

The feature *av* is derived from unsupervised segmentation as in (Zhao and Kit, 2008a), and the *accessor variety* (AV) (Feng et al., 2004) is adopted as the unsupervised segmentation criterion. The AV value of a substring s is defined as

$$AV(s) = \min\{L_{av}(s), R_{av}(s)\},$$

where the left and right AV values $L_{av}(s)$ and $R_{av}(s)$ are defined, respectively, as the numbers of its distinct predecessor and successor characters. In this work, AV values for substrings are derived from unlabeled training and test corpora by substring counting. Multiple features are used to represent substrings of various lengths identified by the AV criterion. Formally put, the feature function for a n-character substring s with a score $AV(s)$ is defined as

$$av_n = t, \text{ if } 2^t \leq AV(s) < 2^{t+1}, \quad (1)$$

where t is an integer to logarithmize the score and taken as the feature value. For an overlap character of several substrings, we only choose the one with the greatest AV score to activate the above feature function for that character.

The feature $preact_n$ returns the previous parsing action type, and the subscript n stands for the action order before the current action.

3.4 Decoding

Without Markovian feature like $preact_{-1}$, a shift-reduce parser can scan through an input sequence in linear time. That is, the decoding of a parsing method for word segmentation will be extremely fast. The time complexity of decoding will be $2L$ for Scheme E, and L for Scheme B, where L is the length of the input sequence.

However, it is somewhat complicated as Markovian features are involved. Following the work of (Duan et al., 2007), the decoding in this case is to search a parsing action sequence with the maximal probability.

$$S_{d_i} = \text{argmax} \prod_i p(d_i|d_{i-1}d_{i-2}...),$$

where S_{d_i} is the object parsing action sequence, $p(d_i|d_{i-1}...)$ is the conditional probability, and d_i is i-th parsing action. We use a beam search algorithm as in (Ratnaparkhi, 1996) to find the object parsing action sequence. The time complexity of this beam search algorithm will be $4BL$ for Scheme E and $3BL$ for Scheme B, where B is the beam width.

3.5 Related Methods

Among character-based learning techniques for word segmentation, we may identify two main types, classification (GOH et al., 2004) and tagging (Low et al., 2005). Both character classification and tagging need to define the position of character inside a word. Traditionally, the four tags, b, m, e, and s stand, respectively, for the *b*eginning, *m*idle, *e*nd of a word, and a *s*ingle-character as word since (Xue, 2003). The following n-gram features from (Xue, 2003; Low et al., 2005) are used as basic features,

(a) $C_n (n = -2, -1, 0, 1, 2)$,

(b) $C_n C_{n+1} (n = -2, -1, 0, 1)$,

(c) $C_{-1} C_1$,

where C stands for a character and the subscripts for the relative order to the current character C_0. In addition, the feature av that is defined in equation (1) is also taken as an option. av_n (n=1,...,5) is applied as feature for the current character.

While word segmentation is conducted as a classification task, each individual character will be simply assigned a tag with the maximal probability given by the classifier. In this case, we restore word boundary only according to two tags b and s. However, the output tag sequence given by character classification may include illegal tag transition (e.g., m is after e.). In (Low et al., 2005), a dynamic programming algorithm is adopted to find a tag sequence with the maximal joint probability from all legal tag sequences. If such a dynamic programming decoding is adopted, then this method for word segmentation is regarded as character tagging [5].

The time complexity of character-based classification method for decoding is L, which is the best result in decoding velocity. As dynamic programming is applied, the time complexity will be $16L$ with four tags.

Recently, conditional random fields (CRFs) becomes popular for word segmentation since it provides slightly better performance than maximum entropy method does (Peng et al., 2004). However, CRFs is a structural learning tool rather than a simple classification framework. As shift-reduce parsing is a typical step-wise method that checks each character one by one, it is reasonable to compare it to a classification method over characters.

[5]Someone may argue that maximum entropy Markov model (MEMM) is truly a tagging tool. Yes, this method was initialized by (Xue, 2003). However, our empirical results show that MEMM never outperforms maximum entropy plus dynamic programming decoding as (Low et al., 2005) in Chinese word segmentation. We also know that the latter reports the best results in Bakeoff-2. This is why MEMM method is excluded from our comparison.

3.6 Evaluation Results

Table 3: Corpus size of Bakeoff-2 in number of words

	AS	CityU	MSRA	PKU
Training(M)	5.45	1.46	2.37	1.1
Test(K)	122	41	107	104

The experiments in this section are performed in all four corpora from Bakeoff-2. Corpus size information is in Table 3.

Traditionally, word segmentation performance is measured by F-score ($F = 2RP/(R + P)$), where the recall (R) and precision (P) are the proportions of the correctly segmented words to all words in, respectively, the gold-standard segmentation and a segmenter's output. To compute the word F-score, all parsing results will be restored to word boundaries according to the direction of output arcs.

Table 4: The results of parsing and classification/tagging approaches using different feature combinations

S.[a]	Feature	AS	CityU	MSRA	PKU
B	Basic[b]	.935	.922	.950	.917
	+AV[c]	.941	.933	.956	.927
	+Prev[d]	.937	.923	.951	.918
	+AV+Prev	.942	.935	.958	.929
E	Basic	.940	.932	.957	.926
	+AV	.948	.947	.964	.942
	+Prev	.944	.940	.962	.931
	+AV+Prev	.949	.951	.967	.943
C[f]	n-gram/c[e]	.933	.923	.948	.923
	+AV/c	.942	.936	.957	.933
	n-gram/d[g]	.945	.938	.956	.936
	+AV/d	.950	.949	.966	.945

[a]Scheme
[b]Features in top two blocks of Table 2.
[c]Five av features are added on the above basic features.
[d]Three Markovian features in Table 2 are added on the above basic features.
[e]/c: Classification
[f]Character classification or tagging using maximum entropy
[g]/d: Only search in legal tag sequences.

Our comparison with existing work will be conducted in closed test of Bakeoff. The rule for the closed test is that no additional information beyond training corpus is allowed, while open test of Bakeoff is without such restrict.

The results with different dependency schemes are in Table 4. As the feature *preact* is involved, a beam search algorithm with width 5 is used to decode, otherwise, a simple shift-reduce decoding is used. We see that the performance given by Scheme E is much better than that by Scheme B. The results of character-based classification and tagging methods are at the bottom of Table 4[6]. It is observed that the parsing method outperforms classification and tagging method without Markovian features or decoding throughout the whole sequence. As full features are used, the former and the latter provide the similar performance.

Due to using a global model like CRFs, our previous work in (Zhao et al., 2006; Zhao and Kit, 2008c) reported the best results over the evaluated corpora of Bakeoff-2 until now[7]. Though those results are slightly better than the results here, we still see that the results of character-level dependency parsing approach (Scheme E) are comparable to those state-of-the-art ones on each evaluated corpus.

4 Character Dependencies inside a Word

We further consider exploiting annotated character dependencies inside a word (internal dependencies). A parsing task for these internal dependencies incorporated with trivial external dependencies [8] that are transformed from common word boundaries are correspondingly proposed using the same parsing way as the previous section.

4.1 Annotation of Internal Dependencies

In Subsection 3.1, we assign trivial character dependencies inside a word for the parsing task of word segmentation, i.e., each character as the head of its predecessor or successor. These trivial formally defined dependencies may be against the syntactic or semantic senses of those characters, as we have discussed in Section 2. Now we will consider human annotated character dependencies inside a word.

As such an corpus with annotated internal dependencies has not been available until now, we launched an annotation job based on UPUC segmented corpus of Bakeoff-3(Bakeoff-2006)(Levow, 2006). The training corpus is with 880K characters and test corpus 270K. However, the essential of the annotation job is actually conducted in a lexicon.

After a lexicon is extracted from CTB segmented corpus, we use a top-down strategy to annotate internal dependencies inside these words from the lexicon. A long word is first split into some smaller constituents, and dependencies among these constituents are determined, character dependencies inside each constituents are then annotated. Some simple rules are adopted to determine dependency relation, e.g., modifiers are kept marking as dependants and the only rest constituent will be marked as head at last. Some words are hard to determine internal dependency relation, such as foreign names, e.g., '葡萄牙'(Portugal) and '马拉多纳'(Maradona), and uninterrupted words (连绵词), e.g., '蚂蚁'(ant) and '苜蓿'(clover). In this case, we simply adopt a series of linear dependencies with the last character as head to mark these words.

In the previous section, we have shown that Scheme E is a better dependency representation for encoding word boundaries. Thus annotated internal dependencies are used to replace those trivial internal dependencies in Scheme E to obtain the corpus that we require. Note that now we cannot distinguish internal and external dependencies only according to the arc direction any more, as both left- and right-arc can appear for internal character dependency representation. Thus two labeled left arcs, external and internal, are used for the annotation disambiguation. As internal dependencies are introduced, we find that some words (about 10%) are constructed by two or more parallel constituent parts according to our annotations, this not only lets two labeled arcs insufficiently distinguish internal- and external dependencies, but also makes parsing extremely difficult, namely, a great amount of non-projective dependencies will appear if we directly introduce these internal dependencies. Again, we adopt a series of linear dependencies with the last character as head to represent internal dependencies for these words by ignoring their parallel constituents. To handle the remained non-projectivities, a strengthened pseudo-projectivization technique as in (Zhao and Kit,

[6]Only the results of open track are reported in (Low et al., 2005), while we give a comparison following closed track rules, so, our results here are not comparable to those of (Low et al., 2005).

[7]As n-gram features are used, F-scores in (Zhao et al., 2006) are, AS:0.953, CityU:0.948, MSRA:0.974,PKU:0.952.

[8]We correspondingly call dependencies that mark word boundary external dependencies that correspond to internal dependencies.

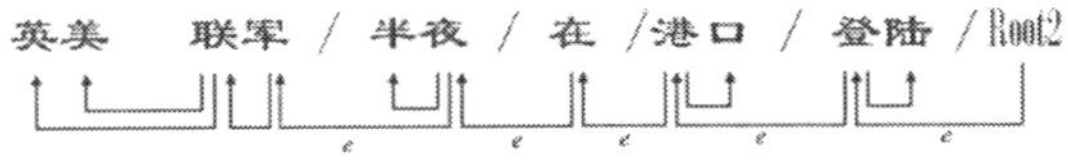

Figure 2: Annotated internal dependencies (Arc label e notes trivial external dependencies.)

Table 5: Features for internal dependency parsing

Basic	Extension
s.char	itself, its next two characters, and all bigrams within the three-character window.
i.char	its previous one and next three characters, and all bigrams within the four-character window.
-	*s.char+i.char*
-	*s.h.char*
-	*s.rm.dprel*
-	*s.curtree*
-	*s.curtree+s.char*
-	s_{-1}*.curtree+s.char*
-	*s.curroot.lm.curtree*
-	s_{-1}*.curroot.lm.curtree*
-	*s.curroot.lm.curtree+s.char*
-	s_{-1}*.curroot.lm.curtree+s.char*
-	*s.curtree+s.curroot.lm.curtree*
-	s_{-1}*.curtree+*s_{-1}*.curroot.lm.curtree*
-	*s.curtree+s.curroot.lm.curtree+s.char*
-	s_{-1}*.curtree+*s_{-1}*.curroot.lm.curtree+s.char*
-	s_{-1}*.curtree+*s_{-1}*.curroot.lm.curtree+i.char*
-	$x.av_n, n = 1, ..., 5$ (x is s or i.)
-	$s.av_n + i.av_n, n = 1, ..., 5$
-	$preact_{-1}$
-	$preact_{-2}$
-	$preact_{-2}+preact_{-1}$

2008b) is used during parsing. An annotated example is illustrated in Figure 2.

4.2 Learning of Internal Dependencies

To demonstrate internal character dependencies are helpful for further processing. A series of similar word segmentation experiments as in Subsection 3.6 are performed. Note that this task is slightly different from the previous one, as it is a five-class parsing action classification task as left arc has two labels to differ internal and external dependencies. Thus a different feature set has to be used. However, all input sequences are still projective.

Features listed in Table 5 are adopted for the parsing task that annotated character dependencies exist inside words. The feature *curtree* in Table 5 is similar to *cnseq* of Table 2. It first greedily searches all connected character started from the given one until an arc with external label is found over some character. Then it collects all characters that has been reached to yield an output substring as feature value.

A comparison of classification/tagging and parsing methods is given in Table 6. To evaluate the results with word F-score, all external dependencies in outputs are restored as word boundaries. There are three models are evaluated in Table 6. It is shown that there is a significant performance enhancement as annotated internal character dependency is introduced. This positive result shows that annotated internal character dependencies are meaningful.

Table 6: Comparison of different methods

Approach [a]	basic	+AV	+Prev [b]	+AV+Prev
Class/Tag [c]	.918	.935	.928	.941
Parsing/wo [d]	.921	.937	.924	.942
Parsing/w [e]	.925	.940	.929	.945

[a] The highest F-score in Bakeoff-3 is 0.933.

[b] As for the tagging method, this means dynamic programming decoding; As for the parsing method, this means three Markovian features.

[c] Character-based classification or tagging method

[d] Using trivial internal dependencies in Scheme E.

[e] Using annotated internal character dependencies.

5 Is Word Still Necessary?

Note that this work is not about joint learning of word boundaries and syntactic dependencies such as (Luo, 2003), where a character-based tagging method is used for syntactic constituent parsing from unsegmented Chinese text. Instead, this work is to explore an alternative way to represent "word-hood" in Chinese, which is based on character-level dependencies instead of traditional word boundaries definition.

Though considering dependencies among words is not novel (Gao and Suzuki, 2004), we recognize that this study is the first work concerned with character dependency. This study originally intends to lead us to consider an alternative way that can play the similar role as word boundary annotations.

In Chinese, not word but character is the actual minimal unit for either writing or speaking. Word-hood has been carefully defined by many means, and this effort results in multi-standard segmented corpora provided by a series of Bakeoff evaluations. However, from the view of linguistics, Bakeoff does not solve the problem but technically skirts round it. As one asks what a Chinese word is, Bakeoff just answers that we have many definitions and each one is fine. Instead, motivated from the results of the previous two sections, we suggest that character dependency representation could present a natural and unified way to alleviate the drawbacks of word boundary representation that is only able to represent the relation of neighbored characters.

Table 7: What we have done for character dependency

Internal	External	Our work
trivial	trivial	Section 3
annotated	trivial	Section 4
annotated		?

If we regard that our current work is stepping into more and more annotated character dependencies as shown in Table 7, then it is natural to extend annotated internal character dependencies to the whole sequence without those unnatural word boundary constraints. In this sense, internal and external character dependency will not need be differed any more. A full character-level dependency tree is illustrated as shown in Figure 3(a)[9] With the help of such a tree, we may define word or even phrase according to what part of subtree is picked up. Word-hood, if we still need this concept, can be freely determined later as further processing purpose requires.

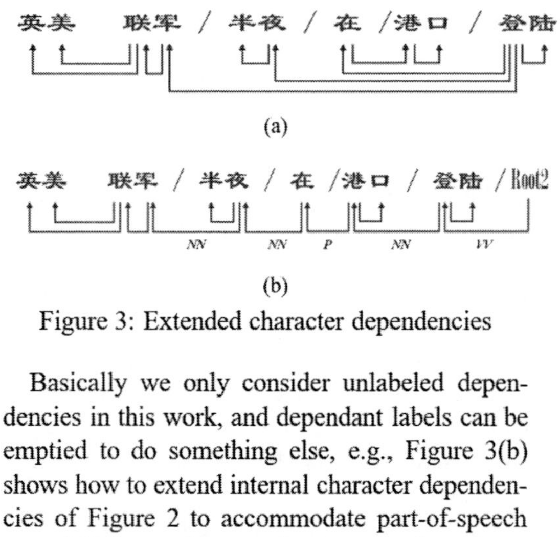

Figure 3: Extended character dependencies

Basically we only consider unlabeled dependencies in this work, and dependant labels can be emptied to do something else, e.g., Figure 3(b) shows how to extend internal character dependencies of Figure 2 to accommodate part-of-speech tags. This extension can also be transplanted to a full character dependency tree of Figure 3(a), then this may leads to a character-based labeled syntactic dependency tree. In brief, we see that character dependencies provide a more general and natural way to reflect character relations within a sequence than word boundary annotations do.

[9] We may easily build such a corpus by embedding annotated internal dependencies into a word-level dependency tree bank. As UPUC corpus of Bakeoff-3 just follows the word segmentation convention of Chinese tree bank, we have built such a full character-level dependency tree corpus.

6 Conclusion and Future Work

In this study, we initially investigate the possibility of exploiting character dependencies for Chinese. To show that character-level dependency can be a good alternative to word boundary representation for Chinese, we carry out a series of parsing experiments. The techniques are developed step by step. Firstly, we show that word segmentation task can be effectively re-formularized character-level dependency parsing. The results of a character-level dependency parser can be comparable with traditional methods. Secondly, we consider annotated character dependencies inside a word. We show that a parser can still effectively capture both these annotated internal character dependencies and trivial external dependencies that are transformed from word boundaries. The experimental results show that annotated internal dependencies even bring performance enhancement and indirectly verify the usefulness of them. Finally, we suggest that a full annotated character dependency tree can be constructed over all possible character pairs within a given sequence, though its usefulness needs to be explored in the future.

Acknowledgements

This work is beneficial from many sources, including three anonymous reviewers. Especially, the authors are grateful to two colleagues, one reviewer from EMNLP-2008 who gave some very insightful comments to help us extend this work, and Mr. SONG Yan who annotated internal dependencies of top frequent 22K words extracted from UPUC segmentation corpus. Of course, it is the duty of the first author if there still exists anything wrong in this work.

References

Michael Collins. 1999. *Head-Driven Statistical Models for Natural Language Parsing*. Ph.D. thesis, University of Pennsylvania.

Xiangyu Duan, Jun Zhao, and Bo Xu. 2007. Probabilistic parsing action models for multi-lingual dependency parsing. In *Proceedings of the CoNLL Shared Task Session of EMNLP-CoNLL 2007*, pages 940–946, Prague, Czech, June 28-30.

Thomas Emerson. 2005. The second international Chinese word segmentation bakeoff. In *Proceedings of the Fourth SIGHAN Workshop on Chinese Language Processing*, pages 123–133, Jeju Island, Korea, October 14-15.

Haodi Feng, Kang Chen, Xiaotie Deng, and Weimin Zheng. 2004. Accessor variety criteria for Chinese word extraction. *Computational Linguistics*, 30(1):75–93.

Jianfeng Gao and Hisami Suzuki. 2004. Capturing long distance dependency in language modeling: An empirical study. In K.-Y. Su, J. Tsujii, J. H. Lee, and O. Y. Kwong, editors, *Natural Language Processing - IJCNLP 2004*, volume 3248 of *Lecture Notes in Computer Science*, pages 396–405, Sanya, Hainan Island, China, March 22-24.

Chooi-Ling GOH, Masayuki Asahara, and Yuji Matsumoto. 2004. Chinese word segmentation by classification of characters. In *ACL SIGHAN Workshop 2004*, pages 57–64, Barcelona, Spain, July. Association for Computational Linguistics.

Johan Hall, Jens Nilsson, Joakim Nivre, Gülsen Eryiğit, Beáta Megyesi, Mattias Nilsson, and Markus Saers. 2007. Single malt or blended? a study in multilingual parser optimization. In *Proceedings of the CoNLL Shared Task Session of EMNLP-CoNLL 2007*, pages 933–939, Prague, Czech, June.

Gina-Anne Levow. 2006. The third international Chinese language processing bakeoff: Word segmentation and named entity recognition. In *Proceedings of the Fifth SIGHAN Workshop on Chinese Language Processing*, pages 108–117, Sydney, Australia, July 22-23.

Jin Kiat Low, Hwee Tou Ng, and Wenyuan Guo. 2005. A maximum entropy approach to Chinese word segmentation. In *Proceedings of the Fourth SIGHAN Workshop on Chinese Language Processing*, pages 161–164, Jeju Island, Korea, October 14-15.

Xiaoqiang Luo. 2003. A maximum entropy chinese character-based parser. In *Proceedings of the 2003 Conference on Empirical Methods in Natural Language Processing (EMNLP 2003)*, pages 192 – 199, Sapporo, Japan, July 11-12.

Ryan McDonald and Joakim Nivre. 2007. Characterizing the errors of data-driven dependency parsing models. In *Proceedings of the 2007 Joint Conference on Empirical Methods in Natural Language Processing and Computational Natural Language Learning (EMNLP-CoNLL 2007)*, pages 122–131, Prague, Czech, June 28-30.

Joakim Nivre and Jens Nilsson. 2005. Pseudo-projective dependency parsing. In *Proceedings of the 43rd Annual Meeting on Association for Computational Linguistics (ACL-2005)*, pages 99–106, Ann Arbor, Michigan, USA, June 25-30.

Joakim Nivre. 2003. An efficient algorithm for projective dependency parsing. In *Proceedings of the 8th International Workshop on Parsing Technologies (IWPT 03)*, pages 149–160, Nancy, France, April 23-25.

Joakim Nivre. 2006. Constraints on non-projective dependency parsing. In *Proceedings of 11th Conference of the European Chapter of the Association for Computational Linguistics (EACL-2006)*, pages 73–80, Trento, Italy, April 3-7.

Fuchun Peng, Fangfang Feng, and Andrew McCallum. 2004. Chinese segmentation and new word detection using conditional random fields. In *COLING 2004*, pages 562–568, Geneva, Switzerland, August 23-27.

Adwait Ratnaparkhi. 1996. A maximum entropy part-of-speech tagger. In *Proceedings of the Empirical Method in Natural Language Processing Conference*, pages 133–142, University of Pennsylvania.

Richard Sproat and Thomas Emerson. 2003. The first international Chinese word segmentation bakeoff. In *The Second SIGHAN Workshop on Chinese Language Processing*, pages 133–143, Sapporo, Japan.

Nianwen Xue. 2003. Chinese word segmentation as character tagging. *Computational Linguistics and Chinese Language Processing*, 8(1):29–48.

Hai Zhao and Chunyu Kit. 2008a. Exploiting unlabeled text with different unsupervised segmentation criteria for chinese word segmentation. In *Research in Computing Science*, volume 33, pages 93–104.

Hai Zhao and Chunyu Kit. 2008b. Parsing syntactic and semantic dependencies with two single-stage maximum entropy models. In *Twelfth Conference on Computational Natural Language Learning (CoNLL-2008)*, pages 203–207, Manchester, UK, August 16-17.

Hai Zhao and Chunyu Kit. 2008c. Unsupervised segmentation helps supervised learning of character tagging for word segmentation and named entity recognition. In *The Sixth SIGHAN Workshop on Chinese Language Processing*, pages 106–111, Hyderabad, India, January 11-12.

Hai Zhao, Chang-Ning Huang, Mu Li, and Bao-Liang Lu. 2006. Effective tag set selection in Chinese word segmentation via conditional random field modeling. In *Proceedings of the 20th Asian Pacific Conference on Language, Information and Computation*, pages 87–94, Wuhan, China, November 1-3.

Author Index

Association for Computational Linguistics
209 N. Eighth Street
Stroudsburg, Pennsylvania 18360

CURRAN ASSOCIATES INC
proceedings.com